Japan

Chris Rowthorn
Andrew Bender, Matthew D Firestone,
Timothy N Hornyak, Benedict Walker, Paul Warham,
Wendy Yanagihara

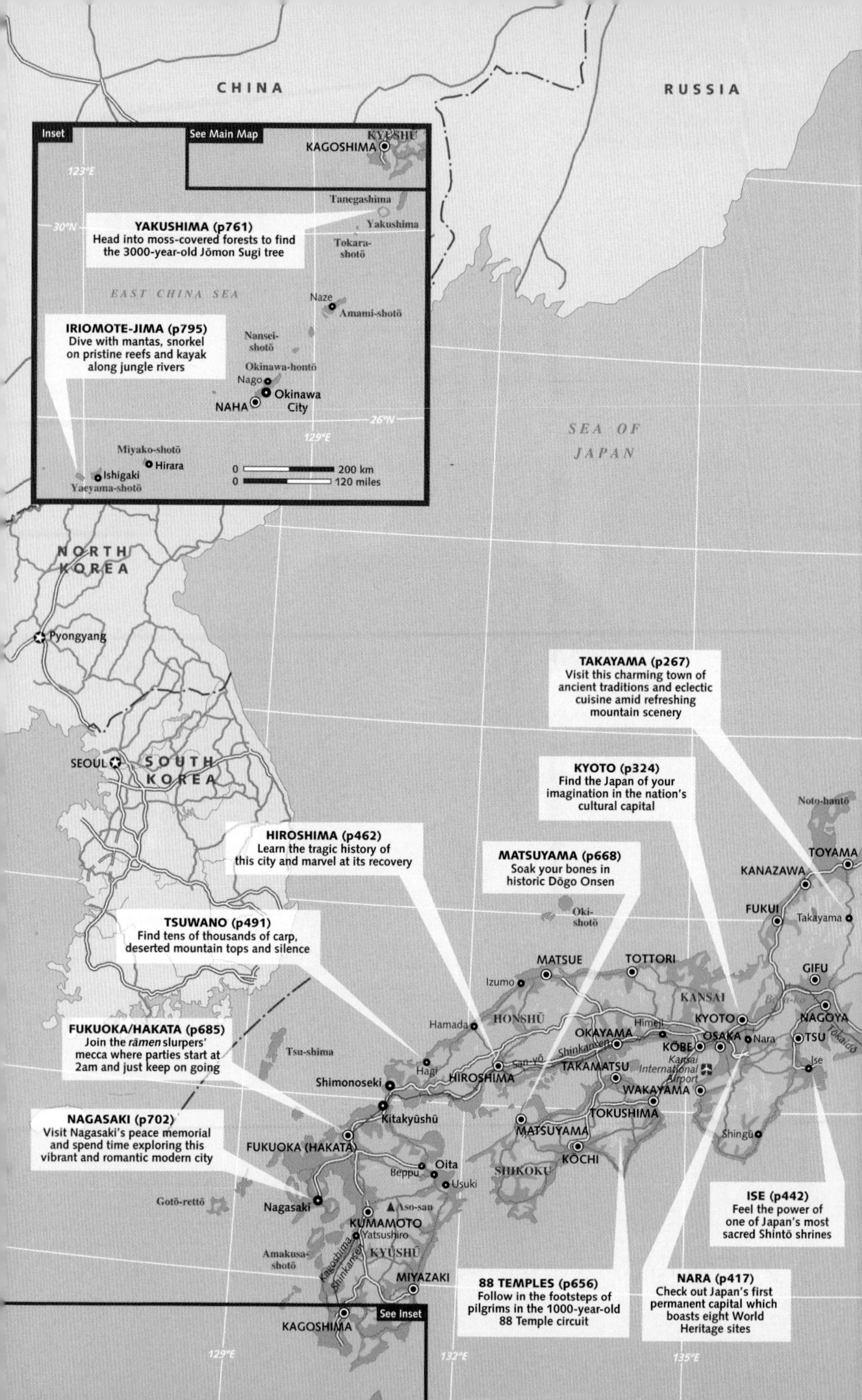

CHINA
RUSSIA
Inset
See Main Map
KYUSHU
KAGOSHIMA
123°E
30°N
Tanegashima
Yakushima
YAKUSHIMA (p761)
Head into moss-covered forests to find the 3000-year-old Jōmon Sugi tree
Tokara-shotō
EAST CHINA SEA
Naze
Amami-shotō
IRIOMOTE-JIMA (p795)
Dive with mantas, snorkel on pristine reefs and kayak along jungle rivers
Nansei-shotō
Okinawa-hontō
Nago
Okinawa City
NAHA
26°N
129°E
Miyako-shotō
Hirara
Ishigaki
Yaeyama-shotō
0 200 km
0 120 miles
SEA OF JAPAN
NORTH KOREA
Pyongyang
SEOUL
SOUTH KOREA
TAKAYAMA (p267)
Visit this charming town of ancient traditions and eclectic cuisine amid refreshing mountain scenery
KYOTO (p324)
Find the Japan of your imagination in the nation's cultural capital
HIROSHIMA (p462)
Learn the tragic history of this city and marvel at its recovery
MATSUYAMA (p668)
Soak your bones in historic Dōgo Onsen
TSUWANO (p491)
Find tens of thousands of carp, deserted mountain tops and silence
Noto-hantō
TOYAMA
KANAZAWA
FUKUI
Takayama
Oki-shotō
GIFU
MATSUE
TOTTORI
Izumo
KANSAI
HONSHŪ
KYOTO
NAGOYA
FUKUOKA/HAKATA (p685)
Join the *rāmen* slurpers' mecca where parties start at 2am and just keep on going
Hamada
Himeji
OKAYAMA
KŌBE
OSAKA
Nara
TSU
Tōkaidō
Tsu-shima
Hagi
San-yō
Shinkansen
Kansai International Airport
Ise
Shimonoseki
HIROSHIMA
TAKAMATSU
WAKAYAMA
NAGASAKI (p702)
Visit Nagasaki's peace memorial and spend time exploring this vibrant and romantic modern city
Kitakyūshū
TOKUSHIMA
MATSUYAMA
Shingū
FUKUOKA (HAKATA)
KŌCHI
Oita
Beppu
SHIKOKU
Usuki
Gotō-rettō
Nagasaki
Aso-san
KUMAMOTO
Yatsushiro
ISE (p442)
Feel the power of one of Japan's most sacred Shintō shrines
Amakusa-shotō
KYŪSHŪ
Kagoshima Shinkansen
MIYAZAKI
88 TEMPLES (p656)
Follow in the footsteps of pilgrims in the 1000-year-old 88 Temple circuit
NARA (p417)
Check out Japan's first permanent capital which boasts eight World Heritage sites
See Inset
KAGOSHIMA
129°E
132°E
135°E

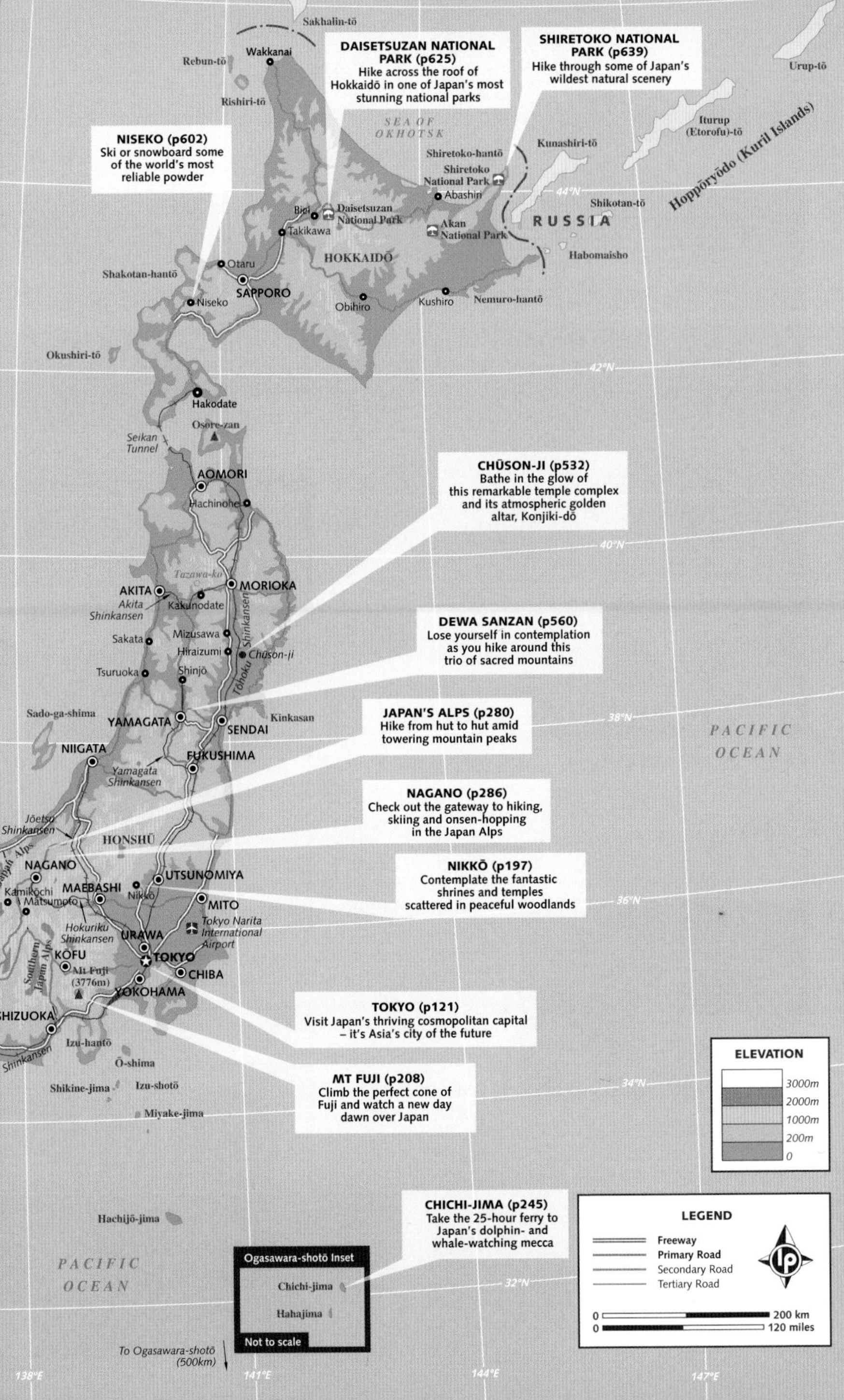

DAISETSUZAN NATIONAL PARK (p625)
Hike across the roof of Hokkaidō in one of Japan's most stunning national parks
SHIRETOKO NATIONAL PARK (p639)
Hike through some of Japan's wildest natural scenery
NISEKO (p602)
Ski or snowboard some of the world's most reliable powder
CHŪSON-JI (p532)
Bathe in the glow of this remarkable temple complex and its atmospheric golden altar, Konjiki-dō
DEWA SANZAN (p560)
Lose yourself in contemplation as you hike around this trio of sacred mountains
JAPAN'S ALPS (p280)
Hike from hut to hut amid towering mountain peaks
NAGANO (p286)
Check out the gateway to hiking, skiing and onsen-hopping in the Japan Alps
NIKKŌ (p197)
Contemplate the fantastic shrines and temples scattered in peaceful woodlands
TOKYO (p121)
Visit Japan's thriving cosmopolitan capital – it's Asia's city of the future
MT FUJI (p208)
Climb the perfect cone of Fuji and watch a new day dawn over Japan
CHICHI-JIMA (p245)
Take the 25-hour ferry to Japan's dolphin- and whale-watching mecca
Sakhalin-tō
Wakkanai
Rebun-tō
Rishiri-tō
SEA OF OKHOTSK
Urup-tō
Iturup (Etorofu)-tō
Kunashiri-tō
Hoppōryōdo (Kuril Islands)
Shiretoko-hantō
Shiretoko National Park
Abashiri
Shikotan-tō
RUSSIA
Habomaisho
Bibai
Daisetsuzan National Park
Takikawa
Akan National Park
HOKKAIDŌ
Otaru
Shakotan-hantō
SAPPORO
Niseko
Obihiro
Kushiro
Nemuro-hantō
Okushiri-tō
Hakodate
Osore-zan
Seikan Tunnel
AOMORI
Hachinohe
Tazawa-ko
AKITA
MORIOKA
Akita Shinkansen
Kakunodate
Sakata
Mizusawa
Hiraizumi
Chūson-ji
Tōhoku Shinkansen
Tsuruoka
Shinjō
Sado-ga-shima
YAMAGATA
SENDAI
Kinkasan
NIIGATA
FUKUSHIMA
Yamagata Shinkansen
Jōetsu Shinkansen
HONSHŪ
Northern Japan Alps
NAGANO
UTSUNOMIYA
Kamikōchi
Matsumoto
MAEBASHI
Nikkō
MITO
Tokyo Narita International Airport
Hokuriku Shinkansen
URAWA
Southern Japan Alps
KŌFU
TOKYO
CHIBA
Mt Fuji (3776m)
YOKOHAMA
SHIZUOKA
Shinkansen
Izu-hantō
Ō-shima
Shikine-jima
Izu-shotō
Miyake-jima
Hachijō-jima
PACIFIC OCEAN
PACIFIC OCEAN
Ogasawara-shotō Inset
Chichi-jima
Hahajima
Not to scale
To Ogasawara-shotō (500km)
44°N
42°N
40°N
38°N
36°N
34°N
32°N
138°E
141°E
144°E
147°E
ELEVATION
3000m
2000m
1000m
200m
0
LEGEND
Freeway
Primary Road
Secondary Road
Tertiary Road
0
200 km
0
120 miles

On the Road

CHRIS ROWTHORN Coordinating Author

This is me at Hōrin-ji (better known as Daruma-dera) in western Kyoto. It's a small temple about 10 minutes' walk northeast of Enmachi station on the JR Sagano Line. My wife took the picture. We were cycling across Kyoto to climb Atago-san, which is in the western mountains above Arashiyama (p359).

BENEDICT WALKER The expense of a night in a good ryokan is definitely justifiable. This photo was taken at Sanga Ryokan (p727) after tearing around the grassy hillsides of Aso on a hot summer day. After a long soak in a private bath, with the river rushing by the open window, you too can enjoy a taste of the real Japan. It feels wonderful.

MATTHEW D FIRESTONE Don't let the swish goggles and sophisticated ski outfit fool you – I'm actually a terrible skier, and spent a good deal of time rolling down black diamond runs on all fours. But, updating ski coverage for Northern Honshū and Hokkaidō was almost as memorable as all the black and blues I picked up along the way!

ANDREW BENDER Although I've been to the Japan Alps dozens of times, I was unprepared for the spectacle at the top of the Shin-Hotaka Ropeway (p284) in January. Someone had kindly carved paths as tall as me into the snowdrifts, and the sun gamely peeked through the pines sagging with snow. And I'm told this was a low snow year!

PAUL WARHAM It's early in the evening, and I'm about to step into a small *izakaya* (pub-eatery). In a few minutes' time, I'll be sitting down with the regulars, asking for tips on sake while the chef behind the counter prepares a plate of fresh locally-caught fish. I can't think of any tastier or more enjoyable way to get to know Japan.

TIMOTHY N HORNYAK I'd sailed all the way down to tropical Haha-jima (p246), over 1000km from Tokyo, and wasn't about to leave without bagging a whale photo. But I'd had a day of snorkelling through tropical fish and tracking dolphins offshore, and it was off-season for whale-watching anyway, so this statue by the pier was good enough!

WENDY YANAGIHARA This was a little detour during research, when my Aunt Shigeko, cousin Kikuyo and her husband Takahide and I went roaming around in Shizuoka one afternoon. I have so many fond memories of staying with my aunt while growing up, and Kikuyo is my closest cousin, so I always cherish my getaways from research with them.

For full author biographies see p860

Japan Highlights

Japan is a whirlwind of dazzling cultural attractions and awesome natural wonders. Wander the ancient Zen gardens of Kyoto; let loose in the neon jungles of Tokyo; ski nose-deep powder snow in Hokkaidō and soak away your cares in steaming natural hot springs; eat mouth-watering sushi in Osaka and wash it down with the best sake you've ever tasted; hike for days in the Japan Alps and never see another hiker; swim with manta rays off Okinawa. These are some of our favourite experiences.

But why not let the experts speak for themselves? Here's what Lonely Planet authors, staff and readers like best about Japan, in no particular order.

CHRISTOPHER GROENHOL

1 KYOTO TEMPLES & GARDENS

From the moss garden at Saihō-ji (p363) to the shining apparition that is Kinkaku-ji (p358), Kyoto is home to the most beautiful temples in all of Japan, and most of them are surrounded by sublime gardens.

Chris Rowthorn, Lonely Planet Author, Japan

LOU JONES

2 HIROSHIMA PEACE MEMORIAL PARK

On a bench in Hiroshima's Peace Memorial Park (p463), a Japanese man sat beside me and asked if he could practise his English with me. He hoped that one day he would speak well enough to share his story with tourists visiting Hiroshima. Hearing his first-hand account of the day of the bomb – when he lost his father, who worked in the city centre, and his younger brother, who was one of many schoolchildren clearing fire zones – and how this park looked the day after, remains one of my most valued life experiences.

Angela Tinson, Lonely Planet Staff, Australia

TIMOTHY N HORNYAK

3 CLASSIC RYOKAN

Staying at a ryokan is a must while in Japan, but don't settle for the ordinary. Classic ryokan, often in secluded rural areas and made from wood, are the best. One of my favourites is Hōshi Onsen Chōjūkan (p206), in northern Gunma-ken. Its legendary bathhouse is over a hundred years old, with deep chestnut-wood tubs, arched windows and – a rarity – mixed bathing.

Timothy N Hornyak, Lonely Planet Author, Japan

OKU-NO-IN, KŌYA-SAN

Far from the neon bustle of Tokyo, this Buddhist cemetery-temple (p435) – filled with beautiful, old moss-covered tombstones in an eerily misty cedar forest – is possibly the most utterly peaceful place on earth. Spend a couple of hours wandering before finishing the day with a vegetarian meal served in a traditional Japanese-style tatami room at your temple lodging, to get a glimpse at the serenity of a monk's life.

Angela Tinson, Lonely Planet Staff, Australia

4

RACHEL LEW

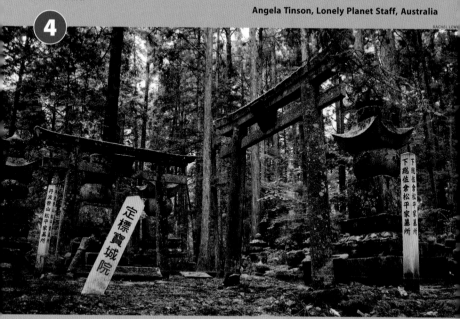

TSUKIJI FISH MARKET

I'm not awake yet, really, since it's before dawn. But the action at Tokyo's wholesale fish market (p150) wakes me up right quick. Motorised carts, loaded with produce and enormous frozen tuna, zip by. This is where fresh seafood of every variety makes its appearance before being shipped to the city's restaurants and shops. For the full experience, I peruse the trays of octopus and sea urchin, then treat myself to the freshest sushi breakfast ever.

Wendy Yanagihara, Lonely Planet Author, USA

5

OLIVER STREW

GREG ELMS

6 SHOPPING IN OMOTE-SANDŌ, TOKYO

A chorus of 'irrashimassssseee' greets me as I enter the store. It begins with a young Japanese boy in tight black jeans, cowboy boots, and a retro shirt. It ends fives voices later. Unable to do anything but smile in response, I let the consumerist fever hit. Before me are boutique adornments and retro one-offs, all immaculately folded and styled. Be warned: Omote-sandō (p155) is always chic, and the sales people impossibly well-groomed, so take care of your wallet.

Stephanie Ong, Traveller, Australia

7 HATTŌJI

The deliciously unspoilt village of Hattōji (p455) in rural Okayama features an old-school, thatched-roof farmhouse where you can enjoy the sunken hearth and drum-shaped *goemonburo* bath. Happily, Hattōji isn't entirely devoid of conveniences – down the road there's a Wild West–themed restaurant where a real Japanese cowboy serves up duck hotpot and karaoke.

Timothy N Hornyak, Lonely Planet Author, Japan

TIMOTHY N HORNYAK

ALI LEMER

8 DŌTOMBORI BY NIGHT

Here's what I saw on my night walk through Osaka's hyperkinetic downtown Dōtombori district (p396): hypnotic, animated neon signs reflecting crazily in the placid river below; slightly drunken fun-seekers staggering around in animal costumes while texting on mobile phones; giant, articulated robot crabs mounted above seafood restaurants; colourful shopfront statues of everything from cute, cartoony raccoons and children, to angry-faced chefs wielding skewers of *tonkatsu* (p85). And that was just a Monday.

Ali Lemer, Lonely Planet Staff, Australia

FROM GAIJIN TO GEISHA

Long fascinated by Japanese culture since childhood, I always wondered what it would be like to dress up as a geisha or a samurai. In Kyoto's Gion district, I was finally able to find out. I stood stock-still as the staff at Maika (p366) slathered my face and neck with thick white make-up, arranged and decorated my hair, and carefully dressed me in the elaborate layers of a *maiko* (apprentice geisha) kimono in deep blue, dotted with cherry blossoms. When I shuffled gracefully into the waiting room, my father didn't even recognise me.

Ali Lemer, Lonely Planet Staff, Australia

9

ALBERT LEMER

RICHARD I'ANSON

10 SUMŌ

Even from these cheap seats, the sumō tournaments (p74) are riveting: the wrestler's elegant rituals of scattering handfuls of salt before him in the ring, squatting and retreating, staring his opponent down. Each short match culminates in both wrestlers leaping forth in a burst of energy – sometimes slapping madly, scrabbling for one another's thick belts, occasionally tossing one another off the platform altogether. I roam around the stadium listening to the murmur of chattering, punctuated by cheers.

Wendy Yanagihara, Lonely Planet Author, USA

JOHN ELK

11 GINKAKU-JI

The gardens of Ginkaku-ji (p354) somehow manage to stand out among the many, many temples around Kyoto. There are few better places to spend a relaxing few hours after a hard morning's walk.

Daniel Corbett, Lonely Planet Staff, Australia

MT FUJI FROM YAMANAKA-KO

On a clear day, this is one of the best ways to view the majestic Mt Fuji. We enjoyed the sunset gliding gracefully on the calm water of the lake (p211).

Ivy Kwan, Traveller, lonelyplanet.com

12

BOB CHARLTON

ONSEN

Making my way through the steam and other naked bodies, I pad self-consciously to the stone pool. Am I doing this right? Is that girl looking at me? Is she staring at my birthmark? My inhibitions, however, soon melt as I touch the water. Snow falls gently on our reddened faces, and a little Japanese boy squeals in delight.

Stephanie Ong, Traveller, Australia

13

JOHN BORTHWICK

TROPICAL JAPAN

Few travellers are aware of Japan's tropical side. If you're after brilliant coral reefs, mangrove swamps and jungle trekking, head to the southern islands of Okinawa (p758). Who would have thought that you could swim with manta rays in Japan?

Chris Rowthorn, Lonely Planet Author, Japan

14

MASON FLORENCE

FOOD, GLORIOUS FOOD!

People simply *love* to eat in Japan. No wonder, since Japanese cuisine delivers an eye-popping variety of options that delight your tastebuds. Popular Japanese dishes include *gyoza*, tempura, *tonkatsu*, *rāmen*, *soba*, yakitori, sukiyaki, *okonomiyaki*, *teppanyaki*, *shabu-shabu* and, of course, sushi (p76). For an additional foodie adventure, head to the basement of any department store; you'll be bedazzled by the best food courts in the world.

Melissa Randall, Traveller, USA

15

GREG ELMS

PHIL WEYMOUT

16

KARAOKE

Although karaoke can be found in lots of bars, the real experience is getting a few friends together and trying out a private room at a karaoke club. Lounge around and belt out the best (and worst) of your musical memories. You can package drinks into the hourly fee making it a cheap place to have a few drinks…provided you don't stay all night!

Adam Stanford, Lonely Planet Staff, Australia

ARASHIYAMA'S BAMBOO FOREST

Walking through the shade of these massive stalks of bamboo at Arashiyama (p359) made me feel like I was in a Japanese fairy tale, where mysterious demons or roaming samurai might be met around any corner.

Ali Lemer, Lonely Planet Staff, Australia

17

ALI LEMER

NISHIKI MARKET

This covered market (p346) in downtown Kyoto crams all sorts of stores into a thin alley that seems to stretch forever. Perfect for picking up everything from silk to unidentifiable foods and, of course, there's a temple hidden away in there, too.

Daniel Corbett, Lonely Planet Staff, Australia

18

PETER PTSCHELINZEW

19

JUDY BOARD / ALAMY

HIKING IN THE JAPAN ALPS

The long traverse over the northern Japan Alps from Kamikōchi (p280) to Tsurugi-dake (the northern terminus of the route) is world-class by any standard. If you've got a strong back, you can take a backpack and camp it; if not, you can stay in the excellent mountain huts. Either way, I guarantee you that it will be one of the great hikes of your life.

Chris Rowthorn, Lonely Planet Author, Japan

TŌDAI-JI

The largest wooden building in the world, Tōdai-ji (p421) also houses the largest enclosed Buddha in the world, the Daibutsu. A must-see.

Anonymous, Traveller, lonelyplanet.com

20

ADINA TOVY AMSEL

EYE OF THE BEHOLDER

Japanese culture rates aesthetics so highly that beauty can be found around every corner. Even underfoot, the maintenance-hole covers in Tokyo's Ueno-kōen (p151) are cast-iron works of art.

Ali Lemer, Lonely Planet Staff, Australia

21

ALI LEMER

JOHN ASHBURNE

22

KENROKU-EN, KANAZAWA

The gardens of Kanazawa are not to be missed. From the meticulous cuttings of the smallest blade of grass to the grand tree supports of the ancient Bonsai, Kenroku-en (p307) is spectacular.

Ilo Orleans, Traveller, USA

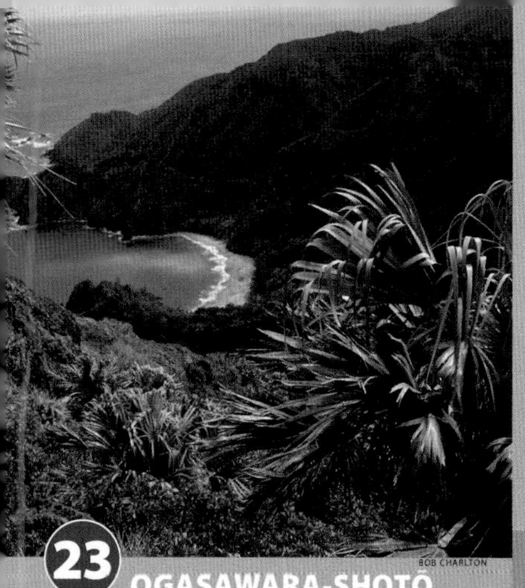

BOB CHARLTON

23 OGASAWARA-SHOTŌ

The 25-hour ferry ride from Tokyo down to the isolated islands of Ogasawara-shotō (p245) is the most unusual and rewarding trip you can take in Japan. It's another world, and few non-Japanese make the trip (although it was originally settled by New England whalers). The hiking, snorkelling, whale-watching and dolphin-swimming here is easily worth the cost of the ferry trip.

Chris Rowthorn, Lonely Planet Author, Japan

24 HIMEJI-JŌ

Japanese castles are pure medieval fantasy, evoking the days of steely samurai and stealthy ninja. Most, though, are postwar ferro-concrete reconstructions. The most spectacular of the authentic fortresses is Himeji-jō (p415), a gem virtually unchanged from four centuries ago. Renowned as the 'white heron' for its shimmering plaster walls, it towers 92m above sea level and boasts 83 buildings, mazelike paths, and stunning architectural aesthetics. The April cherry blossoms here are a delight.

Timothy N Hornyak, Lonely Planet Author, Japan

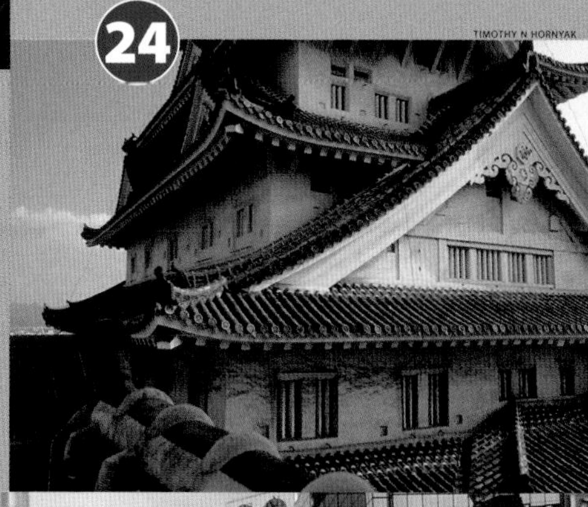

TIMOTHY N HORNYAK

GREG ELMS

25 CROWDS

A high population density is readily apparent throughout Japan, but nowhere more so than at Tokyo's Shinjuku station (p154) during rush hour or Shibuya crossing (p156) at almost any time of day. Trying to navigate the mass humanity is a reminder why group harmony is a defining characteristic of Japanese culture: without consideration for others, nobody would reach their destination without getting run over!

Lou LaGrange, Lonely Planet Staff, USA

FRANK CARTER

26 HANAMI

In springtime, cherry blossoms (p29) bloom across Japan, and the Japanese flock to the best parks to eat, drink and be merry, while contemplating the fragile beauty of the snowy pink blossoms. When the wind blows, it's like a soft-pink snow-flurry.

Anonymous, Traveller, lonelyplanet.com

OSAKA AQUARIUM (KAIYŪKAN)

Ride the vertiginous escalator to the entrance of one of the world's largest aquariums (p400) for all things weird and wonderful. Cruising around the 9m-deep cylinder tank at the heart of the building is the famous whale shark, Kai-Kun. Kids squeal in delight and the cameras come out. But no photos of the charmingly fragile ocean sunfish please – he's shy.

Kate Morgan,
Lonely Planet Staff, Australia

27

KATE MORGA

HIKING FROM MAGOME TO TSUMAGO

This hiking trail (p303) is a must-do if you want to experience the old highway used by ancient travellers between Tokyo and Kyoto. You'll be rewarded with scenery of villages, plantation fields and waterfalls.

Ivy Kwan,
Traveller, lonelyplanet.com

28

SKYE HOHMANN / ALA

Contents

Regional Map Contents

Destination Japan

Japan is a world apart – a wonderful little planet floating off the coast of mainland China. It is a kind of cultural Galapagos, a place where a unique civilisation was allowed to grow and unfold on its own, unmolested by invading powers. And while there has been a lot of input from both Western and Eastern cultures over the millennia, these have always been turned into something distinctly Japanese once they arrived on the archipelago.

Even today, the world struggles to categorise Japan: is it the world's most advanced technological civilisation, or a bastion of traditional Asian culture? Has the country become just another outpost of the West, or is there something decidedly Eastern lurking under the veneer of its familiar modernity? There are no easy answers, but there is plenty of pleasure to be had in looking for them.

First and foremost, Japan is a place of delicious contrasts: ancient temples and futuristic cities; mist-shrouded hills and lightning-fast bullet trains; kimono-clad geisha and suit-clad businesspeople; quaint thatch-roofed villages and pulsating neon urban jungles. This peculiar synthesis of the modern and the traditional is one of the things that makes travel in Japan such a fascinating experience.

For all its uniqueness, Japan shares a lot with the wider world, and this includes the state of the economy. Japan has been severely affected by the worldwide recession that started with the US sub-prime loan crisis of 2008. Japan's export-driven economy has always been sensitive to economic health of its trading partners, particularly the USA. Indeed, it has often been observed that when America sneezes, Japan catches a cold. And this time, Japan has caught a whopper.

As housing prices fell and the stock market tanked in the USA, America's profligate consumers stopped buying Japanese products. The effect on the Japanese economy was almost immediate. Exports in January 2009 were down an astonishing 46% compared to the previous year. For a nation that exports about 20% of its total manufacturing output, this sort of decline can only be termed apocalyptic, and the bursting of Japan's famous 'Bubble Economy' in the late '80s is starting to look tame by comparison.

To add insult to injury, just as the world's consumers have stopped buying Japanese products, the world's currency traders have been snapping up the Japanese yen, making it one of the world's most valuable currencies. This has made Japan's exports even less attractive to foreign buyers. This one-two economic punch has left the nation reeling, and Japanese newspaper headlines are a daily litany of economic woes, from shrinking tax receipts, to massive layoffs, to huge corporate losses. It's too early to tell how all of this will play out in the coming months and years, but one thing is certain: many businesses will probably close (including some listed in the pages of this guide).

To make matters worse, the present economic crisis is unfolding against a backdrop of two other severe problems: Japan's low birth rate (the second-lowest in the industrialised world after Italy) and ageing population. Japan's population peaked in 2006 at 127.46 million and is estimated to have fallen by almost 400,000 people by mid-2009. Experts predict that it may drop as low as 100 million by the year 2050, which begs the question: who will work in the factories and who will take care of the elderly as time passes?

In order to address the problem, Japan has recently been experimenting with a solution familiar to those in Hong Kong: importing workers from

FAST FACTS

Population: 127 million

Female life expectancy: 84.5 years

Literacy rate: 99%

GDP: US$3.7 trillion (estimated)

Latitude of Tokyo: 35.4°N, the same as Tehran, and about the same as Los Angeles (34.05°N) and Crete (35°N)

Islands in the Japanese archipelago: approximately 3900

Number of onsen (hot springs): more than 3000

World's busiest station: Tokyo's Shinjuku Station, servicing 740,000 passengers a day

Money spent on manga (comics) each year in Japan: ¥481 billion (about US$5 billion)

Cruising speed of the *shinkansen* (bullet train): 300km/h

Southeast Asia. Japan recently changed its visa policies to allow nurses from countries such as Indonesia, Vietnam and the Philippines to work in Japan on a temporary basis. Critics have assailed the plan as inherently racist, as these nurses are not eligible for eventual permanent residence. However, many observers see foreign nurses as the first wave of overseas workers who may eventually change Japan's traditionally conservative (some would say xenophobic) attitudes towards immigration.

Changes are also taking place in many other spheres of Japanese life. The traditional foundations of Japanese life – cradle-to-grave employment, age-based promotion, and a strong social safety net – are gradually being abandoned in favour of an economy based on more flexible labour conditions and a tightening of privatised government services (eg in the case of the post office). Now, rather than priding itself on being a country where everyone is a member of the middle class, there is talk of a nation composed of two distinct classes: the '*kachi-gumi*' (winners) and '*make-gumi*' (losers).

Fortunately, it appears that the politicians and corporations behind these changes may have overplayed their hand, and the slightly more progressive Democratic Party of Japan has been gaining ground in the polls recently, based largely on popular discontent with the negative effects of the new economic model.

Relations (or lack thereof) with nearby North Korea continue to be a perpetual source of concern for the Japanese. In 2006 North Korea successfully tested a nuclear bomb. In April 2009 the country launched a rocket over Japan. While the North Koreans insisted the payload was a nonmilitary satellite, many Japanese feared that it was intended to demonstrate the ability of North Korea to lob a warhead over the Sea of Japan (they also feared that jettisoned parts from the rocket would fall on Japan). While American and Japanese analysts later concluded that the test was a failure, this did little to calm Japanese nerves.

Of course, the news is not all bad in Japan. Three Japanese scientists shared the 2008 Nobel Prize in physics, and the Japanese athletes garnered 26 medals in the Beijing Olympics, more than at any previous Olympics. The film *Okuribito* (Departures), by Japanese director Takita Yojiro, won an Oscar for best foreign film, and interest in Japanese manga (comics) and anime continues to soar. Meanwhile, the country continues to expand its brilliant shinkansen (bullet train) system, already the world's most extensive high-speed train network.

Japan's tourist economy has attracted travellers not only from the West, but also from neighbouring Asian countries such as China, Korea, Taiwan and Singapore. Australian skiers have flocked to ski areas like Niseko, so much so that some Japanese have started referring to the area as 'little Australia'. Though tourist numbers have waned in recent times, it seems a safe bet that as the world recovers from recession, Japan will continue to increase in popularity, as more and more people are drawn to a country that manages to be both utterly foreign and incredibly welcoming.

Getting Started

Japan is Asia's most user-friendly country. It's incredibly efficient, clean and safe. Indeed, many travellers will find it easier to travel around Japan than to travel in their home countries. While English is not widely spoken, communication is not as difficult as you might think – more and more Japanese are able to speak some English, and you'll find English signs in train stations, airports and, increasingly, major cities. Another concern is cost: as this book went to press, the yen was soaring versus many world currencies. However, costs within Japan have remained stable for years, and it can actually be cheaper to travel in Japan than in Western Europe and North America.

WHEN TO GO

The best times to visit Japan are the climatically stable seasons of spring (March to May) and autumn (September to November).

See Climate (p810) for more information.

Spring is the time when Japan's famous *sakura* (cherry trees) burst into bloom. Starting from Kyūshū sometime in February or March, the *sakura zensen* (cherry tree blossom line) advances northward, usually passing the main cities of Honshū in early April. Once the *sakura* bloom, their glory is brief, usually lasting only a week.

Autumn is an equally good time to travel, with pleasant temperatures and soothing colours; the autumn foliage pattern reverses that of the *sakura*, starting in the north sometime in October and peaking across most of Honshū in mid- to late November.

Travelling during either winter or summer is a mixed bag – midwinter (December to February) weather can be cold, particularly on the Sea of

DON'T LEAVE HOME WITHOUT...

The clothing you bring will depend not only on the season, but also on where you are planning to go. Japan extends a long way from north to south: the north of Hokkaidō can be under deep snow at the same time Okinawa and Nansei-shotō (the Southwest Islands) are basking in tropical sunshine. If you're going anywhere near the mountains, or are intent on climbing Mt Fuji, you'll need good cold-weather gear, even at the height of summer. And unless you're in Japan on business, you won't need formal or even particularly dressy clothes. Men should keep in mind, however, that trousers are preferable to shorts, especially in restaurants.

You'll also need the following:

- Slip-on shoes – you want shoes that are not only comfortable for walking but are also easy to slip on and off for the frequent occasions where they must be removed.
- Unholey socks – your socks will be on display a lot of the time, so decent socks are a good idea.
- Japan Rail Pass – if you intend to do much train travel at all, you'll save money with a Japan Rail Pass, which *must* be purchased outside Japan; see p840 for details.
- Books – English-language and other foreign-language books are expensive in Japan, and they're not available outside the big cities.
- Medicine – bring any prescription medicine you'll need from home.
- Gifts – a few postcards or some distinctive trinkets from your home country will make good gifts for those you meet along the way.
- International licence – if you appreciate the flexibility of having a rental car, note: most nationalities cannot rent a car in Japan without an international licence (see p834).

SAMPLE DAILY BUDGETS

To help you plan your Japan trip, we've put together these sample daily budgets. Keep in mind that these are rough estimates – it's possible to spend slightly less if you really put your mind to it, and you can spend a heckuva lot more if you want to live large.

Budget

- Youth hostel accommodation (per person): ¥2800
- Two simple restaurant meals: ¥2000
- Train/bus transport: ¥1500
- One average temple/museum admission: ¥500
- Snacks, drinks, sundries: ¥1000
- Total: ¥7800 (about US$80)

Midrange

- Business hotel accommodation (per person): ¥8000
- Two midrange restaurant meals: ¥4000
- Train/bus transport: ¥1500
- Two average temple/museum admissions: ¥1000
- Snacks, drinks, sundries: ¥2000
- Total: ¥16,500 (about US$170)

Japan coasts of Honshū and in Hokkaidō, while the summer months (June to August) are generally hot and often humid. June is also the month of Japan's brief rainy season, which in some years brings daily downpours and in other years is hardly a rainy season at all.

If you're heading to the southern island groups like Okinawa, the islands of southern Kagoshima-ken, the Izu-shotō or the Ogasawara-shotō, keep in mind that typhoons can wreak havoc with your travel plans. They can strike anytime between June and October, with most making a landfall in August, September and early October.

Also keep in mind that peak holiday seasons, particularly Golden Week (late April to early May), which incorporates four major Japanese holidays, and the mid-August O-Bon (Festival of the Dead), are extremely popular for domestic travel and can be problematic in terms of reservations and crowds. Likewise, everything in Japan basically shuts down during Shōgatsu (New Year period).

All that said, it is worth remembering that you can comfortably travel in Japan at any time of year. Indeed, if you come in winter or summer, you'll escape the crowds and probably get better prices for your plane ticket and accommodation.

For information on Japan's festivals and special events, see p813. For public holidays, see p814.

HOW MUCH?

Business hotel accommodation (per person) ¥8000

Midrange meal ¥2000

Local bus ¥220

Temple admission ¥500

Newspaper ¥130

COSTS & MONEY

Japan is generally considered an expensive country in which to travel. Certainly, this is the case if you opt to stay in top-end hotels, take a lot of taxis and eat all your meals in fancy restaurants. But Japan does not have to be expensive; indeed it can be *cheaper* than travelling in other parts of the world if you are careful with your spending (see p26). And in terms of what

IT'S CHEAPER THAN YOU THINK

The fact is, Japan's image as one of the world's most expensive countries is just that: an image. Anyone who has been to Japan recently knows that it can be cheaper to travel in Japan than in parts of Western Europe, the USA, Australia or even the big coastal cities of China. Of course, a lot of this depends on the exchange rate when you travel (as this book went to press, the exchange rate was fluctuating wildly). Prices within the country, however, have barely changed in the last ten years or so (some prices have even gone down due to deflation). Still, there's no denying that Japan is not Thailand. In order to help you stretch those yen, we've put together a list of money-saving tips.

Accommodation

- **Manga Kissa** – These manga (comic book) coffee shops have private cubicles and comfy reclining seats where you can spend the night for only ¥2500. For more details, see Missing the Midnight Train, p163.
- **Capsule Hotels** – A night in a capsule hotel will set you back a mere ¥3000.
- **Guest Houses** – You'll find good, cheap guest houses in many of Japan's cities, where a night's accommodation runs about ¥3500.

Eating

- **Shokudō** – You can get a good filling meal in these all-round Japanese eateries for about ¥700, or US$7, and the tea is free and there's no tipping. For more, see p79.
- **Bentō** – The ubiquitous *bentō* (boxed meal) costs around ¥500 and is both filling and nutritious.
- **Use Your Noodle** – You can get a steaming bowl of tasty *rāmen* (egg noodles) in Japan for as little as ¥500, and ordering is a breeze – you just have to say '*rāmen*' and you're away. *Soba* (buckwheat) and udon (thick white) noodles are even cheaper – as low as ¥350 per bowl.

Shopping

- **Hyaku-en Shops** – *Hyaku-en* means ¥100, and like the name implies, everything in these shops costs only ¥100, or about US$1. You'll be amazed what you can find in these places. Some even sell food.
- **Flea Markets** – A good new kimono costs an average of ¥200,000 (about US$2100), but you can pick up a fine used kimono at a flea market for ¥1000, or about US$10. Whether you're shopping for yourself or for presents for the folks back home, you'll find some incredible bargains at Japan's flea markets.

Transport

- **Japan Rail Pass** – Like the famous Eurail Pass, this is one of the world's great travel bargains. It allows unlimited travel on Japan's brilliant nationwide rail system, including the lightning-fast *shinkansen* (bullet trains). See p840.
- **Seishun Jūhachi Kippu** – For ¥11,500, you get five one-day tickets good for travel on any regular Japan Railways train. You can literally travel from one end of the country to the other for around US$100. See p841.

you get for your money, Japan is good value indeed; see also Sample Daily Budgets (p25) for more practical information.

TRAVEL LITERATURE

Travel books about Japan often end up turning into extended reflections on the eccentricities or uniqueness of the Japanese. One writer who did not fall prey to this temptation was Alan Booth. *The Roads to Sata* (1985)

TOP PICKS

JAPAN IN THE MOVIES

Here are a few excellent films to whet your appetite for your trip.

- *Marusa no Onna* (A Taxing Woman; 1987) Director: Itami Jūzō
- *Tampopo* (1987) Director: Itami Jūzō
- *Osōshiki* (The Funeral; 1987) Director: Itami Jūzō
- *Minbo-no-Onna* (The Anti-Extortion Woman; 1994) Director: Itami Jūzō
- *Tōkyō Monogatari* (Tokyo Story; 1953) Director: Ōzu Yasujirō
- *Maboroshi no Hikari* (Maborosi; 1995) Director: Koreeda Hirokazu
- *Nijushi-no-Hitomi* (Twenty Four Eyes; 1954) Director: Kinoshita Keisuke
- *Lost in Translation* (2003) Director: Sofia Coppola
- *Rashomon* (1950) Director: Kurosawa Akira
- *Okuribito* (Departures; 2008) Director: Takita Yojiro

MOST BEAUTIFUL SIGHTS IN JAPAN

Japan is all about pockets of beauty. It's unfair to single out just a few, but here's a list of some chart toppers.

- Cherry blossoms in Kyoto (p324) – slow pink explosions? Stationary rose-coloured clouds? The English language reveals its poverty when confronted with Kyoto's cherry blossoms.
- Saihō-ji (p363) – is there a garden more beautiful than the one at Kyoto's Saihō-ji temple (otherwise known as Koke-dera or 'Moss Temple')?
- Bamboo dancing on a hillside – you'll see it from the *shinkansen* (bullet train) or when you're hiking in the hills.
- Yaeyama-shotō (p789) – the reefs around Iriomote-jima are as colourful as a Kyoto geisha's kimono.
- Kerama-shotō (p783) – we like our sand white, our water gin-clear and our coral colourful.
- Japan Alps (p280) – there is a sanctuary in the heart of the Japan Alps that will give any part of New Zealand a run for its money.
- Daitoku-ji (p347) – there are 24 temples and subtemples here and countless gardens; it's pointless to pick a favourite – just go see for yourself.

DON'T LEAVE JAPAN WITHOUT TRYING THESE FOODS

Even experienced travellers will be amazed by the sheer diversity, quality and tasty goodness of Japanese food. A note to our vegetarian readers: most of these foods contain meat or fish, but we've included two items that contain no meat, fish or dairy products. For more on Japanese food, see p76.

- Good sushi – not automatic sushi, the proper sit-down-and-order type.
- *Unagi* – eel cooked the Japanese way and served over rice is one of the finer things in life.
- *Wa-gyū* – Kōbe beef is only *the* most famous of the many types of Japanese beef.
- *Kaiseki* – our apologies to the French, but there is simply no food on earth more refined than *kaiseki* (haute cuisine) – especially when you take into account the utensils, plates and setting.
- *Rāmen* – no, not the plastic packets of the stuff you take hiking – the real item served from steaming vats by a guy wearing a headband.
- *Shōjin-ryōri* – Japan's Buddhist vegetarian cuisine may win over a few carnivores; a good place to try it is at Kōya-san (p433), in Kansai.
- *Okonomiyaki* – the so-called 'Japanese pizza' is both delicious and fun (since you help in making it).

is the best of his writings about Japan, and traces a four-month journey on foot from the northern tip of Hokkaidō to Sata, the southern tip of Kyūshū. Booth's *Looking for the Lost – Journeys Through a Vanishing Japan* (1995) was his final book, and again recounts walks in rural Japan. Booth loved Japan, warts and all, and these books reflect his passion and insight into the country.

A more recent account of a trek across the length of Japan is Craig McLachlan's enjoyable *Four Pairs of Boots* (1998). The same author's *Tales of a Summer Henro* (1997) recounts his journey around the 88 Sacred Temples of Shikoku. Both books are light and easy to read, and give an excellent insight into today's Japan.

Alex Kerr's *Lost Japan* (1996) is not strictly a travel book, though he does recount some journeys in it; rather, it's a collection of essays on his long experiences in Japan. Like Booth, Kerr has some great insights into Japan and the Japanese, and his love for the country is only matched by his frustration at some of the things he sees going wrong here.

Donald Richie's *The Inland Sea* (1971) is a classic in this genre. It recounts the author's island-hopping journey across the Seto Inland Sea in the late 1960s. Richie's elegiac account of a vanished Japan makes the reader nostalgic for times gone by. It was re-released in 2002 and is widely available online and in better bookshops.

INTERNET RESOURCES

There's no better place to start your web explorations than at lonelyplanet.com. Here you'll find succinct summaries on travelling to most places on earth, postcards from other travellers and the Thorn Tree bulletin board, where you can ask questions before you go or dispense advice when you get back.

Other websites with useful Japan information and links:

Hyperdia Japan (www.hyperdia.com/cgi-english/hyperWeb.cgi) Get Japan transport information (fares, times etc) in English.

Japan Ministry of Foreign Affairs (MOFA; www.mofa.go.jp) Has useful visa information and embassy/consulate locations under the 'Visa' tab.

Japan National Tourism Organization (JNTO; www.jnto.go.jp) Great information on all aspects of travel in Japan (see also p822).

Japan Rail (www.japanrail.com) Information on rail travel in Japan, with details on the Japan Rail Pass (see also p840).

Kōchi University Weather Home Page (http://weather.is.kochi-u.ac.jp/index-e.html) Weather satellite images of Japan updated several times a day – particularly useful during typhoon season (August, September and October).

Rikai (www.rikai.com/perl/Home.pl) Translate Japanese into English by pasting any bit of Japanese text or webpage into this site.

Tokyo Sights (www.tokyotojp.com) Hours, admission fees, phone numbers and information on most of Tokyo's major sights.

Events Calendar

Japan's calendar is packed with festivities and events from start to finish. It's a safe bet that there is a *matsuri* (festival) happening somewhere in Japan every day of the year. They are often colourful, boisterous and sometimes even wild events. The following is a list of the more interesting *matsuri*, events and seasonal highlights.

JANUARY

SHŌGATSU 31 Dec-3 Jan

New Year's is one of the most important celebrations in Japan and includes plenty of eating and drinking, the sending of auspicious New Year's cards, and the paying of respects to relatives and business associates. The central ritual, *hatsumode*, involves the first visit to the local shrine to pray for health, happiness and prosperity during the coming year.

YAMAYAKI (GRASS BURNING FESTIVAL) early Jan

Held in Nara the day before Seijin-no-hi (below), this festival commemorates a feud between groups of monks of two different temples. An entire mountainside is set alight (it must have been one heckuva feud).

SEIJIN-NO-HI (COMING-OF-AGE DAY) 2nd Mon in Jan

Ceremonies are held for boys and girls who have reached the age of 20. A good place to see the action is at large shrines, where there will be crowds of young folks – girls in beautiful kimono and boys in suits.

FEBRUARY

SETSUBUN MATSURI 3 or 4 Feb

To celebrate the end of winter (one day before the start of spring according to the Japanese lunar calendar) and to drive out evil spirits, the Japanese throw roasted beans while chanting '*oni wa soto, fuku wa uchi*' (out with the demons, in with good luck). Events are often held at local shrines with characters dressed as devils, who act as good targets for beans. See p91 for more details.

MARCH/APRIL

HINA MATSURI 3 Mar

During this festival, old dolls are displayed and young girls are given special *hina* (dolls) that represent ancient figures from the imperial court.

TAGATA HŌNEN SAI FESTIVAL 15 Mar

Held in central Honshū (p265), this festival celebrates the masculine creative force of the universe, which is represented by a giant phallus. The huge member is paraded around the village by joyful villagers. It's both photogenic and fun and guaranteed to make a good 'only in Japan' story.

PLUM BLOSSOM VIEWING late Feb-Mar

Not as famous as the cherries, but quite lovely in their own right, Japan's plum trees bloom from late February into March. Strolling among the plum orchards at places like Kyoto's Kitano-Tenman-gū (p358) is a fine way to spend an early spring day in Japan.

CHERRY BLOSSOM VIEWING late Feb-early Apr

Japan's famous cherry blossoms burst into bloom in the early spring, starting in February in Kyūshū and generally peaking in Honshū in late March or early April. Their moment of glory is brief, generally lasting only a week. Famous spots include Kyoto's Maruyama-kōen (p351) and Tokyo's Ueno-kōen (p151).

MAY

GOLDEN WEEK 29 Apr-5 May

Golden Week takes in Shōwa-no-hi (Shōwa Emperor's Day; 29 April), Kempō Kinem-bi (Constitution Day; 3 May), Midori-no-hi (Green Day; 4 May) and Kodomo-no-hi (Children's Day; 5 May). Transport and lodging in popular holiday areas are often booked solid during this time.

KODOMO-NO-HI 5 May

This is a holiday dedicated to children, especially boys. Families fly paper streamers of *koinobori* (carp), which symbolise male strength.

JULY

TANABATA MATSURI (STAR FESTIVAL) 7 Jul

The two stars meet in the Milky Way on this night, a cosmic meeting that echoes a myth (originally Chinese) of two earthly lovers. From 6 to 8 August, an ornate celebration is held in the city of Sendai (p520).

GION MATSURI 17 Jul

This is the mother of all Japanese festivals. Huge floats are pulled through the streets of Kyoto by teams of chanting citizens. On the three evenings preceding the parade, people stroll through Shijō-dōri dressed in beautiful *yukata* (light cotton kimono). See p367.

FUJI ROCK FESTIVAL late Jul

Held in Naeba (p575), this is Japan's biggest rock festival and it always draws some top-shelf acts from abroad. It's a world-class event and is worth planning a trip around.

AUGUST

NEBUTA MATSURI 2-7 Aug

Held in Aomori (p542), northern Honshū, this is one of Japan's more colourful festivals. On the final day of this festival enormous parade floats are pulled through the city by teams of chanting dancers.

O-BON (FESTIVAL OF THE DEAD) mid-Aug

According to Buddhist tradition, this is a time when ancestors return to earth. Lanterns are lit and floated on rivers, lakes or the sea to signify the return of the departed to the underworld. See also Daimon-ji Gozan Okuribi (below).

DAIMON-JI GOZAN OKURIBI 16 Aug

Commonly known as Daimon-ji Yaki, this is part of the summer O-Bon festival (above) and is one of Japan's most impressive spectacles. See p367 for details.

SUMMER FIREWORKS FESTIVALS Aug

Cities and towns across Japan hold spectacular summer fireworks festivals. You'll be amazed at the quality and duration of some of these incredible displays.

EARTH CELEBRATION 3rd week of Aug

The island of Sado-ga-shima, off the coast of northern Honshū, is the scene of this internationally famous festival of dance, art and music. The festival (p572) is centred on performances by the island's famous *taiko* (Japanese drum) group. This is a must-see if you can make it.

ASAKUSA SAMBA MATSURI late Aug

Brazil comes to Tokyo during this wild samba festival in the streets of Asakusa (see p162). You may find yourself wondering if you're actually in Japan.

SEPTEMBER

KISHIWADA DANJIRI MATSURI 14 & 15 Sep

This is one of Japan's most dangerous festivals. Huge *danjiri* (festival floats) are pulled through the narrow streets of this town south of Osaka (see p401). Much alcohol is consumed and occasionally the *danjiri* go off course and crash into houses.

OCTOBER

KURAMA-NO-HI MATSURI 22 Oct

Huge flaming torches are carried through the streets of the tiny hamlet of Kurama (p364) in the mountains north of Kyoto. This is one of Japan's more primeval festivals.

NOVEMBER

SHICHI-GO-SAN (7-5-3 FESTIVAL) 15 Nov

This is a festival in honour of girls who are aged three and seven and boys who are aged five. Children are dressed in their finest clothes and taken to shrines or temples, where prayers are offered for good fortune.

DECEMBER

BŌNEN-KAI mid-late Dec

Literally 'forget the year' celebrations, these are some of the more festive parties in Japan. They're held by companies, families and anyone who can scrape together enough money for a meal and a couple of drinks to celebrate the end of another successful year.

Itineraries
CLASSIC ROUTES

SKYSCRAPERS TO TEMPLES **One to Two Weeks / Tokyo to Kyoto**

The Tokyo–Kyoto route is the classic Japan route and the best way to get a quick taste of the country. For first-time visitors with only a week or so to look around, a few days in **Tokyo** (p121) sampling the modern Japanese experience and four or five days in the Kansai region exploring the historical sites of **Kyoto** (p324) is the way to go.

In Tokyo, we recommend that you concentrate on the modern side of things, hitting such attractions as **Shinjuku** (p154), **Akihabara** (p189) and **Shibuya** (p156). Kyoto is the place to see traditional Japan, and we recommend such classic attractions as **Nanzen-ji** (p353) and Arashiyama's famous **Bamboo Grove** (p360). If you've got a little more time, consider a side trip down to **Nara** (p417), which has some of Japan's most impressive sights.

The journey between Tokyo and Kyoto is best done by *shinkansen* (bullet train; p839). For a break from cities, we recommend a side trip to **Takayama** (p267), which can be done on the way to or from Kyoto.

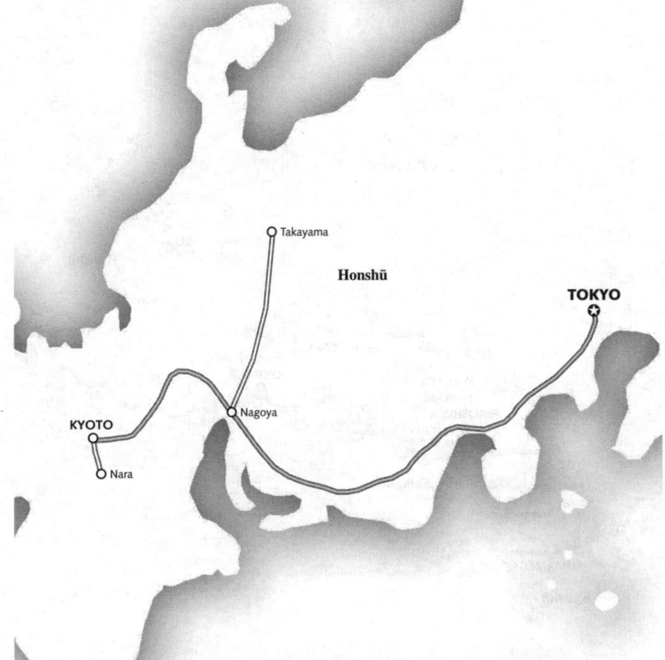

This route involves only one major train journey: the three-hour *shinkansen* trip between Tokyo and Kyoto (the Kyoto–Nara trip takes less than an hour by express train, and the side trip to Takayama adds about five hours of travel time).

CAPITAL SIGHTS & SOUTHERN HOT SPRINGS

Two Weeks to One Month / Tokyo to the Southwest

Travellers with more time to spend in Japan often hang out in Tokyo and Kyoto and then head west across the island of Honshū and down to the southern island of Kyūshū. The advantage of this route is that it can be done even in mid winter, whereas Hokkaidō and Northern Honshū are in the grip of winter from November to March.

Assuming you fly into **Tokyo** (p121), spend a few days exploring the city before heading off to the **Kansai area** (p323), notably **Kyoto** (p324) and **Nara** (p417). A good side trip en route is **Takayama** (p267), which can be reached from Nagoya.

From Kansai, take the San-yō *shinkansen* straight down to **Fukuoka/Hakata** (p685) in Kyūshū. Some of Kyūshū's highlights include **Nagasaki** (p702), **Kumamoto** (p717), natural wonders like **Aso-san** (p723) and the hot-spring town of **Beppu** (p750).

The fastest way to return from Kyūshū to Kansai or Tokyo is by the San-yō *shinkansen* along the Inland Sea side of Western Honshū. Possible stopovers include **Hiroshima** (p462) and **Himeji** (p414), a famous castle town. From Okayama, the seldom-visited island of **Shikoku** (p644) is easily accessible. The Sea of Japan side of Western Honshū is visited less frequently by tourists, and is more rural – notable attractions are the shrine at **Izumo** (Izumo Taisha; p496) and the small cities of **Matsue** (p497) and **Tottori** (p502).

This route involves around 25 hours of train travel and allows you to sample the metropolis of Tokyo, the cultural attractions of Kansai (Kyoto and Nara), and the varied attractions of Kyūshū and Western Honshū.

NORTH BY NORTHEAST THROUGH HONSHŪ

Two Weeks to One month / Tokyo/Kansai & Northern Japan

This route allows you to experience Kyoto and/or Tokyo and then sample the wild, natural side of Japan. The route starts in either **Kyoto** (p324) or **Tokyo** (p121), from where you head to the Japan Alps towns of **Matsumoto** (p297) and **Nagano** (p286), which are excellent bases for hikes in and around places like **Kamikōchi** (p280). From Nagano, you might travel up to **Niigata** (p566) and from there to the island of **Sado-ga-shima** (p571), famous for its *taiko* drummers and Earth Celebration in August. On the other side of Honshū, the city of **Sendai** (p520) provides easy access to **Matsushima** (p527), one of Japan's most celebrated scenic outlooks.

Highlights north of Sendai include peaceful **Kinkasan** (p529) and **Tazawa-ko** (p550), the deepest lake in Japan, **Morioka** (p538), **Hachimantai** (p550) and **Osore-zan** (p545).

Travelling from Northern Honshū to Hokkaidō by train involves a journey from Aomori through the world's longest underwater tunnel, the **Seikan Tunnel** (p599); rail travellers arriving via the Seikan Tunnel might consider a visit (including seafood meals) to the historic fishing port of **Hakodate** (p593). **Sapporo** (p583) is a good base for your Hokkaidō travels. It's particularly lively during its Yuki Matsuri (Snow Festival; see p589).

The real treasures of Hokkaidō are its national parks, which require either more time or your own transport. If you've only got three or four days in Hokkaidō, you might hit **Shiretoko National Park** (p639) and **Akan National Park** (p632). If you've got at least a week, head to **Daisetsuzan National Park** (p625).

This route, which involves around 28 hours of train travel, is for those who want to combine the urban/cultural attractions of Tokyo or Kansai with a few Northern Honshū and Hokkaidō attractions.

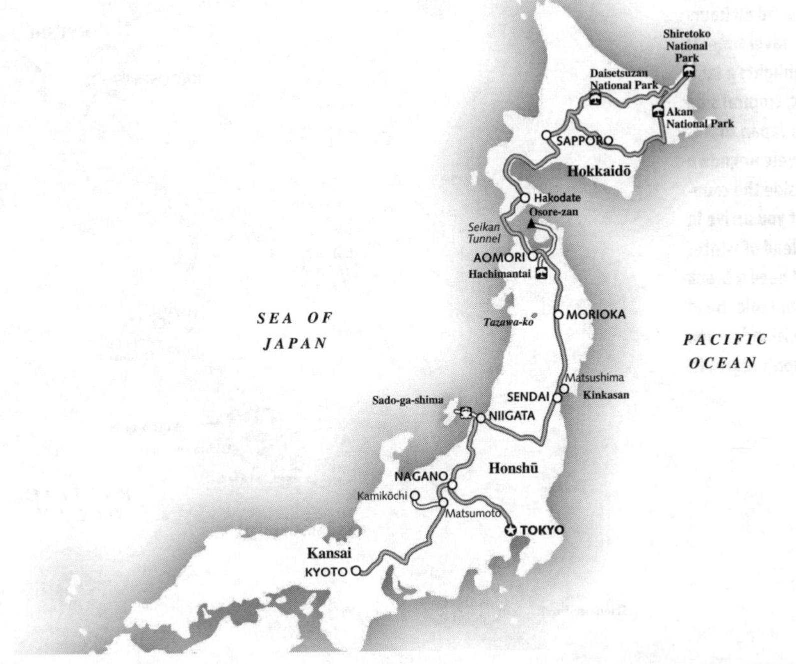

ROADS LESS TRAVELLED

ISLAND HOPPING THROUGH THE SOUTHWEST ISLANDS

Three Weeks to One month / Kyūshū to Iriomote-jima

For those with the time to explore tropical laid-back Japan, this is a great option. The route starts on the southern island of Kyūshū, in the city of **Kagoshima** (p730), where you can catch an overnight ferry to the island of **Amami-Ōshima** (p768), which has some great beaches and semitropical jungles. From Amami-Ōshima, board another ferry and head south to tiny **Yoron-tō** (p772). This little gem of an island is fringed by beaches on all sides. After a few days kicking backing on the beaches of Yoron-tō, hop on another ferry for the short ride to **Naha** (p776), on the island of Okinawa-hontō. First, check out the city for a day or two, and then take the short ferry ride out to **Kerama-shotō** (p783). Here, the tiny island of **Aka-jima** (p783) has some of the best beaches in the entire archipelago.

If you're out of time, you can fly back to the mainland from Naha; otherwise, take a flight down to **Ishigaki-jima** (p792). If you've got scuba certification and you're there between June and October, you'll want to dive the mantas. Next, hop a ferry for the quick journey to jungle-covered **Iriomote-jima** (p795), which has some incredible coral reefs around its shores. From Iriomote-jima, return to Ishigaki-jima for the flight back to the mainland.

This route takes around 60 hours of travel time. It highlights a laid-back, tropical side of Japan that is relatively unknown outside the country. If you arrive in the dead of winter and need a break from the cold, head to the islands – you won't regret it!

THE WILDS OF HOKKAIDŌ

Two Weeks to One Month / Hokkaidō

Whether you're on a JR Pass or flying directly, **Sapporo** (p583) makes a good hub for Hokkaidō excursions. A one- or two-night visit to **Hakodate** (p593) should be first on the list. Jump over to the cherry trees of **Matsumae** (p598) if you have time. Be sure to stop between Hakodate and Sapporo at **Tōya-ko** (p607), where you can soak in one of the area's many onsen (hot springs) and see Usu-zan's smouldering peak. On the route is **Shiraoi** (p614), Hokkaidō's largest Ainu living-history village. Onsen fans may wish to dip in the famed **Noboribetsu Onsen** (p609).

See romantic **Otaru** (p599), an easy day trip out of Sapporo, then head north to **Wakkanai** (p616). Take the ferry to **Rebun-tō** (p621) and check it out for a day, maybe two if you're planning on serious hiking. On the return, see **Sōya-misaki** (p617), Japan's northernmost point. Sip Otokoyama sake in **Asahikawa** (p612); from there jump to **Asahidake Onsen** (p626), and hike around **Daisetsuzan National Park** (p625) for a day or two, possibly doing a day trip to the lavender fields of **Furano** (p623) or **Biei** (p622).

Head to **Abashiri** (p630). Rent a car there or in **Shari** (p639) if you're planning on going to **Shiretoko National Park** (p639). Do the entire eastern part of the island by car. Not including hiking or other stops this will take one night and two days. Check out **Nemuro** (p638) and return your four-wheeled steed in **Kushiro** (p637).

Watch cranes, deer and other wildlife in **Kushiro Shitsugen National Park** (p637), zip up to **Akan National Park** (p632) to see **Mashū-ko** (p634), the most beautiful lake in Japan, and then toodle back towards Sapporo.

This route, which involves around 40 hours of travel, is popular as it allows you to do what you have time for. Use Sapporo as a hub and do day trips or overnight to nearby attractions, then loop out eastward, renting a car for the most remote regions.

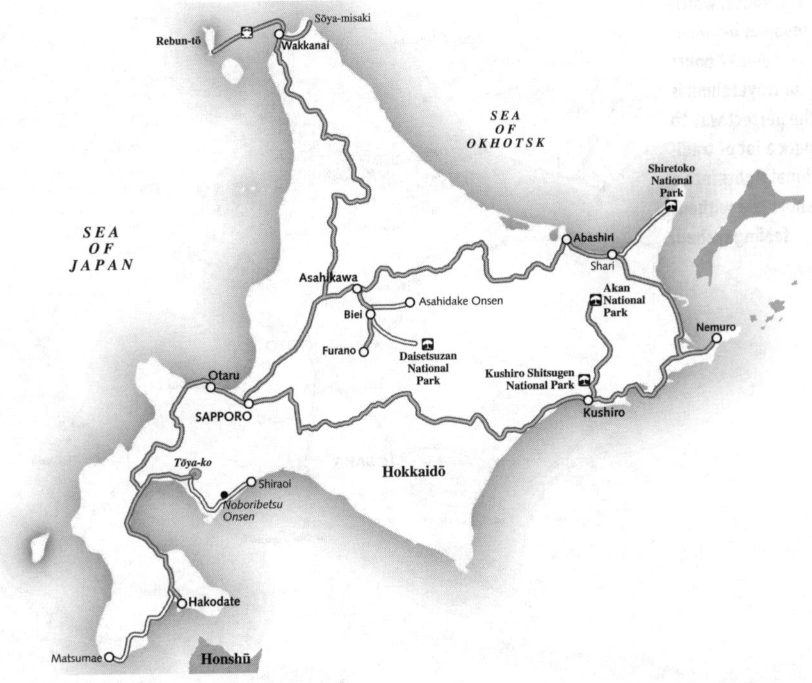

KANSAI IN DEPTH

One to Two Weeks / Kansai

Kansai (p323) contains the thickest concentration of must-see sights in all of Japan. If you want to see a lot of traditional Japanese sights without spending a lot of time in transit, then spending your entire trip in Kansai is a great idea.

Kyoto (p324) is the obvious place to base yourself; it's central and it's got a wide range of excellent accommodation, not to mention the nation's finest temples, gardens and shrines. Spend a day exploring the **Higashiyama Area** (p349), followed by another day strolling through the bamboo groves of **Arashiyama** (p359). Then, hop on a train for a day trip to **Nara** (p417) to see the sights of **Nara-kōen** (p420), including **Tōdai-ji** (p421), with its enormous Buddha figure. Another day trip to see **Ise-jingū** (p443), in the town of Ise, is highly recommended – the ride is quite scenic and the shrine is awe-inspiring.

If you've got the urge to see the modern side of Japan, **Osaka** (p391) is only about 30 minutes by train from Kyoto, and you can combine it with a trip west to see the fantastic castle in **Himeji** (p414). Finally, if you really want to wind down and relax, an overnight trip up to the onsen town of **Kinosaki** (p388) is the perfect way to round off your Kansai experience.

This route, which involves between four and 12 hours of travel time, is the perfect way to pack a lot of traditional sights into a short trip without feeling rushed.

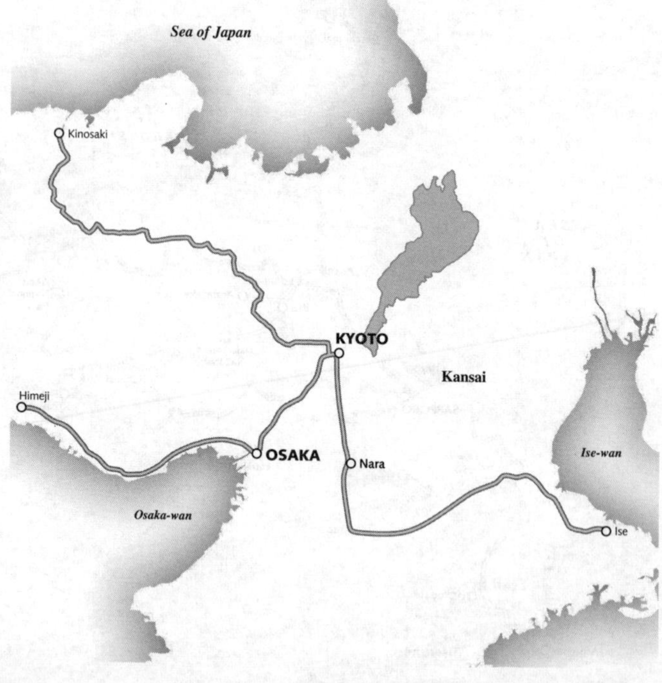

TAILORED TRIPS

FOOD-LOVER'S PARADISE

Japan is a food-lover's paradise and the cuisine runs the gamut from simple *soba* (buckwheat) noodles to multicourse *kaiseki* (haute-cuisine) banquets.

Start in **Tokyo** (p121) and make an early-morning pilgrimage to wander the expanse of **Tsukiji Fish Market** (p150), the world's largest fish market. After taking in the sights and scents of the market, head to one of the nearby sushi restaurants to sample the freshest, and surely tastiest, sushi on earth. **Kyoto** (p324) is the place to sample *kaiseki.* The fresh and seasonal food is superb and the setting is perfect: traditional buildings with lovely gardens to gaze over while you eat. Rough-and-ready locals in **Osaka** (p391) are known for their big appetites and it's hardly surprising that the city's speciality is *okonomiyaki*, savoury pancakes that you cook yourself on a griddle in front of you. The Inland Sea is known for its delectable oysters, and **Hiroshima** (p462) is the place to try them; *kaki-furai* (batter-fried) is just one of the many ways to savour them. Also try *Hiroshima-yaki*, the local version of *okonomiyaki.* **Kyūshū** (p683) is the closest of Japan's major islands to China, which may explain why it's Japan's *rāmen* (egg noodle) mecca. You'll find an incredible variety here, but the locals swear by *tonkotsu rāmen* (noodles in pork-bone broth).

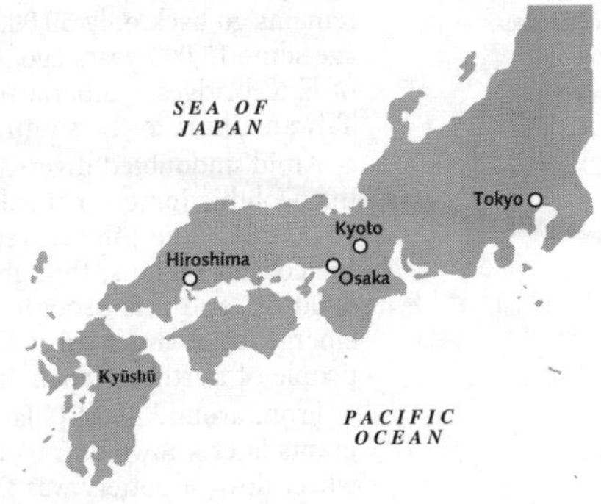

TRADITIONAL CULTURE

A route built around Japan's sublime cultural attractions is a natural choice.

Hidden among the neon and concrete of **Tokyo** (p121) you'll find historical sites, such as **Meiji-jingū** (p155) and **Sensō-ji** (p152). **Kyoto** (p324) is home to the nation's most incredible collection of temples, shrines, gardens and traditional neighbourhoods. For a peek into Japan's ancient religious traditions, a trip to the mountaintop monastery **Kōya-san** (p433) is a must. You can almost feel the power emanating from Japan's most sacred Shintō shrine, **Ise-jingū** (p443), just a day trip by express train from Kyoto. A stop in the town of **Kurashiki** (p456), with its canals and preserved buildings, is a must for those with an interest in old Japan. Head to one of Japan's most iconic sights: the 'floating' torii (Shintō shrine gate) of **Miyajima** (p469). **Izumo Taisha** (p496) in Izumo is the oldest Shintō shrine in Japan.

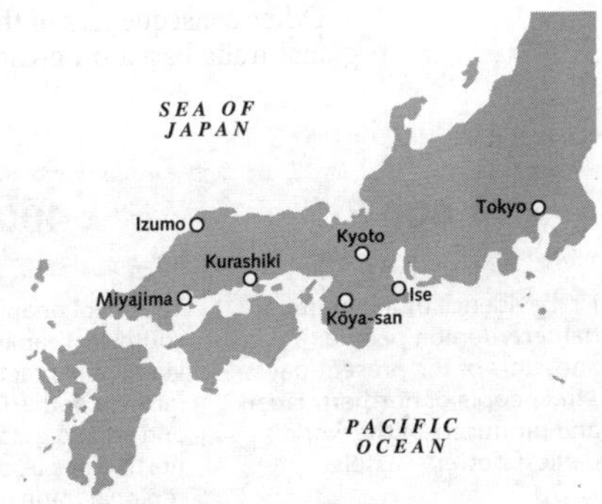

History

Ken Henshall

ANCIENT JAPAN: FROM HUNTER-GATHERERS TO DIVINE RULE

Once upon a time, two deities, the male Izanagi and the female Izanami, came down from Takamagahara (The Plains of High Heaven) to a watery world in order to create land. Droplets from Izanagi's 'spear' solidified into the land now known as Japan. Izanami and Izanagi then populated the new land with gods. One of these was Japan's supreme deity, the sun goddess Amaterasu (Light of Heaven), whose great-great-grandson Jimmu was to become the first emperor of Japan, reputedly in 660 BC.

Ken Henshall teaches Japanese Studies at the University of Canterbury, New Zealand. He is well known for his many books on Japanese history, literature, society and language.

Such is the seminal creation myth of Japan. More certainly, humans were present in Japan at least 200,000 years ago, though the earliest human remains go back only 30,000 years or so. Till around the end of the last ice age some 15,000 years ago, Japan was linked to the continent by a number of land bridges – Siberia to the north, Korea to the west, and probably Taiwan-China to the south – so access was not difficult.

Amid undoubted diversity, the first recognisable culture to emerge was the neolithic Jōmon (named after a 'rope mark' pottery style), from around 13,000 BC. The Jōmon were mostly hunter-gatherers, with a preference for coastal regions, though agriculture started to develop from around 4000 BC and this brought about greater stability in settlement and the emergence of larger tribal communities. The present-day indigenous Ainu people of northern Japan are of Jōmon descent.

From around 400 BC Japan was effectively invaded by waves of immigrants later known as Yayoi (from the site where their distinctive reddish wheel-thrown pottery was first found). They first arrived in the southwest, probably through the Korean Peninsula. Their exact origins are unknown, and may well be diverse, but they brought with them iron and bronze technology, and highly productive wet rice-farming techniques. In general they were taller and less stocky than the Jōmon – though a Chinese document from the 1st century AD nonetheless refers to Japan (by this stage quite heavily peopled by the Yayoi) as 'The Land of the Dwarfs'!

Jōmon pottery vessels dating back some 15,000 years are the oldest known pottery vessels in the world.

Opinion is divided as to the nature of Yayoi relations with the Jōmon, but the latter were gradually displaced and forced ever further north. The Yayoi had spread to the middle of Honshū by the 1st century AD, but Northern Honshū could still be considered 'Jōmon' till at least the 8th century. With the exception of the Ainu, present-day Japanese are overwhelmingly of Yayoi descent.

Other consequences of the Yayoi advent included greater intertribal/regional trade based on greater and more diverse production through new

TIMELINE

c 13,000 BC

First evidence of the hunter-gatherer Jōmon people, ancestors of the present-day Ainu people of northern Japan, and producers of the world's earliest pottery vessels.

c 400 BC

The Yayoi people appear in southwest Japan (probably via Korea), practising wet rice farming and using metal tools, and spread gradually east and north. They also promote inter-regional trade and a sense of territoriality.

3rd century AD

Queen Himiko reigns over Yamatai (Yamato) and is recognised by Chinese visitors as 'over-queen' of Japan, at that time comprising more than a hundred kingdoms. The Yamato clan's dominance continues hereafter.

technologies, but at the same time increased rivalry between tribal/regional groups, often over resources, and greater social stratification.

Agriculture-based fixed settlement led to the consolidation of territory and the establishment of boundaries. According to Chinese sources, by the end of the 1st century AD there were more than a hundred kingdoms in Japan, and by the mid-3rd century these were largely subject to an 'over-queen' named Himiko, whose own territory was known as Yamatai (later Yamato). The location of Yamatai is disputed, with some scholars favouring northwest Kyūshū, but most favouring the Nara region. The Chinese treated Himiko as sovereign of all Japan – the name Yamato eventually being applied to Japan as a whole – and for her part she acknowledged through tribute her allegiance to the Chinese emperor.

On her death in 248 she is said to have been buried – along with a hundred sacrificed slaves – in a massive barrowlike tomb known as a *kofun*, indicative of the importance of status. Other dignitaries chose burial in similar tombs, and so from this point on, till the establishment of Nara as a capital in 710, Japan is usually referred to as being in the Kofun or Yamato period.

The period saw the confirmation of the Yamato as the dominant – indeed imperial – clan in Japan. Their consolidation of power often appears to have been by negotiation and alliance with (or incorporation of) powerful potential foes. This was a practice that Japan was to continue through the ages where possible, though it was less accommodating in the case of perceived weaker foes.

The name of Japan's most famous mountain, Fuji, is an Ainu name for a god of fire.

The first verifiable emperor was Suijin (who died around 318), very likely of the Yamato clan, though some scholars think he may have been the leader of a group of 'horse-riders' who appear to have come into Japan around the start of the 4th century from the Korean Peninsula. The Kofun/Yamato period saw the adoption of writing, based on Chinese but first introduced by scholars from the Korean kingdom of Paekche in the mid-5th century. Scholars from Paekche also introduced Buddhism a century later.

Buddhism was promoted by the Yamato rulers as a means of unification and control of the land. Though Buddhism originated in India it was seen by the Japanese as a Chinese religion, and as such was one of a number of 'things Chinese' that they adopted to achieve recognition – especially by China – as a civilised country. Through emulating powerful China, Japan also hoped it too could become powerful. The desire to learn from the strongest/best is an enduring Japanese characteristic.

In 604 the regent Prince Shōtoku (573–620) enacted a constitution of 17 articles, with a very Chinese and indeed Confucianist flavour, esteeming harmony and hard work. Major Chinese-style reforms followed some decades later in 645, such as centralisation of government, nationalisation and allocation of land, and law codes. To strengthen its regime, under Emperor Temmu (r 673–86) the imperial family initiated the compilation of

c 300

Suijin is the first verifiable emperor of Japan, possibly arriving as the leader of 'horse-riders' from Korea but in any event almost certainly affiliated with the Yamato clan.

Mid-5th century

Writing, in the form of Chinese characters, is introduced into Japan by scholars from the Korean kingdom of Paekche. Using Chinese characters to express spoken Japanese leads to an extremely complex writing system.

Mid-6th century

Scholars from Paekche introduce Buddhism, the texts of which are able to be read by a now literate elite, who use it to unify and control the nation.

HISTORICAL PERIODS

Period	Date
Jōmon	c 13,000 BC–c 400 BC
Yayoi	c 400 BC–c AD 250
Kofun/Yamato	250–710
Nara	710–94
Heian	794–1185
Kamakura	1185–1333
Muromachi	1333–1568
Azuchi-Momoyama	1568–1600
Edo/Tokugawa	1600–1868
Meiji	1868–1912
Taishō	1912–26
Shōwa	1926–89
Heisei	1989–present

historical works such as the *Kojiki* (Record of Old Things; 712) and *Nihon Shoki* (Record of Japan, 720), with the aim of legitimising its power-holding through claimed divine descent. It had the desired effect and, despite a number of perilous moments, Japan continues to have the longest unbroken monarchic line in the world.

Emulation of things Chinese was not indiscriminate. For example, in China Confucianism condoned the removal of an unvirtuous ruler felt to have lost the 'mandate of heaven', but this idea was not promoted in Japan. Nor was the Chinese practice of allowing achievement of high rank through examination, for the Japanese ruling class preferred birth over merit.

Though northern Japan might be excluded at this point, in terms of factors such as effective unification, centralised government, social stratification, systematic administration, external recognition, legitimisation of power, a written constitution and a legal code, Japan, with its estimated five million people, could be said to have formed a nation-state by the early 8th century.

THE AGE OF COURTIERS

In 710 an intended permanent capital was established at Nara (Heijō), built to a Chinese grid pattern. The influence of Buddhism in those days is still seen today in the Tōdai-ji (p421), which houses a huge bronze Buddha and is the world's largest wooden building (and one of the oldest).

In 784 Emperor Kammu (r 781–806) decided to relocate the capital. His reasons are unclear, but may have related to an inauspicious series of disasters following the move to Nara, including a massive smallpox epidemic between 735 and 737 that killed as many as one-third of the population. In 794 the

Early 7th century

Japan tries to emulate China, in 604 drawing up a basic constitution, and in 645 implementing major Chinese-style policies such as centralisation of government, nationalisation of land and codification of law.

710

Japan's first intended permanent capital is established at Nara, based on Chinese models, though this is presently to be deemed inauspicious and the capital relocated. Japan is arguably a nation-state by this stage.

712 & 720

The imperial family traces its 'divine' origins, and hence legitimises its right to rule, through the compilation of two major historical works, *Kojiki* (Record of Old Things; 712) and *Nihon Shoki* (Record of Japan; 720).

capital was transferred to nearby Kyoto (Heian), newly built on a similar grid pattern. It was to remain Japan's capital for more than a thousand years – though not necessarily as the centre of actual power.

It was in Kyoto that, over the next few centuries, courtly life reached a pinnacle of refined artistic pursuits and etiquette, captured famously in the novel *Genji Monogatari* (The Tale of Genji), written by the court-lady Murasaki Shikibu around 1004. It showed a world where courtiers indulged in divertissements such as guessing flowers by their scent and building extravagant follies. On the positive side, it was a world that encouraged aesthetic sensibilities, for example, of *mono no aware* (the bitter-sweetness of things) and *okashisa* (pleasantly surprising incongruity), which were to endure right through to the present. But on the negative side, it was also a world increasingly estranged from the real one. Put bluntly, it lacked muscle. The effeteness of the court was exacerbated by the weakness of the emperors, manipulated over centuries by the intrigues of the notorious and politically powerful Fujiwara family.

The Tale of Genji, written by the court-lady Murasaki Shikibu around 1004, is widely believed to be the world's first novel.

By contrast, while the major nobles immersed themselves in courtly pleasures and/or intrigues, out in the real world of the provinces powerful military forces were developing. They were typically led by minor nobles, often sent out on behalf of court-based major nobles to carry out 'tedious' local gubernatorial and administrative duties. Some were actually distant imperial family members, barred from succession claims – a practice known as 'dynastic shedding' – and often hostile to the court. Their retainers included skilled warriors known as samurai (literally 'retainers').

The two main 'shed' families were the Minamoto (also known as Genji) and the Taira (Heike), who were basically enemies. In 1156 they were employed to assist rival claimants to headship of the Fujiwara family, though these figures soon faded into the background, for it developed into a feud between the Minamoto and the Taira.

The Taira prevailed, under Kiyomori (1118–81), who based himself in the capital and, over the next 20 years or so, fell prey to many of the vices that lurked there. In 1180, following a typical court practice, he enthroned his own two-year-old grandson, Antoku. However, a rival claimant requested the help of the Minamoto, who had regrouped under Yoritomo (1147–99) in Izu. Yoritomo was more than ready to agree.

Both Kiyomori and the claimant died very shortly afterwards, but Yoritomo, with his younger half-brother Yoshitsune (1159–89), continued the campaign against the Taira – a campaign interrupted by a pestilence during the early 1180s. By 1185 Kyoto had fallen and the Taira had been pursued to the western tip of Honshū. A naval battle ensued (at Dan-no-ura), and the Minamoto were victorious. In a well-known tragic tale, Kiyomori's widow clasped her grandson Antoku (now aged seven), and leapt with him

794

Following a series of misfortunes while the capital is at Nara, including a terrible smallpox epidemic, Japan's formal capital is relocated to Heian (present-day Kyoto), and remains there for over a thousand years.

9th–12th centuries

The court develops a high degree of cultural sophistication but becomes increasingly effete and removed from the real world. Actual power comes to lie with provincial military clans.

1156

Two major 'dynastically shed' provincial families, the Taira and the Minamoto, are employed by rival court factions and engage in bitter warfare, with the Taira prevailing under Kiyomori.

into the sea, rather than have him surrender. Minamoto Yoritomo was now the most powerful man in Japan, and was to usher in a martial age.

THE AGE OF WARRIORS

Yoritomo did not seek to become emperor, but rather to have the new emperor confer legitimacy on him through the title of shōgun (generalissimo). This was granted in 1192. Similarly, he left many existing offices and institutions in place, though often modified, and he set up his base at his home territory of Kamakura rather than Kyoto. In theory he represented merely the military arm of the emperor's government, but in practice he was in charge of government in the broad sense. His 'shōgunate' was known in Japanese as the *bakufu*, meaning the tent headquarters of a field general, though it was far from temporary. As an institution, it was to last almost 700 years.

'More ruthless power-seekers would not hesitate to kill family members they saw as threats'

The system of government now became feudal, centred on a lord-vassal system in which loyalty was a key value. It tended to be more personal and more 'familial' than medieval European feudalism, particularly in the extended *oya-ko* relationship (parent-child, in practice father-son). This 'familial hierarchy' was to become another enduring feature of Japan.

But 'families' – even actual blood families – were not always happy, and the more ruthless power-seekers would not hesitate to kill family members they saw as threats. Yoritomo himself, seemingly very suspicious by nature, killed off so many of his own family there were serious problems with the shōgunal succession upon his death in 1199 (following a fall from his horse in suspicious circumstances). One of those he had killed was his half-brother Yoshitsune, who earned an enduring place in Japanese literature and legend as the archetypical tragic hero.

Yoritomo's widow Masako (1157–1225) was a formidable figure, arranging shōgunal regents and controlling the shōgunate for much of her remaining life. Having taken religious vows on her husband's death, she became known as the 'nun shōgun' and one of the most powerful women in Japanese history. She was instrumental in ensuring that her own family, the Hōjō, replaced the Minamoto as shōguns. The Hōjō shōgunate continued to use Kamakura as the shōgunal base, and was to endure till the 1330s.

It was during their shōgunacy that the Mongols twice tried to invade, in 1274 and 1281. The Mongol empire was close to its peak at this time, under Kublai Khan (r 1260–94). After conquering Korea in 1259 he sent requests to Japan to submit to him, but these were ignored.

His expected first attack came in November 1274, allegedly with some 900 vessels carrying around 40,000 men – many of them reluctant Korean conscripts – though these figures may be exaggerated. They landed near Hakata in northwest Kyūshū and, despite spirited Japanese resistance, made progress inland. However, for unclear reasons, they presently re-

1185

The Taira are toppled by Minamoto Yoritomo, who becomes the most powerful man in the land and brings a certain unity to it. A suspicious man, he kills many of his own relatives.

1192

Yoritomo takes the title shōgun (generalissimo) from a largely puppet emperor and establishes the *bakufu* (shōgunate) in his home territory at Kamakura. This is the effective start of feudalism in Japan.

1199

Upon Yoritomo's suspicious death his formidable wife Masako – known as the 'nun shōgun' – becomes the most powerful figure in Japan, establishing her family, the Hōjō, as shōguns. The shōgunate remains based at Kamakura.

treated to their ships. Shortly afterwards a violent storm blew up and damaged around a third of the fleet, after which the remainder returned to Korea.

A more determined attempt was made seven years later, from China. Allegedly, Kublai ordered the construction of a huge fleet of 4400 warships to carry a massive force of 140,000 men – again, questionable figures. They landed once more in northwest Kyūshū, in August 1281, and again met spirited resistance, and had to retire to their vessels. Once again, the weather soon intervened, this time a typhoon, and half of their vessels were destroyed – many of which were actually designed for river use, without keels, and unable to withstand rough conditions. The survivors went back to China, and there was to be no further Mongol attempt to invade Japan.

The 'divine wind' of 1281 is said to have drowned 70,000 Mongol troops, which, if true, would make it the world's worst maritime disaster.

It was the typhoon of 1281 in particular that led to the idea of divine intervention to save Japan, with the coining of the term *shinpū* or *kamikaze* (both meaning 'divine wind'). Later this was used to refer to the Pacific War suicide pilots who, said to be infused with divine spirit, gave their lives in the cause of protecting Japan from invasion. It also led the Japanese to feel that their land was indeed the Land of the Gods.

Despite the successful defence, the Hōjō shōgunate suffered. It was unable to make a number of promised payments to those involved in repelling the Mongols, which brought considerable dissatisfaction towards it, while the payments it did make severely depleted its finances.

It was during the Hōjō shōgunacy that Zen Buddhism was brought from China. Its austerity and self-discipline appealed greatly to the warrior class, and it was also a factor in the appeal of aesthetic values such as *sabi* (elegant simplicity). More popular forms of Buddhism were the Jōdo (Pure Land) and Jōdo Shin (True Pure Land) sects, based on salvation through invocation of Amida Buddha.

Dissatisfaction towards the Hōjō shōgunate came to a head under the unusually assertive emperor Go-Daigo (1288–1339), who, after escaping from exile imposed by the Hōjō, started to muster anti-shōgunal support in Western Honshū. In 1333 the shōgunate dispatched troops to counter this, under one of its most promising generals, the young Ashikaga Takauji (1305–58). However, realising that between them he and Go-Daigo had considerable military strength, and also aware of the dissatisfaction towards the Hōjō, Takauji threw in his lot with the emperor and attacked the shōgunal offices in Kyoto. Others also soon rebelled against the shōgunate in Kamakura itself.

This was the end for the Hōjō shōgunate, but not for the shōgunal institution. Takauji wanted the title of shōgun for himself, but his ally Go-Daigo was reluctant to confer it, fearing it would weaken his own imperial power. A rift developed, and Go-Daigo sent forces to attack Takauji. However, Takauji emerged victorious, and turned on Kyoto, forcing Go-Daigo to flee into the

13th century

Zen Buddhism becomes established in Japan, especially among warriors, who admire in particular its principles of austerity and self-discipline. It also influences Japanese aesthetics. 'Mass appeal' forms of Buddhism are also established.

1274 & 1281

Under Kublai Khan the Mongols twice attempt to invade Japan, but fail due to poor planning, spirited Japanese resistance, and in particular destruction of their fleets by 'divine wind' *(shinpū or kamikaze)* typhoons.

1333

General Ashikaga Takauji, initially in alliance with the unusually assertive emperor Go-Daigo, topples the increasingly unpopular Hōjō shōgunate. Ashikaga requests the title of shōgun, but Go-Daigo is reluctant to confer it, and a rift develops.

hills of Yoshino, some 100km south of the city, where he set up a court in exile. In Kyoto, Takauji installed a puppet emperor from a rival line, who returned the favour by declaring him shōgun in 1338. Thus there were two courts in co-existence, which continued till 1392 when the 'southern court' (at Yoshino) was betrayed by Ashikaga Yoshimitsu (1358–1408), Takauji's grandson and the third Ashikaga shōgun.

Takauji set up his shōgunal base in Kyoto, at Muromachi, which gives its name to the period of the Ashikaga shōgunate. With a few exceptions, such as Takauji himself and his grandson Yoshimitsu, who among other things had Kyoto's famous Kinkaku-ji (Golden Pavilion) built, and once declared himself 'King of Japan', the Ashikaga shōguns were relatively weak. In the absence of strong centralised government and control, the country slipped increasingly into civil war as regional warlords – who came to be known as *daimyō* (big names) – vied with each other in seemingly interminable feuds and power struggles. Eventually, starting with the Ōnin War of 1467–77, the country entered a period of virtually constant civil war for the next hundred years, a time appropriately known as the Sengoku (Warring States) era.

'Presently more Portuguese and other Europeans arrived, bringing with them Christianity and firearms'

Ironically perhaps, it was during the Muromachi period that a new flourishing of the arts took place, such as in the refined nō drama, ikebana (flower arranging) and *chanoyu* (tea ceremony). Key aesthetics were *yūgen* (elegant and tranquil other-worldliness, as seen in nō), *wabi* (subdued taste), *kare* (severe and unadorned) and the earlier-mentioned *sabi*.

The later stages of the period also saw the first arrival of Europeans, specifically three Portuguese traders blown ashore on the island of Tanegashima, south of Kyūshū, in 1543. Presently more Portuguese and other Europeans arrived, bringing with them two important items, Christianity and firearms (mostly arquebuses). They found a land torn apart by warfare, ripe for conversion to Christianity – at least in the eyes of missionaries such as (St) Francis Xavier, who arrived in 1549 – while the Japanese warlords were more interested in the worldly matter of firearms.

REUNIFICATION

One of the most successful warlords to make use of firearms was Oda Nobunaga (1534–82), from what is now Aichi prefecture. Though starting from a relatively minor power base, his skilled and ruthless generalship resulted in a series of victories over rivals. In 1568 he seized Kyoto in support of the shōgunal claim of one of the Ashikaga clan (Yoshiaki), duly installed him, but then in 1573 drove him out and made his own base at Azuchi. Though he did not take the title of shōgun himself, Nobunaga was the supreme power in the land.

Noted for his brutality, he was not a man to cross. In particular he hated Buddhist priests, whom he saw as troublesome, and tolerated Christianity as

1338–92

Takauji installs a puppet emperor who names him shōgun (1338), establishing the Ashikaga shōgunate at Muromachi in Kyoto. Two rival courts and emperors exist till Go-Daigo's line is betrayed by Takauji's grandson Yoshimitsu (1392).

1400s & 1500s

Japan is in almost constant internal warfare, including the particularly fierce Ōnin War of 1467–77. The era (especially from the late 15th to late 16th centuries) is known as the Sengoku (Warring States) period.

1543

Portuguese arrive (by chance) in Japan, the first Westerners, heralding the advent of firearms and Christianity. Firearms prove popular among warlords, while Christianity has a mixed reception that is gradually to become increasingly negative.

a counterbalance to them. His ego was massive, leading him to erect a temple where he could be worshipped, and to declare his birthday a national holiday. His stated aim was 'Tenka Fubu' – 'A Unified Realm under Military Rule' – and he went some way to achieving this unification by policies such as strategic redistribution of territories among the *daimyō*, land surveys, and standardisation of weights and measures.

In 1582 he was betrayed by one of his generals and forced to commit suicide. However, the work of continuing unification was carried on by one of his generals, Toyotomi Hideyoshi (1536–98), a footsoldier who had risen through the ranks to become Nobunaga's favourite. Small and simian in his features, Nobunaga had nicknamed him Saru-chan (Little Monkey), but his huge will for power belied his physical size. He disposed of potential rivals among Nobunaga's sons, took the title of regent, continued Nobunaga's policy of territorial redistribution and also insisted that *daimyō* should surrender their families to him as hostages to be kept in Kyoto – his base being at Momoyama. He also banned weapons for all classes except samurai.

'Toyotomi Hideyoshi banned weapons for all classes except samurai'

Hideyoshi became increasingly paranoid, cruel and megalomaniacal in his later years. Messengers who gave him bad news would be sawn in half, and he had young members of his own family executed for suspected plotting. He also issued the first expulsion order of Christians (1587), whom he suspected of being an advance guard for an invasion. This order was not necessarily enforced, but in 1597 he crucified 26 Christians, of whom nine were Europeans. His grand scheme for power included a pan-Asian conquest, and as a first step he attempted an invasion of Korea in 1592, which failed amid much bloodshed. He tried again in 1597, but the campaign was abandoned when he died of illness in 1598.

On his deathbed Hideyoshi entrusted the safeguarding of the country, and the succession of his young son Hideyori (1593–1615, whom he had unexpectedly fathered late in life), to one of his ablest generals, Tokugawa Ieyasu (1542–1616). However, upon Hideyoshi's death, Ieyasu betrayed that trust. In 1600, in the Battle of Sekigahara, he defeated those who were trying to protect Hideyori, and became effectively the overlord of Japan. In 1603 his power was legitimised when the emperor conferred on him the title of shōgun. His Kantō base, the once tiny fishing village of Edo – later to be renamed Tokyo – now became the real centre of power and government in Japan.

Through these three men, by fair means or more commonly foul, the country had been reunified within three decades.

STABILITY & SECLUSION

Having secured power for the Tokugawa, Ieyasu and his successors were determined to retain it. Their basic strategy was of a linked, twofold nature: enforce the status quo and minimise potential for challenge. Orthodoxy and strict control were key elements.

1568

The warlord Oda Nobunaga seizes Kyoto and soon becomes the supreme power in the land, though he does not take the title of shōgun. He is noted for his massive ego and brutality.

1582

Nobunaga is betrayed and forced to commit suicide. Power then switches to one of his loyal generals, Toyotomi Hideyoshi, who later becomes increasingly paranoid and anti-Christian. Hideyoshi presently takes the title of regent.

1592 & 1597–98

Hideyoshi twice tries unsuccessfully to conquer Korea as part of a grand plan to control Asia, the second attempt ending after his death in 1598. The invasions seriously damage relations between Japan and Korea.

Their policies included tight control over military families in particular, such as requiring authorisation for castle-building and marriages, continuing strategic redistribution (or confiscation) of territory, and, importantly, requiring *daimyō* and their retainers to spend every second year in Edo, with their families kept there permanently as hostages. In addition, the shōgunate directly controlled ports, mines, major towns and other strategic areas. Movement was severely restricted by deliberate destruction of many bridges, the implementation of checkpoints and requirements for written travel authority, the banning of wheeled transport, the strict monitoring of potentially ocean-going vessels, and the banning of overseas travel for Japanese and even the return of those already overseas. Social movement was also banned, with society divided into four main classes: in descending order, *shi* (samurai), *nō* (farmers), *kō* (artisans) and *shō* (merchants). Detailed codes of conduct applied to each of these classes, even down to clothing, food and housing – right down to the siting of the toilet!

Christianity, though not greatly popular, threatened the authority of the shōgunate. Thus Christian missionaries were expelled in 1614. By 1638, following the bloody quelling of the Christian-led Shimabara Uprising (near Nagasaki), which saw Christianity banned and Japanese Christians – probably several hundred thousand – forced into hiding, all Westerners except the Protestant Dutch were expelled. The shōgunate found Protestantism less threatening than Catholicism – among other things it knew the Vatican could muster one of the biggest military forces in the world – and would have been prepared to let the British stay too if the Dutch, showing astute commercial one-upmanship, had not convinced it that Britain was a Catholic country. Nevertheless, the Dutch were confined geographically to a tiny trading base on the man-made island of Dejima, near Nagasaki, and numerically to just a few dozen men.

'Within the isolated and severely prescribed world of Tokugawa Japan, breach of even a trivial law could mean execution'

Thus Japan entered an era of *sakoku* (secluded country) that was to last for more than two centuries. Within the isolated and severely prescribed world of Tokugawa Japan, breach of even a trivial law could mean execution. Even mere 'rude behaviour' was a capital offence, and the definition of this was 'acting in an unexpected manner'. Punishments could be cruel, such as crucifixion, and could be meted out collectively or by proxy (for example, a village headman could be punished for the misdeed of a villager). Secret police were used to report on misdeeds.

As a result, people at large learned the importance of obedience to authority, of collective responsibility and of 'doing the right thing'. These are values still prominent in present-day Japan.

For all of the constraints there was nevertheless a considerable dynamism to the period, especially among the merchants, who as the lowest class were often ignored by the authorities and thus had relative freedom. They pros-

1600

The warlord Tokugawa Ieyasu breaks his earlier promise to the dying Hideyoshi to protect his young son and heir Hideyori, and seizes power for himself at the Battle of Sekigahara.

1603

Ieyasu formally becomes shōgun, leading to policies aimed at maintaining the status quo and minimising potential threat (including foreigners) in order to retain power for the Tokugawa. Orthodoxy and strict control are key elements.

1638

Japanese Christians are massacred by shōgunal forces in the Christian-led Shimabara Uprising. Westerners are by now expelled, except for a small Protestant Dutch presence on a tiny island off Nagasaki.

pered greatly from the services and goods required for the *daimyō* processions to and from Edo, entailing such expense that *daimyō* had to convert much of their domainal produce into cash. This boosted the economy in general.

A largely pleasure-oriented merchant culture thrived, and produced the popular kabuki drama, with its colour and stage effects. Other entertainments included *bunraku* (puppet theatre), haiku (17-syllable poems), popular novels and *ukiyo-e* (wood-block prints), often of female geisha, who came to the fore in this period. (Earlier geisha – meaning 'artistic person' – were male.)

Samurai, for their part, had no major military engagements. Well-educated, most ended up fighting mere paper wars as administrators and managers. Ironically, it was during this period of relative inactivity that the renowned samurai code of *bushidō* (way of the warrior) was formalised, largely to justify the existence of the samurai class – some 6% of the population – by portraying them as moral exemplars. Though much of it was idealism, occasionally the code was put into practice, such as the exemplary loyalty shown by the Forty-Seven Rōnin (masterless samurai) in 1701–03, who waited two years to avenge the unfair enforced suicide by seppuku (disembowelment) of their lord. After killing the man responsible, they in turn were obliged to commit seppuku.

In more general terms, Confucianism was officially encouraged with the apparent aim of reinforcing the idea of hierarchy and status quo – which was not in the best interests of women – but at the same time it encouraged learning, and along with this, literacy. By the end of the period as many as 30% of the population of 30 million were literate – far ahead of the Western norm at the time. In some opposition to the 'Chinese learning' represented by Confucianism, there was also a strong trend of nationalism, centred on Shintō and the ancient texts. This was unhelpful to the shōgunate, as it tended to focus on the primacy of the emperor. Certainly, by the early- to mid-19th century, there was considerable dissatisfaction towards the shōgunate, fanned also by corruption and incompetence among shōgunal officials.

The Japanese religion of Shintō is one of the few religions in the world to have a female sun deity, or a female supreme deity.

It is questionable how much longer the Tokugawa shōgunate and its secluded world could have continued, but as it happened, external forces were to bring about its demise.

MODERNISATION THROUGH WESTERNISATION

Since the start of the 19th century a number of Western vessels had appeared in Japanese waters. Any Westerners who dared to land, even through shipwreck, were almost always met with expulsion or even execution.

This was not acceptable to the Western powers, especially the USA, which was keen to expand its interests across the Pacific and had numerous whaling vessels in the northwest that needed regular reprovisioning. In 1853, and again the following year, US Commodore Matthew Perry steamed into Edo Bay with a show of gunships and demanded the opening of Japan for trade

1600s–1800s

The Tokugawa shōgunate is based at Edo (later renamed Tokyo). Life is tightly controlled, the nation is shut off from most of the world, and society is divided into hierarchical strata. Nonetheless, 'Edo merchant culture' emerges.

1701–03

The mass suicide of the Forty-Seven Rōnin after avenging their lord's death is seen by many as a model for samurai ethics, recently codified as *bushidō* (way of the warrior).

Early 19th century

The shōgunate's policy of national isolation comes under threat from increasing numbers of foreign whalers and other vessels entering Japanese waters. Treatment of those attempting to land, even if shipwrecked, is harsh.

SAMURAI

The prime duty of a samurai, a member of the warrior class from around the 12th century onwards, was to give faithful service to his lord. In fact, the term 'samurai' is derived from a word meaning 'to serve'. Ideally, 'service' meant being prepared to give up one's life for one's lord, though there were many ranks of samurai and, at least in the early days, it was typically only the hereditary retainers who felt such commitment. At the other end of the ranks, samurai were in effect professional mercenaries who were by no means reliable and often defected if it was to their advantage.

The renowned samurai code, *bushidō* (way of the warrior), developed over the centuries but was not formally codified till the 17th century, by which stage there were no real battles to fight. Ironically, the intention of the code appears to have been to show samurai as moral exemplars in order to counter criticism that they were parasitic. It was thus greatly idealised.

Core samurai ideals included *gaman* (endurance), *isshin* (whole-hearted commitment) and *makoto* (sincerity). Samurai were supposed to be men of Zen-like austerity who endured hardship without complaint. Chivalry among samurai was not so dominant as in Europe, and certainly not towards women, even though samurai were often highly educated and sometimes paralleled with European knights. Far from romancing women, most samurai shunned them on the grounds that sexual relations with women (who were Yin/*in*) weakened their maleness *(Yang/yō)*. Most samurai were homosexual or, in many cases, bisexual. There were actually a small number of female samurai, such as Tomoe Gozen (12th century), but they were not given formal recognition.

Warriors who for one reason or another became lordless were known as *rōnin* (wanderers or masterless samurai), acted more like brigands and were a serious social problem.

Samurai who fell from grace were generally required to commit ritual disembowelment, meant to show the purity of the soul, which was believed to reside in the stomach. Westerners typically refer to this as hara-kiri, but the Japanese prefer the term seppuku – though both mean 'stomach cutting'.

The samurai's best-known weapon was the *katana* sword, though in earlier days the bow was also prominent. Arguably the world's finest swordsmen, samurai were formidable opponents in single combat. During modernisation in the late 19th century, the government – itself comprising samurai – realised that a conscript army was more efficient as a unified fighting force, and disestablished the samurai class. However, samurai ideals such as endurance and fighting to the death were revived through propaganda prior to the Pacific War, and underlay the determination of many Japanese soldiers.

and reprovisioning. The shōgunate had little option but to accede to his demands, for it was no match for Perry's firepower. Presently an American consul arrived, and other Western powers followed suit. In a series of humiliating 'unequal treaties' Japan was obliged to give 'most favoured nation' rights to all the powers, and lost control over its own tariffs.

The humiliation of the shōgunate, the nation's supposed military protector, was capitalised on by anti-shōgunal samurai in the outer domains of Satsuma

1853–54

US Commodore Matthew Perry uses 'gunboat diplomacy' to force Japan to open up for trade and reprovisioning, bringing criticism by many Japanese towards the ineffective shōgunate.

1854–67

Opposition to the shōgunate grows, led by samurai from the Satsuma and Chōshū domains. Initially hostile to foreigners, they soon come to realise Japan's defensive limitations.

1867–68

The samurai coup known as the Meiji Restoration disestablishes the shōgunate and in theory restores imperial authority, but 15-year-old emperor Mutsuhito is a puppet, and oligarchs rule. Japan's capital moves to Edo, renamed Tokyo.

(southern Kyūshū) and Chōshū (western Honshū) in particular. A movement arose to 'revere the emperor and expel the barbarians' *(sonnō jōi)*. However, after unsuccessful skirmishing with the Western powers, the reformers realised that expelling the barbarians was not feasible, but restoring the emperor was. Their coup, known as the Meiji (Enlightened Rule) Restoration, was put into effect in late 1867 to early 1868, and the new teenage emperor Mutsuhito (1852–1912, later to be known as Meiji) found himself 'restored', following the convenient death of his stubborn father Kōmei (1831–67). After some initial resistance, the last shōgun, Yoshinobu (1837–1913), retired to Shizuoka to live out his numerous remaining years peacefully. The shōgunal base at Edo became the new imperial base, and was renamed Tokyo (Eastern Capital).

The rickshaw was not developed until 1869, following the lifting of the Tokugawa ban on wheeled transport.

Mutsuhito did as he was told by those who had restored him, though they would claim that everything was done on his behalf and with his sanction. Basically, he was the classic legitimiser. His restorers – driven by both personal ambition and genuine concern for the nation – were largely leading Satsuma/Chōshū samurai in their early 30s. The most prominent of them was Itō Hirobumi (1841–1909), who was to become prime minister on no fewer than four occasions. Fortunately for Japan, they proved a very capable oligarchy.

Japan was also fortunate in that the Western powers were distracted by richer and easier pickings in China and elsewhere and did not seriously seek to occupy or colonise Japan, though Perry does seem to have entertained such thoughts at one stage. Nevertheless, the fear of colonisation made the oligarchs act with great urgency. Far from being colonised, they themselves wanted to be colonisers, and make Japan a major power.

Under the banner of *fukoku kyōhei* (rich country, strong army), the young men who now controlled Japan decided on Westernisation as the best strategy – again showing the apparent Japanese preference for learning from a powerful potential foe. In fact, as another slogan – *oitsuke, oikose* (catch up, overtake) – suggests, they even wanted to outdo their models. Missions were sent overseas to observe a whole range of Western institutions and practices, and Western specialists were brought to Japan to advise in areas from banking to transport to mining.

The disorienting collapse of the regimented Tokugawa world produced a form of mass hysteria called Ee Ja Nai Ka (Who Cares?), with traumatised people dancing naked and giving away possessions.

In the coming decades Japan was to Westernise quite substantially, not just in material terms such as telegraphs and railways and clothing, but also, based on selected models, in the establishment of a modern banking system and economy, a legal code, a constitution and Diet, elections and political parties, and a conscript army.

Existing institutions and practices were disestablished where necessary. *Daimyō* were 'persuaded' to give their domainal land to the government in return for governorships or similar compensation, enabling the implementation of a prefectural system. The four-tier class system was scrapped, and people were now free to choose their occupation and place of residence. This included even the samurai class, phased out by 1876 to pave the way for a

1870s–early 1890s

The oligarchs implement policies of modernisation and Westernisation, such as creating a conscript army (1873), pragmatically disestablishing the samurai (1876), adopting a Western-style constitution (1889) and forming a Diet (1890).

1894–95

Japan starts a war with China, which at this stage is a weak nation and which Japan defeats in the Sino-Japanese War (1895). Japan gains Taiwan as a result, thereby starting its territorial expansion.

1902

Japan signs the Anglo-Japanese Alliance, the first-ever equal alliance between a Western and non-Western nation. This effectively means that Japan has succeeded in becoming a major power.

more efficient conscript army – though there was some armed resistance to this in 1877 under the Satsuma samurai (and oligarch) Saigō Takamori, who ended up committing seppuku when the resistance failed.

To help relations with the Western powers, the ban on Christianity was lifted, though few took advantage of it. Nevertheless, numerous Western ideologies entered the country, one of the most popular being 'self-help' philosophy. This provided a guiding principle for a population newly liberated from a world in which everything had been prescribed for them. But at the same time, too much freedom could lead to an unhelpful type of individualism. The government quickly realised that nationalism could safely and usefully harness these new energies. People were encouraged to make a success for themselves and become strong, and in doing so show the world what a successful and strong nation Japan was. Through educational policies, supported by imperial pronouncements, young people were encouraged to become strong and work for the good of the family-nation.

The government was proactive in many other measures, such as taking responsibility for establishing major industries and then selling them off at bargain rates to chosen 'government-friendly' industrial entrepreneurs – a factor in the formation of huge industrial combines known as *zaibatsu*. The government's actions in this were not really democratic, but this was typical of the day. Another example is the 'transcendental cabinet', which was not responsible to the parliament but only to the emperor, who followed his advisers, who were members of the same cabinet! Meiji Japan was outwardly democratic, but internally it retained many authoritarian features.

The salaries of the foreign specialists invited to Japan in the Meiji period are believed to have amounted to 5% of all government expenditure during the period.

The 'state-guided' economy was helped by a workforce that was well educated, obedient and numerous, as well as traditions of sophisticated commercial practices such as futures markets. In the early years, Japan's main industry was textiles and its main export silk, but later in the Meiji period, with judicious financial support from the government, it moved increasingly into manufacturing and heavy industry, becoming a major world shipbuilder by the end of the period. Improvement in agricultural technology freed up surplus farming labour to move into these manufacturing sectors.

A key element of Japan's aim to become a world power with overseas territory was the military. Following Prussian (army) and British (navy) models, Japan soon built up a formidable military force. Using the same 'gunboat diplomacy' on Korea that Perry had used on the Japanese, in 1876 Japan was able to force on Korea an unequal treaty of its own, and thereafter interfered increasingly in Korean politics. Using Chinese 'interference' in Korea as a justification, in 1894 Japan initiated a war with China – a weak nation at this stage despite its massive size – and easily emerged victorious. As a result it gained Taiwan and the Liaotung Peninsula. Russia put pressure on Japan to renounce the peninsula then a few years later occupied the peninsula itself, leaving the Japanese feeling tricked. This led to the Russo-

1904–05

Japan has an epoch-making victory over Russia in the Russo-Japanese War. Antipathy towards Russia had hardened after the Sino-Japanese War, when Russia pressured Japan into renouncing Chinese territory that Russia itself then occupied.

1910

Now free from any Russian threat, Japan formally annexes Korea, in which it had had an increasing interest since the 1870s. The international community makes no real protest.

1912

Emperor Meiji (Mutsuhito) dies, having seen Japan rise from a remote pre-industrial nation to world-power status in just half a century. His mentally disabled son Yoshihito succeeds him.

Japanese War of 1904–05, from which Japan again emerged victorious. One important benefit was Western recognition of its interests in Korea, which it proceeded to annex in 1910.

By the time of Mutsuhito's death in 1912, Japan was indeed recognised as a world power. In addition to its military victories and territorial acquisitions, in 1902 it had signed the Anglo-Japanese Alliance, the first-ever equal alliance between a Western and non-Western nation. The unequal treaties had also been rectified. Western-style structures were in place. The economy was world-ranking. The Meiji period had been a truly extraordinary half-century of modernisation. But where to now?

GROWING DISSATISFACTION WITH THE WEST

Mutsuhito was succeeded by his son Yoshihito (Taishō), who suffered mental deterioration that led to his own son Hirohito (1901–89) becoming regent in 1921.

On the one hand, the Taishō period (Great Righteousness; 1912–26) saw continued democratisation, with a more liberal line, the extension of the right to vote and a stress on diplomacy. Through WWI Japan was able to benefit economically from the reduced presence of the Western powers, and also politically, for it was allied with Britain (though with little actual involvement) and was able to occupy German possessions in East Asia and the Pacific. On the other hand, using that same reduced Western presence, Japan aggressively sought in 1915 to gain effective control of China with its notorious 'Twenty-One Demands', which were eventually modified.

In Japan at this time there was a growing sense of dissatisfaction towards the West, and a sense of unfair treatment. The Washington Conference of 1921–22 set naval ratios of three capital ships for Japan to five US and five British, which upset the Japanese despite being well ahead of France's 1.75. Around the same time a racial equality clause that Japan proposed to the newly formed League of Nations was rejected. And in 1924 the USA introduced race-based immigration policies that effectively targeted Japanese.

This dissatisfaction was to intensify in the Shōwa period (Illustrious Peace), which started in 1926 with the death of Yoshihito and the formal accession of Hirohito. He was not a strong emperor, and was unable to curb the rising power of the military, who pointed to the growing gap between urban and rural living standards and accused politicians and big businessmen of corruption. The situation was not helped by repercussions from the Great Depression in the late 1920s. For many Japanese it would seem that the ultimate cause of these troubles was the West, with its excessive individualism and liberalism. According to the militarists, Japan needed to look after its own interests, which in extended form meant a resource-rich, Japan-controlled Greater East Asia Co-Prosperity Sphere that even included Australia and New Zealand.

Until it was occupied by the USA and other Allies following WWII, Japan (as a nation) had never been conquered or occupied by a foreign power.

1914–15

Japan utilises the involvement of many Western countries in WWI in Europe to occupy German territory in the Pacific in 1914 (legitimately, as Britain's ally) and in 1915 to aggressively present China with the 'Twenty-One Demands'.

1920s

Japan becomes increasingly disillusioned with much of the West, feeling unfairly treated, such as in the Washington Conference naval ratios (1921–22) and the USA's immigration policies in 1924.

1931

Increasingly defiant of the West, Japan invades Manchuria on a pretext, and withdraws dramatically from the League of Nations after criticism from it. Japan's behaviour becomes more aggressive.

In 1931 Japan invaded Manchuria on a pretext, and presently set up a puppet government. When the League of Nations objected, Japan promptly left the league. It soon turned its attention to China, and in 1937 launched a brutal invasion that saw atrocities such as the notorious Nanjing Massacre of December that year. Casualty figures for Chinese civilians at Nanjing vary between 20,000 (some Japanese sources) and 340,000 (some Chinese sources). Many of the tortures, rapes and murders were filmed and are undeniable, but persistent (though not universal) Japanese attempts to downplay this and other massacres in Asia remain a stumbling block in Japan's relations with many Asian nations, even today.

Japan did not reject all Western nations, however, for it admired the new regimes in Germany and Italy, and in 1940 entered into a tripartite pact with them. This gave it confidence to expand further in Southeast Asia, principally seeking oil, for which it was heavily dependent on US exports. However, the alliance was not to lead to much cooperation, and since Hitler was openly talking of the Japanese as *untermenschen* (lesser beings) and the 'Yellow Peril', Japan was never sure of Germany's commitment. The USA was increasingly concerned about Japan's aggression and applied sanctions. Diplomacy failed, and war seemed inevitable. The USA planned to make the first strike, covertly, through the China-based Flying Tigers (Plan JB355), but there was a delay in assembling an appropriate strike force.

Books and films such as *Letters from Iwo Jima* and *Memoirs of a Geisha* help provide realistic historical context and an increased understanding of other eras and cultures.

So it was that the Japanese struck at Pearl Harbor on 7 December 1941, damaging much of the USA's Pacific Fleet and allegedly catching the USA by surprise, though some scholars believe Roosevelt and others deliberately allowed the attack to happen in order to overcome isolationist sentiment and bring the USA into the war against Japan's ally Germany. Whatever the reality, the USA certainly underestimated Japan and its fierce commitment, which led rapidly to widespread occupation of Pacific islands and parts of continental Asia. Most scholars agree that Japan never expected to beat the USA, but hoped to bring it to the negotiating table and emerge better off.

The tide started to turn against Japan from the Battle of Midway in June 1942, which saw the destruction of much of Japan's carrier fleet. Basically, Japan had overextended itself, and over the next three years was subjected to an island-hopping counter-attack under General Douglas MacArthur. By mid-1945 the Japanese, ignoring the Potsdam Declaration calling for unconditional surrender, were preparing for a final Allied assault on their homelands. On 6 August the world's first atomic bomb was dropped on Hiroshima, with 90,000 civilian deaths. On the 8th, Russia, which Japan had hoped might mediate, declared war. On the 9th another atomic bomb was dropped, on Nagasaki, with another 75,000 deaths. The situation prompted the emperor to formally announce surrender on 15 August. Hirohito prob-

1937

During its attempted occupation of China, Japan perpetrates one of the world's greatest atrocities at Nanjing, torturing and killing around 250,000 people, mostly innocent civilians.

1941

Japan enters WWII by striking Pearl Harbor on 7 December, with no prior warning, destroying much of the USA's Pacific Fleet and thereby bringing the USA into the War.

1942

After early successes, Japan's expansion is thwarted at the Battle of Midway in June, with significant carrier loss. From this point on Japan is largely 'on the back foot'.

ably knew what the bombs were, for Japanese scientists were working on their own atomic bomb, and seem to have had both sufficient expertise and resources, though their state of progress is unclear.

RECOVERY & BEYOND

Following Japan's defeat, a largely US occupation began under General MacArthur. It was benign and constructive, with the twin aims of demilitarisation and democratisation, and with a broader view of making Japan an Americanised bastion against communism in the region. To the puzzlement of many Japanese, Hirohito was not tried as a war criminal but was retained as emperor. This was largely for reasons of expediency, to facilitate and legitimise reconstruction – and with it US policy. It was Americans who drafted Japan's new constitution, with its famous 'no war' clause. US aid was very helpful to the rebuilding of the economy, and so too were procurements from the Korean War of 1950–53. The occupation ended in 1952, though Okinawa was not returned until 1972 and is still home to US military bases. Japan still supports US policy in many regards, such as in amending the law to allow (noncombatant) troops to be sent to Iraq.

The Japanese responded extremely positively in rebuilding their nation, urged on by a comment from the postwar prime minister Yoshida Shigeru that Japan had lost the war but would win the peace. Certainly, in economic terms, through close cooperation between a stable government and well-organised industry, and a sincere nationwide determination to become 'Number One', by the 1970s Japan had effectively achieved this and become an economic superpower, with its 'economic miracle' the subject of admiration and study around the world. Even the Oil Shocks of 1973 and 1979 did not cause serious setback.

The Yamato dynasty is the longest unbroken monarchy in the world, and Hirohito's reign from 1926 to 1989 the longest of any monarch in Japan.

By the late 1980s Japan was by some criteria the richest nation on the planet, of which it occupied a mere 0.3% in terms of area but 16% in terms of economic might and an incredible 60% in terms of real-estate value. Some major Japanese companies had more wealth than many nations' entire GNP.

Hirohito died in January 1989, succeeded by his son Akihito and the new Heisei (Full Peace) period, and he must have ended his extraordinarily eventful life happy at his nation's economic supremacy.

The so-called 'Bubble Economy' may have seemed unstoppable, but the laws of economics eventually prevailed and in the early 1990s it burst from within, having grown beyond a sustainable base. Though Japan was to remain an economic superpower, the consequences were nevertheless severe. Economically, Japan entered a recession of some 10 years, which saw almost zero growth in real terms, plummeting land prices, increased unemployment and even dismissal of managers

1945

After intensive firebombing of Tokyo in March, on 6 August Hiroshima becomes the first-ever victim of an atomic bombing, followed on 9 August by another bombing on Nagasaki, leading Hirohito to announce surrender on 15 August.

1945–52

Japan experiences a US-led occupation, the constructive policies of which revive Japanese morale and facilitate a remarkable and rapid economic recovery. Hirohito is spared from prosecution as a war criminal, puzzling many Japanese.

1970s & 1980s

Japan is widely seen as having achieved an economic miracle and is admired as a model economic superpower, though its 'Bubble Economy' of the late 1980s is seen as fragile and becomes a cause for concern.

who had believed they were guaranteed 'lifetime' employment. Socially, the impact was even greater. The public, whose lives were often based around corporations and assumed economic growth, were disoriented by the effective collapse of corporatism and the economy. Many felt deracinated, confused and even betrayed, their values shaken. In 1993 the Liberal Democratic Party, in power since 1955, found itself out of office, though it soon recovered its position as a sort of resigned apathy seemed to set in among the public.

The situation was not helped by two events in 1995. In January the Kōbe Earthquake struck, killing over 5000 people and earning the government serious criticism for failure to respond promptly and effectively. A few months later the sarin gas subway attack by the AUM religious group killed 12 and injured thousands. Many people, such as the influential novelist Murakami Haruki, saw the ability of this bizarre cult to attract intelligent members as a manifestation of widespread anxiety in Japan, where people had suddenly experienced the collapse of core values and beliefs, and were now left on their own – a situation postmodernists term 'the collapse of the Grand Narrative'.

The collapse of corporatism is reflected in increasing numbers of *freeters* (free arbeiters), who do not commit to any one company but move around in employment, and 'neets' (not in employment or education or training). More people are now seeking their own way in life, which has resulted in greater diversity and more obvious emergence of individuality. On the one hand, this has led to greater extremes of self-expression, as shown by young people and their 'way-out' clothes, hairstyles and hair colour. On the other hand, there is greater 'Western-style' awareness of the rights of the individual, as seen in the recently introduced privacy and official information laws. Direct control by government has also loosened, as seen in the 2004 corporatisation of universities.

'Japan is the world's most rapidly ageing society, with its elderly comprising 21% of the population'

The economy started to recover from around 2002, in part thanks to increased demand from China, and steadied around the 2% to 3% per annum growth mark. The year 2002 was also marked by a successful co-hosting of the soccer World Cup with Korea. However, relations with Asian nations are still far from fully harmonious, with the continued appearance of history textbooks that downplay atrocities such as the Nanjing Massacre, and with controversial visits by Prime Minister Koizumi Junichirō (in office from 2001 to 2006) to Yasukuni Shrine to honour Japanese war dead, including war criminals.

There are other worries for Japan. One is that it is the world's most rapidly ageing society, with the birth rate declining to 1.3 per woman, and with its elderly (65 years plus) comprising 21% of the population while its children (up to 15 years) comprise just 13%. This has serious ramifications economically as well as socially, with a growing ratio of supported to supporter, and increased

1989

Controversial Emperor Hirohito (posthumously Emperor Shōwa) dies after reigning 63 years, and his son Akihito succeeds him, the new reign name being Heisei. This translates literally as 'Full Peace', seemingly in contrast to Hirohito's reign.

1990s–early 2000s

After its 'Bubble Economy' bursts in the early 1990s, Japan enters a decade of economic recession that erodes corporate loyalties and brings about a reorientation of values, including a more 'Western' idea of individual rights.

1995

On 17 January an earthquake with a magnitude of 7.2 hits Kōbe, killing over 5000 people. A few months later the AUM religious group is responsible for a sarin gas attack that kills 12 and injures thousands in a Tokyo subway.

pension and health costs. Along with many ageing Western nations, Japan is doing its best (for example, by introducing nursing insurance schemes), but there is no easy solution in sight, and there are calls to redefine 'elderly' (and concomitant retirement expectations) as 75 years of age rather than 65.

Other social concerns include juvenile crime and a growing problem of social anxiety disorder in young people that can lead to *hikikomori* (withdrawal) from everyday life.

Economically, Japan was hit by the global financial collapse that started in 2008, with its share market losing a third of its value and Toyota announcing its first-ever loss in its 70-year history. Politically, after Koizumi stepped down in September 2006, Japan has had a rapid turnover of prime ministers, with Abe Shinzō and Fukuda Yasuo each resigning after a year. In September 2008 Asō Tarō assumed office, though some feared he was too traditionalist to steer Japan forward. Then on 31 August 2009, the Liberal Democratic Party was ousted for the first time in 54 years. Asō Tarō was replaced by the leader of the successful Democratic Party of Japan, Hatoyama Yukio, who has already signalled a less close relationship with the United States.

Internationally, despite criticism for continued whaling and other issues, contemporary Japan is widely respected in the world. Its cultural exports are popular worldwide, especially its manga (comics) and anime among younger people, and it is seen as a world trendsetter.

2002

Japan's economy starts a sustained recovery, and Japan successfully co-hosts the soccer World Cup with Korea. However, problems such as a rapidly ageing society and less than fully harmonious relations with other Asian nations still remain.

2006

Prince Hisahito is born on 6 September, and is third in line for the throne under current succession laws. His birth makes him the first male child born to the Japanese imperial family since 1965.

2008–09

Japan is hit by the global recession, its share market tumbling and Toyota announcing its first-ever loss. A rapid turnover of prime ministers since 2006 does not bode well for facing a major crisis.

The Culture

THE NATIONAL PSYCHE

The uniqueness and peculiarity of 'the Japanese' is a favourite topic of both Western observers and the Japanese themselves. It's worth starting any discussion of 'the Japanese' by noting that there is no such thing as 'the Japanese'. Rather, there are 127 million individuals in Japan with their own unique characters, interests and habits. And despite popular stereotypes to the contrary, the Japanese are as varied as any people on earth. Just as importantly, Japanese people have more in common with the rest of humanity than they have differences.

Why then the pervasive images of the Japanese as inscrutable or even bizarre? These stereotypes are largely rooted in language: few Japanese are able to speak English as well as, say, your average Singaporean, Hong Kong Chinese or well-educated Indian, not to mention most Europeans. This difficulty with English is largely rooted in the country's appalling English education system, and is compounded by a natural shyness, a perfectionist streak and the nature of the Japanese language itself, which contains fewer sounds than any other major world language (making pronunciation of other languages difficult). Thus, what appears to the casual observer to be a maddening inscrutability is more likely just an inability to communicate effectively. Outsiders who become fluent in Japanese discover a people whose thoughts and feelings are surprisingly – almost boringly – similar to those of folks in other developed nations.

Of course, myths of Japanese uniqueness are quite useful to certain elements of Japanese society, to whom Japanese uniqueness is evidence of Japanese racial superiority. Among this small minority are writers of a class of books known as Nihonjiron (studies of the Japanese people), which contain absurd claims about the Japanese (including the claim that Japanese brains work differently to other people's, and even that Japanese have longer intestines than other races). Some of these beliefs have made headway in general Japanese society, but most well-educated Japanese pay little mind to these essentially racist and unscientific views.

'For almost all of its history, Japan has been a strictly hierarchical place'

All this said, the Japanese do have certain characteristics that reflect their unique history and interaction with their environment. The best way to understand how most modern Japanese people think is to look at these influences. First, Japan is an island nation. Second, until WWII, Japan was never conquered by an outside power, nor was it heavily influenced by Christian missionaries. Third, until the beginning of last century, the majority of Japanese lived in close-knit rural farming communities. Fourth, most of Japan is covered in steep mountains, so the few flat areas of the country are quite crowded – people literally live on top of each other. Finally, for almost all of its history, Japan has been a strictly hierarchical place, with something approximating a caste system during the Edo period.

All of this has produced a people who highly value group identity and smooth social harmony – in a tightly packed city or small farming village, there simply isn't room for colourful individualism. One of the ways harmony is preserved is by forming consensus, and concealing personal opinions and true feelings. Thus, the free-flowing exchange of ideas, debates and even heated arguments that one expects in the West are far less common in Japan. This reticence about sharing innermost thoughts perhaps contributes to the Western image of the Japanese as mysterious.

The Japanese tendency to put social harmony above individual expression is only strengthened by the country's Confucian and Buddhist heritage. The former, inherited from China, stresses duty to parents, teachers, society and ancestors before individual happiness. The latter, inherited from India by way of China, stresses the illusory nature of the self and preaches austerity in all things.

Of course, there is a lot more to the typical Japanese character than just a tendency to prize social harmony. Any visitor to the country will soon discover a people who are remarkably conscientious, meticulous, industrious, honest and technically skilled. A touching shyness and sometimes almost painful self-consciousness are also undoubted features of many Japanese as well. These characteristics result in a society that is a joy for the traveller to experience.

And let us say that any visit to Japan is a good chance to explode the myths about Japan and the Japanese. While you may imagine a nation of suit-clad conformists or inscrutable automatons, a few rounds in a local *izakaya* (pub-eatery) will quickly put all of these notions to rest. More than likely, the salaryman (white-collar worker) next to you will offer to buy you a round and then treat you to a remarkably frank discussion of Japanese politics. Or maybe he'll just bring you up to speed on how the Hanshin Tigers are going this year.

LIFESTYLE

The way most Japanese live today differs greatly from the way they lived before WWII. As the birth rate has dropped and labour demands have drawn more workers to cities, the population has become increasingly urban. At the same time, Japan continues to soak up influences from abroad and the traditional lifestyle of the country is quickly disappearing in the face of a dizzying onslaught of Western pop/material culture. These days, the average young Tokyoite has a lot more in common with her peers in Melbourne or London than she does with her grandmother back in her *furusato* (hometown).

In the City

The overwhelming majority of Japanese live in the bustling urban environments of major cities. These urbanites live famously hectic lives dominated by often-gruelling work schedules and punctuated by lengthy commutes from city centres to more affordable outlying neighbourhoods and suburbs.

Until fairly recently, the nexus of all this activity was the Japanese corporation, which provided lifetime employment to the legions of blue-suited white-collar workers, almost all of them men, who lived, worked, drank, ate and slept in the service of the companies for which they toiled. These days, as the Japanese economy makes the transition from a manufacturing economy to a service economy, the old certainties are vanishing. On the way out are Japan's famous 'cradle-to-grave' employment and age-based promotion system. Now, the recent college graduate is just as likely to become a *furitaa* (part-time worker) as he is to become a salaryman. Needless to say, all this has wide-ranging consequences for Japanese society.

Did you know that there are more than six million vending machines in Tokyo alone?

The majority of families once comprised a father who was a salaryman, a mother who was a housewife, kids who studied dutifully in order to earn a place at one of Japan's elite universities and an elderly in-law who had moved in. Though the days of this traditional model may not be completely over, it has been changing fast in recent years. As in Western countries, *tomobataraki* (both spouses working) is now increasingly common.

The kids in the family probably still study like mad: if they are in junior high, they will be working towards gaining admission to a select high school by attending a cram school, known as a *juku;* if they are already in high school, they will be working furiously towards passing university admission exams.

As for the mother- or father-in-law, who in the past would have expected to be taken care of by the eldest son in the family, she or he may have found that beliefs about filial loyalty have changed substantially since the 1980s, particularly in urban centres. Now, more and more Japanese families are sending elderly parents and in-laws to live out their 'golden years' in *rōjin hōmu* (literally 'old folks homes').

In the Country

Only one in four Japanese live in the small farming and fishing villages that dot the mountains and cling to the rugged coasts. Mass postwar emigration from these rural enclaves has doubtless changed the weave of Japanese social fabric and the texture of its landscape, as the young continue their steady flight to the city, leaving untended rice fields to slide down the hills from neglect.

Today only 15% of farming households continue to make ends meet solely through agriculture, with most rural workers holding down two or three jobs. Though this lifestyle manages to make the incomes of some country dwellers higher than those of their urban counterparts, it also speaks clearly of the crisis that many rural communities are facing in their struggle to maintain their traditional way of life.

The salvation of traditional village life may well rely on the success of the 'I-turn' (moving from urban areas to rural villages) and 'U-turn' (moving from country to city, and back again) movements. Though not wildly successful, these movements have managed to attract young people who work at home, company workers who are willing to put in a number of hours on the train commuting to the nearest city, and retirees looking to spend their golden years among the thatched roofs and rice fields that symbolise a not-so-distant past.

ECONOMY

The Japanese 'economic miracle' is one of the great success stories of the postwar period. In a few short decades, Japan went from a nation in ruins to the world's second-largest economy. The rise of the Japanese economy is even more startling when one considers Japan's almost total lack of major natural resources beyond agricultural and marine products.

'During the 1980s the Japanese economy went into overdrive, leading to a stock market bubble that abruptly burst in early 1990'

There are many reasons for Japan's incredible economic success: a hardworking populace; strong government support for industry; a strategic Pacific-rim location; infusions of cash during the Korean War (during which Japan acted as a staging point for the US military); and, some would say, protectionist trade policies. What is certain is this: when free-market capitalism was planted in the soil of postwar Japan, it was planted in extremely fertile soil.

During the 1980s the country experienced what is now known as the 'Bubble Economy'. The Japanese economy went into overdrive, with easy money supply and soaring real-estate prices leading to a stock market bubble that abruptly burst in early 1990. In the years that followed, Japan flirted with recession, and the jobless rate climbed to 5%, a surprising figure in a country that had always enjoyed near full employment.

The early years of the new millennium saw a strong economic recovery in Japan: in the last three months of 2006, the Japanese economy grew by an impressive 4.8%. There was talk that Japan had finally escaped from the curse of economic stagnation (the so-called 'lost decade').

However, it was not to last. The world economic crisis that started with the collapse of a housing and credit bubble in the USA in late 2008 had dire effects for Japan, which traditionally depended on America's spendthrift consumers to keep its factories running. Japan's exports in January 2009 fell an astonishing 46% compared with a year earlier (including a drop in exports to the USA of 53%). The results were predictable: Japan's economy contracted at an annualised rate of over 12% in the last quarter of 2008. As this book goes to press, unemployment in the country is climbing fast and Japan is running a trade deficit for the first time in years. It's too early to tell what effects this will have on the country, but one thing is certain: it's going to be a time of change for Japan.

POPULATION

Japan has a population of approximately 127 million people (the ninth-largest in the world) and, with 75% of it concentrated in urban centres, population density is extremely high. Areas such as the Tokyo–Kawasaki–Yokohama conurbation are so densely populated that they have almost ceased to be separate cities, running into each other and forming a vast coalescence that, if considered as a whole, would constitute the world's largest city.

One notable feature of Japan's population is its relative ethnic and cultural homogeneity. This is particularly striking for visitors from the USA, Australia and other multicultural nations. The main reason for this ethnic homogeneity is Japan's strict immigration laws, which have ensured that only a small number of foreigners settle in the country.

The largest non-Japanese group in the country is made up of 650,000 *zai-nichi kankoku-jin* (resident Koreans). For most outsiders, Koreans are an invisible minority. Indeed, even the Japanese themselves have no way of knowing that someone is of Korean descent if he or she adopts a Japanese name. Nevertheless, Japanese-born Koreans, who in some cases speak no language other than Japanese, were only recently released from the obligation to carry thumb-printed ID cards at all times, and some still face discrimination in the workplace and other aspects of their daily lives.

Aside from Koreans, most foreigners in Japan are temporary workers from China, Southeast Asia, South America and Western countries. Indigenous groups such as the Ainu have been reduced to very small numbers, due to intermarriage with non-Ainu and government attempts to hasten assimilation of Ainu into general Japanese society. At present, Ainu are concentrated mostly in Hokkaidō, the northernmost of Japan's main islands.

The most notable feature of Japan's population is the fact that it is shrinking. Japan's astonishingly low birth rate of 1.3 births per woman is among the lowest in the developed world and Japan is rapidly becoming a nation of elderly citizens. Experts say that the population began declining in 2007, and will reach 100 million in 2050 and 67 million in 2100. Needless to say, such demographic change will have a major influence on the economy in coming decades (for more information on the Japanese economy, see opposite).

Almost all Japanese babies are born with a Mongolian spot or *mōkohan* on their bottoms or lower backs. This harmless bluish-grey birthmark is composed of melanin-containing cells. Mongolian spots are common in several Asian races, including, as the name suggests, Mongolians, as well as in Native Americans. These birthmarks, which usually fade by the age of five, raise interesting questions about the origins of the Japanese people.

The Ainu

The Ainu, of whom there are roughly 24,000 living in Japan, are the indigenous people of Hokkaidō and, some would argue, the only people who can claim to be natives of Japan. Due to ongoing intermarriage and assimilation, almost all Ainu consider themselves bi-ethnic. Today, fewer than 200 people in Japan can claim both parents with exclusively Ainu descent.

Burakumin

The Burakumin are a largely invisible (to outsiders, at least) group of Japanese whose ancestors performed work that brought them into contact with the contamination of death – butchering, leatherworking and the disposing of corpses. The Burakumin were the outcasts in the social hierarchy (some would say caste system) that existed during the Edo period. While the Burakumin are racially the same as other Japanese, they have traditionally been treated like an inferior people by much of Japanese society. Estimates put the number of hereditary Burakumin in present-day Japan at anywhere from 890,000 to three million.

While discrimination against Burakumin is now technically against the law, there continues to be significant discrimination against Burakumin in such important aspects of Japanese social life as work and marriage. It is common knowledge, though rarely alluded to, that information about any given individual's possible Burakumin origin is available to anyone (generally employers and prospective fathers-in-law) who is prepared to make certain discreet investigations. Many Japanese consider this a very culturally sensitive issue and may prefer to avoid discussion of this topic with foreigners.

MULTICULTURALISM

'There are about 1.9 million foreign residents registered with the Japanese government'

Like many industrialised countries, Japan attracts thousands of workers hoping for high salaries and a better life. At present, there are about 1.9 million foreign residents registered with the government (about 1.5% of the total population of Japan). Of these, 32% are Korean (for more on resident Koreans, see p59), 24% are Chinese or Taiwanese, 14% are Brazilian and 2.5% are from the USA. In addition, it has been estimated that at least another 250,000 unregistered illegal immigrants live and work in Japan.

Due to its ageing population and low birth rate (see p59), Japan is being forced to consider means to increase immigration of skilled workers, something that many Japanese oppose on the grounds that it will disrupt Japan's existing social order. In late 2008 the Japanese government initiated a program to encourage foreign nurses (mostly of Southeast Asian origin). Already critics on both sides of the issue have attacked the program, some claiming the nurses are being subjected to exploitative working conditions, others claiming that the nurses do not posses the language skills to work effectively in Japan. Whatever the case, it seems likely that Japan's reliance on foreign nurses will increase as the society ages.

MEDIA

Like all democratic countries, Japan constitutionally guarantees freedom of the press. In general, journalists do have quite a bit of freedom, though both Japanese and foreign media analysts have noted that exercise of this liberty is not always easy.

For reasons that are not completely clear, many Japanese journalists practise a form of self-censorship, often taking governmental or police reports at face value rather than conducting independent investigations that might reveal what is hidden beneath the official story. Some media analysts have speculated that this practice is symptomatic of journalists working closely, perhaps too closely, with political figures and police chiefs, who may tacitly encourage them to omit details that might conflict with official accounts. The topic of police corruption and the unwillingness of Japanese mainstream media to tackle the issue was one of the themes of director Takahashi Gen's 2006 film *Pochi no kokuhaku* (sadly, unavailable in English).

Added to the problem of self-censorship is that of exclusive press clubs, also known as *kisha* clubs. These clubs provide a privileged few with access to the halls of government. Journalists who are not members of a *kisha* club are unable to obtain key information and thus are shut out of a story. Some reporters have argued that this constitutes a form of information monopoly and have put pressure on the Japanese government to abolish the clubs.

Despite some problems with the free flow of information, the Japanese press is considered trustworthy by most people in Japan. Newspapers enjoy wide circulation, aided perhaps by the nation's incredible 99% literacy rate, and almost all households have TVs. Internet usage is also high: an estimated 87 million Japanese use the internet regularly.

RELIGION

Shintō & Buddhism

The vast majority (about 86%) of Japanese are followers of both Buddhism and Shintō, a fact puzzling to many Westerners, most of whom belong to exclusive monotheistic faiths. The Japanese are fond of saying that Shintō is the religion of this world and this life, while Buddhism is for matters of the soul and the next world. Thus, births, marriages, harvest rituals and business success are considered the province of Shintō, while funerals are exclusively Buddhist affairs. When one looks at the beliefs and metaphysics of each religion, this makes perfect sense, for Shintō is a religion that holds that gods reside in nature itself (this world), while Buddhism stresses the impermanence of the natural world.

Shintō, or 'the way of the gods', is the indigenous religion of Japan. More than a monolithic faith, Shintō is a collection of indigenous folk rituals and practices, many concerned with rice production, and wedded to ancient myths associated with the Yamato clan, the forerunners of the present-day imperial family. It is revealing that Shintō didn't even have a name until one was given to distinguish it from Japan's imported religion, Buddhism.

In Shintō there is a pantheon of gods *(kami)* who are believed to dwell in the natural world. Consisting of thousands of deities, this pantheon includes both local spirits and global gods and goddesses. Shintō gods are often enshrined in religious structures known as *jinja, jingū* or *gū* (usually translated into English as shrine; see the boxed text, p62). The greatest of these is Ise-jingū in Kansai's Mie-ken (p443), which enshrines the most celebrated Shintō deity, Amaterasu-Ōmikami, the goddess of the sun to whom the imperial family of Japan is said to trace its ancestry. At the opposite end of the spectrum,

VISITING A SHRINE

Entering a Japanese shrine can be a bewildering experience for travellers. In order to make the most of the experience, follow these guidelines and do as the Japanese do.

Just past the torii (shrine gate), you'll find a *chōzuya* (trough of water) with *hishaku* (long-handled ladles) perched on a rack above. This is for purifying yourself before entering the sacred precincts of the shrine. Some Japanese forgo this ritual and head directly for the main hall. If you choose to purify yourself, take a ladle, fill it with fresh water from the spigot, pour some over one hand, transfer the spoon and pour water over the other hand, then pour a little water into a cupped hand and rinse your mouth, spitting the water onto the ground beside the trough, *not* into the trough.

Next, head to the *haiden* (hall of worship), which sits in front of the *honden* (main hall) enshrining the *kami* (god of the shrine). Here you'll find a thick rope hanging from a gong, with an offerings box in front. Toss a coin into the box, ring the gong by pulling on the rope (to summon the deity), pray, then clap your hands twice, bow and back away from the shrine. Some Japanese believe that a ¥5 coin is the best for an offering at a temple or shrine, and that the luck engendered by the offering of a ¥10 coin will come further in the future (since 10 can be pronounced *tō* in Japanese, which can mean 'far').

If photography is forbidden at a shrine, it will be posted as such; otherwise, it is permitted and you should simply use your discretion when taking photos.

TEMPLE OR SHRINE?

One of the best ways to distinguish a Buddhist temple from a Shintō shrine is to examine the entrance. The main entrance of a shrine is a torii (shrine gate), usually composed of two upright pillars, joined at the top by two horizontal cross-bars, the upper of which is normally slightly curved. Torii are often painted a bright vermilion, though some are left as bare wood. In contrast, the main entrance gate *(mon)* of a temple is often a much more substantial affair, constructed of several pillars or casements, joined at the top by a multitiered roof, around which there may even be walkways. Temple gates often contain guardian figures, usually Niō (deva kings). Keep in mind, though, that shrines and temples sometimes share the same precincts, and it is not always easy to tell where one begins and the other ends.

you may come across waterfalls, trees or rocks decorated with a sacred rope (known as a *shimenawa*), which essentially declares that these things contain *kami* (and makes them natural shrines in their own right).

In contrast to Shintō, which evolved with the Japanese people, Buddhism arrived from India via China and Korea sometime in the 6th century AD. For most of its history, it has coexisted peacefully with Shintō (the notable exception being the WWII period, during which Buddhism was suppressed as a foreign import). Buddhism, which originated in southern Nepal in the 5th century BC, is sometimes said to be more of a way or method than a religion, since, strictly speaking, there is no god in Buddhism. In practice, the various forms of Buddha and bodhisattvas (beings who have put off entering nirvana to help all other sentient beings enter nirvana) are worshipped like gods in most branches of Buddhism, at least by laypeople.

There are three sacred regalia in Shintō: the sacred mirror (stored in Mie-ken's Ise-jingū; p443), the sacred sword (stored near Nagoya in Atsuta-jingū; p255) and the sacred beads (stored in the Imperial Palace in Tokyo; p127). Some speculate that the sacred treasures were brought over by the continental forerunners of the Yamato clan.

The four noble truths of Buddhism are as follows: 1) life is suffering; 2) the cause of suffering is desire; 3) the cure for suffering is the elimination of desire; and 4) the way to eliminate desire is to follow the Eightfold Path of the Buddha. Thus, Buddhism can be thought of as an operating manual for the human mind when faced with the problem of existence in an impermanent world.

All of the main sects of Japanese Buddhism belong to the Mahayana (Greater Vehicle) strain of Buddhism, which is distinguished from Theravada (Lesser Vehicle) Buddhism by its faith in bodhisattvas. The major sects of Japanese Buddhism include Zen, Tendai, Esoteric, Pure Land and True Pure Land Buddhism. The religious structure in Buddhism is known as a *tera, dera, ji* or *in* (temple; see the boxed text, above).

WOMEN IN JAPAN

Traditional Japanese society restricted the woman's role to the home, where as housekeeper she wielded considerable power, overseeing all financial matters, monitoring the children's education and, in some ways, acting as the head of the household. Even in the early Meiji period, however, the ideal was rarely matched by reality: labour shortfalls often resulted in women taking on factory work, and even before that, women often worked side by side with men in the fields.

As might be expected, the contemporary situation is complex. There are, of course, those who stick to established roles. They tend to opt for shorter college courses, often at women's colleges, and see education as an asset in the marriage market. Once married, they leave the role of breadwinner to their husbands.

Increasingly, however, Japanese women are choosing to forgo or delay marriage in favour of pursuing their own career ambitions. Of course, changing aspirations do not necessarily translate into changing realities, and Japanese women are still significantly underrepresented in upper management and political positions, and there is a disproportionately high number of females employed as OLs (office ladies). Part of the reason for this is the prevalence of gender discrimination in Japanese companies. Societal expectations, however, also play a role: Japanese women are often forced to choose between having a career and having a family. Not only do most companies refuse to hire women for career-track positions, many Japanese men are simply not interested in having a career-woman as a spouse. This makes it very intimidating for a Japanese woman to step out of her traditional gender role and follow a career path.

In 2008 the number of *maiko* (apprentice geisha) in Kyoto topped 100 for the first time in four decades.

Those women who do choose full-time work suffer from one of the worst gender wage gaps in the developed world: Japanese women earn only 66% of what Japanese men earn, compared to 76% in the USA, 83% in the UK and 85% in Australia (according to figures released by the respective governments). In politics, the situation is even worse: Japanese women hold only 10% of seats in the Diet, the nation's governing body.

ARTS

Contemporary Visual Art

In the years that followed WWII, Japanese artists struggled with issues of identity. This was the generation who grappled with duelling philosophies: 'Japanese spirit, Japanese knowledge' versus 'Japanese spirit, Western knowledge'. This group was known for exploring whether Western artistic media and methods could convey the space, light, substance and shadows of the Japanese spirit, or if this essence could only truly be expressed through traditional Japanese artistic genres.

Today's emerging artists and the movements they have generated have no such ambivalence. Gone is the anxiety about coopting, or being coopted by, Western philosophies and aesthetics; in its place is the insouciant celebration of the smooth, cool surface of the future articulated by fantastic colours and shapes. This exuberant, devil-may-care aesthetic is most notably represented by Takashi Murakami, whose work derives much of its energy from *otaku,* the geek culture that worships characters that figure prominently in manga, Japan's ubiquitous comic books (see the boxed text, p349). Murakami's spirited, prankish images and installations have become emblematic of the Japanese aesthetic known as *poku* (a concept that combines pop art with an *otaku* sensibility), and his *Super Flat Manifesto,* which declares that 'the world of the future might be like Japan is today – super flat', can be seen as a primer for contemporary Japanese pop aesthetics.

Beyond the pop scene, artists continue to create works whose textures and topics relay a world that is broader than the frames of a comic book. Three notable artists to look for are Yoshie Sakai, whose ethereal oil paintings, replete with pastel skies and deep waters, leave the viewer unsure whether they are floating or sinking; Noriko Ambe, whose sculptural works with paper can resemble sand dunes shifting in the Sahara, or your high-school biology textbook; and the indomitable Hisashi Tenmyouya, whose work chronicles the themes of contemporary Japanese life, echoing the flat surfaces and deep impressions of wood-block prints while singing a song of the street.

Traditional Visual Art

PAINTING

From 794 to 1600, Japanese painting borrowed from Chinese and Western techniques and media, ultimately transforming them into its own aesthetic ends. By the beginning of the Edo period (1600–1868), which was marked by the enthusiastic patronage of a wide range of painting styles, Japanese art had come completely into its own. The Kanō school, initiated more than a century before the beginning of the Edo era, continued to be in demand for its depiction of subjects connected with Confucianism, mythical Chinese creatures or scenes from nature. The Tosa school, which followed the *yamato-e* style of painting (often used on scrolls during the Heian period, 794–1185), was also kept busy with commissions from the nobility, who were eager to see scenes re-created from classics of Japanese literature.

The screen paintings of Hasegawa Tohaku, painted almost 400 years ago, are said to be the first examples of impressionist art.

The Rimpa school (from 1600) not only absorbed the styles of painting that had preceded it, but progressed beyond well-worn conventions to produce a strikingly decorative and delicately shaded form of painting. The works of art produced by a trio of outstanding artists from this school – Tawaraya Sōtatsu, Hon'ami Kōetsu and Ogata Kōrin – rank among the finest of this period.

CALLIGRAPHY

Shodō (the way of writing) is one of Japan's most valued arts, cultivated by nobles, priests and samurai alike, and still studied by Japanese schoolchildren today as *shūji*. Like the characters of the Japanese language, the art of *shodō* was imported from China. In the Heian period, a fluid, cursive, distinctly Japanese style of *shodō* evolved that was called *wayō,* though the Chinese style remained popular in Japan among Zen priests and the literati for some time.

In both Chinese and Japanese *shodō* there are three important types. Most common is *kaisho,* or block-style script. Due to its clarity, this style is favoured in the media and in applications where readability is key. *Gyōsho,* or running hand, is semicursive, and often used in informal correspondence. *Sōsho,* or grass hand, is a truly cursive style. *Sōsho* abbreviates and links the characters together to create a flowing, graceful effect.

UKIYO-E (WOOD-BLOCK PRINTS)

The term *ukiyo-e* means 'pictures of the floating world' and derives from a Buddhist metaphor for the transient world of fleeting pleasures. The subjects chosen by artists for these wood-block prints were characters and scenes from the tawdry, vivacious 'floating world' of the entertainment quarters in Edo (latter-day Tokyo), Kyoto and Osaka.

The floating world, centred on pleasure districts, such as Edo's Yoshiwara, was a topsy-turvy kingdom, an inversion of the usual social hierarchies that were held in place by the power of the Tokugawa shōgunate. Here, money meant more than rank, actors and artists were the arbiters of style, and prostitutes elevated their art to such a level that their accomplishments matched those of the women of noble families.

The vivid colours, novel composition and flowing lines of *ukiyo-e* caused great excitement in the West, sparking a vogue that one French art critic dubbed 'Japonisme'. *Ukiyo-e* became a key influence on impressionists (for example, Toulouse-Lautrec, Manet and Degas) and postimpressionists. Among the Japanese the prints were hardly given more than passing consideration – millions were produced annually in Edo. They were often thrown away or used as wrapping paper for pottery. For many years, the Japanese continued to be perplexed by the keen interest foreigners took in this art form, which they considered of ephemeral value.

CERAMICS

Ceramics are Japan's oldest art form: Jōmon pottery, with its distinctive cord-like decorative patterns, has been dated back some 15,000 years. When the Jōmon people were displaced by the Yayoi people, starting around 400 BC, a more refined style of pottery appeared on the scene. While Jōmon pottery

FAMOUS CERAMIC CENTRES

The suffix '*-yaki*' denotes a type of pottery. Thus, the term 'Bizen-yaki' refers to a type of pottery made in the Bizen area of Western Honshū. Some of Japan's main ceramic centres include the following:

Arita-yaki Known in the West as Imari, this colourful pottery is produced in the town of Arita (p700), in Kyūshū.

Bizen-yaki The ancient ceramics centre of Bizen (p454) in Okayama-ken, Western Honshū, is famed for its solid unglazed bowls, which turn red through oxidation. Bizen also produces roofing tiles.

Hagi-yaki The town of Hagi (p486) in Western Honshū is renowned for Hagi-yaki, a type of porcelain made with a pallid yellow or pinkish, crackled glaze.

Karatsu-yaki Karatsu (p698), near Fukuoka in northern Kyūshū, produces tea-ceremony utensils that are Korean in style and have a characteristic greyish, crackled glaze.

Kiyomizu-yaki The approach road to the temple Kiyomizu-dera (p350), in Kyoto, is lined with shops selling Kiyomizu-yaki, a style of pottery that can be enamelled, blue-painted or red-painted in appearance.

Kutani-yaki The porcelain from Ishikawa-ken (p312), in Central Honshū, is usually usually green or painted with five distinctive colours.

Satsuma-yaki The most common style of this porcelain, from Kagoshima (p730) in Kyūshū, has a cloudy white, crackled glaze enamelled with gold, red, green and blue.

was an indigenous Japanese form, Yayoi pottery had clear continental influences and techniques. Continental techniques and even artisans continued to dominate Japanese ceramic arts for the next millennia or more: around the 5th century AD, Sue Ware pottery was introduced from Korea, and around the 7th century, Tang Chinese pottery became influential.

In the medieval period, Japan's great ceramic centre was Seto, in Central Honshū. Here, starting in the 12th century, Japanese potters took Chinese forms and adapted them to Japanese tastes and needs to produce a truly distinctive pottery style known as Seto Ware. One Japanese term for pottery and porcelain, *setomono* (literally 'things from Seto'), clearly derives from this still-thriving ceramics centre.

Today, there are more than 100 pottery centres in Japan, with scores of artisans producing everything from exclusive tea utensils to souvenir folklore creatures. Department stores regularly organise exhibitions of ceramics and offer the chance to see some of this fine work up close (for more information, see the boxed text, above).

SHIKKI (LACQUERWARE)

The Japanese have been using lacquer to protect and enhance the beauty of wood since the Jōmon period (13,000–400 BC). In the Meiji era (1868–1912), lacquerware became very popular abroad and it remains one of Japan's best-known products. Known in Japan as *shikki* or *nurimono,* lacquerware is made using the sap from the lacquer tree *(urushi)*, a close relative of poison oak. Raw lacquer is actually toxic and causes severe skin irritation in those who have not developed immunity. Once hardened, however, it becomes inert and extraordinarily durable.

The most common colour of lacquer is an amber or brown colour, but additives have been used to produce black, violet, blue, yellow and even white lacquer. In the better pieces, multiple layers of lacquer are painstakingly applied and left to dry, and finally polished to a luxurious shine.

Contemporary Theatre & Dance

Contemporary theatre and dance are alive and well in Japan, though you'll quickly notice that most major troupes are based in Tokyo. If you're interested in taking in contemporary theatre, your best bet is to enlist the help of a translator and to hit the *shōgekijō* (little theatres; see below) scene. If contemporary dance is what you seek, check the *Japan Times, Metropolis* or the *Tokyo Journal* in Tokyo, or the *Kansai Time Out* in Kansai, to see what's on when you're in town.

UNDERGROUND THEATRE

Theatre the world over spent the 1960s redefining itself, and it was no different in Japan. The *shōgekijō* movement, also called *angura* (underground), has given Japan many of its leading playwrights, directors and actors. It arose as a reaction to the realism and structure of *shingeki* (a 1920s movement that borrowed heavily from Western dramatic forms), and featured surrealistic plays that explored the relationship between human beings and the world. Like their counterparts in the West, these productions took place in any space available – in small theatres, tents, basements, open spaces and street corners.

Tokyo Art Beat (www.tokyoartbeat.com) is a great way to find out about what's happening in the arts while you're in the country.

The first generation of *shōgekijō* directors and writers often included speedy comedy, wordplay and images from popular culture in their works to highlight the lunacy of modern life. More recent *shōgekijō* productions have dealt with realistic and contemporary themes, such as modern Japanese history, war, environmental degradation and social oppression. Changing cultural perceptions have propelled the movement in new directions, notably towards socially and politically critical dramas.

BUTOH

In many ways, butoh is Japan's most accessible (there are no words except for the occasional grunt) and exciting dance form. It is also its newest dance form, dating only to 1959, when Hijikata Tatsumi (1928–86) gave the first butoh performance. Butoh was born out of a rejection of the excessive formalisation that characterises traditional forms of Japanese dance. It also stems from the desire to return to the ancient roots of the Japanese soul, so is also a rejection of Western influences that flooded Japan in the postwar years.

Displays of butoh are best likened to performance art happenings rather than traditional dance performances. During a butoh performance, one or more dancers use their naked or seminaked bodies to express the most elemental and intense human emotions. Nothing is sacred in butoh, and performances often deal with topics such as sexuality and death. For this reason, critics often describe butoh as scandalous, and butoh dancers delight in pushing the boundaries of what can be considered tasteful in artistic performance.

Butoh tends to be more underground than the more established forms of Japanese dance and it is, consequently, harder to catch a performance. The best way to see what's on while you're in town is to check the local English-language media (the *Japan Times, Metropolis* or the *Tokyo Journal* in Tokyo, or the *Kansai Time Out* in Kansai), or to ask at a local tourist information office.

Traditional Theatre & Dance

NŌ

Nō is a hypnotic dance-drama that reflects the minimalist aesthetics of Zen. The movement is glorious, the chorus and music sonorous, the expression subtle. A sparsely furnished cedar stage directs full attention to the performers, who include a chorus, drummers and a flautist. There are two principal characters: the *shite,* who is sometimes a living person but more often a demon, or a ghost whose soul cannot rest; and the *waki,* who leads the main character towards the play's climactic moment. Each nō school has its own repertoire, and the art form continues to evolve and develop.

KABUKI

The first performances of kabuki were staged early in the 17th century by an all-female troupe. The performances were highly erotic and attracted enthusiastic support from the merchant class. In true bureaucratic fashion, Tokugawa officials feared for the people's morality and banned women from the stage in 1629. Since that time, kabuki has been performed exclusively by men, giving rise to the institution of *onnagata,* or *ōyama,* male actors who specialise in female roles.

Over the course of several centuries, kabuki has developed a repertoire that draws on popular themes, such as famous historical accounts and stories of love-suicide, while also borrowing copiously from nō, *kyōgen* (comic vignettes) and *bunraku* (classical puppet theatre). Most kabuki plays border on melodrama, although they vary in mood.

Formalised beauty and stylisation are the central aesthetic principles of kabuki; the acting is a combination of dancing and speaking in conventionalised intonation patterns, and each actor prepares for a role by studying and emulating the style perfected by his predecessors. Kabuki actors are born into the art form, and training begins in childhood. Today, they enjoy great social prestige and their activities on and off the stage attract as much interest as those of popular film and TV stars.

'Kabuki actors are born into the art form, and training begins in childhood'

BUNRAKU

Japan's traditional puppet theatre developed at the same time as kabuki, when the *shamisen* (a three-stringed instrument resembling a lute or a banjo), imported from Okinawa, was combined with traditional puppetry techniques and *joruri* (narrative chanting). *Bunraku,* as it came to be known in the 19th century, addresses many of the same themes as kabuki, and in fact many of the most famous plays in the kabuki repertoire were originally written for puppet theatre. *Bunraku* involves large puppets – nearly two-thirds life-sized – manipulated by up to three black-robed puppeteers. The puppeteers do not speak; a seated narrator tells the story and provides the voices of the characters, expressing their feelings with smiles, weeping and fits of surprise and fear. One of the best places to see *bunraku* is at Osaka's National Bunraku Theatre (p406).

RAKUGO

A traditional Japanese style of comic monologue, *rakugo* (literally 'dropped word') dates back to the Edo period. The performer, usually in kimono, sits on a square cushion on a stage. Props are limited to a fan and hand towel. The monologue begins with a *makura* (prologue), which is followed by the story itself and, finally, the *ochi* (punch line or 'drop', which is another pronunciation of the Chinese character for *raku* in *rakugo*). Many of the monologues in the traditional *rakugo* repertoire date back to the Edo and Meiji periods, and while well known, reflect a social milieu unknown to modern listeners. Accordingly, many practitioners today also write new monologues addressing issues relevant to contemporary life.

MANZAI

Manzai is a comic dialogue, with its origins in the song-and-dance and comedy routines traditionally performed by itinerant entertainers. It is a highly fluid art that continues to draw large audiences to hear snappy duos exchange clever witticisms on up-to-the-minute themes from everyday life. Much of the humour derives from wordplay and double entendre. Needless to say, much of this will be lost on anyone but a truly fluent Japanese speaker.

Still, if you'd like to see a performance, check journals like the *Japan Times, Metropolis* or the *Tokyo Journal* in Tokyo, or the *Kansai Time Out* in Kansai, or ask at a local tourist information office.

Architecture

Running the gamut from rustic rural simplicity to shining modern towers (with vast expanses of forgettable concrete dross in between), Japanese architecture is perhaps the world's most varied. Broadly speaking, the country's structures can be divided into traditional and contemporary, the former being built mostly of wood, bamboo, earth and paper, the latter being built mostly of concrete, steel and glass. In this section, we discuss the main types of Japanese architecture; for more details see p113.

Until Buddhism arrived in Japan in the 6th century AD, Japanese emperors were buried in giant earth and stone burial mounds known as *kofun* (see p430). The largest of these is said to contain more mass than the Great Pyramid at Cheops.

CONTEMPORARY ARCHITECTURE

Contemporary Japanese architecture is currently among the world's most exciting and influential. The traditional preference for simple, natural and harmonious spaces is still evident in the work of modern architects, but this style is now combined with hi-tech materials and the building techniques of the West.

Japan first opened its doors to Western architecture in 1868 during the Meiji Restoration, and its architects immediately responded to the new influence by combining traditional Japanese methods of wood construction with Western designs. Some 20 years later, a nationalistic push against the influence of the West saw a surge in the popularity of traditional Japanese building styles, and Western technique was temporarily shelved.

This resistance to Western architecture continued until after WWI, when foreign architects such as Frank Lloyd Wright came to build the Imperial Hotel in Tokyo. Wright was careful to pay homage to local sensibilities when designing the Imperial's many elegant bridges and unique guest rooms (though he famously used modern, cubic forms to ornament the interiors of the hotel). The building was demolished in 1967 to make way for the current Imperial Hotel, which shows little of Wright's touch.

By WWII many Japanese architects were using Western techniques and materials and blending old styles with the new, and by the mid-1960s had developed a unique style that began to attract attention on the world stage. Japan's most famous postwar architect, Tange Kenzō, was strongly influenced by Le Corbusier. Tange's buildings, including the Kagawa Prefectural Offices at Takamatsu (1958) and the National Gymnasium (completed in 1964), fuse the sculptural influences and materials of Le Corbusier with traditional Japanese characteristics, such as post-and-beam construction and strong geometry. His Tokyo Metropolitan Government Offices (1991; p154), in Nishi-Shinjuku (west Shinjuku), is the tallest building in Tokyo. It may look a little sinister and has been criticised as totalitarian, but it is a remarkable achievement and pulls in around 6000 visitors daily. Those with an interest in Tange's work should also look for the UN University, close to Omote-sandō subway station in Tokyo.

In the 1960s, architects such as Shinohara Kazuo, Kurokawa Kisho, Maki Fumihiko and Kikutake Kiyonori began a movement known as Metabolism, which promoted flexible spaces and functions at the expense of fixed forms in building. Shinohara finally came to design in a style he called Modern Next, incorporating both modern and postmodern design ideas combined with Japanese influences. This style can be seen in his Centennial Hall at Tokyo Institute of Technology, an elegant and uplifting synthesis of clashing forms in a shiny metal cladding. Kurokawa's architecture blends Buddhist building traditions with modern influences, while Maki, the master of minimalism, pursued design in a modernist style while still emphasising the elements of nature – like the roof of his Tokyo Metropolitan Gymnasium (near Sendagaya

Station), which takes on the form of a sleek metal insect. Another Maki design, the Spiral Building (p155), built in Aoyama in 1985, is a favourite with Tokyo residents and its interior is also a treat.

Isozaki Arata, an architect who originally worked under Tange Kenzō, also promoted the Metabolist style before later becoming interested in geometry and postmodernism. His work includes the Cultural Centre (1990) in Mito, which contains a striking, geometrical, snakelike tower clad in different metals.

Kikutake, a contemporary of Isozaki's, designed the Edo-Tokyo Museum (1992; p159) in Sumida-ku, which charts the history of the Edo period, and is arguably his best-known building. It is a truly enormous structure, encompassing almost 50,000 sq metres of built space and reaching 62.2m, which was the height of Edo-jō at its peak. It has been likened in form to a crouching giant and it easily dwarfs its surroundings.

Another influential architect of this generation is Hara Hiroshi. Hara's style defies definition, but the one constant theme is nature. His Umeda Sky Building (1993; p393) in Kita, Osaka, is a sleek, towering structure designed to resemble a garden in the sky. The Yamamoto International Building (1993) on the outskirts of Tokyo is the headquarters of a textile factory. Both of these buildings, though monumental in scale, dissolve down into many smaller units upon closer inspection – just like nature itself.

In the 1980s a second generation of Japanese architects began to gain recognition within the international architecture scene, including Andō Tadao, Hasegawa Itsuko and Toyo Ito. This younger group has continued to explore both modernism and postmodernism, while incorporating a renewed interest in Japan's architectural heritage.

Andō's architecture in particular blends classical modern and native Japanese styles. His buildings often use materials such as concrete and the strong geometric patterns that have so regularly appeared in Japan's traditional architecture. Some critics contend that Andō's work is inhuman and monolithic, while others are taken by the dramatic spaces his buildings create. The most accessible of Andō's work is the Omotesandō Hills shopping complex in Tokyo's Aoyama area (2006; p154).

Fans of modern Tokyo architecture may be surprised to discover that Tokyo's most famous modern building, the Roppongi Hills complex (2003; p157), wasn't designed by a Japanese architect at all – it was designed by the New York–based firm of Kohn Pedersen Fox Associates.

'Simple and refined, the typical house is constructed of post-and-beam timber, with sliding panels of wood or mulberry paper'

TRADITIONAL SECULAR ARCHITECTURE

Houses

With the exception of those on the northern island of Hokkaidō, traditional Japanese houses are built with the broiling heat of summer in mind. They are made of flimsy materials designed to take advantage of even the slightest breeze. Another reason behind the gossamer construction of Japanese houses is the relative frequency of earthquakes, which precludes the use of heavier building materials such as stone or brick.

Principally simple and refined, the typical house is constructed of post-and-beam timber, with sliding panels of wood or mulberry paper (for warmer weather) making up the exterior walls. Movable screens, or *shōji,* divide the interior of the house. There may be a separate area for the tea ceremony – the harmonious atmosphere of this space is of the utmost importance and is usually achieved through the use of natural materials and the careful arrangement of furniture and utensils.

A particularly traditional type of Japanese house is the *machiya* (townhouse), built by merchants in cities such as Kyoto and Tokyo. Until very recently, the older neighbourhoods of Kyoto and some areas of Tokyo were lined with neat, narrow rows of these houses, but most have fallen victim to the current frenzy of construction. These days, the best place to see *machiya* is in Kyoto (p324).

Farmhouses

The most distinctive type of Japanese farmhouse is the thatched-roof *gasshō-zukuri* (see the boxed text, p272), so named for the shape of the rafters, which resemble a pair of praying hands. While these farmhouses look cosy and romantic, bear in mind that they were often home for up to 40 people and occasionally farm animals as well. Furthermore, the black floorboards, soot-covered ceilings and lack of windows guaranteed a cavelike atmosphere. The only weapon against this darkness was a fire built in a central fireplace in the floor, known as an *irori,* which also provided warmth in the cooler months and hot coals for cooking. Multistorey farmhouses were also built to house silkworms for silk production (particularly prevalent during the Meiji era) in the airy upper gables.

Castles

Japan has an abundance of castles, most of them copies of originals destroyed by fire or war or time.

The first castles were simple mountain forts that relied more on natural terrain than structural innovations for defence, making them as frustratingly inaccessible to their defenders as they were to invading armies. The central feature of these edifices was the *donjon* (keep), which was surrounded by several smaller towers. The buildings, which sat atop stone ramparts, were mostly built of wood that was covered with plaster intended to protect against fire.

The wide-ranging wars of the 16th and 17th centuries left Japan with numerous castles, though many of these were later destroyed by the Edo and then the Meiji governments. Half a century later, the 1960s saw a boom in castle reconstructions, most built of concrete and steel; and like Hollywood movie sets they're authentic-looking when viewed from a distance but distinctly modern in appearance when viewed up close.

Some of the best castles to visit today include the dramatic Himeji-jō (p415), also known as *shirasagi* (white heron) castle, and Edo-jō (p127), around which modern Tokyo has grown. Little of Edo-jō actually remains (the grounds are now the site of the Imperial Palace), though its original gate, Ōte-mon, still marks the main entrance.

Literature

Interestingly, much of Japan's early literature was written by women. One reason for this was that men wrote in kanji (imported Chinese characters), while women wrote in hiragana (Japanese script). Thus, while the men were busy copying Chinese styles and texts, the women of the country were producing the first authentic Japanese literature. Among these early female authors is Murasaki Shikibu, who wrote Japan's first great novel, *Genji Monogatari* (The Tale of Genji). This detailed, lengthy tome documents the intrigues and romances of early Japanese court life, and although it is perhaps Japan's most important work of literature, its extreme length probably limits its appeal to all but the most ardent Japanophile or literature buff.

In the exquisite haiku travelogue *Narrow Road to the Deep North,* Matsuo Bashō captures the wonders and contradictions of Honshū's northern region.

Most of Japan's important modern literature has been penned by authors who live in and write of cities. Though these works are sometimes celebratory, many also lament the loss of a traditional rural lifestyle that has given way to the pressures of a modern, industrialised society. *Kokoro,* the modern classic by Sōseki Natsume, outlines these rural/urban tensions, as does *Snow Country,* by Nobel laureate Kawabata Yasunari. These works touch upon

MOBILE-PHONE NOVELS: THE THUMB IS MIGHTIER THAN THE SWORD

Take a subway in any Japanese city and you'll notice that half of the young folks are frantically tapping away on their mobile (cell) phones with their thumbs. It's a safe bet that most of them are sending text messages to their friends, but there's always a chance that you are witnessing the creation of the next Great Japanese Novel. *Keitai shōsetsu* (mobile-phone novels) are all the rage in Japan. In 2007, five of the top 10 best-selling hardcopy novels in Japan started their lives as mobile-phone novels. This is an incredible figure, considering that the first *keitai shōsetsu* was only published in 2003 (a novel called *Deep Love*, written by a writer named Yoshi).

The *keitai* genre is dominated by young women, often writing under one-name pseudonyms. *Keitai* novels often revolve around the themes of love and alienation, written in bleak abbreviated style and infused with techno-pop references. Japanese literary critics are fiercely divided over their merits: some deride them as the puerile musings of lovelorn adolescents, others celebrate them as the wondrous application of a new technology to an ancient art form. Whatever the case, one thing is certain: if Tolstoy were reincarnated as a Japanese 20-something, he'd have one helluva mobile-phone bill!

the tensions between Japan's nostalgia for the past and its rush towards the future, between its rural heartland and its burgeoning cities.

Although Mishima Yukio is probably the most controversial of Japan's modern writers, and is considered unrepresentative of Japanese culture by many Japanese, his work still makes for very interesting reading. *The Sailor Who Fell from Grace* and *After the Banquet* are both compelling. For unsettling beauty, reach for the former; history buffs will want the latter tome, which was at the centre of a court case that became Japan's first privacy lawsuit.

Ōe Kenzaburo, Japan's second Nobel laureate, has produced some of Japan's most disturbing, energetic and enigmatic literature. *A Personal Matter* is the work for which he is most widely known. In this troubling novel, which echoes Ōe's frustrations at having a son with autism, a 27-year-old cram-school teacher's wife gives birth to a brain-damaged child. His life claustrophobic and his marriage failing, he dreams of escaping to Africa while planning the murder of his son.

Of course, not all Japanese fiction can be classified as literature in high-brow terms. Murakami Ryū's *Almost Transparent Blue* is strictly sex and drugs, and his ode to the narcissistic early 1990s, *Coin Locker Babies,* recounts the toxic lives of two boys who have been left to die in coin lockers by their mothers. Like Murakami Ryū, Banana Yoshimoto is known for her ability to convey the prevailing zeitgeist in easily, um, digestible form. In her novel *Kitchen,* she relentlessly chronicles Tokyo's fast-food menus and '80s pop culture, though underlying the superficial digressions are hints of a darker and deeper world of death, loss and loneliness.

Abe Kobo's beautiful novel *Woman in the Dunes* (1962) is a tale of shifting sands and wandering strangers. One of the strangest and most interesting works of Japanese fiction.

Japan's most internationally celebrated living novelist is Murakami Haruki, a former jazz club owner gone literary. His most noted work, *Norwegian Wood,* set in the late '60s against the backdrop of student protests, is both a portrait of the artist as a young man (as recounted by a reminiscent narrator) and an ode to first loves. Another interesting read is his *A Wild Sheep Chase*, in which a mutant sheep with a star on its back inspires a search that takes a 20-something ad man to the mountainous north. The hero eventually confronts the mythical beast while wrestling with his own shadows.

Music

Japan has a huge, shape-shifting music scene supported by a local market of audiophiles who are willing to try almost anything. International artists make a point of swinging through on global tours, and the local scene surfaces every

TRADITIONAL MUSIC & ITS INSTRUMENTS

- *Gagaku* is a throwback to music of the Japanese imperial court. Today, ensembles consist of 16 members and include stringed instruments, such as the *biwa* (lute) and *koto* (13-stringed instrument derived from a Chinese zither that is played flat on the floor), and wind instruments such as the *hichiriki* (Japanese oboe).
- *Shamisen* is a three-stringed instrument resembling a lute or banjo with an extended neck. Popular during the Edo period, particularly in the entertainment districts, it's still used as formal accompaniment in kabuki and *bunraku* (classical puppet theatre) and remains one of the essential skills of a geisha.
- *Shakuhachi* is a wind instrument imported from China in the 7th century. The *shakuhachi* was popularised by wandering Komusō monks in the 16th and 17th centuries, who played it as a means to enlightenment as they walked alone through the woods.
- *Taiko* refers to any of a number of large Japanese drums. Drummers who perform this athletic music often play shirtless to show the rippled movements of their backs.

night in one of thousands of live houses. The jazz scene is enormous, as are the followings for rock, house and electronica. More mainstream gleanings are the *aidoru,* idol singers whose popularity is generated largely through media appearances and is centred on a cute, girl-next-door image. Unless you're aged 15, this last option probably won't interest you.

These days, J-pop (Japan pop) is dominated by female vocalists who borrow heavily from such American pop stars as Mariah Carey. The most famous of these is Utada Hikaru, whose great vocal range and English ability (she peppers her songs with English lyrics) make her a standout from the otherwise drab *aidoru* field.

Another headliner in Japan's modern music scene is a 28-year-old African American singer who goes by the name of Jero (real name: Jerome White). Born and raised in Pittsburgh, Pennsylvania, Jero got a taste for Japanese music by listening to his Japanese grandmother sing *enka* (emotional, sometimes sappy, Japanese songs). He scored a hit in 2008 with his song 'Umi Yuki' (Ocean Snow). Performing on stage dressed in American hip-hop attire, Jero has impressed serious music critics with his excellent voice and mastery of Japanese. Some even think that he might spark a renaissance for this somewhat outdated genre.

Cinema

Japan has a vibrant film industry and proud, critically acclaimed cinematic traditions. Renewed international attention since the mid-1990s has reinforced interest in domestic films, which account for an estimated 40% of box-office receipts, nearly double the level in most European countries. Of course, this includes not only artistically important works, but also films in the science-fiction, horror and 'monster-stomps-Tokyo' genres for which Japan is also known.

At first, Japanese films were merely cinematic versions of traditional theatrical performances, but in the 1920s Japanese directors starting producing films in two distinct genres: *jidaigeki* (period films) and new *gendaigeki* films, which dealt with modern themes. The more realistic storylines of the new films soon reflected back on the traditional films with the introduction of *shin jidaigeki* (new period films). During this era, samurai themes became an enduring staple of Japanese cinema.

The golden age of Japanese cinema arrived with the 1950s and began with the release in 1950 of Kurosawa Akira's *Rashōmon,* winner of the Golden Lion at the 1951 Venice International Film Festival and an Oscar for best foreign film. The increasing realism and high artistic standards of the period are evident in such landmark films as *Tōkyō Monogatari* (Tokyo Story; 1953), by the legendary Ōzu Yasujirō; Mizoguchi Kenji's classics *Ugetsu Monogatari* (Tales of Ugetsu; 1953) and *Saikaku Ichidai Onna* (The Life of Oharu; 1952); and Kurosawa's 1954 masterpiece *Shichinin no Samurai* (Seven Samurai). Annual attendance at the country's cinemas reached 1.1 billion in 1958, and Kyoto, with its large film studios, such as Shōchiku, Daiei and Tōei, and more than 60 cinemas, enjoyed a heyday as Japan's own Hollywood.

Tōkyō Monogatari (Tokyo Story; 1953) is Ōzu Yasujirō's tale of an older couple who come to Tokyo to visit their children, only to find themselves treated with disrespect and indifference.

As it did elsewhere in the world, TV spurred a rapid drop in the number of cinema-goers in Japan in the high-growth decades of the 1960s and '70s. But despite falling attendance, Japanese cinema remained a major artistic force. These decades gave the world such landmark works as Ichikawa Kon's *Chushingura* (47 Samurai; 1962) and Kurosawa's *Yōjimbo* (1961).

The decline in cinema-going continued through the 1980s, reinforced by the popularisation of videos, with annual attendance at cinemas bottoming out at just over 100 million. Yet Japan's cinema was far from dead: Kurosawa garnered acclaim worldwide for *Kagemusha* (1980), which shared the Palme d'Or at Cannes, and *Ran* (1985). Imamura Shōhei's heartrending *Narayama Bushiko* (The Ballad of Narayama) won the Palme d'Or at Cannes in 1983. Itami Jūzō became perhaps the most widely known Japanese director outside Japan after Kurosawa, with such biting satires as *Osōshiki* (The Funeral; 1987), *Tampopo* (Dandelion; 1987) and *Marusa no Onna* (A Taxing Woman; 1987). Ōshima Nagisa, best known for controversial films such as *Ai no Corrida* (In the Realm of the Senses; 1976), scored a critical and popular success with *Senjo no Merry Christmas* (Merry Christmas, Mr Lawrence) in 1983.

The film *Distance* (2001) is a subtle meditation on togetherness and loneliness. Koreeda Hirokazu's sequel to *After Life* tracks four people into the woods as they seek the truth about lovers and friends who belonged to a mysterious cult.

In recent years, Japanese cinema has been enjoying something of a renaissance and foreign audiences and critics have taken note. In 1997 Japanese directors received top honours at two of the world's most prestigious film festivals: *Unagi* (Eel), Imamura Shōhei's black-humoured look at human nature's dark side, won the Palme d'Or at Cannes, making him the only Japanese director to win this award twice; and 'Beat' Takeshi Kitano took the Golden Lion in Venice for *Hana-bi*, a tale of life and death, and the violence and honour that links them. More recently, in 2009, Takita Yojiro's film *Okuribito* (Departures) garnered an Oscar for best foreign film.

ANIME

The term anime, a contraction of the word 'animation', is used worldwide to refer to Japan's highly sophisticated animated films. Unlike its counterparts in other countries, anime occupies a position very near the forefront of the film industry in Japan. Anime films encompass all genres, from science-fiction and action adventure to romance and historical drama.

Anime targets all age and social groups. Anime films include deep explorations of philosophical questions and social issues, humorous entertainment and bizarre fantasies. The films offer breathtakingly realistic visuals, exquisite attention to detail, complex and expressive characters and elaborate plots. Leading directors and voice actors are accorded fame and respect, while characters become popular idols.

Some of the best-known anime include *Akira* (1988), Ōtomo Katsuhiro's psychedelic fantasy set in a future Tokyo inhabited by speed-popping biker gangs and psychic children. Ōtomo also worked on the interesting *Memories* (1995), a three-part anime that includes the mind-bending 'Magnetic Rose' sequence where deep-space garbage collectors happen upon a spaceship

MIYAZAKI HAYAO – THE KING OF ANIME

Miyazaki Hayao, Japan's most famous and critically acclaimed anime director, has given us some of the most memorable images ever to appear on the silver screen. Consider, for example, the island that floated through the sky in his 1986 classic *Laputa*. Or the magical train that travelled across the surface of an aquamarine sea in *Spirited Away* (2001). Or the psychedelic dreamworlds that waited outside the doors of *Howl's Moving Castle* (2004). Watching scenes like this, one can only conclude that Miyazaki is gifted with the ability to travel to the realm of pure imagination and smuggle images back to this world intact and undiluted.

Miyazaki Hayao was born in 1941 in wartime Tokyo. His father was director of a firm that manufactured parts for the famous Japanese Zero fighter plane. This early exposure to flying machines made a deep impression on the young Miyazaki, and one of the hallmarks of his films is skies filled with the most whimsical flying machines imaginable: winged dirigibles, fantastic flying boats and the flying wings of *Nausicaa of the Valley of the Winds* (to see one is to want one).

In high school, Miyazaki saw one of Japan's first anime, *Hakujaden,* and resolved to become an animator himself. After graduating from university in 1963, he joined the powerful Tōei Animation company, where he worked on some of the studio's most famous releases. He left in 1971 to join A Pro studio, where he gained his first directorial experience, working on the now famous (in Japan, at least) *Lupin III* series as co-director. In 1979 he directed *The Castle of Cagliostro,* another *Lupin* film and his first solo directorial credit.

In 1984 Miyazaki wrote and directed *Nausicaa of the Valley of the Winds*. This film is considered by many critics to be the first true Miyazaki film, and it provides a brilliant taste of many of the themes that run through his later work. The film enjoyed critical and commercial success and established Miyazaki as a major force in the world of Japanese anime. Capitalising on this success, Miyazaki founded his own animation studio, Studio Ghibli, through which he has produced all his later works.

In 1988, Studio Ghibli released what many consider to be Miyazaki's masterwork: *My Neighbor Totoro*. Much simpler and less dense than many Miyazaki films, *Totoro* is the tale of a young girl who moves with her family to the Japanese countryside while her mother recuperates from an illness. While living in the country, she befriends a magical creature who lives in the base of a giant camphor tree and is lucky enough to catch a few rides on a roving cat bus (a vehicle of pure imagination if ever there was one). For anyone wishing to make an acquaintance with the world of Miyazaki, this is the perfect introduction.

Serious Miyazaki fans will want to make a pilgrimage to his Ghibli Museum (p207), located in the town of Mitaka, a short day trip out of Tokyo.

containing the memories of a mysterious woman. Finally, there is *Ghost in a Shell* (1995), an Ōishii Mamoru film with a sci-fi plot worthy of Philip K Dick – it involves cyborgs, hackers and the mother of all computer networks.

Of course, one name towers above all others in the world of anime: Miyazaki Hayao, who almost single-handedly brought anime to the attention of the general public in the West (see the boxed text, above).

SPORT
Sumō

A fascinating, highly ritualised activity steeped in Shintō beliefs, sumō is the only traditional Japanese sport that pulls big crowds and dominates primetime TV. The 2000-year-old sport, which is based on an ancient combat form called *sumai* (to struggle), attracts huge crowds on weekends. Because tournaments take place over the span of 15 days, unless you're aiming for a big match on a weekend, you should be able to secure a ticket. Sumō tournaments *(bashō)* take place in January, May and September at Ryōgoku Kokugikan (p188) in Tokyo; in March at the Furitsu Taiiku-kan Gymnasium in Osaka; in July at the Aichi Prefectural Gymnasium (p256) in Nagoya; and in November at the Fukuoka Kokusai Centre in Fukuoka (p692). Most popular are matches where one of the combatants is a *yokozuna* (grand champion). At the moment, sumō is dominated by foreign-born *rikishi* (sumō wrestlers), including Mongolian Asashōryū and Bulgarian Kotoōshū.

'Japan was already soccer crazy when the World Cup came in 2002. Now it's a chronic madness'

Soccer

Japan was already soccer crazy when the World Cup came to Saitama and Yokohama in 2002. Now it's a chronic madness, and five minutes of conversation with any 10-year-old about why they like David Beckham should clear up any doubts you might have to the contrary. Japan's national league, also known as J-League (www.j-league.or.jp/eng), is in season from March to November and can be seen at stadiums around the country.

Baseball

Baseball was introduced to Japan in 1873 and became a fixture in 1934 when the Yomiuri started its own team after Babe Ruth and Lou Gehrig had swung through town. During WWII the game continued unabated, though players were required to wear unnumbered khaki uniforms and to salute each other on the field.

Today, baseball is still widely publicised and very popular, though many fans have begun to worry about the future of the sport in Japan as some of the most talented national players, such as Matsui Hideki, Suzuki Ichirō and Matsuzaka Daisuke, migrate to major league teams in the USA. If you're visiting Japan between April and October and are interested in catching a game, two exciting places to do so are the historic Koshien Stadium (Map p395), which is located just outside Osaka and was built in 1924 as Japan's first stadium, and Tokyo Dome (p188), affectionately known as the 'Big Egg' and home to Japan's most popular team, the Yomiuri Giants.

Food & Drink

Those familiar with *nihon ryōri* (Japanese cuisine) know that eating is half the fun of travelling in Japan, if not perhaps the best part. Even if you've already tried some of Japan's better-known specialities in Japanese restaurants in your own country, you're likely to be surprised by how delicious the original is when served on its home turf. More importantly, the adventurous eater will be delighted to find that Japanese food is far more than just sushi, tempura or sukiyaki. Indeed, it is possible to spend a month in Japan and sample a different speciality restaurant every night.

Lonely Planet's *World Food Japan* (John Ashburne and Yoshi Abe) provides a detailed introduction to Japanese cuisine. It's an excellent supplement to the information in this chapter.

Of course, you may baulk at charging into a restaurant where both the language and the menu are likely to be incomprehensible. The best way to get over this fear is to familiarise yourself with the main types of Japanese restaurants so that you have some idea of what's on offer and how to order it. Those timid of heart should take solace in the fact that the Japanese will go to extraordinary lengths to understand what you want and will help you to order. To help you out further, eating reviews in this book recommend specific dishes where no English menu is available.

With the exception of *shokudō* (all-round restaurants) and *izakaya* (pub-eateries), most Japanese restaurants concentrate on a speciality cuisine. This naturally makes for delicious eating, but does limit your choice. The information under Restaurants & Sample Menus (p79) introduces the main types of Japanese restaurants, along with a sample menu of some of the most common dishes served.

For information on how to eat in a Japanese restaurant, see the boxed text, p79. For information on eating etiquette in Japan, see the tips in the boxed text, opposite.

STAPLES

Despite the mind-boggling variety of dishes throughout the island chain, the staples that make up Japanese cuisine remain the same nationwide: *shōyu* (soy sauce), miso, tofu, *mame* (beans) and above all, the divine crop, *kome* (rice).

Rice (O-kome)

The Japanese don't just consume *kome* (rice) all day, every day. In its uncooked form it is called *o-kome,* the *o-* denoting respect, *kome* meaning rice. Cooked Japanese style, it is called *go-han* (the *go-* prefix is the highest indicator of respect), denoting rice or meal. Truck drivers, however, may use the more informal *meshi,* something akin to 'grub'. When it is included in Western-style meals, it is termed *raisu*. On average, Japanese consume an astonishing 70kg of *kome* per person per year. Culturally, most Japanese feel a meal is simply incomplete without the inclusion of *kome.*

Hakumai is the plain white rice that is used in every dish from the humble *ekiben* (*bentō* lunch box bought at a train station) to the finest *kaiseki* (Japanese haute cuisine). A meal will consist of, for example, a bowl of *hakumai* topped with *tsukudani* (fish and vegetables simmered in *shōyu* and *mirin,* which is a sweet rice wine), served with a bowl of miso soup, accompanied by a side dish of *tsukemono* (pickles). *Genmai,* unpolished, unrefined brown rice, is rarely spotted outside

EATING ETIQUETTE

When it comes to eating in Japan, there are quite a number of implicit rules, but they're fairly easy to remember. If you're worried about putting your foot in it, relax – the Japanese don't expect you to know what to do, and they are unlikely to be offended as long as you follow the standard rules of politeness from your own country. Here are a few major points to keep in mind:

- **Chopsticks in rice** Do not stick your *hashi* (chopsticks) upright in a bowl of rice. This is how rice is offered to the dead in Buddhist rituals. Similarly, do not pass food from your chopsticks to someone else's. This is another funereal ritual.
- **Polite expressions** When eating with other people, especially when you're a guest, it is polite to say '*itadakimasu*' (literally 'I will receive') before digging in. This is as close as the Japanese come to saying grace. Similarly, at the end of the meal, you should thank your host by saying '*gochisō-sama deshita*' which means, 'It was a real feast'.
- **Kampai** It is bad form to fill your own glass. You should fill the glass of the person next to you and wait for them to reciprocate. Raise your glass a little off the table while it is being filled. Once everyone's glass has been filled, the usual starting signal is a chorus of '*kampai*', which means 'cheers!'
- **Slurp** When you eat noodles in Japan, it's perfectly OK, even expected, to slurp them. In fact, one of the best ways to find *rāmen* (egg noodle) restaurants in Japan is to listen for the loud slurping sound that comes out of them!

organic restaurants (with the notable exception of *shōjin-ryōri* – Buddhist vegetarian cuisine) as it lacks that fragrance and glow so desired of simple *hakumai*. Rice is used in *zōsui* (rice soup), *o-chazuke* (where green tea is poured onto white rice), *onigiri* (the ubiquitous rice balls) and vinegared in sushi.

The most important Shintō deity is Inari, the god of the rice harvest.

Mame (Beans)

Given the country's Buddhist history, it's no surprise that Japanese cuisine has long been dependent on beans as a source of protein. Top of the Japanese bean pile is the indispensable soy bean, the *daizu* (literally 'big bean'), which provides the raw material for miso, *shōyu*, tofu, *yuba* (soy milk skin) and the infamous *nattō* (fermented soy beans). It also finds its way into such dishes as *hijiki-mame*, where black spiky seaweed is sautéed in oil, with soy sauce and sugar, and *daizu no nimono*, soy beans cooked with *konbu* (kelp) and dried shiitake mushrooms.

Next is the azuki bean (written with the characters for 'little bean'), used extensively in preparation of *wagashi* (Japanese sweets), often for the tea ceremony, and in the preparation of *seki-han* (red-bean rice), which is used at times of celebration and to commemorate a teenage girl's first menstruation.

The highly prized Japanese *matsutake* mushroom can sell for up to US$2000 per kilogram.

Miso

A precursor of miso arrived on the Japanese mainland from China sometime around AD 600, not long after Buddhism. Its inhabitants have been gargling it down as *misoshiru* (miso soup) ever since, at breakfast, lunch and dinner. Made by mixing steamed soy beans with *kōji* (a fermenting agent) and salt, miso is integral to any Japanese meal, where it is likely to be present as *misoshiru* or as a flavouring. It is also used in *dengaku* (fish and vegetables roasted on skewers), where it is spread on vegetables such as eggplant and *konnyaku* (devil's tongue).

Misoshiru is a brownish soup made from a mixture of *dashi* (stock), miso and shellfish, such as *shijimi* (freshwater clams) or *asari* (short-necked clams);

TASTY TRAVEL

There's one word every food lover should learn before coming to Japan: *meibutsu*. It means 'speciality', as in regional speciality, and despite its small size, Japan has loads of them. In fact, in never hurts to simply ask for the *meibutsu* when you order at a restaurant or *izakaya* (pub-eatery). Like as not, you'll be served something memorable. Here are some of Japan's more famous local specialities.

- Hiroshima: *kaki* (oysters); *Hiroshima-yaki*, which is Hiroshima-style *okonomiyaki* (batter and cabbage cakes cooked on a griddle)
- Hokkaidō: *kani-ryōri* (crab cuisine); salmon
- Kyoto: *kaiseki* (Japanese haute cuisine); *wagashi* (Japanese traditional sweets); *yuba* (the skim off the top of tofu, or soy milk skin); *Kyō-yasai* (Kyoto-style vegetables)
- Kyūshū: *tonkotsu-rāmen* (pork-broth *rāmen*); *Satsuma-imo* (sweet potatoes)
- Northern Honshū: *wanko-soba* (eat-till-you-burst *soba*); *jappa-jiru* (cod soup with Japanese radish and miso)
- Okinawa: *gōya champurū* (bitter melon stir fry); *sōki-soba* (*rāmen* with spare ribs); *mimiga* (pickled pigs' ears)
- Osaka: *tako-yaki* (battered octopus pieces); *okonomiyaki*
- Shikoku: *sansai* (wild mountain vegetables); *Sanuki-udon* (a type of wheat noodles); *katsuo tataki* (lightly seared bonito)
- Tokyo: sushi

assorted vegetables, such as *daikon* (giant white radish), carrot or burdock (especially good for the digestion); pork; or simply tofu. You may see this up to three times a day in Japan, as it accompanies almost every typical Japanese meal. The simple rule is this: if there's a bowl of rice, then a bowl of *misoshiru* is never far behind.

Tofu

Usually made from soy beans, tofu is one of Japan's most sublime creations. Tofu is sold as the soft 'silk' *kinugoshi* and the firm *momen* (or *momengoshi*). The former is mainly used in soups, especially *misoshiru*. The latter is eaten by itself, as *agedashi-dōfu* – deep-fried tofu in a *dashi* broth – or used in the Kyoto classic *yudōfu*, a hotpot dish. Both *momen* and *kinugoshi* take their names from the technique used when the hot soy milk is strained – if the material used is cotton, the resulting firm tofu is *momen*; when silk *(kinu)* is used, it's *kinugoshi*.

A classic way to eat tofu is as *hiyayakko*, cold blocks of tofu covered with soy, grated ginger and finely sliced spring onion. This is a favourite on the menus of *izakaya*.

Abura-age is thinly sliced, especially thick tofu traditionally fried in sesame oil (more recently, however, producers use salad oil or soy bean oil). It is a key ingredient in the celebratory *chirashi-zushi* (sushi rice topped with cooked egg and other tidbits like shrimp, cucumber and ginger) and in *inari-zushi* (where vinegared rice is stuffed into a fried bean-curd pouch).

Yuba is a staple of *shōjin-ryōri* and a speciality of Kyoto. It is a marvellous accompaniment to sake when it is served fresh with grated wasabi (hot green horseradish) and *shōyu tsuyu* (dipping sauce). Its creation is a time- and labour-intensive process in which soy milk is allowed to curdle over a low heat and then the skin is plucked from the surface.

Shōyu (Soy Sauce)

Surprisingly, *shōyu* is a relatively new addition to Japanese cuisine, although a primitive form of it, *hishio,* was made in the Yayoi period by mixing salt and fish. *Shōyu* in its current form dates back to the more recent Muromachi era (1333–1568).

Twentieth-century mass production made a household name out of Kikkōman, but *shōyu* is still made using traditional methods at small companies throughout the country. It comes in two forms: the dark brown, 'thicker taste' *koikuchi-shōyu* and the chestnut-coloured, 'thinner', much saltier *usukuchi-shōyu* (sweetened and lightened by the addition of *mirin*). *Koikuchi* is used for a variety of applications and is perfect for teriyaki, where meat or fish is brushed with *shōyu, mirin* and sugar, and grilled. The aromatic *usukuchi-shōyu,* a favourite of the Kansai region, is best suited to clear soups and white fish. It is especially important in enhancing the colour of a dish's ingredients.

RESTAURANTS & SAMPLE MENUS

Shokudō

A *shokudō* is the most common type of restaurant in Japan, and is found near train stations, tourist spots and just about any other place where people congregate. Easily distinguished by the presence of plastic food displays in the window, these inexpensive places usually serve a variety of *washoku* (Japanese dishes) and *yōshoku* (Western dishes).

At lunch, and sometimes dinner, the easiest meal to order at a *shokudō* is a *teishoku* (set-course meal), which is sometimes also called *ranchi setto* (lunch set) or *kōsu*. This usually includes a main dish of meat or fish, a bowl of rice, *misoshiru*, shredded cabbage and some *tsukemono*. In addition, most *shokudō* serve a fairly standard selection of *donburi-mono* (rice dishes) and *menrui* (noodle dishes). When you order noodles, you can choose between *soba* and udon, both of which are served with a variety of toppings. If you're at a loss as to what to order, simply say *'kyō-no-ranchi'* (today's lunch) and they'll do the rest. Expect to spend from ¥800 to ¥1000 for a meal at a *shokudō*.

EATING IN A JAPANESE RESTAURANT

When you enter a restaurant in Japan, you'll be greeted with a hearty *'irasshaimase'* (Welcome!). In all but the most casual places the waiter will next ask you *'nan-mei sama'* (How many people?). Answer with your fingers, which is what the Japanese do. You will then be led to a table, a place at the counter or a tatami room.

At this point you will be given an *oshibori* (a hot towel), a cup of tea and a menu. The *oshibori* is for wiping your hands and face. When you're done with it, just roll it up and leave it next to your place. Now comes the hard part: ordering. If you don't read Japanese, you can use the romanised translations in this book to help you, or direct the waiter's attention to the Japanese script. If this doesn't work, there are two phrases that may help: *'o-susume wa nan desu ka'* (What do you recommend?) and *'o-makase shimasu'* (Please decide for me). If you're still having problems, you can try pointing at other diners' food or, if the restaurant has them, at the plastic food models in the window.

When you've finished eating, you can signal for the bill by crossing one index finger over the other to form the sign of an 'x'. This is the standard sign for 'bill please'. You can also say *'o-kanjō kudasai'*. Remember there is no tipping in Japan and tea is free of charge. Usually you will be given a bill to take to the cashier at the front of the restaurant. At more upmarket places, the host of the party will discreetly excuse themselves to pay before the group leaves. Unlike some places in the West, one doesn't usually leave cash on the table by way of payment. Only the bigger and more international places take credit cards, so cash is always the surer option.

When leaving, it is polite to say to the restaurant staff, *'gochisō-sama deshita'*, which means 'It was a real feast'. See Useful Words & Phrases (p93) for more restaurant words and phrases.

RICE DISHES

katsu-don	かつ丼	rice topped with a fried pork cutlet
niku-don	牛丼	rice topped with thin slices of cooked beef
oyako-don	親子丼	rice topped with egg and chicken
ten-don	天丼	rice topped with tempura shrimp and vegetables

NOODLE DISHES

kake soba/udon	かけそば/うどん	*soba*/udon noodles in broth
kitsune soba/udon	きつねそば/うどん	*soba*/udon noodles with fried tofu
nagashi-sōmen	流しそうめん	flowing noodles
reimen	冷麺	*soba* noodles served with *kimchi* (spicy Korean pickles)
soba	そば	buckwheat noodles
tempura soba/udon	天ぷらそば/うどん	*soba*/udon noodles with tempura shrimp
tsukimi soba/udon	月見そば/うどん	*soba*/udon noodles with raw egg on top
udon	うどん	thick, white wheat noodles
zaru soba	ざるそば	cold noodles with seaweed strips served on a bamboo tray

Izakaya

An *izakaya* is the Japanese equivalent of a pub-eatery. It's a good place to visit when you want a casual meal, a wide selection of food, a hearty atmosphere and, of course, plenty of beer and sake. When you enter an *izakaya*, you are given the choice of sitting around the counter, at a table or on a tatami floor. You usually order a bit at a time, choosing from a selection of typical Japanese foods, such as *yakitori* (below), sashimi and grilled fish, as well as Japanese interpretations of Western foods like French fries and beef stew.

Harumi's Japanese Cooking (Kurihara Harumi) is a well-illustrated cookbook and a good introduction to Japanese cuisine. If you want to try making some of the dishes you enjoyed while in Japan, this is an excellent choice.

Izakaya can be identified by their rustic facades and the red lanterns outside their doors bearing the kanji for *izakaya* (居酒屋). Since *izakaya* food is casual fare to go with drinking, it is usually fairly inexpensive. Depending on how much you drink, you can expect to get away with spending ¥2500 to ¥5000 per person. See also the boxed text, Ōta Kazuhiko on Japan's Izakaya (p88).

agedashi-dōfu	揚げだし豆腐	deep-fried tofu in a *dashi* broth
chiizu-age	チーズ揚げ	deep-fried cheese
hiyayakko	冷奴	a cold block of tofu with soy sauce and spring onions
jaga-batā	ジャガバター	baked potatoes with butter
kata yaki-soba	固焼きそば	hard fried noodles with meat and vegetables
niku-jaga	肉ジャガ	beef and potato stew
poteto furai	ポテトフライ	French fries
sashimi mori-awase	刺身盛り合わせ	a selection of sliced sashimi
shio-yaki-zakana	塩焼魚	a whole fish grilled with salt
tsuna sarada	ツナサラダ	tuna salad over cabbage
yaki-onigiri	焼きおにぎり	a triangle of grilled rice with *yakitori* sauce
yaki-soba	焼きそば	fried noodles with meat and vegetables

Yakitori

Yakitori (skewers of charcoal-grilled chicken and vegetables) is a popular after-work meal. *Yakitori* is not so much a full meal as an accompaniment for beer and sake. At a *yakitori-ya* (*yakitori* restaurant) you sit around a counter with the other patrons and watch the chef grill your selections over charcoal. The best way to eat here is to order several varieties, then order seconds of the ones you really like. Ordering can be a little confusing since one serving often means two or three skewers (be careful – the price listed on the menu is usually that of a single skewer).

In summer, the beverage of choice at a *yakitori* restaurant is beer or cold sake, while in winter it's hot sake. A few drinks and enough skewers to fill you up should cost ¥3000 to ¥4000 per person. *Yakitori* restaurants are usually small places, often near train stations, and are best identified by a red lantern outside and the smell of grilled chicken.

gyū-niku	牛肉	pieces of beef
hasami/negima	はさみ/ねぎま	pieces of white meat alternating with leek
kawa	皮	chicken skin
piiman	ピーマン	small green peppers
rebā	レバー	chicken livers
sasami	ささみ	skinless chicken-breast pieces
shiitake	しいたけ	Japanese mushrooms
tama-negi	玉ねぎ	round white onions
tebasaki	手羽先	chicken wings
tsukune	つくね	chicken meat balls
yaki-onigiri	焼きおにぎり	a triangle of grilled rice with *yakitori* sauce
yakitori	焼き鳥	plain, grilled white meat

Sushi & Sashimi

Like *yakitori,* sushi is considered an accompaniment for beer and sake. Nonetheless, both Japanese and foreigners often make a meal of it, and it's one of the healthiest meals around. All proper sushi restaurants serve their fish over rice, in which case it's called sushi; without rice, it's called sashimi or *tsukuri* (or, politely, *o-tsukuri*).

There are two main types of sushi: *nigiri-zushi* (served on a small bed of rice – the most common variety) and *maki-zushi* (served in a seaweed roll). Lesser-known varieties include *chirashi-zushi* (a layer of rice covered in egg and fish toppings), *oshi-zushi* (fish pressed in a mould over rice) and *inari-zushi* (rice in a pocket of sweet, fried tofu). Whatever kind of sushi you try, it will be served with lightly vinegared rice. Note that *nigiri-zushi* and *maki-zushi* will contain a bit of wasabi.

Sushi is not difficult to order. If you sit at the counter of a sushi restaurant you can simply point at what you want, as most of the selections are visible in a refrigerated glass case between you and the sushi chef. You can also order à la carte from the menu. When ordering, you usually order *ichi-nin mae* (one portion), which usually means two pieces of sushi. Be careful, since the price on the menu will be that of only one piece. If ordering à la carte is too daunting, you can take care of your whole order with just one or two words by ordering *mori-awase,* an assortment plate of *nigiri-zushi*. These usually come in three grades: *futsū nigiri* (regular *nigiri*), *jō nigiri* (special *nigiri*) and *toku-jō nigiri* (extra-special *nigiri*). The difference is in the type of fish used. Most *mori-awase* contain six or seven pieces of sushi.

The Tsukiji Fish Market in Tokyo is the world's largest. It handles 2246 tonnes of marine products a day (more than 450 kinds of fish!).

Be warned that meals in a good sushi restaurant can cost upwards of ¥10,000, while an average establishment can run from ¥3000 to ¥5000 per person. One way to sample the joy of sushi on the cheap is to try an automatic sushi place, usually called *kaiten-zushi,* where the sushi is served on a conveyor belt that runs along a counter. Here you simply reach up and grab whatever looks good to you (which certainly takes the pain out of ordering). You are charged by the number of plates of sushi that you have eaten. Plates are colour-coded by their price and the cost is written either somewhere on the plate itself or on a sign on the wall. You can usually fill yourself up in one of these places for ¥1000 to ¥2000 per person.

Randy Johnson's 'Sushi a la Carte' (www.ease.com/~randyj/rjsushi.htm) is a must for sushi lovers – it explains everything you need to know about ordering and enjoying sushi.

Before popping the sushi into your mouth, dip it very lightly in *shōyu*, which you pour from a small decanter into a low dish specially provided for the purpose. If you're not good at using *hashi* (chopsticks), don't worry – sushi is one of the few foods in Japan that is perfectly acceptable to eat with your hands. Slices of *gari* (pickled ginger) will also be served to help refresh the palate. The beverage of choice with sushi is beer or sake (hot in winter and cold in summer), with a cup of green tea at the end of the meal.

Note that most of the items on this sample sushi menu can be ordered as sashimi. Just add the words '*no o-tsukuri*' to get the sashimi version (*o-tsukuri* is the more common Japanese expression for sashimi). So, for example, if you wanted some tuna sashimi, you would order '*maguro no o-tsukuri*'. Note that sashimi often appears in other kinds of restaurants, not just sushi specialists. *Shokudō* often serve a sashimi set meal *(o-tsukuri teishoku)*, *izakaya* usually offer a plate of assorted sashimi *(otsukuri moriawase)* and *kaiseki* courses usually feature a few pieces of carefully chosen sashimi. When it's eaten at a sushi restaurant, sashimi is often the first course, a warm-up for the sushi itself. Note that you'll often be served a different soy sauce to accompany your sashimi; if you like wasabi with your sashimi, you add some directly to the soy sauce and stir.

ama-ebi	甘海老	sweet shrimp
awabi	あわび	abalone
ebi	海老	prawn or shrimp
hamachi	はまち	yellowtail
ika	いか	squid
ikura	イクラ	salmon roe
kai-bashira	貝柱	scallop
kani	かに	crab
katsuo	かつお	bonito
maguro	まぐろ	tuna
tai	鯛	sea bream
tamago	たまご	sweetened egg
toro	とろ	the choicest cut of fatty tuna belly
unagi	うなぎ	eel with a sweet sauce
uni	うに	sea urchin roe

Sukiyaki & Shabu-shabu

Restaurants usually specialise in both these dishes. Popular in the West, sukiyaki is a favourite of most foreign visitors to Japan. Sukiyaki consists of thin slices of beef cooked in a broth of *shōyu*, sugar and sake, and accompanied by a variety of vegetables and tofu. After cooking, all the ingredients are dipped in raw egg before being eaten. When made with high-quality beef, like Kōbe beef, it is a sublime experience.

Shabu-shabu consists of thin slices of beef and vegetables cooked by swirling the ingredients in a light broth, then dipping them in a variety of special sesame-seed and citrus-based sauces. Both of these dishes are prepared in a pot over a fire at your private table. Don't fret about preparation – the waiter will usually help you get started, and keep a close watch as you proceed. The key is to take your time, add the ingredients a little at a time and savour the flavours as you go.

Sukiyaki and *shabu-shabu* restaurants usually have traditional Japanese decor and sometimes a picture of a cow to help you identify them. Ordering is not difficult. Simply say sukiyaki or *shabu-shabu* and indicate how many people are dining. Expect to pay from ¥3000 to ¥10,000 per person.

KŌBE BEEF

All meals involving Kōbe beef should come with the following label: warning, consuming this beef will ruin your enjoyment of any other type of beef. We're not kidding, it's that good.

The first thing you should know about Kōbe beef is how to say it: it's pronounced 'ko bay', which rhymes with 'no way'. In Japanese, Kōbe beef is known as *Kōbe-gyū*. Second, Kōbe beef is actually just one regional variety of Japanese beef, which is known as *wa-gyū* (literally 'Japanese beef'). *Wa-gyū* can be any of several breeds of cattle bred for the extreme fatty marbling of their meat (the most common breed is Japanese Black). Kōbe beef is simply *wa-gyū* raised in Hyogō-ken, the prefecture in which the city of Kōbe is located.

There are many urban legends about Kōbe beef, promulgated, we suppose, by the farmers who raise them, or simply imaginative individuals who ascribe to cows the lives they'd like to lead. It is commonly believed that Kōbe beef cattle spend their days drinking beer and receiving regular massages. However, in all our days in Japan, we have never seen a single drunk cow or met a 'cow masseur'. More likely, the marbling pattern of the beef is the result of selective breeding and the cow's diet of alfalfa, corn, barley and wheat straw.

The best way to enjoy Kōbe beef, or any other type of *wa-gyū,* is cooked on a *teppan* (iron hotplate) at a *wa-gyū* specialist, and these restaurants are known as *teppen-yaki-ya*. In the West, a giant steak that hangs off the side of the plate is generally considered a good thing. But due to the intense richness (and price) of a good *wa-gyū* steak, it is usually consumed in relatively small portions, say, smaller than the size of your hand. The meat is usually seared quickly and then cooked to medium rare – cooking a piece of good *wa-gyū* to well done is something akin to making a tuna fish sandwich from the best cut of *toro* (fatty tuna belly) sashimi.

Although Kōbe beef and *wa-gyū* are now all the rage in Western cities, like most Japanese food, the real thing consumed in Japan is far superior to what is available overseas. And – surprise, surprise – it can be cheaper to eat it in Japan than overseas. You can get a fine *wa-gyū* steak course at lunch for around ¥5000, and at dinner for around double that. Of course, the best place for Kōbe beef is – you got it – Kōbe. See our eating reviews for Wakkoqu (p412) and Mouriya (p412) for our favourite beef specialists. Just don't blame us if this puts you off the leathery things they call steaks in the West.

Tempura

Tempura consists of portions of fish, prawns and vegetables cooked in fluffy, nongreasy batter. When you sit down at a tempura restaurant, you will be given a small bowl of *ten-tsuyu* (a light brown sauce) and a plate of grated *daikon* to mix into the sauce. Dip each piece of tempura into this sauce before eating it. Tempura is best when it's hot, so don't wait too long – use the sauce to cool each piece and dig in.

While it's possible to order à la carte, most diners choose to order *teishoku*, which includes rice, *misoshiru* and *tsukemono*. Some tempura restaurants offer courses that include different numbers of tempura pieces.

Expect to pay between ¥2000 and ¥10,000 for a full tempura meal. Finding these restaurants is tricky as they have no distinctive facade or decor. If you look through the window, you'll see customers around the counter watching the chefs as they work over large woks filled with oil.

kaki age	かき揚げ	tempura with shredded vegetables or fish
shōjin age	精進揚げ	vegetarian tempura
tempura moriawase	天ぷら盛り合わせ	a selection of tempura

Rāmen

The Japanese imported this dish from China and put their own spin on it to make what is one of the world's most delicious fast foods. *Rāmen* dishes are big bowls of noodles in a meat broth, served with a variety of toppings, such as sliced pork, bean sprouts and leeks. In some restaurants, particularly in

More than five billion servings of instant *rāmen* are consumed each year in Japan.

Kansai, you may be asked if you'd prefer *kotteri* (thick) or *assari* (thin) soup. Other than this, ordering is simple: just sidle up to the counter and say *rāmen*, or ask for any of the other choices usually on offer (a list follows). Expect to pay between ¥500 and ¥900 for a bowl. Since *rāmen* is derived from Chinese cuisine, some *rāmen* restaurants also serve *chāhan* or *yaki-meshi* (both dishes are fried rice), *gyōza* (dumplings) and *kara-age* (deep-fried chicken pieces).

Rāmen restaurants are easily distinguished by their long counters lined with customers hunched over steaming bowls. You can sometimes *hear* a *rāmen* shop as you wander by – it's considered polite to slurp the noodles and aficionados claim that slurping brings out the full flavour of the broth.

chānpon-men	ちゃんぽん麺	Nagasaki-style *rāmen*
chāshū-men	チャーシュー麺	*rāmen* topped with slices of roasted pork
miso-rāmen	みそラーメン	*rāmen* with miso-flavoured broth
rāmen	ラーメン	soup and noodles with a sprinkling of meat and vegetables
wantan-men	ワンタン麺	*rāmen* with meat dumplings

Soba & Udon

Soba (thin, brown buckwheat noodles) and udon (thick, white wheat noodles) are Japan's answer to Chinese-style *rāmen*. Most Japanese noodle shops serve both *soba* and udon in a variety of ways. Noodles are usually served in a bowl containing a light, bonito-flavoured broth, but you can also order them served cold and piled on a bamboo screen with a cold broth for dipping.

By far the most popular type of cold noodles is *zaru soba*, which is served with bits of *nori* (seaweed) on top. If you order these noodles, you'll receive a small plate of wasabi and sliced spring onions – put these into the cup of broth and eat the noodles by dipping them in this mixture. At the end of your meal, the waiter will give you some hot broth to mix with the leftover sauce, which you drink like a kind of tea. As with *rāmen*, you should feel free to slurp as loudly as you please.

Soba and udon places are usually quite cheap (about ¥900 a dish), but some fancy places can be significantly more expensive (the decor is a good indication of the price). See Noodle Dishes (p80) for more *soba* and udon dishes.

Unagi

Unagi (eel) is an expensive and popular delicacy in Japan. Even if you can't stand the creature when served in your home country, you owe it to yourself to try *unagi* at least once while in Japan. It's cooked over hot coals and brushed with a rich sauce of *shōyu* and sake. Full *unagi* dinners can be expensive, but many *unagi* restaurants offer *unagi bentō* (boxed meals) and lunch sets for around ¥1500. Most *unagi* restaurants display plastic models of their sets in their front windows, and may have barrels of live eels to entice passers-by.

kabayaki	蒲焼き	skewers of grilled eel without rice
una-don	うな丼	grilled eel over a bowl of rice
unagi teishoku	うなぎ定食	full-set *unagi* meal with rice, grilled eel, eel-liver soup and pickles
unajū	うな重	grilled eel over a flat tray of rice

Fugu

The deadly *fugu* (globefish or pufferfish) is eaten more for the thrill than the taste. It's actually rather bland – most people liken the taste to chicken – but is acclaimed for its fine texture. Nonetheless, if you have the money to lay out for a *fugu* dinner (around ¥10,000), it makes a good 'been there, done that' story back home.

Although the danger of *fugu* poisoning is negligible, some Japanese joke that you should always let your dining companion try the first piece – if they are still talking after five minutes, you can consider it safe and have some yourself. If you need a shot of liquid courage in order to get you started, try a glass of *hirezake* (toasted *fugu* tail in hot sake) – the traditional accompaniment to a *fugu* dinner.

In 1997 there were 44 cases of poisoning from eating improperly prepared *fugu* (globefish or pufferfish), resulting in three fatalities.

Fugu is a seasonal delicacy best eaten in winter. *Fugu* restaurants usually serve only *fugu*, and can be identified by a picture of a *fugu* on the sign out the front.

Fugu is the speciality of Western Honshū, and Shimonoseki (p484) is a good place to give it a try. Of course, you can also find *fugu* in other parts of Japan.

fugu chiri	ふぐちり	a stew made from *fugu* and vegetables
fugu sashimi	ふぐ刺身	thinly sliced raw *fugu*
fugu teishoku	ふぐ定食	a set course of *fugu* served several ways, plus rice and soup
yaki fugu	焼きふぐ	*fugu* grilled on a hibachi at your table

Tonkatsu

Tonkatsu is a deep-fried breaded pork cutlet that is served with a special sauce, usually as part of a set meal *(tonkatsu teishoku)*. *Tonkatsu* is served both at speciality restaurants and at *shokudō*. Naturally, the best *tonkatsu* is to be found at the speciality places, where a full set will cost ¥1500 to ¥2500. When ordering *tonkatsu*, you are able to choose between *rōsu* (a fatter cut of pork) and *hire* (a leaner cut).

hire katsu	ヒレかつ	*tonkatsu* fillet
kushikatsu	串かつ	deep-fried pork and vegetables on skewers
minchi katsu	ミンチカツ	minced pork cutlet
tonkatsu teishoku	とんかつ定食	a set meal of *tonkatsu*, rice, *misoshiru* and shredded cabbage

Kushiage & Kushikatsu

This is the fried food to beat all fried foods. *Kushiage* and *kushikatsu* are deep-fried skewers of meat, seafood and vegetables eaten as an accompaniment to beer. *Kushi* means 'skewer' and if food can be fit on one, it's probably on the menu. Cabbage is often eaten with the meal.

You order *kushiage* and *kushikatsu* by the skewer (one skewer is *ippon*, but you can always use your fingers to indicate how many you want). Like *yakitori*, this food is popular with the after-work crowd and students and is fairly inexpensive, though there are upmarket places. Expect to pay ¥2000 to ¥5000 for a full meal and a couple of beers. Not particularly distinctive in appearance, the best *kushiage* and *kushikatsu* places are found by asking a Japanese friend.

ebi	海老	prawn or shrimp
ginnan	銀杏	ginkgo nuts
gyū-niku	牛肉	pieces of beef
ika	いか	squid
imo	いも	potato
renkon	れんこん	lotus root
shiitake	しいたけ	Japanese mushrooms
tama-negi	玉ねぎ	round white onions

Okonomiyaki

The name means 'cook what you like', and an *okonomiyaki* restaurant provides you with an inexpensive opportunity to do just that. Sometimes described as Japanese pizza or pancake, the resemblance is in form only. At an *okonomiyaki* restaurant you sit around a *teppan* (iron hotplate), armed with a spatula and chopsticks to cook your choice of meat, seafood and vegetables in a cabbage and vegetable batter.

Some restaurants will do most of the cooking and bring the nearly finished product over to your hotplate for you to season with *katsuo bushi* (bonito flakes), *shōyu, ao-nori* (an ingredient similar to parsley), Japanese Worcestershire-style sauce and mayonnaise. Cheaper places, however, will simply hand you a bowl filled with the ingredients and expect you to cook it for yourself. If this happens, don't panic. First, mix the batter and filling thoroughly, then place it on the hotplate, flattening it into a pancake shape. After five minutes or so, use the spatula to flip it and cook for another five minutes. Then dig in.

Most *okonomiyaki* places also serve *yaki-soba* (fried noodles with meat and vegetables) and *yasai-itame* (stir-fried vegetables). All of this is washed down with mugs of draught beer.

One final word: don't worry too much about preparation of the food – as a foreigner you will be expected to be awkward, and the waiter will keep a sharp eye on you to make sure no real disasters occur.

gyū okonomiyaki	牛お好み焼き	beef *okonomiyaki*
ika okonomiyaki	いかお好み焼き	squid *okonomiyaki*
mikkusu	ミックスお好み焼き	mixed fillings of seafood, *okonomiyaki* meat and vegetables
modan-yaki	モダン焼き	*okonomiyaki* with *yaki-soba* and a fried egg
negi okonomiyaki	ネギお好み焼き	thin *okonomiyaki* with spring onions

Kaiseki

Kaiseki is the pinnacle of Japanese cuisine, where ingredients, preparation, setting and presentation come together to create a dining experience quite unlike any other. Born as an adjunct to the tea ceremony, *kaiseki* is a largely vegetarian affair (though fish is often served, meat never appears on the *kaiseki* menu). One usually eats *kaiseki* in the private room of a *ryōtei* (an especially elegant style of traditional restaurant), often overlooking a private, tranquil garden. The meal is served in several small courses, giving the diner an opportunity to admire the plates and bowls, which are carefully chosen to complement the food and season. Rice is eaten last (usually with an assortment of pickles) and the drink of choice is sake or beer.

The Japanese Ministry of Agriculture recently created a team to assess the quality of Japanese restaurants abroad. The so-called 'Sushi Police' are intended to put a stop to third-rate restaurants serving poor imitations of real Japanese food. Does this spell the end of the California roll?

All this comes at a steep price – a good *kaiseki* dinner costs upwards of ¥10,000 per person. A cheaper way to sample the delights of *kaiseki* is to visit a *kaiseki* restaurant for lunch. Most places offer a boxed lunch containing a sampling of their dinner fare for around ¥2500.

Unfortunately for foreigners, *kaiseki* restaurants can be intimidating places to enter. If possible, bring a Japanese friend or ask a Japanese friend to call ahead and make arrangements.

bentō	弁当	boxed meal, usually of rice, with a main dish and pickles or salad
kaiseki	懐石	traditional, Kyoto-style haute cuisine
matsu	松	extra-special course
take	竹	special course
ume	梅	regular course

Sweets

Although most restaurants don't serve dessert (plates of sliced fruit are sometimes served at the end of a meal), there is no lack of sweets in Japan. Most sweets (known generically as *wagashi*) are sold in speciality stores for you to eat at home. Many of the more delicate-looking ones are made to balance the strong, bitter taste of the special *matcha* (powdered green tea) served during the tea ceremony.

Some Westerners find Japanese sweets a little challenging, due to the liberal use of a sweet, red azuki-bean paste called *anko*. This unusual filling turns up in even the most innocuous-looking pastries. But don't let anyone make up your mind for you: try a Japanese sweet for yourself.

With such a wide variety of sweets, it's impossible to list all the names. However, you'll probably find many variations on the *anko*-covered-by-*mochi* theme.

Okashi-ya (sweet shops) are easy to spot; they usually have open fronts with their wares laid out in wooden trays to entice passers-by. Buying sweets is simple – just point at what you want and indicate with your fingers how many you'd like.

anko	あんこ	sweet paste or jam made from azuki beans
kashiwa-mochi	柏餅	pounded glutinous rice with a sweet filling, wrapped in an aromatic oak leaf
mochi	餅	pounded rice cakes made of glutinous rice
wagashi	和菓子	Japanese-style sweets
yōkan	ようかん	sweet red-bean jelly

The film *Tampopo* (Itami Jūzō, 1987) is essential preparation for a visit to Japan – especially if you intend to visit a *rāmen* shop while you're here! It's about two fellows who set out to help a *rāmen* shop owner improve her shop, with several food-related subplots woven in for good measure.

DRINKS

Drinking plays a big role in Japanese society, and there are few social occasions where beer or sake is not served. Alcohol (in this case sake) also plays a ceremonial role in various Shintō festivals and rites, including the marriage ceremony. As a visitor to Japan, you'll probably find yourself in lots of situations where you are invited to drink, and tipping back a few beers or glasses of sake is a great way to get to know the locals. However, if you don't drink alcohol, it's no big deal. Simply order *oolong cha* (oolong tea) in place of beer or sake. While some folks might put pressure on you to drink alcohol, you can diffuse this pressure by saying '*sake o nomimasen*' (I don't drink alcohol).

What you pay for your drink depends on where you drink and, in the case of hostess bars, with whom you drink. Hostess bars are the most expensive places to drink (up to ¥10,000 per drink), followed by upmarket traditional Japanese bars, hotel bars, beer halls and casual pubs. If you are not sure about a place, ask about prices and cover charges before sitting down. As a rule, if you are served a small snack (called *o-tsumami*, or charm) with your first round, you'll be paying a cover charge (usually a few hundred yen, but sometimes much more).

Izakaya and *yakitori-ya* are cheap places for beer, sake and food in a casual atmosphere resembling that of a pub. All Japanese cities, whether large or small, will have a few informal bars with reasonable prices. Such places are popular with young Japanese and resident *gaijin* (foreigners), who usually refer to such places as *gaijin* bars. In summer, many department stores and hotels in Japan's big cities open up beer gardens on the roof. Many of these places offer all-you-can-eat/drink specials for around ¥3000 per person. The action usually starts at dusk.

izakaya	居酒屋	pub-eatery
yakitori-ya	焼鳥屋	*yakitori* restaurant

Beer

Introduced at the end of the 1800s, *biiru* (beer) is now the favourite tipple of the Japanese. The quality is generally excellent and the most popular type is light lager, although recently some breweries have been experimenting with darker brews. The major breweries are Kirin, Asahi, Sapporo and Suntory. Beer is dispensed everywhere, from vending machines to beer halls,

ŌTA KAZUHIKO ON JAPAN'S IZAKAYA

Ōta Kazuhiko is considered by many to be Japan's leading authority on *izakaya*, Japan's beloved pub-eateries. Ōta-san travels the length of Japan seeking out the best traditional *izakaya* and he has published his findings in over a dozen books, including one titled *Ōta Kazuhiko no Izakaya Mishuran*, the 'Mishuran' in the title being a play on the famed Michelin restaurant guide series.

What is the definition of an *izakaya*? Simply put, an *izakaya* is a place where you can enjoy sake. More broadly, an *izakaya* is a place where you can enjoy sake and food. In addition, they are places that you can easily enter alone.

What is the history of the *izakaya*? Prior to the Meiji period, *saka-ya* (sake shops) would serve alcohol to customers who dropped by for a drink. The customers would stand around and drink their sake out of *masu* (square wooden boxes used to measure sake). Thus, these places were *tachi-nomiya* (stand-and-drink places). Later, some *saka-ya* turned the sake barrels into seats for their customers, so they could relax and enjoy their drink. Thus, they became '*izakaya*' (the 'i' here means 'to be', which added to *saka-ya* forms *izakaya*, or a *saka-ya* where you can stay and drink). Later on, some places started to serve snacks to go with the sake, and this evolved into proper food to go with the sake.

What role did *izakaya* play in Japanese society? *Izakaya* played an important role in Japanese society. Traditionally, after men finished work at a company, they would go together to an *izakaya*. The older members of the group, or the boss, would often pay for the younger workers. While they drank, they could talk freely about work and also about things outside of work, like their

and even in some temple lodgings. A standard can of beer from a vending machine is about ¥250, although some of the gigantic cans cost more than ¥1000. At bars, a beer starts at ¥500 and the price climbs upwards, depending on the establishment. *Nama biiru* (draught beer) is widely available, as are imported beers.

biiru	ビール	beer
nama biiru	生ビール	draught beer

Shōchū

For those looking for a quick and cheap escape route from the sorrows of the world, *shōchū* is the answer. It's a distilled spirit made from a variety of raw materials, including potato (in which case it's called *imo-jōchū*) and barley (in which case it's called *mugi-jōchū*). It's quite strong, with an alcohol content of about 30%. In recent years it has been resurrected from its previous lowly status (it was used as a disinfectant in the Edo period) to become a trendy drink. You can drink it *oyu-wari* (with hot water) or *chūhai* (in a highball with soda and lemon). A 720mL bottle sells for about ¥600, which makes it a relatively cheap option compared with other spirits.

chūhai	チューハイ	*shōchū* with soda and lemon
oyu-wari	お湯割り	*shōchū* with hot water
shōchū	焼酎	distilled grain liquor

Wine, Imported Drinks & Whisky

Japanese wines are available from areas such as Yamanashi, Nagano, Tōhoku and Hokkaidō. Standard wines are often blended with imports from South America or Eastern Europe. The major producers are Suntory, Mann's and Mercian. Expect to pay at least ¥1000 for a bottle of something drinkable. Imported wines are often stocked by large liquor stores or department stores in the cities. Bargains are sometimes available at ¥600, but most of the quaffable imports cost considerably more.

personal lives and their past. The older guys would teach the young ones how to drink, how to order, and also about the ways of the world. Thus, the *izakaya* served as a place of human and social education, not just drinking places.

What should you order in an *izakaya*? First of all, don't rush. Just have a look around. Maybe start with some *ginjō-shu* (a high-grade sake). Have the first one cold. Then, consider having some hot sake. As for food, seafood is the way to go: sashimi, stewed fish, grilled fish or shellfish. You can also try some chicken dishes. Have a look at what the other customers are eating, or check out the specials board. If you can't speak or read Japanese, you can point at things or bring along a Japanese friend to help you order.

Where can you find good *izakaya*? Well, there are lots of chain *izakaya* near the train stations in most cities, but the best place to look for really good places is in the old *hankagai* (entertainment district), which is usually not where the train station is. The best places have been run for generations by the same family, and the customers have also been coming for generations. So, the master might have watched his customers grow up. These are the places that take pride and their work and are the most reliable.

What is the best thing about *izakaya*? *Izakaya* are places where people show their true selves, their true hearts. The sake allows people to drop their pretensions and let their hair down. *Izakaya* are places where people show their individuality. They bind people together, whether strangers or friends. I think all countries have a place like this, but in Japan, if you want to see the way people really are, the *izakaya* is the place to go.

Prices of imported spirits have been coming down in recent years and bargain liquor stores have been popping up in bigger cities. However, if you really like imported spirits, it is probably a good idea to pick up a duty-free bottle or two on your way through the airport. Whisky is available at most drinking establishments and is usually drunk *mizu-wari* (with water and ice) or *onzarokku* (on the rocks). Local brands, such as Suntory and Nikka, are sensibly priced, and most measure up to foreign standards. Expensive foreign labels are popular as gifts.

Most other imported spirits are available at drinking establishments in Japan. Bars with a large foreign clientele, including hotel bars, can usually mix anything you request. If not, they will certainly tailor a drink to your specifications.

uisukii	ウィスキー	whisky
mizu-wari	水割り	whisky, ice and water
onzarokku	オンザロック	whisky with ice

Nonalcoholic Drinks

Most of the drinks you're used to at home will be available in Japan, with a few colourfully named additions like Pocari Sweat and Calpis Water. One convenient aspect of Japan is the presence of drink-vending machines on virtually every street corner, and at ¥120, refreshment is rarely more than a few steps away.

COFFEE & TEA

Kōhii (coffee) served in a *kissaten* (coffee shop) tends to be expensive in Japan, costing between ¥350 and ¥500 a cup, with some places charging up to ¥1000. A cheap alternative is one of the coffee-restaurant chains like Doutor or Pronto, or doughnut shops like Mr Donut (which offers free refills). An even cheaper alternative is a can of coffee, hot or cold, from a vending machine. Although unpleasantly sweet, at ¥120 the price is hard to beat.

SAKE *Paul Warham*

Brewed from rice, sake has been enjoyed for centuries in Japan, and although it's been overtaken in terms of consumption by beer and *shōchū* (distilled grain liquor) in recent years, it is still regarded by most Japanese people as the national drink. Indeed, what we call 'sake' in the West is more commonly known as *nihonshu* in Japan: the 'drink of Japan'. Sake has traditionally been associated with Shintō and other traditional ceremonies, and you will still see huge barrels of sake (known as *o-miki*) on display at almost every shrine you visit. Although consumption has been on the wane in recent years, it is generally agreed that the quality of sake available is better now than ever, and many of the best have a complexity of flavours and aromas comparable to the fine wines and beers of Europe.

Not surprisingly, sake makes the perfect accompaniment to traditional Japanese food, and sake pubs (see *izakaya*, p80) generally also serve excellent seasonal fish and other foods to go with the booze. Sake is drunk chilled *(reishu)*, at room temperature *(jō-on)*, warmed *(nuru-kan)* or piping hot *(atsu-kan)*, according to the season and personal preference. The top-drawer stuff is normally served well chilled. Sake is traditionally served in a ceramic jug known as a *tokkuri*, and poured into tiny cups known as *o-choko* or *sakazuki*. A traditional measure of sake is one *gō* (一合), a little over 180mL, or 6 fluid oz. In speciality bars, you'll have the option of ordering by the glass, which will often be filled to overflowing and brought to you in a wooden container to catch the overspill. If you're in company, the tradition is to pour for your neighbour first, and then be waited on by them in turn.

Sake is brewed during the winter, in the cold months that follow the rice harvest in September. The main ingredients are rice and yeast, together with a benign mould known as *kōji* that helps to convert the starch in the rice into fermentable sugars. Sake is categorised by law into two main classes: *futsū-shu* (ordinary sake, which makes up the bulk of what's produced), and premium sake known as *tokutei-meishōshu*, further classified by the extent to which the rice is refined before fermentation to remove proteins and oils that interfere with the flavour of the final product. This is generally shown on the label as the *seimai buai*, expressed as the percentage of the original size to which the grain is reduced by polishing before the brewing process starts. As a general rule, the lower this number, the better (or at least, the more expensive) the sake will be. Sake made from rice polished to 60% or less of its original size is known as *ginjō*; rice polished to 50% or less of its original size produces the finest sake of all, known as *dai-ginjō*. Sake made only with rice and *kōji* (without the use of added alcohol) is known as *junmai-shu*, or 'pure rice' sake.

When ordering coffee at a coffee shop in Japan, you'll be asked whether you like it *hotto* (hot) or *aisu* (cold). Black tea also comes hot or cold, with *miruku* (milk) or *remon* (lemon). A good way to start a day of sightseeing in Japan is with a *mōningu setto* (morning set) of tea or coffee, toast and eggs, which costs around ¥400.

American kōhii	アメリカンコーヒー	weak coffee
burendo kōhii	ブレンドコーヒー	blended coffee, fairly strong
kafe ore	カフェオレ	*café au lait*, hot or cold
kōcha	紅茶	black, British-style tea
kōhii	コーヒー	regular coffee
orenji jūsu	オレンジジュース	orange juice

JAPANESE TEA

Unlike black tea, which Westerners are familiar with, most Japanese tea is green and contains a lot of vitamin C and caffeine. The powdered form used in the tea ceremony is called *matcha* (see Japanese Tea Culture, p94) and is drunk after being whipped into a frothy consistency. The more common form, a leafy green tea, is simply called *o-cha*, and is drunk after being steeped in a pot. In addition to green tea, you'll probably drink a lot of a brownish tea called *bancha*, which restaurants serve for free. In summer, a cold beverage called *mugicha* (roasted barley tea) is served in private homes.

Sake is brewed in every prefecture in Japan, with the single exception of Kagoshima in southern Kyūshū, the traditional stronghold of the distilled drink known as *shōchū* (see p88), and there are more than 1500 breweries in operation today. Niigata and other parts of Northern Honshū are particularly famous for the quality of their sake, with Hiroshima and Nada-ku (in Kōbe) also major centres of the brewing industry. Almost everywhere you go in Japan you will have an opportunity to drink sake brewed just a few miles from where you are staying. A foreign visitor who shows an interest in the *jizake* (local brew) is likely to be treated to enthusiastic recommendations and the kind of hospitality that has been known to lead to sore heads the next morning.

ama-kuchi	甘口	sweet flavour
ama-zake	甘酒	sweet sake served at winter festivals
dai-ginjō	大吟醸	sake brewed from rice polished down to at least 50% of its original size
futsū-shu	普通酒	ordinary sake
genshu	原酒	undiluted sake, often with an alcohol content close to 20%
ginjō	吟醸	sake brewed from rice polished down to at least 60% of its original size
jizake	地酒	'local sake', often from small, traditional breweries
junmai-shu	純米酒	pure rice sake, made from only rice, *kōji* and water
kara-kuchi	辛口	dry, sharp flavour
kōji	麹	*kōji* mould
kura, saka-gura	蔵 酒蔵	sake brewery
nama-zake	生酒	fresh, unpasteurised sake
nigori-zake	濁り酒	milky-white 'cloudy sake', often rather sweet
nihonshu	日本酒	Japanese word for sake
o-choko	お猪口	small cups traditionally used for sake
seimai buai	精米歩合	expressed as the percentage of the original size to which the grain is reduced by polishing before the brewing process starts
tokkuri	徳利	traditional ceramic serving vessel
tokutei-meishōshu	特定名称酒	premium sake

bancha	番茶	ordinary-grade green tea, has a brownish colour
matcha	抹茶	powdered green tea used in the tea ceremony
mugicha	麦茶	roasted barley tea
o-cha	お茶	leafy green tea
sencha	煎茶	medium-grade green tea

CELEBRATIONS

When the Japanese celebrate, it must include food and drink, and lots of it, whether it is in a rural festival to appease the rice gods (themselves not averse to the odd glass of sake) or in the party-hard *izakaya* of the big cities. And it's fun. Everyone seems to know about the famous Japanese reserve – everyone, that is, except the Japanese themselves.

The celebratory year begins in homes and restaurants on 1 January, with the multicourse, lavish, colourful *osechi-ryōri* (special New Year's cuisine that involves dishes chosen for their symbolic meaning, including shrimp, fish eggs and cooked vegetables). Served in *jūbako* (four-layered lacquerware boxes), *osechi* originated primarily as a means of giving the overworked Japanese housewife three days' much-needed rest – its ingredients last well.

The 3rd (or 4th) of February sees beans employed not as an ingredient, but as weapons in the fight against evil, at the Setsubun Matsuri. To celebrate the end of winter (last day of winter according to the lunar calendar), events are often held at local shrines throughout the country with characters dressed as devils, who act as good targets for beans. Worshippers and tourists gleefully pepper costumed demons with hard soy beans, to the cry of '*oni wa soto, fuku wa uchi*' (out with the demons, in with good luck). Japanese also eat *maki-zushi* on this day, facing a lucky direction, which changes each year, in addition to eating one bean for each year of their age, plus another for good luck.

Common at many celebrations, but especially at the Hina Matsuri (Girls' Day celebration; 3 March), is *seki-han* (red-bean rice), made from glutinous and nonglutinous rice mixed with the red azuki bean, which gives it its sweetness and characteristic pink colour.

What's What in Japanese Restaurants: A Guide to Ordering, Eating and Enjoying (Robb Satterwhite) is a brilliant guide to what's on offer in Japanese restaurants. With thorough explanations of the various types of Japanese dishes and sample English/Japanese menus, this is a must for those who really want to explore and enjoy Japanese restaurants.

Late March or early April sees the much-anticipated coming of the cherry blossoms. The Japanese gather for *hanami* (flower-viewing parties), which during the brief, glorious reign of the pink blossoms transform every inch of open space into a riot of alcohol-drenched, raucous contemplation of the evanescence of life and beauty. As if the cherry blossoms overhead weren't enough, the Japanese eat a variety of pink and white *mochi* on sticks during these parties, which is supposed to resemble the branches from a cherry tree.

The Japanese summer is long, hot and very humid. Its star festival is Kyoto's July Gion Matsuri (p367), nicknamed Hamo Matsuri, the Pike-conger Festival, for the large quantities of the beast consumed during that time. Pike-conger and eel are famed for their invigorating qualities and their ability to restore flagging appetites.

New Year (Shōgatsu; p29) is one of the most food-centred festivals in Japan, the time when distant family members gather for a three-day bout of feasting and drinking, punctuated with the sacred first visit to the local shrine. Inevitably, it's a freezing midwinter night, and the warm *ama-zake* (sweet sake served at winter festivals) served at the shrine helps keep out the winter chill. The first dish of the year will be *toshi-koshi soba,* long buckwheat noodles symbolising long life and wealth, as *soba* dough was once used by gold traders to collect gold dust. To cries of '*yoi o-toshi o*' (have a happy New Year) and, postmidnight, '*akemashite omedetō gozaimasu*' (happy New Year), the cycle of eating and celebration continues anew…

VEGETARIANS & VEGANS

Travellers who eat fish should have almost no trouble dining in Japan: almost all *shokudō, izakaya* and other common restaurants offer a set meal with fish as the main dish. Vegans and vegetarians who don't eat fish will have to get their protein from tofu and other bean products. Note that most *misoshiru* is made with *dashi* that contains fish, so if you want to avoid fish, you'll also have to avoid *misoshiru.*

Most big cities in Japan have vegetarian and/or organic restaurants that naturally will serve a variety of choices that appeal to vegetarians and vegans. (See the Eating sections of the destination chapters for specific recommendations. Reviews that include the V icon throughout this guide indicate places that have a good vegetarian selection.) In the countryside, you'll have to do your best to find suitable items on the menu, or try to convey your dietary preferences to the restaurant staff. Note that many temples in Japan serve *shōjin-ryōri,* Buddhist vegetarian cuisine, which is made without meat, fish or dairy products. A good place to try this is Kōya-san (p437) in Kansai.

For some ways to express your dietary preferences to restaurant staff, see Useful Words & Phrases (p95).

EATING WITH KIDS

Travelling with children in Japan is easy, as long as you come with the right attitudes, equipment and the usual parental patience. There's such a variety of food on offer that even the most particular eaters can find something to their liking, and if noodles and rice begin to pale there are always Japanese fast-food chains in almost every city, with options including soup, pizza, sandwiches and burgers. At most budget restaurants during the day, you can find '*okosama-ranchi*' (children's special), which is often Western style and actually rather good, though its minihamburgers and wiener sausages won't appeal to non-meat-eaters.

The Useful Words & Phrases section (p96) contains a few phrases that will come in handy when dining out with children in tow.

HABITS & CUSTOMS

Japanese people generally eat breakfast at home, where a few slices of bread and a cup of coffee are quickly taking over from the traditional Japanese breakfast of rice, fish and *misoshuri* as the breakfast of choice. If they don't eat at home, a *mōningu setto* of toast and coffee at a coffee shop is the norm.

The Insider's Guide to Sake (Philip Harper) offers a fine introduction to sake, including information on how to choose a good sake and the history of the drink.

Lunch is often eaten at a *shokudō* or a noodle restaurant, usually in the company of coworkers, but alone if a partner can't be found.

Evening meals can be a mixed bag in Japan. Many people, of course, eat at home, but the stereotype of the salaryman heading out for drinks and dinner every evening after work with his workmates has some basis in fact.

Weekends are when almost everyone, if they can afford it, heads out for dinner with friends and family, and at this time many eateries are packed with groups of people eating, drinking, conversing and generally having a ball.

Mealtimes are pretty much the same as in many parts of the West: breakfast is eaten between 6am and 8am, lunch is eaten between noon and 2pm, and dinner is eaten between 7pm and 9pm.

COOKING COURSES

If you enjoy the food in Japan, why not deepen your appreciation of Japanese cuisine by taking a cooking class? There are good cooking courses available in both Tokyo and Kyoto, and these companies can also arrange market tours:

A Taste of Culture (☎ 03-5716-5751; www.tasteofculture.com; courses from ¥5500) Offers cooking courses, and can create custom courses. For more, see p161.

Uzuki (www.kyotouzuki.com; 3hr class per person ¥3500) Learn how to cook typical Japanese dishes in a Kyoto home. You can request specific dishes, including Japanese sweets. Reserve via website. For more information, see p366.

WAK Japan (☎ 075-212-9993; www.wakjapan.com; 412-506 Iseya-chō, Kamigyō-ku, Kyoto) Offers cooking courses, and can create courses to suit special interests. For more, see p366.

USEFUL WORDS & PHRASES

Eating Out

Table for (one/two/three/…), please.

(hitori/futari/san-nin/… -nin) onegai shimas[u] — (一人/二人/三人/…人), お願いします。

I'd like to reserve a table for eight o'clock (tonight/tomorrow night).

(konban/ashita no ban) hachi-ji ni yoyaku shitai no des[u] ga — (今晩/明日の晩) 八時に予約したいのですが。

JAPANESE TEA CULTURE *Morgan Pitelka, PhD*

Tea came to Japan from China as part of a cultural package that included kanji and Buddhism, but the beverage did not become popular until the medieval period. Buddhist monks drank tea for its medicinal and stimulatory properties, a practice that gradually spread to warrior society and then to commoners. By the 16th century, elite urban commoners such as the merchant and tea master Sen no Rikyû (1522–91) had elevated the preparation, serving and consumption of *matcha* (powdered green tea) to an elaborate performance art. In the 17th century, tea masters established their own schools of tea, and these institutions codified, spread and protected the practice over subsequent centuries.

Although *chanoyu* (literally 'hot water for tea') or *sadō/chadō* (literally 'the way of tea') is usually referred to in English as 'the tea ceremony', the practice has always been more focused on collaboration, pleasure and artistic appreciation than on dutiful ritual. Tea gatherings can be short and spontaneous or long and extremely formal. They might be held to mark an anniversary or the changing of the seasons, or just as an opportunity to see old friends.

Typically, a group of guests arrives at the location of the gathering, perhaps a home or a temple with its own tea house, and waits in the outer garden, a peaceful and meditative space. After entering the tea house, the guests observe while the host arranges the charcoal and serves a special meal known as *kaiseki* cuisine (p86). After the meal, they eat some simple sweets, take a brief intermission and then return for a serving of viscous *koicha* (thick tea) followed, in many cases, by a round of *usucha* (thin tea). The movements of the host and guests are carefully choreographed and rehearsed, making the sharing of the beverage a satisfying mutual performance.

We have a reservation.
yoyaku shimash[i]ta 予約しました。

We don't have a reservation.
yoyaku shiteimasen 予約していません。

What's that?
are wa nan des[u] ka あれは何ですか?

What's the speciality here?
koko no tokubetsu ryōri wa nan des[u] ka ここの特別料理は何ですか?

What do you recommend?
o-susume wa nan des[u] ka おすすめは何ですか?

Do you have ...?
... ga arimas[u] ka …がありますか?

Can I see the menu, please?
menyū o misete kudasai メニューを見せてください。

Do you have a menu in English?
eigo no menyū wa arimas[u] ka 英語のメニューはありますか?

I'd like...	*... o kudasai*	…をください。
Please bring me...	*... o onegai shimas[u]*	…をお願いします。
some/more bread	*pan*	パン
some pepper	*koshō*	コショウ
a plate	*sara*	皿
some salt	*shio*	塩
soy sauce	*shōyu*	醤油
a spoon	*supūn*	スプーン
a beer	*biiru*	ビール
some water	*mizu*	水
some wine	*wain*	ワイン
The (bill/check), please.	*(o-kanjō/o-aiso) o onegai shimas[u]*	(お勘定/おあいそ)をお願いします。

At certain moments during the gathering, the guests have the chance to admire the hanging scroll, the flower arrangement and the host's careful selection of *chadōgu* (tea utensils).

Tea culture has stimulated and supported traditional arts and crafts in Japan for centuries, and utensils – including tea bowls, tea caddies, tea scoops, tea whisks and tea ladles – can be purchased in tea shops, in local galleries or directly from artists. Urban department stores, such as Takashimaya, Daimaru, Seibu and Mitsukoshi, among many others, frequently have whole floors devoted to ceramics, bambooware, lacquerware and other crafts. There are also galleries in which the finest artists hold solo exhibitions and sales. A trip to a town famous for its crafts, such as Bizen (p454), Hagi (p486) or Karatsu (p698), gives travellers further opportunities to buy tea utensils.

Some tea schools, such as Urasenke (www.urasenke.or.jp/texte/index.html), Omotesenke (www.omotesenke.jp/english/tobira.html), Mushanokojisenke and Dai Nippon Chado Gakkai, hold tea gatherings that are open to the public, particularly in large cities. Speciality cafes, such as the confectionary Toraya, also offer a serving of sweets and tea. Museums that specialise in art associated with tea, such as Kyoto's Nomura Art Museum (www.nomura-museum.or.jp), Raku Museum (www.raku-yaki.or.jp), the Kitamura Museum (www.raku-yaki.or.jp/culture/english/kitamura.html) and Tokyo's Gotoh Museum (www.gotoh-museum.or.jp), display historical tea utensils and on occasion serve tea as well.

Morgan Pitelka is the author of Handmade Culture: Raku Potters, Patrons, and Tea Practitioners in Japan.

You May Hear

Welcome/May I help you?
irasshaimase いらっしゃいませ

Welcome!
irasshai いらっしゃい！

By yourself?
o-hitori-sama des[u] ka お一人さまですか?

(Two/Three/Four) persons?
(ni/san/yon) -mei-sama des[u] ka (二名/三名/四名)さまですか?

This way, please.
kochira e dōzo こちらへどうぞ。

May I take your order?
(go-chūmon wa) o-kimari des[u] ka (ご注文は)お決まりですか?

Vegetarian & Special Needs

I'm a vegetarian.
watashi wa bejitarian des[u] 私はベジタリアンです。

I'm a vegan, I don't eat meat or dairy products.
watashi wa saishoku-shugisha des[u] kara, niku ya nyūseihin wa tabemasen 私は菜食主義者ですから, 肉や乳製品は食べません。

Do you have any vegetarian dishes?
bejitarian-ryōri ga arimas(u) ka ベジタリアン料理がありますか?

Is it cooked with pork lard or chicken stock?
kore wa rādo ka tori no dashi o tsukatte imas[u] ka これはラードか鶏のだしを使っていますか?

I don't eat …	*… wa tabemasen*	…は食べません。
meat	*niku*	肉
pork	*buta-niku*	豚肉
seafood	*shiifūdo/kaisanbutsu*	シーフード/海産物

I'm allergic to (peanuts).
watashi wa (pīnattsu) arerugii des[u] 私は(ピーナッツ)アレルギーです。

The superb Tokyo Food Page (www.bento.com) offers explanations of Japanese dishes, great places to eat in Tokyo and much, much more.

Children

Are children allowed?
kodomo-zure demo ii des[u] ka 子供連れでもいいですか?

Is there a children's menu?
kodomo-yō no menyū wa arimas[u] ka 子供用のメニューはありますか?

Do you have a highchair for the baby?
bebii-yō no isu wa arimas[u] ka ベビー用の椅子はありますか?

Environment

Japan may be small, crowded and heavily industrialised, but make no mistake: this mountainous chain of nearly 4000 islands has some of the most breathtaking and varied scenery in the world. Tropical beaches, snowbound mountaintops and hot-spring valleys await those with enough determination to escape the sprawl of Tokyo and Osaka and explore the Japanese countryside. The human impact on the environment in Japan is often brutal, but enough of the country's original beauty remains that even the most jaded travellers may feel inspired.

The classic postcard image of a *shinkansen* (bullet train) speeding past a snowcapped Mt Fuji, perhaps with a bough of cherry blossoms in the foreground, is the Japanese ideal of modern technology in harmony with traditional aesthetics. The reality is that Mt Fuji is a breathtakingly lovely mountain to behold, but its foothills are blighted by an eye-glazing stretch of puffing factories and concrete. Yet viewed from a quiet hiking path away from the traffic corridors, the mountain – like the rest of Japan's natural environment – is quite stunning.

Concrete is an unfortunate theme of Japan's environment. Decades of public works projects have produced a land of mountainsides, embankments, shorelines, rivers and streams covered with concrete or otherwise reinforced. Landslides and erosion are real threats in Japan, but often the countermeasures seem like overkill: witness massive concrete fortifications built up around minuscule brooks.

In 2000 Japan's cement production was around twice the global average, according to the *Japan Times*. Some 5570km of Japan's coastline, or nearly 50%, has been completely or substantially altered by cement.

Fortunately, environmental consciousness is on the rise in Japan, and more effort is being put into recycling, conservation and protection of natural areas. Through this, hopefully some of Japan's remaining areas of beauty will be preserved for future generations.

THE LAND

Japan is an island nation but it has not always been so. As recently as the end of the last ice age, around 10,000 years ago, the level of the sea rose enough to flood a land bridge that connected Japan to the Asian continent. Today, Japan consists of a chain of islands that rides the back of a 3000km-long arc of mountains along the eastern rim of the continent. It stretches from around 25°N at the southern islands of Okinawa to 45°N at the northern end of Hokkaidō. Cities at comparable latitudes are Miami and Cairo in the south and Montreal and Milan in the north. Japan's total land area is 377,435 sq km, and more than 80% of it is mountainous.

Alex Kerr's book *Dogs and Demons: Tales from the Dark Side of Modern Japan* is a primer on the country's addiction to wasteful construction projects. Check out Kerr's website at www.alex-kerr.com.

Japan consists of some 3900 small islands and four major ones: Honshū (slightly larger than Britain), Hokkaidō, Kyūshū and Shikoku. Okinawa, the largest and most significant of Japan's many smaller islands, is about halfway along an archipelago that stretches from the western tip of Honshū almost all the way to Taiwan. It is far enough from the rest of Japan to have developed a culture that differs from that of the 'mainland' in many respects.

There are several disputed islands in the Japanese archipelago. The most important of these are the Kuril Islands, north of Hokkaidō. Seized by Russia at the close of WWII, they have been a source of tension between Japan and Russia ever since. While the Japanese have made some progress towards their return in recent years, they remain part of Russia.

If Japanese culture has been influenced by isolation, it has equally been shaped by the country's mountainous topography. A number of the mountains are volcanic, and more than 100 of these are active, many of them

A MIXED BAG *Timothy N Hornyak*

Japan is known for designing energy-efficient products, and its arts and traditional culture have a deep sensitivity to nature and the seasons. But what's the view on conservation among the Japanese?

It's a mixed bag. Most Japanese cooperate with complex municipal waste policies, and throw away only half as much as Americans do. But it's not unusual to see country roadsides littered with unwanted vehicles and appliances. Old TVs, PCs and other Japanese 'e-waste' often end up in unregulated markets in China and the Philippines, where toxic components enter the environment after they're stripped for valuable metals.

Japanese who live around reactor sites and ports where US nuclear-powered vessels call are extremely sensitive about possible contamination. Others are very fussy about smells, which is why Japan's incinerators (three-quarters of trash is burned) are some of the most sophisticated and odourless on the planet. Dioxins from incineration were a major air contaminant through the late 1990s.

More and more people are using traditional *furoshiki* wrapping cloths or canvas bags for shopping, but for every supermarket trying to help the environment there are thousands of other retailers handing out plastic bags like they're going out of style. Not to mention the 5.5 million vending machines nationwide pumping out plastic bottles and cans.

For every laudable Japanese attitude towards the environment, there's another discouraging practice. When I visited Chichibu-jinja in Saitama-ken outside Tokyo, its priest proudly told me that the shrine was established over a thousand years ago near the base of sacred Mt Bukōzan. He spoke about the importance of nature to Japan's indigenous Shintō religion. I expressed interest in visiting Bukōzan, and the priest was pleased to show me the way.

But when I got there, I was shocked. The entire upper third of the sacred peak looked like a moonscape. It had been strip-mined for limestone by half a dozen concrete factories on its flanks. Peeking through the window of one factory office, I spotted something that symbolised for me Japan's often contradictory attitude towards nature – a small Shintō shrine.

on the southern island of Kyūshū. The Meteorological Agency watches 34 volcanoes in Japan around the clock. One of the latest eruptions was Mt Asama, a volcano northwest of Tokyo that sent smoke 2km into the air and cast ash over parts of the capital in February 2009.

On the plus side, all of this geothermal activity is responsible for Japan's fabulous abundance of onsen (hot springs).

Some Japanese households recycle their bathwater in their laundry machines. Hang-drying clothes in the sun is still favoured over dryers.

Japan has the dubious distinction of being one of the most seismically active regions of the world. More than 1000 earthquakes a year rock the country, most of which are too small to notice. Seismic activity is concentrated in the Kantō region, home to Tokyo. But earthquakes can strike any part of the archipelago, as the citizens of Kōbe discovered in the disastrous earthquake of January 1995, which killed more than 5000 people.

WILDLIFE

The latitudinal spread of the islands of Japan makes for a wide diversity of flora and fauna. The Nansei and Ogasawara archipelagos in the far south are subtropical, and flora and fauna in this region are related to those found on the Malay peninsula. Mainland Japan (Honshū, Kyūshū and Shikoku), on the other hand, shows more similarities with Korea and China, while subarctic northern and central Hokkaidō have their own distinct features.

Animals

Japan's land bridge to the Asian continent allowed the migration of animals from Korea and China. There are species that are unique to Japan, such as the Japanese giant salamander and the Japanese macaque. In addition,

Nansei-shotō, which has been separated from the mainland for longer than the rest of Japan, has a few examples of fauna (eg the Iriomote cat) that are classified by experts as 'living fossils'.

Japan's largest carnivorous mammals are its bears. Two species are found in Japan – the *higuma* (brown bear) of Hokkaidō, and the *tsukinowaguma* (Asiatic brown bear) of Honshū, Shikoku and Kyūshū.

According to a 2006 report by the International Union for Conservation of Nature and Natural Resources (IUCN), there are 132 endangered species in Japan. Endangered species include the Iriomote cat, the Tsushima cat, Blakiston's fish owl and the Japanese river otter.

Japan: The Cycle of Life is a gorgeously illustrated book about how nature and the seasons traditionally have been incorporated into all aspects of life. It is co-authored by CW Nicol, a conservationist and columnist who owns a forest in Nagano-ken.

Plants

The flora of Japan today is not what the Japanese saw hundreds of years ago. This is not just because a lot of Japan's natural landscape has succumbed to modern urban culture, but also because much of Japan's flora is imported. It is thought that 200 to 500 plant species have been introduced to Japan since the Meiji period, mainly from Europe but also from North America. Japanese gardens laid out in the Edo period and earlier are good places to see native Japanese flora, even though they are highly manicured environments.

The cool to temperate zones of Central and Northern Honshū and southern Hokkaidō were home to broad-leaf deciduous forests, and still are, to a certain extent. Nevertheless, large-scale deforestation is a feature of contemporary Japan. Pollution and acid rain have also taken their toll. Fortunately, the sheer inaccessibility of much of Japan's mountainous topography has preserved some areas of great natural beauty – in particular the alpine regions of Central Honshū and the lovely national parks of Hokkaidō.

Twenty-five billion pairs of *waribashi* (disposable chopsticks) are used in Japan annually – equivalent to the timber needed to build 17,000 houses.

According to a 2008 report in the *Proceedings of the Japan Academy*, there are 1690 endangered and threatened species of vascular plants in Japan. For more information, visit the Biodiversity Center of Japan's website at www.biodic.go.jp/index_e.html.

NATIONAL PARKS

Japan has 29 *kokuritsu kōen* (national parks) and 56 *kokutei kōen* (quasi-national parks). Ranging from the far south (Iriomote National Park) to the northern tip of Hokkaidō (Rishiri-Rebun-Sarobetsu National Park), the parks represent an effort to preserve as much as possible of Japan's natural environment. Although national and quasi-national parks account for less

SUSTAINABLE TRAVEL IN JAPAN

As a traveller, there are several ways you can minimise your impact on the Japanese environment.

Cut down on packaging Many Japanese are nuts about packaging – some would say overpackaging. The solution to this is simply to refuse excess packaging. When purchasing goods, you can say *'Fukuro wa irimasen'* (I don't need a bag), or simply *'Kekkō desu'* (That's alright).

Refuse hand towels *Oshibori* are moist hand towels given to customers at restaurants, pubs and bars. They can be reusable cotton or disposable paper. While this hospitality is just the thing for sticky fingers before a meal, it harms the environment through the laundering of used towels, transport and the cutting of trees.

Carry your own chopsticks Carry your own chopsticks around with you and say no to *waribashi* (disposable chopsticks) provided in restaurants. Either keep the first nice pair of *waribashi* that you are given, or visit a convenience store or 100 yen shop and ask for *my hashi* (lacquered, washable chopsticks with a carrying case).

A little less tuna, please When you go to a sushi place, try to stay away from species of fish that are endangered, like *maguro* (tuna), including *toro* (fatty tuna belly). We know, this one hurts!

COOL BIZ, HOT TREND

Japan managed to cut CO_2 emissions by about 1.4 million tons in both summer 2006 and 2007 – roughly equivalent to all emissions generated in the Tokyo area over one month – by making every work day a casual Friday. In a successful public campaign, air-conditioners are used less, office workers dress down and inveterately unstylish bureaucrats look, well, almost hip. Welcome to Cool Biz.

The Cool Biz campaign has made Japan's torrid summers more bearable. Spearheaded by the central government, it runs from early June through September. Office workers are encouraged to leave their suits and neckties at home in favour of short-sleeved shirts and other light garments. This allows for office thermostats to be set at 28°C instead of the average 26.2°C, cutting air-conditioner use and saving electricity.

Launched in 2005 by then Environment Minister Yuriko Koike, Cool Biz was also taken up by Japan's private sector, famous for its hidebound 'salarymen' workers. The change was shocking for these corporate warriors, whose ubiquitous dark suits are an essential part of Japanese business protocol. But Koike had charismatic former prime minister Koizumi Junichirō as an ally. They convinced the establishment that dressing down isn't impolite and it promotes the greater good, something inherently supported in Japan. They were so persuasive that Supreme Court judges and the president of Toyota Motor Corporation were also seen unbuttoned. The powerful Keidanren business lobby reported that 70% of its member companies set their thermostats to 28°C.

Koike organised Cool Biz fashion shows to spread the message. Clothing makers responded by producing a greater variety of lightweight suits and business attire. Salarymen found themselves getting 'global-warming underwear' and Cool Biz haircuts; retailers profited from a boom in sales. Necktie makers, though, were singing the blues.

In winter, the government has promoted the Warm Biz campaign. Offices are encouraged to lower thermostats and workers are asked to wear sweaters and warmer clothing to reduce electricity used for heating. According to a 2007 survey by the Ministry of the Environment, 52% of respondents used heating less, up 21 percentage points from 2005. Sales of hot-water bottles and blankets, some featuring stylish designs, have jumped.

After four summers of Cool Biz, energy-saving wardrobes seem to have become conventional wisdom for doing business. It's an example of Japanese environmental leadership that has inspired similar campaigns in South Korea and Britain and at the United Nations. Japan can be environmentally cool, after all.

than 1% of Japan's total land area, it is estimated that 14% of Japan's land is protected or managed for sustainable use.

Few of the parks have facilities that you might expect in national parks (ranger stations, camping grounds, educational facilities etc). More importantly, national-park status doesn't necessarily mean that the area in question is free from residential, commercial or even urban development.

The highest concentration of national parks and quasi-national parks is in Northern Honshū (Tōhoku) and Hokkaidō, where the population density is relatively low. But there are also national parks and quasi-national parks, such as Chichibu-Tama and Nikkō, within easy striking distance of Tokyo.

For descriptions of Japan's parks, see www.env.go.jp/en/np/index.html.

Toyota Motor Corporation topped the 2008 ranking of Nikkei Inc's greenest manufacturers for the third straight year for its pollution and recycling measures. Toyota has sold over 1.67 million hybrid vehicles worldwide.

ENVIRONMENTAL ISSUES

Japan was the first Asian nation to industrialise. It has also been one of the most successful at cleaning up the resulting mess.

In the early postwar years, there was widespread public ignorance of the problems of pollution, and Japan was more concerned with rebuilding its infrastructure and economy. Industrial pollution was at its worst from the mid-1960s to the mid-1970s. But public awareness of the issue had already been awakened by an outbreak in 1953 of what came to be called Minamata disease, after the town of the same name, in which up to 6000 people were affected by mercury poisoning. It was not until 1968 that the government officially acknowledged the cause of the 'disease'.

In the 1960s laws were passed to curb air and water pollution. These have been reasonably successful, though critics are quick to point out that while toxic matter has been mostly removed from Japanese waters, organic pollution remains a problem. Photochemical smog emerged as a problem in Tokyo in the early 1970s; it remains a problem and also affects other cities.

Under the 1997 Kyoto Protocol, Japan pledged to cut emissions by 6% from 1990 levels, but emissions to 2007 rose by 8%. The government lets companies implement voluntary environmental action plans.

In 1972 the government passed the Nature Conservation Law, which aimed to protect the natural environment and provide recreational space for the public. National parks, quasi-national parks and prefectural parks were established, and it appears that these measures have been successful in increasing wildlife numbers.

More recently, Japan has been facing a new set of problems, including a series of accidents at nuclear reactors. These have forced the government to revise its safety guidelines for the nuclear-power industry. Meanwhile, Japanese automakers have led international efforts to develop and popularise energy-saving vehicles such as hybrid cars.

Since the nation's largest nuclear-power plant was deactivated following a quake in 2007, fossil fuel use has risen, and overall carbon emissions are expected to have increased in 2009. While businesses are not legally compelled to cut emissions, the government has suggested upping Japan's solar-power generation capacity 10 times by 2020 and 40 times by 2030. But as the prolonged global recession bites hard into the Japanese economy, environmental initiatives may be put on the back burner.

The Onsen

Japan is in hot water. Literally. The stuff percolates up out of the ground from one end of the country to the other. The Japanese word for a hot spring is onsen, and there are more than 3000 of them in the country, more than anywhere else on earth – it's like Iceland on steroids. So if your idea of relaxation involves spending a few hours soaking away your aches and cares in a tub of bubbling hot water, then you've definitely come to the right place.

With so many onsen, it's hardly surprising that they come in every size, shape and colour. There is an onsen on an artificial island in Tokyo Bay. There are onsen high up in the Japan Alps that you can only get to by walking for a full day over high mountain peaks. There are onsen bubbling up among the rocks on the coast that only exist when the tide is just right.

Some Japanese will tell you that the only distinctively Japanese aspect of their culture – that is, something that didn't ultimately originate in mainland Asia – is the bath. There are accounts of onsen bathing in Japan's earliest historical records, and it's pretty certain that the Japanese have been bathing in onsen as long as there have been Japanese.

Over the millennia, they have turned the simple act of bathing in an onsen into something like a religion. And, for the average modern Japanese, making a pilgrimage to a famous onsen is the closest he or she will come to a religious pilgrimage.

Today, the ultimate way to experience an onsen is to visit an onsen ryokan, a traditional Japanese inn with its own private hot-spring bath on the premises. At an onsen ryokan you spend all day enjoying the bath, relaxing in your room and eating sumptuous Japanese food.

SO CLOSE TO HEAVEN *Chris Rowthorn*

Takama-ga-hara is a natural sanctuary in the heart of the northern Japan Alps. The name means 'high heaven plain' and it's very apt. Most people take at least two days to walk here from the nearest trailhead. But I had only three days to spend in the mountains, and I wanted to check out the sanctuary and then make it all the way down to Yari-ga-take, a fine peak two days' walk south of there, so I rushed things a bit.

I climbed from the Oritate trailhead, over Taro-san, and walked down the lovely Yakushi-zawa valley. I made it to Yakushi-koya, a hut located at the bottom of the valley. It was already about 2pm. I asked the hut owner if he thought I could make it to Takama-ga-hara and he looked at me like I was mad. Nonetheless, I set out.

Turns out the hut owner was right. The light was fading and I was completely exhausted as I finally arrived at Takama-ga-hara-koya hut. I could barely walk, but I knew the onsen was only another 20 minutes' walk into the forest.

I dropped my bag and made my way along the trail in the fading light. Finally, I heard the sound of a stream rushing down a mountainside. I crossed the river and there it was – Takama-ga-hara Onsen (see also p105) – the simplest of tubs sitting right beside the river. It was deserted and that suited me just fine.

I stripped down, splashed quick buckets over myself and plunged in. It was pure bliss. It took a few minutes to gather my wits. But, when I did, I realised that I was sitting in one of the most spectacular natural baths anywhere. I was smack dab in the middle of the Japan Alps, with mountains forming a perfect circle around me and a fine alpine river cascading by me. And, I had it all to myself. There was no place in the world I would rather have been.

JEWELLERY WARNING

The minerals in certain onsen can discolour jewellery, particularly anything made of silver. However, don't worry too much if you forget to take off your silver wedding ring before jumping in the tub. After a few hours, the discolouration usually fades.

Like many of the best things in life, some of the finest onsen in Japan are free. Just show up with a towel and your birthday suit, splash a little water on yourself and plunge in. No communication hassles, no expenses and no worries. And even if you must pay to enter, it's usually just a minor snip – averaging about ¥700 (US$7) per person.

BEST ONSEN EXPERIENCES

With so many great onsen to choose from in Japan, it's tricky to pick favourites. And no matter how many onsen you try, there's always the suspicion that somewhere out there is the holy grail of onsen just waiting to be discovered. That said, we're going to go way out on a limb here and recommend a few of our favourites, broken up into categories to help you choose. Here goes…

Urban Onsen

Ōedo Onsen Monogatari (Tokyo; p158) Located on the artificial island of Odaiba out in Tokyo Bay, this giant super onsen is modelled on an Edo-period town. There is a huge variety of tubs, including outdoor tubs, as well as restaurants, relaxation rooms and shops. You can even get a massage and spa treatments. You can easily spend a whole day here soaking away your cares.

Ocean-side Onsen

Jinata Onsen (Shikine-jima, Izu-shotō; p242) The setting of this onsen couldn't be more dramatic: it's located in a rocky cleft in the seashore of lovely little Shikine-jima, an island only a few hours' ferry ride from downtown Tokyo. The pools are formed by the seaside rocks and it's one of those onsen that only works when the tide is right. You can spend a few lovely hours here watching the Pacific rollers crashing on the rocks. And, there are two other excellent onsen on the island when you get tired of this one.

Riverside Onsen

Takaragawa Onsen (Gunma-ken; p206) Japanese onsen connoisseurs often pronounce Gunma-ken's onsen to be the best in the country. Difficult for us to argue. Takaragawa means 'treasure river', and its several slate-floored pools sit along several hundred metres of riverbank, surrounded by maple trees and mountains. Most of the pools are mixed bathing, with one ladies-only bath. The alkaline waters are said to cure fatigue, nervous disorders and digestive troubles.

Onsen Town

Kinosaki (Kansai; p388) Kinosaki, on the Sea of Japan coast in northern Kansai, is the quintessential onsen town. With seven public baths and dozens of onsen ryokan, this is the place to sample the onsen ryokan experience, eg Nishimuraya Honkan (p106). You can relax in your accommodation, taking the waters as it pleases you, and when you get tired of your ryokan's bath, you can hit the streets in a *yukata* (light cotton kimono) and *geta* (wooden sandals) and soak in the public baths. It doesn't hurt that the town is extremely atmospheric at night, and the local winter speciality, giant crab, goes down pretty nice after a day of onsen-hopping.

'The local winter speciality, giant crab, goes down pretty nice after a day of onsen-hopping'

Clifftop Onsen

Sawada-kōen Rotemburo onsen (Dōgashima, Izu-hantō; p226) If you like a view with your bath, you won't do any better than this simple *rotemburo* (outdoor bath) perched high on a cliff overlooking the Pacific Ocean. We liked it early in the day, when you can often have it all to yourself. Of course, if you don't mind a crowd, it's a great place to watch the sunset.

Hidden Onsen

Lamp no Yado (Noto-hantō, Central Honshū; p319) The Noto-hantō peninsula is about as far as one can go in Central Honshū, and the seaside is about as far as one can go on Noto-hantō. A country road takes you to a narrow

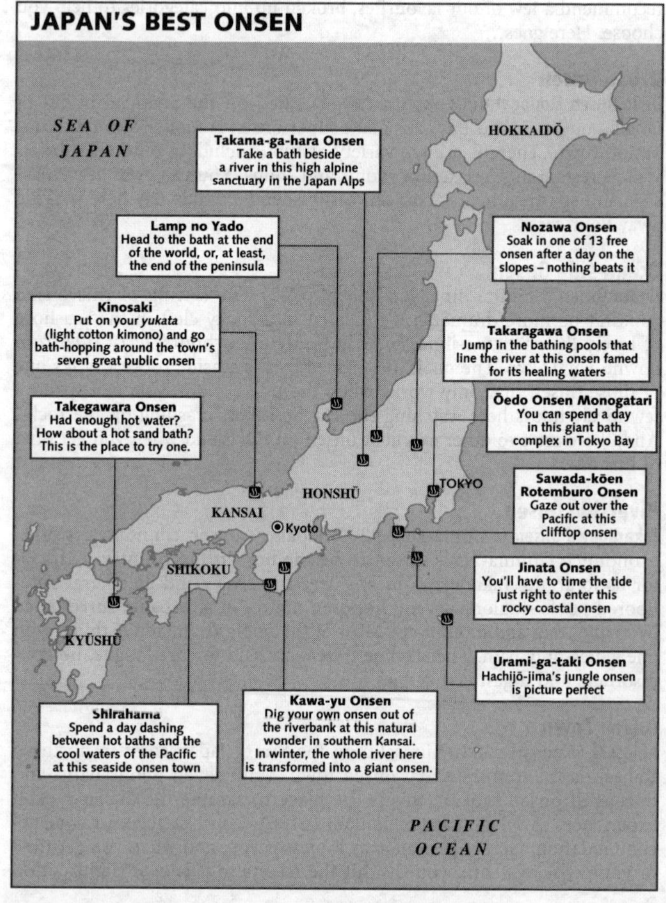

JAPAN'S BEST ONSEN
SEA OF JAPAN
HOKKAIDŌ
Takama-ga-hara Onsen
Take a bath beside a river in this high alpine sanctuary in the Japan Alps
Lamp no Yado
Head to the bath at the end of the world, or, at least, the end of the peninsula
Nozawa Onsen
Soak in one of 13 free onsen after a day on the slopes – nothing beats it
Kinosaki
Put on your *yukata* (light cotton kimono) and go bath-hopping around the town's seven great public onsen
Takaragawa Onsen
Jump in the bathing pools that line the river at this onsen famed for its healing waters
Takegawara Onsen
Had enough hot water? How about a hot sand bath? This is the place to try one.
Ōedo Onsen Monogatari
You can spend a day in this giant bath complex in Tokyo Bay
TOKYO
HONSHŪ
KANSAI
Kyoto
Sawada-kōen Rotemburo Onsen
Gaze out over the Pacific at this clifftop onsen
SHIKOKU
Jinata Onsen
You'll have to time the tide just right to enter this rocky coastal onsen
KYŪSHŪ
Urami-ga-taki Onsen
Hachijō-jima's jungle onsen is picture perfect
Shirahama
Spend a day dashing between hot baths and the cool waters of the Pacific at this seaside onsen town
Kawa-yu Onsen
Dig your own onsen out of the riverbank at this natural wonder in southern Kansai. In winter, the whole river here is transformed into a giant onsen.
PACIFIC OCEAN

TATTOO WARNING

Be warned that if you have any tattoos, you may not be allowed to enter Japanese onsen or *sentō* (public baths). The reason for this is that *yakuza* (Japanese mafia) almost always sport tattoos. Banning people with tattoos is an indirect way of banning gangsters. Unfortunately, to avoid the appearance of unfairness (and because Japan is a country where rules are rigorously adhered to), the no-tattoo rule also applies to foreigners. If your tattoo is small enough to cover with some adhesive bandages, then cover it up and you'll have no problem. Otherwise, ask the people at the front desk if you can go in despite your tattoos. The phrase to use is: *'irezumi wa daijōbu desu ka'* (are tattoos okay?).

1km path, from where you have to climb down a zigzagging hillside path on foot. No wonder this property has been a refuge for centuries of Japanese seeking to cure what ails them. Even if one night here now costs what people would have once spent over weeks, it's a worthy splurge for a dark-wood and tatami room on a cove, with its own *rotemburo* and Sea of Japan views through craggy rocks.

Semitropical Onsen

Urami-ga-taki Onsen (Hachijō-jima, Izu-shotō; p244) Even in a country of lovely onsen, this is a real standout: the perfect little *rotemburo* located next to a waterfall in lush semitropical jungle. It's what they're shooting for at all those resorts on Bali, only this is the real thing. Sitting in the bath as the late-afternoon sunlight pierces the ferns here is a magical experience. Did we mention that it's free?

Onsen/Beach Combination

Shirahama (Shirahama, Wakayama-ken, Kansai; p438) There's something peculiarly pleasing about dashing back and forth between the nippy ocean and a natural hot-spring bath – the contrast in temperature and texture is something we never tire of. At Shirahama, a beach town in southern Kansai, there is a free onsen right on the beach. And, Sakino-yu Onsen (p439) here is just spectacular – it's one of our favourite onsen in all Japan.

Onsen/Sand Bath Combination

Takegawara Onsen (Beppu, Kyūshū; p752) Sometimes simplest is best. This traditional Meiji era onsen first opened in 1859, and its smooth wooden floors transport you back to a Japan of neighbourhood pleasures – unpretentious, relaxing and accessible to all. There are separate (and very hot) baths for men and women. Takegawara also offers heated sand baths in which, wearing a cotton *yukata*, you are buried up to your neck with hot sand for 10 to 15 minutes, followed by a rinse and a soak in an adjacent onsen bath.

Mountain Onsen

Takama-ga-hara Onsen (Northern Japan Alps, Central Honshū; p102) Located high, high up in the Japan Alps, if you want to soak in this wonderful free riverside *rotemburo*, you're going to have to hike for at least a full day. It's located in a lofty natural sanctuary with stunning mountain scenery on all sides. To tell the truth, even if it took three days of walking to get here, it would be worth it. Some Japanese say that this is the highest *rotemburo* in Japan, and it's definitely one of the best. You can spend the night nearby in a creaky old mountain

DO 'YU' SPEAK ONSEN?

yu	ゆ or 湯	hot water
o-yu	お湯	hot water (polite)
dansei-no-yu	男性の湯	male bath
otoko-yu	男湯	male bath (most commonly used)
josei-no-yu	女性の湯	female bath
onna-yu	女湯	female bath (most commonly used)
konyoku	混浴	mixed bath
kazoku-no-yu	家族の湯	family bath
rotemburo	露天風呂	outdoor bath
kake-yu	かけ湯	rinsing one's body
yubune	湯船	bath tub
uchi-yu	内湯	private bath

hut. The onsen is in the middle of the northern Japan Alps, roughly halfway between Murodo, on the Tateyama-kurobe Alpen Route (p305), and Kamikōchi (p280).

Do-It-Yourself Onsen

Kawa-yu Onsen (Kawa-yu, Wakayama-ken, Kansai; p442) If you like doing things your own way, you'll love this natural oddity of an onsen in southern Kansai. Here, the onsen waters bubble up through the rocks of a riverbed. All you have to do is choose a likely spot, dig out a natural hot pot along the riverside, and wait for it to fill with hot water and – *voila* – your own private *rotemburo*. In the winter, it gets even better: they use bulldozers to turn the entire river into a giant 1000-person onsen. It doesn't hurt that the river water is a lovely translucent emerald colour.

Onsen Ryokan

Nishimuraya Honkan (Kinosaki, Kansai; p389) If you want to sample the ultimate in top-end onsen ryokan, this is the place. With several fine indoor and outdoor baths and elegant rooms, your stay here will be a highlight of your trip to Japan, and will shed some light on why the Japanese consider an onsen vacation to the be ultimate in relaxation.

Onsen Ski Town

Nozawa Onsen (Nagano, Central Honshū; p293) What could be better than a day spent on the slopes, followed by a soak in a Jacuzzi? Well, how about a day on the slopes followed by a soak in a real natural hot spring? This is skiing the Japanese way. This fine little ski town boasts some first-rate skiing, reliable snow, ripping alpine views and no fewer than 13 free onsen. Best of all, the onsen here are scalding hot, which is a nice contrast to the snow outside and feels wonderful on tired skier's legs.

ONSEN ETIQUETTE

First: relax. That's what onsen are all about. You'll be relieved to hear that there really is nothing tricky about taking an onsen bath. If you remember just one basic point, you won't go too far wrong. This is the point: the water in the pools and tubs is for soaking in, not washing in, and it should only be entered after you've washed or rinsed your body.

This is the drill. Pay your entry fee, if there is one. Rent a hand towel if you don't have one. Take off your shoes and put them in the lockers or shelves provided. Find the correct changing room/bath for your gender (man: 男; woman: 女). Grab a basket, strip down and put your clothes in the basket. Put the basket in a locker and bring the hand towel in with you.

Once in the bathing area, find a place around the wall (if there is one) to put down your toiletries (if you have them) and wash your body, or, at least, rinse your body. You'll note that some scofflaws dispense with this step and just stride over to the tubs and grab a bucket (there are usually some around) and splash a few scoops over their 'wedding tackle'. Some miscreants can't even be bothered with this step and plunge right into the tubs unwashed and unrinsed. Frankly, we like to think that these people will be reincarnated into a world where there are only cold-water showers for their bathing needs.

Skiing in Japan

With over 600 ski resorts and some of the most reliable snow anywhere, Japan may be the skiing world's best-kept secret – the perfect place to combine some world-class skiing with an exotic vacation. Japan offers stunning mountain vistas, great runs at all levels of difficulty, kilometres of groomed runs along with ripping mogul runs, snowboard parks, friendly locals and good food. And let's not forget Japan's incredible variety of onsen (hot springs) for that all-important après-ski soak.

Easily the best source of online information on skiing in Japan can be found at www.snowjapan.com. This site has extensive resort info, snow reports, transport and accommodation info and booking services, as well as information on English ski lessons. And it's all in English.

With so many ski resorts, you're spoiled for choice in Japan. Powder hounds flock to Hokkaidō's Niseko, which offers the world's most reliable lift-served powder snow. Others head to the sprawling Shiga Kōgen resort in Central Honshū, by some estimations the largest ski resort in the world. Those who want a little European atmosphere head for nearby Nozawa Onsen, which, like its name suggests, offers great hot springs as well as excellent skiing. In addition to headlining places like these, you'll also find plenty of small local areas near the big areas, and these are often great for families.

Skiing in Japan is remarkably reasonable: it actually costs less to ski here than in comparable areas in North America and Europe. For information on costs, see below. It's also quite easy to get from gateways like Tokyo's Narita International Airport and Osaka's Kansai International Airport to the slopes. For details, see Getting to the Slopes (opposite).

COSTS

Many people unfamiliar with skiing in Japan often assume that it will cost an arm and a leg to ski here. But, even after factoring in the international air ticket, it might actually be cheaper to ski for a week in Japan than in your home country. Are we mad? Well, let's check the numbers.

Hokkaidō's Niseko ski area receives a whopping 15m of snow every year.

- **Lift tickets** A full-day lift ticket at most areas in Japan costs around ¥4800 (US$50). This is significantly less than a full day at large resorts in North America or Europe. Many resorts also offer packages including lunch or even a dip in an onsen. Note that you will also have to put down a deposit of ¥1000 for your electronic chip ski pass, which you must scan in the lift line. You will get this back when you're done skiing.
- **Accommodation** You can find plenty of accommodation in the ¥8000 per person (US$82 per person) range at most major areas in Japan, and this will often include one or two meals. This is *less than half* of what you'd expect to pay for similar accommodation in the USA or Europe. The budget traveller will find a variety of backpacker-type hostels near most resorts, and families will be glad to know that younger children (usually under six years of age) are usually included free or at a discount.
- **Food** On-slope meals average around ¥1000 (around US$10). This is less than you'd expect to pay in North America or Europe. The restaurant selection anywhere you go is fantastic, including the likes of 'make-your-own-pizza', kebabs and pitas, *rāmen* (egg noodle) shops, regular curry-rice fare, and even a fast-food chain or two in the main resorts. Beer and snacks are more expensive – better to bring your own to the slopes than to buy from one of the ubiquitous convenience stores if you want to save a few yen.
- **Transport** Airport-to-resort transport in Japan costs no more than in other countries, and is usually faster and more efficient (and unlike in North America, you don't need to rent a car). See Getting to the Slopes (opposite) for more details.

GETTING TO THE SLOPES

Japan's brilliant public transport system makes getting to the slopes a breeze. Take Japan's premier resort, Niseko in Hokkaidō. If you're coming from abroad and want to go straight to the resort, you'll find the journey painless and efficient. First, you fly into Tokyo's Narita International Airport, then change to a domestic flight to Sapporo's New Chitose Airport. Buses to Niseko depart from right outside the arrivals hall here, take a mere 2½ hours and cost only ¥2300 (about US$24) to reach the resort. If you arrive in Sapporo in the morning, you can be skiing that afternoon. Likewise, the journey by train from Tokyo to Nagano, the heart of Japan's Central Honshū ski country, takes only 1¾ hours and costs only ¥7970 (about US$82). And the best part is this: you get to ride on one of the country's ultramodern *shinkansen* (bullet trains). You could literally start the day with a look at Tokyo's incredible Tsukiji Fish Market and be skiing in Nagano that afternoon.

The 1998 Winter Olympics were held at Nagano, in Central Honshū. The downhill events were held at Happō-One resort, the slalom and giant slalom events were held at Shiga Kōgen resort, and the biathlon was held at Nozawa Onsen resort.

WHERE TO SKI

Japan's best ski resorts are found in the Japan Alps region of Central Honshū (mostly in Nagano and Niigata prefectures) and on the northern island of Hokkaidō. The former lays claim to the highest mountains; the latter lays claim to the deepest and most regular snow in the country. Both regions offer first-class skiing.

If you're interested in doing some sightseeing in cities like Kyoto, Nara and Tokyo in addition to your skiing, you might consider hitting the resorts in the Japan Alps. If skiing is your main goal, then Hokkaidō might be the way to go (although, to be fair, the difference is really only one quick internal flight).

What follows is our five best ski areas in Japan. This is just to whet your appetite – there are over 600 more that we don't mention here.

Niseko

As far as most Australian skiers are concerned, 'Niseko' is how you say powder in Japanese. This is understandable, since Niseko receives an average of 15m of snow annually. Niseko, located on Japan's northern island of Hokkaidō, is actually four interconnected ski areas: Hirafu, Higashiyama, An'nupuri and Hanazono. One lift ticket gives access to all 60 runs and 20 ski lifts. Snowboarding is allowed on all slopes. Needless to say, with so many Aussie skiers making a yearly pilgrimage to Niseko, you'll find that communication is a breeze, and if you like Vegemite on your morning toast, you'll find that, too. If you're heading to Niseko in early February, don't miss Sapporo's famous Yuki Matsuri (p589). For more information on Niseko, see p602).

Nearly 90% of foreign skiers at Niseko come from Australia.

Happō-One

Nagano-ken's Happō-One (pronounced hah-poh-oh-nay) is the quintessential Japan Alps ski resort. With the sprawling Hakuba mountain range as

SKI-DŌ: THE JAPANESE WAY OF SKIING

Snow is snow, skis are skis, right? How different can it be to ski in Japan? At first glance, you might conclude that ski areas in Japan are exactly like those at home. But, as Vincent Vega observed in the movie *Pulp Fiction*, 'it's the little differences'. Throughout the day, these little differences will keep reminding you that you're not in, say, New Zealand, Colorado or the Swiss Alps.

- Pop music – often really annoying pop music – is played along ski lifts and in restaurants. Bring an MP3 player if you prefer real music to the latest girl/boy band.
- The signposting is inconsistent and irregular, something you may not expect in Japan. It's a good idea to study the map carefully and plan a central meeting point/time at the beginning of the day.
- Not all resorts use the green/blue/black coding system for difficulty. Some have red, purple, orange, dotted lines, or black numbered runs on the map.
- The majority of Japanese skiers start skiing at 9am, have lunch at exactly 12 noon, and get off the hill by 3pm. If you work on a slightly different schedule, you will avoid a lot of the crowds.
- You will find young Aussies, Kiwis and Canadians working the lifts and restaurants at many Japanese resorts (a popular way for people from these countries to earn money, do a little skiing and see the country). These folks are always a good source of information.
- Snowboarders are everywhere in Japan, but unlike in areas back home, few of them seem to do much snowboarding. In Japan, the usual position for a snowboarder is sitting on his/her bum surrounded by friends doing the same. Consider them natural hazards and give them a wide berth.
- Lift-line management is surprisingly poor in Japan. Skiers are often left to jostle and fend for themselves, and even when it's crowded, singles are allowed to ride triple and quad lifts alone.
- Off-piste and out-of-bounds skiing is often high quality but also highly illegal and potentially dangerous, resulting in the confiscation of your lift pass if caught by the ski patrol. Cut the ropes at your own risk. Every year people go missing in the mountains and have to be rescued at great expense. Additionally, it must be noted that Japan has ideal conditions for avalanches, and the powder isn't worth the risk if you aren't trained in backcountry safety.

SKIING LESSONS IN ENGLISH

The following outfits offer skiing lessons in English for both children and adults (usually with foreign instructors).

- **Canyons Japan** (www.canyons.jp/index_E.html) With a base at Hakuba (p294; close to Happō-One), Canyons offers skiing, backcountry skiing and snowboarding lessons, as well as snowshoeing tours.
- **Evergreen** (www.evergreen-hakuba.com) Also in Hakuba, Evergreen offers skiing, snowboarding, powder skiing and telemark lessons.
- **SAS Snow Sports** (www.sas-net.com) Based in Niseko (p602), SAS offers snowshoe tours.

a backdrop, it offers eye-popping views in addition to excellent and varied skiing. The layout is pretty straightforward here, with plenty of good wide burners heading straight down the fall line from the top of the area. There are both groomed runs and bump runs and you can descend most of the mountain on either. The village at the base of the mountain has several good onsen and lots of foreigner-friendly accommodation. For more information on Happō-One, see p294.

Shiga Kōgen

Also in Central Honshū's Nagano-ken, Shiga Kōgen is the world's largest ski area, with an incredible 21 different interlinked areas, all interconnected by trails and lifts and accessible with one lift ticket. Needless to say, with so many different areas, there is something for (almost) everyone here, including one skier-only area. This is a very family-friendly area, and there's lots of accommodation right at the base of the slopes, so you can ski right from your lodgings. Like most other major resorts in Japan, there are also some good onsen around for soaking out the kinks after a day on the slopes. While you're there, you can make an easy side trip to Yudanaka to see Japan's famous 'snow monkeys' (see p291). For more information on Shiga Kōgen, see p291.

Snowboarding first debuted as an Olympic sport at the 1998 Nagano Winter Olympics.

Nozawa Onsen

This quaint little ski resort/village tucked high up in the Japan Alps of Nagano-ken is the closest thing you'll find to Switzerland in Japan. The only difference is, unlike Switzerland, this village has 13 free onsen scattered around for your entertainment. Of course, skiing is the main reason to visit, and it's excellent here. The area is more compact and easy to get around than Shiga Kōgen, and it has a good variety of runs, including some challenging bump runs. Snowboarders will enjoy the terrain park and half-pipe and there's a cross-country skiing course up on the mountain as well. For more information on Nozawa Onsen, see p293.

The world's longest ski lift, the 'Dragondola', a 5.4km-long gondola, can be found at the Naeba ski resort (p576), in Niigata-ken.

Rusutsu

Hokkaidō's Rusutsu is luring a lot of skiers away from Niseko. It gets regular dumps of deep powder snow, and allows skiers and boarders to enjoy it both on piste and off piste (there are some great tree runs and the management doesn't try to prevent you from enjoying them). Rusutsu tends to be less crowded than Niseko and as long as the lifts aren't shut down due to high winds, you won't often wait in line here. All in all, if you're going to ski in Hokkaidō, we recommend that you at least give one day to Rusutsu – you may like it as much or even more than Niseko. For more information on Rusutsu, see p606.

WHAT TO BRING

With the exception of really large ski boots (see below), almost everything you need is available in Japan. However, due to prices or difficulty in finding some items, it's best to bring the following things from abroad:

- **A small 'around the arm' type case to hold your ski lift chip** You will be scanning this at every lift – having it on your arm is easily the best place to keep it.
- **Goggles** They're very expensive in Japan, so it's best to bring your own.
- **Sunscreen** Sunblock, aspirin, and other pharmacy items you're used to may be hard to track down, so it's best to bring your own favourites.
- **Large-sized ski boots** Rental places at most resorts have boots up to 30cm (which is equivalent to a men's size 12 in the USA, UK or Australia), though boots up to 31cm are available at Happō-One (p110) and Nozawa Onsen (p111). If you have larger feet, you'll have trouble finding your size.
- **Mobile phone(s)** Many of Japan's ski areas are covered by one or more mobile-phone networks, and these are a great way to keep in touch with others in your party. You can easily rent mobile phones in Japan (see p821).

The first Winter Olympics to be held outside of Europe or North America were held at Sapporo in 1972.

Before you start your skiing day, it's also useful to grab a bunch of ¥1000 notes and ¥500 and ¥1000 coins, as many of the rest houses on the mountain have vending machines.

CAN YOU SAY SKI IN JAPANESE?

That's right: it's 'ski' (alright, it's pronounced more like 'sukee'). But the point is, communication won't be much of a problem on your Japan ski trip. Tackling the language barrier has never been easier: most resorts employ a number of English-speaking foreigners on working-holiday visas. They work the lifts and in the cafeterias, and often find work in the hotels or ryokan that are most popular with foreign guests. All major signs and maps are translated into English, and provided you have some experience at large resorts back home, you'll find the layout and organisation of Japanese resorts to be pretty intuitive. The information counter at the base of the mountain always has helpful and polite staff available to answer questions.

Architecture

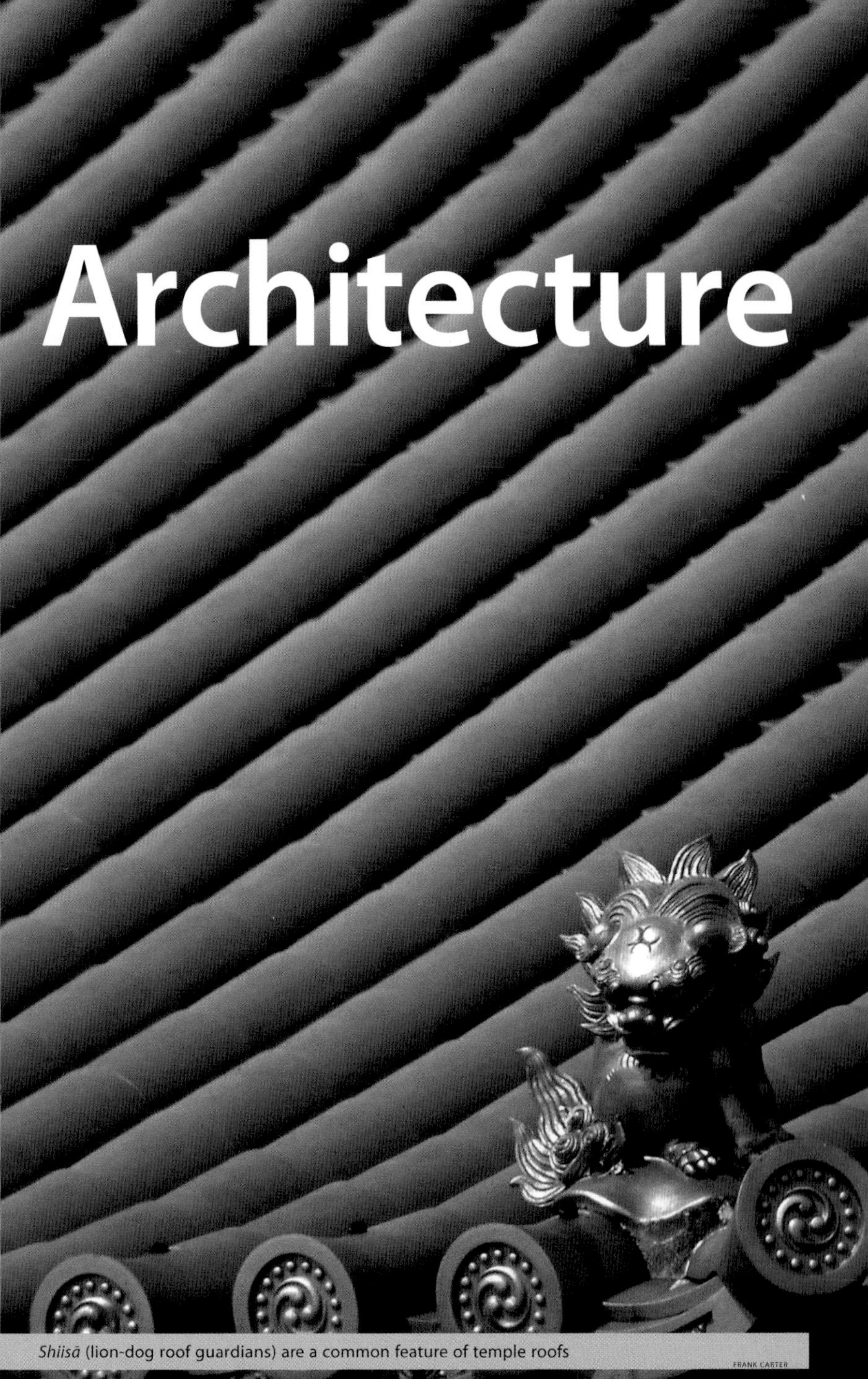

Shiisā (lion-dog roof guardians) are a common feature of temple roofs

FRANK CARTER

Most *Nihon* neophytes liken their first glimpses of Japan to touching down on an alien world. The sounds are different, the smells are different, but it's the sights that truly transport visitors to another planet – a place where glances out of the *shinkansen* (bullet-train) window reveal an awe-inducing alternative universe bubbling over with bright lights and geometric shapes. From the wooden temples hidden in a bamboo forest, to the urban frenzies of metal and glass, Japan offers the ultimate feast of architectural eye candy.

THE ESSENCE OF JAPANESE DESIGN

But what is 'Japanese' design really? It would be horribly cliché for us to say that what defines the Japanese aesthetic is its lack of definability, but alas, 'quintessential Japanese' architecture is a bit ambiguous. This ambiguity of style is exacerbated when contrasted with the fundamentals of Western design, like the Five Orders of classical Greek columns. Many see Japanese style as sleek, minimal and austere; simplicity has been attributed to structures epitomising a Japanese style. Although Japanese architecture historically embraces a simple style, it is difficult to fully reconcile this characteristically unadorned aesthetic with a modern nondescript facade. Traditional Japanese design prioritises the space within, so emphasis should not be placed on the exterior details, but rather the interior function of the building. The function of the space was paramount in traditional Japanese architectural design and the austereness of an edifice encouraged its own disappearance.

Rice-paper doors shield a Kyoto restaurant
FRANK CARTER

There is, however, one other factor at play in the creation of Japan's anything-goes urban centres. For centuries, the Japanese have carefully woven together the fabric of their culture by assimilating foreign ideas, inventions and customs, and modifying them – essentially turning them Japanese. The notion of assimilation and adjustment transcends all aspects of the nation's culture from the importation and reinterpretation of Buddhism to the eclectic assortment of local cuisine. Japan's urban landscape is rife with modern architecture from the West that has been re-envisioned and taken to the next level.

MONKS & TREE TRUNKS

Upon glimpsing the visual chaos of Japan's urban centres, it's hard to believe that once upon a time, the local architectural aesthetic

TOKYO BOUTIQUES

Pop icon Gwen Stefani once described Tokyo's vibrant, fashion-hungry vibe as 'a pedestrian paradise where the catwalk got its claws', and her observation pretty much holds true. Shopping is a national pastime – a competitive sport, even – where Gucci purses and Chanel sunglasses are both a snazzy accessory and a souvenir from a whirlwind day of high-speed purchasing. Chaotic as they may seem, outfits are assembled with the utmost seriousness, from the pattern of safety pins in one's Catholic schoolgirl tartan to the zig-zagging streak of fuchsia accenting a Mohawk coiffure. The result of this fashion fixation is a magnificent parade of sculpture-like boutiques – monuments to the brand names that inhabit them.

- **Dior Omotesandō** (Map p134; 5-9-11 Jingūmae, Shibuya-ku; Chiyoda, Ginza, Hanzōmon lines to Omote-sandō, exit A1) Any architecture buff will recognise Dior Omotesandō's trademark white-box facade designed by SANAA's leading Japanese architects Sejima Kazuyo and Nishizawa Ryūe. The exterior is made entirely of glass and a thin grey sheath acts as a semipermeable veil protecting the refined interior from the urban tangle outside.
- **Prada Aoyama** (Map p134; ☎ 6418 0400; 5-2-6 Minami-Aoyama, Minato-ku; 11am-8pm; Chiyoda, Ginza & Hanzōmon lines to Omote-sandō, exits A4 & A5) The brainchild of the Pritzker Prize–winning designer firm Herzog & de Meuron, this beehive-like concoction has become Tokyo's second-most visited 'attraction' after Tokyo Disneyland.
- **Louis Vuitton** (Map p134; ☎ 3478-2100; 5-7-5 Jingūmae, Chiyoda, Ginza, Hanzōmon lines to Omote-sandō, exit A1) The first powerhouse boutique plunked down along the linden-lined Omote-sandō, Louis Vuitton's flagship store was designed by noted Japanese architect Jun Aoki. The boutique sold over US$1 million dollars of merchandise on the day of its grand opening.
- **Tod's Omotesandō** (Map p134; ☎ 6419-2055; 5-1-15 Jingūmae; Chiyoda, Ginza, Hanzōmon lines to Omote-sandō, exit A1) Designed by local architect Toyo Ito, Tod's secured its spot in Tokyo's retail pantheon with its mesmerising glass facade covered in opaque ribbons that wend their way skyward like the branches of a tree.
- **Bapexclusive Aoyama** (Map p134; ☎ 3407 2145; 5-5-8 Minami-Aoyama, Minato-ku; 11am-7pm; Chiyoda, Ginza, Hanzōmon lines to Omote-sandō, exit A5) Although not as ostentatious as the other superstore slam-dunks, Bapexclusive's boutique, designed by Wonderwall, makes the list for its sterile-yet-swish ambience that feels like hospital for fashion victims.

Pedestrians stroll past the bulbous glass confection of Prada Aoyama, Tokyo

ANTHONY PLUMMER

NINJA-PROOFING

Long before lasers, padlocks and klaxons hampered trespassers, Japanese feudal lords employed a much simpler method of safeguarding their castles from stealth, black-masked assassins. Charged with the difficult task of protecting their masters from things that go bump in the night, court architects devised a straightforward security system known as *uguisubari*, or 'nightingale floors'. These special floorboards were rigged together with nails that would scratch against their clamps making a warbling noise when walked upon. Weathered timber planks usually creak on their own, but these special contraptions would sing like a songbird as people moseyed on by. The creaking floors of Nijō-jō (p358) are an excellent example of this melodic security technique. Tiptoe across the squeaky planks and see how far you can get before the ground starts to sing.

was governed by a preference for understated, back-to-nature design. Long before the Japanese borrowed and bested Western design motifs, the island nation honed its craft and style during two centuries of self-inflicted isolation when Tokugawa Ieyasu defeated the last of his enemies and secured total control for the Tokugawa shōgunate.

Japan's flamboyant temples are undoubtedly the best examples of the nation's early architectural abilities. Important religious complexes were usually quite large and featured a great hall surrounded by smaller buildings like pagodas – the ancient version of the skyscraper – and structures that served as quarters for devotees.

Equally as impressive were the country's collection of feudal castles, although most of the bastions we see today are concrete replicas of the original wooden structures destroyed by war, fire or decay. Initially, the first feudal castles were simple mountain forts that relied more on natural terrain than structural innovation when defending the keep from invaders. Castle construction boomed during the 16th and 17th centuries, each one more impressive than the next, however most were later razed by Edo and Meiji governments. The main castles in Osaka

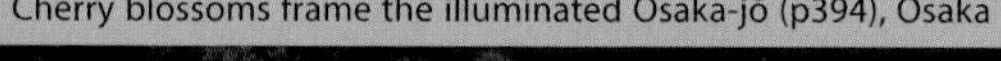

Cherry blossoms frame the illuminated Osaka-jō (p394), Osaka

JOHN BAN

Steps, more steps, and the glorious Niō-mon entrance to Kiyomizu-dera (p350), Kyoto

GREG ELMS

TOP FIVE WOODEN WONDERS

Although Japan is currently known for its eye-popping alien architecture – like the buzzing metallic haze depicted in Sofia Coppola's film *Lost In Translation* – it was the almighty tree that dominated the nation's traditional construction materials. The following structures are among Japan's finest flourishes of timber.

- **Hōryū-ji** (p428) Located in the ancient capital city of Nara, this temple complex is commonly believed to feature the two oldest wooden structures in the world: the pagoda (rising just over 32m) and the *kondō* (golden or main hall). Its full name, *Hōryū Gakumonji,* means 'Learning Temple of the Flourishing Law', a moniker chosen because the grounds were used for sermons and monastic practices.
- **Tōdai-ji** (p421) Tōdai-ji's original Daibutsu-den and giant bronze Buddha were constructed by over two million people during the 8th century. The structure has twice been incinerated and the current incarnation dates back to 1709.
- **Chion-in** (p352) This stunning temple complex is the centre of the Jōdo shū, a sect of Pure Land Buddhism established by Hōnen, a Japanese monk who lived during the 12th century. Chion-in's main gate, known as San-mon is the largest structure of its kind in all of Japan. Several structures in the precinct were incinerated in the 17th century, but were rebuilt by the Tokugawa shōgunate a few years later.
- **Kiyomizu-dera** (p350) One of the most beloved temples in Kyoto, this stunning sanctuary overlooks the city's sea of chestnut-coloured roofs from a privileged hillside position. The temple's pièce de résistance is the main hall with its signature verandah sitting atop a scaffolding-like structure.
- **Byōdō-in** (p362) Originally built as a country estate for the Fujiwara clan in 998, Byōdō-in was transformed into a temple a century later. The Amida-dō (Phoenix Hall; also known as Hōō-dō) is one of the most prized pieces of architecture from the Fujiwara period and is featured on the ¥10 coin. The Byōdō-in complex was duplicated on Hawai'i's island of O'ahu.

(Osaka-jō; p394) and Nagoya (Nagoya-jō; p254) are quite impressive and boast interactive museum spaces, but the country's must-see castle is Himeji-jō (p415), also known as the 'white heron', derived from its stately white form.

Traditional thatched-roofed *gasshō-zukuri*
FRANK CARTER

Principally simple and refined, the typical house was also constructed using post-and-beam timber, with sliding panels of wood or rice paper (for warmer weather) making up the exterior walls. *Shōji* (movable screens), would divide the interior rooms. In more densely populated areas, traditional housing took the form of *machiya* (traditional Japanese townhouse) and were usually built by merchants. Although most of the neat, narrow rows of these structures have been replaced with flashier modern dwellings, one can still stumble across *machiya* in Kyoto. The reasoning behind the gossamer construction of domestic dwellings was twofold: light materials were favourable during broiling summer months, and heavier building products were inadvisable due to the abundance of earthquakes.

The most distinctive type of Japanese farmhouse was the thatched-roofed *gasshō-zukuri,* so named for the shape of the rafters, which resemble a pair of palms pressed together in prayer. While these farmhouses appear cosy and romantic, they were often home for up to 40 people and the occasional farm animal. The dark floorboards, soot-covered ceilings and lack of windows starkly contrasted with the breezy merchant houses in more populated areas.

ROCK, PAPER, SCISSORS

When the Tokugawa shōgunate lost control of the island nation, the Meiji Restoration (1868) opened Japan's doors once more and architectural influences began to change. Josiah Conder, a British architect, was invited to Tokyo to design many structures that embodied the pillars of Western architecture. Conder erected many buildings in Gothic, Renaissance, Moorish and Tudor styles, energising Tokyo's heterogeneous cityscape. Conder was trying to develop an adaptation of Western architecture that could be understood as uniquely Japanese, but the adaptation of numerous Western styles exhibited the difficulty of choosing and propagating a Japanese architecture. The Meiji administration was not pleased. They sought a ubiquitous Western aesthetic rather than a garish mishmash of colonial styles. Offended that Conder tried to impose a synthetic 'Japanisation' of the Western style, the Meiji administration rescinded his contract.

By the end of WWII, Tokyo was a veritable blank slate. The city barely had time to regain its footing in the aftermath of the Great Kantō Earthquake (1923) before being bombed beyond recognition by the Allied forces. The other major metropolises in Japan suffered a similar fate. Through both geological and political phenomena, most of the country had been washed clean of the traditional Tokugawa aesthetic that had sustained the island nation through 200 years of forced isolation.

When TV was introduced as a Western marvel, Japan built its first broadcasting tower in the heart of Tokyo, known as Tokyo Tower. They didn't, however, just build an ordinary beacon; engineers constructed a duplicate of Paris' Eiffel Tower. True to the latent Japanese desire for importation and improvement, the orange-and-white behemoth was built to stand at 333m – 13m higher than the icon of modernity in the City of Lights. In the 1890s Paris' iron tower was an emblem of the incoming age of machines and international progress, but Tokyo Tower, constructed over 60 years later, lacked the 'wow' impact that Eiffel achieved. Instead, the structure felt antiquated – a reminder of the borrowed aesthetic – and it took its place among other proto-modern designs rather than looming over Paris' homogenous cityscape of grey-brick Haussmannian buildings.

WABI-SABI

No, it isn't the spicy green stuff you eat with your sushi; *wabi-sabi* is one of the fundamental visual principles that governs the traditional Japanese idea of beauty. It's a rather lofty concept – most scholars argue that it's undefinable using the English lexicon – but we're gonna take a stab at it anyway. The idea of *wabi-sabi* is an aesthetic that embraces the notion of ephemerality and imperfection as it relates to all facets of Japanese culture.

The term *wabi-sabi* comes from the Japanese *wabi* and (you guessed it) *sabi* – both with quite convoluted definitions. *Wabi* roughly means 'rustic' and connotes the loneliness of the wilderness, while *sabi* can be interpreted as 'weathered', 'waning', or 'altered with age'; so it's no surprise that the Japanese word for 'rust' is also *sabi*. Together the two words signify an object's natural imperfections that arise during its inception and the acknowledgment that the object will evolve as it confronts mortality.

This penchant for impermanence and incompleteness transcends Japanese visual culture from the fragrant cherry blossoms that bloom in spring, to the slightly asymmetric *Hagi-yaki* pottery, but is perhaps most palpable in landscape design and traditional architecture. Japanese tea houses are the paradigm of nuance, and reflect the *wabi-sabi* motifs with their natural construction materials, handmade ceramics and manicured gardens.

Although the origins of *wabi-sabi* can be traced back to ancient Buddhism, these aesthetic ideals are still present in modern Japan and can even be found throughout the imaginative cityscapes we see today.

Ornate roofline of Ōkura Shūkokan (p158), Tokyo
MARTIN MOOS

All eyes were on Japan – the first time since WWII – for the 1964 Summer Olympic Games held in Tokyo. The newly founded Japanese government decided that the new Olympic centre would be built where the American occupation compound had once stood in Yoyogi, a southwestern district of the city. But choosing a site was the easy part. The Olympic planners were faced with the problems of identifying and exemplifying modern Japanese design. The architectural concept for the Olympics had to accomplish two things: first, it should demonstrate modernity through a unique architectural gesture, and second, it must reflect a distinctive sense of Japanese-ness. The Olympic complex would dictate the future language of Japanese design.

Capturing this inherent Japanese-ness and expressing it through architecture proved to be much more difficult than expected, even for native architects. A modern design by Japanese architect Tange Kenzō was ultimately chosen. Tange was a young architect whose ideas were highly influenced by the works of Le Corbusier, although the ideas did not feel reappropriated and improved. The designs for the two large stadiums were like swirling shells plucked from the depths of an alien ocean. The larger structure was shaped as though the hull of a majestic boat had been flipped upside down. The gracious gestures of the design masked the sheer volume required to house thousands of spectators. Indeed, the entire world was captivated by these inspired designs. Tange went on to have a very successful career, and would later design the Tokyo Metropolitan Government Offices (1991; p154), Tokyo's tallest building.

Tokyo Metropolitan Government Offices (p154)
BRENT WINEBRENNER

Tange's contemporaries, such as Shinohara Kazuo and Maki Fumihiko, began a movement known as Metabolism, which promoted flexible spaces and functions at the expense of fixed forms in building. Prioritising function over form was a common theme in traditional Japanese design and Metabolism sought to bring this back to the forefront in a modern context where new materials, such as concrete and glass, were being used.

In the 1980s, a second generation of Japanese architects began to gain recognition within the international architecture scene, including Andō Tadao, Hasegawa Itsuko and Toyo Ito. This younger group continued to explore both modernism and postmodernism, while incorporating a renewed interest in Japan's architectural heritage.

For more information on architecture in Japan, see p68.

Tokyo 東京

You know Tokyo – perhaps from the illustrated pages of *Akira*, or the films of Akira Kurosawa. Maybe your personal style is informed by Harajuku street fashion or the classic avant-garde of Comme des Garçons; maybe your musical taste runs to BoA or the Zazen Boys. Or maybe you only know it in passing, from images of pulsing pedestrian traffic across Shibuya Crossing, stereotypes of buttoned-up businessmen or a clip of an incomprehensibly wacky Japanese game show. This is a city where a macaque can work as a waiter and unconventional individuals find freedom in the anonymity of the city – the Japanese aphorism, *the nail that stands up gets hammered down* doesn't necessarily apply in Tokyo.

Tokyo's bubbling *nabe* (pot) of creativity is a rich, long-simmering brew resulting from the mix of age-old Japanese traditions, a modern uberurban society and novel international ingredients. Likewise, its cuisine, popular culture and psyche are curious blends of old Japan and twists of modern tastes. It's a city torn between the rigidity of rules and etiquette, and the flux of reinvention and fusion – all of which create a flavour that is heady with subtle, fleeting nuances of the recognisable and the totally foreign. The city's massive scale alone means a stunning abundance of idiosyncratic experiences.

So how well can you get to know Tokyo?

HIGHLIGHTS

- Stroll the grounds of **Meiji-jingū** (p155), Tokyo's most impressive Shintō shrine
- Snapshots of goth Lolitas at **Jingū-bashi** (p155), who pose and preen for your photographic pleasure
- Take in high art and low culture in **Roppongi** (p157)
- Dodge flying fish on the floor of **Tsukiji Fish Market** (p150) and feast on early-morning sushi
- Attend the seasonal spectacle of sumō at **Ryōgoku Kokugikan** (p188) for salt-slinging, belly-slapping and solemn ritual
- See how the Edo-half lived at the wonderful **Edo-Tokyo Museum** (p159)

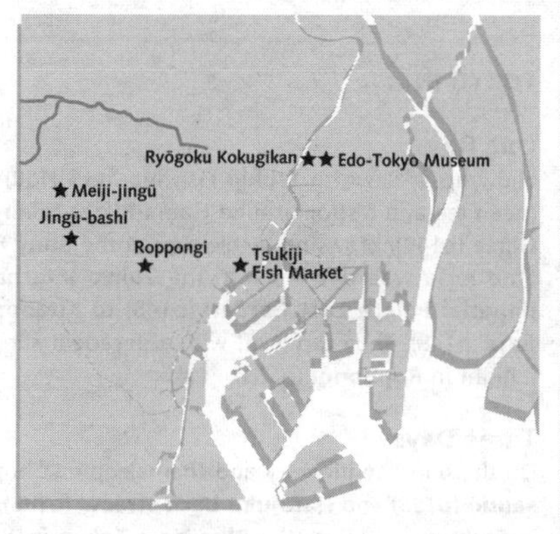

- TELEPHONE CODE: 03
- POPULATION: 12.56 MILLION

HISTORY

Tokyo is something of a miracle, a city that rose from the ashes of WWII to become one of the world's leading economic centres.

Tokyo was formerly known as Edo (literally 'Gate of the River'), so named for its location at the mouth of Sumida-gawa. The city first became significant in 1603, when Tokugawa Ieyasu established his shōgunate (military government) there. Edo grew into a city from which the Tokugawa clan governed the whole of Japan. By the late 18th century it had become the most populous city in the world. When the authority of the emperor was restored in 1868, the capital moved from Kyoto to Edo, which was renamed Tokyo (Eastern Capital).

After more than 250 years of isolation, Tokyo began transforming itself into a modern metropolis. Remarkably, it has succeeded in achieving this despite two major disasters that each practically levelled the city – the Kantō Earthquake and ensuing fires of 1923, and the devastating US air raids of 1944 and 1945.

After the giddy heights of Japan's Bubble Economy of the 1980s burst in the '90s, Tokyo spent much of the interim recovering from the resulting recession. These days, the economy is feeling the pinch again. Apart from economics, Tokyo's cultural exports continue to strongly influence the global scene, with its fashion, music, design, manga and anime, and quirky, uniquely Japanese technology.

ORIENTATION

Tokyo is a vast conurbation spreading out across the Kantō Plain from Tokyo Bay (Tokyo-wan). The central metropolitan area is made up of 23 *ku* (wards), while outlying areas are divided into 27 separate *shi* (cities), a *gun* (county) and four island-districts. Nearly everything of interest to visitors lies on or near the JR Yamanote line, the rail loop that circles central Tokyo. Areas not on the Yamanote line – like Roppongi, Tsukiji and Asakusa – are nonetheless within easy reach, as the central city is crisscrossed by Tokyo's excellent subway system.

In Edo times, Yamanote referred to 'Uptown': the estates and residences of feudal barons, military aristocracy and other Edo elite, in the hilly regions of the city. Shitamachi or 'Downtown' was home to the working classes, merchants and artisans. Even today this distinction persists. The areas west of the Imperial Palace (Kōkyo) are more modernised, housing the commercial and business centres of modern Tokyo; the areas east of the palace retain more of the character of old Edo.

A trip around the JR Yamanote line makes a good introduction to the city. You might start at Tokyo station. Near the station are the Marunouchi and Ōtemachi office districts and the high-class shopping district of Ginza. Continuing north from Tokyo station brings you to Akihabara, the discount electronics centre of Tokyo. Further along is Ueno, home to many of the city's museums. After rounding the top of the loop you descend into Ikebukuro, a shopping and entertainment dis-

TOKYO IN...

One Day

Show up at dawn to **Tsukiji Fish Market** (p150) for a look at the day's catch. Follow this with green tea and a stroll around **Hama-Rikyū-Teien** (p150). Then window-shop along Chūō-dōri in **Ginza** (p149), browsing techie toys at the **Sony Building** (p149) or **Leica Ginza Salon** (p149). Stop for a weekday lunch in the **Tokyo International Forum plaza** (p148), wander through **Imperial Palace East Garden** (p148) to **Kitanomaru-kōen** (p148) and possibly to **Yasukuni-jinja** (p148). Then top it off with a decadent supper at **L'Atelier de Joël Robuchon** (p179) and a night in **Roppongi** (p183).

Three Days

Do the one-day itinerary and then sleep in! Shop high fashion and pop culture along **Omotesandō** (p155) and **Harajuku back streets** (p188), winding up at an all-you-can-eat dessert cafe in **Shibuya** (p177), or the **Blue Note Tokyo** (p186) for top-notch jazz.

On the third day take it easy, poking around the tiny bars, cafes and boutiques of **Daikanyama** (p156), **Kichijōji** (p159) or **Shimo-Kitazawa** (p159).

BOOKS ON TOKYO

If you're planning to stay a while or become a resident of Tokyo, pick up Lonely Planet's *Tokyo,* a comprehensive guide to the city.

Manga and anime fans should check out *The Akiba* by Makoto Nakajima (Japan Publications Trading, 2008). It's a guidebook to Akihabara, actually illustrated manga-style with a cute storyline, detailing Akiba culture, *otaku* (geek), shops and cafes.

Tokyo: Exploring the City of the Shogun by Enbutsu Sumiko (Kodansha, 2007) details walking tours of traditional Tokyo with fascinating historical and cultural detail.

For a deeper understanding of the Tokyo landmark that is Tsukiji Fish Market (p150), have a look at the intricate, insightful *Tsukiji: The Fish Market at the Center of the World* by Theodore C Bestor (University of California Press, 2004).

Investigate *Izakaya: The Japanese Pub Cookbook* by Mark Robinson (Kodansha, 2008). It not only points out specific *izakaya* (pub-eateries) but also gives recipes.

trict. A few stops further on is Shinjuku, a massive shopping, entertainment and business district considered by many the heart of modern Tokyo. From there, trains continue to the youth-oriented, fashionable shopping areas of Harajuku, Shibuya and Ebisu. A swing through Shinagawa at the bottom of the loop then brings you back to Tokyo station.

The information in this chapter is presented in an anticlockwise direction around the JR Yamanote line.

Maps

We strongly recommend you pick up a free copy of the excellent *Tourist Map of Tokyo* from one of the tourist information centres (TICs – see p126); along with detailed insets of Tokyo's major neighbourhoods, it also includes subway and rail maps. For more in-depth exploration of the city, pick up a copy of *Tokyo City Atlas: A Bilingual Atlas* (Kodansha), which includes *banchi* (street address) numbers, which are essential for finding addresses.

Tokyo's train and subway lines are much easier to navigate with the free, colour-coded *Tokyo Metro Guide* map. It's available at subway stations and TICs around town, and we've included it in the colour section of this guide.

INFORMATION

Bookshops

Tokyo's traditional bookshop area is Jimbōchō. Mostly catering to Japanese readers, it's nonetheless a fascinating place to browse for Edo-period maps or gardening manuals. The annual Kanda Furuhon Matsuri (Kanda Secondhand Book Festival) is a bibliophile's paradise, occupying the whole district at the end of October. For places to find manga and anime, see p190.

Aoyama Book Center Roppongi-dōri (Map pp140-1; ☎ 3479-0479; www.aoyamabc.co.jp/43/; 6-1-20 Roppongi, Minato-ku; 🕑 10am-5am Mon-Sat, 10am-10pm Sun, closed 2nd & 3rd Tue each month; 🚇 Hibiya, Toei Ōedo lines to Roppongi, exit 3); Roppongi Hills (Map pp140-1; ☎ 5775-2151; 4th fl, West Walk, Roppongi Hills, 6-10-1 Roppongi, Minato-ku; 🕑 11am-9pm; 🚇 Hibiya line to Roppongi, exit 1c)

Blue Parrot (Map pp128-9; ☎ 3202-3671; www.blueparrottokyo.com; 3rd fl, Obayashi Bldg, 2-14-10 Takadanobaba, Shinjuku-ku; 🕑 11am-9.30pm; 🚇 JR Yamanote line to Takadanobaba, Waseda-dōri exit) One of the best selections of used English-language books in Tokyo.

Good Day Books (Map p136; ☎ 5421-0957; www.gooddaybooks.com; 3rd fl, Asahi Bldg, 1-11-2 Ebisu, Shibuya-ku; 🕑 11am-8pm Mon-Sat, 11am-6pm Sun; 🚇 JR Yamanote line to Ebisu, east exit) Another excellent selection of used English-language books.

Hacknet (Map p136; ☎ 5728-6611; www.hacknet.tv, in Japanese; 1-30-10 Ebisu, Shibuya-ku; 🕑 11am-8pm; 🚇 JR Yamanote line to Ebisu, west exit) Carrying a candy-store array of art and design books in Ebisu's Q-Flagship Building.

Kinokuniya Shinjuku-dōri (Map p131; ☎ 3354-0131; 3-17-7 Shinjuku, Shinjuku-ku; 🕑 10am-9pm; 🚇 JR Yamanote line to Shinjuku, east exit); Takashimaya (Map p131; ☎ 5361-3301; Annexe Bldg, Takashimaya Times Sq, 5-24-2 Sendagaya, Shibuya-ku; 🕑 10am-8pm Sun-Fri, 10am-8.30pm Sat; 🚇 JR Yamanote line to Shinjuku, new south exit) Kinokuniya's Takashimaya Times Square branch has one of Tokyo's largest selections of English-language books on the 6th floor.

Maruzen Marunouchi (Map pp142-3; ☎ 5288-8881; www.maruzen.co.jp, in Japanese; 1st-4th fl, Oazo Bldg, 1-6-4 Marunouchi, Chiyoda-ku; 🕑 9am-9pm; 🚇 JR Yamanote line to Tokyo, Marunouchi north exit) The 4th floor houses foreign-language books, a stationery shop and a cafe; Nihombashi (Map pp142–3; ☎ 6214 2001; 2-3-10 Nihombashi, Chūō-ku; 🕑 9am-8.30pm; 🚇 Ginza, Tōzai & Toei

Asakusa lines to Nihombashi, exit B3) Maruzen's original location is on the Yaesu side of Tokyo Station.

Tower Books (Map p134; ☎ 3496-3661; 7th fl, Tower Records Bldg, 1-22-14 Jinnan, Shibuya-ku; 🕑 10am-11pm; 🚇 JR Yamanote line to Shibuya, Hachikō exit) Carries English-language books and a great array of competitively priced international magazines and newspapers.

Cultural Centres

Cultural centres in Tokyo generally act as focal points of the national groups they represent, and usually have good bulletin boards, events, small libraries and language classes.

British Council (Map pp142-3; ☎ 3235-8031; www.britishcouncil.org/japan.htm; 1-2 Kagurazaka, Shinjuku-ku; 🕑 10.30am-8.30pm Mon-Fri, 9.30am-5.30pm Sat; 🚇 JR Chūō, Sōbu lines to Iidabashi, west exit or Namboku, Tōzai, Yūrakuchō, Toei Ōedo lines to Iidabashi, exit B3) Find it several blocks south along the canal on Sotobori-dōri.

Goethe-Institut Tokyo (Map pp140-1; ☎ 3584-3201; www.goethe.de/tokyo, in Japanese & German; 7-5-56 Akasaka, Minato-ku; 🕑 10am-1pm Tue, 2-5pm Wed, 10am-1pm & 2-3.30pm Fri, closed Mon, Thu, Sat & Sun; 🚇 Ginza, Hanzōmon, Toei Ōedo lines to Aoyama-itchōme, exit A4) Walk eastward on Aoyama-dōri; turn right at Sōgetsu Kaikan and walk one more block to Goethe Institut. See also opposite.

L'Institut Franco-Japonais de Tokyo (Map pp142-3; ☎ 5206-2500; www.institut.jp, in Japanese & French; 15 Ichigaya Funagawarachō, Shinjuku-ku; 🕑 noon-8pm Mon, 9.30am-8pm Tue-Fri, 9.30am-7pm Sat, 9.30am-6pm Sun; 🚇 JR Chūō, Sōbu lines to Iidabashi, west exit or Namboku, Tōzai, Yūrakuchō, Toei Ōedo lines to Iidabashi, exits B2a & B3) Head south along Sotobori-dōri and then hang a right at the stoplight before continuing for about 50m uphill.

Emergency

You should be able to get your point across in simple English. See opposite for more information about dealing with a medical emergency.

Emergency numbers:

Ambulance & fire (☎ 119)

Japan Helpline (☎ 0120-461-997; 🕑 24hr) If you have problems communicating with medical staff, ring this emergency number.

Police (☎ 110)

Immigration Offices

See p813 for information on foreign embassies and consulates in Tokyo.

Tokyo Regional Immigration Bureau (東京入国管理局; off Map pp128-9; ☎ 5796-7112; www.moj.go.jp/ENGLISH/information/iic-01.html; 5-5-30 Kōnan, Minato-ku; 🕑 9am-noon & 1-4pm Mon-Fri; 🚇 Tokyo Monorail to Tennōzu-Isle) A 15-minute walk from Tennōzu-Isle station; board the Tokyo Monorail from Hamamatsuchō station on the JR Yamanote line. Print a map from the web page for a clear route from Tennōzu-Isle station.

Internet Access

In some neighbourhoods it can be rather challenging to find an internet cafe. Your best bet is finding a local *manga kissa* – these are 24-hour manga-reading, DVD-viewing internet cafes dotted around major transport hubs. Though often crowded and smoky, they generally offer inexpensive internet access, cheap eats and a thousand ways to kill time (see the boxed text, p163).

Another option is to look for a FedEx Kinko's, which has branches all over the city. Internet access costs around ¥250 per 10 minutes.

FedEx Kinko's Higashi-Ginza (Map p138; ☎ 5565 0441; 1st fl, Taiyo Ginza Bldg, 7-14-16 Ginza, Chūō-ku; 🕑 24hr; 🚇 Hibiya & Toei Asakusa lines to Higashi-Ginza, exit 4)

FedEx Kinko's Shibuya (Map p134; ☎ 5464 3391; 1st & 2nd fl, Tokyo Tatemono Shibuya Bldg, 3-9-9 Shibuya, Shibuya-ku; 🕑 24hr; 🚇 JR Yamanote line to Shibuya, east exit)

FedEx Kinko's Shinjuku-Minamiguchi (Map p131; ☎ 3377 5711; 3rd fl, Southern Terrace Bldg, 2-2-1 Yoyogi, Shibuya-ku; 🕑 24hr; 🚇 JR Yamanote line to Shinjuku, new south exit)

Internet Resources

There are thousands of websites about Tokyo. Here are five of the most useful:

Metropolis (www.metropolis.co.jp) The best all-round site for Tokyo. Lots of events, places of interest and hip feature articles.

Superfuture (http://superfuture.com/supertravel/supercity/1) This hip city guide is particularly good for fashion-savvy shoppers.

Tokyo Food Page (www.bento.com/tokyofood.html) The authority on Tokyo's dining scene, but be aware that some listings are outdated.

WI-FI

The easiest way to access the internet is at your local *manga kissa* (see the boxed text, p163), but if you're toting your own laptop, free wi-fi is plentiful. Freespot (www.freespot.com/users/map_e.html) lists a bunch of free hotspots, many in cafes.

Tokyo Journal (www.tokyo.to) Has monthly events listings, also interesting articles and interviews from time to time.

Tokyo Q (www.tokyoq.com) Another great all-round Tokyo site for finding places to shop, drink and explore.

Laundry

Most hotels, midrange and up, have laundry services. If you are in a budget ryokan (traditional Japanese inn), ask the staff for the nearest *koin randorii* (laundrette). Costs start from ¥150 for a load of washing, and drying usually costs ¥100 for 10 minutes.

Kuriiningu-yasan (dry-cleaners) are in almost every neighbourhood. The standards are high and some offer a rush service. It's about ¥200 for your basic business shirt.

Left Luggage

Travellers wary of hauling unwieldy luggage through Tokyo subways and stations should take advantage of the *takkyubin* (baggage courier) services operating from Narita airport. For about ¥2000 per large bag, a courier will deliver the goods to your hotel the next day (or pick it up the day before your flight out; call a day ahead of pick-up). At Narita, courier counters are in each terminal hall and are signed in English.

ABC (0120-919-120)

Yamato (0476-324-755)

There are coin lockers in all train and bus stations in Tokyo. Smaller lockers start at ¥300 (you can leave luggage for up to three days). For periods of up to two weeks, you can leave luggage at Tokyo Station's **Rail-Go Service** (3231 0804; B1 fl, Tokyo Station; 9am-8pm). If Tokyo Station is still under construction during your visit, the service desk is only accessible by exiting the station. From the Yaesu south exit, turn right and continue alongside the station until you reach a doorway leading to a lift, which goes downstairs to the desk. Rates start at ¥410 per bag per day (the price doubles after five days).

Libraries

Bibliothèque de la Maison franco-japonaise (Map p136; 5421-7643; www.mfj.gr.jp, in Japanese & French; 3-9-25 Ebisu, Shibuya-ku; 10.30am-6pm Mon-Sat; JR Yamanote line to Ebisu) From Ebisu station, take the Skywalk to the terminus, turn left at the exit and walk two blocks before turning left at the primary school. The public library, with its formidable collection of French volumes, will be on your right.

British Council (Map pp142-3; 3235-8031; www.britishcouncil.org/japan.htm; 1-2 Kagurazaka, Shinjuku-ku; 10.30am-8.30pm Mon-Fri, 9.30am-5.30pm Sat; JR Chūō, Sōbu lines to Iidabashi, west exit or Namboku, Tōzai, Yūrakuchō, Toei Ōedo lines to Iidabashi, exit B3) Comprehensive selection of books and magazines.

Goethe Institut Tokyo Bibliothek (Map pp140-1; 3584-3203; 7-5-56 Akasaka, Minato-ku; 1-6pm Mon-Sat, 10am-3pm Sun) With around 15,000 volumes. See also opposite.

Japan Foundation Library (Map pp128-9; 5369-6086; www.jpf.go.jp/e/jfic/lib/index.html; 4-4-1 Yotsuya, Shinjuku-ku; 10am-7pm Mon-Fri, 10am-5pm 3rd Sat each month, closed 4th Mon & last day each month; Marunouchi line to Yotsuya-sanchōme, exit 1) Has some 30,000 English-language publications.

National Diet Library (Map pp140-1; 3506-3300; www.ndl.go.jp/en/; 1-10-1 Nagatachō, Chiyoda-ku; 9.30am-5pm Mon-Sat; Hanzōmon, Yūrakuchō lines to Nagatachō, exit 2) This small treasure has 1.3 million books in Western languages.

Media

There's plenty of English-language info about Tokyo, starting with the three English-language newspapers (*Japan Times*, *Daily Yomiuri* and *Asahi Shimbun/International Herald Tribune*). The best listings of Tokyo events can be found in Saturday's *Japan Times*.

The *Tokyo Journal*'s Cityscope listings section makes it worth the purchase price, but the free weekly *Metropolis* is the magazine of choice for most Tokyo residents.

Medical Services

All hospitals listed have English-speaking staff and 24-hour emergency departments. Travel insurance is advisable to cover any medical treatment you may need while in Tokyo. Medical treatment is among the best in the world, and reasonably priced for a developed country.

Japanese Red Cross Medical Center (Map pp140-1; Nihon Sekijūjisha Iryō Sentā; 3400-1311; www.med.jrc.or.jp, in Japanese; 4-1-22 Hiro-o, Shibuya-ku; Hibiya line to Hiro-o, exit 3)

Keiō University Hospital (Map pp140-1; 3353-1211; www.hosp.med.keio.ac.jp; 35 Shinanomachi, Shinjuku-ku; JR Sōbu line to Shinanomachi)

St Luke's International Hospital (Map pp128-9; Seiroka Byōin; 3541-5151; www.luke.or.jp/eng/index.html; 9-1 Akashichō, Chūō-ku; Hibiya line to Tsukiji, exit 3)

Money

Banks are open from 9am to 3pm Monday to Friday (some are open until 5pm). Look out for the 'Foreign Exchange' sign outside. Some post offices also offer convenient foreign-exchange services, and most have English-language ATMs.

Tokyo has a reasonable number of ATMs that accept foreign-issued cards, and Citibank has 24-hour ATMs that accept all kinds of cards. 7-Eleven convenience stores also tend to have English-language ATMs.

For lost or stolen credit cards, call the following 24-hour, toll-free numbers within Japan.

American Express (☎ 0120-020-120)
MasterCard (☎ 0053-111-3886)
Visa (☎ 0120-133-173)

Post

The Tokyo central post office, outside Tokyo station, is under construction until 2011. In the interim, the **Azabu Post Office** (Map pp140-1; ☎ 3582-3806; 1-6-19 Azabudai, Minato-ku; 🕑 9am-7pm Mon-Fri; 🚇 Hibiya, Ōedo lines to Roppongi, exits 3 & 5) is accustomed to foreigners and can hold poste restante mail for 30 days.

Telephone & Fax

Almost all public phones in Tokyo take prepaid phone cards. For domestic directory assistance, call ☎ 104 and ask to be transferred to an English speaker. For details on making international calls from a public phone, see p820.

You can send faxes from the front desk of many hotels (some allow nonguests to use their services for a fee), some convenience stores and from FedEx Kinko's (see p124).

Tourist Information

The Japan National Tourism Organization (JNTO) runs two **tourist information centres** (TIC; ☎ 0476-303-383, 0476-345-877; 🕑 8am-8pm) on the arrival floors of both terminals at Narita airport. Staffed by knowledgeable folks who speak English, this centre is a good place to get oriented or to make a hotel booking if you haven't yet figured out where to stay.

TIC offices will make accommodation reservations, but only for hotels and ryokan that are members of the **International Tourism Center of Japan** (formerly Welcome Inn Reservation Center; www.itcj.jp). It can also arrange for tours of the city with volunteer guides.

> **GRUTT PASS**
>
> The magical book of tickets known as the **Grutt Pass** (www.museum.or.jp/grutto/; ¥2000) entitles the bearer to free or discounted entry at over 60 Tokyo museums and zoos. Valid for two months from the first visit, the pass is a terrific deal if you plan on checking out several museums across Tokyo. Pick up a Grutt Pass at participating museums, or at the Tokyo Tourist Information Center (below) in Shinjuku.

Asakusa Tourist Information Center (Map pp146-7; ☎ 3842-5566; 2-18-9 Kaminarimon, Taitō-ku; 🕑 9.30am-8pm; 🚇 Ginza line to Asakusa, exit 2) Stop by the friendly Asakusa centre to arrange free guided tours of the area; show up on the hour to watch the centre's animatronic clock go off.

JNTO Tourist Information Center (TIC; Map p138; ☎ 3201-3331; www.jnto.go.jp; 10th fl, Kōtsu Kaikan Bldg, 2-10-1 Yūrakuchō, Chiyoda-ku; 🕑 9am-5pm; 🚇 JR Yamanote line to Yūrakuchō) The main JNTO-operated TIC is just outside Yūrakuchō station. It has the most comprehensive information on travel in Tokyo and Japan, and is an essential port of call. The Kōtsu Kaikan Building is just opposite the station as you exit to the right.

Tokyo Tourist Information Center (Map p131; ☎ 5321-3077; 1st fl, Tokyo Metropolitan Government Bldg No 1, 2-8-1 Nishi-Shinjuku, Shinjuku-ku; 🕑 9.30am-6.30pm; 🚇 Toei Ōedo line to Tochōmae, exit A4) A good place to pick up a Grutt Pass (see the boxed text, above for more information).

Travel Agencies

In Tokyo there are a number of travel agencies where English is spoken and where discounting on flights and domestic travel is the norm. For an idea of current prices check the *Japan Times* or *Metropolis*.

Four well-established agencies with English-speaking staff:

A'cross Travellers Bureau Ikebukuro (Map p132; ☎ 5391-3227; www.across-travel.com; 3rd fl, Nippon Life Higashi-Ikebukuro Bldg, 1-11-1 Higashi-Ikebukuro, Toshima-ku; 🕑 11am-8pm Mon-Sat, 11am-6pm Sun; 🚇 JR Yamanote line to Ikebukuro, east exit); Shibuya (Map p134; ☎ 5467-0077; 3rd fl, TK Shibuya East Bldg, 1-14-14 Shibuya, Shibuya-ku; 🕑 11am-8pm Mon-Fri, 11am-7pm Sat; 🚇 JR Yamanote line to Shibuya, Hachikō exit); Shinjuku (Map p131; ☎ 3340-1633; 2nd fl, Yamate Shinjuku Bldg, 1-19-6 Nishi-Shinjuku, Shinjuku-ku; 🕑 10am-7pm Mon-Sat, 11am-6pm Sun; 🚇 Toei Shinjuku line to Shinjuku, exit 7)

JTB (Japan Travel Bureau); Akasaka (Map pp140-1; ☎ 3580-4253; 2-14-2 Nagatachō, Chiyoda-ku; 🕑 10.30am-7pm Mon-Fri; 🚇 Ginza & Marunouchi lines to Akasaka-mitsuke, Belle Vie exit); Marunouchi (Map p138; ☎ 3283-1320; www.jtb.co.jp/shop/tl-kokusai forum, in Japanese; 1st fl, C Bldg, Tokyo International Forum, 3-5-1 Marunouchi, Chiyoda-ku; 🕑 10.30am-7.30pm Mon-Fri, 12.30-6pm Sat; 🚇 JR Yamanote line to Yūrakuchō) Can arrange domestic travel; the Marunouchi branch is more reliably staffed with English speakers.

No 1 Travel Ikebukuro (Map p132; ☎ 3986-4690; www.no1-travel.com; 4th fl, Daini Mikasa Bldg, 1-16-10 Nishi-Ikebukuro, Toshima-ku; 🕑 10am-6pm Mon-Fri, 9.30am-3.30pm Sat; 🚇 JR Yamanote line to Ikebukuro, west exit) Just across from the west exit of Ikebukuro JR station, along Azalea-dōri; Shibuya (Map p134; ☎ 3770-1381; 6th fl, Osawa Bldg, 1-20-1 Dōgenzaka, Shibuya-ku; 🕑 10am-6.30pm Mon-Fri, 11am-4.30pm Sat; 🚇 JR Yamanote line to Shibuya, Hachikō exit) Walk north up Jingū-dōri and turn right after Tower Records; Shinjuku (Map p131; ☎ 3205-6073; 7th fl, Don Quixote Bldg, 1-16-5 Kabukichō, Shinjuku-ku; 🕑 10am-6.30pm Mon-Fri, 11am-4.30pm Sat; 🚇 JR Yamanote line to Shinjuku, east exit)

STA Travel (Map p132; ☎ 5391-2922; www.statravel.co.jp; 7th fl, Nukariya Bldg, 1-16-20 Minami-Ikebukuro, Toshima-ku; 🕑 10am-6pm Mon-Fri, 10am-1pm Sat; 🚇 JR Yamanote line to Ikebukuro, south exit)

Useful Organisations & Services

There are innumerable associations for foreign residents and travellers. For the one most suited to your needs and interests, we recommend checking the listings sections of *Metropolis* and *Tokyo Journal*.

Several useful telephone services offer information and support for foreigners in Tokyo.

Foreign Residents' Advisory Center (☎ 5320-7744; 🕑 9.30am-noon & 1-5pm Mon-Fri) For general information.

Japan Helpline (☎ 0120-461-997; 🕑 24hr) A nationwide emergency support number.

JR English Information (☎ 050-2016-1603; 🕑 10am-6pm) Offers information on train schedules and fares.

Tokyo English Lifeline (TELL; ☎ 5774-0992; www.telljp.com; 🕑 9am-11pm) Can help with information and counselling.

DANGERS & ANNOYANCES

Tokyo can be annoying at times but it is rarely dangerous. If possible, avoid the rail network during peak hours – around 8am to 9.30am and 5pm to 7pm – when the surging crowds would try anyone's patience. *Chikan* (gropers) can be a problem, but before you cry *chikan*, be sure it's not just a crowded car.

Some travellers may also be disturbed by the overtly sexual nature of some of the signs and sights in Tokyo's red-light districts, like Shinjuku's Kabukichō and parts of Ikebukuro. Those venturing into hostess clubs should be prepared to spend liberally and to watch their drinks carefully, as both drinks and credit cards of the unwary may be corrupted.

Earthquakes

Check the locations of emergency exits in your hotel and be aware of earthquake safety procedures (see p811). If an earthquake occurs, the Japan Broadcasting Corporation (NHK) will broadcast information and instructions in English on all its TV and radio networks. Tune to channel 1 on your TV, or to NHK (693AM), AFN (810AM) or InterFM (76.1FM) on your radio.

SIGHTS

Hopping on and off the JR Yamanote loop and criss-crossing town on the metro lines, you can easily catch the major sights from wherever you're based in Tokyo.

Kanda & Tokyo Station 神田・東京駅

IMPERIAL PALACE 皇居

The Imperial Palace (Kōkyo; Map pp142–3) occupies the site of the castle Edo-jō, from which the Tokugawa shōgunate ruled Japan. In its heyday the castle was the largest in the world, though little remains of it today apart from the moat and walls. The present palace, completed in 1968, replaced the palace built in 1888 that was destroyed during WWII.

As it's the home of Japan's emperor and imperial family, the palace is closed to the public for all but two days of the year, 2 January and 23 December (the emperor's birthday). Though you can't enter the palace itself, you can wander around its outskirts and visit the gardens.

It's an easy walk from Tokyo station, or from Hibiya or Nijū-bashi-mae subway stations, to Nijū-bashi. Crossing Babasaki Moat and the expansive Imperial Palace Plaza (Kōkyo-mae Hiroba), you'll arrive at a vantage point that gives a picture-postcard view of the palace peeking over its fortifications, behind Nijū-bashi.

(Continued on page 148)

TOKYO

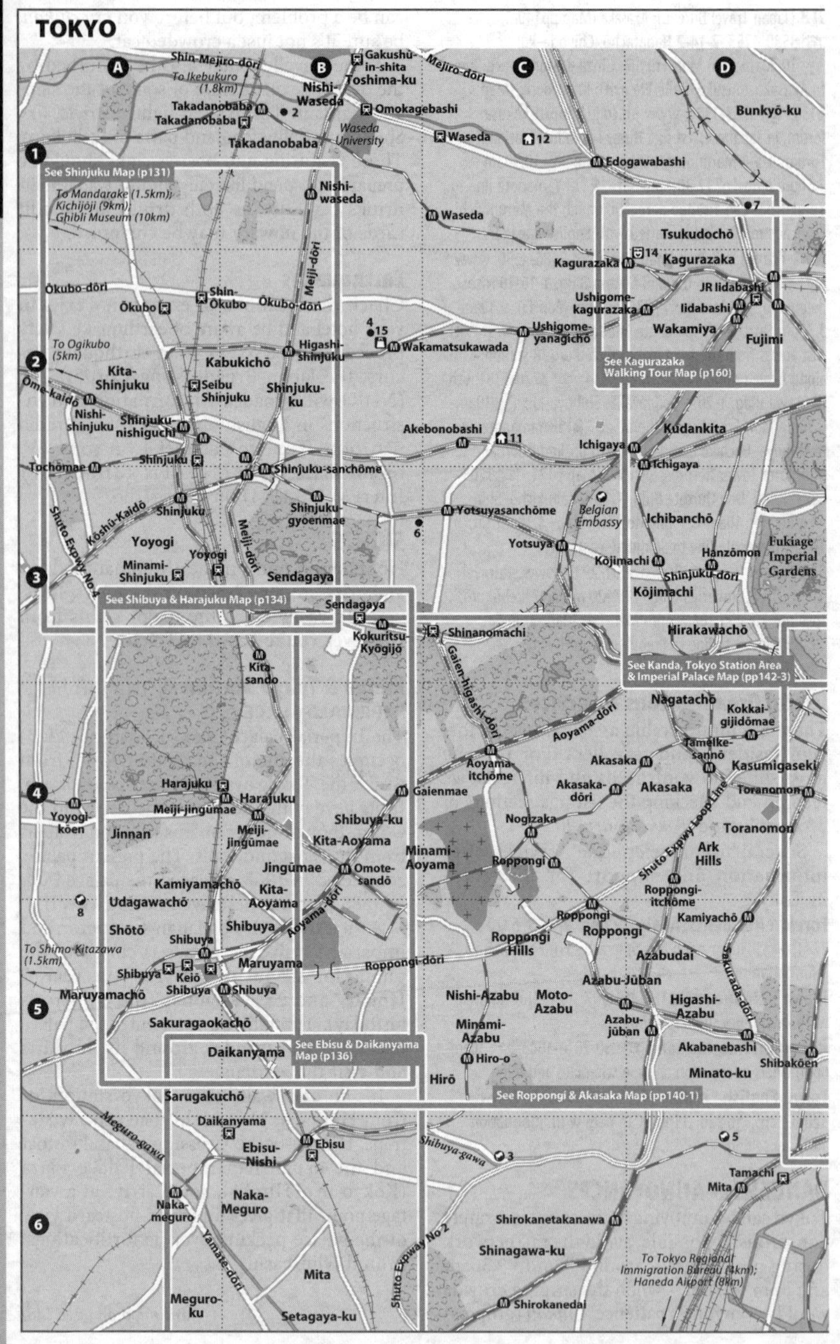

Shin-Mejiro-dōri
To Ikebukuro (1.8km)
Gakushū-in-shita
Toshima-ku
Mejiro-dōri
Nishi-Waseda
Takadanobaba
Omokagebashi
Waseda University
Waseda
Edogawabashi
Bunkyō-ku
See Shinjuku Map (p131)
To Mandarake (1.5km); Kichijōji (9km); Ghibli Museum (10km)
Nishi-waseda
Meiji-dōri
Ōkubo-dōri
Ōkubo
Shin-Ōkubo
To Ogikubo (5km)
Kita-Shinjuku
Kabukichō
Higashi-shinjuku
Wakamatsukawada
Ushigome-yanagichō
Ōme-kaidō
Seibu Shinjuku
Shinjuku-ku
Nishi-shinjuku
Shinjuku-nishiguchi
Tochōmae
Shinjuku
Shinjuku-sanchōme
Shinjuku-gyoenmae
Yotsuyasanchōme
Akebonobashi
Kōshū-Kaidō
Shuto Expwy No 4
Yoyogi
Minami-Shinjuku
Sendagaya
Tsukudochō
Kagurazaka
Ushigome-kagurazaka
JR Iidabashi
Iidabashi
Wakamiya
Fujimi
See Kagurazaka Walking Tour Map (p160)
Kudankita
Ichigaya
Belgian Embassy
Ichibanchō
Yotsuya
Kōjimachi
Hanzōmon
Shinjuku-dōri
Fukiage Imperial Gardens
See Shibuya & Harajuku Map (p134)
Kokuritsu-Kyōgijō
Shinanomachi
Hirakawachō
See Kanda, Tokyo Station Area & Imperial Palace Map (pp142-3)
Kita-sando
Gaien-higashi-dōri
Nagatachō
Kokkai-gijidōmae
Aoyama-dōri
Aoyama-itchōme
Akasaka
Tameike-sannō
Kasumigaseki
Akasaka-dōri
Toranomon
Harajuku
Meiji-jingūmae
Gaienmae
Yoyogi-kōen
Jinnan
Shibuya-ku
Kita-Aoyama
Nogizaka
Minami-Aoyama
Jingūmae
Omote-sandō
Roppongi
Ark Hills
Shuto Expwy Loop Line
Kamiyamachō
Udagawachō
Roppongi-itchōme
Kamiyachō
Shōtō
Shibuya
Roppongi Hills
Azabudai
To Shimo-Kitazawa (1.5km)
Keiō Shibuya
Maruyama
Roppongi-dōri
Sakurada-dōri
Maruyamachō
Nishi-Azabu
Moto-Azabu
Azabu-Jūban
Higashi-Azabu
Sakuragaokachō
Minami-Azabu
Azabu-jūban
Akabanebashi
Shibakōen
Daikanyama
See Ebisu & Daikanyama Map (p136)
Hiro-o
Minato-ku
Hirō
See Roppongi & Akasaka Map (pp140-1)
Sarugakuchō
Meguro-gawa
Ebisu-Nishi
Ebisu
Shibuya-gawa
Tamachi
Mita
Naka-meguro
Naka-Meguro
Shirokanetakanawa
Yamate-dōri
Shinagawa-ku
Shuto Expwy No 2
To Tokyo Regional Immigration Bureau (4km); Haneda Airport (8km)
Meguro-ku
Setagaya-ku
Shirokanedai
A
B
C
D
1
2
3
4
5
6

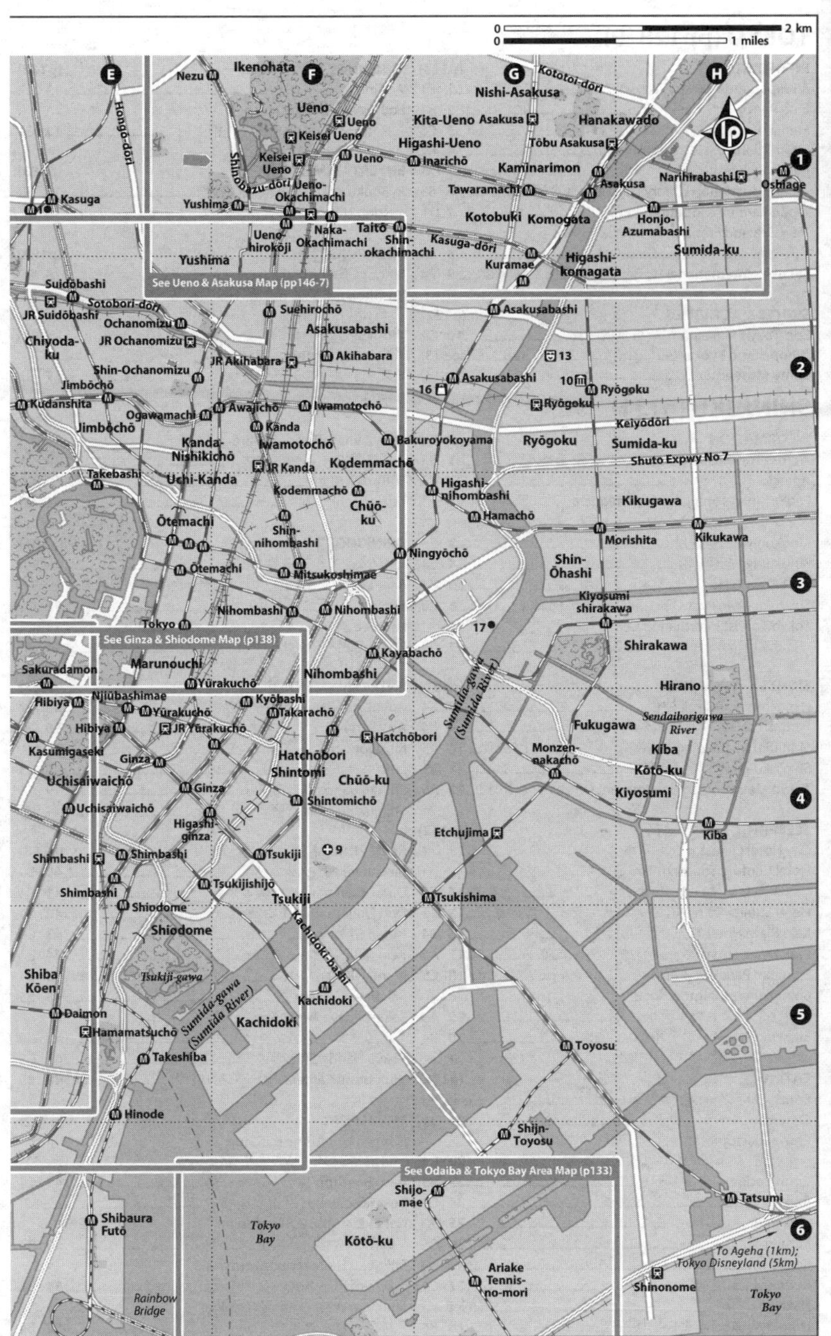
0 2 km
0 1 miles
See Ueno & Asakusa Map (pp146-7)
See Ginza & Shiodome Map (p138)
See Odaiba & Tokyo Bay Area Map (p133)
Ikenohata
Nishi-Asakusa
Kototoi-dōri
Hongō-dōri
Ueno
Kita-Ueno
Higashi-Ueno
Hanakawado
Kaminarimon
Asakusa
Narihirabashi
Oshiage
Kasuga
Yushima
Shinobazu-dōri
Ueno-Okachimachi
Naka-Okachimachi
Ueno-hirokōji
Taitō
Shin-okachimachi
Kasuga-dōri
Tawaramachi
Inarichō
Kotobuki
Komogata
Honjo-Azumabashi
Sumida-ku
Kuramae
Higashi-komagata
Suidōbashi
JR Suidōbashi
Sotobori-dōri
Ochanomizu
JR Ochanomizu
Chiyoda-ku
Suehirochō
Asakusabashi
Akihabara
JR Akihabara
Shin-Ochanomizu
Jimbōchō
Kudanshita
Ogawamachi
Awajichō
Iwamotochō
Kanda
Kanda-Nishikichō
Bakuroyokoyama
Ryōgoku
Keiyōdōri
Shuto Expwy No 7
Takebashi
Uchi-Kanda
JR Kanda
Kodemmachō
Chūō-ku
Higashi-nihombashi
Kikugawa
Ōtemachi
Shin-nihombashi
Hamachō
Morishita
Kikukawa
Ningyōchō
Mitsukoshimae
Shin-Ōhashi
Kiyosumi shirakawa
Nihombashi
Tokyo
Kayabachō
Shirakawa
Sakuradamon
Marunouchi
Yūrakuchō
Hirano
Sumida-gawa (Sumida River)
Hibiya
Njiūbashimae
Kyōbashi
Takarachō
JR Yūrakuchō
Hatchōbori
Fukugawa
Sendaiborigawa River
Kasumigaseki
Ginza
Shintomi
Monzen-nakachō
Kiba
Kōtō-ku
Uchisaiwaichō
Shintomichō
Kiyosumi
Higashi-ginza
Etchujima
Shimbashi
Tsukiji
Tsukijishijō
Tsukishima
Shiodome
Kachidoki-bashi
Shiba Kōen
Tsukiji-gawa
Kachidoki
Daimon
Hamamatsuchō
Toyosu
Takeshiba
Hinode
Shijn-Toyosu
Shijo-mae
Tatsumi
Shibaura Futō
Tokyo Bay
To Ageha (1km); Tokyo Disneyland (5km)
Ariake Tennis-no-mori
Shinonome
Rainbow Bridge

TOKYO (pp128–9)

INFORMATION (p123)
All Japan Jūdō Federation 1 E1
Blue Parrot ブルーパロット 2 B1
French Embassy フランス大使館 3 C6
International Aikidō Federation 4 B2
Italian Embassy イタリア大使館 5 D6
Japan Foundation Library 国際交流基金図書館 6 B3
Japan Karate Association 7 D1
New Zealand Embassy ニュージーランド大使館 8 A5
St Luke's International Hospital 聖路加国際病院 9 F4

SIGHTS & ACTIVITIES (p127)
Edo-Tokyo Museum 江戸東京博物館 10 G2
Nihon Sumō Kyōkai (see 13)
Sumō Museum (see 13)

SLEEPING (p162)
Ace Inn エースイン 11 C2
Four Seasons Chinzan-sō フォーシーズンズホテル椿山荘 12 C1

ENTERTAINMENT (p183)
Ryōgoku Kokugikan 両国国技館 13 G2
Session House セッションハウス 14 D2

SHOPPING (p188)
Bingoya 備後屋 15 B2
Yoshitoku 吉徳 16 G2

TRANSPORT (p192)
Tokyo City Air Terminal (TCAT) 東京シティエアターミナル 17 G3

SHINJUKU (p131)

INFORMATION (p123)
A'cross Travellers Bureau アクロストラベル 1 B5
Aprecio アプレシオ 2 C3
FedEx Kinko's Shinjuku-Minamiguchi フェデックス　キンコーズ (see 14)
Kinokuniya 紀伊國屋 3 C5
Kinokuniya 紀伊國屋 4 C4
No 1 Travel ナンバーワントラベル 5 C4
Shinjuku Main Post Office 新宿中央郵便局 6 B5
Tokyo Tourist Information Center 東京観光案内センター 7 A5

SIGHTS & ACTIVITIES (p127)
Hanazono-jinja 花園神社 8 C4
Pentax Forum ペンタックスフォーラム 9 B4
Shinjuku NS Building 新宿NSビル 10 A5
Shinjuku-gyoen 新宿御苑 11 D5
Tokyo Metropolitan Government Offices 東京都庁 12 A5

SLEEPING (p162)
City Hotel Lonestar シティホテルロンスター 13 D4
Hotel Century Southern Tower ホテルセンチュリー サザンタワー 14 C5
Hotel Sunlite Shinjuku ホテルサンライト新宿 15 D4
Keiō Plaza Hotel 京王プラザホテル 16 B4
Park Hyatt Tokyo パークハイアット東京 17 A5
Shinjuku Park Hotel 新宿パークホテル 18 C5
Shinjuku Washington Hotel 新宿ワシントンホテル 19 A5
Star Hotel スターホテル 20 B4

EATING (p170)
Breizh Café ブレッツカフェ (see 29)
Canard レストランカナル 21 D4
Chaya Macrobiotics チャヤ　マクロビオティックス 22 C4
Court Lodge コートロッジ 23 B5
Ibuki 伊吹 24 C4
Kinkantei きんかん亭 25 D4
Kōmen 光麺 26 C5
Kozue 梢 (see 17)
Kurumaya 車屋別館 27 C4
Nakajima 中嶋 (see 26)
Omoide-yokochō 思い出横丁 28 B4
Takashimaya Times Square 高島屋タイムズスクエア 29 C5
Tōfuro 土風炉 30 C6
Tsunahachi つな八 31 C4

DRINKING (p181)
Albatross アルバトロス (see 28)
Bar Plastic Model バープラスチックモデル (see 32)
Bon's ボンズ 32 C4
La Jetée ラジェッティ 33 C4
Zoetrope ゾートロープ 34 B4

ENTERTAINMENT (p183)
Advocates Bar アドボケイツカフェ 35 D4
Arty Farty アーティファーティ 36 D4
Kinswomyn キンズウミン 37 D4
Loft ロフト 38 C3
Shinjuku Piccadilly 新宿ピカデリー 39 C4
Shinjuku Pit Inn 新宿ピットイン (see 35)

SHOPPING (p188)
Bic Camera ビックカメラ 40 B4
Disk Union ディスクユニオン 41 C4
Don Quijote ドンキホーテ 42 C4
Isetan 伊勢丹 43 C4
Keiō 京王百貨店 44 B4
Marui (O|O|) マルイ 45 C4
Sakuraya Camera さくらやカメラ 46 B5
Takashimaya Times Square 高島屋タイムズスクエア (see 29)
Tōkyū Hands 東急ハンズ 47 C5
Yodobashi Camera ヨドバシカメラ 48 B5

TRANSPORT (p192)
Haneda Limousine Bus Stop 羽田リムジンバス乗り場 (see 51)
Hato Bus Stop はとバス乗り場 49 C4
Keiō Kōsoku Bus 京王高速バス (see 52)
Narita Limousine Bus Stop 成田リムジンバス停 50 B4
Shinjuku Highway Bus Terminal 新宿高速バスターミナル 51 B5
Shinjuku West Exit Bus Terminal 新宿西口バスターミナル 52 B4

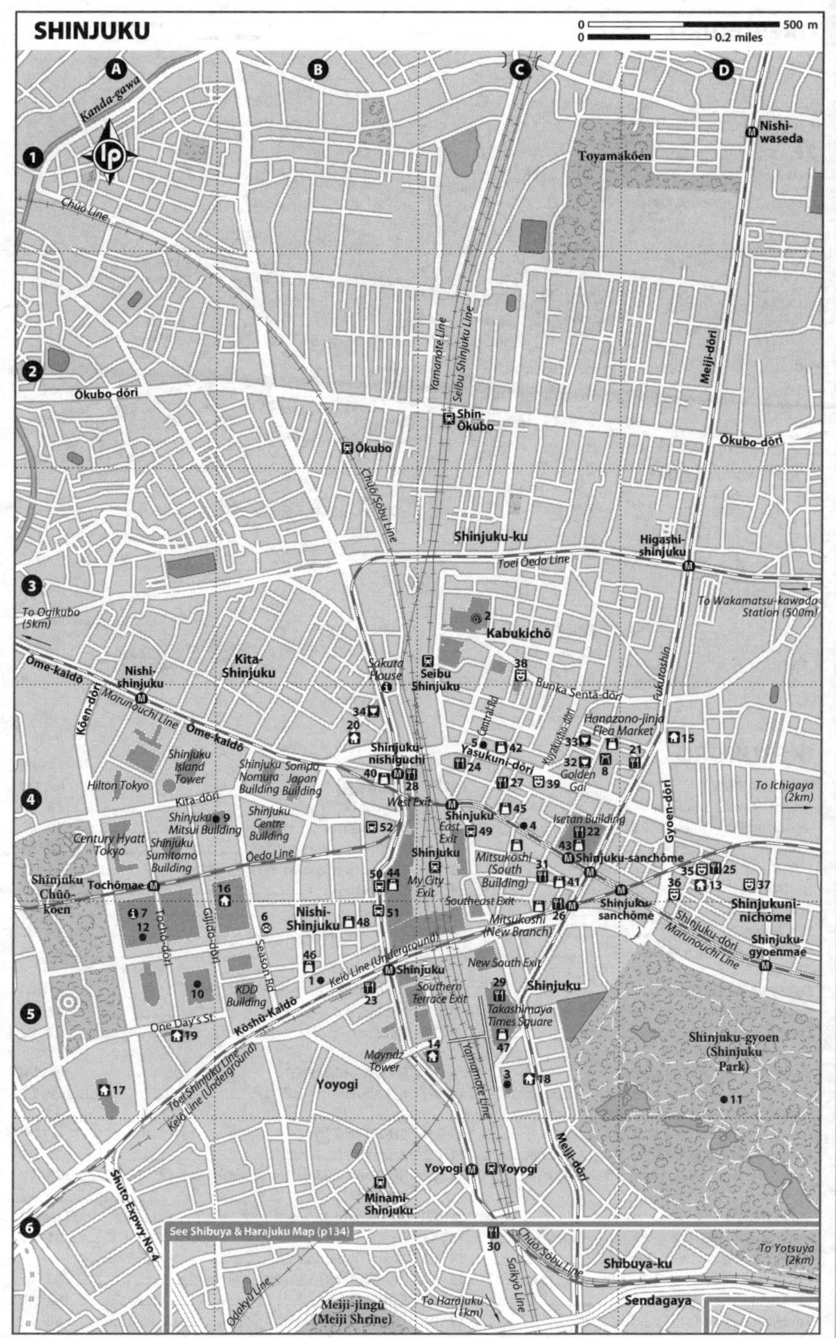
SHINJUKU
0 500 m
0 0.2 miles
A
B
C
D
1
2
3
4
5
6
Kanda-gawa
Chūō Line
Nishi-waseda
Toyamakōen
Yamanote Line
Seibu Shinjuku Line
Meiji-dōri
Ōkubo-dōri
Shin-Ōkubo
Ōkubo
Chūō/Sōbu Line
Shinjuku-ku
Higashi-shinjuku
Toei Ōedo Line
To Ogikubo (5km)
To Wakamatsu-kawada Station (500m)
Kabukichō
Kita-Shinjuku
Nishi-shinjuku
Ōme-kaidō
Kōen-dōri
Marunouchi Line
Sakura House
Seibu Shinjuku
Bunka Sentā-dōri
Central Rd
Kuyakusho-dōri
Fukutoshin
Hanazono-jinja Flea Market
Golden Gai
Shinjuku Island Tower
Shinjuku Nomura Building
Sompo Japan Building
Shinjuku-nishiguchi
Yasukuni-dōri
Hilton Tokyo
Kita-dōri
West Exit
Shinjuku
East Exit
Isetan Building
Gyoen-dōri
To Ichigaya (2km)
Shinjuku Mitsui Building
Shinjuku Centre Building
Century Hyatt Tokyo
Shinjuku Sumitomo Building
Ōedo Line
Mitsukoshi (South Building)
Shinjuku-sanchōme
Shinjuku Chūō-kōen
Tochōmae
My City Exit
Southeast Exit
Shinjukuni-nichōme
Tochō-dōri
Gijidō-dōri
Season Rd
Nishi-Shinjuku
Mitsukoshi (New Branch)
Shinjuku-dōri
Shinjuku-gyoenmae
Keiō Line (Underground)
New South Exit
KDD Building
Kōshū-Kaidō
Southern Terrace Exit
Takashimaya Times Square
One Day's St
Shinjuku-gyoen (Shinjuku Park)
Toei Shinjuku Line
Keiō Line (Underground)
Mayndz Tower
Yoyogi
Yamanote Line
Shuto Expwy No 4
Minami-Shinjuku
See Shibuya & Harajuku Map (p134)
Chūō/Sōbu Line
To Yotsuya (2km)
Shibuya-ku
Saikyō Line
Odakyū Line
To Harajuku (1km)
Sendagaya
Meiji-jingū (Meiji Shrine)
1
2
3
4
5
6
7
8
9
10
11
12
13
14
15
16
17
18
19
20
21
22
23
24
25
26
27
28
29
30
31
32
33
34
35
36
37
38
39
40
41
42
43
44
45
46
47
48
49
50
51
52

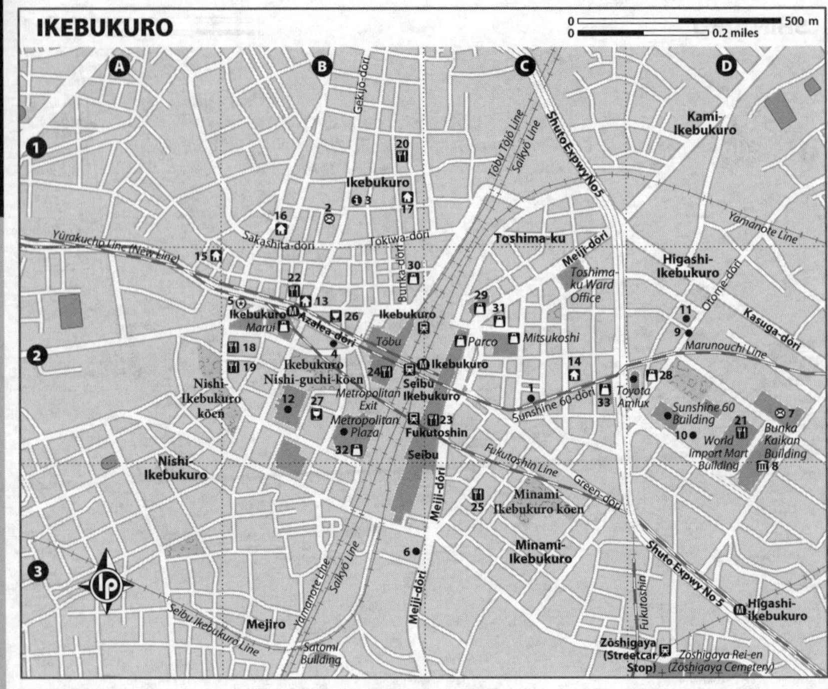

IKEBUKURO

INFORMATION (p123)

A'cross Travellers Bureau アクロストラベル 1 C2
Ikebukuro Post Office 池袋郵便局 2 B1
Kimi Information Center 貴美インフォメーションセンター 3 B1
No 1 Travel ナンバーワントラベル 4 B2
Police 警察署 5 B2
STA Travel STAトラベル 6 B3
Toshima Post Office 豊島郵便局 7 D2

SIGHTS & ACTIVITIES (p127)

Ancient Orient Museum 古代オリエント博物館 8 D3
Otome Road 乙女ロード 9 D2
Sunshine City サンシャインシティ 10 D2
Sunshine International Aquarium サンシャイン国際水族館 (see 21)
Sunshine Planetarium サンシャインプラネタリウム (see 21)
Swallowtail Café 執事喫茶スワロウテイル 11 D2
Tokyo Metropolitan Art Space 東京芸術劇場 12 B2

SLEEPING (p162)

Hotel Strix Tokyo ホテルストリックス東京 13 B2
Hotel Theatre ホテルテアトル 14 C2
House Ikebukuro ハウス池袋 15 A2
Kimi Ryokan 貴美旅館 16 B1
Toyoko Inn 東横イン 17 B1

EATING (p170)

Akiyoshi 秋吉 18 B2
Malaychan マレーチャン 19 B2
Marhaba マルハバ 20 B1
Namco Namjatown ナムコ　ナンジャタウン 21 D2
Sasashū 笹周 22 B2
Seibu 西武 23 C2
Tōbu 東武 24 B2
Tonchin 屯ちん 25 C3

DRINKING (p181)

Bobby's Bar ボビーズバー 26 B2
Dubliners ザダブリナーズ 27 B2

ENTERTAINMENT (p183)

Nekobukuro ねこぶくろ (see 33)

SHOPPING (p188)

Animate 28 D2
Bic Camera (Main Store) ビックカメラ本店 29 C2
Bic Camera ビックカメラ 30 B2
Bic Camera ビックカメラ (see 1)
Bic Camera PC Store ビックカメラＰＣストア 31 C2
Japan Traditional Crafts Center 全国伝統的工芸品センター 32 B2
Loft ロフト (see 23)
Tōykū Hands 東急ハンズ 33 C2

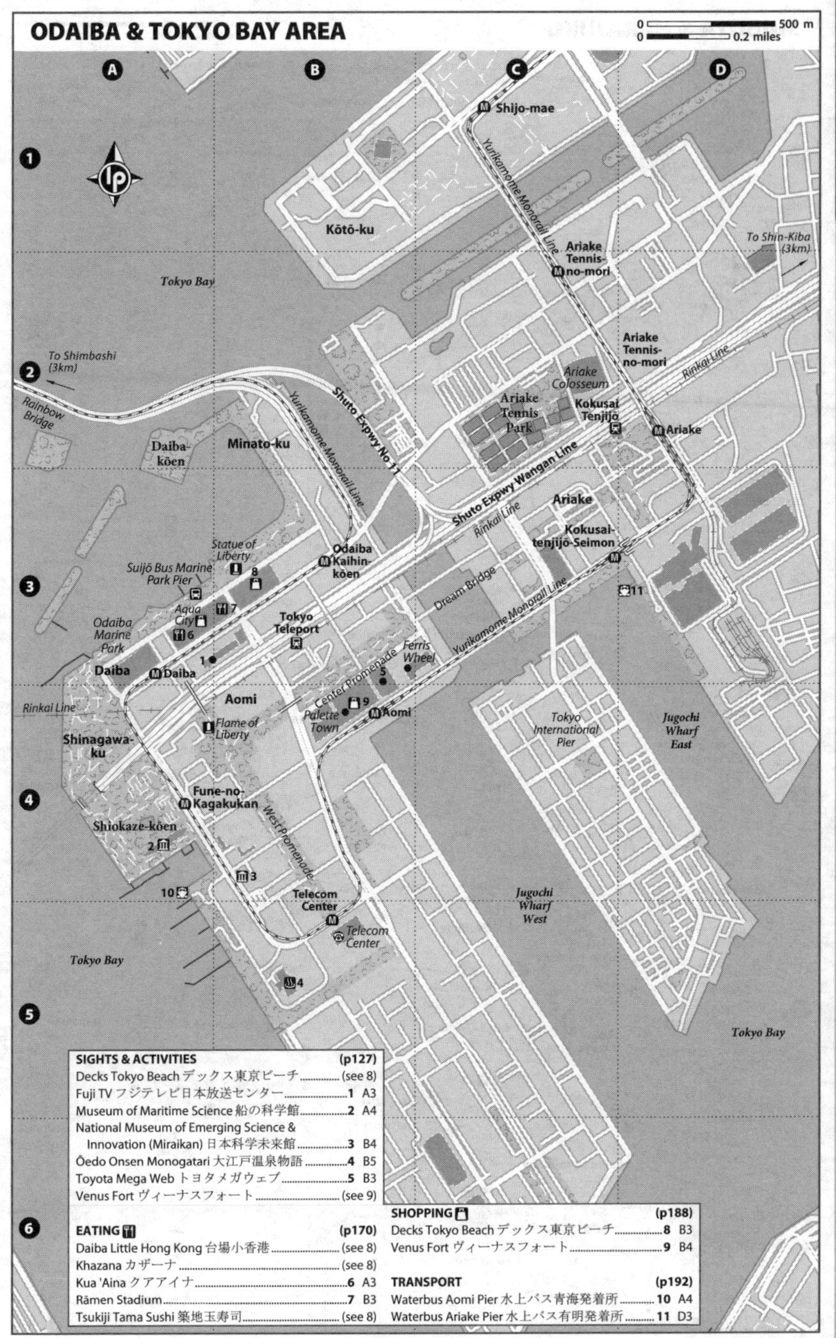
ODAIBA & TOKYO BAY AREA
0 500 m
0 0.2 miles
A
B
C
D
1
2
3
4
5
6
Shijo-mae
Yurikamome Monorail Line
Kōtō-ku
Tokyo Bay
Ariake Tennis-no-mori
To Shin-Kiba (3km)
To Shimbashi (3km)
Rainbow Bridge
Ariake Tennis-no-mori
Rinkai Line
Ariake Colosseum
Shuto Expwy No 11
Ariake Tennis Park
Kokusai Tenjijō
Ariake
Daiba-kōen
Minato-ku
Shuto Expwy Wangan Line
Ariake
Rinkai Line
Kokusai-tenjijō-Seimon
Statue of Liberty
Odaiba Kaihin-kōen
Suijō Bus Marine Park Pier
Dream Bridge
Yurikamome Monorail Line
Aqua City
Tokyo Teleport
Odaiba Marine Park
Ferris Wheel
Center Promenade
Daiba
Daiba
Aomi
Rinkai Line
Palette Town
Aomi
Flame of Liberty
Tokyo International Pier
Jugochi Wharf East
Shinagawa-ku
Fune-no-Kagakukan
Shiokaze-kōen
West Promenade
Telecom Center
Telecom Center
Jugochi Wharf West
Tokyo Bay
Tokyo Bay
SIGHTS & ACTIVITIES (p127)
Decks Tokyo Beach デックス東京ビーチ (see 8)
Fuji TV フジテレビ日本放送センター 1 A3
Museum of Maritime Science 船の科学館 2 A4
National Museum of Emerging Science & Innovation (Miraikan) 日本科学未来館 3 B4
Ōedo Onsen Monogatari 大江戸温泉物語 4 B5
Toyota Mega Web トヨタメガウェブ 5 B3
Venus Fort ヴィーナスフォート (see 9)
EATING (p170)
Daiba Little Hong Kong 台場小香港 (see 8)
Khazana カザーナ (see 8)
Kua 'Aina クアアイナ 6 A3
Rāmen Stadium 7 B3
Tsukiji Tama Sushi 築地玉寿司 (see 8)
SHOPPING (p188)
Decks Tokyo Beach デックス東京ビーチ 8 B3
Venus Fort ヴィーナスフォート 9 B4
TRANSPORT (p192)
Waterbus Aomi Pier 水上バス青海発着所 10 A4
Waterbus Ariake Pier 水上バス有明発着所 11 D3

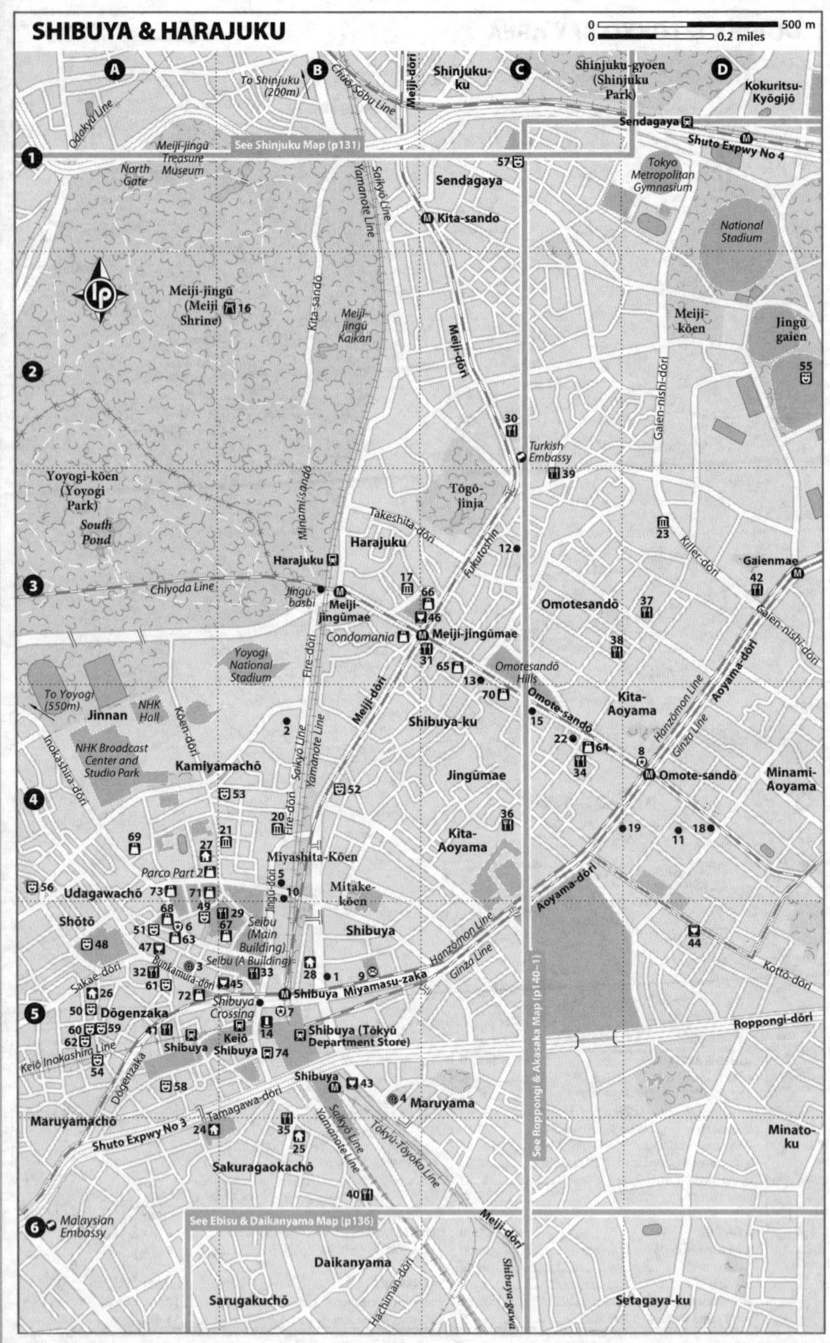

SHIBUYA & HARAJUKU
0 500 m
0 0.2 miles
Shinjuku-gyoen (Shinjuku Park)
Kokuritsu-Kyōgijō
Sendagaya
Shuto Expwy No 4
Tokyo Metropolitan Gymnasium
National Stadium
Meiji-kōen
Jingū gaien
Gaien-nishi-dōri
To Shinjuku (200m)
Chūō-Sōbu Line
Meiji-dōri
Shinjuku-ku
Odakyū Line
See Shinjuku Map (p131)
Meiji-jingū Treasure Museum
North Gate
Sendagaya
Kita-sando
Saikyō Line
Yamanote Line
Meiji-jingū (Meiji Shrine)
Kita-sandō
Meiji-jingū Kaikan
Turkish Embassy
Tōgō-jinja
Yoyogi-kōen (Yoyogi Park)
South Pond
Minami-sandō
Takeshita-dōri
Harajuku
Fukutoshin
Killer-dōri
Gaienmae
Chiyoda Line
Jingū-bashi
Meiji-jingūmae
Omotesandō
Condomania
Yoyogi National Stadium
Omotesandō Hills
Omote-sandō
Kita-Aoyama
Hanzōmon Line
Ginza Line
Aoyama-dōri
To Yoyogi (550m)
Jinnan
NHK Hall
Kōen-dōri
Shibuya-ku
NHK Broadcast Center and Studio Park
Kamiyamachō
Inokashira-dōri
Jingūmae
Omote-sandō
Minami-Aoyama
Kita-Aoyama
Miyashita-Kōen
Parco Part 2
Udagawachō
Mitake-kōen
Shōtō
Seibu (Main Building)
Shibuya
Seibu (A Building)
Sakae-dōri
Bunkamura-dōri
Shibuya
Miyamasu-zaka
Kottō-dōri
Dōgenzaka
Shibuya Crossing
Shibuya (Tōkyū Department Store)
Keiō Shibuya
Roppongi-dōri
Keiō Inokashira Line
Dōgenzaka
Tamagawa-dōri
Maruyama
Maruyamachō
Shuto Expwy No 3
Tōkyū-Tōyoko Line
Sakuragaokachō
See Roppongi & Akasaka Map (p140-1)
Minato-ku
Malaysian Embassy
See Ebisu & Daikanyama Map (p136)
Daikanyama
Hachiman-dōri
Shibuya-gawa
Sarugakuchō
Setagaya-ku

SHIBUYA & HARAJUKU (p134)

INFORMATION **(p123)**

A'cross Travellers Bureau アクロストラベル ... **1** B5
All Nippon Kyūdō Federation ... **2** B4
Bagus Gran Cyber Cafe バグースグランサイバーカフェ ... **3** A5
FedEx Kinko's Shibuya フェデックス　キンコーズ ... **4** B5
MasterCard ... (see 24)
No 1 Travel ナンバーワントラベル ... **5** B4
Police Box 交番 ... **6** A5
Police Box 交番 ... **7** B5
Police Box 交番 ... **8** D4
Shibuya Post Office 渋谷郵便局 ... **9** B5
Tower Books タワーブックス ... **10** B4

SIGHTS & ACTIVITIES **(p127)**

Bapexclusive Aoyama ベイプエクスクルーシヴ ... **11** D4
Design Festa Gallery デザインフェスタギャラリー ... **12** C3
Dior Omotesandō ... **13** C3
Hachikō Statue 八千公像 ... **14** B5
Louis Vuitton ... **15** C4
Meiji-jingū (Meiji Shrine) 明治神宮 ... **16** B2
Ōta Memorial Art Museum 太田記念美術館 ... **17** B3
Prada Aoyama プラダ青山 ... **18** D4
Spiral Building スパイラルビル ... **19** C4
Tepco Electric Energy Museum 電力館 ... **20** B4
Tobacco & Salt Museum たばこと塩の博物館 ... **21** B4
Tod's Omotesandō ... **22** C4
Watari-um (Watari Museum of Contemporary Art) ワタリウム美術館 ... **23** D3

SLEEPING **(p162)**

Cerulean Tower Tōkyū Hotel セルリアンタワー東急ホテル ... **24** A6
Granbell Hotel グランベルホテル ... **25** B6
Shibuya City Hotel 渋谷シティホテル ... **26** A5
Shibuya Tōbu Hotel 渋谷東武ホテル ... **27** A4
Shibuya Tōkyū Inn 渋谷東急イン ... **28** B5

EATING **(p170)**

Bio Café ビオカフェ ... **29** B5
Den Rokuen-Tei デンロクエンテイ ... (see 71)
Fonda de la Madrugada フォンダデラマドゥルガーダ ... **30** C2
Fujimamas フジママス ... **31** C3
Gomaya ごまや ... **32** A5
Hina Sushi 雛鮨 ... **33** B5
Hiroba 広場 ... **34** C4
Kantipur カンティプール ... **35** B6
Las Chicas ラスチカス ... **36** C4
Le Bretagne ル· ブルターニュ ... **37** D3
Maisen まい泉 ... **38** C3
Mominoki House モミノキハウス ... **39** C3
Sakana-tei 酒菜亭 ... (see 26)
Sonoma ソノマ ... (see 61)
Sora-no-Niwa 空ノ庭 ... **40** B6
Toriyoshi Dining 鳥良ダイニング ... **41** A5
Ume-no-hana 梅の花 ... **42** D3

DRINKING **(p181)**

Belgo ベルゴ ... **43** B5
Den Aquaroom デンアクアルーム ... **44** D5
Insomnia 2 インソムニア２ ... **45** B5
Tokyo Apartment Café 東京アパートメントカフェ ... **46** C3
Tsubohachi つぼ八 ... **47** A5

ENTERTAINMENT **(p183)**

Bunkamura Theatre Cocoon 文化村シアターコクーン ... **48** A5
Cerulean Tower Nō Theatre セルリアンタワー能楽堂 ... (see 24)
Cinema Rise シネマライズ ... **49** A5
Club Asia クラブアジア ... **50** A5
Club Quattro クラブクアトロ ... **51** A5
Crocodile クロコダイル ... **52** B4
Eggman エッグマン ... **53** B4
Harlem ハーレム ... **54** A5
Jingū Kyūjō (Jingū Baseball Stadium) 神宮球場 ... **55** D2
JZ Brat ジェイジーブラット ... (see 24)
Kanze Nō-gakudō (Kanze Nō Theatre) 観世能楽堂 ... **56** A4
Kokuritsu Nō-gakudō (National Nō Theatre) 国立能楽堂 ... **57** C1
La.mama ラママ ... **58** A5
O-East オーイースト ... **59** A5
O-West オーウェスト ... **60** A5
Ruby Room ルビールーム ... **61** A5
Womb ウーム ... **62** A5

SHOPPING **(p188)**

Disk Union ディスクユニオン ... **63** A5
Guinness Records ギネスレコード ... (see 69)
Hanae Mori Building ハナエモリビル ... **64** C4
Kiddyland キデイランド ... **65** C3
Laforet ラフォーレ ... **66** C3
Loft ロフト ... **67** B5
Mandarake まんだらけ ... **68** A5
Manhattan Records マンハッタンレコード ... **69** A4
Oriental Bazaar オリエンタルバザー ... **70** C4
Parco Factory パルコファクトリー ... **71** A4
Recofan レコファン ... (see 68)
Shibuya 109 渋谷１０９ ... **72** A5
Tōkyū Hands 東急ハンズ ... **73** A4
Tower Records タワーレコード ... (see 10)

TRANSPORT **(p192)**

Shibuya Bus Terminal 渋谷バスターミナル ... **74** B5

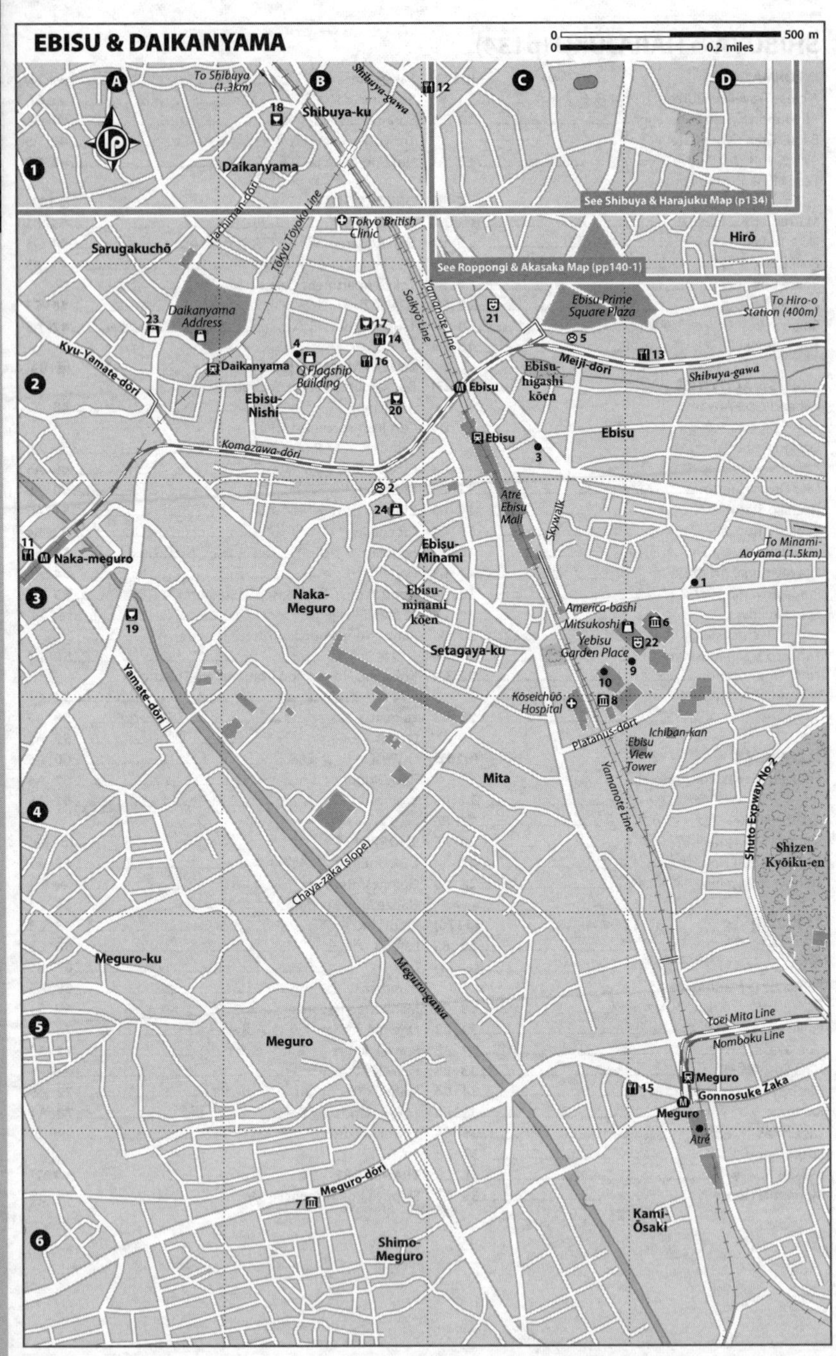
EBISU & DAIKANYAMA
0 500 m
0 0.2 miles
To Shibuya (1.3km)
Shibuya-ku
Daikanyama
Shibuya-gawa
See Shibuya & Harajuku Map (p134)
See Roppongi & Akasaka Map (pp140-1)
Hachiman-dōri
Tōkyū Tōyoko Line
Tokyo British Clinic
Sarugakuchō
Hirō
Yamanote Line
Saikyō Line
Daikanyama Address
Ebisu Prime Square Plaza
To Hiro-o Station (400m)
Kyu-Yamate-dōri
Daikanyama
Q Flagship Building
Meiji-dōri
Ebisu-higashi kōen
Ebisu-Nishi
Ebisu
Komazawa-dōri
Ebisu
Atré Ebisu Mall
Skywalk
To Minami-Aoyama (1.5km)
Naka-meguro
Ebisu-Minami
Naka-Meguro
Ebisu-minami kōen
America-bashi
Mitsukoshi
Yebisu Garden Place
Setagaya-ku
Kōseichūō Hospital
Yamate-dōri
Platanus-dōri
Ichiban-kan
Ebisu View Tower
Mita
Yamanote Line
Shuto Expway No 2
Shizen Kyōiku-en
Chaya-zaka (slope)
Meguro-ku
Meguro-gawa
Toei Mita Line
Nomboku Line
Meguro
Meguro
Gonnosuke Zaka
Atré
Meguro-dōri
Kami-Ōsaki
Shimo-Meguro

EBISU & DAIKANYAMA (p136)

INFORMATION (p123)
Bibliothèque de la Maison franco-japonaise 日仏会館図書室 ... 1 D3
Ebisu Eki-mae Post Office 恵比寿駅前郵便局 ... 2 B3
Good Day Books グッドデイブックス ... 3 C2
Hacknet ハックネット ... 4 B2
Post Office 郵便局 ... 5 C2

SIGHTS & ACTIVITIES (p127)
Beer Museum Yebisu 恵比寿麦酒記念館 ... 6 D3
Meguro Parasitological Museum 目黒寄生虫館 ... 7 B6
Sapporo Breweries サッポロビール本社 ... (see 6)
Tokyo Metropolitan Museum of Photography 東京都写真美術館 ... 8 C4
Yebisu Garden Place 恵比寿ガーデンプレイス ... 9 D3
Yebisu Garden Place Tower 恵比寿ガーデンプレイスタワー ... 10 C3

EATING (p170)
Fujiyama Seimen フジヤマ製麺 ... 11 A3
Good Honest Grub グッドオネストグラブ ... 12 C1
Ippūdō Rāmen 一風堂ラーメン ... 13 D2
Mushroom マッシュルーム ... 14 B2
Tonki とんき ... 15 D5
Ura ウラ ... 16 B2

DRINKING (p181)
Enjoy! House エンジョイハウス ... 17 B2
Frames フレイムス ... 18 B1
Munch-ya マンチャ ... 19 A3
What the Dickens ワットザディケンズ ... 20 B2

ENTERTAINMENT (p183)
Air エアー ... (see 18)
Liquid Room リキッドルーム ... 21 C2
Yebisu Garden Cinema 恵比寿ガーデンシネマ ... 22 D3

SHOPPING (p188)
Kamawanu かまわぬ ... 23 A2
Matsuzakaya 松坂屋 ... 24 B3

GINZA & SHIODOME (p138)

INFORMATION (p123)
Citibank シティバンク ... 1 C2
FedEx Kinko's Higashi Ginza フェデックス キンコーズ ... 2 C3
Ginza Post Office 銀座郵便局 ... 3 C3
Japan Karate-dō Federation ... 4 A3
JNTO Tourist Information Center 日本政府観光局案内所 ... 5 C2
JTB ... (see 15)
Kyōbashi Post Office 京橋郵便局 ... 6 D3

SIGHTS & ACTIVITIES (p127)
Advertising Museum Tokyo アドミュージアム東京 ... 7 C3
Hama-Rikyū-Teien 浜離宮庭園 ... 8 C4
Hato Bus Tours 株式会社はとバス ... 9 B5
Hibiya-koen ... 10 B2
Idemitsu Museum of Arts 出光美術館 ... 11 C1
Kabuki-za 歌舞伎座 ... 12 D3
Leica Ginza Salon ライカ銀座店 ... 13 C2
Sony Building ソニービル ... 14 C2
Tokyo International Forum 東京国際フォーラム ... 15 C1
Tsukiji Fish Market 築地市場 ... 16 D4
Zōjō-ji 増上寺 ... 17 A5

SLEEPING (p162)
Conrad Tokyo コンラッド東京 ... 18 C4
Ginza Nikkō Hotel 銀座日航ホテル ... 19 B3
Ginza Yoshimizu 銀座吉水 ... 20 D2
Hotel Seiyo Ginza ホテル西洋銀座 ... 21 D2
Hotel Villa Fontaine Shiodome ホテルヴィラフォンテーヌ汐留 ... (see 18)
Imperial Hotel 帝国ホテル ... 22 B2
Mercure Hotel Ginza Tokyo メルキュールホテル銀座東京 ... 23 D2
Mitsui Garden Hotel Ginza 三井ガーデンホテル銀座 ... 24 C3
Peninsula Tokyo ペニンシュラ東京 ... 25 B2

EATING (p170)
Birdland バードランド ... 26 C2
Ginza Palmy Building 銀座パルミビル ... 27 C2
Kyūbei 久兵衛 ... 28 C3
L'Osier レストランロオジェ ... 29 C3
Mimiu 美々卯 ... 30 D2
Nair's ナイルレストラン ... 31 C2
Robata 爐端 ... 32 B2
Shin-Hi-no-Moto 新日の基 ... 33 C2
Sushi Zanmai すしざんまい ... 34 D3
Ten-Ichi 天一 ... 35 C2
Yakitori Alley 有楽町焼き鳥横丁 ... 36 C2

DRINKING (p181)
300 Bar 300 バー ... 37 B3
Aux Amis des Vins オザミ·デ·ヴァン ... 38 C2

ENTERTAINMENT (p183)
Kabuki-za 歌舞伎座 ... (see 12)
Takarazuka Gekijō 宝塚劇場 ... 39 B2

SHOPPING (p188)
Hakuhinkan Toy Park 博品館 ... 40 C3
Matsuya 松屋 ... 41 C2
Mitsukoshi 三越 ... 42 C2
Muji 無印良品 ... 43 C2
Takumi Handicrafts たくみ ... 44 B3
Uniqlo ユニクロ ... 45 C2

TRANSPORT (p192)
Hinode Pier ... 46 B6
Water Bus Pier 水上バス乗り場 ... 47 C4

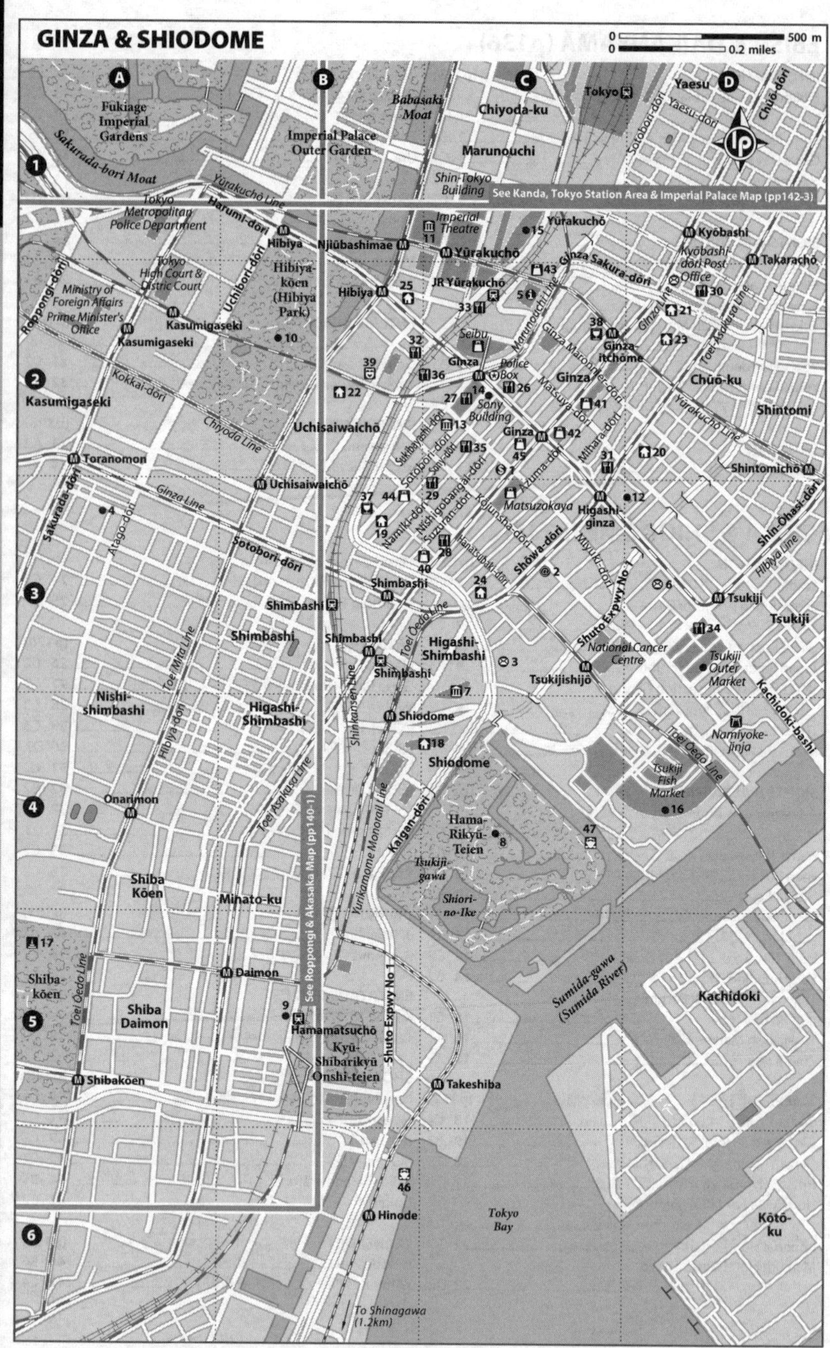
GINZA & SHIODOME
0 500 m
0 0.2 miles
A
B
C
D
1
2
3
4
5
6
Fukiage Imperial Gardens
Sakurada-bori Moat
Imperial Palace Outer Garden
Babasaki Moat
Chiyoda-ku
Marunouchi
Tokyo
Yaesu
Yaesu-dōri
Sotobori-dōri
Chūō-dōri
Shin-Tokyo Building
See Kanda, Tokyo Station Area & Imperial Palace Map (pp142-3)
Yūrakuchō Line
Tokyo Metropolitan Police Department
Harumi-dōri
Hibiya
Njiūbashimae
Imperial Theatre
Yūrakuchō
Kyōbashi
Kyōbashi-dōri Post Office
Takarachō
Ginza Sakura-dōri
Tokyo High Court & Distric Court
Ministry of Foreign Affairs
Prime Minister's Office
Roppongi-dōri
Uchibori-dōri
Hibiya-kōen (Hibiya Park)
Kasumigaseki
JR Yūrakuchō
Marunouchi Line
Ginza Line
Toei Asakusa Line
Seibu
Ginza
Police Box
Sony Building
Ginza Marronnier-dōri
Ginza-itchōme
Matsuya-dōri
Mihara-dōri
Chūō-ku
Shintomi
Kokkai-dōri
Chiyoda Line
Uchisaiwaichō
Toranomon
Sukiyabashi-dōri
Sotobori-dōri
Sony-dōri
Nishigobangai-dōri
Namiki-dōri
Suzuran-dōri
Azuma-dōri
Kōjunsha-dōri
Matsuzakaya
Hanatsubaki-dōri
Higashi-ginza
Miyuki-dōri
Showa-dōri
Shintomichō
Shin-Ohasi-dōri
Hibiya Line
Sakurada-dōri
Atago-dōri
Sotobori-dōri
Shimbashi
Toei Ōedo Line
Higashi-Shimbashi
Shuto Expwy No 1
National Cancer Centre
Tsukiji
Tsukijishijō
Tsukiji Outer Market
Kachidoki-bashi
Namiyoke-jinja
Toei Mita Line
Nishi-shimbashi
Shinkansen Line
Shiodome
Tsukiji Fish Market
Hibiya-dōri
Onarimon
See Roppongi & Akasaka Map (pp140-1)
Yurikamome Monorail Line
Kaigan-dōri
Hama-Rikyū-Teien
Tsukiji-gawa
Shiori-no-Ike
Shiba Kōen
Minato-ku
Shiba-kōen
Daimon
Sumida-gawa (Sumida River)
Kachidoki
Shiba Daimon
Hamamatsuchō
Kyū-Shibarikyū Onshi-teien
Takeshiba
Shibakōen
Hinode
Tokyo Bay
Kōtō-ku
To Shinagawa (1.2km)
1
2
3
4
5
6
7
8
9
10
12
13
14
15
16
17
18
19
20
21
22
23
24
25
26
27
28
29
30
31
32
33
34
35
36
37
38
39
40
41
42
43
44
45
46
47

ROPPONGI & AKASAKA (pp140–1)

INFORMATION (p123)
Akasaka Post Office 赤坂郵便局 **1** E2
Aoyama Book Centre 青山ブックセンター **2** D4
Aoyama Book Centre 青山ブックセンター (see 48)
Australian Embassy オーストラリア大使館 **3** E6
Azabu Post Office **4** F5
Canadian Embassy カナダ大使館 **5** D2
Citibank シティバンク **6** E1
Citibank シティバンク **7** D4
Dutch Embassy オランダ大使館 **8** G4
German Embassy ドイツ大使館 **9** C6
Goethe Institut Tokyo Bibliothek ゲーテインスティトゥート東京 **10** D2
Japanese Red Cross Medical Centre 日本赤十字社医療センター **11** C6
JTB **12** E1
Keiō University Hospital 慶應義塾大学病院 **13** B1
Manga Hiroba まんが広場 **14** E4
National Diet Library 国立国会図書館 **15** F2
Nishi-Azabu Post Office 西麻布郵便局 **16** C5
Police Box 交番 **17** D4
Roppongi Post Office 六本木郵便局 **18** E3
Russian Embassy 在日ロシア連邦大使館 **19** F5
South Korean Embassy 韓国大使館 **20** E6
Tokyo Medical & Surgical Clinic 東京クリニック **21** G5
US Embassy アメリカ大使館 **22** F3

SIGHTS & ACTIVITIES (p127)
Hie-jinja 日枝神社 **23** F2
Mori Art Museum 森美術館 **24** D5
National Art Centre Tokyo 国立新美術館 **25** C4
Ōkura Shūkokan 大倉集古館 **26** F3
Roppongi Hills 六本木ヒルズ **27** D5
Sōgetsu Kaikan 草月会館 **28** D2
Suntory Museum of Art サントリー美術館 (see 77)
Tokyo City View 東京シティビュー (see 24)
Tokyo Midtown 東京ミッドタウン (see 77)
Tokyo Tower 東京タワー **29** F5

SLEEPING (p162)
ANA Intercontinental Tokyo ANAインターコンチネンタルホテル東京 **30** F3
Arca Torre ホテルアルカトーレ六本木 **31** D4
Asia Center of Japan アジア会館 **32** D3
b Akasaka ビー赤坂 **33** D2
Chisun Grand Akasaka チサングランド赤坂 **34** E3
Grand Hyatt Tokyo グランドハイアット東京 **35** D5
Hotel Avanshell ホテルアバンシェル **36** E2
Hotel Ibis ホテルアイビス **37** D4
Hotel Ōkura ホテルオークラ **38** F3
Ritz-Carlton Tokyo リッツカールトン東京 (see 77)

EATING (p170)
Asterix アステリックス **39** E3
Daidaiya 橙家 **40** E1
Eat More Greens イートモアグリーンズ **41** E6
Fukuzushi 福鮨 **42** E4
Gogyō Rāmen 五行ラーメン **43** C4
Gonpachi 権八 **44** C5
Inakaya 田舎家 (see 66)
Jangara Rāmen じゃんがらラーメン **45** E2
Kikunoi 菊乃井 **46** E3
Kushinobō 串の坊 **47** E1
L'Atelier de Joël Robuchon ラトリエドゥジョエルロブション **48** D5
Moti モティ **49** E2
Moti モティ **50** E2
Namban-tei 南蛮亭 **51** E4
Pintokona ぴんとこな **52** D4
Pizzeria 1830 ピッツェリア1830 **53** D3
Salsita サルシータ **54** C6
Seryna 瀬里奈 **55** E4
Sunaba 砂場 **56** E3
Sushi-sei 寿司清 **57** E2
Umaya うまや **58** E2

DRINKING (p181)
A971 **59** D4
Agave アガヴェ **60** D4
Heartland ハートランド **61** D4
Mado Lounge マドラウンジ (see 24)
Maduro マデュロ (see 35)
Mogambo モガンボ **62** D4
SuperDeluxe スーパーデラックス **63** D4

ENTERTAINMENT (p183)
Blue Note Tokyo ブルーノート東京 **64** B4
BuL-Let's ブレッツ **65** C4
Cavern Club キャヴァンクラブ **66** E4
Club 328 三二八 **67** C5
Hotel New Ōtani ホテルニューオータニ **68** E1
Lovenet ラブネット (see 37)
Muse ミューズ **69** C5
New Lex-Edo ニューレックスエドゥー **70** E4
Salsa Sudada サルサスダーダ **71** D4
Smash Hits スマシヒッツ **72** B6
STB 139 (Sweet Basil) スイートベイジル１３９ **73** D4
Tōhō Cinemas Roppongi Hills 東宝シネマズ六本木ヒルズ (see 61)

SHOPPING (p188)
Don Quijote ドンキホーテ **74** E4
Kurofune 黒船 **75** D4
Sou-Sou そうそう **76** B4
Tokyo Midtown 東京ミッドタウン **77** D3

ROPPONGI & AKASAKA

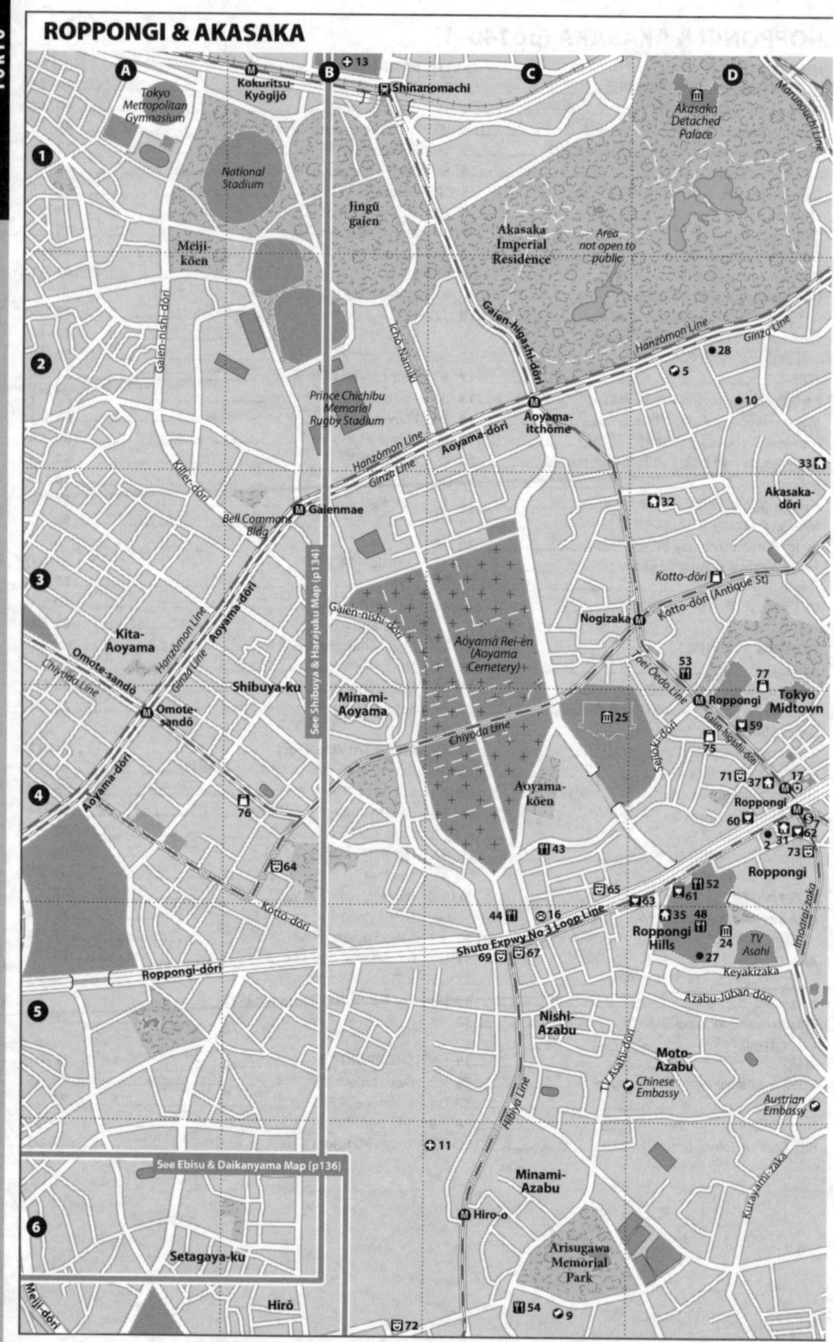

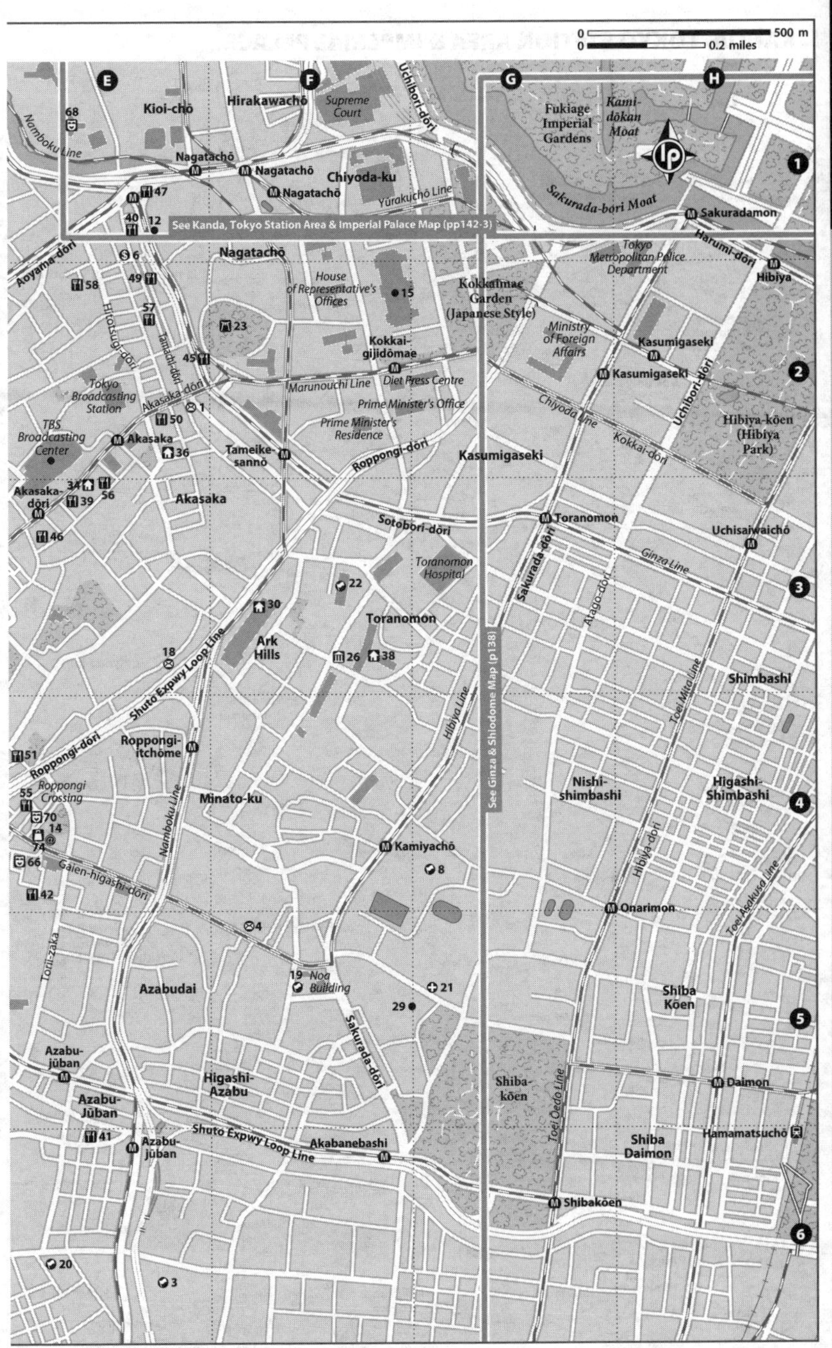
Kioi-chō
Hirakawachō
Supreme Court
Uchibori-dōri
Fukiage Imperial Gardens
Kami-dōkan Moat
Sakurada-bori Moat
Sakuradamon
Namboku Line
Nagatachō
Chiyoda-ku
Yūrakuchō Line
See Kanda, Tokyo Station Area & Imperial Palace Map (pp142-3)
Aoyama-dōri
Harumi-dōri
Tokyo Metropolitan Police Department
Hibiya
House of Representative's Offices
Kokkaimae Garden (Japanese Style)
Ministry of Foreign Affairs
Kasumigaseki
Hitotsugi-dōri
Tamachi-dōri
Kokkai-gijidōmae
Marunouchi Line
Diet Press Centre
Prime Minister's Office
Prime Minister's Residence
Tokyo Broadcasting Station
Akasaka-dōri
TBS Broadcasting Center
Akasaka
Tameike-sannō
Roppongi-dōri
Chiyoda Line
Kokkai-dōri
Hibiya-kōen (Hibiya Park)
Akasaka-dōri
Sotobori-dōri
Toranomon
Uchisaiwaichō
Ginza Line
Toranomon Hospital
Sakurada-dōri
Atago-dōri
Ark Hills
Shuto Expwy Loop Line
Toei Mita Line
Shimbashi
See Ginza & Shiodome Map (p138)
Hibiya Line
Roppongi-itchōme
Roppongi Crossing
Nishi-shimbashi
Higashi-Shimbashi
Minato-ku
Kamiyachō
Gaien-higashi-dōri
Hibiya-dōri
Onarimon
Toei Asakusa Line
Toriizaka
Noa Building
Azabudai
Shiba Kōen
Azabu-jūban
Higashi-Azabu
Shiba-kōen
Toei Oedo Line
Daimon
Hamamatsuchō
Shiba Daimon
Akabanebashi
Shibakōen
0 500 m
0 0.2 miles
E
F
G
H
1
2
3
4
5
6
68
47
40
12
6
58
49
57
23
15
45
1
50
36
34
56
39
46
22
30
18
26
38
51
55
70
14
74
66
42
8
4
19
21
29
41
20
3

KANDA, TOKYO STATION AREA & IMPERIAL PALACE

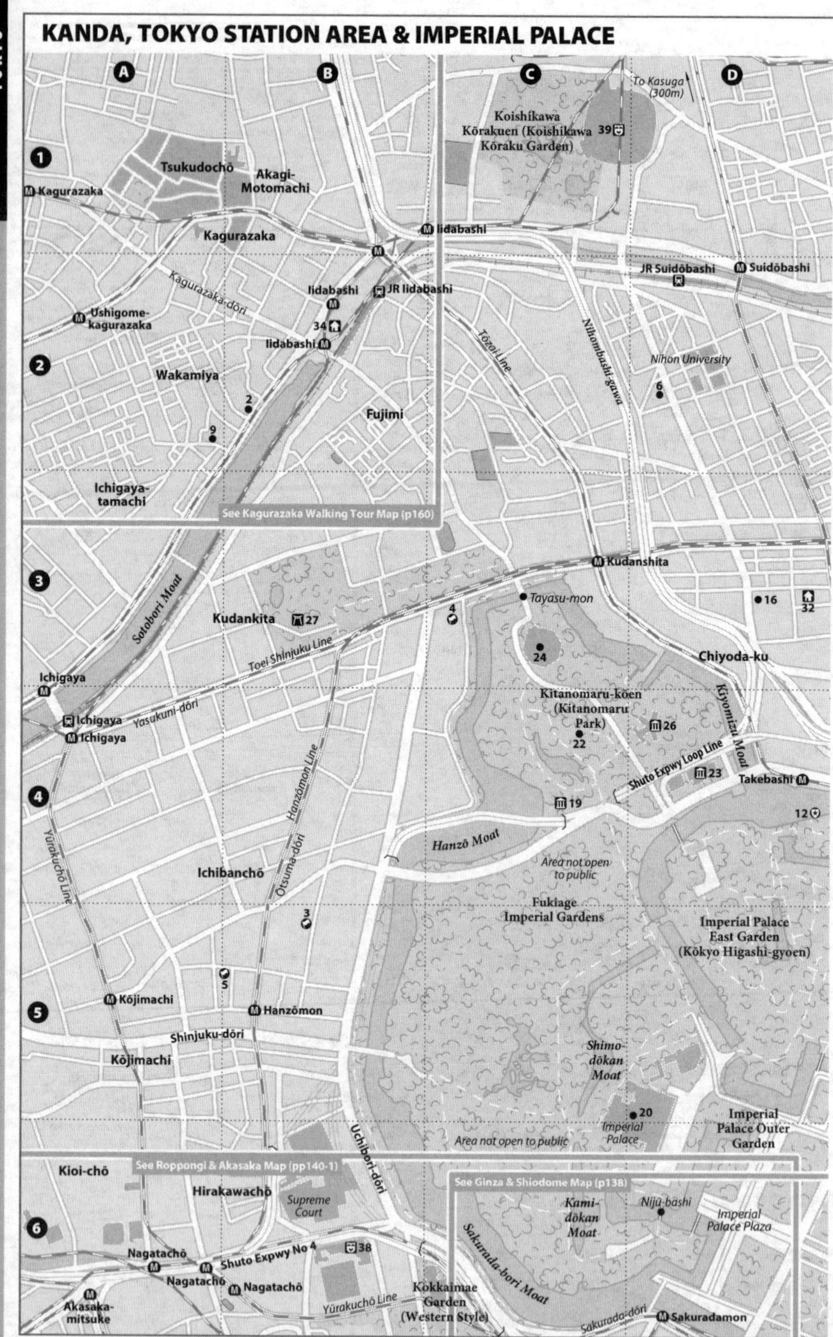

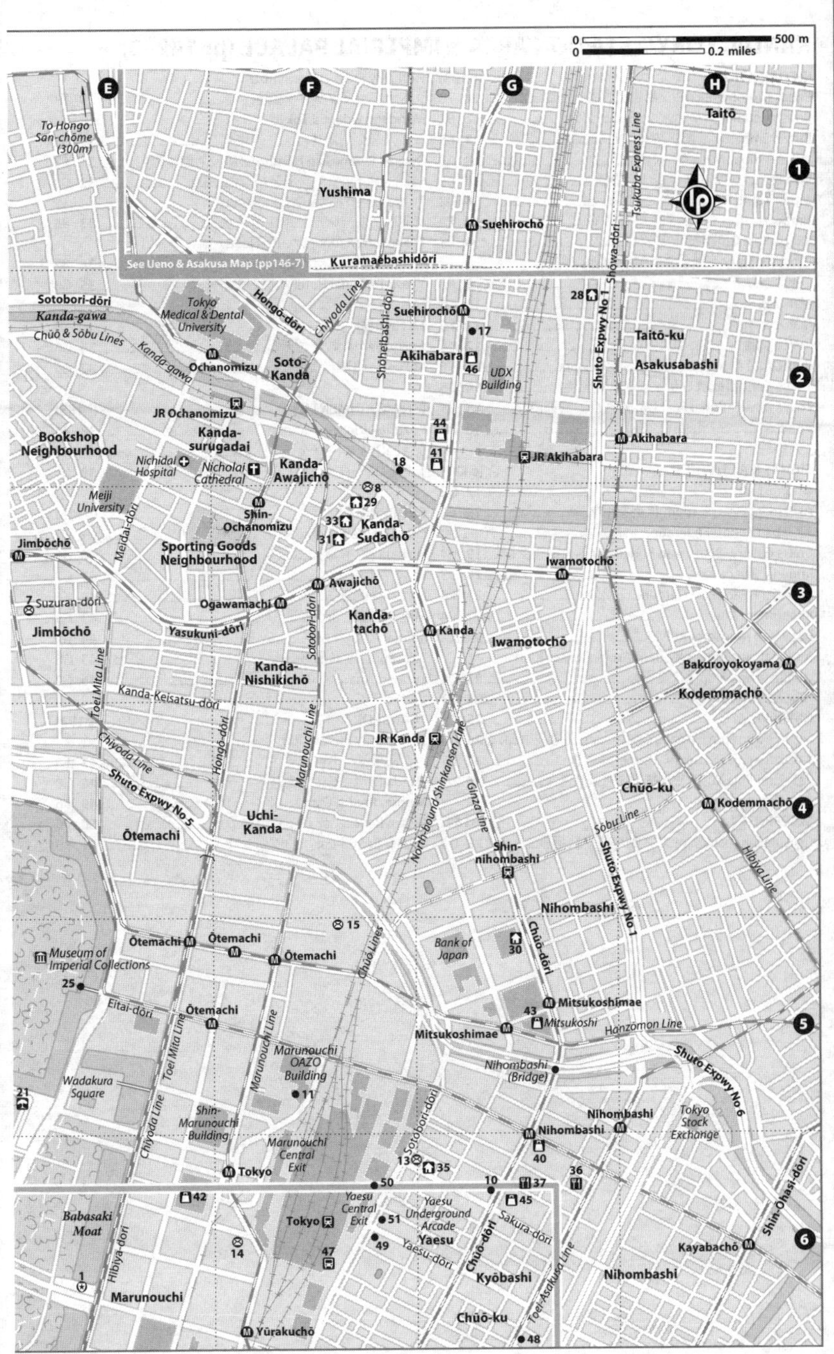
0 500 m
0 0.2 miles
E
F
G
H
To Hongo San-chōme (300m)
Yushima
Suehirochō
Taitō
Tsukuba Express Line
See Ueno & Asakusa Map (pp146-7)
Kuramaebashidōri
Shōwa-dōri
Sotobori-dōri
Kanda-gawa
Chūō & Sōbu Lines
Tokyo Medical & Dental University
Hongō-dōri
Chiyoda Line
Shōheibashi-dōri
Suehirochō
Akihabara
UDX Building
Shuto Expwy No 1
Taitō-ku
Asakusabashi
Ochanomizu
Soto-Kanda
JR Ochanomizu
Kanda-surugadai
Bookshop Neighbourhood
Nichidai Hospital
Nicholai Cathedral
Kanda-Awajichō
Akihabara
JR Akihabara
Meiji University
Meidai-dōri
Shin-Ochanomizu
Kanda-Sudachō
Jimbōchō
Sporting Goods Neighbourhood
Awajichō
Iwamotochō
Suzuran-dōri
Ogawamachi
Jimbōchō
Yasukuni-dōri
Sotobori-dōri
Kanda-tachō
Kanda
Iwamotochō
Kanda-Nishikichō
Bakuroyokoyama
Kodemmachō
Toei Mita Line
Kanda-Keisatsu-dōri
Hongō-dōri
Marunouchi Line
JR Kanda
Chiyoda Line
Shuto Expwy No 5
North-bound Shinkansen Line
Ginza Line
Chūō-ku
Kodemmachō
Uchi-Kanda
Ōtemachi
Sōbu Line
Shin-nihombashi
Shuto Expwy No 1
Hibiya Line
Nihombashi
Chūō Lines
Bank of Japan
Chūō-dōri
Ōtemachi
Ōtemachi
Ōtemachi
Museum of Imperial Collections
Eitai-dōri
Ōtemachi
Toei Mita Line
Marunouchi Line
Mitsukoshimae
Mitsukoshi
Mitsukoshimae
Hanzōmon Line
Marunouchi OAZO Building
Nihombashi (Bridge)
Shuto Expwy No 6
Wadakura Square
Shin-Marunouchi Building
Chiyoda Line
Sotobori-dōri
Nihombashi
Nihombashi
Tokyo Stock Exchange
Marunouchi Central Exit
Tokyo
Shin-Ōhasi-dōri
Babasaki Moat
Yaesu Central Exit
Yaesu Underground Arcade
Tokyo
Yaesu
Sakura-dōri
Yaesu-dōri
Chūō-dōri
Kayabachō
Hibiya-dōri
Toei-Asakusa Line
Kyōbashi
Nihombashi
Marunouchi
Chūō-ku
Yūrakuchō
1
2
3
4
5
6
1
7
8
10
11
13
14
15
17
18
21
25
28
29
30
31
33
35
36
37
40
41
42
43
44
45
46
47
48
49
50
51

KANDA, TOKYO STATION AREA & IMPERIAL PALACE (pp142–3)

INFORMATION **(p123)**

Babasakimon Police Box 馬場先門交番 1 E6
British Council ブリティッシュカウンシル 2 B2
British Embassy イギリス大使館 3 B5
Indian Embassy インド大使館 4 C3
Irish Embassy アイルランド大使館 5 B5
Japan Youth Hostels, Inc 6 D2
Jimbōchō Post Office 神保町郵便局 7 E3
Kanda Post Office 神田郵便局 8 F3
L'Institut Franco-Japonaise de Tokyo 東京日仏学院 9 A2
Maruzen 丸善 10 G6
Maruzen 丸善 11 F5
Police 交番 12 D4
Post Office 郵便局 13 F6
Tokyo Central Post Office 東京中央郵便局 14 F6
Tokyo International Post Office 東京国際郵便局 15 F5
Visa 16 D3

SIGHTS & ACTIVITIES **(p127)**

@home Café アットホームカフェ 17 G2
Akihabara Electric Town 秋葉原電気街 18 F2
All Japan Kendō Federation 全日本剣道連盟 (see 24)
Crafts Gallery (Bijutsukan Kōgeikan) 美術館工芸館 19 C4
Imperial Palace 皇居 20 D5
Imperial Palace East Garden 21 E5
Kitanomaru-kōen 22 C4
Kōrakuen Amusement Park (see 39)
National Museum of Modern Art (Kokuritsu Kindai Bijutsukan) 国立近代美術館 23 D4
Nihon Budōkan 日本武道館 24 C3
Ōte-mon 25 E5
Science Museum (Kagaku Gijutsukan) 科学技術館 26 D4
Yasukuni-jinja (Yasukuni Shrine) 靖国神社 27 B3
Yasukuni-jinja Yūshūkan 靖国神社遊就館 (see 27)

SLEEPING **(p162)**

Capsule Inn Akihabara カプセルイン秋葉原 28 G2
Hotel My Stays Ochanomizu ホテルマイステイズ御茶ノ水 29 F3
Mandarin Oriental Tokyo マンダリンオリエンタル東京 30 G5
Ryokan Ryūmeikan Honten 旅館龍名館本店 31 F3
Sakura Hotel サクラホテル 32 D3
Tokyo Green Hotel Ochanomizu 東京グリーンホテル御茶ノ水 33 F3
Tokyo International Youth Hostel 東京国際ホステル 34 B2
Yaesu Terminal Hotel 八重洲ターミナルホテル 35 G6

EATING **(p170)**

Anago Tamai あなご玉ゐ 36 G6
Mikuniya 美國屋 37 G6

ENTERTAINMENT **(p183)**

Kokuritsu Gekijō (National Theatre) 国立劇場 38 B6
Spa LaQua スパラクーア (see 39)
Tokyo Dome City 東京ドームシティ 39 C1

SHOPPING **(p188)**

Don Quijote Building ドンキホーテビル (see 17)
Haibara はいばら 40 G6
Laox ラオックス 41 G2
Loft ロフト 42 E6
Mitsukoshi 三越 43 G5
Sofmap ソフマップ 44 G2
Takashimaya 高島屋 45 G6
Tora-no-Ana とらのあな 46 G2

TRANSPORT **(p192)**

JR Highway Bus Station ＪＲ高速バスターミナル 47 F6
Mazda Rent-a-Car マツダレンタカー 48 G6
Nippon Rent-a-Car ニッポンレンタカー 49 F6
Nissan Rent-a-Car 日産レンタカー 50 F6
Toyota Rent-a-Car トヨタレンタカー 51 F6

UENO & ASAKUSA (pp146–7)

INFORMATION (p123)

Asakusa Post Office 浅草郵便局 **1** E5
Asakusa Tourist Information Center 浅草文化観光センター **2** F5
Police Box 交番 **3** B2
Post Office **4** F5
Sensōji Hospital 浅草寺病院 **5** F4

SIGHTS & ACTIVITIES (p127)

Ameyoko Arcade アメ横 **6** C5
Asakusa Kannon Onsen 浅草観音温泉 **7** F4
Asakusa-jinja 浅草神社 **8** F4
Children's Playground こどもの広場 **9** B4
Dembō-in 伝法院 **10** F5
Edo Shitamachi Traditional Crafts Museum 江戸下町伝統工芸館 **11** F4
Five-Storey Pagoda 五重塔 **12** B4
Five-Storey Pagoda 五重塔 **13** F4
Jakotsu-yu Onsen 蛇骨湯 **14** E5
Kappabashi-Dōri かっぱ橋通り **15** E5
Nakamise-dōri **16** F5
National Museum of Western Art (Kokuritsu Seiyō Bijutsukan) 国立西洋美術館 **17** C4
National Science Museum (Kokuritsu Kagaku Hakubutsukan) 国立科学博物館 **18** C4
Saigō Takamori Statue 西郷隆盛銅像 **19** B5
Sensō-ji 浅草寺 **20** F4
Shitamachi Museum 下町風俗資料館 **21** B5
Sumida-gawa Cruise 隅田川クルーズル **22** F5
Tokugawa Shōgun Rei-en (Tokugawa Shōgun Cemetery) 徳川将軍家霊所 **23** C3
Tokyo Daigaku (Tokyo University) 東京大学 **24** A4
Tokyo Metropolitan Museum of Art 東京都美術館 **25** B4
Tokyo National Museum (Tokyo Kokuritsu Hakubutsukan) 東京国立博物館 **26** C3
Tōshōgū 東照宮 **27** B4
Ueno Zoo 上野動物園 **28** B4
Ueno-kōen 上野公園 **29** B4

SLEEPING (p162)

Annex Katsutarō Ryokan アネックス勝太郎旅館 **30** A2
Asakusa Ryokan Tōkaisō 旅館東海荘 **31** E5
Asakusa View Hotel 浅草ビューホテル (see 3)
Capsule Hotel Riverside カプセルホテルあさくさリバーサイド **32** F5
Daikokuya 大黒家 (see 39)
Hotel Edoya ホテル江戸屋 **33** B6
Hotel Parkside ホテルパークサイド **34** B5
Khaosan Tokyo Annex カオサン東京アネックス **35** G6
Khaosan Tokyo Guesthouse カオサン東京ゲストハウス **36** F5
K's House ケイズハウス **37** E6
Ryokan Katsutarō 旅館勝太郎 **38** B4
Ryokan Shigetsu 旅館指月 **39** F5
Sakura Hostel サクラホステル **40** F4
Sakura Ryokan 桜旅館 **41** E3
Sawanoya Ryokan 澤の屋旅館 **42** A3
Suigetsu Hotel Ōgaisō 水月ホテル鷗外荘 **43** B4
Sukeroku No Yado Sadachiyo 助六の宿貞千代 **44** F4
Sutton Place Hotel サットンプレイスホテル **45** C4
Taitō Ryokan 台東旅館 **46** E5
Tokyo Ryokan 東京旅館 **47** E5

EATING (p170)

Daikokuya 大黒家 **48** F5
Echikatsu 江知勝 **49** B6
Futaba とんかつ双葉 **50** B5
Ikenohata Yabu Soba 池之端やぶそば **51** B4
Izu-ei 伊豆栄 **52** B5
Kappabashi Coffee 合羽橋珈琲 **53** E4
Komagata Dojō 駒形どじょう **54** F6
Sasa-no-Yuki 笹乃雪 **55** C2
Sometarō 染太郎 **56** E5
Tsukiji Sushi-sen 旅館東海荘 **57** F5
Ueno Yabu Soba 上野やぶそば **58** C5
Vin Chou 萬鳥 **59** E5

DRINKING (p181)

Kamiya Bar 神谷バー **60** F5
Warrior Celt ウォーリアーケルト **61** C5

SHOPPING (p188)

Ameyoko Arcade アメ横 (see 6)

TRANSPORT (p192)

Suijō Bus (Waterbus) Terminal 水上バスターミナル (see 22)

UENO & ASAKUSA

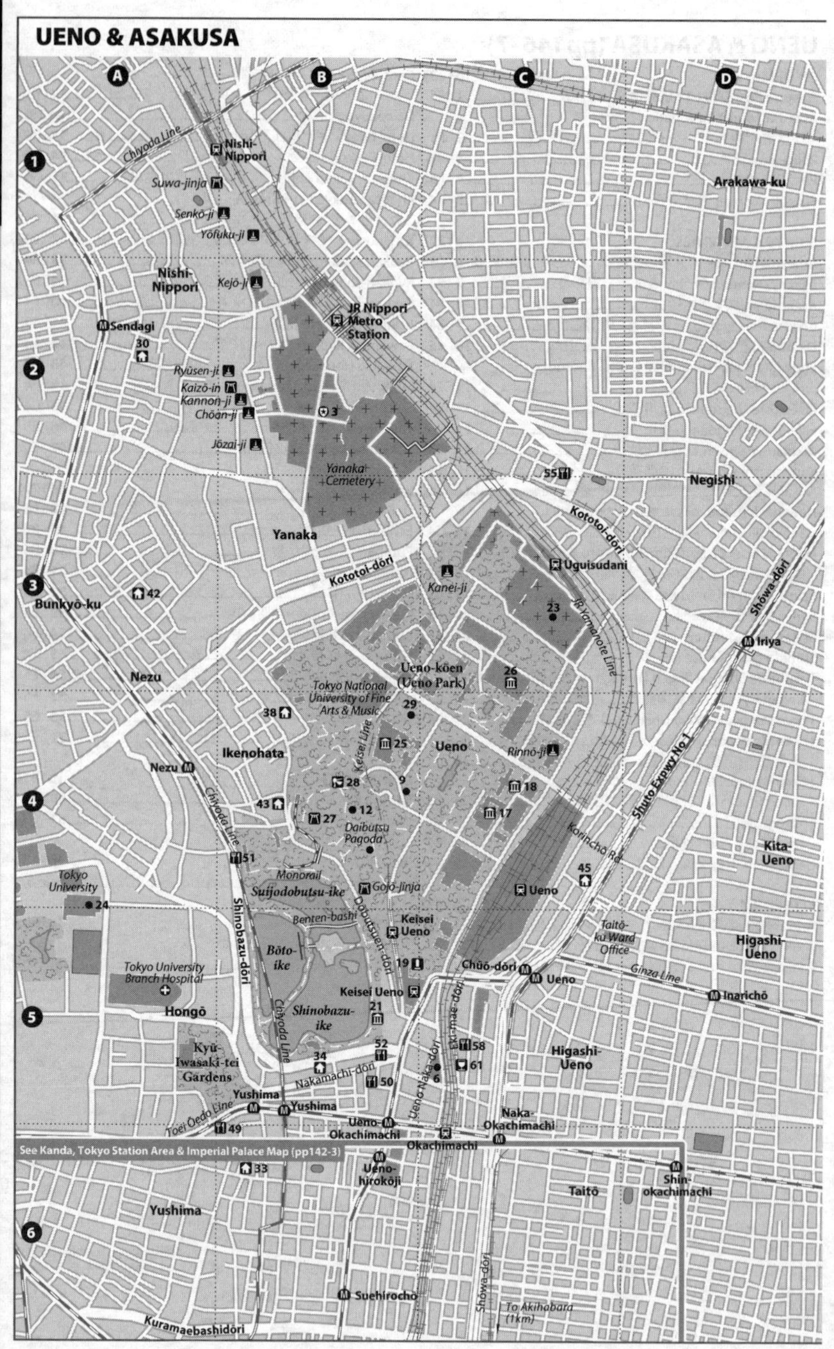

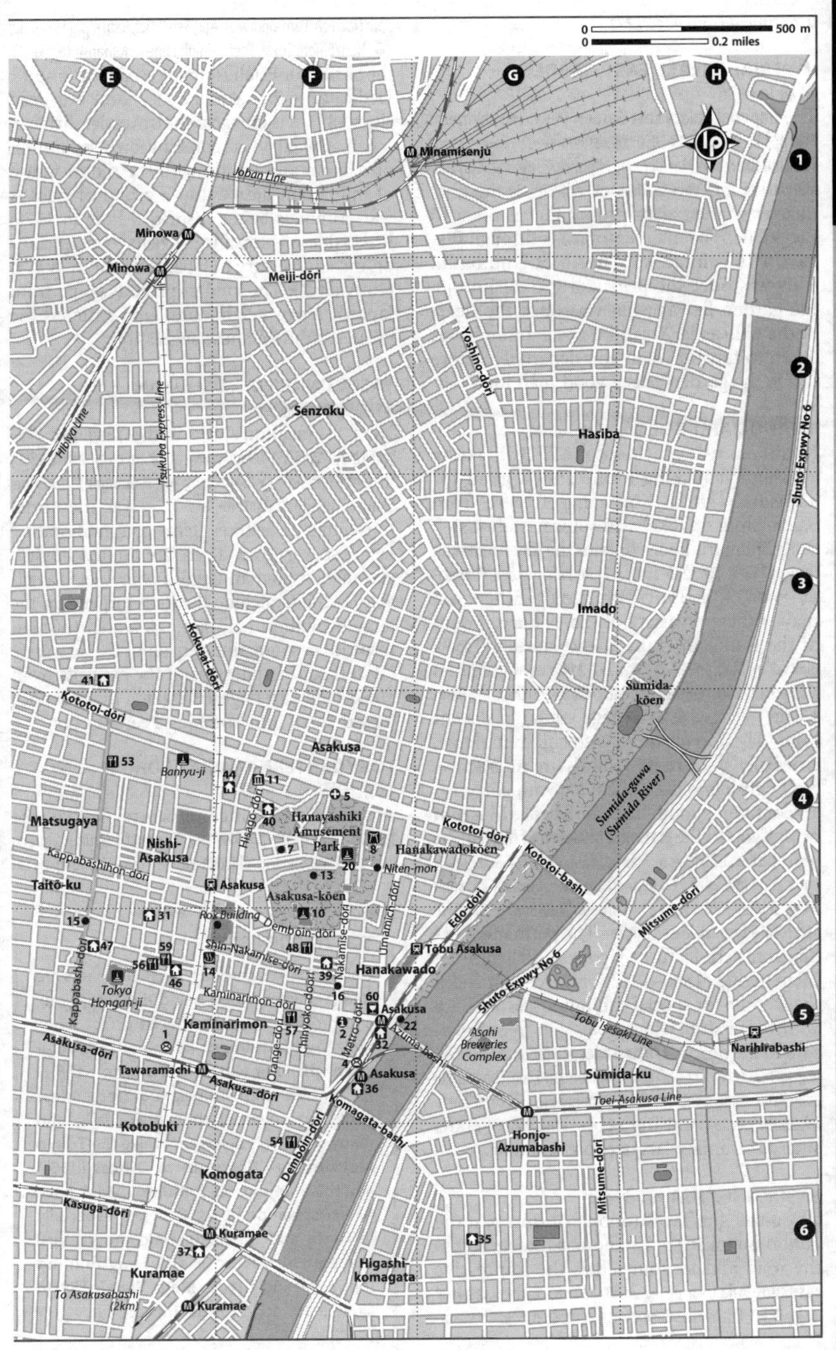
0 500 m
0 0.2 miles
Minamisenju
Joban Line
Minowa
Minowa
Meiji-dōri
Yoshino-dōri
Hibiya Line
Tsukuba Express Line
Senzoku
Hasiba
Shuto Expwy No 6
Imado
Kokusai-dōri
Sumida-kōen
Kototoi-dōri
Asakusa
Banryu-ji
Hisago-dōri
Hanayashiki Amusement Park
Matsugaya
Nishi-Asakusa
Kototoi-dōri
Hanakawadokōen
Sumida-gawa (Sumida River)
Kappabashihon-dōri
Niten-mon
Kototoi-bashi
Taitō-ku
Asakusa
Asakusa-kōen
Umamichi-dōri
Edo-dōri
Mitsume-dōri
Rox Building
Demboin-dōri
Nakamise-dōri
Tōbu Asakusa
Shin-Nakamise-dōri
Hanakawado
Shuto Expwy No 6
Kappabashi-dōri
Tokyo Hongan-ji
Kaminarimon-dōri
Asakusa
Kaminarimon
Orange-dōri
Chinyoko-dōori
Metro-dōri
Azuma-bashi
Asahi Breweries Complex
Tobu Isesaki Line
Narihirabashi
Asakusa-dōri
Tawaramachi
Asakusa-dōri
Asakusa
Sumida-ku
Komagata-bashi
Toei Asakusa Line
Kotobuki
Demboin-dōri
Honjo-Azumabashi
Mitsume-dōri
Komogata
Kasuga-dōri
Kuramae
Kuramae
Higashi-komagata
To Asakusabashi (2km)
Kuramae

(Continued from page 127)

IMPERIAL PALACE EAST GARDEN
皇居東御苑

The **Imperial Palace East Garden** (Kōkyo Higashi-gyoen; Map pp142-3; ☎ 3213-2050; admission free; 9am-4.30pm Tue-Thu, Sat & Sun Mar-Oct, 9am-4pm Nov-Feb; Chiyoda, Marunouchi, Tōzai lines to Ōtemachi, exit C10) is the only quarter of the palace proper that is open to the public. The main entrance is through **Ōte-mon**, a 10-minute walk north of Nijū-bashi. This was once the principal gate of Edo-jō; the garden lies at what was once the heart of the old castle. You'll be given a numbered token to turn in when you depart. The store inside the garden sells a good map for ¥150.

KITANOMARU-KŌEN 北の丸公園

Kitanomaru-kōen (Map pp142–3) makes a pleasant picnicking locale and is good for a leisurely stroll. You can get there from Kudanshita or Takebashi subway stations.

Kitanomaru-kōen contains the **Nihon Budōkan** (Map pp142-3; ☎ 3216-5100; 2-3 Kitanomaru-kōen, Chiyoda-ku; vary; Tōzai line to Takebashi, exit 1a), where you may witness a variety of martial arts. South of the Budōkan is the **Science Museum** (Kagaku Gijutsukan; Map pp142-3; ☎ 3212-2440; www.jsf.or.jp; 2-1 Kitanomaru-kōen, Chiyoda-ku; adult/child ¥600/250; 9am-4.50pm; Tōzai line to Takebashi, exit 1a), a decent rainy-day stop for those with children in tow, especially since most exhibits are interactive. An English booklet is included with entry.

Continuing south from the Science Museum brings you to the **National Museum of Modern Art** (Kokuritsu Kindai Bijutsukan; Map pp142-3; ☎ 5777-8600; www.momat.go.jp/english; 3-1 Kitanomaru-kōen, Chiyoda-ku; adult ¥420, student ¥70-130; 10am-5pm Tue-Sun, to 8pm Fri; Tōzai line to Takebashi, exit 1a). The permanent exhibition here features Japanese art from the Meiji period (1868–1912) onwards, but check the website for special exhibitions. Hold onto your ticket stub, which gives you free admission to the nearby **Crafts Gallery** (Bijutsukan Kōgeikan; Map pp142-3; ☎ 5777-8600; 1-1 Kitanomaru-kōen, Chiyoda-ku; adult ¥200, student ¥40-70; 2-5pm Tue-Fri; Tōzai line to Takebashi, exit 1a), housing a good display of crafts such as ceramics, lacquerware and dolls.

YASUKUNI-JINJA 靖国神社

If you take the Tayasu-mon exit (just past the Nihon Budōkan) of Kitanomaru-kōen, across the road and to your left is the impressive **Yasukuni-jinja** (Map pp142-3; ☎ 3261-8326; www.yasukuni.or.jp; 3-1-1 Kudankita, Chiyoda-ku; admission free; 9am-5pm Nov-Feb, 9am-6pm Mar, Apr, Sep & Oct, 9am-7pm May-Aug; Hanzōmon, Tōzai, Toei Shinjuku line to Kudanshita, exit 1), the Shrine for Establishing Peace in the Empire. Dedicated to the 2.4 million Japanese war-dead since 1853, it is the most controversial shrine in Japan. The Japanese constitutional separation of religion and politics and the renunciation of militarism didn't stop a group of class-A war criminals being enshrined here in 1979; it also doesn't stop annual visits by politicians on the anniversary of Japan's defeat in WWII (15 August). The loudest protests come from Japan's Asian neighbours, who suffered the greatest from Japanese aggression.

YASUKUNI-JINJA YŪSHŪKAN
靖國神社遊就館

Next to Yasukuni-jinja is the **Yūshūkan** (Map pp142-3; ☎ 3261-0996; www.yasukuni.or.jp; adult ¥800, student ¥100-500; 9am-5pm; Hanzōmon, Tōzai, Toei Shinjuku line to Kudanshita, exit 1), a war memorial museum that features items commemorating Japanese war-dead. There are limited English explanations, but an English pamphlet is available. Exhibits include the long torpedo in the large exhibition hall that is a *kaiten* (human torpedo), a submarine version of the *kamikaze* (WWII suicide pilots), and the excerpts from books (some in English) arguing that America forced Japan into bombing Pearl Harbor.

TOKYO INTERNATIONAL FORUM
東京国際フォーラム

A remarkable edifice in central Tokyo, the **forum** (Map p138; ☎ 5221-9000; www.t-i-forum.co.jp/english; 3-5-1 Marunouchi, Chiyoda-ku; 7am-11.30pm; JR

TOKYO FOR FREE

Unlike Tokyo's gardens, most city parks are free (Shinjuku-gyoen being the exception), and provide a peaceful backdrop for a picnic – try **Kitanomaru-kōen** (left), **Yoyogi-kōen** (p155) or **Hibiya-kōen** (Map p138).

Temples and shrines are free unless you'd like to enter their main halls, and many of Tokyo's skyscrapers, like the **Tokyo Metropolitan Government Offices** (p154) and the **Shinjuku NS Building** (p154), have free observation floors. Galleries, especially in Ginza and Harajuku, welcome visitors. Company showrooms like the **Sony Building** (opposite) and **Toyota Mega Web** (p158) in Odaiba are good for gearheads.

MAID CAFES

As the popularity of manga spreads around the world, so does Akihabara culture – maid cafes, for example.

The nationally famous **@home Café** (Map pp142–3; ☎ 3254-7878; www.cafe-athome.com/pics/?lang=en; 5th fl, Don Quijote Bldg, 4-3-3 Soto-Kanda, Chiyoda-ku; 11.30am-10pm Mon-Fri, 10.30am-10pm Sat & Sun; JR Sōbu, Yamanote lines to Akihabara, Electric Town exit), features live singing performances by its adorable staff; and in addition to being served lunch by a maid calling you *'ojō-sama'* (mistress) or *'goshujin-sama'* (master) for the duration, you can also play games with her for prizes and discounts.

Yamanote & Yūrakuchō lines to Yūrakuchō, main exit & exit A4b) is mostly used for conventions and events. Its prominent glass wing looks like a transparent ship plying Tokyo's urban waters. In contrast, the west wing is a boxy affair of cantilevered, overhanging spaces and cavernous atria.

AKIHABARA 秋葉原

Akihabara (Map pp142–3) began its evolution into 'Denki-gai' (Electric Town) post-WWII, when the area around the station became a black market for radio parts. In more recent decades, Akihabara has been widely known as *the* place to hunt for bargains on new and used electronics. Nowadays, you're more likely to hear it called Akiba, the more common nickname among the manga and anime fans who are drawn by its gravitational pull, as Akihabara has morphed into the centre of the known *otaku* (geek) universe. The neighbourhood not only caters to the consumption of comic books and computer games, but also to the R&R of the consumers.

And thus, Akiba has helped to spawn an *otaku* culture of sorts, as maid cafes and *cosplay* (costume play) street performances have become their own phenomena that attract fans of Japan's unique sub-pop cultures. You'll see maids milling around Akihabara station with flyers advertising specialist maid cafes ranging in theme from cutesy pajama-party to (professional) foot massage to Catholic nunnery, but all featuring the staff in some version of the foofy maid uniform.

Ginza & Shiodome 銀座・汐留

GINZA 銀座

Ginza is Tokyo's answer to NYC's Fifth Ave. Back in the 1870s Ginza was one of the first areas to modernise, featuring a large number of novel (for Tokyoites of that era) Western-style brick buildings. Ginza was also home to Tokyo's first department stores, gas lamps and other harbingers of the modern world.

Today, other shopping districts rival Ginza in opulence, vitality and popularity, but it retains a distinct snob value – conspicuous consumption remains big here. It's therefore a superb place to window-shop and browse the galleries (usually free). Saturday afternoons and Sundays are the best, when Chūō-dōri and some smaller streets are closed to vehicles, allowing kimono-clad ladies to amble and toddlers to gambol down the middle of the boulevard.

Sony Building ソニービル

Although essentially a **Sony showroom** (Map p138; ☎ 3573 2371; www.sonybuilding.jp; 5-3-1 Ginza, Chūō-ku; admission free; 11am-7pm; Ginza, Hibiya, Marunouchi line to Ginza, exit B9), this place has hands-on displays of Sony's latest gizmos and gadgets – some that have yet to be released. It's a good place to test-drive Sony's latest digital cameras, laptops and idiosyncratic electronic 'pets'.

Galleries & Museums

Ginza is packed with small galleries and museums, many with a graphic design focus. Though scattered throughout Ginza, they are concentrated in the area south of Harumi-dōri, between Ginza-dōri and Chūō-dōri.

Idemitsu Museum of Arts (Map p138; ☎ 5777-8600; www.idemitsu.co.jp/museum; 9th fl, 3-1-1 Marunouchi, Chiyoda-ku; adult/student ¥1000/700; 10am-5pm Tue-Sun, 10am-7pm Fri; Chiyoda, Toei Mita lines to Hibiya, exits A1 & B3) holds Japanese and Chinese art and is famous for its collection of work by the Zen monk Sengai. It's next door to the Imperial Theatre.

Exhibiting the outstanding work of up-and-coming photographers and long-time professionals, **Leica Ginza Salon** (Map p138; ☎ 6215-7070; www.leica-camera.us/culture/galeries/gallery_tokyo; 1st & 2nd fl, Tokaido Bldg, 6-4-1 Ginza, Chūō-ku; admission free; 11am-7pm Tue-Sun; Ginza, Hibiya & Marunouchi line to Ginza, exit C2) remains one of the best photography galleries in the area.

TSUKIJI MANNERS *Chris Rowthorn*

As this book was being researched, the tuna auction at Tsukiji was temporarily closed to tourists, due to inappropriate behaviour by a small minority of visitors (both foreign and Japanese), some of whom touched the (*very* expensive!) fish or got in the way of the buyers and auctioneers in order to pose for photographs. (Not to mention the general disturbance created by large crowds of tourists milling about the place during working hours.)

As this book went to press, the tuna auction had been reopened, but visitors were confined to a small viewing area. It is unclear what the final policy on visitors to the auction will be, so it's a good idea to ask at your place of accommodation about the current state of affairs before waking up at 4am to see the auction (and do keep in mind that the rest of the market is absolutely great and can be visited freely and you can do so without waking up at an unholy hour).

Whether you visit the tuna auction or just the rest of the market, it's a good idea to keep in mind the following:

- Tsukiji is a working market and not a show for tourists. Please keep out of the way of buyers and sellers as they go about their business.
- Do not touch any of the products for sale.
- Keep a sharp eye out for the motorised carts that prowl the market – especially if you're with small children – getting hit by one of these things would really put a crimp in your vacation.
- Wear shoes you won't mind getting a bit mucky.
- Consider actually buying something – after all, this is a market and not a museum.

Kabuki-za 歌舞伎座

Even distinguished historic structures as **Kabuki-za** (Map p138; ☎ 3541-3131; www.shochiku.co.jp/play/kabukiza/theater/index.html; 4-12-5 Ginza, Chūō-ku; admission ¥2500-17,000; 11am-9pm; Hibiya, Toei Asakusa lines to Higashi-Ginza, exit 3) are shockingly vulnerable to the Tokyo wrecking ball. If you'll be visiting before April 2010, walk by to view the beautifully dramatic exterior of this kabuki theatre, or consider taking in a performance (p187) before the curtain falls. Kabuki-za will reopen after demolition and reconstruction in 2013.

ADVERTISING MUSEUM TOKYO アド・ミュージアム東京

A clean, well-lit setting for ad displays is only fitting for the **Advertising Museum Tokyo** (ADMT; Map p138; ☎ 6218-2500; B1 & B2 fl, Caretta Shiodome Bldg, 1-8-2 Higashi-Shimbashi, Minato-ku; admission free; 11am-6.30pm Tue-Fri, 11am-4.30pm Sat; Toei Ōedo line to Shiodome, JR Shimbashi exit). From cutting-edge pop designs to Edo-period woodcuts presaging advertising to come, the exhibitions are as fascinating as they are eye-catching. Find detailed directions on the website.

HAMA-RIKYŪ-TEIEN 浜離宮庭園

Arguably the loveliest garden in central Tokyo, **Hama-Rikyū-Teien** (Detached Palace Garden; Map p138; ☎ 3541-0200; admission ¥300; 9am-5pm; Toei Ōedo line to Tsukiji-Shijō, exit A2) is incongruously surrounded by gleaming high-rises at the edge of Tokyo Bay. Walk the garden paths along tide-fed ponds for a little peace.

TSUKIJI FISH MARKET 築地市場

Tsukiji Fish Market (Map p138; ☎ 3541-2640; www.tsukiji-market.or.jp; 5-2 Tsukiji, Chūō-ku; closed 2nd & 4th Wed most months, Sun & public holidays; Toei Ōedo line to Tsukiji-Shijō, exits A1 & A2) is the world's biggest seafood market. The day begins very early, with the arrival of the catch and its early-morning wholesale auctioning (see the boxed text, above).

To get to the climate-controlled auction hall, head into the main entrance of the market hall and go all the way to the back. You can pick up an English guide at the market entrance. Of course, the rest of the market is open to the public and is at its best before 8am.

Ueno 上野

Ueno is one of the last areas in Tokyo where the old Shitamachi feel still permeates. Ueno's aging but spry shopping arcade, Ameyoko Arcade (Map pp146–7), remains a bustling market that feels worlds away from the monumental marketplace of Roppongi Hills (p157). But Ueno has no need for fancy shopping malls, for its real draw is Ueno-kōen, which boasts the highest concentration of museums and galleries anywhere in Japan.

UENO-KŌEN 上野公園

Ueno Hill was the site of a last-ditch defence of the Tokugawa shōgunate by about 2000 Tokugawa loyalists in 1868. They were duly dispatched by the imperial army, and the new Meiji government decreed that Ueno Hill would be transformed into Tokyo's first public park. Today, **Ueno-kōen** (Map pp146-7; JR Yamanote line to Ueno, Park exit) may not be the sexiest of Tokyo's parks, but it certainly packs a bigger cultural punch than any others. Across the street from the Park exit is a large map showing the layout of the park and museum complex.

The park is famous as Tokyo's most popular site for *hanami* (blossom-viewing) in early to mid-April – which isn't to say it's the *best* place (see Shinjuku-gyoen, p154 for an altogether quieter *hanami* spot). At the southern end of the park, in all seasons, enormous round lotus leaves blanket Shinobazu-ike (Shinobazu Pond).

Saigō Takamori Statue 西郷隆盛銅像

Near the southern entrance to the park is this unconventional **statue** (Map pp146-7; JR Yamanote line to Ueno, Shinobazu exit) of a samurai walking his dog. Saigō Takamori started out supporting the Meiji Restoration but ended up ritually disembowelling himself in defeated opposition to it. The turnabout in his loyalties occurred when the Meiji government withdrew the powers of the military class to which he belonged (see the boxed text, p733).

Tokyo National Museum 東京国立博物館

The **Tokyo National Museum** (Tokyo Kokuritsu Hakubutsukan; Map pp146-7; ☎ 3822-1111; www.tnm.jp; 13-9 Ueno-kōen, Taitō-ku; adult/student ¥600/400; 9.30am-5pm Tue-Sun Oct-Mar, to 8pm Fri, to 6pm Sat & Sun Apr-Sep; JR Yamanote line to Ueno, Park exit) is the one museum in Tokyo worth a spot on your itinerary. Not only is it Japan's largest, housing some 87,000 items, it also has the world's largest collection of Japanese art. Only a portion of the museum's works is displayed at any one time.

The museum has four galleries, the most important of which is the **Main Hall** (Honkan). It's straight ahead as you enter, and it houses a very impressive array of Japanese art, from sculpture and swords to lacquerware and calligraphy. The **Gallery of Eastern Antiquities** (Tōyō-kan), to the right of the ticket booth, displays a collection of art and archaeological finds from all over Asia. The **Hyōkei-kan**, to the left of the ticket booth, houses Japanese archaeological finds and includes a room devoted to artefacts once used by the Ainu, the indigenous people of Hokkaidō.

Perhaps best of all is the **Gallery of Hōryūji Treasures** (Hōryūji Hōmotsu-kan), which houses some of Japan's most important Buddhist artworks, all from Hōryū-ji in Nara.

Take some air after your museum visit with a stroll around the **Tokugawa Shōgun Reien** (Tokugawa Shōgun Cemetery), behind the museum.

Tokyo Metropolitan Museum of Art 東京都美術館

This **museum of art** (Map pp146-7; ☎ 3823-6921; www.tobikan.jp; 8-36 Ueno-kōen, Taitō-ku; admission varies; 9am-5pm Tue-Sun; JR Yamanote line to Ueno, Park exit) has several galleries that run temporary displays of contemporary Japanese art. Galleries feature both Western-style art and Japanese-style art, such as *sumi-e* (ink brush painting) and ikebana (flower arrangement). Apart from the main gallery, the rental galleries are not curated by the museum, so exhibition standards tend to fluctuate.

National Science Museum 国立科学博物館

Though there's limited interpretive signage in English, this **museum** (Kokuritsu Kagaku Hakubutsukan; Map pp146-7; ☎ 3822-0111 Mon-Fri, 3822-0114 Sat & Sun; www.kahaku.go.jp/english; 7-20 Ueno-kōen, Taitō-ku; adult/child ¥600/free; 9am-5pm Tue-Sun, 9am-8pm Fri; JR Yamanote line to Ueno, Park exit) often installs excellent special exhibitions (extra fees apply) on everything from biodiversity to robots. The interactive exhibits make it a good place to bring kids, especially combined with a trip to the Ueno Zoo.

National Museum of Western Art 国立西洋美術館

The **National Museum of Western Art** (Kokuritsu Seiyō Bijutsukan; Map pp146-7; ☎ 5777-8600; www.nmwa.go.jp; 7-7 Ueno-kōen, Taitō-ku; adult ¥420, student ¥70-130; 9.30am-5.30pm, to 8pm Fri, closed Mon; JR Yamanote line to Ueno, Park exit) has a respectable, though rather indifferently displayed, permanent collection. It frequently hosts special exhibits (admission varies) on loan from other museums of international repute.

Shitamachi Museum 下町風俗資料館

This **museum** (Map pp146-7; ☎ 3823-7451; 2-1 Ueno-kōen, Taitō-ku; adult/student ¥300/100; 9.30am-4.30pm Tue-Sun; JR Yamanote line to Ueno, Hirokōji exit) re-creates life in Edo's Shitamachi, the plebeian downtown quarter of old Tokyo. Exhibits include a sweet shop, the home and business of a copper boilermaker and a tenement house. Docents are on hand to teach games or help you try on the clothes, making for an engaging hands-on visit.

Ueno Zoo 上野動物園

Established in 1882, **Ueno Zoo** (Map pp146-7; ☎ 3828-5171; 9-83 Ueno-kōen, Taitō-ku; adult/student/child ¥600/200/free; 9.30am-5pm Tue-Sun; JR Yamanote line to Ueno, Shinobazu exit) was the first of its kind in Japan. It's a good outing if you have children; otherwise, it can be safely dropped from a busy itinerary.

Tōshōgū 東照宮

This **shrine** (Map pp146-7; ☎ 3822-3455; 9-88 Ueno-kōen, Taitō-ku; admission ¥200; 9am-4.30pm Dec-Feb, to 5.30pm Mar-Nov; JR Yamanote line to Ueno, Shinobazu exit), like its counterpart in Nikkō, is dedicated to Tokugawa Ieyasu, who unified Japan. The shrine, resplendent in gold leaf and ornate details, dates from 1651 and is one of the few extant early-Edo structures, having fortuitously survived Tokyo's innumerable disasters.

Ameyoko Arcade アメ横

This **market** (Ameya-yokochō; Map pp146-7; JR Yamanote line to Okachimachi (north exit) or Ueno (Hirokōji exit), Hibiya line to Naka-Okachimachi, exit A5) has a flavour unlike any other market in Tokyo, resembling noisy, pungent markets elsewhere in Asia. It was famous as a black-market district after WWII, and is still a lively outdoor shopping arcade where bargains abound on sneakers, dried squid and shirts emblazoned with Japanese motifs. Look for its big archway sign opposite Ueno station's south side.

Asakusa 浅草

Long considered the heart of old Shitamachi, Asakusa is an interesting, compact neighbourhood to explore on foot. Asakusa's main attraction is the temple Sensō-ji, also known as Asakusa Kannon-dō. In Edo times, Asakusa was a halfway stop between the city and its most infamous pleasure district, Yoshiwara. Eventually Asakusa developed into a pleasure quarter in its own right, becoming the centre for that most loved of Edo entertainments, kabuki. In the shadow of Sensō-ji a fairground spirit prevailed and a range of secular establishments thrived, from kabuki theatres to brothels.

These days, Asakusa is one of the few areas of Tokyo to have retained the old-fashioned spirit of Shitamachi. Though more a tourist quarter than pleasure district, Asakusa continues to attract crowds not only with the Sensō-ji complex, but also with its bustling marketplaces of **Nakamise-dōri**, where you can find cheesy souvenirs and fancy *geta* (wooden sandals), and **Kappabashi-dōri**, famous for its plastic food models and kitchenware of all kinds.

SENSŌ-JI 浅草寺

This **temple** (Map pp146-7; ☎ 3842-0181; 2-3-1 Asakusa, Taitō-ku; admission free; 24hr; Ginza or Toei Asakusa lines to Asakusa, exits 1 & A5) enshrines a golden image of Kannon (the Buddhist Goddess of Mercy), which, according to legend, was miraculously fished out of the nearby Sumida-gawa by two fishermen in AD 628. The image has remained on the spot ever since, through successive rebuildings of the temple; the present structure dates from 1950.

Approaching Sensō-ji from Asakusa subway station, the entrance is via Kaminarimon (Thunder Gate). The gate's protector gods are Fūjin, the god of wind, on the right; and Raijin, the god of thunder, on the left.

Near Kaminarimon, you'll probably be wooed by *jinrikisha* (pedicab drivers) in traditional dress; they can cart you around on tours (30/60 minutes for ¥5000/9000 per person), providing commentary in English or Japanese.

Straight ahead is Nakamise-dōri, the temple precinct's shopping street, where everything from tourist trinkets to genuine Edo-style crafts is sold. Need a formal wig to wear with your kimono? Here's where to shop.

Nakamise-dōri leads to the main temple compound. Whether the ancient image of Kannon actually exists is a secret, as it's not on public display. This doesn't stop a steady stream of worshippers from travelling to the top of the stairs to bow and clap. In front of the temple is a large incense cauldron: the smoke is said to bestow health and you'll see visitors rubbing it into their bodies through their clothes.

DEMBŌ-IN 伝法院

To the left of the temple precinct is Dembō-in (Map pp146–7). Although the garden of Dembō-in is not open to the public, it is possible to obtain a pass by calling a few days ahead to the **main office** (☎ 3842-0181; 2-3-1 Asakusa, Taitō-ku; admission free; open by appointment, closed for ceremonies; Ginza or Toei Asakusa lines to Asakusa, exits 1 & A5) to the left of the entrance of the Five-Storeyed Pagoda nearby. The garden is one of Tokyo's best, containing a picturesque pond and a replica of a famous Kyoto tea house.

EDO SHITAMACHI TRADITIONAL CRAFTS MUSEUM 江戸下町伝統工芸館
Because Shitamachi is still home to countless traditional workshops – often of the mom-and-pop variety who have been in business for generations – Asakusa is the perfect location for this **museum** (Map pp146-7; ☎ 3842-1990; 2-22-13 Asakusa, Taitō-ku; admission free; 10am-8pm; Ginza line to Tawaramachi, exit 3 or Tsukuba Express to Asakusa, exit A1). Displayed inside are beautifully made handicrafts in wood, straw, ceramic and lacquer, and if you visit on a weekend, local craftspeople demonstrate their expertise.

SUMIDA-GAWA CRUISE 隅田川クルーズ
A Sumida-gawa cruise on the **Suijō Bus** (Waterbus; Map pp146-7; ☎ 0120-977-311; www.suijobus.co.jp; fare to Hama-Rikyū-Teien/Hinode Pier ¥720/760; 9.30am-6pm; Ginza or Toei Asakusa lines to Asakusa, exits 4 & A5) may not be the most scenic you've ever experienced, but it's a great way to get to or from Asakusa. Cruises depart about every half-hour from the pier next to the bridge, Azuma-bashi, and go to Hama-Rikyū-Teien (p150) and Hinode Pier (Map p138). A good way to do the cruise is to buy a ticket to Hama-Rikyū-Teien (where you'll have to pay an additional ¥300 entry fee). After exploring the garden, you can walk into Ginza in about 10 to 15 minutes.

Ikebukuro 池袋

Though Ikebukuro once boasted the world's largest department store, tallest building and longest escalator, these former glories have since been outshined elsewhere. But Ikebukuro's Sunshine City is still perfect for rainy weather, since you could spend 40 days roaming the humongous mall, visiting the aquarium and planetarium and sampling enough ice cream and *gyōza* (Chinese dumplings) to last you a biblical deluge. The neighbourhood shouldn't rate high on a busy schedule unless you're looking for manga and girl-geek culture, in which case you'll want to walk down Otome Rd.

SUNSHINE CITY サンシャインシティ
Billed as a 'city in a building', **Sunshine City** (Map p132; ☎ 3989-3331, 3989-1111; 3-1-1 Higashi-Ikebukuro, Toshima-ku; 10am-10pm; JR Yamanote line to Ikebukuro, east exit) is 60 floors of office space and shopping malls, with a few cultural and entertainment options thrown in, all in east Ikebukuro. If you've got ¥620 to burn, you can take a 35-second lift ride to the **observatory** (10am-9.30pm) on the 60th floor and gaze out on the building blocks below.

On the 7th floor of the Bunka Kaikan Building of Sunshine City is the **Ancient Orient Museum** (☎ 3989-3491; 3-1-4 Higashi-Ikebukuro, Toshima-ku; adult ¥500, student ¥150-400; 10am-5pm), displaying antiquities and art from across Asia.

Also of interest might be the **Sunshine Planetarium** (☎ 3989-3475; 10th fl, World Import Mart Bldg, 3-1-3 Higashi-Ikebukuro, Toshima-ku; adult/child ¥900/500; 11am-6pm Mon-Thu, 8-10pm Fri-Sun), though shows are in Japanese, and the **Sunshine International Aquarium** (☎ 3989-3466; 10th fl, World Import Mart Bldg, 3-1-3 Higashi-Ikebukuro, Toshima-ku; adult/child ¥1800/900; 10am-6pm Mon-Fri, 10am-6.30pm Sat & Sun;), which boasts the distinction of being the highest aquarium in the world. This high-rise water world has tanks full of electric eels, sharks and other intriguing sea life. You can also purchase combination tickets (adult/child ¥2400/1200) for admission to both.

OTOME ROAD 乙女ロード
You won't find it on official maps, as **Otome Rd** (Maiden Rd; Map p132) is only a nickname in honour of the female *otaku* who browse the many manga shops lining this street. Many of the shops specialise in *yaoi* ('boys' love') and beautifully-rendered *dōjinshi* (fan fiction), catering to the girl geeks who love them. And like its overwhelmingly male-centric *otaku* counterpart Akihabara, Otome Rd has its share of 'butler cafes' and similar spinoffs, where customers are waited on by attentive young men (or husky-voiced women in convincing drag).

One such establishment, the **Swallowtail Café** (Map p132; www.butlers-cafe.jp, in Japanese; B1 fl, 3-12-12 Higashi-Ikebukuro, Toshima-ku; 10.30am-9pm Mon-Sat, by appointment only; JR Yamanote line to Ikebukuro, east exit), is so popular you must make reservations days or weeks in advance, so book ahead for your princess-fantasy afternoon tea.

TOKYO METROPOLITAN ART SPACE
東京芸術劇場
Designed to host performances of all kinds, the **Tokyo Metropolitan Art Space** (Map p132; ☎ 5391-2111; www.geigeki.jp/english/index.html; 1-8-1 Nishi-Ikebukuro; JR Yamanote line to Ikebukuro, west exit;) was plonked down just where Tokyo needed it most – on Ikebukuro's west side. The building has four halls as well as shops and cafes. Those without a ticket for anything should treat themselves to the soaring escalator ride – and the thrills just don't stop.

Shinjuku 新宿

Here in Shinjuku, much of what makes Tokyo tick is crammed into one busy district: upscale department stores, anachronistic stand-up bars, buttoned-up government offices, swarming crowds, streetside video screens, hostess clubs, shyly tucked-away shrines and soaring skyscrapers.

Shinjuku is a sprawling civic, commercial and entertainment centre. Every day more than three million people pass through the station alone, making it one of the busiest in the world. On the western side of the station is Tokyo's highest concentration of skyscrapers and, presiding over them, Tange Kenzō's Tokyo Metropolitan Government Offices (right) – massive awe-inspiring structures. The eastern side of the station, by contrast, is a labyrinth of department stores, restaurants, boutiques, neon and a glimpse of Tokyo's underbelly.

EAST SIDE 東新宿

Shinjuku's east side is a great one-stop mash-up of trashy low culture, sedate department stores and one of the city's best cherry-blossom viewing spots, Shinjuku-gyoen.

Kabukichō 歌舞伎町

Tokyo's most notorious red-light district lies east of Seibu Shinjuku station, north of Yasukuni-dōri. This is one of the world's more imaginative red-light districts, with 'soaplands' (massage parlours), love hotels, pink cabarets ('pink' is the Japanese equivalent of 'blue' in English) and strip shows. The streets here are all crackling neon and drunken salarymen. Shady-looking *yakuza* (mafia) and wannabes glare and slouch in sharkskin suits, and *freeters* (part-time workers) earn some yen passing out tissue-pack advertisements.

Kabukichō is not wall-to-wall sex; there are also some straight entertainment options, including cinemas and some good restaurants (p174). For a drink, stroll around the teeny, intriguing alleys of the Golden Gai (p181).

Hanazono-jinja 花園神社

Nestled in the shadow of Kabukichō is this quiet, unassuming shrine, **Hanazono-jinja** (Map p131; ☎ 3200-3093; 5-17-3 Shinjuku, Shinjuku-ku; Marunouchi & Toei Shinjuku lines to Shinjuku-sanchōme, exits B3 & B5). It only takes a few minutes to stroll the grounds, but it's a quiet refuge from the Shinjuku streets and particularly pleasant when it's lit up in the evening.

Shinjuku-gyoen 新宿御苑

One of the city's best escapes and top cherry-blossom viewing spots, **Shinjuku-gyoen** (Map p131; ☎ 3350-0151; Naitochō, Shinjuku-ku; adult/child under 15/child under 6 ¥200/50/free; 9am-4.30pm Tue-Sun; Marunouchi line to Shinjuku-gyoenmae, exit 1) is also one of Tokyo's largest parks at 57.6 hectares (144 acres). It dates back to 1906 and was designed as a European-style park, though it also has a Japanese garden, a hothouse containing tropical plants and a pond with giant carp.

WEST SIDE 西新宿

Shinjuku's west side is mainly administrative, with its attractions mainly centred around the gleaming building interiors and the observation floors of the towering Tokyo Metropolitan Government Offices.

Tokyo Metropolitan Government Offices 東京都庁

These city **offices** (Tokyo Tochō; Map p131; ☎ 5321-1111; 2-8-1 Nishi-Shinjuku, Shinjuku-ku; admission free; observatories 9.30am-11pm Tue-Sun, North Tower closed 2nd & 4th Mon, South Tower closed 1st & 3rd Tue; Toei Ōedo line to Tochōmae, exits A3 & A4) occupy two adjoining buildings worth visiting for their stunning architecture and for the great views from the **twin observation floors**. On really clear days, you might even spot Mt Fuji to the west. To reach the observation floors, take one of the two 1st-floor lifts.

Shinjuku NS Building 新宿 NS ビル

The interior of the **Shinjuku NS Building** (Map p131; 2-4-1 Nishi-Shinjuku, Shinjuku-ku; admission free; 11am-10pm; Toei Ōedo line to Tochōmae, exit A2) is hollow, featuring a 1600-sq-metre atrium illuminated by sunlight that streams in through the glass roof. The atrium features a 29m-tall pendulum clock. The restaurants on the 29th and 30th floors have excellent views over Tokyo, but if you're not hungry the views are still free.

Pentax Forum ペンタックスフォーラム

Set up as an interactive showroom where photography buffs can play with the latest equipment, **Pentax Forum** (Map p131; ☎ 3348-2941; 1st fl, Shinjuku Mitsui Bldg, 2-1-1 Nishi-Shinjuku, Shinjuku-ku; admission free; 10.30am-6.30pm; Toei Ōedo line to Tochōmae, exit B2) is a must for shutterbugs.

Harajuku & Aoyama 原宿・青山

Harajuku and Aoyama (Map p134) are where Tokyoites come to be spendy and trendy. They're enjoyable areas to stroll and watch lo-

COSPLAY

However you know them – as Harajuku girls, goth-Lolis or *cosplay-zoku* (costume play gang) – these reps of Tokyo youth culture are recognisable all over the world.

The *cosplay-zoku* are mostly teenage girls who assemble at Jingū-bashi (p134) on the weekends, bedecked in goth make-up, punk kimono getups, subversive nuns' habits and cartoon-nurse exaggeration.

Cosplay kids are united in their fondness for Japanese visual-*kei* (visual type) bands or anime and manga characters, and a sense of pride in their individual style. Many of the girls are *ijime-ko,* kids bullied in school, who find release and expression in their temporary weekend identities.

The end result is Tokyo's famous weekend circus of excited photographers, bewildered tourists and cultural voyeurs. The girls revel, primp and pose for the cameras until dusk, when they hop on their trains back to 'normal' life in Tokyo or its faceless suburbs.

cals in contented consumer mode. **Takeshita-dōri** buzzes with teenyboppers shopping for hilariously mistranslated T-shirts and fishnet stockings; tree-lined **Omote-sandō**, with its alfresco cafes, is still the closest Tokyo gets to Paris; and the bistro alleys of Aoyama harbour some of the best international cuisine in town.

For snaps of the idiosyncratically clad natives, check out the weekend madness at **Jingū-bashi** (see the boxed text, above).

MEIJI-JINGŪ 明治神宮

Completed in 1920, the **shrine** (Map p134; ☎ 3379-5511; www.meijijingu.or.jp; 1-1 Yoyogi Kamizonochō, Shibuya-ku; admission free; 🕒 dawn-dusk; 🚊 JR Yamanote line to Harajuku, Omote-sandō exit) was built in memory of Emperor Meiji and Empress Shōken, under whose rule Japan ended its long isolation from the outside world. Unfortunately, like much else in Tokyo, the shrine was destroyed in WWII bombing. Rebuilding was completed in 1958.

Meiji-jingū might be a reconstruction of the original but, unlike so many of Japan's postwar reconstructions, it is altogether authentic. The shrine itself was built with Japanese cypress, while the cypress for the huge torii (shrine gate) came from Alishan in Taiwan.

The shrine's inner garden, **Meiji-jingū-gyoen** (adult/child ¥500/200; 🕒 9am-5pm), is almost deserted on weekdays. It's especially beautiful in June, when the irises are in bloom.

YOYOGI-KŌEN 代々木公園

Weekends at **Yoyogi-kōen** (Yoyogi Park; Map p134; 2-1 Yoyogi-Kaminzonochō; admission free; 🕒 dawn-dusk; 🚊 JR Yamanote line to Harajuku, Omote-sandō exit or Chiyoda line to Yoyogi-kōen, exit 4) are prime for stumbling upon the cool and unusual – *shamisen* (three-stringed lute) or punk-rock practice, or fire-eating, for example. At 53.2 hectares (133 acres), its wooded grounds are ringed with walking trails even if there aren't any interesting goings-on. It's at its best on a sunny Sunday in spring or autumn.

ŌTA MEMORIAL ART MUSEUM

太田記念美術館

Pad quietly in slippers through the **Ōta Museum** (Map p134; ☎ 3403-0880; www.ukiyoe-ota-muse.jp/english.html; 1-10-10 Jingūmae, Shibuya-ku; adult/student ¥1000/700; 🕒 10.30am-5.30pm Tue-Sun, closed from 27th to end of each month; 🚊 Chiyoda line to Meiji-jingūmae, exit 5) to view its first-rate collection of *ukiyo-e* (woodblock prints), including works by masters of the art such as Hiroshige. Find it in the alley just northwest of the Laforet Building. Extra charges apply for special exhibits.

GALLERIES

Aoyama is packed with tiny galleries, most of them free. Up Killer-dōri, look for the **Watari-um** (Watari Museum of Contemporary Art; Map p134; ☎ 3402-3001; www.watarium.co.jp; 3-7-6 Jingūmae, Shibuya-ku; adult/student ¥1000/800; 🕒 11am-7pm, to 9pm Wed, closed Mon; 🚊 Ginza line to Gaienmae, exit 3), which hosts cutting-edge contemporary art.

In the heart of Harajuku are the east and west branches of the **Design Festa Gallery** (Map p134; ☎ 3479-1442; www.designfestagallery.com; 3-20-18 Jingūmae, Shibuya-ku; admission free; 🕒 11am-8pm; 🚊 JR Yamanote line to Harajuku, Takeshita exit), where a vibrant mixed bag of art and craftiness is displayed by local creators.

Cross Omote-sandō to find the **Spiral Building** (Map p134; ☎ 3498-1171; 5-6-23 Minami-Aoyama, Minato-ku; admission free; 🕒 11am-8pm; 🚊 Chiyoda, Ginza, Hanzōmon lines to Omote-sandō, exit B1) features changing exhibits, dining and live music. Even more museum-store wares are sold on the 2nd floor.

Just around the corner from the Spiral Building, Kottō-dōri (Antique St) is a good place to seek out both galleries and antique shops.

Shibuya 渋谷

Shibuya Crossing (Map p134) is probably one of the world's most visually famous four-way intersections, where the green light given to pedestrians releases a timed surge of humanity. Mostly of interest as a stupendous youth-oriented shopping district and people-watching hotspot, the goods for sale and energy of Shibuya offer glimpses into the desires and psyche of a certain generation. Especially on weekends, you might get the feeling that the jammed streets are populated solely by fashionable under-25s.

HACHIKŌ STATUE ハチ公像

In the 1920s, a professor who lived near Shibuya station kept a small Akita dog, who would come to the station every afternoon to await his master's return. The professor died in 1925, but Hachikō continued to show up and wait at the station until his own death 11 years later. The poor dog's faithfulness was not lost on the locals, who built a statue to honour his memory.

PARCO FACTORY パルコファクトリー

Shows at the **Parco Factory** (Map p134; ☎ 3477-5873; 6th fl, Parco Part 1, 15-1 Udagawachō, Shibuya-ku; admission varies; 🕑 10am-9pm; 🚇 JR Yamanote line to Shibuya, Hachikō exit) tend to feature contemporary art with a sense of fun, as befits a gallery in Shibuya. Think graphic design and pop culture for an idea of Factory aesthetic.

TOBACCO & SALT MUSEUM
たばこと塩の博物館

This unusual little **museum** (Map p134; ☎ 3476-2041; 1-16-8 Jinnan, Shibuya-ku; adult/child ¥100/50; 🕑 10am-6pm Tue-Sun; 🚇 JR Yamanote line to Shibuya, Hachikō exit) has some fairly interesting exhibits detailing the history of tobacco and the methods of salt production practised in premodern Japan (when Japan harvested all its salt from the sea). While there's little English signage, much of the material is self-explanatory.

TEPCO ELECTRIC ENERGY MUSEUM 電力館

Folks with kids in tow and an interest in electric power might want to stop by the **Tepco Electric Energy Museum** (Denryokukan; Map p134; ☎ 3477-1191; 1-12-10 Jinnan, Shibuya-ku; admission free; 🕑 10am-6pm Thu-Tue; 🚼 ♿; 🚇 JR Yamanote line to Shibuya, Hachikō exit). Displays are well presented and cover everything associated with electricity; English handouts explain the exhibits.

Ebisu & Daikanyama 恵比寿・代官山

Human scale in size and speed, Ebisu and Daikanyama are stylish neighbourhoods that make quick escapes from faster-paced parts of the city. Daikanyama has a slow Euro-Japanese fusion atmosphere, with abundant alfresco cafes and boutiques of imaginative local designers. Neighbouring Ebisu, meanwhile, possesses some of Tokyo's cooler clubs and bars, and the open-air Yebisu Garden Place complex.

YEBISU GARDEN PLACE
恵比寿ガーデンプレイス

This **complex** (Map p136; ☎ 5423-7111; http://gardenplace.jp, in Japanese; 🚇 JR Yamanote line to Ebisu, east exit to Skywalk) of shops, restaurants and a 39-floor tower is surrounded by an open mall area – perfect for hanging out on warmer days, when you might catch live music. And, as you would expect, the restaurants on the 38th and 39th floors of **Yebisu Garden Place Tower** offer expansive city views.

Also located here is the Sapporo Breweries headquarters, which houses the **Beer Museum Yebisu** (☎ 5423-7255; www.sapporobeer.jp/english/guide/yebisu/; 4-20-1 Ebisu, Shibuya-ku; admission free; 🕑 10am-6pm Tue-Sun). Sure, the exhibits are interesting, but the obvious draw is its tasting lounge, where you can sample Sapporo's various brews (¥200 to ¥250 per glass) or a flight of four for ¥400.

Finally, check out the terrific **Tokyo Metropolitan Museum of Photography** (☎ 3280-0099; www.syabi.com; 1-13-3 Mita, Meguro-ku; admission varies; 🕑 10am-6pm Tue, Wed, Sat & Sun, 10am-8pm Thu & Fri), Japan's first large-scale museum devoted entirely to photography. The emphasis here is on Japanese pictures, but international work is also displayed.

MEGURO PARASITOLOGICAL MUSEUM
目黒寄生虫館

Some people will not find exhibits like the 9m-long tapeworm to their liking, but for others, this tiny **museum** (Map p136; ☎ 3716 1264; http://kiseichu.org/english.aspx; 4-1-1 Shimo-Meguro, Meguro-ku; admission free; 🕑 10am-5pm Tue-Sun; 🚇 JR Yamanote line to Meguro, west exit; ♿ 🚼) is gruesomely fascinating. Though there isn't much English signage, kids will get a kick out of the rows of formaldehyde-preserved critters, which are labelled with their Latin names. Upstairs, the gift counter sells parasite-themed keychains and T-shirts.

Roppongi & Akasaka 六本木・赤坂

Roppongi has undergone a renaissance over the last several years, with monumental development changing the urban landscape as well as elevating its respectability quotient. While Roppongi is still the pulsating centre of wild nightlife, it now also claims bragging rights to world-class restaurants, a trio of superb museums collectively making up the **Roppongi Art Triangle** and even some green oases.

Neighbouring Akasaka, mainly a government and business district, has a few notable sights of its own.

ROPPONGI HILLS 六本木ヒルズ

This massive development was no less than 17 years in the making, conceived by developer Mori Minoru, who envisioned improving people's quality of urban life by centralising home, work and leisure into a microcosm of a city. Whether this grand vision has been realised may be a matter of opinion, but the shopping-dining-entertainment-housing complex certainly continues to draw crowds.

Enviably ensconced atop Mori Tower is **Mori Art Museum** (Map pp140-1; ☎ 5777-8600; www.mori.art.museum; 53rd fl, Roppongi Hills Mori Tower, 6-10-1 Roppongi, Minato-ku; admission incl entry to Tokyo City View about ¥1500; 10am-10pm Wed-Mon, to 5pm Tue; Hibiya & Toei Ōedo lines to Roppongi, exits 1c & 3), forming one corner of the Roppongi Art Triangle. Exhibitions at this contemporary art museum tend toward the (mind-bogglingly myriad) multimedia variety and are of a consistently high calibre.

Admission to the museum also gets you into **Tokyo City View** (Map pp140-1; ☎ 6406-6652; www.tokyocityview.com; 52nd fl, Roppongi Hills Mori Tower, 6-10-1 Roppongi, Minato-ku; adult/student/child ¥1500/1000/500; 9-1am, last admission midnight; Hibiya & Toei Ōedo lines to Roppongi, exits 1c & 3) for free. offering 360 degrees' worth of Tokyo. If the floor-to-ceiling windows don't give you enough of an eyeful, there's an open-air deck that's open when weather permits.

TOKYO MIDTOWN 東京ミッドタウン

Roppongi's shiniest new development is **Tokyo Midtown** (Map pp140-1; www.tokyo-midtown.com; 9-7 Akasaka, Minato-ku; ; Hibiya & Toei Ōedo lines to Roppongi, exit 8), classing up the neighbourhood with upscale design-oriented shops, a Ritz-Carlton (see Twenty-five Stars, p170), wine bar, excellent eateries, pet salon and a lovely park area.

Along with a slew of design businesses and boutiques based here, Tokyo Midtown is also home to the **Suntory Museum of Art** (Map pp140-1; ☎ 3479-8600; www.suntory.com/culture-sports/sma/index.html; 9-7-4 Akasaka, Minato-ku; admission ¥1300/1000/free; ; 10am-6pm Sun-Mon, 10am-8pm Wed-Sat; Hibiya & Toei Ōedo lines to Roppongi, exit 8). It's another point of the Art Triangle, with spacious galleries showcasing the museum's collection of Japanese antiques and traditional arts and crafts. Occasionally, the museum also exhibits temporary exhibitions on loan from other institutions.

NATIONAL ART CENTER TOKYO 国立新美術館

When the beautifully curvaceous glass exterior of the **National Art Center Tokyo** (Map pp140-1; ☎ 5777 8600; www.nact.jp; 7-22-2 Roppongi, Minato-ku; admission varies; 10am-6pm Wed & Sat-Mon, 10am-8pm Fri; ; Chiyoda line to Nogizaka, exit 6 or Hibiya & Toei Ōedo lines to Roppongi, exits 4a & 7) glints into view, you'll know you've reached the last point in the Art Triangle. If the current exhibitions don't interest you, the fabulous museum shop is a treasure-trove of unusual, artsy gifts.

HIE-JINJA 日枝神社

This modern shrine is largely cement, but the highlight of **Hie-jinja** (Map pp140-1; ☎ 3581-2471; www.hiejinja.net/jinja/english/index.html; 2-10-5 Nagatachō, Chiyoda-ku; Ginza, Marunouchi lines to Akasaka-mitsuke, Belle Vie exit) is the walk up to the shrine through a 'tunnel' of orange *torii* – a spectacular sight during cherry-blossom season. Walking south on Sotobori-dōri, look for the concrete plaza-style entrance leading up to the shrine gates.

TOKYO TOWER 東京タワー

Nine metres taller than the Eiffel Tower, on which it is based, the 333m **Tokyo Tower** (Map pp140-1; ☎ 3433-5111; www.tokyotower.co.jp/english/; 4-2-8 Shiba-kōen, Minato-ku; main observation deck ¥310-820, special observation deck extra ¥350-600; 9am-10pm; Hibiya line to Kamiyachō, exits 1 & 2) is a pleasantly retro spire from which to look out across Tokyo. Completed in 1958, it stands as a kind of old-school counterpoint to ultramodern Roppongi Hills. While the daytime view is unremarkable, the night view is stellar.

Behind Tokyo Tower, **Zōjō-ji** (Map pp140-1; ☎ 3432-1431; 4-7-35 Shiba-kōen, Minato-ku; dawn-dusk; Toei Ōedo line to Akabanebashi, Akabanebashi exit) was the family temple of the Tokugawas. Visit in the evening, walking to Tokyo Tower from Hamamatsuchō station on the JR Yamanote line. Cut through Zōjō-ji and admire the bizarre juxtaposition of the illuminated tower leaping skyward above the dark shape of the main hall.

ŌKURA SHŪKOKAN 大倉集古館

On the grounds of the venerable Ōkura Hotel, this small **museum** (Map pp140-1; ☎ 3583-0781; 2-10-3 Toranomon, Minato-ku; adult/student/child ¥800/500/free; 🕑 10am-4.30pm Tue-Sun; Ⓢ Ginza line to Tameike-sannō, exit 13) displays a collection of sculpture, lacquer writing boxes and no fewer than three National Treasures, all surrounded by a small but well-populated sculpture garden.

Odaiba & Tokyo Bay お台場・東京湾

Built on reclaimed land in Tokyo Bay, the island of Odaiba stands as another reminder that Tokyo is a waterfront city. Aside from the whole fake-island angle, Odaiba has loads of oddities that trump the views of Tokyo across the bay – including bizarre architecture, a petite Statue of Liberty, and an onsen (hot spring) dressed up as an ersatz Edo-era town.

Get to Odaiba on the driverless Yurikamome monorail, which departs from Shimbashi station, and get around the island on the free shuttle than runs from 11am to 8pm.

SHOPPING MALLS & AMUSEMENT ARCADES

No district of Tokyo would be complete without its shrines to shopping, such as the unironically kitschy **Venus Fort** (Map p133; ☎ 3599-0700; www.venusfort.co.jp; Palette Town, Aomi 1-chōme, Kōtō-ku; 🕑 shops 11am-9pm Sun-Fri, to 10pm Sat; Ⓢ Yurikamome to Aomi or Rinkai line to Tokyo Teleport), complete with 18th-century Italian-style ceiling frescoes. And there's no shortage of fun to be had in megamalls such as **Decks Tokyo Beach** (Map p133; ☎ 3599-6500; www.odaiba-decks.com, in Japanese; 1-6-1 Daiba, Minato-ku; 🕑 11am-9pm; Ⓢ Yurikamome line to Odaiba Kaihin-kōen), which contains a Hong Kong–themed mall, Sega Joypolis amusement centre with virtual-reality rides and Muscle Park for active, physical games.

MUSEUM OF MARITIME SCIENCE
船の科学館

This ship-shaped **museum** (Fune-no-Kagakukan; Map p133; ☎ 5500-1111; www.funenokagakukan.or.jp; 3-1 Higashi-Yashio, Shinagawa-ku; adult/child ¥700/400; ♿ 🚼; 🕑 10am-5pm Tue-Sun; Ⓢ Yurikamome line to Fune-no-Kagakukan) has four floors of displays dealing with every aspect of shipping, with loads of highly detailed models. There are also lots of hands-on exhibits that kids will love.

NATIONAL MUSEUM OF EMERGING SCIENCE & INNOVATION 日本科学未来館

Also known as the **Miraikan** (Map p133; ☎ 3570-9151; www.miraikan.jst.go.jp; 2-41 Aomi, Kōtō-ku; adult/child under 18 ¥500/200, child free on Sat; 🕑 10am-5pm Wed-Mon; ♿ 🚼; Ⓢ Yurikamome line to Fune-no-Kagakukan or Telecom Center), this is undoubtedly Japan's best science museum and terrific for kids. Its hands-on exhibits are fun and genuinely educational, whether you're building your own robot or fathoming how Medaka riverfish could copulate in zero gravity aboard the space shuttle.

ŌEDO ONSEN MONOGATARI
大江戸温泉物語

Modelled on an old Edo town, this **onsen** (Map p133; ☎ 5500-1126; www.ooedoonsen.jp/english; 2-57 Aomi, Kōtō-ku; adult/child ¥2900/1600; 🕑 11am-9am, last entry at 7am; Ⓢ Yurikamome line to Telecom Center) pipes in natural mineral water from 1400m beneath Tokyo Bay. Though it sounds hokey, the place is attractively designed, with lovely mixed-gender (*yukata* – light cotton kimono – required) outdoor pools, traditional baths and spa treatments. Admission fees cover *yukata* and towel rental, and there are old-style restaurants and souvenir shops for a postbath bite and browse. Admission rates fluctuate depending on how late or early you arrive; check the website for details.

TOYOTA MEGA WEB トヨタメガウェブ

Car fiends and kids can get behind the wheel of hybrid and electric cars at **Toyota Mega Web** (Map p133; ☎ 3599-0808; www.megaweb.gr.jp; Palette Town, Aomi 1-chōme, Kōtō-ku; admission free; 🕑 11am-9pm; Ⓢ Yurikamome line to Aomi), one of Toyota's company showrooms. Some attractions close earlier and the whole place closes on varying days, so consult the website before cruising by.

Elsewhere in Tokyo

MUSEUMS & GALLERIES

For a more complete listing of museums and galleries in Tokyo, get hold of the TIC's *Museums & Art Galleries* pamphlet.

The wonderland that is the **Ghibli Museum** (三鷹の森ジブリ美術館; off Map pp128-9; ☎ 0570-055-777; www.ghibli-museum.jp; 1-1-83 Shimo-Renjaku, Mitaka-shi; adult ¥1000, child ¥100-700; 🕑 10am-6pm Wed-Mon; 🚼 ♿; Ⓢ JR Chūō line to Mitaka, south exit) was designed by anime master Miyazaki Hayao with children in mind, but anyone who fell in love with *Princess Mononoke* or *Spirited Away* should consider visiting. Entering the whimsical building, filled with tunnels, spiral staircases and tiny rooms, is akin to walking into a Studio Ghibli animation come to life – the artist's studio replica is papered with

OFF THE BEATEN DŌRI

Not far from the city centre are two of Tokyo's coolest, out-of-the-way neighbourhoods that feel saner and lower-key than some of central Tokyo's more overwhelming districts.

One favourite is **Kichijōji**(吉祥寺; off Map pp128–9), about 10km west of Shinjuku and centred on Inokashira-kōen, which surrounds a large pond that feeds the Kanda River. If you have a ticket to the **Ghibli Museum** (opposite), meander through the park on the way to your appointment with the Cat Bus. On weekends, there's an impromptu arts-and-crafts market and bands playing around the lake. The road leading from station to park is packed with little cafes, shops and bars, making it a wonderful getaway for a few hours, or an entire day and evening. To get there, take the JR Chūō or Sōbu line to Kichijōji and take the park exit. Walk to the Marui department store and hang a left on the road to its right. This road leads down to the park.

Similarly stocked with secondhand shops, bars, cafes and an artsy vibe is **Shimo-Kitazawa** (下北沢; off Map pp128–9), about 2.5km from Shibuya. Take the Keiō Inokashira line from Shibuya to Shimo-Kitazawa and make a circle through the neighbourhood. From the north exit, turn right and wander the boutique-and-cafe-filled alleys before heading back towards the train tracks. Cross the tracks to check out more shops, lively restaurants, tiny clubs and bars. Once you've travelled your loop, find the south entrance to the station on that side of the tracks. Construction on the Odakyū underground rail means that this charming maze of low-rise buildings may be demolished over the next few years, but if the grassroots movement to save Shimo-Kita has its way, this unique neighbourhood may yet survive.

Miyazaki's hand-drawn sketches, and the cat bus is a huge hit with little ones (though sadly, off-limits to adults).

Getting to the Ghibli (pronounced *jiburi*) is part of the adventure, if you haven't booked ahead from your home country; consult the website for details. Within Japan, ticket vouchers can be purchased from ticket machines at Lawson convenience stores. Because the museum imposes a daily visitor quota to provide a quality experience for everyone, you'll have to choose a date and timeframe to visit. The website provides detailed purchase instructions with illustrations. When you arrive at the museum, you'll exchange your voucher for a ticket, which contains an original animation cel from a Studio Ghibli film. Combine the museum visit with a stroll through Inokashira-kōen (see the boxed text, above).

The **Edo-Tokyo Museum** (Map pp128-9; ☎ 3626-9974; www.edo-tokyo-museum.or.jp; 1-4-1 Yokoami, Sumida-ku; adult/child ¥600/free, student ¥300-450; ⏰ 9.30am-5.30pm Tue-Sun, to 7.30pm Sat; 🚻 ♿; 🚆 JR Sōbu line to Ryōgoku, west exit or Toei Ōedo line to Ryōgoku, exit A4) is a gem, with a replica of Nihombashi (the bridge that is the namesake of today's Tokyo neighbourhood) dividing this display of re-creations of Edo-period and Meiji-period Tokyo. Exhibits range from examples of actual Edo infrastructure – a wooden sewage pipe, for one – to exquisite scale models of markets and shops, including such meticulous details as period costumes and stray cats scavenging fish scraps. Volunteer foreign-language guides are sometimes available. The museum is adjacent to Ryōgoku Sumō Stadium.

Near the main entrance of Ryōgoku Sumō Stadium, the **Sumō Museum** (Map pp128-9; ☎ 3622-0366; www.sumo.or.jp; 1-3-28 Yokoami, Sumida-ku; admission free; ⏰ 10am-4.30pm Mon-Fri; 🚆 JR Sōbu line to Ryōgoku, west exit or Toei Ōedo line to Ryōgoku, exit A4) features displays with sumō memorabilia, although there's no interpretive signage in English. During the grand tournaments in January, May and September the museum is open daily, but only to those attending the tournament. See Ryōgoku Kokugikan (p188) for more information.

AMUSEMENT PARKS

Tokyo Disneyland (東京ディズニーランド; off Map pp128-9; ☎ 045-683-3777; www.tokyodisneyresort.co.jp; 1-1 Maihama, Urayasu-shi, Chiba; 1-day ticket adult/youth/child ¥5800/5000/3900; ⏰ vary; 🚆 JR Keiyō line to Maihama) is a near-perfect replica of the original in Anaheim, California, but it has the added attraction of a sister park called Tokyo DisneySea, which is aimed at adults. The resort is open year-round except for about a dozen days a year (most of them in January), and opening hours vary seasonally, so check the website before heading out.

Right in the middle of Tokyo, **Kōrakuen Amusement Park** (Map pp142-3; ☎ 5800-9999; Tokyo Dome City, 1-3-61 Kōraku, Bunkyō-ku; rides ¥200-1000, unlimited rides adult/child ¥3300/2600; 10am-10.30pm Mon-Sat, 9am-10.30pm Sun; JR Chūō, Sōbu lines to Suidobashi or Marunouchi line to Kōrakuen, Kōrakuen exit) has some excellent rollercoasters, such as the Thunder Dolphin, which goes through the Ferris wheel and soars over city streets, made even more exciting by its location smack in the middle of the city. The park also has virtual-reality games if those are more your speed.

ACTIVITIES

Sentō & Onsen

A good soak at a *sentō* (public bath) or onsen is a great way to relax after a day pounding the pavements of Tokyo. Inexpensive *sentō* can be found in every neighbourhood; bring your own towel and look for the hot-water symbol (ゆ or 湯). Tokyo also has quite a few onsen, which pipe their mineral water from deep underneath Tokyo Bay. For a primer on bath etiquette, see p102.

Higher-end destination onsen include the Edo-village 'theme park', Ōedo Onsen Monogatari (p158) in Odaiba, a must-do for lovers of Japanese kitsch. Closer to central Tokyo, **Spa LaQua** (Map pp142-3; 3817-4173; www.laqua.jp; 5th-9th fl, Tokyo Dome City, 1-1-1 Kasuga, Bunkyō-ku; adult/youth ¥2565/1890; 11am-9am; JR Chūō & Toei Mita lines to Suidobashi, west exit & exit A3) at Tokyo Dome City offers a true inner-city onsen experience, where you can bathe in spacious luxury and listen to the shudder of the occasional rollercoaster (and delighted screams) from nearby Kōrakuen Amusement Park over the *rotemburo* (outdoor bath). Be aware that both establishments have strict no-tattoo policies plainly stated in English, but small or discreet tattoos will probably not get you ejected. To be safe, you may want to cover any exposed tattoos when checking in, or temporarily bandage your ink.

For a more authentic neighbourhood bathing experience, Asakusa's **Jakotsu-yu Onsen** (Map pp146-7; 3841-8645; www.jakotsuyu.co.jp, in Japanese; 1-11-11 Asakusa, Taitō-ku; admission ¥450; 1pm-midnight Wed-Mon; Ginza line to Tawaramachi, exit 3) does nicely. One of the hottest in town, with mineral-rich dark water at 45°C, this onsen has a small garden *rotemburo*. From Kokusai-dōri, make a right into the second alley north of Kaminarimon-dōri, then slip into the first narrow alley on the right.

In the same neighbourhood, **Asakusa Kannon Onsen** (Map pp146-7; 3844-4141; 2-7-6 Asakusa, Taitō-ku; admission ¥700; 6.30am-6pm Thu-Tue; Ginza line to Asakusa, exits 1, 3 & 6) is a large old bathhouse, and probably the only place you'd feel OK about getting naked with the *yakuza* – not that we're saying you'd run into any here… Look for its ivy-covered exterior near Sensō-ji.

WALKING TOUR

Mention the name Kagurazaka (Map pp128–9) to a Tokyoite, and it will likely conjure visions of geisha turning down cobbled alleys to tucked-away *ryōtei* (traditional Japanese restaurants). That romantic atmosphere still pervades, surprisingly, in a city known for its hyper-modernity and blasé ease with demolition.

To get there, hop the Tōzai line to Kagurazaka station. From exit 1, turn left and you'll be at the top of Kagurazaka-dōri, a small one-way street leading downhill. Make another immediate left at the stoplight, and at the end of the alley lies the small shrine, **Akagi-jinja** (赤城神社; **1**). Kagurazaka's most famous feature is its maze-like *kakurembo-yokochō* (hide-and-seek alleys; **2**). Enter the alleys with a right turn at the shrine entrance, to find a wealth of tiny bars (some barely big enough to fit two or three patrons), expat-run French cafes and Italian restaurants, and small homes fronted by bonsai. Make your way up to the peaceful grounds of **Tsukudo Hachiman shrine** (筑土八幡神社; **3**), with the oldest torii in Shinjuku-ku.

WALK FACTS

Distance 2km
Duration 1½ hours

KAGURAZAKA WALKING TOUR

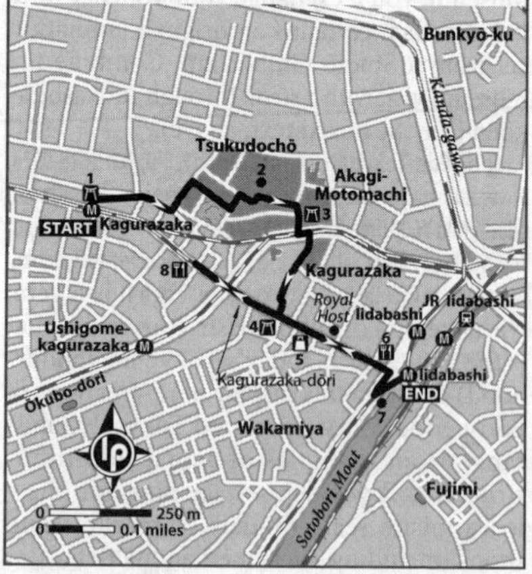

Roaming back to Kagurazaka-dōri, where the slope below Ōkubo-dōri is lined with mom-and-pop groceries and noisy pachinko parlours, have a look at the shrine **Zenkoku-ji** (善国寺; **4**), also known as Bishamonten for its statue of the military god housed in one of its halls. Head down the hill, to browse the parasols, *geta* and other kimono-appropriate accessories at **Sukeroku** (助六; **5**; ☎ 3260-0015; www.bolanet.ne.jp/sukeroku, in Japanese; 3-6 Kagurazaka, Shinjuku-ku; 10.30am-8.30pm). Then stop for an azuki-bean or custard-filled Peko-yaki (grilled pastry shaped like the shop mascot, Peko-chan) at **Fujiya** (不二家; **6**; ☎ 3269-1526; 1-12 Kagurazaka, Shinjuku-ku; 10am-9.30pm Mon-Fri, to 8pm Sat).

Alternatively, work up an appetite by renting a rowboat at **Canal Café** (カナルカフェ; **7**; ☎ 3260-8068; 1-9 Kagurazaka, Shinjuku-ku; 30 min ¥500; 11.30am-sunset) on the canal, and end with a drink here. Or, backtrack up Kagurazaka-dōri, turning left at the first alley, for an *izakaya* (pub-eatery) dinner at **Seigetsu** (霽月; **8**; ☎ 3269-4320; 2nd fl, 6-77-1 Kagurazaka, Shinjuku-ku; 5-11pm) down the alley next to the Family Mart convenience store. Retrace your steps to Kagurazaka station, or return via Iidabashi station, adjacent to the canal.

COURSES

A Taste of Culture (☎ 5716-5751; www.tasteofculture.com; courses from ¥5500) Perhaps your last meal has inspired you to learn how to assemble beautiful, balanced Japanese cuisine yourself? Established by noted Japanese culinary expert Elizabeth Andoh, courses emcompass everything from market tours to culinary classes, all imbued with deep cultural knowledge. Consult the website for current offerings, which include customised courses.

Sōgetsu Kaikan (Map pp140-1; ☎ 3408-1151; www.sogetsu.or.jp/english/index.html; Sōgetsu Kaikan Bldg, 7-2-21 Akasaka, Minato-ku; courses from ¥3800; 10am-5pm, to 8pm Fri, closed Sun; Ginza, Hanzōmon, Toei Ōedo lines to Aoyama-itchōme, exit 4) If you're interested in the art of ikebana (flower arranging), this avant-garde school offers classes taught in English. The school was founded on the idea that there are no limits to when, where or in what style ikebana can be practised. Call ahead for information about classes; prices include flowers and tax.

TOKYO FOR CHILDREN

Tokyo is a dangerous place to bring children, as they'll be doted upon, have all senses bombarded with stimulation, and get accosted by a neverending parade of novel distractions and tempting treats.

Great spots for kids include the National Museum of Emerging Science & Innovation (p158), the Meguro Parasitological Museum (p156) and the Ghibli Museum (p158). Showrooms like the Sony Building (p149) and Toyota Mega Web (p158) have terrific interactive activities. Fair-weather jaunts could include Ueno Zoo (p152), Yoyogi-kōen(p155) and Tokyo's theme parks (p159).

Tokyo's toy shops are always a huge hit, notably Hakuhinkan Toy Park (p190) and Kiddyland (p190).

TOURS

The best way to get under the skin of any city is to have a local show you around, and in Tokyo you can meet up with someone to do just that, even gratis.

Mr Oka (www.homestead.com/mroka; half-day from ¥2000) A wonderful, well-informed English-speaking guide who conducts walking tours around the city.

Tokyo Free Guide (www.tokyofreeguide.com) A group of volunteer tour guides who will tailor walking tours according to your interests. You'll have to pay for any admission, transport fees and meals, but no tips are expected. Guides' language skills may vary, but it's a great way to get around and get to know a friendly Tokyoite. Book before you arrive in town.

Several reliable bus companies offer a wide variety of Tokyo tours, from all-day, city-wide affairs to shorter, half-day tours or evenings taking in sukiyaki dinners and performances at Kabuki-za (p150). All of the following companies provide English-speaking guides and most tours pick up guests at various major hotels around town.

Hato Bus Tours (Map p138; ☎ 3435-6081; www.hatobus.com) Among its variety of tours, the Panoramic Tour (adult/child ¥12,000/8000) takes in most of Tokyo's major sights and includes lunch and a Tokyo Bay cruise. Most tours depart from Hamamatsuchō bus terminal.

Japan Gray Line (☎ 3595-5939; www.jgl.co.jp/inbound/traveler/traveler.htm) The full-day Talk of the Town tour (adult/child ¥8800/6800) includes lunch, pick-up and dropoff.

JTB's Sunrise Tours (☎ 5796-5454; www.jtbgmt.com/sunrisetour; full-day tour adult/child ¥9800/7700) Sunrise's general sightseeing tours are nearly identical to the Hato Bus offerings, including in name.

FESTIVALS & EVENTS

There is a festival of one sort or another every day in Tokyo. Call or visit the JNTO's TIC (p126) for up-to-date information. Some of the major celebrations:

TOKYO

Ganjitsu At New Year, Tokyoites head en masse to Meiji-jingū (p155), Sensō-ji (p152) or Yasukuni-jinja (p148).
Hanami (cherry-blossom viewing) Chaotic at Ueno-kōen (p151), peaceful at Shinjuku-gyoen (p154); early to mid-April.
Sanja Matsuri This massive festival, held the third weekend in May, features 100 *mikoshi* (portable shrines) paraded through Asakusa.
Asakusa Samba Matsuri Asakusa's wild, flesh-baring samba extravaganza happens in late August.
Kanda Furuhon Matsuri (Kanda Secondhand Book Festival) This annual event occupies the whole district or Jimbōchō at the end of October. See also Bookshops (p123).
Bōnen-kai Season This last one isn't an official festival at all, but this is the late-December period leading up to New Year, when the Japanese hold their drink-and-be-merry year-end parties.

SLEEPING

In Tokyo you can choose from the whole range of Japanese accommodation, from capsules to ryokan to luxurious hotels, but accommodation tends to cost a bit more than elsewhere. Prices quoted here are inclusive of taxes, service charges and Tokyo's metropolitan accommodation tax. Top-end establishments typically accept credit cards, but many midrange hotels do not – best to check beforehand. Booking online usually nets significantly discounted rates, particularly at highest-end hotels.

Most midrange hotels in Tokyo are reasonably priced business hotels. Always check what time your hotel locks its doors before heading out at night – though most hotels stay open all night, some ryokan, hostels and smaller hotels lock up around midnight.

If you can make a few concessions to Japanese etiquette, ryokan and *minshuku* (Japanese equivalent of a B&B) are quite inexpensive, with rates from around ¥4500 per person. In Tokyo, unlike elsewhere in Japan, ryokan may offer meals for an extra fee and may not supply basic amenities like towels or toiletries.

At youth hostels and so-called '*gaijin* houses' (foreigner houses) you can get single rates down to ¥3500 per person (about as low as it gets in Tokyo). But youth hostels usually impose a curfew, and *gaijin* houses typically require minimum stays of one month.

The **International Tourism Center of Japan** (formerly Welcome Inn Reservation Center; www.itcj.jp; Narita Airport Terminals 1 & 2; ⏲ 8am-8pm), with another location at the TIC (p126) in central Tokyo, is a free service that will make reservations for you at hotels, ryokan and *minshuku* in the Japan Welcome Inn hotel group.

If you absolutely must find inexpensive accommodation, book before you arrive. Flying into Narita – particularly at night – without accommodation lined up can be hellish. For hotels near Narita airport, see p239.

For more detailed information on capsule hotels, *gaijin* houses, hostels and love hotels, see p803.

Kanda & Tokyo Station 神田・東京駅

If you're pinching yen, you can forget about staying in Ginza, but you can still be near the city centre just a few stops north. Credit cards are accepted at all the following places unless otherwise indicated.

BUDGET

Ace Inn (Map pp128-9; ☎ 3350-6655; www.ace-inn.jp; 5-2 Katamachi, Shinjuku-ku; dm ¥3150-4200; 💻 📶; 🚇 Toei Shinjuku line to Akebonobashi, exit A3) Base yourself at the all-dorm Ace if you don't mind this bargain being a little out of the loop (it's still only a couple of stops from Shinjuku and Akasaka). There's free internet access, Japanese-style rooms, a women-only floor and comfortable common areas.

Sakura Hotel (Map pp142-3; ☎ 3261-3939; www.sakura-hotel.co.jp; 2-21-4 Kanda-Jimbōchō, Chiyoda-ku; dm/s/d ¥3780/7140/8200; ⊠ 💻 📶; 🚇 Hanzōmon, Toei Mita, Toei Shinjuku lines to Jimbōchō, exits A1 & A6) The helpful staff is bilingual at this reliable, sociable spot in the bookshop district. The bar-cafe is open 24 hours and there's a coin-operated laundry. From the A6 exit, walk south and turn right at the *kōban* (police box); the hotel is 200m on the right.

Tokyo International Youth Hostel (Map pp142-3; ☎ 3235-1107; fax 3267-4000; www.tokyo-ih.jp; 18th fl, Ramla Bldg, 1-1 Kagurakashi, Shinjuku-ku; dm ¥3860; ⊠ 💻; 🚇 JR Sōbu line to Iidabashi, west exit or Namboku, Tōzai, Yūrakuchō, Toei Ōedo lines to Iidabashi, B2b exit) No membership is required here, credit cards are accepted and you can book ahead online. The hostel is in the building that towers next to Iidabashi station. Check-in is 3pm to 10pm, and breakfast/dinner costs a paltry ¥450/900. The Narita airport TIC (see p126) has a step-by-step instruction sheet on the cheapest way to get from airport to hostel.

Capsule Inn Akihabara (Map pp142-3; ☎ 3251-0841; www.capsuleinn.com; 6-9 Akihabara, Taitō-ku; capsule ¥4000; 💻 📶; 🚇 JR Yamanote line to Akihabara, Shōwa-dōri exit) A few minutes' walk from the centre of Akihabara, put your feet up in a clean capsule of your own. Men get a *sentō*, while women

MISSING THE MIDNIGHT TRAIN

Cinderellas who've stayed out partying past midnight and found that their last train has turned into a *kabocha* (pumpkin) needn't fret. If dancing the night away doesn't appeal, and an astronomically priced taxi ride doesn't compute, give the capsule hotel a miss and try a *manga kissa* instead.

Kissaten (coffee shops) have long been mainstays for socialising away from home, but the next-generation versions offer a place for watching DVDs, getting some Playstation action, catching up on email or catching some Zs. *Manga kissa* have libraries of DVDs and manga, bottomless cups of coffee and soft drinks, and inexpensive food. Staff make regular rounds to ensure safe surfing and sleeping.

Overnight rates – typically around ¥2500 for eight hours – are a bargain. Check in at the reception desk, prepay for your stay and while away the wee hours in a cosy private cubicle. Try one of these if you're stranded:

Aprecio (Map p131; ☎ 3205-7336; www.aprecio.co.jp/shinjuku/english/service_guide.htm; B1 fl, Hygeia Plaza, 2-44-1 Kabukichō, Shinjuku-ku; overnight package from ¥2400; 24hr; JR Yamanote line to Shinjuku, east exit) This clean, comfortable spot in Kabukichō offers all the usuals in smoking and nonsmoking wings, plus massage and beauty services, billiards and darts.

Bagus Gran Cyber Cafe (Map p134; ☎ 5428-3676; www.bagus-99.com/netcafe, in Japanese; 6th fl, 28-6 Udagawachō, Shibuya-ku; per 8hr ¥1500; 24hr; JR Yamanote line to Shibuya, Hachikō exit) This popular chain has branches all over Tokyo.

Manga Hiroba (Map pp140-1; ☎ 3497-1751; www.mangahiroba.com/e; 2nd fl, Shuwa Roppongi Bldg, 3-14-12 Roppongi, Minato-ku; 1st hr ¥380, 30min thereafter ¥150; 24hr; Hibiya, Toei Ōedo lines to Roppongi, exit 3) Along Gaien-higashi-dōri, this one's handy for pre- or post-party surfing but is always crowded.

make do with showers. But only the women's floors contain suites where several capsules share a common area, perfect for girlfriends travelling together. Check in after 5pm.

MIDRANGE

Tokyo Green Hotel Ochanomizu (Map pp142-3; ☎ 3255-4161; fax 3255-4962; www.greenhotel.co.jp; 2-6 Kanda-Awajichō, Chiyoda-ku; s/d/tw ¥8600/14,200/14,200; ; JR Chūō line to Ochanomizu, Hijiribashi exit or Marunouchi line to Awajichō, exit A5) Though Kanda offers little of interest, this clean, thoughtfully renovated business hotel is a lovely retreat from the surrounding monotonous concrete jungle. Comfortable rooms and friendly staff elevate it from the typical business hotel. Look for its bamboo-covered entryway along Sotobori-dōri.

Hotel Mystays Ochanomizu (Map pp142-3; ☎ 5289-3939; fax 5289-3940; www.mystays.jp in Japanese; 2-10-6 Kanda-Awajichō, Chiyoda-ku; s/d/tw ¥10,100/15,200/16,200; ; JR Chūō line to Ochanomizu, Hijiribashi exit or Marunouchi line to Awajichō, exit A5) A few doors down from the Green Hotel Ochanomizu, this newly-remodelled business hotel is another great deal in the neighbourhood. Though rooms are typically small, the dark wood and subdued grey and cream tones give them a more upmarket feel. Free LAN internet, Simmons beds and electric kettles add to the comforts; there's also a coin laundry. Staff don't speak much English but will do what they can to meet your needs.

Ryokan Ryūmeikan-Honten (Map pp142-3; ☎ 3251-1135; fax 3251-0270; www.ryumeikan.co.jp/honten_e.htm; 3-4 Kanda-Surugadai, Chiyoda-ku; s/d with breakfast from ¥10,100/17,200; ; JR Chūō line to Ochanomizu, Hijiribashi exit or Chiyoda line to Shin-Ochanomizu, exit B3) This little spot is a great choice for its Japanese-style rooms, offered at rates comparable to most Western-style accommodation, including a Japanese breakfast and LAN internet in rooms. Find it across the boulevard from the Sumitomo Mitsui Insurance building.

Yaesu Terminal Hotel (Map pp142-3; ☎ 3281-3771; fax 3281-3089; www.yth.jp; 1-5-14 Yaesu, Chūō-ku; s/d/tw from ¥12,000/17,600/17,600; ; JR Yamanote line to Tokyo, Yaesu north exit or Ginza line to Nihombashi, exit B3) Near Tokyo station, this business hotel sports clean lines. Rooms are quite small, but prices are good for this area and it feels a touch classier than the usual bland business hotel. Rooms have flat-screen TVs and LAN internet access. The pleasant in-house restaurant's wall of plate-glass windows looks onto streetside treetops.

Ginza & Shiodome 銀座・汐留

Along with Akasaka, Ginza is home to the thickest concentration of elite hotels in Tokyo. Prices here reflect the desirable real estate and proximity to several subway lines, great shopping, excellent restaurants, all manner of theatre, and the political and financial districts of the city.

MIDRANGE

Hotel Villa Fontaine Shiodome (Map p138; ☎ 3569-2220; fax 3569-2221; www.hvf.jp; 1-9-2 Higashi-Shimbashi, Minato-ku; s/d/tw from ¥10,000/14,000/18,000; P ⊠ 💻; 🚉 Toei Ōedo line to Shiodome, exit 10) This place is a superb midrange deal with an upscale feel. Lighting in lobby areas is dim and subtly spooky, but the rooms are comfortable and modern, with internet-TV and high-speed LAN. Rooms don't include fridges, but the hotel offers the rarity of a complimentary buffet breakfast. Parking costs ¥2100 per night.

Ginza Nikkō Hotel (Map p138; ☎ 3571-4911; fax 3571-8379; www.ginza-nikko-hotel.com; 8-4-21 Ginza, Chūō-ku; s/d/tw from ¥14,060/29,475/28,320; ⊠ 💻; 🚉 JR Yamanote line to Shimbashi, Ginza exit or Ginza, Marunouchi line to Shimbashi, exit 5) In a prime location right on Sotobori-dōri between Ginza and Shimbashi, this is a business hotel with small, cosy rooms and decently sized bathtubs. Internet access is available with modems provided by the hotel.

TOP END

our pick **Ginza Yoshimizu** (Map p138; ☎ 3248-4432; www.yoshimizu.com; 3-11-3 Ginza, Chūō-ku; s/tw/tr ¥17,000/27,500/31,800; 🚉 Hibiya, Toei Asakusa lines to Higashi-Ginza, exits 3 & A7) Stepping through the bamboo doors of the Yoshimizu means leaving behind phones, TVs, internet access and city din in favour of more natural living. This elegantly simple ryokan features earth walls, bamboo and tatami flooring, organic cotton bedding and a *sentō* made from immaculate granite and *hinoki* (Japanese cypress). Organic meals are served in a peaceful, communal dining room – breakfast is included in room rates, but dinner reservations are a must. Rooms with shared toilet and shower are considerably cheaper; check the website for current rates.

Mitsui Garden Hotel Ginza (Map p138; ☎ 3543-1131; fax 3543-5531; www.gardenhotels.co.jp/eng/ginza.html; 8-13-1 Ginza, Chūō-ku; s/d from ¥19,100/25,600; P ⊠ 💻 ♿; 🚉 JR Yamanote line to Shimbashi, Ginza exit or Ginza, Marunouchi lines to Shimbashi, exit 1) Semi-organic urban decor characterises this sleek hotel. Hardwood trim and a minimalist aesthetic create a spacious, relaxed feeling, with tech comforts like Bose sound systems, flat-screen TVs and free LAN internet in rooms. Six universal rooms accommodate wheelchair users. Parking costs ¥1800 per night.

Mercure Hotel Ginza Tokyo (Map p138; ☎ 4335-1111; fax 4335-1222; www.mercure.com/asia; 2-9-4 Ginza, Chūō-ku; s/d/tw from ¥20,890/32,740/32,740; P ⊠ 💻 ♿; 🚉 Yūrakuchō line to Ginza-itchōme, exit 11) Though it has an upper-end business vibe to it, the Mercure also has a decidedly French hominess about it, with toile accents complementing the neat, modern rooms. LAN internet access, satellite TV, minibar and an excellent Japanese and French buffet breakfast ¥2100 are among the perks here, in addition to its convenient location. Parking is ¥1500 per night.

Imperial Hotel (Map p138; ☎ 3504-1111; fax 3504-9146; www.imperialhotel.co.jp; 1-1-1 Uchisaiwaichō, Chiyoda-ku; s/d from ¥35,700/40,950; P ⊠ 💻 🏊; 🚉 Chiyoda, Hibiya, Toei Mita lines to Hibiya, exit A13) One of Tokyo's grand old hotels, the Imperial is within easy walking distance of the Ginza sights and Hibiya-kōen (Map p138). It has all the amenities of its standard, with large, tastefully appointed rooms with a pleasingly old-fashioned air. Parking is free for guests.

Conrad Hotel (Map p138; ☎ 6388-8000; fax 6388-8001; www.conradtokyo.co.jp; 1-9-1 Higashi-Shimbashi, Minato-ku; s/d from ¥74,000/79,000; ⊠ 💻 🏊 ♿; 🚉 Toei Ōedo line to Shiodome, exit 10) It's big. Whether you choose city or garden views, you'll find varnished hardwoods and cushy elegance. Enormous bathrooms boast rainshower fixtures, free-standing tubs, Shiseido amenities and floor-to-ceiling glass walls facing the windows. Intrahotel mobile phones, a gym overlooking the 25m pool and huge plasma TVs are some of the superlative perks (though luxuries of wireless internet and parking will cost you ¥1500 and ¥3000 per day, respectively).

Ueno 上野

Ueno and the surrounding neighbourhoods may be a bit removed from the bright lights, but they make a great sightseeing base, especially for museum buffs. Additionally, the many budget ryokan in the area are not only inexpensive but also more interesting than bland business hotels. All hotels listed here accept major credit cards.

BUDGET

If you're coming from Narita airport, it's easy and inexpensive to catch a taxi from Ueno station to each of these ryokan, and you can print maps from their websites.

Sawanoya Ryokan (Map pp146-7; ☎ 3822-2251; fax 3822-2252; www.sawanoya.com; 2-3-11 Yanaka, Taitō-ku; s without bathroom ¥5040-5355, d/tr with bathroom ¥10,080/14,490; ⊠ 💻; 🚉 Chiyoda line to Nezu, Yanaka exit) A cosy, family-run ryokan, Sawanoya is a superb choice if you're looking for a home-like atmosphere in a quiet corner of Shitamachi. The spotless *sentō*, overlooking a small garden, was recently remodeled, but the comfortable rooms and common areas remain as welcoming as ever.

Ryokan Katsutarō (Map pp146-7; ☎ 3821-9808; fax 3821-4789; www.katsutaro.com; 4-16-8 Ikenohata, Taitō-ku; s/d/tr without bathroom ¥5200/8400/12,300, d/tr with bathroom ¥9600/13,200; ⊠ 💻; 🚇 Chiyoda line to Nezu, exit 2) A pleasant ramble from Ueno Zoo and Ueno-kōen museums, this small, quaint ryokan is run by the friendly brother of the Annex's manager. Western breakfasts cost an extra ¥800.

Hotel Edoya (Map pp146-7; ☎ 3833-8751; fax 3833-8759; www.hoteledoya.com; 3-20-3 Yushima, Bunkyō-ku; s/d from ¥5890/8540; 💻 📶; 🚇 Chiyoda line to Yushima, exit 5) Hotel Edoya is off the main thoroughfares of Ueno and Akihabara but conveniently located just between, while the hotel itself is a perfect balance of Japanese and Western styles. Most rooms are Japanese style with Western bathrooms, and a complimentary buffet breakfast (Japanese or Western) is included. There's a men's and women's *rotemburo,* coin laundry and common areas for relaxing in front of a small garden or playing some mah-jong.

Annex Katsutarō Ryokan (Map pp146-7; ☎ 3828-2500; fax 3821-5400; www.katsutaro.com; 3-8-4 Yanaka, Taitō-ku; s/d/tr from ¥6300/10,500/14,700; ⊠ 💻; 🚇 Chiyoda line to Sendagi, exit 2) All of the bright, Japanese-style rooms at the spotless Annex have Western-style baths and LAN internet. The ryokan offers a continental breakfast for ¥840, as well as a coin laundry and in-room amenities, such as hairdryer and electric kettle.

Sakura Ryokan (Map pp146-7; ☎ 3876-8118; www.sakura-ryokan.com; 2-6-2 Iriya, Taitō-ku; s/d ¥6600/11,000, without bathroom ¥5500/10,000; 💻; 🚇 Hibiya line to Iriya, exit 1) One stop from Ueno, the modest, family-run Sakura Ryokan is a good base for those interested in staying in contemporary working-class Shitamachi. Definitely opt for a Japanese-style room. Japanese or Western breakfasts cost a reasonable ¥840, and a home-cooked Japanese dinner is offered Monday through Saturday for ¥1680.

MIDRANGE

Suigetsu Hotel Ōgaisō (Map pp146-7; ☎ 3822-4611; fax 3823-4340; www.ohgai.co.jp; 3-3-21 Ikenohata, Taitō-ku; Western-style s/d/tw ¥6820/9870/10,280, Japanese-style s/d/tr ¥12,275/13,850/17,725; ⊠ 💻; 🚇 Chiyoda line to Nezu, exit 2) Writers may find symbolic inspiration here, where this hotel's namesake penned his first novel *Maihime* in 1890. Though set up like a Western hotel, it offers tatami rooms, several large Japanese-style baths and a lovely garden in the centre of the complex. Japanese meals are available, and the hotel is a pleasant walk from Ueno-kōen.

Sutton Place Hotel (Map pp146-7; ☎ 3842-2411; www.thehotel.co.jp/jp/sutton_ueno; 7-8-23 Ueno, Taitō-ku; s/d from ¥7800/11,000; ⊠ 💻; 🚇 JR Yamanote line to Ueno, Iriya exit) The discreet entrance off busy Shōwa-dōri leads to the newly remade, very nicely appointed Sutton Place Hotel. This business hotel shines with thoughtful touches, such as hairdryers, LAN internet access, sliding wooden bathroom doors and all-around sleek styling. Rooms are definitely small, so it's worth springing for a larger twin or suite if you're travelling with someone. A complimentary continental breakfast is included.

Hotel Parkside (Map pp146-7; ☎ 3836-5711; fax 3831-6641; www.parkside.co.jp; 2-11-18 Ueno, Taitō-ku; s/d from ¥9200/15,500, Japanese style d from ¥18,000; 🅿 ⊠ 💻; 🚇 JR Yamanote line to Ueno, Shinobazu exit) Overlooking the gigantic lotus pads of Shinobazu-ike, the Parkside is a good choice in Ueno, if you can get a room on the 4th floor or above. The best spot in the house is the Japanese-style room with private *rotemburo;* Western-style rooms are comfortable but nothing extraordinary. Parking is ¥1050.

Asakusa 浅草

If you don't mind sacrificing central location for unpretentious Shitamachi atmosphere, Asakusa is a fine place to stay, crammed with some of Tokyo's best budget ryokan and hostels. If you're coming from outside of Tokyo, the Tsukuba Express is the fastest line to Asakusa.

BUDGET

Unless otherwise specified, all of the places listed here have detailed maps and directions on their websites, and do not accept credit cards.

Khaosan Tokyo Annex (Map pp146-7; ☎ 5856-6560; www.khaosan-tokyo.com/en/annex; 2-2-5 Higashi-Komagata, Sumida-ku; dm/s/tw from ¥2000/3600/4600, cabins ¥2800; ⊠ 💻 📶; 🚇 Toei Asakusa line to Asakusa, exit A2) One of the several Khaosan guest houses in the neighbourhood, the annex offers novel 'cabin' rooms in addition to the usual dorm beds and private rooms. Cabins come outfitted with cute capsule-like bed pods that have sliding wooden doors for privacy. The Annex offers bike rental, free wireless internet, coin laundry and a free drink each night.

Khaosan Tokyo Guesthouse (Map pp146-7; ☎ 3842-8286; www.khaosan-tokyo.com; 2-1-5 Kaminarimon, Taitō-ku; dm/s/tw ¥2200/3700/5000; ⊠ 💻; 🚇 Ginza, Toei Asakusa lines to Asakusa, exits 4 & A2b) Very friendly, remarkably inexpensive and homey, the Khaosan is a warm intro to Tokyo. Located on the bank of the Sumida-gawa, it has a tiny but cheery kitchen and pleasant rooftop terrace.

our pick **K's House** (Map pp146-7; ☎ 5833-0555; fax 5833-0444; http://kshouse.jp/tokyo-e/index.html; 3-20-10 Kuramae, Taitō-ku; dm/s/d from ¥2800/3400/6800; ; Toei Asakusa, Toei Ōedo lines to Kuramae, exits A2 & A6) This spotless guest house has homey common areas and a well-equipped kitchen. There's also a coin-operated laundry and a rooftop terrace overlooking Sumida-gawa. Internet access is ¥100 for 20 minutes in the relaxed, cosy living area (wi-fi is free) and free LAN access is available in each room. Credit cards are accepted here.

Tokyo Ryokan (Map pp146-7; ☎ 090-8879-3599; www.tokyoryokan.com; 2-4-8 Nishi-Asakusa, Taitō-ku; per person with shared bathroom ¥3000; ; Ginza line to Tawaramachi, exit 3) With only three *hinoki*-walled tatami rooms in this immaculate, intimate ryokan, book well ahead through the website. Internet access is available for ¥10 per minute. The English-speaking owner here is helpful and open, and always happy to talk travel and philosophy.

There are too many good-value budget spots in the area to list exhaustively, but here are a few:

Asakusa Ryokan Tōkaisō (Map pp146-7; ☎ 3844-5618; www.toukaisou.com; 2-16-12 Nishi-Asakusa, Taitō-ku; dm/s/tw from ¥2600/4500/6000; ; Ginza line to Tawaramachi, exit 3) Tucked in a corner of Asakusa, this is a clean, quiet ryokan.

Sakura Hostel (Map pp146-7; ☎ 3847-8111; www.sakura-hostel.co.jp; 2-24-2 Asakusa, Taitō-ku; dm/tw from ¥2940/8295; ; Ginza line to Tawaramachi, exit 3) This bright, clean hostel offers amenities, such as laundry facilities, bike rentals and spacious kitchen; credit cards accepted.

Capsule Hotel Riverside (Map pp146-7; ☎ 3844-5117; fax 3841-6566; www.asakusa-capsule.jp/english; 2-20-4 Kaminarimon, Taitō-ku; capsules ¥3000; Ginza, Toei Asakusa lines to Asakusa, exits 3 & 4) This is one capsule hotel that accepts women; with a women-only floor and *sentō*. Look for the entrance around the back of the building.

Taitō Ryokan (Map pp146-7; ☎ 3843-2822, 090-5321-3599; www.libertyhouse.gr.jp; 2-1-4 Nishi-Asakusa, Taitō-ku; per person with shared bathroom ¥3000; ; Ginza line to Tawaramachi, exit 3) The traditional, creaky Taitō is run by sociable English speakers. Solo travellers should expect to share a room when demand is high.

MIDRANGE

Both of these ryokan accept credit cards:

our pick **Ryokan Shigetsu** (Map pp146-7; ☎ 3843-2345; fax 3843-2348; www.shigetsu.com; 1-31-11 Asakusa, Taitō-ku; Western-style s/tw ¥7665/14,900, Japanese-style s/d from ¥9450/17,200; ; Ginza, Toei Asakusa lines to Asakusa, exits 1 & 2) This ryokan is a gorgeous oasis of Japanese hospitality, just off Nakamise-dōri. Most rooms have bathrooms, but bathing in the *sentō* is a must – both the black granite bath and the *hinoki* one have unique, stunning views. Lovely Japanese breakfasts cost ¥1300.

Sukeroku No Yado Sadachiyo (Map pp146-7; ☎ 3842-6431; fax 3842-6433; www.sadachiyo.co.jp; 2-20-1 Asakusa, Taitō-ku; s/d from ¥14,100/19,400; Ginza line to Tawaramachi, exit 3 or Tsukuba Express to Asakusa, exit A1) Another traditionally elegant spot, just far enough removed from bustling Nakamise-dōri, the Sadachiyo features rooms of *shōji* (movable screens) and tatami, each with a Western-style bath. There's also one wood and one granite *sentō*, and guests can order delicious Japanese breakfasts (¥1500) and dinners (¥7000) to take in the lovely banquet room.

TOP END

Asakusa View Hotel (Map pp146-7; ☎ 3847-1111; fax 3842-2117; www.viewhotels.co.jp/asakusa/english/index.html; 3-17-1 Nishi-Asakusa, Taitō-ku; s/d from ¥17,525/26,800; ; Ginza line to Tawaramachi, exit 3) The ritziest joint in the neighbourhood isn't called the Asakusa View for nothing. While rooms aren't particularly striking, the views are, and they are spacious. Try to swing a room on a higher floor on the east side for beautiful views of Sensō-ji. There's a charge to use the indoor pool (¥3000/2000 per adult/child).

Ikebukuro 池袋

Ikebukuro, though a convenient stop on the JR Yamanote line, is not one of Tokyo's sexiest neighbourhoods – but this low-key district does have its attractions and a certain unflashy appeal.

BUDGET

Book well ahead at these popular ryokan whose websites contain maps and directions; credit cards are not accepted at either.

Kimi Ryokan (Map p132; ☎ 3971-3766; fax 3987-1326; www.kimi-ryokan.jp; 2-36-8 Ikebukuro, Toshima-ku; s ¥4725, d ¥6825-7875; ; JR Yamanote line to Ikebukuro, west exit) Kimi Ryokan is one of Tokyo's best budget accommodation options, with clean tatami rooms and a convivial wood-floored lounge area decorated with the wonderful owner's changing ikebana. The shared bathrooms each has both a shower and a Japanese-style bath.

House Ikebukuro (Map p132; ☎ 3984-3399; fax 3984-3999; www.housejp.com.tw; 2-20-1 Ikebukuro, Toshima-ku; d/tr ¥8000/11,000, s/d/tr without bathroom from ¥5000/6000/8000; 💻; 🚉 JR Yamanote line to Ikebukuro, west exit) Also in west Ikebukuro, this guest house has a variety of smallish tatami rooms, all with shared bathroom and a spotless common kitchen. Also available are the apartment-like suites in the annexe, with kitchenettes and bathrooms.

MIDRANGE

There are innumerable business, love and capsule hotels in the Ikebukuro area. Be aware that the local capsule hotels are not as accustomed to foreign guests as their counterparts in Akasaka and Shinjuku.

Toyoko Inn (Map p132; ☎ 5960-1045; fax 5960-1046; www.toyoko-inn.com/eng; 2-50-5 Ikebukuro, Toshima-ku; s ¥7140, d & tw ¥9240; ⊠ 💻 📶; 🚉 JR Yamanote line to Ikebukuro, north exit) The Toyoko Inn is one of the most appealing of the cheaper business hotels around here. Rooms are tidy, if tiny, and even single rooms have semidouble beds. Japanese-style rooms are available, and the rates even include a Japanese breakfast.

Hotel Theatre (Map p132; ☎ 3988-2251; fax 3988-2260; www.theatres.co.jp/hotel, in Japanese; 1-21-4 Higashi-Ikebukuro, Toshima-ku; s/d/tw from ¥9135/12,600/16,275; ⊠ 💻; 🚉 JR Yamanote line to Ikebukuro, east exit) Located along Sunshine 60-dōri, this centrally located and clean hotel has typical business hotel amenities, such as LAN internet access, electric kettles and vending machines.

Hotel Strix Tokyo (Map p132; ☎ 5396-0111; fax 5396-9815; www.strix.jp, in Japanese; 2-3-1 Ikebukuro, Toshima-ku; s/d from ¥15,000/20,000; ⊠ 💻; 🚉 JR Yamanote line to Ikebukuro, west exit) The most central and stylish option in the neighbourhood, the Strix is styled out in retro-inspired rooms with square furniture and red accents. Rooms and beds are quite spacious by business hotel standards. Look for its teal-coloured dome.

Shinjuku 新宿

Shinjuku is full of business hotels accustomed to foreign guests, and the competition keeps prices reasonable. Near massive Shinjuku station, a hub for nearly every rail line snaking in and around Tokyo, this is a nonstop neighbourhood for travellers who want to be in the middle of all the buzz, and those doing business in the area.

MIDRANGE

Credit cards are accepted at the following hotels unless otherwise indicated:

City Hotel Lonestar (Map p131; ☎ 3356-6511; www.thehotel.co.jp/en/lonestar/index.html; 2-12-12 Shinjuku, Shinjuku-ku; s/d/tw from ¥7350/12,075/13,650; ⊠ 💻; 🚉 Marunouchi, Toei Shinjuku lines to Shinjuku-sanchōme, exit C8) Though the name of this queer-friendly, no-frills hotel in Sanchōme was formerly known as the (much more delightful) Lornstar, the clean, modestly proportioned rooms here are excellent value. A simple continental breakfast is provided.

Shinjuku Park Hotel (Map p131; ☎ 3356-0241; fax 3352-2733; www.shinjukuparkhotel.co.jp; 5-27-9 Sendagaya, Shibuya-ku; s/tw from ¥7900/14,000, Japanese-style r ¥24,800; P ⊠ 💻; 🚉 JR Yamanote line to Shinjuku, new south exit) Just south of Takashimaya Times Sq, this pleasant business hotel has larger rooms than most. Solo travellers should spend up for a B-type single for the bigger bed, but everyone should try booking a room with a park view of Shinjuku-gyoen. Parking is a steal at ¥800 per night, and LAN internet access is free.

Hotel Sunlite Shinjuku (Map p131; ☎ 3356-0391; fax 3356-1223; www.sunlite.co.jp; 5-15-8 Shinjuku, Shinjuku-ku; s/d/tw from ¥8715/12,275/14,375; P 💻; 🚉 Marunouchi, Toei Shinjuku lines to Shinjuku-sanchōme, exit C7) At the lower end of the midrange price scale, the clean and comfortable Sunlite won't break the budget, and it even accepts credit cards. Cosy rooms are well maintained and have LAN internet, and its central location in east Shinjuku puts you near Shinjuku-gyoen, nocturnal life in Kabukichō and Shinjuku shopping. Parking costs ¥2000 per night.

Star Hotel Tokyo (Map p131; ☎ 3361-1111; fax 3369-4216; www.starhotel.co.jp/city/tokyo/index.html; 7-10-5 Nishi-Shinjuku, Shinjuku-ku; s/d from ¥9450/18,250; P ⊠ 💻; 🚉 JR Yamanote line to Shinjuku, west exit) In west Shinjuku, this comfortable but rather average business hotel is very conveniently located and competitively priced. There's free LAN internet access in rooms, and parking available for ¥1500 per night.

Shinjuku Washington Hotel (Map p131; ☎ 3343-3111; fax 3342-2575; www.shinjyuku-wh.com; 3-2-9 Nishi-Shinjuku, Shinjuku-ku; s/d/tw from ¥10,400/15,400/21,200; ⊠ 💻; 🚉 JR Yamanote line to Shinjuku, south exit) This large, efficient business hotel has in-house staff to help foreign travellers get their bearings around Tokyo. Though windows and rooms are small, they come equipped with free LAN internet access, fridge, and psychedelic decor if you're lucky. Several restaurants and a convenience store provide sustenance downstairs.

TOP END

Hotel Century Southern Tower (Map p131; ☎ 5354-0111; fax 5354-0100; www.southerntower.co.jp; 2-2-1 Yoyogi, Shibuya-ku; s/d from ¥18,680/28,120; ; JR Yamanote line to Shinjuku, Southern Tce exit) Graced with expansive views, this Shinjuku monolith is very reasonably priced for the intangible sense of space the windows reveal. If it weren't so central and convenient, the views would be this place's winning hand. The hotel also boasts LAN internet access, a small gym and several restaurants. Reception is on the 20th floor.

Keiō Plaza Hotel (Map p131; ☎ 3344-0111; fax 3345-8269; www.keioplaza.com; 2-2-1 Nishi-Shinjuku, Shinjuku-ku; s/d from ¥26,450/29,800, Japanese-style ste from ¥98,050; P ; JR Yamanote line to Shinjuku, west exit) The Keiō Plaza has 47 floors and a simple, refined style. Rooms provide excellent views over west Shinjuku and there's are more than a dozen restaurants in the lower floors. So-called 'universal' rooms here are exceptionally accessible for those with disabilities.

Park Hyatt Tokyo (Map p131; ☎ 5322-1234; fax 5322-1288; www.tokyo.park.hyatt.com; 3-7-1-2 Nishi-Shinjuku, Shinjuku-ku; r/ste from ¥55,650/68,250; ; JR Yamanote line to Shinjuku, south exit) Views here are legendarily stunning, day and night, and from these serene heights appear to be part of another world. Dignified but relaxed, the stylishly understated rooms are done in naturally finished wood, fabric and marble. Staff is gracefully, discreetly attentive and the restaurants are among Tokyo's best.

Shibuya 渋谷

Around the top of Dōgenzaka is the highest concentration of love hotels (also referred to as 'boutique' hotels) in Japan. Tokyo's love hotels are not as wacky as elsewhere in the country, but you'll find a theme to suit your tastes – anything from pink and girly to bondage-ready. Wander into the lobbies and take a look at the screens picturing the available rooms. Though check-in is usually around 10pm to midnight for a full-night's stay, prices are pretty budget-friendly if you're in a pinch.

MIDRANGE

Pickings are slim in Shibuya for midrange hotels. Less expensive business hotels in Ueno, Ikebukuro and even Shinjuku represent much better value for money, but then you're not in as fun a spot as here.

Shibuya City Hotel (Map p134; ☎ 5489-1010; fax 5489-1030; www.shibuya-city-hotel.com, in Japanese; 1-1 Maruyamachō, Shibuya-ku; s/d from ¥9900/18,300; ; JR Yamanote line to Shibuya, Hachikō exit) Night owls will love this hotel, strategically located on the lower slope of Love Hotel Hill, just a short downhill roll from good live-music venues and clubs. For such a prime location, the prices are a fabulous deal. It has comfortable, spacious rooms with LAN internet access, including one tricked-out wheelchair-friendly room (¥15,000).

Shibuya Tōkyū Inn (Map p134; ☎ 3498-0109; fax 3498-0189; www.tokyuhotels.co.jp/en/TI/TI_SHIBU/index.shtml; 1-24-10 Shibuya, Shibuya-ku; s/d/tw from ¥13,650/21,420/21,840; ; JR Yamanote line to Shibuya, east exit) At a similar standard to the Shibuya Tōbu Hotel, the vaguely mod nonsmoking rooms are the best of the bunch. There's LAN internet access in the comfortable rooms decorated with accents in primary colours.

Shibuya Tōbu Hotel (Map p134; ☎ 3476-0111; fax 3476-0903; www.tobuhotel.co.jp/shibuya; 3-1 Udagawachō, Shibuya-ku; s/d from ¥14,060/20,035; ; JR Yamanote line to Shibuya, Hachikō exit) One of Shibuya's nicest business hotels, the Tōbu has stylish, clean and relatively large rooms with LAN internet access. Common areas are pleasant and sparkly, and the friendly, attentive staff speaks English.

TOP END

our pick **Granbell Hotel** (Map p134; ☎ 5457-2681; fax 5457-2682; www.granbellhotel.jp; 15-17 Sakuragaokachō, Shibuya-ku; s/d/ste from ¥13,100/21,400/55,400; ; JR Yamanote line to Shibuya, south exit) Though the size of the Granbell's rooms are on par for Tokyo, the glass-walled bathrooms and bright tropical colour schemes give the illusion of spaciousness. In addition to amenities like free LAN internet access, English-language TV and hairdryers, rooms in the main building feature curtains with fun Lichtenstein-esque designs and Simmons beds. Suites, such as the two-storey View Bath, are uniquely well-appointed with luxuries like record players (!) and open-air terraces.

Cerulean Tower Tōkyū Hotel (Map p134; ☎ 3476-3000; fax 3476-3001; www.ceruleantower-hotel.com; 26-1 Sakuragaokachō, Shibuya-ku; s/d from ¥32,540/43,135; P ; JR Yamanote line to Shibuya, south exit) Sprawl out on huge beds and drink deeply of the big views of the glittery city, because there's room to breathe in these enormous quarters. Arts fiends take note: quality *nō* (classical stylised dance-drama) and jazz performances take place at the in-house theatre and jazz club, the Cerulean Tower Nō Theatre. Parking is ¥2000 per night, and LAN internet access costs ¥1050 per day.

Roppongi & Akasaka 六本木・赤坂

Akasaka has a high concentration of luxury hotels due to its location: there are loads of good restaurants nearby, the political and business centres are within walking distance, and Roppongi's nightlife is just down the road. Of course, if nightlife features prominently on your agenda, Roppongi has several convenient digs.

MIDRANGE

Asia Center of Japan (Map pp140-1; ☎ 3402-6111; fax 3402-0738; www.asiacenter.or.jp; 8-10-32 Akasaka, Minato-ku; s/d from ¥8610/12,390; P 💻; 🚇 Ginza, Hanzōmon, Toei Ōedo lines to Aoyama-itchōme, exit 4) Down a narrow road in a quiet Akasaka neighbourhood, the Asia Center attracts many long-term stayers. Old-annexe rooms have wood-panelled walls and an airy, simple charm. LAN internet access, laundry facilities, parking (¥1500 per night) and ¥945 breakfast buffet are among the offerings.

Arca Torre (Map pp140-1; ☎ 3404-5111; fax 3404-5115; www.arktower.co.jp/arcatorre; 6-1-23 Roppongi, Minato-ku; s/d from ¥12,755/16,570; ⊠ 💻; 🚇 Hibiya, Toei Ōedo lines to Roppongi, exit 3) Excellently placed yet reasonably priced, the cosy Arca Torre is made for hard partiers and heavy sleepers. Rooms at the back are considerably quieter than those facing the street. Beds are on the hard side, but even standard singles are furnished with semidoubles. All rooms have free LAN internet access.

Hotel Ibis (Map pp140-1; ☎ 3403-4411; fax 3479-0609; www.ibis-hotel.com; 7-14-4 Roppongi, Minato-ku; s/d/tw from ¥13,382/16,285/22,145; ⊠ P; 🚇 Hibiya, Toei Ōedo lines to Roppongi, exit 4a & 7) Just this side of noir, the interior of the Ibis suggests some dark drama lurking underneath. Aesthetics notwithstanding, it's a clean, modern hotel just steps from Roppongi Crossing. Rooms are small, and solo travellers should skip the cramped single rooms in favour of larger semidoubles. There's LAN internet access.

Chisun Grand Akasaka (Map pp140-1; ☎ 5572-7788; fax 5572-7789; www.solarehotels.com/english; 6-3-17 Akasaka, Minato-ku; s/d ¥14,600/17,900; ⊠ 💻; 🚇 Chiyoda line to Akasaka, exits 6 & 7) This business hotel has all of the comforts of its class (like LAN internet) and then some: MP3-player-ready speakers, in-room clothes presses and full-sized beds even in single rooms. Red trim and funky fixtures throw tasteful splashes of personality into the rooms, some of which have balconies.

b Akasaka (Map pp140-1; ☎ 3586-0811; fax 3589-0575; theb-akasaka@ishinhotels.com; 7-6-13 Akasaka, Minato-ku; s/tw from ¥14,600/20,400; ⊠ 💻; 🚇 Chiyoda line to Akasaka, exit 3b) Curvy patterns, like circular windows and rounded shower stalls, characterise the modern rooms at b Akasaka. On a quiet street across from the TBS Broadcasting Center, this lovely business hotel offers free LAN internet, a light buffet breakfast and free coffee and tea 24 hours a day. There's also a spa next door, should you need to unwind after a long day.

Hotel Avanshell (Map pp140-1; ☎ 3568-3456; www.avanshell.com, in Japanese; 2-14-14 Akasaka, Minato-ku; s/d/tw ¥15,750/19,950/25,200; ⊠ 💻; 🚇 Chiyoda line to Akasaka, exits 6 & 7) The cafe in front of the Avanshell gives this hotel more of a European flavour than other business hotels in the neighbourhood. Some of the spacious, modern rooms even have balconies – a rare plus when the environs are relatively quiet at night. There's LAN internet in all the spacious rooms.

TOP END

Hotel Ōkura (Map pp140-1; ☎ 3582-0111, 3582-3707; www.okura.com/tokyo; 2-10-4 Toranomon, Minato-ku; s/d from ¥42,363/48,700; P ⊠ 💻 🏊; 🚇 Ginza line to Tameike-sannō, exit 13) A preferred landing place for visiting dignitaries and businesspeople, the unpretentious but graceful Hotel Ōkura exudes old-school elegance. The inviting feel of the hotel's retro decor and low-lying architecture is complemented by a beautiful Japanese garden. Personable staff, excellent business facilities and top-notch restaurants complete the picture. The hotel grounds also house the Ōkura Shūkokan (p158). LAN internet access is ¥1575 per day.

ANA Intercontinental Tokyo (Map pp140-1; ☎ 3505-1111; fax 3505-1155; www.anaintercontinental-tokyo.jp; 1-12-33 Akasaka, Minato-ku; s/d & tw from ¥31,185/40,425; P ⊠ 💻 🏊 ♿; 🚇 Ginza, Namboku lines to Tameike-sannō, exit 13) Midway between Akasaka and Roppongi, the ANA caters to discerning travelling professionals, and gleams with businesslike glam. Suites come standard with LAN internet (¥1575 per day) and humidifiers accompanied with essential oils. Club rooms also have exclusive access to lounges, private concierges and other perks. Parking is ¥1000

TWENTY-FIVE STARS

Tokyo's wealth of luxury hotels makes it impossible to cover them all, but there's a place for every taste. The following properties are a handful of the city's best, from small boutique spots to luxury towers.

- **Mandarin Oriental Tokyo** (Map pp142-3; ☎ 3270-8800; www.mandarinoriental.com/tokyo; 2-1-1 Nihombashi Muromachi, Chūō-ku; r/ste from ¥39,000/79,000; P ☒ ♿ ; Ginza, Hanzōmon lines to Mitsukoshimae, exit A7) In the heart of Nihombashi, the opulent Mandarin Oriental boasts three restaurants that each earned a Michelin star. Room designs make use of nature-inspired motifs and hi-tech comforts.
- **Four Seasons Chinzan-sō** (Map pp128-9; ☎ 3943-2222; fax 3943-2300; www.fourseasons.com/tokyo; 2-10-8 Sekiguchi, Bunkyō-ku; r/ste from ¥43,000/69,000; P ☒ ♿ ; Yūrakuchō line to Edogawabashi, exit 1a) The mood here is grand and flowery, with no urban sleekness in its sumptuous decor – which explains its popularity as a wedding locale. Spacious rooms surround its famous Japanese garden that dates back to the Meiji period.
- **Hotel Seiyo Ginza** (Map p138; ☎ 3535-1111; fax 3535-1110; www.seiyo-ginza.com; 1-11-2 Ginza, Chūō-ku; r/ste from ¥55,300/69,400; P ☒ ♿ ; Ginza, Yūrakuchō lines to Ginza-itchōme, exit 7) With only 77 rooms, this classic boutique property is the only hotel in Tokyo providing 24-hour personal butler service for each guest. It's discreetly placed with Ginza but only steps away.
- **Peninsula Tokyo** (Map p138; ☎ 6270-2888; fax 6270-2000; www.peninsula.com; 1-8-1 Yūrakuchō, Chiyoda-ku; r/ste from ¥69,000/115,000; P ☒ ♿ ; Chiyoda, Hibiya, Yūrakuchō, Toei Mita lines to Yūrakuchō & Hibiya, exits A6 & A7) Adding to this chain's stellar reputation with its new Tokyo outpost, the Peninsula offers elegant rooms and atmosphere throughout. With easy access to Ginza, the Imperial Palace and the entire city, it provides a relaxing haven when you return.
- **Ritz-Carlton Tokyo** (Map pp140-1; ☎ 3423-8000; fax 3423-8001; www.ritzcarlton.com/en/Properties/Tokyo/Default.htm; Tokyo Midtown Tower, 9-7-1 Akasaka, Minato-ku; r/ste from ¥77,000/126,500; P ☒ ♿ ; Hibiya, Toei Ōedo lines to Roppongi, exits 4a & 8) The Ritz boasts sweeping, unobstructed views and a spectacular pool and spa. Home to a Michelin-rated Japanese restaurant, it also has the excellent dining and high-end shops of Tokyo Midtown just below.

per night; use of the outdoor pool is ¥6000. Several exquisite restaurants and bars serve top-notch sushi, steak, champagne or whisky and cigars.

our pick **Grand Hyatt Tokyo** (Map pp140-1; ☎ 4333-1234; fax 4333-8123; www.tokyo.grand.hyatt.com; 6-10-3 Roppongi, Minato-ku; s/d from ¥50,400/55,650; P ☒ ♿ ; Hibiya, Toei Ōedo lines to Roppongi, exits 1c & 3) Set in uber-desirable Roppongi Hills, the Grand Hyatt gleams with polished refinement. Though the look is decidedly urban, the interior makes liberal use of natural materials, lending an earthy and comfortable feel to this modern hotel with details like rain-shower fixtures and mahogany walls. Hi-tech luxuries include DVD players and flat-screen TVs in the bathrooms, while in-house hotel facilities encompass a spa with wet and dry saunas, large indoor pool and gym, some of Tokyo's best dining and a number of bars. Book the west side for views of Mt Fuji (if the weather cooperates). Parking is ¥3000 per day.

EATING

No city in Asia can match Tokyo for the sheer variety and quality of its restaurants, and in 2008, the Michelin guides sent the culinary world into a tizzy when it awarded Tokyo with a whopping 191 Michelin stars – more than New York and Paris combined.

As well as refined Japanese cuisine, Tokyo covers the global spectrum with superb international restaurants for all budgets. One thing to keep in mind is that Japanese food tends to be cheaper than international food. For ¥750 you can get a good bowl of noodles in a *shokudō* (all-round restaurant); the same money will buy you a plate of spaghetti in one of Tokyo's many cheap Italian places (though a Japanified version of the real stuff). Be prepared to pay a little extra for a more authentic version of any international food.

Whatever you choose, you'll rarely have to look far for sustenance. Check out the upper floors of big department stores for *resutoran-gai* (restaurant 'towns'), which usually have a good selection of Japanese, Chinese and Italian restaurants with inexpensive lunchtime specials. Department stores usually also have *depachika* (food halls) in the basement floors selling *bentō* (boxed meals) amid groceries and gourmet gifts. Train stations are home to *rāmen* (egg noodle) shops, *bentō* and *onigiri* (rice ball) stands and *kareraisu* (curry rice) restaurants.

During the day the best eating areas are the big shopping districts like Shibuya, Shinjuku, Harajuku and Ginza. By night try Aoyama and Roppongi for some of the city's best restaurants. For something more traditional, try an *izakaya* or Yakitori Alley (right), or the down-at-heel eating arcade of Omoide-yokochō (p174) in Shinjuku. If you're not on an expense account, hit a few high-end restaurants at lunchtime (when midday meals are quite reasonably priced) and enjoy dinners at more modest eateries.

The **Tokyo Food Page** (www.bento.com/tokyofood.html) website, a gigantic database of restaurant reviews, is a great place to search for eateries by cuisine or neighbourhood. The database is so huge that listings sometimes go stale, so always go forth and dine with a plan B in mind.

For quick, cheap eats, or a cup of coffee in an air-conditioned (albeit smoky) cafe, chain coffee shops like Doutor and Excelsior dot the city landscape and usually offer sandwiches and snacks at budget prices.

Vegetarian food is less common than you might expect in Tokyo. Luckily, many places that aren't strictly vegetarian – such as Japanese noodle and tofu (bean curd) shops – serve a good variety of no-meat and no-fish dishes. For more information, pick up the TIC's *Vegetarian & Macrobiotic Restaurants in Tokyo* handout. It lists strictly vegetarian restaurants, wholefood shops, *shōjin-ryōri* (Buddhist temple fare) restaurants and Indian restaurants that offer a good selection of vegetarian and vegan dishes.

Kanda & Tokyo Station 神田・東京駅

On weekdays, colourful lunch trucks set up shop in the tree-shaded plaza of the Tokyo International Forum (p148). Cheap eats of an international variety range from falafel to tacos, and most takeaway costs less than ¥1000.

Mimiu (Map p138; ☎ 3567-6571; www.mimiu.co.jp; 3-6-4 Kyōbashi, Chūō-ku; meals ¥1600; 🕑 11.30am-9.30pm Mon-Sat, 11.30am-9pm Sun; 🚇 Ginza line to Kyōbashi, exits 1 & 2) Connoisseurs of udon say that Osaka-style broth is lighter in colour and more delicate in flavour than what Tokyoites favour. Try for yourself at Mimiu, an Osaka original that's said to have invented *udon-suki* (¥3500 per person), udon cooked sukiyaki-style in broth, with seafood, vegetables and meat. There's a picture menu. Look for the stately black corner building.

Mikuniya (Map pp142-3; ☎ 3271-3928; http://unagi3928.com, in Japanese; 2-5-11 Nihombashi, Chūō-ku; meals ¥1800-3000; 🕑 11am-4pm Mon-Sat; 🚇 Ginza, Tōzai, Toei Asakusa lines to Nihombashi, exit B1) The friendly family-run Mikuniya serves tasty *unagi* (eel). *Unagi bentō* comes in three sizes (¥2000, ¥2500 and ¥3200), accompanied by pickled veggies and soup. From exit B1, make a U-turn and go down the alley behind Takashimaya department store – look for the slab of driftwood above the door, embossed with gold kanji.

our pick **Anago Tamai** (Map pp142-3; ☎ 3272-3227; www.anago-tamai.com, in Japanese; 2-9-9 Nihombashi, Chūō-ku; meals ¥2000; 🕑 lunch & dinner; 🚇 Ginza, Tōzai, Toei Asakusa lines to Nihombashi, exit C4) *Anago*, the seafaring eel that is cousin to the more familiar freshwater *unagi*, isn't as fatty and is equally delicious. The English menu will explain this and the finer points of eating *anago*. Choose a *bentō* or *anago* sushi pressed in bamboo moulds; the dining experience is enhanced by this wooden house's old-fashioned interior.

Ginza & Shiodome 銀座・汐留

Lunch deals are competitive in and around Ginza; roam the *resutoran-gai* in the **Ginza Palmy Building** (Map p138; 5-2-1 Ginza, Chuō-ku; 🚇 Ginza, Hibiya, Marunouchi lines to Ginza, exit C3), or in department stores like Matsuzakaya (p189), Matsuya (p189) and Takashimaya (p189). Alternatively, head down to the basement food halls to pick up a *bentō* for later.

Nearby, convivial, atmospheric *yakitori* (skewers of grilled chicken) restaurants light up their grills each evening under the railway tracks in Yūrakuchō's Yakitori Alley (Map p138).

Sushi Zanmai (Map p138; ☎ 3541-1117; 4-11-9 Tsukiji, Chūō-ku; dinner from ¥1500; 24hr; V; Hibiya line to Tsukiji, exit 1) After the sunrise fish auctions of the Tsukiji Fish Market, it serves market-fresh sushi to weary fishermen; then tourists and townsfolk, office workers and retirees. In the evening, it remains open to bar and restaurant trade, and the ladies of the floating world. Zanmai has an English picture menu and English lettering on the sign; there's a proliferation of branches around the market.

Nair's (Map p138; ☎ 3541-8246; www.ginza-nair.co.jp, in Japanese; 4-10-7 Ginza, Chūō-ku; lunch/dinner ¥1500/3000; 11.30am-9.30pm, to 8.30pm Sat & Sun, closed Tue; V; Hibiya, Toei Asakusa lines to Higashi-Ginza, exit A2) Nair's was the first Indian restaurant to open in Tokyo, back in 1949, arriving here by way of Kerala and Manchuria. This still-popular restaurant, just up Shōwa-dōri from Kabuki-za, has an English menu and sign and is a boon for vegetarians in Ginza.

Shin-Hi-no-Moto (Map p138; ☎ 3214-8021; 2-4-4 Yūrakuchō, Chiyoda-ku; meals ¥2500; 5pm-midnight; Yūrakuchō line to Yūrakuchō, exit A5 or Chiyoda, Hibiya, Toei Mita lines to Hibiya, exit A2) Under the tracks in Yūrakuchō, this lively *izakaya* is the perfect blend of authentic and accessible. It's also known as Andy's, after the expat son-in-law of the family, who now runs this friendly joint. There's English-speaking staff and an English menu, but no English sign; look for the Guinness signs and red lantern.

Robata (Map p138; ☎ 3591-1905; 1-3-8 Yūrakuchō, Chiyoda-ku; meals from ¥3500; 5.30-11pm Mon-Sat; Chiyoda, Hibiya, Toei Mita lines to Hibiya, exit A4) Along the alley parallelling the JR tracks, this is one of Tokyo's most celebrated *izakaya*. A little Japanese ability is helpful here, but the point-and-eat method works fine, as the country-style dishes are piled invitingly on the counter. Look for the rustic black shop, huge sign on the 2nd floor and vegetables displayed outside.

Kyūbei (Map p138; ☎ 3571-6523; www.kyubey.jp; 8-7-6 Ginza, Chūō-ku; lunch/dinner from ¥4000/10,000; lunch & dinner Mon-Sat; ⊠; Ginza line to Shimbashi, exit 1) Established in 1936, this superb sushi restaurant continues to earn its reputation as one of Tokyo's best. If you treat yourself to one high-end, raw-fish experience, reserve a place at Kyūbei. An English menu is available online, not in-house, but English-speaking staff can help you order. Its minimalist facade has a discreet flagstone path on the left, one street west of Chūō-dōri.

Ten-Ichi (Map p138; ☎ 3571-1949; www.tenichi.co.jp, in Japanese; 6-6-5 Ginza, Chūō-ku; lunch/dinner from ¥5000/8500; 11.30am-9.30pm; ⊠; Ginza, Hibiya, Marunouchi lines to Ginza, to Ginza, exits A1, B3 & B6) Frying up famously transcendent tempura since 1930, Ten-Ichi is the place to splash out on unbelievably light tempura in elegant surroundings. Reservations are recommended. There's a square lantern out front with the shop's bold kanji on it.

Birdland (Map p138; ☎ 5250-1081; B1 fl, Tsukamoto Sogyo Bldg, 4-2-15 Ginza, Chūō-ku; meals from ¥6000; 5-9pm Tue-Sat; Ginza, Hibiya, Marunouchi lines to Ginza, exit C6) The *yakitori* chefs at Birdland know there's more than one way to skewer a chicken. The resulting preparation of the restaurant's free-range fowl varies from grilled heart kebabs to sashimi, and the respectable wine list honours the humble bird. Only same-day reservations can be made from noon on, and there's an English menu and sign.

L'Osier (Map p138; ☎ 3571-6050; www.shiseido.co.jp/e/losier/top.htm; 7-5-5 Ginza, Chūō-ku; lunch/dinner from ¥6800/19,000; lunch & dinner Mon-Sat; Ginza, Hibiya, Marunouchi lines to Ginza, exit B6) L'Osier has long been considered one of Tokyo's most sublime French restaurants, this idea lately reinforced by the three stars Michelin granted in 2008. Modern takes on classic French cuisine are served in a relaxed and elegant setting – you'll want to dress up for this delicious expedition.

Ueno 上野

Around Ueno, you'll find a good variety of cheap Japanese places in and around Ameyoko Arcade, where you can also pick up takeaway and fruit from vendors.

Ueno Yabu Soba (Map pp146-7; ☎ 3831-4728; 6-9-16 Ueno, Taitō-ku; meals from ¥750; 11.30am-9pm Thu-Tue; JR Yamanote line to Ueno, Hirokōji exit) Near the arcade, this famous *soba* (buckwheat noodles) shop has a peaceful, traditional atmosphere despite its busyness. There's an English picture menu, but if you can't decide, try the filling *nabeyaki soba* (noodles topped with vegetables, egg and tempura shrimp). Look for the black granite sign on the corner shop that says 'Since 1892'.

Futaba (Map pp146-7; ☎ 3831-6483; 2-8-11 Ueno, Taitō-ku; meals ¥1500-3000; lunch & dinner Tue-Fri, 11.30am-6pm Sat & Sun, closed Mon & Thu; JR Yamanote line to Ueno, Hirokōji exit) Though the nondescript beige exterior doesn't look like much, the proof of Futaba's longevity is in its pudding – or rather, its pork cutlets. We found the service to be a bit gruff, but you're keeping it real in Ueno if you head to this corner shop and order a *tonkatsu teishoku* (deep-fried pork cutlet set meal; ¥1500). There's no English menu or sign.

Izu-ei (Map pp146-7; ☎ 3831-0954; 2-12-22 Ueno, Taitō-ku; meals from ¥1785; 11am-10pm; ; JR Yamanote line to Ueno, Hirokōji exit) *Unagi* is believed to improve one's stamina on oppressively humid days, but we enjoy it as much in cooler weather. Izu-ei, which has an English picture menu, offers the added bonus of lovely views of Shinobazu-ike. Stray beyond the usual *bentō*, and try an *unagi kaiseki* (multicourse meal, from ¥7350) in a traditional tatami room. You'll find menus at street level and a traditional black exterior, set back slightly above the street.

Sasa-no-Yuki (Map pp146-7; ☎ 3873-1145; www.sasanoyuki.com, in Japanese; 2-15-10 Negishi, Taitō-ku; meals from ¥1800; 11am-9pm Tue-Sun; V; JR Yamanote line to Uguisudani, north exit) Sasa-no-Yuki opened its doors in Edo times, serving beautifully presented *tōfu-ryōri* (multicourse, tofu-based meals). Friendly staff and the English menu will help you order. To find it, turn right out the station exit, cross the big intersection at Kototoi-dōri and look for the black-walled restaurant on your left about 200m up, past the pedestrian overpass.

Echikatsu (Map pp146-7; ☎ 3811-5293; 2-31-23 Yushima, Bunkyō-ku; meals from ¥7000; 5-9.30pm Mon-Sat, closed Sat in Aug; Chiyoda line to Yushima, exit 5) One of Shitamachi's most attractive qualities is its time-warp from modern Tokyo. Echikatsu is no exception, with its sukiyaki and shabu-shabu bubbling within the bamboo walls of a beautifully maintained traditional house with a Japanese garden. There's an English menu here; reservations are recommended.

Asakusa 浅草

Asakusa's variety of Japanese food makes it difficult to choose where to eat. Poke your head into some of the restaurants in the alleys between Sensō-ji and Kaminarimon-dōri if you can't decide.

Sometarō (Map pp146-7; ☎ 3844-9502; www.sometaro.com, in Japanese; 2-2-2 Nishi-Asakusa, Taitō-ku; meals ¥1000; noon-10pm; ; Ginza line to Tawaramachi, exit 3) Sometaro is a fun, funky place to try DIY *okonomiyaki* (meat, seafood and vegetables in a cabbage-and-vegetable batter). You cook it yourself on a griddle built into your table, and the English menu includes a helpful how-to. Sometarō has a rustic, overgrown facade.

Kappabashi Coffee (Map pp146-7; ☎ 5828-0308; 3-25-11 Nishi-Asakusa, Taitō-ku; meals from ¥1050; 8am-9pm Tue-Fri, to 8pm Sat-Mon; ; Ginza line to Tawaramachi, exit 3) So you're not a Starbucks fan, but you crave a nonsmoky coffeehouse where you can sit a while after shopping for plastic food models along Kappabashi-dōri. This incongruously cool little cafe is your place. Have a cafe au lait and dessert or a simple, inexpensive *bentō* in a modern room centred on an old-fashioned Japanese hearth. Look for the circular logo with the name in English lettering.

Daikokuya (Map pp146-7; ☎ 3844-1111; 1-38-10 Asakusa, Taitō-ku; dishes ¥1500-3000; 11.30am-8.30pm Mon-Fri, to 9pm Sat; ; Ginza, Toei Asakusa lines to Asakusa, exit 1) Near Nakamise-dōri, this is the place to get down-home tempura, an Asakusa speciality. The line out the door usually snakes around the corner at lunchtime, but if it looks unbearably long, try your luck at the branch on the next block. Both have English menus but signs in Japanese; if there's no queue, look for the bench in front of this small, traditional building.

Komagata Dojō (Map pp146-7; ☎ 3842-4001; 1-7-12 Komagata, Taitō-ku; dishes ¥1500-3000; 11am-9pm; Ginza, Toei Asakusa lines to Asakusa, exits 2 & A5) The sixth-generation chef running this marvellous restaurant continues the tradition of turning the simple *dojō* (a small, eel-like river fish) into rich deliciousness. It's all floor seating at the shared low, wooden plank tables, and an English picture menu details your options. If you choose the *nabe* (¥1700), the *dojō* will come on a charcoal-heated dish; heap it with chopped scallions and cook through before eating. Look for the restaurant's traditional facade between modern buildings.

Tsukiji Sushi-sen (Map pp146-7; ☎ 5830-1020; 1st & 2nd fl, 2-16-9 Kaminarimon, Taitō-ku; meals ¥1800; 24hr; ; Ginza, Toei Asakusa lines to Asakusa, exits 2 & A5) A seating charge of ¥315 will be added to your bill here, but it's a small price to pay when you're fiending for good sushi at 4am. As the name implies, this shop traces its lineage back to the Tsukiji Market. If you aren't well-versed in sushi lingo, there's a picture menu, but you can't go wrong with the *tokusen omakase nigiri* (chef's choice assortment; ¥3150). Look for the name in English beneath the kanji on the sign.

Vin Chou (Map pp146-7; ☎ 3845-4430; www.vinchou.jp/r-asakusa/asakusa.html, in Japanese; 2-2-13 Nishi-Asakusa, Taitō-ku; meals from ¥5000; 5-11pm Mon, Tue & Thu-Sat, 4-10pm Sun) In a city enamoured of all things French, this is, *bien sûr*, a French-style *yakitori* joint, offering foie gras with your *tori negi* (chicken and leek). A pleasant novelty for this old-fashioned neighbourhood. It's around the corner from Taitō Ryokan, with an English menu and small sign in French.

Ikebukuro 池袋

Though not a dining destination in itself, Ikebukuro has plenty of fine places to chow down.

Tonchin (Map p132; ☎ 3987-8556; http://tonchin.foodex.ne.jp, in Japanese; 1st fl, 2-26-2 Minami-Ikebukuro, Toshima-ku; meals from ¥600; 11am-4am; JR Yamanote line to Ikebukuro, Seibu east exit) The line out the door could signal mere hype, but the rich *tonkotsu rāmen* (noodles in pork-bone broth) here will show you substance. To order, choose what type of *rāmen* and toppings you want from pictures on the ticket vending machine in front. While you wait, staff will take your ticket so that your *rāmen* is ready when you're seated. Turn up at off-peak hours for a shorter wait.

Marhaba (Map p132; ☎ 3987-1031; 2-63-6 Ikebukuro, Toshima-ku; meals ¥1200-2400; lunch & dinner Mon-Sat, 11.30am-9pm Sun; V; JR Yamanote line to Ikebukuro, north exit) The small green sign indicating the entrance to this Pakistani place is as unassuming as the humble interior, but the smells issuing from the glassed-in kitchen are heavenly. There are few concessions to Japanese tastes, so the brain masala (¥1200) and samosas (¥400) are authentic and pleasantly spicy.

Malaychan (Map p132; ☎ 5391-7638; www.malaychan.jp/NewFiles/contents_E.html; 3-22-6 Nishi-Ikebukuro, Toshima-ku; meals ¥2000; dinner Mon, lunch & dinner Tue-Sat, 11am-11pm Sun; JR Yamanote line to Ikebukuro, west exit) With its sweet location on a corner across from Nishi-Ikebukuro kōen, Malaychan is one of Tokyo's few Malaysian restaurants and serves a huge breadth of dishes spanning the country's multiethnic background. There's an English menu here, and an English sign outside.

Akiyoshi (Map p132; ☎ 3982-0644; 3-30-4 Nishi-Ikebukuro, Toshima-ku; meals ¥3000; 5-11pm; JR Yamanote line to Ikebukuro, west exit) If in the mood for *yakitori*, Akiyoshi's open grill at centre stage ignites a festive, sociable atmosphere. Chefs work quickly to move traffic along, but that doesn't mean you can't sit comfortably through several courses and some conversation with a fellow diner. There's an English menu and an English sign.

Sasashū (Map p132; ☎ 3971-6796; 2-2-6 Ikebukuro, Toshima-ku; meals from ¥6000; dinner Mon-Sat; JR Yamanote line to Ikebukuro, north exit) Sasashū's Japanese-style facade is easy to pick out between the modern concrete strip joints nearby; look for the small gourd-shaped wooden sign lettered in English. This dignified *izakaya* is renowned for its high-quality sake selection and traditional hearths. Some Japanese-language ability (or a Japanese friend) would be helpful here, but consider trying the *kamonabe* (duck stew; ¥3150) or *salmon yaki* (grilled salmon; ¥840), if not an *omakase* meal (chef's recommendation; name your budget).

At lunchtime, don't forget the restaurant floors in Seibu and Tōbu. The eastern side of the Ikebukuro station is crammed with *rāmen* shops and *kaiten-sushi* (conveyor-belt sushi restaurant), and is also the place you'll find **Namco Namjatown** (☎ 5950-0765; 2nd fl, World Import Mart Bldg, 3-1-3 Higashi-Ikebukuro, Toshima-ku; adult/child ¥300/200; 10am-10pm), which houses three food 'theme parks', specialising variously in *gyōza* (Chinese dumplings), desserts and ice cream. Admission only gets you in; you'll have to pay extra for the treats you want to sample.

Shinjuku 新宿

For a taste of Occupation-era Tokyo, meander through Omoide-yokochō (Map p131; Memory Lane), aka 'Piss Alley' (as it's less politely known), where tiny restaurants are packed shoulder to shoulder beside the JR tracks just northwest of Shinjuku station. Here, local workers stop off for *yakitori, oden* (fishcakes, tofu, vegetables and eggs simmered in a kelp-flavoured broth), noodles and beer before braving the trains back home. Most places serve similar things and few have names, so pick the place that appeals to you. What they serve will be piled on the counters; just point to order, and expect to pay about ¥2000 per person. Omoide-yokochō is slated to be razed imminently to make way for new development, so catch it while it's still standing.

Here are a few options in the Shinjuku area:

Nakajima (Map p131; ☎ 3356-7962; http://shinjyuku-nakajima.com, in Japanese; 3-32-5 Shinjuku, Shinjuku-ku; lunch/dinner from ¥800/12,500; lunch & dinner Mon-Sat; Marunouchi line to Shinjuku-sanchōme, exit A1) The speciality of this warmly-lit, immaculate basement restaurant is the *iwashi* (sardine) – simmered in sweet broth with egg, served as sashimi, or delicately fried and laid on a bed of rice. Though there's no English menu, the hostess will explain the options to you in flawless English. Dinners are *kaiseki,* but lunches are fabulously inexpensive. Down the alley next to the Beams building, look for a black building with an outside stairwell leading down to this one-Michelin-star shop.

Kōmen (Map p131; ☎ 5919-1660; www.kohmen.com, in Japanese; 1st & 2nd fl, 3-32-2 Shinjuku, Shinjuku-ku; meals ¥850; 🕑 11am-5am; Ⓜ Marunouchi line to Shinjuku-sanchōme, exit A1) Though *rāmen* lovers have strong opinions on broth, noodles and their favourite shops, Kōmen is a popular chain serving excellent *tonkotsu rāmen*. This two-storey branch has an English menu and a classier, sleeker look than most *rāmen* joints. Look for its huge circular sign above the door near the corner of Meiji-dōri and Kōshū Kaidō.

Tsunahachi (Map p131; ☎ 3352-1012; www.tunahachi.co.jp, in Japanese; 3-31-8 Shinjuku, Shinjuku-ku; meals from ¥1260; 🕑 11am-10pm; Ⓜ JR Yamanote line to Shinjuku, east exit) Tsunahachi keeps them coming with its reasonably priced, tasty tempura. Sit at the counter for the pleasure of watching the efficient chefs fry each course of your dinner and place it on your dish. There's an English menu. From Shinjuku-dōri as you face Mitsukoshi department store, go down the small street to its left; Tsunahachi will be on your left.

Breizh Café (Map p131; ☎ 5361-1335; 13th fl, Takashimaya Times Sq, 5-24-2 Sendagaya, Shibuya-ku; meals from ¥1480; 🕑 lunch & dinner; Ⓜ JR Yamanote line to Shinjuku, new south exit) The Breton-style buckwheat crêpes and savoury galettes are reason enough to dine at this bright crêperie (clearly signed in French), but on sunny days, taking a garden-side table on the outdoor terrace is an added treat. While the French standards are well represented on the English menu, Japanese enhancements keep things interesting – like the dessert crêpe drizzled with *kuro-mitsu* (sweet black sugar), served with green-tea ice cream (¥850).

Canard (Map p131; ☎ 3200-0706; www.jlcjapon.com; B1 fl, 5-17-6 Shinjuku, Shinjuku-ku; lunch/dinner courses from ¥1700/3000; 🕑 lunch & dinner; Ⓜ JR Yamanote line to Shinjuku, east exit) Tucked into a tiny alley near Hanazono-jinja, an equally petite Canard serves homemade, seasonally-changing French food in intimate surroundings. With wine the bill adds up, but the meal is worth every yen. Reservations are highly recommended. There's a menu in English and a French sign.

Chaya Macrobiotics (Map p131; ☎ 3357 0014; 7th fl, Isetan Bldg, 3-14-1 Shinjuku, Shinjuku-ku; meals from ¥2000; 🕑 11am-10pm; Ⓥ; Ⓜ Marunouchi line to Shinjuku-sanchōme, exit A1) Marrying the concepts of Japanese macrobiotics and French cuisine, Chaya offers healthy whole foods alongside lists of organic tea, wine and apple cider. Though the seasonal menu (available in English) is anchored by mostly vegan offerings, such as red rice risotto, seitan-and-millet burgers and seaweed side salads, fish also figures prominently. The signage is all English.

Ibuki (Map p131; ☎ 3352-4787; 3-23-6 Shinjuku, Shinjuku-ku; sukiyaki course ¥3600, shabu-shabu ¥3800; 🕑 4-11.30pm; Ⓜ JR Yamanote line to Shinjuku, east exit) A terrific sukiyaki and shabu-shabu restaurant in Shinjuku, Ibuki gets a lot of foreign trade and has an English menu and sign. This friendly place offers a traditional atmosphere and sociable dining experience, and accepts credit cards.

Tōfuro (Map p131; ☎ 3320-1370; 1-32-1 Yoyogi, Shibuya-ku; meals ¥4000; 🕑 lunch & dinner; Ⓜ JR Yamanote line to Yoyogi, south exit) Even if you're not a fan of tofu, there's lots to eat in this upscale, Edo-style *izakaya*. Small, private rooms are good for groups, who can order set meals consisting of several courses. The traditional cuisine includes homemade tofu and a full menu of grilled meats, fish, soups and *oden*, detailed on an English menu. Look for the traditional shopfront with a well-lit red doorway.

Kozue (Map p131; ☎ 5323-3460; 40th fl, Park Hyatt Tokyo, 3-7-1-2 Nishi-Shinjuku, Shinjuku-ku; set lunch/dinner from ¥4000/12,000; 🕑 lunch & dinner; ⊠; Ⓜ JR Yamanote line to Shinjuku, south exit) With so many places to splurge on a phenomenal supper in this city, the choice can be paralysing. But if you're planning on upmarket Japanese, Kozue delivers in sublime fashion. High up on the 40th floor of the Park Hyatt, the atmosphere is romantically dim for your full-course meal (you can also order à la carte). Either way, nonspeakers of Japanese will appreciate the English menu and knowledgeable bilingual staff, while all tongues will savour the exquisite cuisine prepared here.

If you can't find anything to your liking on the streets, try the *resutoran-gai* of the big department stores. The Isetan building (p189) has a *resutoran-gai* on its 8th floor, while **Takashimaya Times Square** (☎ 5361-3301; 5-24-2 Sendagaya, Shibuya-ku; 🕑 10am-9pm) has a *resutoran-gai* on its 12th to 14th floors. Both also have huge, sparkly *depachika*.

Harajuku & Aoyama 原宿・青山

Harajuku and Aoyama have more bistros, cafes and trattorias than most small European towns. The artery feeding it all is the promenade of Tokyo's young and beautiful:

Omote-sandō. A few Japanese eateries are worth seeking out among the French and faddish restaurants.

Fujimamas (Map p134; 5485-2283; www.fujimamas.com; 6-3-2 Jingūmae, Shibuya-ku; lunch/dinner ¥1100/2000; 11am-11pm; ; Chiyoda line to Meiji-jingūmae, exit 4 or JR Yamanote line to Harajuku, Omote-sandō exit) Once a tatami-maker's workshop, the airy upstairs dining room and breezy, open ground-floor space now echo the freshness and vitality of Fujimamas' fusion food. Generously proportioned dishes come from multi-ethnic backgrounds, as do the clientele, for whom there's an English menu (and kids' menu), and English signage. Reservations are recommended.

Hiroba (Map p134; 3406-6409; B1 fl, Crayon House, 3-8-15 Kita-Aoyama, Minato-ku; lunch buffet ¥1260; 11am-10pm; ; Chiyoda, Ginza, Hanzōmon to Omote-sandō, exits B2 & B4) In the brightly signed Crayon House Building, this cheery little spot does an excellent organic lunch buffet that includes both vegetarian and nonvegetarian options. Though descriptions of dishes are only in Japanese, the signs include cute, helpful drawings of fish or pigs to tell you what kinds of animal ingredients are used.

Le Bretagne (Map p134; 3478-7855; www.le-bretagne.com; 3-5-4 Jingūmae, Shibuya-ku; meals ¥1800; 11.30am-11pm Mon-Sat, to 10pm Sun; Chiyoda, Ginza, Hanzōmon lines to Omote-sandō, exit A2) Authentic and satisfying buckwheat crêpes straight out of Brittany (much like the chefs themselves) are the stars at Le Bretagne. A savoury galette with mixed greens and a ceramic cup of organic cider is a perfect retreat from an afternoon shopping along Omote-sandō. There's an English menu and the name in French on the awning.

Las Chicas (Map p134; 3407-6865; www.vision.co.jp/aoyama/index.html; 5-47-6 Jingūmae, Shibuya-ku; meals from ¥1300; 11.30am-11pm Mon-Thu, 11am-11.30pm Fri & Sat, 11am-11pm Sun; ; Chiyoda, Ginza, Hanzōmon lines to Omote-sandō, exit B2) One of the rare alfresco dining terraces in the city, this almost too-cool-for-school spot offers casual classics like the Caligula salad (Caesar with a twist) enjoyed by the largely foreign fans. The wine list is solid, but you can repair to the basement lounge for cocktails before dinner and browse adjacent designer boutiques afterwards. Signed in English, with an English menu available.

Maisen (Map p134; 3470-0071; 4-8-5 Jingūmae, Shibuya-ku; lunch sets ¥1500; 11am-10pm; ; Chiyoda, Ginza, Hanzōmon lines to Omote-sandō, exit A2) Maisen turns out righteous, crisp *tonkatsu* that draws consistent queues. Thankfully, the place is housed in a converted bathhouse, so there's plenty of room for the many souls craving Kagoshima *kurobuta* (black pork; ¥1260). If you're on the run, pick up a *bentō* at the takeaway window.

Mominoki House (Map p134; 3405-9144; www2.odn.ne.jp/mominoki_house; 1st fl, 2-18-5 Jingūmae, Shibuya-ku; mains around ¥1500; 11am-11pm; JR Yamanote line to Harajuku, Takeshita exit) You might be all *tonkatsu*-ed out, even if you're not of the vegetarian persuasion. Those seeking some relief from deep-fried delicacies can stop into Mominoki House, which turns out excellent macrobiotic food. In this rambling little warren of a space, corners are filled with jazz and happy plants, and the proprietor will stop and chat about Stevie Wonder, pottery and holistic living. There's an English menu and sign outside.

Fonda de la Madrugada (Map p134; 5410-6288; www.fonda-m.com, in Japanese; B1 fl, Villa Blanca, 2-33-12 Jingūmae, Shibuya-ku; lunch/dinner from ¥3800/6000; 5.30pm-2am Sun-Thu, to 5am Fri & Sat; ; JR Yamanote line to Harajuku, Takeshita exit) Head north of the Turkish embassy to this local favourite, serving some of Tokyo's best-loved Mexican food. Everything from the tiles to the strolling mariachi musicians has been imported from Mexico. It ain't cheap (¥900 guacamole?! *ay-ay-ay*), but after a few tequila shots you'll be having too much fun to notice. There's an English menu and sign.

our pick **Ume-no-hana** (Map p134; 3475-8077; 6th fl, Aoyama Bell Commons, 2-14-6 Kita-Aoyama, Minato-ku; dinner ¥7000; lunch & dinner Mon-Sat, dinner Sun; Ginza & Hanzōmon lines to Gaienmae, exit 2) This elegant, traditional restaurant is rightfully well known for its *kaiseki* meals that showcase tofu and yuba (tofu 'skin') in beautifully presented small courses. Both *niku-nashi* (literally 'without meat') and meat-inclusive sets are available; but ordering will be problematic unless you have a Japanese speaker to make the reservation for you and help you decide the best set for you and your party.

Shibuya 渋谷

Take the briefest look around Shibuya and it may occur to you that there must be a lot of restaurants lurking in all those department stores – you are correct. Winners: to collect your prize, proceed to the 7th floor of Parco Part 1 or the 8th floor of the Shibuya 109 building.

Kantipur (Map p134; ☎ 3770-5358; www.kantipur.jp; B1 fl, 16-6 Sakuragaokachō, Shibuya-ku; mains around ¥850; lunch & dinner Mon-Fri, 11.30am-11pm Sat; ; JR Yamanote line to Shibuya, south exit) After crossing the pedestrian overpass above Tamagawa-dōri and spotting its colourful sandwich boards on the street, make your way downstairs into the warmly lit dining room. Kantipur serves generous portions of Nepalese food with a bountiful selection of vegetarian choices, detailed on an English menu.

Hina Sushi (Map p134; ☎ 3462-1003; B2 fl, 21-1 Udagawachō, Shibuya-ku; lunch/dinner from ¥1050/2420; 11am-11pm; ; JR Yamanote line to Shibuya, Hachikō exit) In the basement of the Seibu A Building, Hina Sushi has several *tabehōdai* (all-you-can-eat) and *nomihōdai* (all-you-can-drink) specials on Fridays and Saturdays. It's great value for sushi of this quality, but there's a time limit, so come ravenous. There's an English sign and menu.

Bio Café (Map p134; ☎ 5428-3322; 16-14 Udagawachō, Shibuya-ku; lunch ¥1400; 11am-11pm; ; JR Yamanote line to Shibuya, Hachikō exit) Nestled amid the accessories shops and all-you-can-eat dessert cafes down this winding alley lies the peaceful Bio Café, serving organic, mostly vegetarian meals in a softly lit dining room. Some dishes contain animal products, so strict vegetarians should ask before ordering. Consider sampling the 'alcohol for beautiful skin' cocktail. The sign is in English, and there's an English menu.

Toriyoshi Dining (Map p134; ☎ 5784-3373; B1 fl, 2-10-10 Dōgenzaka, Shibuya-ku; dinner from ¥3000; 5pm-4am; JR Yamanote line to Shibuya, Hachikō exit) This step up from more casual *yakitori* joints is below ground in Shibuya. With a tasteful urban aesthetic, the atmosphere is appealing for an intimate dinner of free-range chicken grilled over *binchō* (high-grade oak) charcoal. Order à la carte or go with full-course meals. There's an English sign and English menu available.

Den Rokuen-tei (Map p134; ☎ 6415-5489; 8th fl, Parco Part 1, 15-1 Udagawachō, Shibuya-ku; meals from ¥3000; 11am-midnight; JR Yamanote line to Shibuya, Hachikō exit) Modern twists on seasonally changing Japanese izakaya dishes are matched with an array of wine, beer and sake cocktails. Private tatami rooms are available, but at this relaxed, stylish perch on the top of Parco 1, the open-air terrace is the prime real estate. There's an English sign and menu available.

Sakana-tei (Map p134; ☎ 3780-1313; 4th fl, Koike Bldg, 2-23-15 Dōgenzaka, Shibuya-ku; meals from ¥3500; 5.30-11pm Mon-Sat; JR Yamanote line to Shibuya, Hachikō exit) This unpretentious, but slightly posh, *izakaya* is a sake specialist much sought after by connoisseurs, and it's great value to boot. There's no English menu; just point at the dishes on the counter to order. Call ahead for reservations, but turn off your mobile phone once you're in. From the Shibuya JR station, take Bunkamura-dōri (to the right of the Shibuya 109 building), and take a left where the road splits. Take your first left, and the Koike Building will be the first on your right.

Gomaya (Map p134; ☎ 3770-8158; B1 fl, Matsubara Bldg, 2-25-13 Dōgenzaka, Shibuya-ku; meals ¥3500; 5pm-midnight; JR Yamanote line to Shibuya, Hachikō exit) Duck into the alley next to McDonald's along Bunkamura-dōri and find the stairwell for Gomaya on your right. The sign is in English, as is a limited menu. Artistically arranged plates will appear in front of you as you order, but a must-try is the house-made *gomadōfu* (black sesame tofu). There's also a six-course, all-you-can-drink special (¥4000, two-hour limit), a terrific deal.

Sora-no-Niwa (Map p134; ☎ 5728-5191; 4-17 Sakuragaokachō, Shibuya-ku; meals ¥4000; 5pm-midnight; JR Yamanote line to Shibuya, New South West exit) Reservations are recommended at this popular tofu restaurant, where you can enjoy not only freshly-made tofu, but try your hand at making yuba at your table. The modern Japanese decor complements the traditional tofu dishes with contemporary twists – tofu tiramisu, for one. There's an English menu and English sign.

Ebisu & Daikanyama 恵比寿・代官山

In Ebisu, have a look around the 6th floor of the Atré building above Ebisu station for all the standard Japanese standbys, or you could venture forth into the neighbourhood for more variety and worthwhile eating establishments serving international food.

Rivalling Harajuku and Aoyama as the centre of Tokyo cafe society, Daikanyama is a chic destination to sip a cappuccino and engage in serious people-watching before perusing the local designer wares. You'll also find plenty of foreign restaurants – some good, some merely fashionable. The Tōkyū Tōyoko line (catch it from Shibuya) stops directly in Daikanyama, but it's also an easy 10-minute walk from Ebisu. From the west exit of Ebisu station, head west along Komazawa-dōri and turn right at the big intersection with Kyu-Yamate-dōri. When you hit the pedestrian overpass, make another right at Hachiman-dōri and you'll soon arrive in the heart of Daikanyama, with the shopping complex Daikanyama Address on your right.

Here are some other neighbourhood options:

our pick **Fujiyama Seimen** (Map p136; ☎ 3473-0088; 1-13-6 Ebisu, Shibuya-ku; meals ¥900; lunch & dinner; Hibiya line to Naka-Meguro, northwest exit) At most *rāmen* shops, you can order *tsukemen* (noodles with the broth on the side), but some outshine others in this presentation, Fujiyama being one of them. The open kitchen and friendly staff create a vibrant atmosphere in this semi-industrial shop alongside the tracks. The noodles are thick and substantial, readily soaking up the flavour of the soup, which has a piquant hint of *yuzu* (Japanese citrus) to it. There's an English sign and menu.

Ippūdō Rāmen (Map p136; ☎ 5420-2225; 1-3-13 Hiro-o, Shibuya-ku; meals ¥900; 11am-4am Mon-Sat, to midnight Sun; JR Yamanote line to Ebisu, east exit) This *rāmen* shop on Meiji-dōri is nationally famous for its Kyūshū-style *rāmen* into which you add fresh garlic and spicy sprouts. There's a big white sign in kanji over the door and a long queue at peak periods – as at any busy *rāmen* shop, you shouldn't linger longer than 20 minutes to eat. There's an English menu.

Ura (Map p136; ☎ 5489 1117; 1-17-1 Ebisu-Nishi, Shibuya-ku; meals ¥1500; noon-4am Tue-Sun, to 11pm Mon; JR Yamanote line to Ebisu, west exit) With so many little cafes and bistros around Daikanyama, it can be hard to decide whether you want to nibble a scone or indulge in an afternoon cocktail. But this cool, casual spot is inviting day or night, with mostly French-style dishes, and is balanced out by well-chosen wines, good espresso and desserts. The seasonally changing menu is in basic English, as is its subtle sign on the wall outside.

Good Honest Grub (Map p136; ☎ 3797-9877; www.goodhonestgrub.com; 2-20-8 Higashi, Shibuya-ku; meals ¥1500; 11.30am-4pm Mon-Fri, 10.30am-4.30pm Sat & Sun; ; Chiyoda line to Meiji-jingūmae, exit 4) Long the place to go for weekend brunches, this Canadian-run, vegetarian-friendly eatery is a sweet place for a healthy bite. Serving smoothies, hearty wraps and sandwiches, it's a welcoming spot to turn up for a nosh. There's an English sign and menu.

Tonki (Map p136; ☎ 3491-9928; 1-1 Shimo-Meguro, Meguro-ku; meals ¥1650; 4-11pm Wed-Mon, closed 3rd Mon each month; JR Yamanote line to Meguro, west exit) You know a place is doing something right when it only offers two choices. Here, it's *tonkatsu* – choose the lean *hire-katsu* or fattier *rōsu-katsu*. The service here is down to an efficient art form, and your perfect *tonkatsu* will arrive (after a wait) with rice, shredded cabbage and miso soup. From the station walk westward down the hill on Meguro-dōri, take a left at the first alley and look for a white sign and *noren* (curtains) across the sliding doors.

Mushroom (Map p136; ☎ 5489-1346; www.mush.jp, in Japanese; 2nd fl, 1-16-3 Ebisu-Nishi, Shibuya-ku; lunch/dinner from ¥2625/5040; ; JR Yamanote line to Ebisu, west exit) Chef Yamaoka's obsession with the taming of the 'shroom has sprouted this very cosy little French bistro, whose decor is dominated by a fungus motif, of course. Three-course meals showcasing mushrooms are amazing value and will transport you without mind-altering side effects – though the gorgeous wines might. There's a daily-changing French menu and English sign.

Roppongi 六本木

It's only logical that there be an abundance of international restaurants in Roppongi, Tokyo's foreign-nightlife playground. From inexpensive burger joints to high-end sushi bars, whatever food you fancy is here. Japanese restaurants tend to be expensive but very accessible to *gaijin*, making it the perfect area for any long-awaited, lavish Japanese meal. But there are also heaps of cheap spots if you just need a quick bite before hitting the bars.

Gogyō Rāmen (Map pp140-1; ☎ 5775-5566; 1-4-36, Nishi-Azabu, Minato-ku; meals ¥900; 11.30am-4pm & 5pm-3am Mon-Sat, to midnight Sun; Hibiya, Toei Ōedo lines to Roppongi, exits 2 & 3) Open late, this sleek place is famous for its *kogashi-miso rāmen* (blackened miso *rāmen*, ¥850), a strange black soup unlike any other you're likely to try in Tokyo. The awning has the shop's name in English, and there's an English menu.

Salsita (Map pp140-1; ☎ 3280-1145; http://salsita-tokyo.com; B1 fl, 4-5-65 Minami-Azabu, Minato-ku; meals ¥1500; lunch & dinner Tue-Sun; to Hiro-o, exit 1) It's worth going out of your way to Salsita for reasonably priced, respectably authentic Mexican food. It's a colourful little spot where the tortillas and chorizo are homemade and the *cochinita* *pibil* (Yucatan-style roasted pork; ¥1900) is particularly tender and delicious. There's an English menu and Spanish sign.

Eat More Greens (Map pp140-1; ☎ 3798-3191; www.eatmoregreens.jp; 2-2-5 Azabu-Jūban, Minato-ku; meals ¥1500; 11am-11pm Mon-Fri, 9am-11pm Sat & Sun; ; Namboku line to Azabu-jūban, exit 4) For all the healthiness of Japanese food, there's often a dearth of greens on restaurant plates in Tokyo. Inspired, interestingly, by the greengrocers and farmers markets of NYC, this shop holds its own farmers market on Saturdays. Choose the airy interior or outdoor patio to enjoy seasonally changing vegetarian and vegan dishes. It has an English menu and English sign.

Gonpachi (Map pp140-1; ☎ 5771-0170; www.gonpachi.jp; 1-13-11 Nishi-Azabu, Minato-ku; lunch/dinner ¥2000/4000; 11.30am-5am; ; Hibiya, Toei Ōedo lines to Roppongi, exit 2) The Edo-village decor and urban buzz in the air makes Gonpachi a great place for celebratory dinners, but do you need a reason to thrill your palate with a dozen new-to-you Japanese morsels? Upstairs you can order everything on the menu (in English), plus sushi. Book ahead on its website; the rock-wall exterior should give it away, but there's also an English sign.

Pizzeria 1830 (Map pp140-1; ☎ 3402-1830; 9-6-28 Akasaka, Minato-ku; meals ¥2500; lunch & dinner; Chiyoda line to Nogizaka, exit 3) Pizza catering to Japanese tastes can be found all over Tokyo, but the real beast – with wood-fired crust hand-tossed by an Italian *pizzaiolo* – is more elusive. Find the real Neapolitan deal at 1830. Other treats, such as tender gnocchi, melt-in-your-mouth tiramisu and a strong wine list also await. There's an English menu and signage.

Pintokona (Map pp140-1; ☎ 5771-1133; B2 fl, Metrohat, Roppongi Hills, 6-4-1 Roppongi, Minato-ku; meals ¥2500; 11am-11pm; Hibiya, Toei Ōedo lines to Roppongi, exits 1c & 3) Taking its name from a kabuki term, this *kaiten-sushi* at Roppongi Hills plays up the kabuki aesthetic and kicks the conveyor-belt standards up a notch. Accordingly, the prices are slightly higher, but it's good-quality stuff with hi-tech touches like microchipped dishes that signal when sushi has been in rotation for too long (30 minutes). There's an English menu and sign.

L'Atelier de Joël Robuchon (Map pp140-1; ☎ 5772-7500; 2nd fl, Hillside, Roppongi Hills, 6-10-1 Roppongi, Minato-ku; lunch/dinner ¥5000/15,000; lunch & dinner; Hibiya, Toei Ōedo lines to Roppongi, exits 1c & 3) Another two-star Michelin standout, L'Atelier is an upscale French diner whose main counter is fashioned after a sushi bar. Sip on wine or a cocktail from the well-rounded list as you watch the chefs, clad in black, working their magic in the open kitchen. The divine fusion cuisine combines Japanese, French and Spanish elements with refined style, and is best sampled in one of the tasting menus. The menu is in French and Japanese, but the servers speak English.

Seryna (Map pp140-1 ☎ 3402-1051; www.seryna.co.jp; 3-12-2 Roppongi, Minato-ku; lunch/dinner ¥6000/15,000; noon-11.30pm Mon-Fri, to 10.30pm Sat & Sun; Hibiya, Toei Ōedo lines to Roppongi, exits 3 & 5) Seryna is the go-to stalwart for those wishing to try Kōbe *(wa-gyū)* beef. With several eateries under its roof, you can try shabu-shabu and sukiyaki, or opt for a slab of steak and *teppanyaki* (table-top grilling). The restaurant surrounds a pretty rock garden. There's an English sign and menu.

Inakaya (Map pp140-1; ☎ 3408-5040; www.roppongiinakaya.jp; 5-3-4 Roppongi, Minato-ku; meals from ¥10,000; dinner; Hibiya, Toei Ōedo lines to Roppongi, exits 2 & 3) Once you're bombarded with greetings at the door, the action doesn't stop at this old-guard *robatayaki* (rustic bar-restaurant serving charcoal-grilled food that goes beautifully with booze; literally 'hearthside cooking'). Point at what you'd like to eat (there's no English menu, though prices are listed on the website) and it will be grilled for you. It's boisterous and joyous – the attitude one must have when the bill arrives.

Fukuzushi (Map pp140-1; ☎ 3402-4116; 5-7-8 Roppongi, Minato-ku; meals around ¥10,000; lunch & dinner Mon-Sat; Hibiya, Toei Ōedo lines to Roppongi, exits 3 & 5) This is one of the best, most accessible sushi bars in Roppongi, with an upscale atmosphere that's decidedly more relaxed than more traditional places in Ginza. The fish here is fresh, the portions are large and there are cocktails to boot. It's in the alley beyond the Hard Rock Café, and has an English picture menu and English sign.

Akasaka 赤坂

Along with nearby Roppongi, Akasaka is one of Tokyo's more cosmopolitan neighbourhoods. While most of the evening action shuts down on the early side, a stroll through the narrow streets just west of Akasaka-mitsuke subway station will turn up a number of good lunch bargains.

Jangara Rāmen (Map pp140-1; ☎ 3595-2130; 2-12-8 Nagatachō, Minato-ku; meals from ¥580; 11am-2am, to 3.30am Fri, to 1am Sun; Chiyoda line to Akasaka, exit 2) Near the entrance to Hie-jinja, colourful

Jangara is a popular place for a great, inexpensive bowl of *rāmen*. Live a little and order the *zenbu-iri rāmen* (all-in *rāmen;* ¥1000) – it comes topped with hard-boiled egg, slices of pork and fish cake (among other goodies). There's no English menu.

Moti (Map pp140-1; ☎ 3582-3620; 2nd fl, 3-8-8 Akasaka, Minato-ku; lunch/dinner ¥800/2000; 11.30am-11pm; V; Ginza, Marunouchi lines to Akasaka-mitsuke, Belle Vie exit) Moti, probably Tokyo's most popular chain of Indian restaurants, has two branches in Akasaka, each just a few minutes' walk from Akasaka or Akasaka-mitsuke subway stations. Both are cosy and friendly, serving inexpensive and tasty Indian food. It has English signs and menus.

Kushinobō (Map pp140-1; ☎ 3581-5056; 3rd fl, Akasaka Tōkyū Plaza, 2-14-3 Nagatachō, Minato-ku; lunch/dinner from ¥1050/2100; lunch & dinner Mon-Fri, dinner Sat & Sun; Ginza, Marunouchi lines to Akasaka-mitsuke, Belle Vie exit) Sometimes it's necessary to give in to those dark cravings for something deep fried, and because these lunches are fairly inexpensive, you can at least console yourself with your budgetary virtue. Come to Kushinobō at times like these for *kushiage* (skewers of deep-fried meat, seafood and vegetables). There's an English menu and sign here.

Umaya (Map pp140-1; ☎ 6229-1661; 4-2-32 Akasaka, Minato-ku; lunch/dinner from ¥1100/3000; lunch & dinner Mon-Sat; Ginza, Marunouchi lines to Akasaka-mitsuke, Belle Vie exit) This lovely, traditionally styled restaurant serves a variety of Japanese dishes, incorporating free-range chicken and house-made tofu. There's no lunch menu in English, but servers can explain the seasonally changing *teishoku*. To find it from Hitotsugi-dōri, head for Akasaka-fudōson-jinja but turn left just inside the shrine gate. A small path leads under another small gate to the restaurant.

Sunaba (Map pp140-1; ☎ 3583-7670; 6-3-5 Akasaka, Minato-ku; meals ¥1200; 11am-7.30pm Mon-Fri, to 7pm Sat; Chiyoda line to Akasaka, exit 6) Sunaba has some of the city's finest buckwheat noodles. It invented tempura *soba* (¥1550), and serves it in an exquisite, smoky *tsuyu* (dipping sauce). It's next to the Kokusai Shin-Akasaka building, and it has a sister shop in Nihombashi. There's a limited picture menu in English.

Asterix (Map pp140-1; ☎ 5561-0980; B1 fl, 6-3-16 Akasaka, Minato-ku; lunch/dinner from ¥1500/3000; lunch & dinner Mon-Sat; Chiyoda line to Akasaka, exit 7) A French lunch at Asterix is a smashing deal. But dinner has its own merits – not as rushed, so you can linger over your wine. Portions are large but the dining room is tiny, so reservations are advised. The menu is in French (as is the sign); the server can translate into English if necessary.

Daidaiya (Map pp140-1; ☎ 3588-5087; 9th fl, Belle Vie, 3-1-6 Akasaka, Minato-ku; lunch/dinner ¥1500/6000; 11.30am-2.30pm & 5pm-midnight Mon-Fri, 5-11pm Sat & Sun; Ginza, Marunouchi lines to Akasaka-mitsuke, Belle Vie exit) The dark, modern decor of this fusion *izakaya* could hint at pretentious drama, but you'll soon see that the mood is fun and festive. Mixing up salmon roe and pine nuts, balsamic vinegar and sea urchin, the menu uses seasonal ingredients to artistic and delicious effect – and the backdrop adds to the flavour. There's an English menu.

Sushi-sei (Map pp140-1; ☎ 3582-9503; 3-11-14 Akasaka, Minato-ku; lunch/dinner ¥1700/4500; 11.30am-2pm & 5-10.30pm Mon-Fri, 11.45am-2pm & 4.30-10pm Sat; Ginza, Marunouchi lines to Akasaka-mitsuke, Belle Vie exit) This branch of the famous Tsukiji sushi chain won't disappoint; with its reputation, you can be sure you're eating some of the freshest fish around. Choose from a picture menu or try a reasonably-priced sushi set (the *nigiri omakase* is ¥2625). The low-profile shop is set back slightly from the street and there's no English sign.

Kikunoi (Map pp140-1; ☎ 3568-6055; 6-13-8 Akasaka, Minato-ku; dinners from ¥20,000; dinner Mon-Sat; Chiyoda line to Akasaka, exit 6) This Kyoto-based *kaiseki* restaurant has built its reputation over three generations, and its fame has expanded to international recognition after being awarded with two Michelin stars in 2008. Exquisitely prepared seasonal dishes are as beautiful as they are delicious. The restaurant's Chef Murata has also written a book on *kaiseki*, and the staff helpfully use the book to explain the dishes you are served. There's no English menu, and reservations are essential.

Odaiba お台場

Odaiba makes a beautiful backdrop for enjoying a romantic meal, as most of the restaurants have good views of Tokyo Bay.

Khazana (Map p133; ☎ 3359-6551; 5th fl, Decks Tokyo Beach, 1-6-1 Daiba, Minato-ku; lunch/dinner ¥1000/2000; 11am-11pm; V; Yurikamome line to Odaiba Kaihin-kōen, main exit) Khazana's Odaiba outpost is a welcoming perch for taking in the bay views and tucking into the eight-dish Rainbow special (¥3000). The staff are warm and the environment pleasantly laid-back. It has an English restaurant and sign.

Kua 'Aina (Map p133; ☎ 3599-2800; 4th fl, Aqua City, 1-7-1 Daiba, Minato-ku; meals ¥1400; ☒; 11am-11pm; Yurikamome line to Daiba, main exit) A good burger is hard to find (in Tokyo). What a welcome sight, then, to find a branch of this Hawaiian chain, which serves fat (one-third to half-pound) burgers with avocado or bacon. On the side you can also nosh on American sides like fries and onion rings, and wash it all down with an imported Kona beer. There are other branches around Tokyo, all with English signage and menus.

Tsukiji Tama Sushi (Map p133; ☎ 3599-6556; 5th fl, Decks Tokyo Beach, 1-6-1 Daiba, Minato-ku; meals ¥2000-4000; 🕑 11am-11pm; 🚉 Yurikamome line to Odaiba Kaihin-kōen, main exit) Settle yourself near the windows and sip from a huge, earthy cup of green tea while you wait for your sushi, which will come immaculately presented and perfectly fresh. It has an English menu and also offers an all-you-can-eat sushi special (men/women ¥3675/3045).

For fun – and a little dim sum (yum cha) – check out the array of Hong Kong–style eateries at **Daiba Little Hong Kong** (Map p133; www.odaiba-decks.com, in Japanese; 6th & 7th fl, 1-6-1 Daiba, Minato-ku; 🕑 breakfast, lunch & dinner; 🚉 Yurikamome line to Odaiba Kaihin-kōen, main exit). *Rāmen* lovers will want to check out the **Rāmen Stadium** (Map p133; 5th fl, Aqua City, 1-7-1 Daiba, Minato-ku; 🕑 11am-11pm; 🚉 Yurikamome line to Daiba, main exit).

DRINKING

Bar and club life being what it is, the venue of the moment might be passé come tomorrow morning. The following is a rundown on bars and clubs that have shown some staying power and were going strong at the time of writing. For up-to-the-minute listings, check the websites noted on p124.

For a true Japanese drinking experience, round up a few people and check out an *izakaya;* chains like **Tsubohachi** (Map p134; ☎ 3464-5681; B1 fl, 33-1 Udagawachō, Shibuya-ku; meals ¥3500; 🕑 5pm-midnight Sun-Thu, to 3am Fri & Sat; 🚉 JR Yamanote line to Shibuya, Hachikō exit) have branches all over Tokyo and huge picture menus to choose what to eat with your *nama-biiru* (draught beer). During the summer, many of the large department stores like Keiō (p189) in Shinjuku or Matsuya (p189) in Ginza open up their rooftop beer gardens, a treat on hot summer evenings. Join the salarymen after work and hoist a few on these open-air terraces.

And of course, most high-rise hotels have bars with stupendous views over the city. Try the New York Bar at the Park Hyatt (p168), the Bello Visto at the Cerulean Tower Tōkyū Hotel (p168), or Lobby Bar at the Ritz-Carlton (see the boxed text, p170).

Ginza & Shiodome 銀座・汐留

Business folk meet for after-work drinks at local *izakaya* and cement collegial relationships at fancy lounges in these neighbourhoods. Though not a party zone, there are some nice places for a drink or two.

300 Bar (Map p138; ☎ 3571-8300; www.300bar-8chome.com; B1 fl, No 2 Column Bldg, 8-3-12 Ginza, Chūō-ku; 🕑 5pm-2am Mon-Sat, 5-11pm Sun; 🚉 JR Yamanote line to Shimbashi, Ginza exit) One of the few places in Ginza that can truthfully say it offers a bargain, this bar charges ¥300 for every drink or snack (tax not included). There's no cover at this friendly standing bar.

Aux Amis des Vins (Map p138; ☎ 3567-4120; www.auxamis.com/desvins, in Japanese; 2-5-6 Ginza, Chūō-ku; 🕑 5.30pm-2am Mon-Fri, noon-midnight Sat; 🚉 Yūrakuchō line to Ginza itchōme, exits 5 & 8) Both the informal indoor and a small outdoor seating area at this wine bar feel welcoming in all seasons. A solid selection of mostly French wines comes by the glass (¥800) or by the bottle. You can also order small plates or full prix-fixe dinners.

Ueno & Asakusa 上野 浅草

Yawn – definitely not the neighbourhoods for a wild night out. But if you're in Asakusa, try the beer halls in the Asahi Breweries complex (look up and follow the Flamme D'Or – aka the 'Golden Turd' – to the east side of the Sumida-gawa).

Kamiya Bar (Map pp146-7; ☎ 3841-5400; 1-1-1 Asakusa, Taitō-ku; 🕑 11.30am-10pm Wed-Mon; 🚉 Ginza, Toei Asakusa lines to Asakusa, exits 3 & A5) Spend an evening at this Shitamachi bar, which opened in 1880 and is said to be the oldest Western-style bar in Japan. There's a smoky beer hall on the ground floor, where you order and pay for beer and food as you enter.

Warrior Celt (Map pp146-7; ☎ 3836-8588; www.warriorcelt.com; 3rd fl, Ito Bldg, 6-9-22 Ueno, Taitō-ku; 🕑 5pm-5am Tue-Sat, to midnight Sun & Mon; 🚉 JR Yamanote line to Ueno, south central exit) If you do find yourself hanging around old Shitamachi at night, head to this pub in Ueno, where drinks are only ¥600 from 5pm to 7pm. It's a fun, friendly place with a good selection of English and Irish brews, as well as free live music several nights a week.

Shinjuku 新宿

Gaudy Shinjuku is awash with nightspots of every shape and size, many of which fall into the sordid category and don't cater to foreigners. That said, there's still plenty to do here at night if you have a high tolerance for neon and blitzed salarymen.

One of the city's most interesting night zones, the Golden Gai, is here in Shinjuku. Even if you don't feel like a drink, take an evening stroll through this maze of tightly packed little establishments, just to soak in the low-slung moodiness – the whole place seems suspended in a time warp. Many of these miniscule bars do not welcome *gaijin* and/or non-Japanese speakers and may charge you a hefty cover for entering, but the first three establishments listed here are friendly to strangers. An easy way to get there is to find Hanazono-jinja (p154) and then walk around to the steps at the back of the shrine, which lead right into the Golden Gai.

Albatross (Map p131; ☎ 3342-5758; www.alba-s.com, 1-2-11 Nishi-Shinjuku, Shinjuku-ku; 🕒 5pm-2am; 🚇 Marunouchi, Toei Shinjuku lines to Shinjuku-sanchōme, exit B5) Though it has three floors, this tiny, atmospheric bar takes up little space in Omoide-yokochō (p174). Don't be daunted if it looks full; order a drink on the 1st floor and keep heading upward to see if there's space on the 3rd-floor terrace.

Bar Plastic Model (Map p131; ☎ 5273-8441; www.plastic-model.net, in Japanese; 1-1-10 Kabukichō, Shinjuku-ku; admission ¥700; 🕒 8pm-5am Mon-Sat, to 2am Sun; 🚇 Marunouchi, Toei Shinjuku lines to Shinjuku-sanchōme, exit B5) There's a new generation of creative bar owners converting old Golden Gai bars into incarnations of their own visions. This is one such concoction, decorated with tchotchkes c 1980, and sometimes with a DJ spinning beats.

Bon's (Map p131; ☎ 3209-6334; 1-1-10 Kabukichō, Shinjuku-ku; admission ¥900; 🕒 7pm-5am; 🚇 Marunouchi, Toei Shinjuku lines to Shinjuku-sanchōme, exit B5) Drinks start at ¥700 at this friendly spot in the Golden Gai. Look for its corner location with 'Old Fashioned American Style Pub' painted across its exterior wall.

La Jetée (Map p131; ☎ 3208-9645; 1-1-8 Kabukichō, Shinjuku-ku; admission ¥700; 🕒 7pm-late Mon-Sat; 🚇 Marunouchi, Toei Shinjuku lines to Shinjuku-sanchōme, exit B5) A favourite among cineastes (and run by one), this tidy little haven is the namesake for a film much admired by its French-speaking proprietor and a good introduction to these alleys.

Zoetrope (Map p131; ☎ 3363-0162; http://homepage2.nifty.com/zoetrope; 3rd fl, Gaia Bldg, 7-10-14 Nishi-Shinjuku, Shinjuku-ku; 🕒 7pm-4am Mon-Sat; 🚇 Toei Ōedo line to Shinjuku-nishiguchi, exit D5) Spend a sociable, relaxed evening at this cosy bar, which features more than 300 kinds of Japanese whisky and screens silent films on the wall. An English menu will help you taste your way around.

Shibuya & Harajuku 原宿・渋谷

These adjoining areas are a good option when the Roppongi crush is too much to bear. Harajuku and Aoyama are more about cafe culture, and you can spend an evening drinking beer and wine in them rather than mashing yourself into a smoky basement bar.

Belgo (Map p134; ☎ 3409-4442; B1 fl, 3-18-7 Shibuya, Shibuya-ku; 🕒 5.30pm-2am, to 4.30am Fri, 4pm-midnight Sun) Pouring over 100 kinds of beer, including Guinness and Chimay on draught, Belgo rounds out its liquid offerings with quality Euro-style pub fare like classic fish and chips.

Den Aquaroom (Map p134; ☎ 5778-2090; B1 fl, 5-13-3 Minami-Aoyama, Minato-ku; admission ¥700; 🕒 6pm-2am Mon-Sat, 6-11pm Sun; 🚇 Chiyoda, Ginza, Hanzōmon lines to Omote-sandō, exit B1) Darting fish within the walls of back-lit, blue aquariums make a visual counterpoint to the bop of jazz basslines. Even prettier than the dark decor is the chic clientele floating around here.

Insomnia 2 (Map p134; ☎ 3476-2735; B1 fl, 26-5 Udagawachō, Shibuya-ku; 🕒 6pm-5am; 🚇 JR Yamanote line to Shibuya, Hachikō exit) Insomnia is that rare Shibuya find: a bar for grown-ups. Good food (and the kitchen's open late), low music and an inviting red interior make it the kind of place to come when you want to hear your conversation.

Las Chicas (Map p134; ☎ 3407-6865; www.vision.co.jp/aoyama/index.html; 5-47-6 Jingūmae, Shibuya-ku; 🕒 11.30am-11pm Mon-Thu, 11am-11.30pm Fri & Sat, 11am-11pm Sun; ⊠; 🚇 Chiyoda, Ginza, Hanzōmon lines to Omote-sandō, exit B2) A great place to plant yourself for the night (see p176).

Tokyo Apartment Café (Map p134; ☎ 3401-4101; 1-11-11 Jingūmae, Shibuya-ku; 🕒 11-4am; 🚇 Chiyoda line to Meiji-jingūmae, exit 5 or JR Yamanote line to Harajuku, Omote-sandō exit) The Apartment Café is a pleasant afternoon refuge for spring rolls, a glass of wine or even Fruits Conscious Frozen. But in the evenings it transforms into a cocktail lounge, good for chilling with the locals.

Ebisu & Daikanyama 恵比寿・代官山

These two neighbourhoods are excellent choices for a night out in Tokyo, striking the balance between hip and unpretentious.

Enjoy! House (Map p136; ☎ 5489-1591; 2nd fl, Kokuto Bldg, 2-9-9 Ebisu-Nishi, Shibuya-ku; 🕒 1pm-2am Tue, Thu & Sun, to 4am Fri & Sat, closed Mon & 1st Sun each month; 🚇 JR Yamanote line to Ebisu, west exit) A multilayered world of sparkly, '70s retro funkiness awaits inside the gleefully named Enjoy! House. The free-spirited dude who runs this joint will elevate your mood.

Frames (Map p136; ☎ 5784-3384; 1st fl, Hikawa Bldg, 2-11 Sarugakuchō, Shibuya-ku; 11.30am-3am Sun-Thu, to 5am Fri & Sat; Tōkyū Tōyoko to Daikanyama, main exit, or JR Yamanote line to Shibuya, south exit) Kick back with a glass of wine in this airy Daikanyama bar-restaurant. It's a dog-friendly establishment, so the pup-watching is as interesting as the human kind.

Munch-ya (Map p136; ☎ 5722-1333; 1-10-23 Naka-Meguro, Meguro-ku; noon-3pm & 6pm-4am Mon-Fri, 6pm-4am Sat & Sun; Hibiya line to Naka-Meguro) This casual little canal-side bar in Naka-Meguro serves beer and wine, as well as Japanese small plates, for around ¥500 a pop. From the exit, turn right on Yamate-dōri, make a left on Komazawa-dōri and then a right along the cafe pathway next to the river.

What the Dickens (Map p136; ☎ 3780-2099; www.whatthedickens.jp; 4th fl, Roob 6 Bldg, 1-13-3 Ebisu-Nishi, Shibuya-ku; 5pm-late Tue-Sat, to midnight Sun; JR Yamanote line to Ebisu, west exit) Live music, British beers, pub grub and a good time in Ebisu – a combo that works, as the happy crowd will attest. Live music, spanning a variety of genres, happens almost every night.

Roppongi 六本木

Roppongi is a floating entity apart from Japan – it's like Mardi Gras in Asia, where *gaijin* and locals mix it up and boozily schmooze until the first trains at dawn. Tokyo nightlife is most intensely concentrated here. There are loads of shot bars and cheap dives in which to get wasted, and those will be obvious to you when you emerge at Roppongi Crossing. But plenty of bars here offer style as well as stiff drinks.

A971 (Map pp140-1; ☎ 5413-3210; www.a971.com; Tokyo Midtown, 9-7-2 Roppongi, Minato-ku; 10-5am Mon-Thu, to 5am Fri & Sat, to midnight Sun; Hibiya, Toei Ōedo lines to Roppongi, exits 4a & 8) The ¥500 beers are a big draw to this corner bar at Tokyo Midtown, but the outdoor terrace is also enticing. A good mix of locals and *gaijin* hang out here.

Agave (Map pp140-1; ☎ 3497-0229; B1 fl, 7-15-10 Roppongi, Minato-ku; 6.30pm-2am Mon-Thu, to 4am Fri & Sat; Hibiya, Toei Ōedo lines to Roppongi, exit 2) This amiable spot, all dolled up in warm Mexican hues and design, is more about savouring the subtleties of its 400-plus types of tequila rather than tossing back shots of Cuervo. Walking west from Roppongi Crossing, find it on the small alley on the north side of the street.

Heartland (Map pp140-1; ☎ 5772-7600; www.heartland.jp; 1st fl, West Walk, Roppongi Hills, 6-10-1 Roppongi, Minato-ku; 5pm-4am; Hibiya, Toei Ōedo lines to Roppongi, exits 1c & 3) At the foot of Roppongi Hills and thus removed from the sloshed amateurs around Roppongi Crossing, Heartland is a good choice for starting your evening. Order a Heartland beer (¥500) and observe the foreign male and Japanese female social dynamic for a primer on Roppongi relations.

Mado Lounge (Map pp140-1; ☎ 3470-0052; www.ma-do.jp; 52nd fl, Mori Tower, Roppongi Hills, 6-10-1 Roppongi, Minato-ku; admission Sun-Thu ¥500, Fri & Sat ¥2000; 10am-11.30pm Sun-Thu, to 3am Fri & Sat; Hibiya, Toei Ōedo lines to Roppongi, exits 1c & 3) On the 52nd floor of Mori Tower, the views are indeed stunning from this very cool lounge. To get in, you must first pay admission to the Mori Art Museum (p157) and/or Tokyo City View (p157), so it's only worth the additional cover if you're here anyway.

Maduro (Map pp140-1; ☎ 4333-8888; 4th fl, Grand Hyatt Tokyo, 6-10-3 Roppongi, Minato-ku; admission around ¥1500; 6pm-2am Sun-Thu, to 3am Fri & Sat; Hibiya, Toei Ōedo lines to Roppongi, exits 1c & 3) Inside the labyrinthine Grand Hyatt Tokyo, this sleek, swanky lounge is a chic spot to kick off your evening with a champagne or scotch. There's live music nightly, but arrive before 9pm to avoid the cover.

Mogambo (Map pp140-1; ☎ 3403-4833; www.mogambo.net; 1st fl, Osawa Bldg, 6-1-7 Roppongi, Minato-ku; 6pm-6am Mon-Fri, 7pm-6am Sat; Hibiya, Toei Ōedo lines to Roppongi, exits 2 & 3) A small shot bar with a campy jungle theme, Mogambo attracts an international crowd with its long list of cocktails. It's on the southern side of Roppongi-dōri, a block south of Roppongi Crossing.

our pick **SuperDeluxe** (Map pp140-1; ☎ 5412 0515; www.super-deluxe.com; B1 fl, 3-1-25 Nishi-Azabu, Minato-ku; admission varies; 6pm-late Mon-Sat; Hibiya & Toei Ōedo lines to Roppongi, exits 1b & 3) Hard to categorise, easy to love, SuperDeluxe morphs from lounge to gallery to club to performance space from night to night. Check the website for current events to see what's on, but you're guaranteed to run into a fabulous mix of creative types from Tokyo and beyond.

ENTERTAINMENT

Tokyo is very much the centre of the Japanese arts world, with the best of everything. On the nightlife front, there are those who maintain that Osaka is more cutting edge, but then Osaka offers nowhere near the diversity of entertainment options available in Tokyo – from kabuki to avant-garde theatre, cinemas, live houses, pubs and bars. See p65 for more information on Japanese theatre.

Cinemas

Going to the cinema in Tokyo can be surprisingly expensive. You can save several hundred yen by buying discounted tickets at convenience stores, but most theatres offer steep discounts on admission (¥1000 rather than ¥1800, for example) on the first day of the month, and a similar 'ladies' day' discount on Wednesdays. Check the *Japan Times, Metropolis* or the *Tokyo Journal* to see what's playing while you're in town. Imported films are usually subtitled in Japanese, so the sound tends to be in the original language.

Cinema Rise (Map p134; ☎ 3464-0051; www.cinemarise.com, in Japanese; 13-17 Udagawachō, Shibuya-ku; 🚇 JR Yamanote line to Shibuya, Hachikō exit) Screening international indie cinema.

Shinjuku Piccadilly (Map p131; ☎ 5367-1144; www.shinjukupiccadilly.com, in Japanese; 3-15-15 Shinjuku, Shinjuku-ku; 🕑 10am-midnight; 🚇 Marunouchi & Toei Shinjuku lines to Shinjuku-sanchōme, exits B7 & B8) With more than 600 seats, including several two-person private viewing booths outfitted with surround sound and leather sofas (¥30,000 per screening).

Tōhō Cinemas Roppongi Hills (Map pp140-1; ☎ 5775-6090; 6-10-2 Roppongi, Minato-ku; adult ¥1800-3000, child ¥1000; 🕑 10am-midnight Sun-Wed, to 5am Thu-Sat; 🚇 Hibiya, Toei Ōedo lines to Roppongi, exit 3) Nine-screen mainstream multiplex with luxurious reclining seats and all-night weekend screenings.

Yebisu Garden Cinema (Map p136; ☎ 5420-6161; Yebisu Garden Pl, 4-20-2 Ebisu, Shibuya-ku; 🕑 10am-11pm; 🚇 JR Yamanote line to Ebisu, east exit to Skywalk) Screens mainstream and independent films. Tickets are numbered as they're sold and theatregoers are called in by number, preventing competition for seats.

Music

In Tokyo, you might have the luxury of seeing up-and-coming performers playing in intimate venues. Check the latest issue of *Metropolis* or *Tokyo Journal* or pick up some flyers at record shops (p191) in Shibuya to see who's playing around town. Ticket prices generally range from ¥5000 to ¥8000, depending on performer and venue.

DANCE CLUBS

You'll find the greatest concentration and diversity of clubs in Roppongi; if you can find a flyer at local record shops or on club websites, most clubs will knock ¥500 to ¥1000 off the cover. Cover charges usually include a drink or two. If IDs are required, the minimum age is usually 20.

Ageha (揚羽; off Map pp128-9; ☎ 5534-1515; www.ageha.com; 2-2-10 Shin-Kiba, Kōtō-ku; admission ¥3000-4000; 🕑 10pm-5am Tue-Sat; 🚇 Yūrakuchō line to Shin-Kiba, main exit) This ginormous club on the water rivals any you'd find in LA or Ibiza. Headliner international and Japanese DJs appear here, and counterbalancing the thumping beats are chillout rooms and a small pool area. Free shuttles (ID required) run every half-hour between the club and Shibuya station's east side bus terminal on Roppongi-dōri.

Air (Map p136; ☎ 5784-3386; www.air-tokyo.com; B1 & B2 fl, Hikawa Bldg, 2-11 Sarugakuchō, Shibuya-ku; admission ¥3000-4000; 🕑 10pm-5am, closed Tue, Wed & Sun; 🚇 Tōkyū Tōyoko to Daikanyama, main exit, or JR Yamanote line to Shibuya, south exit) DJs spin mostly house here, and the crowd tends to be happy and friendly – though not huge on dancing. You can find a decent map on its website. The entrance to the basement is inside Frames (p183). Bring your ID.

BuL-Let's (Map pp140-1; ☎ 3401-4844; www.bul-lets.com; B1 fl, Kasumi Bldg, 1-7-11 Nishi-Azabu, Minato-ku; admission from ¥1500; 🕑 from around 7pm; 🚇 Hibiya, Toei Ōedo lines to Roppongi, exit 2) This mellow basement space plays worldwide trance and ambient sounds for barefoot patrons. Beds and sofas furnish this carpeted club, but don't get the wrong idea – it's not all tranquillity and deadbeats.

our pick **Club 328** (Map pp140-1; ☎ 3401-4968; www.3-2-8.jp; B1 fl, Kotsu Anzen Center Bldg, 3-24-20 Nishi-Azabu, Minato-ku; admission ¥2000-2500; 🕑 8pm-5am; 🚇 Hibiya, Toei Ōedo lines to Roppongi, exits 1b & 3) DJs at San-ni-pa (Japanese for the numbers 3-2-8) spin a quality mix, from funk to reggae to R&B. With its refreshing un-Roppongi feel and a cool crowd of Japanese and *gaijin*, 328 is a good place to boogie 'til the break of dawn. Admission includes two drinks. It's on Roppongi-dōri just off Nishi-Azabu Crossing.

Club Asia (Map p134; ☎ 5458-2551; www.clubasia.co.jp, in Japanese; 1-8 Maruyamachō, Shibuya-ku; admission ¥2500; 🕑 5pm-5am; 🚇 JR Yamanote line to Shibuya, Hachikō exit) This massive techno-soul club is popular with those on the younger end of 20-something. Events here are usually jam-packed no matter what night it is. There's also an OK restaurant serving Southeast Asian food.

Harlem (Map p134; ☎ 3461-8806; www.harlem.co.jp; 2nd & 3rd fl, Dr Jeekahn's Bldg, 2-4 Maruyamachō, Shibuya-ku; admission ¥2000-3000; 🕑 10pm-5am Tue-Sat; 🚇 JR Yamanote line to Shibuya, Hachikō exit) Bust a few hip-hop moves with Tokyo B-boys and B-girls. Be aware that Harlem maintains a (questionable) policy of not admitting groups of foreign males, so guys, come with a girlfriend.

Muse (Map pp140-1; ☎ 5467-1188; www.muse-web.com; 4-1-1 Nishi-Azabu, Minato-ku; admission ¥3000; 🕑 9pm-late Sat & Tue-Thu, 8pm-late Fri, 7pm-late Sun & Mon; 🚇 Hibiya, Toei Ōedo lines to Roppongi, exits 1b & 3) With a friendly, international crowd, multilevel Muse has something for everyone – packed dance floor, several bar areas, cosy alcoves big enough for two – but also pool tables, darts and karaoke. Women usually don't pay a cover, which includes a drink or two. Near the Hobson's on the corner of Nishi-Azabu Crossing there's a neon 'Bar' sign marking the entrance.

New Lex-Edo (Map pp140-1; ☎ 3479-7477; www.newlex-edo.com; B1 fl, Gotō Bldg, 3-13-14 Roppongi, Minato-ku; admission women/men ¥3000/4000; 🕑 8pm-5am; 🚇 Hibiya, Toei Ōedo lines to Roppongi, exit 3) The Lex was one of Roppongi's first discos and recently had a facelift. It's still the place where visiting celebrities – who get in for free – end up, but even noncelebs get three free drinks.

Ruby Room (Map p134; ☎ 3780-3022; www.rubyroomtokyo.com; 2nd fl, Kasumi Bldg, 2-25-17 Dōgenzaka, Shibuya-ku; admission ¥2000; 🕑 9pm-late; 🚇 JR Yamanote line to Shibuya, Hachikō exit) This dark, sparkly cocktail lounge is on a hill behind the Shibuya 109 building. The Ruby Room hosts both DJed and live music, and is a fun place for older kids hanging in Shibuya. If you dine at Sonoma, the restaurant downstairs, you get in for free.

Salsa Sudada (Map pp140-1; ☎ 5474-8806; www.salsasudada.org; 3rd fl, La Palette Bldg, 7-13-8 Roppongi, Minato-ku; 🕑 6pm-6am; 🚇 Hibiya, Toei Ōedo lines to Roppongi, exit 3) Experienced salsa dancers can kick up their heels here for hours, while beginners can take lessons offered on Sunday nights. International dancers flock regularly to this place from Tokyo and beyond for salsa and merengue.

Womb (Map p134; ☎ 5459-0039; www.womb.co.jp; 2-16 Maruyamachō, Shibuya-ku; admission ¥1500-4000; 🕑 8pm-late; 🚇 JR Yamanote line to Shibuya, Hachikō exit) A perennial favourite, 'Oomu' (as pronounced in Japanese) has DJs spinning house, techno and drum 'n' bass, and the four floors get packed on weekends. Picture ID required at the door.

KARAOKE

Karaoke is ever popular in the land of its birth, and Tokyoites love belting out a few tunes at their local karaoke bars. There's no shortage of them in Tokyo, and most offer at least a limited selection of songs in English and even a few in Spanish, French and Chinese. Oh, by the way, it's not 'carry-okie' in this country, so watch your pronunciation if you're asking the way to 'kah-rah-oh-kay'.

Lovenet (Map pp140-1; ☎ 5771-5511; www.lovenet-jp.com; 3rd fl, Hotel Ibis, 7-14-4 Roppongi, Minato-ku; private ste ¥4000-60,000; 🕑 6pm-5am; 🚇 Hibiya, Toei Ōedo lines to Roppongi, exit 4a) If you're going for a more unique, upmarket experience, you can rent one of the gajillion-themed rooms at Lovenet – one even has a hot tub from which you can warble.

Smash Hits (Map pp140-1; ☎ 3444-0432; www.smashhits.jp; B1 fl, M2 Bldg, 5-2-26 Hiro-o, Shibuya-ku; admission ¥3500; 🕑 7pm-3am Mon-Sat; 🚇 Hibiya line to Hiro-o, exit B2) You're spoilt for choice at Smash Hits, where it has thousands of songs to choose from. There's no time limit, and entry includes two drinks.

LIVE MUSIC

Tokyo's homegrown live music scene has turned out some good live acts, often found playing around Shibuya and Ebisu. If you're willing to wander a bit farther, tiny bars and clubs in Shimo-Kitazawa and Kichijōji (see Off the Beaten Dōri, p159) often have live shows featuring local talent.

Cavern Club (Map pp140-1; ☎ 3405-5207; www.cavernclub.jp; 1st fl, Saito Bldg, 5-3-2 Roppongi, Minato-ku; admission women/men ¥1575/1890; 🕑 6pm-2.30am; 🚇 Hibiya, Toei Ōedo lines to Roppongi, exit 3) Eerily flawless renditions of Beatles covers have to be heard to be believed, sung by four Japanese mop-heads at this club named for the place the originals first appeared at in Liverpool. It's best to reserve a table.

Crocodile (Map p134; ☎ 3499-5205; B1 fl, New Sekiguchi Bldg, 6-18-8 Jingūmae, Shibuya-ku; admission from ¥2000; 🕑 6pm-2am; 🚇 Chiyoda line to Meiji-jingūmae, exit 4) Crocodile has live music seven nights a week, with enough room for dancing if the music moves you – though you may be the only one. Tunes cover the gamut from one night to night, be it jazz, reggae or rock and roll. Admission includes one drink. It's directly on Meiji-dōri.

Eggman (Map p134; ☎ 3496-1561; www.eggman.jp; 1-6-8 Jinnan, Shibuya-ku; admission ¥1000-3000; 🕑 6.30pm-late; 🚇 JR Yamanote line to Shibuya, Hachikō exit) Follow the spiral staircase down to this basement spot to hear blues, rock or hip-hop. A smaller venue compared with Shibuya's bigger clubs, Eggman features a good mixed bag of mostly local musicians.

La.mama (Map p134; ☎ 3464-0801; www.lamama.net; B1 fl, Primera Dōgenzaka Bldg, 1-15-3 Dōgenzaka, Shibuya-ku; admission from ¥2000; 🕑 6pm-late; 🚇 JR Yamanote line to Shibuya, Hachikō exit) For a dose of current local-centric music, this is a good bet for catching live, mainstream Japanese acts

GAY & LESBIAN TOKYO

Tokyo's gay and lesbian enclave is Shinjuku-nichōme, the area east of Shinjuku sanchōme station's C8 exit. There are lots of little bars here; the following venues have been around a while and are friendly. For more options, check out www.utopia-asia.com or www.fridae.com.

If you're in Tokyo during the summer, the **Tokyo International Lesbian & Gay Film Festival** (www.tokyo-lgff.org) hits screens in July.

Advocates Bar (Map p131; ☎ 3358-3988; 1st fl, 7th Tenka Bldg, 2-18-1 Shinjuku, Shinjuku-ku; 🕑 8pm-5am Mon-Sat, to 1am Sun; 🚇 Marunouchi, Toei Shinjuku lines to Shinjuku-sanchōme, exit C8) Advocates Bar is so small that as the crowd gets bigger during the course of an evening, it becomes more like a block party and takes to the streets. Family of all genders are welcome here.

Arty Farty (Map p131; ☎ 5362-9720; www.arty-farty.net; 2nd fl, 2-11-7 Shinjuku, Shinjuku-ku; 🕑 7pm-late Mon-Sat, 5pm-3am Sun; 🚇 Marunouchi, Toei Shinjuku lines to Shinjuku-sanchōme, exit C8) Arty Farty is a long-standing place to meet people, with fabulous all-you-can-drink specials and a mixed crowd. It's a good place to start your evening and find out about the area's other hot spots.

Kinswomyn (Map p131; ☎ 3354-8720; 3rd fl, 2-15-10 Shinjuku, Shinjuku-ku; 🕑 8pm-4am Wed-Mon; 🚇 Marunouchi, Toei Shinjuku lines to Shinjuku-sanchōme, exit C8) Another well-established bar, Kinswomyn is a welcoming, women-only spot for Japanese and foreign women alike. The bar mistress Tara is friendly, as are the ladies hanging out here.

who've arrived or are rocking their way up. The room is fairly spacious, and even when the place gets crowded you'll never be far from the stage.

Loft (Map p131; ☎ 5272-0382; www.loft-prj.co.jp/LOFT/index.html; B2 fl, Tatehana Bldg, 1-12-9 Kabukichō, Shinjuku-ku; admission from ¥2500; 🕑 5pm-late; 🚇 JR Yamanote line to Shinjuku, east exit) Had they been Japanese, the Rolling Stones would have played here long before they cut their first single. This Shinjuku institution is smoky, loud and lots of fun on a good night. Head into Kabukichō and find Loft a block east of the Koma Theater complex.

These bigger clubs draw brighter stars, so you'll need to book tickets, rather than turn up in the hope of getting in on the night of a show:

Club Quattro (Map p134; ☎ 3477-8750; www.clubquattro.com; 4th & 5th fl, Parco Quattro Bldg, 32-13 Udagawachō, Shibuya-ku; admission from ¥3500; 🕑 from 6pm; 🚇 JR Yamanote line to Shibuya, Hachikō exit)

Liquid Room (Map p136; ☎ 5464-0800; www.liquidroom.net; 3-16-6 Higashi, Shibuya-ku; admission from ¥3000; 🕑 7pm-late; 🚇 JR Yamanote line to Ebisu, east exit)

O-East (Map p134; ☎ 5458-4681; www.shibuya-o.com, in Japanese; 2-14-8 Dōgenzaka, Shibuya-ku; admission from ¥2500; 🕑 from 6pm; 🚇 JR Yamanote line to Shibuya, Hachikō exit)

O-West (Map p134; ☎ 5784-7088; www.shibuya-o.com, in Japanese; 2-3 Maruyamachō, Shibuya-ku; admission from ¥2500; 🕑 from 5.30pm; 🚇 JR Yamanote line to Shibuya, Hachikō exit)

JAZZ

People in this city take their jazz seriously. For listings of performances, check the latest issue of *Tokyo Journal* or *Metropolis*.

Blue Note Tokyo (Map pp140-1; ☎ 5485-0088; www.bluenote.co.jp; Raika Bldg, 6-3-16 Minami-Aoyama, Minato-ku; admission ¥6000-10,000; 🕑 5.30pm-1am Mon-Sat, 5pm-1.30am Sun; 🚇 Chiyoda, Ginza, Hanzōmon lines to Omote-sandō, exit B3) Tokyo's marquee jazz venue in Minami-Aoyama allows aficionados the opportunity to listen up close and personal to greats like Chick Corea and Maceo Parker. You can print out an English map from its website.

JZ Brat (Map p134; ☎ 5728-0168; www.jzbrat.com, in Japanese; 2nd fl, Cerulean Tower Tōkyū Hotel, 26-1 Sakuragaokachō, Shibuya-ku; admission varies; 🕑 from 6pm Mon-Sat; 🚇 JR Yamanote line to Shibuya, south exit) This sleek club is an intimate venue with a sophisticated vibe, hosting performances not limited solely to jazz. Touring performers of folk and electronica also pass through; check local listings to find out what's on.

our pick **STB 139** (Sweet Basil; Map pp140-1; ☎ 5474-1395; http://stb139.co.jp; 6-7-11 Roppongi, Minato-ku; admission ¥3000-7000; 🕑 6-11pm Mon-Sat; 🚇 Hibiya, Toei Ōedo lines to Roppongi, exit 3) This is a large, comfortable space that draws big-name domestic and international acts, with performances covering the gamut of jazz genres. Call for reservations between 11am and 8pm.

Shinjuku Pit Inn (Map p131; ☎ 3354-2024; www.pit-inn.com; B1 fl, Accord Shinjuku Bldg, 2-12-4 Shinjuku, Shinjuku-ku; admission ¥1300-4000; 🕑 from 2pm; 🚇 Marunouchi, Toei Shinjuku lines to Shinjuku-sanchōme, exit C8) This club has been going strong for around 40 years now. It's an intimate space hosting day and evening performances by mostly Japanese jazz musicians.

Theatre & Dance

BUNRAKU

Kokuritsu Gekijō (National Theatre; Map pp142-3; ☎ 3230-3000; www.ntj.jac.go.jp/english/index.html; 4-1 Hayabusachō, Chiyoda-ku; admission ¥1500-12,000; reservations 10am-6pm; Namboku, Yūrakuchō lines to Nagatachō, exit 4) Performances are staged several times a year here, even though Osaka is the home of *bunraku* (classical puppet theatre). Check the English-language website for a performance schedule.

DANCE

Bunkamura Theatre Cocoon (Map p134; ☎ 3477-9111; www.bunkamura.co.jp/english; 2-24-1 Dōgenzaka, Shibuya-ku; tickets from ¥4000; 10am-7pm Sun-Thu, to 9pm Fri & Sat; JR Yamanote line to Shibuya, Hachikō exit) This behemoth of an arts centre houses a cinema, theatre, concert hall and art gallery. Theatre Cocoon hosts innovative, offbeat and traditional musical and theatrical performances; check the website for information on current productions.

Session House (Map pp128-9; ☎ 3266-0461; 158 Yaraichō, Shinjuku-ku; admission varies; performances 7pm; Tōzai line to Kagurazaka, exit 1) Dance aficionados consider Session House one of the best traditional, folk and modern dance spaces in the city. The theatre seats only 100 people, ensuring an intimate and memorable performance. Exit right from Kagurazaka Station, make a right into the first narrow alley, and turn left where it dead-ends. Session House will be a few metres on your right.

KABUKI

Kabuki-za (Map p138; ☎ 3541-3131; www.shochiku.co.jp/play/kabukiza/theater/index.html; 4-12-5 Ginza, Chūō-ku; admission ¥2500-17,000; 11am-9pm; Hibiya, Toei Asakusa lines to Higashi-Ginza, exit 3) If you visit before April 2010, take in a last kabuki performance at historic Kabuki-za before the theatre is demolished (see p150). Performances and times vary from month to month, so consult the website or contact the theatre directly for program information. Audio guides providing commentary in English are available for ¥650 plus a ¥1000 deposit. Kabuki performances can be quite a marathon, lasting from four to five hours. If you're not up to it, you can get tickets for the 4th floor from ¥600 to ¥1000 and watch only part of the show (ask for *hitomakumi*; one act, audio guides not available). Tickets can be bought on the day of the performance; there are generally two performances, starting at around 11am and 4pm.

Kokuritsu Gekijō (left), Japan's national theatre, also has kabuki performances, with a range of seat prices. Audio guides are available. Check with the theatre for performance times.

NŌ

Nō (classical stylised Japanese dance-drama) performances are held at various locations around Tokyo. Tickets cost between ¥2100 and ¥15,000, and it's best to get them at the theatre itself. Check with the TIC or the appropriate theatre for performance information.

Kanze Nō-gakudō (Map p134; ☎ 3469-5241; www.kanze.net, in Japanese; 1-16-4 Shōtō, Shibuya-ku; tickets from ¥3000; JR Yamanote line to Shibuya, Hachikō exit) One of the oldest and most highly respected schools of *nō* in Tokyo, Kanze Nō-gakudō is about a 15-minute walk west from Shibuya station.

Kokuritsu Nō-gakudō (National Nō Theatre; Map p134; ☎ 3423-1331; www.ntj.jac.go.jp/nou/index.html, in Japanese; 4-18-1 Sendagaya, Shibuya-ku; admission ¥2800-5600; reservations 10am-6pm; JR Chūō, Sōbu lines to Sendagaya, main exit) The National Nō Theatre stages its own productions (for which written English synopses are provided), but also hosts privately sponsored *nō* performances. To get there, exit Sendagaya station with Shinjuku to your left and follow the road that hugs the railway tracks. The theatre is on the left.

TAKARAZUKA GEKIJŌ

Kabuki kicked women out of the tradition, but the ladies have taken the ball and run with it at the **Takarazuka Gekijō** (Takarazuka Revue; Map p138; ☎ 5251-2001; http://kageki.hankyu.co.jp/english; 1-1-3 Yūrakuchō, Chiyoda-ku; admission ¥3500-10,000; vary; Chiyoda, Hibiya, Toei Mita lines to Hibiya, exits A5 & A13), founded in 1913. The extensively trained, all-female cast puts on an equally grand – if drastically different – show, with women in drag playing the male roles. These musical productions tend toward the soap-operatic and attract a disproportionate percentage of swooning female fans.

Tea Ceremonies

A few hotels in Tokyo hold tea ceremonies that you can see and occasionally participate in for a fee. Call ahead to make reservations.

Hotel New Ōtani (Map pp140-1; ☎ 3265-1111; 4-1 Kioi-chō, Chiyoda-ku; tea ceremony ¥1050; ceremonies 11am & 1pm Thu-Sat; Ginza & Marunouchi lines to Akasakamitsuke, Belle Vie exit or Hanzōmon & Yūrakuchō lines to Nagatachō, exit 7)

Hotel Ōkura (Map pp140-1; ☎ 3582-0111; www.okura.com/tokyo; 2-10-4 Toranomon, Minato-ku; tea ceremony ¥1050; 11am-4pm Mon-Sat; Ginza line to Tameike-sannō, exit 13) See also p169.

Imperial Hotel (Map p138; ☎ 3504-1111; www.imperialhotel.co.jp; 1-1-1 Uchisaiwaichō, Chiyoda-ku; tea ceremony ¥1500; 10am-4pm Mon-Sat; Chiyoda, Hibiya, Toei Mita lines to Hibiya, exit A13) See also p164.

Sports

BASEBALL

…and Japan's national love affair with baseball continues. Of the two professional leagues – Central and Pacific – several teams are based in the Tokyo area. Within Tokyo, the Yomiuri Giants and Yakult Swallows are crosstown rivals. Going to a ballgame is a uniquely Japanese spectator-sport experience, what with its teams of cheerleading fans, beer girls with kegs strapped to their backs and the polite crowd bursting into song – big fun. Baseball season runs from April through the end of October. Check the *Japan Times* to see who's playing while you're in town. The cheapest unreserved outfield seats start at ¥1000.

Tokyo Dome (Big Egg; Map pp142-3; ☎ 5800-9999; 1-3-61 Kōraku, Bunkyō-ku; JR Chūō, Sōbu lines to Suidobashi, west exit or Marunouchi line to Kōrakuen, Kōrakuen exit) Home to Japan's favourite baseball team, the Yomiuri Giants, Tokyo Dome is next to Kōrakuen Amusement Park (p159). Though it's a covered dome, a little dirigible camera motors around inside.

Jingū Kyūjo (Jingū Baseball Stadium; Map p134; ☎ 3404-8999; 13 Kasumigaoka, Shinjuku-ku; Ginza line to Gaienmae, north exit) Jingū Baseball Stadium was originally built to host the 1964 Olympics, and is where the Yakult Swallows are based.

SUMŌ

Travellers who visit Tokyo in January, May or September should not miss their chance to attend a Grand Tournament at Tokyo's **Ryōgoku Kokugikan** (Ryōgoku Sumō Stadium; Map pp128-9; ☎ 3622-1100; www.sumo.or.jp; 1-3-28 Yokoami, Sumida-ku; 10am-4pm; JR Sōbu line to Ryōgoku, west exit or Toei Ōedo line to Ryōgoku, exit A4). The best seats are all bought up by those with the right connections, but if you don't mind standing, you can get in for around ¥500. Tickets can be purchased up to a month prior to the tournament, or you can simply turn up on the day (you'll have to arrive very early, say 6am, to be assured of seats during the last days of a tournament). See also the Sumō Museum, p159.

If you can't attend in person, NHK televises sumō from 3.30pm daily during each tournament. If you aren't in town during a tournament, you could pick up a handbook at the stadium and take a self-guided walking tour of the neighbourhood, which houses several *sumō-beya* (sumō stables).

SHOPPING

Tokyo is not as notoriously expensive as it once was, and shopping is one of the great pastimes of local residents. Shopping may not normally interest you, but the city's seductive wares may sway you.

Antiques

In Aoyama, the street Kotto-dōri (Antiques Street; Map p134) takes its name from the antique shops doing business there, making it a logical place to poke around for wares with character.

Hanae Mori Building (Map p134; B1 fl, 3-6-1 Kita-Aoyama, Minato-ku; 11am-7pm; Chiyoda, Ginza, Hanzōmon lines to Omote-sandō, exit A1) One great place to look for antiques and eccentric souvenirs is in the basement of this Harajuku building, which has more than 30 antique shops hawking everything from over-the-hill kewpie dolls to antique obi ornaments.

Kurofune (Map pp140-1; ☎ 3479-1552; www.kurofuneantiques.com; 7-7-4 Roppongi, Minato-ku; 10am-6pm Mon-Sat; Toei Ōedo line to Roppongi, exits 4a & 7) Kurofune, run for the past quarter-century by a friendly American collector, carries an awesome treasure-trove of Japanese antiques. Correspondingly impressive amounts of cash are necessary to acquire such items, like painstakingly constructed antique *tansu* (Japanese chests of drawers), but it's a nice place to window-shop.

Clothes

Harajuku (Map p134) has reached iconic proportions internationally, having become synonymous with Tokyo street fashion. While established houses of haute couture, such as Vuitton, Comme les Garçons and Prada, line Omote-sandō; Ura-Hara (the Harajuku backstreets) is where the small boutiques and studios represent the indie designers. Wander the alleys snaking off either side of Omote-sandō and check out the boutiques and second-hand shops. Farther south, Aoyama (Map p134) caters to more sophisticated mainstream (and expensive) tastes.

Department stores like **Laforet** (Map p134; ☎ 3475-0411; 1-11-6 Jingūmae, Shibuya-ku; 🕑 11am-8pm; 🚇 Chiyoda line to Meiji-jingūmae, exit 5) or the **Shibuya 109 building** (Ichimarukyū; Map p134; ☎ 3477-5111; 2-29-1 Dōgenzaka, Shibuya-ku; 🕑 10am-9pm Mon-Fri, 11am-10.30pm Sat & Sun; 🚇 JR Yamanote line to Shibuya, Hachikō exit) are good places to dig up the latest hot look you're seeing on the chic young things strutting around town. Daikanyama (Map p136) is another wonderfully stylish neighbourhood in which to admire the locals' individualistic senses of fashion, and shop the boutiques of budding and established fashion designers.

If unexpected changes in weather mean that you've packed all the wrong clothes, pop into **Uniqlo** (Map p138; ☎ 3569-6781; 5-7-7 Ginza, Chūō-ku; 🕑 11am-9pm; 🚇 Ginza, Hibiya, Marunouchi lines to Ginza, exits A2 & A3), full of inexpensive Gap-like basics for men, women and children. This flagship store is in Ginza, but there are branches all over Tokyo.

Department Stores

Tokyo's big *depāto* (department stores), opulent shrines to consumerism, are worth a look for sheer scale and inventory. Department stores close at least one day each month, usually a Monday or Wednesday. Some of the best things about them are not necessarily the wares, but the eats – with their rooftop beer gardens, *resutoran-gai* and elaborately stocked *depachika*. Following is a necessarily selective list of *depāto* in Tokyo.

Isetan (Map p131; ☎ 3352-1111; 3-14-1 Shinjuku, Shinjuku-ku; 🕑 10am-8pm; 🚇 Marunouchi, Toei Shinjuku lines to Shinjuku-sanchōme, exit A1) In addition to having a stunning food basement, Isetan offers a free service called I-club, matching English-speaking staff to visiting shoppers; the membership desk is on the 6th floor of the main Isetan building.

Keiō (Map p131; ☎ 3342-2111; 1-1-4 Nishi-Shinjuku, Shinjuku-ku; 🕑 10am-8pm, closed some Thu; 🚇 JR Yamanote line to Shinjuku, west exit) Opens its rooftop beer garden during the summer.

Marui (Map p131; ☎ 3354-0101; 3-18-1 Shinjuku, Shinjuku-ku; 🕑 11am-9pm; 🚇 JR Yamanote line to Shinjuku, east exit) Targeted toward a younger audience, with unmistakable presences in Shinjuku and Shibuya.

Matsuya (Map p138; ☎ 3567-1211; 3-6-1 Ginza, Chūō-ku; 🕑 10.30am-7.30pm; 🚇 Ginza, Hibiya, Marunouchi lines to Ginza, exits A12 & A13) Also opens its beer garden during the summer and has a good *depachika*.

Matsuzakaya (Map p138; ☎ 3572-1111; 6-10-1 Ginza, Chūō-ku; 🕑 10am-7.30pm Sun-Wed, to 8pm Thu-Sat; 🚇 Ginza, Hibiya, Marunouchi lines to Ginza, exit A3) How many department stores besides this one can say they've been around for almost 400 years?

Mitsukoshi (Map p138; ☎ 3562-1111; 4-6-16 Ginza, Chūō-ku; 🕑 10am-8pm; 🚇 Ginza, Hibiya, Marunouchi lines to Ginza, exits A7 & A11) Look for the Mitsukoshi lion at the corner entrance at this Ginza stalwart.

Takashimaya (Map pp142-3; ☎ 3211-4111; 2-4-1 Nihombashi, Chūō-ku; 🕑 10am-7.30pm; 🚇 Ginza, Tōzai, Toei Asakusa lines to Nihombashi, exit B1 & B2) This is one of the more venerable old establishments, where primly dressed, white-gloved attendants operate old-fashioned elevators; have a look at the rooftop patio. There's another branch in Ginza.

Electronics

Akihabara (p149), Tokyo's discount electronics neighbourhood, carries a huge range of electrical appliances in a highly concentrated area – hence the nickname Denki-gai (Electric Town). While prices may be competitive with those in your home country, it's unusual to find bargains like you would in Hong Kong or Singapore. Some larger stores (like those listed here) have tax-free departments with export models of various appliances and gadgets for sale – remember to double-check that they're compatible with your home country's system, and bring your passport.

Laox (Map pp142-3; ☎ 3253-7111; 1-2-9 Soto-Kanda, Chiyoda-ku; 🕑 10am-9pm; 🚇 JR Sōbu, Yamanote lines to Akihabara, Electric Town exit) Multilingual staff can help you work out voltage compatibility; Laox has several branches in Akihabara.

Sofmap (Map pp142-3; ☎ 3253-1111; 4-1-1 Soto-Kanda, Chiyoda-ku; 🕑 11am-9pm; 🚇 JR Sōbu, Yamanote lines to Akihabara, Electric Town exit) Another electronics shop with a dozen outlets scattered all over Akihabara.

Handicrafts & Souvenirs

While toy shops and department stores sell fun, futuristic and only-in-Japan types of goodies, there's also a wealth of more traditional gifts and souvenirs to be found in Tokyo. All the major department stores also have a section devoted to *washi*.

Bingoya (Map pp128-9; ☎ 3202-8778; www.quasar.nu/bingoya; 10-6 Wakamatsuchō, Shinjuku-ku; 🕑 10am-7pm Tue-Sun; 🚇 Toei Ōedo line to Wakamatsu-Kawada, Kawadachō exit) Regional ceramics, vibrant batik textiles, richly dyed *washi* (handmade paper), handmade glassware and tatami mats fill out the five floors of this wonderful handicrafts shop.

Haibara (Map pp142-3; ☎ 3272-3801; www.haibara.co.jp, in Japanese; 2-7-6 Nihombashi, Chūō-ku; 10am-6.30pm Mon-Fri, to 5pm Sat; Ginza, Tōzai, Toei Asakusa lines to Nihombashi, exits B8 & C3) East of Tokyo station, Haibara stocks a quality range of *washi* and paper handicrafts, such as reproductions of famous woodcuts, handbound notebooks and unique stationery.

Japan Traditional Crafts Center (Map p132; ☎ 5954-6066; www.kougei.or.jp/english/center.html; 1st-3rd fl, Metropolitan Plaza Bldg, 1-11-1 Nishi-Ikebukuro, Toshima-ku; 11am-7pm; JR Yamanote line to Ikebukuro, Metropolitan exit) Demonstrations and temporary exhibitions of handmade crafts, such as weavings, mosaics, ceramics and *washi* are held on the 3rd floor of this centre. High-quality folk arts and handicrafts are available for purchase on the 1st and 2nd floors.

Kamawanu (Map p136; ☎ 3780-0182; www.kamawanu.co.jp, in Japanese; 23-1 Sarugakuchō, Shibuya-ku; 11am-7pm; JR Yamanote line to Ebisu, west exit) In Daikanyama, this shop specialises in beautifully dyed *tenugui*, those ubiquitous Japanese handtowels used for everything from *bentō* carriers to handkerchiefs. Designs come in a spectrum of colours, incorporating traditional abstract patterns and representations of natural elements.

Kappabashi-dōri (Map pp146-7; Ginza line to Tawaramachi, all exits) This is where to go if you're setting up a restaurant or setting up house. Custom-made *noren* (doorway curtains), crockery, chopsticks and, most importantly, plastic food models. They are carefully crafted and not cheap, but they do make quirky souvenirs for the fridge back home. Kappabashi-dōri is a five-minute walk northwest of Tawaramachi station.

Oriental Bazaar (Map p134; ☎ 3400-3933; 5-9-13 Jingūmae, Shibuya-ku; 10am-7pm Fri-Wed; Chiyoda, Ginza, Hanzōmon lines to Omote-sandō, exit 4) Oriental Bazaar is a good one-stop shop for gifts and souvenirs, with a wide range of items such as fans, folding screens, *yukata* and pottery – many at very affordable prices.

Takumi Handicrafts (Map p138; ☎ 3571-2017; www.ginza-takumi.co.jp, in Japanese; 8-4-2 Ginza, Chūō-ku; 11am-7pm Mon-Sat; JR Yamanote line to Shimbashi, Ginza exit) Takumi offers an elegant selection of toys, textiles, ceramics and other traditional folk crafts from around Japan. The shop also encloses information detailing the origin and background of pieces you purchase.

Yoshitoku (Map pp128-9; ☎ 3863-4419; 1-9-14 Asakusabashi, Taitō-ku; 9.30am-6pm; JR Sōbu or Toei Asakusa lines to Asakusabashi, main exit or exit A2) Near the JR Asakusabashi station, Yoshitoku is the most famous of the many traditional *ningyō* (doll) shops lining Edo-dōri. This dollmaker has been crafting exquisite *ningyō* since 1711 and is now owned by its 11th-generation descendant, who also stocks *ningyō* made by other dollmakers.

Kids Stuff

Are you fascinated by all the wonderfully weird and totally charming *stuff* created by the Japanese? Just think how mind-blowing it is for kids.

Kiddyland (Map p134; ☎ 3409-3431; www.kiddyland.co.jp; 6-1-9 Jingūmae, Shibuya-ku; 10am-8pm, closed 3rd Tue of each month; Chiyoda line to Meiji-jingūmae, exit 4) Prepare to overdose on the six floors of *kawaii* (cute), here on Omote-sandō in Harajuku. This store is stuffed with toys for kids from age zero onward. You might want to avoid it on the weekends, when teenagers descend in droves.

Hakuhinkan Toy Park (Map p138; ☎ 3571-8008; www.hakuhinkan.co.jp; 8-8-11 Ginza, Chūō-ku; 11am-8pm; JR Yamanote line to Shimbashi, Ginza exit) This multilevel toy shop along Chūō-dōri in Ginza is another great one, full of distractions and objects of desire, with an 8th-floor theatre and two floors of child-friendly restaurants.

Manga & Anime

Along with electronics, Akihabara (p149) overflows with shops selling manga and anime. Be sure to wander the shops along Otome Rd (p153) in Ikebukuro, the most visible of which are the many branches of **K-Books** (www.k-books.co.jp, in Japanese), each of which specialise in anime, specific genres and multimedia.

Animate (Map p132; ☎ 3988-1351; www.animate.co.jp; 3-2-1 Higashi-Ikebukuro, Toshima-ku; 10am-8.30pm Mon-Sat, 10am-8pm Sun; JR Yamanote line to Ikebukuro, east exit) Across from the western street-level entrance of Sunshine City, Animate marks the first stop girl geeks and manga freaks will want to make.

Mandarake Shibuya (Map p134; ☎ 3477-0777; www.mandarake.co.jp; B2 fl, Shibuya Beam Bldg, 31-2 Udagawachō, Shibuya-ku; noon-8pm; JR Yamanote line to Shibuya, Hachikō exit); Nakano (まんだらけ; off Map pp128-9; ☎ 3228-0007; 2nd-4th fl, Nakano Broadway Bldg, 5-52-15 Nakano, Nakano-ku; noon-8pm; JR Chūō line to Nakano, north exit) Mandarake's Shibuya Beam branch carries a range of new manga and also hosts performances by real, live *cosplay* kids in full-on anime character drag. The huge flagship store in Nakano has three floors packed with new and used manga, anime, games and character figures.

Tora-no-Ana (Map pp142-3; ☎ 5294-0123; www.toranoana.co.jp, in Japanese; 4-3-1 Soto-Kanda, Chiyoda-ku; 🕑 10am-10pm; 🚉 JR Sōbu, Yamanote lines to Akihabara, Electric Town exit) Keep your eyes peeled for the cute illustrated tiger-girl on the top of this building, which has seven floors of manga and anime. Tora-no-Ana has other branches in Shinjuku and Ikebukuro.

Music

Shibuya, that nexus of Tokyo's pop culture, is a logical place to hunt for music. Udagawachō (Map p134; take the JR Yamanote line to Shibuya, Hachikō exit), the area northwest of Shibuya station, has a clutch of music stores all in one compact area. Most of these shops specialise in certain genres and stock rare and used CDs and vinyl.

Here's a selection of music outlets:

Disk Union Shibuya (Map p134; ☎ 3476-2627; http://diskunion.net, in Japanese; Antenna 21 Bldg, 30-7 Udagawachō, Shibuya-ku; 🕑 11.30am-9pm); Shinjuku (Map p131; ☎ 3352-2691; http://diskunion.net, in Japanese; 3-31-4 Shinjuku, Shinjuku-ku; 🕑 11am-9pm Mon-Sat, 11am-8pm Sun; 🚉 JR Yamanote line, east exit) Used and new records, each floor specialising in a different genre.

Guinness Records (Map p134; ☎ 3464-7752; www.guinness-records.com, in Japanese; 4th fl, 10-2 Udagawachō, Shibuya-ku; 🕑 1-8.30pm) Guinness specialises in hip-hop, soul, R&B and jazz.

Manhattan Records (Map p134; ☎ 3477-7737; 1st fl, 10-1 Udagawachō, Shibuya-ku; 🕑 noon-9pm) Bounce into Manhattan for hip-hop.

Recofan (Map p134; ☎ 5454-0161; www.recofan.co.jp; 4th fl, Beam Bldg, 31-2 Udagawachō, Shibuya-ku; 🕑 11.30am-9pm) Of several branches around town, this place stocks a wide variety of music, including folk, soul, J-pop and reggae.

Tower Records (Map p134; ☎ 3496-3661; 1-22-14 Jinnan, Shibuya-ku; 🕑 10am-11pm; 🚉 JR Yamanote line to Shibuya, Hachikō exit) has a massive branch in Shibuya, with the most extensive range in Tokyo and lots of listening stations. Tower and HMV have several branches in Tokyo.

Photographic Equipment

Photographers, take note: the area behind the Keiō department store on the west side of Shinjuku station is home to Tokyo's largest camera stores, Yodobashi (right) and Sakuraya (right). They carry practically everything photography-related that you could possibly want, including MP3 players, computers and electronics of all kinds, all at quite reasonable prices. Be sure to shop around for the best deals.

Some options:

Bic Camera Shinjuku (Map p131; ☎ 5326-1111; 1-5-1 Nishi-Shinjuku, Shinjuku-ku; 🕑 10am-8.30pm; 🚉 JR Yamanote line to Shinjuku, west exit); Ikebukuro (Map p132; ☎ 5396 1111; 1-41-5 Higashi-Ikebukuro, Toshima-ku; 🕑 10am-9pm; 🚉 JR Yamanote line to Ikebukuro, east exit) See if you can come out of here without getting the Bic song stuck in your head. There are branches all over Tokyo.

Sakuraya Camera (Map p131; ☎ 3346-3939; 1-16-4 Nishi-Shinjuku, Shinjuku-ku; 🕑 10am-8.30pm; 🚉 JR Yamanote line to Shinjuku, west exit) One of the biggest camera shops in town.

Yodobashi Camera (Map p131; ☎ 3346-1010; 1-11-1 Nishi-Shinjuku, Shinjuku-ku; 🕑 9.30am-9.30pm; 🚉 JR Yamanote line to Shinjuku, west exit) Bring your passport and the consumption tax will be waived.

Variety Stores

Perhaps, like certain authors, you hate shopping. But shopping is a major recreational pastime in Tokyo, and even the stingiest of spenders will be seduced by some oddball novelty here, especially if they enter that one must-visit store, Tōkyū Hands (below).

A selection of variety stores:

Don Quijote (Map p131; ☎ 5291-9211; www.donki.com; 1-16-5 Kabukichō, Shinjuku-ku; 🕑 24hr; 🚉 JR Yamanote line to Shinjuku, east exit) This fluorescent-lit, trashy cousin of Tōkyū Hands is filled to the gills with weird loot: knock-off designer goods, packaged snacks and sex toys. There are branches all over Tokyo, though not all are open 24 hours.

Loft Shibuya (Map p134; ☎ 3462-3807; www.loft.co.jp, in Japanese; 21-1 Udagawachō, Shibuya-ku; 🕑 10am-9pm; 🚉 JR Yamanote line to Shibuya, Hachikō exit); Ikebukuro (Map p132; ☎ 5949 3880; 1-28-1 Minami-Ikebukuro, Toshima-ku; 🕑 10am-9pm Mon-Sat, 10am-8pm Sun; 🚉 JR Yamanote line to Ikebukuro, east exit); Marunouchi (Map pp142–3; Marunouchi Bldg, 2-4-1 Marunouchi, Chiyoda-ku; 🕑 11am-9pm Mon-Sat, 11am-8pm Sun; 🚉 Marunouchi line to Tokyo, exit 4) The bias here is more towards fun rather than function, and it's a good place to look for cool housewares, gifts and toys for big kids.

Muji (Map p138; ☎ 5208-8241; 2nd & 3rd fl, 3-8-3 Marunouchi, Chiyoda-ku; 🕑 10am-9pm; 🚉 JR Yamanote line to Yūrakuchō, main exit or Yūrakuchō line to Yūrakuchō, exit A4b) The flagship store of this 'no-name brand' is full of beautifully and simply designed wares, from tea sets to toddler clothing to travel gear. Other branches can be found all over Tokyo.

Tōkyū Hands Shinjuku (Map p131; ☎ 5361-3111; Takashimaya Times Sq, 5-24-2 Sendagaya, Shibuya-ku; 🕑 10am-8.30pm; 🚉 JR Yamanote line to Shinjuku, new south exit); Ikebukuro (Map p132; ☎ 3980 6111; 1-28-10 Higashi-Ikebukuro, Toshima-ku; 🕑 10am-9pm; 🚉 JR

Yamanote line to Ikebukuro, east exit); Shibuya (Map p134; ☎ 5489 5111; 12-18 Udagawachō, Shibuya-ku; 🕑 10am-8.30pm; 🚇 JR Yamanote line to Shibuya, Hachikō exit) Ostensibly a DIY home-improvement emporium, Tōkyū Hands sells everything you never knew you needed – from lumber to designer humidifiers to mobile-phone bling.

GETTING THERE & AWAY

Air

With the exception of a few Asian airlines, all international flights arrive at Narita International Airport (p827) rather than the more conveniently located Haneda airport (p194).

Immigration and customs procedures are usually straightforward, but they can be time-consuming. Note that Japanese customs officials are probably the most scrupulous in Asia; backpackers arriving from anywhere even remotely considered as a developing country (the Philippines, Thailand etc) can expect some questions and perhaps a thorough search.

You can change money in the customs hall after having cleared customs, and in the arrival hall. The rates are the same as those offered in town.

Narita has two terminals, Nos 1 and 2, both of which have train stations that are connected to JR and Keisei lines. The one you arrive at will depend on the airline you are flying with. Both terminals have clear English signposting for train and limousine bus services. See opposite for more details.

Be sure to check which terminal your flight departs from, and give yourself plenty of time to get out to Narita – the trip can take from 50 minutes to two hours.

Boat

A ferry journey can be a great, relatively inexpensive way to get from Tokyo to other parts of the country. Prices given here are for 2nd-class travel. Though we've listed phone numbers here, most lines are not staffed by English-speaking operators. It's easiest to book passage through a local travel agency or the JNTO (p126).

From Tokyo, the long-distance **Ocean Tōkyū Ferry** (オーシャン東九フェリー; ☎ 5148-0109; www.otf.jp) goes to Tokushima (¥9900, 18 hours) in Shikoku and to Kitakyūshū (¥14,000, 34 hours) in Northern Kyūshū. **Maruei Ferry/A Line** (☎ 03-5643-6170, in Naha 861-1886; www.aline-ferry.com, in Japanese) operates four or five ferries a month between Tokyo and Naha (¥24,500, 46 hours). Long-distance ferry services to Hokkaidō are no longer available from Tokyo; however, **Shosen Mitsui Ferry** (☎ 029-267-4133) has departures from Ibaraki prefecture to Tomakomai in Hokkaidō (¥8500, 19 hours).

Bus

Long-distance buses are generally little or no cheaper than trains, but are sometimes a good alternative for long-distance trips to areas serviced by expressways.

There are a number of express buses running between Tokyo, Kyoto and Osaka. Overnight JR buses leave at 10pm from the Yaesu side of Tokyo station and arrive at Kyoto and Osaka between 6am and 7am the following day. They cost from ¥7270 to ¥8550 (you'll save money by buying a return ticket if you intend on coming back). Tickets can be booked at one of the green windows at a JR station. For a list of typical bus services from Tokyo see p834.

From Shinjuku station Keiō runs buses to the Fuji and Hakone regions, including, for Mt Fuji climbers, express services to the 5th station (see p210). The long-distance bus station is across from the west exit of Shinjuku station, next to the Keiō department store.

Train

All major JR lines radiate from Tokyo station; northbound trains stop at Ueno station, which, like Tokyo station, is on the convenient JR Yamanote line. Private lines – often cheaper and quicker for making day trips out of Tokyo – start from various stations around Tokyo. With the exception of the Tōbu Nikkō line, which starts in Asakusa, all private lines originate somewhere on the Yamanote line.

For fares to major cities from Tokyo, see p839.

SHINKANSEN

There are three *shinkansen* (bullet train) lines that connect Tokyo with the rest of Japan: the Tōkaidō line, which passes through Central Honshū, changing its name along the way to the Sanyō line before terminating at Hakata in Northern Kyūshū; the Tōhoku line, which runs northeast via Utsunomiya and Sendai as far as Morioka, with the Yamagata branch heading from Fukushima to Yamagata and the Akita branch heading from Morioka to Akita; and the Jōetsu line, which runs north to Niigata, with the Nagano branch heading from Takasaki to Nagano-shi. All three *shinkansen* lines start at Tokyo station, though the Tōhoku and Jōetsu lines make a stop at Ueno station, and the Tōkaidō line now stops at Shinagawa station in southcentral Tokyo.

Of these lines, the one most likely to be used by visitors to Japan is the Tōkaidō line, as it passes through Kyoto and Osaka. Nozomi (super express) trains between Tokyo and Kyoto (¥13,520, 2½ hours) are fastest, as they make only a few stops. Buy tickets at the green JR windows; the way to *shinkansen* platforms in Tokyo station are clearly signposted in English.

PRIVATE LINES

The private lines generally service Tokyo's sprawling suburbia. The most useful are the Tōkyū Tōyoko line, running between Shibuya station and Yokohama; the Odakyū line, running from Shinjuku to Odawara and the Hakone region; the Tōbu Nikkō line, running from Asakusa to Nikkō; and the Seibu Shinjuku line from Ikebukuro to Kawagoe.

OTHER JR LINES

The regular Tōkaidō line serves the stations that the Tōkaidō *shinkansen* line zips through without stopping. Trains start at Tokyo station and pass through Shimbashi and Shinagawa stations on the way out of town. There are *kyūkyō* (express) services to Yokohama and to Izu-hantō via Atami, and from there trains continue – very slowly – to Nagoya, Kyoto and Osaka.

Northbound trains start in Ueno. The Takasaki line goes to Kumagaya and, of course, Takasaki, with onward connections from Takasaki to Niigata. The Tōhoku line follows the Takasaki line as far north as Ōmiya, from where it heads to the far north of Honshū via Sendai and Aomori. Getting to Sendai without paying any express surcharges will involve changes at Utsunomiya and Fukushima. For those intent on saving the expense of a night's accommodation, there are also overnight services.

GETTING AROUND

Tokyo has an excellent public transport system, with everything of note conveniently close to a subway or JR station. Bus services are difficult to use if you don't read kanji, but the average visitor to Tokyo won't need the buses anyway.

To/From Narita Airport

Narita airport is 66km from central Tokyo, and is used by almost all the international airlines and a small number of domestic operators. Travel to or from Tokyo takes from 50 minutes to two hours, depending on your mode of transport and destination in town.

Depending on where you're headed, it's generally cheaper and faster to travel into Tokyo by train than by limousine bus. However, rail users will probably need to change trains somewhere, and this can be confusing on a jetlagged first visit. Limousine buses provide a hassle-free direct route to a number of Tokyo's top hotels, and you don't have to be a hotel guest to use the buses.

If you're seriously desperate or have money to burn, taxis from Narita will run you a cool ¥30,000 or so.

TRAIN

Two railway lines run between Tokyo and both terminals at Narita airport: the private **Keisei line** (☎ 3621-2232; www.keisei.co.jp) and **JR East** (☎ 050-2016-1603; www.jreast.co.jp/ e/nex/index.html).

At the time of writing, the Keisei line has two services and will add a third in 2010. The Keisei Skyliner does the trip between Narita and Ueno (¥1920, 56 minutes) or Nippori (¥1920, 51 minutes). It's worth noting that it's much easier to transfer to the Yamanote line at Nippori station. Keisei *tokkyū* (limited express; ¥1000) services are much more frequent than the Skyliner, and add another 15 or so minutes to the trip (to Ueno, it's 71 minutes; to Nippori, 67 minutes). The third, highly anticipated service is the Skyliner Airport Express, which at 160km/h will whisk passengers from Narita to Tokyo station in a mere 36 minutes (check www.keisei.co.jp for current fare information).

JR East runs the Narita Express (N'EX) to Tokyo station (¥2940, 53 minutes), to Shinjuku station (¥3110, 1½ hours), to or from Ikebukuro station (¥3110, one hour and 40 minutes) and to or from Yokohama station (¥4180, 1½ hours). The N'EX services are fast, comfortable, and include amenities like drink-dispensing machines and telephones. N'EX services run approximately half-hourly between 7am and 10pm, but Ikebukuro services are infrequent; in most cases you're better off heading to Shinjuku and taking the Yamanote line from there. Seats are reserved only, but can be bought immediately before departure if they are available. 'Airport Narita' trains cost ¥1280 and take 1½ hours to or from Tokyo. Trains only run approximately once an hour.

The Keikyū rail line runs between Narita and Haneda airports (¥1560, two hours), but you'll have to transfer to or from the Keisei line at Aoto station.

LIMOUSINE BUS

Airport Limousine Bus (www.limousinebus.co.jp/en) actually runs ordinary buses that take 1½ to two hours to travel between Narita airport and a number of major hotels. Check departure times before buying your ticket, as services are not all that frequent. The fare to or from hotels around Asakusa, to or from Ikebukuro, Akasaka, Ginza, Shiba, Shinagawa, Shinjuku or Haneda airport costs around ¥3000. There's also direct service between Narita airport and Yokohama (¥3500, two hours).

To/From Haneda Airport

Most domestic flights and JAL, ANA, China Eastern Airlines, Shanghai Airlines and Air China use the convenient Haneda airport.

Transport to or from Haneda airport is a simple matter, as the **Tokyo Monorail** (www.tokyo-monorail.co.jp) runs from 5.15am to 11.15pm between the airport and Hamamatsuchō station on the JR Yamanote line (¥470, 22 minutes, every 10 minutes).

Taxis from the airport to places around central Tokyo cost around ¥6000. Limousine buses connect Haneda with the Tokyo City Air Terminal (TCAT; ¥900), Tokyo station (¥900), Ikebukuro and Shinjuku (¥1200), and several other destinations in Tokyo.

There is a direct bus service between Haneda and Narita airports (¥3000, 1¼ hours).

Bus

Pick up a copy of the free *TOEI Bus Route Guide* from the TIC. When using a bus, have the name of your destination written in Japanese so you can either show the driver or match up the kanji with the route map yourself (there's very little English signposting on buses or at bus stops). It's a flat ¥200 for city destinations.

Car

If you plan to rent a car, you must obtain an International Driving Permit before arriving in Japan; bring the permit and your passport with you to rent a car. Several rental agencies have counters at Narita Airport, as well as offices or rental desks just outside, or near, the Yaesu central exit at Tokyo station (Map pp142–3). The agencies listed here usually have English speakers on hand. Prices quoted are average costs for sedans, and usually include unlimited mileage.

Mazda Rent-a-Car (Map pp142-3; ☎ 3564-5656, overseas reservations 0120-08-5656 ⏲ 9am-5.30pm; www.mazda-rentacar.co.jp; 1-17-11 Kyōbashi, Chūō-ku; per day/week ¥12,600/69,300; ⏲ 8am-8pm) Insurance is an extra ¥1050 per day. From the Yaesu underground central exit, take exit 24.

Nippon Rent-a-Car (Map pp142-3; ☎ English line 3271-6643; ⏲ 9am-5pm Mon-Fri; www.nipponrentacar.co.jp; B2 fl, 2-1- Yaesu, Chūō-ku; per day/week ¥9555/57,435; ⏲ 7am-10pm Mon-Fri, 8am-8pm Sat & Sun) Insurance is an extra ¥1050 per day. The desk is at the Yaesu West Parking Lot, in the basement that is accessible when you come to the entrance of the underground mall.

Nissan Rent-a-Car (Map pp142-3; ☎ 3274-4501, overseas reservations ☎ 0120-00-4123; http://nissan-rentacar.com; 1-8 Yaesu, Chūō-ku; per day/week ¥9923/68,460; ⏲ 24hr) Insurance is included. From the Yaesu underground central exit, take exit 19.

Toyota Rent-a-Car (Map pp142-3; ☎ 3278-0100, overseas reservations 0800-7000-815; http://rent.toyota.co.jp; per day/week ¥9450/56,700; ⏲ 7am-10pm) Insurance is included. From the entrance to the Yaesu underground mall, pass the post office and make a right down the stairs for the Yaesu East Parking Lot. The office is on the B2 floor, on the left.

Taxi

Taxis are so expensive that you should only use them when there's no alternative. Flagfall is ¥710, which gives you 2km (1.5km after 11pm), after which the meter starts to clock an additional ¥100 for every 350m; you also click up ¥100 for every two minutes you sit idly gazing at the scenery in a Tokyo traffic jam. If you don't speak Japanese, taxi drivers can plug a venue's telephone number into the GPS system to find its location.

Train

Tokyo has a crowded but otherwise awesome rail network. Between the JR and private above-ground and subway lines, you can get to almost anywhere in town quickly and cheaply. But night owls beware: it closes from around midnight until 5am or 6am. If you do miss your midnight train, see p163.

Avoiding Tokyo's rush hour is not often possible, though things tend to quiet down from 10am to 4pm.

DAY TRIPPING FROM NARITA

If you face a long layover at Narita airport, consider these alternatives to dazed, interminable hours in the terminals.

Assuming you have several hours to kill – including at least 2½ hours to get out, away and back into the airport – make a quick detour into Narita town. The town's highlight is its impressive temple, **Naritasan Shinshōji** (成田山新勝寺; ☎ 0476-222-111; 1 Narita, Narita-shi, Chiba-ken), surrounded by a pretty park laced with walking paths, trees and ponds. Along Omote-sandō, the main road leading from station to temple, explore the little shops and restaurants in town. To get there, take a limited express Keisei or JR train to Narita station (¥250, 10 minutes). Pick up a Narita map from the friendly TIC outside the east exit of the JR station.

If your layover is longer than eight hours, you can spend a couple of those hours discovering Tokyo. Hit the airport ATM for at least ¥10,000, check your bag through or stow it in a left-luggage locker, and catch the next JR Narita Express (p193) or Keisei Skyliner (p193) into Tokyo. To save time later, buy a round-trip ticket that departs from Tokyo at least three hours before your flight. Stick to one neighbourhood on the Yamanote line and make sure you don't miss your train back to the airport!

JR LINES

Undoubtedly, the most useful line in Tokyo is the JR Yamanote line, which does a 35km-long loop around the city, taking in most of the important areas. Another useful aboveground JR route is the Chūō line, which cuts across the city centre between Shinjuku and Akihabara. Tickets are transferable on all JR lines.

The major JR stations (Tokyo, Shibuya, Shinjuku, Ikebukuro and Ueno) are massive places with thronging crowds and never enough English signposting. Just working out how to buy a ticket can drive a newcomer to the edge of madness. If it's a JR train you're taking, look for the JR sign (usually green) and the rows of vending machines. If you don't know the fare, put in the minimum ¥130 and push the top left-hand button (the one with no price on it). When you get to your destination you can pay the balance at a fare adjustment machine, found near the ticket gates. English signposting points the way to the railway platforms.

Travellers planning to spend an extended period of time in Tokyo might consider getting a Suica smart card – the Suica card can be swiped without being removed from a wallet, and they can be recharged at any JR vending machine. They can not only be used on most other metropolitan railway lines in addition to JR lines, but can even be used as debit cards at convenience stores and restaurants in the stations. Suica cards require a ¥500 deposit, refundable when you return it to a JR window.

For English-language train information, you can call the **JR English Information line** (☎ 050-2016-1603; 10am-6pm Mon-Fri).

SUBWAY LINES

Ticket prices on the Tokyo Metro start at ¥160 (¥170 on TOEI lines) for short hops, but if your trip involves a change of train, it will probably cost upwards of ¥190. As with the JR system, if you're in doubt at all (there are still subway stations where the only pricing maps are in Japanese), buy the cheapest ticket and do a fare adjustment at your destination.

There are 13 subway lines in Tokyo, of which nine are Tokyo Metro lines and four are TOEI lines. This is not particularly important to remember, as the subway services are essentially the same and have good connections from one to another. However, you'll need a special transfer ticket to switch between Tokyo Metro and TOEI subway lines. If you can't read Japanese, the easiest way around this is to buy a Pasmo card, which works in the same way as a Suica card but is sold by the Tokyo Metro system. The Pasmo card can be used on Tokyo Metro, JR and most other metropolitan lines, saving you time, money and confusion when switching between the various systems.

DISCOUNT TICKETS & TRAIN PASSES

There are no massively discounted tickets available for travel around Tokyo. The best deal is the Tokyo Combination Ticket (¥1580), which allows travel on any subway, tram, TOEI bus or JR train in the metropolitan area until the last train of the day. It's available from subway and JR stations and post offices.

Around Tokyo
東京近郊

If you've never spotted Mt Fuji from Tokyo, it can take your breath away. Japan's tallest peak looms over the distant Tanzawa mountains, hinting at amazing outdoor experiences right on Tokyo's doorstep. In summer, you can climb through forests towards the jagged summit of Japan's national symbol, as pilgrims have done for centuries, or the towns of Hakone or the Fuji Go-ko (Fuji Five Lakes) make for ideal hiking and soaking in onsen (hot springs) anytime of year.

North of the capital, Nikkō's gilded shrines and exquisitely crafted temples are spectacularly set amid verdant woodlands. Further north and west, Gunma-ken is the nation's hot-spring capital, with river-bank onsen, mountain onsen, even onsen with mixed bathing!

South of Tokyo, Japan's ancient capital Kamakura boasts a treasury of temples and sylvan hiking trails. Nearby Yokohama has grown from a blip 150 years ago to Japan's second-largest city, with crackling entertainment districts, shopping galore and longstanding foreign influence.

Continuing south, the Izu peninsula has charming seaside towns, lovely windswept beaches and cliff-top onsen overlooking the Pacific. And you needn't leave Tokyo Prefecture for an island getaway; Izu-shotō are a chain of volcanic peaks tapering to white-sand beaches and lush subtropical landscapes for hiking. The Ogasawara-shotō, 25 hours by ferry, form a pristine national park where you can frolic with dolphins year-round.

HIGHLIGHTS

- Watch the sunrise from the majestic **Mt Fuji** (p208), Japan's highest mountain and national symbol
- Find your spiritual centre while exploring the dazzling temples of **Nikkō** (opposite)
- Recover from the madness of the metropolis at idyllic onsen on **Izu-hantō** (p226) or in **Gunma-ken** (p205)
- Truly get away from it all (except the dolphins) on pristine **Chichi-jima** (p245)
- Relax in a natural seaside onsen while gazing over the Pacific on one of the easily accessible islands in the **Izu-shotō** group (p240)

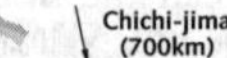

NORTH OF TOKYO

Resisting the urge to take the *shinkansen* (bullet train) south to Kyoto, you can experience the postcard splendour of Japan's mountains – Nikkō with its amazing shrines and, further north and west, Gunma-ken, home to numerous hot-spring resorts.

NIKKŌ 日光

☎ 0288 / pop 93,000

Ancient moss clinging to a stone wall, rows of perfectly aligned stone lanterns, vermillion gates and towering cedars: this is only a pathway in Nikkō, a sanctuary that enshrines the glories of the Edo period (1600–1868). Scattered among hilly woodlands, Nikkō is one of Japan's major attractions. If there's any drawback, it's that plenty of other people have discovered it too; peak season (summer and autumn) and weekends can be extremely crowded. Although Nikkō is certainly possible as a day trip from Tokyo, try to spend at least one night here so that the following morning you arrive at its World Heritage shrines and temples before the crowds do. Gorgeous natural scenery west of the city merits another night.

History

Nikkō's religious history dates back to the middle of the 8th century, when the Buddhist priest Shōdō Shōnin (735–817) established a hermitage here. It was a training centre for Buddhist monks before it eventually declined into obscurity. Nikkō became famous when chosen as the site for the mausoleum of Tokugawa Ieyasu, the warlord who took control of Japan and established the shōgunate that ruled for more than 250 years, until the Meiji Restoration ended the feudal era.

Ieyasu was laid to rest among Nikkō's towering cedars in 1617, and in 1634 his grandson, Tokugawa Iemitsu, commenced work on the shrine that can be seen today. The original shrine, Tōshō-gū, was completely rebuilt using an army of some 15,000 artisans from across Japan, taking two years to complete the shrine and mausoleum. Whatever one's opinion of Ieyasu, the grandeur at Nikkō is awesome, a display of wealth and power by a family that for two-and-a-half centuries was Japan's supreme arbiter of power.

Orientation

Both JR Nikkō Station and the nearby Tōbu Nikkō Station lie within a block of Nikkō's main road (Rte 119, the old Nikkō-kaidō), southeast of the town centre. From here, it's a 30-minute walk uphill to the shrine area, past restaurants, hotels and the main tourist information centre. From the stations to the shrines, you can take buses to the Shin-kyō bus stop for ¥190. The area north of the Daiya-gawa from the town centre is greener but not as well served by public transport.

Information

The *Tourist Guide of Nikkō* has about everything you need, and the bilingual *Central Nikko* shows the small streets. Hikers should pick up a copy of *Yumoto-Chūzenji Area Hiking Guide* (¥150), which has maps and information on local flora and fauna. The small *Guidebook for Walking Trails* (¥150) is useful for short walks.

Kawai i-in Clinic (☎ 54-1125; ⏰ irregular hr) On the main road, three blocks southeast of the Kyōdo Centre tourist information office. Has an English speaker; call first for an appointment.

Kyōdo Center tourist information office (☎ 54-2496; internet per 15min ¥50; ⏰ 9am-5pm) Has maps and English speakers. You can also arrange for free guided tours in English. There are several computers available for internet use.

Nikko Perfect Guide (www.nikko-jp.org/english/index.html) This website to the city also has a print version available from the Kyōdo Center tourist information office for ¥1575.

Post office On the main road, three blocks northwest of the Kyōdo Center tourist information office. Has an international ATM and currency exchange.

Tōbu Nikkō Station tourist information desk (☎ 53-4511; ⏰ 8.30am-5pm)

Sights

The World Heritage Sites around Tōshō-gū are Nikkō's centrepiece. A ¥1000 'combination ticket', valid for two days and available at booths in the area, covers entry to Rinnō-ji, Tōshō-gū and Futarasan-jinja, but not the Nemuri-Neko (Sleeping Cat) in Tōshō-gū and Ieyasu's tomb. Separate admission tickets to these sights are available.

Most sites are open from 8am to 5pm (until 4pm from November to March). To avoid the hordes, visit early on a weekday. Be sure to bring a map, as finding the English signposts to the shrines and temples can be tricky.

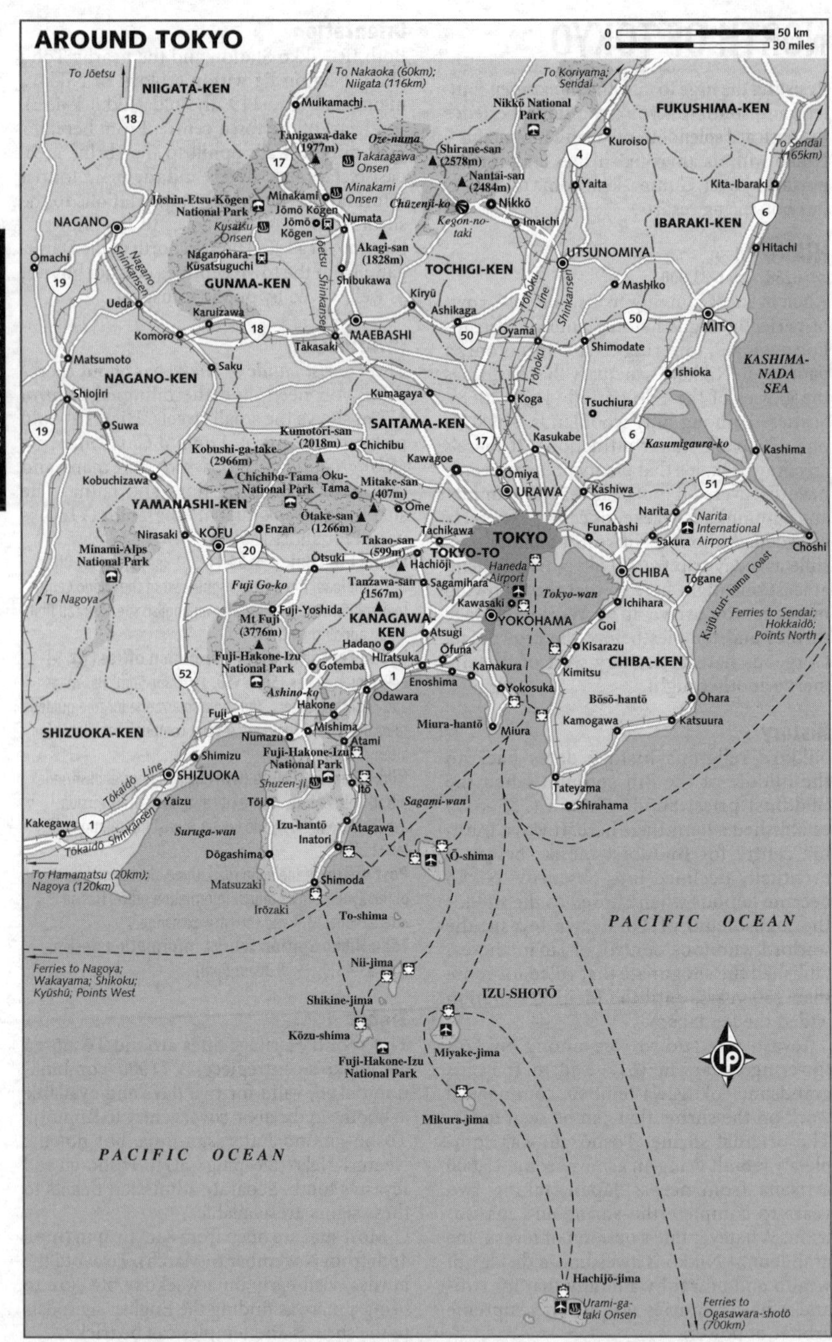

AROUND TOKYO
0 50 km
0 30 miles
To Jōetsu
NIIGATA-KEN
To Nakaoka (60km); Niigata (116km)
To Koriyama; Sendai
FUKUSHIMA-KEN
Nikkō National Park
Muikamachi
Tanigawa-dake (1977m)
Oze-numa
Takaragawa Onsen
Shirane-san (2578m)
Nantai-san (2484m)
Kuroiso
To Sendai (165km)
Yaita
Kita-Ibaraki
Minakami
Minakami Onsen
Jōshin-Etsu-Kōgen National Park
Jōmō Kōgen
Jōmō Kōgen
Chūzenji-ko
Nikkō
Kegon-no-taki
Imaichi
NAGANO
Kusatsu Onsen
Numata
IBARAKI-KEN
Akagi-san (1828m)
Hitachi
Ōmachi
Naganohara-Kusatsuguchi
UTSUNOMIYA
Nagano Shinkansen
GUNMA-KEN
Jōetsu Shinkansen
Shibukawa
TOCHIGI-KEN
Mashiko
Tōhoku Line
Tōhoku Shinkansen
Kiryū
Ueda
Ashikaga
Karuizawa
MITO
MAEBASHI
Komoro
Takasaki
Oyama
Shimodate
Matsumoto
KASHIMA-NADA SEA
NAGANO-KEN
Saku
Ishioka
Kumagaya
Shiojiri
Koga
Tsuchiura
SAITAMA-KEN
Suwa
Kumotori-san (2018m)
Kasukabe
Kasumigaura-ko
Kobushi-ga-take (2966m)
Chichibu
Kashima
Kawagoe
Chichibu-Tama National Park
Oku-Tama
Mitake-san (407m)
Ōmiya
Kobuchizawa
URAWA
Kashiwa
YAMANASHI-KEN
Ōme
Ōtake-san (1266m)
Narita
Narita International Airport
Nirasaki
KŌFU
Enzan
Tachikawa
TOKYO
Funabashi
Minami-Alps National Park
TOKYO-TO
Sakura
Chōshi
Takao-san (599m)
Ōtsuki
Hachiōji
Haneda Airport
CHIBA
To Nagoya
Fuji Go-ko
Tanzawa-san (1567m)
Sagamihara
Tōgane
Tokyo-wan
Fuji-Yoshida
Kawasaki
Ichihara
KANAGAWA-KEN
YOKOHAMA
Ferries to Sendai; Hokkaidō; Points North
Mt Fuji (3776m)
Kujū kuri-hama Coast
Atsugi
Goi
Hadano
Kisarazu
Ōfuna
Fuji-Hakone-Izu National Park
Hiratsuka
CHIBA-KEN
Gotemba
Kamakura
Kimitsu
Enoshima
Ashino-ko
Yokosuka
Odawara
Bōsō-hantō
Ōhara
Hakone
Fuji
Miura-hantō
Kamogawa
Katsuura
SHIZUOKA-KEN
Mishima
Miura
Numazu
Atami
Shimizu
Fuji-Hakone-Izu National Park
Tōkaidō Line
SHIZUOKA
Shuzen-ji
Itō
Tateyama
Yaizu
Sagami-wan
Shirahama
Tōi
Kakegawa
Suruga-wan
Izu-hantō
Atagawa
Inatori
Tōkaidō Shinkansen
Dōgashima
Ō-shima
To Hamamatsu (20km); Nagoya (120km)
Matsuzaki
Shimoda
Irōzaki
To-shima
PACIFIC OCEAN
Ferries to Nagoya; Wakayama; Shikoku; Kyūshū; Points West
Nii-jima
Shikine-jima
IZU-SHOTŌ
Kōzu-shima
Miyake-jima
Fuji-Hakone-Izu National Park
Mikura-jima
PACIFIC OCEAN
Hachijō-jima
Urami-ga-taki Onsen
Ferries to Ogasawara-shotō (700km)

SHIN-KYŌ 神橋

The lovely red sacred **bridge** (☎ 54-0535; crossing fee ¥300; 🕑 8am-4pm Jun-Aug, 9am-5pm Dec-Feb) over the Daiya-gawa is a much-photographed reconstruction of the 17th-century original. Its location is famed as the spot where Shōdō Shōnin was carried across the river on the backs of two giant serpents.

RINNŌ-JI 輪王寺

This Tendai-sect **temple** was founded 1200 years ago by Shōdō Shōnin, and today some 360m of zelkova trees make up the pillars in the current building. The three 8m gilded images in the Sambutsu-dō (Three Buddha Hall) are the largest wooden Buddhas in Japan. The central image is Amida Nyorai (one of the primal deities in the Mahayana Buddhist cannon) flanked by Senjū (1000-armed Kannon, deity of mercy and compassion) and Batō (a horse-headed Kannon), whose special domain is the animal kingdom. A room to the side contains a healing Buddha, holding his ring finger over a medicine bowl, and said to be the origin of the Japanese name for this finger (*kusuri-yubi* means 'medicine finger').

Rinnō-ji's **Hōmotsu-den** (Treasure Hall; admission ¥300) houses some 6000 treasures associated with the temple; admission is not included in the combination ticket (p197).

Next to Rinnō-ji is the 15m-high, 3m-circumference pillar Sōrintō, built by Iemitsu in 1643. Inside are 1000 volumes of sutras.

TŌSHŌ-GŪ 東照宮

A huge stone torii is a fittingly grand entrance to this storied **Shintō shrine**. To the left is a **five-storey pagoda** (34.3m) dating from 1650 and reconstructed in 1818. The pagoda has no foundations but contains a long suspended pole that swings like a pendulum, maintaining equilibrium in the event of an earthquake.

The entrance to the main shrine is through the torii at **Omote-mon**, a gate protected on either side by Deva kings. Just inside are the **Sanjinko** (Three Sacred Storehouses). On the upper storey of the last storehouse are imaginative relief carvings of elephants by an artist who famously had never seen the real thing. To the left of the entrance is **Shinkyūsha** (Sacred Stable), a plain building housing a carved white horse. The stable is adorned with allegorical relief carvings of monkeys, including the famous 'hear no evil, see no evil, speak no evil' monkeys, demonstrating three principles of Tendai Buddhism.

Just beyond the stable is a granite font at which, in accordance with Shintō practice, worshippers cleanse themselves by washing their hands and rinsing their mouths. Next to the gate is a sacred library containing 7000 Buddhist scrolls and books; it's closed to the public.

Pass through another torii, climb another flight of stairs, and on the left and right are a drum tower and a belfry. To the left of the drum tower is **Honji-dō** (Yakushido). This hall is best known for the painting on its ceiling of

ROAD-TRIPPING, EDO-STYLE

You know that old chestnut about all roads leading to Rome? Well, in Edo-era Japan all of the important roads literally led to the shōgun's capital.

Under a system called *sankin-kotai, daimyō* (feudal lords) were required to maintain residences in Edo as well as in their home provinces and go back and forth to attend to affairs in both places. Their families, meanwhile, remained in Edo in order to suppress temptation towards insurrection. Travel to the provinces was via main 'trunk' roads, including the Tōkaidō ('Eastern Sea road', connecting Edo to Heian-kyō, now Kyoto), the Nikkō-kaidō (Nikkō road) and the Nakasendō ('Central Mountain road', most notably through Nagano-ken).

These roads became celebrated, notably through Hiroshige's series of *ukiyo-e* (wood-block prints) entitled *53 Stations of the Tōkaidō*. At the 'stations', inns thrived and nobles and their retainers could unwind after long days. Strategically located stations housed checkpoints, 50 in all, called *sekisho*. Travelling commoners had to present a *tegata* (a wooden plaque that served as a passport) and subject themselves to inspection for contraband, such as weaponry. Violation of these rules – including trying to circumnavigate the *sekisho* – could bring severe penalties including a particularly ghastly form of crucifixion. The *sekisho* at Hakone and Kiso-Fukushima were among the most important and remain the best preserved. Other atmospheric station towns are Arimatsu (p264) on the Tōkaidō and Tsumago (p302) on the Nakasendō.

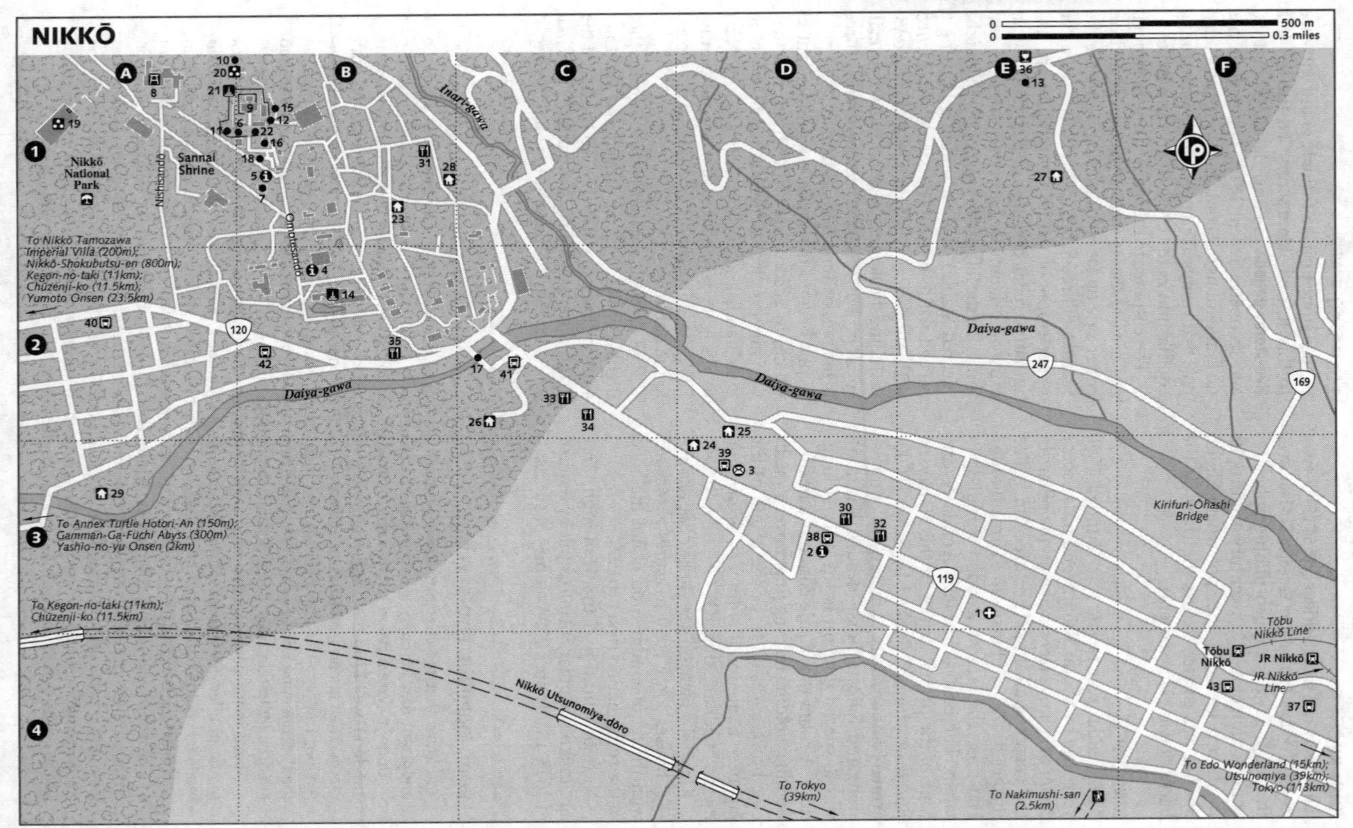
NIKKŌ
500 m
0.3 miles
Nikkō National Park
Sannai Shrine
Nishisandō
Omotesandō
Inari-gawa
Daiya-gawa
Kirifuri-Ōhashi Bridge
Tōbu Nikkō Line
JR Nikkō Line
Tōbu Nikkō
JR Nikkō
Nikkō Utsunomiya-dōro
To Nikkō Tamozawa Imperial Villa (200m); Nikkō-Shokubutsu-en (800m); Kegon-no-taki (11km); Chūzenji-ko (11.5km); Yumoto Onsen (23.5km)
To Annex Turtle Hotori-An (150m); Gamman-Ga-Fuchi Abyss (300m) Yashio-no-yu Onsen (2km)
To Kegon-no-taki (11km); Chūzenji-ko (11.5km)
To Tokyo (39km)
To Nakimushi-san (2.5km)
To Edo Wonderland (15km); Utsunomiya (39km); Tokyo (113km)

the Nakiryū (Crying Dragon). Monks demonstrate the acoustical properties of this hall by clapping two sticks together. The dragon 'roars' (a bit of a stretch) when the sticks are clapped beneath the dragon's mouth, but not elsewhere.

Next comes **Yōmei-mon** (Sunset Gate), dazzlingly decorated with glimmering gold leaf and intricate, coloured carvings and paintings of flowers, dancing girls, mythical beasts and Chinese sages. Worrying that its perfection might arouse envy in the gods, those responsible for its construction had the final supporting pillar placed upside down as a deliberate error. Although the style is more Chinese than Japanese and some critics deride it as gaudy, it's a grand spectacle.

To the left of Yōmei-mon is **Jin-yōsha**, the storage for the *mikoshi* (portable shrines) used during festivals.

Tōshō-gū's **Honden** (Main Hall) and **Haiden** (Hall of Worship) are across the enclosure. Inside (open only to *daimyō* during the Edo period) are paintings of the 36 immortal poets of Kyoto, and a ceiling-painting pattern from the Momoyama period; note the 100 dragons, each different. *Fusuma* (sliding door) paintings depict a *kirin* (a mythical beast that's part giraffe and part dragon). It's said that it will appear only when the world is at peace.

Through Yōmei-mon and to the right is **Nemuri-Neko**, a small wooden sculpture of a sleeping cat that's famous throughout Japan for its life-like appearance (though admittedly the attraction is lost on some visitors). From here, **Sakashita-mon** opens onto an uphill path through towering cedars to **Ieyasu's tomb**, appropriately solemn. There's a separate entry fee (¥520) to see the cat and the tomb.

FUTARASAN-JINJA 二荒山神社

Shōdō Shōnin founded this **shrine**; the current building dates from 1619, making it Nikkō's oldest. It's the protector shrine of Nikkō itself, dedicated to the nearby mountain, Nantai-san (2484m), the mountain's consort, Nyotai-san, and their mountainous progeny, Tarō. There are other shrine branches on Nantai-san and by Chūzenji-ko (p204).

TAIYŪIN-BYŌ 大猷院廟

Enshrining Ieyasu's grandson Iemitsu (1604–51) is **Taiyūin-byō**. Though it houses many of the same elements as Tōshō-gū (storehouses, drum tower, Chinese-style gates etc), its smaller, more intimate scale and setting in a cryptomeria forest make it very appealing. It's unusual in that it's both a Buddhist temple and a mausoleum.

Among Taiyūin-byō's many structures, look for dozens of lanterns donated by *daimyō*, and the gate Niō-mon, whose guardian deities have a hand up (to welcome those with pure hearts) and a hand down (to suppress impure hearts). Inside the main hall, 140 dragons painted on the ceiling are said to carry prayers

INFORMATION

Kawai i-in Clinic 河合医院 ... 1 E3
Kyōdo Center Tourist Information Office 日光郷土センター ... 2 D3
Post Office 日光郵便局 ... 3 D3
Ticket Office きっぷ売り場 ... 4 B2
Ticket Office きっぷ売り場 ... 5 B1

SIGHTS & ACTIVITIES

Drum Tower 鼓楼 ... 6 B1
Five-storey Pagoda 五重塔 ... 7 B1
Futarasan-jinja 二荒山神社 ... 8 A1
Haiden 拝殿 ... 9 B1
Hōmotsu-den 宝物殿 ... (see 14)
Honden 本殿 ... 10 A1
Honji-dō 本地堂 ... 11 A1
Nemuri-Neko 眠猫 ... 12 B1
Nikkō Woodcarving Center 日光木彫りの里工芸センター ... 13 E1
Rinnō-ji 輪王寺 ... 14 B2
Sakashita-mon 坂下門 ... 15 B1
Sanjinko 三神庫 ... 16 B1
Shin-kyō 神橋 ... 17 C2
Shinkyūsha 神厩舎 ... 18 B1
Taiyūin-byō 大猷院廟 ... 19 A1
Tomb of Ieyasu 奥社（徳川家康の墓） ... 20 A1
Tōshō-gū 東照宮 ... 21 A1
Yōmei-mon 陽明門 ... 22 B1

SLEEPING

Hotel Seikōen ホテル清晃苑 ... 23 B1
Jōhsyū-ya Ryokan 上州屋旅館 ... 24 D3
Nikkō Daiyagawa Youth Hostel 日光大谷川ユースホステル ... 25 D2
Nikkō Kanaya Hotel 日光金谷ホテル ... 26 C2
Nikkō Park Lodge 日光パークロッジ ... 27 E1
Nikkō Tōkan-sō Ryokan 日光東観荘 ... 28 B1
Turtle Inn Nikkō タートルイン日光 ... 29 A3

EATING

Gusto ガスト ... 30 D3
Gyōshintei 尭心亭 ... 31 B1
Hi no Kuruma ひの車 ... 32 D3
Hippari Dako ひっぱり凧 ... 33 C2
Kikō きこう ... 34 C2
Yuba Yūzen ゆば遊膳 ... 35 B2

DRINKING

Nikkō Beer 日光ビール ... 36 E1

TRANSPORT

JR Nikkō Station Bus Stop (No 1) ＪＲ日光駅前バス停 ... 37 F4
Nikkō Kyōdo Center-mae Bus Stop 日光郷土センター前バス停 ... 38 D3
Nikkō Shishō-mae (City Hall branch office) Bus Stop ... 39 D3
Nishi-sandō Bus Stop 西参道バス停 ... 40 A2
Shin-Kyō Bus Stop 神橋バス停 ... 41 C2
Sōgō-kaikan-mae Bus Stop 総合会館前バス停 ... 42 B2
Tōbu Nikkō Station Bus Stops (No2A-2D) 東武日光駅前バス停 ... 43 F4

to the heavens; those holding pearls are on their way up, and those without are returning to gather more prayers.

GAMMAN-GA-FUCHI ABYSS 含満ヶ淵

If the crowds of Nikkō leave you yearning for a little quiet, take the 20-minute walk to **Gamman-Ga-Fuchi Abyss**, a collection of *jizō* statues (the small stone statues of the Buddhist protector of travellers and children) set along a wooded path. One of the statues midway along is known as the Bake-jizō, who mocks travellers foolish enough to try to count all of the *jizō* (they're said to be uncountable). Take a left after crossing the Shin-kyō bridge and follow the river for about 800m, crossing another bridge en route.

NIKKŌ TAMOZAWA IMPERIAL VILLA 日光田母沢御用邸

The 1899 **Nikkō Tamozawa Goyōtei** (☎ 53-6767; adult/child ¥500/250; ⌚ 9am-4pm Wed-Mon) was the largest wooden imperial villa (106 rooms) in two generations of emperors, and it was where Emperor Shōwa (aka Hirohito) spent WWII. It has been painstakingly restored to its former glory and is well worth a visit. It's about 1km west of the Shin-kyō bridge.

NIKKŌ WOODCARVING CENTER 日光木彫りの里

The workshop and sales shop of **Nikkō woodcarving center** (☎ 53-0070; 2848 Tokorono; admission free; ⌚ 9am-5pm, closed Thu Nov-Apr) have contemporary and utilitarian pieces in the local woodcarving tradition. Exhibits on the 2nd floor include *yatai* (festival floats) and *tansu* (wooden chests). You can try your own hand with a week's notice (fax 53-0310; fee varies).

Festivals & Events

Yayoi Matsuri Procession of *mikoshi* held at Futarasan-jinja on 16 and 17 April.

Tōshō-gū Grand Festival Nikkō's most important annual festival is held on 17 and 18 May and features horseback archery on the first day and a 1000-strong costumed re-enactment of the delivery of Ieyasu's remains to Nikkō on the second.

Tōshō-gū Autumn Festival Autumnal repeat on 16 and 17 October of the May festival, minus the equestrian archery.

Sleeping

BUDGET

Nikkō Daiyagawa Youth Hostel (☎/fax 54-1974; www5.ocn.ne.jp/~daiyayh; 1075 Nakahatsuishi-machi; dm ¥2730; ⊠) This four-room, 24-bed hostel earns commendations for its hospitable hostess. It's a four-minute walk from the Nikkō/Shishō-mae (City Hall branch office) bus stop, behind the post office and overlooking the river. Breakfast/dinner is ¥420/840.

Jōhsyū-ya Ryokan (☎ 54-0155; fax 53-2000; www.johsyu-ya.co.jp; 911 Nakahatsuishi; r per person ¥3900; P) This very tidy inn on the main road beside the post office is just good honest value. No private facilities and there's little English spoken, but there's a hot-spring bath. Breakfast/dinner from ¥800/1500.

Nikkō Park Lodge (☎ 53-1201; fax 53-4332; www.nikkoparklodge.com; 28285 Tokorono; dm from ¥3990; P) Friendly, cute, unpretentious and well kept, with pick-up available between 3pm and 5pm. It's mostly twin and double rooms, plus a couple of dorms, run by English-speaking Zen Buddhist monks; look for yoga classes. Breakfast/dinner is ¥395/1500.

MIDRANGE

Turtle Inn Nikkō (☎ 53-3168; fax 53-3883; www.turtle-nikko.com; 2-16 Takumi-chō; s/d without bathroom ¥4800/9000, s/d with bathroom ¥5600/10,600; P 💻) Here you'll find large Japanese- and Western-style rooms, some English-speaking staff and hearty meals (breakfast/dinner ¥1050/2100). Take a bus to Sōgō-kaikan-mae, backtrack about 50m, turn right along the river and walk for about five minutes; you'll see the turtle sign on the left.

Annex Turtle Hotori-An (☎ 53-3663; fax 53-3883; www.turtle-nikko.com; 8-28 Takumi-chō; s/d ¥6500/12,400; P 💻) The Turtle Inn's newer Annex is a more modern, pleasant option. It has a windowed dining room (breakfast/dinner ¥1050/2100), well-tended tatami and Western-style rooms, and greenery surrounding the onsen (plus in-room baths).

Nikkō Tōkan-sō Ryokan (☎ 54-0611; fax 53-3914; www.tokanso.com; 2335 Sannai; r per person incl 2 meals ¥8400-14,000, min 2 people; P) Clean and spacious, Tōkan-sō provides a welcoming (if not luxurious) ryokan experience; it's popular with tour and school groups. From the Shin-kyō bus stop, continue uphill, cross the street, turn right and bear left again uphill.

TOP END

Hotel Seikōen (☎ 53-5555; fax 53-5554; www.hotel-seikoen.com; 2350 Sannai; d per person incl 2 meals from ¥13,650) This 25-room hotel was built in the 1980s but somehow looks older. That's forgotten in the neat rooms (mostly Japanese style) and alkali onsen, including indoor and outdoor baths and sauna. It's past Tōkan-sō Ryokan, about 100m on the left-hand side.

our pick **Nikkō Kanaya Hotel** (☎ 54-0001; fax 53-2487; www.kanayahotel.co.jp; 1300 Kami-Hatsuishi-machi; tw from ¥17,325; P 🖳) One of the finest heritage Western hotels in Japan, this grand lady from 1893 wears her history like a fine dress. The best rooms have excellent vistas, spacious quarters and private bathrooms. The lobby bar is deliciously dark and amenable to drinking scotch. Rates do not include meals and rise steeply in peak seasons.

Eating & Drinking

A local speciality is *yuba* (the skin that forms when making tofu) cut into strips; better than it sounds, it's a staple of *shōjin ryōri* (Buddhist vegetarian cuisine).

Hippari Dako (☎ 53-2933; meals ¥500-850; 🕑 11am-8pm) With English menus, this three-table shop is an institution among foreign travellers, as years of business cards tacked to the walls testify. It serves filling sets, including *yakitori* (chicken on skewers) and *yaki* udon (fried noodles). It's a white building on the left side of Rte 119, and has an English sign.

Gusto (☎ 50-1232; mains ¥500-1000; 🕑 10am-2am Mon-Fri, 7am-2am Sat & Sun) Nikkō's only late-night restaurant makes up for what it lacks in individuality with value and variety. There's a detailed picture menu, and offerings include pizzas, pasta and *ribu rosu suteeki* (rib roast steak; ¥899). Look for the red circle sign.

Hi no Kuruma (☎ 54-2062; mains ¥500-1500; 🕑 lunch & dinner Thu-Tue) A local favourite for *okonomiyaki* (savoury pancakes), which you cook yourself on a *teppan* (hot-steel table). Most choices are under ¥1000, or splurge on the works: pork, squid, beef, shrimp, corn etc (¥1500). There's an English menu. Look for the small parking lot and red-black-and-white Japanese sign.

Kikō (☎ 53-3320; mains ¥700-1300; 🕑 lunch & dinner) Welcoming, home-style spot for Korean dishes, like *ishiyaki bibimpa* (rice with beef and vegetables in a hot stone bowl), *chapchae* (fried clear noodles with vegetables) and *kimchi rāmen* (noodles with spicy Korean pickles). It's a few doors downhill from Hippari Dako, with a scrolling electronic sign. An English menu is available.

Yuba Yūzen (☎ 53-0355; sets ¥2700-3200; 🕑 lunch Thu-Tue) This *yuba* speciality house serves it sashimi-style, with tofu and soy milk, and with a variety of seasonal side dishes. There's no English menu, but there are only two choices for sets: ¥2700 if you're hungry and ¥3200 if you're really hungry. Look for the two-storey tan building across from the first left turn after Shin-kyō.

Gyōshintei (☎ 53-3751; set courses ¥3000-8000; 🕑 lunch & dinner Fri-Wed) For *shōjin ryōri* in a setting to die for, Gyōshintei is worth the splurge. Set courses and prices change with the season, but a safe bet is the *omakase kaiseki* (chef's choice *kaiseki*; price varies). This elegant, traditional eatery overlooks a carefully tended garden, around 250m north of the Shin-kyō bridge. There's a three-peaked emblem on the door curtain.

Nikkō Beer (☎ 54-3005; beer & snacks from ¥525; 🕑 9am-6pm) Sample the local brew in the hills above town, a light lager-style Pilsner that's won beer competitions both internationally and in Japan. Snacks include *go-shurui sōseji* (five-variety sausage set; ¥800). There's a picture menu and an English sign.

Getting There & Away

Nikkō is best reached from Tokyo via the Tōbu Nikkō line from Asakusa Station. You can usually get last-minute seats on reserved *tokkyū* (limited express) trains (¥2620, one hour 50 minutes) about every 30 minutes from 7.30am to 10am, hourly thereafter. *Kaisoku* (rapid) trains (¥1320, 2½ hours, hourly from 6.20am to 4.30pm) require no reservation. For either train, you may have to change at Shimo-imaichi. Be sure to ride in the first two cars to reach Nikkō (some cars may separate at an intermediate stop).

JR trains connect Nikkō and Tokyo's Shinjuku and Ikebukuro Stations (¥4310) in about two hours. Otherwise, travelling by JR is time-consuming and costly without a JR Pass. Take the *shinkansen* from Tokyo to Utsunomiya (¥4290, 54 minutes) and change there for an ordinary train to Nikkō (¥740, 45 minutes).

TRAIN/BUS PASSES

Tōbu Railway offers two passes covering rail transport from Asakusa to Nikkō (though not the *tokkyū* surcharge, from ¥1040) and unlimited hop-on-hop-off bus services around Nikkō. The All Nikko Pass (adult/child ¥4400/2210) is valid for four days and includes buses to Chūzenji-ko and Yumoto Onsen. The World Heritage

Pass (Sekai-isan Meguri Pass; adult/child/junior-high student/senior-high student ¥3600/1700/3000/3200), valid for two days, includes buses to the World Heritage sights, plus admission to Tōshō-gū, Rinnō-ji and Futarasan-jinja. Purchase these passes at the Tōbu **Sightseeing Service Center** (8am-2.30pm) in Asakusa Station. Bus stops are announced in English.

TŌBU NIKKŌ BUS FREE PASS

If you've already got your rail ticket, two-day bus-only passes are available and allow unlimited rides between Nikkō and Yumoto Onsen (adult/child ¥3000/1500) or Nikkō and Chūzenji Onsen (adult/child ¥2000/1000), including the World Heritage Sites. Alternatively, the Sekai-isan-meguri (World Heritage Bus Pass; adult/child ¥500/250) covers the area between the stations and shrine precincts. Buy these at Tōbu Nikkō Station.

AROUND NIKKŌ 日光周辺

Nikkō is part of the Nikkō National Park, 1402 sq km sprawling over Fukushima, Tochigi, Gunma and Niigata prefectures. This mountainous region features extinct volcanoes, lakes, waterfalls and marshlands. There are good hiking opportunities and some remote hot-spring resorts.

Edo Wonderland 日光江戸村

Thirty minutes by bus from Nikkō is Edo Wonderland Nikko Edomura, a kitschy but fun **theme park** (0288-77-1777; www.edowonderland.net; half-day pass adult/child ¥3900/2000; 9am-5pm Thu-Tue 20 Mar-30 Nov, 9.30am-4pm 1 Dec-19 Mar, closed 25 Jan-7 Feb;) where kids can watch ninjas battle, geishas strut and magicians astound in a re-created town of the Edo period. There are three free shuttle buses daily from JR Nikkō Station.

Yashio-no-yu Onsen やしおの湯温泉

A 5km bus ride from central Nikkō, this modern **onsen** (0288-53-6611; adult/child ¥500/300; 10am-8.30pm Fri-Wed) has various baths including a *rotemburo* (outdoor bath). Take a Chūzenji-bound bus from either train station in Nikkō and get off at the Kiyotaki Itchōme stop. The onsen is across the river from the bus stop; walk back towards Nikkō, under the Rte 120 bypass and across the bridge.

TOP FIVE ONSEN

- **Hōshi Onsen Chōjūkan** (p206)
- **Jinata Onsen** (p242)
- **Takaragawa Onsen** (p206)
- **Shuzen-ji Onsen** (p226)
- **Yunohama Onsen** (p242)

Chūzenji-ko 中禅寺湖

This highland area 11.5km west of Nikkō offers some natural seclusion and striking views of Nantai-san (2484m) from Chūzenji-ko lake. The big-ticket attraction is the billowing, 97m-high **Kegon-no-taki** (Kegon falls; 華厳滝; 0288-55-0030; adult/child return ¥530/320; 7.30am-6pm May-Sep, 9am-4.30pm Dec-Feb, sliding hours rest of year). Take the elevator down to a platform to observe the full force of the plunging water. **Futarasan-jinja** (二荒山神社; 0288-55-0017; 8am-5pm Apr-Oct, 9am-4pm Nov-Mar) complements the shrines at Tōshō-gū. The shrine is about 1km west of the falls, along the lake's north shore. The eponymous temple **Chūzen-ji Tachiki-kannon** (中禅寺立木観音; 0288-55-0013; adult/child ¥500/200; 8am-5pm Apr-Oct, to 4pm Nov-Mar), located on the lake's eastern shore, was founded in the 8th century and houses a 6m-tall Kannon statue from then.

For good views of the lake and Kegon-no-taki, get off the bus at the Akechi-daira bus stop (the stop before Chūzenji Onsen) and take the **Akechi-daira Ropeway** (Akechi Plateau Cable Car; 明智平ロープウェイ; 0288-55-0331; one way/return adult ¥390/710, child ¥190/360; 9am-4pm, closed 1-15 Mar) up to a viewing platform. From here, it's a pleasant 1.5km walk across the Chanoki-daira to a vantage point with great views over the lake, the falls and Nantai-san. From here you can walk down to the lake and Chūzenji Onsen.

Chūzenji-ko has the usual flotilla of sightseeing boats at the dock (prices vary). The lake (161m deep) is a fabulous shade of deep blue in good weather, with a mountainous backdrop.

SLEEPING

Chūzenji Pension (中禅寺ペンション; 0288-55-0888; fax 55-0721; www8.ocn.ne.jp/~chuzn-pn, in Japanese; s with/without meals from ¥8925/5250; P) This pink hostelry set back from the lake's eastern shore has nine mostly Western-style rooms that feel a bit like grandma's house. There's a cosy fireplace, two baths and bike rental (per day ¥3000) available.

Hotel Fūga (楓雅; ☎ 0288-55-1122; fax 55-1100; www.nikko-hotelfuga.com, in Japanese; d per person incl 2 meals from ¥23,000; P) The common baths here are enormous, the building is fitted with contemporary art and hallways are lined with carpets you may want to dive into. All 30 palatial Japanese-style rooms have lake views. It's 150m beyond Chūzenji Pension.

GETTING THERE & AWAY

Buses run from Tōbu Nikkō Station to Chūzenji Onsen (¥1100, 45 minutes). It's most economical to use a Tōbu Nikkō Bus free pass (see opposite).

Yumoto Onsen 湯元温泉

From Chūzenji-ko, you might continue on to the quieter hot-springs resort of Yumoto Onsen by bus (¥840, 30 minutes) or reach it by a rewarding three-hour hike on the **Senjōgahara Shizen-kenkyu-rō** (Senjōgahara Plain Nature Trail; 戦場ヶ原自然研究路).

From Chūzenji Onsen, take a Yumoto-bound bus and get off at Ryūzu-no-taki (竜頭ノ滝; ¥410, 20 minutes), which is the start of the hike. The hike follows the Yu-gawa across the picturesque marshland of Senjōgahara (partially on wooden plank paths), alongside the 75m-high falls of Yu-daki (湯滝) to the lake Yu-no-ko (湯の湖), then around the lake to Yumoto Onsen and the bus stop to Nikkō (¥1650, 1½ hours).

Before leaving Yumoto Onsen, you might stop off for a bath at the hot-spring temple **Onsen-ji** (温泉時; adult/child ¥500/300; 9am-4pm late Apr-Nov), a good spot to rest hiking-weary muscles.

To hike downhill, take the bus to Yumoto and follow this route in reverse.

GUNMA-KEN 群馬県

The Japanese archipelago is filled with onsen, but the star in the Kanto area hot-spring firmament is Gunma-ken. Mineral baths seem to bubble out of the ground at every turn in this mountainous landscape, and some small towns feel delightfully traditional. Here's just a small selection.

Kusatsu Onsen 草津温泉

☎ 0279 / pop 7000

Kusatsu has been famous for its waters since the Kamakura period and is a heavily touristed bath town. Their source is Yubatake (湯畑, 'hot water field') in the town centre, flowing at 5000L per minute and topped with wooden tanks from which Kusatsu's ryokan fill their baths. A stroll here in your *yukata* (cotton bathrobe) is a must. Kusatsu's waters are relatively heavy with sulphuric acid, which sounds scary until you realise that it destroys harmful microbes.

Stop in or phone the **city hall tourist section** (☎ 88-0001; 8.30am-5.30pm Mon-Fri), next to the bus station (there's an English speaker on hand).

There are plenty of onsen open to the public, including **Ōtakinoyu** (大瀧乃湯; ☎ 88-2600; adult/child ¥800/400; 9am-9pm), known for its tubs at a variety of temperatures; try different ones for an experience known as *awase-yu* (mix-and-match waters). West of town in Saino Kawara kōen is **Sai-no-kawara Rotemburo** (西の河露天風呂; ☎ 88-6167; adult/child ¥500/300; 7am-8pm Apr-Nov, 9am-8pm Dec-Mar), a 500-sq-metre outdoor bath that can fit 100 people. It's a 20-minute ride (¥100) on community buses leaving the Kusatsu bus terminal. Ask for the 'A course' bus.

Kusatsu also offers a touristy but unique opportunity to see *yumomi*, in which local women stir the waters to cool them while singing folk songs. It's next to Yubatake at the bathhouse **Netsu no Yu** (熱の湯; ☎ 88-3613; adult/child ¥500/250; 4-5 shows daily from 10am 1 Apr-30 Nov).

For a bite to eat, immediately west of Yubatake is **Yurakutei** (湯楽亭; ☎ 88-3001; mains ¥700-1300; 9.30am-11pm), a 2nd-floor spot that serves up hearty *okonomiyaki* crepes (¥720). Look for the wooden, tower-like structure.

Inns in the town centre are mostly pretty expensive, but the 12-room, Alpine-vibe **Pension Segawa** (ペンションセガワ; ☎ 88-1288; fax 88-1377; http://scty.net/segawa/, in Japanese; r per person incl 2 meals from ¥8025; P) is a 10-minute walk from the bus terminal (or the owners will pick you up). Choose a Western- or Japanese-style room and three different bathtubs, and look for fresh-baked bread.

Though you might not know from looking at its tower next to Yubatake, **Hotel Ichii** (ホテル一井; ☎ 88-0011; fax 88-0111; www.hotel-ichii.co.jp; r per person incl 2 meals from ¥13,500; P) has been a Kusatsu institution in business for 300-plus years. This is a rambling, retro-decor place featuring indoor and outdoor baths. Expect *sansai* (mountain vegetable) cuisine. In winter, ask about complimentary lift tickets for Kusatsu Kokusai ski resort.

Transport to Kusatsu Onsen is by bus from Naganohara-Kusatsuguchi Station. From Ueno, *tokkyū* Kusatsu trains take about 2½ hours (¥4620) to Naganohara-Kusatsuguchi Station, then take the local bus to Kusatsu Onsen (¥670, 25 minutes). Alternatively, take the *shinkansen* to Takasaki and transfer to the JR Agatsuma line (¥5140, 2½ hours). **JR Highway Buses** (www.jrbuskanto.co.jp) from Shinjuku Station's New South Exit cost ¥3200/5600 (one way/return) and take three to four hours each way; reservations required.

Minakami & Takaragawa Onsen 水上温泉・宝川温泉

☎ 0278

In eastern Gunma-ken, Minakami is a thriving, sprawling onsen town with outdoor activities to match. The town of Minakami also encompasses Takaragawa Onsen (about 30 minutes away by road), a riverside spa oft-voted the nation's best.

The train station is in the village of Minakami Onsen, as are most of Minakami's lodgings. **Minakami Tourist Information Centre** (水上観光協会; ☎ 72-2611; www.minakami-onsen.com; ⌚ 9am-5pm) is across from the station, has English pamphlets and can make accommodation reservations (in Japanese). Ask which inns in town have *higaeri nyuyoku* (day-use baths) open when you visit.

our pick **Hōshi Onsen Chōjūkan** (法師温泉長寿館; ☎ 66-0005; fax 66-0003; www.houshi-onsen.jp, in Japanese; r per person incl 2 meals from ¥13,800), on the southwestern fringes of Minakami town, is one of Japan's finest onsen inns. To reach this perfectly rustic, supremely photogenic lodging, take a bus to Jōmō Kōgen Station (20 minutes), then another bus for Sarugakyō Onsen (35 minutes). At the last stop, take another bus for Hōshi Onsen (25 minutes). Be sure to check schedules at the tourist information centre.

Tanigawadake Ropeway (谷川岳ロープウエイ; ☎ 72-3575; return ¥2000; ⌚ 8am-5pm Mon-Fri, 7am-5pm Sat & Sun) takes you via gondola to the peak of Tenjin-daira, from where hiking trips, ranging from a couple of hours to all day, are available from May to November. There's skiing and snowboarding in winter. From Minakami Station, take a 20-minute bus to Ropeway-Eki-mae bus stop (¥650, about hourly).

A number of operators lead rafting and kayaking trips in warmer months, and winter expeditions such as snowshoeing, from about ¥6000 for a half-day. Enquire at the tourist information centre. **Max** (☎ 72-4844) is a typical outlet, with English-speaking guides.

Takaragawa Onsen (☎ 75-2611; adult/child ¥1500/1000; ⌚ 9am-5pm) is idyllic and rangey. Most of its several pools on the river-banks (with slate, not natural, flooring) are mixed-bathing, and there's a women-only bath. Women are allowed to take modesty towels into the mixed baths. A fascinating antiques shop on the way down to the baths is full of junk and gems ranging from lacquered teapots to Buddha heads and abacuses.

The inn on the other side of the river, **Ōsenkaku** (汪泉閣; ☎ 75-2121; fax 75-2038; www.takaragawa.com; r per person incl 2 meals from ¥11,700) is spectacular, with gorgeous riverfront rooms over several buildings, a mighty old-style feel and 24-hour use of the outdoor onsen. Prices rise steeply for nicer rooms with better views, but aim for the 1930s-vintage No 1 annex. Note, the menu features bear-meat soup.

To reach Minakami Station, take the *shinkansen* from Ueno to Takasaki and transfer to the Jōetsu line (¥5140, two hours), or *tokkyū* Minakami trains run direct (¥4620, 2½ hours). You can also catch the *shinkansen* to Jōmō Kōgen (1¼ hours) from Tokyo/Ueno (¥5240/5040), from where buses run to Minakami (¥600) and Takaragawa Onsen (¥1450, April to early December). Buses to Takaragawa Onsen also run from Minakami Station (¥1100, year-round).

MITO 水戸

☎ 029 / pop 264,000

Capital of Ibaraki Prefecture and a one-time castle town, Mito is best known for **Kairaku-en** (偕楽園; ☎ 244-5454; garden/Kobuntei pavilion free/¥190; ⌚ garden 6am-7pm Mar-Sep, 7am-6pm Oct-Feb, pavilion 9am-4.30pm). It's one of the three most-celebrated landscape gardens in Japan; the other two are Kenroku-en (p307) in Kanazawa and Kōraku-en in Okayama (p448).

The 18-acre Kairaku-en dates back to 1842 when it was built by the *daimyō* of the Mito *han* (domain), a member of the clan of the Tokugawa shōgun. 'Kairaku-en' means 'the garden to enjoy with people', and it was one of the first gardens in the nation to open to the public.

The gardens remain popular for their 3000 *ume* (plum blossom) trees, some 100 varieties of which bloom in late February or early

March. A plum-blossom festival takes place here around this time; contact the **tourist office** (☎ 232-9189) for dates. Other flowering trees (azaleas, camellias, cherry etc) make for impressive viewing in other seasons, and the hillside setting allows broad views. The three-storey pavilion Kobun-tei is a faithful 1950s reproduction of the *daimyo's* villa (the original was destroyed during WWII).

From Tokyo, JR Jōban line trains depart from Ueno Station for Mito (*tokkyū;* ¥3510, 80 minutes); during the plum-blossom festival, connect by local train to Kairaku-en Station (¥180, five minutes), otherwise take a bus to Kairaku-en bus stop (¥230, 15 minutes) or walk (about 30 minutes) from the station's south exit along the lake Senba-ko.

WEST OF TOKYO

The western part of Tokyo-to (Tokyo Prefecture) and the surrounding region offer many rewarding outdoor activities, with cedar-lined hiking trails and bubbling hot springs. South and west of the capital are the scenic Fuji Go-ko region, Mt Fuji itself, the tourist mecca of Hakone, and the onsen and beach resorts of the Izu-hantō.

GHIBLI MUSEUM 三鷹の森ジブリ美術館

If you saw *Spirited Away*, by Miyazaki Hayao (or *Princess Mononoke*, *Howl's Moving Castle*, *My Neighbor Totoro* and so on), you probably fell in love with its mythical themes, fanciful characters and outrageous landscapes. So did every kid in Japan, which means you need to arrange tickets long before you arrive at this **museum** (☎ 0570-055777; www.ghibli-museum.jp; 1-1-83 Shimorenjaku, Mitaka-shi; adult ¥1000, child ¥100-700; 🕑 10am-6pm Wed-Mon) of the work of Ghibli, Miyazaki's animation studio (for more on Miyazaki see the boxed text, p74). In Japan, tickets can only be had through Lawson convenience stores. See the museum's website for details; you may need the help of a Japanese speaker when purchasing.

Exhibits cover the animation process from concept to screen (English-speaking docents are usually on hand, but don't expect English labels). There's a zoetrope presentation of a half-dozen Ghibli characters in motion, a mini-theatre presenting short films (in Japanese but easy enough to follow), a rooftop robot from *Castle in the Sky* and a gift shop.

The museum is in Tokyo's Mitaka City. From the south exit of Mitaka Station on the JR Chūō line (from Shinjuku: ¥210, 17 minutes), follow the signs along the Tamagawa waterway for 15 minutes to Inokashira Park and turn right. Alternatively, a community bus (one way/return ¥200/300, approximately every 10 minutes) goes directly to the museum from the station.

TAKAO-SAN 高尾山

☎ 042

Easily reached from Shinjuku Station, gentle Takao-san is one of Tokyo's most popular day trips. Although it's often busy on weekends and holidays and rather built up compared to other regional hikes, it can make for a perfect family outing.

One of the chief attractions on this 599m mountain is the temple **Yaku-ō-in** (薬王院; ☎ 661-1115; 🕑 24hr), best known for the Hi-watari Matsuri (fire-crossing ceremony), which takes place on the second Sunday in March, at 1pm near Takaosanguchi Station). Priests walk across hot coals with bare feet amid the ceremonial blowing of conch shells. The public is also welcome to participate.

The rest of the year, Takao-san offers nature hikes with six trails. Keio line offices have free trail maps in English. The most popular trail (No 1) leads you past the temple; allow about 3¼ hours return for the 400m ascent. Alternatively, a cable car and a chair lift can take you part of the way up (one way adult/child ¥470/230, return ¥900/450).

From Shinjuku Station, take the Keio line (*jun-tokkyū;* ¥370, 47 minutes) to Takaosanguchi. The tourist village (with snack and souvenir shops), trail entrances, cable car and chairlift are a few minutes away to the right. JR Pass holders can travel to Takao Station on the JR Chūō line (48 minutes) and transfer to the Keio line to Takaosanguchi (¥120, two minutes).

OKU-TAMA REGION 奥多摩周辺

Oku-Tama is Tokyo's best spot for hiking getaways. Here, the Tama-gawa runs through magnificent mountains with waterfalls, woodlands and hiking trails, ideal for day trips or overnight stays. The lofty shrine of Musashi Mitake-jinja and the quaint village surrounding it is a hidden gem of Tokyo.

Mitake-san 御岳山

Mitake is a charming old-world mountain hamlet that seems light years from Tokyo's bustle. Try to spot a flying squirrel or simply breathe the fresh air redolent of cedar. Access is easiest by cable car, and about 20 minutes on foot from the terminus, up dozens of steps, is **Musashi Mitake-jinja** (武蔵御嶽神社; ☎ 0428-78-8500; ⏲ 24hr), a Shintō shrine and pilgrimage site said to date back some 1200 years. The site commands stunning views of the surrounding mountains. Pick up maps at the **Mitake Visitors Centre** (御岳ビジターセンター; ☎ 0428-78-9363; ⏲ 9am-4.30pm Tue-Sun), 250m beyond the cable car, near the start of the village.

Ōtake-san Hike 大岳山

If you've got time, the five-hour round-trip hike from Musashi Mitake-jinja to the summit of Ōtake-san (1266m) is highly recommended. Although there's some climbing involved, it's a fairly easy hike and the views from the summit are excellent – Mt Fuji is visible on clear days. On the way, you can detour to Nanoyono-taki falls, Ganseki-en rock garden and Ayahirono-taki falls.

If you're not spending the night on Mitake-san, be sure to note the hours of the cable car before setting out.

Sleeping & Eating

The following places are all near Musashi Mitake-jinja.

Mitake Youth Hostel (御嶽ユースホステル; ☎ 0428-78-8501; fax 78-8774; www.jyh.or.jp; dm with/without 2 meals ¥4550/2880, extra ¥1000 for nonmembers) This comfortable hostel has fine tatami rooms inside a handsome old building that used to be a pilgrims' lodge. It's midway between the top of the cable car and Musashi Mitake-jinja, about a minute beyond the visitors centre.

Komadori San-sō (駒鳥山荘; ☎ 0428-78-8472; fax 78-8472; www.hkr.ne.jp/~komadori; r per person from ¥4500; 💻) Below the shrine near the back end of the village, this 10-room inn brims with bric-a-brac, and the owners are friendly and at ease with foreigners. There's a balcony with mountain views, and gigantic cypress bathtubs.

Reiunso (嶺雲荘; ☎ 0428-78-8501; fax 78-8774; www.reiunsou.com, in Japanese; r per person incl 2 meals from ¥8400) In the same building as the Mitake Youth Hostel, Reiunso has upgraded facilities and more elaborate meals featuring seasonal mountain vegetables.

Momiji-ya (紅葉屋; ☎ 0428-78-8475; mains ¥735-1155; ⏲ noon-5pm, closed irregularly) This *soba* (buckwheat noodles) shop near the shrine gate has views out the back windows and items like *kamonanban soba* (noodles in hearty duck broth; ¥1155). There's a picture menu. Look for the brown-and-white curtain outside.

Getting There & Away

To reach Mitake-san, take the JR Chūō line from Shinjuku Station, changing to the JR Ōme line at Tachikawa Station or Ōme Station depending on the service, and get off at Mitake (¥890, 90 minutes). Buses (¥270, 10 minutes) run from Mitake Station to Takimoto, where a cable car takes you near Mitake village (elevation 831m, one way/return ¥570/1090, six minutes, 7.30am to 6.30pm); on foot, the climb takes about one hour.

MT FUJI AREA 富士山周辺

Always breathtaking, iconic Mt Fuji dominates the region west of Tokyo. Climbing this volcano is a tradition with sacred overtones, though many visitors are content to view it from its foothills. Hakone is the most famous spot for Fuji viewing, but the scenic Fuji Go-ko region offers similar views and fewer crowds.

Mt Fuji 富士山

On clear days, particularly in winter, Mt Fuji (Fuji-san in Japanese) is visible from as far as Tokyo, 100km away. When Japan's highest mountain (3776m) is capped with snow, it's a picture-postcard perfect volcanic cone. For much of the year you need to be closer, and even then the notoriously shy mountain is often covered in haze or cloud. Winter and spring are your next best bets for Fuji-spotting, yet even during these times the mountain may be visible only in the morning before it retreats behind its cloud curtain.

ORIENTATION

If Mt Fuji is the centre of this region, other attractions radiate around it like the numerals on a clock. At 5 o'clock is Izu-hantō, while 4 o'clock points you towards Hakone. The Fuji Go-ko (Fuji Five Lakes) region begins at about 2 o'clock and heads west, through the towns of Fuji-Kawaguchi-ko, continuing along the mountain's northern flank to the lovely, remote lake Motosu-ko at about 10.30 on the clock. Much of this land is part of the noncontiguous Fuji-Hakone-Izu National Park.

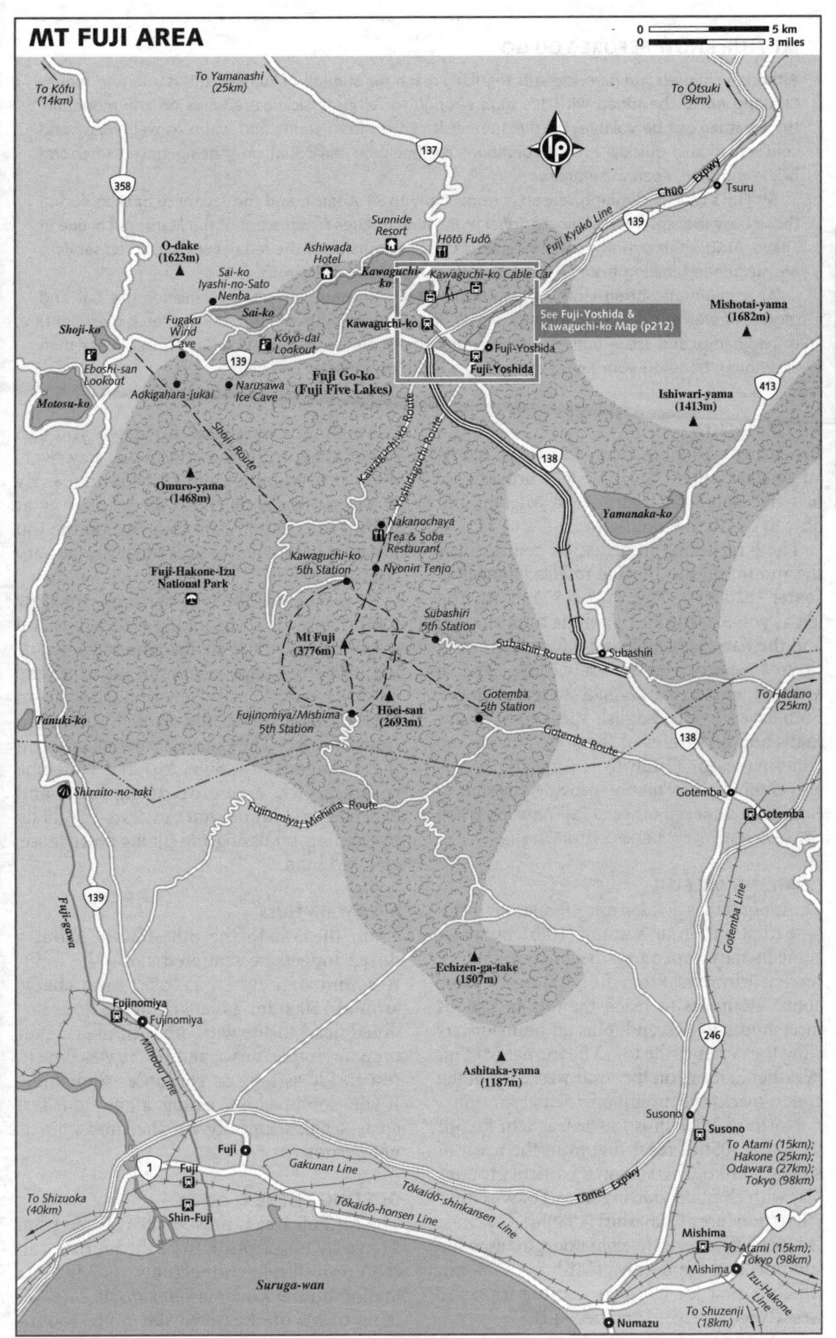
MT FUJI AREA
0 5 km
0 3 miles
To Kōfu (14km)
To Yamanashi (25km)
To Ōtsuki (9km)
Tsuru
Chūō Expwy
Fuji Kyūkō Line
Sunnide Resort
Ashiwada Hotel
Hōtō Fudō
O-dake (1623m)
Sai-ko Iyashi-no-Sato Nenba
Kawaguchi-ko
Kawaguchi-ko Cable Car
Sai-ko
Shoji-ko
Fugaku Wind Cave
Kōyō-dai Lookout
See Fuji-Yoshida & Kawaguchi-ko Map (p212)
Mishotai-yama (1682m)
Eboshi-san Lookout
Fuji-Yoshida
Motosu-ko
Aokigahara-jukai
Narusawa Ice Cave
Fuji Go-ko (Fuji Five Lakes)
Ishiwari-yama (1413m)
Shoji Route
Kawaguchi-ko Route
Yoshidaguchi Route
Omuro-yama (1468m)
Yamanaka-ko
Nakanochaya Tea & Soba Restaurant
Kawaguchi-ko 5th Station
Nyonin Tenjo
Fuji-Hakone-Izu National Park
Subashiri 5th Station
Mt Fuji (3776m)
Subashiri Route
Subashiri
To Hadano (25km)
Gotemba 5th Station
Fujinomiya/Mishima 5th Station
Hōei-san (2693m)
Tanuki-ko
Gotemba Route
Shiraito-no-taki
Gotemba
Fujinomiya/Mishima Route
Fuji-gawa
Gotemba Line
Echizen-ga-take (1507m)
Fujinomiya
Minobu Line
Ashitaka-yama (1187m)
Susono
Fuji
To Atami (15km); Hakone (25km); Odawara (27km); Tokyo (98km)
Gakunan Line
Tōmei Expwy
To Shizuoka (40km)
Shin-Fuji
Tōkaidō-shinkansen Line
Tōkaidō-honsen Line
Mishima
To Atami (15km); Tokyo (98km)
Suruga-wan
Izu-Hakone Line
To Shuzenji (18km)
Numazu
AROUND TOKYO

MT FUJI: KNOW BEFORE YOU GO

Although children and grandparents regularly reach the summit of Fuji-san, this is a serious mountain and not to be trifled with. It's high enough for altitude sickness and, as on any mountain, the weather can be volatile. On the summit it can go from sunny and warm to wet, windy and cold remarkably quickly. Even if conditions are fine, you can count on it being close to freezing in the morning, even in summer.

Mt Fuji's official climbing season is from 1 July to 31 August, and the Japanese pack in during those busy months, meaning occasional night-time queues reminiscent of the Marunouchi line in Tokyo. Authorities strongly caution against climbing outside of the regular season, when services are suspended; hiking from October to May can be very dangerous.

At a minimum, bring clothing appropriate for cold and wet weather, including a hat and gloves, as well as drinking water and snacks. If you're climbing at night, bring a torch (flashlight) or headlamp, and spare batteries. Descending the mountain is much harder on the knees than ascending; bending your knees and using your thigh muscles can help.

INFORMATION

Brochures available from the **Tokyo Tourist Information Center** (☎ 03-5321-3077) provide exhaustive detail on transport to Mt Fuji and how to climb the mountain.

The best tourist information centres near the mountain are the **Fuji-Yoshida Information Center** (☎ 0555-22-7000; 🕑 9am-5.30pm), to the left as you exit the Fuji-Yoshida train station, and the **Kawaguchi-ko Tourist Information Center** (☎ 0555-72-6700; 🕑 9am-5pm Sun-Fri, 8.30am-6.30pm Sat & holidays), next to Kawaguchi-ko train station. Both have friendly, English-speaking staff and maps and brochures of the area. During the climbing season (1 July to 31 August), there is also climbing information provided by staff in English at a special office at **Fuji-Yoshida city hall** (☎ 0555-24-1236; 🕑 8.30am-5.15pm Mon-Fri).

CLIMBING MT FUJI

The mountain is divided into 10 'stations' from base (first station) to summit (10th), but most climbers start from one of the four 5th stations, reachable by road. From the 5th stations, allow about 4½ hours to reach the top and about three hours to descend, plus an hour for circling the crater at the top. The former Mt Fuji Weather Station, on the southwest edge of the crater, marks the mountain's actual summit.

North of Mt Fuji is the Kawaguchi-ko 5th station (2305m), reachable from the town of Kawaguchi-ko. This station is particularly popular with climbers starting from Tokyo. Other 5th stations are at Subashiri (1980m), Gotemba (1440m; allow seven to eight hours to reach the summit) and Fujinomiya (Mishima; 2380m), which is best for climbers coming from the west (Nagoya, Kyoto and beyond).

To time your arrival for dawn you can either start up in the afternoon, stay overnight in a mountain hut and continue early in the morning, or climb the whole way at night. You do not want to arrive on the top too long before dawn, as it's likely to be very cold and windy.

Trails below the 5th stations are now used mainly as short hiking routes, but you might consider the challenging but rewarding hike from base to summit on either the Yoshidaguchi Trail (see opposite) from Fuji-Yoshida or on the Shoji Route from near Shoji-ko. There are alternative trails on the Kawaguchi-ko, Subashiri and Gotemba routes, which, assuming strong knees and expendable clothing, you can descend rapidly by running, schussing and sliding down loose, clay-red sand.

Mountain Huts

From the 5th to the 8th station, about a dozen lodges are scattered along the trails. Accommodation here is basic: most charge around ¥5000 for a blanket on the floor sardined head-to-toe with other climbers. Staff prepare simple meals, and you're welcome to rest inside as long as you order something. If you don't feel like eating, a one-hour rest costs ¥500. Camping on the mountain is not permitted.

GETTING THERE & AWAY

The Mt Fuji area is most easily reached from Tokyo by bus; from Kansai the journey can require multiple connections via Mishima Station on the Kodama *shinkansen*. The two main towns on the north side of the mountain, Fuji-Yoshida and Kawaguchi-ko, are the principal gateways. See Fuji Go-ko (Fuji Five Lakes), right.

From 1 July to 31 August, direct buses (¥2600, 2½ hours) run from Shinjuku bus terminal to the Kawaguchi-ko 5th station. For details call **Keiō Dentetsu Bus** (☎ 03-5376-2217). This is by far the fastest and cheapest way of getting from Tokyo to the 5th station. If you take two trains and a bus, the same trip can cost nearly ¥6000. If you're already in Kawaguchi-ko, there are bus services up to Kawaguchi-ko 5th station (¥1500, 55 minutes) from 1 July to 31 August. The schedule varies considerably during the shoulder period – call **Fuji Kyūkō bus** (☎ 0555-72-6877) for details. At the height of the climbing season, there are buses until 9.15pm – ideal for climbers intending to make an overnight ascent. Taxis operate from Kawaguchi-ko train station to the Kawaguchi-ko 5th station for around ¥10,000, plus tolls.

Coming from western Japan, buses run from the *shinkansen* stations at Shin-Fuji (¥2400) and Mishima (¥2390) to Fujinomiya (Mishima) 5th station in just over two hours. There are reservation centres in **Tokyo** (☎ 03-5376-2217) and **Fuji** (☎ 0555-72-5111).

Fuji Go-ko 富士五湖

☎ 555

The Fuji Go-ko (Fuji Five Lakes) region is a postcard-like area around Fuji's northern foothills; its lakes provide perfect reflecting pools for the mountain's majesty. Yamanaka-ko is the largest and easternmost lake, followed by Kawaguchi-ko, Sai-ko, Shoji-ko (the smallest) and Motosu-ko. Particularly during

THE YOSHIDAGUCHI TRAIL UP MT FUJI

Before the construction of the road to the 5th station, Fuji pilgrims began at Sengen-jinja near present-day Fuji-Yoshida, walking among towering cryptomeria trees and old stone lanterns, paying their homage to the shrine gods, and beginning their 19km ascent up Japan's most sacred mountain. Today, this path offers climbers a chance to participate in this centuries-old tradition. Purists feel this is the best way to climb, saying that the lower reaches are the most beautiful, through lush forests along an isolated path. Through sunset, the sunrise and a night in a mountain hut, you'll perhaps get a sense of that elusive spirit so deeply sought by pilgrims in the past.

Of all the routes up Mt Fuji, the Yoshidaguchi trail is the oldest. To reach the trail from Sengen-jinja, veer to the right before the main building and turn left onto the main road. This is paved, and you'll soon see a walking path alongside the road. When this roadside trail ends, take the first turn to the right to meet up with the woodland path.

After about 1¼ hours of walking you'll reach **Nakanochaya**, an ancient site marked by carved stones left by previous climbers. You'll also find a quaint **tea and soba restaurant** here (the last place to refuel before the 5th station). From here you enter Fuji's lush forests.

Around 90 minutes later is Umagaeshi, which once housed the old stables where horses were left before pilgrims entered the sacred area of the mountain. A big yellow sign to your left marks the path. Follow this through the torii with monkeys on either side, as it continues uphill. Another 20 minutes and you'll pass the 1st station.

Between the 2nd and the 3rd stations, just a bit of navigation is required. The Fuji path meets up with the **Nyonin Tenjo** (Women's Holy Ground), which until 1832 was as far up as women were allowed to go. All that remains is an altar, hidden in the forest. Just before entering you'll cross through a set of posts. Take a right, walk for 150m and look for the posts on the left, which mark the continuation of the path. Around an hour later, the path meets up with the 5th station road. You'll find the Fuji path 150m on, cutting up to the right. You can stay at one of the 5th stations in the vicinity or if you still have energy, continue up another two hours to one of the 7th station huts.

It takes about five hours to reach the 5th station from Sengen-jinja. The next day, you'll have a much harder 4½-hour ascent up the scarred, barren mountain. Many rise at midnight and climb in darkness, but you can let the crowds go, get up at 4.30am and complete the ascent as the sun peeks through the clouds. On the descent, you can catch a bus at the Kawaguchi-ko 5th station, which will take you to Kawaguchi-ko station.

Pick up maps and get the latest climbing information from the **Fuji-Yoshida Information Center** (☎ 0555-22-7000; 🕑 9am-5.30pm). The *Climbing Mt Fuji* brochure is invaluable.

the autumn *kōyō* (foliage) season, the lakes make a good overnight trip out of Tokyo, for a stroll or a drive, and the energetic can hike in nearby mountains.

SIGHTS & ACTIVITIES

Although adjacent, Fuji-Yoshida and Kawaguchi-ko are separate administrative districts, with separate visitor facilities.

Fuji-Yoshida 富士吉田

Fuji-Yoshida's *oshi no ie* (pilgrims' inns) have served visitors to the mountain since the days when climbing Mt Fuji was a pilgrimage rather than a tourist event. A necessary preliminary to the ascent was a visit to the deeply wooded, atmospheric **Sengen-jinja** (1615; thought to have been the site of a shrine as early as 788), which is still worth a visit for its 1000-year-old cedar, the main gate, which is rebuilt every 60 years (slightly larger each time), and the two one-tonne *mikoshi* used in the annual Yoshida no Hi Himatsuri (Yoshida Fire Festival).

From Fuji-Yoshida Station you can walk (15 minutes) or take a bus to Sengen-jinja-mae bus stop (¥150, five minutes).

Central Fuji-Yoshida's **Gekkō-ji district** (月江寺) feels like the little town that time forgot, with original mid-20th century facades. Inside are some surprisingly hip cafes and shops, and it's worthwhile getting a little lost here.

One stop west of Fuji-Yoshida Station is **Fuji-Q Highland** (☎ 23-2111; admission only adult/child ¥1200/600, day pass ¥4800/3500; ⏰ 9am-5pm Mon-Fri, to

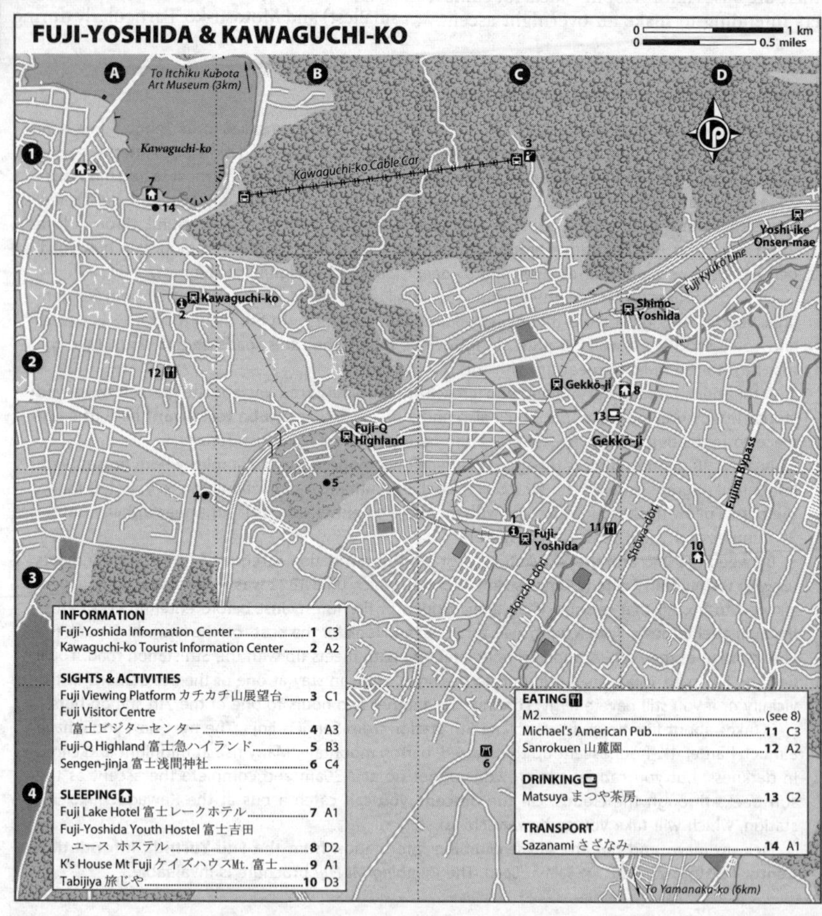

8pm Sat & Sun), an amusement park with roller coasters, bumper cars, Gundam and Thomas the Tank Engine attractions, and more.

Kawaguchi-ko 河口湖

On the lake of the same name, the sleepy town of Fuji-Kawaguchi-ko is closest to four of the five lakes and a popular departure point for climbing the mountain. Around 600m north of Kawaguchi-ko Station, on the lower eastern edge of the lake, is the **Kawaguchi-ko cable car** (☎ 72-0363; one way/return ¥400/700) to the Fuji Viewing Platform (1104m). Ask at Kawaguchi-ko Tourist Information Center (p210) for a map.

Near the north shore of the lake, the unique **Itchiku Kubota Art Museum** (久保田一竹美術館; ☎ 76-8811; admission ¥1300; 🕑 10am-5pm Dec-Mar, 9.30am-5pm Apr-Nov) presents lavishly dyed kimonos by Itchiku Kubota, whose lifework of continuous landscapes is displayed in a grand hall made of cypress.

If Mt Fuji isn't visible, **Fuji Visitor Center** (富士ビジターセンター; ☎ 72-0259; admission free; 🕑 8.30am-10pm late Jul-late Aug, to 4.30pm Dec-Feb, sliding closing time rest of year) shows what you've missed. An English video gives a great summary of the mountain and its geological history.

The western lakes are relatively undeveloped. At Sai-ko, **Sai-ko Iyashi-no-Sato Nenba** (西湖いやしの里根場; ☎ 20-4677; adult/child ¥200/100; 🕑 9am-5pm) opened in 2006 on the site of some historic thatched-roof houses, washed away in a typhoon 40 years earlier. Inside these dozen reconstructed frames are demonstrations of silk and paper crafts; restaurants specialise in *soba* and *konyakku* (arrowroot gelatin).

There are good views of Mt Fuji from the western end of the lake and from the **Kōyō-dai lookout**, near the main road. Close to the road are the **Narusawa Ice Cave** and the **Fugaku Wind Cave**, both formed by lava flows from a prehistoric eruption of Mt Fuji.

Further west, tiny Shoji-ko is said to be the prettiest of the Fuji Go-ko, though it has no view of Mt Fuji. However, you can continue to **Eboshi-san**, a one- to 1½-hour climb from the road, for a fine view of the mountain over the Aokigahara-jukai (Sea of Trees). The last lake along is Motosu-ko, the deepest and least visited of the lakes.

FESTIVALS & EVENTS

The **Yoshida no Hi Matsuri** (Yoshida Fire Festival; 26 to 27 August) is an annual festival held to mark the end of the climbing season and to offer thanks for the safety of the year's climbers. The first day involves a *mikoshi* procession and the lighting of bonfires on the town's main street. On the second day, festivals are held at Sengen-jinja (opposite).

SLEEPING

If you're not overnighting in a mountain hut, Fuji-Yoshida and Kawaguchi-ko make good bases. Their respective tourist information offices (see p210) can make reservations for you.

Fuji-Yoshida

Fuji-Yoshida Youth Hostel (☎ 22-0533; www.jyh.or.jp; member/nonmember dm ¥2900/3400; ⊠) This is a popular old lodging in Fuji-Yoshida's old town. Some of these Japanese-style rooms have mountain views. The hostel is around 600m south of Shimo-Yoshida Station; walk down the main street, going through three sets of lights and turning down the small alley on the right.

Tabijiya (☎ 20-0500; fax 24-0200; www.tabijiya.jp, in Japanese; s/d/tw from ¥5900/11,000/12,000; ⊠ 💻) This clean, family-run business hotel is about 25 minutes' walk from the town centre behind Keiyo drugstore and MOS Burger. A large breakfast is ¥950.

Kawaguchi-ko

Most inns far from Kawaguchi-ko Station offer free pick-up.

K's House Mt. Fuji (☎ 83-5556; fax 83-5557; kshouse.jp; dm from ¥2500, r from ¥3400; 💻) This clean, new hostel near the lake is in a renovated building with a cheery, welcoming atmosphere. There's a fully loaded kitchen, mountain bikes for hire and no curfew. Staff will pick you up for free.

Sunnide Resort (サニーデリゾート; ☎ 76-6004; fax 76-7706; www.sunnide.com, in Japanese; r per person ¥6300, cottages from ¥16,000; 💻) A bit remote but with the best Fuji views in town, friendly Sunnide has hotel rooms and rental cottages with a delicious outdoor bath. Splash out in the stylish premium suites with private balcony baths or ask for the discounted 'backpacker' rates (¥4200) if same-day rooms are available. Breakfast/dinner is ¥1050/2100 (¥1575 for the backpacker dinner).

Ashiwada Hotel (足和田ホテル; ☎ 82-2321; fax 82-2548; www.asiwadahotel.co.jp, in Japanese; s/d ¥7350/12,000; Ⓟ ⊠ 💻) This dated but friendly hotel boasts impressive views of Kawaguchi-ko and generously proportioned, mostly Japanese-style rooms with private bath. There are also well-kept common baths and *rotemburo*. It's at the western end of the lake, in a more residential neighbourhood.

Fuji Lake Hotel (☎ 72-2209; fax 73-2700; www.fujilake.co.jp; r per person with 2 meals from ¥10,500; P ⊠ 💻 ♿) Just off from the town centre and right on the lakefront, this seven-storey historic (1935) hostelry offers mountain and lake views from its Japanese-Western combo rooms. In addition to private facilities (some rooms have their own *rotemburo*), there are common onsen, too.

EATING & DRINKING

Fuji-Yoshida is known for its *teuchi udon* (homemade, white wheat noodles); some 60 shops sell it! Try yours with tempura, *kitsune* (fried tofu) and *niku* (beef). The **Fuji-Yoshida Information Center** (☎ 22-7000; 🕑 9am-5.30pm) has a map and list of restaurants (with dishes around ¥500).

Kawaguchi-ko's local noodles are *hōtō*, sturdy, hand-cut and served in a thick miso stew with pumpkin, sweet potato and other vegetables.

Fuji-Yoshida

M2 (☎ 23-9309; mains ¥700-1350; 🕑 11am-10pm; 💻) A block from the Fuji-Yoshida Youth Hostel, this quaint cafe with an English menu serves Western and Japanese dishes such as curry rice and pork sauté. The shelves of comics, miniature toys and kitschy artwork add to the charm. Look for the 'M2' sign.

Michael's American Pub (☎ 24-3917; meals ¥800-1100; 🕑 8pm-2am Fri-Wed, lunch Sun-Fri) For traditional Americana – burgers, pizzas and brew – drop by this expat and local favourite. From Fuji-Yoshida Station, walk north to the main road (Akafuji-dōri) and take a right. At a shop called Nojima, take a left and it's a bit down the road on the right in a little strip mall. There's an English menu and sign.

Matsuya (☎ 22-5185; 🕑 11am-8pm Tue-Sun; 💻) A fitting emblem for arty Gekkō-ji, this charming cafe is also a craft store. Come for coffee, tea or a chat with the equally charming English-speaking owner. Snacks include *chiri to biinzu tōsuto* (chili and toast; ¥400) It's on the main drag; look for an old hanging wooden sign.

Kawaguchi-ko

Hōtō Fudō (ほうとう不動; ☎ 76-7800; hōtō ¥1050; 🕑 11am-7pm) Three branches around town serve this massive stew bubbling in its own cast-iron pot. For the adventurous, *basashi* (raw horse meat; ¥1050) is also on the menu. The *honten* (main branch) is a brown-and-white barn of a restaurant north of the lake, near the Kawaguchi-ko Art Museum via retro-bus.

Sanrokuen (☎ 73-1000; set meals ¥2100-4200; 🕑 10am-7.30pm Fri-Wed) With a picture menu, this charming, barn-like *irori* (fireplace) restaurant allows diners to grill their own meals (skewers of fish, chicken, tofu, steak and veggies) around charcoal pits set in the floor. From Kawaguchi-ko Station, turn left, left again after the 7-Eleven and after 600m you'll see the thatched roof on the right.

GETTING THERE & AWAY

Buses (¥1700, 1¾ hours) operate directly to Kawaguchi-ko from outside the western exit of Shinjuku Station in Tokyo. There are departures up to 16 times daily at the height of the Fuji climbing season. Some continue on to Yamanaka-ko and Motosu-ko. In Tokyo, call **Keiō Kōsoku Bus** (Map p131; ☎ 03-5376-2217) for reservations and schedule info. In Kawaguchi-ko, make reservations through **Tōmei Highway Bus** (☎ 72-2922).

Trains take longer and cost more. JR Chūō line trains go from Shinjuku to Ōtsuki (*tokkyū*, ¥2980, one hour; *futsū*, ¥1280, 1½ hours), where you transfer to the Fuji Kyūkō line to Kawaguchi-ko (*futsū*, ¥1110, 50 minutes).

GETTING AROUND

The Fuji-Kawaguchi-ko sightseeing bus (the 'retro-bus') has hop-on-hop-off service to all of the sightseeing spots in the western lakes area. One route (two-day passes adult/child ¥1000/500) follows Kawaguchi-ko's northern shore, and the other (¥1300/650) heads south and around Sai-ko and Aokigahara.

Rental bicycles (hour/half-day ¥500/1500) and rowboats (per person ¥2500, plus ¥1000 per hour) are available at **Sazanami** (☎ 72-0041; 🕑 9am-6pm) on Kawaguchi-ko's southeast shore.

Buses run from Fuji-Yoshida Station to Fujinomiya (¥2050, 80 minutes) via the four smaller lakes and around the mountain. From Kawaguchi-ko, there are nine to 11 buses daily to the *shinkansen* stop of Mishima (¥2130, two hours).

HAKONE REGION 箱根

☎ 0460 / pop 13,511

If you only have a day or two outside Tokyo, Hakone can give you almost everything you could desire from the Japanese countryside – spectacular mountain scenery crowned by Mt Fuji, art museums, onsen, traditional inns and the opportunity to ride a variety of transport.

During holidays, Hakone can be quite busy and feel highly packaged. To beat the crowds, plan your trip during the week. For more information, try www.hakone.or.jp/english.

FESTIVALS & EVENTS

Ashino-ko Kosui Matsuri At Hakone-jinja near Moto-Hakone, this festival on 31 July features firework displays over Hakone's landmark lake.

Hakone Daimonji-yaki Matsuri During this summer festival on 16 August, the torches are lit on Myojoga-take so that they form the shape of the Chinese character for 'big' or 'great'.

Hakone Daimyō Gyoretsu Parade On the national Culture Day holiday on 3 November, 400 costumed locals re-enact a feudal lord's procession.

GETTING THERE & AWAY

Bus

Odakyū's express bus service runs directly from the west exit of Shinjuku Station to Hakone-machi (¥1950, two hours, 20 daily), but you lose the fun of the combination of rail, cable and water-borne conveyances.

Train

The private **Odakyū line** (www.odakyu.jp) from Shinjuku Station takes you directly into Hakone-Yumoto, the region's transit hub. If you are travelling on a JR Pass, you can save the intercity fare by taking the JR train to Odawara and changing trains for Hakone-Yumoto.

Odakyū's Hakone Freepass (箱根フリーパス), available at Odakyū stations and Odakyū Travel branches, is an excellent deal for the standard Hakone circuit, covering the return fare to Hakone and unlimited use of most modes of transport within the region, plus other discounts. It's available as a two-day pass (adult/child from Shinjuku ¥5000/1500, from Odawara ¥3900/1000) or a three-day pass (adult/child from Shinjuku ¥5500/1750, from Odawara ¥4400/1250).

Transport prices in this section are without the Freepass, except as noted.

The most convenient service is Odakyū's charmingly named Romance Car to Hakone-Yumoto (with/without Freepass ¥870/2020, 85 minutes). There is also *kyūkō* (regular express) service (¥1150, two hours), although you may have to change trains at Odawara.

JR trains run between Shinjuku and Odawara (¥1450, 80 minutes). From Tokyo Station, take the Kodama *shinkansen* (¥3130, 35 minutes) or the JR Tōkaidō line (*futsū*, ¥1450, 1¼ hours; *tokkyū*, ¥2350, one hour).

At Odawara, change to the narrow-gauge, switchback Hakone-Tōzan line, via Hakone-Yumoto to Gōra (¥650, one hour). If you've arrived in Hakone-Yumoto on the Odakyū line, you can change to the Hakone-Tōzan line (¥390 to Gōra, 40 minutes) in the same station.

GETTING AROUND

Part of Hakone's popularity comes from the chance to ride assorted *norimono* (modes of transport): switchback train (from Hakone-Yumoto to Gōra), funicular, ropeway (gondola), ship and bus. Check out www.odakyu.jp, which describes this circuit. Stops along the way have snack and souvenir shops.

Boat

From Tōgendai, sightseeing boats crisscross Ashino-ko to Hakone-machi and Moto-Hakone (¥970, 30 minutes). The boats look like pirate ships and Mississippi River paddlewheelers – tourist kitsch but fun all the same.

Bus

The Hakone-Tōzan and Izu Hakone bus companies service the Hakone area, linking up most of the sights. Hakone-Tōzan bus routes are included in the Hakone Freepass. If you finish in Hakone-machi, Hakone-Tōzan buses run between here and Odawara for ¥1150 and take 45 minutes. Hakone-en to Odawara costs ¥1270. Buses run from Moto-Hakone to Hakone-Yumoto for ¥930, taking 35 minutes, every 30 minutes from 10am to 3pm.

Cable Car & Ropeway

Gōra is the terminus of the Hakone-Tōzan railway and the beginning of the cable car (funicular) to Sōun-zan, from where you can catch the Hakone Ropeway (gondola) line to Ōwakudani and Tōgendai.

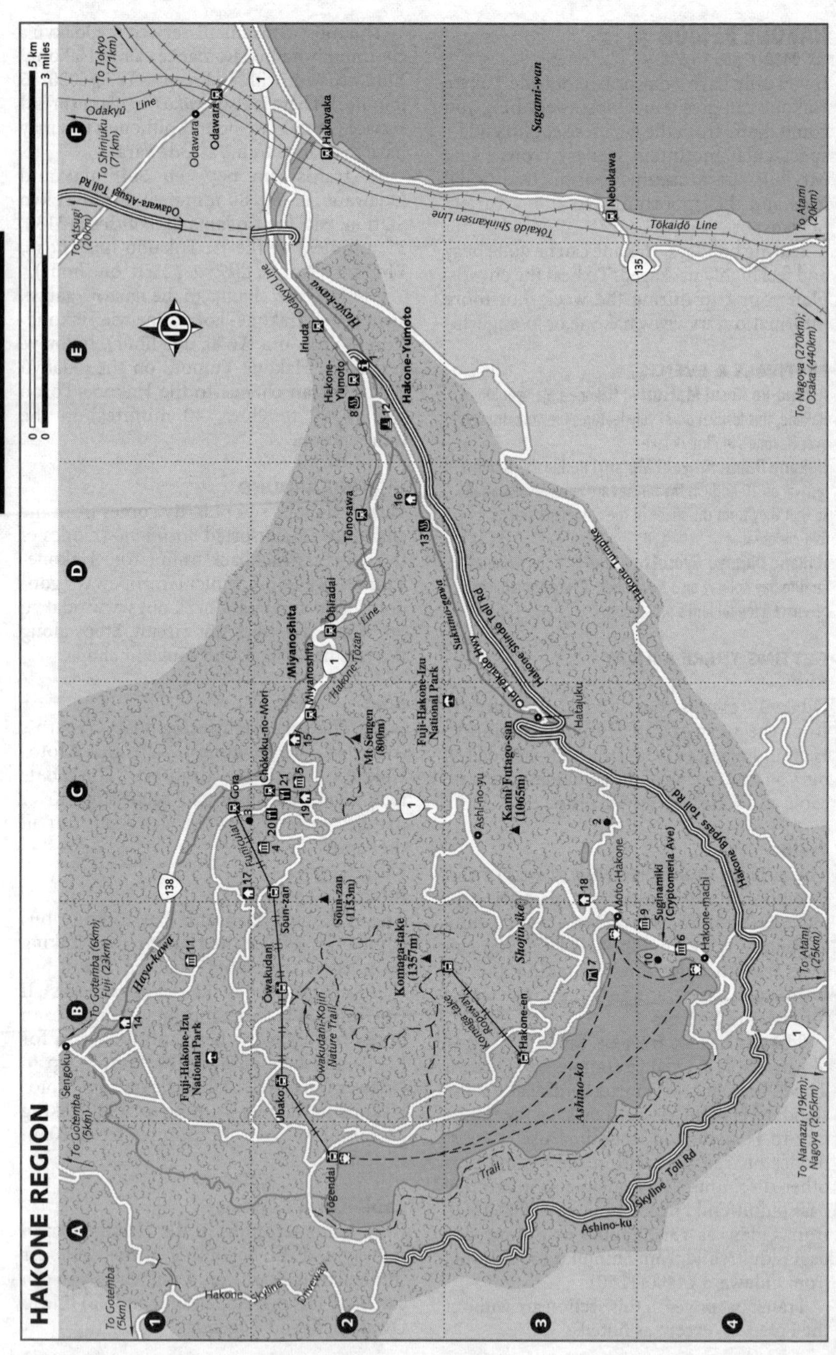
HAKONE REGION
0 5 km
0 3 miles
To Gotemba (5km)
To Gotemba (5km)
Sengoku
To Gotemba (6km); Fuji (23km)
To Atsugi (20km)
To Shinjuku (71km)
To Tokyo (71km)
Odakyū Line
Odawara-Atsugi Toll Rd
Odawara
Odawara
Hakayaka
Sagami-wan
Nebukawa
Tōkaidō Shinkansen Line
Tōkaidō Line
To Atami (20km)
To Nagoya (270km); Osaka (440km)
Odakyū Line
Haya-kawa
Iriuda
Hakone-Yumoto
Hakone-Yumoto
Tōnosawa
Ōhiradai
Miyanoshita
Miyanoshita
Hakone-Tōzan Line
Chōkoku-no-Mori
Gora
Funicular
Sōun-zan
Sōun-zan (1153m)
Ōwakudani
Ōwakudani-Kojiri Nature Trail
Ubako
Tōgendai
Haya-kawa
Fuji-Hakone-Izu National Park
Fuji-Hakone-Izu National Park
Mt Sengen (800m)
Sukumo-gawa
Hakone Shindō Toll Rd
Old Tōkaidō Hwy
Hatajuku
Hakone Turnpike
Ashi-no-yu
Kami Futago-san (1065m)
Komaga-take (1357m)
Komaga-take Ropeway
Hakone-en
Shōjin-ike
Moto-Hakone
Suginamiki (Cryptomeria Ave)
Hakone-machi
Hakone Bypass Toll Rd
Ashino-ko
Trail
Ashino-ku Skyline Toll Rd
Hakone Skyline Driveway
To Atami (25km)
To Numazu (19km); Nagoya (265km)
138
135

INFORMATION		
Tourist Information Center 箱根観光案内所	1	E2
SIGHTS & ACTIVITIES		
Amazake-jaya Teahouse 甘酒茶屋	2	C3
Hakone Gōra-kōen 箱根強羅公園	3	C1
Hakone Museum of Art 箱根美術館	4	C2
Hakone Open-Air Museum 彫刻の森美術館	5	C2
Hakone Sekisho 箱根関所	6	B4
Hakone-jinja 箱根神社	7	B3
Kappa Tengoku Rotemburo かっぱ天国	8	E2
Narukawa Art Museum 成川美術館	9	B4
Onshi Hakone Kōen 恩賜箱根公園	10	B4
Pola Museum of Art ポーラ美術館	11	B1
Sōun-ji 早雲寺	12	E2
Tenzan Tōji-kyō 天山湯治郷	13	D2
SLEEPING		
Fuji Hakone Guest House 富士箱根ゲストハウス	14	B1
Fujiya Hotel 富士屋ホテル	15	C2
Hakone Sengokuhara Youth Hostel 箱根仙石原ユースホステル	(see 14)	
Hotel Okada ホテルおかだ	16	D2
Hyatt Regency Hakone Resort and Spa ハイアット リージェンシー 箱根	17	C1
Moto-Hakone Guesthouse 元箱根ゲストハウス	18	C3
Yudokoro Chōraku 湯処長楽	19	C2
EATING		
Gyōza Center 餃子センター	20	C2
Kappeizushi かつ平寿し	21	C2

Luggage Forwarding

At Hakone-Yumoto Station, deposit your luggage with **Hakone Baggage Service** (箱根キャリーサービス; ☎ 86-4140; baggage per piece from ¥600; 🕑 8.30am-7pm) by noon, and it will be delivered to your inn within Hakone from 3pm. From inns, pick-up is at 10am for a 1pm delivery at Hakone-Yumoto. Hakone Freepass holders get ¥100 discount per bag.

Hakone-Yumoto Onsen 箱根湯元温泉

Hakone-Yumoto is the starting point for most visits to Hakone, and it can be very busy. If the weather looks dodgy, it makes sense to stop off between Odawara and the Tōzan railway and spend the day soaking in the baths. You can also approach the town on foot from Moto-Hakone via the Old Tōkaidō Hwy (see p219).

Pick up local and regional maps and info at the excellent **Tourist Information Center** (☎ 85-5700; 🕑 9am-5.45pm), by the bus stops across the main road from the train station.

Onsen are the main attraction of Hakone-Yumoto. **Kappa Tengoku Rotemburo** (☎ 85-6121; adult/child ¥750/400; 🕑 10am-10pm), behind and above the station, is a popular outdoor bath, worth a dip if the crowds aren't too bad; it's three minutes on foot up from Hakone-Yumoto Station. More upmarket are the fantastic onsen of **Tenzan Tōji-kyō** (☎ 86-4126; admission ¥1200; 🕑 9am-10pm), which has a larger selection of indoor and outdoor baths. To get here, take the B Course shuttle bus from the bridge outside the station.

SLEEPING

Hotel Okada (☎ 85-6000; fax 85-5774; www.hotel-okada.co.jp/eng/; r per person incl 2 meals from ¥17,000; P 🖳) Try this rambling hotel on the edge of the Sukumo-gawa for a bit of pampering. It has excellent Japanese- and Western-style rooms and baths including the large Yu no Sato complex (also open to day trippers, from ¥1000) above the cheaper Pension Okada wing (which has rooms per person from ¥5930). Take bus A from the train station (¥100, 10 minutes).

Miyanoshita 宮ノ下

The first worthwhile stop on the Hakone-Tōzan railway towards Gōra, this village has antique shops along the main road (head down the hill from the station), some splendid ryokan, and a pleasant hiking trail skirting up 800m Mt Sengen. The trailhead is 20m from the road from the station, up an incline.

our pick **Fujiya Hotel** (☎ 82-2211; fax 82-2210; www.fujiyahotel.jp; d from ¥18,870) is one of Japan's finest hotels. Opened in 1878, it's one of the first Western-style hotels in the nation. Now sprawled across several wings, it remains dreamily elegant for the woodwork in its old-world lounge areas, dining room, a hillside garden, historic hot-spring baths and guest rooms with hot-spring water. It's worth a visit to soak up the atmosphere and have tea in the lounge. Foreign travellers should enquire about the weekday special of roughly US$130 for double rooms (you can pay the equivalent sum in yen). The hotel is around 250m west of the station.

If you don't fancy paying resort prices for dinners at the Fujiya, a short walk away is the friendly sushi shop with English menu, **Miyafuji** (鮨みやふじ; ☎ 82-2139; most dishes ¥1575-2310; 🕑 lunch & dinner Wed-Mon), known for its *aji-don* (brook trout over rice). Look for the door curtain with a circular crest.

Chōkoku-no-Mori 彫刻の森

Two stops beyond Miyanoshita is the excellent **Hakone Open-Air Museum** (☎ 82-1161; www.hakone-oam.or.jp; adult/child/college & high-school student

¥1600/800/1100; 9am-4.30pm). Although tickets are pricey, there's an impressive selection of 19th- and 20th-century Japanese and Western sculptures (including Henry Moore, Rodin, Maillol and Miro) in a soaring hillside setting. There's also a Picasso pavilion and paintings by Takamura Kotaro and other Japanese artists. Decent restaurants and a tea house are inside. Hakone Freepass holders get ¥200 off.

A charming ryokan lies 300m uphill from the museum on the left. **Yudokoro Chōraku** (82-2192; fax 82-4533; r per person from ¥5150; P) has simple but nicely maintained tatami rooms with kitchenettes and private toilet. There's an onsen on the 1st floor (available for day use for ¥550).

For exquisite sushi and sashimi, don't miss **Kappeizushi** (82-3278; mixed sushi around ¥1500; 9am-8pm Wed-Mon). A picture menu is available. It's just downhill from the museum with a blue-white door curtain and wooden signboard.

Gōra 強羅

Gōra is the terminus of the Hakone-Tōzan line and the starting point for the funicular and cable-car trip to Tōgendai on Ashino-ko. The town also has a couple of its own attractions that may be of minor interest to travellers.

Just a short walk beside the funicular tracks towards Sōun-zan is **Hakone Gōra-kōen** (82-2825; adult with/without Freepass free/¥500, child free; 9am-5pm), a park with a rock garden, alpine and seasonal plants, a fountain and several greenhouses with tropical flowers. Adjacent to the park, **Hakone Museum of Art** (82-2623; adult/junior-high student & younger/student ¥900/free/400; 9.30am-4pm Apr-Nov, to 3.30pm Dec-Mar) has a stately collection of Japanese ceramics from as far back as the Jōmon period (10,000 years ago).

Pola Museum of Art (84-2111; www.polamuseum.or.jp; adult/junior-high & elementary school student/university & high-school student ¥1800/700/1300; 9am-4.30pm) is a worthy detour from Gōra. The collection comprises some 9500 works of European and Japanese painting from the impressionists onwards, as well as ceramics and glass art, in changing displays. Admission is free for elementary and junior-high school students on Saturdays. From Gōra Station, take the sightseeing shuttle bus to Shissei-kaen (¥290, 13 minutes).

The newly built **Hyatt Regency Hakone Resort and Spa** (82-2000; fax 82-2001; hakone.regency.hyatt.com; tw from ¥43,900; P) is an exquisite retreat with large, ultra-deluxe rooms featuring private terraces and excellent views of the valley. A spa and onsen here offers exclusive de-stressing courses and enormous baths, but you can also just kick back around the large open fireplace in the stylish central lounge.

Gyōza Center (82-3457; mains ¥735-945, set meals ¥1155-1365; lunch daily, dinner Fri-Wed) is famous for its *gyōza* (dumplings) a dozen different ways, including in soup *(sui-gyōza)*, in soup with *kimchi (kimchi sui-gyōza)* and plain pan-fried *(nōmaru)*. It's between Gōra and Chōkoku-no-Mori Stations, with a small English sign and English menu.

SLEEPING

In addition to places listed in other individual destination sections there are these long-time favourites.

Hakone Sengokuhara Youth Hostel (84-8966; fax 84-6578; http://hakone.syuriken.jp/YH/; members/nonmembers dm ¥3200/3800, r per person ¥4800/5000; P) This pleasant hostel is directly behind the Fuji Hakone Guest House and is run by the same family. It has Japanese-style dorms and private rooms, hot-spring baths, cooking facilities and English-speaking staff.

Fuji Hakone Guest House (84-6577; fax 84-6578; http://hakone.syuriken.jp/hakone/; r per person ¥5250-6300; P) Run by a welcoming, English-speaking family, the guest house has handsome tatami rooms and a cosy onsen. Expect rates to increase by between ¥1000 and ¥2000 per person at busy times. Take the stop No 4 bus from Odawara Station to Senkyōrō-mae bus stop (50 minutes). There's an English sign close by.

Sōun-zan & Ōwakudani 早雲山・大桶谷

From Gōra, continue to near the 1153m-high summit of Sōun-zan by funicular (¥410, 10 minutes).

From Sōun-zan, there are several hiking trails including one to Mt Kami (1¾ hours) and another up to Ōwakudani (1¼ hours). The latter is sometimes closed due to the mountain's toxic gases. Check at the tourist information office.

Sōun-zan is the starting point for the Hakone Ropeway, a 30-minute, 4km gondola ride to Tōgendai (one way/return ¥1330/2340), stopping at Ōwakudani en route. In fine weather Mt Fuji looks fabulous from here.

Ōwakudani is a volcanic cauldron of steam, bubbling mud and mysterious smells. The **Ōwakudani-Kojiri Nature Trail** (Ōwakudani Kojiri Shizen Tanshō Hodō; 大涌谷湖尻自然探勝歩道) leads uphill through the charred, somewhat apocalyptic landscape to some of the boiling pits. Here you can buy boiled eggs, turned black in the sulphurous waters. Don't linger as the gases are poisonous.

Ashino-ko 芦ノ湖

Between Tōgendai, Hakone-machi and Moto-Hakone, this leg-shaped lake is touted as the primary attraction of the Hakone region; but it's Mt Fuji, with its snow-clad slopes glimmering in reflection on the water, that lends the lake its poetry. If the venerable mountain is hidden behind clouds (as often happens), you have the consolation of a trip across the lake with recorded commentary in English about the history and natural surroundings. See p215 for details about lake transport.

Hakone-machi & Moto-Hakone 箱根町・元箱根

The sightseeing boats across Ashino-ko deposit you at either of these two towns, both well touristed and with sights of historical interest. The main attraction in Hakone-machi is the **Hakone Sekisho** (Hakone Checkpoint Museum; ☎ 83-6635; adult/child ¥500/250; ⏲ 9am-5pm), a recent reconstruction of the feudal-era checkpoint on the Old Tōkaidō Hwy. Be sure to check out the museum with Darth Vader–like armour and grisly implements used on lawbreakers, but don't expect English explanations. On a small peninsula nearby is a scenic park, **Onshi Hakone Kōen** (☎ 83-7484; admission free; ⏲ 9am-4.30pm). Its elegant Western-style building was once used by the imperial family, and has Fuji views across the lake.

Suginamiki (杉並木; Cryptomeria Ave) is a 2km stone path beside the busy lakeside road connecting Hakone-machi and Moto-Hakone, lined with some 400 cryptomeria cedars that were planted nearly 400 years ago. Between the cedars and Moto-Hakone is the **Narukawa Art Museum** (☎ 83-6828; adult/child ¥1200/600; ⏲ 9am-5pm), which houses an impressive collection of modern Japanes paintings.

It is impossible to miss Moto-Hakone's **Hakone-jinja** (☎ 83-7213; treasure hall ¥500; ⏲ 9am-4pm) with its signature red torii rising from the lake. A pleasant stroll around the lake to the torii leads along a path lined with huge cedars. A wooded grove surrounds the shrine.

For a bit more exercise, a 3½-hour walk leads you back to Hakone-Yumoto along the Old Tōkaidō Hwy. Start up the hill from the lakeside Moto-Hakone bus stop, and along the way you'll pass the 350-year-old **Amazake-jaya Teahouse** (☎ 83-6418; ⏲ 7am-5.30pm), an isolated, traditional-looking building where you can enjoy a cup of *amazake* (warm, sweet sake; ¥400). You can also stop in the small village of Hatajuku, and end your walk at the historic temple of **Sōun-ji** near Hakone-Yumoto Station.

SLEEPING

Moto-Hakone Guesthouse (☎ 83-7880; fax 84-6578; www.fujihakone.com; r per person ¥5250; Ⓟ) A popular spot with foreign tourists, this place offers simple but pleasant Japanese-style rooms without private facilities, and an informative website. From Hakone-machi or Moto-Hakone, take an Odawara-bound bus to Ashinokōen-mae (adult/child ¥210/160, 10 minutes), from where the guest house is a one-minute walk.

IZU-HANTŌ 伊豆半島

The Izu-hantō (Izu peninsula), about 100km southwest of Tokyo in Shizuoka-ken, has a cool surfer vibe backed by plenty of history, particularly the famed Black Ships of US Commodore Perry (p47). It also packs lush greenery, rugged coastlines, abundant onsen, and foods such as *himono* (sun-dried fish) and *mikan* (mandarin oranges). Weekends and holidays can be very crowded on the east coast, particularly in summer. It's always quieter on the west coast, which has Mt Fuji views over the bay of Suruga-wan.

An easy loop takes you by train to Itō on the east coast (reachable by JR from Tokyo), from where you can enjoy drop-dead coastal views on the train or bus to historic Shimoda. Then journey by bus across a landscape of hilly countryside, farms and rural townships to Matsuzaki and Dōgashima on Izu's west coast. Finish at the intimate onsen village of Shuzen-ji before catching the Izu-Hakone Tetsudō line to Mishima to connect back to the JR.

Atami 熱海

☎ 0557 / pop 40,000

Atami may be the gateway to Izu, but this overdeveloped hot-springs resort has little to detain foreign travellers, aside from its museum. Overlooking the coastline, the sleek

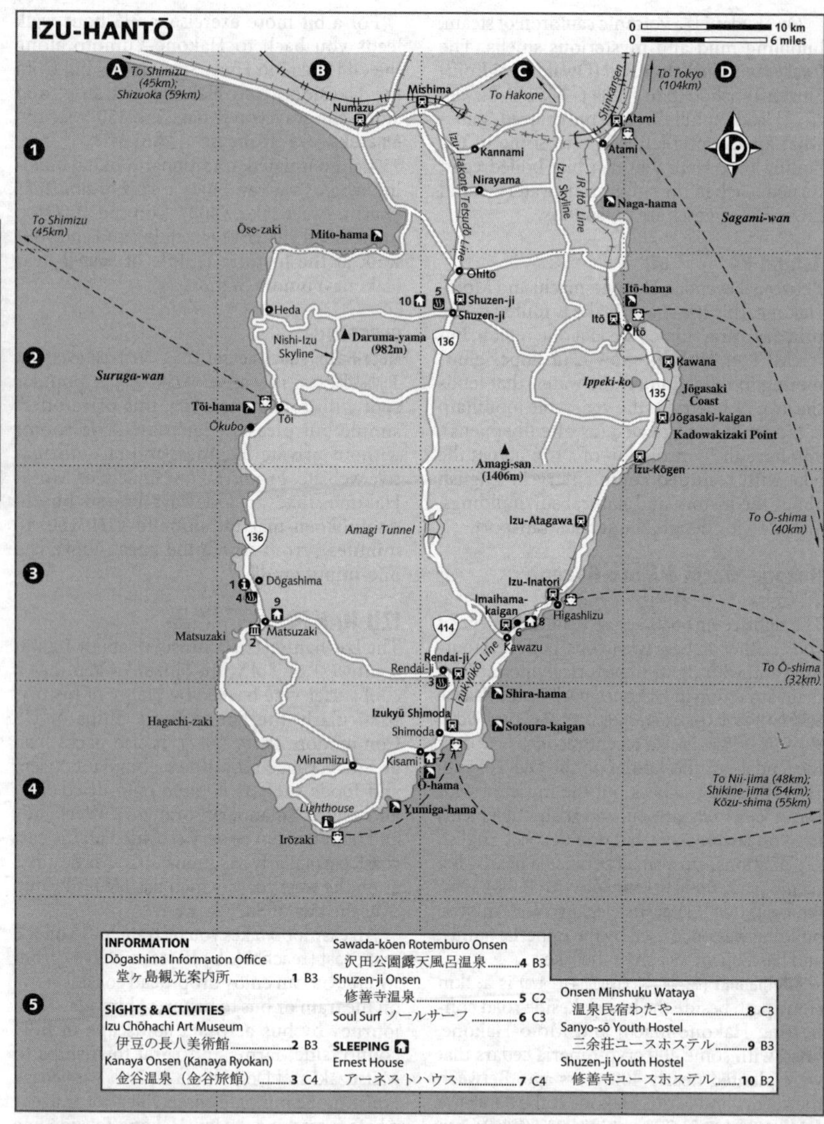

MOA Museum of Art (MOA美術館; ☎ 84-2511; www.moaart.or.jp; adult/student ¥1600/800; ⏰ 9.30am-4pm Fri-Wed, closed 4-14 Jan & 25-31 Dec) has a collection of Japanese and Chinese paintings, ceramics, calligraphy and sculpture, spanning over 1000 years and including national treasures. Take the bus from stop 4 outside Atami Station to the last stop (¥160, eight minutes).

Discount tickets to the museum (¥1300) and town information are available at the **tourist office** (☎ 81-5297; ⏰ 9.30am-5.30pm), at the station building.

Because of Atami's popularity with domestic tourists, rooms are overpriced; head down to Itō or Shimoda to find more reasonable lodgings.

GETTING THERE & AWAY

JR trains run from Tokyo Station to Atami on the Tōkaidō line (Kodama *shinkansen* ¥3570, 46 minutes; Odoriko ¥3190, 1¼ hours; Acty *kaisoku* ¥1890, 1½ hours).

Itō & Jōgasaki 伊東・城ヶ崎

☎ 0557

Itō is another hot-springs resort and is notably famous as the place where Anjin-san (William Adams), the hero of James Clavell's book *Shogun,* built a ship for the Tokugawa shōgunate. It is said that this resort town was so popular that 100 geisha entertained here a century ago, although these days it's a commendably relaxed place. Itō Station has a **Tourist Information Center** (☎ 37-6105; 9am-5pm).

A seven-minute walk south of the station is the lovingly crafted **Tōkaikan** (東海館; ☎ 36-2004; adult/child ¥200/100; 9am-9pm, closed 3rd Tue of the month), a 1920s inn and now a national monument for its elegant woodwork, each of its three storeys designed by a different architect. Its large **bath** (adult/child ¥500/300; 11am-7pm) is still open to bathers.

South of Itō is the striking Jōgasaki coast, with its windswept cliffs formed by lava. A harrowing 48m-long suspension bridge leads over Kadowakizaki Point, with waves crashing 23m below. It's a popular location for film and TV shoots, particularly suicide scenes. If you have time, there's a moderately strenuous cliffside hike with volcanic rock and pine forests, south of the 17m-tall lighthouse.

Yamaki Ryokan (山喜旅館; ☎ 37-4123, in Japanese; fax 38-8123; www.ito-yamaki.co.jp; r per person incl 2 meals ¥8550), a block east of Tōkaikan, is a charming 15-room inn from the 1940s that testifies to Itō's rich woodworking tradition. The owner is very friendly but has limited English. Ask for reservations at the Tourist Information Center.

GETTING THERE & AWAY

Itō is connected to Atami by the JR Itō line (¥320, 25 minutes). The JR limited express Odoriko service also runs from Tokyo Station to Itō (¥3510, 1¾ hours). From Itō to Jōgasaki, take the Izukyūkō (aka Izukyū) line to Jōgasaki-kaigan (¥560, 18 minutes) and walk downhill about 1.5km; buses are also available but take longer and cost more. Izukyū also continues on to Shimoda.

Shimoda 下田

☎ 0558 / pop 25,000

Shimoda's laid-back vibe is perfectly suited for an exploration of its beaches and history. It holds a pivotal place in Japan's evolution as the spot where the nation officially opened to the outside world after centuries of isolation. Following the opening of Japan by the *Kurofune* (Black Ships) under Commodore Matthew Perry, the American Townsend Harris opened the first Western consulate here.

INFORMATION

Main post office (☎ 22-1531; 10am-5pm) The main post office has an international ATM; it's a few blocks from Perry Rd.

Shelly's English School & Café (☎ 27-2686; 11am-6pm Tue-Sat) This kid-friendly snack bar northeast of Izukyū Shimoda Station along the river has info, free internet, book swapping and yummy taco wraps. Look for the red stairs.

Shimoda Tourist Association (☎ 22-1531; 10am-5pm) Pick up the useful *Shimoda Walking Map* and book accommodation. From the station, take a left, walk to the first intersection and you'll see it on the southeast corner.

Volunteer English Guide Association (☎ 23-5151; maimai-h@i-younet.ne.jp; 8.30am-5.15pm Tue-Sun) Offers free guided tours.

SIGHTS & ACTIVITIES

Ryōsen-ji & Chōraku-ji 了仙寺・長楽寺

A 25-minute walk south of Shimoda Station is **Ryōsen-ji** (☎ 22-0657), site of another treaty, supplementary to the Treaty of Kanagawa, signed by Commodore Perry and representatives of the Tokugawa shōgunate.

The temple's **Black Ship Art Gallery** (Hōmotsukan; ☎ 22-0657; adult/child ¥500/150; 8.30am-5pm, closed 1-3 Aug & 24-26 Dec) includes more than 2800 artefacts relating to Perry, the Black Ships, and Japan as seen through foreign eyes and vice versa. Exhibits change about five times per year.

Behind and up the steps from Ryōsen-ji is **Chōraku-ji**, where a Russo-Japanese treaty was signed in 1854; look for the cemetery and *namako-kabe* (black-and-white lattice-patterned) walls.

Hōfuku-ji 宝福寺

In the centre of town is Hōfuku-ji, a temple that is chiefly a **museum** (☎ 22-0960; admission ¥300; 8am-5pm) memorialising the life of Okichi (see the boxed text, p224).

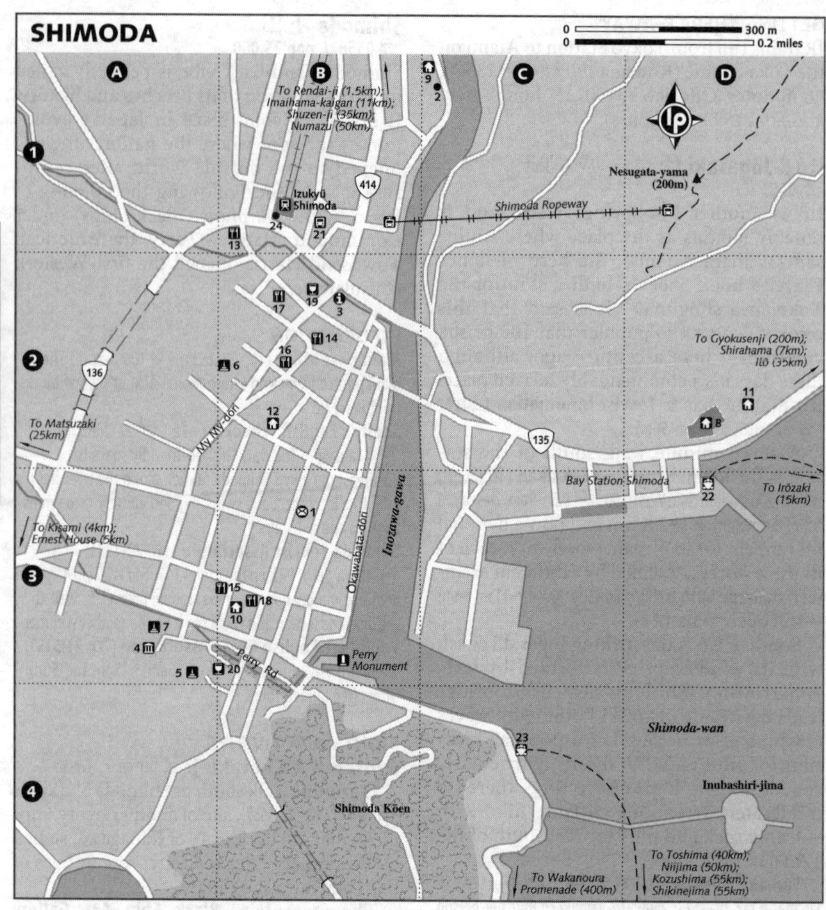

The museum is filled with scenes and artefacts from the various movie adaptations of her life on stage and screen. Okichi's grave is also here, in the far corner of the back garden, next to a faded copper statue. Other graves in this garden are dedicated to her, with the names of actors who played her.

Gyokusenji 玉泉寺

Founded in 1590, this **temple** (☎ 22-1287; admission free, Harris museum adult/child ¥300/150; 🕑 8am-5pm) is most famous as the first Western consulate in Japan, in 1856. The museum here is filled with artefacts of the life of Townsend Harris, the first consul general, and life-size models of him and Okichi (see the boxed text, p224). The bas-relief of a cow in front of the temple refers to the fact that Harris requested milk to recover from an illness; Japan had no custom of milk drinking at the time, which changed after seeing the results here.

Shimoda Kōen & Wakanoura Promenade 下田公園・和歌の浦遊歩道

If you keep walking east from Perry Rd, you'll reach the pleasant hillside park of Shimoda Kōen, which overlooks the bay. It's loveliest in June, when the hydrangeas are in bloom. Before entering the park, the coastal road is also a fine place to walk. If you have an hour or so, keep following it around the bay, passing an overpriced aquarium, and eventually you'll meet up with the 2km-

INFORMATION
Main Post Office 下田郵便局 1 B3
Shelly's English School & Café 2 C1
Shimoda Tourist Association 観光案内所 3 B2
Volunteer English Guide Association .... (see 3)

SIGHTS & ACTIVITIES
Black Ship Art Gallery (Hōmotsukan) 了仙寺宝物館 4 A3
Chōraku-ji 長楽寺 5 A3
Hōfuku-ji 宝福寺 6 B2
Ryōsen-ji 了仙寺 7 A3

SLEEPING
Kurofune Hotel 黒船ホテル 8 D2
Nansuisō 南水荘 9 C1
Ōizu Ryokan 大伊豆旅館 10 B3
Shimoda Bay Kuroshio 下田ベイクロシオ 11 D2
Yamane Ryokan やまね旅館 12 B2

EATING
Dining Log Shimoda ダイニング ログ 下田 13 B1
Gorosaya ごろさや 14 B2
Hiranoya 平野屋 15 B3
Isoka-tei 磯華亭 16 B2
Musashi むさし 17 B2
Porto Caro ポルトカーロ 18 B3

DRINKING
Cheshire Cat Jazz House チェシャーキャット 19 B2
Ja Jah ジャジャ 20 B3

TRANSPORT
Bus Stop バス停 21 B1
Izu Cruise 伊豆クルーズ 22 D3
Tōkai Kisen ferry 東海汽船 フェリー 23 C4
Toyota Rent-a-Car トヨタレンタカー 24 B1

long Wakanoura Promenade, a stone path along a peaceful stretch of beach. Turn right when you meet up with the road to return to Perry Rd.

Nesugata-yama 寝姿山

About 200m east of Izukyū Shimoda Station is the cable-car station to Nesugata-yama (Mt Nesugata; 200m). The **Shimoda Ropeway** (☎ 22-1211; adult/child return, incl park admission ¥1200/600; ⏰ 9am-5pm) runs cable cars every 10 minutes to a mountain-top park, where the temple Aizendō houses a Kamakura period Buddha statue; some 150 Jizō statues get amazing views of the bay. There's also a hedge maze and an underwhelming museum of early photographic equipment included in the ticket.

Beaches

There are good beaches around Shimoda, particularly around Kisami, south of town. Take an Irōzaki-bound bus (bus 3 or 4; ¥340); ask to be dropped at Kisami and walk 10 minutes towards the coast. North of Shimoda is the lovely white-sand beach of Shira-hama (bus 9; ¥320), which can get packed in July and August.

Bay Cruises

Several cruises depart from the Shimoda harbour area. Most popular with Japanese tourists is the *Kurofune* (Black Ships) cruise around the bay (adult/child ¥1000/500, 20 minutes), which departs every 30 minutes (approximately) from 9.10am to 3.30pm.

Three boats a day (9.40am, 11.20am and 2pm) travel to Irōzaki. You can leave the boat at Irōzaki (adult/child ¥1600/800, 40 minutes) and head northwards up the peninsula by bus, or stay on the boat to return to Shimoda.

FESTIVALS & EVENTS

Kurofune Matsuri (Black Ships Festival) On Friday, Saturday and Sunday around the 3rd Saturday in May, Shimoda commemorates the first landing of Commodore Perry with parades by the US Navy Marine band and firework displays.

Shimoda Taiko Matsuri (Drum Festival) On 14 and 15 August there is a spectacular parade of *dashi* floats and some serious Japanese-style drumming.

SLEEPING

The **Shimoda Tourist Association** (☎ 22-1531; ⏰ 10am-5pm) can help with reservations.

Ōizu Ryokan (☎ 22-0123; r per person ¥3500; P) Popular with international travellers for its excellent prices, Ōizu has plain but comfy Japanese-style rooms with TV, and a two-seater onsen. It's at the southern end of town, two blocks north of Perry Rd. Check-in is from 3pm. It's often closed on weekdays, so phone ahead.

Nansuisō (☎ 22-2039; fax 22-4027; r per person ¥4000; P) This quiet old inn along the river is simple but features a large bath fed by real hot-spring water. There are six Japanese-style rooms, without private bathrooms. It's a pretty spot in spring, when the riverside cherry trees are in bloom.

Yamane Ryokan (☎ 22-0482; r per person from ¥5000; P) Conveniently located between Shimoda Station and Perry Rd, this simple, recently built inn has tidy Japanese-style rooms, shared bathrooms and a friendly manager. Breakfast is available for ¥1000.

Ernest House (☎ 22-5880; fax 23-3906; www.ernest-house.com; s from ¥6300; P 💻) A great escape, two minutes' walk from the beach in Kisami Ō-hama, down the coast from Shimoda. In a Western-style house named after Hemingway, this 13-room pension has hardwood furniture, a restaurant, cafe and a youthful vibe. Dinners

THE LEGEND OF OKICHI

Shimoda is famous in international affairs, but an affair of the heart remains this town's most enduring melodrama. Like all good stories, there are many versions.

Saito Kichi (the 'O' was later added as an honorific) was born a carpenter's daughter in Shimoda. Some accounts say that her exceptional beauty and talent for music led her poor family to sell her to a geisha house at age seven. Others skip directly to 1854, when the Black Ships arrived in Shimoda and a devastating earthquake destroyed Okichi's home and possessions.

Okichi's home was rebuilt by a long-time admirer named Tsurumatsu, and the two fell in love. But in 1856, when Townsend Harris became America's first consul in Shimoda, he needed a maid, and local authorities assigned the task to Okichi, then in her late teens. Despite her initial refusal, authorities prevailed on her to sacrifice her love of Tsurumatsu for the good of the nation. Tsurumatsu received a position with the shōgunate in Edo (now Tokyo).

Okichi gradually developed respect for Harris, even reportedly protecting him from an assassination attempt. Some versions of the story say that Harris forced her to fulfil his needs as well, and locals began taunting her as *'tōjin* Okichi' (the foreigner's concubine), driving her to drink.

Following Harris's departure in 1858, Okichi moved briefly to Kyoto before heading to Edo to find Tsurumatsu. Together they lived in Yokohama until Tsurumatsu's untimely death.

Okichi returned to Shimoda and opened a restaurant (some say it was a brothel). But drink had taken its hold, the business went bankrupt and she wandered the streets before eventually drowning herself in a river.

Okichi's story has been dramatised in just about every form of Japanese drama. Outside Japan, the best-known version of this story is *The Barbarian and the Geisha,* the 1958 film starring John Wayne, which, no surprise, tells the story its own way.

cost ¥2625. Reservations are recommended, and note that rates can more than double at peak times. From Izukyū Shimoda Station, take an Irōzaki-bound bus (stop 3 or 4; ¥360); ask to be dropped off at the Kisami stop, from where it's a 15-minute walk towards the coast.

Shimoda Bay Kuroshio (☎ 27-2111; fax 27-2115; www.baykuro.co.jp; r per person from ¥10,500; Ⓟ) This futuristic 42-room hotel gleams above Shimoda-wan. Texas-sized rooms are festooned with textiles, woodworked headboards, designer bedspreads, and relics, shells and fossils inlaid in its poured-in-place concrete. Outside: *rotemburo* (naturally) and summer barbecues.

Kurofune Hotel (☎ 22-1234; fax 22-1801; www.kurofune-hotel.com, in Japanese; r per person incl 2 meals from ¥15,000; Ⓟ) On the hillside across from Shimoda's boat dock and with dead-on bay views, this old-line hotel has both Japanese- and Western-style rooms – some have their own *rotemburo* – plus heaping seafood meals and huge common onsen with *rotemburo*. The lobby decor is a little over the top, but squint as you walk through and you'll be fine.

EATING

Seafood is the speciality in Shimoda.

Musashi (☎ 22-0934; mains ¥630-1000; 🕑 lunch) This casual spot serves tasty Japanese *shokudō* (cafeteria-style) favourites, including *kamo nabeyaki udon* (duck hotpot; ¥950). Take a left out of the station, turn right down the narrow lane and take the first left. Look for the giant badger.

Dining Log Shimoda (☎ 22-3457; sets from ¥1000; 🕑 11.30am-8.30pm Wed-Mon) This recently opened, log-framed resto has decent French-Italian-Japanese dishes like *mentaiko* (pollock roe) pasta (¥900). There's a picture menu and an English sign.

Porto Caro (☎ 22-5514; mains ¥1050-1360; 🕑 lunch & dinner Thu-Tue) A second-floor trattoria serving tasty pastas, pizzas (at night) and other Italian fare. Try seafood pasta with local wasabi, or paella (¥3000). It's two blocks north of Perry Rd, on the same road as the post office; English menu and sign.

Isoka-tei (☎ 23-1200; meals ¥1155-2100; 🕑 11.30am-3pm & 5.30-9pm) This friendly spot serves hearty seafood sets like *torotoro donburi* (tuna belly on rice, ¥1890). From the Tourist Association, head three blocks down My My-dōri, take a left and it'll be on the next corner, with a fish and crab drawing in the overhead sign. There's a picture menu.

Hiranoya (☎ 22-2525; meals ¥1260-3150; 🕑 lunch & dinner Wed-Mon) A former private home, filled with antiques, elegant woodwork and funky

Western-style seating. With an English menu, it serves steaks, sandwiches, burgers and curry. Look for the *namako-kabe* (lattice-pattern walls).

Gorosaya (☎ 23-5638; lunch/dinner ¥1575/3150; ⏰ lunch & dinner Fri-Wed) Elegant, understated ambience and fantastic seafood. The *Isōjiru* soup is made from over a dozen varieties of shellfish. From the Tourist Association, head two blocks down My My-dōri, take a left and it's on your left. Look for the wooden fish decorating the entrance of the blue-and-white building. There's an English menu.

DRINKING

Ja Jah (☎ 27-1611; drinks from ¥700; ⏰ 7pm-2am Tue-Sun) This cosy bar is a good place to kick back with fun tunes and friendly people. DJs sometimes spin (R&B, soul, hip-hop) on weekends. Look for the English sign.

Cheshire Cat Jazz House (☎ 23-3239; drinks from ¥500; ⏰ 11am-1am Thu-Sun) For live jazz, visit this low-key spot on My My-dōri. It's easily spotted by its English sign.

GETTING THERE & AWAY

Shimoda is as far as you can go by train on the Izu-hantō. You can take the Odoriko *tokkyū* from Tokyo Station (¥5480, 2¾ hours) or Atami (¥3400, 80 minutes). From Itō, Izukyūkō trains run from Itō Station (¥1570, one hour). Trains also run from Atami (¥1890, 1½ hours). Try to catch Izukyū's Resort 21 train cars, with sideways-facing seats for full-on sea views.

South and west, transit is by Tōkai Bus to Dōgashima (¥1360, one hour) or Shuzen-ji (¥2140, two hours, one daily).

Car rental is available at **Toyota Rent-a-Car** (☎ 27-0100) by the train station.

Tōkai Kisen ferry (☎ 22-2626) serves the Izu-shotō islands Kōzushima, Shikinejima and Niijima (all ¥3740).

Around Shimoda

IMAIHAMA 今井浜

This relaxing seaside village is one of Izu's few towns with a sandy beach and a laid-back surfer vibe. Just what the doctor ordered for an overdose of culture and history.

You can rent body boards or fins from ¥1500 a day at **Soul Surf** (☎ 0558-32-1826) on the main street. **Onsen Minshuku Wataya** (☎ 0558-32-1055; fax 32-2058; http://wataya.biz, in Japanese; s/d incl 2 meals ¥9075/1650) is a kindly, family-run, eight-room place facing the beach, with tiny sea-view *rotemburo* and 24-hour indoor baths. Look for the Kirin beer sign about 100m past the surf shop.

Imaihama-kaigan Station is on the Izukyū line between Itō (¥1330, 45 minutes) and Izukyū Shimoda (¥480, 20 minutes).

RENDAI-JI & KANAYA ONSEN

蓮台寺・金谷温泉

The town of Rendai-ji is home to one of the best onsen on the peninsula, **Kanaya Onsen** (admission ¥1000; ⏰ 9am-10pm). Its rangey, rambling building houses the biggest all-wood bath in the nation (on the men's side), called the *sennin-furo* (1000-person bath, a vast exaggeration). The women's bath is nothing to sneeze at, and both sides have private outdoor baths as well. BYO towel, or buy one for ¥200.

The same building also houses the fabulously traditional **Kanaya Ryokan** (☎ 0558-22-0325; fax 23-6078; r per person with/without meals from ¥15,750/7350), which was built in 1929 and feels like it. Some of the tatami rooms are simple, while others are vast suites with private toilet. There are no restaurants nearby, so go for the inn's meals or pack you own.

From Izukyū Shimoda Station take the Izukyū line to Rendai-ji Station (¥160, five minutes), go straight across the river and main road to the T-junction and turn left; the onsen is 50m on the right.

IRŌZAKI 石廊崎

The southernmost point of the peninsula is noted for its cliffs and lighthouse and some fairly good beaches. You can get to the cape from Shimoda by boat (see p223) or by bus (¥930, 45 minutes) from bus 4 platform. **Izu Cruise** (☎ 0558-22-1151; adult/child ¥1000/500) runs frequent 25-minute cruises around the harbour.

Matsuzaki 松崎

☎ 0558

Things are much quieter on the west coast. The sleepy port of Matsuzaki is known for its streetscapes: some 200 traditional houses with *namako-kabe* walls. They're concentrated in the south of town, on the far side of the river. There is no tourist information in English.

The **Izu Chōhachi Art Museum** (☎ 42-2540; adult/child ¥500/free; ⏰ 9am-5pm) showcases the work of Irie Chōhachi (1815–99). His plaster, fresco and stucco paintings are unimaginably detailed. Each colour, no matter how intricate the design (be it a pine needle or a stitch on a kimono), gets its own layer of plaster. You'll want to use a magnifying glass (supplied by staff) to examine the works in detail.

Amid rice fields 3km east of town is the delightfully antique **Sanyo-sō Youth Hostel** (☎/fax 42-0408; www.jyh.or.jp; dm member/nonmember ¥3360/3960), a former landowner's home with fine (shared) tatami rooms. If this building was not a hostel, it would probably be some kind of important cultural property. From Shimoda take a Dōgashima-bound bus and get off at the Yūsu-hosteru-mae bus stop (¥1160, 50 minutes); it's another ¥240 to Matsuzaki.

To central Matsuzaki, the bus fare from Shimoda is ¥1230; from Dōgashima it's ¥260.

Dōgashima 堂ヶ島

For help booking accommodation and info on onward transport, stop by the **information office** (☎0558-52-1268; 8.30am-5pm Mon-Sat), in front of the bus stop and above the tourist jetty. Staff will also lend you a bicycle for free.

The main attraction at Dōgashima is the dramatic rock formations that line the seashore. The park just across the street from the bus stop has some of the best views. It's also possible to take a return boat trip (for 20/50 minutes ¥920/1880) from the nearby jetty to visit the town's famous shoreline cave. The cave has a natural window in the roof that allows light to pour in. You can look down into the cave from paths in the aforementioned park.

About 700m south of the bus stop and on the water, you'll find the small but stunning **Sawada-kōen Rotemburo onsen** (admission ¥500; 7am-7pm Wed-Mon Sep-Jul, 6am-8pm Wed-Mon Aug) perched high on a cliff overlooking the Pacific. Go early in the day if possible; around sunset it's standing room only for these tiny segregated baths.

GETTING THERE & AWAY

Buses to Dōgashima (¥1360, one hour) leave from platform 5 in front of Shimoda Station. From Dōgashima you can catch a bus onward to Shuzen-ji (¥1970, 1½ hours), complete with fantastic views over Suruga-wan to Mt Fuji. When the air is clear and the mountain is blanketed by snow, you'll swear you're looking at a Hokusai print. The best views are between Ōkubo (大久保) and Tōi (土肥).

Shuzen-ji Onsen 修善寺温泉

☎0558

Inland Shuzen-ji Onsen is Izu-hantō's most charming town, a hot-spring village in a lush valley bisected by the rushing Katsura-gawa. Some of Japan's finest onsen ryokan inns are here as well. There are some fine places to stroll, and at dusk the town bells play 'Moon River'. There's a **tourist information office** (☎55-0412; 8.30am-5pm) at Shuzen-ji Station. Shuzen-ji Onsen is a 10-minute bus ride from the station.

SIGHTS & ACTIVITIES

In the middle of Shuzen-ji Onsen is the tranquil namesake temple **Shuzen-ji** (☎72-0053; admission free; 8.30am-4pm), which celebrated the 1200th anniversary of its founding in 2007. It's said to have been founded by Kōbō Daishi, the Heian-period priest credited with spreading Buddhism throughout much of Japan. The present structure dates from 1489.

The real reason to visit Shuzen-ji is to take a dip in one of its famous onsen. Right on the river is a foot bath called **Tokko-no-yu** (独鈷の湯; iron-club waters; admission free; 24hr), said to be Izu's oldest hot spring. Its name comes from a legend that its waters sprung from the rock when it was struck by Kōbō Daishi himself.

Inns around town offer day-use bathing, or try **Hako-yu** (筥湯; ☎72-5282; admission ¥350; noon-8.30pm), an elegant facility identified by its wonderful wooden tower; bring your own soap.

SLEEPING & EATING

Shuzen-ji Youth Hostel (☎72-1222; www.jyh.or.jp; dm member/nonmember ¥3360/3960; P ⊠ 🖳) In the hills west of town, this large (100-bed) hostel feels a little institutional but a good choice nonetheless, featuring tasty meals (breakfast/dinner ¥630/1500), decent rooms and a peaceful setting. It's a 12-minute bus ride from Shuzen-ji Station; take a bus from platform 6 at Shuzen-ji Station to the New Town-guchi stop (last bus 6.45pm). It's a five-minute walk from the bus stop.

Goyōkan (五葉間; ☎72-2066; fax 72-8212; www.goyokan.co.jp; r per person without/with breakfast ¥6450/7500; P) A midrange *minshuku* (B&B-style lodging) in the centre of everything, with river views. There are no private facilities, but the shared (indoor) baths are made of stone and *hinoki* cypress. Some English is spoken.

our pick Yukairo Kikuya (湯回廊菊屋; ☎ 72-2000; fax 72-2002; www.yukairou-kikuya.net, in Japanese; per person with meals from ¥23,000; P) Spanning the Katsura-gawa, this splendid, romantic ryokan, recently renovated, has been an inn since the mid-17th century and is one of the finest in the country. The blend of Japanese and European furnishings here is delightful. Deluxe rooms feature *wa-beds* (futons on platforms), and, unusual for *kaiseki* cuisine, you get to choose your own meals. Naturally, the baths are splendid, too.

Arai Ryokan (新井旅館; ☎ 72-2007; fax 72-5119; www.arairyokan.net; r per person with meals from ¥24,300; P) Long beloved by Japanese artists and writers, this gem of an inn was founded in 1872 and has kept its traditional, wood-crafted heritage. Riverside rooms are magnificent in autumn, when the maples are ablaze. The large outdoor bath is a perfect spot to admire Shuzen-ji's greenery.

Tokko Café (独鈷茶屋; ☎ 72-6112; meals & snacks ¥400-1250; 9.30am-5pm Fri-Wed) This stylish new cafe-gallery right by Tokko-no-yu features local woodcrafts, homemade cakes and *bentō* lunch sets of tofu, rice and seasonal veggies for ¥1250. There's usually a rickshaw parked outside.

Zendera Soba (禅寺そば; ☎ 72-0007; meals ¥630-1890; lunch Fri-Wed) This cosy local institution serves *zaru soba* (cold soba) and the speciality namesake Zendera *soba* (¥1260), served with your own stalk of wasabi root to grate. It's steps from the bus station on the river side of the street, and has white and black banners. There's an English menu.

GETTING THERE & AWAY

From Tokyo, access to Shuzen-ji is via Mishima on the Tōkaidō line (Kodama *shinkansen* ¥4400, one hour) and then Izu-Hakone Tetsudō trains between Mishima and Shuzen-ji (¥500, 35 minutes). Buses connect Shuzen-ji Station and Shuzen-ji Onsen (¥210, 10 minutes). Buses run between Shuzen-ji and Shimoda (¥2140, two hours) and Shuzen-ji and Dōgashima (¥2140, 1½ hours).

SOUTH OF TOKYO

It's easy to breeze by this area on the *shinkansen* going to Kansai, but it's packed with history and cultural attractions, particularly the fascinating old capital of Kamakura, often called a Little Kyoto for its wealth of Buddhist temples and Shintō shrines. The vibrant port of Yokohama is Japan's second-largest city, though it's a much less chaotic metropolis than its big sister to the north.

YOKOHAMA 横浜

☎ 045 / pop 3,655,000

Celebrating its 150th anniversary in 2009, Yokohama prides itself on its role as an early gateway to the West. Home to barely 600 people at the time of the Black Ships, today it's Japan's second-largest metropolis, and has a breezy atmosphere and great historical spots. Unlike most Japanese cities, it's also a city of distinct neighbourhoods, including Chinatown, the historic Motomachi and Yamate districts, and the recent seaside development of Minato Mirai 21.

Yokohama is barely 20 minutes from central Tokyo, which means it's an easy day trip or night-time excursion. Among Japanese it's a popular date spot.

History

For most of history, Yokohama was an unnoticed fishing village near a rest stop called Kanagawa on the Tōkaidō. Its fate changed abruptly in 1853–54, when the American fleet under Commodore Matthew Perry arrived off the coast to persuade Japan to open to foreign trade; in 1858 this little village was designated an international port.

Westerners were first relegated to an area within a moat in a district called Kannai ('inside the barrier') but later began to own property up the mountainside (Yamate). A Chinese community burgeoned as well, and the city expanded on reclaimed land, eventually encompassing the original Kanagawa rest stop.

Although Yokohama is unquestionably Japanese, foreign influence is in its blood. Among Yokohama's firsts-in-Japan: a daily newspaper, gaslamps and a train terminus (connected to Shimbashi, in Tokyo).

The Great Kantō Earthquake of 1923 destroyed much of the city, with the rubble used to reclaim more land, including Yamashita-kōen. The city was devastated yet again in WWII air raids; occupation forces were initially based here but later moved down the coast to Yokosuka. The late 20th century saw redevelopment of the harbour area, including some fancy skyscrapers, and in 2002 Yokohama hosted the finals of the FIFA World Cup. In 2009 the city marked 150 years

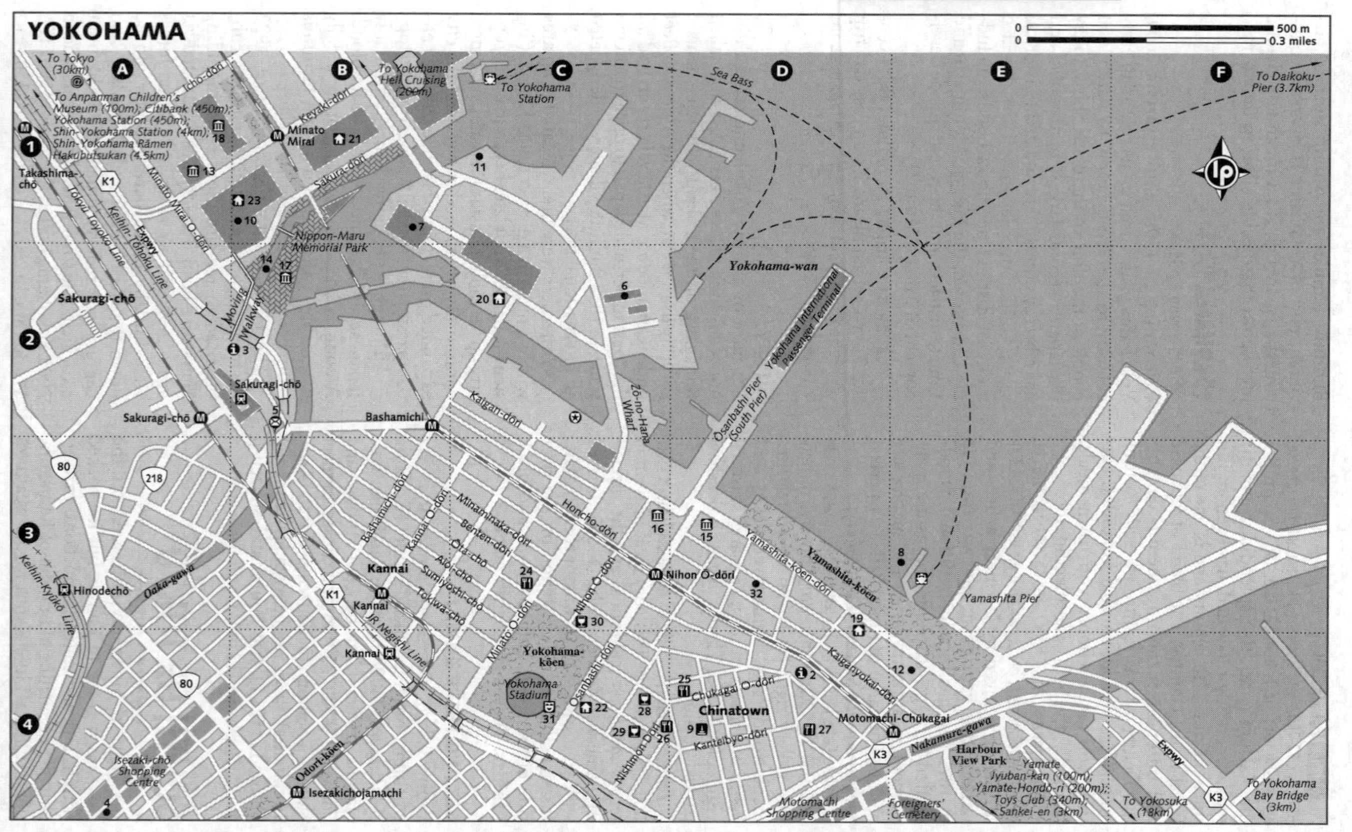
YOKOHAMA
0 500 m
0 0.3 miles
To Tokyo (30km)
To Anpanman Children's Museum (100m); Citibank (450m); Yokohama Station (450m); Shin-Yokohama Station (4km); Shin-Yokohama Rāmen Hakubutsukan (4.5km)
To Yokohama Heli Cruising (200m)
To Yokohama Station
Sea Bass
To Daikoku Pier (3.7km)
Icho-dōri
Keyaki-dōri
Minato Mirai
Takashima-chō
Tōkyū Tōyoko Line
Keihin-Tōhoku Line
Expwy
Minato Mirai Ō-dōri
Sakura-dōri
Nippon-Maru Memorial Park
Sakuragi-chō
Moving Walkway
Bashamichi
Kaigan-dōri
Zō-no-Hana Wharf
Ōsanbashi Pier (South Pier)
Yokohama International Passenger Terminal
Yokohama-wan
Honcho-dōri
Bashamichi-dōri
Kannai Ō-dōri
Minaminaka-dōri
Benten-dōri
Ōta-chō
Aioi-chō
Sumiyoshi-chō
Tokiwa-chō
Kannai
JR Negishi Line
Minato Ō-dōri
Nihon Ō-dōri
Yamashita-kōen-dōri
Yamashita-kōen
Yamashita Pier
Hinodechō
Keihin-Kyūkō Line
Ōoka-gawa
Yokohama-kōen
Yokohama Stadium
Ōsanbashi-dōri
Chukagai Ō-dōri
Chinatown
Nishimon Dōri
Kanteibyō-dōri
Kaiganyokai-dōri
Motomachi-Chūkagai
Nakamura-gawa
Harbour View Park
Yamate Jyuban-kan (100m); Yamate-Hondō-ri (200m); Toys Club (340m); Sankei-en (3km)
To Yokosuka (18km)
To Yokohama Bay Bridge (3km)
Isezaki-chō Shopping Centre
Odori-kōen
Isezakichojamachi
Motomachi Shopping Centre
Foreigners' Cemetery
K1
K3
80
218

since it opened as a treaty port with a host of events including the World Table Tennis Championships and the reopening of Marine Tower and the Zō-no-Hana quay area.

Orientation

Central Yokohama sits on the southern side of the western part of Tokyo-wan (here called Yokohama-wan). Most of the sights are within about 1km of the water, near Sakuragi-chō, Kannai and Ishikawa-chō Stations on the JR Negishi line, or Minato Mirai or Motomachi-Chūkagai Stations on the Minato Mirai line.

Information

Information about Yokohama is available on the web at www.welcome.city.yokohama.jp/eng/tourism.

Animi (☎ 222-3316; 4-2-7 Minato Mirai; per hr ¥100; 🕑 10am-6pm) Internet access. Walk 15 minutes northwest of Minato Mirai 21 Station.

Chinatown 80 Information Center (☎ 662-1252; Honcho-dōri; 🕑 10am-10pm) For the latest goings-on in Chinatown, the centre is a few blocks from the Motomachi subway station.

Citibank (🕑 24hr) An international ATM is outside the western exit of Yokohama Station, on the 2nd floor of the First Building, to the left of the Yokohama Bay Sheraton.

Minato Mirai 21 Information Center (☎ 211-0111; 1-1-62 Sakuragi-chō; 🕑 9am-7pm) English speakers here can provide a wealth of information, including the free *Yokohama Visitors' Map* or the more detailed *Yokohama Guide Book*. It's outside the northern exit of Sakuragi-chō Station.

No 1 Travel (☎ 231-0751; Isezaki-chō Royal Bldg, 5-127-13 Isezaki-chō; 🕑 10am-6.30pm Mon-Fri, to 4.30pm Sat) For discount international travel; about 10 blocks southwest of Kannai Station at Isezaki Shopping Centre.

Post office A block east of Sakuragi-chō Station, with foreign ATM service.

Yokohama Station Tourist Information Center (☎ 441-7300; 2-16-1 Takashima; 🕑 9am-7pm) This small booth is in the east–west corridor.

Sights & Activities

MINATO MIRAI 21 みなとみらい 21

This district of man-made **islands** (🚇 Sakuragi-chō, Minato Mirai, Bashamichi) used to be shipping docks, but the last two decades have transformed them into a metropolis-of-the-future ('Minato Mirai' means 'port future'), with a buzzing street scene by day and glowing towers by night (eg Landmark Tower and the three-towered Queens Sq). In addition to the attractions listed here, there's one of the world's largest convention complexes, several hotels and lots of shopping and dining options.

The following sights are arranged as a possible walking tour.

Landmark Tower ランドマークタワ

Japan's tallest building (70 storeys, 296m) has one of the world's fastest lifts (45km/h). The

INFORMATION
Animi あにみ 1 A1
Chinatown 80 Information Center 横浜中華街80 .... 2 D4
Minato Mirai 21 Information Center みなとみらい 21 .... 3 B2
No 1 Travel 4 A4
Post Office 郵便局 5 B2

SIGHTS & ACTIVITIES
Akarenga Sōko 横浜赤レンガ倉庫 6 C2
Cosmo World 横浜コスモワールド 7 B1
Hikawa Maru 氷川丸 8 E3
Kantei-byō 関帝廟 9 D4
Landmark Tower ランドマークタワ 10 B1
Manyō Club 万葉倶楽部 11 C1
Marine Tower マリンタワー 12 E4
Mitsubishi Minato Mirai Industrial Museum 三菱みなとみらい技術館 13 A1
Nippon Maru Sailing Ship 日本丸 14 B2
Silk Museum シルク博物館 15 D3
Yokohama Archives of History 横浜開港資料館 16 C3
Yokohama Maritime Museum 横浜マリタイム ミュージアム 17 B2
Yokohama Museum of Art 横浜美術館 18 A1

SLEEPING
Hotel New Grand ホテルニューグランド 19 D3
Navios Yokohama ナビオス横浜 20 C2
Pan Pacific Yokohama Bay パン パシフィック 横浜ベイホテル 21 B1
Toyoko Inn Sutajium-mae 東横インスタジアム前 22 C4
Yokohama Royal Park Hotel 横浜ロイヤルパークホテル 23 B1

EATING
Baikōtei 梅香亭 24 C3
Chano-ma チャノマ .... (see 6)
Manchinrō Honten 萬珍樓本店 25 D4
Ryūsen 馬さんの店 龍仙 26 C4
Yokohama Daisekai 横浜大世界 27 D4

DRINKING
Cable Car ケーブルカー 28 C4
Nana's Green Tea ナナズ·グリーンティー .... (see 6)
Sirius シリウス .... (see 23)
Windjammer ウィンドジャマー 29 C4
Zaim Café ザイムカフェ 30 C3

ENTERTAINMENT
Motion Blue モーション· .... (see 6)
Yokohama Stadium Ticket Office 横浜スタジアム きっぷ売り場 31 C4

SHOPPING
Queen's Square クイーンズスクエア .... (see 21)

TRANSPORT
Green Style グリーンスタイル 32 D3

Landmark Tower Sky Garden (☎ 222-5030; 2-2-1-1 Minato Mirai; adult/child/senior & student ¥1000/500/800; 10am-9pm Sep-Jun, to 10pm Sat, to 10pm 19 Jul-31 Aug; Minato Mirai) observatory is on the 69th floor; on clear days there are views to Tokyo, Izuhantō and Mt Fuji.

Yokohama Museum of Art 横浜美術館

Behind Landmark Tower, this modern **art museum** (☎ 221-0306; 3-4-1 Minato Mirai; adult/elementary-school student/junior -high student/college & high-school student ¥500/free/100/300; 10am-6pm Fri-Wed; Minato Mirai) has a decent collection featuring Picasso and Yokoyama Taikan displayed in changing exhibitions. It's noted for its building, designed by Pritzker Prize winner Tange Kenzō (1989).

Anpanman Children's Museum
横浜アンパンマンこどもミュージアム

This **kids' mall** (☎ 227-8855; 4-3-1 Minato Mirai; mall/museum free/¥1000; museum 10am-5pm, mall 10am-8pm Apr-Sep & 10am-6pm Oct-Mar; ; Takashimachō) is a celebration of Anpanman, the anime character made of baked-bean jam and beloved by all Japanese under (and over) 12. There's an Anpanman hair salon, museum and, natch, a bakery.

Mitsubishi Minato Mirai Industrial Museum 三菱みなとみらい技術館

This is one of Japan's better science and technology **museums** (☎ 224-9031; 3-3-1 Minato Mirai; adult/child/junior & high school student ¥300/100/200; 10am-5.30pm Tue-Sun; Minato Mirai), with robots, a wildly enjoyable helicopter simulator and good hands-on exhibits. See also Yokohama Heli Cruising (right).

Yokohama Maritime Museum
横浜マリタイムミュージアム

On the harbour in front of Landmark Tower, this fan-shaped **museum** (☎ 221-0280; 2-1-1 Minato Mirai; museum & ship adult/child ¥600/300; 10am-6.30pm Tue-Sun Jul & Aug, to 5pm Tue-Sun Sep-Jun; Minato Mirai) is largely dedicated to the *Nippon Maru* sailing ship docked adjacent. The four-masted barque (built in 1930) retains many original fittings, including the captain's and officers' rooms and the engine room.

Cosmo World 横浜コスモワールド

Next to the Maritime Museum, this **amusement park** (☎ 641-6591; 2-8-1 Shinkō; rides ¥300-700; 11am-9pm Mon-Fri, to 10pm Sat & Sun 21 Mar-30 Nov, 11am-8pm Mon-Fri, to 9pm Sat & Sun 1 Dec-20 Mar; Minato Mirai) features one of the world's tallest – at 112.5m – Ferris wheels, **Cosmo Clock 21** (admission ¥700).

Manyō Club 万葉倶楽部

This new **hot-spring facility** (☎ 663-4126; 2-7-1 Shinkō; adult/child ¥2720/1470; 10am-9am) trucks in water daily from Atami and gives you five storeys' worth of ways to enjoy them: pool to pool, sauna to sauna in your custom *yukata*. Spa treatments are available (extra charge), and 'relax rooms' have hundreds of TVs in front of hundreds of comfy chairs. Check-in is on the 7th floor. There are shuttle buses to Shin-Yokohama Station from here.

Akarenga Sōkō 横浜赤レンガ倉庫

Akarenga Sōkō refers to red-brick **warehouses** (☎ 211-1515; 1-1-2 Shinkō; admission free; 11am-8pm, some restaurants later), and these century-old structures have been refurbished into chichi speciality shops, restaurants, cafes and event spaces. Worth a look if you're in the area.

Yokohama Heli Cruising
横浜ヘリクルージング

For a less-simulated airborne adventure, take a helicopter tour of Yokohama. **Yokohama Heli Cruising** (☎ 380-5555; 1-7 Minato Mirai; flight per 5/10min from ¥4000/10,500; Fri-Sun & holidays) offers short but exhilarating flights from its heliport in Rinko Park, a seven-minute walk northeast of Queen's Sq. Flights depart around sunset.

YAMASHITA-KŌEN AREA 山下公園周辺

Moored alongside this seaside **park** (Motomachi-Chūkagai) you'll find the **Hikawa Maru** (☎ 641-4362; Yamashita-kōen; adult/child & senior ¥200/100; 10am-4.30pm Tue-Sun), a retired 1930 passenger liner (one of the staterooms was used by Charlie Chaplin) that was renovated and reopened in 2008.

Across the street, the **Silk Museum** (☎ 641-0841; 1 Yamashita-kōen-dōri; adult/child/student/senior ¥500/100/200/300; 9am-4.30pm Tue-Sun) pays tribute to Yokohama's history as a silk trading port, with all aspects of silk production and some lovely kimono and *obi* (sashes). The nearby **Yokohama Archives of History** (☎ 201-2100; 3 Nihon Ō-dōri; adult/child ¥200/100; 9.30am-5pm Tue-Sun; Nihon-ō-dōri) chronicles the city (with displays in English) from the opening of Japan to the mid-20th century; it's inside the former British consulate. **Marine Tower** (☎ 664-1100; adult ¥750, child ¥200-500; 10am-10pm; Motomachi-Chūkagai) is one of the world's tallest inland lighthouses (106m).

MOTOMACHI & YAMATE 元町・山手

South of Yamashita-kōen, the areas of **Motomachi** and **Yamate** (Motomachi-Chūkagai, Ishikawa-chō) combines the gentle intimacy of Motomachi's shopping street with early-20th-century Western-style architecture and fantastic views from the brick sidewalks of Yamate-hon-dōri ('Bluff St'). Private homes and churches here are still in use. Attractions include Harbour View Park and the Foreigners' Cemetery, final resting place of 4000 foreign residents and visitors – the headstones carry some fascinating inscriptions. A stroll from near Yamashita-kōen to Ishikawa-chō Station should take about one hour. Near the cemetery is the delightful **Toys Club** (621-8710; 239 Yamate-chō; adult/child ¥200/100; 9.30am-6pm, to 7pm Sat & Sun), a collection of old tin playthings including inspirations for the 1995 film *Toy Story*. Follow the signs on Yamate-hon-dōri.

CHINATOWN 中華街

Yokohama's **Chinatown** (Chūkagai; Motomachi-Chūkagai, Ishikawa-chō) has the sights, sounds, aromas of Hong Kong, and rivals Minato Mirai in popularity. Within its 10 elaborately painted gates are all manner of Chinese speciality shops and some 500 food shops and (often expensive) restaurants. Chinatown's heart is the Chinese temple **Kantei-byō** (226-2636; 140 Yamashita-chō; admission free; 9am-7pm), dedicated to Kanwu, the god of business. For information about Yokohama Daisekai, a Chinese theme park, see the boxed text (p232).

SANKEI-EN 三渓園

Opened to the public in 1906, the beautifully landscaped gardens of **Sankei-en** (621-0634; www.sankeien.or.jp; 58-1 Honmoku-sannotani; adult/child ¥500/200; 9am-4.30pm) feature walking paths among ponds, 17th-century buildings, several fine tea-ceremony houses and a 500-year-old, three-storey pagoda. The inner garden is a fine example of traditional Japanese-garden landscaping. From Yokohama or Sakuragi-chō Station, take bus 8 to Honmoku Sankei-en-mae bus stop (10 minutes).

Sleeping

Toyoko Inn Sutajium-mae (228-0045; fax 228-0046; www.toyoko-inn.com/eng; 205-1 Yamashita-chō; s/d ¥6090/8400; Kannai;) Simple but nicely outfitted business hotel with small, comfortable rooms in a main building (Honkan) and marginally nicer new building (Shinkan). Rates include breakfast and internet.

Navios Yokohama (633-6000; fax 633-6001; www.navios-yokohama.com; 2-2-1 Shinkō; s/tw from ¥8400/15,750; Bashamichi;) In Minato Mirai, it's Yokohama's best deal in this price range; rooms are spacious, spotless and central. Choose city views (across the harbour to Landmark Tower or sea views towards Akarenga Sōkō).

Hotel New Grand (681-1841; fax 681-1895; www.hotel-newgrand.co.jp; 10 Yamashita-kōen-dōri; s/tw from ¥13,860/28,000; Motomachi-Chūkagai;) This old-line (1927) hotel with 251 rooms has a prime waterfront location and was once a favourite of visiting foreign dignitaries (check out the timeless original lobby). Now it's a classy, upmarket option with some old-world charm, despite the addition of a tower in 1992.

Yokohama Royal Park Hotel (221-1111; fax 224-5153; www.yrph.com; 2-2-1-3 Minato Mirai; s/tw & d from ¥31,500/36,750;) You can't get any higher than this, on the upper floors of Landmark Tower, and it hardly gets more luxe either, with a fitness centre, a pool, oodles of space, marble, burl wood, automatic blackout curtains and an aromatherapy salon.

Pan Pacific Yokohama Bay (682-2222; fax 682-2223; http://pphy.co.jp; 2-3-7 Minato Mirai; tw from ¥42,000; Minatomirai;) Right by the convention centre, this superbly glitzy hotel boasts designer furnishings, rooms with balconies, excellent views and butlers for the higher-end suites, and several good but pricey restaurants.

Eating

Chinatown offers the most interesting food options in town. Plan on spending about ¥5000 per person for a fancy dinner and perhaps half that for lunch (look for set menus), although there are certainly less expensive eateries. For an eclectic mix of cuisines, visit the restaurant floors of Landmark Tower and Queen's Sq.

Chano-ma (650-8228; 3rd fl, Akarenga Sōkō Bldg 2; mains from ¥700; 11am-4am, to 5am Fri & Sat) Dine on sushi, salads and croquettes at high tables with high chairs or on mattresses arranged around an open kitchen, while serious club beats play under tall ceilings; English menu.

Baikōtei (681-4870; 1-1 Aioicho; mains ¥800-1300; 11am-8.30pm Mon-Sat; Kannai or Nihon Ō-dōri) This weathered classic with red-velour

IT'S A RESTAURANT! IT'S A THEME PARK!

Yokohama loves food and Yokohama loves fun. Put them together and you get the food theme park! An industry pioneer is the **Shin-Yokohama Rāmen Hakubutsukan** (新横浜ラーメン博物館; ☎ 471-0503; 2-14-21 Shinyokohama; adult/child ¥300/100, most meals from ¥900; 🕑 11am-10pm). This museum of *rāmen* continues to show the history and culture of these Chinese-style noodles that (it's fair to say) Japan is bonkers about. Downstairs, nine *rāmen* restaurants from around the country were hand-picked to sell their wares in a replica of a 1958 *shitamachi* (downtown district).

The concept has been copied many times since, not least here in Yokohama. In Chinatown, the eight-storey **Yokohama Daisekai** (Daska; ☎ 681-5588; 97 Yamashita-chō; adult/child ¥500/300, mains from ¥900; 🕑 10am-9pm) models itself on Shanghai's gilded age of the 1920s and '30s, with silks, carvings and crafts, performances of jazz and Chinese opera, and three floors of restaurants. To beat the crowds, visit on weekdays.

seating is famed for its Hayashi rice (with meat, vegetables and demi-glace), and a mean *katsu-don* (pork cutlet). Look for the sign that announces Baikō Emmies; there's an English menu available.

Ryūsen (☎ 651-0758; 218-5 Yamashita-chō; mains ¥900-1500; 🕑 7am-3am; 🚇 Ishikawa-chō) You can't miss friendly old Mr Ma sitting outside his small but welcoming Cantonese and Shanghai-style eatery with red awning and English menus, as he has done for years. The walls outside and inside are covered with photos of reasonably priced, tasty-looking dishes like fried cashew nuts and chicken (¥1050).

Manchinrō Honten (☎ 681-4004; 153 Yamashita-chō; mains from ¥1100, dinner for 2 ¥8400; 🕑 11am-10pm) One of Chinatown's oldest and most popular Cantonese restaurants, with a respected Hong Kong chef. Expect specialities like wok-fried seafood with XO sauce and shrimp with mayonnaise, plus yum cha (dim sum; ¥480 to ¥700). Look for the stone lions out the front; there's an English menu.

Yamate Jyuban-kan (山手十番館; ☎ 621-4466; 247 Yamatechō; mains/courses from ¥2000/3500; 🕑 11am-9pm) Overlooking the Foreigners' Cemetery in Yamate, this French restaurant with English menus serves consistently good cuisine in a building that's like a mansion from the American south. A casual cafe occupies the 1st floor, while upstairs is the classic restaurant, dishing out longstanding favourites like the Kaika steak set. Reservations recommended; look for the French flag outside.

Drinking & Entertainment

Cable Car (☎ 662-5303; 200 Yamashita-chō; drinks from ¥650; 🕑 6pm-2am Mon-Thu, to 4am Fri & Sat, to midnight Sun; 🚇 Nihon Ō-dōri) The idea is a bar from 1890s San Francisco, with polished wood surfaces, a long bar and 300 cocktails. Pub-style food options include Cajun-style *ebi-furai* (deep-fried shrimp; ¥1350). There's an English sign.

Windjammer (☎ 662-3966; 215 Yamashita-chō; live-music cover ¥400-600, drinks from ¥650; 🕑 5pm-1.30am; 🚇 Kannai) The setting feels like the inside of a yacht (especially after the potent Jacktar cocktail, ¥1050). All the better to listen to live jazz nightly, from 8pm; look for the English sign.

Zaim Café (☎ 227-8051; 34 Nihon Ō-dōri; drinks from ¥600; 🕑 11.30am-11pm; 🚇 Nihon Ō-dōri) This bohemian space in a 1920s-era Japan Cotton Corp building run by the Yokohama Arts Foundation often has live blues and jazz acts to enjoy from the comfort of an eclectic group of old sofas. The menu includes light meals like *maguro don* (tuna on rice, ¥1000). There's an English sign.

Motion Blue (☎ 226-1919; 3rd fl, Akarenga Sōkō Bldg 2; most tickets free-¥8200; 🕑 5-11.30pm Mon-Sat, 4-10.30pm Sun; 🚇 Bashamichi) Yokohama's hottest music club books jazz, fusion, world music, J-pop and more. It's in the Akarenga Sōkō.

Nana's Green Tea (☎ 664-2707; Akarenga Sōkō Bldg 2; drinks around ¥550; 🕑 11am-9pm) Contemporary takes on traditional Japanese drinks: latte of frozen *maccha* (powdered green tea; ¥450) with whipped cream, drinks with azuki beans, and a steaming bowl of *zensai* (azuki-bean soup).

Sirius (☎ 221-1111; 2-2-1-3 Minato Mirai; cover charge after 5/7pm ¥1050/2100; 🕑 7am-1am; 🚇 Sakuragi-chō) Elegant cocktail lounge on the top (70th floor) of the Yokohama Royal Park Hotel. The place to go for a view over cocktails such as the Two Hearts, with apple and cherry syrups, Calpis and fresh apple, topped with champagne (¥1900). Also open for breakfast and lunch buffets.

Getting There & Away

Frequent JR and private-line trains from Tokyo serve JR Yokohama Station, where you can change for Sakuragi-chō (¥130, three minutes), Kannai (¥130, five minutes), Ishikawa-chō (¥150, eight minutes) or the more expensive local subway. Take the Keihin Kyūkō line from Shinagawa Station (¥290, 18 minutes), or the Tōkyū Tōyoko line from Shibuya Station (¥260, about 25 minutes), which becomes the Minato Mirai subway line to Minatomirai (¥440, 28 minutes) and Motomachi-Chūkagai (¥460, 30 minutes).

From Tokyo Station, JR's Keihin Tōhoku and Tōkaidō lines stop at Yokohama Station (¥450, 30 minutes); some continue on to Sakuragi-chō, Kannai and Ishikawa-chō (all ¥540). The Tōkaidō *shinkansen* stops at Shin-Yokohama Station, northwest of town, connected to the city centre by the Yokohama line.

TO/FROM THE AIRPORT

Yokohama Station has connections to Narita airport via Narita Express trains (N'EX; ¥4180, 1½ hours) or Keihin Kyūkō Airport Narita line (¥1450, two hours, including transfers) and limousine buses to/from the Yokohama City Air Terminal (YCAT, Sky Building east of Yokohama Station, next to Sogō department store; Narita airport ¥3500, two hours; Haneda airport ¥560, 35 minutes).

Getting Around

BICYCLE

The stylish staff at **Green Style** (☎ 662-1414; 2-5-8 Yamashita-chō; per 3hr ¥1000; ⏰ 11am-8pm Fri-Tue) rents bicycles on a back street near Yamashita-kōen.

BOAT

Sea Bass (☎ 671-7719) ferries connect Yokohama Station, Minato Mirai 21 and Yamashita-kōen. Boats run between approximately 10am and 7pm. Full fare from Yokohama Station to Yamashita-kōen is ¥700 (20 minutes). **Suijō Bus** (☎ 201-0821; 1-1 Kaigan-dōri; adult/child ¥500/200; ⏰ 1-5pm Tue-Fri, noon-6pm Sat & Sun) runs ferries between Minato Mirai, Ōsanbashi and Renga Park.

BUS

Although trains are more convenient, Yokohama has an extensive bus network (adult/child ¥210/110 per ride). A special Akai-kutsu (red shoe) bus loops every 30 minutes during the day through the tourist areas for ¥100 per ride or from ¥500 to ¥830 for a day pass.

KAMAKURA 鎌倉

☎ 0467 / pop 173,000

The capital of Japan from 1185 to 1333, Kamakura rivals Nikkō as the most culturally rewarding day trip from Tokyo and is often less crowded. Many Buddhist temples and the occasional Shintō shrine dot the surrounding countryside here. If you start early you can cover a lot of ground in a day, but two days will also allow you to visit the temples of East Kamakura and take some nice walks – even a swim at the beach! Kamakura does tend to get packed on weekends and in holiday periods, so plan accordingly.

History

The end of the Heian period was marked by a legendary feud between two great warrior families, the Minamoto (Genji) and the Taira (Heike). After the Taira routed the Minamoto, the third son of the Minamoto clan, called Yoritomo, was sent to live at a temple in Izu-hantō. When the boy grew old enough, he began to gather support for a counterattack on his clan's old rivals. In 1180 Yoritomo set up his base at Kamakura, far away from the debilitating influences of Kyoto court life, close to other clans loyal to the Minamoto and, having the sea on one side and densely wooded hills on the others, easy to defend.

After victories over the Taira, Minamoto Yoritomo was appointed shōgun in 1192 and governed Japan from Kamakura. When he died without an heir, power passed to the Hōjō, the family of Yoritomo's wife.

The Hōjō clan ruled Japan from Kamakura for more than a century until, in 1333, weakened by the cost of maintaining defences against threats of attack from Kublai Khan in China, the Hōjō clan was defeated by Emperor Go-Daigo. Kyoto once again became the capital.

Orientation

Kamakura's main attractions can be covered on foot, with the occasional bus ride. Cycling is also practical (see p238 for details). Most sights are signposted in English and Japanese. You can start at Kamakura Station and travel around the area in a circle (Komachi-dōri

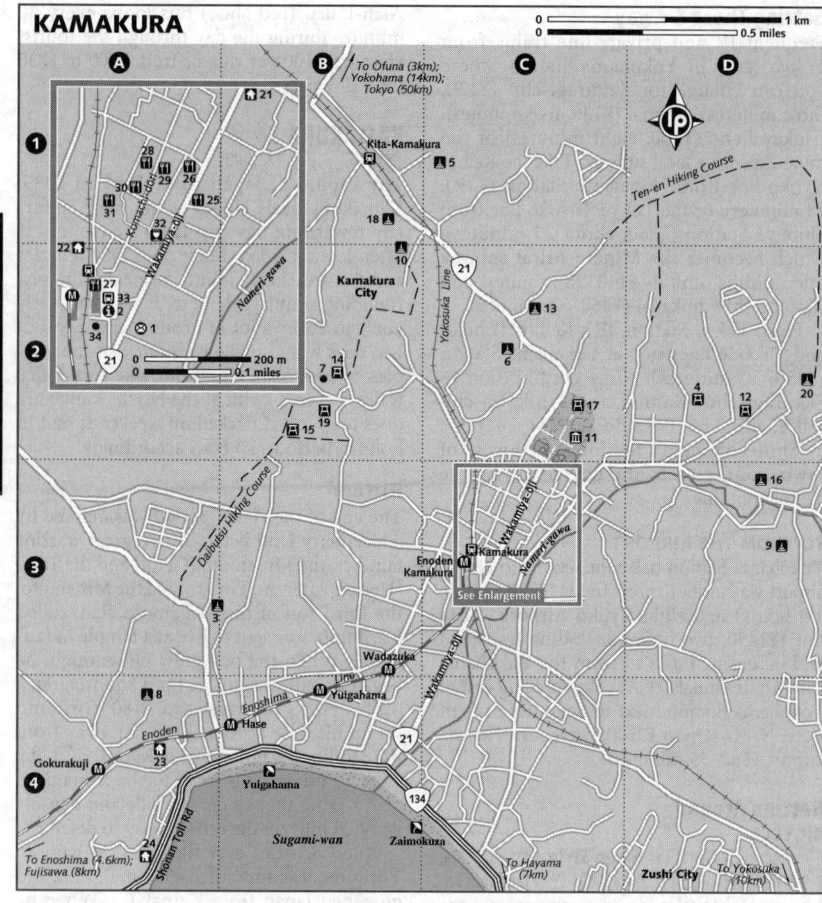

'shopping town' and broad Wakamiya-ōji are the main streets east of the station), or start one station north at Kita-Kamakura and visit the temples between there and Kamakura Station on foot. The itinerary in this section follows the latter route.

Information

Kamakura Green Net (http://guide.city.kamakura.kanagawa.jp) Has an English section with useful information about both living and sightseeing in Kamakura.

Post office (1-10-3 Komachi; 9am-7pm Mon-Fri, to 3pm Sat) With ATMs; a short walk from Kamakura Station's east exit.

Tourist Information Center (☎ 22-3350; 9am-5.30pm Apr-Sep, to 5pm Oct-Mar) Just outside Kamakura Station's east exit, this helpful tourist office distributes maps and brochures, such as the English guide *Oshiete Kamakura,* and can also make bookings for same-day accommodation.

Sights & Activities

ENGAKU-JI 円覚寺

Engaku-ji (☎ 22-0478; adult/child ¥300/100; 8am-5pm Apr-Oct, to 4pm Nov-Mar) is on the left as you exit Kita-Kamakura Station. It is one of the five main Rinzai Zen temples in Kamakura. Engaku-ji was founded in 1282, allegedly as a place where Zen monks might pray for soldiers who lost their lives defending Japan against Kublai Khan. Today, the only real reminder of the temple's former magnificence and antiquity is the gate San-mon, a 1780 reconstruction. At the top of the long flight

INFORMATION

Post Office 郵便局 ... 1 A2
Tourist Information Center 観光案内センター ... 2 A2

SIGHTS & ACTIVITIES

Daibutsu (Great Buddha) 大仏 ... 3 A3
Egara Ten-jin ... 4 D2
Engaku-ji 円覚寺 ... 5 C1
Ennō-ji 円応寺 ... 6 C2
Genjiyama-kōen 源氏山公園 ... 7 B2
Hase-dera 長谷寺 ... 8 A4
Hōkoku-ji 報国寺 ... 9 D3
Jōchi-ji 浄智寺 ... 10 B2
Kamakura Museum 鎌倉国宝館 ... 11 C2
Kamakura-gu ... 12 D2
Kenchō-ji 建長寺 ... 13 C2
Kuzuharaoka-jinja 葛原岡神社 ... 14 B2
Sasuke-inari jinja 佐助稲荷神社 ... 15 B2
Sugimoto-dera 杉本寺 ... 16 D3
Tsurugaoka Hachiman-gū 鶴岡八幡宮 ... 17 C2
Tōkei-ji 東慶寺 ... 18 B1
Zeniarai-benten 銭洗弁天 ... 19 B2
Zuisen-ji 瑞泉寺 ... 20 D2

SLEEPING

Classical Hotel Ajisai ホテルあじさい ... 21 B1
Hotel New Kamakura ホテルニューカマクラ ... 22 A2
Kamakura Hase Youth Hostel 鎌倉はせユースホステル ... 23 A4
Kamakura Park Hotel 鎌倉パークホテル ... 24 A4

EATING

Bowls Donburi Café 鎌倉どんぶりカフェ Bowls ... 25 A1
Caraway キャラウェイ ... 26 A1
Fūrin 風凜 ... 27 A2
HoretarŸ 惚太郎 ... 28 A1
Imo-no-kichikan 芋の吉館 ... 29 A1
Kamakura Ichibanya 鎌倉壱番屋 ... 30 A1
Milk Hall ミルクホール ... 31 A1

DRINKING

Bar Ram バーラム ... 32 A1

TRANSPORT

Bus Station バス停 ... 33 A2
Rent-a-Cycle Kurarin レンタサイクル ... 34 A2

of stairs through the gate is the Engaku-ji bell, the largest bell in Kamakura, cast in 1301. The Hondō (Main Hall) inside San-mon is a recent reconstruction, dating from the mid-1960s. Public Zen meditation sessions are held on the second and fourth Sunday every month from 9am.

TŌKEI-JI 東慶寺

Across the railway tracks from Engaku-ji, **Tōkei-ji** (☎ 22-1663; admission ¥100; 8.30am-5pm Mar-Oct, to 4.30pm Nov-Feb) is notable for its lush grounds as much as for the temple itself. On weekdays, when visitors are few, it can be a pleasantly relaxing place.

Historically, the temple is famed as having served as a women's refuge. A woman could be officially recognised as divorced after three years as a nun in the temple precincts. Today, there are no nuns; the grave of the last abbess can be found in the cemetery, shrouded by cypress trees.

JŌCHI-JI 浄智寺

A couple of minutes further on from Tōkei-ji is **Jōchi-ji** (☎ 22-3943; adult/child ¥200/100; 9am-4.30pm Mar-Oct, to 4pm Nov-Feb), another temple with pleasant grounds. Founded in 1283, this is considered one of Kamakura's five great Zen temples, prized for its moss-covered entry, its bell tower and for the flowers that seem to explode here each spring.

DAIBUTSU HIKING COURSE

If time permits, consider taking the Daibutsu Hiking Course, which begins at the steps just up the lane from Jōchi-ji and follows a wooded path for 3km to the Daibutsu (allow about 1½ hours). Along the course you'll pass the small shrine of **Kuzuharagaoka-jinja**, from which you'll see signs to the landscaped park of **Genjiyama-kōen** (where you'll see a statue of Minamoto Yoritomo). From here, head down the stairs, keep going down the hill and take a right to reach **Zeniarai-benten** (Money-washing Shrine; ☎ 25-1081; admission free; 8am-5pm), one of Kamakura's most alluring Shintō shrines. A cave-like entrance leads to a clearing where visitors come to bathe their money in natural springs with the hope of bringing financial success. You can either return back up the steps to the path or continue down the paved road, turning right at the first intersection, walking along a path lined with cryptomeria and ascending up through the shrine of **Sasuke-inari jinja** (typical of inari shrines, it's recognised by the succession of torii gates) before meeting up with the Daibutsu path once again.

KENCHŌ-JI 建長寺

Continuing towards Kamakura along the main road from Jōchi-ji, on the left you'll pass the turn-off to this **temple** (☎ 22-0981; adult/child ¥300/100; 8.30am-4.30pm), the first-ranked of the five great Zen temples. Founded in 1253, Kenchō-ji once comprised seven buildings and 49 subtemples, most of which were destroyed in the fires of the 14th and 15th centuries. However, the 17th and 18th centuries saw its restoration, and you can still get a sense of its splendour. Today, Kenchō-ji functions as a working monastery with 10 subtemples. Among the highlights are the **Butsuden** (Buddha hall), brought piece by piece from Kyoto; the painstakingly landscaped **Zen garden**, shaped like the kanji for 'mind'; and the **juniper grove**, believed to have sprouted from seeds brought from China by Kenchō-ji's founder some seven centuries ago. Public Zen meditation sessions are held Fridays and Saturdays from 4.45pm.

TEN-EN HIKING COURSE

Another excellent walk through the countryside begins by walking around Kenchō-ji's Hojo (Main Hall) and up the steps to the entrance of the Ten-en Hiking Course. From here it's a two-hour walk to Zuisen-ji, along one of the most scenic spots in Kanagawa-ken; those with less time can take a shorter (80-minute) trail to Kamakura-gū.

ENNŌ-JI 円応寺

Across the road from Kenchō-ji is **Ennō-ji** (☎ 25-1905; admission ¥200; 🕑 9am-4pm Mar-Nov, to 3.30pm Dec-Feb), which is distinguished primarily by its collection of statues depicting the judges of hell. Presiding over them is a statue of Emma (Sanskrit name is Yama; an Important Cultural Property), an ancient Hindu deity and ruler of the hell's 10 kings. The statue is noted for its fierce gaze meant for the wicked (hopefully you won't have anything to worry about).

TSURUGAOKA HACHIMAN-GŪ 鶴岡八幡宮

Further down the road, where it turns towards Kamakura Station, is **Tsurugaoka Hachiman-gū** (☎ 22-0315; treasure hall admission adult/child ¥200/100; 🕑 6am-8.30pm), the main Shintō shrine of Kamakura. It was founded by Minamoto Yoriyoshi, of the same Minamoto clan that ruled Japan from Kamakura. This shrine's sprawl, with elongated paths, broad vistas and lotus ponds, presents the visitor with an atmosphere drastically different to the repose of the Zen temples clustered around Kita-Kamakura Station. The Gempei Pond (the name comes from the kanji for the Genji and Heike clans) is divided by bridges, said to symbolise the rift between the clans. Behind the pond is the **Kamakura Museum** (☎ 22-0753; adult/child ¥300/100; 🕑 9am-4pm), housing remarkable Zen Buddhist sculptures from the 12th to 16th centuries.

DAIBUTSU 大仏

The Kamakura **Daibutsu** (Great Buddha; ☎ 22-0703; adult/child ¥200/150; 🕑 7am-6pm Apr-Sep, to 5.30pm Oct-Mar) is at Kōtoku-in temple. Completed in 1252, it is Japan's second-largest Buddha image and Kamakura's most famous sight. Once housed in a huge hall, today the statue sits in the open, the hall having been washed away by a tsunami in 1495. Cast in bronze and weighing close to 850 tonnes, the statue is 11.4m tall. Its construction is said to have been inspired by Yoritomo's visit to Nara (where Japan's biggest Daibutsu holds court) after the Minamoto clan's victory over the Taira clan. Even though Kamakura's Daibutsu doesn't quite match Nara's in stature, it is commonly agreed that it is artistically superior.

The Buddha itself is the Amida Buddha (*amitābha* in Sanskrit), worshipped by followers of the Jōdo school as a figure of salvation.

Buses from stops 1 to 6 in front of Kamakura Station run to the Daibutsu-mae stop. Alternatively, take the Enoden Enoshima line to Hase Station and walk north for about five minutes. Better yet, take the Daibutsu Hiking Course.

HASE-DERA 長谷寺

About 10 minutes' walk from the Daibutsu, **Hase-dera** (Hase Kannon; ☎ 22-6300; adult/child ¥300/100; 🕑 8am-5pm Mar-Sep, to 4.30pm Oct-Feb) is one of the most popular temples in the Kantō region.

The walls of the staircases leading up to the main hall are lined with thousands of tiny statues of Jizō; ranked like a small army of urchins, many of them are clothed to keep them warm. It's quite charming until you realise that Jizō is the patron bodhisattva of travellers and departed children, and the statues were placed there by women who lost children through miscarriage or abortion.

The focal point of the temple's main hall is the Kannon statue. Kannon (*avalokiteshvara* in Sanskrit), the goddess of mercy, is the bodhisattva of infinite compassion and, along with Jizō, is one of Japan's most popular Buddhist deities. This 9m-high carved wooden *jūichimen* (11-faced Kannon) is believed to date from the 8th century. The temple dates back to AD 736, when it is said the statue washed up on the shore near Kamakura.

OTHER SHRINES & TEMPLES

If you're still in the mood for temples, there are plenty more in and around Kamakura, which has some 60 more temples and shrines.

From the Daibutsu it is best to return to Kita-Kamakura Station by bus and take another bus out to the temples in the peaceful eastern part of town. While these temples lack the grandeur of Kamakura's more famous temples, they more than make up for it with their charm and lack of crowds.

The grounds of **Zuisen-ji** (☎ 22-1191; adult/child ¥200/100; 9am-4.30pm), a secluded Zen temple, make for a pleasant stroll and include gardens laid out by Musō Soseki, the temple's esteemed founder. It is possible to get here from the Egara Ten-jin shrine on foot in about 10 to 15 minutes; turn right where the bus turns left in front of the shrine, take the next left and keep following the road. From Zuisen-ji you can access the Ten-en Hiking Course.

The small **Sugimoto-dera** (☎ 22-3463; adult/child ¥200/100; 8am-4.30pm), founded in AD 734, is reputed to be the oldest in Kamakura. Its ferocious-looking guardian deities and a statue of Kannon are its main draw. Take a bus from stop 5 at Kamakura Station to the Sugimoto Kannon bus stop.

Down the road (away from Kamakura Station) from Sugimoto-dera, on the right-hand side, **Hōkoku-ji** (☎ 22-0762; bamboo garden admission ¥200; 9am-4pm) is a Rinzai Zen temple with quiet, landscaped gardens where you can relax under a red parasol with a cup of Japanese tea. This is one of the more active Zen temples in Kamakura, regularly holding *zazen* (Soto-school meditation) classes for beginners; public sessions are held Sundays from 7.30am. Take a bus from stop 5 at Kamakura Station (¥190, 10 minutes) to Jōmyōji.

Festivals & Events

Bonbori Matsuri From 6 to 9 August, hundreds of lanterns are strung up around Tsurugaoka Hachiman-gū.

Reitai Matsuri Festivities between 14 and 16 September include a procession of *mikoshi* (portable shrines) and, on the last day, a display of horseback archery.

Kamakura Matsuri A week of celebrations held from the second Sunday to the third Sunday in April. It includes a wide range of activities, most of which are centred on Tsurugaoka Hachiman-gū.

Sleeping

Kamakura Hase Youth Hostel (☎/fax 24-3390; www1.kamakuranet.ne.jp/hase_yh/; dm member/nonmember ¥3000/4000; P) Three beds and three minutes from both Hase-dera and the beach, and 10 minutes from the Great Buddha. Simple, but contemporary and tidy, this hostel is mostly bunk beds. From Kamakura Station take an Enoden Enoshima train to Hase Station.

Classical Hotel Ajisai (☎ 22-3492; www.beniya-ajisai.co.jp/hotel.html, in Japanese; r per person from ¥6830; P) Across from Tsurugaoka Hachiman-gū, the 11-room Ajisai is a businesslike, affordable option with basic Western-style rooms and a friendly, no-nonsense host. Fourth-floor rooms have shrine views. Breakfast (¥1050) is *kamameshi* (rice in a hot pot; vegetarian version available).

Hotel New Kamakura (☎ 22-2230; fax 22-0233; www.newkamakura.com; s/d without bathrooms from ¥4200/11,000; P) This handsome hotel dating from 1924 is in two buildings. It has Western- and Japanese-style rooms with large windows, dark-wood floors, exposed beams and comfortable furnishings. Exit west from Kamakura Station and take a sharp right down the alley. It's at the car park. Avoid rooms off the old lobby, which can be noisy.

Kamakura Park Hotel (☎ 25-5121; fax 25-3778; www.kamakuraparkhotel.co.jp; s/tw from ¥12,705/24,200; P) Recently renovated, this marble-tiled, Western-style hotel by the sea is glitzy and breezy. The decor still looks 1980s plush, but every room is large, with ocean views. There's a shuttle bus to Kamakura Station (only weekdays), or it's a 12-minute walk from Hase Station on the Enoden Enoshima line.

Eating & Drinking

Milk Hall (☎ 22-1179; most dishes ¥600-1050; 11am-10.30pm) Sweet! This quaint cafe-bar-antique shop with English menus serves light meals (small plates like boiled sausages or baked camembert), coffees and cocktails, and it features live jazz some nights. From Kamakura Station's east exit, head two blocks down Komachi-dōri, take a left and then another left down the first alley; the door has an English sign.

Caraway (☎ 25-0927; dishes ¥630-940; 11.30am-7.30pm Tue-Sun) This Japanese-style curry shop has an old-world charm and some unusual preparations. Go for the classic beef curry, or spring for chicken curry with Edam cheese; there's an English menu. It's a white building with a tile fringe over the door.

Fūrin (☎ 0120-86-4411; most dishes ¥700-1890; 11am-10.30pm) Upstairs from Kamakura Station, Fūrin is a smart sushi joint where sake and spirits flow at night and very filling sashimi sets go for ¥1600. Weekday lunch specials include sliced tuna sets (¥1365) and tempura bowls (¥950); an English menu is available.

Bowls Donburi Café (☎ 61-3501; most meals ¥750-1250; 11am-midnight) The owner of this jazzy new spot with English menus believes anything can be a *donburi* (rice bowl), and he has turned this humble dish into an art form. You'll find yummy rice toppings like sashimi, ginger pork, and salmon avocado here (there are vegetarian options too) – plus, you get a discount if you discover the word *atari* in the bowl, underneath the food. There's an English sign over the doors.

Horetarō (☎ 23-8622; most dishes ¥1000-1300, all-you-can-eat from ¥1575; ⌚ lunch & dinner Tue-Sun) *Okonomiyaki* and *monjayaki* (Osaka- and Tokyo-style savoury pancakes, respectively) are the thing here; grill them yourself. All-you-can-eat-and-drink sets, including alcoholic drinks, are ¥3150 for 2½ hours. There's an English menu. Look for the traditional banners and lanterns outside.

Snackers will love Komachi-dōri. **Kamakura Ichibanya** (☎ 22-6156; ⌚ 9am-6.30pm) specialises in *sembei* (rice crackers); watch staff grilling them in the window or buy some 70 packaged varieties, including curry, garlic, *mentaiko* (spicy cod roe) or *uni* (sea urchin); look for the baskets on the corner. **Imo-no-kichikan** (☎ 25-6038; ⌚ 10am-6pm) is famous for soft-serve sweet-potato ice cream (¥295). Look for the giant plastic cone with lavender-hued ice cream.

Bar Ram (☎ 60-5156; drinks from ¥500; ⌚ 7pm until late) Kamakura is pretty monastic at night, but this hole in the wall in the lanes off Komachi-dōri is a *tachinomiya* (drink-while-standing bar) with plenty of old Rolling Stones vinyls and friendly banter. Look for the English sign.

Getting There & Away

JR Yokosuka line trains run to Kamakura from Tokyo (¥890, 56 minutes) and Shinagawa stations, via Yokohama (¥330, 27 minutes). Alternatively, the Shōnan Shinjuku line runs from the west side of Tokyo (Shibuya, Shinjuku and Ikebukuro, all ¥890) in about one hour, though some trains require a transfer at Ōfuna, one stop before Kita-Kamakura.

The JR Kamakura-Enoshima Free Pass (from Tokyo/Yokohama ¥1970/1130) is valid for two days, covering the trip to and from Tokyo/Yokohama and unlimited use of JR trains around Kamakura, the Shōnan monorail between Ōfuna and Enoshima, and the Enoden Enoshima line. The Odakyū Enoshima/Kamakura Free Pass (from Shinjuku/Machida ¥1430/990) is valid for one day but goes to Katase-Enoshima Station and Fujisawa Station (where it meets the Enoden line), not Kamakura Station.

Getting Around

You can walk to most temples and shrines from Kamakura or Kita-Kamakura Station. Sites in the west, like the Daibutsu, can be reached via the Enoden Enoshima line from Kamakura Station to Hase (¥190) or bus from Kamakura Station stops 1 to 6. Bus trips around the area cost either ¥170 or ¥190. Another good option is renting a bicycle; **Rent-a-Cycle Kurarin** (☎ 24-2319; per hr/day ¥600/1600; ⌚ 8.30am-5pm) is outside the east exit of Kamakura Station, and right up the incline. Local rickshaw rides start at ¥2000 per person for 10 minutes.

EAST OF TOKYO

Chiba-ken, east and southeast of Tokyo, has few attractions for travellers, save some decent beaches on the Pacific side of the Bōsō-hantō peninsula near Ōhara. An overlooked destination in Chiba-ken is the city of Narita, which most visitors will pass through from its airport.

NARITA 成田

☎ 0476 / pop 125,000

Narita is chiefly known as the home of Japan's main international airport, but the older part of the city is a surprisingly pleasant stop. Its quiet streets lead to a 1000-year-old temple with lush gardens – perfect for unwinding before or after a long flight or if you have a layover of a half-day or more.

Orientation

Both the Keisei Narita and JR Narita lines stop in Narita, a couple of hundred metres apart. Both are within a block of Omotesandō, the town's very pleasant main drag lined with restaurants and shops. It winds like an eel downhill to Narita's main attractions, Narita-san-kōen and Narita-san Shinshō-ji.

Information

You can pick up a copy of the Narita map/pamphlet at the **Narita Tourist Information Center** (☎ 24-3198; ⌚ 8.30am-5.30pm) just outside the eastern exit of JR Narita Station, or at the tourist information counters at Narita International Airport (p827). Maps, which include locations of local restaurants, are available at the tourist info center by the station. You might also stop by the **Narita Tourist**

Pavilion (☎ 24-3232; Omotesandō; ⏲ 9am-5pm Tue-Sun Oct-May, 10am-6pm Jun-Sep) for exhibits on local history. Either of the offices in town can book accommodation.

Sights

The town's centrepiece is the impressive **Narita-san Shinshō-ji** (成田山新勝寺; ☎ 22-2111; admission free; ⏲ 24hr) and the attractive park around it, **Narita-san-kōen** (成田山公園). While the temple was founded in 1070 (five of its buildings are Important Cultural Properties), the main hall is a 1968 reconstruction. The temple itself remains an important centre of the Shingon sect of Buddhism and attracts as many as 10 million visitors annually, particularly around New Year's.

Amid the 165,000 sq metres of ponds and greenery of Narita-san-kōen (be sure to stroll around the ponds), you'll find two museums good for real aficionados: the **Narita-san Calligraphy Museum** (成田山書道美物館; ☎ 24-0774; adult/child ¥500/300; ⏲ 9am-4pm Tue-Sun), which has a good collection of *shodō* (calligraphy), and the **Reikōkan Historical Material Museum** (成田山霊光館; ☎ 22-0234; adult/child ¥300/150; ⏲ 9am-4pm Tue-Sun), under the temple's upper pagoda, with artefacts from 18th-century Japanese life and various temple treasures.

Festivals & Events

Hatsumōde On New Year's Day, when a large proportion of the Japanese populace visits shrines and temples to receive blessing for the new year, things get hectic at Narita-san Shinshō-ji. A high level of crowd-tolerance is a must.

Setsubun Another notable festival at Narita-san Shinshō-ji, on 3 February, commemorating the last day of winter in the Japanese lunar calendar.

Taiko Matsuri (Drum Festival) On the first Saturday and Sunday in April, some 30 to 40 drumming troupes from all over Japan converge on the city for a noisy, energetic weekend.

Gion Festival Held for three days at the beginning of July, this 300-year-old festival is Narita's most spectacular, featuring colourful floats and costumed processions.

Unagi Festival During this celebration of eel cuisine from 12 July to 17 August, dig in to a yummy grilled eel set meal *(unajū)*, advertised at many restaurants.

Sleeping

Narita lodging is both in the town centre (accessible by train) and closer to the airport (with airport shuttle service).

Comfort Hotel Narita (コンフォートホテル成田; ☎ 24-6311; fax 24-6321; www.choice-hotels.jp/cfnarita/; s/d/tw ¥5800/8000/10,000; P ⊠ 💻) Right outside the east exit of Keisei Narita Station, this business hotel's rooms are small but spotless, staff have English-language maps to restaurants, there's a coin laundry, and breakfast and internet connections are free.

Kirinoya Ryokan (桐之屋旅館; ☎ 22-0724; fax 22-1245; www.naritakanko.jp/kirinoya; s/d ¥5000/9000; P 💻) Remote and underwhelming from outside, this inn is actually a museum in disguise. The owner can trace his lineage back 50 generations, and his simple ryokan is filled with samurai armour, swords and art. It's on Higashi-sando; take the first left after passing the entrance to Narita-san-kōen, follow the road for the next 400m and it's on the left. Meals are available.

Ohgiya Ryokan (扇屋旅館; ☎ 22-1161; fax 24-1663; www.naritakanko.jp/ohgiya; s/d ¥7350/13,650, without bathroom ¥6300/10,500; P 💻) This 27-room Japanese inn has comfortable rooms; some have traditional art and woodwork and open onto a lovely garden. It's a 10-minute walk from JR Narita or Keisei Narita Stations, down Omotesandō towards the temple, but forking to the left just before the Tourist Pavilion. It's 200m further on the left.

Airport hotels are typically big chains. For the following, it's best to go to the airport and then take the shuttle bus to your hotel.

Hilton Tokyo Narita Airport (ヒルトン成田; ☎ 33-1121; fax 33-0369; www.hilton.com; s/d from ¥8000/12000; P ⊠ 💻 🏊 ♿) The 548 modern, spacious guest rooms here are the best bet among the large chains, and staff here stand out for their welcome and professionalism. It's a 10-minute shuttle bus ride to the airport and train stations.

Narita Excel Hotel Tokyū (成田エクセルホテル東急; ☎ 33-0109; fax 33-0148; www.tokyuhotels.co.jp/en/TE/TE_NARIT/index.html; s/d from ¥13,860/23,100; P ⊠ 💻 🏊) Ten minutes by taxi from the airport and train stations along the Shin-Kūkō expressway, this better-quality business hotel has refurbished rooms, common baths and saunas as well as a tennis court and swimming pool (open midsummer only). Women-only rooms are available.

Eating & Drinking

Grill House Hero's (弘's; ☎ 22-9002; most dishes ¥630-890; ⏲ dinner) The English menu of this *izakaya* (pub-eatery) careens from *okonomiyaki* to sausages, in a large room with dark beams. From JR Narita Station east exit, turn where you see Mr Donut. Passing the Tsukuba Hotel, you'll see the restaurant at the bottom of a hill. There's a red *yakiniku* (grilled beef) joint outside.

Kikuya (菊屋; ☎ 22-0236; sets ¥1050-2310; ⏲ lunch & dinner) A simple place on Omotesandō across from the Tourist Pavilion. It serves a variety of lunch and dinner sets on the English menu, including sashimi, grilled eel sets (¥1500 to ¥2000) and other Japanese fare. Look for a lady in a kimono greeting customers outside.

Kawatoyo Honten (川豊本店; ☎ 22-2711; meals ¥1260-1890; ⏲ 10am-5pm Tue-Sun) This landmark eel house with a wooden signboard over the door is across from the Tourist Pavilion. The most popular preparation on the English menu is *unajū* (¥1500), grilled, sauced and served over rice in a lacquer box.

Barge Inn (バージイン; ☎ 23-2546; meals around ¥1500, drinks from ¥400; ⏲ 4pm-2am Mon-Thu, 11am-2am Fri & Sat) A popular gathering spot for expats (especially flight crews), this sprawling, nicely aged British-style pub features billiards, a live music space with dance floor, and eclectic English eats on the English menu. There's a large English sign over the door.

Getting There & Away

From Narita International Airport you can take either the private Keisei line (¥250, five minutes) or JR (¥190/230 from Terminal 2/1, five minutes). From Tokyo, the easiest way to get to Narita is via the Keisei line from Keisei Ueno Station, taking the Skyliner limited express (¥1920, 56 minutes), or the express (*kyūkō* ¥810, 65 minutes). JR trains from central Tokyo usually involve a transfer at Chiba and Sakura (¥1110, 1½ hours). Note that most JR Narita Express trains do not stop at Narita. For more information, see p193.

Getting Around

The Narita Circle Bus (adult/child ¥200/100) connects the airport hotels with the train stations and Narita-san Shinshō-ji.

IZU-SHOTŌ 伊豆諸島

Known in English as the Izu Seven Islands, Izu-shotō are refreshing, worthwhile getaways from the grind of Japan's big cities. They're peaks of a submerged volcanic chain extending 300km into the Pacific. Although easily reached by ferry from Tokyo, they feel worlds away. Five of the seven islands are suitable for tourism, and each is different – with excellent connections you could spend an enjoyable week island-hopping. No matter which oneyou visit, you're sure to find yourself thinking: 'Can I really be only a few hours from downtown Tokyo?'

Soaking in an onsen while gazing at the Pacific is the classic Izu-shotō activity. There is also excellent hiking up the *mostly* dormant volcanoes. The islands can be crowded in the summer high season – it's often better to visit just outside this season, but typhoons can wreak havoc with your plans from late summer into early fall and you'll need to plan for delays.

Getting There & Away

Tōkai Kisen Ferry Company (東海汽船; ☎ 03-5472-9999, in Japanese; www.tokaikisen.co.jp, in Japanese) operates ferries between Tokyo and the Izu-shotō.

The inner group of islands (Ō-shima, To-shima, Nii-jima, Shikine-jima and Kōzu-shima) is serviced by high-speed hydrofoils departing mornings from Tokyo (usually around 8am) and returning from the islands to Tokyo that same afternoon. Fares and travel times to/from Tokyo are as follows: Ō-shima ¥8430, two hours; Nii-jima ¥10,880, 3¼ hours; Shikine-jima ¥10,880, 3¼ hours; and Kōzu-shima ¥11,700, four hours.

The inner islands are also serviced by the large passenger ferry *Camellia-maru*, which departs around 11pm and arrives at the islands early the next morning (it stops at all of the islands from north to south). It returns to Tokyo the same evening. Fares (2nd class) and travel times are as follows: Ō-shima ¥5180, 6¼ hours; Nii-jima ¥6960, 8¾ hours; Shikine-jima ¥6960, 9¼ hours; and Kōzu-shima ¥7380, 10¼ hours. Some of these islands are also serviced by ferries from Izu-hantō.

The outer group of islands (Miyake-jima, Mikura-jima and Hachijō-jima) is serviced by the large passenger ferry *Salvia-maru*, departing daily around 10.30pm and arriving at the islands the following morning, returning to Tokyo late the same evening. The journey between Tokyo and Hachijō-jima takes 10 hours and costs ¥9760 in 2nd class.

Ferries sail to/from Tokyo's Takeshiba Pier, a 10-minute walk from the north exit of Hamamatsu-chō Station.

ANA (全日空グループ エアーニッポン; ☎ 0120-02-9222; www.air-nippon.co.jp, in Japanese) has flights between Tokyo's Haneda airport and Ō-shima (¥13,100, 35 minutes) and Hachijō-jima (¥19,800, 45 minutes). **Shinchūō Kōku** (新中央航空; ☎ 0422-31-4191; www.central-air.co.jp, in Japanese) has flights between Chōfu airport (on the Keiō line about 20 minutes from Shinjuku) and Ō-shima (¥9500, 35 minutes), Nii-jima (¥13,700, 45 minutes) and Kōzu-shima (¥14,900, 55 minutes). **Tokyo Ai Land Shuttle** (東京愛らんどシャトル; ☎ 0499-62-5222; www.tohoair.co.jp, in Japanese) flies helicopters between Miyake-jima and Ō-shima (¥11,340, 20 minutes).

Getting Around

Island hopping is easy on the daily ferries that run up and down the island chains. In addition, three ferries daily between Nii-jima and Shikine-jima (¥420, 10 minutes) make day trips possible.

Buses run on the larger islands, though they are infrequent. Hitching, while possible, is not that easy. Scooters (around ¥3000 per day) are ideal, though you'll need an international license to rent them. Bicycle rentals are widely available.

Ō-SHIMA 大島

☎ 04992

The largest of the Izu islands and closest to Tokyo, Ō-shima makes an easy overnight trip out of the city while maintaining a strong island vibe. It is dominated by 754m Mihara-san (三原山), a semidormant volcano that last erupted in 1986. The south coast has some good beaches, and you can round out your stay with a dip in one of the island's fine onsen. It's most beautiful when the camellia flowers are in bloom in late winter.

Information

The **Ō-shima Tourist Association** (大島観光協会; ☎ 2-2177; ⌚ 8.30am-5.15pm) is located near the pier in Motomachi.

Sights & Activities

If you've never peered into the maw of a recently erupted volcano, then we highly recommend a trip to the summit of **Mihara-san**. It's an awesome experience, and the concrete eruption shelters that line the path to the crater add a certain frisson to the approach. To get there, take a bus from Motomachi port to Mihara-sancho-guchi (¥860, 25 minutes, five departures daily) and walk to the Kaguchi-tenbōdai observation point (about 45 minutes).

Ō-shima's southernmost point, **Toushiki-no-hana** (トウシキの鼻) is rocky and wave-beaten, with good swimming in sheltered pools below Tōshiki Camp-jō. Don't even try to swim when the waves are high. To get there, take a Seminaa-bound bus from Motomachi port to Minami-kōkō-mae (¥620, 35 minutes). About 5km east of this point is the island's best beach, Suna-no-hama (砂の浜), a fine stretch of black volcanic sand. Take a Seminaa-bound bus from Motomachi port to Suna-no-hama-iriguchi (¥420, 20 minutes).

Onsen are Ō-shima's other main attraction. **Motomachi Hama-no-yu** (元町浜の湯; ☎ 2-2870; admission ¥400; ⌚ 1-7pm, from 11am Jul & Aug), 10 minutes' walk north of the port, is a fine outdoor onsen with great ocean views. It's mixed bathing, so swimsuits are mandatory, and it can be crowded in summer. The more institutional, glitzy place next door is **Gojinka Onsen** (御神火温泉; ☎ 2-0909; admission ¥1000; ⌚ 9am-9pm), which has baths, a swimming pool and relaxation areas.

The southeastern end of the island has the charmingly nostalgic port of **Habu** (波浮), full of old buildings like the venerable **Ryokan Minato-ya** (旧港屋旅館; admission free; ⌚ 9am-4pm), now a museum with mannequins in period attire.

Sleeping & Eating

Tōshiki Camp-jō (トウシキキャンプ場; camp sites free) Very close to the Minami-kōkō-mae stop, this camp site has a nice location right near the sea, as well as showers and a communal cooking area.

Ryokan Kifune (旅館喜船; ☎ 2-1171; fax 2-2853; r per person incl 2 meals ¥7350) They call it a ryokan, but it's actually a collection of small, retro cabins with a communal dining area. It's midway between Motomachi and Okadakō. Call in Japanese and the owners will pick you up at the pier.

Hotel Shiraiwa (ホテル白岩; ☎ 2-2571; fax 2-1864; www.h-shiraiwa.com, in Japanese; s from ¥9600; Ⓟ 💻) Retro is the watchword at this large hotel above Motomachi port. It seems stuck in the 1960s, but the Japanese- and Western-style rooms are still comfortable, some with harbour views. Large common baths are a plus.

Otomodachi (おともだち; ☎ 2-0026; mains ¥650-2000; ⌚ lunch & dinner, closed irregularly) This simple *shokudō* located 50m north of the Motomachi pier serves set meals like *jōsashimi teishoku* (special sashimi set; ¥1200). Look for the red shingles and large white signboard out front.

NII-JIMA 新島

☎ 04992

Nii-jima competes with neighbouring Shikine-jima as the most appealing island in the Izu-shotō. It's got a ripping white-sand beach, two fine onsen and an easy laid-back vibe that'll make you think they hauled a bit of Okinawa right to the doorstep of Tokyo. And there's a great camping ground within walking distance of the beach!

Information

The **Nii-jima Tourist Association** (新島観光協会; ☎ 5-0001; 8am-4pm) is about 200m south of the pier.

Sights & Activities

The best beach anywhere near Tokyo is Nii-jima's fantastic Habushi-ura, a blazing 6.5km stretch of white sand that runs over half the length of the island. Although it's really just a beach break, it attracts surfers from all over Kantō. Careful, though, because the waves and tide are very strong here. On the port side of the island, Mae-hama stretches 4km and is a good alternative.

The island's other main attraction is one of Japan's most whimsical onsen: **Yunohama Onsen** (湯の浜温泉; admission free; 24hr). This onsen consists of several outdoor tubs built into the rocks overlooking the Pacific Ocean with a few Parthenon-inspired columns. It's a lot of fun and it's only five minutes' walk south of the Tourist Association. Bathing suits are required. About five minutes' walk south, **Mamashita Onsen** (まました温泉; ☎ 5-0240; regular/sand bath ¥300/700; 10am-9.30pm Thu-Tue) has a good indoor bath and a sand bath – you're buried in hot sand and you lie there sweating and feeling like you're being crushed. Sounds awful, but we felt good when it was over!

Nii-jima's other attractions include the **Niijima Modern Glass Art Museum** (新島現代ガラスアートミュージアム; ☎ 5-1840; www.niijimaglass.com; admission ¥300; 9am-4.30pm), 1km south of the port. There's some fine work made from naturally magnetic Koga stone (which is found only on Nii-jima and in Sicily). You can often see glassblowers in action.

Sleeping & Eating

Habushi-ura Camp-jo (羽伏浦キャンプ場; camp sites free; P) With a stunning mountain backdrop and spacious grassy sites, this camp site is a winner, and it's only about 10 minutes' walk to the beach. There are showers, a cooking area and fresh water.

Nii-jima Grand Hotel (新島グランドホテル; ☎ 5-1661; fax 5-1668; www15.ocn.ne.jp/~nghotel, in Japanese; r per person incl 2 meals from ¥6800; P) The island's only proper hotel, only 15 minutes' walk from Habushi-ura, has pleasant, large, clean rooms with private bathrooms and friendly young staff. The large communal bath is also a winner.

Minshuku Hamashō (民宿浜庄; ☎ 5-0524; fax 5-1318; r per person incl 2 meals from ¥7800; P) Very close to Mae-hama beach, this rambling *minshuku* has friendly owners, good seafood and a great location. We were bitten by the pet dog here, however, so watch out!

Sakaezushi (栄寿司; ☎ 5-0134; mains ¥650-2000; dinner, closed irregularly) About five blocks from Mae-hama beach on the road to Habushi-ura, this popular fishermen's pub has sets like *shima-zushi* (island-style sushi; ¥1850). It's a white building with a renovated wing to the left; look for the blue door curtain.

SHIKINE-JIMA 式根島

☎ 04992

About 6km south of Nii-jima is tiny Shikine-jima, only 3.8 sq km. What this island lacks in size, it more than makes up for in charm. It's got a couple of great seaside onsen (all of which are free and require bathing suits) and several good little beaches. You can easily make your way around the island on foot, or on *mama-charis* (granny bikes) that can be rented on the island.

Information

The **Shikine-jima Tourist Association** (式根島観光協会; ☎ 7-0170; 8am-5pm) is at the pier.

Sights & Activities

Jinata Onsen (地鉈温泉; admission free; 24hr) is one of the most dramatically located onsen we've seen in Japan: at the end of a narrow cleft in the rocky coastline, it looks like the work of an angry axe-wielding giant. Try to go midway between high tide and low tide, when the temperature is ideal. Pick up a map at the Tourist Association and look for the stone sign with red arrows at the access road.

Near Ashitsuki Port, you'll find another onsen: picturesque **Matsugashita Miyabi-yu** (松が下雅湯; admission free; 24hr). It's not affected by the tide and the view of the harbour is great; look for the entrance near the boat ramp. A minute or so further down the coast is **Ashizuki Onsen** (足付温泉; admission free; 24hr), another fine onsen built into the rocks right at the water's edge. Like Jinata Onsen, the water temperature depends on the tide.

Tomarikō-kaigan (泊港海岸) is a picturesque little beach in a sheltered cove with calm waters perfect for children. It's about 500m northwest of the ferry port, up and over the hill. **Naka-no-ura** (中の浦海岸) and **Ō-ura** (大浦海岸) beaches are an easy walk along the same coast.

Sleeping

Kamanoshita Camp-jo (釜の下キャンプ場; camp sites free; Jun-Sep; P) Right near a fine little beach and two free onsen, this little camping ground is great, especially in the quieter times of year, when you might have it to yourself. No showers here.

Ō-ura Camp-jo (大浦キャンプ場; camp sites free; Jul & Aug; P) Right on a good beach, this camping ground is rather cramped and not well maintained, but the location is hard to beat. There are showers.

La Mer (ラ・メール; ☎ 7-0240; fax 7-0036; www.shikine.com, in Japanese; r from ¥11,550; P) Right uphill from the ferry port, this small pension and separate Early Bird group of bungalows are great for small groups of travellers, though the decor is basically nonexistent. Rental bicycles are available.

KŌZU-SHIMA 神津島

☎ 04992

Dominated by 572m **Tenjō-san** (天上山), a table-topped mountain that takes up the entire northern end of the island, Kōzu-shima has a couple of decent beaches, one good onsen and some of the best hiking in the Izu-shotō. For thrill seekers, the island's airport, on a plateau on the southern end of the island, is the closest most of us will ever get to flying off an aircraft carrier.

Information

Located near the pier is the **Kōzu-shima Tourist Association** (神津島観光協会; ☎ 8-0321; 8.30am-5.30pm).

Sights & Activities

Hiking around the summit area of Tenjō-san is Kōzu-shima's main draw. The Tourist Association has excellent Japanese-language hiking maps. The hike up to the 524m **Kuroshima-Tenbō-Dai** (黒島展望台) point is a three-hour roundtrip; on clear days you'll be rewarded with a fine view of Mt Fuji. From the point, you can continue along the summit plateau to **Ura-Sabaku** (裏砂漠), a sandy 'desert', and **Babaa-Ike** (ババア池), a small pond.

Back at sea level, about 1km north of the pier, the fine **Kōzu-shima Onsen** (神津島温泉; admission ¥800; 10am-9pm Thu-Tue) has three excellent outdoor baths built into the wild rocks of the coast, plus some indoor baths. You'll need a swimsuit to enter the outdoor baths.

About 2km north of the onsen, along the coastal road, you'll find **Akazaki-no Yūhodō** (赤崎の遊歩道; admission free; 24hr), a fantasy land of wooden walkways, bridges, diving platforms and observation towers built around a great natural swimming inlet in the craggy coast. It's the sort of place you'd see more of if the world was ruled by children.

Sleeping & Eating

Nagahama Camp-jo (長浜キャンプ場; camp sites free; P) Right on the beach, with showers and barbecue grills, this camping ground is fairly close to the onsen, about 2km north of the pier.

Hotel Kōzukan (ホテル神津館; ☎ 8-1321; fax 8-1323; www.kozukan.yad.jp, in Japanese; r per person from ¥6300; P) The island's only hotel has both Japanese- and Western-style rooms, with private toilets but shared bathrooms. A friendly family runs the place. Rooms are fairly spacious and there are sunset views.

Ryokan Shūsō (旅館秀蒼; ☎ 8-0883; fax 8-0884; www.syuso.jp, in Japanese; r per person incl 2 meals from ¥7500; P) At the top of the village, near the trailhead for Tenjō-san, this very modern home run by an English-speaking lady has baths with views of the valley, and excellent food. Call for a pick-up.

Daijinko (だいじんこ; ☎ 8-1763; snacks ¥300-900; 10am-4pm Fri & Mon-Wed, to 5pm Sat & Sun) Perched on a cliff overlooking the harbour, this cafe is a trek up from town (unless you're scootering), but boasts unbeatable views. It has light snacks like *chīzu tōsuto kōhī setto* (cheese on toast with coffee; ¥700). Ask for a map and directions at the Tourist Association.

MIYAKE-JIMA 三宅島

☎ 04994

Miyake-jima, 180km south of Tokyo, is one of the spookiest places in all of Japan. In 2000 its volcano O-yama (雄山) erupted again, forcing a temporary evacuation of the island's residents and destroying many trees. Despite its desolate appearance, Miyake has a good onsen, as well as snorkelling and diving. Tourist facilities remain limited, however.

Information

Miyake-jima Tourism Association (三宅島観光協会; ☎ 5-1144; ⏲ 8am-5pm) is just up from the ferry pier at Sabi-ga-Hama and on the right. Check here for maps and volcanic gas warnings affecting parts of the island.

Sights & Activities

Since O-yama still emits gas, most of it is off-limits. Entire villages in gas zones, such as **Miike** (三池) on the east coast near the airport, have been abandoned but they make for fine apocalyptic scenery if you're scootering through; it's unsafe to linger. You can contemplate the devastation of lava flows from 1983, preserved at the **Ako Junior and Middle School Ruins** (旧阿古小中学校跡), a 15-minute walk north of the ferry pier. Nearby is the onsen **Furusato-no-Yu** (ふるさとの湯; ☎ 5-0630; adult/child ¥500/250; ⏲ 11am-9pm Thu-Tue Apr-Sep, to 8pm Thu-Tue Oct-Mar), which has an excellent outdoor bath overlooking the sea and a restaurant. There's a decent black-sand beach, a picturesque fishing village and diving points at Ōkubo (大久保) on the north shore. On the south side of Miyake, naturalists and twitchers may enjoy the bird sanctuary **Tairo-ike** (大路池) and nature centre **Akakokko-kan** (アカコッコ館; ☎ 6-0410; adult/child ¥200/free; ⏲ 9am-4.30pm), named for the rare Izu-shotō thrush *(Turdus celaenops)*.

Sleeping

Camping is not permitted on the island. **Santomo** (サントモ; ☎ 5-0532; fax 5-0527; www.asahi-net.or.jp/~di5a-okym/top.html, in Japanese; r from ¥8000; Ⓟ 📶) is a cheery pension and dive shop, a 10-minute walk north of the ferry pier along the main road. It has nine well-kept Japanese and Western-style rooms, and Japanese breakfasts for ¥800. Dive tours start at ¥6000.

HACHIJŌ-JIMA 八丈島

☎ 04996

About 290km south of Tokyo, Hachijō-jima is the second-largest and next-to-last island in the Izu-shotō chain. Basically two dormant volcanoes connected by a flat strip of land, it's a relaxing place to spend a few days away from the Tokyo rat race. The highlight here is climbing Mt Hachijō-Fuji, an easy hike that offers stunning views.

Information

In the centre of the island, **Hachijōjima Tourism Association** (八丈島観光協会; ☎ 2-1377; ⏲ 8.15am-5.15pm) is next to the town hall on the main road. Maps (in Japanese) are available.

Sights & Activities

The island is dominated by two dormant volcanoes, 854m **Hachijō-Fuji** (八丈富士) and 701m **Mihara-yama** (三原山), covered with lush semitropical vegetation. The best hike is the three-hour trip up Hachijō-Fuji. The one-hour walk around the crater rim is awesome, but watch for the large holes along the trail. On the Mihara-yama end of the island, try the hike to **Kara-taki** (唐滝), a lovely waterfall about an hour's hike inland and uphill from the settlement of Kashidate. The best snorkelling is by the rocks at **Nambara** (南原), on the west coast.

Urami-ga-taki Onsen (裏見ケ滝温泉; admission free; ⏲ 10am-9pm) is not to be missed. Just below the road, it overlooks a waterfall – pure magic in the early evening. You'll need a swimsuit since it's mixed bathing. Take a Sueyoshi-bound bus from the port (you may have to change at Kashitate Onsen Mae) to Nakata-Shōten-mae and walk 20 minutes towards the ocean. Before you enter the onsen, take the trail from the road above and follow it upstream for a few minutes to the lovely waterfall of **Urami-ga-taki** (裏見ケ滝).

A 15-minute walk below Urami-ga-taki Onsen, towards the sea, is **Nakanogō-Onsen Yasuragi-no-yu** (中之郷温泉 やすらぎの湯; ☎ 7-0779; admission ¥300; ⏲ 10am-9pm Fri-Wed), a quaint local onsen with a fine view over the Pacific from its inside baths.

Project WAVE (☎ 2-5407; www3.ocn.ne.jp/~p-wave, in Japanese) offers a variety of ecotourism options, including hiking, birdwatching, sea kayaking and scuba diving. Its owner, Iwasaki-san, speaks English.

Sleeping & Eating

Sokodo Camp-jō (底土キャンプ場; ☎ 2-1121; camp sites free; Ⓟ) This excellent camping ground is 500m north of Sokodo pier. Toilets, cold showers and cooking facilities are available and there are two beaches nearby. You must reserve by telephone (in Japanese only) a spot at the ward office.

Kokuminshukusha San Marina (国民宿舎サンマリーナ; ☎ 2-3010; fax 2-0952; www6.ocn.ne.jp/~marina-6, in Japanese; r per person incl 2 meals from ¥7875; Ⓟ 💻) This is a very tidy, breezy guest house with good food and a convenient location, about 500m north of Sokodo pier. Turn left off the coastal road at a sign that reads 'Ocean Boulevard' and look for a big whitish building.

Hachijō View Hotel (八丈ビューホテル; ☎ 2-3221; fax 2-3225; www.hachijo-v.co.jp, in Japanese; s/d from ¥17,850/12,600; Ⓟ) This contemporary hotel just west of the airport on the slopes of Mt Hachijō-Fuji has terrace dining, common baths looking out over the sea, and an outdoor whirlpool.

Ryōzanpaku (梁山泊; ☎ 2-0631; mains from ¥1500; 🕒 dinner Mon-Sat) This *izakaya* on the main road between the airport and the ferry port serves up delicious appetisers on the English menu, such as taro croquettes (¥800), as well as sashimi sets (¥1500). Look for the white vertical sign and sliding wooden doors.

OGASAWARA-SHOTŌ 小笠原諸島

You won't believe you're still in Japan, much less Tokyo! About 1000km south of downtown in the middle of the Pacific Ocean, this far-flung outpost of Tokyo Prefecture has pristine beaches and star-studded night skies. Ogasawara is a nature-lover's paradise surrounded by tropical waters and coral reefs. Snorkelling, whale-watching, swimming with dolphins, and hiking are all on the bill.

The only way to get here is by a 25-hour ferry ride from Tokyo. The ferry docks at Chichi-jima (父島; Father Island), the main island of the group. A smaller ferry connects this island to Haha-jima (母島), the other inhabited island.

The islands see few Western visitors, despite the fact that the earliest inhabitants were Westerners who set up provisioning stations for whaling ships working the Japan whaling grounds. You still see the occasional Western family name and face. You'll also see disused gun emplacements at the ends of most of the islands' beaches, built by the Japanese in hopes of repelling an anticipated Allied invasion in WWII (the big battles were fought further south on Iwo-jima).

Given the islands' nature, history and location, a trip here is one of Japan's great little adventures. When your boat sails from Chichi-jima and the entire island turns out to wave you off, you'll know you've done something special.

CHICHI-JIMA 父島

☎ 04998

Beautifully preserved, gorgeous Chichi-jima has plenty of accommodation, restaurants, even a bit of tame nightlife. But the real attractions are the excellent beaches and outdoor activities.

Information

Chichi-jima Tourism Association (父島観光協会; ☎ 2-2587; 🕒 9am-5pm) In the B-Ship building, about 250m west of the pier, near the post office. Ask for the helpful *Guide Map of Chichi-jima*.

Ogasawara Visitor Center (小笠原ビジターセンター; ☎ 2-3001; 🕒 8am-5pm) Right on the beach past the village office, it has displays about the local ecosystem and history (there's an English guidebook).

Sights & Activities

The two best beaches for snorkelling are on the north side of the island, a short walk over the hill from the village. **Miya-no-ura** (宮之浦) has decent coral and is sheltered, making it suitable for beginners. About 500m along the coast (more easily accessed from town) is **Tsuri-hama** (釣浜), a rocky beach that has better coral but is more exposed.

Good swimming beaches line the west side of the island, getting better the further south you go. **Kominato-kaigan** (小港海岸) is the best, easily accessible on this side by bus from town, or some try hitching. From here, you can walk over the hill and along the coast to the excellent Jinny and John beaches, but note that it's a two-hour walk in each direction and there is no drinking water – bring at least 3L per person. Another fine beach, Copepe, is a short hike north of Kominato.

On Chichi-jima's east side is the uncrowded **Hatsune-ura** (初寝浦), a beach at the bottom of a 1.2km trail with a 200m vertical drop.

ONLY IN OGASAWARA

When scientists photographed the fabled giant squid *Architeuthis* for the first time ever in 2004, no wonder it was just off the Ogasawaras. The chain is home to some 60 endangered species, such as the Bonin flying fox. While you're most likely to run into feral goats and hermit crabs, going jungle-trekking, snorkelling, diving, sea kayaking or on a dolphin cruise virtually guarantees an exciting wildlife experience. Timing is the key: from January to April, humpback whales can come within 500m of shore. And keep looking up! On a clear night, from the top deck of the *Ogasawara-maru* ferry, you'll see the Milky Way stretching from horizon to horizon through a breathtaking field of stars. The spectacle makes the Ogasawara islands all the more special.

Going by scooter to the trailhead is the best bet (some also try hitching).

Many operators, including **Chichijima Taxi** (父島タクシー; ☎ 2-3311, in Japanese) offer dolphin swimming and whale-watching, as well as trips to Minami-jima, an uninhabited island with a magical secret beach called **Ōgi-ike** (扇池). Stanley Minami, skipper of the **Pink Dolphin** (☎ 2-2096; www15.ocn.ne.jp/~pdolphin, in Japanese) runs full-day tours to Minami-jima and Haha-jima for ¥13,500, including snorkelling and dolphin-watching.

Rental scooter is the best way to get around the island (from ¥3000 per day).

Sleeping & Eating

Camping is not permitted on the island.

Banana Inn (バナナ荘; ☎ 2-2051; r from ¥4200) Steps from the ferry pier, this humble inn has very basic Japanese- and Western-style rooms but lots of hospitality from owner John Washington, an Ernest Hemingway type who enjoys discussing local history.

Ogasawara Youth Hostel (小笠原ユースホステル; ☎ 2-2692; fax 2-2692; www.oyh.jp, in Japanese; dm members/nonmembers incl 2 meals ¥5150/5750; Ⓟ 💻) This is a clean, well-run, regimented hostel about 400m southwest of the pier, near the post office. Be sure to book early as it fills up quickly.

Chichi-jima View Hotel (父島ビューホテル; ☎ 2-7845; fax 2-7846; www16.ocn.ne.jp/~view1; r per person from ¥10,000; Ⓟ) Just a minute's walk west of the pier, this hotel has large, airy rooms with private bathroom and kitchen. It's one of the more upscale places on the island, with super views of the bay from guestroom balconies.

Marujō-shokudō (丸丈食堂; ☎ 2-3030; set meals from ¥800) This simple *shokudō* is where the locals come for simple but tasty set meals, such as the sashimi set (¥840, ask for *kyō no sashimi teishoku*). It's in a blue-and-white building next to a gift shop.

Yankee Town (ヤンキータウン; ☎ 2-3042; drinks ¥700-1200; 🕑 8pm-2am Thu-Tue) A 15-minute walk east of the main pier, by the Okumua Sports Ground, this driftwood bar is the perfect spot to chill with a pina colada. Go through the tunnel facing the pier, continue straight until the road bends to the right and you'll see it on the left with a barbecue pit out front.

Getting There & Away

The *Ogasawara-maru* sails about once a week between Tokyo's Takeshiba Pier (10 minutes from Hamamatsu-chō Station) and Chichi-jima (2nd class from ¥28,000 in July and August, from ¥22,000 September to June, 25 hours). Contact **Ogasawara Kaiun** (小笠原海運; ☎ 03-3451-5171; www.ogasawarakaiun.co.jp, in Japanese).

HAHA-JIMA 母島

☎ 04998

Haha-jima is a quieter, less developed version of Chichi-jima, with some fine beaches on its west side and good hiking along its spine. Certain bays along the east coast are particularly good for dolphin-watching. If you really want to get away from it all, this is the place.

Information

Haha-jima Tourist Association (母島観光協会; ☎ 3-2300; 🕑 8am-5pm) is in the passenger waiting room at the pier.

Sights & Activities

A road runs south from the village to the start of the **Minami-zaki Yūhodō** (南崎遊歩道), a hiking course that continues all the way to the **Minami-zaki** (南崎; literally, 'southern point'). Along the way you'll find **Hōraine-kaigan** (蓬莢根海岸), a narrow beach with a decent offshore coral garden, Wai Beach, the best beach on the island, with a drop-off that sometimes attracts eagle rays, and finally, Minami-zaki itself, which has a rocky, coral-strewn beach with ripping views of smaller islands to the south. Above Minami-zaki you'll find **Kofuji** (小富士), an 86m-high mini Mt Fuji with fantastic views in all directions. Scooter is the best way to get around the island (from ¥3000 per day).

Sleeping & Eating

Camping is not permitted on the island.

Anna Beach Haha-jima Youth Hostel (アンナビーチ母島ユースホステル; ☎ 3-2468; fax 3-2371; www.k4.dion.ne.jp/~annayh, in Japanese; dm members/nonmembers incl 2 meals ¥5320/5920) A young family runs this tidy, cheery youth hostel in a cosy Canadian-style house overlooking the fishing port.

Minshuku Nanpū (民宿ナンプー; ☎ 3-2462; fax 3-2458; r per person incl 2 meals ¥8400) This clean, new *minshuku* is about 500m northeast of the pier, with friendly owners, good food, five rooms with large beds, and a nice jet bath.

Club Noah Haha-jima (クラブノア母島; ☎ 3-2442; http://noah88.web.fc2.com, in Japanese; snacks from ¥500; lunch) Dive shop Club Noah runs jungle-trekking and marine-life ecotours. The menu includes light meals like *shima-zakana no soboro-don* (grated fish on rice set; ¥900). It's in a white building on the far side of the fishing port.

Getting There & Away

The *Hahajima-maru* sails about five times a week between Chichi-jima and Haha-jima (¥3780, two hours). Contact **Ogasawara Kaiun** (小笠原海運; ☎ 03-3451-5171; www.ogasawarakaiun.co.jp, in Japanese). Other operators run day cruises from Chichi-jima.

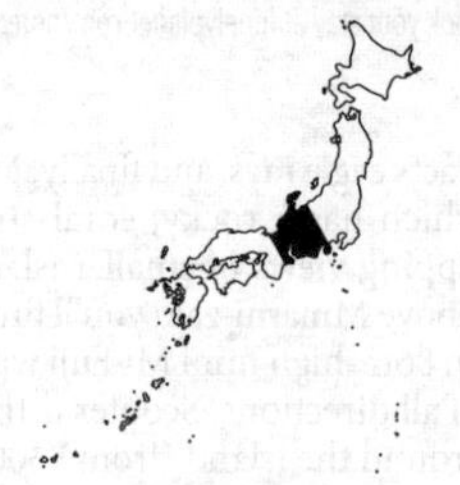

Central Honshū

本州中部

Japan's heartland in both geography and attitude, Central Honshū stretches between the two great megalopolises of Kantō (Greater Tokyo) and Kansai (Osaka, Kyoto and Kōbe), between the Pacific Ocean and the Sea of Japan. This region is filled with modern commercial centres and traditional towns, the majestic Japan Alps and the rugged northern coastline.

In Central Honshū's southern prefectures, called 'Chūbu' in Japanese, hiking takes you through the Japan Alps National Park, and onsen (hot-spring) villages offer welcome recovery for skiers drawn to the Olympic slopes of Nagano-ken. The Sea of Japan side of this region ('Hokuriku' in Japanese) boasts clifftop vistas, remarkable temples and incredibly fresh seafood.

Busy Nagoya, Japan's fourth-largest city, is the nation's industrial heart, with a can-do spirit and unique foods. Hokuriku's hub is Kanazawa, a historic yet thriving city where handsomely preserved streets once housed samurai and geisha. Lovely Takayama is admired for its traditional riverside houses, wood crafts, delicious cuisine and verdant countryside. Matsumoto is another favourite with visitors for its striking 16th-century black-and-white castle and many galleries.

The mountainous Unesco World Heritage Sites of Shirakawa-gō and Gokayama showcase Japan's rich architectural tradition, and Central Honshū is traversed by the Nakasendō, the Edo-period trunk road through the mountains.

HIGHLIGHTS

- Stroll the streets of **Takayama** (p267), with its traditional architecture and skilled woodworkers
- Hike amid the stunning mountain scenery of **Kamikōchi** (p280)
- Step back in time at the National Treasure castles **Inuyama-jō** (p263) and **Matsumoto-jō** (p297)
- Discover the rugged beauty of **Noto-hantō** (p314), a windswept peninsula of fishing hamlets and seafood feasts
- Ski, ski, ski at the Olympic resorts of **Shiga Kōgen** (p291), **Nozawa Onsen** (p293) and **Hakuba** (p294)
- Take in arts in Kanazawa, from the ancient garden **Kenroku-en** (p307) to the daring **21st Century Museum of Contemporary Art** (p307)
- Train with Zen Buddhist monks in the 13th-century **Eihei-ji** (p320) or be awed by Nagano's **Zenkō-ji** (p286)
- Sleep in a thatch-roofed house in **Shirakawa-gō** (p278)

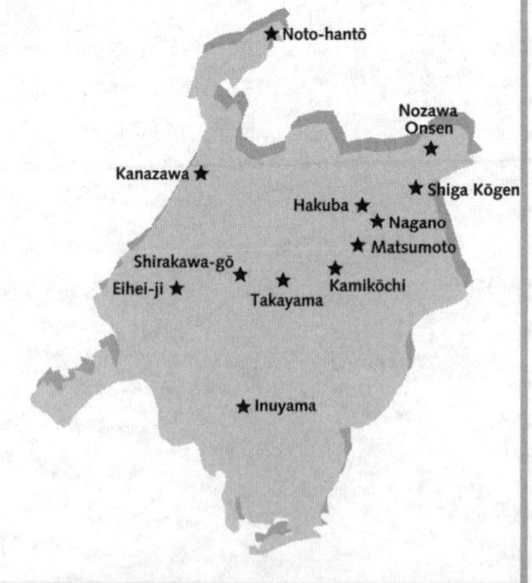

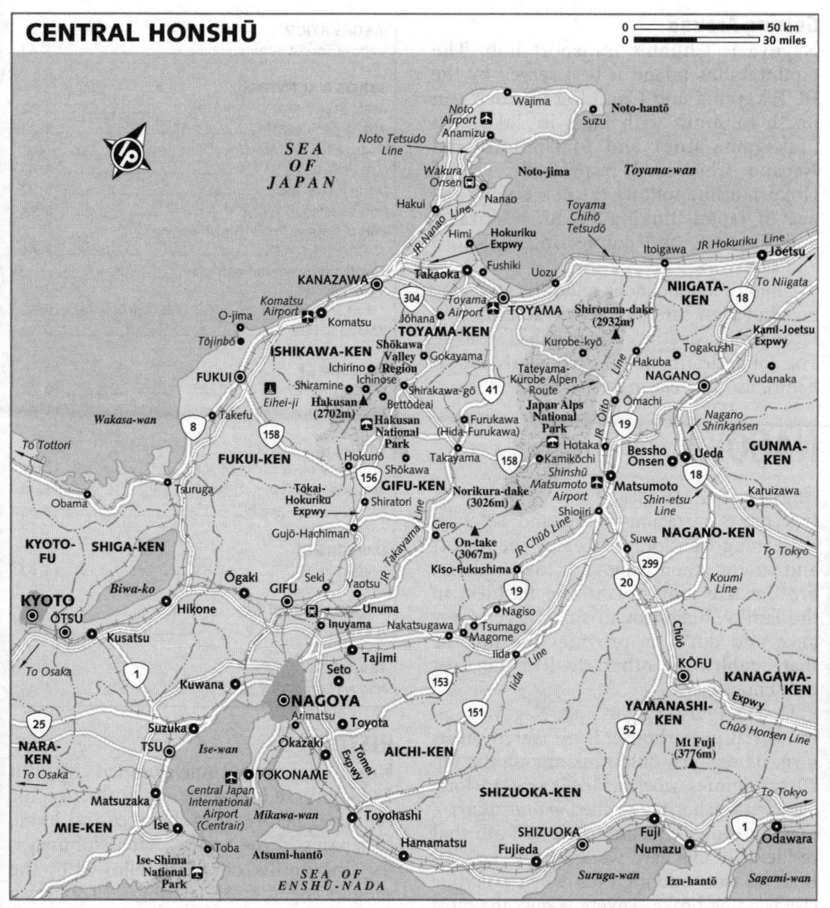

Climate

Central Honshū's climate varies with its landscape. In the lowlands the best times to visit are April and May or late September to early November; temperatures are mild and clear sunny skies are the norm. Expect heavy rains in the *tsuyu* (monsoon) season (typically a few weeks beginning in mid-June), followed by sticky summers (through mid-September) capped with a typhoon season. In the Japan Alps, November to March are cold and snowy. Many roads are impassable then, and the highest peaks might remain snow-covered until June. July and August tend to be most agreeable for mountain hikers; snows are generally melted and temperatures warmest.

Getting There & Away

Central Japan International Airport (NGO), near Nagoya, provides easy access from abroad, and there are limited international flights into Komatsu (near Kanazawa; see p313) and Toyama (p304). Nagoya is a hub for rail travel nationwide, and a *shinkansen* (bullet train) line links Tokyo with Nagano.

For travellers coming from Russia by sea, **FKK Air Service** (☎ 0766-22-2212; http://fkk-air.toyama-net.com, in Japanese) operates ferries between Fushiki in Toyama-ken and Vladivostok (one way adult/child from ¥44,000/33,000). Ferries depart Vladivostok on Monday at 9pm and arrive at 9am on Wednesday in Fushiki. Ferries depart Japan on Friday at 6pm, arriving in Russia at 9.30am on Sunday.

Getting Around

Nagoya is Chūbu's transport hub. The mountainous inland is best served by the JR Takayama and Chūō lines, which run north to south with hubs in Takayama (Takayama line) and Matsumoto and Nagano (Chūō line), respectively. The JR Hokuriku line follows the coast along the Sea of Japan, linking Fukui, Kanazawa and Toyama, and connecting to Kyoto and Osaka.

Chūbu's mountainous middle is served by bus, but plan carefully as schedules can be inconvenient or stop entirely in bad weather. For some destinations, particularly Noto-hantō, hiring a car makes sense.

NAGOYA 名古屋

☎ 052 / pop 2.24 million

If Kyoto is a gracious geisha and Tokyo is a preening teen forever seeking the newest and coolest, then Nagoya is their stalwart brother. He may not be the flashiest in the family, but through smarts, perseverance and duty, he provides the fortune that enables the others to live the lives they choose.

Japan's fourth-largest city, Nagoya is an industrial powerhouse; if measured on its own, its region would rank among the top 20 economies worldwide. It started long ago, with a heritage called *monozukuri* – making things. It's an article of faith that residents of this hard-working city can continue to earn a living even when everyone else is going broke. Toyota is only the most famous of the many manufacturers based here. It's even the birthplace of pachinko (Japanese pinball).

None of this marks Nagoya as a top-rank tourist destination, but since you're likely to pass through (Nagoya's a major transit hub), it's worth a detour for its impressive castle, important shrine and temples, unique and accessible cuisine, attractive port, and urban amusement on a far more relaxed scale than Tokyo or Osaka. Locals and expats alike take pride in the hometown character of this friendly city.

Nagoya also makes a useful base for day trips. From factory visits to ceramic villages to cormorant fishing, there's plenty in the region to keep you – need we say it? – busy.

INFORMATION

Nagoya Tourist Information	1	A3

SIGHTS & ACTIVITIES

Asahi Beer アサヒビール工場	2	B2
Atsuta-jingū 熱田神宮	3	A3
Nagoya/Boston Museum of Fine Arts 名古屋ボストン美術館	4	A3
Nittai-ji 日泰寺	5	B2
Port Building 名古屋ポートビル	6	A4
Port of Nagoya Public Aquarium 名古屋港水族館	7	A4
Toyota Commemorative Museum of Industry & Technology トヨタテクノミュージアム産業技術記念館	8	A2
Yōki-sō 揚揮荘	9	B3

SLEEPING

Petit Ryokan Ichifuji プチ旅館いちふじ	10	A2
Tsuchiya Hotel つちやホテル	11	A2

EATING

Atsuta Hōraiken あつた蓬莱軒	12	A3
Atsuta Hōraiken あつた蓬莱軒	(see 3)	
Eikoku-ya えいこく屋	13	B3

DRINKING

Ichirin いち倫	14	B2

ENTERTAINMENT

Nagoya Dome ナゴヤドーム	15	B2

TRANSPORT

Nagoya Port 名古屋港	16	A4

HISTORY

Nagoya did not become a unified city until 1889, but it had a strong influence for centuries before. It is the ancestral home of Japan's 'three heroes': Oda Nobunaga, the first unifier of Japan, followed by the shōgun Toyotomi Hideyoshi and Tokugawa Ieyasu, whose dictatorial reign from Edo also ushered in an era of peace, prosperity and the arts. Ieyasu ordered the construction of Nagoya-jō, which became an important outpost for 16 generations of the Tokugawa family in this region, known as the Owari clan.

Nagoya grew into a centre of commerce, finance, industry, transport and shipping; during WWII some 10,000 Zero fighter planes were produced here. Manufacturing prominence led to massive Allied bombing – citizens were evacuated and roughly one quarter of the city was obliterated. The resulting blank slate allowed officials to plan the city you see today: wide avenues, subways, gleaming skyscrapers and green space.

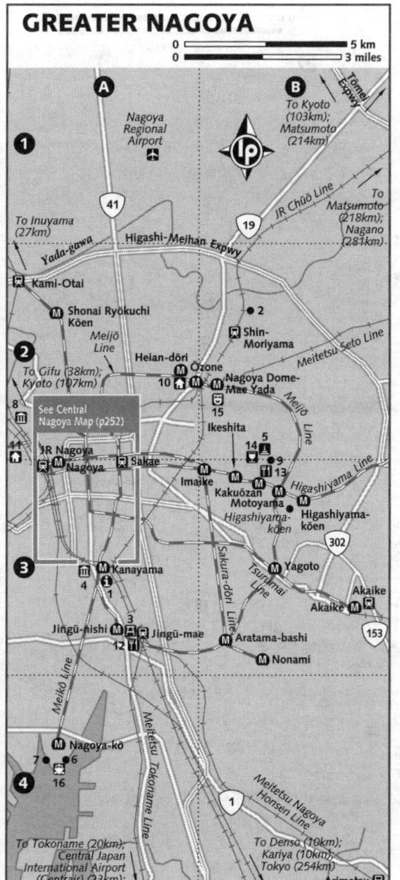

Today, Nagoya continues as a worldwide leader in automobiles, machinery, electronics and ceramics. One look at Nagoya's many department stores shows the city's thriving commercial sector, though it's a mark of the severity of the current global economic downturn that even Nagoyans are tightening their belts.

ORIENTATION

On the western edge of the city centre, JR Nagoya Station (known locally as Meieki) is a city in itself, with department stores, boutiques, restaurants, hotels and observation decks on skyscrapers. Several train lines converge here, including *shinkansen* and the private regional lines Meitetsu and Kintetsu, and there are also subway and bus stations. Nagoya Station is quite large and confusing, so don't plan on a quick transfer.

From the east exit, Sakura-dōri runs towards the massive Eiffel Towerish TV tower, in the centre of the narrow Hisaya-ōdōri-kōen (Central Park). South and west of the TV tower are the Sakae and Nishiki districts, more atmospheric than Meieki and booming with shopping, dining and nightlife; the atmospheric Kakuōzan district is a few subway stops east of Sakae. The castle, Nagoya-jō, is just north of the city centre, while the Ōsu Kannon and, much further, Nagoya Port areas are to the south.

English-language signage and a convenient subway system make navigating Nagoya relatively easy.

INFORMATION

Bookshops

The following shops carry English-language titles.

Kinokuniya Books (Map p252; ☎ 585-7526; 5th fl, 1-2-1 Meieki; 🕑 10am-8pm; Ⓡ Nagoya) In the Meitetsu Men's-kan building, south of Nagoya Station.

Maruzen (Map p252; ☎ 261-2251; 3-2-7 Sakae; Ⓡ Sakae) On busy Hirokoji-dōri.

Emergency

Ambulance & fire (☎ 119)

Nagoya International Centre (Map p252; ☎ 581-0100; 1-47-1 Nagono; 🕑 9am-7pm Tue-Sun; Ⓡ Kokusai Centre) Provides information in English, including referrals.

Police (☎ 110)

Internet Access

Chikōraku (Map p252; ☎ 587-2528; 1-25-2 Meieki; 1st hr ¥490; 🕑 24hr; Ⓡ Nagoya) In the basement of the Meitetsu Lejac building.

FedEx Kinko's (Map p252; ☎ 231-9211; 2-3-31 Sakae; 1st 10min ¥250, 1st hr ¥1250; 🕑 24hr; Ⓡ Fushimi)

Nagoya International Centre (Map p252; ☎ 581-0100; 1-47-1 Nagono; per 15min ¥100; 🕑 9am-7pm Tue-Sun; Ⓡ Kokusai Centre)

Internet Resources

Nagoya Convention and Visitors Bureau (www.ncvb.or.jp) Good general website for visitors.

Nagoya International Centre (www.nic-nagoya.or.jp) Up-to-date event listings, plus practical info for residents.

Medical Services

Nagoya's prefecture, **Aichi-ken** (☎ 249-9799; www.qq.pref.aichi.jp), has a list of medical institutions with English-speaking staff, including specialities and hours of operation.

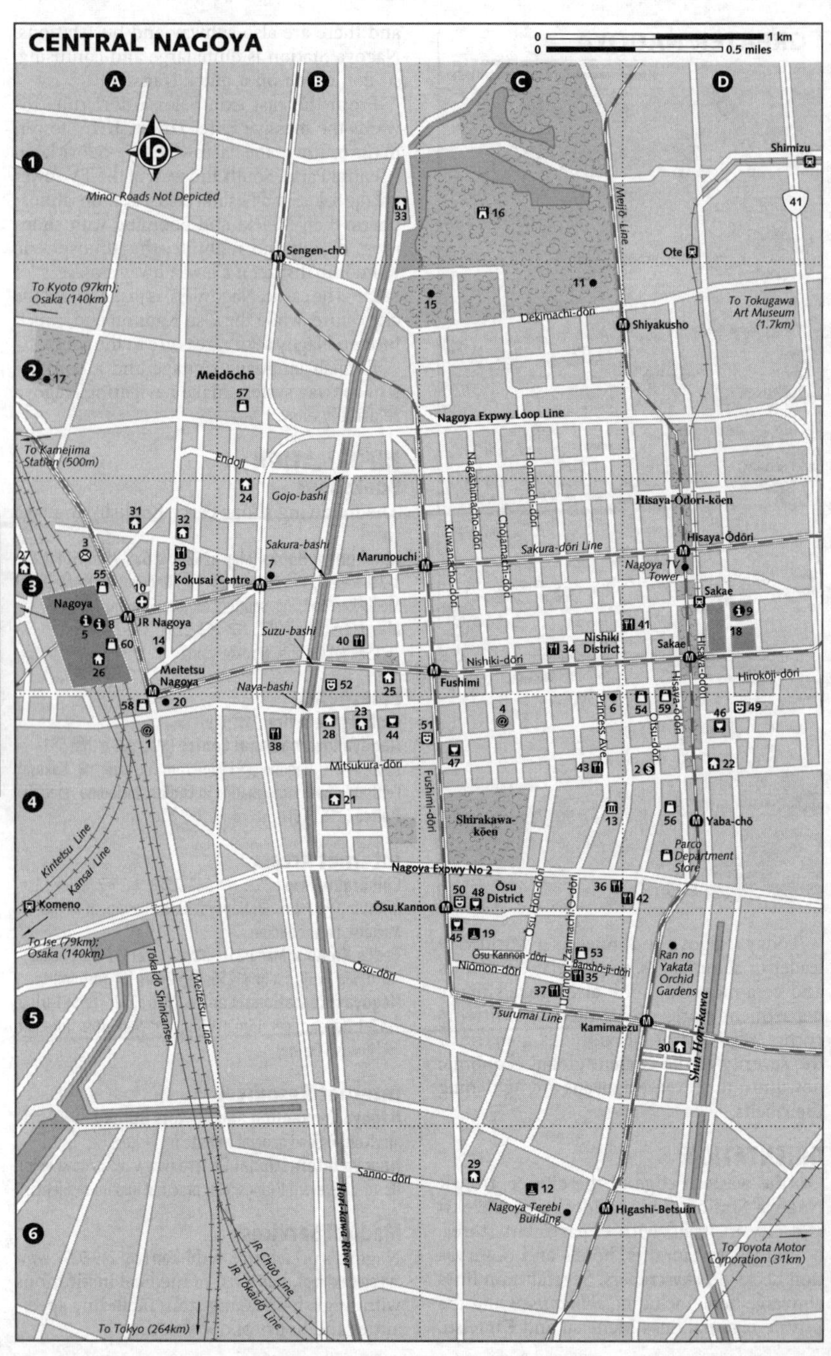
CENTRAL NAGOYA
0 1 km
0 0.5 miles
Minor Roads Not Depicted
Sengen-chō
To Kyoto (97km); Osaka (140km)
Dekimachi-dōri
Shiyakusho
Shimizu
Ote
Meijō Line
To Tokugawa Art Museum (1.7km)
Meidōchō
Nagoya Expwy Loop Line
To Kamejima Station (500m)
Endoji
Gojo-bashi
Nagashimacho-dōri
Honmachi-dōri
Chōjamachi-dōri
Kuwanacho-dōri
Hisaya-Ōdori-kōen
Hisaya-Ōdori
Sakura-bashi
Sakura-dōri Line
Marunouchi
Nagoya TV Tower
Kokusai Centre
Sakae
Nagoya
JR Nagoya
Suzu-bashi
Nishiki District
Nishiki-dōri
Fushimi
Meitetsu Nagoya
Naya-bashi
Hirokōji-dōri
Princess Ave
Hisaya-dōri
Ōtsu-dōri
Mitsukura-dōri
Fushimi-dōri
Shirakawa-kōen
Yaba-chō
Parco Department Store
Kintetsu Line
Kansai Line
Nagoya Expwy No 2
Ōsu District
Ōsu Kannon
Komeno
Ōsu Hon-dōri
Uramon-Zenmachi-Ō-dōri
To Ise (79km); Osaka (140km)
Ōsu Kannon-dōri
Banshō-ji-dōri
Niōmon-dōri
Ōsu-dōri
Ran no Yakata Orchid Gardens
Tōkaidō Shinkansen
Meitetsu Line
Tsurumai Line
Kamimaezu
Shin Hori-kawa
Sanno-dōri
Nagoya Terebi Building
Higashi-Betsuin
To Toyota Motor Corporation (31km)
Hori-kawa River
JR Chūō Line
JR Tōkaidō Line
To Tokyo (264km)

INFORMATION
- Chikōraku 知好楽 1 A4
- Citibank ATM シティバンク 2 D4
- Eki-mae Post Office 駅前郵便局 3 A3
- FedEx Kinko's フェデックスキンコーズ 4 C4
- Kinokuniya Books 紀伊国屋 (see 58)
- KNT Tourist KNTツーリスト 5 A3
- Maruzen 丸善 6 C4
- Nagoya International Centre 国際センター 7 B3
- Nagoya Station Post Office 郵便局名古屋駅支店 (see 60)
- Nagoya Tourist Information 名古屋市観光案内所 8 A3
- Nagoya Tourist Information 名古屋市観光案内所 9 D3
- Tachino Clinic たちのクリニック 10 A3

SIGHTS & ACTIVITIES
- Aichi Prefectural Gymnasium 愛知県立体育館 11 C2
- Higashi Betsuin 12 C6
- International Design Centre Nagoya (Nadya Park Building) 国際デザインセンター 13 C4
- Midland Square ミッドランドスクエアー 14 A3
- Nagoya Noh Theatre 名古屋能楽堂 15 C2
- Nagoya-jō 名古屋城 16 C1
- Noritake Garden ノリタケの森 17 A2
- OASIS 21 オアシス２１ 18 D3
- Ōsu Kannon Temple 大須観音 19 C5
- Sky Promenade (see 14)
- Spiral Towers 20 A4

SLEEPING
- Aichi-ken Seinen-kaikan Youth Hostel 愛知県青年会館ユースホステル 21 B4
- B Nagoya ザB名古屋 22 D4
- Hilton Nagoya ヒルトン名古屋 23 B4
- Kimiya Ryokan きみや旅館 24 B3
- Nagoya Kankō Hotel 名古屋観光ホテル 25 B3
- Nagoya Marriott Associa Hotel 名古屋マリオットアソシアホテル 26 A3
- Natural Hotel Elséreine ナチュラルホテルエルセラーン 27 A3
- Richmond Hotel Nagoya Nayabashi リチモンドホテル名古屋納屋橋 28 B4
- Ryokan Marutame 旅館丸為 29 C6
- Ryokan Meiryū 旅館名龍 30 D5
- Sofitel the Cypress Nagoya ソフィテルザサイプレス名古屋 31 A3
- Tōyoko Inn Nagoya-eki Sakura-dōri-guchi Shinkan 東横イン名古屋駅桜通り口新館 32 A3
- Westin Nagoya Castle ウエスティン名古屋キャッスル 33 B1

EATING
- Ebisuya えびすや 34 C3
- Lee's Taiwan Kitchen 李さんの台湾名物屋台 35 C5
- Misen 味仙 36 C4
- Osso Brasil オッソブラジル 37 C5
- Sekai no Yamachan 世界の山ちゃん 38 B4
- Tarafuku たら福 39 A3
- Tiger Café タイガーカフェ 40 B3
- Torigin Honten 鳥銀本店 41 D3
- Yabaton 矢場とん 42 D4
- Yamamotoya Sōhonke 山本屋総本家 43 C4

DRINKING
- Elephant's Nest エレファントネスト 44 B4
- Eric Life エリックライフ 45 C5
- Red Rock Bar & Grill レッドロック 46 D4
- Shooters シューターズ 47 C4
- Smash Head スマッシュヘッド 48 C4

ENTERTAINMENT
- Club JB's クラブＪＢ'ｓ 49 D4
- Electric Lady Land エレクトリックレディランド 50 C4
- Misono-za 御園座 51 C4
- Shu シュー 52 B3

SHOPPING
- Flea Market (see 12)
- Komehyō コメ兵 53 C5
- Loft ロフト (see 13)
- Maruei 丸栄 54 D4
- Matsuzakaya 松坂屋デパート 55 A3
- Matsuzakaya 松坂屋デパート 56 D4
- Meidōchō 明道町 57 B2
- Meitetsu & Kintetsu Department Stores 名鉄、近鉄デパート 58 A4
- Mitsukoshi 三越デパート 59 D4
- Momijiya もみじや (see 35)
- Takashimaya 高島屋 60 A3
- Takashimaya 高島屋 (see 26)

TRANSPORT
- Bus Terminal バスターミナル (see 9)
- City Bus Station 市バスターミナル (see 55)
- Meitetsu Bus Centre めいてつバスセンター (see 58)

Tachino Clinic (Map p252; ☎ 541-9130; Dai-Nagoya Bldg, 3-28-12 Meieki; Nagoya) Opposite the east exit of Nagoya Station, with English-speaking staff.

Money & Post

Citibank has 24-hour Cirrus ATMs on the 1st floor of the Sugi building (Sakae, exit 7) and in the arrival lobby at Central Japan International Airport.

Eki-mae post office (Map p252; Nagoya) North of the station's east exit.

Nagoya Station post office (Map p252) Off the main concourse.

Tourist Information

English-language street and subway maps are widely available at information centres and hotels – the Convention & Visitors Bureau's free *Live Map Nagoya* covers the basics. English-language listings publications include *Japanzine*, *Avenues* and *Nagoya Calendar*.

Nagoya International Centre (Map p252; ☎ 581-0100; 1-47-1 Nagono; 9am-7pm Tue-Sun; Kokusai Centre) Has helpful English-speaking staff and information on both Nagoya and regional destinations. There's a library, overseas-TV newscasts and a bulletin board for postings.

Nagoya Tourist Information Nagoya Station (Map p252; ☎ 541-4301; 9am-7pm; Nagoya, in the central concourse); Kanayama Station (Map p251; ☎ 323-0161; 9am-8pm; Kanayama); Sakae (Map p252; ☎ 963-5252; Oasis 21 Bldg; 10am-8pm; Sakae) All locations have plenty of info and at least one English speaker on hand.

HIKING THE JAPAN ALPS

Central Honshū is blessed, in the Shintō sense and every other way, with half of the nation's 100 famous mountains across many national parks, making it a key destination for hiking. This chapter presents some of the more popular destinations; enthusiastic hikers should pick up Lonely Planet's *Hiking in Japan* (2009) by David Joll, Craig McLachlan and Richard Ryall.

For info on onward transportation, there is English-speaking staff at JR Nagoya Station's ticket windows, or try the travel agency **KNT Tourist** (Map p252; ☎ 541-8686; 1-2-2 Meieki; 🕑 10am-8pm Mon-Fri, to 6pm Sat & Sun; 🚇 Nagoya).

SIGHTS

Nagoya Station Area

MIDLAND SQUARE ミッドランドスクエア

In 2007 Toyota Motor Corporation moved its headquarters to this skyscraper (247m), Nagoya's tallest and the fifth-tallest in Japan, just across from Nagoya Station. If you've seen Tokyo Midtown, you get the idea. There is a chichi shopping centre on the lower floors, offices occupy the middle floors, and the top floors comprise the **Sky Promenade** (Map p252; ☎ 527-8877; www.noritake-elec.com/garden; 4-7-1 Meieki; garden adult/child/senior ¥700/300/500; 🕑 10am-10pm; 🚇 Nagoya), home of Japan's tallest outdoor observation deck (closed in bad weather), reached via passageways with some adventurously designed light murals.

Architecture fans should check out the exterior of the new **Spiral Towers** (Map p252), a couple of blocks south. It's an amazing structure, as if someone has tried to peel London's landmark 'Gherkin' (Swiss Re Tower).

NORITAKE GARDEN ノリタケの森

Take a stroll around **Noritake Garden** (Map p252; ☎ 561-7290; www.noritake-elec.com/garden; 3-1-36 Noritake-shinmachi; garden admission free; 🚇 Kamejima), the tree-planted grounds of the original 1904 factory of one of Japan's best-known porcelain makers. The **craft centre** (☎ 561-7114; adult/child & senior/high-school student ¥500/free/300; 🕑 10am-5pm) offers a peek at the production process and a museum of old Noritake pieces, plus a chance to glaze your own dish (¥1500). The **Noritake Gallery** (☎ 562-9811; 🕑 10am-6pm Tue-Sun) has changing exhibitions of paintings, sculpture and ceramic works. Signage is in English throughout, and look for an early kiln and some atmospheric old chimneys, the remains of a 1933 tunnel kiln.

Naturally there are shopping opportunities, including the Box outlet store (open 10am to 6pm), with 30% to 40% discounts on discontinued items.

TOYOTA COMMEMORATIVE MUSEUM OF INDUSTRY & TECHNOLOGY
トヨタテクノミュージアム産業技術記念館

Toyota, the world's largest automobile maker, started in another very Japanese industry: weaving. About 10 minutes' walk northwest of Noritake Garden, this **museum** (Map p251; ☎ 551-6115; www.tcmit.org; 4-1-35 Noritake-shinmachi; adult/child ¥500/300; 🕑 9.30am-5pm Tue-Sat; 🚇 Sako, Meitetsu Nagoya line) is on the site of the company's original Nagoya weaving plant (1911). It's filled with displays and demonstrations of metal processing and textile machinery, and hands-on experiences with principles of force, electronics and such, but the rubber meets the road in the 7900-sq-metre automotive pavilion. There's English signage, and an English-language audio guide for ¥200. See the boxed text (p261) for information on factory tours.

Nagoya Castle Area

NAGOYA-JŌ 名古屋城

Tokugawa Ieyasu ordered **Nagoya-jō** (Nagoya Castle; Map p252; ☎ 231-1700; 1-1 Honmaru; adult/child under 15 ¥500/100; 🕑 9am-4.30pm; 🚇 Shiyakusho, exit 7) to be built for his ninth son, from 1610 to 1614. Although it was destroyed in WWII and replaced in 1959 with a Ferro concrete replica, it's worth a visit for the fine museum inside featuring armour, treasures and histories of the Oda, Toyotomi and Tokugawa families. A lift will save you climbing stairs. Note the 3m-long replicas of *shachi-hoko* (gilded dolphin-like sea creatures) at either end of the roof (and in every souvenir shop).

Within the castle grounds, the garden, Ninomaru-en (二の丸園), has a tea house in an attractive setting. It's a sight during the cherry-blossom season (around early April), and on Fridays **ceremonial tea** (¥525; 🕑 9.30am-4pm Fri) is served here from a golden urn.

Nearby is the stately **Nagoya Noh Theatre** (Map p252; ☎ 231-0088; 1-1-1 San-no-maru; admission free; 🕑 9am-5pm), which has a small museum containing kimono, masks, fans and art related to nō, the world's oldest continuously performed art.

TOKUGAWA ART MUSEUM 徳川美術館

A must for anyone with even a passing interest in Japanese culture and history, this **museum** (off Map p252; ☎ 935-6262; www.tokugawa-art-museum.jp; 1017 Tokugawa-chō; adult/child under 7/child/student/senior ¥1200/free/500/700/1000; 🕑 10am-5pm Tue-Sun) has a 10,000-plus piece collection that includes National Treasures and Important Cultural Properties that once belonged to the shōgunal family: furnishings, arms and armour, tea-ceremony implements, calligraphy, painted scrolls, lacquerware, and masks and costumes from nō theatre. A priceless 12th-century scroll depicting *The Tale of Genji* (see p70) is locked away except for a short stint in late November; the rest of the year, visitors must remain content with a video.

The museum is three minutes' walk from the Tokugawaen-Shindeki bus stop, east of Nagoya-jō.

Sakae & East

While Sakae doesn't have big-name attractions, it's ground zero for shopping and people-watching. The wide central park in the middle of Hisaya-ōdōri is busy all day, and Sakae's side streets are packed with revellers well into the night. For more classic sights, head a few subway stops east of Sakae to Kakuōzan, a historic temple town.

INTERNATIONAL DESIGN CENTRE NAGOYA 国際デザインセンター

Just a short walk from Sakae, the futuristic, swooping Nadya Park skyscraper houses the **International Design Centre Nagoya** (Map p252; ☎ 265-2106; 4th fl, 3-18-1 Sakae; adult/student/child under 16 ¥300/200/free; 🕑 11am-8pm Wed-Mon; Ⓜ Yaba-chō, exit 5 or 6). It's a secular shrine to the deities of conceptualisation, form and function, from art deco to the present, from Electrolux to Isamu Noguchi, and from Arne Jacobsen to the Mini Cooper. Signage is in English.

Also in Nadya Park is the Loft department store, which design-shoppers will find equally alluring. Nadya Park is about five minutes' walk from Yaba-chō Station.

OASIS 21 オアシス

Yes, it's a bus terminal, but if all the world's bus terminals were as interesting as OASIS 21 (Map p252), recipient of good-design awards, everyone would take public transport. The 'galaxy platform', a fantastical glass disk, seems to hover storeys above the ground, and you can climb it via stairs and go for a walk about, particularly at night when it's adventurously lit.

KAKUŌZAN & NITTAI-JI 覚王山日泰寺

The Kakuōzan neighbourhood, a few subway stops away from Sakae, is an old-style spot that you might expect to see in the country-side instead of in flashy Nagoya, and perhaps that's why it was chosen as the site of **Nittai-ji** (Map p251; ☎ 751-2121; 1-1 Hōō-chō, Chikusa-ku; admission free; 🕑 9am-2.30pm; ♿; Ⓜ Kakuōzan, exit 1). Nittai-ji means 'Japan Thailand temple', and it is here that, in 1904, Thai King Chulalongkorn chose Nagoya over Kyoto to bestow a Buddha relic and a 1000-year-old Buddha statue (the relic is kept elsewhere); Thai royalty continue to visit here on trips to Japan. The temple was rebuilt in 1984 and is, rare for Japan, accessible for travellers with disabilities.

Daily *otsutome* (Buddhist worship) is held at 12.30pm. On the 21st of each month, the street leading to the temple, Kakuōzan-Nittai-ji-dōri, bustles with a street fair with stalls selling food, ceramics, tea, knives and crafts.

Nearby is **Yōki-sō** (Map p251; ☎ 759-4450; 2-5-21 Hōō-chō, Chikusa-ku; admission free; 🕑 gardens 9.30am-4.30pm; Ⓜ Kakuōzan, exit 1), a pretty villa that hosted students from Southeast Asia during the early 20th century. The building is open only limited hours by tour only, but the garden in a ravine is modelled after Shūgaku-in Rikyū in Kyoto (p357). From Nittai-ji, face away from the main hall, turn left before the five-storey pagoda, head downhill, turn right at the street and take the first driveway.

South of the City Centre

ŌSU KANNON AREA 大須観音周辺

The much-visited **Ōsu Kannon temple** (Map p252; admission free; 🕑 5.30am-7pm; Ⓜ Ōsu Kannon, exit 2) traces its roots back to 1333 and was considered so auspicious that Tokugawa Ieyasu ordered it moved here around 1610. Although the current buildings are 20th-century reconstructions, it still retains a traditional atmosphere. Chanting is often piped throughout the temple grounds.

Ōsu is equally famous for the vibrant shopping district just east, which draws bargain hunters. See p260 for more on shopping.

ATSUTA-JINGŪ 熱田神宮

Hidden among 1000-year-old cypress trees, the 1900-year-old **Atsuta-jingū** (Map p251; ☎ 671-4151; www.atsutajingu.or.jp; 1-1-1 Jingū; admission free;

24hr; Jingū-mae, Meitetsu Nagoya line or Jingū-nishi, exit 2) is one of the most sacred shrines in all of Shintō. It houses the *kusanagi-no-tsurugi* (sacred sword; literally the 'grass-cutting sword'), one of the *sanshu no jingi* (three regalia) that were, according to legend, handed down to the imperial family by the sun goddess Amaterasu-Ōmikami. (The other two are the curved jewels at the Imperial Palace in Tokyo, p127, and the sacred mirror housed at Ise-jingū, p444.) You won't be able to view the regalia, but don't feel left out; no one but the emperor and a few selected Shintō priests ever get to see them.

There is a small **museum** (Treasure Hall; Hōmotsukan; adult/child ¥300/150; 9am-4.30pm, closed last Wed & Thu of each month), housing a changing collection of Tokugawa-era swords, masks and paintings, including some Important Cultural Properties.

The shrine is about three minutes' walk west from Jingū-mae Station on the Meitetsu Nagoya line, or five minutes' walk east from Jingū-nishi Station on the Meijō subway line.

NAGOYA/BOSTON MUSEUM OF FINE ARTS 名古屋ボストン美術館

This excellent **museum** (Map p251; ☎ 684-0786; www.nagoya-boston.or.jp; 1-1-1 Kanayama-chō; special & long-term exhibitions adult/child/senior & student ¥1200/free/900; 10am-7pm Tue-Fri, to 5pm Sat & Sun; Kanayama via JR, Meitetsu or Meijō subway lines) is a collaborative effort between Japanese backers and the Museum of Fine Arts, Boston. Rotating exhibitions showcase both Japanese and non-Japanese masterpieces, and have good English signage.

The museum is to the right of the south exit of Kanayama Station.

NAGOYA PORT AREA 名古屋港

Nagoya's cargo port has been attractively redeveloped and now boasts several high-profile attractions. The hi-tech **Port of Nagoya Public Aquarium** (Map p251; ☎ 654-7000; www.nagoyaaqua.jp; 1-3 Minatomachi; adult/child ¥2000/1000; 9.30am-8pm Tue-Sun 21 Jul-31 Aug, to 5.30pm Apr-20 Jul & Sep-Nov, to 5pm rest of year; Nagoya-kō) is one of Japan's largest aquariums and is generally a hit with kids. The observation deck of the **Port Building** (Map p251; ☎ 652-1111; 1-3 Minatomachi; 9.30am-5pm Tue-Sun; Nagoya-kō) seems to be balanced on giant pistons and offers good views of the harbour and Ise Bay from 53m up. There's a Maritime Museum on the 3rd floor and the Fuji Antarctic Exploration Ship outside. Admission to any of the Port Building attractions is ¥300/200 (adult/child) individually, ¥700/400 for all three, or ¥2400/1200 including the aquarium. Attractions are signposted in English.

Nagoya Port is reached via the Meikō subway line. From central Nagoya, change trains at Kanayama. From Nagoya Station, the journey to Nagoya Port takes approximately 30 minutes.

FESTIVALS & EVENTS

Atsuta Matsuri Displays of martial arts, sumō and fireworks on 5 June at Atsuta-jingū (p255).

Dekimachi Tennō-sai On the first Saturday and Sunday of June there's a parade of floats with large *karakuri* (mechanical puppets) around the shrine, Susano-o-jinja, near the Tokugawa Art Museum (p255).

Nagoya Basho sumō tournament One of six annual championship tournaments, over two weeks in July at Aichi Prefectural Gymnasium (Map p252; ☎ 962-9300; 1-1 Honmaru; tickets from ¥1500). Arrive early in the afternoon to watch the lower-ranked wrestlers up close.

Minato Matsuri Street parade in Nagoya Port, around the third Sunday in July. There's a traditional parade, street dancers, fireworks and a water-logging contest that dates back to the Edo period.

Nagoya Matsuri Nagoya's big annual event takes place in mid-October at Hisaya-ōdōri-kōen. It includes costume parades, processions of floats with *karakuri* puppets, folk dancing, music and a parade of flower-decorated cars.

Kiku-no-hana Taikai Chrysanthemum exhibition at Nagoya-jō in late October to late November. A *ningyō* (doll) pavilion incorporates flowers into scenes from Japanese history and legend.

SLEEPING

Accommodation in Nagoya is clustered around Nagoya Station and Sakae. Ryokan listed here do not have en-suite toilet or bath, except where noted. All Western-style hotels listed provide LAN cables for in-room internet access.

Budget

Aichi-ken Seinen-kaikan Youth Hostel (Map p252; ☎ 221-6001; www.jyh.or.jp; 1-18-8 Sakae; dm ¥2992; ; Fushimi, exit 7) This central, 50-bed hostel feels institutional, and there are no elevator or meals. Still, it's usually the first budget place to fill up. Most options are Japanese-style dorms, while HI members can enjoy private, Western-style rooms (¥4147 double occupancy) with private toilet. Baths are communal and are only available at night. From the station, walk west and take a left after the Hilton, from where it's two blocks further south. There is an 11pm curfew.

Kimiya Ryokan (Map p252; ☎ 551-0498; hott@hotmail.com; 2-20-16 Nagono; r per person ¥4500, with breakfast/dinner ¥5000/6000; Kokusai Centre, exit 1) This friendly, 14-room, family-run ryokan is good value for its tatami rooms. The best ones overlook the garden. Not much English is spoken, but the owners dispense a helpful map and prepare Japanese meals. From the subway, walk north about five minutes. It's on the left, with English signage, before Endōji shopping arcade.

Tsuchiya Hotel (Map p251; ☎ 451-0028, toll-free 0120-144-028; www.tsuchiya-hotel.co.jp; 2-16-2 Noritake; r per person from ¥4800; ; Nagoya, west exit) In business for generations, the Tsuchiya oozes character despite its nondescript neighbourhood. Craft-style tiles line the hallways to Japanese-style rooms. Some have private facilities, but you'll want to use the common baths: a pottery tub in this region's famous *Mino-yaki* style for the ladies or stone for the gents. Meals are available with advance notice.

B Nagoya (Map p252; ☎ 241-1500; www.ishinhotels.com; 4-15-23 Sakae; s/d & tw from ¥5000/7500; ; Sakae, exit 13) A business hotel in Sakae that's as stylish as it is functional. Rooms make up in panache (think PJs with piping and embroidered logos) for what they lack in space. Look online for rates including breakfast.

Ryokan Meiryū (Map p252; ☎ 331-8686; www.japan-net.ne.jp/~meiryu; 2-4-21 Kamimaezu; s/d/tr ¥5250/8400/11,025; ; Kamimaezu, exit 3) This 22-room ryokan doesn't look like much from the outside, but inside it's quite professional, with some English-speaking staff, coin laundry, women's communal bath and a sauna in the men's. Home-style Japanese meals are available by reservation. From the station, walk along the street and take the first left. It's 1½ blocks down, on the left.

Ryokan Marutame (Map p252; ☎ 321-7130; www.jin.ne.jp/marutame; 2-6-17 Tachibana; s/tw ¥5250/8450; Higashi-Betsuin, exit 4) Narrow staircases testify to this ryokan's 50-plus-year history, yet it's modern with clean but basic Japanese rooms, English-speaking staff, coin-operated laundry and simple Japanese meals (breakfast/dinner ¥500/1200). Try for the lovely private *hanare* (apart) room in the back garden. From the station, cross the street, walk past the Nagoya Terebi building and Higashi Betsuin temple and turn right. It's on the left.

Midrange

Petit Ryokan Ichifuji (Map p251; ☎ 914-2867; www.jin.ne.jp/ichifuji; 1-7 Saikōbashi-dōri, kita-ku; s/d with breakfast from ¥6100/9600; ; Heian-dōri, exit 2 via elevator) Well worth the 20-minute subway ride from Nagoya Station. It's dramatically lit, clean and comfortable, with designer basins and a communal cypress-wood bath. Japanese-Western fusion dinner (from ¥2480) is available with advance notice; after dinner the dining room turns into a little bar. From the station, walk south for three minutes. The ryokan is signposted in English, down a gravel alley across from the Pola store.

Tōyoko Inn Nagoya-eki Sakura-dōri-guchi Shinkan (Map p252; ☎ 562-1045; www.toyoko-inn.com; 3-9-16 Meieki; s/d & tw ¥6615/8715; ; Nagoya, Sakura-dōri exit) Everyone likes free stuff, and this business hotel offers it: simple Japanese breakfast, water and coffee, internet access and even short phone calls…all before you leave the lobby. It's almost enough to make up for the microscopic rooms. Note: this is the *shinkan* (new building); the *honkan* (original building) is diagonally across the street.

Richmond Hotel Nagoya Nayabashi (Map p252; ☎ 212-1055; www.richmondhotel.jp; 1-2-7 Sakae; s/d/tw from ¥7800/10,800/15,500; ; Fushimi, exit 7) This business hotel offers relatively large, spick-and-span rooms in a minimalist shell, with dark-wood furniture, hi-tech desk lamps and English-language news on flat-panel TVs. Rates quoted here are 'member' rates; if you're not already a member, become one on registration (¥500).

Natural Hotel Elséreine (Map p252; ☎ 459-5344, toll-free 0120-793-489; fax 453-7188; 1-23 Tsubaki-chō; s/tw from ¥11,500/18,480; ; Nagoya, west exit) Walk past the drab business hotels out Meieki's west exit to this gracious, nonsmoking hotel. Beds of flowering plants grace the lobby. Rooms, while not breaking any size records, are comfy and sparkling clean.

Top End

Nagoya Kankō Hotel (Map p252; ☎ 231-7407; www.nagoyakankohotel.co.jp; 1-19-30 Nishiki; s/d from ¥15,015/23,100; ; Fushimi) This 1970s edifice was recently renovated and now is the kind of place where you're likely to see politicians followed around by camera crews. There's an understated Euro elegance to the renovated rooms, which have marble bathrooms, though the unrenovated rooms are less expensive. There's a fitness centre.

Westin Nagoya Castle (Map p252; ☎ 521-2121; www.castle.co.jp; 3-19 Hinokuchi-chō; s/d from ¥16,000/34,000; ; Sengen-chō) You can't get closer to Nagoya-jō than this, located across the moat. The Castle is popular for its 'heavenly beds', spacious bathrooms, fitness facilities and restaurants. Look for website-only specials. There's a shuttle bus to/from Nagoya Station.

Hilton Nagoya (Map p252; ☎ 212-1111, toll-free 0120-489-852; www.hilton.com; 1-3-3 Sakae; s/d from ¥16,500/24,500; ; Fushimi, exit 7) A soaring lobby with a piano player and manicured shrubs is your entree to Western-style rooms with Japanese touches such as *shōji* (rice-paper screens) and blackout panels on the windows. There's a well-equipped fitness centre and great views from the top-storey bar.

Sofitel the Cypress Nagoya (Map p252; ☎ 571-0111; www.sofitelthecypress.com; 2-43-6 Meieki; s/d from ¥20,000/25,000; ; Nagoya) A quiet atmosphere prevails in this 115-room, European-style hotel with a swanky bar in the basement. Deluxe doubles offer extra space and interesting layouts. From Nagoya Station, exit on the Sakura-dōri side, turn left and cross by the post office.

our pick **Nagoya Marriott Associa Hotel** (Map p252; ☎ 584-1111; www.associa.com/english/nma; 1-1-2 Meieki; s/d from ¥22,000/30,000; ; Nagoya) The Marriott literally tops other hotels in town. The palmy lobby (accessed via an elevator from Nagoya Station) is on the 15th floor, and 774 spacious rooms start from the 20th, fitted with deluxe, well, everything. The 18th-storey gym has views across the city.

EATING

Nagoya is famous for bold-flavoured local specialities, which, unlike in many other places in Japan, are also instantly palatable to non-Japanese tastes. *Kishimen* are flat, handmade wheat noodles, similar to udon (thick white noodles) and nicely chewy; *miso-nikomi udon* are noodles in hearty miso broth; and *miso-katsu* is breaded, fried pork cutlet with miso sauce. *Kōchin* (free-range chicken) is another local speciality, as are *tebasaki* (chicken wings). *Hitsumabushi* (charcoal-grilled eel sets) are also popular.

Sekai no Yamachan (Map p252; ☎ 581-1711 in Yanagibashi; 1-5-16 Meieki-Minami; small plates ¥360-630; 11am-midnight Sun-Thu, to 3am Fri & Sat; Nagoya) This is a cheap and cheerful local chain that's an institution for *tebasaki*. The house standard is *maboroshino tebasaki* (fried chicken wings heady with black pepper; there are five to an order); other small plates include *renkon* (lotus-root) chips, daikon salad and *kimumayo omuretsu* (omelette with kimchi and mayonnaise). An English menu is available. Ask at your hotel for the closest branch.

Tarafuku (Map p252; ☎ 566-5600; 3-17-26 Meieki; dishes ¥400-800; dinner; Nagoya) Ambitious, young gourmets have turned the *izakaya* (pub-eatery) concept on its head, installing a stainless-steel kitchen in what looks from the outside like a falling-down house. East-west fusion dishes might include airy potato croquettes in a fried tofu crust; tomato and eggplant au gratin; house-cured ham, or beef, in wine sauce; plus wine and cocktail lists. There is an *omakase* (chef's recommendation) course from ¥3000. No English menu is available, but the staff is game to help. Tarafuku is located diagonally across from both Tōyoko Inns.

Misen (Map p252; ☎ 238-7357; 3-6-3 Ōsu; dishes ¥580-1680; lunch & dinner, until 2am Fri & Sat; Yaba-chō, exit 4) Around the corner from Yabaton, Misen has little atmosphere and no English menu, but the *Taiwan rāmen* (egg noodles; ¥580) induces rapture – it's a spicy concoction of ground meat, chilli, garlic and green onion, served over noodles in a hearty clear broth. Other faves include *gomoku mame-itame* (stir-fried green beans with meat; ¥800) and *mabō-dōfu* (tofu in spicy meat sauce; ¥700).

Tiger Café (Map p252; ☎ 220-0031; 1-8-26 Nishiki; mains ¥600-2000, specials from ¥850; 11am-3am Mon-Sat, to 11pm Sun; Fushimi) Fashionistas grace the windows of this faithful re-creation of an old-style Parisian bistro, with tiled floors, white-shirted staff, sidewalk seating, art deco details and people smoking (even though you can't smoke in Paris bistros anymore). The smoked-salmon sandwich and *croque-monsieur* (toasted ham and cheese sandwich) are favourites, as are the good-value lunch specials.

Ebisuya (Map p252; ☎ 961-3412; 3-20-7 Sakae; dishes from ¥650; lunch & dinner Mon-Sat; Sakae) One of the city's best-known *kishimen* chains, Ebisuya has a laid-back atmosphere and tasty, inexpensive bowls of noodles, which you can often catch the chefs making. There's a picture menu available.

Yabaton (Map p252; ☎ 252-8810; 3-6-18 Ōsu; dishes ¥735-1575; lunch & dinner Tue-Sun; Yaba-chō, exit 4) Throw dietary caution to the wind at this spotless, workmanlike institution for *miso-katsu,* which has been around since 1947. *Waraji-tonkatsu* is a cutlet flattened to as big as your head, or try *kani-korokke* (crab croquettes). *Yabaton-salada* (boiled pork with miso sesame sauce over vegetables) is kinda sorta good for you. Look for the pig-in-an-apron logo and English menu.

Torigin Honten (Map p252; ☎ 973-3000; 3-14-22 Nishiki; dishes ¥750-1950; dinner; Sakae) For top *kōchin,* Torigin has been going strong for decades. Chicken is served in many forms, including *kushiyaki* (skewered), *kara-age* (deep-fried pieces), *zōsui* (mild rice hotpot) and sashimi (what you think it is). Individual dishes are a bit dainty for the price, but *teishoku* (set menus; from ¥3000) are more substantial. It's next door to St James Gate Irish pub. A menu in English is available.

Eikoku-ya (Map p251; ☎ 763-2788; 2-58 Kakuōzan; mains ¥950-1600; 8am-9.30pm Wed-Mon; Kakuōzan) You'll smell the aroma of curry several doors down from this Indian chai-and-curry shop, at the heart of Kakuōzan's shopping street. Curries and mixed grills are served in a room from a bygone era. Look for the elephant statues out front.

Yamamotoya Sōhonke (Map p252; ☎ 241-5617; 3-12-19 Sakae; dishes ¥976-1554; lunch & dinner; Sakae, Yaba-chō) This *miso-nikomi udon* shop has been in business since 1925, thanks to a lot of repeat customers. The basic dish costs ¥976. It's not really close to any subway station; it's a couple of blocks east of Shirakawa-kōen.

OUR PICK **Atsuta Hōraiken** (Map p251; ☎ 671-8686; 503 Kōbe-chō, Honten; mains ¥1575-4305; lunch & dinner, closed Mon; Temma-chō) This *hitsumabushi* shop, in business since 1873, is revered with good reason. Expect long queues during the summer peak season for *hitsumabushi*, basted in a secret *tare* (sauce) and served atop rice in a covered lacquered bowl (¥2730); add green onion, wasabi and *dashi* (fish broth) to your taste. Other *teishoku* include chicken, tempura and steak. There's another branch (Map p251; ☎ 682-5598; 2-10-26 Jingū, Atsuta-ku; open lunch and dinner, closed Tuesday; the nearest station is Jingū-minami) a few blocks away, near Atsuta-jingū. The main branch has more atmosphere but also more smokers.

For cheap, informal, international eats, head to the Ōsu district. Expect to hear Portuguese at **Osso Brasil** (Map p252; ☎ 238-5151; 3-41-13 Ōsu; mains ¥700-1500; 10.30am-9pm Tue-Sun; Kamimaezu, exit 8), a storefront serving Brazilian grills at lunchtime (all-you-can-eat on weekends, ¥1600) and snacks, while **Lee's Taiwan Kitchen** (Map p252; ☎ 251-8992; 3-21-8 Ōsu; mains around ¥450; noon-8pm, closed 3rd Wed each month; Kamimaezu, exit 8) does a big trade in take-out crackly *kara-age*. Other stands run from kebabs to crêpes to *okonomiyaki* (savoury pancakes).

DRINKING

Eric Life (Map p252; ☎ 222-1555; 2-11-18 Ōsu; noon-midnight Thu-Tue; Ōsu Kannon, exit 2) Minimalist, kitsch-free and a teeny bit artsy, this cafe behind Ōsu Kannon temple is perfect for chilling over a coffee, cocktail or snack. Being in the Ōsu district, it draws a youngish crowd.

Smash Head (Map p252; ☎ 201-2790; 2-21-90 Ōsu; noon-midnight Wed-Mon; Ōsu Kannon, exit 2) Just north of Ōsu Kannon temple, this low-key spot is both a pub and a motorcycle repair shop (no, really), where Guinness is the beverage of choice. But don't drink and ride or you may end up a…you know…

Shooters (Map p252; ☎ 202-7077; www.shooters-nagoya.com; 2-9-26 Sakae; 5pm-3am Mon-Fri, 11.30am-3am Sat & Sun; Fushimi, exit 5) This US-style sports bar with over a dozen screens attracts a mostly *gaijin* (foreign), mostly raucous crowd. Japanese and foreign staff pour daily drink specials, and the menu includes burgers, pasta and Tex-Mex. It's on the 2nd floor of the Pola Building, diagonally across from Misono-za.

Elephant's Nest (Map p252; ☎ 232-4360; 1-4-3 Sakae; 5.30pm-1am Sun-Thu, to 2am Fri & Sat; Fushimi, exit 7) Near the Hilton, Elephant's Nest is a favourite expat haunt, with a welcoming vibe, darts and traditional English fare. It's on the 2nd floor.

Red Rock Bar & Grill (Map p252; ☎ 262-7893; www.theredrock.jp; 4-14-6 Sakae; 5.30pm-late Tue-Sun; Sakae, exit 13) On a Sakae side street, the Aussie-owned Red Rock has a warm ambience and plenty of pub food. Look for happy hours and specials such as Ladies' Night and Quiz Night.

Ichirin (Map p251; ☎ 751-1953; 1-58 Yamamoto-chō Ōsu; 10am-5pm Wed-Sun; Kakuōzan, exit 1) Around the left-hand side of Nittai-ji is this hillside cafe in a private home c 1940, filled with antiques and crafts and looking out over a garden that could be in a Kyoto temple. Drinks and snacks will set you back ¥500 to ¥700. The calm: priceless.

ENTERTAINMENT

Nagoya's nightlife might not match Tokyo's or Osaka's in scale but makes it up in ebullience. Check English-language listings magazines for dates and times.

Misono-za (Map p252; ☎ 222-1481; www.misonoza.co.jp, in Japanese; 1-6-14 Sakae; Fushimi, exit 6) This is the city's venue for kabuki theatre in April and October, although it does not have the translation facilities of theatres in other cities.

Nagoya Dome (Map p251; ☎ 719-2121; Nagoya Dome-mae Yada) Baseball fans will want to visit this 45,000-seat stadium, home of the Chunichi Dragons baseball team. It's also a venue for large concerts.

Electric Lady Land (Map p252; ☎ 201-5004; www.ell.co.jp, in Japanese; 2-10-43 Ōsu; Ōsu Kannon, exit 2) An intimate concert venue purveying the underground music scene in a cool, postindustrial setting. Nationally known bands perform in the 1st-floor hall, while the 3rd floor sees more up-and-coming acts.

Club JB's (Map p252; ☎ 241-2234; www.club-jbs.jp; 4-3-15 Sakae; Sakae, exit 13) Club kids (aged 20 and over) come for an excellent sound system and famous DJs.

Shu (Map p252; ☎ 223-3788; www.geocities.com/mensbar_shu_japan; 10-15 Nishiki 1-chōme; Wed-Mon; Fushimi, exit 7) Nagoya doesn't have a whole lot of options for gay visitors from overseas (most operate as private clubs), but this tiny, chatty bar for gay men welcomes all ages and nationalities.

SHOPPING

Both Meieki and Sakae boast gargantuan malls and department stores, good for clothing, crafts and foods. Look for the department stores Maruei and Mitsukoshi in Sakae; Takashimaya, Meitetsu and Kintetsu near Nagoya Station; and Matsuzakaya in Sakae and near Nagoya Station. Regional crafts include *Arimatsu-narumi shibori* (elegant tie-dying; see p264), cloisonné, ceramics and Seki blades (swords, knives, scissors etc).

A youthful energy fills vintage clothing shops, electronics and music shops, cafes and a hodge-podge of old and new in the Ōsu district, east of the temple around Ōsu Kannon-dōri and its continuation, Banshō-ji-dōri. **Komehyō** (Map p252; 2-20-25 Ōsu, Naka-ku) is a multistorey discounter that's recently taken over much of the real estate, selling electronics, fashion, jewellery, house wares, used kimono etc. Inside, the ingenious **yen=g** (☎ 218-2122) sells used clothing by weight. **Momijiya** (Map p252; ☎ 251-1313; 3-37-46 Ōsu) creates clothing and accessories patterned after antique kimono fabric, though look closely for its own cute, contemporary twists.

Just east of Ōsu, Ōtsu-dōri is called the Akihabara of Nagoya for its proliferation of manga shops. Ōsu Kannon temple itself hosts a colourful antique market on the 18th and 28th of each month, while Higashi Betsuin has a **flea market** (Map p252; ☎ 321-9201; 9am-2pm; Higashi-Betsuin, exit 4) on the 12th of each month.

The speciality in the Meidōchō district, by the expressway overpass north of Meieki and west of Nagoya-jō, is *okashi*, which are Japanese snacks and penny nibbles, including *sembei* rice crackers, sweet-potato sticks, dried fish and sponge cake, plus small toys like action figures, beads and balloons (imagine a kiddie party). Dozens of wholesalers display their wares in a manner that may dispel any notion of Japanese neatness.

GETTING THERE & AWAY

Air

Many Nagoyans go to **Central Japan International Airport** (Centrair; NGO; off Map p251; ☎ 0569-38-1195; www.centrair.jp/en), opened in 2005 on a manmade island in Ise-wan (Ise Bay) 35km south of the city, for an afternoon out. On the 4th floor are dozens of Japanese and Western shopping and dining options (at out-of-airport prices), plane-spotting from the observation deck, and **Fū-no-yu** (風の湯; ☎ 0569-38-7070; adult/child with towel ¥1000/600; 8am-10pm), hot-spring baths with *rotemburo* (outdoor bath), which are admittedly a little institutional.

Some 30 airlines connect Centrair with around 30 international cities (in Europe, North America, Australia and especially Asia) and 20 Japanese cities, though some are faster reached by train.

Boat

Taiheiyo ferry (☎ 398-1023) runs between Nagoya and Tomakomai (Hokkaidō, from ¥10,500, 38½ hours) via Sendai (from ¥7000, 21 hours) every second evening at 8pm. Take the Meikō subway line to Nagoya-kō Station and head for Nagoya Port.

Bus

JR and **Meitetsu Highway buses** (☎ 563-0489) operate services between Nagoya and Kyoto (¥2500, 2½ hours, hourly), Osaka (¥2900,

CENTRAL HONSHŪ

three hours, hourly), Kanazawa (¥4060, four hours, 10 daily) and Tokyo (¥5100, six hours, 14 daily). Overnight buses run to Hiroshima (¥8400, nine hours).

Train

Nagoya is a major *shinkansen* hub, connecting with Tokyo (¥10,580, 1¾ hours), Shin-Osaka (¥6180, 50 minutes), Kyoto (¥5440, 35 minutes) and Hiroshima (¥13,630, 2½ hours). The private Meitetsu line is your best bet within the region.

To the Japan Alps, you can take the JR Chūō line to Nagano (Shinano *tokkyū*, ¥7330, 2¾ hours) via Matsumoto (¥5670, two hours). A separate line serves Takayama (Hida *tokkyū*, ¥5670, 2¼ hours).

GETTING AROUND

To/From the Airport

Central Japan International Airport is accessible from Nagoya Station via the Meitetsu Kūkō (Airport) line (*tokkyū*, ¥870, 28 minutes). A taxi from central Nagoya costs upwards of ¥13,000.

Bus

The **Me~guru bus** (www.ncvb.or.jp/routebus/en/index.html; day pass adult/child ¥500/250; 9.30am-5pm, hourly Tue-Fri, twice hourly Sat & Sun) makes a convenient loop (close) to attractions in the Meieki, Sakae and castle areas, and offers discounted admission.

Subway & Train

Nagoya's **Transportation Bureau** (www.kotsu.city.nagoya.jp/english/index.html) operates an excellent subway system with six lines, clearly signposted in English and Japanese. The most useful lines for visitors are the Meijō (purple), Higashiyama (yellow) and Sakura-dōri (red) lines. The last two serve Nagoya Station, and the Meijō line has a spur to the Meikō line to Nagoya Port. Fares cost ¥200 to ¥320 depending on distance. One-day passes (¥740, ¥850 including city buses), available at ticket machines, include subway transport and discounted admission to many attractions. On Saturday and Sunday the *donichi eco-kippu* (Saturday-Sunday eco-ticket) gives the same benefits for ¥600 per day.

Meitetsu Nagoya Station is cramped and confusing. Trains for different destinations come at rapid-fire pace on its four underground platforms. Departures are colour-coded on platform signage.

AROUND NAGOYA

名古屋近辺

This region, consisting of outlying Aichi-ken and southern Gifu-ken, offers plenty of easy day trips. The commuter towns of Tokoname and Arimatsu are historic centres for ceramics and tie-dyeing. Or for some 21st-century *monozukuri*, check out the factories making

CENTRAL HONSHŪ

FAMOUS FACTORIES FOR FREE

Nagoya is the hub of a major industrial centre and visitors have a unique opportunity to visit some of the world's leading manufacturers. Bookings are required.

Two-hour tours of Toyota Motor Corporation's main plant in Toyota city depart from the **Toyota Kaikan Exhibition Hall** (☎ 0565-23-3922; www.toyota.co.jp/en/about_toyota/facility/toyota_kaikan; 11am Mon-Fri). Book online up to three months in advance. Allow at least one hour to get to Toyota city from central Nagoya; check the website for directions. See also the Toyota Commemorative Museum of Industry & Technology (p254).

Denso (off Map p251; ☎ 0566-61-7215; www.globaldenso.com/en/aboutdenso/hall/gallery; Kariya City; 9.30am-5pm Mon-Fri) is a company whose products you've used even if you don't know its name: its backbone is automotive components, but there are also industrial robots. Short visits (up to one hour) take place in the Denso Gallery, or you can visit the plant on a 2½-hour tour. It's a seven-minute walk from Kariya Station on the JR Tōkaidō line.

The Nagoya brewery of **Asahi Beer** (Map p251; ☎ 052-792-8966; 9.30am-3pm, closed irregularly) welcomes visitors for 1¼-hour tours. Sample the wares for the tour's final 20 minutes – woo-hoo! Request about one month in advance for English guidance. Take the JR Chūō line to Shin-Moriyama Station; it's a 15-minute walk.

If none of that starts your motor, visit www.sangyokanko.jp for more ideas.

household-name brands (see the boxed text, p261). Easygoing Inuyama boasts National Treasures – its castle and tea house – as well as side trips to an architecturally historical theme park and some rather randy shrines. Both Inuyama and Gifu city are famed for *ukai* (cormorant fishing), in which the trained birds, with cords around their necks, dive for river trout and smelts.

TOKONAME 常滑

☎ 0569 / pop 52,800

Clay beneath the ground of this bayside community has made Tokoname a hub for ceramic-making for centuries – during its height some 400 chimneys rose above its centre. Today, Tokoname still produces some ¥60 trillion in ceramics annually. Most of that is for plumbing and tiles, but teapots and *maneki-neko* (welcoming cat figurines at the entrance to shops and restaurants) are also signature designs. It all makes Tokoname's historic centre a visually interesting day trip from Nagoya or a quick detour from Central Japan International Airport. Pick up a map in English at **Tokoname Tourist Information** (常滑市観光案内所; ☎ 34-8888; 9am-5.30pm), inside Tokoname Station.

Yakimono Sanpo Michi (やきもの散歩道; Pottery Footpath) is a handsome 1.8km paved trail looping up and down hills around the town's historic centre. Lining the path are locally produced ceramics from historic pipes to roofing tiles and plaques decorated by school kids. Numbered plaques corresponding to the tourist office map indicate the stops along the way, and you'll pass kilns and chimneys, cafes and galleries selling the works of some 100 local ceramic artists, some at bargain prices. The pipe-and-jug-lined lane **Dokanzaka** (土管坂; stop 9) is particularly photogenic, and go around the back at **Noborigama-hiroba** (登窯広場; Climbing Kiln Sq; stop 13) for a peek at the 10 square chimneys that served the gigantic, 1887 kiln. The restored **Takita-ke** (滝田家; Takita residence; ☎ 36-2031; stop 8; admission ¥300; 9am-4.30pm Tue-Sun), c 1850, was the home of a shipping magnate family and exhibits a replica of the local trading ships called *bishu-kaisen*, and displays of ceramics, lacquer, furniture and oil lamps. Look for the *suikinkutsu*, a ceramic jar buried in the ground so that it rings like a *koto* (13-stringed instrument derived from a Chinese zither that is played flat on the floor) when water drips into it. A video is available with English translation.

With a little more time, visit **Inax Live Museum** (イナックスライブミュージアム; ☎ 34-8282; adult/child/student ¥600/200/400; 10am-6pm, closed 3rd Wed of month), a cluster of buildings about a five-minute detour from the Pottery Footpath. Inax is one of Japan's top plumbing-equipment manufacturers. On the 2nd floor of Inax Kiln Plaza are some 150 Meiji- and Taisho-era toilets that are elaborately decorated. There are also small exhibits of tiles from around the world, and a workshop where you can try your own hand at tile-making (at an extra charge).

You won't have trouble finding cafes along the Pottery Footpath. **Koyōan** (古窯庵; ☎ 35-8350; mains ¥880-1800; 11.30am-5pm Tue-Sun, dinner by reservation) serves homemade *soba* (buckwheat noodles) on handsome ceramic-ware dishes, surrounded by wood-beamed ceilings and inlaid tiles. There's no English menu, but specialities include *teuchi soba* (handmade *soba*, ¥880) and tempura *soba* (¥1780); set menus are available from ¥2100.

Many visitors cap their day with a side trip to Central Japan International Airport (p260) for restaurants, shopping and onsen-ing.

Getting There & Around

The private Meitetsu line connects Tokoname with Meitetsu Nagoya (*kyūkō*, ¥650, 40 minutes; *tokkyū* ¥1000, 30 minutes) and Central Japan International Airport (¥300, five minutes). Once in town, the Pottery Footpath is a few hundred metres from the train station.

INUYAMA 犬山

☎ 0568 / pop 75,700

Dubbed the 'Japanese Rhine' since the 19th century, Inuyama's Kiso-gawa sets a pretty scene beneath its castle, a National Treasure. By day, the castle, quaint streets, manicured Uraku-en and 17th-century Jo-an Teahouse make for a pleasant ramble, while at night the scene becomes cinematic as fishermen practise *ukai* in season. Nearby attractions include architecture at Museum Meiji-mura, shooting the rapids down the Kiso-gawa and some rather racy shrines.

Orientation & Information

Inuyama's **tourist information office** (☎ 61-6000; 9am-5pm) is in Inuyama Station. It dispenses useful English-language pamphlets and maps and can book accommodation and make referrals to river activities such as rafting. The castle and *ukai* area are closer to Inuyama-

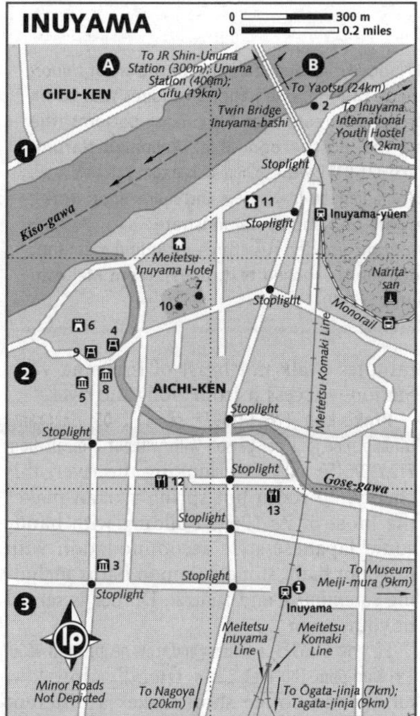

INFORMATION
Tourist Information Office 観光案内所 1 B3

SIGHTS & ACTIVITIES
Cormorant-Fishing Pier 鵜飼桟橋 2 B1
Dondenkan どんでん館 3 A3
Haritsuna Jinja 針綱神社 4 A2
Inuyama Castle Historical Museum 犬山市文化資料館 5 A2
Inuyama-jō 犬山城 6 A2
Jo-an Teahouse 茶室如安 7 A2
Kisogawa Kankō .... (see 2)
Marionette (Karakuri) Exhibition Room からくり展示館 8 A2
Sankō-Inari Jinja 三光稲荷神社 9 A2
Uraku-en 有楽園 10 A2

SLEEPING
Rinkō-kan 臨江館 11 B1

EATING
Fū ふう 12 A2
Narita なり多 13 B3

yūen Station, one stop north or about 15 minutes on foot. On the web, visit www.city.inuyama.aichi.jp/english/index.html.

Sights & Activities

INUYAMA-JŌ 犬山城

A National Treasure, Japan's oldest standing **castle** (☎ 61-1711; adult/child ¥500/100; 🕑 9am-5pm) is said to have originated with a fort in 1440; the current *donjon* (main keep) dates from 1537 and has withstood war, earthquake and restoration to remain an excellent example of Momoyama-period architecture. Stone walls reach 5m high, and inside are narrow, steep staircases and military displays. There's a fine view of mountains and plains from the top storey.

Just south are the shrines **Haritsuna Jinja** and **Sankō-Inari Jinja**, the latter with interesting statues of *komainu* (protective dogs).

MARIONETTE (KARAKURI) EXHIBITION ROOM & INUYAMA CASTLE HISTORICAL MUSEUM
からくり展示館・犬山市文化資料館

Included in your admission ticket to Inuyama-jō are the following two collections.

One block south of Haritsuna Jinja and Sankō-Inari Jinja, the **Marionette (Karakuri) Exhibition Room** (☎ 61-3932; admission purchased separately ¥100; 🕑 9am-5pm) contains a small display of Edo- and Meiji-era puppets. On Saturday and Sunday you can see the wooden characters in action (at 10.30am and 2pm).

To see the puppets as they were meant to be used, visit during **Inuyama Matsuri** (Inuyama Festival, on the first Saturday and Sunday in April), designated an Intangible Cultural Asset by the Japanese government. Dating back to 1635, the festival features a parade of 13 three-tiered floats decked out with lanterns and *karakuri*, which perform to music.

Nearby, the **Inuyama Castle Historical Museum** (☎ 65-1728; admission purchased separately ¥100; 🕑 9am-5pm) has two of the festival floats on display. Four more of the current floats are on exhibit at **Dondenkan** (☎ 61-1800; adult/child ¥200/100; 🕑 9am-5pm) a few blocks south, accessed via a street of wood-built buildings.

URAKU-EN & JO-AN TEAHOUSE
有楽園・茶室如安

The garden **Uraku-en** (☎ 61-4608; admission ¥1000; 🕑 9am-5pm Mar-Nov, to 4pm Dec-Feb) is 300m east of Inuyama-jō, in a corner of the grounds of the Meitetsu Inuyama Hotel. One of the finest tea houses in Japan and a National Treasure, Jo-an was built in 1618 in Kyoto by Oda Urakusai, a younger brother of Oda Nobunaga, and was relocated here in 1972.

TIE ME UP, TIE ME DOWN

The suburb of Arimatsu (有松), southeast of central Nagoya, has been famous for the art of *shibori* (tie-dyeing) for centuries. No 1960s flower-power here, though; one kimono requires four to six months of painstaking work. Artisans tie cotton threads to create over 100 precise patterns (the tiny boxes of the *kanoko* – fawn spot – pattern are the most recognisable). **Arimatsu-Narumi Shibori Kaikan** (有松鳴海絞会館; Tie-Dyeing Museum; ☎ 621-0111; www.shibori-kaikan.com/kaikan-e.html; admission free, film & exhibitions adult/child ¥300/100; 🕑 9.30am-5pm Thu-Tue) shows and sells *shibori* works; a video in English explains the process and artisans are on hand to demonstrate.

Arimatsu's main street boasts a smattering of Edo-period wooden structures, including merchant homes, from when it was a stop along the Tōkaidō (see the boxed text, p199). From Meitetsu Nagoya Station, the trip to Arimatsu takes 20 minutes (¥340).

Urakusai was a renowned tea master who founded his own tea-ceremony school. He was also a closet Christian whose adopted name (the Portuguese 'João') was bestowed on the tea house. Visitors may peek into the tea house but are not allowed inside except for four days in spring (March to May) and autumn. You can enjoy tea on the grounds for ¥500.

CORMORANT FISHING 鵜飼い

Ukai takes place close to Inuyama-yūen Station, by Twin Bridge Inuyama-bashi. Book your ticket at the tourist information office or **Kisogawa Kankō** (☎ 61-0057; adult/child Jul & Aug from ¥2800/1400, May-Jun & Sep-Oct from ¥2500/1250), near the cormorant-fishing pier.

Boats depart nightly at 6pm from May to August, with the show starting around 7.45pm. In September and October, boats depart at 5.30pm, with things kicking off at 7.15pm.

Festivals & Events

In addition to **Inuyama Matsuri** (see p263), the city also hosts the summer **Nihon Rhine Festival**, every 10 August on the banks of the river, culminating in fireworks.

Sleeping & Eating

Inuyama International Youth Hostel (犬山国際ユースホステル; ☎ 61-1111; fax 61-2770; www.inuyama-iyh.com; s/d/tr ¥3300/6200/8700; 💻) This modern and well-kept hostel offers large, comfortable, Japanese- and Western-style rooms, friendly staff and a stone common bath (BYOT). Reservations are recommended. Meals (breakfast/dinner ¥840/1580, choice of Japanese or Western) are available with advance notice – and recommended, as there are no restaurants nearby. It's 25 minutes' walk northeast of Inuyama-yūen Station – access it from along the river.

Rinkō-kan (☎ 61-0977; fax 61-2505; rinkokan@triton.ocn.ne.jp; r per person with/without 2 meals from ¥12,750/6450; 💻) Overlooking the river, this cheery, 20-room hot-spring ryokan makes the most of its 1960s building with handsome Japanese-style accommodation with in-room bath, stone common baths including *rotemburo*, and jacuzzi. Dinner is served in your room.

Fū (☎ 61-6515; a-fuusan@md.ccnw.ne.jp; lunch ¥600; 🕑 8am-6pm Thu-Tue) This friendly, low-key, family-run coffee shop makes a different simple lunch daily and serves it until supplies run out. Phone (in Japanese) or email to enquire or reserve, and do not flake (bad karma). Or just enjoy coffee and cake. There's occasional live music.

Narita (☎ 65-2447; 5-course meal from ¥2940; 🕑 lunch & dinner) This is a chichi French restaurant in a traditional Japanese building with attractive garden, specialising in five-course set meals. It's a block west of the Inuyama Miyako Hotel.

Getting There & Away

Inuyama is connected with Nagoya (¥540, 30 minutes) and Meitetsu-Gifu Station in Gifu city (¥440, 35 minutes) via the Meitetsu Inuyama line. JR travellers can connect via Gifu to Unuma (¥320, 20 minutes) and walk across the Kiso-gawa to Inuyama.

AROUND INUYAMA 犬山近辺

Museum Meiji-mura 明治村

Few Meiji-period buildings have survived war, earthquake or rabid development, but this open-air **museum** (☎ 0568-67-0314; www.meijimura.com; 1 Uchiyama; adult/elementary & junior-high-school student/student/senior ¥1600/600/1000/1200; 🕑 9.30am-5pm

CENTRAL HONSHŪ

Mar-Oct, to 4pm Nov-Feb, closed Mon Dec-Feb) has brought together over 60 of them from all over Japan to a lakeside 'village'. On exhibit are one-time public offices, private homes, banks and a sake brewery, as well as some forms of transport. Among them are the entryway designed by Frank Lloyd Wright for Tokyo's Imperial Hotel, the home of novelist Sōseki Natsume (who wrote *I am a Cat* and *Botchan*) and early Kyoto trams. Note the coming-together of Western and Japanese architectural styles, which is indicative of this era. Allow at least half a day to enjoy it at an easy pace.

A bus to Meiji-mura (¥410, 20 minutes) departs every 30 minutes from Inuyama Station's east exit.

Ōgata-jinja 大縣神社

This 2000-year-old **shrine** (☎ 0568-67-1017) is dedicated to the female Shintō deity Izanami and draws women devotees seeking marriage or fertility. The precincts of the shrine contain rocks and other items resembling female genitals.

The popular **Hime-no-Miya Grand Festival** takes place here on the Sunday before 15 March (or on 15 March if it's a Sunday). Locals pray for good harvests and prosperity by parading through the streets bearing a *mikoshi* (portable shrine) with replicas of female genitals.

Ōgata-jinja is a 25-minute walk southeast of Gakuden Station on the Meitetsu Komaki line (¥220 from Inuyama, seven minutes).

Tagata-jinja 田県神社

Izanagi, the male counterpart of Izanami, is commemorated at this **shrine** (☎ 0568-76-2906). The main hall has a side building containing images of phalluses, left as offerings by grateful worshippers.

The **Tagata Hōnen Sai Festival** takes place on 15 March at Tagata-jinja, when the highly photogenic, 2m-long, 60kg 'sacred object' is paraded, amid much mirth, around the neighbourhood. Arrive well before the procession starts at 2pm.

Tagata-jinja is five minutes' walk west of Tagata-jinja-mae Station on the Meitetsu Komaki line (¥290 from Inuyama, nine minutes).

Yaotsu 八百津

☎ 0574 / pop 13,500

This Kiso-gawa town has become a pilgrimage site as the birthplace of Sugihara Chiune (1900–86), Japan's consul in Lithuania during early WWII. Sugihara saved some 6000 Jews from the Nazis by issuing transit visas against Japanese government orders; the 'Sugihara survivors' escaped to Kōbe and Japanese-controlled Shanghai and, later, to other countries. The story was commemorated in the 1997 Academy Award–winning film *Visas and Virtue*.

On Yaotsu's **Jindō-no-oka** (Hill of Humanity; 人道の丘) is a **museum** (adult/child ¥300/100; 🕒 9.30am-5pm Tue-Sun) with photos and thought-provoking exhibits about this inspiring story. For more information, visit www.town.yaotsu.gifu.jp or contact the **city office** (☎ 43-2111, ext 2253), which has an English speaker available.

Yaotsu is easiest reached by car, but from Inuyama you can take the Meitetsu Hiromi line to Akechi (¥440, 30 minutes) via Shin-Kani, then transfer to the Yao bus to Yaotsu (¥400, 25 minutes); it's a short bus (¥300) or taxi ride to the museum.

GIFU 岐阜

☎ 058 / pop 413,000

Historically, Gifu has a strong association with Oda Nobunaga (p44), *daimyō* (domain lord) of the castle and bestower of the city's name in 1567. It was later visited by famed haiku poet Matsuō Bashō, who witnessed *ukai* here in 1688; Charlie Chaplin did the same in his day.

Contemporary Gifu shows little evidence of those historic times, due to a colossal earthquake in 1891 and a thorough drubbing in WWII. Still, the Nagara-gawa remains a popular destination for *ukai,* there's a reconstruction of the castle Gifu-jō atop the riverside mountain, Kinka-zan (329m), and a spiffed-up business district. Gifu is also known for handicrafts.

Orientation & Information

JR Gifu Station and Meitetsu-Gifu Station are a few minutes' walk apart in the southern city centre. Most of the sights are about 4km north, near Nagara-gawa and Kinka-zan, easily reachable by bus (see p266).

The **tourist information office** (☎ 262-4415; 🕒 9am-7pm Mar-Dec, to 6pm Jan-Feb) on the 2nd floor of JR Gifu Station provides useful English-language city maps and can make same-day hotel reservations. Some English is spoken.

Sights & Activities

CORMORANT FISHING 鵜飼い

During Gifu's cormorant fishing season (11 May to 15 October), boats depart nightly (except after flooding or on the night of a full moon) from the bridge, Nagara-bashi, or you can view the action from a distance by walking along the river east of the bridge.

Bookings are strongly advised. Tickets are sold at hotels or, if any tickets remain after 6pm, at the **booking office** (☎ 262-0104 for advance reservations; adult/child ¥3300/2900; ⏲ departures 6.15pm, 6.45pm & 7.15pm) just below Nagara-bashi. Food and drink are not provided on the boats; you can bring food aboard the first departure of the evening but not on later departures. On Monday to Friday, fares for the two later departures are ¥3000/2600 per adult/child. Take the bus to the Nagara-bashi stop.

GIFU-KŌEN 岐阜公園

At the foot of Kinka-zan, this is one of the loveliest city parks in Japan, with plenty of water and trees set into the hillside. Inside are the **Gifu City History Museum** (岐阜市歴史博物館; ☎ 265-0010; 2-18-1 Ōmiya-chō; adult/child ¥300/150; ⏲ 9am-5pm Tue-Sun), the site of Oda Nobunaga's home, and **Kinka-zan Ropeway** (金華山ロープウエー; ☎ 262-6784; 257 Senjōjiki-shita; return adult/child ¥1050/520; ⏲ 9am-5pm mid-Oct–mid-Mar, to 10.30pm late Jul-Aug, to 6pm mid-Mar–late Jul & Sep–mid-Oct), a cable car to the summit. From here you can check out **Gifu-jō** (岐阜城; ☎ 263-4853; 18 Kinka-zan, Tenshukaku; adult/child ¥200/100; ⏲ 9.30am-30min before ropeway closure), a small but scenic modern reconstruction of the original castle. Those who'd rather huff it can hike to the castle (one hour).

Take the bus to the Gifu-kōen Rekishi Hakubutsukan-mae stop.

SHŌHŌ-JI 正法寺

The main attraction of this orange-and-white **temple** (☎ 264-2760; 8 Daibutsu-chō; admission ¥150; ⏲ 9am-5pm) is the papier-mâché *daibutsu* (Great Buddha; 1832), which is nearly 14m tall and is said to have been fashioned over 38 years using about a tonne of paper Sutras. The temple is a short walk southwest of Gifu-kōen. Get off at the Daibutsu-mae bus stop (from Gifu-kōen only).

Sleeping & Eating

Comfort Hotel Gifu (コンフォートホテル岐阜; ☎ 267-1311; fax 267-1312; s/tw with breakfast ¥6090/11,550; ⊠ 💻 📶) Across from JR Gifu Station, this unpretentious, 219-room business hotel offers LCD TVs with CNN, wireless internet access from rooms and a coin laundry. Breakfast is a simple but plentiful Japanese/continental buffet.

Daiwa Roynet Hotel Gifu (ダイワロイネットホテル岐阜; ☎ 212-0055; fax 212-0056; s/d from ¥7500/15,000; ⊠ 💻) A posher choice, with a minimalist design, nice linens, and rooms outfitted with LAN cables for your computer. It's steps from Meitetsu-Gifu Station.

The narrow streets between Nagarabashi-dōri and Kinka-zan-dōri (between the train stations) provide happy hunting for cafes, restaurants and *izakaya*. For a nightcap, join expats and locals at the *wabi-sabi*-cool **Bier Hall** (ビアホール; ☎ 266-8868; ⏲ 5.30pm-1am, closed 1st & 3rd Sun of month), which specialises in Guinness, pizzas, fried snacks and Thai curry. It's a few doors behind the clothing shop 'Bad'.

Shopping

Gifu's craft tradition includes *wagasa* (oiled paper parasols/umbrellas) and *chōchin* (paper lanterns) elegantly painted with landscapes etc, though the number of artisans is a mere fraction of their golden age (600 umbrella-makers then compared to a handful now). Souvenir shops sell mass-produced versions, or the tourist information office has a map of high-quality makers and/or sellers. Expect to pay ¥10,000-plus for a quality *wagasa* or *chōchin*. Shops keep irregular hours, so it's worth phoning ahead to make sure they're open.

Sakaida Eikichi Honten (坂井田永吉本店; ☎ 271-6958) makes and sells *wagasa*. It's a 10-minute walk from JR Gifu Station. Turn left from the south exit, and turn right at the second stoplight. Sakaida is at the next corner.

For Gifu *chōchin*, try **Ozeki Chōchin** (小関提灯; ☎ 263-0111). From Ken-Sōgōchōsha-mae bus stop, walk east. It's by the temple Higashi Betsuin.

Getting There & Around

From Nagoya, take the JR Tōkaidō line (*tokkyū*, ¥1180, 20 minutes; *futsū*, ¥450, 30 minutes) to Gifu or the Meitetsu line to Meitetsu-Gifu (¥540, 35 minutes). Meitetsu trains also serve Inuyama (¥440, 35 minutes).

Buses to sights (¥200) depart from stops 11 and 12 of the bus terminal by JR Gifu Station's Nagara exit, stopping at Meitetsu-Gifu en route. However, ask before boarding as not all buses make all stops.

GUJŌ-HACHIMAN 郡上八幡

☎ 0575 / pop 16,000

Nestled in the mountains at the confluence of several rivers, Gujō-Hachiman is a small, pleasant town famed for its **Gujō Odori**, Japan's third-largest folk dance festival, and as the place where all of those plastic food models you see in restaurant windows come from.

The **tourist office** (観光協会; ☎ 67-0002; 8.30am-5pm) is by Shin-bashi in the centre of town, about five minutes' walk from the Jōka-machi Plaza bus terminal.

The festival first: following a tradition dating to the 1590s, townsfolk engage in frenzied dancing on 32 nights between mid-July and early September. Visitor participation is encouraged, especially during *tetsuya odori*, the four main days of the festival (13 to 16 August), when the dancing goes all night.

At other times of the year the town's sparkling rivers, narrow lanes and stone bridges make for a relaxing stopover.

Those incredibly realistic food models are one of life's great mysteries, and here's your chance to suss them out. In an old *machiya* (merchant house), **Shokuhin Sample Kōbō Sōsakukan** (食品サンプル工房創作館; ☎ 67-1870; admission free; 9am-5pm daily late Jul-Aug, closed Thu rest of year) lets you view the goodies and try creating them yourself (reservation required). Tempura (¥1000 for three pieces) and lettuce (free) make memorable souvenirs. It's about five minutes' walk from Jōka-machi Plaza.

Gujō-Hachiman's other attractions include the tiny hilltop castle **Gujō Hachiman-jō** (郡上八幡城; ☎ 65-5839; adult/child ¥300/150; 8am-6pm Jun-Aug, 9am-5pm Sep-Nov & Mar-May, 9am-4.30pm Dec-Feb), which had been a humble fortress dating back to about 1600; the current, grander building dates from only 1933. It contains weapons, armour and the like, and offers fine views. From the bus terminal it's about 20 minutes' walk.

The town is also known for its waterways. A famous spring, **Sōgi-sui**, near the centre of town, is something of a pilgrimage site, named for a Momoyama-era poet. People who rank such things place Sōgi-sui at the top of the list for clarity.

Gujō Tōsen-ji Youth Hostel (郡上洞泉寺ユースホステル; ☎ 67-0290; fax 67-0549; dm ¥3300; closed mid-Aug; ☒) is an attractively refurnished hostel with private rooms pleasantly situated on the grounds of a temple. There is no bath on the premises, but there's a *sentō* (public bath) nearby. Breakfast is ¥500.

Bizenya Ryokan (備前屋旅館; ☎ 65-2068; fax 67-0007; r per person with 2 meals from ¥11,550; ☒) boasts large rooms, some with private facilities, around a handsome garden. This 30-bed ryokan provides a relaxing, quietly upscale experience. It's located between the bus terminal and tourist office.

The most convenient access to Gujō-Hachiman is via bus from Gifu (¥1560, one hour, hourly). The private Nagaragawa Tetsudō line serves Gujō-Hachiman from Mino-Ōta (¥1320, 80 minutes, hourly), with connections via the JR Takayama line to Nagoya (¥1110, one hour) and Takayama (*tokkyū*, ¥4180, 1¾ hours; *futsū*, ¥1890, three hours). Buses also journey from Nagoya (¥3500, three hours). Central Gujō-Hachiman is easily walkable, or bicycles are available for rent (¥300/1500 per hour/day).

HIDA DISTRICT 飛騨地域

The centrepiece of this ancient, mountainous region is the handsome town of Takayama, known for merchant houses, temples and a strong craft tradition. Hida's signature architectural style is the thatch-roofed *gasshō-zukuri* (see the boxed text, p272), while its culinary fame rests in Hida-*gyū* (local beef), *hoba-miso* (sweet miso paste grilled at the table on a magnolia leaf) and *soba*.

TAKAYAMA 高山

☎ 0577 / pop 95,300

With its old inns, shops and sake breweries, Takayama is a rarity: a 21st-century city (admittedly a small one) that's also retained its traditional charm. Vibrant morning markets, hillside shrines and a laid-back populace add to the town's allure, and it should be a high priority on any visit to Central Honshū. Give yourself at least two days to enjoy the place; it's easily tackled on foot or bicycle.

Takayama was established in the late 16th century as the castle town of the Kanamori clan, but in 1692 it was placed under direct control of the *bakufu* (shōgunate) in Edo. The present layout dates from the Kanamori period, and its sights include more than a dozen museums, galleries and exhibitions

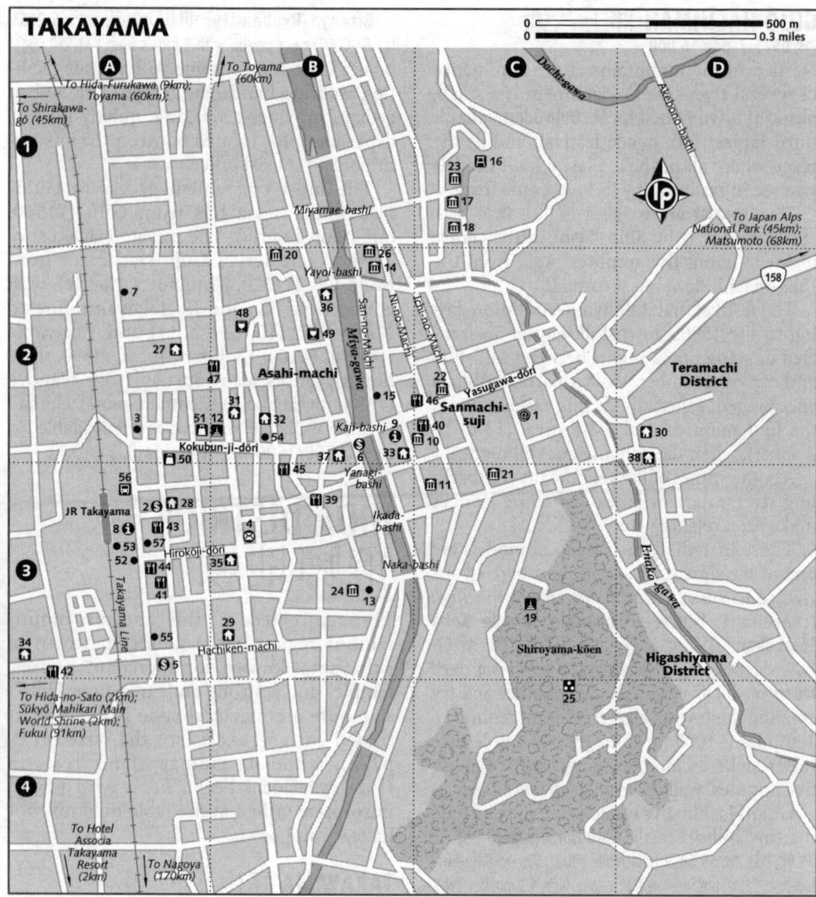

that cover lacquer and lion masks, folk craft and architecture.

Takayama remains the region's administrative and transport hub, and it makes a good base for trips around Hida and Japan Alps National Park (p280).

Orientation

All of the main sights except Hida-no-Sato (Hida Folk Village) are in the centre of town, within walking distance of the station. Northeast of the station, Kokubun-ji-dōri, the main street, heads east, across the Miya-gawa (about 10 minutes' walk), where it becomes Yasugawa-dōri. South of Yasugawa-dōri is the historic, picturesque Sanmachi-suji (Sanmachi district) of immaculately preserved old homes. On signage, look for 古い町並み *(furui machinami)* or 'Old Private Homes' in English.

Hida-no-Sato is a 10-minute bus ride west of the station.

Information

Takayama's main **tourist information office** (☎ 32-5328; 🕑 8.30am-5pm Nov-Mar, to 6.30pm Apr-Oct), directly in front of JR Takayama Station, has knowledgeable English-speaking staff, as well as English-language maps and information on sights (the *Hida Takayama* pamphlet is a good start), accommodation, special local events and regional transit. A **tourist information office branch** (☎ 32-2177; Kami-san-no-machi; 🕑 10am-4pm) is in the centre of Sanmachi-suji and is use-

INFORMATION
City Library 図書館 ... 1 C2
International Affairs Office 国際情報センター ... (see 7)
Jūroku Bank 十六銀行 ... 2 A3
Kinki Nippon Tourist ... 3 A2
Main Post Office 高山郵便局 ... 4 B3
Ōgaki Kyōritsu Bank ATM 大垣共立銀行 ... 5 A3
Ōgaki Kyōritsu Bank ATM 大垣共立銀行 ... 6 B2
Takayama Municipal Office 高山市役所 ... 7 A2
Tourist Information Office 観光案内所 ... 8 A3
Tourist Information Office Branch 観光案内所 ... 9 B2

SIGHTS & ACTIVITIES
Fujii Folkcraft Art Gallery 藤井美術民芸館 ... 10 C2
Hida Folk Archaeological Museum 飛騨民族考古館 ... 11 C3
Hida Kokubun-ji 飛騨国分寺 ... 12 B2
Jinya-mae Morning Market 陣屋前朝市 ... 13 B3
Kusakabe Mingeikan 日下部民芸館 ... 14 B2
Miya-gawa Morning Market 宮川朝市 ... 15 B2
Sakurakaya Hachiman-gū 桜山八幡宮 ... 16 C1
Sakurayama Nikkō-kan 日光館 ... 17 C1
Shishi Kaikan (Lion Mask Exhibition Hall) 獅子会館 ... 18 C1
Shōren-ji 照蓮寺 ... 19 C3
Shunkei Kaikan (Lacquerware Exhibition Hall) 春慶会館 ... 20 B2
Takayama Museum of Local History 高山市郷土館 ... 21 C3
Takayama Shōwa-kan 高山昭和館 ... 22 C2
Takayama Yatai Kaikan (Festival Floats Exhibition Hall) 高山屋台会館 ... 23 C1
Takayama-jinya 高山陣屋 ... 24 B3
Takayama-jō Ruins 高山城跡 ... 25 C4
Yoshijima-ke 吉島家住宅 ... 26 B2

SLEEPING
Asunaro Ryokan あすなろ ... 27 A2
Best Western Hotel ベストウェスタンホテル ... 28 A3
Hida Takayama Temple Inn Zenkō-ji 飛騨高山善光寺宿坊 ... 29 B3
Hida Takayama Tenshō-ji Youth Hostel 飛騨高山天照寺ユースホステル ... 30 D2
Minshuku Kuwataniya 民宿桑谷屋 ... 31 B2
Rickshaw Inn 力車イン ... 32 B2
Ryokan Gōdo 旅館河渡 ... 33 B2
Sōsuke 惣助 ... 34 A3
Spa Hotel Alpina スパホテルアルピナ ... 35 B3
Sumiyoshi Ryokan 寿美吉旅館 ... 36 B2
Tanabe Ryokan 田辺旅館 ... 37 B2
Yamakyū 山久 ... 38 D2

EATING
Chapala チャパラ ... 39 B3
Ebisu-honten 恵比寿本店 ... 40 C2
Holy Grail ホリーグレール ... 41 A3
Jingoro Rāmen 甚五郎ラーメン ... 42 A3
Myōgaya 若荷舎 ... 43 A3
Origin おりぎん ... 44 A3
Suzuya 寿々や ... 45 B3
Takumi-ya 匠家 ... 46 C2
Yamatake-Shōten 山武商店 ... 47 B2

DRINKING
Red Hill Pub レッドヒルパブ ... 48 B2
Tonio トニオ ... 49 B2

SHOPPING
Mori no Kotoba 森のことば ... 50 A2
Suzuki Chōkoku 鈴木彫刻 ... 51 A2

TRANSPORT
Daily Yamazaki デイリーヤマザキ ... 52 A3
Eki Rent-a-Car System 駅レンタカー ... 53 A3
Hara Cycle ハラサイクル ... 54 B2
Mazda Rent-a-Car マツダレンタカー ... 55 A3
Takayama Bus Station 高山バスターミナル ... 56 A3
Toyota Rent-a-Car トヨタレンタカー ... 57 A3

ful for quick enquiries. On the web, head to www.hidatakayama.or.jp.

To arrange a home visit, home stay or volunteer interpreter for non-Japanese languages (including sign language), contact the city's **International Affairs Office** (☎ 32-3333, ext 2407; 2-18 Hanaoka), located inside the Takayama Municipal Office building, one month in advance.

Internet access is available at the **city library** (☎ 32-3096; 9.30am-9.30pm), east of Sanmachi-suji, and **Takayama Municipal Office** (2-18 Hanaoka; 9am-5pm Mon-Fri), which has two computers.

Jūroku Bank can change cash or travellers cheques. For ATM users, the **main post office** (Hirokōji-dōri) is located a few blocks east of the station, and Ōgaki Kyōritsu Bank, with foreign-card ATMs, is southeast of the station and also near the Miya-gawa Morning Market.

For onward bus or train reservations within Japan, try **Kinki Nippon Tourist** (☎ 32-6901; 1-17 Hanaoka-machi).

Sights & Activities

SANMACHI-SUJI 三町筋

The centre of the old town, this district of three main streets (Ichi-no-Machi, Ni-no-Machi and San-no-Machi) is lined with traditional shops, restaurants and museums. Sake breweries are easily recognised by the spheres of cedar fronds: some open to the public in January and early February (the schedule is available at tourist offices); most of the year they just sell their wares. For beautiful night-time shots, bring a tripod and set your camera's exposure to long.

Fujii Folkcraft Art Gallery (Fujii Bijutsu Minzoku-kan; ☎ 35-3778; 69 San-no-Machi; adult/child ¥700/350; 9am-5pm, often closed Tue-Fri early Dec-early Mar) is a private collection in an old merchant's house, with folk craft and ceramics, particularly from the Muromachi and Edo periods. **Hida Folk Archaeological Museum** (Hida Minzoku Kōko-kan; ☎ 32-1980; 82 San-no-Machi; adult/child/high- & junior-high-school student ¥500/200/300; 8.30am-5pm Mar-Nov, 9am-4.30pm Dec-Feb) is a former samurai house boasting interesting secret passageways and an old well in the courtyard.

Takayama Museum of Local History (☎ 32-1205; 75 Ichi-no-Machi; adult/child ¥300/150; ⌚ 8.30am-5pm Mar-Nov, 9am-4.30pm Tue-Sun Dec-Feb) is devoted to the crafts and traditions of the region, with images carved by Enkū, a woodcarving priest who wandered the region in the 17th century. There are also several small but nicely maintained gardens.

TAKAYAMA-JINYA 高山陣屋

These sprawling grounds south of the Sanmachi district house the only remaining prefectural office building of the Tokugawa shōgunate. **Takayama-jinya** (Historical Government House; ☎ 32-0643; 1-5 Hachiken-machi; adult/child ¥420/free; ⌚ 8.45am-5pm Mar-Oct, to 4.30pm Nov-Feb) was originally built in 1615 as the administrative centre for the Kanamori clan but was later taken over by the *bakufu*. The main gate was once reserved for high officials. The present main building dates back to 1816 and it was used as the local government office until 1969.

As well as government offices, a rice granary and a garden, there's a torture chamber with explanatory detail. Free guided tours in English are available (reservations advised). Takayama-jinya is a 15-minute walk east of the train station.

MERCHANT HOUSES 吉島家・日下部民芸館

North of Sanmachi are two excellent examples of Edo-period merchants' homes, with the living quarters in one section and the commercial/warehouse areas in another. Design buffs shouldn't miss **Yoshijima-ke** (Yoshijima house; ☎ 32-0038; 1-51 Ōshinmachi; adult/child ¥500/300; ⌚ 9am-5pm Mar-Nov, to 4.30pm Wed-Sun Dec-Feb), which is well covered in architectural publications. Its lack of ornamentation allows you to focus on the spare lines, soaring roof and skylight. Admission includes a cup of delicious shiitake tea, which you can also purchase for ¥600 per can.

Down the block, **Kusakabe Mingeikan** (Kusakabe Folk Art Museum; ☎ 32-0072; 1-52 Ōshinmachi; adult/child ¥500/300; ⌚ 9am-4.30pm Mar-Nov, to 4pm Wed-Mon Dec-Feb), built during the 1890s, showcases the striking craftsmanship of traditional Takayama carpenters. Inside is a collection of folk art.

TAKAYAMA YATAI KAIKAN 高山屋台会館

A rotating selection of four of the 23 multi-tiered *yatai* (floats) used in the Takayama Matsuri can be seen at **Takayama Yatai Kaikan** (Festival Floats Exhibition Hall; ☎ 32-5100; 178 Sakura-machi; adult/child/high-school student ¥820/410/510; ⌚ 8.30am-5pm Mar-Nov, 9am-4.30pm Dec-Feb). These spectacular creations, some dating from the 17th century, are prized for their flamboyant carvings, metalwork and lacquerwork. A famous feature of some floats is *karakuri*, mechanical puppets that perform amazing tricks and acrobatics courtesy of eight accomplished puppeteers using 36 strings. A video gives a sense of the festival. The stately, hillside **Sakurayama Jinja** is just around the back.

The Yatai Kaikan is on the grounds of the stately hillside shrine **Sakurayama Hachiman-gū**; the shrine's main buildings are behind the Yatai Kaikan. Dedicated to the protection of Takayama, the shrine also oversees the festival.

Your ticket also admits you to the **Sakurayama Nikkō-kan** diagonally across from the shrine, with intricate models of the famous shrines at Nikkō (p197). Lighting takes you from dawn to dusk and back again, allowing you to witness these sites in different kinds of light.

You might pass some unusual slender garages around town with three-storey doors; these house the *yatai* that are not in the museum.

SHISHI KAIKAN 獅子会館

Just south of Sakurayama Nikkō-kan is the **Shishi Kaikan** (Lion Mask Exhibition Hall; ☎ 32-0881; 53-1 Sakura-machi; adult/child ¥600/400; ⌚ 8.30am-5.30pm Apr-Nov, 9am-5pm Dec-Mar). It displays over 800 lion masks and musical instruments connected with the lion dances performed at festivals in central and northern Japan, as well as art pieces such as scrolls and folding screens. The real reason to visit, though, is the twice-hourly demonstrations of *karakuri*. You can view these marvellous puppets in action and go backstage to see how it's done.

SHUNKEI KAIKAN 飛騨高山春慶会館

Shunkei lacquerware was introduced from Kyoto several centuries ago but has become Takayama's signature style, used to produce boxes, trays and flower vases. West of Takayama Yatai Kaikan and across the river, **Shunkei Kaikan** (Lacquerware Exhibition Hall; ☎ 32-3373; 1-88 Kando-chō; adult/child ¥300/200; ⌚ 8am-5.30pm Apr-Oct, 9am-5pm Nov-Mar) has more than 1000 pieces, including some dating from the 17th century. Unlike many other Japanese lacquer styles, *shunkei* is designed to show off the wood grain. A display shows production techniques, and the shop has occasional specials.

HIDA KOKUBUN-JI 飛騨国分寺

Takayama's oldest temple, **Hida Kokubun-ji** (☎ 32-1395; 1-83 Sōwa-chō; treasure hall adult/child ¥300/250; 🕒 9am-4pm) was originally built in the 8th century and subsequently ravaged by fire; the oldest of the present buildings dates from the 16th century. The temple's treasure hall houses some Important Cultural Properties, and the courtyard boasts a three-storey pagoda and an impressively gnarled gingko tree, which is in remarkably good shape considering it's believed to be 1200 years old.

TAKAYAMA SHŌWA-KAN 高山昭和館

Nostalgia for the mid-20th century is all the rage in Japan these days, and **Takayama Shōwa-kan** (exhibition hall; ☎ 33-7836; 6 Shimo-ichi-no-machi; adult/child ¥500/300; 🕒 9am-6pm Apr-Oct, to 5pm Nov-Mar) feels like a nostalgia bonanza from the era of Shōwa, the Japanese name for the previous emperor, known elsewhere as Hirohito. Though Shōwa ruled from 1926 to 1989, the museum concentrates on the period between 1955 and 1965, a time of great optimism between Japan's postwar malaise and pre-Titan boom. Lose yourself among the vehicles and movie posters, recreated storefronts, beauty salon and classroom.

MORNING MARKETS 朝市

Asa-ichi (morning markets) take place every morning from 7am to noon, starting an hour earlier from April to October. The **Jinya-mae Morning Market** is in front of Takayama-jinya; the **Miya-gawa Morning Market** is larger, situated along the east bank of the Miya-gawa, between Kaji-bashi and Yayoi-bashi. The markets provide a pleasant way to start the day, with a stroll past rugged farm-folk at their vegetable stands and stalls selling crafts of wood or fabric, pickles, souvenirs and that all-important steaming cuppa joe (or beer or sake for the hearty).

TERAMACHI & SHIROYAMA-KŌEN 寺町・城山公園

The hilly districts in the east of town are linked by a walking trail, which is particularly enjoyable in the early morning or late afternoon. Teramachi has over a dozen temples (one houses a youth hostel) and shrines that you can wander around before taking in the greenery of Shiroyama-kōen. Various trails lead through the park and up the mountainside to the ruins of the castle, **Takayama-jō**. As you descend, take a look at **Shōren-ji**, a temple that was transferred to this site from the Shōkawa Valley when a dam was built there in 1960.

The walk takes a leisurely two hours, plus a 10-minute walk back to the centre of town. Get a map and temple descriptions at the tourist information office.

HIDA-NO-SATO 飛騨の里

The large, open-air **Hida-no-Sato** (Hida Folk Village; ☎ 34-4711; 1-590 Okamoto-chō; adult/child ¥700/200; 🕒 8.30am-5pm) is highly recommended for its dozens of traditional houses, dismantled at their original sites throughout the region and rebuilt here. Allow at least three hours. During clear weather, there are good views across the town to the peaks of the Japan Alps.

Hida-no-Sato is in two sections. The western section features 12 old houses and a complex of traditional buildings (see the boxed text, p272). Displays are well presented and offer an excellent chance to see what rural life was like in previous centuries.

The eastern section of the village is centred on Omoide Taikenkan, where you can try your hand at making things such as candles and *sembei* (rice crackers). Other buildings include the Go-kura Storehouse (used for storage of rice as payment of taxes) and the Museum of Mountain Life.

Hida-no-Sato is a 30-minute walk west from Takayama Station, but the route is not enjoyable. Either hire a bicycle, or catch a bus from Takayama bus station (¥200, 10 minutes). The 'Hida-no-Sato setto ken' ticket combines return fare and admission to the park for ¥900. Be sure to check return times for the bus.

SŪKYŌ MAHIKARI MAIN WORLD SHRINE 崇教真光世界総本山

Gleaming above Takayama's western skyline is the golden roof of the **Main World Shrine** (☎ 34-7008; admission free; 🕒 8.30am-4.30pm, except during religious observances) of Sūkyō Mahikari, a new religion whose teachings are said to include healing via training courses and amulets that transmit divine light rays. Guided tours are available (call in advance for an English-speaking guide).

GASSHŌ-ZUKURI ARCHITECTURE

Winter in the Hida region can be fierce, and inhabitants faced snow and cold long before the advent of propane heaters and 4WD vehicles. One of the most visible symbols of that adaptability is *gasshō-zukuri* architecture, seen in the steeply slanted straw-roofed homes that still dot the landscape around the region.

The sharply angled roofs were designed to prevent heavy snow accumulation, a serious concern in a region where nearly all mountain roads close from December to April. The name *gasshō* comes from the Japanese word for praying, because the shape of the roofs was thought to resemble two hands clasped in prayer. *Gasshō* buildings often featured pillars crafted from stout cedars to lend extra support. The attic areas were ideal for silk cultivation.

Larger *gasshō-zukuri* buildings were inhabited by wealthy families, with up to 30 people under one roof. Peasant families lived in huts of the size that are now used as tool sheds.

Development has made the *gasshō-zukuri* building an endangered species. Most examples have been gathered and preserved in folk villages, including Hida-no-Sato in Takayama (p271) and in Shirakawa-gō (p277) and Gokayama (p278). So, two homes that are now neighbours may once have been separated by several days of travel on foot or sled. Local authorities have worked hard to recreate their natural surroundings, making it possible to imagine a bygone life in the Hida hills.

Festivals & Events

One of Japan's greatest festivals, the **Takayama Matsuri**, is in two parts. On 14 and 15 April is the **Sannō Matsuri**; a dozen *yatai*, decorated with carvings, dolls, colourful curtains and blinds, are paraded through the town. In the evening the floats are decked out with lanterns and the procession is accompanied by sacred music. **Hachiman Matsuri**, on 9 and 10 October, is a slightly smaller version (see p270).

From January to early February several of the sake breweries in Sanmachi-suji (p269), many dating back to the Edo period, arrange tours and tastings.

Sleeping

One of Takayama's pleasures is its variety of high-quality accommodation, both Japanese and Western, for all budgets. If visiting during festival times, book accommodation months in advance and expect to pay a 20% premium, or just commute in. The tourist information office can assist with lodging information.

BUDGET

Hida Takayama Temple Inn Zenkō-ji (☎ 32-8470; www.geocities.jp/zenkojitakayama; 4-3 Tenman-chō; dm/r per person ¥2500/3000) At this temple (a branch of Nagano's famous Zenkō-ji, p286), private-use rooms are generously proportioned around a courtyard garden, and even the dorm-style rooms are handsome. There's a kitchen for guest use, no curfew and a master who speaks excellent English. If you want, you can practise Jōdō-style meditation in the main hall.

Hida Takayama Tenshō-ji Youth Hostel (☎ 32-6345; fax 32-6392; 83 Tenshōji-machi; dm members/non-members ¥3150/3500; ⊠ 💻) This peaceful hostel (with a rather early 9.45pm curfew) occupies an attractive hillside temple in Teramachi. Rooms are Japanese-style, you have a choice of shower near the rooms or small bath on the other side of the temple, and breakfast is available (¥630). Add ¥1000 per room to have it to yourself (subject to availability). The hostel is a 20-minute walk from the train station, or there's an infrequent bus service.

Rickshaw Inn (☎ 32-2890; www.rickshawinn.com; 54 Suehiro-chō; s without bathroom from ¥4900, tw with/without bathroom from ¥11,900/10,200; ⊠ 💻) Excellent value and a travellers' favourite, with pleasant Japanese- and Western-style rooms, a small kitchen, laundry facilities and a cosy lounge. Friendly English-speaking owners are founts of information about Takayama. Book well in advance.

Sōsuke (☎ 32-0818; fax 33-5570; www.irori-sosuke.com; 1-64 Okamoto-machi; r per person ¥5040; 💻) West of the train station, Sōsuke has 13 pleasant tatami rooms, some with skylights and paper lanterns. English-speaking staff prepares excellent dinners (¥2100) and breakfasts (¥645), served at *hori-kotatsu* (low tables with a well beneath for your feet), including meals for vegetarians. The handsomely updated building dates from the 1800s and includes an *irori* (hearth). It's across a busy road from the hulking Takayama Green Hotel.

MIDRANGE

our pick **Spa Hotel Alpina** (☎ 33-0033; www.spa-hotel-alpina.com, in Japanese; 5-41 Nada-cho; s/tw from ¥6300/11,000; ⊠ 💻) This business hotel, which opened in 2008, is minimalist without being cold – crisp bedding, modular bathrooms and a variety of room types. The best part, though, is the onsen baths on the top floor, including *rotemburo,* with views across the city. The breakfast buffet is ¥700. Some of the staff members speak English and can respond to email enquiries sent via the website. LAN cable is available.

Minshuku Kuwataniya (☎ 32-5021; fax 36-3835; www.kuwataniya.com; 1-50-30 Sowa-machi; r per person with/without bathroom ¥6450/4350; 💻) Takayama's longest-running *minshuku* (home-style accommodation; since the 1920s) has both Japanese- and Western-style rooms, high-def TVs (Japanese channels), simple onsen baths and free bicycle use. Dinner (available for ¥2310) features Hida's famed beef (vegetarian options are available with advance notice), and breakfast is ¥840. It's half a block north of Hida Kokubun-ji.

Ryokan Gōdo (☎/fax 33-0870; San-no-Machi; r per person from ¥6825) The very traditional five-room Gōdo lies in the heart of Sanmachi-suji, positioning you perfectly for this district's dramatic nightscapes (you can borrow an oiled paper umbrella if it's raining). There's a low door at the entry and eclectic touches throughout. Rooms have no private facilities, though the common bath is of stone and *hinoki* cypress. No English is spoken.

Yamakyū (☎ 32-3756; www.takayama-yamakyu.com; 58 Tenshōji; r with 2 meals ¥7980; 💻) This hillside inn, near the temples on the eastern side of town, is lined with antique-filled curio cabinets (glassware, tea bowls, the occasional bit of kitsch). Thanks to a recent makeover, each of its 20 comfy tatami rooms has a sink and toilet, while bathing is in the signature water-wheel common baths. Some English is spoken. Yamakyū's about 20 minutes' walk from the station; staff can arrange for luggage pick-up with a couple of days' notice.

Best Western Hotel (☎ 37-2000; www.bestwestern.co.jp; 6-6 Hanasato-machi; s/d/tw from ¥9500/13,000/18,000; ⊠ 💻 📶) Very popular among overseas guests, this 78-room Western-style hotel offers crisp service and spacious, comfortably furnished rooms. There's a lounge and restaurant on-site, and LAN access from rooms. It's a block from the station.

Sumiyoshi Ryokan (☎ 32-0228; www.sumiyoshi-ryokan.com; 4-21 Hon-machi; r per person with 2 meals from ¥11,550; 💻) This delightfully traditional inn is set in an old merchant's house from the late Meiji period and is filled with antiques. Some rooms have river views through windows of antique glass, and the common baths are made of wood and slate tiles. One room has a private bath (¥13,650).

TOP END

Hotel Associa Takayama Resort (ホテルアソシア高山リゾート; ☎ 36-0001; www.associa.com/tky; 1134 Echigo-chō; s/tw with breakfast from ¥13,800/21,600; ⊠) If you find Takayama too historic, the Associa's three towers south of town provide an escape back to the 21st century. The 290 rooms are either Western or Japanese style, as are the restaurants (dinner is approximately ¥6000 per person). The real showpiece is the three-storey, valley-view onsen baths and *rotemburo*. The Associa's about 10 minutes from town, and there's a shuttle-bus service. Guests can deposit luggage at the hotel's Café Scenery, just outside the station exit, for transport to the hotel.

Tanabe Ryokan (☎ 32-0529; fax 35-1955; www.tanabe-ryokan.jp; 58 Aioi-chō; r per person with 2 meals from ¥15,000; ⊠ 💻) Central, family-run inn with sweet, welcoming staff. There's art throughout, stone paths line the carpeted hallways, the 21 rooms are spacious, and dinner is *kaiseki*-style Hida cuisine. Rooms have en-suite bath, but the common baths with their beamed ceilings are worth a try. Some English is spoken.

Asunaro Ryokan (☎ 33-5551, toll-free 0120-052-536; www.yado-asunaro.com; 2-96 Hatsuda-machi; r per person with 2 meals with/without bathroom from ¥15,750/13,650; 💻) This excellent ryokan has handsome tatami rooms, a spacious onsen bath and decadent dinners and breakfasts. Several rooms have *irori,* and some have private bathrooms (all have toilets). The staff speaks some English.

Eating

Takayama's specialities include *soba, hoba-miso, sansai* (mountain vegetables) and Hida-*gyū*, among Japan's top grades. You're likely to find many of these in meals at your inn. Street foods include *mitarashi-dango* (skewers of grilled riceballs seasoned with soy sauce), *shio-sembei* (salty rice crackers), and Hida-*gyū* served up on *kushiyaki* (skewers) and in *korokke* (croquettes) and *niku-man* (steamed buns).

Origin (☎ 36-4655; 4-108 Hanasato-chō; most dishes ¥315-819; ⏲ dinner) This wonderful local *izakaya* located a minute from the station has the usual *kushiyaki* and tofu steak, plus original dishes like sardines rolled in *yuba* (tofu skin), or big-as-a-beer-can grilled daikon in miso sauce. Or go for broke with Hida beef (¥1575). Look for the bamboo poles out the front. There's an English menu.

Jingoro Rāmen (☎ 34-5565; mains from ¥600; ⏲ 10.30am-2.30pm & 8pm-2am, closed dinner Sun & some Mon) Like a roadhouse south of the station, Takayama's most venerable *rāmen* restaurant is a simple affair – broth, noodles and pork (or not) – but the savoury results are extremely satisfying. An English menu is available.

Chapala (☎ 34-9800; mains ¥600-980; ⏲ dinner Mon-Sat, closed 1st Mon of each month) Mexico is about as far from Japan as can be, but this little shop run by a Japanese enthusiast makes a fair stab at it. The taste and dainty portions of tacos, quesadillas and guac' and chips might not pass muster in California, Texas or Guadalajara, but the place is adorable and the owners earnest. Plus, you get to eat Mexican with chopsticks while swilling Coronas and margaritas. The menu comes in English.

Takumi-ya (☎ 36-2989; 2 Shimo-Ni-no-Machi; mains downstairs ¥680-980, upstairs from ¥1280; ⏲ lunch & dinner Thu-Tue) Hida beef on a burger budget. Adjacent to Takumi-ya's butcher shop is a casual restaurant (open 10am to 4pm) specialising in *rāmen* in Hida-beef broth and Hida *gyū-don* (beef and onion over rice; *gyū-don* and mini-*rāmen* combo for ¥1000). The upstairs restaurant serves *yakiniku* (Korean-style barbecue). It's next to the shop selling 'Total Fashion'.

Holy Grail (☎ 35-3393; 4-68 Hanasato-chō; mains ¥730-1250; ⏲ lunch Mon & Wed-Sat, dinner Wed-Mon) Italian trattoria-style dishes in a hardwood, home-style setting. A husband-and-wife team creates crostini, handmade pizzas, pastas and more. Lunch specials start at ¥550, and inexpensive house wines are available by the bottle. An English menu is available.

Ebisu-Honten (☎ 32-0209; 46 Kami-Ni-no-Machi; soba dishes ¥830-1530; ⏲ 10am-5pm Thu-Tue; V) This Sanmachi shop has been making *teuchi* (handmade) *soba* since 1898. The menu explains the *soba*-making process. Go for *zaru* (cold) *soba* for the real flavour of the buckwheat, or try curry or *miso-nikomi* (in miso broth) style.

Myōgaya (☎ 32-0426; 5-15 Hanasato-chō; mains around ¥1000; ⏲ 8-10.30am, 11.30am-3pm & 5-7pm Wed-Sun; ⊠ V) A good-for-you vibe pervades this tiny, organic restaurant and food shop that's adorned with natural fibres, located a block east of the train station. Look for tasty vegetarian curry with brown rice, samosas, fruit juices, dandelion tea and coffees. Reservations are requested on Saturdays.

Suzuya (☎ 32-2484; 24 Hanakawa-chō; sets ¥1155-3100; ⏲ 11am-3pm & 5-8pm Wed-Mon) In the centre of town, Suzuya is one of Takayama's long-standing favourites, and it's highly recommended for local specialities like Hida beef, *hoba-miso* and various stews. The menu is available in English.

Yamatake-Shōten (☎ 32-0571; 1-70 Sōwa-chō; meals per person from around ¥3500; ⏲ lunch & dinner Thu-Tue, closed 3rd Thu of month) This is a workmanlike butcher shop with a restaurant upstairs, and is an excellent place to sample Hida-*gyū*. Here's the drill: choose your own cut (pay by weight, from ¥1380 per 100g), which is plated and brought to the table for you to cook on an inset charcoal grill. Vegetables and simple desserts are included. Sides like kimchi and *gyū tataki* (marinated raw beef) are also for sale.

Drinking

Asahi-machi, north of Kokubun-ji-dōri and west of the Miya-gawa, is Takayama's bar district, though don't go expecting a raucous time. The places listed here will point you in the right direction, or feel free to wander.

Tonio (☎ 32-1677; ⏲ 7pm-2am Mon-Sat) This welcoming English-style pub dates from 1956 and feels like a time warp. Locals and visitors mingle over kitsch and antiques; there's Guinness on tap and imported whiskies.

Red Hill Pub (☎ 33-8139; ⏲ 7pm-midnight, closed irregularly) Locals and expats gather at this welcoming bar. There are snacks such as pita bread and *karai rāmen* (spicy *rāmen*), an excellent selection of domestic and imported brews and an eclectic mix of tunes.

Shopping

Takayama is renowned for crafts. *Ichii ittobori* (woodcarvings) are fashioned from yew and can be seen as intricate components of *yatai* or in shops around town. **Suzuki Chōkoku** (☎ 32-1367; ⏲ 9am-7pm Wed-Mon) is helmed by the one-time head of the local *ittobori* association and sells figurines and accessories priced from ¥750 to *how much?* Woodworking also extends to furniture shops such as **Mori no Kotoba** (Words from the Forest; ☎ 36-7005; ⏲ 9am-6pm Thu-Tue).

Takayama is also known for its *shunkei* lacquerware. Around Shunkei Kaikan (p270) are shops with outstanding lacquerware and porcelain and, occasionally, good deals.

Local pottery styles include the rustic *Yamada-yaki* and the decorative *Shibukusa-yaki* styles.

Takayama's most ubiquitous souvenirs are *saru-bobo* (monkey babies), dolls of red cloth dressed in blue fabric, with pointy limbs and featureless faces, recalling the days when *obāsan* (grandmas) in this once-impoverished town fashioned dolls for kids out of readily available materials.

Getting There & Away

From Tokyo or Kansai, Takayama is most efficiently reached via Nagoya on the JR Takayama line (Hida *tokkyū*, ¥5670, 2¼ hours); the mountainous train ride along the Hida-gawa is *gorge*-ous. The same train continues to Toyama (¥3480, 90 minutes), with connections to Kanazawa (additional ¥2050, 40 minutes).

Highway buses (☎ 32-1688; www.nouhibus.co.jp/english) connect Takayama and Tokyo's Shinjuku (¥6500, 5½ hours, several daily, reservations required). Takayama's bus station is adjacent to the train station. Many roads in this region close during winter, so bus schedules vary seasonally and buses don't run at all in winter on some routes. Check with tourist offices for details.

For trips to Shirakawa-gō and the Japan Alps National Park, see p277 and p280, respectively.

You'll find **Eki Rent-a-Car System** (☎ 33-3522), **Toyota Rent-a-Car** (☎ 36-6110) and **Mazda Rent-a-Car** (☎ 36-1515) all near the station.

Getting Around

Most sights in Takayama except Hida-no-Sato can be covered easily on foot. You can amble from the train station across to Teramachi in about 20 minutes.

Takayama is bicycle-friendly. Some lodgings lend cycles, or you can hire one (per hour/same day about ¥300/1300) from **Eki Rent-a-Car System** (above); the convenience store **Daily Yamazaki** (☎ 34-1183), next to the train station; or **Hara Cycle** (☎ 32-1657; Kokubun-ji-dōri).

HIDA-FURUKAWA 飛騨古川

☎ 0577 / pop 16,000

Just 15 minutes by train from Takayama, Hida-Furukawa is a relaxing riverside town with photogenic streetscapes, peaceful temples and interesting museums, all framed against mountains. It's also famous for Hadaka Matsuri (known as Naked Festival – *woo hoo!*), held each April.

Orientation & Information

Hida-Furukawa train and bus stations adjoin each other east of the town centre. Sights are within 10 minutes' walk. There's an **information office** (観光案内所; ☎ 73-3180; 8.30am-5pm) at the bus station, dispensing the English *Hida Furukawa Stroll Map*, which is sufficient for most visitors. No English is spoken, though Takayama's tourist information office (p268) can help.

Sights

From the train station, walk right (north) two blocks and turn left towards the historic canal district **Setokawa to Shirakabe-dōzō** (瀬戸川と白壁土蔵街, Seto River and White Wall Clay Storehouse Quarter), one of the region's prettiest strolls. Its handsome streets boast white- and dark-wood-walled shops, storehouses and private homes. Carp-filled waterways course through the district. You can buy fish food for ¥50.

Along the way, **Hida Furukawa Matsuri Kaikan** (飛騨古川まつり会館; Festival Exhibition Hall; ☎ 73-3511; adult/child/high-school student ¥800/400/700; 9am-5pm Mar-Nov, to 4.30pm Dec-Feb) shows Furukawa's festival in all its glory. You can don 3-D glasses to watch a video of the festivities (with free English narration via iPod), see three of the *yatai* that are paraded through the streets, and watch a *karakuri* show. You can also try manipulating *karakuri* like those used on the *yatai*, and watch craftsmen demonstrating *kirie* (paper cut-outs) or *ittobori*. Drums used in the festival are on view in the barnlike structure diagonally to the left as you exit the exhibition hall.

Across the square, **Takumi-Bunkakan** (匠文化館; Hida Craft Museum; ☎ 73-3321; adult/child ¥300/100; 9am-4.45pm Mar-Nov, to 4.30pm Tue-Sun Dec-Feb) is a must for woodworkers, craftspeople and design fans. In a hands-on room, you can try assembling blocks of wood cut into different joint patterns – not as easy as it sounds.

Follow the canal street westward for three blocks, then turn right to reach the riverside **Honkō-ji** (本光寺), an intricately carved temple that showcases Furukawa's fine craftsmanship. It is Hida's largest wood-built temple. Though the temple was established in 1532, the current buildings are reconstructions from 1913 after the original design, following a fire that destroyed 90% of the town.

From the temple, instead of retracing your steps, walk back along Ichi-no-Machi, a street sprinkled with shops selling woodworking and handcrafted toys, sake breweries (marked by the large balls of cedar fronds above the entrance) and traditional storehouses. Among them is **Mishima Wa-rosoku Ten** (三島和ろうそく店; ☎ 73-4109; 🕑 9am-6pm Thu-Tue), a shop that has made traditional candles for over two centuries.

Festivals & Events

Furukawa Matsuri, as Hadaka Matsuri is formally known (it's also known as Naked Festival), takes place every 19 and 20 April with parades of *yatai*. The highlight is an event known as Okoshi Daiko in which, on the night of the 19th, squads of boisterous young men dressed in *fundoshi* (loincloths) parade through town, competing to place small drums atop a stage bearing a giant drum. OK, it's not *naked*-naked, but we didn't make up the name.

During **Kitsune-bi Matsuri** (Fox Fire Festival) on the fourth Saturday in September, locals dress up as foxes, parade through the town by lantern light and enact a wedding at Okura Inari-jinja. The ceremony, deemed to bring good fortune, climaxes with a bonfire.

Sleeping & Eating

Hida Furukawa Youth Hostel (飛騨古川ユースホステル; ☎/fax 75-2979; www.jyh.or.jp/english/toukai/hidafuru/index.html; dm ¥3300, with 2 meals ¥4900; 🕑 closed 30 Mar-10 Apr; ⊠ 💻) A friendly and attractive 22-bed hostel, across from Shinrin-kōen. It's about 6km from the town centre, or 1.2km west of Hida-Hosoe Station (two stops north of Hida-Furukawa). In winter the hostel can help guests get set up for telemark skiing. Pick-up from the station is available after 6pm with advance notice. Both Japanese- and Western-style rooms are available.

Kitchen Kyabingu (キッチンきゃびんぐ; ☎ 73-4706; mains ¥850-2200; 🕑 lunch & dinner Tue-Sun) This cosy lunch spot in the historic district serves Hida-*gyū*. Order the beef curry with rice (¥1050) or the *kyabingu teishoku* (¥2600), starring sizzling steak on a hot iron plate.

Getting There & Around

Some 20 daily trains run each way between Takayama and Furukawa. Hida-Furukawa train station is three stops north of Takayama (*futsū*, ¥230, 15 minutes), or you can bus it (¥360, 30 minutes). Central Furukawa is an easy stroll, or hire bikes at the taxi office **Miyagawa** (☎ 73-2321; per hr ¥200), near the station. Staff here can also store your luggage for ¥200 each day or a portion thereof.

SHIRAKAWA-GŌ & GOKAYAMA 白川郷・五箇山

These remote, dramatically mountainous districts between Takayama and Kanazawa are best known for farmhouses in the thatched, A-frame style called *gasshō-zukuri* (see the boxed text, p272). They're rustic and lovely, particularly in clear weather or in the region's copious snows, and they hold a special place in the Japanese heart.

In the 12th century the region's remoteness is said to have attracted stragglers from the Taira (Heike) clan, virtually wiped out by the Minamoto (Genji) clan in a brutal battle in 1185. During feudal times Shirakawa-gō, like the rest of Hida, was under direct control of the Kanamori clan, connected to the Tokugawa shōgun, while Gokayama was a centre for the production of gunpowder for the Kaga region, under the ruling Maeda clan (see p306).

Fast-forward to the 1960s: when construction of the gigantic Miboro Dam over the river Shōkawa was about to submerge some local villages, many *gasshō* houses were moved to their current sites for safekeeping. Although much of what you'll find has been specially preserved for, and supported by, tourism, it still presents a view of rural life found in few other parts of Japan.

Most of Shirakawa-gō's sights are in the heavily visited community of Ogimachi; a new expressway from Takayama has made it even more crowded. In less-crowded Gokayama (technically not in Hida but in Toyama-ken), the community of Ainokura has the greatest concentration of attractions; other sights are spread throughout hamlets over many kilometres along Rte 156. Ogimachi and Ainokura are Unesco World Heritage Sites (as is the Gokayama settlement of Suganuma).

Even locals recognise that the community is becoming overrun with tour buses, traffic and souvenir-seekers, and there's passionate debate as to what to do about it. For you, the best advice is to avoid weekends, holidays, and cherry-blossom and autumn-foliage seasons.

Better, stay overnight in a *gasshō-zukuri* house that's been turned into an inn. Advance reservations are highly recommended; the Shirakawa-gō tourist information office by the parking area in Ogimachi can help with bookings (in Japanese), or via email in English at info@shirakawa-go.go.jp. Don't expect rooms with private facilities, though some inns have *irori* for guests to eat around.

Shirakawa-gō 白川郷

☎ 05769

The region's central settlement, **Ogimachi**, has some 600 residents and over 110 *gasshō-zukuri* buildings, and is the most convenient place to orient yourself for tourist information and transport.

Ogimachi's **main tourist office** (Deai no Yakata; ☎ 6-1013; www.shirakawa-go.org; 9am-5pm) is near the Shirakawa-gō bus stop. There's a free English map of Ogimachi. Limited English is spoken. There's a smaller tourist information office near the Ogimachi car park.

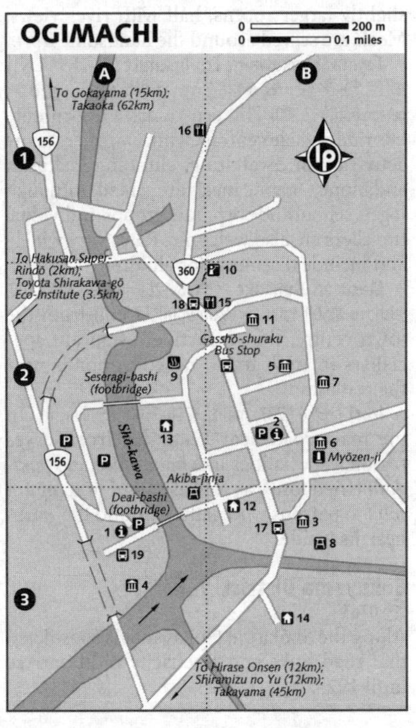

SIGHTS & ACTIVITIES

On the site of the former castle, **Shiroyama Tenbōdai** (observation point) provides a lovely overview of the valley. It's a 15-minute walk via the road behind the east side of town. You can climb the path (five minutes) from near the intersection of Rtes 156 and 360, or there's a shuttle bus (¥200 one way) from the Shirakawa-gō bus stop.

Gasshō-zukuri Minka-en (☎ 6-1231; adult/child ¥500/300; 8.40am-5pm Apr-Jul & Sep-Nov, 8am-5.30pm Aug, 9am-4pm Fri-Wed Dec-Mar) features over two dozen relocated *gasshō-zukuri* buildings, reconstructed in this open-air museum amid seasonal flowers. Several houses are used for demonstrating regional crafts such as woodwork, straw handicrafts and ceramics; many items are for sale.

You can wander away from the houses for a pleasant stroll through the trees further up the mountain. Feel free to take a picnic, but obey Shirakawa-gō custom and carry your rubbish out of town.

Opening hours listed here are subject to change, as some of the old houses close irregularly. Check ahead to avoid disappointment.

INFORMATION

Main Tourist Office 観光案内所 1 A3
Tourist Information Office 観光案内所 2 B2

SIGHTS & ACTIVITIES

Doburoku Matsuri Exhibition Hall どぶろく祭りの館 3 B3
Gasshō-zukuri Minka-en 合掌造り民家園 4 A3
Kanda-ke 神田家 5 B2
Myōzen-ji Folk Museum 明善寺 6 B2
Nagase-ke 長瀬家 7 B2
Shirakawa Hachiman-jinja 8 B3
Shirakawa-gō no Yu 白川郷の湯 9 A2
Shiroyama Tenbōdai (observation point) 城山展望台 10 B2
Wada-ke 和田家 11 B2

SLEEPING

Kōemon 幸エ門 12 B3
Magoemon 孫右エ門 13 A2
Shimizu 志みづ 14 B3

EATING

Irori いろり 15 B2
Masu-en Bunsuke ます園文助 16 A1

TRANSPORT

Jinja-mae Bus Stop 神社前バス停 17 B3
Ogimachi Bus Stop 荻町バス停 18 A2
Shirakawa-gō Bus Stop 白川郷バス停 19 A3

Shirakawa-gō's largest *gasshō* house, **Wada-ke** (☎ 6-1058; adult/child ¥300/150; ⌚ 9am-5pm) is a designated National Treasure. It once belonged to a wealthy silk-trading family and dates back to the mid-Edo period. Upstairs are silk-harvesting equipment and a valuable lacquerware collection.

Of the other *gasshō* houses, **Kanda-ke** (☎ 6-1072; adult/child ¥300/150; ⌚ 9am-5pm) is the least cluttered with exhibits, which leaves you to appreciate the architectural details – enjoy a cup of herb tea in the 36-mat living room on the ground floor. **Nagase-ke** (☎ 6-1047; adult/child ¥300/150; ⌚ 9am-5pm) was the home of the doctors to the Maeda clan; look for displays of herbal medicine equipment. The *butsudan* (Buddhist altar) dates from the Muromachi period. In the attic, you can get an up-close look at the construction of the roof, which took 530 people to re-thatch.

Next door to Ogimachi's small temple, **Myōzen-ji Folk Museum** (☎ 6-1009; adult/child ¥300/150; ⌚ 8.30am-5pm Apr-Nov, 9am-4pm Dec-Mar) displays the traditional paraphernalia of daily rural life.

Shirakawa-gō's big festival is held on 14 and 15 October at **Shirakawa Hachiman-jinja** (other festivals continue until the 19th), and features groups of dancing locals, taking part in the lion dance and *niwaka* (improvised buffoonery). The star is *doburoku*, a very potent unrefined sake. **Doburoku Matsuri Exhibition Hall** (☎ 6-1655; adult/child ¥300/150; ⌚ 9am-4pm Apr-Nov) shows a video of the festival (in Japanese).

There are several onsen around Shirakawa-gō. In central Ogimachi, **Shirakawa-gō no Yu** (☎ 6-0026; adult/child ¥700/300; ⌚ 10am-9.30pm) boasts a sauna, small *rotemburo* and large bath. Visitors staying at lodgings in town get a ¥200 discount. About 12km south of Ogimachi, off Rte 156 in Hirase Onsen, **Shiramizu no Yu** (しらみずの湯; ☎ 5-4126; adult/child ¥600/400; ⌚ 10am-9pm Tue-Sun) is a new onsen facility with views across the river valley, a treat during the autumn-foliage season; its waters are said to be beneficial for fertility. About another 40km up the Ōshirakawa river (via a mountain road with blind curves and no public transport), **Ōshirakawa Rotemburo** (大白川露天風呂; ☎ 090-2770-2893, 052-683-9248 in Nagoya; admission ¥300; ⌚ 8.30am-5pm mid-Jun–Oct, to 6pm Jul & Aug) is much admired for its middle-of-nowhere setting and views of an emerald-green lake set amid the mountains. Getting there requires a private vehicle or taxi (90 minutes) from Ogimachi.

SLEEPING & EATING

Some Japanese is helpful in making reservations at one of Ogimachi's many *gasshō-zukuri* inns, originally private houses that now let out rooms. Rates include two meals. Expect a nightly heating surcharge (¥400 and up) during cold weather. Ogimachi has a few casual restaurants (look for *soba* or *hoba-miso*); most open only for lunch.

Kōemon (☎ 6-1446; fax 6-1748; r per person ¥8400) In the town centre, atmospheric Kōemon has five rooms with heated floors, dark-wood panelling and shared bathrooms. The fifth-generation owner speaks English and his love of Shirakawa-gō is infectious. Try to book the room facing the pond.

Shimizu (☎ 6-1914; www.shimizuinn.com; r per person ¥8400) Its location, a little removed from the town centre, means more quiet and a home-style feel; arrange for pick-up in advance in bad weather or if you have large baggage. Its three rooms have six tatami each and are comfortably furnished, though the bath is tiny and guests often choose instead to go to the public onsen. Some English is spoken.

Magoemon (☎ 6-1167; fax 6-1851; r per person ¥9800) Another friendly place, Magoemon has six slightly larger rooms, half with river views. Meals are served around the handsome *irori*.

Toyota Shirakawa-gō Eco-Institute (トヨタ白川郷自然学校; ☎ 6-1187; www.toyota.eco-inst.jp; d per person from ¥12,200) This eco-resort, a five-minute bus ride outside central Ogimachi, offers many activities: birdwatching, climbing Hakusan and more. Organic meals are served. Although it gets school and corporate groups, individual travellers are also welcome. Rates vary widely and include discounts for children.

Masu-en Bunsuke (☎ 6-1268; dishes ¥300-500, teishoku ¥1500-4000; ⌚ 9am-9pm) Uphill from the town centre, this attractive restaurant specialises in fresh trout, raised in ponds near the restaurant.

Irori (☎ 6-1737; mains ¥700-1500; ⌚ lunch) On the main road near Wada-ke, Irori serves regional specialities like *hoba-miso* and *yaki-dofu* (fried tofu), as well as *sansai* or *tempura soba* to patrons who gather around the warm hearths inside.

Gokayama District 五箇山

☎ 0763

Along the Shōkawa, Gokayama is so isolated that road links and electricity didn't arrive until 1925.

Villages with varying numbers of *gasshō-zukuri* buildings are scattered over many kilometres along Rte 156. The following briefly describes some of the communities you'll come across as you travel north from Shirakawa-gō or the Gokayama exit from the Tōkai-Hokuriku Expressway; if your time is limited, head straight for Ainokura.

SUGANUMA 菅沼

This riverside World Heritage Site (www.gokayama.jp/english/index.html), 15km north of Ogimachi and down a steep hill, features an attractive group of nine *gasshō-zukuri* houses. The **Minzoku-kan** (民族館; Folklore Museum; ☎ 67-3652; adult/child ¥300/150; ⏰ 9am-4pm) consists of two houses, with items from traditional life, and displays illustrating traditional gunpowder production.

About 1km further up Rte 156, **Kuroba Onsen** (くろば温泉; ☎ 67-3741; adult/child ¥600/300; ⏰ 10.30am-9pm Wed-Mon Apr-Nov, 11am-9pm Wed-Mon Dec-Mar) is a complex of indoor-outdoor baths overlooking the river, with fine mountain views from its different storeys. Its low-alkaline waters are good for fatigue and sore muscles.

KAMINASHI 上梨

About 5km beyond Suganuma, the house museum **Murakami-ke** (村上家; ☎ 66-2711; adult/child ¥300/150; ⏰ 8.30am-5pm Apr-Nov, 9am-4pm Dec-Mar, closed 2nd & 4th Wed of each month) is one of the oldest in the region (dating from 1578). The proud owner shows visitors around and then sits them beside the *irori* and sings local folk songs. An English-language leaflet is available.

Also close by is the shrine **Hakusan-gū**. The main hall dates from 1502 and has been designated an Important Cultural Property. Its **Kokiriko Festival** (25 and 26 September) features costumed dancers performing with rattles that move like snakes. On the second day everyone joins in.

AINOKURA 相倉

This World Heritage Site is the most impressive of Gokayama's villages, with over 20 *gasshō* buildings in an agricultural valley amid splendid mountain views. It's less equipped for visitors than Ogimachi, which can be either a drawback or a selling point. Pick up an English pamphlet at the booth by the central car park.

Stroll through the village to the **Ainokura Museum of Life** (相倉民族館; ☎ 66-2732; admission ¥200; ⏰ 8.30am-5pm), with displays of local crafts and paper.

Continue along Rte 156 for several kilometres until **Gokayama Washi-no-Sato** (五箇山和紙の里; Gokayama Japanese Paper Village; ☎ 66-2223; adult/child ¥200/150; ⏰ 8.30am-5pm), where you will find displays of *washi* (Japanese handmade paper) art and a chance to make your own (from ¥500, reservations required, limited English spoken). It's inside the *michi-no-eki*, a sort of public rest station.

Sleeping

Ainokura is a great place for a *gasshō-zukuri* farmhouse stay. Have a Japanese speaker contact the inns directly for reservations, or approach them yourself; all cost about ¥8000 per person, including two meals. Try the welcoming four-room **Yomoshiro** (与茂四郎; ☎ 66-2377; fax 66-2387); **Goyomon** (五ヨ門; ☎ 66-2154; fax 66-2227), with excellent views from the 2nd storey; or **Chōyomon** (長ヨ門民宿; ☎ 66-2755; fax 66-2765), with its atmospheric dark-wood sliding doors. Ainokura also has a **camping ground** (☎ 66-2123; per person ¥500; ⏰ mid-Apr–late Oct), which is closed if there's snow.

Getting There & Away

Nōhi Bus Company (☎ 0577-32-1688, Japanese only; www.nouhibus.co.jp/english) operates seven buses daily linking Shirakawa-gō with Takayama (one way/return ¥2400/4300, 50 minutes). Some buses require a reservation. Two buses a day connect Kanazawa from Takayama (¥3300/5900, 2¼ hours), from Shirakawa-go (¥1800/3200, 1¼ hours). Weather delays and cancellations are possible between December and March.

Just before Ainokura, buses divert from Rte 156 for Rte 304 towards Kanazawa. From the Ainokura-guchi bus stop it's about 400m uphill to Ainokura.

Kaetsuno Bus (☎ 0766-22-4888) operates at least four buses a day between Takaoka on the JR Hokuriku line, Ainokura (¥1450, 90 minutes) and Ogimachi (¥2350, 2½ hours), stopping at all major sights. If you want to get off at unofficial stops (eg Kuroba Onsen), tell the driver.

By car, this region is about 50 minutes from Takayama, with interchanges at Gokayama and Shōkawa. From Hakusan, the scenic toll road Hakusan Super-Rindō ends near Ogimachi (cars ¥3150). In colder months, check conditions in advance with regional tourist offices.

JAPAN ALPS NATIONAL PARK 中部山岳国立公園

Boasting some of Japan's most dramatic scenery, this mountain-studded park – also called Chūbu-Sangaku National Park – is a favourite of alp-lovers. Highlights include hiking the valleys and peaks of Kamikōchi and Shin-Hotaka Onsen, and soaking up the splendour of Shirahone Onsen or Hirayu Onsen. The northern part of the park extends to the Tateyama-Kurobe Alpen Route (p305).

Orientation & Information

The park straddles the border between Gifu-ken and Nagano-ken. Several maps and pamphlets are published in English by the Japan National Tourism Organization (JNTO) and local tourist authorities, with more detailed hiking maps in Japanese.

There are no banks in the park, and the only ATM in the communities listed in this section is at Hirayu Onsen's post office, which keeps shorter hours than most ATMs nationwide. Be sure you have enough cash on hand before setting out.

Getting There & Around

The main gateway cities are Takayama to the west and Matsumoto to the east. Service from Takayama is by bus, while most travellers from Matsumoto catch the private Matsumoto Dentetsu train to Shin-Shimashima Station (¥680, 30 minutes) and transfer to buses – the ride in from either side is breathtaking. Within the park, the main transit hubs are Hirayu Onsen (Gifu-ken side) and Kamikōchi (Nagano-ken side). Bus schedules short-change visits to some areas and *long*-change others. Check schedules before setting out. See the boxed text, opposite, for fares and travel times.

Hiring a car may save money, time and nerves. However, some popular routes, particularly the road between Naka-no-yu and Kamikōchi, are open only to buses and taxis.

KAMIKŌCHI 上高地

☎ 0263

The park's biggest drawcard, Kamikōchi offers some of Japan's most spectacular scenery along the rushing Azusa-gawa, and a variety of hiking trails from which to see it.

In the late 19th century, foreigners 'discovered' this mountainous region and coined the term 'Japan Alps'. A British missionary, Reverend Walter Weston, toiled from peak to peak and sparked Japanese interest in mountaineering as a sport. He is now honoured with a festival (on the first Sunday in June, the official opening of the hiking season), and Kamikōchi has become a base for strollers, hikers and climbers. It's a pleasure just to meander Kamikōchi's riverside paths lined with *sasa* (bamboo grass).

Kamikōchi is closed from mid-November to late April, and in peak times (late July to late August, and during the foliage season in October) can seem busier than Shinjuku Station. Arrive early in the day, especially during the foliage season. June to mid-July is the rainy season, making outdoor pursuits depressingly soggy. It's perfectly feasible to visit Kamikōchi as a day trip, but you'll miss out on the pleasures of staying in the mountains and taking uncrowded early-morning or late-afternoon walks.

Orientation

Visitors arrive at Kamikōchi at the bus station, which is surrounded by visitor facilities. A 10-minute walk from the bus station along the Azusa-gawa takes you to the bridge Kappa-bashi, named for a water sprite of Japanese legend, where most of the hiking trails start.

Information

The **Kankō Ryokan Kumiai** (Ryokan Association; ☎ 95-2405; 🕒 9am-5pm late Apr–mid-Nov) at the Kamikōchi bus station is geared to booking accommodation, though non-Japanese speakers may want to book through the tourist information office in Matsumoto (p297) for Kamikōchi and Shirahone Onsen as it has English-speaking staff.

A little bit further along and to the left, the **Kamikōchi Information Centre** (☎ 95-2433; 🕒 8am-5pm late Apr–mid-Nov) provides hiking instructions and info on weather conditions, and also distributes the useful English *Kamikōchi Pocket Guide* with a map of the main walking tracks.

A 10-minute walk from the bus station along the main trail, the spiffy **Kamikōchi Visitor Centre** (☎ 95-2606; 🕒 8am-5pm late Apr–mid-Nov) has displays on Kamikōchi's flora and fauna, and explanations of its geological history.

Serious hikers and climbers might consider getting **insurance** (*hoken;* ¥1000 per person per day), available from window 3 at the Kamikōchi bus station. Weigh the benefits for yourself, but know that the out-of-pocket cost for a rescue 'copter starts at ¥800,000.

Sights & Activities

HIKING & CLIMBING

The river valley offers mostly level, short-distance walks. A four-hour round trip starts east of Kappa-bashi along the right-hand side of the river past Myōjin-bashi (one hour) to Tokusawa (another hour) before returning. By Myōjin-bashi is the idyllic **Myōjin-ike** (admission ¥300), a pond whose clear waters mark the innermost shrine of **Hotaka-jinja**. There's also a track on the left-hand side of the river, though it's partly a service road.

West of Kappa-bashi, you can amble along the right-hand side of the river to **Weston Relief** (a monument to Kamikōchi's most famous hiker, Walter Weston; 15 minutes) or keep to the left-hand side of the river and walk to the pond **Taishō-ike** (40 minutes).

The visitor centre offers **guided walks** (per person ¥500) to destinations including Taishō-ike and Myōjin-ike. **Nature guides** (per hr approx ¥2000) and **climbing guides** (per day approx ¥30,000) may also be requested. It is always wise to request guides in advance, though English speakers cannot be guaranteed. Other popular hikes include the mountain hut at Dakesawa (2½ hours up) and Yakedake (four hours up, starting about 20 minutes west of the Weston Relief, at Hodaka-bashi). From the peaks, it's possible to see all the way to Mt Fuji in clear weather.

Dozens of long-distance options vary in duration from a couple of days to a week. Japanese-language maps of the area show routes and average hiking times between huts, major peaks and landmarks. Favourite hikes and climbs (which can mean human traffic jams during peak seasons) include Yariga-take (3180m) and Hotaka-dake (3190m) – also known as Oku-Hotaka-dake.

A steep but worthwhile hike connects Kamikōchi and Shin-Hotaka (p284). The trail from Kappa-bashi crosses the ridge below Nishi Hotaka-dake (2909m) at Nishi Hotaka San-sō (Nishi Hotaka Mountain Cottage; three hours) and continues on to Nishi Hotaka-guchi, which is the top station of the Shin-Hotaka Ropeway. The hike takes nearly four hours (because of a steep ascent).

SAMPLE BUS ROUTES & DISCOUNTS: JAPAN ALPS NATIONAL PARK

Within the park, bus fares and schedules change seasonally and annually; the following are fares and travel times on common bus routes. If you are doing a lot of back-and-forth travel, consider the three-day 'Free Coupon' (¥6400) for unlimited bus transport within the park and to Matsumoto and Takayama. From Takayama, the 'Marugoto Value Kippu' is a great deal: ¥5000 buys you two days' passage anywhere between Takayama and Shin-Hotaka, a ride on the Shin-Hotaka Ropeway and a soak in the *rotemburo* (outdoor bath) at Hirayu Onsen bus station. Find current fares and schedules at tourist offices in Matsumoto and Takayama, or at www.alpico.co.jp/access/route_k/honsen/info_e.html or www.nouhibus.co.jp/english.

Bus Fares

From	To	Fare (¥; one way or one way/return)	Duration (min; one way)
Takayama	Hirayu Onsen	1530	55
	Kamikōchi	2000	80
	Shin-Hotaka	2100	90
Matsumoto	Shin-Shimashima	680 (train)	30
	Kamikōchi	2400/4400	95
Shin-Shimashima	Naka-no-yu	1550	50
	Kamikōchi	1900/3300	70
	Shirahone Onsen	1400/2300	75
Kamikōchi	Naka-no-yu	600	15
	Hirayu Onsen	1050/1800	25
	Shirahone Onsen	1350	35
Hirayu Onsen	Naka-no-yu	540	45
	Shin-Hotaka	870	30

Or you could save an hour of sweat by hiking in the opposite direction. To reach the ropeway, take a bus from Takayama or Hirayu Onsen to Shin-Hotaka.

Other more distant hiking destinations include Nakabusa Onsen (allow three days) and Murodō (allow five days), which is on the Tateyama-Kurobe Alpen Route (p305). This allows you to indulge in a soak en route in Takama-ga-hara Onsen, one of the finest in Japan.

For long-distance hikes there are mountain huts available; enquire at the information centre for details. Hikers and climbers should be well prepared. Even during summer, temperatures can plummet, or the whole area can be covered in sleeting rain or blinding fog, and in thunderstorms there is no refuge on the peaks.

ONSEN

On cold or drizzly days, the hot baths at the **Kamikōchi Onsen Hotel** (☎ 95-2311; admission ¥600; 🕑 7-9am & 12.30-3.30pm) are a refreshing respite.

The area's most unusual onsen is **Bokuden-no-yu** (☎ 95-2341; admission ¥700; 🕑 7am-5pm), a tiny cave bath dripping with minerals. It's at the intersection at Naka-no-yu, just before the bus-only tunnel towards Kamikōchi proper. Enter the small shop next to the Naka-no-yu bus stop, pay and get the key to the little mountain hut housing the onsen. It is yours privately for up to 30 minutes.

Sleeping & Eating

Accommodation in Kamikōchi is pricey and advance reservations are essential. Except for camping, rates quoted here include two meals. Some lodgings shut down their electricity generators in the middle of the night (emergency lighting stays on).

Tokusawa-en (☎ 95-2508; camp sites/dm/r per person ¥500/9450/13,650) A marvellously secluded place, in a wooded dell about 3km northeast of Kappa-bashi. It's both a camping ground and a lodge, and has Japanese-style rooms (shared facilities) and hearty meals served in a busy dining hall.

Kamikōchi Konashidaira Kyampu-jō (☎ 95-2321; camp sites per person from ¥700, tents/bungalows from ¥2000/6000; 🕑 office 7am-7pm) About 200m past the visitor centre, this camping ground can get packed with tents. Rental tents (in July and August) and bungalows are available, and there's a small shop and restaurant (open until 6pm).

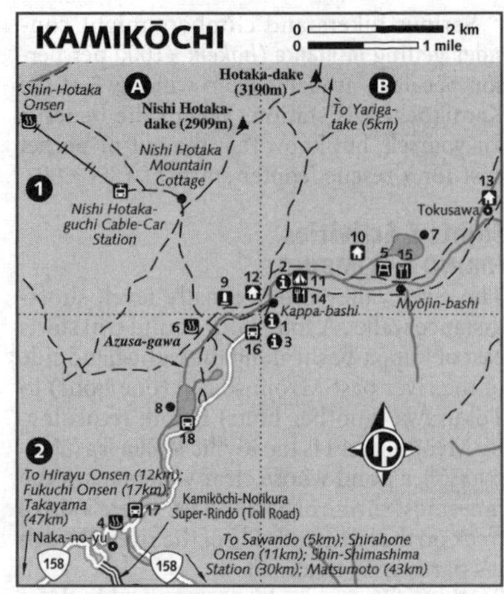

Kamikōchi Nishiitoya San-sō (☎ 95-2206; fax 95-2208; www.nishiitoya.com; dm ¥8000, d per person ¥10,550) Recently refurbished, this friendly lodge with a cosy lounge dates from the early 20th century. Rooms are a mix of Japanese and Western styles, all with toilet and shared bath: a large onsen facing the Hotaka mountains. It's just west of Kappa-bashi.

Kamikōchi Gosenjaku Lodge (☎ 95-2221; fax 95-2511; www.gosenjaku.co.jp; 'skier's bed' per person ¥10,500, d/tr/q ¥17,850/16,800/15,750) This is a polished little place. Its 34 rooms are mostly Japanese-style plus some 'skier's beds', which are basically curtained-off bunk beds. Rooms all have sink and toilet, but baths are shared. Buffet-style meals are Japanese, Chinese and Western.

Dotted along the trails and around the mountains are dozens of spartan *yama-goya* (mountain huts), which provide two meals and a futon from around ¥8000 per person; some also serve simple lunches. Enquire before setting out to make sure there's one on your intended route.

Kamikōchi's signature dish is *iwana* (river trout) grilled over an *irori*. Some trail huts serve it (along with the usual noodles and curry rice), but **Kamonji-goya** (☎ 95-2418; dishes ¥600-2000; 🕑 8.30am-4pm) is worth seeking out. The *iwana* set is ¥1500, or there's *oden* (fish-cake stew), *soba* and *koru-sake* (dried *iwana* in sake) served in a lovely ceramic bowl. It's near Myōjin-bashi, just outside the entrance to Myōjin-ike.

There's a shop at the bus station with cheap trail snacks or, at the other end of the spectrum, **Kamikōchi Gosenjaku Hotel** (☎ 95-2111) has

INFORMATION
Kamikōchi Information Centre 上高地インフォメーションセンター 1 B2
Kamikōchi Visitor Centre 上高地ビジターセンター 2 B1
Kankō Centre 観光センター 3 B2
Kankō Ryokan Kumiai .... (see 16)

SIGHTS & ACTIVITIES
Bokuden-no-yu ト伝の湯 4 A2
Hotaka-jinja 穂高神社 5 B1
Kamikōchi Onsen Hotel 上高地温泉ホテル 6 A2
Myōjin-ike 明神池 7 B1
Taishō-ike 8 A2
Weston Relief ウェストン像 9 A1

SLEEPING
Kamikōchi Gosenjaku Lodge 上高地五千尺ロッヂ 10 B1
Kamikōchi Konashidaira Kyampu-jō 上高地小梨平キャンプ場 11 B1
Kamikōchi Nishiitoya San-sō 上高地西糸屋山荘 12 A1
Tokusawa-en 徳沢園 13 B1

EATING
Kamikōchi Gosenjaku Hotel 上高地五千尺ホテル 14 B1
Kamonoji-goya 嘉門次小屋 15 B1

TRANSPORT
Kamikōchi Bus Station 16 A2
Naka-no-yu Bus Stop 中の湯バス亭 17 A2
Taishō-ike Bus Stop 大正池バス停 18 A2

pricey restaurants with French food and fancy cakes like Camembert torte with apples (¥630 per slice).

Getting Around

Private vehicles are prohibited between Naka-no-yu and Kamikōchi; access is only by bus or taxi, and then only as far as the Kamikōchi bus station. Those with private cars can use car parks en route to Naka-no-yu in the hamlet of Sawando for ¥500 per day; shuttle buses (¥1800 return) run a few times per hour.

Buses run via Naka-no-yu and Taishō-ike to the bus station. Hiking trails commence at Kappa-bashi, which is a short walk from the bus station.

SHIRAHONE ONSEN 白骨温泉

☎ 0263

Intimate, dramatic and straddling a deep gorge, this onsen resort town is easily the park's most beautiful. During the autumn-foliage season, and especially in the snow, it is just this side of heaven. All around the gorge are traditional inns (some more traditional than others) with open-air baths. Shirahone Onsen could also be a base for trips into Kamikōchi.

Shirahone means 'white bone', and it is said that bathing in the milky-blue hydrogen-sulphide waters here for three days ensures three years without a cold; the waters have a wonderful silky feel. The riverside **kōshū rotemburo** (公衆露天風呂; public outdoor bath; admission ¥500; 8.30am-5pm Apr-Oct), deep within the gorge, is separated by gender; the entrance is by the bus stop. Diagonally opposite, the **tourist information office** (観光案内所; ☎ 93-3251; 9am-5pm, irregular closures) maintains a list of inns that have opened their baths (admission from ¥600) to the public that day.

Budget travellers may wish to dip and move on; nightly rates start at ¥9000 with two meals. Advance reservations are highly recommended.

Tsuruya Ryokan (つるや旅館; ☎ 93-2331; fax 93-2029; www.tsuruya-ryokan.jp, in Japanese; r per person with 2 meals from ¥10,650) has both contemporary and traditional touches and great indoor and outdoor baths. Each of its 28 rooms has lovely views of the gorge; rooms with private toilet and sink are available for an extra charge.

our pick **Awanoyu Ryokan** (泡の湯旅館; ☎ 93-2101; www.awanoyu-ryokan.com; r per person incl 2 meals from ¥25,150) may be what you have in mind when you think onsen ryokan. Up the hill from most of Shirahone, it's been an inn since 1912 (the current building dates from 1940). It has private facilities in each room as well as single-sex common baths. There's also *kon-yoku* (mixed bathing), but not to worry: the waters are so milky that you can't see below the surface.

Note: many visitors find the bus ride up along the narrow cliffside roads from the Sawando junction either a thrill ride or a reason to take their happy pills.

HIRAYU ONSEN 平湯温泉

☎ 0578

This onsen village is a hub for bus transport on the Takayama side of the park and makes a convenient base for excursions elsewhere. There's a pleasant, low-to-the-ground cluster of onsen lodgings, about half of which open for day-bathers; even the bus station has a rooftop **rotemburo** (admission ¥600; 8.30am-5pm). The **information office** (☎ 89-3030; 9.30am-5.30pm), opposite the bus station, has leaflets and maps and can book accommodation. No English is spoken.

Ryosō Tsuyukusa (旅荘つゆくさ; ☎ 89-2620; fax 89-3581; r per person with 2 meals ¥7500) is a recently redone eight-room mum 'n' dad *minshuku* with decent tatami rooms and a cosy mountain-view *rotemburo* of *hinoki* cypress. Go downhill from the bus station and left at the first narrow street. It's on the left before the road curves.

Practically in its own forest uphill from the bus station, the sprawling onsen ryokan **Hirayu-no-mori** (ひらゆの森; ☎ 89-3338; www.hirayunomori.co.jp; r per person with 2 meals from ¥8000, bath day use ¥500) boasts 16 different *rotemburo* pools (gender separate), plus indoor and private baths. After 9pm, they're exclusively for overnight guests. Rooms are Japanese-style, and meals are hearty and local.

The dignified **Hirayu-kan** (平湯館; ☎ 89-3111; www.hirayukan.com; r per person with 2 meals from ¥13,800) has 60 rooms (Japanese, Western and combination style), plus a splendid garden and dreamy indoor and outdoor baths. All rooms have private facilities. It's a short walk past the turn-off for Tsuyukusa.

To reach the small **Hirayu Camping Ground** (平湯キャンプ場; ☎ 89-2610; fax 89-2130; camp sites per adult/child ¥600/400, parking ¥1500; end Apr-Oct), turn right out of the station, and it's about 700m ahead on the left.

CENTRAL HONSHŪ

FUKUCHI ONSEN 福地温泉

☎ 0578

This relatively untouristed onsen town, a short ride north of Hirayu Onsen, has rural charm, a morning market and two outstanding baths.

our pick **Yumoto Chōza** (湯元長座; ☎ 89-0099; fax 89-2010; www.cyouza.com, in Japanese; r per person with 2 meals from ¥21,150), one of Central Honshū's finest onsen ryokan, is reached by a long, rustic, covered walkway. Exquisite mountain cuisine is served at *irori* and you're surrounded by elegant traditional architecture and five indoor and two outdoor pools. Half of the 32 rooms have en-suite *irori*. Reservations are essential. By bus, get off at Fukuchi-Onsen-shimo.

A restaurant-cum-onsen, **Mukashibanashi-no-sato** (昔ばなしの里; ☎ 89-2793; bath ¥500; 8am-5pm, closed irregularly) is set back from the street in a traditional farmhouse with fine indoor and outdoor baths, free on the 26th of each month. Out the front, there's an **asa-ichi** (morning market; 6-10am daily Apr-Nov, Sat & Sun Dec-Mar). By bus, get off at Fukuchi-Onsen-kami bus stop.

SHIN-HOTAKA ONSEN 新穂高温泉

☎ 0578

The reason to visit Shin-Hotaka Onsen, north of Fukuchi Onsen, is the **Shin-Hotaka Ropeway** (新穂高ロープウェイ; ☎ 89-2252; www.okuhi.jp/rop/frtop.html; one way/return ¥1500/2800; 6am-5.15pm 1 Aug-last Sun in Aug, 8.30am-4.45pm late Aug-Jul, additional hours at peak times). At 1308m, this two-stage cable car is Japan's – some say Asia's – longest, whisking you 2156m up Nishi Hotaka-dake (2909m). The entrance is a few minutes' walk uphill from Shin-Hotaka Onsen bus station.

Assuming clear weather, views from the top are spectacular, from observation decks and walking trails – in winter, snows can easily be shoulder deep. In season (only, please!), fit, properly equipped hikers with ample time can choose longer hiking options from the top cable-car station, Nishi Hotaka-guchi, including over to **Kamikōchi** (p280, three hours), which is *much* easier than going the other way.

Adjacent to the bus terminal is a spartan **public onsen** (新穂高温泉アルペン浴場; admission free; 9.30am-4pm). During summer it's crowded with tourists, but in the off-season your only company is likely to be a few weary shift workers from the nearby hydroelectric plant.

Information is available at **Oku-Hida Spa Tourist Information Centre** (奥飛騨温泉郷観光案内所; ☎ 89-2458; 10am-5pm) by the bus terminal. There is only one (unappealing) hotel in Shin-Hotaka; visitors are better off bussing in from Kamikōchi, Fukuchi Onsen or Hirayu Onsen. For transit info, see the boxed text (p281).

NAGANO-KEN 長野県

Known as Shinshū in earlier days, Nagano-ken is one of Japan's most enjoyable visits, for the beauty of its mountainous terrain (it claims the title 'Roof of Japan'), traditional architecture, cultural offerings and unique foods.

Japan Alps National Park is the big draw, along with several quasi national parks that attract skiers, campers, hikers, mountaineers and onsen aficionados. Nagano, the prefectural capital, boasts a nationally important temple and makes a useful base for day trips, while Nagano-ken's second city, Matsumoto, mixes culture, outdoor pursuits and a National Treasure castle.

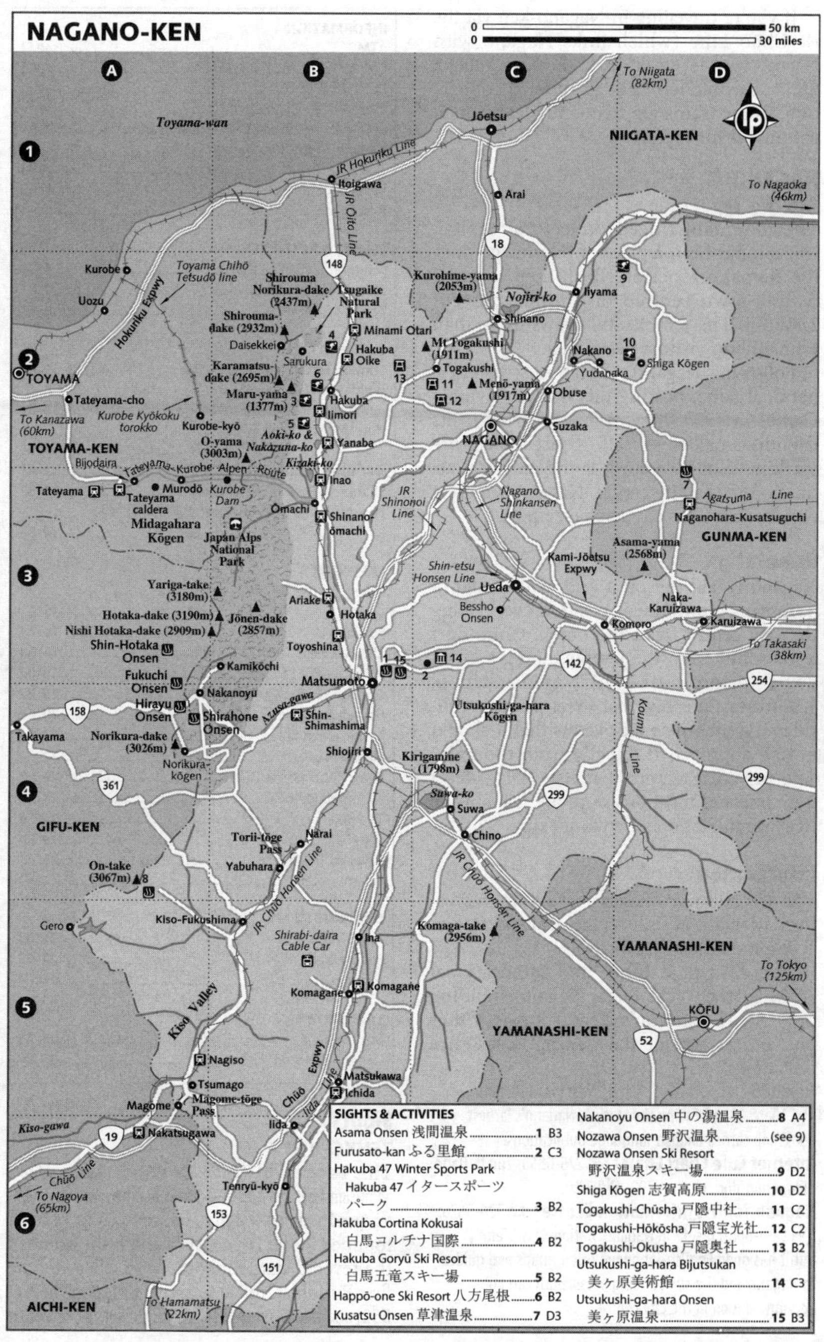
NAGANO-KEN
0 50 km
0 30 miles
Toyama-wan
To Niigata (82km)
Jōetsu
NIIGATA-KEN
JR Hokuriku Line
Itoigawa
JR Ōito Line
Arai
To Nagaoka (46km)
Kurobe
Uozu
Toyama Chihō Tetsudō line
Hokuriku Expwy
Shirouma Norikura-dake (2437m)
Tsugaike Natural Park
Kurohime-yama (2053m)
Nojiri-ko
Iiyama
Shinano
Shirouma-dake (2932m)
Minami Otari
Mt Togakushi (1911m)
Daisekkei
Sarukura
Hakuba Oike
Togakushi
Nakano
Yudanaka
Shiga Kōgen
TOYAMA
Karamatsu-dake (2695m)
Menō-yama (1917m)
Obuse
Tateyama-cho
Maru-yama (1377m)
Hakuba
Iimori
To Kanazawa (60km)
Kurobe Kyōkoku torokko
Kurobe-kyō
NAGANO
Suzaka
TOYAMA-KEN
O-yama (3003m)
Aoki-ko & Nakazuna-ko
Yanaba
Bijodaira
Tateyama-Kurobe Alpen Route
Kizaki-ko
Tateyama
Murodō
Kurobe Dam
Inao
Tateyama caldera
JR Shinonoi Line
Nagano Shinkansen Line
Agatsuma Line
Naganohara-Kusatsuguchi
Ōmachi
Shinano-ōmachi
Midagahara Kōgen
Japan Alps National Park
GUNMA-KEN
Asama-yama (2568m)
Kami-Jōetsu Expwy
Shin-etsu Honsen Line
Ueda
Yariga-take (3180m)
Ariake
Bessho Onsen
Naka-Karuizawa
Hotaka-dake (3190m)
Jōnen-dake (2857m)
Hotaka
Komoro
Karuizawa
Nishi Hotaka-dake (2909m)
Toyoshina
To Takasaki (38km)
Shin-Hotaka Onsen
Kamikōchi
Fukuchi Onsen
Nakanoyu
Matsumoto
Hirayu Onsen
Shirahone Onsen
Azusa-gawa
Shin-Shimashima
Utsukushi-ga-hara Kōgen
Koumi Line
Takayama
Norikura-dake (3026m)
Norikura-kōgen
Shiojiri
Kirigamine (1798m)
Suwa-ko
Suwa
Chino
GIFU-KEN
Torii-tōge Pass
Narai
Yabuhara
JR Chūō Honsen Line
On-take (3067m)
Gero
Kiso-Fukushima
Komaga-take (2956m)
Shirabi-daira Cable Car
Ina
YAMANASHI-KEN
To Tokyo (125km)
Komagane
Kiso Valley
KŌFU
Chūō Expwy
Nagiso
Tsumago
Matsukawa
Ichida
Magome
Magome-tōge Pass
Iida Line
Kiso-gawa
Iida
Nakatsugawa
Chūō Line
To Nagoya (65km)
Tenryū-kyō
AICHI-KEN
To Hamamatsu (22km)
SIGHTS & ACTIVITIES
Asama Onsen 浅間温泉 1 B3
Furusato-kan ふる里館 2 C3
Hakuba 47 Winter Sports Park Hakuba 47 イタースポーツパーク 3 B2
Hakuba Cortina Kokusai 白馬コルチナ国際 4 B2
Hakuba Goryū Ski Resort 白馬五竜スキー場 5 B2
Happō-one Ski Resort 八方尾根 6 B2
Kusatsu Onsen 草津温泉 7 D3
Nakanoyu Onsen 中の湯温泉 8 A4
Nozawa Onsen 野沢温泉 (see 9)
Nozawa Onsen Ski Resort 野沢温泉スキー場 9 D2
Shiga Kōgen 志賀高原 10 D2
Togakushi-Chūsha 戸隠中社 11 C2
Togakushi-Hōkōsha 戸隠宝光社 12 C2
Togakushi-Okusha 戸隠奥社 13 B2
Utsukushi-ga-hara Bijutsukan 美ヶ原美術館 14 C3
Utsukushi-ga-hara Onsen 美ヶ原温泉 15 B3

If you're travelling in Nagano-ken via the JR Chūō Line (which links Nagano with Nagoya via Matsumoto and the Kiso Valley), don't schedule too tight an onward connection, as the trains are frequently late (which is unusual for Japan).

NAGANO 長野

☎ 026 / pop 377,000

The mountain-ringed prefectural capital, Nagano has been a place of pilgrimage since the Kamakura period. Back then it was a temple town centred on the magnificent Zenkō-ji. The temple still draws more than four million visitors every year.

Following Nagano's flirtation with international fame, hosting the Winter Olympic Games in 1998, the city has reverted to its friendly small-town self, if just a bit more worldly. While Zenkō-ji is the only real attraction in the city centre, Nagano is a great regional base for day trips (see p290).

Orientation

Nagano is laid out on a grid, with Zenkō-ji occupying a prominent position overlooking the city centre from the north. Chūō-dōri leads south from the temple, doing a quick dogleg before hitting JR Nagano Station, 1.8km away; it is said that street-planners considered Zenkō-ji so auspicious that it should not be approached directly from the train. The private Nagano Dentetsu ('Nagaden') train line and most bus stops are just outside JR Nagano Station's Zenkō-ji exit.

Information

The website www.nagano-cvb.or.jp has information about sightseeing, transportation, accommodation and festivals.

There's a post office and international ATM in the West Plaza Nagano building opposite the station's Zenkō-ji exit. Other post offices include the Central Post Office on Chūō-dōri.

Heiandō (☎ 224-4545; 4th fl, West Plaza Nagano; 10am-10pm) Facing the station, Nagano's largest bookshop carries English-language publications.

Internet Cafe Chari Chari (☎ 226-0850; 2nd fl, Daito Bldg, Chūō-dōri; per hr ¥390; 24hr)

Nagano Tourist Information Centre (☎ 226-5626; 9am-6pm) Inside JR Nagano Station, this friendly outfit has good English-language colour maps and guides to Nagano and the surrounding areas. Staff can book accommodation in the city centre.

INFORMATION

ATM ... (see 5)
Central Post Office 中央郵便局 ... 1 A3
Heiandō 平安堂 ... (see 5)
Internet Cafe Chari Chari インターネットカフェ茶里茶里 ... 2 A4
Nagano Tourist Information Centre 長野観光案内所 ... 3 B4
Post Office 郵便局 ... 4 A2
Post Office 郵便局 ... 5 A4

SIGHTS & ACTIVITIES

Niō-mon 仁王門 ... 6 B1
Sanmon 三門 ... 7 B1
Zenkō-ji 善光寺 ... 8 A1

SLEEPING

Comfort Hotel Nagano コンフォートホテル長野 ... 9 B4
Holiday Inn Express Nagano ホリデイインエキスプレッス長野 ... 10 B4
Hotel Metropolitan Nagano ホテルメトロポリタン長野 ... 11 B4
Matsuya Ryokan 松屋旅館 ... 12 A1
Shimizuya Ryokan 清水屋旅館 ... 13 B2
Zenkō-ji Kyōju-in Youth Hostel 善光寺教授院ユースホステル ... 14 B1

EATING

Bakery's Street & Café ベーカリーズストリートカフェ ... 15 A3
Bosco ボスコ ... 16 A4
Chō Bali Bali チョーバリバリ ... 17 A4
Fujiki-an 藤木庵 ... 18 B2
Gohonjin Fujiya 御本陣藤屋 ... 19 B2
Gomeikan 五明館 ... 20 A2
Kashin Miwa 菓心美和 ... 21 B1
Marusei 丸清 ... 22 A1
Oyaki Kōbō お焼き工房 ... (see 24)
Patio Daimon ぱてぃお大門 ... 23 B2
Tilia Building ティリア ... 24 B4
Tofu Café Gorokutei とうふかふぇ五六亭 ... (see 23)
Yayoi-za 弥生座 ... 25 A2
Yukimura-tei ... (see 24)

DRINKING

Asian Night Market アジアンナイトマーケット ... 26 B3
Bistro Liberty ビストロリバティー ... 27 B3
Groovy グルービー ... 28 B4

TRANSPORT

Bus Terminal バスターミナル ... 29 A4
Daimon Bus Stop 大門バス停 ... 30 B2

Sights

ZENKŌ-JI 善光寺

This **temple** (☎ 186-026-234-3591; 491 Motoyoshi-chō; admission free; 4.30am-4.30pm summer, 6am-4pm winter, varied hours rest of year) is believed to have been founded in the 7th century and is the home of the revered statue Ikkō-Sanzon, allegedly the first Buddhist image to arrive in Japan (in AD 552; see the boxed text, p288). Don't expect to

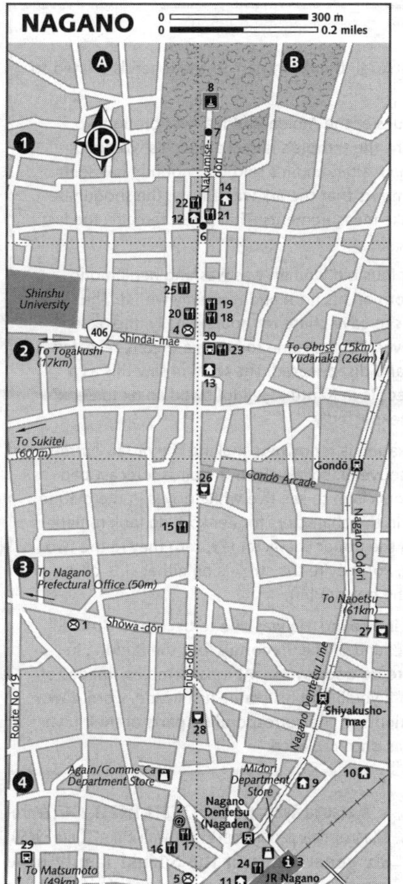

see it, however; it is said that 37 generations of emperors have not seen the image, though millions of visitors flock here to view a copy every six years during the Gokaichō Matsuri (see right).

Zenkō-ji's immense popularity stems partly from its liberal welcoming of believers from all Buddhist sects, including women; its chief officiants are both a priest and a priestess.

The original site was south of the current temple, off what's now the busy shopping street Nakamise-dōri; however, in that location it was destroyed 11 times by fires originating in neighbouring homes and businesses – and rebuilt each time with donations from believers throughout Japan. Finally, the Tokugawa shōgunate decreed that the temple be moved to its present, safer location. The current building dates from 1707 and is a National Treasure.

Visitors ascend to the temple via Nakamise-dōri and the impressive gates **Niō-mon** and **Sanmon**. In the *hondō* (main hall), the Ikkō-Sanzon image is in an ark left of the central altar, behind a dragon-embroidered curtain. To the right of the altar, visitors may descend a staircase to **Okaidan** (admission ¥500), a pitch-black tunnel that symbolises death and rebirth and provides the closest access to the hidden image (taller visitors: watch your head!). As you navigate the twisting tunnel, dangle your arm along the right-hand wall until you feel something heavy, moveable and metallic – said to be the key to salvation, a bargain for the admission price.

It's worth getting to the temple shortly after it opens to witness the morning service and the *ojuzu chodai,* in which the priest or priestess touches the Buddhist holy beads to the heads of all who line up and kneel. Check with the tourist information centre or the Zenkō-ji office for the times.

Any bus from bus stop 1 in front of JR Nagano Station's Zenkō-ji exit will get you to the temple (¥100, about 10 minutes; alight at the Daimon bus stop).

Festivals & Events

Gokaichō Matsuri Five million pilgrims come to Zenkō-ji every six years from early April to mid-May, to view a copy of Zenkō-ji's sacred Buddha image – the only time it can be seen. The next festival is in 2015.

Enka Taikai A fireworks festival with street food on 23 November.

Sleeping

Near Zenkō-ji are several traditional and very old ryokan. The station area is mostly uninspiring business hotels; listed here are some of the better options. Perhaps the most Nagano way to stay is in a *shukubō* (temple lodging) at one of Zenkō-ji's subtemples. Contact **Zenkō-ji** (☎ 186-026-234-3591) to book, at least one day in advance. Be sure to dial the '186' to permit caller ID, without which staff might not pick up the phone. Expect to pay ¥7000 to ¥10,000 per person with two meals.

Zenkō-ji Kyōju-in Youth Hostel (☎ 232-2768; fax 232-2767; 479 Motoyoshi-chō; dm from ¥4000) This atmospheric hostel is housed in a 100-plus-

ZENKŌ-JI LEGENDS

Few Japanese temples have the fascination of Zenkō-ji, thanks in part to the legends related to it. The following are just a few:

- **Ikkō-Sanzon** This image, containing three statues of the Amida Buddha, was brought to Japan from Korea in the 6th century and remains the temple's raison d'être. It's wrapped like a mummy and kept in an ark behind the main altar, and it's said that nobody has seen it for 1000 years. However, in 1702, to quell rumours that the ark was empty, the shōgunate ordered a priest to confirm its existence and take measurements. That priest remains the last confirmed person to have viewed it.
- **Following an Ox to Zenkō-ji** Long ago, an impious old woman was washing her kimono when an ox appeared, caught a piece of the cloth on his horn and ran away with it. The woman was as stingy as she was impious, and she gave chase for hours. Finally, the ox led her to Zenkō-ji, and she fell asleep under its eaves. The ox came to her in a dream, revealed himself to be the image of the Amida Buddha and disappeared. The woman saw this as a miracle and became a pious believer. Today, people in Kantō say, 'I followed an ox to Zenkō-ji', to mean that something good happened unexpectedly.
- **The Doves of Sanmon** Zenkō-ji's pigeon population is renowned, making the rattan *hatto-guruma* (wheeled pigeon) a favourite Nagano souvenir. Locals claim the birds forecast bad weather by roosting on the Sanmon gate. Visitors claim to see five white doves in the plaque above the central portal; the five short strokes in the characters for Zenkō-ji do look remarkably dove-like. See if you can spot them too. In the upper character (善, zen) they're the two uppermost strokes; in the middle character (光, kō) they're the strokes on either side of the top; and in the 'ji' (寺) it's the short stroke on the bottom left.
- **Binzuru** A follower of Buddha, Binzuru trained in healing. He was due to become a Bosatsu (bodhisattva, or enlightened one) and go to the land of the immortals, but the Buddha instructed him to remain on earth and continue to do good works. At most temples, images of Binzuru are outside the main hall, but at Zenkō-ji you'll find his statue just inside, worn down where visitors have touched it to help heal ailments of the corresponding parts of their own bodies; you can see the lines where the face was once replaced.

year-old subtemple of Zenkō-ji, with mostly private rooms. Be sure to book ahead. No meals are served.

Shimizuya Ryokan (☎ 232-2580; fax 234-5911; 49 Daimon-chō; r per person from ¥4725) On Chūō-dōri, a few blocks south of Zenkō-ji, this friendly, family-run ryokan offers good value, with a smoky dark-wood interior, spotless tatami rooms (no private facilities), laundry machines and lots of ins, outs, ups, downs, nooks and crannies. It's been in the family for 130 years. No meals are served.

Comfort Hotel Nagano (☎ 268-1611; fax 268-1621; www.choice-hotels.com; 1-12-4 Minami-Chitose; s/d/tw from ¥4820/7350/9870; ⊠ 💻) Of the many business hotels near the station, this one has the best combination of value and welcome. Rooms are teeny tiny, but rates include a simple breakfast and internet access in the lobby. From the station, head northeast along Nagano Ōdōri.

Matsuya Ryokan (☎ 232-2811; fax 233-2047; Zenkō-ji Kannai; r per person from ¥5250, with 2 meals from ¥9450) Six generations of the Suzuki family have run this traditional inn just inside Zenkō-ji's Niō-mon. Even if the communal baths are a bit aged, the rest of the ryokan is exceedingly well maintained. Meals are seasonal *kaiseki* (Japanese haute cuisine). Add ¥1000 per person for rooms with private facilities. It's next to the statue of Enmei Jizō.

Holiday Inn Express Nagano (☎ 264-6000; fax 264-5511; www.ichotelsgroup.com; 2-17-1 Minami-Chitose; s/d/tw from ¥8800/16,000/17,000; ⊠ 💻) Built for the Olympics to cater to guests of overseas proportions, this professional 137-room hotel is a good deal for its large, Western-style rooms with LAN cable access. Breakfast is a Japanese-Western buffet (¥1100).

Hotel Metropolitan Nagano (☎ 291-7000; www.metro-n.co.jp; 1346 Minami-Ishido-chō; s/d/tw from ¥9240/18,480/19,635) An excellent choice by the station. The modern, elegant Metropolitan features airy, comfortable rooms, and there's a cafe, restaurant and top-floor lounge with broad views. Japan Rail Pass holders get a 20% discount. It's just outside the station's Zenkō-ji exit; sensitive sleepers should reserve a room facing away from the tracks.

Eating

Chō Bali Bali (☎ 229-5226; 1366-1 Ishidō-machi; mains from ¥600; 🕑 noon-2.30pm & 6pm-midnight Tue-Sun; Ⓥ) This stylish space gathers lively crowds most nights and serves eclectic dishes from Indonesia, Thailand and Vietnam, with a touch of Italian for good measure; *yam-un-sen* is spicy Thai salad with vermicelli. Highly recommended.

Marusei (☎ 232-5776; 486 Motoyoshi-chō; dishes ¥600-1800; 🕑 11am-6pm Thu-Tue) A stone's throw from the temple on Nakamise-dōri, tiny, unassuming Marusei serves *soba* and a well-liked *tonkatsu* (deep-fried breaded pork cutlet); the Marusei *bentō* (boxed meal; ¥1300) lets you try both.

Gohonjin Fujiya (☎ 232-1241; 80 Daimon-chō; mains ¥700-2700, courses from ¥2500; 🕑 lunch Mon-Fri, dinner nightly) Until recently, this was Nagano's most venerable hotel (since 1648 – look for 'Hotel Fujiya' on signage), but it quit the hotel business and is now the city's most venerable Western restaurant. Try potato gnocchi with gorgonzola sauce or *wa-gyū* (Japanese beef) sirloin Florentine. The imposing 1923 building mixes Japanese and art deco motifs. An English menu is available.

Fujiki-an (☎ 232-2531; 67 Daimon-chō; mains ¥800-1500; 🕑 noon-2.30pm & 6pm-midnight Tue-Sun) The clean, contemporary setting belies this *soba* shop's history (since 1827) of making fresh *soba* from the north of Nagano-ken. There's no English menu but a picture menu: *seiro-mori soba* (cold *soba* on a bamboo mat; ¥900) lets the flavour shine; other favourites are with *sansai*, *kinoko* (mushroom) tempura (¥1400) or *nishin* (herring; ¥1200).

Bosco (☎ 264-6270; 2nd fl, 1358 Suehiro-chō; mains ¥800-1600; 🕑 lunch & dinner Wed-Mon) Brush up on your katakana to dine at this comfortably modern Italian trattoria, Nagano's best. Although the writing may be unfamiliar, the cooking is like an old friend: airy crusted pizzas and generously proportioned pastas. Dark woods, walls of bright tile and an open kitchen provide a snappy backdrop.

Yayoi-za (☎ 232-2311; 503 Daimon-chō; mains ¥945-2650; 🕑 lunch & dinner, closed Tue & 2nd Wed each month) A homey 150-year-old shop specialising in *seiro-mushi* (ingredients steamed in a wood and bamboo box). The standard is *monzen seiro-mushi* (local beef and vegetables; ¥1680), while vegetarians can enjoy *onyasai salada* (steamed vegetables in sesame sauce). For dessert, try *kuri-an cream* (chestnut-paste mousse; ¥525).

Gomeikan (☎ 232-1221; 515 Daimon-chō; mains from ¥1200; 🕑 11am-8pm Thu-Tue) If you can't decide on one style of cooking, this long-standing generalist restaurant serves *tonkatsu*, vegetarian Indian curry, beefsteak, and coffee and cake in an old renovated building next to the post office on Chūō-dōri.

Sukitei (すき亭; ☎ 234-1123; 112-1 Tsumashina; lunch sets ¥1150-2950, sukiyaki from ¥2500; 🕑 lunch & dinner Tue-Sun) Tops in town for succulent sukiyaki. Set menus include udon, *gyusashi* (beef sashimi) and more. The price of the top-grade beef is sky-high, but if you try it you may never go back to the cheaper stuff.

Patio Daimon, an open-air collection of small buildings constructed like a village of *kura* (storehouses), by the Daimon bus stop, houses several casual eateries and boutiques, including **Tofu Café Gorokutei** (☎ 233-0356; 125-1 Higashi-machi; mains ¥600-1200; 🕑 lunch & dinner; Ⓥ), where just about everything is made from Japan's favourite protein.

For a quick bite next to Nagano Station's Zenkō-ji exit, the Tilia building has a half-dozen restaurants. On the ground floor, **Oyaki Kōbō** (☎ 223-4537; oyaki each around ¥140; 🕑 8.30am-7.30pm; Ⓥ) sells the local speciality *oyaki* (little baked or steamed wheat buns) with tasty fillings like pumpkin, mushroom and eggplant. Of the chain restaurants, **Yukimura-tei** (☎ 225-7878; mains ¥620-1080; 🕑 11am-11pm) serves heaping bowls of righteous *rāmen* – we like *moyashi miso* flavour (bean sprouts with miso broth). There's a picture menu.

Other quick bites:

Kashin Miwa (☎ 238-3041; 483 Motoyoshi-cho; ice cream ¥250; 🕑 9am-5pm) Ice cream made with *soba* (only in Nagano!), near Zenkō-ji's Niō-mon.

Bakery's Street & Café (☎ 232-0269; 1283 Toigosho; mains from ¥480; 🕑 7.30am-7pm; Ⓥ) Dozens of bakeries from around Shinshū take turns supplying the wares. On Chūō-dōri, en route to Zenkō-ji.

Drinking

Asian Night Market (☎ 214-5656; http://asian-night-market.net; 2-1 Higashi Go-chō; 🕑 noon-11pm; 💻) Part cafe, part humble-jumble Thai clothing and knick-knack shop, this storefront is at once sweet and hip. There's English-speaking staff, beer, cocktails, soft drinks including Thai coffee, Thai food (most dishes under ¥1000), and nooks and crannies for browsing and assignations.

Groovy (☎ 227-0480; http://nagano.cool.ne.jp/jazzgroovy; 1398 Kita-ishidō-machi; cover ¥1000-3500) A music spot popular with jazz lovers for its live shows; check the website for schedule info. It's upstairs on Chūō-dōri, a six-minute walk from the train station.

Bistro Liberty (☎ 235-1050; 1602 Midori-chō; 11.30am-4pm & 6pm-1am, closed Tue) Nagano's most popular *gaijin* pub has Guinness on tap, decent pub food and a friendly crowd. From JR Nagano Station, take a right on busy Nagano-Ōdōri and another right (at the second stoplight) on Shōwa-dōri.

Getting There & Away

Nagano *shinkansen* run twice hourly from Tokyo Station (Asama, ¥7970, 1¾ hours). The JR Shinonoi line connects Nagano with Matsumoto (Shinano *tokkyū*, ¥2970, 50 minutes) and Nagoya (Shinano *tokkyū*, ¥7330, 2¾ hours).

TOGAKUSHI 戸隠

☎ 026

This mountainous, forested region northwest of Nagano makes an excellent day trip. Hikers enjoy the refreshing alpine scenery from late spring to autumn, while winter belongs to the skiers. Togakushi has been famed for *soba* for centuries. Pick up English-language maps from the Nagano Tourist Information Centre.

Three subshrines (Togakushi-Hōkōsha 宝光社, Togakushi-Chūsha 中社 and Togakushi-Okusha 奥社), each a few kilometres apart, together make up the **Togakushi Shrine**, which honours the 1911m-high Mt Togakushi. Intimate Chūsha is the most easily accessible; one tree here is said to be 700 years old. There's a little village by Chūsha with shops, restaurants and ryokan, and in winter there's the smallish, 10-lift **Togakushi Ski Park** (戸隠スキー場; ☎ 254-2106; day pass ¥4000), which has a local following.

Okusha, the innermost shrine, can be reached via bus or hiking trail. The direct path from Chūsha to Okusha bus stop takes about 25 minutes, or there's a longer route via **Kagami-ike** (鏡池; Mirror Pond) and the **Togakushi Botanic Garden** (森林植物園). From Okusha bus stop it's another 2km (40 minutes) to the shrine buildings, partially via a 500m-long, cedar-lined path (杉並木; *suginamiki*), planted in 1612.

From Okusha, avid alpinists can make the strenuous climb to the top of Mt Togakushi. In winter, Okusha is inaccessible except for hearty snowshoers, and attractions and businesses here are closed.

On the hill above the Okusha bus stop, the highlight of the **Togakushi Minzoku-kan** (戸隠民俗館; ☎ 254-2395; adult/child ¥500/350; 9am-5pm mid-Apr–mid-Nov) is the 'ninja house', cleverly concocted with trick doors, hidden staircases, a room that slopes upwards and others from which there is seemingly *NO ESCAPE!* It pays tribute to the days when *yamabushi* (mountain monks) practised here, at what became the forerunner to *ninpo* (the art of stealth, as practised by ninja). Other buildings at Minzoku-kan contain museums of *ninpo* and local folklore.

In Chūsha, **Yokokura Ryokan** (横倉旅館; ☎ 254-2030; dm ¥3045, with 2 meals ¥5065, r per person incl 2 meals from ¥7200) is in a thatch-roofed building from the early Meiji era, about 150m from the steps up to Chūsha. It's both a hostel and a ryokan, with tatami-room dorms (gender-separate) and private rooms. **Uzura Soba** (うずら家そば; ☎ 254-2219; dishes ¥800-1700; lunch) serves handmade *soba* noodles until they run out. It's directly across from the steps to the shrine.

By Okusha bus stop, **Okusha no Chaya** (奥社の茶屋; ☎ 254-2222; mains ¥530-1480; 10am-4.30pm late Apr-late Nov; ⊠) serves fresh *soba* in a minimalist, contemporary setting behind a glass wall that overlooks the forest; ice cream comes in seasonal flavours such as tomato, chestnut and wasabi.

Buses via the scenic routes from Nagano depart approximately hourly (7am to 7pm) and arrive at Chūsha-Miyamae bus stop by Chūsha shrine in about an hour (one way/return ¥1160/2100). To Okusha the one-way/return fare is ¥1280/2300. The Togakushi Kōgen Free Kippu pass (¥2500) gives unlimited rides on buses to and around Togakushi for three days. Buy tickets at **Kawanakajima Bus Co** (☎ 229-6200), inside the Alpico Bus office by bus stop 7 in front of Nagano Station's Zenkō-ji exit.

OBUSE 小布施

☎ 026 / pop 11,600

This little town northeast of Nagano occupies a big place in Japanese art history.

The famed *ukiyo-e* (wood-block print) artist Hokusai (1760–1849) worked here during his last years. Obuse is also noted for its *kuri* (chestnuts), which you can sample steamed with rice or in ice cream or sweets.

The first stop should be **Hokusai-kan** (北斎館; ☎ 247-5206; adult/child/high-school student ¥500/free/300; 🕒 9am-6pm Apr-Sep, to 5pm Oct-Mar), displaying some 30 of Hokusai's inspiring prints at any one time, as well as several colourful floats decorated with his imaginative ceiling panels. From the train station, cross the street and walk down the road perpendicular to the station; take the second right, then look for signs to the museum. It's a 10-minute walk from the station.

A block away, Hokusai's patron, Takai Kōzan, is commemorated in the **Takai Kōzan Kinenkan** (高井鴻山記念館; ☎ 247-4049; admission ¥300; 🕒 9am-6pm Apr-Sep, to 5pm Oct-Mar). This businessman was also an accomplished artist, albeit of more classical forms than Hokusai's; look for elegant Chinese-style landscapes.

Among Obuse's nine other museums, **Nihon no Akari Hakubutsukan** (日本のあかり博物館; Japanese Lamp & Lighting Museum; ☎ 247-5669; adult/child/student ¥500/300/400; 🕒 9am-5pm late Mar-late Nov, 9.30am-4.30pm late Nov-late Mar, closed Wed except May, Aug, Oct, Nov) showcases lighting through Japanese history, including oil lamps and lanterns that will flip the switches of design fans. **Taikan Bonsai Museum** (盆栽美術館大観; ☎ 247-3000; adult/child ¥500/300 Apr-Nov, ¥300/free Dec-Mar; 🕒 9am-5pm) displays rare species and represents different Japanese landscapes.

Sample chestnut confections at **Chikufūdō** (竹風堂; ☎ 247-2569; 🕒 8am-7pm), established in 1893. *Dorayakisan* (chestnut paste in pancake dumplings) are the standard.

Obuse is reached via the Nagano Dentetsu (Nagaden) line from Nagano (*tokkyū*, ¥750, 22 minutes; *futsū*, ¥650, 35 minutes). Obtain maps and info and hire bikes (¥400 per half-day) at **Obuse Guide Centre** (おぶせガイドセンター; ☎ 247-5050; 🕒 9am-5pm), en route to the museums from the station.

YUDANAKA 湯田中

☎ 0269

This onsen village is known as the home of Japan's famous 'snow monkeys', a troop of some 200 Japanese macaques who live in and around the onsen baths. The monkeys and their mountain hot tub can be found at **Jigokudani Yaen-kōen** (地獄谷野猿公苑; Jigokudani Monkey Park; ☎ 33-4379; www.jigokudani-yaenkoen.co.jp; adult/child ¥500/250; 🕒 8.30am-5pm Apr-Oct, 9am-4pm Nov-Mar). The park has been operating since 1964, so the monkeys can no longer be described as truly wild, and they're often lured into the tub to gather food that's been placed there. Still, it's a unique chance to see them up close. It's a popular day trip from Nagano, and in winter it can be combined with a ski excursion to nearby Shiga Kōgen (below).

Across the river from Jigokudani, **Kōraku-kan** (後楽館; ☎ 33-4376; r per person with 2 meals from ¥10,545, onsen only adult/child ¥500/250; 🕒 8-10am & noon-3.30pm) is a simple onsen hotel. Accommodation is basic, with small but clean-swept tatami rooms. Aside from the mountain vegetable tempura for overnight visitors, the highlight is the indoor and concrete riverside outdoor onsen. Bathe in the great outdoors, and some uninvited guests – of the decidedly hairy variety – may join you.

In peaceful central Yudanaka, **Uotoshi Ryokan** (魚歳旅館; ☎ 33-1215; www.avis.ne.jp/~miyasaka/; s/d/tr/q from ¥4300/7980/11,970/15,960; 💻) is basic but commendably hospitable. The English-speaking owner will demonstrate and let you try *kyūdō* (Japanese archery), pick you up at Yudanaka Station, or drop you off near the start of the Monkey Park trail on request. Dinner (from ¥2520) and breakfast (from ¥530) are available. From the station (seven minutes), walk left and follow the road over the river; when the road ends turn right. It's 20m further on.

From Nagano, take the Nagano Dentetsu (Nagaden) line to Yudanaka terminus (*tokkyū*, ¥1230, 45 minutes; *futsū*, ¥1130, 1¼ hours); note that not all trains go all the way to Yudanaka. For Jigokudani Monkey Park, take the bus for Kanbayashi Onsen Guchi and get off at Kanbayashi Onsen (¥220, 15 minutes, eight daily), walk uphill along the road about 400m, and you'll see a sign reading 'Monkey Park' at the start of a tree-lined 1.6km walk.

SHIGA KŌGEN 志賀高原

☎ 0269

The site of several events in the 1998 Nagano Olympics, **Shiga Kōgen** (☎ 34-2404; www.shigakogen.gr.jp/english; 1-day lift ticket ¥4800; 🕒 8.30am-4.30pm Dec-Apr) is Japan's largest ski resort and one of the largest in the world: 21 linked areas

SHINSHŪ CUISINE: A ROGUE'S GALLERY

Nagano-ken is renowned for foods from the familiar to the, shall we say, challenging. You'll know a food is local if the name is preceded by Shinshū (信州), the region's ancient name. From the tamest, look for the following:

- *ringo* (りんご): apples, often as big as grapefruits. Ubiquitous in autumn.
- *kuri* (栗): chestnuts, especially in Obuse (p290).
- *soba* (そば): buckwheat noodles, handmade from 100% buckwheat in speciality shops (ordinary *soba* contains as little as 50% buckwheat). These can be eaten either cold (*zaru-soba;* with wasabi and soy-based dipping sauce) or hot (*kake-soba;* in broth).
- *oyaki* (おやき): little wheat buns filled with vegetables, baked or steamed.
- wasabi (わさび): Japanese horseradish, grown in bogs particularly in Hotaka (p301). You know grated wasabi from sushi and *soba*, and locals parboil the greens as drinking snacks. Some shops sell wasabi in cakes and ice cream.
- *basashi* (馬刺し): raw horse meat
- *hachinoko* (鉢の子): bee larvae
- *inago* (稲子): crickets

covering 80 runs. One lift ticket gives access to all areas as well as the shuttle bus between the various base lodges. There is a huge variety of terrain for all skill levels, as well as ski-only areas. **Shiga Kōgen Tourist Office** (志賀高原観光協会; ☎ 34-2323; ⌚ 9am-5pm) has English speakers who can help you navigate the slopes and can book accommodation. It's in front of the Shiga Kōgen ropeway station.

Due to its sprawling size, skiers will need to plan carefully or spend their first day at the resort making a full reconnaissance, and then spend the following days at their favourite spots. If you've got limited time, base yourself somewhere central like the Ichinose Family Ski Area, which has a central location and wide variety of accommodation and restaurants. You could also start at the Yakebitai area and work your way gradually down the length of the entire resort, taking the bus back up when you're done.

The Nishitateyama area has good wide runs and generally ungroomed terrain. The Terakoya area is a little hard to get to but it is generally uncrowded and has good short runs and a pleasant atmosphere. Skiers who don't play well with snowboarders will be happiest at the Kumanoyu area.

During the rest of the year, the mountains' lakes, ponds and overlooks make an excellent destination for hikers.

Sleeping & Eating

Hotels are scattered the length of Shiga Kōgen, clustered at the bases of the different areas. It makes sense to choose one near the base of your favourite area. **Hotel Shirakabasō** (ホテル白樺荘; ☎ 34-3311; www.shirakaba.co.jp/english/index.html; r per person with 2 meals from ¥11,700; 📶), close to the cable-car base station and the Sun Valley ski area, is a pleasant little hotel with a variety of rooms and its own indoor and outdoor onsen baths. Near the base of the Kumanoyu ski area, the large **Hotel Heights Shiga Kōgen** (ホテルハイツ志賀高原; ☎ 34-3030; www.shigakogen.jp/heights/english/index.htm; r per person with 2 meals from ¥9500) boasts clean Japanese- and Western-style rooms and its own onsen. Staff are used to foreign guests and, upon request, make some concessions to foreign palates in the dining room.

Another place that caters to a Western crowd is the **Hotel Sunroute Shiga Kōgen** (ホテルサンルート志賀高原; ☎ 34-2020; www.shigakogen.com/hotel/sunroute, in Japanese; r per person with 2 meals from ¥10,500). It's located in the Ichinose village, only a three-minute walk to the Ichinose Diamond ski lift, with great access to other ski areas. The rooms are Western style with en-suite baths, and some have mountain views.

Villa Ichinose (ヴィラ・一の瀬; ☎ 34-2704; www.villa101.biz/english/index.htm; r per person from ¥4800; 📶) is popular with foreigners, and its location in front of the Ichinose bus stop can't be beat. There are Japanese-style rooms (toilet only), and Western-style rooms with a bathroom. There is wireless internet in the lobby and a 24-hour public bath on the 2nd floor. It has English-speaking staff and a friendly atmosphere.

Also convenient to the slopes is the **Chalet Shiga** (シャレー志賀; ☎ 34-2235; www.shigakogen.jp/chalet; r per person with 2 meals from ¥11,500), a nice place with clean Western- and Japanese-style rooms and a popular sports bar.

Getting There & Away

Direct buses run between Nagano Station and Shiga Kōgen, with frequent departures in ski season (¥1600, 70 minutes). You can also take a train from Nagano to Yudanaka (p291) and continue to Shiga Kōgen by bus – take a Hase-ike-bound bus and get off at the last stop (¥760, approximately 40 minutes).

NOZAWA ONSEN 野沢温泉

☎ 0269 / pop 4050

A compact town that is tucked into a corner of the eastern Japan Alps, Nozawa Onsen is the quintessential Japanese onsen/ski resort. Nozawa feels like a Swiss ski resort, and you may wonder where you are – until you see a sign written entirely in kanji. Although Nozawa is worth visiting any time of year, skiing is the main attraction for foreign visitors.

On 15 January there is the **'Dosojin' fire festival**, one of the three most famous fire festivals in Japan, to pray for good fortune and a plentiful harvest in the coming year.

Sights & Activities

NOZAWA ONSEN SKI RESORT

野沢温泉スキー場

The town is dominated by the **Nozawa Onsen Ski Resort** (☎ 85-3166; www.nozawaski.com/winter/en/; 1-day lift ticket ¥4600; 🕑 Dec-Apr), which is one of Honshū's best. The ski area here is more compact than, say, nearby Shiga Kōgen, and it's relatively easy to navigate and enjoy. The main base area is right around the Higake gondola station. There is a good variety of terrain at all levels, and snowboarders should try the Karasawa terrain park or the half-pipe at Uenotaira. Advanced skiers will enjoy the steep and often mogulled Schneider Course, while beginners and families will enjoy the Higake Course.

For on-slope refreshments, try the rest house at Uenotaira gondola station, which has a standard-issue restaurant and snack bar. There's another restaurant at the top of the Nagasaka gondola. There are ski-hire places near the base of both gondolas, and boots of up to 31cm are available.

Snowshoe tours are available from the end of January, organised by the **Nozawa Onsen ski school** (☎ 85-2623; tours per person ¥4000, snowshoe rental ¥1000; 🕑 Tue, Thu & Sat 20 Jan-31 Mar), and there is a **snow bus tour** (☎ 85-2506; ¥500; six times daily) from 5 January to 29 March from the rest house at Yunomine.

ONSEN

After skiing or hiking, check out the 13 free **onsen** (🕑 6am-11pm) dotted about the town. Our favourite is Ō-yu, with its fine wooden building, followed by the scalding-hot Shin-yu, and the atmospheric old Kuma-no-tearai (Bear's Bathroom). The locals like to say about some of these that they're so hot 'humans can't even enter'. If you have silver jewellery, leave it in your room unless you don't mind it turning black for a day or so.

The baths are said to have a variety of healing powers and they're sure to fit the bill after a day on the slopes. If you plan on making a full circuit of all the onsen, leave valuables in your room and wear easy-on/easy-off clothes, such as a *yukata* (light summer cotton kimono), and slip-on shoes or sandals. If you go to one of the free baths just before or after dinner you can expect a crowd, but try one in the mid-morning or later in the evening, and you're likely to have it to yourself.

Sleeping & Eating

The **Minshuku Information Office** (野沢温泉民宿組合事務所; ☎ 85-2068; 🕑 8.30am-5.30pm), in the centre of town, can help with accommodation, and has English-speaking staff.

Lodge Nagano (ロッジながの; ☎ 090-8670-9597; www.lodgenagano.com; r per person with breakfast from ¥4000, r in summer from ¥2500; wi-fi) This is a popular foreign-run guest house that attracts a lot of Aussie skiers and, with Vegemite in the dining room, makes them feel right at home. It's a friendly, fun place with both bunk- and Japanese-style rooms, some with private bath. There's wi-fi and a house computer as well.

Villa Nozawa (ヴィラ野沢; ☎ 85-3163; www.nozawaholidays.com; r per person with breakfast from ¥6000, child under 15 half-price; wi-fi) This place caters to families, couples and small groups. It's next to the free Nakao Onsen and has 14 Japanese-style rooms, a large kitchen and laundry facilities.

Lodge Matsuya (ロッヂ まつや; ☎ 85-2082; fax 85-3694; r per person with breakfast from ¥6000, with 2 meals from ¥8000) In the centre of town is this large, friendly, family-run place with both Western- and Japanese-style rooms.

Pension Schnee (ペンションシュネー; ☎ 85-2012; www.pensionschnee.com; r per person with 2 meals from ¥8400) On the slopes near the Higake gondola base, this European-style hotel enjoys the best location in town. It's a ski-in/ski-out place with comfortable pension-style rooms and a woodsy dining room.

Haus St Anton (サンアントンの家; ☎ 85-3597; http://nozawa.com/stanton; r per person with 2 meals with/without bathroom from ¥14,000/11,550) In the centre of the village, this is a comfortable inn with an Austrian theme and very helpful, friendly staff. It has six attractive Western-style bedrooms in a variety of themes, and a dining area/bar with a woody, warm atmosphere. It is also very close to the supermarket and main shopping street.

Drinking

For nightlife, try **Main Street Bar Foot** (マインストリトバーフット; ☎ 85-4004), right on the main drag. It's a casual place for an after-ski drink, with free internet and table soccer. **Stay** (ステイ; ☎ 85-3404; www.seisenso.com), on the basement floor of the same building, is open late and run by a music-loving Japanese man who has lived abroad. The older crowd will prefer **Minato Bar** (みなと; ☎ 85-2609), also easy to find in the northern part of town, near the base of the gondola. It's a Japanese-style place that seats 50 and also offers karaoke next door.

Getting There & Away

There are direct buses between Nagano Station's east exit and Nozawa Onsen (¥1400, 90 minutes, six buses per day in winter, three buses per day in summer). Alternatively, take a JR Iiyama-line train between Nagano and Togari Nozawa Onsen Station (¥740, 55 minutes). Regular buses connect Togari Nozawa Onsen Station and Nozawa Onsen (¥300, 15 minutes, nine per day). The bus station/ticket office is about 200m from the main bus stop, which is directly in the middle of town. This can be a little confusing, but there are staff around to help get people where they need to be.

HAKUBA 白馬

☎ 0261

At the base of one of the highest sections of the northern Japan Alps, Hakuba is one of Japan's main ski and hiking centres. In winter, skiers from all over Japan and increasingly from overseas flock to Hakuba's seven ski resorts. In summer, the region is crowded with hikers drawn by easy access to the high peaks. There are many onsen in and around Hakuba-mura, the main village, and a long soak after a day of action is the perfect way to ease your muscles.

For information, maps and lodging assistance, visit the **Hakuba Shukuhaku Jōhō Centre** (白馬宿泊情報センター; ☎ 72-6900; www.hakuba1.com, in Japanese; ⏲ 7am-6pm), to the right of the Hakuba train/bus station, or **Hakuba-mura Kankō Kyōkai Annai-jo** (白馬村観光協会案内所; ☎ 72-2279; ⏲ 8.30am-5.15pm), just outside the station to the right (look for the 'i' symbol). Online, visit www.vill.hakuba.nagano.jp/e/index.htm.

Sights & Activities

HAPPŌ-ONE SKI RESORT 八方尾根

Host of the men's and women's downhill races at the 1998 Winter Olympics, **Happō-One** (☎ 72-3066; www.hakuba-happo.or.jp, in Japanese; 1-day lift ticket ¥4800; ⏲ Dec-Apr) is one of Japan's best ski areas. The mountain views here are superb – the entire Hakuba massif looks close enough to touch with your ski poles. Beginner, intermediate and advanced runs cater to skiers and snowboarders.

Most runs go right down the face of the mountain, with several good burners descending from Usagidaira 109, the mountain's centrepoint. Above this, two chairlifts run to the top, worth visiting for the views alone. On busy days, you can usually avoid lift-line bottlenecks by heading to areas like the Skyline 2.

The rest house at Usagidaira 109 is the largest eating establishment. There's a *rāmen* restaurant, a kebab shop, a McDonald's and the usual curry-rice-type selections. The modern Virgin Café Hakuba has upscale ambience, decent food, wait service, cappuccino etc. Café Kurobishi has excellent mountain views to the north and cafeteria-style seating.

There are plenty of hire places in the streets around the base of the mountain, some with boots up to 31cm. All have roughly the same selection and prices (¥2500 to ¥3000 per day for skis/board and boots), with modern carving skis, snowboards, short skis and accessories.

From Hakuba Station, a five-minute bus ride (¥260) takes you into the middle of Hakuba-mura; from there it's a 10-minute walk to the base of Happō-One and the main 'Adam' gondola base station. In winter, a shuttle bus makes the rounds of the village, lodges and ski base.

HAKUBA 47 WINTER SPORTS PARK & HAKUBA GORYŪ SKI RESORT HAKUBA 47

ウイタースポーツパーク & 白馬五竜スキー場

The interlinked areas of **Hakuba 47 Winter Sports Park** (☎ 75-3533; www.hakuba47.co.jp/index_en.php) and **Goryū Ski Resort** (☎ 75-3700; www.hakubagoryu.com/e/index.html) form the second major ski resort (one-day lift ticket ¥4800; open December to April) in the Hakuba area. There's a good variety of terrain at both areas, but you'll have to be at least an intermediate skier to ski the runs linking the two. Like Happō-One, this area boasts fantastic mountain views; the restaurant Alps 360 is the place to enjoy them. The Genki Go shuttle bus from Hakuba-mura and Hakuba-eki provides the easiest access.

HAKUBA CORTINA KOKUSAI

白馬コルチナ国際

This smaller **ski area** (☎ 82-2236; http://hakubacortina.jp/ski/index.html, in Japanese; 1-day lift ticket ¥3300; ⌚ Dec-Apr) at the north end of the Hakuba valley is popular both with those wanting a break from the main ski areas, and with the richer crowd from Tokyo who want the resort experience. It also caters to more advanced skiers, but can be icy when there isn't new snow. Its main building is a massive European gothic structure in red, white and black, with hotel, restaurants, ski rental and even a brand-new deluxe onsen all under one roof. You can also get a combined ticket with neighbouring Norikura resort for more skiing terrain. When the snow is fresh it's an uncrowded alternative to Happō-One, and the lift/lunch option is great value at less than ¥4000. Try the make-your-own pizza option in the main restaurant for a lunch to remember.

ONSEN

There are many onsen in and around Hakuba-mura, and a long soak after a day of skiing or hiking is the perfect way to ease your muscles. By far the best of these is **Obuya** (おぶや; ☎ 75-3311; 21396 Kamishiro, Hakuba, Kita azumi-gun; www.obuya.jp/english.html; adult/child ¥800/400; ⌚ 11am-10pm, enter by 9.30pm), just off the main road near the turn-off to Goryū Ski Resort, notable for its outdoor steam sauna and expansive *rotemburo*. **Mimizuku-no-yu** (みみずくの湯; ☎ 72-6542; adult/child ¥500/250; ⌚ 10am-9.30pm, enter by 9pm), near the Hakuba Tokyu Hotel, has some of the best mountain views from the tub.

SUMMER ACTIVITIES

In summer, take the gondola and the two upper chairlifts, and then hike along a trail for an hour or so to the pond Happō-ike on a ridge below Karamatsu-dake. From here, follow a trail for an hour up to Maru-yama, continue for 1½ hours to the Karamatsu-dake San-sō (mountain hut) and then climb to the peak of **Karamatsu-dake** (唐松岳; 2695m) in about 30 minutes. The return fare is ¥2340 if purchased at the Hakuba tourist office, ¥2600 otherwise.

Other popular hikes include the four-hour ascent of **Shirouma-dake** (白馬岳; 2932m), which offers spectacular views on clear days. Mountain huts provide meals and clean, basic accommodation (around ¥9000 per person with two meals) and are within an hour from the summit. **Yari Onsen** (鑓温泉; ☎ 72-2002; onsen ¥300, r per person with 2 meals ¥9000) is another popular hike for Japan's highest *rotemburo* (2100m) and more breathtaking views.

Buses leave Hakuba Station for the trailhead at Sarukura (¥980, 30 minutes, between late May and September). From here you can hike west to Shirouma-dake in about six hours. A track southwest of Sarukura leads uphill for three hours to Yari Onsen.

Ask at tourist offices for information about **Tsugaike Natural Park** (栂池自然園), renowned for its alpine flora, and **Nishina San-ko** (仁科三湖; literally 'Three Lakes of Nishina', which are Aoki-ko, Nakazuna-ko and Kizaki-ko), which offer pleasant hiking.

Evergreen Outdoor Centre (www.evergreen-hakuba.com) offers an array of half-day adventures with English-speaking guides from about ¥5000 year-round, including canyoning and mountain biking, as well as snowshoeing and backcountry treks in the winter.

Sleeping & Eating

The village of Hakuba-mura has a huge selection of accommodation. The Hakuba Shukuhaku Jōhō Centre (opposite) can help arrange accommodation if you arrive without reservations.

Snowbeds (スノーベッズ; ☎ 72-5242; www.snowbedsjapan.com; r per person from ¥3900) One of Hakuba's cheapest, with fairly cramped bunk rooms and a nice communal area with a wood stove. It's foreign-run, so communication is no problem, and it's close to some good nightlife options.

CENTRAL HONSHŪ

Hotel Viola (ホテルヴィオラ; ☎ toll-free 0120-89-8193; www.hotel-viola.com; d per person with 2 meals from ¥8000) About 15 minutes' walk from the gondola, this friendly place is a favourite of Aussie skiers and has clean, well-maintained rooms, English-speaking staff and a friendly atmosphere.

Hakuba Highland Hotel (白馬ハイランドホテル; ☎ 72-3450; fax 72-3067; r per person with 2 meals from ¥8400) Located at the base of the Hakuba Highland ski area, this family-friendly hotel boasts a sensational view over the Hakuba range, clean and fairly spacious rooms and a great indoor-outdoor onsen.

Hakuba Tokyu Hotel (白馬東急ホテル; ☎ 72-3001; www.tokyuhotelsjapan.com/en/TR/TR_HAKUB/index.html; per person with breakfast from ¥13,000) This is a deluxe hotel with all the amenities. The rooms are formal, with great views. The Grand Spa boasts the highest alkaline content in the area, and the hotel also has a gift shop, bar and restaurant with French and Japanese cuisine.

Uncle Steven's Mexican Food (☎ 72-7569; www15.ocn.ne.jp/~ustevens/index-e.html; Happō Gondola Rd; dinner meals ¥1000-1600; 🕑 11am-10.30pm) This is one of the most popular restaurants in Hakuba. The Steven's Burrito, chimichanga and enchiladas are all quite authentic and the portions are big, though you may find it a little on the expensive side.

Canada-Tei (金田邸; ☎ 75-2698) This delicious and popular *izakaya* is located on the road to Goryū Ski Resort area, with food cooked right in front of you. It's run by an interesting and well-travelled character.

Drinking & Entertainment

As you might expect, the town of Hakuba bustles with nightlife during the winter season, and it isn't hard to find what you like for food, drink and music.

Tracks Bar (☎ 75-4366; www.tracksbar.com; 22200-7 Kitashiro, Hakuba-mura, Kita Azumi-gun; drinks from ¥500; 🕑 5pm-midnight, closed irregularly) Located between Kamishiro Station and the base of Hakuba 47 Winter Sports Park/Goryū Ski Resort area, this is one of the favourite night spots for the younger, foreign crowd, with live music, sports on a huge screen and regular events. There is also budget accommodation in the area.

The Pub (☎ 72-4453) For a few drinks after a day on the slopes, try this British-style pub in the Mominoki Hotel. It offers pub food, live music and events and is just five minutes from the base of the hill in Hakuba village.

Getting There & Away

Hakuba is connected with Matsumoto by the JR Ōito line (*tokkyū*, ¥2770, 56 minutes; *futsū*, ¥1110, 99 minutes). Continuing north, change trains at Minami Otari to meet the JR Hokuriku line at Itoigawa, with connections to Niigata, Toyama and Kanazawa. From Nagano, buses leave from Nagano Station (¥1500, approximately 70 minutes). There are also buses between Shinjuku Nishi-guchi, in Tokyo, and Hakuba (¥4700, 4½ hours).

BESSHO ONSEN 別所温泉

☎ 0268

This intimate, mountain-ringed onsen town, bisected by a gentle stream, is known as 'Little Kamakura' for its dramatic temples and the fact that it served as an administrative centre during the Kamakura period (1185–1333). It was also mentioned in *The Pillow Book* by the Heian-era poetess Sei Shōnagon and was later a retreat for writers, including Kawabata Yasunari.

Bessho's excellent waters, reputed to cure diabetes and constipation while beautifying your complexion, bring in tourists aplenty, but overall it feels undervisited. Web information is available at www.bessho-spa.jp/j_en glish/english_fls.htm.

Bessho Onsen Ryokan Association (別所温泉旅館組合; ☎ 38-2020; 🕑 9am-5pm) is the local tourist office – at the train station. English speakers will be marginally better off enquiring at the **tourist office** (☎ 26-5001; 🕑 9am-6pm) in Ueda Station en route to Bessho; staff can book same-day accommodation in Bessho.

The National Treasure temple **Anraku-ji** (安楽時; ☎ 38-2062; adult/child ¥300/100; 🕑 8am-5pm Mar-Oct, to 4pm Nov-Feb), from AD 824–34 and renowned for its octagonal pagoda, is 10 minutes on foot from Bessho Onsen Station. The Tendai temple **Kitamuki Kannon** (北向観音; ☎ 38-2023; admission free; 🕑 24hr) is a few minutes' walk away, with some prodigiously old trees, sweeping views across the valley and a pavilion on stilts that's like a tiny version of Kyoto's Kiyomizu-dera. Its name comes from the fact that this Kannon image faces north, a counterpart to the south-facing image at Zenkō-ji in Nagano. About a 5km hike away are the temples **Chūzen-ji** (☎ 38-4538; adult/child ¥200/50; 🕑 9am-4pm) and **Zenzan-ji** (☎ 38-2855; adult/child ¥200/100; 🕑 9am-4pm, occasional winter closures), which feel like a real escape.

There are three central **public baths** (admission ¥150; ⏰ 6am-10pm): Ō-yu (大湯) has a small *rotemburo;* Ishi-yu (石湯) is famed for its stone bath; and Daishi-yu (大師湯), most frequented by the locals, is known for being relatively cool.

The 13-bed **Mahoroba Youth Hostel** (上田まほろばユースホステル; ☎ 38-5229; fax 38-1714; dm ¥3200, with 2 meals ¥4950) is comfortable and secluded, surrounded by lush scenery, but doesn't have an onsen. It's an eight-minute walk south from the train station.

Uematsu-ya (上松屋; ☎ 38-2300; fax 38-8501; www.uematsuya.com, in Japanese; r per person with 2 meals from ¥10,500) is neither historical nor traditional but kindly, well kept and good value. Its 33 rooms (both Japanese and Western style) are up nine storeys. There's an all-you-can-drink plan (females/males ¥2100/3150), plus indoor and outdoor baths. Some English is spoken.

The traditional **Ryokan Hanaya** (旅館花屋; ☎ 38-3131; fax 38-7923; r per person with 2 meals from ¥15,750) is among lovely, manicured gardens. Spacious tatami rooms open onto the scenery. Some rooms have private onsen baths attached; guests without enjoy pleasant indoor and outdoor baths. Book far in advance.

Access to Bessho Onsen is via Ueda, on the JR Nagano *shinkansen* (from Tokyo ¥6490, 1½ hours; from Nagano ¥2870, 13 minutes) or the private Shinano Tetsudō line from Nagano (¥740, about 35 minutes). At Ueda, change to the private Ueda Dentetsu line to Bessho Onsen (¥570, 30 minutes, approximately hourly).

MATSUMOTO 松本

☎ 0263 / pop 227,000

A traveller's favourite, Matsumoto has a superb castle, some pretty streets and an atmosphere that's both laid-back and surprisingly cosmopolitan.

Nagano-ken's second-largest city has been around since at least the 8th century. Formerly known as Fukashi, it was the castle town of the Ogasawara clan during the 14th and 15th centuries, and it continued to prosper through the Edo period. Today, Matsumoto's street aesthetic combines the black and white of its castle with *namako-kabe* (lattice-pattern-walled) *kura* and Edo-period streetscapes in the Nakamachi district, and some smart 21st-century Japanese architecture. Plus, views of the Japan Alps are never much further than around the corner. The areas by the Metoba-gawa and Nakamachi boast galleries, comfortable cafes and reasonably priced, high-quality accommodation.

Utsukushi-ga-hara and Asama Onsens and the Utsukushi-ga-hara plateau are day trips, while Hotaka can be either a day trip or the start of a hiking route. Matsumoto is also a transit hub for Japan Alps National Park and the Kiso Valley.

Orientation & Information

For a castle town, Matsumoto is relatively easy to get around. Although small streets radiate somewhat confusingly from the train station, soon you're on a grid. Any place on the Matsumoto map in this book is within 20 minutes' walk of the train station.

The main post office is located on Honmachi-dōri. For web information, visit www.city.matsumoto.nagano.jp.

Matsumoto's **tourist information office** (☎ 32-2814; 1-1-1 Fukashi; ⏰ 9.30am-5.45pm), inside Matsumoto Station, has English-language pamphlets and maps, and can book accommodation. For train and bus reservations, try **JTB** (☎ 35-3311; 1-2-11 Fukashi).

Sights & Activities

MATSUMOTO-JŌ 松本城

Even if you spend only a couple of hours in Matsumoto, be sure to visit **Matsumoto-jō** (☎ 32-2902; 4-1 Marunōchi; adult/child ¥600/300; ⏰ 8.30am-5pm early-Sep–mid-Jul, to 6pm mid-Jul & Aug), Japan's oldest wooden castle and one of four castles designated National Treasures – the others are Hikone (p385), Himeji (p415) and Inuyama (p263).

The magnificent three-turreted *donjon* was built c 1595, in contrasting black and white, leading to the nickname Karasu-jō (Crow Castle). Steep steps lead up six storeys, with impressive views from each level. Lower floors display guns, bombs and gadgets with which to storm castles, and a delightful *tsukimi yagura* (moon-viewing pavilion). It has a tranquil moat full of carp, with the occasional swan gliding beneath the red bridges. The basics are explained over loudspeakers in English and Japanese. You can also ask at the entrance about a free tour in English (subject to availability), or call the **Goodwill Guide Group** (☎ 32-7140), which gives free one-hour tours by reservation.

The castle grounds (and your admission ticket) also include the **Matsumoto City**

INFORMATION
JTB 1 A3
Main Post Office 中央郵便局 2 B2
Tourist Information Office 観光案内所 3 A3

SIGHTS & ACTIVITIES
Matsumoto City Museum/Japan Folklore Museum 松本市立博物館 4 B1
Matsumoto-jō 松本城 5 B1
Nakamachi Kura-Chic-Kan 中町蔵シック館 6 B2

SLEEPING
Hotel Buena Vista ホテルブエナビスタ 7 A3
Marumo まるも旅館 8 B2
Nunoya 旅館ぬのや 9 B2
Richmond Hotel リチモンドホテル 10 A2
Tōyoko Inn Matsumoto Ekimae Honmachi 東横イン松本駅前本町 11 A2

EATING
Kura 蔵 12 A2
Nomugi 野麦 13 B2
Robata Shōya 炉ばた庄屋 14 A2
Shizuka しづか 15 B1
Vamonos バモノス 16 A2

DRINKING
Coat メインバーコート 17 A2
Old Rock オールドロック 18 A2

SHOPPING
Berami (Belle Amie) ベラミ 19 B2
Parco Department Store パルコ 20 A2

TRANSPORT
Matsumoto Bus Station 松本バスターミナル 21 A3

Museum/Japan Folklore Museum (☎ 32-0133; 4-1 Marunōchi; ⌚ 8.30am-4.30pm), with small displays relating to the region's history and folklore, including *tanabata* dolls (wood or cardboard cut-outs dressed in paper) and the wooden phalluses that play a prominent role in the September Dōsojin Matsuri (opposite).

NAKAMACHI 中町

The narrow streets of this former merchant district make a fine setting for a stroll, as most of its storehouses have been transformed into cafes, galleries and craft shops specialising in wood, glass, fabric, ceramics and antiques. **Nakamachi Kura-Chic-Kan** ('Classic-kan'; ☎ 36-3053; 2-9-15 Chūō; ⌚ 9am-10pm) is just one option, showcasing locally produced arts and crafts, with a relaxing coffee house next door.

MATSUMOTO PERFORMING ARTS CENTRE
まつもと市民芸術館

Architect Itō Toyō has broken all the rules with this 2004 building. Undulating exterior walls are punctuated with frosted glass cut-outs that look like rocks – impressive at night. Among other performance spaces, the **Matsumoto Performing Arts Centre** (☎ 33-3800; 3-10-1 Fukashi) is the key venue for the Saitō Kinen Festival (opposite). Heading east on Ekimae-dōri from the city centre, it's just off the map on the right.

MATSUMOTO CITY MUSEUM OF ART
松本市美術館

This sleek **museum** (☎ 39-7400; 4-2-22 Chūō; adult/child/high-school & college student ¥400/free/200; ⌚ 9am-5pm Tue-Sun) has a good collection of Japanese artists, many of whom hail from Matsumoto or depict scenes of the surrounding countryside. Highlights include the striking avant-garde works of Kusama Yayoi (look for the 'Infinity Mirrored Room'), the finely crafted landscapes of Tamura Kazuo, the calligraphy of Kamijo Shinzan and temporary exhibitions. The striking contemporary building (2002) borrows motifs (black facade, stone walls, impressive greenery and minimoat) from the castle. It's about 100m past the Performing Arts Centre, across the street.

JAPAN UKIYO-E MUSEUM
日本浮世絵美術館

Several generations of the Sakai family have collected more than 100,000 wood-block prints, paintings, screens and old books to create reputedly the largest private collection in the world. This **museum** (☎ 47-4440; 2206-1 Koshiba, Shimadachi; adult/child ¥1050/530; ⌚ 10am-5pm Tue-Sun) exhibits a minuscule fraction of the collection at any one time, in a contemporary building. English signage is minimal, but an explanatory leaflet in English is provided.

The museum is approximately 3km from Matsumoto Station, 15 minutes' walk from Ōniwa Station on the Matsumoto Dentetsu line (¥170, six minutes), or about ¥2000 by taxi.

UTSUKUSHI-GA-HARA & ASAMA ONSENS
美ヶ原温泉・浅間温泉

These two onsen resort towns are northeast of town. Utsukushi-ga-hara Onsen (not to be confused with Utsukushi-ga-hara Kōgen) is the more beautiful of the two, with a quaint main street and views across the valley, while Asama Onsen's history is said to date back to the 10th century and includes writers and poets, though it looks quite generic now. The waters in both places are said to be good for gastrointestinal and skin troubles, and women's disorders. **Hot Plaza Asama** (ホットプラザ浅間; ☎ 46-6278; adult/child ¥840/420; ⌚ 10am-8pm

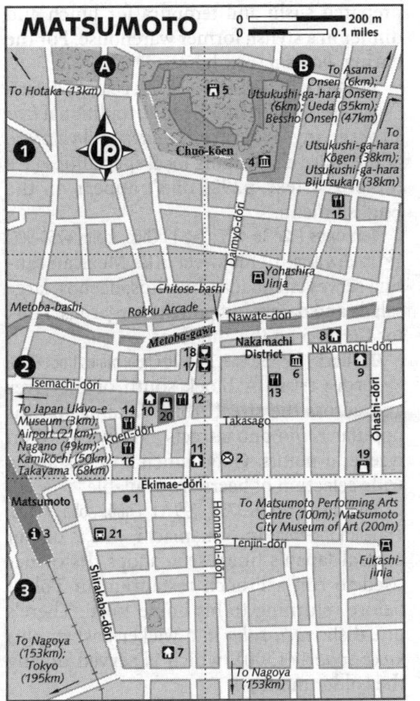

Wed-Mon) feels like a neighbourhood *sentō* but boasts many pools and sauna.

Both towns are easily reached by bus from Matsumoto's bus terminal (Utsukushi-ga-hara Onsen: ¥330, 18 minutes, twice hourly; Asama Onsen: ¥350, 23 minutes, hourly).

UTSUKUSHI-GA-HARA KŌGEN 美ヶ原高原

Not to be confused with Utsukushi-ga-hara Onsen, this alpine plateau (2000m) is a popular warm-weather excursion from Matsumoto, reached via an ooh-and-ahh drive on twisty mountain roads called Azalea Line and Venus Line.

Utsukushi-ga-hara Bijutsukan (美ヶ原美術館; Utsukushi-ga-hara Open-Air Museum; ☎ 86-2331; adult/child/student ¥1000/700/800; ⌚ 9am-5pm late-Apr–mid-Nov), in the same vein (with the same owner) as the Hakone Open-Air Museum (p217), is a large sculpture garden (some 350 pieces, mostly by Japanese sculptors), and the surrounding mountains provide an inspiring backdrop in clear weather.

Nearby are pleasant walks and the opportunity to see cows in pasture (a constant source of fascination in Japan). **Furusato-kan** (ふる里館; ☎ 0268-86-2311), the shop at the hilltop farm, sells ice cream made from local *kokemomo* (lingonberries).

Most Japanese visitors reach the museum by car. Buses (¥1300, 80 minutes) run several times daily in midsummer, with spotty-to-nonexistent service the rest of the season; check before you go. Taxis to the museum are upwards of ¥10,000 each way, so renting a car may make sense. See p301 for information on car hire.

Festivals & Events

Matsumoto-jō Sakura Matsuri Cherry-blossom time (late April) coincides with mood lighting at the castle.

Tenjin Matsuri The festival at Fukashi-jinja on 23 and 24 July features elaborately decorated *yatai*.

Takigi Nō Matsuri This atmospheric festival during August features nō performances by torchlight, outdoors on a stage in the park below the castle.

Saitō Kinen Festival About a dozen classical music concerts in memory of revered Japanese conductor and music educator Saitō Hideo (1902–72) held in mid-August to mid-September. Ozawa Seiji, conductor emeritus of the Boston Symphony Orchestra, is festival director.

Dōsojin Matsuri On the fourth Saturday in September, phallic merriment is to be had at the festival held in honour of *dōsojin* (roadside guardians) at Utsukushi-ga-hara Onsen.

Yohashira Jinja Matsuri This festival (aka Shintōsai) occurs around the beginning of October, featuring fireworks and large dolls.

Taimatsu Matsuri Around the start of October, Asama Onsen celebrates the spectacular fire festival with torch-lit parades that are accompanied by drumming.

Oshiro Matsuri The Castle Festival, from mid-October to 3 November, is a cultural jamboree that includes costume parades, puppet displays and flower shows.

Sleeping

Get away from the station (mostly cramped and charmless business hotels) for the many worthwhile lodgings within 10 minutes' walk, especially in Nakamachi.

Nunoya (☎/fax 32-0545; 3-5-7 Chūō; r per person from ¥4500) Few inns have more heart than this pleasantly traditional charmer, with shiny wood floors and quality tatami rooms with shared bathrooms. No meals are served, but the cafes (and shops and galleries) of Nakamachi are just outside.

Marumo (☎ 32-0115; fax 35-2251; 3-3-10 Chūō; r per person ¥5250, with breakfast ¥6300) Between Nakamachi and the rushing Metoba-gawa, this beautiful wooden ryokan dates from 1868 and has lots of traditional charm, including a bamboo garden and coffee shop. Although rooms aren't huge and don't have private facilities, it's quite popular, so book ahead.

Tōyoko Inn Matsumoto Ekimae Honmachi (☎ 36-1045; www.toyoko-inn.com; 2-1-23 Chūō; s/d & tw from ¥5460/8190; ⊠ 💻) Bargain business hotel in the centre of everything. Rooms are functional, spotless and cramped, but freebies include quick phone calls from the lobby, LAN cable access and a simple Japanese breakfast.

Richmond Hotel (☎ 37-5000; www.richmondhotel.jp/e/matsumoto; 1-10-7 Chūō; s/d from ¥6400/8800; ⊠ 💻) Central and crisp, this 240-room business hotel offers decent-sized rooms, a minimum of fuss and LAN cable access. Rates are for *kai-in* (members); to become one, fill out a form and pay a one-time ¥500 charge at check-in. Even cheaper rates are often available online.

Hotel Buena Vista (☎ 37-0111; www.buena-vista.co.jp; 1-2-1 Honjo; s/tw from ¥9240/19,645; ⊠ 💻) Long Matsumoto's sharpest Western hotel, the Buena Vista has been given a chic Barcelona-style makeover in its public spaces: dark woods, stone, mood lighting and world beats in the lobby. Rooms were slo-o-wly being renovated as we went to press. The Salon de Fuego lounge on the top (14th) floor has the city's best views. LAN cable access and frequent internet specials are available.

UTSUKUSHI-GA-HARA ONSEN

Sugimoto (☎ 32-3379; 451-7 Satoyamabe; r per person from ¥15,000) You might want two nights in this fabulous ryokan on Utsukushi-ga-hara's main street: one to get acquainted with the facilities – onsen baths, jacuzzi, *mingei* (folk art) collection, tea room, underground passage, bar stocked with single malts etc – and the second to enjoy them. Rooms range in size and decor (Japanese, Western and mixed), but all are ineffably stylish. Lunch or dinner (¥6000, by reservation) includes bath admission.

Eating & Drinking

Robata Shōya (☎ 37-1000; 11-1 Chūō; dishes ¥150-900; 🕑 dinner) On a corner in the town centre is this classic, lively *yakitori-ya* (restaurant specialising in *yakitori*, which are skewers of grilled chicken), with a large selection of grills, seasonal specials and a (sort of) English menu.

Kura (☎ 33-6444; 1-10-22 Chūō; dishes from ¥300, teishoku ¥945-2100; 🕑 lunch & dinner Thu-Tue) Located near Nakamachi, Kura serves meticulously prepared sushi and tempura for lunch and dinner in a stylish former warehouse. For the daring: *basashi* (raw horse meat).

Shizuka (☎ 32-0547; 4-10-8 Ōte; dishes ¥525-1365; 🕑 lunch & dinner Mon-Sat) Friendly, traditional *izakaya* serving favourites like *oden* and *yakitori*. Some more challenging local specialities (see the boxed text, p292) don't appear on the English menu.

Vamonos (☎ 36-4878; 1-4-13 Chūō; mains ¥750-900; 🕑 lunch & dinner) This sweet little Mexican cantina serves enchiladas, burritos, nachos, large salads and dainty but potent margaritas. Look for the sign on the 2nd floor.

Old Rock (☎ 38-0069; 2-30-20 Chūō; mains from ¥750; 🕑 lunch & dinner) A block south of the river and across the street from Nakamachi, this popular *gaijin* pub attracts a lively crowd on weekend nights. Good lunch specials and a wide selection of beers are available.

Nomugi (☎ 36-3753; 2-9-11 Chūō; soba ¥1100; 🕑 lunch Thu-Mon) In Nakamachi, this is one of central Japan's finest *soba* shops. Its owner used to run a French restaurant in Tokyo before returning to his home town. There's one dish: *zaru-soba* in a wicker basket; plus *kake-soba* (¥1300), which is served during the colder months.

Coat (☎ 34-7133; 2-3-24 Chūō; 🕑 4pm-12.30am Tue-Sun) This sophisticated little bar is home to Matsumoto's most famous bartender. Hayashi-san's inventive *otomenadeshiko* cocktail won first prize at the Japan Bartenders Association competition early this decade.

For a quick coffee and cake, cafes line the banks of the Metoba-gawa and Nawate-dōri.

Shopping

Matsumoto is synonymous with *temari* (embroidered balls) and doll-making. You can find both at **Berami** (Belle Amie; ☎ 33-1314; 3-7-23 Chūō; 🕑 9am-7pm Mon, Tue, Thu, Fri & Sat, 10am-6pm Sun). Doll styles include *tanabata* and *oshie-bina* (dressed in fine cloth). Takasago street, one block south of Nakamachi, also has several doll shops.

In addition to Nakamachi's galleries, Nawate-dōri north of the river is a colourful place for souvenirs and cafes. Parco department store has pride of place in the city centre.

Getting There & Away

AIR

Shinshū Matsumoto airport has flights to Fukuoka, Osaka and Sapporo.

BUS

Alpico (☎ 35-7400) runs buses between Matsumoto and Shinjuku in Tokyo (¥3400, 3¼ hours, 18 daily), Osaka (¥5710, 5¼ hours, two daily), Nagoya (¥3460, 3½ hours, six daily) and Takayama (¥3100, 2½ hours, four daily). Reservations are advised. Matsumoto's bus station is in the basement of the Espa building across from the train station.

CAR

Hiring a car is often the best way to do side trips, and there are several agencies around the train station. Rates start at about ¥5250 for a half-day.

TRAIN

Matsumoto is connected with Tokyo's Shinjuku Station (*tokkyū*, ¥6510, 2¾ hours, hourly), Nagoya (*tokkyū*, ¥5670, two hours) and Nagano (Shinano *tokkyū*, ¥2970, 50 minutes; *futsū*, ¥1110, 70 minutes).

Getting Around

The castle and the city centre are easily covered on foot, or free bicycles are available for loan; enquire at the tourist information office. Three 'town sneaker' bus routes loop through the centre between 9am and 6pm from April to November (to 5.30pm December to March) for ¥100/300 per ride/day; the blue and orange routes cover the castle and Nakamachi.

An airport shuttle bus connects Shinshū Matsumoto airport with the city centre (¥540, 25 minutes). Buses are timed to flights. A taxi costs around ¥4500.

HOTAKA 穂高

☎ 0263

Not to be confused with Shin-Hotaka in Japan Alps National Park, Hotaka is home to Japan's largest wasabi (Japanese horseradish) farm. It is an easy day trip from Matsumoto and a popular starting point for mountain hikes.

The **tourist office** (観光案内所; ☎ 82-9363; 🕒 9am-5pm Apr-Nov, 10am-4pm Dec-Mar) and **bicycle hire** (per hr from ¥200), the recommended way to get around, are outside the Hotaka Station exit. Both have basic maps, and the tourist office has some English-speaking staff and can make lodging reservations.

Sights & Activities

DAI-Ō WASABI-NŌJO 大王わさび農場

A visit to the **Dai-ō Wasabi-Nōjo** (Dai-ō Wasabi Farm; ☎ 82-2118; admission free; 🕒 8.30am-5.30pm Jul & Aug, shorter hours rest of year) is de rigueur for wasabi lovers, and even wasabi haters may have fun. An English map guides you among wasabi plants (wasabi is grown in flooded fields), restaurants, shops and workspaces, all set amid rolling hills. There are lots of free sampling and purchasing opportunities; wasabi finds its way into everything from wine to rice crackers, ice cream to chocolate.

The farm is about a 15-minute bike ride from Hotaka Station. There are also some calmer municipal wasabi fields.

ROKUZAN BIJUTSUKAN 碌山美術館

Ten minutes' walk from the station, **Rokuzan Bijutsukan** (Rokuzan Art Museum; ☎ 82-2094; adult/child/student ¥700/150/300; 🕒 9am-5.10pm Mar-Oct, to 4.10pm Nov-Feb, closed Mon Nov-Apr) showcases the work of Meiji-era sculptor Rokuzan Ogiwara (whom the Japanese have labelled the 'Rodin of the Orient') and his Japanese contemporaries. Strolling through the four buildings and garden, you may be struck by how much cross-cultural flow there was between East and West.

NAKABUSA ONSEN 中房温泉

Seasonal buses (late April to mid-November) from Hotaka Station (¥1610, 50 minutes) serve these remote onsen. If no bus is available, taxis start at about ¥7000. From Nakabusa Onsen, there are several extended mountain hikes, served by two seasonal inns.

JŌNEN-DAKE 常念岳

From Hotaka Station, it takes about 30 minutes by taxi (about ¥4800) to reach Ichi-no-sawa, from where experienced hikers can climb Jōnen-dake (2857m); the ascent takes about 5½ hours. There are many options for mountain hikes extending over several days in the region, but you must be properly prepared. Hiking maps and information are available at regional tourist information offices, although the more detailed maps are in Japanese. Get the taxi's *meishi* (business card) to phone for your return trip.

Sleeping & Eating

Azumino Pastoral Youth Hostel (安曇野パストラルユースホステル; ☎ 83-6170; pastoral@ai.wakwak.com; dm ¥3960, with 2 meals from ¥5900) Amid farmland, 4km west of Hotaka Station (a one-hour walk), this pleasant hostel has plenty of rustic charm and rooms that sleep three to five people. It occasionally closes during the off season (typically in winter).

Ariake-so Kokuminshukusha (有明荘国民宿舎; ☎ 090-2321-9991; r per person with 2 meals from ¥9500; ⌚ late Apr-late Nov) Nestled up near Nakabusa Onsen, this is a seasonal 95-person lodge with basic rooms and a nourishing onsen (day use ¥600).

Getting There & Away

Hotaka is about 30 minutes (¥320) from Matsumoto on the JR Ōito line.

KISO VALLEY REGION 木曽

☎ 0264

Thickly forested and alpine, southwest Nagano-ken is traversed by the twisting, craggy former post road, the Nakasendō (see the boxed text, p199). Like the more famous Tōkaidō, the Nakasendō connected Edo (present-day Tokyo) with Kyoto, enriching the towns along the way. Today, several small towns feature carefully preserved architecture of those days, making this a highly recommended visit.

It was not always so. Kiso *hinoki* (cypress) was so prized that it was used in the construction of the Edo and Nagoya castles (it is still used for the reconstruction of Ise-jingū, p443, Shintō's most revered shrine, every 20 years). To protect this asset, the region was placed under control of the Tokugawa shōgunate, and locals could be put to death for cutting down even their own trees; restrictions remained in effect well after the Meiji Restoration. The resulting lack of maintenance left many local buildings beyond repair or unreconstructed after fires. Further economic decline came with the introduction of new roads and commercial centres to the north; the construction of the Chūō train line effectively cut the region off.

However, the 1960s saw a move to preserve the post towns' architecture, and tourism has become a major source of income. Even if most of the remaining buildings are technically Meiji- and Taishō-era reconstructions, the streetscapes are pure Edo and the effect is dramatic.

Tsumago & Magome 妻籠・馬篭

These are two of the most attractive Nakasendō towns. Both close their main streets to vehicular traffic and they're connected by an agreeable hike.

Tsumago feels like an open-air museum, about 15 minutes' walk from end to end. It was designated by the government as a protected area for the preservation of traditional buildings, so no modern developments such as telephone poles are allowed to mar the scene. The dark-wood glory of its lattice-fronted houses and gently sloping tile roofs is particularly beautiful in early morning mist. Many films and TV shows have been shot on its main street.

Tsumago's **tourist information office** (観光案内館; ☎ 57-3123; fax 57-4036; ⌚ 8.30am-5pm) is in the centre of town, by the antique phone booth. Some English is spoken and there's English-language literature.

Down the street and across, **Waki-honjin** (脇本陣; ☎ 57-3322; adult/child ¥600/300; ⌚ 9am-5pm) is a former rest stop for retainers of *daimyō* on the Nakasendō. Reconstructed in 1877 under special dispensation from the emperor Meiji, it contains a lovely moss garden and a special toilet built in case Meiji happened to show up (apparently he never did). If some elements remind you of Japanese castles, that's because Waki-honjin was built by a former castle builder, out of work due to Meiji's anti-feudal policies. The **Shiryōkan** (資料館; local history museum) here houses elegant exhibitions about Kiso and the Nakasendō, with some English signage.

Across from Shiryōkan, **Tsumago Honjin** (妻籠本陣; ☎ 57-3322; adult/child ¥300/150; ⌚ 9am-5pm) is where the *daimyō* themselves spent the night, though this building is more noteworthy for its architecture than its exhibits. A combined ticket (¥700/350) gives you admission to Waki-honjin and Shiryōkan as well.

Kisoji-kan (木曽路館; ☎ 58-2046; baths ¥700; ⌚ 10am-8pm), a few hilly kilometres above Tsumago, is a tourist facility with a raging souvenir shop. The real reason to visit is the *rotemburo* with panoramic mountain vistas. Some Tsumago lodgings offer discount tickets, and there's a free shuttle bus to/from Tsumago's car park No 1 (10 minutes, approximately hourly) and Nagiso (opposite).

On 23 November, the **Fuzoku Emaki Parade** is held along the Nakasendō in Tsumago, featuring townsfolk in Edo-period costume.

Magome, the next post town south, is more modern, with houses, restaurants, inns (and souvenir shops) lining a steep, cobblestone pedestrian road. Even if only some structures are Edo-style, Magome and its mountain views are undeniably pretty. At the **tourist information office** (観光案内館; ☎ 59-2336; fax 59-2653; ⌚ 8.30am-5pm mid-Mar–mid-Dec, 9am-5pm mid-Dec–mid-Mar), about halfway up the hill on the right, you can pick up maps, and staff will book accommodation.

Magome was the birthplace of the author Shimazaki Tōson (1872–1943). His masterpiece, *Ie* (The Family), records the decline of two provincial Kiso families. A **museum** (藤村記念館; ☎ 59-2047; admission ¥500; ⌚ 8.30am-4.45pm Apr-Oct, to 4.15pm Nov-Mar, closed 2nd Tue, Wed & Thu Dec) is devoted to his life and times, though it's pretty impenetrable for non-Japanese speakers.

Good gifts from both towns include toys, crafts and household implements made from Kiso *hinoki*.

The 7.8km **hike** connecting Tsumago and Magome peaks at the top of the steep pass, Magome-tōge (elevation 801m). From here, the trail to/from Tsumago passes waterfalls, forest and farmland, while the Magome approach is largely on paved road. It takes around 2½ hours to hike between these towns. It's easier from Magome (elevation 600m) to Tsumago (elevation 420m) than the other way. English signage marks the way. The Magome–Tsumago bus (¥600, 30 minutes, at least three daily in each direction, except Monday to Friday from December to February) also stops at the pass.

If you're hiking between Magome and Tsumago, the towns offer a handy **baggage-forwarding service** (per bag ¥500; ⌚ daily late Jul-Aug, Sat, Sun & holidays late Mar-late Nov) from either tourist office to the other. Deposit your bags between 8.30am and 11.30am for delivery by 1pm.

SLEEPING & EATING

It's worth a stay in these towns, particularly Tsumago, to have them to yourself once the day-trippers clear out. Both tourist information offices can help book accommodation at numerous ryokan (from around ¥9000 per person) and *minshuku* (from around ¥7000); prices include two meals. Don't expect en-suite bath or toilet, but you will get heaps of atmosphere. For street foods, look for *gohei-mochi,* skewered rice dumplings coated with sesame-walnut sauce, and in autumn you can't miss *kuri-kinton* (chestnut dumplings).

Magome-Chaya (馬籠茶屋; ☎ 59-2038; www.magomechaya.com; s/d ¥5250/8190) This friendly, well-kept restaurant and *minshuku* is in the centre of Magome, near the water wheel. Japanese-style meals (reservations recommended; breakfast ¥1050, dinner ¥3150) are quite large.

Minshuku Daikichi (大吉旅館; ☎ 57-2595; fax 57-2203; r per person ¥9000) Popular with foreign visitors, this place feels very traditional – with handsome tatami rooms and fine wood features – despite its 1970s construction. All rooms have a view. It's at the edge of Tsumago (take the right-hand fork uphill from the centre).

Matsushiro-ya (松代屋旅館; ☎ 57-3022; fax 57-3386; r per person ¥10,500; ⌚ Thu-Tue) One of Tsumago's most historic lodgings (parts date from 1804), Matsushiro-ya sits on the village's most picturesque street and offers large tatami rooms.

our pick **Fujioto** (藤乙; ☎ 57-3009; www.takenet.or.jp/~fujioto; r per person ¥11,550) Another much-photographed, excellent ryokan, this place has impressive old-style rooms and a graceful garden, which you can enjoy over lunch such as Kiso Valley trout (*teishoku* ¥1500). It's a few doors down from the Waki-honjin in Tsumago.

Stalls throughout Tsumago sell street foods, and there are a few little *shokudō* (all-round restaurants) near the path to the car park. **Yoshimura-ya** (吉村屋; ☎ 57-3265; dishes ¥700-1500; ⌚ lunch, closed Thu) is typical and has an English menu; its speciality is handmade *soba* – try it with tempura.

GETTING THERE & AWAY

Nakatsugawa and Nagiso Stations on the JR Chūō line serve Magome and Tsumago, respectively, though both are still at some distance. Nakatsugawa is connected with Nagoya (*tokkyū*, ¥2740, 47 minutes) and Matsumoto (*tokkyū*, ¥3980, 1¼ hours). A few *tokkyū* daily stop in Nagiso (from Nagoya ¥3080, one hour); otherwise change at Nakatsugawa (*futsū* ¥320, 20 minutes).

Buses leave hourly from Nakatsugawa Station for Magome (¥540, 30 minutes). There's also an infrequent bus service between Magome and Tsumago (¥600, 25 minutes), via Magome-tōge.

Buses run between Tsumago and Nagiso Station (¥270, 10 minutes, eight per day), or it's an hour's walk.

Highway buses operate between Magome and Nagoya's Meitetsu Bus Centre (¥1810, 1½ hours), as well as Tokyo's Shinjuku Station (¥4500, 4½ hours). These stop at the nearby interchange (Magome Intah, 馬籠インター), from where it's about 1.3km on foot uphill, unless it's timed with the bus from Nakatsugawa.

Kiso-Fukushima 木曽福島

North of Tsumago and Magome and considerably more developed, Kiso-Fukushima's historical significance makes it a worthy few-hour side trip en route to these towns or from Matsumoto. It was an important checkpoint on the Nakasendō, and the town centre boasts a picturesque district of old residences.

From the station, cross the street and pick up an English map at the simple **tourist office** (木曽町観光協会; Kisomachi Kankō Kyōkai; ☎ 22-4000; ⏲ 9am-4.45pm), and head down the hill towards the town centre. Sights are well signposted. To your right, between the Kiso-gawa and the train tracks, is **Ue-no-dan** (上の段), the old historic district full of atmospheric houses, many of which now serve as shops, cafes and galleries.

Another several minutes' walk leads you to the **Fukushima Sekisho-ato** (福島関所跡; Fukushima Checkpoint Site; ☎ 23-2595; adult/child ¥300/150; ⏲ 8am-5.30pm Apr-Oct, 8.30am-4.30pm Nov-Mar), a reconstruction of one of the most significant checkpoints on the Edo-period trunk roads (see the boxed text, p199). From its perch above the river valley, it's easy to see the barrier's strategic importance. Displays inside show the implements used to maintain order, including weaponry and *tegata* (wooden travel passes), as well as the special treatment women travellers received.

Kurumaya Honten (くるまや本店; ☎ 22-2200; mains ¥577-1575; ⏲ 10am-5pm Thu-Tue) is one of Japan's most renowned *soba* shops. The classic presentation is cold *mori* (plain) or *zaru* (with strips of nori seaweed) on lacquer trays with a sweetish dipping sauce, or try it with *daikon orishi* (grated daikon radish) or hot with *jidori* (free-range chicken). It's just before the first bridge at the bottom of the hill from the station – look for the gears above the doorway.

In Ue-no-dan, **Bistro Matsushima-tei** (ビストロ松島体; ☎ 23-3625; mains ¥1155-1900, lunch sets ¥1200-1800; ⏲ lunch & dinner daily Jul-Oct, closed Wed Nov-Jun) serves a changing selection of handmade pizzas and pastas in a chichi-atmospheric setting befitting the building's history – a nice date spot. Or stop in for coffee and cake.

Kiso-Fukushima is a stop on the JR Chūō line (Shinano *tokkyū*), easily reached from Matsumoto (¥2610, 35 minutes), Nakatsugawa (¥2610, 35 minutes) and Nagoya (¥4500, 1½ hours).

Two daily buses travel each way (¥4500, 4¼ hours) between Kiso-Fukushima and Tokyo's Shinjuku Station (west exit).

TOYAMA-KEN 富山県

TOYAMA 富山

☎ 076 / pop 421,000

Toyama is big in pharmaceuticals, zipper manufacturing and mountains. Visitors come for the latter, the Tateyama range, to the city's east and south. Toyama is also a transit hub on the Hokuriku coast.

The helpful **information office** (観光案内所; ☎ 432-9751; ⏲ 8.30am-8pm), outside Toyama Station's south exit, stocks maps and pamphlets on the city and Tateyama-Kurobe Alpen Route (opposite). Some English is spoken. Most lodgings and restaurants are outside the station's south exit, and sights are easily reachable by tram or bus.

Toyama Municipal Folkcraft Village (富山市民俗民芸村; ☎ 433-8270; adult/child ¥500/250; ⏲ 9am-5pm) exhibits folk art, ceramics, tea ceremony implements, *sumi-e* (ink brush) paintings and more, in a variety of buildings snaking up a hillside. Atop the hill, the temple **Chōkei-ji** (長慶寺; ☎ 441-5451; admission free; ⏲ 24hr) offers awesome mountain views and 500-plus statues of *rakan* (Buddha's disciples) draped in colourful sashes. Toyama's free Museum Bus takes you to the Folkcraft Village (10 minutes, hourly from 10.30am to 4.30pm), from in front of the Toyama Excel Hotel Tōkyū.

North of the city centre is the bayside **Iwase** (岩瀬) neighbourhood, the well-preserved main street of the former shipping business district. Now it's filled with shops and private homes; even the banks look interesting. Take the Portram light rail line from Toyama Station's north exit to the terminus, Iwase-hama (¥200, 25 minutes), make a sharp left to cross the canal via Iwase-bashi (岩瀬橋) and you'll see signs in English. Rather than backtrack, you can return via Higashi-Iwase Station on the Portram.

There are many lodgings within a few minutes' walk of the train station's south exit. **Toyama Excel Hotel Tōkyū** (富山エクセルホテ

ル東急; ☎ 441-0109; www.tokyuhotels.co.jp; s/d from ¥10,972/18,480;), located above the landmark CIC shopping centre, has large-ish singles, small twin rooms and LAN internet access. **Comfort Hotel Toyama Eki-mae** (コンフォートホテル富山駅前; ☎ 433-6811; www.choice-hotels.jp; s/d with breakfast from ¥5800/8500;) is a new business hotel. Neutral-palette rooms feature good beds, and buffet breakfast is decent for the price. It's across the street and to the right as you exit the station.

Small wonder that *yakuzen-ryōri*, cuisine made from medicinal herbs, thrives in this city of pharmaceuticals. Try it at **Yakuto** (薬都; ☎ 425-1873; courses from ¥2100; lunch Thu-Tue), by the Nishi-chō tram stop, 10 minutes' ride from the station (¥200). Make a reservation.

Shiroebi (white shrimp about 6cm long) are another regional speciality. **Shiroebi-tei** (白えび亭; ☎ 432-7575; mains ¥730-2200; 10am-8pm) and its *shiroebi ten-don* (*shiroebi tempura* over rice; ¥730), on the 3rd floor of Toyama Station, may be workmanlike, but locals swear by it. Next to the station, the Marier (マリエ) shopping building has restaurants on its 6th floor, and the streets around CIC boast many *izakaya*. *Masu-no-sushi* (ますのすし; sliced trout pressed onto rice; from ¥150) is ubiquitous at *bentō* stands, and the cinnamon cream puffs at **Maple House** (メープルハウス; ☎ 441-1193; each ¥150; 10am-8pm) inside the station are irresistible.

Daily flights operate between Toyama and major Japanese cities, with less-frequent flights to Seoul, Shanghai and Vladivostok.

The JR Takayama line runs south to Takayama (*tokkyū*, ¥3480, 90 minutes; *futsū*, ¥1620, two hours) and Nagoya (*tokkyū*, ¥7640, four hours). JR's Hokuriku line runs west to Kanazawa (*tokkyū*, ¥2810, 35 minutes; *futsū*, ¥950, 70 minutes), Kyoto (*tokkyū*, ¥7960, three hours) and Osaka (¥8690, 3½ hours), and northeast to Naoetsu (¥4380, 1¼ hours) and Niigata (¥7330, three hours).

TATEYAMA-KUROBE ALPEN ROUTE
立山黒部アルペンルート

This seasonal, 90km route, popular with tourists, connects Toyama with Shinano-ōmachi in Nagano-ken via a sacred mountain, a deep gorge, a boiling-hot spring and glory-hallelujah mountain scenery. It is divided into nine sections with different modes of transport: train, ropeway, cable car, bus, trolley bus and your own two feet. Travel is possible in either direction; instructions here are from Toyama. The website www.alpen-route.com/english/index.html has details.

The fare for the entire route is ¥10,560/17,730 one way/return; individual tickets are available. The route can be completed in under six hours one way, although you'll probably want to stop en route; some visitors find that a trip as far as Murodō, the route's highest point, is sufficient (¥6530 return). The route is open from mid-April to mid-November. Precise dates vary, so check with a tourist office. During peak season (August to October), transport and accommodation reservations are strongly advised.

From Toyama Station take the chug-a-lug regional Chitetsu line (¥1170, one hour) through rural scenery to **Tateyama** (立山; 475m). There are plenty of ryokan in Tateyama if you make an early start or late finish.

From Tateyama, take the cable car (¥700, seven minutes) to **Bijodaira** (美女平) and then the bus (¥1660, 50 minutes) via the spectacular alpine plateau of Midagahara Kōgen to **Murodō** (室堂; 2450m). You can break the trip at Midagahara and do the 15-minute walk to see **Tateyama caldera** (立山カルデラ), the largest nonactive crater in Japan. The upper part of the plateau is often covered with deep snow until late into the summer; the road is kept clear by piling up the snow to form a virtual tunnel (great fun to drive through).

Murodō's beauty has been somewhat spoilt by a monstrous bus station, but short hikes take you back to nature. Just 10 minutes' walk north is the pond **Mikuri-ga-ike** (みくりが池). Twenty minutes further on is **Jigokudani Onsen** (Hell Valley Hot Springs): no bathing here, the waters are boiling! To the east, you can hike for about two hours – including a very steep final section – to the peak of **O-yama** (雄山; 3003m) for an astounding panorama. Keen long-distance hikers with several days or a week to spare can continue south to Kamikōchi (p280).

Continuing on the route from Murodō, there's a bus ride (¥2100, 10 minutes) via a tunnel dug through Tateyama to **Daikanbō** (大観峰), where you can pause to admire the view before taking the cable car (¥1260, seven minutes) to Kurobe-daira, where another cable car whisks you down (¥840, five minutes) to Kurobeko beside the vast **Kurobe Dam** (黒部ダム).

There's a 15-minute walk from Kurobeko to the dam, where you can descend to the water for a cruise, or climb up to a lookout point, before taking the trolley bus to **Ogizawa** (扇沢; ¥1260, 16 minutes). From here, a bus ride (¥1330, 40 minutes) takes you down to Shinano-ōmachi Station (712m). From here there are frequent trains to Matsumoto (one hour), from where you can connect with trains for Tokyo, Nagoya and Nagano.

ISHIKAWA-KEN 石川県

This prefecture, made up of the former Kaga and Noto fiefs, offers a blend of cultural and historical sights and natural beauty. Kanazawa, the Kaga capital and power base of the feudal Maeda clan, boasts traditional architecture and one of Japan's most famous gardens. To the north, the peninsula, Noto-hantō, has sweeping seascapes, rolling hills, crashing waves and quiet fishing villages. Hakusan National Park, near the southern tip of the prefecture, offers great hiking, though it can be tough to reach even during peak season.

You can find good overviews at www.hot-is hikawa.jp.

KANAZAWA 金沢

☎076 / pop 456,000

Kanazawa's wealth of cultural attractions makes it a highlight for visitors to Hokuriku. It is most famed for Kenroku-en, the fine former castle garden that dates from the 17th century. The experience is rounded out by handsome streetscapes of the former geisha and samurai districts, attractive temples and a great number of museums for a city of its size.

The city's main sights can be seen in a leisurely two days, and side trips to Noto-hantō are highly recommended.

History

Kanazawa means 'golden marsh', which is appropriate given its history. During the 15th century, Kanazawa was under the control of an autonomous Buddhist government, which was ousted in 1583 by Maeda Toshiie, head of the powerful Maeda clan of retainers to the shōgun.

Then the fun started.

Three centuries of bountiful rice production made the Kaga region Japan's wealthiest; it was known as Kaga-Hyaku-Man-Goku for the million *koku* (about five million bushels) of rice produced annually. Wealth allowed the Maeda to patronise cultural and artistic pursuits (see the boxed text, p312), and today Kanazawa is one of Japan's key cultural centres. During WWII, the absence of military targets spared Kanazawa from destruction, preserving its historical and cultural sites, although it is an undeniably modern city with its share of functional (and some fanciful) contemporary architecture.

Orientation

Kanazawa's labyrinthine layout befits its castle-town past, but bus service makes it easy to get from the train station to the main sightseeing districts, which can then be covered on foot.

The site of the former Kanazawa-jō (Kanazawa Castle) and its gardens, including Kenroku-en, occupy the centre of town. The Katamachi district, just south, is Kanazawa's commercial and business hub, around the Kōrinbō 109 department store; its busiest intersection is known as the Scramble. The Nagamachi samurai district is a short walk west from Kōrinbō 109. Northeast of the castle, across the Asano-gawa, is the picturesque Higashi Chaya-gai (east geisha district); the hills of Higashiyama to its east offer walks and city views. Just south of Katamachi, across the Sai-gawa, is the Teramachi temple district.

Information

There are post offices in Katamachi and in Kanazawa Station, and several coin-operated laundries, including in Higashi Chaya-gai and Katamachi. For information on the city, visit www.city.kanazawa.ishikawa.jp.

Ishikawa Prefectural International Exchange Center (☎262-5931; 1-5-3 Honmachi; 🕑9am-6pm Mon-Fri, to 5pm Sat & Sun) Offers information, a library, satellite-TV news and free internet access. It's on the 3rd floor of the Rifare building, a few minutes' walk southeast of the train station.

Kanazawa Goodwill Guide Network (KGGN; ☎232-3933; 🕑10am-6pm) Inside the tourist information office at Kanazawa Station, it provides helpful English-language information and can help book hotels. Two weeks' notice is requested for free guiding in English.

Kanazawa tourist information office (☎232-6200; 1 Hiro-oka-machi; 🕑9am-7pm) Friendly office inside Kanazawa Station. Pick up the bilingual map

Kanazawa Japan (with details of sights, crafts and local specialities) and the English-language *Eye On Kanazawa,* which focuses on restaurants.
Libro Books (☎ 232-6202; 1-5-3 Honmachi; 🕑 10am-8pm) Located downstairs from Ishikawa Prefectural International Exchange Center, Libro sells English-language books and magazines.

Sights & Activities

The following information is arranged in geographical order, and can be used as a walking tour. If time is limited, must-sees are Kenroku-en, the 21st Century Museum of Contemporary Art, the Nagamachi and Higashi Chaya-gai districts and Ōmichō Market.

NAGAMACHI DISTRICT 長町

Once inhabited by samurai, this attractive, well-preserved district (Nagamachi Buke Yashiki) framed by two canals features winding streets lined with tile-roofed mud walls. **Nomura Samurai House** (☎ 221-3553; 1-3-32 Nagamachi; adult/child/student ¥500/250/400; 🕑 8.30am-5.30pm Apr-Sep, to 4.30pm Oct-Mar), though partly transplanted from outside Kanazawa, is worth a visit for its decorative garden.

Towards Sai-gawa, **Shinise Kinenkan** (☎ 220-2524; 2-2-45 Nagamachi; adult/child ¥100/free; 🕑 9.30am-5pm) offers a peek at a former pharmacy and, upstairs, a moderate assortment of local traditional products. If the flowering tree made entirely of candy gives you a sweet tooth, slake it at *wagashi* (Japanese sweet) shops. **Tarō** (☎ 223-2838; 🕑 8.30am-5.30pm), next to the Nomura Samurai House, makes unusual flavours of *yōkan* (bean-paste gelatin) – our favourite is choco. **Murakami** (☎ 264-4223; 🕑 8.30am-5pm), across the canal, makes *fukusamochi* (red-bean paste and pounded rice in a crêpe) and *kakiho* (*kinako* ie soybean flour, rolled in *kurogoma,* which are black sesame seeds).

In a nonhistoric building just outside Nagamachi (about 250m from the Nomura Samurai House), **Nagamachi Yūzen-kan** (☎ 264-2811; admission ¥350; 🕑 9am-noon & 1-4.30pm Fri-Wed) displays some splendid examples of *Kaga yūzen* kimono-dyeing (see the boxed text, p312) and demonstrates the process. Enquire ahead about trying the silk-dyeing process yourself (¥4000).

21ST CENTURY MUSEUM OF CONTEMPORARY ART 金沢21世紀美術館

Designed by the acclaimed Tokyo architecture firm SANAA, this ultramodern **museum** (☎ 220-2800; www.kanazawa21.jp; 1-2-1 Hirosaka; permanent collection adult/high-school student & child/university student & senior ¥350/free/280; 🕑 10am-6pm Tue-Thu & Sun, to 8pm Fri & Sat) opened in late 2004 and instantly became an 'it' building. A low-slung glass cylinder, 113m in diameter, forms the perimeter, and inside galleries and auditoria are arranged like boxes on a tray. Nongallery portions of the building are open daily from 9am to 10pm.

Oh yes, there's art too: temporary exhibits by leading contemporary artists from Japan and abroad, plus occasional music and dance performances. Check the website for events; admission charges may increase up to ¥1000 during special exhibitions.

KANAZAWA NOH MUSEUM 金沢能楽美術館

This modern **museum** (☎ 220-2790; 1-2-25 Hirosaka; adult/child/senior ¥300/free/200; 🕑 10am-6pm Tue-Sun) gives a basic introduction to the mysterious art form of nō, the world's oldest continually performed art, with special emphasis on Kaga-style performance. Changing exhibits (costumes, masks etc) complement the ground floor, which is marked with an outline of a nō stage. Enthusiasts should also visit the Ishikawa Prefectural Nō Theatre (p313).

KANAZAWA CASTLE PARK 金沢城公園

Originally built in 1580, **Kanazawa-jō** (Kanazawa Castle; ☎ 234-3800; 1-1 Marunouchi; grounds/building admission free/¥300; 🕑 grounds 5am-6pm Mar-15 Oct, 6am-4.30pm 16 Oct-Feb, castle 9am-4.30pm) housed the Maeda clan for 14 generations; this massive structure was called the castle of 1000 tatami. That castle was destroyed by fire, but some reconstruction has taken place inside its moated walls, now rechristened Kanazawa Castle Park (Kanazawa-jō Kōen). The elegant gate **Ishikawa-mon**, rebuilt in 1788, provides a dramatic entry from Kenroku-en; holes in its turret were designed for *ishi-otoshi* (hurling rocks at invaders). Two additional buildings, the **Hishi-yagura** (diamond-shaped turret) and **Gojikken-Nagaya** (armoury), were reconstructed in 2001, offering a glimpse of the castle's unique wood-frame construction.

KENROKU-EN 兼六園

Kanazawa's star attraction, **Kenroku-en** (☎ 234-3800; 1-1 Marunouchi; adult/senior/child ¥300/free/100; 🕑 7am-6pm Mar-15 Oct, 8am-4.30pm 16 Oct-Feb) is ranked as one of the great gardens of the Edo

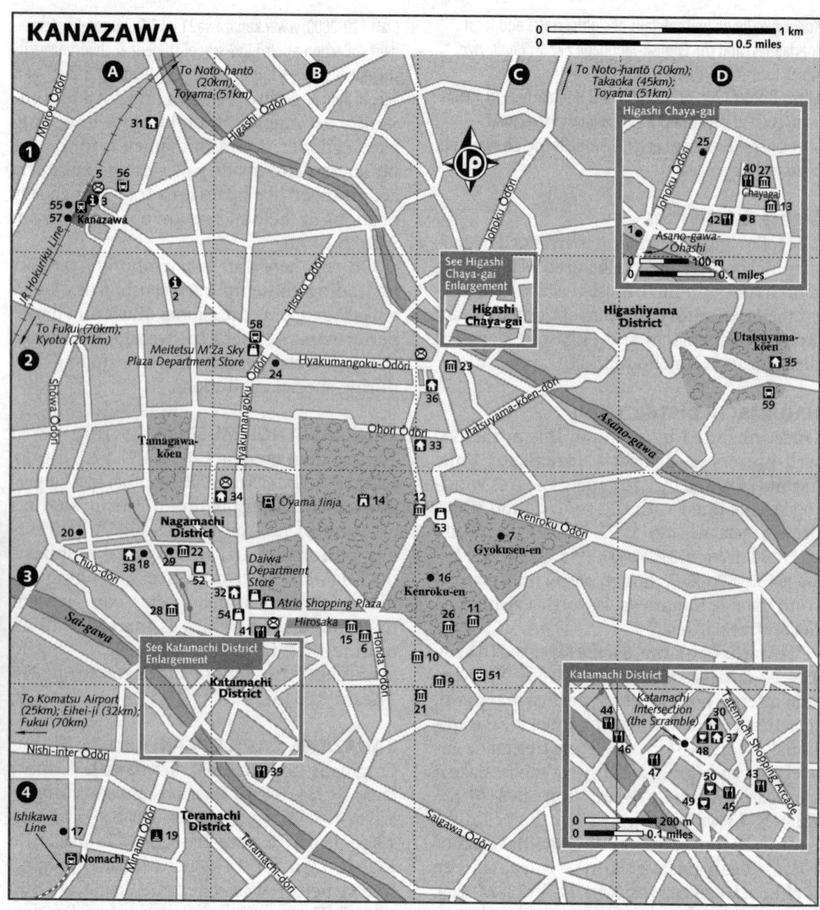

period and one of the top three gardens in Japan (the other two are Kairaku-en in Mito, p206, and Kōraku-en in Okayama, p448).

The name (*kenroku* means 'combined six') refers to a renowned garden from Sung-dynasty China that required six attributes for perfection: seclusion, spaciousness, artificiality, antiquity, abundant water and broad views (on clear days you can see to the Sea of Japan). In 1676 Kenroku-en started as the garden of an outer villa of Kanazawa-jō, but later it was enlarged to serve the castle itself, reaching completion in the early 19th century; the garden opened to the public in 1871. In winter the branches of Kenroku-en's trees are famously suspended with ropes via a post at each tree's centre, forming elegant conical shapes that protect the trees from breaking under Kanazawa's heavy snows. In spring, irises turn Kenroku-en's waterways into rivers of purple.

Inside the park, **Seison-kaku** (☎ 221-0580; 2-1 Dewa-machi; adult/elementary-school student/student ¥700/250/300; 9am-5pm Thu-Tue) is a retirement villa built by a Maeda lord for his mother in 1863. Elegant chambers named for trees and animals are filled with furniture, clothing and furnishings. A detailed English-language pamphlet is available.

Kenroku-en is certainly attractive, but enormous crowds can diminish its intimacy. Visit at opening time and you'll have the place to yourself.

INFORMATION
Coin Laundry コインランドリー 1 D1
Ishikawa Prefectural International Exchange Centre 石川県国際交流センター 2 A2
Kanazawa Goodwill Guide Network ....(see 3)
Kanazawa Tourist Information Office 観光案内所 3 A1
Libro Books リブロ ....(see 2)
Post Office 郵便局 4 B3
Post Office 郵便局 5 A1

SIGHTS & ACTIVITIES
21st Century Museum of Contemporary Art 金沢 21 世紀 美術館 6 B3
Gojikken-nagaya ５０間長屋 ..(see 14)
Gyokusen-en 玉泉園 7 C3
Higashi-yu 東湯 8 D1
Hishi-yagura 菱櫓 ....(see 14)
Honda Museum 本多蔵品館 9 C3
Ishikawa Prefectural Art Museum 石川県立美術館 10 C3
Ishikawa Prefectural Museum of Traditional Products & Crafts 石川県立伝統産業工芸館 11 C3
Ishikawa-mon 石川門 12 C3
Kaikarō 懐花楼 13 D1
Kanazawa Castle Park 金沢城公園 14 B3
Kanazawa Noh Museum 金沢能楽美術館 15 B3
Kenroku-en 兼六園 16 C3
Kutani Kosen Gama Kiln 久谷光仙窯 17 A4
Murakami 菓子の村上 18 A3
Myōryū-ji (Ninja-dera) 妙竜寺（忍者寺） 19 A4
Nagamachi Yūzen-kan 長町友禅館 20 A3
Nakamura Memorial Museum 中村記念美術館 21 C4
Nomura Samurai House 野村家跡 22 A3
Ōhi Pottery Museum 大樋美術館 23 C2
Ōmichō Market 近江町市場 24 B2
Sakuda Gold Leaf Company 作田金箔 25 D1
Seison-kaku 成巽閣 26 C3
Shima 志摩 27 D1
Shinise Kinenkan 老舗記念館 28 A3
Tarō たろう 29 A3

SLEEPING
APA Hotel Kanazawa Chūō APA ホテル金沢 30 D4
Hotel Dormy Inn Kanazawa ホテルドーミイン金沢 31 A1
Kanazawa Excel Hotel Tokyū 金沢エクセルホテル 32 B3
Kanazawa Hakuchōro Hotel 金沢白鳥路ホテル 33 C2
Kanazawa New Grand Hotel Annex 金沢ニューグランドホテル別館 34 B3
Kanazawa Youth Hostel 金沢ユースホステル 35 D2
Matsumoto まつ本 36 C2
Murataya Ryokan 村田屋旅館 37 D4
Yamadaya 山田家 38 A3

EATING
Bistro Yuiga ビストロユイガ 39 B4
Hotaruya 蛍屋 40 D1
Janome-sushi Honten 蛇の目寿司本店 41 B3
Jiyūken 自由軒 42 D1
Kōtatsu 香立 43 D4
Legian レギャン 44 C4
Oden Miyuki Honten おでん美幸本店 45 D4
Osteria del Campagne オステリアデルカンパーニュ 46 D4
Tamazushi 玉寿司 47 D4

DRINKING
Baby Rick ベビーリック 48 D4
I no Ichiban いの一番 49 D4
Pilsen ぴるぜん 50 D4
Polé Polé ポレポレ ....(see 44)

ENTERTAINMENT
Ishikawa Prefectural Nō Theatre 石川県立能楽堂 51 C3

SHOPPING
Kanazawa Kutani Museum 九谷ミュウジャム 52 A3
Kankō Bussankan (Ishikawa Local Products Shop) 石川観光物産館 53 C3
Kōrinbō 109 香林坊 １０９ ....54 B3

TRANSPORT
Hokutetsu Bicycle Rental 北鉄自転車レンタル 55 A1
Hokutetsu Bus Company 北鉄観光バスターミナル 56 A1
JR Kanazawa Station Rent-a-Cycle JRレンタサイクル 57 A1
Musashi-ga-tsuji Bus Stop 武蔵ヶ辻バス停 58 B2
Yūsu-Hosteru-mae Bus Stop ユースホステル前バス停 59 D2

ISHIKAWA PREFECTURAL MUSEUM OF TRADITIONAL PRODUCTS & CRAFTS
石川県立伝統産業工芸館

Behind Seison-kaku, this **museum** (☎ 262-2020; 2-1 Kenroku-machi; adult/child/senior ¥250/100/200; 9am-5pm, closed 3rd Thu of month Apr-Nov, closed Thu Dec-Mar) is not flashy but offers fine displays of over 20 regional crafts. Pick up the free English-language headphone guide.

ISHIKAWA PREFECTURAL ART MUSEUM
石川県立美術館

This **museum** (☎ 231-7580; 2-1 Dewa-machi; adult/child/university student ¥350/free/280; 9.30am-5pm) specialises in antique exhibitions of traditional arts, with special emphasis on colourful Kutani porcelain, Japanese painting and *Kaga yūzen* (silk-dyed) fabrics and costumes. Admission prices are higher during special exhibitions.

NAKAMURA MEMORIAL MUSEUM
中村記念美術館

Rotating exhibitions from the 600-piece collection of this **museum** (☎ 221-0751; 3-2-29 Honda-machi; adult/child/senior ¥300/free/200; 9.30am-5pm) usually include *chanoyu* (tea ceremony) utensils, calligraphy and traditional crafts from the collection of a wealthy sake brewer, Nakamura Eishun. You can enjoy a bowl of powdered tea for ¥100. Reached via a narrow flight of steps below the Ishikawa Prefectural Art Museum.

HONDA MUSEUM 本多蔵品館

The Honda family were chief retainers to the Maeda clan, and this **museum** (☎ 261-0500; 3-1 Dewa-machi; admission ¥500; 9am-5pm daily Mar-Oct, Fri-Wed Nov-Feb) exhibits the family collection of armour, household utensils and works of art. The bulletproof coat and the family vase are particularly interesting, and there's a detailed catalogue in English.

GYOKUSEN-EN 玉泉園

For more intimacy and fewer crowds than Kenroku-en, this Edo-period **garden** (☎ 221-0181; 1-1 Marunouchi; adult/child ¥500/350; 9am-4pm Mar–mid-Nov) rises up a steep slope. Enjoy a cup of tea here for an additional ¥700, while contemplating the tranquil setting.

ŌHI POTTERY MUSEUM 大樋美術館

This **museum** (☎ 221-2397; Hashiba-chō; adult/child ¥700/500; 9am-5pm) was established by the Chōzaemon family, now in its 10th generation. The first Chōzaemon developed this style in nearby Ōhi village, using a special slow-fired amber glaze, specifically for use in *chanoyu*. See the boxed text, p312, for more information.

HIGASHI CHAYA-GAI 東茶屋街

North of the Ōhi Pottery Museum and across Asano-gawa, Higashi chaya-gai (Higashi Geisha District) is an enclave of narrow streets that was established early in the 19th century as a centre for geisha to entertain wealthy patrons. The slatted wooden facades of the geisha houses are romantically preserved.

One famous, traditional former geisha house is **Shima** (☎ 252-5675; 1-13-21 Higashiyama; adult/child ¥400/300; 9am-6pm), dating from 1820. Note the case of elaborate combs and *shamisen* (three-stringed traditional instrument) picks. Across the street, **Kaikarō** (☎ 253-0591; 1-14-8 Higashiyama; admission ¥700; 9am-5pm) is an early-19th-century geisha house refinished with contemporary fittings and art, including a red lacquered staircase.

The **Sakuda Gold Leaf Company** (☎ 251-6777; 1-3-27 Higashiyama; admission free; 9am-6pm) is a good place to observe the *kinpaku* (gold leaf) process and pick up gilded souvenirs (including pottery, lacquerware and, er, golf balls). The tea served here contains flecks of gold leaf, meant to be good for rheumatism. Even the walls of the loos are lined with gold and platinum.

On most nights you can visit the local *sentō,* **Higashi-yu** (☎ 252-5410; 1-13-2 Higashiyama; admission ¥370; 2pm-12.30am Mon & Wed-Sat, 1pm-12.30am Sun).

TERAMACHI DISTRICT 寺町

This hilly neighbourhood across Sai-gawa, southwest of the centre, was established as a first line of defence and contains dozens of temples. **Myōryū-ji** (Ninja-dera; ☎ 241-0888; 1-2-12 Nomachi; admission ¥800; 9am-4.30pm Mar-Nov, to 4pm Dec-Feb, reservations required) is a five-minute walk from the river. Completed in 1643, it was designed as a hideout in case of attack, and contains hidden stairways, escape routes, secret chambers, concealed tunnels and trick doors. The popular name refers to the temple's connection with ninja. Admission is by tour only – it's in Japanese but visual enough. Take Minami Ō-dōri across the river, take a left at the first major intersection, then the first right.

Nearby, **Kutani Kosen Gama Kiln** (☎ 241-0902; 5-3-3 Nomachi; admission free; 9am-5pm) is a must for pottery lovers. Short tours give a glimpse of the process and history of this fine craft. Try decorating porcelain yourself from ¥1050.

ŌMICHŌ MARKET 近江町市場

A warren of several hundred shops and restaurants, many of which specialise in seafood, this **market** (35 Ōmichō; 9am-5pm) bustles all day and is a great place for a break from sightseeing and to watch everyday people in action. Ōmichō functions like the outer market of Tokyo's Tsukiji Fish Market, but thanks to a recent makeover it's a lot more orderly and polished. It's between Katamachi district and Kanazawa Station. The nearest bus stop is Musashi-ga-tsuji.

Festivals & Events

Kagatobi Dezomeshiki In early January, scantily clad firemen brave the cold, imbibe sake and demonstrate ancient fire-fighting skills on ladders.

Asano-gawa Enyūkai Performances of traditional Japanese dance and music are held on the banks of the Asano-gawa during the second weekend of April.

Hyakumangoku Matsuri In early June, Kanazawa's main annual festival commemorates the first time the region's rice production hit 1 million *koku* (around 150,000 tonnes). There's a parade of townsfolk in 16th-century costumes, *takigi nō* (torch-lit performances of nō drama), *tōrō nagashi* (lanterns floated down the river at dusk) and a special *chanoyu;* at Kenroku-en.

Sleeping

All Western-style hotels provide LAN cable access.

BUDGET

Kanazawa Youth Hostel (☎ 252-3414; fax 252-8590; www.jyh.or.jp; 37 Suehiro-machi; dm ¥3150; closed early Feb) Commanding a superb position in the hills to the east of the city, this strict, 80-bed hostel has Japanese- and Western-style rooms, with some private rooms available (extra charge). Unfortunately, bus services are infrequent. From the station, take bus 90 for Utatsuyama (not Senjūkaku) and get off after about 25 minutes at Yūsu-Hosteru-mae.

Yamadaya (☎/fax 261-0065; 2-3-28 Nagamachi; r per person ¥4000; 💻) This friendly place offers decent tatami rooms in a former samurai house in Nagamachi. No English is spoken. It's on a side street just west of the Nomura Samurai House.

Murataya Ryokan (☎ 263-0455; fax 263-0456; murataya@spacelan.ne.jp; 1-5-2 Katamachi; s/tw ¥4700/9000; ⊠ 💻) Eleven well-kept rooms with friendly hosts await at this travellers' favourite in Katamachi, convenient to restaurants and nightlife; there's an English-language map of local establishments.

MIDRANGE

APA Hotel Kanazawa Chūō (☎ 235-2111; www.apahotel.com; 1-5-24 Katamachi; s/d/tw from ¥8000/11,000/15,000; ⊠ 💻) Towering above Katamachi, this 500-plus-room business hotel offers nicely appointed if cramped rooms. Guests have use of indoor and outdoor onsen baths on the 14th floor. Pick up an origami crane.

Hotel Dormy Inn Kanazawa (☎ 263-9888; fax 263-9312; www.hotespa.net, in Japanese; 2-25 Horikawa-shinmachi; s/d/tw ¥8500/12,000/15,000; ⊠ 💻) This brand-new hotel steps from the station is filled with futuristic art. Most of its 304 rooms are singles and have an inner door to keep out extraneous noise. There's a naturium- and calcium-rich onsen *rotemburo* on the top floor, and a coin laundry.

Kanazawa New Grand Hotel Annex (☎ 233-7000; fax 265-6655; www.new-grand.co.jp, in Japanese; 1-50 Takaoka-machi; s/d & tw from ¥9817/18,480; ⊠) Near both Nagamachi and Katamachi, this business hotel has nice-sized, up-to-date rooms. It's next door to the New Grand main building; you can reserve at either, but the Annex is newer and more polished.

TOP END

Kanazawa Hakuchōrō Hotel (☎ 222-1212; www.hakuchoro.com; 6-3 Marunouchi; s/tw with breakfast from ¥14,000/22,000; ⊠) East meets West with room design (and dimensions) that could be from France or Germany and only-in-Japan touches like sashes across the beds and display cases of local crafts. Its out-of-the-way location means lots of quiet. Common onsen baths are available.

Kanazawa Excel Hotel Tokyū (☎ 231-2411; www.tokyuhotels.co.jp; 2-1-1 Kōrinbo; s/d/tw from ¥14,400/21,900/24,200; ⊠ 💻 📶) At 15 storeys (try for a room with views across the city to Hakusan National Park), Kanazawa city's most stylish hotel has sleek rooms, a slightly '80s retro design and plenty of amenities (including BBC on the telly). It's also a winner for its central location in the heart of Katamachi.

Matsumoto (☎ 221-0302; fax 221-0303; 1-7-2 Owari-chō; r per person with 2 meals ¥25,000) This upscale inn bills itself as a *ryōri* (cuisine) ryokan; expect a culinary treat of local specialities. Huge rooms have private bathrooms. It's near the intersection of Hyakumangoku-ōdōri and Jūhoku-dōri, down a narrow street across from the post office. No English is spoken.

Eating

Seafood is the staple of Kanazawa's *Kaga ryōri* (Kaga cuisine); even the most humble train-station *bentō* nearly all feature some type of fish. *Oshi-zushi,* a thin layer of fish pressed atop vinegared rice, is said to be the precursor to modern sushi. Another favourite is *jibuni,* which is flour-coated duck or chicken stewed with shiitake and green vegetables. The Katamachi district and Ōmichō market are great for browsing, packed with locals and visitors alike. Many restaurants have English menus. One Ōmichō speciality is seafood *donburi* (seafood served atop a deep bowl of rice). *Teishoku* cost ¥800 to ¥1200. Ōmichō's restaurants close around 7pm or 8pm.

Oden Miyuki Honten (☎ 222-6117; 1-10-3 Katamachi; oden ¥100-400, most other dishes ¥400-600; 🕑 dinner Mon-Sat) For fish in another form (ground and pressed into cakes and served in broth), *oden* is very satisfying, especially on chilly nights. Fans include Ishikawa's most famous son, New York Yankees baseball star Hideki Matsui. Counter seats let you watch all the action. Some of the staff are English-speaking.

Legian (☎ 262-6510; 2-31-30 Katamachi; most dishes ¥600-1000; 🕑 dinner; Ⓥ) For popular, authentic Indonesian cuisine head to this tiny spot by the river. Staff make annual trips to Indonesia to bone up on technique, and are happy to make vegetarian versions. Good lunch specials are available.

Osteria del Campagne (☎ 261-2156; 2-31-33 Katamachi; mains ¥650-1950, set menus from ¥2500; 🕑 dinner Mon-Sat) This cosy, quietly fashionable Italian bistro serves lovely set menus, including house-made focaccia, salads, pastas

GET LACQUERED, GO TO POT, DYE & BE GILDED

Much as the Medici family was the patron of some of the great artists of the Italian Renaissance, during the Edo period Kanazawa's ruling Maeda family fuelled the growth of important crafts. Many of these crafts are still practised today.

Kanazawa & Wajima Lacquerware

This luminous black lacquerware starts with hard, durable wood, such as *keyaki* (zelkova), or Japanese chestnut, finely carved with any defects removed or filled. Many layers of undercoating and middle coating are applied, each rubbed down with *washi* (Japanese paper) before the next application. Before the final topcoat, decoration is applied through *maki-e* (painting) or gilding. With the last coat of lacquer, artists must take great care that dust does not settle on the final product.

Ōhi Pottery

An aesthetic central to the tea ceremony is *wabi-sabi:* introspective, humble and understated, yet profound and prepared with great thought. The deliberately simple, almost primitive designs, rough surfaces, irregular shapes and monochromatic glazes of Ōhi pottery have long been favoured by tea practitioners. The same family, with the professional name Chōzaemon, has been keeper of the Ōhi tradition since the early Edo period.

Kutani Porcelain

Known for elegant shapes, graceful designs and bold hues of red, blue, yellow, purple and green, this underglaze ware could hardly be more different from Ōhi pottery. It is said to date back to the early Edo period, and shares design characteristics with Chinese porcelain and Japanese Imari ware. Typical motifs include birds, flowers, trees and landscapes.

Kaga Yūzen Silk Dyeing

This kimono-dyeing technique is characterised by sharp colours (red, ochre, green, indigo and purple) and realistic depictions of nature, such as flower petals that have begun to brown around the edges.

It's highly specialised, labour-intensive work. A pattern is drawn on the fabric with grey-blue ink from spiderwort flowers and the lines are traced over with rice paste using a cone like a fine pastry tube; this keeps the dyes from running as they are painted onto the silk. The colours are filled in and coated with more rice paste and then the entire sheet of silk is dyed with the kimono's background colour.

Only then is the fabric rinsed clean (traditionally in a river) and steamed to fix the colours. White lines between the elements, where the initial spiderwort ink has washed away, are a characteristic of *Kaga yūzen*. To dye the fabric for one kimono takes about three months.

Gold Leaf

It starts with a lump of pure gold the size of a ¥10 coin, which is rolled to the size of a tatami mat, as little as 0.0001mm thick. The gold leaf is cut into squares of 10.9cm – the size used for mounting on walls, murals or paintings – or then cut again for gilding on lacquerware or pottery. Tiny particles find their way into tea, sweets and hand lotion. Kanazawa makes over 98% of Japan's gold leaf.

and desserts, plus hors d'oeuvres you can eat with chopsticks. There's an English menu and friendly, professional staff.

Kōtatsu (☎ 261-6310; 32-1 Daiku-machi; mains ¥700-900; ⏲ dinner Mon-Sat) More sophisticated than your everyday *okonomiyaki* place, there's a dark atmosphere and an assortment of sake and *shōchū*, *and* they'll cook your *okonomiyaki* for you. Salads are also available, and there's an English menu. It's beneath Arroz Spanish restaurant.

Jiyūken (☎ 252-1996; 1-6-6 Higashiyama; most mains ¥785-2990; ⏲ lunch & dinner, closed Tue & 3rd Wed of month) By Higashi Chaya-gai, this simple but welcoming spot has been serving *yō-shoku* (Japanese takes on Western cuisine; eg beef stew, grilled chicken, omelettes) since 1909. The *teishoku* is a steal at ¥920. There are plastic models in the window. Look for the stone front.

Janome-sushi Honten (☎ 231-0093; 1-1-12 Kōrinbō; mains ¥1200-3400, Kaga ryōri sets from ¥4000; 🕑 lunch & dinner Thu-Tue) Highly regarded for sashimi and Kaga cuisine. One of our Japanese friends says that when he eats here, he knows he's really in Kanazawa. It's across a little stream from Siena clothing store.

Tamazushi (☎ 221-2644; 2-14-9 Katamachi; mains ¥1300-3300; 🕑 dinner Mon-Sat) Down near Saigawa in Katamachi, this classic sushi counter, backed by a painting of a nō stage, is one of Kanazawa's best. No English is spoken, but there's a picture menu. It's on your right as you enter from the main street.

Bistro Yuiga (☎ 261-0978; 4-1 Mizutamemachi; sets from ¥2575; 🕑 lunch Mon, Tue, Thu & Fri, dinner Thu-Tue) There's a gentle jazz soundtrack to accompany elegantly prepared French delicacies in this one-time private home. Set menus include treats like raw ham and – because this is Kanazawa – seafood. It's a short walk off the main street from Katamachi, down the street opposite Kōtatsu. An English menu is available.

Hotaruya (☎ 251-8585; 1-13-24 Higashiyama; lunch/dinner courses from ¥3675/6300; 🕑 lunch & dinner) To splurge on *Kaga ryōri* and step back in time, visit this shop in Higashi Chaya-gai. You'll be rewarded with wood-beam and tatami room surroundings, and understated, standard-setting course dinners.

Drinking

Most of Kanazawa's bars and clubs are holes-in-the-wall, jam-packed into high-rises in Katamachi. Some are straightforward bars, others are barely disguised girlie clubs. Here are some of the former. Weekdays can be slow, but weekends tend to hop. For a quieter scene, peek into the lovely little bars of Higashi Chaya-gai.

Polé Polé (☎ 260-1138; 2-31-30 Katamachi; 🕑 7pm-5am) In the same building (and sharing the same owners) as Legian restaurant, this dark, grungy and friendly bar has been an institution for decades for *gaijin* and locals – look for the signatures of foreign exchange students. The narrow floor is littered with peanut shells (proceeds from peanut sales go to charity), and the music (reggae) is loud.

Baby Rick (☎ 263-5063; 1-5-20 Katamachi; 🕑 5pm-3am) This classy little shot bar has a billiard table, jazz and whisky (the good kind), and you can get dishes like spaghetti carbonara and homemade pizzas. It's in the basement level beneath Shidax karaoke. There's a ¥500 cover after 10pm.

I no Ichiban (☎ 261-0001; 1-9-20 Katamachi; 🕑 6pm-3am Mon-Sat, to midnight Sun) This slender *izakaya* serves plenty of cocktails and has ambience in spades – so much so that it's almost unrecognisable from the street. Look for the wood-panel screen and tiny stand of bamboo.

Pilsen (☎ 221-0688; 1-9-20 Katamachi; dishes ¥600-1800; 🕑 5.30pm-midnight) Munich by the Katamachi Scramble, this German-style place serves lots of beers and a fascinating hybrid menu: where else can you get a sausage plate *and* warm tofu-mushroom salad in the same meal?

Entertainment

Nō theatre is alive and well in Kanazawa, and performances are held weekly during summer at **Ishikawa Prefectural Nō Theatre** (☎ 264-2598; 3-1 Dewa-machi; admission free, performance tickets extra; 🕑 9am-4.30pm Tue-Sun).

Shopping

For a quick view of Kanazawa crafts, you can visit **Kankō Bussankan** (Ishikawa Local Products Shop; ☎ 222-7788). The Hirosaka shopping street, between Kōrinbō 109 department store and Kenroku-en, has some upmarket craft shops on its south side; department stores carry crafts too. At the Sakuda Gold Leaf Company (p310) you can find business-card holders, mirrors, chopstick rests and Buddhist prayer bells among many objects covered in gold leaf.

On a corner in the Nagamachi samurai district in a wonderful old house with a garden, the **Kanazawa Kutani Museum** (☎ 221-6666; 1-3-16 Nagamachi; 🕑 9am-10pm Mon-Sat, to 6pm Sun) is a lovely place if a bit of a misnomer; it's really a shop selling mostly high-end ceramic ware with a small museum of historic Kutani ware in the old storehouse and a cafe.

At the other end of the spectrum, Tatemachi is to Kanazawa what Teramachi is to Kyoto: a young, trendy, pedestrian shopping street blaring with music.

Getting There & Away

AIR

Nearby **Komatsu airport** (KMQ; www.komatsuairport.jp) has air connections with major Japanese cities, as well as Seoul, Shanghai and Taipei.

BUS

JR Highway Bus (☎ 234-0111; ⏲ reservations 9am-7pm) operates express buses from in front of Kanazawa Station's east exit, to Tokyo (¥7840, Ikebukuro seven hours, Shinjuku 7½ hours) and Kyoto (¥4060, 4¼ hours). **Hokutetsu Bus** (☎ 234-0123; ⏲ reservations 8am-7pm) serves Nagoya (¥4060, four hours).

TRAIN

The JR Hokuriku line links Kanazawa with Fukui (*tokkyū*, ¥2940, 50 minutes; *futsū*, ¥1280, 1½ hours), Kyoto (*tokkyū*, ¥6710, 2¼ hours), Osaka (*tokkyū*, ¥7440, 2¾ hours) and Toyama (*tokkyū*, ¥2810, 35 minutes), with connections to Takayama (total ¥5840, additional 90 minutes). From Tokyo take the Jōetsu *shinkansen* and change at Echigo-Yuzawa in Northern Honshū (¥12,710, four hours).

Getting Around

Airport buses (¥1100, 40 minutes) are timed to aeroplane departures and arrivals, leaving from stop 6 in front of Kanazawa Station's east exit. Some buses also stop at Katamachi and Kōrinbō 109 department store but take one hour to reach the airport.

Hire bikes from **JR Kanazawa Station Rent-a-Cycle** (☎ 261-1721; per hr/day ¥200/1200; ⏲ 8am-8.30pm) – take an immediate left from Kanazawa Station's west exit – and **Hokutetsu Bicycle Rental** (☎ 263-0919; per 4hr/day ¥630/1050; ⏲ 8am-5.30pm), by stop 4 out the west exit.

Any bus from station stop 7, 8 or 9 will take you to the city centre (¥200, day pass ¥900). The Kanazawa Loop Bus (single ride/day pass ¥200/500, every 15 minutes from 8.30am to 6pm) circles the major tourist attractions in 45 minutes. On Saturday, Sunday and holidays, the Machi-bus goes to Kōrinbō for ¥100.

Cars can be hired at rental agencies around the station.

NOTO-HANTŌ 能登半島

With rugged seascapes, traditional rural life, fresh seafood and a light diet of cultural sights, this peninsula atop Ishikawa-ken is highly recommended. Noto juts out from Honshū like a boomerang, with sights dotting its flat west coast. The lacquer-making town of Wajima is the hub of the rugged north, known as Oku-Noto, and the best place to stay overnight. Famous products include *Wajima-nuri* lacquerware, renowned for its durability and rich colours, Suzu-style pottery and locally harvested sea salt and *iwanori* seaweed.

Day trips from Kanazawa, while possible, don't do the peninsula justice; buzzing through the sights leaves little time to savour the day-to-day pace. Unless you're under your own power, a speedy trip may not be an option anyway: public transport is infrequent. If staying overnight, be sure to reserve; accommodation fills up in summer, and many lodgings close in winter.

Kanazawa's **tourist information office** (☎ 076-232-6200) stocks the *Unforgettable Ishikawa* map and guide, which includes the peninsula. On the peninsula, the most user-friendly tourist office is in Wajima.

GETTING THERE & AROUND

In the centre of Oku-Noto, **Noto airport** (NTQ; ☎ 0768-26-2100) connects the peninsula with Tokyo's Haneda airport. **ANA** (☎ 0120-029-222) offers two return flights daily (one way ¥19,800, 65 minutes). **Furusato Taxi** (☎ 0768-22-7411) is a van service to locations around the peninsula. Fares start at ¥700 to nearby communities including Wajima (about 30 minutes).

Although there are trains, most sights can be reached by road only. For the west Noto coast, get off the JR Nanao Line at Hakui (*tokkyū*, ¥1370; *futsū*, ¥740), and connect to buses. For Oku-Noto, trains continue to Wakura Onsen, connecting to less frequent buses. Check departure and arrival times with the bus company **Hokutetsu** (☎ 076-234-0123 in Kanazawa) to avoid long waits. Hokutetsu also runs express buses between Kanazawa and Wajima (¥2200, two hours, 10 daily), with a couple continuing to Sosogi (¥2510, 2¾ hours). Buses leave from outside Kanazawa Station.

Daily tour buses from Kanazawa (¥7200, 8.10am to 3.30pm) include Wajima's morning market (p318), Ganmon and more, plus lunch, a Japanese-speaking guide and admission fees, with a very quick turnaround.

Driving has become a popular option. The 83km Noto Yūryo (能登有料; Noto Toll Rd) speeds you as far as Anamizu (toll ¥1180); allow two hours to complete the journey to Wajima via Rte 1. The toll road does not serve most of Noto's west-coast sights, so allow a day to see those sights en route to Wajima.

Noto's mostly flat west coast appeals to cyclists. However, cycling is not recommended on the Noto-kongō coast and east because of steep, blind curves.

West Noto Coast

☎ 0767

KITA-KE 喜多家

During the Edo period, the Kita family administered over 200 villages from this **house** (☎ 28-2546; adult/child ¥500/200; 8.30am-5pm Apr-Oct, to 4pm Nov-Mar), at the pivotal crossroads of the Kaga, Etchū and Noto fiefs. Inside this splendid, sprawling home and adjacent museum, still in the hands of the same family (about 400 years), are displays of weapons, ceramics, farming tools, fine and folk art, and documents. The garden has been called the Moss Temple of Noto.

Kita-ke is about 1km from the Komedashi exit on the Noto Toll Rd. By train, take the JR Nanao line to Menden Station; it's about 20 minutes' walk.

CHIRIHAMA NAGISA DRIVEWAY

千里浜なぎさドライブウエイ

At times the 8km beach, in the Chirihama district of Hakui City (羽咋), resembles an early Daytona, as buses, motorcycles and cars roar past the breakers. Hakui is Noto's western transit hub, with frequent train connections to Kanazawa and less frequent bus connections along Noto's west coast.

KETA-TAISHA 気多大社

About 4km north of central Hakui, this **shrine** (☎ 22-0602; admission free; 8.30am-4.30pm), set in a wooded grove with sea views from its hillside, is said to be one of Japan's four largest shrines. It was allegedly founded in the 1st century BC and dedicated to the *kami* (god) of this region. The architectural style of the present wooden buildings varies, but the oldest (Wakamiya-sha) dates from 1569.

Take a Togi-bound bus from Hakui to the Ichinomiya bus stop (¥240, 10 minutes, approximately 15 buses daily).

KITA KAZUKO, OWNER OF KITA-KE, NOTO-HANTŌ

I am the 12th generation of the Kita family in this place. Actually, we trace our ancestry back 28 generations, to the Kamakura-period samurai Nitta Yoshisada, who fought on the side of the emperor Go-Daigo against the Ashikaga warlords (see p42). Centuries later, one of his descendants found himself an orphan, penniless and stranded, when a local from Noto took a liking to him and invited him here.

It was around that time that the Hyaku-man-goku (see p306) Maeda family took over as *daimyō* (domain lords) of the Kaga fief (p306) and became familiar with the hard work of the Kita family. A Maeda lord presented our ancestors with a thatched-roof gate, which still stands today as the entryway to this house.

The Maeda and Kita families became so close that we were eventually given a special title of *tomurayaku,* overseeing a total of 203 villages from this property, now 13,000 *tsubo* (42,900 sq m). The title of *tomurayaku* was unique to the Kaga fief. Normally, the *daimyō* himself oversaw his region, but we are at the junction of three provinces (Kaga, Noto and Etchū), and the *tomurayaku* was a private nobleman whose job was to oversee villages in all three fiefs. In order not to be confused for a castle and arouse the suspicion of the Tokugawa shōgunate, our house was built down a hill and concealed behind a forest. [Castles were typically built on a plain or a hilltop.]

Our lineage is very different from that of samurai, who could pass their titles to the next generation regardless of merit. The position of *tomurayaku* was based on effectiveness, and we retained it for 170 years.

And so, through the generations, the house was passed on to us. Nowadays we don't have any official role, but we tell the story of our ancestors and keep the house clean and in good condition. It's a 400-year-old house, so the posts and windows are very delicate. It's not the kind of thing where just anyone can come in and clean or repair it. It needs to be treated with respect, or something could easily be broken. I think that our ancestors are here with us, giving us the strength to protect and preserve this house.

We were put here courtesy of our ancestors, and I always feel a great sense of responsibility.

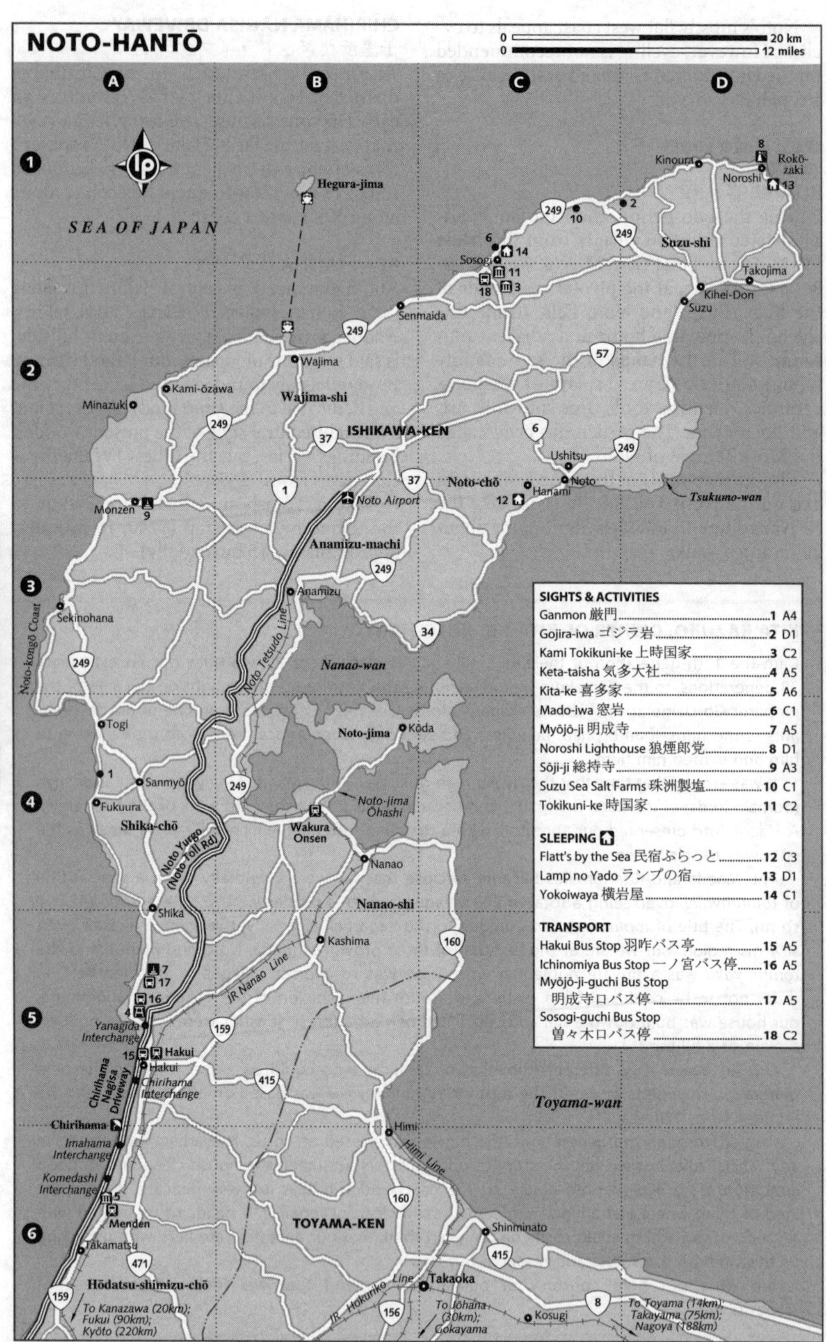
NOTO-HANTŌ
0 20 km
0 12 miles
SEA OF JAPAN
Hegura-jima
Kinoura
Rokō-zaki
Noroshi
Sosogi
Senmaida
Suzu-shi
Takojima
Kihei-Don
Suzu
Wajima
Kami-ōzawa
Minazuki
Wajima-shi
ISHIKAWA-KEN
Ushitsu
Noto
Hanami
Noto-chō
Tsukumo-wan
Monzen
Noto Airport
Anamizu-machi
Anamizu
Sekinohana
Noto-kongō Coast
Noto Tetsudo Line
Nanao-wan
Togi
Noto-jima
Kōda
Sanmyō
Fukuura
Shika-chō
Noto-jima Ōhashi
Wakura Onsen
Noto Yurgo (Noto Toll Rd)
Nanao
Nanao-shi
Shika
Kashima
JR Nanao Line
Yanagida Interchange
Hakui
Chirihama Nagisa Driveway
Chirihama Interchange
Chirihama
Imahama Interchange
Komedashi Interchange
Menden
Takamatsu
Hōdatsu-shimizu-chō
To Kanazawa (20km); Fukui (90km); Kyōto (220km)
Toyama-wan
Himi
Himi Line
TOYAMA-KEN
Shinminato
Takaoka
JR Hokuriko Line
To Johana (30km); Gokayama
Kosugi
To Toyama (14km); Takayama (75km); Nagoya (188km)
SIGHTS & ACTIVITIES
Ganmon 厳門 1 A4
Gojira-iwa ゴジラ岩 2 D1
Kami Tokikuni-ke 上時国家 3 C2
Keta-taisha 気多大社 4 A5
Kita-ke 喜多家 5 A6
Mado-iwa 窓岩 6 C1
Myōjō-ji 明成寺 7 A5
Noroshi Lighthouse 狼煙郎党 8 D1
Sōji-ji 総持寺 9 A3
Suzu Sea Salt Farms 珠洲製塩 10 C1
Tokikuni-ke 時国家 11 C2
SLEEPING
Flatt's by the Sea 民宿ふらっと 12 C3
Lamp no Yado ランプの宿 13 D1
Yokoiwaya 横岩屋 14 C1
TRANSPORT
Hakui Bus Stop 羽咋バス亭 15 A5
Ichinomiya Bus Stop 一ノ宮バス停 16 A5
Myōjō-ji-guchi Bus Stop 明成寺口バス停 17 A5
Sosogi-guchi Bus Stop 曽々木口バス停 18 C2

MYŌJŌ-JI 妙成寺
Founded in 1294 by Nichizō, a disciple of Nichiren, the imposing **Myōjō-ji** (☎ 27-1226; admission ¥500; 🕑 8am-5pm Apr-Oct, to 4.30pm Nov-Mar) remains an important temple for the sect. The grounds comprise many buildings, including 10 Important Cultural Properties, notably the strikingly elegant **Gojū-no-tō** (Five-Storeyed Pagoda). Pick up an English-language pamphlet.

The Togi-bound bus from Hakui Station can drop you at Myōjō-ji-guchi bus stop (¥420, 18 minutes); from here, it's under 10 minutes' walk.

Noto-kongō Coast 能登金剛

☎ 0768

This rocky, cliff-lined shoreline extends for about 16km between Fukuura and Sekinohana, and is set with dramatic rock formations like the gate-shaped **Ganmon** (best reached under your own power, or by tour bus with the usual caveats).

The manicured little town of Monzen, about 25km northeast of Ganmon, is home to majestic **Sōji-ji** (☎ 42-0005, dial 186 for caller ID; fax 42-1002; adult/child/high-school student ¥400/150/300; 🕑 8am-5pm), the temple established in 1321 as the head of the Sōtō school of Zen. After a fire severely damaged the buildings in 1898 the temple was restored, but it now functions as a branch temple; the main temple is now in Yokohama. Sōji-ji welcomes visitors to experience one hour of *zazen* (seated meditation; ¥300; 9am to 3pm) and serves *shōjin-ryōri* (Buddhist vegetarian cuisine; ¥2500 to ¥3500); reserve at least two days in advance.

Monzen is a bus hub with service to Kanazawa (¥2200, 2½ hours), Hakui (¥1510, 1½ hours) and Wajima (¥740, 35 minutes). For the temple, tell the driver 'Sōji-ji-mae'.

Wajima 輪島

☎ 0768 / pop 31,500

About 20km from Monzen, this fishing port on the north coast is the largest town in Oku-Noto and a historic centre for the production of *Wajima-nuri* (Wajima lacquerware) and, now, tourism. There's a prettily refurbished town centre and a lively morning market.

The **tourist information office** (☎ 22-1503; 🕑 8am-7pm) at the former Wajima train station (now called Michi-no-eki, 道の駅, still the bus station) provides English leaflets and maps, and staff can book accommodation. Limited English is spoken.

SIGHTS & ACTIVITIES

Wajima Shikki Shiryōkan/Shikki Kaikan
輪島漆器会館
In the centre of town next to Shin-bashi is **Wajima Shikki Shiryōkan/Shikki Kaikan** (☎ 22-2155; admission ¥200; 🕑 8.30am-5pm), a lacquerware hall and museum. The 2nd-floor museum displays lacquerware production techniques and some prodigiously old pieces, including bowls that were being swilled out of when Hideyoshi was struggling to unify Japan 500 years ago. There's a **shop** (admission free) downstairs where you can purchase contemporary works. Not cheap, but beautiful.

Ishikawa Wajima Urushi Art Museum
石川輪島漆芸美術館
In the southwest corner of the town centre, this stately contemporary **museum** (☎ 22-9788; adult/junior-high & elementary-school student/student ¥600/150/300; 🕑 9am-5pm) has a large, rotating collection of lacquerware in galleries on two floors; works are both Japanese and foreign, ancient and contemporary. It's about a 15-minute walk west of the train station. Phone ahead, as this museum closes between exhibitions.

Kiriko Kaikan キリコ会館
A selection of the impressive illuminated lacquered floats used in the Wajima Taisai (p318) and other regional festivals is on display in this **hall** (☎ 22-7100; adult/junior-high & elementary-school student/high-school student ¥600/350/450; 🕑 8am-6pm mid-Jul–Aug, to 5pm Sep–mid-Jul). Some of the floats are up to 15m tall. From Wajima Station, it is 20 minutes on foot, or you can take the bus to Tsukada bus stop (¥150, six minutes).

AND IT WAS THIIIIIS BIG...

Wajima is home to the world's largest lacquerware mural. Called *Umi no Uta* (Song of the Sea), this ocean scene is composed of 15 panels, each 2.6m by 1.2m; gold dust was applied to the wet lacquer to create the patterns. See it in the **Wajima-shi Bunka Kaikan** (輪島市文化会館; Wajima Culture Hall; admission free; 🕑 daytime hr), behind the former Wajima station.

CENTRAL HONSHŪ

Hegura-jima 舳倉島

This island with a lighthouse, several shrines and no traffic is a relaxing day trip. Birdwatchers flock here during the Golden Week holidays (29 April to 6 May) and in autumn for the astounding array of birds during the migratory season. If you want to extend your island stay, there are a couple of *minshuku*.

Weather permitting, Hegura Kōro operates a daily **ferry** (☎ 22-4381; one way ¥2200). It's a 1½-hour trip, departing Wajima at 9am and Hegura-jima at 3pm (March to October) or 2pm (November to February), taking a week off in January for maintenance.

FESTIVALS & EVENTS

Gojinjō Daikō Nabune Matsuri This festival culminating on 31 July features wild drumming by performers wearing demon masks and seaweed headgear.

Wajima Taisai See Wajima's famous, towering, illuminated *kiriko* festival floats (late August).

SLEEPING & EATING

Wajima has dozens of *minshuku* known for seafood meals worth staying in for. There are also some lovely restaurants by the harbour, though some close by early evening.

Sodegahama Camping Ground (袖が浜キャンプ場; ☎ 23-1146; fax 23-1855; camp sites per person ¥1000; ⌚ late-Apr–mid-Aug, office 4pm-9am) This camping ground is about 10 minutes west of town by bus. Take the local *noranke* bus (umi course, ¥100) or Nishiho bus (direction Zōza 雑座) to Sodegahama or hike for 20 minutes.

Fukasan (深三; ☎ 22-9933; fukasan@crux.ocn.ne.jp; r per person with 2 meals ¥7800) By the harbour, this contemporary *minshuku* offers mood-lit rustic elegance, dark beams, high ceilings, an onsen and waves crashing outside your window.

Wajima (わじま; ☎ 22-4243; sakaguti@quartz.ocn.ne.jp; s/d per person with 2 meals ¥7875/7350) This 10-room *minshuku* has subdued woodwork, a mineral onsen and *Wajima-nuri* bowls and chopsticks for eating your home-grown rice and catch of the day. It's across Futatsuya-bashi, south of the city centre.

Madara-yakata (まだら館; ☎ 22-3453; mains ¥800-2100; ⌚ lunch & dinner, closed irregularly) This restaurant serves local specialities, including *zosui* (rice hotpot), *yaki-zakana* (grilled fish) and seasonal seafood, surrounded by folk crafts. It's near the morning market street.

Shinpuku (伸幅; ☎ 22-8133; sushi per piece from ¥150, sets ¥1000-2500; ⌚ lunch & dinner, closed irregularly but mostly Wed) This tiny, assiduously local sushi shop serves fabulously fresh fish and seafood, and *iwanori* seaweed in the miso soup. Sets are a sure bet, and *asa-ichi-don* is a selection from the morning market. It's on the main street, one block east of the Cosmo petrol station. There's a picture menu.

SHOPPING

The **asa-ichi** (morning market; ⌚ 8am-noon, closed 10th & 25th of month) is highly entertaining, though undeniably touristy. Some 200 fishwives ply their wares – seafood, crafts etc – with sass and humour that cuts across the language barrier. To find the market, walk north along the river from the Wajima Shikki Shiryōkan and turn right just before Iroha-bashi.

GETTING THERE & AWAY

See p314 for information on Hokutetsu buses to Wajima (☎ 22-2314). Buses to Monzen (¥740, 35 minutes) leave every one to two hours.

Suzu & Noto-chō 珠洲・能登町

☎ 0768

Heading east from central Wajima towards the end of the peninsula, you'll pass the famous slivered *dandan-batake* (rice terraces) at **Senmaida** (千枚田) before arriving in the coastal village of **Sosogi** (曽木). After the Taira were defeated in 1185 (see p40), one of the few survivors, Taira Tokitada, was exiled to this region. The Tokikuni family, which claims descent from Tokitada, eventually divided into two clans and established separate family residences here, both now Important Cultural Properties. From Wajima, buses bound for Ushitsu stop in Sosogi (¥740, 40 minutes).

The first residence, **Tokikuni-ke** (Tokikuni Residence; ☎ 32-0075; adult/junior high-school student/high-school student ¥600/300/400; ⌚ 8.30am-5pm daily Apr-Dec, Sat & Sun Jan-Mar), was built in 1590 in the style of the Kamakura period and has a *meishō tei-en* (famous garden). A few minutes' walk away, **Kami Tokikuni-ke** (Upper Tokikuni Residence; ☎ 32-0171; adult/child ¥500/400; ⌚ 8.30am-5.30pm Jul-Sep, to 5pm Oct-Jun), with its impressive thatched roof and elegant interior, was constructed early in the 19th century. Entry to either home includes a leaflet in English.

Several hiking trails are close by, and the rock formation **mado-iwa** (window rock) is about 1km up the coast, just offshore. In winter, look for *nami-no-hana* (flowers of the waves), masses of foam that form when waves gnash Sosogi's rocky shore. Across from Mado-iwa Pocket Park, the well-kept, seven-room *minshuku* **Yokoiwaya** (☎ 32-0603; fax 32-0663; r per person with 2 meals from ¥8350) has welcomed guests for 150 years with comfortable rooms, onsen baths and outstanding seafood dinners; in most Japanese cities the dinner alone would easily cost this much. Look for the paper lantern, or request pick-up from Sosogi-guchi bus stop.

The road northeast from Sosogi village leads past the **sea salt farms** and **Gojira-iwa** (Godzilla rock, for its shape) into the town of Suzu and the remote cape Rokō-zaki, the peninsula's furthest point. At the cape, you can amble up to the lighthouse in the village of **Noroshi** (狼煙); a signpost marks the distances to faraway cities (302km to Tokyo, 1598km to Shanghai). A coastal **hiking trail** runs west along the cape. It is rustic scenery, especially on weekdays when tourist buses run less frequently and Noroshi reverts to its sleepy fishing-village self.

As you head south, the road circles around the tip of the peninsula towards less dramatic scenery on the eastern coast, and, reluctantly, back towards Kanazawa.

our pick **Lamp no Yado** (☎ 86-8000; www.lampnoyado.co.jp; r per person with 2 meals from ¥19,000;), in remote Suzu, is a place that sparkles. This 14-room wood-built waterside village, far from the main drag, has been an inn since the 1970s, but the building goes back four centuries, to when people would escape to its curative waters for weeks at a time. Rooms (some two-storey) have private bathrooms and their own *rotemburo*. The pool is almost superfluous. A very worthy splurge; reservations are required.

An Australian-Japanese couple runs the seaside inn-restaurant-bakery **Flatt's by the Sea** (Minshuku Flatto; ☎ 62-1900; www.flatts.jp; r per person with 2 meals ¥8500; Thu-Tue). It has just a few tables, serving Italian-Japanese cuisine, and the three 10-mat *minshuku* rooms have bang-on water views from across the street. For nonguests, meals are by reservation only, or just visit Flatt's bakery and cafe (closed Wednesday and Thursday) for basics or adventurous creations like chorizo rolls. It's near the inner elbow of Noto, in the town of Hanami.

HAKUSAN NATIONAL PARK
白山国立公園

For travellers with a thirst for exercise and time on their hands, this national park straddles four prefectures: Ishikawa, Fukui, Toyama and Gifu. The park has several peaks above 2500m; the tallest is Hakusan (2702m), a sacred mountain that, along with Mt Fuji, has been worshipped since ancient times. In summer, hiking and scrambling uphill to catch mountain sunrises are the main activities, while in winter skiing and onsen bathing take over.

For information, phone **Hakusan Murodō Reservation Centre** (白山室堂予約センター; ☎ 076-273-1001) or **Shiramine Town Hall** (白山市白峰支所; ☎ 076-259-2011) in Japanese.

The alpine section of the park is criss-crossed with trails, offering treks of up to 25km. For hikers who are well equipped and in no hurry, there is a 26km trek to Ogimachi (p277) in Shōkawa Valley.

Those looking to hike on and around the peaks are required to stay overnight, mostly in giant dorms at either **Murodō Centre** (dm with 2 meals ¥7700; 1 May-15 Oct) or **Nanryū Sansō** (南竜; Nanryū Mountain Lodge; ☎ 076-259-2022; dm with 2 meals ¥7600, camp sites ¥300, tent rental ¥2200, 5-person cabins ¥12,000; Jul-Sep). Getting to either of these requires a hike of 3½ to five hours, and when the lodges are full, each person gets about one tatami mat's worth of sleeping space. Camping is prohibited in the park except at Nanryū Sansō camping ground; there are several camping grounds outside the park. That doesn't stop the park from swarming with visitors, however. Reservations are recommended at least one week in advance.

The closest access point is Bettōdeai. From here it's 6km to Murodō (about 4½ hours' walk) and 5km to Nanryū (3½ hours). Ichirino, Chūgū Onsen, Shiramine and Ichinose have *minshuku*, ryokan and camping. Rates per person start from around ¥300 for camp sites, or around ¥7500 for inns with two meals.

Getting There & Away

This is not easily done, even during the peak summer period. The main mode of transport is the **Hokutetsu Kankō** (☎ 076-237-5115) bus from Kanazawa Station to Bettōdeai. From late June to mid-October, up to three buses operate daily (¥2000, two hours). Return fares include a coupon for a stay at Murodō Centre (¥10,600).

If you're driving from the Shōkawa Valley, you can take the spectacular toll road, Hakusan Super-Rindō (cars ¥3150).

FUKUI-KEN 福井県

FUKUI 福井

☎ 0776 / pop 268,000

Thanks to a drubbing in WWII and an earthquake in 1948, Fukui, the prefectural capital, doesn't bubble over with big-name attractions like other Hokuriku towns, yet this friendly, down-to-earth city makes a useful sightseeing base.

Fukui Tourist Information Centre (☎ 20-5348; 8.30am-7pm) dispenses English information and maps from beside the ticket gate at Fukui Station. If you are planning to visit both Eihei-ji (right) and Tōjinbō (opposite), enquire here about a Free Pass (¥2000), offering unlimited bus transport to these destinations for two days.

In the city, just north of the station, are the business district and the walls and moats of what was once Fukui castle, which now house the prefectural government (*kenchō*, 県庁). About 300m further on, **Yōkōkan** (養浩館; ☎ 21-2906; adult/child ¥210/100; 9am-7pm Mar-early Nov, to 5pm early Nov-Feb) is the reconstructed villa of Fukui's Edo-period *daimyō* Matsudaira clan; its stroll garden was recently rated one of Japan's top three in a gardening journal. Between 19 and 21 May, Fukui celebrates the **Mikuni Matsuri** with a parade of giant warrior dolls.

Hotel Route Inn Fukui-Ekimae (ホテルルートイン福井駅前; ☎ 30-2130; fax 30-2170; www.route-inn.co.jp; s/d/tw with breakfast ¥6200/8300/10,300; ⊠ 💻) is a crisp, new business hotel a minute's walk from Fukui Station, behind Tōyoko Inn. Minimalist design mitigates the smallness of the rooms, as do Japanese/Western breakfast, LAN internet access and common baths on the top floor.

Ten minutes' walk west of the station, **Hotel Riverge Akebono** (ホテルリバージュアケボノ; ☎ 22-1000, 0120-291-489; fax 22-8023; s/tw from ¥7161/12,705; ⊠ 💻 📶) is on the bank of the Asuwa-gawa, which is very dramatic at cherry-blossom time. Staff is genteel, and conventional rooms have private facilities and LAN cable access, plus top-floor common baths with a view. From the station, walk down Chūō-dōri, which is lined with a modern glass arcade; turn left after Ace Inn.

Miyoshiya (見吉屋; ☎ 23-3448; mains ¥500-1400; lunch & dinner Mon-Sat) is a much-loved shop serving a varied menu but known for Fukui-ken's most famous dish, *oroshi soba* (*soba* noodles topped with grated daikon and shaved bonito flakes; ¥500). It's about five minutes' walk from Fukui Station down Chūō-dōri, behind Fukui Bank (福井銀行), at the corner of Phoenix-dōri.

The simple corner shop **Yōroppa-ken** (ヨーロッパ軒; ☎ 26-4681; mains ¥850-1350; lunch & dinner Wed-Mon) creates another beloved Fukui speciality, *sōsu katsu-don* (breaded, fried pork cutlet dipped in a Worcestershire-based sauce, over rice; ¥850), which is surprisingly light. Add ¥200 for a set with salad and miso soup. It's on the same side of the street as Miyoshiya, about 200m further from the station.

The ingenious *izakaya* **Ori-Ori-ya** (織屋; ☎ 27-4004; skewers ¥100-300, dishes ¥380-980; dinner) lets you select your own ingredients and grill them yourself at the table. It's near Hotel Riverge Akebono.

JR trains connect Fukui with Kanazawa (*tokkyū*, ¥2940, 50 minutes; *futsū*, ¥1280, 1½ hours), Tsuruga (*tokkyū*, ¥2610, 35 minutes; *futsū*, ¥950, 55 minutes), Kyoto (¥4810, 1½ hours) and Osaka (¥5870, 1¾ hours).

EIHEI-JI 永平寺

☎ 0776

In 1244 the great Zen master Dōgen (1200–53), founder of the Sōtō sect of Zen Buddhism, established Eihei-ji in a forest near Fukui. Today it's one of Sōtō's two head temples, one of the world's most influential Zen centres and a palpably spiritual place amid mountains, mosses and ancient cedars. Serious students of Zen should consider a retreat here – there are commonly some 150 priests and disciples in residence – but all are welcome to visit.

The **temple** (☎ 63-3102; adult/child ¥500/200; 9am-5pm) receives huge numbers of visitors as sightseers or for rigorous Zen training. Among the approximately 70 buildings, the standard circuit concentrates on seven major ones: Sanmon (main gate), Butsuden (Buddha Hall), Hattō (Dharma Hall), Sō-dō (Priests' Hall), plus the *daikuin* (kitchen), *yokushitsu* (bath) and, yes, *tōsu* (lavatory). You walk among the buildings on wooden walkways in your stockinged feet (pretty chilly in cold weather). The Shōbōkaku exhibits many Eihei-ji treasures.

The temple is often closed for periods varying from a week to 10 days for religious observance. Before setting out, be sure to check www.sotozen-net.or.jp/kokusai/list/eiheiji.htm or with tourist offices.

You can attend the temple's four-day, three-night **sanzen program** (religious trainee program; ☎ 63-3640; fax 63-3631; www.sotozen-net.or.jp/kokusai/list/eiheiji.htm; fee ¥12,000), which follows the monks' training schedule, complete with 3.50am prayers, cleaning, *zazen* and ritual meals in which not a grain of rice may be left behind. Japanese ability is not necessary, but it helps to be able to sit in the half-lotus position. Everyone we've spoken to who has completed this course agreea it is a remarkable experience. Book at least one month in advance. A single night's stay, *sanrō*, is also possible for ¥8000 (with two meals). Day visitors can eat a lunch of *shōjin-ryōri* (¥3000) by reservation.

To get to Eihei-ji from Fukui, take the Keifuku bus (¥720, 35 minutes, at least three daily) from stop 5, a couple of blocks from Fukui; buses (¥720, 35 minutes) depart from the east exit of Fukui Station. See opposite for the Free Pass that also covers Tōjinbō.

TŌJINBŌ 東尋坊

On the coast about 25km northwest of Fukui are these towering **rock columns** and **cliffs**, a too-popular tourist destination that's also a place of legend: one says that Tōjinbō was an evil Buddhist priest who was cast off the cliff by angry villagers in 1182; the sea surged for 49 days thereafter, a demonstration of the priest's fury from beyond his watery grave.

Visitors can take a boat trip (¥1010, 30 minutes) to view the rock formations or travel further up the coast to **O-jima**, a small island with a shrine that is joined to the mainland by a bridge.

The most convenient connection to Tōjinbō is by bus via Awara Onsen Station (from Fukui: *tokkyū*, ¥1560, 10 minutes). *Futsū* trains are less expensive (¥320, 16 minutes), but less frequent. Buses to Tōjinbō depart Awara Onsen Station at 40 minutes past the hour (¥730, 40 minutes). See opposite for information on the Free Pass that also covers Tōjinbō, and note that the Free Pass is not valid on trains.

TSURUGA 敦賀

Tsuruga, south of Fukui and north of Biwa-ko, is a thriving port and train junction. **Shin Nihonkai ferry company** (☎ 0770-23-2222; www.snf.co.jp, in Japanese) operates 11 sailings a week to Tomakomai, Hokkaidō (2nd class from ¥9300, 19¼ hours nonstop, 30½ hours with stops). Several of these stop en route at Niigata (¥5100, 13¼ hours) and Akita (¥6700, 22¾ hours). Buses timed to ferry departures serve Tsuruga-kō port from Tsuruga Station (¥340, 20 minutes).

OBAMA 小浜

☎ 0770 / pop 32,000

Under two hours from Fukui or Kyoto, this little seaside town recently received a big PR boost when a certain world leader made history, but

ELECTION DAY IN OBAMA *Chris Rowthorn*

Obama Japan is a sleepy little fishing town on the Sea of Japan coast. It's a fair bet that citizens of the town generally didn't usually pay much attention to American politics. That all changed in 2008, when it became increasingly clear that Barack Obama was going to become the next president of the USA. The town was swept up in Obama fever and citizens watched the campaign with great interest.

Several young ladies in the town formed a hula dance troupe and called themselves the 'Obama Girls' (I guess they were celebrating the fact that Obama had grown up in Hawaii). Local musicians formed a whacky Japanese band that included a character dressed in a Power Rangers outfit. Town bakers started turning out Japanese bean cakes bearing the likeness of Barack Obama (actually, the back of his head – it was considered bad luck to put his face on the cakes until he was elected). The town's chopstick manufacturers even produced a limited series of Obama chopsticks.

On 5 November (Japan is 12 hours ahead of the States, where the election was held on 4 November), I took a train up to Obama from my home in Kyoto to watch the election returns with the citizens of Obama. The atmosphere was electric. As the Obama Girls danced, a squad of older Obama supporters waved placards in the air, and one of the town bigwigs kept up a running patter, trying his best to interpret the CNN reports for the assembled mass.

Around noon, as one of the bands was performing another Obama-inspired number, a shout suddenly emerged from a group of young American Democrats stationed near the TV: CNN had called the election for Obama. The place went mad. Caught up in the excitement, Obama housewives embraced joyous American English teachers, half-drunk *ojisans* (older guys) high-fived foreign reporters, and the Obama Girls jumped for joy, their grass skirts waving in the air. The crowd took up the chant: 'Obama! Obama! Obama!'

We had a lot to celebrate.

it's got quite a history of its own. For centuries its close proximity to the capital (Heian-kyō, now Kyoto) and river-fed bay (Wakasa-wan) made it a primary source of fresh food, particularly *saba* (mackerel), to the imperial court. Locals still identify more with the Kyoto area than with the rest of Fukui-ken, in speech, manner and outlook. Obama's 144 temples constitute Japan's most per capita (it's nicknamed 'Little Nara'), and its craft heritage includes lacquerware chopsticks inlaid with patterns of eggshell and abalone, as well as roofing tiles.

Wakasa Obama tourist information office (若狭おばま観光案内所; ☎ 53-2042; ⏰ 9am-5pm Mon-Sat, 10am-4pm Sun, closed Sun Dec-Mar) is next to Obama Station. Bicycle rental (two/four/eight hours ¥300/500/1000), located by the station, makes an easy way to get around town.

Miketsukuni Wakasa Obama Food Culture Museum (御食国若狭おばま食文化会館; ☎ 53-1000; admission free; ⏰ 9am-6pm) shows off the region's food heritage with extensive displays (in Japanese) and occasional cooking demonstrations on the ground floor. Upstairs is a workshop where you can put the finishing touches on your own *Wakasa-nuri* (Wakasa lacquer) chopsticks (¥900) or imprint a design on a *kawara* (clay tile; ¥700). The *sentō* on the premises, **Hama-no-yu** (濱の湯; with/without towel ¥800/600; ⏰ 10am-midnight, closed 3rd Wed of month), offers views of the bay from the bath as well as from its restaurant **Hama-tei** (濱亭; mains ¥650-850; ⏰ 11am-11pm). Look for *negi-toro-don* (fatty tuna and green onion over rice; ¥650) or the Hama-no-yu *teishoku* (¥850 with local *saba*).

Outside of the town centre are two important temples. The hilltop **Haga-ji** (羽賀寺; ☎ 52-4502; adult/child ¥400/200; ⏰ 8am-5pm Mar-Nov, 9am-4pm Dec-Feb) traces its history to AD 716 and features a peace bell rung seven times at community celebrations, notably for the inauguration of the current US president. A 4km bike ride through rice fields from Higashi-Obama Station (¥180, five minutes), **Myōtsū-ji** (明通寺; ☎ 57-1355; adult/child ¥400/200; ⏰ 8am-5pm Mar-Nov, 9am-4.30pm Dec-Feb) was established in AD 806 by a shōgun seeking to console the souls of those he defeated in war. The late-13th-century three-storey pagoda and *hondō* (main hall) are both National Treasures. Note: bicycles are not allowed on the train between the two stations, but rentals are available at both.

Obama is a stop on the JR Obama line from Tsuruga (*futsū*, ¥950, 65 minutes).

Kansai 関西

Kansai is the heart of Japan. It is here that a truly distinctive Japanese culture came into being, and with it, those things that so many of us associate with Japan: ancient temples, colourful shrines and peaceful Zen gardens. Indeed, nowhere else in the country can you find so much of historical interest in such a compact area. And, since plenty of international carriers fly into Kansai International Airport, it is perfectly possible to make Kansai your first port of call in Japan.

Kansai's major drawcards are Kyoto and Nara. Kyoto was the imperial capital between 794 and 1868, and is still considered by many to be the cultural heart of Japan. Nara predates Kyoto as an imperial capital and also has an impressive array of temples, burial mounds and relics.

Osaka is a great place to sample Japanese city life in all its mind-boggling intensity, while Kōbe is one of Japan's most cosmopolitan and attractive cities. Further west, Himeji has the best of Japan's many feudal castles.

Other prefectures in Kansai include Mie-ken, which is home to Ise-jingū, Japan's most sacred Shintō shrine, and Wakayama-ken, which offers onsen (hot springs), a rugged coastline and the temple complex of Kōya-san, Japan's most important Buddhist centre. Finally, the northern coast of Kansai has some fabulous scenery, several good beaches and the lovely Tango-hantō (Tango Peninsula).

Kyoto is the logical base for an exploration of Kansai, but you could also base yourself in Osaka or Nara. Wherever you stay, you will find that Kansai is the perfect place to sample both modern and traditional Japan without spending too much time moving from place to place.

HIGHLIGHTS

- Immerse yourself in **Kyoto** (p324), Japan's cultural capital, with more than 2000 temples and shrines
- Delve into the roots of Japanese culture in **Nara** (p417), the country's ancient capital
- Be dazzled by the incredible nightscapes of **Osaka** (p391), Kansai's down-to-earth urban heart
- Feel the spiritual power emanating from Japan's most sacred shrine: **Ise-jingū** (p443)
- Ascend to the Buddhist sanctuary of **Kōya-san** (p433)
- Soak in a riverside onsen in the heart of the **Kii-hantō** (p441)

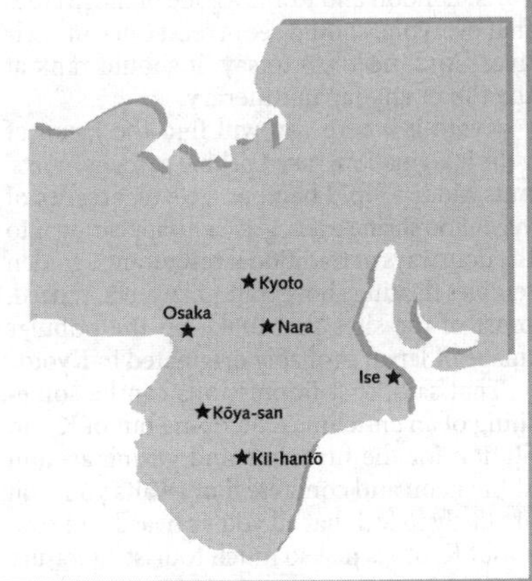

Climate

For information on the climate of Kansai, see p326.

Getting There & Away

Travel between Kansai and other parts of Japan is a breeze. Kansai is served by the Tōkaidō and San-yō *shinkansen* (bullet train) lines, several JR main lines and a few private rail lines. It is also possible to travel to/from Kansai and other parts of Honshū, Shikoku and Kyūshū by long-distance highway buses. Ferries sail between Kōbe/Osaka and other parts of Honshū, Kyūshū, Shikoku and Okinawa. In addition, ferries run between Higashi-Maizuru, on the Sea of Japan coast in northern Kyoto-fu, and Otaru, in Hokkaidō. Finally, Kansai has several airports, most notably Osaka's Itami Airport (ITM), which has flights to/from many of Japan's major cities, and Kansai International Airport (KIX), which has flights to dozens of foreign cities (as well as some domestic destinations). For more information, see p381.

KYOTO 京都

☎ 075 / pop 1.47 million

Kyoto is the storehouse of Japan's traditional culture and the stage on which much of Japanese history was played out. With 17 Unesco World Heritage Sites (see the boxed text, p328), more than 1600 Buddhist temples and over 400 Shintō shrines, Kyoto is also one of the world's most culturally rich cities. Indeed, it is fair to say that Kyoto ranks with Paris, London and Rome as one of those cities that everyone should see at least once in their lives. And, needless to say, it should rank at the top of any Japan itinerary.

Kyoto is where you will find the Japan of your imagination: raked pebble gardens, poets' huts hidden amid bamboo groves, arcades of vermilion shrine gates, geisha disappearing into the doorways of traditional restaurants, golden temples floating above tranquil waters. Indeed, most of the sites that make up the popular image of Japan probably originated in Kyoto.

That said, first impressions can be something of an anticlimax. Stepping out of Kyoto Station for the first time and gazing around at the neon and concrete that awaits you, you are likely to feel that all you've heard and read about Kyoto is just so much tourist-literature hype. We can only advise you to be patient, for the beauty of Kyoto is largely hidden from casual view: it lies behind walls, doors, curtains and facades. But if you take a little time to explore, you will discover that there are hundreds, perhaps thousands of pockets of incredible beauty scattered across the city. And, the closer you look, the more there is to see.

HISTORY

The Kyoto basin was first settled in the 7th century, and by 794 it had become Heian-kyō, the capital of Japan. Like Nara, a previous capital, the city was laid out in a grid pattern modelled on the Chinese Tang-dynasty capital, Chang'an (contemporary Xi'an). Although the city was to serve as home to the Japanese imperial family from 794 to 1868 (when the Meiji Restoration took the imperial family to the new capital, Tokyo), the city was not always the focus of Japanese political power. During the Kamakura period (1185–1333), Kamakura served as the national capital, and during the Edo period (1600–1867), the Tokugawa shōgunate ruled Japan from Edo (now Tokyo).

The problem was that from the 9th century, the imperial family was increasingly isolated from the mechanics of political power and the country was ruled primarily by military families, or shōgunates. While Kyoto still remained capital in name and was the cultural focus of the nation, imperial power was, for the most part, symbolic and the business of running state affairs was often carried out elsewhere.

Just as imperial fortunes have waxed and waned, the fortunes of the city itself have fluctuated dramatically. During the Ōnin War (1466–67), which marked the close of the Muromachi period, the Kyoto Gosho (Imperial Palace) and most of the city were destroyed. Much of what can be seen in Kyoto today dates from the Edo period. Although political power resided in Edo, Kyoto was rebuilt and flourished as a cultural, religious and economic centre. Fortunately Kyoto was spared the aerial bombing that razed other Japanese urban centres in the closing months of WWII.

Today, Kyoto remains an important cultural and educational centre. It has some 20% of Japan's National Treasures and 15% of Japan's Important Cultural Properties, as well as dozens of museums and universities. The city also retains a lot of the industries that grew up to service the needs of the imperial court, and Kyoto remains the headquarters for

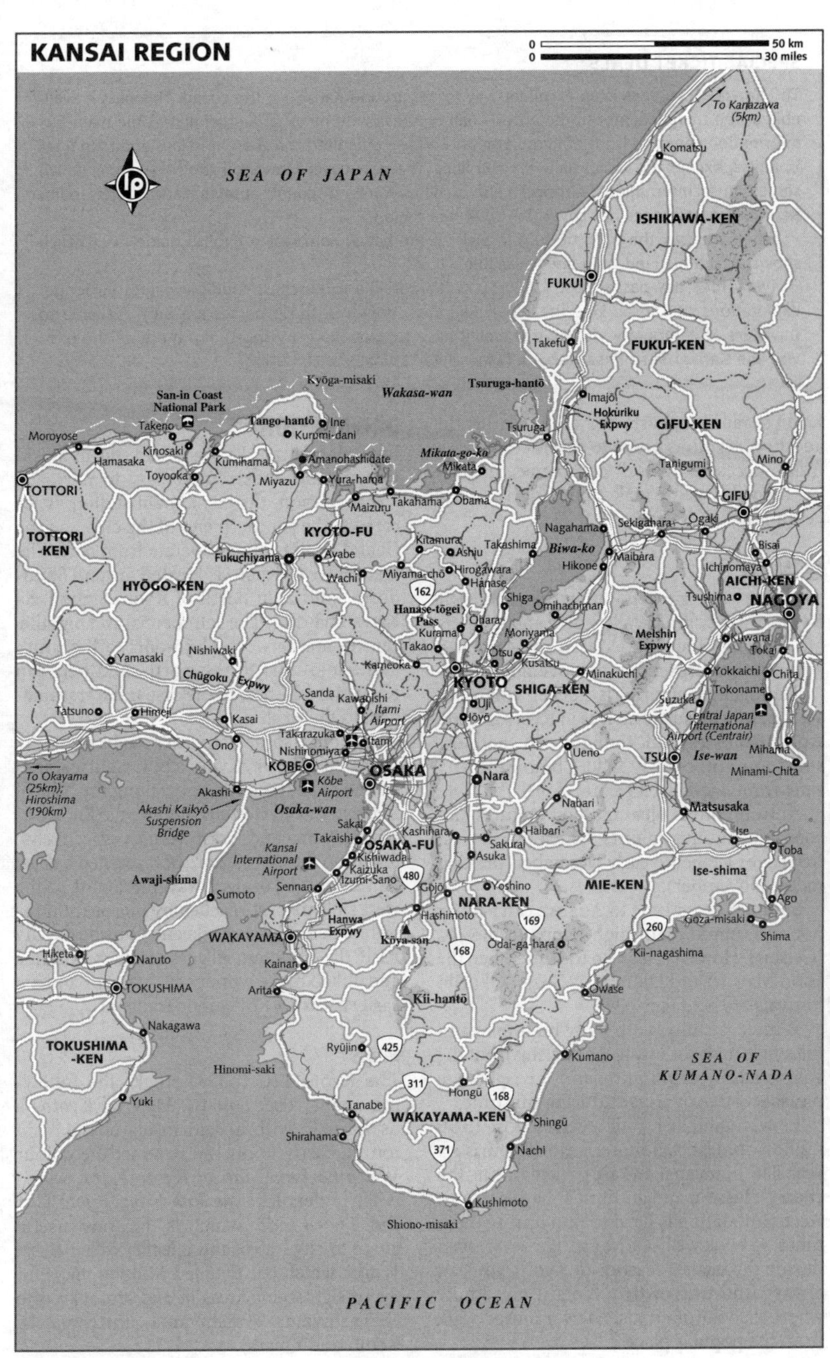

KANSAI REGION
0 50 km
0 30 miles
SEA OF JAPAN
To Kanazawa (5km)
Komatsu
ISHIKAWA-KEN
FUKUI
Takefu
FUKUI-KEN
Kyōga-misaki
Wakasa-wan
Tsuruga-hantō
Imajō
Hokuriku Expwy
San-in Coast National Park
Tango-hantō
Ine
Kurumi-dani
Takeno
Moroyose
Kinosaki
Hamasaka
Kumihama
Amanohashidate
Mikata-go-ko
Mikata
Tsuruga
GIFU-KEN
Tanigumi
Mino
Toyooka
Miyazu
Yura-hama
TOTTORI
Maizuru
Takahama
Obama
GIFU
TOTTORI -KEN
KYOTO-FU
Nagahama
Sekigahara
Ōgaki
Kitamura
Takashima
Biwa-ko
Ashiu
Maibara
Bisai
Fukuchiyama
Ayabe
Hikone
Ichinomaya
HYŌGO-KEN
Wachi
Miyama-chō
Hirogawara
Hanase
AICHI-KEN
162
Tsushima
NAGOYA
Shiga
Hanase-tōgei Pass
Ōmihachiman
Kurama
Ohara
Moriyama
Meishin Expwy
Kuwana
Takao
Tokai
Nishiwaki
Yamasaki
Kameoka
Ōtsu
Kusatsu
KYOTO
Minakuchi
Yokkaichi
Chita
Chūgoku Expwy
SHIGA-KEN
Sanda
Kawanishi
Itami Airport
Uji
Tokoname
Suzuka
Tatsuno
Himeji
Kasai
Jōyō
Central Japan International Airport (Centrair)
Takarazuka
Itami
Ono
Ueno
Nishinomiya
Mihama
TSU
Ise-wan
KOBE
OSAKA
Nara
Minami-Chita
To Okayama (25km); Hiroshima (190km)
Kōbe Airport
Akashi
Nabari
Akashi Kaikyō Suspension Bridge
Osaka-wan
Matsusaka
Sakai
Kashihara
Haibari
Takaishi
OSAKA-FU
Sakurai
Ise
Toba
Kansai International Airport
Kishiwada
Asuka
Kaizuka
Ise-shima
Izumi-Sano
480
Awaji-shima
Sennan
Gojō
Yoshino
MIE-KEN
Sumoto
NARA-KEN
Ago
Hanwa Expwy
Hashimoto
169
Goza-misaki
WAKAYAMA
260
Kōya-san
Shima
Ōdai-ga-hara
168
Hiketa
Naruto
Kii-nagashima
Kainan
TOKUSHIMA
Arita
Owase
Kii-hantō
Nakagawa
TOKUSHIMA -KEN
Ryūjin
425
Kumano
SEA OF KUMANO-NADA
Hinomi-saki
311
Hongū
168
Yuki
Tanabe
WAKAYAMA-KEN
Shingū
Shirahama
371
Nachi
Kushimoto
Shiono-misaki
PACIFIC OCEAN

KANSAI

SPECIAL TICKET DEALS

The **Kansai Thru Pass** is an excellent way to get around Kansai on the cheap. This pass – available at the travel counter in the arrivals hall of Kansai International Airport and at the main bus information centre in front of Kyoto Station – allows unlimited travel on most bus and train lines in Kansai except the Japan Railways (JR) line. (The pass covers travel on the Nankai line, which serves Kansai International Airport.) It also qualifies you for discounts at several attractions around Kansai. The pass does not cover the Ise-Shima region.

When you buy the pass, be sure to pick up the handy companion English guide-map, which shows all the bus and train lines available.

Two-/three-day passes cost ¥3800/5000. It's possible to purchase multiple passes for longer explorations of Kansai. Like the Japan Rail Pass, however, these passes are only available to travellers on temporary visitor visas (you'll have to show your passport). For more on the pass, visit the **Kansai Thru Pass website** (www.surutto.com/conts/ticket/3dayeng).

Japan's traditional arts and crafts worlds. In addition, Kyoto is home to several of Japan's most successful hi-tech companies, including the video-game maker Nintendo and the ceramics giant Kyocera.

CLIMATE

The best and most popular times to visit Kyoto are the climatically stable and temperate seasons of spring (March to May) and autumn (late September to November).

The highlight of spring is the cherry-blossom season, which usually arrives in Kyoto in early April. Bear in mind, though, that the blossoms are notoriously fickle, blooming any time from late March to mid-April.

Autumn offers pleasant temperatures and soothing autumn colours, which usually last from late October to early December (peaking in late November).

Summer, from June to August, can be very hot and humid, with high temps in the 30s (Celsius). However, it's also the time when the Gion Matsuri and Daimon-ji Gozan Okuribi festivals are held (see p366).

Winter is chilly, with daily high temps in the single digits or low teens (Celsius), but the cold is hardly debilitating and the sights are pleasantly free of crowds during this time.

Be warned that Kyoto receives close to 50 million domestic and international tourists a year. The popular sights are packed during the cherry-blossom and autumn-foliage seasons. Accommodation is hard to find during these times, so book well in advance. However, even during the busiest seasons in Kyoto, you can always find uncrowded spots if you know where to look (often just a few minutes' walk from the popular places).

ORIENTATION

Like Manhattan, Kyoto is laid out in a grid pattern and is extremely easy to navigate. Kyoto Station, the city's main station, is located at the southern end of the city, and the JR and Kintetsu lines operate from here. The real centre of Kyoto is located around Shijō-dōri, about 2km north of Kyoto Station via Karasuma-dōri. The commercial and nightlife centres are between Shijō-dōri to the south and Sanjō-dōri to the north, and between Kawaramachi-dōri to the east and Karasuma-dōri to the west.

Although some of Kyoto's major sights are in the city centre, Kyoto's best sightseeing is on the outskirts of the city, along the base of the eastern and western mountains (known as Higashiyama and Arashiyama, respectively). Sights on the east side are best reached by bus, bicycle or the Tōzai subway line. Sights on the west side are best reached by bus or train (or by bicycle if you're very keen). Outside the city itself, the mountain villages of Ōhara, Kurama and Takao make wonderful day trips and are easily accessible by public transport.

Maps

The Kyoto TIC (p328) stocks the following maps: the *Tourist Map of Kyoto,* a useful map with decent insets of the main tourist districts on the reverse; the colour *Welcome Inns Map of Kyoto/Nara,* which is fairly detailed; the *Bus Navi: Kyoto City Bus Travel map,* which is the most useful guide to city buses; and a leaflet called *Kyoto Walks,* which has detailed walking maps for major sightseeing areas in and around Kyoto (Higashiyama, Arashiyama, northwestern Kyoto and Ōhara).

INFORMATION

Bookshops

Junkudō (Map p336; ☎ 253-6460; Kyoto BAL Bldg, 2 Yamazaki-chō, Sanjō sagaru, Kawaramachi-dōri, Nakagyō-ku; 🕑 11am-8pm) In the BAL Building, this shop has a great selection of English-language books on the 5th 8th floors. This is Kyoto's best bookshop now that the old Maruzen and Random Walk bookshops have closed (you may remember these shops if you visited in the past).

Emergency

Ambulance (☎ 119)
Fire (☎ 119)
Police (☎ 110)

Immigration Offices

Osaka Regional Immigration Bureau Kyoto Branch (Map pp340-1; ☎ 752-5997; 2F Kyoto Second Local Joint Government Bldg, 34-12 Marutamachi Kawabata Higashi iru, Higashi Marutamachi, Sakyō-ku; 🕑 9am-noon & 1-4pm Mon-Fri)

Internet Access

Kinko's (Map p336; ☎ 213-6802; 651-1 Tearaimizu-chō, Takoyakushi sagaru, Karasuma-dōri, Nakagyō-ku; first 10min ¥262, then every 10min ¥210; 🕑 24hr)
Kyoto International Community House (KICH; Map pp340-1; ☎ 752-3010; 2-1 Torii-chō, Awataguchi, Sakyō-ku; per 30min ¥200; 🕑 9am-9pm Tue-Sun, closed Tue when Mon is a holiday) The machines here have Japanese keyboards and allow access to only a limited number of sites.
Kyoto Prefectural International Centre (Map p335; ☎ 342-5000; 9F Kyoto Eki Bldg, Karasuma-dōri Shiokōji sagaru, Shimogyō-ku; per 15min ¥100; 🕑 10am-6pm, closed 2nd & 4th Tue each month) This is a good place to log on in the Kyoto Station area. Note that this will move to the Suvaco shopping area in spring 2010 (for details, see p328).
Media Café Popeye (Map p336; ☎ 253-5300; www.mediacafe.jp/branch/sanjokawaramachi/index.html, in Japanese; Kawaramachi-dōri Sanjō sagaru, Nakagyō-ku; per hr ¥420; 🕑 24hr) This is convenient when you're downtown.
Tops Café (Map p335; ☎ 681-9270; www.topsnet.co.jp, in Japanese; Kyoto-eki, Hachijō-guchi; per 15min ¥120, plus ¥200 registration fee; 🕑 24hr) This is an all-night manga/internet cafe where you can actually spend the night in the booths if you want. It's just outside the south (Hachijō) exit of Kyoto Station.

Internet Resources

Kyoto Temple Admission Fees (www.templefees.com)
Kyoto Visitor's Guide (www.kyotoguide.com)

Media

The free *Kyoto Visitor's Guide* is the best source of information on upcoming events. It has restaurant reviews, day walks, detailed maps, useful information sections and feature articles about various aspects of the city. Pick up a copy as soon as you arrive in Kyoto. It's available at the TIC, Kyoto International Community House and most major hotels.

Another excellent source of information about Kyoto and the rest of the Kansai area is *Kansai Time Out*, a monthly English-language listings magazine. Apart from lively articles, it has a large section of ads for employment, travel agencies, meetings etc. It's available at the bookshops listed in this section (left) and at the TIC (p328).

Medical Services

Kyoto University Hospital (Map pp340-1; ☎ 751-3111; 54 Shōgoinkawara-chō, Sakyō-ku; 🕑 reception 8.30-11am, medical examination starts at 9am) Best hospital in Kyoto. There is an information counter near the entrance that can point you in the right direction.

Money

Most of the major banks are near the Shijō-Karasuma intersection, two stops north of Kyoto Station on the Karasuma line subway.

International transactions (like wire transfers) can be made at **Bank of Tokyo-Mitsubishi UFJ** (Map p336; ☎ 221-7161; 🕑 9am-3pm Mon-Fri, ATM 7am-11pm Mon-Fri, to 9pm Sat, Sun & holidays), which is at the southeast corner of this intersection. There is another branch one block southwest of the intersection. Other international transactions can be made at **Citibank** (Map p336; ☎ 212-5387; 🕑 office 9am-3pm Mon-Fri, ATM 24hr), just west of this intersection. Finally, you can change travellers cheques at most post offices around town, including the Kyoto Central Post Office (p328) next to Kyoto Station.

INTERNATIONAL ATMS

Post offices have ATMs that accept most foreign-issued cards. If your card doesn't work at postal ATMs, try the ATMs in 7-Eleven convenience stores. Failing that, try the following:

Citibank (Map p336; ☎ 212-5387; 🕑 office 9am-3pm Mon-Fri, ATM 24hr) Has a 24-hour ATM that accepts most foreign-issued cards.

KYOTO UNESCO WORLD HERITAGE SITES

In 1994 13 of Kyoto's Buddhist temples, three Shintō shrines and one castle met the criteria to be designated World Heritage Sites by the UN. Each of the 17 sites has buildings or gardens of immeasurable historical value and all are open for public viewing.

Castle

- Nijō-jō (p358)

Shrines

- Kamigamo-jinja (p348)
- Shimogamo-jinja (p348)
- Ujigami-jinja in Uji (p362)

Temples

- Byōdō-in (p362)
- Daigo-ji (p362)
- Enryaku-ji (p357)
- Ginkaku-ji (p354)
- Kinkaku-ji (p358)
- Kiyomizu-dera (p350)
- Kōzan-ji (p365)
- Ninna-ji (p359)
- Nishi Hongan-ji (opposite)
- Ryōan-ji (p358)
- Saihō-ji (p363)
- Tenryū-ji (p360)
- Tō-ji (p348)

Post

Kyoto Central Post Office (Map p335; ☎ 365-2471; 843-12 Higashishiokōji-chō, Shimogyō-ku; ⏲ 9am-9pm Mon-Fri, to 7pm Sat, Sun & holidays, ATMs 12.05am-11.55pm Mon-Sat, to 8pm Sun) Conveniently located next to Kyoto Station (take the Karasuma exit, as the post office is on the northwestern side of the station). There's an after-hours service counter on the southern side of the post office, which is open 24 hours a day, 365 days a year. Also, the ATMs here are open *almost* 24 hours a day.

Tourist Information

Note that the following two information centres (along with the Welcome Inn Reservation counter, and the Prefectural International Centre) will move to the Suvaco shopping complex in spring 2010. Suvaco is on the 2nd floor of Kyoto Station, in the main concourse between the north side of the station and the *shinkansen* gates. It is just to the left (south) of the main entrance of Isetan department store.

Kyoto City Tourist Information (Map p335; ☎ 343-6655; ⏲ 8.30am-7pm) Inside the new Kyoto Station building, on the 2nd floor just across from Café du Monde. Though it's geared towards Japanese visitors, an English-speaking staff member is usually on hand and it's easier to find than the following.

Kyoto Tourist Information Center (TIC; Map p335; ☎ 344-3300; ⏲ 10am-6pm, closed 2nd & 4th Tue of each month & new-year holidays) The best source of information on Kyoto, this is located on the 9th floor of the Kyoto Station building. To get there from the main concourse of the station, take the west escalator to the 2nd floor, enter Isetan department store and take an immediate left, then look for the elevator on your left and take it to the 9th floor. It's right outside the elevator, inside the Kyoto Prefectural International Centre. There is a Welcome Inn Reservation counter here that can help with accommodation bookings.

Travel Agencies

IACE TRAVEL (Map p336; ☎ 212-8944; 4F Dai15 Hase Bldg, 688 Takanna-chō, Shijo agaru, Karasuma dōri, Nakagyō-ku; ⏲ office 10am-7pm Mon-Fri, to 5pm Sat)

KNT (Map p336; ☎ 255-0489; 437 Ebisu-chō, Sanjo agaru, Kawaramachi dōri, Nakagyō-ku; ⏲ office 10.30am-7pm Mon-Fri, to 6.30pm Sat, Sun & holidays)

Useful Organisations

Kyoto International Community House (KICH; Map pp340-1; ☎ 752-3010; 2-1 Torii-chō, Awataguchi, Sakyō-ku; ⏲ 9am-9pm, closed Mon, open Mon when Mon is a national holiday, closed Tue when preceding Mon is a national holiday) An essential stop for those planning a long-term stay in Kyoto, but it can also be quite useful for short-term visitors. Here you can rent typewriters, send and receive faxes, and use the internet. It has a library with maps, books, newspapers and magazines from around the world, and a noticeboard displaying messages regarding work, accommodation, rummage sales etc. KICH is in eastern Kyoto. Take the Tōzai line subway from central Kyoto and get off at Keage Station, from which it's a 350m (five-minute) walk downhill.

SIGHTS

Kyoto Station Area

Although most of Kyoto's attractions are further north, there are a few attractions within walking distance of the station (Map p335). The most impressive sight in this area is the vast Higashi Hongan-ji, but don't forget the station building itself – it's an attraction in its own right.

KYOTO TOWER 京都タワー

If you want to orient yourself and get an idea of the layout of Kyoto as soon as you arrive in town, **Kyoto Tower** (Map p335; ☎ 361-3215; Shichijō sagaru, Karasuma, Shimogyō-ku; admission ¥770; ⌚ 9am-9pm) is the place to do it. Located right outside the Karasuma (north) gate of the station, this retro tower looks like a rocket perched atop the Kyoto Tower Hotel. The tower provides excellent views in all directions and you can really see why Kyotoites describe their city as a *bonchi* (a flat tray with raised edges). There are free mounted binoculars to use, and these allow ripping views over to Kiyomizu-dera (p350) and as far south as Osaka. Last entry is 8.40pm.

HIGASHI HONGAN-JI 東本願寺

A short walk north of Kyoto Station, this **temple** (Map p335; ☎ 371-9181; Shichijō agaru, Karasuma-dōri, Shimogyō-ku; admission free; ⌚ 5.50am-5.30pm Mar-Oct, 6.20am-4.30pm Nov-Feb) is the last word in all things grand and gaudy. Considering the proximity to the station, the free admission, the awesome structures and the dazzling interiors, this temple is an obvious spot to visit if you find yourself near the station.

In 1602, when Tokugawa Ieyasu engineered the rift in the Jōdo Shin-shū school, he founded this temple as a competitor to Nishi Hongan-ji (see following). Rebuilt in 1895 after a series of fires destroyed all of the original structures, the temple is now the headquarters of the Ōtani branch of Jōdo Shin-shū.

In the corridor between the two main buildings you'll find a curious item encased in glass: a tremendous coil of rope made from human hair. Following the destruction of the temple in the 1880s, an eager group of female temple devotees donated their locks to make the ropes that hauled the massive timbers used for reconstruction.

The enormous Goei-dō main hall is one of the world's largest wooden structures, standing 38m high, 76m long and 58m wide. At the time of writing, this hall was being restored, but it should be open by the time this book goes to print. The adjoining Amida-dō hall will undergo restoration following completion of the Goei-dō.

NISHI HONGAN-JI 西本願寺

In 1591 Toyotomi Hideyoshi built this **temple** (Map p335; ☎ 371-5181; Hanaya-chō sagaru, Horikawa-dōri, Shimogyō-ku; admission free; ⌚ 6am-5pm Nov-Feb, 5.30am-5.30pm Mar, Apr, Sep & Oct, to 6pm May-Aug), known as Hongan-ji, as the new headquarters for the Jōdo Shin-shū (True Pure Land) school of Buddhism, which had accumulated immense power. Later, Tokugawa Ieyasu saw this power as a threat and sought to weaken it by encouraging a breakaway faction of this school to found Higashi Hongan-ji (*higashi* means 'east') in 1602. The original Hongan-ji then became known as Nishi Hongan-ji (*nishi* means 'west'). It now functions as the headquarters of the Hongan-ji branch of the Jōdo Shin-shū school, with over 10,000 temples and 12 million followers worldwide.

The temple contains five buildings, featuring some of the finest examples of architecture and artistic achievement from the Azuchi-Momoyama period (1568–1600). The **Goei-dō** (Main Hall) has just been restored and is a marvellous sight. Another must-see building is the **Daisho-in Hall**, which has sumptuous paintings, carvings and metal ornamentation. A small garden and two nō (stylised Japanese dance-drama) stages are connected with the hall. The dazzling **Kara-mon** has intricate ornamental carvings.

KYOTO STATION 京都駅

Kyoto's **station building** (Map p335; Higashishiokō-ji-chō, Shiokōji sagaru, Karasuma-dōri, Shimogyō-ku) is a striking steel-and-glass structure – a futuristic cathedral for the transport age. Take some time to explore the many levels of the station, all the way up to the 15th-floor observation level. If you don't suffer from fear of heights, try riding the escalator from the 7th floor on the eastern side of the building up to the 11th-floor aerial skywalk, high over the main concourse.

In the station building you'll find several food courts (see p372), the Kyoto Prefectural International Centre (see p327), a performance space and Isetan department store.

SHŌSEI-EN 涉成園

About five minutes' walk east of Higashi Hongan-ji, the garden **Shōsei-en** (Map p335; ☎ 371-9181; Shichijō agaru, Karasuma-dōri, Shimogyō-ku; admission free; ⌚ 9am-3.30pm) is a nice place for a stroll when you're in the station area. The lovely grounds, incorporating the Kikoku-tei villa, were completed in 1657. Bring a picnic (and some bread to feed the carp) or just stroll around the beautiful Ingetsu-ike pond.

(Continued on page 346)

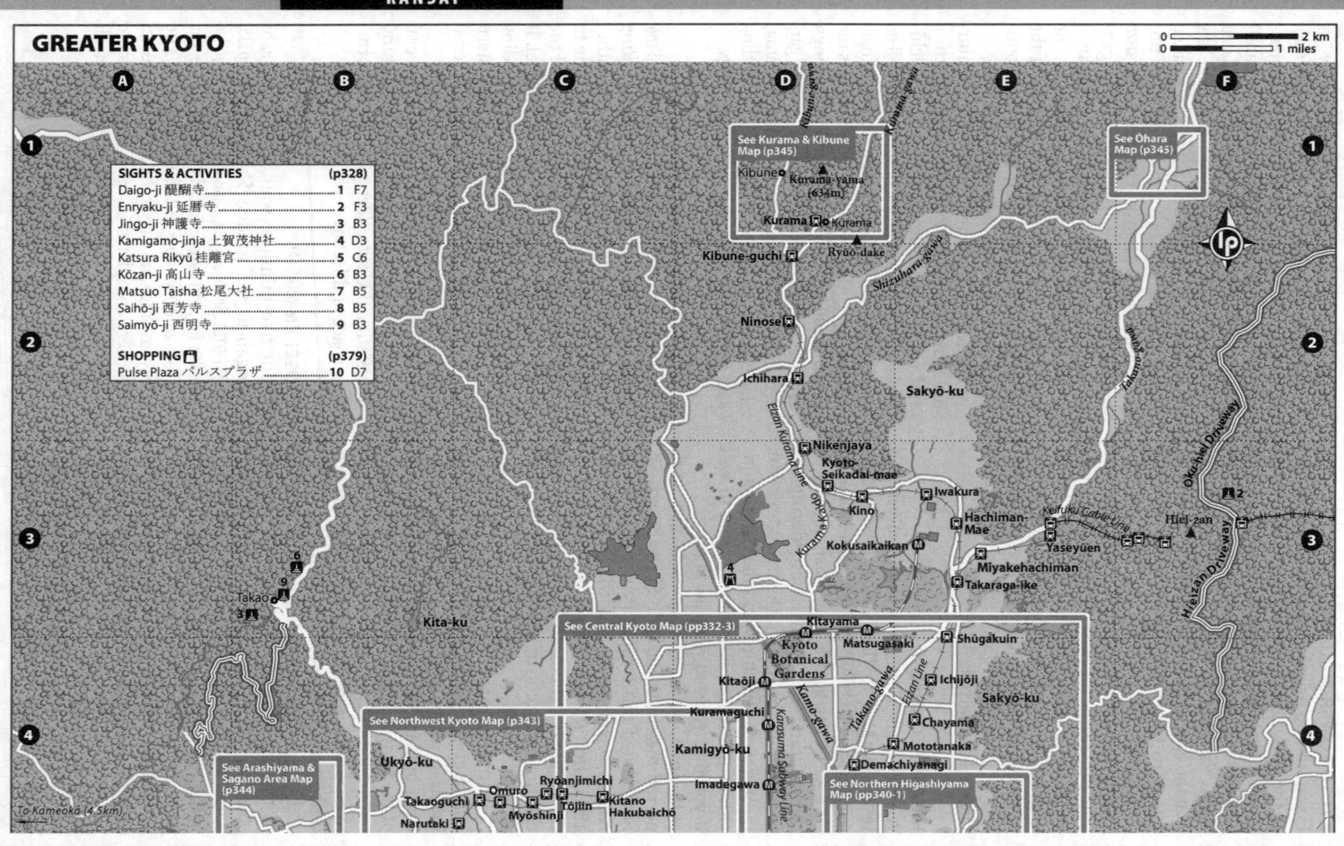
GREATER KYOTO
0 2 km
0 1 miles
SIGHTS & ACTIVITIES (p328)
Daigo-ji 醍醐寺 1 F7
Enryaku-ji 延暦寺 2 F3
Jingo-ji 神護寺 3 B3
Kamigamo-jinja 上賀茂神社 4 D3
Katsura Rikyū 桂離宮 5 C6
Kōzan-ji 高山寺 6 B3
Matsuo Taisha 松尾大社 7 B5
Saihō-ji 西芳寺 8 B5
Saimyō-ji 西明寺 9 B3
SHOPPING (p379)
Pulse Plaza パルスプラザ 10 D7
See Kurama & Kibune Map (p345)
Kibune
Kurama-yama (634m)
Kurama
Kibune-gawa
Kurama-gawa
See Ōhara Map (p345)
Kibune-guchi
Ryūō-dake
Shizuhara-gawa
Ninose
Ichihara
Sakyō-ku
Takano-gawa
Oku-hiei Driveway
Hiei-zan
Hieizan Driveway
Keifuku Cable Line
Elzan Kurama Line
Nikenjaya
Kyoto-Seikadai-mae
Kino
Iwakura
Hachiman-Mae
Yaseyūen
Kurama Kaidō
Kokusaikaikan
Miyakehachiman
Takaraga-ike
Takao
Kita-ku
See Central Kyoto Map (pp332-3)
Kitayama
Matsugasaki
Shūgakuin
Kyoto Botanical Gardens
Kitaōji
Ichijōji
Kamo-gawa
Takano-gawa
Elzan Line
Sakyō-ku
Kuramaguchi
Karasuma Subway Line
Chayama
Mototanaka
Kamigyō-ku
Demachiyanagi
Imadegawa
See Northern Higashiyama Map (pp340-1)
See Northwest Kyoto Map (p343)
Ukyō-ku
Ryōanjimichi
Omuro
Takaoguchi
Tōjiin
Kitano Hakubaichō
Myōshinji
Narutaki
See Arashiyama & Sagano Area Map (p344)
To Kameoka (4.5km)

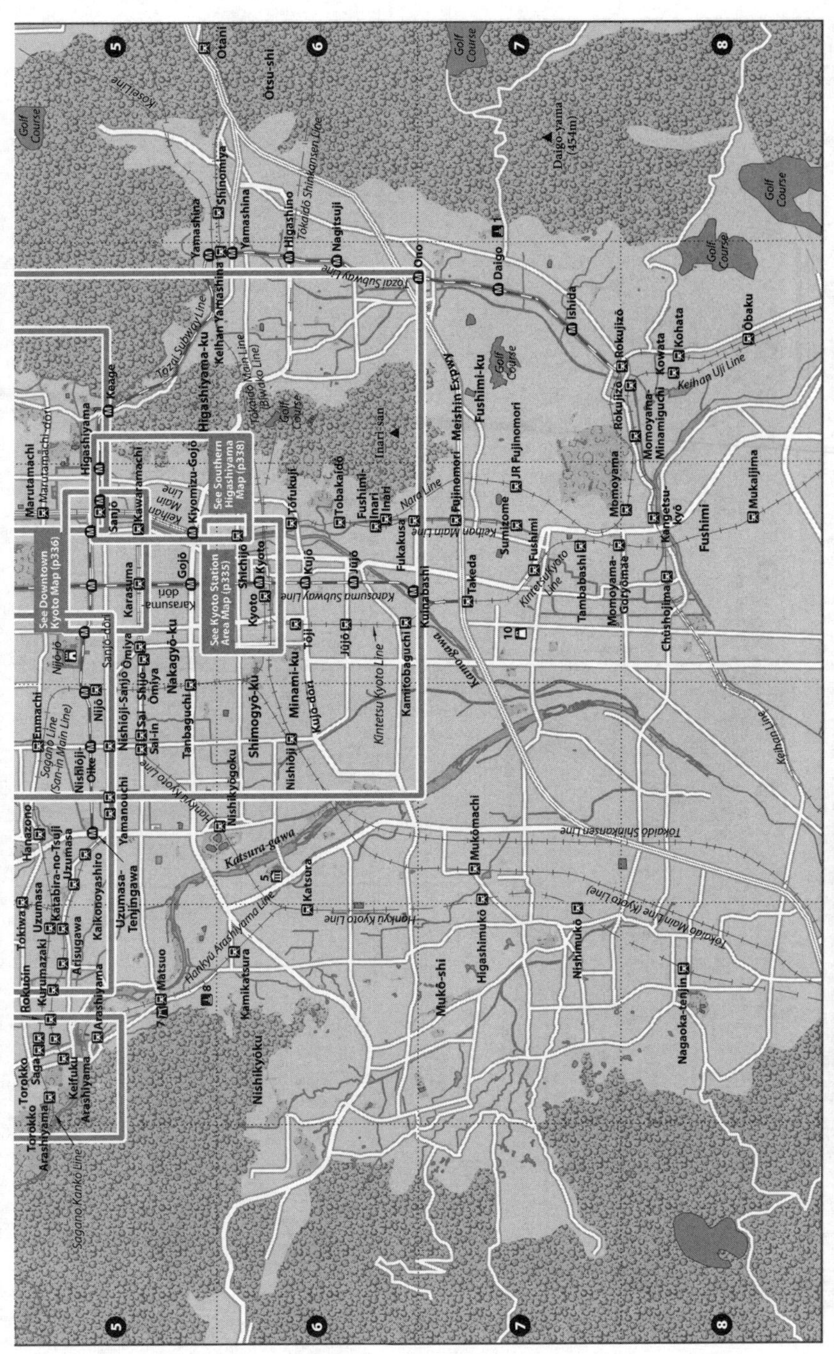
Golf Course
Ōtsu-shi
Ōtani
Kosei Line
Shinomiya
Yamashina
Higashino
Tōkaidō Shinkansen Line
Nagitsuji
Tōzai Subway Line
Ono
Daigo
Daigo-yama (454m)
Ishida
Rokujizō
Kowata
Kohata
Ōbaku
Keihan Uji Line
Keihan Yamashina
Higashiyama-ku
Tōkaidō Main Line (Biwako Line)
Keage
Higashiyama
Marutamachi
Marutamachi-dōri
Sanjō
Kawaramachi
Keihan Main Line
Kiyomizu-Gojō
See Southern Higashiyama Map (p338)
See Downtown Kyoto Map (p336)
Karasuma
Karasuma-dōri
Gojō
See Kyoto Station Area Map (p335)
Shichijō
Kyoto
Tōfukuji
Tōbakaidō
Fushimi-Inari
Inari
Inari-san
Kujō
Jūjō
Fukakusa
Nara Line
Fujinomori
Meishin Expwy
Fushimi-ku
Sumizome
JR Fujinomori
Fushimi
Kintetsu Kyoto Line
Takeda
Kuinabashi
Karasuma Subway Line
Tambabashi
Momoyama-Goryōmae
Momoyama
Momoyama-Minamiguchi
Kangetsukyō
Chūshojima
Mukaijima
Keihan Line
Tōji
Kamitobaguchi
Kamo-gawa
Minami-ku
Kujō-dōri
Nishiōji
Shimogyō-ku
Nishikyōgoku
Nakagyō-ku
Tanbaguchi
Sai-in
Nishiōji-Sanjō
Ōmiya
Shijō-Ōmiya
Nijō
Nijō-jō
Sanjō-dōri
Enmachi
Sagano Line (San-in Main Line)
Nishiōji-Oike
Yamanouchi
Hankyū Kyoto Line
Hanazono
Uzumasa
Katabira-no-Tsuji
Kaikonoyashiro
Uzumasa-Tenjingawa
Tokiwa
Kurumazaki
Arisugawa
Arashiyama
Rokuōin
Torokko Saga
Keifuku Arashiyama
Torokko Arashiyama
Sagano Kankō Line
Matsuo
Katsura-gawa
Katsura
Hankyū Arashiyama Line
Kamikatsura
Nishikyō-ku
Mukō-shi
Mukōmachi
Higashimukō
Nishimukō
Tōkaidō Main Line (Kyoto Line)
Nagaoka-tenjin

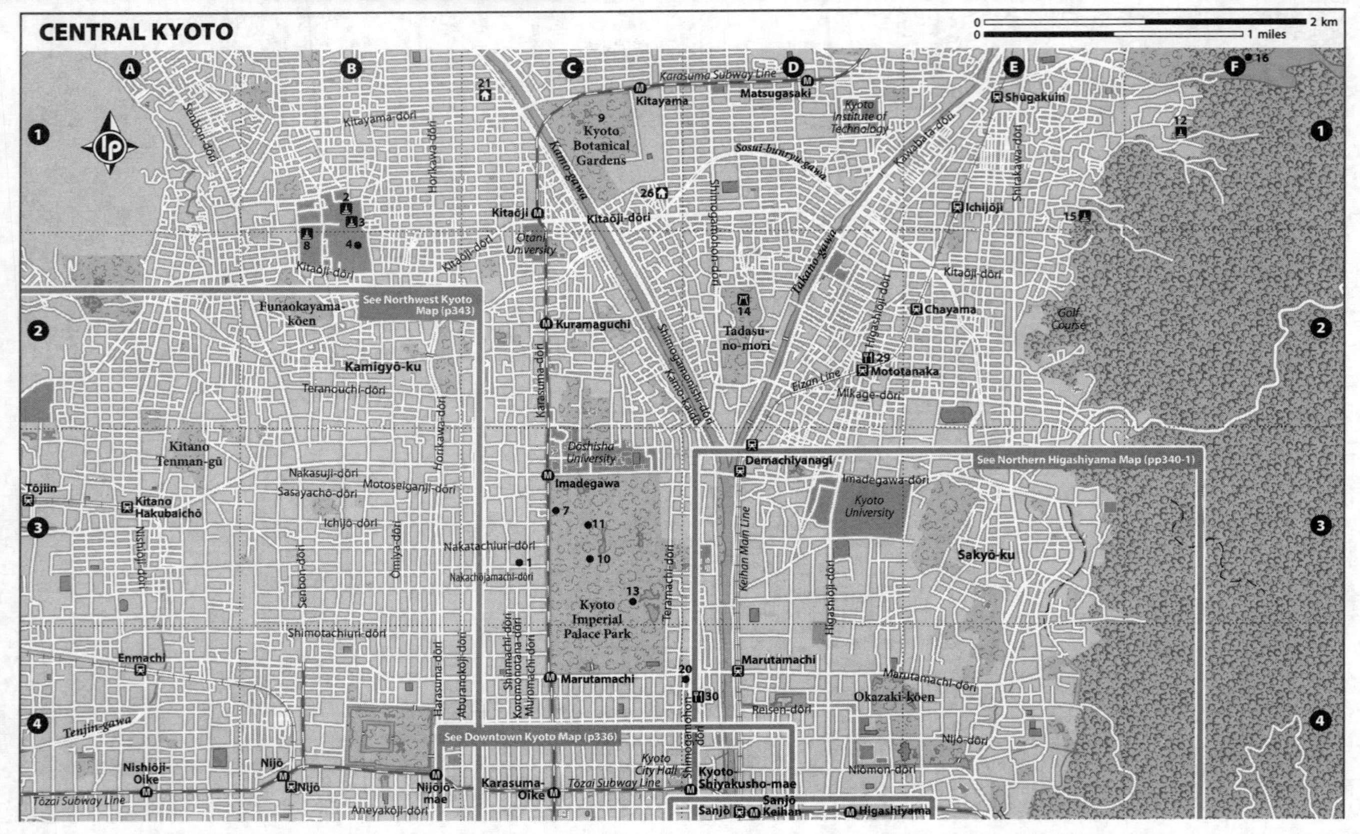
CENTRAL KYOTO
0 2 km
0 1 miles
See Northern Higashiyama Map (pp340-1)
See Northwest Kyoto Map (p343)
See Downtown Kyoto Map (p336)
Shūgakuin
Ichijōji
Chayama
Mototanaka
Matsugasaki
Kitayama
Kitaōji
Kuramaguchi
Imadegawa
Marutamachi
Demachiyanagi
Karasuma-Oike
Kyoto-Shiyakusho-mae
Sanjō
Sanjō Keihan
Higashiyama
Nijōjō-mae
Nijō
Nishiōji-Oike
Enmachi
Kitano Hakubaichō
Tōjiin
Kyoto Botanical Gardens
Kyoto Institute of Technology
Otani University
Doshisha University
Kyoto University
Kyoto Imperial Palace Park
Tadasu-no-mori
Okazaki-kōen
Funaokayama-kōen
Kitano Tenman-gū
Kamigyō-ku
Sakyō-ku
Kamo-gawa
Takano-gawa
Sosui-bunryu-gawa
Tenjin-gawa
Karasuma Subway Line
Tōzai Subway Line
Eizan Line
Keihan Main Line
Kyoto City Hall
Golf Course
Kitaōji-dōri
Kitayama-dōri
Shimogamohon-dōri
Shimogamonishi-dōri
Kamo-kaidō
Kawabata-dōri
Shirakawa-dōri
Higashiōji-dōri
Mikage-dōri
Imadegawa-dōri
Marutamachi-dōri
Nijō-dōri
Niōmon-dōri
Reisen-dōri
Teramachi-dōri
Karasuma-dōri
Koromonotana-dōri
Muromachi-dōri
Shinmachi-dōri
Aburanokōji-dōri
Horikawa-dōri
Nakatachiuri-dōri
Nakachōjamachi-dōri
Ōmiya-dōri
Ichijō-dōri
Senbon-dōri
Shimotachiuri-dōri
Teranouchi-dōri
Motoseiganji-dōri
Sasayachō-dōri
Nakasuji-dōri
Nishiōji-dōri
Aneyakōji-dōri
Harasuma-dōri

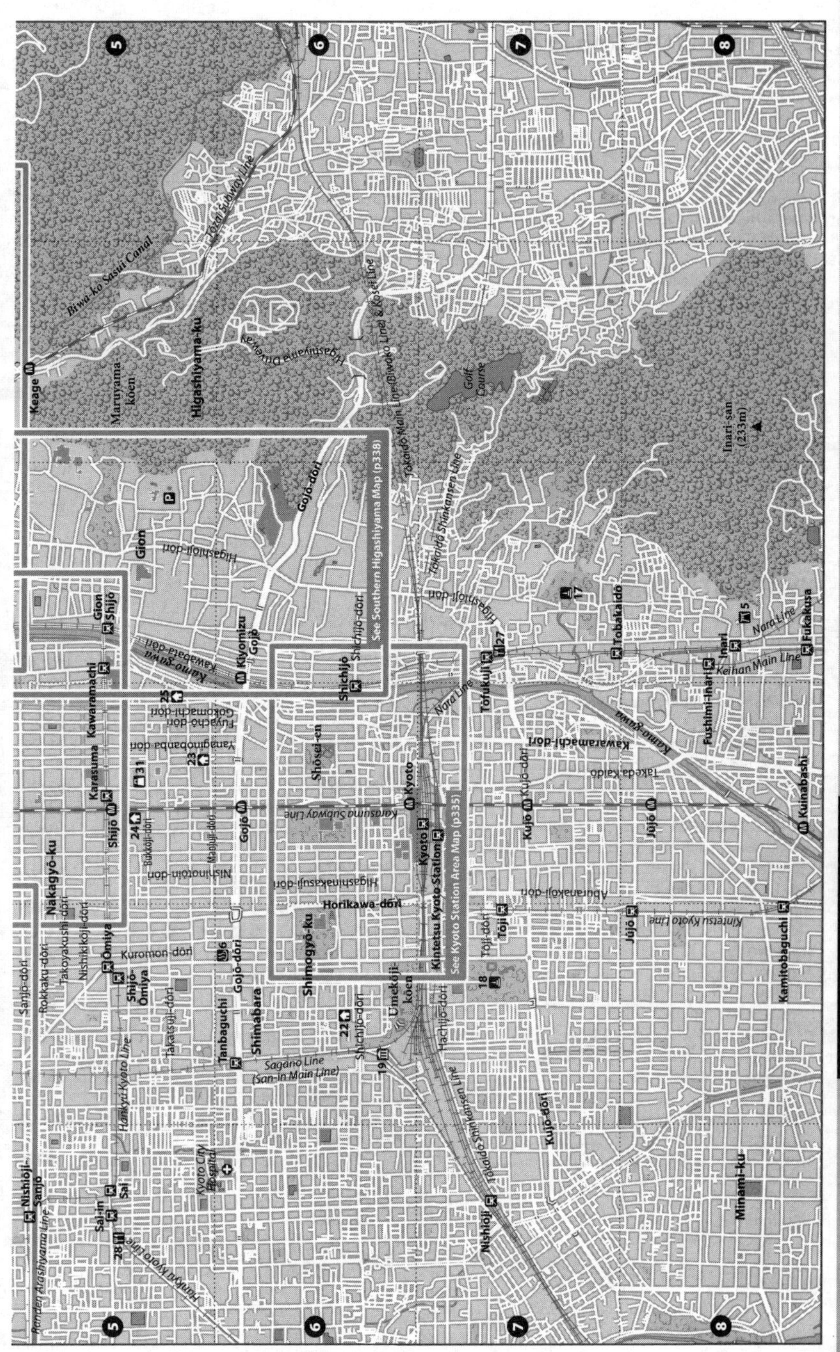
Keage
Maruyama-kōen
Higashiyama-ku
Biwa-ko Sosui Canal
Tōzai Subway Line
Higashiyama Driveway
Tōkaidō Main Line (Biwako Line) & Kosei Line
Tōkaidō Shinkansen Line
Golf Course
Inari-san (233m)
See Southern Higashiyama Map (p338)
Gojō-dōri
Gion
Higashiōji-dōri
Gion Shijō
Kawaramachi
Kamo-gawa
Kawabata-dōri
Kiyomizu Gojō
Shichijō
Shichijō-dōri
Karasuma
Shijō
Fuyachō-dōri
Gokomachi-dōri
Yanaginobanba-dōri
Shōsei-en
Karasuma Subway Line
Kyoto
Nara Line
Tōfukuji
Kawaramachi-dōri
Takeda-kaidō
Kujō-dōri
Kujō
Jūjō
Tobakaidō
Inari
Fushimi-Inari
Keihan Main Line
Fukakusa
Kuinabashi
Nakagyō-ku
Bukkōji-dōri
Nishinotōin-dōri
Gojō
Higashinakasuji-dōri
Horikawa-dōri
Kyoto
Kintetsu Kyoto Station
See Kyoto Station Area Map (p335)
Aburanokōji-dōri
Tōji
Tōji-dōri
Kintetsu Kyoto Line
Kamitobaguchi
Sanjō-dōri
Rokkaku-dōri
Takoyakushi-dōri
Nishikikōji-dōri
Ōmiya
Shijō-Ōmiya
Kuromon-dōri
Takatsuji-dōri
Tanbaguchi
Shimabara
Shimogyō-ku
Umekōji-kōen
Hachijō-dōri
Sagano Line (San-in Main Line)
Hankyū Kyoto Line
Kyoto City Hospital
Nishiōji-Sanjō
Sai-in
Sai
Randen Arashiyama Line
Tōkaidō Shinkansen Line
Nishiōji
Minami-ku
5
6
7
8
KANSAI

CENTRAL KYOTO (pp332–3)

SIGHTS & ACTIVITIES (p328)
Club Ōkitsu Kyoto クラブオクツ京都 1 C3
Daisen-in 大仙院 2 B1
Daitoku-ji 大徳寺 3 B1
Daitoku-ji Main Gate 大徳寺総門 4 B2
Fushimi-Inari Taisha 伏見稲荷大社 5 D8
Gokō-yu 五香湯 6 B6
Imperial Household Agency 宮内庁京都事務所 7 C3
Kōtō-in 高桐院 8 B2
Kyoto Botanical Gardens 京都府立植物園 9 C1
Kyoto Imperial Palace (Kyoto Gosho) 京都御所 10 C3
Kyoto Imperial Palace Park 京都御苑 11 C3
Manshu-in 曼殊院 12 F1
Sentō Gosho Palace 仙洞御所 13 C3
Shimogamo-jinja 下鴨神社 14 D2
Shisen-dō 詩仙堂 15 E1
Shūgaku-in Rikyū 修学院離宮 16 F1
Tōfuku-ji 東福寺 17 D7
Tō-ji 東寺 18 B7
Umekōji Steam Locomotive Museum 梅小路蒸気機関車館 19 B6
WAK Japan WAKジャパン 20 D4

SLEEPING (p367)
Casa de Natsu Casa de 夏 21 C1
Crossroads Inn クロスロードイン 22 B6
Furnished Apartment ザファーニシュドアパートメント 23 C5
Karasuma Kyoto Hotel からすま京都ホテル 24 C5
Ryokan Hinomoto 旅館ひのもと 25 C5
Ryokan Rakuchō 旅館洛頂 26 C1

EATING (p372)
Cocohana ここはな 27 D7
Den Shichi 傳七 28 A5
Didi ディディ 29 D2
Manzara Honten まんざら本店 30 D4

SHOPPING (p379)
Kōbō-san Market 弘法さん（東寺露天市） ....(see 18)
Morita Washi 森田和紙 31 C5

KYOTO STATION AREA (p335)

INFORMATION (p327)
Kyoto Central Post Office 京都中央郵便局 1 C3
Kyoto City Tourist Information Center 京都市観光案内所 2 C3
Kyoto Prefectural International Centre 京都府国際センター ....(see 3)
Kyoto Tourist Information Center (TIC) 京都ツーリストインフォメーション 3 C4
Tops Café トップスカフェ 4 C4

SIGHTS & ACTIVITIES (p328)
Higashi Hongan-ji 東本願寺 5 C2
Kyoto Tower 京都タワー 6 D3
Nishi Hongan-ji 西本願寺 7 A2
Shōsei-en 渉成園 8 D2

SLEEPING (p367)
APA Hotel Kyoto Ekimae アパ ホテル 9 B3
Budget Inn バジェットイン 10 B3
Hotel Granvia Kyoto ホテルグランヴィア京都 11 D4
K's House Kyoto ケイズハウス京都 12 E2
Kyōraku 京らく 13 D2
Matsubaya 松葉家 14 D2
Nihonkan 日本館 15 C2
Rihga Royal Hotel Kyoto リーガロイヤルホテル京都 16 B3
Ryokan Shimizu 旅館しみず 17 C2
Tour Club 旅倶楽部 18 B2

EATING (p372)
Café du Monde カフェデュモンド 19 C3
Cube キューブ 20 C3
Eat Paradise イートパラダイス ....(see 20)
Iimura いいむら 21 D2

SHOPPING (p379)
Bic Camera ビックカメラ 22 B3
Isetan Department Store 伊勢丹百貨店 ....(see 3)

TRANSPORT (p381)
Airport Limousine Bus Stop 京都八条口アバンティ前バス停 23 D4
Bicycle Parking Lot 京都駅前自転車駐車場 24 C3
Kyoto Bus Information Centre 京都バス案内書 25 D3
Kyoto Cycling Tour Project 京都サイクリングツアープロジェクト 26 B3
Kyoto Station Bus Terminal 京都駅前バスターミナル 27 C3
Kyoto Station Taxi Stand (North) 京都駅前タクシーのりば〈北〉 28 D3
Kyoto Station Taxi Stand (South) 京都駅前タクシーのりば〈南〉 29 C4
Tōkai Discount Ticket Shop トーカイ格安きっぷ売り場 30 D3

KANSAI

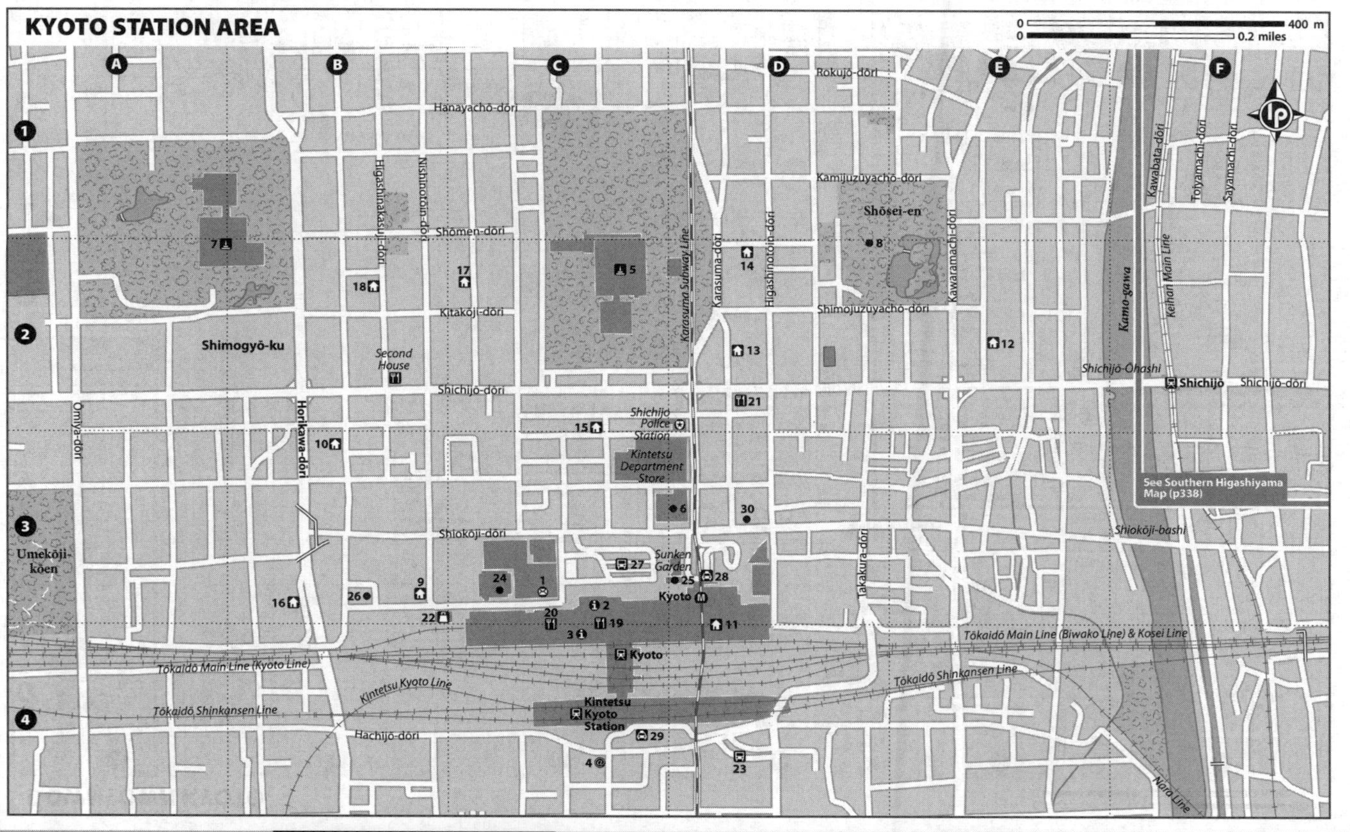
KYOTO STATION AREA
400 m
0.2 miles
Rokujō-dōri
Hanayachō-dōri
Kamijuzuyachō-dōri
Shōsei-en
Shōmen-dōri
Higashinakasuji-dōri
Nishinotōin-dōri
Karasuma Subway Line
Karasuma-dōri
Higashinotōin-dōri
Kawaramachi-dōri
Kawabata-dōri
Toiyamachi-dōri
Sayamachi-dōri
Kamo-gawa
Keihan Main Line
Kitakōji-dōri
Shimojuzuyachō-dōri
Shimogyō-ku
Second House
Shichijō-Ōhashi
Shichijō
Shichijō-dōri
Ōmiya-dōri
Horikawa-dōri
Shichijō Police Station
Kintetsu Department Store
See Southern Higashiyama Map (p338)
Shiokōji-dōri
Shiokōji-bashi
Umekōji-kōen
Sunken Garden
Takakura-dōri
Kyoto
Tōkaidō Main Line (Biwako Line) & Kosei Line
Tōkaidō Main Line (Kyoto Line)
Kintetsu Kyoto Line
Tōkaidō Shinkansen Line
Kintetsu Kyoto Station
Hachijō-dōri
Nara Line

KANSAI

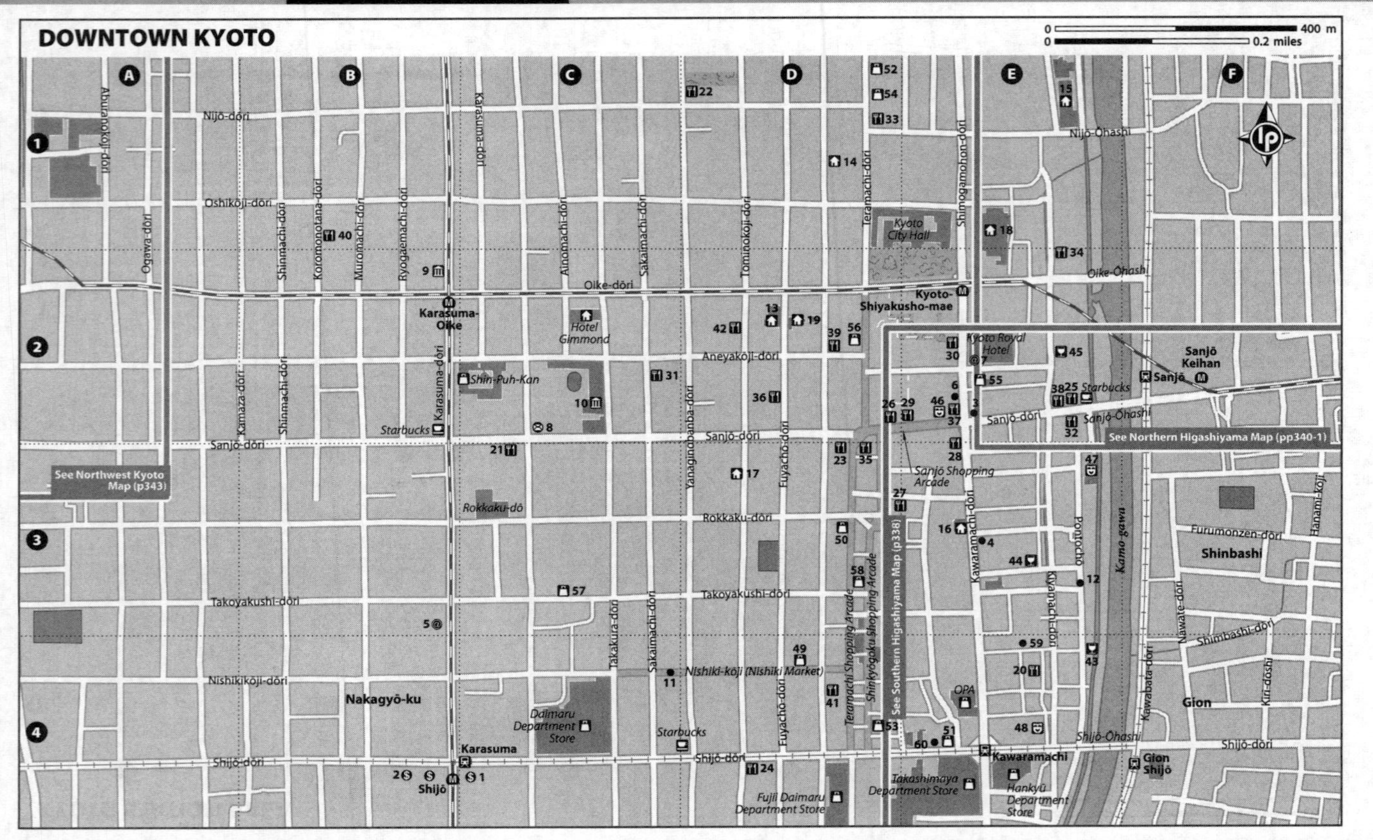
DOWNTOWN KYOTO
400 m
0.2 miles
See Northwest Kyoto Map (p343)
See Northern Higashiyama Map (pp340-1)
See Southern Higashiyama Map (p338)
Aburanokōji-dōri
Ogawa-dōri
Nijō-dōri
Oshikōji-dōri
Shinmachi-dōri
Koromonotana-dōri
Muromachi-dōri
Ryogaemachi-dōri
Karasuma-dōri
Ainomachi-dōri
Sakaimachi-dōri
Tominokōji-dōri
Teramachi-dōri
Shimogamohon-dōri
Oike-dōri
Oike-Ōhashi
Nijō-Ōhashi
Aneyakōji-dōri
Sanjō-dōri
Sanjō-Ōhashi
Kamaza-dōri
Yanaginobanba-dōri
Fuyachō-dōri
Rokkaku-dōri
Rokkaku-dō
Takoyakushi-dōri
Takakura-dōri
Nishikikōji-dōri
Nishiki-kōji (Nishiki Market)
Shijō-dōri
Shijō-Ōhashi
Kawaramachi-dōri
Kiyamachi-dōri
Pontochō
Kawabata-dōri
Kamo-gawa
Nawate-dōri
Hanami-kōji
Furumonzen-dōri
Shinbashi-dōri
Kiri-dōshi
Shinbashi
Gion
Gion Shijō
Sanjō Keihan
Sanjō
Kyoto-Shiyakusho-mae
Karasuma-Oike
Karasuma
Shijō
Kawaramachi
Kyoto City Hall
Kyoto Royal Hotel
Hotel Gimmond
Shin-Puh-Kan
Starbucks
Sanjō Shopping Arcade
Shinkyōgoku Shopping Arcade
Teramachi Shopping Arcade
OPA
Hankyū Department Store
Takashimaya Department Store
Fujii Daimaru Department Store
Daimaru Department Store
Nakagyō-ku

DOWNTOWN KYOTO (p336)

INFORMATION (p327)
Bank of Tokyo-Mitsubishi UFJ 東京三菱UFJ銀行 **1** C4
Citibank シティバンク **2** B4
IACE Travel IACEトラベル **3** E2
Junkudō ジュンク堂書店 **4** E3
Kinko's キンコーズ **5** B3
KNT 近畿日本ツーリスト **6** E2
Media Café Popeye ポパイ **7** E2
Nakagyō Post Office 中京郵便局 **8** C2

SIGHTS & ACTIVITIES (p328)
Kyoto International Manga Museum 京都国際マンガミュージアム **9** B2
Museum of Kyoto 京都文化博物館 **10** C2
Nishiki Market 錦市場 **11** C4
Pontochō 先斗町 **12** E3

SLEEPING (p367)
Hiiragiya 柊屋旅館 **13** D2
Hiiragiya Bekkan (Annex) 柊屋旅館別館 **14** D1
Hotel Fujita Kyoto ホテルフジタ京都 **15** E1
Hotel Unizo ホテルユニゾ **16** E3
Kinsuikan 錦水館 **17** D3
Kyoto Hotel Ōkura 京都ホテルオークラ **18** E1
Tawaraya 俵屋旅館 **19** D2

EATING (p372)
A-Bar ア バー **20** E4
Biotei びお亭 **21** C3
Café Bibliotec HELLO! カフェビブリオテックハロー **22** D1
Café Independants カフェ アンデパンダン **23** D3
Doutor Coffee ドトールコーヒー **24** D4
Ganko Zushi がんこ寿司 **25** E2
Honke Tagoto 本家田毎 **26** D2
Kane-yo かねよ **27** D3
Karafuneya Coffee Honten からふねや珈琲本店 **28** E3
Katsu Kura かつくら **29** E2
Kerala ケララ **30** E2
Kōsendō-sumi 光泉洞寿み **31** C2
Kyo-Hayashi-ya 京はやしや **32** E2
Le Bouchon ル ブション **33** D1
Merry Island Café メリーアイランド カフェ **34** E2
Mishima-tei 三嶋亭 **35** D3
Misoka-an Kawamichi-ya 晦庵河道屋 **36** D2
Musashi Sushi むさし寿司 **37** E2
Ootoya 大戸屋 **38** E2
Park Café パークカフェ **39** D2
Shizenha Restaurant Obanzai 自然派レストランおばんざい **40** B1
Yak & Yeti ヤック＆イェティ **41** D4
Yoshikawa 吉川 **42** D2

DRINKING (p378)
Atlantis アトランティス **43** E4
Ing イング **44** E3
McLoughlin's Irish Bar & Restaurant マクラクランズアイリッシュ バー & レストラン **45** E2

ENTERTAINMENT (p378)
Jumbo Karaoke Hiroba ジャンボカラオケ広場 **46** E2
Pontochō Kaburen-jō Theatre 先斗町歌舞練場 **47** E3
World ワールド **48** E4

SHOPPING (p379)
Aritsugu 有次 **49** D4
Chicago シカゴ **50** D3
Erizen ゑり善 **51** E4
Ippo-dō 一保堂 **52** D1
Iwai 井和井 **53** D4
Kamiji Kakimoto 紙司柿本 **54** D1
Koj-Kōjitsu Sansō コージツ **55** E2
Kyūkyo-dō 鳩居堂 **56** D2
Rakushikan 楽紙館 **57** C3
Teramachi Shōten 寺町商店 **58** D3

TRANSPORT (p381)
Bicycle Parking Lot 駐輪場 **59** E4
Discount Ticket Shop 格安きっぷ売り場 **60** E4

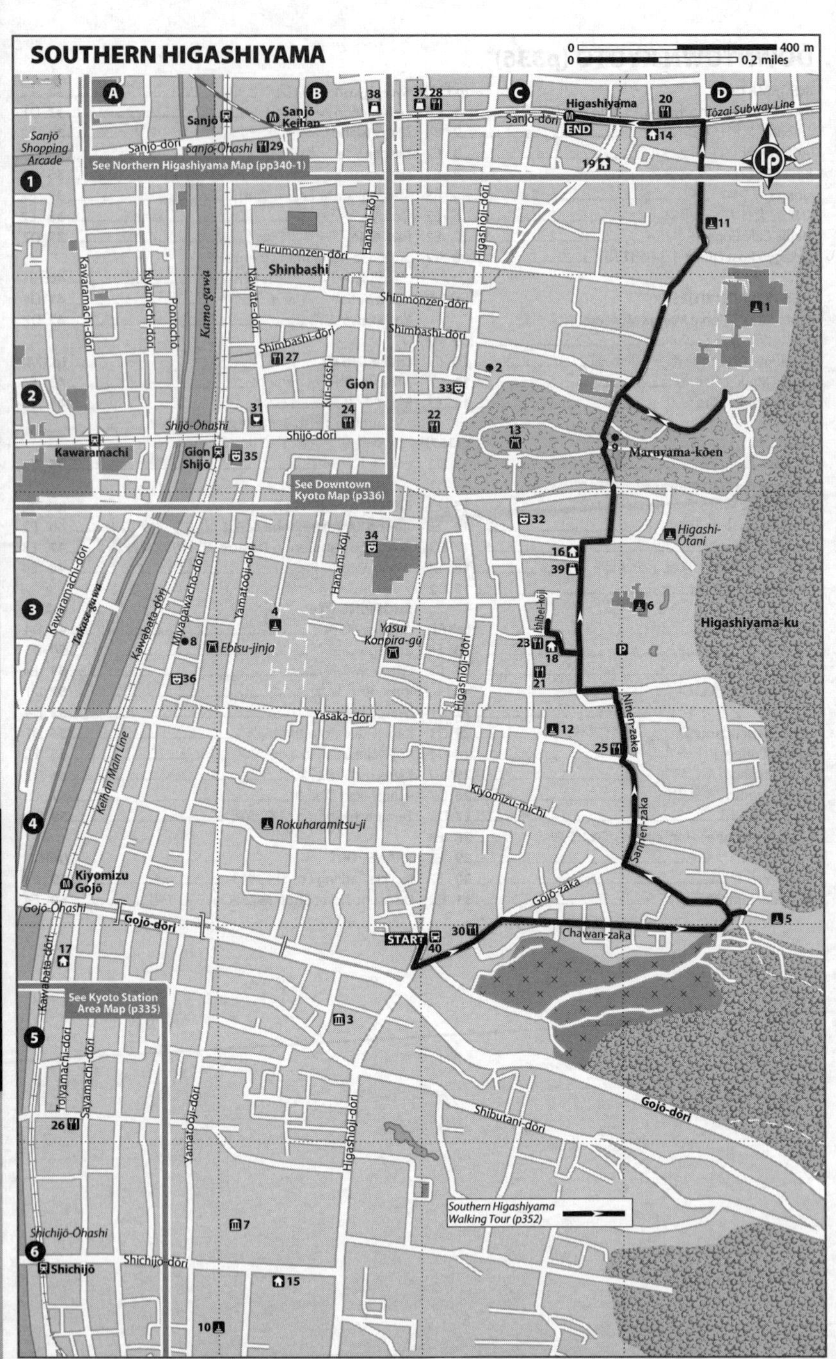
SOUTHERN HIGASHIYAMA
0 400 m
0 0.2 miles
A
B
C
D
1
2
3
4
5
6
Sanjō Shopping Arcade
Sanjō
Sanjō Keihan
Sanjō-dōri
Sanjō-Ōhashi
See Northern Higashiyama Map (pp340-1)
Higashiyama
END
Tōzai Subway Line
Furumonzen-dōri
Shinbashi
Shinmonzen-dōri
Shimbashi-dōri
Hanami-kōji
Higashiōji-dōri
Kawaramachi-dōri
Kiyamachi-dōri
Pontochō
Kamo-gawa
Nawate-dōri
Kiri-dōshi
Gion
Shijō-Ōhashi
Shijō-dōri
Kawaramachi
Gion Shijō
See Downtown Kyoto Map (p336)
Maruyama-kōen
Higashi-Ōtani
Higashiyama-ku
Ishibei-kōji
Kawaramachi-dōri
Takase-gawa
Kawabata-dōri
Miyagawachō-dōri
Yamatooji-dōri
Ebisu-jinja
Yasui Konpira-gū
Yasaka-dōri
Ninen-zaka
Kiyomizu-michi
Sannen-zaka
Keihan Main Line
Rokuharamitsu-ji
Kiyomizu Gojō
Gojō-Ōhashi
Gojō-dōri
Gojō-zaka
Chawan-zaka
START
See Kyoto Station Area Map (p335)
Kawabata-dōri
Toiyamachi-dōri
Sayamachi-dōri
Yamatooji-dōri
Higashiōji-dōri
Shibutani-dōri
Gojō-dōri
Southern Higashiyama Walking Tour (p352)
Shichijō-Ōhashi
Shichijō
Shichijō-dōri
KANSAI

SOUTHERN HIGASHIYAMA (p338)

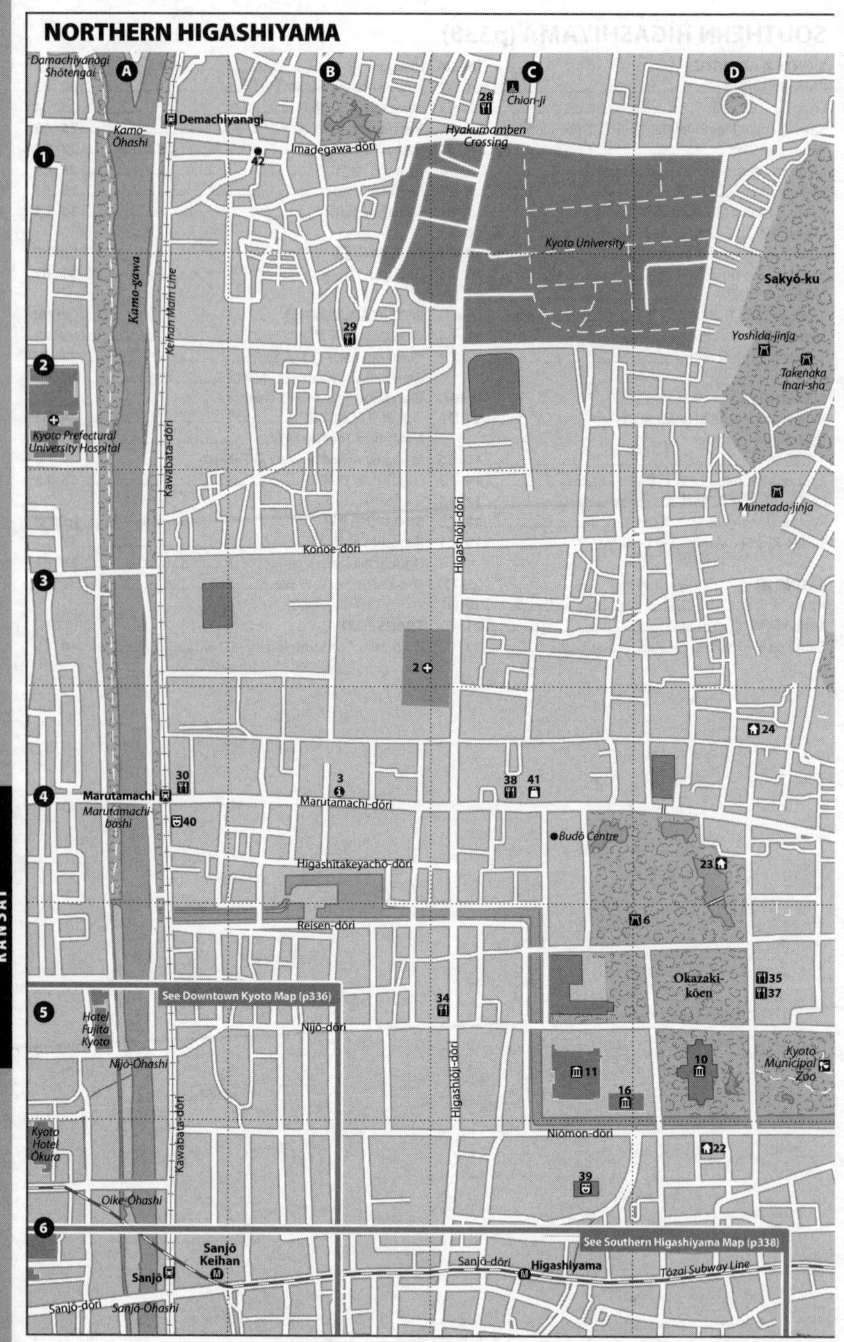
NORTHERN HIGASHIYAMA
A
B
C
D
1
2
3
4
5
6
Damachiyanagi Shotengai
Demachiyanagi
Kamo-Ōhashi
Imadegawa-dōri
Hyakumamben Crossing
Chion-ji
28
42
Kyoto University
Kamo-gawa
Keihan Main Line
Sakyō-ku
29
Yoshida-jinja
Takenaka Inari-sha
Kyoto Prefectural University Hospital
Kawabata-dōri
Munetada-jinja
Konoe-dōri
Higashiōji-dōri
2
24
30
3
38
41
Marutamachi
Marutamachi-bashi
Marutamachi-dōri
40
Budō Centre
23
Higashitakeyachō-dōri
Reisen-dōri
6
Okazaki-kōen
35
37
See Downtown Kyoto Map (p336)
34
Hotel Fujita Kyoto
Nijō-dōri
Nijō-Ōhashi
Higashiōji-dōri
11
10
Kyoto Municipal Zoo
16
Niōmon-dōri
Kyoto Hotel Ōkura
Kawabata-dōri
22
39
Oike-Ōhashi
See Southern Higashiyama Map (p338)
Sanjō Keihan
Sanjō
Sanjō-dōri
Higashiyama
Tōzai Subway Line
Sanjō-dōri
Sanjō-Ōhashi
KANSAI

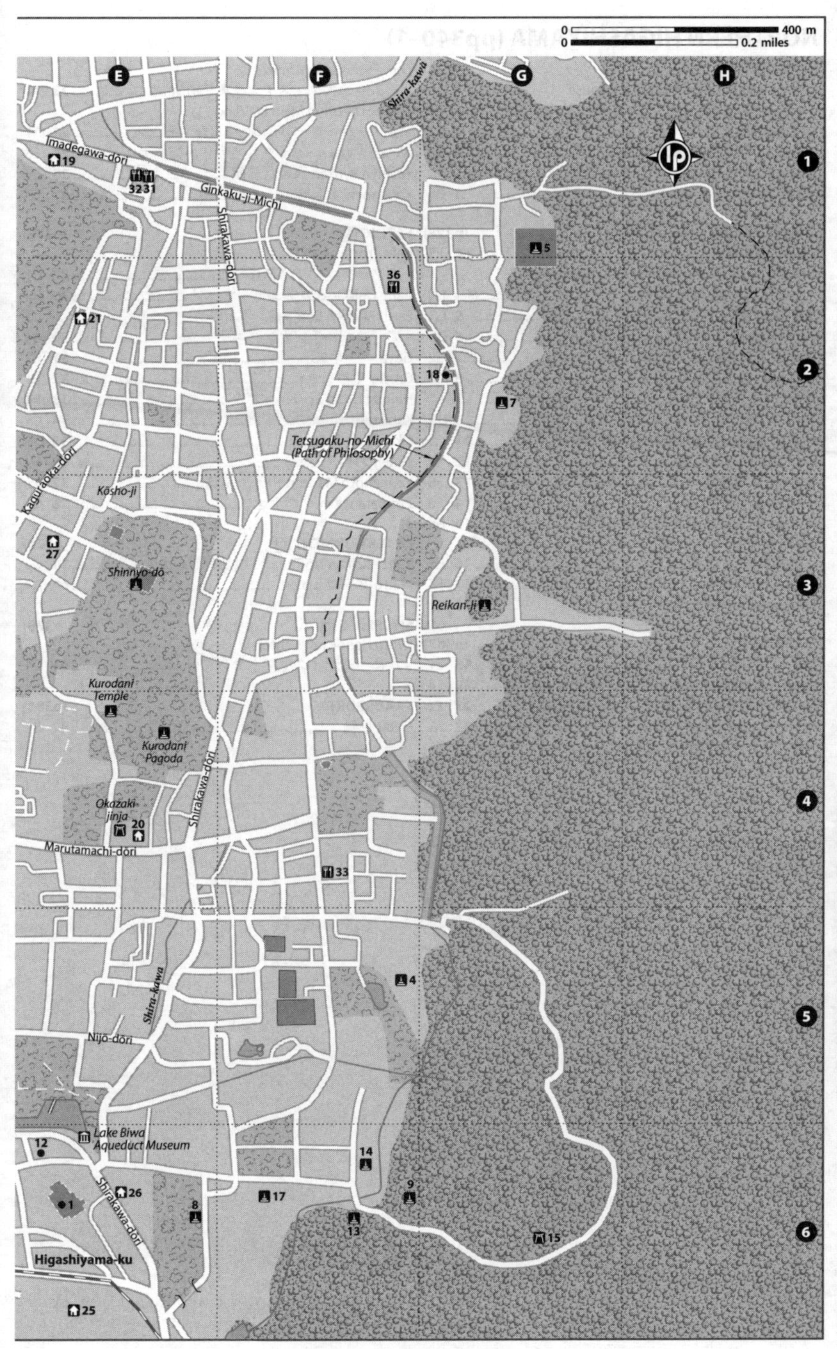

0 400 m
0 0.2 miles
E
F
G
H
1
2
3
4
5
6
Imadegawa-dōri
19
32 31
Ginkaku-ji-Michi
Shirakawa-dōri
Shira-kawa
5
36
21
18
7
Tetsugaku-no-Michi
(Path of Philosophy)
Kaguraoka-dōri
Kōsho-ji
27
Shinnyo-dō
Reikan-ji
Kurodani
Temple
Kurodani
Pagoda
Okazaki-
jinja
20
Marutamachi-dōri
33
Shirakawa-dōri
4
Shira-kawa
Nijō-dōri
Lake Biwa
Aqueduct Museum
12
14
9
26
1
8
17
13
15
Shirakawa-dōri
Higashiyama-ku
25

NORTHERN HIGASHIYAMA (pp340–1)

INFORMATION (p327)
Kyoto International Community House 京都市国際交流会館 1 E6
Kyoto University Hospital 京都大学医学部附属病院 2 B3
Osaka Regional Immigration Bureau Kyoto Branch 大阪入国管理局京都出張所 3 B4

SIGHTS & ACTIVITIES (p328)
Eikan-dō 永観堂 4 F5
Fureai-kan Kyoto Museum of Traditional Crafts 京都伝統産業ふれあい館 (see 11)
Ginkaku-ji 銀閣寺 5 G1
Heian-jingū 平安神宮 6 D5
Hōnen-in 法然院 7 G2
Konchi-in 金地院 8 E6
Kōtoku-an 高徳庵 9 F6
Kyoto Municipal Museum of Art 京都市美術館 10 D5
Miyako Messe みやこめっせ 11 C5
Murin-an Villa 無鄰菴 12 E6
Nanzen-in 南禅院 13 F6
Nanzen-ji 南禅寺 14 F6
Nanzen-ji Oku-no-in 南禅寺奥の院 15 G6
National Museum of Modern Art 京都国立近代美術館 16 C5
Tenju-an 天授庵 17 F6
Tetsugaku-no-Michi 哲学の道 18 G2

SLEEPING (p367)
B&B Juno B&B じゅの 19 E1
Hotel Heian No Mori Kyoto ホテル平安の森京都 20 E4
Kaguraya B&B かぐらや 21 E2
Kyoto Traveller's Inn 京都トラベラーズイン 22 D6
Three Sisters Inn Annex スリーシスターズイン洛東荘別館 23 D4
Three Sisters Inn Main Building スリーシスターズイン 洛東荘本館 24 D4
Westin Miyako Hotel ウエスティン都ホテル 25 E6
Yachiyo Ryokan 八千代旅館 26 E6
Yonbanchi 4 番地 27 E3

EATING (p372)
Café Proverbs 15:17 カフェプロバーブズ15:17 28 C1
Caffé Dell'Orso カフェデルオーソ 29 B2
Earth Kitchen Company アースキッチンカンパニー 30 A4
Goya ゴーヤ 31 E1
Grotto ぐろっと 32 E1
Hinode Udon 日の出うどん 33 F4
Karako 唐子 34 C5
Okakita おかきた 35 D5
Omen おめん 36 F2
Yamamoto Menzou 山元めん蔵 37 D5
Zac Baran ザックバラン 38 C4

ENTERTAINMENT (p378)
Kanze Kaikan Nō Theatre 観世会館 39 C6
Metro メトロ 40 A4

SHOPPING (p379)
Kyoto Handicraft Center 京都ハンディクラフトセンター 41 C4

TRANSPORT (p381)
Ei Rin 栄輪 42 B1

KANSAI

NORTHWEST KYOTO

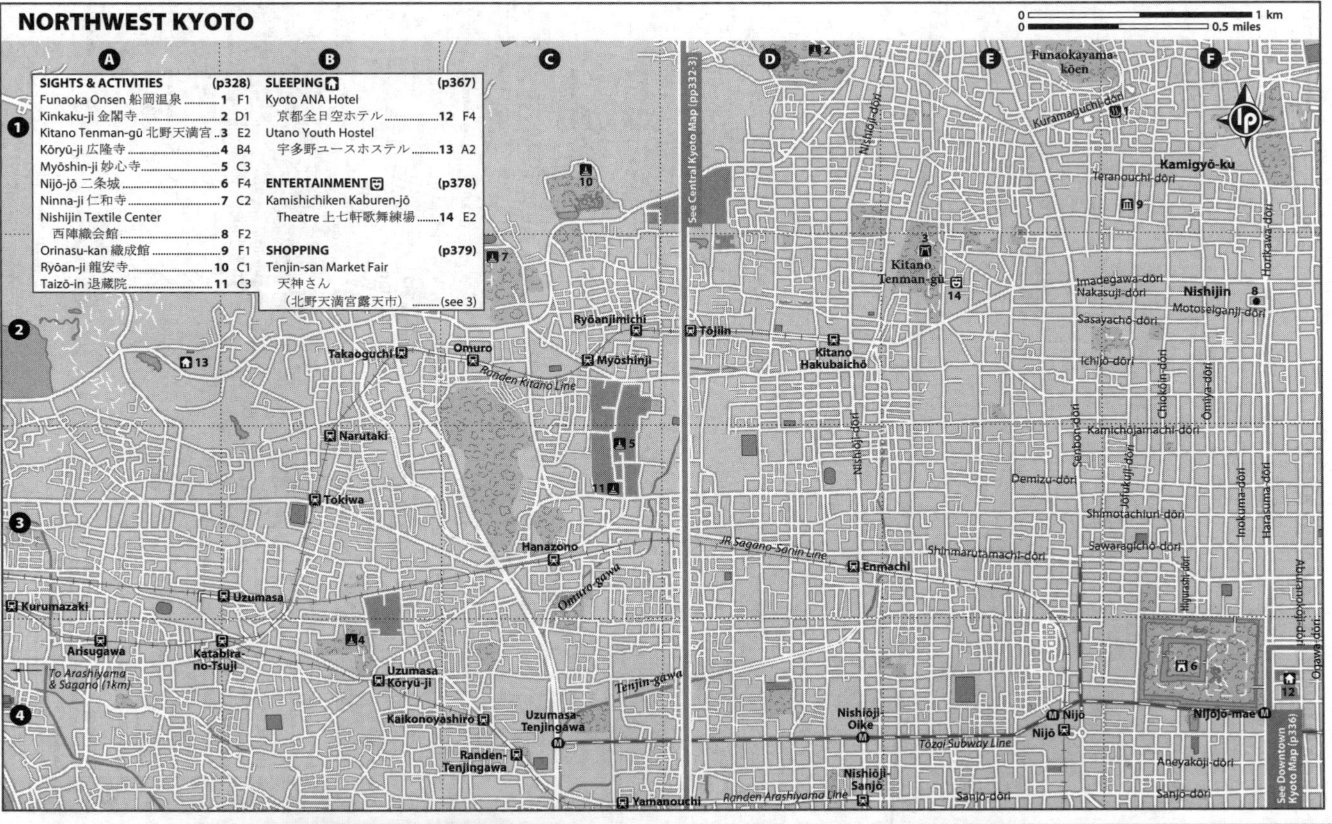

KANSAI

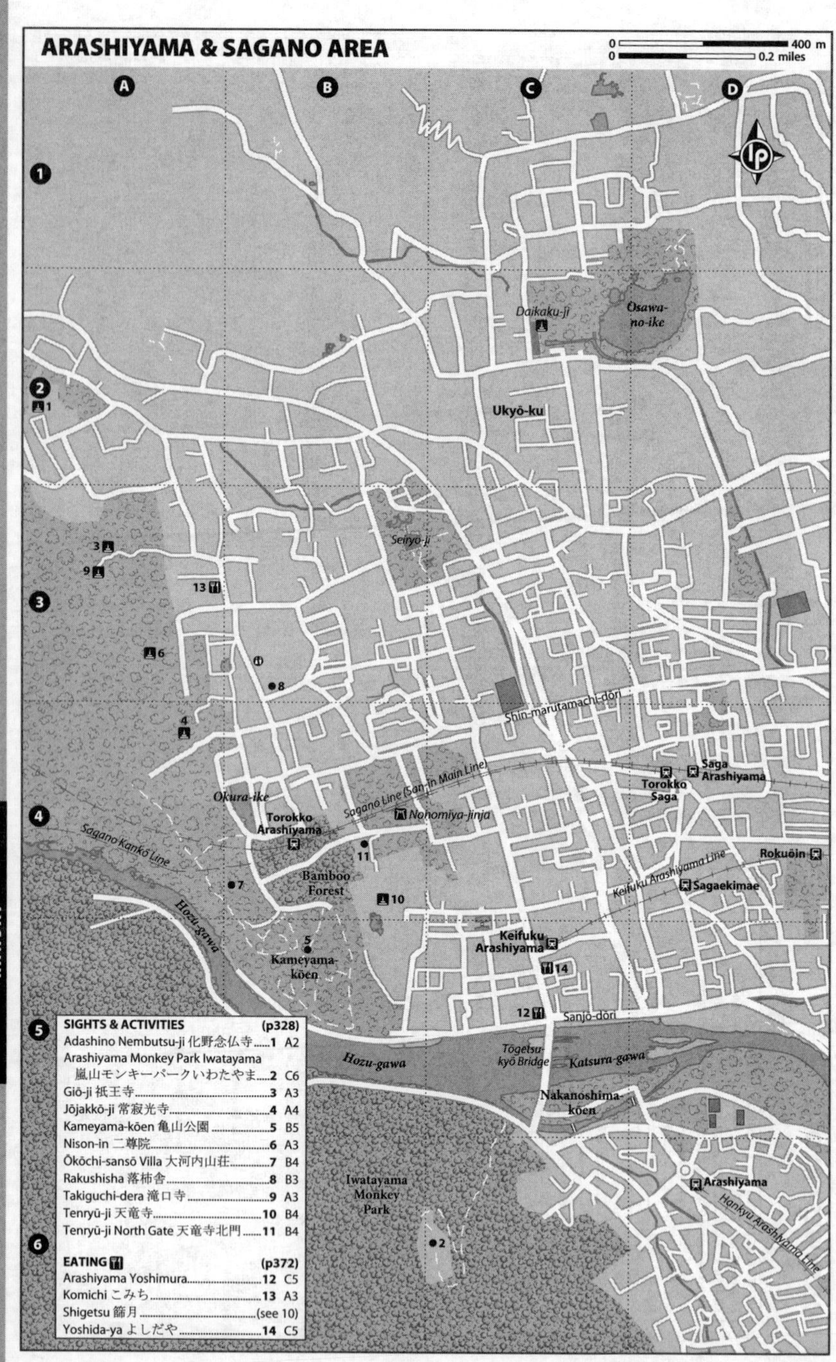
ARASHIYAMA & SAGANO AREA
0 400 m
0 0.2 miles
Daikaku-ji
Osawa-no-ike
Ukyō-ku
Seiryō-ji
Shin-marutamachi-dōri
Saga Arashiyama
Torokko Saga
Sagano Line (San-in Main Line)
Okura-ike
Torokko Arashiyama
Nonomiya-jinja
Sagano Kankō Line
Rokuōin
Keifuku Arashiyama Line
Sagaekimae
Bamboo Forest
Hozu-gawa
Keifuku Arashiyama
Kameyama-kōen
Sanjō-dōri
Togetsu-kyō Bridge
Katsura-gawa
Hozu-gawa
Nakanoshima-kōen
Iwatayama Monkey Park
Arashiyama
Hankyū Arashiyama Line
SIGHTS & ACTIVITIES (p328)
Adashino Nembutsu-ji 化野念仏寺 1 A2
Arashiyama Monkey Park Iwatayama 嵐山モンキーパークいわたやま 2 C6
Giō-ji 祇王寺 3 A3
Jōjakkō-ji 常寂光寺 4 A4
Kameyama-kōen 亀山公園 5 B5
Nison-in 二尊院 6 A3
Ōkōchi-sansō Villa 大河内山荘 7 B4
Rakushisha 落柿舎 8 B3
Takiguchi-dera 滝口寺 9 A3
Tenryū-ji 天竜寺 10 B4
Tenryū-ji North Gate 天竜寺北門 11 B4
EATING (p372)
Arashiyama Yoshimura 12 C5
Komichi こみち 13 A3
Shigetsu 篩月 (see 10)
Yoshida-ya よしだや 14 C5

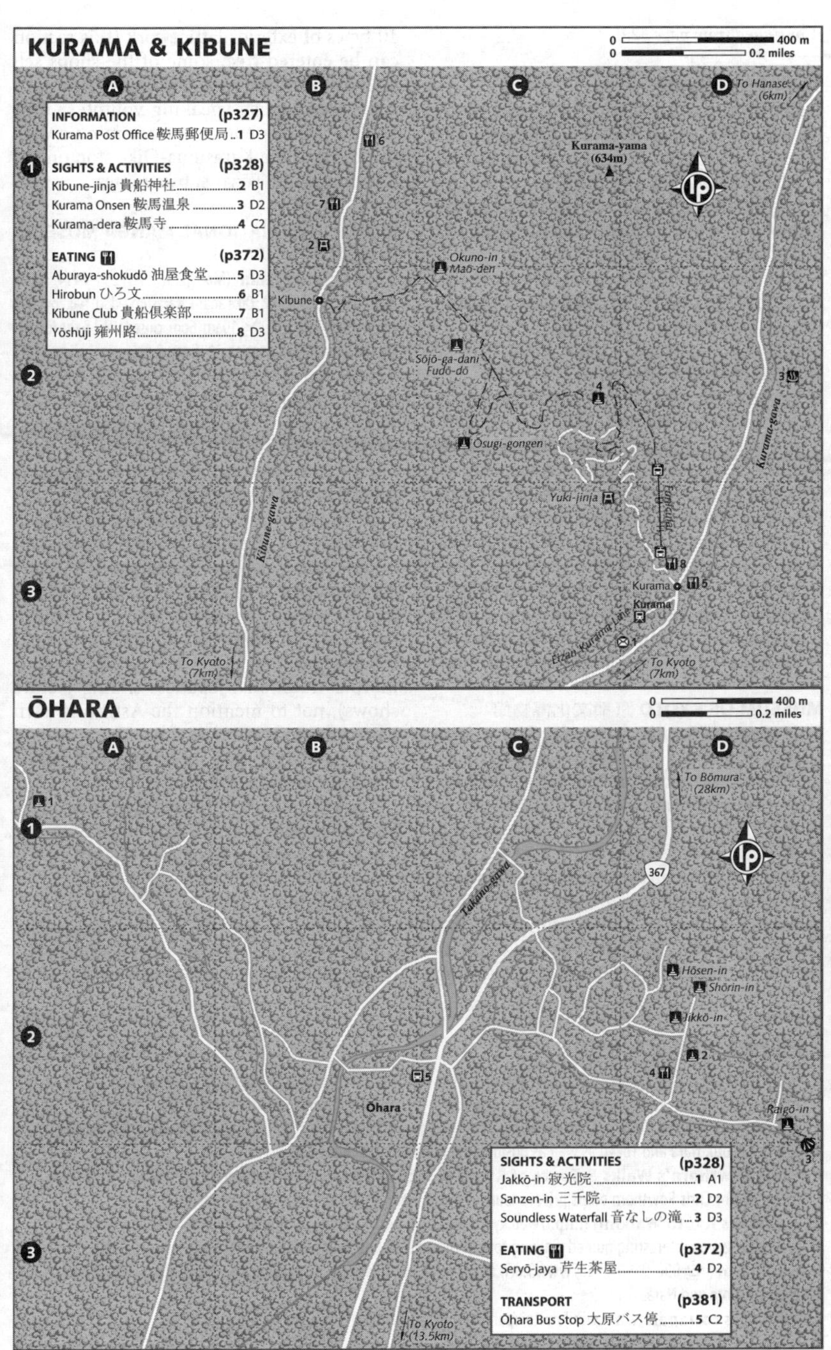
KURAMA & KIBUNE
0 400 m
0 0.2 miles
INFORMATION (p327)
Kurama Post Office 鞍馬郵便局 ..1 D3
SIGHTS & ACTIVITIES (p328)
Kibune-jinja 貴船神社 2 B1
Kurama Onsen 鞍馬温泉 3 D2
Kurama-dera 鞍馬寺 4 C2
EATING (p372)
Aburaya-shokudō 油屋食堂 5 D3
Hirobun ひろ文 6 B1
Kibune Club 貴船倶楽部 7 B1
Yōshūji 雍州路 8 D3
To Hanase (6km)
Kurama-yama (634m)
Okuno-in Maō-den
Kibune
Sōjō-ga-dani Fudō-dō
Ōsugi-gongen
Yuki-jinja
Funicular
Kurama-gawa
Kibune-gawa
Kurama
Eizan Kurama Line
To Kyoto (7km)
To Kyoto (7km)
ŌHARA
0 400 m
0 0.2 miles
To Bōmura (28km)
367
Takano-gawa
Hōsen-in
Shōrin-in
Jikkō-in
Ōhara
Raigō-in
To Kyoto (13.5km)
SIGHTS & ACTIVITIES (p328)
Jakkō-in 寂光院 1 A1
Sanzen-in 三千院 2 D2
Soundless Waterfall 音なしの滝 ... 3 D3
EATING (p372)
Seryō-jaya 芹生茶屋 4 D2
TRANSPORT (p381)
Ōhara Bus Stop 大原バス停 5 C2

(Continued from page 329)

Downtown Kyoto

Downtown Kyoto (Map p336) looks much like any other Japanese city, but there are some excellent attractions to be found here, including Nishiki Market, the Museum of Kyoto, the Kyoto International Manga Museum and Ponto-chō. If you'd like a break from temples and shrines, then downtown Kyoto can be a welcome change. It's also good on a rainy day, because of the number of covered arcades and indoor attractions.

NISHIKI MARKET 錦市場

If you are interested in seeing all the really weird and wonderful foods that go into Kyoto cuisine, wander through **Nishiki Market** (Map p336; ☎ 211-3882; Nishikikōji-dōri btwn Teramachi & Takakura; 🕑 9am-5pm, varies for individual stalls, some shops closed on Wed). It's in the centre of town, one block north of (and parallel to) Shijō-dōri. This market is a great place to visit on a rainy day or if you need a break from temple-hopping. The variety of foods on display is staggering, and the frequent cries of *Irasshaimase!* (Welcome!) are heart-warming.

MUSEUM OF KYOTO 京都文化博物館

This **museum** (Map p336; ☎ 222-0888; Takakura, Sanjō, Nakagyō-ku; admission ¥500, extra for special exhibitions; 🕑 10am-7.30pm, special exhibitions to 6pm, closed Mon or following day if Mon is a holiday, & 28 Dec-3 Jan) is worth visiting if a special exhibition is on or if you need a break from temples. The regular exhibits consist of models of ancient Kyoto, audiovisual presentations and a small gallery dedicated to Kyoto's film industry. On the 1st floor, the Roji Tempō is a reconstructed Edo-period merchant area showing 10 types of exterior latticework (this section can be entered free; some of the shops sell souvenirs and serve local dishes). The museum has English-speaking volunteer tour guides. The museum is a three-minute walk southeast of the Karasuma-Oike stop on the Karasuma and Tōzai subway lines.

KYOTO INTERNATIONAL MANGA MUSEUM 京都国際マンガミュージアム

This fine **museum** (Map p336; ☎ 254-7414; www.kyotomm.com/english; Oike agaru, Karasuma-dōri, Nakagyō-ku; adult/child ¥500/100; 🕑 10am-6pm, closed Wed & the following Thu when Wed is a national holiday, & new-year holiday) has a collection of some 300,000 manga (Japanese comic books). Located in an old elementary school building, the museum is the perfect introduction to the art of manga. While most of the manga and displays are in Japanese, the collection of translated works is growing.

In addition to the galleries that show both the historical development of manga and original artwork done in manga style, there are beginners' workshops and portrait drawings on weekends. Visitors with children will appreciate the children's library and the occasional performances of *kami-shibai* (humorous traditional Japanese sliding-picture shows), not to mention the Astroturf lawn where the kids can run free. The museum hosts six month-long special exhibits yearly: check the website for details.

It's a short walk from the Karasuma-Oike Station on the Karuma line subway or the Tōzai line subway. Enter by 5.30pm.

PONTO-CHŌ 先斗町

A traditional nightlife district, Ponto-chō (Map p336) is a narrow alley running between Sanjō-dōri and Shijō-dōri just west of

PRIVATE TOURS OF KYOTO

A private tour is a great way to see the sights and learn about the city without having to worry about transport and logistics. There's a variety of private tours on offer in Kyoto.

All Japan Private Tours & Speciality Services (www.kyotoguide.com/yjpt) This company offers private tours of Kyoto, Nara and Tokyo as well as business coordination and related services.

Chris Rowthorn's Walks & Tours of Kyoto & Japan (www.chrisrowthorn.com) Lonely Planet *Kyoto* and *Japan* author Chris Rowthorn offers private tours of Kyoto, Nara, Osaka and other parts of Japan.

Johnnie's Kyoto Walking (http://web.kyoto-inet.or.jp/people/h-s-love) Hirooka Hajime, aka Johnnie Hillwalker, offers an interesting guided walking tour of the area around Kyoto Station and the Higashiyama area.

Naoki Doi (☎ 090-9596-5546; www3.ocn.ne.jp/~doitaxi) This English-speaking taxi driver offers private taxi tours of Kyoto and Nara.

Windows to Japan (www.windowstojapan.com) Offers custom tours of Kyoto and Japan.

Kamo-gawa. It's best visited in the evening, when the traditional wooden buildings and hanging lanterns create a wonderful atmosphere of old Japan. It makes a nice stroll in the evening, perhaps combined with a walk in nearby Gion.

Central Kyoto

KYOTO IMPERIAL PALACE PARK 京都御所

The Kyoto Gosho is surrounded by the spacious **Kyoto Imperial Palace Park** (Kamigyō-ku Kyoto gyoen; Map pp332-3; admission free; dawn-dusk), which is planted with a huge variety of flowering trees and open fields. It's perfect for picnics, strolls and just about any sport you can think of. Take some time to visit the pond at the park's southern end, which contains gorgeous carp. The park is most beautiful in the plum- and cherry-blossom seasons (late February and late March, respectively). The plum arbour is located about midway along the park on the west side. The best cherries can be found at the north end. The park is between Teramachi-dōri and Karasuma-dōri (to the east and west) and Imadegawa-dōri and Marutamachi-dōri (to the north and south).

KYOTO IMPERIAL PALACE (KYOTO GOSHO) 京都御所

The original imperial palace (Map pp332–3) was built in 794 and was replaced numerous times after destruction by fire. The present building, on a different site and smaller than the original, was constructed in 1855. Enthronement of a new emperor and other state ceremonies are still held there.

The Gosho does not rate highly in comparison with other attractions in Kyoto and you must apply for permission to visit (see following). However, you shouldn't miss the park surrounding the Gosho (see preceding).

To get there, take the Karasuma line subway to Imadegawa or a bus to the Karasuma-Imadegawa stop and walk 600m southeast.

Reservation & Admission

Permission to visit the Gosho is granted by the Kunaichō, the **Imperial Household Agency** (Map pp332-3; ☎ 211-1215; 8.30am-5.30pm Mon-Fri), which is inside the walled park surrounding the palace, a short walk from Imadegawa Station on the Karasuma line. You have to fill out an application form and show your passport. Children can visit if accompanied by adults over 20 years of age (but are forbidden entry to the other three imperial properties of Katsura Rikyū, Sentō Gosho and Shūgaku-in Rikyū). Permission to tour the palace is usually granted the same day (try to arrive at the office at least 30 minutes before the start of the tour you'd like to join). Guided tours, sometimes in English, are given at 10am and 2pm from Monday to Friday. The tour lasts about 50 minutes.

The Gosho can be visited without reservation during two periods each year, once in the spring and once in the autumn. The dates vary each year, but as a general guide, the spring opening is around the last week of April and the autumn opening is in the middle of November. Check with the TIC for exact dates.

The Imperial Household Agency is also the place to make advance reservations to see the Sentō Gosho, Katsura Rikyū and Shūgaku-in Rikyū.

SENTŌ GOSHO PALACE 仙洞御所

The **palace** (Map pp332-3; ☎ 211-1215; Kamigyō-ku Kyoto gyoen) is a few hundred metres southeast of the main Kyoto Gosho. It was originally built in 1630 during the reign of Emperor Go-Mizunō as a residence for retired emperors. The palace was repeatedly destroyed by fire and reconstructed but served its purpose until a final blaze in 1854 (it was never rebuilt).

The gardens, which were laid out in 1630 by Kobori Enshū, are superb. The route takes you past lovely ponds and pathways and, in many ways, a visit here is more enjoyable than a visit to the Gosho, especially if you are a fan of Japanese gardens. Visitors must obtain advance permission from the Imperial Household Agency (see preceding) and be over 20 years old. Tours (in Japanese) start at 11am and 1.30pm.

DAITOKU-JI 大徳寺

Daitoku-ji is a separate world within Kyoto – a collection of Zen temples, raked gravel gardens and wandering lanes. It is one of the most rewarding destinations in this part of the city, particularly for those with an interest in Japanese gardens. The name Daitoku-ji confusingly refers to both the main temple here and the entire complex, which contains a total of 24 temples and subtemples. We discuss three of them here, but another five are open to the public.

The eponymous **Daitoku-ji** (Map pp332-3; ☎ 491-0019; 53 Daitokuji-chō, Murasakino, Kita-ku; admission free; dawn-dusk) is on the eastern side of the grounds. It was founded in 1319, burnt down in the next century and rebuilt in the 16th century. The **San-mon** contains an image of the famous tea master Sen-no-Rikyū on the 2nd storey. If you enter via the main gate on the east side of the complex, Daitoku-ji will be on your right, a short walk north.

Just north of Daitoku-ji, **Daisen-in** (Map pp332-3; ☎ 491-8346; 54-1 Daitokuji-chō, Murasakino, Kita-ku; admission ¥400; 9am-5pm Mar-Nov, to 4.30pm Dec-Feb) is famous for its two small gardens. At the western edge of the complex, **Kōtō-in** (Map pp332-3; ☎ 492-0068; 73-1 Daitokuji-chō, Murasakino, Kita-ku; admission ¥400; 9am-4.30pm) is famous for its stunning bamboo-lined approach and the maple trees in its main garden (try to visit in the foliage season).

The temple bus stop is Daitoku-ji-mae and convenient buses from Kyoto Station are buses 205 and 206. Daitoku-ji is also a short walk west of Kitaō-ji subway station on the Karasuma line.

SHIMOGAMO-JINJA 下鴨神社

This **shrine** (Map pp332-3; ☎ 781-0010; 59 Izumigawa-chō, Shimogamo, Sakyō-ku; admission free; 6.30am-5pm) dates from the 8th century and is a Unesco World Heritage Site. It is nestled in the fork of the Kamo-gawa and Takano-gawa rivers, and is approached along a shady path through the lovely Tadasu-no-mori. This wooded area is said to be a place where lies cannot be concealed and is considered a prime location to sort out disputes.

The shrine is dedicated to the god of harvest. Traditionally, pure water was drawn from the nearby rivers for purification and agricultural ceremonies. The *hondō* (main hall) dates from 1863 and, like the Haiden hall at its sister shrine, Kamigamo-jinja, is an excellent example of *nagare*-style shrine architecture.

The shrine is only a one-minute walk from Shimogamo-jinja-mae bus stop; take bus 205 from Kyoto Station.

KANSAI

KYOTO BOTANICAL GARDENS
京都府立植物園

The **Kyoto Botanical Gardens** (Map pp332-3; ☎ 701-0141; Shimogamohangi-chō, Sakyō-ku; gardens adult ¥200, child ¥80-150, greenhouse ¥200, ¥80-150; 9am-5pm, closed new-year holidays), opened in 1914, occupy 240,000 sq metres and feature 12,000 plants, flowers and trees. It is pleasant to stroll through the rose, cherry and herb gardens or see the rows of camphor trees and the large tropical greenhouse. This is a good spot for a picnic or a bit of Frisbee throwing. The gardens are a two-minute walk from Kitayama subway station (Karasuma line). Enter by 4.30pm.

KAMIGAMO-JINJA 上賀茂神社

This **shrine** (Map pp330-1; ☎ 781-0011; 339 Motoyama, Kamigamo, Kita-ku; admission free; 8am-5.30pm) is one of Japan's oldest shrines and predates the founding of Kyoto. Established in 679, it is dedicated to Raijin, the god of thunder, and is one of Kyoto's 17 Unesco World Heritage Sites. The present buildings (over 40 in all), including the impressive Haiden hall, are exact reproductions of the originals, dating from the 17th to 19th centuries. The shrine is entered from a long approach through two torii (shrine gates). The two large conical white-sand mounds in front of Hosodono hall are said to represent mountains sculpted for gods to descend upon.

The shrine is a five-minute walk from Kamigamo-misonobashi bus stop; take bus 9 from Kyoto Station.

TŌ-JI 東寺

This **temple** (Map pp332-3; ☎ 691-3325; 1 Kujō-chō, Minami-ku; admission to grounds free, Kondō & Treasure Hall ¥500; 8.30am-5.30pm, to 4.30pm 20 Sep-19 Mar) was established in 794 by imperial decree to protect the city. In 818 the emperor handed the temple over to Kūkai, the founder of the Shingon school of Buddhism. Many of the buildings were destroyed by fire or fighting during the 15th century; most of those that remain date from the 17th century.

The **Kōdō** (Lecture Hall) contains 21 images representing a Mikkyō (Esoteric Buddhism) mandala. The **Kondō** (Main Hall) contains statues depicting the Yakushi (Healing Buddha) trinity. In the southern part of the garden stands the five-storey pagoda, which burnt down five times, was rebuilt in 1643 and is now the highest pagoda in Japan, standing 57m tall.

The **Kōbō-san market-fair** is held here on the 21st of each month. The fairs held in December and January are particularly lively.

Tō-ji is a 15-minute walk southwest of Kyoto Station or a five-minute walk from Tōji Station on the Kintetsu line.

UMEKŌJI STEAM LOCOMOTIVE MUSEUM
梅小路蒸気機関車館

A hit with steam-train buffs and kids, this **museum** (Map pp332-3; ☎ 314-2996; Kannon-ji-chō, Shimogyō-

MANGA – JAPANESE COMICS

Despite the recent popularity of graphic novels in the West, it's fair to say that comics occupy a fairly humble position in the Western literary world. In Japan, however, manga stand shoulder to shoulder with traditional text-based books. Indeed, hop on any morning train in Japan and you could be excused for thinking that the Japanese refuse to read anything that isn't accompanied by eye-popping graphics, long-legged doe-eyed heroines, and the Japanese equivalents of words like 'POW!' and 'BLAM!'

Manga, written with the Japanese characters for 'random' and 'picture', have their roots way back in Japanese history – some would say as early as the 12th century, when ink-brush painters drew humorous pictures of humans and animals (these pictures are known as *chōjū jinbutsu giga*). The direct antecedents of manga, however, are the *ukiyo-e* (wood-block prints) of the 18th century. Following WWII, Japanese artists worked with Western artists to produce the first true manga. These were sometimes called *ponchi-e,* a reference to the British magazine *Punch,* which often ran comics of a political or satirical nature.

The father of modern manga was Tezuka Osamu, who, in the late 1940s, began working cinematic effects based on European movies into his cartoons – pioneering multipanel movements, perspectives that brought the reader into the action, close-ups, curious angles and a host of movielike techniques. His adventurous stories quickly became movie-length comic strips – essentially films drawn on paper. What Tezuka started took off in a big way once weekly magazines realised they could boost sales by including manga in their pages. Tezuka's most famous works include *Tetsuwan Atomu* (Astro Boy), *Black Jack* and *Rion Kōtei* (*Jungle Emperor Leo*, which Disney adapted to make the film *The Lion King*).

These days manga have proliferated and diversified to an almost unimaginable degree, and there is literally no topic that manga do not explore. There are manga for young boys and girls, manga for white-collar workers, manga for studying, historical manga and even high literary manga. And let's not forget the inevitable *sukebe* manga (pornographic manga), which contain some truly bizarre and often disturbing sexual images.

Unfortunately, almost all manga available in Japan are written in Japanese. These days, however, some of Japan's better English-language bookshops stock English translations of famous Japanese manga. Try the Kyoto branch of Junkudō bookshop (p327) or the giant Kinokuniya bookshop in Tokyo's Shinjuku area (p123).

If you want to get a quick taste of what's out there in the manga world, drop into any Japanese convenience store and check out the magazine rack. If you want to delve deeper, head for a *manga kissa* (manga coffee shop), where buying one drink will give you access to a huge library of manga (and internet access to boot). Finally, real manga fans will want to check out Kyoto's International Manga Museum (p346).

ku; adult/child ¥400/100, train ride ¥200/100; 9.30am-5pm, admission by 4.30pm, closed Mon) features 18 vintage steam locomotives (dating from 1914 to 1948) and related displays. It's in the former Nijō Station building, which was recently relocated here and carefully reconstructed. For an extra few yen, you can take a 10-minute ride on one of the fabulous old trains (departures at 11am, 1.30pm and 3.30pm).

From Kyoto Station, take bus 33, 205 or 208 to the Umekō-ji Kōen-mae stop (make sure you take a westbound bus).

Southern Higashiyama

The Higashiyama district, which runs along the base of the Higashiyama mountains (Eastern Mountains), is the main sightseeing district in Kyoto and it should be at the top of your Kyoto itinerary. It is thick with impressive sights: fine temples, shrines, gardens, museums, traditional neighbourhoods and parks. In this guide, we divide the Higashiyama district into two sections: Southern Higashiyama and Northern Higashiyama (p353).

This section starts at the southern end, around Shichijō-dōri, and works north, to Sanjō-dōri. You could cover these in the order presented in a fairly long day. The best way to see the highlights here is to take our Southern Higashiyama Walking Tour (p352).

SANJŪSANGEN-DŌ 三十三間堂

The original **Sanjūsangen-dō** (Map p338; ☎ 525-0033; 657 Sanjūsangendōmawari-chō, Higashiyama-ku; admission ¥600; 8am-4.30pm, 9am-3.30pm 16 Nov-16 Mar) was built in 1164 at the request of the retired emperor Go-shirakawa. The temple burnt to the ground in 1249 but a faithful copy was constructed in 1266.

The temple's name refers to the 33 *(sanjūsan)* bays between the pillars of this long, narrow building that houses 1001 statues of the 1000-armed Kannon (the Buddhist goddess of mercy). The largest Kannon is flanked on either side by 500 smaller Kannon images, neatly lined up in rows.

There are an awful lot of arms, but if you're picky and think the 1000-armed statues don't have the required number of limbs, then you should remember to calculate according to the nifty Buddhist mathematical formula that holds that 40 arms are the equivalent of 1000 arms, because each saves 25 worlds.

At the back of the hall are 28 guardian statues in a great variety of expressive poses. The gallery on the western side of the hall is famous for the annual **Tōshi-ya Matsuri**, held on 15 January, during which archers shoot arrows the length of the hall. The ceremony dates back to the Edo period, when an annual contest was held to see how many arrows could be shot from the southern end to the northern end in 24 hours. The all-time record was set in 1686, when an archer successfully landed over 8000 arrows at the northern end.

The temple is a 1.5km walk east of Kyoto Station; alternatively, take bus 206 or 208 and get off at the Sanjūsangen-dō-mae stop. It's also very close to Keihan Shichijō Station.

KYOTO NATIONAL MUSEUM
京都国立博物館

The **Kyoto National Museum** (Map p338; ☎ 531-7509; www.kyohaku.go.jp/eng/index_top.html; 527 Chaya-machi, Higashiyama-ku; adult/student ¥500/250, extra for special exhibitions; 9.30am-5pm, closed Mon) is housed in two buildings opposite Sanjūsangen-dō temple. It was founded in 1895 as an imperial repository for art and treasures from local temples and shrines. There are 17 rooms with displays of over a thousand artworks, historical artefacts and handicrafts. However, the excellent permanent collection is closed for renovation until 2013. Until that time, the museum is open only when a special exhibition is on.

KAWAI KANJIRŌ MEMORIAL HALL
河井寛次郎博物館

This **museum** (Map p338; ☎ 561-3585; 569 Kanei-chō, Gojō-zaka, Higashiyama-ku; admission ¥900; 10am-5pm, closed Mon & around 10-20 Aug & 24 Dec-7 Jan, dates vary each year) is one of Kyoto's overlooked little gems, especially for those with an interest in Japanese crafts like pottery and furniture. The hall was the home and workshop of one of Japan's most famous potters, Kawai Kanjirō (1890–1966). The 1937 house is built in rural style and contains examples of Kanjirō's work, his collection of folk art and ceramics, and his workshop and a fascinating *nobori-gama* (a stepped kiln).

The hall is a 10-minute walk north of the Kyoto National Museum. Alternatively, take bus 206 or 207 from Kyoto Station and get off at the Umamachi stop. Enter by 4.30pm.

KIYOMIZU-DERA 清水寺

This ancient **temple** (Map p338; ☎ 551-1234; 1-294 Kiyomizu, Higashiyama-ku; admission ¥300; 6am-6pm) was first built in 798, but the present buildings are reconstructions dating from 1633. As an affiliate of the Hossō school of Buddhism, which originated in Nara, it has successfully survived the many intrigues of local Kyoto schools of Buddhism through the centuries and is now one of the most famous landmarks of the city (for which reason it can get very crowded during spring and autumn).

The main hall has a huge verandah that is supported by hundreds of pillars and juts out over the hillside. Just below this hall is the waterfall **Otowa-no-taki**, where visitors drink sacred waters believed to have therapeutic properties. Dotted around the precincts are other halls and shrines. At Jishu-jinja, the shrine on the grounds, visitors try to ensure success in love by closing their eyes and walking about 18m between a pair of stones – if you miss the stone, your desire for love won't be fulfilled!

Before you enter the actual temple precincts, check out the **Tainai-meguri** (admission ¥100; 9am-4pm), the entrance to which is just to the left (north) of the pagoda that is located in front of the main entrance to the temple (you may have to ask a temple official as there is no English sign). We won't tell you too much about it as it will ruin the experience. Suffice to say that by entering the Tainai-meguri, you are symbolically entering the womb of a female bodhisattva. When you get to the rock in the darkness, spin it in either direction to make a wish.

The steep approach to the temple is known as Chawan-zaka (Teapot Lane) and is lined with shops selling Kyoto handicrafts, local snacks and souvenirs.

To get there from Kyoto Station take bus 206 and get off at either the Kiyōmizu-michi or Gojō-zaka stop and plod up the hill for 10 minutes.

NINEN-ZAKA & SANNEI-ZAKA/ SANNEN-ZAKA
二年坂・産寧坂/三年坂

Just below and slightly to the north of Kiyomizu-dera, you will find one of Kyoto's loveliest restored neighbourhoods, the Ninen-zaka-Sannen-zaka area. The name refers to the two main streets of the area: Ninen-zaka and Sannen-zaka, literally 'Two-Year Hill' and 'Three-Year Hill'. These two charming streets are lined with old wooden houses, traditional shops and restaurants. If you fancy a break, there are many tea houses and cafes along these lanes.

KŌDAI-JI 高台寺

This **temple** (Map p338; ☎ 561-9966; 526 Shimokawara-chō, Kōdai-ji, Higashiyama-ku; admission ¥600; 9am-5pm) was founded in 1605 by Kita-no-Mandokoro in memory of her late husband, Toyotomi Hideyoshi. The extensive grounds include gardens designed by the famed landscape architect Kobori Enshū, and tea houses designed by the renowned master of the tea ceremony, Sen-no-Rikyū.

The temple is a 10-minute walk north of Kiyomizu-dera (opposite). Check at the TIC for the scheduling of special night-time illuminations of the temple (when the gardens are lit by multicoloured spotlights).

MARUYAMA-KŌEN 円山公園

This **park** (Map p338; Maruyama-chō, Higashiyama-ku) is a great place to escape the bustle of the city centre and amble around gardens, ponds, souvenir shops and restaurants. Peaceful paths meander through the trees and carp glide through the waters of a small pond in the centre of the park.

For two weeks in late March/early April, when the park's many cherry trees come into bloom, the calm atmosphere of the park is shattered by hordes of revellers enjoying *hanami* (blossom-viewing). For those who don't mind crowds, this is a good place to observe the Japanese at their most uninhibited. It is best to arrive early and claim a good spot high on the eastern side of the park, from which point you can safely peer down on the mayhem below.

The park is a five-minute walk east of the Shijō-Higashiōji intersection. To get there from Kyoto Station, take bus 206 and get off at the Gion stop.

YASAKA-JINJA 八坂神社

This colourful **shrine** (Map p338; ☎ 561-6155; Gion-machi, Higashiyama-ku; admission free; 24hr) is just down the hill from Maruyama-kōen. It's considered the guardian shrine of neighbouring Gion and is sometimes endearingly referred to as 'Gion-san'. This shrine is particularly popular as a spot for *hatsu-mōde* (the first shrine visit of the new year). If you don't mind a stampede, come here around midnight on New Year's Eve or over the next few days. Surviving the crush is proof that you're blessed by the gods! Yasaka-jinja also sponsors Kyoto's biggest festival, Gion Matsuri (p367).

GION 祇園周辺

Gion is Kyoto's famous entertainment and geisha district on the eastern bank of the Kamo-gawa. Modern architecture, congested traffic and contemporary nightlife establishments rob the area of some of its historical beauty, but there are still some lovely places left for a stroll. Gion falls roughly between Sanjō-dōri and Gojō-dōri (north and south, respectively) and Higashiyama-dōri and Kawabata-dōri (east and west, respectively).

Hanami-kōji is the main north–south avenue of Gion, and the section south of Shijō-dōri is lined with 17th-century restaurants and tea houses, many of which are exclusive establishments for geisha entertainment. If you wander around here in the late afternoon or early evening, you may glimpse geisha or *maiko* (apprentice geisha) on their way to or from appointments.

Another must-see spot in Gion is **Shimbashi** (sometimes called Shirakawa Minami-dōri), which is one of Kyoto's most beautiful streets, and, arguably, the most beautiful street in all of Asia, especially in the evening and during cherry-blossom season. To get there, start at the intersection of Shijō-dōri and Hanami-kōji and walk north, then take the third left.

Gion is very close to Gion Shijō Station on the Keihan line.

KENIN-JI 建仁寺

Founded in 1202 by the monk Eisai, **Kenin-ji** (Map p338; ☎ 561-6363; Higashiyama-ku, Shijo-sagaru; admission ¥500; 10am-4pm) is the oldest Zen temple in Kyoto. It's an island of peace and calm on

SOUTHERN HIGASHIYAMA WALKING TOUR

- Start: Gojō-zaka bus stop on Higashiōji-dōri, serviced by buses 18, 100, 206 and 207 (see Map p338)
- End: Higashiyama Station on the Tōzai subway line
- Distance: About 5km
- Duration: Half-day

If you had only one day in Kyoto, this walk would be the best way to sample several of Kyoto's most important sights and neighbourhoods. It's pretty much a must-see route, heading right through the heart of Kyoto's premier sightseeing district. Be warned, though, that almost every visitor to Kyoto, both Japanese and foreign, eventually makes their way here, so you'll have to hit it very early in the day to avoid the crush.

The walk begins at Gojō-zaka bus stop (Map p338) on Higashiōji-dōri. From here, walk south for a few metres and turn up Gojō-zaka slope (there is an old noodle shop and pharmacy at the bottom of this street). Head uphill until you reach the first fork in the road; bear right and continue up **Chawan-zaka** (Teapot Lane). At the top of the hill you'll come to **Kiyomizu-dera** (p350), with its unmistakable pagoda rising against the skyline. Before you enter the main complex of Kiyomizu-dera, we recommend that you pay ¥100 to descend into the **Tainai-meguri**, the entrance to which is just to the left of the main temple entrance.

After touring Kiyomizu-dera, exit down Kiyomizu-michi, the busy approach to the temple. Walk down the hill for about 200m until you reach a four-way intersection; go right here down the stone-paved steps. This is **Sannen-zaka** (p351), a charming street lined with old wooden houses, traditional shops and restaurants. There are many tea houses and cafes along this stretch.

the border of the boisterous Gion nightlife district and it makes a fine counterpoint to the worldly pleasures of that area. The highlight here is the fine and expansive *kare-sansui* (dry landscape) garden. The painting of the twin dragons on the roof of the Hōdō hall is also fantastic; access to this hall is via two gates with rather puzzling English operating instructions (you'll see what we mean).

CHION-IN 知恩院

In 1234 **Chion-in** (Map p338; ☎ 531-2111; 400 Rinka-chō, Higashiyama-ku; admission to grounds/inner buildings & garden free/¥400; 9am-4pm Mar-Nov, to 3.40pm Dec-Feb) was built on the site where a famous priest by the name of Hōnen had taught and eventually fasted to death. Today it is still the headquarters of the Jōdo (Pure Land) school of Buddhism, which was founded by Hōnen, and a hive of activity. For visitors with a taste for the grand, this temple is sure to satisfy.

The oldest of the present buildings date back to the 17th century. The two-storey **San-mon**, a Buddhist temple gate at the main entrance, is the largest temple gate in Japan and prepares you for the massive scale of the temple. The immense main hall contains an image of Hōnen. It's connected to another hall, the Dai Hōjō, by a 'nightingale' floor (that sings and squeaks at every move, making it difficult for intruders to move about quietly).

Up a flight of steps southeast of the main hall is the temple's giant **bell**, which was cast in 1633 and weighs 74 tonnes. It is the largest bell in Japan. The combined muscle-power of 17 monks is needed to make the bell ring for the famous ceremony that heralds the new year.

The temple is close to the northeastern corner of Maruyama-kōen. From Kyoto Station take bus 206 and get off at the Chion-in-mae stop, or walk up (east) from Gion Shijō Station on the Keihan line.

SHŌREN-IN 青蓮院

This **temple** (Map p338; ☎ 561-2345; Sanjōbō-chō, Awataguchi, Higashiyama-ku; admission ¥500; 9am-5pm) is hard to miss, with the giant camphor trees growing just outside its walls. Shōren-in was originally the residence of the chief abbot of the Tendai school of Buddhism. The present building dates from 1895, but the main hall has sliding screens with paintings from the 16th and 17th centuries. Often overlooked by the crowds that descend on

Halfway down Sannen-zaka, the road curves to the left. Follow it a short distance, then go right down a flight of steps into **Ninen-zaka** (p351), another quaint street lined with historic houses, shops and tea houses. At the end of Ninen-zaka zigzag left (at the vending machines), then right (just past the parking lot), and continue north. Very soon, on your left, you'll come to the entrance to **Ishibei-kōji** – perhaps the most beautiful street in Kyoto, though it's actually a cobbled alley lined on both sides with elegant, traditional Japanese inns and restaurants. Take a detour to explore this, then retrace your steps and continue north, passing almost immediately the entrance to **Kōdai-ji** (p351) on the right up a long flight of stairs.

After Kōdai-ji continue north to the T-intersection; turn right at this junction and then take a quick left. You'll cross the wide pedestrian arcade and then descend into **Maruyama-kōen** (p351), a pleasant park in which to take a rest. In the centre of the park, you'll see the giant Gion *shidare-zakura,* Kyoto's most famous cherry tree. Opposite the tree there's a bridge that leads across a carp pond to the lovely upper reaches of the park – this is a good place for a picnic, but you'll have to have brought something with you to eat, since the offerings in the park are limited to junk food.

From the park, you can head west (downhill) into the grounds of **Yasaka-jinja** (p351) and descend from the shrine to Shijō-dōri and Gion and make your way home (it's about a 400m walk to Keihan Shijō Station from here). However, if you've got the energy, it's best to return back through the park and head north to tour the grounds of the impressive **Chion-in** (opposite). From here it's a quick walk to **Shōren-in** (opposite), which is famous for its enormous camphor trees out the front. From Shōren-in descend to Sanjō-dōri (you'll see the giant shrine gate of **Heian-jingū**, p356, in the distance). By going left on Sanjō-dōri, you'll soon come to the Jingū-michi bus stop, where you can catch bus 5 or 100 to Kyoto Station, or continue west a little further on Sanjō-dōri and you'll soon come to the Higashiyama-Sanjō Station on the Tōzai line.

other Higashiyama temples, this is a pleasant place to sit and think while gazing out over the beautiful gardens.

The temple is a five-minute walk north of Chion-in (opposite).

Northern Higashiyama

This area at the base of the Higashiyama mountains is one of the city's richest areas for sightseeing. It includes such first-rate attractions as Ginkaku-ji, Hōnen-in, Shūgaku-in Rikyū, Shisen-dō and Manshu-in. You can spend a wonderful day walking from Keage Station on the Tōzai subway line all the way north to Ginkaku-ji via the Tetsugaku-no-Michi (the Path of Philosophy), stopping in the countless temples and shrines en route. Sights further north should be tackled separately, as they are a little harder to reach.

NANZEN-JI 南禅寺

This is one of our favourite **temples** (Map pp340-1; ☎ 771-0365; http://nanzenji.com/english/index.html; Fukuchi-chō, Nanzen-ji, Sakyō-ku; admission to grounds/Hōjō garden/San-mon gate free/¥500/300; 🕑 8.40am-5pm Mar-Nov, to 4.30pm Dec-Feb) in Kyoto, with its expansive grounds and numerous subtemples. It began as a retirement villa for Emperor Kameyama but was dedicated as a Zen temple on his death in 1291. Civil war in the 15th century destroyed most of the temple; the present buildings date from the 17th century. It operates now as headquarters for the Rinzai school of Zen.

At its entrance stands the massive **San-mon**. Steps lead up to the 2nd storey, which has a fine view over the city. Beyond the gate is the main hall of the temple, above which you will find the **Hōjō**, where the **Leaping Tiger Garden** is a classic Zen garden well worth a look. (Try to ignore the annoying taped explanation of the garden.) While you're in the Hōjō, you can enjoy a cup of tea while gazing at a small waterfall (¥400, ask at the reception desk of the Hōjō).

Dotted around the grounds of Nanzen-ji are several subtemples that are often skipped by the crowds.

To get to Nanzen-ji from JR Kyoto or Keihan Sanjō Station, take bus 5 and get off at the Nanzen-ji Eikan-dō-michi stop. You can also take the Tōzai subway line from the city centre to Keage and walk for five minutes downhill. Turn right (east, towards the mountains) opposite the police box and walk slightly uphill and you will arrive at the main gate of the temple.

Nanzen-ji Oku-no-in 南禅寺奥の院

Perhaps the best part of Nanzen-ji is overlooked by most visitors: **Oku-no-in** (Map pp340-1; admission free; ⏲ dawn-dusk), a small shrine-temple hidden in a forested hollow behind the main precinct. To get there, walk up to the red-brick aqueduct in front of the subtemple of Nanzen-in. Follow the road that runs parallel to the aqueduct up into the hills, past several brightly coloured torii, until you reach a waterfall in a beautiful mountain glen. Keep in mind that this is a sacred spot and worshippers come here to pray in peace. Please try to maintain a respectful silence.

Tenju-an 天授庵

This **temple** (Map pp340-1; ☎ 771-0744; 86-8 Fukuchi-chō, Nanzen-ji, Sakyō-ku; admission ¥400; ⏲ 9am-5pm Mar-Nov, to 4.30pm Dec-Feb) stands at the side of the San-mon, a four-minute walk west of Nanzen-in. Built in 1337, the temple has a splendid garden and a great collection of carp in its pond.

Konchi-in 金地院

Just west of the main gate to Nanzen-ji (up some steps and down a side street), you will find **Konchi-in** (Map pp340-1; admission ¥400; ⏲ 8.30am-5pm Mar-Nov, to 4.30pm Dec-Feb), which has a dry garden designed by the master landscape designer Kobori Enshū. This garden is a good example of *shakkei*, or borrowed scenery; note how the mountains behind are drawn into the design.

MURIN-AN VILLA 無鄰庵

This elegant **villa** (Map pp340-1; ☎ 771-3909; Kusakawa-chō, Nanzen-ji, Sakyō-ku; admission ¥350; ⏲ 9am-5pm) was the home of prominent statesman Yamagata Aritomo (1838–1922) and the site of a pivotal 1902 political conference as Japan was heading into the Russo-Japanese War. Enter by 4.30pm.

Built in 1896, the grounds contain well-preserved wooden buildings including a fine Japanese tearoom. The Western-style annexe is characteristic of Meiji-period architecture and the serene garden features small streams that draw water from the Biwa-ko Sosui canal. For ¥300 you can savour a bowl of frothy *matcha* (powdered green tea) while viewing the backdrop of the Higashiyama mountains.

Murin-an is a seven-minute walk from Keage Station on the Tōzai subway line.

EIKAN-DŌ 永観堂

Eikan-dō (Map pp340-1; ☎ 761-0007; www.eikando.or.jp/english/index_eng.htm; 48 Eikandō-chō, Sakyō-ku; admission ¥600; ⏲ 9am-5pm) is a large temple famed for its varied architecture, gardens and works of art. It was founded in 855 by the priest Shinshō, but the name was changed to Eikan-dō in the 11th century to honour the philanthropic priest Eikan.

In the Amida-dō Hall, at the southern end of the complex, is the statue of Mikaeri Amida (Buddha Glancing Backwards). From the Amida-dō Hall, head north to the end of the covered walkway. Change into the sandals provided, then climb the steep steps up the mountainside to the **Tahō-tō** (Tahō Pagoda), where there's a fine view across the city.

The temple is a 10-minute walk north of Nanzen-ji (p353). Enter by 4pm.

TETSUGAKU-NO-MICHI (PATH OF PHILOSOPHY) 哲学の道

The **Tetsugaku-no-Michi** (Map pp340-1; Sakyō-ku Ginkaku-ji) is a pedestrian path that runs along a canal near the base of the Higashiyama. It's lined with cherry trees and a host of other blooming trees and flowers. It takes its name from one of its most famous strollers: 20th-century philosopher Nishida Kitarō, who is said to have meandered along the path lost in thought. It only takes 30 minutes to complete the walk, which starts just north of Eikan-dō (left) and ends at Ginkaku-ji (below).

HŌNEN-IN 法然院

This fine **temple** (Map pp340-1; ☎ 771-2420; 30 Goshonodan-chō, Shishigatani, Sakyō-ku; admission free; ⏲ 6am-4pm) was established in 1680 to honour Hōnen, the charismatic founder of the Jōdo school. This is a lovely, secluded temple with carefully raked gardens set back in the woods. Be sure to visit in early April for the cherry blossoms and early November for the maple leaves, when the main hall is opened for a special viewing.

The temple is a 10-minute walk from Ginkaku-ji (below), on a side street that is accessible from the Tetsugaku-no-Michi (above); heading south on the path, look for the English sign on your left, then cross the bridge over the canal and follow the road uphill.

GINKAKU-JI 銀閣寺

Ginkaku-ji (Map pp340-1; ☎ 771-5725; 2 Ginkaku-ji-chō, Sakyō-ku; admission ¥500; ⏲ 8.30am-5pm Mar-Nov, 9am-4.30pm Dec-Feb) is one of Kyoto's premier sights. In 1482 Shōgun Ashikaga Yoshimasa constructed a villa here as a genteel retreat from the turmoil of civil war. The villa's name translates as 'Silver Pavilion', but the shōgun's

THE LIVING ART OF THE GEISHA

Behind the closed doors of the exclusive tea houses and restaurants that dot the backstreets of Kyoto, women of exquisite grace and refinement entertain gentlemen of considerable means. Patrons may pay more than US$3000 to spend an evening in the company of two or three geisha – kimono-clad women versed in an array of visual and performing arts, including playing the three-stringed *shamisen*, singing old tea-house ballads and dancing.

An evening in a Gion tea house begins with an exquisite *kaiseki* (Japanese cuisine that obeys very strict rules of etiquette for every detail of the meal, including the setting) meal. While their customers eat, the geisha or *maiko* (apprentice geisha) enter the room and introduce themselves in Kyoto dialect.

A *shamisen* performance, followed by a traditional fan dance, is often given, and all the while the geisha and *maiko* pour drinks, light cigarettes and engage in charming banter.

It is virtually impossible to enter a Gion tea house and witness a geisha performance without the introduction of an established patron. With the exception of public performances at annual festivals or dance presentations, they perform only for select customers. Geisha are not prostitutes, and those who decide to open their own tea houses once they retire at 50 or so may receive financial backing from well-to-do clients.

Knowledgeable sources estimate that there are perhaps 80 *maiko* and just over 100 geisha in Kyoto. Although their numbers are ever decreasing, geisha (*geiko* in the Kyoto dialect) and *maiko* can still be seen in some parts of Kyoto, especially after dusk in the back streets between the Kamo-gawa and Yasaka-jinja and along the narrow Ponto-chō alley. Geisha and *maiko* can also be found in other parts of the country, most notably Tokyo. However, it is thought that there are fewer than 1000 geisha and *maiko* remaining in all Japan.

Geisha and *maiko* entertainment can be arranged through top-end hotels, ryokan and some private tour operators in Kyoto.

ambition to cover the building with silver was never realised. After Yoshimasa's death, the villa was converted into a temple.

You approach the main gate between tall hedges, before turning sharply into the extensive grounds. Walkways lead through the gardens, which include meticulously raked cones of white sand (said to be symbolic of a mountain and a lake), tall pines and a pond in front of the temple. A path also leads up the mountainside through the trees.

Note that Ginkaku-ji is one of the city's most popular sites, and it is almost always crowded, especially during the spring and autumn. We strongly recommend visiting right after it opens or just before it closes.

From JR Kyoto or Keihan Sanjō Station, take bus 5 and get off at the Ginkaku-ji-michi stop. From Demachiyanagi Station or Shijō Station, take bus 203 to the same stop.

OKAZAKI-KŌEN AREA 岡崎公園

Right in the heart of the northern Higashiyama area, you'll find Okazaki-kōen (Map pp340–1), which is Kyoto's museum district, and the home of one of Kyoto's most popular and important shrines, Heian-jingū.

Take bus 5 from Kyoto Station or Keihan Sanjō Station and get off at the Kyoto Kaikan Bijutsu-kan-mae stop and walk north, or walk up from Keihan Sanjō Station (15 minutes). All the sights listed here are within five minutes' walk of this stop.

Kyoto Municipal Museum of Art
京都市美術館

The **Kyoto Municipal Museum of Art** (Map pp340-1; ☎ 771-4107; 124 Enshōji-chō, Okazaki, Sakyō-ku; admission varies by exhibition; 🕒 9am-5pm, closed Mon) organises several major exhibitions a year, including the excellent Kyoten exhibition, which showcases Japan's best living artists. It's held from late May until early June most years (check with the TIC for exact dates). These exhibitions are drawn from its vast collection of post-Meiji-era artworks. Kyoto-related works form a significant portion of this near-modern and modern collection. Last entry 4pm.

National Museum of Modern Art
京都国立近代美術館

This **museum** (Map pp340-1; ☎ 761-4111; www.momak.go.jp/English; Enshōji-chō, Okazaki, Sakyō-ku; admission ¥420; 🕒 9.30am-5pm, closed Mon) is renowned for its

GEISHA MANNERS

There's no doubt that catching a glimpse of a geisha is an once-in-a-lifetime Japanese experience. Unfortunately, some people take things a little too far. Groups of camera-wielding tourists – both Japanese and foreign – gather each evening on Hanami-kōji in Gion, hoping to do a little 'geisha-spotting'. While most are content with just a quick look or a photo snapped from a polite distance, a small minority of people actually chase the geisha, and some have even grabbed their kimono in hopes of stopping them for a picture.

Needless to say, this causes a lot of distress for Kyoto's geisha and residents of Gion. Eventually, such behaviour will likely cause the geisha to go elsewhere, or avoid going outside altogether. Thus, we recommend that visitors to Gion keep a few simple things in mind when exploring the area:

- Geisha should not be pursued or interfered with.
- Geisha are usually on a tight schedule and they do not have time to stop and pose for pictures.
- It is never acceptable to touch or grab a geisha, or physically block their progress.
- It is important to treat geisha with respect. No one likes being mobbed by photographers or hounded as they walk down the street. It's best to observe them from a polite distance and leave it at that.
- If you really want to get close to a geisha, private tour agencies and high-end ryokan/hotels can arrange geisha entertainment; see the boxed text, p355.
- Finally, if you are intent on getting a few photos of geisha, you will find plenty of 'tourist geisha' in the streets of Higashiyama during the daytime. These are tourists who have paid to be made up as geisha. They look pretty much like the real thing and they are usually more than happy to pose for pictures.

compact collection of contemporary Japanese ceramics and paintings. Check to see what's on while you're in town. Last entry 4.30pm.

Miyako Messe & Fureai-Kan Kyoto Museum of Traditional Crafts
みやこめっせ・京都伝統産業ふれあい館

The **museum** (Map pp340-1; ☎ 762-2670; 9-1 Seishōji-chō, Okazaki, Sakyō-ku; admission free; 🕑 9am-5pm, closed Dec 29-Jan 3) has exhibits covering things like wood-block prints, lacquerware, bamboo goods and gold-leaf work. It's in the basement of the Miyako Messe (Kyoto International Exhibition Hall). Last entry 4.30pm.

Heian-jingū 平安神宮

This impressive **shrine complex** (Map pp340-1; ☎ 761-0221; Nishitennō-chō, Okazaki, Sakyō-ku; admission to shrine precincts/garden free/¥600; 🕑 6am-6pm, slightly earlier/later depending on the season) was built in 1895 to commemorate the 1100th anniversary of the founding of Kyoto. The buildings are colourful replicas, reduced to two-thirds of the size of the Kyoto Gosho of the Heian period.

The spacious garden, with its large pond and Chinese-inspired bridge, is also meant to represent the kind of garden that was popular in the Heian period. About 500m in front of the shrine there is a massive steel torii. Although it appears to be entirely separate from the shrine, this is actually considered the main entrance to the shrine itself.

Two major events are held at the shrine: Jidai Matsuri (Festival of the Ages; p367), on 22 October, and *takigi nō* (p423), from 1 to 2 June.

SHISEN-DŌ 詩仙堂

This **temple** (Map pp332-3; ☎ 781-2954; 27 Monkuchi-chō, Ichijō-ji, Sakyō-ku; admission ¥500; 🕑 9am-5pm) was built in 1641 by Jōzan, a scholar of Chinese classics and a landscape architect, who wanted a place to retire to at the end of his life. The garden is a fine place to relax, with only the rhythmic 'thwack' of a bamboo *sōzu* (animal scarer) to interrupt your snooze.

The temple is a five-minute walk from the Ichijōji-sagarimatsu-mae bus stop on the bus 5 route.

MANSHU-IN 曼殊院

Founded by Saichō on Hiei-zan, this **temple** (Map pp332-3; ☎ 781-5010; 42 Takenouchi-chō, Ichijō-ji, Sakyō-ku; admission ¥600; 🕑 9am-5pm) was relocated here at the beginning of the Edo period. The architecture, works of art and garden are impressive. The temple is situated around 30 minutes' walk (approximately 3km) to the north of Shisen-dō. Last entry 4.30pm.

SHŪGAKU-IN RIKYŪ 修学院離宮

This imperial **villa** (Map pp332-3; ☎ 211-1215; Yabusoe, Shūgakuin, Sakyō-ku; admission free) was begun in the 1650s by the abdicated emperor Go-Mizunoo, and work was continued after his death in 1680 by his daughter Akenomiya.

Designed as an imperial retreat, the villa grounds are divided into three large garden areas on a hillside: lower, middle and upper. The gardens' reputation rests on their ponds, pathways and impressive use of 'borrowed scenery' in the form of the surrounding hills; the view from the Rinun-tei Teahouse in the upper garden is particularly impressive.

Tours, in Japanese, start at 9am, 10am, 11am, 1.30pm and 3pm (50 minutes). Admission is free, but you must make advance reservations through the Imperial Household Agency (see p347 for details). An audio guide is available for non-Japanese speakers.

From Kyoto Station, take bus 5 and get off at the Shūgaku-in Rikyū-michi stop. The trip takes about an hour. From the bus stop it's a 15-minute walk (about 1km) to the villa. You can also take the Eiden Eizan line from Demachiyanagi Station to the Shūgaku-in stop and walk east about 25 minutes (about 1.5km) towards the mountains.

HIEI-ZAN & ENRYAKU-JI 比叡山・延暦寺

A visit to 848m-high Hiei-zan and the vast **Enryaku-ji complex** (Map p386; ☎ 077-578-0001; 4220 Honmachi, Sakamoto, Ōtsu city, Shiga; admission ¥550; ⏲ 8.30am-4.30pm, 9am-4pm in winter) is a good way to spend half a day hiking, poking around temples and enjoying the atmosphere of a key site in Japanese history.

Enryaku-ji was founded in 788 by Saichō, also known as Dengyō-daishi, the priest who established the Tendai school. From the 8th century the temple grew in power; at its height it possessed some 3000 buildings and an army of thousands of *sōhei,* or warrior monks. In 1571 Oda Nobunaga saw the temple's power as a threat to his aims of unifying the nation and he destroyed most of the buildings, along with the monks inside. This school did not receive imperial recognition until 1823. Today only three pagodas and 120 minor temples remain.

The complex is divided into three sections – Tōtō, Saitō and Yokawa. The **Tōtō** (eastern pagoda section) contains the Kompon Chū-dō (primary central hall), which is the most important building in the complex. The flames on the three Dharma (the law, in Sanskrit) lamps in front of the altar have been kept lit for over 1200 years. The Daikō-dō (great lecture hall) displays life-sized wooden statues of the founders of various Buddhist schools. This part of the temple is heavily geared to group access, with large expanses of asphalt for parking.

The **Saitō** (western pagoda section) contains the Shaka-dō, which dates from 1595 and houses a rare Buddha sculpture of the Shaka Nyorai (Historical Buddha). The Saitō, with its stone paths winding through forests of tall trees, temples shrouded in mist and the sound of distant gongs, is the most atmospheric part of the temple. Hold onto your ticket from the Tōtō section, as you may need to show it here.

The **Yokawa** is of minimal interest and a 4km bus ride away from the Saitō area. The Chū-dō here was originally built in 848. It was destroyed by fire several times and has undergone repeated reconstructions (most recently in 1971). If you plan to visit here, as well as Tōtō and Saitō, allow a full day for in-depth exploration.

Getting There & Away

You can reach Hiei-zan and Enryaku-ji by either train or bus. The most interesting way is the train–cable car–ropeway route.

By train, take the Keihan line north to the last stop, Demachiyanagi, and change to the Yase-yūen/Hiei-bound Eizan Dentetsu Eizan-line train (be careful not to board the Kurama-bound train that sometimes leaves from the same platform). At the last stop, Yase-yūen (¥260), board the cable car (¥530, nine minutes) and then the ropeway (¥310, three minutes) to the peak, then walk down to the temples.

Alternatively, if you want to save money (by avoiding the cable car and ropeway), there are direct Kyoto buses from Kyoto and Keihan Sanjō Stations to Enryaku-ji, which take about 70 and 50 minutes, respectively (both cost ¥800).

Northwest Kyoto

Northwest Kyoto has many excellent sights spread over a large swath of Kyoto. Highlights include Nijō-jō, a shōgun's castle; Kinkaku-ji, the famed Golden Pavilion; and Ryōan-ji, with its mysterious stone garden. Note that three of the area's main sites – Kinkaku-ji, Ryōan-ji and Ninna-ji – can easily be linked together to form a great half-day tour out of the city centre.

NIJŌ-JŌ 二条城

This **castle** (Map p343; ☎ 841-0096; 541 Nijōjō-chō, Horikawa Nishi iru, Nijō-dōri, Nakagyō-ku; admission ¥600; 8.45am-5pm, closed Tue in Dec, Jan, Jul & Aug, closed 26 Dec-4 Jan) was built in 1603 as the official Kyoto residence of the first Tokugawa shōgun, Ieyasu. The ostentatious style of construction was intended as a demonstration of Ieyasu's prestige and to signal the demise of the emperor's power. As a safeguard against treachery, Ieyasu had the interior fitted with 'nightingale' floors and concealed chambers where bodyguards could keep watch.

After passing through the grand **Karamon** gate, you enter **Ninomaru Palace**, which is divided into five buildings with numerous chambers. The Ohiroma Yon-no-Ma (Fourth Chamber) has spectacular screen paintings. Don't miss the excellent **Ninomaru Palace Garden**, which was designed by the tea master and landscape architect Kobori Enshū.

To reach the castle, take bus 9 from Kyoto Station to the Nijō-jō-mae stop. Alternatively, take the Tōzai subway line to the Nijō-jō-mae Station. Enter by 4pm.

NISHIJIN 西陣

The Nishijin district (Map p343) is the home of Kyoto's textile industry, the source of the fantastically ornate kimonos and obi (ornamental kimono belts) for which the city is famous. It's one of Kyoto's more traditional districts, and there are still lots of good old *machiya* (traditional town houses) scattered about. To reach Nishijin, take bus 9 from Kyoto Station to the Horikawa Imadegawa stop.

Nishijin Textile Center 西陣織会館

In the heart of the Nishijin textile district, this **centre** (Map p343; ☎ 451-9231; Imadegawa Minami iru, Horikawa-dōri, Kamigyō-ku; admission free; 9am-5pm) is a good place to observe the weaving of fabrics used in kimono and obi. There are also displays of completed fabrics and kimono, as well as weaving demonstrations and occasional kimono fashion shows. It's on the southwest corner of the Horikawa-dōri and Imadegawa-dōri intersection.

Orinasu-kan 織成館

This **museum** (Map p343; ☎ 431-0020; 693 Daikoku-chō, Kamigyō-ku; adult/child ¥500/350; 10am-4pm, closed Mon) is housed in a Nishijin weaving factory. It has impressive exhibits of Nishijin textiles. The Susamei-sha building next door is also open to the public and worth a look. With advance reservations, traditional weaving workshops can be attended. It's a short walk north of the Nishijin Textile Center (left).

KITANO TENMAN-GŪ 北野天満宮

This **shrine** (Map p343; ☎ 461-0005; Bakuro-chō, Kamigyō-ku; admission free; 5am-dusk, 5am-6pm Jun-Aug, 5.30am-5.30pm Dec-Feb) is a fine and spacious shrine on Imadegawa-dōri. If you're in town on the 25th of any month, be sure to catch the **Tenjin-san market-fair** held here. This is one of Kyoto's two biggest markets and is a great place to pick up some interesting souvenirs. The markets held in December and January are particularly colourful.

From Kyoto Station, take bus 50 and get off at the Kitano-Tenmangū-mae stop. From Keihan Sanjō Station, take bus 10 to the same stop.

KINKAKU-JI 金閣寺

Kyoto's famed 'Golden Pavilion', **Kinkaku-ji** (Map p343; ☎ 461-0013; 1 Kinkaku-ji-chō, Kita-ku; admission ¥400; 9am-5pm) is one of Japan's best-known sights. The original building was built in 1397 as a retirement villa for Shōgun Ashikaga Yoshimitsu. His son converted it into a temple.

In 1950 a young monk consummated his obsession with the temple by burning it to the ground. The monk's story was fictionalised in Mishima Yukio's *The Golden Pavilion*. In 1955 a full reconstruction was completed that exactly followed the original design, but the gold-foil covering was extended to the lower floors.

Note that this temple can be packed almost any day of the year. We recommend going early in the day or just before closing.

To get to the temple from Kyoto Station, take bus 205 and get off at the Kinkaku-ji-michi stop. From Keihan Sanjō, take bus 59 and get off at the Kinkaku-ji-mae stop.

RYŌAN-JI 龍安寺

This **temple** (Map p343; ☎ 463-2216; 13 Goryōnoshitamachi, Ryōan-ji, Ukyō-ku; admission ¥500; 8am-5pm Mar-Nov, 8.30am-4.30pm Dec-Feb) belongs to the Rinzai school of Zen and was founded

KANSAI

in 1450. The main attraction is the garden arranged in the *kare-sansui* style. An austere collection of 15 rocks, apparently adrift in a sea of sand, is enclosed by an earthen wall. The designer, who remains unknown, provided no explanation.

The viewing platform for the garden can be packed solid but the other parts of the temple grounds are also interesting and less crowded. Among these, Kyoyo-chi pond is perhaps the most beautiful, particularly in autumn. If you want to enjoy the *kare-sansui* garden without the crowds, try to come right at opening time.

From Keihan Sanjō Station, take bus 59 to the Ryōan-ji-mae stop. Alternatively, you can walk to Ryōan-ji from Kinkaku-ji (see preceding) in about half an hour.

NINNA-JI 仁和寺

This **temple** (Map p343; ☎ 461-1155; 33 Omuroōuchi, Ukyō-ku; admission to grounds free, admission to Kondō Hall & Treasure Hall ¥500; 🕑 9am-4.30pm) was built in 842 and is the head temple of the Omura branch of the Shingon school of Buddhism. The present temple buildings, including a five-storey pagoda, are from the 17th century. The extensive grounds are full of cherry trees that bloom in early April.

Admission to most of the grounds is free, but separate admission fees are charged for some of the temple's buildings, many of which are closed most of the year. To get there, take bus 59 from Keihan Sanjō Station and get off at the Omuro Ninna-ji stop. From Kyoto Station take bus 26.

MYŌSHIN-JI 妙心寺

The vast temple complex **Myōshin-ji** (Map p343; ☎ 461-5226; 64 Myoshin-ji-chō, Hanazono, Ukyō-ku; admission to main temple/other areas of the complex ¥500/free; 🕑 9.10-11.40am, closed irregularly) is a separate world within Kyoto, a walled-off complex of temples and subtemples that invites lazy strolling. Myōshin-ji dates back to 1342, and belongs to the Rinzai school. There are 47 subtemples, but only a few are open to the public.

From the north gate, follow the broad stone avenue flanked by rows of temples to the southern part of the complex. The eponymous Myōshin-ji is roughly in the middle of the complex. Your entry fee here entitles you to a tour of several of the buildings of the temple. The ceiling of the *hattō* (lecture hall) here features Tanyū Kanō's unnerving painting *Unryūzu* (meaning 'dragon glaring in eight directions'). Your guide will invite you to stand directly beneath the dragon; doing so makes it appear that it's spiralling up or down.

Another highlight of the complex is the wonderful garden of **Taizō-in** (admission ¥500; 🕑 9am-5pm), a subtemple in the southwestern corner of the grounds.

The northern gate of Myōshin-ji is an easy 10-minute walk south of Ninna-ji; or take bus 10 from Keihan Sanjō Station to the Myōshin-ji Kita-mon-mae stop.

KŌRYŪ-JI 広隆寺

A bit out of the way in northwest Kyoto, **Kōryū-ji** (Map p343; ☎ 861-1461; 32 Hachioka-chō, Uzumasa, Ukyō-ku; admission ¥700; 🕑 9am-5pm Mar-Nov, to 4.30pm Dec-Feb) is easily paired with nearby Myōshin-ji to form a half-day tour for those with an interest in Japanese Buddhism. It is one of the oldest temples in Japan, and was founded in 622 to honour Prince Shōto-ku, an enthusiastic early promoter of Buddhism.

The Reihōkan hall contains numerous fine Buddhist statues, including the Naki Miroku (Crying Miroku) and the renowned Miroku Bosatsu, which is extraordinarily expressive. A national upset occurred in 1960 when an enraptured university student embraced the statue in a fit of passion (at least, that was his excuse) and inadvertently snapped off its little finger.

The *hattō* to the right of the main gate houses a magnificent trio of 9th-century statues: Buddha, flanked by manifestations of Kannon.

Take bus 11 from Keihan Sanjō Station, get off at the Ukyō-ku Sogo-chosha-mae stop and walk north. The temple is also close to Uzumasa Station on the Keifuku Arashiyama line.

Arashiyama & Sagano Area

Arashiyama and Sagano, at the base of Kyoto's western mountains (known as the Arashiyama), is Kyoto's second-most important sightseeing district after Higashiyama. On first sight, you may wonder what all the fuss is about: the main street and the area around the famous Tōgetsu-kyō bridge are a classic Japanese tourist circus. But once you head up the hills to the temples hidden in the greenery, you'll understand the appeal.

Arashiyama's most stunning sight is the famous **bamboo grove**, which begins just outside the north gate of Tenryū-ji (p360). Walking through this expanse of swaying bamboo is like entering another world and it ranks high on the list of must-do experiences to be had in Japan.

Bus 28 links Kyoto Station with Arashiyama. Bus 11 connects Keihan Sanjō Station with Arashiyama. The most convenient rail connection is the ride from Shijō-Ōmiya Station on the Keifuku-Arashiyama line to Arashiyama Station (take the Hankyū train from downtown to get to Shijō-Ōmiya). You can also take the JR San-in line from Kyoto Station or Nijō Station and get off at Saga Arashiyama Station (be careful to take only the local train, as the express does not stop in Arashiyama).

The sites in this section are all within walking distance of Arashiyama Station. We suggest walking from this station to Tenryū-ji, exiting the north gate, checking out the bamboo grove, visiting Ōkōchi Sansō, then walking north to Giō-ji or Adashino Nembutsu-ji. If you have time for only one temple in the area, we recommend Tenryū-ji. If you have time for two, we suggest adding Giō-ji.

KAMEYAMA-KŌEN 亀山公園

Southwest of Tenryū-ji, this park (Map p344) is a nice place to escape the crowds of Arashiyama. It's laced with trails, the best of which leads to a lookout over Katsura-gawa and up into the Arashiyama mountains. Keep an eye out for the monkeys; and keep children well away from the occasionally nasty critters.

TENRYŪ-JI 天龍寺

One of the major temples of the Rinzai school of Zen, **Tenryū-ji** (Map p344; ☎ 881-1235; 68 Susukinobaba-chō, Saga Tenryū-ji, Ukyō-ku; admission ¥600; 🕑 8.30am-5.30pm, with slight seasonal variations) was built in 1339 on the former site of Emperor Go-Daigo's villa after a priest had dreamt of a dragon rising from the nearby river. The dream was interpreted as a sign that the emperor's spirit was uneasy and the temple was constructed as appeasement – hence the name *tenryū* (heavenly dragon). The present buildings date from 1900, but the main attraction is the 14th-century Zen garden.

Arashiyama's famous **bamboo grove** lies just outside the north gate of the temple.

ŌKŌCHI SANSŌ 大河内山荘

This **villa** (Map p344; ☎ 872-2233; 8 Tabuchiyama-chō, Ogurayama, Saga, Ukyō-ku; admission ¥1000; 🕑 9am-5pm) is the home of Ōkōchi Denjiro, an actor in samurai films. The superb gardens allow fine views over the city and are open to visitors. The gardens are particularly lovely during the autumn foliage season. The admission fee is hefty but includes tea and a cake (save the tea/cake ticket that comes with your admission). The villa is a 10-minute walk through the bamboo grove north of Tenryū-ji.

JŌJAKKŌ-JI 常寂光寺

If you continue north of Ōkōchi Sansō, the narrow road soon passes stone steps on your left that lead up to the pleasant grounds of **Jōjakkō-ji** (Map p344; ☎ 861-0435; 3 Ogura-chō, Ogurayama, Saga, Ukyō-ku; admission ¥400; 🕑 9am-5pm). The temple is famous for its maple leaves and the Tahōtō pagoda. The upper area of the temple precinct affords good views east over Kyoto. The temple is a 10-minute walk north of Ōkōchi Sansō. Last entry by 4.30pm.

RAKUSHISHA 落柿舎

This **hut** (Map p344; ☎ 881-1953; 20 Hinomyōjin-chō, Ogurayama, Saga, Ukyō-ku; admission ¥200; 🕑 9am-5pm Mar-Dec, 10am-4pm Jan & Feb) belonged to Mukai Kyorai, the best-known disciple of illustrious haiku (17-syllable poem) poet Bashō. Literally meaning 'House of the Fallen Persimmons', legend holds that Kyorai dubbed the house Rakushisha after waking one morning after a storm to find the persimmons he had planned to sell from the garden's trees scattered on the ground. The hut is a short walk downhill and to the north of Jōjakkō-ji.

NISON-IN 二尊院

Near Jōjakkō-ji, **Nison-in** (Map p344; ☎ 861-0687; 27 Monzenchōjin-chō, Nison-in, Saga, Ukyō-ku; admission ¥500; 🕑 9am-4.30pm) is in an attractive setting up the wooded hillside. The long approach to the temple, which is lined with lovely maple trees, is the biggest drawcard. The temple is a short walk north of Jōjakkō-ji.

TAKIGUCHI-DERA 滝口寺

The history of this temple reads like a Romeo and Juliet romance. **Takiguchi-dera** (Map p344; ☎ 871-3929; 10 Kameyama-chō, Saga, Ukyō-ku; admission ¥300; 🕑 9am-5pm) was founded by Heian-era nobleman Takiguchi Nyūdō, who entered the priesthood after being forbidden by his father to marry his peasant consort Yokobue. One day Yokobue came to the temple with her flute to serenade Takiguchi, but was again refused by him; she wrote a farewell love sonnet on a stone (in her own blood) before throwing herself into the river to perish. The stone remains at the temple. The temple is about 10 minutes' walk north of Nison-in.

GIŌ-JI 祇王寺

This quiet **temple** (Map p344; ☎ 861-3574; 32 Kozaka, Toriimoto, Saga, Ukyō-ku; admission ¥300; ⏰ 9am-4.30pm, with seasonal variations) was named for a Heian-era *shirabyōshi* (traditional dancer) named Giō. Aged 21, Giō committed herself here as a nun after her romance with Taira-no-Kiyomori, the commander of the Heike clan. She was usurped by a fellow entertainer, Hotoke Gozen (who later left Kiyomori to join Giō at the temple). Enshrined in the main hall are five statues: these are Giō, Hotoke Gozen, Kiyomori, and Giō's mother and sister (who were also nuns at the temple). It's next to Takiguchi-dera.

ADASHINO NEMBUTSU-JI 化野念仏寺

This rather unusual **temple** (Map p344; ☎ 861-2221; 17 Adashino-chō, Toriimoto, Saga, Ukyō-ku; admission ¥500; ⏰ 9am-4.30pm, with seasonal variations) is where the abandoned bones of paupers and destitutes without next of kin were gathered. Thousands of stone images are crammed into the temple grounds, and these abandoned souls are remembered each year with candles here in the **Sentō Kuyō ceremony** held on the evenings of 23 and 24 August. The temple is about 15 minutes' walk north of Giō-ji.

ARASHIYAMA MONKEY PARK IWATAYAMA 嵐山モンキーパークいわたやま

Home to some 200 Japanese monkeys of all sizes and ages, this **park** (Map p344; ☎ 861-1616; 8 Genrokuzan-chō, Arashiyama, Nishikyō-ku; adult/child ¥550/250; ⏰ 9am-5pm 15 Mar-15 Nov, to 4pm winter) is fun for kids and animal lovers of all ages.

Though it is common to spot wild monkeys in the nearby mountains, here you can see them close up. It makes for an excellent photo opportunity, not only for the monkeys but for the panoramic view over Kyoto. Refreshingly, it is the animals who are free to roam while the humans who feed them are caged in a box!

Just be warned: it's a steep climb up the hill to get to the monkeys. If it's a hot day, you're going to be drenched by the time you get to the spot where they gather.

The entrance to the park is up a flight of steps just upstream of the Tōgetsu-kyō bridge (near the orange torii of Ichitani-jinja). Buy your tickets from the machine to the left of the shrine at the top of the steps.

HOZU-GAWA TRIP 保津川下り

The **Hozu-gawa river trip** (☎ 0771-22-5846; 1 Shimonakajima, Hozu-chō, Kameoka-shi; adult/age 4-12 ¥3900/2500; ⏰ 9am-3.30pm, closed 29 Dec-4 Jan) is a great way to enjoy the beauty of Kyoto's western mountains without any strain on the legs. The river winds through steep, forested mountain canyons before it arrives at its destination, Arashiyama. Between 10 March and 30 November, there are seven trips (from 9am to 3.30pm) per day. During the winter, the number of trips is reduced to four per day and the boats are heated.

The ride lasts two hours and covers 16km between Kameoka and Arashiyama, through occasional sections of tame white water – a scenic jaunt with minimal danger. The boats depart from a dock that is eight minutes on foot from Kameoka Station. Kameoka is accessible by rail from Kyoto Station or Nijō Station on the JR San-in (Sagano) main line. The train fare from Kyoto to Kameoka is ¥400 one way by *futsū* (local train).

Southeast Kyoto

TŌFUKU-JI 東福寺

Founded in 1236 by the priest Enni, **Tōfuku-ji** (Map pp332-3; ☎ 561-0087; 15-778 Honmahi, Higashiyama-ku; admission to garden/grounds ¥400/free; ⏰ 9am-4pm Dec-Oct, 8.30am-4.30pm Nov) belongs to the Rinzai sect of Zen Buddhism. As this temple was intended to compare with Tōdai-ji and Kōfuku-ji in Nara, it was given a name combining characters from the names of each of these temples. Enter by 30 minutes before closing.

The huge **San-mon** is the oldest Zen main gate in Japan. The *tōsu* (lavatory) and *yokushitsu* (bathroom) date from the 14th century. The present temple complex includes 24 subtemples; at one time there were 53.

The **Hōjō** was reconstructed in 1890. The gardens, laid out in 1938, are well worth a visit. The northern garden has stones and moss neatly arranged in a chequerboard pattern. From a viewing platform at the back of the gardens, you can observe the Tsūten-kyō (Bridge to Heaven), which spans a valley filled with maples.

Note that Tōfuku-ji is one of Kyoto's most famous autumn-foliage spots, and it is invariably packed during the peak of colours in November. Otherwise, it's often very quiet.

Tōfuku-ji is a 20-minute walk (2km) southeast of Kyoto Station. You can also take a local train on the JR Nara line and get off at JR Tōfukuji Station, from which it's a 10-minute walk southeast. Alternatively, you can take the Keihan line to Keihan Tōfukuji Station, from which it's also a 10-minute walk.

FUSHIMI-INARI TAISHA 伏見稲荷大社

This intriguing **shrine** (Map pp332-3; ☎ 641-7331; 68 Yabunouchi-chō, Fukakusa, Fushimi-ku; admission free; ⌚ dawn-dusk) was dedicated to the gods of rice and sake by the Hata family in the 8th century. As the role of agriculture diminished, deities were enrolled to ensure prosperity in business. Nowadays the shrine is one of Japan's most popular, and is the head shrine for some 30,000 Inari shrines scattered the length and breadth of Japan.

The entire complex consisting of five shrines sprawls across the wooded slopes of Inari-yama. A pathway wanders 4km up the mountain and is lined with hundreds of red torii. There are also dozens of stone foxes. The fox is considered the messenger of Inari, the god of the rice harvest (and, later on, business). The Japanese traditionally see the fox as a sacred, somewhat mysterious figure capable of 'possessing' humans. The key often seen in the fox's mouth is for the rice granary.

The walk around the upper precincts of the shrine is a pleasant day hike. It also makes for a very eerie stroll in the late afternoon and early evening, when the various graveyards and miniature shrines along the path take on a mysterious air.

To get to the shrine from Kyoto Station, take a JR Nara line train to Inari Station. From Keihan Sanjō Station take the Keihan line to Fushimi-Inari Station. The shrine is just east of both of these stations.

DAIGO-JI 醍醐寺

Daigo-ji (Map pp330-1; ☎ 571-0002; 22 Higashiōji-chō, Daigo, Fushimi-ku; admission to grounds most of year/during cherry-blossom & autumn-foliage seasons free/¥600, to Sampō-in ¥600; ⌚ 9am-5pm Mar-Dec, to 4pm Jan & Feb) was founded in 874 by the priest Shobo, who gave it the name of Daigo. This refers to the five periods of Buddha's teaching, which were often compared to the five forms of milk prepared in India, the highest form of which is called *daigo* (ultimate essence of milk).

The temple was expanded into a vast complex of buildings on two levels – Shimo Daigo (Lower Daigo) and Kami Daigo (Upper Daigo). During the 15th century, the lower-level buildings were destroyed, with the sole exception of the five-storey pagoda. Built in 951, this pagoda still stands and is lovingly noted as the oldest of its kind in Japan and the oldest existing building in Kyoto.

The subtemple **Sampō-in** is a fine example of the amazing opulence of that period. The Kanō paintings and the garden are special features.

Daigo-yama, the mountain that forms the backdrop to the temple, is a steep climb that is enjoyable if you're in good shape and the weather is cool. From Sampō-in, walk up the large avenue of cherry trees, go through the Niō-mon gate and past the pagoda. From there you can continue for a steep climb through the upper part of Daigo-yama, browsing temples and shrines on the way. Allow at least 50 minutes to reach the top. Unfortunately, one of the main halls, the Juntei-dō, burned to the ground recently. However, it's still a worthwhile hike.

To get to Daigo-ji, take the Tōzai subway line from central Kyoto to the last stop, Daigo, and walk east (towards the mountains) for about 10 minutes. Make sure that the train you board is bound for Daigo, as some head to Hama-Ōtsu instead.

UJI 宇治

Uji is a small city to the south of Kyoto. Its main claims to fame are Byōdō-in and tea cultivation. The stone bridge at Uji – the oldest of its kind in Japan – has been the scene of many bitter clashes in previous centuries.

Uji is also home to Ujigami-jinja, a Unesco World Heritage Site. Despite this status, it's not one of the Kyoto area's more interesting sights. Those who wish to see it can find it by crossing the river (using the bridge near Byōdō-in) and walking about 10 minutes uphill (there are signs).

Uji can be reached by rail in about 40 minutes from Kyoto on the Keihan Uji line or JR Nara line.

When arriving in Uji by Keihan train, leave the station, cross the river via the first bridge on the right, and then turn left to find Byōdō-in. When coming by JR, the temple is about 10 minutes' walk east (towards the river) of Uji Station.

Byōdō-in 平等院

This **Buddhist temple** (☎ 0774-21-2861; 116 Uji renge, Uji-shi; admission ¥600; ⌚ 8.30am-5.30pm) was converted from a Fujiwara villa in 1052. The Hōō-dō (Phoenix Hall), more properly known as the Amida-dō, was built in 1053 and is the only original remaining building. The phoenix was a popular mythical bird in China and was revered by the Japanese as a protector of Buddha. The architecture of the building resembles the shape of the bird, and there are two bronze phoenixes perched opposite each other on the roof.

The building was originally intended to represent Amida's heavenly palace in the Pure Land. This building is one of the few extant examples of Heian-period architecture, and its graceful lines make one wish that far more of its type had survived to the present day. For a preview, take a look at the ¥10 coin.

Inside the hall is the famous statue of Amida and 52 Bosatsu (bodhisattvas) dating from the 11th century and attributed to the priest-sculptor Jōchō. Enter by 5.15pm.

Southwest Kyoto

SAIHŌ-JI 西芳寺

The main attraction at this **temple** (Map pp330-1; ☎ 391-3631; 56 Jingatani-chō, Matsuo, Nishikyō-ku; admission ¥3000, entry as part of tour only, advance reservation required) is the heart-shaped garden designed in 1339 by Musō Kokushi. The garden is famous for its luxuriant moss, hence the temple's other name, Koke-dera (Moss Temple). While the reservation procedure is troublesome and the entry fee rather steep, a visit to the temple is highly recommended – the lush, shady garden is among the best in Kyoto.

Before you visit the garden, you will be asked to copy a Sutra using a Japanese ink brush. It's not as hard as it sounds, as you can trace the faint letters on the page – and don't worry about finishing. Once in the garden, you're free to move about as you wish.

Take bus 28 from Kyoto Station to the Matsuo-taisha-mae stop and walk 15 minutes southwest. From Keihan Sanjō Station, take Kyoto bus 63 to Koke-dera, the last stop, and walk for two minutes.

Reservations

To visit Saihō-ji, you must make a reservation. Send a postcard at least one week before the date you wish to visit and include details of your name, number of visitors, address in Japan, occupation, age (you must be over 18) and desired date (choice of alternative dates preferred). The address:

Saihō-ji,
56 Kamigaya-chō,
Matsuo, Nishikyō-ku,
Kyoto-shi 615-8286,
JAPAN

Enclose a stamped, self-addressed postcard for a reply to your Japanese address. You might find it convenient to buy an Ōfuku-hagaki (send-and-return postcard set) at a Japanese post office.

KATSURA RIKYŪ 桂離宮

This **palace** (Katsura Detached Palace; Map pp330-1; ☎ 211-1215; Katsura Misono, Nishikyō-ku; admission free) is considered to be one of the finest examples of Japanese traditional architecture. It was built in 1624 for the emperor's brother, Prince Toshihito. Every conceivable detail of the villa, the tea houses, the large pond with islets and the surrounding garden has been given meticulous attention.

Tours (around 40 minutes), in Japanese, commence at 10am, 11am, 2pm and 3pm. You should be there 20 minutes beforehand. An explanatory video is shown in the waiting room and a leaflet is provided in English. You must make advance reservations with the Imperial Household Agency (see p347 for details). Visitors must be over 20 years of age.

To get to the villa from Kyoto Station, take bus 33 and get off at the Katsura Rikyū-mae stop, which is a five-minute walk from the villa. The easiest access from the city centre is to take a Hankyū line train from Hankyū Kawaramachi Station to Hankyū Katsura Station, which is a 15-minute walk from the villa. Note that some *tokkyū* (express) trains don't stop in Katsura.

Kitayama Area

Starting on the north side of Kyoto city and stretching almost all the way to the Sea of Japan, the Kitayama (Northern Mountains) are a natural escape prized by Kyoto city dwellers. Attractions here include the village of Ōhara, with its pastoral beauty, the fine mountain temple at Kurama, the river dining platforms at Kibune, and the trio of mountain temples in Takao.

ŌHARA 大原

Since ancient times Ōhara (Map p345), a quiet farming town about 10km north of Kyoto, has been regarded as a holy site by followers of the Jōdo school of Buddhism. The region provides a charming glimpse of rural Japan, along with the picturesque Sanzen-in, Jakkō-in and several other fine temples. It's most popular in autumn, when the maple leaves change colour and the mountain views are spectacular. During the peak foliage season of November, this area can get very crowded, especially on weekends.

Sanzen-in 三千院

Founded in 784 by the priest Saichō, **Sanzen-in** (Map p345; ☎ 744-2531; 540 Raigōin-chō, Ōhara, Sakyō-ku; admission ¥700; ⏲ 8.30am-5pm Mar-Nov, to 4.30pm Dec-Feb) belongs to the Tendai sect of Buddhism. Saichō, considered one of the great patriarchs of Buddhism in Japan, also founded Enryaku-ji (Map p386) on nearby Hiei-zan. The temple's Yusei-en is one of the most photographed gardens in Japan, and rightly so.

After seeing Yusei-en, head off to the Ojogokuraku Hall (Temple of Rebirth in Paradise) to see the impressive Amitabha trinity, a large Amida image flanked by attendants Kannon, goddess of mercy, and Seishi, god of wisdom. After this, walk up to the hydrangea garden at the back of the temple, where in late spring and summer you can walk among hectares of blooming hydrangeas.

If you feel like a short hike after leaving the temple, head up the hill around the right side of the temple to the **Soundless Waterfall** (you'll note that it sounds pretty much like any other waterfall). The sound of this waterfall is said to have inspired Shomyo Buddhist chanting.

To get to Sanzen-in, follow the signs from Ōhara's main bus stop up the hill past a long arcade of souvenir stalls. The entrance is on your left as you crest the hill.

Jakkō-in 寂光院

The history of **Jakkō-in** (Map p345; ☎ 744-2545; 676 Kusao-chō, Ōhara, Sakyō-ku; admission ¥600; ⏲ 9am-5pm Mar-Nov, to 4.30pm Dec-Feb) is exceedingly tragic. The actual founding date of the temple is subject to some debate (somewhere between the 6th and 11th centuries), but it gained fame as the temple that harboured Kenrei Mon-in, a lady of the Taira clan. In 1185 the Taira were soundly defeated in a sea battle with the Minamoto clan at Dan-no-ura. With the entire Taira clan slaughtered or drowned, Kenrei Mon-in threw herself into the waves with her grandson Antoku, the infant emperor; she was fished out – the only member of the clan to survive.

She was returned to Kyoto, where she became a nun living in a bare hut until it collapsed during an earthquake. Kenrei Mon-in was accepted into Jakkō-in and stayed there, immersed in prayer and sorrowful memories, until her death 27 years later. Her tomb is located high on the hill behind the temple.

Unfortunately the main building of the temple burned down in May 2000 and the newly reconstructed main hall is lacking some of the charm of the original. Nonetheless, it's a nice spot and the walk there is pleasant.

Jakkō-in lies to the west of Ōhara. Walk out of the bus station up the road to the traffic lights, then follow the small road to the left. Since it's easy to get lost on the way, we recommend familiarising yourself with the kanji for Jakkō-in (see p345) and following the Japanese signs.

KURAMA & KIBUNE 鞍馬・貴船

Only 30 minutes north of Kyoto on the Eiden Eizan main line, Kurama and Kibune (Map p345) are a pair of tranquil valleys long favoured by Kyotoites as places to escape the crowds and stresses of the city below. Kurama's main attractions are its mountain temple and its onsen (hot springs). Kibune, over the ridge, is a cluster of ryokan overlooking a mountain stream. It is best enjoyed in the summer, when the ryokan serve dinner on platforms built over the rushing waters of the Kibune-gawa, providing welcome relief from the summer heat.

The two valleys lend themselves to being explored together. In the winter one can start from Kibune, walk for an hour or so over the ridge, visit Kurama-dera and then soak in the onsen before heading back to Kyoto. In the summer the reverse is best; start from Kurama, walk up to the temple, then down the other side to Kibune to enjoy a meal suspended above the cool river.

If you happen to be in Kyoto on the night of 22 October, be sure not to miss the **Kurama-no-hi Matsuri** (Kurama Fire Festival; p367), one of the most exciting festivals in the Kyoto area.

To get to Kurama and Kibune, take the Eiden Eizan line from Kyoto's Demachiyanagi Station. For Kibune, get off at the second-to-last stop, Kibune Guchi, take a right out of the station and walk about 20 minutes up the hill. For Kurama, go to the last stop, Kurama, and walk straight out of the station. Both destinations are ¥410 and take about 30 minutes to reach.

Kurama-dera 鞍馬寺

This **temple** (Map p345; ☎ 741-2003; 1074 Honmachi, Kurama, Sakyō-ku; admission ¥200; ⏲ 9am-4.30pm) was established in 770 by the monk Gantei from Nara's Tōshōdai-ji. After seeing a vision of the deity Bishamon-ten, guardian of the northern quarter of the Buddhist heaven, he established Kurama-dera just below the peak of Kurama-yama. Originally under the Tendai sect, Kurama has been independent since 1949, describing its own brand of Buddhism as Kurama Kyō.

The entrance to the temple is just up the hill from the Eiden Eizan main line's Kurama Station. A tram goes to the top for ¥100; alternatively, hike up by following the main path past the tram station. The trail is worth taking if it's not too hot, as it winds through a forest of towering old-growth *sugi* (cryptomeria) trees. At the top there is a courtyard dominated by the *honden* (main hall). Behind the *honden*, a trail leads off to the mountain's peak.

At the top, you can take a brief detour across the ridge to Ōsugi-gongen, a quiet shrine in a grove of trees. Those who want to continue to Kibune can take the trail down the other side. It's a 1.2km, 30-minute hike from the *honden* to the valley floor of Kibune. On the way down are two pleasant mountain shrines, Sōjō-gadani Fudō-dō and Okuno-in Maō-den.

Kurama Onsen 鞍馬温泉

One of the few onsen within easy reach of Kyoto, **Kurama Onsen** (Map p345; ☎ 741-2131; 520 Honmachi, Kurama, Sakyō-ku; admission to outdoor/indoor bath ¥1100/2300; 10am-9pm) is a great place to relax after a hike. The outdoor bath has a fine view of Kurama-yama; even with the use of sauna and locker thrown in, it's difficult to imagine why one would opt for the indoor bath. For both, buy a ticket from the machine outside the door of the main building (instructions are in Japanese and English).

To get to Kurama Onsen, walk straight out of Kurama Station, turn left up the main road and follow it for about 10 minutes. You'll see the baths down on your right. There's also a free shuttle bus that runs between the station and the onsen, leaving approximately every 30 minutes.

Kibune-jinja 貴船神社

This **shrine** (Map p345; ☎ 741-2016; 180 Kibune-chō Kurama, Sakyō-ku; admission free; 6am-8pm, earlier Dec-Feb), halfway up the valley-town of Kibune, is worth a quick look, particularly if you can ignore the unfortunate plastic horse statue at its entrance. From Kibune you can hike over the mountain to Kurama-dera, along a trail that starts halfway up the village on the eastern side (or vice versa – see opposite).

TAKAO 高雄

Takao (Map pp330–1) is a secluded mountain village tucked far away in the northwestern part of Kyoto. It is famed for autumn foliage and the temples of Jingo-ji, Saimyō-ji and Kōzan-ji.

Jingo-ji (神護寺; Map pp330-1; ☎ 861-1769; 5 Umegahata Takao-chō, Ukyō-ku; admission ¥500; 9am-4pm) is the best of the three temples in the Takao area. This mountain temple sits at the top of a long flight of stairs that stretch up from Kiyotaki-gawa to the temple's main gate. The Kondō (Gold Hall) is the most impressive of the temple's structures; it's roughly in the middle of the grounds, at the top of another flight of stairs.

After visiting the Kondō, head in the opposite direction along a wooded path to an open area overlooking the valley. Don't be surprised if you see people tossing small discs over the railing into the chasm below. These are *kawarakenage* – light clay discs that people throw to rid themselves of their bad karma. Be careful: it's addictive, and at ¥100 for two, it can become expensive. You can buy the discs at a nearby stall. The trick is to flick the discs very gently, convex side up, like a Frisbee. When you get it right, they sail all the way down the valley, taking all that bad karma away with them.

The other two temples are within easy walking distance of Jingo-ji; **Saimyō-ji** (西明寺; Map pp330-1; ☎ 861-1770; 2 Umegahata Toganoo-chō, Ukyō-ku; admission ¥400; 9am-5pm) is the better of the two. It's about five minutes' walk north of the base of the steps that lead up to Jingo-ji (follow the river upstream). To get to **Kōzan-ji** (高山寺; Map pp330-1; ☎ 861-4204; Umegahata Toganoo-chō, Ukyō-ku; admission ¥600; 8am-5pm) you must walk back up to the main road and follow it north for about 10 minutes.

There are two options for buses to Takao: an hourly JR bus from Kyoto Station, which takes about an hour to reach the Takao stop (get off at the Yamashiro-Takao stop); and Kyoto city bus 8 from Shijō-Karasuma (get off at the Takao stop). To get to Jingo-ji from these bus stops, walk down to the river, then look for the steps on the other side.

ACTIVITIES
Baths
FUNAOKA ONSEN 船岡温泉

This old **bath** (Map p343; ☎ 441-3735; 82-1 Minami-Funaoka-chō-Murasakino Kita-ku; admission ¥410; 3pm-1am Mon-Sat, 8am-1am Sun & holidays) on

KANSAI

Kuramaguchi-dōri is Kyoto's best. It boasts an outdoor bath, a sauna, a cypress-wood tub, an electric bath, a herbal bath and a few more for good measure. Be sure to check out the *ranma* (carved wooden panels) in the changing room. Carved during Japan's invasion of Manchuria, the panels offer insight into the prevailing mindset of that era. (Note the panels do contain some violent imagery, which may disturb some visitors.)

To find the bath, head west about 400m on Kuramaguchi-dōri from the Kuramaguchi-Horiikawa intersection. It's on the left, not far past Lawson convenience store. Look for the large rocks out the front.

GOKŌ-YU 五香湯

This popular **bath** (Map pp332-3; ☎ 812-1126; 590-1 Kakinomoto-chō-Gojō agaru Kuromon-dōri; admission ¥410; 2.30pm-midnight Tue-Sat, 7am-midnight Sun, 11am-midnight holidays, closed Mon and 3rd Tue) is another excellent choice. It has several good tubs and two saunas; one is merely hot, the other is roughly the same temperature as the centre of the sun.

Cooking Classes

If you want to learn how to cook some of the delightful foods you've tried in Kyoto, we highly recommend **Uzuki** (www.kyotouzuki.com; 3hr class per person ¥3500), a small cooking class conducted in a Japanese home for groups of two to four people. You will learn how to cook a variety of dishes and then sit down and enjoy the fruits of your labour. You can consult beforehand if you have particular dishes you'd like to cook. The fee includes all ingredients. Reserve via website.

Geisha & Maiko Costume

If you ever wondered how you might look as a geisha, Kyoto has several shops that offer *maiko-henshin* (geisha transformation). **Maika** (Map p338; ☎ 551-1661; www.maica.net; Higashiyama-ku, Miyagawa suji; maiko/geisha from ¥6500/8000) is a popular *maiko-henshin* shop in Gion. If you don't mind spending a bit extra, it's possible to head out in costume for a stroll through Gion (and be stared at like never before!). The process takes about an hour. Call to reserve at least one day in advance.

Japanese Culture

Kyoto is a fine place to get a taste of traditional Japanese culture, and there are several organisations that offer introductions to various aspects of Japanese culture, including the following.

WAK Japan (Map pp332-3; ☎ 212-9993; www.wakjapan.com; 412-506 Iseya-chō, Kamigyō-ku) offers a wide variety of excellent introductions to Japanese culture: tea ceremony, ikebana (Japanese flower arrangement), trying on kimonos, home visits, Japanese cooking, calligraphy, origami etc. Presenters/instructors speak English or interpreters are provided. Pick-up service is available from your lodgings.

Club Ōkitsu Kyoto (Map pp332-3; ☎ 411-8585; www.okitsu-kyoto.com; 524-1 Mototsuchimikado-chō, Shinmachi, Kamigyō-ku) offers an upscale introduction to various aspects of Japanese culture including tea ceremony, incense ceremony and traditional Japanese games. The introduction is performed in an exquisite Japanese villa near the Kyoto Gosho and participants get a real sense of the elegance and refinement of traditional Japanese culture.

En (Map p338; ☎ 080-3782-2706; 272 Matsubara-chō, Higashiyama-ku; tea ceremony per person ¥2000; 1-6pm, closed Wed) is a small tea house near Gion where you can experience the Japanese tea ceremony with a minimum of fuss or expense. English explanations are provided and no reservations are needed: just show up at 1pm, 2.30pm, 4pm, 5pm or 6pm (check the website for latest times, as these may change). Groups of up to eight people can be accommodated. It's a little tricky to find: it's located down a little alley off Higashiōji-dōri – look for the sign just south of Tenkaippin Rāmen.

FESTIVALS & EVENTS

There are hundreds of festivals in Kyoto throughout the year. Listings can be found in the *Kyoto Visitor's Guide* or *Kansai Time Out*. The following are some of the major and most spectacular festivals. These attract hordes of spectators from out of town, so book accommodation well in advance.

February

Setsubun Matsuri at Yoshida-jinja This festival is held on the day of *setsubun* (2, 3 or 4 February; check with the TIC), which marks the last day of winter in the Japanese lunar calendar. In this festival, people climb up to Yoshida-jinja (pp340–1) in the northern Higashiyama area to watch a huge bonfire (in which old good luck charms are burned). It's one of Kyoto's more dramatic festivals. The action starts at dusk.

May

Aoi Matsuri (Hollyhock Festival) This festival dates back to the 6th century and commemorates the successful prayers of the people for the gods to stop calamitous weather. Today the procession involves imperial messengers in ox carts and a retinue of 600 people dressed in traditional costume. The procession leaves at around 10am on 15 May from the Kyoto Gosho (p347) and heads for Shimogamo-jinja (p348).

July

Gion Matsuri Perhaps the most renowned of all Japanese festivals, this one reaches a climax on 17 July with a parade of over 30 floats depicting ancient themes and decked out in incredible finery. On the three evenings preceding the main day, people gather on Shijō-dōri (p336), many dressed in beautiful *yukata* (light summer kimonos), to look at the floats and carouse from one street stall to the next.

August

Daimon-ji Gozan Okuribi This festival, commonly known as Daimon-ji Yaki, is performed to bid farewell to the souls of ancestors on 16 August. Enormous fires are lit on five mountains in the form of Chinese characters or other shapes. The largest fire is burned on Daimon-ji-yama, just above Ginkaku-ji (p354), in northern Higashiyama. The fires start at 8pm and it is best to watch from the banks of the Kamo-gawa or pay for a rooftop view from a hotel.

October

Jidai Matsuri (Festival of the Ages) This festival is of recent origin, only dating back to 1895. More than 2000 people, dressed in costumes ranging from the 8th century to the 19th century, parade from Kyoto Gosho (p347) to Heian-jingū (p356) on 22 October.

Kurama-no-hi Matsuri (Kurama Fire Festival) In perhaps Kyoto's most dramatic festival, huge flaming torches are carried through the streets of Kurama (p364) by men in loincloths on 22 October (the same day as the Jidai Matsuri).

SLEEPING

The most convenient areas in which to be based, in terms of easy access to shopping, dining and sightseeing attractions, are downtown Kyoto and the Higashiyama area. The Kyoto Station area is also a good place to be based, with excellent access to transport and plenty of shops and restaurants about. Transport information in the following listings is from Kyoto Station unless otherwise noted.

Kyoto Station Area

BUDGET

Guest Houses

K's House Kyoto (Map p335; ☎ 342-2444; http://kshouse.jp/kyoto-e/index.html; 418 Naya-chō, Shichijō agaru, Dotemachi-dōri, Shimogyō-ku; dm from ¥2300, s/d/tw per person from ¥3500/2900/2900; ⊠ 💻 📶; 🚇 Kyoto Station, Karasuma central gate) K's House is a large Western-style backpacker's guest house with both private and dorm rooms. The rooms are simple but adequate and there are spacious common areas. There's also an on-site restaurant that serves cheap cafe drinks, alcohol and snacks. There are coin-operated internet terminals and free wi-fi. The staff can help arrange inexpensive onward travel around Japan. It's about a 10-minute walk from Kyoto Station.

Tour Club (Map p335; ☎ 353-6968; www.kyotojp.com; 362 Momiji-chō, Higashinakasuji, Shōmen-sagaru, Shimogyō-ku; dm ¥2450, d ¥6980-7770, tr ¥8880-9720; ⊠ 💻 📶; 🚇 Kyoto Station, Karasuma central gate) Run by a charming and informative young couple, this clean, well-maintained guest house is a favourite of many foreign visitors. Facilities include bicycle rentals, laundry and free tea and coffee. Most private rooms have a bathroom, and there is a spacious quad room for families. This is probably the best choice in this price bracket. It's a 10-minute walk from Kyoto Station; turn north off Shichijō-dōri at the Second House coffee shop (looks like a bank) and keep an eye out for the English sign.

Budget Inn (Map p335; ☎ 344-1510; www.budgetinnjp.com; 295 Aburanokōji-chō, Shichijō sagaru, Shimogyō-ku; dm/tr/q/5-person r ¥2500/10,980/12,980/14,980; ⊠ 💻 📶; 🚇 Kyoto Station, Karasuma central gate) This well-run guest house is an excellent choice. It's got two dorm rooms and six Japanese-style private rooms, all of which are clean and well maintained. All rooms have their own bathroom, and there is a spacious quad room which is good for families. The staff here is very helpful and friendly, and laundry and bicycle rental are available. All in all, this is a great choice in this price range. It's a seven-minute walk from Kyoto Station; from the station, walk west on Shiokōji-dōri, turn north one street before Horikawa and look for the English-language sign out front.

Ryokan

Nihonkan (Map p335; ☎ 371-3125; Karasuma-dōri Shichijō sagaru nishi iru, Shimogyō-ku; r per person from ¥4000; 🚇 Kyoto Station, Karasuma central gate) If you want a taste of an old-school budget-traveller's ryokan, then walk north from Kyoto Station for about two minutes and you'll come to the humble Nihonkan. Rooms are simple but adequate and there are big common baths (sort of like those in a public bath).

Matsubaya (Map p335; ☎ 351-3727; www.matsubayainn.com; Nishi-iru Higashinotoin, Kamijizuyamachi-dōri, Shimogyō-ku; r per person from ¥4200; 💻; 🚇 Kyoto Station, Karasuma central gate) A short walk from Kyoto Station, this newly renovated ryokan has clean, well-kept rooms and a management that is used to foreign guests. Some rooms on the 1st floor look out on small gardens. There are internet terminals and LAN cable-access points in rooms. Average room rates here run about ¥6500 per person. Matsubaya also has several serviced apartments in its adjoining Bamboo House section – these would be great for anyone planning a longer stay in the city.

Kyōraku (Map p335; ☎ 371-1260; www.ryokankyoraku.jp; 231 Kogawa-chō, Shichijō agaru, Akezu-dōri, Shimogyō-ku; r per person from ¥5200; 💻; 🚇 Kyoto Station, Karasuma central gate) About 10 minutes' walk from Kyoto Station and a stone's throw from Higashi Hongan-ji, Kyōraku is a friendly little ryokan with nice traditional rooms (some with bathroom). The free internet terminal in the lobby is a nice touch.

Ryokan Shimizu (Map p335; ☎ 371-5538; www.kyoto-shimizu.net; 644 Kagiya-chō, Shichijō-dōri, Wakamiya agaru, Shimogyō-ku; r per person from ¥5250; ⊠ 💻; 🚇 Kyoto Station, Karasuma central gate) A short walk north of Kyoto Station, this fine ryokan is quickly building a loyal following of foreign guests, and for good reason: it's clean, well run and friendly. Rooms are standard ryokan style with one difference: all have bathrooms. Bicycle rental is available.

MIDRANGE

APA Hotel Kyoto Ekimae (Map p335; ☎ 365-4111; www.apahotel.com/hotel_e/ah_kyotoekimae/index.html; Shiokōji sagaru, Nishinotōin-dōri, Shimogyō-ku; s/tw from ¥10,500/20,000; ⊠ 💻 📶; 🚇 Kyoto Station, Karasuma central gate) Only five minutes on foot from Kyoto Station, this efficient business hotel is a good choice for those who want the convenience of a nearly stationside location. Rooms are adequate, with firm, clean beds and unit bathrooms. The staff is professional and is used to dealing with foreign guests. There is LAN cable internet in rooms and wi-fi in the lobby.

TOP END

Hotel Granvia Kyoto (Map p335; ☎ 344-8888; www.granvia-kyoto.co.jp/e/index.html; Shiokōji sagaru, Karasuma-dōri, Shimogyō-ku; d/tw from ¥23,100/25,410; ⊠ 💻 🏊; 🚇 Kyoto Station, Karasuma central gate) Imagine stepping straight out of bed and into the *shinkansen*. This is almost possible when you stay at the Granvia, an excellent hotel located directly above Kyoto Station. Rooms are clean, spacious and well appointed, with deep bathtubs. This is a very professional operation with some good on-site restaurants, some of which have good views over the city. There is LAN cable internet in rooms.

Rihga Royal Hotel Kyoto (Map p335; ☎ 341-1121; fax 341-3073; www.rihga.com/kyoto; Horikawa-Shiokōji, Shimogyō-ku; s/d/tw from ¥16,170/26,565/25,410; ⊠ 💻; 🚇 Kyoto Station, Karasuma central gate) Though a little dated and too large for some people's taste, this long-running hotel has all the facilities that you'd expect from an international hotel, including a revolving rooftop restaurant. The location is fairly convenient for Kyoto Station. There is LAN cable internet in rooms (it costs ¥1050 for 24 hours).

Downtown Kyoto

BUDGET

Kinsuikan (Map p336; ☎ 255-3930; Tominokōji Sanjō sagaru, Nakagyō-ku; r per person from ¥4200; 💻 📶; 🚇 Tōzai & Karasuma subway lines to Karasuma-Oike Station, exit 3) They don't make locations much more convenient than this: Kinsuikan is located right in the middle of the downtown shopping-restaurant district. It's a simple ryokan that's used to welcoming foreign travellers. There is a wide variety of rooms, some of which have bathrooms and toilets. Wi-fi is in the lobby and you can take a soak in the large common baths downstairs.

MIDRANGE

Hotel Unizo (Map p336; ☎ 241-3351; www.sun-hotel.co.jp/ky_index.htm, in Japanese; Kawaramachi-dōri-Sanjō sagaru, Nakagyō-ku; s/d/tw from ¥7350/13,650/12,810; ⊠; 🚌 bus 5 to Kawaramachi-Sanjō stop) They don't get more central than this downtown business hotel: it's smack-dab in the middle of Kyoto's nightlife, shopping and dining district and you can walk to hundreds of restaurants and shops within five minutes. It's a standard-issue business hotel, with small but adequate rooms and unit bathrooms. Considering the location and the condition of the rooms, it's great value.

Hotel Fujita Kyoto (Map pp332-3; ☎ 222-1511; www.fujita-kyoto.com/e; Nijō-Ōhashi Hotori, Kamogawa, Nakagyō-ku; s/d/tw from ¥10,395/26,565/16,170; ⊠ 💻; 🚇 Tōzai subway line to Shiyakusho-mae Station, exit 2) Located on the banks of the Kamo-gawa, this hotel has rooms that are slightly larger than those you'd find in a business hotel. Rooms on the east side have great views over the river to the

Higashiyama mountains. There are several good on-site restaurants and a nice bar. It's an easy walk to the downtown area.

TOP END

Hiiragiya Bekkan (Annex) (Map p336; ☎ 231-0151; fax 231-0153; www.hiiragiya.com/index-e.html; Gokōmachi-dōri, Nijō sagaru, Nakagyō-ku; r per person with 2 meals from ¥16,800; ; Tōzai subway line to Shiyakusho-mae Station, exit North-10) Not far from the Hiiragiya main building (below), the Hiiragiya Bekkan Annex offers the traditional ryokan experience at slightly more affordable rates. The *kaiseki* (Japanese haute cuisine) served here is delicious, and the gardens are lovely. Rooms have en-suite bathrooms, but bathtubs are shared (there are four lovely bathtubs). There is LAN cable access in the lobby.

Kyoto Hotel Ōkura (Map p336; ☎ 211-5111; fax 254-2529; www.kyotohotel.co.jp/khokura/english/index.html; Kawaramachi-dōri, Oike, Nakagyō-ku; s/d/tw from ¥21,945/31,185/31,185; ; Tōzai subway line to Shiyakusho-mae Station, exit 3) This towering hotel in the centre of town has some of the best views in the city. Rooms here are clean, spacious and comfortable. There are several excellent on-site restaurants and bars, along with hundreds within easy walking distance of the hotel. If you exhaust the possibilities in and around the hotel, you can walk downstairs and hop right onto the subway. There is LAN cable internet in rooms.

Hiiragiya (Map p336; ☎ 221-1136; fax 221-139; www.hiiragiya.co.jp/en; Anekōji-agaru, Fuya-chō, Nakagyō-ku; r per person with 2 meals ¥30,000-60,000; ; Tōzai & Karasuma subway lines to Karasuma-Oike Station, exit 3) This classic ryokan is favoured by celebrities from around the world. From the decorations to the service to the food, everything at the Hiiragiya is the best available. Rooms in the old wing have great old Japan style, while those in the new wing are pristine and comfortable. It's centrally located downtown within easy walk of two subway stations and lots of good restaurants. There is LAN cable internet access in the new wing.

Tawaraya (Map p336; ☎ 211-5566; fax 221-2204; Fuyachō-Oike sagaru, Nakagyō-ku; r per person with 2 meals ¥42,263-84,525; ; Tōzai & Karasuma subway lines to Karasuma-Oike Station, exit 3) Tawaraya has been operating for over three centuries and is classed as one of the finest places to stay in the world. Entering this ryokan is like entering another world and you just might not want to leave. The ryokan has an intimate, private feeling and all rooms have bathrooms. The gardens are sublime and the cosy study is the perfect place to linger with a book. A night here is sure to be memorable.

Central Kyoto

BUDGET

Crossroads Inn (Map pp332-3; ☎ 354-3066; fax 354-3022; www.rose.sannet.ne.jp/c-inn; Ebisu Banba-chō- Shimogyō-ku; r per person cash/credit card from ¥3800/4000; ; bus 205 to Umekōji-kōen-mae stop) Crossroads Inn is a charming little guest house with clean, well-maintained rooms and a friendly owner. The entire inn is nonsmoking. It's good value but a little hard to find: turn north off Shichijō-dōri just west of the Umekōji-kōen-mae bus stop across from the Daily Yamazaki convenience store. Reservations are by email only.

Ryokan Hinomoto (Map pp332-3; ☎ 351-4563; fax 351-3932; Matsubara agaru-Kawaramachi-dōri; s/d from ¥4200/8400; ; bus 17 or 205 to Kawaramachi-Matsubara stop) This cute little ryokan is very conveniently located for shopping and dining in downtown Kyoto, as well as sightseeing on the east side of town. It's got a nice wooden bathtub and simple rooms. It's a nice, cosy place to stay and there is LAN cable internet access.

Casa de Natsu (Map pp332-3; ☎ 491-2549; casadenatsu@gmail.com; 27 Koyamamotomachi, Kita-ku; r per person ¥4500; ; Karasuma subway line to Kitayama Station, exit 4) Up in the north of town, this cosy little Japanese-style guest house is a good spot for those who want to escape the hubbub of downtown. There are two rooms, each decorated in the traditional style, and a fine little garden. A light breakfast is served.

Ryokan Rakuchō (Map pp332-3; ☎ 721-2174; fax 791-7202; 67 Higashi hangi chō, Shimogamo, Sakyō-ku; s/tw/tr ¥5300/9240/12,600; ; Karasuma subway line to Kitaōji Station; bus 205, Furitsudaigaku-mae stop) There is a lot to like about this fine little foreigner-friendly ryokan in the northern part of town: it's entirely nonsmoking, there is a nice little garden and the rooms are clean and simple. Meals aren't served, but the owners can supply a good map of local eateries. Wi-fi sweetens the deal for travellers.

MIDRANGE

Karasuma Kyoto Hotel (Map pp332-3; ☎ 371-0111; fax 371-2424; www.kyotohotel.co.jp/karasuma/index_e.html; Karasuma-dōri, Shijō sagaru, Shimogyō-ku; s/d/tw from ¥10,164/23,100/18,480; ; Karasuma subway line to Shijō Station, exit South-6) This busy downtown hotel occupies the middle ground between a business hotel and a standard hotel, with decent rooms and efficient staff. It's very popular with businesspeople and travellers, many of whom like the convenience of a Starbucks right in the lobby. There is LAN cable internet access.

Southern Higashiyama

BUDGET

Higashiyama Youth Hostel (Map p338; ☎ 761-8135; fax 761-8138; www.syukuhaku.jp/youth-hostel-kyoto; 112 Gokenmachi, Shirakawabashi, Sanjō-dōri, Higashiyama-ku; dm from ¥3960; ⊠ 💻; 🚇 Tōzai subway line to Higashiyama Station, exit 1) This YH is very close to the sights of Higashiyama. It's regimented, but if you're the early-to-bed-early-to-rise type, it might suit.

MIDRANGE

Ryokan Uemura (Map p338; ☎ /fax 561-0377; Ishibe-kōji, Shimogawara, Higashiyama-ku; r with breakfast per person ¥9000; ⊠; 🚌 bus 206 to Yasui stop) This beautiful little ryokan is at ease with foreign guests. It's on a quaint cobblestone alley, just down the hill from Kōdai-ji. Rates include breakfast, and there is a 10pm curfew. Book well in advance, as there are only three rooms. Note that the manager prefers bookings by fax and asks that cancellations also be made by fax (with so few rooms, it can be costly when bookings are broken without notice).

Suisen-Kyo Shirakawa (Map p338; ☎ 712-7023; www.suisenkyo.com; 473-15 Umemiya-chō, Higashiyama-ku; house per night ¥12,000-16,000, depending on group size; 📶; 🚇 Tōzai subway line to Higashiyama Station) Located near the prime sightseeing area of Kyoto, this small private house is available for short-term rental. It's perfect for families and small groups and there are two bedrooms (one Japanese-style, one Western-style). There's a Western toilet, kitchen, bathtub, small garden, and a washing machine.

TOP END

Ryokan Motonago (Map p338; ☎ 561-2087; fax 561-2655; www.motonago.com; 511 Washio-chō, Kōdaiji-michi, Higashiyama-ku; r per person with 2 meals from ¥17,850; ⊠ 💻; 🚌 bus 206 to Gion stop) This ryokan may have the best location of any ryokan in the city: right on Nene-no-Michi in the heart of the Higashiyama sightseeing district. It's got traditional decor, friendly service, nice bathtubs and a few small Japanese gardens.

Hyatt Regency Kyoto (Map p338; ☎ 541-1234; fax 541-2203; www.kyoto.regency.hyatt.com; 644-2 Sanjūsangendō-mawari, Higashiyama-ku; r Y£22,000-46,000; ⊠ 💻 📶; 🚇 5min walk from Keihan Shichijō Station) The new Hyatt Regency is an excellent, stylish, foreigner-friendly hotel at the southern end of Kyoto's southern Higashiyama sightseeing district. Many travellers consider this the best hotel in Kyoto, and almost all mention the great restaurants and bar and the highly professional staff. The stylish rooms and bathrooms have lots of neat touches. The concierges are helpful and they'll even lend you a laptop to check your email if you don't have your own.

Ryokan Seikōrō (Map p338; ☎ 561-0771; fax 541-5481; www.seikoro.com/top-e.htm; 467 Nishi Tachibana-chō, 3 chō-me, Gojō sagaru, Tonyamachi-dōri, Higashiyama-ku; r per person with 2 meals from ¥28,875; ⊠ 💻 📶; 🚌 bus 17 or 205 to Kawaramachi-Gojō stop) The Seikōrō is a classic ryokan with sumptuous rooms and a grandly decorated lobby. It's fairly spacious, with excellent, comfortable rooms, attentive service and a fairly convenient midtown location. Wi-fi is in the lobby.

Northern Higashiyama

BUDGET

Yonbanchi (Map pp340-1; www.thedivyam.com; 4 Shinnyo-chō; r ¥10,000; ⊠ 💻 📶; 🚌 bus 5 to Kinrinshako-mae stop) Yonbanchi is a charming B&B ideally located for sightseeing in the Ginkakuji-Yoshida-Yama area. One of the two guest rooms looks out over a small Japanese garden. The house is a late-Edo-period samurai house located just outside the main gate of Shinnyo-dō, a temple famed for its maple leaves and cherry blossoms. There is a private entrance and no curfew. Reservations by email only.

B&B Juno (Map pp340-1; www.gotokandk.com; Jōdo-ji-Nishida-chō; r per person ¥5000; 📶; 🚌 bus 17 to Shirakawa-mae stop) Located close to Ginkaku-ji, on the east side of Kyoto University, this large B&B-home, in an old private compound, has three bright Japanese-style rooms on the 2nd floor. It is run by a charming international couple with a wealth of inside information on Kyoto. Reservations by email only.

Kaguraya B&B (Map pp340-1; kaguraya@me.com; Yoshidakaguraoka-cho 8 banchi, Sakyō-ku; B&B per person double occupancy ¥5000) Kaguraya is a 100-year-old traditional Japanese house, with a garden and panoramic views of the eastern hills of Kyoto. Two large rooms are available. A Western breakfast is provided by the helpful owners. Reservation is via email only.

MIDRANGE

Kyoto Traveller's Inn (Map pp340-1; ☎ 771-0225; fax 771-0226; www.k-travelersinn.com/english/index.php; 91 Enshō-ji-chō, Okazaki, Sakyō-ku; s/tw from ¥5775/10,500;

KANSAI

⊠ 💻; 🚌 bus 5 to Kyōto Kaikan Bijyutsukan-mae stop) This small business hotel is very close to Heian-jingū. It offers Western- and Japanese-style rooms. The restaurant on the 1st floor is open till 10pm. It's good value for the price and the location is dynamite for exploring the Higashiyama area.

Three Sisters Inn Main Building (Rakutō-sō Honkan; Map pp340-1; ☎ 761-6336; fax 761-6338; 18 Higashifukunokawa-chō, Okazaki, Sakyō-ku; s/d/tr ¥10280/15,014/22,521; ⊠; 🚌 bus 5, Dōbutsuen-mae stop) This is a good foreigner-friendly ryokan with a loyal following of foreign guests. It's well situated in Okazaki for exploring the Higashiyama area.

Three Sisters Inn Annex (Rakutō-so Bekkan; Map pp340-1; ☎ 761-6333; fax 761-6338; 89 Irie-chō, Okazaki, Sakyō-ku; s/d/tr ¥10,810/18,170/23,805, s/d without bathroom ¥5635/11,270; ⊠ 💻 📶; 🚌 bus 5, Dōbutsuen-mae stop) In the same neighbourhood, this is run by another one of the three eponymous sisters, and is a good choice. The features are similar to the main building, but it's somewhat more intimate and the garden walkway adds to the atmosphere.

TOP END

Hotel Heian No Mori Kyoto (Map pp340-1; ☎ 761-3130; fax 761-1333; www.heiannomori.co.jp, in Japanese; 51 Higashitennō-chō, Okazaki, Sakyō-ku; d/tw from ¥17,325/18,480; ⊠ 📶; 🚌 bus 5 to Tennōchō stop) This large, pleasant hotel is located close to Ginkaku-ji, Nanzen-ji and the Tetsugaku-no-michi (Path of Philosophy). Rooms are average size for the class and there are some on-site restaurants. The rooftop beer garden has a great view of the city in summer. Wi-fi is in the lobby.

Yachiyo Ryokan (Map pp340-1; ☎ 771-4148; fax 771-4140; www.ryokan-yachiyo.com/top/englishtop.html; 34 Fukuji-chō, Nanzen-ji, Sakyō-ku; r per person with 2 meals from ¥23,100; ⊠ 📶; 🚇 Tōzai subway line to Keage Station, exit 2) Located just down the street from Nanzen-ji temple, this large ryokan is at home with foreign guests. Rooms are spacious and clean, and some look out over private gardens. There is an excellent on-site restaurant with a choice of tatami (woven floor matting) and table seating. For convenient evening strolling, this is a good bet. Wi-fi is in the lobby.

Westin Miyako Hotel (Map pp340-1; ☎ 771-7111; fax 751-2490; www.westinmiyako-kyoto.com/english/index.html; Keage, Sanjō-dōri, Higashiyama-ku; s/d/tw from ¥26,600/33,500/33,500, Japanese-style r from ¥53,000; ⊠ 💻 📶 🏊; 🚇 Tōzai subway line to Keage Station, exit 2) This sprawling complex is perched atop the Higashiyama area, making it one of the best locations for sightseeing in Kyoto. Rooms are clean, well maintained and tastefully decorated, and the staff is at home with foreign guests. Rooms on the north side have great views over the city to the Kitayama mountains. There is a fitness centre, as well as a private garden and walking trail. Rooms have LAN cable internet and wi-fi is in the lobby.

Northwest Kyoto

BUDGET

Utano Youth Hostel (Map p343; ☎ 462-2288; http://web.kyoto-inet.or.jp/org/utano-yh/index.html; 9 Nakayama-chō, Uzumasa, Ukyō-ku; dm ¥3300; ⊠ 💻 📶; 🚌 bus 10 or 59 to Yuusu-hosteru-mae stop) This is the best youth hostel in Kyoto. Bear in mind, though, that while it is conveniently located for touring sights in northwest Kyoto, it's something of a hike to those in other areas of the city. Wi-fi is in the lobby.

MIDRANGE

Kyoto ANA Hotel (Map pp332-3; ☎ 231-1155; fax 231-5333; www.ichotelsgroup.com/h/d/6c/1/en/hd/kstna; Nijō-jō-mae, Horikawa-dōri, Nakagyō-ku; s/d/tw from ¥10,515/24,255/26,565; ⊠ 💻 🏊; 🚇 Tōzai subway line to Nijōjō-mae Station, exit 2) Directly opposite Nijō-jō on the west side of downtown, this large hotel gets plenty of foreign guests. Rooms are fairly spacious and some have good views over the castle, there are all the usual on-site facilities (pool, restaurants and bars) and rooms have LAN cable internet.

Long-Term Rentals

There is a variety of long-term rental situations in Kyoto, ranging from cramped '*gaijin* (foreigner) houses' to proper apartments and houses. The best place to look for long-term accommodation is on the message board at the Kyoto International Community House (p328). One good option in central Kyoto is the following.

Furnished Apartment (Map pp332-3; ☎ 090-8523-2053; www.kyotojp.com/furnished-apt.html; 34 Hinoshitachō, Matsubara-sagaru, Takakura-dōri, Shimogyō-ku; apt per month from ¥78,000; 🚇 Karasuma subway line to Gojō) Located in the middle of Kyoto, these apartments have everything you need for a longer stay in Kyoto, including simple kitchens, bathrooms and basic furniture. They're within walking distance of the shops and restaurants of downtown.

EATING

Kyoto is a great place to make a full exploration of Japanese cuisine and you'll find good restaurants in every budget bracket. If you tire of Japanese food, there are plenty of excellent international restaurants to choose from. You'll find the thickest concentration of eateries in downtown Kyoto, but also plenty of choice in southern Higashiyama/Gion and in and around Kyoto Station.

Because Kyoto gets a lot of foreign travellers, you'll find a surprising number of English menus, and most places are quite comfortable with foreign guests – it's rare to see waiters running for the exits at the first sign of a foreign face.

Kyoto Station Area

The new Kyoto Station building is chock-a-block with restaurants, and if you find yourself anywhere near the station around mealtime, this is probably your best bet in terms of variety and price. For a quick cuppa while waiting for a train try Café du Monde (Map p335) on the 2nd floor overlooking the central atrium.

For more substantial meals there are several food courts scattered about. The best of these can be found on the 11th floor on the west side of the building: the Cube food court and Isetan department store's Eat Paradise food court. In Eat Paradise, we like Tonkatsu Wako for *tonkatsu* (deep-fried breaded pork cutlet), Tenichi for sublime tempura, and Wakuden for approachable *kaiseki* fare. To get to these food courts, take the west escalators from the main concourse all the way up to the 11th floor and look for the Cube on your left and Eat Paradise straight in front of you.

Other options in the station include Kyoto Rāmen Koji, a collection of seven *rāmen* (egg noodle) restaurants on the 10th floor (underneath the Cube). Buy tickets for *rāmen* from the machines, which don't have English but have pictures on the buttons. In addition to *rāmen,* you can get green-tea ice cream and other Japanese desserts at Chasen, and *takoyaki* (battered octopus pieces) at Miyako.

If you're departing by train or bus from Kyoto Station and want to pick up some nibblies for the ride, head downstairs to the B1 floor Porta underground shopping arcade. Here, you can purchase excellent sushi *bentō* (boxed meals) at Kyōtaru and good bread and pastries at Shinshindō. Both are near the *kita* (north) entrance/exit of the Karasuma subway line.

Outside the station building, there are also lots of good places to eat.

Iimura (Map p335; ☎ 351-8023; 216 Maoya-chō, Shimogyō-ku (Shichijō-dōri-Higashinotōin); set lunch ¥650; 🕑 11.30am-until they run out of food) About 10 minutes' walk north of the station, this is a classic little restaurant that's popular with locals who come for its ever-changing set Japanese lunch. Just say '*kyō no ranchi*' (today's lunch) and you should be fine. It's in a traditional Japanese house, set back a bit from the street. English menu (for dinner only).

Downtown Kyoto

Downtown Kyoto has the best variety of approachable Japanese and international restaurants. In addition to the choices listed here, don't forget the restaurant floors of the major department stores, which contain many easy-to-enter restaurants of all descriptions.

BUDGET

Musashi Sushi (Map p336; ☎ 222-0634; Kawaramachi-dōri, Sanjō agaru, Nakagyō-ku; all plates ¥130; 🕑 11am-10pm) This is the place to go to try *kaiten-zushi* (conveyor-belt sushi). Sure, it's not the best sushi in the world, but it's cheap, easy and fun. Look for the mini sushi conveyor belt in the window. It's just outside the entrance to the Sanjō covered arcade.

Park Café (Map p336; ☎ 211-8954; 1F Gion Bldg, 340-1 Aneyakō-ji kado, Gokomachi-dōri, Nakagyō-ku; drinks from ¥400; 🕑 noon-midnight) This hip little cafe always reminds us of a Melbourne coffee shop. It's on the edge of the downtown shopping district and a convenient place to take a break.

Café Independants (Map p336; ☎ 255-4312; B1F 1928 Bldg, Sanjō Gokomachi kado, Nakagyō-ku; salads/sandwiches from ¥400/800; 🕑 11.30am-midnight) Located beneath a gallery, the cool subterranean cafe offers a range of light meals and good cafe drinks in a bohemian atmosphere. A lot of the food offerings are laid out on display for you to choose from – with the emphasis on healthy sandwiches and salads. Take the stairs on your left before the gallery.

A-Bar (Map p336; ☎ 213-2129; Nishikiyamachi-dōri; dishes from ¥500; 🕑 5-11pm) This student *izakaya* (pub-eatery) with a log-cabin interior is popular with expats and Japanese students for a raucous night out. The food is fairly typical *izakaya* fare, with plenty of fried items and some decent salads. It's a little tough to find – look for the small black-and-white sign at the top of a flight of steps. Last orders 10.30pm.

Kyō-Hayashi-ya (Map p336; ☎ 231-3198; 6F Takase Bldg, 105 Nakajima-chō, Kawaramachi Higashi iru, Sanjō-dōri, Nakagyō-ku; green tea ¥600; 11.30am-9.30pm) If you feel like a change from international coffee chains and want to try some good Japanese green tea and enjoy a nice view over the mountains while you're at it, this is the place. English menu.

Ootoya (Map p336; ☎ 255-4811; Sanjō-dō, Kawaramachi higashi iru, Nakagyō-ku; meals around ¥700; 10am-11pm) Ootoya is a clean, modern Japanese restaurant that serves a range of standard Japanese dishes at bargain-basement prices. It's popular with Kyoto students and young office workers. The large picture menu makes ordering a breeze. Look for the English sign just west of Ganko Sushi.

Misoka-an Kawamichi-ya (Map p336; ☎ 221-2525; Sanjō agaru, Fuyachō-dōri, Nakagyō-ku; dishes ¥700-4000; 11am-8pm, closed Thu) This is the place to head for a taste of some of Kyoto's best *soba* (buckwheat) noodles in traditional surroundings. They've been handmaking noodles here for 300 years. Try a simple bowl of *nishin soba* (*soba* topped with fish), or the more elaborate *nabe* dishes (cooked in a special cast-iron pot). Look for the *noren* (Japanese curtains) and the traditional Japanese exterior. English menu.

Yak & Yeti (Map p336; ☎ 213-7919; 403-2 Dainichi-chō, Nishikikōji sagaru, Gokomachi-dōri, Nakagyō-ku; curry lunch sets from ¥750; 11.30am-3pm & 5-10pm) This is a little Nepali place that serves reliably good curry sets for lunch and tasty à la carte dinners. English menu. Last lunch orders 2.25pm.

Biotei (Map p336; ☎ 255-0086; 2F M&I Bldg, 28 Umetada-chō, Higashinotōin Nishi iru, Sanjō-dōri, Nakagyō-ku; lunch from ¥750; 11.30am-2pm & 5-8.30pm Tue-Fri, dinner Tue, Wed, Fri, Sat, closed Sun, Mon & holidays; V) Located diagonally across from the Nakagyō post office, this is a favourite of Kyoto vegetarians. Best for lunch, it serves a daily set of Japanese vegetarian food (the occasional bit of meat is offered as an option, but you'll be asked your preference). It's up the metal spiral steps. English menu.

Karafuneya Coffee Honten (Map p336; ☎ 254-8774; Kawaramachi-dōri Sanjō sagaru, Nakagyō-ku; simple meals around ¥800; 9am-1pm) Japan is famous for its plastic food models, but this place takes them to a whole new level – it's like some futuristic dessert museum. We like the centrepiece of the display: the mother of all sundaes that goes for ¥18,000 and requires advance reservation to order. Lesser mortals can try the tasty *matcha* parfait for ¥780 or any of the cafe drinks and light meals on offer. English menu.

Shizenha Restaurant Obanzai (Map p336; ☎ 223-6623; 199 Shimomyōkaku-ji-chō, Oike agaru, Koromonotana-dōri, Nakagyō-ku; lunch/dinner ¥840/2100; 11am-2pm & 5-9pm, closed dinner Wed; V) A little out of the way but good value, Obanzai serves a good buffet-style lunch/dinner of mostly organic vegetarian food. It's northwest of the Karasuma-Oike crossing, set back from the street a bit.

Kerala (Map p336; ☎ 251-0141; 2F KUS Bldg, Sanjō agaru, Kawaramachi, Nakagyō-ku; lunch/dinner from ¥850/2500; 11.30am-2pm & 5-9pm, closed irregularly) This is where we go for reliable Indian lunch sets – great *thalis* that include two curries, good naan bread, some rice, a small salad etc. Dinners are à la carte and run closer to ¥2500 per person. It's on the 2nd floor; look for the display of food in the glass case on street level. English menu.

Honke Tagoto (Map p336; ☎ 221-3030; 12 Ishibashi-chō, Kawaramachi Nishi iru, Sanjō-dōri, Nakagyō-ku; noodle dishes from ¥840; 11am-9pm) One of Kyoto's oldest and most revered *soba* restaurants makes a good break for those who have overdosed on *rāmen*. It's in the Sanjō covered arcade and you can see inside to the tables. English menu.

Café Bibliotec HELLO! (Map pp332-3; ☎ 231-8625; 650 Seimei-chō, Yanaginobanba higashi iru, Nijō, Nakagyō-ku; food from ¥850, coffee ¥450; 11.30am-11pm, closed irregularly) Like its name suggests, books line the walls of this cool cafe located in a converted *machiya*. You can get the usual range of coffee and tea drinks here, as well as light cafe lunches. Overall, this may be our favourite cafe in Kyoto, and it's worth the walk from the centre of town. Look for the plants out front. English menu.

Katsu Kura (Map p336; ☎ 212-3581; Sanjō Higashi iru Teramachi-dōri, Nakagyō-ku; tonkatsu from ¥890; 11am-9.30pm) This restaurant in the Sanjō covered arcade is a good place to sample *tonkatsu*. It's not the best in Kyoto, but it's relatively cheap and casual. English menu. Last orders 9pm.

Kōsendō-sumi (Map p336; ☎ 241-7377; Aneyakōji Higashi iru, Sakaimachi-dōri, Nakagyō-ku; lunch from ¥900; 11.30am-3pm Mon-Sat) A good pick for a pleasant lunch while in the city centre. Kōsendō-sumi is in an old Japanese house and serves a daily set lunch of simple Japanese fare. It's near the Museum of Kyoto.

Kane-yo (Map p336; ☎ 221-0669; Rokkaku, Shinkyōgoku, Nakagyō-ku; unagi over rice from ¥950; 11.30am-9pm) This is a good place to try *unagi* (eel). You can sit downstairs with a nice view of the waterfall or upstairs on the tatami. The *kane-yo donburi* set (¥950) is great value; it's served until 3pm. Look for the barrels of live eels outside and the wooden facade. English menu.

Le Bouchon (Map pp332-3; ☎ 211-5220; 71-1 Enoki-chō, NIjō sagaru, Teramachi-dōri, Nakagyō-ku; lunch/dinner from ¥980/2500; 11.30am-2.30pm & 5.30-9.30pm, closed Thu) This reliable French place serves good lunch and dinner sets and has a pleasant, casual atmosphere. The kitchen does very good work with fish, salads and desserts. The owner speaks English and French as well as Japanese, and will make you feel right at home.

MIDRANGE & TOP END

Merry Island Café (Map p336; ☎ 213-0214; Oike agaru, Kiyamachi-dōri, Nakagyō-ku; weekend lunch from ¥1000; 2pm-midnight Tue-Fri, 11.30am-midnight Sat, Sun & holidays, closed Mon) This popular lunch/dinner restaurant strives to create the atmosphere of a tropical resort. The menu is *mukokuseki* (without nationality) and most of what is on offer is pretty tasty. It does a good risotto and occasionally has a nice piece of Japanese steak. In warm weather the front doors are opened and the place takes on the air of a sidewalk cafe. English menu.

Ganko Zushi (Map p336; ☎ 255-1128; 101 Nakajima-chō, Kawaramachi Higashi iru, Sanjō-dōri, Nakagyō-ku; lunch/dinner ¥1000/3000; 11am-11pm) Near Sanjō-ōhashi bridge, this is a good place for sushi or just about anything else. There are plenty of sets to choose from, but we recommend ordering sushi à la carte. There's a full English menu, the kitchen is fast and they are used to foreigners. Look for the large display of plastic food models in the window.

Yoshikawa (Map p336; ☎ 221-5544; Oike sagaru, Tominokōji, Nakagyō-ku; lunch ¥3000-25,000, dinner ¥8000-25,000; 11am-2pm & 5-8.30pm) This is the place to go for delectable tempura. It offers table seating, but it's much more interesting to sit and eat around the small counter and observe the chefs at work. It's near Oike-dōri in a fine traditional Japanese-style building. Reservation required for tatami room; counter and table seating unavailable on Sunday.

Mishima-tei (Map p336; ☎ 221-0003; 405 Sakurano-chō, Sanjō sagaru, Teramachi-dōri, Nakagyō-ku; sukiyaki lunch ¥8663-26,250, dinner ¥12,705-26,250, special lunch ¥3350 until 3pm; 11.30am-10pm, closed Wed) In the Sanjō covered arcade, this is an inexpensive place to sample sukiyaki: there is even a discount for foreign travellers! English menu; last orders 9pm.

Finally, you'll find a few branches of the coffee chain Doutor in the downtown area, including one set back just off Kawaramachi-dōri, between Shijō and Sanjō.

Central Kyoto

This section covers a large swath of Kyoto, and includes our options that fall in the centre of the city, but that don't fall on the Kyoto Station Area or Downtown Kyoto maps.

Didi (Map pp332-3; ☎ 791-8226; 22 Tanaka Ōkubo-chō, Sakyō-ku; meals from ¥900; 11am-10pm, to 5pm Thu, closed Wed; V) On Higashiōji-dōri, north of Mikage-dōri, you'll find this friendly little smoke-free restaurant serving tasty Indian lunch/dinner sets. There are plenty of vegetarian choices on the menu. It's easy to spot from the street. English menu.

Cocohana (Map pp332-3; ☎ 525-5587; 13-243-1 Honmachi, Higashiyama-ku; lunch ¥1000-1200; 10am-5.30pm) This place is one of a kind: a Korean cafe in a converted old Japanese house. Dishes here include *bibimbap* (a Korean rice dish) and *kimchi* (Korean pickles). A full range of coffee and tea drinks is also available. It's a woody rustic place with both table and tatami seating. This makes a great stop while exploring southeastern Kyoto (Tōfuku-ji etc). English menu.

Den Shichi (Map pp332-3; ☎ 323-0700; 4-1 Tatsumi-chō, Saiin, Ukyō-ku; sushi dinners from ¥2500; 11.30am-2pm & 5-11pm, closed Mon) A little out of the way, but well worth the trip, this is one of our favourite sushi restaurants in Kyoto. It's great for dinner, but it also serves excellent and cheap lunches. In terms of price and quality, Den Shichi is always a good bet. Look for the black-and-white sign about 100m west of Hankyū Saiin Station on Shijō-dōri.

Manzara Honten (Map pp332-3; ☎ 253-1558; 321 Sashimono-chō, Ebisugawa agaru, Kawaramachi-dōri, Nakagyō-ku; dinner courses from ¥5000; 5pm-midnight) Manzara is located in a converted *machiya*. The fare here is creative modern Japanese and the surroundings are decidedly stylish. The *omakase* (chef's recommendation) course is good value, with eight dishes for ¥5000. English menu; last order is 11.30pm.

Southern Higashiyama

BUDGET

Gion Koishi (Map p338; ☎ 531-0331; 286-2 Gion machi Kita gawa, Higashiyama-ku; tea from ¥600; 10.30am-7.30pm) This is where we go when we want to cool down on a hot summer day in Gion. The speciality here is *uji kintoki* (¥900), a mountain of shaved ice flavoured with green tea, sweetened milk and sweet beans (it tastes a lot better than it sounds, trust us). This is only available in the summer months. Look for the models of the sweets and tea out the front. English menu.

Kasagi-ya (Map p338; ☎ 561-9562; 349 Masuya chō, Kōdai-ji, Higashiyama-ku; 🕑 11am-6pm, closed Tue) At Kasagi-ya, on the Ninen-zaka slope near Kiyomizu-dera, this funky old wooden shop has atmosphere to boot and friendly staff. It's a great place for a cup of green tea and a Japanese sweet to power you through a day of sightseeing in Higashiyama. *Matcha* tea with a sweet costs ¥700. It's hard to spot; you may have to ask someone in the area to point it out. English menu; last entry 5.30pm.

Santōka (Map p338; ☎ 532-1335; 137 Daikoku-chō, Sanjō sagaru, Yamatoōji-dōri, Higashiyama-ku; rāmen from ¥790; 🕑 11am-midnight) The young chefs at this popular restaurant dish out some seriously good Hokkaidō-style *rāmen*. You'll be given a choice of three kinds of soup when you order: *shio* (salt), *shōyu* (soy sauce) and miso. It's on the east side/ground floor of the new Kyōen restaurant-shopping complex. English menu.

Machapuchare (Map p338; ☎ 525-1330; 290 Kamihoritsume-chō, Sayamachi-dōri Shōmen sagaru, Higashiyama-ku; obanzai lunch set ¥840; 🕑 11.30am-8pm, closed Tue; Ⓥ) This organic vegetarian restaurant serves a sublime vegetarian *obanzai* set (Kyoto home-style cooking). The problem is, the restaurant keeps somewhat irregular hours and the *obanzai* is not always available. Get a Japanese speaker to call and check before trekking here.

Asuka (Map p338; ☎ 751-9809; 144 Nishi-machi, Jingū-michi Nishi iru, Sanjō-dōri, Higashiyama-ku; meals from ¥850; 🕑 11am-10pm, closed Mon) With an English menu, and a staff of old Kyoto *mama-sans* at home with foreign customers, this is a great place for a cheap lunch or dinner while sightseeing in the Higashiyama area. The tempura *moriawase* (assorted tempura set) is a big pile of tempura for only ¥1000. Look for the red lantern and the pictures of the set meals. English menu.

Kagizen Yoshifusa (Map p338; ☎ 561-1818; 264 Gion machi Kita gawa, Higashiyama-ku; kuzukiri ¥900; 🕑 9.30am-6pm, closed Mon) One of Kyoto's oldest and best-known *okashi-ya* (sweet shops) sells a variety of traditional sweets and has a cosy tearoom upstairs where you can sample cold *kuzukiri* (transparent arrowroot noodles), served with a *kuro-mitsu* (sweet black sugar) dipping sauce. It's in a traditional *machiya* up a flight of stone steps. English menu. Last orders 5.45pm.

Hisago (Map p338; ☎ 561-2109; 484 Shimokawara-chō, Higashiyama-ku; 🕑 11.30am-7.30pm, closed Mon) If you need a quick meal while in the main southern Higashiyama sightseeing district, this simple noodle and rice restaurant is a good bet. It's within easy walking distance of Kiyomizu-dera and Maruyama-kōen. *Oyako-donburi* (chicken and egg over rice; ¥980) is the speciality of the house. There is no English sign; look for the traditional front and the small collection of food models on display. In the busy seasons, there's almost always a queue outside. English menu.

MIDRANGE & TOP END

Shibazaki (Map p338; ☎ 525-3600; 4-190-3 Kiyomizu, Higashiyama-ku; soba from ¥1000; 🕑 11am-9pm, closed Tue) For excellent *soba* noodles and well-presented tempura sets (among other things) in the area of Kiyomizu-dera, try this comfortable and spacious restaurant. After your meal, head upstairs to check out the sublime collection of Japanese lacquerware – it's the best we've seen anywhere. There's an English menu. Look for the low stone wall and the *noren* curtains hanging in the entryway.

Ryūmon (Map p338; ☎ 752-8181; Kita gawa, Higashiōji Nishi iru, Sanjō-dōri, Higashiyama-ku; dinner from ¥1500; 🕑 5pm-5am) The place looks like a total dive, but the food is reliable and authentic, as the crowds of Kyoto Chinese residents will attest. There's no English menu, but there is a picture menu and some of the waiters can speak English. Decor is strictly Chinese kitsch, with the exception of the deer head over the cash register – we're still trying to figure that one out.

Aunbo (Map p338; ☎ 525-2900; Shimokawara-chō, Yasaka Torii mae sagaru, Higashiyama-ku; lunch from ¥2625, lunch course ¥6615, dinner course ¥6615-11,025; 🕑 noon-2pm & 5.30-10pm, closed Wed) Aunbo serves elegant, creative Japanese cooking in traditional Japanese surroundings. Dishes include sashimi, tempura-battered offerings and creative vegetable dishes. Aunbo takes reservations in the evening. There's a small English sign and an English menu.

Ōzawa (Map p338; ☎ 561-2052; Minami gawa, Gion Shirakawa Nawate Higashi iru, Higashiyama-ku; meals from ¥3900; 🕑 5-10pm, closed Thu, lunch available on advance request) On a beautiful street in Gion, this restaurant offers good tempura in traditional Japanese surroundings. Unless you choose a private tatami room, you'll sit at the counter and watch as the chef prepares each piece of tempura. English menu. Last orders 9pm.

Northern Higashiyama

BUDGET

Hinode Udon (Map pp340-1; ☎ 751-9251; 36 Kitanobō-chō, Nanzenji, Sakyō-ku; noodle dishes from ¥400; 🕑 11am-6pm, closed Sun) Filling noodle and rice dishes are served at this pleasant little shop with an English menu. Plain udon (thick white noodles) here is only ¥400, but we recommend you spring for the *nabeyaki udon* (pot-baked udon in broth) for ¥800. This is a good spot for lunch when temple-hopping near Ginkaku-ji or Nanzen-ji. English menu.

Karako (Map pp340-1; ☎ 752-8234; 12-3 Tokusei-chō, Okazaki, Sakyō-ku; rāmen from ¥650; 🕑 11.30am-2pm & 6pm-2am, closed Tue) This is our favourite *rāmen* restaurant in Kyoto. While it's not much on atmosphere, Karako has excellent *rāmen* – the soup is thick and rich and the *chāshū* (pork slices) melt in your mouth. We recommend the *kotteri* (thick soup) *rāmen*. Look for the red lantern outside.

Zac Baran (Map pp340-1; ☎ 751-9748; 18 Sannō-chō, Shōgo-in, Sakyō-ku; dishes from ¥500; 🕑 noon-3am) Near the Kyoto Handicraft Centre, this is a good spot for a light meal or a drink. It serves a variety of spaghetti dishes, as well as a good lunch special. It's down a flight of steps.

Earth Kitchen Company (Map pp340-1; ☎ 771-1897; 9-7 Higashi Maruta-chō, Kawabata, Marutamachi, Sakyō-ku; lunch ¥700; 🕑 10.30am-6.30pm Mon-Fri, to 3.30pm Sat, closed Sun) Located on Marutamachi-dōri near the Kamo-gawa, this is a tiny spot that seats just two people but does a bustling business serving tasty takeaway lunch *bentō*. If you fancy a picnic lunch for your temple-hopping, this is the place.

Cafe Proverbs 15:17 (Map pp340-1; ☎ 707-6856; Domus Hyakumanben 3F, 28-20 Tanakamonzen-chō, Sakyō-ku; drinks/food from ¥300/700; 🕑 11am-10pm, from noon Sun, to 6pm Wed, closed Mon; Ⓥ) This is a pleasant spot for a cuppa or a light vegetarian meal. Lunch sets include green curry, sandwiches and Japanese fare. It's on the 3rd floor but there's a small sign on street level. English menu.

Goya (Map pp340-1; ☎ 752-1158; 114-6 Nishida-chō, Jōdo-ji, Sakyō-ku; 🕑 noon-5pm & 6pm-midnight, closed Wed) We love this Okinawan-style restaurant for its tasty food, stylish interior and comfortable upstairs seating. It's the perfect place for lunch while exploring northern Higashiyama and it's just a short walk from Ginkaku-ji. At lunch they serve simple things like taco rice (¥880) and *gōya champurū* (bitter melon stir-fry; ¥680), while dinners are more à la carte affairs with a wide range of *izakaya* fare, much of it with an Okinawan twist. There's an English sign and menu.

MIDRANGE

Okakita (Map pp340-1; ☎ 771-4831; 34 Minamigosho-chō, Okazaki, Sakyō-ku; 🕑 11am-8pm, closed Tue) For a civilised bowl of excellent *soba* noodles, try this elegant place in Okazaki, not far from the museum district and Heian-jingū. If you can manage to get a table (it's very popular), you'll be able to sample such dishes as tempura *soba* (¥1200). There is no English sign but there is a simple English menu; look for the traditional latticework on the front.

Yamamoto Menzou (Map pp340-1; ☎ 751-0677; 34 Minamigosho-chō, Okazaki, Sakyō-ku; 🕑 lunch 11am-2.30pm, dinner 5.30-9pm, lunch only Wed, closed Thu & 4th Wed) Right next door to Okakita, this place serves a great bowl of udon noodles (about ¥900 per bowl) with a variety of toppings. We like to pair them with a plate of *tsuchi gobō* tempura (burdock-root fries; ¥265). Like its neighbour, it's very popular, but worth the wait. The name is written in English in small letters on the sign.

Caffe' Dell'Orso (Map pp340-1; ☎ 761-7600; 36-13 Naka Adachi-chō, Yoshida, Sakyō-ku; lunch/dinner ¥1000/2500; 🕑 11.30am-10pm, closed Sun & 2nd Mon) If you find yourself in the area of Kyoto University, this casual and friendly Italian cafe is a great spot for a meal or a drink. They serve excellent pasta and homemade foccacia at a long counter or tables. English is spoken. Look for the blue awning.

Omen (Map pp340-1; ☎ 771-8994; 74 Jōdo-ji Ishibashi-cho, Sakyō-ku; noodles from ¥1050; 🕑 11am-10pm, closed Thu) This noodle shop is named after the thick, white noodles served in a hot broth with a selection of seven fresh vegetables. Just say '*omen*' and you'll be given your choice of hot or cold noodles, a bowl of soup to dip them in and a plate of vegetables (you put these into the soup along with some sesame seeds). It's a great bowl of noodles but don't stop there: the à la carte menu is also fantastic – ranging from exellent tempura to healthy vegetable dishes. It's about five minutes' walk from Ginkaku-ji in a traditional Japanese house with a lantern outside. English menu.

TOP END

Grotto (Map pp340-1; ☎ 771-0606; 114 Jōdo-ji Nishida-chō, Sakyō-ku; dinner course ¥4750; 🕑 6pm-midnight, closed Sun) This stylish little place along Imadegawa-dōri serves a killer dinner set menu that will take you through the major tastes in the Japanese gastronomy. It's a great way to spend two or three hours with someone special. Reservations are recommended. The master speaks English and there's an English menu. Last orders 10pm.

Arashiyama & Sagano Area

Komichi (Map p344; ☎ 872-5313; 23 Ōjōin-chō, Nison-in Monzen, Ukyō-ku, Saga; matcha ¥600; 🕑 10am-5pm, closed Wed) This friendly little tea house is perfectly located along the Arashiyama tourist trail. In addition to hot and cold tea/coffee drinks, they serve *uji kintoki* (sweet *matcha* over shaved ice, sweetened milk and sweet beans – sort of a Japanese Italian ice) in summer and a variety of light noodle dishes year-round. The picture menu helps with ordering. The sign is green and black on a white background.

Yoshida-ya (Map p344; ☎ 861-0213; 20-24 Tsukurimichi-chō, Saga Tenryū-ji, Ukyō-ku; lunch from ¥800; 🕑 10am-6pm, closed Wed) This quaint and friendly little *teishoku-ya* (set-meal restaurant) is the perfect place to grab a simple lunch while in Arashiyama. All the standard *teishoku* favourites are on offer, including things like *oyako-donburi* for ¥850. You can also cool off here with a refreshing *uji kintoki* (¥650). It's the first place south of the station and it's got a rustic front.

Arashiyama Yoshimura (Map p344; ☎ 863-5700; Tōgetsu-kyō kita, Ukyō-ku; soba dishes from ¥1050, set meals from ¥1575; 🕑 11am-5pm) For a tasty bowl of *soba* noodles and a million-dollar view over the Arashiyama mountains and the Tōgetsu-kyō bridge, head to this extremely popular eatery just north of the famous bridge, overlooking the Katsura-gawa. There's an English menu but no English sign; look for the big glass windows and the stone wall.

Shigetsu (Map p344; ☎ 882-9725; 68 Susukinobaba-chō, Saga Tenryū-ji, Ukyō-ku; lunch sets ¥3500, ¥5500 & ¥7500; 🕑 11am-2pm) To sample *shōjin-ryōri* (Buddhist vegetarian cuisine) try Shigetsu in the precinct of Tenryū-ji. It has beautiful garden views.

Ōhara

Seryō-jaya (Map p345; ☎ 744-2301; Ōhara Sanzenin hotori, Sakyō-ku; lunch sets from ¥2756; 🕑 11am-6pm) Just by the entry gate to Sanzen-in, Seryō-jaya serves tasty *soba* noodles and other fare. There is outdoor seating in the warmer months. Look for the food models. Enter by 4pm.

Kurama

Aburaya-shokudō (Map p345; ☎ 741-2009; 252 Honmachi, Kurama, Sakyō-ku; udon & soba from ¥550; 🕑 10am-4.30pm, closed irregularly) Just down the steps from the main gate of Kurama-dera, this classic old-style *shokudō* (all-round restaurant) reminds us of what Japan was like before it got rich. The *sansai teishoku* (¥1700) is a delightful selection of vegetables, rice and *soba* topped with grated yam.

Yōshūji (Map p345; ☎ 741-2848; 1074 Honmachi, Kurama, Sakyō-ku; meals from ¥1050; 🕑 9am-6pm, closed Tue) Yōshūji serves superb *shōjin-ryōri* in a delightful old Japanese farmhouse with an *irori* (open hearth). The house special, a sumptuous selection of vegetarian dishes served in red lacquered bowls, is called *kurama-yama shōjin zen* (¥2600). Or if you just feel like a quick bite, try the *uzu-soba* (*soba* topped with mountain vegetables; ¥1050). It's halfway up the steps leading to the main gate of Kurama-dera; look for the orange lanterns out the front. English menu.

Kibune

Visitors to Kibune from June to September should not miss the chance to cool down by dining at one of the picturesque restaurants beside the Kibune-gawa. Meals are served here on platforms (known as *kawa-doko*) suspended over the river as cool water flows just underneath. Most of the restaurants offer some kind of lunch special for around ¥3000. For a full *kaiseki* dinner spread (¥5000 to ¥10,000) have a Japanese speaker call to reserve in advance.

Kibune Club (Map p345; ☎ 741-2146; 76 Kibune-chō, Kurama, Sakyō-ku; 🕑 11.30am-6pm; coffee from ¥450) The exposed wooden beams and open, airy feel of this rustic cafe make it a great spot for a cuppa while exploring Kibune. In the winter, they sometimes crank up the wood stove, which makes the place rather cosy. It's easy to spot.

Hirobun (Map p345; ☎ 741-2147; 87 Kibune-chō, Kurama, Sakyō-ku; noodles from ¥1200, kaiseki courses from ¥8400; 🕑 11am-9pm) If you don't feel like breaking the bank on a snazzy course lunch, head for this place where you can sample *nagashi-sōmen* (¥1200), thin white noodles that flow to you in globs down a split bamboo gutter; just pluck them out and slurp away (it is served until 5pm). Look for the black-and-white sign and the lantern. Reserve for dinner.

DRINKING

Kyoto has a great variety of bars, clubs and discos, all of which are good places to meet Japanese folks. And if you happen to be in Kyoto in the summer, many hotels and department stores operate rooftop beer gardens with all-you-can-eat-and-drink deals and good views of the city. Check the *Kyoto Visitor's Guide* for details.

Bars

Ing (Map p336; ☎ 255-5087; Nishikiyamachi-dōri, Takoyakushi agaru, Nakagyō-ku; meals ¥250-700, drinks from ¥600; 🕑 6pm-2am Mon-Thu, to 5am Fri-Sun) One of our favourite spots, this little joint is the place for cheap bar snacks and drinks, good music and friendly company. It's on the 2nd floor of the Royal building.

Atlantis (Map p336; ☎ 241-1621; 161 Matsumoto-chō, Shijō agaru, Ponto-chō, Nakagyō-ku; drinks from ¥730; 🕑 6pm-2am Mon-Sat, to 1am Sun) This bar is one of the few on Ponto-chō that foreigners can walk into without a Japanese friend. It's a slick, trendy place that draws a fair smattering of Kyoto's beautiful and wannabe beautiful people. In summer you can sit outside on a platform looking over the Kamo-gawa. Drinks average ¥900 to ¥1000.

McLoughlin's Irish Bar & Restaurant (Map p336; ☎ 212-6339; 8F The Empire Bldg, Kiyamachi, Sanjō-agaru, Nakagyō-ku; 🕑 6pm-midnight, closed Tue; 💻 📶) With a fine view over the city, great beer on tap, good food and an open feeling, this bar is a nice place to spend an evening in Kyoto. It's also a good place to meet local expats and Japanese. It hosts some great music events as well. There is wi-fi internet access in case you want to do some surfing with your beer.

Gael Irish Pub (Map pp340-1; ☎ 525-0680; Nijūikken-chō, Yamatoōji-dōri agaru, Shijō, Higashiyama-ku; drinks from ¥500; 🕑 5pm-1am, later Thu-Sun) A cosy little Irish bar on the doorstep of Gion. It offers good food, excellent beer and friendly staff, as well as occasional live music. It's a great place to meet local expats and see what's going on in town. It's up a flight of steps.

KANSAI

ENTERTAINMENT

Most of Kyoto's cultural entertainment is of an occasional nature, and you'll need to check with the TIC or a magazine like *Kansai Time Out* to find out whether anything interesting coincides with your visit. Regular cultural events are generally geared towards the tourist market and tend to be expensive and, naturally, somewhat touristy.

Clubs

Metro (Map pp340-1; ☎ 752-4765; BF Ebisu Bldg., Marutamachi sagaru, Kawabata, Sakyō-ku; admission ¥500-5000, varies daily; 🕑 about 10pm-3am) This is one of the most popular and vibrant clubs in town. It holds a variety of themed events and occasional live bands or international DJ events. It's inside exit 2 of the Keihan Marutamachi Station.

World (Map p336; ☎ 213-4119; Nishikiyamachi-dōri-Shijō agaru; admission ¥2500-3000, drinks from ¥500; 🕑 about 10pm-5am, Fri, Sat & day before holiday only) World is Kyoto's biggest club and it naturally hosts some of the biggest events. It has two floors, a dance floor and lockers where you can leave your stuff while you dance the night away. Events include everything from deep soul to reggae to techno to salsa.

Geisha Dances

Annually in autumn and spring, geisha and their *maiko* apprentices from Kyoto's five geisha districts dress elaborately to perform traditional dances in praise of the seasons. The cheapest tickets cost about ¥1650 (unreserved on tatami mats), better seats cost ¥3000 to ¥3800, and spending an extra ¥500 includes participation in a quick tea ceremony. We highly recommend seeing one of these dances if you are in town when they are being held. Dates and times vary, so check with the TIC.

Gion Odori (祇園をどり; ☎ 561-0224; Higashi-yama-ku-Gion; admission/with tea ¥3500/4000; 🕑 shows 1pm & 3.30pm) Held at Gion Kaikan Theatre (Map p338) near Yasaka-jinja; 1 to 10 November.

Kamogawa Odori (鴨川をどり; ☎ 221-2025; Ponto-chō-Sanjō sagaru; normal/special seat/special seat with tea ¥2000/3800/4300; 🕑 shows 12.30pm, 2.20pm & 4.10pm) Held at Ponto-chō Kaburen-jō Theatre (Map p336), Ponto-chō; 1 to 24 May.

Kitano Odori (北野をどり; ☎ 461-0148; Imade-gawa-dōri-Nishihonmatsu nishi iru; admission/with tea ¥3800/4300; 🕑 shows 1pm & 3pm) At Kamishichiken Kaburen-jō Theatre (Map p343), east of Kitano-Tenman-gū; 15 to 25 April.

Kyō Odori (京をどり; ☎ 561-1151; Kawabata-dōri-Shijō sagaru; admission/with tea ¥3800/4300; 🕑 shows 12.30pm, 2.30pm & 4.30pm) Held at Miyagawa-chō Kaburen-jō Theatre (Map p338), east of the Kamo-gawa between Shijō-dōri and Gojō-dōri; from the first to the third Sunday in April.

HOTEL BARS

Some of the best bars in Kyoto are inside hotels. These are usually very easy to enter and you will have no communication problems. Here are our favourites:

- **Orizzonte** (Kyoto Hotel Okura; p369) This is a restaurant by day, lounge by night (usually from 7pm to 11pm). The view over Kyoto here is stunning.
- **Sekisui** (Hotel Fujita Kyoto; p368) Open from 5pm until 1am, this basement-floor bar really looks out over water falling onto stones (hence the name, which means 'stone and water').
- **Tōzan Bar** (Hyatt Regency Kyoto; p370) We love this cosy and cool underground retreat below one of Kyoto's best hotels. It's worth it to go just to marvel at the design. It's open from 5pm until midnight.

Miyako Odori (都をどり; ☎ 561-1115; Higashiyama-ku-Gion-chō South; seat reserved/nonreserved/reserved with tea ¥3800/1900/4300; shows 12.30pm, 2pm, 3.30pm & 4.50pm) At Gion Kōbu Kaburen-jō Theatre (Map p338), near Gion Corner; throughout April.

Geisha Entertainment

If you want to see geisha up close and personal, one of the best ways is at Gion Hatanaka (Map p338), which offers the **Kyoto Cuisine & Maiko Evening** (☎ 541-5315; www.kyoto-maiko.jp; Yasaka Jinja Minamimon-mae, 505 Minamigawa, Gion-machi, Higashiyama-ku; per person ¥18,000; start time 6pm, every Mon, Wed, Fri, Sat & selected dates). Here, you can enjoy elegant Kyoto *kaiseki* food while being entertained by real Kyoto *geiko* and *maiko* (geisha and apprentice geisha).

Kabuki

Minami-za Theatre (Map p338; ☎ 561-0160; Shijō-Ōhashi; performances ¥4200-12,600; irregular) In Gion, this is the oldest kabuki (stylised Japanese theatre) venue in Japan. The major event of the year is the Kao-mise Festival (1 to 26 December), which features Japan's finest kabuki actors. Other performances take place on an irregular basis. Those interested should check with the TIC. The most likely months for performances are May, June and September.

Karaoke

Jumbo Karaoke Hiroba Kawaramachi Branch (Map p336; ☎ 231-6777; 29-1 Ishibashi-chō, Sanjō dōri, Kawaramachi Nishi iru, Nakagyō-ku; per person per 30min by/after 7pm from ¥140/340; 11am-6am) If you feel like giving the vocal chords a workout with the Japanese national pastime (karaoke), then head to this popular 'karaoke box' in the Sanjō shopping arcade. They've got enough English songs to keep foreign guests entertained.

Musical Performances

Musical performances featuring the koto, *shamisen* and *shakuhachi* are held in Kyoto on an irregular basis. Traditional performances of *bugaku* (court music and dance) are often held at Kyoto shrines during festival periods. Occasionally contemporary butoh dance is also performed in Kyoto. Check with the TIC to see if any performances are scheduled to be held while you are visiting the city.

Nō

Kanze Kaikan Nō Theatre (Map pp340-1; ☎ 771-6114; Sakyō-ku-Okazaki; admission free-¥8000; 9am-5pm Tue-Sun) This is the main theatre for performances of nō. *Takigi nō* is a picturesque form of nō performed in the light of blazing fires. In Kyoto this takes place on the evenings of 1 and 2 June at Heian-jingū – tickets cost ¥2000 if you pay in advance (ask at the TIC for the location of ticket agencies) or you can pay ¥3300 at the entrance gate.

Traditional Dance, Theatre & Music

Gion Corner (Map p338; ☎ 561-1119; Gion-Hanamikōji-dōri; admission ¥2800; performances nightly at 7.40pm & 8.40pm 1 Mar-29 Nov, closed 16 Aug) The shows presented here are a sort of crash course in Japanese traditional arts. You get a chance to see snippets of the tea ceremony, koto music, ikebana, *gagaku* (court music), *kyōgen* (ancient comic plays), *Kyōmai* (Kyoto-style dance) and *bunraku* (puppet plays).

SHOPPING

The heart of Kyoto's shopping district is around the intersection of Shijō-dōri and Kawaramachi-dōri. The blocks to the north and west of here are packed with stores selling both traditional and modern goods.

Kyoto's largest department stores (Hankyū, Takashimaya, Daimaru and Fujii Daimaru) are grouped together in this area.

Some of the best shopping and people-watching can be had along Kyoto's three downtown shopping arcades: Shinkyōgoku shopping arcade, Teramachi shopping arcade and Nishiki Market (right). Teramachi and Shinkyōgoku run parallel to each other in the heart of downtown. The former has a mix of tasteful and tacky shops; the latter specialises in tacky stuff for the hoards of schoolkids who visit Kyoto every year. Nishiki branches off Shinkyōgoku to the west, about 100m north of Shijō-dōri.

Antiques

The place to look for antiques in Kyoto is Shinmonzen-dōri, in Gion (Map p338). The street is lined with great old shops, many of them specialising in one thing or another (furniture, pottery, scrolls, prints etc). You can easily spend an afternoon strolling from shop to shop here, but be warned: if something strikes your fancy you're going to have to break out the credit card – prices here are steep!

Camping & Outdoor Equipment

Kōjitsu Sansō (Map p336; ☎ 257-7050; B1 Kyoto Asahi Kaikan, 427 Ebisu-chō, Sanjō agaru, Kawaramachi-dōri, Nakagyō-ku; ⏲ 10.30am-8pm) If you plan to do some hiking or camping while in Japan, you can stock up on equipment at this excellent little shop on Kawaramachi.

Clothing

Teramachi Shōten (Map p336; ☎ 213-3131; B1 Teramachi Shōtengai Takoyakushi agaru, Nakagyō-ku; ⏲ 11am-8pm) A T-shirt with your name written in kanji, katakana or hiragana across the chest is a memorable souvenir, and this place can make them in just a few minutes. If you don't fancy your own name on the shirt, you can also get the name of your country or choose from a variety of Japanese words and slogans. Look for the T-shirts displayed outside.

Electronics & Cameras

Bic Camera (Map p335; ☎ 353-1111; 927 Higashi Shiokōji-chō, Shimogyō-ku; ⏲ 10am-9pm) This vast new electronics/camera shop is directly connected to Kyoto Station via the Nishinotōin gate; otherwise, it's accessed by leaving the north (Karasuma) gate and walking west. You will be amazed by the sheer amount of goods they have on display. Just be sure that an English operating manual is available. For computer parts, keep in mind that not all items on offer will work with English operating systems.

Food & Kitchen Utensils

Nishiki Market (Map p336), in the centre of town, is Kyoto's most fascinating food market (see p346).

If you do choose to visit, be sure to stop into the knife shop **Aritsugu** (Map p336; ☎ 221-1091; 219 Kajiya-chō, Gokōmachi nishi iru, Nishikikōji-dōri, Nakagyō-ku; ⏲ 9am-5.30pm) near the eastern end of the market. Here you can find some of the best kitchen knives available in the world, as well as a variety of other kitchenware.

For an even more impressive display of food, check the basements of any of the big department stores on Shijō-dōri (perhaps Daimaru has the largest selection). It's difficult to believe the variety of food on display, or some of the prices (check out the ¥10,000 melons or the Kōbe beef, for example).

MARKETS

If you're in town when one of the following markets is on, by all means go! Markets are the best places to find antiques and bric-a-brac at reasonable prices and are the only places in Japan where you can actually bargain for a better price.

On the 21st of each month, **Kōbō-san Market** is held at Tō-ji (Map pp332–3) to commemorate the death of Kōbō Daishi (Kūkai), who in 823 was appointed abbot of the temple.

Another major market, **Tenjin-san Market**, is held on the 25th of each month at Kitano Tenman-gū (Map p343), marking the day of the birth (and, coincidentally, the death) of the Heian-era statesman Sugawara Michizane (845–903).

If you're not in Kyoto on the 21st, there's also a regular antiques fair at Tō-ji on the first Sunday of each month. In addition, the **Antique Grand Fair** is a major event, with over 100 dealers selling a wide range of Japanese and foreign curios. It is held thrice-yearly at Pulse Plaza (Map pp330–1) in Fushimi (southern Kyoto). Ask at the TIC for more details as times vary each year.

Japanese Arts & Crafts

The paved streets of Ninnen-zaka and Sannen-zaka (close to Kiyomizu-dera), in eastern Kyoto (Map p338), are renowned for their crafts and antiques. You'll also find lots of pottery shops along Gojō-dōri, between Kawabata-dōri and Higashiōji-dōri.

North of the city hall, Teramachi-dōri, between Oike-dōri (Map p336) and Marutamachi-dōri (Map pp332–3), has a number of classic old Kyoto shops, and this area is pleasant for strolling around and window-shopping.

Kamiji Kakimoto (Map p336; ☎ 211-3481; 54 Tokiwagi-chō, Nijō agaru, Teramachi, Nakagyō-ku; 🕑 9am-6pm Mon-Sat, 10am-5pm Sun & holidays) This place sells a good selection of *washi* (Japanese paper). It's not as good as Morita Washi, but it's great for things like *washi* computer paper.

Morita Washi (Map pp332-3; ☎ 341-1419; 1F Kajioha Bldg, 298 Ōgisakaya-chō, Bukkō-ji agaru, Higashinotōin-dōri, Shimogyō-ku; 🕑 9.30am-5.30pm, to 4.30pm Sat, closed Sun & holidays) Not far from Shijo-Karasuma, it sells a fabulous variety of handmade *washi* for reasonable prices.

Rakushikan (Map p336; ☎ 221-1070; Takoyakushi-dōri Takakura nishi iru, Nakagyō-ku; 🕑 10.30am-6pm, closed Mon) This downtown Kyoto paper specialist carries an incredible variety of *washi* and other paper products in its spacious new store. You can also try your hand at making your own *washi* here (ask at the counter for details).

Kyūkyo-dō (Map p336; ☎ 231-0510; 520 Shimohonnōjimae-chō, Aneyakōji agaru, Teramachi, Nakagyō-ku; 🕑 10am-6pm Mon-Sat, closed Sun & 1-3 Jan) This old shop in the Teramachi covered arcade sells a selection of incense, *shodō* (calligraphy) goods, tea-ceremony supplies and *washi*. Prices are on the high side but the quality is good.

Ippo-dō (Map pp332-3; ☎ 211-3421; Teramachi-dōri, Nijō, Nakagyō-ku; 🕑 9am-7pm Mon-Sat, to 6pm Sun & holidays, cafe 11am-5pm) This is an old-fashioned tea shop selling all sorts of Japanese tea. You can ask to sample the tea before buying.

Kyoto Handicraft Center (Map pp340-1; ☎ 761-5080; 21 Entomi-chō, Shōgoin, Sakyō-ku; 🕑 10am-6pm, closed 1-3 Jan) Just north of the Heian-jingū, this is a huge cooperative that sells, demonstrates and exhibits crafts (wood-block prints and *yukata* are a good buy here). It's the best spot in town for buying Japanese souvenirs and is highly recommended.

Kagoshin (Map p338; ☎ 771-0209; 4 chō-me, Sanjō-Ōhashi higashi, Higashiyama-ku; 🕑 9am-6pm, closed Mon) This small shop sells a wide variety of inexpensive bamboo products like flower holders and baskets.

Onouechikuzaiten (Map p338; ☎ 751-2444; 3-39 Sanjō-dōri, Higashiyama-ku; 🕑 10am-7pm) Just a few doors from the previous, it's almost a carbon copy.

Tessai-dō (Map p338; ☎ 531-9566; Kōdai-ji Kitamonzen-dōri, Higashiyama-ku (west side on Nene-no-Michi); 🕑 10am-5pm) Just outside Kōdai-ji, this small shop deals in original wood-block prints. Prices average ¥10,000 per piece.

Iwai (Map p336; ☎ 221-0314; Shijō agaru, Shinkyōgoku, Nakagyō-ku; 🕑 10.30am-9pm Mon-Fri, 10am-9pm Sat, Sun & holidays) At the southern end of the Shinkyōgoku shopping arcade, you'll find this excellent little all-round souvenir shop, which handles all manner of inexpensive Japanalia, from paper to incense to used kimonos.

GETTING THERE & AWAY

Air

Kyoto is served by Osaka Itami airport, which principally handles domestic traffic, and the new Kansai International Airport (KIX), which principally handles international flights. There are frequent flights between Tokyo and Itami (¥22,600, 65 minutes), but unless you're very lucky with airport connections you'll probably find it as quick and more convenient to take the *shinkansen*. There are ample connections to/from both airports, though the trip to/from Kansai International Airport takes longer and costs more.

Bus

The overnight bus (JR Dream Kyoto Go) runs between Tokyo Station (Yaesu-guchi long-distance bus stop) and Kyoto Station Bus Terminal (Map p335).

The trip takes about eight hours and there are usually two departures nightly in either direction, at 10pm (Friday, Saturday, Sunday and holidays) and 11pm (daily). The fare is ¥8180/14,480 one way/return. You should be able to grab some sleep in the reclining seats. There is a similar service to/from Shinjuku Station's Shin-minami-guchi in Tokyo.

Other JR bus transport possibilities include Kanazawa (one way/return ¥4060/6600) and Hiroshima (¥5500/10,000).

Hitching

Although we never recommend it, for long-distance hitching head for the Kyoto-Minami Interchange of the Meishin Expressway (Map pp330–1), about 4km south of Kyoto Station. Take bus 19 from Kyoto Station and get off when you reach the Meishin Expressway signs. From here you can hitch east towards Tokyo or west to southern Japan.

Train

SHINKANSEN (TOKYO, OSAKA, NAGOYA & HAKATA)

Kyoto is on the Tōkaidō-San-yō *shinkansen* line, which runs between Tokyo and northern Kyūshū, with stops at places like Nagoya, Osaka, Kōbe, Himeji and Hiroshima en route. Fares and times for Hikari (the second-fastest type of *shinkansen*) between Kyoto and the following cities are as follows: Tokyo (¥13,220, two hours 43 minutes); Nagoya (¥5440, 40 minutes); Osaka (¥2730, 15 minutes); Hiroshima (¥9540, 1½ hours); and Hakata (¥15,210, three hours 22 minutes). The *shinkansen* operates to/from Kyoto Station (Kyoto's main train station). On the Tokyo end, it operates from Tokyo, Shinagawa and Shin-Yokohama Stations.

NARA

The private Kintetsu line (sometimes written in English as the Kinki Nippon railway) links Kyoto (Kintetsu Kyoto Station, on the south side of the main Kyoto Station building) and Nara (Kintetsu Nara Station). There are fast direct *tokkyū* (¥1110, 33 minutes) and ordinary express trains (¥610, 40 minutes), which may require a change at Saidai-ji.

The JR Nara line also connects Kyoto Station with JR Nara Station (express, ¥690, 41 minutes), and this is a great option for Japan Rail Pass holders.

OSAKA

The fastest train other than the *shinkansen* between Kyoto Station and Osaka is the JR *shinkaisoku* (special rapid train), which takes 29 minutes (¥540). In Osaka, the train stops at both Shin-Osaka and Osaka Stations.

There is also the cheaper private Hankyū line, which runs between Hankyū Kawaramachi, Karasuma and Ōmiya Stations in Kyoto and Hankyū Umeda Station in Osaka (*tokkyū* or limited express Umeda–Kawaramachi, ¥390, 40 minutes). These trains are usually more comfortable than the JR trains, and if you board at Kawaramachi or Umeda, you can usually get a seat.

Alternatively, you can take the Keihan main line between Demachiyanagi, Sanjō, Shijō or Shichijō Stations in Kyoto and Keihan Yodoyabashi Station in Osaka (*tokkyū* to/from Sanjō ¥400, 51 minutes). Yodoyabashi is on the Midō-suji subway line. Again, these are more comfortable than JR trains and you can usually get a seat if you board in Demachiyanagi or Yodoyabashi.

TOKYO

The *shinkansen* line has the fastest and most frequent rail links. The journey can also be undertaken by a series of regular JR express trains, but keep in mind that it takes around eight hours and involves at least two (often three or four) changes along the way. The fare is ¥7980. Get the staff at the ticket counter to write down the exact details of each transfer for you when you buy your ticket.

GETTING AROUND

To/From the Airport

OSAKA ITAMI AIRPORT 大阪伊丹空港

There are frequent limousine buses between Osaka Itami airport (Map p325) and Kyoto Station (the Kyoto Station airport bus stop is opposite the south side of the station, in front of Avanti department store). Buses also run between the airport and various hotels around town, but on a less regular basis (check with your hotel). The journey should take around 55 minutes and the cost is ¥1280. Be sure to allow extra time in case of traffic.

At Itami, the stand for these buses is outside the arrivals hall; buy your tickets from the machines and ask one of the attendants which stand is for Kyoto (hint: you've got a better chance of getting a seat if you board at the South Terminal).

MK Taxi Sky Gate Shuttle limousine van service (☎ 778-5489) also offers limousine van service to/from the airport for ¥2300. Call at least two days in advance to reserve, or ask at the information counter in the arrivals hall on arrival in Osaka.

KANSAI INTERNATIONAL AIRPORT (KIX) 関西国際空港

The fastest, most convenient way to travel between KIX (Map p325) and Kyoto is on the special Haruka airport express, which makes the trip in about 78 minutes. Most seats are reserved (¥3290) but there are usually two cars on each train with unreserved seats (¥2980). Open seats are almost always available, so you don't have to purchase tickets in advance. First and last departures from Kyoto to KIX are

5.46am and 8.15pm; first and last departures from KIX to Kyoto are 6.34am and 10.18pm.

If you have time to spare, you can save some money by taking the *kankū kaisoku* (Kansai airport express) between the airport and Osaka Station and taking a regular *shinkaisoku* to/from Kyoto. The total journey by this method takes about 92 minutes with good connections and costs ¥1830, making it the cheapest option.

It's also possible to travel by limousine bus between Kyoto and KIX (¥2300, about 105 minutes). In Kyoto, the bus departs from the same place as the Itami-bound bus (see opposite).

A final option is the **MK Taxi Sky Gate Shuttle limousine van service** (☎ 778-5489), which will pick you up anywhere in Kyoto city and deliver you to KIX for ¥3500. Call at least two days in advance to reserve. The advantage of this method is that you are delivered from door to door and you don't have to lug your baggage through the train station. MK has a counter in the arrivals hall of KIX, and if there's room they'll put you on the next van to Kyoto. A similar service is offered by **Yasaka Taxi** (☎ 803-4800).

Bicycle

Kyoto is a great city to explore on a bicycle; with the exception of outlying areas it's mostly flat and there is a bike path running the length of the Kamo-gawa.

Unfortunately, Kyoto must rank near the top in having the world's worst public facilities for bike parking and the city regularly impounds bikes parked outside of regulation bike-parking areas. If your bike does disappear, check for a poster in the vicinity (in both Japanese and English) indicating the time of seizure and the inconvenient place you'll have to go to pay a ¥2000 fine and retrieve your bike.

There are two bicycle-parking lots in town that are convenient for tourists: one in front of Kyoto Station and another on Kiyamachi-dōri, halfway between Sanjō-dōri and Shijō-dōri (Map p336). It costs ¥150 per day to park your bicycle here. Be sure to hang onto the ticket you pick up as you enter.

BICYCLE PURCHASE

If you plan on spending more than a week or so exploring Kyoto by bicycle, it might make sense to purchase a used bicycle. A simple *mama chari* (shopping bike) can be had for as little as ¥3000. Try the used-cycle shop **Ei Rin** (Map pp340-1; ☎ 752-0292; 28-4 Sekiden-chō, Tanaka, Sakyō-ku (on Imadegawa-dōri); 🕑 9.30am-7.30pm) near Kyoto University. Otherwise, you'll find a good selection of used bikes advertised for sale on the message board of the Kyoto International Community House (see p127).

BICYCLE RENTAL

A great place to rent a bike is **Kyoto Cycling Tour Project** (KCTP; Map p335; ☎ 354-3636; www.kctp.net/en/index.html; 🕑 9am-7pm). These folk rent bikes (¥1000 per day) that are perfect for getting around the city. KCTP also conducts a variety of excellent bicycle tours of Kyoto with English-speaking guides. These are a great way to see the city (check the website for details).

Most rental outfits require you to leave ID such as a passport or driver's licence.

Bus

Kyoto has an extensive network of bus routes providing an efficient way of getting around at moderate cost. Many of the routes used by visitors have announcements in English. The core timetable for buses is between 7am and 9pm, though a few run earlier or later.

The main bus terminals are Kyoto Station on the JR and Kintetsu lines, Sanjō Station on the Keihan line/Tōzai subway line, Karasuma-Shijō Station on the Hankyū line/Karasuma subway line, and Kitaōji Station on the Karasuma subway line. The bus terminal at Kyoto Station is on the north side and has three main departure bays (departure points are indicated by the letter of the bay and number of the stop within that bay).

The TIC (p328) stocks the *Bus Navi: Kyoto City Bus Sightseeing Map*, which is a good map of the city's main bus lines. This map is not exhaustive. If you can read a little Japanese, pick up a copy of the regular (and more detailed) Japanese bus map available at major bus terminals throughout the city.

Bus stops usually display a map of destinations from that stop on the top section. On the bottom section there's a timetable for the buses serving that stop. Unfortunately, all of this information is in Japanese, and nonspeakers will simply have to ask locals for help.

Entry to the bus is usually through the back door and exit is via the front door. Inner-city buses charge a flat fare (¥220), which you drop into the clear plastic receptacle on top of the machine next to the driver on your way out. A separate machine gives change for ¥100 and ¥500 coins or ¥1000 notes.

KYOTO BUS/SUBWAY PASSES

To save time and money, you can buy a *kaisū-ken* (book of five tickets) for ¥1000. There's also a one-day card *(shi-basu senyō ichinichi jōshaken cādo)* valid for unlimited travel on city buses, which costs ¥500. A similar pass *(Kyoto kankō ichinichi jōsha-ken)* that allows unlimited use of the bus and subway costs ¥1200. A two-day bus/subway pass *(Kyoto kankō futsuka jōsha-ken)* costs ¥2000. *Kaisū-ken* can be purchased directly from bus drivers. The other passes and cards can be purchased at major bus terminals and at the bus information centre (Map p335).

On buses serving the outer areas, you take a numbered ticket *(seiri-ken)* when entering. When you leave, an electronic board above the driver displays the fare corresponding to your ticket number (drop the *seiri-ken* into the ticket box with your fare).

The main bus information centre (Map p335) is located in front of Kyoto Station. Here you can pick up bus maps, purchase bus tickets and passes (on all lines, including highway buses), and get additional information. Nearby, there's a convenient English/Japanese bus-information computer terminal; just enter your intended destination and it will tell you the correct bus and bus stop.

Three-digit numbers written against a red background denote loop lines: bus 204 runs around the northern part of the city and buses 205 and 206 circle the city via Kyoto Station. Buses with route numbers on a blue background take other routes.

When heading for locations outside the city centre, be careful which bus you board. Kyoto city buses are green, Kyoto buses are tan and Keihan buses are red and white.

Scooter

Scooters are a good way to get around the city. Just be sure you have a valid international licence. **Kyoto Rental Scooters** (☎ 864-1635; http://kyotorentalscooter.com/e.htm) rents 50cc scooters for ¥4000/14,000 per day/week.

Subway

Kyoto has two efficient subway lines, which operate from 5.30am to 11.30pm. The minimum fare is ¥210 (children ¥110).

The quickest way to travel between the north and south of the city is the Karasuma subway line. The line has 15 stops and runs from Takeda in the far south, via Kyoto Station, to the Kyoto International Conference Hall (Kokusaikaikan Station) in the north.

The east–west Tōzai subway line traverses Kyoto from Uzumasa-Tenjingawa in the west, meeting the Karasuma subway line at Karasuma-Oike Station, and continuing east to Sanjō Keihan, Yamashina and Rokujizō, in the east and southeast.

Taxi

Kyoto taxi fares start at ¥640 for the first 2km. The exception is **MK Taxis** (☎ 778-4141), whose fares start at ¥580.

MK Taxis also provides tours of the city with English-speaking drivers. For a group of up to four, prices start at ¥21,800 for a three-hour tour. Another company offering a similar service is **Kyōren Taxi Service** (☎ 672-5111).

Most Kyoto taxis are equipped with satellite navigation systems. If you are going somewhere unusual, it will help the driver if you have the address or phone number of your destination, as both of these can be programmed into the system.

SHIGA-KEN 滋賀県

Just across the Higashiyama mountains from Kyoto is Shiga-ken, a small prefecture dominated by Biwa-ko, Japan's largest lake. The prefecture has a variety of attractions that are easily visited as day trips from Kyoto. The major attractions here are the towns of Nagahama, with its Kurokabe Square neighbourhood of glass artisans, and Hikone, with its fine original castle. Other worthwhile destinations include temples like Mii-dera and Ishiyama-dera, and the Miho Museum, which is worth a trip just to see the building and the compound in which it is located.

ŌTSU 大津

☎ 077 / pop 333,800

Ōtsu has developed from a 7th-century imperial residence (the city was capital of Japan for just five years) into a lake port and major post station on the Tōkaidō highway between eastern and western Japan. It is now the capital of Shiga-ken.

The **information office** (☎ 522-3830; ⏲ 8.40am-5.25pm) is at JR Ōtsu Station.

Mii-dera 三井寺

Mii-dera (☎ 522-2238; 246 Onjōji-chō; admission ¥500; 8am-5pm) is a short walk northwest from Keihan Hama-Ōtsu Station. The temple, founded in the late 7th century, is the head branch of the Jimon branch of Tendai Buddhism. It started its days as a branch of Enryaku-ji on Hiei-zan, but later the two fell into conflict, and Mii-dera was repeatedly razed by Enryaku-ji's warrior monks. The Niō-mon gate here is unusual for its roof, made of layers of tree bark, rather than tiles. It looks particularly fine when framed by the cherry trees in early April. Last entry 4.30pm.

Festivals & Events

Ōtsu Dai Hanabi Taikai (Ōtsu Grand Fireworks Festival) If you're in town on 8 August, be sure to catch this. Starting at dusk, the best spots to watch are along the waterfront near Keihan Hama-Ōtsu Station. Be warned that trains to and from Kyoto are packed for hours before and after the event.

Ōtsu Matsuri Takes place in early–mid-October at Tenson-jinja, close to JR Ōtsu Station. Ornate floats are displayed on the first day and paraded around the town on the second day.

Getting There & Away

From Kyoto, take the JR Tōkaidō line from JR Kyoto Station to JR Ōtsu Station (¥190, nine minutes), or travel on the Kyoto Tōzai subway line to Hama-Ōtsu Station (¥410, 21 minutes from Sanjō Keihan Station).

ISHIYAMA-DERA 石山寺

This Shingon-sect **temple** (☎ 077-537-0013; 1-1-1 Ishiyama-dera; admission ¥500; 8am-4.30pm) was founded in the 8th century. The room beside the *hondō* is famed as the place where Lady Murasaki wrote *The Tale of Genji*. The temple precincts are in a lovely forest with lots of good trails to explore, including the one that leads up to Tsukimitei hall, from which there are great views over Biwa-ko.

The temple is a 10-minute walk from Keihan Ishiyama-dera Station (continue along the road in the direction that the train was travelling). Take the Kyoto Tōzai line subway from Sanjō Keihan Station in Kyoto to Keihan Hama-Ōtsu and change there to a Keihan-line Ishiyama-dera-bound *futsū* (¥540, 33 minutes). Alternatively, take the JR Tōkaidō line from JR Kyoto Station to JR Ishiyama-dera Station (*kaisoku* or *futsū* trains only, ¥230, 13 minutes) and switch to the Keihan line for the short journey to Keihan Ishiyama-dera Station (¥160).

MIHO MUSEUM

This **museum** (☎ 0748-82-3411; www.miho.or.jp; 300, Momodani, Shigaraki; adult/child ¥1000/300; 10am-5pm, closed Mon mid-Mar–mid-Jun, mid-Jul–mid-Aug & Sep–mid-Dec) is visually stunning, located in the countryside of Shiga-ken near the village of Shigaraki. The IM Pei–designed museum houses the Shumei Family art collection, which includes examples of Japanese, Middle Eastern, Chinese and south Asian art.

A visit to the museum is something like a visit to the secret hideout of an archvillain in a James Bond film, and there is no doubt that the facility is at least as impressive as the collection. Since a trip to the museum from Kyoto or Osaka can take the better part of a day, we highly recommend calling the museum to check what's on before making the trip. Last entry 4pm.

To get there, take the JR Tōkaidō line from Kyoto or Osaka to Ishiyama Station, and change to a **Teisan Bus** (Tanakami Eigyōsho; ☎ 562-3020; www.teisan-bus.co.jp/index.php, in Japanese) bound for the museum (¥800, approximately 50 minutes).

HIKONE 彦根

☎ 0749 / pop 111,800

Hikone is the second-largest city in the prefecture and of special interest to visitors for its lovely castle, which dominates the town. The adjoining garden is also a classic and is a must-see after your visit to the castle.

Orientation & Information

There is a good **tourist information office** (☎ 22-2954; 9am-5pm), which is on your left at the bottom of the steps as you exit the west exit of Hikone Station. It stocks the excellent *Street Map & Guide to Hikone*.

The castle is a 10-minute walk straight up the street from the station (take a left before the shrine, then a quick right).

Hikone-jō 彦根城

This **castle** (☎ 22-2742; 1-1 Konki-chō; admission ¥500; 8.30am-5pm) was completed in 1622 by the Ii family, who ruled as *daimyō* (domain lords) over Hikone. It is rightly considered one of the finest castles in Japan. Much of it is original, and you can get a great view across the lake from the upper storeys. Surrounded by more than 1000 cherry trees, the castle is a very popular spot for springtime *hanami* activities.

After visiting the castle, don't miss nearby **Genkyū-en** (admission incl in castle ticket; 8.30am-5pm), a lovely Chinese-influenced garden

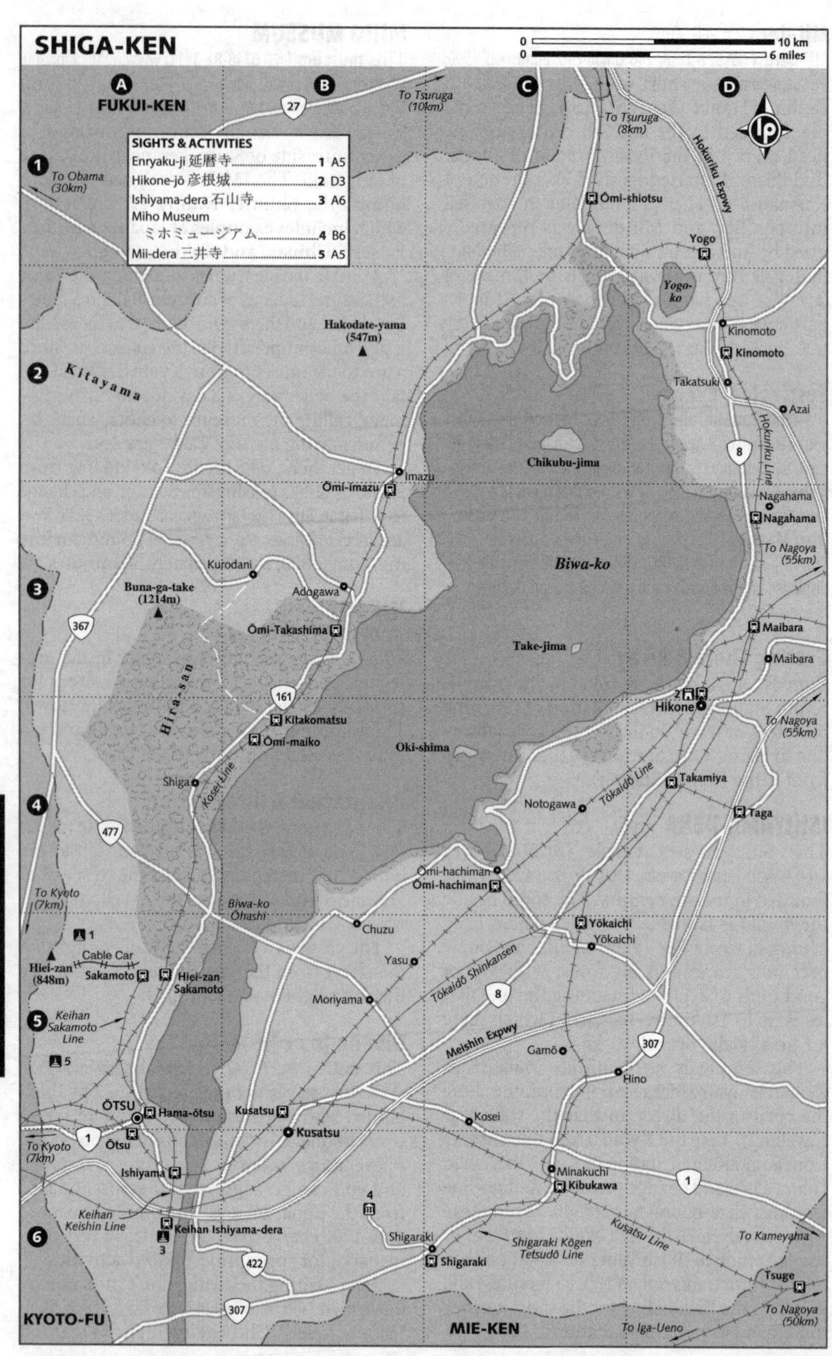
SHIGA-KEN
0 10 km
0 6 miles
SIGHTS & ACTIVITIES
Enryaku-ji 延暦寺 1 A5
Hikone-jō 彦根城 2 D3
Ishiyama-dera 石山寺 3 A6
Miho Museum ミホミュージアム 4 B6
Mii-dera 三井寺 5 A5
FUKUI-KEN
To Tsuruga (10km)
To Tsuruga (8km)
To Obama (30km)
Hokuriku Expwy
Ōmi-shiotsu
Yogo
Yogo-ko
Kinomoto
Takatsuki
Azai
Hokuriku Line
Hakodate-yama (547m)
Kitayama
Chikubu-jima
Imazu
Ōmi-imazu
Nagahama
To Nagoya (55km)
Kurodani
Adogawa
Biwa-ko
Buna-ga-take (1214m)
Ōmi-Takashima
Maibara
Take-jima
Hira-san
Hikone
Kitakomatsu
Ōmi-maiko
Oki-shima
Kosei Line
Shiga
Tōkaidō Line
Takamiya
Notogawa
Taga
Ōmi-hachiman
To Kyoto (7km)
Biwa-ko Ōhashi
Chuzu
Yōkaichi
Cable Car
Hiei-zan (848m)
Sakamoto
Hiei-zan Sakamoto
Yasu
Tōkaidō Shinkansen
Moriyama
Keihan Sakamoto Line
Meishin Expwy
Gamō
Hino
ŌTSU
Hama-ōtsu
Kusatsu
Kosei
Ōtsu
Ishiyama
Minakuchi
Kibukawa
Keihan Keishin Line
Keihan Ishiyama-dera
Shigaraki
Shigaraki Kōgen Tetsudō Line
Kusatsu Line
To Kameyama
Tsuge
To Nagoya (50km)
KYOTO-FU
MIE-KEN
To Iga-Ueno
KANSAI

that was completed in 1677. Ask someone at the castle to point you in the right direction. There's a tea house in the garden where ¥500 gets you a cup of *matcha* and a sweet to enjoy as you gaze over the scenery.

Yumekyō-bashi Castle Road 夢京橋キャッスルロード

About 400m southwest of the castle (marked on the *Street Map & Guide to Hikone* map and accessible via the Omote-mon gate or the Ōte-mon gate of the castle), this street of traditional shops and restaurants is the ideal spot for lunch after exploring the castle, and a browse in the shops is a nice way to round out the day.

Our favourite spot for a bite here is **Monzen-ya** (もんぜんや; ☎ 24-2297; soba around ¥800; 🕒 11am-7pm, closed Tue), a great little *soba* place that serves such things as *nishin-soba* (*soba* noodles with herring; ¥880). Starting from the castle end of the street, it's about 100m on the left – look for the white *noren* curtain with black lettering in the doorway.

Festivals & Events

The **Birdman Contest**, held in summer (dates differ every year) at Matsubara Beach in Hikone, is a fantastic celebration of the human desire to fly – ideally without the use of fossil fuels. Here you will find contestants launching themselves over Biwa-ko in all manner of flimsy human-powered flying machines.

Getting There & Away

Hikone is about an hour (*shinkaisoku*, ¥1110) from Kyoto on the JR Tōkaidō line. If you have a JR Rail Pass or are in a hurry, you can take the *shinkansen* to Maibara (¥3100, 18 minutes from Kyoto) and then backtrack from there on the JR Tōkaidō line to Hikone (¥180, five minutes).

NAGAHAMA 長浜

☎ 0749 / pop 85,350

Nagahama is a surprisingly appealing little town on the northeast shore of Biwa-ko, which can easily be teamed up with a trip to Hikone. The main attraction here is the **Kurokabe Square** neighbourhood northeast of the station.

If you're in the area from 14 to 16 April, check out the **Nagahama Hikiyama Matsuri**, in which costumed children perform Hikiyama *kyōgen* on top of a dozen festival floats decked out with elaborate ornamentation.

Kurokabe Square 黒壁スクエア

Many of the old *machiya* and *kura* (storehouses) in this attractive old neighbourhood have been converted into shops and galleries highlighting the town's traditional (and modern) glass industry. Exit the east side of Nagahama Station and take the first left after Shiga Bank; after about 50m on your right (at the corner), you will find the **Kurokabe Information Centre** (黒壁インフォメーションセンター; ☎ 65-8055; 🕒 10am-6pm, to 5pm Nov-Mar), which has maps of the area.

We like the small collection of glass *objets* at the **Kurokabe Museum of Glass Art** (黒壁美術館; ☎ 62-6364; admission ¥600; 🕒 10am-5pm). While you're there, ask them to demonstrate the *suikinkutsu*, a strange 'musical instrument' formed from an overturned urn into which water is dripped. It's about 50m north of the information centre, on the opposite side of the street. Last entry 4.30pm.

Our hands-down favourite attraction in Kurokabe Square is the **Giant Kaleidoscope** (巨大万華鏡; kyodaimangekyō; admission free; 🕒 dawn-dusk), which is located off a shopping arcade north of the Kurokabe Museum of Glass Art. From the museum, walk north to the next street and take a right. About 30m after entering the arcade, you will see a sign reading 'Antique Gallery London'. It's in an open area behind this shop.

Not far from the Giant Kaleidoscope is **Daitsū-ji** (大通寺; ☎ 62-0054; admission to garden/grounds ¥500/free; 🕒 9am-4.30pm, closed year-end/new-year holidays), a Jodo-Shin-sect temple that's worth a quick look (we don't recommend paying to enter the garden, though).

Eating

Torikita (鳥善多; ☎ 62-1964; dishes from ¥470; 🕒 11.30am-2pm & 4.30-7pm, closed Tue) This place specialises in one dish: *oyako-donburi* (chicken and egg over a bowl of rice; ¥580). If you don't like raw egg, ask for *oyako-donburi nama tamago nashi de*. It's 200m down the main street east of the station, opposite Shiga Bank; look for the traditional front and white *noren* curtain in the doorway.

Getting There & Away

Nagahama is on the JR Tōkaidō line (*shinkaisoku*, ¥1280, 62 minutes from Kyoto). Be aware that not all *shinkaisoku* from Kyoto go all the way to Nagahama; you may have to change in Maibara, which is a 10-minute ride south of Nagahama by *shinkaisoku* (¥190). If you've got a JR Rail Pass, you can take the *shinkansen* to Maibara (¥3100, 18 minutes from Kyoto) and then switch to a local JR train for the short trip to Nagahama.

NORTHERN KANSAI 関西北部

The spectacular coastline of northern Kansai is known for its sandy beaches, rugged headlands, rocky islets and laid-back atmosphere. The JR San-in line runs the length of the area, but it spends a fair bit of time inland and in tunnels. The best way to see the coastline is on wheels, whether it be a rental car, a motorbike, a bicycle or by thumb.

MOROYOSE 諸寄

Moroyose, in Hyōgo-ken, near the border with Tottori-ken, is a pleasant little seaside town with a decent sand beach. **Youth Hostel Moroyose-sō** (諸寄荘ユースホステル; ☎ 0796-82-3614; 461 Moroyose; r without meals per person ¥3225) is a good spot to stay for backpackers, with fairly large rooms for a YH and breakfast/dinner for ¥525/945. It's a 10-minute climb uphill from the eastern end of the beach. Moroyose is on the JR San-in line; the station is in the centre of town, very close to the beach.

TAKENO 竹野

Takeno is a pleasant little fishing village and summer resort with two good sandy beaches: **Benten-hama** (弁天浜) to the west and **Takeno-hama** (竹野浜) to the east. To get to Benten-hama, exit Takeno Station and turn left at the first light and walk straight for about 15 minutes (you will cross one big street en route). To get to Takeno-hama, go straight out of the station and walk for around 20 minutes. There is an **information office** (☎ 0796-47-1080; 🕑 8.30am-5pm) on the beachfront at Takeno-hama in an orange brick building. This office can help with accommodation in local *minshuku* (B&B-style accommodation) and ryokan.

Bentenhama camping area (弁天浜キャンプ場; ☎ 0796-47-0888; camp sites per adult/child ¥1000/500; 🕑 Jul & August only) is on the seafront at Benten-hama. It's a decent, if crowded, spot to pitch a tent. **Kitamaekan** (北前館; ☎ 0796-47-2020; onsen adult/child ¥400/250; 🕑 11am-10pm) is an onsen complex where the baths are on the 2nd floor with a great view of the beach and sea. It's at Takeno-hama, in a large grey building about 150m west of the information office.

Takeno Station is on the JR San-in line, an easy trip from Kinosaki (¥190, nine minutes). The train trip is a good chance to enjoy some of the coastal scenery.

KINOSAKI 城崎

☎ 0796 / pop 4140

Kinosaki is one of the best places in Japan to sample the classic Japanese onsen experience. A willow-lined canal runs through the centre of this town and many of the houses, shops and restaurants retain something of their traditional charm. Add to this the delights of crab fresh from the Sea of Japan in winter, and you'll understand why this is one of our favourite overnight trips from the cities of Kansai.

Information

Opposite the station is an **accommodation information office** (お宿案内所; ☎ 32-4141; 🕑 9am-6pm) where the staff will gladly help you find a place to stay and make bookings, as well as provide maps to the town. The same office has rental bicycles available for ¥400/800 per two hours/day (return by 5pm).

Sights & Activities

Kinosaki's biggest attraction is its seven **onsen.** Guests staying in town stroll the canal from bath to bath wearing *yukata* and *geta* (wooden sandals). Most of the ryokan and hotels in town have their own *uchi-yu* (private baths), but also provide their guests with free tickets to the ones outside *(soto-yu)*.

Here is the full list of Kinosaki's onsen, in order of preference (get a map from the information office or your lodgings):

Sato-no-yu (さとの湯; admission ¥800; 🕑 7am-11pm, closed 2nd & 4th Thu) Fantastic variety of baths, including Arab-themed saunas, rooftop *rotemburo* (outdoor bath) and a 'Penguin Sauna' (basically a walk-in freezer – the only one we've seen anywhere – good after a hot bath). Women's and men's baths shift floors daily, so you'll have to go two days in a row to sample all of the offerings.

Gosho-no-yu (御所の湯; admission ¥800; 🕑 7am-11pm, closed irregularly) Lovely log construction, a nice two-level *rotemburo* and fine maple colours in autumn.

KANSAI

The entry area is decorated like the Kyoto Gosho (Imperial Palace).

Kou-no-yu (鴻の湯; admission ¥600; 7am-11pm, closed irregularly) Nothing fancy, but a good *rotemburo* and pleasant inside baths.

Ichi-no-yu (一の湯; admission ¥600; 7am-11pm, closed irregularly) Wonderful 'cave' bath.

Yanagi-yu (柳湯; admission ¥600; 3-11pm, closed irregularly) Worth a quick soak as you make your way around town. Nice wooden construction.

Mandara-yu (まんだら湯; admission ¥600; 3-11pm, closed irregularly) Small wooden *rotemburo*.

Jizo-yu (地蔵湯; admission ¥600; 7am-11pm, closed irregularly) Spacious main inside tub but no *rotemburo*. Good if others are crowded.

In addition to the town's great onsen, visitors might want to have a peek at the **Kinosaki Mugiwarazaikudenshokan** (城崎麦わら細工伝承館; admission ¥300; 9am-5pm, closed last Wed of every month), which has displays on one of the local handicrafts known as *mugiwarazaiku*, a decorative technique that employs barley straw cut into tiny pieces and applied to wood to form incredibly beautiful patterns. It's located off the canal, a short walk north of Mandara-yu onsen.

Sleeping

Mikuniya (三国屋; 32-2414; www.kinosaki3928.com, in Japanese; r per person with 2 meals from ¥18,900;) About 150m on the right on the street heading into town from the station, this ryokan is a good choice. The rooms are clean, with nice Japanese decorations, and the onsen bath is soothing. There is an English sign.

Suishōen (水翔苑; 32-4571; www.suisyou.com, in Japanese; r per person with 2 meals from ¥21,675, r per person without meals Sun-Fri ¥7875, r per person without meals Sat ¥9450;) This excellent modern ryokan is a short drive from the town centre, but they'll whisk you straight to the onsen of your choice in their own London taxi and pick you up when you're done. It's a strangely pleasant feeling to ride in the back wearing nothing but a *yukata*! The rooms are clean and well kept and the private onsen is great, with indoor and outdoor baths. Taking the price into consideration, it's great value.

Nishimuraya Honkan (西村屋本館; 32-2211; honkan@nishimuraya.ne.jp; r per person with 2 meals from ¥37,950;) This is a classic and the ultimate of inns here. If you would like to try the high-class ryokan experience, this is a good place. The two onsen baths here are exquisite and most of the rooms look out over private gardens. The excellent food is the final touch. There is LAN cable internet access.

Eating

Crab from the Sea of Japan is a speciality in Kinosaki during the winter months. It's called *kani* and the way to enjoy it is in *kani-suki,* cooked in broth with vegetables right at your table.

Daikō Shōten (大幸商店; 32-3684; 10am-9pm, to 11pm in summer, closed irregularly) This seafood shop/*izakaya* is a great place to try freshly caught local seafood in a casual atmosphere. From November until mid-April (the busy tourist season for Kinosaki), the restaurant section is upstairs, while the downstairs is given over to selling vast quantities of crabs and other delights. For the rest of the year, the restaurant is on the ground floor. *Teishoku* (set meals) are available from ¥1380, but you'll never go wrong by just asking for the master's *osusume* (recommendations). It's diagonally across from Mikuniya (left).

Heihachirō (32-0086; 11.30am-2pm & 6-11pm, closed Wed) This is a great place to try *kani-suki* (¥4500) in winter. It also serves the usual *izakaya* fare, along with beer and sake. It's a little past Gosho-no-yu, on the opposite side of the street; look for a stone wall and a small English sign that reads 'Dining Bar Heihachiro'.

Oritsuru (32-2203; sushi dinner average ¥3000; lunch & dinner, closed Tue) For decent sushi and crab dishes, try this popular local sushi restaurant on the main street. You can get a *jō-nigiri* (superior sushi set; ¥3700) or try their crab dishes in the winter. It's between Ichi-no-yu and Gosho-no-yu, on the opposite side of the street. There is a small English sign about the door.

For simpler meals, try Yamayoshi (山よし), a simple *shokudō* outside the station on the 2nd floor (look for the pictures and food models out the front). It serves the usual set meals as well as some local specialities like crab.

Note that most restaurants in Kinosaki shut down very early. This is because most people opt for the two-meal option at their accommodation. You should consider doing the same.

Getting There & Away

Kinosaki is on the JR San-in line and there are a few daily *tokkyū* from Kyoto (¥4510, two hours 22 minutes) and Osaka (¥5250, two hours 42 minutes).

TANGO-HANTŌ 丹後半島

Tango-hantō is a peninsula that juts up into the Sea of Japan on the north coast of Kansai. The inside of the peninsula is covered with thick forest, idyllic mountain villages and babbling streams, while the serrated coast alternates between good sand beaches and rocky points.

The private Kita-kinki Tango Tetsudō rail line runs between Toyooka and Nishi-Maizuru, cutting across the southern base of the peninsula and stopping en route at Amanohashidate (below). Thus, if you want to check out the rest of the peninsula you'll have to go by road. A bus runs around the peninsula, passing a small number of scenic fishing ports (Tango Ōkoku Romance gō; Tankai Bus ☎ 0772-42-0321; from ¥4400). A large car park and restaurant mark the start of the 40-minute round-trip walk (about 3km) to the **Kyōga-misaki Lighthouse** (経ヶ岬灯台).

The village of **Ine** (伊根), on a perfect little bay on the eastern side of the Tango-hantō, is particularly interesting. There are *funaya* houses that are built right out over the water, under which boats are drawn in, as if in a carport. The best way to check it out is by boat, and **Ine-wan Meguri** (☎ 0772-42-0321) tour boats putter around the bay (¥660, 30 minutes) from March to December. Buses (¥910) reach Ine in half an hour from Amanohashidate.

Sleeping

One of the best ways to see Tango-hantō is with **Two to Tango** (www.thedivyam.com; lodging & 2½-day all-inclusive tour per person ¥100,000), an exclusive tour of the Tango peninsula offered by a French resident of Kyoto-fu. Guests stay in a secluded farmhouse in Kurumi-dani (a six-house hamlet in the heart of Tango-hantō) and drive over scenic roads to beautiful onsen, excellent restaurants and lovely beaches. Everything is taken care of, including driving and guiding. The tour gives you an intimate look at a side of Japan rarely glimpsed by foreign travellers.

There are several fine *minshuku* in the small village of Ine, including **Yoza-sō** (与謝荘; ☎ 0772-32-0278; 507 Hirata; per person with 2 meals from ¥9000).

AMANOHASHIDATE 天橋立

☎ 0772 / pop 21,000

Amanohashidate (the Bridge to Heaven) is rated as one of Japan's 'three great views'. The 'bridge' is really a long, narrow, tree-covered (8000 pine trees!) sand-spit, 3.5km in length. There is good swimming, as well as beach showers, toilet facilities and covered rest areas, the length of the spit. It's a good example of a Japanese tourist circus, but it is pleasant enough and there are some decent attractions like Ine (left) in the vicinity.

The town of Amanohashidate consists of two separate parts, one at each end of the spit. At the southern end there are a number of hotels, ryokan and restaurants, a popular temple and Amanohashidate Station. There's an **information counter** (☎ 22-8030; 10am-6pm) at the station. To get to the bridge from the station, take a right out of the station and walk along the main road for 200m to the first light and take a sharp left.

At the southern end of the bridge, **Amanohashidate View Land** (天橋立ビューランド; chairlift/monorail round-trip ¥850; 9.10am-5pm, 8.40am-6pm Jul 21-Aug 20) is serviced by chairlift and monorail. From here, you are supposed to view Amanohashidate by turning your back to it, bending over and observing it framed between your legs! (It supposedly makes Amanohashidate look like it is 'floating'.)

At the northern end, **Kasamatsu-kōen** (傘松公園; funicular/chairlift round-trip ¥640; 8am-4.30pm) offers similar views and another chance to view the world from between your legs.

Sleeping & Eating

Amanohashidate Youth Hostel (天橋立ユースホステル; ☎ 27-0121; per person with/without 2 meals ¥4500/2950;) This fine YH has good views down towards Amanohashidate, friendly owners, well-kept rooms and an excellent hillside location. To get there take a bus (¥510, 20 minutes) from JR Amanohashidate Station and get off at the Jinja-mae bus stop. From the stop, walk to the main hall of the shrine, take a right and leave the shrine precinct then turn left up the hill and walk 50m, take a right and follow the sign for Manai Shrine. Turn at the stone torii, walk 200m uphill and it's on the right.

Amanohashidate Hotel (天橋立ホテル; ☎ 22-4111; per person with 2 meals from ¥20,000;) This hotel about 100m west of the station commands the best views of Amanohashidate. Rooms are mixed Japanese/Western style and there are several good communal baths that afford views of Amanohashidate and the bay.

The hotel serves special crab cuisine in winter. Wi-fi is in the lobby.

There are several decent but slightly overpriced *shokudō* at the southern end of Amanohashidate, including **Resutoran Monju** (れすとらん文珠; ☎ 22-2805; meals from ¥1000; 🕑 9.30am-4pm, closed Thu), which has *asari udon* (udon noodles with clams), a local speciality, for ¥1000. Look for the red-and-white sign as you approach Chion-ji (the temple at the southern end of Amanohashidate).

Getting There & Away

The Kita-kinki Tango Tetsudō line runs between JR stations at Toyooka to the west and Nishi-Maizuru to the east. Amanohashidate Station is on this line, 1¼ hours from Toyooka (*futsū*, ¥1160) and 40 minutes from Nishi-Maizuru (*futsū*, ¥620). There are several direct trains from Kyoto daily, but JR pass holders will have to fork out for the Kita-kinki Tango Tetsudō part of the route (from Kyoto ¥4180, two hours; from Osaka ¥5040, 2¼ hours).

Getting Around

You can cross Amanohashidate on foot, by bicycle or on a motorcycle of less than 125cc capacity. Bicycles can be hired at a number of places for ¥400/1600 for two hours/a day.

MAIZURU 舞鶴

There's nothing overly appealing about the two ports of Nishi-Maizuru and Higashi-Maizuru, but they play an important part in the area's transport networks. If you've come from the west on the Kita-kinki Tango Tetsudō trains, Nishi-Maizuru is the end of the line and where the JR Obama line comes out to meet the coast. If you're on your way to Amanohashidate, this is where you'll have to change to the private line.

There are regular ferry services between Higashi-Maizuru and Otaru in Hokkaidō (2nd class ¥9300, 20 hours). Call **Shin-Nihonkai Ferry** (☎ 06-6345-2921; www.snf.co.jp, in Japanese) for details.

OSAKA 大阪

☎ 06 / pop 2.65 million

Osaka is the working heart of Kansai. Famous for the gruff manners of its citizens and the colourful *Kansai-ben* (Kansai dialect) they speak, it's a good counterpart to the refined atmosphere of Kyoto. First and foremost, Osaka is famous for good eating: the phrase *kuidaore* (eat 'til you drop) was coined to describe Osakans' love for good food. Osaka is also a good place to experience a modern Japanese city: it's only surpassed by Tokyo as a showcase of the Japanese urban phenomenon.

This isn't to say that Osaka is an attractive city; almost bombed flat in WWII, it appears an endless expanse of concrete boxes, pachinko (pinball) parlours and elevated highways. But the city somehow manages to rise above this and exert a peculiar charm. At night, Osaka really comes into its own; this is when all those drab streets come alive with flashing neon, beckoning residents and travellers alike with promises of tasty food and good times.

Osaka's highlights include Osaka-jō and its surrounding park, Osaka Aquarium with its enormous whale sharks and manta rays, the *Blade Runner* nightscapes of the Dōtombori area, and the wonderful Open-Air Museum of Old Japanese Farmhouses. But Osaka has more to offer than its specific sights; like Tokyo, Osaka is a city to be experienced in its totality, and casual strolls are likely to be just as rewarding as structured sightseeing tours.

HISTORY

Osaka has been a major port and mercantile centre from the beginning of Japan's recorded history. It was also briefly the first capital of Japan (before the establishment of a permanent capital at Nara). During its early days, Osaka was Japan's centre for trade with Korea and China, a role which it shares today with Kōbe and Yokohama.

In the late 16th century, Osaka rose to prominence when Toyotomi Hideyoshi, having unified all of Japan, chose Osaka as the site for his castle. Merchants set up around the castle and the city grew into a busy economic centre. This development was further encouraged by the Tokugawa shōgunate, which adopted a hands-off approach to the city, allowing merchants to prosper unhindered by government interference.

In the modern period, Tokyo has usurped Osaka's position as economic centre of Japan, and most of the companies formerly headquartered in Osaka have moved east. Osaka is still an economic powerhouse, however, and the city is ringed by factories churning out the latest in electronics and hi-tech products. Unfortunately, Osaka has been hit hard by the recent worldwide recession and the ranks of homeless are growing in the city.

ORIENTATION

Osaka is usually divided into two areas: Kita and Minami. Kita (Japanese for 'north') is the city's main business and administrative centre and contains two of its biggest train stations, JR Osaka and Hankyū Umeda Stations.

Minami (Japanese for 'south') is the city's entertainment district and contains the bustling shopping and nightlife zones of Namba and Shinsaibashi. It's also home to two major train stations, JR Namba and Nankai Namba Stations.

The dividing line between Kita and Minami is formed by two rivers, the Dōjima-gawa and the Tosabori-gawa, between which you'll find Nakano-shima, a relatively peaceful island that is home to the Museum of Oriental Ceramics. About 1km southeast of Nakano-shima you'll find Osaka-jō and its surrounding park, Osaka-jō-kōen.

To the south of the Minami area you'll find another group of sights clustered around Tennō-ji Station. These include Shitennō-ji, Tennō-ji-kōen, Den-den Town (the electronics neighbourhood) and the retro entertainment district of Shin-Sekai.

The bay area, to the west of the city centre, is home to another set of attractions including the excellent Osaka Aquarium and Universal Studios Japan theme park.

Keep in mind that, while JR Osaka Station is centrally located in the Kita area, if you're coming from Tokyo by *shinkansen* you will arrive at Shin-Osaka Station, which is three stops (about five minutes) north of Osaka Station on the Midō-suji subway line.

Maps

At the visitor information offices (see right), pick up a free copy of the first-rate *Osaka City Map*, which has insets of the city's most important areas and a map of the excellent subway/tram/train system. You'll find detailed route maps at every subway station, and this book contains a full Osaka subway/tram map; see p512.

INFORMATION

Bookshops

Athens (Map p399; ☎ 6253-0185; 🕑 10am-10pm; Ⓜ Midō-suji subway line to Shinsaibashi) This Minami bookshop has a good selection of English books and magazines on its 4th floor.

Junkudō (Map p397; ☎ 4799-1090; 🕑 10am-9pm; Ⓜ JR line to Osaka) This giant bookstore has the best selection of foreign and Japanese-language books in Osaka. It's inside the Dōjima Avanza Building in Kita, about 10 minutes' walk from Osaka Station. Most English-language books are on the 3rd floor along with a cafe, and English travel guides, including a good selection of Lonely Planet guides, are on the 2nd floor.

Kinokuniya (Map p397; ☎ 6372-5821; 🕑 10am-10pm; Ⓜ Hankyū line to Umeda) Also in Kita, inside Hankyū Umeda Station, this shop has a decent selection of foreign books and magazines.

Immigration Offices

Osaka Immigration Office (Map p395; ☎ 6941-0771; www.immi-moj.go.jp/english/soshiki/kikou/osaka.html; 🕑 9am-5pm Mon-Fri; Ⓜ Tanimachi subway line to Temmabashi) The main office for the Kansai region is a three-minute walk from exit 3 of Temmabashi Station on the Keihan main line.

Internet Access

Aprecio (Map p399; ☎ 6634-0199; www.aprecio.co.jp/namba/index.php, in Japanese; Minami; per 30min from ¥360; 🕑 24hr; Ⓜ Midō-suji subway line to Namba)

Kinko's (off Map p399; ☎ 6266-0565; per 10min from ¥262; 🕑 24hr; Ⓜ Midō-suji subway line to Honmachi)

Media Café Popeye (Map p397; ☎ 6292-3800; www2.media-cafe.ne.jp/branch/Umedadd/index.html, in Japanese; B1 fl, DD House Bldg, Kita; per 60min from ¥400; 🕑 24hr; Ⓜ Hankyū line to Umeda)

Money

Citibank Osaka Ekimae (Map p397; ☎ 6344-8608; www.citibank.co.jp/en/bankingservice/branch_atm/kansai/br_osakaekimae.html; 🕑 9am-3pm Mon-Fri, ATM 24hr; Ⓜ Hankyū line to Umeda or JR line to Osaka); Shinsaibashi (Map p399; ☎ 6213-2731; www.citibank.co.jp/en/bankingservice/branch_atm/kansai/br_shinsaibashi.html; 🕑 9am-3pm Mon-Fri, ATM 24hr; Ⓜ Midō-suji subway line to Shinsaibashi); Umeda (Map p397; ☎ 4802-0277; www.citibank.co.jp/en/bankingservice/branch_atm/kansai/br_umeda.html; 🕑 9am-3pm Mon-Fri, ATM 8am-10pm; Ⓜ Hankyū line to Umeda or JR line to Osaka)

Post

Osaka Central Post Office (Map p397; ☎ 6347-8097; Ⓜ JR line to Osaka) Next to JR Osaka Station. Has a 24-hour service window.

Tourist Information

All the offices listed here can help book accommodation if you visit in person. For information on upcoming events, pick up a copy of *Kansai Time Out* magazine at any of the bookstores listed earlier (see left).

Umeda Visitors Information Office (Map p397; ☎ 6345-2189; Kita; ⌚ 8am-8pm, closed 31 Dec-3 Jan) is the main tourist information office in Osaka. It's a little tricky to find: from JR Osaka Station, exit the Midō-suji ticket gate/exit, turn right, and walk about 50m. The office is just outside the station, beneath a pedestrian overpass. From the subway, go out exit 9, and look for it outside the station, beside the bus terminal. Note that the station is presently under construction and there is word that this office might move again.

Other similar offices (hours are the same) include the following:

Namba Station Visitors Information Office (Map p399; ☎ 6211-3551; Minami)

Shin-Osaka Station Visitors Information Office (Map p395; ☎ 6305-3311)

Tennō-ji Station Visitors Information Office (Map p395; ☎ 6774-3077)

Osaka Itami and Kansai International Airports also have information counters:

Kansai International Airport Information Center (☎ 07-2455-2500; 2F/North, 1F&4F/North, South & Central zones; ⌚ 24hr)

Osaka Itami Airport Information Center (☎ 6856-6781; 1F Terminal Arrival Lobby, North & South zones; ⌚ North zone 8am-9.15pm, South zone 6.30am-9.15pm).

Travel Agency

No 1 Travel Osaka (Map p397; ☎ 6345-4700; www.no1-travel.com/kix/no1air/index.htm; Kyo-Tomi Bldg 3F, 1-3-16 Sonezake-Shinchi, Kita-ku; ⌚ 10am-6.30pm Mon-Fri, 11am-5pm Sat; 🚉 JR line to Osaka) Located in Umeda, this helpful travel agency has English speakers and competitive prices.

SIGHTS & ACTIVITIES

Kita Area キタ

By day, Osaka's centre of gravity is the Kita area (Map p397). While Kita doesn't have any great attractions to detain the traveller, it does have a few good department stores, lots of places to eat and the eye-catching Umeda Sky building.

UMEDA SKY BUILDING 梅田スカイビル

Just northwest of Osaka Station, the Umeda Sky building is Osaka's most dramatic piece of modern architecture. The twin-tower complex looks like a space-age version of Paris' Arc de Triomphe. The view from the top is impressive, particularly after sunset, when the lights of the Osaka-Kōbe conurbation spread out like a magical carpet in all directions.

There are two observation galleries: one outdoors on the roof and one indoors on the floor below. Getting to the top is half the fun as you take a glassed-in escalator for the final five storeys (definitely not for vertigo sufferers). Tickets for the **observation decks** (Map p397; ☎ 6440-3855; 1-1-88 Ōyodonaka, Kita-ku; admission ¥700; ⌚ 10am-10.30pm; 🚉 JR line to Osaka) include the escalator ride and can be purchased on the 3rd floor of the east tower. Last entry 10pm.

Below the towers, you'll find **Takimi-kōji Alley** (Map p397), a re-creation of an early Shōwa-era market street crammed with restaurants and *izakaya*.

The building is reached via an underground passage that starts just north of both Osaka and Umeda Stations.

OSAKA MUSEUM OF HOUSING & LIVING

大阪くらしの今昔館

Two subway stops from Umeda is the **Osaka Museum of Housing & Living** (Map p395; ☎ 6242-1170; 6-4-20 Tenjinbashi, Kita-ku; admission ¥600; ⌚ 10am-5pm, closed Tue; 🚉 Tanimachi subway line to Tenjinbashisuji Rokuchōme, exit 3), which contains a life-sized reproduction of an entire 1830s Edo-period Osaka neighbourhood. You can enter and inspect shophouses, meeting halls, drug stores and even an old-style *sentō* (public bath). The rooms and houses are dimly lit in order to re-create the ambience of pre-electric Osaka. The museum also contains a room filled with dioramas of post-Meiji Osaka neighbourhoods, including an interesting community of buses that were converted into homes following WWII.

To get there, from the station's exit 3 go through the glass doors to the left of the escalator and take the elevator to the 8th floor. There's no English sign.

Central Osaka

OSAKA MUSEUM OF HISTORY

大阪歴史博物館

Just southwest of Osaka-jō, the **Osaka Museum of History** (Osaka Rekishi Hakubutsukan; Map p395; ☎ 6946-5728; 4-1-32 Ōtemae, Chūō-ku; admission ¥600; ⌚ 9.30am-5pm, to 8pm Fri; 🚉 Tanimachi subway line to Tanimachi-yonchōme) is housed in a fantastic new sail-shaped building adjoining the Osaka NHK Broadcast Center. The display floors of the museum occupy the 7th to the 10th floors.

The displays are broken into four sections by floor; you start at the top and work your way down, passing in time from the past to the present. The displays are very well done and there are plenty of English explanations; taped tours are available.

The museum is a two-minute walk northeast of Tanimachi-yonchōme Station.

OSAKA-JŌ 大阪城

This **castle** (Map p395; ☎ 6941-3044; 1-1 Osaka-jō, Chūō-ku; admission grounds/castle keep free/¥600; 🕒 9am-5pm, to 8pm Aug; 🚇 JR Osaka Loop line to Osaka-jō-kōen) was built as a display of power by Toyotomi Hideyoshi after he achieved his goal of unifying Japan. One hundred thousand workers toiled for three years to construct an 'impregnable' granite castle, finishing the job in 1583. However, it was destroyed just 32 years later, in 1615, by the armies of Tokugawa Ieyasu.

Within 10 years the castle had been rebuilt by the Tokugawa forces, but it was to suffer a further calamity when another generation of the Tokugawa clan razed it rather than let it fall to the forces of the Meiji Restoration in 1868.

The present structure is a 1931 concrete reconstruction of the original, which was refurbished in 1997. The interior of the castle houses an excellent collection of displays relating to the castle, Toyotomi Hideyoshi and the city of Osaka. On the 8th floor there is an observation deck offering 360-degree views of Osaka and surrounding areas.

The castle and park are at their best in the spring-cherry-blossom and autumn-foliage seasons. Enter by 30 minutes before closing.

The Ōte-mon gate, which serves as the main entrance to the park, is a 10-minute walk northeast of Tanimachi-yonchōme Station (sometimes written as Tanimachi 4-chome) on the Chūō and Tanimachi subway lines. You can also take the Osaka Loop line, get off at Osaka-jō-kōen Station and enter through the back of the castle.

MODERN TRANSPORTATION MUSEUM
交通科学博物館

If you've got kids in tow or just love those trains, then you'll want to check out the small but interesting **Modern Transportation Museum** (off Map p395; ☎ 6581-5771; 3 Namiyoke, Minato-ku; adult/child ¥400/100; 🕒 9am-5.30pm, closed Mon & year-end/new-year holidays; 🚇 JR Osaka Loop line to Bentenchō, south exit), which is on the west side of town, easily accessed by the JR Osaka Loop line. The displays focus mostly on trains, but there are also some great models of ships and aircraft, several decent interactive displays, as well as life-sized *shinkansen* that you can climb inside to check out what things look like from the engineer's seat. Outside, there are several real steam and electric engines and passenger cars that you can climb inside (one is a working restaurant car). Finally, don't miss the great model-train layout at the far end of the building.

To get there from the station, take a hard left out of the turnstiles and it's across the street.

Nakano-shima 中之島

Sandwiched between Dōjima-gawa and Tosabori-gawa, this island (Map p395) is a pleasant oasis of trees and riverside walkways in the midst of Osaka's unrelenting grey. It's also home to **Osaka City Hall**, the Museum of Oriental Ceramics and **Nakano-shima-kōen**. The latter park, on the eastern end of the island, is a good place for an afternoon stroll or picnic lunch. If you're coming from Kyoto, Nakano-shima is just north of Yodoyabashi Station, the terminus of the Keihan line.

INFORMATION
- Osaka Immigration Office 大阪入国管理局 1 C4
- Shin-osaka Station Visitors Information Office 大阪市ビジターズインフォメーションセンター·新大阪 2 B1
- Tennō-ji Station Visitors Information Office 大阪市ビジターズインフォメーションセンター·天王寺 3 C6

SIGHTS & ACTIVITIES
- Imamiya Ebisu-jinja 今宮戎神社 4 B6
- Museum of Oriental Ceramics 大阪市立陶芸美術館 5 B3
- Nakano-shima-kōen 中之島公園 6 C3
- Osaka City Hall 大阪市役所 7 B3
- Osaka Museum of History 大阪歴史博物館 8 C4
- Osaka Museum of Housing & Living 大阪くらしの今昔館 9 C2
- Osaka-jō 大阪城 10 C4
- Shitennō-ji 四天王寺 11 C6
- Spa World フェスティバルゲート；スパワールド 12 B6

SLEEPING
- Imperial Hotel Osaka 帝国ホテル大阪 13 C3
- Shin-Osaka Youth Hostel 新大阪ユースホステル 14 B1

ENTERTAINMENT
- National Bunraku Theatre 国立文楽劇場 15 C5

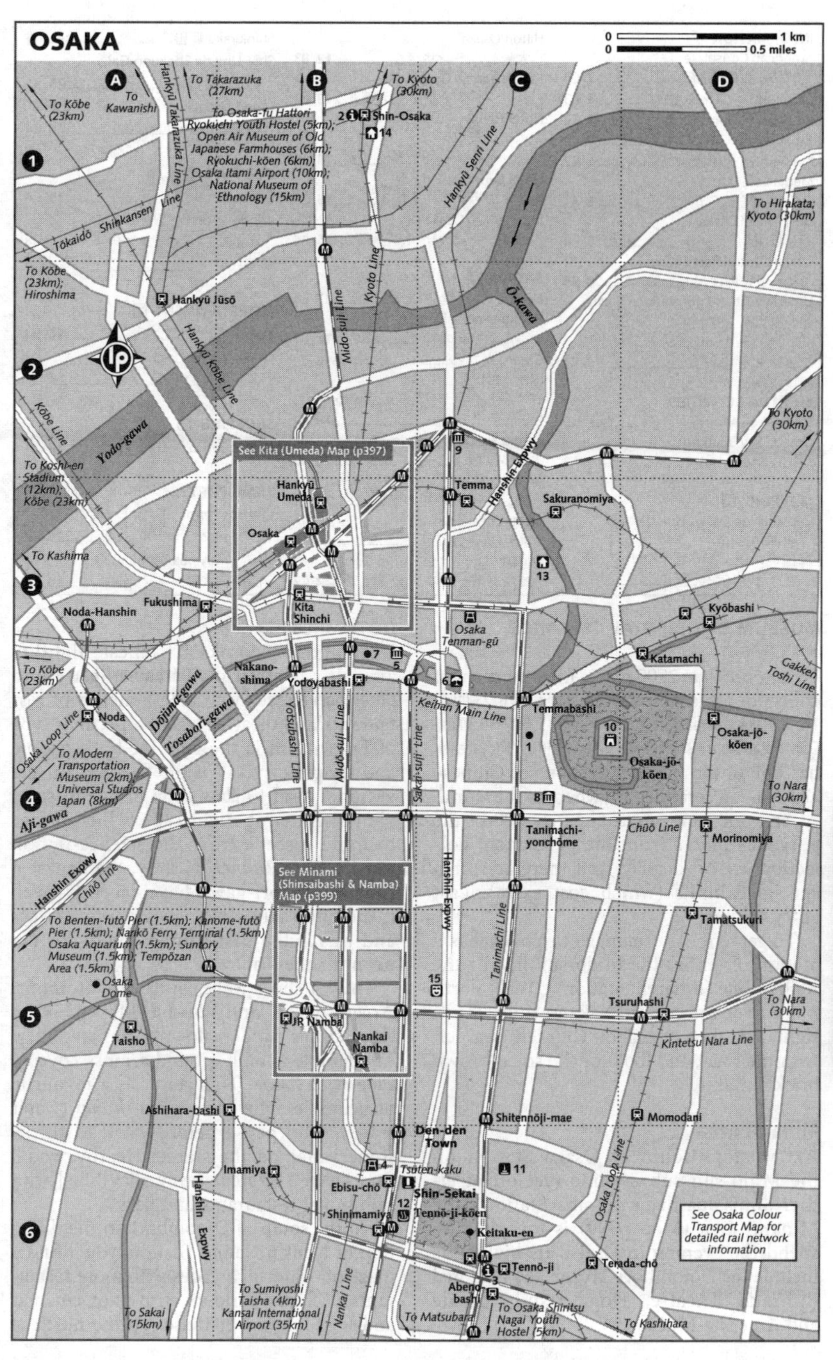
OSAKA
0 1 km
0 0.5 miles
To Kōbe (23km)
To Kawanishi
Hankyū Takarazuka Line
To Takarazuka (27km)
To Osaka-fu Hattori Ryokuchi Youth Hostel (5km); Open Air Museum of Old Japanese Farmhouses (6km); Ryokuchi-kōen (6km); Osaka Itami Airport (10km); National Museum of Ethnology (15km)
Shin-Osaka
To Kyoto (30km)
Hankyū Senri Line
Tōkaidō Shinkansen Line
To Kōbe (23km); Hiroshima
Kyoto Line
Mido-suji Line
Hankyū Jūsō
Hankyū Kōbe Line
Ō-kawa
To Hirakata; Kyoto (30km)
Kōbe Line
Yodo-gawa
To Kyoto (30km)
See Kita (Umeda) Map (p397)
Hankyū Umeda
Osaka
Kita Shinchi
Temma
Hanshin Expwy
Sakuranomiya
To Koshi-en Stadium (12km); Kōbe (23km)
To Kashima
Fukushima
Noda-Hanshin
Osaka Tenman-gū
Kyōbashi
Katamachi
To Kōbe (23km)
Nakanoshima
Yodoyabashi
Gakken Toshi Line
Noda
Dōjima-gawa
Tosabori-gawa
Keihan Main Line
Temmabashi
Osaka-jō-kōen
Osaka Loop Line
To Modern Transportation Museum (2km); Universal Studios Japan (8km)
Yotsubashi Line
Mido-suji Line
Sakai-suji Line
Osaka-jō-kōen
To Nara (30km)
Aji-gawa
Tanimachi-yonchōme
Chūō Line
Morinomiya
Hanshin Expwy
Chūō Line
See Minami (Shinsaibashi & Namba) Map (p399)
Hanshin Expwy
Tanimachi Line
To Benten-futō Pier (1.5km); Kanome-futō Pier (1.5km); Nankō Ferry Terminal (1.5km); Osaka Aquarium (1.5km); Suntory Museum (1.5km); Tempōzan Area (1.5km)
Tamatsukuri
Osaka Dome
JR Namba
Nankai Namba
Tsuruhashi
To Nara (30km)
Taisho
Kintetsu Nara Line
Ashihara-bashi
Shitennōji-mae
Momodani
Den-den Town
Osaka Loop Line
Imamiya
Tsūten-kaku
Ebisu-chō
Shin-Sekai
Hanshin Expwy
Shinimamiya
Tennō-ji-kōen
Keitaku-en
See Osaka Colour Transport Map for detailed rail network information
Tennō-ji
Terada-chō
To Sumiyoshi Taisha (4km); Kansai International Airport (35km)
Nankai Line
Abeno-bashi
To Sakai (15km)
To Matsubara
To Osaka Shiritsu Nagai Youth Hostel (5km)
To Kashihara

KANSAI

INFORMATION
American Consulate アメリカ領事館 1 C4
Citibank シティバンク 2 B3
Citibank シティバンク 3 C2
Junkudō ジュンク堂書店 4 B4
Kinokuniya 紀伊國屋書 5 B2
Media Café Popeye メディアカフェポパイ 6 B1
No 1 Travel Osaka 大阪No1トラベル 7 B4
Osaka Central Post Office 大阪中央郵便局 8 B3
Umeda Visitors Information Office 大阪市ビジターズインフォメーションセンター·梅田 9 B3

SIGHTS & ACTIVITIES
Takimi-kōji Alley 滝見小路 .... (see 10)
Umeda Sky Building 梅田スカイビル 10 A2

SLEEPING
Capsule Inn Osaka/Umeda New Japan Sauna 梅田ニュージャパンサウナ カプセルイン大阪 11 D2
Hilton Osaka 大阪ヒルトンホテル 12 B3
Hotel Granvia Osaka ホテルグランヴィア大阪 13 B3
Hotel Hankyū International ホテル阪急インターナショナル 14 C1
Hotel Sunroute Umeda ホテルサンルート梅田 15 C1
Ritz-Carlton Osaka ザ·リッツ·カールトン大阪 16 A4

EATING
Dōjima Hana 堂島花 17 B4
Ganko Umeda Honten がんこ梅田本店 18 B1
Gataro がたろ .... (see 20)
Hilton Plaza ヒルトンプラザ .... (see 12)
Isaribi 漁火 19 B2
Kappa Yokochō Arcade かっぱ横丁 20 B1
Monsoon Café モンスーンカフェ 21 B1
Okonomiyaki Sakura お好み焼きさくら .... (see 23)
Organic Life オルグオーガニックライフ 22 C2
Shinkiraku 新善楽 .... (see 12)
Shin-Umeda Shokudō-Gai 新梅田食道街 23 B2
Umeda Hagakure 梅田はがくれ 24 C4

DRINKING
Canopy キャノピー 25 C4
Windows on the World ウィンドーズオン ザ ワールド .... (see 12)

ENTERTAINMENT
Karma カーマ 26 B4
Osaka Nōgaku Hall 大阪能楽会館 27 D2

SHOPPING
Kōjitsu Sansō 好日山荘 28 C4

TRANSPORT
City Bus Terminal 市バスターミナル 29 B3
JR Highway Bus Terminal JR高速バスターミナル 30 B3

MUSEUM OF ORIENTAL CERAMICS 東洋陶磁美術館

With more than 2700 pieces in its permanent collection, this **museum** (Map p395; ☎ 6223-0055; 1-1-26 Nakanoshima, Kita-ku; admission ¥500; 9.30am-5pm, closed Mon; Midō-suji subway line to Yodoyabashi) has one of the finest collections of Chinese and Korean ceramics anywhere in the world. At any one time, approximately 300 of the gorgeous pieces from the permanent collection are on display, and there are often special exhibits (which cost extra). Last entry 4.30pm.

To get to the museum, go to Yodoyabashi Station on either the Midō-suji line or the Keihan line (different stations). Walk north to the river and cross to Nakano-shima. Turn right, pass the city hall on your left, bear left with the road, and look for the squat brown brick building.

Minami Area ミナミ

A few stops south of Osaka Station on the Midō-suji subway line (get off at either Shinsaibashi or Namba Station), the Minami area (Map p399) is the place to spend the evening in Osaka. Its highlights include the Dōtombori Arcade, the National Bunraku Theatre, Dōguya-suji Arcade and Amerika-Mura.

DŌTOMBORI 道頓堀

Dōtombori is Osaka's liveliest nightlife area. It's centred on **Dōtombori-gawa** and **Dōtombori Arcade** (Map p399), a strip of restaurants and theatres where a peculiar type of Darwinism is the rule for both people and shops: survival of the flashiest. In the evening, head to **Ebisu-bashi** bridge to sample the glittering nightscape, which brings to mind a scene from the science-fiction movie *Blade Runner*. Nearby, the banks of the Dōtombori-gawa have recently been turned into attractive pedestrian walkways and this is the best vantage point for the neon madness above.

Only a short walk south of Dōtombori Arcade you'll find **Hōzen-ji** (Map p399), a tiny temple hidden down a narrow alley. The temple is built around a moss-covered **Fudō-myōō statue**. This statue is a favourite of people employed in *mizu shōbai* (water trade), who pause before work to throw some water on the statue. Nearby, you'll find **Hōzen-ji Yokochō**, a tiny alley filled with traditional restaurants and bars.

To the south of Dōtombori, in the direction of Nankai Namba Station, you'll find a maze of colourful arcades with more restaurants, pachinko parlours, strip clubs, cinemas and who knows what else. To the north of

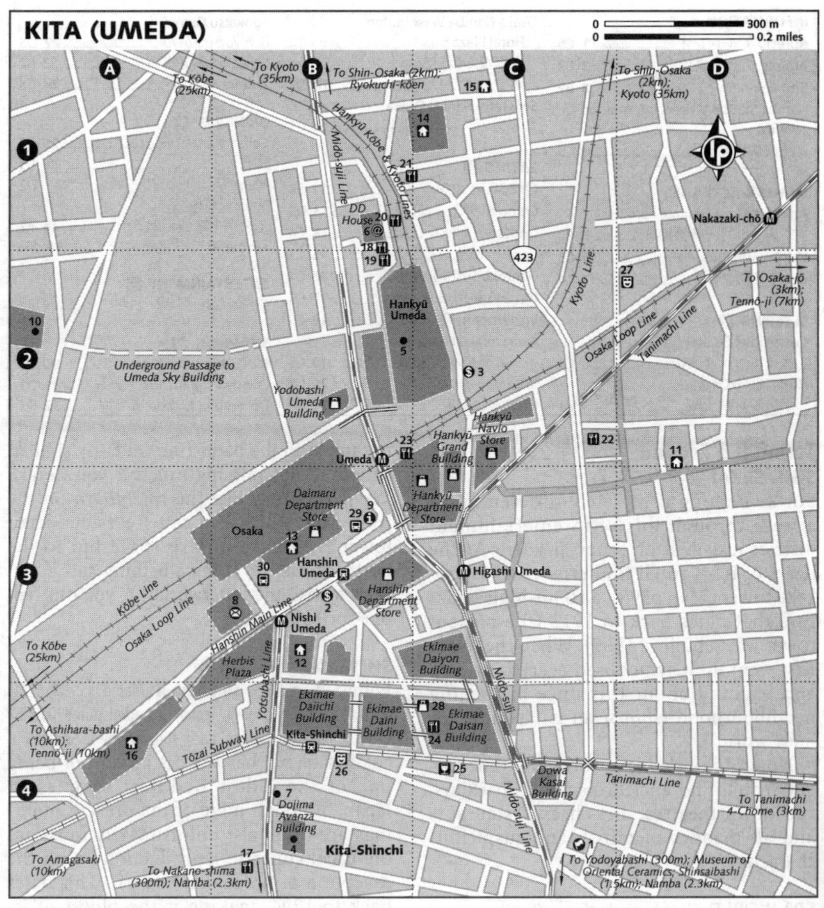

Dōtombori, between Midō-suji and Sakai-suji, the narrow streets are crowded with hostess bars, discos and pubs.

DŌGUYA-SUJI ARCADE 道具屋筋

If you desperately need a *tako-yaki* (octopus piece) fryer, a red lantern to hang outside your shop or plastic food models to lure the customers in, this shopping arcade (Map p399) is the place to go. You'll also find endless knives, pots, pans and just about anything else that's even remotely related to the preparation and consumption of food.

AMERIKA-MURA アメリカ村

Amerika-Mura (America Village; Map p399) is a compact enclave of trendy shops and restaurants, with a few discreet love hotels thrown in for good measure. The best reason to come is to check out the hordes of colourful Japanese teens living out the myth of America. These days, the look is hip-hop for guys and dark tans and tiny shorts for the girls. The peculiar name, by the way, comes from the presence of several shops that sprang up here after the war and sold various bits of Americana, like Zippo lighters and American T-shirts.

In the middle of it all is **Amerika-Mura Triangle Park**, an all-concrete park with benches where you can sit and watch the parade of fashion victims. Amerika-Mura is one or two blocks west of Midō-suji, bounded on the north by Suomachi-suji and on the south by Dōtombori-gawa.

INFORMATION
Aprecio アルレシオ 1 C5
Athens アテネ書店 2 C2
Citibank シティバンク 3 B2
Namba Station Visitors Information Office 難波駅観光案内 4 C5

SIGHTS & ACTIVITIES
Amerika-Mura Triangle Park アメリカ村三角公園 5 B2
Ebisū-bashi Bridge 戎橋 6 C3
Hōzen-ji 法善寺 7 C4

SLEEPING
Cross Hotel Osaka クロスホテル大阪 8 C3
Hotel Nikkō Osaka ホテル日航大阪 9 B1
Osaka Namba Washington Hotel Plaza 大阪なんばワシントンホテルプラザ 10 D3
Swissotel Nankai Osaka スイスホテル南海大阪 11 C5

EATING
Café Slices カフェスライセス 12 B3
Chibō 千房 13 D3
Doutor ドトール 14 C4
Ganko Zushi がんこ寿司 15 C3
Genroku Sushi 元禄寿司 16 C4
Gin Sen 銀扇 17 C3
Imai Honten 今井本店 18 C3
Kani Dōraku Honten かに道楽本店 19 C3
Krungtep クンテープ 20 C3
Nishiya にし家 21 C1
Tonkatsu Ganko とんかつがんこ 22 D5
Ume no Hana 梅の花 23 B2
Zuboraya づぼらや 24 C3

DRINKING
Cellar ザ セラー 25 B3
Hub ハッブ 26 C3
Murphy's マーフィーズ 27 D2
SoulFuckTry ソウルファクトリー 28 A2
Tavola 36 タヴォラ３６ .... (see 11)

ENTERTAINMENT
Grand Café グランドカフェ 29 B2

SHOPPING
Bic Camera ビックカメラ 30 C4
Dōguya-suji Arcade 道具屋筋 31 D5
Dōtombori Arcade 道頓堀 32 D3

Tennō-ji & Around 天王寺公園

SHIN-SEKAI 新世界

For something completely different, take a walk through this retro entertainment district just west of Tennō-ji-kōen. At the heart of it all you'll find crusty old **Tsūten-kaku** tower (Map p395), a 103m-high structure that dates back to 1912 (the present tower was rebuilt in 1969). When the tower first went up it symbolised everything new and exciting about this once-happening neighbourhood (*shin-sekai* is Japanese for 'new world').

Now, Shin-Sekai is a world that time forgot. You'll find ancient pachinko parlours, run-down theatres, dirt-cheap restaurants and all manner of raffish and suspicious characters.

SPA WORLD スパワールド

At the southern edge of Shin-Sekai is the superspa known as **Spa World** (Map p395; ☎ 6631-0001; 3-4-24 Ebisu higashi, Naniwa-ku; per 3hr/full day Mon-Fri ¥2400/2700, Sat, Sun & holidays ¥2700/3000; 24hr, no entry 8.45-10am; Sakai-suji or Midō-suji subway line to Dōbutsuen-mae). Billed as the world's largest spa complex, it consists of two floors of baths, one Asian themed and one European themed, and a fabulous rooftop waterworld with pools and waterslides, along with restaurants and relaxation areas.

The Asian and European bath floors are segregated by sex; one month the ladies get the Asian bath floor and the men have the European bath floor, and then it switches to the opposite, so you will have to visit twice to sample all the baths (they're fairly similar, so you're not missing much if you don't). We particularly like the *rotemburo* on the roof, from which you can see Tsūten-kaku tower rising like a retro spaceship to the north. Be sure to bring a bathing suit if you want to visit the waterworld (or you can rent one for ¥300).

SHITENNŌ-JI 四天王寺

Founded in 593, **Shitennō-ji** (Map p395; ☎ 6771-0066; 1-11-18 Shitennō-ji, Tennōji-ku; admission ¥200-300; 8.30am-4pm; Tanimachi subway line to Shitennōji-mae, southern exit) has the distinction of being one of the oldest Buddhist temples in Japan, although none of the present buildings are originals; unfortunately most are the usual concrete reproductions, with the exception of the big stone torii. This dates back to 1294, making it the oldest of its kind in Japan. Apart from the torii, there is little of real historical significance, and the absence of greenery in the raked-gravel grounds makes for a rather desolate atmosphere. The adjoining **museum** (admission ¥200) is of limited interest.

Take the southern exit from the station, cross to the left side of the road and take the small road that goes off at an angle away from the subway station. The entrance to the temple is on the left.

SUMIYOSHI TAISHA 住吉大社

This **shrine** (off Map p395; ☎ 6672-0753; 2-9-89 Sumiyoshi, Sumiyoshi-ku; admission free; dawn-dusk; Nankai main line to Sumiyoshi-taisha) is dedicated to Shintō deities associated

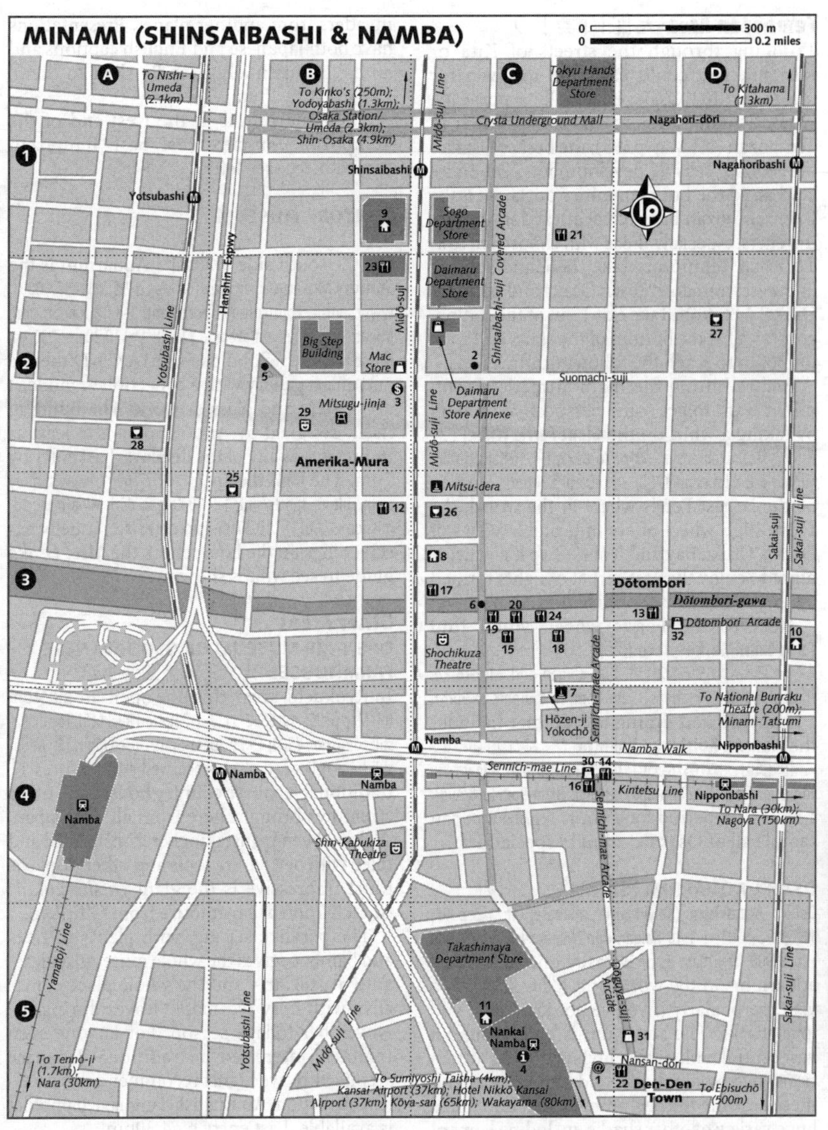

with the sea and sea travel, in commemoration of a safe passage to Korea by a 3rd-century empress.

Having survived the bombing in WWII, Sumiyoshi Taisha actually has a couple of buildings that date back to 1810. The shrine was founded in the early 3rd century and the buildings that can be seen today are faithful replicas of the originals. They offer a rare opportunity to see a Shintō shrine that predates the influence of Chinese Buddhist architectural styles.

It's next to both Sumiyoshi-taisha Station on the Nankai main line and Sumiyoshi-torimae Station on the Hankai line (the tram line that leaves from Tennō-ji Station).

Tempōzan Area 天保山エリア

Trudging through the streets of Kita or Minami, you could easily be forgiven for forgetting that Osaka is actually a port city. A good remedy for this is a trip down to Tempōzan (off Map p395), the best of Osaka's burgeoning seaside developments. On an island amid the busy container ports of Osaka Bay, Tempōzan has several attractions to lure travellers, especially those with children in tow. To reach Tempōzan, take the Chūō subway line west from downtown Osaka and get off at Osakakō Station. Take exit 1 out of the station, go straight at the bottom of the stairs and walk for 300m to reach the following attractions.

Before hitting the main attractions, you might want to get some perspective on it all by taking a whirl on the **Giant Ferris Wheel** (大観覧車; Daikanransha; ☎ 6576-6222; 1-1-10 Kaigan-dōri, Minato-ku; admission ¥700; ⏰ 10am-9.30pm). Said to be the largest Ferris wheel in the world, the 112m-high wheel offers unbeatable views of Osaka, Osaka Bay and Kōbe. Give it a whirl at night to enjoy the vast carpet of lights formed by the Osaka/Kōbe conurbation.

Next to the Ferris wheel, you'll find **Tempōzan Marketplace** (天保山マーケットプレース; ☎ 6576-5501; 1-1-10 Kaigan-dōri, Minato-ku; admission free; ⏰ shops 11am-8pm, restaurants to 9pm), a shopping and dining arcade that includes the **Naniwa Kuishinbō Yokochō** (なにわ食いしんぼ横丁; ☎ 6576-5501; 1-1-10 Kaigan-dōri, Minato-ku; admission free; ⏰ 11am-8pm Sep-Jun, 10am-9pm Jul & Aug), a faux-Edo-period food court where you can sample all of Osaka's culinary specialities.

OSAKA AQUARIUM 海遊館

Osaka Aquarium (Kaiyūkan in Japanese; off Map p395; ☎ 6576-5501; 1-1-10 Kaigan-dōri, Minato-ku; adult/child ¥2000/900; ⏰ 10am-8pm) is easily one of the best aquariums in the world and it's well worth a visit, particularly if you've got kids, or if you love sharks. The aquarium is built around a vast central tank, which houses the star attractions: two whale sharks and two mantas. But these are only the beginning: you'll also find a huge variety of other sharks, including leopard sharks, zebra sharks, hammerhead sharks and even a tiger shark (the only one we've ever seen in an aquarium). There are also countless other species of rays and other fish.

A walkway winds its way around the main tank and past displays of life found on eight different ocean levels. The giant spider crabs in the Japan Ocean Deeps section look like alien invaders from another planet. Presentations have both Japanese and English captions and an environmentally friendly slant to them. Last entry by 7pm.

The aquarium is at the west end of the Tempōzan complex, just past Tempōzan Marketplace (see left).

SUNTORY MUSEUM サントリーミュージアム

On the south side of Osaka Aquarium is the **Suntory Museum complex** (off Map p395; ☎ 6577-0001; www.suntory.com/culture-sports/smt; 1-5-10 Kaigan-dōri, Minato-ku; admission average ¥1000; ⏰ 10.30am-7.30pm, closed Mon), which holds an IMAX 3-D theatre and an art gallery with a collection of modern art posters and glass artwork. The building itself, designed by Andō Tadao, is at least as impressive as any of the displays. Last entry by 7pm. The **IMAX theatre** (☎ 6577-0001; www.suntory.com/culture-sports/smt; 1-5-10 Kaigan-dōri, Minato-ku; admission ¥1000; ⏰ 10.30am-8pm, closed Mon) usually has screenings on the hour; check the *Meet Osaka* guide to see what's showing.

Other Areas

OPEN-AIR MUSEUM OF OLD JAPANESE FARMHOUSES 日本民家集落博物館

In Ryokuchi-kōen, this fine open-air **museum** (off Map p395; ☎ 6862-3137; 1-2 Hattori Ryokuchi, Toyonaka-shi; admission ¥500; ⏰ 9.30am-5pm, closed Mon; 🚇 Midō-suji subway line to Ryokuchi-kōen, west exit) features 11 traditional Japanese country houses and other structures brought here from all over Japan. All have been painstakingly reconstructed and filled with period-era tools and other displays. Most impressive is the giant *gasshō-zukuri* (thatch-roofed) farmhouse from Gifu-ken.

The parklike setting, with plenty of trees and bamboo, gives the whole museum a pleasantly rustic air – and the whole place comes alive with fiery red maple leaves during the November foliage season. For anyone even remotely interested in traditional Japanese architecture, we highly recommend this excellent attraction. An English-language pamphlet is available. Last entry by 4.30pm.

To get there, walk northwest from the station into the park.

UNIVERSAL STUDIOS JAPAN ユニバーサルスタジオジャパン

Universal Studios Japan (off Map p395; ☎ 6465-3000; Universal City; adult/child ¥5800/3900; ⏰ 10am-5pm Mon-Fri, to 6pm Sat, Sun & holidays, with seasonal variations; 🚇 JR

Osaka Loop line to Universal City) is Osaka's answer to Tokyo Disneyland. Closely based on its two sister parks in the USA, the park features a wide variety of rides, shows, restaurants and other attractions.

To get there, take the JR Loop line to Nishikujō Station, switch to one of the distinctively painted Universal Studio shuttle trains and get off at Universal City Station. From Osaka Station the trip costs ¥170 and takes about 20 minutes. There are also some direct trains from Osaka Station (ask at the tourist office for times; the price is the same).

NATIONAL MUSEUM OF ETHNOLOGY
国立民族学博物館

Located in Osaka Banpaku-kōen (World Expo Park), this **museum** (off Map p395; ☎ 6876-2151; 10-1 Senri Expo Park, Suita; admission ¥420; ⌚ 10am-5pm, closed Wed, closed Thu if the preceding Wed is a national holiday; 🚇 Midō-suji subway line to Senri-chūō, then east on Osaka Monorail to Banpaku-kinen-kōen) is arguably Osaka's best, and it's worth the trip from downtown Osaka or Kyoto, especially if there's a good special exhibit on (check the *Kansai Time Out* for upcoming exhibits).

The museum provides a whirlwind tour through the cultural artefacts of many of the world's cultures. Exhibits range from Bollywood movie posters to Thai túk-túk (motorised transport), with Ainu textiles, Bhutanese mandalas and Japanese festival floats in between. There is little English signage, but most of the materials are self-explanatory. You can also borrow a sheet of English explanations from the reception desk. Last entry by 4.30pm.

From the station, go left, cross the bridge over the highway, buy a ticket from the machines, go through the turnstile and walk towards the huge Tower of the Sun statue. Once past the statue, you will see the museum about 250m in front of you to the northwest (it's got several towers on its roof that resemble cooling towers). From Kyoto, you can take the Hankyū line to Minami Ibaraki Station and change there to the Osaka Monorail.

FESTIVALS & EVENTS

Tōka Ebisu Huge crowds of more than a million people flock to the Imamiya Ebisu-jinja (Map p395) to receive bamboo branches hung with auspicious tokens from 9 to 11 January. The shrine is near Imamiya Ebisu Station on the Nankai line.

Tenjin Matsuri Held on 24 and 25 July, this is one of Japan's three biggest festivals. Try to make the second day, when processions of *mikoshi* (portable shrines) and people in traditional attire start at Osaka Temman-gū and end up in O-kawa (in boats). As night falls, the festival is marked with a huge fireworks display.

Kishiwada Danjiri Matsuri Osaka's wildest festival on 14 and 15 September, a kind of running of the bulls except with *danjiri* (festival floats), many weighing over 3000kg. The *danjiri* are hauled through the streets by hundreds of people using ropes, and in all the excitement there have been a couple of deaths – take care and stand back. Most of the action takes place on the second day. The best place to see it is west of Kishiwada Station on the Nankai Honsen line (from Nankai Station).

SLEEPING

There are plenty of places to stay in and around the two centres of Kita and Minami. You can also explore Osaka from a base in Kyoto, and you'll find more budget accommodation in the old capital, which is only about 40 minutes away by train. Keep in mind, however, that the trains stop running a little before midnight (party-goers take note).

Kita Area

BUDGET

Capsule Inn Osaka/Umeda New Japan Sauna (Map p397; ☎ 6314-2100; 9-5 Dōyama-chō, Kita-ku; men-only capsules ¥2600; 💻; 🚇 Hankyū line to Umeda or JR line to Osaka) Located in one of Kita's busiest entertainment districts, this is the place to stay if you miss the last train. It's fairly clean and well maintained, with sauna (from ¥525), Jacuzzi and optional massage services. Note that it's men-only, and if you're over 180cm tall you won't be able to lie flat out.

MIDRANGE

Hotel Sunroute Umeda (Map p397; ☎ 6373-1111; www.sunroute.jp/SunrouteTopHLE.html; 3-9-1 Toyosaki, Kita-ku; s/d/tw from ¥8820/12,600/15,750; 💻; 🚇 Midō-suji subway line to Nakatsu) A good business hotel, and perhaps the best value in this price range, the Sunroute hits all the right notes: clean rooms, efficient check-in and excellent location. Some of the rooms even have great views over Osaka. It's just north of Hankyū Umeda. Cable LAN available in rooms.

TOP END

Hotel Granvia Osaka (Map p397; ☎ 6344-1235; www.granvia-osaka.jp/english/index.html; 3-1-1 Umeda, Kita-ku; s/d/tw ¥16,170/26,565/27,720; 💻; 🚇 JR line to Osaka) This hotel can't be beaten for convenience: it's located directly over Osaka Station. Rooms and facilities are of a high standard and the views from the restaurants on the upper floors of the building are superb. Cable LAN available in rooms.

Hilton Osaka (Map p397; ☎ 6347-7111; 1-8-8 Umeda, Kita-ku; s ¥18,000-36,000, d & tw ¥22,000-40,000; ; JR line to Osaka) Just south of JR Osaka Station, this is an excellent hotel at home with foreign guests. The rooms are clean and light, with a Japanese touch, and there's a 15m pool in the fitness centre. The views from the 35th-floor Windows on the World bar here are awesome, and there are two floors of great restaurants below the hotel. Cable LAN available in rooms.

Ritz-Carlton Osaka (Map p397; ☎ 6343-7000; www.ritzcarlton.com/en/Properties/Osaka/Default.htm; 2-5-25 Umeda, Kita-ku; s/d/tw from ¥31,000/37,000/37,000; ; Hanshin line to Umeda, west exit, or JR line to Osaka, Sakurabashi exit) A short walk from JR Osaka and Hankyū Umeda Stations in Kita, the Ritz Carlton is one of the best hotels in the city. Rooms are well appointed, comfortable and spacious, and the staff is polite and efficient. There is a pool, fitness centre and 24-hour business centre, as well as six on-site restaurants.

Hotel Hankyū International (Map p397; ☎ 6377-2100; www.hhi.co.jp/new2002/e-index.html; 19-19 Chayamachi, Kita-ku; s/d/tw from ¥34,650/46,200/48,510; ; Midō-suji subway line to Nakatsu or Hankyū line to Umeda) North of Hankyū Umeda Station, this is a good choice for comfort near the station. Rooms are Western size and everything is polished, right down to the marble bathrooms. The *hinoki* (cypress) wooden bathtubs in the Japanese suites are a special touch. Cable LAN available in rooms.

Minami Area

MIDRANGE

Osaka Namba Washington Hotel Plaza (Map p399; ☎ 6212-2555; http://nanba.wh-at.com, in Japanese; 1-1-13 Nihonbashi, Chūō-ku; s/d/tw from ¥6900/13,000/14,000; Sakai-suji subway line, Sennichimae subway line & Kintetsu Nara line to Nihonmashi) The Washington Hotel Plaza chain is a reliable and relatively comfortable nationwide business-hotel chain and its Namba branch stays true to form: rooms are small but sufficient and well kept. The hotel is within walking distance of the chaos of Minami, but (fortunately) not right in the thick of things.

Cross Hotel Osaka (Map p399; ☎ 6213-8281; www.crosshotel.com/eng_osaka/index.html; 2-5-15 Shinsaibashisuji, Chūō-ku; s/d/tw from ¥16,170/24,255/27,720; ; Midō-suji subway line to Namba) Located just a short walk from the Dōtombori area, this is a decent deal if you want to be based in the heart of Minami. The hotel has just been refurbished and the rooms are fairly spacious for this price bracket. Cable LAN available in rooms.

TOP END

Hotel Nikkō Osaka (Map p399; ☎ 6244-1281; www.hno.co.jp/english/index_e.html; 1-3-3 Nishi-Shinsaibashi, Chūō-ku; s/d/tw from ¥21,945/34,650/34,650; ; Midō-suji subway line to Shinsaibashi) In Shinsaibashi, this is a good choice, with excellent facilities and a convenient location. All the rooms here are Western style and very clean, including the bathrooms. There is direct access to Shinsaibashi subway station. Cable LAN available in rooms.

Swissotel Nankai Osaka (Map p399; ☎ 6646-1111; http://osaka.swissotel.com; 5-1-60 Namba, Chūō-ku; d/tw from ¥34,650/48,510; ; Midō-suji subway line to Namba) Minami's most elegant hotel, with stunning views and direct connections to KIX via Nankai-line trains that depart from Namba Station below the hotel. Rooms are clean and well appointed. There is a gym and excellent dining options on-site and nearby. Cable LAN available in rooms.

Other Areas

BUDGET

Osaka-fu Hattori Ryokuchi Youth Hostel (大阪府服部緑地ユースホステル; off Map p395; ☎ 6862-0600; www.osakaymca.or.jp/shisetsu/hattori/hattori.html; 1-3 Hattori Ryokuchi, Toyonaka-shi; dm ¥2500; Midō-suji subway line to Ryokuchi-kōen Station, western exit) Located in Ryokuchi-kōen, this youth hostel is a little long in the tooth and not quite as welcoming as the other two listed here. However, if you fancy a little fresh air in the evening, this is a good choice. No membership is necessary here. It's approximately 15 minutes from Kita or 30 minutes from Minami. Leave the station, enter the park and follow the path past a fountain and around to the right alongside the pond.

Osaka Shiritsu Nagai Youth Hostel (大阪市立長居ユースホステル; off Map p395; ☎ 6699-5631; www.nagaiyh.com/english/index.html; 1-1 Nagai-kōen, Higashisumiyoshi-ku; dm from ¥2950, s ¥3450; ; JR Hanwa line to Tsurugaoka) This is another good youth hostel, although it's somewhat less conveniently located than the Shin-Osaka Youth Hostel. It's clean, well run and smoke-free. There are private rooms and a family room for up to four people. Take the Midō-suji subway line south from the centre of town to Nagai Station, go out exit 1 and walk for 10 minutes towards the stadium. The hostel is at the back of the stadium. Or (for Japan Rail Pass holders), take the JR Hanwa line to Tsurugaoka Station and walk southeast for five minutes.

Shin-Osaka Youth Hostel (新大阪ユースホステル; Map p395; ☎ 6370-5427; www.osaka-yha.com/shin-osaka; 1-13-13 Higashinakajima, Higashiyodogawa-ku; dm ¥3300, tw per person ¥4500; 💻 📶; 🚆 JR line to Shin-Osaka, east exit) Five minutes' walk from Shin-Osaka Station, this fine new youth hostel is the closest hostel to the centre of town. The rooms are clean and well taken care of and there are great views across the city. A variety of private rooms are available, including one barrier-free room. The east exit out of Shin-Osaka Station is only marked from the upper floors of the station; cross the road and go left, passing a small convenience store and a sushi restaurant; turn right just past the sushi restaurant and walk 200m and you will see the large building on your left. Elevators are at the back.

TOP END

Hotel Nikkō Kansai Airport (☎ 0724-55-1111; www.nikkokix.com/e/top.html; 1 Senshū Kūkō kita, Izumisano-shi; s/d/tw ¥21,945/32,340/32,340; 💻 🏊; 🚆 JR Kansai Kūkō line to Kansai Kūkō) This is the only hotel at KIX and it charges accordingly. But, if you can live with that, it's a good place. The rooms are spacious with some good views. Note that check-in can be slow when a lot of flights are arriving at once. There is cable LAN internet in rooms.

Imperial Hotel Osaka (Map p395; ☎ 6881-1111; 8-50, Temmabashi 1-chōme, Kita-ku; s/d/tw from ¥32,340/38,115/53,130; 💻 🏊; 🚆 JR Osaka Loop line to Sakuranomiya) Within easy walking distance of Osaka-jō, this classic hotel has fairly spacious and well-appointed rooms. There is a fitness club and 25m pool. The standard of service is very high here and all staff speaks English. The location is not particularly convenient, unless you plan to concentrate on Osaka-jō, but there is a shuttle bus to JR Osaka Station. There is cable LAN internet in rooms.

EATING

Kita

JAPANESE

Umeda Hagakure (Map p397; ☎ 6341-1409; 1-1-3 Umeda; noodles ¥500-600; 🕑 lunch & dinner, lunch only Sat & Sun; 🚆 JR line to Osaka) Locals line up outside this place for the fantastic udon noodles. It's on the B2 floor of the Ekimae Daisan building. Take the central escalator to the B2 floor, take a right, walk 25m and take another right. It is on the left with a small English sign. There are pictures outside to help with ordering. Our pick here is *tenzaru* (udon served on a plate with tempura; ¥1100). Whatever you do, don't go on a weekday between noon and 1pm (this is when the white-collar workers line up for lunch).

Ganko Umeda Honten (Map p397; ☎ 6376-2001; 1-5-11 Shibata; lunch meals from ¥780; 🕑 11.30am-4am; 🚆 Hankyū line to Umeda) Big is the operative word at this giant dining hall alongside Hankyū Umeda Station that serves a wide variety of Japanese dishes starting with sushi (if you want just sushi, you can sit at the counter and order à la carte). It's very approachable and has an English picture menu. Look for the picture of the guy with the headband; it's just south of the DD House complex.

Dōjima Hana (Map p397; ☎ 6345-0141; 2-1-31 Dōjima, Kita-ku; meals from ¥819; 🕑 11am-11pm; 🚆 JR line to Osaka) If you crave something a little *kotteri* (rich and fatty), we recommend the tasty *tonkatsu* at this approachable restaurant a stone's throw from the excellent Junkudō bookstore. We recommend the *rōsukatsu teishoku* (pork cutlet roast *teishoku*, regular/large; ¥924/1134). There is a limited picture menu and an English sign.

Isaribi (Map p397; ☎ 6373-2969; 1-5-12 Shibata; dinner average per person ¥2000-3000; 🕑 5-11pm Mon-Fri, 4.30-11pm Sat, Sun & holidays; 🚆 Hankyū line to Umeda) This is a great *robatayaki* (a restaurant where the food is arrayed in front of diners and cooked in front of them; literally 'hearthside cooking'), down a flight of white-tile stairs outside Hankyū Umeda Station. Like *yakitori*, this is drinking food, and *nama beeru* (draught beer) really flows at this place. It's a little tricky to spot; it's just south of Ganko Umeda Honten (see above).

A great place for a cheap lunch or dinner while in Kita is the Shin-Umeda Shokudō-Gai (Map p397), which is located down the escalators and to the right of the main exit of Hankyū Umeda Station (just past the McDonald's). There are heaps of good restaurants here that vie for the lunch/dinner custom with cheap set meals, many of which are displayed outside, making ordering easy.

One excellent place here is **Okonomiyaki Sakura** (Map p397; ☎ 6364-7521; 9-10 Kakuda-chō; okonomiyaki under ¥1000; 🕑 11am-11pm; 🚆 Hankyū line to Umeda), a foreigner-friendly *okonomiyaki* (Japanese savoury pancake) specialist with an English menu. There is a map in the middle of the food court, and Okonomiyaki Sakura is No 10 on the map. Look for the glass sliding doors and the counter.

Another good food court in Kita is the Kappa Yokochō Arcade (marked 'Kappa Plaza' in English) just north of Hankyū Umeda Station. Here you'll find **Gataro** (Map p397; ☎ 6373-1484; 1-7-2 Shibata; dinner per person around ¥3500-4000; 4-11pm; Hankyū line to Umeda), a cosy little spot that does creative twists on standard *izakaya* themes. Look for the glass front with credit-card stickers on the left as you head north in the arcade. Unlike most *izakaya*, this one has an English menu.

Another top food court is Hilton Plaza, on the B2 floor beneath the Osaka Hilton. Here, you will find the excellent **Shinkiraku** (Map p397; ☎ 6345-3461; 1-8-16 Umeda, Kita-ku; meals from around ¥800; 11am-2.30pm & 4-11pm Mon-Fri, 11am-2.30pm & 5-10pm Sat, Sun & holidays; JR line to Osaka), a favourite tempura specialist that packs 'em in at lunchtime. At lunch try the *ebishio-tendon* (shrimp tempura over rice; ¥880) and at dinner try the *osusume-gozen* (tempura full set; ¥2079). Take the escalator to the B2 floor, go right and look for the small English sign.

INTERNATIONAL

Org…Organic Life (Map p397; ☎ 6312-0529; 7-7 Dōyama-chō, Kita-ku; drinks from ¥500, meals ¥1000-2500; 11am-11pm; Hankyū line to Umeda, JR line to Osaka or Tanimachi subway line to Higashi Umeda) At this open-plan, casual cafe you can grab a light meal or a quick pick-me-up while exploring Kita. You can get a pasta or risotto lunch for ¥900, and finish it off with cake and coffee. It's easy to spot, with an English sign. There's no English menu, but there is a picture menu and 'pasta lunch' or 'risotto lunch' will get your point across.

Monsoon Café (Map p397; ☎ 6292-0010; 15-22 Chayamachi, Kita-ku; meals average ¥1000; 11.30am-4am; Hankyū line to Umeda) For a fun night with decent pan-Asian cuisine and a casual international atmosphere, try the Osaka branch of this nationwide chain. It's in the Urban Terrace building (the westernmost of the three buildings), which is across from the Hotel Hankyū International. English menu.

Minami

JAPANESE

You will find lots of good Japanese choices in Minami, including a bunch of giant dining halls in Dōtombori Arcade.

Nishiya (Map p399; ☎ 6241-9221; 1-18-18 Higashi Shinsaibashi, Chūō-ku; noodle dishes from ¥630, dinner average ¥3000-4000; lunch & dinner; Midō-suji, Yotsubashi or Nagahori Tsurumiryokuchi subway line to Shinsaibashi) An Osaka landmark that serves udon noodles and a variety of hearty *nabe* (iron pot) dishes for reasonable prices, including a tempura udon (¥1155). Look for the semirustic facade and the food models. English menu.

Tonkatsu Ganko (Map p399; ☎ 6646-4129; 2-2-16 Nambanaka, Naniwa-ku; meals from ¥880; lunch & dinner; Nankai Main line or Midō-suji, Yotsubashi or Sennichi-mae subway line to Namba) Sometimes you need something a little heavier than noodles and rice, and *tonkatsu* may be the call. This popular *tonkatsu* specialist near Namba Station is easy to spot with food models in the glass case out front (next to an NTT Docomo shop). There's a picture menu and an English menu.

Gin Sen (Map p399; ☎ 6213-2898; 2-4-2 Shinsaibashi-suji, Chūō-ku; all-you-can-eat kushikatsu lunch/dinner ¥2380/2680; 11.30am-11pm; Midō-suji, Yotsubashi or Sennichi-mae subway line to Namba) This casual, approachable place serves delicious *kushikatsu* (meat and veggies deep-fried on skewers), a greasy but tasty treat. It's on the 2nd floor of the Gurukas building; there's a Lawson convenience store on the ground floor. English menu.

Ume no Hana (Map p399; ☎ 6258-3766; OPA Bldg, 11th fl, 1-4-3 Nishi-Shinsaibashi, Chūō-ku; dinner from ¥4100; 11am-3pm & 5-9pm; Midō-suji subway line to Shinsaibashi) This is part of an upscale chain that serves a variety of tofu-based dishes. It's on the 11th floor of the OPA building. The elevator is on the southeast side of the building (entry from the street – look for the sign reading 'OPA Restaurant & Café'). English menu.

Of course, Minami is all about *shōtengai* (shopping arcades) and the Sennichi-mae Arcade is one of the biggest. In addition to all the pachinko parlours here, you'll find lots of cheap, casual restaurants like **Genroku Sushi** (Map p399; ☎ 6644-4908; 2-11-4 Sennichi-mae; 10am-11.10pm; Midō-suji, Yotsubashi or Sennichi-mae subway line to Namba), a bustling automatic sushi place where plates of sushi cost a mere ¥130.

Dōtombori Arcade (Map p399; Dōtombori, Chūō-ku; Midō-suji, Yotsubashi or Sennichi-mae subway line to Namba) is the heart of Minami, and it's crammed with eateries. This is not the place to go for refined dining, but if you want heaping portions of tasty food in a very casual atmosphere, it can be a lot of fun. And because it sees a lot of tourists, most of the big restaurants here have English menus. Here is a quick list of our favourite spots:

Imai Honten (Map p399; ☎ 6211-0319; 1-7-22 Dōtombori, Chūō-ku; noodles from ¥577; 🕑 11am-10pm, closed Wed) One of the area's oldest and most revered udon specialists and our favourite place on the strip. It's an oasis of calm amid the chaos (their no-mobile-phone policy ensures quiet). Try the *tendon* (tempura over rice; ¥1575). It's sandwiched between two pachinko parlours. There's no English sign, but the traditional front stands out among the glitter. English menu.

Chibō (Map p399; ☎ 6212-2211; 1-5-5 Dōtombori, Chūō-ku; okonomiyaki from ¥850; 🕑 11am-1am Mon-Thu, to 3am Fri & Sat, to midnight Sun) A great *okonomiyaki* specialist. There's an English sign in addition to the English menu. Try the house special *Dōtombori yaki,* a toothsome treat with pork, beef, squid, shrimp and cheese for ¥1550. Some tables look out over the canal. Last orders an hour before closing.

Ganko Zushi (Map p399; ☎ 6212-1705; 1-8-24 Dōtombori, Chūō-ku; set meals from ¥1000; 🕑 11.30am-11pm) Giant sushi restaurant (can order à la carte at counter) that serves just about everything else. English menu.

Zuboraya (Map p399; ☎ 6211-0181; 1-6-10 Dōtombori, Chūō-ku; fugu sashimi ¥1400, full dinners from ¥3000; 🕑 11am-11pm) A huge *fugu* (Japanese pufferfish) specialist with a good picture menu. Look for the giant *fugu* out front. Some English on menu.

Kani Dōraku Honten (Map p399; ☎ 6211-8975; 1-6-18 Dōtombori, Chūō-ku; lunch/dinner from ¥1995/4620; 🕑 11am-11pm) Popular crab specialist; look for giant crab on storefront. Limited English menu.

INTERNATIONAL

Café Slices (Map p399; ☎ 6211-2231; 2-3-21 Nishi-Shinsaibashi, Chūō-ku; pizza slices/whole from ¥400/2500; 🕑 11am-late; Ⓜ Midō-suji subway line to Namba or Shinsaibashi) If you need a break from Japanese food and want something casual and easy, stop into this foreigner-friendly pizza joint for a slice or two. In addition to pizza, they serve wraps, bagels, salads and fries. There's a big English sign.

Krungtep (Map p399; ☎ 4708-0088; 1-6-14 Dōtombori, Chūō-ku; lunch buffet ¥1200, dinner dishes from ¥1000; 🕑 lunch & dinner; Ⓜ Midō-suji, Yotsubashi or Sennichi-mae subway line to Namba) Dōtombori's most popular Thai place serves fairly authentic versions of the standard favourites like green curry and fried noodles. Look for the small English sign – it's on the B1 floor.

Finally, if you just feel like a Western-style sandwich or a quick cup of coffee, drop into the Doutor (Map p399) at the mouth of the Sennichi-mae Arcade. There's a picture menu here.

DRINKING

Osaka is a hard-working city, but when quitting time rolls around Osakans know how to party. Take a stroll through Minami on a Friday night and you'd be excused for thinking that there is one bar for every resident of the city. Whatever your taste, you're sure to find something to your liking among this vast array of bars and clubs.

Kita キタ

Although Minami is Osaka's real nightlife district, there are plenty of bars, clubs and *izakaya* in the neighbourhoods to the south and east of Osaka Station.

Canopy (Map p397; ☎ 6341-0339; 1-11-20 Sonezakishinchi, Kita-ku; 🕑 5pm-6am Mon-Sat, to midnight Sun; Ⓜ JR Tōzai line to Kitashinchi) Cafe-style bar that pulls in a crowd of local expats for after-work snacks and drinks. The happy-hour special here is a good and popular deal.

Windows on the World (Map p397; ☎ 6347-7111; 1-8-8 Umeda, Kita-ku; 🕑 11.30am-12.30am; Ⓜ JR line to Osaka) An unbeatable spot for drinks with a view – it's on the 35th floor of the Hilton Osaka. Be warned that there's a ¥1750-per-person table charge and drinks average ¥2000.

Minami ミナミ

This is the place for a wild night out in Osaka. You simply won't believe the number of bars, clubs and restaurants they've packed into the narrow streets and alleys of Dōtombori, Shinsaibashi, Namba and Amerika-Mura.

Hub (Map p399; ☎ 6211-8286; 2F Across Bldg, 2-6-14 Shinsaibashi-suji, Chūō-ku; average cost per person ¥700-1000; 🕑 5pm-midnight Sun-Thu, to 2am Fri, Sat & the day before holidays; Ⓜ Midō-suji subway line to Namba or Shinsaibashi) Previous visitors to Osaka and expats will remember this as the location of the old Shinsaibashi Pig & Whistle. The Hub is a slightly more Americanised *gaijin* bar, but the main ingredients haven't changed: pub grub, cheap beer and a crowd of expats, travellers and internationally minded Japanese.

Murphy's (Map p399; ☎ 6282-0677; 1-6-31 Higashi-Shinsaibashi, Chūō-ku; average cost per person ¥700-1000; 🕑 5pm-1am Sun-Thu, to 4am Fri & Sat; Ⓜ Sakaisuji subway line to Nagahoribashi) This is one of the oldest Irish-style pubs in Japan, and a good place to rub shoulders with local expats and Japanese. It's on the 6th floor of the Reed Plaza Shinsaibashi building, a futuristic building with what looks like a rocket moulded into the front.

SoulFuckTry (Map p399; ☎ 6539-1032; 1-9-14 Minami Horie, Nishi-ku; drinks from ¥700; Ⓜ Yotsubashi subway line to Yotsubashi) This interestingly named bar-club describes itself as a soul disco, and that pretty much nails it. It attracts some interesting DJs and recently played host to Japanese turntable wunderkinds Sara and Ryusei. Turn down the narrow street opposite Eneos gas station.

Cellar (Map p399; ☎ 6212-6437; B1 Shin-sumiya Bldg, 2-17-13 Nishi-Shinsaibashi, Chūō-ku; Ⓜ Midō-suji subway line to Shinsaibashi) Live music is often the draw at this popular basement bar on the west side of Nishi-Shinsaibashi. Look for the entrance to the stairs a few metres north of the corner.

Tavola 36 (Map p399; ☎ 6646-5125; 5-1-60 Namba, Chūō-ku; 🕒 11.30am-11.30pm Mon-Thu, to midnight Fri, 11am-midnight Sat, to 11.30pm Sun & holidays; Ⓜ Nankai Main line to Namba) If you want drinks, a killer view and upscale surroundings, this is the place to be in Minami. It's an Italian restaurant-bar on the 36th floor of the Swissotel Nankai Osaka. There's a ¥1260-per-person table charge after 6pm and drinks start at ¥1200.

ENTERTAINMENT

For up-to-date listings of forthcoming club events, check *Kansai Time Out*.

Clubs

Karma (Map p397; ☎ 6344-6181; 1-5-18 Sonezakishinchi, Kita-ku; Ⓜ JR line to Osaka) A long-standing club in Kita that is popular with Japanese and foreigners alike. On weekends it usually hosts techno events with cover charges averaging ¥2500.

Grand Café (Map p399; ☎ 6213-8637; 2-10-21 Nishi-Shinsaibashi, Chūō-ku; Ⓜ Midō-suji or Yotsubashi subway line to Shinsaibashi) This hip underground club hosts a variety of electronica-DJ events. There's a comfy seating area and several dance floors. Look for the blue sign at street level.

KANSAI

Traditional Japanese Entertainment

Unfortunately, neither of the following places has regularly scheduled shows. The best thing is to check with the tourist information offices about current shows, check the listings in the *Meet Osaka* guide or look in *Kansai Time Out*.

National Bunraku Theatre (Map p395; ☎ 6212-2531; 1-12-10 Nipponbashi, Chūō-ku; Ⓜ Sennichi-mae or Sakai-suji subway line to Nipponbashi) Although *bunraku*, or puppet theatre, did not originate in Osaka, the art form was popularised at this theatre. The most famous *bunraku* playwright, Chikametsu Monzaemon (1653–1724), wrote plays set in Osaka concerning the classes that traditionally had no place in Japanese art: merchants and the denizens of the pleasure quarters. Not surprisingly, *bunraku* found a wide audience among these people, and a theatre was established to put on the plays of Chikametsu in Dōtombori. Today's theatre is an attempt to revive the fortunes of *bunraku*. Performances are only held at certain times of the year: check with the tourist info offices. Tickets normally start at around ¥2500; earphones and program guides in English are available. This is probably the best place in Japan to see *bunraku*. Just be warned that performances sell out quickly.

Osaka Nōgaku Hall (Map p397; ☎ 6373-1726; 2-3-17 Nakasakinishi, Kita-ku; Ⓜ JR line to Osaka) A five-minute walk east of Osaka Station, this hall holds nō shows about twice a month, most of which cost ¥5000 to ¥6000.

SHOPPING

Osaka has almost as many shops as it has restaurants. The major department stores are clustered around JR Osaka and Umeda Stations in Kita. High-end fashion shops and international luxury brands have their outlets along Midō-suji, the main street of Minami, between Shinsaibashi and Namba subway stations.

Osaka's speciality is electronics, and Den Den Town (Map p399) is Osaka's version of Tokyo's Akihabara. Taking its name from the Japanese word for electricity, *denki*, Den Den Town is an area of shops almost exclusively devoted to electronic goods. To avoid sales tax, check if the store has a 'Tax Free' sign outside and bring your passport. Most stores are closed on Wednesday. Take the Sakai-suji subway line to Ebisu-chō Station and take exit 1 or exit 2. Alternatively, it's a 15-minute walk south of Nankai Namba Station.

For anything related to cooking and eating, head to the Dōguya-suji Arcade in Minami (p397).

Kōjitsu Sansō (Map p397; ☎ 6442-5267; Osaka Ekimae Daisan Bldg, 1-3 Umeda, Kita-ku; 🕒 10.30am-8pm; Ⓜ JR line to Osaka) If you need a new backpack or any other kind of outdoor gear, head to this excellent shop on the ground floor at the northwest corner of the Ekimae Daisan building.

Bic Camera (Map p399; ☎ 6634-1111; 2-10-1 Sennichimae, Chūō-ku; 🕒 10am-9pm; Ⓜ JR line, Kintetsu line, Midō-suji, Sennichi-mae, Nankai Honsen, Kūkō, Kōya subway lines to Namba) Bic Camera is a one-stop shop for everything related to cameras, electronics and computers (but note that many computer-related items are designed for operation with a Japanese system). You'll find some of the best prices in the city at this vast shop.

GETTING THERE & AWAY

Air

Osaka is served by two airports: Osaka Itami Airport (ITM), which handles only domestic traffic, and the newer Kansai International Airport (KIX), which handles all international and some domestic flights. Itami is conveniently located right in Osaka itself; KIX is on an artificial island in Wakayama-ken (see p408 for transport details).

Boat

The **Japan China International Ferry Company** (☎ in Japan 6536-6541, in China 021-6325-7642; www.shinganjin.com, in Japanese) connects Shanghai and Osaka/Kōbe (one way 2nd class ¥20,000/CNY1300, around 48 hours). A similar service at similar prices is provided by the **Shanghai Ferry Company** (☎ in Japan 6243-6345, in China 021-6537-5111; www.shanghai-ferry.co.jp, in Japanese). These ferries operate from the Osaka Nankō international ferry terminal, which can be reached by taking the New Tram service from Suminoe-kōen Station to Nankoguchi Station.

Domestic ferries operate from Nankō ferry terminal and Kanome-futō and Benten-futō piers for various destinations around Honshū, Kyūshū and Shikoku. Destinations (2nd-class fares) include Beppu (from ¥10,000, 11½ hours), Miyazaki (from ¥10,800, 12¾ hours), Shibushi (from ¥11,500, 14¾ hours) and Shinmoji (from ¥6420, 12 hours) in Kyūshū; and Shōdo-shima (from ¥3800, 4½ hours), Matsuyama (from ¥7500, 9¼ hours) and Niihama (from ¥5700, 9¼ hours) in Shikoku.

For detailed information about sailing schedules and bookings contact the tourist information offices (p392).

Bus

There is a long-distance highway bus service between Osaka and cities all across Honshū, Shikoku and some cities in Kyūshū. Destinations include Tokyo (from ¥4300, eight hours), Nagasaki (¥11,000, 10 hours) and Kagoshima (¥12,000, 11 hours 54 minutes). Most buses depart from JR Osaka Station (Map p397); check with the tourist information offices (p392) for more details.

Train

SHINKANSEN

Osaka is on the Tōkaidō-San-yō *shinkansen* line that runs between Tokyo and Hakata (Kyūshū): Hikari *shinkansen* run to/from Tokyo (¥13,550, three hours) and to/from Hakata (¥14,390, three hours). Other cities on this line include Hiroshima, Kyoto, Kōbe and Okayama.

KYOTO

The *shinkansen* is the fastest way to travel between Kyoto and Osaka (¥2730, 15 minutes). The second-fastest way is a JR *shinkaisoku* train between JR Kyoto Station and JR Osaka Station (Map p397; ¥540, 28 minutes).

Another choice is the cheaper but more comfortable private Hankyū line that runs between Hankyū Umeda Station in Osaka and Hankyū Kawaramachi, Karasuma and Ōmiya Stations in Kyoto (*tokkyū* to Kawaramachi ¥390, 44 minutes).

Alternatively, you can take the private Keihan main line between Sanjō, Shijō or Shichijō Stations in Kyoto and Keihan Yodoyabashi Station in Osaka (*tokkyū* to Sanjō ¥400, 51 minutes). Yodoyabashi is on the Midō-suji subway line.

KŌBE

The *shinkansen* is the fastest way to travel between Kōbe and Osaka (¥2810, 13 minutes, from Shin-Kōbe Station to Shin-Osaka Station). The second-fastest way between Kōbe and Osaka is a JR *shinkaisoku* train between JR Osaka Station and Kōbe's Sannomiya and Kōbe Stations (¥390, 24 minutes).

There is also the private Hankyū line, which takes a little more time but is cheaper and usually less crowded/more comfortable. It runs from Osaka's Hankyū Umeda Station (Map p397) to Kōbe's Sannomiya Station (*tokkyū*, ¥310, 29 minutes).

NARA

The JR Kansai line links Osaka (Namba and Tennō-ji Stations) and Nara (JR Nara Station) via Hōryū-ji (*yamatoji kaisoku*, ¥780, 42 minutes).

The private Kintetsu Nara line also connects Osaka (Kintetsu Namba Station) with Nara (Kintetsu Nara Station). *Kyūkō* (express) and *futsū* services take about 36 minutes and cost ¥540. *Tokkyū* trains do the journey in five minutes' less time but at almost double the cost, making them a poor option.

GETTING AROUND

To/From the Airport

OSAKA ITAMI AIRPORT

There are frequent **limousine buses** (Osaka Airport Transport Co; ☎ 6844-1124; www.okkbus.co.jp/eng/index.html) running between the airport and various parts of Osaka. Buses run to/from Shin-Osaka Station every 20 minutes from about 8am to 9pm (¥490, 25 minutes). Buses run at about the same frequency to/from Osaka and Namba Stations (¥620, 25 minutes). At Itami, buy your tickets from the machine outside the arrivals hall. (Hint: you've got a better chance of getting a seat if you board at the South Terminal.)

KANSAI INTERNATIONAL AIRPORT (KIX)

The fastest way between KIX and Osaka is the private Nankai express Rapit, which runs to/from Nankai Namba Station on the Midō-suji subway line (¥1390, 35 minutes). The JR Haruka limited airport express runs between KIX and Tennō-ji Station (¥2070, 29 minutes) and Shin-Osaka Station (¥2780, 45 minutes).

Regular JR express trains called *kankū kaisoku* also run between KIX and Osaka (¥1160, 63 minutes), Kyōbashi (¥1160, 70 minutes), Tennō-ji (¥1030, 49 minutes) and JR Namba (¥1030, 56 minutes) Stations.

The Osaka City Air Terminal (OCAT), in JR Namba Station, allows passengers on Japanese and some other airlines to check in and deposit baggage before boarding trains to the airport. Check with your airline for details.

There are a variety of bus routes between KIX and Osaka. **Limousine buses** (Kansai Airport Transportation Enterprise; ☎ 0724-61-1374; www.kate.co.jp/pc/index_e.html) travel to/from Osaka Umeda, OCAT Namba, Uehonmachi and Nankō (Cosmo Sq) Stations. The fare is ¥1300 (¥880 OCAT) for most routes and the journeys take an average of 50 minutes, depending on traffic conditions.

Bus

Osaka does have a bus system, but it is nowhere near as easy to use as the rail network. Japanese-language bus maps are available from the tourist offices.

Train & Subway

Osaka has a good subway network and, like Tokyo, a JR loop line (known in Japanese as the JR Kanjō-sen) that circles the city area. In fact, there should be no need to use any other form of transport while you are in Osaka unless you stay out late and miss the last train.

There are eight subway lines, but the one that most short-term visitors are likely to find most useful is the Midō-suji line, which runs north to south, stopping at Shin-Osaka, Umeda (next to Osaka Station), Shinsaibashi, Namba and Tennō-ji Stations. Most rides cost between ¥200 and ¥300. This book contains a full Osaka subway/tram map; see p512.

If you plan a lot of subway rides, consider buying a 'one-day free ticket' *(kyōtsū ichinichi jōsha ken)*. For ¥850 (or ¥600 on Fridays and the 20th of every month) you get unlimited travel on any subway, the New Tram line and all city buses (but not the JR line). These tickets can be purchased from some of the ticket machines in most subway stations; push the button for 'one-day free ticket' *(kyōtsū ichinichi jōsha ken)* then press the illuminated button reading '¥850'.

KŌBE 神戸

☎ 078 / pop 1.53 million

Perched on a hillside overlooking the sea, Kōbe is one of Japan's most attractive cities. It's also one of the country's most cosmopolitan, having served as a maritime gateway to Kansai from the earliest days of trade with China. To this day, there are significant populations of other Asian nationalities in Kōbe, as well as plenty of Westerners, many of whom work in nearby Osaka.

One of Kōbe's best features is its relatively small size – most of the sights can be reached on foot from the main train stations. Of course, it must be noted that none of these sights are must-sees: Kōbe is likely to appeal more to Japan residents than to travellers. However, it does have some good restaurants, cafes and bars and is a good place for a night out in Kansai if you just can't face the mayhem of Osaka.

ORIENTATION

Kōbe's two main entry points are Sannomiya and Shin-Kōbe Stations. Shin-Kōbe Station, in the northeast of town, is where the *shinkansen* stops. A subway (¥200, two minutes) runs from here to the downtown Sannomiya Station, which has frequent rail connections with Osaka and Kyoto. It's possible to walk between the two stations in around 20 minutes. Sannomiya Station marks the city centre, although a spate of development in Kōbe Harbor Land is starting to swing the city's centre of gravity to the southwest. Before starting your exploration of Kōbe, pick up a copy of the *Kōbe City Map* at one of the two information offices.

INFORMATION

The city's main **tourist information office** (☎ 322-0220; 9am-7pm) is on the ground floor on the south side of JR Sannomiya Station's west gate (follow the signs for Santica, a shopping mall). There's a smaller information counter on the 2nd floor of Shin-Kōbe Station, right outside the main *shinkansen* gate. Both information centres carry the free *Kōbe City Map*.

Citibank (☎ 392-4122; 9am-3pm Mon-Fri, ATM 24hr; Hankyū Kōbe line, Hanshin Main line or JR Kōbe line to Sannomiya) Behind Kōbe City Hall; ATM accepts international cards.

HIS Motomachi Branch (☎ 335-2505; 10.30am-7pm, 11am-6pm Sat, Sun & holidays, closed Thu; Hanshin Main line or JR Kōbe line to Motomachi) Travel agency on the 2nd floor near the corner, diagonally across from Motomachi Station.

rw books (☎ 332-9200; 11am-7pm; JR Kōbe line to Motomachi) Small English-language bookshop on 2nd floor in shopping street.

SIGHTS

Kitano 北野

Twenty minutes' walk north of Sannomiya is the pleasant hillside neighbourhood of Kitano, where local tourists come to enjoy the feeling of foreign travel without leaving Japanese soil. A European-American atmosphere is created by the winding streets and *ijinkan* (literally 'foreigners' houses') that housed some of Kōbe's early Western residents. Admission to some is free, to others ¥300 to ¥700, and most are open from 9am to 5pm daily. Although these brick and weatherboard dwellings may not hold the same fascination for Western travellers that they hold for local tourists, the area itself is pleasant to stroll around and is dotted with good cafes and restaurants.

Shin-Kōbe Cable Car & Nunobiki Hābu-kōen 新神戸ロープウェイ・布引ハーブ公園

The **Shin-Kōbe cable car** (Shin-Kōbe Ropeway; one way/return ¥550/1000; 9.30am-5.30pm, later in Jun-Aug; Seishin-Yamate subway line to Shin-Kōbe) leaves from behind the Crowne Plaza Kōbe hotel near Shin-Kōbe Station and ascends to a mountain ridge 400m above the city. The views from the top over Kōbe and the bay are particularly pretty after sunset. There's a complex of gardens, restaurants and shops below the top station known as the **Nunobiki Hābu-kōen** (Nunobiki Herb Garden; admission ¥200; 10am-5pm, until later Jun-Aug; Shin-Kōbe cable car to Nunobiki Hābu-kōen). Note that you can easily walk down to the bottom station from the Herb Garden in about 30 minutes.

Kōbe City Museum 神戸市立博物館

This **museum** (Kōbe Shiritsu Hakubutsukan; ☎ 391-0035; 24 Kyō-machi, Chūō-ku; admission ¥200 plus varying exhibition fees; 10am-5pm, closed Mon; JR Kōbe line to Sannomiya) has a collection of so-called *namban* (literally 'southern barbarian') art and occasional special exhibits. *Namban* art is a school of painting that developed under the influence of early Jesuit missionaries in Japan, many of whom taught Western painting techniques to Japanese students. The entrance is on the east side of the building. Last entry by 4.30pm.

Nankinmachi (Chinatown) 南京町

Nankinmachi, Kōbe's Chinatown, is a gaudy, bustling, unabashedly touristy collection of Chinese restaurants and stores that should be familiar to anyone who's visited Chinatowns elsewhere in the world. The restaurants here tend to be overpriced and may disappoint sophisticated palates, but the place is fun for a stroll, particularly in the evening when the lights of the area illuminate the gaudily painted facades of the shops. If you fancy a bite while touring the area, we recommend a plate of *gyōza* (dumplings) and we list two good choices (see p412).

Kōbe Harbor Land & Meriken Park 神戸ハーバーランド

Five minutes' walk southeast of Kōbe Station, Kōbe Harbor Land is awash with megamall shopping and dining developments. This may not appeal to foreign travellers the way it does to the local youth, but it's still a nice place for a stroll in the afternoon.

A five-minute walk to the east of Harbor Land you'll find Meriken Park, on a spit of reclaimed land jutting out into the bay. The main attraction here is the **Kōbe Maritime Museum** (Kōbe Kaiyō Hakubutsukan; ☎ 327-8983; 2-2 Hatoba-chō, Chūō-ku; admission ¥500; 10am-5pm, closed Mon; JR Kōbe line to Motomachi). The museum has a small collection of ship models and displays, with some English explanations. Last entry by 4.30pm.

Hakutsuru Sake Brewery Museum 白鶴記念造酒資料館

The Nada-ku area of Kōbe is one of Japan's major sake-brewing centres and the dominant brewer here is the famous Hakutsuru company. The **Hakutsuru Sake Brewery Museum** (☎ 822-8907; 4-5-5 Sumiyoshi Minami-machi, Higashinada-ku; admission free; 9.30am-4.30pm, closed Mon, new year & O-Bon; Hanshin Main line to Sumiyoshi) provides a fascinating look into traditional sake-making methods. There is not much in the way of English explanations, but the free English pamphlet should get you started. Free sake tasting is possible after you tour the facilities (ask at the counter).

Take the Hanshin line eight stops east from Sannomiya (¥180, six minutes, express trains do not stop) and get off at Hanshin Sumiyoshi Station. Exit the station, walk south to the elevated highway and cross the pedestrian overpass; take a right at the bottom of the steps; take your first left, then a right and look for it on the right (there is no English sign). You have to sign in at the gate. Use the blue-and-white crane logo atop the modern wing of the factory as your guide.

FESTIVALS & EVENTS

Luminarie, Kōbe's biggest yearly event, is held every evening from around 4 to 15 December to celebrate the city's miraculous recovery from a 1995 earthquake that killed over 6000 people (check with the Kōbe tourist information office as the exact dates change slightly every year). The streets southwest of Kōbe City Hall are decorated with countless illuminated metal archways, which when viewed from within look like the interior of some otherworldly cathedral.

SLEEPING

B Kōbe (☎ 333-4880; fax 333-4876; www.ishinhotels.com/theb-kobe/en/index.html; s/d/tw from ¥8400/16,800/18,900; ; Seishin-Yamate subway line to Sannomiya) The centrally located B Kōbe is a good utilitarian choice if you've got business in Kōbe or just want a clean place to lay your head in the evening. The windows are tiny and there's not much light, but if you're only there at night this shouldn't matter too much. LAN cable internet in rooms.

Hotel Tor Road (☎ 391-6691; fax 391-6570; www.hoteltorroad.co.jp, in Japanese; s/d/tw from ¥8400/17,850/17,850; ; JR Kōbe line to Sannomiya or Motomachi) A step up from the typical business hotel, this Tor Road hotel is a good choice for those who want a little more comfort. Beds are larger than normal for this sort of hotel and quite clean. LAN cable internet in rooms.

Crowne Plaza Hotel Kōbe (☎ 291-1121; fax 291-1151; www.ichotelsgroup.com/h/d/cp/1/en/hotel/osakb; s/d/tw from ¥15,015/27,720/27,720; ; Seishin-Yamate subway line or JR Sanyō shinkansen to Shin-Kōbe) You'll feel on top of the world as you survey the bright lights of Kōbe from this perch atop the city. Conveniently located near JR Shin-Kōbe Station, this first-class hotel offers clean and fairly spacious rooms and has an English-speaking staff. Downstairs in the Avenue shopping centre, you'll find several good restaurants to choose from. LAN cable internet in rooms.

Hotel Ōkura Kōbe (☎ 333-0111; fax 333-6673; www.okura.com/hotels/kobe/index.html; s/d/tw from ¥18,480/22,050/28,875; ; ; JR Kōbe line to Motomachi) The Ōkura is the most comfortable and polished hotel in the city, and the harbourside location can't be beat. The rooms are clean, spacious and well maintained. Avoid

KANSAI

INFORMATION
- Citibank シティバンク 1 C5
- HIS Motomachi Branch HIS元町支店 2 B6
- rw books ｒｗブックス 3 B6
- South Korea Consulate 大韓民国大使館 4 B4
- Tourist Information Office 観光案内所 5 C5

SIGHTS & ACTIVITIES
- Kōbe City Museum 神戸市立博物館 6 C6
- Nankinmachi Square 南京町 7 B6
- Shin-Kōbe Cable Car 新神戸ロープウェイ 8 B1

SLEEPING
- B Kōbe ザ・ビー神戸 9 B5
- Crowne Plaza Hotel Kōbe クラウンプラザ神戸 10 B1
- Hotel Tor Road ホテルトアロード 11 A4
- Kōbe Kitano Hotel 神戸北野ホテル 12 A4

EATING
- Court Lodge コートロッジ 13 B3
- Ganko Sushi がんこ寿司 14 B5
- Ganso Gyōza-en がんそぎょうざ苑 15 B6
- Kintoki 金時 16 B6
- Mikami 味加味 17 B2
- Modernark Pharm モダナークファーム 18 B5
- Mon もん 19 B5
- Mouriya モーリヤ 20 B5
- Nailey's Café ネイリーズ カフェ 21 B2
- Sona Rupa ショナルパ 22 B5
- Tanoshiya 楽舎 23 B3
- Toritetsu とり鉄 24 B4
- Wakkoqu 和黒 .... (see 10)

DRINKING
- New Munchen Club ニューミュンヘンクラブ 25 B6

SHOPPING
- Avenue Shopping Centre アベニュー .... (see 10)

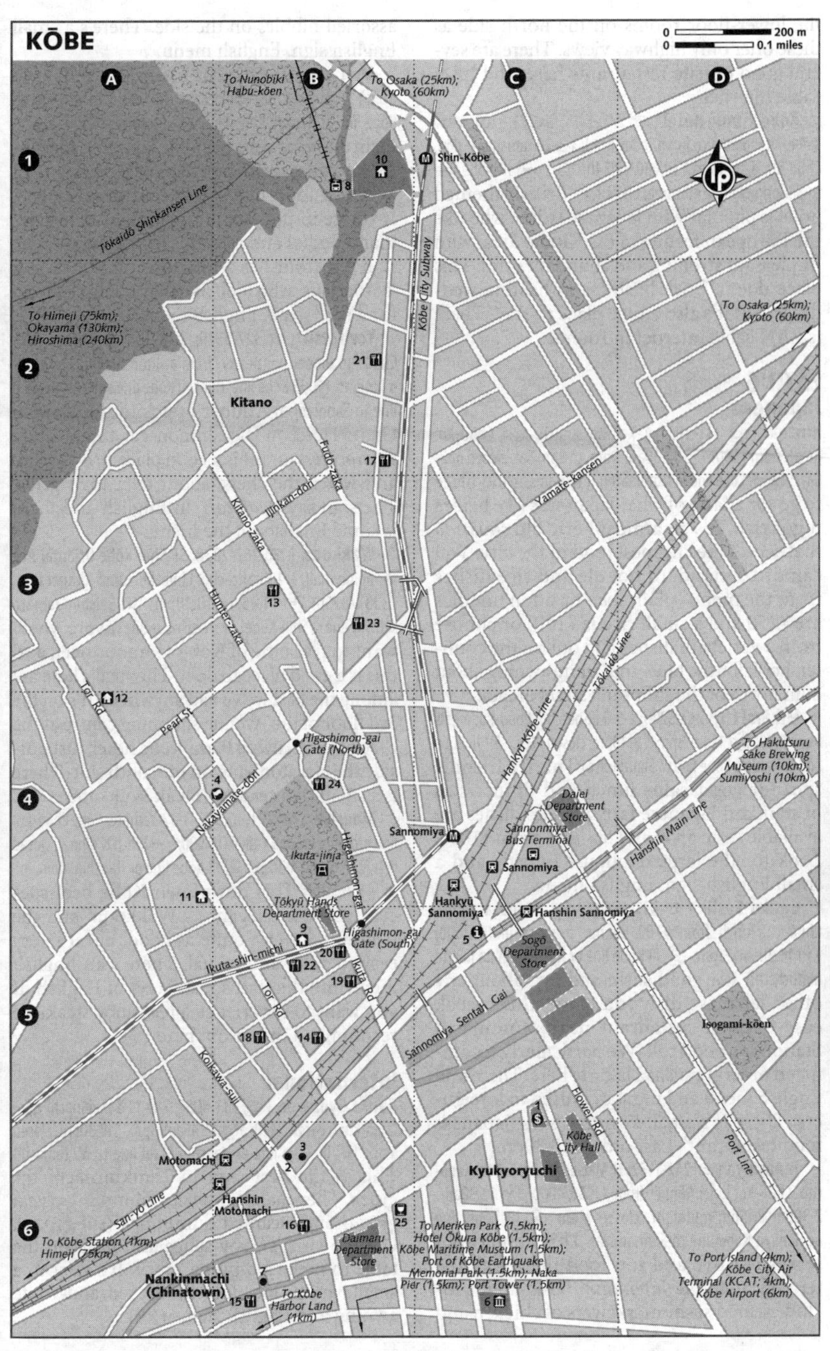
KŌBE
0 200 m
0 0.1 miles
A
B
C
D
1
2
3
4
5
6
To Nunobiki Habu-kōen
To Osaka (25km); Kyoto (60km)
Shin-Kōbe
Tōkaidō Shinkansen Line
To Himeji (75km); Okayama (130km); Hiroshima (240km)
Kōbe City Subway
To Osaka (25km); Kyoto (60km)
Kitano
Fudō-zaka
Ijinkan-dōri
Kitano-zaka
Yamate-kansen
Hunter-zaka
Tōkaidō Line
Tor Rd
Pearl St
Hankyū Kōbe Line
Higashimon-gai Gate (North)
To Hakutsuru Sake Brewing Museum (10km); Sumiyoshi (10km)
Nakayamate-dōri
Daiei Department Store
Hanshin Main Line
Sannomiya
Sannonmiya Bus Terminal
Higashimon-gai
Ikuta-jinja
Sannomiya
Hankyū Sannomiya
Hanshin Sannomiya
Tōkyū Hands Department Store
Higashimon-gai Gate (South)
Sogō Department Store
Ikuta-shin-michi
Ikuta Rd
Tor Rd
Sannomiya Sentah Gai
Isogami-kōen
Koikawa-suji
Flower Rd
Kōbe City Hall
Port Line
Motomachi
Kyukyoryuchi
Hanshin Motomachi
San-yō Line
To Kōbe Station (1km); Himeji (75km)
To Meriken Park (1.5km); Hotel Ōkura Kōbe (1.5km); Kōbe Maritime Museum (1.5km); Port of Kōbe Earthquake Memorial Park (1.5km); Naka Pier (1.5km); Port Tower (1.5km)
Daimaru Department Store
To Port Island (4km); Kōbe City Air Terminal (KCAT; 4km); Kōbe Airport (6km)
Nankinmachi (Chinatown)
To Kōbe Harbor Land (1km)
KANSAI

the lower-floor rooms on the north side as these offer only highway views. There are several good on-site restaurants here, and LAN cable internet.

Kōbe Kitano Hotel (☎ 271-3711; fax 271-3700; www.kobe-kitanohotel.co.jp/en/index.html; 3-3-20 Yamamoto-dōri, Chūō-ku; d/tw from ¥30,030/32,340; 💻; 🚊 JR Kōbe line to Sannnomiya or Motomachi) This British-themed hotel is popular with Japanese ladies, who like the European feeling of the Kitano area, with its pleasant strolling and abundant cafes. This place does a brisk business in hosting weddings, but it's also a nice place to stay. There is LAN cable internet in rooms.

EATING

Japanese

Kintoki (☎ 331-1037; 1-7-2 Motomachi-dōri, Chūō-ku; meals from ¥500; 🕑 10.30am-9pm, to 8pm Sat, closed holidays; 🚊 JR Kōbe line to Motomachi) This is a good place to go for a taste of what Japan was like before it got rich. It's an atmospheric old *shokudō* that serves the cheapest food in the city. You can order standard noodle and rice dishes from the menu (plain *soba* or udon noodles are ¥250 and a small rice is ¥160) or choose from a variety of dishes laid out on the counter. Look for the blue-and-white awning about 20m north of the shopping street arcade.

Mikami (☎ 242-5200; 2-5-9 Kanō-chō, Chūō-ku; meals from ¥500; 🕑 11am-3pm & 5-10pm, closed Wed; 🚊 JR Kōbe line or Hankyū Kōbe line to Sannomiya) This is a friendly spot for good-value lunch and dinner sets of standard Japanese fare. Noodle dishes are available from ¥500 and *teishoku* from ¥1000. Look for the large doghouse outside and a small English sign. English menu.

Ganko Sushi (☎ 331-6868; 2-5-1 Kitanagasa-dōri, Chūō-ku; lunch from ¥700, dinner from around ¥2000; 🕑 11.30am-11pm; 🚊 JR Kōbe line or Hanshin Main line to Motomachi) For good sushi and just about any other Japanese dish you crave, this casual, easy-to-enter restaurant near Motomachi Station is a good call. We particularly recommend ordering sushi à la carte here. There's an English menu and the staff is used to foreigners. There is a small sign that says 'Japanese food restaurant'. Last orders 10.30pm.

Tanoshiya (☎ 242-1132; 1F Matsuda Bldg, 3-14-8 Kanō-chō, Chūō-ku; lunch/dinner from ¥1050/4000; 🕑 11.30am-2.30pm & 5pm-midnight, closed Mon; 🚊 JR Kōbe line or Hankyū Kōbe line to Sannomiya) This casual spot serves creative and fun food that might be termed *'nouvelle Japonaise'*. This might include seared sashimi, skewers of chicken and assorted nibbles on the side. There's a small English sign. English menu.

Mon (☎ 331-0372; 2-12-2 Ikatsuji, Chūō-ku; meals from ¥1100; 🕑 11am-9pm, closed 3rd Mon of month; 🚊 JR Kōbe line or Hankyū Kōbe line to Sannomiya) This Kōbe institution serves a peculiar Japanese speciality known as *yōshoku:* Japanese versions of Western food like steaks and pork cutlets. If you're in the mood for something heavier than noodles and rice, this might satisfy. The sign out front has a hilarious picture of two 'barbarians' who look like they could really go for a nice steak. English menu.

Toritetsu (☎ 327-5529; 1-16-12 Nakayamate-dōri, Chūō-ku; dinner per person from around ¥3000; 🕑 5pm-midnight; 🚊 JR Kōbe line, Hankyū Kōbe line or Hanshin Main line to Sannomiya) Almost opposite the Daiichi Grand Hotel on Higashimon-gai, this bustling *yakitori* restaurant is a good place to eat, drink and watch the chefs labour over their grills. The sign says *'yakitori'* in English and there is some English on the menu.

Wakkoqu (☎ 262-2838; 3F Shin Kōbe Oriental Ave shopping mall, 1-1 Kitano-chō, Chūō-ku; lunch/dinner from ¥3234/8250; 🕑 11.45am-10.30pm; 🚊 Seishin-Yamate subway line to Shin-Kōbe) If you're a carnivore, you'll want to try some of Kōbe's famous beef, and this is a good place to do it. The steaks here are among the best we've had anywhere. It's on the 3rd floor of the Avenue shopping centre at the base of the Crowne Plaza Kōbe hotel, just outside the elevator bank on the south side. There is a small sign reading 'Steak Wakkaqu'.

Mouriya (☎ 391-4603; 2-1-17 Yamate-dōri, Chūō-ku; lunch/dinner around ¥4800/10,000; 🕑 lunch & dinner, closed first Mon of the month; 🚊 JR Kōbe line or Hanshin Main line to Motomachi) This downtown Kōbe beef specialist isn't as elegant as Wakkoqu, and the trimmings aren't quite as good, but it's very easy to enter and casual. There's an English menu and the staff speaks a bit of English. If you want to experience a real juicy steak, we recommend the sirloin here.

International

Ganso Gyōza-en (☎ 331-4096; 2-8-11 Sakaemachi-dōri, Chūō-ku; 6 gyōza ¥420; 🕑 11.45am-3pm, 5-8.30pm, closed Mon; 🚊 JR Kōbe line or Hanshin Main line to Motomachi) This is the best spot in Nankinmachi for *gyōza*. They make both fried dumplings *(yaki gyōza)* and steamed dumplings *(sui gyōza)*. Use the vinegar, soy sauce and *miso* on the table to make a dipping sauce. It's next to a small parking lot – look for the red-and-white awning and English sign.

Modernark Pharm (☎ 391-3060; 3-11-15 Kitanagasa-dōri, Chūō-ku; lunch & dinner from ¥850; ⏲ 11.30am-10.30pm, to 10pm Sun, closed irregularly; 🚉 JR Kōbe line to Motomachi) This interesting little restaurant serves tasty sets of Japanese and Western dishes, including burritos and rice dishes. There are some veggie choices here. Look for the plants. English menu.

Sona Rupa (☎ 322-0252; 2-2-9 Yamate-dōri, Chūō-ku; lunch/dinner from ¥850/3500; ⏲ 11.30am-2.30pm & 5.30-10pm, closed Wed; 🚉 JR Kōbe line, Hankyū Kōbe line or Hanshin Main line to Sannomiya) We like this small Indian restaurant for its crispy naan bread, tasty curries and tranquil atmosphere. It's on the 3rd floor, with a sign at street level. English menu.

Court Lodge (☎ 222-5504; 1-23-16 Nakayamate-dōri, Chūō-ku; meals ¥1000-2000; ⏲ 11am-10.30pm; 🚉 JR Kōbe line, Hankyū Kōbe line or Hanshin Main line to Sannomiya). If you feel like eating right in the heart of Kitano, this Sri Lankan place serves tasty set meals and delicious Ceylon tea.

Nailey's Café (☎ 231-2008; 2-8-12 Kanō-chō, Chūō-ku; coffee from ¥430, lunch/dinner from ¥1050/1200; ⏲ 11.30am-midnight, to 2am Fri & Sat, closed Tue lunch; 🚉 Seishin-Yamate subway line to Shin-Kōbe) This hip little cafe serves espresso, light lunches and dinners. The menu here is Europe influenced and includes such things as pizza, pasta and salads. This is a good spot for an evening drink. English menu.

DRINKING

Kōbe has a large foreign community and a number of bars that see mixed Japanese and foreign crowds. For Japanese-style drinking establishments, try the *izakaya* in the neighbourhood between the JR tracks and Ikuta-jinja. Also bear in mind that a lot of Kōbe's nightlife is centred around the city's many cafes, most of which transform into bars come evening.

New Munchen Club (☎ 335-0170; 47 Akashi-chō, Chūō-ku; ⏲ 11am-11pm; 🚉 JR Kōbe line to Motomachi) A decent German-style pub that draws its share of foreign residents. It's got a picture menu for food. It can be a little smoky, but the beer is good and it's easy to enter. It's close to Daimaru department store, on the basement floor.

GETTING THERE & AWAY

Boat

China Express Line (☎ in Japan 321-5791, in China 022-2420-5777; www.celkobe.co.jp, in Japanese) operates a ferry (2nd class from ¥22,000, around 48 hours) between Kōbe and Tientsin. It departs Kōbe every Thursday at midnight.

There are regular ferries between Kōbe and Shikoku (Imabari and Matsuyama) and Kyūshū (Ōita). Most ferries depart from Rokkō Island and are operated by **Diamond Ferry Company** (☎ 857-1988; www.diamond-ferry.co.jp, in Japanese). The cheapest fares are as follows: Imabari ¥6600, Matsuyama ¥7500 and Ōita ¥10,000.

Bus

Buses run between Kōbe (Sannomiya Bus Terminal) and Tokyo (Shinjuku highway bus terminal and JR highway bus terminal at Tokyo Station). The journey costs ¥8690 and takes around 9½ hours. Buses depart in the evening and arrive early the following day.

Train

Kōbe's JR Sannomiya Station is on the JR Tōkaidō line. A JR *shinkaisoku* train on this line is the fastest way between Kōbe and Osaka Station (¥390, 24 minutes) or Kyoto (¥1050, 54 minutes).

Two private lines, the Hankyū line and Hanshin line, also connect Kōbe and Osaka. The Hankyū line is the more convenient of the two, running between Kōbe's Hankyū Sannomiya Station and Osaka's Hankyū Umeda Station (*tokkyū*, ¥310, 29 minutes). The Hankyū line also has connections between Kyoto and Osaka, so you can travel between Kyoto and Kōbe (*tokkyū*, ¥600, 65 minutes, change at Jūsō or Umeda).

Shin-Kōbe Station is on the Tōkaidō to San-yō *shinkansen* line. The Hikari *shinkansen* goes to/from Fukuoka (¥14,070, two hours 52 minutes) and to/from Tokyo (¥21,520, six hours seven minutes). Other stations on this line include Osaka, Kyoto, Nagoya and Hiroshima.

Note that there are several discount ticket shops near Hankyū Sannomiya Station.

GETTING AROUND

To/From the Airport

ITAMI OSAKA AIRPORT

There are direct limousine buses to/from Osaka's Itami airport (¥1020, 40 minutes). In Kōbe, the buses stop on the southwestern side of Sannomiya Station.

KŌBE AIRPORT

The easiest way to get to/from Kōbe's spanking-new airport is with the Portliner, which makes the trip between Sannomiya (downtown Kōbe) and the airport in 18 minutes and costs ¥320. A taxi will cost between ¥2500 and ¥3000 and take 15 to 20 minutes.

KANSAI INTERNATIONAL AIRPORT (KIX)

There are a number of routes between Kōbe and KIX. By train, the fastest way is the JR *shinkaisoku* to/from Osaka Station, and the JR *kanku kaisoku* between Osaka Station and the airport (total cost ¥1550, total time 87 minutes with good connections). There is also a direct limousine bus to/from the airport (¥1800, 1¼ hours) and this is more convenient if you have a lot of luggage. The Kōbe airport bus stop is on the southwestern side of Sannomiya Station.

Public Transport

Kōbe is small enough to travel around on foot. The JR, Hankyū and Hanshin railway lines run east to west across Kōbe, providing access to most of Kōbe's more distant sights. A subway line also connects Shin-Kōbe Station with Sannomiya Station (¥200, two minutes). There is also a city-loop bus service that makes a grand-circle tour of most of the city's sightseeing spots (per ride/all-day pass ¥200/600). The bus stops at both Sannomiya and Shin-Kōbe Stations; look for the retro-style green buses.

HIMEJI 姫路

☎ 079 / pop 536,500

Himeji-jō, the finest castle in all Japan, towers over the small city of Himeji, a quiet city on the *shinkansen* route between Osaka and Okayama. In addition to the castle, the city is home to the Hyōgo Prefectural Museum of History and Kōko-en, a small garden alongside the castle. If you're a fan of castles a visit to Himeji is a must, and you can visit it as a day trip from cities like Kyoto, Nara or Osaka, or as a stopover between these cities and places like Hiroshima.

ORIENTATION & INFORMATION

In Himeji Station, you'll find a **tourist information counter** (☎ 285-3792; 🕘 9am-5pm) on the ground floor to the left as you exit the central exit on the north side of the station. Between 10am and 3pm, an English-speaking staff is on duty. The castle is a 15-minute walk (1200m) straight up the main road from the north exit of the station. If you

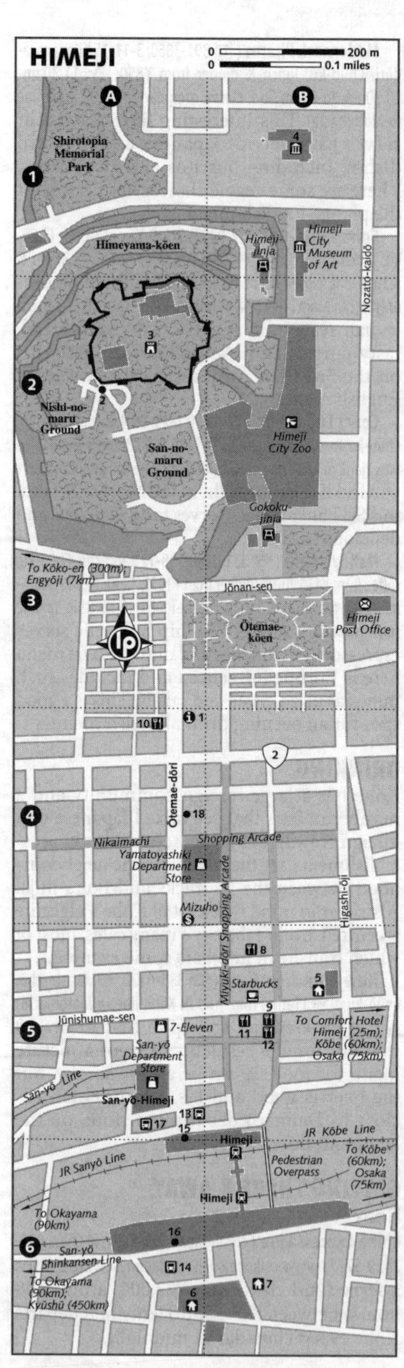

INFORMATION
Himeji Tourist Information 姫路観光なびポート 1 A4

SIGHTS & ACTIVITIES
Castle Ticket Office 姫路城切符売り場 2 A2
Himeji-jō 姫路城 3 A2
Hyōgo Prefectural Museum of History 兵庫県立歴史博物館 4 B1

SLEEPING
Himeji Washington Hotel Plaza 姫路ワシントンホテルプラザ 5 B5
Hotel Nikkō Himeji ホテル日航姫路 6 A6
Tōyoko Inn 東横イン 7 B6

EATING
Fukutei ふく亭 8 B5
Len レン 9 B5
Me-n-me めんめ 10 A4
Rāmen-no-Hōryū ラーメンの寶龍 11 B5
Uottori うおっとり 12 B5

TRANSPORT
City Bus Terminal 市バスターミナル 13 A5
City South Bus Terminal 市バス南ターミナル 14 A6
Himeji North Exit 北口 15 A5
Himeji South Exit 南口 16 A6
Shinki Bus Terminal 神姫バスターミナル 17 A5
Underground Bicycle Parking Lot 地下駐輪場 18 A4

don't feel like walking, free rental cycles are available from an underground parking area halfway between the station and the castle; enquire at the information counter.

On the way to the castle you'll find **Himeji Tourist Information** (☎ 287-3658; 9am-5pm), which has information on movies filmed in Himeji, public toilets, a fantastic model of the castle and free rental bicycles.

SIGHTS

Himeji-jō 姫路城

This **castle** (☎ 285-1146; 68 Honmachi; adult/child ¥600/200; 9am-5pm Sep-May, to 6pm Jun-Aug) is the most magnificent castle in Japan. It's also one of only a handful of original castles in Japan (most others are modern concrete reconstructions). In Japanese the castle is sometimes called *shirasagi*, or 'white heron', a title that derives from the castle's stately white form. Although there have been fortifications in Himeji since 1333, today's castle was built in 1580 by Toyotomi Hideyoshi and enlarged some 30 years later by Ikeda Terumasa. Ikeda was awarded the castle by Tokugawa Ieyasu when the latter's forces defeated the Toyotomi armies. In the following centuries the castle was home to 48 successive lords.

The castle has a five-storey main *donjon* (heavily fortified central tower) and three smaller *donjon*, and the entire structure is surrounded by moats and defensive walls punctuated with rectangular, circular and triangular openings for firing guns and shooting arrows. The walls of the *donjon* also feature *ishiotoshi* – openings that allowed defenders to pour boiling water or oil onto anyone who made it past the defensive slits and was thinking of scaling the walls. All things considered, visitors are recommended to pay the admission charge and enter the castle by legitimate means.

It takes around 1½ hours to follow the arrow-marked route around the castle. Free volunteer English-speaking guides are sometimes available at the castle ticket office. Unfortunately, reservations aren't accepted and there is no regular schedule – ask at the counter and hope for the best. Enter by an hour before closing.

Kōko-en 好古園

Just across the moat on the western side of Himeji-jō, you'll find **Kōko-en** (☎ 289-4120; 68 Honmachi; admission ¥300; 9am-5pm, later in Jun-Aug, closed Dec 29 & 30), a reconstruction of the former samurai quarters of the castle. There are nine separate Edo-style gardens, two ponds, a stream, a tea arbour (¥500 for *matcha* and a Japanese sweet) and the restaurant **Kassui-ken**, where you can enjoy a *bentō* (¥1500) of *anago* (conger eel, a local speciality) while gazing over the gardens. While the garden doesn't have the subtle beauty of some of Japan's older gardens, it is well done and especially lovely in the autumn-foliage season.

Note that a joint ticket to both the Kōko-en and Himeji-jō costs only ¥720, a saving of ¥180. These can be purchased at both the entrance to Kōko-en and Himeji-jō. Enter by 30 minutes before closing.

Hyōgo Prefectural Museum of History 兵庫県立歴史博物館

This **museum** (Hyōgo Kenritsu Rekishi Hakubutsukan; ☎ 288-9011; 68 Honmachi; admission ¥200; 10am-5pm, closed Mon & the day after national holidays) has good displays on Himeji-jō and other castles around Japan. In addition, the museum covers the main periods of Japanese history with some English explanations. At 10.30am, 1.30pm and 3.30pm, one lucky person can even try on a suit of samurai armour or a kimono (ask at the front desk to be included in the lottery).

The museum is a five-minute walk north of the castle. Enter by 30 minutes before closing.

Engyōji 円教寺

Around 8km northwest of Himeji Station, this mountaintop **temple complex** (☎ 266-3327; 2968 Shosha, Himeji-shi; admission ¥300; 🕑 8.30am-5pm) is well worth a visit if you've got time after visiting the castle. The temple and surrounding area are most beautiful in the April cherry-blossom season or November *momiji* (maple-leaf) season.

From the top cable-car station, it's about a 25-minute walk (about 2km) to the Maniden, one of the main structures of the complex, which is dedicated to Kannon (the Goddess of Mercy). Five minutes further on brings you to the Daikō-dō, a lovely wooden auditorium where parts of *The Last Samurai* were filmed. The path to both of these buildings is lined with Senjū-Kannon (Thousand-Armed Kannon) figures.

To get there, take bus 8 from Himeji Station (bus terminal East; ¥260, 28 minutes). Get off at 'Shosha Ropeway', and board the cable car (one way/return ¥500/900). The trip takes about half a day from downtown Himeji.

FESTIVALS & EVENTS

The **Nada-no-Kenka Matsuri**, held on 14 and 15 October, involves a battle between three *mikoshi* that are battered against each other until one smashes. Try to go on the second day, when the festival reaches its peak (around noon). The festival is held five minutes' walk from Shirahamanomiya Station (10 minutes from Himeji Station on the Sanyō-Dentetsu line); follow the crowds. The train company lays on extra trains on the day of the *matsuri*.

SLEEPING

Himeji is best visited as a day trip from other parts of Kansai. If you'd like to stay, however, there are plenty of choices.

Tōyoko Inn (☎ 284-1045; 97 Minamiekimae-chō; s/d/tw ¥5880/7980/7980; 💻) This new business hotel is a good choice if you want to be close to the station. The rooms are serviceable, well maintained and, as usual in a business hotel, fairly small. There is LAN internet.

Himeji Washington Hotel Plaza (☎ 225-0111; 98 Higashiekimae-chō; s/d ¥5800/11,000; 💻) This centrally located business hotel is pretty much everything a good hotel should be: well run and clean with reasonable-sized rooms (for a business hotel, that is). It's within easy walking distance of the castle and lots of restaurants. There is free LAN internet and rental computers are available.

Comfort Hotel Himeji (☎ 286-8511; 1-50-3 Hojoguchi; d/tw ¥8500/10,000; 📶) Three blocks from the main entrances to Himeji's shopping arcades, this three-year-old business hotel is one of the cheapest and most convenient in town. The rooms have free wi-fi and a free continental breakfast is served downstairs. Rooms are small but well designed, with all the newest Japanese hotel gadgetry (flat-screen TV, hi-tech toilet, eco shampoo-dispensers).

Hotel Nikkō Himeji (☎ 222-2231; 100 Minamiekimae-chō; s/d/tw ¥10,925/20,700/20,700; 💻) A stone's throw from the south side of the station, this hotel has stylish and fairly spacious rooms and is the best choice for those who want something nicer than a business hotel. The rooms are larger than in the preceding business hotels and the bathtubs have almost enough room to stretch out. Some of the upper rooms on the north side have views of the top of the castle. There is LAN internet.

EATING

The food court in the underground mall at JR Himeji Station has all the usual Western and Japanese dishes. It's just to the right as you exit the north ticket gate of the station. Otherwise, you'll find the following choices in the streets between the station and the castle.

Me-n-me (☎ 225-0118; 68 Honmachi; noodles from ¥550; 🕑 11.30am-6pm, closed Wed) They make their own noodles at this homey little noodle joint a few minutes' walk from the castle. It's not fancy, but if you want an honest, tasty bowl of udon to power you through the day, this

> **HIMEJI-JŌ RENOVATION**
>
> Visitors to Himeji should note that the city's castle, Himeji-jō, will be undergoing a massive renovation from late 2009 until early 2014. During most of this period, the main keep of the castle will be covered by a scaffoldlike structure that will obscure the keep from view. The rest of the castle will not be covered by any structure. It will be possible to enter the castle during the reconstruction period, although some areas may be closed to the public from time to time.

is the spot. They usually put an English sign on the street. English menu.

Rāmen-no-Hōryū (☎ 288-1230; 316 Eki-mae-chō; buta miso rāmen ¥990; 🕑 11.30am-midnight Mon-Sat, to 11pm Sun & holidays) For good *gyōza* and hearty bowls of *buta miso rāmen* (pork *miso rāmen*), we recommend this friendly *rāmen* joint near the station. Buy your tickets from the machine. It's roughly opposite Starbucks – look for the faux wooden facade painted with large white swirls.

Len (☎ 225-5505; 324 Eki-mae-chō; lunch/dinner from ¥1000/3000; 🕑 11.30am-3pm & 4.45-11.30pm, closed 3rd Mon & 1 Jan) If you find yourself in Himeji in the evening and feel like a good meal of pan-Asian *izakaya* fare, then try Len. Dishes include things like Indonesian *yaki soba* (fried noodles; ¥850) and Chinese fried chicken (¥780). There's a blue sign in English.

Fukutei (☎ 222-8150; 75 Kamei-chō; lunch/dinner from ¥1500/3000; 🕑 11.30am-2.30pm & 5-9pm Mon-Sat, 11.30am-2.30pm & 5-8pm Sun & holidays) This stylish, approachable restaurant is a great lunch choice if you want something a little civilised. The fare here is casual *kaiseki:* a little sashimi, some tempura and the usual nibbles on the side. At lunch try the excellent *omakese-zen* (tasting set; ¥1500). There's a small English sign that reads 'Omotenashi Dining Fukutei'. English menu.

Uottori (☎ 225-2729; 325 Eki-mae-chō; meals from ¥2000; 🕑 11.30am-2pm, 5pm-midnight) This friendly Japanese chicken and fish specialist offers the usual *yakitori* and sashimi assortments as well as a few Himeji specialities. *Oden* flavoured with ginger soy sauce is a tasty local dish (¥80 per piece). Minced chicken baked in bamboo tubes pleases both the mouth and ears, as the bamboo squeaks and squeals as it splits from the heat (¥700). It's just left of Len (above); look for the beige stucco facade. An ageing English menu is available.

GETTING THERE & AWAY

A *shinkaisoku* on the JR Tōkaidō line is the best way to reach Himeji from Kyoto (¥2210, 91 minutes), Osaka (¥1450, 61 minutes) and Kōbe (¥950, 37 minutes). From Okayama, to the west, a *tokkyū* JR train on the San-yō line takes 82 minutes and costs ¥1450. You can also reach Himeji from these cities via the Tōkaidō/San-yō *shinkansen* line, and this is a good option for Japan Rail Pass holders or those in a hurry.

On the way to Himeji, take a look out the train window at the newly constructed Akashi Kaikyō Suspension Bridge. Its 3910m span links the island of Honshū with Awaji-shima, making it the longest suspension bridge in the world. It comes into view on the southern side of the train approximately 10km west of Kōbe.

NARA 奈良

☎ 0742 / pop 369,000

The first permanent capital of Japan, Nara is one of the most rewarding destinations in the country. Indeed, with eight Unesco World Heritage Sites, Nara is second only to Kyoto as a repository of Japan's cultural legacy. The centrepiece is, of course, the Diabutsu, or Great Buddha, which rivals Mt Fuji and Kyoto's Golden Pavilion (Kinkaku-ji) as Japan's single most impressive sight. The Great Buddha is housed in Tōdai-ji, a soaring temple that presides over Nara-kōen, a park filled with other fascinating sights that lends itself to relaxed strolling amid the greenery and tame deer.

Nara's best feature is its small size: it's quite possible to pack the most worthwhile sights into one full day. Many people visit Nara as a side trip from Kyoto – comfortable express trains link the cities in about half an hour. Of course, it's preferable to spend at least two days here if you can. If your schedule allows for two days in Nara, you might spend one in Nara-kōen and the other seeing the sights in western and southwestern Nara.

HISTORY

Nara is at the northern end of the Yamato Plain, where members of the Yamato clan rose to power as the original emperors of Japan. The remains of these early emperors are contained in *kofun* (burial mounds), some of which date back to the 3rd century AD.

Until the 7th century, however, Japan had no permanent capital, as Shintō taboos concerning death stipulated that the capital be moved with the passing of each emperor. This practice died out under the influence of Buddhism and with the Taika reforms of 646, when the entire country came under imperial control.

At this time it was decreed that a permanent capital be built. Two locations were tried before a permanent capital was finally

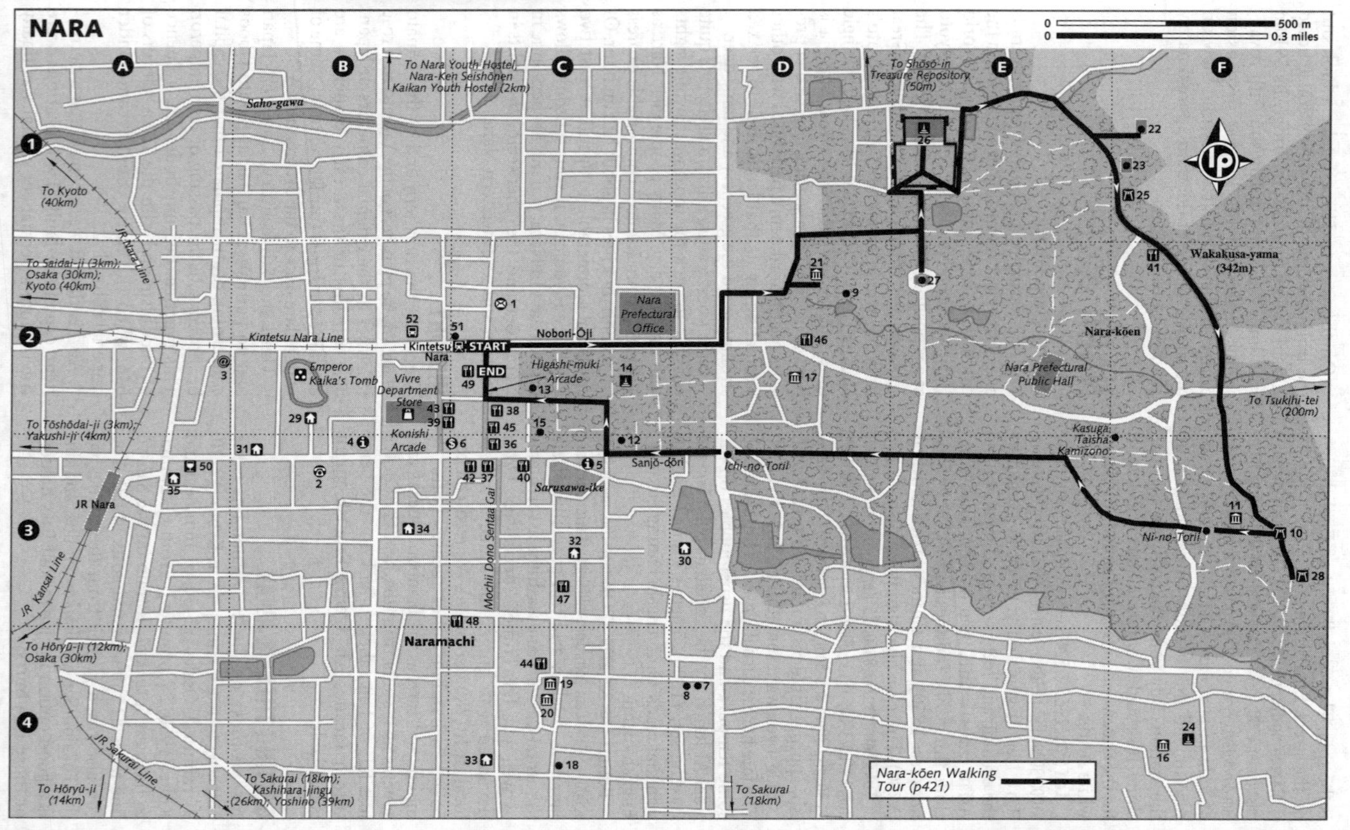
NARA
500 m
0.3 miles
Saho-gawa
To Kyoto (40km)
JR Nara Line
To Saidai-ji (3km); Osaka (30km); Kyoto (40km)
To Nara Youth Hostel, Nara-Ken Seishōnen Kaikan Youth Hostel (2km)
To Shōsō-in Treasure Repository (50m)
Kintetsu Nara Line
Kintetsu Nara
START
END
Nobori-Ōji
Nara Prefectural Office
Emperor Kaika's Tomb
Vivre Department Store
Higashi-muki Arcade
Konishi Arcade
To Tōshōdai-ji (3km); Yakushi-ji (4km)
Sanjō-dōri
Ichi-no-Torii
Sarusawa-ike
Mochii Dono Sentaa Gai
JR Nara
JR Kansai Line
Naramachi
To Hōryū-ji (12km); Osaka (30km)
JR Sakurai Line
To Hōryū-ji (14km)
To Sakurai (18km); Kashihara-jingu (26km); Yoshino (39km)
To Sakurai (18km)
Wakakusa-yama (342m)
Nara-kōen
Nara Prefectural Public Hall
To Tsukihi-tei (200m)
Kasuga Taisha Kamizono
Ni-no-Torii
Nara-kōen Walking Tour (p421)

INFORMATION

Higashi-Muki Post Office 東向郵便局 1 C2
International Phone 国際電話 2 B3
Internet Café Suien 水煙 3 A2
Nara City Tourist Center 奈良市観光センター 4 B3
Sarusawa Tourist Information Office 猿沢観光案内所 5 C3
SMBC Bank 三井住友銀行 6 C3

SIGHTS & ACTIVITIES

Imanishi Seibei Shōten 今西清兵衛商店 7 D4
Imanishike Shoin 今西家書院 8 D4
Isui-en 依水園 9 D2
Kasuga Taisha 春日大社 10 F3
Kasuga Taisha Hōmotsu-den 春日大社宝物殿 11 F3
Kōfuku-ji Five-Storey Pagoda 興福寺五重塔 12 C3
Kōfuku-ji Hokuen-do Hall 興福寺北円堂 13 C2
Kōfuku-ji Nanen-do Hall 興福寺南円堂 14 C2
Kōfuku-ji National Treasure Hall 興福寺国宝館 15 C2
Nara City Museum of Photography 奈良市写真美術館 16 F4
Nara National Museum 奈良国立博物館 17 D2
Naramachi Koushi-no-Ie ならまち資料館 18 C4
Naramachi Monogatari-kan 奈良町物語館 19 C4
Naramachi Shiryō-kan Museum 奈良町資料館 20 C4
Neiraku Art Museum 寧楽美術館 21 D2
Nigatsu-dō Hall 二月堂 22 F1
Sangatsu-dō Hall 三月堂 23 F1
Shin-Yakushi-ji 新薬師寺 24 F4
Tamukeyama-hachimangū 手向山八幡宮 25 F1
Tōdai-ji Daibutsu-den 東大寺大仏殿 26 E1
Tōdai-ji Nandai-mon 東大寺南大門 27 E2
Wakamiya-jinja 若宮神社 28 F3

SLEEPING

Hotel Fujita Nara ホテルフジタ奈良 29 B2
Nara Hotel 奈良ホテル 30 D3
Nara Washington Hotel Plaza 奈良ワシントンホテルプラザ 31 B3
Ryokan Matsumae 旅館松前 32 C3
Ryokan Seikan-sō 旅館静観荘 33 C4
Ryokan Tsubakisō 旅館椿荘 34 B3
Super Hotel スーパーホテル 35 A3

EATING

Beni-e べに江 36 C3
Bikkuri Udon Miyoshino びっくりうどん三好野 37 C3
Don どん 38 C2
Doutor ドトール 39 B2
Drink Drank ドリンク ドランク 40 C3
Kasugano 春日野 41 F2
Kyōshō-An 京匠庵 42 C3
Mellow Café メロー カフェ 43 B2
Nonohana Ohka ののはな黄花 44 C4
Okaru おかる 45 C2
Shizuka 志津香 46 D2
Tempura Asuka 天ぷら飛鳥 47 C3
Ten Ten Café テンテンカフェ 48 C3
Tonkatsu Ganko とんかつがんこ 49 C2

DRINKING

Woo Koo BAR ウークーバー 50 A3

TRANSPORT

Highway Bus Tickets エアポートリムジン切符売り場 51 C2
Local Bus Stop 市バス停 52 B2

established at Nara (which was then known as Heijōkyō) in 710. Permanent status, however, lasted a mere 75 years. When a priest by the name of Dōkyō managed to seduce an empress and nearly usurp the throne, it was decided to move the court to a new location, out of reach of Nara's increasingly powerful clergy. This led to the new capital being established at Kyoto, where it remained until 1868.

Although brief, the Nara period was extraordinarily vigorous in its absorption of influences from China, a process that laid the foundations of Japanese culture and civilisation. The adoption of Buddhism as a national religion made a lasting impact on government, arts, literature and architecture.

With the exception of an assault on the area by the Taira clan in the 12th century, Nara was subsequently spared the periodic bouts of destruction wreaked upon Kyoto, and a number of magnificent buildings have survived.

ORIENTATION

Nara retains the grid pattern of streets laid out in Chinese style during the 8th century. There are two main train stations: JR Nara Station and Kintetsu Nara Station. JR Nara Station is a little west of the city centre (but still within walking distance of the sights), while Kintetsu Nara is central. Nara-kōen, which contains most of the important sights, is on the eastern side, against the bare flank of Wakakusa-yama. Most of the other sights are southwest of the city and are best reached by buses that leave from both train stations (or by train in the case of Hōryū-ji). It's easy to cover the city centre and the major attractions in nearby Nara-kōen on foot, though some may prefer to rent a bicycle (see p426).

Maps

Nara tourist information offices stock the useful *Welcome to Nara Sight Seeing Map*.

INFORMATION

The main **Nara City Tourist Center** (☎ 22-3900; 23-4 Kamisanjō-chō; 🕑 9am-9pm, closed year-end/new-year holidays) is worth a stop if you start your sightseeing from JR Nara Station. If you start from Kintetsu Nara Station, try the helpful **Kintetsu Nara Station information office** (☎ 24-4858; 🕑 9am-5pm), which is near the top of the stairs above exit 3 from the station.

KANSAI

NARA UNESCO WORLD HERITAGE SITES

In 1998 eight sites in Nara were designated as World Heritage Sites by the UN. They are the Buddhist temples of Tōdai-ji, Kōfuku-ji, Gango-ji, Yakushi-ji and Tōshōdai-ji; the shrine, Kasuga Taisha; Kasuga-yama Primeval Forest; and the remains of Heijō-kyō Palace. Five are covered in detail in the text; of the remaining three, Kasuga-yama Primeval Forest is directly behind Kasuga Taisha, Gango-ji is in Naramachi, and the Heijō-kyō Palace ruins are 10 minutes' walk east of Saidai-ji Station on the Kintetsu line.

There are two other information offices in Nara: the **JR Nara Station office** (☎ 22-9821; 9am-5pm) and the **Sarusawa Tourist Information Office** (☎ 26-1991; 9am-5pm).

The information centres can put you in touch with volunteer guides who speak English and other foreign languages, but you must book at least one day in advance. Two of these services are the **YMCA Goodwill Guides** (☎ 45-5920; www.geocities.com/egg_nara) and **Nara Student Guides** (☎ 26-4753; www.narastudentguide.org).

Outside the NTT telephone company office on Sanjō-dōri there is an IC Card international phone. For internet, try the following place:

Internet Café Suien (☎ 22-2577; 1-58 Aburasaka-chō; internet per hr ¥200, 2hr with one drink ¥500; 7.30am-11pm) Inside Hotel Asyl Nara.

SIGHTS

Nara-kōen Area 奈良公園

Many of Nara's most important sites are located in Nara-kōen, a fine park that occupies much of the east side of the city. The park is home to about 1200 deer, which in pre-Buddhist times were considered messengers of the gods and today enjoy the status of National Treasures. They roam the park and surrounding areas in search of handouts from tourists, often descending on petrified children who have the misfortune to be carrying food. You can buy *shika-sembei* (deer biscuits) from vendors for ¥150 to feed to the deer. Note: don't eat them yourself, as we saw one misguided foreign tourist doing.

Our Nara-kōen walking tour (see the boxed text, opposite) is the best way to take in all the major sights in a day.

NARA NATIONAL MUSEUM
奈良国立博物館

The **Nara National Museum** (Nara Kokuritsu Hakubutsukan; ☎ 22-7771; 50 Noborioji-chō; admission ¥500; 9.30am-5pm) is devoted to Buddhist art and is divided into two wings. The western gallery has a fine collection of *butsu-zō* (statues of Buddhas and bodhisattvas), while the new eastern gallery displays sculptures, paintings and calligraphy.

A special exhibition featuring the treasures of the Shōsō-in Hall, which holds the treasures of Tōdai-ji, is held here in May, as well as from 21 October to 8 November (call the Nara City Tourist Center to check, as these dates vary slightly each year). The exhibits include priceless items from the cultures along the Silk Road. If you are in Nara during these periods and are a fan of Japanese antiquities, you should make a point of visiting the museum, but be prepared for crowds. Enter by 4.30pm.

KŌFUKU-JI 興福寺

This temple was transferred here from Kyoto in 710 as the main temple for the Fujiwara family. Although the original temple complex had 175 buildings, fires and destruction as a result of power struggles have left only a dozen standing. There are two **pagodas** – three storeys and five storeys – dating from 1143 and 1426, respectively. The taller of the two is the second-tallest in Japan, outclassed by the one at Kyoto's Tō-ji by a few centimetres.

The **Kōfuku-ji National Treasure Hall** (☎ 22-7755; 48 Noborioji-chō, Kokuhō-kan; admission ¥500; 9am-5pm) contains a variety of statues and art objects salvaged from previous structures. Enter by 4pm.

ISUI-EN & NEIRAKU ART MUSEUM
依水園・寧楽美術館

This **garden** (☎ 25-0781; 74 Suimon-chō; admission museum & garden ¥650; 9.30am-4pm, closed Tue & year-end/new-year holidays), dating from the Meiji era, is beautifully laid out and features abundant greenery and a pond with ornamental carp. It's without a doubt the best garden in the city and well worth a visit. For ¥450 you can enjoy a cup of tea on tatami mats overlooking the garden.

The adjoining art museum, Neiraku Bijutsukan, displays Chinese and Korean ceramics and bronzes (admission is included in garden entry).

There is no English sign outside the garden; look for the imposing wooden gate.

TŌDAI-JI 東大寺

Nara's famous Daibutsu (Great Buddha) is housed in the Daibutsu-den Hall of this grand temple. It's Nara's star attraction and can often be packed with tour groups and schoolchildren from across the country, but it's big enough to absorb huge crowds and it belongs at the top of any Nara itinerary.

Before you enter the temple be sure to check out the **Nandai-mon**, an enormous gate containing two fierce-looking **Niō guardians**. These recently restored wooden images, carved in the 13th century by the sculptor Unkei, are some of the finest wooden statues in all of Japan, if not the world. They are truly dramatic works of art and seem ready to spring to life at any moment. The gate is about 200m south of the temple enclosure.

Note that most of Tōdai-ji's grounds can be visited free of charge, with the exception of the main hall: the Daibutsu-den Hall.

Daibutsu-den Hall 大仏殿

Tōdai-ji's **Daibutsu-den** (Hall of the Great Buddha; ☎ 22-5511; 406-1 Zōshi-chō; admission ¥500; ⏲ 8am-4.30pm Nov-Feb, to 5pm Mar, 7.30am-5.30pm Apr-Sep, to 5pm Oct) is the largest wooden building in the world. Unbelievably, the present structure, rebuilt in 1709, is a mere two-thirds of the size of the original! The Daibutsu (Great Buddha) contained within is one of the largest bronze figures in the world and was originally cast in 746. The present statue, recast in the Edo period, stands just over 16m high and consists of 437 tonnes of bronze and 130kg of gold.

NARA-KŌEN WALKING TOUR

- Start: Kintetsu Nara Station (see Map p418)
- End: Kintetsu Nara Station
- Distance: about 5km
- Duration: half a day

This walk meanders through the pleasantly wooded hills of Nara-kōen, taking in some of Nara's most important sights along the way. Start at Kintetsu Nara Station. Walk straight up Nobori-Ōji, passing **Kōfuku-ji** (opposite) on your right (you can visit it now, or leave it until the return leg). After Kōfuku-ji, go left and visit **Isui-en** (opposite), one of Nara's finest gardens. After enjoying the garden, walk north from the garden entrance and take the next major right after about 100m and walk east. This brings you out in front of Tōdai-ji. Go right to inspect the the massive **Nandai-mon**, the main gate of **Tōdai-ji** (above). Stop in the gate to admire the Niō guardians and then continue to the temple.

After visiting Tōdai-ji, exit via the southeast exit, take a hard left and walk along the temple enclosure. Just past the pond, take a right up the hill following the stone-paved path. This leads to an incredibly atmospheric stretch that takes you up to an open plaza in front of **Nigatsu-dō** and **Sangatsu-dō** halls (p422). Climb the steps to Nigatsu-do to enjoy the view from the verandah, which takes in the graceful curves of the Daibutsu-den and most of the Nara plain.

Return to the plaza and exit the plaza heading south, passing between a log-cabinlike structure and gaudy **Tamukeyama-hachimangū**. Follow the broad path through the woods, descend two staircases and follow the signs reading 'Kasuga Shrine'. You'll come to a road that leads uphill to the left; follow it along, passing under the bare slopes of Wakakusa-yama. At Musashino Ryokan (look for the small English sign), walk straight down the steps, cross a bridge, jog left, and at the T-intersection take a left up to **Kasuga Taisha** (p422; you'll have to work around the side of it to find the main entrance).

After visiting the shrine, leave via the main entrance and bear left up the path to **Wakamiya-jinja**, passing several small shrines on the way. After seeing the shrine, retrace your steps towards Kasuga Taisha, and take a left down the steps which lead back towards the centre of town. You'll pass first through **Ni-no-Torii** and then continue down the broad wooded arcade to **Ichi-no-Torii**. Cross the street and you'll soon see the pagoda of **Kōfuku-ji** (opposite). Walk through the Kōfuku-ji grounds, passing between the **Nanen-dō** and **Hokuen-dō** halls, and take the narrow lane that leads down to **Higashi-muki Arcade**. A quick right here will bring you back to where you started.

The Daibutsu is an image of Dainichi Buddha, the cosmic Buddha believed to give rise to all worlds and their respective Buddhas. Historians believe that Emperor Shōmu ordered the building of the Buddha as a charm against smallpox, which ravaged Japan in preceding years. Over the centuries the statue took quite a beating from earthquakes and fires, losing its head a couple of times (note the slight difference in colour between the head and the body).

As you circle the statue towards the back, you'll see a wooden column with a hole through its base. Popular belief maintains that those who can squeeze through the hole, which is exactly the same size as one of the Great Buddha's nostrils, are ensured of enlightenment. There's usually a line of children waiting to give it a try and parents waiting to snap their pictures. Adults sometimes try it, but it's really something for the kids. A hint for big kids: it's a lot easier to go through with both arms held above your head – and someone on either end to push and pull helps, too.

Nigatsu-dō & Sangatsu-dō
二月堂・三月堂

The Nigatsu-dō and Sangatsu-dō are halls (almost subtemples) of Tōdai-ji. They are an easy walk east (uphill from the Daibutsu-den). You can walk straight east up the hill, but we recommend taking a hard left out of the Daibutsu-den exit, following the enclosure past the pond and turning up the hill. This pathway is among the most scenic walks in all of Nara. For details, see the Nara-kōen Walking Tour (p421).

As you reach the plaza at the top of the hill, the **Nigatsu-dō** (☎ 22-5511; 406-1 Zōshi-chō; admission free) is the temple hall with the verandah overlooking the plaza. This is where Nara's Omizutori Matsuri (see opposite) is held. The verandah affords a great view over Nara, especially at dusk. Opening hours here are the same as those of the Daibutsu-den.

A short walk south of Nigatsu-dō is **Sangatsu-dō** (admission ¥500), which is the oldest building in the Tōdai-ji complex. This hall contains a small collection of fine statues from the Nara period. It's open the same hours as the Daibutsu-den.

KASUGA TAISHA 春日大社

This **shrine** (☎ 22-7788; 160 Kasugano-chō; admission free; 🕑 dawn-dusk) was founded in the 8th century by the Fujiwara family and was completely rebuilt every 20 years according to Shintō tradition until the end of the 19th century. It lies at the foot of the hill in a pleasant, wooded setting with herds of sacred deer awaiting handouts. As with similar shrines in Japan, you will find several subshrines around the main hall.

The approaches to the shrine are lined with hundreds of lanterns, and there are many hundreds more in the shrine itself. The **lantern festivals** held twice a year at the shrine are a major attraction (for details see Mantōrō, opposite).

The **Hōmotsu-den** (Treasure Hall; admission ¥420; 🕑 9am-4pm) is just north of the entrance torii for the shrine. The hall displays Shintō ceremonial regalia and equipment used in *bugaku*, nō and *gagaku* performances.

While you're in the area, it's worth walking a few minutes south to nearby Wakamiya-jinja.

SHIN-YAKUSHI-JI 新薬師寺

This **temple** (☎ 22-3736; 1352 Takabatake-chō; admission ¥600; 🕑 9am-5pm) was founded by Empress Kōmyō in 747 in thanks for her husband's recovery from an eye disease. Most of the buildings were destroyed or have been reconstructed, but the present main hall dates from the 8th century. The hall contains sculptures of Yakushi Nyorai (Healing Buddha) and a set of 12 divine generals.

It's about 15 minutes' walk from Kasuga Taisha/Wakamiya-jinja (see left); follow the trail south through the woods. When you come to the main street, look for the small signs in English leading up (south) into a suburban neighbourhood.

NARA CITY MUSEUM OF PHOTOGRAPHY
奈良市写真美術館

Around the corner from Shin-Yakushi-ji, this small **museum** (Nara-shi Shashin Bijutsukan; ☎ 22-9811; 600-1 Takabatake-chō; admission ¥500; 🕑 9.30am-5pm, closed Mon) is worth a visit if you are in the area or interested in a particular exhibit (there is no permanent collection). Ask at any of the tourist offices before making the trek. See Shin-Yakushi-ji for directions. Enter by 4.30pm.

Naramachi 奈良町

South of Sanjō-dōri and Sarusawa-ike pond you will find Naramachi, with many well-preserved *machiya* and *kura*. It's a nice place for a stroll before or after hitting the big sights of Nara-kōen, and there are several good restaurants in the area to entice the hungry traveller.

Highlights of Naramachi include the **Naramachi Shiryō-kan Museum** (☎ 22-5509; 14 Nishishinya-chō; admission free; 10am-4pm Sat & Sun), which has a decent collection of bric-a-brac from the area, including a display of old Japanese coins and bills. **Naramachi Koushi-no-Ie** (☎ 23-4820; 44 Gangōji-chō; admission free; 9am-5pm, closed Mon) is a traditional Japanese house that you can enter and explore.

While you're in the neighbourhood, check out the **Naramachi Monogatari-kan** (☎ 26-3476; 2-1 Nakanoshinya-chō; admission free; 10am-5pm), an interesting little gallery that holds some worthwhile exhibitions.

Imanishike Shoin (☎ 23-2256; 24-3 Fukuchiin-chō; admission ¥350; 10am-4pm, closed Mon) is a lovely old house dating to the Muromachi period and is built in the *shoin*, or library, style. There are a few small gardens here that are well framed by the house itself. Tea is served here. If you are a fan of sake, stop in next door at the **Imanishi Seibei Shōten**, an old sake merchant where for ¥400 you can sample five kinds of sake. Enter by 3.30pm.

TOURS

Nara Kōtsū (☎ 22-5263) runs daily bus tours on a variety of routes, two of which include Nara city sights only and two of which include more distant sights like Hōryū-ji and the burial mounds around Asuka (see p430). Prices for the all-day trips range from ¥2000 to ¥9000 for adults (including all temple fees and an English audio guide). Nara Kōtsū has offices in JR Nara Station and across the street from Kintetsu Nara Station. For something more intimate, try one of the private tours operated by one of the Kyoto-based private tour operators (see p346) or one of the city's volunteer guide organisations (see p420).

FESTIVALS & EVENTS

The following is a brief list of Nara's most important festivals. Because the dates for some of these festivals vary, it's best to check with the Nara or Kyoto tourist information offices.

January

Yamayaki (Grass Burning Festival) In early January (the day before Seijin-no-hi or Coming-of-Age Day), this festival commemorates a feud many centuries ago between the monks of Tōdai-ji and Kōfuku-ji: Wakakusa-yama is set alight at 6pm, with an accompanying display of fireworks.

February

Mantōrō (Lantern Festival) Held in early February at Kasuga Taisha at 6pm, this festival involves the lighting of 3000 stone and bronze lanterns around Kasuga Taisha – it's impossibly atmospheric, as you can imagine. A *bugaku* dance also takes place in the Apple Garden on the last day. This festival is also held around 14 August in the O-Bon holiday period.

March

Omizutori (Water-Drawing Ceremony) On the evening of 12 March, the monks of Tōdai-ji parade huge flaming torches around the balcony of Nigatsu-dō and rain down embers on the spectators to purify them. The water-drawing ceremony is performed after midnight.

May

Takigi Onō (Firelight nō performances) Open-air performances of nō held after dark by the light of blazing torches at Kōfuku-ji and Kasuga Taisha, on 11 and 12 May.

October

Shika-no-Tsunokiri (Deer Antler Cutting) Those deer in Nara-kōen are pursued in a type of elegant rodeo into the Roku-en (deer enclosure) close to Kasuga Taisha on Sundays and holidays in October. They are then wrestled to the ground and their antlers sawn off. Tourist brochures hint that this is to avoid personal harm, though it's not clear whether they are referring to the deer fighting each other or the deer mugging the tourists.

SLEEPING

Although Nara is often visited as a day trip from Kyoto, it is pleasant to spend the night here and this allows for a more relaxing pace.

Budget

Nara-ken Seishōnen Kaikan Youth Hostel (☎/fax 22-5540; www6.ocn.ne.jp/~naseikan, in Japanese; 1-3-1 Hōren Sahoyama; dm from ¥2650;) This YH is older and less pristine than the Nara Youth Hostel (following), but the warm and friendly staff more than makes up for this. The rooms are large and fairly well maintained; breakfast/dinner is ¥300/900. From bus stand 9 at JR Nara Station or bus stand 13 at Kintetsu Nara Station, take bus 12, 13, 131 or 140 and get off at the Ikuei-gakuen bus stop, from which it's a five-minute walk. The information offices have maps and directions.

Nara Youth Hostel (☎ 22-1334; www.jyh.gr.jp/nara/english/neweng.html; 4-3-2 Hōren Sahoyama; dm from ¥3150;) This clean YH is easy to get to and well run. The reception here is efficient and the place is a relatively convenient base for exploring Nara. From bus stand 7 at JR Nara Station or bus stand 13 at Kintetsu Nara Station, take bus 108, 109, 111, 113 or 115 and get off at the Shieikyūjō-mae bus stop – the hostel is almost directly next to the stop.

Ryokan Seikansō (☎/fax 22-2670; 29 Higashikitsuji-chō; per person without bathroom from ¥4200; 💻) This traditional ryokan has reasonable rates and a good Naramachi location. The rooms are clean and spacious with shared bathrooms and a large communal bathtub. The management is used to foreign guests. The lovely Japanese garden is the icing on the cake here.

Ryokan Matsumae (☎ 22-3686; fax 26-3927; www.matsumae.co.jp/english/index_e.html; 28-1 Higashiterahayashi-chō; per person without bathroom from ¥5250; 💻) This friendly little ryokan lays claim to an incredibly convenient location in Naramachi, a short walk from all the sights. The rooms are typical of a ryokan: tatami mats, low tables, TVs and futons. Some of the rooms are a little dark, but the feeling here is warm and relaxing. English is spoken here.

Midrange

Super Hotel (☎ 20-9000; fax 20-9008; www.superhotel.co.jp/s_hotels/jrnara/jrnara.html, in Japanese; 500-1 Sanjō-chō; s/d ¥5280/7280; 💻) Directly across from JR Nara Station, the Super Hotel is part of a no-frills hotel chain that offers clean, small, business-hotel rooms at very reasonable prices. As with other business hotels, all rooms have small en-suite bathrooms. If all you need is a clean place to lay your head, this is a good choice. LAN internet access.

Nara Washington Hotel Plaza (☎ 27-0410; http://nara.wh-at.com; 31-1 Shimosanjō-chō; s/d/tw from ¥6900/12,000/12,000; 💻) Also very conveniently located right downtown, this reliable hotel is another excellent choice in this price range. Rooms are clean and comfortable and there is LAN internet access. Right outside are endless restaurants to choose from.

Hotel Fujita Nara (☎ 23-8111; fax 22-0255; www.fujita-nara.com/e/index.html; 47-1 Shimosanjō-chō; s/d/tw from ¥7500/11,000/12,600; 💻) Right smack in downtown Nara and close to both main train stations, this efficient midrange hotel hits all the right notes: clean rooms, reasonable prices and some English-speaking staff. It's a good choice for those who want a conveniently located hotel. LAN internet access.

Top End

HOTELS

Nara Hotel (☎ 26-3300; fax 23-5252; www.narahotel.co.jp/english/index.html; 1096 Takabatake-chō; s/tw from ¥18,480/33,495; 💻) This grande dame of Nara hotels is a classic, with high ceilings and the smell of polished wood all around. All the rooms are spacious and comfortable with big beds. Unfortunately, some of the bathrooms have cramped unit baths. The rooms in the Shinkan (new wing) are nice, but we recommend the Honkan (main building) for its great retro atmosphere. LAN internet access.

RYOKAN

Ryokan Tsubakisō (☎ 22-5330; fax 27-3811; 35 Tsubai-chō; per person with breakfast from ¥13,000; 💻) Popular with foreign guests, this excellent ryokan is a homey and wonderful place to stay in Nara. The bedrooms and bathrooms are clean and well maintained and the owner can prepare vegetarian meals upon request.

Tsukihi-tei (☎ 26-2021; fax 20-3003; http://homepage3.nifty.com/tukihitei, in Japanese; 158 Kasugano-chō; per person with 2 meals from ¥31,500; 💻) Hidden in a valley above Nara-kōen, this traditional high-class ryokan offers fine rooms and excellent service. If you don't mind being a bit of a distance from the centre of town, this hideaway is a tempting choice. LAN internet access.

EATING

Nara is chock-a-block with good restaurants, most of which are located in the area around Kintetsu Nara Station. There aren't as many good choices in Nara-kōen, but we list one spot halfway between Tōdai-ji and Kasuga Taisha.

Don (☎ 27-7080; 13-2 Higashimukiminami-machi; donburi from ¥480; 🕑 11am-8pm) In the Higashimuki Arcade, the Don serves the eponymous *donburi* (rice bowl with various toppings) for absurdly low prices. It's healthy Japanese fast food and there's a picture menu to make ordering easier. It's opposite McDonald's, in more ways than one. English menu.

Nonohana Ohka (☎ 22-1139; 13 Nakashinya-chō; meals from ¥1000, coffee & tea average ¥500-600; 🕑 11am-5pm, closed Mon) With indoor and outdoor garden seating, this cafe is one of our favourite places for a drink or a light meal when in Naramachi. The cakes are usually very good here and they go down a treat with the excellent tea. It's easy to spot, with a glass front. English menu.

KANSAI

Kasugano (☎ 26-3311; 494 Zōshi-chō; meals from ¥600; 9am-5pm; V) If you're exploring Nara-kōen, lunchtime often finds you somewhere between Tōdai-ji and Kasuga Taisha. A good choice in this area is Kasugano, a restaurant–souvenir shop at the base of Wakakusa-yama. Take a seat in the woodsy annexe cafe section here rather than at the main tables in the shop area (the menu is the same). Dishes include things like tempura *soba* (¥800). There is an English and vegetarian menu. It's the third shop house from the northern end of this strip.

Kyōshō-An (☎ 27-7715; 26-3 Hashimoto-chō; green tea & sweets from ¥650; 11am-7.30pm, closed Mon) This simple shop is a great place to sample Japanese tea and sweets. In the hot months, we recommend an *Uji gōri* (sweetened green tea over shaved ice; ¥600). It's opposite Nanto Bank, up a flight of white steps – look for the pictures of tea and sweets. English menu.

Okaru (☎ 24-3686; 13-2 Higashimukiminami-machi; okonomiyaki from ¥680; 11am-10pm, closed Wed) We like this homey spot in the Higashi-muki Arcade for simple *okonomiyaki*. If you can't decide what to order, look at the food models in the window. It's not far from the Don (opposite) – look for a small English sign.

Tonkatsu Ganko (☎ 25-4129; 19-2 Higashimukinaka-machi; meals from ¥680; 11am-10pm) This popular *tonkatsu* specialist is in the Higashi-muki Arcade, around the corner from Kintetsu Nara. We recommend the *hirekatsu zen* (fillet pork cutlet set; ¥1080 lunchtime, ¥1280 dinnertime). Refills of rice, cabbage and pickles are free. It's next to Mr Donuts and there's an English menu.

Drink Drank (☎ 27-6206; 8 Hashimoto-chō; smoothies from ¥650, lunch sets ¥750-1000; 11am-8pm, closed Wed) This modern cafe-eatery serves a variety of fresh-fruit drinks and light lunches including sandwiches and soup. If you want a break from Japanese food and feel like something light and casual, this might be the move. English menu.

Ten Ten Café (☎ 26-6770; 19 Wakido-chō; meals from ¥700; 11.30am-6pm) Operated by a singer-songwriter, and venue for lots of live-music happenings, this open and airy cafe is a fine spot for a relaxing drink or light meal in the Naramachi area. It serves a daily lunch special for ¥750. Look for the English sign and plants out front. English menu.

Shizuka (☎ 27-8030; 59-11 Noboriōji-chō; rice dishes from ¥892; 11am-8pm, closed Tue) Shizuka is a cosy little traditional restaurant that serves a Nara speciality known as *kamameshi* (rice cooked in a small iron pot with various vegetables, meat or fish thrown in). It's in a two-storey building that looks like a private home, with a white-and-black paper lantern-sign. English menu.

Mellow Café (☎ 27-9099; 1-8 Konishi-chō; lunch from ¥980; 11am-11.30pm) Located down a narrow alley (look for the palm tree), this open-plan cafe attempts to create the ambience of a South Seas resort in downtown Nara. Offerings include international and pan-Asian cuisine. Lunch specials are displayed in front to help you choose and order. There's an English sign and menu.

Bikkuri Udon Miyoshino (☎ 22-5239; 27 Hashimoto-chō; meals average no more than ¥1000; 11am-8.30pm, closed Wed) Miyoshino does good-value sets of typical Japanese fare – noodles and rice dishes predominate. Stop by and check the daily lunch specials on display outside. English menu.

Tempura Asuka (☎ 26-4308; 11 Shōnami-chō; meals ¥1500-5000; 11.30am-2.30pm & 5-9.30pm, closed Mon) This reliable restaurant serves attractive tempura and sashimi sets in a relatively casual atmosphere. At lunchtime try its nicely presented *yumei-dono bentō* (a box filled with a variety of tasty Japanese foods) for ¥1600. There is an English sign/menu.

Beni-e (☎ 22-9493; 1 Higashimukiminami-machi; meals from ¥1600; 11.30am-2.30pm & 5-9pm, closed Mon) If you want tempura without a lot of distractions, this tiny downtown tempura specialist is likely to satisfy. It serves good tempura sets for ¥1600/2100/2600 (*hana*, *tsuki* and *yuki* lunch sets, respectively). It's located a little back from Higashi-muki Arcade, behind Regal Shoes; go down the alley and look for the red writing above the door. English menu.

Lastly, if you just need a quick cuppa or an eat-in or takeaway sandwich, there is a branch of the coffee shop Doutor in the Konishi Arcade (a five-minute walk from Kintetsu Nara).

DRINKING

Woo Koo BAR (☎ 27-5959; 499-1 Sanjō-chō; 6pm-late) If you want to meet the locals (both Japanese and expats), this friendly pub is a good choice. They serve a variety of beer including Guinness and Belgian brews, as well as bar food like fish and chips. Happy hour runs from 6pm to 7pm. Look for the sign at street level.

GETTING THERE & AWAY

Bus

There is an overnight bus service between Tokyo's Shinjuku (Shinjuku highway bus terminal) and Nara (one way/return ¥8400/15,120). In Nara, call **Nara Kōtsū Bus** (☎ 22-5110; www.narakotsu.co.jp/kousoku/index.html, in Japanese) or check with the Nara City Tourist Center for more details. In Tokyo, call **Kantō Bus** (☎ 03-3371-1225; www.kanto-bus.co.jp, in Japanese) or visit the Shinjuku highway bus terminal in person.

Train

KYOTO

The Kintetsu line, which runs between Kintetsu Kyoto Station (in Kyoto Station) and Kintetsu Nara Station, is the fastest and most convenient way to travel between Nara and Kyoto. There are *tokkyū* (¥1110, 33 minutes) and *kyūkō* (¥610, 40 minutes). The *tokkyū* trains run directly and are very comfortable; the *kyūkō* usually require a change at Saidai-ji.

The JR Nara line also connects JR Kyoto Station with JR Nara Station (*JR miyakoji kaisoku,* ¥690, 41 minutes) and there are several departures an hour during the day.

OSAKA

The Kintetsu Nara line connects Osaka (Kintetsu Namba Station) with Nara (Kintetsu Nara Station). *Kaisoku* and *futsū* services take about 36 minutes and cost ¥540. *Tokkyū* services do the journey in five minutes less but cost almost double, making them a poor option.

The JR Kansai line links Osaka (Namba and Tennō-ji Stations) and Nara (JR Nara Station). A *kaisoku* connects Namba and JR Nara Station (¥540, 36 minutes) and Tennō-ji and JR Nara Station (¥450, 30 minutes).

GETTING AROUND

To/From the Airport

Nara is served by Kansai International Airport (KIX). There is a **limousine bus service** (Nara Kōtsū; ☎ 22-5110; www.narakotsu.co.jp/kousoku/limousine/nara_kanku.html, in Japanese) between Nara and the airport with departures roughly every hour in both directions (¥1800, 85 minutes). At Kansai International Airport ask at the information counter in the arrivals hall, and in Nara visit the ticket office in the building across from Kintetsu Nara Station. Reservations are a good idea.

For domestic flights, there are **limousine buses** (Nara Kōtsū; ☎ 22-5110; www.narakotsu.co.jp/kousoku/limousine/nara_itami.html, in Japanese) to/from Osaka's Itami airport (¥1440, 65 minutes).

Bicycle

Nara is a convenient size for getting around on a bicycle. **Eki Renta Car Kansai** (☎ 26-3929; 1-1 Honmachi, Sanjō; 8am-8pm) rents regular bicycles for ¥500 a day. At the time of writing, Nara Station was being rebuilt; it's uncertain where the Eki Renta Car office will be, so ask at the tourist information office in the station.

Bus

Most of the area around Nara-kōen is covered by two circular bus routes: bus 1 runs anticlockwise and bus 2 runs clockwise. There's a ¥180 flat fare. You can easily see the main sights in the park on foot and use the bus as an option if you are pushed for time or get tired of walking. If you plan to ride a lot, the one-day Free Pass costs ¥500.

AROUND NARA
奈良周辺

Southern Nara-ken was the birthplace of imperial rule and is rich in historical sites that are easily accessible as day trips from Osaka, Kyoto or Nara, provided that you make an early start. Of particular historical interest are the *kofun* that mark the graves of Japan's first emperors; these are concentrated around Asuka. There are also several isolated temples where you can escape the crowds that plague Nara's city centre. Further afield, the mountaintop town of Yoshino is one of Japan's cherry-blossom meccas.

Easily reached by rail, Yamato-Yagi and Sakurai serve as useful transport hubs for the region. Keep in mind that the Kintetsu line is far more convenient than JR for most of the destinations in this section. Kintetsu sells a variety of special tickets that may be useful to those planning extensive travel in the area, including the Nara Sekkai Isan Furii Kippu (Nara World Heritage Free Ticket) that allows unlimited travel on Kintetsu trains in the area for a period of three days. The cost is ¥3000/2800/4848 when travel

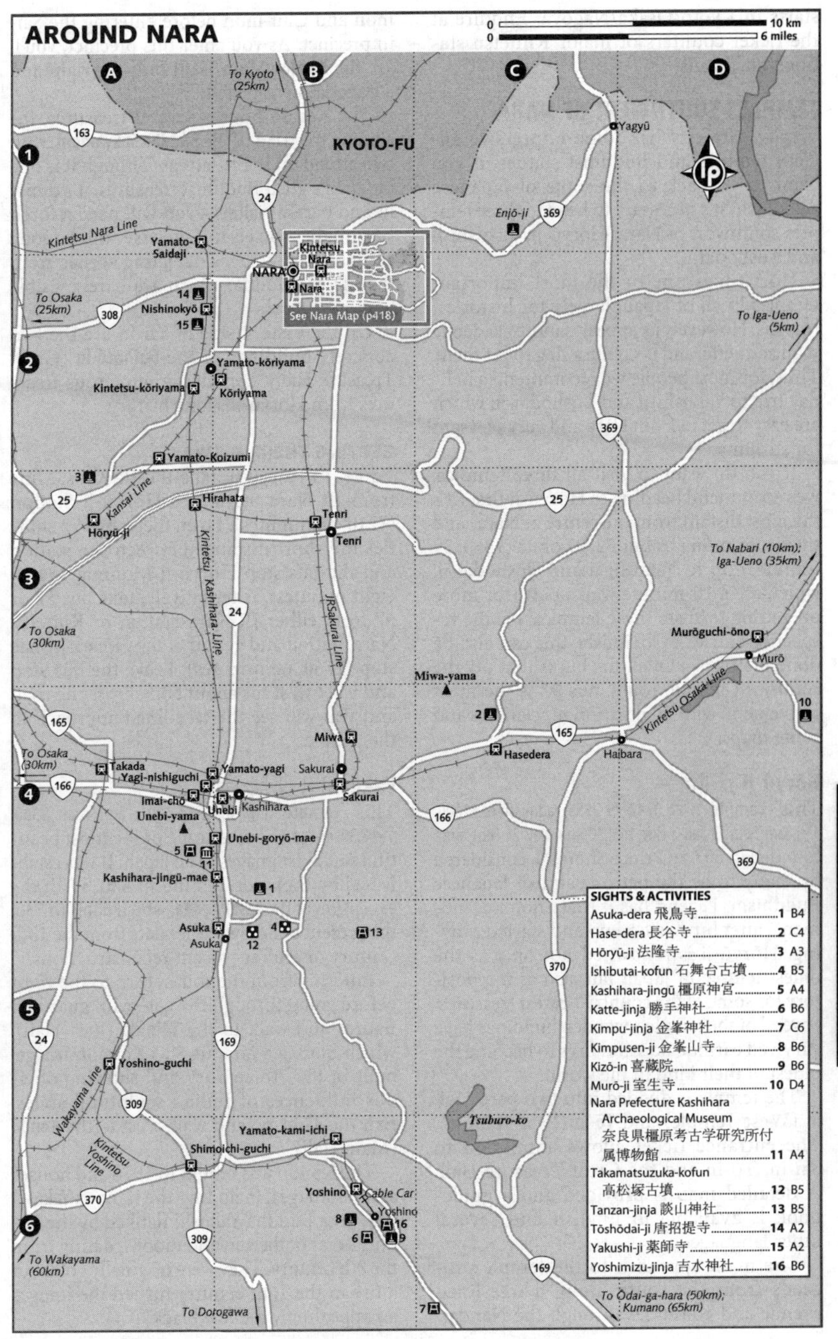

SIGHTS & ACTIVITIES

- Asuka-dera 飛鳥寺 1 B4
- Hase-dera 長谷寺 2 C4
- Hōryū-ji 法隆寺 3 A3
- Ishibutai-kofun 石舞台古墳 4 B5
- Kashihara-jingū 橿原神宮 5 A4
- Katte-jinja 勝手神社 6 B6
- Kimpu-jinja 金峯神社 7 C6
- Kimpusen-ji 金峯山寺 8 B6
- Kizō-in 喜蔵院 9 B6
- Murō-ji 室生寺 10 D4
- Nara Prefecture Kashihara Archaeological Museum 奈良県橿原考古学研究所付属博物館 11 A4
- Takamatsuzuka-kofun 高松塚古墳 12 B5
- Tanzan-jinja 談山神社 13 B5
- Tōshōdai-ji 唐招提寺 14 A2
- Yakushi-ji 薬師寺 15 A2
- Yoshimizu-jinja 吉水神社 16 B6

starts in Kyoto/Osaka/Nagoya. Enquire at the ticket counters of major Kintetsu stations for details.

TEMPLES SOUTHWEST OF NARA

While Nara city has some impressive ancient temples and Buddhist statues, if you want to go back to the roots of Japanese Buddhism it's necessary to head to three temples southwest of Nara: Hōryū-ji, Yakushi-ji and Tōshōdai-ji.

Hōryū-ji is one of the most important temples in all of Japan, largely for historical reasons. However, its appeal is more academic than aesthetic, and it's quite a slog to get there. Thus, for most people we recommend a half-day trip to Yakushi-ji and Tōshōdai-ji, which are easy to get to from Nara and very pleasant for strolling.

If you do want to visit all three temples, we recommend heading to Hōryū-ji first (it's the most distant from the centre of Nara) and then continuing by bus 52, 97 or 98 (¥560, 39 minutes) up to Yakushi-ji and Tōshōdai-ji, which are a 10-minute walk apart (for more on getting to/from these temples, see the respective entries). Obviously, this can also be done in reverse. Of all the buses that ply the southwest temple route, bus 97 is the most convenient, with English announcements and route maps.

Hōryū-ji 法隆寺

This **temple** (☎ 0742-75-2555; admission ¥1000; ⌚ 8am-5pm 22 Feb-3 Nov, to 4.30pm 4 Nov-21 Feb) was founded in 607 by Prince Shōtoku, considered by many to be the patron saint of Japanese Buddhism. Legend has it that Shōtoku, moments after birth, stood up and started praying. Hōryū-ji is renowned not only as the oldest temple in Japan but also as a repository for some of the country's rarest treasures. Several of the temple's wooden buildings have survived earthquakes and fires to become the oldest of their kind in the world.

The temple is divided into two parts, **Sai-in** (West Temple) and **Tō-in** (East Temple). The entrance ticket allows admission to Sai-in, Tō-in and the Great Treasure Hall. A detailed map is provided and a guidebook is available in English and several other languages.

The main approach to the temple proceeds from the south along a tree-lined avenue and continues through the Nandai-mon and Chū-mon before entering the Sai-in precinct. As you enter this precinct, you'll see the **Kondō** (Main Hall) on your right and a pagoda on your left.

The Kondō houses several treasures, including the triad of the **Buddha Sakyamuni**, with two attendant bodhisattvas. Though it is one of Japan's great Buddhist treasures, it's dimly lit and barely visible – you will need a torch (flashlight) to see it. Likewise, the pagoda contains clay images depicting scenes from the life of Buddha, which are barely visible without a torch.

On the eastern side of Sai-in are the two concrete buildings of the **Daihōzō-in** (Great Treasure Hall), containing numerous treasures from Hōryū-ji's long history.

GETTING THERE & AWAY

To get to Hōryū-ji, take the JR Kansai line from JR Nara Station to Hōryū-ji Station (¥210, 10 minutes). From there, bus 72 shuttles the short distance between the station and the bus stop Hōryū-ji Monmae (¥170, eight minutes). Alternatively, take bus 52 or 97 from either JR Nara Station or Kintetsu Nara Station and get off at the Hōryū-ji-mae stop (¥760, 60 minutes). Leave the bus stop and walk west for about 50m, cross the road and you will see the tree-lined approach to the temple.

Yakushi-ji 薬師寺

This **temple** (☎ 0742-33-6001; admission ¥500; ⌚ 8.30am-5pm) houses some of the most beautiful Buddhist images in all Japan. It was established by Emperor Temmu in 680. With the exception of the **East Pagoda**, which dates to 730, the present buildings either date from the 13th century or are very recent reconstructions.

Entering from the south, turn to the right before going through the gate with guardian figures and walk to the **Tōin-dō** (East Hall), which houses a famous Shō-Kannon image, built in the 7th century and showing obvious influences of Indian sculptural styles. Exit the Tōin-dō and walk west to the **Kondō** (Main Hall).

The Kondō was rebuilt in 1976 and houses several images, including the famous **Yakushi Triad** (the Buddha Yakushi flanked by the bodhisattvas of the sun and moon), dating from the 8th century. They were originally gold, but a fire in the 16th century turned the images an appealingly mellow black.

Behind (north of) the Kondō is the Kō-dō (Lecture Hall), which houses yet another fine Buddhist trinity, this time Miroku Buddha with two bodhisattva attendants. You can exit to the north behind this hall and make your way to Tōshōdai-ji.

GETTING THERE & AWAY

To get to Yakushi-ji, take bus 52, 63, 70, 88, 89 or 97 from either JR Nara Station or Kintetsu Nara Station and get off at either the Yakushi-ji Higashiguchi stop or the Yakushi-ji stop (¥240, 22 minutes). From the stop, walk 100m south (same direction the bus was travelling) to a Mobil station, cross the road to the west, and walk west across a canal. From the main road it's 250m to the temple's south entrance.

You can also take a *futsū* on the Kintetsu Kashihara line and get off at Nishinokyō Station, which is about 200m walk northwest of Yakushi-ji (and 600m walk south of Tōshōdai-ji). If you're coming from Nara, you will have to change trains at Yamato-Saidaiji (¥200, five minutes; *kyūkō* and *tokkyū* do not stop at Nishinokyō).

Tōshōdai-ji 唐招提寺

This **temple** (☎ 0742-33-7900; admission ¥600; 🕒 8.30am-5pm) was established in 759 by the Chinese priest Ganjin (Jian Zhen), who had been recruited by Emperor Shōmu to reform Buddhism in Japan. Ganjin didn't have much luck with his travel arrangements from China to Japan: five attempts were thwarted by shipwreck, storms and bureaucracy. Despite being blinded by eye disease, he finally made it on the sixth attempt and spread his teachings to Japan. The lacquer sculpture in the Miei-dō Hall is a moving tribute to Ganjin: blind and rock steady. It is shown only once a year, on 6 June – the anniversary of Ganjin's death. Last entry by 4.30pm.

The **Kondō** (Golden Hall) of the temple, which is the main hall of the temple, is presently under reconstruction and is scheduled to reopen in November 2009.

Tōshōdai-ji is a 600m walk north of Yakushi-ji's northern gate; see above for transport details from Nara.

AROUND YAMATO-YAGI 大和八木周辺

Easily reached on the Kintetsu line from Osaka, Kyoto or Nara, Yamato-Yagi is the most convenient transport hub for sights in southern Nara-ken. From Kyoto take the Kintetsu Nara/Kashihara line direct (*kyūkō*, ¥860, 57 minutes). From Nara take the Kintetsu Nara line to Saidaiji and change to the Kintetsu Kashihara line (*kyūkō*, ¥430, 27 minutes). From Osaka's Uehonmachi Station, take the Kintetsu Osaka line direct (*kyūkō*, ¥540, 34 minutes).

Kashihara 橿原

Three stops south of Yamato-Yagi, on the Kintetsu Kashihara line, is Kashihara-jingū-mae Station (¥200 from Yamato-Yagi, five minutes, all trains stop). There are a couple of interesting sights within easy walking distance of this station.

KASHIHARA-JINGŪ 橿原神宮

This **shrine** (☎ 0744-22-3271; admission free), at the foot of Unebi-yama, dates back to 1889, when many of the buildings were moved here from Kyoto Gosho (Kyoto Imperial Palace). The shrine buildings are built in the same style as those of Ise-jingū's Grand Shrine and are a good example of classical Shintō architecture. The shrine is dedicated to Japan's mythical first emperor, Jimmu, and an annual festival is held here on 11 February, the legendary date of Jimmu's enthronement. The vast, parklike grounds are pleasant to stroll around. The shrine is five minutes' walk from Kashihara-jingū-mae Station; take the central exit out of the station and follow the main street in the direction of the mountain.

NARA PREFECTURE KASHIHARA ARCHAEOLOGICAL MUSEUM

奈良県橿原考古学研究所付属博物館

This **museum** (Nara Ken-ritsu Kashihara Kōkogaku Kenkyūjo Fuzoku Hakubutsukan; ☎ 0744-24-1185; admission ¥400, foreign passport holders free; 🕒 9am-5pm, closed Mon) is highly recommended for those with an interest in the history of the Japanese people. The objects on display come from various archaeological sites in the area, including several *kofun*. Although most of the explanations are in Japanese, there's enough English to give you an idea of what's going on and a decent English pamphlet is available on entry. Foreigners can enter free, but you'll need your passport to take advantage of this great deal. Last entry by 4.30pm.

To get there from Kashihara-jingū, walk out the northern gate of the shrine (to your left when you stand with your back to the main hall), follow the wooded avenue for five minutes, cross the main road and continue on in the same direction for 100m before turning left at the first intersection. It's on the left soon after this turn.

ASUKA 飛鳥

☎ 0744 / pop 6330

The Yamato Plain in central Nara-ken is where the forerunners of Japan's ruling Yamato dynasty cemented their grip on power. In these pre-Buddhist days, huge earthen burial mounds were used to entomb deceased emperors. Some of the best examples of these burial mounds, or *kofun*, can be found around the town of Asuka, an hour or so south of Nara on the Kintetsu line.

The best way to explore the area is by bicycle, which can be rented from one of several rental shops outside the station (per day weekday/weekend ¥900/1000). There's a **tourist information office** (☎ 54-3624; 🕒 8.30am-5pm, closed year-end/new-year holidays) outside Asuka Station, which stocks an excellent pamphlet with a suggested bicycle route of the area.

Two tombs worth seeing are **Takamatsuzuka-kofun** (高松塚古墳) and **Ishibutai-kofun** (石舞台古墳; admission ¥250; 🕒 8.30am-5pm). Takamatsuzuka-kofun, which was excavated in 1972, is closed to the public but can be observed from outside. Unfortunately, it's once again being excavated and it looks very much like a construction site (and work won't be completed until 2019). Luckily, the Ishibutai-kofun is open to the public and is not being excavated. It is said to have housed the remains of Soga no Umako but is now completely empty.

If you have time left after visiting the earlier sights, take a look at **Asuka-dera** (飛鳥寺; ☎ 54-2126; admission ¥350; 🕒 9am-4.45pm), which dates from 596 and is considered the first true temple in all of Japan. Housed within is the oldest remaining image of Buddha in Japan – it looks pretty good considering it's been around for more than 1300 years.

Lastly, if you'd like a bite to eat while in Asuka, try **Café Rest Ashibi** (あしびの郷; ☎ 0742-26-6662; simple meals from ¥1000; 🕒 10am-6pm, lunch until 2pm). To get there, exit the station and follow the canal to the right for about 150m.

Asuka is five stops south of Yamato-Yagi (change at Kashihara-jingū-mae) and two stops south of Kashihara-jingū-mae on the Kintetsu Yoshino line (¥220 from Yamato-Yagi, 10 minutes, *tokkyū* stops at Asuka).

KANSAI

AROUND SAKURAI 桜井周辺

There are a few interesting places to visit close to the town of Sakurai, which can be reached directly from Nara on the JR Sakurai line (*futsū*, ¥320, 28 minutes). To reach Sakurai via Yamato-Yagi (when coming from Kyoto or Osaka), take the Kintetsu Osaka line from Yamato-Yagi (*junkyū*, ¥200, seven minutes).

Tanzan-jinja 談山神社

South of Sakurai, this **shrine** (☎ 0744-49-0001; admission ¥500; 🕒 8.30am-4.30pm) can be reached by bus 14 from stand 1 outside the southern exit of Sakurai Station (¥460, 24 minutes). Enshrined here is Nakatomi no Kamatari, patriarch of the Fujiwara line, which effectively ruled Japan for nearly 500 years. Legend has it that Nakatomi met here secretly with Prince Naka no Ōe over games of kickball to discuss the overthrow of the ruling Soga clan. This event is commemorated on the second Sunday in November by priests playing a game of kickball.

The central structure of the shrine is an attractive 13-storey pagoda best viewed against a backdrop of maple trees ablaze with autumn colours.

Hase-dera 長谷寺

Two stops east of Sakurai on the Kintetsu Osaka line is Hasedera Station. From the station, it's a 20-minute walk to lovely **Hase-dera** (☎ 0744-47-7001; admission ¥500; 🕒 9am-4.30pm). After a long climb up seemingly endless steps, you enter the main hall and are rewarded with a splendid view from the gallery, which juts out on stilts over the mountainside. Inside the top hall, the huge Kannon image is well worth a look. The best times to visit this temple are in the spring, when the way is lined with blooming peonies, and in autumn, when the temple's maple trees turn a vivid red. From the station, walk down through the archway, cross the river and turn right onto the main street that leads to the temple.

Murō-ji 室生寺

Founded in the 9th century, this **temple** (☎ 0745-93-2003; admission ¥600; 🕒 8am-5pm, 8.30am-4pm Dec-Feb) has strong connections with Esoteric Buddhism (the Shingon sect). Women were never excluded from Murō-ji as they were from other Shingon temples, and it is for this reason that it came to be known as 'the Woman's Koya'. Unfortunately, the temple's lovely five-storey pagoda, which dates from the 8th or 9th century, was severely damaged in a typhoon in the summer of 1999. The newly rebuilt pagoda lacks some of the rustic charm of the old one. Nonetheless, Murō-ji is a secluded place in thick forest and is well worth a visit. Enter by 30 minutes before closing.

After visiting the main hall, walk up to the pagoda and then continue on behind the pagoda in the direction of **Oku-no-in**, a hall of the temple located at the top of a very steep flight of steps. If you don't feel like making the climb, at least go about 100m past the pagoda to see the mammoth cedar tree growing over a huge rock here.

Murōguchi-ōno Station on the Kintetsu Osaka line is two stops east of Hasedera Station. It's a 14-minute bus ride from Murōguchi-ōno Station to Murō-ji on bus 43, 44, 45 or 46 (¥400). In spring, there is a direct bus between Hase-dera and Murō-ji (¥830, end of April to early May, one or two buses per hour between 11am and 3pm).

YOSHINO 吉野

☎ 0746 / pop 9600

Yoshino is Japan's top cherry-blossom destination, and for a few weeks in early to mid-April the blossoms of thousands of cherry trees form a floral carpet gradually ascending the mountainsides. It's definitely a sight worth seeing, but the narrow streets of the village become jammed tight with thousands of visitors at this time, and you'll have to be content with a day trip unless you've booked accommodation long in advance. Once the cherry-blossom petals fall, the crowds depart and Yoshino reverts to a sleepy village with a handful of shrines and a couple of temples to entertain day-trippers.

Information

Yoshino Visitors Center (☎ 32-3081; 🕑 9am-5pm, closed Jan & Feb) is about 500m up the main street from the top cable-car station, on your right just after Kimpusen-ji (look for the large tan-and-white building). It can help with *minshuku* bookings if necessary. The **Yoshino town webpage** (www.town.yoshino.nara.jp/sakura_off/kaika/index.htm, in Japanese) has the best information on when the trees will bloom.

Sights

Walk about 400m uphill from the cable-car station and you will come to the stone steps leading to the Niō-mon gate of **Kimpusen-ji** (金峯山寺; ☎ 32-8371; admission ¥400; 🕑 8.30am-4.30pm). Check out the fearsome **Kongō Rikishi** (guardian figure statues) in the gate and then continue on to the massive **Zaō-dō Hall** of the temple. Said to be the second-largest wooden building in Japan, the hall is most interesting for its unfinished wooden columns. For many centuries Kimpusen-ji has been one of the major centres for Shugendō, and pilgrims have often stopped here to pray for good fortune on the journey to Ōmine-san.

Continuing another 300m up the street brings you to a side road to the left (the first turn past the post office) that leads to **Yoshimizu-jinja** (吉水神社), a small shrine that has a good view back to Kimpusen-ji and the *hito-me-sen-bon* (1000 trees in a glance) viewpoint. The shrine has played host to several important historical figures. Minamoto Yoshitsune, a legendary swordsman and general, fled here after incurring the wrath of his brother, the first Kamakura shōgun. Emperor Go-Daigo set up a rival southern court in Yoshino after a dispute for succession broke out in Kyoto. He stayed here while his palace was being built and the shrine displays a collection of scrolls, armour and painted murals from his stay (admission ¥400). It also entertained Toyotomi Hideyoshi and his 5000-person *hanami* party in 1594.

Another 150m up the street is the dilapidated **Katte-jinja** (勝手神社). The road forks just above this shrine. The left fork leads to **Nyoirin-ji** (如意輪時; ☎ 32-3008; admission ¥400; 🕑 9am-4pm), a temple that preserves both the relics of Emperor Go-Daigo's unlucky court and his tomb itself. Of particular interest are some old swords and a door upon which Masatsura Kusunoki, leader of the Emperor's army, scratched a poem with an arrowhead before going to battle and his death. The right fork leads uphill, where you will soon pass **Kizō-in** (喜蔵院) on your left and come to **Chikurin-in** (竹林院) on the right, which has a wonderful garden (see p432).

A few minutes' walk further on there is another fork, where you'll find a wooden torii and some steps leading up to a shrine. Take the left fork and the next right up the hill for the 3km hike to **Kimpu-jinja** (金峯神社), a small shrine in a pleasantly wooded mountain setting. If you don't fancy this somewhat strenuous uphill hike, there are plenty of smaller shrines on the streets and alleys off Yoshino's main street.

Sleeping

Yoshino-yama Kizō-in (吉野山喜蔵院; ☎ 32-3014; per person with 2 meals, dm HI members/nonmembers ¥5000/8000, temple stay ¥10,000; ⏰ Mar-Dec) This temple, Kizō-in, doubles as the local youth hostel and is the cheapest option in town. It's a pleasant place to stay, and several of the hostel's rooms look out across the valley. See p431 for directions to the temple.

Chikurin-in Gumpo en (竹林院群芳園; ☎ 32-8081; www.chikurin.co.jp/e/home.htm; r per person with 2 meals with/without bathroom from ¥21,000/15,750; 💻) Not far past Kizō-in, on the opposite side of the street, this is an exquisite temple that now operates primarily as a ryokan. Both present and previous emperors have stayed here, and a look at the view afforded by some of the rooms explains why. Reservations are essential for the cherry-blossom season, and a good idea at all other times. Even if you don't plan to stay at the temple, you should at least visit its splendid garden (admission ¥300).

Eating

Hōkon-an (芳魂庵; ☎ 32-8207; ⏰ 9am-5pm, closed irregularly) This is an atmospheric little tea house, where you can sip your tea while enjoying a lovely view over the valley. The *matcha* (¥650) comes with a homemade Japanese sweet. Look for the rustic wooden facade and large ceramic urn on the left, just past the post office.

Nakai Shunpūdō (中井春風堂; ☎ 32-3043; ⏰ 9am-5pm, closed irregularly) With a limited picture menu, this restaurant serves a *kamameshi teishoku* (rice cooked in an iron pot; ¥1500) and other typical lunch favourites; the view from the windows is great. It's about 5m past the information office, on the opposite side – look for the ceramic *tanuki* (Japanese raccoon dog) figure out front.

Nishizawaya (西澤屋; ☎ 32-8600; ⏰ 9am-5pm) Run by a bunch of friendly ladies, this homey restaurant serves things like the *shizuka gozen* set, which includes a broiled *ayu* (sweetfish) and a small hotpot filled with vegetables and tofu (¥1500). It's directly across the street from Katte-jinja: look for the plastic food on display. English menu.

Getting There & Away

Visitors to Yoshino first arrive at Yoshino Station, and then make their way up to the village proper by cable car or on foot. The cable car costs ¥350/600 one way/return. The walk takes about 15 minutes; follow the path that leaves from beside the cable-car station. Note that the cable car stops running at 5pm – plan your day accordingly or you'll have to walk down.

To get to Yoshino Station from Kyoto or Nara, take the Kintetsu Nara-Kashihara line to Kashihara-jingū-mae (*kyūkō* from Kyoto, ¥860, 66 minutes; *kyūkō* from Nara, ¥480, 36 minutes) and change to the Kintetsu Yoshino line (*kyūkō*, ¥460, 52 minutes).

You can take a direct train on the Kintetsu Minami–Osaka–Yoshino line from Osaka (Abenobashi Station, close to Tennō-ji Station) to Yoshino (*kyūkō*, ¥950, 89 minutes; *tokkyū* ¥1450, 75 minutes).

The closest JR station to Yoshino is Yoshino-guchi, where you can transfer to trains to/from Nara, Osaka and Wakayama.

KII-HANTŌ 紀伊半島

The remote and mountainous Kii-hantō (Kii Peninsula) is a far cry from central Kansai's bustling urban sprawl. Most of the peninsula's attractions are found in Wakayama-ken, including the mountaintop temple complex of Kōya-san, one of Japan's most important Buddhist centres. Other Wakayama-ken attractions include the onsen clustered around the village of Hongū, in the centre of the peninsula, the beachside onsen resort of Shirahama, on the west coast of the peninsula, and the rugged coastline of Shiono-misaki and Kii-Ōshima, at the southern tip of the peninsula.

The JR Kii main line (Kinokuni line) runs around the coast of the Kii-hantō, linking Shin-Osaka and Nagoya Stations (some trains originate/terminate at Kyoto Station). Special Kuroshio and Nankii *tokkyū* trains can get you around the peninsula fairly quickly, but once you step off these express trains you're at the mercy of slow local trains and buses, so plan accordingly. For this reason, renting a car is a good option for exploring this area.

We present the information in this section anticlockwise, working from Wakayama-shi around the horn to Mie-ken, but it's perfectly possible to do this the other way round (perhaps starting in Ise).

WAKAYAMA 和歌山

☎ 073 / pop 371,100

Wakayama, the prefectural capital, is a pleasant little city useful as a transport hub for travellers heading to other parts of the prefecture. The main attraction here is the city's rebuilt castle, a short walk west of the station.

There is a useful **tourist information counter** (☎ 422-5831; 8.30am-7pm Mon-Sat, to 5.15pm Sun & holidays) inside JR Wakayama Station, which stocks copies of the excellent *Wakayama City Guide* map.

Sights & Activities

WAKAYAMA-JŌ 和歌山城

The city's main attraction is **Wakayama-jō** (☎ 435-1044; 3 Ichiban-chō; admission to grounds/castle keep free/¥350; 9am-4.30pm). The original castle was built in 1585 by Toyotomi Hideyoshi and destroyed by bombing in WWII. The present structure is a concrete postwar reconstruction; it's picturesque from afar and unprepossessing up close. However, the gardens surrounding the castle are well worth a stroll if you're in the area. Last entry by 4pm.

The castle is a 20-minute walk (about 1.8km) west of JR Wakayama Station. Alternatively, it's about a 10-minute walk (about 1km) south of Wakayama-shi Station.

MUSEUM OF MODERN ART WAKAYAMA 和歌山県立近代美術館

A short walk from the castle, this **museum** (☎ 436-8690; 1-4-14 Fukiage; admission ¥310, extra for special exhibitions; 9.30am-5pm, closed Mon) is worth a visit for its unique building and small but interesting collection of Japanese and Western 20th-century art. The collection contains, among other things, 4000 block prints, and works by Picasso, Miró and Klee. The museum is across the street south of the castle.

Sleeping & Eating

Hotel Granvia Wakayama (ホテルグランヴィア和歌山; ☎ 425-3333; hotel@granvia-wakayama.co.jp; 5-18 Tomoda-chō; s/d/tw ¥10,164/17,902/19,635; 💻) This place is right outside the station and offers new, clean rooms. It's centrally located and fairly convenient to the sights and restaurants. There is LAN cable internet in rooms.

Mendori-tei (めんどり亭; ☎ 422-3355; 478 Yoshida; 10am-10pm) For a bite to eat, head to the restaurant arcade on the basement floor beneath JR Wakayama Station. Mendori-tei is one of our favourites here. It serves excellent *tonkatsu* dishes (try the *tonkatsu teishoku* for ¥980). Look for the brown curtains and the all-counter seating. If you fancy something a little lighter, there are several choices nearby.

Getting There & Away

Wakayama is serviced by JR *tokkyū* trains from Shin-Osaka and Kyoto, but unless you've got a Japan Rail Pass it's cheaper to take a local train on the JR Hanwa line from Osaka's Tennō-ji Station (*kaisoku,* ¥830, 65 minutes). From Osaka's Namba Station you can also take the private Nankai line to Wakayama-shi Station (*kyūkō,* ¥890, 63 minutes), which is linked to JR Wakayama Station by the JR Kisei main line (*futsū,* ¥180, six minutes).

KŌYA-SAN 高野山

☎ 0736 / pop 4090

Kōya-san is a raised tableland in northern Wakayama-ken covered with thick forests and surrounded by eight peaks. The major attraction here is the Kōya-san monastic complex, which is the headquarters of the Shingon school of Esoteric Buddhism. Though not quite the Shangri-la it's occasionally described as, Kōya-san is one of the most rewarding places to visit in Kansai, not just for the natural setting of the area but also as an opportunity to stay in temples and get a glimpse of long-held traditions of Japanese religious life.

Although it is just possible to visit Kōya-san as a day trip from Nara, Kyoto or Osaka, it's much better to reduce the travel stress and stay overnight in one of the town's excellent *shukubō* (temple lodgings). Keep in mind that Kōya-san tends to be around 5°C colder than down on the plains, so bring warm clothes if you're visiting in winter, spring or autumn.

Whenever you go, you'll find that getting there is half the fun – the train winds through a series of tight valleys with mountains soaring on all sides, and the final vertiginous cable-car leg is not for the faint of heart.

History

The founder of the Shingon school of Esoteric Buddhism, Kūkai (known after his death as Kōbō Daishi), established a religious community here in 816. Kōbō Daishi travelled as a young priest to China and returned after two years to found the school. He is one of Japan's most famous religious figures and

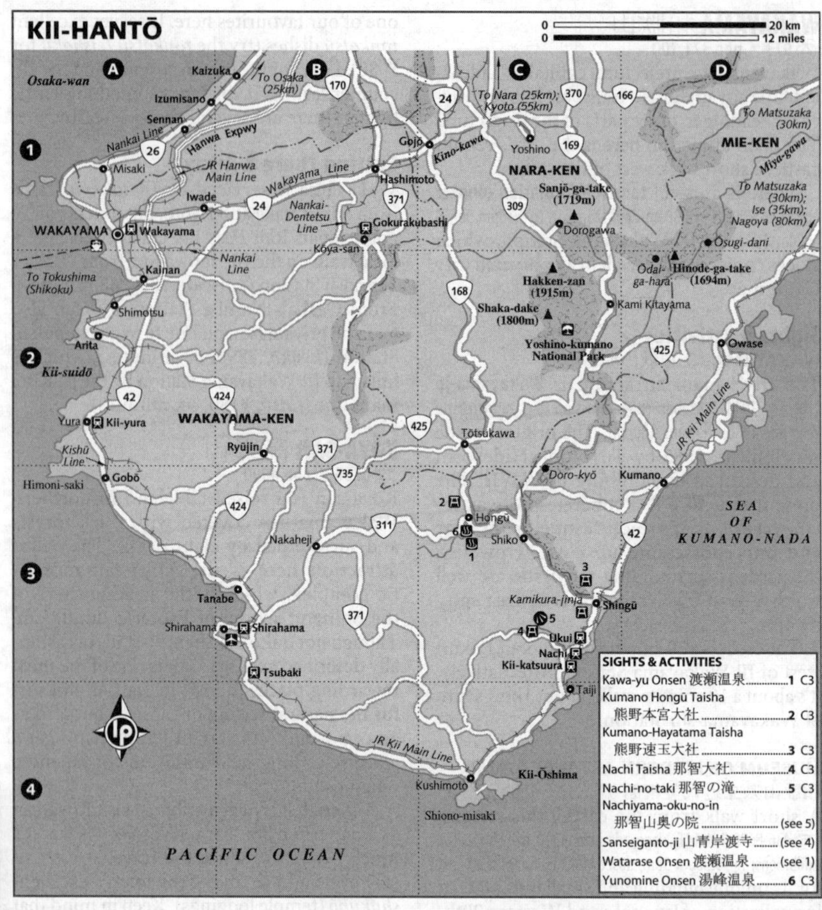

is revered as a bodhisattva, calligrapher, scholar, and inventor of the Japanese *kana* syllabary.

Followers of Shingon believe that Kōbō Daishi is not dead, but rather that he is meditating in his tomb in Kōya-san's Oku-no-in Cemetery, awaiting the arrival of Miroku (Maitreya, the future Buddha). Food is ritually offered in front of the tomb daily to sustain him during this meditation. When Miroku returns, it is thought that only Kōbō Daishi will be able to interpret his heavenly message for humanity. Thus, the vast cemetery here is like an amphitheatre crowded with souls gathered in expectation of this heavenly sermon.

Over the centuries the temple complex grew in size and attracted many followers of the Jōdo (Pure Land) school of Buddhism. During the 11th century, it became popular with both nobles and commoners to leave hair or ashes from deceased relatives close to Kōbō Daishi's tomb.

In the 16th century Oda Nobunaga asserted his destructive power by slaughtering large numbers of monks at Kōya-san. The community subsequently suffered the confiscation of their lands and narrowly escaped invasion by Toyotomi Hideyoshi. At one stage Kōya-san numbered about 1500 monasteries and many thousands of monks. The members of the community were divided into *gakuryō* (clergy), *gyōnin* (lay priests) and *hijiri* (followers of Pure Land Buddhism).

In the 17th century the Tokugawa shōgunate smashed the economic power of the lay priests, who managed considerable estates in the region. Their temples were destroyed, their leaders banished and the followers of Pure Land Buddhism were bluntly pressed into the Shingon school. During the Edo period, the government favoured the practice of Shintō and confiscated the lands that supported Kōya-san's monastic community. Women were barred from entry to Kōya-san until 1872.

Kōya-san is now a thriving centre for Japanese Buddhism, with more than 110 temples remaining and a large population. It is the headquarters of the Shingon school, which numbers 10 million members and presides over nearly 4000 temples all over Japan.

Orientation

The precincts of Kōya-san are divided into two main areas: the Garan (Sacred Precinct) in the west, where you will find interesting temples and pagodas, and the Oku-no-in, with its vast cemetery, in the east. We recommend visiting both sites.

Information

There is a joint ticket (*shodōkyōtsu-naihaiken;* ¥1500) that covers entry to Kongōbu-ji, the Kondō, Dai-tō, Treasure Museum and Tokugawa Mausoleum. It can be purchased at the following information office.

Kōya-san Tourist Association (☎ 56-2616; fax 56-2889; ⏲ 8.30am-5.30pm Jul & Aug, to 4.30pm Sep-Jun) In the centre of town in front of the Senjūin-bashi bus stop, this tourist information centre stocks maps and brochures and English speakers are usually on hand.

Kōyasan Interpreter Guide Club (☎ 080-6148-2588; www.geocities.jp/koyasan_i_g_c) This club offers four-hour private tours of Kōya-san for ¥5000 per group for up to five people. It also offers regularly scheduled tours on Wednesday from April to September for ¥1000 per person. The morning tour meets at Ichi-no-hashi at 8.30am, lasts three hours and covers Oku-no-in, Garan and Kongōbu-ji. The afternoon tour meets at Kongōbu-ji at 1pm, takes three hours, and covers Kongōbu-ji, Garan and Oku-no-in.

Sights

OKU-NO-IN 奥の院

Any Buddhist worth their salt in Japan has had their remains, or just a lock or two of hair, interred in this **cemetery-temple** to ensure pole position when Miroku Buddha comes to earth.

The best way to approach Oku-no-in is to walk or take the bus east to Ichi-no-hashi-mae bus stop. From here you cross the bridge, **Ichi-no-hashi**, and enter the cemetery grounds along a winding, cobbled path lined by tall cedar trees and thousands of tombs. As the trees close in and the mist swirls the atmosphere can be enchanting, especially as night falls.

One of the more interesting monuments to look out for is the **White Ant Memorial**, built by a pesticide company to expiate its guilt for the murder of legions of the little critters.

At the northern end of the graveyard, you will find the **Tōrō-dō** (Lantern Hall), which is the main building of the complex. It houses hundreds of lamps, including two believed to have been burning for more than 900 years. Behind the hall you can see the closed doors of the Kūkai mausoleum.

On the way to the Lantern Hall is the bridge **Mimyo-no-hashi**. Worshippers ladle water from the river and pour it over the nearby Jizō statues as an offering for the dead. The inscribed wooden plaques in the river are in memory of aborted babies and those who died by drowning.

Between the bridge and the Tōrō-dō is a small wooden building the size of a large phone booth, which contains the **Miroku-ishi**. Pilgrims reach through the holes in the wall to try to lift a large, smooth boulder onto a shelf. The weight of the stone is supposed to change according to your weight of sin. We can only report that the thing was damn heavy!

Buses return to the centre of town from the Oku-no-mae bus stop, or you can walk back in about 30 minutes.

KONGŌBU-JI 金剛峯寺

This is the headquarters of the Shingon school and the residence of Kōya-san's abbot. The present **structure** (☎ 56-2011; admission ¥500; ⏲ 8.30am-5pm) dates from the 19th century and is definitely worth a visit.

The main hall's Ohiro-ma room has ornate screens painted by Kanō Tanyu in the 16th century. The Yanagi-no-ma (Willow Room) has equally pretty screen paintings of willows but the rather grisly distinction of being the place where Toyotomi Hidetsugu committed *seppuku* (ritual suicide by disembowelment).

The rock garden is interesting for the sheer number of rocks used in its composition, giving the effect of a throng of petrified worshippers eagerly listening to a monk's sermon.

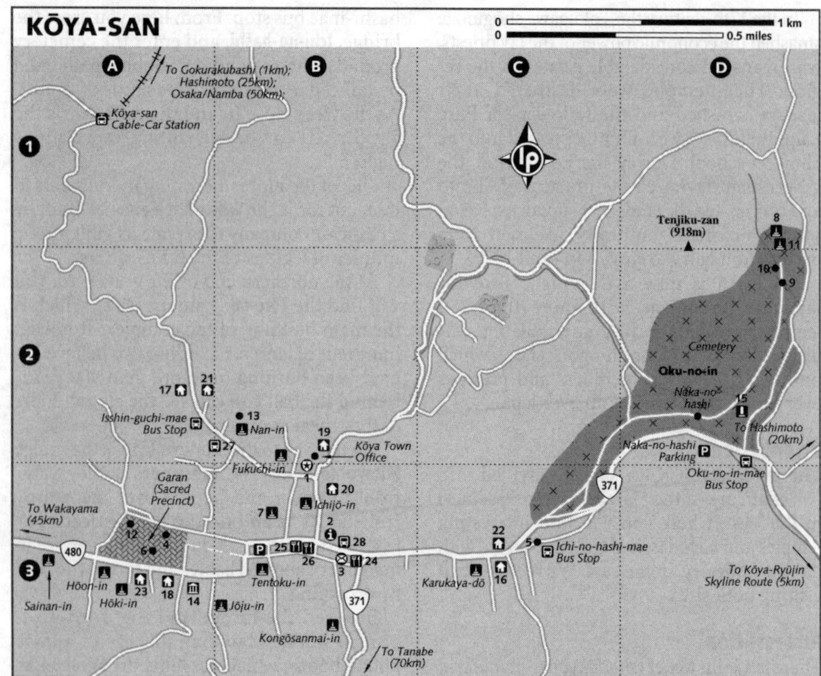

Admission includes tea and rice cakes served beside the stone garden. Last entry 4.30pm.

GARAN 伽藍

This is a **temple complex** (☎ 56-2011; admission to each bldg ¥200; 8.30am-5pm) of several halls and pagodas. The most important buildings are the **Dai-tō** (Great Pagoda) and **Kondō** (Main Hall). The Dai-tō, rebuilt in 1934 after a fire, is said to be the centre of the lotus-flower mandala formed by the eight mountains around Kōya-san. It's well worth entering the Dai-tō to see the Dainichi-nyōrai (Cosmic Buddha) and his four attendant Buddhas. It's been repainted recently and is an awesome sight. The nearby **Sai-tō** (Western Pagoda) was most recently rebuilt in 1834 and is more subdued. Last entry 4.30pm.

TREASURE MUSEUM 霊宝館

The **Treasure Museum** (Reihōkan; admission ¥600; 8.30am-5.30pm May-Oct, to 4.30pm Nov-Apr) has a compact display of Buddhist works of art, all collected in Kōya-san. There are some very fine statues, painted scrolls and mandalas.

TOKUGAWA MAUSOLEUM 徳川家霊台

Built in 1643, the **Tokugawa Mausoleum** (Tokugawa-ke Reidai; admission without joint ticket ¥200; 8.30am-5pm, to 4pm Nov-Apr) consists of two adjoining structures that serve as the mausoleums of Tokugawa Ieyasu (on the right) and Tokugawa Hidetada (on the left), the first and second Tokugawa shōguns, respectively. They are ornately decorated, as with most structures associated with the Tokugawa shōguns. See p435 for details of the joint ticket. The mausoleum is not far from the Namikiri-fudō-mae bus stop.

Festivals & Events

Aoba Matsuri Held on 15 June to celebrate the birth of Kōbō Daishi. Various traditional ceremonies are performed at the temples around town.

Rōsoku Matsuri (Candle Festival) This more interesting festival is held on 13 August in remembrance of departed souls. Thousands of mourners light candles along the approaches to Oku-no-in.

Sleeping

There are more than 50 temples in Kōya-san offering *shukubō*. It's worth staying the night at a temple here, especially to try *shōjin-ryōri*

KANSAI

INFORMATION		
Kōya Police Station 高野警察署	1	B3
Kōya-san Tourist Association 高野山観光協会	2	B3
Post Office 郵便局	3	B3
SIGHTS & ACTIVITIES		
Dai-tō 大塔	4	A3
Ichi-no-hashi 一の橋	5	C3
Kondō (Main Hall) 金堂	6	A3
Kongōbu-ji 金剛峯寺	7	B3
Kūkai Mausoleum 空海の墓	8	D1
Mimyo-no-hashi 御廟橋	9	D2
Miroku-ishi みろく石	10	D2
Oku-no-in 奥の院	11	D1
Sai-tō 西塔	12	A3
Tokugawa Mausoleum 徳川家霊台	13	B2
Tōrō-dō 灯ろう堂	(see 11)	
Treasure Museum 霊宝館	14	A3
White Ant Memorial 白蟻墓	15	D2
SLEEPING		
Ekō-in 永光院	16	C3
Haryō-in 巴陵院	17	A2
Henjōson-in 遍照尊院	18	A3
Kōya-san Youth Hostel 高野ユースホステル	19	B2
Muryōkō-in 無量光院	20	B3
Rengejō-in 蓮華定院	21	A2
Shojōshin-in 清浄心院	22	C3
Yōchi-in 桜池院	23	A3
EATING		
Hanabishi Honten 花菱本店	24	B3
Maruman 丸万	25	B3
Nankai Shokudo 南海食堂	26	B3
TRANSPORT		
Namikiri-fudō-mae Bus Stop 波切不動前バス亭	27	B2
Senjūin-bashi Bus Stop 千手院橋前バス停	28	B3

(Buddhist vegetarian food – no meat, fish, onions or garlic). Because *shukubō* is intended for religious pilgrims, in the morning you may be asked to participate in morning Buddhist prayer. While participation is not mandatory, taking part enables you to appreciate the daily workings of a Japanese temple.

Most lodgings *start* at ¥9500 per person including two meals. There is a lot of variation in prices, not just between temples, but also within temples, depending upon room, meals and season (needless to say, the more you pay, the better the room and the meals).

Make advance reservations by fax through the Kōya-san Tourist Association (p435) or directly with the temples (getting a Japanese speaker to help will make this easier). Even if you contact the temples directly, you will usually be asked to go to the Tourist Association to pick up a reservation slip–voucher.

Kōya-san Youth Hostel (☎ 56-3889; fax 56-3889; dm ¥4160; 💻) This YH is a friendly and comfortable budget choice if the prices at the temples are out of your range. It's closed for parts of December and January. Call ahead for reservations.

Haryō-in (☎ 56-2702; fax 56-2936; r per person with 2 meals from ¥6825) This temple is one of the cheaper *shukubō* and functions as a *kokumin-shukusha* (people's lodge).

Rengejō-in (☎ 56-2233; fax 56-4743; r per person with 2 meals from ¥9500, single travellers ¥11,550) This lovely temple has superb rooms, many with garden views, fine painted *fusuma* (sliding doors) and interesting art on display. English is spoken here and sometimes explanation of Buddhist practices and meditation is available. It is highly recommended.

Ekō-in (☎ 56-2514; fax 56-2891; ekoin@mbox.co.jp; r per person with 2 meals from ¥10,000; 💻) One of the nicer temples in town, Ekō-in is run by a friendly bunch of young monks and the rooms look onto beautiful gardens. This is also one of the two temples in town (the other is Kongōbu-ji) where you can study *zazen* (seated meditation). Call ahead to make arrangements.

Yōchi-in (☎ 56-2003; fax 56-3628; r per person with 2 meals from ¥11,000) This simple temple is a welcoming and friendly place with a nice garden outside its entryway. It's very close to the Garan and the centre of town.

Henjōson-in (☎ 56-2434; fax 56-3641; r per person with 2 meals from ¥15,750) This is another good choice. The rooms here also have good garden views and are quite spacious. High-quality meals are served in the dining hall. The communal bathtubs here are huge and have nice views. And the flowers in the entryway are usually stunning.

Other good choices:

Muryōkō-in (☎ 56-2104; fax 56-4555; r per person with 2 meals ¥9500) A fine place with an interesting morning Buddhist ceremony.

Shōjōshin-in (☎ 56-2006; fax 56-4770; r per person with 2 meals from ¥11,100) Friendly spot.

Eating

The culinary speciality of Kōya-san is *shōjin-ryōri*, which you can sample at your temple lodgings. Two tasty tofu specialities are *goma-tōfu* (sesame tofu) and *kōya-tōfu* (local tofu). If you're just in town for the day, you can try *shōjin-ryōri* at any of the temples that offer *shukubō*. Ask at the Kōya-san Tourist Association office (p435) and staff will call ahead to make reservations. Prices are fixed at ¥2700, ¥3700 and ¥5300, depending on how many courses you have.

There are various coffee shops and *shokudō* dotted around town where you can have breakfast or lunch (most close before dinnertime).

Maruman (☎ 56-2049; noodle dishes from ¥370; ⌚ 9am-5pm, closed irregularly) This simple *shokudō* is a good spot for lunch. All the standard lunch items are represented by plastic food models in the window. *Katsu-don* is ¥820. It's just west of the tourist office on the main street – look for the food models in the window. If this is full or doesn't suit, the Nankai Shokudō next door is similar.

Hanabishi Honten (☎ 56-2236; 769 Kōyasan; lunch ¥2100-5250, dinner ¥2100-16,000; ⌚ 11am-6pm, closed irregularly) If you fancy something a little nicer than a *shokudō*, you could try this slightly overpriced restaurant. At lunch, the *sankozen* set (a variety of vegetarian dishes; ¥2100) is a good choice. Look for the grey facade and the food models in the window (which will also help with ordering, if necessary). English menu; reserve after 6pm.

Getting There & Away

Unless you have a rental car, the best way to Kōya-san is the Nankai-Dentetsu line from Osaka's Namba Station to Kōya-san. The trains terminate at Gokurakubashi, at the base of the mountain, where you board a funicular railway (five minutes, price included in train tickets) up to Kōya-san itself. From the cable-car station, you take a bus into the centre of town (walking is prohibited on the connecting road).

From Osaka (Namba Station) you can travel directly on a Nankai-Dentetsu line *kyūkō* to Kōya-san (¥1230, 100 minutes). For the slightly faster *tokkyū* service with reserved seats you pay a supplement (¥760).

From Wakayama you can go by rail on the JR Wakayama line to Hashimoto (¥820, one hour) and then continue on the Nankai-Dentetsu line to Gokurakubashi Station (¥430, 38 minutes).

From Kyoto go via Namba in Osaka. From Nara you can take the JR line to Hashimoto, changing at Sakurai and Takadate en route.

Getting Around

Buses run on three routes from the top cable-car station via the centre of town to Ichi-no-hashi and Oku-no-in. The fare to the tourist office in the centre of town at Senjūin-bashi is ¥280. The fare to the final stop, Oku-no-in, is ¥400. An all-day bus pass (*ichi-nichi furee kippu*; ¥800) is available from the bus office outside the top cable-car station, but once you get into the centre of town you can reach most destinations quite easily on foot (including Oku-no-in, which takes about 30 minutes). Note that buses run infrequently, so you should make a note of the schedule before setting out to see the sights.

If you don't feel like walking, bicycles can be rented (per hour/day ¥400/1200) at the Kōya-san Tourist Association office (p435).

SHIRAHAMA 白浜

☎ 0739 / pop 22,980

Shirahama, on the southwest coast of the Kii-hantō, is Kansai's leading beach resort and has all the trappings of a major Japanese tourist attraction – huge resort hotels, aquariums, amusement parks etc. However, it also has several good onsen, a great white-sand beach and rugged coastal scenery.

Because the Japanese like to do things according to the rules – and the rules say the only time you can swim in the ocean is from late July to the end of August – the place is almost deserted outside the peak season. Thus, this is a great place to visit in, say, June or September, and we've swum in the sea here as late as mid-October.

There's a **tourist information office** (☎ 42-2900; ⌚ 9.30am-6pm) in the station, where you can pick up a map to the main sights and accommodation. Since the station is a fair distance from the main sights, you'll need to take a bus (one way/all-day pass ¥330/1000, 12 minutes to the beach) or rent a bicycle if you arrive by rail. The JR office at the station rents bicycles (¥500 per day); unfortunately, no one would describe these as performance vehicles.

Sights & Activities

SHIRARA-HAMA BEACH 白良浜

Shirara-hama, the town's main beach, is famous for its white sand. If it reminds you of Australia don't be surprised – the town had to import sand from Down Under after the original stuff washed away. This place is packed during July and August. In the off-peak season, it can actually be quite pleasant. The beach is hard to miss, as it dominates the western side of town.

ONSEN

In addition to its great beach, Shirahama has some of Japan's oldest developed onsen (they're even mentioned in the *Nihon Shoki*, one of Japan's earliest literary texts).

Shirasuna-yu (しらすな湯; ☎ 43-1126; 864 Shirahama-chō, Nishimuro-gun; 10am-3pm Oct-Jun, to 7pm Jul-Sep, closed Mon 16 Sep-30 Jun) is a free open-air onsen off the boardwalk in the middle of Shirara-hama beach. You can soak here and then dash into the ocean to cool off – not a bad way to spend an afternoon.

Sakino-yu Onsen (崎の湯温泉; ☎ 42-3016; 1688 Shirahama-chō, Nishimuro-gun; admission ¥300; 7am-7pm Thu-Tue Jul & Aug, 8am-5pm Thu-Tue Sep-Jun) is sensational. It's built on a rocky point with great views of the Pacific Ocean (and you can climb down the rocks to cool off if the waves aren't too big). Come early in the day to beat the crowds. It's 1km south of the main beach; walk along the seafront road and look for the point below the big Hotel Seymor. The baths are segregated by sex.

Other baths include **Shirara-yu** (白良湯; ☎ 43-2614; 3313-1 Shirahama-chō, Nishimuro-gun; admission ¥300; 7am-11pm Wed-Mon, noon-11pm Tue), a pleasant bath right on the north end of Shirara-hama (the main beach), and **Murono-yu** (牟婁の湯; ☎ 43-0686; 1665 Shirahama-chō, Nishimuro-gun; admission ¥300; noon-11pm Thu, 7am-11pm Fri-Wed), a simple onsen not far from Sakino-yu, in front of Shirahama post office, on the way to Sakino-yu. Enter by 10.30pm.

SENJŌ-JIKI, SANDAN-HEKI & ISOGI-KŌEN
千畳敷・三段壁・いそぎ公園

Just around the point south of the Sakino-yu Onsen are two of Shirahama's natural wonders: Senjō-jiki and Sandan-heki. **Senjō-jiki** (Thousand Tatami Mat Point) is a wildly eroded point with stratified layers that actually resemble the thousand tatami mats it is named for.

More impressive is the 50m cliff face of **Sandan-heki** (Three-Step Cliff), which drops away vertiginously into the sea. While you can pay ¥1200 to take a lift down to a cave at the base of the cliff, it's better simply to clamber along the rocks to the north of the cliff – it's stunning, particularly when the big rollers are pounding in from the Pacific.

If you'd like to enjoy more rugged coastal scenery, walk south along the coast another 1km from Sandan-heki to **Isogi-kōen**, where the crowds are likely to be thinner and the scenery just as impressive.

These attractions can be reached on foot or bicycle from the main beach in around 30 minutes, or you can take a bus from the station (¥430, 20 minutes to Senjō-jiki, bus stop 'Senjō-guchi'), from which you can walk to the others.

Sleeping

Minshuku Katsuya (民宿かつ屋; ☎ 42-3814; fax 42-3817; 3118-5 Shirahama-chō, Nishimuro-gun; r per person without meals ¥4000) Katsuya is the best-value *minshuku* in town and it's very central, only two minutes' walk from the main beach. It's built around a small Japanese garden and has its own natural onsen bath. There is red-and-white Japanese writing on the building and faint English on a small sign.

Kokumin-shukusha Hotel Shirahama (国民宿舎ホテルシラハマ; ☎ 42-3039; fax 42-4643; 813 Shirahama-chō, Nishimuro-gun; r per person with 2 meals ¥6870) This is a good bet if Katsuya is full, and offers similar rates. It's a little dark and showing its age, but the rooms are spacious and there is an onsen bath. It's just off Miyuki-dōri, 100m past the post office towards the beach (look for a parking lot and the black-blue-red-and-white sign). The tourist information office at the station has maps to both places.

Hotel Marquise (ホテルマーキーズ; ☎ 42-4010; fax 43-2720; www.aikis.or.jp/~marquise, in Japanese; 1905 Yuzaki, Shirahama-chō; r per person with 2 meals from ¥16,800) Very close to Sakino-yu Onsen, this hotel has excellent sea-view rooms, some with balconies. The Japanese-style rooms are spacious and clean. This hotel is popular with female guests and the ladies' bath is larger than the men's (something of a rarity in Japan).

Eating

There are many restaurants in the streets just in from the beach.

Kiraku (喜楽; ☎ 42-3916; 890-48 Shirahama-chō, Nishimuro-gun; 11am-2pm & 4-9pm, closed Tue) There is nothing fancy about this friendly little *shokudō* that serves standard *teishoku* for around ¥1200. There is a limited picture menu to help with ordering. It's about 5m in from Miyuki-dōri, on the beach side, close to a coin laundry (look for the plants out the front).

If you'd like to self-cater, Sakae Supermarket is five minutes' walk from the main beach.

Getting There & Away

Shirahama is on the JR Kii main line. There are *tokkyū* trains from Shin-Osaka Station (¥5450, 132 minutes). There also *futsū* trains on the same line (¥3260, 207 minutes). The same line also connects Shirahama to other cities on Kii-hantō such as Kushimoto, Nachi, Shingū and Wakayama city. A cheaper alternative is offered by **Meikō Bus** (☎ 42-3008; www13.ocn.ne.jp/~meikobus, in Japanese; 🕑 9am-6pm), which runs buses between JR Osaka Station and Shirahama (one way/return ¥2700/5000, about 3½ hours).

KUSHIMOTO, SHIONO-MISAKI & KII-ŌSHIMA
串本・潮岬・紀伊大島

☎ 0735

The southern tip of Kii-hantō has some stunning coastal scenery. Shiono-misaki, connected to the mainland by a narrow isthmus, has some fine rocky vistas, but the real action is over on Kii-Ōshima, a rocky island accessible by bridge.

The main attraction on Kii-Ōshima is the coastal cliffs at the eastern end of the island, which can be viewed from the park around **Kashino-zaki Lighthouse** (樫野崎灯台). Just before the park, you'll find the **Toruko-Kinenkan Museum** (トルコ記念館; ☎ 65-0628; 1025-25 Kashino, Kushimoto-chō, Higashimuro-gun; admission ¥250; 🕑 9am-5pm), which commemorates the sinking of the Turkish ship *Ertugrul* in 1890.

Backtracking about 1km towards the bridge, there are small English signs to the **Japan-US Memorial Museum** (日米修交記念館; ☎ 65-0099; 1033 Kashino, Kushimoto-chō, Nishimuro-gun; admission ¥250; 🕑 9am-4pm), which commemorates the visit of the US ship *Lady Washington* in 1791, a full 62 years before Commodore Perry's much more famous landing in Yokohama in 1853. There is a lookout just beyond the museum from which you can see the magnificent **Umi-kongō** (海金剛) formations along the eastern point of the island.

If you're without your own transport, the best way to explore Kii-Ōshima is by renting a bicycle at Kushimoto Station (per four hours/full day ¥600/1000, discount for JR ticket holders), but be warned that there are a few big hills en route and these bikes are better suited to shopping than cruising. Otherwise, there are buses from the station, but take note of schedules as departures are few and far between.

Misaki Lodge Youth Hostel (みさきロッジユースホステル; ☎ 62-1474; fax 62-0529; 2864-1 Shionomisaki, Kushimoto-chō; per person dm without meals/minshuku with 2 meals from ¥4200/7350) is the best place to stay in the area. It's in a good position, on the southern side of the cape overlooking the Pacific. It's also a *minshuku,* offering large rooms and two meals. Take a Shiono-misaki-bound bus from Kushimoto Station (20 minutes) and get off at Koroshio-mae.

Kushimoto is one hour from Shirahama by JR *tokkyū,* and 3½ hours (¥6280) from Shin-Osaka. *Futsū* services are significantly cheaper but take almost twice as long.

NACHI & KII-KATSUURA
那智・紀伊勝浦

The Nachi and Kii-Katsuura area has several sights grouped around the sacred **Nachi-no-taki** (那智の滝), Japan's highest waterfall (133m). **Nachi Taisha** (那智大社), near the waterfall, was built in homage to the waterfall's *kami* (Shintō spirit god). It is one of the three great shrines of Kii-hantō, and it's worth the climb up the steep steps to get there. Next to the shrine, **Sanseiganto-ji** (山青岸渡寺) is a fine old temple that is well worth a look.

The most atmospheric approach to the falls and the shrine is the fantastic tree-lined arcade of **Daimon-zaka**. To get to Daimon-zaka, take a bus from Nachi or Kii-Katsuura Station, and get off at the Daimon-zaka stop (ask the bus driver to drop you at Daimon-zaka and he'll point you in the right direction from the stop). The way isn't marked in English, but it's roughly straight uphill just in from the road. From the bus stop to the shrine is roughly 800m, most of it uphill. It's fine in winter, but in summer you'll get soaked, so consider doing it in reverse (check bus schedules carefully before setting out).

Daimon-zaka takes you up to the steps at the base of the shrine. After visiting the shrine, walk down to the falls. At the base of the falls you will find **Nachiyama-oku-no-in** (那智山奥の院), where you can pay ¥200 to hike up to a lookout that affords a better view of the falls.

The **Nachi-no-Hi Matsuri** (Fire Festival) takes place at the falls on 14 July. During this lively event *mikoshi* are brought down from the mountain and met by groups bearing flaming torches.

Buses to the waterfall and shrine leave from Nachi Station (¥470, 25 minutes) and from Kii-Katsuura Station (¥600, 30 minutes). Buses to the Daimon-zaka stop leave from Nachi Station (¥330, 15 minutes) and from Kii-Katsuura Station (¥410, 20 minutes).

Sleeping

There are a few places to stay near Nachi Station and Kii-Katsuura Station.

Hotel Ura-Shima (ホテル浦島; ☎0735-52-1011; www.hotelurashima.co.jp, in Japanese; r per person with 2 meals from ¥10,650;) Laying claim to an entire peninsula in Katsuura-wan, this vast hotel-onsen complex is either a lot of fun or an overpriced tourist trap, depending upon your mood. It's got two fantastic baths built into caves looking out over the Pacific, and two others located high atop the peninsula, reached by the longest escalator we've ever seen. The fun of the baths is offset by uninspiring food, ageing rooms, and the noisy announcements in the hallways.

Getting There & Away

Nachi and Kii-Katsuura (the stations are only two stops apart) can be reached by JR Kii main-line trains from Shin-Osaka Station (*tokkyū*, ¥6700, 216 minutes; *futsū*, ¥4310, 332 minutes) and from Nagoya Station (*tokkyū*, ¥7510, 213 minutes; *futsū*, ¥3920, 327 minutes). *Futsū* are significantly cheaper but take almost twice as long.

SHINGŪ 新宮

☎0735 / pop 33,070

Shingū functions as a useful transport hub for access to the **Kumano Sanzan**, the three major Shintō shrines of the Kii-hantō. The first of these, **Kumano Hayatama Taisha** (熊野速玉大社), is actually in Shingū itself, a 15-minute walk northwest of Shingū Station. The other two are Kumano Hongū Taisha (right) and Nachi Taisha (opposite). There's a helpful **information office** (☎22-2840; 9am-5.30pm) at the station.

Station Hotel Shingū (ステーションホテル新宮; ☎21-2200; fax 21-1067; station@rifnet.or.jp; s/d/tw from ¥4900/10,000/10,000;), a small business hotel, has decent Western-style rooms. It's 200m southeast of the station. The whitish building is visible from outside Shingū Station. Ask for a room in the *shinkan* (new wing).

A two-minute walk north of the station, **Hase Ryokan** (長谷旅館; ☎22-2185; fax 21-6677; r per person with 2 meals from ¥6300) is a comfortable and reasonable choice for those who prefer Japanese-style accommodation. Call from the station and someone will collect you, or ask at the information office for a map.

The JR Kii main line connects Shingū with Nagoya Station (*tokkyū*, ¥7190, three hours) and Shin-Osaka Station (*tokkyū*, ¥7010, four hours).

There are buses between Shingū and Hongū, about half of which make a loop of the three surrounding onsen (Watarase, Yunomine and Kawa-yu). See Hongū (below) for details.

HONGŪ 本宮

Hongū itself isn't particularly interesting but it makes a good starting point for the onsen nearby. Hongū is also home to **Kumano Hongū Taisha** (熊野本宮大社), one of the three famous shrines of the Kumano Sanzan. The shrine is close to the Ōmiya Taisha-mae bus stop (the buses listed in this section stop there).

Buses leave for Hongū from JR Gojō Station and Kintetsu Yamato-Yagi Station in the north (¥4000, 283 minutes), Kii-Tanabe in the west (¥2000, two hours) and Shingū in the southeast (¥1500, 80 minutes). Shingū is the most convenient of these three access points (departures are most frequent from there). Most Hongū buses also stop at Kawa-yu, Watarase and Yunomine onsen (in that order), but be sure to ask before boarding. Keep in mind that departures are few in any direction, so jot down the times and plan accordingly.

YUNOMINE, WATARASE & KAWA-YU ONSEN

These three onsen are among the best in all of Kansai. Because each has its own distinct character, it's worth doing a circuit of all three. There are several ryokan and *minshuku* in the area, but if you are on a tight budget it's possible to camp on the riverbanks above and below Kumano Hongū Taisha. See Hongū (above) for transport details.

Note that you can walk between the three onsen in this section relatively easily. The tunnel at the west end of the village at Kawa-yu connects to Watarase Onsen (the total journey is a little less than 1km). From Watarase Onsen, it's about 3km west along Rte 311 to reach Yunomine.

Yunomine Onsen 湯峰温泉

The town of Yunomine is nestled around a narrow river in a wooded valley. Most of the town's onsen are contained inside ryokan or *minshuku* but charming little **Tsubo-yu Onsen** (つぼ湯温泉; admission ¥250; 6am-9.30pm) is open to all. It's right in the middle of town, inside a tiny wooden shack built on an island in the river. Buy a ticket at the *sentō* next to

Tōkō-ji (東光寺), the temple in the middle of town. The *sentō* itself is open the same hours as the onsen and entry is ¥300; of the two baths at the *sentō,* we suggest the *kusuri-yu* (medicine water; ¥380), which is 100% pure hot-spring water.

SLEEPING

Yunomine has plenty of *minshuku* and ryokan for you to choose from.

Minshuku Yunotanisō (民宿湯の谷荘; ☎ 0735-42-1620; r per person with 2 meals ¥8000) At the upper end of the village, this *minshuku* is exactly what a *minshuku* should be: simple, clean and welcoming. The food is very good and there's an excellent onsen bath on the premises.

Ryokan Yoshino-ya (旅館よしのや; ☎ 0735-42-0101; r per person with 2 meals from ¥8970) Located very close to Tsubo-yu, this is a slightly more upscale place with a lovely *rotemburo*. It's fairly new and the location can't be beat. Like Yunotanisō, it's a friendly and well-run spot.

Kawa-yu Onsen 川湯温泉

Kawa-yu Onsen is a natural wonder, where geothermally heated water percolates up through the gravel banks of the river that runs through the middle of the town. You can make your own private bath here by digging out some of the stones and letting the hole fill with hot water; you can then spend the rest of the day jumping back and forth between the bath and the cool waters of the river. Admission is free and the best spots along the river are in front of Fujiya ryokan. We suggest bringing a bathing suit unless you fancy putting on a 'naked *gaijin*' show for the whole town.

In the winter, from November to 28 February, bulldozers are used to turn the river into a giant *rotemburo*. Known as the **Sennin Buro** (仙人風呂; admission free; ⏲ 6.30am-10pm), the name is a play on the word for 'thousand', a reference to the fact that you could just about squeeze 1000 bathers into this open-air tub. It's a lot of fun and you can dazzle locals by jumping into the main flow of the river to cool off.

SLEEPING

Pension Ashita-no-Mori (ペンションあしたの森; ☎ 0735-42-1525; fax 0735-42-1333; ashitanomori-kawayu@za.ztv.ne.jp; r per person with 2 meals from ¥8550) This is in a pleasant wooden building with a good riverside location. Rooms are adequate in size and well maintained. It's got its own private onsen bath. Inside baths are all onsen as well.

Fujiya (冨士屋; ☎ 0735-42-0007; fax 0735-42-1115; www.fuziya.co.jp/english/index.html; r per person with 2 meals from ¥15,900) Next door, this is a more upmarket ryokan with tasteful rooms: spacious, clean and tastefully decorated. For a very civilised place to stay after a day in the river baths, this is the spot. Needless to say, it's got its own private onsen bath as well.

Watarase Onsen わたらせ温泉

This **onsen** (☎ 0735-42-1185; admission ¥700; ⏲ 6am-9.30pm) is built around a bend in the river directly between Yunomine Onsen and Kawa-yu Onsen. It's not as interesting as its neighbours, but does boast a nice collection of *rotemburo*. Baths get progressively cooler as you work your way out from the inside bath. Buy tickets from the machine outside the change room. The onsen itself has a restaurant, but you'll find better choices at the adjoining Watarase Onsen Sasayuri Hotel (わたらせ温泉ホテルささゆり), which has a restaurant with a picture menu.

ISE-SHIMA 伊勢志摩

The Ise-Shima region, on Mie-ken's Shima-hantō, is most famous for Ise-jingū, Japan's most sacred Shintō shrine. The shrine is located in Ise-shi, the main city of the region. Ise-Shima also encompasses the tourist circus of Toba and some pleasant coastal scenery around Kashikojima and Goza. Ise-Shima is easily reached from Nagoya, Kyoto or Osaka and makes a good two-day trip from any of these cities (although you can even do it as a day trip from these cities if you take Kintetsu express trains).

ISE 伊勢

☎ **0596 / pop 135,250**

Although the city of Ise-shi is rather drab, it's worth making the trip here to visit the spectacular Ise-jingū. This is arguably Japan's most impressive shrine; its only rival to this claim is Nikkō's Tōshō-gū, which is as gaudy as Ise-jingū is austere. Ise is also home to a lovely traditional street, Kawasaki Kaiwai.

Sights & Activities

If you have some time to kill in town after visiting the shrines, take a stroll down atmospheric **Kawasaki Kaiwai** (河崎界隈), a street lined with traditional Japanese houses and shops. It's a little tricky to find: start at the Ise City Hotel (see p444), cross the street, go down the side street that runs next to and behind Eddy's Supermarket (yes, that's the name), and take a left down the street just before the canal; Kawasaki Kaiwai parallels this canal, on its west side. It's about a five-minute walk to the beginning of the traditional section of the street.

ISE-JINGŪ 伊勢神宮

Dating back to the 3rd century, Ise-jingū is the most venerated Shintō **shrine** (admission free; sunrise-sunset) in Japan. Shintō tradition has dictated for centuries that the shrine buildings be replaced every 20 years with exact imitations built on adjacent sites according to ancient techniques – no nails, only wooden dowels and interlocking joints.

Upon completion of the new buildings, the god of the shrine is ritually transferred to its new home in the Sengū No Gi ceremony, first witnessed by Western eyes in 1953. The wood from the old shrine is then used to reconstruct the torii at the shrine's entrance or is sent to shrines around Japan for use in rebuilding their structures. The present buildings were rebuilt in 1993 (for the 61st time) at a cost exceeding ¥5 billion. They'll next be rebuilt in 2013.

You may be surprised to discover that the main shrine buildings are almost completely hidden from view behind wooden fences. Only members of the imperial family and

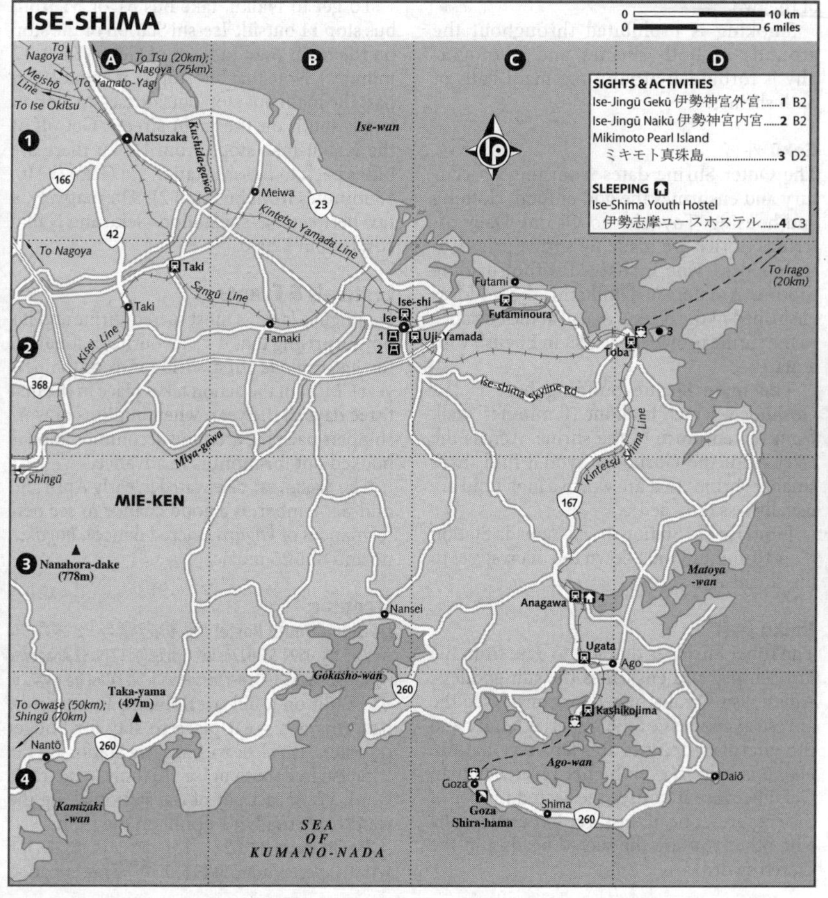

certain shrine priests are allowed to enter the sacred inner sanctum. This is unfortunate, as the buildings are stunning examples of pre-Buddhist Japanese architecture. Don't despair, though, as determined neck craning over fences allows glimpses of the upper parts of buildings (at least if you're tall). You can get a good idea of the shrine's architecture by looking at any of the lesser shrines nearby, which are exact replicas built on a smaller scale.

There are two parts to the shrine, **Gekū** (Outer Shrine) and **Naikū** (Inner Shrine). The former is an easy 10-minute walk from Ise-shi Station; the latter is accessible by bus from the station or from the stop outside Gekū (below). If you only have time to visit one of the shrines, Naikū is the more impressive of the two.

Smoking is prohibited throughout the grounds of both shrines and photography is forbidden around the main halls of both shrines.

Gekū 外宮

The Outer Shrine dates from the 5th century and enshrines the god of food, clothing and housing, Toyouke-no-Ōkami. Daily offerings of rice are made by shrine priests to the goddess, who is charged with providing food to Amaterasu-Ōmikami, the goddess enshrined in the Naikū. A stall at the entrance to the shrine provides a leaflet in English with a map.

The main shrine building here is the Goshōden, which is about 10 minutes' walk from the entrance to the shrine. Across the river from the Goshōden, you'll find three smaller shrines that are worth a look (and are usually less crowded).

From Ise-shi Station or Uji-Yamada Station it's a 10-minute walk down the main street to the shrine entrance.

Naikū 内宮

The Inner Shrine is thought to date from the 3rd century and enshrines the sun goddess, Amaterasu-Ōmikami, who is considered the ancestral goddess of the imperial family and the guardian deity of the Japanese nation. Naikū is held in even higher reverence than Gekū because it houses the sacred mirror of the emperor, one of the three imperial regalia (the other two are the sacred beads and the sacred sword).

A stall just before the entrance to the shrine provides the same English leaflet given out at Gekū. Next to this stall is the Uji-bashi, which leads over the crystal-clear Isuzu-gawa into the shrine. Just off the main gravel path is a Mitarashi, the place for pilgrims to purify themselves in the river before entering the shrine.

The path continues along an avenue lined with towering cryptomeria trees to the Goshōden, the main shrine building. As at Gekū, you can only catch a glimpse of the top of the structure here, as four rows of wooden fences obstruct the view. If you're tempted to jump the fence when nobody's around, think again – they're watching you on closed-circuit TV cameras not so cleverly disguised as trees!

To get to Naikū, take bus 51 or 55 from bus stop 11 outside Ise-shi Station or the stop on the main road in front of Gekū (¥410, 12 minutes). Note that bus stop 11 is about 100m past the main bus stop outside Ise-shi Station (walk south on the main street). Get off at the Naikū-mae stop. From Naikū there are buses back to Ise-shi Station via Gekū (¥410, 18 minutes from bus stop 2). Alternatively, a taxi between Ise-shi Station/Gekū and Naikū costs about ¥2000.

Festivals & Events

Ise-jingū is Japan's most sacred shrine and it's not surprising that it's a favourite destination for *hatsu-mōde* (first shrine visit of the new year). Most of the action takes place in the first three days of the year, when millions of worshippers pack the area and accommodation is booked out for months in advance.

The **Kagura-sai**, celebrated in early April and mid-September, is a good chance to see performances of *kagura* (sacred dance), *bugaku*, nō and Shintō music.

Sleeping

Ise-Shima Youth Hostel (伊勢志摩ユースホステル; ☎ 0599-55-0226; ise@jyh.gr.jp; 1219-82 Anagawa, Isobe-chō, Shima-shi; r per person with breakfast from ¥4620; 💻) Built on a hill overlooking an attractive bay, this is a great place to stay for budget travellers. It's close to Anagawa Station on the Kintetsu line south of Ise-shi (only *futsū* trains stop). Walk east out of the station along the waterfront road; it's uphill on the right.

Ise City Hotel (伊勢シティホテル; ☎ 28-2111; 1-11-31 Fukiage; s/tw ¥6510/13,650; 📶) This is a good

KANSAI

business hotel with small, clean rooms and a convenient location less than 10 minutes' walk from the station. Some staff members speak a bit of English. To get there from Ise-shi Station, take a left (east) outside the station, walk past a JTB travel agency, take a left at the first traffic light, and cross the tracks. You'll see it on the left.

Hoshide-kan (星出館; ☎ 28-2377; fax 27-2830; 2-15-2 Kawasaki; r per person with/without 2 meals ¥7500/5000; 💻) Also in Ise-shi, this is a quaint wooden ryokan with some nice traditional touches. Go straight past Ise City Hotel, and it's on the right (there is a small English sign). It's at the second light (400m) past the train tracks. Look for the large traditional building with cedars poking out of tiny gardens. Free internet.

Ise Pearl Pier Hotel (パールピアホテル; ☎ 26-1111; www.pearlpier.com; 2-26-22 Miyajiri; s/d/tw ¥7875/12,600/16,800; 📶) Next to the Ise City Hotel (opposite), the Pearl Pier is a little newer, a little more spacious and a little more expensive. The 'deluxe' rooms (single/twin ¥8400/18,900) may be worth the cash if you've been feeling cramped in business hotels.

Eating & Drinking

Daiki (大善; ☎ 28-0281; meals from ¥1500; 🕒 11am-9pm) Our favourite place to eat in Ise-shi bills itself as 'Japan's most famous restaurant'. It's a great place to sample seafood, including *ise-ebi* (Japanese lobsters), served as set meals for ¥5000; ask for the *ise-ebi teishoku* and specify *yaki* (grilled), *niita* (boiled) or *sashimi* (raw). Simpler meals include tempura *teishoku* (¥1500). It's outside and to the right of Uji-Yamada Station; there's a small English sign reading 'Kappo Daiki' and 'Royal Family Endorsed'. English menu.

Tamaya (珠家; ☎ 24-0105; 2-17-23 Kawasaki; 🕒 7pm-midnight, closed Mon & 3rd Thu every month) In the Kawasaki Kaiwai district, you'll find this excellent bar-restaurant in an old *kura*. This is a friendly spot for a drink or a light meal. It's just down a narrow street off Kawasaki Kaiwai on the left as you walk north (look for a white-and-red sign on a utility pole that reads 'Tamaya The Lounge'). English menu.

At Naikū you'll find plenty of good restaurants in the Okage-yokochō Arcade, just outside the shrine (when walking from the bus stop towards the shrine, look to the left and you will see the covered arcade).

In the arcade **Nikōdōshiten** (二光堂支店; ☎ 24-4409; 19 Ujiimazaike-chō; 🕒 11am-4pm, closed Thu) is a good place to try some of the local specialities in a rough, roadhouse atmosphere. *Ise-udon* (thick noodles in a dark broth; small/large bowl ¥420/570) is the speciality. For a bigger meal, try the *ise-udon teishoku* (*ise-udon* with rice and side dishes; ¥1000). The restaurant is 100m up from the southern (shrine) end of the arcade.

Also in the Okage-yokochō, **Isuzugawa Café** (五十鈴川; ☎ 23-9002; 52 Ujiimazaike-chō; 🕒 10am-5pm) is an attractive cafe overlooking the Isuzu-gawa. The tatami seating makes it a relaxing spot to sit with a cup of coffee and watch the birds swim past. Coffee is 'strong', 'mild' or 'ice' (¥400) and cakes start at ¥200. It's about four minutes' walk from the shrine end of the arcade, on the right. Look for a low English sign; it's in the building just before a camphor tree.

Getting There & Away

There are rail connections between Ise-shi and Nagoya, Osaka and Kyoto on both the JR and the Kintetsu lines. For those without a Japan Rail Pass, the Kintetsu line is by far the most convenient way to go and the *tokkyū* are comfortable and fast.

Kintetsu fares and travel times to/from Ise-shi include Nagoya (*tokkyū,* ¥2690, 81 minutes), Osaka (Uehonmachi or Namba Stations, *tokkyū,* ¥3030, 106 minutes) and Kyoto (*tokkyū,* ¥3520, 123 minutes).

There are two stations in Ise: Ise-shi Station and Uji-Yamada Station, which are only a few hundred metres apart (most trains stop at both). Get off at Ise-shi Station for destinations and accommodation described in this section.

TOBA 鳥羽

The serrated coast of the Shima-hantō is perfect for the cultivation of pearls and Toba is one of the main centres of Japan's pearl industry. It's also a popular spot for city folk to soak up a bit of coastal ambience. The two main attractions here are Toba Aquarium and Mikimoto Pearl Island. There's no denying that Toba is touristy, but it can be fun if you're in the mood.

Toba Aquarium (鳥羽水族館; Toba Suizoku-kan; ☎ 0599-25-2555; 3-3-6 Toba; admission ¥2400; 🕒 9am-4.30pm) has some interesting fish and marine-mammal displays and some good shows. It would make a good destination for those with children or if the rain puts a damper on outdoor activities. It's about 10 minutes' walk southeast of the Kintetsu and JR Toba Stations; it's on the seafront, across the main road (Rte 42).

Mikimoto Pearl Island (ミキモト真珠島; ☎ 0599-25-2028; 1-7-1 Toba; admission ¥1500; ⏲ 8.30am-5pm, 9am-4.30pm Dec) is a monument to Kokichi Michimoto, who devoted his life to producing cultured pearls. The demonstration halls show all the oyster tricks from growing and seeding to selecting, drilling and threading the finished product. The island is across a bridge about five minutes' walk southeast of Kintetsu and JR Toba Stations.

Ise-wan Ferry Co Ltd (☎ 0599-26-3335; www.isewanferry.co.jp) has ferry connections from Toba-ko port to Irako on Atsumi-hantō in Aichi-ken (¥1500, 55 minutes). Boats leave from Ise-wan ferry terminal. Toba can be reached from Ise in 16 minutes by the Kintetsu line (*kyūkō*, ¥320) or the JR line (*futsū*, ¥230).

AGO-WAN, KASHIKOJIMA & GOZA 英虞湾・賢島・御座

A short train ride south of Ise-shi, Ago-wan is a scenic bay festooned with islands and inlets. Kashikojima, the main island in the bay, is the terminus of the Kintetsu line. From Ise-shi Station, a *futsū* costs ¥1170 and takes about 50 minutes. There is no JR service. Kashikojima itself is probably of little interest to foreign travellers as it is dominated by large resort hotels, but it's the jumping-off point for exploration of the bay.

Those in search of peace and quiet might want to take a ferry to Goza on the other side of the bay (¥600, 25 minutes). The ferry terminal is right outside Kashikojima Station (buy your tickets from the Kinki Kankōsen office near the terminal). The ride is a good way to see the sights in the bay. There are also sightseeing boats that do a loop around the bay for ¥1500.

Goza is a sleepy fishing community with a fine white-sand beach, Goza Shirahama. There are small signs in English from the ferry pier to the beach; just follow the main road over the hill and across the peninsula. The beach is mobbed in late July and early August but almost deserted at other times.

If you'd like to stay in Goza, there are plenty of *minshuku*, some of which close down outside of summer. **Shiojisō** (潮路荘; ☎ 0599-88-3232; r per person with 2 meals from ¥7875, single travellers not accepted), just off the beach (look for the sign reading 'Marine Lodge Shiojisō' in English), is one of the better *minshuku*.

SOUTH OF KASHIKOJIMA 賢島以南

If you want to continue down the Kii-hantō from here, backtrack to Ise-shi and take the JR line to Taki, then switch to the JR Kisei main line. This line crosses from Mie-ken into Wakayama-ken and continues down to Shingū on its way round Kii-hantō, finally ending up in Osaka's Tennō-ji Station.

Western Honshū 本州西部

A land of ceramics and mountain villages, Western Honshū has much to offer the traveller. The Inland Sea coasts of Okayama-ken and Hiroshima-Ken are dotted with charming villages, attractive islands, and cities with room to breathe. In Kurashiki, elegant 18th-century warehouses line a shady canal. Down the road, Bizen is the proud heir of one of the oldest ceramics traditions in Japan. In Yamaguchi-ken, Shimonoseki is a prime destination for any fan of fresh seafood. The Inland Sea, meanwhile, contains a galaxy of little islands, ringed by the twinkling lights of Honshū and Shikoku.

Shimane and Tottori prefectures, once disparaged as 'the back of Japan', are especially welcoming. Although former gateways for continental culture, they now enjoy a slower pace of life, marked by onsen (hot spring) villages and mountain towns. Highlights of this area include Matsue (the castle town that was Lafcadio Hearn's first home in Japan), and Izumo Taisha, one of the oldest and most important shrines in Japan, where the Shintō gods get together to discuss the state of the world once a year.

The Chūgoku mountain range divides Western Honshū. On the southern San-yō coast (literally, 'the sunny side of the mountains'), the mild Inland Sea weather supports populous cities; to the north, the San-in coast (literally, 'in the shade of the mountains') is on the cooler Sea of Japan, and is much less densely populated.

HIGHLIGHTS

- Enjoy a night out in cosmopolitan **Hiroshima** (p462), and visit the floating Itsukushima-jinja (Itsukushima Shrine) on nearby **Miyajima** (p469)
- Admire stunning sea views from the ancient fishing port of **Tomo-no-ura** (p459)
- Slow down and listen to the waves on **Manabe-shima** (Manabe Island; p476) in the Inland Sea
- Explore the village of **Ōmori** (p495) and the historic Iwami Ginzan silver mines
- Hire a bike and pedal yourself from Honshū to Shikoku over the **Shimanami Kaidō** (p476)
- See where the gods go on holiday at **Izumo Taisha** (p496)
- Have your mind bent pleasantly out of shape at the art installations of Honmura on **Naoshima** (p474)

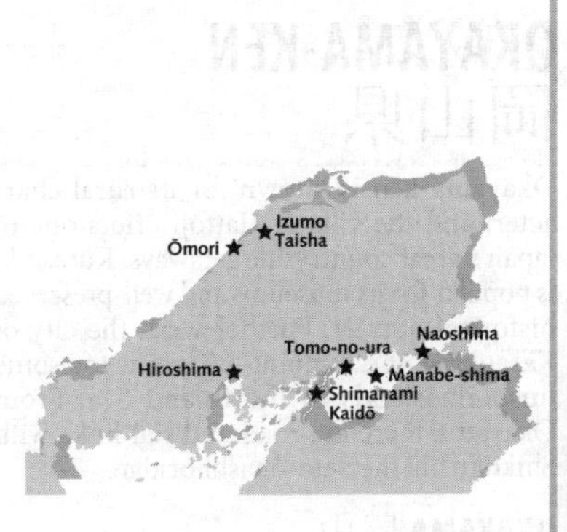

History

Because of its proximity to the Korean peninsula and China, the Western Honshū region has long been a gateway for continental influences. Buddhism and the Chinese writing system entered Japan through this part of the country in the 6th century. During his Korean peninsula campaigns in 1592 and 1598, Toyotomi Hideyoshi abducted whole families of potters as growing interest in the tea ceremony generated desire for the finest Korean ceramics. The firing techniques brought over all those centuries ago live on in Japanese ceramics today.

Climate

The Western Honshū region is generally mild and comfortable. On the San-in coast by the Sea of Japan the temperatures are cooler than on the San-yō coast of the Inland Sea, and winters can be snowy. The Inland Sea coast is known as the *hare no kuni* (land of sunshine) thanks to its moderate temperatures and low rainfall.

Getting There & Away

The *shinkansen* (bullet train) along the San-yō coast is the fastest way to get around. On the San-in coast, the *shinkansen* is not an option, though *tokkyū* (limited express) trains will limit changes and shorten travel times by up to half. Between the San-yō and San-in coasts it's often quicker to go by bus. The major rail link between the two coasts runs between Okayama on the Inland Sea coast and Yonago in Tottori-ken on the Sea of Japan.

OKAYAMA-KEN

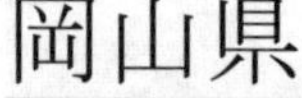

岡山県

Okayama-ken is known for its rural character, and the villa at Hattōji offers one of Japan's great countryside getaways. Kurashiki is popular for its museums and well-preserved historical quarter. Further west, the city of Kasaoka is the jumping-off point for some unspoilt islands in the Inland Sea. From Okayama there are road and rail links with Shikoku via the Seto-ōhashi bridge.

OKAYAMA 岡山

☎ 086 / pop 630,000

The laid-back capital is a major transportation hub, an important regional city, and of interest to travellers as the location of the Kōraku-en, one of Japan's top three gardens, overlooked by the city's castle. The city prides itself on its connection to Momotarō, the demon-quelling boy hero of one of Japan's best-known folktales, whose smiling face beams out at you all over town. Okayama makes a good base for day trips out to the well-preserved merchant town of Kurashiki, and to the ancient pottery area of Bizen, and for cycle excursions to the countryside of the Kibi Plain.

Orientation

The main street, Momotarō-Ōdōri, leads eastward from the station to the castle and the famous garden, Kōraku-en, about 1.5km away. Trams (¥100 for the castle area) run down the middle of the street.

Information

Bank of Tokyo-Mitsubishi UFJ (☎ 223-9211; 6-36 Honmachi; 🕑 9am-3pm Mon-Fri) Cashes travellers cheques.

Club Mont Blanc (☎ 224-7050; 6th fl, Dai-ichi Central Bldg, 6-30 Honmachi; internet per 1st 30min ¥290, per extra 15min ¥100; 🕑 24hr) Opposite the station, to the right as you exit.

JTB Travel (☎ 232-3810; 1-7-36 Omote-chō; 🕑 10am-6pm) This travel agency is around by the Kenchō-dōri tram stop.

Maruzen (☎ 233-4640; 1-5-1 Omote-chō; 🕑 10am-8pm) This bookshop is on the ground floor of the Symphony Building. Has a good selection of books in English.

Okayama Central Post Office (☎ 227-2757; 2-1-1 Naka Sange; 🕑 9am-7pm Mon-Fri, to 5pm Sat, to 12.30pm Sun) At the corner of Yanagawa-suji and Kenchō-dōri.

Okayama International Centre (☎ 256-2914; www.opief.or.jp/english; 2-2-1 Hōkan-chō; 🕑 9am-5pm Mon-Sat) Has information in English on sights throughout Okayama prefecture.

Tourist Information Counter (☎ 222-2912; 1-1 Ekimoto-machi; 🕑 9am-6pm) In the station, by the entrance to the Shinkansen tracks.

Sights

KŌRAKU-EN 後楽園

Overlooked by the castle and built on the orders of the *daimyō* (regional lord) Ikeda Tsunemasa, **Kōraku-en** (☎ 272-1148; 1-5 Kōraku-en; admission ¥350; 🕑 7.30am-6pm Apr-Sep, 8am-5pm Oct-Mar; Ⓟ) has enjoyed a reputation as one of the three most beautiful gardens in Japan since its completion in 1700. Unusually for a Japanese garden, most of the park is taken up by expansive lawns, which are broken up by ponds, tea houses and other Edo-period buildings, including a nō

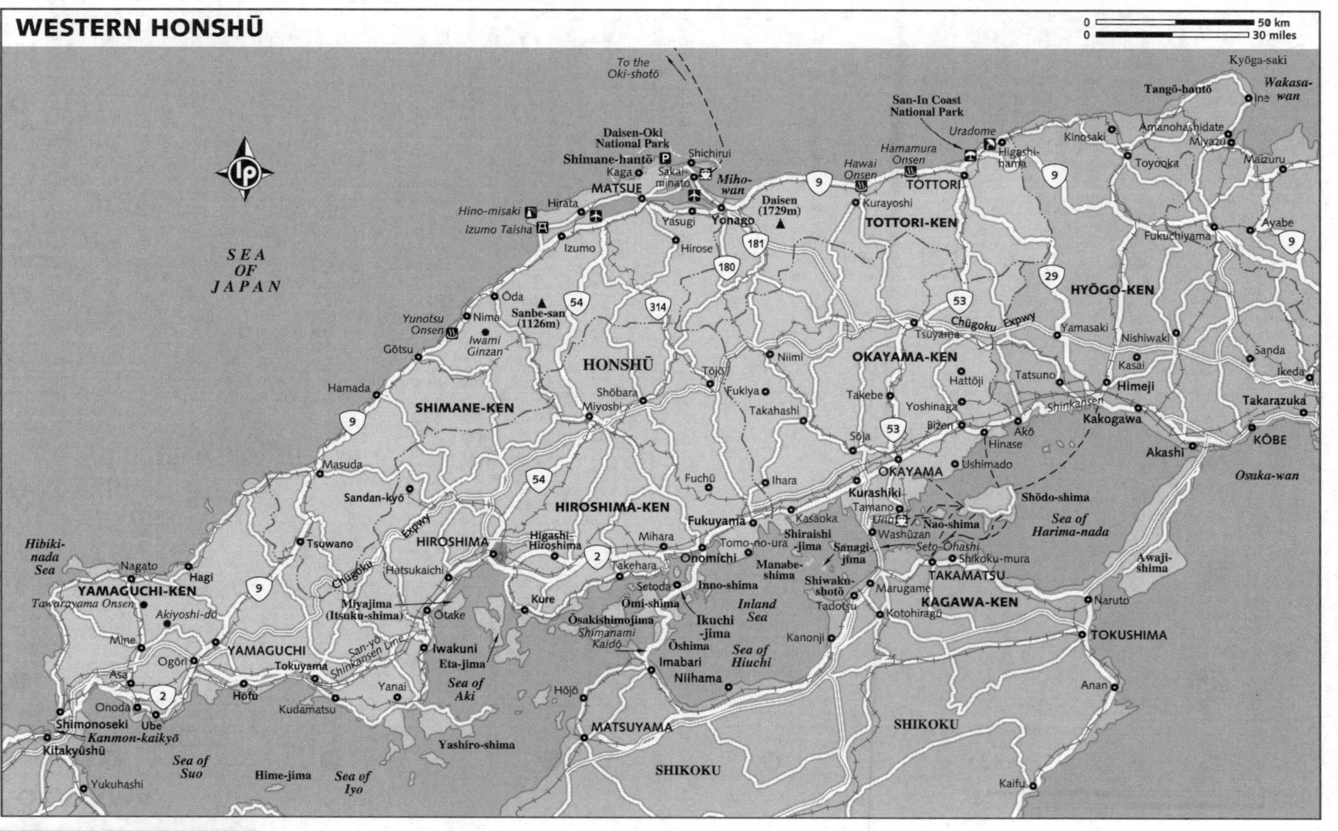
WESTERN HONSHŪ
0 — 50 km
0 — 30 miles
SEA OF JAPAN
To the Oki-shotō
Kyōga-saki
Tangō-hantō
Wakasa-wan
Ine
San-In Coast National Park
Uradome
Amanohashidate
Miyazu
Kinosaki
Toyooka
Maizuru
Higashi-hama
Hamamura Onsen
Hawai Onsen
TOTTORI
Daisen-Oki National Park
Shimane-hantō
Shichirui
Kaga
Sakai-minato
Miho-wan
MATSUE
Daisen (1729m)
Kurayoshi
Hino-misaki
Hirata
Yasugi
Yonago
TOTTORI-KEN
Izumo Taisha
Izumo
Hirose
Fukuchiyama
Ayabe
HYŌGO-KEN
Ōda
Nima
Sanbe-san (1126m)
Yunotsu Onsen
Iwami Ginzan
Chūgoku Expwy
Tsuyama
Yamasaki
Nishiwaki
Sanda
Gōtsu
Niimi
OKAYAMA-KEN
Kasai
Ikeda
HONSHŪ
Tōjō
Hattōji
Tatsuno
Himeji
Hamada
Fukiya
Takebe
Takarazuka
Shōbara
SHIMANE-KEN
Miyoshi
Takahashi
Yoshinaga
Shinkansen
Kakogawa
Bizen
Akō
KŌBE
Sōja
Hinase
Akashi
Masuda
Ushimado
OKAYAMA
Osaka-wan
Fuchū
Ihara
Sandan-kyō
Kurashiki
Shōdo-shima
HIROSHIMA-KEN
Tamano
Kasaoka
Sea of Harima-nada
Fukuyama
Uno
Nao-shima
Shiraishi-jima
Washūzan
HIROSHIMA
Higashi-Hiroshima
Mihara
Tomo-no-ura
Sanagi-jima
Seto-Ōhashi
Tsuwano
Hibiki-nada Sea
Onomichi
Manabe-shima
Shikoku-mura
Awaji-shima
Nagato
Hagi
Hatsukaichi
Takehara
Shiwaku-shotō
TAKAMATSU
YAMAGUCHI-KEN
Setoda
Inno-shima
Marugame
Tawarayama Onsen
Miyajima (Itsuku-shima)
Kure
Ōmi-shima
Inland Sea
KAGAWA-KEN
Naruto
Akiyoshi-dō
Ōtake
Ōsakishimojima
Tadotsu
Kotohiragū
Shimanami Kaidō
Ikuchi-jima
Mine
YAMAGUCHI
San-yō Shinkansen Line
Iwakuni
Kanonji
TOKUSHIMA
Ogōri
Ōshima
Sea of Hiuchi
Tokuyama
Eta-jima
Imabari
Asa
Yanai
Sea of Aki
Niihama
Anan
Hōfu
Hōjō
Onoda
Kudamatsu
Ube
Shimonoseki
MATSUYAMA
SHIKOKU
Kanmon-kaikyō
Kitakyūshū
Yashiro-shima
Sea of Suo
Hime-jima
Sea of Iyo
SHIKOKU
Yukuhashi
Kaifu

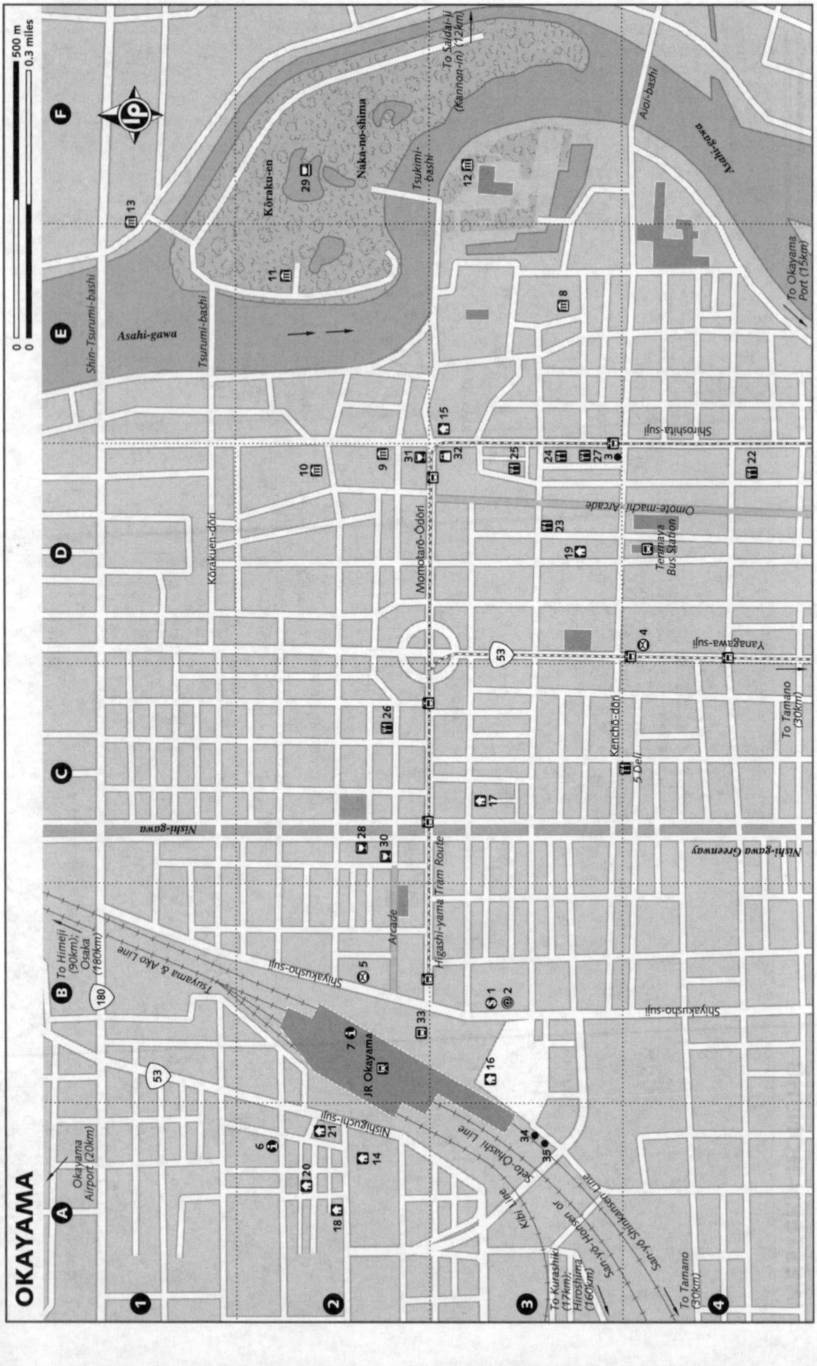

WESTERN HONSHŪ

OKAYAMA

Asahi-gawa
Shin-Tsurumi-bashi
Tsurumi-bashi
Kōraku-en
Naka-no-shima
Tsukimi-bashi
To Saidai-ji (Kannon-in) (12km)
Aioi-bashi
To Okayama Port (15km)
Kōrakuen-dōri
Momotarō-Ōdōri
Shiroshita-suji
Omote-machi Arcade
Tenmaya Bus Station
Yanagawa-suji
Kenchō-dōri
5 Deli
To Tamano (30km)
Nishi-gawa
Nishi-gawa Greenway
Higashi-yama Tram Route
Arcade
Shiyakusho-suji
Tsuyama & Ako Line
To Himeji (90km); Osaka (180km)
JR Okayama
Nishiguchi-suji
Seto-Ōhashi Line
Kibi Line
San-yō-Honsen or San-yō Shinkansen Line
To Kurashiki (17km); Hiroshima (160km)
To Tamano (30km)
Okayama Airport (20km)
500 m
0.3 miles

INFORMATION
Bank of Tokyo-Mitsubishi UFJ 三菱東京UFJ銀行 1 B3
Club Mont Blanc クラブモンブラン 2 B3
JTB 3 D3
Maruzen 丸善 .... (see 32)
Okayama Central Post Office 岡山中央郵便局 4 D4
Okayama Ekimae Post Office 岡山駅前郵便局 5 B2
Okayama International Centre 岡山国際交流センター 6 A2
Tourist Information Counter 観光案内所 7 B2

SIGHTS & ACTIVITIES
Hayashibara Museum of Art 林原美術館 8 E3
Okayama Orient Museum 市立オリエント美術館 9 D2
Okayama Prefectural Museum of Art 県立美術館 10 D2
Okayama Prefectural Museum 県立博物館 11 E2
Okayama-jō 岡山城 12 F3
Yumeji Art Museum 夢二郷土美術館 13 F1

SLEEPING
ANA Hotel Okayama 岡山全日空ホテル 14 A2
Comfort Hotel Okayama コンフォートホテル岡山 15 E3
Hotel Granvia Okayama 16 B3
Kōraku Hotel 後楽ホテル 17 C3
Matsunoki Ryokan まつのき旅館 18 A2
Okayama View Hotel 岡山ビューホテル 19 D3
Saiwai-sō 幸荘 20 A2
Tōyoko Inn Nishi-Guchi Hiroba 東横イン西口広場 21 A2

EATING
Biroku Omote-chō Koroku 美禄表町ころく 22 D4
Okabe おかべ 23 D3
Padang Padang パダンパダン 24 D3
Quiet Village Curry Shop クワィエットビレッジカレーショップ 25 D3
Sakuraya 佐久良家 26 C2
Tori-soba Ōta 元祖岡山とりそば太田 27 D3

DRINKING
Aussie Bar オージーバー 28 C2
Fukuda Chaya 29 F2
Izayoi No Tsuki 佐久良家 30 C2
Saudade Na Yoru サウダーヂな夜 31 D2

SHOPPING
Okayama-ken Kankō Bussan Centre 岡山県観光物産センター 32 D3

TRANSPORT
Buses to the Port & Airport 33 B2
Eki Rent-a-Car 駅レンタカー 34 A3
JR Eki-Rinkun Rent-a-cycle 駅リンくんレンタサイクル 35 A3

(stylised dance drama) stage. Despite suffering major damage during floods in the 1930s and air-raids in the 1940s, Kōraku-en remains much as it was in feudal times, when it was the private playground of the *daimyō* and his favoured retainers. The park was opened to the public in 1884, and has been a favourite destination for large crowds of locals and tourists ever since.

Several stalls around the park offer drinks and an opportunity to try Momotarō's favourite snack – sweet white millet cakes known as *kibi-dango*. For a tea house experience on the island of Naka-no-shima, see Drinking, p453.

The park is a 20-minute walk up Momotarō-Ōdōri from the station. Alternatively, take the Higashi-yama tram to the Shiroshita stop (¥100) in front of the cylindrical Okayama Symphony Hall building. From here, it's a short walk – there are signs to point you in the right direction.

OKAYAMA-JŌ 岡山城

Known to locals as U-jō (烏城; Crow Castle), the striking black **Okayama-jō** (Okayama Castle; ☎ 225-2096; 2-3-1 Marunouchi; admission ¥300, additional charge for special exhibitions; 9am-5pm) was built by Ukita Hideie, the *daimyō* who was one of the most powerful men in the country for a brief period in the late 16th century. Completed in 1597, the castle was one of the largest in Japan, boasting 35 turrets and 21 gates and reaching as far as Yanagawa-suji, traversed by the tram system today. Over the next three centuries, it served as the seat of power for 15 successive lords. Much of the castle was taken down after the Meiji Restoration, and most of what remained burned down during Allied air-raids at the end of WWII, with only the stone walls and the small *tsukima-yagura* (moon-viewing turret) surviving intact. The castle was rebuilt in 1966. The interiors may strike purists as too modern, but the outside of the building is an impressive sight, and there are good views of Kōraku-en from the top of the central keep.

MUSEUMS

Probably the most interesting of the museums spread around Okayama's culture zone is the **Okayama Orient Museum** (☎ 232-3636; 9-31 Tenjin-chō; admission ¥300; 9am-5pm, closed Mon), north of the end of Momotarō-Ōdōri, where the tram line turns south. The museum houses 3000 artefacts from the ancient Middle East, and holds regular special exhibitions. It's a short walk from the Shiroshita tram stop.

Close to the back entrance of the castle, near the corner of the moat, the **Hayashibara Museum of Art** (☎ 223-1733; 2-7-15 Marunouchi; admission ¥300; 9am-5pm, closed Mon; P) exhibits items from a collection of calligraphy, armour, and paintings that was once the property of the Ikeda clan (who ruled Okayama for much of the Edo period). Opposite the main entrance to Kōraku-en is the slightly run-down **Okayama Prefectural Museum** (☎ 272-1149; 1-5 Kōraku-en;

MOMOTARŌ, THE PEACH BOY

Okayama-ken and Kagawa-ken on the island of Shikoku are linked by the legend of Momotarō, the Peach Boy, who emerged from the stone of a peach and, backed up by a monkey, a pheasant and a dog, defeated a three-eyed, three-toed people-eating demon. There are statues of Momotarō at JR Okayama station, and the city's biggest street is named after him. The island of Megi-jima, off Takamatsu in Shikoku, is said to be the site of the clash with the demon.

Momotarō may actually have been a Yamato prince who was deified as Kibitsuhiko. His shrine, Kibitsu-jinja, lies along the route of the Kibi Plain bicycle ride (see boxed text, p454).

admission ¥200; 9am-6pm Apr-Sep, 9.30am-5pm Oct-Mar, closed Mon; P), which has Japanese-only displays on local history, including swords and some old Bizen pottery.

North of Kōraku-en is the **Yumeji Art Museum** (271-1000; 2-1-32 Hama; admission ¥700; 9am-5pm, closed Mon; P), displaying works by local poet and artist Takehisa Yumeji (1884–1934). Not far away, on the main road, the **Okayama Prefectural Museum of Art** (225-4800; 8-48 Tenjin-chō; admission ¥300; 9am-5pm, closed Mon; P) was recently refurbished and has now re-opened. Local Okayama art is on display, supplemented by temporary exhibits.

Festivals & Events

The **Saidai-ji Eyō**, also known as the Hadaka Matsuri (Naked Festival), takes place on the third Saturday in February at the Kannon-in temple in Saidai-ji. A chaotic crowd of around 10,000 men in loincloths and *tabi* (split-toed Japanese socks) fight over two sacred *shingi* (wooden batons) while freezing water is poured over them. The fun kicks off at 10pm.

Sleeping

Matsunoki Ryokan (253-4111; www.matunoki.com; 19-1 Ekimoto-chō; s/tw with 2 meals ¥4200/6000, without bath ¥3900/5800; P) A short walk from the station, Matsunoki has both Japanese- and Western-style rooms, most with private bathrooms.

Saiwai-sō (254-0020; http://w150.j.fiw-web.net, in Japanese; 24-8 Ekimoto-chō; s/tw from ¥4200/7600; P) A five-minute walk west of the station, Okayama's 'first business hotel' offers comfortable rooms, some with shared bathrooms. Look for the lilac building.

Okayama View Hotel (224-2000; www.okaview.jp, in Japanese; 1-11-17 Naka Sange; s/tw from ¥5800/8400; P). Comfortable place between the station and castle with facilities a cut above the average, including 'fusion' rooms with Western beds and Japanese fittings.

Comfort Hotel Okayama (801-9411; www.choice-hotels.jp/cfoka; 1-1-13 Marunouchi; s/tw with breakfast from ¥5800/8500; P) A well-appointed business hotel close to the castle and park.

Tōyoko Inn Nishi-Guchi Hiroba (251-1045; www.toyoko-inn.com; 22-10 Ekimoto-chō; s/tw with breakfast from ¥6090/8200; P) Dependable chain hotel a couple of minutes from the station, providing all the usual business-hotel comforts, including LAN internet in all rooms.

Kōraku Hotel (221-7111; www.hotel.kooraku.co.jp; 5-1 Heiwa-chō; s/tw from ¥6930/9200; P) A five-minute walk from the station, this luxurious midrange hotel offers comfortably sized rooms and welcoming staff. A convenience store and restaurant are on site, and there's also a business centre with free internet access.

Hotel Granvia Okayama (234-7000; www.granvia-oka.co.jp; 1-5 Ekimoto-chō; s/tw from ¥9817/18,480; P) This landmark building on top of the station has decent-sized rooms with LAN internet. There are several restaurants on site, as well as a gym and pool. This is where Okayama comes to get married on weekends.

ANA Hotel Okayama (898-1111; www.anahotel-okayama.com, in Japanese; 15-1 Ekimoto-chō; s/tw from ¥13,860/24,255; P) A luxurious modern hotel less than a minute's walk from the west exit of the station, featuring gorgeous rooms (with LAN internet) as well as several restaurants and bars – there are great views from the 'Sky Bar' on the 20th floor.

Eating

Tori-soba Ōta (236-0310; 1-7-24 Omote-chō; dishes ¥650-990; 11am-8pm) The name of this little countertop restaurant is also its trademark dish: *tori-soba* (steaming bowls of noodles packed with chicken and served in a tasty broth; ¥650). Has Japanese menu only. Look for the big blue canvas *noren* (the sign indicating that the restaurant is open) opposite Chūgoku Bank.

Quiet Village Curry Shop (231-4100; 1-6-43 Omote-chō; dishes ¥780-1000; 11.30am-7pm, closed Mon) This tiny curry restaurant consists of one long table, where the Japanese-only menu is disguised as an Indian book. Some English is spoken. Chicken curry and dahl each cost ¥780.

Okabe (☎ 222-1404; 1-10-1 Omote-chō; dishes ¥800-850; ⏰ 11.30am-2.30pm, closed Sun) This street-corner tofu restaurant is recognisable by the big illustration of a heavily laden tofu seller in a straw hat. Squeeze in at the counter and watch the team of women chopping and frying as you wait. There are only two things on the menu: an *okabe teishoku* (set meal with several types of tofu; ¥800) and a *nama yuba don teishoku* (dried 'tofu skin' on rice, with soup; ¥850).

Biroku Omote-chō Koroku (☎ 227-0569; 2-4-56 Omote-chō; dishes ¥800-1500; ⏰ 5-11pm, closed Tue) A relaxed little *izakaya* (pub-eatery) on a quiet street off Shiroshita-suji. The friendly owners serve excellent fish from the Inland Sea, including *anago* tempura (salt-water eel cooked in batter; ¥1000) and *shimesaba* (vinegared mackerel; ¥800). There's also *otsukuri moriawase* (a selection of sashimi) from around ¥1500. Turn right at the end of Momotarō-Ōdōri by the Comfort Inn, then right again at the second set of traffic lights. Take the first left, and it's on the left.

Sakuraya (☎ 223-5318; 1-8-21 Nodaya-chō; dishes ¥800-1800; ⏰ 5-10.30pm, closed Sun) A brightly lit *izakaya* attached to a more formal restaurant next door. Superlative fish from the Inland Sea dominates the Japanese-only menu here, along with tempura, *kara-age* (deep-fried chicken pieces) and other standards. There's also *sashimi tenko mori* (a selection of sashimi) from ¥1000 per person, and there are around 40 different *jizake* (local sakes) available, from ¥500 yen. It's a small glass-fronted place.

Padang Padang (☎ 223-6665; 1-7-10 Omote-chō; dishes ¥1000-2000; ⏰ 6pm-midnight, closed Tue) Despite its name, this mellow restaurant focuses on French and Italian fusion dishes, like *Iberiko-buta hone-tsuki rōsu* (roast Iberico pork; ¥1880). Close to the castle on Shiroshita-suji, it's a good spot for a glass of wine after a day of sightseeing. Look for the glass-fronted ground-floor building on the right as you walk away from the castle.

Drinking

Izayoi No Tsuki (☎ 222-2422; 1-10-2 Ekimae-chō; ⏰ 5pm-midnight) An atmospheric *izakaya* on a street corner in the Sky Mall arcade, five minutes' walk from the station. It has a menu listing 150 different sakes from Okayama prefecture (from around ¥450) and several beers from local microbreweries. The name of the bar is written in large characters on the wall, on the left as you head away from the station.

Aussie Bar (☎ 223-5930; 1-10-21 Ekimae-chō; ⏰ 7pm-3am) A laid-back expat-run watering hole that's popular with the city's English-speaking population and their Japanese hangers-on. Drinks include Coopers Sparking Ale from Adelaide (¥600).

Saudade Na Yoru (☎ 234-5306; 2nd fl, Shiroshita bldg, 10-16 Tenjin-chō; dishes ¥650-1000; ⏰ 6pm-3am) A chic 2nd-floor lounge bar overlooking the Symphony Hall building. Most drinks are around ¥700; a limited food menu is also available (pastas and curry rice from ¥700 to ¥800). A ¥300 cover charge applies after 9pm.

Fukuda Chaya (1-5 Kōraku-en; ⏰ 7.30am-6pm Apr-Sep, 8am-5pm Oct-Mar) An old tea house is on the small island of Naka-no-shima within Kōraku-en, where you can enjoy *matcha* (powdered green tea) for ¥800 per person.

Shopping

Okayama-ken Kankō Bussan Centre (☎ 234-2270; ⏰ 10am-8pm, closed 2nd Tue of each month) Found in the Symphony Hall, this centre has a good range of souvenirs from around the prefecture, including Bizen-yaki pottery, handicrafts, and sake.

Getting There & Away

Okayama airport (☎ 294-1811; 1277 Nichiyōji; www.okayama-airport.org/en/) is 20km northwest of the station. There are flights to Kagoshima (¥29,500, one hour and 25 minutes), Naha (¥34,200, two hours), Sapporo (¥44,000, one hour and 45 minutes) and Tokyo (¥30,200, one hour and 10 minutes), as well as Beijing, Guam, Seoul and Shanghai. Buses (¥680, 30 minutes) run to the airport from Okayama Station.

Ferries to Shōdo-shima leave hourly from the port (新岡山港; ¥1000, 70 minutes), which is about 40 minutes by bus from the city centre. Buses leave from bus stop 8 in front of the station (¥480, two to four per hour).

With regular departures on the San-yō *shinkansen* line, Okayama is connected to Hiroshima (¥5350, 35 minutes) and Hakata (Fukuoka; ¥11,550, two hours) to the west; and to Osaka (¥5350, 45 minutes), Kyoto (¥6820, one hour) and Tokyo (¥15,850, 3½ hours). The JR Hakubi line runs between Okayama and Yonago (¥4620, two hours), in Tottori-ken. There are regular trains to Takamatsu in Shikoku; the most convenient is the *kaisoku* (rapid train; ¥1470, one hour), which runs two to three times per hour.

Getting Around

The Higashi-yama tram route will take you to all the main attractions. You'll pay ¥100 to travel by tram anywhere in the central area.

JR Eki-Rinkun Rent-a-cycle (☎ 223-7081; 🕑 7am-11pm) rents out bikes for ¥300 per day. **Eki Rent-a-Car** (☎ 224-1363; 1-1 Ekimoto-chō; 🕑 8am-8pm) is next door and has 24-hour rentals from ¥5770.

BIZEN 備前

☎ 0869 / pop 42,000

The Bizen region has been renowned for its ceramics since the Kamakura period (1185–1333). The pottery produced here tends to be earthy and subdued, and has been prized by dedicated tea-ceremony aficionados for centuries. The tradition continues to thrive today, and travellers with an interest in pottery may find the gritty town of Imbe and its kilns a worthwhile side trip from Okayama.

Bizen 'city' is a sprawling administrative area covering the mountains, rice paddies and small towns east of Okayama. Most of the places of ceramic interest are within easy walking distance of Imbe (伊部) Station, easily reached via the Akō line from Okayama. An **information counter** (☎ 64-1100; 🕑 9am-6pm). on the left as you exit the station dispenses maps and pamphlets

On the 2nd floor of the station building is a gallery run by the **Friends of Bizen-yaki Ceramics Society** (岡山県備前焼陶友会; ☎ 64-1001; admission free; 🕑 9.30am-5.30pm, closed Tue). A wide range of ceramics by contemporary potters is available for purchase here.

In the multistorey concrete building directly to the right as you exit the station is the **Okayama Prefectural Bizen Ceramics Art Museum** (岡山県備前陶芸美術館; ☎ 64-

KIBI PLAIN BICYCLE ROUTE

This cycling course through the countryside around Okayama takes in several interesting temples and shrines, an ancient burial mound, and an old sake brewery. To get to the starting point, take a local JR Kibi line train from Okayama for three stops to Bizen Ichinomiya (備前一宮). From here, the route runs west for roughly 15km to the station at Sōja (総社), where you can drop off your bike and take a train back to Okayama. Most of the course follows a cycling path that's closed to traffic.

Uedo Rent-a-Cycle (☎ 086-284-2311; 🕑 9am-6pm) is immediately outside JR Bizen Ichinomiya station. Pick up your bike (¥1000) and Japanese-language route map here. Turn right and then right again across the tracks and you'll come to the **Kibitsuhiko-jinja** (吉備津彦神社), a shrine fronted by a small pond. From here you'll soon pick up the bicycle path, which follows a canal through the fields until it rejoins the road just before the Fukudenkai temple (福田海本部). From here, it's another 200m to **Kibitsu-jinja** (吉備津神社). This major shrine is dedicated to an ancient warrior who subdued a local bandit/demon called Ura and brought the area under central control. Many people believe that these exploits were the ultimate source of the Momotarō legend (see boxed text, p452). You'll see Momotarō's peachy features looking out at you from the votive tablets in front of the shrine.

Pedalling on, you'll pass the **Koikui-jinja** (鯉喰神社), slightly off the main route by the river. Further along is the 5th-century **Tsukuriyama-kofun** (造山古墳), rising like a gentle hill from the surrounding plain. The fourth-biggest *kofun* tomb in Japan, this is thought to mark the final resting place of a local king who ruled the Kibi region when this area was a rival power to the Yamato court (which eventually came to rule all of Japan).

The next major stop on the trail is the **Bitchū Kokobun-ji** (備中国分寺) temple with its picturesque five-storey pagoda. The oldest buildings here date from the Edo period, but the first temple on this site was built in the 8th century. You pass by some excavated remains of the original structure on your way towards the main gate. Across the road from the temple is the **Miyake Sake Brewery Museum** (三宅酒造資料館; ☎ 086-692-0075; admission ¥400; 🕑 9am-4.30pm, closed Mon). Look for the large white building. The brewery has been in the same family for over 100 years, and there is a small museum of old brewing paraphernalia, as well as opportunities to taste and buy.

From here, it's a few kilometres Sōja, where you can return your bicycle at **Araki Rent-a-Cycle** (☎ 086-692-0233; 🕑 9am-6pm), in front of the station.

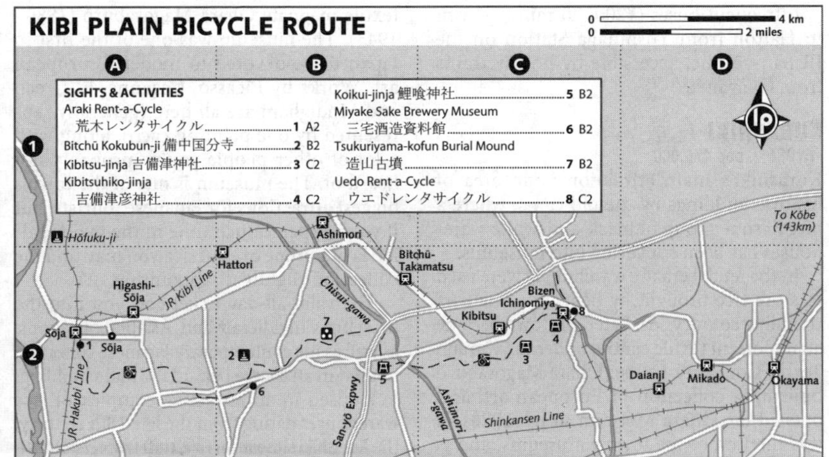

1400; admission ¥500; ⌚ 9.30am-5pm, closed Mon). The museum's collection includes pieces dating from the Muromachi (1333–1568) and Momoyama (1568–1600) periods; the 3rd floor is given over to pieces by several modern artists who have been designated as 'Living National Treasures'.

The chimney of the **Tōkei-dō** (桃蹊堂; ☎ 64-2147; 1527 Imbe; admission free; ⌚ 10am-4pm) kiln is visible from the station, straight ahead on the main road that leads north from the station. There are several galleries on this street, and many more right and left at the end of it. Turning right at the end of this street brings you to **Amatsu-jinja** (天津神社), the area's shrine, decorated with Bizen-yaki figures of the animals of the Chinese zodiac.

Several kilns in the area offer the chance to try your hand at making your own masterpiece. Advance reservations are required. Some English is spoken at **Bishū Gama** (備州窯; ☎ 64-1160; bisyu@gift.or.jp; 302-2 Imbe Bizen-shi; ⌚ 9am-3pm), where a spin on the wheel will set you back between ¥2625 and ¥3675. To get here, turn right out of the station and then walk about 800m until you come to the intersection with the next main road – the kiln is to the left of the intersection on a smaller road. It takes between an hour and 90 minutes to sculpt your piece, but you'll need to arrange to have it shipped to you after it's been fired. Back at the station, the **Bizen-yaki Traditional Industries Hall** (備前焼伝統産業会館; classes ¥3150-3675; ⌚ 10am-5pm) also has classes on weekends and public holidays.

There is one direct train an hour to Imbe from Okayama (¥570, 40 minutes) on the Akō line (赤穂線), bound for Banshū-Akō (播州赤穂) and Aioi (相生).

HATTŌJI 八塔寺

☎ 0869 / pop 42,000

Hattōji is a tranquil farming village on a plateau in the east of the prefecture. It's many miles from the nearest town, and coming here feels a bit like going back in time. There are no shops, or traffic, and there's no noise.

The **Hattōji International Villa** (八塔寺国際交流ヴィラ; ☎ 85-0254; 1193 Kagami Yoshinaga-chō Bizen-shi) is a restored farmhouse that was one of several places established by the prefectural government in the late 1980s as tourist accommodation for foreigners. The project became the victim of budget cuts in spring 2009, but the popular villa will remain open. For reservations, contact the **International Villa Group** (☎ 086-256-2535; fax 086-256-2576; www.harenet.ne.jp/villa) in Okayama. Rates are ¥3500 per person.

Accommodation is also available at **Hattōji Furusatokan** (八塔寺ふるさと館; ☎ 85-0333; cottages per person ¥3500), where there is a restaurant. The only other place at which to eat is **Nozomigaoka** (望ヶ丘; ☎ 85-0252; ⌚ sporadic hours, closed evenings), run by a Japanese cowboy, where the duck *nabe* (hotpot) has a good reputation. If you're staying at the villa, you'll want to stock up on food in Yoshinaga.

Infrequent buses (¥200, 30 minutes) run to Hattōji from Yoshinaga Station on the JR San-yō line, accessible by hourly trains from Okayama.

KURASHIKI 倉敷

☎ 086 / pop 476,000

Kurashiki's main attraction is an area of historic buildings by the old canal, where a picturesque group of black-and-white warehouses has been converted into museums.

In the feudal era the warehouses were used to store rice brought by boat from the surrounding countryside. Later, the town became an important textile centre, under the Kurabō Textile Company. Owner Ōhara Magosaburō built up a collection of European art, and opened the Ōhara Museum in the 1920s. It was the first of the town's museums, and is still the best. Many of Kurashiki's attractions are closed on Mondays.

Orientation

It's about 1km from the station to the historic Bikan quarter (美観地区), where all the old buildings and museums are clustered. All the tourist attractions are within a few minutes' walk of each other, along the canal.

Information

Just out of the station and to the right, the **tourist information counter** (☎ 424-1220; 2nd fl, Kurashiki City Plaza, 1-7-2 Achi; ⏲ 9am-7pm) has English-speaking staff and free internet access. The **Kurashikikan** (☎ 422-0542; 1-4-8 Chuō; ⏲ 9am-6pm Apr-Oct, 9am-5.15pm Nov-Mar), by the Naka-bashi bridge at the bend in the canal, also has a tourist information office and rest area.

Sights

Between the station and the canal area is the beautifully restored **Ōhashi House** (Ōhashi-ke Jūtaku; ☎ 422-0007; 3-21-31 Achi; admission ¥500; ⏲ 9am-5pm, closed Mon), built in 1793. The house belonged to one of Kurashiki's richest families, and was built at a time when prosperous merchants were beginning to claim privileges that had previously been the preserve of the samurai. The house's design contains several elements theoretically reserved for members of the ruling class.

Marked by its grand classical facade, the **Ōhara Museum of Art** (☎ 422-0005; 1-1-15 Chuō; admission ¥1000; ⏲ 9am-5pm, closed Mon) is Kurashiki's premier museum, housing the predominantly European art collection amassed by local textile magnate Ōhara Magosaburō (1880–1943). The museum was one of the first in Japan to be devoted to modern European art. Works by Picasso, Cézanne, El Greco and Modigliani are all here (generally represented by one painting each), along with a lot of other people you've probably not heard of. The museum is one of the town's biggest attractions for Japanese tourists, but if you've spent much time in the major galleries of Europe or America you may find the collection slightly disappointing.

The valid-all-day ticket gets you into the museum's handicraft and Asiatic collections, as well as the contemporary Japanese collection housed in an **annexe** behind the main building.

Housed in an attractive complex of rice warehouses dating from the late 18th century, the **Kurashiki Museum of Folk-craft** (☎ 422-1637; 1-4-11 Chuō; admission ¥700; ⏲ 9am-5pm Mar-Nov, 9am-4.15pm Dec-Feb, closed Mon) features interesting exhibits of ceramics, glassware, textiles and furniture.

A little further down the same street is the **Japan Rural Toy Museum** (☎ 422-8058; 1-4-16 Chuō; admission ¥400; ⏲ 9am-5pm), where four rooms are crammed with traditional kites, dolls and spinning tops from all over Japan.

A short walk from the canal area are the steep stone steps that lead up to **Achi-jinja** (☎ 425-4898; 12-1 Honmachi) and the **Tsurugata-yama-kōen**, a park that overlooks the old area of town.

IVY SQUARE アイビースクエア

This was once the site of Ōhara's Kurabō textile factories. The company moved into more modern premises a long time ago, and the red-brick factory buildings (dating from 1889) now house a hotel, restaurants, shops and yet more museums. You've come to the right place if you've been dying to hear **mechanical music-box concerts** (Kurashiki Ivy Square Orgel Musée; ticket ¥500; ⏲ hourly from 10am), or itching to learn all about the history of the Japanese textile industry – which you'll discover at **Kurabō Memorial Museum** (☎ 422-0011; admission ¥300; ⏲ 9am-5pm) – or yearning to learn about Kojima Torajirō, the European-style painter who helped Ōhara build up his art collection; head to **Kojima Torajirō Memorial Museum** (☎ 422-0005; admission ¥500; ⏲ 9am-5pm, closed Mon;) to immerse yourself in his life.

Sleeping

Kurashiki is a good place to experience a night in a ryokan (traditional Japanese inn). Alternatively, it's just 14 minutes by train

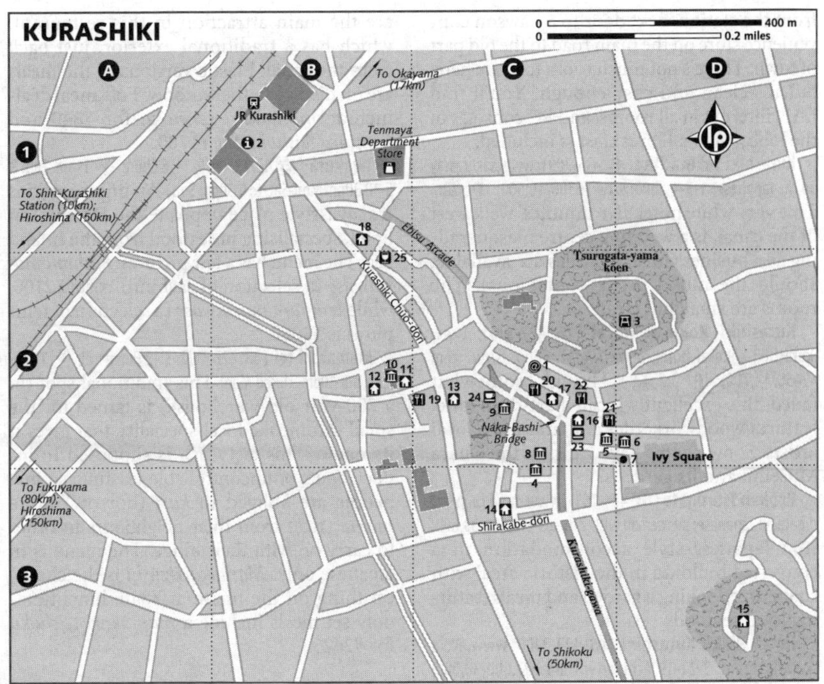

INFORMATION
Kurashikikan Information Centre 倉敷館観光案内所 1 C2
Tourist Information Counter 光案内所 2 B1

SIGHTS & ACTIVITIES
Achi-jinja 阿智神社 3 D2
Japan Rural Toy Museum 日本郷土玩具館 4 C3
Kojima Torajirō Memorial Museum 島虎次郎記念館 5 C2
Kurabō Memorial Museum 倉紡記念館 6 D2
Kurashiki Ivy Square Orgel Musée 倉敷アイビースクエアオルゴールミュゼ 7 D2
Kurashiki Museum of Folk-craft 倉敷民芸館 8 C2
Mechanical Music-Box Concerts .... (see 7)
Ōhara Museum of Art 大原美術館 9 C2
Ōhashi House (Ōhashi-ke Jūtaku) 大橋家住宅 10 B2

SLEEPING
Dormy Inn Kurashiki ドーミーイン倉敷 11 B2
Hotel Nikkō Kurashiki ホテル日航倉敷 12 B2
Kurashiki Kokusai Hotel 倉敷国際ホテル 13 C2
Kurashiki Sakura Stay ホテル倉敷サクラステイ 14 C3
Kurashiki Youth Hostel 倉敷ユースホステル 15 D3
Ryokan Kurashiki 旅館くらしき 16 C2
Ryokan Tsurugata 旅館鶴形 17 C2
Tōyoko Inn 東横イン 18 B1

EATING
Iwakura いわ倉 19 C2
Kamoi Restaurant カモ井 20 C2
Kana Izumi かな泉 21 C2
Mamakari-tei ままかり亭 22 C2

DRINKING
Coffee-Kan 珈琲館 23 C2
El Greco エルグレコ 24 C2
SWLABR 25 B2

to Okayama, where there's a wide range of accommodation and eating options available.

Kurashiki Youth Hostel (☎ 422-7355; www.jyh.or.jp/english/chugoku/kurasiki/index.html; 1537-1 Mukōyama; dm members/nonmembers ¥2940/3540; P ⊠) South of the canal area and a steep 25-minute climb from Ivy Sq, this tidy hostel's hilltop location overlooks the Bikan area. Meals are available. From the station, take bus 6 and get off at Shimin-kaikan-mae (市民会館前), then walk up through the cemetery.

Dormy Inn Kurashiki (☎ 426-5489; fax 426-5455; in-kurashiki@dormy-hotels.com; 3-21-11 Achi; s/tw from ¥5000/8000; P ⊠ 💻) A new hotel between the station and tourist district. Comfy rooms are complemented by an onsen on the top floor.

Tōyoko Inn (☎ 430-1045; www.toyoko-inn.com; 2-10-20 Achi; s/tw ¥5250/6300; P ⊠ 💻) A short walk from the station, next door to a Lawson convenience store on the main road to the old part of town. There's not much room to spare here, but it's clean and cosy enough. You'll find LAN internet in all rooms, and PC consoles in the lobby. A small breakfast is included.

Kurashiki Sakura Stay (☎ 435-7001; www.sakurastay.jp, in Japanese; 1-9-4 Chūō; s/tw ¥6300/10,500; P) This very white hotel, five minutes' walk west of the canal, is a wedding centre masquerading as a business hotel (candles are available, should the mood prove contagious). The rooms are small but clean.

Kurashiki Kokusai Hotel (☎ 422-5141; www.kurashiki-kokusai-hotel.co.jp; 1-44-1 Chūō; s/tw from ¥9450/14,700; P) Though somewhat faded, this excellently located art-deco hotel features woodwork, tiles and murals by local artists. Some rooms have views of the Ōhara Museum and its gardens.

Ryokan Tsurugata (☎ 424-1635; www.mmd.co.jp/tsurugata, in Japanese; per person with 2 meals ¥13,800-33,600; P) Japanese-style accommodation in a converted building in the historic area, with rooms overlooking a garden and meals featuring local seafood.

Hotel Nikkō Kurashiki (☎ 423-2400; www.nikko-kurashiki.com; 3-21-19 Achi; s/tw from ¥22,000/30,000; P) A modern high-rise towering over Ōhashi House a short walk from the historic quarter, this top-end business hotel has comfortable, spacious rooms with good city views, and several restaurants and bars on site.

Ryokan Kurashiki (☎ 422-0730; fax 422-0990; www.ryokan-kurashiki.jp; 4-1 Honmachi; per person with 2 meals from ¥28,000; P) Right by the canal in the heart of the historic district, and incorporating several beautifully restored Edo-period buildings, this is probably the best ryokan in town. There's a pleasant cafe overlooking a garden, and dinner is a multicourse *kaiseki* (Japanese haute cuisine)-style affair featuring delicacies from the Inland Sea.

Eating

Kamoi Restaurant (☎ 422-0606; 1-3-17 Chūō; 10am-6pm, closed Wed) A pleasant canalside restaurant opposite the Ōhara Museum. Meals, from a photo menu, include a *sashimi teishoku* (sashimi set meal; ¥2100), *unajū* (grilled eel on rice, ¥1890) and *mamakari-zushi* (sushi featuring the local sardine-like speciality; ¥1050).

Kana Izumi (☎ 421-7254; 8-33 Honmachi; 11am-8pm, closed Mon) *Sanuki-udon* (a type of wheat noodle) dishes such as *tempura udon* (¥780) are the main attraction in this restaurant, which has a traditional exterior, just back from the canal. Plastic versions of the meals are on display in the window. Full-meal deals include *mamakari teishoku* for ¥840 and *tempura teishoku* for ¥1780.

Iwakura (☎ 427-3100; 2-1-18 Chūō; 11am-2pm & 5-10.30pm Mon-Sat, to 9.30pm Sun) An unpretentious *izakaya*-style place opposite the Dormy Inn hotel, specialising in seafood from the Inland Sea. The menu has a few pictures. *Sashimi moriawase* (a selection of sashimi) costs ¥2100, while *tempura moriawase* (a selection of tempura) is ¥1050.

Mamakari-tei (☎ 427-7112; 3-12 Honmachi; 11am-2pm & 5-10pm, closed Mon) This traditional spot (in a 200-year-old warehouse) is famed for the small sardinelike local speciality that gives it its name. This tasty fish is supposed to induce bouts of uncontrollable feasting, so that people are obliged to *kari* (borrow) more *mama* (rice) from their neighbours in order to carry on with their binge. The menu is in Japanese only. *Mamakari-zushi* is the cheapest thing on the menu at ¥840; lunchtime-only set meals include a *mamakari teishoku* for ¥2625.

Drinking

El Greco (☎ 422-0297; 1-1-11 Chuō; coffees from ¥500; 10am-5pm, closed Mon) Right next to Ōhara Museum (you can't miss the cafe's ivy-clad walls), this relaxed, roomy spot is popular for coffee and cakes.

Coffee-Kan (☎ 424-5516; 4-1 Honmachi; coffees ¥500-850; 10am-5pm Tue-Sun) With its brick interior, this cavernous caffeine-lovers' paradise is thick with the aroma of freshly roasted coffee. There's an English menu, but no food is served. It's on the canal, just down from Ryokan Kurashiki.

SWLABR (☎ 434-3099; 2-18-2 Achi; 11.30am-3am, closed Thu) After the Bikan area closes down, relax with the good music and friendly staff at SWLABR. The food stops at 6pm, but the cosy bar-lounge keeps going until late. It's the green weatherboard house on the corner, a couple of blocks southeast of the station. A BLT sandwich costs ¥800, and cocktails cost from ¥600.

Getting There & Away

Kurashiki is just 17km southwest of Okayama. Regular trains on the San-yō line from Okayama make the journey in 14 minutes

(¥320). From Kurashiki it's 40 minutes to Fukuyama (¥740) in Hiroshima-ken.

Getting Around

It's a 15-minute walk from the station to the canal area, where almost everything is within a few minutes' stroll. Walking is best for Kurashiki.

HIROSHIMA-KEN 広島県

In addition to the sights of the prefecture's cosmopolitan capital city, Hiroshima-ken is notable for the island of Miyajima and its famous shrine; the postcard-pretty fishing village of Tomo-no-ura; and, in the north of the prefecture, the spectacular Sandan-kyō gorge.

SOUTHERN HIROSHIMA-KEN 広島県南部

Fukuyama 福山

☎ 084 / pop 462,000

Fukuyama is a large industrial city without much to attract the traveller. Its convenient location on the main *shinkansen* route makes it a good jumping-off point for the fishing port of Tomo-no-ura (¥530, 30 minutes by bus) or Onomichi (¥400, 20 minutes by train), a gateway to the Inland Sea.

If timetables conspire to keep you in Fukuyama, you can while away a few hours in one of the city's museums or at the reconstructed castle outside the station. There's a **tourist information office** (☎ 922-2869; 8.30am-5.15pm) in the main station. The **Japan Footwear Museum** (日本はきもの博物館; ☎ 934-6644; 4-16-27 Matsunaga-chō; admission ¥1000; 9am-5pm), five minutes' walk from the nearby Matsunaga Station, chronicles footwear from sandals to moon boots. If you can wear it on your feet, you'll find it in here somewhere. A 5-minute walk from the station is the **Fukuyama Auto and Clock Museum** (福山自動車時計博物館; ☎ 922-8188; 3-1-22 Kita-Yoshizu; admission ¥900; 9am-6pm), where you can mess around with old trucks, buses and antique cars.

Tomo-no-ura 鞆の浦

☎ 084 / pop 5000

The delightful fishing port of Tomo-no-ura, with its picturesque old streets and temples, is just 30 minutes south of Fukuyama Station by bus. Perfectly situated in the middle of the Inland Sea coast, Tomo-no-ura flourished for centuries as a stopping-off point for boats travelling between western Japan and the capital, until the arrival of steam put an end to the town's glory days in the late 19th century. Not a lot has happened here since.

The town is not completely unspoiled – several large concrete hotels, for instance, have done little to improve the skyline – but the old harbour and the narrow, winding streets that surround it retain much of the flavour of the town's Edo-period heyday. The sublime view out to sea has hardly changed at all since a visiting Korean envoy described it in 1711 as 'the finest in all Japan'.

Brochures and maps are available at JR Fukuyama Station and at various hotels in Tomo-no-ura itself. Bikes can be hired (¥300 for two hours) from a booth next to the ferry terminal; the town is small enough to be seen on foot in half a day.

Five minutes away by regular ferry is Sensui-jima, where there is a camping ground, a couple of hotels and some good views, especially at sunset (¥240 return, five minutes).

SIGHTS

At the top of the hill behind the ferry pier is the **Tomo-no-Ura Historical Museum** (鞆の浦歴史民俗資料館; ☎ 982-1121; admission ¥150; 9am-5pm, closed Mon) and the site of the old castle, of which nothing remains but a few foundation stones. Stone steps lead down from here to a network of narrow streets lined with old houses and shops, which then leads towards the harbour. Close to the ferry pier is **Fukuzenji temple** (福禅寺), which dates back to the 10th century. Adjoining the temple is **Taichōrō** (対潮楼; admission ¥200; 8am-5pm), built in the 1690s. This is where you go for a classic view out across a narrow channel to the uninhabited island of Benten-jima, and its shrine. The road along the shoreline from here leads to the main harbour area, dominated by the stone lantern that used to serve as a lighthouse, known as the Jōyatō (常夜燈). Close to the lantern is the former **Ōta Residence** (太田家住宅; ☎ 982-3553; admission ¥400; 10am-5pm, closed Tue), a fine collection of restored buildings from the mid-18th century. Guided tours take you through the impressive family residence and workplace. There is an English pamphlet.

Around the harbour and inland slightly from here are a dozen or so temples. Up a steep hill to the west of the harbour, **Iō-ji** (医王寺) was reputedly founded by Kōbō Daishi in the 900s. A path leads from the temple to the top of a bluff, from where there are more great views. The town's main Shintō shrine is the **Nunakuma-jinja** (沼名前神社). The shrine dates back to the Heian period, but the present building is a modern reconstruction. There are a few interesting bits and pieces in the grounds, including a nō stage that once belonged to warlord Toyotomi Hideyoshi. The component pieces of the stage are numbered to allow easy dismantling – apparently to allow the stage to be taken apart and carried to the battlefield for a bit of light half-time entertainment. To the right of the main shrine is a collection of huge mill-stones with Chinese characters on them. The haulers who loaded and unloaded the boats in the harbour would compete to lift these at festival times.

The **Amo Chinmi Processed Seafoods Company** (阿藻珍味) has its factory and shop at the far western end of the harbour. Walk along the shoreline for about 10 minutes from the harbour until you come to the kindergarten (鞆平保育所) on your left. Look for the large building on the right marked with kanji that has a circle round it. In the factory premises, **Uonosato** (うをの里; ☎ 982-3333; 1567-1 Ushiroji Tomo-chō; admission free, food lessons from ¥600; 🕑 9am-5pm, closed Mon) processes much of the locally caught fish. You can watch the workers making prawn *sembei* (rice crackers) and *chikuwa* (processed fish sausages), and even have a go at making them yourself. Tomo-no-ura is also famous for *homei-shu* (保命酒), a medicinal liquor made from rice, *shōchū* (a distilled spirit made from potato and barley) and 16 different types of herbs. Four breweries are still in operation; among the houses a few blocks back from the waterfront you can find stalls offering samples.

SLEEPING & EATING

Tomo Seaside Hotel (鞆シーサイドホテル; ☎ 983-5111; www.tomonoura.co.jp, in Japanese; per person with/without 2 meals from ¥6800/4179; Ⓟ) Close to the sights on the mainland, this hotel is slightly rundown and caters mainly to families and bingo-playing tour groups. All rooms are tatami (woven floor matting) style, and there's an onsen downstairs.

Kokuminshukusha Sensui-jima (国民宿舎仙酔島; ☎ 970-5050; www.tomonoura.co.jp, in Japanese; 3373-2 Ushiroji Tomo-chō; per person with meals from ¥7800; Ⓟ ⊠) Right on the beach, this is the most reasonably priced accommodation on nearby Sensui-jima. There are Japanese- and Western-style rooms and wonderful baths.

Keishōkan Sazanami-tei (景勝館漣亭; ☎ 982-2121; www.keishokan.com, in Japanese; 421 Tomo Tomo-chō; per person with 2 meals from ¥17,850) On the seafront, not far from the ferry pier, this luxurious ryokan offers an impressive array of baths in which to soak, and fresh fish from the Inland Sea. There's a spa on site, and some rooms come with their own outdoor *rotemburo* (outdoor baths).

@Cafe (☎ 982-0131; Jōyatōmae Tomo-chō; meals ¥400-900; 🕑 11am-8pm Thu-Tue) Attractive and airy modern cafe in a 150-year-old building beside the stone lighthouse in the harbour. There's a small menu of pasta dishes and other meals for around ¥1000. Anchovy and olive pasta is ¥900.

Tabuchiya (田渕屋; ☎ 983-5085; 838 Tomo Tomo-chō; 🕑 9am-6.30pm Thu-Tue) Coffee (¥400) and light meals including *hayashi raisu* (beef in sauce on rice; ¥1000) are served in this coffee shop on a corner just back from the harbour. Walk past the Ōta residence away from the harbour and look for the green *noren* on your left.

Chitose (千とせ; ☎ 982-3165; 552-7 Tomo Tomo-chō; 🕑 lunch & dinner, closed Tue) Just past the Tomo Seaside Hotel heading away from the ferry pier. Set meals featuring local fish start at ¥1300. An English menu is available.

GETTING THERE & AWAY

It's only 14km from Fukuyama to Tomo-no-ura; buses run every 15 minutes from bus stop 11 outside JR Fukuyama Station (¥530, 30 minutes).

Onomichi 尾道

☎ 0848 / pop 150,000

Onomichi is a gritty, old-timey seaport town whose hills are full of temples and literary sites. Film director Ōbayashi Nobuhiko was born in Onomichi, and the town has featured in a number of Japanese movies, notably Ozu's *Tokyo Story*. There are connections from here to the Inland Sea and on to Imabari in Ehime-ken via the Shimanami Kaidō system of road bridges. If you've got energy to burn, you can bike all the way to Shikoku from here (p476). The **tourist information office** (☎ 20-0005; 🕑 9am-6pm) is inside Onomichi Station.

SIGHTS

The modern town stretches east from the station along a thin corridor between the railway tracks and the sea. Most of the places of interest are on the other side of the tracks, in the series of steep flag-stoned streets that ladder the hillside. The **Historical Temple Walk** (古寺めぐり) is a well-signed trail that takes in 25 old temples scattered along the hillside. The start of the trail is just east of the station: take the inland road from the station and cross the railway tracks by the statue of local author Hayashi Fumiko. Close to the fourth temple along, Hōdo-ji, is **Onomichi Literature Museum** (文学記念室; 13-28 Tsuchidō; ☎ 22-4102; admission with Shiga Naoya residence ¥300; ⏰ 9am-5pm Nov-Mar, 9am-6pm Apr-Oct, closed Tue, Dec-Feb), where there are displays on the lives and works of Hayashi Fumiko and other writers connected with Onomichi. It's all in Japanese, but the proprietor speaks English and will delight in taking you through it all at length, if you give him half a chance. Around the corner is **Shiga Naoya residence** (志賀直哉旧居; ☎ 23-6243; 8-28 Tsuchi-dō;; admission with Onomichi Literature Museum ¥300; ⏰ 9am-5pm Nov-Mar, 9am-6pm Apr-Oct, closed Tue, Dec-Feb), where another of Japan's major 20th-century writers lived, from 1912 to 1913. About a third of the way along the temple route is a **cable car** (one way/return ¥280/440; ⏰ every 15min) that whisks you up to the hilltop Senkō-ji, the best-known and most impressive of Onomichi's temples, and its pleasant park.

SLEEPING & EATING

Onomichi Royal Hotel (尾道ロイヤルホテル; ☎ 23-2111; www.kokusai-hotel.com, in Japanese; 2-9-27 Tsuchido; s/tw from ¥5300/10,500; Ⓟ) On the coastal road, about a 15-minute walk from the station (turn left and head along the waterfront), this simple business hotel is a decent place to crash for the night.

Alpha-1 (アルファワン; ☎ 25-5600; www.alpha-1.co.jp/onomichi/, in Japanese; 1-1 Nishi Gosho-machi; s/tw from ¥5400/10,000; Ⓟ ☒ 💻) A comfortable business hotel a short walk from the station. Turn right out of the station; it's behind the Fukuya shopping arcade. LAN internet is in all rooms, and laptop rental service is available, as well as free bike hire.

Green Hill Hotel Onomichi (グリーンヒルホテル尾道; ☎ 24-0100; http://gho.hotwire.jp/index_e.html; 9-1 Higashi Gosho-machi; s/tw from ¥7875/15,750; Ⓟ 💻) Directly above the ferry port and a minute's walk from the station, this comfortable, well-appointed hotel could hardly be better located. LAN internet in all rooms.

Uonobu Ryokan (魚信旅館; ☎ 37-4175; fax 37-3849; www.uonobu.jp, in Japanese; 2-27-6 Kubo; per person with meals from ¥16,800; Ⓟ) Right on the waterfront, this elegantly old-fashioned place is renowned for its seafood. Nonguests can eat here too, but you'll need to reserve by 5pm the previous day. It's a good 20-minute walk from the station. Look for the imposing traditional building on the right just after the city hall (市役所). There are paper lanterns outside.

Common (茶房こもん; ☎ 37-2905; 1-2-2 Nagae; ⏰ 9am-7pm, closed Tue; ☒) Decked out in black and white, this pleasant coffee-and-waffles cafe at the foot of the cable car makes an excellent place to stop and refuel halfway through the temple circuit. Various coffee-and-waffle sets cost ¥800.

Onomichi Rāmen Ichibankan (尾道ラーメン壱番館; ☎ 21-1119; 2-9-26 Tsuchidō; ⏰ 11am-8pm, closed Fri) Opposite the Sumiyoshi shrine on the waterfront, a 15-minute walk from the station, this popular noodle shop is a good place to try Onomichi's *rāmen* (soup and noodles), characterised by thick slabs of juicy pork. Its best seller is the *kaku-ni rāmen* (角煮ラーメン; noodles with eggs and tender cuts of fatty pork) for ¥890. There is a picture menu.

Yamaneko (やまねこ; ☎ 21-5355; 2-9-33 Tsuchidō; ⏰ 11.30am-10pm, to midnight Sat & Sun, closed Mon) A relaxed and deliberately scruffy cafe on a corner along the waterfront road, a 15-minute walk from the station, just before Royal Hotel. There's an English sign; look for the cats. Drinks start at ¥500, and the menu includes sandwiches and pasta. Pasta carbonara is ¥900.

Yasuhiro Sushi (保広寿司; ☎ 22-5639; 1-10-12 Tsuchidō; ⏰ lunch & dinner, closed Mon) Enjoy excellent local seafood in this cosy sushi restaurant on the seafront. It's a white building with black tiling, five to 10 minutes' walk from the station. Lunchtime deals include *sashimi teishoku* and *anago-don* (saltwater eel on rice), both for ¥1600.

GETTING THERE & AWAY

Onomichi is at the Honshū end of the island-hopping Shimanami-Kaidō bridge system to Imabari in Shikoku (p476. As such, it's a gateway to Inno-shima (p476) and Ikuchi-jima (p476), both of which are officially part of Onomichi city. There are nine ferries a day to the port of Setoda on Ikuchi-jima (¥800, 40 minutes, 7.20am–7.30pm) via Inno-shima (¥400). Sixteen buses a day run from Onomichi all the way across to Imabari in Shikoku, with a change of buses at Inno-shima (¥2200, 6.40am–

4.50pm) – travel time is less than two hours, but connection times vary; check the timetables in advance. **Bike hire** (☎ 22-5332; per day ¥500, deposit ¥1000; 🕑 9am-6pm) is available in the large car park attached to the ferry terminal.

The Shin-Onomichi *shinkansen* station is 3km north of the JR San-yō line station. Buses connect the two stations, but it's easier to reach Onomichi on the JR San-yō line and change to the *shinkansen* line either at Fukuyama or Mihara.

NORTHERN HIROSHIMA-KEN 広島県北部

Sandan-kyō 三段峡

The Sandan-kyō gorge, about 50km northwest of Hiroshima, is an area that you could get lost in for a few days. A mostly paved trail follows the Shiki-gawa through an 11km gorge, providing visitors with access to fresh air, waterfalls and forests. The hike is very popular in autumn, when the leaves change colour. Pick up a copy of Lonely Planet's *Hiking in Japan* for details.

A dozen buses a day run from the Hiroshima bus centre to Sandan-kyō Station (¥1200 to ¥1400, 1½ hours), at the southern end of the gorge. There is no longer a rail service. The gorge is also accessible by car from Shimane-ken along Rte 191.

HIROSHIMA 広島

☎ 082 / pop 1,154,000

Although it's a prosperous and attractive city with excellent nightlife and a cosmopolitan population, to most people, Hiroshima means just one thing. The city will forever be remembered for the terrible instant on 6 August 1945 when it became the target of the world's first atomic-bomb attack. Hiroshima's Peace Memorial Park is a constant reminder of that day, and it attracts visitors from all over the world. But Hiroshima is a far from depressing place; its citizens have recovered from nuclear holocaust to build a thriving and internationally minded community. It's worth spending a night or two here and seeing the city at its vibrant best.

The city's history goes back to 1589, when Mōri Terumoto established his castle here.

Orientation

Hiroshima is built on a series of sandy islands in the Ōta-gawa delta. JR Hiroshima Station is east of the city centre. The city's main island is traversed east–west by the busy Aioi-dōri (with the main tram lines from the station). South of this is another east–west boulevard, Heiwa-Ōdōri. Between these two major roads is the Hon-dōri covered arcade, along with most of the shops, bars and restaurants.

The A-Bomb Dome and Peace Memorial Park are at the western end of Aioi-dōri.

Information

BOOKSHOPS

Book Nook (☎ 244-8145; 5-17 Kamiya-chō; 🕑 noon-9pm Mon-Thu, to 11pm Fri & Sat; 💻) A decent selection of secondhand English paperbacks and an internet cafe (¥200 for 15 minutes). It's in a language school called Outsider, behind Iyo Bank and Yamaha music store. Look for the 2nd-floor sign.

INTERNET ACCESS

Futaba@Cafe (☎ 568-4792; 2-22 Matsubara-chō; membership fee ¥105, 1st 30min ¥300; 🕑 24hr) On the 6th floor of a book and CD store, with a yellow sign to the left as you exit the station.

International Exchange Lounge (Peace Memorial Park; 🕑 9am-7pm Apr-Sep, 9am-6pm Oct-Mar) Has free internet access.

MONEY

The central post office changes money during the week, and on weekends the major international hotels have exchange services. Hiroshima Rest House (see Tourist Information, opposite) has an extensive list of banks and post offices that change money and travellers cheques.

POST

Central post office (広島中央郵便局; ☎ 245-5335; 1-4-1 Kokutaiji-chō, Naka-ku; 🕑 9am-7pm Mon-Fri, to 5pm Sat, to 12.30pm Sun) Near the Shiyakusho-mae tram stop. You can change money here between 9am and 4pm from Monday to Friday.

Higashi Post Office (☎ 261-6401; 2-62 Matsubara-chō, Minami-ku; 🕑 9am-7pm Mon-Fri, to 5pm Sat, to 12.30pm Sun) Near the southern exit of the station, this branch is more convenient than the 'Central'.

Naka Post Office (☎ 222-1314; 6-36 Motomachi, Naka-ku; 🕑 9am-7pm Mon-Fri, to 3pm Sat) Next to the Sogō department store.

TOURIST INFORMATION

Check out www.gethiroshima.com for good food and nightlife recommendations, and insights into the local culture that aren't covered by the tourist brochures.

Hiroshima Rest House (☎ 247-6738; 1-1 Nakajima-machi, Naka-ku; 🕑 9.30am-6pm Apr-Sep, 8.30am-5pm Oct-Mar) In the Peace Memorial Park, next to Motoyasu-bashi. Comprehensive information about the city and the island of Miyajima.

Tourist information office JR Hiroshima Station South (☎ 261-1877; 🕑 9am-5.30pm) JR Hiroshima Station North (☎ 263-6822; 🕑 9am-5.30pm) There's also another branch downstairs.

Sights

A-BOMB DOME 原爆ドーム

Perhaps the starkest reminder of the destruction visited upon Hiroshima is the **A-Bomb Dome** (Gembaku Dōmu), across the river from Peace Memorial Park. Built by a Czech architect in 1915, the building served as the Industrial Promotion Hall until the bomb exploded almost directly above it. Everyone inside was killed, but the building itself was one of very few left standing anywhere near the epicentre. Despite local misgivings, a decision was taken after the war to preserve the shell of the building as a memorial. Declared a Unesco World Heritage Site in December 1996, the propped-up ruins are floodlit at night, and have become a grim symbol of the city's tragic past.

PEACE MEMORIAL PARK 平和記念公園

From the A-Bomb Dome, cross over into **Peace Memorial Park** (Heiwa-kōen), which is dotted with memorials, including the **cenotaph** that contains the names of all the known victims of the bomb. The cenotaph frames the **Flame of Peace**, which will only be extinguished once the last nuclear weapon on earth has been destroyed, and the A-Bomb Dome across the river.

Just north of the road crossing through the park is the **Children's Peace Monument**, inspired by leukaemia victim Sadako Sasaki. When Sadako developed leukaemia at 11 years of age in 1955 she decided to fold 1000 paper cranes. In Japan, the crane is the symbol of longevity and happiness, and she was convinced that if she could achieve that target she would recover. She died before reaching her goal, but her classmates folded the rest. The story inspired a nationwide bout of paper-crane folding that continues to this day.

Nearby is the recently relocated **Korean A-Bomb Memorial**. Many Koreans were shipped over to work as slave labourers during WWII, and Koreans accounted for more than one in 10 of those killed by the atomic bomb.

PEACE MEMORIAL MUSEUM 平和記念資料館

Hiroshima's **Peace Memorial Museum** (☎ 241-4004; 1-2 Nakajima-chō, Naka-ku; admission ¥50; 🕑 8.30am-5pm, to 6pm Mar-Nov, to 7pm Aug) presents a balanced narrative of events leading up to the war and the bombing. There are some harrowing exhibits documenting the horror of what happened on 6 August 1945, and a depressing display showing the development of even more destructive weapons in the years since. A visit to the museum can be an overwhelming experience.

HIROSHIMA NATIONAL PEACE MEMORIAL HALL FOR THE ATOMIC BOMB VICTIMS 国立広島原爆死没者追悼平和祈念館

Opened in August 2002, **Peace Memorial Hall** (☎ 543-6271; 1-6 Nakajima-chō, Naka-ku; admission free; 🕑 8.30am-6pm Mar-Jul, to 7pm Aug, to 6pm Sep-Nov, 8.30am-5pm Dec-Feb) contains a contemplative underground hall of remembrance and a room where the names and photographs of atomic-bomb victims are kept, along with survivors' testimonies in several languages. It was built by architect Tange Kenzō, who also designed the museum, cenotaph and eternal flame. These testimonies, which can be viewed on video, vividly evoke the chaos of the time. It's worth taking time here to get first-hand accounts of the after-effects of the bomb.

HIROSHIMA-JŌ 広島城

Also known as Carp Castle (Rijō; 鯉城), **Hiroshima-jō** (Hiroshima Castle; ☎ 221-7512; 21-1 Moto-machi, Naka-ku; admission ¥360; 🕑 9am-6pm Mar-Nov, to 5pm Dec-Feb) was originally constructed in 1589, but much of it was dismantled following the Meiji Restoration, leaving only the donjon, main gates and turrets. The remainder was totally destroyed by the bomb and rebuilt in 1958. There's not a lot to see inside, but the surrounding park is a pleasant place for a stroll.

SHUKKEI-EN 縮景園

Modelled after Xi Hu (West Lake) in Hangzhou, China, **Shukkei-en** (2-11 Kami-nobori-chō; admission ¥250, combined ticket with museum ¥600; 🕑 9am-6pm Apr-Sep, to 5pm Oct-Mar) was built in 1620 for *daimyō* Asano Nagaakira. The garden's name means 'contracted view', and it attempts to re-create grand vistas in miniature. It was totally destroyed by the bomb, though many of the trees and plants survived to blossom again the following year, and the

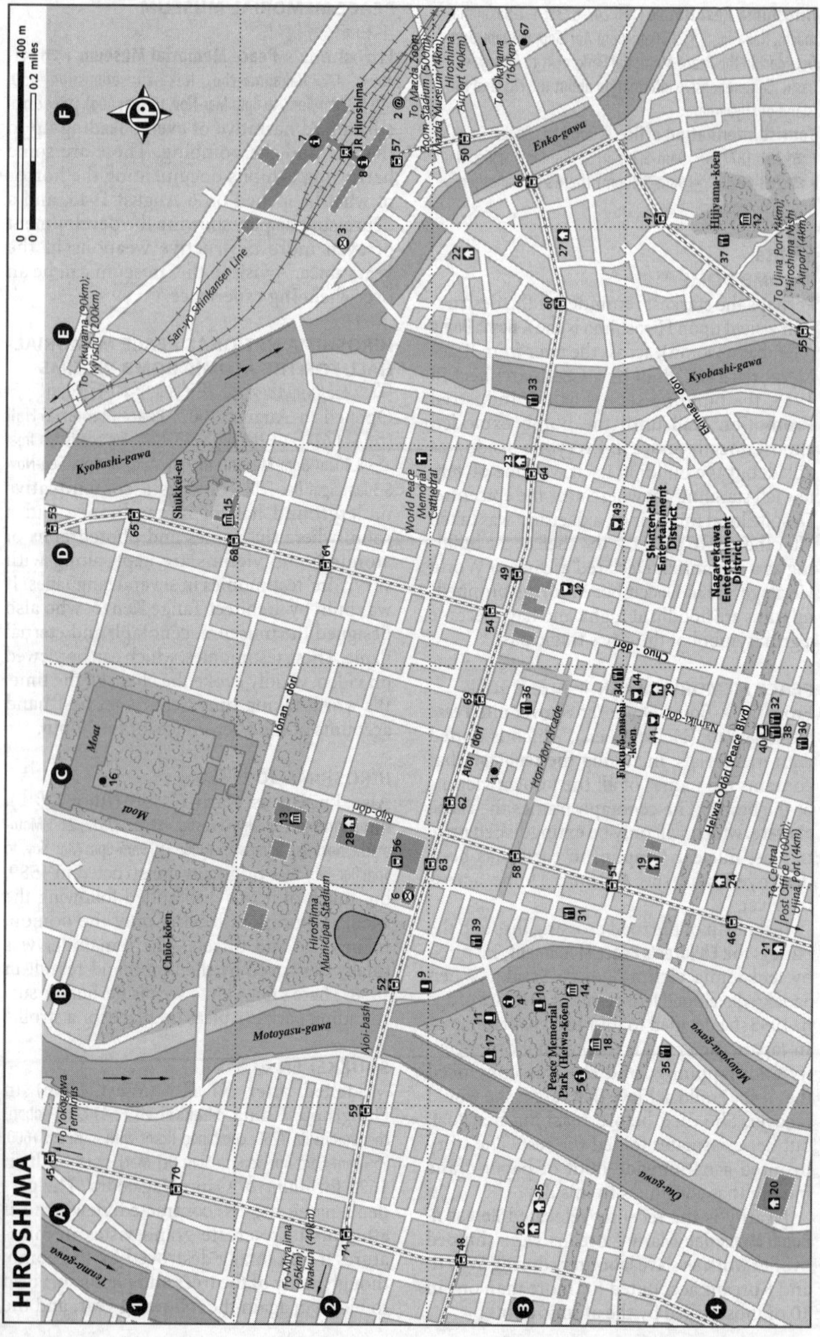

HIROSHIMA

0 400 m
0 0.2 miles

Tenma-gawa
To Yokogawa Terminus
Motoyasu-gawa
Chūō-kōen
Moat
Kyobashi-gawa
Shukkei-en
To Tokuyama (90km); Kyūshū (200km)
San-yo Shinkansen Line
JR Hiroshima
To Mazda Zoom-Zoom Stadium (500m); Mazda Museum (4km); Hiroshima Airport (40km)
To Okayama (160km)
Enko-gawa
Hijiyama-kōen
To Ujina Port (4km); Hiroshima Nishi Airport (4km)
Kyobashi-gawa
Ekimae-dōri
Shintenchi Entertainment District
Nagarekawa Entertainment District
Chuo-dōri
Namiki-dōri
Heiwa-Ōdōri (Peace Blvd)
To Central Post Office (160m); Ujina Port (4km)
Fukuro-machi-kōen
Hon-dōri Arcade
Aioi-dōri
Rijo-dōri
Jōnan-dōri
World Peace Memorial Cathedral
Hiroshima Municipal Stadium
Aioi-bashi
Peace Memorial Park (Heiwa-kōen)
Motoyasu-gawa
Ota-gawa
To Miyajima (25km); Iwakuni (40km)

INFORMATION

Book Nook ブックヌック 1 C3
Futaba@Cafe フタバ@アットカフェ 2 F2
Higashi Post Office 東郵便局 3 E2
Hiroshima Rest House 広島市レストハウス 4 B3
International Exchange Lounge 国際交流ラウンジ 5 B3
Naka Post Office 中郵便局 6 B2
Tourist Information Office 観光案内所 7 F2
Tourist Information Office 観光案内所 8 F2

SIGHTS & ACTIVITIES

A-Bomb Dome 原爆ドーム 9 B2
Cenotaph 原爆慰霊碑 10 B3
Children`s Peace Monument 原爆の子像 11 B3
Flame of Peace 平和の灯 (see 10)
Hiroshima City Museum of Contemporary Art 広島現代美術館 12 F4
Hiroshima Museum of Art ひろしま美術館 13 C2
Hiroshima National Peace Memorial Hall for the Atomic Bomb Victims 国立広島原爆死没者追悼平和祈念館 14 B3
Hiroshima Prefectural Art Museum 広島県立美術館 15 D1
Hiroshima-jō 広島城 16 C1
Korean A-Bomb Memorial 韓国人原爆犠牲者慰霊碑 17 B3
Peace Memorial Museum 広島平和記念資料館 18 B3

SLEEPING

ANA Crowne Plaza Hiroshima ANA クラウンプラザホテル広島 19 C4
Aster Plaza International Youth House 広島市国際青年会館 20 A4
Comfort Hotel Hiroshima Ōtemachi コンフォートホテル広島大手町 21 B4
Hiroshima Grand Intelligent Hotel 広島グランドインテリジェントホテル 22 E3
Hotel Active! ホテルアクティブ！広島 23 D3
Hotel Dormy Inn Hiroshima ドーミーイン広島 24 C4
Ikawa Ryokan いかわ旅館 25 A3
J-Hoppers Hiroshima ジェイホッパーズ広島 26 A3
K's House Hiroshima ケイズハウス広島 27 E3
Rihga Royal Hotel Hiroshima リーガロイヤルホテル広島 28 C2
Sera Bekkan 世羅別館 29 C4

EATING

Bakudanya ばくだん屋 30 C4
Cha Cha Ni Moon 茶茶貳ムーン 31 B3
Hassei 八誠 32 C4
Kaki-tei 牡蠣亭 33 E3
Okonomi-mura お好み村 34 C3
Ristorante Mario リストランテマリオ 35 B4
Spicy Bar Lal's スパイシーバーラルズ 36 C3
Tōshō 豆匠 37 E4
Wein Izakaya Banzai ワイン居酒屋ばんざい 38 C4
Zucchini ズッキーニ 39 B3

DRINKING

J-Café ジェイカフェ 40 C4
Koba コバ 41 C4
Kuro-sawa 黒澤 42 D3
Lotus ロータス (see 44)
Nawanai なわない 43 D3
Opium オピウム 44 C4

TRANSPORT

Betsuin-mae 別院前 45 A1
Chūden-mae 中電前 46 B4
Danbara 1 chome 段原一丁目 47 F4
Dobashi 土橋 48 A3
Ebisu-chō 胡町 49 D3
Enkōbashi-chō 猿猴橋町 50 F3
Fukuro-machi 袋町 51 C3
Genbaku Domu-mae (A-Bomb Dome) 原爆ドーム前 52 B2
Hakushima Line Terminus 白島 53 D1
Hatchō-bori 八丁堀 54 D3
Hijiyama-shita 比治山下 55 E4
Hiroshima Bus Centre 広島バスセンター 56 C2
Hiroshima Eki 広島駅 57 F2
Hon-dōri 本通 58 C3
Honkawa-chō 本川町 59 A2
Inari-machi 稲荷町 60 E3
Jogakuin-mae 女学院前 61 D2
Kamiya-chō-higashi 紙屋町東 62 C3
Kamiya-chō-nishi 紙屋町西 63 C3
Kanayama-chō 銀山町 64 D3
Katei Saibansho-mae 家庭裁判所前 65 D1
Matoba-chō 的場町 66 F3
Nippon Rent-a-car ニッポンレンタカー 67 F3
Shukkeien-mae 縮景園前 68 D1
Tate-machi 立町 69 C3
Tera-machi 寺町 70 A1
Tōkaichimachi 十日市町 71 A2

park and its buildings have long since been restored to their original splendour.

Next to the garden is the **Hiroshima Prefectural Art Museum** (2-22 Kami-nobori-chō; admission ¥500, combined ticket with garden ¥600; 9am-5pm, to 7pm Sat, closed Mon), where the highlight is Salvador Dali's *Dream of Venus*. If you have a combined ticket you can enter the museum via the garden.

OTHER SIGHTS

Hijiyama-kōen, a park noted for its cherry blossoms in spring, is a 20-minute walk south of JR Hiroshima station. Inside the park is the **Hiroshima City Museum of Contemporary Art** (☎ 264-1121; 1-1 Hijiyama-kōen, Minami-ku; admission ¥360, additional fee for temporary exhibits; 10am-5pm, closed Mon), which has frequently changing exhibits by modern Japanese and international artists.

The **Hiroshima Museum of Art** (☎ 223-2530; 3-2 Moto-machi, Naka-ku; admission ¥1000; 9am-5pm) is in an interesting 1970s building that was built by the Hiroshima Bank. It has a decent collection of minor works by well-known painters, including Picasso, Gaughin, Monet and Van Gogh. The museum is in Hanover Park, just southwest of the castle.

The **Mazda Museum** (マツダミュージアム; www.mazda.com/mazdaspirit/museum; ☎ 252-5050; English tours 1pm Mon-Fri) is quite popular, because you get to see the 7km assembly line – the longest in the world. Details are available on the English-language website. Reservations are required. The museum is a short walk from

JR Mukainada (向洋) Station, two stops from Hiroshima on the San-yō line.

Activities

A love of **baseball** is not a prerequisite for having a great time at a Hiroshima Carp game (www.carp.co.jp, in Japanese). It's just as much fun watching the rowdy, organised enthusiasm of the crowd, especially when the despised Tokyo Giants come to town. After playing for decades in the heart of the city near the A-Bomb Dome, in spring 2009 the Carp moved to the new Mazda Zoom-Zoom Stadium, a short walk southeast of the station.

Miyajima (p469), 25km west of the city, makes an easy **day trip** from Hiroshima, possibly combined with Iwakuni in Yamaguchi-ken (p478).

A variety of lunch and dinner **cruises** run from Hiroshima to Miyajima and back. On weekdays from March to September day cruises operate through the Inland Sea. Tickets can be bought through Japan Travel Bureau (JTB) or online at www.setonaikaikisen.co.jp, in Japanese.

Festivals & Events

On 6 August, the anniversary of the atomic bombing, a **memorial service** is held in Peace Memorial Park and thousands of paper lanterns for the souls of the dead are floated down the Ōta-gawa from in front of the A-Bomb Dome.

Sleeping

BUDGET

J-Hoppers Hiroshima (☎ 233-1360; http://hiroshima.j-hoppers.com/; 5-16 Dobashi-chō, Naka-ku; dm/tw per person with shared bathroom ¥2300/3000; P ⊠ 💻) Friendly and popular backpackers hostel, with dorm beds and private tatami rooms. Internet access is available in the common room, and bikes can be rented (¥500 per day). The young staff are a good source of local information.

K's House Hiroshima (☎ 568-7244; http://kshouse.jp/hiroshima-e/; 1-8-9 Matoba-chō; dm/s/d ¥2500/5500/7800; 💻 ⊠) Opened in September 2008 near the station, this is an excellent budget option, with small dorms as well as private singles and doubles. There are internet-ready computers in common areas, along with a kitchen and rooftop terrace.

Aster Plaza International Youth House (☎ 247-8700; http://hiyh.pr.arena.ne.jp/Hp_eng/indexeng.htm; 4-17 Kako-machi Naka-ku; s/tw ¥3620/6260; P 💻) On the top floors of a huge municipal building, this city-run hotel south of Peace Memorial Park represents excellent value for foreign travellers, who get large rooms and complimentary breakfast at the 'peace study' rates. There's a midnight curfew.

Ikawa Ryokan (☎ 231-5058; fax 231-5995; ikawa1961@go.enjoy.ne.jp; 5-11 Dobashi-chō, Naka-ku; s/tw from ¥4725/8400; P 💻) This is a friendly, family-run complex consisting of several wings with recently renovated rooms. It's a modern hotel with Japanese- and Western-style rooms, all very clean, and meals are available in the cafeteria. There's a computer with internet access, and some English is spoken.

MIDRANGE

Hotel Dormy Inn Hiroshima (☎ 240-1177; fax 240-1755; www.hotespa.net/hotels/hiroshima, in Japanese; 3-28 Komachi Naka-ku; s/tw from ¥6000/9000; P ⊠ 💻) Conveniently located on Heiwa-Ōdōri, the Dormy Inn has comfortable rooms and a wide range of amenities including a large onsen. There's LAN internet in all rooms, and there are consoles in the lobby.

Hotel Active! (☎ 212-0001; fax 211-3121; www.hotel-active.com, in Japanese; 15-3 Nobori-chō Naka-ku; s/d with breakfast ¥6279/7875; P ⊠ 💻) This very chic hotel has designer couches, satiny coverlets and onsen baths. It's right in the heart of things, within stumbling distance of the entertainment district. Free internet in the lobby.

Hiroshima Grand Intelligent Hotel (☎ 263-5111; fax 262-2403; www.intelligenthotel.co.jp, in Japanese; 1-4 Kyōbashi-chō; s/tw ¥6300/7300; P ⊠ 💻) A recently renovated business hotel–style place a short walk from the station, with a suit of armour standing to attention as you enter. Comfortable rooms have all the mod cons, including LAN internet. There are computers in the lobby, and there's a pleasant coffee shop.

Comfort Hotel Hiroshima Ōtemachi (☎ 545-7811; fax 545-7812; www.choicehotels.com; 3-7-9 Ōtemachi Naka-ku; s/tw with buffet breakfast ¥6500/8500; P ⊠ 💻) Attractively designed, this great business hotel has internet access via the computers in the lobby.

Sera Bekkan (☎ 248-2251; fax 248-2768; www.yado.to, in Japanese; 4-20 Mikawa-chō Naka-ku; per person with/without meals ¥8400/12,600; P) A very friendly traditional ryokan near Fukurō-machi-kōen. There are large baths, and a peaceful garden on the 2nd floor.

TOP END

Rihga Royal Hotel Hiroshima (☎ 502-1121; www.rihga.com/en/hiroshima/; 6-78 Moto-machi; s/tw ¥16,170/24,255;

(P ⊠ 💻). Conveniently located for all the sights and nightlife, this top-class hotel is the tallest building in town, with fantastic views out over the city at night. You'll have to cough up a surcharge if you want to use the pool or gym.

ANA Crowne Plaza Hiroshima (☎ 241-1111; www.anacrowneplaza-hiroshima.jp/en/index.html; 7-20 Naka-machi Naka-ku; s/tw ¥16,170/23,677; P ⊠ 💻) There are large rooms at this luxury hotel in the centre of town, as well as French, Chinese and Japanese restaurants. There's a gym and swimming pool on the 6th floor, for an additional charge.

Eating

Hiroshima is famous for oysters and *okonomiyaki* (savoury pancakes; with vegetables and seafood or meat cooked on a griddle), served Hiroshima-style with noodles. There's a decent selection of restaurants on the 6th floor of the Asse department store inside the station compound (all with picture menus and plastic food displays), including a couple of places to try the local oysters.

Bakudanya (☎ 245-5885; 6-13 Fujimi-chō Naka-ku; ⏲ 11.30am-3pm & 6pm-midnight, to 1am Fri & Sat, all day Sat & Sun) This simple street-corner stall is a good place to try another famous Hiroshima dish: *tsukemen,* a cold *rāmen*-like dish in which noodles and soup come separately. You can choose the size of your serving and the spiciness of your dipping sauce. This is the original outlet; the chain has now spread across the country. A *nami* (medium-sized) serving of *tsukemen* is ¥750. It's under a green awning on Jizō-dori.

Zucchini (☎ 546-0777; 1-5-18 Otemachi Naka-ku; meals ¥400-2800; ⏲ 5.30pm-1am) Very lively Spanish-style tapas restaurant serving all the usual ham, cheese and fish goodies and paellas from ¥1400. It's a two-storey glass-fronted affair on the corner – you can't miss it. There's an English menu.

Hassei (☎ 242-8123; 4-17 Fujimi-chō Naka-ku; dishes ¥450-1200; ⏲ lunch & dinner, dinner only Sun, closed Mon) The walls of this popular *okonomiyaki* joint are covered in the signatures of celebrity visitors. There's an English menu. Unless you're a sumō wrestler who hasn't eaten for a week, you'll probably find a half-order more than enough to be getting on with at lunchtime. The *shīfūdo supeshiaru* (seafood special; ¥1300) is stuffed with squid, shrimp and octopus. Look for the rising-sun pattern on the sign over the door.

Spicy Bar Lal's (☎ 504-6328; 5-12 Tatemachi Naka-ku; dishes ¥500-4200; ⏲ lunch & dinner) This colourful Indian and Nepalese restaurant serves filling lunch specials from ¥920. Tasty curries, naans and a Bollywood soundtrack make this a nice change, if you ever get tired of *okonomiyaki.* There is an English menu.

Wein Izakaya Banzai (☎ 245-3403; 4-20 Fujimi-chō; ¥650-1200; ⏲ 5-11pm, to midnight Fri & Sat) What do you mean you didn't come all the way to Japan to eat pig's knuckle? The picture menu features an impressive selection of sausages and German-style cold meats. Wallerstein dark lagers are ¥1030; Nuremberger sausages are ¥280 each.

Okonomi-mura (☎ 241-2210; 5-13 Shintenchi Naka-ku; dishes ¥700-1000; ⏲ 11am-2am) Twenty-five stalls spread over three floors, all of them serving the same thing – this Hiroshima institution is an atmospheric place to get acquainted with the local speciality of *okonomiyaki.* It's close to the Parco department store; the entrance is decorated with dozens of red-and-white lanterns, and the name is written in red illuminated characters.

Ristorante Mario (☎ 248-4956; 4-11 Nakajima-chō Naka-ku; dishes ¥1000-2000; ⏲ lunch & dinner, 11.30am-11.30pm Sat & Sun) A cosy ivy-walled place across the road from the Peace Memorial Museum (close to the roadside sculptures), serving good, honest Italian food. Lunch courses start at ¥1900, and there is an English (though largely Italian!) menu. Try to reserve on weekends.

Kaki-tei (☎ 090-8062-0378; 11 Hashimoto-chō Naka-ku; ⏲ lunch & dinner, closed Tue) This intimate bistro on the riverbank specialises in oysters prepared in a variety of mouthwatering ways. Grilled options include *champagne cream yaki* (¥850 for two). The daily oyster lunch is ¥1200. There's no English menu, but the friendly staff will help you figure things out. Look for the green *noren* decorated with oysters and the words 'Oyster Conclave' in English.

Tōshō (☎ 506-1028; 6-24 Hijiyama-chō Minami-ku; lunch/dinner menus from ¥1575/3000; ⏲ lunch & dinner) In a traditional wooden building overlooking a delightful pond and garden, Tōshō specialises in delicious homemade tofu (the menu has some pictures). It's a short walk from Danbara 1 chōme tram stop, left uphill after the Hijiyama shrine.

Cha Cha Ni Moon (☎ 241-7444; 2-6-26 Otemachi Naka-ku; dishes from ¥3000; ⏲ 5-11.30pm) Sophisticated minimalist chic prevails in this softly lit old house. There's a cosy bar downstairs and two floors of intimate semiprivate dining rooms upstairs. The beautifully presented dishes here are based on traditional Kyoto cuisine. Look for the tiny 'Moon' sign across from the small park.

Drinking

The city's lively entertainment district is made up of hundreds of bars, restaurants and karaoke joints crowding the lanes between Aioi-dōri and Heiwa-Ōdōri in the city centre.

Nawanai (☎ 248-0588; Fujimi Bldg, 12-10 Kanayama-chō Naka-ku; 🕑 6pm-midnight) This lively basement *izakaya* is an atmospheric place to mingle with locals over fresh fish and a range of local sakes. Try *ko-iwashi* (baby sardines), available either as sashimi or tempura (¥600). There is no English menu, but it's a welcoming spot and the owners will make sure you don't go home hungry – or thirsty. Look for the illuminated sign in Japanese pointing down into the basement.

Opium (☎ 504-0255; 3rd fl, Namiki Curl Bldg, 3-12 Mikawa-chō; dishes from ¥500; 🕑 6pm-4am) Groovy minimalist spot with good views out onto the street below. Cocktails start at ¥600, and happy hour is from 6pm to 9pm. Snacks, pizza and pasta dishes are available from an English menu. There's a bright purple sign on the wall outside.

Lotus (☎ 246-0104; 5th fl, Namiki Curl Bldg, 3-12 Mikawa-chō; drinks from ¥500; 🕑 6pm-3am) Two floors above Opium (see above) is Lotus, a stylish, Zen-like space where you can take off your shoes and relax on the raised floor amid cushions, or sip ¥600 cocktails from the English menu at the bar.

Koba (☎ 249-6556; 3rd fl, Rego Bldg, 1-4 Naka-machi; dishes ¥700-1200; 🕑 6pm-2am, closed Wed) Friendly Koba is an extremely chilled place to enjoy a few drinks and a curry, along with an eclectic range of music. It's in a concrete building with a pool of water by the entrance, just behind Stussy.

Kuro-sawa (☎ 247-7750; 5th fl, Tenmaya Ebisuclub, 3-20 Horikawa-chō Naka-ku; dishes under ¥1000; 🕑 6pm-2.30am Mon-Thu, to 3.30am Fri & Sat, to 12.30am Sun) A swish and trendy 'Japanese style public house' hewn from bare concrete, with seating at the bar or on velvet chairs in a raised red-carpet area. All the usual *izakaya* standards are available from an English menu. Don't forget to visit the remarkable bathrooms. From Nagarekawa-dōri, turn right into the Ebisu-dōri arcade. It's in the third building on the left, marked by a small red sign, opposite the Italian Tomato Café.

J-Café (☎ 242-1234; 4-20 Fujimi-chō Naka-ku; 🕑 noon-2am, to 3am Fri & Sat) Sophisticated boutique cafe with plush red sofas and graffiti art adorning the walls. Old cartoons flicker from the wall above the bar. A wide range of delicious crepes (¥600) and other snacks are on offer. There's an English menu. The sign outside has a stylised 'j' that looks like an ampersand.

Getting There & Away

Hiroshima's main **airport** (☎ 0848-86-8151; www.hij.airport.jp; 64-31 Zennyūji, Hongō-chō, Mihara-shi) is 40km east of the city, with bus connections to/from Hiroshima Station (¥1300, 48 minutes). There are flights to/from Tokyo (¥30,800, one hour and 15 minutes), Sapporo (¥45,700, one hour and 50 minutes), Sendai (¥39,000, one hour and 20 minutes) and Naha (¥32,000, two hours), as well as flights to Seoul, Dalian, Beijing, Shanghai, Taipei (all daily), Bangkok (Monday and Friday) and Guam (Monday and Thursday). **Hiroshima Nishi airport** (☎ 822-95-2650; www.hij.airport.jp/nishi/, in Japanese; 4-10-2 Kannon Shin-machi, Nishi-ku), 4km southwest of the city centre on the coast, has daily flights to Miyazaki (¥23,700, one hour) and Kagoshima (¥23,700, one hour) in Kyūshū. There are regular buses to/from Hiroshima Station (¥240, 20 minutes).

Hiroshima is an important stop on the Tokyo–Osaka–Hakata *shinkansen* route. The trip from Hiroshima to Hakata (Fukuoka) takes roughly 1¼ hours (¥8190); to Osaka, it's 1½ hours (¥9470), and to Tokyo it's four hours (¥17,540).

The JR San-yō line passes through Hiroshima westwards to Shimonoseki, hugging the coastline much of the way. The ordinary local services move along fairly quickly and are the best way to visit the nearby attractions of Miyajima and Iwakuni. Long-distance buses connect Hiroshima with all the major cities. Buses depart from the Hiroshima Bus Centre, located on the 3rd floor between the Sogo and AQ'A shopping centres by the Kamiya-cho Nishi tram stop.

There are regular connections to Matsuyama in Shikoku across the Inland Sea. The Hiroshima-to-Matsuyama ferry (¥3500, 2¾ hours, 10 daily) and hydrofoil (¥6900, one hour and 15 minutes, 14 daily) services leave from Ujina (宇品). The port (広島港) is the last stop on tram lines 1, 3 and 5 from the station.

Getting Around

Hiroshima has an extensive tram service that will get you almost anywhere you want to go for a flat fare of ¥150. There's even a tram that runs all the way to Miyajima port (¥270). If you have to change trams to get to your destination, you should ask for a *norikae-ken* (transfer ticket). Pay when you get off. A day pass covering unlimited travel on the tram network is ¥600.

Two bicycles are available for rent at **Nippon Rent-a-car** (☎ 264-0919; 3-14 Kojin-machi; 24hr), four blocks southeast of the station. Bike rental costs ¥263 per two hours, ¥735 per day.

MIYAJIMA 宮島

☎ 0829 / pop 1970

The small island of Miyajima is a Unesco World Heritage Site and one of Japan's biggest tourist attractions. The vermilion torii (shrine gate) of the Itsukushima-jinja is one of the most photographed sites in the country, and has traditionally been ranked as one of the three best views in Japan. The shrine itself seems to float on the waves at high tide. Besides the main shrine, there are some good hikes on Mt Misen, and large numbers of cheeky deer that wander the streets hitting up tourists for something (anything!) to eat.

Information

There's a **tourist information counter** (☎ 44-2011; 1162-18 Miyajima-chō; 9am-5pm) in the ferry terminal. Turn right as you emerge and follow the waterfront for 10 minutes to get to the shrine. The shopping street, packed with souvenir outlets and restaurants, as well as the world's largest *shakushi* (rice scoop), is a block back from the waterfront.

Sights

ITSUKUSHIMA-JINJA 厳島神社

Going back as far as the late 6th century, **Itsukushima-jinja** (☎ 44-2020; 1-1 Miyajima-chō; admission ¥300; 6.30am-6pm Mar–mid-Oct, to 5.30pm mid-Oct–Nov, Jan & Feb, to 5pm Dec) gives the island its real name. The shrine's present form dates from 1168, when it was rebuilt under the patronage of Taira no Kiyomori, head of the doomed Heike clan. Its pier-like construction is a result of the island's holy status: commoners were not allowed to set foot on the island and had to approach the shrine by boat through the **floating torii** out in the bay. Much of the time, however, the shrine and torii are surrounded by mud: to get the classic view of the torii that adorns the brochures, you'll need to come at high tide.

On one side of the floating shrine is a **floating nō stage** built by local lord Asano Tsunanaga in 1680 and still used for performances every year from 16 to 18 April. The famous torii, dating in its present form from 1875, is floodlit at night.

The **Treasure House** (admission ¥300; 8am-5pm), just outside the main shrine complex, has an unimpressive collection of relics and swords that is only for the incurably curious.

TEMPLES & HISTORICAL BUILDINGS

Dominating the hill immediately to the north of Itsukushima-jinja is **Senjō-kaku** (☎ 44-2020; 1-1 Miyajima-chō; admission ¥100; 8.30am-4.30pm), a huge pavilion built in 1587 by Toyotomi Hideyoshi. The atmospheric hall is constructed with massive pillars and beams, and the ceiling is hung with paintings. It looks out onto a colourful five-storey pagoda (五重塔) dating from 1407. Senjō-kaku was left unfinished when Toyotomi died in 1598.

Miyajima has several important Buddhist temples, including the 1201 **Daigan-ji** (☎ 44-0179; 3 Miyajima-chō; 9am-5pm), just south of the shrine, which dates back to the Heian period and is dedicated to Benzaiten, the Japanese name for Saraswati (the Hindu goddess of good fortune). The seated image of Yakushi Nyorai here is said to have been carved by Kōbō Daishi. The impressive **Daishō-in** (☎ 44-0111; 210 Miyajima-chō; 8am-5pm), just south of town at the foot of Mt Misen, is a worthwhile stopping point on the way up or down the mountain p470. This Shingon temple is crowded with interesting things to look at: from Buddhist images and prayer wheels to sharp-beaked *tengu* (bird-like demons) and a cave containing images from each of the 88 Shikoku pilgrimage temples. An informative English pamphlet is available. South of Itsukushima-jinja is the picturesque pagoda **Tahō-tō**.

MIYAJIMA HISTORY & FOLKLORE MUSEUM 歴史民俗資料館

Set in a fine garden, this **museum** (☎ 44-2019; 57 Miyajima-chō; admission ¥210; 8.30am-5pm, closed Mon) combines a 19th-century merchant house with exhibitions on trade in the Edo period, as well as displays connected with the island.

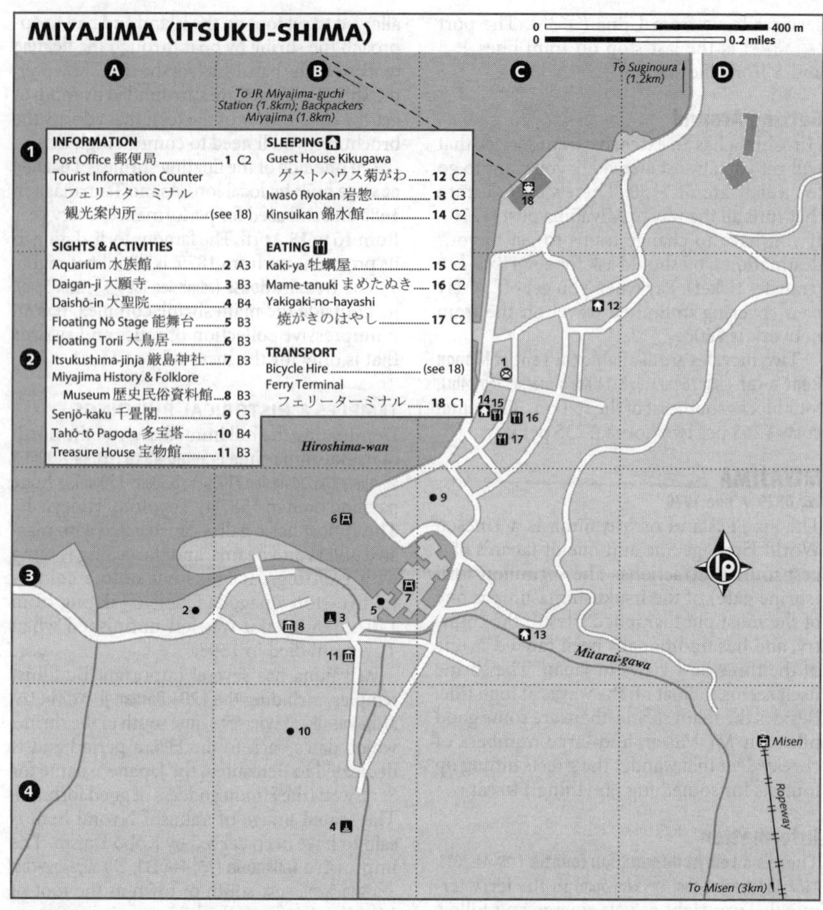

MISEN 弥山

The ascent of Misen (530m) is the island's finest walk. You can avoid most of the uphill part of the climb by taking the two-stage **ropeway** (one way/return ¥1000/1800), which leaves you with a 20-minute walk to the top. There are monkeys and deer around the cable-car station, and some fantastic views – on clear days you can see across to the mountain ranges of Shikoku. Close to the summit is a temple where Kōbō Daishi meditated for 100 days following his return from China in the 9th century. Next to the main temple hall close to the summit is a flame that's been burning continually since Kōbō Daishi lit it 1200 years ago. From the temple, a path leads down the hillside to Daishō-in and Itsukushima-jinja. The descent takes a little over an hour. A four-hour hike of Misen is detailed in Lonely Planet's *Hiking in Japan*.

OTHER SIGHTS

The Miyajima **aquarium** (www.sunameri.jp/eng/index.html) is closed for renovations, and is due to reopen in August 2011.

Festivals & Events

Festivals include **fire-walking rites** by the island's monks on 15 April and 15 November, and the **Kangensai Boat Festival** in summer (held on the 17th of the sixth lunar-calendar month).

Sleeping & Eating

It's well worth staying on the island, if you can afford it – you'll be able to enjoy the evening quiet after the day-trippers have left. There are plenty of restaurants on Miyajima, though most of them shut down after the crowds go home.

Backpackers Miyajima (☎ 56-3650; www.backpackers-miyajima.com/index_e.html; dm ¥2500-3000; ⊠ 💻) Opened in November 2008, this friendly budget hostel is a short walk from the mainland ferry terminal in Miyajima-guchi. Internet costs ¥100 for 20 minutes.

Guest House Kikugawa (☎ 44-0039; fax 44-2773; www.kikugawa.ne.jp; 796 Miyajima-chō; s/tw from ¥6615/11,550; Ⓟ) This charming inn is comfortable and tastefully decorated, with attractive wooden interiors. There are six Western-style rooms and two slightly larger Japanese-style rooms. Meals are available. Look for the white building with the red *noren*. It's across the road from the small Zonkō-ji (存光寺) temple.

Kinsuikan (☎ 44-2131; www.kinsuikan.jp; 1133 Miyajima-chō; s/d from ¥8500/12,000; Ⓟ) A large ryokan-style hotel between the ferry terminal and the main shrine, with a wide range of accommodation options available (including a few Western-style rooms), local seafood, onsen baths and good views out across the Inland Sea.

our pick Iwasō Ryokan (☎ 44-2233; www.iwaso.com; Momijidani Miyajima-chō; per person with 2 meals from ¥19,950; Ⓟ) The Iwasō, open since 1854, offers the grand ryokan experience in exquisite gardens, a few minutes' walk from the throng. It's worth the splurge, especially in autumn when Momiji-dani (Maple Valley) explodes with colour. There's a relaxing onsen in the main building.

Yakigaki-no-hayashi (☎ 44-0335; 505-1 Miyajima-chō; dishes ¥700-1400; 🕑 10.30am-4.30pm) The oysters in the tank and on the barbecue outside are what everyone is eating here. A plate of *namagaki* (raw oysters) is ¥1300. There's a plastic food display outside, and an English menu.

Kaki-ya (☎ 44-2747; 539 Miyajima-chō; plate of 4 oysters ¥1000; 🕑 11am-6pm) A sophisticated oyster bar in a converted building on the main street. It serves delicious local oysters freshly grilled on the barbecue by the entrance, along with beers and wines by the glass. There is an English menu.

Mame-tanuki (☎ 44-2131; 1113 Miyajima-chō; 🕑 lunch & 5-11pm) This friendly *izakaya* on the main shopping street is one of the few places that stays open late. There are several set meals to choose from, including *anago meshi* (steamed conger eel with rice; ¥1575). There is an English menu.

Getting There & Away

The mainland ferry terminal for Miyajima is a short walk from Miyajima-guchi station on the JR San-yō line, halfway between Hiroshima and Iwakuni. Miyajima trams from Hiroshima terminate at the Hiroden-Miyajima-guchi stop by the ferry terminal. Trams from Hiroshima (¥270, 70 minutes) take longer than *futsū* (slowest trains that stop at all stations; ¥400, 25 minutes), but can be boarded in central Hiroshima.

Regular ferries shuttle across from Miyajima-guchi (¥170, 10 minutes). JR passholders should use the one operated by JR. High-speed ferries (¥1800, 30 minutes, six to eight daily) operate direct to Miyajima from Hiroshima's Ujina port. Another ferry (¥1900, 45 minutes, 12 daily) runs between Miyajima and Peace Memorial Park in Hiroshima.

Getting Around

Bicycles can be hired from the JR office in the ferry terminal. Alternatively, everywhere on the island is within easy walking distance.

INLAND SEA
瀬戸内海

The beautiful Inland Sea (Seto-nai-kai) offers travellers a chance to experience a part of Japan that is much slower-paced than the metropolitan centres. The most interesting area of the Inland Sea is the island-crowded stretch from Shōdo-shima (accessible from Okayama and Takamatsu) and Miyajima, near Hiroshima. There are said to be more than 3000 islands and islets in all, most of them uninhabited.

The Inland Sea can be explored by ferry from the main islands. There are now three bridge systems linking Honshū with Shikoku; the westernmost, known as Seto-Uchi Shimanami Kaidō, comprises 10 bridges and crosses nine islands.

Information

Brochures, maps and general tourist information are readily available, but Donald Richie's classic *The Inland Sea*, originally published in 1971, makes an excellent introduction to the region.

The following Inland Sea section starts with its second-largest island, Shōdo-shima, and moves west. Occasionally, an island closely associated with a particular place on the mainland appears in that place's chapter. Miyajima, for example, is included in the Hiroshima section, and Megi-jima appears in the Takamatsu section of the Shikoku chapter.

Getting Around

Besides the regular ferry services between Honshū, Shikoku and the various islands, **SKK** (Seto Naikai-kisen; 瀬戸内海汽船; ☎ 082-253-1212; ⏲ ticket office 7am-9pm) offers day cruises on the Inland Sea from Hiroshima. The trips take around 2½ hours and include a brief stop to admire the famous shrine gates at Miyajima. Cruises with lunch/dinner cost from ¥4800/7500.

The Japan Travel Bureau (JTB) and other tour operators also run seasonal cruises in the Inland Sea.

SHŌDO-SHIMA 小豆島

☎ 0879 / pop 33,000

Famed for its olive groves and as the setting of the classic film *Nijūshi-no-hitomi* (*Twenty-Four Eyes*; it tells the story of a village school teacher and her young charges), Shōdo-shima is a mountainous island with a number of interesting places to visit, and it makes an enjoyable escape from big-city Japan. It's a popular destination for Japanese tourists during the summer and when the autumn leaves are at their peak in October and November.

Orientation & Information

Tonoshō, at the western end of the island, is the biggest town and the usual point of arrival from Takamatsu or Okayama. Tonoshō has a small **tourist information booth** (☎ 62-5300; ⏲ 8.30am-5.15pm) inside the ferry terminal, and another among the souvenir stalls a couple of minutes' walk inland.

Sights & Activities

AROUND THE COAST

Heading anticlockwise from Tonoshō along the south coast, the first point of interest is the **Shōdo-shima Olive Park** (小豆島オリーブ公園; ☎ 82-2200; Nishimura-misaki 1941-1; admission free; ⏲ 8.30am-5pm), where the island's olive-growing activities are celebrated with several white-washed buildings, some fake Grecian ruins and a souvenir stand selling olive-flavoured chocolates and olive-themed Hello Kitty key rings. Past the Greek windmill and the **Olive Museum** (オリーブ記念館; admission free; ⏲ 8.30am-5pm) is the **Sun Olive Onsen** (サン・オリーブ温泉; ☎ 82-2200; admission ¥700; ⏲ noon-9pm, closed Wed), where you can enjoy views of the Japanese Aegean from a variety of herbal baths.

Shōdo-shima's first olives were planted in 1908, but the island was famous for its soy beans long before that, and several old soy-sauce companies are still in business here (as frequent whiffs around the island will remind you). The **Marukin Soy Sauce Historical Museum** (マルキン醤油記念館; ☎ 82-0047; Nouma; admission ¥210; ⏲ 9am-4pm) is in an old building on the main road between Kusakabe and Sakate. There are good English explanations to guide you through the brewing process, and souvenirs include soy sauce–flavoured ice cream.

Just north of Sakate is the turn-off to the picturesque fishing village of **Tanoura** (田ノ浦), site of the village school featured in the film *Twenty-Four Eyes*. The film was based on a novel by local writer Tsuboi Sakae and was a huge hit in postwar Japan. The set used in the 1980s remake of the original B&W film is now open as the **Twenty-Four Eyes Movie Village** (二十四の瞳映画村; ☎ 82-2455; Tanoura; admission ¥630, combined ticket with the old school ¥750; ⏲ 9am-5pm), where bus loads of tourists gather to wallow in nostalgia and stock up on souvenirs before sitting down to watch old clips from the film. Also worth seeing is the perfectly preserved 1902 **school building** (岬の分教場; admission ¥200, combined ticket with the movie village ¥750; ⏲ 9am-5pm), a short walk from the Movie Village on the road back to Sakate.

CENTRAL MOUNTAINS

The **Kanka-kei cable car** (寒霞渓ロープウエイ; one way/return ¥700/1250; ⏲ 8.30am-5pm, 8am-5pm late Oct-late Nov, 8.30am-4.30pm late Dec-late Mar) is the main attraction in the central mountains, making a spectacular trip up through the Kanka-kei gorge. There are some breathtaking views out across the Inland Sea from the top. An alternative for keen walkers is to climb up the Omote 12 Views (表十二景) track from the bottom of the ropeway, and back down via the Ura Eight Views (裏八景) trail. From the cable car's arrival point at the top of the gorge, you can hike to the eastern peak of Hoshigajō-yama (星ヶ城東峰; 817m) in an hour. There are seven buses a day from Kusakabe port to the Kōuntei (紅雲亭) cable-car station (¥350, last from Kusakabe at 3.40pm, last return at 3.55pm), and three

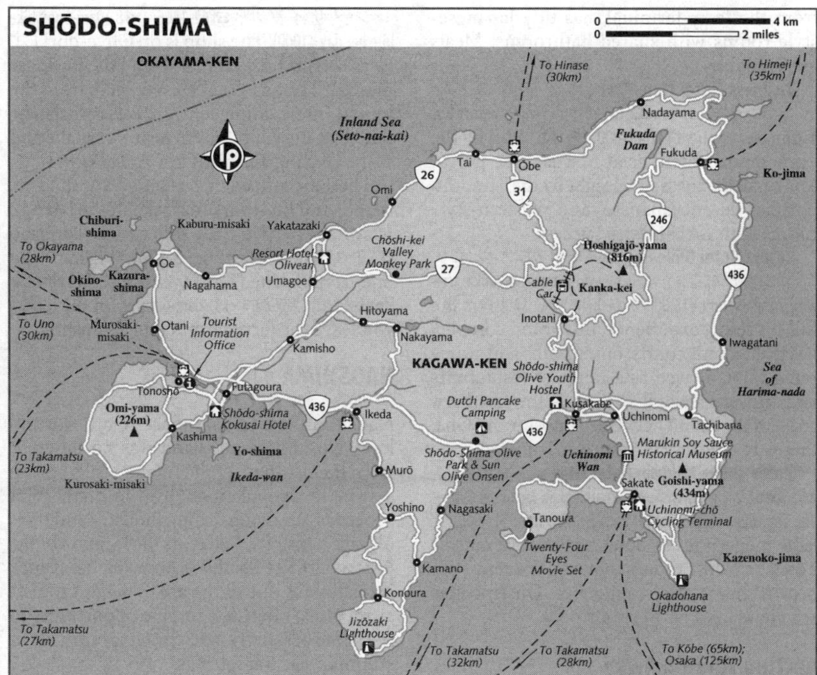

a day between Kanka-kei and Tonoshō port (¥840, last from Tonoshō at 1.30pm, last from Kanka-kei at 4.20pm). Neither of these bus services runs out of season.

The bus from Tonoshō to Kanka-kei stops for 30 minutes at the **Chōshi-kei Valley Monkey Park** (銚子渓お猿の国; ☎ 62-0768; Nouma; admission ¥370; ⏰ 8.10am-4.50pm), where large troupes of monkeys come to squabble for food – they're used to people and will come right up to you.

Festivals & Events

Shōdo-shima was famous during the Edo period for its tradition of **rural kabuki drama** (農村歌舞伎). Two 17th-century thatched theatres survive in the mountain villages east of Tonoshō, and performances are held on 3 May at the Rikyū Hachiman Shrine in Hitoyama (肥土山) and on the second Sunday in October at the Kasuga Shrine in Nakayama (中山).

Sleeping & Eating

Tonoshō has a variety of hotels and simple places to eat, particularly along the road running straight back from the waterfront. For the youth hostel and Dutch Pancake Camping, the nearest port is at Kusakabe.

Dutch Pancake Camping (ダッチ・パンケーキ・キャンピング; ☎ 82-4616; ww8.tiki.ne.jp/~dpc-/; 1765-7 Nishimura Otsu, Shōdoshima-chō; tents per person ¥1800; Ⓟ) Run by a Dutchman and his Japanese wife, this friendly spot is in an idyllic setting on a small road behind the Sun Olive onsen, with great views out to sea. Full price details are on the website. The Dutch Café Cupid and Cotton, in a cosy windmill just behind the campsite, serves tasty pancakes and coffee. The cafe is open from 11am to 5pm but is closed on Wednesday. Lunches are around ¥850, and there's an English menu.

Shōdo-shima Olive Youth Hostel (小豆島オリーブユースホステル; ☎ 82-6161; www4.ocn.ne.jp/~olive-yh/, in Japanese; 1072 Nishimura, Uchinomi-chō; dm members/nonmembers ¥3255/3885; Ⓟ ⊠) On the south coast, this pleasant hostel has bunk-bed dorms and Japanese- and Western-style rooms. Meals and bike rental are available.

Minshuku Maruse (民宿マルセ; ☎ 62-2385; http://new-port.biz/maruse/1.htm, in Japanese; Tonoshō-kō; s/tw ¥3650/7000; Ⓟ) This neatly kept place next to Tonoshō's post office, a short walk from the ferry terminal, has tidy Japanese-style rooms with shared bathrooms. Meals are available.

Business Hotel New Port (ビジネスホテル・ニューポート; ☎ 62-6310; www.new-port.biz, in Japanese; s/tw from ¥4200/7800; P 💻) Run by the same management as at Maruse (see p473), this small business hotel right by the Tonoshō port has decent Japanese- and Western-style rooms with LAN internet access.

Resort Hotel Olivean (リゾートホテルオリビアン; ☎ 65-2311; www.olivean.com; Yū-higaoka; s/tw with 2 meals from ¥13,600/23,000; P ⊠ 💻) For the full-on resort experience, this grand complex has it all: tennis courts, onsen baths and swimming pool, as well as a range of restaurants and sunset views. It's towards the northern coast of the island between Tonoshō and Ōbe; there are courtesy buses from Tonoshō.

Shōdo-shima Kokusai Hotel (国際ホテル小豆島; ☎ 62-2111; www.shodoshima-kh.jp, in Japanese; Gimpaura, Tonoshō-chō; per person with 2 meals from ¥14,000) A large modern resort hotel on the coast outside Tonoshō. Most rooms combine Western-style beds with a tatami seating area. Onsen baths, sea views, and an open-air pool.

Getting There & Away

High-speed (¥1140, 30 minutes, 17 daily) and regular (¥670, one hour, 15 daily) ferries run regularly between Takamatsu and Tonoshō (土庄). There are also frequent connections from Takamatsu to Kusakabe (草壁) and Ikeda (池田).

It is also possible to get to Tonoshō from Okayama (¥1000, one hour and 10 minutes, 13 daily) and Uno (宇野) on Honshū (¥1200, 1½ hours, seven daily). There are trains from Uno to Okayama.

There are several boats a day from Himeji to Fukuda (福田) port, and infrequent sailings between Kōbe/Ōsaka and Sakate (坂手) with **Kansai Kisen** (☎ 06-6572-5181; www.kanki.co.jp) during the summer.

Getting Around

If you have plenty of time and don't mind all the hills, cycling can be an enjoyable way to get around the island. **Yoshida Rent-a-cycle** (吉田レンタサイクル; ☎ 62-0423; gearless shopping bikes per day ¥1000; 🕑 8.30am-5pm) is inside the tall Asahiya Hotel (旭屋), opposite the post office, a short walk from the Tonoshō ferry terminal. For bikes with gears (and motorbikes), it's worth making the trek to **Ishii Rent-a-Cycle** (石井レンタサイクル; ☎ 62-1866; 🕑 8.30am-5pm; bike hire per day ¥1000). The shop is on Olive-dōri (オリーブ通り), and is marked on the Japanese maps of Tonoshō that are available from the tourist information centre. Bikes can also be rented at the youth hostel near Kusakabe and at the Cycling Terminal in Sakate Port.

There are infrequent bus services around the island, and bus tours that take in the island's major sites – two daily tours from Tonoshō (¥3280/3980, departing 12.40pm/9.40am) and one from Sakate (¥2500, 1.20pm). **Nippon Car Rental** (☎ 62-0680; 🕑 8.30am-6pm) is on the left as you leave the ferry terminal in Tonoshō.

NAOSHIMA 直島

☎ 087 / pop 3500

Naoshima is a special place. Until not too long ago, this small island was no different from many others in the Inland Sea: home to a dwindling population subsisting on the joint proceeds of a dying fishing industry and their old-age pensions. Today, as the location of the **Benesse Art Site Naoshima** (www.naoshima-is.co.jp), Naoshima is one of the area's biggest tourist attractions, offering a unique opportunity to see some of Japan's best contemporary art in stunning natural settings.

The project started in the early '90s, when the Benesse Corporation chose Naoshima as the setting for its growing collection of modern art. Award-winning architect Andō Tadao was hired to design the company's **Benesse House** (ベネッセハウス; ☎ 892-2030; Gotanji Nao-shima-chō; admission ¥1000; 🕑 8am-9pm), a stunning museum and hotel on the south coast of the island. There are works here by Andy Warhol, David Hockney and Jasper Johns, among many others.

A short walk away is the **Chichū Art Museum** (地中美術館; ☎ 892-3755; www.chichu.jp; 3449-1 Naoshima; admission ¥2000; 🕑 10am-6pm Mar-Sep, to 5pm Oct-Feb, closed Mon), another Andō creation completed in 2004. Largely underground, yet lit entirely by natural light, the museum provides a remarkable setting for several Monet 'Water Lilies', some monumental sculptures by Walter de Maria and three unforgettable installations by James Turrell.

At the **Art House Project** (家プロジェクト; ☎ 892-2030; combined ticket ¥1000; 🕑 10am-4.30pm, closed Mon), in the old fishing village of Honmura (本村), half-a-dozen traditional buildings have been restored and turned over to contemporary artists to use as the setting for some impressive installations. In a converted fisherman's house called **Kadoya**, Miyajima Tatsuo's red, yellow and green LEDs float serenely on a pond where you would expect to find tatami mats. Another of James Turrell's experiments with light occupies **Minami-dera**, where the viewer sits in total darkness for up to 10 minutes before the eyes grow used to the dim light and the art slowly starts to reveal itself. Elsewhere, Sugimoto Hiroshi's glass staircase and underground 'Stone Chamber' make striking use of the traditional **Go'o Shrine**.

In addition to the main sites, numerous works of outdoor art are situated around the coast, including the **pumpkin sculpture** by Kusama Yayoi that has become a symbol of the island.

With an early ferry from Takamatsu or Uno it's possible to cover the sights as a day trip, but there is a growing range of accommodation options available for those who want to soak up the special atmosphere of the island overnight. Close to the ferry port in Miyanoura, bare-bones dormitory accommodation is available at **Dormitory in Kūron** (ドミトリーin九龍; ☎ 892-2424; www.kawloon.gozaru.jp/index.html; dm ¥2800). **Minshuku Oyaji-no-umi** (民宿おやじの海; ☎ 892-2269; http://mypage.odn.ne.jp/home/stone_ocean/; per person with breakfast ¥4200) is in an old house close to the Art House Project in Honmura. **Tsutsuji-sō** (つつじ荘; ☎ 892-2838; fax 892-3871; per person from ¥3675; P) is an encampment of Mongolian-style pao tents by the beach, not far from the two museums. Meals are available.

For upmarket accommodation, there's **Benesse House** (☎ 892-2030; www.naoshima-is.co.jp/english/benessehouse/index.html; r from ¥30,000; P ☒) itself, where guests can view the artworks at leisure, 24 hours a day.

In Honmura, close to the Art House Project buildings, **Café Maruya** (まるや; ☎ 892-2714; lunch special ¥800; 11am-6pm, closed Mon) is a civilised spot for coffee or *higawari ranchi* (daily lunch special).

The **tourist information desk** (☎ 892-2299; www.naoshima.net/en/accommodations/index.html; 9am-7pm) in the Marine Station by the ferry port has a full list of accommodation options (also outlined on the website) and a useful bilingual map of the island.

Minibuses link the sights (¥100), and **bike hire** (per day ¥500; 9am- 7pm) is available at the ferry port. The main areas of interest are easily covered on foot.

There are six to seven ferries a day to the main port of Miyaura from Takamatsu (高松; ¥510, one hour, 8.10am to 8.05pm) in Shikoku and 15 from Uno (宇野) in Okayama-ken (¥280, 20 minutes, 6.10am to 8.25pm). Uno is at the end of the JR Uno line, about an hour from Okayama (¥570). You may have to change trains at Chaya-machi (茶屋町). Travelling via Naoshima is a good way to get from Honshū to Shikoku, or vice versa.

KASAOKA ISLANDS 笠岡諸島

Located between Kurashiki and Fukuyama, the port of Kasaoka is the jumping-off point for a collection of six small islands connected to the mainland only by boat. In particular, the islands of Shiraishi-jima and Manabe-shima are ideal places in which to enjoy a taste of the slower pace of life as it used to be lived all over the Inland Sea.

By train, Kasaoka is 40 minutes west of Okayama, 25 minutes west of Kurashiki or 15 minutes east of Fukuyama on the JR San-yō line. From the station, it's a five-minute stroll down to the port and the ferry terminal. There are eight boats a day with the **Sanyō Kisen** (三洋汽船; ☎ 0865-62-2866) ferry company to Shiraishi-jima and Manabe-shima.

Shiraishi-jima 白石島

☎ 0865 / pop 750

Sleepy Shiraishi-jima is popular in the summer for its beaches, and is an excellent year-round place on which to slow down. There are some good walking paths around the island. Go-everywhere Buddhist saint Kōbō Daishi stopped off here on his way back from China in 806; the temple associated with him, **Kairyū-ji** (開龍寺), incorporates a trail of small shrines leading to a huge boulder on top of the hill, where there are some breathtaking views out to sea.

Visitors can stay at **International Villa** (per person ¥3500), where communal accommodation is available on a hillside overlooking the beach. For reservations, contact **International Villa Group** (☎ 086-256-2535; fax 086-256-2576; www.harenet.ne.jp/villa) in Okayama.

Alternatively, there are several *minshuku* (family-run budget accommodations) on the beach. **San-chan** (民宿さんちゃん; ☎ 68-3169; per person with/without 2 meals ¥6000/2500) is open year round, and has no-frills Japanese-style rooms with shared bathrooms. Simple meals are also available in San-chan's mellow waterfront **restaurant** (11am-10pm); there's an English menu.

Resident expat Amy Chavez runs the Mooo! Bar on the beach (open during the summer only) and can arrange sailing trips to other islands in the Inland Sea (starting from ¥2500 per person for two hours).

During the Buddhist festival of O-bon (13 to 16 August), traditional **Shiraishi-odori** dances take place on the beach.

There are eight boats a day from Kasaoka with Sanyō Kisen (¥650 to ¥1130, 20 to 35 minutes, 7.25am to 5.50pm), plus four car ferries run by the Shiraishi Ferry company, a 15-minute walk left along the coast from the Sanyō Ferry terminal.

Manabe-shima

☎ 0865 / pop 300

This tranquil, slow-paced island in the middle of the Inland Sea is little more than an hour by boat from the mainland, but in terms of atmosphere it's a thousand miles – and a hundred years – from the bustle of the big cities. The island's one small town is home to more cats than people, and is an atmospheric maze of old wooden houses, a solitary village shop that has been in business since the Meiji period (and looks it) and an old-fashioned school with just 14 pupils. As with everywhere in this part of Japan, Kōbō Daishi got here first – the great man spent time at the **Enpukuji** (円福寺) temple.

The beachside **Santora Youth Hostel** (三虎ユースホステル; ☎ 68-3515; fax 68-3516; 2224 Manabe-shima; per person with 2 meals ¥5770) offers comfortable accommodation in private tatami rooms. The ryokan on the same premises offers more-upmarket rooms with meals from ¥10,500 per person. Reservations are required at **Ryōka** (漁火; ☎ 68-3519; courses from ¥5000; 🕑 11am-6pm), a restaurant on the waterfront (where the ferry arrives) – the fisherman-turned-restaurateur owner serves up some dauntingly fresh seafood. There's no menu; you get whatever the day's catch has turned up. If you're not comfortable with the idea of food that wriggles in your chopsticks, **Nagisa** (渚; ☎ 68-3771), uphill from the school, serves good *okonomiyaki* (¥600) and has views out to sea.

There are eight boats a day from Kasaoka (¥760 to ¥1360, 44 minutes to one hour and 10 minutes, 7.25am to 5.50pm). On Tuesday, Thursday and Saturday there's a ferry to Sanagi-jima (¥250, 15 minutes, 3.05pm), where transfer is available to Tadotsu on Shikoku (¥780, 50 minutes).

SETO-UCHI SHIMANAMI KAIDŌ 瀬戸内しまなみ海道

Opened in May 1999, the Shimanami Kaidō is a chain of bridges linking Onomichi in Hiroshima-ken with Imabari in Ehime-ken on Shikoku via six islands, three of which are featured in this section. Separate bicycle lanes are provided on all the bridges, making it possible to cover the 70km distance between Honshū and Shikoku entirely on bike, travelling through some impressive scenery. Bikes (which can be dropped off anywhere along the route) can be rented near the ferry terminal in Onomichi, in Imabari, and at least one location on each of the islands. Rates are ¥500 per day plus a ¥1000 deposit, which you get back if you return the bike to the same place where you rented it, but not if you drop the bike off at another of the rental places along the route.

Tourist information offices on the islands have maps and information. If you don't feel like biking the whole way, a good option is to take a ferry to Setoda on Ikuchi-jima and bike from there to Ō---, where there are regular boats and buses to Imabari on Shikoku.

INNO-SHIMA 因島

☎ 0845 / pop 27,000

Famed for its flowers and fruit, Inno-shima is connected by bridge to Mukai-shima (facing Ono-michi) to the east and Ikuchi-jima to the west. During the Middle Ages, the island was the base of one of the three Murakami pirate clans, who, between them, controlled shipping throughout the Inland Sea until the beginning of the Edo period. The island's past is commemorated at the **pirate castle** (因島水軍城; ☎ 24-0936; 3228-2 Nakanosho; admission ¥310; 🕑 9.30am-5pm, closed Thu), a modern replica built in the 1980s. Atop Shirataki-yama (白滝山) is a collection of sculptures of the 500 Rakan disciples of the Buddha. On the last Saturday and Sunday in August, the lively **Suigun Furusato Matsuri** features bonfires, drumming and boat races that commemorate the island's pirate past.

IKUCHI-JIMA 生口島

☎ 0845 / pop 10,900

Ikuchi-jima is known for its citrus groves and beaches, including Sunset Beach on the west coast. It is also home to Kōsan-ji, a colourful display of Buddhist kitsch put up by a businessman-turned-priest in memory of his mother. Bike hire and tourist information are available in front of **Bel Canto Hall** (☎ 27-0051;

(9am-5pm) – to get here, head right out of the ferry terminal, turn left down the main shopping street and then left again at the intersection in front of Kōsan-ji.

Sights

The main attraction in sleepy Setoda, the island's main town, is the remarkable temple complex of **Kōsan-ji** (耕三寺; ☎ 27-0800; 553-2 Setoda; admission ¥1200; 9am-5pm). Shortly after the death of his beloved mother in 1934, local steel-tube magnate and arms manufacturer Kanemoto Kōzō decided to become a Buddhist priest. He grew his hair long, bought himself the rights to a priesthood and the name of a temple in Niigata, and spent much of the next 30 years sinking his fortune into a series of garishly coloured temple buildings, among them several colourful replicas of Japan's most important ancient temples. The complex is a chaos of over-the-top Buddhist kitsch, consisting of some 2000 exhibits.

Admission to Kōsan-ji includes entrance to the **Art Museum**, **1000 Buddhas Cave**, **Treasure House** and **Choseikaku Villa**, where Kōzō's mother lived in an elegant mixture of Japanese and European-inspired splendour. The extraordinary 1000 Buddhas Cave includes a series of graphically illustrated hells. Across the road, the Treasure House has a collection of Buddhist images from the Heian and Kamakura periods.

To get to the temple, turn right as you leave the boat landing, then turn left up the shop-lined main street. Halfway up the same street is a sign in Japanese pointing you left towards the hillside **Chōon-zan Kōen** (潮音山公園) and its several temples and shrines. Further up the hill is the early-15th-century **Kōjō-ji** (向上寺), with a three-storey pagoda designated as a national treasure, and some fine views over the island. Just past Kōsan-ji is the **Hirayama Ikuo Museum** (平山郁夫美術館; ☎ 27-3800; admission ¥700; 9am-5pm), dedicated to the life and work of the famous artist, who grew up in Setoda.

Sleeping & Eating

Setoda Shimanami Guest House (瀬戸田しまなみゲストハウス; ☎ 27-3137; www.d1.dion.ne.jp/~sunami/youth/, in Japanese; 58-1 Tarumi Setoda-chō; per person ¥3000; P) Right on Sunset Beach, this friendly hostel is popular with cyclists. Accommodation is in individual tatami rooms. The hostel has its own onsen, and meals are available.

Ryokan Tsutsui (旅館つつ井; ☎ 27-2221; fax 27-2137; www.tsutsui.yad.jp, in Japanese; 216 Setoda Setoda-chō; per person with 2 meals from ¥10,500; P) This recently renovated ryokan-style hotel, right in front of the ferry terminal, is the grandest of the relatively limited options in Setoda itself. The Japanese-style rooms are spacious, and the gorgeous new wooden baths offer great views.

Keima (桂馬; ☎ 27-1989; Setoda 251; sushi from ¥1260; lunch & dinner, closed Thu) This simple sushi place in the main shopping street serves filling meals in a friendly atmosphere. It's close to the ferry terminal, and is one of the first buildings on the left as you walk down the main shopping street away from the sea. Set meals include *sashimi teishoku* for ¥1890 and *taikamameshi* (sea bream on rice) for ¥1680.

Getting There & Away

Ferries to Setoda run from Onomichi (¥800, 40 minutes, nine daily) and Mihara (¥800, 20 minutes, 18 daily) in Hiroshima-ken.

ŌMI-SHIMA 大三島

☎ 0897 / pop 7500

Across the border in Ehime-ken, this mountainous island is home to one of the oldest Shintō shrines in western Japan, **Ōyamazumi-jinja** (大山祇神社; ☎ 82-0032; 3327 Miyaura; admission Treasure Hall & Kaiji Museum ¥1000; 8.30am-5pm). The deity enshrined here is the brother of Amaterasu, the sun goddess, revered as the guardian deity of the mountains and seas. The present structure was built in 1378, but the history of the shrine goes back much further. In the courtyard is a camphor tree that is 2600 years old, reputedly planted here during the visit of Jimmu, the legendary first emperor of Japan. As the home of the country's most important protective deity, Ōyamazumi-jinja was a popular place for warriors to come and pray before going into battle. The shrine's treasure hall contains the most important collection of ancient weapons found anywhere in Japan. Around 80% of the armour and helmets designated as National Treasures are held here. In an adjacent building known as **Kaiji Museum** (海事博物館) there's a boat that was used by Emperor Hirohito in his marine-science investigations, along with a natural-history exhibit.

Miyaura port (宮浦港) is a short walk from the shrine. There's a tourist information counter in the roadside **Shimanami no eki mishima** (しまなみの駅御島; ☎ 82-0002; 3260

Miyaura; 8.30am-5pm), just past the shrine, and another **tourist information counter** (☎ 87-3855; Tatara Shimanami Kōen; 9am-5pm) by the Tatara Bridge to Ikuchi-jima in the east of the island. Bicycle rental and help with local *minshuku* reservations are available at both.

Getting There & Away

Ferries link Miyaura port near the shrine with Imabari on Shikoku (¥990 to ¥1050, one to 1½ hours, five daily). There are also regular buses to Imabari (¥1140, one hour, 17 daily), where you can transfer to Matsuyama. There are no longer boats to Ōmi-shima from Honshū. The Shimanami Liner bus links Ōmi-shima with Honshū via Ikuchi-jima. Alternatively, take a ferry from Onomichi or Mihara to Setoda on Ikuchi-jima (see p476) and cross over to Ōmi-shima by rental bike.

YAMAGUCHI-KEN 山口県

Yamaguchi, at the western end of Honshū, straddles both the southern San-yō coast and the northern San-in coast. The Kintai-kyō bridge at Iwakuni is a southern highlight; in the west, Shimonoseki acts as the gateway to Kyūshū and Korea. The northern stretch includes the historically important town of Hagi and, in the central mountains, the vast cave at Akiyoshi-dai. The section of the coast from Tottori eastwards to Wakasa-wan is included in the Kansai chapter (see p388).

IWAKUNI 岩国

☎ 0827 / pop 151,000

The five-arched Kintai-kyō bridge is Iwakuni's major attraction, but this relaxed city has a number of points of interest in the nearby Kikkō-kōen area. The main sights can be seen in a couple of hours.

Orientation & Information

Iwakuni is made up of three widely separated areas. To the far west is the Shin-Iwakuni *shinkansen* station, half an hour by bus from the rest of town. The reconstructed castle and the museums are in the old samurai area, on the western bank of the river across the Kintaikyō bridge. The mainline JR station is a 20-minute bus ride east of the river in the modern part of town, along with a few hotels and restaurants.

Tourist information (shinkansen station ☎ 46-0655; 1055-1 Mishō; 10.30am-3.30pm, closed Wed; JR station ☎ 21-6050; 1-1-1 Marifu-machi; 10am-5pm, closed Mon) is available at the train stations.

Sights

KINTAI-KYŌ 錦帯橋

Iwakuni's chief claim to fame is the impressive five-arched **Kintai-kyō** (Brocade Sash Bridge), built in 1673 during the rule of feudal lord Kikkawa Hiroyoshi. It has been restored several times since then, most recently in 2003–4. In the feudal era only members of the ruling class were allowed to use the bridge, which linked the samurai quarters on the west bank of the Nishiki-gawa with the rest of the town. Today, anyone can cross over for a ¥300 fee. The ticket office at the entrance to the bridge also sells an all-inclusive *setto-ken* (combination ticket; ¥930) covering the bridge, the return cable-car trip and entry to the castle – a saving of ¥170 compared to buying all the tickets separately. The combination ticket also gets you a reduction at the Art Museum and the History Museum.

SAMURAI QUARTER

What remains of the old samurai quarter now forms pleasant Kikkō-Kōen (吉香公園) on the west bank of the river, across the bridge from the modern town. To the right of the big fountain is the **Mekata Family Residence** (旧目加田住宅; ☎ 41-0452; admission free; 9.30am-4.30pm, closed Mon), the former home of a middle-ranking samurai family from the mid-Edo period. Next door is the small **White Snake Viewing Facility** (白蛇観覧所; ☎ 43-4888; 2-6 Yokoyama; admission ¥100; 9am-5pm), where several of the bizarre albino snakes unique to Iwakuni are on display.

Beside the cable-car station is the **Iwakuni Art Museum** (岩国美術館; ☎ 41-0506; 2-10-27 Yokoyama; admission ¥800; 9am-5pm Mar-Nov, to 4pm Dec-Feb, closed Thu), which features a collection of armour and swords on the 2nd floor and screens and lacquerware on the 3rd. The **Kikkawa Historical Museum** (吉川資料館; ☎ 41-1010; 2-7-3 Yokoyama; admission ¥500; 9am-5pm, closed Wed) holds an extensive collection of artworks and historical pieces connected with the Kikkawa family that ruled Iwakuni during feudal times.

IWAKUNI-JŌ 岩国城

The original **Iwakuni-jō** (Iwakuni Castle; ☎ 41-0633; admission ¥260; 9am-4.45pm, closed mid–end Dec) was built by Hiroie, the first of the Kikkawa lords, between 1603 and 1608. Just seven years later, the Tokugawa shogunate passed a law limiting the number of castles *daimyō* were allowed to build, and the castle at Iwakuni was demolished. It was rebuilt not far from its original setting in 1960 as part of Japan's great castle-reconstruction movement. There is nothing much of interest inside, but there are good views from the hilltop setting.

You can get to the castle by **cable car** (one way/return ¥320/540; every 20min 9am-5pm) or on foot via the pleasant path beside the youth hostel.

OTHER SIGHTS

Ukai (cormorant fishing; ☎ 28-2877; Yokoyama 2-7-3; per person ¥3500; noon & 6.30pm Jun-Aug) takes place at Kintai-kyō daily in the summer, except when rain makes the water muddy, or on nights with a full moon.

Sleeping & Eating

Iwakuni Youth Hostel (岩国ユースホステル; ☎ 43-1092; fax 43-0123; www.geocities.jp/iwakuniyouth/englishtop.html; 1-10-46 Yokoyama; dm members/nonmembers ¥2835/3835) This large hostel is in a tranquil spot close to the sights on the west bank of the river. There's a path outside that makes for a nice walk up to the castle area. Meals are available.

Alpha-One Iwakuni (☎ 21-2244; fax 21-2245; www.alpha-1.co.jp/iwakuni/index.html, in Japanese; 4-8-2 Marifu-machi; s/tw ¥5100/8000; P) A large business hotel in the modern part of town, a short walk down the main road in front of the mainline JR station. LAN internet is available in all rooms, and computers are also available to rent. Free bike rental.

Hangetsu-an (半月庵; ☎ 41-0021; fax 43-0121; www.gambo-ad.com/iwakuni/hotel/hangetsuan/info.htm, in Japanese; 1-17-27 Iwakuni; per person with 2 meals from ¥9900; P) Built as a tea house in the early Meiji period, this traditional place has well-maintained tatami rooms, and local food. It's on the opposite bank from the castle and the samurai town, down the street continuing from the bridge; look for the traditional gateway on the left as you head away from the river.

Midori-no-sato (緑の里; ☎ 41-1370; 1-4-10 Iwakuni; meals ¥630-1050; 10am-6pm) Found behind a cake shop, this pleasant no-smoking restaurant has set menus including *iwakuni-zushi* (Iwakuni-style sushi; ¥1050), and *niku udon* (noodles with meat; ¥630). Crossing the Kintai-kyō bridge from the samurai part of town (with the musuems), carry straight on after you cross the bridge and it's on the right after a minute.

Campagne (カンパーニュ; ☎ 43-4477; 2-7-25 Kawanishi; meals ¥1000-3800; 11am-11pm) One of the few restaurants open late near the old part of town, this Italian place is about 1.5km from the Kintai-kyō bridge. From the bridge, head south and cross the Garyō-bashi (臥龍橋) to the mountain side of the river, then turn left and continue to the intersection before Kawanishi station. There's an English menu.

Getting There & Away

Iwakuni is only 40km from Hiroshima. Shin-Iwakuni station is on the *shinkansen* line, while JR Iwakuni Station is on the JR San-yō line. Kintai-kyō is about 5km from either. Buses shuttle between JR Iwakuni Station and Shin-Iwakuni (¥440, 25 minutes), stopping at the bridge on the way (¥220, 15 minutes).

YAMAGUCHI 山口

☎ 083 / pop 192,000

During the 100 years of civil war that bedevilled Japan until the country was reunited under the Tokugawa in the early 17th century, Yamaguchi prospered as an alternative capital to chaotic Kyoto. In 1550 Jesuit missionary Francis Xavier paused for two months in Yamaguchi on his way to the imperial capital, but quickly returned to the safety of this provincial centre when he was unable even to find the emperor in Kyoto! Today this surprisingly small and laid-back prefectural capital is a peaceful town with several interesting attractions.

Orientation & Information

Eki-dōri is the main shopping street, running straight up from the station and crossing the main shopping arcade before reaching Rte 9. The helpful **tourist information office** (☎ 933-0090; 2-1 Sodayu-chō; 9am-12.30pm & 1.30-6pm) is on the 2nd floor of the station. Yuda Onsen is one stop away on the local train line; there are regular buses.

Sights

ST FRANCIS XAVIER MEMORIAL CHURCH
ザビエル記念聖堂

Yamaguchi was a major centre of Christian missionary activity before the religion was outlawed in 1589. The **church** overlooks the town centre from a hilltop in Kameyama-kōen.

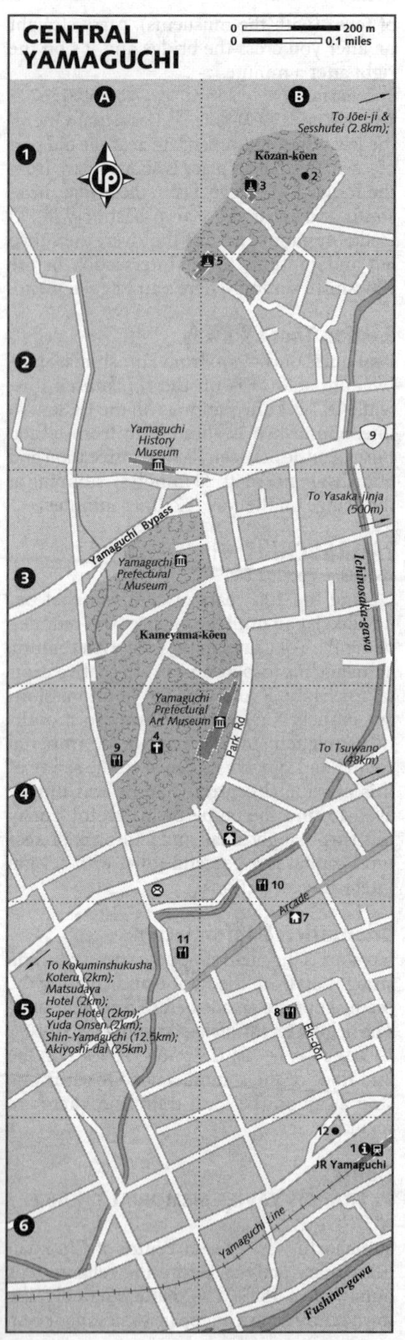

Built in 1952 in honour of St Francis Xavier, it burned down in 1991 and was rebuilt in 1998. The ground-floor **Christian museum** (☎ 920-1549; 4-1 Kameyama-chō; admission ¥300; 🕒 9am-5.30pm, closed Wed) contains exhibits on the life of Xavier and the early history of Christianity in Japan, most of it in Japanese only.

KŌZAN-KŌEN & RURIKŌ-JI
香山公園 瑠璃光寺

North of the town centre is **Kōzan-kōen**, where the impressive **five-storey pagoda** of **Rurikō-ji**, a National Treasure dating from 1404, is picturesquely situated beside a small lake. The park is also the site of the **Tōshun-ji** and the graves of the Mōri lords.

JŌEI-JI 常栄寺

About 4km northeast of the JR station, **Jōei-ji** is notable for its Zen garden, **Sesshutei** (☎ 922-2272; 2001 Miyano-shimo; admission ¥300; 🕒 8am-5pm), designed by the painter Sesshū. From the garden, a pleasant trail leads uphill through the woods to several more shrines.

YUDA ONSEN

Just west of the city is the 800-year-old **Yuda Onsen**, said to have been discovered when a white fox healed its injured legs in the waters here. Today the area is covered in a rash of hotels and bathing facilities aimed at Japanese tour groups. There's a **tourist information office** (☎ 901-0150; 2-1-23 Yuda Onsen; 🕒 9am-7pm) on the

INFORMATION
Tourist Information Office 観光案内所 1 B6

SIGHTS & ACTIVITIES
Five-Storey Pagoda 五重塔 2 B1
Rurikō-ji 瑠璃光寺 3 B1
St Francis Xavier Memorial Church
ザビエル記念聖堂 4 A4
Tōshun-ji 洞春寺 5 B2

SLEEPING
Sunroute Kokusai Hotel Yamaguchi
サンルート国際ホテル山口 6 B4
Taiyō-dō Ryokan 太陽堂旅館 7 B5

EATING
Frank フランク 8 B5
La Francesca ラフランチェスカ 9 A4
Renkon 蓮根 10 B4
Sabō Kō 茶房 幸 11 A5

TRANSPORT
Fukutake Rōho Bicycle Rental
福武老舗 貸自転車 12 B6

main road about 600m northwest of Yuda Onsen Station. Take the road straight ahead as you leave the station to reach the main road, where most of the hotels and baths are located. There are some impressive facilities, including massage baths, at **Onsen no Mori** (温泉の森; ☎ 920-1126; 4-7-17 Yuda Onsen; admission ¥1000; ⏲ 10am-midnight). You can also use the baths at the large **Hotel Kamefuku** (ホテルかめ福; ☎ 922-7000; 4-5 Yuda Onsen; admission ¥800; ⏲ 11.30am-10pm), the less-crowded **Kokuminshukusha Koteru** (国民宿舎小てる; ☎ 922-3240; 4-3-15 Yuda Onsen; admission ¥400; ⏲ 8am-noon & 3-10pm) and, for a taste of luxury, the traditional ryokan **Umenoya** (梅乃屋; ☎ 922-0051; 4-3-19 Yuda Onsen; admission ¥800; ⏲ 1pm-midnight). Buses run regularly to Yuda Onsen bus stop from Yamaguchi Station (¥190, 10 minutes). It's one stop on the local train line (¥140).

Festivals & Events

During **Gion Matsuri**, which takes place on 20, 24 and 27 July, the Sagi no mai (Egret Dance) is held at Yasaka-jinja. From 6 to 7 August, during **Tanabata Chōchin Matsuri**, 10,000 decorated lanterns illuminate the city.

Sleeping

Taiyō-dō Ryokan (☎ 922-0897; fax 922-1152; 2-3 Komeya-chō; per person from ¥3500) On the shopping arcade just off Eki-dōri and beside a bakery with a green peaked roof, the Taiyō-dō has comfortable rooms. The place is quite old, but it has character. It's seven minutes' walk from Yamaguchi Station.

Super Hotel (☎ 921-9000; fax 921-9002; www.superhotel.co.jp; 4-1-5 Yuda Onsen; s/d from ¥4980/6980; Ⓟ ⊠ 🖳) This business hotel in Yuda Onsen is nothing to write home about, but it has all the facilities you would expect. Guests have access to the Kame no Yu onsen for ¥200. LAN access in all rooms.

Sunroute Kokusai Hotel Yamaguchi (☎ 923-3610; fax 923-2379; www.sunroute.jp; 1-1 Nakagawara-chō; s/tw from ¥6825/12,180; Ⓟ ⊠ 🖳) Central to the sights in the middle of town and a 10-minute walk from the station, this hotel has cheerful staff and stylish rooms and an Indian restaurant on the ground floor.

Kokuminshukusha Koteru (国民宿舎小てる; ☎ 922-3240; fax 928-6177; 4-3-15 Yuda Onsen; per person with/without meals ¥7500/5400; Ⓟ) Two blocks north of the main street in Yuda Onsen, this is a good-value family-run place with Japanese-style rooms and cheery staff. The entrance to the baths is on the side of the building.

Matsudaya Hotel (ホテル松田屋; ☎ 922-0125; fax 925-6111; www.matsudayahotel.co.jp, in Japanese; 3-6-7 Yuda Onsen; s & tw with 2 meals from ¥21,150; Ⓟ) The rooms and gardens in this centuries-old ryokan are gorgeous, with service to match. The Matsudaya is about 800m north of Yuda Onsen Station along the main drag in Yuda Onsen.

Eating

Sabō Kō (☎ 928-5522; 1-2-39 Dōjōmonzen; dishes ¥300-900; ⏲ 11.30am-7pm closed Tue) A hushed and cosy atmosphere prevails in this crowded little coffee shop, where goldfish swim in bowls on the counter. The speciality on the Japanese-only menu is *wafū omuraisu* (Japanese-style rice omelette; ¥800). The building's outside is covered in wood, and there are plants in pots outside.

Frank (☎ 932-4836; 2nd fl, 2-4-19 Dōjōmonzen; meals ¥700-900; ⏲ noon-11pm, closed Tue) Overlooking the main shopping street, this spacious cafe has sofas, drinks and good daily lunch sets from ¥700. Look for the red 'F' by the door, around the corner from the main street.

La Francesca (☎ 934-1888; 7-1 Kameyama; ⏲ lunch & dinner; ⊠) Excellent Italian food is the main attraction at this elegant Tuscan villa, on the left as you head up the hill to the St Francis Xavier Memorial Church. Set-course options include the *Pranzo* (¥1575) at lunchtime and *Cena* (¥5250) in the evenings.

Renkon (☎ 921-3550; 1-3 Komeyachō; ⏲ 5pm-midnight) A wooden bar dominates the interior of this upmarket *izakaya*-style restaurant, where the Japanese-only menu includes such treats as *gyū rebā sashi* (raw calf's liver; ¥900) and *sashimi moriawase* (¥1200). Look for the illuminated sign between the arcade and the Sunroute Hotel.

Getting There & Away

The Yamaguchi *futsū* service connects the city with Shin-Yamaguchi (¥230, 25 minutes). Shin-Yamaguchi is 10km southwest of Yamaguchi in Ogōri, at the junction of the San-yō Osaka–Hakata *shinkansen* line and the JR Yamaguchi line, which passes through Yamaguchi and continues on to Tsuwano and Masuda on the San-in coast.

JR and Bōchō Kōtsū buses run to/from Yamaguchi to Hagi (¥1680, one hour and 10 minutes) and Akiyoshi-dai (¥1130, 55 minutes).

The *SL Yamaguchi-gō* steam locomotive stops at Yamaguchi and Yuda Onsen Stations from March to November (see p494).

Getting Around

Yamaguchi's sights are quite spread out – it's 8km from the station to Jōei-ji and back. Bicycles can be hired opposite the station at **Fukutake Rōho** (☎ 922-0915; Eki-dōri 1-4-6; hire 1st 2hr ¥300, per additional hr ¥100; ⏰ 8am-7pm).

AKIYOSHI-DAI 秋吉台

☎ 0837

The rolling Akiyoshi-dai tablelands lie halfway between Yamaguchi and Hagi on the northern San-in coast. In this unusual landscape, the fields are dotted with curious rock spires. Beneath this picturesque plateau are hundreds of limestone caverns, the largest of which, **Akiyoshi-dō** (秋芳洞; ☎ 62-0304; admission ¥1200; ⏰ 8.30am-4.30pm), is open to the public.

Akiyoshi-dō is the largest limestone cave in Japan, and some of the layered limestone pools inside are quite remarkable. In all, the cave extends about 10km, at some points 100m wide, with a river flowing through it. Public access is limited to a small well-paved 1km section. At the midpoint of the cave trail you can take an elevator up to the surface, where there is a lookout over the surrounding country.

Sleeping

There is not much in the way of accommodation around the cave area; you'd be better off staying in Hagi or Yamaguchi and visiting Akiyoshi-dai as a day trip.

Akiyoshi Royal Hotel (秋芳ロイヤルホテル; ☎ 62-0311; fax 62-0231; www.shuhokan.co.jp; Akiyoshi-dai; per person with 2 meals ¥11,550; Ⓟ) This large hotel caters to group tours visiting the plateau. Spacious Japanese- and Western-style rooms are available, and there are onsen baths with views of the plain. It's about 1.5km along the main road north of the main entrance to the cave, or a short walk from the elevator exit halfway through the cave.

Getting There & Away

It takes around an hour by bus to reach the cave from Yamaguchi (¥1130, 55 minutes, 10 daily) or Higashi-Hagi (¥1710, one hour and 10 minutes, 10.50am and 1.35pm). Buses also run from Shin-Yamaguchi (¥1140, 45 minutes, nine daily) and Shimonoseki (¥1730, two hours, eight daily). With the exception of the JR bus from Yamaguchi, all other routes are run by the Bōchō Bus Company (防長バス). There are also buses to Mine (美祢; ¥600) on the JR Mine line, which runs north to Nagato and south to Asa. Get off at Nagato Yumoto Station for transfer by bus to Tawarayama Onsen.

SHIMONOSEKI 下関

☎ 0832 / pop 288,000

Shimonoseki is an important crossroads. At the extreme western tip of Honshū, it's separated from Kyūshū by a narrow strait, famous for a decisive 12th-century clash between rival samurai clans. The expressway crosses the Kanmon-kaikyō strait on the Kanmon-bashi, while another road, the *shinkansen* railway line and the JR railway line all tunnel underneath. You can even walk to Kyūshū through a tunnel under the water. Shimonoseki is also an important connecting point to South Korea, with a daily ferry service to Busan. The town is famous for its seafood, particularly *fugu*, the potentially lethal pufferfish.

Orientation

Beside JR Shimonoseki Station is the large Sea Mall Shimonoseki shopping centre, and just east is the Kaikyō Yume Tower. The main road from the station leads to the Karato fish market, the Dan-no-ura Memorial and on to the old samurai part of town in Chōfu.

Information

There's a **tourist information office** (☎ 32-8383; 4-3-1 Takezaki-chō; ⏰ 9am-7pm) in JR Shimonoseki Station and another **tourist office** (☎ 56-3422; 1-11-1 Akine Minami-machi; ⏰ 9am-7pm) in the Shin-Shimonoseki *shinkansen* station, two stops north of the JR station on the JR San-yō line.

Internet access and a small library are available at the **International Exchange Room Global Salon** (☎ 31-5770; 3-3-1 Buzenda-chō; internet access per 30min ¥100; ⏰ 10am-8pm, closed Mon), on the 4th floor of the International Trade Building, which is by the Kaikyō Yume Tower. There's an **internet cafe** (☎ 28-1638; 1-15-33 Takezaki-chō; per 30min ¥400; ⏰ 10am-10pm) on the 1st floor of Hotel 38 Shimonoseki, a two-minute walk from the station.

If you're arriving from Korea, note that there are no currency-exchange counters in the ferry terminal. The information office in the station can give you a list of international ATMs and places where you can change money; one is the **Shimonoseki Post Office** (☎ 22-0957; 2-12-12 Takezaki-chō; ⏰ 9am-4pm), which takes cash and travellers cheques.

Sights & Activities

KARATO ICHIBA 唐戸市場

A highlight of any trip to Shimonoseki is an early-morning visit to the **Karato Ichiba fish market** (☎ 31-0001; 5-50 Karato; 4am-3pm Mon-Sat, 7am-3pm Sun; P). The market kicks off at 2am for those in the industry, but the public is welcome from 4am – the earlier you get there, the better. It's a great opportunity to try sashimi for breakfast or lunch, and the fish doesn't get any fresher – a fair bit of it will still be moving.

The market is in Karato, halfway between central Shimonoseki and Hino-yama. The first bus leaves from outside the station at 5.55am during the week and at 6.14 on Saturday – it costs ¥190 and takes seven minutes. The markets are occasionally closed on Wednesday.

Also in Karato, the impressive **Kaikyō-kan aquarium** (☎ 28-1100; 6-1 Arukapōto; admission ¥1800; 9.30am-5.30pm; P) has stacks of fish, dolphin and sea-lion shows, a blue-whale skeleton and several tanks of *fugu*.

The Meiji-era former **British Consulate building** (☎ 31-1238; 4-11 Karato; admission free; 9am-5pm) is across the road from the market. There's a small museum inside, with the consul's desk still in place. There's a unique coffee house, Shimonoseki Ijinkan, at the rear (see p484).

KAIKYŌ YUME TOWER

The 153m **Kaikyō Yume Tower** (admission ¥600; 9.30am-9.30pm) is a midget skyscraper, topped by a futuristic billiard ball. The entrance ticket to the tower gets you to the **observatory** (☎ 31-5600; 3-3-1 Buzenda-chō; 9.30am-9.30pm) for some impressive 360-degree views.

AKAMA-JINGŪ 赤間神宮

Bright vermilion, **Akama-jinjū** (☎ 31-4138; 4-1 Amidaiji-chō; 24hr) is a shrine dedicated to the seven-year-old emperor Antoku, who died in 1185 in the battle of Dan-no-ura. In the Hōichi Hall stands a statue of Miminashi Hōichi (Earless Hōichi), the blind bard whose musical talents get him into trouble with ghosts in a story made famous by Lafcadio Hearn (for more about Hearn, see boxed text, p500). The shrine is between Karato and Hino-yama. Get off the bus (¥230, 10 minutes) at the Akama-jingū-mae bus stop. Close to the Hōichi statue there is a small **exhibit** (admission ¥100) of scrolls and manuscripts relating to the Heike story.

The **Sentei Festival** (2 to 4 May) is held here to remember the Heike women who worked as prostitutes to pay for rites for their fallen relatives. On 3 May women dressed as Heian-era courtesans form a colourful procession at the shrine.

HINO-YAMA 火の山

About 5km northeast of JR Shimonoseki Station there are superb views over the Kanmon-kaikyō from the top of 268m-high **Hino-yama**. To get to the **ropeway** (☎ 31-1351; one-way fare ¥300; 10am-5pm, closed Tue & Thu), get off the bus at Mimosusōgawa (御裳川) stop, by the Dan-no-ura memorial (¥230). The ropeway is closed for periods over winter, so call to confirm it's open, if visiting at this time. For a free 780m submarine walk to Kyūshū, head down to a cross-strait **walking tunnel** that's popular with local joggers – there are lifts (open 6am to 10pm) down to the tunnel by the Mimosusōgawa-kōen bus stop.

Across the road from the same bus stop is the **Dan-no-ura Memorial**, marking the spot where the decisive clash between the Minamoto and Taira clans took place in 1185. This is where Taira no Tokiko plunged into the sea with the young emperor Antoku in her arms, rather than surrender to the enemy. The statues depict Yoshitsune (the victorious Minamoto general) and Taira no Tomomori, who tied an anchor to his feet and leapt into the sea at Dan-no-ura when it became clear that his side had lost. Local legend holds that the Heike crabs that live in these waters and have strange face-like patternings on their shells are the reincarnations of angry Taira warriors.

CHŌFU 長府

Chōfu is the old castle town area and, while little remains of the castle itself, there are earth walls and samurai gates, along with a museum and several temples and shrines.

The **Shimonoseki City Art Museum** (下関市立美術館; ☎ 45-4131; Chōfu Kuromon Higashi-machi 1-1; admission ¥200; 9.30am-5pm, closed Mon) houses an eclectic collection of local art and temporary exhibits. At the time of writing, renovations were scheduled for early 2010, so call to see if it's reopened. Opposite the art museum is **Chōfu-teien** (長府庭園; ☎ 46-4120; Chōfu Kuromon Higashi-machi 8-11; admission ¥200; 9am-5pm), a garden famous for its flowers in spring and autumn. Head along the coast from here on the main road until you come to a small channel that heads inland. Following this brings you to national treasure **Kōzan-ji** (功山時; ☎ 45-0258;

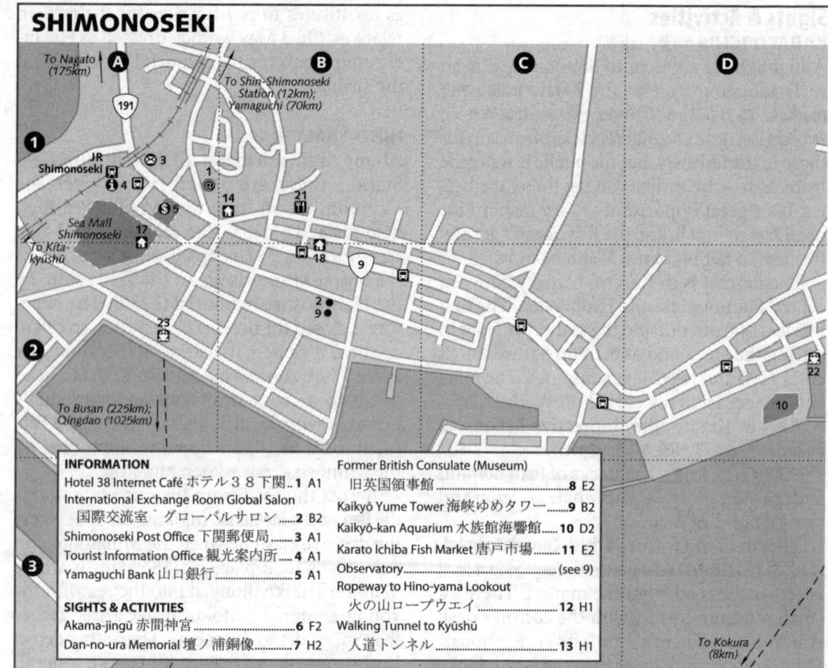

1-2-3 Chōfu Kawabata; 9am-5pm), the family burial temple of the local Mōri lords, with a Zen-style hall dating from 1327. The **Chōfu Museum** (長府博物館; ☎ 45-0555; admission ¥200; 9.30am-5pm, closed Mon) is also in the temple grounds.

Sleeping

Hinoyama Youth Hostel (☎ 22-3753; www.e-yh.net/shimonoseki; 3-47 Mimosusogawa-chō; d ¥3200; P) Amazing views of the strait and relaxed service make this one of the best youth hostels in Western Honshū. You can take a Hino-yama bus from the station (¥230, 26 minutes). Meals are available.

Green Hotel Shimonoseki (☎ 31-1007; fax 31-3603; www.greenhotelshimonoseki.jp, in Japanese; 1-16-13 Takezaki-chō; s/tw ¥4800/8800; P) Singles in this bright, friendly little chain hotel are small, but it's well kept and a short walk from the station and ferry terminal. A free lobby computer is available.

Tōyoko Inn (☎ 34-1045; fax 34-1046; www.toyoko-inn.com; 2-7-10 Buzenda-chō; s/tw ¥5565/8190; P) Not far from the station, this is a decent chain hotel with all the usual amenities. There's LAN internet access in all rooms and there are computer terminals in the lobby.

Shimonoseki Tōkyū Inn (☎ 33-0109; fax 23-0285; www.tokyuhotels.co.jp; 4-4-1 Takezaki-chō; s/tw ¥6825/12,600; P) Ideally located just a minute's walk from the station and ferry terminal, this smart business hotel has comfortable rooms (with LAN internet in all rooms) and wireless access in the lobby.

Kaikyō View Shimonoseki (☎ 29-0117; fax 29-0114; www.kv-shimonoseki.com, in Japanese; 3-58 Mimosusogawa-chō; per person with 2 meals from ¥9975; P) On Hino-yama, Kaikyō View has great views and professional service. Japanese- and Western-style rooms overlook the strait. There's an onsen, which has sea views, and is open to nonguests from 11am to 3pm (for ¥700).

Eating & Drinking

Shimonoseki Ijinkan (☎ 22-2262; 4-11 Karato; drinks ¥500-1500; 9.30am-9pm, closed Mon) Tucked away in the British consulate courtyard, the Ijinkan coffee house is famous for the theatrical ministrations of bow-tied 'coffee meister' Kunio Kanegae. It's worth ordering a *café au lait* (¥1050) for the show alone – but you'll have to be quick. The performance takes so much out of him that orders are limited to just 10 per day.

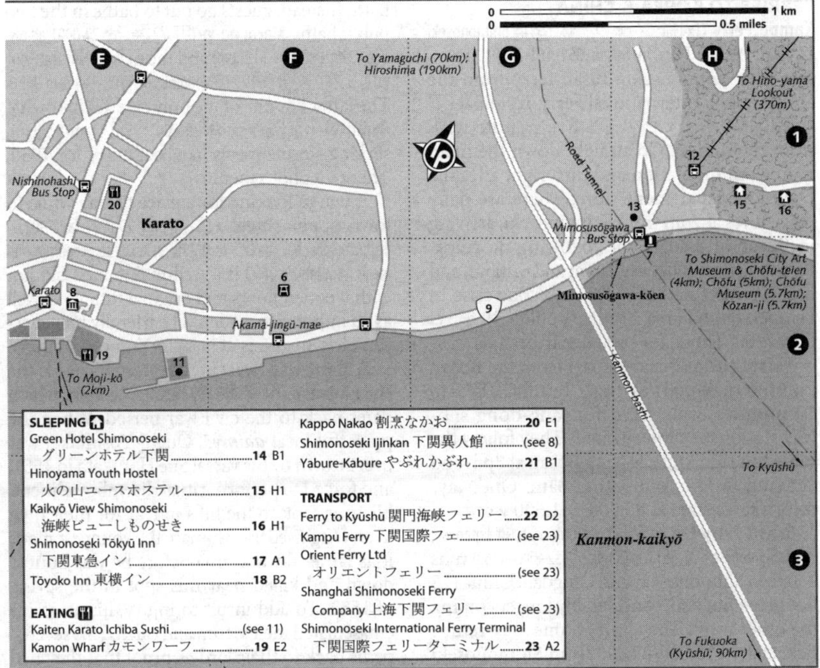

Kaiten Karato Ichiba Sushi (☎ 33-2611; 2F 5-50 Karato; per plate from ¥105; ⏰ lunch & dinner) This revolving sushi restaurant in the heart of the fish market is a great place to get your hands on the freshest fish without needing to know what they're all called. There are normally over 60 different kinds of fish available.

Yabure-Kabure (☎ 34-3711; 2-2-5 Buzenda-chō; lunch/dinner set menu from ¥3150/5250; ⏰ lunch & dinner) There's only one thing on the menu in this boisterous, pufferfish-themed spot: pick from a range of *fugu* set menus, such as the Ebisu course (¥5250), which features the cute little puffer in raw, seared, fried and drowned-in-sake incarnations. A lunchtime *sashimi setto* (sashimi set meal) is ¥3150. There is no English menu, but you can't go wrong here. Look for the blue-and-white pufferfish outside.

Kappō Nakao (割烹奈可超; ☎ 31-4129; 4-6 Akama-chō; meals ¥3800-26,250; ⏰ lunch & dinner Nov-Mar, closed Mon Apr-Oct) Five minutes' walk from the Karato market, this sophisticated *fugu* restaurant offers graceful service and splendidly prepared dishes. Courses start at ¥8400, though there are cheaper deals available at lunchtime. Look for the stone lantern and wooden gate out the front.

Close to the fish market is Kamon Wharf, a collection of restaurants and shops specialising in the local goodies – seekers of only-in-Japan culinary experiences can look out for the *uni* (sea-urchin)-flavoured ice cream (うにソフトクリーム; ¥300) and *fugu* burgers (ふぐバーガー; ¥350).

Getting There & Away

Shinkansen trains stop at Shin-Shimonoseki Station, two stops from JR Shimonoseki. From Shimonoseki, a bridge and tunnels connect Honshū with Kyūshū. Eastbound road users can take Rte 191 along the northern San-in coast, Rte 2 along the southern San-yō coast or the Chūgoku Expressway through central Honshū.

Kanmon Kisen (☎ 083-222-1488) ferries run two or three times hourly from the Karato area of Shimonoseki to Moji in Kyūshū (¥390, five minutes). Kanmon Kaikyō ferries ply the route between Karato and Kokura in Kyūshū (¥200, 13 minutes). From Shin-moji in Kita-Kyūshū there are ferries to Kōbe and Osaka and to Tokyo.

FERRIES TO KOREA & CHINA

Kampu Ferry (関釜フェリー; ☎ in Shimonoseki 24-3000, Pukwan Ferry in Busan 051-464-2700) operates the Shimonoseki–Busan ferry from the Shimonoseki International Ferry Terminal (下関港国際ターミナル), a five-minute walk from the station. Go straight down the main road from the station and turn right after the Daimaru department store. There are daily departures at 7pm from Shimonoseki, arriving in Busan at 8.30am the following morning. Boarding time is between 6pm and 6.20pm, and one-way fares start at ¥9000 for second class, in an open tatami area. Students under 30 travel for ¥7200. There is a ¥600 departure tax.

Ferries from Busan depart from the Busan Port International Passenger Terminal, five- to 10-minutes' walk from Jungang-dong subway station on subway line 1. They follow the same time schedule, leaving Busan at 8pm and arriving in Shimonoseki at 8am. One-way/return fares start at 85,000/161,500 won.

Orient Ferry Ltd (www.orientferry.co.jp, in Japanese; ☎ in Shimonoseki 32-6615, in Qingdao 0532-8387-1160) runs between Shimonoseki and Qingdao, China (28 hours to Qingdao, considerably longer coming the other way). The cheapest one-way/return tickets are ¥15,000/27,000 from Shimonoseki (leaving noon Wednesday and Saturday, arriving at 4pm the following day), and 1100/1980 yuan from Qingdao, departing from the port ferry terminal north of Qingdao Station at 8pm on Monday and Thursday (arriving in Shimonoseki at 9.30am two days later).

The **Shanghai Shimonoseki Ferry Company** (上海下関フェリー; ☎ in Shimonoseki 32-9677, in Taicang 512-53-186686; www.ssferry.co.jp, in Japanese) sails once a week to Taicang in Suzhou, near Shanghai. Second-class fares start at ¥15,000 one way. The ferry departs Shimonoseki at 5pm on Sunday (arriving in Taicang at 8am on Tuesday), and from Taicang at 8pm on Tuesday (arrives in Shimonoseki at 8.30am on Thursday).

TAWARAYAMA ONSEN 俵山温泉

☎ 0837

Nestled in the mountains, Tawarayama Onsen is a small village that has escaped developers and maintained its reputation as a favoured hidden spa for *tōji* (curative bathing). It's serious about its purpose: there are no karaoke bars, no neon – and almost no restaurants. Bathers come here for their health, usually staying from four days to a week in the 40-odd ryokan. This onsen is so old-style that none of the ryokan has its own bath. Instead, guests go out to bathe in the two public baths: **Machi-no-yu** (町の湯; ☎ 29-0001; admission ¥390; ⌚ 6am-10.30pm) and the newer **Hakuen-no-yu** (白猿の湯; ☎ 29-0036; admission ¥700; ⌚ 7am-9pm). The latter has one of the only eateries in town – **Ryōfūtei** (涼風亭; ☎ 29-0001; ⌚ 11am-8.30pm), serving simple meals like beef curry for ¥950. There's a photo menu.

If you're looking for a place to stay while in town, popular **Izumiya** (泉屋; ☎ 29-0231; fax 29-0232; http://member.hot-cha.tv/~htc02178/, in Japanese; per person with meals from ¥8925; Ⓟ) is a well-maintained old inn with wooden floors and original fittings as well as an impressive garden. The friendly managers can pick up guests at Nagato-Yumoto station.

A short walk west of the onsen village is the **Mara Kannon (麻羅観音) fertility temple**, which dates back to the civil war period. When the powerful local *daimyō*, Ōuchi Yoshitaka, was overthrown by his vassal Sue Harukata in 1551, and forced to perform ritual disembowelment, his sons took to the hills in fear for their own lives. Disguised as a woman, the youngest made it as far as Tawarayama before he was hunted down and killed near this spot in the spring of 1552. To add insult to injury, his assassins emasculated their victim and carried his severed penis back to their lord as proof that they had got their man. Local villagers built the shrine to appease the dead man's spirit. Today, the small wooden temple and its lingam-strewn grounds are popular with couples trying to conceive.

Take a local train on the JR Mine line from Asa to the south or Nagato to the north to Nagato-Yumoto. From here, there is one bus an hour to Tawarayama Onsen (¥510, 25 minutes). There's also a direct bus from Shimonoseki (¥1610, one hour and 45 minutes, nine per day).

HAGI 萩

☎ 0838 / pop 56,000

Hagi is an attractive city with a well-preserved old samurai quarter. The ceramics made here are among the finest in Japan. During the feudal period, Hagi was the castle town of the Chōshū domain, which, together with Satsuma (corresponding to modern Kagoshima in southern Kyūshū), was instrumental in defeating the Tokugawa government and ushering in a new age after the Meiji Restoration.

Orientation & Information

Western and central Hagi are effectively an island created by the two rivers Hashimoto-gawa and Matsumoto-gawa; eastern Hagi (with the major JR station Higashi-Hagi) lies on the eastern bank of the Matsumoto-gawa. Get off at JR Higashi-Hagi for the main sights.

The main road through central Hagi starts from JR Hagi Station in the south and runs north, past the bus centre in the middle of town. West of this central area is the *jōkamachi* (城下町; old samurai quarter), with its picturesque streets and old buildings.

Hagi City Library (☎ 25-6355; 2nd fl, 552-26 Emukai; 9.30am-5.30pm Tue-Sun) Free internet access.

Tourist information office (☎ 25-3145; 2997-3 Chintō; 9am-5pm) Located inside Higashi-Hagi Station. There's another near Hagi station.

Sights

HAGI POTTERY & KILNS

Connoisseurs of Japanese ceramics rank *hagi-yaki* as some of the best. As in other Japanese pottery centres, the craft came from Korea when Korean potters were abducted during Toyotomi Hideyoshi's unsuccessful invasion in the late 1500s. At a number of shops and kilns you can see the pottery being made, and browse the finished products. *Hagi-yaki* is noted for its fine glazes and delicate pastel colours.

Hagi-jō Kiln (☎ 22-5226; 2-5 Horiuchi; 8am-5pm) in Horiuchi (within the walls of the old castle ruins) has some fine pieces. The western end of Hagi has several interesting pottery kilns near the park, Shizuki-kōen. You can also try your hand at making *hagi-yaki* at the crafts centre **Jōzan** (☎ 25-1666; 31-15 Horiuchi Nishi-no-hama; lessons ¥1680; 8am-4pm).

Swede **Bertil Persson** (☎ 25-2693), who has lived in Hagi for over 30 years, has his own kiln and is happy to meet anyone seriously interested in ceramics.

HAGI-JŌ RUINS & SHIZUKI-KŌEN 萩城跡指月公園

There's not much of the old Hagi-jō to see, apart from the typically imposing outer walls and the surrounding moat. The **castle** (☎ 25-1826; Horiuchi Shizuki-kōen-nai; admission with Asa Mōri House ¥210; 8am-6.30pm Apr-Oct, to 4.30pm Nov-Feb, to 6pm March) was built in 1604 and dismantled in 1874 following the Meiji Restoration.

Now the grounds are a pleasant park, with the **Shizukiyama-jinja**, the **Hanano-e Tea House** (Hanano-e Chatei; tea ¥500) from the mid-19th century, and other buildings. From the castle ruins you can climb the hillside to the 143m peak of Shizuki-yama.

ASA MŌRI HOUSE 旧厚狭毛利家萩屋敷長屋

South of the park is **Asa Mōri House** (☎ 25-2304; Horiuchi Shizuki-Kōen; admission with Hagi-jō ruins ¥210; 8am-6.30pm Apr-Aug, 8.30am-4.30pm Nov-Feb, to 6pm Mar), a *nagaya* (type of Japanese long house) that belonged to a branch of the Mōri family, which ruled the region during the feudal period. There's not a lot to see beyond a few pieces of old armour. To the south of the samurai house is the **Catholic Martyrs' Memorial Park**. Here, a monument and graves commemorate 40 of the 'hidden Christians' who died for their faith when they were exiled in Hagi from Nagasaki in the early years of the Meiji period.

JŌKAMACHI, HORIUCHI & TERAMACHI AREAS 城下町•堀内•寺町

Between the town centre and the moat that separates western Hagi from central Hagi is the old samurai residential area, with many streets lined with whitewashed walls. This area is fascinating to wander around and has a number of interesting houses.

The Kikuya family were merchants rather than samurai, but they were the most important merchants in town. As official merchants to the *daimyō* their wealth and connections allowed them to build a house well above their station. **Kikuya House** (☎ 25-8282; 1-1 Gofuku-machi; admission ¥500; 9am-5.30pm) dates from 1604 and has a fine gate, attractive gardens and numerous construction details and materials that would normally have been forbidden to the merchant class. Across the street is **Kubota House** (☎ 25-3139; 1-3 Gofuku-machi; admission ¥100; 9am-5pm), a renovated residence from the late Edo period that served as a clothing store and sake brewery.

At the southern perimeter of the Jōkamachi district, before you reach the little canal, is the green tea–coloured **Ishii Chawan Museum** (☎ 22-1211; 33-3 Minamifuruhagi-machi; admission ¥500; 9am-noon, 1-4.45pm, closed Mon & Dec-Feb), which has an extensive collection of tea-ceremony bowls and utensils. From the museum, go east, cross the canal and turn south to reach the **Hagi Uragami Museum** (☎ 24-2400; 586-1 Hiyako; admission ¥1000; 9am-4.30pm, closed Mon). This superb collection consists of ceramics and wood-block prints. There are fine works by Katsushika Hokusai and Utamaro Kitagawa.

At the main entrance to the Horiuchi district is the **Hagi Museum** (☎ 25-6447; 355 Horiuchi; admission ¥500; 9am-5pm), which has exhibitions on Hagi's history as a castle town and the role it

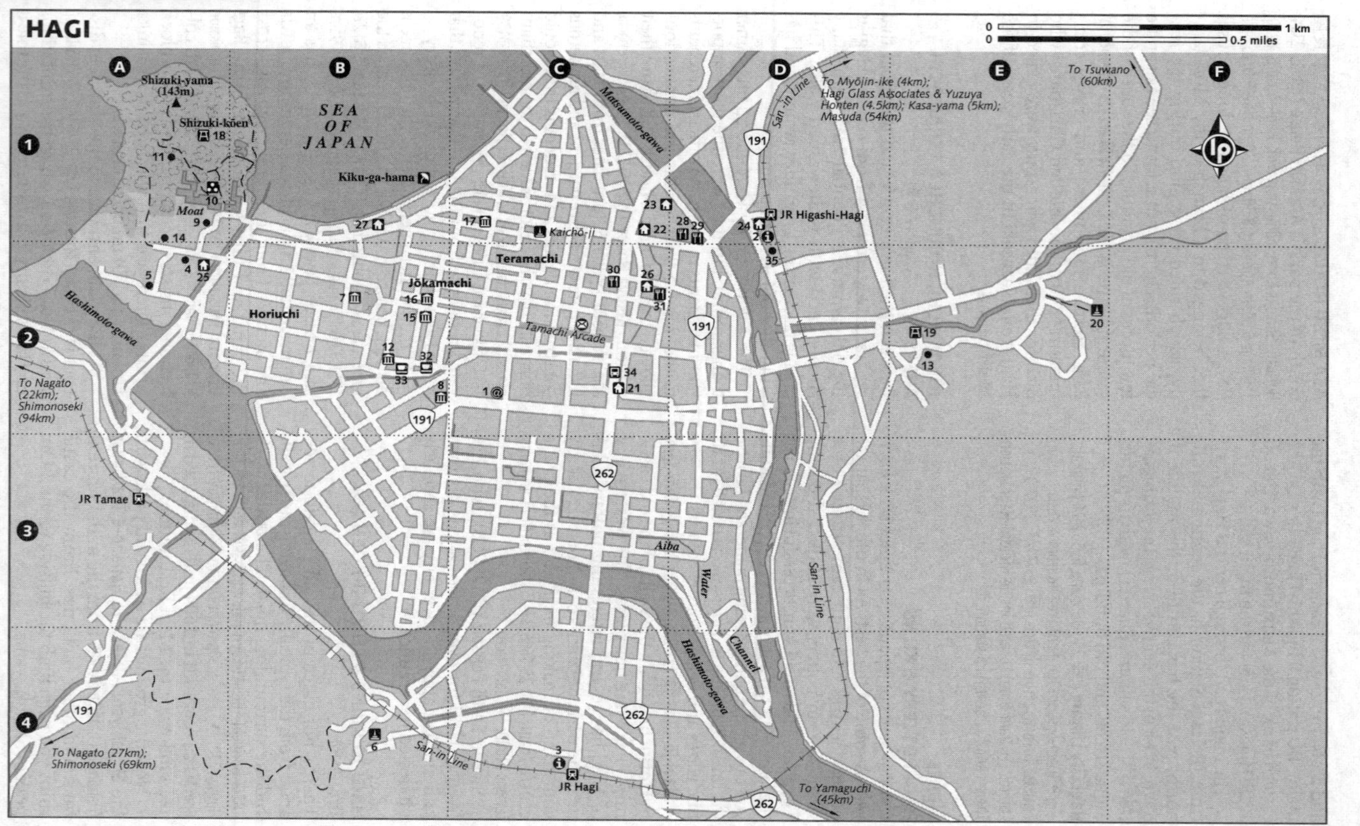
HAGI
0 1 km
0 0.5 miles
SEA OF JAPAN
Kiku-ga-hama
Shizuki-yama (143m)
Shizuki-kōen
Moat
Horiuchi
Jōkamachi
Teramachi
Kaichō-ji
Tamachi Arcade
Matsumoto-gawa
Hashimoto-gawa
Aiba
Water
Channel
San-in Line
JR Higashi-Hagi
JR Hagi
JR Tamae
To Tsuwano (60km)
To Myōjin-ike (4km); Hagi Glass Associates & Yuzuya Honten (4.5km); Kasa-yama (5km); Masuda (54km)
To Yamaguchi (45km)
To Nagato (22km); Shimonoseki (94km)
To Nagato (27km); Shimonoseki (69km)

INFORMATION
Hagi City Library 萩市立図書館 ... 1 C2
Tourist Information Office 観光案内所 ... 2 D1
Tourist Information Office 観光案内所 ... 3 C4

SIGHTS & ACTIVITIES
Asa Mōri House 旧厚狭毛利家萩屋敷長屋 ... 4 A2
Catholic Martyrs' Memorial Park 萩キリシタン殉教者記念公園 ... 5 A2
Daishō-in 大照院 ... 6 B4
Hagi Museum 萩博物館 ... 7 B2
Hagi Uragami Museum 萩浦上美術館 ... 8 B2
Hagi-jō Kiln 萩城窯 ... 9 A1
Hagi-jō Ruins 萩城跡 ... 10 A1
Hanano-e Tea House 花江茶亭 ... 11 A1
Ishii Chawan Museum 石井茶碗美術館 ... 12 B2
Itō Hirobumi House 伊藤博文旧宅 ... 13 E2
Jōzan 城山 ... 14 A1
Kikuya House 菊屋家住宅 ... 15 B2
Kubota House 久保田家 ... 16 B2
Kumaya Art Museum 熊谷美術館 ... 17 C1
Shizukiyama-jinja 指月山神社 ... 18 A1
Shōin-jinja 松陰神社 ... 19 E2
Tōkō-ji 東光寺 ... 20 E2

SLEEPING
Business Hotel Hasegawa ビジネスホテル長谷川 ... 21 C2
Hagi Grand Hotel Tenkū 萩グランドホテル天空 ... 22 C1
Hagi no Yado Tomoe 萩の宿 常茂恵 ... 23 C1
Hagi Royal Intelligent Hotel 萩ロイヤルインテリジェントホテル ... 24 D1
Hagi Youth Hostel 萩ユースホステル ... 25 A2
Nakamura 中村旅館 ... 26 C2
Well Heart Pia Hagi ウェルハートピア萩 ... 27 B1

EATING
Don Don Udonya どんどんうどん屋 ... 28 D1
Hagi Shinkai 萩心海 ... 29 D1
Maru マル ... 30 C2
Nakamura 中村 ... 31 C2

DRINKING
Cafeteria Ijinkan カフェテリア異人館 ... 32 B2
Kurumayado Tenjuppei 俥宿天十平 ... 33 B2

TRANSPORT
Hagi Bus Centre 萩バスセンター ... 34 C2
Hagi Rainbow Cycles 萩レインボーサイクル ... 35 D2

played in the Meiji Restoration. Unfortunately, there are no English explanations.

Kumaya Art Museum (☎ 25-5535; 47 Imauono Tanamachi; admission ¥700; 9am-5pm, closed Mon & Dec–mid-Mar), in Jōkamachi, has a limited collection including tea bowls, screens and other items, displayed in a series of small warehouses dating from 1768. The Kumaya family ran the salt trade for the Mōri family, and spent part of their fortune on the ceramics, screens and other objects of art that form the bulk of the collection.

SHŌIN-JINJA 松陰神社

This shrine was founded in 1890 and is dedicated to Meiji Restoration movement leader Yoshida Shōin. His old house and the school where he agitated against the shogunate in the years leading up to the revolution are also here. A Treasure House is set to open in late 2009. South of the shrine is the **Itō Hirobumi House** (伊藤博文旧宅; admission ¥100; 9am-5pm), the thatched early home of the four-term prime minister who was a follower of Yoshida Shōin, and who later drafted the Meiji Constitution. The impressive mansion he lived in during his years in Tokyo is next door, built in 1907 and moved to Hagi after his death.

TŌKŌ-JI 東光寺

East of the river stands pretty Zen **Tōkō-ji** (☎ 26-1052; admission ¥300; 1647 Chintō; 8.30am-5pm), built in 1691 and home to the tombs of five Mōri lords. The stone walkways on the hillside behind the temple are flanked by almost 500 stone lanterns, erected by the lords' servants.

DAISHŌ-IN 大照院

South of the centre, near JR Hagi Station, the funerary temple **Daishō-in** (☎ 22-2124; 4132 Ōmi; admission ¥200; 8am-5pm Apr-Nov, to 4.30pm Dec-Mar) was built in 1656 and dedicated to the first Mōri lord, Hidenari. The graves of the first two lords are here, along with all the even-numbered generations after that. There are 52 graves in the mausoleum, including those of several retainers who performed *junshi* – a ritual suicide by disembowelment that was performed so they could join their masters in death.

MYŌJIN-IKE & KASA-YAMA 明神池•笠山

About 5km east of the town is the 112m dormant volcano **Kasa-yama**. The pond at the mountain's base, **Myōjin-ike**, is connected to the sea, and shelters a variety of saltwater fish.

Further up the mountain is **Hagi Glass Associates** (萩ガラス工房; ☎ 26-2555; Myōjin-ike Koshigahama; admission free; 9am-6pm, demonstrations 9am-noon & 1-4.30pm), where quartz basalt from the volcano is used to make extremely tough Hagi glassware. There is a showroom and a shop, and visitors can make their own piece of glassware (glass-blowing classes ¥3150). Next door is Hagi's own beer and citrus juice factory, **Yuzuya Honten** (柚子屋本店; ☎ 25-7511; Myojin-ike Koshigahama; admission free; 9am-5pm).

The road continues to the top of Kasa-yama, from where there are fine views along the coast and a tiny 30m-deep crater. Kasayama is close enough to make a good bicycle ride from Hagi.

Sleeping

Hagi Youth Hostel (☎ 22-0733; fax 22-3558; www.jyh.or.jp/yhguide/chugoku/hagi/index.html, in Japanese; 109-22 Horiuchi; dm members/nonmembers ¥2940/3540; closed mid-Jan–mid-Feb; P) Close to the castle at the western end of town, the hostel is a 15-minute walk from JR Tamae station. The hostel is cold and bare, but the manager is very attentive. Bicycles can be rented for ¥500 a day and meals are available.

Nakamura Ryokan (☎ 22-0303; fax 26-0303; nakamura-r.ftw.jp, in Japanese; 56 Furuhagi-machi; s/tw ¥5250/8400; P) The Nakamura is a friendly place divided into modern and older buildings. It has large tatami rooms and there's a big pine by the tiled-roof *genkan* (entrance).

Business Hotel Hasegawa (☎ 22-0450; fax 22-4884; www.hagi.ne.jp/004_hasegawa, in Japanese; 17 Karahi-machi; s/tw ¥5500/10,500; P) Between the station and the sights near Hagi castle, the Hasegawa has sunny and good-sized Western- and Japanese-style rooms. It's right by the bus centre. There is LAN internet in the rooms, and a computer in the lobby downstairs.

Hagi Royal Intelligent Hotel (☎ 21-4589; fax 21-4488; http://hrih.jp, in Japanese; 3000-5 Chintō; s/tw ¥5900/7400; P) Immediately to the left as you exit Higashi-Hagi Station, this new hotel has large, comfortably appointed rooms with little extras like felt dartboards. There is an onsen downstairs, and a computer centre with free internet access.

Hagi Grand Hotel Tenkū (☎ 25-1211; fax 25-4422; www.hagi-gh.com, in Japanese; 25 Furuhagi-machi; s/tw ¥9450/17,325; P) A huge, slightly faded tourist hotel with large rooms and an extensive onsen complex at the back. There is a market on the ground floor that sells all kinds of tasty local treats.

Well Heart Pia Hagi (☎ 22-7580; fax 25-7931; www.kjp.or.jp/hp_109, in Japanese; 485-2 Horiuchi; per person with meals from ¥9800; P) Five minutes' walk east of Hagi castle, this large modern facility has huge rooms with views of Kiku-ga-hama beach. The onsen baths are also open to nonguests (¥500, from 10am to 9pm Thursday to Tuesday, and from 3pm to 9pm Wednesday). Bike hire is available for ¥1000 per day.

Hagi no Yado Tomoe (☎ 22-0150; fax 25-0152; www.tomoehagi.jp/english01.html; 608-53 Kōbō-ji Hijiwara; per person from ¥10,500; P) The finest inn in Hagi, the historic Tomoe has gorgeous Japanese rooms with garden views, beautifully prepared cuisine and luxurious baths.

Eating & Drinking

Don Don Udonya (☎ 22-7537; 377 San-ku Hijiwara; dishes ¥390-700; 9am-9pm) A popular spot serving tasty udon, with plastic models in the window. *Tempura udon* goes for ¥450. It's in a big black-and-white building on the right as you head away from the station.

Maru (☎ 26-5060; 78 Yoshida-chō; meals ¥700-1200; 5-11pm, closed Sun) A relaxed and modern young people's *izakaya*, Maru features the local beef, *kenran-gyū* (見蘭牛), available as sashimi (¥850), sushi (¥1000) or garlic steak (¥650). It also serves all the usual *izakaya* favourites (no English menu). Try the *Hagi no kuramoto udedameshi setto* (¥1000) for a tasting set from six local sake breweries. Maru has a large wooden door marked with a circle and the words 'Maru Barrel House' written in English.

Nakamura (☎ 22-6619; 394 Hijiwara; meals ¥1500-5000; lunch & dinner, closed Wed) *Unidon* (sea urchin on rice; from ¥2639) is the house speciality here. Fronted by bushes, this old fashioned–looking restaurant is behind a car park by a small canal.

Hagi Shinkai (☎ 26-1221; 370-71 Hijiwara; set meals ¥4000-6000; lunch & dinner) This popular place, a few minutes' walk from Higashi-Hagi station, specialises in seafood served fresh from tanks. *Teishoku* options from the Japanese-only menu include *sashimi teishoku* (¥2415), *hotate teishoku* (scallops; ¥3675) and *uni teishoku* (sea urchin; ¥3990). Look for the white building with the lighthouse jutting out from the roof.

Kurumayado Tenjuppei (☎ 26-6474; 33-5 Minamifuruhagi-machi; 9am-6pm) This charming gallery and tearoom is in a late–Edo period house with a large garden. Pots of tea go for ¥600; a plate of scones is ¥400. It's down a little lane after Cafeteria Ijinkan (see below), through a gate on the right.

Cafeteria Ijinkan (☎ 25-6334; 2-61 Gofuku-machi; 9.30am-9.30pm) The Ijinkan is a brick-walled Japanese-style coffee house complete with floral carpets, chandeliers and waitresses in French-maid outfits. The Japanese-only menu features simple meals such as *yakisoba* (fried noodles with meat and vegetables, ¥650) and pizza (¥800).

Getting There & Away

The JR San-in line runs along the north coast through Tottori, Matsue, and Hagi to Shimonoseki. Local services between Shimonoseki and Higashi-Hagi (¥1890) take up to three hours, depending on transfers.

Long-distance buses connect Hagi with Shin-Yamaguchi (¥1970, 1½ hours, 21 daily), south of Hagi on the Tokyo–Osaka–Hakata *shinkansen* line. Buses run to Tsuwano (¥2080, one hour and 45 minutes) to the east in Shimane-ken, and also to Tokyo (¥12,640, 12 hours), Osaka (¥6920, 11 hours) and Hiroshima (¥3700, four hours). There are buses to Hagi from Yamaguchi (¥1680, one hour).

Hagi is served by Iwami airport, an hour to the northeast near Masuda in Shimane-ken. There are daily flights to/from Tokyo (¥35,800, one hour and 20 minutes, two daily) and Osaka (¥25,800, one hour, one daily). A bus (¥1560, one hour and 10 minutes) from in front of Higashi-Hagi Station or the Hagi bus centre connects Hagi with all flights.

If you're going to Tsuwano, there's a direct bus from Hagi (¥2080, one hour and 45 minutes, five daily), but if you've got a JR pass you'll want to go by train up the coast to Masuda, then change to the JR Yamaguchi line for Tsuwano.

Getting Around

Hagi is a good place to explore by bicycle and there are plenty of hire places, including one at the youth hostel and several around the castle and JR Higashi-Hagi Station. To the left as you exit the station is **Hagi Rainbow Cycles** (☎ 25-0067; 2960-19 Chintō; hire per hr/day ¥150/1000; ⌚ 8am-5pm).

The handy *māru basu* (まぁーるバス; circle bus) takes in Hagi's main attractions. There are east- (東回り) and west-bound (西回り) loops, with two services per hour at each stop. One trip costs ¥100, and one-/two-day passes cost ¥500/700.

SHIMANE-KEN 島根県

Along the northern San-in coastline on the Sea of Japan, Shimane-ken may be off the beaten track, but there is no shortage of reasons to visit. Cities are few and far between, the pace of life is decidedly slower than on the San-yō coast, and the people are particularly friendly towards visitors. Highlights include Tsuwano, a quiet mountain town; the great shrine at Izumo; and Matsue, where the writer Lafcadio Hearn lived.

TSUWANO 津和野

☎ 0856 / pop 9,500

Tsuwano is a relaxing, 700-year-old mountain town with an important shrine, a ruined castle, and an evocative samurai quarter. It's in the far west of, about 60km by road east of Hagi, and has a wonderful collection of carp swimming in the roadside water channels – in fact, there are far more carp here than people!

Orientation & Information

Tsuwano is a long, narrow town wedged into a deep north–south valley. Tsuwano-kawa, the JR Yamaguchi line and the main road all run down the middle of the valley. The **tourist information office** (☎ 72-1771; Ekimae; ⌚ 9am-5pm) is immediately to the right as you exit the station.

Sights & Activities

TSUWANO-JŌ 津和野城

The broken walls of **Tsuwano-jō** brood over the valley. The castle was originally constructed in 1295 and remained in use until the Meiji Restoration. An old single-seater chairlift takes you up the hillside for ¥450, and there's a further 15-minute walk to the castle ruins. There's nothing here but the walls, but there are good views over the town and the valleys.

TAIKODANI-INARI-JINJA 太鼓谷稲成神社

Just above the castle chairlift station, thriving **Taikodani-Inari-jinja** (☎ 72-0219; Tsuwano; ⌚ 8am-4.30pm), built in 1773 by the seventh lord Kamei Norisada, is one of the five major Inari shrines in Japan. You can walk up to it from the main road through a tunnel created by hundreds of *torii* (lit up beautifully at night). Inari is the god of rice and prosperity in business, and festivals are held here on 15 May and 15 November.

TONOMACHI DISTRICT 殿町

Only the walls and some fine old gates from the former **samurai quarter** of Tonomachi remain. The water channels that run alongside the picturesque Tonomachi road are home to numerous carp, bred to provide food in the case of emergency.

The Tsuwano **Catholic Church** (☎ 72-0251; Tonomachi; ⌚ 8am-5.30pm Apr-Nov, to 5pm Dec-Mar) is a reminder of the town's Christian history. Hidden Christians from Nagasaki were exiled here in the early Meiji period. Instead of pews, the church has tatami mats. Just north of the river is the **Yōrō-kan**, a school for young samurai originally dating from 1786 and rebuilt on this site after a fire in 1855. The building houses the **Folk Museum** (☎ 72-1000; Tonomachi; admission ¥250; 🕑 8.30am-5pm Mar-Nov), a small folk-art museum with all sorts of farming and cooking equipment.

Near the post office, the **Katsushika Hokusai Museum** (☎ 72-1850; 254 Ushiroda-guchi; admission ¥500; 🕑 9.30am-5pm) features a small collection by the Edo-period painter and his disciples, and, interestingly, shows the wood-block process plate by plate.

CHAPEL OF ST MARIA マリア聖堂

The tiny **Maria-dō** (Mary Chapel) dates from 1951, and was built as a memorial to the Christians who died here during the final period of persecution. More than 150 'hidden Christians' were imprisoned in a Buddhist temple on this site after their discovery in Nagasaki in the early years of the Meiji Restoration. Thirty-six of them died for their faith before a law allowing freedom of religion was passed in 1873. A procession is held here on 3 May to commemorate the martyrs.

OTHER SIGHTS

South of town and just a short walk from each other, are the beautiful former residences of **Nishi Amane** (Ushiroda; admission free; ☎ 9am-5pm), a philosopher and political scientist prominent in the Meiji government, and **Mori Ōgai**, a highly regarded novelist who served as a physician in the Imperial Japanese Army. At the rear of the latter is the **Mori Ōgai Memorial Museum** (☎ 72-3210; 238 Machida; museum ¥600, residence grounds ¥100; 🕑 9am-5pm, closed Mon Dec-Mar), a modern building housing many of the writer's personal effects. There are no English explanations.

The **Morijuku Museum** (☎ 72-3200; 542 Morimura; admission ¥300; 🕑 9.30am-4.30pm) is an impressive building that once served as the home of a *shōya* (village headman), with a room of bullfight sketches by Goya and paintings by local artists. Make sure you see the pinhole camera feature on the 2nd floor (the proprietor will gladly show you). **Tsuwano Dentō Kōgeisha** (☎ 72-1518; 8-7 Ushiroda; admission free; 🕑 9am-5pm, closed Tue) is a traditional craft shop where *washi* (Japanese handmade paper) is made. You can watch the paper being made and also have a go at it yourself (¥600 to ¥1000).

Kuwabara Shisei Photography Museum (☎ 72-3171; 71-2 Ushiroda; admission ¥300; 🕑 9am-4.45pm) has a small collection dedicated to the work of Kuwabara Shisei, a photojournalist born near Tsuwano in 1936. It's in the same building as the information office, next to the station. Across the street is the **Anno Mitsumasa Art Museum** (☎ 72-4155; Ekimae; admission ¥800; 🕑 9am-5pm), showing works by the local artist.

Along the main street in Tonomachi are three old sake breweries. First on the left as you head away from the station is **Kasen** (☎ 72-0036; 221 Ushiroda); further up the same street is **Furuhashi** (☎ 72-0048; 196 Ushiroda), home to the Uijin (初陣) brand. In between is **Hashimoto** (☎ 72-0055; 218 Ushiroda), which has been in the same family since 1717, although no brewing takes place on-site now.

South of the town is the shrine **Washibara Hachiman-gū**, about 4km from the station, where **yabusame** (archery contests) on horseback are held on the second Sunday in April.

If you fancy a soak, head to **Nagomi-no-sato** (なごみの里; ☎ 72-4122; 256 Washibara; admission ¥600; 🕑 10am-9pm, closed Thu), an onsen complex that is a 15-minute walk along the main road south of the Mori museum.

Festivals & Events

The **Sagi Mai Matsuri** (Heron Dance Festival), which includes a procession of dancers dressed as herons, is performed on 20 and 27 July. The festival procession takes in the major route from the station through Tonomachi to Yasaka Jinja near the Inari Shrine.

Sleeping

Hoshi Ryokan (☎ 72-0136; fax 72-0241; 53-6 Ushiroda; per person with meals ¥6500; P) The Hoshi Ryokan is a friendly *minshuku* located opposite the bicycle shop, less than a minute's walk from the station. Accommodation is in spacious tatami rooms that include shared bathrooms.

Wakasagi-no-yado Minshuku (☎/fax 72-1146; http://gambo-ad.com/tsuwano/hotel/wakasagi/index.htm, in Japanese; 98-6 Morimura-guchi; per person with 2 meals ¥7500; P) This well-kept *minshuku* is on the main road between Tonomachi and the Mori Ōgai house. Walking from the station, look for the white building on the left with a checked-tile design, and the curtain with a picture of a heron.

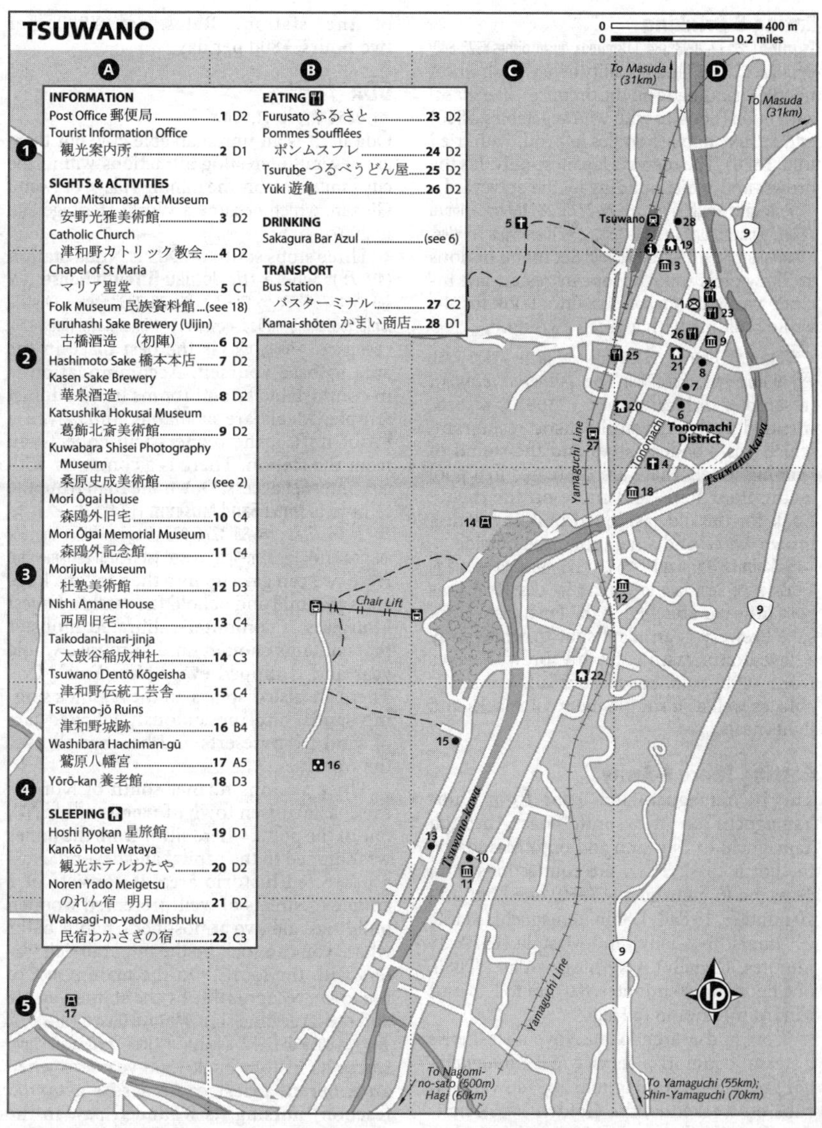

Noren Yado Meigetsu (☎ 72-0685; fax 72-0637; http://gambo-ad.com/tsuwano/hotel/meigetsu/, in Japanese; 665 Ushiroda-guchi; per person with 2 meals from ¥10,500; Ⓟ) The Noren Yado Meigetsu is a traditional ryokan located on a narrow lane off Tonomachi. The ryokan has a warm and welcoming service and the well-kept rooms overlook an attractive garden. Look for the old-fashioned gate with a tiled roof outside the white building.

Kankō Hotel Wataya (☎ 72-0333; fax 72-1543; www.tsuwano.jp, in Japanese; 82-3 Ushiroda-guchi; per person with 2 meals ¥13,650; Ⓟ) The Wataya is a modern, sophisticated onsen complex with Western- and Japanese-style rooms and some very stylish bathing facilities.

Eating & Drinking

Tsurube (☎ 72-2098; 384-1 Ushoroda-guchi; dishes ¥520-840; 11am-6.30pm) The speciality here is fresh wheat noodles handmade on the premises, like *sansai zaru udon* (noodles with wild vegetables; ¥840) and *kitsune udon* (noodles in broth with fried tofu; ¥630). The menu is Japanese only. It's the brown-and-white building by the graveyard.

Pommes Soufflées (☎ 72-2778; 284 Ushiroda; lunch ¥1200, dinner courses ¥2000-3000; 10am-9pm Fri-Wed, bar to midnight Fri & Sat, closed Thu) Set menu options at Tsuwano's only European restaurant include pasta, pizzas, and risotto. Look for the white building with a green awning.

Yūki (☎ 72-0162; 271-4 Ushiroda; meals ¥1300-3000; 10.30am-7pm, closed Thu) The *Tsuwano teishoku* (a sampler of local dishes; ¥2300) is recommended at this elegantly rustic restaurant, which has wooden tables and the sound of running water. There are *koi* (carp) in a pool in the floor here, and more on the menu. Look for the old-fashioned building with a brown *noren* and small pine tree outside.

Sakagura Bar Azul (☎ 72-3355; Tsuwano Honmachi 1-chōme; 5pm-2am, to 4am Fri & Sat, closed Sun) This cosy little bar attached to the Furuhashi Uijin sake brewery is an ideal spot to while away a few hours tasting freshly brewed sakes from ¥400. Sake-based cocktails are available, as well as a simple menu of snacks and light meals.

Getting There & Away

The JR Yamaguchi line runs from Shin-Yamaguchi on the south coast through Yamaguchi to Tsuwano and onto Masuda on the north coast. There are connections from Tsuwano to Yamaguchi (¥950, one hour and 10 minutes, 13 daily), Shin-Yamaguchi (¥1150, 1¾ hours, five daily) and Masuda (¥570, 35 minutes, 12 daily). Five buses a day (¥2080, one hour and 40 minutes, 8.07am to 5.07pm) run from Tsuwano to Hagi.

From mid-March to late November there's a steam locomotive service *(SL Yamaguchi-gō)* from Shin-Yamaguchi to Tsuwano. It runs on weekends, the Golden Week holiday (late April to early May) and from late July to late August. The trip costs ¥1620 and takes two hours. Ask for up-to-date details and book well ahead at JR and tourist information offices.

Getting Around

Rental bicycles are available at **Kamai-shōten** (☎ 72-0342; 8am-7pm), in front of the station. Rates are ¥500 per two hours, ¥800 per day.

ŌDA 大田

☎ 0854 / pop 41,000

Ōda itself is an unremarkable city, but there are several interesting attractions within the city limits, notably the mining village of Iwami Ginzan, which became a World Heritage Site in 2007.

Three stops south of Ōda is Nima Station (仁万), where the **Jōfuku-ji Youth House** (城福寺ユースハウス; ☎ 88-2233; www14.plala.or.jp/joufukuji/, in Japanese; 1114 Nima-machi Nima-chō; r per person ¥3000;) is the best place in the area to base yourself. Accommodation is in comfortable tatami rooms in a Buddhist temple. Meals are available, and, given a bit of notice, the owners will collect you from the station. There is a computer with free internet access. Down the road from the temple is **Nima Sand Museum** (仁摩サンドミュージアム; ☎ 88-3776; 975Amagōchi Nima-chō; admission ¥700; 9am-5pm, closed 1st Wed of each month). Here you can gaze up into the roof of a huge glass pyramid and behold the world's largest hourglass, a computer-calibrated monster that contains enough sand to count a whole year and is flipped every New Year's Eve. There are also displays on the region's singing sands, and meticulously labelled jars of sand from deserts and beaches all over the world.

Three stations further south of Nima is the coastal onsen town of **Yunotsu** (温泉津), one of the ports, where silver from the mines was shipped to the capital and beyond. Now a protected historic area, it consists of a couple of streets of well-preserved wooden buildings and two atmospheric public baths where you can soak up the mineral-rich waters with the locals. On the main street of the town, recognisable by the statue outside and the large blue sign, **Motoyu Onsen** (元湯温泉; ☎ 0855-65-2052; admission ¥300; 5.30am-9pm) traces its history back 1300 years, to when an itinerant priest came across a *tanuki* (racoon) nursing its wounded paw in the waters here. A short walk away on the other side of the street is the relatively modern **Yakushinoyu Onsen** (薬師湯温泉; ☎ 0855-65-4894; admission ¥300; 5am-9pm), discovered when hot water bubbled up from the ground after an earthquake in 1872. There are a number of places to stay here, including the 100-year-old **Ryokan Masuya** (☎ 0855-65-2515; fax 0855-65-2516; www.ryokan-masuya.com; per person with

2 meals from ¥10,600; P), down the street towards the sea from the two public baths. Some English is spoken, and accommodation is in tatami rooms (one Western-style room is available).

Iwami Ginzan 石見銀山

About 6km inland from Nima Station is the old **Iwami Ginzan Silver Mine**. In the early 17th century, the mine produced as much as 38 tonnes of silver annually, making it the most important mine in the country at a time when Japan was producing around a third of the world's silver every year. The Tokugawa shogunate had direct control over the 500 or so mines in the area.

Ōmori is a small town near the mines, with carefully restored houses lining the main street. At the southernmost end of the street is the **Iwami Ginzan Museum** (石見銀山資料館; ☎ 89-0846; admission ¥500; 9am-5pm, to 4pm Dec-Feb), inside the **Ōmori Daikansho Ato** (大森代官所跡; Former Magistrate's Office). Not far up the old road on the left is the lovingly restored **Kumagai Residence** (熊谷家住宅; ☎ 89-9003; admission ¥500; 9.30am-5pm), rebuilt in 1801 after an earthquake destroyed most of the town the previous year. The house belonged to a merchant family who made their fortune as officials in the silver trade. To the left off the main road is an interesting temple, **Rakan-ji** (羅漢寺; ☎ 89-0005; 804 Ōmori-chō; admission ¥500; 8am-5pm), where 500 stone statues of the Buddha's disciples crowd into two small caves beside stone bridges opposite the main temple building. The collection was completed in 1766, after 25 years of work.

A little over 2km further up the main street is the the **Ryūgenji Mabu Shaft** (龍源寺間歩; ☎ 89-0347; admission ¥400; 9am-5pm, to 4pm 24 Nov-19 Mar), which has been widened substantially from its original size. One glance at the original tunnel that stretches beyond the fence at the end of the accessible area should be enough to make most people glad they weren't born as 17th-century miners. Past the Ryūgenji mine shaft, a hiking trail leads 12km to Yunotsu on the coast, following the old route along which silver was hauled to port.

The **Iwami Ginzan World Heritage Centre** (石見銀山世界遺産センター; ☎ 89-0183; 1597-3 Ōmori-chō; admission ¥300; 8.30am-5pm) has exhibits on the history of the mines and the surrounding area. Tours leave from here to the larger **Ōkubo mineshaft** (大久保間歩; ☎ 84-0750; tours ¥3800; 9.30am, 10am, 1.30pm & 2pm Fri-Sun & holidays Mar-Nov).

A good place for a break is **Gungendō** (群言堂; ☎ 89-0077; 183 Ōmori-chō Ōda-shi; coffee & tart set ¥1000; 10am-6pm, closed Wed), a swish cafe on the main street just before the Rakan-ji turning. It's a large building on the corner with an orange post box outside. Close to the bus stop opposite the Daikansho-ato, **O-shokuji-dokoro Ōmori** (お食事処大森; ☎ 89-0106; 44-1 Ōmori-chō; ⊠) is a good spot for lunch, where the *daikan soba* (¥1100) set features *warigo soba* (buckwheat noodles) and tempura.

The **tourist information office** (☎ 89-0333; 9am-5pm May-Sep, to 4pm Oct-Apr) is by the car park close to Rakan-ji. Buses run to the Daikansho-ato from Ōda (¥560, 25 minutes, 18 per day) and Nima (¥390, 15 minutes, five per day) Stations; some buses continue on to the World Heritage Center. Within the mine area, shuttle buses connect the Daikansho-ato and the World Heritage Center every 15 minutes (¥200).

Sanbe-san 三瓶山

About 20km inland from Ōda is Sanbe-san, an old volcano with grassy slopes that reaches 1126m. It takes about an hour to climb from **Sanbe Onsen** and five hours to walk around the caldera. You can have a dip in the onsen on your return. Day-trippers can try the outdoor baths at **Kokuminshukusha Sanbesō** (国民宿舎さんべ荘; ☎ 83-2011; www.komachi-web.com/sanbe/, in Japanese; Shigaku Sanbe-chō Ōda-shi; baths ¥500, r per person from ¥7400; 10.30am-9pm; P), where accommodation is available. The area is a popular ski centre in winter. Buses run between Ōda and Sanbe Onsen (¥830, 40 minutes).

IZUMO 出雲

☎ 0853 / pop 148,000

Only 38km west of Matsue, Izumo has one major attraction – the great **Izumo Taisha shrine** (出雲大社; ☎ 53-3100; 195 Kizuki Higashi Taisha-chō; 6am-8pm), which ranks with Ise-jingū (p443) as one of the most important shrines in Japan.

Orientation & Information

Izumo Taisha is 8km northwest of central Izumo. The shrine area, basically one sleepy street, is accessible from the Ichibata Line Taisha Ekimae Station and runs right up the shrine gates. Izumo Taisha can be visited easily as a day trip from Matsue. The **tourist information office** (☎ 53-2298; 1346-9 Kizuki Minami Shinmondōri Taisha-chō; 9am-5.30pm) is located in the station building, and has pamphlets and maps.

Sights

IZUMO TAISHA 出雲大社

Perhaps the oldest Shintō shrine of all, Izumo is second in importance only to Ise-jingū, the home of the sun goddess Amaterasu. The shrine is as old as Japanese history – there are references to Izumo in the *Kojiki,* Japan's oldest book – and its origins stretch back into the age of the gods. Impressive as the structure is today, it was once even bigger. Records dating from AD 970 describe the shrine as the tallest building in the country; there is evidence that the shrine towered as high as 48m above the ground during the Heian period. It may well have been too high for its own good – the structure collapsed five times between 1061 and 1225, and the roofs today are a more modest 24m.

The current appearance of the main shrine dates from 1744. The main hall is currently undergoing one of its periodic rebuildings, and from April 2008 to May 2013 the deity will take up residence in a temporary shrine in front of the main hall.

The shrine is dedicated to Ōkuninushi, who, according to tradition, ceded control over Izumo to the sun goddess' line – he did this on the condition that a huge temple would be built in his honour, one that would reach as high as the heavens. Long revered as a bringer of good fortune, Ōkuninushi is worshipped as the god of marriage, and visitors to the shrine summon the deity by clapping four times rather than the usual two.

Huge *shimenawa* (twisted straw ropes) hang over the entry to the main buildings. Those who can toss and lodge a coin in them are said to be blessed with good fortune. Visitors are not allowed inside the main shrine precinct, most of which is hidden behind huge wooden fences. Ranged along the sides of the compound are the *jūku-sha,* which are long shelters where Japan's myriad deities stay when they come for their annual conference.

On the southeastern side of the compound is **Shinko-den** (神祜殿; Treasure House; admission ¥150; 8.30am-4.30pm), with a collection of shrine paraphernalia.

Just to the right of the shrine's front gate is **Shimane Museum of Ancient Izumo** (島根県立古代出雲歴史博物館; ☎ 53-8600; 99-4 Kizuki Higashi Taisha-chō; admission ¥600, foreigners with ID ¥300; 9am-6pm, to 5pm Nov-Feb, closed 3rd Tue of month; P), containing exhibits on local history. These include reconstructions of the shrine in its pomp, and recordings of the annual ceremonies held to welcome the gods to Izumo. The museum also houses a superb collection of bronze from the ancient Yayoi period, excavated nearby in 1996.

To get an idea of the original size of Izumo Taisha, check out the **Kodai Izumo Ōyashiro Mokei Tenjikan** (古代出雲大社模型展示館; Ancient Izumo Shrine Model Hall; ☎ 53-3100; admission free; 8.30am-4.30pm), where there is a scale model of the shrine as it was about 800 years ago.

HINO-MISAKI 日御碕

It's less than 10km from Izumo Taisha to **Hino-misaki** cape, where you'll find a beautiful lighthouse, some fine views and another shrine. On the way you'll pass the pleasant **Inasa-no-hama**, a good swimming beach just 2km from Taisha Ekimae Station. This is where the gods arrive by sea for their annual powwow in the 10th month of the lunar calendar; a team of priests escorts them by night to their temporary lodgings at Izumo Taisha. Buses run from the station to the cape via the beach (¥530, 35 minutes, 13 per day). Bright-orange **Hinomisaki-jinja**, near the bus terminal, is an ancient shrine dedicated to Amaterasu and her brother Susa-no-o. The present structure was built on the orders of Tokugawa Iemitsu (1604–1651), the third Tokugawa shogun. Coastal paths head north and south from the car park, offering fine views, particularly from the top of the 1903 **lighthouse** (日御碕灯台; admission ¥200; 9am-4.30pm).

Festivals & Events

The 10th month of the lunar calendar is known throughout Japan as Kan-na-zuki (Month without Gods). In Izumo, however, it is known as Kami-ari-zuki (Month with Gods), for this is the month when all the Shintō gods congregate at Izumo Taisha.

The **Kamiari-sai** festival is a series of events to mark the arrival of the gods in Izumo. It runs from the 11th to the 17th of the 10th month according to the old calendar; exact dates vary from year to year.

Sleeping & Eating

Izumo has 'day trip' written all over it: the area around the shrine is devoid of life after sunset. There's slightly more going on in downtown Izumo, half an hour away by bus or train. If you're determined to spend the night near the shrine, there are several inns around, including **Fujiwara Ryokan** (藤原旅館;

(☎ 53-2009; fax 53-2524; Seimonmae Taisha-chō; s/tw with 2 meals ¥10,500/21,000; P), close to the shrine gates. It's on the left as you walk from the station towards the shrine. Look for the large pine tree outside. There is the usual clutch of business hotels around the JR station in downtown Izumo, including **Tōyoko Inn** (東横イン; ☎ 25-1044; fax 25-2046; www.toyoko-inn.com; 971-13 Imaichi-chō; s/d ¥5250/7350; P ⊠ 💻), where internet access is available in the lobby.

Yashiroya (☎ 53-2596; 72-5 Kizuki-higashi Taisha-chō; ⏲ 10am-7pm, closed Tue), opposite the museum, is a good place to try the local *warigo soba* (¥700). It's the white building with a tiled roof. In Izumo city, **Hanaman** (華満; ☎ 21-3913; 928-12 Imaichi-chō; ⏲ lunch & dinner, closed Wed) is a pleasant *izakaya*-style place with fresh fish and local sakes. It's on the right as you head down the main street away from the station; look for the name of the restaurant in big black characters.

Getting There & Away

The private Ichibata line starts from Matsue Shinjiko-onsen Station in Matsue and runs along the northern side of Shinji-ko (Lake Shinsji) to Taisha Ekimae Station (¥790, one hour, with a transfer at Kawato, 川跡). The JR line runs from JR Matsue Station to JR Izumo-shi Station (¥570, 42 minutes), where you can transfer to an Ichibata train to Izumo Taisha (¥480). There are also buses to the shrine from Izumo-shi Station (¥490, 25 minutes).

Izumo airport has daily flights to/from Tokyo (¥31,400, one hour and 20 minutes), Osaka (¥19,200, 55 minutes), Fukuoka (¥25,300, one hour and 10 minutes) and the Oki Islands (¥12,300, 30 minutes).

MATSUE 松江

☎ 0852 / pop 194,000

With its fine castle and spectacular sunsets over Shinji-ko (Lake Shinji), Matsue is a pleasant, laid-back city with some interesting historical attractions. The city straddles the Ōhashi-gawa, which connects Shinji-ko with Nakanoumi, a saline lake. Most of the sites are in a compact area in the north, where you'll find the castle, a samurai residence and the house of Lafcadio Hearn.

Information

Shimane International Centre (☎ 31-5056; 3rd fl, Town Plaza Shimane, 8-3 Tonomachi; ⏲ 9am-7pm Mon-Fri, closed Sat, to 5pm Sun). Here you'll find information, a small library and internet access.

Tourist information office (☎ 21-4034; 665 Asahi-machi; ⏲ 9am-6pm) Directly in front of JR Matsue Station.

Sights

MATSUE-JŌ 松江城

Dating from 1611, picturesque **Matsue-jō** (Matsue Castle; ☎ 21-4030; 1-5 Tonomachi; admission ¥550, foreigners with ID ¥280; ⏲ 8.30am-6.30pm Apr-Sep, to 5pm Oct-Mar) has a wooden interior showcasing treasures belonging to the Matsudaira clan. Known as Plover Castle for the graceful shape of its gable ornaments, Matsue-jō is one of only 12 original keeps left in Japan.

Horikawa Pleasure Boat tours (☎ 27-0417; ¥1200, foreigners with ID ¥800; ⏲ every 15-20min 9am-5pm Mar-Jun & Sep–mid-Oct, to 6pm Jul & Aug, to 4pm mid-Oct–Feb) circumnavigate the castle moat and then zip around the city's canals and beneath a series of bridges.

KOIZUMI YAKUMO (LAFCADIO HEARN) RESIDENCE 小泉八雲旧宅

Matsue's favourite Irishman lived in this house with its attractive garden for 15 months shortly after his arrival in Japan. The view from his study is little changed since Hearn described it in his 1892 essay 'In a Japanese Garden'. The former **residence** (admission ¥350; ⏲ 9am-4.30pm) is at the northern end of Shiomi Nawate.

KOIZUMI YAKUMO (LAFCADIO HEARN) MEMORIAL MUSEUM 小泉八雲記念館

Next door to Hearn's former home is this **memorial museum** (☎ 21-2147; 322 Okudani-chō; admission ¥300, foreigners with ID ¥150; ⏲ 8.30am-6.30pm Apr-Sep, to 5pm Oct-Mar), which has displays on Hearn's life and work as well as personal effects – including his dumb-bells, his spectacles, and a stack of Japanese newspapers on which Hearn wrote words and phrases to teach English to his son. You can also see some of the letters that Hearn and his wife wrote to each other – all written painstakingly in the phonetic syllabary, since Hearn (despite all his other achievements) never learned how to read Japanese properly.

TANABE ART MUSEUM 田部美術館

This **museum** (☎ 26-2211; 310-5 Kitahori-chō; admission ¥600; ⏲ 9am-4.30pm Tue-Sun) exhibits a collection of bowls, scrolls and other items relating to the tea ceremony, and many of the items are associated with the Matsudaira family who ruled Matsue during the Edo period.

BUKE YASHIKI SAMURAI RESIDENCE 武家屋敷

Built for a middle-ranking samurai family during the early 18th century, **Buke Yashiki**

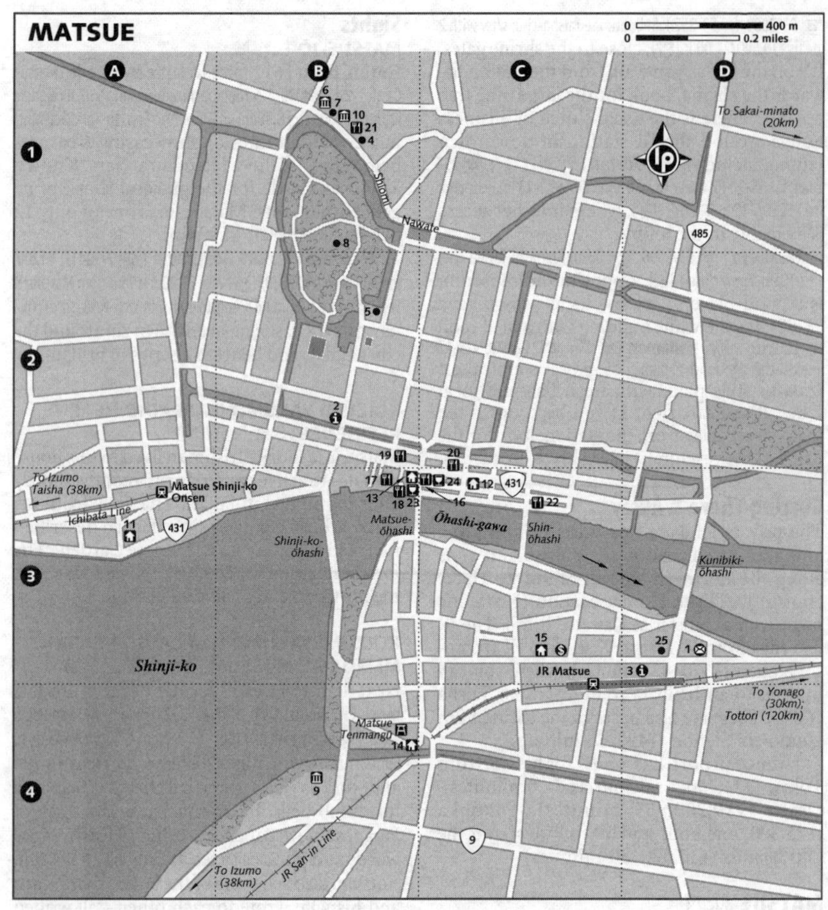

(☎ 22-2243; 305 Kitahori-chō; admission ¥300, foreigners with ID ¥150; 🕓 8.30am-6.30pm Apr-Sep, to 5pm Oct-Mar) is an immaculately preserved house and garden.

SHIMANE PREFECTURAL ART MUSEUM
島根県立博物館

This impressive **museum** (☎ 55-4700; 1-5 Sodeshi-chō; admission ¥300; 🕓 10am-6.30pm, to 30min after sunset Mar-Sep, closed Tue; P) displays rotating exhibits from its collection of European paintings, wood-block prints and contemporary art. It's in a perfect spot overlooking the lake, and is famous for the sunset views from the 2nd-floor viewing platform or outside by the water. The museum is a 15-minute walk west of the station.

Sleeping

Terazuya (☎ 21-3480; fax 21-3422; www.mable.ne.jp/~terazuya/english; 60-3 Tenjin-machi; per person with/without 2 meals ¥7000/4000; P 💻) This friendly ryokan, next to Matsue Tenmangū shrine, is a great budget option. Some English is spoken, and there's free internet access. Accommodation is in smart tatami rooms with shared bathrooms.

Matsue City Hotel (☎ 25-4100; fax 25-4102; www2.crosstalk.or.jp/sobido/dalian/ctyhote.html, in Japanese; 31 Suetsugu Honmachi; s/tw ¥3900/5500; P 💻) Right by Matsue-ōhashi bridge, this recently renovated hotel is housed in an old-fashioned building and has antique clocks on every floor. Look for the clocktower on the left-hand side as you cross the bridge away from the station.

INFORMATION
- Post Office 郵便局 1 D3
- Shimane International Centre しまね国際センター 2 B2
- Tourist Information Office 観光案内所 3 D3

SIGHTS & ACTIVITIES
- Buke Yashiki Samurai Residence 武家屋敷 4 B1
- Horikawa Pleasure Boat Tours 堀川めぐり 5 B2
- Koizumi Yakumo (Lafcadio Hearn) Memorial Museum 小泉八雲記念館 6 B1
- Koizumi Yakumo (Lafcadio Hearn) Residence 小泉八雲旧宅 7 B1
- Matsue-jō 松江城 8 B1
- Shimane Prefectural Art Museum 島根県立美術館 9 B4
- Tanabe Art Museum 田部美術館 10 B1

SLEEPING
- Hotel Ichibata ホテル一畑 11 A3
- Hotel Route Inn Matsue ホテルルートイン松江 12 C3
- Matsue City Hotel 松江シティホテル 13 B3
- Terazuya 旅館寺津屋 14 B4
- Tōyoko Inn Matsue Ekimae 東横イン松江駅前 15 C3

EATING
- Kawa-kyō 川京 16 C3
- Minamikan 皆美館 17 B3
- Naniwa なにわ 18 B3
- Pasta Factory パスタファクトリー 19 B2
- Tsurumaru 鶴丸 20 C2
- Yakumo-an 八雲庵 21 B1
- Yamaichi やまいち 22 C3

DRINKING
- Cafe Bar EAD カフェバーEAD 23 B3
- Filaments フィラメンツ 24 C3

TRANSPORT
- Mazda Rent-a-Car マツダレンタカー 25 D3

Tōyoko Inn Matsue Ekimae (☎ 60-1045; fax 60-1046; www.toyoko-inn.com; 498-10 Asahi-machi; s/tw with breakfast ¥5040/7700; P) The ever-dependable Tōyoko Inn is close to the station and has small but comfortable rooms with LAN internet and terminals in the lobby.

Hotel Route Inn Matsue (☎ 20-6211; fax 20-6215; www.route-inn.co.jp/english/pref/shimane.html/matsue; 2-22 Higashi Honmachi; s/tw ¥5000/10,500; P) Across the river from JR Matsue Station in the entertainment district, this hotel has views of the downtown area. There is LAN internet in all rooms, and there are consoles in the lobby.

Hotel Ichibata (☎ 22-0188; fax 22-0230; www.ichibata.co.jp/hotel, in Japanese; 30 Chidōri-chō; s/tw ¥9390/17,100; P) Located on the lakeside close to the Matsue Shinjiko-onsen Station, the luxurious Ichibata has great views and impeccable service. There's an onsen with outdoor baths and fine views. There is LAN internet in the rooms, and wireless access in the lobby.

Eating

Pasta Factory (☎ 28-0101; 82 Suetsugu Honmachi; 11.30am-10pm) A swish glass-fronted deli specialising in pasta and sandwiches. The daily pasta lunch ¥980, and the daily hot sandwich is ¥880. There is some English on the menu.

Yakumo-an (☎ 22-2400; 308 Kita Horiuchi; 9am-4.30pm) Next door to the samurai house, this *soba* (buckwheat noodle) restaurant and its beautiful grounds are an excellent place to sample the local *warigo soba*. A combination of noodles with *kamo nanban* (noodles with slices of duck in broth) is ¥1130. Look for the large gate topped by a lantern; there is an English menu.

Tsurumaru (☎ 22-4887; 1-79 Higashi Honmachi; dishes ¥600-1050; 5.30-10.30pm, closed Sun) The smell of fish grilling over coals permeates this restaurant, which specialises in the cuisine of the Oki Islands. The (Japanese-only) menu features things like *eri-yaki konabe* (hot spicy soup cooked over a flame at your table; ¥630). *Sashimi moriawase* is ¥1260. You'll know it by the *noren* with the crane on it, and the rustic folk-singing that plays into the street.

Kawa-kyō (☎ 22-1312; 65 Suetsugu Honmachi; meals ¥800-1300; 6-10.30pm, closed Sun) You can count on a friendly welcome at this *izakaya*-style restaurant that specialises in the 'seven delicacies' from Shinji-ko (see p501). The daughter of the family speaks good English, and an English menu is available. Look for the lantern hanging outside with 川京 on it.

Yamaichi (☎ 23-0223; 4-1 Higashi Honmachi; 4.30-9.30pm, to 9pm Sun) This atmospheric *izakaya* is a good place to try the local specialities. It's an old-fashioned little place with a small Shintō shrine above the bar. The 'seven delicacies' are available here, along with other options such as a *sashimi moriawase* (at market price). The menu is handwritten above the counter in Japanese only. It's immediately on the right after you cross over the Shin-ōhashi bridge; there is a white sign with the name of the restaurant in black: やまいち.

Minamikan (☎ 21-5131; 14 Suetsugu Honmachi; meals ¥1500-10,000; lunch & dinner) Top-quality Japanese food in an exquisite ryokan set directly on the river. *Kisetsu bentō* (seasonal *bentō*) go for around ¥3360; the *tai meshi gozen* (sea-bream course; ¥3780) is another beautifully arranged treat. Lunchtime deals start at ¥1575. The menu has some pictures. Look for a driveway leading to the entrance.

Naniwa (☎ 21-2835; 21 Suetsugu Honmachi; lunch & dinner) Next to Matsue-ōhashi bridge, this bright restaurant is an elegant spot for *unameshi* (eel and rice; ¥2625). Courses featuring the local specialities start at ¥4200 for a *Shinji-ko* course.

Drinking

Filaments (☎ 24-8984; 5 Hakkenya-chō; drinks from ¥600; ⏰ 7.30pm-late) This mellow little bar near the river is a good spot to chill out and chat with the owner into the early hours.

Cafe Bar EAD (☎ 28-3130; 36 Suetsugu Honmachi; drinks from ¥525; ⏰ 5pm-midnight Thu & Mon, to 1am Fri-Sun) There are great river views from the terrace of this relaxed spot, found as you head away from the bridge. Snacks include homemade pizzas (such as tomato and anchovy for ¥735). Take the stairs beside the EAD used-clothing shop by the bridge and climb to the 3rd floor.

Getting There & Away

Matsue is on the JR San-in line, which runs along the San-in coast. You can get to Okayama via Yonago on the JR Hakubi line. It's ¥480 to Yonago (35 minutes), then ¥4620 to Okayama by *tokkyū* (two hours and 15 minutes).

Matsue is served by Izumo and Yonago airports. There are flights to Tokyo, Osaka, Nagoya, Fukuoka, the Oki Islands and Seoul. Highway buses operate to Japan's major cities.

Getting Around

The red streetcar-like Lake Line buses follow a set route around the city's attractions every 20 minutes from 8.40am to 5.40pm. One ride costs ¥200, or a day pass is available for ¥500.

Matsue is a good place to explore by bicycle; these can be rented close to Matsue station at **Mazda Rent-a-Car** (☎ 26-8787; 466-1 Asahimachi; ⏰ 8.30am-6pm). Rates are ¥300 per day.

JAPAN'S ADOPTED SON

Mention Lafcadio Hearn (1850–1904) to people in the English-speaking world today, and you're likely to be met with blank stares. But in Japan, where he's known as Koizumi Yakumo, he's a superstar. More than 100 years after his death, Hearn remains a beloved figure in his adopted homeland, his books cherished for providing glimpses of life in Japan during the early years of the country's emergence as a modern power – a vanished world as alien to the inhabitants of Osaka and Tokyo today as his was to original readers in Boston and London 100 years ago.

At the turn of the 20th century, Lafcadio Hearn was synonymous with Japan. Indeed, for many people in the West, Lafcadio Hearn *was* Japan – but his life would have been a remarkable one even if he'd never set foot in the 'fairyland' that made him famous. Born to a Greek mother and an Anglo-Irish army surgeon on the island of Lefkada in the Ionian Sea, Patrick Lafcadio Hearn grew up in Dublin and studied in England before being packed off at 19 with a one-way ticket to America and instructions to try his luck in the New World. An odd-looking misfit of a man with atrocious eyesight and the paranoia of a born outsider, he eventually found work as a journalist in Cincinnati – until he scandalised acquaintances by marrying a black woman and found himself cast out from polite society. Hearn fled to New Orleans, where he wrote about voodoo and began to develop the taste for the exotic that would characterise his writing on Japan. After two years in the French West Indies, Hearn accepted an assignment from *Harper's* magazine to travel to Japan. He landed in Yokohama in 1890, and never left the country again.

Hearn arrived at the height of one of the Western world's periodic bouts of infatuation with Japan, and soon became famous for the articles and books in which he introduced the wonders of this faraway land to the English-speaking world. Eager to stay on after his contract with *Harper's* ran out, Hearn did what many others have done since, and took a job teaching English. For 15 idyllic months he lived in the provincial castle town of Matsue, where he married Koizumi Setsu, the daughter of a local samurai family. The house where they lived is now one of the most popular tourist destinations in western Japan. After a stint in Kumamoto and a period as a journalist in Kobe, he finally settled in Tokyo – 'the most horrible place in Japan' – where he was appointed professor of English Literature at Tokyo Imperial University. He became a naturalised citizen in 1895 and died less than 10 years later, at the age of 54.

Although Japan has changed almost beyond recognition in the century or so since Hearn lived here, his best pieces have stood the test of time and many of them are well worth reading today. His first Japan-themed collection, *Glimpses of Unfamiliar Japan* (1894), contains his famous essay on Matsue – 'Chief City of the Province of the Gods', as well as an account of his trip to Izumo (p496), where he was the first European allowed inside the gates of the ancient shrine. *Kwaidan,* a collection of ghost stories, was made into a successful film by Kobayashi Masaki in 1964.

AROUND MATSUE & IZUMO

Shimane-hantō 島根半島

North of Matsue, the coastline of the Shimane-hantō (Shimane Peninsula) has some spectacular scenery, particularly around Kaga. From April to October, 50-minute boat tours run from **Marine Plaza Shimane** (☎ 0852-85-9111; tour per person ¥1200, minimum 3 people) to the sea cave at Kaga-no-Kukedo. Take an Ichibata bus from Matsue Station to Marine Gate, where you can change for another bus to the Marine Plaza.

Adachi Art Museum 足立美術館

East of Matsue in Yasugi is this excellent **museum** (☎ 0854-28-7111; 320 Furukawa-chō, Yasugi-shi; admission ¥2200, foreigners with ID ¥1100; 9am-5.30pm, to 5pm Oct-Mar; P). Founded by local businessman and art collector Adachi Zenkō, the collection here includes more than 100 paintings by Yokoyama Taikan (1868–1958) and a good selection of works by other major Japanese painters of the 20th century. But the real attraction is the stunning gardens, regularly voted among the best in Japan. Take the JR line to Yasugi (安来), where there's a free shuttle bus to the museum (nine daily from 9.40am to 4.05pm).

OKI-SHOTŌ 隠岐諸島

☎ 08512 / pop 24,000

North of Matsue are the Oki-shotō (Oki Islands), with spectacular scenery and steep cliffs. Strictly for those who want to get away from it all, they were once used to exile prisoners (as well as two emperors) who came out on the losing side of political squabbles. The group consists of several islands, including the three Dōzen islands and the larger Dōgo. The 7km-long cliffs of the Oki Kuniga coast of **Nishi-no-shima**, at times falling 250 sheer metres into the sea, are particularly noteworthy. **Kokobun-ji** on Dōgo dates from the 8th century. **Bullfights** are an attraction on Dōgo during the summer months – not man versus bull, but bull versus bull.

If you're keen to go, allow at least a couple of days and pop into the information office at Matsue Station to make any necessary bookings and get information before you head off. Pick up the simple English-language brochure and map of the islands called *Oki National Park*. There's also the Japanese-only website www.e-oki.net.

The islands have some *minshuku* and other forms of accommodation, and places to camp.

Ferry services to the Oki Islands from Shichirui and Sakai-minato, which are north-east of Matsue, are operated by **Oki Kisen** (☎ 0851-22-1122). For Dōgo-shima, from Matsue bus terminal take the 7.55am bus to Shichirui (七類; ¥1000, 40 minutes), then the 9am ferry (¥3050, 2½ hours). Another ferry leaves Shichirui in the afternoon; the timetable varies depending on the time of year. There are flights to Dōgo from Izumo and Osaka.

DELICACIES FROM THE LAKE

Matsue's *kyodo ryōri* (regional cuisine) includes the 'seven delicacies' from Shinji-ko.

- *suzuki* or *hōsho yaki* – steam-baked and paper-wrapped bass
- *shirauo* – whitebait tempura or sashimi
- *amasagi* – sweet tempura or teriyaki
- *shijimi* – freshwater clams in miso soup
- *moroge ebi* – steamed shrimp
- *koi* – baked carp
- *unagi* – grilled freshwater eel

TOTTORI-KEN 鳥取県

Although Tottori is the least populous of Japan's 47 prefectures, it has a wealth of spectacular coastal scenery, sand dunes, onsen and volcanoes. Summer is the best time to visit. The large city of Yonago (米子) is a major transport hub, with trains heading south to Okayama on the San-yō coast.

DAISEN 大山

☎ 0859

Although it's not one of Japan's highest mountains, at 1729m Daisen looks impressive because it rises straight from sea level – its summit is only about 10km from the coast.

The popular climb up the volcano is a five-to six-hour return trip from **Daisen-ji** (大山寺) temple. Up a stone path is **Ōgamiyama-jinja** (大神山神社) shrine, the oldest building in western Tottori-ken. From the summit, there are fine views over the coast and, in perfect conditions, all the way to the Oki-shotō. Pick up a copy of Lonely Planet's *Hiking in Japan* for detailed information on hiking Daisen.

Buses run to the temple from Yonago (¥800, 50 minutes, eight daily from 7.20am to 6.10pm). At the temple is the **Daisen-ji Tourist**

Information Centre (☎ 52-2502; ⏲ 8.30am-5pm Mon-Fri, to 6.30pm Sat & Sun), with brochures, maps and hiking information. Staff can arrange bookings at the local ryokan.

The mountain catches the northwest monsoon winds in the winter, bringing lots of snow to western Japan's top skiing area. **Daisen Kokusai Ski Resort** (大山国際スキー場; ☎ 52-2321; www.daisen.net) is one of four linked ski hills on the lower slopes.

ALONG THE COAST TO TOTTORI

About 6km north of Kurayoshi (倉吉) Station is **Lake Tōgo**, with **Hawai Onsen** on its western side and **Tōgo Onsen** on its eastern side. There are buses from Kurayoshi Station, where the **tourist information office** (⏲ 8.30am-5pm, closed Wed) has free bikes for hire. There is plenty of accommodation at Hawai Onsen, including **Bōkorō** (望湖楼; ☎ 0858-35-2221; fax 0858-35-2675; www.bokoro.com; 4-25 Hawai Onsen; per person with 2 meals from ¥12,600), a large resort-style hotel on the lake with Japanese-style rooms and swish indoor and outdoor baths. Nearby is a friendly local *sentō* (public bath) with a glass ceiling called **Hawai Yūtown** (ハワイゆ〜たうん; ☎ 0858-35-4919; admission ¥350; ⏲ 9am-9pm, closed Tue). The likeness of the town's name to the popular Pacific islands is not lost on the people of Hawai, but – although there's a nice beach – it's not Waimea Bay.

Travelling eastwards there's a succession of impressive **swimming beaches** split by rocky headlands all the way to Tottori city, notably Ishiwaki, Ide-ga-hama, Aoya and Hakuto. You can also take a dip at **Hamamura Onsen Kan** (浜村温泉館; ☎ 0857-82-4567; admission ¥420; ⏲ 10am-10pm, closed 1st Wed of month). From Hamamura Station, head straight and take the first major turning on the right; it's on the left, a seven-minute walk from the station, with delightful indoor and outdoor baths.

TOTTORI 鳥取

☎ 0857 / pop 201,000

Tottori is a medium-sized Japanese city where crowds of Japanese tourists come to take pictures of each other next to camels on the famous sand dunes. There is a **tourist information booth** (☎ 22-3318; ⏲ 9.30am-6.30pm) inside the station, with English-language pamphlets and maps. For internet access, try **Comic Buster Dorothy** (☎ 27-7775; 2-27 Tomiyasu; 1st 30min ¥260, each additional 15min ¥100; ⏲ 24hr), south-east of the station.

Sights

Most of Tottori's attractions are concentrated in a compact little group about 1.5km north-east of the station at the foot of Mt Kyūshō.

Tottori-jō once overlooked the town, but now only the castle's foundations remain. Below is the elegant **Jinpū-kaku Villa** (☎ 26-3595; 2-121 Higashi-machi; admission ¥150; ⏲ 9am-5pm, closed Mon), built as accommodation for the Taishō emperor when he visited as Crown Prince in 1907, and now used as a museum.

The small **Folkcraft Museum** (☎ 26-2367; 651 Sakae-machi; admission ¥500; ⏲ 10am-5pm, closed Wed), a five-minute walk from the JR station, has some attractive antique furniture and kimono fabrics. East of the station is the 17th-century temple and garden **Kannon-in** (☎ 24-5641; 162 Ue-machi; admission with matcha tea ¥600; ⏲ 9am-5pm; Ⓟ).

There are a number of inner-city onsen within a short walk of the station. If you can brave the scorching hot waters, try soaking with the locals at the *sentō* **Hinomaru Onsen** (☎ 22-2648; 401 Suehiro Onsen-chō; admission ¥350; ⏲ 6am-midnight, closed 2nd Mon of month except Jan & Aug), in the heart of the entertainment district.

TOTTORI-SAKYŪ (THE DUNES) 鳥取砂丘

Used as the location for Teshigahara Hiroshi's classic 1964 film *Woman in the Dunes*, the Tottori sand dunes are on the coast about 5km from the city. There's a viewing point on a hillside overlooking the dunes, along with a car park and the usual array of tourist schlock. The dunes stretch for over 10km along the coast and, at some points, can be about 2km wide. You can even get a 'Lawrence of Arabia' photo of yourself accompanied by a camel. There are maps and pamphlets at the **Sand Pal Tottori Information Centre** (☎ 20-2231; 2083-17 Yūyama, Fukube-chō; ⏲ 9am-6pm), which has bikes for hire (¥310 for four hours).

Regular buses sail out to the dunes from Tottori Station (¥360, 20 minutes). The closest stop to the dunes is Sakyū-Sentā (砂丘センター; Dunes Centre).

Sleeping

Matsuya-sō (☎ 22-4891; 3-814 Yoshikata Onsen; s/tw ¥3500/6000; Ⓟ) About a 15-minute walk from the station and behind a high-rise apartment building, this *minshuku*-style lodging is friendly and comfortable. It has simple Japanese rooms and shared bathrooms. From the station, go straight

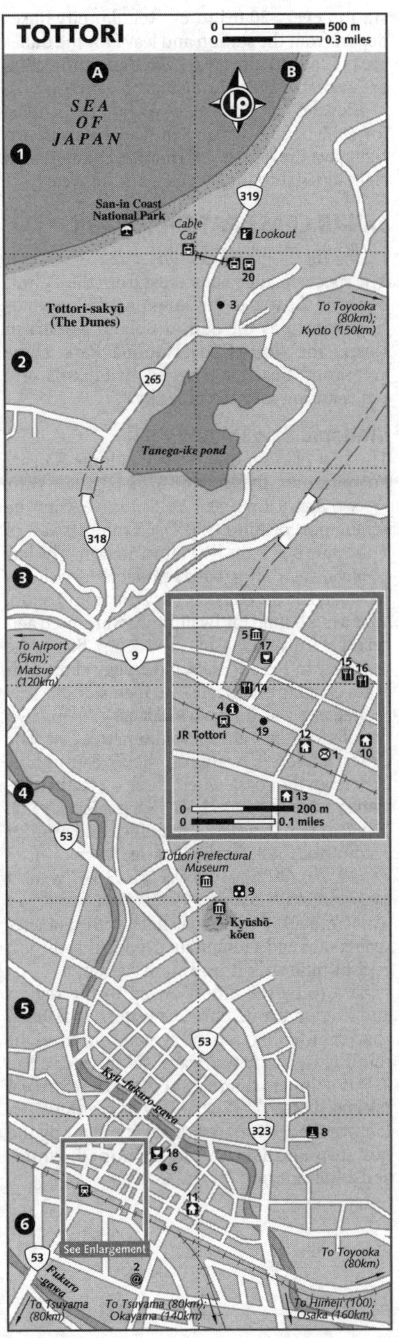

and turn right onto Eiraku-dōri (永楽通り). Look for the yellowish sign on the left.

Tōyoko Inn Tottori Eki Minami-guchi (☎ 36-1045; www.toyoko-inn.com; 2-153-3 Tomiyasu; s/tw with breakfast ¥5460/7560; P ⊠ ◻) A good, clean business hotel a minute from the station with internet access via the terminals in the lobby.

Tottori Washington Hotel Plaza (☎ 27-8111; fax 27-8125; 102 Higashi Honji-chō; s/tw from ¥6900/13,500; P ⊠ ◻) Comfortable rooms are on offer in this large white building by the station. If you have your own computer, there is LAN internet access in all rooms.

Hotel Monarque (☎ 20-0101; fax 27-8181; http://hotel-monarque.jp/, in Japanese; 403 Eiraku Onsen-chō; s/tw from ¥7080/18,780; P ⊠ ◻) This swish weddings-and-reunions type place is a short walk from the station, and has its own onsen on the ground floor. There's LAN internet in all rooms.

Eating & Drinking

Daizen (☎ 27-6574; 715 Sakae-machi; 🕑 11am-midnight) This cheap and cheerful young people's *izakaya* by the station has all the usual favourites

INFORMATION

Central Post Office 鳥取中央郵便局	1	B4
Comic Buster Dorothy コミックバスタードロシー	2	A6
Sand Pal Tottori Information Centre サンドパルとっとり	3	B2
Tourist Information Booth 観光案内所	4	B4

SIGHTS & ACTIVITIES

Folkcraft Museum 民芸美術館	5	B3
Hinomaru Onsen 日乃丸温泉	6	A6
Jinpū-kaku Villa & Museum 仁風閣	7	B5
Kannon-in 観音院	8	B6
Tottori-jō Ruins 鳥取城跡	9	B4

SLEEPING

Hotel Monarque ホテルモナーク鳥取	10	B4
Matsuya-sō 松屋荘	11	A6
Tottori Washington Hotel Plaza 鳥取ワシントンホテル	12	B4
Tōyoko Inn Tottori Eki Minami-guchi 東横イン鳥取駅南口	13	B4

EATING

Daizen 大善	14	B4
Jujuan ジュジュアン	15	B3
Tottori-ya とっ鳥屋	16	B3

DRINKING

Chocolate チョコレート	17	B3
Falkenstein ファルケンシュタイン	18	A6

TRANSPORT

Bike Rental レンタサイクル	19	B4
Sakyū-Sentā Bus Stop (Dunes Centre) 砂丘センター	20	B2

on the Japanese-only menu, including *tempura moriawase* (¥735) and *honjitsu no o-tsukuri san-ten* (three types of sashimi; ¥945). It's on the right as you enter the covered shopping arcade opposite the station; look for the lanterns and banners out the front.

Tottori-ya (☎ 26-5858; 585-1 Yamane; 🕑 5pm-midnight) This bustling *yakitori* (skewers of grilled chicken) place in the heart of the entertainment district has *yakikushi moriawase* (grilled chicken assortments) at ¥609 for six sticks, or ¥1207 for 12. Look for the wooden exterior with a *nawa-noren* (rope curtain) hanging over the door.

Jujuan (☎ 21-1919; 751 Suehiro Onsen-chō; 🕑 lunch & dinner) Fresh seafood and local beef *sumibiyaki* (charcoal grilled) are the specialities in this airy restaurant. Options include *awabi* (abalone; ¥2000) and *shira-ika* (squid; ¥800). It's in the entertainment district, close to the station – look for a white building with a sloped roof on the right as you head away from the station.

Chocolate (☎ 37-2227; 611 Sakae-machi; drinks from ¥550; 🕑 10am-midnight, to 2am Fri & Sat, closed Tue) This long and narrow cafe-bar is a good place to unwind. Meals include pasta carbonara (¥800) and *ebi-iri nama harumaki* (spring rolls with shrimp; ¥600).

Falkenstein (☎ 27-4610; 318 Suehiro Onsen-chō; 🕑 6pm-midnight, closed Sun) This cosy German pub, run for 30 years by an expat from Kiel, is a friendly place to kick back and catch up on the football. German beers from ¥680; sausages from ¥850.

Getting There & Away

The coastal JR San-in line runs through Tottori from Matsue (¥2210, 2¼ hours) and on to Toyooka (*futsū;* ¥1450, 2½ hours) and Kyoto. Express services connect Tottori and Okayama (¥4270, two hours) via Yonago.

Tottori's **airport** (☎ 28-1150; 4-110-5 Koyama-chō Nishi) is just northwest of town, with four daily flights to/from Tokyo. Buses run from Tottori station to the airport (¥450).

Getting Around

A Loop Bus (¥300/600 per ride/day pass) operates on weekends, holidays and from 20 July to 31 August. It connects the station with the dunes. Red- and blue-roofed minibuses (¥100 per ride) ply smaller, inner-city loops from the station every 20 minutes. Regular city buses depart from the station and leave for the dunes area (¥360, 20 minutes). Maps and timetables are available at the information office.

Bicycles can be rented outside the station for ¥500 per day (from 8am to 6.30pm). Turn right past the tourist information counter, then right again into the bicycle parking area.

SAN-IN COAST NATIONAL PARK 山陰海岸国立公園

The spectacular coastline east from the Tottori dunes all the way to the Tango-hantō in Kyoto-fu is known as the San-in Kaigan Kokuritsu Kōen – the San-in Coast National Park. There are sandy beaches, rugged headlands and pines jutting into the blue sky.

Uradome Kaigan 浦富海岸

The first place of interest is Uradome Kaigan. Forty-minute **cruises** (☎ 0857-73-1212; cruise ¥1200; 🕑 every 20min 9.10am-4.10pm Mar-Nov) leave from the fishing port of Ajiro (網代), 35 minutes east of Tottori by bus from JR Tottori Station. The bus goes via the dunes, so it's possible to visit the dunes and do the cruise as a day trip from Tottori. Take a bus bound for Iwami and Iwai Onsen and get off at Kutsui-Ōhashi (沓井大橋). Boat is the only way to see the islets and craggy cliffs, with pines clinging precariously to their sides.

Uradome (浦富) and **Makidani** (牧谷), two popular beaches, are a few kilometres east. The closest station is Iwami on the JR San-in line, 2km from the coast, where there's a **tourist information office** (☎ 0857-72-3481; 🕑 9am-6pm Tue-Sun). You can rent bicycles at the office and arrange accommodation. **Seaside Uradome** (シーサイドうらどめ; ☎ 0857-73-1555; fax 0857-73-1557; www.seasideuradome.com, in Japanese; 2475-18 Uradome Iwamichō; per person from ¥4200; Ⓟ) is a small hotel with Japanese-style rooms and a restaurant overlooking the sea, a 15-minute walk from Iwami station.

Said to be the oldest onsen in the region and known for its curative waters, **Iwai Onsen** is a small collection of ryokan about eight minutes by bus from Iwami station along Rte 9. Day-trippers can relax at modern *sentō* **Iwai Yukamuri Onsen** (岩井ゆかむり温泉; ☎ 0857-73-1670; admission ¥300; 🕑 6am-10pm). It's right by the bus stop and has an old-fashioned, white-and-blue exterior.

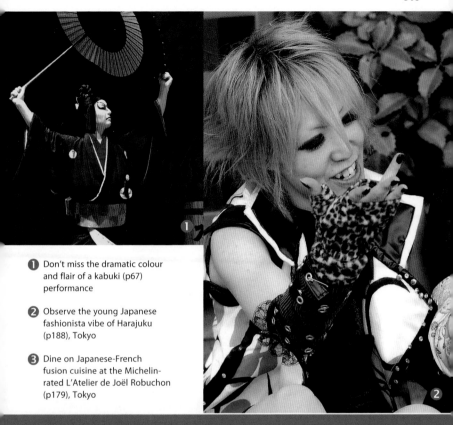

❶ Don't miss the dramatic colour and flair of a kabuki (p67) performance

❷ Observe the young Japanese fashionista vibe of Harajuku (p188), Tokyo

❸ Dine on Japanese-French fusion cuisine at the Michelin-rated L'Atelier de Joël Robuchon (p179), Tokyo

City Life

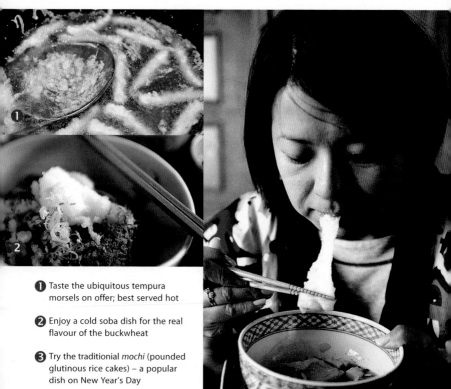

❶ Taste the ubiquitous tempura morsels on offer; best served hot

❷ Enjoy a cold soba dish for the real flavour of the buckwheat

❸ Try the traditionial *mochi* (pounded glutinous rice cakes) – a popular dish on New Year's Day

❹ Sample some delicate sashimi – a quintessential Japanese delicacy

Culinary Delights

Outdoor Activities

1. Soak your bones in the mineral-rich milky waters of Tsuru-no-yu Onsen (p552), Tazawa-ko

2. Hike the spectacular track to Rausu-dake (p640), Shiretoko National Park

3. Enjoy the snow-blanketed slopes while skiing in Hakuba (p294), Japan Alps

Japan's Islands

1 Explore the dense interior jungles and watering holes of Iriomote-jima (p795), Okinawa

2 Delight in some brightly painted toy dragons for sale streetside

3 Take in the relaxing views from the coral-fringed islet of Taketomi-jima (p798), Okinawa

KYOTO TRANSPORT MAP

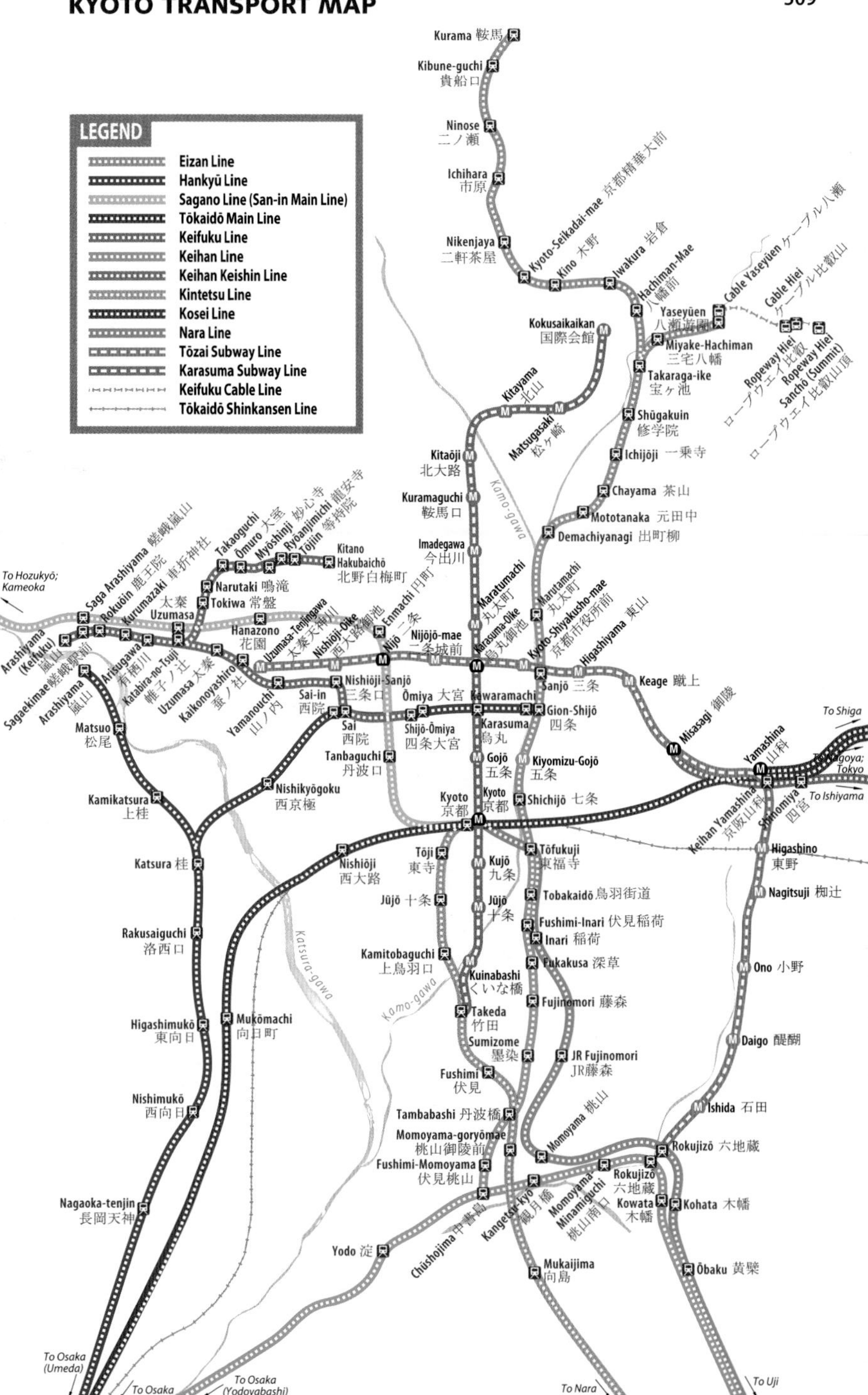

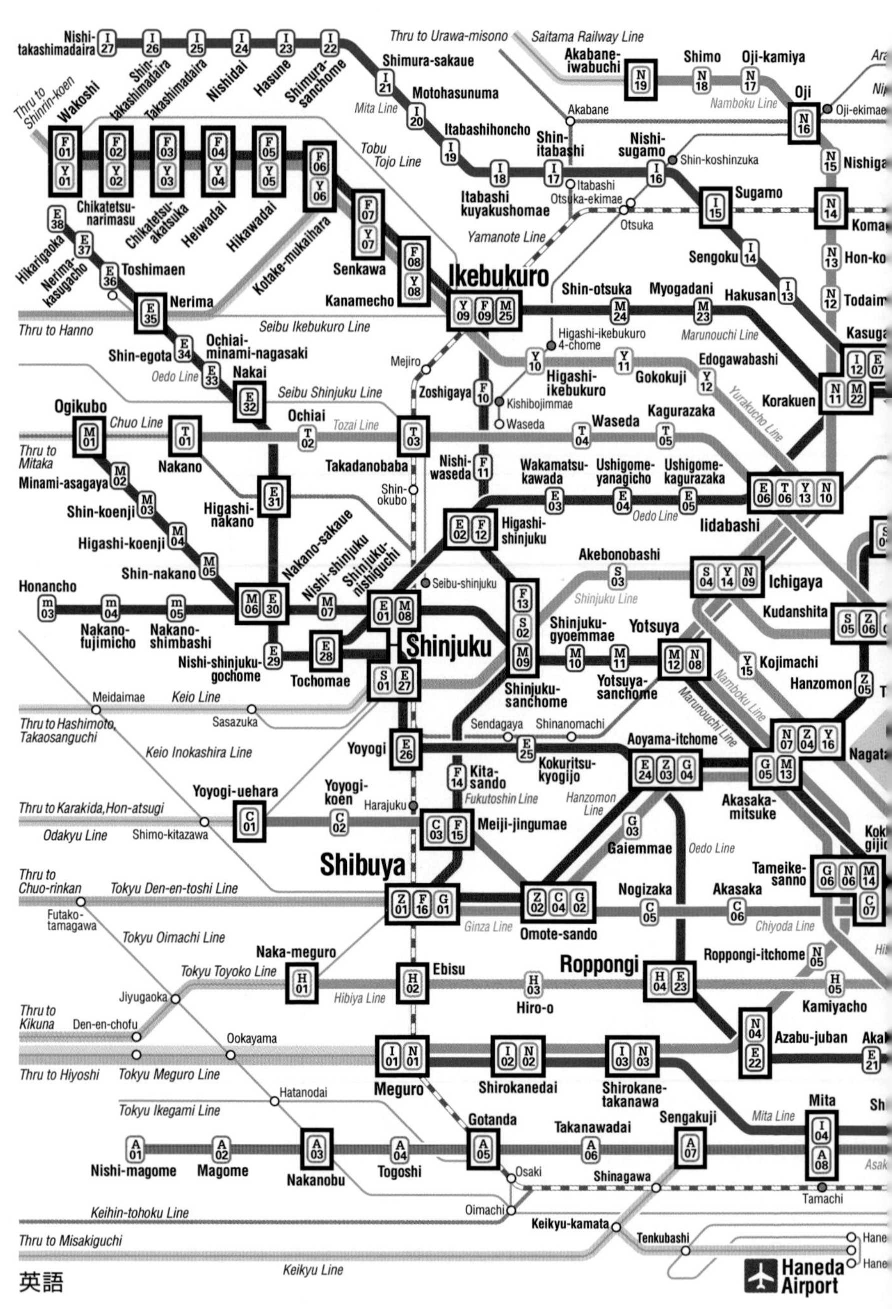

Nishi-takashimadaira
Thru to Shinrin-koen
Wakoshi
Shin-takashimadaira
Takashimadaira
Nishidai
Hasune
Shimura-sanchome
Shimura-sakaue
Thru to Urawa-misono
Saitama Railway Line
Akabane-iwabuchi
Shimo
Oji-kamiya
Oji
Oji-ekimae
Namboku Line
Motohasunuma
Mita Line
Akabane
Itabashihoncho
Tobu Tojo Line
Shin-itabashi
Nishi-sugamo
Shin-koshinzuka
Nishigahara
Itabashi
Otsuka-ekimae
Itabashi kuyakushomae
Sugamo
Otsuka
Komagome
Chikatetsu-narimasu
Chikatetsu-akatsuka
Heiwadai
Hikawadai
Kotake-mukaihara
Senkawa
Yamanote Line
Sengoku
Hon-komagome
Hikarigaoka
Nerima-kasugacho
Toshimaen
Nerima
Kanamecho
Ikebukuro
Shin-otsuka
Myogadani
Hakusan
Todaimae
Thru to Hanno
Seibu Ikebukuro Line
Higashi-ikebukuro 4-chome
Marunouchi Line
Kasuga
Shin-egota
Ochiai-minami-nagasaki
Mejiro
Higashi-ikebukuro
Gokokuji
Edogawabashi
Oedo Line
Nakai
Seibu Shinjuku Line
Zoshigaya
Kishibojimmae
Yurakucho Line
Korakuen
Ogikubo
Chuo Line
Ochiai
Tozai Line
Waseda
Kagurazaka
Thru to Mitaka
Nakano
Takadanobaba
Nishi-waseda
Wakamatsu-kawada
Ushigome-yanagicho
Ushigome-kagurazaka
Minami-asagaya
Shin-okubo
Iidabashi
Shin-koenji
Higashi-nakano
Higashi-shinjuku
Higashi-koenji
Nakano-sakaue
Nishi-shinjuku
Shinjuku-nishiguchi
Akebonobashi
Shin-nakano
Seibu-shinjuku
Ichigaya
Honancho
Shinjuku Line
Kudanshita
Nakano-fujimicho
Nakano-shimbashi
Shinjuku
Shinjuku-gyoemmae
Yotsuya
Nishi-shinjuku-gochome
Tochomae
Kojimachi
Hanzomon
Shinjuku-sanchome
Yotsuya-sanchome
Meidaimae
Keio Line
Thru to Hashimoto, Takaosanguchi
Sasazuka
Sendagaya
Shinanomachi
Keio Inokashira Line
Yoyogi
Aoyama-itchome
Kokuritsu-kyogijo
Nagatacho
Kita-sando
Fukutoshin Line
Hanzomon Line
Yoyogi-uehara
Yoyogi-koen
Harajuku
Akasaka-mitsuke
Thru to Karakida, Hon-atsugi
Odakyu Line
Shimo-kitazawa
Meiji-jingumae
Gaiemmae
Oedo Line
Shibuya
Tameike-sanno
Thru to Chuo-rinkan
Tokyu Den-en-toshi Line
Nogizaka
Akasaka
Futako-tamagawa
Ginza Line
Omote-sando
Chiyoda Line
Tokyu Oimachi Line
Naka-meguro
Roppongi-itchome
Tokyu Toyoko Line
Ebisu
Roppongi
Hibiya Line
Hiro-o
Kamiyacho
Jiyugaoka
Thru to Kikuna
Den-en-chofu
Azabu-juban
Ookayama
Thru to Hiyoshi
Tokyu Meguro Line
Meguro
Shirokanedai
Shirokane-takanawa
Mita
Hatanodai
Tokyu Ikegami Line
Gotanda
Takanawadai
Sengakuji
Mita Line
Nishi-magome
Magome
Nakanobu
Togoshi
Osaki
Shinagawa
Tamachi
Keihin-tohoku Line
Oimachi
Keikyu-kamata
Thru to Misakiguchi
Tenkubashi
Keikyu Line
Haneda Airport

英語

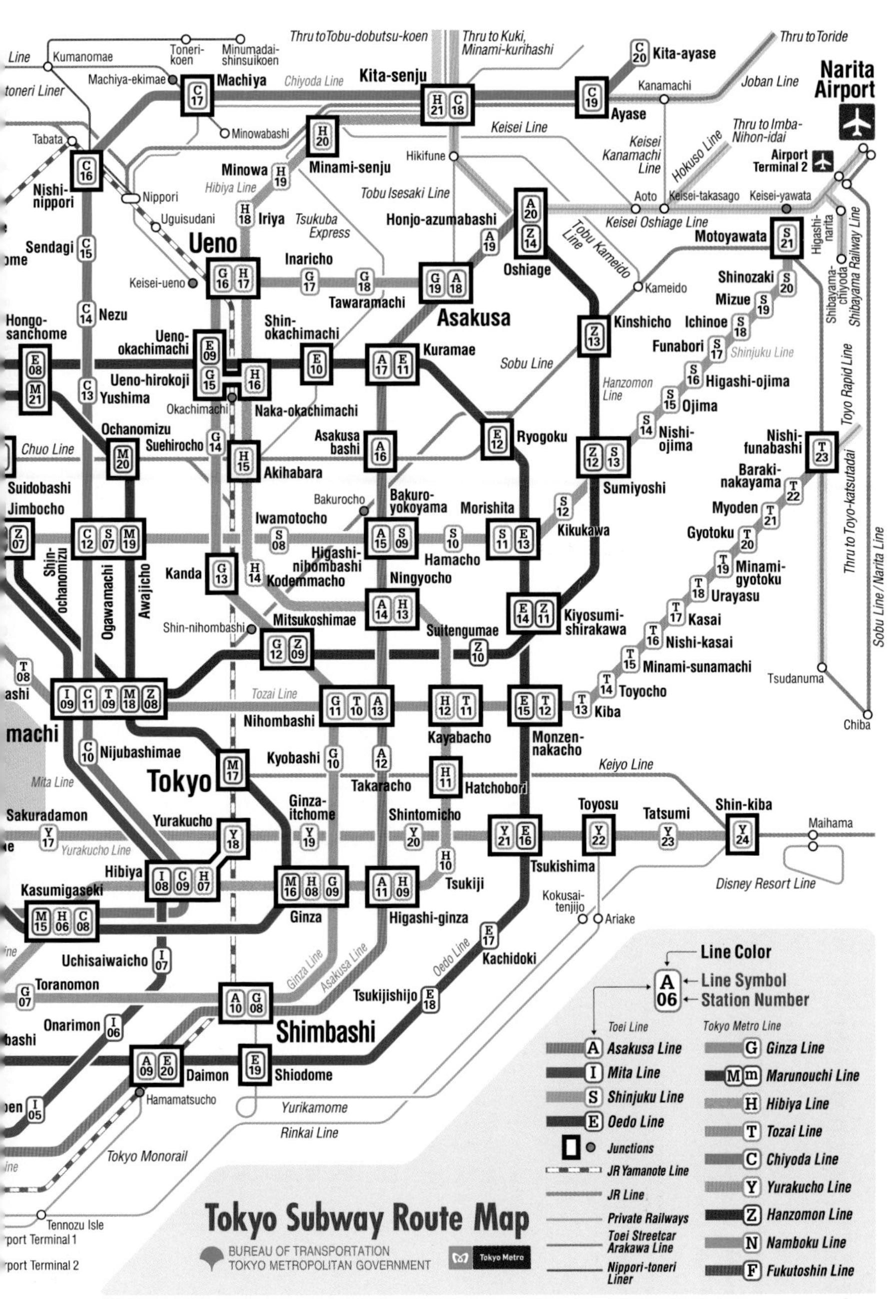

Thru to Tobu-dobutsu-koen
Thru to Kuki, Minami-kurihashi
Thru to Toride
Line
Kumanomae
Toneri-koen
Minumadai-shinsuikoen
C 20 Kita-ayase
Narita Airport
Machiya-ekimae
C 17 Machiya
Chiyoda Line
Kita-senju
H 21 C 18
C 19 Ayase
Kanamachi
Joban Line
toneri Liner
Minowabashi
H 20 Minami-senju
Keisei Line
Thru to Imba-Nihon-idai
Tabata
Keisei Kanamachi Line
Hokuso Line
Airport Terminal 2
C 16 Nishi-nippori
Nippori
Minowa H 19
Hibiya Line
Hikifune
Tobu Isesaki Line
Aoto
Keisei-takasago
Keisei-yawata
Uguisudani
H 18 Iriya
Tsukuba Express
Honjo-azumabashi
A 20 Z 14 Oshiage
Tobu Kameido Line
Keisei Oshiage Line
Motoyawata S 21
Higashi-narita
Shibayama-chiyoda
Shibayama Railway Line
Sendagi C 15
Ueno
A 19
Inaricho
Keisei-ueno
G 16 H 17
G 17
G 18
G 19 A 18
Tawaramachi
Asakusa
Kameido
Shinozaki S 20
Mizue S 19
Hongo-sanchome
C 14 Nezu
Ueno-okachimachi
Shin-okachimachi
Kinshicho
Z 13
Ichinoe S 18
Funabori S 17
Shinjuku Line
E 08 M 21
E 09 G 15
H 16
Ueno-hirokoji
E 10
A 17 E 11 Kuramae
Sobu Line
Hanzomon Line
S 16 Higashi-ojima
S 15 Ojima
Toyo Rapid Line
C 13 Yushima
Okachimachi
Naka-okachimachi
S 14 Nishi-ojima
Ochanomizu
Chuo Line
M 20
Suehirocho G 14
H 15 Akihabara
Asakusabashi A 16
E 12 Ryogoku
Z 12 S 13 Sumiyoshi
Nishi-funabashi T 23
Baraki-nakayama T 22
Suidobashi
Jimbocho
Bakurocho
Bakuro-yokoyama
Morishita
Iwamotocho
S 12
Kikukawa
Myoden T 21
Gyotoku T 20
Thru to Toyo-katsutadai
Sobu Line / Narita Line
Z 07
C 12 S 07 M 19
S 08
A 15 S 09
S 10
S 11 E 13
Shin-ochanomizu
Ogawamachi
Awajicho
Kanda G 13
Higashi-nihombashi
Hamacho
H 14 Kodemmacho
Ningyocho
T 19 Minami-gyotoku
T 18 Urayasu
A 14 H 13
E 14 Z 11 Kiyosumi-shirakawa
T 17 Kasai
Mitsukoshimae
Shin-nihombashi
Suitengumae
T 16 Nishi-kasai
T 15 Minami-sunamachi
G 12 Z 09
Z 10
T 08
ashi
I 09 C 11 T 09 M 18 Z 08
Tozai Line
G 11 T 10 A 13
H 12 T 11
E 15 T 12
T 13 Kiba
T 14 Toyocho
Tsudanuma
Chiba
machi
Nihombashi
Kayabacho
Monzen-nakacho
C 10 Nijubashimae
Kyobashi G 10
A 12
Keiyo Line
Mita Line
Tokyo
M 17
Takaracho
H 11 Hatchobori
Ginza-itchome
Shintomicho
Toyosu
Tatsumi
Shin-kiba
Sakuradamon
Yurakucho
Maihama
Y 17
Y 18
Y 19
Y 20
Y 21 E 16
Y 22
Y 23
Y 24
Yurakucho Line
H 10
Tsukishima
Hibiya
I 08 C 09 H 07
Kasumigaseki
M 16 H 08 G 09
A 11 H 09
Tsukiji
Disney Resort Line
M 15 H 06 C 08
Ginza
Higashi-ginza
Kokusai-tenjijo
Ariake
E 17
Kachidoki
Uchisaiwaicho I 07
Ginza Line
Asakusa Line
Oedo Line
Line Color
Line Symbol
Station Number
G 07 Toranomon
A 10 G 08
Tsukijishijo E 18
Onarimon I 06
bashi
Shimbashi
Toei Line
Tokyo Metro Line
A 09 E 20
Daimon
E 19 Shiodome
A Asakusa Line
G Ginza Line
I Mita Line
M m Marunouchi Line
S Shinjuku Line
H Hibiya Line
E Oedo Line
T Tozai Line
Hamamatsucho
I 05
Yurikamome
Rinkai Line
Junctions
C Chiyoda Line
Tokyo Monorail
JR Yamanote Line
Y Yurakucho Line
JR Line
Z Hanzomon Line
Private Railways
Tokyo Subway Route Map
Toei Streetcar Arakawa Line
N Namboku Line
Tennozu Isle
port Terminal 1
port Terminal 2
BUREAU OF TRANSPORTATION TOKYO METROPOLITAN GOVERNMENT
Tokyo Metro
Nippori-toneri Liner
F Fukutoshin Line
BUREAU OF TRANSPORTATION TOKYO METROPOLITAN GOVERNMENT Tokyo Metro Co., Ltd. © 2008.6

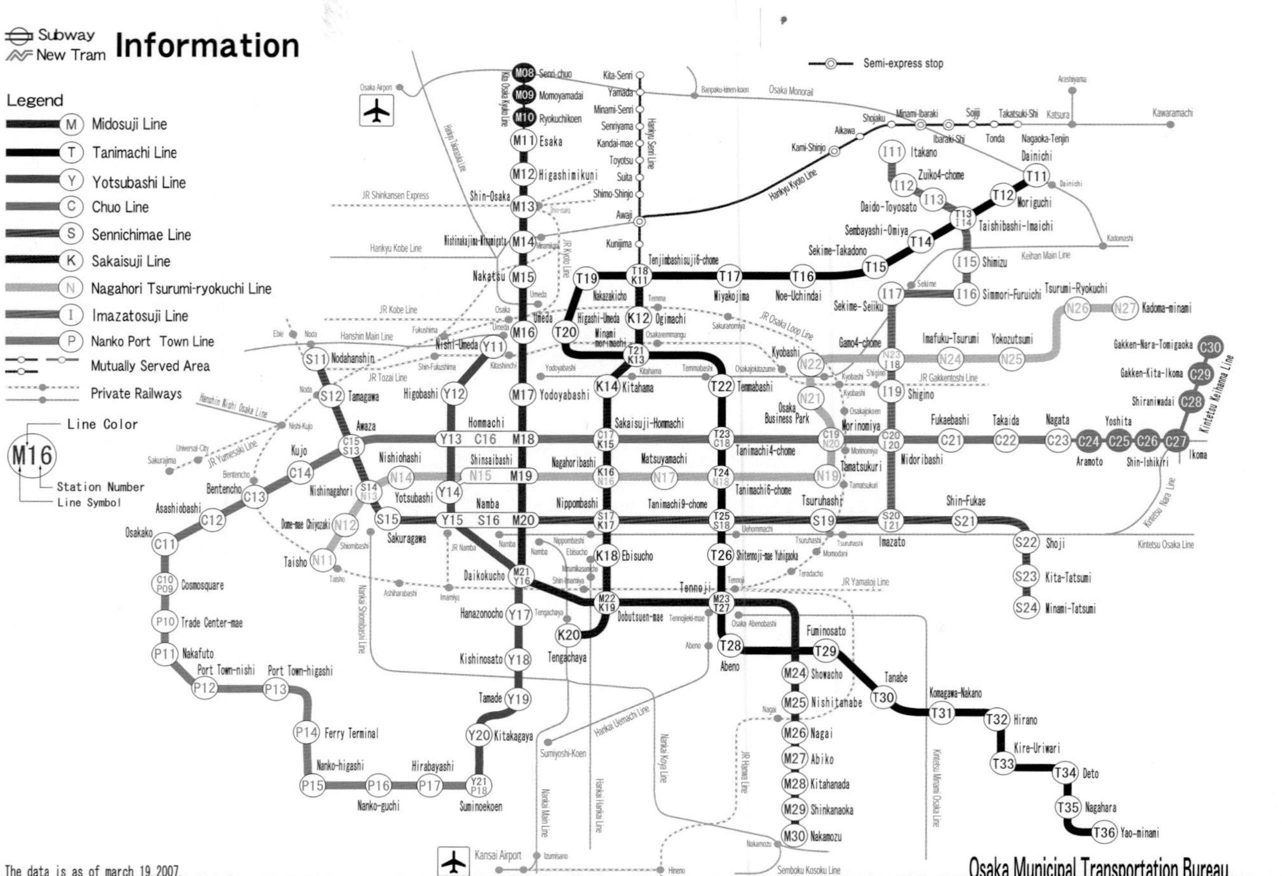
Information
Subway
New Tram
Legend
M Midosuji Line
T Tanimachi Line
Y Yotsubashi Line
C Chuo Line
S Sennichimae Line
K Sakaisuji Line
N Nagahori Tsurumi-ryokuchi Line
I Imazatosuji Line
P Nanko Port Town Line
Mutually Served Area
Private Railways
Line Color
Station Number
Line Symbol
M16
Semi-express stop
Osaka Municipal Transportation Bureau
The data is as of march 19, 2007.
Kita Osaka Kyuko Line
M08 Senri-chuo
M09 Momoyamadai
M10 Ryokuchikoen
M11 Esaka
M12 Higashimikuni
M13 Shin-Osaka
M14 Nishinakajima-Minamigata
M15 Nakatsu
M16 Umeda
M17 Yodoyabashi
M18 Hommachi
M19 Shinsaibashi
M20 Namba
M21 Daikokucho
M22 Dobutsuen-mae
M23 Tennoji
M24 Showacho
M25 Nishitanabe
M26 Nagai
M27 Abiko
M28 Kitahanada
M29 Shinkanaoka
M30 Nakamozu
T11 Dainichi
T12 Moriguchi
T13 Taishibashi-Imaichi
T14 Sembayashi-Omiya
T15 Sekime-Takadono
T16 Noe-Uchindai
T17 Miyakojima
T18 Tenjimbashisuji6-chome
T19 Nakazakicho
T20 Higashi-Umeda
T21 Minami-morimachi
T22 Temmabashi
T23 Tanimachi4-chome
T24 Tanimachi6-chome
T25 Tanimachi9-chome
T26 Shitennoji-mae Yuhigaoka
T27 Tennoji
T28 Abeno
T29 Fuminosato
T30 Tanabe
T31 Komagawa-Nakano
T32 Hirano
T33 Kire-Uriwari
T34 Deto
T35 Nagahara
T36 Yao-minami
Y11 Nishi-Umeda
Y12 Higobashi
Y13 Hommachi
Y14 Yotsubashi
Y15 Namba
Y16 Daikokucho
Y17 Hanazonocho
Y18 Kishinosato
Y19 Tamade
Y20 Kitakagaya
Y21 Suminoekoen
C11 Osakako
C12 Asashiobashi
C13 Bentencho
C14 Kujo
C15 Awaza
C16 Hommachi
C17 Sakaisuji-Hommachi
C18 Tanimachi4-chome
C19 Morinomiya
C20 Midoribashi
C21 Fukaebashi
C22 Takaida
C23 Nagata
C24 Aramoto
C25 Yoshita
C26 Shin-Ishikiri
C27 Ikoma
C28 Shiraniwadai
C29 Gakken-Kita-Ikoma
C30 Gakken-Nara-Tomigaoka
Kintetsu Keihanna Line
S11 Nodahanshin
S12 Tamagawa
S13 Awaza
S14 Nishinagahori
S15 Sakuragawa
S16 Namba
S17 Nippombashi
S18 Tanimachi9-chome
S19 Tsuruhashi
S20 Imazato
S21 Shin-Fukae
S22 Shoji
S23 Kita-Tatsumi
S24 Minami-Tatsumi
K11 Tenjimbashisuji6-chome
K12 Ogimachi
K13 Minami-morimachi
K14 Kitahama
K15 Sakaisuji-Hommachi
K16 Nagahoribashi
K17 Nippombashi
K18 Ebisucho
K19 Dobutsuen-mae
K20 Tengachaya
N11 Taisho
N12 Dome-mae Chiyozaki
N13 Nishinagahori
N14 Nishiohashi
N15 Shinsaibashi
N16 Nagahoribashi
N17 Matsuyamachi
N18 Tanimachi6-chome
N19 Tamatsukuri
N20 Morinomiya
N21 Osaka Business Park
N22 Kyobashi
N23 Gamo4-chome
N24 Imafuku-Tsurumi
N25 Yokozutsumi
N26 Tsurumi-Ryokuchi
N27 Kadoma-minami
I11 Itakano
I12 Zuiko4-chome
I13 Daido-Toyosato
I14 Taishibashi-Imaichi
I15 Shimizu
I16 Simmori-Furuichi
I17 Sekime-Seiiku
I18 Gamo4-chome
I19 Shigino
I20 Midoribashi
I21 Imazato
P09 Cosmosquare
P10 Trade Center-mae
P11 Nakafuto
P12 Port Town-nishi
P13 Port Town-higashi
P14 Ferry Terminal
P15 Nanko-higashi
P16 Nanko-guchi
P17 Hirabayashi
P18 Suminoekoen
Hankyu Senri Line
Hankyu Kyoto Line
Hankyu Takarazuka Line
Hankyu Kobe Line
Osaka Monorail
Keihan Main Line
JR Kyoto Line
JR Kobe Line
JR Tozai Line
JR Osaka Loop Line
JR Gakkentoshi Line
JR Yamatoji Line
JR Hanwa Line
JR Yumesaki Line
JR Shinkansen Express
Hanshin Main Line
Hanshin Nishi Osaka Line
Kintetsu Nara Line
Kintetsu Osaka Line
Kintetsu Minami Osaka Line
Nankai Koya Line
Nankai Main Line
Nankai Shiomibashi Line
Hankai Hankai Line
Hankai Uemachi Line
Semboku Kosoku Line
Osaka Airport
Kansai Airport
Kita-Senri
Yamada
Minami-Senri
Senriyama
Kandai-mae
Toyotsu
Suita
Shimo-Shinjo
Awaji
Kunijima
Kami-Shinjo
Aikawa
Shojaku
Minami-Ibaraki
Ibaraki-Shi
Sojiji
Tonda
Takatsuki-Shi
Nagaoka-Tenjin
Katsura
Kawaramachi

Northern Honshū
本州の北部

The rough sea, stretching out towards Sado, the Milky Way.

Matsuo Bashō, The Narrow Road to the Deep North (1689)

From the old city of Edo, the narrow road to the deep north winds precipitously through rugged mountains and remote valleys, terminating at the very tip of Japan's main island. This time-honoured travellers' route runs alongside ancient watercourses that feed fertile rice paddies, and around hulking volcanic massifs that fuel natural onsen (hot springs). In the days of Matsuo Bashō, the legendary itinerant haiku poet, a trip to the farthest reaches of Honshū was synonymous with walking to the ends of the Earth.

The *shinkansen* (bullet train) has accelerated the development and modernisation of northern Honshū, commonly known as Tōhoku, though you only need to step away from the tracks to find yourself in the midst of untamed nature. From hiking and skiing to rafting and onsen-hopping, Tōhoku provides a natural complement to the ordered neon chaos of Tokyo. Indeed, northern Honshū is separated from the frenetic capital by a train ride of several hours, and proud locals wouldn't have it any other way.

English is not widely spoken in Tōhoku, and the region's unique dialect is impenetrable even to many native Japanese. However, kind denizens of the deep north will happily go out of their way to assist a traveller in need. And also, thanks to an excellent network of local trains and highways, Tōhoku is remarkably more accessible than you might think, either by express train or rental car.

HIGHLIGHTS

- Get away from the mainland crush on **Sado-ga-shima** (p571), a former island of exile that can be explored on foot or by rental car
- Go cycling in the **Tōno valley** (p534), but keep an eye out for mythological little goblins known as *kappa*
- Dodge ice-covered trees known as 'snow monsters' at **Zaō Onsen** (p563), or at any of the region's other **ski slopes** (p564)
- Soak your worries away in **Sukayu Onsen Ryokan** (p544), a lemony, 1000-person bath, or at any of the region's other steamy **onsen** (p526)
- Go hiking through the sacred trio of peaks that comprise **Dewa Sanzan** (p560), and seek out tutorage from the famed *yamabushi* (mountain priests)
- Sample a small but remarkable taste of Hiraizumi's former glory at **Chūson-ji** (p532)
- Compose a haiku while scanning the scenery at **Matsushima** (p527), the famous bay immortalised by the poet Bashō

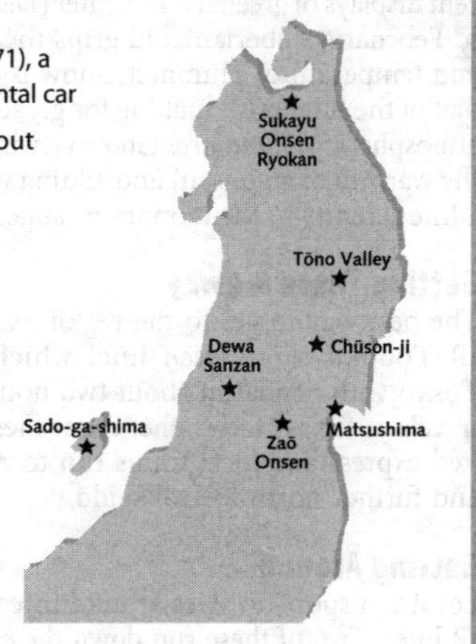

History

Originally inhabited by the Ezo people, who are believed to have been related to the Ainu of Hokkaidō, Tōhoku was settled during the 7th to 9th centuries, when Japanese from the south spread northward, searching for arable new land.

In the 11th century the Northern Fujiwara clan ruled from Hiraizumi, a settlement reputed to have rivalled Kyoto in its majesty and opulence. Aizu-Wakamatsu and Morioka were also important feudal towns.

The great *daimyō* (domain lord) Date Masamune (1567–1636) represents the cornerstone of Tōhoku's feudal history. In 1601 construction commenced on Date's castle at the former fishing village of Sendai; the clan would go on to rule for close to 300 years, a reign that ushered in Tōhoku's Golden Age.

Unfortunately, Tōhoku faded into obscurity when the Meiji Restoration wiped out clan rule. It subsequently suffered years of neglect, a trend that was reversed only after WWII and the subsequent drive for development heavily based on industrial growth. These days, tourism is a major player in the region's economic health.

Climate

Depending on when you come, northern Honshū will either be very comfortable or bone-chillingly cold. Summers (June to August) are mild and considerably more comfortable than in the south, producing magnificent displays of greenery. In winter (December to February), Siberian cold grips the region and temperatures plummet. Snow is at least half of the fun here – making for great skiing, atmospheric *yukimiburos* (snow viewing from the warmth of an onsen) and adding winter's white serenity to the mountain ranges.

Getting There & Away

The best way to get to the region is via the JR Tōhoku *shinkansen* line, which links Tokyo with Sendai in about two hours, and travels as far as Hachinohe. From there, limited express and local trains run to Aomori and further north to Hokkaidō.

Getting Around

Local transport revolves around three major JR lines. Two of these run down the east and west coasts, and the third snakes down between them in the centre, closely following the Tōhoku *shinkansen* line. Transport connections in the region have been accelerated with the opening of the Akita *shinkansen* line from Morioka to Akita and the extension of the Yamagata *shinkansen* line north to Shinjō.

Exploration of the more remote parts of Tōhoku is generally possible with local train and bus connections, but car rental is preferable as there is little traffic and most rentals include GPS positioning, making navigation a breeze. Roads and connections can be severely affected by winter weather, which can change quickly.

Those without JR Passes should consider investing in the JR East Pass (p840), which provides unlimited travel by JR rail in the Tōhoku region for four flexible days, or five or 10 consecutive days, and – unlike the JR Pass – this one can be purchased after you arrive.

FUKUSHIMA-KEN 福島県

Fukushima-ken, Japan's third-largest prefecture, serves as the gateway to Tōhoku. While it boasts fewer sites of tourist value than its northern neighbours, you shouldn't just blaze through here on the *shinkansen*. There is plenty of hiking and skiing that is worth seeking out, as well as a number of high-profile local sakes that certainly benefit from a slow sipping. The city of Fukushima serves as the region's administrative capital, but the medieval capital of Aizu-Wakamatsu, with its reconstructed castle, is a much more appealing place to base yourself.

AIZU-WAKAMATSU 会津若松

☎ 0242 / pop 120,000

During the Edo period, Aizu-Wakamatsu was the capital of the Aizu clan, a reign that came to an end in the Bōshin Civil War in 1868 when Tsuruga castle fell after the clan sided with the Tokugawa shōgunate against the imperial faction. The event is known throughout Japan due to the actions of the *Byakkotai* (White Tigers), a group of teenage samurai who committed *seppuku* (ritual suicide by disembowelment) when they saw that the castle was shrouded in smoke.

In reality, it was the surrounding area that was ablaze, and it would be weeks before the Aizu clan would fall; this tragi-comic tale

NORTHERN HONSHŪ

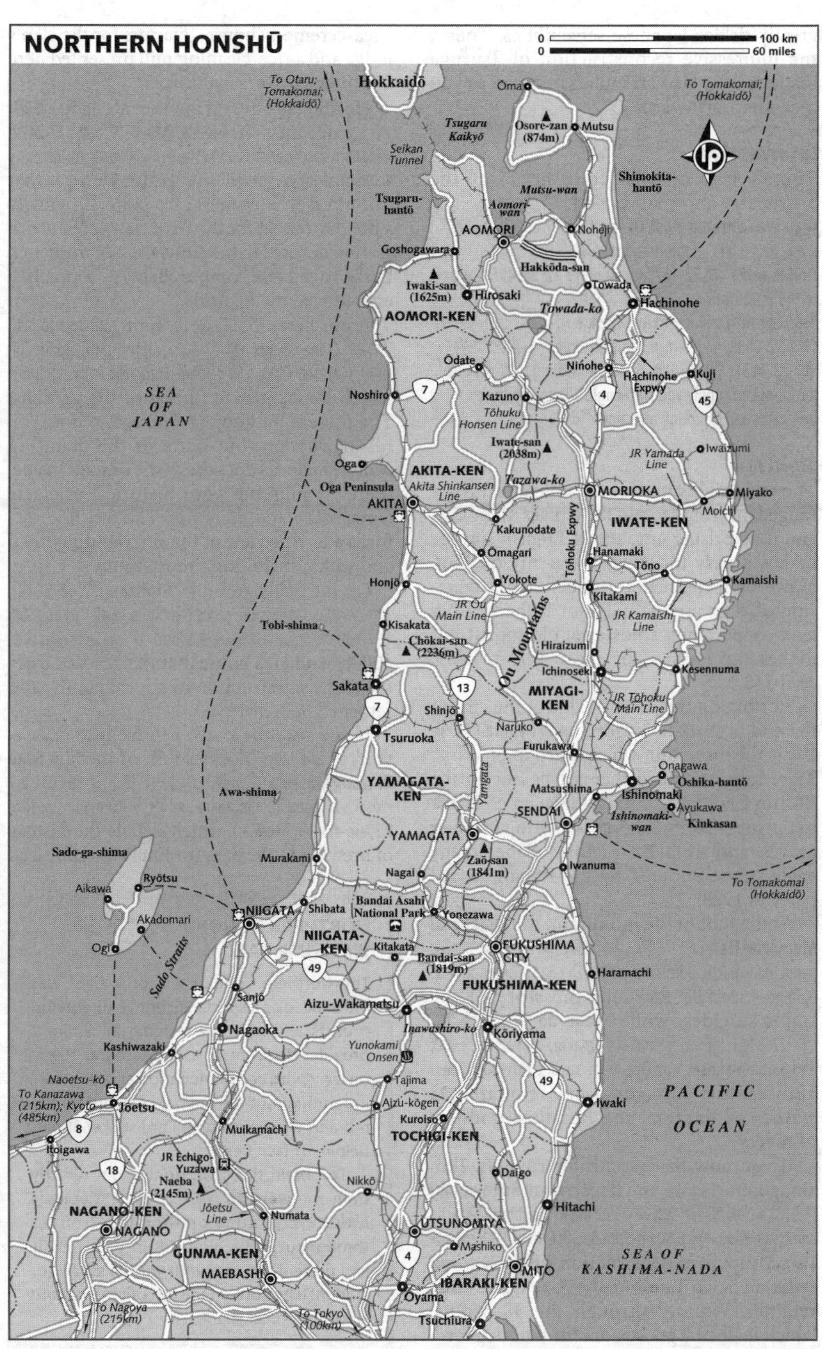

greatly tickles Japanese sensibilities. Today, the impressive reconstruction of Tsuruga castle makes Aizu an interesting stop as you meander northward.

Information

There's free internet (one hour) at the Tsuruga-jō information desk.

Aizu Wakamatsu Post Office (1-2-17 Chūō) On the main street; has an international ATM.

Police box (☎ 22-1877, main office 22-5454) Right next to the train station.

Sightseeing information desk Aizu-Wakamatsu station (☎ 32-0688; 9am-5.30pm); Tsuruga-jō (鶴ケ城; ☎ 29-1151; 8.30am-5pm) The willing staff at both locations can supply you with English-language maps, brochures and thorough directions.

Sights

The main sights in Aizu are conveniently arranged in a ring around the fringes of the city, and a surprising amount of English signage makes it easy to navigate the city on foot. However, if you're not confident in the precision of your internal GPS, or if the weather isn't cooperating, a nostalgic old tourist bus makes the loop – for more information, see p518.

Starting on the eastern edge of the city, at the end of Byakkotai-dori, **Iimori-yama** (飯盛山) is the mountain where a group of White Tiger samurai killed themselves during the Bōshin Civil War. You can take an escalator to the top (¥250; 8am-5pm Mar-Nov) to visit their graves, and to take a picture of the creepy eagle statue donated by the Italian Fascist party in 1928.

At the foot of the mountain, the **Byakkotai Memorial Hall** (白虎隊記念館; ☎ 24-9170; Iimori-yama, Ikki-machi; admission ¥400; 8am-5pm Apr-Nov, 8.30am-4.30pm Dec-Mar) tells the story of the tragic suicides, while **Sazae-dō** (さざえ堂; ☎ 22-3163; Iimori-yama, Ikki-machi; admission ¥400; 8.15am-sunset Apr-Oct, 9am-sunset Nov-Mar), an 18th-century hexagonal hall, contains 33 statues of Kannon, the Buddhist goddess of mercy.

If you now head south for roughly 2km along Iimori-dori, you'll reach **Aizu Bukeyashiki** (会津武家屋敷; ☎ 28-2525; Innai Higashiyama-machi; admission ¥850; 8.30am-5pm Apr-Oct, 9am-4.30pm Nov-Mar), a superb reconstruction of the *yashiki* (villa) of Saigō Tanomo, the Aizu clan's chief retainer. Wander through the 38 rooms, which include a guestroom for the Aizu lord, a tea-ceremony house, quarters for the clan's judge and a rice-cleaning mill presented here in full, noisy working order.

Heading northwest for 1km along Rte 325, you can't miss **Oyaku-en** (御薬園; ☎ 27-2472; Hanaharu-machi; admission ¥310; 8.30am-5pm, last entry 4.30pm), a large meditative garden complex that is centred on a tranquil carp pond. Originally a holiday retreat for the Aizu clan, it features a section devoted to the cultivation of medicinal herbs (available for purchase) – a practice encouraged by the lords.

From here, it's easy to spot **Tsuruga-jō** (鶴ケ城; Crane Castle; ☎ 27-4005; Oute-machi; admission ¥400, with tea ¥500; 8.30am-5pm, last entry 4.30pm), which looms just southeast of the gardens. The present building of Tsuruga-jō is a 1965 reconstruction, but parts of the daunting walls remain, as does the castle's moat. Inside, there's a museum with historical artefacts from battle and daily life. The 5th floor affords a terrific view of the surrounding town and valley, including Iimori-yama.

On the castle grounds, **Rinkaku** (茶室麟閣; ☎ 27-4005; admission ¥200, combined castle ticket ¥500; 8.30am-5pm, last entry 4.30pm) is an evocative, 400-year-old tea house that was rescued from the castle's destruction by a local family, and returned here in 1990.

If you take the north exit from the castle, you're just two blocks south of the **Aizu Sake Brewing Museum** (会津酒造歴史館; ☎ 26-0031; 8-7 Higashisakae-machi; admission ¥300; 8.30am-5pm Apr-Nov, 9.30am-4.30pm Dec-Mar), which details the history of brewing in the area (in English). Life-sized

NORTHERN TŌHOKU WELCOME CARD

The Northern Tōhoku Welcome Card was introduced as a special incentive for foreign tourists and students residing in Japan. It provides discounts – usually around 10% – on transport, accommodation and sightseeing throughout the region. Look out for the red-and-white Welcome Card sticker at participating facilities.

To obtain the card, print it out directly from the **website** (www.northern-tohoku.gr.jp/welcome) or pick up a form from tourist offices throughout the region. Fill in your details and present the card with your passport (or student ID) to obtain the discount – the card is valid for one year.

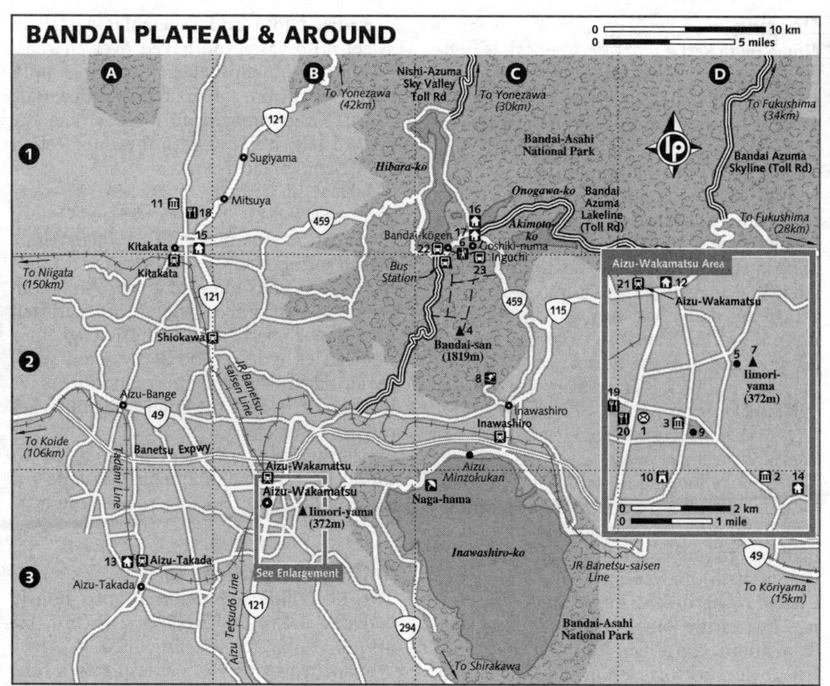

INFORMATION
Aizu Wakamatsu Post Office 郵便局 1 D2
Police Station 警察署 .... (see 21)
Sightseeing Information Desk 観光案内所 .... (see 10)
Sightseeing Information Desk 観光案内所 .... (see 21)

SIGHTS & ACTIVITIES
Aizu Bukeyashiki 会津武家屋敷 2 D3
Aizu Sake Brewing Museum 会津酒造歴史館 3 D2
Bandai-san 磐梯山 4 C2
Byakkotai Memorial Hall 白虎隊記念館 5 D2
Goshiki-numa Nature Trail 五色沼 自然歩道 6 C1
Iimori-yama 飯盛山 7 D2
Inawashiro-Sukī-Jō-Chūō 猪苗代湖スキー場中央 8 C2
Oyaku-en 御薬園 9 D2
Sazae-dō さざえ堂 .... (see 5)
Tsuruga-jō 鶴ヶ城 10 D3
Yamatogawa Sake Brewing Museum 大和川酒造北方風土館 11 A1

SLEEPING
Aizu Wakamatsu Washington Hotel 会津若松ワシントンホテル 12 D2
Aizuno Youth Hostel 会津野ユースホステル 13 A3
Minshuku Takaku 民宿多賀来 14 D3
Sasaya Ryokan 笹屋旅館 15 A1
Urabandai Royal Hotel 裏磐梯ロイヤルホテル 16 C1
Urabandai Youth Hoste 裏磐梯ユースホステル 17 C1

EATING
Genraiken 源来軒 18 A1
Mitsutaya 満田屋 19 C2
Takino 田季野 20 D2

TRANSPORT
Aizu Town Bus まちなか周遊 .... (see 21)
Aizu Wakamatsu Station 裏磐梯ロイヤルホテル 21 D2
Bandai-kōgen Bus Stop 番台高原 バス停 22 C1
Goshiki-numa Iriguchi Bus Stop 五色沼入りロバス停 23 C2

dioramas and old sake advertisements add to the charm. Naturally, you can sample the famous tipple for the price of admission.

Festivals & Events

Aizu-Wakamatsu holds four main festivals, coordinated according to season. The most prominent is the three-day **Aizu Autumn Festival** (会津秋祭り) from 22 to 24 September, an extravagant procession that threads through the city to Tsuruga-jō, accompanied by a drum-and-fife band, a children's parade and an evening lantern parade. There's also the **Higanjishi** on the spring equinox, the **Summer Festival** during the first Saturday in August and winter's **Sainokami**, held on 14 January.

Sleeping

Aizuno Youth Hostel (会津野ユースホステル; ☎ 55-1020; fax 55-1320; www.aizuno.com, in Japanese; 88 Kakiyashiki, Terasaki Aizu-Takada-chō; dm/r from ¥3200/4200) One of the best budget options in the region, Aizuno thrives amidst a pleasant rural setting far from the congestion of Aizu's centre. The spick-and-span hostel, which offers both dormitory and private rooms, is located about 20 minutes by foot from Aizu-Takada station along the Tadami line from Aizu-Wakamatsu (¥230, 20 minutes). Seven trains run daily, but only one in the afternoon. Find out your train's arrival time in advance and give the hostel notice – a staff member will pick you up from the station.

Minshuku Takaku (民宿多賀来; ☎ 26-6299; fax 26-6116; www.naf.co.jp/takaku, in Japanese; 104 Innai Higashiyama-machi; r with/without 2 meals from ¥6300/4200; 💻) If you're looking for traditional Japanese lodging, this mid-sized *minshuku* (Japanese-style B&B) offers modest tatami (woven floor matting) rooms, a small but pleasant *sentō* (public bath) and an attractive dining area framed by hardwood furnishings. Takaku is just east of the Aizu Bukeyashiki bus stop; from there, continue along the road, turn left at the post office and it's just behind, on the left.

Aizu Wakamatsu Washington Hotel (会津若松ワシントンホテル; ☎ 22-6111; fax 24-7535; www.aizu-wh.com, in Japanese; 201 Byakko-machi; s/d from ¥7350/13,650; P 💻 wi-fi) There is no shortage of business hotels around the station, though the Washington is our top pick, offering no-nonsense rooms that are sweetened with a whole host of onsite amenities from high-speed wi-fi to sophisticatd bars and restaurants. The Washington is located just three minutes' walk east of the train station along Byakkotai-dori; look for the tall building with the English sign on the left-hand side of the road. LAN cable internet available.

Eating

Aizu is famous for *wappa meshi*, steamed fish over rice, prepared in a round container made from tree bark, giving a woody fragrance to the contents.

Mitsutaya (満田屋; ☎ 27-1345; 1-1-25 Ōmachi; skewers from ¥200; 🕑 10am-5pm, closed 1st & 3rd Wed of each month & every Wed Jan-Mar) A former bean-paste mill that dates from 1834, this place is an Aizu landmark. The speciality here is *dengaku*, which are bamboo skewers with deep-fried tofu and vegetables basted in sweet *miso* paste and baked over charcoal (the picture menu helps clear things up!). Facing west from the main post office, walk down Nanokomachi-dōri, then take the second left; it's just near the intersection with Nanokomachi-dōri.

Takino (田季野; ☎ 25-0808; 5-31 Sakae-machi; wappa meshi from ¥1420; 🕑 lunch & dinner) One of the most famous places to try the sublime *wappa meshi*, offers several versions including salmon, crab and wild mushroom. From the main post office, facing south, turn left onto Nanokomachi-dōri, at the first light turn right; go left at the second alleyway, and you'll see an old farm house on the right which is the location of Takino. An English menu makes ordering a breeze.

Alternatively, head on over at lunch- or dinnertime to neighbouring Kitakata for some of the most delicious *rāmen* (egg noodles) in Japan.

Getting There & Around

The JR Tōhoku *shinkansen* runs hourly between Tokyo and Kōriyama (¥7970, 1¼ hours). Kōriyama is connected to Aizu-Wakamatsu by the JR Banetsu-saisen line; hourly *kaisoku* (rapid) trains (¥1110, 1¼ hours) ply this scenic route.

There are a couple of daily *kaisoku* on the JR Bansetsu and Shinetsu lines between Aizu-Wakamatsu and Niigata (¥2210, 2¾ hours). If you miss any of these trains, there are also four to six daily express buses (¥2000, 1¾ hours) between both cities (the buses run between the stations in both towns and are operated by JR).

The historic **Aizu Town Bus** (まちなか周遊バスハイカラさん; single/day pass ¥200/500) departs from outside the train station and does a slow loop of the main sights. The tourist information desks can also help you arrange bike rental (per day ¥1500).

If you're driving, the Tōhoku Expressway (東北自動車道) runs between Tokyo and Kōriyama, while the Banetsu Expressway (磐越自動車道) connects Kōriyama and Aizu-Wakamatsu.

KITAKATA 喜多方

☎ 0241 / pop 55,000

An old Kitakata saying reflects this town's view towards commerce: 'A man is not a man unless he has built at least one *kura* (a mud-walled storehouse)'. These days, the town's 2500-plus colourful *kura* – now functioning as living quarters, sake breweries and workshops – are a perennial tourist attraction, as are Kitakata's 120-plus *rāmen* shops.

The **tourist information kiosk** (☎ 24-2633; 8.30am-5.15pm), left of the station exit, provides colourful English-language maps. These are essential in finding the listings below, which are hidden in the mazes of Kitakata's back streets.

Sample the excellent local sake at **Yamatogawa Sake Brewing Museum** (大和川酒造北方風土館; ☎ 22-2233; Teramachi; admission free; 9am-4.30pm, closed irregularly), five minutes' walk north of the station behind the post office.

While the *kura*-lined streets are certainly atmospheric, Kitakata is really all about the *rāmen*. The most famous spot in town is **Genraiken** (源来軒; ☎ 22-0091; 7745 Ippongiue Kitakata City; sets from ¥550; 10am-8pm Wed-Mon, last orders 7.30pm), which boasts a 75-year history, and a detailed picture menu outlining its original creations. Find it one block north and one block east of the station – look for the red façade as well as the crowds of people queuing outside.

Of course, if you want to buck tradition, just follow your nose to any one of Kitakata's competing *rāmen* joints. Kitakata's signature noodles are thick and curly, and served up in a hearty pork and fish broth that makes use of local spring water, soy sauce and sake. Delicious.

Most visitors to Kitakata head back to Aizu for the night, but you can extend your visit by sleeping at **Sasaya Ryokan** (笹屋旅館; ☎ 22-0008; Chūō-dōri; r per person with/without 2 meals from ¥8800/5500;), a traditional two-storey Japanese house offering a handful of private tatami rooms. It's only about a 10-minute walk northeast of the station, though it's best to have the staff at the tourist information centre mark it for you on the map.

Kitakata is a relatively easy trip from Aizu-Wakamatsu, accessible by frequent trains along the JR Banetsu-saisen line (¥320, 25 minutes). For drivers, Rte 121 runs between Aizu and Kitakata.

Bicycle rental (per two hours/day ¥500/1500) is available outside Kitakata station, while a **horse-drawn carriage** (☎ 24-4111; tours on demand ¥1300) shaped like a *kura* departs from the train station for an 80-minute tour of the more interesting storehouses.

BANDAI PLATEAU 磐梯高原

☎ 0241 / pop 4000

On 15 July 1888 **Bandai-san** (磐梯山; 1819m), a once-dormant volcano, suddenly erupted, spewing forth a tremendous amount of debris that's said to have lowered the mountain's height by 600m. The force of the eruption destroyed dozens of villages, claimed more than 400 lives and completely rearranged the landscape, resulting in the vast lake-dotted plateau now known as Bandai-kōgen. Today, this massive wilderness area, which is hemmed in by the Fukushima, Niigata and Yamagata prefectural boundaries, attracts hikers, climbers, fishing enthusiasts, skiers and snowboarders with its spectacular scenery and vast potential for independent exploration.

Orientation & Information

Bandai-kōgen comprises the southern part of **Bandai-Asahi National Park** (磐梯朝日国立公園), which is the second-largest protected area in Japan.

There are trailheads located at the Goshiki-numa Iriguchi and Bandai-kōgen bus stops, the main transport hubs on the edge of Hibara-ko. This route is serviced by buses that depart from the town of Inawashiro.

There's a **visitors centre** (☎ 32-2850; 9am-4pm Wed-Mon Dec-Mar, to 5pm Wed-Mon Apr-Nov) not far from the Goshiki-numa Iriguchi trailhead, and a **tourist information office** (☎ 0242-62-2048; 8.30am-5pm) to the left outside JR Inawashiro station.

Sights & Activities

HIKING

The most popular walk starts from Goshiki-numa Iriguchi bus stop, and follows a 3.7km nature trail around **Goshiki-numa** (五色沼), an area of around a dozen bodies of water that are known as Five Colours Lakes. Mineral deposits from the eruption imparted various hues to the waters – cobalt blue, emerald green, reddish brown and so on – that change depending on the weather.

Bandai-san can be climbed in a day with an early start; the most popular route starts from the Bandai-kōgen bus stop, and climbs up through the skiing grounds to the summit. The descending trail takes you down to the town of Inawashiro.

SKIING & SNOWBOARDING

The most popular ski area in the Bandai plateau is the **Inawashiro-sukī-jō-chūō** (☎ 62-3800; www.g-jmt.com/inawashiro/eng/index.php; 1-day lift ticket weekday/weekend ¥3000/3500; Dec-Apr), which has 15 runs in total. The majority of the trails are beginner and intermediate, and are largely devoid of large trees and moguls. There are two black diamond chutes if you want to get your kicks. There are also a number of restaurants on the premises, with plenty of English signage. Inawashiro-sukī-jō-chūō is located in the hills above Inawashiro town. During the ski season, frequent shuttle buses run between Inawashiro station and the resort (¥380, 20 minutes).

Sleeping & Eating

Urabandai Youth Hostel (☎ 32-2811; http://homepage3.nifty.com/urabandai/indexe.html; camping from ¥1000, dm with/without 2 meals from ¥4400/2900; cabin from ¥5000; late Apr-Nov; P) One of the region's classic mountaineering institutions, the Ura Bandai Youth Hostel is supremely located next to the Goshiki-numa trailhead, approximately seven minutes walk from the Goshiki-numa Iriguchi bus stop (you can follow the signs). Choose one of the dorm rooms for a social atmosphere, grab a camping spot if you want to rough it or share a romantic cabin in the woods with your better half.

Urabandai Royal Hotel (☎ 32-3111; fax 32-3130; www.daiwaresort.co.jp/english/04_uraba.html; r with full board per person from ¥12,600; P) Far and beyond the smartest option in the area, the Royal Hotel offers full package deals that vary with the seasons – contact it in advance as you can sometimes score some cheaper rates. Plush rooms have sweeping views of the national park, while the sophisticated restaurants highlight the best in local and seasonal cuisine. There is also an onsite open-air onsen that is free for guests, or ¥500 for anyone who happens to stop by. LAN cable internet available.

Getting There & Away

Frequent express *kaisoku* run along the JR Banetsu-saisen line (¥480, 30 minutes) between Aizu-Wakamatsu and Inawashiro. From outside Inawashiro station, frequent buses depart from stop 3, and pass by the Goshiki-numa Iriguchi stop (¥750, 25 minutes), heading onto the Bandai-kōgen stop (¥820, 30 minutes).

MIYAGI-KEN 宮城県

Miyagi-ken is something of a buffer zone between the rural hinterlands of the far north and the massive urban development that typifies much of Honshū to the south. Its capital, Sendai, is Tohokū's most cosmopolitan city, boasting excellent tourist infrastructure, a sophisticated restaurant scene, raucous nightlife and plenty of cultural attractions to boot. Of course, if you want to escape the urban trappings, and get back to the nature that most likely brought you up this way, then don't miss the healing waters of Naruko Onsen, 'Golden Mountain' hiking and Matsushima, a worthy contender for the title of Japan's most beautiful bay.

SENDAI 仙台

☎ 022 / pop 1,020,000

Established by Date Masamune, Sendai or the city of '1000 generations' was once a feudal capital that controlled trade routes, salt supplies and grain milling throughout much of Tōhoku. Although Masamune was eventually passed over for the role of shōgunate, his supporters remained loyal to the samurai's vision. Even today, Masamune continues to reign over the city – the roof of Miyagi Stadium's west stand is modelled after the unique crescent symbol that the *daimyō* wore on his helmet, while his mausoleum and ruined castle also pay tribute to his overarching presence.

Sendai was largely demolished by Allied bombing during WWII. The city was rebuilt with wide, tree-lined streets that make for relaxing strolls. As the largest and most commercially important city in the region, Sendai serves as one of Tōhoku's principle transportation hubs.

Even if you never actually spend the night here, be sure to take some time between catching trains to explore this compact and relaxed city. And of course it's worth pointing out that Sendai's justifiably famous Tanabata Matsuri is definitely one of the best festivals in both Tōhoku and Japan.

Orientation

From Sendai station, located east of most of the action, the broad sweep of Aoba-dōri, lined with many of the major department stores, banks and hotels, leads west to a park, Aoba-yama. The main shopping areas are the

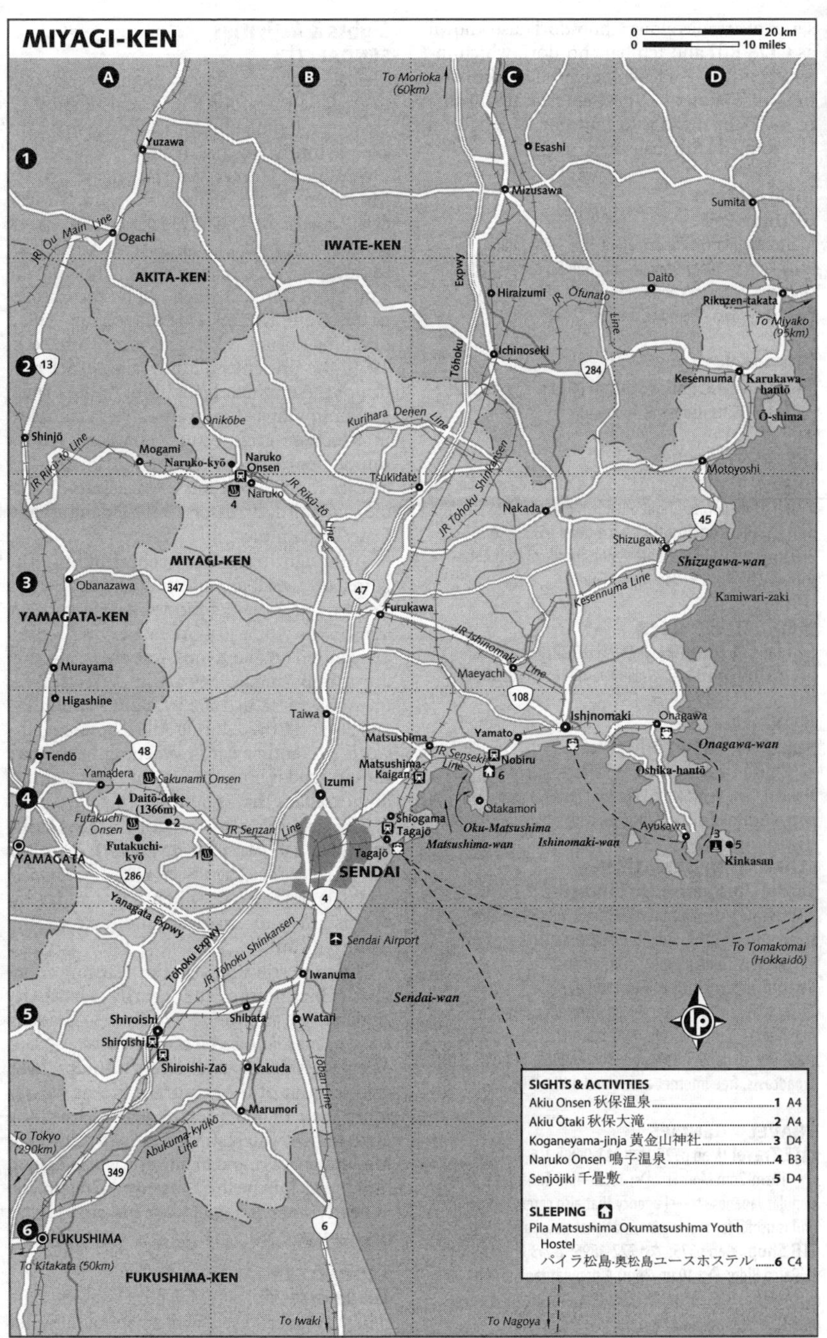
MIYAGI-KEN
0 20 km
0 10 miles
To Morioka (60km)
Yuzawa
Esashi
Mizusawa
Sumita
JR Ōu Main Line
Ogachi
IWATE-KEN
AKITA-KEN
Expwy
Hiraizumi
JR Ōfunato Line
Daitō
Rikuzen-takata
To Miyako (95km)
Tōhoku
Ichinoseki
284
13
Kesennuma
Karukawa-hantō
Ō-shima
Onikōbe
Kurihara Denen Line
Shinjō
JR Rikū-tō Line
Mogami
Naruko-kyō
Naruko Onsen
Naruko
JR Tōhoku Shinkansen
Tsukidate
Motoyoshi
Nakada
45
Shizugawa
Shizugawa-wan
MIYAGI-KEN
Obanazawa
347
47
Kesennuma Line
Kamiwari-zaki
YAMAGATA-KEN
Furukawa
JR Ishinomaki Line
Murayama
Maeyachi
Higashine
108
Taiwa
Ishinomaki
Onagawa
Yamato
Onagawa-wan
Matsushima
Tendō
48
Yamadera
JR Senseki Line
Nobiru
Matsushima-Kaigan
Oshika-hantō
Sakunami Onsen
Izumi
Daitō-dake (1366m)
Otakamori
Futakuchi Onsen
Shiogama
Oku-Matsushima
Tagajō
Ishinomaki-wan
Ayukawa
JR Senzan Line
Matsushima-wan
Futakuchi-kyō
Kinkasan
YAMAGATA
SENDAI
286
4
Yanagata Expwy
Tōhoku Expwy
Sendai Airport
To Tomakomai (Hokkaidō)
JR Tōhoku Shinkansen
Iwanuma
Sendai-wan
Shiroishi
Shibata
Watari
Shiroishi-Zaō
Kakuda
Jōban Line
Marumori
To Tokyo (290km)
Abukuma-kyūkō Line
349
FUKUSHIMA
6
To Kitakata (50km)
FUKUSHIMA-KEN
To Iwaki
To Nagoya
SIGHTS & ACTIVITIES
Akiu Onsen 秋保温泉 1 A4
Akiu Ōtaki 秋保大滝 2 A4
Koganeyama-jinja 黄金山神社 3 D4
Naruko Onsen 鳴子温泉 4 B3
Senjōjiki 千畳敷 5 D4
SLEEPING
Pila Matsushima Okumatsushima Youth Hostel パイラ松島·奥松島ユースホステル 6 C4

series of arcades along Chūō-dōri (also known as CLIS Rd) and Ichibanchō-dōri, which intersect just east of Kokubunchō-dōri, the main drag of Tōhoku's largest entertainment district. To the north is Jozenji-dōri, a delightful street lined with lush trees.

Information

BOOKSHOPS

Maruzen (Map p525; ☎ 264-0151; 1-3-1 Chūō, Aoba-ku; 🕑 10am-9pm, to 8pm Sun & holidays) English-language magazines and books on the AER building's 1st floor, steps away from the station.

EMERGENCY

Sendai Central Police Station (Map p523; ☎ 222-7171; 1-3-19 Itsutsubashi, Aoba-ku)

INTERNET ACCESS

Internet kiosks (Map p525; 2nd fl, JR Sendai station; per 15min ¥100) Located right outside the tourist info booth.

Sendai International Centre (Map p523; ☎ 265-2450; www.sira.or.jp/icenter/english/index.html; Aoba-yama, Aoba-ku; 🕑 9am-8pm) Free!

MEDICAL SERVICES

Sendai City Hospital (仙台市立病院; ☎ 266-7111; 3-1 Shimizu-kōji, Wakabayashi-ku; 🕑 7am-6pm)

MONEY & POST

Sendai Central Post Office (Map p523; ☎ 267-8035; 1-7 Kitame-machi, Aoba-ku; 🕑 ATM service 7am-11pm Mon-Fri, 9am-9pm Sat, to 7pm Sun) Also a branch on the 1st floor of Sendai station (Map p525) with international ATM.

TOURIST INFORMATION

Sendai City Information Office (Map p525; ☎ 222-4069; www.stcb.or.jp/eng/tbic.html; 2nd fl, JR Sendai station; 🕑 8.30am-8pm) Inside the station's west exit, it has possibly Tōhoku's most efficient staff.

Sendai International Centre (Map p523; ☎ 265-2471; www.sira.or.jp/icenter/english/index.html; Aoba-yama, Aoba-ku; 🕑 9am-8pm) English-speaking staff, international newspaper library, bulletin board, CNN broadcasts, free internet access and a Visa ATM.

TRAVEL AGENCIES

IACE Travel (Map p525; ☎ 211-0489; 1-6-24 Chūō; 🕑 10am-7pm Mon-Fri, 🕑 10am-4pm Sat, closed Sun) A popular Japanese travel agency that also caters to foreigners and is useful for making international travel arrangements.

JTB Shop (Map p525; ☎ 722-1895; 1-2-3 Chūō-ku, 5th fl, Parco Bldg; 🕑 10am-7pm) A popular Japanese travel agency that is useful for making domestic travel arrangements, including plane and train bookings.

Sights & Activities

SENDAI CITY

Sendai's sights are close enough to each other to make an on-foot tour a real possibility. However, if time is money, take a spin on the Loople tourist bus (see p526).

Sendai's largest tourist drawcard is Masamune Date's mausoleum, namely **Zuihō-den** (Map p523; ☎ 262-6250; 23-2 Otamayashita, Aoba-ku; admission ¥550; 🕑 9am-4.30pm Feb-Nov, to 4pm Dec & Jan; Loople stop 4), which sits majestically atop the summit of a tree-covered hill by the Hirose-gawa. Built in 1637, destroyed by Allied bombing during WWII and reconstructed in 1979, the present building is an exact replica of the original. It's faithful to the ornate and sumptuous Momoyama style: a complex, interlocking architecture, characterised by multicoloured woodcarvings. Also atop the hill are the mausoleums of Masamune's second and third successors, Date Tadamune and Date Tsunamune.

Although it receives second billing, the ruins of **Sendai-jō Ato** (Map p523; admission free; 🕑 24hr; Loople stop 6, regular bus stop 'Sendai Jō Ato Minami'), or Aoba-jō (Green Leaves Castle), are centred on giant, moss-covered walls that are as imposing as they are impressive. Built on Aoba-yama in 1602 by Date Masamune, and also destroyed during Allied bombing, the castle presently awards sweeping views over the city, and is home to a statue of Masamune on horseback that is quite stirring.

The grounds also contain the **Aoba Castle Exhibition Hall** (Map p523; ☎ 227-7077; Aobajō Ato, Tenshudai, Aoba-ku, admission ¥700; 🕑 9am-5pm Apr-Oct, to 4pm Nov-Mar), which helps add a bit of insight and historical context to the hallowed ruins.

If you're still interested in learning more about Masamune, the nearby **Sendai City Museum** (Map p523; ☎ 225-3074; Sendai Jō Sannomaru Ato, 26 Kawauchi, Aoba-ku; admission ¥400; 🕑 9am-4.45pm Tue-Sun; Loople stop 5) offers a comprehensive account of the samurai's life, as well as more than 13,000 artefacts loaned from the Date family. Interestingly enough, although Masamune was blind in one eye, which earned him the nickname the 'One-Eyed Dragon', he is nearly always depicted in his portraits as having two eyes!

AROUND SENDAI

Akiu Onsen (秋保温泉; Map p521) was the Date clan's favourite onsen, with a natural saltwater

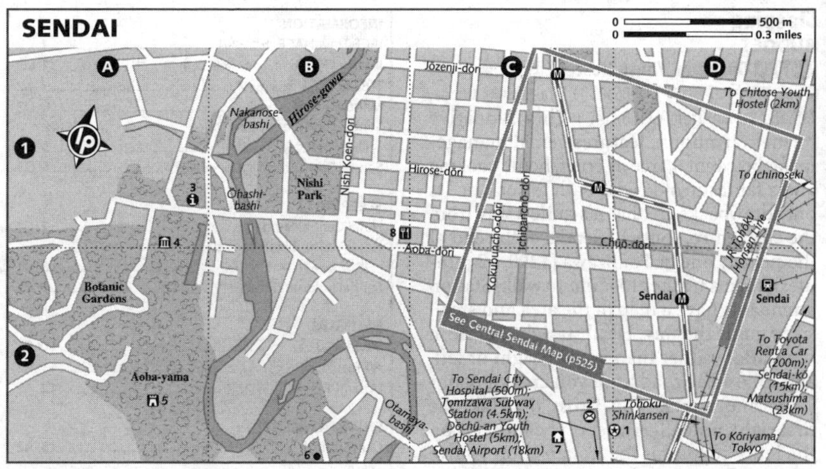

INFORMATION

Sendai Central Police Station 仙台中央警察署 1 D2
Sendai Central Post Office 仙台中央郵便局 2 C2
Sendai International Centre 仙台国際センター 3 A1

SIGHTS & ACTIVITIES

Aoba Castle Exhibition Hall 青葉城資料展示館 ......(see 5)
Sendai City Museum 仙台市博物館........4 A1
Sendai-jō Ato 仙台城跡........5 A2
Zuihō-den 瑞鳳殿........6 B2

SLEEPING

Aisaki Ryokan 相崎旅館........7 C2

EATING

Yabuya Honten やぶ屋本店........8 B1

spring that's said to be a curative for back pain and arthritis.

The village is a good base for side trips into the mountains to see **Akiu Ōtaki** (秋保大滝; Map p521), a 6m-wide, 55m-high waterfall, which is itself designated as one of Japan's three most famous waterfalls (Japanese do love those famous sets of three!). You can view the falls from a scenic outlook or down by the basin.

Akiu Onsen is also convenient for access to the gorge, **Futakuchi-kyō** (二口渓), with its banji-iwa (rock columns). There are hiking trails along the river valley and a trail from Futakuchi Onsen to the summit of Daitō-dake (1366m) that takes about three hours.

A list of the bathhouses and hiking maps are available at Akiu Onsen's **tourist information office** (☎ 398-2323; 🕑 9.30am-6pm), located adjacent to the village's bus stop.

Akiu Onsen is an easy day trip from Sendai, though there are a number of small inns and guest houses in town if you want to slow down and soak up the atmosphere.

Buses leave hourly from stop 8 at Sendai station's west bus pool for Akiu Onsen (¥780, 50 minutes), but only a few continue to Akiu Ōtaki (¥1070, 1 ½ hours).

Festivals & Events

Donto-sai (どんと祭) On 14 January men brave subzero weather conditions to hop around almost naked, a ritual supposed to bring good fortune for the new year.

Sendai Tanabata Matsuri (仙台七夕まつり; Star Festival) Sendai's major event, held from 6 to 8 August, celebrates a Chinese legend about the stars Vega and Altair. Vega was the king's daughter who fell in love with and married Altair, a common herder. The king disapproved, so he formed the Milky Way between them. Once a year magpies are supposed to spread their wings across the universe so that the lovers can meet – traditionally on 7 July. Sendai celebrates in grand style by decorating the main streets with bamboo poles festooned with multicoloured streamers, and holding afternoon parades on Jōzenji-dōri. A couple of million visitors ensure that accommodation is booked solid at this time of year.

Jōzenji Street Jazz Festival (定禅寺ストリートジャズフェスティバル) During the second weekend in September, 600 buskers from across Japan perform in Sendai's streets and arcades. Again, book rooms way, way in advance.

Sendai Pageant of Starlight (SENDAI光のページェント) Illuminates Aoba-dōri and Jōzenji-dōri with festive lights on 12 to 31 December.

INFORMATION		
IACE Travel IACE トラベル	1	C2
Internet Kiosks インターネットコーナ	2	D3
JTB Shop JTB ショップ	3	B2
Maruzen 丸善	4	D2
Sendai City Information Office 仙台市総合観光案内所	5	D4
Sendai Post Office 仙台中央郵便局	6	D3
SLEEPING		
Hotel Central Sendai ホテルセントラル仙台	7	C4
Hotel Metropolitan Sendai ホテルメトロポリタン仙台	8	D4
Sendai Kokusai Hotel 仙台国際ホテル	9	C4
EATING		
30View 30ヴュー	10	C4
Aji Tasuke 味太助	11	A2
Umami Tasuke 旨味太助	12	A2
ENTERTAINMENT		
Club Shaft クラブ　シャフト	13	A2
TRANSPORT		
Airport Limousine Stops 空港 リムジン停	(see 15)	
Bus Stop 34 バス乗り場34番	14	D3
Loople Tourist Bus るーぷる観光バス	(see 15)	
West Bus Terminal 西バスターミナル	15	D3

Sleeping

BUDGET

OUR PICK **Dōchū-an Youth Hostel** (道中庵ユースホステル; ☎ 247-0511; 31 Kita-yashiki, Ōnoda, Taihaku-ku; dm from ¥3150; 💻) This evocative former farmhouse features genial management, bike rental, free internet, home cooking and a fantastic old cedar bath to soak in. Its only drawbacks are that it's quite a way from the city centre, south of Sendai at the end of the subway line in Tomizawa (¥290, 12 minutes), then a further 15-minute walk. Station attendants have a map of the area and small signs guide the way. Head straight out from the station rather than veering right or left, and follow the road until you cross a major (four-lane) intersection. Cross, then take the first right, a smallish street. The hostel is on the left – if you hit the *rāmen* shop you've gone too far.

Sendai Chitose Youth Hostel (仙台千登勢ユースホステル; ☎ 222-6329; 6-3-8 Odawara, Aoba-ku; dm from ¥3255; 💻) If you want budget digs that are closer to the city centre, this snug little hostel with Japanese-style rooms is a 20-minute walk from Sendai station's west exit. Take any bus going via Miyamachi from stop 17 at the west bus pool and get off at Miyamachi 2 Chōme bus stop. The hostel is tucked down a small side street three blocks east of the bus stop.

MIDRANGE

Aisaki Ryokan (Map p523; ☎ 264-0700; fax 227-6067; http://aisakiryokan.com, in Japanese; 5-6 Kitame-machi, Aoba-ku; s/d/tw ¥3990/6720/7350) If you're not intimidated by cramped and claustrophobic spaces, this budget ryokan (traditional Japanese inn) offers simple yet functional Japanese-style rooms with clean and modern furnishings. It's also within easy walking distance of the station; Aisaki occupies a narrow side street just behind the post office.

Hotel Central Sendai (Map p525; ☎ 711-4111; fax 711-4110; www.hotel-central.co.jp/english.html; 4-2-6 Chūō, Aoba-ku; s/d from ¥7140/12600; 💻) As its name implies, the Hotel Central Sendai is conveniently located in central Sendai, just two blocks west of the Hotel Metropolitan Sendai and JR Sendai station. While fairly standard as far as business hotels go, it's a good choice for privacy seekers, and a much cheaper alternative to Sendai's more famous brand-name accommodation options. LAN cable internet available.

TOP END

Sendai Kokusai Hotel (Map p525; ☎ 268-1112; www.tobu-skh.co.jp/english/english.htm; 4-6-1 Chūō, Aoba-ku; s/d from ¥13,282/20,790; 💻) The Sendai Kokusai Hotel is centred on a sumptuous baroque dining area, decked out in soothing brown and cream tones, and highlighted by European-inspired rooms. The hotel is just a few blocks west of the station, next to the easy-to-spot SS30 building, Sendai's second-tallest building. LAN cable internet available.

Hotel Metropolitan Sendai (Map p525; ☎ 268-2525; www.s-metro.stbl.co.jp/english/index.html; 1-1-1 Chūō, Aoba-ku; s/tw/d from ¥14,437/25,410/27,142; 💻 📶) No surprises here at the Metropolitan, Sendai's signature luxury hotel, which is part of the Sendai station complex. Rooms are smart, well appointed and comfortably plush, and cosmopolitan dining and drinking options sweeten the deal. LAN cable internet available.

Eating & Drinking

Gyūtan (cow tongue) is much loved by Sendai locals. Apparently the tradition derived from hard times (as so many Tōhoku traditions do) – in the immediate post-war years, meat was scarce, so cow tongue became a coveted source of protein. Despite its humble origins, cow tongue is a surprisingly tender cut of meat that is low in fat and high in flavour.

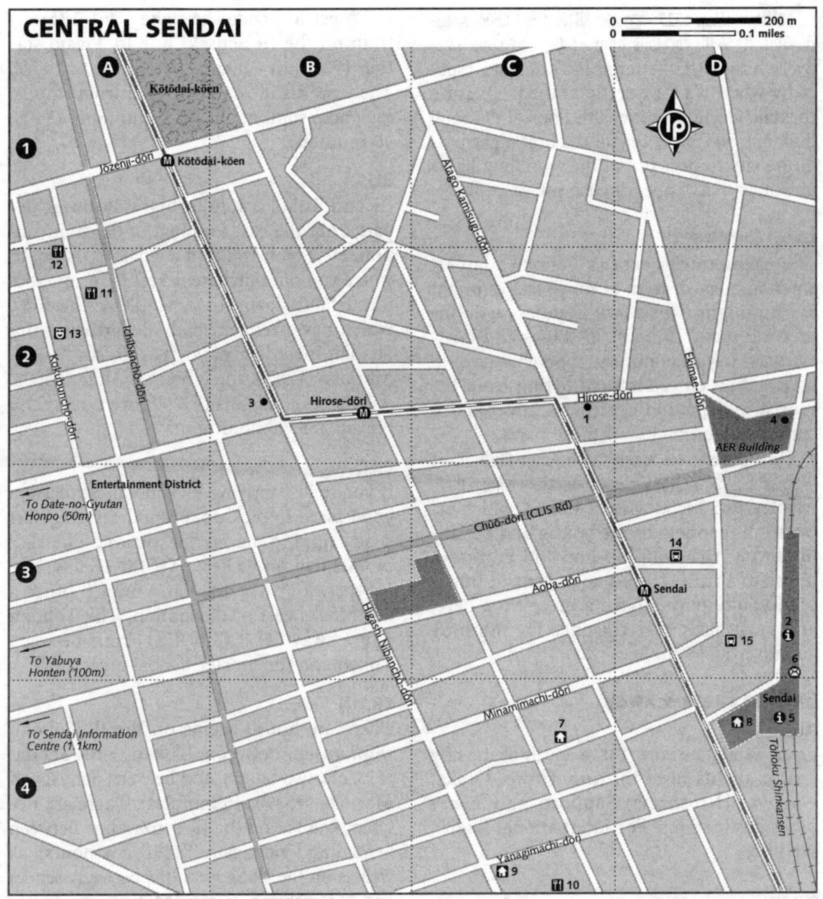

There's a clutch of restaurants and bars that cover the gamut of price ranges at the top of SS30, any of which is a great place to survey the land and scope out the night skies. Also check out the underground mall in JR Sendai station, which is home to the aptly named 'Restaurant Avenue,' a row of various Japanese and international eateries.

Yabuya Honten (Map p523; ☎ 222-5002; 2-2-24 Ōmachi, Aoba-ku; mains from ¥400; 11.30am-6pm Mon-Sat) A much-loved *soba* (buckwheat noodles) specialist, Yabuya Honten has been around since 1847 – more than enough time to perfect its craft. The *kamo-zaru soba* (¥600) variation, served with duck, is just as delicious as it sounds. Located off Aoba-dōri, just before it curves into the park.

Umami Tasuke (Map p525; ☎ 262-2539; 1st fl, Sen chimatsushima Bldg, 2-11-11 Kokubunchō, Aoba-ku; gyūtan from ¥800; 11.30am-10pm Tue-Sun) You're in luck, as one of the most famous places in Sendai to sample *gyūtan* happens to offer an easy-to-use English menu. Just outside the covered market of Ichibanchō-dori, this restaurant generally has a queue.

Aji Tasuke (Map p525; ☎ 225-4641; 4-4-13 Ichibanchō, Aoba-ku; gyūtan from ¥900; lunch & dinner Wed-Mon) If you can't get enough *gyūtan* – cooked over charcoal, this is some seriously tasty stuff – try this other landmark Sendai eatery where you can score a *teishoku* (set meal) for ¥1400. It's outside the market Ichibanchō-dori, right next to the small *torii* (shrine gate).

30View (Map p525; ☎ 267-8818; 4-6-1 Chūō, Aoba-ku, 30th fl, SS30; cocktails from ¥1000; ⏰ 11am-1am) Everything tastes better at lofty heights, especially when it's a perfectly crafted signature cocktail. Occupying the 30th floor of the SS30 Building, 30View is one of the best nightspots in the city to peer out at the twinkling lights of Sendai's cityscape. English menu available.

Entertainment

The Kokubunchō area is Tōhoku's largest entertainment district, as noisy and as bright as you might expect, with endless hole-in-the-wall seedy clubs, strip shows and hostess bars. If you're not the type who pays to play, get an entertainment listing from the tourist information centre as clubs tend to come and go quickly in these parts.

One perennial party venue is **Club Shaft** (Map p525; ☎ 722-5651; www.clubshaft.com; 4th fl, Yoshiokaya Dai 3 Bldg, Kokubunchō, Aoba-ku), which attracts all manners of the young and beautiful. From American hip-hop and European house to British cheese and crunked-out J-pop, you're gonna have a great time here, and most likely regret it once the morning hangover kicks in.

Getting There & Away

AIR

From Sendai airport, 18km south of the city centre, flights head to/from Tokyo, Osaka, Nagoya, Hiroshima, Sapporo and many other destinations. For international flights, see p828.

BOAT

From the port of Sendai-kō, **Taiheyo Ferry** (☎ 259-0211) runs one daily ferry to Tomakomai on Hokkaidō (from ¥8100, 15 hours), and three to four ferries per week to Nagano (from ¥72,000, 21 hours). There is a small ticket office at the pier.

HOT HONSHŪ ONSEN

- **Naruko Onsen** (p530)
- **Sukayu Onsen** (p544)
- **Nyūtō Onsen** (p552)
- **Zaō Onsen** (p563)
- **Echigo-Yuzawa Onsen** (p576)

To get to Sendai-kō, take a *futsū* (local) train on the JR Senseki line to Tagajō station (¥230); it's then a 10-minute taxi ride. There are also five direct buses from stop 34 at Sendai station, but only until 6pm (¥490, 40 minutes).

BUS

JR and Tohoku Kyuko highway buses depart from the east terminal of the train station. Here, you will find a small ticket booth where you can purchase tickets to major cities throughout Japan. Some sample destinations, which have frequent daily departures from Sendai, include: Tokyo (¥6210, six hours), Morioka (¥2850, three hours), Akita (¥4000, four hours), Aomori (¥5700, five hours) and Niigata (¥4500, four hours).

CAR

If you're just arriving in Tohokū, Sendai is a good place to pick up a rental car and start road-tripping across the region. The recommended **Toyota Rent a Car** (☎ 291-0100; 2-4-8 Tsutsujygaoka; ⏰ 8am-8pm) has a branch office a few blocks east of the station. The Tōhoku Expressway (東北自動車道) runs between Tokyo and the greater Sendai area.

TRAIN

There are hourly trains on the JR Tōhoku *shinkansen* between Tokyo and Sendai (¥10,590, two hours), and between Sendai and Morioka (¥6290, 45 minutes). There are frequent *kaisoku* on the JR Senzan line between Sendai and Yamagata (¥1110, 1¼ hours), as well as on the JR Senseki line between Sendai and Matsushima-kaigan (¥400, 35 minutes).

Getting Around

Airport limousines (¥700, 40 minutes) depart from the JR Sendai station frequently for the airport between 6.25am and 6.40pm.

The Loople tourist trolley leaves from the west bus pool's stop 15-3 every 30 minutes from 9am to 4pm, taking a useful loop around the city in a clockwise direction (¥250 per ride). A one-day pass costs ¥600 and comes with an English-language booklet detailing the bus route and sightseeing discounts for pass holders. Passes can be purchased from the station.

Sendai's single subway line runs from Izumi-chūō in the north to Tomizawa in the south but doesn't cover any tourist attractions; single tickets cost ¥200 to ¥350.

MATSUSHIMA & OKU-MATSUSHIMA
松島・奥松島

☎ 022 / pop 20,000

Centuries ago, the haiku poet Bashō had initial misgivings about journeying through Tōhoku. Although he famously lamented: 'I may as well be travelling to the ends of the earth', the north's special charms eventually rendered him lost for words. Upon his encounter with Matsushima Bay, Bashō wrote: 'Matsushima, ah! Matsushima! Matsushima!'

It's easy to see why Bashō was so taken by Matsushima. The bay features around 250 islands covered in pines that have been shaped by the wind, and rock formations that have been shaped by the ceaseless slapping of waves, resulting in spectacular monuments to natural forces. This conglomeration is one of Japan's *Nihon Sankei* (Three Great Sights) – the other two are the floating *torii* of Miyajima Island and the sand-spit at Amanohashidate.

As a result of this distinguished reputation, Matsushima is heavily touristed. Yet it is undeniably picturesque, with a peculiar charm. Masamune Date was so smitten with one of the rock formations that he offered a reward to anyone who could deliver it to castle headquarters. No one could.

On the eastern curve of the bay, Oku-Matsushima is less touristed and offers several trails for exploration by bicycle or on foot.

Orientation & Information

There's a Matsushima station, but Matsushima-kaigan is the one you want – it's closer to the main sights. Outside, the **tourist information office** (☎ 354-2618; ⏲ 8.30am-5pm Apr-Nov, to 4.30pm Dec-Mar) provides maps.

Inside Oku-Matsushima's Nobiru station, the **tourist information office** (☎ 588-2611; ⏲ 9am-6pm) has a few bicycles for rent.

Sights & Activities

MATSUSHIMA

Matsushima is essentially a small village, which means that the following sights are within quick and easy walking distance of one another.

Zuigan-ji (admission ¥1000; ⏲ 8am-3.30pm Jan & Dec, to 4pm Feb & Nov, to 4.30pm Mar & Oct, to 5pm Apr-Sep), one of Tōhoku's finest Zen temples, was founded in AD 828. The present buildings were constructed in 1606 by Date Masamune to serve as a family temple. Look out for **Seiryū-den** (青龍殿; Treasure Hall), displaying works of art associated with the Date family. The temple is accessed via an avenue lined with tall cedars, with weathered Buddhas and altars to the sides – a frequently spooky, deeply contemplative approach.

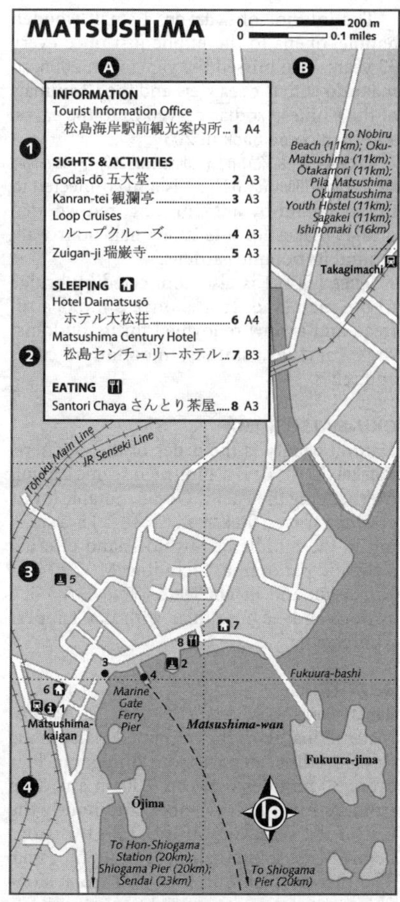

The **Kanran-tei** (admission ¥200; ⏲ 8.30am-5pm Apr-Oct, to 4.30pm Nov-Mar) pavilion was presented to the Date family by Toyotomi Hideyoshi in the late 16th century. It served as a genteel venue for tea ceremonies and moon viewing – the name means 'a place to view ripples on the water'. Today *matcha* (powdered green tea) is served here, and the garden includes the **Matsushima Hakubutsukan**, a small museum housing a collection of relics from the Date family.

The interior of **Godai-dō**, a small wooden temple, opens to the public just once every 33 years. You missed the viewing in 2006, so make do with the sea view and the 12 animals of the Chinese zodiac carved in to the eaves, and then come back in 2039.

Fukuura-jima (福浦島; admission ¥200; 8am-5pm Mar-Oct, to 4.30pm Nov-Feb), an island connected to the mainland by a 252m-long, red wooden bridge, makes for a leisurely half-hour walk around its botanic gardens.

Ōjima (雄島) is also connected by bridge to the mainland. It was once a monk's retreat, and is now renowned for its Buddhist rock carvings, statues, meditation caves and relics.

OKU-MATSUSHIMA

Natural beauty is the order of the day here. **Sagakei** (嵯峨渓) is a 40m-high scenic canyon overhanging the Pacific Ocean, notable for its crashing waves; **Ōtakamori** (大高森) is a small hill in the middle of Miyato Island offering a terrific panorama, including Mt Zaō and Kinkasan; and **Nobiru Beach** (野蒜海岸) is a swimming beach popular with day trippers from Sendai.

BOAT TRIPS

Boats (lower/upper deck ¥1420/2220, 50 min) to Matsushima, along the celebrated Matsushima Bay coastline, depart from Shiogama Pier every 30 minutes between 9.30am and 3pm from 21 April to November, and hourly the rest of the year. Get off the train two stops before Matsushima-kaigan at Hon-Shiogama. The pier is 10 minutes on foot from Hon-Shiogama station – turn right as you exit.

Otherwise there are **loop cruises** that depart from the Marine Gate Ferry Pier in Matsushima (¥1400, 50 minutes) between 9.30am and 3pm, though these are often overrun with sightseers, especially on weekends and holidays.

Festivals & Events

Matsushima Kaki Matsuri (松島牡蠣祭り; Matsushima Oyster Festival) Bivalve aficionados will appreciate this festival held the first weekend in February, where you can purchase oysters and cook them on a 100m-long grill.

Zuigan-ji Tōdō The approach to Zuigan-ji is enhanced from 6 to 8 August, when candlesticks are lit along the path for the event, which honours this ancient shrine.

Matsushima Tōrō Nagashi Hanabi Taikai On 17 August, the souls of the departed are honoured with the O-Bon (Festival of the Dead) ritual, when lighted lanterns are floated out to sea accompanied by an extensive fireworks display.

Sleeping & Eating

Pila Matsushima Okumatsushima Youth Hostel (Map p521; ☎ 0225-88-2220; 89-48 Minami-Akazaki, Nobiru, Matsushima; dm from ¥4905; P) Set in a lovely location just near the beach at Oku-Matsushima, this is a great base if you want to tackle some of the nearby hiking and biking trails, especially if you meet a few new friends in the dormitories. To get to the hostel from Nobiru station, walk across the bridge and towards the ocean for about 15 minutes until you reach an intersection with a blue youth-hostel sign pointing down the road to the right. From there it's about 800m. Staff at the tourist information office can give you a map with directions.

Hotel Daimatsusō (☎ 354-3601; fax 354-6154; www.daimatsuso.co.jp, in Japanese; 25 Matsushima; per person incl 2 meals from ¥8400; P) Just steps away from the station (to the left as you exit, at the end of the car park), with welcoming potted plants to greet you. Not as fancy as some places, but clean and convenient with good food and service, and the upper floors have nice views of the bay.

Matsushima Century Hotel (☎ 354-4111; www.centuryhotel.co.jp, in Japanese; 8 Aza-Senzui; d from ¥12,700; P) The pick of the resorts, the Century enjoys a stunning location, resting elegantly on one of the islands in Matsushima Bay. Western- and Japanese-style rooms vary in price depending on their furnishings and location (upmarket rooms have sea-view balconies), though everyone can enjoy the panoramic vistas from the on-site communal bath. LAN cable internet available.

Santori Chaya (☎ 353-2622; dinner mains ¥1500-2500; lunch & dinner Thu-Tue, closed 2nd & 4th Wed of month;) A small, intimate, Japanese-style eatery favoured by locals, Santori Chaya is great for *kaki yaki* (fried oysters; ¥650) or *sanma sashimi* (raw saury; ¥750) in season. From Matsushima-kaigan station, go left out of the car park and follow the main road to the third set of lights. You'll find Santori Chaya on the left side of the big parking lot. LAN cable internet available.

Getting There & Away

There are frequent *kaisoku* on the JR Senseki line between Sendai and Matsushima-kaigan (¥400, 35 minutes). To reach Oku-Matsushima from Matsushima-kaigan station, take the JR

MATSUO BASHŌ

Another year is gone, a traveller's shade on my head, straw sandals at my feet.

Matsuo Bashō, *Account of Exposure to the Fields* (1685)

Regarded as Japan's master of haiku, Matsuo Bashō (1644–94) is credited with elevating its status from comic relief to Zen-infused enlightenment.

Bashō was born into a samurai family, and served the feudal lord Yoshitada in his late teenage years. Moving first to Kyoto, and then to Edo, Bashō found success as a published poet, but ultimately found the acclaim to be spiritually unsettling. He eventually turned to Zen, and the philosophy had a deep impact on his work. In fact, comparisons have been made between his haiku and Zen *kōan* (short riddles), intended to bring about a sudden flash of insight in the listener.

Bashō was also influenced by the natural philosophy of the Chinese Taoist sage Chuangzi, and began to examine nature uncritically. Later he developed his own poetic principle by drawing on the concept of *sabi,* a kind of spare, lonely beauty.

When he reached his 40s, Bashō decided to give his career away in favour of travelling throughout Japan, seeking to build friendships and commune with nature as he went. He published evocative accounts of his travels, including *The Records of a Weather-Beaten Skeleton* and *The Records of a Travel-Worn Satchel,* but his collection *The Narrow Road to the Deep North,* detailing his journey throughout Tōhoku in 1689, is probably the most famous.

Senseki line six stations east (two stops by *kaisoku*) to Nobiru (¥230, 10 minutes).

For drivers, Matsushima can be reached from Sendai via the Sendai Matsushima Hwy (仙台松島道路).

ISHINOMAKI 石巻

☎ 0225 / pop 170,000

Manga-maniacs should be sure to put Ishinomaki on their to-do list – the town is littered with tributes to cartoonist Shōtarō Ishinomori, a local hero who created some of Japan's best-loved manga characters. Aside from that, and its use as a launching pad for Kinkasan, there isn't much else going on here.

The **tourist information office** (☎ 93-6448; 9am-5.30pm) is just outside the station, and has combo bus-and-ferry timetables for the Kinkasan-bound. Also, be sure to pick up a manga-themed map of the city, which is helpful, as the sights listed here are scattered about. With Sendai and Matushima close by, there's no compelling reason to stay here.

The spaceship-style **Ishinomaki Mangattan Museum** (石ノ森萬画館; ☎ 96-5055; 2-7 Nakase; admission 1st & 3rd fl free, 2nd fl ¥800; 9am-6pm Mar-Nov, to 5pm Wed-Mon Dec-Feb, closed 3rd Tue Mar-Nov) is mostly devoted to Shōtarō Ishinomori's work and will appeal most to folks already familiar with the comics *Cyborg 009,* one of Ishinomori's many cartoon creations.

Old Ishinomaki Orthodox Church (旧石巻ハリストス正教会教会堂; ☎ 95-1111; 3-18 Nakase; admission free; 9am-5pm Apr-Oct, to 4pm Mon-Fri Nov-Mar) is Japan's oldest wooden church (dating from 1880, but no longer in use). Advance reservation (by phone) is mandatory.

An impressive replica of the galleon **San Juan Bautista** (宮城県慶長使節船ミュージアム; ☎ 24-2210; www.santjuan.or.jp, in Japanese; 30-2 Ōmori Watanoha; admission ¥700; 9.30am-4.30pm Wed-Mon) is near the wharf. The San Juan is a monument to Date Masamune's forward-thinking rule; with an envoy of 20, it sailed to Rome as Japan's first diplomatic mission.

Frequent *kaisoku* run along the JR Senseki line between Sendai and Ishinomaki (¥820, 1¼ hours) via Matsushima-kaigan and Nobiru. Rental bikes, which are available right outside the station, make a great way to see the town, even though most of the sights are within walking distance.

KINKASAN 金華山

☎ 0225

The island of Kinkasan, or 'Golden Mountain', was an ancient site for gold prospecting, and it's said that if you pay a visit three years running, you can kiss your money worries goodbye for the rest of your life. Of course, the vein has long since been tapped dry, though Kinkasan still attracts a steady stream of visitors eager for some good fortune to rub off. Interestingly enough, women were banned on

Kinkasan until the late 19th century. Today, for both sexes, an overnight stay is ideal for those seeking wide-open spaces, fresh air and plenty of peace and tranquillity.

Orientation & Information

Kinkasan is accessed by ferry from Ayukawa, a small port town that is technically part of Ishinomaki. There's no tourist information, or much else for that matter on Kinkasan, so it's best to collect pamphlets and timetables at the Ishinomaki tourist information office before making the journey

Sights & Activities

Before setting out on foot, take heed: the dirt trail that once circled the entire island (24km) along the shore is no longer safe at the northern edge because of a landslip – only the southern side is considered safe. If you get lost, head south and downhill towards the sea.

Turning left from the boat dock, it's a steep 20-minute walk uphill to **Koganeyama-jinja** (黄金山神社), built in AD 794 by Emperor Shōmu as thanks for finding the gold used to finish the Great Buddha at Nara's Tōdai-ji.

From Koganeyama-jinja it's a 50-minute hike downhill to **Senjōjiki** (千畳敷; 1000 Tatami Mats Rock), a large formation of white rock on the eastern shore of the island, and a further hour to the lighthouse propping up the southeast corner.

It takes roughly 1½ hours to follow the dirt trail along the shore and cross back over the summit to the dock area.

Festivals & Events

Ryūjin Matsuri (龍神祭り; Dragon Festival) On the last weekend in July; features giant dragon floats supported by up to 50 dancers.

Antler-cutting ceremony On the first and second Sunday in October; this tradition is meant to help stop the deer from injuring each other during mating season.

Sleeping & Eating

Most visitors to Kinkasan are day trippers, which means the island is delightfully deserted in the early morning, late afternoon and evening. Note that phoning ahead and making a reservation is a good idea as there are only a few places to stay and no places to eat on the island. If you don't speak Japanese, the staff at the tourist information office in Ishinomaki can help you.

Koganeyama-jinja (黄金山神社; ☎ 45-2301; dm per person ¥5000) There is basic lodging in shared tatami rooms at the temple, and simple vegetarian meals are available (from ¥500). If you're awake before 6am, you can attend morning prayers.

Minshuku Shiokaze (民宿!潮風; ☎ 45-2666; fax 45-2244; r per person with 2 meals ¥6300) This *minshuku*, located 500m south along the headland from the pier, is a more comfortable – but less atmospheric – option than the temple. Simple but airy rooms overlook the sea, while the friendly owners can fill you up with hearty local cuisine before giving you tips on the island's best hiking routes. .

If you get stuck in Ayukawa, **Minami-sō** (みなみ荘; ☎ 45-2501; r per person with/without 2 meals from ¥6300/4200), behind the Ayukawa bus station, is a basic *minshuku* where you can get some rest and catch either the bus or the ferry in the morning.

Getting There & Away

There are seven daily buses between JR Ishinomaki station and Ayukawa port (¥1460, 1½ hours). During the summer months, **Dream** (☎ 44-1055) operates ferries between Ayukawa and Kinkasan (one way ¥900, 25 minutes). Ferries run almost hourly between 8.30am and 3.45pm; the last return ferry is at 4pm. Service is greatly reduced the rest of the year.

NARUKO ONSEN 鳴子温泉

☎ 0229 / pop 8570

Come to Naruko Onsen (Map p521) to hear the clip-clop of *geta* (Japanese clogs) as *yukata* (Japanese robe)–clad bathers trot between spring-fed baths. Breathe in and smell the sulphurous steam as it rises from street culverts. Stop and soak tired feet in the (free!) *ashiyu* (foot baths), or go for the full wash in sulphurous onsen said to possess distinct healing qualities. Simply put, Naruko's charms are quiet, simple and rejuvenating.

The helpful **tourist information office** (☎ 83-3441; 🕑 8.30am-6pm), inside JR Naruko Onsen station, has useful English-language maps and brochures, and can also help book your accommodation.

Taki-no-yu (滝の湯; admission ¥150; 🕑 7.30am-10pm) is a sheer delight – a fabulously atmospheric wooden bathhouse that's hardly changed in 150 years. Water gushes in from *hinoki* (Japanese cypress) channels, carrying with it various elements and minerals including sulphur, sodium bicarbonate and sodium chloride. This particular onsen is famous for its therapeutic relief of high blood pressure and hardened arteries.

Naruko-kyō (鳴子峡), a scenic, 100m-deep gorge, can be reached in 20 minutes (Bashō time, that is) on foot from Naruko Onsen station. Alternatively, buses (¥200, five minutes) run from 8.50am to 4pm. From the gorge entrance, a pleasant 4km trail leads along the river valley to Nakayama-daira. If you turn right just after the bridge, but before reaching the gorge, you'll find the historical Shitomae checkpoint, the start of a quiet 5km country path along the route Bashō once walked. The last bus back to the station leaves at around 4.30pm.

The **Japan Kokeshi Museum** (日本こけし館; ☎ 83-3600; admission ¥320; ⏲ 8.30am-5pm Apr-Nov, 9am-4pm Dec) features around 5000 *kokeshi* dolls (which look like typical Japanese dolls – simply adorned with soft lines and traditional fabrics – but they're distinguished by the symbology surrounding them) from around the country. During the Meiji era, Tōhoku was almost totally neglected, with the result that a flood of men and women moved south to find work. Some say that *kokeshi* dolls were symbolic representations of those lost girls, who were often snatched away at a young age.

While there is no shortage of hot springs hotels to choose from, we particularly like **Yusaya Ryokan** (ゆさや旅館; ☎ 83-2565; www.yusaya.co.jp, in Japanese; s/d with meals from ¥13,800/23,400; Ⓟ), a small and intimate traditional-style inn that is centred on a stunning *rotemburo* (outdoor bath) overlooking a dense thicket of trees.

Another rustic charmer is **Gin-no-shō** (吟の庄; ☎ 83-4355; www.hds-net.jp/ginnosho, in Japanese; r with meals from ¥18,900; Ⓟ), which is built out of natural materials to provide a relaxed and minimalist ambience.

Both accommodation options, as well as a few more modern options, are within easy walking distance of the station – ask the staff at the tourist information centre to point the way.

Getting There & Away

There are hourly trains on the JR Tōhoku *shinkansen* between Sendai and Furukawa (¥2300, 15 minutes). Hourly trains run on the JR Rikū-tō line between Furukawa and Naruko Onsen (¥1750, 45 minutes). There are also infrequent trains between Naruko Onsen and Shinjō (¥950, 1¼ hours), where you can pick up the Yamagata *shinkansen* line and a few local trains.

IWATE-KEN 岩手県

Japan's second-largest prefecture, Iwate-ken is a quiet and bucolic place that is largely characterised by rich farmland, sleepy valleys and some pretty serious mountain ranges. Although the region once played host to warring states and feudal rule, there are few remnants of this turbulent past, aside from the magnificent temples at Hiraizumi. Indeed, Iwate-ken feels more provincial – in the best of ways – and stopping in places like the Tōno valley, which influenced a rich collection of folkloric tales, can seem almost like turning back time.

HIRAIZUMI 平泉

☎ 0191 / pop 9000

Hiraizumi's grandeur once rivalled Kyoto's, and the tale of its ruin is one of the most bittersweet sagas in Tōhoku's history. From 1089 to 1189, three generations of the Fujiwara family, headed by Fujiwara Kiyohira, created a political and cultural centre in Hiraizumi. Kiyohira had made his fortune from local gold mines and, at the behest of Kyoto priests, he used his wealth and power to commence work on the creation of a 'paradise on earth', devoted to the principles of Buddhist thought as a reaction against the feudal wars that were plaguing the land.

Although his son and grandson continued along this path, Kiyohira's great-grandson, Yoshihira, yielding to both internal and external pressures, brought this short century of fame and prosperity to an abrupt end. Today only a few sights scattered around this rural town bear testament to Hiraizumi's faded glory, though they do represent a singular experience, and remain a regional highlight.

Information

Turning right outside Hiraizumi station, the **tourist information office** (☎ 46-2110; ⏲ 8.30am-5pm) has English-language pamphlets. The post office, with an international ATM, is 400m northwest of the station heading towards

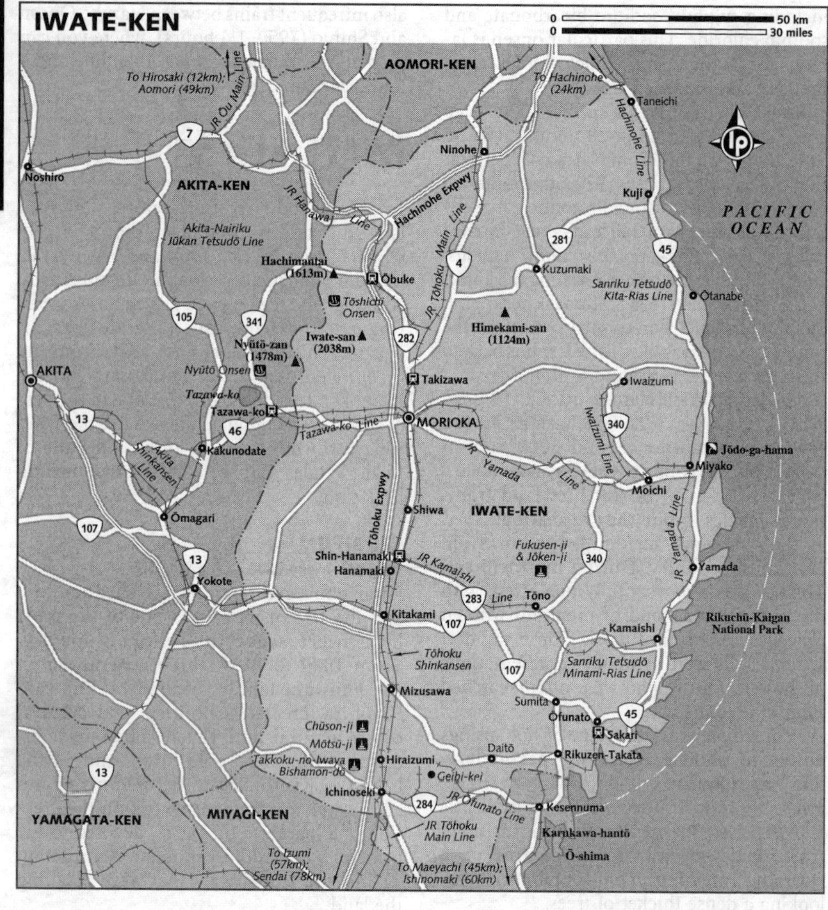

Mōtsū-ji. Free internet access is available at the public library (open 9am to 5pm Tuesday to Sunday), 1500m southwest of the station.

Sights & Activities

Note that Hiraizumi is very small and easily walkable, though cycling will help cut down some of the distances between sights (see p535 for bike-rental details). Navigation is also a cinch as directions to major sights are signposted in English.

CHŪSON-JI 中尊寺

This **temple complex** (☎ 46-2211; admission incl Konjiki-dō, Sankōzō & Kyōzō ¥800; 🕒 8am-5pm Apr-Oct, 8.30am-4.30pm Nov-Mar) was established in AD 850 by the priest Ennin, though it was Fujiwara Kiyohira who decided in the early 12th century to expand the complex into a site with around 300 buildings, including 40 temples. Ironically, in the face of the grand scheme to build a Buddhist utopia, Hiraizumi was never far from tragedy: a massive fire here in 1337 destroyed most of the buildings, although two of the original constructions remain alongside the newer temples. The site is accessed via a steep approach along an avenue lined with trees and Jizō statues.

The approach snakes past the **Hon-dō** (Main Hall) to an enclosed area featuring the splendid **Konjiki-dō** (金色堂; Golden Hall; 🕒 8am-4.30pm Apr-Oct, 8.30am-4pm Nov-Mar). Built in 1124, Konjiki-dō is quite a sight, packed with gold detailing, black lacquerwork and inlaid mother-of-pearl (the region was known for its gold and lacquer resources). The centrepiece of the hall is the fabulously ornate statue of the Amida Buddha, along with attendants. Beneath the three side altars are the mummified remains of three generations of the Fujiwara family.

Beside the Konjiki-dō, the temple treasury, **Sankōzō**, contains the coffins and funeral finery of the Fujiwara clan – scrolls, swords and images transferred from long-vanished halls and temples. The sutra treasury **Kyōzō**, built in 1108, is the oldest structure in the complex.

MŌTSŪ-JI 毛越寺

Dating from AD 850, **Mōtsū-ji** (☎ 46-2331; admission ¥500; 🕑 8.30am-5pm Apr-Oct, to 4.30pm Nov-Mar) once surpassed Chūson-ji as Tōhoku's largest temple complex; it too was established by Ennin. Now the temples are long gone and only the beautiful gardens remain, a so-called Pure Land garden from the Heian era, designed with the Buddhist notion of preserving 'paradise' in mind.

TAKKOKU-NO-IWAYA BISHAMON-DŌ 達谷窟毘沙門堂

Five kilometres southwest of Mōtsū-ji, **Takkoku-no-Iwaya Bishamon-dō** (☎ 46-4931; admission ¥300; 🕑 8am-5pm, varies per season) is a small picturesque cave temple dedicated to the deity Bishamon (the Buddhist guardian of warriors) by the famous general Sakanoue no Tamuramaro. It was built in AD 801 after Sakanoue's victory against the Ezo, the original inhabitants of Northern Honshū; the present structure is a 1961 replica. You can cycle to the cave along a paved path from Mōtsū-ji in about 30 minutes.

TAKADACHI GIKEI-DŌ 高館義経堂

A small memorial honouring Minamoto Yoshitsune, **Takadachi Gikei-dō** (☎ 46-3300; admission ¥200; 🕑 8.30am-5pm Apr-Oct, to 4.30pm Nov-Mar) includes a monument inscribed with Bashō's 'summer grass' lament. The hall is at the top of a small hill with fine views of the Kitakami-gawa, about 700m from the entrance to Chūson-ji.

GEIBI-KEI 猊鼻渓

A huge natural gorge, **Geibi-kei** features sheer 100m-high cliffs. Singing boatmen on flat-bottomed **boats** (☎ 47-2341; per 90min ¥1500; 🕑 8.30am-4.30pm Apr-Oct, 9am-3pm Nov-Mar, varies per season) regale passengers with local folk songs that echo along the cliffs. Take the bus from stop 7 outside Ichinoseki station (¥620, 40 minutes, hourly) or the train from Ichinoseki to Geibi-kei station on the JR Ōfunato line (*kaisoku* ¥480, 30 minutes).

Festivals & Events

Haru-no-Fujiwara Matsuri (春の藤原まつり; Spring Fujiwara Festival) From 1 to 5 May; features a costumed procession, performances of *nō* (classical Japanese dance-drama), traditional *ennen-no-mai* (longevity dances) and an enormous rice cake–carrying competition.

Aki-no-Fujiwara Matsuri (秋の藤原まつり; Autumn Fujiwara Festival) A similar festival takes place from 1 to 3 November.

Sleeping & Eating

Mōtsū-ji Youth Hostel (☎ 46-2331; 58 Ōsawa; dm/r from ¥2800/4200; 💻) Despite the youth hostel moniker, this accommodation is actually part of the

Mōtsu-ji temple grounds, and allows guests to attend morning prayers and *zazen* (seated meditation) sessions. Facilities are shared, there's a strict 9pm curfew and proper manner is expected, though the serene ground can calm even the most rowdy of temperaments.

Hotel Musashibō (☎ 46-2241; fax 46-2250; www.musasibou.co.jp, in Japanese; r per person incl 2 meals from ¥8550; 💻) If you're looking for a bit more privacy, the Musashibō is something of a cross between a business hotel and a ryokan, offering Japanese-style rooms, an onsen bath, formal sit-down dinners and an informal snack bar. From the station, walk straight for 500m and turn right, pass the temple, then look on the corner after the second road on the left. LAN cable internet available.

Ekimae-bashōkan (☎ 46-5555; soba sets from ¥1050; 🕑 lunch & dinner) A nice little noodle shop that is literally in front of the train station (look for the blue-tiled roof), Ekimae-bashōkan is a great place to try *wanko-soba* (¥1750). A speciality of nearby Morioka, tiny bowls of *soba* are served one after another alongside a tray of accompaniments (note: true *wanko-soba* aficionados skip the fixings and focus solely on racking up their bowl count!).

Getting There & Away

Hourly trains run along the JR Tōhoku *shinkansen* between Sendai and Ichinoseki (¥3320, 30 minutes). Local trains run about every hour or two on the JR Tōhoku Main line between Ichinoseki and Hiraizumi (¥190, 10 minutes). There are also frequent local buses running between Ichinoseki and Chūson-ji (¥350, 20 minutes) via JR Hiraizumi station.

Ichinoseki is connected to Morioka by the JR Tōhoku *shinkansen* (¥3920, 40 minutes) and the JR Tōhoku Main line (*futsū*, ¥1620, 1½ hours).

If you're driving, the Tōhoku Expressway (東北自動車道) runs between Sendai and Hiraizumi.

Getting Around

In addition to the local buses running between JR Hiraizumi station and Chūson-ji, there is **bicycle rental** (per day ¥1000; 🕑 9am-4pm Apr-Nov) available at a small kiosk next to the station.

TŌNO VALLEY 遠野

☎ 0198 / pop 31,000

The Tōno valley, surrounded by verdant rice fields and dramatic mountains, is the heartland of some of Japan's most cherished folk tales. A comparatively poor area that has suffered from devastating famines and droughts throughout the centuries, Tōno has always been subject to the whims of nature. Given this harsh history, superstitious residents have a healthy mix of fear and admiration for the natural world, which has led to the creation of a whole assortment of wild creatures that run the gamut from the odd to the perverse (see the boxed text, p537).

The merging of eight traditional farming villages formed the present city, and much of that rural flavour is preserved today. There are still some examples of the local architectural style of L-shaped farmhouses, known as *magariya*, where farm-folk and their prized horses lived under one roof, albeit in different sections (unlike the fertility goddess, Oshira-sama; see the boxed text, p537). Tōno is also reportedly home to the country's largest concentration of *kappa*, which are mischievous water spirits that figure prominently in Japanese mythology.

If you have a vivid imagination, and are longing for some clean country air, the

INFORMATION

Tourist Information Office 総合観光案内所	1 B1
Tōno City Library 遠野市立図書館	2 A2
Tōno Post Office 遠野郵便局	3 B2

SIGHTS & ACTIVITIES

Chiba Family Magariya 南部曲り家千葉家	4 A3
Denshōen 伝承園	5 D2
Fukusen-ji 福泉寺	6 D1
Gohyaku Rakan 五百羅漢	7 C3
Jōken-ji 常堅寺	8 D2
Kappa-buchi Pool カッパ淵	9 D2
Tsuzuki Ishi 続き石	10 A3
Tōno Furusato-mura 遠野ふるさと村	11 C1
Tōno Mukashibanashi-mura とおの昔話村	12 A2
Tōno Municipal Museum 遠野市立博物館	(see 2)
Unedori-sama Shrine 卯子酉様	13 C3

SLEEPING

Folkloro Tōno フォルクローロ遠野	14 B1
Minshuku Magariya 民宿曲り屋	15 B3
Minshuku Tōno 民宿とおの	16 B1
Tōno Youth Hostel 遠野ユースホステル	17 D2

EATING

Ichiriki 一力	18 B2
Topia Department Store トピアデパート	19 B1
Umenoya うめのや	20 B1

TRANSPORT

Bicycle Rental 自転車レンタル	(see 1)
Kankō Rent-a-Car 観光レンタカー	21 B1

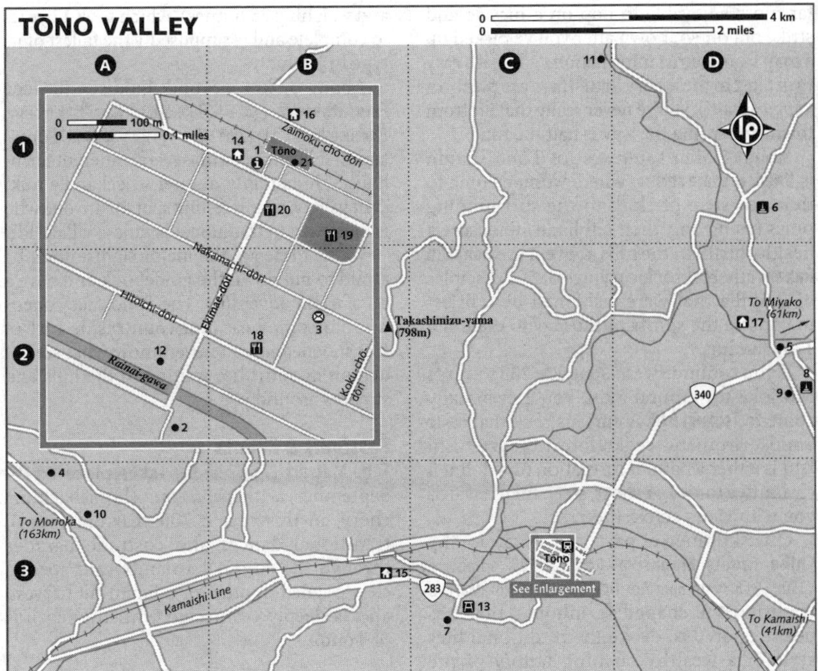

Tōno valley is a wonderful place to explore on bicycle, assuming of course you've got at least two days to leave behind the trappings of civilisation.

One last thing – if you do happen to come across a *kappa*, remember to bow – Japanese to the core, *kappa* will return the gesture, thus spilling out the water they store in their head, and rendering them temporarily powerless!

Orientation & Information

You'll need some form of transport to make the most of your stay, as there is not much in the town itself to hold your attention for long. A beautiful way to see the countryside is by bicycle, made easier by a fantastic bike trail that runs alongside the river. Renting a car is another option, and bus tours are sporadically available – ask at the tourist information office before making plans.

Tōno City Library (☎ 62-2340; ⏲ 9am-5pm Tue-Sun) Offers free internet access.

Tōno post office (遠野郵便局; ☎ 62-2830; 6-10 Chūō-dōri) Has an international ATM.

Tourist information office (☎ 62-1333; ⏲ 8am-6pm Apr-Oct, 8.30am-5.30pm Nov-Mar) To the right as you exit Tōno station; staff speak some English and supply a useful English-language brochure and a map of the three main cycling routes.

Sights

TŌNO TOWN

These two sights are within easy walking distance of the JR Tōno station.

On the upper floors of the city library, the **Tōno Municipal Museum** (☎ 62-2340; 3-9 Higashidate-chō; admission ¥310, combined entrance to Tōno Mukashibanashi-mura ¥520; ⏲ 9am-5pm, closed last day of each month) has exhibits of folklore and traditional life, and some engaging audio-visual presentations of the various legends of Tōno.

Tōno Mukashibanashi-mura (☎ 62-7887; 2-11 Chūō-dōri; admission ¥310, combined entrance to Tōno Municipal Museum ¥520; ⏲ 9am-5pm) is a folk village with a restored ryokan, where Kunio Yanagita (see the boxed text, p537) once stayed, as well as an exhibition hall for folk art.

TŌNO VALLEY

While technically some of the sights listed here can be accessed by infrequent local buses, it's far more enjoyable to hop on a bicycle and strike out on your own after you've picked up a map from tourist information. While it's easy to get lost in these parts (and there are plenty of *kappa* about!), you're never really that far from town, and losing the way is half the fun.

About 2.5km southwest of Tōno station is **Unedori-sama shrine**, where women come to tie a red strip of cloth to the surrounding pines (using only their left hand) to ensure a healthy birth. In the hills above it are **Gohyaku Rakan**, ethereal rock carvings of 500 disciples of Buddha that were fashioned by a priest to console the spirits of those who died in a 1754 famine.

If you continue west along Rte 283 towards Morioka for around 8km, you'll eventually come to **Tsuzuki Ishi.** A curious rock that rests amidst aromatic cedar forest, Tsuzukushi Ishi is either a natural formation or a dolmen (primitive tomb). A short, steep hike rewards you with views across the valley.

One kilometre past the rock is the **Chiba Family Magariya** (☎ 62-9529; admission ¥350; ⏲ 8.30am-5pm Apr-Oct, 9am-4pm Nov-Mar), a traditional L-shaped farmhouse that has been restored to evoke the traditional lifestyle of a wealthy farming family of the 18th century.

Approximately 6km northwest of Tōno station, along Rte 340 towards Miyako, is **Denshōen** (☎ 62-8655; admission ¥520; ⏲ 9am-5pm, last entry 4.30pm), a small folk village featuring a hall with 1000 Oshira-sama dolls.

A few hundred metres southeast of Denshōen is **Jōken-ji**, a peaceful little temple dedicated to the deity image of Obinzuru-sama – some believe it will cure their illness if they rub the parts of its body corresponding to the location of their ailment.

Behind the temple is the **Kappa-buchi** pool. Legend has it that *kappa*, belying their impish nature, once put out a fire in the temple; the lion statue was erected as a gesture of thanks to honour this good deed. It is said that if pregnant women worship at the shrine on the riverbank they'll produce plenty of milk, but only if they first produce a breast-shaped offering. The tiny temple is filled with small cloth bags, either red or white, most replete with nipple.

About 2.5km north of Denshōen along local roads is **Fukusen-ji** (☎ 62-3822; 7-57 Komagi, Matsuzaki; admission ¥300; ⏲ 8am-4.30pm Apr-Dec). Founded in 1912, the temple's major claim to fame is the wooden Fukusen-ji Kannon statue (17m high and weighing 25 tonnes), which took 12 years to complete and is supposedly the tallest of its type in Japan.

About 3.5km beyond Fukusen-ji, **Tōno Furusato-mura** (☎ 64-2300; 5-89-1 Kami-tsukimoushi, Tsukimoushi-chō; admission ¥520; ⏲ 9am-5pm) is Tōno's largest folk village, with several different farmhouses, restaurants, a water wheel and a folkcraft gallery, an interesting spot for anyone who is interested in traditional Japanese village life.

While these are the major sights, don't be afraid to put down the guidebook and have a bit of a DIY adventure. The Tōno valley opens up into some beautiful countryside east of Denshōen, and you never know what sort of demon or spirit lies waiting in the hills and streams around you.

Festivals & Events

Tōno Matsuri (遠野祭り) takes place on 14 September, with *yabusame* (horseback archery, in this case a 700-year-old event), traditional dances and costume parades through the city. It's a flamboyant spectacle, designed to pray for a bountiful harvest, and is deeply connected with the legends of Tōno.

Sleeping & Eating

Note that aside from the youth hostel, prices in the Tōno valley vary considerably according to the day of the week and the season.

our pick **Tōno Youth Hostel** (☎ 62-8736; www1.odn.ne.jp/tono-yh/index-e.htm; 13-39-5 Tsuchibuchi, Tsuchibuchi-chō; dm from ¥3200; P) A spick-and-span, two-storey hostel that's a super base for exploring the valley. The manager speaks some English and is well versed in the local legends (there's a detailed report nightly). Bicycle rental is available, there's no curfew and there's an extensive manga library. Meals are available (breakfast/dinner ¥550/1150). From Tōno station, take a bus bound for Sakanoshita to the Nitagai stop (¥290, 12 minutes). From there, it's a 10-minute walk; the hostel is clearly signposted – minute-by-minute – along the way.

Minshuku Tōno (☎ 62-4395; fax 62-4365; www.minshuku-tono.com; 2-17 Zaimoku-chō; r per person incl 2 meals from ¥6300) There are several cheapie places to bed down in Tōno village, but this dignified *minshuku* behind the station is the best. While not as remote and atmospheric as Magariya, it's still a quiet little spot, and the owners are keen on using fresh local produce in their home cooking.

THE CURIOUS CUSTOMS OF TŌHOKU

At the beginning of the 20th century, a collection of regional folk tales was published under the title *Tōno Monogatari* (Legends of Tōno). They were compiled by Kunio Yanagita (1875–1962), a prominent writer and scholar who is regarded as the father of Japanese folklore. The collection was based on interviews with Tōno resident Kyōseki Sasaki, who was born into a peasant family and who had committed to memory more than 100 *densetsu* (local legends). What Yanagita and Sasaki unearthed immediately captured the nation's imagination, bringing into rich focus the oral storytelling traditions of a region hitherto almost completely ignored.

The cast of characters and situations is truly weird and wonderful, and draws heavily on the concept of animism, a system of belief that attributes a personal spirit to everything that exists, including animals and inanimate objects. One of the more striking tales concerns a simple village girl who married her horse. As you might imagine, this was against her father's wishes, so the father hung the horse from a mulberry tree and beheaded it. The girl, clutching the horse's head, then flew off to heaven where she became Oshira-sama, the fertility goddess. Today, Oshira-sama dolls are still important ceremonial objects for *itako* (mediums); see p545.

Elsewhere, there are shape-shifting foxes; elderly folk who are cast off into the wilderness to die; impish water spirits called *kappa,* who sumō-wrestle passers-by to the ground and who like to pull their victim's intestines out through their anus; *zashiki warashi* spirits, who live in the corners of houses and play tricks on the residents; and wild men who live in the hills and eat children. Throughout all of them is a common theme: the battle with nature and the struggle to tame the elements – everyday features of rural life, of which Tōno is an exemplar.

Legends of Tōno is available, in English, for ¥2000 from the souvenir shop next to the Tōno tourist information office.

Folkloro Tōno (☎ 62-0700; fax 62-0800; 5-7 Shinkoku-chō; r per person incl 2 meals ¥8800) A standard business hotel that is curiously located right above the JR Tōno station, so it's a good choice if you want a central home base, or if you're partial to Western-style rooms. The train is infrequent, but when it comes, you'll certainly know.

Minshuku Magariya (☎ 62-4564; 30-58-3 Niisato, Ayaori-chō; r per person incl 2 meals from ¥9750; Ⓟ) If you came to Tōno to escape urban Japan, then head to this pastoral farmhouse and inn, located about 3km southwest of the station along Rte 283 – if you don't have a car, take a taxi (around ¥1000). True to its roots, Magariya is centred on a large hearth where guests congregate for hearty country cooking, while old-fashioned tatami rooms practically open up into the forest.

Umenoya (☎ 62-2622; meals from ¥650; 🕑 11.30am-8pm) On the main road in front of the train station, Umenoya is a popular place for a light meal or just a small snack. Grab a picture menu and choose from *rāmen, soba,* udon, omelettes, curry rice and sandwiches.

Ichiriki (☎ 62-2008; meals from ¥800; 🕑 11am-8pm, closed irregularly) With its cosy interior covered with advisory posters on the walls for those wishing to go *kappa* hunting, this traditional spot four blocks south of the station is a great spot to try *hitsuko soba* (¥1000), a local dish of handmade noodles, chicken, raw egg and veggies.

If you want to prepare a picnic lunch or *bentō* (boxed meal), check out the food shops in the Topia department store in front of the station.

Getting There & Around

Hourly trains run on the JR Tōhoku line between Hiraizumi and Hanamaki (¥820, 45 minutes). The JR Kamaishi line connects Hanamaki to Tōno (¥1330, one hour), while the JR Tohoku line connects Hanamaki to Morioka (¥650, 45 minutes).

There are several trains every hour on the *shinkansen* line between Sendai and Shin-hanamaki (¥5550, one hour). The JR Kamaishi line connects Shin-hanamaki to Tōno (¥1250, 45 minutes), while the *shinkansen* line connects Shin-hanamaki to Morioka (¥2950, 15 minutes).

Tōno is one place where car rental might be a good idea, though you'll definitely need the car's navigation computer to find your way around – try **Kankō Rent-a-Car** (☎ 62-1375), inside the train station. Bicycle rental is available from the tourist office at ¥1000 per day, or from the youth hostel.

MORIOKA 盛岡

☎ 019 / pop 305,000

The historical seat of power for the Nambu clan, as well as the present-day capital of Iwate-ken, Morioka is a beautiful old castle town framed by three flowing rivers and a brooding volcano. Serving as one of Tōhoku's major transport hubs, you'll most likely whiz through Morioka at some point during your travels, though it's certainly worth getting off the train and having a look around. In addition to providing access to the trails on Mt Iwate, Morioka is also the birthplace of *wanko-soba,* an all-you-can-eat noodle extravaganza that needs to be experienced to be believed.

Orientation

The city centre is east of the station, which lies on the southwest corner of the action, on the other side of the Kitakami-gawa. Ōdōri, which heads over the Kaiun-bashi up to Iwate-kōen, is the main shopping street.

Information

INTERNET ACCESS

Iwate International Plaza and Morioka Tourist Information Centre provide free access.

MEDICAL SERVICES

Iwate Medical University Hospital (☎ 651-5111; 19-1 Uchi-maru)

MONEY & POST

Morioka Central Post Office (盛岡中央郵便局; ☎ 624-5353; 1-13-45 Chūō-dōri; 9am-7pm Mon-Fri, to 5pm Sat, to 12.30pm Sun, ATM 7am-11pm Mon-Fri, 9am-9pm Sat, to 7pm Sun) Has an international ATM.

TOURIST INFORMATION

Iwate International Plaza (☎ 654-8900; 5th fl, AIINA, 1-7-1 Moriokaekinishi-dōri; 9am-9.30pm) An excellent resource for visitors and residents, with helpful staff, a foreign-newspaper library, local 'what's on' information and free internet.

Morioka Tourist Information Centre (☎ 604-3305; 1-1-10 Nakanohashi-dōri; 9am-8pm, closed 2nd Tue of each month) On the 2nd floor of Odette Plaza. Provides free internet access, tourist brochures, phonecards and stamps.

Northern Tōhoku Tourist Information Centre (☎ 625-2090; 9am-5.30pm) On the 2nd floor of Morioka station at the north exit, next to the *shinkansen* ticket gate. Highly efficient, English-speaking staff and a good supply of regional brochures.

Sights

MORIOKA CITY

Morioka is small enough to navigate on foot, though there is a tourist bus (see p541) that makes a convenient loop between the major sights listed below.

If you head east on foot from the station along Kaiun-bashi for about 20 minutes, you'll eventually come to **Iwate-kōen**, the park where Morioka-jō once stood. Only the castle's moss-covered stone foundation walls remain as a testament to Edo-period life, though the park has pleasant views over the city. Also look out for the totem pole, which was presented by Morioka's sister city in British Columbia, and was a collaboration between a Native North American chief and a local woodcarver.

A few blocks north of the park in front of the Morioka District Court is the **Rock-Splitting Cherry Tree**, a much beloved local attraction. This 300-year-old tree, which sprouted from the crack in a huge granite boulder, has the locals claiming that it's pushed its way through over time. That's

INFORMATION
- Iwate Medical University Hospital 岩手医科大学附属病院 1 C2
- Morioka Central Post Office 盛岡中央郵便局 2 C1
- Morioka Tourist Information Centre 盛岡観光案内所 3 D3
- Northern Tōhoku Information Centre 北東北観光案内所 4 A3

SIGHTS & ACTIVITIES
- Iwate-kōen 岩手公園 5 C2
- Rock-Splitting Cherry Tree 石割桜 6 C2

SLEEPING
- Hotel Metropolitan Morioka ホテルメトロポリタン盛岡 7 A2
- Kumagai Ryokan 熊ケ井旅館 8 B3
- Morioka New City Hotel 盛岡ニューシティホテル 9 A2

EATING
- Azumaya Honten 東家本店 10 D3
- Chokurian 直利庵 11 D3
- Hot JaJa ホットジャジャ 12 A2

DRINKING
- Fukakusa 深草 13 D3

SHOPPING
- Kamasada Honten 釜定本店 14 D2

TRANSPORT
- Dendenmushi Bus Stop でんでんむし号バス乗り場 ..... (see 15)
- JR Bus Station ＪＲバス乗り場 15 A2

clearly an impossible feat, but it makes for a very charming story, and is nevertheless a stunning sight to behold.

Heading north along the same street for another 1.5km will bring you to Morioka's *teramachi* (temple district). The district is centred on **Hōon-ji** (報恩寺), a quiet Zen defined by its impressive San-mon (Main Gate), and **Rakan-dō** (羅漢堂; donation ¥300; 9am-4pm), a small hall containing 18th-century statues of the 500 disciples of Buddha.

AROUND MORIOKA

Iwate-San 岩手山

The jagged molar of Iwate-san (2038m) is a dominating landmark northwest of Morioka, and was at one time a popular destination for mountaineers. In theory, seven walking trails are open between July and October, though they're frequently closed due to intense volcanic activity. If the mountain is accessible, buses depart JR Morioka station for the various trail-heads – check with tourist information in Morioka for the latest mountain conditions and transport info.

Festivals & Events

Chagu-Chagu Umakko Matsuri On the second Saturday of June, features a parade of brightly decorated horses and children in traditional dress.

Hachiman-gū Matsuri During the festival from 14 to 16 September, portable shrines and colourful floats are paraded to the rhythm of *taiko* (Japanese drums).

Sleeping

Kumagai Ryokan (651-3020; fax 626-0096; http://kumagairyokan.com; 3-2-5 Ōsawakawara; s/d from ¥4700/8400;) A very foreigner-friendly, Japanese-style inn that is located about eight minutes on foot east of the station (behind the large church). Kumagai offers clean and tidy rooms as well as a pleasant Japanese garden and folk-craft displays.

Morioka New City Hotel (654-5161; fax 654-5168; www.moriokacityhotel.co.jp/newcity, in Japanese; 13-10 Ekimae-dōri; r from ¥5670;) Conveniently located across the road from the station, this relaxed business hotel caters primarily for single travellers. Rooms are simple but more than adequate, and the subdued restaurants help you to feel at home. LAN cable internet available.

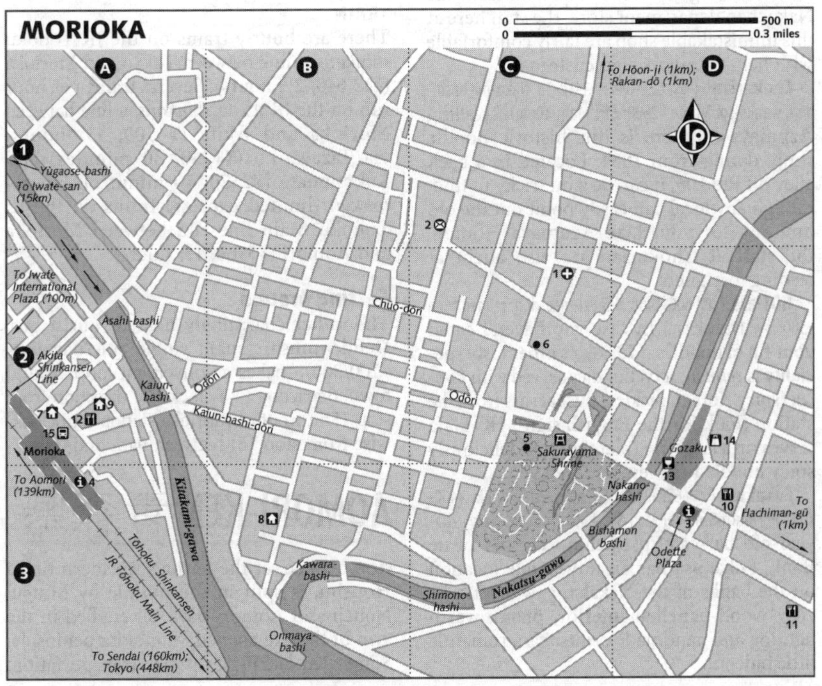

Hotel Metropolitan Morioka (☎ 625-1211; fax 625 1210; www.metro-morioka.co.jp/morioka/index.html; 1-44 Ekimae-dōri; s/d incl breakfast from ¥9240/17,325) Business hotels cluster around the east exit of the station, though this upmarket offering adjacent to the Fezan department store is in a class of its own. Plush rooms with ultramodern amenities are enhanced by impeccable service, as well as a great range of onsite bars, restaurants and lounges. LAN cable internet available.

Eating & Drinking

Famished? Let's see you eat hundreds of bowls of the local noodle dish, *wanko-soba*. More of a competition between you and the waitress (who tries to refill your bowl faster than you can say you're full), it's a fun culinary tradition that is well worth doing once. Of course, you're going to need practice if you want to break the record and top 550-plus bowls of *soba*!

Azumaya Honten (☎ 622-2252; 2nd fl, Miurabiru Bldg, 1-8-3 Naka-no-hashi-dōri; wanko-soba from ¥2600; 11am-8pm) Try notching up your noodle-bowl count at this famous noodle shop, with a history dating back more than 100 years. Just east of the Nakatsu-gawa across the street from the Nakachan department store, the staff here at this unmistakable shop are fairly comfortable with helping out foreign customers.

Chokurian (☎ 624-0441; 1-12-13 Naka-no-hashi-dōri; wanko-soba from ¥2600; 11am-10pm) Rivalling Azumaya Honten, is this historic noodle shop, dating from 1884. Located in a back alley off Rte 106, it can be a bit tricky to find, though any local can easily point out the old building for you. Like Azumaya Honten, the staff at Chokurian are also adept at feeding foreigners.

HOTJaJa (☎ 606-1068; 9-5 Eki-mae-dōri; reimen from ¥580; 11am-10pm) In case you haven't eaten your fill of noodles, Morioka's other tasty speciality is *reimen*, *soba* noodles served with *kimchi* (spicy Korean pickles). Just across from the station (look for the English sign), HOTJaJa serves up a large *dai* (plate) of this deliciously spicy noodle for a few hundred yen.

Fukakusa (☎ 622-2353; 1-2 Konya-chō; drinks ¥400-700; lunch & dinner Mon-Sat, lunch Sun) A tiny, 40-year-old bar-cafe just behind the old Iwate Bank, Fukakusa has an unbeatable location on the banks of the Nakatsu-gawa. With its cosy wood-panelled interior, piano, warm lighting and handmade prints, it's a romantic little hideout.

Shopping

The Morioka region is famous for its *nanbu tetsubin* (cast ironware).

Kamasada Honten (☎ 622-3911; 2-5 Konya-chō; 9am-5.30pm Mon-Sat) A fine exponent of *nanbu tetsubin*, selling affordable gift items alongside tea kettles that cost as much as a small car. It's across the Nakatsu-gawa near Gozaku, a traditional merchant's area of *kura* (mud-walled) warehouses, coffee shops and craft studios.

Getting There & Away

BUS

JR highway buses depart from an organised terminal across from the train station. There's a booth here where you can purchase tickets to major cities throughout Japan. Some sample destinations, which have frequent daily departures from Morioka, include Tokyo (¥7800, six hours), Sendai (¥2850, three hours) and Hirosaki (¥2930, 2½ hours).

CAR

If you're driving, the Tōhoku Expressway (東北自動車道) runs between Tokyo and the greater Morioka area.

TRAIN

There are hourly trains on the JR Tōhoku *shinkansen* line between Tokyo and Morioka (¥13,640, 2½ hours). Several trains per hour run on the JR Akita *shinkansen* line between Morioka and Akita (¥4300, 1½ hours) via Tazawa-ko (¥1780, 30 minutes) and Kakunodate (¥2570, 50 minutes). Hourly *tokkyū* (limited express) trains on the JR Tōhoku Main line run between Morioka and Aomori (¥5960, 1¾ hours).

Getting Around

The rather charmingly named tourist bus, Dendenmushi (snail; single ride/day pass ¥100/300), makes a convenient loop around town, departing in a clockwise direction from stop 15 in front of Morioka station (anticlockwise from stop 16) between 9am and 7pm.

AOMORI-KEN 青森県

Aomori-ken, at the curious northern tip of Honshū, is split in the middle by Mutsu, Noheji and Aomori bays, all cradled in the arm of the axe-shaped Shimokita peninsula. Somewhat lacking in public transportation,

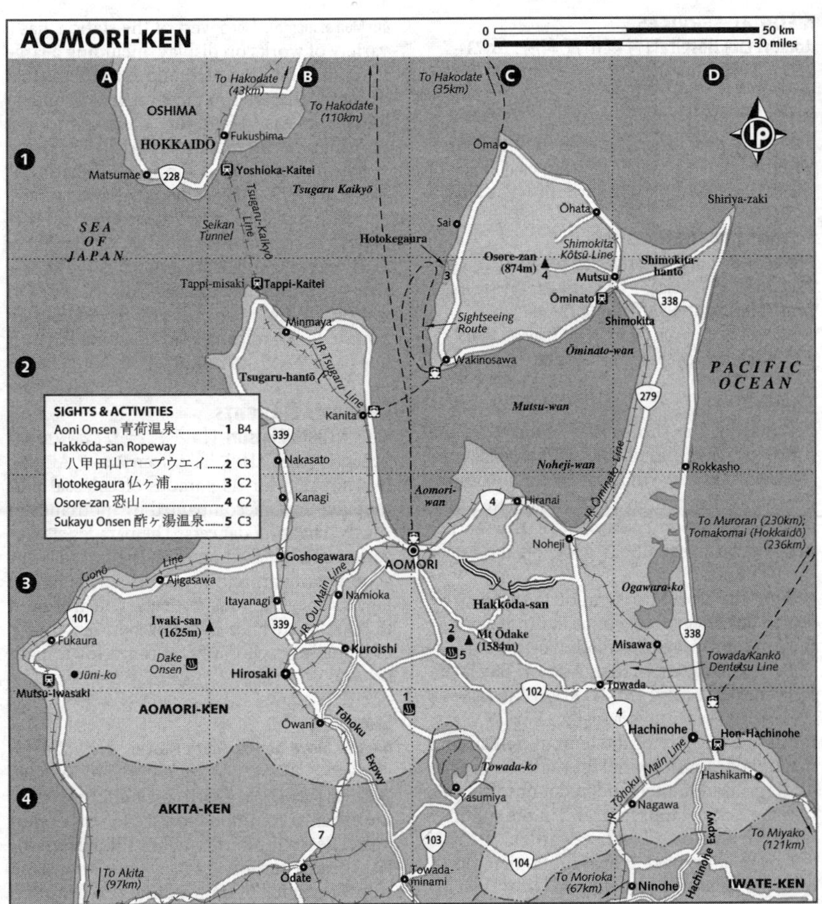

this is a prefecture where having a rental car will really open up some of Japan's most remote and wildly exotic areas. The ethereal volcanic landscapes around Osore-zan are where Aomori's people come to commune with the dead, though the verdant nature clinging to the shores of Towada-ko is definitely more rooted in this world.

AOMORI 青森

☎ 017 / pop 315,000

Virtually wiped off the map by Allied bombing during WWII, Aomori exists today as a thoroughly modern (and somewhat boring…) transport hub – it serves mainly as a rest stop for travellers breaking up the journey between Tokyo and Hokkaidō, and as a jumping off point for destinations around the prefecture.

All of this changes during the Nebuta Matsuri in the first week of August, when traditional floats parade down the streets, followed by raucous merrymakers. If you're not able to attend one of Japan's top celebrations, a decent consolation prize is a few hours spent visiting the city's humble but engaging museums.

Information

EMERGENCY

Aomori Police Station (☎ 723-4211; 2-3-1 Shinmachi)

INTERNET ACCESS

Ai Plaza (☎ 734-1111; www.city.aomori.aomori.jp/contents/english/01-1location.html; 1-3-7 Shin-machi; per 1hr free; 🕑 10am-9pm) On the 4th floor of the AUGA building. Also provides some tourist information.

MEDICAL SERVICES

Aomori City Hospital (青森市民病院; ☎ 734-2171; 1-14-20 Katsuda)

POST

The main post office is east of the city centre, while a smaller branch is within easy reach of the station. Both have international ATMs.

TOURIST INFORMATION

Prefectural tourist information counter (☎ 734-2500; 2nd fl, ASPAM Bldg, 1-1-40 Yasukata; 🕑 9am-6pm)

Tourist information office (☎ 723-4670; 🕑 8.30am-5.30pm) On the left of the station's central exit; English-language pamphlets and a city map.

Sights

Perched on the shores of Aomori Bay, the futuristic, pyramid-shaped **ASPAM building** (1-1-40 Yasukata) is the symbol of modern Aomori. On the top floor, there is a **viewing plaza** (admission ¥400, with panoramic slideshow ¥800), though the perspective is equally as good on the lower (free!) floors.

The city's second symbol is the nearby **Aomori Bay Bridge** – climb the stairs at the station end for more top-notch views.

Permanently moored in Aomori Bay is the ferry **Hakkōda-maru** (☎ 735-8150; admission ¥500; 🕑 9am-5pm Nov-Mar, to 6pm Apr-Oct). For 25 years, it was the flagship of the famous Seikan line that linked Honshū with Hokkaidō, before the underground tunnel rendered it obsolete. It's now a maritime museum, and in the summer it becomes an excellent beer garden.

If you can't make it to Nebuta, then don't miss the **Nebuta-no-sato Museum** (ねぶたの里; ☎ 738-1230; 1 Yaegiku, Yokouchi; admission ¥630; 🕑 9am-5.30pm), which tells the story of Aomori's legendary festival. Buses to the museum, 9km south of town, leave frequently from stop 9 outside the train station for the Nebuta-no-sato Iriguchi stop (¥450, 30 minutes).

The **Munakata Shikō Memorial Museum** (棟方志功記念館; ☎ 777-4567; 2-1-2 Matsubara; admission ¥500; 🕑 9.30am-5pm Tue-Sun), about 5km east of the station, houses a collection of prints, paintings and calligraphy by Munakata Shikō, an Aomori native who won international fame. Buses bound for Nakatsutui leave from stop 2 outside the train station for the Munakata Shikō Kinenkan-dōri stop (¥190, 15 minutes).

The **Aomori Museum of Art** (青森県立美術館; ☎ 783-3000; 185 Yasuta-Aza Chikano; admission ¥500; 🕑 9am-6pm Jun-Sep, 9.30am-5pm Oct-May, closed 2nd & 4th Mon of month), 1km west of the station, has a variety of works on display, including a large outdoor exhibition of Jōmon-era replicas that bring the lifestyles of these ancient people to life. It's an easy 15-minute walk, and tourist information can mark it for you on its map.

South of the city is the **Shōwa Daibutsu** (昭和大仏; ☎ 726-2312; 458 Yamazaki, Kuwabara; admission ¥400; 🕑 8am-5.30pm Apr-Oct, 9am-4.30pm Nov-Mar), Japan's largest outdoor Buddha. At a height of 21m, and weighing 220 tonnes, it is an impressive sight. Five daily buses from JR Aomori station are timed so that you have about an hour to look around before catching the next bus back (¥540, 45 minutes).

Festivals & Events

The **Nebuta Matsuri** (ねぶた祭り; www.nebuta.or.jp/english/index_e.htm), held from 2 to 7 August, is renowned for its parades of colossal illuminated floats accompanied by thousands of rowdy, chanting dancers. The parades start at sunset and last for hours; on the final day the action starts around noon. As this is one of Japan's most famous festivals, you will need to book in advance if you harbour any hopes of actually scoring a hotel room for a night or two.

Sleeping

Aomori Moya Kogen Youth Hostel (青森雲谷高原ユースホステル; ☎ 764-2888; 9-5 Yamabuki, Moya; dm from ¥3360; 💻) A nice alternative to the urban accommodation scene, this homey hostel lies in the 'burbs, about 12km from the JR Aomori station – buses departing from stop 9 outside the train station can drop you off outside the hostel (¥590, 40 minutes, last bus 8.20pm). The English-speaking owner loves Ireland, and is quick to welcome guests with a frothy pint of Guinness.

Tako Ryokan (☎ 722-4825; Yasukata 2-chōme; r per person incl 2 meals from ¥6800) Located about 1km east of the train station, and one block south of police headquarters, this easily identifiable traditional Japanese inn offers good-sized tatami rooms in addition to some serious seafood dinners.

Aomori Grand Hotel (☎ 723-1011; www.agh.co.jp; 1-1-23 Shin-machi; s/d from ¥6500/10,000; 💻 📶) Just east of the station, across from Ai Plaza, this midrange business hotel is by far the best value in town. Spacious rooms, some with sea views, are regally appointed with modern furnishings, and you really can't beat the central location. LAN cable internet available.

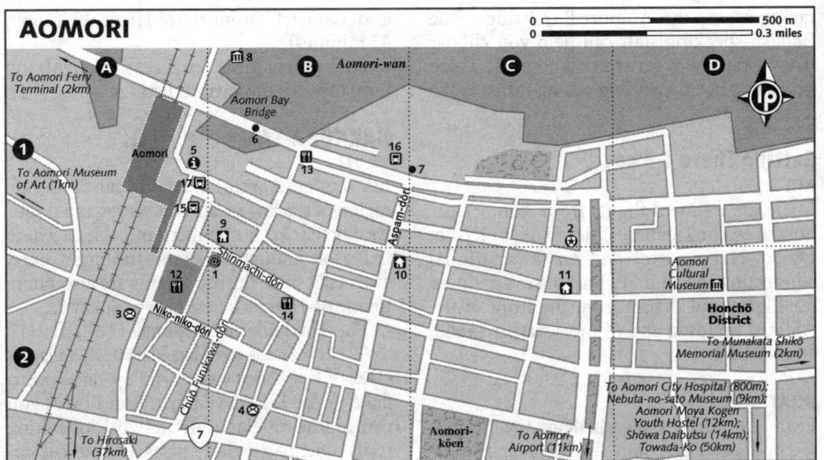

INFORMATION
Ai Plaza アイプラザ 1 B2
Aomori Police Station 青森県警察 2 C1
Branch Post Office 郵便局 3 A2
Main Post Office 中央郵便局 4 B2
Prefectural Tourist Information 青森県観光案内所 ....(see 7)
Tourist Information Office 観光案内所 5 A1

SIGHTS & ACTIVITIES
Aomori Bay Bridge 青森ベイブリッジ 6 B1
ASPAM Building アスパム 7 C1
Hakkōda-maru 八甲田丸 8 B1

SLEEPING
Aomori Grand Hotel 青森グランドホテル 9 B1
Hotel JAL City Aomori ホテルJALシティ青森 10 B2
Tako Ryokan 田子旅館 11 C2

EATING
Fish & Fresh Food Market 市場 12 A2
Jintako 甚太古 13 B1
Kakigen 柿源 14 B2
Nishimura 西村 ....(see 7)

TRANSPORT
Aomori City Buses 青森駅前市営バス停 15 A1
Bus Stand バス乗り場 16 B1
JR Highway Bus Stop JR ハイウエイ バス乗り場 17 A1

Hotel JAL City Aomori (☎ 732-2580; fax 735-2584; http://jalhotels.com; 2-4-12 Yasukata; s/tw ¥9400/16,100; 💻 📶) If it is good enough for the Japan Airlines flight attendants, it is certainly good enough for us! Just a few blocks south of ASPAM, Aomori's most luxurious offering is surprisingly affordable. Everything from the comfortable Western-style rooms to the business facilities are, not surprisingly, swish and sophisticated. LAN cable internet available.

Eating

The best place in Aomori to grab a snack is the **fish and fresh food market** (🕒 5am-6.30pm) in the Auga building near the station. Aomori is famous for a number of local and regional speciality items including apples, pickled vegetables, scallops, codfish and many, many others. You can easily spend an hour perusing all of the food stalls, stopping here and there to sample the bounty from land and sea.

Kakigen (☎ 727-2933; 1-8-9 Shinmachi; dishes from ¥1300; 🕒 10.30am-9pm) This little hole-in-the-wall on the main thoroughfare next to the Hotel Sunroute is a famous spot for Aomori scallops – the picture menu looks almost as tasty as the real plates.

Jintako (☎ 722-7727; 1-6-16 Yasukata; set meal ¥5000; 🕒 dinner, closed 1st & 3rd Sun) Housed in an unassuming beige building (look for the wooden sign) on the waterfront, this restaurant serves formal seafood dinners set to the tune of the *tsugaru jamisen*, a version of the traditional three-stringed *shamisen* (guitar). Advance reservations are necessary – if you don't speak Japanese, ask the staff at tourist information to call for you.

Nishimura (☎ 734-5353; 10th fl, ASPAM, 1-1-40 Yasukata; set meals from ¥1500; 🕒 lunch & dinner) You can't beat the stunning views from this restaurant near the top of the ASPAM building, especially when the multicoloured lights start racing across the Aomori Bay Bridge. The English-speaking staff can help you choose from a variety of set seafood courses, which range in price depending on the rarity of the featured catch.

Getting There & Away

AIR

There are frequent flights from Aomori airport to major Japanese cities (Tokyo, Kyoto, Osaka, Nagoya etc) and an international connection to Seoul. Airport buses are timed for flights and depart from the front of the ASPAM building and Aomori station (¥560, 40 minutes).

BOAT

From Aomori-kō, **Higashi Nihon** (☎ 0120-756-564) operates eight daily ferries (year-round) between Aomori and Hakodate (from ¥2150, 3¾ hours). The company also operates one daily ferry from April to December that leaves Aomori at around 1.30pm, and arrives in Muroran at 8pm the same day (from ¥3460). The ferry terminal, where you also buy your tickets, is on the western side of the city – it's a 10-minute taxi ride from Aomori station (around ¥1300).

BUS

Convenient JR highway buses depart from the well-organised bus stop across from the JR Aomori train station, while tickets can be purchased at a small counter inside the station. Some sample destinations, which have frequent daily departures from Aomori, include Tokyo (¥10,000, eight hours) and Sendai (¥5700, five hours). There are also regional buses to Shimokita-hantō, Hakkōda and Towada-ko – see each section for more information.

TRAIN

Frequent *tokkyū* on the JR Tsugaru Kaikyō line run between Aomori and Hakodate on Hokkaidō (¥5140, two hours), via the Seikan Tunnel (see the boxed text, p599). There are also frequent trains on the JR Tōhoku Main line running between Morioka and Aomori (¥5960, 1¾ hours).

There are several daily departures on the *Kamoshika* limited express train that runs on the JR Ōu Main line between Aomori and Akita (¥5250, 2¾ hours). Slower *futsū* trains also ply this same route (¥3570, 3¾ hours), and connect Aomori to Hirosaki (¥650, 45 minutes).

For information on accessing sights by local bus, see the various listings.

HAKKŌDA-SAN 八甲田山

☎ 017

Just south of Aomori, Hakkōda-san is a scenic region of soaring peaks that serves as a popular day trip for both hikers and skiers. There is reason enough to spend the night here, especially since the mountains are also home to one of Tōhoku's best onsen, Sukayu.

The Hakkōda-san **ropeway** (八甲田山ロープウエイ; one way/return ¥1150/1800, 5-trip pass ¥4900; ⏲ 9am-4.20pm) whisks you up Tamoyachi-dake to the 1324m summit. From there you can follow an elaborate network of hiking trails. One particularly pleasant route scales the three peaks of Akakura-dake (1548m), Ido-dake (1550m) and Ōdake (1584m), and then winds its way down to Sukayu Onsen. This 8km hike can be done in a leisurely four hours.

During the winter, you can rent ski or snowboarding equipment (¥3500 per day) at the top of Tamoyachi-dake. Compared with other ski mountains across Tōhoku and Hokkaidō, Hakkōda-san is fairly modest in scope, though you can expect frozen fir trees, piles of wet snow and little to no crowds, as well as fairly limited goods and services. The runs are mostly intermediate.

our pick **Sukayu Onsen Ryokan** (酸ヶ湯温泉; ☎ 738-6400; www.sukayu.jp, in Japanese; r per person with/without 2 meals from ¥9600/5925, bath-only admission ¥600; ⏲ 7am-5.30pm; **P**) is a place plucked right out of an *ukiyo-e* wood-block painting – a delight for all five senses. Look at the dark wood, milky water and steam; listen to the gurgle of the water; feel its penetrating heat or massage tired shoulders with its *utase-yu* (massaging stream of water); smell the sulphur; and, if you dare, taste the water itself – it's lemony, almost like *ponzu* (citrusy sauce). On a cold day, relaxing here is hard to beat, and one of the baths is rumoured to hold up to 1000 people (though you'll rarely see more than 25 at any one time).

Two daily buses leave from stop 8 outside Aomori station, pass by the Hakkōda Ropeway-eki stop (¥1070, 50 minutes), and terminate at the next stop, Sukayu Onsen (¥1300, one hour). Once again, having a car will make it easier to access the area as public transport is extremely limited.

SHIMOKITA-HANTŌ 下北半島

☎ **0175 / pop 120,000**

Also called Masakari-hantō (Axe peninsula) because of its unmistakable shape, this isolated peninsula has long stretches of sparsely inhabited coastline and remote mountain valleys. At the centre lies Osore-zan (874m), a barren volcanic mountain that is regarded as one of the most sacred places in all of Japan. With the yellow sulphur tributaries running into **Usori-ko** (宇曽利湖), and ravens swarming about, it's an appropriate setting for Buddhist purgatory – even the name, Osore, means fear or dread.

Unlike the rest of the country, however, Shimokita-hantō might as well be off the grid – stock up with supplies before heading to the peninsula as facilities are extremely limited. While public transport does run (however infrequent it might be), this is one destination where having your own rental car will make all the difference.

Orientation & Information

Shimikita's main hub, the town of Mutsu, is accessible by train from Aomori. From here, bus services operate across the peninsula. To the east is the cape, Shiriya-zaki, and to the west, Ōma, Honshū's northernmost point. At the bottom tip of the peninsula is Wakinosawa, which is connected to Aomori by ferry.

The tiny **tourist information office** (☎ 22-0909; 9am-6pm daily May-Oct, 9am-6pm Wed-Mon Nov-Apr) inside the Masakari Plaza in Mutsu has few resources; comprehensive information is available in the Aomori tourist information office.

Sights & Activities

OSORE-ZAN 恐山

This holy mountain, with its holy shrine **Osorezan-bodaiji** (恐山菩提寺; admission ¥500; 6am-6pm May-Oct), is a somewhat terrifying, strangely atmospheric place that's popular with pilgrims seeking to commune with the dead. Several stone statues of the child-guardian deity, Jizō, overlook hills of craggy, sulphur-strewn rocks and hissing vapour; visitors help lost souls with their underworld penance by adding stones to the cairns. You can bathe on hell's doorstep at free onsen to the side as you approach the main hall (sex-segregated options are on the left).

HOTOKEGAURA 仏ヶ浦

The western edge of the peninsula is a spectacular stretch of coastline dotted with 100m-tall wind-carved cliffs, which are said to resemble Buddhas. Between April and October, round-trip sightseeing boats for Hotokegaura depart from Wakinosawa at 10.45am and 2.45pm (¥3800, two hours), though services are often suspended in poor weather.

WATCHING WILDLIFE

The peninsula is home to the world's most northerly population of primates – these 'snow monkeys' or Japanese macaques number around 400, and are most commonly seen in the winter months when they move closer to the towns and villages in search of food. Locals, particularly those in the tourism industry, tend to keep pretty good tabs on the whereabouts of the colonies – ask around, and you might get lucky and spot a troop or two.

Festivals & Events

The two annual **Osore-zan Taisai festivals** (20 to 24 July and 9 to 11 October) attract huge crowds who come to consult *itako* (mediums) and try to contact dead family members.

Sleeping & Eating

Murai Ryokan (むらい旅館; ☎ 22-4755; 9-30 Tanabu-chō, Mutsu; r incl 2 meals from ¥7000) Next to Masakari Plaza in Mutsu, this is a basic place with fairly standard tatami rooms, though you can count on a hot meal and some local hospitality before striking out for the wilds.

our pick **Wakinosawa Youth Hostel** (脇野沢ユースホステル; ☎ 44-2341; 41 Wakinosawasenokawame, Mutsu; dm from ¥3990, breakfast/dinner ¥525/945; P) Charmingly perched on a hillside at Wakinosawa village, about 15 minutes west of the ferry pier (call ahead for a pick-up if you don't have a car). Both Western- and Japanese-style dormitory rooms are available, each of which are decked out in rich hardwoods and country stylings. The extremely accommodating owners can drive you to a local onsen before dinner, and conduct excursions to observe snow monkeys in the nearby forests.

Getting There & Around

BUS

There are a few daily direct buses between JR Aomori station and the bus terminal in Mutsu (¥2520, 2½ hours).

CAR

You really need a rental vehicle to get the most out of Shimokita-hantō, and a well-maintained (if somewhat minimal) network of roads provides access to some stunning coastal drives. Since facilities are extremely limited, you're going to need to pick up your wheels in points further south.

FERRY

There are several daily *kaisoku* on the JR Tsugaru line between Aomori and Kanita (¥1290, 25 minutes). **Mutsuwan** (☎ 422-3020) runs two to three daily ferries between Kanita and Wakinosawa (¥1420, one hour). **Higashi Nihon** (☎ 0120-756-564) runs two to three daily ferries between Hakodate on Hokkaidō and Ōma (¥1370, 1¾ hours).

TRAIN

There are several daily *kaisoku* on the JR Ōminato line between Aomori and Shimokita (¥2700, 2½ to four hours) via Noheji. Local buses connect JR Shimokita station and the bus terminal in Mutsu (¥230, 10 minutes).

LOCAL TRANSPORT

Buses to destinations across the peninsula run from the Mutsu bus terminal, though services are cut severely during the winter months. The three main routes for travellers without wheels connect Mutsu to Wakinosawa (¥1790, 1½ hours), Osore-zan (¥750, 40 minutes) and Ōma (¥1880, two hours).

HIROSAKI 弘前

☎ 0172 / pop 185,000

Founded in the 17th century by Lord Tsugaru Tamenobu, the town of Hirosaki was once one of Tōhoku's leading cultural centres. During the Meiji Restoration, however, Tsugaru's territories were combined with those of the Nambu clan, and power was shifted to Aomori. As history would have it, Aomori, and not Hirosaki, was resultantly targeted by allied bombing campaigns, which inadvertently led to the preservation of Tsugaru's feudal stronghold.

Today, Hirosaki is centred on its castle grounds, complete with extant keeps and towers, and highlighted by its beautiful canopies of majestic cherry trees. The town also serves as a convenient jumping-off point for an invigorating and equally spiritual trek up Iwaki-san.

Information

Hirosaki Sightseeing Information Centre (☎ 37-5501; ⏲ 9am-6pm) Inside the Kankōkan (tourism building) on the south side of Hirosaki-kōen.

Main post office (☎ 232-4104; 18-1 Kita Kawarake-chō) Has an international ATM.

Tourist information office (☎ 26-3600; ⏲ 8.45am-6pm) To the right as you exit Hirosaki station; offers free internet access.

Sights & Activities

HIROSAKI TOWN

The main thoroughfare from the JR Hirosaki station runs for just under 1km west to a block before **Hirosaki-kōen** (弘前公園), an expansive public park that has been shaped over the centuries by three castle moats, and landscaped by overhanging cherry trees (more than 5000 in total). You can either burn a bit of shoe leather hiking out here, or take any local bus from stop 2 to Shiyaku-shomae (¥100, 20 minutes), which is right across from the park.

At the heart of the park lies the ancient remains of **Hirosaki-jō**, which was originally constructed in 1611. Only 16 years later, in 1627, the castle was burnt to the ground after being struck by lightning. Two centuries on, one of the corner towers was rebuilt, and it presently contains a small **museum** (admission ¥300; ⏲ 9am-5pm Apr-Nov), housing samurai weaponry.

At the northeastern corner of the park is the **Neputa-mura** (☎ 39-1511; 61 Kamenoko-machi; admission ¥500; ⏲ 9am-5pm Apr-Nov, to 4pm Dec-Mar), a fun-filled interactive museum with extensive displays on Hirasaki's famous Neputa Matsuri (see p548).

Just beyond the southwest corner of the park is **Fujita Kinen Tei-en** (☎ 37-5525; admission ¥300; ⏲ 9am-5pm Tue-Sun Apr-Nov), an impeccably manicured formal Japanese garden that was originally laid out in 1919 for a wealthy local businessman.

Aside from Hirosaki-kōen, the town's other main attraction is the **Zenrin-gai** (禅林街) **temple district**, a 10-minute walk southwest of the castle ruins (follow English signs for Chōshō Temple). An atmospheric spot redolent of Old Japan, the district follows the central avenue flanked by temples to **Chōshō-ji** (長勝寺; admission ¥500; ⏲ 8am-5pm Apr-Oct, 9am-4pm Nov–mid-Dec), which harbours rows of mausoleums built for the early rulers of the Tsugaru clan.

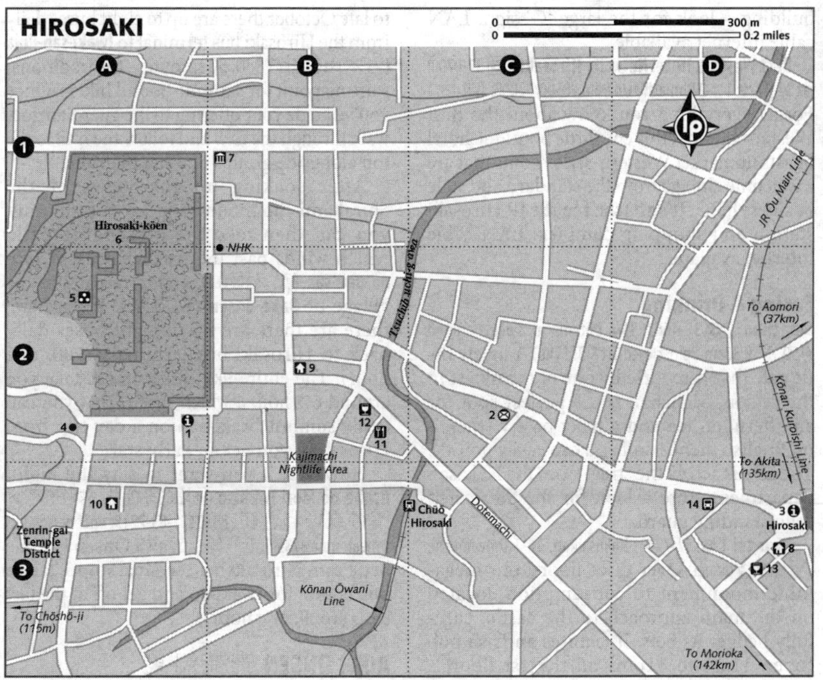

INFORMATION
Hirosaki Sightseeing Information Centre 観光館 1 A2
Main Post Office 弘前郵便局 2 C2
Tourist Information Office 旅行案内所 3 D3

SIGHTS & ACTIVITIES
Fujita Kinen Tei-en 藤田記念庭園 4 A2
Hirosaki-Jō 弘前城 5 A2
Hirosaki-kōen 弘前公園 6 A1
Neputa-mura ねぷた村 7 B1

SLEEPING
Best Western Hotel New City Hirosaki ベストウェスタンホテルニューシティ弘前 8 D3
Hirosaki Grand Hotel 弘前グランドホテル 9 B2
Hirosaki Youth Hostel ひろさきユースホステル 10 A3

EATING
Manchan 万茶ん 11 B2

DRINKING
Bīru-tei びいる亭 12 B2
Live House Yamauta ライブハウス山唄 13 D3

TRANSPORT
Hirosaki Bus Terminal 弘前バスターミナル 14 D3

Festivals & Events

From 1 to 7 August Hirosaki celebrates its **Neputa Matsuri**, a festival famous for its illuminated floats parading every evening to the accompaniment of flutes and drums. The festival is generally said to signify ceremonial preparation for battle, expressing sentiments of bravery for what lies ahead and of heartache for what lies behind.

Sleeping

Hirosaki Youth Hostel (☎ 33-7066; 11 Mori-machi; dm from ¥3045; 💻) Tucked away on a side street two blocks south of the outer moat, this hostel is identifiable by the large 'YH' sign on the exterior. A friendly, but somewhat institutional, place, Hirosaki's youth hostel is nevertheless smack in the middle of the town's main sights.

Hirosaki Grand Hotel (☎ 32-1515; fax 32-1810; www.ehotel.co.jp/hotels/hirosaki/index.html; 1 Ichiban-chō; s/d from ¥6000/9000; 💻) A very affordable business hotel with good service, decent restaurants and moderate-sized rooms, the Hirosaki Grand Hotel is within easy walking distance of the castle. It's a fairly nondescript grey building – look for the large 'G' sign. LAN cable internet available.

Best Western Hotel New City Hirosaki (☎ 37-0700; fax 37-1229; 1-1-2 Ohmachi; s/d from ¥8500/12000; 💻 📶) Forget everything you know about the Best Western brand – this chic little boutique hotel boasts upmarket Western-style rooms that are a welcome change from the standard and stale business hotel. It's attached to the JR Hirosaki station and shopping complex. LAN cable internet available.

Eating & Drinking

Manchan (☎ 35-4663; 36-6 Dotemachi; sweets around ¥750 🕑 9.30am-8pm, closed 1st & 3rd Thu) A lovely little cafe that is reportedly one of the oldest in the region, Manchan is the perfect spot for an afternoon tea and a flaky pastry (there's no English menus, but you can easily point!). The cafe is across the street from the Nakasan department store – look for the bifurcated cello standing guard.

Bīru-tei (☎ 37-7741; Hokusaikan, 26-1 Dote-machi; 🕑 lunch & dinner) Over three floors, this megalithic monument to consumption, located on the main approach to the castle, carefully hedges its bets. It features an Irish pub (open 11am to 11pm) on the 1st floor, a *Cheers*-style bar with a comprehensive international-beer menu on the 2nd and an *izakaya* (pub-eatery; open noon to 1am) on the 3rd. The English menu makes it all the more foreigner-friendly.

Live House Yamauta (☎ 36-1835; 1-2-7 Ōmachi; dinner/show per person from ¥3000; 🕑 5-11pm, closed alternate Mon) Just a few steps down the road from the station (look for the English sign), this popular venue offers nightly performances of traditional Japanese folk music alongside locally influenced *izakaya* dishes. Call ahead for reservations – the staff caters well for foreign guests.

Getting There & Away

Hourly *tokkyū* on the JR Ōu Main line run between Aomori and Hirosaki (¥1460, 35 minutes), and Hirosaki and Akita (¥4130, two hours). Regular buses also run from the terminal adjacent to Itō Yōkadō department store to Aomori (¥2930, 2½ hours).

IWAKI-SAN 岩木山

Soaring above Hirosaki is the sacred volcano of **Iwaki-san** (岩木山; 1625m), a popular peak for both pilgrims and hikers. From early April to late October there are up to eight buses daily from the Hirosaki bus terminal to **Iwaki-san-jinja** (岩木山神社; ¥880, 50 minutes), the traditional starting point for summit-bound hikers. Once you've made your offering to the guardian god, walk through the *torii* and follow the trail to the top alongside groups of other pilgrims.

After soaking up the views of the Shirakami mountain range at the summit, you can then take the descending path, which winds past the smaller peak of **Tori-no-umi-san** (鳥ノ海山), and terminates in the village of **Dake-onsen** (岳温泉). From here, there are there are up to eight buses daily back to Hirosaki bus terminal (¥900, one hour). The entire 9km hike should take you around 6½ hours, which means that you can easily summit Iwaki-san on a day trip from Hirosaki if you get an early start.

However, if you want to stay the night, **Asobe no Mori Iwakisō** (国民宿舎岩木荘 アソベの森いわき荘; ☎ 0172-83-2215; r per person incl 2 meals from ¥7350), in Hyakuzawa Onsen is a safe bet. From Hirosaki bus terminal stop 3, take a bus bound for Iwaki-sō and get off at the last stop (¥660, one hour).

AONI ONSEN 青荷温泉

A seriously atmospheric, but seriously isolated, onsen, **Aoni Onsen Ryokan** (青荷温泉旅館; ☎ 0172-54-8588; fax 54-2655; www.yo.rim.or.jp/~aoni/html/index.htm, in Japanese; r per person incl 2 meals from ¥9600, bath ¥500; 🅿) seems to exist in a time warp. Here, alongside Rte 102 between Hirosaki and Towada-ko, oil lamps replace electricity, open hearths replace kitchen appliances and bathing is elevated to a fine art. Note that advanced reservations are mandatory.

If you don't have your own car, you're going to have to work to get out here, though the journey helps filter out the true onsen buffs. By public transport, take the private Kounan Tetsudō line from Hirosaki to Kuroishi (¥420, 30 minutes, six daily); Kounan buses connect with arriving passengers for Niji-no-ko (¥750, 10 minutes), from where shuttle buses run to Aoni (free, 30 minutes, six daily).

TOWADA-KO 十和田湖

☎ 0176 / pop 6000

There's no denying that this 327m-deep **crater lake** (52km in circumference) has impressive scenery and famously transparent waters, though it is a bit difficult to access without your own car, and it's much less developed

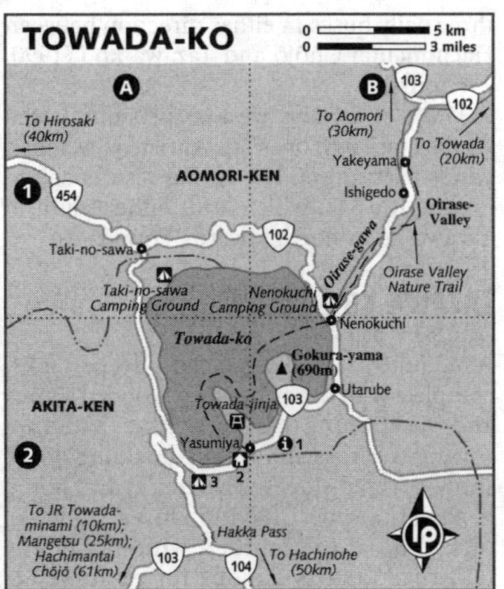

INFORMATION
Tourist Information Center 観光案内所 1 B2

SLEEPING
Hakubutsukan Youth Hostel 博物館ユースホステル .... (see 2)
Towada-ko Grand Hotel 十和田湖グランドホテル 2 A2
Towada-ko Oide Camping Ground 十和田湖生出キャンプ場 3 A2

for tourism than nearby Tazawa-ko. With that said, it's a lovely place for a scenic drive if you need a break from the highway, or for a relatively quiet lakeside amble if you need a break from the crowds.

Nenokuchi, a small tourist outpost on the eastern shore of the lake, marks the entrance to the 14km **Oirase Valley Nature Trail**, a three-hour hike along the lakeshore; you might want to hike it in the early morning or late afternoon to avoid the coach parties. The path ends at Yakeyama, from where relatively frequent buses return to Nenokuchi (¥660, 30 minutes) and Yasumiya (¥1100, one hour).

The tourist hub, Yasumiya, offers numerous boat tours of the lake, the best of which is the one-hour cruise between Yasumiya and Nenokuchi (one way ¥1400). Boats leave roughly every hour from April to early November between 8am and 4pm. You can also rent mountain bikes at the dock for ¥1500 per day from April to November.

The hole-in-the-wall **tourist information centre** (☎ 75-2425; ⏰ 8am-5pm), just north of the JR bus station, can help arrange accommodation.

There are several camping grounds around the edge of the lake, including **Towada-ko Oide Camping Ground** (☎ 75-2368; camp sites ¥300; ⏰ 25 Apr–5 Nov; Ⓟ), about 4km west of Yasumiya.

South of the ferry pier in Yasumiya is the **Towada-ko Grand Hotel** (☎ 75-1111; Yasumiya-sanbashi-mae, Towada-kohan, Towada-chō, Kamikita-gun; r per person incl 2 meals from ¥6800; Ⓟ), a pleasant cross between a European chalet and a Japanese country inn.

A somewhat cheaper option is the **Hakubutsukan Youth Hostel** (☎ 75-2002; dm from ¥3360; Ⓟ), which offers dorm beds squeezed into the old wing of the Towada-ko Grand Hotel.

Minshuku line the track leading out of Yasumiya away from the lake, but almost all of them close from November through March.

A great place for handmade soba noodles, tempura and other Japanese meals, **Mangetsu** (満月; ☎ 0186-37-3340; 20-1 Towada Ōyu Kaminoyu, Kazunoshi; meals from ¥650; ⏰ lunch & dinner Tue-Sun) is run by a young chef. There's no English menu, but a very helpful, warm staff make dining here a pleasure. It's 25km towards Akita-ken on Route 103.

Getting There & Around

Frequent *kaisoku* on the JR Hanawa line run between Towada-minami and Morioka (¥2080, 2½ hours) and between Towada-minami and Hachinmantai (¥230, 20 minutes). Infrequent local buses connect Towada-minami to Yasumiya (¥330, one hour).

From April to November, JR buses run between Aomori and Yasumiya (¥3000, three hours), and Morioka and Yasumiya (¥2420, 2¼ hours).

Buses can drop you off at any of the camping grounds or the Towda-ko Grand Hotel, though limited transport options really necessitate having your own wheels.

AKITA-KEN 秋田県

Japan's sixth-largest prefecture, Akita-ken is shaped by the Ōu and Dewa mountain ranges, which harbour some of the region's holiest peaks and shrines, and can be accessed by a series of high alpine trails. At lower altitudes, towns and cities have sprung up around the therapeutic waters of onsen. The prefecture is also firmly rooted in its

SCENIC DRIVES

- **Tōno valley** (p534)
- **Shimokita-hantō** (p545)
- **Towada-ko** (p548)
- **Tazawa-ko** (right)
- **Sado-ga-shima** (p571)

feudal history, especially in towns such as Kakunodate, which serve as veritable living museums of samurai culture.

HACHIMANTAI 八幡平

Like a row of giant molars, the peaks of this volcanic plateau south of Towada-ko are popular with hikers and onsen enthusiasts. Difficult access keeps the crowds away, but there are opportunities here for some rough and rugged back-country hiking, or a scramble to the top of **Hachimantai-san** (八幡平山; 1613m).

There's a small **visitors centre** (☎ 0186-31-2714; 🕒 9am-5pm, closed Nov-Apr) next to the car park at Hachimantai Chōjō. However, the best place for English-language information is at the tourist office in Morioka (p538).

From **Hachimantai Chōjō**, the main access point for Hachimantai-san, it's a fairly gentle hour-long hike to the summit. If you're looking for more challenging multiday treks – assuming you've got the appropriate gear and topographic maps – there is a complex network of trails across the Hachimantai plateau originating from **Tōshichi Onsen**, a 2km walk downhill from the Hachimantai Chōjō car park.

If you have a rental car, the mountain lodge **Yuki-no-Koya** (ゆきの小舎; ☎ 0186-31-2118; dm incl 2 meals ¥5550; 🕒 closed mid-Nov–Christmas & Feb–late Apr; Ⓟ) is a warm and welcoming place constructed entirely of local materials, and set in a quiet riverside location at **Shibari Onsen**, on Rte 341, north of the turn-off for the Aspite Line Hwy to Hachimantai.

If you're relying on public transport, the more modern **Hachimantai Youth Hostel** (☎ 0195-78-2031; 5-2 Midorigaoka, Matsuo-mura; dm from ¥3360, breakfast/dinner ¥760/1260; Ⓟ) is 20 minutes by bus east of the summit – ask the driver to drop you off at the Hachimantai Kankō Hoteru-mae stop.

From April to October, there are five daily buses in either direction between Hachimantai Chōjō and Morioka (¥1320, two hours), and three daily buses in either direction between Hachimantai Chōjō and Tazawa-ko (¥1990, 2¼ hours).

If you're driving, west of the summit, the Aspite Line Hwy, open late April to November, winds past several hot-spring resorts before joining Rte 341, which leads either south to Tazawa-ko or north towards Towada-ko.

TAZAWA-KO 田沢湖

☎ 0187 / pop 13,000

At 423m, Tazawa-ko is Japan's deepest lake, complete with sandy beaches, wooded shores and vacationing families either paddling rowboats across still waters or skiing down snow-covered slopes. The area is also home to the atmospheric Nyūtō Onsen, which is tucked up at the top of a winding mountain road, and is famous for its mineral-enriched milky white water. As if all of this isn't enough of a hard sell, consider the fact that Tazawa-ko also has its own *shinkansen* station, which makes it an easy-to-access rural getaway.

Orientation & Information

JR Tazawa-ko station is located a few kilometres southeast of the lake, and serves as the area's access point. Buses connect the station to Tazawa Kohan, a small transport hub on the eastern shores of the lake. From here, it takes about 40 minutes travelling northwesterly by bus or car to reach Nyūtō Onsen and the ski slopes. Tazawa Kohan is also the jumping-off point for hikes up Akita Komaga-take.

Inside the train station, **Folake** (☎ 43-2111; 🕒 8.30am-6.30pm) is a tourist information office that has excellent bilingual maps and free internet.

A 20km perimeter road surrounds the lake, and you can rent bicycles (¥400 per hour) or scooters (¥1200 per hour) in Tazawa Kohan. A car makes getting around easier, though there is a decent public transport network here.

SIGHTS & ACTIVITIES

Nyūtō Onsen 乳頭温泉	1	D3
Tazawako-Sukī-Jō たざわ湖スキー場	2	C3

SLEEPING

Cafe+Inn That Sounds Good! カフェ+イン ザッツサウンドグッド！	3	C3
Hachimantai Youth Hostel 八幡平ユースホステル	4	D3
Nyūtō Camping Ground	(see 1)	
Tazawa-ko Youth Hostel 田沢湖ユースホステル	5	C3
Yuki-no-Koya ゆきの小舎	6	D2

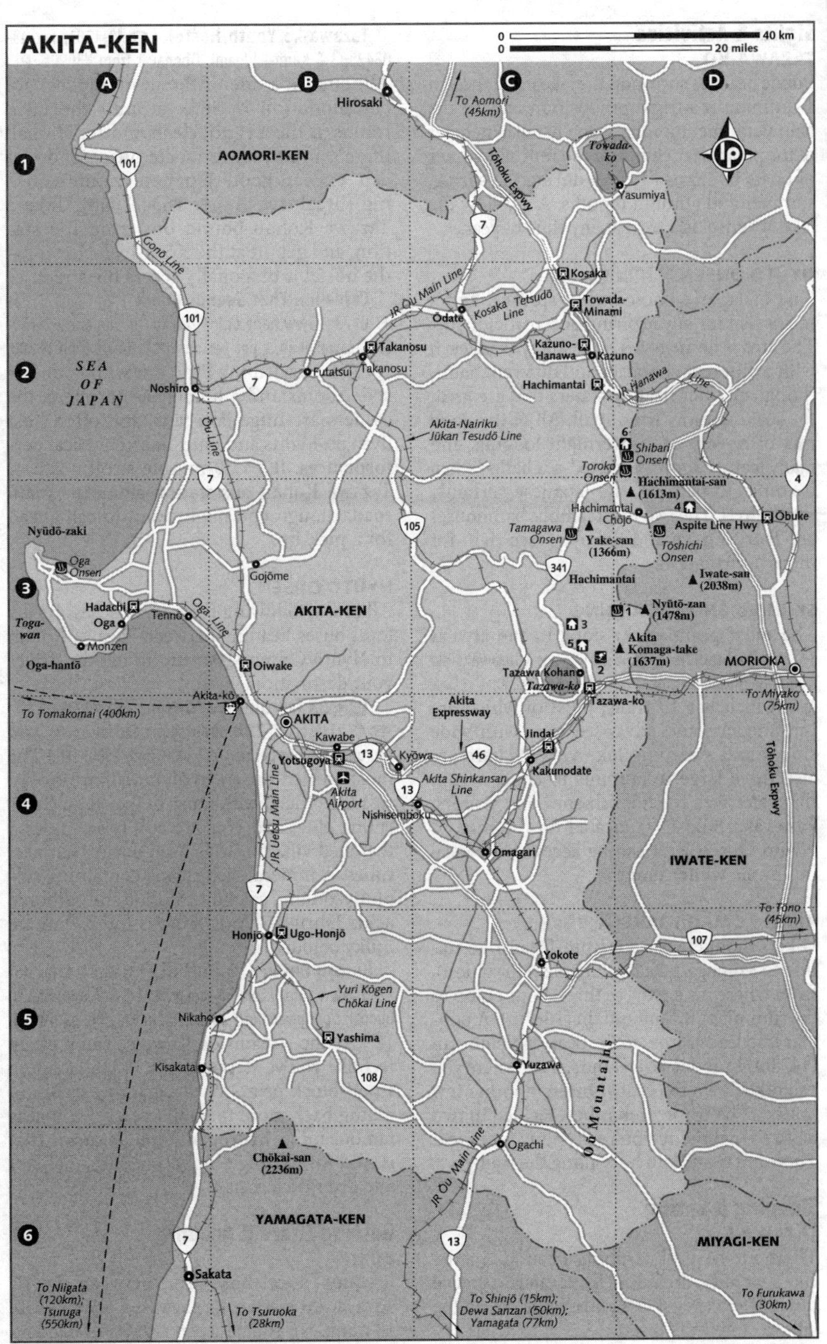
AKITA-KEN
0 40 km
0 20 miles
Hirosaki
To Aomori (45km)
AOMORI-KEN
Towada-ko
Yasumiya
Tōhoku Expwy
Gonō Line
JR Ōu Main Line
Kosaka
Towada-Minami
Ōdate
Kosaka Tetsudō Line
Kazuno-Hanawa
Kazuno
Takanosu
Futatsui
Hachimantai
JR Hanawa Line
SEA OF JAPAN
Noshiro
Ōu Line
Akita-Nairiku Jūkan Tesudō Line
Shibari Onsen
Toroko Onsen
Hachimantai-san (1613m)
Hachimantai Chōjō
Aspite Line Hwy
Ōbuke
Nyūdō-zaki
Oga Onsen
Gojōme
Tamagawa Onsen
Yake-san (1366m)
Tōshichi Onsen
Hachimantai
Iwate-san (2038m)
Toga-wan
Hadachi
Oga
Tennō
Oga Line
AKITA-KEN
Nyūtō-zan (1478m)
Akita Komaga-take (1637m)
Monzen
Oga-hantō
Oiwake
Tazawa Kohan
Tazawa-ko
MORIOKA
To Miyako (75km)
Akita-kō
To Tomakomai (400km)
AKITA
Akita Expressway
Jindai
Kawabe
Kyōwa
Yotsugoya
Kakunodate
Akita Airport
Akita Shinkansan Line
Nishisemboku
Tōhoku Expwy
JR Uetsu Main Line
Ōmagari
IWATE-KEN
To Tōno (45km)
Honjō
Ugo-Honjō
Yokote
Yuri Kōgen Chōkai Line
Nikaho
Yashima
Kisakata
Yuzawa
Ōu Mountains
Chōkai-san (2236m)
Ogachi
JR Ōu Main Line
YAMAGATA-KEN
MIYAGI-KEN
Sakata
To Niigata (120km); Tsuruga (550km)
To Tsuruoka (28km)
To Shinjō (15km); Dewa Sanzan (50km); Yamagata (77km)
To Furukawa (30km)

Sights & Activities

TAZAWA-KO

Public beaches surround the lake itself, though swimming is a frigid proposition outside the balmy summer months. If you're not a member of the polar-bear club, you can rent all manner of boats in Tazawa Kohan during the spring, summer and autumn months. A stroll by the lake at sunset is a treat at any time of year.

NYŪTŌ ONSEN 乳頭温泉

One of Japan's choicest hot springs, and a must-visit for any aspiring onsen aficionado. The area is home to seven rustic ryokan, each with a different character and different baths, though all offer healing waters that are great for soaking away from it all. All of the good mix of ryokan offer overnight lodging, and many feature *konyoku,* mixed-sex baths (when it comes to bathing, the Japanese certainly aren't shy!). The two most famous bathhouses are Tsuru-no-Yu and Kuroyu – see right for more information.

SKIING & SNOWBOARDING

The most popular ski slope in the area is **Tazawako-Sukī-Jō** (☎ 46-2011; www.tazawako-ski.com/engligh/index.html; 1-day lift ticket ¥4200; 🕒 Dec-Apr), which has 13 trails, most of which are intermediate and advanced runs with wide slopes and sweeping lake views. There are also three large restaurants to choose from that cater well for English-speaking visitors. Tazawako-Sukī-Jō is located on the road to Nyūtō Onsen, and can be accessed by local bus in the winter months.

AKITA KOMAGA-TAKE 秋田駒ヶ岳

Hikers should take a bus from Tazawa-ko station to Komaga-take Hachigōme (8th station), from where it's a two- to three-hour climb to the summit of this mountain (1637m). A popular trail leads across to the peak of Nyūtō-zan (1478m) in about seven hours, from where you can hike down to Nyūtō Onsen (another few hours). The whole trek is best tackled in two days, so make sure you're properly prepared. There are mountain huts along the trail.

Sleeping & Eating

TAZAWA-KO

There are several camping grounds in the lake's vicinity, including **Nyūtō camping ground** (☎ 46-2244; camp sites ¥1000, plus per person ¥500) in the village of Nyūtō Onsen.

Tazawa-ko Youth Hostel (☎ 43-1281; fax 43-0842; 33-8 Kami-Ishigami, Obonai; r from ¥3090; Ⓟ) Although it's one of the more modest accommodation options around the lake, rooms at the YH are clean and functional, there's an attractive onsite onsen and you can expect good Japanese home-cooking (breakfast/dinner ¥630/1050). Take a Tazawa Kohan-bound bus from the station, and get off at the Kōen-iriguchi stop – the hostel is diagonally across the street.

Cafe+Inn That Sounds Good! (☎ 43-0127; fax 43-0578; www.hana.or.jp/~takko, in Japanese; 160-58 Tazawakohan; r per person incl 2 meals from ¥8800; Ⓟ 💻) A charming little inn with country-style rooms and a homely atmosphere, the owners are huge jazz fans, and often host live jazz nights and impromptu musical performances. It's a 30-minute stroll north of Tazawa Kohan bus station along the main road, though you might want to call ahead for a pick-up.

NYŪTŌ ONSEN

All of the following ryokan are accessible by local buses heading between Tazawa Kohan to Nyūtō Onsen – be sure to tell the driver your destination.

our pick **Tsuru-no-yu Onsen** (鶴の湯温泉; ☎ 46-2139; fax 46-2100; 50 Kokuyurin, Sendatsuzawa; www.tsurunoyu.com; r per person ¥8400, bath ¥500; Ⓟ) The most storied onsen in Nyūtō, Tsuru-no-yu was the official bathhouse of the Akita clan's ruling elite, and you can still relax under a thatched villa that was used during samurai times. A mineral-rich spring containing sulphur, sodium, calcium chloride and carbonic acid, Tsuru-no-yu is famous for its unique milky colour.

Kuroyu Onsen (黒湯温泉; ☎ 46-2214; fax 46-2280, www.kuroyu.com, in Japanese; 2-1 Aza-kuroyuzawa, Obonai; r per person incl 2 meals from ¥11,700, bath ¥500; Ⓟ) At the streamside Kuroyu, you'll easily feel like you've stepped back into a Japanese wood-block print. With a bathing tradition dating back more than 300 years, Kuroyu is famous for its hydrogen sulphide spring that is said to ease high blood pressure, diabetes and arteriosclerosis.

Getting There & Around

BUS

Frequent local buses run between the JR Tazawa-ko station to Tazawa Kohan (¥350, 10 minutes), and between Tazawa Kohan and

Nyūtō Onsen (¥650, 40 minutes). Note that these services terminate after sunset.

From April to October, there are three daily buses in either direction between JR Tazawa-ko station and Hachimantai Chōjō (¥1990, 2¼ hours), and six daily buses in either direction between the station and Komaga-take Hachigōme (¥1000, one hour).

CAR

If you're driving, a well-maintained network of local roads branches off the Akita Expressway (秋田自動車道) running between Morioka and Akita.

TRAIN

Several hourly trains on the Akita *shinkansen* line run between Tazawa-ko and Tokyo (¥14,900, three hours) via Morioka (¥13,640, 2½ hours), and between Tazawa-ko and Akita (¥3080, one hour) via Kakunodate (¥1360, 15 minutes). Infrequent local trains also run on the JR Tazawako line between Tazawa-ko and Kakunodate (¥320, 25 minutes).

KAKUNODATE 角館

☎ 0187 / pop 30,000

Established in 1620 by Ashina Yoshikatsu, the lord of the Satake clan, Kakunodate is known as 'Little Kyoto', and presents a thoughtful, immersive experience for anyone interested in catching a glimpse of old Japan. While the original castle that once guarded over the feudal town is no more, the *bukeyashiki* – or samurai district – is splendidly preserved. A veritable living museum of Japanese culture and history, the *bukeyashiki* consists of original samurai mansions surrounded by cherry trees and lush garden expanses. It takes an hour or so to stroll through the district, which makes Kakunodate a pleasant stopover en route between Tazawa-ko and Akita.

Orientation & Information

The *bukeyashiki* is a 15-minute walk northwest from Kakunodate station. If you don't feel like walking, you can hire a **bicycle** (per hr ¥300) at the taxi office across from the station.

Library (Sōgō Jōhō Centre; 9am-5pm Tue-Sun) Free internet access.

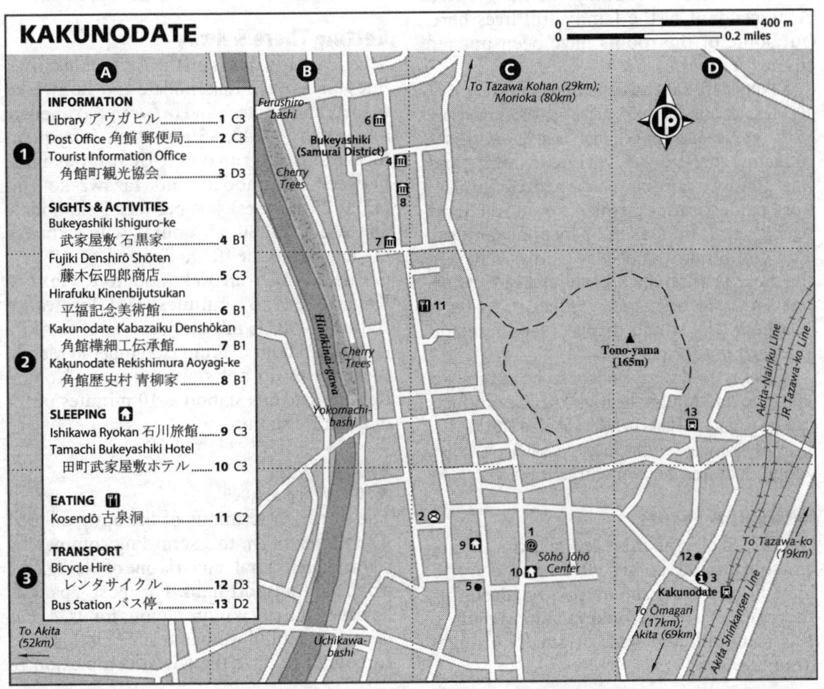

Post office (☎ 54-1400) Has an international ATM.

Tourist information office (☎ 54-2700; 🕐 9am-6pm mid-Apr–Sep, to 5.30pm Oct–mid-Apr) Outside the station in a small building shaped like a *kura*. There are English maps, and some staff speak English.

Sights

Pick up an English-language map from the tourist information centre, and then set out either on foot or bike. You can see everything in a short time, but it's best to go slow and soak up the ancient atmosphere.

Each of the samurai mansions is impressive in its own right, though the highlight of the district is the **Kakunodate Rekishimura Aoyagi-ke** (☎ 54-3257; www.samuraiworld.com/english/index.html; 3 Omotemachi, Shimochō; admission ¥500; 🕐 9am-5pm Apr-Oct, to 4pm Nov-Mar). This agglomeration of mini-museums exhibits everything from Aoyagi family heirlooms and folk art to valuable antiques including old-time cameras, gramophones and classic jazz records.

Built in 1809, the **Bukeyashiki Ishiguro-ke** (☎ 55-1496; Omotemachi; admission ¥300; 🕐 9am-5pm) was the residence of the Isihiguro family, advisers to the Satake clan, and remains one of the oldest buildings in the district. A descendant of the family still lives here, but some of the rooms have been opened to the public.

Kakunodate Kabazaiku Denshōkan (☎ 54-1700; 10-1 Omotemachi Shimochō; admission ¥300, combined ¥510; 🕐 9am-5pm Apr-Oct, to 4.30pm Nov-Mar) is a museum that houses various exhibits and has demonstrations of *kabazaiku* (household or decorative items covered in cherry bark), a craft first taken up by poor samurai. The combined ticket also allows entry to the nearby **Hirafuku Kinenbijutsukan** (☎ 54-3888; 4-4 Kamichō Omotemachi; 🕐 9am-5pm Apr-Oct, to 4.30pm Nov-Mar), which displays Japanese and Western modern art.

There is no shortage of cheap *kabazaiku* for sale in town, though the high-quality products can be found at **Fujiki Denshirō Shōten** (☎ 54-1151; 45 Shimoshinmachi; 🕐 9am-5.30pm, closed Sun in winter), which operates its own workshop.

Festivals & Events

On the river embankment, a 2km 'cherry blossom tunnel' comes alive around April/May. Some of the *shidarezakura* (drooping cherry) trees in the bukeyashiki are up to 300 years old, and were originally brought from Kyōtō.

From 7 to 9 September, Kakunodate celebrates the **Hikiyama Matsuri**, in which participants haul around enormous seven-tonne *yama* (wooden carts) to pray for peaceful times, accompanied by folk music and dancing.

Sleeping & Eating

The majority of travellers stay in either Tazawa-ko or Akita, and visit Kakunodate in a day trip. However, there are some attractive spots to stay for the night.

Ishikawa Ryokan (☎ 54-2030; 32 Iwasemachi; r incl 2 meals from ¥9000) This atmospheric, Edo-period ryokan continues to operate just as it did in the time of travelling samurai.

Tamachi Bukeyashiki Hotel (☎ 52-2030; fax 52-1701; www.bukeyashiki.jp, in Japanese; 52 Tamachi; r with/without 2 meals from ¥17,850/13,125) A Western-style hotel of mind-blowing opulence that preserves the original character and structure of the samurai mansion.

Several of the old houses in the *bukeyashiki* serve noodles, though the town's most historically significant lunch spot is **Kosendō** (☎ 53-2902; noodles from ¥750; 🕐 lunch & dinner), an old wooden schoolhouse – try the *inaniwa udon* (udon noodles in a clear mushroom soup; ¥850).

Getting There & Away

Several hourly trains on the Akita *shinkansen* line run between Kakunodate and Tazawa-ko (¥1360, 15 minutes), and between Kakunodate and Akita (¥2740, 45 minutes). Infrequent local trains also run on the JR Tazawako line between Kakunodate and Tazawa-ko and (¥320, 25 minutes), and between Kakunodate and Akita (¥1280, 1¾ hours), with a change at Ōmagari to the JR Ōu line.

Buses run from Kakunodate to Tazawa Kohan (¥840, 52 minutes) and Tazawa-ko station (¥490, 35 minutes), as well as to Akita (¥1330, 1½ hours). From December to March, these buses do not stop at Tazawa Kohan. Kakunodate bus station is 10 minutes north of the train station.

AKITA 秋田

☎ 018 / pop 336,000

The northern terminus of the aptly dubbed Akita *shinkansen*, this sprawling commercial city and prefectural capital is one of the region's principal transport hubs. For most Japanese, however, the city is more famous for its '*Akita-bijin*' (a beautiful woman from Akita), who is rumoured to have the fairest complexion in

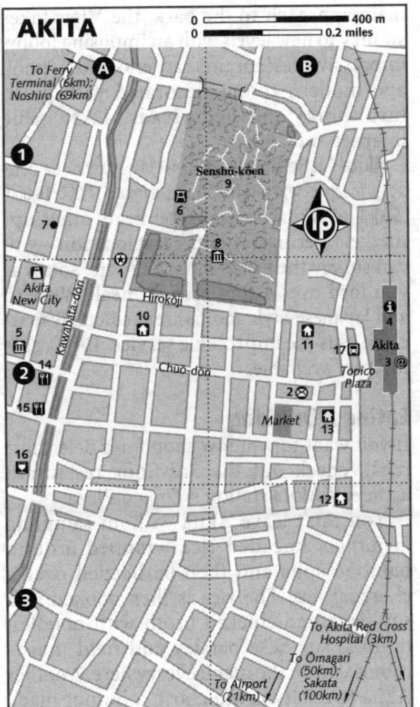

INFORMATION

Akita Central Police Station 秋田中央警察署 1 A2
Akita Central Post Office 秋田中央郵便局 2 B2
Comic Buster コミックバスター 3 B2
Tourist Information Office 秋田観光案内所 4 B2

SIGHTS & ACTIVITIES

Akarengakan Museum 赤れんが郷土館 5 A2
Hachiman Akita-jinja 八幡秋田神社 6 A1
Kantō Festival Centre 秋田市民俗芸能伝承館 ねぶり流し館 7 A1
Masakichi Hirano Art Museum 平野政吉美術館 8 B1
Senshū-kōen 千秋公園 9 B1

SLEEPING

Akita Castle Hotel 秋田キャッスルホテル 10 A2
Akita View Hotel 秋田ビューホテル 11 B2
Naniwa Hotel ホテルなにわ 12 B3
Ryokan Chikuba-sō 旅館 竹馬荘 13 B2

EATING

Bekkan 別館 14 A2
Otafuku お多福 15 A2

DRINKING

Green Pocket グリーンポケット 16 A2

TRANSPORT

Bus Station バス乗り場 17 B2

the country. This is somewhat ironic given how ugly the city itself can be – it was virtually destroyed by Allied bombing during WWII – though things brighten up during the famous Kantō Matsuri in August. You're likely to pass through Akita once or twice during your travels, and the good local food is another bonus.

Information

Akita Central Police Station (☎ 835-1111; 1-9 Meitoku-chō, Senshū)

Akita central post office (秋田中央郵便局; ☎ 823-2900; 5-1 Hodono Teppōmachi) Five minutes west of the train station's west exit, in the backstreets near the market.

Akita Red Cross Hospital (秋田赤十字病院; ☎ 829-5000; 222-1 Naeshirosawa Aza Kamikitatesaruta)

Comic Buster (☎ 884-7472; 2nd fl, ALVE Bldg, 4-1 Higashidōri Nakamachi; internet per 30min ¥320; 24hr) Connected to the east exit of the JR station; the building is pronounced 'Aroo-vay'.

Tourist information office (☎ 832-7941; www.akitafan.com/language/en/index.html; 9am-7pm) Opposite the *shinkansen* tracks on the 2nd floor of Akita station.

Sights

Akita's few sights cluster in the city centre near the train station, so you can easily get around on foot without fear of getting too lost.

Originally constructed in 1604, Akita's castle, **Kubota-jō**, was destroyed with other feudal relics during the Meiji 'enlightenment'. However, the hallowed ruins still frame **Senshū-kōen** (千秋公園), a leafy park just 10 minutes due west of the station. The park protects a few odd walls, turrets, guardhouses and an observation platform that delivers appealing views of the city.

At the heart of the park also lies the **Masakichi Hirano Art Museum** (☎ 833-5809; 3-7 Senshū Meitoku-chō; admission ¥610; 10am-5.30pm Tue-Sun May-Sep, to 5pm Tue-Sun Oct-Apr), which is noted for its enormous painting, *Events of Akita*. Reputed to be the world's largest canvas painting, it measures 3.65m by 20.5m and depicts traditional Akita life throughout the seasons.

The city's last two major sights can be reached by exiting the park to the west, crossing over the river, walking two blocks and turning south. You should now see the **Kantō Festival Centre** (☎ 866-7091; Neburi Nagashi-kan; admission ¥100; 9.30am-4.30pm, 9am-9pm during festivals), which has exhibitions and videos of Akita's famous Kantō Matsuri. Here, you can try to heft the famous *kantō* poles. It won't be easy – these babies are 10m long and weigh around 60kg!

Continue south past the Akita New City department store until you come to the **Akarengakan Museum** (☎ 864-6851; 3-3-21 Ōmachi; admission ¥200; 🕑 9.30am-4.30pm), a Meiji-era, Renaissance-style, red-brick building. Inside, you'll find wood-block prints of traditional Akita life by self-taught folk artist Katsuhira Tokushi. A combined ticket with the Kantō Festival Centre is available at either place for ¥250.

Festivals & Events

From 3 to 6 August, Akita celebrates the visually stunning **Akita Kantō Matsuri** (秋田竿燈まつり; Pole Lantern Festival; www.kantou.gr.jp/english/index.htm). Starting in the evening along Kantō Ōdori, more than 160 men skilfully balance giant poles, weighing 60kg and hung with illuminated lanterns, on their heads, chins, hips and shoulders, to the beat of *taiko* drumming groups. As the aim of the festival is to pray for a good harvest, the arrangement of the lanterns is designed to resemble an ear of rice. During the day, exhibitions of music and pole balancing are held in Senshū-kōen. Book accommodation well in advance.

Sleeping

Cheap business hotels cluster near the station if you find yourself in a pinch, though the accommodation options listed are above and beyond.

Naniwa Hotel (☎ 832-4570; www.hotel-naniwa.jp, in Japanese; 6-18-27 Nakadōri; d per person with/without 2 meals ¥6200/3500; 💻) This family-run hotel consists of cutesy and cosy tatami rooms as well as appealing extras including free massage chairs, a beautiful 24-hour *hinoki* (Japanese cyprus) bath and meals made with the owners' own home-grown rice. From the station, turn left at the Topico plaza, and head south until you hit the major throughway – it's the red building with a wooden entrance.

Ryokan Chikuba-sō (☎ 832-6446; 4-14-9 Nakadōri; r per person with/without 2 meals ¥6800/4200) This comfortable, welcoming inn offers Japanese-style rooms with enough leg room, and an affordable meal plan featuring hearty local favourites. It's convenient to the station's west exit.

Akita View Hotel (☎ 832-1111; www.akitaviewhotel.jp; 2-6-1 Naka-dōri; s/tw from ¥9500/18,000; 💻 📶 🏊) Next to the Seibu department store on the main approach to the park, the View takes swanky to new levels with an imposing lobby, impressive restaurants, an enormous pool, and modern rooms decorated with plush furnishings and bedspreads. LAN cable internet available.

Akita Castle Hotel (☎ 834-1141; www.castle-hotel.co.jp, in Japanese; 1-3-5 Nakadōri; s/d from ¥11,000/18,000; 💻) The Akita Castel Hotel beats other upmarket offerings with its great location – you can survey the castle moat from the south as you lord over a fine French meal. Western and Japanese-style rooms are predictably first-class, as is the impeccable service. LAN cable internet available.

Eating & Drinking

If you want to window shop for a delectable meal, check out the 3rd-floor restaurant arcade of Akita station's Topico Plaza.

You can't leave Akita without sampling *kiritanpo*, kneaded rice wrapped around bamboo spits and then barbecued over a charcoal fire. The rice is then cooked in a soy-flavoured chicken broth with noodles, onions, Japanese parsley and field mushrooms. It's on the menu everywhere. Another Akita specialty is *shottsuru*, a hotpot made with salted and fermented *hatahata* (a local fish), green onions and tofu.

Kawabata-dōri, which runs parallel to the river of the same name, serves as Akita's main nightlife area and pleasure quarter.

Otafuku (☎ 862-0802; 4-2-25 Ōmachi; kiritanpo from ¥2000; 🕑 lunch & dinner) Specialising in *kiritanpo-nabe* (¥2520), a masterful hotpot of sticky rice stew, this restaurant is in a traditional black and beige wooden building on the western banks of the Kawabata-gawa.

Bekkan (☎ 62-7481; 4-2-11 Ōmachi; set meals around ¥3000; 🕑 lunch & dinner) You can try *shottsuru* as well as *kiritanpo* and other regional specialties at the justifiably famous Bekkan. Ordering can be a bit tricky here, though if you say the name of the dish you want to try, the wait staff will do their best to accommodate you. The restaurant is housed in a traditional wooden structure on the opposite bank of the Albert Hotel.

Green Pocket (☎ 863-6917; 5-1-7 Ōmachi; 🕑 7pm-midnight Mon-Sat) One place that definitely bucks the neon trend of Kawabata-dōri, is this little gem at the street's southern end. Decked out in authentic period panelling, there's an old-time piano in the corner, Vivien Leigh prints on the walls and a fabulously decadent selection of scotch whiskies and fine wines – classy.

Getting There & Away

AIR

From Akita airport, 21km south of the city centre, there are domestic flights to various destinations, such as Tokyo, Osaka, Nagoya, Sapporo and others. Frequent buses run between JR Akita station and the airport (¥890, 40 minutes).

BOAT

From the port of Akita-kō, **Shin Nihonkai** (☎ 880-2600) ferries run at 7am on Tuesday, Wednesday, Friday, Saturday and Sunday to Tomakomai on Hokkaidō (from ¥4300, 12½ hours). At 9am on Tuesday, Wednesday, Thursday, Saturday and Sunday, ferries run to Niigata (from ¥3900, 8½ hours), with the Sunday and Wednesday ferries continuing on to Tsuruga (from ¥6600, 20½ hours). One bus daily at 6.05am runs from the JR Akita station to Akita-kō, 8km northwest of the station (¥390, 30 minutes). There is a small ticket office at the pier.

BUS

JR highway night buses depart from the bus station in front of the east exit of the train station daily at 9.20pm, and arrive in Tokyo's Nihombashi station the next morning at 6am (¥9100). Buses from Tokyo arrive at this bus station, too.

CAR

If you're driving, the Akita Expressway (秋田自動車道) runs between Morioka and Akita.

TRAIN

Several hourly trains on the JR Akita *shinkansen* run between the northern terminus of Akita and the southern terminus of Tokyo (¥16,470, four hours) via Morioka (¥4300, 1½ hours), Tazawako (¥3080, one hour) and Kakunodate (¥2740, 45 minutes). Infrequent local trains also run on the JR Ōu line between Akita and Kakunodate (¥1280, 1¾ hours), with a change at Ōmagari to the JR Tazawako line. Finally, there are a few *tokkyū* each day on the JR Uetsu line connecting Akita with Niigata (¥6820, 3¾ hours).

YAMAGATA-KEN 山形県

While it's not as famous as its neighbouring prefectures, Yamagata-ken is home to a couple of Tōhoku's top attractions. At the top of the list is tiny but tranquil Zaō Onsen, famous for its enormous *rotemburo* and challenging ski slopes. A close second is the sacred trio of peaks at Dewa Sanzan, which are revered by *yamabushi* (mountain priests) and hikers alike. Yamadera offers temple buffs and Bashō fans some spectacular photo opportunities, while quieter places like Tobi-shima and Tendō have charm all of their own.

TOBI-SHIMA 飛島

☎ 0234

You're gonna have to work hard to get out to this tiny island floating in the Sea of Japan, though your reward will be time spent on a lonely landmass defined by rugged sea cliffs and expansive sea caves. Only 8 sq km in size, and home to less than 100 people inhabiting small fishing villages, the nature here is pristine, especially if you're a fan of birdwatching, wilderness beaches and snorkelling (in the summertime only!).

There aren't too many places to stay on the island, though a long-standing spot is the **Sawaguchi Ryokan** (沢口旅館; ☎ 95-2246; fax 96-3052; 73 Ko-katsūra; r per person incl 2 meals from ¥8400), a modest Japanese-style inn where you can feast on some serious seafood spreads. Sawaguchi is located approximately five minutes on foot from the ferry pier (the building is marked by a red ship's wheel). Islanders are friendly, and can easily point the way, though you can always call ahead for a pick-up.

The jumping-off point for Tobi-shima is the coastal town of Sakata, which is easiest to access by rail. A few daily *tokkyū* on the JR Uetsu Main line run between Akita and Sakata (¥3500, 1½ hours), and between Sakata and Niigata (¥4930, 2¼ hours) via Tsuruoka (¥1290, 20 minutes). There are also a few daily *futsū* running on the same line between Akita and Sakata (¥1890, two hours), and between Sakata and Tsuruoka (¥480, 45 minutes).

There is a small but helpful **tourist information centre** (☎ 24-2233; 🕑 9am-6pm) at the station that can give you information on the ferries, and call ahead to reserve tickets.

YAMAGATA-KEN

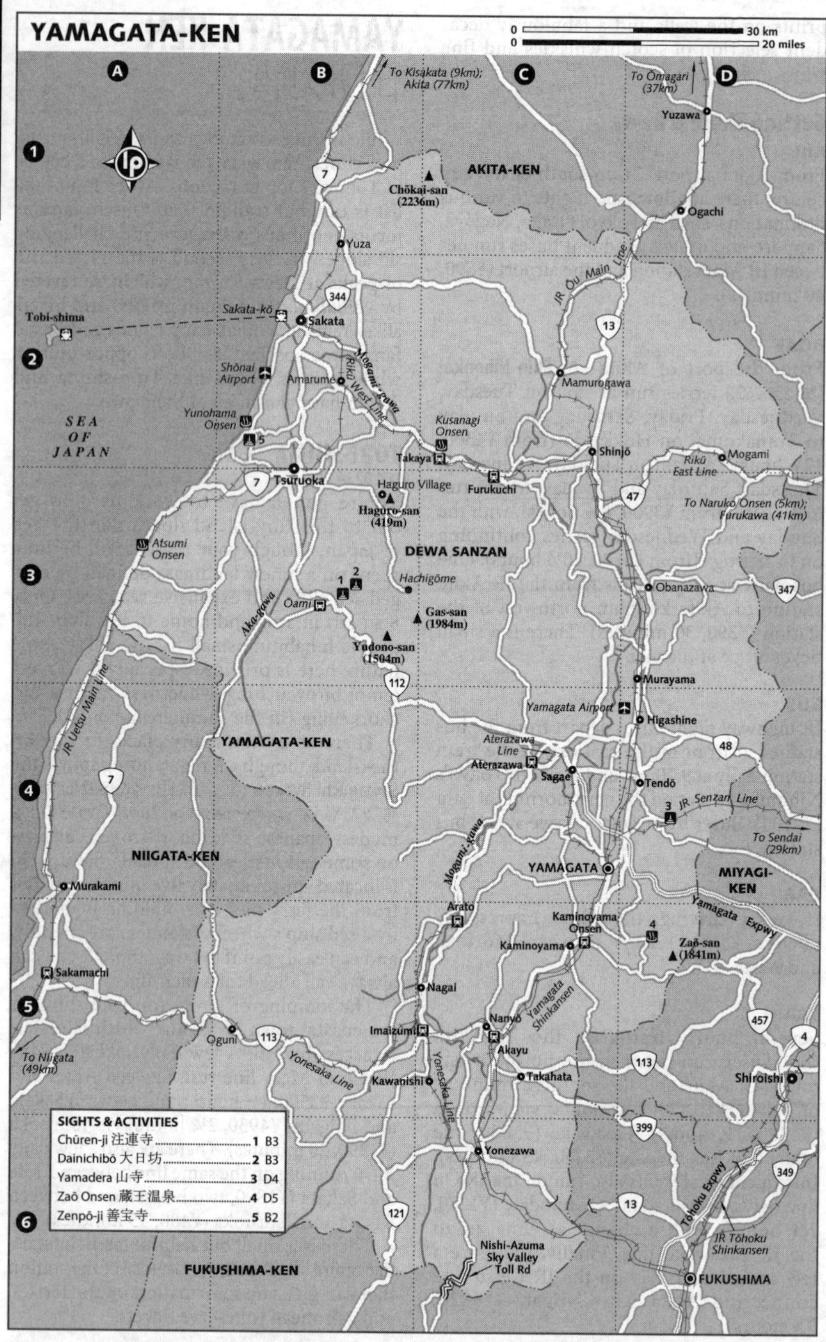

SIGHTS & ACTIVITIES

Chūren-ji 注連寺	1	B3
Dainichibō 大日坊	2	B3
Yamadera 山寺	3	D4
Zaō Onsen 蔵王温泉	4	D5
Zenpō-ji 善宝寺	5	B2

New Tobishima (☎ 22-3911) runs at least once (often twice) daily in both directions between the port of Sakata-kō and the island (¥2040, 1½ hours). You should make advanced reservations in the summer, though other times you can buy your tickets at the port. Fairly regular local buses connect the JR Sakata station to Sakata-kō (¥100, 10 minutes), or you can simply take a taxi (around ¥1000).

TSURUOKA 鶴岡

☎ 0235 / pop 144,000

Tsuruoka is a pleasant enough place to spend the night and get some rest, which is a good thing as you're going to need it if you plan on tackling nearby Dewa Sanzan. Indeed, Tsuruoka serves as the take-off point for Tōhoku's most famous trio of mountains, though this former castle town in the middle of the Shōnai plain was once an important city in its own right. Established by the Sakai clan, one of feudal Yamagata's most important families, Tsuruoka continues to hold on to a few relics of its proud past.

Information

Internet access (鶴岡市ネットワークコミュニティセンター; ☎ 29-7775; 1hr free; 🕑 9am-7.30pm) On the 3rd floor of the Marica building, opposite JR Tsuruoka station.

Post office With ATM service, 300m south of the station.

Tourist information office (☎ 25-7678; 🕑 10am-5pm Nov-Feb, 9.30am-5.30pm Mar-Oct) To the right as you exit JR Tsuruoka station; can book accommodation and has information about Dewa Sanzan.

Sights & Activities

CHIDŌ HAKUBUTSUKAN 致道博物館

Founded in 1950 by the former Lord Shōnai in order to develop and preserve local culture, this **museum** (☎ 22-1199; 10-18 Kachū-shinmachi; admission ¥700; 🕑 9am-4.30pm) features Sakai family artefacts, a family residence, two Meiji-era buildings, a traditional storehouse and a *kabuto-zukuri* (a farmhouse with a thatched roof shaped like a samurai helmet).

The museum is on the southwest corner of Tsuruoka-kōen, the sight of the former Sakai castle. You can either walk for about 15 minutes southwesterly from the JR Tsuruoka station, or take a bus from stop 1 – frequent buses bound for Yunohama Onsen pass by the Chidō Hakubutsukan-mae stop (¥200, 10 minutes).

ZENPŌ-JI 善寶寺

Seven kilometres west of Tsuruoka you'll find this Zen-Buddhist **temple**, complete with a five-tier pagoda and large gateway. It dates from the 10th century, when it was dedicated to the Dragon King, guardian of the seas. Near the temple is a more contemporary attraction, the famous *jinmen-gyo* (human-faced carp). When viewed from above, these curious fish actually do appear to have human faces. From the station, take a bus bound for Yunohama Onsen to the Zenpō-ji stop (¥580, 30 minutes).

Festivals & Events

Tenjin Matsuri Tsuruoka's best-known festival, on 25 May, is also known as the Bakemono Matsuri (Masked Faces Festival). People stroll around in masks and costume for three days, serving sake and keeping an eye out for friends and acquaintances. The object is to make it through three festivals in a row without anyone recognising you, whereupon local lore states you'll have good luck for the rest of your life.

Sleeping & Eating

Narakan (奈良館; ☎ 22-1202; 2-35 Hiyoshimachi; r per person incl 2 meals from ¥6300) Head five minutes south along the main street leading out from the station to reach this modern Western-style inn (look for the tall chimney). Rooms are a bit on the small side, but you'll eat well – and you need the calories before hitting Dewa Sanzan.

Tsuruoka Washington Hotel (鶴岡ワシントンホテル; ☎ 25-0111; fax 25-0110; www.tsuruoka-wh.com, in Japanese; 5-20 Suehiro-machi; s/d from ¥6930/10,972; 💻) Directly outside the station's south exit, Tsuruoka's instalment of the Washington Hotel is true to the brand name, offering affordable, well-maintained rooms and a convenient location. LAN cable internet available.

Tokyo Daiichi Hotel Tsuruoka (東京第一ホテル鶴岡; ☎ 24-7662; fax 24-7610; www.tdh-tsuruoka.co.jp, in Japanese; 2-10 Nishiki Machi; s/d from ¥8662/12,705; 💻) A huge yellow brick building just one minute southwest of the station next to bus station, this upmarket business hotel has spacious and well-lit rooms as well as an attractive open-air onsen and sauna. LAN cable internet available.

Sanmaian (三昧庵; ☎ 24-3632; 10-18 Kachū-shinmachi; set meals around ¥1000; 🕑 9am-4.30pm) Adjacent to the Chidō Hakubutsukan, this small noodle shop has set meals that are perfect for a light lunch or afternoon snack. The *soba setto* or *udon setto* changes daily, but either is always fairly priced.

Getting There & Away

BUS

Shoko night buses run between the Tokyo Dai-ichi Hotel in Tsuruoka and Shibuya Mark City in Tokyo (¥7390, eight hours). There are also a few buses each day between Tsuruoka and Yamagata (¥2400, 1¾ hours), though services are often cut back during the winter months due to snowdrifts.

For detailed information on accessing Dewa Sanzan, see p562.

TRAIN

A few daily *tokkyū* on the JR Uetsu Main line run between Tsuruoka and Akita (¥3820, 1¾ hours), and between Tsuruoka and Niigata (¥4130, 1¾ hours). There are also a few daily *futsū* running on the same line between Tsuruoka and Akita (¥2210, 2¾ hours) via Sakata (¥480, 35 minutes).

DEWA SANZAN 出羽三山

☎ 0235

Dewa Sanzan is the collective title for three sacred peaks – Haguro-san, Gas-san and Yudono-san – which are believed to represent birth, death and rebirth, respectively. Together, they have been worshipped for centuries by *yamabushi* and followers of the Shugendō sect. During the annual pilgrimage seasons, you can see white-clad pilgrims equipped with wooden staff, sandals and straw hat, and fleece-clad hikers equipped with poles, trekking boots and bandana.

Of course, it is the *yamabushi*, with their unmistakable conch shells, checked jackets and voluminous white pantaloons, that keep the tradition alive. Whether stomping along precipitous trails or sitting under icy waterfalls, these devoted mountain men embrace severe ascetic exercises to discipline both body and spirit.

Orientation & Information

Theoretically, if you hiked at a military pace and timed the buses perfectly, you might be able to cover all three peaks in one day. However, this would leave you no time to enjoy the scenery, and the chances of missing a key bus connection are very high. If you want to tackle all three mountains, it's best to devote two or three days, especially if you eschew buses in favour of foot leather.

Before setting out, it's recommended that you book accommodation, and stock up on maps, at the tourist information office in Tsuruoka. Also note that transport can grind to a halt once the snow starts to pile up – it's best to time your visit between July and September when all three mountains are open to hikers.

Sights & Activities

Tradition dictates that you start at Haguro-san and finish at Yudono-san, which is why we're presenting the pilgrimage in this order. However, feel free to follow the circuit in the opposite direction, which is certainly one way of going against the crowd.

HAGURO-SAN 羽黒山

Because it has the easiest access, Haguro-san (419m) attracts a steady flow of tourists. At the base of the mountain is Haguro village, consisting of *shukubō* (temple lodgings) and the **Ideha Bunka Kinenkan** (☎ 62-4727; admission ¥400; 🕑 9am-4.30pm Wed-Mon Apr-Nov, 9.30am-4pm Wed-Mon Dec-Mar), a small history museum featuring films of *yamabushi* rites and festivals.

The orthodox approach to the shrine on the summit requires pilgrims to climb 2446 steps, but buses run straight to the top. The climb can be done in a leisurely hour, though you might be lapped by gaggles of sprightly senior citizens.

From the Haguro Centre bus stop, walk straight ahead through the *torii*, and continue across the bridge. En route you'll pass **Gojū-no-tō**, a weather-beaten, five-storey pagoda dating from the 14th century. Then comes a very long slog up the hundreds of stone steps arranged in steep sections. Pause halfway at the **tea house** (🕑 8.30am-5pm Apr-Nov) for refreshment and breathtaking views. If you detour to the right, just past the tea house, you'll come upon the temple ruins of **Betsu-in**, visited by Bashō during his pilgrimage here.

The scene at the summit can be a bit anticlimactic if the crowds are thick. However, you can still have a contemplative moment in front of the **Gosaiden**, a vivid red hall that enshrines the deities of all three mountains.

At the top of Haguro-san, you have a number of options to consider. In summer, there are a couple of morning buses that travel directly from the summit to the 8th station of Gas-san. If you miss these buses, you can walk back down to the village, or spend the night at Saikan (see p563). Alternatively, purists can follow the 20km ridge hike to the peak of Gas-san.

GAS-SAN 月山

Accessible from July to September, Gas-san (1984m) is the highest of the three sacred mountains. Coming from Haguro-san, the peak is usually accessed from the trailhead at **Hachigōme** (8th station). This route then passes through an alpine plateau to **Kyūgōme** (9th station) in 1¾ hours, and then grinds uphill for another 1¼ hours. At the summit, pilgrims flock to **Gassan-jinja** (admission with ritual purification ¥500; 6am-5pm), though not without first being purified: bow your head to receive a priest's benediction before rubbing your head and shoulders with sacred paper, which is then placed in the fountain.

From the summit, you could retrace your steps to 8th station, though almost everybody will be pressing on with the steep descent to Yudono-san-jinja. This takes another three hours or so, and you'll have to carefully descend rusty ladders chained to the cliff sides, and pick your way down through a slippery streambed at the end of the trail.

YUDONO-SAN 湯殿山

Accessible from May to October, Yudono-san (1504m) is the spiritual culmination of the Dewa Sanzan trek. Coming from Gas-san, it's just a short walk from the streambed at the end of the down climb to **Yudono-san-jinja** (admission ¥500; 6am-5pm, closed Nov-Apr). This sacred shrine is not a building, but rather a large orange rock continuously lapped by water from a hot spring. It has the strictest rituals of the three, with pilgrims required to perform a barefoot circuit of the rock, paddling through the cascading water.

To finish the pilgrimage, it's a mere 10-minute hike further down the mountain to the trailhead at **Yudono-san-sanrōsho**, which is marked by a *torii*, or you can give your feet a break by taking a shuttle bus.

From here, you have a number of options: spend the night at Yudono-san Sanrōjo (see p563), catch a direct bus back to Tsuruoka, catch the bus or walk along the 3km toll road to the Yudono-san Hotel, or take a detour to Dainichibō and Chūren-ji.

DAINICHIBŌ & CHŪREN-JI 大日坊・注連寺

Off Rte 112, halfway between Yudono-san and Tsuruoka in the village of Ōami, these two seemingly ordinary country temples house the mummies of priests who have become 'living Buddhas.' The ascetic practice of self-mummification, outlawed since the 19th century, involved coming as close to death as possible through starvation, before being buried alive while meditating.

Both temples are located close to the Ōami bus stop, and there are colourful signs to follow. The mummy at **Dainichibō** (admission ¥500; 8am-5pm) is dressed in bright reddish-orange robes, and is looking rather ghoulish with his leathery skin. From the bus stop, head into the village, make a left at the post office, and continue walking for about 10 minutes.

The **Chūren-ji** (admission ¥500; 8.30am-5pm) mummy, which is no less freakish looking, is allegedly a reformed murderer who became a powerful Buddhist priest. From the bus stop, head north along the road, carefully following signs at all of the junctions. Appropriately enough, the temple is after the graveyard.

Buses are spaced about two hours apart, which leaves you enough time to look around, and still make your connection back to Tsuruoka.

Festivals & Events

The peak of Haguro-san is the site of several major festivals. During the **Hassaku Matsuri** (八朔祭り), *yamabushi* perform ancient fire rites to pray for a bountiful harvest (31 August and 1 September). During the **Shōrei-sai** (松例祭) festival on New Year's Eve, they perform similar rituals in competition with each other after completing 100-day-long austerities.

Courses

If you haven't yet found your calling, consider becoming a *yamabushi*.

Dewa Sanzan-jinja (☎ 62-2355) This temple at the top of Haguro-san is where you should enquire about becoming a 'real' *yamabushi*. Note that these courses are extremely intense, not for the faint of heart and only really a viable option if you have a decent command of Japanese, and a good bit of time and money to burn.

Ideha Bunka Kinenkan (☎ 62-4727) For those who are happy being just a *yamabushi* 'in-training', this centre in Haguro village runs minicourses that include fasting, mountain sprints and morning wake-up calls. Again, you need to have a decent command of Japanese – phone ahead to enquire about dates and prices.

Sleeping & Eating

There are more than 30 *shukubō* in the Tōge district of Haguro village, as well as a few places on Haguro-san and around Yudosan-jinja, all charging around ¥7000 to ¥8000 per person including two meals. It's also possible for nonguests to score a tasty vegetarian lunch for around ¥1500 (reservations recommended).

Saikan (☎ 62-2357; r per person incl 2 meals ¥7350) The most famous *shukubō*, located at the top of Haguro-san, this atmospheric lodging has sweeping views over the valley below, and is a good spot to spend the night and break up the hike.

Yudono-san Sanrōjo (☎ 54-6131; r per person incl 2 meals from ¥7350; ⏲ closed Nov-Apr) At the end of your second day, consider staying here. It's conveniently located next to Sennin-zawa bus terminal and is a fun spot to unwind with other successful pilgrims.

Yudono-san Hotel (☎ 54-6231; r per person from ¥8500) Alternatively, you can catch the bus or hike down the road to this hotel, a much more modern option than the temple lodgings. A hot bath and a cold beer at the end of a hike is close enough to nirvana.

Getting There & Around

The following transport information is subject to change due to the area's variable weather conditions. For this reason, it is advised that you get the latest bus timetables from tourist information in Tsuruoka before setting out.

Note that directions are given in the same sequence as the trek.

Hourly buses run from Tsuruoka to the Haguro Centre bus stop (¥680, 45 minutes), several of which then continue on to Haguro-sanchō (Haguro summit; ¥990, one hour).

From early July to late August, and then on weekends and holidays until late September, there are up to four daily buses from Haguro-sanchō to Gas-san as far as Hachigōme (¥1240, one hour).

Between June and early November, there are up to four daily buses from the Yudono-san Sanrōjo trailhead at Yudono-san to Tsuruoka (¥1480, 1½ hours), which also passes by the Yudono-san Hotel (¥100, five minutes) and Ōami (¥910, 45 minutes). Regular buses between Tsuruoka and Yamagata also run via the Yudono-san Hotel.

YAMAGATA 山形

☎ 023 / pop 255,000

Yamagata is a thriving industrial city with a sizable student population, making for a more youthful vibe than in comparable *inaka* (rural) cities. While it's a bit short on sights, Yamagata is a good base for day trips to Yamadera, Tendō and Yonezawa, and serves as the main access point for Zaō Onsen.

Information

Prefectural tourism information office (やまがた観光情報センター; ☎ 647-2333; www.yamagatakanko.com/english/index.html; ⏲ 10am-6pm) On the 1st floor of the Kajō Central building; joined to the station complex by walkways.

Tourist information office (山形市観光案内センター; ☎ 647-2266; ⏲ 8.30am-8pm) On the 2nd floor of Yamagata station, in a small glass booth.

WIP (☎ 615-0788; www.wip-fe.com/yamagata, in Japanese; per hr ¥410; ⏲ 24hr) Internet access, just outside the east exit of the Akita JR station, diagonally to the left.

Yamagata Post Office (山形郵便局; ☎ 622-9600) Has an international ATM; on the 1st floor of the Kajō Central building.

Sights & Activities

The recently revived kilns of the **Hirashimizu Pottery District** (平清水陶器地域), along the Hazukashi-kawa (Embarrassed River), turn out beautiful bluish-grey spotted-glaze pieces, nicknamed *nashi-seiji* (pear skin), which are displayed for sale in attached workshops. The renowned **Shichiemon-gama** (七右エ門窯; ☎ 642-7777; 153 Hirachimizu; ⏲ 8.30am-5.30pm, pottery making 9am-3pm) offers formal instruction (in Japanese) in pottery making. To get there, buses bound for Nishi-Zaō or Geikō-dai run hourly or half-hourly from stop 5 outside Yamagata station to the Hirashimizu stop (¥200, 15 minutes).

Festivals & Events

Hanagasa Matsuri In early August; features large crowds of dancers wearing *hanagasa* (flower-laden straw hats) and singing folk songs.

Yamagata International Documentary Film Festival (www.yidff.jp) This biennial event takes place over one week in October, and screens films from over 70 countries screen, along with retrospectives, symposiums and a Japanese panorama.

Sleeping & Eating

Tōyoko Inn Yamagata Eki Nishiguchi (東横イン山形駅西口; ☎ 644-1045; 1-18-13 Jōnan-machi; s/d ¥5250/7770; 💻) Business hotels cluster around the JR Yamagata station, but this is the best value for your money. Just a minute's walk from the station's west exit, this reliable chain offers the standard-issue Japanese business hotel room. LAN cable internet available.

Hotel Metropolitan Yamagata (ホテルメトロポリタン山形; ☎ 628-1111; fax 628-1166; www.jrhotelgroup.com/eng/hotel/eng108.htm; 1-1-1 Kasumicho; s/d ¥10,972/19,635; 💻 📶) A more upmarket option is this notable business hotel that is conveniently squashed between the station and the S-PAL shopping centre. LAN cable internet available.

Sakaeya Honten (栄屋本店; ☎ 623-0766; 2-3-21 Honchō; hiyashi rāmen ¥700; 🕒 11.30am-7.30pm Thu-Tue) A tasty Yamagata specialty is *hiyashi rāmen* (chilled soup noodles), and it is served up in huge doses here. Facing east from the AZ store, take the first side street to your right.

Getting There & Away

There are several hourly trains on the JR Yamagata and Tōhoku *shinkansen* lines between Tokyo and Yamagata (¥11,030, three hours) via Yonezawa (¥2060, 35 minutes). There are also frequent *kaisoku* on the JR Senzan line between Yamagata and Sendai (¥1110, 1¼ hours), and between Yamagata and Yamadera (¥230, 20 minutes). Finally, there are regular *futsū* on the JR Ōu line between Yamagata and Yonezawa (¥820, 45 minutes), and between Yamagata and Tendo (¥230, 20 minutes).

There are a few buses each day between the JR Yamagata station and Tsuruoka (¥2400, 1¾ hours), and between Yamagata and Zaō Onsen (¥860, 40 minutes).

TENDŌ 天童

☎ 023 / pop 62,000

Tendō, an interesting half-day excursion from Yamagata, produces around 90% of Japan's chess pieces annually. This exquisite art was started by poor samurai during the Edo period, who had fallen upon hard times after their salaries were cut by the Tendō lord.

The **tourist information centre** (天童市観光物産協会; ☎ 653-1680; 🕒 9am-6pm, closed every 3rd Mon), on the 2nd floor of JR Tendō station, has details of local attractions, including the eccentric **Tendō Mingeikan** (天童民芸館; ☎ 653-5749; admission ¥500; 🕒 9am-5pm), a folk craft museum housed in a *gasshō-zukuri* (thatched 'praying' roof) farmhouse. The **Tendō Shōgi Museum** (天童市将棋資料館; ☎ 653-1690; 1-1-1 Hon-chō; admission ¥300; 🕒 9am-6pm Thu-Tue) is part of JR Tendō station and displays chess sets from Japan and abroad.

You can see chess pieces being made at **Eishundō** (栄春堂; ☎ 653-2843; 1-3-28 Kamatahonchō; admission free; 🕒 8am-6pm Wed-Mon), a 15-minute walk straight out from the station, just past the Tendō Park Hotel. Across the street, the **Hiroshige Art Museum** (広重美術館; ☎ 654-6555; 1-2-1 Kamatahonchō; admission ¥600; 🕒 8.30am-5.30pm Wed-Mon Apr-Oct, 9am-4.30pm Wed-Mon Nov-Mar) displays wood-block prints by famous Edo-period master Hiroshige.

On the last weekend in April, Tendō-kōen hosts the theatrical **Ningen Shōgi**, when outdoor chess matches are played using real people as pieces.

There are regular *futsū* on the JR Ōu line between Yamagata and Tendō (¥820, 45 minutes).

ZAŌ ONSEN 蔵王温泉

☎ 023 / pop 14,000

The centrepiece of Zaō Quasi National Park, Zaō Onsen is a small hot-springs town with some of the best skiing in the region. While there are bigger and badder runs further north in Hokkaidō, Zaō Onsen is famous for its 'snow monsters', which are huge conifers that have been frozen solid by Siberian winds. Other times of the year, Zaō attracts visitors with great hiking opportunities, a relaxed atmosphere, and – of course – the chance to soak in the *dai-rotemburo*, a tub so big that it can literally hold hundreds of bathers.

Orientation & Information

Near Zaō bus terminal, the **tourist information office** (☎ 694-9328; 🕒 9am-5.30pm) can advise on accommodation, skiing and transport options. Zaō has a complex network of 14 ski runs and more than 30 chairlifts – pick up *The Skier's Guide* (in Japanese), which has colourful maps to help you get your bearing.

Skiing starts in December and runs through April, while the *dai-rotemburo* is open from May to October.

Sights & Activities

SKIING & SNOWBOARDING

Zaō may be relatively small, but there is plenty here for beginner and intermediate skiers, in addition to a few challenging black-diamond runs. Regardless of your level, you're primarily

> **SKIING**
>
> For wo stats, maps and reviews, check out www.snowjapan.com/e/index.php.
>
> - **Bandai Plateau** (p519)
> - **Tazawa-ko** (p550)
> - **Zaō Onsen** (p563)
> - **Myōkō Kōgen** (p570)
> - **Naeba p576**
> - **Echigo-Yuzawa Onsen** (p576)

here to ski or (snowboard) through fields of snow monsters, which at times can be a truly surreal experience. Snow monsters are at their best in February, and reach their greatest density in the **Juhyō Kōgen** (樹氷高原) or 'Ice Monster Plateau.'

One-day passes start at ¥4800, and grant you access to the slopes and lifts as well as the free shuttle buses running between them. The **Zaō-san Ropeway** (蔵王山ロープウェイ; one way/return ¥750/1400; ⏲ 8.30am-5pm), a 10-minute walk southeast of the bus station, runs to Juhyō-kōgen, providing a bird's-eye view of the snow monsters. Note that passes do not cover the ropeways or the sky cable.

HIKING

In the summer, you can hike up to **Okama** (御釜), a volcanic crater of shimmering cobalt blue that sits atop Zaō-san. Hiking around the lake is a joy, with Buddhist statues and monuments hidden among the greenery.

The most convenient access is via Katta Chūsha-jōcar park, where the **Zaō Sky Cable** (蔵王スカイケーブル; one way/return ¥750/1200; ⏲ 8.30am-5pm) takes you to within spitting distance of the Okama overlook.

ONSEN

In the winter, onsen action is a private affair that takes place either back at the hotel, or at several small bathhouses scattered around the town. In the summer, however, hikers congregate en masse for a soak at the **Zaō Onsen Dai-rotenburo** (蔵王温泉大露天風呂; admission ¥450; ⏲ 6am-7pm May-Oct), where each outdoor hot-spring pool can hold up to 200 people. The sulphur-stained rocks set the stage for the spectacle that is hundreds of complete strangers bathing naked together.

Sleeping & Eating

Accommodation abounds, but advance reservations are essential if visiting during the ski season or on weekends in summer. If you speak Japanese, it pays to call ahead – alternatively, have tourist information phone around for a vacancy.

Ginrei Honten (銀嶺本店; ☎ 694-9120; www.community-i.com/zao/ginrey.html; 940-5 Zaō Onsen; r per person with/without meals ¥6500/3500; Ⓟ) A great budget option offering simple rooms with shared facilities, this casual *minshuku* is run by welcoming owners dedicated to fostering a warm, communal atmosphere. Find it by going right from the bus station, cross the bridge and it's on the right corner, just before a large hotel car park.

Lodge Chitoseya (ロッジちとせや; ☎ 694-9145; fax 694-9145; 954 Zaō Onsen; r per person with/without 2 meals from ¥6825/4515; Ⓟ 💻) Right near the bus station, this relaxed lodge is also very budget-friendly, and attracts a youthful crowd of skiers and hikers. You'll also eat very well here as the delightful couple in charge serve up original meals that are a mix of Japanese-inspired and fusion favourites.

Pension Boku-no-Uchi (ペンションぼくのうち; ☎ 694-9542; www.bokunouchi.com; 904 Zaō Onsen; r per person incl 2 meals from ¥7200; Ⓟ) Next to the Lawson convenience store, this family-run place is the perfect compromise between Western and Japanese-style accommodation. Guests can scrub down in the 24-hour sulphur bath, take their meals in the ski lodge-esque dining room and then turn down for the night in the inviting tatami rooms.

our pick **Takamiya** (高見屋; ☎ 694-9333; fax 694-2166; www.zao.co.jp/takamiya; 54 Zaō Onsen; r per person incl 2 meals from ¥15,900; Ⓟ) There is no shortage of upmarket ryokan in town, though Takamiya gets our pick for its emphasis on the classics. Meals are incredibly opulent *kaiseki ryōri* (traditional Japanese formal banquet served in multiple courses) affairs that span a couple of hours, while intimate bathing takes places in one of several nostalgic onsen that are hundreds of years old. Rooms vary according to price, though each one is an artful blend of antique rustic stylings with carefully placed modern flourishes.

Shinzaemon-no-Yu (新左衛門の湯; ☎ 693-1212; www.zaospa.co.jp/top.html; 905 Kawa-mae Zaō Onsen; bath ¥600, meals from ¥1500; ⏲ onsen 10am-9.30pm, lunch & dinner, closed irregularly) Luxurious bath-cum-banquet – come here to soak those ski pains away, and then feast on the winter warmer that is *shabu-shabu* (thin slices of beef boiled in water with fresh vegetables; ¥3600) in simple, natural-wood elegance. The restaurant occupies a traditional wooden building across from the ropeway.

Getting There & Away

Frequent hourly buses run between the bus terminal in Zaō Onsen and the JR Yamagata station (¥860, 40 minutes). To cope with the demand during winter – when there are more than a million visitors to the region – night buses depart Tokyo's Hamamatsuchō station at 10pm, arrive in Zaō the next morning at around 6.30am, and head back to Tokyo at 2pm (return ¥9500).

YAMADERA 山寺

☎ 023 / pop 1500

> Stillness, seeps into the stones, the cry of cicadas.
> Matsuo Bashō, *The Narrow Road to the Deep North (1689)*

The stunning temple complex of **Risshaku-ji** (立石寺; ⏲ 8am-5pm; admission ¥300), more commonly known as Yamadera, is an atmospheric cluster of buildings and shrines perched on lush and wooded slopes. Founded in AD 860 by priests who carried with them the sacred flame from Enryaku-ji near Kyoto – supposedly the same flame is still alight today – it is believed that Yamadera's rock faces are the boundaries between this world and the next.

Each twist and turn of the mountain path holds a new place with a character all its own, though the complex is often besieged with tourists. For a measure of the meditative bliss that so inspired Bashō, visit on a day trip from Yamagata early in the morning or late afternoon.

There is a small **tourist information office** (☎ 695-2816; ⏲ 9am-5pm) near the bridge, where you can pick up English-language pamphlets.

Once you've navigated the tourist gauntlet, pass through the **San-mon** (山門) gate, and start the steep climb up hundreds of steps through the trees. At the top is the **Oku-no-in** (奥の院) or Inner Sanctuary, from where trails lead off on either side to small shrines and lookout points.

Before heading back to Yamagata, pay a visit to the **Bashō Kinenkan** (山寺芭蕉記念館; ☎ 695-2221; admission ¥400; ⏲ 9am-4.30pm, closed Mon Dec-Feb), back down in the village near the train station. This worthwhile museum exhibits scrolls and calligraphy related to Bashō's famous northern journey, as well as documentary videos of the places he visited.

There are frequent *kaisoku* on the JR Senzan line between Yamadera and Yamagata (¥230, 20 minutes).

YONEZAWA 米沢

☎ 0238 / pop 91,000

Carnivores should come here on a day trip from Yamagata to chow down on Yonezawa beef, famous for its tenderness and flavour, and arguably rivalling Kobe's own. Yonezawa is also home to the ruined 17th-century castle of the Uegugi clan, which developed the feudal town into a major centre for silk weaving.

You can pick up maps and information at the **tourist information office** (☎ 24-2965; ⏲ 8am-6pm) inside the station. Rental bicycles (per day ¥1000) are available outside, which will help you reach the outer moats of the castle, about 1km due east from the station. Alternatively, local buses bound for Shirabu Onsen depart stop 2 from outside the station, and stop at the Uesugi-jinja-mae stop (¥190, 10 minutes).

The foundations of the castle now form the boundaries of **Matsugasaki-kōen** (松ヶ崎公園), a tiny but attractive park framed by a placid moat. Inside the park is the **Uesugi Museum** (米沢市上杉博物館; ☎ 26-8001; admission ¥400; ⏲ 9am-4.30pm, closed every 4th Wed, closed Mon Dec-Mar), which displays Uesugi clan artefacts, **Uesugi-jinja** (上杉神社), a small temple dating from 1923, and the **Keishō-den**, (稽照殿; ☎ 22-3189, ⏲ 9am-4pm), a treasury displaying armour and works of art belonging to several generations of the Uesugi family.

Festivals & Events

The **Uesugi Matsuri** starts off with folk singing on 29 April and mock ceremonial preparation for battle in Matsugasaki-kōen on the evening of 2 May. The real action takes place on 3 May with a re-enactment of the titanic Battle of Kawanakajima, featuring more than 2000 participants.

Sleeping & Eating

Most visitors come to Yonezawa in the late afternoon to visit the castle, and then to gnaw on some seriously gourmet beef before returning to Yamagata.

Hotel Otowa (ホテルおとわ; ☎ 22-0124; www.hotel-otowa.com; s/tw ¥4500/8400; 💻) Just a few minutes east of the station along the main road, Otowa is a magnificent castle-like building with more than 100 years of history – it was the only inn in town not destroyed at the end of WWII.

Tokiwagyū-nikuten (登起波牛肉店; ☎ 24-5400; 2-3 Chūō; meals from ¥3500; ⏰ lunch & dinner) Yonezawa beef is on the menu everywhere, but this is the most famous place to sample the delightfully marbled meat. This Edo-period restaurant specialises in *shabu-shabu* (¥3700) and sukiyaki (¥4500). While the historic building is easy enough to spot from the street, it's located in the northern Chūō district, so have tourist information mark the location on your map.

Getting There & Away

Regular *futsū* run on the JR Ōu line between Yonezawa and Yamagata (¥820, 45 minutes).

NIIGATA-KEN 新潟県

While not technically part of Tōhoku proper, Niigata-ken serves as a wonderful steppingstone to these beautiful northern lands, and offers the full compliment of outdoor activities you'd expect to find in Northern Honshū. The onsen town of Echigo-Yuzawa was the setting for Kawabata's acclaimed novel *Snow Country*, while Myōkō Kōgen is the mother of all Tōhoku ski destinations. Of course, the star in Niigata-ken's tourism crown is undeniably the persimmon-peppered island of Sado-ga-shima, a former penal colony that is today one of the region's top outdoors destinations.

NIIGATA 新潟

☎ 025 / pop 813,900

For most travellers, the prefectural capital of Niigata is regarded as little more than a transport hub and a springboard to nearby Sado-ga-shima. Though there's little to keep you here for more than the time it takes to change trains or board a ferry, Niigata is an attractive city that is bisected by the Shinano River, which generates a great swathe of blue sky wherever you look. Niigata is also famous for the quality of its rice, seafood and sake, so be sure to treat yourself to a nice meal before pushing on.

Orientation

The Niigata JR station is in the middle of the city; much of the tourist action is between the station and the Shinano River. Higashi Ōdori is the main thoroughfare leading north from the station. Across the Bandai-bashi, Furumachi is the downtown shopping district and home to the vibrant Honchō market area.

Information

Niigata central post office (☎ 244-3429; 2-6-26 Higashi Ōdori; ⏰ 7am-11pm Mon-Fri, 9am-7pm Sat, Sun & holidays) Offers postal and ATM cash services.

Niigata International Friendship Centre (☎ 225-2777; Kurosuparu Niigata Bldg, 3-2086 Ishizuechōdōri; ⏰ 9am-9.30pm Mon-Sat, to 5pm Sun & holidays, closed every 4th Mon) Has a small library and helpful staff for general tourist information.

Niigata University Medical & Dental Hospital (☎ 223-6161; 1-757 Asahimachi-dōri)

Stock + Nigata (☎ 246-1370; www.stockplus-n.com, in Japanese; 1-2-23 Ōdōri; internet per 15min ¥157; ⏰ 9.30am-6pm Mon-Fri)

Tourist information centre (☎ 241-7914; ⏰ 9am-6pm) To the left of Niigata station's Bandai exit. The best place for information on Sado-ga-shima.

Sights

The city centre is easily covered on foot. Otherwise, a flat-rate fare of ¥180 operates on city buses. If the weather is cooperating, the banks of the Shinano-gawa serve as popular people-watching spots.

If you cross over the Shinano-gawa via Shōwa-ōhashi-bashi, you'll arrive at the **Niigata Prefectural Government Memorial Hall** (admission free; ⏰ 9am-4.30pm, closed irregularly), a beautiful old building that survived the tsunami of 1964, which destroyed much of the city. Take the buses from stop 13 at the station to Showa Ōhashi (15 minutes), in the direction of Irihonechō.

Just beyond the memorial hall is **Hakusan-kōen** (⏰ dawn-dusk), a small park containing a shrine, Hakusan-jinja, to the local god of marriage. The grounds also preserve a fine lotus pond and the historic Meiji-era tea house **Enkikan** (admission free, tea ¥300; ⏰ 9am-5pm), which was transplanted from Kyoto and reconstructed here.

The **Northern Culture Museum** (北方文化博物館; ☎ 385-2001; 2-15-25 Sōmi; admission ¥800; ⏰ 9am-5pm Apr-Nov, to 4.30pm Dec-Mar), located

10km southeast of Niigata, is set in an attractive landscaped garden complex containing traditional earthen warehouses and individual tea arbours. Buses leave roughly every hour from stop 7 at the Bandai bus centre (not the train station) for the Nishi Ohata stop outside the museum (¥500, 45 minutes).

Festivals & Events

Sake-no-jin (酒の陣) Sake aficionados won't want to miss this event, held on the third weekend each March. It's a mammoth bacchanal, highlighting over 175 different varieties of sake from all over Japan are available. *Kanpai!*

Niigata Matsuri (新潟祭り) From the first or second weekend (varies yearly) in August, the streets are filled with afternoon parades of colourful floats and shrines. At night thousands of folk dancers parade across the Bandai Bridge. A bumper fireworks display on the final night lights up the Shinano-gawa, as a passage of decorated boats carries the shrine of the local god of the sea.

Sleeping

Ueda Ryokan (☎ 225-1111; fax 225-1110; www.uedaryokan.com, in Japanese; 2120 Yonnochō; r per person with/without meals from ¥7350/3780; 💻) A pleasant alternative to all of the run-of-the-mill business hotels clustering the station exits, this basic but all-around pleasant Japanese-style inn occupies a quiet spot on the northern banks of the river. From the Lawson near the Bandai Bridge, cross Ōdōri, and follow the small side street past three intersections. When the road narrows, turn right at the next street and Ueda will be on your left, about halfway down.

Dormy Inn Niigata (☎ 247-7755; fax 247-7789; 1-7-14 Akashi; s/d from ¥4500/7350; 💻) Just a few minutes walk from the train station, across the street from the NTT Building, the Dormy Inn is pioneering a great concept for budget business hotels. Prices are kept low by offering rooms that are tight, relatively featureless and lacking in bathrooms, though guests take advantage of the fabulous onsite onsen and sauna, as well as the large and surprisingly sociable cafeteria. LAN cable internet available.

Hotel Okura Niigata (☎ 244-6111; fax 224-7060; www.okura-niigata.com/english/index.html; 53 Kawabata-cho; s/d from ¥8925/14,700; 💻 📶) Arguably the finest hotel in Niigata, the Hotel Okura has a picturesque location next to the Bandai Bridge, and offers sweeping views of the Shinano-gawa, particularly from the formal French restaurant on the 15th floor. Accommodation is in classically stylish rooms that are well decorated without being overbearing. LAN cable internet available.

Eating & Drinking

Honchō Market (本町市場; 🕑 10am-5pm, closed irregualry) If you want a feast for both the eyes and the stomach, check out this market, which occupies several pedestrian arcades running off of Masa-koji. While it's primarily a produce and seafood market, there are plenty of little hole-in-the-wall places here where you can dine on Niigata's justifiably famous cuisine.

Inakaya (☎ 223-1266; 1457 Kyūban-chō; dishes from ¥800; 🕑 lunch & dinner) A famous seafood joint that packs in blue-collar locals, Inakaya specialises in *wappa meshi* or steamed fish over rice served up in a wooden container. There is a picture menu here to help the uninitiated, though you can't go wrong as Niigata's seas are incredibly bountiful. Located on a small street in the eating district Furu-machi, Inakaya is located directly across the street from a Daily Yamazaki convenience store.

Kurumiya (☎ 290-6556; 1st fl, Tōkyū Inn, 1-2-4 Benten; dishes from ¥800; 🕑 lunch & dinner) Right next to the train station (look for the wooden English sign), this place has a comprehensive selection of local sakes, terribly tempting seafood set menus and an eclectic assortment of local and regional specialities. Ordering can be a bit tricky, so best to ask the waiter for an *osusume* (recommendation) or simply point to other diners' dishes.

Immigrant's Cafe (☎ 242-2722; www.immigrantscafe.com, 1-7-10 Higashi Ōdori; drinks from ¥600; 🕑 5.30pm-close) Catering well to local expats and internationally minded locals, this bilingual spot in the basement of the Niigata Central Building mixes light electronic beats, Mexican eats and a comprehensive drinks list to keep everyone juiced up.

Entertainment

Ryūtopia (☎ 224-5622; www.ryutopia.or.jp, in Japanese; 3-2 Ichibanbori-dōri; 🕑 9am-10pm, closed 2nd & 4th Mon of each month) The city's snazziest attraction is a major performing arts centre with a 1900-seat concert hall, a 900-seat theatre and a 400-seat *nō* (classical Japanese drama performed on a bare stage) theatre. Enquire for more details at the tourist information office.

Getting There & Away

AIR

From Niigata airport, 13km north of the city centre, domestic destinations include Tokyo, Osaka, Fukuoka and many others. For international flights, see p828. Buses run from stop 11 outside Niigata station to the airport every half-hour from 6.40am to 6.40pm (¥370, 25 minutes), while a taxi should cost around ¥2000.

BOAT

From the port of Niigata-kō, **Shin-Nihonkai** (☎ 273-2171) ferries run at 10.30am daily except Monday to Otaru on Hokkaidō (¥6200, 18 hours), returning every day except Monday. To get to Niigata-ko, take any buses bound for Rinko-nichōme from stop 3 at Niigata station – get off at Suehiro-bashi (¥200, 20 minutes). There is a small ticket office at the pier.

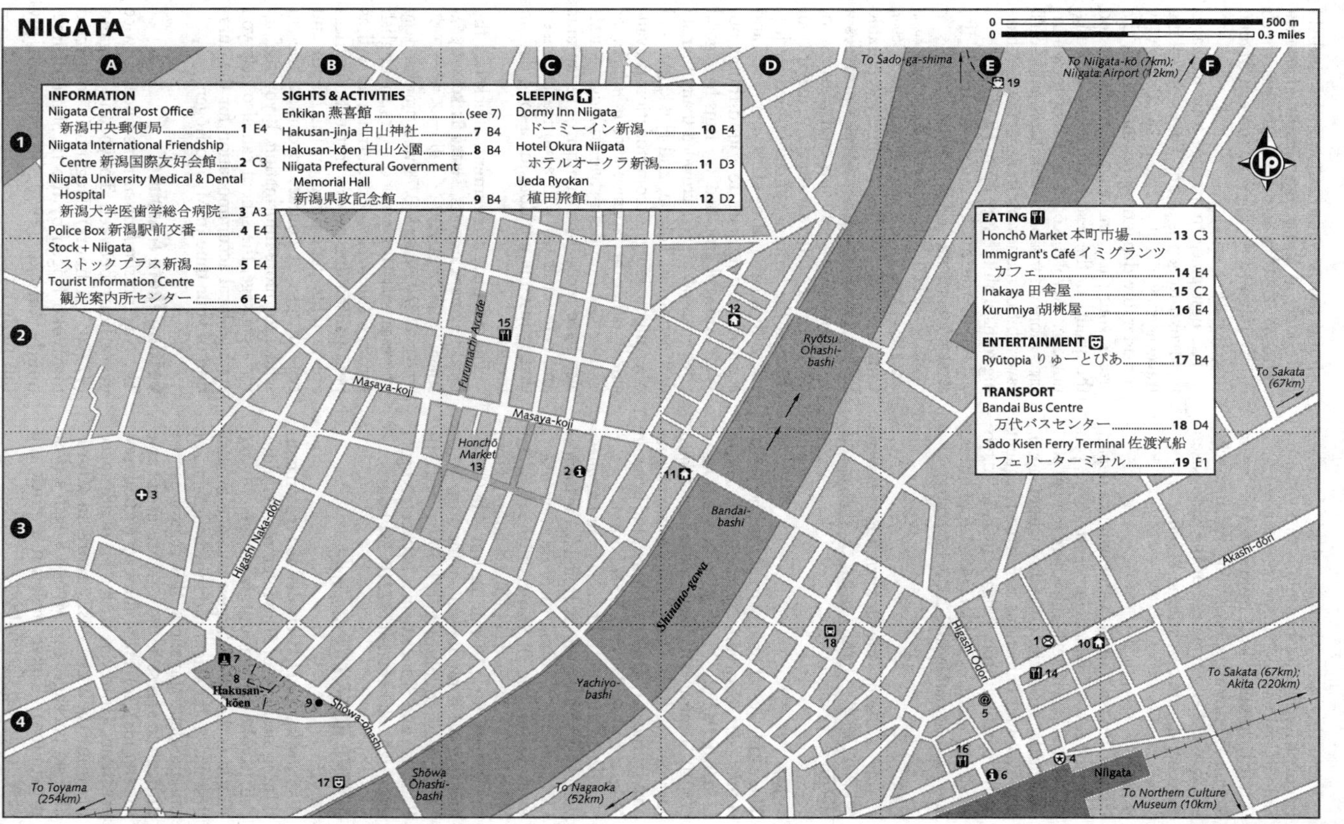
NIIGATA
INFORMATION
Niigata Central Post Office 新潟中央郵便局 1 E4
Niigata International Friendship Centre 新潟国際友好会館 2 C3
Niigata University Medical & Dental Hospital 新潟大学医歯学総合病院 3 A3
Police Box 新潟駅前交番 4 E4
Stock + Niigata ストックプラス新潟 5 E4
Tourist Information Centre 観光案内所センター 6 E4
SIGHTS & ACTIVITIES
Enkikan 燕喜館 (see 7)
Hakusan-jinja 白山神社 7 B4
Hakusan-kōen 白山公園 8 B4
Niigata Prefectural Government Memorial Hall 新潟県政記念館 9 B4
SLEEPING
Dormy Inn Niigata ドーミーイン新潟 10 E4
Hotel Okura Niigata ホテルオークラ新潟 11 D3
Ueda Ryokan 植田旅館 12 D2
EATING
Honchō Market 本町市場 13 C3
Immigrant's Café イミグランツカフェ 14 E4
Inakaya 田舎屋 15 C2
Kurumiya 胡桃屋 16 E4
ENTERTAINMENT
Ryūtopia りゅーとぴあ 17 B4
TRANSPORT
Bandai Bus Centre 万代バスセンター 18 D4
Sado Kisen Ferry Terminal 佐渡汽船フェリーターミナル 19 E1
500 m
0.3 miles
To Sado-ga-shima
To Niigata-kō (7km); Niigata Airport (12km)
To Sakata (67km)
Akashi-dōri
To Sakata (67km); Akita (220km)
To Northern Culture Museum (10km)
Niigata
Higashi Ōdori
Ryōtsu Ōhashi-bashi
Bandai-bashi
Shinano-gawa
Yachiyo-bashi
To Nagaoka (52km)
Masaya-koji
Furumachi Arcade
Honchō Market
Shōwa Ōhashi-bashi
Shōwa-ōhashi
Hakusan-kōen
Higashi Naka-dōri
To Toyama (254km)

From the Sado Kisen terminal, there are frequent ferries and hydrofoils to Ryōtsu on Sado-ga-shima (p575). Buses to the terminal (¥200, 15 minutes) leave from stop 6 at Niigata station 45 minutes before sailing. Alternatively, a taxi to either Niigata-kō or the Sado Kisen terminal should cost around ¥1200.

BUS

Niigata Transit and JR highway buses depart from the covered Bandai bus centre. Here, you will find a small ticket booth where you can purchase tickets to major cities throughout Japan. Some sample destinations, which have frequent daily departures from Niigata, include Tokyo (¥5250, six hours), Sendai (¥4500, four hours) and Aizu-Wakamatsu (¥2000, 1¾ hours).

CAR

If you're driving, the Hokuriku Expressway (北陸自動車道) runs between Tokyo and the greater Niigata area.

TRAIN

There are several hourly trains on the Jōetsu *shinkansen* between Niigata and Tokyo (¥10,070, 2¼ hours) via Echigo-Yuzawa Onsen (¥5040, 50 minutes). There are also a few *tokkyū* each day on the JR Uetsu line between Niigata and Tsuruoka (¥4130, 1¾ hours), and between Niigata and Akita (¥6820, 3¾ hours).

For accessing the port of Naoetsu-kō, where you can grab a ferry or hydrofoil to the town of Ogi on Sado-ga-Shima, there are a few *tokkyū* each day on the JR Shinetsu line between Niigata and Naoetsu (¥4300, 1¾ hours). From the station, it's a 10-minute bus ride (¥160) and then a 15-minute walk to the port.

There are couple of daily *kaisoku* on the JR Bansetsu and Shinetsu lines between Niigata and Aizu-Wakamatsu (¥2210, 2¾ hours).

MYŌKŌ KŌGEN 妙高高原

☎ 0255

A sprawling and loosely defined region containing more than 50 winter resorts along the Myōkō-shi mountain range, Myōkō Kōgen is the area's largest package-holiday destination for skiers and snowboarders. For independent travellers, this region can be difficult to access as most resorts aren't able to cater for guests who show up without reservations. However, with a bit of advanced planning, you can easily score an affordable ski package, and Myōkō Kōgen's close proximity to Tokyo makes it a quick and easy-to-access destination.

Local tourist information, maps and ski reports are at **Myōkō Kōgen Tourist Information** (☎ 86-3911; 291-1 Ōaza Taguchi; 8.30am-6pm), which is just 100m to the right as you exit Myōkō Kōgen station.

The best place to arrange tour packages to Myōkō Kōgen is at any English-speaking travel agency in Tokyo (see p126). Prices vary considerably depending on the season, the size of your party, the length of your stay and the quality of the resort. Generally speaking, however, Myōkō Kōgen is one of the country's more affordable destinations, and you'll save a bit of money on transport by not having to haul all the way up to Hokkaidō.

One of the most famous resorts is the **Myōkō Suginohara Sukī-jō** (妙高杉の原スキー場; ☎ 86-6211; http://ski.princehotels.co.jp/myoko, in Japanese; r per person incl meals & lift ticket from ¥9600), which is run by the extremely reputable Prince Hotel chain. Mt Myōkō provides a towering backdrop to this enormous resort, which has 17 different runs, the majority of them at the beginner and intermediate levels, with a handful of black diamonds and a snowboarding park to round things off. Wide and well groomed, the runs have good powder snow, are less crowded than other ski destinations in Tōhoku and Hokkaidō, and offer night skiing. Accommodation is available in either the Japanese-style *minshuku*, or in the more European-style ski lodge. Guests also have access to a number of restaurants and cafe-terias, as well as a nearby onsen that is just the antidote for a long day on the trails.

For off-piste excitement, check out the local telemark experts, **Myōkō Backcountry Ski School** (妙高バックカントリースキースクール; ☎ 87-2392; fax 87-3278; www.myokokogen.org/mbss/english.php) for guided tours in English through the backwoods terrain, as well as personalised one-on-one instruction. Prices are variable depending on the length and type of tour or course, so contact the ski school for more information. If you sign up for a package, the school can also help you arrange local accommodation for the duration of your time in Myōkō Kōgen.

Getting There & Around

The Nagano *shinkansen* runs once or twice every hour between Tokyo and Nagano (¥7770, 1¾ hours). Nagano is connected to Myōkō Kōgen by the JR Shinetsu line; hourly *kaisoku* (¥960, 45 minutes) ply this route.

From Myōkō Kōgen JR station, shuttle buses run to the various ski resorts. If you have your own car, there is a network of narrow but decent roads running along the Myōkō-shi mountain range.

SADO-GA-SHIMA 佐渡島

☎ 0259 / pop 69,500

Japan's sixth-largest island, Sado-ga-shima has always been something of a far-flung destination, albeit not always a voluntary one. During the feudal era, Sado-ga-shima was a notorious penal colony where out-of-favour intellectuals were forever banished. The illustrious list of former prisoners includes Emperor Juntoku, *nō* master Ze-Ami, and Nichiren, the founder of one of Japan's most influential Buddhist sects. When gold was discovered near the village of Aikawa in 1601, there was a sudden influx of gold-diggers, who were often vagrants press-ganged from the mainland and made to work like slaves.

Despite this history of ill repute, Sado is now one of Tōhoku's top tourist destinations. Compared to Honshū, the island is relatively undeveloped, and is characterised by rugged natural beauty and eccentric reminders of its rich and evocative past. While a good number of hikers descend on the island in the warmer months, crowds peak during the third week in August for the three-day Earth Celebration, which is headlined by the world-famous Kodo Drummers.

SIGHTS & ACTIVITIES

- Aikawa Kyōdo Hakubutsukan 相川郷土博物館 1 A3
- Kokubun-ji 国分寺 2 B3
- Konpon-ji 根本寺 3 B3
- Mano Go-ryō 真野御陵 4 A3
- Myōsen-ji 妙宣寺 5 A3
- Sado Kinzan Gold Mine 佐渡金山 6 A3
- Sado Nōgaku-no-sato 佐渡能楽の里 7 B3
- Sado Rekishi Densetsukan 佐渡歴史伝承館 8 A3

SLEEPING

- Green Village グリーンビレッジ 9 B3
- Kunimisō 国見荘 10 B3
- Minshukū Sakaya 民宿 さかや 11 A4
- Sado Belle Mer Youth Hostel 佐渡ベルメールユースホステル 12 A2
- Sado Seaside Hotel 佐渡 シーサイドホテル 13 B2
- Silver Village Sado シルバービレッジ佐渡 14 A1
- Sotokaifu Youth Hostel 外海府ユースホステル 15 B1
- Tōkaen 桃華園 16 A2

Even if you're not an avid hiker, Sado is still an alluring destination of incredible rural beauty. Framed by mountainous backdrops, vast orchards of persimmon trees stretch across cultivated fields, while small fishing villages bustle with life along the rocky shores of the Sea of Japan. Wind your way across ocean-side roads and lofty mountain passes, and pause to soak up panoramic vistas of old Japan, much of which have long since disappeared from the mainland.

Sado is a large island home to southern and northern mountain ranges that run parallel and are separated by a vast fertile plain. Small fishing villages dot the island's ring road, though much of

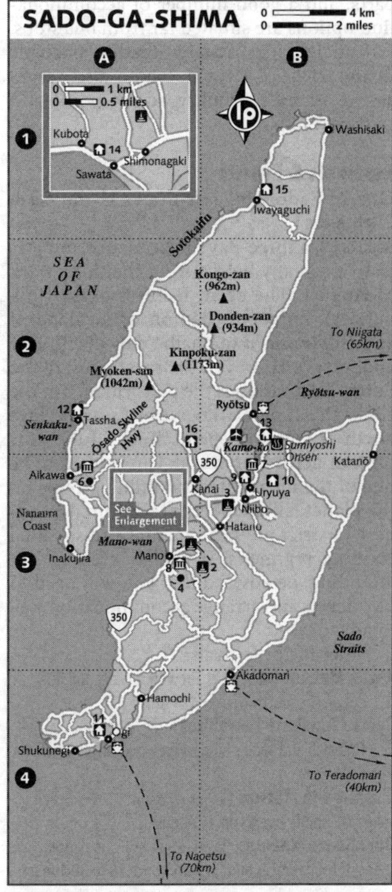

the population is confined to the central agricultural region.

The best time to visit is between late April and mid-October. During the harsh winter, the weather will be foul, much of the accommodation will be closed and transport will be slashed to a bare minimum.

Sado is well furnished with guest houses, youth hostels and camping, though booking accommodation in advance is a good idea during the hectic summer months. Ask the tourist information offices for help if necessary as only a few of the many options are listed here.

While there is a comprehensive and fairly regular bus network between major towns on Sado-ga-shima, you really need a private vehicle to access the island's most scenic parts, and a good number of accommodation options are situated far from bus stops. Fortunately, car rental is readily available in the town of Ryōtsu, which also serves as the island's primary access point and transport hub.

Festivals & Events

One of Sado's biggest draws is the **Earth Celebration** (アースセレブレーション; www.kodo.or.jp), a three-day music, dance and arts festival usually held during the third week in August. The event features *okesa* (folk dances), *onidaiko* (demon drum dances) and *tsuburosashi* (a phallic dance with two goddesses). However, the focal point of the Earth Celebration is the performance of the Kodo Drummers, who live in a small village north of Ogi, but spend much of the year on tour across the world. Considered to be one of the most elite drumming groups on the planet, all members are required to adhere to strict physical, mental and spiritual training regimens. If you're interested in attending, be advised that you will need to buy tickets and arrange accommodation well in advance.

Other major festivals:

Kōzan Matsuri (鉱山祭) Fireworks, *okesa* and float parades on the fourth weekend of July.

Ryōtsu Tanabata Kawabiraki (両津七夕・川開き) Onidaiko and Sado's biggest fireworks display, held on 7 and 8 August.

Shishi-ga-jō Matsuri (獅子ケ城まつり) Beach volleyball and fireworks on 11 August.

Ogi Minato Matsuri (小木港祭り) Lion dances, folk songs, tub-boat races and fireworks from 28 to 30 August.

Ryōtsu & Around 両津

Considering that Ryōtsu is essentially a port town, Sado's main hub is surprisingly beautiful, and serves as an excellent introduction to the rustic splendour of the island. While there isn't too much here in the way of sights, Ryōtsu is where you can get your bearings, make onward arrangements and get a good night's rest.

The island's main **tourist information centre** (☎ 23-3300; ⌚ 8.30am-5pm, to 6.50pm Jun-Aug) is in Ryōtsu, in the street behind the coffee and souvenir shops across from the ferry terminal. Be sure to stock up on comprehensive maps, bus timetables and tourist pamphlets for the entire island.

Check internet at tiny **Clever Cat** (☎ 23-3158; 138-1 Minato; 30min incl 1 drink from ¥500; ⌚ 10am-9pm Wed-Mon), near the ferry terminal.

A nice introduction to the island's ancient culture is the **Sado Nōgaku-no-sato** (☎ 23-5000; ⌚ 8.30am-5pm; admission ¥500), about 3km out of Ryōtsu; it's a hi-tech museum of *nō* drama, with displays of masks and costumes as well as performances of *nō* enacted by a cast of animatronic actors. A few kilometres further west is **Konpon-ji** (admission ¥300; ⌚ 8am-4pm), a temple that occupies the location where Nichiren was first brought when exiled to Sado in 1271. Any bus on the Minami line between Ryōtsu and Sawata can drop you off at the Nōgaku-no-sato-mae and Konpon-ji-mae bus stops.

Kunimisō (☎ 22-2316; Niibo-Shomyōji; per person incl 2 meals from ¥7000; Ⓟ) is one of Sado's most popular *minshuku*, due to its collection of *bunya* puppets, which the owner likes to demonstrate to guests. It's 15 minutes by bus from Ryōtsu to the Uryūya bus stop, then a long walk along a country road to this small house (follow signs). Alternatively, phone ahead for a pick-up from the ferry terminal, or get directions from tourist information if you're driving.

Located about 2km from Ryōtsu at Sumiyoshi Onsen (look for the large white building), **Sado Seaside Hotel** (☎ 27-7211; fax 27-2713; http://sadoseasidehotel.yuyado.net, in Japanese; 80 Sumiyoshi; s/d from ¥5925/10,800, breakfast/dinner ¥840/1575; Ⓟ 💻) is a Western-style drive-up motel with sea-view rooms, an attractive onsen, free internet and an obliging free shuttle service to and from the port.

Small restaurants and cafes line Ryōtsu's main street, and feature seasonal specialities from the sea. Persimmons are also everywhere, and *hoshi-gaki* (dried winter persimmon) is a common food, even appearing in the traditional *yōkan* (bean jelly) sweets – some flecked with real gold.

For detailed transport information on accessing Ryōtsu and Sado-ga-shima by ferry, see p575.

Sawata & Around 佐和田

Some 15km southwest of Ryōtsu, Sawata serves as the island's main administrative and population centre. With the cessation of Kyokushin Air in early 2008, the airport is looking a bit forlorn these days, though the town itself is still a relaxed and pleasant base for exploring the island.

Near the bus terminal in Sawata, **Silver Village Sado** (☎ 52-3961; fax 52-3963; 981-3 Kubotahama; r incl 2 meals from ¥7500; P 💻) is a centrally located resort hotel with a low-key ambiance, manicured grounds and country-comfort inspired Western rooms. The Silver Village also stages traditional puppet performances (¥750; open to nonguests) on a daily basis during the summer tourist season.

One of our favourite spots on the island is the OUR PICK **Green Village** (☎ 22-2719; www.e-sadonet.tv/~gvyh/eng/index.html; 750-4 Niibo Uryuya; s/d from ¥4100/7200, meals ¥700-1500; P 💻), an adorable little cottage that looks like it was scooped up from some far-flung European hamlet, and plopped down in the middle of Sado. The wonderfully accommodating hosts can help you arrange all manners of activities, and stuff you full of home-baked apple pie before sending you on your way. From Ryōtsu, regular buses on the Minami line heading towards Sawata can drop you off at the Uryūya stop, from where you need to continue for 10 minutes and turn left at the first bend. If you tell the driver you're going to Green Village, he'll drop you off a bit closer.

A great little *minshuku* is **Tōkaen** (☎ 63-2221; fax 61-1051; www.on.rim.or.jp/~toukaen, in Japanese; 1636-1 Otsu; s with/without 2 meals from ¥8400/4200; P), which has an attractive but isolated location in the middle of the central plains. However, it's a nice escape, especially since the owners are avid outdoors folk who know every trail on the island, and will let you unwind in their *shiogama-buro* (rock-salt bath) at the end of a long, hard day. Any bus on the Hon line between Ryōtsu and Aikawa via Kanai can drop you off at the Shinbo Undōkōen-mae stop, from where it's another 3km north on foot. Again, if you tell the driver you're going to Tōkaen, he'll drop you off a bit closer.

Regular buses run on the Minami line run between Ryōtsu and Sawata (¥570, 40 minutes), and on the Hon line between Aikawa and Sawata (¥390, 20 minutes).

Mano & Around 真野

Although Mano was the provincial capital and cultural centre of the island from early times until the 14th century, it has since played younger sibling to nearby Sawata. However, a vast wealth of historical attractions is located in the countryside surrounding this tiny and unpretentious village.

Mano's **tourist information office** (☎ 55-3589; 🕑 9am-5.30pm Apr-Oct), located at the junction of Rtes 350 and 65, can provide information on hikes and temples in the near vicinity.

The entrance to a peaceful 7km-long nature trail is located just west of Konpon-ji along the Minami bus route between Ryōtsu and Sawata, near the Danpū-jōbus stop. From the trailhead, it's a short walk to **Myōsen-ji** (admission free; 🕑 9am-4pm), which was founded by one of Nichiren's disciples, and features a distinctive five-storey pagoda.

The trail then passes through rice fields and up old wooden steps set into the hillside to **Kokubun-ji** (admission free; 🕑 8am-4pm), Sado-ga-shima's oldest temple, dating from AD 741. Another 3km takes you past marvellous lookout points to **Mano Go-ryō**, the tomb of Emperor Juntoku.

From there, it's a short walk down to **Sado Rekishi Densetsukan** (☎ 55-2525; admission ¥700; 🕑 8am-5.30pm Apr-Nov, to 5pm Dec-Mar), where more tireless robots illustrate dioramas of Sado's history and festivals. Next door is **Mano-gū**, a small shrine dedicated to Emperor Juntoku. It's a 15-minute walk back to the main road.

Regular buses run on the Minami line between Mano and Ryōtsu (¥630, 45 minutes), and between Mano and Sawata (¥260, 13 minutes). There are also regular buses between Mano and Ogi (¥810, 50 minutes).

Ogi 小木

Although it's the famed home of the Kodo Drummers, Ogi is little more than a minor port that sees much less ferry traffic than

Ryōtsu. During the Earth Celebration, Ogi does become something of a heaving metropolis, though for the rest of the year it's a drowsy village, home to some unique tourist attractions.

The **tourist office** (☎ 86-3200; 🕑 9am-5.30pm Apr-Oct) is a few minutes' walk west of the bus terminal.

For Japanese visitors, Ogi is famous for its *taraibune,* which are boats made from huge barrels that are rowed by women in traditional fisher folk costumes. In the olden days, they were used for collecting shellfish, though today they're mainly used for giving **rides** (¥450, 10 minutes, from 8.30am to 4.30pm) to tourists. Tickets are available at the marine terminal.

If you want to cover a bit more ground, you can take a **sightseeing boat** (¥1400, 45 minutes, from 8.30am to 4.30pm April to November) on a circle tour that runs from the marine terminal to the Sawa-zaki lighthouse and back.

For travellers who are more independent, the coastal areas in these parts are riddled with remote caves and coves, which can be accessed either by bike or rental car.

If you're catching a ferry back to Honshū, the **Minshukū Sakaya** (☎ 86-2535; fax 86-2145; 1991 Ogi-chō; r per person incl 2 meals ¥7350; Ⓟ) is conveniently located just a few minutes' walk east of the Ogi ferry terminal. It's a fairly basic and unassuming spot, but the seafood dinners are delicious and the staff is delightful.

While it's certainly a bit bleak from the exterior, the five-storey **Hotel New Kihachiya** (ホテルニュー喜八屋; ☎ 86-3131; www.kihachiya.com, in Japanese; 1935-21 Ogi-chō; r per person incl meals from ¥10,000; Ⓟ 💻) in the centre of town is a surprisingly upmarket spot. Large and lovely Japanese- and Western-style rooms – some with sea views – are complemented by a sparkling onsen and a large dining room hosting nightly formal feasts.

Regular buses run on the Ogi line between Ogi and Sawata (¥910, 1¼ hours) via Mano (¥810, 50 minutes).

For detailed transport information on accessing Ogi and Sado-ga-shima by ferry, see opposite.

Aikawa 相川

From a tiny hamlet, Aikawa grew almost overnight into a 100,000-person boomtown when gold was discovered nearby in 1601. Private mining amidst some incredibly rough and rugged conditions continued until the end of the Edo period. Today, this dwindling town is a fraction of its former size and significance.

There's a small **tourist information centre** (☎ 74-2220; 🕑 9am-5.30pm Apr-Oct) beside the bus terminal.

From Aikawa bus terminal, it's a 40-minute walk up a steep mountain (buses run occasionally in the high season) to the bountiful **Sado Kinzan Gold Mine** (☎ 74-2389; 1305 Shimoaikawa; admission ¥700; 🕑 8am-5pm Apr-Oct, 8.30am-4.30pm Nov-Mar), which produced large quantities of gold and silver until its demise in 1989. Descend into the chilly depths where you'll encounter robots that dramatise the tough existence of former miners. A further 300m up the mountain is Dōyū-no-Wareto, the original opencast mine where you can still see the remains of the workings.

It takes around 30 minutes to return on foot down the mountain road to Aikawa. On the way you'll pass several temples and **Aikawa Kyōdo Hakubutsukan** (☎ 74-4312; Sakashita Machi; admission ¥300; 🕑 8.30am-5pm), a folk museum with more exhibits putting face and shape to the old mine town.

Along the town's southern waterfront is the **Hotel Ōsado** (ホテル大佐渡; ☎ 74-3300; www.oosado.com; 288-2 Aikawakabuse; r per person incl meals from ¥9000; Ⓟ 💻), where you can soak up sunsets over the Sea of Japan while you soak away in a *rotemburo*. Accommodation is in a variety of different Western- and Japanese-style rooms, the best of which are also awash with ocean views.

Regular buses run on the Nanaura Kaigan line between Aikawa and Ryōtsu (¥780, one hour) via Sawata (¥390, 20 minutes).

Sotokaifu 外海府

Known as Sotokaifu, Sado's rugged northern coast is a dramatic landscape of sheer sea cliffs dropping off into deep blue waters. Roads are narrow and windy, which lead to both harrowing bus rides and exhilarating coastal drives. Indeed, this is one area in Sado where having a rental car will make a big difference.

In order to truly appreciate the beauty of the region, you're going to have to head out into the bay. During the summer months, glass-bottom boats depart from the village of **Tassha** (達者), and embark on a 30-minute cruise of **Senkaku-wan** (尖閣湾, ¥850).

ROCK FESTIVALS IN JAPAN *Simon Bartz*

Music lovers head to Japan in late July for the **Fuji Rock Festival** (www.fujirockfestival.com). There's no better location than the ski resort in Naeba, Niigata Prefecture: mountains rise on both sides of a forested valley, littered with several stages. Here you'll find foreign and home-grown rock, hip-hop, experimental jazz, techno, punk and reggae, all just a two-hour train ride from Tokyo.

More than 100,000 people attend Fuji Rock, and most camp up on a mountain as accommodation tends to be booked out. What to bring? You won't need your skis so much as some sunscreen and, yes, sturdy boots. Most years see two days of blue skies and sun followed by rain. You may find yourself swimming in mud.

Held in late September, the two-day **Asagiri Jam** (www.asagirijams.org, in Japanese) festival is perhaps more deserving of the name 'Fuji Rock Festival' – it's located in the beautiful foothills that surround Mt Fuji. Asagiri Jam is low-key, and the line-up isn't announced beforehand. The emphasis is more on creating a good vibe rather than pulling in big names. Dub, techno, jazz and, of course, rock are featured. There are no hotels around here, so bring a tent or stay up all night.

The two-day **Summer Sonic** (www.summersonic.com, in Japanese) draws major international acts and is held during early August in Chiba, next to Tokyo, and Osaka. Chiba's line-up plays the next day in Osaka, and vice-versa.

Then there's the three-day **Rock in Japan** (www.rock-net.jp, in Japanese) festival, set in acres of green fields in Ibaraki Prefecture, a two-hour train ride from Tokyo. In many ways, this festival epitomises the Japanese music scene today – all performers are Japanese – and it spans J-Pop stars to ageing crooners.

There are some wonderful youth hostels along this stretch of coast. In the fishing village of **Iwayaguchi** (岩谷口), just south of the bus stop, you'll find the **Sotokaifu Youth Hostel** (☎ 78-2911; fax 78-2931; 131 Iwayaguchi; dm from ¥3360, breakfast/dinner ¥760/1260; Ⓟ), which is a traditional Sado-style house that has been converted into a very chilled-out accommodation spot.

Another great option is the **Sado Belle Mer Youth Hostel** (☎ 75-2011; http://sado.bellemer.jp, in Japanese; 369-4 Himezu; dm from ¥3360, breakfast/dinner ¥760/1260; Ⓟ), a more modern building that is scenically perched near the shore about five-minutes on foot from the Minami-Himezu bus stop.

A few daily buses run on the Kaifu line between Iwayaguchi and Aikawa (¥1010, 70 minutes).

Getting There & Away

Sado Kisen (☎ 03-5390-0550) passenger ferries and hydrofoils run between Niigata and Ryōtsu. There are up to six regular ferries daily (one way from ¥3170, 2½ hours). As many as 10 jetfoils zip across daily in merely an hour (one way/return ¥6340/11,490), but service is greatly reduced between December and February. Before embarking, you need to buy a ticket from the vending machines and to fill in a white passenger ID form.

From Naoetsu-kō, about 90km southwest of Niigata, there are ferry and hydrofoil services to Ogi, in the southwest part of Sado-ga-shima. Between April and late November, there are four or more ferry departures daily (2½ hours) and two hydrofoils (one hour). During the rest of the year, the hydrofoil service is suspended, and ferries run only twice daily. Fares are the same as for the Niigata–Ryōtsu service. From JR Naoetsu station, it's a 10-minute bus ride (¥160) and then a 15-minute walk to the port.

Getting Around

Local buses are fine on the main routes, though services to other parts of the island are often restricted to two or three a day, and sharply restricted in the winter.

To explore less-touristed areas, car rental is desirable. There are numerous car-rental firms close to the Ryōtsu terminal; rates start from ¥7000/9000 per day/24 hours. Tell the proprietor your plan, as construction, unpassable bridges or snow may mean the map's routes are unavailable.

If you plan to make extended use of local buses, there's an English-language timetable available from the ferry terminals and tourist information offices. The ¥2000 unlimited-ride bus pass, also in English, is a good-value option valid for two consecutive days on weekends only.

Cycling is an enjoyable way to get off the beaten track. Bicycle rental is available at various locations in all major towns (per day ¥400 to ¥1500).

NAEBA 苗場

☎ 025

Home to the Fuji Rock Festival and some of Tōhoku's best skiing, Naeba is a little town with a lot going on.

Naeba is also connected to the ski resort **Tashiro** (田代) by one of the world's longest gondolas (5481m!), which means that you sort of get two ski resorts for the price of one. The **Dragondola** (トラゴンドラ; return ¥2000), as it is called, can speed up to eight people to dry, light powder that makes for great trips down the slopes for skiers of all skill levels. Snowboarders will also want to check out the biggest half-pipe within a day's trip from Tokyo. Unfortunately, due to Naeba's proximity to Tokyo, you may find long waits in lift lines and at the restaurants.

If you come in late July, the **Fuji Rock Festival** (www.fujirockfestival.com; admission from ¥42,000) is three-days of musical madness – like Woodstock, only with toilets and less mud – and up to 100,000 people show up to hang out, listen to great bands and enjoy the party atmosphere. While pricey, it's like a trip to J-Mecca for music lovers.

All of the action in Naeba centres around the **Prince Hotel Naeba** (プリンスホテル苗場; ☎ 789-2211; fax 789-3140; www.princehotels.co.jp/naeba; San-goku; r per person incl 2 meals & lift ticket from ¥14,000; P 💻), a monolithic ski resort that caters to your every whim and fancy, offering a range of luxury rooms and suites adjacent to a whole slew of restaurants and upmarket facilities. Prices vary considerably, and advanced reservations are essential. The best place to arrange tour packages is at any English-speaking travel agency in Tokyo (see p126). LAN cable internet available.

There are several hourly trains on the Jōetsu *shinkansen* between Tokyo and Echigo-Yuzawa Onsen (¥5980, 1½ hours), and between Niigata and Echigo-Yuzawa Onsen (¥5040, 55 minutes). Echigo-Yuzawa Onsen is connected to Naeba by regular local buses (¥1600, 40 minutes). Free shuttle buses to the Prince Hotel also run this route, though you will need to be a registered guest to take advantage of this service.

ECHIGO-YUZAWA ONSEN 越後湯沢温泉

☎ 025 / pop 8660

Echigo-Yuzawa was the setting for Nobel Prize–winning writer Kawabata Yasunari's *Snow Country*, a novel about decadent onsen geisha. Not surprisingly, steaming hot springs and Kawabata memorabilia are major tourist drawcards, as are the town's lofty ski slopes and fine collection of rustic inns.

Echigo-Yuzawa's JR station features the usual **tourist information office** (☎ 785-5505; 🕑 9am-5.30pm), as well as the more unusual **onsen** (¥800; 🕑 9am-6pm Apr–22 Dec, 9am-8pm 23 Dec–Mar) and **sake tasting bar** (ぽんしゅ館; ☎ 784-3758; www.ponshukan.com, in Japanese; sets from ¥500).

The **Yukiguni-kan** (雪国館; History & Folk Museum; ☎ 784-3965; admission ¥500; 🕑 9am-4.30pm Thu-Tue), 500m north of the station, is a wonderful little museum that displays memorabilia from the life of Kawabata, as well as some interesting displays that bring his classic book to life.

Gala Yuzawa (ガーラ湯沢スキー場; ☎ 785-6543; www.galaresort.jp/winter/english; day lift ticket ¥4300; 🕑 Dec-May) is one of the area's premier ski resorts, though advanced skiers will have to settle for the easy runs on offer. Lack of difficulty aside, this is a massive complex complete with its own onsen and fitness spa, as well as multiple bars and restaurants at the base and on top of the mountain. Shuttle buses run between the JR Echigo-Yuzawa Onsen and Gala Yuzawa.

If you come here in the summer months, there is some attractive wilderness hiking to be had around **Yuzawa Kōgen** (湯沢高原), an alpine plateau accessed via ropeway (cable car; return ¥1300) from the town.

Right outside the little rotary of the station's west exit is the luxurious **Hatago Isen** (旅籠井仙; ☎ 784-3361; www.isen.co.jp, in Japanese; r per person incl 2 meals from ¥11,550; P 💻), a beautiful ryokan with extremely tasteful decor designed to re-create the feel of an old traveller's lodge. The details make all the difference, whether it be artful screens placed to conceal a plasma TV, or a simple flower in a ceramic vase.

Overlooking the town and its own skiing grounds, **NASPA New Ōtani** (NASPAニューオータニ; ☎ 780-6111, 0120-227-021; www.naspa.co.jp/english; r from ¥8000 per person; P 💻) has luxurious Western-style rooms with excellent views. A small *rotemburo* is a great way to soak the soreness away. Free shuttles run between the station and the resort and, in winter, to many major ski areas, making it a superb choice for skiers. LAN cable internet available.

Asahikan (あさひ館; ☎ 787-3205; www.asahikan-yuzawa.com/english.html; 1760 Tsuchitaru, Yuzawa-machi, Minamiuonuma-gun; r per person incl 2 meals from ¥8000; P) is a friendly *minshuku* in an old-style Japanese house. Home-cooked meals, tea and coffee, and close proximity to the Yuzawa Park Ski Jō, are all reasons to stay here. Pick-up is possible if you call ahead.

There are several hourly trains on the Jōetsu *shinkansen* between Echigo-Yuzawa Onsen and Tokyo (¥6690, 1½ hours), and between Niigata and Echigo-Yuzawa Onsen (¥5040, 55 minutes).

Hokkaidō 北海道

Comprising one-fifth of the country's total land mass, yet home to only 5% of the population, Hokkaidō is where all of your preconceived notions of Japan will be shattered. A frozen hinterland with a wild frontier spirit, Hokkaidō is defined by everything that Japan's southern islands are not. Aside from a few major cities, the untamed north country is a hauntingly beautiful wilderness, on par with the Canadian Rockies or New Zealand's South Island.

Carved by a network of glorious highways, the island attracts all manner of adventurer, drifter or escapist. In fact, the image of cruising across Hokkaidō's dramatic landscapes is often associated with unfettered freedom in the minds of the Japanese.

For the thrill-seeking traveller in search of sweeping vistas, amazing wildlife, wide open roads and overwhelming emptiness, Hokkaidō is a refreshing contrast to the often claustrophobic density of Honshū. From November to March, a Siberian cold descends on the island, providing some of the best skiing in both Japan and the eastern hemisphere. When Hokkaidō thaws, and the bears awaken from their hibernation, the island lures hikers in search of rugged backcountry terrain and remote onsen (hot springs).

Hokkaidō is best travelled by car – or better yet motorcycle – which is fortunate as public transport here leaves a lot to be desired. You'll need lots of time to tackle this largely undeveloped landmass, but you'll be rewarded with an outdoor experience unlike any other in Japan.

HIGHLIGHTS

- Drink freshly tapped beer straight from the source in **Sapporo** (p583)
- Carve some serious volumes of perfect powder on the slopes at **Niseko** (p602), or at any of the island's other **ski slopes** (p603)
- Chart a path through the wilderness in the massive national park of **Daisetsuzan** (p625)
- Say goodbye to stress as you steam in sulphurous spas at **Noboribetsu Onsen** (p609) or at any of the region's other **onsen** (p604)
- Discover enormous and ancient balls of algae known as *marimo* in the mysterious caldera lakes of **Akan National Park** (p632)
- Stroll through 19th-century streetscapes in historic **Hakodate** (p593) and **Otaru** (p599)
- Head to the 'end of the world' in **Shiretoko National Park** (p639)
- Take a plane or ferry out to the far-flung islands of **Rishiri-Rebun-Sarobetsu National Park** (p618) to photograph the summer wildflowers

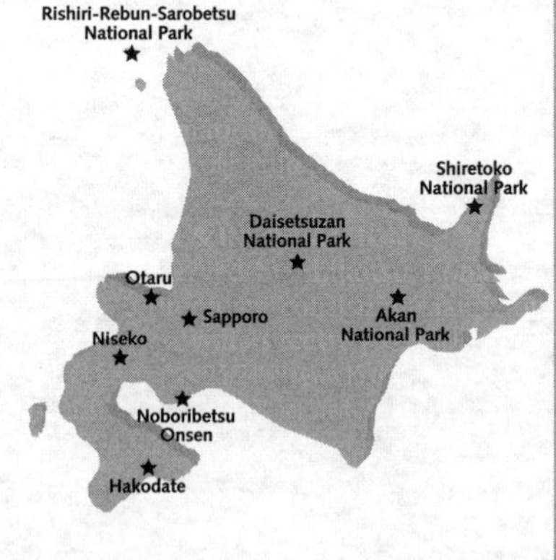

History

The Ainu, Hokkaidō's indigenous people, have shaped this island's history.

After the glaciers receded, the Ainu settled here and called the land Ainu Moshiri – Ainu meaning 'human' and Moshiri meaning 'world'. Until the Edo period (1600–1868), the Ainu and Japanese remarkably had relatively little contact with each other. However, this changed when the Matsumae clan established a major foothold in southwestern Hokkaidō, and successfully bargained with the Ainu. They succeeded in creating a trade monopoly, which was lucrative for the clan, but would ultimately prove disastrous to the Ainu people.

By the end of the Edo period, trade and colonisation had begun in earnest, and by the time the Meiji Restoration began in 1868, the Ainu culture was under attack. Many Ainu customs were banned, women were forbidden to get tattoos, men were prohibited from wearing earrings and the *Kaitakushi* (Colonial Office) was created to encourage mainland Japanese people to migrate northward. When the Meiji period ended, the Ainu had become de facto second-class citizens, and by the start of the 20th century, the mainland Japanese population on the island topped one million.

With world attention focused on Hokkaidō when Sapporo hosted the 1972 Winter Olympics, Japan felt the need to ease restrictions on the Ainu. Sadly, however, it would take another 26 years before significant protections were written into law. Though marginalised for much of the past century, the Ainu have recently won recognition as an important part of Japanese cultural heritage, and are re-establishing themselves. Today, the Ainu are proudly continuing their traditions while still fighting for further recognition of their unique culture.

Hokkaidō's main industries are forestry and agriculture. One look at the rolling farmlands and fields will convince anyone familiar with New England or Europe that Western farming styles were adopted. True enough, in some areas of Hokkaidō, you'd be forgiven for thinking that you were in the pastoral West rather than in Japan. The island is also a top supplier of some of Japan's most revered delicacies, such as snow crab, salmon roe and sea urchin, and scenic kelp production is a major part of many small towns' economies.

And, of course, Hokkaidō is a thriving tourist destination year-round!

Climate

Hokkaidō's temperature ranges from warm and pleasant in summer to subzero and frigid in winter. Spring and early summer can be wet and miserable. The hiking season runs from May through to October, with a peak in July and August when the leaves begin to change colour. Prices tend to be 20% to 30% higher during this time, and many of the popular areas will be booked solid. Typhoons, though a lot less common in Hokkaidō, start to hit Japan in mid-August, and can continue through to the end of October, causing train delays, power outages and even landslides. September and October are chilly, particularly in the mountains, and by November winter has come, bringing heavy snows and very cold temperatures. Bring plenty of layers and plan on bundling up, particularly on the exposed ski slopes.

National Parks

Hokkaidō boasts some of Japan's oldest and most beautiful national parks. Daisetsuzan National Park, centrally located near Asahikawa city, is a must see. This stunning expanse of mountain ranges, volcanoes, onsen, lakes and hiking tracks is Japan's largest, covering 2309 sq km. Skiing and hiking are the main attractions; if you want to escape off the beaten track you should allow a few extra days.

Akan National Park, near Kushiro, has onsen, volcanoes and hiking. In spring, thousands of cranes flock to Kushiro Shitsugen National Park, one of Japan's largest marshlands; deer, foxes, *shima-risu* (none other than the humble chipmunk!) and a host of birds are abundant. The northern islands of Rebun and Rishiri offer superb hiking and views of seaside cliffs, volcanic mountains and (in season) hillsides of flowers.

Shiretoko National Park, in the northeast, is as remote as it gets: two-thirds of it doesn't have roads. Ponds as glassy as reflecting pools, rivers with brown bears munching salmon, waterfalls more delicate than rice-paper paintings – the scenery is stunning, but tourists are told quite plainly that if they venture into restricted areas they will be fined, eaten by Higuma bears... or both.

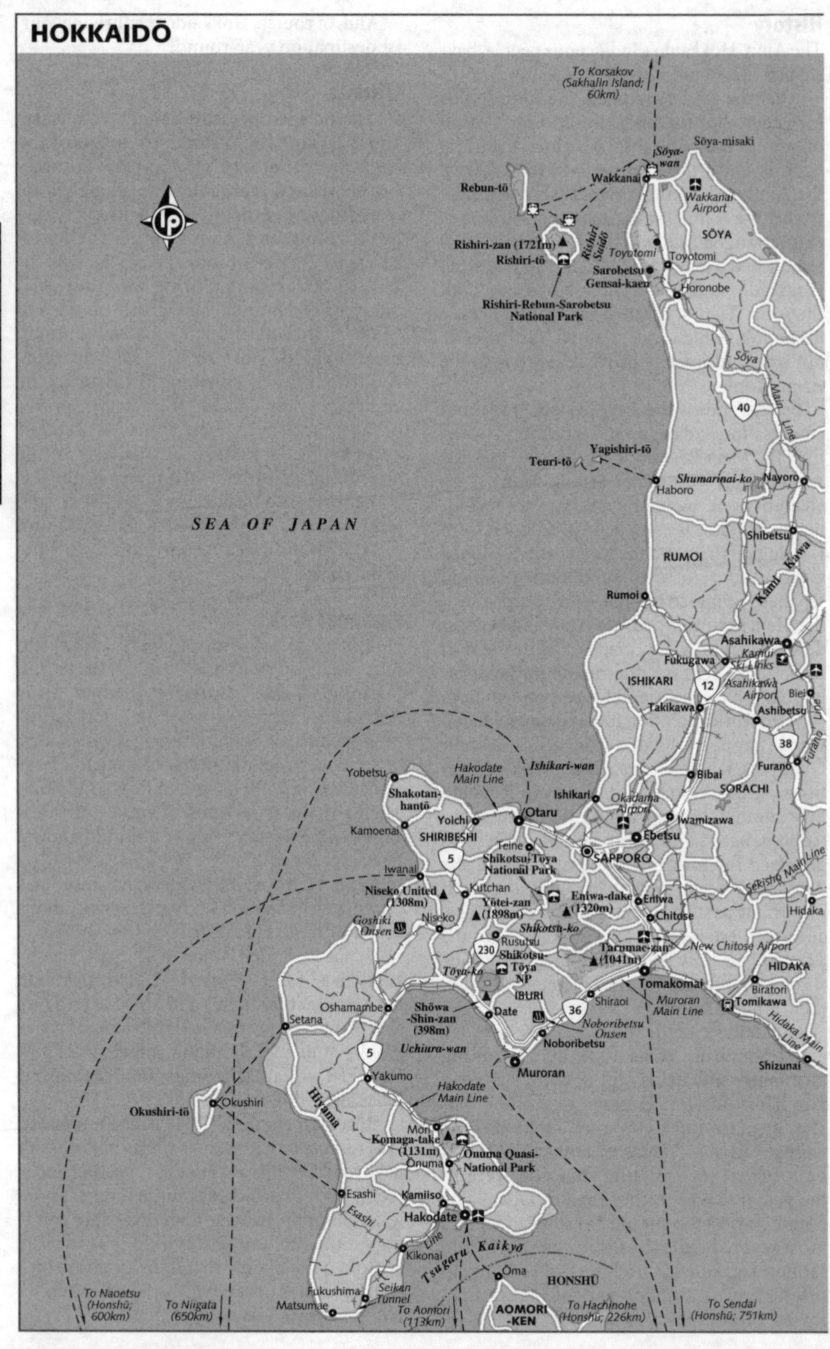
HOKKAIDŌ
To Korsakov (Sakhalin Island; 60km)
Sōya-misaki
Sōya-wan
Wakkanai
Wakkanai Airport
Rebun-tō
SŌYA
Rishiri-zan (1721m)
Rishiri-tō
Rishiri Suidō
Toyotomi
Sarobetsu Gensai-kaen
Horonobe
Rishiri-Rebun-Sarobetsu National Park
Sōya Main Line
40
Yagishiri-tō
Teuri-tō
Shumarinai-ko
Nayoro
Haboro
SEA OF JAPAN
Shibetsu
RUMOI
Kamui Kawa
Rumoi
Asahikawa
Kamui Ski Links
Fukugawa
ISHIKARI
12
Asahikawa Airport
Biei
Takikawa
Ashibetsu
Furano Line
38
Furano
Ishikari-wan
Hakodate Main Line
Yobetsu
Bibai
SORACHI
Shakotan-hantō
Ishikari
Okadama Airport
Iwamizawa
Yoichi
Otaru
Kamoenai
SHIRIBESHI
Ebetsu
Teine
SAPPORO
5
Shikotsu-Tōya National Park
Iwanai
Sekishō Main Line
Niseko United (1308m)
Kutchan
Eniwa-dake (1320m)
Eniwa
Yōtei-zan (1898m)
Chitose
Hidaka
Goshiki Onsen
Niseko
Shikotsu-ko
Rusutsu
New Chitose Airport
230
Shikotsu-Tōya NP
Tarumae-zan (1041m)
Tōya-ko
HIDAKA
Tomakomai
Biratori
IBURI
Tomikawa
Oshamambe
Shōwa -Shin-zan (398m)
Shiraoi
Muroran Main Line
Setana
Date
36
Noboribetsu Onsen
Hidaka Main Line
Noboribetsu
Uchiura-wan
5
Shizunai
Muroran
Yakumo
Hakodate Main Line
Okushiri-tō
Okushiri
Hiyama
Mori
Komaga-take (1131m)
Onuma Quasi-National Park
Onuma
Esashi
Kamiiso
Esashi Line
Hakodate
Kikonai
Tsugaru Kaikyō
Ōma
HONSHŪ
Fukushima
Seikan Tunnel
Matsumae
To Naoetsu (Honshū; 600km)
To Niigata (650km)
To Aomori (113km)
AOMORI -KEN
To Hachinohe (Honshū; 226km)
To Sendai (Honshū; 751km)

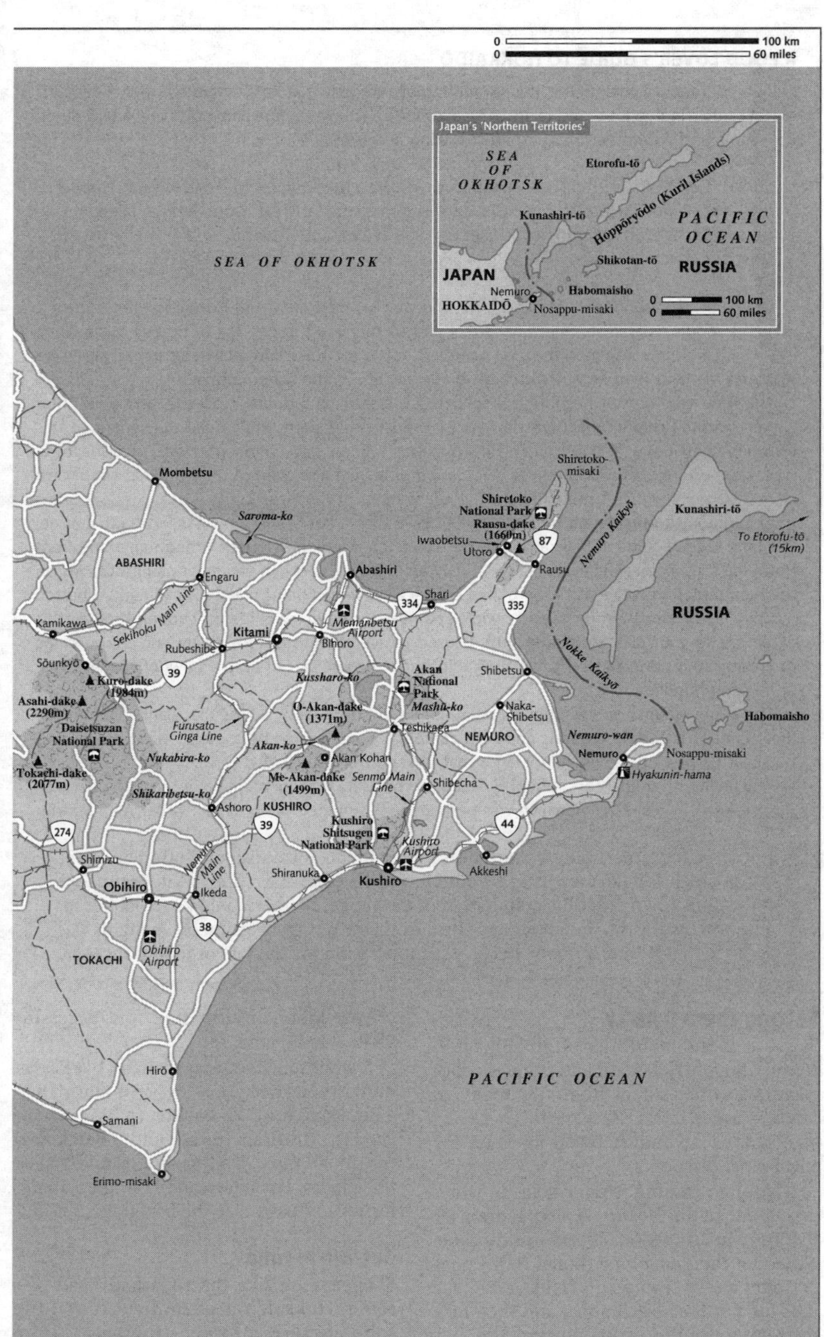
Japan's 'Northern Territories'
SEA OF OKHOTSK
Etorofu-tō
Hoppōryōdo (Kuril Islands)
Kunashiri-tō
PACIFIC OCEAN
Shikotan-tō
JAPAN
RUSSIA
Nemuro
Habomaisho
HOKKAIDŌ
Nosappu-misaki
SEA OF OKHOTSK
Shiretoko-misaki
Shiretoko National Park
Rausu-dake (1660m)
Iwaobetsu
Utoro
Rausu
Nemuro Kaikyō
Kunashiri-tō
To Etorofu-tō (15km)
Mombetsu
Saroma-ko
ABASHIRI
Engaru
Abashiri
Shari
Sekihoku Main Line
Kamikawa
Memanbetsu Airport
Kitami
Bihoro
Rubeshibe
RUSSIA
Sōunkyō
Kuro-dake (1984m)
Kussharo-ko
Akan National Park
Shibetsu
Nokke Kaikyō
Asahi-dake (2290m)
O-Akan-dake (1371m)
Mashū-ko
Naka-Shibetsu
Habomaisho
Daisetsuzan National Park
Furusato-Ginga Line
Teshikaga
NEMURO
Nemuro-wan
Akan-ko
Nemuro
Nosappu-misaki
Nukabira-ko
Akan Kohan
Hyakunin-hama
Tokachi-dake (2077m)
Me-Akan-dake (1499m)
Senmō Main Line
Shibecha
Shikaribetsu-ko
Ashoro
KUSHIRO
Kushiro Shitsugen National Park
Kushiro Airport
Akkeshi
Shimizu
Nemuro Main Line
Shiranuka
Kushiro
Obihiro
Ikeda
TOKACHI
Obihiro Airport
PACIFIC OCEAN
Hirō
Samani
Erimo-misaki
HOKKAIDŌ

A FOOD LOVER'S GUIDE TO HOKKAIDŌ

From a gourmand's perspective, it is something of a tragedy that little tangible evidence remains of Hokkaidō's indigenous cuisine. In 1878, a Yorkshire woman by the name of Isabella Bird dined with Ainu, and wrote the following lip-smacking account:

> Soon, the evening meal was prepared by the chief's principal wife, who tipped into a soot pot swinging over the flames a mixture of wild roots, beans, seaweed, shredded fish, dried venison, millet paste, water and fish oil, and left the lot to stew for three hours.

Of course, the frontier spirit is still alive and well on the island, and Hokkaidō does remain a veritable foodie's paradise. One Ainu dish that has survived the passage of time is **ruibe** (ルイベ), which is simply a salmon that has been left out in the Hokkaidō midwinter freeze, sliced up sashimi style, and then served with high-grade soy sauce and water peppers.

The Ainu tradition of hotpots is also being fostered by modern Japanese, and you'll find winter-warming **nabemono** (鍋物) all across the island. A particularly delicious variant of this dish is **ishikari-nabe** (石狩鍋), a rich stew of cubed salmon, miso, mirin, potatoes, cabbage, tofu, leek, kelp, wild mushrooms and sea salt. Sapporo-ites are also fond of their original **sūpu-karē** (スープカレー), which is quite literally a soupy variant of Japanese curry.

In addition to salmon, another cold-water speciality is **kani-ryōri** (かに料理) or crab cuisine. The long-legged crabs of Wakkanai and Kushiro fetch the highest prices, though anything from Hokkaidō's icy waters will be packed with flavour. Crab appears in a variety of manifestations on the menu, though we're partial to boiled crustaceans served alongside a dish of melted butter.

Dairy cows flourish in the island's wide-open expanses, which is reason enough to add a bit of lactose to your diet. **Hokkaidō milk** is used in everything from ice cream and cappuccinos to creamy soups and sauces, while Hokkaidō butter is best served atop a bowl of **rāmen** (ラーメン; soup noodles).

There are variants on everybody's favourite soup noodle dish across the island, though the most famous is the miso-based **Sapporo rāmen**. If you want to be a purist, wash down your bowl with a pint of the legendary lager that is **Sapporo bīru** (札幌ビール).

And finally, no culinary account of Hokkaidō is complete without mention of Sapporo's beloved **jingisu-kan** (ジンギスカン), which was perhaps best summed up by British writer Alan Booth:

> I ordered the largest mug of draft beer on the menu and a dish of mutton and cabbage, which the Japanese find so outlandish that they have dubbed it *jingisu kan* (Ghenghis Khan) after the grandfather of the greatest barbarian they ever jabbed at. The beer, as always, was about one-third froth, but a single portion of Ghenghis was so huge that it took an hour to eat – compensation for the loss of fluid ounces...

Getting There & Away

Sapporo is the main hub of all Hokkaidō traffic, though Hakodate and other smaller cities also offer direct flights to many of Japan's larger cities. Be sure to check internet deals or budget travel agencies for substantial discounts.

If you are coming from Tokyo, consider taking either the *Hokutosei* sleeper train or the more luxurious *Cassiopeia* to save time. Note that the *shinkansen* (bullet train) does not offer a service direct to Hokkaidō – take it as far north as Hachinohe, and then take the *tokkyū* (limited express) from there.

For more information on accessing Hokkaidō by train, see p592.

For those without Japan Rail (JR) Passes, domestic ferries are a low-cost alternative. They arrive at Hakodate (p598), Otaru (p602), Muroran (p612) and Tomakomai (p612), all three of which are relatively close to Sapporo. For information on international ferries to Russia, see the boxed text, p617.

Getting Around

Shaped a bit like the squashed head of a squid, Hokkaidō is often divided into five subprefectures: Dō-nan (southern), Dō-ō (central), Dō-hoku (northern), Dō-tō (eastern) and Tokachi.

Sapporo has flights to all major Hokkaidō locations, but rail, car or motorcycle are recommended as the island's beauty is in its landscapes. With that said, distances in Hokkaidō can be deceiving, so make a point of travelling early on in the day, especially in the winter months.

Trains run frequently on the trunk lines, but reaching remote locations involves infrequent trains and pricey buses. The foreigner-only Hokkaidō Rail Pass is also available: a three-/five-day pass costs ¥14,000/18,000.

Within cities, buses are convenient and usually cheap. Ask about a *norihō dai* (all day) pass if you're going to use them a lot – it's often a substantial discount.

If you have brought an International Driving Permit (you must get it from your home country prior to arrival in Japan), renting a car or motorcycle may save time. Car-rental rates vary, but if you walk in off the street expect to pay about ¥7000 per day, plus the cost of fuel (which can certainly add up!).

For fans of greener ways to get around, Hokkaidō is a good place to tour by bike. *Charida* (bicycle riders) are a common sight on major roads. Rider houses or cycling terminals (see p807) are also cheap, common and great places to meet other cyclists as well as bikers.

SAPPORO 札幌

☎ 011 / pop 1.89 million

Japan's fifth-largest city, and the prefectural capital of Hokkaidō, Sapporo is a surprisingly dynamic and cosmopolitan urban centre that pulses with energy despite its extreme northerly latitude. Designed by European and American architects in the late 19th century, Sapporo is defined by its wide grid of tree-lined streets and ample public-park space, which contribute to the city's surprising level of liveability. Even if you get cold easily, you can always get your energy back over a hot meal, a great proposition given Sapporo's wholly deserved gastronomic reputation.

As the island's main access point and transport hub, Sapporo serves as an excellent base for striking out into the wilds that lie just beyond the city limits. But, while it might be hard to resist the pull of Hokkaidō's world-class national parks, especially after travelling this far north, don't give Sapporo a quick pass – on the contrary, you'll most definitely be surprised by how good life can be in the capital of the north country. Sapporo is a major tourist destination itself, especially for those partial to the delicious liquid gold that is Sapporo beer. And, if you're planning long periods of time hiking in isolation, you might want to first indulge in a bit of the raucous nightlife of the Susukino district.

In February, the city also hosts the world-famous Snow Festival, which is highlighted by huge ice sculptures of everything from brown bears and tanuki to Hello Kitty and Doraemon.

History

Sapporo is one of Japan's newest cities, and lacks the temples and castles found in its more southerly neighbours. However, it has a long history of occupation by the Ainu, who first named the area *Sari-poro-betsu* or 'a river which runs along a plain filled with reeds.'

The present-day metropolis was once nothing but a quiet hunting and fishing town in the Ishikari Plain of Hokkaidō. While the Ainu were left alone until 1821, everything changed when the Tokugawa shōgunate (military government) created an official trading post that would eventually become Sapporo. The city was declared the capital of Hokkaidō in 1868, and – unlike much of mainland Japan – its growth was carefully planned. In 1880, Japan's third major railway was constructed, linking Sapporo and the port city of Otaru.

In the 20th century Sapporo emerged as a major producer of agricultural products. Sapporo Beer (see p588), the country's first brewery, was founded in 1876, and quickly became synonymous with the city itself. In 1972, Sapporo hosted the Winter Olympics, and the city's annual Snow Festival, begun in 1950, attracts more than two million visitors.

In recent years, Sapporo has experienced something of a cultural and spiritual renaissance, especially as more and more youths are choosing to flee their lives in the Tokyo and Osaka areas in search of a new start.

Orientation

Sapporo, laid out in a Western-style grid pattern, is relatively easy to navigate. Blocks are labelled East, West, North and South in

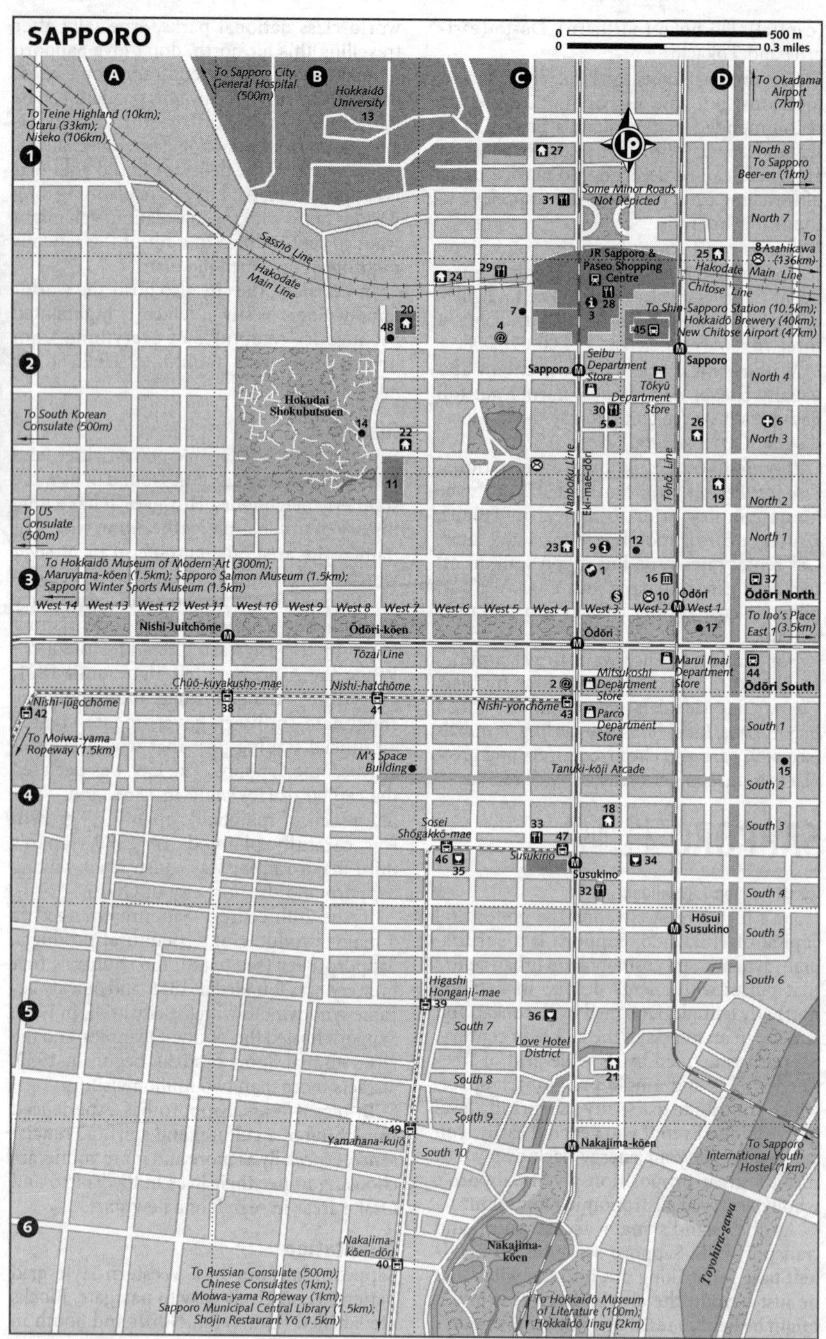
SAPPORO
0 500 m
0 0.3 miles
To Sapporo City General Hospital (500m)
Hokkaidō University
To Teine Highland (10km); Otaru (33km); Niseko (106km)
To Okadama Airport (7km)
North 8
To Sapporo Beer-en (1km)
Some Minor Roads Not Depicted
North 7
To Asahikawa (136km)
Sasshō Line
Hakodate Main Line
JR Sapporo & Paseo Shopping Centre
Chitose Line
To Shin-Sapporo Station (10.5km); Hokkaidō Brewery (40km); New Chitose Airport (47km)
Seibu Department Store
Sapporo
Tōkyū Department Store
North 4
Hokudai Shokubutsuen
To South Korean Consulate (500m)
North 3
Nanboku Line
Eki-mae-dōri
Tōhō Line
North 2
To US Consulate (500m)
North 1
To Hokkaidō Museum of Modern Art (300m); Maruyama-kōen (1.5km); Sapporo Salmon Museum (1.5km); Sapporo Winter Sports Museum (1.5km)
West 14
West 13
West 12
West 11
West 10
West 9
West 8
West 7
West 6
West 5
West 4
West 3
West 2
West 1
Ōdōri
Ōdōri North
To Ino's Place (3.5km)
East 1
Nishi-Juitchōme
Ōdōri-kōen
Tōzai Line
Marui Imai Department Store
Chūō-kuyakusho-mae
Nishi-hatchōme
Mitsukoshi Department Store
Ōdōri South
Nishi-jūgochōme
Nishi-yonchōme
Parco Department Store
To Moiwa-yama Ropeway (1.5km)
South 1
M's Space Building
Tanuki-kōji Arcade
South 2
South 3
Sosei Shōgakkō-mae
Susukino
South 4
Hōsui Susukino
South 5
South 6
Higashi Honganji-mae
South 7
Love Hotel District
South 8
South 9
Yamahana-kujō
South 10
Nakajima-kōen
To Sapporo International Youth Hostel (1km)
Nakajima-kōen-dōri
Nakajima-kōen
Toyohira-gawa
To Russian Consulate (500m); Chinese Consulates (1km); Moiwa-yama Ropeway (1km); Sapporo Municipal Central Library (1.5km); Shojin Restaurant Yō (1.5km)
To Hokkaidō Museum of Literature (100m); Hokkaidō Jingū (2km)

INFORMATION
Australian Consulate
オーストラリア領事館 1 C3
Comic Land
コミックランド三越前店 2 C3
Hokkaidō-Sapporo Food & Tourist Information Centre
北海道さっぽろ食観光情報館 3 C2
i-café アイ·カフェ札幌センチュリーイヤルホテル店 4 C2
IACE Travel IACEトラベル 5 C2
JR Sapporo Railway Hospital
ＪＲ札幌中央鉄道病院 6 D2
JTB Shop JTBショップ .... (see 5)
Kinokuniya
紀伊國屋書店札幌本店 7 C2
Medical Plaza Sapporo
メディカルプラザ札幌 .... (see 3)
Sapporo Chūō Post Office
札幌中央郵便局 8 D1
Sapporo International Communication Plaza Foundation
札幌国際プラザ 9 C3
Sapporo Ōdōri Post Office
札幌大通郵便局 10 D3

SIGHTS & ACTIVITIES
Ainu Association of Hokkaidō
社団法人北海道ウタリ協会 11 B3
Clock Tower 札幌市時計台 12 D3
Hokkaidō University
北海道大学 13 B1
Hokudai Shokubutsuen
北大植物園 14 B2
Ni-jō Fish Market 二条市場 15 D4
Sapporo City Hall 札幌市役所 16 D3
Sapporo TV Tower
さっぽろテレビ塔 17 D3

SLEEPING
Capsule Inn Sapporo
カプセル·イン札幌 18 C4
Hotel Monterey Edelhof Sapporo
ホテルモントレエーデホフ札幌 19 D3
Keiō Plaza Hotel Sapporo
京王プラザホテル札幌 20 B2
Marks Inn Sapporo
マークスイン札幌 21 C5
Nakamuraya Ryokan
中村屋旅館 22 B2
Sapporo Grand Hotel
札幌グランドホテル 23 C3
Sapporo House Youth Hostel
札幌ハウスユースホステル 24 C2
Tōyoko Inn Sapporo-eki Kita-guchi
東横イン札幌駅北口 25 D1
Tōyoko Inn Sapporo-eki Minami-guchi
東横イン札幌駅南口 26 D2
Tōyoko Inn Sapporo-eki Nishi-guchi Hokudai-mae
東横イン札幌駅西口北大前 27 C1

EATING
Esta エスタ 28 C2
Hirihiri-dō スープカレー工房ひりひり堂 29 C2
Kanihonke 札幌かに本家 30 C2
Kushidori 串鳥 31 C1
Ni-jō Fish Market 二条市場 .... (see 15)
Rāmen Yokochō
元祖札幌ラーメン横丁 32 C4
Yosora-no-Jingisukan
夜空のジンギスカン 33 C4

DRINKING
500 Bar ファイブハンドレッドバー 34 D4
alife アライフ 35 C4
Booty ブーティー 36 C5

TRANSPORT
Chūō Bus Terminal
中央バスターミナル 37 D3
Chūō-kuyakusho-mae
中央区役所前 38 B4
Higashi Honganji-mae
東本願寺前 39 C5
Nakajima-kōen-dōri
中島公園通 40 B6
Nishi-hatchōme 西8丁目 41 B4
Nishi-jūgochōme 西15丁目 42 A4
Nishi-yonchōme 西4丁目 43 C4
Ōdōri Bus Terminal
大通ターミナル 44 D3
Sapporo Eki-mae Bus Terminal
札幌駅前バスターミナル 45 D2
Sosei Shōgakkō-mae
創成小学校前 46 C4
Susukino すすきの 47 C4
Toyota Rent a Car
トヨタレンタカー 48 B2
Yamahana-kujō 山鼻９条 49 B6

relation to a central point near the TV Tower in the city centre. For example, the famous landmark Tokei-dai (Clock Tower) is in the block of North 1, West 2 (Kita Ichi-jo, Nishi Ni-chōme) – N1W1. Ōdōri-kōen, a narrow grass-covered section ending at the TV Tower, is a major city feature, dividing the city east–west, into north–south halves. South of Ōdōri is the downtown shopping district with shops and arcades. Susukino, the club and entertainment district, is located mainly between the South 2 and South 6 blocks.

Information

BOOKSHOPS

Kinokuniya (☎ 231-2131; N5W7 Chūō-ku, 5-7 Kita-Gojō-nishi, Chūō-ku) A stone's throw from the south exit of JR Sapporo station. Look to the right as you leave; it's across the street. Foreign books are on the 2nd floor.

Sapporo Municipal Central Library (札幌中央図書館; ☎ 512-7320; www.city.sapporo.jp/tosyokan/ht/english.html; S22W13 Chūō-ku; 9.15am-8pm Mon-Fri, 9.15am-5pm Sat & Sun, closed every 2nd & 4th Wed) Several thousand English-language titles as well as newspapers and magazines. Take the Chūō-Toshokan-mae tram stop.

INTERNET ACCESS

Internet is also available at the tourist information centres (¥100, 10 minutes).

Comic Land (☎ 200-3003; 2nd fl, Hinode Bldg, S1W4 Chūō-ku; per 30min from ¥200; 24hr) Has showers and offers fixed fees as well as half-hourly rates.

i-café (☎ 221-3440; http://sapporocrh.i-cafe.ne.jp, in Japanese; N5W5 Gochōme 2-12, Chūō-ku; per 30min from ¥200; 24hr) Next to the station, with free snacks in addition to the usual coffee/drinks. Heading south, look to the right side, near Kinokuniya bookshop.

MEDICAL SERVICES

Dial ☎ 119 for a medical emergency. JR Sapporo and Sapporo City hospitals require that nonemergency patients arrive before noon.

JR Sapporo Railway Hospital (JR札幌鉄道病院; ☎ 241-4971; N3E1 Chūō-ku) Close to JR Sapporo station, but no emergency room.

Medical Plaza Sapporo (☎ 209-5410; N5W2 Chūō-ku) Conveniently located on the 7th and 8th floors of the JR Tower in JR Sapporo station. Open until 7pm.

Sapporo City General Hospital (市立札幌病院; ☎ 726-2211; N11W13 1-1 Chūō-ku) Offers 24-hour emergency care as well as the usual gamut of health services.

MONEY

ATMs on the street do not accept non-Japanese issued cards, so the best place to get money is at any postal ATMs – there is even an English 'Visitor Withdrawal' option to make getting yen even easier.

POST

Sapporo Chūō Post Office (☎ 748-2313; N6E1-2-1 Higashi-ku) This branch is located just east of Sapporo JR station. Take the north exit, turn right, walk towards the giant white bowling pin and the building is right across the first major intersection. Like many larger post offices, it is open evenings and weekends and offers a variety of services. The ATMs stay open longer than the window.

Sapporo Ōdōri Post Office (☎ 221-4280; 2-9 Ōdōri-nishi, Chūō-ku) Adjacent to Sapporo City Hall on the edge of Ōdōri-kōen.

TOURIST INFORMATION

Hokkaidō-Sapporo Food & Tourism Information Centre (北海道さっぽろ食と観光情報館; ☎ 213-5088; fax 213-5089; www.welcome.city.sapporo.jp/english/index.html; N5W3 Chūō-ku, JR Sapporo station Nishi-dōri Kita-guchi; ⏲ 8.30am-8pm) Located on the 1st floor of Sapporo Stellar Place, inside JR Sapporo station. This is the island's mother load of tourist information, so stock up on maps, timetables, brochures and pamphlets, and be sure to make use of the friendly and helpful bilingual staff.

Sapporo International Communication Plaza Foundation (☎ 211-3670; www.plaza-sapporo.or.jp/english/index_e.html; 1st fl, MN Bldg, N1W3 Chūō-ku; ⏲ 9am-5.30pm) An extensive list of English resources, as well as free internet access; just opposite the Clock Tower (Tokei-dai).

TRAVEL AGENCIES

IACE Travel (☎ 219-2796; fax 219-2766; N3W3 Chūō-ku, 9th fl, Kita San Jō Bldg; ⏲ 10am-7pm Mon-Fri, 10am-4pm Sat, closed Sun) A popular Japanese travel agency that also caters to foreigners, and is useful for making international travel arrangements.

JTB Shop (☎ 241-6201; N3W3 Chūō-ku; ⏲ 10am-7pm) This popular Japanese travel agency is useful for making domestic travel arrangements, including plane and train bookings.

Sights

We're not going to lie to you – Sapporo can be bitterly cold, especially when the Arctic winds are blowing and the snow is piling up. However, if you dress appropriately (and maybe get a beer or two into your system), Sapporo is actually a very walkable city. The gridded streets, which are most definitely a rarity in Japan, make for very simply navigation, and most of the major sights are clustered together in the city centre. Of course, if your body starts to go numb, you can always take advantage of the city's subway, tram and bus lines; see p593 for more information.

HOKUDAI SHOKUBUTSUEN 北大植物園

One of Sapporo's must sees, this beautiful **botanical garden** (☎ 221-0066; N3W8 Chūō-ku; adult ¥400; ⏲ 9am-4.30pm Apr-Sep, 9am-3.30pm Oct-Nov) boasts over 4000 varieties of plants, all attractively set on a meandering 14-hectare plot just 10 minutes on foot southwest of the station. The park suffered from serious typhoon damage in 2004, but has since made a near total recovery.

In addition to the obvious outdoor sights, the Hokudai is also home to two museums: the **Natural History Museum**, a grand, old building dating from 1882 that has a comprehensive taxidermy collection of the island's wildlife, and the smaller **Ainu Museum**, which displays extensive anthropological artefacts from Hokkaidō's indigenous inhabitants.

During the winter months, the botanical gardens are frozen over and the museums are closed, though you can still head to the **greenhouse** (admission ¥110; ⏲ 10am-3pm Mon-Fri, 10am-noon Sat, closed Sun) for some hothouse flowers.

Across the street from the botanical gardens, the **Ainu Association of Hokkaidō** (☎ 221-0462, 221-0672; www.ainu-assn.or.jp/english/eabout01.html; 7th fl, Kaderu 2.7 Community Centre, N2W7 Chūō-ku; ⏲ 9am-5pm Mon-Sat) advocates for increased Ainu rights throughout Japan. The building is open to visitors, and offers an interesting display room of robes, tools and historical information.

CLOCK TOWER 札幌市時計台

While it may not be at the top of your list, no Japanese tourist can leave Sapporo without snapping a photo of the city's signature landmark, the **Clock Tower** (Tokei-dai; ☎ 231-0838; www.15.ocn.ne.jp/~tokeidai/english.html; N1W2 Chūō-ku; admission ¥200; ⏲ 8.45am-5pm Tue-Sun). Built in 1878, the clock has never missed tolling the hour for more than 130 years. Impressive – though the clock tower is also known as one of Japan's top three *gakkari* (disappointing) spots, mainly because the brochure photos often remove the urban metropolis that dwarfs the small building. The clock tower is just two minutes on foot from exit 7 of Ōdōri station – careful as you might walk by before realising it's right in front of you.

SAPPORO TV TOWER さっぽろテレビ塔

There's no way you'll miss this Eiffel Tower–shaped affair at the east of Ōdōri-kōen, which stands alongside Tokyo Tower (p157) in the category of misplaced monuments. Still, the views from the top of the 90m-tall **TV Tower** (☎ 241-1131; www.tv-tower.co.jp/en/index.html; Ōdōri-nishi 1-chōme, Chūō-ku; admission ¥700; 🕑 9.30am-10pm Apr, 9am-10pm May-Oct, 9.30am-9.30pm Nov-Mar) are very impressive, especially when the sun drops below the horizon and Sapporo lights up for the night.

If you're counting your yen, the city hall's **viewing deck** (Kita 1-jo Nishi 2-chōme, Chūō-ku; 🕑 9.30am-4.30pm Mon-Fri May-Nov) is free – it's just northwest of the TV Tower, on the 19th floor.

HOKKAIDŌ UNIVERSITY 北海道大学

Established in 1876, this **university** (www.hokudai.ac.jp/en/index.html; 🕑 dawn-dusk) is a scenic place to meander, and has a number of unique buildings within its grounds. The bust of William S Clark, the founding vice-president of the university, is a famous landmark. Upon his departure in 1877, Professor Clark famously told his students: 'Boys, be ambitious!' Many of the tallest and oldest trees on campus were damaged in 2004 by a severe typhoon, though much of the damage has since been repaired. The Furukawa Memorial Hall and the Seikatei are architecturally noteworthy, and several campus museums are open to the public.

NIJŌ FISH MARKET 二条市場

Buy a bowl of rice and select your own sashimi toppings, gawk at the fresh delicacies or sit down at a shop in **Nijō Fish Market** (S3E1&2 Chūō-ku; 🕑 7am-6pm), one of Hokkaidō's best. Sea urchin and salmon roe are favourites; as is Hokkaidō's version of Mother and Child *(oyakodon)*, a bowl of rice topped with salmon and roe. Get there early for the freshest selections and the most variety; things close up by 6pm and individual restaurants have their own hours.

SAPPORO WINTER SPORTS MUSEUM 札幌ウィンタースポーツミュージアム

Housed in the ski-jump stadium built for the Sapporo Olympics, this highly amusing **museum** (☎ 631-2000; www.sapporowintersportsmuseum.com, in Japanese; 1274 Miyano-mori Chūō-ku; admission ¥600; 🕑 8.30am-6pm Apr-Oct, 9am-5pm Nov-Mar) includes a computerised ski-jump simulator that allows you to try your skills without potentially breaking every bone in your body. Even if you do land a few virtual jumps, a chairlift ride (¥500) to the launch point of the actual ski jump used in the 1972 games should serve as a quick reality check. To reach the museum, take the Tozai line to Maruyama, and then take exit 2 for the Maruyama bus terminal. Next, take bus 14 to Okurayama-iriguchi (15 minutes, ¥200); from here, it's a 10-minute walk uphill to the stadium.

MOIWA-YAMA ROPEWAY 藻岩ロープウェイ

Panoramic views of Sapporo can be had from this ropeway (☎ 561-8177; www.sapporo-dc.co.jp/eng; ticket ¥600; 🕑 10.30am-9.30pm 9 Apr-May & 1 Oct-19 Nov, 10.30am-10pm Jun-Sep, 11am-8pm 10 Dec-Mar, closed 1-8 Apr, subject to weather conditions), which runs 1200m up the slopes of Moiwa-san. You can easily access the ropeway by taking the tram to the Rōpuwei-iriguchi stop, and then walking west towards the hill for around 10 minutes.

HOKKAIDŌ JINGU 北海道神宮

This **temple** (☎ 611-0261; www.hokkaidojingu.or.jp/eng/index.html; admission free) is nestled in a forest so dense that it's easy to forget that the city is just beyond the grounds. Attention has been paid to labelling the natural surroundings: a large plaque lists a number of local birds and the largest trees have identification signs. The temple lies a few blocks east of Maruyama-kōen station (exit 1).

OTHER MUSEUMS

The **Hokkaidō Museum of Literature** (北海道立文学館; ☎ 511-7655; www.h-bungaku.or.jp, in Japanese; Nakashima-kōen 1-4 Chūō-ku; admission ¥250; 🕑 Tue-Sun) offers the opportunity to see the private side of many of Japan's famous novelists, primarily those with a Hokkaidō connection. Letters, memorabilia, books and short films all help viewers understand why these writers have earned a place in the canon of Japanese literature. The museum is scenically located in Nakajima park in the southern district.

SAPPORO BEER

Let's face it: 'Sapporo' means beer. After visiting Germany (and being favourably impressed), Kihachirō Ōkura returned and selected Sapporo as the lucky place to start what would become Japan's first beer brewery, founded in 1876.

Part museum and part beer garden, **Sapporo Beer-En** (サッポロビール園; ☎ museum 731-4368, beer garden 0120-15-0550; www.sapporo-bier-garten.jp; N7E9 Higashi-ku; ⏰ beer garden 11.30am-10pm, tours 9am-3.40pm) is located in the original Sapporo Beer brewery, almost due east of JR Sapporo station. Visitors wanting to belly up to the trough should take the free one-hour tour (recorded English commentary is provided), which includes a tasting (per beer ¥200), and most likely a slight buzz! The adjoining beer garden has four restaurants spanning a variety of cuisines – though purists should note that pints of frothy Sapporo were meant to be enjoyed with the local grilled lamb speciality, *jingisu-kan* (Genghis Khan). There is also a great little gift shop where you can snag a few reprints of nostalgic beer posters dating back to the early 20th century.

To get here take the Tōhō subway to the Higashi-Kuyakusho-mae stop and take Exit 4. Head south along Higashi-Nana-Chōme-dōri to N8E8 (about 10 minutes) and look to the left. The large brick chimney with the distinct Sapporo trademark star is unmistakable. The building itself is at N7E9. By bus, take the Chūō Bus Higashi 63 and get off at the Kitahachi Higashinana (N8E7) stop. The building will be right in front of you. Note that while tour reservations aren't essential, they're not a bad idea – if you don't speak Japanese, ask tourist information or your hotel staff to phone ahead for you.

Diehard fans will want to take the 40-minute train ride out to the current brewing and bottling facility, **Hokkaidō Brewery** (サッポロビール北海道工場; ☎ 0123-32-5811; Toiso 542-1 Eniwa-shi; ⏰ tours 9am-3.30pm, irregularly closed). This mammoth production plant seems more like something out of a James Bond movie rather than a place where beer is made: technicians in white lab coats peer into test tubes; immaculate stainless-steel tanks are covered with computerised gauges and dials; and video cameras monitor the bottles as they whizz by. The 40-minute tour is self-guided and English is minimal, but you'll be rewarded with a refreshing 20 minutes to tipple at the end. Admission is free, but you need to make reservations a few weeks in advance.

Take the JR Chitose line towards the airport, and get off at the Sapporo Beer Teien station. Head away from the tracks towards the giant white silos with the Sapporo logo; the entrance is a 10-minute walk away.

The fascinating **Sapporo Salmon Museum** (豊平さけ科学館; ☎ 582-7555; 2-1 Makomanai-kōen; www.sapporo-park.or.jp/sake/english/e_index.html; admission free; ⏰ 9.15am-4.45pm Tue-Sun) is a tribute to one of the world's most delicious fish. Check out more than 20 different species of salmon in varying stages of development, as well as a few odd salamanders, turtles and frogs. It's located across the street from the Sapporo Winter Sports Museum – bring the kids!

The **Hokkaidō Museum of Modern Art** (北海道立近代美術館; ☎ 644-6881; N1W17 Chūō-ku; adult/student ¥450/220; ⏰ 9.30am-5pm Tue-Sun) has a comprehensive collection of modern works by primarily Japanese artists. The museum is a few blocks north of Nishi-18-chōme station (exit 4) on the Tozai line.

Activities

SKIING & SNOWBOARDING

With the famed Niseko (p602) just around the corner, true hard-core skiers aren't too keen on spending any more time in Sapporo than they have to. But, if you want to practice a bit on the bunny slopes to perfect your moves before hitting the real mountains, there are ski slopes literally on the edge of the city.

Teine Highland (サッポロテイネ; ☎ 681-3191; www.sapporo-teine.com, in Japanese; day pass ¥4600; ⏰ 9am-4pm) is a modestly sized affair with just over a dozen lifts and runs, though it's certainly much more suited to families with children rather than true die-hard alpine extremists. Just 10 minutes from Sapporo by local train, Teine can get very, very crowded. It's still a pleasant day out if you're itching for some powder, or if you're still getting used to your skis or snowboard. Frequent trains on the JR Hakodate line run between Sapporo and Teine (¥260, 10 minutes). From JR Teine station, shuttle buses conveniently whisk you back and forth to Teine Highland's slopes.

Festivals & Events

our pick **Sapporo Yuki Matsuri** (さっぽろ雪まつり; Snow Festival; www.snowfes.com/english) Drawing more than two million visitors, the annual Sapporo Yuki Matsuri takes place in February, and is arguably one of Japan's top festivals. The humble origins of the festival date back to 1950 when local high school students built six snow statues in Ōdori-kōen. Five years later, the Japan Self-Defence Force from the nearby Makomanai base upped the ante by building the city's first gigantic snow sculptures. By 1974, the event had grown into an international contest attracting teams from more than a dozen countries. Taking weeks and weeks to carve, past snow sculptures have included life-sized statues of Hideki Matsui, entire frozen stages for visiting musical acts, ice slides and mazes for the kiddies and – of course – the obligatory Hello Kitty statue or two. You can view these icy behemoths in Ōdori-kōen as well as in other locations around the city. The Snow Festival also highlights the best in regional food and drink from across the island, and you can expect all kinds of wild and drunken revelry, particularly once the sun sets (at these latitudes, it's quite early!). Finding reasonably priced accommodation can be extremely difficult, so book as far in advance as possible.

Ōdōri Nōryō Garden (大通納涼ガーデン) The summer beer festival (mid-July to mid-August) is held in Ōdōri Kōen. Sapporo, Asahi and microbrewers set up outdoor beer gardens, offering a variety of beers and other beverages, as well as food and snacks.

Hokkai Bonodori (北海盆踊り) Families welcome back the spirits of the dead in mid-August. The festival provides viewers with glimpses of traditional songs, dances and summer *yukata* (light, cotton kimonos).

Sleeping

If you're just looking for a place to crash in an emergency, internet cafes (see p585) are open 24 hours, offer reclining chairs and hot showers, and are often cheaper than even the cheapest of hotels. Love hotels in Susukino are another colourful if slightly promiscuous option, and are as clean as (or cleaner than!) budget hostels and hotels. Check in after 11pm for the lowest rates.

BUDGET

Capsule Inn Sapporo (☎ 251-5571; www.capsuleinn-s.com/english.html; S3W3-7 Chūō-ku; per person ¥3200) If you're a man of simple needs that doesn't suffer from claustrophobia, this XY-chromosome-only capsule hotel offers your standard berth plus a sauna, large bathroom, coin laundry and even a 'book corner' with reclining chairs. It's located a stone's throw from the Susukino subway station on the Nanboku line. Take Exit 1, go to the KFC and turn right on the side street – you should see the inn on the left, about halfway down. A 6am to 6pm 'rest' is also an option (¥1200).

Sapporo International Youth Hostel (札幌国際ユースホステル; ☎ 825-3120; www.youthhostel.or.jp/kokusai; 6-5-35 Toyohira-ku; dm/s/tw from ¥3200/3800/6600; 💻 📶) Housed in a surprisingly modern and stylish building that could give most business hotels a run for their money, this well-conceived youth hostel has perfected the basics by offering simple but sparkling rooms to budget travellers. Both Western- and Japanese-style private rooms are available, as well as so-called 'dorm-rooms' featuring four full-sized beds. The closest subway stop is Gakuen-mae (Exit 2) on the Toho line; the hostel is just two minutes from the station behind the Sapporo International Student Center. Note that twin rooms are only for married couples.

our pick **Ino's Place** (イノーズプレイス; ☎ 832-1828; http://inos-place.com/e/; dm/s/d from ¥3400/4800/8600; 💻 📶) While youth hostels in Japan are often stale and sterilised affairs with strict rules and little to no English on hand, Ino's Place is a true backpackers' spot with all the fixings. Friendly and bilingual staff are on hand to make your stay warm and welcome, while clean rooms, private lockers, free internet, no curfew, a steamy Japanese bath, laundry facilities, a kitchen and communal lounge space sweeten the deal. To reach Ino's, take the Tōzai line to the Shiroishi stop (four past Ōdōri); take Exit 1 and walk straight for a few minutes along the main street in the direction of the Eneos petrol station. Turn right at the Marue supermarket and you'll see a detached two-storey white building – you've arrived!

Sapporo House Youth Hostel (☎ 726-4235; www.youthhostel.or.jp/English/c_sapporohouse.htm; N6W6-3-1 Kita-ku; dm from ¥3750; 💻) Although it's conveniently located just a few minutes on foot west of the JR Sapporo station, it's also annoyingly located just beside the train tracks. Noise is a factor, and the dorm rooms here are much older than previously listed options, though it'll certainly do in a pinch, especially if the Snow Festival is in town and vacancies are scarce.

MIDRANGE

Marks Inn Sapporo (☎ 512-5001; www.marks-inn.com/sapporo/english.html; S8W3 Chūō-ku; s/d from ¥4500/6000; 💻) If you want private accommodation, you really can't get cheaper than this business hotel on the edge of the Susukino entertainment district, right across from the canal. Rooms are a bit cramped, but the feathery beds are soft, and become even softer if you party too hard in Susukino, and stumble back in the wee hours of the morning. LAN cable internet available.

Tōyoko Inn Sapporo-eki Kita-guchi (☎ 728-1045; fax 728-1046; www.toyoko-inn.com/e_hotel/00066; N6W1-4-3 Kita-ku; s/d Nov-May ¥4800/6800, Jun-Oct ¥6800/8800; 💻 📶) A convenient clutch of Tōyoko Inns grace the JR station environs, any of which is an affordable and reliable option for the night. One of the newer ones is this brown and grey tower block near the north exit, which considerably discounts its chock-a-block business rooms in the winter months. LAN cable internet available.

Nakamuraya Ryokan (☎ 241-2111, 241-2118; www.nakamura-ya.com/english.html; N3W7-1 Chūō-ku r per person high season from ¥7875, low season ¥7350; 💻 📶) Located directly across from the botanical gardens, this charming little Japanese-style inn is a wonderful introduction to the pleasures of the island. A variety of different plans are available, featuring tatami rooms of varying shapes and sizes, as well as lavish feasts incorporating the unique flavours of Hokkaidō. All guests can also relax in the large onsite bath, and the owner-managers are well equipped to deal with the needs of foreigner travellers.

Keiō Plaza Hotel Sapporo (☎ 271-0111; www.keioplaza-sapporo.co.jp/english/index2.html; N5W7 Chūō-ku; s/d from ¥7000/11,000; ⊠ 💻 🏊) One of the more stylish options in this price bracket, the Keiō Plaza lies at the northeast corner of the botanical gardens, and boasts some impressive amenities including a full-sized swimming pool, sauna complex and athletic training room. Rooms increase in price as you ascend the tower, though you can easily stick to your budget by choosing a standard room on the 12th floor or below. LAN cable internet available.

Alternative Tōyoko options if the Kita-guchi hotel is full:

Tōyoko Inn Sapporo-eki Nishi-guchi Hokudai-mae (☎ 717-1045; fax 717-1046; www.toyoko-inn.com/e_hotel/00018; N8W4 Chūō-ku; s/d Nov-May ¥4200/6600, Jun-Oct ¥6200/8300; 💻 📶) LAN cable internet available.

Tōyoko Inn Sapporo-eki Minami-guchi (☎ 222-1045; fax 222-1046; www.toyoko-inn.com/e_hotel/00059; N3W1 Chūō-ku; s/d Nov-May ¥4800/6800, Jun-Oct ¥6800/8800; 💻 📶) LAN cable internet available.

TOP END

The following hotels can be booked in advance through their English-language websites; this is recommended as rates can dramatically increase if you just show up without a reservation.

Sapporo Grand Hotel (☎ 261-3311; fax 231-0388; www.grand1934.com/english/index.html; N1W4 Chūō-ku; s/d from ¥14,000/17,000; 💻 📶) Established in 1934 as the first European-style hotel in Sapporo, this grand old dame now occupies three adjacent buildings that lie at the southeast corner of the former Hokkaidō government building. Fairly subdued rooms vary considerably in price and style, though all guests are seemingly treated to VIP service from arrival to check-out. LAN cable internet available.

Hotel Monterey Edelhof Sapporo (☎ 242-7111; fax 232-1212; www.hotelmonterey.co.jp/eng/index.htm; N2W1 Chūō-ku; s/d from ¥17,000/32,340; 💻 📶) A few minutes south of the station, opposite the JR Sapporo Railway Hospital, this seemingly modern hotel lords over the street like a concrete monolith, though the interior is fully decked out in a bizarre but surprisingly amenable Austrian-theme. While the opulent lobby and lavish rooms are Continental-inspired, the various dining rooms and onsen are Japanese through and through. LAN cable internet available.

JR Tower Hotel Nikko Sapporo (JRタワーホテル日航札幌; ☎ 251-2222; fax 251-6370; www.jrhotelgroup.com/eng/hotel/eng101.htm; N5W2 Chūō-ku; s/d from ¥18,000/26,000; 💻 📶) You can't beat the location at this soaring tower, which is firmly attached to the JR Sapporo station. Taking advantage of such great heights, the Hotel Nikko Sapporo offers plush rooms priced by floor, a spa with a view on the 22nd floor, and both Western and Japanese restaurants perched at the top on the 35th floor. LAN cable internet available.

Eating

In addition to beer, Sapporo is famous for its miso-based *rāmen* (soup noodles), which makes use of Hokkaidō's delicious butter and fresh corn. The city also serves up some truly incredible seafood, winter-warming stews and *jingisukan*, an easy-to-love dish of roasted lamb that pays tribute to everybody's favourite Mongol warlord, Genghis Khan.

For a complete rundown of the island's unique cuisine, see the boxed text, p582.

One of the best places in town for sushi and sashimi so fresh it's still twitching is the Nijō Fish Market – for more information, see p587.

HOKKAIDŌ

For fussy eaters who like to window shop, head straight to **Esta** (7am-9pm), a giant restaurant floor that forms part of the Paseo Shopping Centre at JR Sapporo Station; one major path to the subway leads right through it. Listen for the singsong '*Ikagadeshou~~ka*?' (Take a look?) and you'll know you've arrived.

Rāmen Yokochō (11am-3am) This famous alleyway in the Susukino entertainment district is crammed with dozens of *rāmen* noodle shops, and you'll most likely wind up here in a noble attempt to vanquish your hangover. Anyone with a yen for *rāmen* shouldn't miss it, but it can be difficult to find. Take the Nanboku line to Susukino and walk south to the first crossroad. Turn left (east); Rāmen Yokochō is halfway down on the right. If you can't find it just ask – it's one place people *will* know. Hours and holidays vary for different shops.

Kushidori (758-2989; www.sapnet.ne.jp/kusidori, in Japanese; N7W4-8-3, Kita-ku; skewers from ¥150, beer ¥500; 4.30pm-12.30am) A famous Sapporo-only chain serving a variety of *yakitori* (skewers of grilled chicken) and grilled vegetables, Kushidori is usually packed with boisterous college kids and 20-somethings. While there is no English menu, you can simply point at what you want, and the chef will grill it for you – choose from either *tare* (sauce) or *shio* (salt). There are locations all around the city, including one just a few blocks north of JR Sapporo station (look for the English sign).

Hirihiri-dō (643-1710; N2-27-5W2 Nishu-ku; 2-27 5 chōme Kotoni Nijō Nishi-ku; soups from ¥850; lunch & dinner Tue-Sun) A Sapporo staple, soup curry is an inventive way to warm the body and spice up your palette, especially on a blistery winter day. As its name implies, soup curry is quite simply a soupier version of Japanese curry – there is no English menu here, but it's easy enough to trust your nose and point to the best-smelling vat. The restaurant is located just outside the JR Sapporo station's west exit – look for the English sign that says 'soup curry'.

Yosora-no-Jingisukan (219-1529; 10th fl, S4W4 Chūō-ku; plates from ¥850; 5pm-2.30am) Genghis Khan is on the menu everywhere, though at this speciality restaurant, located on the 10th floor of the My Plaza building, across from a 7-Eleven, you can grill up tender slices of locally raised lamb, as well as more exotic cuts from far-flung destinations including Australia and Iceland. There is no English, though the handy picture-menu makes ordering a breeze.

Shōjin Restaurant Yō (精進レストラン葉; 562-7020; S17W7-2-12 Chūō-ku; dishes from ¥1000; 11.30am-4.30pm Mon & Tue, 11.30am-8pm Thu-Sun) Macrobiotic, organic and vegan fare that's attractively presented and very tasty. The shop is beautifully done with brown paper lanterns, a sushi-style bar and Zen-style flower arrangements – there is even an English menu to boot. To get here, take the Nanboku line and get off at Horohirabashi. Go left out of the station and veer right at the first traffic signal. The road curves, passing a park (on the right). Go straight through the next signal and turn left when you hit the next one (at the tram line); the restaurant is a few doors down on the right.

Kani-honke (222-0018; N3W2 Chūō-ku; set course from ¥3625; 11.30am-10pm) The frigid seas surrounding Hokkaidō are extremely bountiful and yield some of the tastiest crustaceans on the planet. There is no better place to dine on all manner of exotic crab than at the famous Kani-honke, which serves up elaborate *kaiseki-ryōri* (Japanese cuisine following strict rules of etiquette) centred on these juicy little critters. Seasonal set courses are priced according to the size and rarity of the crab, so simply choose depending on how much you want to spend.

Drinking & Entertainment

Sapporo-ites are famous for their love of the drink, though you can hardly blame them as the beer here really does seem to taste better. While there are literally hundreds of bars and clubs scattered throughout the city, all of the action and nightlife revolves around Susukino, the largest entertainment district north of Tokyo.

The places listed following are all within easy stumbling distance of the Susukino subway station, and are something of Sapporo party landmarks, though you can always simply follow the crowds to whatever is new and trendy. Generally, some bars and most clubs have a cover charge of ¥1000 to ¥3000 on Friday and Saturday nights, which often includes one or two drinks.

If you want to drink delicious Sapporo lager straight from the source, don't miss Sapporo Beer-En – for more information, see the boxed text, p588.

500 Bar (☎ 562-2556; 1st fl, Hoshi Bldg, S4W2 Chūō-ku; 6pm-5am Mon-Sat, 6pm-2am Sun & holidays) Usually packed, even on weekdays, with a mix of foreign and local clientele, every drink on the menu here is ¥500, hence the name (pronounced 'gohyakubaa'). This is one of the franchise's several locations in Sapporo, right across the street from the Susukino subway station's Nanboku line.

Booty (☎ 521-2366; www.booty-disco.com; S7W4 Chūō-ku; 8pm-close) There's plenty of booty to be had at this discotheque and lounge bar, which serves up Western-style fast foods alongside urban beats. The rotating schedule incorporates the best in hip-hop, R&B and reggae, which attracts a young and clubby crowd.

alife (☎ 533-6633; www.alife.jp/pc; B1F Tailki Bldg, S4W6 Chūō-ku; 8pm-close) This ultraplush and ubersophisticated club brings a bit of the Tokyo high life to the far north. Although the thermometer might be dropping outside, it's always hot and heavy in this cavernous joint, so dress to impress!

Getting There & Away

AIR

Sapporo's main airport is **New Chitose Airport** (新千歳空港; Shin-Chitose Kūkō), about 40km south of the city. Domestic destinations include Tokyo, Osaka, Nagoya, Hiroshima, Sapporo and many others. See p828 for details of international flights.

There's a smaller airport at **Okadama** (丘珠空港; Okadama Kūkō), about 10km north of the city, which has limited service to cities in Hokkaidō.

BUS

Highway buses connect Sapporo with the rest of Hokkaidō, and are generally cheaper than trains and even time-competitive on some routes. Sapporo Eki-mae is the main bus station, just southeast of JR Sapporo station, beneath Esta. The Chūō bus station (southeast of JR Sapporo station) and Ōdōri bus centre are also departure spots. At all three departure points, you will find ticket booths from where you can purchase tickets to major cities throughout Hokkaidō.

Some sample destinations, which have frequent daily departures from Sapporo Eki-mae bus terminal, include Wakkanai (¥6000, six hours), Asahikawa (¥2000, two hours), Muroran (¥2250, 2¼ hours), Noboribetsu Onsen (¥1900, two hours), Tōya-ko Onsen (¥2700, 2¾ hours), Niseko (¥2300, three hours), Furano (¥2100, three hours) and Otaru (¥590, one hour).

From the Chūō bus station there are a few departures a day to Obihiro (¥3670, 4¼ hours) and Abashiri (¥6210, 6¼ hours). Buses to Hakodate depart from both the Chūō and Ōdōri bus stations (¥4680, 5¼ hours).

Discounted round-trip tickets are available for most routes.

CAR

The best place in Hokkaidō to pick up a rental car is at the New Chitose Airport. While you might have to backtrack a bit if you're heading north, some people find this preferable to picking up a vehicle in Sapporo, and subsequently navigating through the busy city centre. There are just under a dozen different companies located in the arrivals area on the first floor, which makes it easy to shop around the various booths and quickly compare prices.

If you'd prefer to pick up your vehicle in Sapporo, it's recommended that you deal with **Toyota Rent a Car** (☎ 281-0100; N5E2-1 Chūō-ku; 8am-10pm). In addition to being conveniently located near JR Sapporo station, the company is a bit better at dealing with foreigners than most rental car dealers. There's no guarantee the staff will speak English – if you have problems, you can always try to make arrangements in advance through the tourist information centre.

TRAIN

The *Hokutosei* (北斗星) is a *tokkyū* (limited express) sleeper train that runs between Tokyo's JR Ueno station and JR Sapporo station. There are two departures in both directions every evening, and the total journey time is around 16½ hours, which puts you in your destination the following morning. Ticket prices vary depending on the distance travelled, as well as the type of accommodation you choose.

The base fare for a journey between Tokyo and Sapporo is ¥16,080, plus an additional ¥2890 limited-express train charge. On top of this, you need to pay an additional fee for accommodation – prices range from ¥6300 for a private sleeping berth to ¥17,180 for the 'royal room'. Note that this flat fee is charged regardless of starting or ending location. If you're travelling on a JR Pass, you do not have to pay the base fare and limited-express charge, but you will have to pay the accommodation fare. Full-on French and formal Japanese meals are available on board with advanced reservation, though meal service is not included in the ticket price.

A much more luxurious option is the *Cassiopeia* (カシオペア), a *tokkyū* sleeper train that runs three times a week between Tokyo and Sapporo. There are three evening departures in both directions every week, and the total journey time is also around 16½ hours. Base fares and limited-express train charges are equivalent to the *Hokutosei*, and are again waived if you have a JR Pass, though accommodation is more expensive, ranging from ¥13,350 for a twin room to ¥25,490 for a full-on suite. These prices are on par with an upmarket hotel, and sleeper cars on the *Cassiopeia* are something akin to a four-star resort on wheels. The night train also has sophisticated dining cars offering Michelin-star quality meals, which are not included in the ticket price, and must be booked in advance. Note that single travellers must pay for the full price of a room, so it's advised that you have a travel companion.

Reservations for both the *Hokutosei* and the *Cassiopeia* can be made at any JR ticket counter or travel agency. These trains are very popular and often booked solid, particularly in the summer months, so make a reservation as far in advance as possible.

Additionally there are hourly trains on the JR Tōhoku *shinkansen* between Tokyo and Hachinohe (¥15,150, three hours). Hachinohe is connected to Sapporo by the JR Tsugaru Kaikyō line and Hakodate lines – hourly *tokkyū* trains run through the Seikan Tunnel between Hachinohe and Hakodate (¥7030, three hours), and between Hakodate and Sapporo (¥8390, 3½ hours).

There are hourly *kaisoku* (rapid) trains on the JR Hakodate line between Sapporo and Otaru (¥620, 40 minutes). Finally, Super Kamui *tokkyū* trains run twice an hour between Sapporo and Asahikawa (¥4480, 1½ hours).

Getting Around

TO/FROM THE AIRPORTS

New Chitose Airport is accessible from Sapporo by *kaisoku* (rapid) train (¥1340, 35 minutes) or bus (¥1000, 1¼ hours). There are convenient bus services connecting the airport to various Hokkaidō destinations including Shikotsu-ko, Tōya-ko Onsen, Noboribetsu Onsen and Niseko.

For Okadama airport, buses leave every 20 minutes or so from in front of the ANA ticket offices, opposite JR Sapporo station (¥400, 30 minutes).

BUS & TRAM

JR Sapporo station is the main terminus for local buses. From late April to early November, tourist buses loop through major sights and attractions between 9am and 5.30pm; a one-day pass costs ¥750, single trips are ¥200 (basic fee).

There is a single tram line that heads west from Ōdori, turns south, then loops back to Susukino. The fare is a flat ¥170.

SUBWAY

Sapporo's three subways are efficient. Fares start at ¥200 and one-day passes cost ¥800 (per day ¥500 weekend only). There are also ¥1000 day passes that include the tram and buses as well. Or get a pay-in-advance With You card (various denominations available), which can be used on subways, buses, trams, Jōtetsu and Chūō buses; unlike the one-day passes, the With You card does not expire at midnight.

DŌ-NAN 道南

Southern Hokkaidō is often bypassed entirely by Sapporo-bound travellers, who use the capital's transport network as a springboard for more remote destinations. This is unfortunate, as Hakodate, a prominent Meiji-era port, is by far the most atmospheric city in Hokkaidō. Dō-nan is also home to a couple of small but historically significant towns, which bear striking architectural reminders of the Edo period.

HAKODATE 函館

☎0138 / pop 288,000

Built on a narrow strip of land between Hakodate Harbour to the west and Tsugaru Channel to the east, hourglass-shaped Hakodate is the southern gateway to the island of Hokkaidō. Under the Kanagawa Treaty of 1854, the city was one of the first ports to open up to international trade, and as such hosted a small foreign community. Much of that influence can still be seen in the Motomachi district, a steep hillside that is sprinkled with wooden buildings and brick churches. You can also get a sense of history by riding nostalgic trams through the orderly streets, or by watching the squid boats, with their traditional lantern lights, bob gently in the bay.

Orientation & Information

Spread out along the water's edge, the city is best accessed by its trams; most of the sights can be walked to from stops along the way. Buses, trams and trains leave the station regularly. Head west, towards Mt Hakodate and the Motomachi district, to find most historical sites; Goryō-kaku, Japan's first Western-style fort, is to the east.

Hakodate Tourist Information Centre (Map p596; ☎ 23-5440; www.city.hakodate.hokkaido.jp/kikaku/english; ⌚ 9am-7pm Apr-Oct, 9am-5pm Nov-Mar) Inside JR Hakodate station; provides handy English maps of the Motomachi district.

Hot Web cafe (Map p596; ☎ 26-3591; www.hotweb.or.jp/cafe/shop.html in Japanese; ⌚ 10am-8pm Wed-Mon; per hr incl 1 drink ¥400) Internet access; head straight out from the station (keep going past WAKO, but before Lotteria).

Sights

MOTOMACHI DISTRICT 元町

On Mt Hakodate's lower slopes, this area is home to the lion's share of 19th-century sites, and commands stunning panoramic views of the bay. All of the following sights are located in close proximity to one another, and are easily reached on foot.

There's a beautiful old **Russian Orthodox Church** (Map p472; ☎ 23-7387; 3-13 Motomachi; admission ¥200; ⌚ 10am-5pm Mon-Fri, 10am-4pm Sat, 1-4pm Sun) that dates from 1916, and is adorned with distinctive copper domes and spires.

Hakodate City Museum of Northern Peoples (Map p472; ☎ 22-4128; 21-7 Suehiro-chō; admission ¥300; ⌚ 9am-7pm Apr-Oct, 9am-5pm Nov-Mar) is a good place to learn about the Ainu and their material culture. English signs have been added to some exhibits.

The **Old Public Hall of Hakodate Ward** (☎ 22-1001; 11-13 Motomachi; admission ¥300; ⌚ 9am-7pm Apr-Oct, 9am-5pm Nov-Mar) is an ornate mansion awash in pale blues and yellows that reigns regally over the district. Inside are items of historical interest relating to the city, though the main appeal is the wonderful colonial-style architecture.

> **QUIRKY HOKKAIDŌ EVENTS**
>
> - **Yuki Matsuri** (Snow Festival) in Sapporo – spectacular ice sculptures grace the streets (p589)
> - **Marimo Matsuri** in Akan Kohan – return fuzzballs of algae to Akan-ko (p636)
> - **Orochon-no-hi** (Fire Festival) in Abashiri – fire dancers gyrate in flames (p631)
> - **Japan Cup National Dogsled Races** in Wakkanai – watch as dogs dash and fur flies (p617)
> - **Kyōkoku Hi Matsuri** (Fire Festival) at Sōunkyō Onsen – flaming arrows are shot into a gorge (p629)
> - **Come Back Salmon Night** in Abashiri – grill seafood while watching salmon return to spawn (p631)
> - **Heso Matsuri** (Navel Festival) in Furano – celebrate innies and outies in style (p624)

English-style tea-time at the **Old British Consulate** (Map p472; ☎ 27-8159; 33-14 Motomachi; admission ¥300, afternoon tea from ¥550; ⌚ 9am-7pm Apr-Oct, 9am-5pm Nov-Mar) makes a relaxing afternoon that much more enjoyable.

The **Foreigners' Cemetery** (Map p472), an interesting slice of local history, has the graves of sailors, clergy and others who unfortunately died far away from their homelands. Many of the graves have English, Russian or French inscriptions.

To get to Motomachi, take tram 5 from the station and get off at the Suehirō-chō stop, then walk uphill for 10 minutes. Alternatively, get off at the end of the line and walk along the waterfront first, visit the cemetery, then stop at the buildings as you walk uphill to Suehirō-chō.

HAKODATE-YAMA 函館山

This small mountain (334m) offers a memorable view of Hakodate, especially at night when the twinkling city lights contrast the dark waters. A **ropeway** (Map p472; ☎ 23-6288; www.334.co.jp/en/index.html; one way/return ¥640/1160; ⌚ 10am-10pm May-Oct, to 9pm Nov-Apr) whisks you to the top in a few minutes.

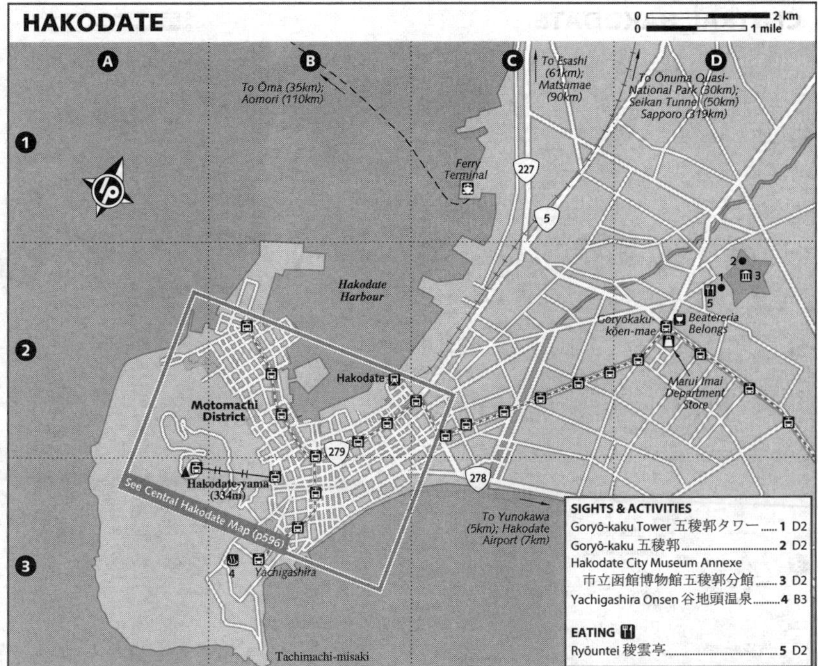

Take tram 2 or 5 to the Jūjigai stop, and walk a few minutes uphill to the ropeway platform. Alternatively, a summit-bound bus (¥360, 30 minutes) leaves directly from the station, and stops at several viewing places as it winds to the top. Those wanting to rough it old-style can take the hiking track (from May to late October).

A 10-minute walk from the summit is Tsutsuji-yama car park, a hot date spot at night, but relatively crowd-free by day. At its far end there is an overgrown path that leads to moss-covered walls and buttresses, the ruins of an old fort, **Hakodateyama Yōsai**. This one is refreshingly deserted, and you can happily clamber around, Indiana Jones–style, among ferns with fronds the size of palm leaves.

YACHIGASHIRA ONSEN 谷地頭温泉

On the southern edge of Hakodate-yama is this enormous **hot spring** (Map p595; ☎ 22-8371; 20-7 Yachigashira; admission ¥390; 6am-9.30pm, closed every 2nd & 4th Tue), one of Hokkaidō's oldest, with dark iron-laden water. To get here, take tram 2 to Yachigashira, the final stop. On foot, continue to the first intersection and then turn right – you'll see the public bathhouse complex on the left shortly after you turn.

GORYŌ-KAKU 五稜郭

Japan's first Western-style **fort** (Map p471;) was built in 1864 in the shape of a five-pointed star (*goryō-kaku* means 'five-sided fort'), and was designed to trap attackers in deadly crossfire. Nothing remains of the actual fort structure, but the landscaped grounds and moat are picturesque, and the moss-covered walls are quite fun to scramble upon.

The nearby **Hakodate City Museum Annexe** (Map p471; ☎ 51-2548; 44-2 Goryōkakumachi; admission ¥100; 9am-4.30pm Tue-Sun Apr-Oct, 9am-4pm Tue-Sun Nov-Mar) offers a taste of the fort's history, including weaponry and bloodstained uniforms.

For a bird's eye view, the modern **Goryō-kaku Tower** (Map p471; ☎ 51-4785; 43-9 Goryōkakumachi; admission ¥840; 8am-7pm Apr-Oct, 9am-6pm Nov & Mar, 9am-7pm Dec-Feb) surveys the fort below and the surrounding city.

To reach the fort, take tram 2 or 5 to the Goryōkaku-kōen-mae stop. From there it's a 10-minute walk.

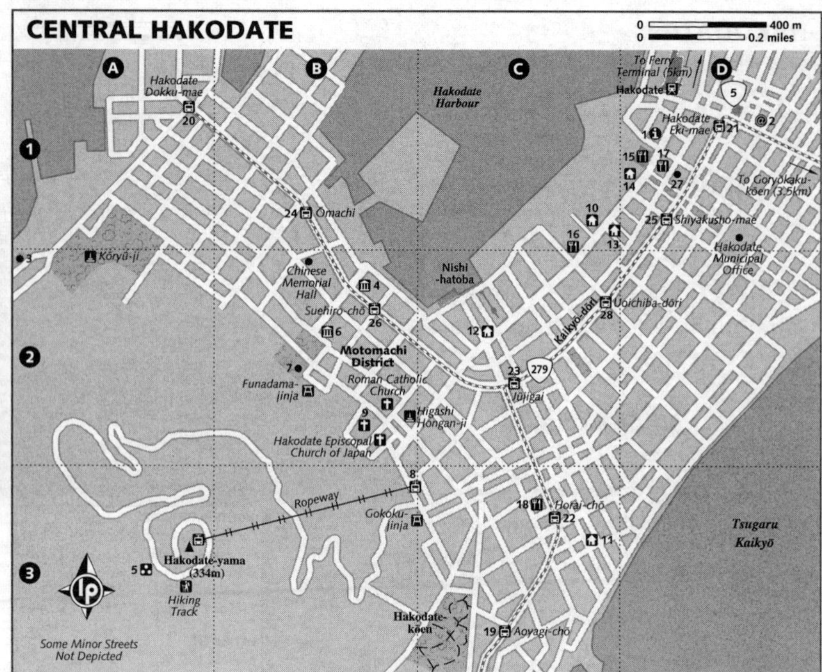

AROUND HAKODATE

If you have your own car, **Ōnuma Quasi-National Park** (大沼国定公園) is just northeast of the city, and is centred on a large lake and surrounding swamplands that offers scenic canoeing, fishing and hiking. Many of the nearby hills have hidden hot springs, but finding them can be difficult – your best bet is to ask a local for directions to their favourite gem.

The historic Edo towns of **Esashi** and **Matsumae** are great day trips from Hakodate – for more information, see p599.

Festivals & Events

Hakodate Goryōkaku Matsuri (函館五稜郭祭り) Held on the third weekend in May, this festival features a parade of townsfolk dressed in the uniforms of the soldiers who took part in the Meiji Restoration battle of 1868.

Hakodate Minato Matsuri (函館港祭り; Hakodate Port Festival) During this festival in early August, groups of seafood-fortified locals (reportedly 10,000 of them) move like waves doing an energetic squid dance.

Sleeping

Niceday Inn (Map p596; ☎ 22-5919; 9-11 Ōtemachi; dm from ¥3000) Near the Asa-ichi morning market, this petite hotel offers bunk-style rooms, and is run by a wonderfully welcoming matron. While you shouldn't expect much more than a bed and a hot shower, it's nevertheless a great place to pinch pennies. Niceday is directly opposite the Kokusai Hotel in a small, nondescript alley.

Hakodate Youth Guesthouse (Map p596; ☎ 26-7892; www12.ocn.ne.jp/~hakodate, in Japanese; 17-6 Hōraimachi; dm Oct-Jun ¥3800, Jul & Sep ¥4200, Aug ¥4500) Wholesome, family friendly accommodation complete with 9am homemade ice-cream parties and 11pm curfews, the Hakodate Youth Guesthouse is a relaxed and affordable base for budget travellers. It's conveniently located near the Hōrai-chō tram stop – after getting off the tram, turn left at the first light, then go past two more lights and turn right. The guest house is across the street from a supermarket and car park.

Kokian (Map p596; ☎ 26-5753; 13-2 Suehirochō; r per person with/without meals from ¥8000/4000) Built in 1897, this well-preserved structure is a living example of Meiji-era architecture, complete with a Japanese-style facade and more Western-influenced inner chambers.

INFORMATION
Hakodate Tourist Information Centre 函館観光案内所 ... 1 D1
Hot Web café ホットウェブカフェー ... 2 D1

SIGHTS & ACTIVITIES
Foreigners' Cemetery 外人墓地 ... 3 A2
Hakodate City Museum of Northern Peoples 函館市北方民族資料館 ... 4 B2
Hakodateyama Yōsai 函館山要塞 ... 5 A3
Old British Consulate 旧イギリス領事館 ... 6 B2
Old Public Hall of Hakodate Ward 旧函館区公会堂 ... 7 B2
Ropeway ロープウェイ ... 8 B3
Russian Orthodox Church ハリストス正教会 ... 9 B2

SLEEPING
Hakodate Kokusai Hotel 函館国際ホテル ... 10 C1
Hakodate Youth Guesthouse 函館ユースゲストハウス ... 11 C3
Kokian 古稀庵 ... 12 C2
Niceday Inn ナイスディイン ... 13 C1
Tōyoko Inn Hakodate Eki-mae Asaichi 東横イン函館駅前朝市 ... 14 D1

EATING
Asa-Ichi (Morning Market) 朝市 ... 15 D1
Hakodate Beer はこだてビール ... 16 C1
Hakodate Rāmen Kamome かもめラーメン ... 17 D1
Hishī ひし伊 ... 18 C3

TRANSPORT
Aoyagi-chō 青柳町 ... 19 C3
Hakodate Dokku-mae 函館どっく前 ... 20 A1
Hakodate Eki-mae 函館駅前 ... 21 D1
Horai-chō 宝来町 ... 22 C3
Jūjigai 十字街 ... 23 C2
Ōmachi 大町 ... 24 B1
Shiyakusho-mae 市役所前 ... 25 D1
Suehiro-chō 末広町 ... 26 B2
Toyota Rent a Car 函館トヨタレンタカー ... 27 D1
Uoichiba-dōri 魚市場通 ... 28 C2

Rooms are definitely on the smallish side, but are certainly not lacking in personality. Kokian is just a two-minute walk from Jūjigai tram station. You should walk three blocks towards the water (dock area) after getting off the tram; the inn is behind one of the old warehouses.

Tōyoko Inn Hakodate Eki-mae Asaichi (Map p596; ☎ 23-1045; www.toyoko-inn.com/e_hotel/00063/index.html; 22-7 Ōtemachi; s/d Nov-May ¥4600/6800, Jun-Oct ¥5600/7800; P 💻 📶) While it's positively characterless in comparison to Kokian, this Tōyoko clone remains the best choice for business-orientated travellers in need of private space and reliable internet access. It's located just steps away from the Asa-ichi market, and only three minutes' walk from Hakodate station. LAN cable internet available.

Hakodate Kokusai Hotel (Map p596; ☎ 23-5151, 23-0239; www.hakodate-kokusai.jp; 5-10 Ōtemachi; s/tw ¥11,500/23,000; P 💻 📶) Hokodate's premier hotel is a relatively modest affair in comparison to Sapporo's upmarket offerings. Still, it's a modern and well-heeled place, highlighted by its stylishly elegant Sky Lounge, which is the place to sip a late-night something – stop by even if you're not staying here. Rooms are fairly generic; LAN cable internet is available.

Eating & Drinking

A trendy district for fine dining is Nishi-hatoba (Map p596), a waterfront district with a variety of eateries in converted warehouses and English-style buildings.

Asa-ichi (morning market; Map p596; 🕓 5am-noon) Located just to the right of Hakodate station, this market is a great place for hungry seafood-lovers. Like tightly packed ammo, freshly caught squid glisten in ice-stuffed Styrofoam. Most of the commerce is over by 8am, after which the tourists come for shopping, snacks and souvenirs.

Hishī (Map p596; ☎ 27-3300; 9-4 Hōraichō; snacks from ¥525; 🕓 10am-5pm) Hishi-sabō, part cafe, part antique shop, is an unmistakable ivy-covered *kura* (mud-walled storehouse) that is situated just one block west from the Hoari-chō tram stop. Even if you are not in the market for a used kimono, you cannot go wrong with a cup of English tea and a tasty gourmet waffle (*waffuru-setto* ¥890) – go slow and take in the building's 80-year-long history while you enjoy your snack.

Hakodate Rāmen Kamome (Map p596; ☎ 22-1727; 8-2 Wakamatsuchō; rāmen from ¥580; 🕓 6.30am-3.30pm) A famous noodle shop (look for the blue awning) where you can put your culinary skills to the test – start with a basic bowl of miso *rāmen* (¥580), and add *kani* (crab), *ebi* (shrimp), *ika* (squid), *hotate* (scallops) and/or *uni* (sea urchin roe) for a few hundred extra yen. The shop is located across the street from the fish market, so you know everything here is fresh.

Ryōuntei (Map p595; ☎ 54-3221; 8-20 Honchō; dishes ¥650-1250; 🕓 lunch & dinner Mon-Sat) Not far from the Goryō-kaku tower is this *izakaya* (pub-eatery), which specialises in fresh seafood from the surrounding seas. Grab a seat at the counter or on the tatami, and order whatever looks good off the picture menu. Here's a tip: anything with *ika* (squid) comes in fresh from the harbour, so give it try either raw or grilled.

Hakodate Beer (Map p596; ☎ 23-8000; 5-22 Ōtemachi; dishes from ¥650; ⏲ 11am-10pm) Next to the Hakodate Kokusai Hotel, this expansive place has live music and boisterous crowds. Scan the English menu, and choose from a variety of microbrews – from cold ales and golden wheat beers to dark stouts – to complement homemade pizzas and various items from the grill.

Getting There & Away

AIR

From Hakodate airport, just a few kilometres east of the city centre, there are international flights to Seoul, and domestic flights to various destinations including Sapporo, Tokyo, Kansai and others.

Frequent buses run direct between Hakodate Airport and JR Hakodate station (¥300, 20 minutes), or you can simply take a taxi (¥2000).

BOAT

From Hakodate-kō, **Higashi Nihon** (☎ 0120-756-564) operates eight daily ferries (departing year-round) between Aomori and Hakodate (from ¥2150, 3¾ hours), and two to three daily ferries between Hakodate and Ōma (¥1370, 1¾ hours) on Shimokita-hantō. The ferry terminal, where you also buy your tickets, is on the northeast corner of Hakodate Harbour.

Regular shuttle buses (¥250, 15 minutes) as well as taxis (¥1500) run between the ferry terminal and the train station.

BUSES

There are five to six daily buses between JR Hakodate train station and Sapporo's Chūō bus station and Ōdōri bus centre (¥4680, 5¼ hours).

For more transport details, also see Matsumae (right) and Esashi (opposite).

CAR

If you've just arrived in Hokkaidō, Hakodate is a good place to pick up a rental car and start your road-tripping adventure across the island. The recommended **Toyota Rent a Car** (Map p472; ☎ 26-0100; 19-2 Ōtemachi; ⏲ 8am-8pm) has a branch office a few blocks southwest of the station, next to the Aqua Garden Hotel. Matsumae and Esashi are an easy-day trip from Hakodate if you have a rental car.

TRAINS

Frequent *tokkyū* on the JR Tsugaru Kaikyō line run between Hakodate and Aomori (¥5140, two hours) via the Seikan Tunnel (see the boxed text, opposite). There are also frequent *tokkyū* on the JR Hakodate line between Hakodate and Sapporo (¥8390, 3½ hours). Finally, a combination of *tokkyū* and *kaisoku* (rapid) trains run on the JR Hakodate line between Hakodate and Niseko via Oshamambe (¥5410, 3½ hours).

For information on trains between Hakodate and Tokyo, see p592.

Getting Around

Single-trip fares on trams and buses are generally between ¥200 and ¥250, and are determined by how long you ride. One-day (¥1000) and two-day (¥1700) passes offer unlimited rides on both trams and buses (¥600 for tram alone), and are available at the tourist information centre or from the drivers. These passes are also good for the bus to the peak of Hakodate-yama.

MATSUMAE 松前

☎ 01394 / pop 10,000

Prior to the start of the Meiji era, this town was the stronghold of the Matsumae clan, and the centre of Japanese political power in Hokkaidō. As a result, Matsumae is home to the only castle on the island, **Matsumae-jō** (松前城; ☎ 42-2216; admission ¥270; ⏲ 9am-5pm mid-Apr–Dec). The present structure is from the 19th century, and currently houses feudal relics and a small collection of Ainu items.

Uphill is a 17th-century temple district and the burial ground of the Matsumae clan. Further along is **Matsumaehan Yashiki** (松前藩屋敷; admission ¥350; ⏲ 9am-4.30pm mid-Apr–Dec), an interesting replica of an Edo-period village, built using authentic materials and construction techniques.

Frequent *tokkyū* on the JR Esashi line run between Hakodate and Kikionai (¥1620, 35 minutes). Regular buses run between the JR Kikonai station and Matsumae (¥1220, 1½ hours). The sights listed here are accessible from the Matsumae-jō stop; buses terminate at Matsumae bus terminal, from where you can grab a bus to Esashi between April and November (¥2720; two hours; four daily).

ESASHI 江差

☎0139 / pop 10,000

If Matsumae was Hokkaidō's Edo-period political centre, then Esashi was its economic centre. Prior to the depletion of fishing stocks in the early 20th century, a number of *nishingoten* (herring barons' homes) dominated the shoreline, though several remain and are quite well preserved. **Yokoyama House** (横山家; ☎ 52-0018; admission ¥300; 9am-5pm) and **Nakamura House** (旧中村家住宅; ☎ 52-1617; admission ¥300; 9am-5pm) are good places to start. Both are open year-round, but closed on Monday during winter. Call ahead for an appointment at Yokoyama House from November to April.

Listen to performances of Esashi Oiwake, a nationally known music style, at **Esashi Oiwake Museum** (江差追分会館; ☎ 52-0920; admission ¥500; closed Mon in winter). Shows are held at 11am, 1pm and 2.30pm. It's high-pitched, nasal singing that will either fascinate you or make you want to cover your ears.

Esashi holds an annual festival, the **Ubagami Matsuri** (姥神祭り; 9 to 11 August), when streets fill with antique floats in honour of Ubagami Daijingu, the oldest shrine in Hokkaidō, which was built to invoke a successful herring catch more than 350 years ago.

Frequent *tokkyū* on the JR Esashi line run between Hakodate and Kikonai (¥1620, 35 minutes). Kikonai is also connected to Esahi by the JR Esahi line – a few daily *kaisoku* ply this route (¥900, 1¼ hours).

Buses run year-round between Hakodate and Esashi (¥1830, 2¼ hours, frequent), and infrequently from April to November between Esashi and Matsumae (¥2720, two hours, four daily).

From Esashi station, it's a 20-minute walk downhill to the tourist sites.

DŌ-Ō 道央

Central Hokkaidō is where Hokkaidō garners its much deserved reputation for stunning national parks, world-class ski slopes and rustic onsen towns. Although the scenic port town of Otaru is the region's largest population centre, the focus is firmly on Niseko, where legendary powder attracts skiers and snowboarders from across the globe. And, while the French might have invented *après-ski*, it is the Japanese who have elevated this concept to an art form. After a long day on the frozen slopes, retire to a steamy onsen while nursing a fine bottle of sake – bliss!

OTARU 小樽

☎0134 / pop 138,000

Resist the temptation to beeline straight for Niseko, and escape to Otaru for a weekend, a day or even an afternoon. One of Hokkaidō's most popular tourist destinations for Japanese visitors, Otaru is a romantic port town steeped in a rich history that dates back to its glory days as a major herring centre. Otaru was the terminal station for Hokkaidō's first railroad, and today nostalgic warehouses still line the picturesque canal district. Whether you stroll through the snow while holding your sweetheart's hand, or pace off the perfect shot while steadying your Nikon, Otaru will be a memorable visit.

Orientation & Information

The main part of town is small enough to tackle on foot, though tourist buses loop through the city taking in most of the sights

Net Cafe La Fille (カフェ・ラ・フィーユ; ☎ 32-1234; Inaho 1-12-5; per 30min ¥400; 9am-6pm Wed-Mon) Internet access; find it by turning right out

SEIKAN TUNNEL 青函トンネル

A modern marvel of Japanese engineering, this railway tunnel travels beneath the Tsugaru Strait, connecting the islands of Honshū and Hokkaidō. With a total length of 53.85km, including a 240m-deep and 23.3km-long undersea portion, the Seikan Tunnel is the deepest and longest undersea tunnel in the world. Prior to 2006, you could actually get off the train, and take a seriously claustrophobic tour of the tunnel's inner workings. However, since the Hokkaidō *shinkansen* is currently under construction, and scheduled for completion in 2015, tours are unlikely to recommence any time soon. Because of all the construction, this site is closed off to private tours. But, once everything concludes and the bullet train starts running, it is likely that they will allow people to disembark the train and tour the station as in the past.

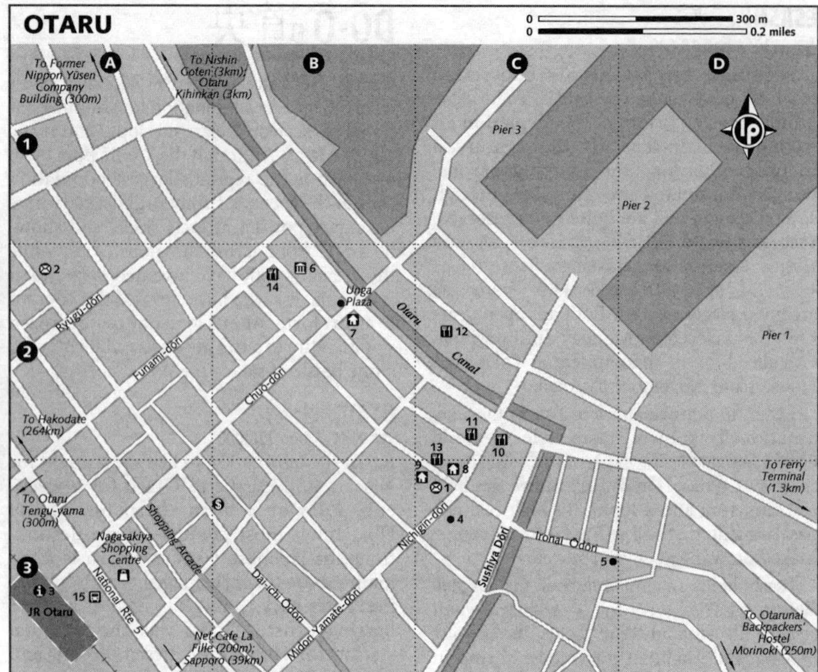

of the station, pass four sets of lights, then look for it on the right just after the pedestrian bridge.

Tourist information office (☎ 29-1333; 🕑 9am-6pm) Located inside the JR Otaru station.

Sights

Walk beneath the old Victorian-style gas lamps lining the **Otaru Canal** (小樽運河), and admire the charismatic old warehouses dating from the Meiji and Taisho eras – many of them are labelled in Japanese, English and Russian.

The **Otaru Museum** (☎ 33-2439; admission ¥300; 🕑 9.30am-5pm) is housed in a restored warehouse dating from 1893. It's small, but has displays on Hokkaidō's natural history, some Ainu relics, and various special exhibitions on herring, ceramics and literature.

At the northern end of the canal, behind the park, is the **Former Nippon Yūsen Company Building** (旧日本郵船株式会社小樽支店; ☎ 22-3316; admission ¥300; 🕑 9.30am-5pm Tue-Sun). At one time, much of Hokkaidō's shipping orders were processed in this very building, which has been tastefully restored to its former grandeur.

More historic buildings can be seen along **Nichigin-dōri** (日銀道り), once known as the 'Wall Street of the North. Don't miss the **Bank of Japan** (☎ 21-1111; admission free; 🕑 9.30am-5pm Tue-Sun), a classically elegant brick building that was designed by the same architect responsible for Tokyo Station. The exterior is marked by owl keystones, which pay homage to the Ainu guardian deity, while an impressive 100m-high ceiling highlights the interior.

Self-styled as the Venice of Japan, Otaru is also trying to build a name for itself as a glass-blowing town. **K's Blowing** (☎ 31-5454; www.ks-blowing.net; lessons ¥1800-2500; 🕑 9am-4.30pm) is a famous gallery and studio where you can take a short lesson (in English). Prices are based on what you want to make – simple but elegant cups, bowls and vases are all within your capacity. And you can always shop around the neighbouring area of craft shops if your project turns out to be a failure.

From late April to mid-October you can take a sightseeing boat from Otaru's Pier 3 (¥1550, 85 minutes), which cruises around the shoreline and returns to the pier. It can also

INFORMATION
Main Post Office 中央郵便局 1 C3
Post Office 郵便局 2 A2
Tourist Information Office 観光案内所 3 A3

SIGHTS & ACTIVITIES
Bank of Japan 日本銀行 4 C3
K's Blowing ケーズブローイング堺町工房 5 C3
Otaru Museum 小樽市博物館 6 B2

SLEEPING
Hotel Nord Otaru ホテルノルド小樽 7 B2
Hotel Vibrant Otaru ホテルヴィブラントオタル 8 C3
Otaru Grand Hotel Classic 小樽グランドホテルクラシック 9 C3

EATING
Denuki-kōji 出抜小路 10 C2
Kita no Ice Cream Yasan 北のアイスクリーム屋さん 11 C2
Otaru Sōko No 1 小樽倉庫 No 1 .... 12 C2
Sushi-toku すし徳 13 C2
Uminekoya 海猫屋 14 B2

TRANSPORT
Bus Station バスターミナル 15 A3

drop you off at the village of Shukutsu, from where you can catch a bus back to town.

A few kilometres north of Otaru, along the coast in the village of Shukutsu, the **Otaru Kihinkan** (小樽貴賓館; ☎ 24-0024; www.otaru-kihinkan.jp, in Japanese; admission ¥1000; 9am-6pm Apr-Oct, 9am-5pm Nov-Mar) is a herring-money mansion, built by the Aoyama family in 1918. This amazing Japanese-style building has all the trimmings: an *uguisu-bari* (squeaking corridor designed to reveal intruders), a lavish 100-tatami room, ornate woodwork and even opulent Arita porcelain pit toilets.

A short walk from the mansion brings you to the **Nishin Goten** (鰊御殿; ☎ 22-1038; admission ¥300; 9am-5pm mid-Apr–Nov), an enormous complex that housed herring-industry barons and their seasonal labourers during the Meiji and Taishō eras.

Bus 11 runs between the JR Otaru station and the Otaru Kihinkan and the Nishin Goten – get off at the last stop, which is the Otaru-suizokukan (Otaru Aquarium, ¥200, 25 minutes).

Sleeping

There are several rider houses and cycling terminals in and around Otaru, which offer cheap accommodation in the ¥1000 to ¥1500 range. Ask at the tourist information centres for detailed directions as they can sometimes be a bit difficult to find.

Otarunai Backpackers' Hostel Morinoki (おたるないバックパッカーズホステル杜の樹; ☎ 23-2175; 4-15 Aioi-chō; http://backpackers-hostel.infotaru.net; dm ¥3200;) Catering specifically to 'free and independent travellers', this is a great little backpacker spot that is worlds apart from your usual Japan YH offerings. Accommodation is in fairly simple male and female dormitories, though guests are treated to kitchen, laundry and internet facilities, as well as bilingual staff, communal lounges and a laid-back and congenial vibe. The hostel is about a 20-minute walk from the JR Otaru station – exit, turn right and head straight through a series of traffic lights until you see the au mobile shop on the left-hand side. Turn left here, and continue straight until you see the big stone gate; make a right and you'll see the hostel on your left-hand side after about 100m.

Otaru Tengu-yama (小樽天狗山; ☎ 33-6944; www.tengu.co.jp/english/index.html; 2-13-1 Mogami; r per person from ¥3800;) A bit outside the city centre, three adjacent properties – the Honkan, the Villa and the Sanrokukan – are all run by the Otaru Tengu-yama association. All three buildings are slightly different in character, though the theme is constant throughout, namely cheap but pleasant accommodation aimed at nonfussy budget travellers. Take bus 9 from JR Otaru station to the final stop (¥200, 20 minutes), which drops you off right near the property at the foot of Mt. Tengu – ask the driver to point it out to you.

our pick **Hotel Vibrant Otaru** (☎ 31-3939; www.vibrant-otaru.jp; 1-3-1 Ironai; s/d from ¥5500/6500, vault r from ¥10,500;) A stylish renovation of a historic Otaru bank resulted in this justifiably 'vibrant hotel', which is located across the road from the main post office. The lobby is very attractive with period-piece furniture including wrought-iron tables, while the rooms themselves are priced according to their size and shape. For a memorable night's stay, shell out a bit of extra cash and bed down in the old bank vault! LAN cable internet available.

Hotel Nord Otaru (☎ 24-0500; www.hotelnord.co.jp/english/index.htm; 1-4-16 Ironai; s/d from ¥7350/12,600;) A charismatic European-style hotel that overlooks the warehouses along Otaru Canal, the upmarket Hotel Nord offers a variety of rooms with soft lighting and clean lines. The hotel is also home to a fabulous Mediterranean restaurant that makes proper use of Otaru's legendary seafood. LAN cable internet available.

Otaru Grand Hotel Classic (☎ 22-6500; http://otaru-grand-hotel.tabite.jp, in Japanese; 1-8-25 Ironai; s/d from ¥8400/16,800; 💻 📶) Another former bank turned hotel, the Otaru Grand Hotel Classic is adjacent to the post office, and is its own slice of history. As one of the first foreign-friendly hotels in town, the building offers tastefully styled Western rooms that are accented with nostalgia-inducing leaded glass windows overlooking the city streets. LAN cable internet available.To get here, exit the station, turn right and head straight through a series of traffic lights until you see the intersection between the tracks and the road. Turn left just before, and continue straight until you see the Otaru Grand hotel.

Eating & Drinking

If you're the type of person who enjoys scouting out good eateries before sitting down at the table, check out the **Denuki-kōji** (1-1 Ironai; 🕑 10am-8pm), located on the southern banks of Asakusa-bashi. This tourist-friendly complex contains a dozen or so restaurants spanning a variety of cuisines – most have plastic models out front to help attract indecisive diners.

our pick **Kita no Ice Cream Yasan** (☎ 23-8983; 1-2-18 Ironai; ice cream from ¥350; 🕑 9.30am-7pm) A legendary Otaru institution across from Denuki-kōji (look for the English sign), Kita no Ice Cream Yasan scoops some seriously stomach-turning flavours including *nattō* (fermented soy beans), tofu, crab, beer…even sea urchin. Squid ink – jet black – is about as bizarre as ice cream gets. Menu is in English, Japanese and Korean, which certainly reflects the store's increasing international fan base.

Sushi-toku (すし徳; ☎ 22-3457; 1-4-23 Hanazono; sushi set from ¥630; 🕑 11am-9pm) For Japanese travellers, eating Otaru is *all* about sushi – Hokkaidō specialities include *sake* (salmon), *ikura* (salmon roe), *uni* (sea urchin roe) and *kani* (crab). Picture menus list the various sets available, which vary according to whatever is fresh and in season. The restaurant is directly across the street from the Otaru Grand Hotel Classic (above).

Uminekoya (☎ 32-2914; Ironai 2-2-14; dishes from ¥750; 🕑 lunch & dinner) Housed in a crumbling brick warehouse laced with vines of ivy, this famous bar-restaurant across from the museum has been the setting for several novels of Japanese literary fame. The English menu helps with the ordering, though it's best to ask the waiter for their *osusume* (recommendation) as the catch of the day and some local sake or beer is generally what you're after here.

Otaru Sōko No 1 (☎ 21-2323; 5-4 Minato-machi; dishes from ¥800; 🕑 11am-10pm) A nice microbrewery with a selection of fresh brews on tap, plus both German and Japanese fare to complement its Bavarian decor. Potatoes and sausages are a big hit, though you're free to choose something a little more heart-healthy from the English menu. There is live music here occasionally to provide some background accompaniment to your meal. An 'Otaru Beer' sign marks the brewery, which is along the banks of the canal.

Getting There & Away

BUS

Buses run frequently to Sapporo (¥590, one hour), and less often to Niseko (¥1600, 1¾ hours, three daily).

BOAT

From the port of Otaru-kō, **Shin-Nihonkai** (☎ 22-6191) ferries run at 10.30am from Tuesday to Saturday, and at 7.30pm on Sunday, to Niigata (from ¥6200, 18 hours), returning every day but Monday. Ferries also run daily between Otaru and Maizuru (from ¥9600, 20 hours), just north of Kyoto. To get to the ferry terminal, take the bus from stop 4 in front of JR Otaru Station (¥210, 30 minutes). There is a small ticket office at the pier.

CAR

If you're driving, the Sapporo Expressway (札幌自動車道) runs between Otaru and the greater Sapporo area.

TRAIN

There are hourly *kaisoku* on the JR Hakodate line between Otaru and Sapporo (¥620, 40 minutes), and occasional *kaisoku* between Otaru and Niseko (¥1410, two hours).

NISEKO ニセコ

☎ 0136 / pop 6000

Hokkaidō is dotted with world-class ski resorts, but the reigning prince of powder is unquestionably Niseko. Despite its village status, Niseko boasts four interconnected resorts, namely Hirafu, Higashiyama, An'nupuri and Hanazono, which together contain more than 800 skiable hectares. Because of its blessed location, Niseko experiences northwest to southeast Siberian weather fronts, which produce a soft and light powdery snow that skiers and snowboarders love to carve. In fact, Niseko was recently named the world's second snowiest ski resort, with an annual average snowfall of more than 15m! (Pipped at the post by Mt Baker Ski Area in Washington State, USA, according to *Forbes* magazine.)

Of course, the secret is out, and Niseko is currently experiencing an unprecedented boom, primarily fuelled by Australians and Singaporeans. Property values are soaring, new resorts and condos are springing up left and right, and the tiny village of Hirafu is rapidly becoming an international hotspot. Depending on whom you ask, Niseko is either losing its traditional Japanese character and in danger of rapid overdevelopment, or becoming floridly cosmopolitan in light of increased foreign investment. Regardless of your opinion, however, skiing at Niseko, with its jaw-dropping views of mountains, is unequalled.

Orientation

The ski resorts of Hirafu, Higashiyama, An'nupuri and Hanazono are run together as a single administrative unit, appropriately dubbed Niseko United. At the base of the ski slopes lie several towns and villages that comprise Niseko's population centre. Most of the hotels, restaurants, bars and tourists are clustered together in **Hirafu** (ひらふ), while Higashiyama, An'nupuri and Hanazono are much quieter and less developed.

Further east are **Kutchan** (倶知安) and **Niseko** (ニセコ) proper, which are more permanent population centres that remain decidedly Japanese. While there is a JR Hirafu station, it is far from the town and poorly serviced by infrequent buses. As a result, incoming passengers on the train disembark at either JR Kutchan or JR Niseko stations, and then switch to local buses. During the ski season, there are also direct buses connecting the Welcome Centre in Hirafu village to Sapporo's New Chitose Airport.

To the east of the valley lies **Yōtei-zan** (羊蹄山), a perfectly conical volcano reminiscent of Fuji-san. Yōtei-zan draws its fair share of hikers in the summer months, though there is something almost holy about the snow-covered crater on a chilly winter day.

> **SKIING**
>
> For up-to-the-minute stats, maps and reviews, check out www.snowjapan.com/e/index.php.
>
> - **Niseko** (opposite)
> - **Furano** (p623)
> - **Rusustu** (p606)
> - **Abashiri** (p630)
> - **Sapporo** (p588)

Information

There are very small **tourist information offices** (Niseko ☎ 44-2468, Kutchan 22-5151; www.niseko.gr.jp/eigo.html; 🕑 10am-7pm) in both JR Niseko and Kutchan stations that can provide pamphlets, maps, bus timetables and help with bookings.

To meet the winter crush, the **Hirafu Welcome Centre** (ひらふウエルカムセンター; ☎ 22-0109; www.grand-hirafu.jp/winter/en/index.html; 🕑 8.30am-9pm), which is where direct buses to/from New Chitose Airport originate and terminate, also provides English-language information.

The Niseko area is packed throughout the ski season. If you're coming from Sapporo, it is recommended that you first visit one of the larger regional tourist information centres, and try to arrange accommodation in advance. Most of the accommodation places in Niseko are very internet savvy, which means that it's also fairly easy to make all of your reservations online well ahead of your trip.

Alternatively, consider visiting a Japanese travel agency to see if you can snag a discounted package holiday. Even if you're a fiercely independent traveller, you can save some serious cash and sometimes land yourself in an affordable room in a generally unaffordable hotel.

Sights & Activities

SKIING & SNOWBOARDING

Niseko United (www.niseko.ne.jp/en; 🕑 day 8.30am-4.30pm, night 4.30-9pm, Nov-Apr) is the umbrella name for four resorts: Niseko An'nupuri, Niseko Higashiyama, Niseko Grand Hirafu and the Hanazono area.

What makes Niseko United stand out from the competition is that you can access all four ski slopes by purchasing a single **All-Mountain**

Pass (day/night ¥4300/1900). This electronic tag gives you access to 20 different lifts and gondolas, as well as free rides on the intermountain shuttle bus. If you're planning on skiing for several days, a week or even the season, you can also buy discounted multiday passes.

Rental equipment is of very high quality, and can be picked up virtually everywhere at fairly standard but affordable prices. In fact, a good number of rental shops will deliver and pick up equipment straight to your accommodation. As with the All-Mountain Pass, you can save a bit of money by renting equipment over a longer period of time.

Niseko caters for skiers and snowboarders of all skill levels, and it's possible to spend several days here without repeating the same course. In total there are around 60 different beginner, intermediate and advanced runs with a 2m to 3m snow base that wind through varied terrain. While it's difficult to generalise such a massive area, Niseko United is arguably some of the finest skiing in Japan and Asia, and the whole world for that matter.

Downsides include long queues – particularly in Grand Hirafu and Higashiyama – and the usual piped music over loudspeakers, but it's all fairly standard for skiing in Japan. And, of course, you can always head out to An'nupuri and Hanazono if you want a little more space on the slopes.

Be sure to check the *Local Rules Guide* (available from the information centre), as accidents do happen and avalanches are a possibility after heavy snows. Note that Australian and New Zealand walkie-talkies are banned in Niseko United as they interfere with local television transmitters – you will be fined heavily if you are caught using one.

HIKING

While the mild summer months may be low season in Niseko, this is the best time of the year to tackle some of the area's challenging wilderness hikes.

There is a 16km circuit that starts just west of the summit of Niseko An'nupuri at **Goshiki Onsen** (五色温泉), and traverses several summits in the western Niseko range. This hike can be tackled in six to seven hours, and the trailhead is accessible by local bus lines.

From Goshiki Onsen, you can also trek east for two hours up the summit of **Niseko An'nupuri** (ニセコアンヌプリ; 1308m). If it's a clear day, the panorama at the top will be of the Niseko United ski resort as well as neighbouring Yōtei-zan.

One of the toughest day hikes around is a trek to the top of the perfect conical volcano **Yōtei-zan** (1893m). Known as 'Ezo Fuji' in recognition of its more famous southerly cousin, Yōtei-zan is covered in alpine flowers during the summer, though you're going to face a 10-hour, 10km slog to the top to see them. The trailhead for Yōtei-zan is at Yōtei-zan Tozan-guchi, which is south of Kutchan near JR Hirafu station, and is accessible by local bus lines.

ADVENTURE SPORTS

While skiing and snowboarding are Niseko's principal drawcards, you can also come here for ice climbing, snowshoeing and dog sledding, as well as canoeing, kayaking and river rafting in the summer. The **Niseko Outdoor Centre** (ニセコアウトドアセンター; ☎ 44-1133; www.noc-hokkaido.jp/e/index.html), near the An'nupuri ski slope, and the **Niseko Adventure Centre** (ニセコアドベンチャーセンター; ☎ 23-2093; www.nac-web.com/e_index.htm), in the village of Hirafu, can organise activities.

ONSEN

Trust us – there is nothing quite like the feeling of stepping out of your skis or snowboard, stripping off all of your clothing and jumping into a steamy hot onsen. Most hotels either have a hot spring on the premises, or can point you in the direction of the nearest bathhouse.

If you're waiting for a bus or train at the JR Niseko station, walk across the street to **Kiranoyu** (綺羅乃湯; ☎ 44-1100; bath ¥500; ⏰ 10am-9.30pm Thu-Tue), where you can scrub down in your choice of *hinoki* (cypress) or rock baths before catching an onward connection.

ONSEN

- **Tōya-ko Onsen** (p607)
- **Noboribetsu Onsen** (p609)
- **Asahidake Onsen** (p626)
- **Sōunkyō Onsen** (p628)
- **Kawayu Onsen** (p633)

Sleeping & Eating

Niseko is spread out, with nothing close to the stations. Most places will provide pick-up and drop-off, or you can take buses and shuttles to move about. The closer you get to the slopes themselves, the more options you'll have. Near the lifts, if you basically walk in a straight line, you'll run into a pension or two.

Note that our list is by no means comprehensive. While we have tried to select perennial travellers' favourites, there are dozens and dozens of recommended accommodation options in the Niseko area.

Niseko Kōgen Youth Hostel (ニセコ高原ユースホステル; Pooh's House; ☎/fax 44-1171; http://www13.ocn.ne.jp/~kogenyh/index2.html, in Japanese; 336 Aza Niseko; dm winter/summer ¥3200/3000, breakfast/dinner ¥500/1000; P 💻) This *Winnie the Pooh*–themed hostel occupies a converted schoolhouse, and is famous among travellers for the owner's incredible accordion solos. It's 5km from Niseko Station and about 1km west of the slopes at An'nupuri, though the staff will pick you up and drop you off wherever you need to go.

Niseko Tourist Home (ニセコツーリストホーム; ☎44-2517; http://niseko-th.com, in Japanese; dm Nov-Apr/Mar-Oct ¥3500/2500, incl 2 meals ¥5500/4500; P 💻) A clean and inexpensive wooden A-frame about 4km from Niseko station, the always-popular Tourist Home is a great budget base. Attracting a more Japanese crowd than the internationally minded youth hostels, the delightful owners have a lot of pride in their small ski town.

Niseko Annupuri Youth Hostel (ニセコアンヌプリユースホステル; ☎58-2084; www.annupuri-yh.com, in Japanese; 470-4 Niseko; dm incl 2 meals ¥5380; P) This mountain lodge with classic Continental airs sits conveniently close to the An'nupuri ski grounds. In between powder-perfect runs, guests congregate in front of the fire, swapping ski tips and tucking into delicious meals.

Jam Garden (ジャムガーデン; ☎22-6676; www.jamgarden.com, in Japanese; 37-89 Kabayama, Kucchan-chō; r per person incl 2 meals ¥7000, group discounts available) Right near the ski lift at Hirafu, this deluxe farmhouse comes complete with its own Jacuzzi and sauna. Western-style rooms and country cooking are also on offer once you pry yourself away from the nearby slopes of Hirafu.

Pension Forest Green (ペンションフォレストグリーン; ☎44-2868; www3.ocn.ne.jp/~forest-g, in Japanese; per person incl 2 meals ¥7000; P) This rustic five-room pension set amidst the forest green offers memorable Chinese feasts as part of the lodging package, as well as a nice little pool table where you can bond with other guests. The owners are avid anglers, and can arrange fly-fishing trips in the summer.

Hilton Niseko Village (ニセコヒルトンヴィレジ; ☎44-1111; fax 44-3224; www.hiltonworldresorts.com/Resorts/Niseko; Higashiyama Onsen; r from ¥19,000; P 💻 wi-fi) There is no shortage of resort hotels in Niseko, though the Hilton enjoys the best location of all – it is quite literally attached to the Niseko Gondola in Higashiyama. As you might expect from the luxury moniker, Western-style rooms at the Hilton are complimented by a whole slew of amenities spread out across a veritable village. Check the website before arriving as special deals are usually available. LAN cable internet available.

Annupuri Village (アンヌプリ・ヴィレジ; ☎59-2111; fax 59-2112; www.annupurivillage.com; 432-21 Niseko; 4-8 person ski chalet from ¥74,000-98,000; P 💻 wi-fi) If you're travelling with a large group of friends, consider giving the resort hotels a pass, and renting an immaculately designed ski chalet in Annupuri Village, located at the base of the An'nupuri ski slopes. Natural hardwoods and picture windows are featured prominently from floor to ceiling, while rich stone fireplaces, spa-quality bathroom fixtures, professional kitchens and plasma TVs add a touch of modern class. Summer discounts available.

Many of the lodges and ryokan offer great meals cooked to order, and the slopes have plenty of snacks, pizza, *rāmen* and other goodies to stave off the munchies while you're in your gear. After hours, things are tricky because lodging is spread out and buses are surprisingly inconvenient, though there are plenty of watering holes in Hirafu that are usually packed with boisterous and fun-loving Aussies.

Getting There & Away

BUS

During the ski season, a couple of companies run regular highway buses from JR Sapporo station and New Chitose Airport to Niseko, a few of which stop in Rusutsu. The trip takes 3¼ hours, costs ¥2300 (return ¥3850) and provides the most direct access to the various slopes.

Reservations are necessary, and it's recommended that you book well ahead of your departure date. If you don't speak Japanese, ask the staff at the tourist information centres or your accommodation to make a reservation for you.

Chūō Bus (☎ 011-231-0500; www.chuo-bus.co.jp, in Japanese)

Donan Bus (☎ 0123-46-5701; www.donanbus.co.jp, in Japanese)

Hokkaidō Resort Liner (☎ 011-219-4411)

Trans Orbit Hokkaidō (☎ 011-242-2040)

CAR

Scenic Rte 5 winds from Sapporo to Otaru around the coast, and then cuts inland through the mountains down to Niseko. Having a car will certainly make it easier to move between the various ski slopes. In the summer (low season), public transport drops off, which provides more incentive to pick up a car in Sapporo.

TRAINS

Frequent *futsū* run on the JR Hakodate line between Sapporo and Otaru (¥620, 40 minutes), and between Otaru and Niseko (¥1410, 1½ hours) via Kutchan (¥1040, 1¼ hours). In the peak of the ski season, there are also a few daily *tokkyū* between Niseko and Sapporo (¥4560, two hours).

While there is a JR Hirafu station, it is far from the town itself, and is not well serviced by local buses. From JR Niseko and JR Kutchan stations, you will need to switch to local buses to access the villages at the base of the ski slopes.

Getting Around

There are twice-hourly local buses linking JR Kutchan and JR Niseko stations to Hirafu, Higashiyama and An'nupuri villages. Pick up a schedule from the tourist information centres so that you don't miss your connection.

If you've purchased an All-Mountain Pass, you can ride the free hourly shuttle bus between Hirafu, Higashiyama and An'nupuri.

RUSUTSU ルスツ

☎ 0136 / pop 2000

Compared to neighbouring Niseko, Rusutsu is something akin to the runt of the litter. Although some Japanese argue that the skiing here doesn't get any better, Rusutsu is much, much less developed than Niseko, and vastly pales in size and scope. On the flip side, the slopes aren't nearly as crowded, and the lack of foreigners results in a decidedly more traditional ambiance.

SIGHTS & ACTIVITIES	
Itō Onsen いとう温泉	1 D1
Koke-no-dōmon 苔の洞門	2 D1
Kompira Promenade 金比羅散策路	(see 8)
Mimatsu Masao Memorial Museum 三松正夫記念館	3 A3
Nishiyama Crater Promenade 西山火口散策路	4 A3
Noboribetsu Onsen 登別温泉	5 C3
Tōya-ko Onsen 洞 爺 湖 温 泉	6 A3
Tōya-ko Sightseeing Cruises 洞爺湖観光クルーズ	7 A2
Volcanic Science Museum 火山科学館	8 A3
Whale Watching 鯨ウオッチング	(see 13)
SLEEPING	
Muroran Youth Hostel 室蘭ユースホステル	9 B4
Naka-tōya Camping Ground 中洞爺キャンプ場	10 B2
Shōwa Shin-zan Youth Hostel 昭和新山ユースホステル	11 A3
Windsor Hotel International ザ・ウィンザーホテル	12 A2
TRANSPORT	
Muroran-kō ferry terminal	13 B4

There is some serious powder waiting for you at **Rusutsu Resort** (ルスツリゾート; ☎ 46-3111; http://en.rusutsu.co.jp; lift ticket day/night ¥5100/2000; ⌚ day 9am-5pm, night 4-9pm, Nov-Apr), which boasts well-groomed trails and fantastic tree runs – at times, you're often the first person passing through the powder! The resort caters equally to skiers and snowboarders, has trails of all difficulty levels, 18 lifts, a 100m half pipe and numerous off-piste options. There are also three restaurants offering bilingual menus, so you can get your energy back by feasting on anything from *rāmen* and sushi to burgers and curry rice.

The cheapest yet most conveniently located option is the **Rusutsu Powder Lodge** (ルスツパウダーロッジ; ☎ 22-4611; fax 22-4613; dm ¥3150; Ⓟ), which has firm beds and crisp linens, shared bathrooms and a communal ski-bum atmosphere. It is located just seconds from the slopes next to the Seicomart shop.

A more upmarket option is the **Pension Lilla Huset** (ペンションリッラヒューセット; ☎ 46-3676; fax 46-3435; www.youtei.org/selection/english/english.htm; per person incl 2 meals from ¥7000; Ⓟ 💻), a red-panelled Western-style inn offering basic rooms and simple meals. Things here aren't fancy by any stretch of the imagination, though you can't beat the location right at the bottom of the lifts.

During the ski season, several companies run highway buses from Sapporo and New Chitose Airport to Niseko via Rusutsu (¥1990,

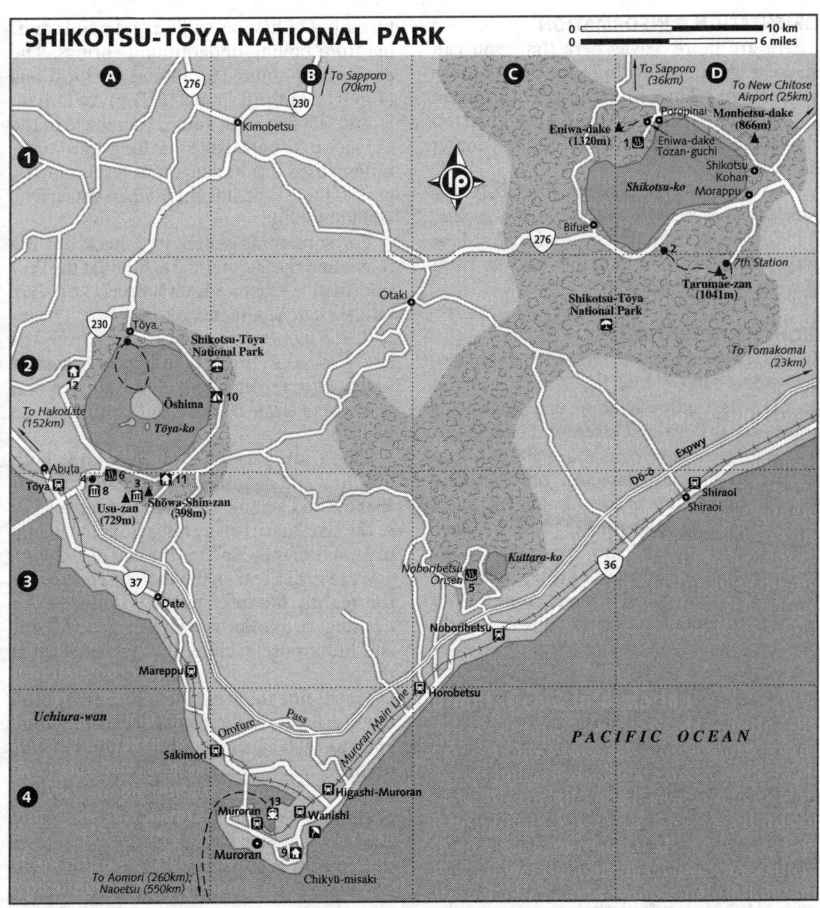

two hours). For information on how to make a booking, see p605.

If you're driving, Rte 230 runs between Sapporo and Tōya-ko via Rusutsu village.

SHIKOTSU-TŌYA NATIONAL PARK 支笏洞爺国立公園

☎0142

Shikotsu-tōya (993 sq km) is much more developed than other national parks on the island, and is relatively easy to access via both public and private transport. Shikotsu-tōya is largely mountainous wilderness that is criss-crossed by rugged hiking trails, marked by two picturesque caldera lakes, and home to two of Hokkaidō's premiere hot-spring towns.

Tōya-ko Onsen 洞爺湖温泉

Tōya-ko, a rather touristy hot-spring resort sprawling along the shores of Lake Tōya, garnered a share of the international spotlight in 2008 by hosting the 34th G8 Summit, though things have calmed down considerably since then. As the closest onsen town to Sapporo and New Chitose Airport, however, Lake Tōya remains one of Hokkaidō's most popular spots for scenic soaking. Then again, it might be a bit hard to relax and enjoy your surroundings, especially when you're staring down active volcanoes that could blow their tops without a moment's notice – at least you'll be fresh and clean when you go!

ORIENTATION & INFORMATION

There are more Tōyas here than you can shake a stick at, but don't let that confuse you. There's Tōya JR station, Tōya Onsen (on the south of the lake) and Tōya town, on the north side. And of course, don't forget Tōya-ko itself.

The Tōya-ko Onsen **tourist office** (☎ 75-2446; www.laketoya.com/en; 144 Tōyako Onsen; 🕑 9am-5pm Mon-Fri) is downhill from the bus station; head towards the lake, then look for it across from the Hotel Grand Tōya.

SIGHTS & ACTIVITIES

In 1943, after a series of violent earthquakes, **Shōwa-Shin-zan** (昭和新山; 398m) emerged as an upstart bump in some vegetable fields southeast of Tōya-ko Onsen, and surged upwards for two more years to reach its present height. At the time, Japanese officials were keen to hush it up as they thought it was a bad omen, and might portend an inauspicious end to WWII. They even urged locals to douse the volcanic flames (they obviously didn't!) so that Allied aircraft couldn't use them for orientation. Shōwa-Shin-zan is still belching sulphurous fumes, creating an awesome spectacle for visitors and keeping local officials nervous about its next move.

Nearby, **Usu-zan** (有珠山; 729m), a taller and more formidable volcano, erupted quite violently in 2000, sending boulders thousands of feet into the air. The ash cloud that rained down on Tōya-ko was 2700m high, and volcanic bombs threatened to down circling news helicopters. For a closer look, there's a **ropeway** (有珠山ロープウェイ; ☎ 75-2401; return ¥1450; 🕑 8am-5pm) that runs from the base of Usu-zan (past the tourist shops) to a small viewing platform overlooking the steaming crater.

Near the ropeway, you should definitely check out the **Mimatsu Masao Memorial Museum** (☎ 75-2365; admission ¥300; 🕑 8am-5pm Apr-Oct, 9am-4pm Nov-Mar), which is devoted to the local postmaster who actually purchased Shōwa-Shin-zan in 1946, and subsequently saved it from greedy mining companies. He spent years diagramming its growth using an ingenious method that has become a standard among volcanologists today. English signage in the museum is limited.

The **Nishiyama Crater Promenade** (admission free; 🕑 closed 10 Nov-20 Apr) is a bit like walking through an area after a bomb blast. Steam hisses out of fissures while azure ponds bubble from boiling underground springs. The entrance is about 10 minutes by local bus (¥160) from the terminal in Tōya-ko Onsen; it costs ¥300 to park your own vehicle in the expansive car park. Note that the area is sometimes closed due to dangerous levels of toxic gas – if there is no one there when you arrive, you know why!

For something sedentary, check out the movie and the audiovisual exhibits at the very informative **Volcanic Science Museum** (☎ 75-2555; www.toyako-vc.jp/en/volcano; admission ¥600; 🕑 9am-5pm). It's just two minutes on foot from the bus terminal, in front of the **Kompira Promenade** (admission free; 🕑 closed 10 Nov-20 Apr), an area that was laid to waste by the eruption of Usu-zan in 2000.

The 37km perimeter of Tōya-ko is both beautiful and daunting – **cruises** (¥1320; 🕑 8am-4pm) out to Ōshima, the island in the middle of the lake, depart every hour from the pier in town. From mid-April to the end of October, you can grab a seat on the shoreline and watch the nightly **fireworks** (roughly 🕑 8.45-9pm). An evening fireworks-viewing cruise (¥1500) is a little more exciting; get your tickets at the pier.

Hotels line the waterfront, and many offer day-use access to their **baths**. Rates vary from ¥500 to ¥1000; bring your own towel to save on the hire fee.

SLEEPING

Naka-tōya Camping Ground (☎ 66-7022; camp sites per person from ¥330; 🕑 May-Sep; Ⓟ) On the eastern edge of the lake, several kilometres from Tōya-ko Onsen. Buses from Toya JR station are infrequent, stopping here only two or three times each day, which means that camping is only really an option for those with their own car. This is a basic camp site with grassy pitches and shared facilities with hot water. Camping equipment is available for rent here.

Shōwa-Shin-zan Youth Hostel (☎ 75-2283; fax 75-2872; 103 Soubetsu-onsen, Soubetsu-chō, Usu-gun; dm from ¥3150; Ⓟ) With comfortable shared-room accommodation, a small onsite hot spring and spic-and-span cooking facilities, this is a great option for shoestring travellers in search of a social atmosphere. The hostel is on the road leading up to Usu-zan. By bus it's eight minutes from Tōya-ko Onsen; get off at the Tozan-guchi stop, from where it's just a one-minute walk. Bicycles are ¥1000 per day, and are a great way to cover ground around town.

Hotel Grand Tōya (ホテルグランドトーヤ; ☎ 75-2288; fax 75-3434; www.grandtoya.com; 144 Tōyako Onsen, Tōyako-chō, Abuta-gun; r per person incl 2 meals ¥7900; P 💻) You can't beat the location of this large, concrete resort hotel, smack bang in the middle of town. Japanese- and Western-style rooms have lake views, and there is a colourful, open-air bath, and a tiny cafe with al fresco seating in the summer months.

our pick **Windsor Hotel International** (☎ 0120--29-0500; www.windsor-hotels.co.jp/en/toya; Shimizu Abuta-chō; low-/high-season d from ¥35,700/46,200; P 💻) A member of the prestigious group 'The Leading Hotels of the World,' and the location of the 34th G8 Summit, this cruise ship–shaped resort on the northwestern shores of the lake is quite possibly the finest upmarket accommodation in all of Hokkaidō. Rooms vary considerably in size and price, and some of the larger suites are more than a US$1000 a night, but everything here is predictably a class act. The highlight of the Windsor is its impressive restaurant offerings – no less than a dozen different options in total – including a Michelin three-star bistro by French chef Michel Bras. Free shuttle buses run between the JR Tōya station and the hotel and LAN cable internet is available.

GETTING THERE & AROUND

Frequent *tokkyū* run on the JR Muroran line between JR Tōya station and Hakodate (¥5340, 1¾ hours), between Tōya and Sapporo (¥5760, 1¾ hours), and between Tōya and Noboribetsu (¥2650, 35 minutes). Local buses run every 30 minutes between JR Tōya station and Tōya-ko Onsen (¥320, 25 minutes).

Highway buses are a less expensive option, running frequently between Tōya and Sapporo (¥2700, 2¾ hours), and between Tōya and Muroran (¥1170, 1¾ hours).

From April to November, regular buses also run between Tōya and Noboribetsu Onsen ¥1530, 1¼ hours) via the scenic Orofure pass; some continue onwards to New Chitose Airport (¥2140, 2½ hours).

If you're driving, a well-maintained network of local roads branches off of the Dō-ō Expressway (道央自動車道) running between Sapporo and Hakodate.

Noboribetsu Onsen 登別温泉

☎ 0143

Nobiribetsu is the most popular onsen resort on the island, boasting over 30 bathhouses clustered tightly together along a narrow, winding street. Unfortunately, it's not nearly as atmospheric as you might expect – unsightly convenience stores, concrete hotels and garish souvenir shops lend a tacky Disneyland-esque atmosphere to an otherwise rustic hot-springs town. However, if you can get over the mass commercialisation of Nobiribetsu, you're in for an onsen experience par excellence. The rejuvenating water here originates from a volcanic sulphurous 'hell' not far above, and some of the higher-end spas are among Hokkaidō's best.

INFORMATION

The **tourist association office** (☎ 84-3311; 60 Noboribetsu onsen-machi; ⏲ 9am-6pm Mon-Fri, 10am-4pm Sat & Sun) has English maps, hotel locations and good English info on the bathing hours.

SIGHTS & ACTIVITIES

The granddaddy of onsen resorts is **Dai-ichi Takimoto-kan** (第一滝本館; ☎ 84-3322; www.takimotokan.co.jp/english; onsen bath ¥2000; ⏲ 9am-5pm). Although it's a bit over the top for some, this massive and unmistakable compound has more than 15 different kinds of baths, ranging from take-your-skin-off scalding to cryogenic freeze-inducing cold. Several outdoor *rotemburo* (open-air baths) offer beautiful views of the valley, and there's even a swimming pool (where you will require a swimsuit).

For half the price, you'll get much of the same luxury (minus the view) at the **Noboribetsu Grand Hotel** (登別グランドホテル; ☎ 717-8899; www.nobogura.co.jp/english; onsen bath ¥1000; ⏲ 12.30-5pm & 6.30-8pm), a few steps away from the bus station. The star attraction is the beautiful *hinoki* bath, and a domed ceiling to give the spacious impression of a Roman-era bath. Men's and women's areas alternate during the day to give each gender the chance to see both bathing areas.

Jigokudani (地獄谷; Hell Valley) is a short walk uphill, offering viewers a peek at what may await us in the afterlife: sulphurous gases, hissing vents and vividly coloured rocks. Pools of scalding water can be seen from **Ōyu-numa** (大湯沼; Boiling Water Swamp). For those of us who are far from heaven-bound, it's good to know that hell (if the Japanese have anything to say about it!) will surely include a lot of onsen.

The simple **public bath** (夢元さぎり湯; ☎ 84-2050; 60 Noboribetsu onsen-machi; onsen bath ¥390; 🕑 7am-10pm), on the 1st floor of an office building next to the tourist association office has three spartan baths if you want a quick soap and scrub without having to peel a ¥1000 bill or two out of your wallet.

SLEEPING

Dai-ichi Takimoto-kan (☎ 84-3322; www.takimotokan.co.jp/english; 55 Noboritsu Onsen; r incl 2 meals from ¥11,175; P 🖳) The town's most famous hot spring also doubles as a resort hotel, offering Western- and Japanese-style rooms in several wings of varying luxury. Meals, which vary seasonally, are offered either buffet-style in the main dining room, or brought straight to your room, and guests receive complimentary 24-hour access to the hot springs complex. Check the internet before arriving as you can sometimes score some big discounts, especially during weekdays and off-season.

Noboribetsu Grand Hotel (☎ 717-8899; fax 84-2543; www.nobogura.co.jp, in Japanese; 154 Noboritsu Onsen; r per person incl 2 meals from ¥12,600 P 🖳) A slightly more refined alternative to the Takimoto-kan, the Grand Hotel was once a favourite of the Imperial family, though today it principally caters to package travellers on the tour-bus circuit. Still, there are some beautiful Western- and Japanese-style rooms here, and having 24-hour access to the beautiful baths is a treat in itself. If you can read Japanese, again, check the internet before arriving as there are sometimes some big discounts on offer.

Kashōtei Hanaya (花鐘亭はなや; ☎ 84-2521; fax 84-2240; www.kashoutei-hanaya.co.jp/english/index.htm; 134 Noboritsu Onsen; r per person incl 2 meals from ¥12,750; P 🖳) A great midrange ryokan with Japanese-style rooms (some overlook the river), Kashōtei Hanaya is a more intimate option to the larger and occasionally overwhelming hot-springs hotels. It's located near the southern end of the resort drag, and features its own charming little onsen that is only open to guests.

Ryotei Hanayura (旅亭花ゆら; ☎ 84-2322; fax 84-2035; http:\\hanayura.com/en/index.html; 100 Noboritsu Onsen; r incl 2 meals from ¥23,000; P 🖳) While it's double the price of other accommodation in town, Hanayura is the embodiment of what you imagine a hot-springs resort to be. Classically Japanese in style and service, the emphasis here is on personalised attention and subdued luxury, which isn't too hard given that there are only 37 rooms, some of which feature private outdoor baths. The hotel is located near the northern end of the resort drag, though with advanced reservations, they'll pick you up in Sapporo.

GETTING THERE & AWAY

Frequent *tokkyū* run on the JR Muroran line between JR Noboribetsu station and Hakodate (¥6700, 2½ hours), between Noboribetsu and Sapporo (¥4360, 1¼ hours), and between Noboribetsu and JR Tōya station (¥2650, 35 minutes). Local buses run every 30 minutes between JR Noboribetsu station and Noboribetsu Onsen (¥330, 15 minutes).

Highway buses are a less expensive option, running frequently between Noboribetsu and Sapporo (¥1900, two hours), and between Noboribetsu and Muroran (¥710, 1¼ hours).

From April to November, regular buses also run between Noboribetsu and Tōya (¥1530, 1¼ hours) via the scenic Orofure pass; some continue onwards to New Chitose Airport (¥1330, 1¼ hours).

If you're driving, Noboribetsu is easily accessed by the Dō-ō Expressway (道央自動車道) running between Sapporo and Hakodate.

Shikotsu-ko 支笏湖

☎ 0123

Completely surrounded by soaring volcanoes, Shikotsu-ko is the second largest caldera lake in Japan, though it perennially plays second fiddle to Tōya-ko. As a result, Shikotsu-ko is much less developed than its spotlight-grabbing sibling, and attracts a more independent crowd of outdoor enthusiasts. While onsen activity is a bit more subdued here, Shikotsu-ko does provide some of the best hiking opportunities in the whole of the national park, and there is a refreshing lack of rampant commercialism.

ORIENTATION & INFORMATION

The area is served by Shikotsu Kohan (支笏湖畔), a tiny town consisting mainly of a bus station, a **visitors centre** (支笏湖ビジターセンター; ☎ 25-2404; www15.ocn.ne.jp/~sikotuvc, in Japanese; 🕑 9.30am-5.30pm Wed-Mon Apr-Oct, 9.30am-4.30pm Wed-Mon Nov-Mar), a boat pier, a few souvenir shops and restaurants.

Morappu (モラップ), 7km south, has a few more spots for dining, sleeping, shopping etc, though it's a bit inconvenient to access as there are no local buses around the lake – Shikotsu-ko is one destination where having your own car will really make a difference.

SIGHTS & ACTIVITIES

Hiking is one of the area's most popular activities, but check first with staff at the visitors centre since trails are frequently closed due to bad weather and erosion. Japanese walkers all wear bear bells in this area, which is an obvious sign that you should stay on the main tracks to avoid an unexpected encounter.

Monbetsu-dake (紋別岳; 866m) is one of the easiest hikes in the area. The trail starts at the northern end of Shikotsu Kohan, and it should take you around 1½ hours to reach the summit.

A much more challenging ascent is **Eniwa-dake** (恵庭岳; 1320m), which lies on the northwestern side of the lake. A 3½-hour hike will bring you to the crater, though enquire locally as trail conditions near the top can be dangerous.

On the southern side of the lake is **Tarumae-zan** (樽前山; 1041m), an active volcano that is the area's most popular trek. Due to poisonous gases, the crater itself is usually closed, but you can reach the rim from the seventh station (only accessible by private car) in about 40 minutes.

A spectacular, mossy gorge, **Koke-no-dōmon** (Map p607; 9am-5pm Jun-Oct) has unfortunately suffered from erosion, which means that visitors are now only allowed to view it from the roped-off area.

You can also take a one-hour walk on the nature trail between the pier and Morappu, which goes through a wild bird forest with two birdwatching blinds. There are birding ID boards along the trail to help you get acquainted with the local avians.

When you're ready to take a break from all the hiking, **Itō Onsen** (☎ 25-2620; admission ¥700; 10am-4pm) on the northern shores of the lake is a great place to quite literally soak up the atmosphere. This modest onsen is famous for its unobstructed views of the lake, so feel free to let it all hang out and embrace Mother Nature.

Freshwater scuba diving in the lake can be arranged through **Blue Note** (ブルーノート; ☎ 0120-43-3340; 107 Shikotsuko Onsen; www2.ocn.ne.jp/~bluenote; 1-/2-tank dive ¥12,390/17,640, dry suit rental ¥9240). Waterflowers, 100m cliffs and numerous freshwater fish can be seen, and you'll be nice and warm if you spring for the dry suit. Some English spoken.

Finally, touristy but all-together enjoyable **sightseeing cruises** (☎ 25-2031; per person ¥1100; Apr-Nov) leave regularly from Shikotsu Kohan's pier.

SLEEPING

Morappu Camping Ground (モラップキャンプ場; ☎ 25-2439; camp sites from ¥500; late Apr–late Oct) If you're car-camping, this is a clean and convenient spot in Morappu that is situated right beside the lake.

Shikotsu-ko Youth Hostel (支笏湖ユースホステル; ☎ 25-2311; fax 25-2312; dm from ¥2900; P) This European-styled alpine lodge offers rustic dormitories and private rooms for travelling families. The extras sweeten the deal: home-cooked meals (breakfast/dinner costs ¥600/1000), a private onsen, bike rental and cross-country skiing tours in the winter. To reach the hostel head away from the visitors centre; after about a three-minute walk, it's on the other side of a car park.

Lapland (ラップランド; ☎ 25-2239; www.north-wind.ne.jp/~lapland, in Japanese; dm/r incl 2 meals ¥4900/5900; P) While you're certainly a long way from Scandinavia, this positively adorable log cabin feels right at home at these northerly latitudes. Guests can bed down in either private rooms or dormitories, and take advantage of the simple *rotemburo*. Located in Morappu, the friendly owners provide personalised service, and can bring you back and forth to the bus station and to the various trailheads.

Log Bear (ログベアー; ☎ 25-2738; http://web.mac.com/logbear; r per person incl 1/2 meals ¥5000/7000; P) Another picture-perfect log cabin, sitting in the centre of Shikotsu Kohan, the owner speaks fluent English, makes an excellent cup of coffee and can cook up some seriously gourmet meals. Appropriately enough, Log Bear is both a B&B and a coffeehouse that caters equally well to Japanese and foreign travellers. Walk straight (east) from the visitors centre to the small alley directly across the street. Log Bear is on the left, just after Tonton (a restaurant). If you reach Tōya-ko Kankō Hotel, you've gone too far.

Shikotsu-sō (支笏荘; ☎ 25-2718; www.shikotsuko.com/s-shikotsusou.htm, in Japanese; r per person incl 2 meals ¥5800; P) A cheerful *minshuku* (Japanese-style B&B) right behind the bus station, the owner's hobby is pressing wildflowers, from which she

HOKKAIDŌ

makes postcards, plates and other souvenirs that are available for purchase. For guests, accommodation is in warm and cosy Japanese-style rooms, and meals featuring local fish and vegetables are served in a laid-back dining hall. There is also a small *rāmen* shop here serving Sapporo-style *miso-rāmen* (¥650).

GETTING THERE & AWAY

Between mid-June and mid-October there are three to four buses a day in both directions between JR Sapporo station and Shikotsu Kohan (¥1330, 1½ hours). More-frequent buses run all year round between Shikotsu Kohan and New Chitose Airport (¥920, 55 minutes).

If you're driving, Rtes 276, 78 and 453 hug the lake's perimeter. Since there are no local buses, you really need your own wheels to get the most out of the area.

HOKKAIDŌ

MURORAN 室蘭

☎0143 / pop 96,000

This dwindling industrial city is in the process of reinventing itself, and is something of a work in progress. Still, Muroran is conveniently connected by ferry to Honshū, has a dramatic coastline that's perfect for a scenic drive, and offers whale-watching tours in the summer months.

While the industrialised section of the valley is definitely less than scenic, the shoreline between Wanishi (where the Muroran Youth Hostel is) and **Cape Chikyū** (地球岬) is quite stunning. A well-marked road parallels the shore and leads to several observation areas where you can stop and admire the view. Cape Chikyū is known for its returning pair of *hayabusa* (peregrine falcons) and for its almost 360-degree panoramic views of the sea.

A whale-watching boat run by **KK Elm** (KKエルム; ☎27-1822; www.kk-elm.jp/index.htm, in Japanese; per 3hr ¥6000) leaves from the pier three times daily in summer. Whales, dolphins, porpoises and seals are best viewed from May to July, and tours are often booked solid weeks ahead.

Institutional and old, but clean and practical, the **Muroran Youth Hostel** (☎44-3357; www.jyh.gr.jp/muroran in Japanese; dm ¥3990; Ⓟ 💻) affords fantastic views of the bay and easy access to hiking tracks along the cliff top. The black-sand beach behind the youth hostel is gorgeous, a perfect place for an early morning walk as you watch the sunrise. From Wanishi station, turn left and follow Rte 36 until you see the Lawson convenience store on the right. Turn right and follow this road all the way until it ends after a steep climb uphill. Look diagonally across the street to the left and you will see a small sign for the hostel. From there it's a three-minute walk to the hostel driveway.

Getting There & Away

Long-distance trains arrive/depart from Higashi-Muroran station, three stops east of Muroran itself; transfer to central Muroran is included in long-distance fares. Frequent *tokkyū* on the JR Muroran line run between Muroran and Hakodate (¥6180, 2¾ hours), and between Muroran and Sapporo (¥4680, 1¾ hours).

Regular highway buses connect the bus terminal in Muroran to Sapporo (¥2250, 2¼ hours), Tōya-ko Onsen (¥1170, 1¾ hours) and Noboribetsu Onsen (¥710, 1¼ hours).

From Muroran-kō, **Higashi Nihon** (☎0120-756-564) operates one daily ferry from April to December that leaves Muroran at around 11.30pm and arrives in Aomori the next day at 6.30am (from ¥3460). The ferry terminal, where you also buy your tickets, is about a 10-minute walk from JR Muroran station.

Shosen Mitsui Ferry (☎029-267-4133) has departures from Ibaraki prefecture to Tomakomai in Hokkaidō (¥8500, 19 hours).

DŌ-HOKU 道北

Northern Hokkaidō is where the last trappings of civilisation give way to the majestic grandeur of the natural world. Southeast of Asahikawa, the second-largest city on the island, Daisetsuzan National Park is a raw and virgin landscape of enormous proportions. West of Wakkanai, in the shadow of Siberia, Rishiri-Rebun-Sarobetsu National Park is a dramatic islandscape famous for its wildflower blooms. And, in case you still need a few reminders of human settlement, Furano is one of Hokkaidō's most famous ski resorts, and home to one of the world's only bellybutton-appreciation festivals!

ASAHIKAWA 旭川

☎0166 / pop 355,000

Asahikawa lies on a flat plain along the Ishikari River, and was once one of the biggest Ainu settlements. It also carries the dual honour of having the most days with

INFORMATION
Asahikawa Chūō Post Office 旭川中央郵便局 1 B1
Compa37 コンパ３７ .... 2 A2
Information Counter 観光案内所 3 A3

SLEEPING
Asahikawa Terminal Hotel 旭川ターミナルホテル 4 A3
Loisir Hotel Asahikawa ロワジールホテル旭川 5 B1
Tokiya Ryokan 時屋旅館 6 B2
Tōyoko Inn Asahikawa Ekimae 東横イン旭川駅前 7 B2

EATING
Ganso Asahikawa Rāmen Ichikura 元祖旭川らーめん一蔵 8 A2
Saroma-ko サロマ湖 9 A2

DRINKING
Den ザデン 10 A2

TRANSPORT
Toyota Rent a Car トヨタレンタカー 11 B3

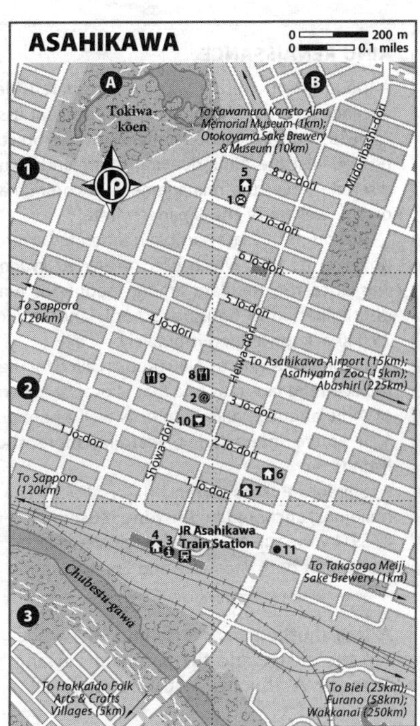

snowfall in all of Japan, as well as the record for the coldest temperature (-40°C). During the Meiji era, Asahikawa became one of the island's major industrial cities, and its principal sake-brewing centre.

Less picturesque than other Hokkaidō cities, Asahikawa is mainly used by travellers as a transit point for Wakkanai to the north, Daisetsuzan National Park to the southeast, and Biei and Furano to the south. However, you'll probably spend the night here at some point, and there are some noteworthy museums and breweries to visit before pressing on.

Orientation & Information

JR Asahikawa station is on the south side of the city. A large pedestrian avenue extends out for a few blocks, and most of the hotels and restaurants listed here are within easy walking distance. Museums and sights, on the other hand, are spread out across the city and will often require a bus ride.

The **information counter** (☎ 22-6704; 8.30am-7pm Jul-Sep, 10am-5.30pm Oct-Jun) inside Asahikawa station provides English pamphlets and sightseeing brochures – be sure to ask for the very useful bus-stop map.

International ATMs are available at the **Asahikawa Chūō Post Office** (☎ 26-2141; 6-28-1 Rokujō).

Internet cafes cluster the station, including **Compa37** (☎ 21-3249; 7-5 Sanjō; per 30min from ¥250; 24hr), which also offers night packages if you need to crash on the cheap.

Sights & Activities

HOKKAIDŌ FOLK ARTS & CRAFTS VILLAGE

北海道伝統美術工芸村

This collection of three **museums** (www.yukaraori.co.jp, in Japanese; 3-1-1 Minamigaoka; combined ticket ¥1200), about 5km southwest of the train station, provides a wonderful overview of the island's traditional folk arts.

The **International Dyeing & Weaving Art Museum** (国際染織美術館; ☎ 61-6161; admission ¥550; 9am-5pm Apr-Nov) displays textiles from around the world, as well as Japanese specialities including embroidered Ainu wood-bark cloth and a number of spectacular silk kimonos.

The **Yukara Ori Folk Craft Museum** (優佳良織工芸館; ☎ 62-8811; admission ¥450; 9am-5.30pm Apr-Nov, 9am-5pm Dec-Mar) focuses primarily on local weaving styles, and has a number of interesting examples of Ainu cloth.

The **Snow Crystal Museum** (雪の美術館; ☎ 63-2211; admission ¥650; 9am-5.30pm Apr-Nov, 9am-5pm Dec-Mar) has the dainty appearance of a European castle, and some wickedly cold walk-in freezers with metre-long icicles.

AINU RENAISSANCE

Although Ainu culture was once declared 'dead' by the Japanese government, the past few decades have seen people of Ainu descent assert their ethnicity both politically and culturally.

In 1899 the Hokkaidō Former Natives Protection Act formalised decades of Meiji-era discrimination against the Ainu, denying them land ownership and giving the governor of Hokkaidō sole discretion over the management of communal Ainu funds. Thus, the Ainu became dependent on the welfare of the Japanese state.

Although this law had been amended over the years, many Ainu people objected to it, right down to its title, which used the word *kyūdo-jin* ('dirt' or 'earth' people) to describe them. It was once the standard among people of Ainu descent to hide their ethnicity out of fear of discrimination in housing, schools and employment; out of an estimated 100,000 Ainu, only 25,000 acknowledged it publicly.

In the 1980s various Ainu groups called for the law's repeal, and in 1998 the Japanese government replaced the law with one that allocated government funds for Ainu research and the promotion of Ainu language and culture, as well as better education about Ainu traditions in state schools.

If you're interested in learning more about the Ainu, we recommended the following listings:

Shiraoi's **Poroto Kotan** (ポロトコタン) is a lakeside village of reconstructed traditional Ainu buildings, anchored by the **Ainu Museum** (アイヌ民族博物館; Ainu Minzoku Hakubutsukan; ☎ 0144-82-3914; www.ainu-museum.or.jp/english/english.html; admission ¥750; 🕑 8.45am-5pm). Museum exhibits are labelled in both Japanese and English, and in the village you might catch demonstrations of

A free shuttle runs every hour or two between the village and the Kureyon Parking, next to the Asahikawa Washington Hotel.

KAWAMURA KANETO AINU MEMORIAL MUSEUM 川村カ子トアイヌ記念館

Kaneto Kawamura, an Ainu chief, became a master surveyor and helped to lay the tracks for several of Hokkaidō's railways. In 1916, after eye problems forced him to retire, he used his accumulated wealth to create the first **Ainu museum** (☎ 51-2461; 11 Kitamonchō; admission ¥500; 🕑 8am-6pm Jul & Aug, 9am-5pm Sep-Jun). The ticket office sells a great English-language booklet, *Living in the Ainu Moshir* by Kawamura Shinrit Eoripak Ainu, the present curator and the son of the museum's founder. Take bus 24 from bus stop 14 in front of the station to the Ainu Kinenkan-mae stop (¥170, 15 minutes).

BREWERIES

If you want a free tipple, take the 30-minute tour of **Otokoyama Sake Brewery & Museum** (男山酒造; ☎ 48-1931; www.otokoyama.com/english/index.html; 2-7 Nagayama; 🕑 9am-5pm), a legendary brewery that appears in old *ukiyoe* (wood-block prints) and historic literature. Take either bus 67, 68, 70, 71, 667 or 669 from bus stop 18 in front of the station, and get off at Nagayama 2-jō 6-chōme (¥200, 20 minutes); from there it's a two-minute walk (look for the large white cube that rests on the roof of the building).

If you want to turn the afternoon into a sake crawl, the **Takasago Meiji Sake Brewery** (高砂明治酒造; ☎ 23-2251; http://takasagoshuzo.com, in Japanese; 17 Miyashitadōri; 🕑 9am-5.30pm Mon-Sat, 🕑 9am-5.30pm) has a 30-minute free tour of its own. From January to March it also has an *aisudōmu,* a sake-filled ice dome where you can warm up with a drink. Take bus 1, 3 or 17 from bus stop 17 in front of the station to 1-jō 18-chōme (¥150, 10 minutes) It's a large white-washed building with a cedar ball hanging outside the door.

Even if you don't speak Japanese, English pamphlets and friendly staff help make both tours worthwhile.

ASAHIYAMA ZOO 旭山動物園

The country's northernmost **zoo** (☎ 36-1104; http://www5.city.asahikawa.hokkaido.jp/asahiyamazoo/zoo/English/top.html; Kuranuma; admission ¥800; 🕑 9.30am-5.15pm May-Oct, 10.30am-3.30pm Nov-Apr) attracts even more visitors than Tokyo's Ueno Zoo. As you might imagine, the star attractions here are cold-weather animals, including the ever-popular polar bears, penguins and seals. As far as zoos go, Asahiyama gets good marks for its attempts to create naturally styled enclosures for the animals. Buses 41, 42 or 47 run between bus stop 5 in front of

Ainu crafts and cultural performances. Frequent *tokkyū* and *kaisoku* on the JR Muroran line run between Shiraoi and Sapporo (¥3400, 1 hour) via Noboribetsu (¥350, 20 minutes).

In the village of Nibutani, which is located in the northern outskirts of Biratori village, **Nibutani Ainu Culture Museum** (二風谷アイヌ文化博物館; ☎ 01457-2-2892; www.ainu-museum-nibutani.org, in Japanese; admission ¥400; 🕑 9am-5pm mid-Apr–mid-Nov, 9am-5pm Tue-Sun mid-Nov–mid-Apr, closed mid-Dec–mid-Jan) has arguably better collections and more attractive displays, although most information is in Japanese only. Visitors could easily spend half a day watching documentary videos about Ainu folk crafts, traditional dances, epic songs and traditional ceremonies. Other highlights include a loom for weaving traditional tree-bark cloth and some enormous canoes hewn from entire tree trunks.

Across Nibutani's main street, amid some traditional huts, the **Kayano Shigeru Ainu Memorial Museum** (萱野茂二風谷アイヌ資料館; ☎ 01457-2-3215; admission ¥400; 🕑 9am-5pm Apr-Nov, by appointment Dec-Mar) houses the private collection of Kayano Shigeru, the first person of Ainu descent to be elected to the Japanese Diet.

A combined ticket for both Nibutani museums costs ¥700. Unfortunately, access to Nibutani is a trial on public transport, though it's a quick and easy trip by car – Rte 237 runs straight to the town.

Other useful sources of information include the **Foundation for the Research & Promotion of Ainu Culture** (アイヌ文化振興研究推進機構; ☎ 011-271-4171; www.frpac.or.jp/eng/index.html) in Sapporo, the **Ainu Culture Centre** (アイヌ文化交流センター; ☎ 03-3245-9831) in Tokyo and the **Ainu Association of Hokkaidō** (北海道ウタリ協会; ☎ 011-221-0462) in Sapporo.

the station and the entrance to Asahiyama Zoo (¥400, 40 minutes).

Festivals & Events

Yuki Matsuri (雪祭り) Held in Asahikawa every February. While second to the one in Sapporo (p589), it is still impressive, with ice sculptures, food and fun seasonal events.

Kotan Matsuri (コタン祭り) Takes place in late September on the banks of the Chubestu-gawa, south of the city. During the festival you can see traditional dances, music and *kamui-nomi* and *inau-shiki*, prayer ceremonies offered to the deities of fire, the river, *kotan* (the village) and the mountains.

Sleeping

As with most major Japanese cities, there are a number of business hotels clustering around the JR station.

Tōyoko Inn Asahikawa Ekimae (☎ 27-1045; fax 27-1046; www.toyoko-inn.com/e_hotel/00069/index.html; Ichijō-dōri 9-164-1; s/d high season ¥6400/8800, low season ¥4800/6800; 💻) This popular chain's clean and convenient Asahikawa clone. LAN cable internet available.

Asahikawa Terminal Hotel (旭川ターミナルホテル; ☎ 24-0111; fax 21-2133; www.asahikawa-th.com/contents/intl/Index_english.htm; 7 Miyashita; s/d from ¥5800/7600; 💻) A reliable spot, conveniently located inside the JR Asahikawa station. LAN cable internet is available.

Tokiya Ryokan (☎ 23-2237; fax 26-3874; www.tokiya.net/tokiyaryokan2.html; Nijō-dōri 9-6; r per person with shared/private bathroom ¥4725/5250, incl 2 meals ¥6300/7350; 💻) North of the station, on the opposite side of the street from the Asahikawa bank, this traditional inn is very well priced, and is a much more atmospheric choice than the standard business hotels. Well-decorated Japanese-style rooms have either shared or private facilities, though all guests can scrub down in the small but refreshing *sento* (public bath).

Loisir Hotel Asahikawa (☎ 25-8811; fax 25-8200; www.solarehotels.com/english/loisir/hotel-asahikawa/guestroom/detail.html; Nanajō-dōri; s/d from high season ¥16,800/18,900, low season ¥9800/11,400; Ⓟ 💻 📶) An easy-to-spot, white tower block overlooking the city's park, the Loisir is Asahikawa's finest hotel, offering minimalist rooms decked out in soft hues and natural shades. First-class amenities include a large gym and spa, as well as four sophisticated restaurants including their signature 15th-floor French bistro. LAN cable internet available.

Eating & Drinking

There is a *rāmen* shop on virtually every street in Asahikawa. This is welcome news given that the city's home-grown blend is a light but flavourful variation of the *shōyu* (soy sauce) variety.

Ganso Asahikawa Rāmen Ichikura (☎ 24-8887; 7-3 Sanjō, Yamada Bldg 1F; noodles from ¥700; 11am-4am, closed Wed) One of the more popular shops in town, the *shōyu-rāmen* (¥700) comes with plenty of scallions, and it's open late – really late – if you need a bite before stumbling home. It's opposite a 7-Eleven, though you'll catch a savoury whiff before you see it!

our pick **Saroma-ko** (☎ 22-6426; 6-1 Sanjō; small plates from ¥500; dinner) Come here for the freshest seafood prepared with care by a chef who's not afraid to close the restaurant if the shellfish doesn't meet his finicky standards. Try the *hotate-no-sashimi* (scallop sashimi) or the *kaki-no-sakemushi* (oysters steamed in sake). Prices vary depending on the quality and the season (and it can quickly get pricey), but if the owner is driving a four-hour round trip daily to get the freshest scallops from Saroma Lake, it's worth it. The restaurant is easily found by looking for the string of traditional Japanese lanterns.

Den (☎ 27-0999; 5th fl, Yoshitake 2 Bldg, Nijō-dori; drinks from ¥500; 5.30pm-1am) This is a highly recommended Australian-run international bar where you can have some drinks, meet some peeps and party the night away. The owner is a long-time resident of Hokkaidō, and can give you some tips about the island. The bar is on the 5th floor, though a large English sign on the street marks the entrance.

Getting There & Around

For information on accessing Daisetsuzan National Park, see p625.

AIR

Asahikawa's small airport is located about 15km outside the city. From here, there are domestic flights to various destinations including Tokyo, Osaka, Nagoya and others. Buses between the airport and JR Asahikawa station (¥570, 35 minutes) are timed to connect with arrivals and departures.

BUS

Some sample destinations, which have frequent daily departures from the bus stops in front of the JR Asahikawa station, include Sapporo (¥2000, two hours), Furano (¥860, 1½ hours), Biei (¥520, 50 minutes) and Wakkanai (¥4700, 4¾ hours).

CAR

If you want to pick up a car before heading either north, south or east, the recommended **Toyota Rent a Car** (☎ 23-0100; 9-396-2 Miyashitadōri 8am-8pm Apr-Oct, 8am-7pm Nov-Mar); 19-2 Ōtemachi 8am-8pm) has a branch office right outside the station.

TRAIN

Super Kamui *tokkyū* run twice an hour between Asahikawa and Sapporo (¥4480, 1½ hours). There are just a couple of *tokkyū* on the JR Sōya line each day between Asahikawa and Wakkanai (¥8070, 3¾ hours), and on the JR Sekihoku line between Asahikawa and Abashiri (¥7750, four hours). Finally, there are regular *kaisoku* on the JR Furano line between Asahikawa and Furano (¥1040, 1¼ hours) via Biei (¥530, 40 minutes).

WAKKANAI 稚内

☎ 0162 / pop 41,000

Wakkanai, Japan's most northern mainland city, changes wildly with the seasons. From November to March, it's something akin to a remote Siberian outpost, home to hearty fishermen, kelp farmers and a harp-seal colony. Outside the winter months, it's a pleasantly mild port city that serves as a departure point for ferries to Rishiri-tō and Rebun-tō, two dramatic wildflower-dotted islands that rank amongst Hokkaidō's highlights, and – assuming you have your visa in order – the Russian city of Karsakov.

Orientation & Information

JR Wakkanai station is right next to the bus terminal, and both are just 10 minutes on foot to the ferry port. If you're heading out to the islands (or Russia), it's wise to stock up on money – an international ATM is available at the **post office** (8.45am-7pm Mon-Fri, 9am-5pm Sat & Sun). Also be sure to pick up maps and get your bearings at the **tourist information counter** (☎ 22-1216; www.welcome.wakkanai.hokkaido.jp, in Japanese; 10am-6pm) inside the train station.

Wakkanai is small enough for most of the sights to be reached on foot or bicycle. Bikes are available for ¥500 per day (June to September) through the **Wakkanai Town Management Organization** (TMO; ☎ 29-0277; 9.30am-5.30pm Mon-Fri). Pick one up during the week from the TMO office in the shopping arcade two blocks north of the station, and on Saturdays and Sundays at the eyeglass shop **Megane-no-Nagano** (長野めがね; ☎ 22-7070; 10am-5pm), also in the arcade.

FERRY TO/FROM RUSSIA

From mid-May to late-October, an unusual excursion from Wakkanai is a ferry trip to the city of Korsakov on Sakhalin Island in Russia. Most Japanese tourists make this journey with a tour group, but with a little advanced planning, it's fairly easy to go on your own.

In order to qualify for a Russian tourist visa, you will need to obtain an invitation letter from a hotel or tourist agency in the country. With an advanced reservation, this letter can usually be emailed to you without any hassle.

You can then apply for the visa at either the **Russian Embassy** (Map pp140-1; ☎ 03-3583-4445; www.rusconsul.jp; 2-1-1, Azabudai, Minato-ku, Tokyo; 🕐 9.30am-12.30pm Mon-Fri) in Tokyo or at the **Russian Consulate** (在札幌ロシア連邦総領事館; ☎ 064-0914; Nishi 12-chōme Minami 14-jo, Chūō-ku; 🕐 9.30am-12.30pm Mon-Fri) in Sapporo. Note that fees vary considerably depending on your nationality, and waits of up to two weeks are not uncommon.

From Wakkanai-kō, **Heartland Ferry** (ハートランドフェリー; ☎ 011-233-8010) operates four to nine monthly ferries (May to October) in both directions between Wakkanai and Karsakov (7½ hours). Tickets can be purchased at the office beside the ferry pier. A 2nd-class one-way/return ticket costs ¥24,000/38,000 – if you're not returning to Japan, you may be asked to show an onward ticket at customs in Russia.

Sights & Activities

Atop a grassy hill a few blocks from the train station, **Wakkanai-kōen** (稚内公園; 🕐 dawn-dusk) is a grassy park centred on the **Centennial Memorial Tower** (稚内開基百年記念塔; ☎ 24-4019; admission ¥400; 🕐 closed Nov-Apr). At the top of the tower on a clear day you can see Russia, just like Alaskan Governor Sarah Palin! The park is also home to a small monument dedicated to the 22 dogs that accompanied Japan's first South Pole expedition.

Noshappu-misaki (Map p619), the second most northern point in mainland Japan, is a nice place for a picture or a picnic, or just to watch the water for a while. If it's a clear day, look for the green flash as the sun slips below the horizon. The cape is a pleasant walk (35 minutes) or bike ride (15 minutes) away from town – along the way, look out for the **kelp drying yards** (they look like gravel-covered car parks if they're not covered with kelp) along the shoreline.

Sōya-misaki (Map p619), 30km from Wakkanai, is the real thing: mainland Japan's most northern point. Among Cape Sōya's various monuments is one dedicated to the victims of Korean Airlines flight 007, shot down in 1983 by a Soviet fighter jet. Birdwatchers will love seeing hawks sitting side by side with seagulls and terns on the wave-washed black sand. There are four return buses each day, departing from the JR Wakkanai station (¥2430, one hour each way).

Harp seal viewing (Map p619) is possible in Bakkai, where a few hundred harp seals arrive each year and stay from November to the end of March. A basic viewing hut (free) provides shelter, a toilet and some information about the seals. Frequent *futsū* run on the JR Sōya line between Wakkanai and Bakkai (¥260, 15 minutes). Dress warmly as the hut is a 30-minute walk from JR Bakkai station, and temperatures can be well below freezing.

While technically part of Rishiri-Rebun-Sarobetsu National Park (p618), the **Sarobetsu Genya** (サロベツ原; Map p619) is best accessed from Wakkanai. These marshlands, approximately 35km south of town, erupt in colour every spring, with dramatic blooms of rhododendrons, irises, lilies and many other types of flowers. Frequent *futsū* on the JR Sōya line run between Wakkanai and Toyotomi (¥900, 45 minutes). Toyotomi is connected to the park entrance by regular local buses (¥430, 15 minutes).

Festivals & Events

In late February, Wakkanai hosts the **Japan Cup National Dogsled Race** (全国犬ぞり稚内大会), the biggest event of this kind in Japan. The race winds through some truly inhospitable frozen terrain, though everyone warms up back in the city where festivities carry well into the night.

Sleeping & Eating

The youth hostels are occasionally closed in the winter, so best to phone ahead.

Wakkanai Youth Hostel (Map p619; ☎ 23-7162; www7.plala.or.jp/komadori-house; 3-9-1 Komadori; dm from ¥3360). The best accommodation in town, the Wakkanai

Youth Hostel is perched on top of a hill, and has a beautiful, commanding view of the surrounding town and ocean. While still a youth hostel, it feels more homey, almost like a *minshuku* rather than an institution. Breakfast/dinner costs ¥630/1050. It's a 15-minute walk from Minami-Wakkanai station – follow the signs.

Wakkanai Moshiripa Youth Hostel (Map p619; ☎ 24-0180; www.moshiripa.net in Japanese; 2-9-5 Chūō; dm/r from ¥3360/4200, breakfast/dinner ¥630/1000) Located between the Wakkanai station and the ferry port (look for the dark-blue, three-storey building), dormitories and private rooms are very basic. But the management is warm and friendly, even if the temperatures outside are cold and unforgiving.

Saihate Ryokan (Map p619; ☎ 23-3556; 2-11-16 Chūō; per person incl/excl 2 meals from ¥6500/3700) Right next to the bus and ferry terminals, this is a very convenient place to bed down for the night before hopping on a ship out to Rishiri-Reburn-Sarobetsu. Although it can get a bit noisy, simple Japanese- and Western-style rooms are well-maintained, and meals usually feature the area's famous sea urchin and salmon roe.

ANA Hotel Wakkanai (Map p619; ☎ 23-8111; www.ana-hotel-wakkanai.co.jp, in Japanese; r per person from ¥7000; P 💻 📶) Tall, sleek and stylish, this place seems a bit out of place in Wakkanai – walk to the waterfront and you can't miss it. While this level of luxury is a bit incongruous, the ANA does good business with travellers who like to live it up in rough places. If you can read Japanese, check the internet as discounted rooms may be available depending on the season. LAN cable internet available.

Takechan (竹ちゃん; ☎ 22-7130; 2-8-7 Chūō; sets from ¥1000; 🕒 lunch & dinner) This is a famous Wakkanai restaurant where you can sample *tako-shabu*, an octopus variant of traditional *shabu-shabu*. Choose a set from the picture menu, and then start dipping slices of tentacles into steaming broth. Exit the JR Wakkanai station, walk straight through the first light, and then turn right at the next corner. Walk for two more blocks, and you'll see a white wooden building with black trim on your left-hand side.

Getting There & Around

AIR

From Wakkanai airport, about 10km east of the city centre, there are a couple of flights a day to Sapporo and Tokyo. Regular buses run between the JR Wakkanai station and the airport (¥590, 35 minutes).

SIGHTS & ACTIVITIES

Harp Seal Viewing あざらし観察所 1 D2
Noshappu-misaki ノシャップ岬 2 D1
Rishiri-Fuji Onsen 利尻富士温泉 3 B2
Sarobetsu Genya サロベツ原 4 D3
Wakkanai-kōen 稚内公園 5 D1

SLEEPING

ANA Hotel Wakkanai 稚内全日空ホテル 6 D1
Field Inn Seikan-sō フィールドイン星観荘 7 A1
Hana Rebun 花れぶん 8 A2
Hokuroku Camping Ground 北麓キャンプ場 9 B2
Island Inn Rishiri アイランドインリシリ .... (see 11)
Kushukohan Camping Ground 久種湖畔キャンプ場 10 A1
Kutsugata-Misaki Camping Ground 沓形岬キャンプ場 11 A3
Kāchan Yado かあちゃん宿 12 A2
Momoiwa-sō Youth Hostel 桃岩荘ユースホステル 13 A2
Pension Misaki ペンション岬 14 B2
Rishiri Fuji Kankō Hotel 利尻富士観光ホテル 15 B2
Rishiri Green Hill Youth Hostel 利尻グリーンユースホステル 16 B2
Saihate Ryokan さいはて旅館 17 D1
Wakkanai Moshiripa Youth Hostel 稚内モシリパユースホステル 18 D1
Wakkanai Youth Hostel 稚内ユースホステル 19 D1

BUS

There are a couple of daily buses in either direction between Wakkanai station and Sapporo (¥5500, six hours), as well as Asahikawa (¥4700, 4¾ hours).

BOAT

For information on ferries to Rishiri-tō and Rebun-tō, see p621 and p622, respectively.

For details about a trip to Russia, see the boxed text p617.

CAR

Long and lonely Rte 40 runs between Asahikawi and Wakkanai. If you're heading out to Rishiri-Rebun-Sarobetsu National Park, parking is available at the ferry terminal for ¥1000 per night.

TRAIN

There are just a couple of *tokkyū* each day on the JR Sōya line between Asahikawa and Wakkanai (¥8070, 3¾ hours).

RISHIRI-REBUN-SAROBETSU NATIONAL PARK 利尻礼文サロベツ国立公園

In case mainland Hokkaidō isn't remote enough for you, take a trip out to the islands of Rishiri-tō and Rebun-tō, which lie just off

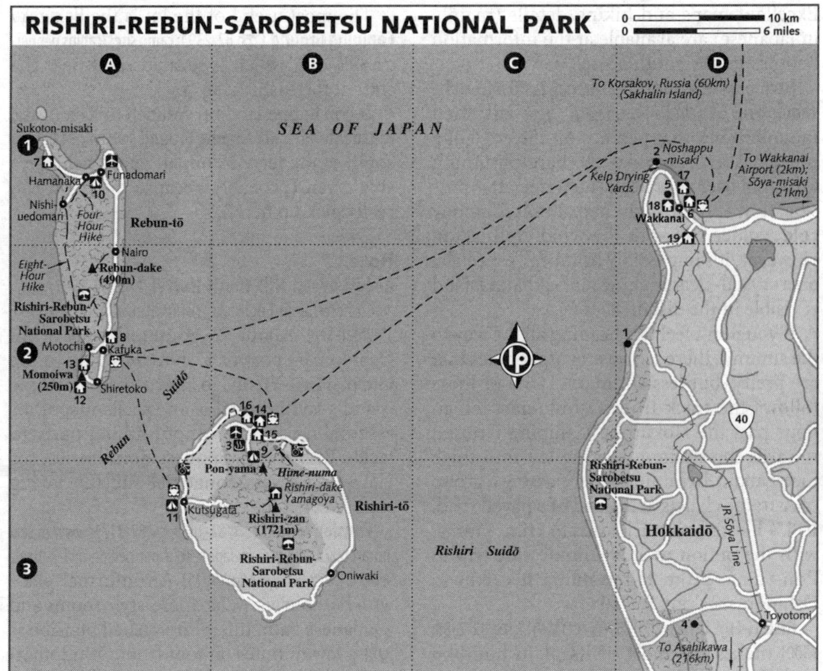

the coast of Wakkanai, and are the centrepiece of this popular national park. While the islands are virtually abandoned in the winter months, from May through August Rishiri-tō and Rebun-tō burst to life with colourful wildflower blooms drawing visitors by the boatload. Peak viewing time is in June and July, which are also the best months to summit Rishiri-zan (1721m), a near-perfect cinder cone rising like a miniature Mt Fuji from the surrounding sea. Note that the park also includes the Sarobetsu Genya (a natural flower garden), which is best accessed from Wakkanai.

Rishiri-tō 利尻島

☎ 0163 / pop 5000

While Rishiri-tō might not have the same concentration of wildflowers as its more popular sibling, the island is home to an extremely rewarding trek to the top of a Fuji-clone. If you're feeling energetic – and the weather is cooperating – you can hike up and down the summit in a day, though it's worth extending your trip and hiking all across this far-flung islet floating in the Sea of Japan.

INFORMATION

A road encircles the island, and a local bus service links the small fishing villages on the way. Oshidomari and Kutsugata are Rishiri-tō's main ports; both have ferry services and **information booths** (Oshidomari ☎ 82-2201; 8am-5.30pm 15 Apr-15 Oct; Kutsugata ☎ 84-3622; 10am-4.30pm May-Sep) that provide maps and details about transport, sights and hiking. Staff can also help you book accommodation, which is recommended during the tourist-packed summer months.

ACTIVITIES

The two most reliable **hiking tracks** to the summit of **Rishiri-zan** start about 3km from town (from the ferry port) at Oshidomari and Kutsugata. A limited bus service runs to the start of each track; otherwise you must walk, hitch, take a taxi or ask your lodgings if they can drop you off.

Prepare properly for a mountain hike and pay particular attention to the season and weather – late June through mid-September is best. Aim for an early start and allow about five hours each for the ascent and descent.

HOKKAIDŌ

Excellent maps and hiking details (mainly in Japanese) are available at the information booths and the youth hostel.

Just past the eighth station is **Rishiri-dake Yamagoya** (利尻岳山小屋), an unstaffed mountain hut that perches on the edge of a precipice, and provides the bare minimum for a roof over your head (no water). It is possible to spend the night here, but it is bloody cold, colder still with the wind-chill factor. However, it's impossibly beautiful, especially on a crystal-clear night when Sakhalin Island is visible in the distance.

If you don't feel like heading all the way to the summit, there are several other hikes that are pretty, but less strenuous. One of these follows the track from Oshidomari for an hour past the Hokuroku Camping Ground towards the summit, veering left into thick forest about 10 minutes after passing a group of A-frame chalets at the end of a paved road. In 1¾ hours, this track leads to Hime-numa, with the option of a 30-minute side trip to Pon-yama. From Hime-numa it's 6km to Oshidomari along Rte 108.

Rishiri-Fuji Onsen (利尻富士温泉; ☎ 82-2388; ¥500) makes the most of its plain building with Jacuzzis, mountain-view *rotemburo*, saunas and indoor baths. The onsen is a 30-minute walk from Oshidomari en route to the Horuroku camping ground and start of the Rishiri-zan track; a couple of buses a day (¥150, 10 minutes) pass here from Oshidomari.

Bicycling is a great way to see the island – rent them from the youth hostels or shops near the Oshidomari ferry terminal – a leisurely circuit of the island (56km) takes anywhere from five to seven hours. There is also a 29km cycling path that runs through woods and coastal plains from Oshidomari past Kutsugata.

SLEEPING & EATING

It's best to phone ahead in the winter months as the places listed here are closed irregularly. Note that eating is best done at the various hotels as restaurants are limited on the island.

Camping

Rishiri-tō has about a half-dozen camping grounds: all are open from May to October, and some are even free.

The most useful of the lot is the **Hokuroku Camping Ground** (☎ 82-2394; camp sites/cabins per person ¥300/3000), which is located right near the start of the Rishiri-zan track.

If you happen to find yourself in Kutsugata, **Kutsugata-Misaki Camping Ground** (☎ 84-2345), just south of the ferry terminal, doesn't charge a single yen (probably because the wind can really pick up here!).

Hotels

Rishiri Green Hill Youth Hostel (☎ 82-2507; www.youthhostel.or.jp/English/n_rishiri.htm; dm from ¥3360; ⌚ Mar-Sep) About 25 minutes' walk from Oshidomari port or a short bus ride to the Gurīn-Hiru-Yūsu-Hosuteru-mae stop, the island's youth hostel is an excellent spot for assembling an impromptu hiking party to tackle Rishiri-zan. Spotless dormitories, sea views and a very congenial and fun-loving staff sweeten the deal.

Pension Misaki (☎ 82-1659; fax 82-2176; www.misaki.burari.biz/sub01.htm in Japanese; r per person incl 2 meals Sep-May ¥7875, Jun-Aug ¥8925) An informal place with harbour-view, Japanese-style rooms and a Japanese bath, this whitewashed pension is just a few minutes on foot from Oshidomari port. While it's definitely not the fanciest place on the island, it is a decent midrange option where you can expect good service and hearty seafood dinners.

Rishiri Fuji Kankō Hotel (☎ 82-1531; fax 82-1897; www15.plala.or.jp/fujikan in Japanese; per person incl 2 meals from ¥15,900; ⌚ closed Dec-Feb; 💻) Just two minutes on foot from the port, Oshidomari's most upmarket offering is a firm favourite for package holiday makers. Although the Fuji Kankō can be positively swamped during summer months, it offers low-key but luxurious Western- and Japanese-style rooms, as well as full resort amenities. LAN cable internet available.

Island Inn Rishiri (☎ 84-3002; fax 84-3340; www.island-inn-rishiri.com in Japanese; r per person incl 2 meals ¥16,500; 💻) Few tourists pass through Kutsugata, though this surprisingly sophisticated resort hotel is reason enough to make a temporary base here. Just behind the ferry terminal, the Island Inn offers Western-style rooms with either ocean or mountain views, in addition to a banquet hall serving traditional Japanese-style meals, and a wonderfully invigorating onsen-fed bath. LAN cable internet available.

GETTING THERE & AROUND

Air

From Rishiri-tō airport, just a few kilometres west of Oshidomari, there are a couple of flights a day to Wakkanai, more in the summer tourist season. Local buses run infrequently by the airport, which means you're better off taking a cab into town for around ¥1200.

Boat

From Wakkanai-kō, **Heartland Ferry** (ハートランドフェリー; ☎ 011-233-8010) operates two to four daily ferries (year-round) between Wakkanai and Oshidomari (from ¥1980, 1¾ hours). Slightly less frequent ferries run in both direction from Oshidomari-kō and Kutsugata-kō to Kafuka (¥780, 45 minutes) on Rebun-tō. All ferry tickets are available for purchase at the various ports.

Bus

Regular local buses run in both directions around the island's perimeter, completing a circuit in about two hours (¥2200). The trip from Oshidomari to Kutsugata (¥730) takes 30 to 50 minutes, depending on whether the bus stops at the airport and/or the onsen.

Rebun-tō 礼文島

☎ 0163 / pop 3300

Shaped like an arrowhead (or a dock-dried squid), Rebun island is a naturalist's dream. From May through August, fields of over 300 species of wildflower explode in an eruption of colour. The terrain is also varied, and each walking track is unique in its own right. The beaches also harbour all sorts of cool finds, from interesting (and edible!) marine animals to semiprecious stones.

INFORMATION

The only main town is the small port of Kafuka, where the ferry arrives several times a day. From there, several of the hiking tracks are within walking distance, and someone at the **tourist information counter** (☎ 86-2655; 8am-5pm mid-Apr–Oct) in the ferry terminal will point out the best routes or discuss your options in detail, as well as give you maps and schedules in English.

ACTIVITIES

Most people come to Rebun-tō to **hike**, whether it is the eight-hour version or some of the tamer three-hour counterparts. It's a good idea to take a bus to the northern tip of the island, Cape Sukoton, and hike your way back past breathtaking cliffside vistas, fields of flowers and dwarf bamboo, thick forests and tiny fishing villages tucked tightly into the island's many coves. Anyone injured has to be rescued by boat, so group hiking is encouraged.

A four-hour hike runs from Cape Sukoton to Nishi-uedomari, then northeast to the bus stop at Hamanaka. The common route is from north to south. Momoiwa-sō Youth Hostel and other lodgings have info about the nearby hiking options and how to get to trailheads.

Another popular hike is from Nairo, halfway down the east coast, to the top of Rebun-dake (490m). The peak is modest by any standards, but the hike is a pleasant 3½ hours return. Near the port in Kafuka there is a wildflower loop leading across a backbone of spectacular highlands to Momoiwa (enigmatically named Peach Rock, as it bears far more resemblance to a breast than to its namesake fruit) and then down through flower fields and dwarf bamboo to the lighthouse at Cape Shiretoko. It's a great two-hour taste of the island's beauty for those without a lot of time.

Watch the weather carefully and plan ahead. Warm layers and rain gear are recommended. Do *not*, under any circumstances, drink unpurified water, as fox faeces now contaminate the streams (foxes were introduced from Russia in the 1930s).

SLEEPING & EATING

It's best to phone ahead in the winter months as the places listed here are closed irregularly. Note that eating is best done at the various hotels as restaurants are limited on the island. Also, you can usually arrange to be collected from the port or the airport if you call ahead to any of these accommodation listings.

There are less options on Rebun-tō for camping, though the **Kushukohan camping ground** (☎ 87-3110; admission per person ¥600, tent ¥500, 4-person cabins ¥2000; May-Oct) offers attractive lakeside camping and woodsy cabins.

our pick **Momoiwa-sō Youth Hostel** (☎ 86-1421; dm ¥3045, breakfast/dinner 630/1050; Jun-Sep) Famous for hard hikes by day and camp songs and craziness until lights out at 10pm, this eclectic youth hostel (located in an old herring house) has quite a devoted following. With an absolutely stunning location on Rebun's southwest side, it's just a few minutes' walk from several hiking tracks and has easy access to the rock-strewn sea. Beds are a combination of Japanese-style dorms (on tatami mats) and bunks. Staff can pick you up when the ferry docks: look for the flags and the enthusiastic guys yelling '*okaerinasai!*' (welcome home!). If you're coming by yourself, you can take a Motochi-bound bus and get off at the Yūsu-mae station (15 minutes), from where it's another 15-minute walk.

Field Inn Seikan-sō (☎ 87-2818; http://homepage1.nifty.com/seikanso/main/p030000.htm, in Japanese; dm incl 2 meals ¥6000; ⌚ May-Oct) This dormitory-style accommodation is more peaceful than Momoiwa-sō, is very convenient for hiking and has an amusing field-station theme throughout. Take a bus to Cape Sukoton (ask the driver to let you off at Seikan-sō). After getting off the bus, take the unpaved road to the west. Staff can pick you up at the ferry if you phone ahead.

Kāchan Yado (☎ 86-1406; fax 86-2188; http://web-kutsurogi.net/kaachan/index.html, in Japanese; r per person incl 2 meals ¥8000; ⌚ Jun-Aug) Translating to Mum's Place, this warm and cosy inn has that personal touch missing at so many *minshuku* in Japan. Japanese-style tatami rooms and – of course – Mum's home-cooking are on the menu here. Get off the bus at the Shiretoko stop, walk a further five minutes along the road, and the inn is on your right.

Hana Rebun (☎ 86-1177; www.hanarebun.com, in Japanese; r incl 2 meals from ¥17,850; 💻) For honeymooners who really want to remember something special, this superluxury hotel offers balcony *rotemburo* in each room (a choice of porcelain or slightly pricier *hinoki* – an aromatic Japanese cypress wood often used in high-end onsen baths) that look out at Rishiri-tō, sunken *kotatsu* (a heated table with a cover over it to keep the legs and lower body warm) surrounded by beautiful tatami, and exquisite meals. Head right as you leave the port and Hana Rebun is about 10 minutes' walk on the left.

GETTING THERE & AROUND

Air

From Rebun-tō airport, at the very northern tip of the island, there are a couple of flights a day to Wakkanai, more in the summer tourist season. The closest bus stop to the airport is Kūkō-shita ('Below the Airport'), which means you'll still need to walk 15 minutes to the terminal.

Boat

From Wakkanai-kō, **Heartland Ferry** (ハートランドフェリー; ☎ 011-233-8010) operates two to five daily ferries (year-round) between Wakkanai and Kafuka (from ¥2200, two hours). Slightly less frequent ferries run in both direction from Kafuka to Oshidomari-kō and Kutsugata-kō (¥780, 45 minutes) on Rebun-tō. All ferry tickets are available for purchase at the various ports.

Bus

Up to five buses per day run along the island's main road from Kafuka in the south to Cape Sukoton in the north (¥1180, 70 minutes). There are also bus routes from Kafula to Shiretoko (¥280, 13 minutes) and Motochi (¥440, 16 minutes) – check the timetable at the Kafuka ferry terminal on arrival.

BIEI 美瑛

☎ 0166 / pop 11,000

With the dramatic mountains of Daisetsuzan National Park (see p625) in the background, Biei is an artist's and nature-lover's mecca. The open fields, often covered in lavender or poppies, are so different from the rest of the mainland that you'll wonder if you have left Japan and somehow ended up in rural France. The ubiquitous tour buses will quickly bring you back to reality, particularly in late June and July when the flowers peak. Still, Biei is a fun place to visit any time: walking and cycling the dirt roads in summer, enjoying the autumn leaves and late spring blooms, and even cross-country skiing and snowshoeing in the dead of winter.

Information

The **tourist information building** (☎ 92-4378; www.biei-hokkaido.jp, in Japanese; ⌚ 8.30am-7pm May-Oct, 8.30am-5pm Nov-Apr) is outside JR Biei station. Staff here can supply you with maps and tourist books, and help you find accommodation in town as well as in other destinations around Daisetsuzan National Park.

Sights & Activities

There are numerous art galleries and museums in the area. One of the most famous is **Takushinkan** (拓真館; Map p626; ☎ 92-3355; admission free; ⌚ 9am-5pm May-Oct, 10am-4pm Nov-Apr), a lovely museum dedicated to the internationally known photographer Shinzō Maeda

(1922–98), whose stunning photographs of the Tokachi area are famous for their unusual colour and composition. The museum is a 10km drive by car or taxi from Biei in the direction of Bibaushi. The road is full of panoramic vistas of pretty hills covered at different times of year with sunflowers, lavender, white birches or snow.

Of course, the real appeal of Biei is simply exploring and getting lost in the beautiful nature surrounding the town. Whether you walk or ride, stick to the paths and roadsides: don't tramp through the farmers' fields or steal tastes of the produce that people's livelihoods depend upon.

Bike rental is available at several places, including **Gaido no Yamagoya** (ガイドの山小屋; ☎ 95-2277; www.yamagoya.jp; 🕑 8am-6pm), right outside the station, which has electrically assisted bicycles (great for those up-down hills!) for ¥600 per hour, as well as normal bikes for ¥200 per hour. If the snow is falling, it also arranges cross-country skiing and snowshoeing tours, starting at ¥2500 per person excluding equipment rental.

Sleeping & Eating

Most of the lodgings are set in gorgeous areas among fields or flowers, but they're not particularly close to the station. Most will arrange to pick you up at the station if you call ahead, which is a good idea as navigating the area can be a bit tricky.

our pick **Biei Potato-no-Oka Youth Hostel** (美瑛ポテトの丘; ☎ 92-3255; www.potatovillage.com/eng/top.html; dm/r per person from ¥4620/6080, 4-person cottage ¥19,950, 3-5 person log house ¥13,650/18,900; Ⓟ) Perched at the top of a field of potatoes (hence the cutesy name) about 15 minutes on foot west of the station, this highly recommended youth hostel has friendly, English-speaking staff that help to foster a warm communal environment. A variety of accommodation options are available in dormitories, private ensuite rooms and positively adorable cottages and log houses, though everyone congregates at night for dinners (extra cost) featuring local produce, most notably potatoes! The real attraction here, however, is the grocery-list of activities on offer, including hiking, biking, skiing, snowshoeing and even nightly stargazing.

Hotel L'Avenir (ホテルラヴニール; ☎ 92-5555; www.biei-lavenir.com, in Japanese; 1-9-21 Honchō, s/d incl 2 meals from ¥6000/11,000; Ⓟ 💻) This Western-style hotel is a nice cross between an American roadside motel and a European country cottage. Modern and business-friendly rooms balance out folksier, hands-on crafts and activities, such as making your own butter, cheese, bread or ice cream. Turn left out of JR Biei station, pass the tourist info booth and L'Avenir is just beyond. LAN cable internet available.

Auberge Hermitage (オーベルジュ・エルミタージュ; ☎ 92-0991; http://lilac.hokkai.net/~erumi, in Japanese; r per person incl 2 meals from ¥18,375; Ⓟ) A comfortable place plopped in the middle of gorgeous fields southeast of the station. Sophisticated, and with lovely Western-style rooms, it also has delicious aromas wafting from the kitchen (all of the meals are homemade by the chef on premises). The 24-hour Jacuzzi with a large picture window is a swanky addition, made better by the fact that you can reserve it for private use. This upscale hotel only has six rooms, so book ahead.

Niji (Map p626; ☎ 95-2492; meals from ¥800; 🕑 lunch & dinner Fri-Wed) Surely a great example of the international ideal: an American-style log cabin up on the Biei farmland hills, serving authentic Korean dishes: sizzling stone *bibimbap* or spicy soups. It has great views, too. No English menu, but the owner gladly makes suggestions or points out daily specials. Niji is past Bibaushi station.

Getting There & Away

There are frequent *futsū* on the JR Furano line between Biei and Asahikawa (¥530, 40 minutes), and between Biei and Furano (¥620, 30 minutes). Frequent highway buses also run between Biei and Asahikawa (¥520, 50 minutes). For drivers, Rte 237 runs between Asahikawa and Biei, though be extremely careful in the winter months as this route can be icy and treacherous.

FURANO 富良野

☎ 0167 / pop 25,230

Humorously known as *Heso-no-machi* (Bellybutton Town), Furano is in the centre of Hokkaidō: the middle. This geographical distinction has given rise to the town's famous bellybutton festival, though there is much more to Furano than bare navels. One of Japan's most inland towns, Furano receives extreme amounts of powdery snow, and is ranked as one the country's top skiing and snowboarding destinations.

Surprisingly, however, a continental climate descends on the area outside the winter months, fostering a burgeoning wine industry, producing award-winning cheeses and enabling sprawling fields of lavender to spring to life. For Japanese tourists who can't spring the time and money to visit the south of France, Furano is regarded as something of a close second.

Orientation & Information

In the winter months, all of the action is centred on the Furano Prince and New Furano Prince hotels (see p501). If it's not ski-season, all eyes shift to the dramatic landscape surrounding the town, which is best explored by car or bike.

Outside JR Furano station is the **tourist information office** (☎ 23-3388; www.furanotourism.com/english/home.htm; 🕒 9am-6pm), where you can stock up on maps and pamphlets, get some last-minute help booking accommodation, rent bicycles and even check your internet for free.

Sights & Activities

The countryside around Furano is stunning in its own right, though there are a number of gourmand attractions worth checking out. Frequent shuttle buses leave from bus stop 4 across from the JR Furano station, stopping at the various sights listed here (per trip ¥150).

As a word of caution, Furano's roads have the highest rate of traffic fatalities in the country, so take care if you're driving or biking, especially if the roads are icy. Also, be sure to pick up a good map from tourist information as it's very easy to get lost in the mountains.

If you're not going skiing or getting behind the wheel, the **Furano Wine Factory** (Map p626; ☎ 22-3242; 🕒 9am-4.30pm, closed weekends Nov-Apr), about 4km northwest of the station, gives tours explaining the wine-making process and offers the complimentary tipple.

If you're going skiing or getting behind the wheel, the nearby **Furano Grape Juice Factory** (Map p626; ☎ 23-3033; 🕒 9am-4.30pm, closed weekends Sep-May), about 1.5km away, gives tours explaining the grape juice-making process and offers the complimentary nonalcholic tipple.

Foodies could then continue on to the **Furano Cheese Factory** (Map p626; ☎ 23-1156; 🕒 9am-5pm May-Oct, 9am-4pm Nov-Apr, closed 1st & 3rd Sat & Sun of month Nov-Apr), which has select tastes – try the squid ink brie, among others. Adjacent is the **Furano Ice Milk Factory** (Map p626), which offers cool treats to beat the summer heat.

From roughly June to September, JR actually opens up a temporary station to accommodate the influx of tourists, namely **Lavender Batake** (Lavender Farm; Map p626). Occasional trains between Biei and Furano stop here, providing easy access to the stunning lavender fields at **Farm Tomita** (Map p626; ☎ 39-3939; www.farm-tomita.co.jp/en; admission free; 🕒 9am-4.30pm Oct-late Apr, 8.30am-6pm late Apr-Sep).

SKIING & SNOWBOARDING

The FIS World Cup and Snowboarding World Cup are held here yearly at the **Furano Ski-jō** (Map p626; ☎ 22-1111; www.princehotels.co.jp/ski/furano_e/index.html; lift tickets full day/night only ¥4000/1500; 🕒 day 8.30am-5pm, night 5-9pm), which lies between the two Prince hotels. The slopes are a mix between beginner and intermediate, with a small section devoted to advanced. The fastest gondola in Japan whisks you to the top, where 24 runs cover three mountainsides, all with perfect powder snow. Night skiing is available, and snowboarding is allowed on all slopes.

Furano is not nearly as expansive as Niseko (p602), and you're likely to be disappointed by the lack of off-piste skiing and comparative lack of advanced runs. However, Furano is comparatively undiscovered by foreigners, and retains a much more authentic Japanese atmosphere. The two Prince hotels, in addition to providing the usual equal rental services, also provide a wonderful après-ski atmosphere of fine dining and lively drinking.

Festivals & Events

Heso Matsuri (へそ祭り; Navel Festival) On 28 and 29 July, this is Furano's signature festival. If you've been pining for a place where you can strip off your shirt and have a traditional mask painted onto your torso before you go revelling, you've come to the right festival. *Tobiiri odori* ('jump right in') dancing is part of the fun; as with sumō, it helps to be a bit on the heavy side!

Furano Wine Festival (富良野ウィン祭り) Coinciding with the grape harvest every September, this festival offers tastings and bacchanal merriment. A barbecue lets you buy local produce and then grill it for yourself, while costumed revellers stamp barefoot on grapes in a barrel.

Sleeping & Eating

Alpine Backpackers (アルパインバックパッカーズ; ☎ 22-1311; fax 23-4385; www.alpn.co.jp/english/index.html; dm Apr-Oct/Dec-Mar ¥2500/2700; Ⓟ 💻) The perfect crash pad for anyone with plans to spend every waking moment on the slopes, Alpine Backpackers is conveniently located just a few minutes' walk from the Kitanomine lift near the Prince Hotel. True to its moniker, backpackers are well catered for with cooking facilities, laundry machines and a boiling onsen that gets the aches and pains out after skiing.

Furano Youth Hostel (富良野ユースホステル; off Map p626; ☎ 44-4441; www4.ocn.ne.jp/~furanoyh/english.htm; 3-20 Okamati Naka-Furano-Cho; dm/s/d incl breakfast & dinner ¥3360/5460/8820; P 💻) Just west of the JR Naka-furano station, the Furano Youth Hostel occupies a big farmhouse complete with an expansive deck overlooking the countryside. The best part of staying here is the free breakfast and dinner (except Monday night – the chef takes a break!), which are simple but tasty self-service meals featuring local produce.

Rokugō Furarin Youth Hostel (ろくごうふらりんユースホステル; Map p626; ☎ 29-2172; www.furalin.jp, in Japanese; dm incl 2 meals from ¥5040; P 💻) Another great youth hostel, this place really feels like home. It's airy and un-institutional with simple decorations that seem more like a kid's room than a hostel. Once again, meals are buffet-style, with an emphasis on fresh, organic and local. From Furano station it's a 15-minute bus ride to the terminus at Rokugō (the bus leaves from in front of the station), but you can get a free lift from the station if you phone ahead.

If you're planning a ski trip, the two most convenient (and nicest!) places to stay are at the **Prince Furano Hotel** (Map p626; ☎ 23-4111; fax 22-3430; www5.princehotels.co.jp/en/furano; r per person from ¥16,000; P 💻 📶) and the **New Furano Prince Hotel** (Map p626; ☎ 22-1111; http://www5.princehotels.co.jp/en/newfurano/; r per person from ¥18,000; P 💻 📶). Lying at opposite ends of the ski slopes, near gondolas, both Prince hotels are snazzy places with a variety of restaurants, bars, and lounge areas. Note that published prices can be slashed significantly if you book in advance through a travel agent – cheap packages are usually available, which include lift tickets, accommodation and even train fare. LAN cable internet available at both properties.

Drinking

Bars and restaurants abound both in the town centre, and closer to the slopes in the vicinity of the Prince hotels. A local landmark that's always a great night out is the **Furano Bar Bocco** (☎ 22-1010; www10.plala.or.jp/bocco/English/index.htm; 12-1 Hinode-cho; cocktails from ¥500; 🕑 8pm-2am Mon-Sat), a few blocks east of the station along the main drag, which is a fun little watering hole with a great international vibe. English is spoken.

Getting There & Away

BUS

Frequent buses run between Furano and Sapporo (¥2100, three hours), as well as between Furano and Asahikawa (¥860, 1½ hours).

CAR

Rte 237 runs between Asahikawa and Furano. Once again, be extremely careful in the winter months as this route can be icy and treacherous.

TRAIN

There are frequent *kaisoku* on the JR Furano line between Furano and Asahikawa (¥1040, 1¼ hours) via Biei (¥530, 40 minutes). There are also frequent *futsū* on the JR Nemuro line between Furano and Takikawa (¥1040, one hour) – hourly Super Kamui *tokkyū* run between Takikawa and Sapporo (¥3210, 50 minutes). A *Lavender Express* special seasonal train also runs direct between Furano and Sapporo (from ¥4340, two hours) daily from early June to 31 August, and on weekends and holidays from September to the end of October.

DAISETSUZAN NATIONAL PARK 大雪山国立公園

Known as Nutakukamushupe in Ainu, Daisetsuzan or Big Snow Mountain is Japan's largest national park, covering more than 2300 sq km. A vast wilderness area of soaring mountains, active volcanoes, remote onsen, clear lakes and dense forests, Daisetsuzan is the kind of place that stressed-out workers in Tokyo and Osaka dream about on their daily commute.

Virtually untouched by human hands, tourism in the park is minimal, with most visitors basing themselves in the hot-spring villages on the periphery. From the comfort of your onsen hotel, you can make small forays into the park's interior, summiting peaks and trekking through valleys on challenging day hikes.

However, if you're properly equipped with the right gear, and you've done a bit of advanced planning, you can tackle

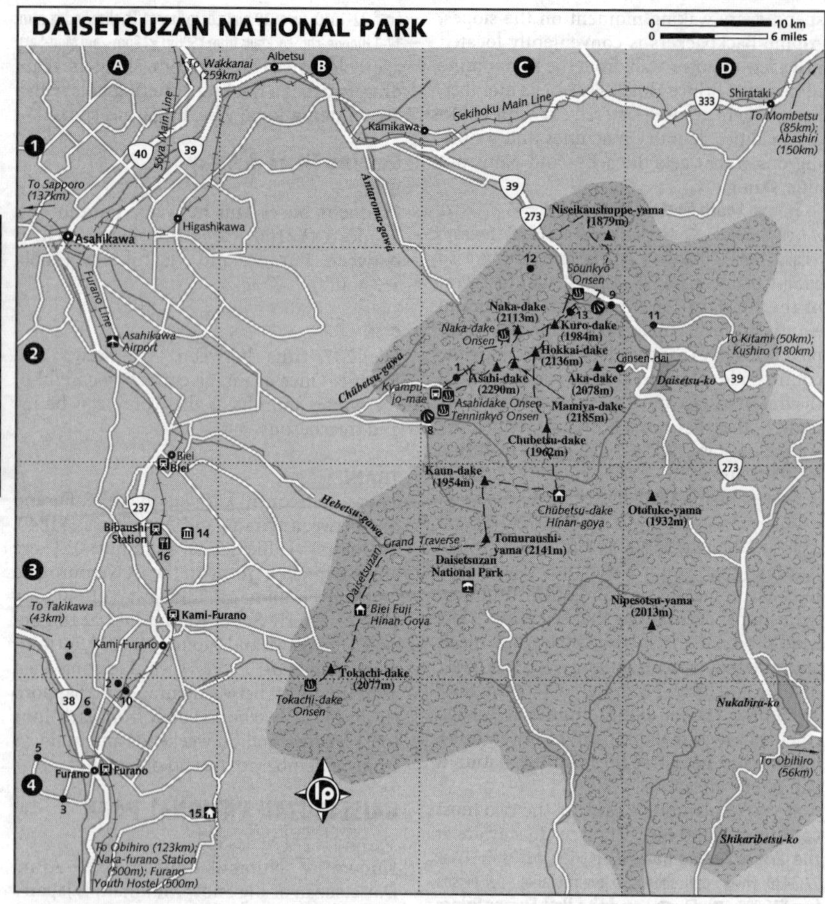

Japan's most hardcore multiday trek, the Daisetsuzan Grand Traverse (see the boxed text, p628). No matter how far you venture into the park, though, any notions you have of Japan being small and densely packed will be shattered.

Asahidake Onsen 旭岳温泉

☎ 0166

This forested hot-springs resort consists of around a dozen or so small inns lying at the base of Asahi-dake. Serious hikers head here for the start of the Daisetsuzan Grand Traverse, though are plenty of other hiking options, many of which wind through unique terrain offering a mix of volcanic activity, fields and foliage. Whether you're here for full-on trek or just a few day hikes, be good to your body by spending ample time luxuriating in the area's healing onsen.

INFORMATION

Hikers should pay a visit to the **Asahidake Visitors Centre** (☎ 97-2153; www.town.higashikawa.hokkaido.jp/vc, in Japanese; 9am-5pm daily Jun-Oct, 9am-4pm Tue-Sun Nov-May), which has excellent maps that the staff will mark with daily track conditions. An onsen map is also available here, which lists the locations, prices and hours of the various baths.

From June to August the flowers are at their peak; foliage turns the hills crimson and then gold shortly after, peaking in mid- to late September. Compared to other onsen towns

SIGHTS & ACTIVITIES

Asahidake Ropeway 朝日岳ロープウェイ	1 C2
Farm Tomita ファーム富田	2 A4
Furano Cheese Factory 富良野チーズ工房	3 A4
Furano Grape Juice Factory ふらのぶどう果汁工場	4 A3
Furano Ice Milk Factory ふらのアイスミルク工場	(see 3)
Furano Ski-jō 富良野スキー場	5 A4
Furano Wine Factory ふらのワイン工場	6 A4
Ginga-no-taki 銀河の滝	7 C2
Hagoromo-no-taki 羽衣の滝	8 C2
Kobako 小箱	9 C2
Lavendar Batake ラベンダー畑	10 A4
Oba-Ōbako 大箱	11 D2
Ryūsei-no-taki 流星の滝	(see 7)
Soūbakudai	(see 7)
Sōunkyō Gorge 層雲峡	12 C2
Sōunkyō Ropeway 層雲峡ロープウェイ	13 C2
Takushinkan 拓真館	14 A3

SLEEPING

Furano Prince Hotel 富良野プリンスホテル	(see 5)
New Furano Prince Hotel	(see 5)
Rokugō Furarin Youth Hostel ろくごうふらりんユースホステル	15 A4

EATING

Niji 虹	16 A3

in Japan, Asahidake Onsen is not overdeveloped, though it can become quite crowded during these times.

SIGHTS & ACTIVITIES

Hiking

At the base of Asahidake, the **Asahidake ropeway** (☎ 68-9111; one way/return Jul–mid-Oct ¥1500/2800, mid-Oct–Jun ¥1000/1800; 6am-4.30pm Jul–mid-Oct, 9am-4pm mid-Oct–Jun) runs to within easy hiking distance of the peak.

Once you've climbed Asahidake, you can either return to the ropeway, embark on the Daisetsuzan Grand Traverse or descend to Sōunkyō Onsen. There is also a 1.7km loop track that leads for about 50 minutes around the area before returning to the ropeway's upper terminal.

There are *rotemburo* off the northern route at Nakadake Onsen; branch left at Nakadake-bunki just before ascending Nakadake. Beware: the water in Yudoku Onsen is poisonous – don't touch it.

From Asahidake Onsen there's also a 5.5km track leading through the forest in about two hours to Tenninkyō Onsen, a small hot-springs resort with a scenic gorge and the beautiful **Hagoromo-no-taki** (Angel's Robe Waterfall).

Onsen

Most onsen, even at the higher-end hotels, are open for day use to the general public, but times and prices vary considerably. Prices range from ¥500 up to ¥1500. Bringing your own wash cloth and towel can shave ¥200 to ¥500 off the price.

SLEEPING & EATING

Daisetsuzan Shirakaba-sō (大雪山白樺荘; ☎ 97-2246; fax 97-2247; http://park19.wakwak.com/~shirakaba/english.html; dm ¥5720, dm/r per person incl 2 meals ¥6890/7940; P) Something of a cross between a youth hostel and a ryokan, this mountain lodge near the ropeway's lower terminal offers comfortable Japanese- and Western-style rooms and hot-spring baths. There is a large kitchen available if you're self-catering, though it's worth going for the full-meal plan as the English-speaking staff specialises in heart-healthy meals.

Lodge Nutapukaushipe (ロッジ・ヌタプカウシペ; ☎ 97-2150; r per person incl 2 meals from ¥7500, rāmen from ¥750; P) Next door to Shirakaba-sō, this log-cabin style accommodation is an intimate choice, offering just a handful of private rooms. The property is also highlighted by a wonderful onsen built from rich woods, as well as a *rāmen* shop that tops traditional noodle blends with local vegetables – the menu changes seasonally, so ask for the *osusume* (recommendation).

Hotel Beamonte (ホテルベアモンテ; ☎ 97-2321; www.bearmonte.jp, in Japanese; r per person incl 2 meals from ¥10,650; P) Across from the visitors centre, Asahidake's most sophisticated accommodation is this European-style resort hotel, which combines elegant rooms (some with polished wooden floors) with a stunner of an onsen, offering a variety of indoor and outdoor rock tubs. Prices vary substantially depending on the season, and it can be quite full at times; calling ahead is a good plan. Visiting the bath only is possible for ¥1500.

GETTING THERE & AWAY

From 15 June to October, there are five buses in both directions between bus stop 4 at the in front of the JR station in Asahikawa and Asahidake Onsen (¥1320, 1½ hours). The first bus, which leaves Asahikawa and Asahidake at 9.10am and 9.15am, respectively, is direct, while all others require a quick transfer in Higashikawa. All other times of the year, there are only one or two daily buses in both directions.

HOKKAIDŌ

DAISETSUZAN GRAND TRAVERSE

Hokkaidō's ultimate outdoor experience, the **Daisetsuzan Grand Traverse** is roughly a five-day, 55-km hike connecting two active volcanoes, **Asahi-dake** (旭岳; 2290m) and **Tokachi-dake** (十勝岳; 2077m), which lie at the northern and southern areas of the park, respectively. While the route follows a clearly marked trek, you will need to be entirely self-sufficient as the various shelters lining the way are unstaffed. You should also be in relatively good physical condition, as this is considered to be a very, very challenging hike.

The hiking season runs from early July to late October, and there are guaranteed sources of fresh water (sometimes snow!) throughout this time frame. A tent and camping gear are preferable to the extremely bare-bones huts, and you'll need to carry in your own food and cooking supplies. This is also bear country, so be smart and tie a bell to your rucksack. You should also pick up a topographic map of the area – we recommend anything by the Japanese company Yama-to-kogen-chizu (山と高原地図) – and be sure to talk to the staff at the Asahidake Visitors Centre (see p626).

The grand traverse starts from atop the ropeway in the village of **Asahidake Onsen**, and leads up and over Asahi-dake, the tallest mountain in Hokkaidō, on the first day. You can spend the night at the base of **Kuro-dake** (黒岳; 1984m), and either continue on the second day to **Chūbetsu-dake Hinan-goya** (忠別岳避難小屋), or cut the hike short by taking a combination of a ropeway and chairlift down to the village of **Sōunkyō Onsen** (see below).

On the third day, you continue south, spending the night at the base of **Tomuraushi-yama** (トムラウシ山; 2141m), one of Japan's famous 100 mountains that is seemingly an enormous pile of boulders. The fourth day is a 17km slog to **Biei Fuji Hinan Goya** (美瑛富士避難小屋) that's notoriously difficult, and can be broken down into two shorter days if you bring enough food.

Finally, on the last day, you tackle Tokachi-dake before descending into the village of **Tokachi-dake Onsen** (see opposite), where you can reward yourself with a much-needed soak in the hot springs. Happy trails!

If you're driving, follow Rtes 237, 213 and 160 from Asahikawa to Asahidake Onsen. Note that these roads are very dangerous in the snowy winter months, so drive with extreme caution.

Sōunkyō Onsen 層雲峡温泉

☎ 01658

Daisetsuzan's second major gateway is this onsen town on the park's northeastern edge, which provides secondary access to the Grand Traverse (see the boxed text, above). Once again, even if you're not hiking through the length of the park, Sōunkyō Onsen is still a nice base for shorter forays into the park's interior, and there are some impressive natural attractions in the area that are worth seeking out between dips in the hot springs.

INFORMATION

The **tourist information office** (☎ 5-3350; www.sounkyo.net/english/index.html; ⏲ 8.30am-5pm), on the first floor of the public bath Kurodake-no-yu, has several maps and English-language pamphlets. Its booking service may be useful if you arrive in high season. Next to the ropeway terminus, the park **visitor centre** (☎ 9-4400; http://sounkyovc.town.kamikawa.hokkaido.jp, in Japanese; ⏲ 8am-5.30pm daily Jun-Oct, 9am-5pm Tue-Sun Nov-May) can provide information on park conditions.

SIGHTS & ACTIVITIES

Sōunkyō 層雲峡

This **gorge** stretches for about 8km beyond Sōunkyō Onsen, and is renowned for its waterfalls – **Ryūsei-no-taki** (流星の滝; Shooting Stars Falls) and **Ginga-no-taki** (Milky Way Falls) are the main ones – and for two sections of perpendicular rock columns that give an enclosed feeling; hence their names, **Ōbako** (Big Box) and **Kobako** (小箱; Little Box). If you don't have a rental car, a number of shops along the main street rent **mountain-bikes** (¥2000 per day).

Hiking

The combination of the **Sōunkyō Ropeway and chairlift** (☎ 5-3031) provides fast access to **Kuro-dake** (黒岳; 1984m) for hikers and sightseers. One-way/return tickets on the ropeway cost ¥900/1750 and on the chairlift ¥400/600.

Hours of operation vary seasonally (8am to 7pm in July and August, closed intermittently in winter).

From July to the end of September, one bus a day goes to Ginsen-dai, where the trailhead **Aka-dake** (赤岳; 2078m) is located. The bus leaves Sōunkyō Onsen at 6am and returns from Ginsen-dai at 2.15pm (¥800, one hour), leaving you plenty of time for your ascent and descent.

A short, steep and very pretty track runs up to Soūbakudai, a scenic overlook of the two waterfalls, Ryūsei-no-taki and Ginga-no-taki. Look for the steps leading up the hill directly behind where the bus stops. It takes about 20 minutes to reach the top.

After a hard day of cycling or hiking, **Kurodake-no-yu** (黒岳の湯; ☎ 5-3333; admission ¥600; ⏰ 10am-9pm Thu-Tue) offers handsome hot-spring baths (including *rotemburo*). It's on the town's main pedestrian street. You can also soothe your aching feet in the free **ashi-no-yu** (foot bath), next to the Ginsenkaku Hotel.

FESTIVALS & EVENTS

Hyōbaku Matsuri (氷瀑まつり; Ice-Waterfall Festival) From the end of January to the end of March, this festival features ice sculptures, tunnels and domes, some lit up.

Kyōkoku Hi Matsuri (峡谷火まつり; Kyōkoku Fire Festival) This celebration on the last Saturday in July is meant to purify the hot springs and appease the mountain and fire deities. Revellers perform traditional Ainu owl dances and drumming, climaxing with archers shooting flaming arrows into the gorge.

SLEEPING

Sōunkyō Youth Hostel (層雲峡ユースホステル; ☎ 5-3418; www.youthhostel.or.jp/sounkyo; dm per person with/without 2 meals ¥4830/3150; ⏰ Jun-Oct; Ⓟ) Dwarfed by the larger block-style resorts, this humble wooden hostel is about a 10-minute walk uphill from the bus station. Offering bunk-bed accommodation, as well as basic but filling meals, this is a great place to meet other hikers before braving the elements and heading into the park.

Ginsenkaku (銀泉閣; ☎ 5-3003; www.ginsenkaku.com in Japanese; r per person incl 2 meals high/low season from ¥15,900/10,500; Ⓟ) A Japanese style-inn with the appearance of an alpine chalet, Ginsenkaku is a very professional operation located in the centre of the village. Traditionally minded tatami rooms are the scene of lavish nightly feasts, though not before you give yourself a good scrub down in the steamy common baths, including a *rotemburo* with a view.

GETTING THERE & AWAY

There are up to seven buses a day in both directions between Sōunkyō Onsen and Asahikawa (¥1950, 1¾ hours) via Kamikawa. JR Rail Pass holders can travel for free between Asahikawa and Kamikawa, and then catch the bus between Kamikawa and Sōunkyō Onsen (¥800, 35 minutes). These buses also run between Sōunkyō Onsen and Akan Kohan (¥3260, 3½ hours) in Akan National Park.

There are also a couple of buses a day to Kushiro (¥4790, 5¼ hours) via Akan Kohan (¥3260, 3½ hours). Finally, there are two buses a day to Obihiro (¥2200, 80 minutes), which follow a scenic route via Nukabira-ko.

If you're driving, Rte 39 connects Sōunkyō Onsen to Asahikawa in the west and Abashiri in the east.

Tokachi-dake Onsen 十勝岳温泉

Northeast of Furano, this remote hot-spring village is the traditional end point for the Grand Traverse (see the boxed text, opposite). It is much less crowded than Asahidake and Sōunkyō Onsen, but still serves as a good base for hikes into Daisetsuzan National Park. For instance, if you're not embarking on the entirety of the Grand Traverse, you can still climb the peak **Tokachi-dake** (十勝岳; 2077m) in a long day.

With Furano so close by, most travellers choose to press onwards as accommodation in Tokachi-dake is very limited. However, an excellent upmarket spot were you can unwind in luxury after a multiday trek is **Kamihoro-sō** (カミホロ荘; ☎ 0167-45-2970; http://tokachidake.com/kamihoro, in Japanese; s/d incl 2 meals from ¥15,700/25,400; Ⓟ), which has large Japanese-style rooms and pleasant hot-spring baths with a great view of the surrounding mountains. If coming by bus, get off at Kokumin-shukusha-mae, which is almost right in front of Kamihoro-sō.

Frequent *futsū* run on the JR Furano line between Furano and Kami-Furano. Kami-Furano station is connected to Tokachi-dake Onsen by regular buses (¥500, 20 minutes). If you're driving, just take it slow along windy Rte 291.

HOKKAIDŌ

DŌ-TŌ 道東

Eastern Hokkaidō is the Japanese equivalent of Canada's Yukon Territory, a harsh yet hauntingly beautiful landscape that has been shaped by vast temperature extremes. In the winter months, dramatic ice flows off the coast of Abashiri can be seen from the decks of icebreakers. However, Akan Kohan, an Ainu cultural stronghold, and Shiretoko, a pristine national park, are best explored during the mild summers, which is coincidentally when all of the bears that live here are most active!

ABASHIRI 網走

☎0152 / pop 40,000

To most Japanese, Abashiri is as synonymous with the word prison as Alcatraz is to Westerners, and mention of the prison (still in operation) sends chills through the spines of even the most hardened individuals. Winters here are as harsh as they come, yet this is exactly why the area's become a tourist attraction.

Looking out at a snow-white plain of frozen floes from the deck of an icebreaker is a surreal experience, and the sound of bergs grinding together from the force of the sea's currents make a deep impression on all who hear it.

Up to 80% of the sea is ice-clogged during the dead of winter, but Abashiri is still a popular destination other times of the year. A ski resort operates from December through to April, and the city is inundated with tourists when the coral grass blooms in September. As the closest major city to Shiretoko National Park, Abashiri is also a good base for hikers.

Information

The **tourist information office** (☎ 44-5849; 🕑 9am-5pm) outside Abashiri station has English-language maps and a wide offering of pamphlets on eastern Hokkaidō.

Sights & Activities

Tento-zan, the main mountain presiding over Abashiri (207m), is steep enough that its 5km climb will leave you winded unless you're going by bus or car. At the top are some excellent views, a park and several interesting museums.

> **SCENIC DRIVES**
>
> - **Hakodate** (p593) to **Sapporo** (p583)
> - **Shikotsu-Tōya National Park** (p607)
> - **Asahikawap612** to **Wakkanaip616**
> - Around **Biei** (p622) and **Furano** (p623)
> - Pretty much anywhere in **Dō-tō** (Eastern Hokkaidō; left)

A cycling road runs for 25km from Abashiri proper to the coral-grass viewing areas (see opposite) and beyond, providing some beautiful views of the area's lakes, forests and pumpkin fields.

In summer, the northern coastal areas are perfect for pretty, easy walking, with lots of sand dollars and other small shells.

ICEBREAKER SIGHTSEEING BOATS 流氷観光砕氷船

From roughly late January to mid-March, the **Aurora** (オーロラ; ☎ 43-6000; cruises ¥3000) departs four to six times a day from Abashiri port for one-hour cruises into the frozen Sea of Okhotsk. Slicing through frozen seas on a behemoth of an icebreaker is an unforgettable experience. As you might imagine, dressing warmly is essential if you want to enjoy this Siberian cruise.

SIGHTSEEING TRAIN 観光列車

Running concurrently with the Aurora is the **Ryūhyō Norokko-gō** (流氷ノロッコ号; admission ¥810), which putters along twice a day from Abashiri to Shari through a field of utter white snow. Stare out at this frozen landscape while eating toasted *surume* (squid) and nursing a can of Sapporo lager.

SKIING & SNOWBOARDING

If you're looking to spend a day on the slopes, you'll find powder at **Kamui Ski Links** (カムイスキーリンクス; ☎ 72-2311; www.kamui-skilinks.com, in Japanese; lift ticket ¥3000; 🕑 9am-5pm Dec-Apr). This top-rated resort is the site of several snowboarding competitions and has an even mix of beginner, intermediate and advanced slopes, including one of Japan's longest – 3500m. Eight lifts and 10 courses help to keep crowds down. There's no night skiing here, but Kamui is less pricey than some of its southern competitors, and much less crowded than any of the resorts outside Sapporo.

MUSEUMS

A ¥900 ticket gives all-day entry on a tourist-loop bus, which connects the bus and train stations to the various museums.

Abashiri Prison Museum (網走監獄博物館; ☎ 45-2411; www.kangoku.jp/world/index.htm; admission ¥1050; 🕑 8am-6pm Apr-Oct, 9am-5pm Nov-Mar) details many of the reasons that this prison was so feared. Inmates braved brutally cold winters with thin bedding and very little heat: one lone pipe ran the length of the corridors, providing almost no heat for cell-bound prisoners.

Abashiri Prison (網走刑務所), across the river, and still a working penitentiary, has a **gift shop and tiny museum** (☎ 43-3167; 🕑 9am-4pm) where crafts made by inmates can be purchased. It's also possible to walk around outside the prison walls, though further entry and photographs are prohibited.

Near the prison museum is the unique **Okhotsk Ryūhyō Museum** (オホーツク流氷館; Museum of Ice Floes; ☎ 43-5951; www.ryuhyokan.com, in Japanese; admission ¥520; 🕑 8am-6pm Apr-Oct, 9am-4.30pm Nov-Mar) has odd ice-related exhibits. One of the more interesting is a display relating to the tiny *kurione* (Sea Angels), a funky relative of the sea slug, which is sort of an Abashiri mascot.

A few minutes' walk downhill from the summit of Tento-zan is the **Museum of Northern Peoples** (北方民族博物館; ☎ 45-3888; www.hoppohm.org/english/index.htm; admission ¥450; 🕑 9.30am-4.30pm Tue-Sun). This is a state-of-the-art place with numerous exhibits of Ainu culture, as well as of Native American, Aleutian and other indigenous peoples.

CORAL-GRASS VIEWING サンゴ草群落地

Known as salt pickle or glasswort in other parts of the world, this humble marsh plant gets its 15 minutes of fame in mid-September, when it turns bright red. Busloads of tourists flock to a few boardwalk-viewing spots. Nature lovers will enjoy the bird life, as the marshes attract not only seagulls, but curlews, terns, egrets, herons and more.

DIVING

If you want to see what is beneath the ice, and possibly come face to face with the odd mollusc that is the *kurione*, **Tartaruga** (タルタルーガ; ☎ 61-5201; www.tar2uga.co.jp; 2 dives ¥30,000) offers blood-pumping scuba dives in the Sea of Okhotsk.

Festivals & Events

Orochon-no-hi (オロチョンの火) A fire festival held on the last Saturday in July, derived from the shamanistic rites of the indigenous Gilyak people, who once lived in the Abashiri area.

Come Back Salmon Night (カムバックサーモンナイト) A welcome to the lake's most famous (and delicious!) fish. Each year (mid-October to mid-December, depending on the fishes' schedule) the salmon run upstream, greeted by bright spotlights that illuminate the fish as they pass into Abashiri Lake. Nearby grilling stations serve *sanma* (a dark, oily and delicious seasonal fish that's distantly related to mackerel, but smaller), scallops, squid and venison, often with free tastes. Salmon – the guest of honour – is *not* served…not *that* night anyway.

Sleeping

Abashiri Gensei-kaen Youth Hostel (網走原生花園ユースホステル; ☎ 46-2630; http://sapporo.cool.ne.jp/genseikaen, in Japanese; dm per person incl breakfast from ¥4600; 🕑 closed Nov-Jan; Ⓟ 💻) This rural farmhouse turned youth hostel is located in the middle of the Wakka Gensei-kaen (ワッカ原生花園), a coastal wildflower garden that is 20km long, 700m wide and boasts more than 300 species. It's about a 15-minute drive east of Abashiri in the village of Kitahama, or you can take a *futsū* on the JR Senmō line from Abashiri to Kitahama (¥260, 20 minutes). The hostel is a 10-minute walk or a quick drive southeast from the station.

Hotel Route Inn (ホテルルートイン; ☎ 44-5511; fax 44-5512; www.route-inn.co.jp/search/hotel/index.php?hotel_id=502, in Japanese; 1-2-13 Shin-chō; s/d ¥6000/10,000; Ⓟ 💻) Directly across from the JR Abashiri station, this instalment of the Route Inn chain offers the usual cookie-cutter business rooms. However, a nice perk here aside from its convenient location is the large winter-warming onsen open to guests only. LAN cable internet available.

Abashiri Central Hotel (網走セントラルホテル; ☎ 44-5151; www.abashirich.com; Minami-ni-jō-nishi, San-chōme; s/tw ¥7350/12,000; Ⓟ 💻) A few minutes' walk east of the station in front of Chūō bridge, the Abashiri Central is the city's best hotel. Rooms are decked out in soft and muted colours to provide for a relaxing stay, while the recommended restaurant serves up seasonal offerings from Abashiri's bountiful seas in pleasantly relaxed surroundings. LAN cable internet available.

Eating & Drinking

Kandō Asa-ichi fish market (感動朝市; ☎ 43-7670; 6.30-9.30am Mon-Fri, 6.30-10.30am Sat & Sun mid-Jul–15 Oct) A great option for fresh-fish lovers: select your own seafood and cook it on one of the open-air grills. Shuttles leave from several major hotels to the market, located on the outskirts of the town; ask your lodging for details.

Murakami (むらかみ; ☎ 43-1147; www.drive-net.com/murakami, in Japanese; Minami-san-jō-nishi, Ni-chōme; platters from ¥1000; lunch & dinner) Two blocks east and one block south of the Central Hotel is this small sushi bar (look for the red-and-blue sign), which is locally famous for its high-quality fish. The owner changes the menu daily based on what's fresh from the boat, so best to just ask for his *osusume* (recommendation).

Abashiri Bīru-kan (網走ビール館; www.takahasi.co.jp/beer/yakiniku/index.html, in Japanese; ☎ 45-5100; Minami-ni-jō-nishi, Yon-chōme; meals from ¥750, beers from ¥375; lunch & dinner) A famous Hokkaidō microbrewery with various flavours on tap, the Abashiri Beer Hall offers refreshing taster sets that are the perfect accompaniment to either German- or Japanese-inspired meals. There is no English, but the mouth-watering picture menu makes things easy.

Getting There & Away

AIR

From Memanbetsu airport, about 15km south of the city centre, there are domestic flights to various destinations including Sapporo, Tokyo and Osaka. Airport buses (¥750, 30 minutes) are approximately timed to flights and run from the bus station via Abashiri station to the airport.

BUS

There are a few highway buses each day in both directions between the bus terminal in Abashiri (1km east of the train station), and the Chūō bus station in Sapporo (¥6210, 6¼ hours). Between June and mid-October there are three daily buses from Memanbetsu airport via Abashiri bus terminal to Utoro in Shiretoko National Park (¥3000, 2½ hours). Finally, there is one direct bus daily linking Abashiri and Shiretoko-shari (¥1120, 1¼ hours).

CAR

Hiring a car is the best option for those who want to get to the more remote sections of Shiretoko and Akan National Parks. Various car-rental agencies, including **JR Hokkaido Rent a Lease** (ジェイアール北海道レンタリース; ☎ 43-6197; 8am-6pm Jan-Apr & Nov-Dec, 8am-8pm May-Oct), are located in front of the station.

TRAIN

Frequent *tokkyū* on the JR Sekihoku line run between Abashiri and Asahikawa (¥7750, four hours) via Bihoro (¥530, 35 minutes), where you can catch onward buses to Akan National Park. There are just a couple of *futsū* each day on the JR Senmō main line between Abashiri and Kushiro (¥3570, 3½ hours) via Shiretoko-shari (¥810, 50 minutes).

Getting Around

Regular bus lines connect the station to various points in town including Tento-zan. There is no bike rental, and the 25km cycling road is for people who have proper cruising bikes.

AKAN NATIONAL PARK 阿寒国立公園

This expansive park (905 sq km) contains volcanic peaks, large caldera lakes, thick forests and rejuvenating onsen, though the six million or so visitors who come here each year are more interested in snapping photos of algae. Of course, we're not talking about any old clump of green slime, but rather *marimo (Cladophora aegagropila)*, a surprisingly cute and increasingly rare spherical form of algae that has been declared a national treasure. Even if the appeal of *marimo* is lost on you, Akan is big enough that even at peak times, it easy to get away from it all, particularly if you're looking to hike or meander around isolated forest and mountain tracks.

Orientation & Information

The main access points are Bihoro and Abashiri to the north, and Kushiro to the south. Inside the park itself, you can base yourself in the towns of Kawayu Onsen and Akan Kohan, while Teshikaga (aka Mashū Onsen) serves as a useful transport hub. While it is possible to access the area by public transport, having your own car will make it much easier to get around and visit the various sights. If you're hiking, be advised that bear activity is high, though you're more likely to see common and cunning foxes, which often steal unguarded food or even sleeping bags.

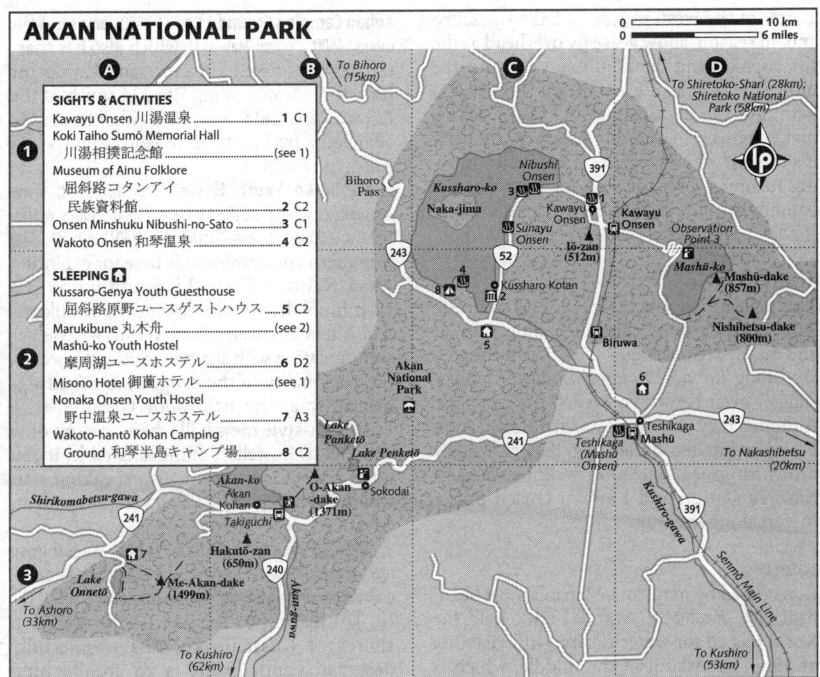

Kawayu Onsen 川湯温泉

☎ 015

Kawayu is a quiet onsen town that is home to more than two dozen hot springs, though it's the surrounding area where Akan National Park really comes to life. From errant monster sightings in crater lakes to hard-boiled eggs in sulphurous pools, there is plenty here to keep you busy between bath times.

ORIENTATION & INFORMATION

The **tourist information office** (☎ 483-2255; www.kawayuonsen.com, in Japanese; 9am-6.30pm Jun-Sep, 9am-5pm Oct-May), about 10 minutes on foot from the bus station in the village of Kawayu Onsen, is a good source of information, and provides free internet access and bike rental. Cycling is a good way to get around, but check distances carefully before a lengthy ride.

Another useful little spot in the village is the **Kawayu Eco-Museum Centre** (川湯エコミュージアムセンター; ☎ 483-4100; www6.marimo.or.jp/k_emc, in Japanese; 8am-5pm May-Oct, 9am-4pm Nov-Apr), which is something akin to a park visitors centre. Here, you can pick up handy hiking maps (in Japanese), and get some tips on exploring the area on foot.

Kawayu Onsen bus station is 10 minutes by bus from JR Kawayu Onsen station, one of the main access points for the national park. JR Mashū station and the adjacent town of Teshikaga, a little further south, is an alternative access point for some of the attractions listed following.

SIGHTS & ACTIVITIES

Onsen

All of the onsen in Kawayu Onsen charge between ¥200 and ¥1000 for admission, though you can save a bit of money if bring along your own waist towel and soap.

Any of the hot springs is good for a bit of clean fun, though make a point of visiting **Wakoto Onsen**. Special not for what it has, but for what it doesn't, Wakoto is merely a scalding hot pool in the middle of nowhere on the southern shore of a beautiful lake. Best reached by car or bicycle, Wakoto Onsen has none of the razzle-dazzle of most spa resorts. There's no electricity, no soap, no buckets, not even any doors on the bathhouse: you just strip, dip and enjoy. Not for everyone, but true onsen buffs will appreciate it. It has a view of the western side of Lake Kussahro and, in season, snow geese fly overhead as the sun slips behind the mountains. Not for the modest either, as it's a *konyoku* (mixed sex) bath and there's algae on the rocks, which makes getting in and out a slippery affair. If it's too hot when you stick a toe in, try moving further away (towards the lake, not the bathhouse) and you'll find it's a slightly cooler shade of scalding.

Iō-zan 硫黄山

This hellish **mountain** (512m) comes complete with steaming vents, sunshine-yellow sulphur and onsen-steamed eggs. You'll hear the sellers calling *Tamago! Tamago! Tamago! Tamago!* (Eggs!) even before you reach the car park. Although they don't taste much different from a regular kitchen-boiled egg, they're a sickly brownish-green. The 4km walk between JR Kawayu station and Kawayu Onsen passes Iō-zan along the way.

Lakes

Considered by many to be Japan's most beautiful lake, **Mashū-ko** (摩周湖) once held the world record for water clarity, with visibility of 35m. The island in the middle, which is hauntingly beautiful, was known by the Ainu as the Isle of the Gods.

Kussharo-ko (屈斜路湖), the other major lake, is famous for its swimming, boating and volcanically warmed sands. Naka-jima is the aptly named 'middle island' that's in the centre of the lake, which has its own version of the Loch Ness monster, named Kusshi. No one has yet claimed it to be a hoax, so if you're a Nessie fan, at least here in Hokkaidō you still have hope.

Museums

Sumō fans will enjoy **Koki Taiho Sumō Memorial Hall** (川湯相撲記念館; ☎ 483-2924; admission ¥400; 🕑 9am-9pm Jun-Sep, 9am-5pm Oct-May), a small museum in Kawayu Onsen dedicated to a hometown hero.

The **Museum of Ainu Folklore** (屈斜路コタンアイヌ民族資料館; ☎ 484-2128; admission ¥310; 🕑 9am-5pm mid-Apr–Oct) in the village of Kussharo Kotan displays tools and crafts.

SLEEPING & EATING

Camping is a good option as there are manicured camping grounds located throughout the park. One of the nicest is **Wakoto-hantō Kohan Camping Ground** (☎ 484-2350; camp sites ¥450, cabins ¥4500; 🕑 mid-May–Oct), which also has spartan cabins, as well as canoes and kayaks for hire. It is located along Rte 234 south of the Bihoro Pass, and is accessible either by private vehicle or by bus from Mashū, Bihoro and Kawayu Onsen.

Mashū-ko Youth Hostel (☎ 482-3098; www.masyuko.co.jp/english/yhe.htm; dm ¥3000-3500, s ¥4500-7400, d ¥5000-9000, breakfast/dinner ¥760/1260; P 💻) A modern and comfortable base for exploring Akan National Park, this youth hostel is a 10-minute drive from downtown Teshikaga, and offers fairly standard Western-style accommodation with shared facilities. However, the personality of the property is raised significantly at the next-door Great Bear, a European-style mess hall where you can dine with fellow hostellers at the long table. If you don't have a car, the English-speaking staff will pick you up at JR Mashū station with an advanced reservation.

our pick **Kussharo-Genya Youth Guesthouse** (☎ 484-2609; www.gogogenya.com/intro/e-intro.htm; dm/r per person from ¥4700/5200, breakfast/dinner ¥600/1300; P 💻) Just off of Rte 243 on the southern shores of Kussharo-ko, this wonderfully designed youth hostel is an architectural treat, both inside and out. Reminiscent of a large wooden church lording over fields of vegetables, Kussharo-Genya charms guests with vaulted ceilings, lofty skylights and polished wooden floors; keeps them busy with a constantly changing list of activities; and sends them away stuffed to the brim with veritable gourmet meals centred on Hokkaidō delicacies. Once again, if you don't have a car, the English-speaking staff will pick you up at JR Mashū station with an advanced reservation.

Onsen Minshuku Nibushi-no-Sato (☎ 483-2294; www1.ocn.ne.jp/~kussie; r per person incl 2 meals ¥8550; P 💻 📶) This family-run *minshuku* sits on the northwestern shores of Kussharo-ko off of Rte 52, and is very accommodating to foreign travellers. The property has a casual log-cabin feel complete with a small but sublime private onsen, and the owners can point out some great local walks, bike trails and birdwatching spots. Nibushi-no-Sato is a short drive from Kawayu Onsen bus station, or you can call ahead for a pick-up.

Misono Hotel (御薗ホテル; ☎ 483-2511; www.misonohotel.com, in Japanese; r high/low season incl 2 meals from ¥10,650/8550; P 💻) This luxurious ryokan

HOKKAIDŌ

sits in the middle of Kawayu village, and is marked by a free *ashiyu* (foot bath) that is a nice little appetiser for the main course to follow. Western- and Japanese-style rooms are large and loungy, though most of your quality time will be spent in the indoor and outdoor sulphur springs, which are reported to help ease muscle pain, stiffness and fatigue.

Marukibune (丸木舟; ☎ 484-2644; dishes from ¥650; 🕑 11am-7.30pm) Next door to the Museum of Ainu Folklore in Kussharo Kotan, this popular restaurant has a variety of local specialities including *howaito-rāmen* (noodles in milk broth; ¥1000) and the sashimi of *parimono* (a local river fish; ¥1000), which is so fresh that the head arrives still moving. Ainu music performances (¥3000) are given on certain Saturday nights: be sure to call for a reservation as seating is limited.

GETTING THERE & AROUND

Bus

Depending on the season – services drop off in the winter – there are up to three buses a day between Kawayu Onsen bus station and Bihoro (¥1920, 2½ hours), which run via the scenic Bihoro Pass.

Between May and October, a sightseeing bus service runs four times a day from Kawayu Onsen bus station via the main sights in the park to Akan Kohan (from ¥2100, 2¼ hours). It stops for sightseeing and picture taking – if you're low on time and don't mind the package-tour atmosphere, this is a nice way to see the area without shelling out for a rental car.

Car

Kawayu Onsen is accessed by Rte 319, which runs north–south between Abashiri and Kushiro. Between Mashū station and Akan Kohan on Rte 241 is a particularly scenic stretch with an outstanding lookout at Sokodai that overlooks the lakes Penketō and Panketō.

Train

Frequent *tokkyū* on the JR Sekihoku line run between Abashiri and Bihoro (¥1640, 25 minutes), and between Asahikawa and Bihoro (¥7020, 3½ hours). From Bihoro, you can catch onward buses to Kawayu bus station.

Frequent *kaisoku* run north on the JR Senmō main line between Kawayu Onsen and Shiretoko-shari (¥900, 45 minutes), and south between Kawayu Onsen and Kushiro (¥1790, 1¾ hours) via Mashū (¥350, 15 minutes).

JR Kawayu Onsen station is a 10-minute bus ride from the town centre (¥280); buses are timed to meet most of the trains.

Akan Kohan 阿寒湖畔

☎ 0154

The resort town of Akan Kohan has one of the largest Ainu *kotan* (village) in Hokkaidō, and is a hot spot for anyone interested in this ancient culture. It's also where you catch a glimpse of *marimo*, the most famous algae ever to bob to the surface, and then quickly leave behind the tourist throngs on a hike into the national park.

ORIENTATION & INFORMATION

Tourists arrive at Akan Kohan bus terminal on the eastern edge of the village. Here, you'll find a **tourist information office** (☎ 67-3200; www.lake-akan.com/en/index.html; 2-1-15 Akan-ko Onsen; 🕑 9am-6pm) that stocks pamphlets about the park in English, including excellent alpine trail guides with contour maps of O-Akan-dake and Me-Akan-dake.

SIGHTS & ACTIVITIES

Ainu Kotan アイヌコタン

Although it's definitely a tourist-orientated affair, the *kotan* on the western edge of the village is in fact inhabited by one of the largest remaining Ainu communities in Hokkaidō. Generally speaking, however, the Ainu are virtually indistinguishable in appearance from the Japanese due to generations of intermarriage, though there are material signs of their rich culture. The most obvious of these are the woodcrafts, leatherwork and other handmade items, which are on sale at shops throughout the *kotan*.

At the top of the hill is the **Ainu Seikatsu Kinenkan** (アイヌ生活記念館; Ainu Lifestyle Memorial Hall; ☎ 67-2727; admission ¥300; 🕑 10am-10pm May-Oct), but it's small – perhaps a disappointment if you've already seen other Ainu exhibitions elsewhere.

Next door and better value is the **Onnechise** (オンネチセ; admission ¥1000), where Ainu dance performances take place six times a day in the high season. Shows are at 11am, 1pm, 3pm, 8pm, 9pm and 10pm from April to October, and at least once a day the rest of the year.

HOKKAIDŌ

The **Akan Forest & Lake Culture Museum** (森と湖の藝術館; ☎ 67-2001; admission ¥500; ⏲ 10am-5pm May-Oct) has more displays and exhibits on the history and culture of both the Ainu and the Akan National Park area.

Marimo Viewing まりも観光

Akan-ko is famous for *marimo (Cladophora aegagropila)*, spheres of algae that are both biologically interesting – it takes as much as 200 years for them to grow to the size of a baseball – and very, very *kawaii* (cute). Only growing in a few places in the world, Akan *marimo* became endangered after being designated a national treasure: suddenly, everyone in Japan wanted one. The building of a power plant (which lowered the lake level several inches) did not help the plight of these green benthic fuzzballs.

The Ainu finally came to the rescue by starting the **Marimo Matsuri** (まりも祭り), held in mid-October, which returns *marimo* to Akan-ko, one by one. Their numbers are growing but they are sometimes affected by natural disasters – typhoons can push as much as 50% of them out of the lake. Luckily, locals quickly return them to the water as soon as the winds have subsided. On that note, please try to resist the urge to buy a bottled *marimo* on a keychain, even though they're widely available throughout Akan Kohan – and all of Hokkaidō for that matter.

The **Akan Kohan Eco-Museum Centre** (阿寒湖畔エコミュージアムセンター; ☎ 67-4100; admission free; ⏲ 9am-5pm Wed-Mon) on the eastern edge of town has well-maintained exhibits with lots of photographs, and a number of *marimo* in aquarium tanks. It also has hiking maps and displays about the local flora and fauna. The *bokke* (bubbling clay pools) walk starts from the museum, and makes a shaded, breezy loop out to the lake and back through some pine forest, with views of obliging tufted-eared squirrels, chipmunks and birds.

The best way to actually get up close and personal with *marimo* is to take a **sightseeing cruise** (☎ 67-2511; www.akankisen.com/_eng/index.html, in Japanese; 1hr trip ¥1750), which makes a 45-minute loop from the docks around the lake. All boats stop for a somewhat meagre 15 minutes at the Marimo Exhibition and Observation Center, where you can hopefully spot a few balls of algae photosynthesising on the surface of the water.

Hiking

About 6km east of Akan Kohan is **O-Akan-dake** (雄阿寒岳; Male Mountain; 1371m). Buses to Kushiro pass the Takiguchi trail entrance five minutes out of Akan Kohan. The ascent takes a fairly arduous 3½ hours, and the descent takes about another 2½ hours. From the peak there are very fine views of the lakes Penketō and Panketō, and on clear days you can see as far as Daisetsuzan National Park.

The highest mountain in the park, **Me-Akan-dake** (雌阿寒岳; Female Mountain; 1499m), is an active volcano that is usually closed due to emissions of poisonous gas. Ask at the tourist information office about current conditions.

The shorter climb to the observation platform on **Hakutō-zan** (白湯山; 650m) affords fine views of the lakes and the surrounding peaks. Starting 2km south of town, the ascent takes about an hour, winding through birch and fir forests and past several groups of bubbling sulphur hot springs (too hot to bathe in: don't try!).

SLEEPING

As in Kawayu Onsen, camping in and around Akan Kohan is a good option. There are several places to choose from, though the most convenient is **Akan Lakeside Campsite** (阿寒湖畔キャンプ場; ☎ 67-3263; 5-1 Akan Onsen; camp sites per person ¥630; ⏲ Jun-Sep; Ⓟ), about a five-minute walk west of the village centre. Here, you'll find plenty of shady pitches, and even an *ashiyu* for cleaning off those muddy feet.

Nonaka Onsen Youth Hostel (☎ 0156-29-7454; http://www.youthhostel.or.jp/English/e_nonaka.htm; Ashoro-chō Moashoro 159; dm from ¥2835, breakfast/dinner ¥630/1050; Ⓟ) Complete with its own onsen, this is a very popular spot that's often booked solid by hikers in the busy summer months. The remote hostel is snuggled between a forested hillside and the shores of Onneto-ko off of Rte 241. It's preferable that you have your own car if you stay here, though buses bound for Meakan Onsen can drop you if you ask the driver

Yamaguchi (山口; ☎ 67-2555; www.tabi-hokkaido.co.jp/~yamaguchi/english; 5-3-2 Akan Onsen; r per person incl 2 meals ¥5925; Ⓟ) This family run Japanese-style inn, located in downtown Akan Kohan, is surprisingly affordable and caters well to foreign travellers. The secret to success here is focusing solely on the basics: traditional Japanese cooking following a therapeutic soak in high mineral content hot spring-fed baths.

New Akan Hotel Shangri-la (ニュー阿寒ホテルシャングリラ; ☎ 67-2121; http://www.newakanhotel.co.jp/english/index.htm; d incl 2 meals from ¥12,000; P 💻) One of the largest hotels in town, the pretentious sounding Shangri-la lacks the personality of the smaller inns, though its luxurious multipooled baths are some of the best around. The fake planetarium in the lobby – though impressive – is a bit over the top. Note that prices vary considerably according to season and availability.

our pick **Akan Yuku-no-sato** (阿寒遊久の里; ☎ 67-2531; http://www.tsuruga-g.com/english/01tsuruga/01tsuru-facility.html; 4-6-10, Akan Onsen; r per person incl 2 meals from ¥12,600; P 💻) If you're looking for a worthwhile splurge, this stunner of a ryokan offers refined elegance in the truest Japanese sense. A variety of tatami rooms are on offer, some of which feature private soaking tubs, rocking chairs in front of picture windows and silk cushions strategically strewn about hewn-wooden floors. Banquet meals are a regal affair featuring never-ending courses of edible art, while two floors of onsen bliss run the gamut from ceramic tubs to open-air rock garden baths.

GETTING THERE & AWAY

There are up to seven buses a day in both directions between Asahikawa and Akan Kohan (¥5210, 4½ hours) via Sōunkyō Onsen (¥3260, 3½ hours) in Daisetsuzan National Park. There are also a couple of buses a day between Akan Kohan and Kushiro (¥4790, 5¼ hours).

Between May and October, a sightseeing bus service runs four times a day from Akan Kohan bus station via the main sights in the park to Kawayu Onsen (from ¥2100, 2¼ hours).

If you're driving, Akan Kohan runs along Rte 240, which (of course!) has been renamed **Marimo Kokudō** (まりも国道).

KUSHIRO 釧路

☎ 0154 / pop 189,000

A large and rather unsightly port city, Kushiro fails to captivate tourists, though it does serve as the southern gateway to Akan National Park, as well as the jumping off point for **Kushiro Shitsugen National Park** (釧路湿原国立公園). Japan's largest expanse of undeveloped wetland (269 sq km), Kushiro Shitsugen is nearly the size of Tokyo, and provides shelter for thousands of different species of wildlife.

To reach Kushiro Shitsugen, you can take trains from Kushiro to the **Hosooka Observatory** (細岡展望台; ☎ 40-4455; admission free; 🕑 9am-7pm summer, 9am-5pm winter) on the eastern side of the park, or a bus (¥660, 40 minutes) to the **Kushiro Observatory** (釧路湿原展望台; ☎ 56-2424; admission ¥360; 🕑 8.30am-6pm summer, 9am-5pm winter) on the west. The former is atop an overlook where you can easily appreciate the grand scale of this wetland preserve.

Kushiro station also has an **information booth** (☎ 22-8294; www.kushiro-kankou.or.jp/english; 🕑 9am-5.30pm) and a **postal ATM** (🕑 9am-7pm Mon-Fri, 9am-5pm Sat & Sun).

Most Japanese visitors to Kushiro Shitsugen are keen on spotting a *tanchō-zuru* (red-crested white crane), the traditional symbol of both longevity and Japan. They're also just plain cool, and several viewing areas let you watch these enormous birds in relative comfort as they land, feed, tend their young or do their mating dance. The peak crane season is winter to early spring, but even in August a few stragglers may be around if you're lucky.

Deer are also so common in this area that the trains have a special *shika-bue* (deer whistle) to scare them off. Foxes also dart around the undergrowth in search of prey, so keep your eyes peeled – it's very fortunate to spot a *kitsune* in the wild as they were revered as gods in ancient Japan!

Around the corner from the JR Kushiro Shitsugen station is the **Kushiro Shitsugen Tōro Youth Hostel** (釧路湿原とうろユースホステル; ☎ 87-2510; www.sip.or.jp/~tohro/sub1.htm, in Japanese; dm from ¥ 3360), which offers delicious and affordable meals (breakfast/dinner costs ¥630/1050), bunk-style rooms that are big enough not to feel cramped, and a great viewing deck from which you can survey the national park.

Next to the train station in Kushiro is the **Kushiro Royal Inn** (釧路ロイヤルイン; ☎ 31-2121; www.royalinn.jp, in Japanese; s/d from ¥5100/7300; P 💻), a small but efficient business hotel highlighted by an attractive dining room on the top floor.

Just to the right of Kushiro station on the corner after Lawson convenience store, the impressive **Washō Market** (和商市場; ☎ 22-3226; www.washoichiba.com, in Japanese; 25-13 Kurokane-chō; items from ¥200; 🕑 8am-6pm Mon-Sat) features every possible seafood one can imagine, plus a food court with *bentō* (boxed meal) and other prepared dishes.

WHY DO YOU LOVE HOKKAIDŌ? *Matthew D Firestone*

While updating the Hokkaidō chapter for this guidebook, I spent a good deal of time talking to random strangers. As you might imagine, gathering and fact-checking travel information takes a lot of time and energy, though it's a great way to pick the brains of all the locals you meet. In fact, I made a point to ask everybody I met the same simple question: 'Why do you love Hokkaidō?' Residents of the island provided me with some truly notable quotables, a few of which are listed here:

Hokkaidō isn't Japan. Seriously. I mean, have you ever walked to the bus stop in Tokyo, and wondered whether or not you would cross paths with a bear?

Tomo from Furano

Have you tasted our crab? It's the best in world. I've never been to Alaska, but I don't need to go. We catch it right here, and eat it right here, and that's why it's the best.

Daisuke from Wakkanai

Do you have *uni* (sea urchin roe) in your country? I love to buy *uni* fresh from the market, and than mix it with cream and eat it with pasta. It's delicious!

Mariko from Otaru

We invented beer, right here in Sapporo! Well, I guess maybe it came from Germany first, but the Japanese were drinking *sake* before we came to the rescue!

Haruki from Sapporo

This island makes you tough. Tokyoites complain when the rains soaks their shoes. We complain when the snow buries our houses.

Ichiro from Kushiro

HOKKAIDŌ

Getting There & Away

AIR

Kushiro's small airport is located about 10km northwest of the city. From here, there are domestic flights to various destinations including Tokyo, Osaka, Nagoya and others. Buses between the airport and JR Kushiro station (¥910, 45 minutes) are timed to connect with arrivals and departures.

BUS

There are a couple of buses a day between Sōunkyō Onsen and Kushiro (¥4790, 5¼ hours) via Akan Kohan (¥1530, 2¼ hours).

CAR

Rte 319 runs north–south between Abashiri and Kushiro.

TRAIN

There are just a couple of *futsū* each day on the JR Senmō main line between Kushiro and Abashiri (¥3570, 3½ hours) via Shiretoko-shari (¥2730, 2½ hours), Kawayu Onsen (¥1790, 1½ hours) and Kushiro Shitsugen (¥350, 20 minutes).

Nemuro 根室

☎ 0153 / pop 3100

This tiny town's main attraction is its view of several islands that currently belong to Russia, despite being the subject of heated debate. On a clear day you get a view of the Hoppōryōdo (Kuril Islands), which are in dispute mainly because of their prime fishing grounds below the surface. English signage is limited, mainly plaques protesting the donation of these lands to Russia. It's the easternmost part of Japan, so those travellers who like to collect '-mosts' should be sure to come here.

At the tip, Nosappu-misaki, you will find some pricey souvenir shops, a **museum centre** (根室市観光物産センター; ☎ 28-2445; 🕑 9am-5pm Mar-Oct, 9am-4pm Nov-Feb) with a brief history of the area (in Japanese), monuments near the cliffside, a **viewing tower** (ノサップ岬平和の塔; ☎ 28-3333; admission ¥900; 🕑 8.30am-15 min after sunset) and a few restaurants.

The bus between Nemuro JR station and Nosappu-misaki passes a number of interesting **kelp-drying areas**, which are self-explanatory if kelp is being dried: it looks like black strips of twisted leather stretched in rows on the ground; otherwise, these areas look like well-maintained gravel car parks.

There are a few *futsū* each day on the JR Nemuro line between Kushiro and Nemuru (¥2420, 2½ hours). Buses, which are timed with train arrivals, bring you from the train station out to Nosappu-misaki (one way/return ¥1040/1900, 50 minutes). Buses leave Nosappu-misaki about every two hours until 6.35pm.

Shari 斜里

☎0152 / pop 13,000

Shari is the closest major settlement to Shiretoko National Park, and there is little reason not to continue pressing on to the park. Before you do, however, the **tourist information office** (☎23-2424; 17 Minato-machi; 10am-5pm mid-Apr–mid-Oct) helps supplement the information given at the park's nature centre. Shari's bus centre is to the left as you exit the JR Shiretoko-shari station.

Koshimizu Gensei Kaen (小清水原生花園; ☎63-4187; admission free; closed Nov-Apr) is an 8km stretch of wildflowers along the coast, only 20 minutes from Shari. Visit in late June with your own wheels and catch it at its peak: over 40 different species of flowers simultaneously blooming.

If you need to spend the night, there are a few convenient options right near the station. The **Ryokan Tanakaya** (旅館たなかや; ☎23-3165; r per person incl 2 meals from ¥7350; P) is a very simple but adequate Japanese-style inn, while the **Shari Central Hotel** (斜里セントラルホテル; ☎23-2355; r per person from ¥5800) offers a more scaled down version of your typical business hotel room.

GETTING THERE & AWAY

Bus

There is one direct bus daily linking Abashiri and Shari (¥1120, 1¼ hours). There are between five and nine buses daily between Shari and Utoro (¥1490, 50 minutes), but only three in summer that continue on as far as Iwaobetsu (¥1770, 1¼ hours).

Car

Surprisingly well-maintained Rte 334 runs up the coast from Abashiri to Shari, and continues to the village of Iwaobetsu.

Train

There are just a couple of *futsū* each day on the JR Senmō main line between Shari and Abashiri (¥810, 50 minutes), and between Shari and Kushiro via Teshikaga (¥2730, 2½ hours).

SHIRETOKO NATIONAL PARK 知床国立公園

Shiretoko-hantō, the peninsula that makes up Shiretoko National Park, was known in Ainu as 'the end of the world.' As remote as Japan gets, this magnificent stretch of land has virtually no sealed roads within its boundaries. Hiking tracks are present, though they're remote, poorly maintained, wind over slippery boulders and disappear at times on cliff sides. If the weather turns frigid or you slip and break an ankle, you'll need to hope that a passing fishing boat spots you – before the bears do.

Indeed, you need to be properly equipped to tackle one of Japan's last true wilderness areas, and you shouldn't underestimate the difficulty of the terrain that awaits you. However, the reward is obvious – Shiretoko boasts some of the best hiking that the country can offer, as evidenced by its recent designation as a Unesco World Heritage Site.

Orientation & Information

There are no sealed roads within the park's boundaries, save for a short northwest–southeast road that connects the town of Utoro (on the northwestern edge) with Rausu (on the southern side); two-thirds of the park has no roads at all.

Hiking must be arranged in advance: there are steep fines for anyone caught hiking off limits or after hours. Be sure to register at the **Shiretoko Nature Centre** (☎24-2114; www.shiretoko.or.jp/snc_eng/en_about.htm; slide show ¥500; 8am-5.40pm mid-Apr–mid-Oct, 9am-4pm mid-Oct–mid-Apr), which offers maps, hiking info and a 20-minute slide show about the peninsula.

Danger & Annoyances

So few people come here that humans haven't ruined it yet: hikers will see pristine forests, remote vistas without a sign of habitation and lots of wildlife, including bears and foxes. The latter can be dangerous too, so don't take any chances: some have been known to steal food or sleeping bags. In addition, fox faeces have contaminated the water with the parasite echinococcus, which can be deadly. Don't drink any water that hasn't been properly purified.

Sights & Activities

The fishing village of **Rausu** (羅臼) once grew wealthy on the herring industry, though there's not much here now, other than a few very beautiful hikes. A challenging but well-marked track to **Rausu-dake** (羅臼岳; 1661m) starts a few kilometres outside of town towards Shiretoko-Toge, near the (free) camping ground at **Kuma-no-yu Onsen** (熊の湯温泉) – yes, that's 'Bear's Boiled Water', you heard right!

From Rausu, to get to Rausu-dake head towards the tip along the marked trail and keep an eye out for a large overhang on the left, marked by a small car park. Peek under the overhang at **phosphorescent moss**, which humbly glows a bright shade of green and is visible even in daylight.

Note that hiking out to the extreme tip of the peninsula is no longer possible: you will be heavily fined if rangers catch you on the unmaintained track, which is often eroded beyond recognition.

The surrounding **Shiretoko-go-ko** (知床岬; Shiretoko Five Lakes) region offers hiking with beautiful views of the ponds and mountains behind them.

Boat rides (☎ 24-2147; trips ¥6000, 3½hr) departing from the pier in the village of **Utoro** (ウトロ) are an option for those who want to see the cape as well as the spectacular cliffs that Shiretoko is famous for. Otherwise, postcards will have to suffice.

SHIRETOKO-HANTŌ

INFORMATION		
Shiretoko Nature Centre 知床ネイチャーセンター	1	A3
SIGHTS & ACTIVITIES		
Boat Rides 遊覧船	2	A3
SLEEPING		
Kinoshita-goya 木下小屋	3	A2
Marumi まるみ	4	B3
Shiretoko Iwaobetsu Youth Hostel	5	A2

Sleeping

Shiretoko Iwaobetsu Youth Hostel (☎ 24-2311; www4.ocn.ne.jp/~iwayh, in Japanese; dm from ¥1800; Mar-Nov) In the small village of Iwaobetsu, just off of Rte 334, this hostel is a popular base for hikers as it provides easy access to the Shiretoko-go-ko region. As well as organising hiking parties, it also provides numerous chances to spot wildlife. Bear, deer and fox are all regulars in the surrounding woods, and the staff know exactly where and when is the best time to see them.

Marumi (☎ 88-1313; www.shiretoko-rausu.com, in Japanese; r per person incl 2 meals ¥9300;) There are not many reasons to stay overnight in Rausu, but right by the seaside is the well-regarded ryokan which features attractive tatami rooms, lovely seafood meals, a *rotemburo* and even a sauna. This is also a great place to build up your energy either before or after you summit Rausu-dake.

Kinoshita-goya (木下小屋; ☎ 24-2824; dm ¥1575; Jun-Sep) If you happen to get tired during the hike to Rausu-dake, you can always overnight at a mountain hut offering spartan accommodation right at the Rausu-dake trailhead. It is often booked solid in the summer months, so call ahead.

Getting There & Around

There are between five and nine buses daily between Shari and Utoro (¥1490, 50 minutes), but only three in summer that continue on as far as Iwaobetsu (¥1770, 1¼ hours).

From late April to October, buses run four times daily from Utoro (¥900, 50 minutes) along

WARNING: BEAR ACTIVITY

The peninsula of Shiretoko-hantō is home to around 600 brown bears, one of the largest bear populations in Japan. Park pamphlets warn visitors that, once they enter Shiretoko National Park, they should assume that bears could appear at any time. Favourite bear haunts include Shiretoko-go-ko (知床岬; Shiretoko Five Lakes) and the falls of Kamuiwakka-no-taki.

Hikers are strongly advised not to go into the forest in the early morning or at dusk, and to avoid hiking alone. Carrying a bell or some other noise-making device is also recommended (bears don't like surprises). If you're camping, tie up your food and do not bury your rubbish. Bear activity picks up noticeably during early autumn, when the creatures are actively foraging for food ahead of their winter hibernation. Visitors should be especially cautious at this time.

the northern side of the peninsula, passing the nature centre, the youth hostel, Shiretoko-go-ko and Kamuiwakka-no-taki before terminating at Shiretoko-ōhashi. During this time frame, there are also buses four times daily between Utoro and Rausu via the dramatic Shiretoko-Toge pass (¥1310, 55 minutes).

Finally, there are up to five daily buses between Rausu and Kushiro (¥4740, 3½ hours).

While not essential, having a car will make it easier to access the park, and to move up and down the coastline, though again, be advised that the vast majority of Shiretoko does not have any roads.

TOKACHI 十勝

The name Tokachi is as synonymous with wine in Japan as Beaujolais is for Westerners. While its name doesn't fit neatly in with the cardinal monikers of Hokkaidō's other subprefectures, Tokachi was a historic but short-lived province that was established in the late 19th century. Today, the region is largely agricultural and has few major tourists draws, though it does boast some lively wine-scented countryside that's worth exploring if you have some time at the end of your trip.

OBIHIRO 帯広

☎ 0155 / pop 171,000

A former Ainu stronghold, the modern city of Obihiro was founded in 1883 by the *Banseisha*, a group of colonial settlers from Shizuoka Prefecture. Squeezed in between the Hidaka and Daisetsuzan mountain ranges, Obihiro is a friendly, laid-back city without much for tourists, though you're likely to pass through en route to Ikeda or Erimo-misaki.

Tokachi Tourist Information (☎ 23-6403; 🕑 9am-7pm) is on the 2nd floor of the Esta shopping mall at the JR Obihiro station, and is your best source of information on Tokachi – stock up on pamphlets and brochures in English.

Toipirka Kitaobihiro Youth Hostel (トイピルカ北帯広ユースホステル; ☎ 30-4165; http://homepage1.nifty.com/TOIPIRKA/english/main_eng.htm; dm from ¥3200, breakfast/dinner ¥600/1000; Ⓟ) is an attractive log house with Western-style beds and nightly tea time. It's near Tokachigawa Onsen, a cluster of resort-style onsens and hotels along the Tokachi River. If you phone ahead, the staff can pick you up from the station in Obihiro.

If you want to stay in Obihiro proper, just step outside the station and look up – just about every popular chain has an Obihiro location, and almost all are within sight of the station.

Butadonburi butadonburi (barbecued pork over rice) is an area speciality. **Panchō** (ぱんちょう; ☎ 22-1974; dishes from ¥850) is across from the station, and is all that's on the picture menu.

Getting There & Away

AIR

Obihiro's tiny airport is located about 25km southwest of the city. From here, there are domestic flights to various destinations including Tokyo, Osaka, Nagoya and others. Buses between the airport and JR Obihiro station (¥1000, 45 minutes) are timed to connect with arrivals and departures.

BUS

There are a few departures in both directions between the bus terminal adjacent to the station in Obihiro and the Chūō bus station in Sapporo (¥3670, 4¼ hours). There are also regular buses running between Obihiro and Kushiro (¥2240, 2½ hours), Asahikawa (¥3150, 3¾ hours), Sōunkyō Onsen (¥2200, 80 minutes), and Ikeda (¥590, one hour).

CAR

Rte 274 runs between Sapporo and Obihiro, while Rte 38 connects Obihiro to Kushiro.

TRAIN

Frequent *tokkyū* run on the JR Nemuro line between Obihiro and Sapporo (¥7020, 2½ hours), and between Obihiro and Kushiro (¥4680, 1½ hours). *Kaisoku* run on the same line between Obihiro and Ikeda (¥440, 30 minutes),

IKEDA 池田

☎015 / pop 8470

Located amidst the grape fields of the eastern Tokachi plain, Ikeda is a small farming town that became famous in the 1960s when the municipal government started experimented with winemaking. While conservative oenophiles might not consider Japanese wines in the same league as Old World classics and other New World upstarts, pull out a bottle of Ikeda and decide for yourself. Judging by the giant corkscrew sculpture in the station, the folks here hope you will.

Town maps are available at the **tourist information desk** (☎572-2024; 🕑10am-5pm Apr-Oct) inside the JR Ikeda station.

In our humble opinion, some excellent wines are made at **Wain-jō** (ワイン城; Wine Castle; ☎572-2467; www.tokachi-wine.com, in Japanese; 83 Kiyomi, Ikeda-chō; admission free; 🕑factory tours 9am-5pm), set on a hillside overlooking the town. A tour guides you through the production process (in Japanese only) and there's a tasting afterwards. To get here head south along the train track from the station; you'll see the hill on your left shortly afterwards (look for the Ferris wheel).

What goes well with wine? Cheese of course! The rather optimistically named **Happiness Dairy** (ハッピネスデーリィ; ☎572-2001; http://happiness.presen.to/index.html, in Japanese; 104-2 Kiyomi, Ikeda-chō; admission free; 🕑9.30am-5.30pm Mon-Fri, 9.30am-6pm Sat, Sun & holidays in summer, 9.30am-5pm Mon-Fri, 9.30am-5.30pm Sat, Sun & holidays in winter) takes you through the entire process, from walking in the wheat fields with the milk cows to tasting the final product, be it fresh cheese or rum-raisin gelato. From Wain-jō head east on Rte 39 about 200m, then turn left at the T-junction, head 500m north and turn right at the cross section. Go 300m, and the shop is on your right.

There is also a burgeoning artists' community in Ikeda that produces some lovely craft goods. The **Moon Face Gallery & Cafe** (画廊喫茶ムーンフェイス; ☎572-2198; 132 Kiyomi, Ikeda-chō; admission free; 🕑10am-6pm Wed-Mon) displays works by locals while serving up tasty cappuccinos and espressos, while the **Spinner's Farm Tanaka** (スピナーズファーム・タナカ; ☎572-2848; www12.plala.or.jp/spinner, in Japanese; admission free; 🕑10am-6pm Apr-Oct, 10am-5.30pm Nov-Mar, closed 2nd Sat of each month) is a wool-weaving workshop.

Friendly management and delicious dinners including a complimentary glass of local wine make **Ikeda Kita no Kotan Youth Hostel** (池田北のコタンユースホステル; ☎572-3666; www11.plala.or.jp/kitanokotan, in Japanese; dm incl 2 meals from ¥5000; Ⓟ ⊠) a real treat. The hostel is within easy walking distance of the Toshibetsu station, one stop west of Ikeda (¥200, five minutes). From the station take the main road south, turn left at the first intersection and the hostel is where the road ends.

Frequent *futsū* run on the JR Nemuro line between Obihiro and Ikeda (¥440, 30 minutes).

ERIMO-MISAKI 襟裳岬

☎01466

This remote cape is far off the beaten path, but with its windswept cliffs and dramatic ocean vistas, and kelp strung up to dry like giant shoelaces, it's a good day trip for anyone with their own wheels and a little extra time.

The history of this unique place is something of an ecological miracle. Beginning in the Meiji era, the hills surrounding this kelp-farming community were gradually deforested, so by the 1950s it was nicknamed Erimo Desert. Sand blew into the ocean, destroying the kelp, and the community faced a stark choice: reforest or leave. Thanks to the locals' perseverance and a vast number of seedlings, the hills now boast a Japanese black pine forest.

Those same great offshore winds and Pacific swell make for spectacular surfing breaks for anyone daring enough to bring along a board and wetsuit, but check with locals about rips and safety before paddling out into the waves. Across from the deserted JR bus stop there's a small bluff that makes a good spot to take a snapshot of the fishing boats below. A lone post office and postal ATM is near the city hall.

Ten minutes' drive further, at the cape itself, is an entire museum dedicated to wind, namely **Kaze-no-Yakata** (襟裳岬 風の館; ☎ 3-1133; www9.ocn.ne.jp/~kaze, in Japanese; 366-3 Tōyō, Erimo-chō; admission ¥1000; ⏲ 8.30am-6pm May-Sep, 9am-5pm Oct-Apr, closed Dec-Feb). There are plenty of weather-related films and displays, though the highlight is being blasted by gale-force winds inside a manmade wind tunnel.

Kuril seals, which bask all year round on the rocks below, are called *zenigata-azarashi* (money shaped) because the white spots on their black bodies are reminiscent of old Japanese coins. Here, you can also pick out your own crab or conch and have it grilled at the restaurant-shacks beside the car park. Bring a windbreaker: outside feels just as gusty as the wind tunnel does.

When things warm up a bit outside the winter months, there is a **camping ground** (百人浜オートキャンプ場; ☎ 4-2168; camp sites per person ¥300; ⏲ 20 Apr–20 Oct) on the beach at Hyakunin-hama, 8km northeast of the cape, right near the lighthouse.

At the tip of the cape, just around the corner from the wind museum, you will find **Minshuku Misaki-sō** (民宿みさき荘; ☎ 3-1316; www.goodinns.com/misakiso, in Japanese; Erimo-misaki Tōdaimoto, Erimo-chō; r per person with/without 2 meals ¥6300/4200; Ⓟ). This place is a surprisingly homey option given its far-flung location.

Shikoku 四国

For more than 1000 years, pilgrims have walked clockwise around Shikoku in the footsteps of the Buddhist saint Kōbō Daishi (774–835), who achieved enlightenment on the island of his birth. Known as the '88 Temples of Shikoku', the 1400km journey is Japan's best known pilgrimage and its oldest tourist trail.

In the days before guidebooks and reliable maps, pilgrims frequently disappeared forever in Shikoku's rugged and mountainous interior. Today, hardship is not the factor it once was, with many pilgrims buzzing merrily around the island in air-conditioned vehicles. In recent years, however, growing numbers of people have been striking out on foot along the age-old trails, in search of meaning and self-realisation.

Shikoku is not quite the rural wilderness it's often made out to be. The northern coast is linked to Honshū by bridges, and the cities of Matsuyama and Takamatsu are vibrant and intoxicating examples of the modern Japanese urban experience. Away from the towns, though, life still moves at a slower pace than elsewhere in Japan. In the countryside, single-carriage trains trundle through rice fields and mountainous valleys, and down by the capes there are (remarkably for Japan) no trains at all.

Relatively few foreigners visit Shikoku, and those who do can expect a friendly welcome. In addition to all the temples and some excellent seafood (and the famous *Sanuki udon* of Kagawa prefecture), Shikoku offers opportunities for hiking, rafting, surfing and whale-watching, as well as the chance to discover glimpses of an older Japan that can be hard to find among the glitter and fumes of the cities.

HIGHLIGHTS

- Follow time-worn paths along the pilgrimage of the **88 Temples** (p656)
- Get off the beaten path in the **Iya Valley** (p652)
- Take a soak in the historic **Dōgo Onsen** (p674) in the castle-town metropolis of Matsuyama
- Trek up 1368 stone steps to pay homage to the god of sea-farers at **Kompira-san** (p676) in the town of Kotohira
- Walk off Japan's most famous noodles with a stroll through Takamatsu's exquisite Edo-period garden, **Ritsurin-kōen** (p678)

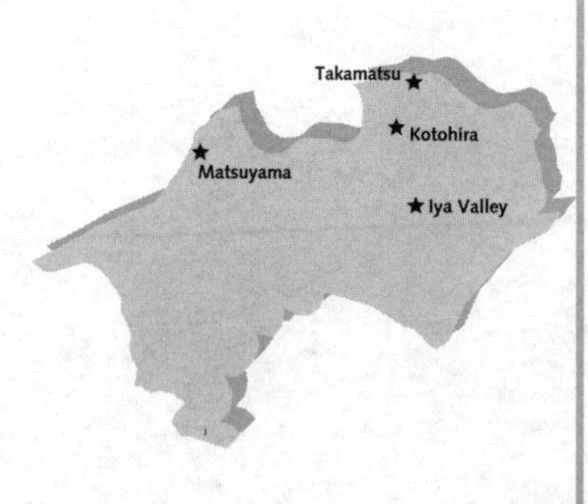

SHIKOKU

History

For most of Japan's history, the island of Shikoku has been divided into four regions – hence the name *shi* (four) and *koku* (provinces). After the Meiji Restoration in 1868, the ancient provinces of Awa, Tosa, Iyo and Sanuki became the modern-day prefectures of Tokushima-ken, Kōchi-ken, Ehime-ken and Kagawa-ken. The old names are still in common use.

Despite its proximity to the historical centres of power of Osaka and Kyoto, Shikoku has always been considered somewhat remote. It's also a rugged land. In the 12th century, defeated Heike (Taira) warriors disappeared into the mountainous interiors to escape their Genji (Minamoto) pursuers after decisive sea battles at Yashima (p681) and Dan-no-ura (p483). Until very recently, the 88 Temples pilgrims returned from Shikoku with stories of extreme hardship that had to be overcome in their search for enlightenment.

Climate

Shikoku enjoys a mild climate, with temperatures typically several degrees warmer than those experienced in Tokyo. Spring and autumn are the best times to come – summers can be stiflingly hot, and typhoons frequently pound the Pacific coast from June until October. Although there is plenty of rain, snow is rare (except in the mountains).

Getting There & Away

Until 20 years ago, if you wanted to get to Shikoku you had to fly or take a boat. Today, there are three bridge systems linking Shikoku with Honshū. In the east, the Akashi Kaikyō-ōhashi connects Tokushima with Kōbe in Hyōgo-ken via Awaji-shima (Awaji Island). The Seto-ōhashi bridge runs from Okayama to Sakaide, west of Takamatsu. This is the only one of the bridges to carry trains. Towards the western end of the north coast, the Shimanami Kaidō (p476) is an island-hopping series of nine bridges (with bike paths!) leading from Imabari in Ehime-ken to Onomichi near Hiroshima.

As a result of the improved bridge infrastructure, ferry services are on the decline, though there are still boats to a few major ports on Kyūshū and the southern coast of Honshū. Most visitors arrive on the island by train from Okayama or by highway bus from Osaka, Kyoto and Tokyo. Air services connect major cities in Shikoku with Tokyo, Osaka and other major centres.

Getting Around

This chapter's coverage follows the same order that most of Shikoku's visitors have used to travel around the island over the past 1000 years – in a loop around the island starting in Tokushima and moving clockwise through Kōchi, Ehime and Kagawa prefectures.

For more information on visiting the 88 Temples of Shikoku, see the boxed text, p656.

TOKUSHIMA-KEN 徳島県

The traditional starting point from which generations of pilgrims have set out on their tour around the island, Tokushima-ken is home to the first 23 of the 88 Temples. Notable attractions include the lively Awa-odori Matsuri (Awa-odori Festival), which takes place in Tokushima in August; the mighty whirlpools of the Naruto Channel between Tokushima and Awaji-shima; the dramatic scenery of the Iya Valley; and the surf beaches of the southern coast.

TOKUSHIMA 徳島

☎ 088 / pop 270,000

Flanked by mountains and centred on a palm-lined promenade, the modern city of Tokushima is best known for the Awa-odori festival in August. The city is also a convenient base for exploring the nearby Naruto whirlpools. To pilgrims, Tokushima serves as the gateway to the island, and the jumping-off point for the first group of temples.

Orientation

Tokushima's main landmark is Mt Bizan (眉山), which dominates the city from the west. The remains of the old castle now form a pleasant park directly behind the railway station. The main road runs from the station to the Mt Bizan cable car, crossing the Shinmachi-gawa (Shinmachi River) on the way. The main entertainment district is across the river in Akita-machi.

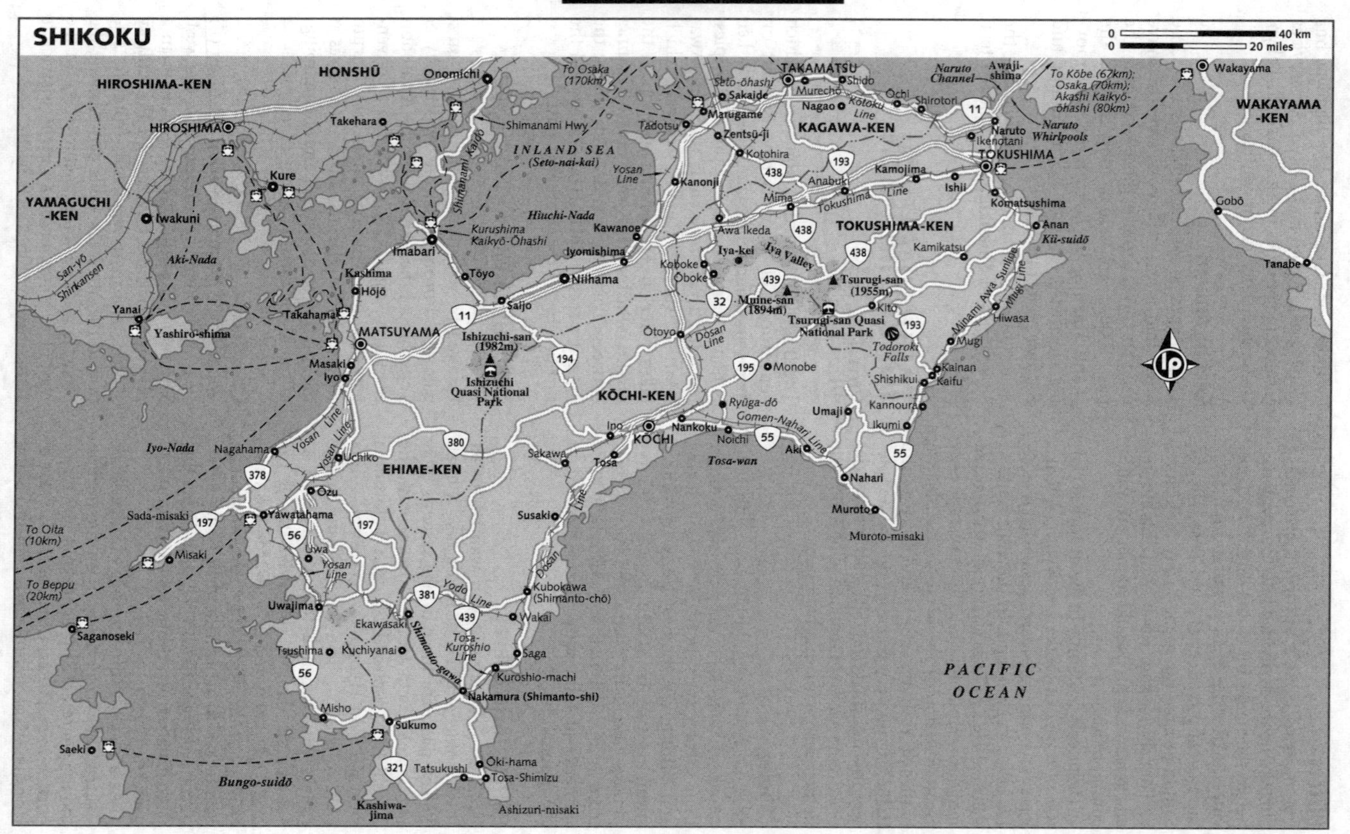
SHIKOKU
0 40 km
0 20 miles
HIROSHIMA-KEN
HONSHŪ
Onomichi
To Osaka (170km)
TAKAMATSU
Shido
Naruto Channel
Awaji-shima
To Kōbe (67km); Osaka (70km); Akashi Kaikyō-ōhashi (80km)
Wakayama
WAKAYAMA -KEN
Seto-ōhashi
Sakaide
Murechō
Ōchi
Shirotori
Marugame
Nagao
Kōtoku Line
Takehara
HIROSHIMA
Shimanami Hwy
Tadotsu
Zentsū-ji
KAGAWA-KEN
Naruto
Ikenotani
Naruto Whirlpools
INLAND SEA (Seto-nai-kai)
Kotohira
Kure
Yosan Line
Kanonji
Anabuki
Kamojima
Ishii
TOKUSHIMA
Shimanami Kaidō
Mima
Tokushima Line
Komatsushima
YAMAGUCHI -KEN
Iwakuni
Hiuchi-Nada
Kurushima Kaikyō-Ōhashi
Kawanoe
Awa Ikeda
TOKUSHIMA-KEN
Anan
Kii-suidō
Gobō
Aki-Nada
Imabari
Iyomishima
Iya-kei
Iya Valley
Kamikatsu
Tanabe
San-yō Shinkansen
Kashima
Tōyo
Niihama
Koboke
Ōboke
Tsurugi-san (1955m)
Minami Awa Sunline
Mugi Line
Yanai
Hōjō
Saijō
Miune-san (1894m)
Kito
Hiwasa
Takahama
Yashiro-shima
MATSUYAMA
Ishizuchi-san (1982m)
Ōtoyo
Dosan Line
Tsurugi-san Quasi National Park
Mugi
Todoroki Falls
Masaki
Iyo
Monobe
Kainan
Kaifu
Shishikui
Ishizuchi Quasi National Park
KŌCHI-KEN
Ryūga-dō
Umaji
Kannoura
Gomen-Nahari Line
Ikumi
Ino
KŌCHI
Nankoku
Noichi
Iyo-Nada
Nagahama
Yosan Line
Uchiko
EHIME-KEN
Sakawa
Tosa
Aki
Tosa-wan
Nahari
Ōzu
Sada-misaki
Yawatahama
Susaki
Muroto
To Oita (10km)
Muroto-misaki
Uwa
Misaki
Yosan Line
To Beppu (20km)
Dosan Line
Yodo Line
Kubokawa (Shimanto-chō)
Uwajima
Saganoseki
Ekawasaki
Wakai
Tsushima
Kuchiyanai
Tosa-Kuroshio Line
Shimanto-gawa
Saga
Kuroshio-machi
PACIFIC OCEAN
Nakamura (Shimanto-shi)
Misho
Sukumo
Saeki
Ōki-hama
Tatsukushi
Tosa-Shimizu
Bungo-suidō
Kashiwa-jima
Ashizuri-misaki

Information

There are coin lockers at the station, and the ATMs at the post office accept international cards.

JTB (Japan Travel Bureau; ☎ 623-3181; 1-29 Ryōgoku Honmachi; 🕑 10am-6pm closed Wed) Travel agency located near Tōyoko Inn.

Tokushima Prefecture International Exchange Association (TOPIA; ☎ 656-3303; www.topia.ne.jp; 🕑 10am-6pm) This extremely helpful place is on the 6th floor of the station building, and has English-speaking staff. Internet access is available (¥50 for 10 minutes), and you can leave your bags here during the day.

Tourist information office (☎ 622-8556; 🕑 9am-8pm) In a booth outside the station. Has English brochures and maps.

Sights & Activities

BIZAN 眉山

At the southwestern end of Shinmachibashi-dōri is **Awa Odori Kaikan** (☎ 611-1611; 2-20 Shinmachibashi; admission ¥300; 🕑 9am-5pm, closed 2nd & 4th Wed), which features extensive exhibits relating to the Awa-odori festival and dance. You can see the dance performed throughout the year at 2pm, 3pm and 4pm daily (with an additional performance at 11am on weekends), with a nightly performance at 8pm (afternoon/evening performances ¥500/700). From the 5th floor, a **cable car** (☎ 652-3617; one way/return Nov-Mar ¥600/1000, return Apr-Oct ¥600; 🕑 9am-5.30pm Nov-Mar, to 9pm Apr-Oct & during cherry-blossom season, to 10pm during Awa-odori festival) whizzes you to the 280m-high summit for fine views over the city. A combined ticket covering the museum, cable car and dance show is ¥1500.

At the top of the hill is a small park centred on a peace pagoda, and the **Wenceslao de Moraes Museum** (☎ 623-5342; Mosukegahara Bizan-chō; admission ¥200, free with cable-car ticket; 🕑 9.30am-5pm, closed 2nd & 4th Wed of the month). Moraes was a Portuguese naval commander who served as consul in Kobe and lived in Tokushima from 1813 until his death in 1929. He wrote a number of books on Tokushima and its traditions. Some rocky trails lead back down to the bottom of the hill, taking about 20 minutes.

AWA PUPPET THEATRE 人形浄瑠璃

For hundreds of years, puppet theatre thrived in the farming communities around Tokushima. Most of the theatres have long since gone, but the traditional dramas can still be seen at **Awa Jūrobei Yashiki** (阿波十郎兵衛屋敷; ☎ 665-2202; 184 Honura; museum admission ¥400; 🕑 9.30am-5pm). This small museum, which contains displays of puppets, and English explanations on the history of the drama. It's in the former residence of Bandō Jūrobei, a samurai who allowed himself to be executed for a crime he didn't commit, in order to preserve the good name of his master. The tale provided inspiration for the drama *Keisei Awa no Naruto*, first performed in 1768. Sections from the play are performed at 11am daily, and at 11am and 2pm on weekends. More puppets can be seen at nearby **Awa Deko Ningyō Kaikan** (阿波木偶人形会館; Awa Puppet Hall; ☎ 665-5600; 1-84 Honura; admission ¥400; 🕑 9am-5pm, closed 1st & 3rd Wed of the month).

To get to the museum, take a bus for Tomiyoshi Danchi (富吉団地) from Tokushima station and get off at the Jūrobei Yashiki-mae stop (¥270, 20 minutes).

CHŪŌ-KŌEN 中央公園

Northeast of the train station, on the slopes of Shiroyama, is **Chūō-kōen**, where you'll find the ruins of Tokushima-jō (Tokushima Castle). Built in 1585 for Hachisuka Iemasa after he was granted the fiefdom of Awa by Toyotomi Hideyoshi, most of the castle was destroyed in 1875 following the Meiji Restoration. A few ramparts and the moat are pretty much all that's left, along with an attractive garden that once formed part of the *daimyō*'s (domain lords') pleasure quarters. The pleasant park is a popular spot for walkers and joggers. If you're having problems imagining the former grandeur of the site, **Tokushima Castle Museum** (☎ 656-2525; 1-8 Jōnai; admission ¥300; 🕑 9am-5pm, closed Mon) contains an impressive reconstruction of the castle town at its peak, as well as the *daimyō's* boat, some displays of armour, and letters to the local lord from Hideyoshi and the first Tokugawa shogun, Ieyasu. The displays are all in Japanese. Just south of the ruins is attractive **Senshūkaku-teien** (千秋閣庭園; admission ¥50, included in museum ticket), an intimate garden that was laid out in the late 16th century.

Tours

On weekends from mid-March to mid-October (and daily from 20 July to 31 August), boats cruise the river around the 'gourd-shaped' Hyōtan-jima (Hyōtan Island) that makes up central Tokushima – a pleasant way to get your bearings. The free 25-minute tours leave from Ryōgoku-bashi (両国橋; Ryōgoku Bridge) on the Shinmachi-gawa. Boats

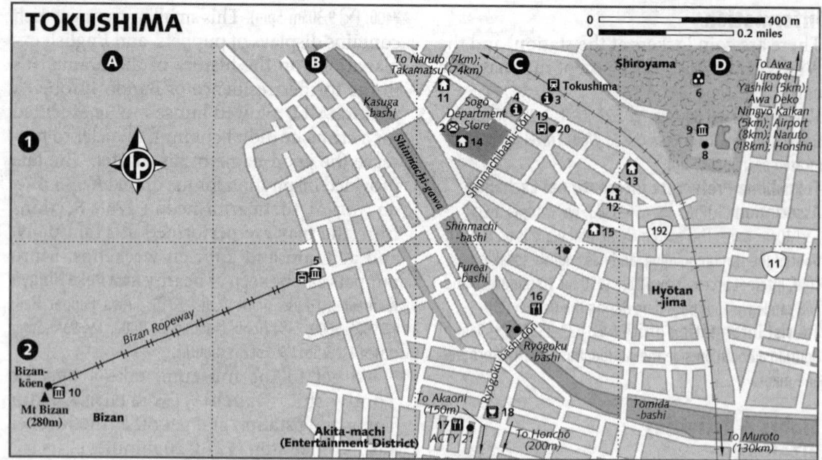

depart every 20 minutes from 1pm to 3.40pm on Saturday and Sunday from mid-March to mid-October, and daily from 20 July to 31 August. In July and August there are additional departures every 40 minutes from 5pm to 7.40pm.

Festivals & Events

Every August Tokushima is the location for one of the biggest parties in Japan, when the **Awa-odori Matsuri** (Awa-odori Festival; 阿波踊り) takes place to mark the O-bon holidays. The Awa-odori is the largest and most famous *bon* dance in Japan. Every night from 12 to 15 August, men, women and children don *yukata* (light cotton kimono) and straw hats and take to the streets to dance to the samba-like rhythm of the theme song 'Awa Yoshikono', accompanied by the sounds of *shamisen* (three-stringed guitars), *taiko* (drums) and *fue* (flutes). You'll need to plan ahead if you want to be a part of it: more than a million people descend on Tokushima for the festival every year, and accommodation is at a premium.

Sleeping

Sakura-sō (☎ 652-9575; fax 652-2220; 1-25 Terashima-honchō-higashi; per person without bathroom ¥3300; P) The best budget option in town is close to the railway tracks, a few blocks east of the station. This friendly *minshuku* (guest house) has good Japanese-style rooms. It's opposite a car park, a short walk from the station. Look for the sign on the right, in Japanese: さくら荘.

Dai-ichi Hotel (☎ 655-5005; fax 655-5003; www.tokushima-daiichihotel.co.jp, in Japanese; s/tw ¥5200/7300; P) A good business-hotel option a short walk left after the bus terminal that's in front of the station. LAN internet in all rooms, and consoles in the lobby.

Tōyoko Inn (☎ 657-1045; fax 657-1046; www.toyoko-inn.com; 1-5 Ryōgoku Honchō; s/tw with small breakfast ¥6300/8400; P) This newly opened hotel is a good option, with small but clean and comfortable rooms. There is LAN internet access in rooms, and there are computer consoles in the lobby.

Agnes Hotel Tokushima (☎ 626-2222; fax 626-3788; www.agneshotel.jp, in Japanese; 1-28 Terashima-honchō-nishi; s/d from ¥6300/12,600; P) This chic hotel a few blocks from the station has large rooms with modern, minimalist designs, and an elegant pastry cafe that's perfect for a lazy breakfast. There's internet access in the lobby, and LAN access in all rooms.

Tokushima Tōkyū Inn (☎ 626-0109; fax 626-0686; www.tokyuhotelsjapan.com; 1-24 Motomachi; s/d from ¥7600/13,000; P) This reliable business hotel, part of the popular Tōkyū Inn chain, is next to the Sogō department store. Western-style rooms are small but functional. There is LAN internet access in all rooms, and there are coin-operated terminals in the lobby.

Hotel Clement Tokushima (☎ 656-3111; www.hotelclement.co.jp; 1-61 Terashima-honchō-nishi; s/d ¥10,164/19,635; P) Directly on top of the station building, luxurious Hotel Clement boasts 18 floors and 250 comfortable, spacious Western-style rooms. Although it's

INFORMATION
- JTB ... 1 C2
- Post Office 郵便局 ... 2 C1
- Tokushima Prefecture International Exchange Association 徳島県国際交流センター ... 3 C1
- Tourist Information Office 駅前観光案内所 ... 4 C1

SIGHTS & ACTIVITIES
- Awa Odori Kaikan 阿波踊り会館 ... 5 B2
- Chūō-kōen 中央公園 ... 6 D1
- Hyōtan-jima Boats ひょうたん島一周遊覧船 ... 7 C2
- Senshūkaku-teien 千秋閣庭園 ... 8 D1
- Tokushima Castle Museum 徳島城博物館 ... 9 D1
- Wenceslao de Moraes Museum モラエス記念館 ... 10 A2

SLEEPING
- Agnes Hotel Tokushima アグネスホテル徳島 ... 11 C1
- Dai-ichi Hotel 徳島駅前第一ホテル ... 12 C1
- Hotel Clement Tokushima ホテルクレメント徳島 ... (see 3)
- Sakura-sō さくら荘 ... 13 D1
- Tokushima Tōkyū Inn 徳島東急イン ... 14 C1
- Tōyoko Inn 東横イン ... 15 C1

EATING
- Masala マサラ ... (see 3)
- Tori-kō 鳥甲 ... 16 C2
- Uoroman ... 17 C2

DRINKING
- Hung Loose ハングルース ... (see 18)
- Ray Charles レイチャールズ ... 18 C2

TRANSPORT
- Bus Terminal バスターミナル ... 19 C1
- Rental Bicycles 貸し自転車 ... 20 C1
- Rental Bicycles 貸し自転車 ... (see 5)

more expensive than other business hotels, the extra yen gets you a whole smattering of amenities including a spa and a range of restaurants and bars.

Eating & Drinking

Tokushima's main entertainment district is in Akita-machi across the river, along the streets around the landmark ACTY 21 Building.

Masala (☎ 654-7122; Terashima-honchō-nishi; 11am-9.30pm) On the 5th floor of the Clement Plaza, this curry restaurant has Indian staff and cheap lunches (from ¥750). There is an English menu.

Tori-kō (☎ 657-0125; 2-19 Ryōgoku Honchō; 4-10.30pm, closed Mon) This atmospheric spot is thick with the smell of delicious local chicken grilling on coals. Orders like *tsukune* (chicken meat balls) and *tebasaki* (chicken wings) are ¥300 for two sticks; the *Awa-odori Sanmai* course (a selection of different cuts of the local gourmet chicken) is ¥3000. Look for the wooden menu boards covering the walls outside.

Honchō (ほんちょう; ☎ 622-1239; 1-25-1 Chūō-dōri; 4-11pm, closed Sun) A traditional *izakaya* (pub-eatery) specialising in local sake and fresh seafood, with half a dozen seats at the counter and a tiny tatami area to the side. *Otsukuri moriawase* (a selection of seasonal sashimi; ¥2000) goes well with a glass of Hōsui or one of the other *jizake* (local sake) options from the fridge behind the bar. From the Ryōgoku bridge, take the third left after the ACTY 21 Building, then left again. Look for the sign on the left that advertises the restaurant's name in Japanese.

Uoroman (☎ 657-7477; 12-1 Konya-machi; 5pm-1am) A cheerful place not far from ACTY 21, and popular with crowds of young people. It specialises in reasonably priced fish. There is no English menu, but most of the waitstaff are young and speak some English. *Honjitsu no sashimi san-shu mori* (a daily selection of sashimi) is ¥980. Look for the wooden exterior with big photos of fish and a cartoon of a mischievous-looking fisherman.

Akaoni (赤鬼; ☎ 652-5099; 2-34 Akita-machi; 5pm-3am) The name of this friendly *izakaya* means 'Red Devil', and you'll know you've come to the right place when you see the plastic statue of a particularly vicious-looking devil standing outside. The usual *izakaya* dishes start at around ¥600; some English is spoken here.

Ray Charles (☎ 652-0878; 3F Tōjō Bldg, 20-1 Ryōgokubashi; 7pm-3am, to 4am Fri & Sat) A dimly lit bar where people drift in to shoot the breeze with the bow-tied bartenders and listen to American oldies. Draft Carlsberg is ¥700. It's in a building diagonally across from ACTY 21.

Hung Loose (☎ 623-3255; 3F Tōjō Bldg, 20-1 Ryōgokubashi; cocktails ¥650; 9am-6am) On the 2nd floor of the building that houses Ray Charles (see above), this surfers' bar comes complete with surfboards and tables that have escaped from a tropical beach somewhere.

Getting There & Away

Tokushima's **airport** (☎ 699-2831; www.tokushima-airport.co.jp) is reached by bus (¥430, 25 minutes, buses timed to coincide with flights) from in front of the station. There are flights to Tokyo (¥29,600, one hour and 15 minutes, six daily), Nagoya (¥19,900, one hour, two daily) and Fukuoka (¥24,700, one hour and 10 minutes, two daily).

Tokushima is just over an hour by train from Takamatsu (¥2560 by *tokkyū* – limited express). For the Iya Valley and Kōchi, change trains at Awa Ikeda (阿波池田, ¥1580, 1½ hours).

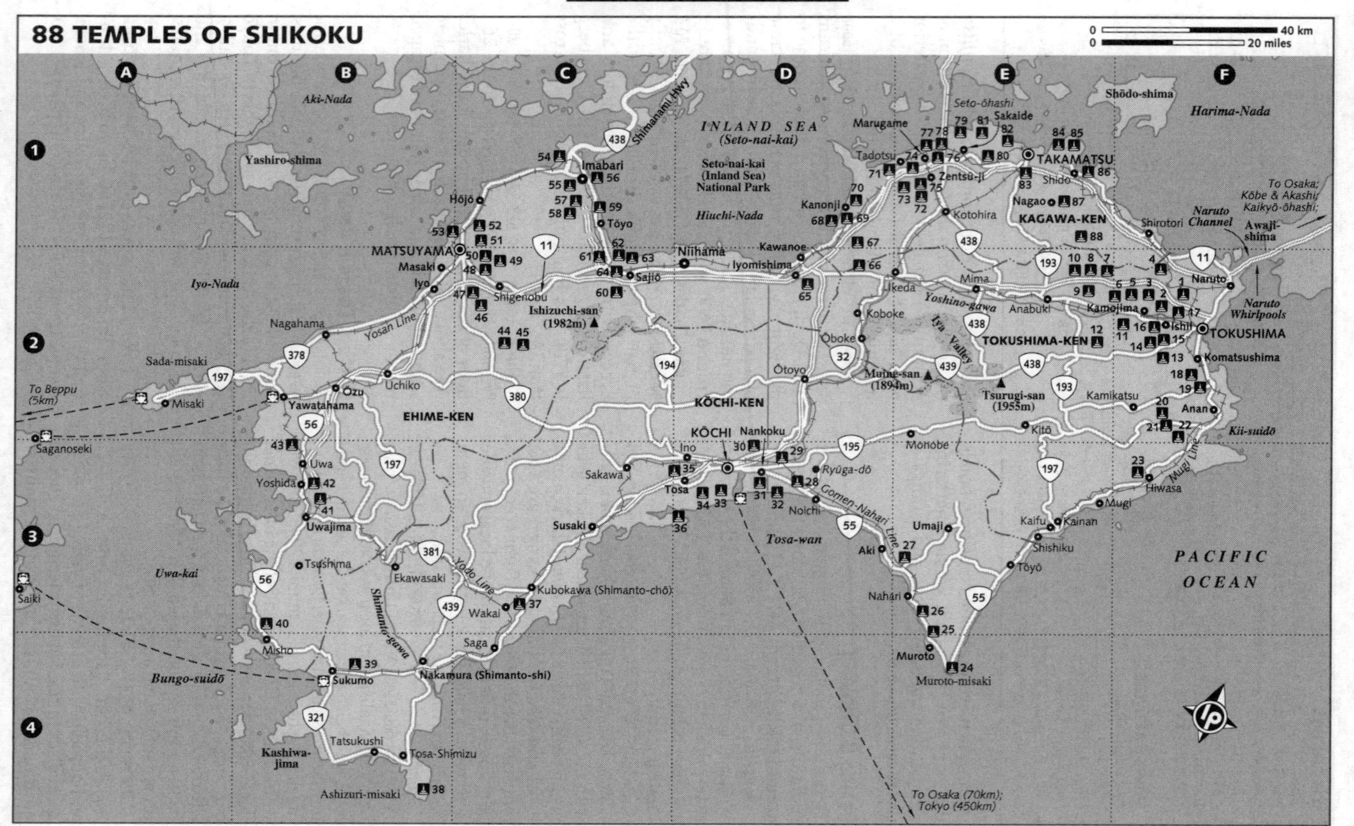
88 TEMPLES OF SHIKOKU
0 40 km
0 20 miles
Aki-Nada
Yashiro-shima
Iyo-Nada
Shimanami Hwy
INLAND SEA (Seto-nai-kai)
Seto-nai-kai (Inland Sea) National Park
Hiuchi-Nada
Seto-ōhashi
Sakaide
Marugame
Tadotsu
Zentsū-ji
Kotohira
Kanonji
Kawanoe
Iyomishima
Niihama
Imabari
Tōyo
Hōjō
MATSUYAMA
Masaki
Iyo
Shigenobu
Ishizuchi-san (1982m)
Saijō
Nagahama
Yosan Line
Sada-misaki
Misaki
To Beppu (5km)
Saganoseki
Yawatahama
Ōzu
Uchiko
EHIME-KEN
Uwa
Yoshida
Uwajima
Tsushima
Uwa-kai
Saiki
Ekawasaki
Shimanto-gawa
Yodo Line
Wakai
Kubokawa (Shimanto-chō)
Saga
Mishō
Sukumo
Bungo-suidō
Nakamura (Shimanto-shi)
Tatsukushi
Tosa-Shimizu
Kashiwa-jima
Ashizuri-misaki
Susaki
Sakawa
Ino
Tosa
KŌCHI
KŌCHI-KEN
Nankoku
Ryūga-dō
Noichi
Gomen-Nahari Line
Tosa-wan
Aki
Nahari
Muroto
Muroto-misaki
To Osaka (70km); Tokyo (450km)
Umaji
Monobe
Ōtoyo
Ōboke
Koboke
Ikeda
Miune-san (1894m)
Iya Valley
Yoshino-gawa
Mima
Anabuki
Tsurugi-san (1955m)
TOKUSHIMA-KEN
Kamikatsu
Kitō
Kamojima
Ishii
TAKAMATSU
Shido
Nagao
KAGAWA-KEN
Shōdo-shima
Harima-Nada
Shirotori
Naruto Channel
Awaji-shima
To Osaka; Kōbe & Akashi Kaikyō-ōhashi
Naruto
Naruto Whirlpools
TOKUSHIMA
Komatsushima
Anan
Kii-suidō
Mugi Line
Hiwasa
Mugi
Kaifu
Kainan
Shishiku
Tōyō
PACIFIC OCEAN

JR highway buses connect Tokushima with Tokyo (¥10,000, nine hours) and Nagoya (¥6600, 4½ hours); there are also buses to Takamatsu (¥1600, 1½ hours), Hiroshima (¥6000, 3¾ hours, two daily) and Kansai airport (¥4000, 2¾ hours).

There are daily connections between Tokushima and Wakayama (¥2400, two hours, eight daily) with **Nankai Ferry** (南海フェリー; ☎ 636-0750; www.nankai-ferry.co.jp). There is one sailing daily to/from Tokyo with **Ocean Tōkyū Ferry** (オーシャン東九フェリー; ☎ 662-0489; www.otf.jp), with 1st class/2nd class/private cabin costing ¥19,290/9900/22,350 (18 hours). Ferries depart and arrive at Okinosu (沖洲) port, 3km east of the town centre, and are linked to the station by bus (¥200, 30 minutes).

Getting Around

It's easy enough to get around Tokushima on foot – it's less than 1km from the station to the Bizan cable-car station. **Rental bicycles** (地下自転車駐輪所; per half/full day ¥300/500, deposit ¥3000; 9am-5pm) are available from the underground bike-park to the left as you leave the station, and bikes are available at **Awa Odori Kaikan** (per half/full day ¥500/1000; 9.30am-5pm); see p454 for details.

AROUND TOKUSHIMA

Naruto Whirlpools 鳴門のうず潮

At the change of tides, sea water whisks through the narrow channel between Shikoku and Awaji-shima at such speed that ferocious **whirlpools** are created. The Naruto-no-Uzushio are one of the region's most famous attractions. The tourist information centre in Tokushima can provide you with a timetable detailing the fluctuating tides: the whirlpools are active twice a day, and are at their most impressive when there's a full moon.

For an up-close and personal view of the whirlpools, you can venture out into the Naruto Channel on one of the **tourist boats** that depart from the waterfront in Naruto. **Naruto**

SIGHTS & ACTIVITIES

- Temple 1 (Ryōzen-ji) 霊山寺 1 F2
- Temple 2 (Gokuraku-ji) 極楽寺 2 F2
- Temple 3 (Konsen-ji) 金泉寺 3 F2
- Temple 4 (Dainichi-ji) 大日寺 4 F2
- Temple 5 (Jizō-ji) 地蔵寺 5 F2
- Temple 6 (Anraku-ji) 安楽寺 6 F2
- Temple 7 (Juraku-ji) 十楽寺 7 E2
- Temple 8 (Kumadani-ji) 熊谷寺 8 E2
- Temple 9 (Hōrin-ji) 法輪寺 9 E2
- Temple 10 (Kirihata-ji) 切幡寺 10 E2
- Temple 11 (Fujii-dera) 藤井寺 11 F2
- Temple 12 (Shōzan-ji) 焼山寺 12 E2
- Temple 13 (Dainichi-ji) 大日寺 13 F2
- Temple 14 (Jōraku-ji) 常楽寺 14 F2
- Temple 15 (Kokubun-ji) 国分寺 15 F2
- Temple 16 (Kannon-ji) 観音寺 16 F2
- Temple 17 (Ido-ji) 井戸寺 17 F2
- Temple 18 (Onzan-ji) 恩山寺 18 F2
- Temple 19 (Tatsue-ji) 立江寺 19 F2
- Temple 20 (Kakurin-ji) 鶴林寺 20 F2
- Temple 21 (Tairyō-ji) 太龍寺 21 F2
- Temple 22 (Byōdō-ji) 平等寺 22 F2
- Temple 23 (Yakuō-ji) 薬王寺 23 F3
- Temple 24 (Hotsumisaki-ji) 最御崎寺 24 E4
- Temple 25 (Shinshō-ji) 津照寺 25 E3
- Temple 26 (Kongōchō-ji) 金剛頂寺 26 E3
- Temple 27 (Kōnomine-ji) 神峯寺 27 E3
- Temple 28 (Dainichi-ji) 大日寺 28 D3
- Temple 29 (Kokubun-ji) 国分寺 29 D3
- Temple 30 (Zenraku-ji) 善楽寺 30 D3
- Temple 31 (Chikurin-ji) 竹林寺 31 D3
- Temple 32 (Zenjibu-ji) 禅師峰寺 32 D3
- Temple 33 (Sekkei-ji) 雪蹊寺 33 D3
- Temple 34 (Tanema-ji) 種間寺 34 D3
- Temple 35 (Kiyotaki-ji) 清滝寺 35 D3
- Temple 36 (Shōryū-ji) 青龍寺 36 D3
- Temple 37 (Iwamoto-ji) 岩本寺 37 C3
- Temple 38 (Kongōfuku-ji) 金剛福寺 38 B4
- Temple 39 (Enkō-ji) 延光寺 39 B4
- Temple 40 (Kanjizai-ji) 観自在寺 40 B3
- Temple 41 (Ryūkō-ji) 龍光寺 41 B3
- Temple 42 (Butsumoku-ji) 仏木寺 42 B3
- Temple 43 (Meiseki-ji) 明石寺 43 B3
- Temple 44 (Taihō-ji) 大宝寺 44 C2
- Temple 45 (Iwaya-ji) 岩屋寺 45 C2
- Temple 46 (Jōruri-ji) 浄瑠璃寺 46 C2
- Temple 47 (Yasaka-ji) 八坂寺 47 C2
- Temple 48 (Sairin-ji) 西林寺 48 C2
- Temple 49 (Jōdo-ji) 浄土寺 49 C2
- Temple 50 (Hanta-ji) 繁多寺 50 C2
- Temple 51 (Ishite-ji) 石手寺 51 C1
- Temple 52 (Taisan-ji) 太山寺 52 C1
- Temple 53 (Enmyō-ji) 円明寺 53 B1
- Temple 54 (Enmei-ji) 延命寺 54 C1
- Temple 55 (Nankō-bō) 南光坊 55 C1
- Temple 56 (Taisan-ji) 泰山寺 56 C1
- Temple 57 (Eifuku-ji) 栄福寺 57 C1
- Temple 58 (Senyū-ji) 仙遊寺 58 C1
- Temple 59 (Kokubun-ji) 国分寺 59 C1
- Temple 60 (Yokomine-ji) 横峰寺 60 C2
- Temple 61 (Kōon-ji) 香園寺 61 C2
- Temple 62 (Hōju-ji) 宝寿寺 62 C2
- Temple 63 (Kisshō-ji) 吉祥寺 63 C2
- Temple 64 (Maegami-ji) 前神寺 64 C2
- Temple 65 (Sankaku-ji) 三角寺 65 D2
- Temple 66 (Unpen-ji) 雲辺寺 66 D2
- Temple 67 (Daikō-ji) 大興寺（小松尾寺） 67 D1
- Temple 68 (Jinne-in) 神恵寺 68 D1
- Temple 69 (Kanon-ji) 観音寺 69 D1
- Temple 70 (Motoyama-ji) 本山寺 70 D1
- Temple 71 (Iyadani-ji) 弥谷寺 71 D1
- Temple 72 (Mandara-ji) 曼陀羅寺 72 E1
- Temple 73 (Shusshaka-ji) 出釈迦寺 73 E1
- Temple 74 (Kōyama-ji) 甲山寺 74 E1
- Temple 75 (Zentsū-ji) 善通寺 75 E1
- Temple 76 (Konzō-ji) 金倉寺 76 E1
- Temple 77 (Dōryū-ji) 道隆寺 77 E1
- Temple 78 (Gōshō-ji) 郷照寺 78 E1
- Temple 79 (Kōshō-in) 高照院（天皇寺） 79 E1
- Temple 80 (Kokubun-ji) 国分寺 80 E1
- Temple 81 (Shiramine-ji) 白峰寺 81 E1
- Temple 82 (Negoro-ji) 根香寺 82 E1
- Temple 83 (Ichinomiya-ji) 一宮寺 83 E1
- Temple 84 (Yashima-ji) 屋島寺 84 E1
- Temple 85 (Yakuri-ji) 八栗寺 85 E1
- Temple 86 (Shido-ji) 志度寺 86 E1
- Temple 87 (Nagao-ji) 長尾寺 87 E1
- Temple 88 (Ōkubo-ji) 大窪寺 88 E1

Kankō Kisen (鳴門観光汽船; ☎ 088-687-0101; per person ¥1530-2200) is one of several companies making regular trips out (every 20 minutes from 9am to 4.20pm) from the port, close to the Naruto Kankō-kō bus stop. For a bird's-eye view, you can walk out along **Uzu-no-michi** (渦の道; ☎ 088-683-6262; admission ¥500; 9am-6pm, to 5pm Oct-Feb), a 500m-long walkway underneath the Naruto-ōhashi, which puts you directly above the action.

The best way to get to the whirlpools is to take a bus bound for Naruto-kōen (鳴門公園) from bus stop 1 in front of Tokushima station (¥600, one hour, hourly from 9am) and get off at Naruto Kankō-kō (鳴門観光港). Alternatively, take a local train from Tokushima to Naruto station (¥350, 40 to 50 minutes, sometimes with a change at Ikenotani), and transfer to a bus there.

The First Five Temples: Ryōzen-ji to Jizō-ji

In addition to its whirlpools, Naruto is famous as the starting point for Shikoku's 88-temple pilgrimage. The first five temples are all within easy walking distance of each other, making it possible to get a taste of the *henro* (pilgrims on the 88-temple circuit) trail on a day-trip from Tokushima.

To get to Temple 1, **Ryōzen-ji** (霊山寺), take a local train from Tokushima to Bandō (板東; ¥260, 25 minutes). The temple is a 10- to 15-minute walk (about 700m) along the main road; the map at Bandō station should point you in the right direction. Ryōzen-ji is an attractive temple built on the orders of Emperor Shōmu in the 8th century, with a main hall lit by hundreds of lanterns. Kōbō Daishi is said to have spent several weeks in meditation here. This is where pilgrims stock up for the trip: you will see several stores with mannequins outside that are kitted out in white robes and straw hats – this clothing marks out a person as a pilgrim on the trail.

From Ryōzen-ji it's a short walk along the main road from the first temple to the second, **Gokuraku-ji** (極楽寺), and another 2km from here to Temple 3, **Konsen-ji** (金泉寺). There are more-or-less regular signposts (in Japanese) pointing the way. Look for the signs by the roadside marked *henro-michi* (へんろ道 or 遍路道), often decorated with a red picture of a *henro* in silhouette. From here, it's about 5km along an increasingly rural path to **Dainichi-ji** (大日寺), and another 2km to **Jizō-ji** (地蔵寺), where there's an impressive **collection of statues** (admission ¥200) of the 500 Rakan disciples of the Buddha. From the Rakan (羅漢) bus stop on the main road in front of the temple you can catch a bus to Itano (板野) station, where a train will take you back to Tokushima (¥350, 30 minutes).

IYA VALLEY 祖谷渓

The remote Iya Valley is a world away from the hustle and bustle of urban Japan. With its rugged mountain scenery and dramatic gorges, the Iya Valley has long been a refuge for people looking to disappear from the world.

The earliest records of the valley describe a group of shamans fleeing from persecution in Nara in the 9th century. At the end of the 12th century, Iya famously became the last refuge for members of the vanquished Heike clan following their defeat at the hands of the Minamoto in the Gempei Wars. Their descendants are believed to live in the valley to this day.

The Iya region is a nature-lover's paradise, with some superb hiking around Mt Tsurugi and white-water rafting in the stunning Ōboke and Koboke Gorges. Worn-out travellers can reward themselves at the end of the day by soaking in top-notch onsen (hot springs) and sampling the local Iya *soba* (buckwheat noodles).

Access to the area is via Ōboke station, reached by train from Takamatsu, Kōchi or Tokushima with a change at Awa Ikeda. Getting around the valley itself involves some planning, because Iya's sights are widespread, and public transport is sporadic at the best of times. Infrequent buses travel between Awa Ikeda, Ōboke and Iya, but the best way to explore the region is with your own wheels – rental cars are available in Shikoku's larger cities.

Ōboke & Koboke 大歩危・小歩危

Ōboke and Koboke are two scenic gorges on the Yoshino-gawa. South of Ikeda on Old Rte 32 between Koboke and Ōboke, white-water rafting and kayaking trips run from April to late November. Aussie-run **Happy Raft** (☎ 0887-75-0500; www.happyraft.com), close to JR Tosa Iwahara station across the border in Kōchi-ken, operates daily trips with English-speaking guides (half-day ¥5500 to ¥7500, full day ¥10,000 to ¥15,500).

A great place to warm up after a chilling plunge is **Iya Onsen** (☎ 0883-75-2311; Matsuo Matsumoto 367-2; admission ¥1500; 7.30am-5pm), on Old Rte 32, where a cable car descends a steep cliff-face to some sulphurous open-air baths overlooking the river. **Accommodation** (www.iyaonsen.co.jp, in Japanese; per person incl meals ¥16,950) is available. Infrequent buses run from Awa Ikeda station, bound for the Kazura-bashi.

Lapis Ōboke (☎ 0883-84-1489; admission ¥500; 9am-5pm), just north of JR Ōboke station, is a geology museum that doubles as a tourist information centre.

Excellent budget accommodation is available 3km from JR Ōboke station at riverside **Ku-Nel-Asob** (☎ 090-9778-7133; www.k-n-a.com; dm ¥2600; P). Accommodation is in simple but attractive communal tatami rooms, and the friendly English-speaking owners can provide free pick-ups/drop-offs at JR Ōboke station. A kitchen is available, and food can be bought at Bokemart, 30m from the train station. Since the house doesn't have a bath, a ride to nearby Iya Onsen is offered for ¥500, including entry to the onsen.

Another option is **Awa Ikeda Youth Hostel** (☎ 0883-72-5277; dm nonmembers ¥3850; P), part of the Mitsugon-ji mountain-temple that's complex about 5km from the station in Awa Ikeda. It's quite isolated, and the tatami rooms are a bit on the spartan side, but the real appeal here is the ambience provided by the attached mountain-temple. Book ahead if you need a pick-up at JR Awa Ikeda station (6pm only). Meals are available.

There is spectacular scenery in the deep canyons along Old Rte 32 – infrequent public buses (¥880, 55 minutes, 7.15, 10.15am and 12.15pm) ply this narrow route between Awa Ikeda and the Iya Valley. However, if you have your own wheels, you can go at your own pace and really appreciate the beauty of the region.

Nishi Iya 西祖谷

The highlight in Nishi Iya is **Kazura-bashi** (admission ¥500; sunrise-sunset), a vine bridge that's one of only three left in the valley (the other two are further east in Higashi Iya). Nearby, **Biwa-no-taki** is an impressive, 50m-high waterfall.

Kazura-bashi Camping Village (☎ 090-1571-5258; camp sites ¥500 plus per person ¥200, 4–5-person bungalows from ¥5200; Apr-Nov; P) is a camping ground 500m upriver from the vine bridge. The atmosphere is rustic, and the basic facilities are well cared for.

For more-upscale accommodation, try **Hotel Kazura-bashi** (☎ 0883-87-2171; www.kazurabashi.co.jp; per person with meals from ¥15,900; P), about a kilometre north of the bridge. The comfortable tatami rooms have terrific mountain views and there's a hilltop onsen.

For a taste of local Iya *soba*, try **Iya Bijin Keikoku-ten** (☎ 0883-87-2009; 9-3 Zentoku; meals ¥600-1000; 8am-5pm), in an attractive black-and-white building with lanterns hanging out the front. A plate of *zaru soba* (cold noodles with seaweed strips) is ¥700.

Higashi Iya 東祖谷

To escape the throngs at the vine bridge in Nishi Iya, head 30km east to the spectacular **Oku Iya Ni-jū Kazura-bashi** (admission ¥500, sunrise-sunset) in Higashi Iya, where two secluded vine bridges hang side by side high over the river. A self-propelled wooden cable-cart is another fun way to cross the river; there's a small public camping area on the other side.

The **Higashi Iya Folk Museum** (☎ 0883-88-2286; admission ¥300; 9.30am-5pm) is in a large red building in Kyōjō, displaying historic artefacts and items relating to the Heike legend.

Several kilometres up a narrow, winding road near Kyōjō, **Buke Yashiki** (☎ 0883-88-2893; admission ¥300; 9am-5pm, closed Tue & Dec-Mar) is a thatched-roof samurai-house museum commanding spectacular views of the valley. Beside the house is a Shintō shrine that is home to a massive cedar tree dating back more than 800 years.

Iyashi no Onsen-kyō (☎ 0883-88-2975; fax 0883-76-7080; www.sobanoyado.jp, in Japanese; per person with meals from ¥13,800, bungalows per person from ¥4350; P), off the main road between Kyōjō and the Higashi Iya vine bridges, is a hotel and hot-springs complex with six Japanese-style and six Western-style rooms, a bungalow and a restaurant. Nonguests can use the onsen (open 8.30am to 3.30pm October and November, to 4pm April to September, closed Wednesday) for ¥1500. During the summer months a monorail runs up the mountainside from the hotel grounds.

At **Soba Dōjō** (☎ 0883-88-2577; 11am-5pm Fri-Wed), also on Rte 438, you can sample a bowl of *zaru soba* (¥800) and even make your own (¥2500; reservation required). The restaurant has a reddish roof, and a yellow curtain hanging over the door.

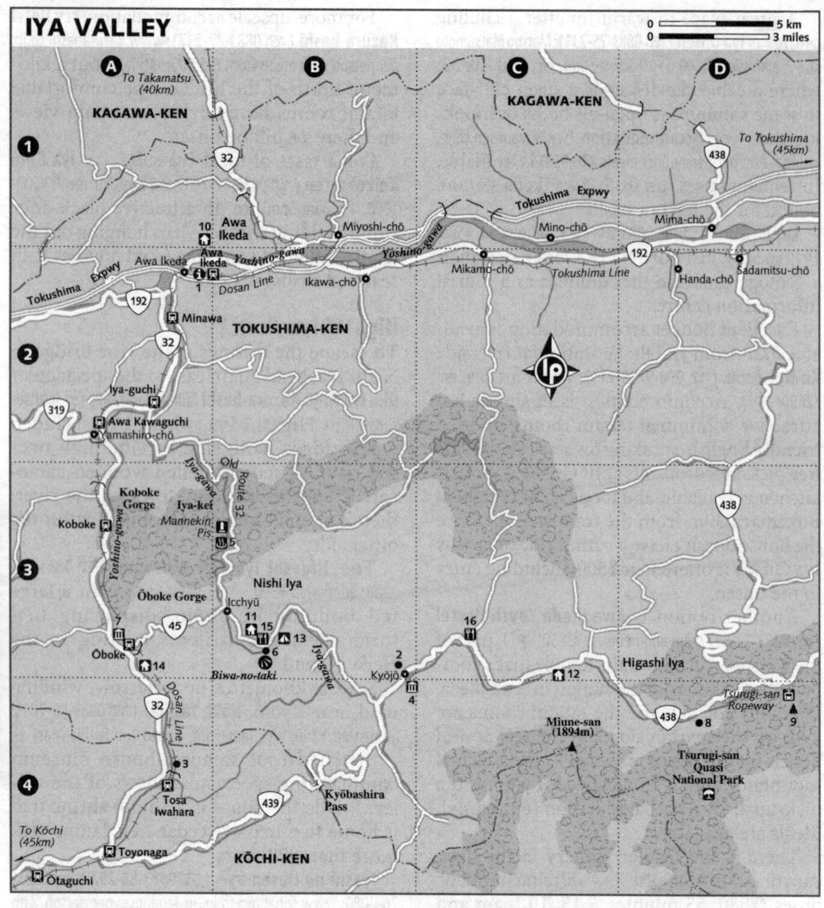

Tsurugi-san 剣山

At 1955m, Tsurugi-san is the second-highest mountain in Shikoku and provides excellent hiking opportunities, as well as snowboarding in winter December to February. A chairlift goes most of the way up, after which it is a leisurely 30-minute walk to the summit. If you decide to climb all the way, you'll pass the Tsurugi-jinja (Tsurugi Shrine) en route, which is close to a natural spring of drinkable water.

Information on the popular multiday hike between Tsurugi-san and Miune-san (1894m), as well as mountain-top accommodation and other detailed regional hiking information, can be found in Lonely Planet's *Hiking in Japan*.

SOUTHERN TOKUSHIMA-KEN 徳島県南部

Tokushima's spectacular southern coastline is highlighted by rocky scenery, white-sand beaches and picturesque fishing villages. In addition to the last temple in Tokushima, the region is also home to several of the island's best surf spots.

The JR Mugi line runs down the coast as far as Kaifu, just short of the border. From Kaifu, the private Asa Kaigan railway runs two stops further to Kannoura, just across the border. From here, you can continue by bus or thumb to the cape at Muroto-misaki and on to Kōchi city. Coming the other way, trains run from Kōchi as far as Nahari – but you'll have to rely on buses to get you around the cape.

INFORMATION
Tourist Information Office
阿波池田駅観光案内所 1 A2

SIGHTS & ACTIVITIES
Buke Yashiki
武家屋敷「喜多家」 2 B3
Happy Raft ハッピーラフト 3 A4
Higashi Iya Folk Museum
東祖谷民族資料館 4 B4
Iya Onsen 祖谷温泉 5 B3
Kazura-bashi かずら橋 6 B3
Lapis Ōboke ラピス大歩危 7 A3
Oku Iya Ni-jū Kazura-bashi
奥祖谷二重かずら橋 8 D4
Tsurugi-san 剣山 9 D4

SLEEPING
Awa Ikeda Youth Hostel
阿波池田ユースホステル 10 A1
Hotel Kazura-bashi
ホテルかずら橋 11 B3
Iyashi no Onsen-kyō
いやしの温泉郷 12 C3
Kazura-bashi Camping Village
かずら橋キャンプ村 13 B3
Ku-Nel-Asob 空音遊 14 A3

EATING
Iya Bijin Keikoku-ten
祖谷美人渓谷店 15 B3
Soba Dōjō そば道場 16 C3

Hiwasa 日和佐

☎ 0884

The major attraction in the small coastal town of Hiwasa is **Yakuō-ji** (薬王寺), Temple 23 and the last temple in Tokushima-ken. Yakuō-ji dates back to the year 726, and is famous as a yakuyoke no tera (a temple with special powers to ward off ill fortune during unlucky years). The unluckiest age for men is 42; for women, 33 is the one to watch out for. Kōbō Daishi is said to have visited in 815, the year of his own 42nd birthday. The long set of stone steps leading up to the main temple building comes in two stages: 33 steps for the women, followed by another 42 for the men. The tradition is for pilgrims to put a coin on each step – if you come when it's busy, you may find the steps practically overflowing with one-yen coins.

About a mile from the centre of town is Ōhama (大浜) beach, a long stretch of sand where sea turtles come to lay their eggs from May to August each year. Next to the beach you'll find **Hiwasa Chelonian Museum Caretta** (日和佐うみがめ博物館カレッタ; ☎ 77-1110; admission ¥600; 9am-5pm, closed Mon), which has some underwhelming exhibits, and turtles both young and old on display. The town's reconstructed castle is currently closed to visitors.

The best accommodation option is at Yakuō-ji's **shukubō** (☎ 77-1105; fax 77-1486; per person with meals ¥7300; P). The tatami rooms here are spacious and well kept, and filling meals are served. It's in a modern building across the road from the temple.

South to Muroto-misaki

A short train ride south from Hiwasa is the sleepy fishing town of **Mugi** (牟岐), where the winding streets of the old fishing port make an interesting stopover if you've a few hours to spare on your way south. A 45-minute (3km) walk along the coast past the fishing port is **Mollusc Mugi Shell Museum** (貝の資料館モラスコむぎ; ☎ 0884-72-2520; admission ¥400; 9am-4.30pm, closed Mon), where there's an impressive collection of shells and tropical fish in an idyllic setting on a quiet beach. There is an old Hachiman shrine in the centre of the town, and boats run out to the off-shore island of Teba-jima (出羽島).

The JR line ends at Kaifu (海部); the private Asa Kaigan line runs further south to Shishikui (宍喰) and Kannoura (甲浦).

This stretch of coast is 'surf central' as far as Shikoku is concerned, with several good beaches and some great scenery. Surfing equipment is available for hire at numerous places in the laid-back, one-street beach-bum town of Ikumi (生見), where you'll find most of the best places to stay. For money, there is a post office with an international ATM in Kaifu, and another in Kannoura.

Glass-bottomed boats tour the waters around Takegashima island near Shishikui, run by **Blue Marine** (ブルーマリン; ☎ 0884-76-3100; cruises ¥1800; 9am-4pm, closed Tue). **Sea kayaking** (マリンジャム; ☎ 0884-76-1401; per person ¥2500; 10am & 2pm) is available at the same place, inside the Marine Jam Building.

There are plenty of places to stay along the coast. At Kannoura, **Shirahama White Beach Hotel** (白浜ホワイトビーチホテル; ☎ 0887-29-3344; www.wbhotel.net, in Japanese; per person from ¥6000) is a slightly faded modern resort hotel that's directly on the beach. In the summer, camping is available on the beach next to the hotel. For food and a beer, try nearby **Aunt Dinah** (☎ 0887-29-2080; meals ¥750-1500; 9.30am-9.30pm, closed Tue), where there's old-time country music and a range of curries available (such as seafood curry for ¥890).

In Shishikui, Western- and Japanese-style rooms are available at upmarket **Hotel Riviera** (ホテルリビエラししくい; ☎ 0884-76-3300; fax 0884-76-3910; www.hotel-riviera.co.jp, in Japanese; per person with meals from ¥12,000), where nonguests can use the sea-view onsen baths (¥600; from 11am to 10pm).

THE HENRO TRAIL *Paul Warham*

The walking pilgrim is one of the most distinctive sights of any trip to Shikoku. They're everywhere you go, striding along busy city highways, cresting hills in remote mountain valleys, and tapping their colourful walking sticks – lonely figures in white, trudging purposefully through heat haze and monsoonal downpour alike on their way from temple to temple. Who are these people, and what drives them to leave the comforts of home for months at a time in order to make a journey of more than 1400km on foot?

Before I set off on a dilettante trip of my own – a mere dipping of toes into the holy waters – I have a vague idea of them as modern-day renunciates, otherworldly figures on a solitary quest for enlightenment. It's not long before I'm relieved of this idea. Among the first *henro* (pilgrims on the 88 Temple circuit) I meet is a young student couple from Tokyo. We arrive at our temple lodgings at the same time, and the woman who checks us in allocates the youngsters separate rooms at opposite ends of the compound. The next morning I'm standing under the eaves of the temple waiting for the rain to stop when I see the two young lovers emerge from the same room and set out under a shared umbrella for the next temple.

I meet only one person who comes anywhere close to meeting my initial expectations: a man from Kawasaki with a bald head that glistens like wet soap in the sun as we walk. He responds to all my questions with a beatific smile and an 'ah' that sounds like a sigh, and then answers all kinds of questions I haven't asked. As we cross a bridge he launches into a lecture on the history of the pilgrimage and of Kōbō Daishi, who, to this day, sleeps in a meditative state of suspended animation on the slopes of Kōya-san (Mt Kōya). Do I know that the sticks the travellers carry are believed to be the embodiment of the Daishi? That it is considered sacrilege to use a knife to smooth a road-battered staff? That pilgrims must never tap their sticks on the ground while crossing a bridge, lest they disturb the spirit of the Daishi, who often used to sleep under bridges on his own journeys?

For many, the trip represents the culmination of years of planning. One night in Kagawa-ken I meet a retired man (originally from Kotohira) who has come home, at last, to finish the pilgrimage. Now in his late 70s, he's been undertaking the trail in small bites over several years. Now that he's nearly finished, he's ready to bring down the curtain on his life, he says matter of factly.

For others, the chief attraction may be the physical challenge. This could explain the behaviour of two Osaka students I room with one night. They have just bought new bikes, and have

SHIKOKU

At Ikumi, just across the border into Kōchi-ken, **Minami Kaze** (南風; ☎ 0887-29-3638; per person ¥3675) is right on the beach, and has basic Japanese-style rooms with shared toilets and showers. Meals are available. **Minshuku Michishio** (民宿みちしお; ☎ 0887-29-3471; fax 0887-29-3470; per person with meals from ¥5775) is another good option on the beach, with Japanese- and Western-style rooms and a restaurant serving tasty *okonomiyaki* (savoury pancakes; butter and cabbage cooked with seafood or meat on a griddle). Close by is **White Beach Hotel Ikumi** (ホワイトビーチホテル生見; ☎ 0887-29-3018; www.wbhotel.net/ikumi, in Japanese; per person ¥4000-5000), which has Japanese- and Western-style rooms and a beachfront restaurant called Oluolu (it has meals from ¥800, and is open for lunch and dinner – a picture menu is available).

Trains run as far south as Kannoura. There are also buses from Mugi to Kannoura (¥770, 45 minutes, 14 per day), stopping at Kaifu and Shishikui on the way. Seven buses a day run from Kannoura to Muroto-misaki, via Ikumi (¥1390, 40 minutes). Buses run as far as Aki (安芸; ¥2880, two hours), where you can transfer to a train to Kōchi. For the last 40km to the cape, the road hugs the coast, hemmed in by mountains on one side and the sea on the other.

KŌCHI-KEN 高知県

The largest of Shikoku's four prefectures, Kōchi-ken spans the entire Pacific coastline between the two capes of Muroto-misaki and Ashizuri-misaki. Cut off from the rest of Japan by the mountains and sea, the province of Tosa was traditionally regarded as one of the wildest and remotest places in the country.

Although the trip through Tosa makes up more than a third of the pilgrimage, only 16 of the 88 Temples are located in the prov-

decided to break them in by completing a circuit of all 88 Temples in a week. Maybe they're about to set some kind of record, I suggest. They smile at the thought, and vow to look into it online when they get back home.

At Hiwasa (p655) I come across a stricken-looking woman practically crawling down the corridor towards the beer vending machine (yes, Japanese temples have beer machines). The next morning I'm not much surprised when she turns out to be the only other person having 'late' breakfast with me at 7am. She's from Yamagata, and is trying to complete her circuit during the low season at the ski resort she runs. Don't they have temples up in Yamagata? Ah, but Shikoku is a special place. She tells me how she went to a local surgery the day before, seeking treatment for injuries she'd sustained by walking too far, too quickly. 'And they wouldn't accept any payment. *O-settai*. Because they could see I was a *henro*. I knew it was a good sign when I saw they had the Daishi's picture on the wall in the waiting room. That's when I knew for sure that he was really watching over me.'

Although pilgrims' backgrounds (and perhaps motives) may differ widely, the pattern and routine of life on the road is very similar for everyone who undertakes the trail. The dress is uniform, too: *hakue* (white garments) to signify sincerity of purpose and purity of mind; the *sugegasa* (straw hat) that has protected pilgrims against sun and rain since time immemorial; and the *kongōzue* (colourful staff). Pilgrims believe that the *kongōzue* is an embodiment of the Daishi himself, who accompanies all pilgrims on their journey – hence the inscription on so many pilgrims' backpacks and other paraphernalia: 同行二人 *(dōgyō ninin),* meaning 'two people on the same journey'. The routine at each temple is mostly the same, too: a bang on the bell and a chant of the Heart Sutra at the Daishi-dō (one of the two main buildings in each temple compound), before filing off to the *nōkyōsho* (desk), where the pilgrims' book is inscribed with beautiful characters detailing the name of the temple and the date of the pilgrimage.

If you're eager to become an *aruki henro* (walking pilgrim) yourself, you'll need to budget around 60 days (allowing for an average distance of 25km a day) to complete the circuit. Travellers who don't have the time or inclination for the whole thing can get a taste of what it's all about by following one of the *henro*-for-a-day minicircuits mentioned in the Around Tokushima (p652) and Uwajima (p664) sections. Other cities with concentrations of temples within easy reach of each other include Matsuyama (p668) in Ehime-ken and Zentsū-ji (p675) in Kagawa-ken.

SHIKOKU

ince. In fact, it's 84km from the last temple in Tokushima-ken at Hiwasa before you get to the first temple in Kōchi-ken at Muroto-misaki. The longest distance between temples is also in Kōchi: a crippling 87km from Temple 37 (Iwamoto-ji) in Kubokawa to Temple 38 (Kongōfuku-ji) at Ashizuri-misaki. Since there are few places this remote in all of Japan, many pilgrims tend to breathe a sigh of relief once they put Kōchi behind them.

Kōchi-ken is a good place for outdoor types. Whale-watching, rafting, hiking and camping are all options here. Kōchi-ken brims with scenic spots, especially along the Shimanto-gawa, one of the last undammed rivers in Japan.

TOKUSHIMA TO KŌCHI

Muroto-misaki 室戸岬

☎ 0887

Famous as one of the wildest spots anywhere in the country, and as the doorway to the land of the dead, Muroto-misaki is one of the two great capes that jut out into the Pacific from the southern coast. To pilgrims, it is the place where Kōbō Daishi achieved enlightenment. On a calm day, the Pacific is like a millpond; in bad weather the cape is pounded by huge waves and buffeted by the wind. Visitors can explore Kōbō Daishi's bathing hole among the rock pools, and the Shinmeikutsu cave (神明窟) where he once meditated.

A huge white statue of the saint stares out to sea just north of the cape. Temple 24, **Hotsumisaki-ji** (最御崎寺; also known as Higashi-dera) was founded by Kōbō Daishi in the early 9th century. It's at the top of a steep hill directly above the point. Next to the temple, accommodation is available at **shukubō temple lodgings** (☎ 23-0024; per person with/without meals ¥5775/3885), a modern building with spotless tatami rooms.

SHIKOKU

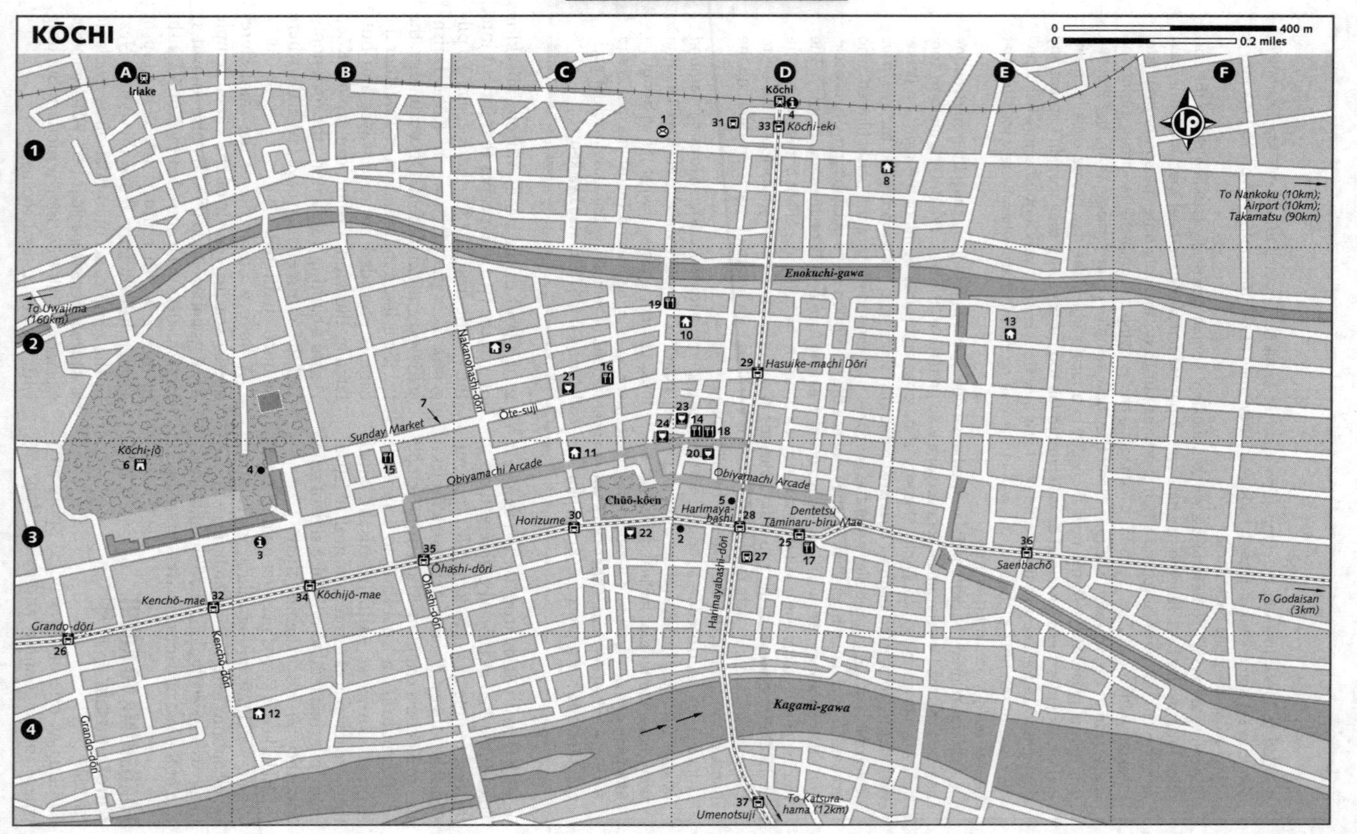
KŌCHI
0 400 m
0 0.2 miles
Iriake
Kōchi
Kōchi-eki
To Nankoku (10km); Airport (10km); Takamatsu (90km)
To Uwajima (160km)
Enokuchi-gawa
Nakanohashi-dōri
Hasuike-machi Dōri
Ōte-suji
Sunday Market
Kōchi-jō
Obiyamachi Arcade
Chūō-kōen
Harimaya-bashi
Dentetsu Tāminaru-biru Mae
Horizume
Ōhashi-dōri
Kenchō-mae
Kōchijō-mae
Grando-dōri
Kenchō-dōri
Harimayabashi-dōri
Saenbachō
To Godaisan (3km)
Kagami-gawa
Umenotsuji
To Katsura-hama (12km)

Seven buses a day run west from the cape to Nahari or Aki (安芸; ¥1300, 1½ hours), where you can change to the JR line for a train to Kōchi (one hour). Trains between Aki to Kochi take anywhere between 45 minutes and 1½ hours, depending on connections at Gomen (tickets cost between ¥1150 and ¥1460). There are also buses up the east coast to Kannoura and Mugi in Tokushima-ken.

Ryūga-dō 龍河洞

☎ 0887

Accessible by bus from Tosa-Yamada station on the Dosan line is the limestone cave **Ryūga-dō** (☎ 53-2144; www.ryugadou.or.jp, in Japanese; admission ¥1000; 🕑 8.30am-5pm, to 4.30pm Dec-Feb). Designated as a national natural monument, the cave has some interesting stalactites and stalagmites, and traces of prehistoric habitation. The route gets quite steep in places. About 1km of the 4km cave is toured in the standard visit. Advance reservations and an additional ¥500 are required for the *bōken kōsu* (adventure course; 冒険コース), where you get to don helmet and overalls and follow a guide for a 90-minute exploration of the inner reaches of the cave.

There are five buses a day to Ryūga-dō from Tosa-Yamada station (¥440, 20 minutes). Tosa-Yamada station is 30 minutes from Kōchi by local train (¥350), or 15 minutes by *tokkyū* (¥600).

KŌCHI 高知

☎ 088 / pop 335,000

The prefectural capital is a pleasant city with excellent nightlife, and it has one of Japan's few castles to have survived with most of its original buildings intact. The city played an important role during the Meiji Restoration, when a young samurai named Sakamoto Ryōma was instrumental in bringing down the feudal government. He's the serious-looking young man in samurai garb whose picture you will see all over town.

Orientation

Harimayabashi-dōri is the main road that leads straight ahead from the station. Trams travel along this road, passing the Obiyamachi arcade before intersecting with the main east–west road tram line at Harimaya-bashi.

Information

Coin lockers and a left-luggage office are in the station, and international ATMs are available at the post office next to the station.

JTB (☎ 823-2321; 1-21 Sakai-chō; 🕑 10am-6pm, closed Wed) Close to the Harimayabashi intersection.

Kōchi International Association (☎ 875-0022; www.kochi-kia.or.jp; 4-1-37 Honmachi; 🕑 8.30am-5.30pm, closed Sun) On the south side of the castle, this office is worth visiting for local information and friendly advice. It offers free internet access, a library and English newspapers.

Tourist information office (☎ 826-3337; 🕑 9am-5pm) This helpful office is inside JR Kōchi station.

Sights & Activities

KŌCHI-JŌ 高知城

Unlike many of Japan's modern concrete reconstructions, **Kōchi-jō** (Kōchi Castle; ☎ 824-5701; 1-2-1 Marunouchi; admission ¥400; 🕑 9am-5pm) is the

INFORMATION
- Central Post Office 中央郵便局 1 C1
- JTB 2 D3
- Kōchi International Association 高知国際交流センター 3 B3
- Tourist Information Office 駅観光案内所 4 D1

SIGHTS & ACTIVITIES
- Harimaya-bashi はりまや橋 5 D3
- Kōchi-jō 高知城 6 A3
- Sunday Market 日曜市 7 B2

SLEEPING
- Comfort Hotel コンフォートホテル 8 D1
- Hotel No 1 Kōchi ホテルNo 1高知 9 C2
- Kōchi Palace Hotel 高知パレスホテル 10 D2
- Richmond Hotel リチモンドホテル 11 C3
- Sansuien 三翠園 12 B4
- Tosa Bekkan 土佐別館 13 E2

EATING
- Hakobe はこべ 14 D2
- Hirome Ichiba ひろめ市場 15 B3
- Jidorian 地鶏庵 16 C2
- Tokugetsurō 得月楼 17 D3
- Tosa-han 土佐藩 18 D2
- Uofuku 魚福 19 C2

DRINKING
- Amontillado Pub アモンティラード 20 D3
- Boston Cafe Bar ボストン 21 C2
- Habotan 葉牡丹 22 C3
- Tonchan とんちゃん 23 D2
- Tosa-no-izakaya Ippon-zuri 土佐の居酒屋一本釣り 24 C2

TRANSPORT
- Dentetsu Tāminaru-biru Mae デンテツターミナルビル前 25 D3
- Grando-dōri グランドどおり 26 A4
- Harimaya-bashi Bus Terminal はりまや橋バスターミナル 27 D3
- Harimaya-bashi はりまや橋 28 D3
- Hasuike-machi Dōri 蓮池町通り 29 D2
- Horizume 堀詰 30 C3
- JR Kōchi Station Bus Terminal 高知駅バスターミナル 31 D1
- Kenchō-mae 県庁前 32 A3
- Kōchi-eki 高知駅 33 D1
- Kōchijō-mae 高知城前 34 B3
- Ōhashi-dōri 35 B3
- Saenbachō 菜園場町 36 E3
- Umenotsuji 梅の辻 37 D4

real thing – one of just a dozen in Japan to have survived with its original *tenshu-kaku* (keep) intact. The castle was originally built during the first decade of the 17th century by Yamanouchi Katsutoyo, who was appointed *daimyō* by Tokugawa Ieyasu after he fought on the victorious Tokugawa side in the Battle of Sekigahara in 1600. A major fire destroyed much of the original structure in 1727, and the castle was largely rebuilt between 1748 and 1753.

The graceful appearance of the castle's design perhaps reflects the fact that, in its present form, it was the product of an age of peace – the castle never came under attack, and for the remainder of the Tokugawa period it was more like a stately home than a military fortress. Inside the castle are exhibits on the history and development of the castle and the city that grew up around it – all in Japanese only. Many of the modern streets in this part of town follow their historic routes, and from the top of the castle it's still easy to make out the traditional layout of a Tokugawa-period castle town.

SHIKOKU

GODAISAN 五台山

Several kilometres east of the town centre is the mountain of Godaisan, where there are excellent views out over the city from a lookout point (展望台) in a park. A short walk away at the top of the hill is **Chikurin-ji** (竹林寺; ☎ 882-3085), Temple 31 of the 88, where the main hall was built by the second Tosa *daimyō*, Yamanouchi Tadayoshi, in 1644. The extensive grounds also feature a five-storey pagoda and thousands of statues of the Bodhisattva Jizō, guardian deity of children and travellers. The **Treasure House** (宝物館; admission ¥400; 🕑 9am-5pm) hosts an impressive collection of Buddhist sculpture from the Heian and Kamakura periods; the same ticket gets you into the lovely late-Kamakura-period garden opposite. Descending the steps by the Treasure Hall brings you to the entrance gates of the **Kōchi Prefectural Makino Botanical Gardens** (高知県立牧野植物園; ☎ 882-2601; admission ¥500; 🕑 9am-5pm), a beautiful network of gardens, greenhouses and parkland featuring more than 3000 different plant species. The gardens are named for Makino Tomitarō, the 'Father of Japanese Botany'. Tomitarō was born in Kōchi-ken and compiled the first scientific encyclopedia of Japanese plantlife, eventually naming more than 2500 species. The **My-Yū** circular bus stops at Godaisan on its way to Katsura-hama from Kōchi station (day ticket ¥600, 25 minutes). The bus usually operates on weekends only, but runs daily during Golden Week (19 July to 31 August) and during the New Year holidays. When not operating, you'll need to take a taxi.

KATSURA-HAMA 桂浜

Katsura-hama is a popular **beach** 13km south of central Kōchi at the point where Kōchi's harbour empties out into the bay. Just before you get to the beach itself is **Sakamoto Ryōma Memorial Museum** (坂本龍馬記念館; ☎ 841-0001; 830 Jōsan; admission ¥400; 🕑 9am-5pm), where the exhibits are dedicated to the life of a local hero who was instrumental in bringing about the Meiji Restoration in the 1860s. Born in Kōchi in 1835, Ryōma brought about the alliance between the Satsuma (modern Kagoshima) and Chōshū (Yamaguchi) domains that eventually brought down the Tokugawa shogunate. He was killed in Kyoto in 1867, aged 32. The museum has a few of his belongings and copies of his letters, but there's nothing in English and if you don't read Japanese, you probably won't get much out of a trip here – though there are some impressive views out to sea from the 2nd floor. A bronze statue of Ryōma stands near the beach, and his grim-looking visage appears on countless postcards and the other bits of tourist paraphernalia that spill out of the souvenir stands around the bus top.

There is an **aquarium** (桂浜水族館; ☎ 841-2437; admission ¥1100; 🕑 9am-5.30pm) on the beach, and a small shrine on the hillside overlooking the ocean. Buses run to Katsura-hama from Kōchi station (¥610, 30 minutes, six daily) and Harimaya-bashi (¥560, 25 minutes, frequent).

SUNDAY MARKET 日曜市

If you're in Kōchi on a Sunday, don't miss the colourful **street market** (🕑 5am-6pm Sun Apr-Sep, 6am-5pm Sun Oct-Mar) along Ōte-suji, the main road leading to the castle. The market, which has been going for some 300 years, has everything from fruit, vegetables and goldfish to antiques, knives and large garden stones.

Festivals

Kōchi's lively **Yosakoi Matsuri** (Yosakoi Festival; よさこい祭り) on 10 and 11 August perfectly complements Tokushima's Awa-odori Matsuri (12 to 15 August; see p648). There's a night-before event on 9 August and night-after effort on 12 August, but 10 and 11 August are the big days.

Sleeping

Tosa Bekkan (とさ別館; ☎ 883-5685; fax 884-9523; 1-11-34 Sakura-chō; per person ¥3800; P) The best deal in town is this homey *minshuku* in a quiet residential area 15 minutes' walk (900m) from the station. It's run by a welcoming family and features spacious Japanese-style rooms. To get here, follow the tram lines straight ahead from the station and turn left when you see Green Hotel on your right. Look out for signs on the telegraph posts with the name in Japanese.

Comfort Inn (☎ 883-1441; fax 884-3692; 2-2-12 Kita-Honmachi; s/tw with breakfast ¥5400/7200; P ⊠ 💻 wi-fi) The rooms are standard business-hotel fare, but this place is well run and comfortable, and just a couple of minutes' walk from the station. There are consoles with internet in the lobby.

Hotel No 1 Kōchi (☎ 873-3333; fax 875-9999; www.hotelno1.jp/kochi/, in Japanese; 16-8 Nijūdai-machi; s/tw ¥5140/7870; P ⊠ 💻 wi-fi) This business hotel is in a quiet area between the station and the castle. Western-style rooms are on the small side, but the rooftop onsen is a nice touch. There is LAN access in all rooms, and there are internet consoles in the lobby.

Kōchi Palace Hotel (☎ 825-0100; www.kochipalace.co.jp, in Japanese; 1-18 Nijūdai-machi; s/d ¥6500/8500; P 💻 wi-fi) This large hotel has comfortable rooms with a French restaurant and beer bar on site. It towers above everything else, two blocks west of the Harimayabashi-dōri tram line on the south side of the river. There's LAN internet access in all rooms.

Richmond Hotel (☎ 820-1122; www.richmondhotel.jp/e/kochi/index.htm; 9-4 Obiyamachi; s ¥11,000, d ¥16,000-20,000; P ⊠ 💻 wi-fi) This elegant hotel with immaculate rooms and professional service is a cut above most other places in this price range, and is just off the main shopping arcade in the heart of the city. There are public consoles with free internet access; rental laptops are also available and LAN access is in all rooms.

Sansuien (☎ 822-0131; www.sansuien.co.jp, in Japanese; 1-3-35 Takajō-machi; per person with meals from ¥13,800; P) Three blocks south of the castle along Kenchō-mae Dōri is this classy multistorey hotel with luxurious onsen baths and a garden incorporating a series of buildings that once formed part of the *daimyō's* residence. Nonguests can use the baths from 10am to 4pm (¥900).

Eating

Kōchi's main entertainment district is in the area around the Obiyamachi arcade and the Harimaya-bashi junction where the tram lines meet. Local specialities include *katsuo tataki* (lightly seared bonito fish), which is on the menu of just about every restaurant in town.

Hirome Ichiba (☎ 822-5287; 2-3-1 Obiyamachi; 🕑 8am-11pm, from 7am Sun) This lively collection of food stalls just east of the castle is a good spot for cheap eats and drinks. Be on the lookout for *gomoku rāmen*, which is a hearty mix of *rāmen* (noodles) and Kōchi's abundant fresh seafood.

Jidorian (☎ 871-5008; 1-7-27 Ōte-suji; 🕑 6pm-1am) A popular *yakitori* (skewers of grilled chicken) joint animated by the sounds of jazz and sizzling chicken. Good options include the *yakitori moriawase* (seven kinds of chicken skewers; ¥740). It's on the corner of Green Rd, a small street lined at night with open-air noodle stalls.

Hakobe (☎ 823-0084; 1-2-5 Obiyamachi; 🕑 11am-midnight) In the Obiyamachi arcade, this simple place is good for a cheap and filling meal. Take your pick of *okonomiyaki* (¥630) with *buta* (pork), *ika* (squid), *ebi* (shrimp) or *tori* (chicken) and cook it yourself on the hotplate at your table. There's a picture menu, and there are plastic food displays in the window.

Uofuku (☎ 824-1129; 2-13 Nijūdai-chō; 🕑 5-11pm, closed Sun) Sit at one of the tables in the small raised tatami area or squeeze in at the counter of this friendly *izakaya*, where the fish comes from a large tank by the door. The menu is a mess of kanji; try the *katsuo tataki* (around ¥1200) or ask for *osusume* (a recommendation). This is a good place for adventurous eaters to try *shutō* – the pickled and fermented innards of the bonito fish (¥450), which locals regard as a delicacy.

Tosa-han (☎ 821-0002; 1-2-2 Obiyamachi; 🕑 11.30am-10pm) This smart restaurant in the Obiyamachi arcade is a good place to try the traditional cuisine. *Bentō* (boxed meals) start at around ¥900; *katsuo* (bonito) is prepared in different ways, including as *sashimi* (raw; ¥1200) and *katsuo tataki* (seared; ¥1300). There is a wide variety of fresh fish from all along the coast, and a picture menu to help you choose. There's a picture of Sakamoto Ryōma looking typically purposeful on the sign outside.

Tokugetsurō (☎ 882-0101; 1-17-3 Minami-harimaya-chō; 🕑 lunch & dinner) Open since 1870, this traditional restaurant is an elegant place to try local *Tosa-ryōri* (Tosa cuisine) in tatami rooms overlooking a garden. The menu consists of a short list of set courses featuring local fish such as bonito and sea bream, according to what's in season. If the thought of eating whale meat is offensive to you, keep away from menu items featuring *kujira* (鯨), which is the Japanese word for whale. The restaurant is in a building with an imposing wooden facade across from the Dentetsu Tāminaru-biru Mae tram stop. If you're on a budget, *bentō* specials start at ¥2625; expect to pay at least twice as much in the evening.

Drinking

Tosa-no-izakaya Ippon-zuri (☎ 825-3676; 2F Sunshine Fujiwara Bldg, 1-5-5 Obiyamachi; ⌚ 5pm-midnight) In the Obiyamachi shopping arcade (look for the lanterns and menu boards outside), this popular *izakaya* has a good selection of local specialities (such as *katuso tataki* for ¥980) and sakes from breweries around Kōchi-ken starting at ¥440 – look for the page labelled 'Tosa no Ji-zake' (土佐の地酒).

Tonchan (☎ 823-6204; 1-3-8 Obiyamachi; ⌚ 5-11pm, closed Sun) Smoke and steam, conversation and laughter fill the air in this timeless place, where the regulars crowd round a horseshoe-shaped bar, and the ladies in charge bustle about warming sake and sending food orders upstairs via an antiquated system of levers and pullies. Snack options include *tsukemono moriawase* (selection of pickles; ¥320), *tan* (ox tongue; ¥420), *wafū sarada* (Japanese salad; ¥480) and *eda-mame* (boiled and lightly salted young soy beans; ¥320). It's a two-storey wooden building on the corner.

Habotan (☎ 872-1330; 2-21 Sakai-machi; ⌚ 11am-11pm) Red lanterns mark out this locals' *izakaya*. There's a large counter as you enter, and booths and tables further back. The menu, plastered over the walls, is in Japanese, but the food is under glass on the counter, so you can always point. *Sashimi moriawase* (a selection of sashimi) is ¥1050. Local booze includes Tosa-tsuru sake and Dabada Hiburi, a *shōchū* (distilled grain liquor) made from chestnuts. It's opposite Chūō Kōen, near several banks.

Amontillado Pub (☎ 875-0899; 1-1-17 Obiyamachi; ⌚ 5pm-1am) This Irish bar has a dartboard, and pints of Guinness for ¥900. It occasionally hosts live Irish music; the rest of the time you'll have to put up with the Cranberries.

Boston Cafe Bar (☎ 875-7730; 1-7-9 Ōte-suji; ⌚ 5.30pm-2am, to after 2am Sat & Sun) This cosy Japanese take on the American neighbourhood bar has baseball on the TV and friendly young staff behind the bar. A draught beer is ¥600, while a bacon pizza is ¥700.

Getting There & Away

Kōchi's Ryōma airport, 10km east of the city, is accessible by bus (¥700, 35 minutes) from the station. There are flights to/from Tokyo (¥31,500, one hour and 20 minutes, eight daily), Nagoya (¥25,800, one hour, two daily), Osaka (¥17,500, 45 minutes, six daily) and Fukuoka (¥23,700, 45 minutes, three daily).

Kōchi is on the JR Dosan line, and is connected to Takamatsu (*tokkyū* ¥4760, two hours and 10 minutes) via Awa Ikeda (*tokkyū* ¥2730, one hour and nine minutes), a jumping-off point for the Iya Valley in Tokushima-ken. Trains also run west to Kubokawa (*tokkyū* ¥2560, one hour), where you can change for Nakamura (for the Shimanto-gawa) and Uwajima on the west coast.

Getting Around

Kōchi's colourful tram service (¥190 per trip) has been running since 1904. There are two lines: the north–south line from the station intersects with the east–west tram route at the Harimaya-bashi junction. Pay when you get off, and ask for a *norikae-ken* (transfer ticket) if you have to change lines.

The My-Yū circular bus (see Godaisan, p660) runs to Godaisan and Katsurahama from Kōchi station.

KŌCHI TO ASHIZURI-MISAKI

The quiet stretch of coast between Kōchi and Ashizuri-misaki offers a number of interesting diversions. Tosa-wan (Tosa Bay) was once a major whaling centre; today, whale-watching is increasingly popular along the coast. There are kayaking opportunities along the Shimanto-gawa, one of the last free-flowing rivers in Japan, and an exquisite beach at Ōkihama. At the cape itself, there's some rugged scenery and Temple 38 on the Shikoku pilgrim trail.

The train line from Kōchi parts at Wakai. The JR Yodo line heads northwest through the mountains to Uwajima in Ehime-ken, while the private Tosa-Kuroshio line heads around to Nakamura and ends at Sukumo. There is also a bus service to Ashizuri-misaki from Nakamura station (¥1930, one hour and 40 minutes, nine daily). You can continue around the cape to Sukumo and Uwajima by bus or thumb (for more on hitching, see p837).

Between spring and mid-September, whale-watching trips are offered at several places along the coast. In the town of Kuroshio-machi not far from Nakamura, **Ōgata Whale Watching** (☎ 0880-43-1058; fax 0880-43-1527; http://sunabi.com/kujira, in Japanese; per person ¥5000) runs three four-hour trips daily between late April and October, leaving at 8am, 10am and 1pm. You'll need to reserve in advance, since the company uses three different ports. Tosa Irino and Tosa Kamikawaguchi are the closest stations to Kuroshio-machi on the Tosa-Kuroshio railway line.

The region's best accommodation option is superbly situated **Shimanto-gawa Youth Hostel** (四万十川ユースホステル; ☎ 0880-54-1352; www16.plala.or.jp/shimanto-yh, in Japanese; nonmembers per person with 2 meals ¥5980; Ⓟ ☒). Accommodation is in shared bedrooms, and the cosy hostel is perfectly situated on the banks of the peaceful Shimanto-gawa. The owners run regular canoeing trips on the river (¥8400 for a regular day's touring; cheaper introductory courses are available for beginners).

The youth hostel is 4.5km away from Kuchiyanai (口屋内), accessible by (infrequent) buses from Ekawasaki station and Nakamura. Given enough notice, the manager will come and pick you up.

Nakamura 中村

☎ 0880 / pop 37,900

Nakamura, as it's still commonly referred to (its official name is now Shimanto-shi, ie Shimanto City after it merged with the village of Nishitosa in 2005), is a good place to organise trips on the beautiful **Shimanto-gawa** (四万十川), one of the last free-flowing rivers in Japan. Staff at the **tourist information office** (☎ 35-4171; 🕑 8.30am-5pm) opposite Nakamura station can provide information on kayaking and canoe trips, and camping and outdoor activities. A number of companies offer river cruises on traditional fishing boats called Yakata-bune (¥2000 for 50 minutes); the tourist information centre has a full list. Bike rental is available here (per five hours/one day ¥600/1000), allowing you to scoot out to the river under your own steam.

Dragonfly lovers may enjoy a trip out to **Shimanto-gawa Gakuyūkan** (四万十川学遊館; ☎ 37-4111; admission ¥840; 🕑 9am-5pm, closed Mon), several kilometres from Nakamura station. It's a dragonfly museum that's full of dead insects for an up-close experience, while outside are six hectares of overgrown ponds, with dragonflies (live ones) flitting about everywhere.

In front of the station, decent Western-style rooms are available at the **Dai-ichi Hotel Nakamura** (第一ホテル中村; ☎ 0880-34-7211; fax 0880-34-7463; s/d ¥5000/10,500). A post office with international ATM is a short walk away.

About 40 minutes south of Nakamura, on the bus to Ashizuri-misaki, is **Ōki-hama** (大岐浜), an attractive 2km-long stretch of sandy white beach backed by pine trees. It's a popular surfing spot, but there is no accommodation available nearby.

ASHIZURI-MISAKI 足摺岬

☎ 0880

Like Muroto-misaki, Ashizuri-misaki is a wild, picturesque promontory that's famous for its other-worldly appearance and violent weather.

On the cape at Ashizuri-misaki there's an imposing statue of locally born hero John Manjirō. Born in 1836 as Nakahama Manjirō, the young fisherman was swept onto the desolate shores of Tori-shima, 600km from Tokyo Bay, in 1841. Five months later, he and his shipmates were rescued by a US whaler passing by, and granted safe passage to Hawaii. After moving to Massachusetts and learning English, 'John' returned to Japan and later played a leading role in diplomatic negotiations with the United States and other countries at the end of the Tokugawa period.

Ashizuri-misaki is also home to Temple 38, **Kongōfuku-ji** (金剛福寺; ☎ 88-0038), which has breathtaking views of the promontory and the Pacific Ocean. If you want to linger in these desolate and lonely surroundings, **Ashizuri Youth Hostel** (足摺ユースホステル; ☎ 88-0324; per person ¥3960; Ⓟ) is a short walk away, with basic but well-cared-for tatami rooms. With advance notice, meals are available. More upmarket is **Ashizuri Kokusai Hotel** (足摺国際ホテル; ☎ 0880-88-0201; fax 0880-88-1135; www.ashizuri.co.jp, in Japanese; per person with meals from ¥13,650), which has onsen baths overlooking the sea.

EHIME-KEN 愛媛県

Occupying the western region of Shikoku, Ehime-ken has the largest number (27) of pilgrimage temples. Like Tosa, the southern part of the prefecture has always been considered wild and remote; by the time pilgrims arrive in Shikoku's largest city, Matsuyama, they know that the hard work has been done. There are large clusters of temples around Matsuyama and the Shimanami-kaidō bridge system, which links Shikoku with Honshū.

Prefectural highlights include the sex museum and shrine in Uwajima, the immaculately preserved feudal castle and historic Dōgo Onsen in Matsuyama, and the sacred peak of Ishizuchi-san (1982m), the tallest mountain in western Japan.

UWAJIMA 宇和島

☎ 0895 / pop 62,000

Uwajima is a charming rural town that's famous among foreign travellers for a graphic sex museum, attached to a small Shintō fertility shrine. Uwajima is also noteworthy as a centre for traditional bull fighting, and for its excellent seafood.

Information

There are coin lockers at the station and international ATMs at the post office that's next to the tourist information office.

Tourist information office (☎ 22-3934; ⏰ 8.30am-5pm Mon-Fri, 9am-5pm Sat & Sun) Across the road from JR Uwajima station, and offers free internet access.

Sights & Activities

TAGA-JINJA & SEX MUSEUM 多賀神社

Once upon a time, many Shintō shrines had a connection to fertility rites. Of those that remain, **Taga-jinja** is one of the best known. The grounds of the shrine are strewn with tree-trunk phalluses and numerous statues and stone carvings, but the star attraction is the three-storey **sex museum** (☎ 22-3444; www3.ocn.ne.jp/~dekoboko, in Japanese; admission ¥800; ⏰ 8am-5pm).

Inside, the museum is packed floor to ceiling with everything from explicit Peruvian pottery to Greek vases; from the illustrated *Kamasutra* to Tibetan Tantric sculptures; from South Pacific fertility gods to a showcase full of leather S&M gear; and from early Japanese *shunga* (explicit erotic prints) to their European Victorian equivalents, not to mention a collection of modern porn magazines.

The shrine is just across the bridge over the Suka-gawa.

UWAJIMA-JŌ 宇和島城

Dating from 1601, **Uwajima-jō** (☎ 22-2832; admission ¥200; ⏰ 9am-4pm) is a small three-storey castle on an 80m-high hill in the centre of town. The present structure was rebuilt in 1666 by the *daimyō* Date Munetoshi. The castle once stood by the sea, and still provides good views over the town. The *donjon* (main keep) is one of only 12 originals left in Japan; there is nothing much to see inside. The surrounding park, **Shiroyama Kōen** (城山公園), is open from sunrise to sunset, and is a pleasant place for a stroll.

DATE MUSEUM 伊達博物館

The well-presented exhibits at the excellent **Date Museum** (☎ 22-776; 9-14 Goten-machi; admission ¥500; ⏰ 9am-5pm, closed Mon) are dedicated to the Date family, who ruled Uwajima from the castle for 250 years during the Tokugawa period. The explanations are mostly in Japanese, but most of the stuff on display – swords, armour, palanquins and lacquerware – is pretty self-explanatory.

BULLFIGHTS 闘牛

Tōgyū is a sort of bovine sumō. Victory is achieved when one animal forces the other to its knees, or when one turns tail and flees from the ring. Fights are held at Uwajima's **municipal bullfighting ring** (admission ¥3000) on 2 January, the first Sunday of April, 24 July, 14 August and the fourth Sunday of October. Directions to the ring are available at the tourist information office.

TEMPLES 41–42

A great way to get a taste of the 88 Temple pilgrimage without having to slog it out along busy main roads is to take a bus from Uwajima station direct to Temple 42, **Butsumoku-ji** (仏木寺; ¥510, 40 minutes). After admiring the thatched bell-house and the statues of the seven gods of good fortune, follow the clearly marked *henro* trail back through picturesque farming villages and rice paddies to Temple 41, **Ryūkō-ji** (龍光寺). Here, a steep stone staircase leads up to a pleasant temple and shrine overlooking the fields. It's a little over 5km in all. From outside Ryūkō-ji there are signs to Muden

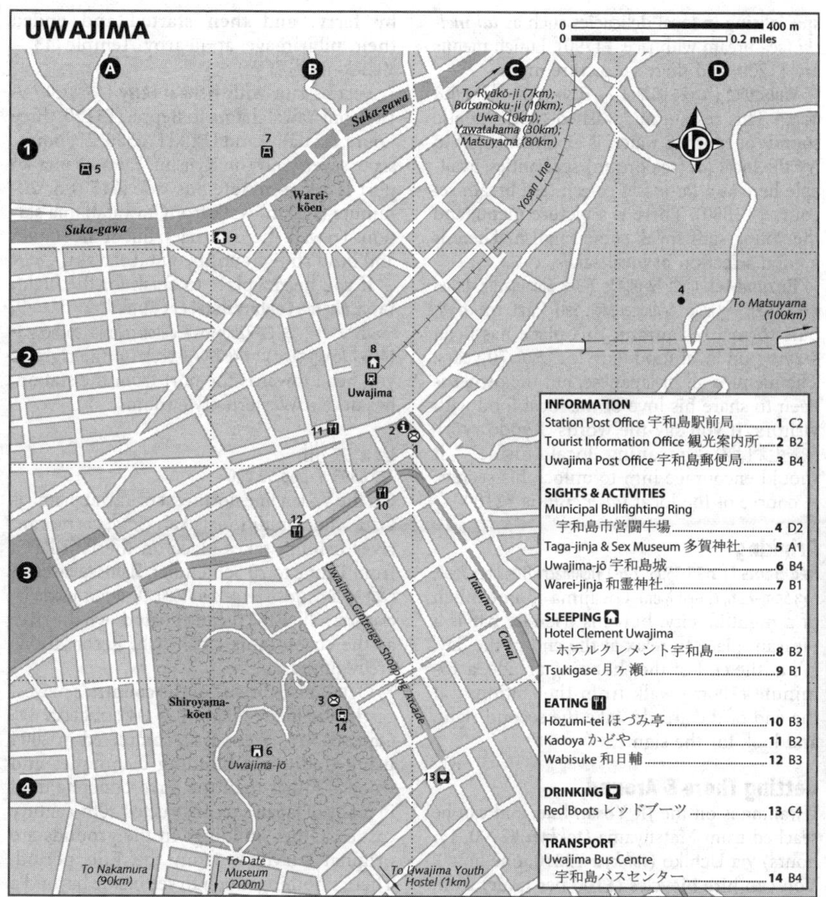

station (務田駅), a 15-minute (800m) walk away. From here, you can catch a train or bus back to Uwajima.

Sleeping & Eating

Uwajima Youth Hostel (宇和島ユースホステル; ☎ 22-7177; fax 22-7176; www2.odn.ne.jp/~cfm91130; dm foreign traveller special rate ¥2100; P ⊠ 💻) Although it's a 2km hike from the station, this friendly spot has clean four-bed dorms, some nice hilltop views and a tranquil location near a clutch of temples. To reach the hostel, follow any of the town's main throughways southeast until you reach Uwatsuhiko-jinja (English sign). From here, a small path leads up the hill to the hostel. There is free internet access and free bike rental.

Hotel Clement Uwajima (☎ 23-6111; fax 23-6666; www.shikoku.ne.jp/clement-uwajima/index.shtml, in Japanese; s/d ¥6930/8662; P ⊠ 💻 wi-fi) Located within the station complex, this smart business hotel has comfortable Western rooms and a rooftop beer garden. LAN internet access is available in all rooms.

Tsukigase (☎ 22-4788; fax 22-4787; per person with/without meals from ¥10,000/6000; P) Between Warei-kōen and the bridge to Taga-jinja is this family-run ryokan, which features traditionally decorated tatami rooms. Guests can take advantage of the stunning on-site onsen complete with mountain views, as well as some excellent food in the adjacent restaurant.

Kadoya (☎ 22-1543; ⏲ lunch & dinner; ⊠) A short walk from the station is this popular spot specialising in local delicacies such as *tai-meishi* (sea bream with rice; ¥1790). Lunch menus are ¥1200, and there's a picture menu.

Wabisuke (☎ 24-0028; 1-2-6 Ebisu-machi; ⏰ lunch & dinner) This restaurant, washed by the gentle sounds of running water, is an elegant spot to try the local *tai* (sea bream) specialities, available here as a *tai-meshi go-zen* (sea bream set course; ¥1880). There is a picture menu, and the young staff speak some English. There is a good selection of local sakes.

Hozumi-tei (☎ 22-0041; 2-3-8 Shinmachi; dishes ¥750-1500; ⏰ lunch & dinner Mon-Sat) Part *izakaya*, part formal restaurant, this place has been serving up local food here for over 70 years. The menu is all in Japanese, but the owner is keen to share his love of the local food with visitors. If you say the words 'Kyōdo ryōri' (郷土料理) – meaning 'local cuisine' – it should encourage him to unlock his secrets. A course of the local *tai-meishi* is ¥2100.

SHIKOKU

Drinking

Red Boots (☎ 25-3506; 2-6-1 Honmachi Ōte; beer ¥600; ⏰ 5pm-2am, closed Mon) Uwajima is not much of a nightlife city, but this friendly bar is a pleasant place to relax at the end of the day. It's at the end of the shopping arcade, a 15-minute (700m) walk from the station – at the end of the arcade, take the second right, and look for the sign.

Getting There & Around

Uwajima is on the JR Yosan line, and can be reached from Matsuyama (*tokkyū* ¥2900, 1½ hours) via Uchiko (*tokkyū* ¥2210, one hour). You can hire bicycles (¥100 per hour) from the tourist information office.

UWAJIMA TO MATSUYAMA

There are several worthwhile stops along the western coast between Uwajima and Matsuyama, including Ōzu, with its recently reconstructed castle, and Uchiko, a town that grew rich on wax in the 19th century and is home to several elegant old buildings. If you've come from further south, you're back in the land of trains. From Uwajima, the JR Yodo line runs to Kubokawa and Kōchi; the JR Yosan line heads north to Matsuyama.

Yawatahama 八幡浜

☎ 0894 / pop 41,200

Throughout the centuries, pilgrims from Kyūshū traditionally arrived in Yawatahama by ferry, and then started and ended their pilgrimage at nearby Temple 43 – **Meiseki-ji** (明石寺).

Ferries run with **Nankai Ferry** (☎ 0120-732-156) from Yawatahama to Beppu (¥3120, three hours, six daily) and Usuki (¥2320, 2¼ hours, six to seven daily) on Kyūshū. Yawatahama-kō port is a five-minute bus ride (¥150) or 20-minute (1.5km) walk from Yawatahama station. To walk there, turn left out of the station and head straight until you hit the sea.

If you need a place to crash for the night, **Yawatahama Century Hotel** (八幡浜センチュリーホテル; ☎ 22-2200; www.c-itoh.com, in Japanese; 1-1460-7 Tenjin-dōri; s/tw ¥6090/10,080), on the right as you head towards the port from the station, has decent Western-style rooms.

Ōzu 大洲

☎ 0893 / pop 50,000

On the Yosan line northeast of Yawatahama is Ōzu, where traditional **ukai** (鵜飼; cormorant river fishing) takes place on the Hiji-kawa from 1 June to 20 September. **Sightseeing boats** (☎ 24-2029; cruises per person ¥3000; ⏰ depart 6.30pm, return 9pm) follow the fishing boats down the river as the cormorants catch fish. Reservations are required.

Ōzu is also the site of the country's newest castle, **Ōzu-jō** (大洲城; ☎ 24-1146; joint ticket with Garyūsansō ¥800; ⏰ 9am-5pm), completed in 2004 using traditional building techniques and wood – rather than the ferro-concrete used in many of Japan's reconstructed 20th-century castles. Other buildings in the grounds are original survivals from the Edo period. There's nothing much to see inside beyond a diorama showing life in the castle town during feudal times. The castle itself is an impressive sight above the river, especially when it is lit at night.

Garyūsansō (臥龍山荘; admission ¥500, or joint ticket with Ōzu-jō ¥800; ⏰ 9am-5pm), across town from the castle, is an elegant Meiji-period tea house and garden in an idyllic spot overlooking the river. There is an excellent English pamphlet.

The best place at which to stay is family-run **Ōzu Kyōdokan Youth Hostel** (大洲郷土館ユースホステル; ☎ 24-2258; http://homepage3.nifty.com/ozuyh; San-no-maru; per person ¥3200), which has huge tatami rooms and a folklore museum full of interesting little curios from the town's boom years as a Tokugawa-period castle town. The hostel is directly below the castle.

Uchiko 内子

☎0893 / pop 20,300

During the late Edo and early Meiji periods, Uchiko boomed as a major producer of wax. As the town prospered, rich merchants built a number of exquisite houses along a street called Yōkaichi – many of these houses are still standing today.

INFORMATION

There are coin lockers at the station.

Tourist information booth (☎43-1450; 🕒9.30am-5pm Thu-Tue) You can pick up an English map at this booth, located on your right as you leave JR Uchiko station.

SIGHTS

Uchiko-za 内子座

About halfway between the station and Yōkaichi is **Uchiko-za** (☎44-2840; admission ¥300; 🕒9am-4.30pm), a magnificent traditional kabuki theatre. Originally constructed in 1916, the theatre was completely restored in 1985, complete with a revolving stage. Performances are still held at the theatre; call ahead for a schedule.

Museum of Commerce & Domestic Life 商いと暮らし博物館

A few minutes' walk further north along the main road from Uchiko-za (see above) is **Museum of Commerce & Domestic Life** (☎44-5220; admission ¥200; 🕒9am-4.30pm), which exhibits historical materials and wax figures portraying a typical merchant scene of the early 20th century.

Yōkaichi 八日市

Uchiko's picturesque main street has a number of interesting buildings, many now serving as museums, souvenir stalls, craft shops and charming tea houses. The old buildings typically have cream-coloured plaster walls and 'wings' under the eaves that serve to prevent fire spreading from house to house. In recent years, residents have banded together to preserve the street, and to make sure that any renovations are sympathetic to the traditional characteristics of the buildings.

On the left as you walk up the street, look for **Ōmori Rōsoku** (☎43-0385; 🕒9am-5pm, closed Mon & Fri), Uchiko's last remaining candle manufacturer. The candles are still made by hand here, according to traditional methods, and you can watch the candle-makers at work.

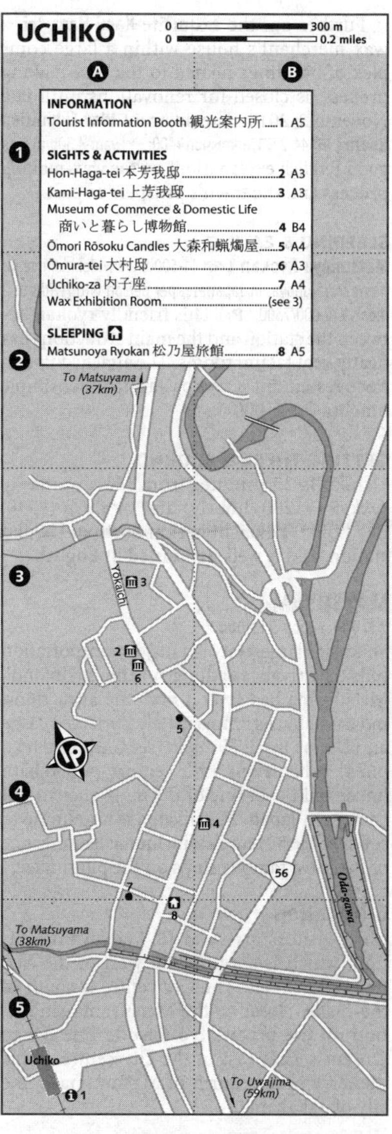

As the road makes a slight bend, several well-preserved Edo-era buildings come into view, including **Ōmura-tei** and **Hon-Haga-tei**, the latter of which is a fine example of a rich merchant's home. The Hon-Haga family established the production of fine wax in Uchiko, winning awards at World Expositions in Chicago (1893) and Paris (1900).

Further on, the exquisite **Kami-Haga-tei**, a wax merchant's house within a large complex of buildings related to the wax-making process, is closed for renovations until late November 2010. The adjacent **Wax Exhibition Room** (☎ 44-2771; admission ¥400; 🕑 9am-4.30pm) has good English explanations on the wax-making process and the town's prosperous past.

SLEEPING & EATING

Matsunoya Ryokan (☎ 44-5000; www.dokidoki.ne.jp/home2/matunoya, in Japanese; per person with/without 2 meals ¥12,600/7500; P) This friendly ryokan between the station and the main attractions has neatly kept tatami rooms. The attached Poco a Poco restaurant serves pasta and other simple lunches for ¥1000.

GETTING THERE & AROUND

Uchiko is 25 minutes from Matsuyama by *tokkyū* (¥1250, hourly) and by *futsu* (¥740, one hour). Yōkaichi is 1km north of Uchiko station, and is well signposted in English.

SHIKOKU

MATSUYAMA 松山

☎ **089 / pop 513,000**

Shikoku's largest city is a major transportation hub that rivals anything on the 'mainland'. Matsuyama has several first-rate attractions, most notably its immaculately preserved castle and Dōgo Onsen Honkan (see the boxed text, p674), a luxurious 19th-century public bath house built over one of the most ancient hot springs in Japan. Matsuyama is also home to seven of the 88 temples, including Ishite-ji, one of the most famous stops on the pilgrimage.

Orientation

Most visitors arrive at JR Matsuyama station, which is about 500m west of the castle's outer moat. The city centre is south of the castle, closer to the Matsuyama-shi station on the private Iyo-tetsudō line. Dōgo Onsen is 2km east of the city centre, while the ferry port is north of Matsuyama in the city of Takahama.

Information

ATMs accepting international cards can be found at the central post office and at the post office that's a couple of minutes' walk north of JR Matsuyama station.

Ehime Prefectural International Centre (EPIC; ☎ 943-6688; www.epic.or.jp; 1-1 Dōgo Ichiman; 🕑 8.30am-5pm, closed Sun) Provides advice, internet access and bike rental. EPIC is near the Minami-machi or Kenmin Bunkakaikan-mae tram stop. Look for the red question mark.

JTB (☎ 931-2281; 4-12-10 Sanbanchō; 🕑 10am-6pm, closed Sun) In the centre of town.

Tourist information office JR Matsuyama station (☎ 931-3914; 🕑 8.30am-8.30pm) Dōgo Onsen-mae (☎ 921-3708; 🕑 8am-4.45pm) The main office is located inside JR Matsuyama station, while a branch office is near the tram terminus for Dōgo Onsen.

Sights

MATSUYAMA-JŌ 松山城

Perched on top of Mt Katsuyama in the centre of town, the castle dominates the city, as it has for centuries. **Matsuyama-jō** (☎ 921-4873; admission ¥500; 🕑 9am-5pm, to 5.30pm Aug, to 4.30pm Dec & Jan) is one of Japan's finest surviving castles, and one of the very few with anything interesting to look at inside: there are excellent displays on the history of the city and the castle from which it was ruled (much of the information has been translated uncommonly well into English).

A ropeway (one way/return ¥260/500) is on hand to whisk you up the hill, though there is a pleasant pathway if you prefer to walk. It's worth walking down via the back slopes of the castle and stopping off at **Ninomaru Shiseki Tei-en** (admission ¥100; 🕑 9am-5pm, to 5.30pm Aug, to 4.30pm Dec & Jan) in the outer citadel of the fort, consisting of old gardens and modern water features. From here it's a short wander to underwhelming **Ehime Museum of Art** (☎ 932-0010; Horinouchi; admission ¥3; 🕑 9.40am-6.30pm, closed Mon), which features a solitary Monet and lots of European-style works by local painters.

ISHITE-JI 石手寺

East of Dōgo Onsen is **Ishite-ji**, 51st of the 88 Temples, and one of the largest and most impressive in the circuit. *Ishite* means 'stone hand' and comes from a legend associated with Kōbō Daishi (see the boxed text, p673). A statue of Kōbō Daishi overlooks the temple from the hillside.

OTHER SIGHTS

Just south of Matsuyama-shi station, in the temple grounds of Shōjūzen-ji, is **Shiki-dō** (☎ 945-0400; 16-3 Suehiro-chō; admission ¥50; 🕑 8.30am-5pm), part of the house where famous haiku poet Shiki Masaoka (1867–1902) spent the first 17 years of his life. A more in-depth treatment of his life and work is on offer at

Shiki Memorial Museum (☎ 931-5566; 1-30 Dōgo-kōen; admission ¥400; 🕑 9am-6pm, to 5pm Nov-Apr, closed Mon), in the grounds of Dōgo-kōen, a short walk east of the tram stop. The museum contains excellent displays and videos on the poet and his literary friend Natsume Sōseki, but there is no English here besides a simple pamphlet. English-speaking volunteer guides can sometimes be arranged by calling in advance the day before your visit.

Dōgo-kōen (道後公園) is a small park containing the site of Yuzuki-jō, the former residence of the Kōno clan that ruled Iyo province in feudal times. Articles unearthed during recent excavations are on display in **Yuzuki-jō Museum** (☎ 941-1480; admission free; 🕑 9am-5pm, closed Mon), near the west entrance of the park.

Isaniwa-jinja (☎ 947-7447), a short walk east of Dōgo Onsen, was built in 1667. Designated a national treasure, the shrine was modelled on Kyoto's Iwashimizu-Hachimangū.

Sleeping

BUDGET

Matsuyama Youth Hostel (☎ 933-6366; www.matsuyama-yh.com/english/index.html; 22-3 Dōgo-himezuka; dm ¥2625, private r per person ¥3360; P ⊠ 💻) This excellent hilltop hostel is famous for its immaculate dorms, stellar service and friendly, communal atmosphere. It's also a great base for multiple visits to Dōgo Onsen, since it's a 10-minute walk up the hill east of the complex. It's a good idea to reserve in advance here. Meals are available.

Check Inn Matsuyama (☎ 998-7000; fax 998-7801; www.checkin.co.jp/matsuyama, in Japanese; 2-7-3 Sanban-chō; s/tw from ¥4380/7700; P ⊠ 💻) This swish hotel is excellent value for money, with well-equipped modern rooms, chandeliers in the lobby, and an onsen on the roof. A short walk from the Ōkaidō arcade, the hotel is convenient to the city's nightlife and restaurants. LAN internet is in all rooms and there are consoles in the lobby.

Tōyoko Inn (☎ 941-1045; fax 941-2046; www.toyoko-in.com; 1-10-8 Ichiban-chō; s/d with breakfast ¥5460/8190; P ⊠ 💻) A chain hotel with somewhat small but comfortable rooms. One minute from the Katsuyama-chō stop on the tram line, and a short walk from the restaurants and bars. There is LAN access in all rooms, and there are terminals in the lobby.

Terminal Hotel Matsuyama (☎ 947-5388; fax 947-6457; www.th-matsuyama.jp, in Japanese; 9-1 Miyata-chō; s/tw ¥5775/10,500; P ⊠ 💻) Slap bang in front of the station, this faded business hotel has large(ish) rooms and all the usual facilities, including internet access from a computer in the lobby. It's a good option if you have an early train to catch.

MIDRANGE

Millennia Hotel Matsuyama (☎ 943-1011; fax 921-4111; 2-5-5 Honmachi; s/tw ¥6800/10,900) Spacious and comfortable rooms, along with satellite TV and a dim-sum restaurant, make this hotel near the castle moat a good option. It's directly opposite the Honmachi 3-chōme tram stop.

TOP END

Reservations at the following ryokan are mandatory.

Dōgo Kan (☎ 941-7777; www.dogokan.co.jp, in Japanese; 7-26 Dōgo Takōchō; per person with meals Mon-Fri from ¥15,000, Sat & Sun from ¥21,000; P) On a slope behind the Tsubaki-no-yu public baths, multistorey Dōgo Kan hotel offers world-class sophistication with a healthy smattering of opulence. Elegant tatami rooms and luxurious baths are the order of the day here, though a few Western-style rooms are available at somewhat cheaper rates.

Funaya (☎ 947-0278; fax 943-2139; www.dogo-funaya.co.jp, in Japanese; 1-33 Dōgo Yunomachi; per person with meals from ¥22,050; P) A short walk from the Dōgo Onsen tram station along the road that leads up to Isaniwa-jinja, this luxurious hotel has been in business for more than 350 years. Natsume Sōseki and various members of the royal family are among the famous people who have stayed here. Despite its unpromising exterior, Funaya is centred on an exquisite garden and features elegant tatami rooms (and a few Western-style rooms) and private onsen that draw their water from the famous spring.

Eating

The area around the Ginten-gai and Ōkaidō shopping arcades in central Matsuyama is full of places at which to eat and drink.

Goshiki Sōmen Morikawa (☎ 933-3838; 3-5-4 Sanban-chō; meals ¥700-1500; 🕑 11am-8.30pm) Next to the central post office is this elegant Matsuyama institution, which specialises in *goshiki sōmen* (thin noodles in five different colours). You'll recognise it by the piles of colourful noodles in the window waiting to be snapped up and taken home as souvenirs. Set meals are around ¥1500; there is a picture menu.

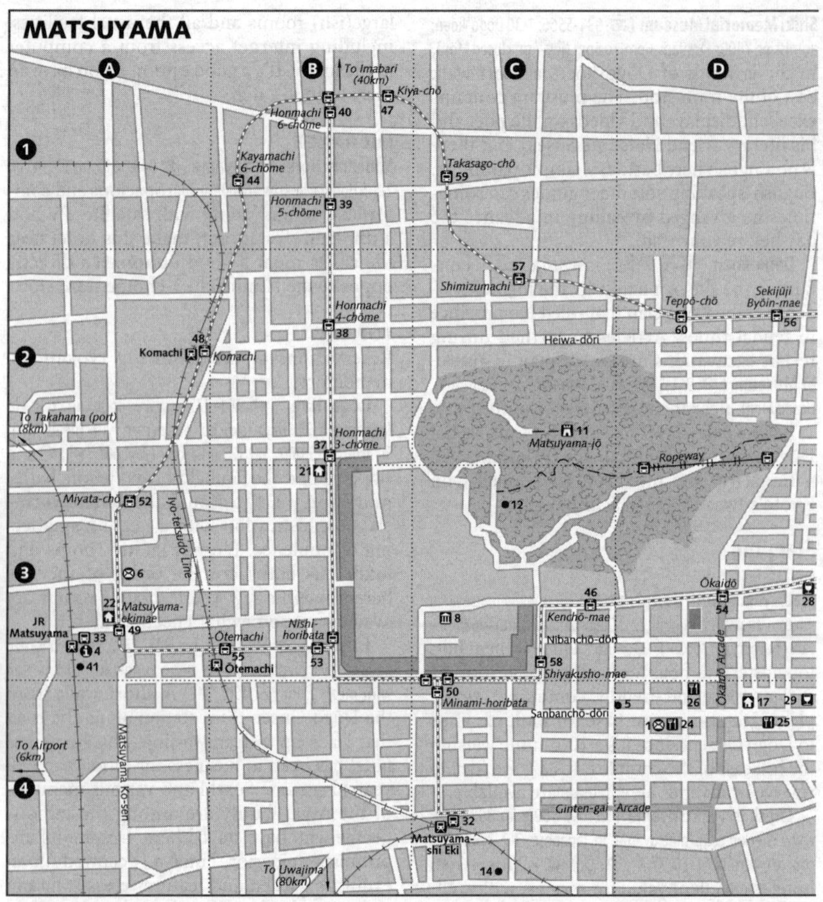

Tori-sen (☎ 908-5565; 3-2-22 Niban-chō; 🕔 5.30pm-midnight) *Yakitori* fans will love this free-range gourmet-chicken take on Japan's favourite beer snack. It's in a crowded street full of restaurants and bars parallel to the Ōkaidō arcade. There's a huge range of choices, and although there's no English menu, the enthusiastic staff are eager to help. The *tori sashimi* (raw chicken sashimi selection; ¥2000) is tastier than you might expect; the *Kōchin setto* (gourmet chicken set; ¥2000) is another good option. Look for the red curtain over the door that has the Japanese character for chicken on it: 鶏.

Tengu no Kakurega (☎ 931-1009; 2-5-17 Sanban-chō; 🕔 5pm-midnight, to 1am Fri & Sat) A chic young people's *izakaya* serving *yakitori* and other dishes in a pleasant setting. Paper screens give onto a little garden at the back. There is no English menu; *yakitori* options include *tsukune* (chicken meat balls; ¥150), *asupara-maki* (chicken with asparagus; ¥200), *nira-maki* (chicken with shallots; ¥150) and *uzura* (quail's eggs; ¥150). It has 100 different types of sake and *shōchū*. It's tucked away and a little hard to find – heading away from the post office, look for the small sign on the right in the second block after the Ōkaidō arcade.

Drinking

There is an overwhelming number of drinking establishments in Matsuyama, the bulk of them concentrated in Ichiban-chō and Niban-

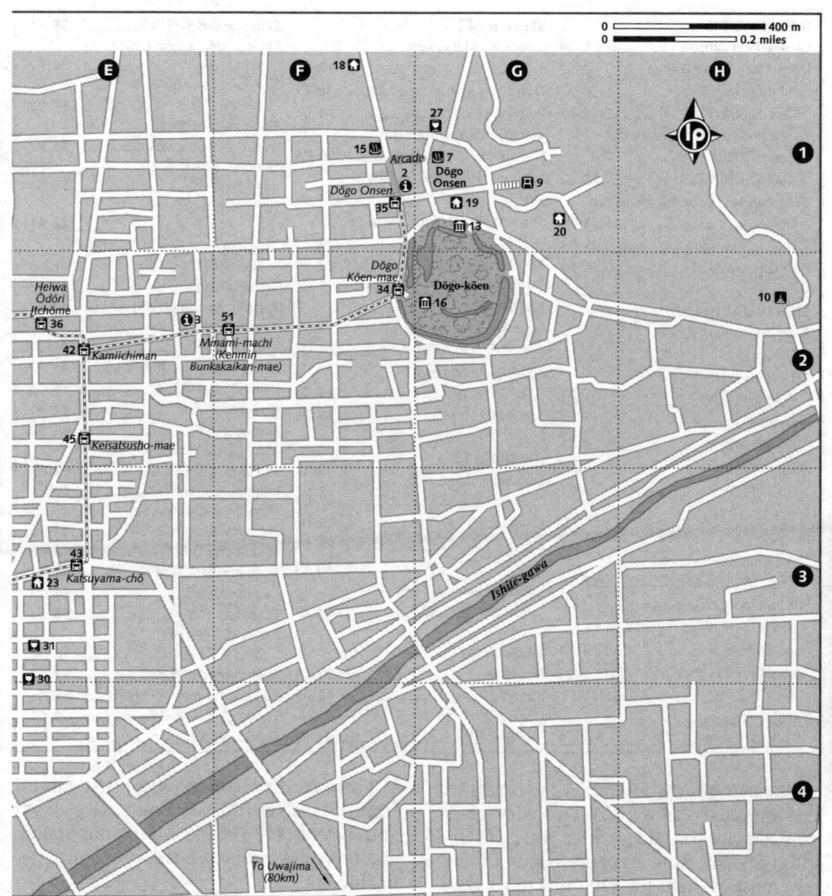

chō amid the network of neon-lit streets either side of the Ōkaidō arcade. You won't die of thirst in Matsuyama, that's for sure.

Rockbar Hoshizora Jett (☎ 933-0001; 1-8-4 Nibanchō; drinks from ¥500; ⌚ 5.30pm-4am) This pleasantly seedy-looking bar plays American rock, and there's a good chance that you can catch live music here on the weekends. It's near the Washington Hotel, up the street towards the Ōkaidō arcade. There's an English sign.

Monk (☎ 945-9512; 2F Aihara Bldg, 1-10-16 Sanban-chō; drinks from ¥700; ⌚ 6pm-2am) This is a mellow place to sink a few with the friendly musician-owner over selections from his huge jazz collection. There are regular live-music nights.

Peggy Sue Saloon (☎ 934-5701; 2F, 1-2-9 Nibanchō; drinks from ¥700; ⌚ 8.30pm-3am, closed Mon) Run by a music nut with a fondness for country music, this friendly bar is a treasure trove of cowboy-themed Americana. There's a Wurlitzer jukebox, and several guitars and mandolins on the walls that are just waiting for someone to take them down and start picking. The 2nd-floor sign is visible from street level.

Dōgo Biiru-kan (☎ 945-6866; 20-13 Dōgo Yunomachi; ⌚ 11am-10pm) Right by Dōgo Onsen Honkan, this place brews its own beer, and is a good spot for a drink and a bite to eat after a relaxing soak. The names of the beers are allusions to Natsume Sōseki and his famous novel: there's a Botchan kölsch, a Madonna alt, and a Sōseki stout (all ¥840). There's also a decent range of food available from a picture menu (such as *iwashi no karaage* – fried sardines – for ¥550).

INFORMATION
Central Post Office 1 D4
Dōgo Onsen-mae Tourist Information Office 道後温泉観光案内所 2 F1
Ehime Prefectural International Centre (EPIC) 愛媛県国際交流センター 3 E2
JR Matsuyama Tourist Information Office 4 A3
JTB 5 D4
Post Office 郵便局 6 A3

SIGHTS & ACTIVITIES
Botchan Karakuri Clock 坊ちゃんからくり時計 .... (see 2)
Dōgo Onsen Honkan 道後温泉本館 7 G1
Ehime Museum of Art 愛媛県美術館 8 C3
Isaniwa-jinja 伊佐爾波神社 9 G1
Ishite-ji 石手寺 10 H2
Matsuyama-jō 松山城 11 C2
Ninomaru Shiseki Tei-en 二之丸史跡庭園 12 C3
Shiki Memorial Museum 松山市立子規記念博物館 13 G1
Shiki-dō 子規堂 14 C4
Tsubaki-no-yu Onsen 椿の湯温泉 15 F1
Yuzuki-jō Museum 湯築城博物館 16 G2

SLEEPING
Check Inn Matsuyama チェックイン松山 17 D4
Dōgo Kan 道後館 18 F1
Funaya ふなや 19 G1
Matsuyama Youth Hostel 松山ユースホステル 20 G1
Millennia Hotel Matsuyama ミレニアホテル松山 21 B3
Terminal Hotel Matsuyama ターミナルホテル松山 22 A3
Tōyoko Inn 東横イン 23 E3

EATING
Goshiki Sōmen Morikawa 五色そうめん森川 24 D4
Tengu no Kakurega てんぐの隠れ家 25 D4
Tori-sen とり泉 26 D4

DRINKING
Dōgo Biiru-kan 道後麦酒館 27 G1
Kuramoto-ya 蔵元屋 28 D3
Monk モンク 29 D4
Peggy Sue ペギースー 30 E3
Rockbar Hoshizora Jett Rockbar 星空 JETT 31 E3

TRANSPORT
Bus stop 32 C4
Bus stop 33 A3
Dōgo Kōen-mae 道後公園前 34 F2
Dōgo Onsen 道後温泉 35 F1
Heiwa Ōdōri Itchōme 平和大通り一丁目 36 E2
Honmachi 3-chōme 本町三丁目 37 B2
Honmachi 4-chōme 本町四丁目 38 B2
Honmachi 5-chōme 本町五丁目 39 B1
Honmachi 6-chōme 本町六丁目 40 B1
JR Matsuyama Rental Bicycles JR松山駅レンタサイクル 41 A3
Kamiichiman 上一万 42 E2
Katsuyama-chō 勝山町 43 E3
Kayamachi 6-chōme 萱町六丁目 44 B1
Keisatsusho-mae 警察署前 45 E2
Kenchō-mae 県庁前 46 C3
Kiya-chō 木屋町 47 B1
Komachi 古町 48 A2
Matsuyama-ekimae ＪＲ松山駅前 49 A3
Minami-horibata 南堀端 50 C4
Minami-machi (Kenmin Bunkakaikan-mae) 南町 51 F2
Miyata-chō 宮田町 52 A3
Nishi-horibata 西堀端 53 B3
Ōkaidō 大街道 54 D3
Ōtemachi 大手町 55 B3
Sekijūji Byōin-mae 赤十字病院前 56 D2
Shimizumachi 清水町 57 C2
Shiyakusho-mae 市役所前 58 C3
Takasago-chō 高砂町 59 C1
Teppō-chō 鉄砲町 60 D2

Kuramoto-ya (☎ 934-5701; 1-11-7 Ichiban-chō; noon-9pm, closed Mon;) This airy glass-fronted place has tables where you can stand and enjoy sake from every brewery in Ehime-ken, most of them for ¥100 to ¥200 a glass. There's no English, but the bottles are on clear display and everyone's eager to help you find what you're looking for.

Getting There & Away

Matsuyama's airport, 6km west of the city, is easily reached by bus (¥330, 20 minutes, hourly) from the front of the JR Matsuyama station. There are direct flights to/from Tokyo (¥32,000, one hour and 25 minutes, 10 daily), Nagoya (¥23,700, one hour, three daily), Osaka (¥17,000, 50 minutes, 15 daily) and Fukuoka (¥28,000, 50 minutes, three daily).

The JR Yosan line connects Matsuyama with Takamatsu (*tokkyū* ¥5500, 2½ hours), and there are also services across the Seto-ōhashi to Okayama (*tokkyū* ¥6120, 2¾ hours) on Honshū.

There are JR Highway buses that run to/from Osaka (¥6700, 5½ hours, five daily) and Tokyo (¥12,200, 12 hours, one daily), and there are frequent buses to major cities in Shikoku.

The superjet hydrofoil, run by the **Setonaikai Kisen ferry** (☎ 082-253-1212., Matsuyama booking office 089-953-1003; 9am-7pm), has regular hydrofoil connections between Matsuyama and Hiroshima (¥6300, 1¼ hours, 14 daily). The Hiroshima-to-Matsuyama ferry (¥2900, 2¾ hours, 10 daily) is also a popular way of getting to/from Shikoku. Matsuyama is also a stopping point for ferries run by **Diamond Ferry company** (☎ 951-0167; www.diamond-ferry.co.jp) between Osaka and Kōbe, and Ōita (Kyūshū). There is one sailing a day each way. To Honshū, the ferry leaves Matsuyama at 8.30pm (2nd class, ¥7500) – to Kōbe it's nine hours and 20 minutes; to Osaka it's 12 hours. For Ōita, the boat leaves Matsuyama at 8.30am and arrives at 12.05pm (2nd class, ¥3800). To reach Matsuyama port, take the Iyo-tetsudō private train line from Matsuyama-shi or Ōtemachi stations to the end of the line at Takahama (¥400, 25 minutes, hourly). From Takahama, a connecting bus (free) whisks you to the port.

Getting Around

Matsuyama has an excellent tram service that costs a flat ¥150 for each trip (pay when you get off). A day pass costs ¥300. Trams to the terminus at Dōgo Onsen leave from outside both JR and Matsuyama-shi stations. The Ōkaidō stop outside the Mitsukoshi department store is a good central stopping point.

Lines 1 and 2 are loop lines, running clockwise and anticlockwise around Katsuyama (the castle mountain). Line 3 runs from Matsuyama-shi station to Dōgo Onsen, line 5 goes from JR Matsuyama station to Dōgo Onsen, and line 6 from Kiya-chō to Dōgo Onsen.

If you're lucky with timing, you can ride the Botchan Ressha (坊ちゃん列車), small trains that were imported from Germany in 1887. Named for Natsume Sōseki's famous novel, they ran up and down Matsuyama's streets for 67 years, and they're back in occasional use.

Bike rental (per day ¥300; 9am-6pm Mon-Sat) is available at the large bicycle park to the right as you exit the JR station.

AROUND MATSUYAMA

Ishizuchi-san 石鎚山

At 1982m, Ishizuchi-san is the highest peak in western Japan, and was traditionally considered to be a holy mountain. Ishizuchi attracts pilgrims and climbers alike, particularly during the July and August climbing season. During the winter (late December to late March), Ishizuchi also serves as a popular local ski slope.

To get to the Nishi-no-kawa cable-car station (on the northern side of the mountain), take the direct bus (¥990, 55 minutes, four daily) from Iyo-Saijo station.

You can climb up one way and down the other or make a complete circuit from Nishi-no-kawa to the summit, down to Tsuchi-goya and then back to Nishi-no-kawa. Allow all day and an early start for the circuit. For detailed information on hiking Ishizuchi-san, see Lonely Planet's *Hiking in Japan*.

KAGAWA-KEN 香川県

Formerly known as Sanuki, Kagawa-ken is the smallest of Shikoku's four regions, and the second smallest of the country's 47 prefectures.

The region's hospitable weather and welcoming people have always been a comfort to pilgrims as they come to the end of their journey. Today, it's an important point of arrival, too, since the only rail link with Honshū is via the Seto-ōhashi bridge to Okayama. Highlights of the region include the celebrated shrine of Kompira-san at

SO THE STORY GOES...

Matsuyama's Ishite-ji (Ishite Temple; *Ishite* means 'stone hand') is so named because of a legend relating to Kōbō Daishi. A rich man named Emon Saburō repeatedly refused to give alms when the great man came to beg at his door, and one day even used violence against the saint and sent him on his way. Shortly afterwards, the man's sons began to die. Seven of them died before it occurred to Saburō that he had acted unwisely in treating the Daishi with so little respect. Repenting of what he had done and desperate for forgiveness, he set off on a long journey around Shikoku, searching desperately for the only man who could help, Kōbō Daishi.

Saburō completed several circuits of the pilgrimage before he managed to track down his man, and by the time he found him, Saburō was ready to breathe his last.

But before he died, he begged a favour of Kōbō Daishi and asked to be reborn as the lord of Iyo province (now Ehime prefecture), so that he might attain merit by serving the common people and atoning for the evil he had done in this life. Kōbō Daishi wrote Saburō's name on a stone and thrust it into his hands. Saburō died with the stone in his hand. Several days later, a baby boy was born to the first wife of the lord of the domain, his hand clasped tight shut. A priest was called in and commanded to use the most powerful prayers in his arsenal to unlock the boy's fist. When the boy finally did release his grip, his astonished parents found clasped between his fingers the stone inscribed with the dead man's name.

AN INSIDER'S GUIDE TO DŌGO ONSEN

According to legend, Dōgo Onsen (道後温泉) was discovered during the age of the gods when a white heron was found healing itself in the spring. Since then, Dōgo has featured prominently in a number of literary classics, and won itself a reputation for the curative powers of its waters. The mono-alkaline spring contains sulphur, and is believed to be particularly effective at treating rheumatism, neuralgia and hysteria.

The main building, **Dōgo Onsen Honkan** (道後温泉本館; ☎ 089-921-5141; 5-6 Dōgo-yunomachi; ⌚ 6am-11pm), was constructed in 1894, and designated as an important cultural site in 1994. The three-storey, castle-style building incorporates traditional design elements, and is crowned by a statue of a white heron to commemorate its legendary origins. Although countless famous people have passed through its doors, Dōgo Onsen Honkan is perhaps best known for its inclusion in the famous 1906 novel *Botchan* by Natsume Sōseki, the greatest literary figure of Japan's modern age, who based his novel on his time as a schoolteacher in Matsuyama in the early 20th century.

Even if you're well versed in onsen (hot springs) culture, Dōgo can be a bit confusing as there are two separate baths (and four pricing options) from which to choose. The larger and more popular of the two baths is *kami-no-yu* (神の湯; water of the gods), which is separated by gender and adorned with heron mosaics. A basic bath costs ¥400, while a bath followed by tea and *senbei* (rice crackers) in the 2nd-floor tatami room costs ¥800, and includes a rental *yukata* (light cotton kimono). A rental towel and soap will set you back a further ¥50. The smaller and more private of the two baths is the *tama-no-yu* (魂の湯; water of the spirit), which is also separated by gender and adorned with simple tiles. A bath followed by tea and *dango* (sweet dumplings) in the 2nd-floor tatami room costs ¥1200, while the top price of ¥1500 allows you to enjoy your snack in a private tatami room on the 3rd floor.

Although there are English-language pamphlets on hand to clarify the correct sequence of steps, Dōgo Onsen can be a bit intimidating if you don't speak Japanese. After paying your money outside, you should enter the building and leave your shoes in a locker. If you've paid ¥400, go to the *kami-no-yu* changing room (signposted in English), where you can use the free lockers

Kotohira, the beautiful garden of Ritsurin-kōen in Takamatsu, and the remarkable Inland Sea island of Naoshima (p474).

MATSUYAMA TO TAKAMATSU

This stretch of country is home to several noteworthy temples on the pilgrimage circuit, including the twin temples at Kanonji, and the important town of Zentsū-ji, the boyhood home of Kōbō Daishi.

The JR Yosan line runs around the coast between Takamatsu and Matsuyama. At Tadotsu, the JR Dosan line splits off and runs south to Zentsū-ji and Kotohira, through the Iya Valley (p652) and eventually to Kōchi (p659).

Kanonji 観音寺

☎ 0875 / pop 65,000

Coming east from Ehime-ken, the first town of consequence in Kagawa-ken is Kanonji, notable as the only spot on the pilgrimage trail to have two of the 88 Temples on the same grounds: Temple 68, **Jinne-in** (神恵院), and Temple 69, **Kanon-ji** (観音寺). It's also known for the odd **Zenigata** (銭形), a 350m-circumference coin-shaped sculpture in the sand dating from 1633. The coin and its inscription are formed by huge trenches dug in the sand, and are said to have been dug overnight by the local population as a welcome present to their feudal lord. For the best views of the sculpture, you'll need to climb the hill in Kotohiki-kōen, 1.9km northwest of Kanonji station (not far from the two temples). A small **tourist information office** (☎ 25-3839), over the bridge from the station, has maps. Kanonji is considerably closer to Takamatsu (*tokkyū* ¥2210, 48 minutes) than Matsuyama (*tokkyū* ¥4130, one hour and 38 minutes).

Marugame 丸亀

☎ 0877 / pop 110,700

An interesting detour from the 88-Temple circuit is in Marugame, home to **Marugame-jō** (丸亀城; ☎ 24-8816; admission ¥200; ⌚ 9am-4.30pm). The castle dates from 1597, and is one of only 12 castles in Japan to have its original wooden *donjon* intact.

for your clothing. If you've paid ¥800 or ¥1200, first go upstairs to receive your *yukata*, and then return to either the *kami-no-yu* or *tama-no-yu* (also signposted in English) changing room. After your bath, you should don your *yukata* and retire to the 2nd-floor tatami room to sip your tea and gaze down on the bath-hoppers clip-clopping by in *geta* (traditional wooden sandals). If you've paid top whack, head directly to the 3rd floor, where you will be escorted to your private tatami room. Here, you can change into your *yukata* before heading to the *tama-no-yu* changing room, and also return after your bath to sip tea in complete isolation.

Regardless of which option you choose, you are allowed to explore the building after taking your bath. On the 2nd floor, there is a small **exhibition room** displaying artefacts relating to the bathhouse, including traditional wooden admission tickets. If you've taken one of the pricier upstairs options, you can also take a guided tour (in Japanese) of the private **imperial baths**, last used by the royal family in 1950. On the 3rd floor, the corner tatami room (which was the favourite of Natsume Sōseki) has a small **display** (in Japanese) on the life of the writer.

Dōgo Onsen is 2km east of the city centre, and can be reached by the regular tram service, which terminates at the start of the spa's shopping arcade. This arcade is lined with small restaurants and souvenir stores, and leads directly to the front of the Honkan.

Dōgo can get quite crowded, especially on weekends and holidays, although at dinner time it's usually empty, because most Japanese tourists will be having dinner in their inns. If you want to escape the crowds, one minute on foot from the Honkan (through the shopping arcade) is **Tsubaki-no-yu** (椿の湯; admission ¥360; 6am-11pm), Dōgo Onsen's hot-spring annexe, frequented primarily by locals. If you don't want a full bath, there are also nine free **ashi-yu** (足湯; foot baths) scattered around Dōgo Onsen where you can take off your shoes and socks, and warm your feet. The most famous one is located just opposite the station at the start of the arcade. Here, you can also check out **Botchan Karakuri Clock** (坊ちゃんからくり時計), which was erected as part of Dōgo Onsen Honkan's centennial in 1994. It features figures based on the main characters from *Botchan*, who emerge to take a turn on the hour from 8am to 10pm.

At **Uchiwa-no-Minato Museum** (うちわの港ミュージアム; ☎ 24-7055; admission free; 9.30am-5pm, closed Mon) there are displays and craft demonstrations showing how uchiwa (traditional paper fans) are made. Marugame is responsible for about 90% of the country's paper-fan output, making it a logical place to pick one up. The museum is in the harbour, a few minutes' walk from the station.

Bike hire (☎ 25-1127; per day ¥200, deposit ¥500) is available from the bicycle park across from the station. By bike, it is less than an hour from Marugame to Zentsū-ji (see below). Maps are available at the tourist information counter at the station. Marugame is easily covered as a day trip from Takamatsu (*tokkyū* ¥1050, 25 minutes).

Zentsū-ji 善通寺

☎ 0877 / pop 34,000

Temple 75 of the 88 Temples, **Zentsū-ji** (善通寺; ☎ 62-0111) holds a special significance as the place where Kōbō Daishi was born. It is also the largest temple – most of the other 88 could fit comfortably into the car park here. The temple boasts a truly magnificent five-storey pagoda and giant camphor trees that are said to date back as far as Daishi's childhood. Visitors can venture into the basement of the **Mie-dō** (御影堂; admission ¥500) building and traverse a 100m-long passageway (戒壇めぐり) in pitch darkness: by moving carefully along with your hand pressed to the wall (painted with mandalas, angels and lotus flowers), you are said to be safely following Buddha's way. There is a small shrine halfway through, where Kōbō Daishi himself welcomes pilgrims, in a booming voice, to his childhood home. If you're on a bike, there are several other pilgrimage temples within easy reach of this one, including Temple 73, **Shusshaka-ji** (出釈迦寺). It's at Shusshaka-ji that a seven-year-old Kūkai flung himself from a cliff, vowing to devote his life to saving souls if the Buddha preserved him. A team of guardian angels duly arrived in time to guarantee him a soft landing.

Kotohira 琴平

☎ 0877 / pop 10,900

The small mountain village of Kotohira is home to Kompira-san, a Shintō shrine dedicated to the god of seafarers. The shrine is one of Shikoku's most famous tourist attractions. If you mention to a Japanese person that you've visited Kotohira, you will almost certainly be asked if you made it to the top. There are 1368 steep stone steps leading up to the top. Sellers of walking sticks and drinks are on hand to help you out.

ORIENTATION

Kotohira is a small town, and all roads lead to the shrine. Starting a few streets southeast of the two stations, a busy street lined with the inevitable souvenir shops stretches to the bottom of the long stone staircase that leads up to the shrine.

INFORMATION

There are coin lockers at the station, and the ATMs at the post office accept international cards.

Tourist information centre (☎ 75-3500; 9.30am-8pm) Found along the main road between JR Kotohira station and Kotoden Kotohira station. Has local maps, and bikes available for hire (¥100/500 per hour/day).

SHIKOKU

SIGHTS

Kompira-san 金刀比羅宮

Kompira-san or, more formally, Kotohira-gū, was originally a Buddhist and Shintō temple dedicated to the guardian of mariners. It became exclusively a Shintō shrine after the Meiji Restoration. The shrine's hilltop position affords superb views over the countryside, and there are some interesting reminders of its maritime connections.

A lot of fuss is made about how strenuous the climb (1368 steps) to the top is, but if you've made it this far in Japan, you've probably completed a few long ascents to shrines already. If you really blanch at the thought of climbing all those steps, you can always dish out ¥6500 and be carried up and down in a palanquin.

The first notable landmark on the long climb is **Ō-mon**, a stone gateway that leads to **Hōmotsu-kan** (Treasure House; admission ¥500; 8.30am-5pm), where the collection of treasures is pretty underwhelming for such a major shrine. Nearby you will find five traditional-sweets vendors at tables shaded by large white parasols. A symbol of ancient times, the vendors (the Gonin Byakushō – Five Farmers), are descendants of the original families that were permitted to trade within the grounds of the shrine. Further uphill is **Shoin** (Reception Hall; admission ¥500; 8.30am-4.30pm), a designated National Treasure that dates from 1659 and has some interesting screen paintings and a small garden.

Continuing the ascent, you eventually reach large **Asahino Yashiro** (Shrine of the Rising Sun). Built in 1837, this large hall is dedicated to the sun goddess Amaterasu, and is noted for its ornate wood-carving. From here, the short final ascent, which is the most beautiful leg of the walk, brings you to **Gohonsha** (Gohon Hall) and **Ema-dō** (Ema Pavilion). The latter is filled with maritime offerings ranging from pictures of ships and models to modern ship engines. There's also a one-man sailboat hull made out of 22,000 recycled aluminium cans and powered by solar panels – its owner donated it to the shrine after he sailed in it from Ecuador to Tokyo in 1996. From this level, there are spectacular views that extend right down to the coast and over the Inland Sea.

Incurable climbers can continue for another 500 or so steps up to **Oku-sha** (Inner Shrine), which features stone carvings of *tengu* (long-nosed mountain demons) on the cliff.

Other Sights

Built in 1835, **Kanamaru-za** (☎ 73-3846; admission ¥500; 9am-5pm) is Japan's oldest kabuki playhouse, though it had a lengthy stint as a cinema before falling out of use. It was lovingly restored in 2003. Inside, you can wander backstage and see the revolving-stage mechanism, basement trap doors and a tunnel out to the front of the theatre. The playhouse is 200m east of the main approach to Kompira-san.

Kinryō-no-Sato (☎ 73-4133; admission ¥310; 9am-5pm) sake museum, located along the main approach to the shrine, is in the old premises of a brewery that has owned the building since 1789. Brewing now takes place in more-modern facilities in Tadotsu. There are model dioramas illustrating the brewing process, and a lot of old equipment on display. At the end of the tour you can try three different Kinryō sakes for ¥100 a glass.

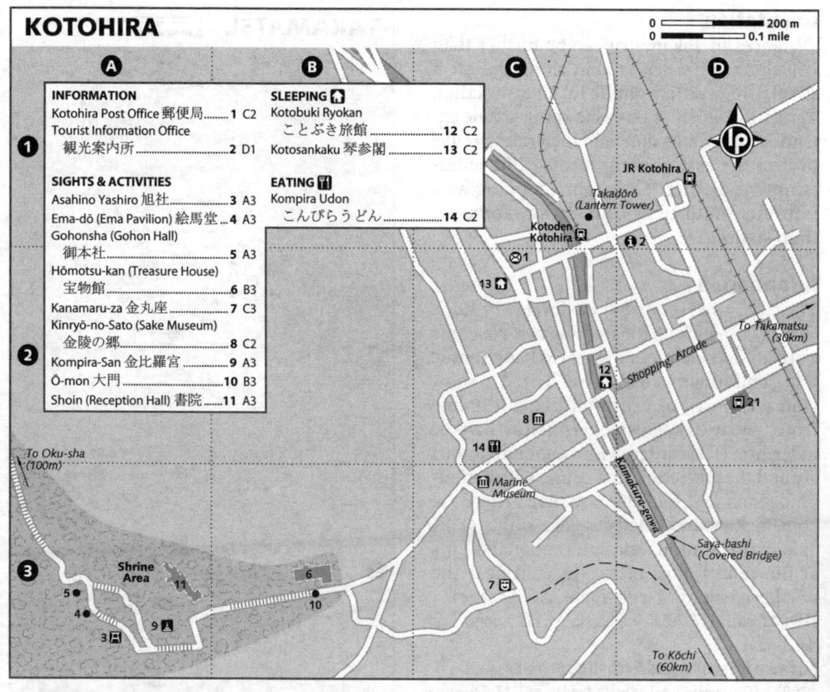

SLEEPING & EATING

Kotobuki Ryokan (☎ 73-3872; per person with 2 meals ¥6800; P) Conveniently situated by the riverside a short walk from the shrine, this friendly family-run place has comfortable tatami rooms with shared bathrooms. If you do stay the night, you'll want to eat in your ryokan; the streets of Kotohira are pretty dead after dark.

Kotosankaku (☎ 75-1000; fax 75-0600; www.kotosankaku.jp/index_en.html; per person Mon-Fri from ¥9600, Sat & Sun from ¥17,850; P) Weighing in at nearly 225 rooms, this elegant place is one of the biggest ryokans in Shikoku. Attractive Japanese- and Western-style rooms are complemented by a pool (summer only) and a stunner of an onsen complex (open to non-guests for ¥1200, from 10.30am to 3pm).

Kompira Udon (☎ 73-5785; meals ¥500-950; 8am-5pm) Just short of the first set of steps leading up Kompira-san, this is one of dozens of *Sanuki udon* (see the boxed text, p680) joints in Kotohira. The house speciality is *shōyu udon* (thick white noodles served with a special soy sauce). Look for the giant udon bowl outside.

GETTING THERE & AWAY

You can travel to Kotohira on the JR Dosan line from Kōchi (*tokkyū* ¥3810, one hour and 38 minutes) and Ōboke. For Takamatsu and other places on the north coast, change trains at Tadotsu. The private Kotoden line has regular direct trains from Takamatsu (¥610, one hour). JR Kotohira station is about 500m north and east of the town centre, while the Kotoden station is conveniently just 200m west of the JR station.

TAKAMATSU 高松

☎ 087 / pop 425,000

Thanks to its rail link to Honshū, the former castle town of Takamatsu is a popular entry point for Shikoku, and serves as a good jumping-off point for destinations around the island. The city's biggest attraction is Ritsurin-kōen, one of the country's most spectacular and delightful gardens. The city also serves as a base for a number of unique day trips, notably to the olive groves of Shōdo-shima and the island of Naoshima (p474) in the Inland Sea.

Orientation

Distances in Takamatsu can be further than you think – it's nearly 2km along the main street, Chūō-dōri, from JR Takamatsu station to Ritsurin-kōen. A busy shopping arcade extends across Chūō-dōri, and then runs parallel to it to the east, passing through the entertainment district. The main shopping area is further south, near Kotoden Kawaramachi train station.

Information

The city is well set up to help foreign visitors. Visitors can pick up the free Kagawa Welcome Card at Kagawa International Exchange or the tourist information office (you'll need to show your passport), or can print one out online from www.21kagawa.com/visitor/kanko/index.htm. The card provides minor discounts around the prefecture, and comes with a mini-guidebook and fold-out city map. There are coin lockers and a left-luggage office at JR Takamatsu station, and international ATMs at the central post office (located near the northern exit of Marugamemachi Arcade).

JTB (☎ 851-2117; 7-6 Kajiyamachi; 🕙 10am-6pm, closed Sun)

Kagawa International Exchange (I-PAL Kagawa; ☎ 837-5901; www.i-pal.or.jp, in Japanese; 1-11-63 Banchō; 🕙 9am-6pm Tue-Sun) In the northwest corner of Chūō-kōen, with a small library, satellite TV and internet access.

Tourist information office (☎ 851-2009; 🕙 9am-6pm) In the plaza outside the station.

Sights

RITSURIN-KŌEN 栗林公園

One of the most beautiful gardens in the country, **Ritsurin-kōen** (☎ 833-7411; 1-20-16 Ritsurinchō; admission ¥400; 🕙 sunrise-sunset) dates from the mid-1600s and took more than a century to complete. Designed as a walking garden for the *daimyō's* enjoyment, the park winds around a series of ponds, tearooms, bridges and islands. To the west, Shiun-zan (Mt Shiun) forms an impressive backdrop to the garden. The classic view of Engetsu-kyō bridge with the mountain in the background is one of the finest in Japan.

Enclosed by the garden are a number of interesting sights, including **Sanuki Folkcraft Museum** (admission free; 🕙 8.45am-4.30pm), which displays local crafts dating back to the Tokugawa dynasty. If you're a fan of *matcha* (powdered green tea) and traditional sweets, there are a number of tea houses in the park, including 17th-century **Kikugetsu-tei**, where you can have *matcha* for ¥710, and the lovely thatched-roof **Higurashi-tei**, which dates from 1898.

The easiest way to reach Ritsurin-kōen is by taking the frequent direct bus (¥230, 15 minutes) from JR Takamatsu station.

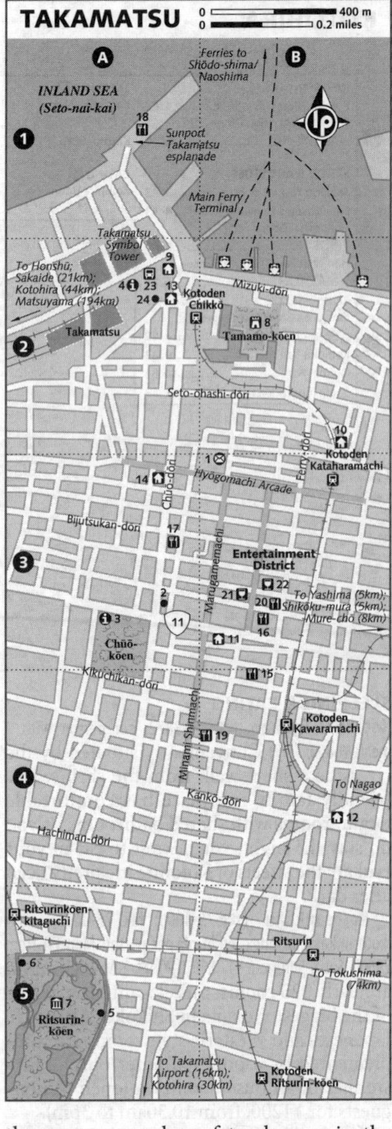

INFORMATION
Central Post Office 中央郵便局 1 B3
JTB 2 A3
Kagawa International Exchange (I-PAL Kagawa)
アイパル香川 国際交流会館 3 A3
Tourist Information Office 観光案内所 4 A2

SIGHTS & ACTIVITIES
Ritsurin-kōen East Gate 栗林公園東門 5 A5
Ritsurin-kōen North Gate 栗林公園北門 6 A5
Sanuki Folkcraft Museum 讃岐民芸館 7 A5
Takamatsu-jō 高松城 8 B2

SLEEPING
ANA Hotel Clement Takamatsu
全日空ホテルクレメント高松 9 A2
Castle Hotel Takamatsu キャッスルホテル高松 10 B2
Dormy Inn Takamatsu ドーミーイン高松 11 B3
Hotel No 1 Takamatsu ホテル No1 高松 12 B4
Takamatsu Station Hotel
高松ステーションホテル 13 A2
Tōyoko Inn Hyōgomachi 東横イン兵庫町 14 A3

EATING
Bijin-tei 美人亭 15 B4
Goemon 五右衛門 16 B3
Kanaizumi かな泉 17 A3
Mikayla ミケイラ 18 A1
Tokiwa Saryō ときわ茶寮 19 B4
Tsurumaru 鶴丸 20 B3

DRINKING
Anbar アンバー 21 B3
Cancun カンクーン 22 B3

TRANSPORT
Bus Terminal バスターミナル 23 A2
Takamatsu-shi Rental Cycles
高松市レンタサイクル 24 A2

TAKAMATSU-JŌ 高松城

The site of Takamatsu's castle now forms delightful **Tamamo-kōen** (玉藻公園; ☎ 851-1521; 2-1 Tamamo-chō; admission ¥200; sunrise-sunset), a park where the walls and moat (filled with sea water) survive, along with several of the original turrets. The original castle was built in 1588 for Itoma Chikamasa, and was the home of the region's military rulers until the Meiji Restoration nearly 300 years later. In 2008 work began on a reconstruction of the main keep, which should be completed in 2010. The park is a short walk from the main JR station.

Sleeping

Castle Hotel Takamatsu (☎ 851-0606; fax 851-0607; 4-8 Tsuruya-machi; s/d ¥3990/5250; P) Near Kataharamachi station on the Kotoden line, this older hotel is slightly rough around the edges, and its common areas are certainly no match for the sparkle of the chain hotels. However, the Japanese- and Western-style rooms are large and comfortable, and represent good value for the price. There's LAN internet access in all rooms.

Takamatsu Station Hotel (☎ 821-6989; fax 851-5575; 1-1 Kotobukichō; s/d ¥5000/8000; P) The building is starting to show its age, and the bare rooms are certainly nothing to write home about, but it's in a perfect location for an early-morning start – a minute's walk from the station and the ferry terminal.

Hotel No 1 Takamatsu (☎ 812-2222; fax 812-0002; www.hotelno1.jp/takamatsu, in Japanese; 2-4-1 Kankō-dōri; s/d ¥5140/7870; P) Three blocks east and three blocks south of Kotoden Kawaramachi station, this is a sparkling business hotel with standard rooms and a rooftop men-only *rotemburo* (outdoor bath) with sweeping views of the city (the women's baths are on the 2nd floor). There is internet access in the lobby, and there are LAN connections in all rooms.

Tōyoko Inn Hyōgomachi (☎ 821-1045; fax 821-1046; www.toyoko-inn.com; 3-1 Hyōgomachi; s/tw ¥6090/8190; P) About a five-minute walk from the station, this is a good business hotel with cosy rooms, complimentary breakfast, and free internet access in the lobby.

Dormy Inn Takamatsu (☎ 832-5489; fax 835-5657; www.hotespa.net/hotels/takamatsu, in Japanese; 1-10-10 Kawaramachi; s/d ¥6500/9000; P) Opened in summer 2008, this immaculate hotel has spacious and well-appointed rooms and an onsen and *rotemburo* on the top floor. A location within easy distance of the city's restaurants and bars makes this an ideal option. There are computers with internet access in the lobby, and there's LAN access in all rooms.

ANA Hotel Clement Takamatsu (☎ 811-1111; fax 811-1100; www.anaclement.com; 1-1 Hamano-chō; s/d ¥12,474/23,100; P) This eye-catching ultramodern hotel is one of the first buildings you see as you exit JR Takamatsu station. The rooms are spacious, and there's a good selection of bars and restaurants with sweeping views of the Inland Sea.

Eating

Restaurants and bars are clustered in the covered arcades and entertainment district to the west side of the tracks between Kotoden Kataharamachi and Kawaramachi stations.

SHIKOKU

SANUKI UDON

People in Takamatsu are serious about their udon (delicious, thick white noodles made from wheat), and no trip here would be complete without at least one bowl of the famous speciality, *Sanuki udon*. Why 'Sanuki'? It's the old name for the province that's now modern Kagawa-ken.

As with most things in this part of Japan, there is a Kōbō Daishi connection: according to tradition, the great saint was the first to bring the noodles to Japan when he returned from Tang China 1200 years ago. There are udon shops on just about every corner, and you don't have to stay here long before you start to recognise the characters for the words *te-uchi udon* (手打ちうどん), meaning 'handmade noodles'.

SHIKOKU

UDON RESTAURANTS

Goemon (☎ 821-2711; 13-15 Furubaba-chō; 6pm-3am, closed Sun) The Japanese-only menu at this no-nonsense spot in the heart of the entertainment district has a long list of udon dishes to choose from, including *tsukimi udon* (udon with raw egg on top; ¥600) and *asari udon* (udon with clams; ¥700). It's opposite a club called Heaven's Door (with an English sign) and there's an illuminated sign outside advertising 'te-uchi udon'.

Kanaizumi (☎ 822-0123; 9-3 Konyamachi; 9.30am-5pm) A popular self-service place by the Takamatsu art museum, where you choose between *shō* (small), *chū* (medium) or *dai* (large) helpings of *kake udon* (udon in broth) or *zaru udon* (cold udon, with a dipping sauce), and then help yourself to a wide variety of toppings. A medium serving of noodles with two toppings comes to less than ¥500.

Tsurumaru (☎ 821-3780; 9-34 Furubaba-chō; 8pm-3am, closed Sun) Sit at the counter and watch the noodles being pounded by hand in this popular spot, which is busy with the bar-hopping crowd until late into the night. The delicious *karē udon* (curry udon; ¥700) is the most popular choice here. Look for the curtain over the door with a picture of a crane on it.

OTHER

Bijin-tei (☎ 861-0275; 2-2-10 Kawara-machi; 5-10pm, closed Sun) An unpretentious *izakaya* with bags of local flavour, the Bijin-tei serves up excellent seafood, bought fresh every morning by the friendly owner. As a result, there's no menu to speak of – but most of the fish is within pointing range on top of the counter, and you can be sure that whatever you plump for will be beautifully prepared and fairly priced. It's on the ground floor of a building containing several snack bars and karaoke joints. Look for the sign with the shop's name on it in kanji: 美人亭.

Mikayla (☎ 811-5357; 8-40 Sunport; set courses from ¥4200; 11am-10pm) A romantic spot on the Sunport Takamatsu esplanade north of the station, this seaside restaurant-bar is the perfect place for a sundowner overlooking the Inland Sea. The food is mostly European-accented seafood, and an English menu is available.

Tokiwa Saryō (☎ 861-5577; 1-8-2 Tokiwa-chō; lunch & dinner) This former ryokan is an elegant spot for lunch or dinner, with tatami rooms set around a beautiful garden and pond. The Japanese-only menu has some pictures, and focuses on local seafood. *O-susume kōsu* (chef's courses) are in the ¥3500 to ¥4500 range, and there are several *Seto sashimi moriawase* (selections of seasonal sashimi from the Seto Inland Sea; ¥1800). Enter the Tokiwa arcade from Ferry Dōri and take the second left; it's the building on the right with the big white lantern.

Drinking

Anbar (☎ 822-1339; 1F Dai-ichi Bldg, 8-15 Furubaba-chō; 8pm-midnight, closed Thu) This mellow feline-themed bar has an impressive collection of whiskies. There's an English sign outside.

Cancun (☎ 821-1550; 6-23 Furubaba-chō; 6pm-3am, closed Sun) Every inch of space is crammed with knick-knacks and paraphernalia in this relaxed bar in the heart of the entertainment district. There's a wide range of drinks (most ¥700 to ¥800), and the friendly young bar-staff speak some English.

Getting There & Away

Takamatsu airport, 16km south of the city, is easily reached by bus (¥740, 35 minutes, hourly from the front of JR Takamatsu station). There are direct flights to/from Tokyo (¥29,600, 1¼ hours, 10 daily).

Thanks to the Seto-ōhashi bridge, completed in 1988, Takamatsu is the only city in Shikoku with regular rail links to Honshū. There are frequent trains to Okayama (¥1470,

55 minutes, every half-hour), where you can connect to *shinkansen* (bullet train) services that will whizz you to any of the major cities in just a few hours.

From Takamatsu, *tokkyū* trains on the JR Kōtoku line run southeast to Tokushima (¥2560, one hour and seven minutes, hourly); the JR Yosan line runs west to Matsuyama (¥5500, 2½ hours, hourly); and the JR Dosan line runs to Kōchi (¥4760, 2½ hours, hourly). The private Kotoden line also runs direct to Kotohira (¥610, one hour, frequent).

There are bus services to/from Tokyo (¥10,000, 9½ hours, one daily), Nagoya (¥6800, 5½ hours), Kyoto (¥4,800, three hours and 40 minutes) and most other major cities.

There are ferries with **Jumbo Ferry** (☎ 811-6688) between Takamatsu and Kōbe (¥1800, three hours and 40 minutes, five daily). Ferries depart from Takamatsu port, just east of the town centre, reached by a free shuttle bus that leaves from in front of the JR Takamatsu station 30 minutes before the ferry's scheduled departure time. Ferries to the Inland Sea islands of Naoshima, Shōdo-shima and Megi-jima leave from the Sunport terminal, close to the JR station.

Getting Around

The easiest way to navigate the city is by using local trains. The main Kotoden junction is Kotoden Kawaramachi, although the line ends at Kotoden Chikkō, near JR Takamatsu station.

Takamatsu is flat, and excellent for biking. The city offers a great deal on its 'blue bicycles' (¥200 per day; photo ID is required), which can be picked up at **Takamatsu-shi Rental Cycles** (☎ 821-0400; ⏰ 7am-10pm) in the underground bicycle park outside JR Takamatsu station. (There are several spots around town where you can pick up a bike, but this spot is the most convenient.)

AROUND TAKAMATSU

There are a number of interesting day trips from Takamatsu. In addition to those listed here, Takamatsu is also an excellent stepping-off point for the olive groves of Shōdo-shima (p472) and the wonderful art of Naoshima (p474) in the Inland Sea, both less than an hour by boat from the ferry port close to Takamatsu station.

Yashima 屋島

About 5km east of Takamatsu is the 292m-high tabletop plateau of Yashima, where you'll find **Yashima-ji** (屋島寺; ☎ 087-841-9418), number 84 of the 88 Temples. This was the site of a decisive battle between the Genji and Heike clans in the late 12th century, and the temple's **Treasure House** (admission ¥500; ⏰ 9am-5pm) exhibits artefacts relating to the battle. Just behind the Treasure House is the **Pond of Blood**, where victorious Genji warriors washed the blood from their swords.

At the bottom of Yashima, about 500m north of the station, is **Shikoku-mura** (四国村; ☎ 087-843-3111; 9-1 Shimanaka; admission ¥800; ⏰ 8.30am-6pm, to 5.30pm Nov-Mar), an excellent village museum that houses old buildings brought from all over Shikoku and neighbouring islands. The village's fine kabuki stage came from Shōdo-shima (p473), which is famous for its traditional farmers' kabuki performances. Other interesting structures include a border guardhouse from the Tokugawa era (a time when travel was tightly restricted), a vine bridge similar to those you can see in the Iya Valley, and several Meiji-era lighthouses. There is also an excellent restaurant serving *Sanuki udon* (what else?) in an old farmhouse building.

Yashima is six stops from Kawaramachi on the private Kotoden line (¥270). Shuttle buses run from the station to the top of the mountain (¥100) – departures are at half-past the hour from 9.30am to 4.30pm, and the last bus back down leaves at 5.20pm. The funicular railway up the mountain closed down in 2004.

Isamu Noguchi Garden Museum イサムノグチ庭園美術館

It's worth considering an excursion to the town of Murechō, east of Takamatsu, to witness the fascinating legacy of noted sculptor Isamu Noguchi (1904–88). Born in Los Angeles to a Japanese poet and an American writer, Noguchi set up a studio and residence here in 1970. Today the **complex** (☎ 087-870-1500; www.isamunoguchi.or.jp; 3-5-19 Murechō; tours ¥2100; ⏰ 1hr tours 10am, 1pm & 3pm Tue, Thu & Sat, by appointment) is filled with hundreds of Noguchi's works, and holds its own as an impressive art installation. Inspiring sculptures are on display in the beautifully restored Japanese buildings and in the surrounding landscape.

If you want to visit here, you have to get your act together early. Visitors should fax or email ahead for reservations, preferably two weeks or more in advance (see the website for reservations and access details).

Megi-jima 女木島

Just offshore from Yashima is the small island of Megi-jima (population 250), also known as Oni-ga-shima (Demon Island). It was here that Momotarō, the legendary Peach Boy (see boxed text, p452), met and conquered the mythical demons. You can tour the impressive **caves** (☎ 087-873-0728; admission ¥500; ⏲ 8.30am-5pm) where the demons are said to have hidden. Today the caves are inhabited by large multicoloured plastic demons pulling scary faces at each other. Five or six boats a day run to Megi-jima from Takamatsu (¥720 return, 20 minutes), departing from the docks on the northern edge of the city. A shuttle bus meets the boat and whisks you straight to the cave (¥600). You'll be on and off the island in not much more than an hour. There are some good views from the hillside by the caves, and if it's a nice day the ferry ride is quite pleasant, too – but this is not an island for which it's worth going far out of your way.

Kyūshū 九州

Kyūshū has long been internationally aware. It was from here that young intellectuals of the Meiji Restoration carried a resistant Japan towards modernity, closing a long chapter of feudal history and ending the way of the Samurai. Today, burgeoning Fukuoka is a multicultural, street-chic metropolis and significant Asian hub. To the west, picturesque Nagasaki, Japan's original gateway to the world beyond, offers a message of hope from a tragic story.

Kyūshū's geothermal core warms a fertile terrain. Rolling hills of lush grasses give way to rugged peaks and the craters of several active volcanoes. Hiking and photographic opportunities abound in Kyūshū's four national parks. If the otherworldly landscape of the Aso caldera doesn't tempt, smouldering Sakurajima, looming over Kagoshima, probably will – frequently showering the city with the kind of fine ash put to good use in the pottery towns of Karatsu and Arita.

Coastal Beppu is Japan's hot-spring mecca, but Yufuin, Kurokawa Onsen and Unzen also promise tranquil forests and a chance to soak. The southern cities of Kagoshima and Miyazaki have a vibe of their own, with glimpses of alternative lifestyles in otherwise structured Japan.

Sadly, Kyūshū's smaller cities are depopulating rapidly. Young people are drawn to the bright lights of Fukuoka, Osaka and Tokyo, and the risk of losing traditional ways of living in this ancient region is increasing. Some foresight, however, has led to the establishment of galleries and museums in most large towns, sharing centuries of culture and storytelling.

Nationally, Kyūshū is known for its warm climate, friendly people and the quality of the local brew, *shō-chū*.

HIGHLIGHTS

- Join the night owls for beer and *yakitori* at a **Fukuoka** (p693) *yatai* (hawker-style food stall)
- Let the volcanic antics of **Sakurajima** (p738) put life in perspective
- Soak in a **Beppu** (p752) hillside onsen *au naturale*
- Hike among rare azaleas and stunning vistas in the **Kirishima-Yaku National Park** (p727)
- Allow **Nagasaki** (p702) to touch your heart and open your mind
- Recharge your batteries in tranquil **Unzen** (p714)
- Get buried in warm volcanic sand in **Ibusuki** (p740)
- Chill out in **Aoshima** (p745) and the Nichinan coast
- Drink distilled sweet-potato *shō-chū* in **Kagoshima** (p737)

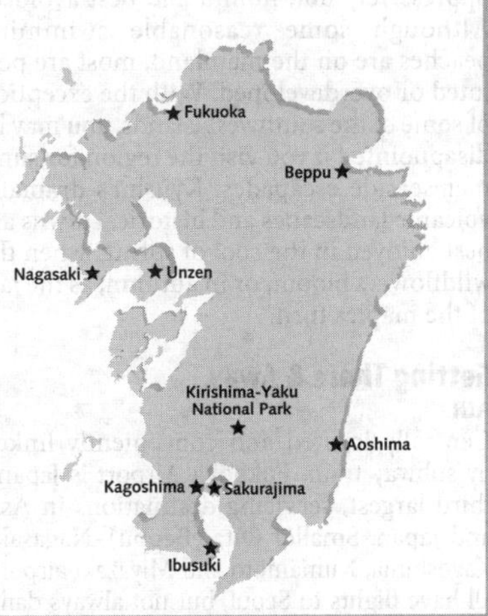

History

Excavations near Kagoshima dating to around 10,000 BC indicate southern Kyūshū was the likely entry point of the Jōmon culture, which gradually crept north.

Japan's centuries-old trade with China and Korea began in Kyūshū. The arrival of Portuguese ships in 1543 initiated Japan's at-times thorny relationship with the West and heralded the beginning of its 'Christian Century' (1549–1650). Over the next few hundred years, Kyūshū had a significant role in the changing face of the nation. With Christianity, the Portuguese also brought gunpowder weaponry, heralding the ultimate decline of the samurai tradition.

In 1868 the Meiji Restoration ended the military shōgunate's policy of isolation, marking the birth of modern Japan. During the ensuing Meiji Era (1868–1912), rapid industrialisation caused profound social and political change.

Sadly, this historically rich region is best known for one day in history – 9 August 1945, the day Nagasaki became the last city to be decimated by an act of atomic warfare.

Climate

Kyūshū is the largest southernmost of Japan's four main islands and enjoys a warm, subtropical climate, yet winter in the mountains frequently registers subzero temperatures and heavy snowfalls. During the rainy season the island is inundated with heavy rainfall, and the months of July and August are oppressively hot, humid and best avoided! Although some reasonable swimming beaches are on the mainland, most are polluted or overdeveloped. With the exception of some of the southwest islands, you may be disappointed if you visit the region for summer seaside escapades. Kyūshū's dramatic volcanic landscapes and historical towns are best enjoyed in the cool of spring, when the wildflowers bloom, or in autumn, as the last of the maples turn.

Getting There & Away

AIR

Centrally located and conveniently linked by subway train, Fukuoka Airport is Japan's third largest, servicing destinations in Asia and Japan. Smaller Ōita (Beppu), Nagasaki, Kagoshima, Kumamoto and Miyazaki airports all have flights to Seoul, but not always daily. It's possible to fly into Hong Kong (from Kagoshima), Shanghai (from Kagoshima, Nagasaki and Kitakyūshū) and Guangzhou (from Kitakyūshū). All of Kyūshū's airports have limited domestic connections. There are also flights to islands off the coast of Kyūshū and to the southwest islands from Fukuoka (to Amakusa, Gotō-Fukue, Naha, Tsushima), Nagasaki (to Iki, Naha), Kumamoto (to Amakusa) and Kagoshima (to Amamioshima, Kikaijima, Naha, Tanegashima, Yakushima, Kikaijima and Tokunoshima).

BOAT

There are sea connections to Kyūshū from Honshū (Tokyo, Osaka, Kobe), Shikoku (Tokushima), Hokkaido (Muroran via Naoetsu) and Okinawa. Local ferry services operate between Kyūshū and islands off the northwest and southern coasts. A high speed ferry service shuttles between Fukuoka and Busan, in South Korea.

TRAIN

The *shinkansen* (bullet train) line from Tokyo and Osaka crosses to Kyūshū from Shimonoseki and ends at Hakata Station (Fukuoka).

Getting Around

Major cities in Kyūshū are connected by *tokkyū* (limited express) train services, and an extensive highway bus system. The Kyūshū *shinkansen* line between Hakata and Kagoshima is partly operational, scheduled for completion in 2011. If you can afford it, a combination of rail travel and car rental is your best option. It's easy to drive here, and the satellite navigation systems in most rental cars, although in Japanese, don't take long to get used to. Without a car, you'll miss out on many of the best-preserved and least-known of the island's diverse and most impressive landscapes.

FUKUOKA-KEN 福岡県

The northern prefecture of Fukuoka is the arrival point for most visitors to Kyūshū. The bland industrial city of Kitakyūshū (population 990,585) is northernmost, but most travellers head straight to Fukuoka.

FUKUOKA 福岡・(HAKATA 博多)

☎092 / pop 1,414,420

Fukuoka is the largest city in Kyūshū and growing fast. Once two separate towns, the lordly Fukuoka castle town on the west bank of the Naka-gawa, and the common folk's Hakata on the east, the two merged in 1889. The name Fukuoka was applied to both towns, but subsequent development has mainly been in Hakata and many residents still refer to the town that way. The airport is known as Fukuoka, the train station as Hakata.

After dark, this youthful, user-friendly metropolis reveals a cosmopolitan charm, peppered with the flavours of its east-Asian neighbours; Seoul and Shanghai are among the nearest. Its attractions are contemporary – art, architecture, shopping and cuisine are the prime drawcards.

In Japan, the city is famed for its 'Hakata *bijin*' (beautiful women), its much-loved baseball team and hearty Hakata *rāmen* (noodles).

Orientation

JR Hakata Station is surrounded by hotels, with the better selection on the Chikushi-*guchi* (gate) side. Three subway stops away, Fukuoka's beating heart is the Tenjin district, where the boutiques, eateries and some good accommodation are found. Above ground, Tenjin follows Watanabe-dōri. Underground, the microcosm of Tenjin Chikagai, a sprawling shopping thoroughfare, runs parallel. Dim lighting and cast-ironwork ceilings set this apart from similar urban projects and it's a cool refuge from the summer heat. Tenjin subway station, the Nishitetsu Tenjin bus centre and Nishitetsu Fukuoka Station, terminus of the private Nishitetsu Ōmuta line, are here.

West of Tenjin is trendy Daimyo, Fukuoka's homage to Tokyo's Omote-sandō (p154), minus the crowds. It's easy to wander here and easier still to spend.

Crossed by a number of bridges, the smelly Naka-gawa and the now-indiscernible island of Nakasu – a mish-mash of strip clubs, hostess bars and *yatai* (food stalls) – separate Tenjin to the west, from Hakata to the east.

MAPS

Fukuoka International Association's **Rainbow Plaza** (☎733-2220; www.rainbowfia.or.jp; 8F, IMS Bldg, 1-7-11 Tenjin, Tenjin; 🕑10am-8pm) has a variety of maps. The tourist information desk at JR Hakata Station has a bilingual walking map of Fukuoka (¥30).

Information

BOOKSHOPS

Junkudō Fukuoka (☎738-3322; 1st-4th fl, Media Mall, Tenjin; 🕑10am-8.30pm) Sells foreign paperbacks.

Kinokuniya (☎434-3100; 6th fl, Fukuoka Kōtsū Centre Bldg, Hakata-eki; 🕑10am-9pm) Has a huge selection of Japanese- and English-language books, magazines and DVDs.

Maruzen (☎731-9000; 2nd-3rd fl, Fukuoka Bldg, Tenjin; 🕑9.30am-10pm) Stocks foreign-language and language-learning books.

INTERNET ACCESS

Fukuoka is wired. Wi-fi hot spots are dotted around town. Most large cybercafés have reclining chairs, snack bars and some have showers. It's not uncommon to crash for the night if you need to.

Cybac Café (☎739-1500; www.cybac.com, in Japanese; 2nd fl, Kawamura Bldg, 3-2-22 Tenjin; registration fee ¥300, per 1st 30min/subsequent 15min ¥300/100; 🕑24hr) A 12-hour unlimited-access pack is ¥1980, available all day, every day.

FedEx Kinko's Akasaka (☎724-7177; 1st fl, Akasaka Sangyo Bldg, 2-12-12 Daimyo; 🕑24hr); Chikushi-guchi (☎414-3399; 2-5-28 Hakata-eki higashi; 🕑24hr); Hakata-ekimae (☎473-2677; 2-19-24 Hakata-ekimae; 🕑8am-10pm) Offers 10-minute access for ¥210.

Media Café Popeye (www.media-cafe.net, in Japanese) Hakata-ekimae (☎432-8788; 8th fl, Fukuoka Kōtsū Centre Bldg; 🕑24hr); Nakasu (☎283-9393; 8th fl, Spoon Bldg, 5-1-7 Nakasu; 🕑24hr); Tenjin (☎737-7744; 2nd fl, Nishitetsu Imaizumi Bldg, 1-12-23 Imaizumi; 🕑24hr) Each has a free soft-drink bar, massage chairs and couples' booths. Offers ¥230 for the first 30 minutes, ¥60 per subsequent 10 minutes.

MEDIA

Broadcasting from Tenjin, Love 76.1FM offers programming in 10 languages. Cross 78.7FM and Free Wave 77.7FM have bilingual DJs and entertainment news.

Fukuoka Now (www.fukuoka-now.com) An indispensable monthly English-language street mag with detailed city maps. It should be the first thing you source to find out what's on.

MEDICAL SERVICES

International Clinic Tojin-machi (☎717-1000; http://internationalclinic.org; 1-4-6 Jigyo, Chūō-ku;

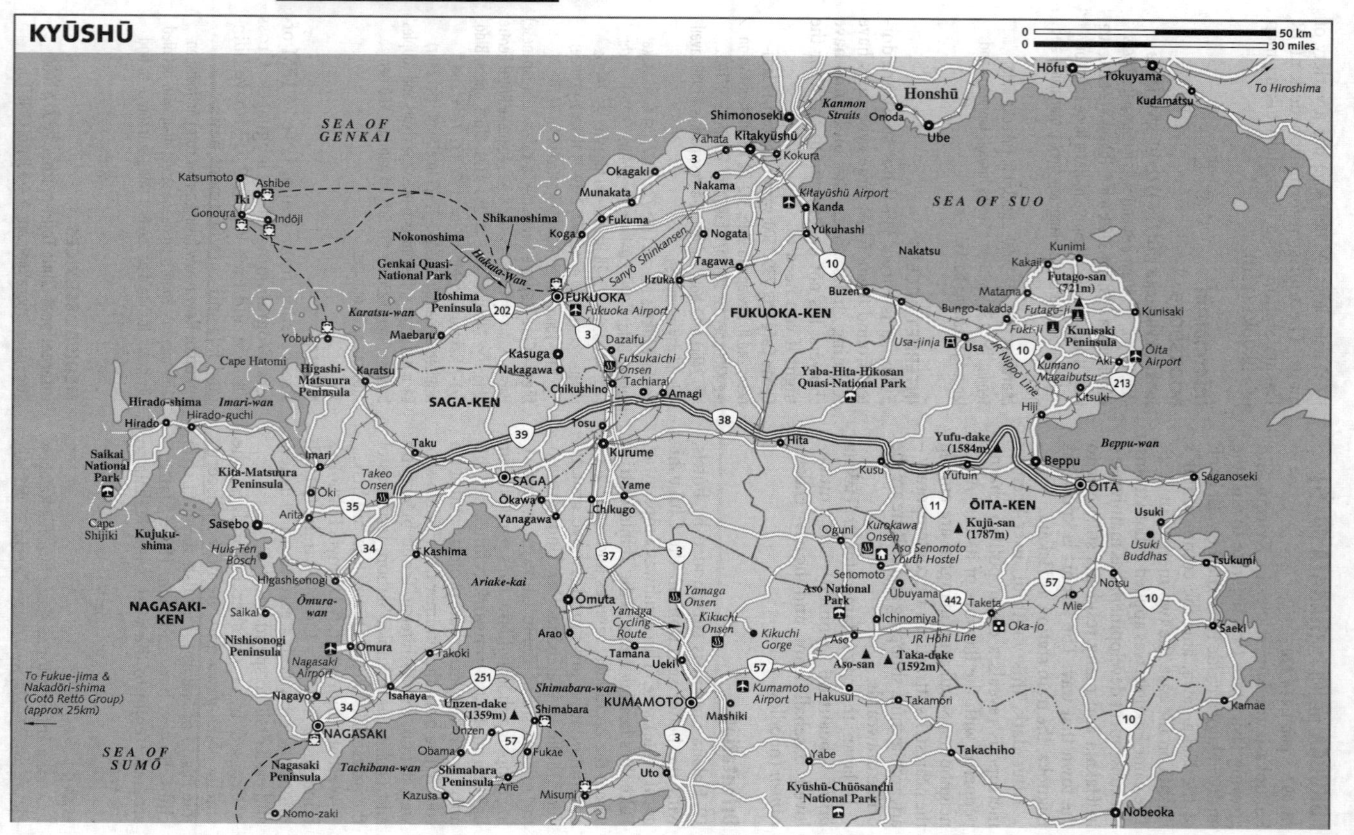
KYŪSHŪ
0 50 km
0 30 miles
To Hiroshima
Honshū
Hōfu
Tokuyama
Kudamatsu
Ube
Onoda
Kanmon Straits
Shimonoseki
SEA OF SUO
SEA OF GENKAI
Kitayūshū Airport
Kanda
Kokura
Kitakyūshū
Yahata
Nakama
Nogata
Yukuhashi
Tagawa
Iizuka
Okagaki
Munakata
Fukuma
Koga
Sanyō Shinkansen
Shikanoshima
Nokonoshima
Hakata-Wan
Genkai Quasi-National Park
FUKUOKA
Fukuoka Airport
Dazaifu
Futsukaichi Onsen
Chikushino
Tachiarai
Amagi
Kasuga
Nakagawa
Itoshima Peninsula
Maebaru
Karatsu-wan
Karatsu
Higashi-Matsuura Peninsula
Yobuko
Cape Hatomi
Imari-wan
Imari
Katsumoto
Ashibe
Iki
Gonoura
Indōji
Hirado-shima
Hirado-guchi
Hirado
Saikai National Park
Cape Shijiki
Kujuku-shima
Kita-Matsuura Peninsula
Sasebo
Huis Ten Bosch
Arita
Ōki
Takeo Onsen
Higashisonogi
Ōmura-wan
Ōmura
Nagasaki Airport
Saikai
Nishisonogi Peninsula
NAGASAKI-KEN
To Fukue-jima & Nakadōri-shima (Gotō Rettō Group) (approx 25km)
Nagayo
NAGASAKI
SEA OF SUMŌ
Nagasaki Peninsula
Nomo-zaki
Tachibana-wan
Isahaya
Takaki
Unzen-dake (1359m)
Unzen
Obama
Shimabara Peninsula
Kazusa
Arie
Fukae
Shimabara
Shimabara-wan
Misumi
Ariake-kai
Kashima
Taku
SAGA-KEN
SAGA
Ōkawa
Yanagawa
Tosu
Kurume
Chikugo
Yame
Ōmuta
Arao
Tamana
Yamaga Cycling Route
Ueki
Yamaga Onsen
Kikuchi Onsen
Kikuchi Gorge
KUMAMOTO
Kumamoto Airport
Mashiki
Uto
FUKUOKA-KEN
Buzen
Nakatsu
Yaba-Hita-Hikosan Quasi-National Park
Usa-jinja
Usa
Bungo-takada
Matama
Kakaji
Kunimi
Futago-san (721m)
Futago-ji
Fuki-ji
Kunisaki Peninsula
Kunisaki
Kumano Magaibutsu
Aki
Ōita Airport
Kitsuki
Hiji
JR Nippō Line
Beppu-wan
Beppu
ŌITA
Saganoseki
Yufu-dake (1584m)
Yufuin
Hita
Kusu
ŌITA-KEN
Kujū-san (1787m)
Oguni
Kurokawa Onsen
Aso Senomoto Youth Hostel
Senomoto
Aso National Park
Ubuyama
Ichinomiya
Aso
Aso-san
Taka-dake (1592m)
JR Hōhi Line
Hakusui
Takamori
Taketa
Oka-jo
Mie
Notsu
Usuki
Usuki Buddhas
Tsukumi
Saeki
Kamae
Nobeoka
Takachiho
Yabe
Kyūshū-Chūōsanchi National Park
3
10
38
39
202
35
34
37
57
251
11
442
213

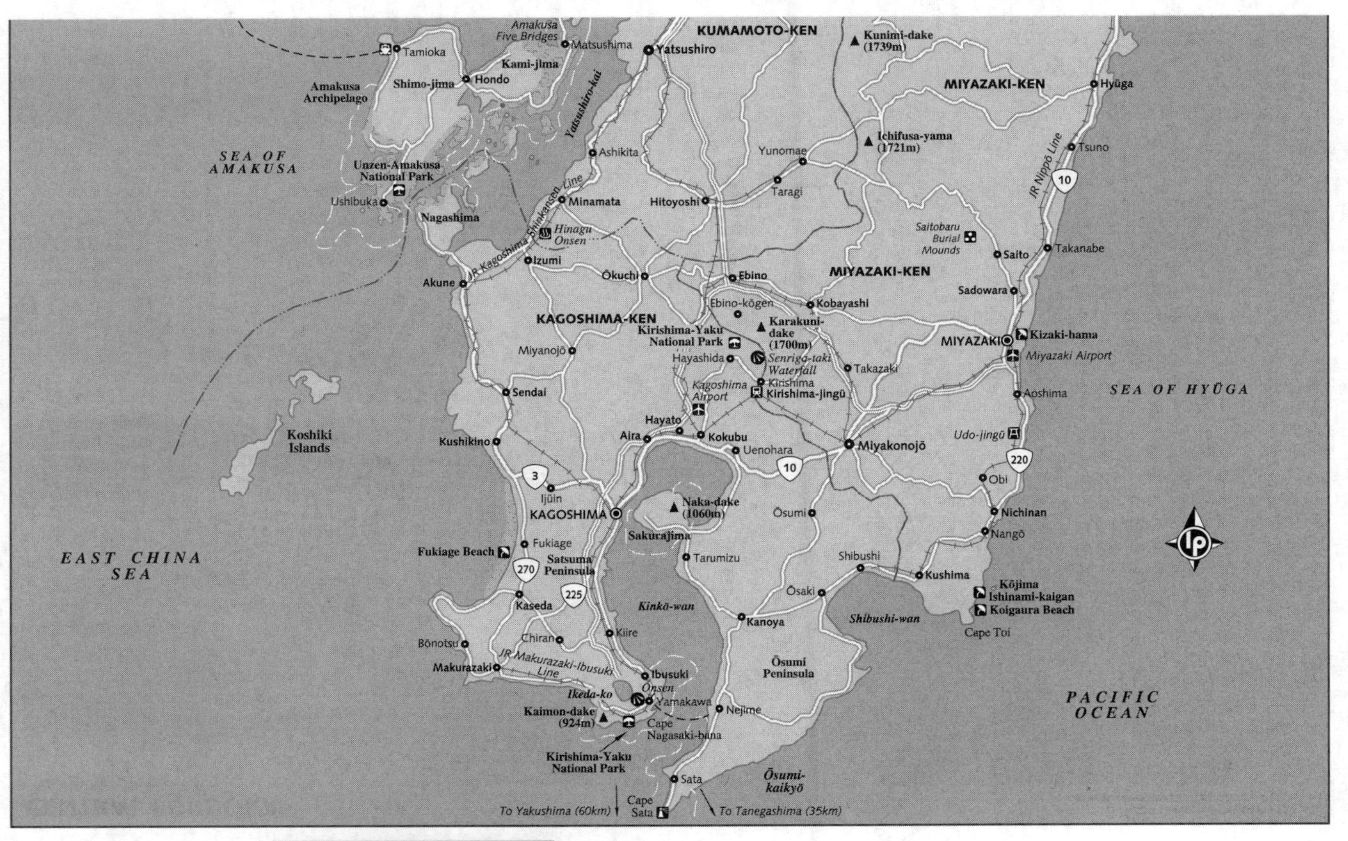
KUMAMOTO-KEN
MIYAZAKI-KEN
MIYAZAKI-KEN
KAGOSHIMA-KEN
SEA OF AMAKUSA
EAST CHINA SEA
SEA OF HYŪGA
PACIFIC OCEAN
Amakusa Five Bridges
Matsushima
Yatsushiro
Kunimi-dake (1739m)
Tamioka
Kami-jima
Shimo-jima
Hondo
Amakusa Archipelago
Yatsushiro-kai
Hyūga
Ichifusa-yama (1721m)
Tsuno
Ashikita
Yunomae
JR Nippō Line
10
Unzen-Amakusa National Park
Taragi
Ushibuka
Minamata
Hitoyoshi
JR Kagoshima Shinkansen Line
Nagashima
Hinagu Onsen
Saitobaru Burial Mounds
Saito
Takanabe
Izumi
Ōkuchi
Ebino
Akune
Sadowara
Ebino-kōgen
Kobayashi
Karakuni-dake (1700m)
Kirishima-Yaku National Park
Kizaki-hama
MIYAZAKI
Miyazaki Airport
Miyanojō
Hayashida
Senriga-taki Waterfall
Takazaki
Kagoshima Airport
Kirishima
Kirishima-jingū
Sendai
Aoshima
Koshiki Islands
Hayato
Aira
Kokubu
Udo-jingū
Kushikino
Uenohara
Miyakonojō
10
220
3
Obi
Ijūin
Naka-dake (1060m)
KAGOSHIMA
Ōsumi
Nichinan
Nangō
Sakurajima
Fukiage
Fukiage Beach
Tarumizu
Satsuma Peninsula
270
Shibushi
Kushima
Kōjima
Ishinami-kaigan
Koigaura Beach
225
Ōsaki
Kaseda
Kinkō-wan
Kanoya
Shibushi-wan
Cape Toi
Kiire
Chiran
Bōnotsu
Makurazaki
JR Makurazaki-Ibusuki Line
Ibusuki
Ōsumi Peninsula
Ikeda-ko
Onsen
Yamakawa
Nejime
Kaimon-dake (924m)
Cape Nagasaki-bana
Kirishima-Yaku National Park
Sata
Ōsumi-kaikyō
Cape Sata
To Yakushima (60km)
To Tanegashima (35km)

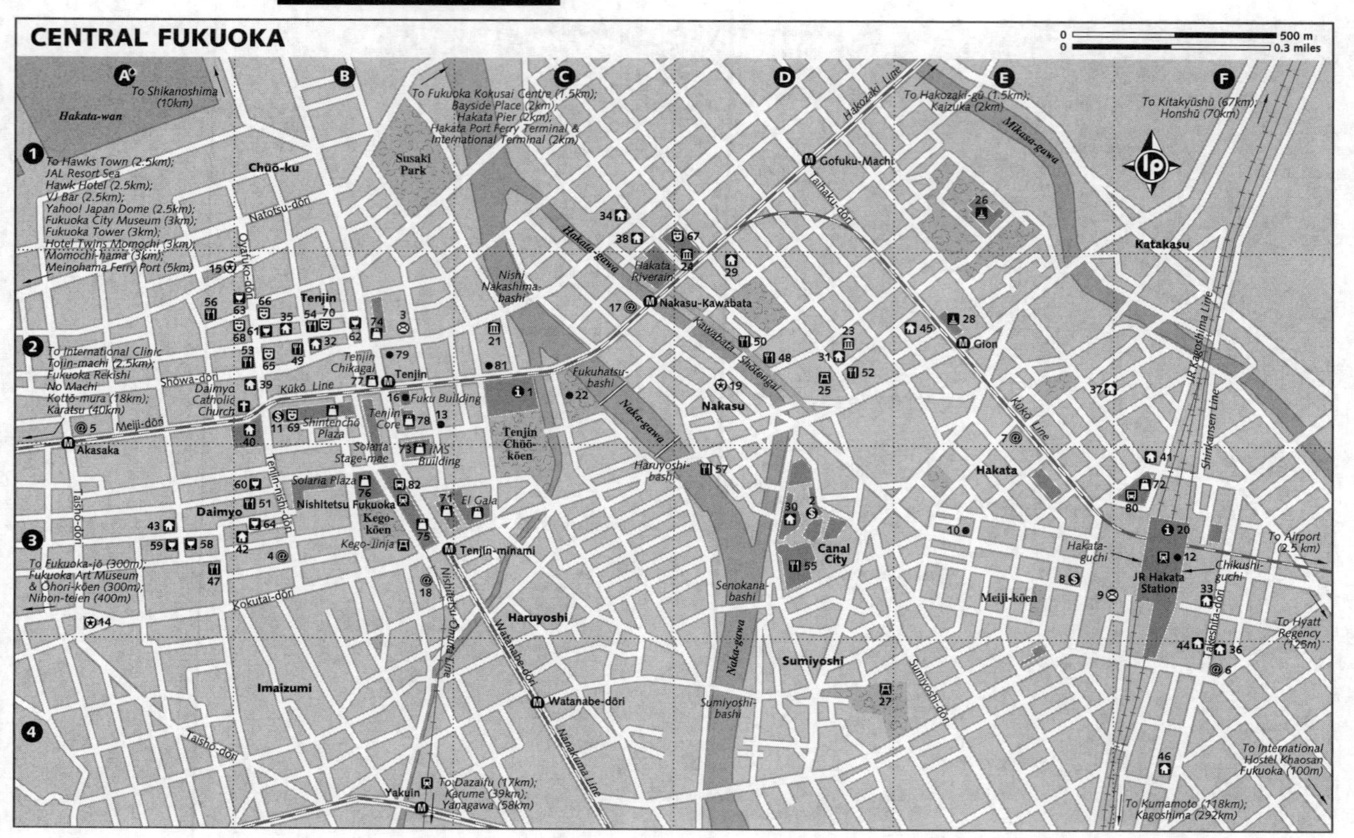
CENTRAL FUKUOKA
500 m
0.3 miles
To Shikanoshima (10km)
Hakata-wan
To Hawks Town (2.5km); JAL Resort Sea Hawk Hotel (2.5km); VJ Bar (2.5km); Yahoo! Japan Dome (2.5km); Fukuoka City Museum (3km); Fukuoka Tower (3km); Hotel Twins Momochi (3km); Momochi-hama (3km); Meinohama Ferry Port (5km)
To Fukuoka Kokusai Centre (1.5km); Bayside Place (2km); Hakata Pier (2km); Hakata Port Ferry Terminal & International Terminal (2km)
To Hakozaki-gū (1.5km); Kaizuka (2km)
To Kitakyūshū (67km); Honshū (70km)
To International Clinic Tojin-machi (2.5km); Fukuoka Rekishi No Machi
Kottō-mura (18km); Karatsu (40km)
To Fukuoka-jō (300m); Fukuoka Art Museum & Ōhori-kōen (300m); Nihon-teien (400m)
To Dazaifu (17km); Karume (39km); Yanagawa (58km)
To Airport (2.5 km)
To Hyatt Regency (125m)
To International Hostel Khaosan Fukuoka (100m)
To Kumamoto (118km); Kagoshima (292km)
Chūō-ku
Susaki Park
Tenjin
Tenjin Chikagai
Daimyo Catholic Church
Shintenchō Plaza
Solaria Stage-mae
Solaria Plaza
Tenjin Core
Fuku Building
IMS Building
El Gala
Nishitetsu Fukuoka
Kego-kōen
Kego-Jinja
Tenjin-minami
Tenjin Chūō-kōen
Akasaka
Daimyo
Haruyoshi
Imaizumi
Yakuin
Watanabe-dōri
Nishi Nakashima-bashi
Fukuhatsu-bashi
Haruyoshi-bashi
Senokana-bashi
Sumiyoshi-bashi
Hakata-gawa
Naka-gawa
Mikasa-gawa
Hakata Riverain
Nakasu-Kawabata
Kawabata Shōtengai
Nakasu
Canal City
Sumiyoshi
Gofuku-Machi
Gion
Hakata
Katakasu
Meiji-kōen
Hakata-guchi
Chikushi-guchi
JR Hakata Station
Natotsu-dōri
Oyafuko-dōri
Shōwa-dōri
Kūkō Line
Meiji-dōri
Taishō-dōri
Tenjin-nishi-dōri
Kokutai-dōri
Nishitetsu-Ōmuta Line
Nanakuma Line
Hakozaki Line
Taihaku-dōri
Sumiyoshi-dōri
Takeshita-dōri
JR Kagoshima Line
Shinkansen Line

INFORMATION

ACROS Fukuoka アクロス福岡 1 C2
ATM 2 D3
Central Post Office 福岡中央郵便局 3 B2
Citibank 24-hour ATM シティバンク ATM (see 11)
Cybac Café サイバックカフェ 4 B3
FedEx Kinko's Akasaka キンコーズ赤坂店 5 A2
FedEx Kinko's Chikushi-guchi キンコーズ筑紫口店 6 F4
FedEx Kinko's Hakata-ekimae キンコーズ博多駅前店 7 E2
Fukuoka Ginkō 福岡銀行 8 E3
Hakata Post Office 博多郵便局 9 E3
HIS Travel 10 E3
International & Postal ATMs 郵便局ATM 11 B2
Joy Road ジョイロード 12 F3
Junkudō Fukuoka ジュンク堂書店 13 B2
Kego Police Box 警固派出所 14 A3
Kinokuniya 紀伊國屋 (see 72)
Maizuru Police Box 舞鶴交番 15 A2
Maruzen 丸善 16 B2
Media Café Popeye Hakata-ekimae メディアカフェポパイ博多 (see 72)
Media Café Popeye Nakasu メディアカフェポパイ中州店 17 C2
Media Café Popeye Tenjin メディアカフェポパイ天神店 18 B3
Nakasu Police Box 中洲交番 19 D2
No 1 Travel ナンバーワントラベル (see 1)
Rainbow Plaza レインボープラザ (see 73)
Tourist Information Desk 観光案内所 20 F3

SIGHTS & ACTIVITIES

Akarenga Cultural Centre 赤煉瓦文化館 21 C2
Former Prefectural Hall & Official Guest House 元福岡県庁グストハウス 22 C2
Fukuoka Asian Art Museum 福岡アジア美術館 (see 24)
Hakata Machiya Furusato-kan 博多町家ふるさと館 23 D2
Hakata Riverain 博多リバレイン 24 D2
Kushida-jinja 櫛田神社 25 D2
Rakusuien 楽水園 (see 27)
Shōfuku-ji 聖福寺 26 E1
Sumiyoshi-jinja 住吉神社 27 D4
Tōchō-ji 東長寺 28 E2

SLEEPING

Amenity Hotel in Hakata アメニティホテルイン博多 29 D2
Grand Hyatt Fukuoka グランドハイアット福岡 30 D3
Hakata JBB 博多ＪＢＢホテル 31 D2
Hotel Ascent ホテルアセント福岡 32 B2
Hotel Century Art ホテルセンチューリーアート 33 F3
Hotel Éclair ホテルエクレール博多 34 C1
Hotel Etwas Tenjin ホテルエトワス天神 35 B2
Hotel Leopalace Hakata ホテルレオパレス博多 36 F4
Hotel New Simple ホテルニューシンプル 37 E2
Hotel Okura ホテルオークラ 38 C1
La Soeur Hotel Monterey ホテルモントレラスール福岡 39 B2
Nishitetsu Grand Hotel 西鉄グランドホテル 40 B2
Nishitetsu Inn Hakata 西鉄イン博多 41 F3
Plaza Hotel Premier プラザホテルプレミエ 42 B3
Plaza Hotel Tenjin プラザホテル天神 43 A3
Richmond Hotel Hakata Station リッチモンドホテル博多駅前 44 F4
Ryokan Kashima Honkan 旅館鹿島本館 45 E2
With the Style ウィズザスタイル福岡 46 F4

EATING

Alohana アロハナ 47 A3
CHINA チャイナ (see 30)
Curry Honpo 伽哩本舗 48 D2
Hakata Ramen Shibaraku 博多ラーメンしばらく 49 B2
Hakata-ya 博多屋 50 D2
Jet Diner ジェットダイナー 51 B3
Murata 信州そばむらた 52 D2
Nanak's Indian ナーナック福岡店 53 B2
No No Budo 野の葡萄 (see 73)
Pik's Coffee Shop ピックズコーヒーショップ 54 B2
Rāmen Stadium ラーメンスタジアム。 55 D3
Yamasaki 山崎 56 A2
Yatai food stalls 屋台 57 D3

DRINKING

Ashok's Bar 2 (see 65)
Bar Garasu バーガラス 58 A3
Bar Oscar バーオスカー 59 A3
British Pub Morris 60 B3
Craic & Porter Beer Bar 61 B2
International Bar インターナショナルバー 62 B2
Off Broadway オフブロードウエー 63 B2
Small Spaces 64 B3

ENTERTAINMENT

Dark Room ダークルーム 65 B2
FUBAR 66 B2
Hakata-za 博多座 67 D1
Juke Joint ジュークジョイント 68 B2
Sam & Dave サム&ディブ 69 B2
Voodoo Lounge ブ-ドゥーラウンジ 70 B2

SHOPPING

Daimaru 大丸 71 B3
Daisou ダイソウ 72 F3
IMS Building 天神イムズビル 73 B3
mina tenjin 74 B2
Mitsukoshi 三越 75 B3
Solaria Plaza ソラリアプラザ 76 B3
Tenjin Chikagai 天神地下街 77 B2
Tenjin Core 天神コア 78 B2

TRANSPORT

ANA 全日空 79 B2
Fukuoka Kōtsū Centre 福岡交通センター 80 F3
JAL 日本航空 81 C2
Nishitetsu Tenjin Bus Terminal 西鉄天神バスターミナル 82 B3

(Kūkō line 3 stops from Tenjin to Tōjin-machi, exit 1) Contact this fluent multilingual clinic for general medical services and emergencies. From the station walk up the stairs and continue in the same direction for two blocks.

MONEY

Post office and Seven Bank ATMs (found in 7-Eleven-branded convenience stores) are the easiest way to withdraw cash, in English, from foreign cards bearing the Visa, MasterCard, Plus, Maestro or Cirrus symbols.

At Fukuoka airport, a number of banks and ATMs offer currency exchange. There's a 24-hour Citibank ATM in Tenjin. Most banks around JR Hakata Station and Tenjin handle foreign-exchange services.

POST

The central post office is one block north-east of Tenjin subway station and Hakata post office is just outside JR Hakata Station's Hakata-guchi.

TOURIST INFORMATION

ACROS Fukuoka (☎ 725-9100; www.acros.or.jp/r_facilities/information.html, in Japanese; Cultural Information Centre, 2nd fl, ACROS Bldg, 1-1-1 Tenjin; 10am-6pm, closed 29 Dec–3 Jan) Has plenty of English-language information on the prefecture. If you're into architecture, the building itself is worth a look.

Information desks (International terminal ☎ 621-0303, domestic terminal ☎ 621-6059; 8am-9.30pm or last flight) These desks on the ground floor at Fukuoka airport handle hotel reservations and car rentals.

Rainbow Plaza (☎ 733-2220; www.rainbowfia.or.jp; 8F, IMS Bldg, 1-7-11 Tenjin; 10am-8pm) The Fukuoka International Association's Rainbow Plaza has bilingual staff, free internet and a plenty of foreign-language resources.

Tourist information desk (JR Hakata Station; 8am-8pm) Has everything you need. Ask for the free *Fukuoka Welcome Card Guide Book* containing maps and discounts at participating hotels, attractions, shops and restaurants.

TRAVEL AGENCIES

HIS Travel (☎ 415-6121; 1st fl, FK Bldg, 2-6-10 Hakata-ekimae; 10am-6.30pm Mon-Fri, 11am-4.30pm Sat) Discount international and domestic arrangements can be made by the Hakata branch of this international chain.

Joy Road (☎ 431-6215; 1-1 Chuo-gai, Hakata-eki; 10am-8pm Mon-Fri, to 6pm weekends) Provides travel booking and advice for within Kyūshū and Japan. Located within JR Hakata Station.

No 1 Travel (☎ 761-9203; www.no1-travel.com/fuk/index.html; 3rd fl, ACROS Fukuoka Bldg, 1-1-1 Tenjin; 10am-6.30pm Mon-Fri, 11am-4.30pm Sat) For discount international airfares and reliable information in English.

Rakubus (www.rakubus.jp/english) An excellent website handling highway bus reservations.

Sights & Activities

CANAL CITY キャナルシティ

Adjacent to Nakasu, once-futuristic **Canal City** (☎ 282-2525; www.canalcity.co.jp/world/english/urban.html; 1-2 Sumiyoshi) is already showing its age, Overlooking an artificial canal with an illuminated fountain symphony are the Grand Hyatt hotel, a multiplex cinema, playhouse, and a few hundred boutiques, bars and bistros. It's about a 15-minute walk from JR Hakata Station, the Gion or Nakasu-Kawabata subway stations, or you can take one of the '¥100 city loop' buses to Canal City-mae.

TENJIN 天神

Tenjin has all the big names and thousands of smaller boutiques and eateries. Catch the subway from Hakata Station, emerge into Tenjin-Chikagai, find a point of reference, then wander. It's a safe, easy, fun place to explore and not as intimidating in scale as similar areas of Tokyo or Osaka.

Tenjin also has some attractive historic Western architecture. The French Renaissance-styled **Former Prefectural Hall & Official Guest House** (☎ 751-4416; 6-29 Nishi-nakasu; admission ¥240; 9am-5pm, closed Mon & 29 Dec–3 Jan) in Tenjin Chūō-kōen was built in 1910. The copper-turreted **Akarenga Cultural Centre** (Akarenga Bunka-kan; ☎ 722-4666; Tenjin; admission free; 9am-9pm, closed Mon & 28 Dec–3 Jan) was built in 1909 by the same architect who designed Tokyo Station. It has some simple historical exhibits and a nice coffee shop.

HAKATA RIVERAIN 博多リバレイン

This stylish **shopping & cultural complex** (☎ 282-1300; www.riverain.co.jp/english.html; Hakata Riverain, 3-1 Shimokawabata-machi), above the Nakasu-Kawabata subway station, houses over 70 boutiques and restaurants, an atrium garden, the Hotel Okura, a museum and a theatre.

On the upper floors, the **Fukuoka Asian Art Museum** (☎ 263-1100; http://faam.city.fukuoka.lg.jp/eng/home.html; 7th & 8th fl, Riverain Centre Bldg, 3-1 Shimokawabata-machi; admission ¥200, special exhibitions vary; 10am-8pm, closed Wed) houses the permanent, world-renowned Asia Gallery and additional galleries for special exhibits and artists-in-residence.

The **Hakata-za Theatre** (☎ 263-5858; www.hakataza.co.jp, in Japanese; Riverain Centre Bldg, 3-1 Shimokawabata-machi) is one of Japan's finest kabuki (stylised Japanese theatre) stages, but also holds concerts and Japanese versions of Broadway musicals. See p695.

HAKATA MACHIYA FURUSATO-KAN 博多町家ふるさと館

This small **folk museum** (☎ 281-7761; www.hakatamachiya.com, in Japanese; 6-10 Reisen-machi; admission ¥200; 10am-5.30pm, closed 29-31 Dec) opposite Kushida Shrine re-creates a late-Meiji-era Hakata village. The replica buildings house historical photos and displays of traditional Hakata culture, including recordings of impenetrable Hakata-ben (dialect).

FUKUOKA REKISHI NO MACHI KOTTŌ-MURA 福岡歴史の町骨董村

This rustic **historical village & antiques cooperative** (☎ 806-0505; 439-120 Tokunaga, Nishi-ku; admission free; 10am-6pm, closed Mon; JR Chikuhi line from Tenjin to Kyūdai-gakkentoshi) gathers over 30 working potters, weavers and paper-makers to exhibit and sell their wares. It's out of the way, but a nice diversion with bargains to be found. It's a 15-minute cab ride from Kyūdai-gakkentoshi Station.

SHRINES & TEMPLES

Tōchō-ji has the largest wooden Buddha in Japan and some impressively carved Kannon (goddess of mercy) statues.

Shōfuku-ji is a Zen temple founded in 1195 by Eisai, who introduced Zen and tea to Japan.

Kushida-jinja home of the Hakata Gion Yamakasa festival, has float displays and a local **history museum** (☎ 291-2951; 1-41 Kami-kawabata; admission ¥300; 10am-4.30pm).

Sumiyoshi-jinja (☎ 262-6665; 2-10-7 Sumiyoshi, Hakata) is said to be the original of the Sumiyoshi Taisha shrines in Japan. On its north side is **Rakusuien** (admission ¥100; 9am-4.30pm, closed Tue), a pretty garden and tea house built by a Meiji-era merchant. You can participate in an outdoor tea ceremony here.

FUKUOKA-JŌ & ŌHORI-KŌEN 福岡城・大濠公園

Only the walls of Fukuoka-jō remain in what is now Maizuru-kōen, but the castle's hilltop site provides good views of the city.

Ōhori-kōen, adjacent to the castle grounds, has a traditionally styled Japanese garden, **Nihon-teien** (☎ 741-8377; admission ¥240; 9am-4.45pm Sep-May, closed Mon, to 5.45pm, Jun-Aug, closed Mon).

Nearby, the **Fukuoka Art Museum** (☎ 714-6051; www.fukuoka-art-museum.jp/english; 1-6 Ōhori-kōen, Chūō-ku; admission ¥200; 9.30am-5pm Sep-May, closed Mon, 9.30am-7pm Tue-Sat, to 5pm Sun Jul & Aug) has ancient pottery and Buddhist guardians on one floor, works by Andy Warhol and Salvador Dalí upstairs, and an interior garden to help soften the transition.

MOMOCHI DISTRICT 百道浜

West of the city you'll find the 234m-tall **Fukuoka Tower** (☎ 823-0234; www.fukuokatower.co.jp/english/index.html; 2-3-26 Momochi-hama, Sawara-ku; admission ¥800; 9.30am-10pm Apr-Sep, to 9pm Oct-Mar). At 120m, the classy **Sky Lounge Refuge** (☎ 833-8255) cafe is a great place to soak in the views, especially from dusk.

The **Fukuoka City Museum** (☎ 845-5011; http://museum.city.fukuoka.jp/english/index_e.html; 3-1-1 Momochi-hama, Sawara-ku; admission ¥200; 9.30am-5pm, closed Mon) displays artefacts of local history and culture, the pride of the museum being an ancient golden snake seal with an inscription proving Japan's historic ties to China.

HAWKS TOWN ホークスタウン

This seaside **entertainment & shopping complex** (www.hawkstown.com/eng/index.html) is built on reclaimed land near Momochi-kōen. It's home to the luxury **JAL Resort Sea Hawk Hotel** and the giant **Yahoo! Japan Dome**. Hawks Town is less than 1km northwest of Tōjin-machi Station. Frequent direct buses go to Yahoo! Dome from Tenjin bus station (about 15 minutes).

OFFSHORE ISLANDS

Often overlooked, pretty **Nokonoshima** (能古島) has a swimming **beach** and **camping ground** at the northern end of the island and fields of wildflowers. Buses 300 and 301 depart frequently from Nishitetsu Tenjin bus centre (¥360, 20 minutes). Ferries depart from Meinohama Municipal Ferry Port, west of the city centre near Meinohama Station (¥220, 10 minutes).

Ferries to delightfully rural **Shikanoshima** (志賀島), where fresh seafood restaurants line the harbourside streets, depart hourly (¥650, 33 minutes) from Bayside Place, along with seasonal sightseeing cruises around Hakata Bay. Shikanoshima also has a **fishing shrine** (志賀海神社; ☎ 603-6501) decorated with deer antlers and a popular **beach** about 5km east of the shrine.

Festivals & Events

Hakozaki-gū Tamatorisai (Tamaseseri) (箱崎宮玉取祭(玉せせり)) On 3 January, two groups of young men clad in loincloths raucously chase a wooden ball in the name of good fortune, at Hakozaki-gū shrine.

Hakata Dontaku Matsuri (博多どんたく祭り) On 3 and 4 May, Fukuoka's Meiji-dōri vibrates to the percussive shock of *shamoji* (wooden serving spoons) being banged together like castanets with *shamisen* (three-stringed instrument) accompaniment. Dontaku, from the Dutch word *zontag,* meaning 'holiday', was added to the name during the Meiji period.

Hakata Gion Yamakasa Matsuri (博多祇園山笠祭り) The city's main festival is held from 1 to 15 July, climaxing at 4.59am on the 15th, when seven groups of men converge at Kushida-jinja, just north of Canal City, then race on a 5km-long course carrying huge *mikoshi* (portable shrines). According to legend, the festival originated after a 13th-century Buddhist priest was carried aloft, sprinkling holy water over victims of a plague.

Kyūshū Bashō sumō tournament (大相撲九州場所) Held over two weeks at the Fukuoka Kokusai Centre during mid-November. Limited same-day tickets (*tōjitsu-ken;* ¥3400 to ¥15,000) are available from 8am but spectators start lining up at dawn.

Sleeping

Fukuoka is popular for business and pleasure. There's plenty of good-value accommodation. Stay near JR Hakata Station for convenience if railing around, but Tenjin is a better bet if you plan to spend a few days and like to shop and play.

BUDGET

International Hostel Khaosan Fukuoka (☎ 404-6035; www.khaosan-fukuoka.com; 11-34 Hiemachi, Hakata-ku; dm/s/tw from ¥2400/3500/5200; ⊠ 💻) This 19-room hostel is a great place to meet fellow travellers. Rooms are basic but light and airy.

Hotel New Simple (☎ 411-4311; fax 411-4312; www.hotel-newsimple.jp; 1-23-11 Hakata-ekimae; dm/s/tw ¥3000/4200/7140) One of Fukuoka's cheapest hotels, about 10 minutes' walk from Hakata Station. Rooms are clean and there's a family room to accommodate up to six.

Hakata JBB (☎ 263-8300; fax 263-8301; 6-5-1 Reisen-machi, Hakata-ku; s/d ¥4725/6000) This small private hotel is homey, friendly and some English is spoken. The decor is a little dated, but it's in a nice area close to Kushida shrine and Nakasu.

Amenity Hotel in Hakata (☎ 282-0041; fax 282-0044; www.amenityhotel.com; 14-25 Kami-kawabata; r with continental breakfast from ¥4900; ⊠ 💻) A standard business hotel, well located to Hakata Riverain and the subway. Free LAN cable internet access.

Hotel Etwas Tenjin (☎ 737-3233; fax 737-3266; 3-5-18 Tenjin; s/d ¥5800/7800 with light breakfast; ⊠ 💻) Recently refurbished, this business hotel is an excellent choice for smart, quiet accommodation in the heart of Tenjin, with lively Oyafuko-dōri around the corner. All rooms have LCD TVs. Some have LAN cable internet access.

Ryokan Kashima Honkan (☎ 291-0746; fax 271-7995; 3-11 Reisen-machi; r per person without bathroom from ¥6000; 💻) In the Gion district near Canal City, this charmingly creaky, unpretentious ryokan (traditional Japanese inn) is pleasantly faded and focused around an enclosed Meiji-era garden. Oozing atmosphere, it's a great place to sample traditional Japan. The friendly owners love LP readers, and communicate well in English.

Hotel Century Art (☎ 473-2111; fax 473-2112; 5-15 Chuo-gai, Hakata-eki; s/d/tw from ¥6500/9900/12,000; ⊠ 💻; 🚉 JR Hakata, Chikushi-gate) Behind JR Hakata Station (Chikushi-gate), this older property has decent-sized rooms and lots of marble. Some rooms have LAN cable internet access.

Hotel Éclair (☎ 283-2000; fax 283-6292; 1-1 Susaki-machi, Hakata-ku; s/tw from ¥6800/13,500; ⊠ 💻) Opposite Hotel Okura (opposite), this modern private hotel has light-filled rooms and a nice imitation Irish pub downstairs. Free LAN cable internet and rental laptops available.

Nishitetsu Inn Hakata (☎ 413-5454; fax 413-5466; 1-17-6 Hakata-ekimae; s/tw from ¥6900/13,300; ⊠ 💻) This shiny 500-room transit hotel next door to the Fukuoka Kōtsū Centre has a sauna and mineral bath and rooms have LAN cable internet.

MIDRANGE

Hotel Twins Momochi (☎ 852-4800; fax 845-8637; www.twinsmomochi.jp, in Japanese; 1-7-4 Momochi-hama, Sawara-ku; s/d from ¥5800/7800; P ⊠ 💻) Near Yahoo! Dome, you'll find this great-value couple- and family-friendly hotel, perhaps inspired by Ikea. Room types vary but all have refreshingly personal touches. There's a coin laundry and shared kitchenettes.

Hotel Ascent (☎ 711-1300; fax 711-1717; 3-3-14 Tenjin; s/d from ¥7245/13,650; ⊠ 💻) This large, neat hotel in the heart of Tenjin is good value for the single traveller, though little Japanese is spoken. Some rooms have LAN cable internet.

Richmond Hotel Hakata Station (☎ 433-0011; fax 433-0166; 6-17 Chuo-gai, Hakata-eki; s/d/tw from ¥7900/10,800/14,800; ⊠ 💻; 🚉 JR Hakata, Chikushi-gate) A business hotel with a little more style, behind the station near Yodobashi Camera. All rooms have free LAN cable internet.

Plaza Hotel Tenjin (☎ 752-7600; fax 752-7550; www.plaza-hotel.net; 1-9-63 Daimyo, Chūō-ku; s/tw from ¥7300/12,000; P ⊠ 💻) Don't be fooled into thinking the room styling follows the lead of the schmick common areas – it doesn't. But this is still an excellent choice for a nice price and cool location. Rooms have cable internet.

our pick Plaza Hotel Premier (☎ 734-7600; fax 734-7601; www.plaza-hotel.net; 1-14-13 Daimyo, Chūō-ku; s/tw from ¥8200/14,000; P ⊠ 💻) Located in trendy Daimyō, big brother of nearby Plaza Hotel Tenjin, the Premier is a smooth operator rivalling far pricier hotels. The night vibe on the street outside is uber-cool and its Trattoria Bal Musette could be straight out of Paris.

KYŪSHŪ

Hotel Leopalace Hakata (482-1212; fax 482-1289; www.leopalacehotels.jp/hakata_top.html; 2-5-33 Hakataeki-higashi; s/d from ¥12,000/15,000; JR Hakata, Chikushi-gate) This trendy new hotel near the station is targeted at young Japanese professionals. It has a slick, minimalist foyer leading to sleek, hi-tech rooms, all with LCD TVs and free cable internet. Some have floor-to-ceiling windows. There's a coin laundry and Italian restaurant, but little English is spoken.

TOP END

If you can afford a splurge when in Kyūshū, Fukuoka is the place to do it.

Nishitetsu Grand Hotel (771-7171; fax 751-8224; www.grand-h.jp/english/index.html; 2-6-60 Daimyo; s/tw/d from ¥12,705/25,410/27,720) One of Fukuoka's originals, this massive property appeals primarily to the Japanese, but its location, scale and service levels all rate highly. Rooms have cable internet.

La Soeur Hotel Monterey (726-7111; fax 726-7100; https://www.hotelmonterey.co.jp/eng/index.html; 2-8-27 Daimyo; s/tw & d from ¥13,860/19,635) A popular wedding spot, this property has a prime location and comfortable, well-appointed rooms, with cable-internet jacks. Check the website for online, pay-in-advance bargains and avoid weekends.

Hyatt Regency (412-1234; fax 414-2490 www.hyatt.com; 2-14-1 Hakataeki-higashi, Hakata-ku; d/tw from ¥18,000) Five minutes' walk from JR Hakata Station, you'll find the imposing building. Inside, plush, well-appointed guestrooms and lounges are synonymous with the Hyatt brand. It's even better when the rates are discounted online.

Hotel Okura (262-1111; fax 262-7701; www.okura.com; 3-2 Shimokawabata-machi; s/d/ste from ¥19,950/25,200/84,000) Rooms are large and suitably appointed, but this enormous Japanese five-star is all about the service. It is well located as part of the Hakata Riverain complex.

Grand Hyatt Fukuoka (282-1234, 282-2817; http://fukuoka.grand.hyatt.com; 1-2-82 Sumiyoshi; d/tw from ¥20,000, ste poa) This massive yet sumptuous property adjacent to Canal City is Fukuoka's truest international five-star. Warm, light-filled rooms synthesise traditional Japanese aesthetics with contemporary comforts. Western and Japanese suites are magnificent, decadent and appropriately expensive.

our pick With the Style (433-3900; www.withthestyle.com; 1-9-18 Hakataeki-minami; d/ste with breakfast, minibar & welcome drinks from ¥31,185/63,525) This sexy designer hotel will be a little wasted if you are flying solo. Each of the 16 rooms exudes rock-star cool and guests are invited to reserve complimentary private use of the rooftop spa or penthouse bar during their stay. The sushi bar, restaurant and cocktail bar each cater impeccably to the discerning adult. An inner-city retreat to savour.

Eating

To most Japanese, Hakata means *tonkotsu-rāmen* – specifically, noodles in a distinctive broth made from pork bones. Fukuoka is also famed for *yatai* – movable hawker-style food stalls. The majority of the *yatai* are by the river in Nakasu, in front of Canal City and scattered around Tenjin, especially where Oyafuko-dōri meets Shōwa-dōri. They open at dusk and soon most seats are taken. Let the aromas and the chatty conversation guide you.

Hakata-ya (291-3080; 9-151 Kami-kawabata; dishes from ¥290; 24hr) On a corner just off the Kawabata-*shōtengai* (shopping street) you'll find the cheapest *rāmen* in town. It's a '70s-looking shop with a red-and-yellow sign between two exhaust fans pumping tasty aromas onto the street. The *rāmen teishoku* (noodle set meal) is an unbeatable ¥580 and comprises a noodle bowl, rice, pickles and five Hakata *gyōza* (dumplings) – made bite-sized so dainty Hakata women don't have to open their mouths too wide to eat them.

Hakata Rāmen Shibaraku (714-0489; 3-2-13 Tenjin; rāmen from ¥600; lunch & dinner) Opposite the Hotel Ascent, this friendly, spotlessly clean and refreshingly spacious vendor has *wantanmen* (*rāmen* in *tonkotsu* pork broth loaded with wontons) for ¥930 and cold beer.

If you fancy something other than *rāmen*, the following may help.

Jet Diner (716-9070; 101 CePa Bldg, 1-12-52 Daimyo; burgers from ¥400; lunch 11am-3am) Juicy burgers with a twist, hot dogs, soup and salads are the theme of this slick and shiny retro diner, in a great spot off Nishi-dōri, opposite Beans. It also serves cocktails – so it's popular with 20-somethings, and often packed. A hamburger with fries and coleslaw is ¥680.

Pik's Coffee Shop (781-0246; http://members3.jcom.home.ne.jp/piks; 3-2-18 Tenjin; meals from ¥495; 12pm-1am Mon-Fri, 6pm-2am Sat, closed Sun) For meals à la Americana, and the closest thing to a bacon-and-egg breakfast you can get in

Japan, head for this fun retro diner where everything is straight out of Kansas City, but for the people.

Murata (☎ 291-0894; 2-9-1 Reisen-machi; soba from ¥550; 🕑 11.30am-8.30pm, closed Sun; Ⓥ) Opposite Hakata JBB hotel, this lovely eatery serves delicious *soba* (buckwheat noodles) from the Shinshū area of central Japan, prepared in a variety of ways. Try the *oroshi-soba* (cold noodles topped with grated daikon) for ¥950.

Curry Honpo (☎ 262-0010; www.curry-honpo.com; 6-135 Kami-kawabata; curry from ¥670; 🕑 lunch & dinner; Ⓥ) People flock to this Kawabata-shōtengai eatery for the delicious combustion curries with a Japanese twist. Try the *pooku no yaki karee* (pork combustion curry) for ¥870. There's an amusing 'Japanenglish' menu and the fake wood–panelled storefront is easy to find in the arcade.

Nanak's Indian (☎ 713-7900; 1-1-14 Maizuru; curries from ¥680; 🕑 lunch & dinner; Ⓥ) All your favourites are here in a typical setting, in English. The aromas wafting down to the bustling intersection of Oyafuko-dōri and Shōwa-dōri, below, are difficult to resist.

Yamasaki (☎ 762-6668; 1F Chestnut Bldg, 1-8-11 Maizuru; meals from ¥1500; 🕑 lunch & dinner) Come off busy Oyafuko-dōri, for excellent fish, salads and *teishoku* (set meals). Grilled *sanma* (mackerel) or *netsuke* (red snapper), a salad and beer will cost you about ¥1750. There's no English sign; look for the small 'Chestnut' signboard. A picture menu is available.

CHINA (☎ 282-1234; 1st fl, Grand Hyatt Hotel, Canal City; dim sum weekdays/weekends ¥2900/3300; 🕑 lunch) A delightful Cantonese banquet hall offering all-you-can-eat dim sum, cooked to order from an English menu and served in the style of a five-star hotel.

The **IMS building** (1-7-11 Tenjin) has prime skyline views from its 12th- and 13th-floor restaurants, including **No No Budo** (☎ 714-1441; buffet lunch/dinner ¥1575/2100; 🕑 lunch & dinner; Ⓥ), a busy self-serve gourmet buffet, with Japanese and Western fresh-fish and meat dishes, noodles, salads, soups and desserts. An extra ¥1400 buys all you can drink: beer, wine and some cocktails for two hours. **Rāmen Stadium** (☎ 282-2525; 5F, Canal City; 🕑 11am-10.30pm) is an entire floor of *rāmen* vendors with styles from the length and breadth of the land.

The department stores off Tenjin-Chikagai have their own food courts and restaurants, usually on the basement and top floors.

DAIMYO DISTRICT 大名地区

The narrow lanes of Daimyo are home to Fukuoka's most stylish bars and restaurants. **Bar Garasu** (☎ 712-8251; 1-12-28 Daimyo) draws a hip, hole-in-the-wall crowd; nearby **Alohana** (☎ 724-0111; Donpa Bldg, 1-11-4 Daimyo) serves up Hawaiian-Japanese (yes!) fusion plates, or if you're feeling swanky, head to the elegant **Bar Oscar** (☎ 7721-5352; 6th fl, 1-10-29 Daimyo), named after jazz luminary Oscar Peterson.

Drinking

The weekend starts on Thursday in multicultural and party-friendly Fukuoka. Most venues stay open until 3am. The main drag, Oyafuko-dōri, roughly translates to 'street of unruly children' – because of the cram schools that once lined the road. In a way, the cap still fits. Tenjin and Daimyo's maze of streets is safe and easy to explore, and great for people-watching. Gay travellers hoping to make new friends will have to search a little harder, but most of the action is south of Nakasu and Canal City in the Sumiyoshi ward. The internet is the best resource for this cloistered scene.

International Bar (☎ 714-2179; 4th fl, Urashima Bldg, 3-1-13 Tenjin) There's free karaoke on Tuesdays at this tiny international bar, Fukuoka's first, now showing its age.

Off Broadway (☎ 724-5383; www.offbroadwayjapan.com; 2nd fl, Beans Bldg, 1-8-40 Maizuru) One of Fukuoka's originals and still one of the nicest, looking down on Oyafuko-dōri. The staff and crowd are friendly, and there's a full bar menu with a good selection of Americana.

Craic & Porter Beer Bar (☎ 090-4514-9516; http://craic.mine.nu; 3-5-16 Tenjin) A tiny taste of Ireland with open windows and premium import beers on tap. Owner Mike is a friendly character, with plenty of experience in Japan. Opposite FUBAR, above ABC flower shop on Oyafuko-dōri.

British Pub Morris (☎ 771-4774; 7th fl, Stage 1 Nishidōri Bldg, 2-1-4 Daimyo; 🕑 from 5pm; 💻) One of the better pubs in Japan, attracting a nice mix of Japanese and *gaijin* (foreigner) punters. There's a good beer selection, including Cooper's Pale, tasty pub food and lots of space. The awesome outdoor patio perched high above trendy Daimyo is a great place to begin your evening, especially with happy-hour cocktails from ¥250 between 5pm and 7pm daily.

Small Spaces (☎ 724-3443; 1-13-12 Daimyo) While this bar may be a little tricky if you can't speak Japanese, it's worth a look. Cool by definition, Small Spaces is all about young Japanese doing their own thing. The cosy glow spills out onto the street through the open door and white-shuttered windows of this little wooden shack on the corner among the big-brand boutiques. There's a blue vinyl sign. Peace, man.

VJ Bar (☎ 844-8000; 34th fl, JAL Resort Sea Hawk Hotel Fukuoka, 2-2-3 Jigyo-hama, Chuo-ku; 🕑 6pm-1am; drinks from ¥800) If you have time, money and good company, the incredible views and tasty international treats tend to justify the expense at this sleek multilevel hotel bar 123m above ground.

The spacious original **Ashok's Bar** (☎ 522-0663; 2nd fl, Sakura Bldg, Sun-road Shōtengai, 1-10-19 Kiyokawa), established by Nepali expat Ashok, was one of the first international bars in Fukuoka, and its little brother, newer and more central **Ashok's Bar2** (☎ 732-3281; 203 Tenjin Bacchus-kan, 3-4-15 Tenjin) both serve Nepalese and Japanese food. Now largely favoured by Japanese, these are good spots to meet locals. Both close Sunday.

Entertainment

CLUBS

Somewhat-sleazy Nakasu island is one of the most popular entertainment districts in Japan, but you need to know what you are looking for. The area around Oyafuko-dōri is a better bet for a night on the tiles. Generally, clubs have a weekend cover charge of ¥1000 to ¥3000, with a free drink or two.

Juke Joint (☎ 762-5596; http://juke-records.net/juke joint, in Japanese; 1-9-23 Maizuru) Funsters can select the tunes at this Fukuoka original DJ lounge. The eclectic music collection is the work of record-shop owner 'Kinky' Ko Matsumoto. Drinks start at ¥500, plus spicy seafood gumbo (that's right) and no cover charge.

Dark Room (☎ 725-2989; www.thedarkroom.biz; 8th fl, Tenjin Bacchus-kan, 3-4-15 Tenjin; 🕑 6pm-2am) Dark, rocky and loud, this is a cool urban rock-oasis with a killer sound system, pool table, foosball, friendly dudes behind the bar and a spiral staircase leading to a fun, summer-only rooftop patio.

Voodoo Lounge (☎ 732-4662; 3rd fl, Tenjin Centre Bldg, Tenjin; 🕑 9pm-3am) Chilled-out and spacious, Voodoo Lounge is known for quality drinks and live bands or DJs most nights.

Sam & Dave (☎ 713-2223; www.samanddave.jp; 3rd fl, West Side Bldg, Tenjin Nishidōri) Like its sister bars around Japan, Sam & Dave's vacillates between being somewhere fun to shake your ass, and just another boozy big-beat meat-market nightclub. Hope for a good crowd and you could be lucky, whatever you fancy.

FUBAR (☎ 722-3006; 4th fl, Okabi Bldg II, 3-6-12 Tenjin, Chūō-ku) More about the music and less of a pick-up joint, this compact club next to Family Mart on Oyafuko-dōri grooves till the wee hours.

KABUKI

Hakata-za (☎ 263-5858; www.hakataza.co.jp, in Japanese; Riverain Centre Bldg, 3-1 Shimokawabata-machi; admission ¥5000-18,600; 🕑 performance times vary) Fans of classical kabuki will swoon over this 1500-seat state-of-the-art theatre, one of Japan's finest, located at Hakata Riverain, above Nakasu-Kawabata subway station.

Shopping

Clay Hakata *ningyō* (Hakata dolls) depicting women, children, samurai and geisha are a popular Fukuoka craft. Hakata *obi* (silk sashes worn with kimonos) are another speciality. Try the Mitsukoshi or Daimaru department stores in Tenjin.

Daisou (4th fl, Fukuoka Kōtsū Centre Bldg; 🕑 10am-10pm) For last-minute bargain gift shopping, head for this sprawling ¥100 (and upwards) shop next to JR Hakata Station (Hakata-guchi).

Shopping in Tenjin's high-rises and underground labyrinths is a popular pastime for many. Packed along a three-block section of Watanabe-dōri, **Tenjin Core** (☎ 721-7755), **Mitsukoshi** (☎ 724-3111), **Daimaru** (☎ 712-8181), **Solaria Plaza** (☎ 733-7004), subterranean **Tenjin Chikagai** (☎ 721-8436), **mina tenjin** (☎ 713-3711) and **IMS building** (☎ 733-2001) are all favourites.

Getting There & Away

AIR

Fukuoka is an international hub into Asia. Domestic routes include Tokyo (¥36,700, 1½ hours, from Haneda airport/Narita International Airport 45/four flights daily), Osaka (¥21,900, one hour, six flights daily) and Okinawa (Naha, from ¥27,500, 1½ hours, 12 flights daily). Both ANA and JAL have offices here.

Japan's only independent cut-rate carrier, **Skymark** (www.skymark.co.jp/en; ☎ 736-3131, in Tokyo 03-3433-7026) flies to Tokyo's Haneda airport (from ¥12,000, 10 flights daily).

BOAT

Ferry services from Hakata connect to Okinawa and other islands off Kyūshū. An international high-speed hydrofoil service called **Beetle** (☎ in Japan 092-281-2315, in Korea 051-465-6111; www.jrbeetle.co.jp/english) connects Fukuoka with Busan in Korea (¥13,000, three hours, four daily). The **Camellia line** (☎ in Japan 092-262-2323, in Korea 051-466-7799; www.camellia-line.co.jp, in Japanese & Korean) has a regular ferry service from Fukuoka to Busan (¥9000, six hours, daily at noon). In Fukuoka, the Beetle and the Camellia depart from Hakata Port Ferry Terminal via bus 11, 19 or 50 from JR Hakata Station (¥220), or bus 80 from Tenjin (Solaria Stage-mae; ¥180). From Busan, both the Beetle (Won 9000, three hours, four daily) and the Camellia (Won 80,000, 7¾ hours, overnight) depart from the International Terminal, approximately 200m from Jungang-dong subway station.

BUS

Long-distance buses (English information ☎ 733-3333) depart from the Fukuoka Kōtsū Centre Building next to JR Hakata Station (Hakata-gate) and also from the Tenjin bus centre. Destinations include Tokyo (¥15,000, 14½ hours), Osaka (from ¥7000, 9½ hours), Nagoya (¥10,500, 11 hours) and many towns in Kyūshū. There's an excellent website (www.rakubus.jp/english).

TRAIN

JR Hakata Station (☎ English information 471-8111, JR English info-line 03-3423-0111) is the western terminus of the Tokyo–Osaka–Hakata *shinkansen*. Services operate to/from Tokyo (¥21,210, five hours), Osaka (¥14,690, 2½ to three hours) and Hiroshima (¥8900, 1½ hours).

Within Kyūshū, the Nippō line runs through Beppu and Miyazaki; the Kagoshima line through Kumamoto to Kagoshima; the Sasebo line runs Saga to Sasebo, and the Nagasaki line, to Nagasaki. The Kyūshū *shinkansen* runs from Shin-Yatsushiro to Kagoshima (¥5490, one hour); eventually it will extend to Hakata. You can also travel by subway and JR train to Karatsu and continue to Nagasaki by train.

Getting Around

TO/FROM THE AIRPORT

Fukuoka airport is conveniently close to the city centre. The airport has three domestic terminals and an international terminal, all connected by a free shuttle bus.

The subway from the domestic terminals takes just five minutes to reach JR Hakata Station (¥250) and 11 minutes to Tenjin (¥250). Buses run frequently between JR Hakata Station and the international terminal.

Airport taxis cost around ¥1600 to Tenjin/Hakata.

BUS

City bus services operate from the Fukuoka Kōtsū Centre Building adjacent to JR Hakata Station and from the Nishitetsu Tenjin Bus Terminal. Many stop in front of the station (Hakata-guchi). Specially marked Nishitetsu buses have a flat ¥100 rate for city-centre rides.

From stand E at the Fukuoka Kōtsū Centre Building, bus 11 or 19 goes to Hakata Pier International Terminal (¥220), while bus 47 or 48 reaches Bayside Place for ferries to islands.

SUBWAY

Fukuoka has three subway lines. The Kūkō (airport) line runs from Fukuoka domestic airport terminal to Meinohama Station via Hakata, Nakasu-Kawabata and Tenjin Stations. The Hakozaki line runs from Nakasu-Kawabata Station to Kaizuka. The Nanakuma line runs from Tenjin-minami to Hashimoto. Fares around town start at ¥200; a one-day pass costs ¥600/300 per adult/child six to 11. Trains run from 5.30am to 12.25am.

DAZAIFU 太宰府

☎ 092 / pop 67,830

Dazaifu, former governmental centre of Kyūshū, now home to Japan's newest national museum, has a beautiful cluster of temples and a famous shrine. It's a pleasant day trip from Fukuoka. The **tourist information office** (☎ 925-1880; ⏲ 9am-5.30pm) at Nishitetsu-Dazaifu Station has helpful staff and an English-language map.

Sights

KYŪSHŪ NATIONAL MUSEUM

九州国立博物館

Japan's fourth national **museum** (☎ 918-2807; www.kyuhaku.com; 4-7-2 Ishizaka, Dazaifu City; adult/student

¥420/210; ⌚ 9.30am-5pm, closed Mon) opened in 2005, the country's first since 1900. This striking structure in the tranquil hills of Dazaifu resembles a massive space station for the arts. Highlights include a fascinating Silk Road exhibit, stone carvings of AD 1st-century women with spears on horseback and a delicate 13th-century oil-spot *tenmoku* tea bowl. Self-guided audio tours and HD video theatre are free.

TENMAN-GŪ 天満宮

Poet and scholar Sugawara-no-Michizane was a distinguished figure in the Kyoto court until he fell foul of political intrigue and was exiled to distant Dazaifu, where he died two years later. Subsequent disasters that struck Kyoto were blamed on his unfair dismissal and he became deified as Tenman Tenjin, the god of culture and scholars. **Tenman-gū** (☎ 922-8225; www.dazaifutenmangu.or.jp; 4-7-1 Saifu), his shrine and burial place, attracts countless visitors, among them students in hope of passing their college entrance exams. The Hondō (main hall) was rebuilt in 1591.

Behind the shrine is the **Kankō Historical Museum** (菅公歴史館; admission ¥200; ⌚ 9am-4.30pm Wed-Mon), with dioramas showing events in Tenjin's life, and the **treasure house** (宝物殿; admission ¥300; ⌚ 9am-4.30pm, closed Mon) has artefacts from his life.

Every second month the shrine hosts an *omoshiro-ichi* (interesting market), selling everything from antique kimonos to Mickey Mouse telephones. Dates vary, but it's a great chance to find some treasure – check with tourist information at the station.

KŌMYŌZEN-JI 光明禅寺

Secreted away on the southern edge of Dazaifu inside this small **temple** (☎ 922-4053; admission by donation ¥200; ⌚ 9am-4.30pm) is an exquisite jewel of a Zen garden. It's a peaceful contrast to the crowds at the nearby shrine.

OTHER SIGHTS

The **Kyūshū Historical Museum** (九州歴史資料館; ☎ 923-0404; admission free; ⌚ 9am-4pm, closed Mon), not far beyond Kōmyōzen-ji (above), showcases artefacts from the Stone to Middle Ages.

Nestled among rice paddies, **Kaidan-in** (戒壇院) dates from 761 and was one of the most important ordination monasteries in Japan. Adjacent **Kanzeon-ji** (観世音寺; ☎ 922-1811) dates from 746 but only the great bell, said to be the oldest in Japan, remains from the original construction. Its **treasure hall** (宝蔵; admission ¥500; ⌚ 9am-4.30pm) has an impressive collection of statuary, most of it wood, dating from the 10th to 12th centuries. Many of the items show Indian or Tibetan influence.

Dazaifu Exhibition Hall (大宰府展示館; ☎ 922-7811; admission ¥150; ⌚ 9am-4.30pm, closed Mon) displays finds from local archaeological excavations. Nearby are the **Tofurō ruins** (都府楼), foundations of the ancient government buildings. **Enoki-sha** (榎社) is where Sugawara-no-Michizane died. His body was transported from here to its burial place, now Tenman-gū, on the ox cart that appears in so many local depictions.

Getting There & Around

The private Nishitetsu line connects Nishitetsu-Fukuoka (Tenjin; opposite) with Dazaifu (¥390, 25 minutes). Change trains at Nishitetsu-Futsukaichi Station. Bicycles can be rented (per three hours/day ¥300/500) at Nishitetsu Dazaifu Station.

FUTSUKAICHI ONSEN 二日市温泉

☎ 092

About 300m south of JR Futsukaichi Station, this unassuming onsen (hot springs) town has public baths grouped together in the old main street. Favoured by traditionalists, **Gozen-yu** (御前湯; ☎ 928-1126; admission ¥200; ⌚ 9am-9pm, closed 1st & 3rd Wed) is the most characteristic. From JR Futsukaichi Station, cross back over the tracks, then follow the road under the *torii* (shrine gate) and across the stream.

TACHIARAI 大刀洗

☎ 0942

Many locals don't know about **Tachiarai Heiwa Kinenkan** (太刀洗平和記念館; ☎ 23-1227; admission ¥500; ⌚ 9.30am-5pm), a tiny memorial museum established by ex-aviators and residents of Tachiarai, a small farmland village near Ogōri. The museum commemorates Japanese killed in WWII, including kamikaze pilots and townspeople who died during a USAF B-29 bombing on 27 March 1945.

Although little is labelled in English, it's a strangely affecting place, with wartime memorabilia and a Japanese fighter plane, retrieved from Hakata Bay where it crashed in 1942.

KURUME 久留米

☎ 0942

The town of Kurume, south of Dazaifu, is known for splash-dyed indigo textiles, papermaking, lacquerware and bamboo work, and Bridgestone rubber.

Narita-san (成田山; ☎ 21-7500; 7am-5pm), a branch of the temple outside Tokyo (see p239), is the town's biggest attraction. Its 62m-high statue of the goddess of mercy, Kannon, stands beside a miniaturised replica of Borobudur. Inside the statue you can climb up past Buddhist treasures and religious dioramas right into the divine forehead.

Ishibashi Museum of Art (石橋美術館; ☎ 39-1131; www.ishibashi-museum.gr.jp; adult/child ¥500/300; 10am-5pm, closed Mon) boasts a private collection of Asian and Western art assembled by the founder of Bridgestone, who felt strongly that art should be accessible to everybody. The museum is 1km from the Nishitetsu-Kurume Station.

Kurume is 40 minutes from Fukuoka on the JR Kagoshima line (¥720).

SAGA-KEN 佐賀県

Karatsu is at the base of the scenic Higashi-Matsūra Peninsula, whose dramatic coastline has been pounded into shape by the waves of the Sea of Genkai.

KARATSU 唐津

☎ 0955 / pop 130,150

It's saddening to say that seaside Karatsu, a world-renowned pottery town, is noticeably suffering the strain of depopulation. Unless you're a pottery fanatic, you may be disappointed by Karatsu's failure to deliver as the promising tourist destination it once was.

Historically, Karatsu's Korean influences elevated the town's craft from useful ceramicware to art. It's true that Karatsu ware is of the finest quality, but the beach is grotty, the castle a reconstruction and the town is at the end of the line. At JR Karatsu Station, the **tourist information office** (☎ 72-4963; 9am-5pm) has a selection of English-language tourist maps and brochures, but little English is spoken and, although staff can book accommodation, there's not much to write home about.

Sights & Activities

Karatsu-jō (☎ 72-5697; admission ¥400; 9am-5pm) is picturesquely perched on a hill overlooking the sea, but is a modern reconstruction.

INFORMATION

- Tourist Information Office 旅行案内所 1 A3

SIGHTS & ACTIVITIES

- Hikiyama Festival Float Exhibition Hall 曳山展示場 2 A2
- Karatsu Ware Federation Exhibition Hall 唐津市ふるさと会館アルピノ·ホール 3 B3
- Karatsu-jinja 唐津神社 4 A2
- Karatsu-jō 唐津城 5 B1
- Nakazato Tarōemon 中里太郎右衛門窯 6 B3

SLEEPING

- Business Hotel SOLA ビジネスホテル宙 7 A3
- Niji-no-Matsubara Hotel 虹の松原ホテル 8 D1

EATING

- Aijdokoro Sakamoto 味どころ坂本 9 D1
- Kawashima Tōfu 川島豆腐 10 B3
- Kiage きあげ .... (see 1)
- Mambō マンボ .... (see 1)
- Morning Market 朝市 11 C1

TRANSPORT

- Eki-mae Rent-a-Car 駅前レンタカー 12 A3
- Ōtemachi Bus Centre 大手町バスセンター 13 A2

It houses antique ceramics, samurai armour and archaeological displays.

Karatsu-jinja (☎ 72-2264) is a scenic shrine in the centre of the city, near the **Hikiyama Festival Float Exhibition Hall** (☎ 72-8278; admission ¥300), which contains the 14 floats used in the Karatsu Kunchi Matsuri (below). Designs include the Aka-jishi (Red Lion), samurai helmets, a dragon and a chicken.

Around town are a number of **kilns and studios** where you can see local potters at work, and there are also ceramic shops along the street between Karatsu Station and the town centre. The **Nakazato Tarōemon** (☎ 72-8171; admission free) kiln-gallery is about 350m southeast of the station.

Adjacent to Karatsu Station, **Karatsu Ware Federation Exhibition Hall** (☎ 73-4888; 2nd fl, Arupino Bldg) displays local potters' works and provides contact information. Many of the items on display are for sale from ¥500.

A **bicycle track** cuts through the pine trees planted behind the 5km-long Niji-no Matsubara Beach.

Festivals & Events

Doyō-yoichi (土曜夜市; Saturday-night market) Held in the town centre over four consecutive Saturdays from late July.

Karatsu Kunchi Matsuri (唐津くんち祭り) From 2 to 4 November, Karatsu comes to life in this spectacular festival, designated a festival of national

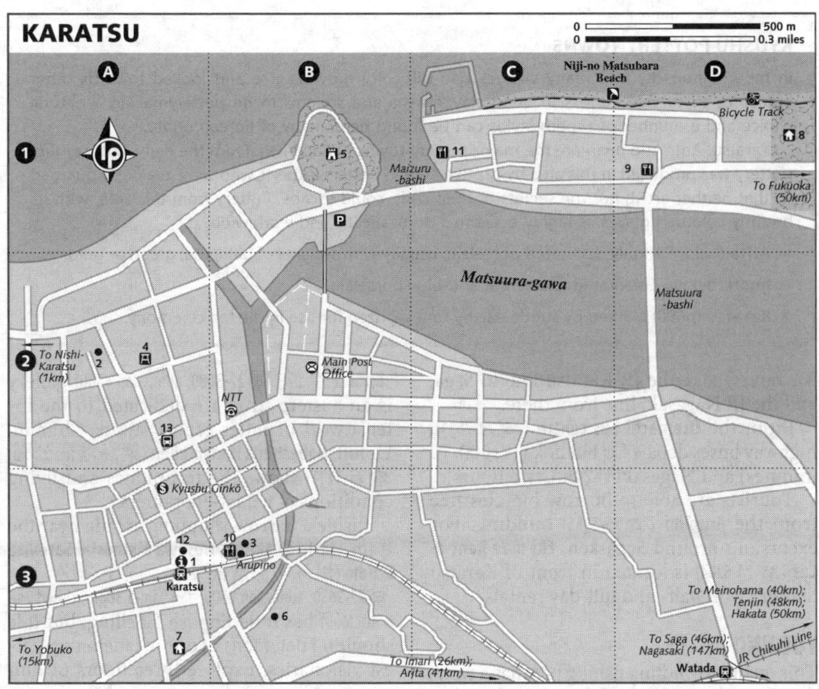

cultural importance, dating from 1592. At the highlight of the celebrations, townsfolk carrying massive, exquisitely decorated *hikiyama* (floats) parade from Nishinohama beach into town.

Sleeping & Eating

Business Hotel SOLA (☎ 72-3003; www.hotel-sola.com, in Japanese; s with breakfast buffet ¥4900; P ⊠ 💻) This bland business hotel offers single rooms only. LAN cable internet is available.

Niji-no-Matsubara Hotel (☎ 73-9111, 0120-73-9100; fax 75-9991; s/d/tw from ¥5000/8400/10,500; P ⊠ 💻) Location is everything, but the beach out the front of this once-bargain property needs attention, as do the rooms. All have a nice outlook facing the beach or the pine forest. It's a short bus (¥160) or taxi (¥900) ride from Karatsu Station. The hotel has free bike rental, as long as you return by 6pm.

Kiage (☎ 73-8080; Karatsu Station; 🕑 lunch & dinner) Next to the turnstiles, Kiage serves up tasty noodles, *gyōza* and other hearty station fare. A massive *rāmen* and fried rice combo costs ¥750. Picture menu.

Mambō (☎ 75-1881; Karatsu Station; dishes from ¥800; 🕑 lunch & dinner) Pick up a boxed meal for the train, or sit down for the *tenzaru udon* (tempura and chilled noodles, ¥1260) at this eatery with food displays.

Ajidokoro Sakamoto (☎ 72-2842; 4-2-19 Higashi-Karatsu, dishes from ¥600; 🕑 dinner) All the regulars are here; *tempura, katsudon,* sushi and sashimi. There's a picture menu and the friendly owners of this quiet eatery aren't unused to foreigners walking in from the nearby hotels.

Kawashima Tōfu (☎ 72-2423; www.zarudoufu.co.jp, in Japanese; set meals ¥1575-2675; 🕑 8am-noon) Close to the station, Kawashima Tōfu has been in business since the Edo period. Zaru-dōfu, its speciality, is scooped like ice cream and served exquisitely in set meals on Karatsu-yaki plates (see p700). A sampler course starts at ¥1575. Reservation only, maximum 10 people.

There's usually a **morning market** at the west end of the beach, from dawn until 9am.

Getting There & Around

From Fukuoka (p685), take the Kūkō subway line from Hakata or Tenjin to the end of the line at Meinohama, then change to the JR Chikuhi line to reach Karatsu (¥1110, 70 minutes). From Karatsu to Nagasaki (¥2420,

KYŪSHŪ POTTERY TOWNS

In mountainous Kyūshū many villages had difficulty growing rice and looked towards other industries to survive. Access to good clay, forests and streams made potterymaking a natural choice and a number of superb styles can be found here, many of Korean origin.

Karatsu, Arita and Imari are the major pottery towns of Saga-ken. From the early 17th century pottery was produced in this area by captive Korean potters, experts who were zealously guarded so that neither artist, nor the secrets of their craft, could escape. Pottery from this area, with its brightly coloured glazes, is highly esteemed domestically and worldwide.

- **Arita** (below) Highly decorated porcelain, usually with squares of blue, red, green or gold.
- **Imari** (below) Celebrated fine, white-and-blue porcelain.
- **Karatsu** (p698) Marked by subtle earthy tones, prized for use in the tea ceremony.

3½ hours) take the JR Karatsu line to Saga, and the JR Nagasaki line from there.

From the **Ōtemachi bus centre** (☎ 73-7511), highway buses depart for Fukuoka (¥1000, 70 minutes) and Nagasaki (¥2400, two hours).

Tourists are able to borrow bicycles free from the **Arupino** (☎ 75-5155) building. For excursions around Saga-ken, **Eki-mae Rent-a-Car** (☎ 74-6204) is located in front of Karatsu Station, with half- and full-day rentals.

YOBUKO 呼子

This quaint dwindling fishing port has a wonderful **morning market** for fish and produce, but the main action is over by 8am. A series of wooden ryokan, charging from around ¥9500 per person (including meals) lines a narrow lane alongside the waterfront; rooms look out onto the bay, where nightly you can watch the flickering lights of the departing fishing boats heading out to sea. Local delicacies include squid sashimi and tempura. Shōwa buses run from Karatsu to Yobuko (¥730, 30 minutes).

IMARI 伊万里

☎ 0955 / pop 57,900

Imari is the name commonly associated with pottery from this area, which is actually produced outside the town. Tourist brochures are available at **Imari City Information** (☎ 23-3479; 8.30am-6pm) at JR Imari Station.

Ōkawachiyama (大川内山), with 20 working pottery kilns, is a 20-minute bus ride from Imari (¥150). Buses operate weekdays only. Arrive by midday to allow time for exploring. The **bridge** entering Ōkawachiyama is decorated with pottery shards. The bus stops near the bridge, and the village is on the hillsides on either side of the river. At the bottom of the hill **Kataoka Tsurutarō Kōgeikan** (片岡鶴太郎工芸館; ☎ 22-3080; admission ¥300) gallery is an austere structure dedicated to the intense work of potter-genius Sawada Chitōjin. Uphill, **Nabeshima Hanyō-kōen** (鍋島藩窯公園; ☎ 23-1111) shows the techniques and living conditions of feudal-era potters.

Inside a narrow shopping arcade near the train station, **Akira Kurosawa Memorial Satellite Studio** (黒澤明記念館サテライトスタジオ; ☎ 22-9630; admission ¥500; 9am-5.30pm, closed 2nd & 4th Mon) has little English labelling, but this shouldn't deter fans of one of cinema's greatest visionaries. Explore three floors of film memorabilia and glimpse behind-the-scenes documentaries and rare footage. There's also a lunch and wine bar.

Karatsu is connected with Imari (¥630, 50 minutes) by the JR Chikuhi line. Local buses to Ōkawachiyama depart from the main bus terminal, a few blocks west of the train station, where you can also catch direct buses to Fukuoka (¥2250, two hours).

ARITA 有田

☎ 0955 / pop 21,390

Kaolin clay was discovered here in 1615 by Ri Sampei, a naturalised Korean potter, enabling the manufacture of fine porcelain in Japan for the first time. By the mid-17th century it was being exported to Europe. The town of Arita is a beautiful example of how tourism can support the preservation of history and culture. The friendly staff at the tiny **tourist information desk** (☎ 42-4052; www.arita.or.jp/index_e.html; 9am-5pm) inside Arita Station can assist with maps, timetables and accommodation, predominantly small private *minshuku* (Japanese guest houses) and ryokan.

An annual **pottery fair** is held from 29 April to 5 May.

Shops line the main street leading out from the station towards the **Kyūshū Ceramics Museum** (九州陶磁文化館; ☎ 43-3681; admission free; ⏰ 9am-4.30pm, closed Mon), a converted warehouse showcasing the development of ceramic arts in Kyūshū. Pottery connoisseurs are sure to find **Imaemon Gallery** (今衛門ギャラリー; ☎ 42-5550; admission ¥300; ⏰ 9.30am-4.30pm, closed Mon), **Kakiemon Kiln** (柿右衛門窯; ☎ 43-2267; admission free; ⏰ 9am-5pm) and **Genemon Kiln** (源衛門窯; ☎ 42-4164; admission free; ⏰ 8am-5.30pm Mon-Sat) interesting, and there are dozens of other workshops and pottery stores to visit.

For the full pottery treatment, join the Japanese package tours at **Arita Porcelain Park** (有田ポーセリンパーク; ☎ 41-0030; adult/student ¥1000/500; ⏰ 10am-5pm Mar-Nov, to 4pm Dec-Feb), a 10-minute bus ride (¥150) from the train station, or shop for **Fukagawa** porcelain at **China on the Park Gallery** (チャイナオンザパーク; ☎ 46-3900; ⏰ 9am-5.30pm), 5km west of town on Rte 202 where you can also watch the firing process. An Arita bus (¥150, four daily from 9.30am) can take you out to the clay mines, from where you can walk back to the station in about an hour or so, if the numerous galleries don't tempt you inside. Along the way, check out the house walls in some of the back streets: leftover pottery was often used in bricks and construction and some of the older buildings show this recycling well.

A short hop east of Arita, **Takeo Onsen** (武雄温泉) is a modern hot-springs town. The traditional baths are said to have refreshed the armies of Toyotomi Hideyoshi. Look for the lacquered Chinese-style gate, which was built without nails.

Takeo Onsen Youth Hostel (武雄温泉ユースホステル; ☎ 0954-22-2490; fax 0954-20-1208; dm with breakfast member/nonmember ¥3300/3900) is comfortable, but the last bus to the hostel (¥250) leaves Takeo Onsen Station at 4pm.

From outside Arita Station, private Matsūra-tetsudō trains depart for Imari (¥410, 25 minutes). JR *tokkyū* trains between Hakata (¥2690, 80 minutes) and Sasebo (¥1050, 30 minutes) stop at Arita and Takeo Onsen. Takeo Onsen is also connected to Arita by local trains (¥270, 20 minutes). Around town, community bus routes (¥150) cover most sights, departing hourly from Arita Station, where you can also rent bicycles (¥300 per day).

NORTHWEST ISLANDS

Five large and many smaller islands lie to the northwest of Kyūshū and are accessible from Fukuoka, Sasebo and Nagasaki, but reaching them is not cheap. Some are part of Saga-ken, but all below are part of Nagasaki-ken. Visit if you want to get away from it all, but if you are looking for the elusive *Lost Japan*, prepare for some level of disappointment.

IKI 壱岐

☎ 09204 / pop 32,310

Iki, off Kyūshū's northern coast, has an area of 138 sq km and lies closer to Karatsu than Fukuoka. As well as having some nice beaches, it's relatively flat and a decent place for cyclists. Toyotomi Hideyoshi fortified **Gonoura**, the busiest port and a base for exploring the island. **Ondake-jinja**, north of Ashibe, features stone statues dedicated to a half-monkey deity. These eroded figures were carved by a local lord, and were intended to bring health to the island's livestock. **Yunomoto Onsen** on the west coast is the island's only hot spring. Other minor sights include burial mounds, Buddhist rock carvings and historic ruins.

The little **beach** near Katsumoto on the island's north side has a camping ground nearby. At the hot springs, the *kokumin-shukusha* (people's lodge) **Ikishima-sō** (壱岐島荘; ☎ 43-0124; r with 2 meals ¥6660) is good value. Otherwise, try **Tomita-sō** (とみた荘; ☎ 47-0011; r with 2 meals ¥5800) if in Gonoura. At Gonoura ferry terminal, the **information desk** (☎ 47-3700) can help book other accommodation around the island.

ORC Air has flights from Nagasaki to Iki (¥9300, 30 minutes, two daily). Jetfoils run year-round from Hakata to Gonoura or Ashibe (¥4900, 70 minutes, three daily) on Iki. Ordinary car-ferry services take twice that long (¥2400, two daily). On Iki, rental cars start at ¥3000 per three hours, costing ¥10,000 for two days. They can be rented at all of the ferry ports. Try friendly **Genkai Kōtsū Rent-a-Car** (☎ 44-5658). Bike rental is possible from **Kawabe Motors** (☎ 44-6636; ¥1000), near the ferry terminal; for an extra ¥1000 you can have the bike dropped to you anywhere on the island.

HIRADO-SHIMA 平戸島

☎ 0950 / pop 39,080

Hirado-shima's proximity to the mainland makes it accessible and affordable. The local government encourages tourism, though accommodation is limited and the population is dwindling. The island, joined to Kyūshū at Hirado-guchi by a Golden Gate–lookalike toll bridge (¥100), has a fascinating history. Portuguese ships first landed in 1549 and in 1584 the Portuguese established a trading post, followed by the Dutch and the British. By 1618, the Japanese had to restore law and order on the island!

The **tourist information centre** (☎ 22-2015; 8am-5pm) nearby the bus terminal has lots of English-language materials and can book accommodation.

The main town, Hirado, is small enough to navigate on foot. The **Matsūra Historical Museum** (松浦史料博物館; ☎ 22-2236; admission ¥500; 8am-5.30pm) is housed in the stunning residence of the Matsuura clan, who ruled the island from the 11th to the 19th centuries. Among the treasures is **Kanun-tei**, a *chanoyu* (tea ceremony) house for the unusual Chinshin-ryū warrior-style tea ceremony that is still practised on the island. **Hirado Christian Museum** (平戸切支丹資料館; ☎ 28-0176; admission ¥200; 8am-5pm Jan-Nov) exhibits items including a Maria-Kannon statue that the 'hidden Christians' used in place of the Virgin Mary.

Hirado-jō (平戸城; ☎ 22-2201; admission ¥500; 8.30am-5.30pm) presides over the town, with an enormous number of rebuilt structures. Inside you'll see traditional armour and clothing, and a few artefacts from the hidden-Christian era. There are fine views over the islands of the Gotō-rettō from **Cape Shijiki**. About midway down the beautiful west coast of the island, **Neshiko Beach** is a lovely, long stretch of sand, while **Senri-ga-hama** is renowned for windsurfing. **Hotel Ranpū** (ホテル蘭風; ☎ 23-2111), near the beach, rents windsurfing gear.

KYŪSHŪ

Jangara Matsuri (ジャンガラ祭り), a folk festival held on 18 August, is particularly colourful. It is quite different from mainland festivals and is reminiscent of Okinawa or Korea. Arrive in Hirado by late morning, if possible, for the afternoon events. From 24 to 27 October, the **Okunchi Matsuri** (おくんち祭り) has dragon and lion dancing at Kameoka-jinja.

In Hirado-guchi, the closest mainland town, there's an excellent **youth hostel** (たびら平戸ロユースホステル; ☎ 57-1443; dm ¥3360; P 💻) with two lovely *rotemburo* (outdoor baths) and a sprawling grassy campground. There are private rooms (from ¥8400) and a restaurant.

Hirado-guchi (aka Tabira) is accessible by bus from Sasebo (¥1300, 1¼ hours), and by train (¥1190, 1½ hours). Local buses cross the bridge to Hirado town (¥260, 10 minutes). Express buses (¥1450, 1½ hours) and trains (¥1600, 1½ hours) run from Nagasaki to Sasebo.

GOTŌ-RETTŌ 五島列島

The two main islands in the Gotō-rettō group are **Fukue-jima** and **Nakadōri-shima**, but there are over 100 small islands and islets. Historically, these islands were a refuge for Japanese Christians fleeing the Edo government's anti-Christian repression; today the main attraction is their natural beauty. If you have the time, money and inclination, they are isolated enough to be worth the effort.

Fukue, the fishing port on the island of the same name, is the main town in the group. The town's castle **Ishida-jō** was rebuilt in the 1860s. There's a street of samurai houses nearby. **Ondake**, about 800m from Fukue, is a cotyloid (cup-shaped) volcano (315m) covered by grass and with an astronomical observatory. **Dozaki Tenshudō** (堂崎天主堂; ☎ 0959-73-0705; admission ¥300; 9am-4.30pm) has exhibits of artefacts from the 'hidden Christian' era, and is the oldest church in the Gotō islands. It's a 30-minute bus ride from Fukue. The island's most popular **beaches** are on the north central coast.

All Nippon Koku (ANK) has flights to Gotō-Fukue airport from Fukuoka (¥18,380, 35 minutes, three daily). Jetfoils leave Nagasaki for Fukue two to five times daily (¥7070, 1½ hours); regular car ferry services depart three times daily (¥2700, 3½ hours). Bicycles and cars can be rented on Fukue-jima.

NAGASAKI-KEN 長崎県

NAGASAKI 長崎

☎ 095 / pop 451,740

The tragedy of Nagasaki's atomic devastation overshadows the story of its colourful trading history. Today Nagasaki has plenty to offer visitors – an array of museums with content ranging from the fascinating to the profound. There are churches, shrines and temples, culinary delights and a landscape that rivals far more visited parts of Japan. Schedule at least a few days here to meet the people and get a sense of the spirit of this unique and embracing place.

History

Nagasaki's role in Japan's emergence as a modern nation is layered and tragic. The arrival of an off-course Chinese ship in 1543, with guns and Portuguese adventurers aboard, heralded the beginning of the long period where Nagasaki was Japan's principal connection with Asia and the West. The first visitors were followed by the missionary St Francis Xavier in 1560, then many others, in the dramatic period that became known as Japan's 'Christian Century' (1549–1650).

Although their visits were brief, these Portuguese contacts were to have far-reaching effects. Among the first Japanese to be converted to Christianity was a minor *daimyō* (regional lord), Ōmura Sumitada, who established Nagasaki as the principal trading port. Although the Portuguese acted as intermediaries between Japan, China and Korea, the trade was mutually profitable and Nagasaki quickly became a fashionable and wealthy city.

By 1587, Japanese authorities who'd begun to see Christianity as a threat began to expel the Jesuits, and in 1597 ceremoniously crucified 26 European and Japanese Christians. Catholic Portuguese and Spanish traders were expelled in favour of the Protestant Dutch, who were thought of as being more interested in trade and less in religion. Christianity was officially banned in 1614.

The final chapter of the 'Christian Century' was the Shimabara peasant uprising of 1637–38, perceived as a Christian revolt at the time, resulting in the authorities forbidding any contact with foreigners and banning all travel outside Japan. The single exception, however, was the closely watched Dutch enclave of Dejima in Nagasaki harbour. Via this small outpost, a trickle of Western science and culture found its way into Japan. When in 1859, it reopened its doors to the West, Nagasaki was a major economic force, particularly in shipbuilding, the industry that ultimately led to its tragic destruction on 9 August 1945 (for details, see the boxed text, p706).

Orientation

About 2km southeast of JR Nagasaki Station, the Hamano-machi arcade and Shianbashi entertainment district are where the locals go to shop and eat. Nagasaki's sights are scattered over a broad area, but it's feasible to walk from Shianbashi through Chinatown, all the way south to the Dutch slopes and Glover Garden. The atomic bomb hypocentre is in the opposite direction in the suburb of Urakami, about 2.5km north of JR Nagasaki Station.

Information

BOOKSHOPS

Kinokuniya (Map p704; ☎ 811-4919; 4th fl, Yume-saito Bldg, 10-1 Motofune-chō) Has English and foreign-language titles, plus CDs, DVDs and maps.

INTERNET ACCESS

Chikyū-shimin Hiroba (Map p704; ☎ 842-2002; www1.city.nagasaki.nagasaki.jp/kokusai/people_hiroba/people_hiroba_e.html; 2nd fl, Nagasaki Brick Hall, 2-38 Morimachi; per hr ¥100; 🕑 9am-8pm, closed 29 Dec–3 Jan) The 'Global Citizens Room' was established to promote cultural exchange. It's a five-minute walk from Urakami Station, behind Mirai Cocowalk Nagasaki.

Cybac Café (Map p708; ☎ 818-8050; 3rd & 4th fl, Hashimoto Bldg, 2-46 Aburaya-chō; registration fee ¥300 then 1st 30/subsequent 15min ¥300/100) This enormous internet cafe has showers, darts, drinks and more.

Internet Café Shin (Map p708; ☎ 822-7824; 5-25 Furukawamachi, Hamano-machi; per 30min ¥210; 🕑 8am-8pm) This quiet internet cafe opposite Minato Park near Chinatown is famed for its Turkish omelette topped with *tonkatsu* (deep-fried pork cutlets) and demisauce.

Kinko's (Map p704; ☎ 818-2522; 1st fl, Amu Plaza, 1-1 Onoue-machi; per 10min ¥210; 🕑 8am-10pm Sat-Mon, 24hr Tue-Fri) Next to 18-Bank.

MONEY

All postal savings and Seven Bank ATMs allow you to withdraw cash in English from foreign cards bearing the Visa, MasterCard, Plus, Maestro or Cirrus symbols. Several branches of the 18-Bank (Map p708) handle foreign-currency exchange.

TOURIST INFORMATION

Nagasaki Prefectural Convention & Visitors Bureau (Map p704; ☎ 828-7875; 8th fl,14-10 Motofuna-machi; 🕑 9am-5.30pm, closed 27 Dec–3 Jan) Has detailed information on the city and prefecture and helpful English-speaking staff.

Nagasaki Tourist Information Centre (Map p704; www.at-nagasaki.jp/foreign/english; ☎ 823-3631; 1st fl,

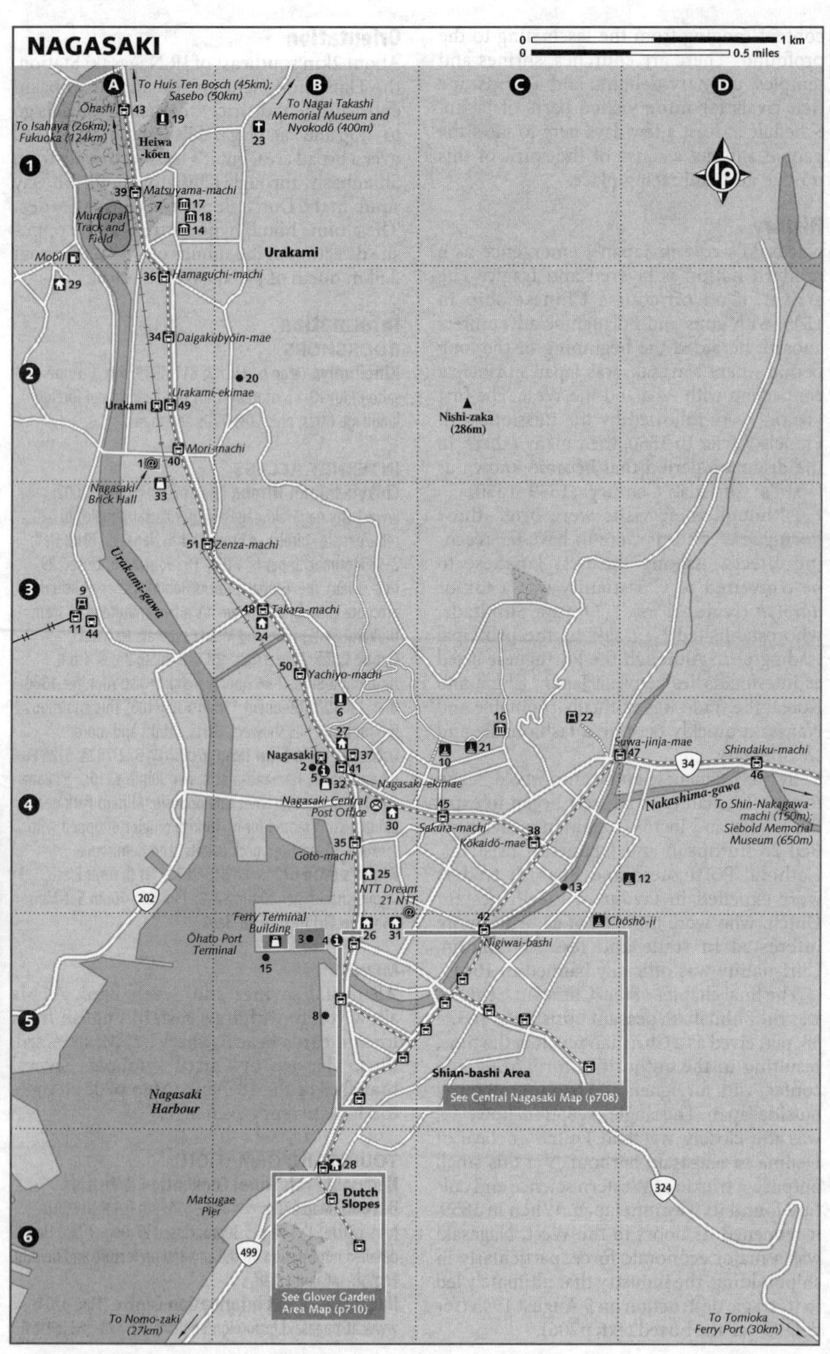

NAGASAKI
0 1 km
0 0.5 miles
To Huis Ten Bosch (45km); Sasebo (50km)
To Nagai Takashi Memorial Museum and Nyokodō (400m)
To Isahaya (26km); Fukuoka (124km)
Ōhashi
Heiwa-kōen
Matsuyama-machi
Municipal Track and Field
Mobil
Urakami
Hamaguchi-machi
Daigakubyōin-mae
Urakami-ekimae
Urakami
Mori-machi
Nagasaki Brick Hall
Zenza-machi
Urakami-gawa
Nishi-zaka (286m)
Takara-machi
Yachiyo-machi
Nagasaki
Nagasaki-ekimae
Nagasaki Central Post Office
Sakura-machi
Kōkaidō-mae
Gotō-machi
Suwa-jinja-mae
Shindaiku-machi
Nakashima-gawa
To Shin-Nakagawa-machi (150m); Siebold Memorial Museum (650m)
NTT Dream 21 NTT
Ferry Terminal Building
Ōhato Port Terminal
Chōshō-ji
Nigiwai-bashi
Shian-bashi Area
See Central Nagasaki Map (p708)
Nagasaki Harbour
Dutch Slopes
Matsugae Pier
See Glover Garden Area Map (p710)
To Nomo-zaki (27km)
To Tomioka Ferry Port (30km)
KYŪSHŪ

INFORMATION
Chikyū-shimin Hiroba 地球市民ひろば 1 A2
Joy Road Nagasaki ジョイロード長崎 2 B4
Kinko's キンコーズ .... (see 32)
Kinokuniya 紀伊國屋書店 3 B5
Nagasaki Prefectural Convention and Visitors Bureau 長崎県観光振興推進本部 4 B5
Nagasaki Tourist Infomation Centre 長崎市総合観光案内所 5 B4

SIGHTS & ACTIVITIES
26 Martyrs Memorial 日本二十六聖人殉教地 6 B4
Atomic Bomb Hypocentre Park 長崎爆心地公園 7 A1
Dejima Wharf 出島 8 B5
Fuchi-jinja 淵神社 9 A3
Fukusai-ji Kannon 福済寺・長崎観音 10 C4
Inasa-yama Cable Car 稲佐山ロープウェイ 11 A3
Kanzen-ji 観善寺 .... (see 21)
Kōfuku-ji 興福寺 12 D4
Megane-bashi めがね橋 13 C4
Nagasaki Atomic Bomb Museum 長崎原爆資料館 14 A1
Nagasaki Harbour Cruises 長崎港クルーズ 15 B5
Nagasaki Museum of History & Culture 長崎歴史文化博物館 16 C4
Nagasaki Museum of History & Folklore 長崎市歴史民俗資料館 17 A1
Nagasaki National Peace Memorial Hall for the Atomic Bomb Victims 国立長崎原爆死没者追悼平和祈念館 18 A1
Nagasaki Peace Statue 平和祈念像 19 A1
One-Pillar Torii (Sanno Shintō Shrine) 一本柱鳥居 20 B2
Shōfuku-ji 聖福寺 21 C4
Suwa-jinja 諏訪神社 22 C4
Urakami Cathedral 浦上天主堂 23 B1

SLEEPING
Best Western Premier Hotel Nagasaki ベストウェスタンプレミアホテル 24 B3
Chisun Grand Nagasaki チサングランド長崎 25 B4
Hotel BelleView ホテルベルビュー長崎 26 B5
Hotel Cuore ホテルクオーレ 27 B4
Hotel Monterey Nagasaki ホテルモントレ長崎 28 B6
Hotel New Nagasaki ホテルニュー長崎 .... (see 32)
JR Kyūshū Hotel Nagasaki ＪＲ九州ホテル .... (see 32)
Minshuku Tanpopo 民宿たんぽぽ 29 A2
Nagasaki Ebisu Youth Hostel 長崎えびすユースホステル 30 B4
Sakamoto-ya 料亭旅館坂本屋 31 B5

EATING
Amu Plaza アミュプラザ .... (see 32)

SHOPPING
Amu Plaza アミュプラザ 32 B4
Mirai Cocowalk みらいココウォーク長崎 33 A3

TRANSPORT
Daigakubyōin-mae 大学病院前 34 A2
Goto-machi 五島町 35 B4
Hamaguchi-machi 浜口町 36 A2
Kenei Bus Terminal 県営バスターミナル 37 B4
Kōkaidō-mae 公会堂前 38 C4
Matsuyama-machi 松山町 39 A1
Mori-machi 茂里町 40 A2
Nagasaki-ekimae 長崎駅前 41 B4
Nigiwai-bashi 賑橋 42 C5
Ōhashi 大橋 43 A1
Ropeway-mae ロープウエイ前 44 A3
Sakura-machi 桜町 45 C4
Shindaiku-machi 新大工町 46 D4
Suwa-jinja-mae 諏訪神社前 47 C4
Takara-machi 宝町 48 B3
Urakami-ekimae 浦上駅前 49 A2
Yachiyo-machi 八千代町 50 B3
Zenza-machi 銭座町 51 A3

JR Nagasaki Station; 8am-8pm) Can assist with finding accommodation and has a swag of brochures and maps in English.

TRAVEL AGENCIES

Joy Road Nagasak (Map p704; ☎ 822-4813; JR Nagasaki Station; 10am-5.30pm) Handles domestic travel and hotel arrangements.

Sights

URAKAMI 浦上

Urakami, the hypocentre of the atomic explosion, is a prosperous, peaceful suburb with shops, eateries and even a couple of love hotels just a few steps from the hypocentre. Nuclear ruin seems comfortably far away.

The **Atomic Bomb Hypocentre Park** (Map p704) has a smooth, black stone column marking the point above which the bomb exploded. Nearby are bomb-blasted relics, including a section of the wall of the Urakami Cathedral. The nearest tram stop is Matsuyama-cho.

Nagasaki Atomic Bomb Museum (Map p704; ☎ 844-1231; www1.city.nagasaki.nagasaki.jp/na-bomb/museum/museume01.html; 7-8 Hirano-machi; admission ¥200, audioguide rental ¥150; 8.30am-5pm; closed 29-31 Dec) An essential experience for visitors to Nagasaki, this sombre place graphically recounts the city's destruction and loss of human life. The exhibits also cover Japan's 15 years of military prewar aggression, chronicle the postbombing struggle for nuclear disarmament and conclude with a frightening illustration of which nations still bear nuclear arms.

Nagasaki National Peace Memorial Hall for the Atomic Bomb Victims (Map p704; ☎ 814-0055; www.peace-nagasaki.go.jp; 7-8 Hirano-machi; admission free; 8.30am-5.30pm Sep-Apr, to 6.30pm May-Aug, to 8pm 7-9 Aug, closed 29-31 Dec) Adjacent to the Atomic Bomb Museum and completed in 2003, this deeply symbolic memorial for those whose lives were lost from the effects of the blast is a profoundly moving place. It is best approached by quietly reading the carved inscriptions and walking around the sculpted

THE ATOMIC EXPLOSION

When USAF B-29 bomber *Bock's Car* set off from the Marianas to drop a second atomic bomb on Japan, the target was Kokura on Kyūshū's northeastern coast. Due to poor visibility, the crew diverted to the secondary target, Nagasaki. It was 9 August 1945.

The B-29 arrived over Nagasaki at 10.58am amid heavy cloud. When a momentary gap appeared and the Mitsubishi Arms Factory was sighted, the 4.57-tonne 'Fat Man' bomb, with an explosive power equivalent to 21.3 kilotonnes of TNT (almost twice that of Hiroshima's 'Little Boy'), was released on the people of Nagasaki.

The bomb missed its intended target and exploded at 11.02am, at an altitude of 500m, almost directly above the largest Catholic church in Asia (Urakami Cathedral; below). In an instant, it annihilated the suburb of Urakami and 75,000 of Nagasaki's 240,000 people. Most victims were women, children and senior citizens, as well as 13,000 conscripted Korean labourers and 200 allied POWs. Another 75,000 people were horribly injured and it is estimated that as many people again have died as a result of the blast. Everything within a 1km radius of the explosion was destroyed and after the fires burned out, a third of the city was gone.

water basin above before entering the hall below. Be prepared for tears.

Nagasaki Museum of History & Folklore (Map p704; ☎ 847-9245; 7-8 Hirano-machi; admission free; 9am-4.30pm, closed Mon) Antique items relating to daily life are exhibited in this museum within the Nagasaki Peace Hall building. A hands-on room allows children of all ages to play around.

Heiwa-kōen (平和公園; Peace Park), north of the hypocentre, is presided over by the **Nagasaki Peace Statue** (Map p704) and includes the Peace Symbol Zone, an unusual sculpture garden with contributions from around the world. On 9 August, a rowdy antinuclear protest is held within earshot of the more respectful official memorial ceremony for those lost to the bomb.

Urakami Cathedral (Map p704; 浦上天主堂; ☎ 844-1777; 1-79 Motō-machi; 9am-5pm, closed Mon), once the largest church in Asia, was completed in 1914 after three decades and flattened in three seconds. The replacement cathedral was completed in 1959. Unlike the Ōura Catholic Church, admission is free.

The extraordinary courage and faith of one man in the face of overwhelming adversity is the subject of the quietly moving **Nagai Takashi Memorial Museum** (永井隆記念館; off Map p704; ☎ 844-3496; 22-6 Ueno-chō; admission ¥100; 9am-5pm). Dr Nagai, already suffering from leukaemia, survived the atomic explosion but lost his wife to it. He immediately devoted himself to the treatment of bomb victims until his death in 1951. In his final days, he continued to write prolifically and secure donations for survivors and orphans. Next door, **Nyokodō** (如己堂; off Map p704), the simple hut from which he worked, is preserved as a memorial to this local hero.

The **One-Pillar Torii** (Map p704) is 800m southeast of the hypocentre. The blast knocked down half of the stone entrance arch to the Sanno-jinja shrine, but the other pillar remains.

NAGASAKI STATION AREA

The **26 Martyrs Memorial** (Map p704) features reliefs commemorating the six Spanish and 20 Japanese crucified in 1597, when authorities cracked down on practising Christians. The youngest killed were boys aged 12 and 13. Behind the memorial is a simple Christianity-related **museum** (☎ 822-6000; 7-8 Nishisaka-machi; admission ¥250). The memorial is five minutes' walk from JR Nagasaki Station.

Fukusai-ji Kannon (Nagasaki Universal Kannon Temple; Map p704; ☎ 823-2663; 2-56 Chikugo-machi; admission ¥200; 8am-4pm) is in the form of a huge astral turtle carrying an 18m-high figure of the goddess Kannon. Inside, a Foucault pendulum, demonstrating the rotation of the earth, hangs from the top. It's the third-largest such pendulum in the world and only dwarfed by those in St Petersburg and Paris. The original temple, built in 1628, was completely burnt by the A-bomb fire. The replacement was built in 1976. The temple bell tolls at 11.02am daily, the exact time of the explosion (see above).

Nearby, the gardens of the temple **Shōfuku-ji** (Map p704; ☎ 823-0282; 3-77 Tamazono-machi), not to be confused with Sōfuku-ji (see opposite), contain an arched stone gate dating from 1657. The main building was reconstructed in 1715 in the ornate Chinese style of the time. The *onigawara* (ogre-covered wall) is particularly interesting, as is the book-burning kiln. There are clear views of Nagasaki port.

Just west of here is another temple, **Kanzen-ji** (Map p704), with one of the biggest camphor trees in Nagasaki.

SUWA-JINJA 諏訪神社

This enormous **shrine** (Map p704; ☎ 824-0445; 18-15 Kaminishiyama-machi), situated on a forested hilltop, was established in 1625. Between 7 and 9 October each year, the shrine comes to life with the dragon dance of Kunchi Matsuri (p711), Nagasaki's most important annual celebration. Inside you will find a number of cutesy *komainu* (prayer dogs). Be sure to see the *kappa-komainu* (water-sprite dog), which you pray to by dribbling water on the plate on its head, and the *gan-kake komainu* (turn-table dog), which was often called on by prostitutes, who prayed that storms would arrive, forcing the sailors to stay at the port another day. Tram lines 3, 4 and 5 run to the Suwa-jinja-mae stop.

TERA-MACHI (TEMPLE ROW) 寺町

Between Shianbashi and Nakajima-gawa, the smaller of the city's two rivers, justly famous Tera-machi is anchored at either end by Nagasaki's two best-known temples, Sōfuku-ji and Kōfuku-ji, both Chinese in origin. The path connecting them is home to several smaller temples and famous gravesites and makes for a relaxing and fascinating stroll. Despite the Chinese influences, it feels thoroughly Japanese here.

An Ōbaku (the third-largest Zen sect after Rinzai and Sōtō) temple, **Sōfuku-ji** (Map p708; ☎ 823-2645; 7-5 Kajiya-machi; admission ¥300; 🕑 8am-5pm) was built in 1629 by Chinese monk Chaonian. Its red entrance gate (Daiippo-mon) exemplifies Ming dynasty architecture. Inside the temple is a huge cauldron that was used to prepare food for famine victims in 1681, and a statue of Maso, goddess of the sea.

Continuing north along the path from Sōfuku-ji, steep steps lead up to **Daikō-ji** (Map p708; ☎ 822-2877; 5-74 Kajiya-machi), founded in 1614 and since famous for avoiding fires (even atomic ones). Near the bottom of the road, turn right and take a few steps to the **Hosshin-ji bell** (Map p708; ☎ 823-2892; 5-84 Kajiya-machi), the oldest temple bell in Nagasaki, cast in 1438. Then climb the stairs to the huge *kuroganemochi* tree at the entrance to **Daion-ji** (Map p708; ☎ 824-2367; 5-87 Kajiya-machi) and follow the path that heads to the grave of Matsudaira Zushonokami, the famous magistrate who in 1808, unable to oppose the British, capitulated to their demands for supplies then promptly disembowelled himself.

A short distance further, turn down the path to **Kōtai-ji** (Map p708; ☎ 823-7211; 1-1 Tera-machi), the only temple in Nagasaki with active monks-in-training and a favourite with local artists; it has a notable bell dating from 1702. The final temple along the walk, **Kōfuku-ji** (Map p704; ☎ 822-1076; 4-32 Tera-machi; admission ¥200; 🕑 6am-6pm), dates from the 1620s and is noted for the Ming architecture of the main hall. Like Sōfuku-ji, it is an Ōbaku Zen temple – and the oldest in Japan.

Parallel to Tera-machi, the Nakajima-gawa is crossed by a picturesque collection of 17th-century stone bridges. At one time, each bridge was the distinct entranceway to a separate temple. The best known is the double-arched **Megane-bashi** (めがね橋; Spectacles Bridge; Map p704), so-called because the reflection of the arches in the water looks like a pair of Meiji-era spectacles! Six of the 10 bridges, including Megane-bashi, were washed away by flooding in 1982, but restored using the recovered stones.

NAGASAKI MUSEUM OF HISTORY & CULTURE 長崎歴史文化博物館

Just east of Shōfuku-ji temple you'll find this handsome **museum** (Map p704; ☎ 818-8366; www.nmhc.jp; 1-1-1 Tateyama; admission ¥600; 🕑 8.30am-7pm, closed 3rd Tue of month). Opened in 2005, its focus is on Nagasaki's proud history of overseas exchange and the main gallery is a fabulous reconstruction of a section of the Edo-period Nagasaki Magistrate's Office, which controlled trade and diplomacy. There's a free English audio guide. The closest tram stop is Sakura-machi.

SHIANBASHI 思案橋

The Shianbashi tram stop marks the site of the former bridge that pleasure seekers would cross to enter the Shianbashi (loosely meaning 'Bridge of Consideration') quarter. Men might stop here and contemplate a night of pleasure versus the journey home. The bridge and the elegant old brothels are long gone but the district is still at the heart of nightlife in Nagasaki.

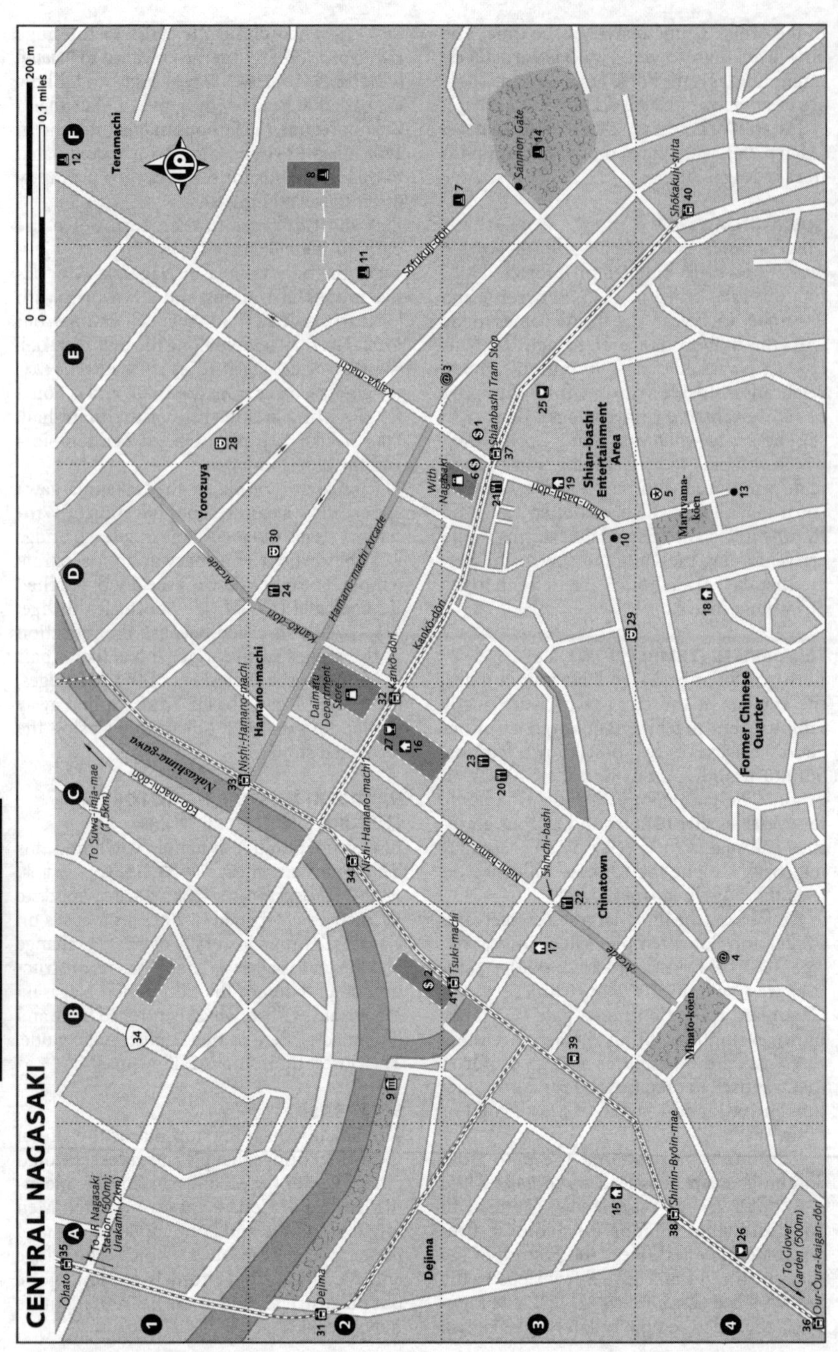
CENTRAL NAGASAKI
0.1 miles
200 m
Teramachi
Yorozuya
Hamano-machi
Hamano-machi Arcade
Kankō-dōri
Kajiya-machi
Sōfukuji-dōri
Sanmon Gate
Shōkakuji-shita
Shianbashi Tram Stop
Shian-bashi-dōri
Shian-bashi Entertainment Area
Maruyama-kōen
Former Chinese Quarter
With Nagasaki
Daimaru Department Store
Nishi-Hamano-machi
Nakashima-gawa
Edo-machi-dōri
To Suwa-jinja-mae (1.5km)
Nishi-hama-dōri
Shinchi-bashi
Chinatown
Arcade
Minato-kōen
Tsuki-machi
Shimin-Byōin-mae
To Glover Garden (500m)
Ōura-kaigan-dōri
Dejima
Ohato
To JR Nagasaki Station (500m); Urakami (2km)

INFORMATION

18 Bank 十八銀行 ... 1 E3
18 Bank 十八銀行 ... 2 B2
Cybac Café サイバックカフェ ... 3 E3
Internet Café Shin しん ... 4 B4
Maruyama Police Box 丸山町交番 ... 5 D4
Shinwa Ginkō 親和銀行 ... 6 D3

SIGHTS & ACTIVITIES

Daikō-ji 大光寺 ... 7 F3
Daion-ji 大音寺 ... 8 F2
Dejima Museum 出島資料館 ... 9 B2
Fukusaya Castella Cake Shop 福砂屋本家 ... 10 D3
Hosshin-ji Bell 発心寺 ... 11 E2
Kōtai-ji 晧台寺 ... 12 F1
Ryōtei Kagetsu 料亭花月 ... 13 D4
Sōfuku-ji 崇福寺 ... 14 F3

SLEEPING

Fukumoto Ryokan 福本旅館 ... 15 A3
Holiday Inn Nagasaki ホリデイイン長崎 ... 16 C2
Nagasaki Washington Hotel 長崎ワシントンホテル ... 17 B3
Nishiki-sō Bekkan にしき荘別館 ... 18 D4
Richmond Hotel Nagasaki Shianbashi リチモンドホテル長崎思案橋 ... 19 D3

EATING

Ginnabe 銀鍋 ... 20 C3
Hyōuntei 宝雲亭 ... 21 D3
Kairaku-en 会楽園 ... 22 C3
Ryōtei Kagetsu 料亭花月 ... (see 13)
Sweet Marjoram スイートマジョラム ... 23 C3
Yosso 吉宗 ... 24 D2

DRINKING

Country Road カントリーロード ... 25 E3
Hotel New Tanda Beer Garden ホテルニュータンダ ... 26 A4
Vingt et Un バンテアン ... 27 C2

ENTERTAINMENT

Ayer's Rock エアーズ·ロック ... 28 E1
International Club Sparkle インターナショナルクラブスパークル ... 29 D3
Panic Paradise パニックパラダイス ... 30 D2

TRANSPORT

Dejima 出島 ... 31 A2
Kankō-dōri 観光通り ... 32 C2
Nishi-Hamano-machi 西浜町 ... 33 C1
Nishi-Hamano-machi1 西浜町 ... 34 C2
Ōhato 大波止 ... 35 A1
Ōura-kaigan-dōri 大浦海岸通り ... 36 A4
Shianbashi Tram Stop 思案橋 ... 37 E3
Shimin-Byōin-mae 市民病院前 ... 38 A4
Shinchi Bus Terminal 新地バスターミナル ... 39 B3
Shōkakuji-shita 正覚寺下 ... 40 F4
Tsuki-machi 築町 ... 41 B3

Modern Shianbashi still has a few reminders of its colourful past. Just south of Shianbashi tram stop, you'll find **Fukusaya Castella Cake Shop** (Map p708; ☎ 821-2938; www.castella.co.jp, in Japanese; 3-1 Funadaiku-machi), trading since 1624! It's a must for history buffs and those with a sweet tooth. Left at this junction, past the police box, you'll find the driveway to **Ryōtei Kagetsu** (p712), now an elegant and expensive restaurant but once an even more expensive brothel.

DEJIMA 出島

From the mid-17th century until 1855, the small Dutch trading post of Dejima provided Japan with its sole peephole to the world outside. Resident and itinerant Dutch were segregated here and their only contact was with Japanese trading partners and courtesans. The area around **Dejima Wharf** (Map p704) was the focal point for this activity, and was recently converted into a picturesque collection of open-air restaurants, bars and galleries.

Dejima Museum (Map p708; ☎ 822-2207; www1.city.nagasaki.nagasaki.jp/dejima/main.html, in Japanese; 8-21 Dejima; admission ¥300; 9am-5pm) has exhibits on Nagasaki's trading history. Although the island was submerged during 19th-century land-reclamation projects, the trading post, now a national historic site, has been restored.

SHINCHI CHINATOWN 新地中華街

During Japan's long period of seclusion, Chinese traders were theoretically just as restricted as the Dutch, but in practice they were relatively free. Only a couple of buildings remain from the old area (Map p708), but Nagasaki still has an energetic Chinese community, evident in the city's culture, architecture, festivals and cuisine. Visitors come from far and wide to eat here.

GLOVER GARDEN グラバー園

At the southern end of Nagasaki, some former homes of the city's pioneering Meiji-period European residents have been reassembled in this hillside **garden** (Map p710; ☎ 822-8223; www.glover-garden.jp; 8-1 Minami-yamatemachi; adult/student ¥600/300; 8am-9.30pm 27 Apr–9 Oct, to 6pm 10 Oct–26 Apr), named after Thomas Glover (1838–1911), who built Japan's first railway, helped establish the shipbuilding industry and whose arms-importing operations influenced the course of the Meiji Restoration.

The best way to explore the steep garden is to take the moving walkways to the top of the hill then walk back down. The **Mitsubishi No 2 Dock building** is highest, with displays about the city's shipyard, before **Walker House**, the **Ringer** and **Alt Houses**, and finally **Glover House**. Halfway down is a **statue** of Japanese opera singer Tamaki Miura, often referred to as Madame Butterfly. You exit the garden through the **Nagasaki Traditional Performing Arts Museum**, which has a display of dragons and floats used in the colourful Kunchi Matsuri.

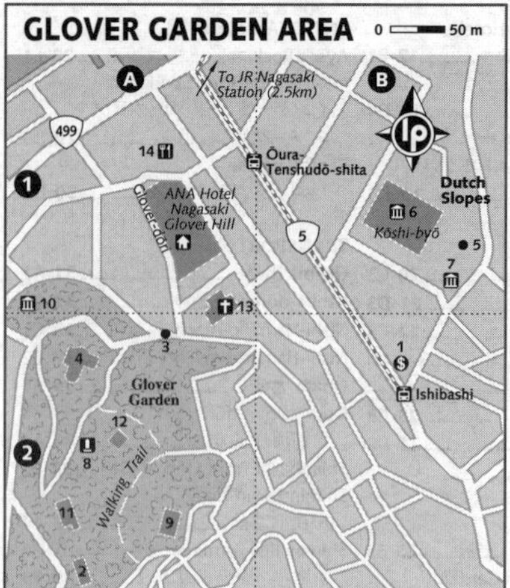

INFORMATION

18 Bank 十八銀行 1 B2

SIGHTS & ACTIVITIES

Alt House 旧オルト住宅 2 A2
Glover Garden Entrance グラバー園入り口 3 A2
Glover House 旧グラバー住宅 4 A2
Higashi-yamate Chikyu-kan 東山手地球館 5 B1
Historical Museum of China 中国歴史博物館 6 B1
Ko-shashin-shiryōkan & Maizō-shiryōkan 古写真資料館 - 埋蔵資料館 7 B1
Madame Butterfly Statue 三浦環像 8 A2
Mitsubishi No 2 Dock Building 旧三菱第２ドックハウス 9 A2
Nagasaki Traditional Performing Arts Museum 長崎伝統芸能館 10 A1
Ringer 旧リンガー住宅 11 A2
Walker House 旧ウォーカー住宅 12 A2
Ōura Catholic Church 大浦天主堂 13 A1

EATING

Shikairō 四海楼 14 A1
Higashi-yamate Chikyu-kan 東山手地球館 .... (see 5)

ŌURA CATHOLIC CHURCH 大浦天主堂

Soon after this hilltop **church** (Map p710; ☎ 823-2628; admission ¥300; 🕑 8.30am-5pm) opened its doors to Nagasaki's foreign residents in 1864, a group of Japanese arrived to announce that Christianity had been secretly practised among the Urakami community throughout the 250 years it had been banned. The government was still anxious about Western contact, and when this news leaked out, thousands of Urakami residents were exiled to other parts of Japan until Christianity was legalised in 1873. The church is dedicated to the 26 Christians crucified in 1597 (see p703 for more information). It's more like a museum than a place of worship and an admission fee is charged. To pray for free, use the regular church just opposite.

DUTCH SLOPES オランダ坂

The gently inclined flagstone streets known as the Dutch Slopes (Oranda-zaka; Map p710) were once lined with wooden **Dutch houses**. Several buildings have been beautifully restored and offer glimpses of Japan's early interest in the West. Quaint **Koshashin-shiryōkan** and **Maizō-shiryōkan** (Map p710; ☎ 820-3386; 6-25 Higashi-yamatemachi; combined admission ¥100; 🕑 9am-5pm, closed Mon) have a collection of vintage photographs and archaeological artefacts between them, but the wonderful **Higashi-yamate Chikyūkan** (www.h3.dion.ne.jp/~chikyu/e_frame.htm; ☎ 820-3386) has a fabulous 'World Foods Restaurant'. Here, each day, a different chef comes to prepare and share an inexpensive meal from his/her home country. This little gem, borne of good intent, is what travel and cultural exchange is all about.

Behind the jauntily coloured **Kōshi-byō**, a Confucian shrine, the **Historical Museum of China** (Map p710; ☎ 824-4022; 10-36 Ōuramachi; admission ¥525; 🕑 8.30am-5pm) has exhibits on loan from Beijing. The original shrine dates from 1893, but was destroyed in the fires following the A-bomb explosion.

SIEBOLD MEMORIAL MUSEUM シーボルト記念館

Beyond Shin-Nakagawa-machi tram stop by 500m is the site of **Dr Siebold's house** (off Map p704; ☎ 823-0707; 2-7-40 Narutaki; admission ¥100; 🕑 9am-5pm, closed Mon), an imposing Western-style home set in a leafy neighbourhood of narrow lanes and flowerboxes. The doctor helped introduce Western science and medicine to Japan in the 1820s, but was later expelled for trying to smuggle Japanese goods. His daughter Ine was one of Japan's first female obstetricians.

INASA-YAMA LOOKOUT 稲左山展望台

From the western side of the harbour, a **cable car** (ropeway; Map p704; ☎ 861-6321; return ¥1200; 🕑 9am-10pm Mar-Nov, to 9pm Dec-Feb) ascends every 20 minutes to the top of 333m-high Inasa-yama, offering superb views over Nagasaki, particularly at night. Buses 3 and 4 leave from outside JR Nagasaki Station;

get off at the Ropeway-mae stop and walk up the stone steps through the grounds of Fuchi-jinja.

Tours

Nagasaki Harbour Cruises (Map p704; ☎ 822-5002; Nagasaki Harbour Terminal Bldg) offers a great way to glimpse picturesque Nagasaki (adult/child ¥1980/1300 with discount, one hour). Check at the ferry terminal for up-to-date schedules.

Festivals & Events

Peiron dragon boat races Colourful races introduced by the Chinese in the mid-1600s, and held to appease the god of the sea, still take place in Nagasaki Harbour in late July.

Shōrō-nagashi On 15 August in this beautiful event, lantern-lit floats are carried down to the harbour in honour of one's ancestors. The boats are handcrafted from a variety of items (bamboo, wood, rice stems etc) and vary in size depending on the family or individual. Eventually they are carried out to sea and destroyed by the waves. The best viewpoint is at Ōhato (Map p708).

Kunchi Matsuri Held 7–9 October, an energetic festival that features more Chinese dragons, this time dancing all around the city but especially at Suwa-jinja (Map p704). The festival is marked by elaborate costumes, fireworks, cymbals and giant dragon puppets on poles.

Sleeping

Wherever you choose to stay, you won't be too far from things to do. The JR Nagasaki Station and Shianbashi areas are good for walking and public transport, while the southern extent of the city near Chinatown and Glover Garden has a lovely atmosphere.

BUDGET

Nagasaki Ebisu Youth Hostel (Map p704; ☎ 824-3823; www5a.biglobe.ne.jp/~urakami; 6-10 Ebisumachi; dm with/without meals from ¥4300/2500; 💻) A tiny youth hostel with three Japanese-style dorm rooms, a bunk room and an 11pm curfew. It's run by a friendly family with years of experience helping travellers.

Minshuku Tanpopo (Map p704; ☎ 861-6230; www.tanpopo-group.biz/tanpopo; 21-7 Hoeimachi; s/d/tr without bathroom ¥4000/7000/9000; 💻) Towards Urakami and the Peace Park, this canary yellow–painted Japanese Inn Group member is cheap and cheery. Breakfast (¥600) and dinner (¥1500) are optional.

Fukumoto Ryokan (Map p708; ☎ 821-0478; 3-8 Dejimamachi; r with/without 2 meals from ¥6500/4500) An older property with both Japanese- and Western-style rooms in the Dejima area. It's near the Shiminbyōin-mae tram stop.

our pick Nishiki-sō Bekkan (Map p708; ☎ 826-6371; 1-2-7 Nishikojima; s/tw with breakfast from ¥4500/8925) It's easy to love this creaky inn perched on a crag and run by the kind and easy-going Ōmura family, whose pride in their home and city is evident. You'll feel like a guest in a Japanese house, but with the privacy of a hotel. There's a communal bath and laundry, but rooms with private facilities are available and the delights of Shianbashi are at your doorstep.

Hotel BelleView (Map p704; ☎ 826-5030; www.hotel-belleview.com, in Japanese; 1-20 Edo-machi; s/d/tw from ¥5800/7000/10,000; ⊠ 💻) Just off the main drag near Dejima and Chinatown, this refurbished business hotel has flat-screen TVs, a breakfast bar and LAN cable internet access.

Hotel Cuore (Map p704; ☎ 818-9000; www.hotel-cuore.com, in Japanese; 7-3 Daikoku-chō; s/d/tw from ¥6100/8000/10,000; 💻; 🚉 JR Nagasaki) Great value, directly opposite JR Nagasaki Station and offers free LAN cable internet and light breakfast.

MIDRANGE

Nagasaki Washington Hotel (Map p708; ☎ 825-8023; www.nagasaki-wh.com, in Japanese; 9-1 Shinchi; s/d from ¥6800/13,000; Ⓟ ⊠ 💻) Adjacent to Chinatown, this multistorey hotel offers great value, with high-speed internet connectivity and tasteful decor.

JR Kyushu Hotel Nagasaki (Map p704; ☎ 832-8000; fax 832-8001; www.jrhotelgroup.com/eng/hotel/eng148.htm; 1-1 Onoue-chō; s/tw/tr ¥6900/12,600/16,200; Ⓟ ⊠ 💻; 🚉 JR Nagasaki) Adjacent to the station and AMU Plaza, many of the otherwise-standard rooms have good views over Nagasaki.

our pick Hotel Monterey Nagasaki (Map p704; ☎ 827-7111; www.hotelmonterey.co.jp/nagasaki, in Japanese; 1-22 Ōura-machi; s/d from ¥9000/18,000; ⊠ 💻) Excellent rates for this lovely Portuguese-themed hotel near the Dutch Slopes and Glover Garden can be found online. Rooms are spacious and light filled, the beds are comfy and there's free internet via LAN cable. The staff is courteous and used to the vagaries of foreign guests.

Holiday Inn Nagasaki (Map p708; ☎ 828-1234; fax 828-0178; 6-24 Dōza-machi; s/d/tw from ¥10,000/14,000/15,000; Ⓟ ⊠ 💻) Close to Shianbashi yet on a quiet laneway, this aging chain property still offers good value and has a great coffee shop-bar. LAN cable internet access is available.

Richmond Hotel Nagasaki Shianbashi (Map p708; ☎ 832-2525; fax 832-2526; www.richmondhotel.jp/e/nagasaki/index.htm; 6-38 Motoshikkui-chō; d from ¥11,000; ⊠ 💻) You can't be closer to the heart of Shianbashi than here. Completed in 2007, rooms are ultramodern with dark tones, flat-screen TVs and LAN internet connectivity. Deluxe rooms are large by Japanese standards and have feature walls.

Chisun Grand Nagasaki (Map p704; ☎ 826-1211; fax 826-1238; www.solarehotels.com/english/chisun/grand-nagasaki/guestroom/detail.html; 35-5 Goto-chō; s/d from ¥12,000/16,000; ⊠ 💻) This new hotel on the main drag just up from JR Nagasaki Station has sleek, small rooms with dark wood and modern styling. All rooms have flat screen TV and free high speed internet via LAN cable.

TOP END

Best Western Premier Hotel Nagasaki (Map p704; ☎ 821-1111; www.bestwestern.com/premier; 2-26 Takara-machi; s/d/ste from ¥15,000/23,000/45,000; P ⊠) Nagasaki's most extravagant hotel has a vast marble lobby, and many of the comfortable rooms have harbour views, though better value can be found elsewhere. LAN cable internet is available. It's opposite the Takara-machi tram stop.

Sakamoto-ya (Map p704; ☎ 826-8210; www.sakamotoya.co.jp; 2-13 Kanaya-machi; r per person with 2 meals from ¥15,750) A magnificent old and well-kept ryokan, with traditional touches, a beautiful garden and only 12 rooms.

Hotel New Nagasaki (Map p704; ☎ 826-8000; www.newnaga.com; s/d/tw from ¥21,700/27,700/30,000; P ⊠ 💻 🏊; 🚊 JR Nagasaki) Next to JR Nagasaki Station, this well-regarded hotel has large rooms, many with bay or hillside views, and some fantastic, though pricey, Japanese-style rooms. There's an excellent swimming pool and a number of restaurants.

KYŪSHŪ

Eating

Nagasaki is a culinary crossroads. The city's Chinese and Portuguese influences converge in *shippoku-ryōri,* a banquet style best enjoyed in a group. *Champon,* the local take on *rāmen,* features squid, octopus, pork and vegetables in a white, salty broth. *Sara-udon* is the stir-fried equivalent.

Hyōuntei (Map p708; ☎ 821-9333; 1-8 Motoshikkui-machi; plate of gyōza ¥300; 🕑 dinner) This tidy *izakaya* (pub-eatery) near Shianbashi tram stop is noticeable for its rustic wooden facade. Inside, there's more of the same styling, mouth-watering *gyōza* and cold beer. Also try the *butaniratoji* (pork and shallots cooked omelette style) for ¥520. There's an English menu if you ask.

Kairaku-en (Map p708; ☎ 822-4261; 10-16 Shinchi-chō; dishes ¥700-1000) Has been serving southern Chinese cuisine since 1950 and there's a distinct possibility that some of the wonderful black-dressed, starched white aproned–servers have been there since. Expect to pay ¥1500 to ¥3000 for a few dishes or splurge on the Peking duck with miso for ¥5000. Most dishes are displayed in the window. It's just inside the Chinatown North gate.

Shikairō (Map p710; ☎ 822-1296; 4-5 Matsugae-machi; champon ¥950) This huge freestanding Chinese restaurant near Glover Garden is credited as the creator of *champon* and has been in operation since 1899. *Sara-udon* is ¥900. English menus.

Sweet Marjoram (Map p708; ☎ 821-3700; 7-9 Dōza-machi; pizza from ¥1000; 🕑 lunch & dinner) Well-priced lunch sets and tasty pastas make this central trattoria a safe bet if you're craving Italian. Pasta set lunches including soup and salad start at ¥1000 and there's a wine menu.

Yosso (Map p708; ☎ 821-0001; 8-9 Hama-machi; set meals from ¥1350; 🕑 lunch & dinner, closed 2nd & 4th Tue; 👶 V) People have been coming to eat the *chawanmushi teishoku* (Japanese egg custard set meal; ¥1785) since 1866. Look for the string of red lanterns and the traditional shopfront.

Ginnabe (Map p708; ☎ 821-8213; www.ginnabe.com/home.html, in Japanese; 7 Dōza-machi; set meals from ¥1500; 🕑 lunch & dinner) Combining modern and traditional, Ginnabe is a large affair, just up from the Hamano-machi arcade, with picture menus and generous *teishoku* starting at ¥1365.

Ryōtei Kagetsu (Map p708; www.ryoutei-kagetsu.co.jp, in Japanese; ☎ 822-0191; 2-1 Maruyama-machi; set meals ¥5200-15,000; 🕑 lunch & dinner) A *shippoku* restaurant dating to 1642 when it was a high-class brothel. If you have Japanese skills or a chaperone, dining companions and a love of food, you might not flinch at the price. A *kaiseki* (degustation) experience in true Japanese style and setting is ¥18,900. It's less than 500m south of Shianbashi tram stop, past the Richmond hotel.

Adjacent to JR Nagasaki Station, Amu Plaza (Map p704) has a good restaurant arcade, Gourmet World, located on the 5th floor. **Sushi Katsu** (☎ 808-1501; 5th fl, Amu Plaza; sushi plates from ¥200) has a fresh sushi train – look for the white lanterns out the front. **Daichi no Table** (☎ 818-2388; 5th fl, Amu Plaza; lunch/dinner ¥1200/1500; 🕑 lunch

& dinner; ⊠ ♿ V) is a bustling, all-you-can-eat buffet featuring sashimi, *champon*, soups, and a variety of healthy vegetable dishes and salads. Kōjōkō has a huge selection of more-ish Cantonese delicacies. If you're craving something from home, **Dragon Deli** (Basement, Amu Plaza) is an import-grocery shop selling goodies from across Asia and the West.

Drinking

Nagasaki isn't the bustling town it ought to be after dark, but there's still some interesting nightlife around the narrow lanes of Hamano-machi.

Country Road (Map p708; ☎ 827-2090; 7-34 Maruyama-machi; drinks from ¥400; ⏰ 6pm-midnight) This cosy family-run country-music bar oozes Americana with a Japanese twist. You'll feel welcome here and the tasty Western bar snacks are likely to tempt.

Vingt et Un (Map p708; ☎ 828-1234; 1st fl, Holiday Inn Nagasaki, 6-24 Dōza-machi; drinks from ¥400; ⏰ 10am-11.30pm, happy hour 6-8pm) More than just a hotel bar, this cafe by day/bar by night is known to locals and expats for its friendly atmosphere and nightly happy hour. Used to a changing crowd, the professional Japanese staff make great cocktails while dispersing local knowledge.

Hotel New Tanda Beer Garden (Map p708; ☎ 827-6121; Rooftop, Hotel New Tanda, 2-24 Tokiwa-machi; ⏰ 6-9pm May-Sep) Everybody loves a rooftop beer garden overlooking the bay! Extremely popular with local Japanese and complete with wonderful views, this is a great way to spend a hot summer's afternoon; ¥3800 buys you two hours of all-you-can-drink draught beer, *chuhai* (alcoholic soda), and soft drinks and a diverse buffet of well-matched, moreish morsels.

Entertainment

Panic Paradise (Map p708; ☎ 824-6167; Basement, Nagatoshokai Bldg, 5-33 Yorozuya-machi; drinks from ¥600; ⏰ 9pm-late) Cool but friendly, this dark basement bar is a bit of a local icon, cluttered with rock memorabilia. There's a huge collection of tunes, cosy booths with dim lamps and the staff has pride in the environment. You'll have a good time here.

Ayer's Rock (Map p708; ☎ 828-0505; basement, Hananoki Bldg, 6-17 Marya-machi; admission Fri & Sat ¥1500; ⏰ 8pm-late) Another basement bar, thumping with DJs, bongos and beer. Popular with local musos, it's a good place to scope out the scene, but starts late.

International Club Sparkle (Map p708; ☎ 824-2676; 2nd fl, NK Kagomachi Bldg, 9-31 Kagomachi; drinks from ¥600; ⏰ 9pm-late) Tricky to find the first time, it's worth the effort to visit this massive new club if you're in the mood to party. The cool concrete interior is minimalist, but has a pool table, low sofas, high stools and space to shake your thang. The music is predominantly hip-hop and R&B.

Shopping

Some local crafts and products are around and opposite JR Nagasaki Station, as well as in lots of shops along busy Hamano-machi shopping arcade. Do your best to ignore Nagasaki's tortoiseshell crafts: turtles actually need their shells. AMU Plaza at the station is nice and easy.

Opened in October 2008, **Mirai Cocowalk Nagasaki** (Map p704; ☎ 848-5599; www.cocowalk.jp, in Japanese; 1-55 Morimachi; ⏰ 10am-9pm), a massive shopping and entertainment complex, has Nagasaki's first permanent Ferris wheel with its apex a whopping 70m above ground. The rotation takes about 11 minutes and will cost you ¥500. Otherwise, state-of-the-art cinemas and a few hundred speciality shops and restaurants will tempt you indoors. The closest tram stop is Mori-machi and JR Urakami Station is just around the corner. You can't miss the place.

Getting There & Away

There are flights between Nagasaki and Tokyo (Haneda airport; ¥38,900), Osaka (Itami airport; ¥25,700), Okinawa (¥28,500) and Nagoya (¥31,900).

From the Kenei bus station opposite JR Nagasaki Station, buses depart for Unzen (¥1900, 1¾ hours), Sasebo (¥1450, 1½ hours), Fukuoka (¥2500, 2¾ hours), Kumamoto (¥3600, three hours) and Beppu (¥4500, 3½ hours). Night buses for Osaka (¥11,000, 10 hours) leave from both the Kenei bus station and the highway bus station next to the Irie-machi tram stop.

JR lines from Nagasaki head for Sasebo (*kaisoku;* ¥1600, 1¾ hours) or Fukuoka (*tokkyū;* ¥4410, two hours).

Ferries sail from a few places around Nagasaki, including Ōhato terminal, south of JR Nagasaki Station.

To travel between here and the Amakusa Archipelago, take bus 10 to Mogi port from the South Exit at JR Nagasaki Station (¥160, 30 minutes), then the ferry to Tomioka on Amakusa island (one way ¥1600, 70 minutes).

Getting Around

TO/FROM THE AIRPORT

Nagasaki's airport is about 40km from the city. Airport buses (¥800, 45 minutes) operate from stand 4 of the Kenei bus station opposite JR Nagasaki Station (Map p704). A taxi costs about ¥9000.

BICYCLE

Bicycles can be rented (40% discount for JR Pass holders) from **JR Nagasaki Station** (Map p704; ☎ 826-0480) at the Eki Rent-a-Car. Some are even electric powered. Rates are reasonable (per two hours/day ¥500/1500).

BUS

A greater area is covered by buses than trams, but the bus service is less user-friendly for non-Japanese.

TRAM

The best way of getting around Nagasaki is by tram. There are four colour-coded routes numbered 1, 3, 4 and 5 (No 2 is for special events) and stops are signposted in English. It costs ¥100 to travel anywhere in town, but you can only transfer for free at the Tsuki-machi stop if you have a ¥500 all-day pass for unlimited travel, available from the Nagasaki Tourist Information Centre (p703) and many hotels. Most trams stop running before 11.30pm.

AROUND NAGASAKI

Huis Ten Bosch ハウステンボス

This 'virtual-Holland' **theme park** (off Map p704; ☎ 095-627-0526; http://english.huistenbosch.co.jp; adult/child/student from ¥3200/1000/2000; ⏲ 9am-9pm) exemplifies Japan's long fascination with the West. Huis Ten Bosch (House in the Forest), although impressive in scale and detail, with its horse-drawn carriages and windmills, is probably not the reason you find yourself in Japan.

KYŪSHŪ

SHIMABARA PENINSULA 島原半島

The most popular route between Nagasaki and Kumamoto is via the hilly roads of Shimabara *hondō* (main route). Local bus services connect with ferries from Shimabara to the Kumamoto coast, and tour buses operating between Nagasaki and Kumamoto explore the peninsula.

An uprising here led to the suppression of Christianity in Japan and the country's subsequent two centuries of seclusion from the West. Peasant rebels made their final stand against overwhelming odds (37,000 versus 120,000) at Hara-jō, at almost the southern tip of the peninsula. The rebels held out for 80 days before being slaughtered.

On 3 June 1991, the 1359m peak of Unzen-dake erupted after lying dormant for 199 years, taking the lives of 43 journalists and scientists. Over 12,000 people were evacuated from nearby villages before the lava flow reached the outskirts of Shimabara.

UNZEN 雲仙

☎ 0957 / pop 49,460

Unzen is an active volcanic centre. Home to **Unzen-Amakusa National Park**, Japan's first, Unzen's woodsy walks and paths are clearly signposted in English. You can explore the town and nearby trails in an afternoon. The park is great for hiking and the village is a peaceful place to spend a night – the smell of sulphur soon dissipates! Day-trippers disappear by 6pm and it's lovely to walk around the quiet streets, in summer or snow. For town maps and accommodation bookings, consult the **Unzen Tourist Association** (雲仙観光協会; ☎ 73-3434; ⏲ 9am-5pm).

The bubbling *jigoku* (hells; boiling mineral hot springs) currently only boil eggs, known as onsen *tamago;* but a few centuries ago the same fate was reserved for 30 Christian martyrs who were tossed into bubbly Oito Jigoku.

There's some wonderful accommodation here, most with *rotemburo*. Day-trippers may prefer the three public baths, all within walking distance of the bus station:

Kojigoku (小地獄温泉館; ☎ 73-3273; admission ¥400; ⏲ 9am-9pm)

Shin-yu (新湯温泉; ☎ 73-3545; admission ¥100; ⏲ 9am-11pm, closed Wed)

Yunosato (湯の里温泉; ☎ 73-2576; admission ¥100; ⏲ 9am-10.30pm, closed 10th & 20th each month)

Sights & Activities

The **Unzen Spa House** (雲仙スパハウス; ☎ 73-3131; admission ¥800; ⏲ 9am-6pm), next to the Unzen Tourist Association office, also has a glass-blowing workshop (lessons ¥2000 to ¥3000 per 10 to 15 minutes, enough time to make something to break on your way home).

From the town, popular walks to Kinugasa, Takaiwa-san and Yadake are all situated within the national park. The **Unzen Visitors Centre** (雲仙お山の情報館; ☎ 73-3636; 🕑 7am-6pm 10 Apr–2 Nov, 9am-5pm 3 Nov–9 Apr, closed Thu), opposite the Kyūshū Hotel, has displays on flora and fauna and information in English. Around town, the 1300-year-old temple **Manmyō-ji** (満明寺; ☎ 73-3422), rebuilt in 1638, and the screeching, geyserlike **Daikyōkan Jigoku** are worth seeing.

Outside town, reached via Nita Pass, is **Fugen-dake** (1359m), part of the Unzen-dake range, with its popular hiking trail. The views of the lava flow from the summit are incredible.

The bus to Nita-tōge parking area, the starting point for the Fugen-dake walk, operates regularly between 9am and 3pm (¥370, 20 minutes) from Unzen's **Shimatetsu bus station** (☎ 74-3131); the last bus back to Unzen leaves the Nita Pass car park at 4.30pm. A **cable car** (ropeway; ☎ 73-3572; ticket each way ¥610; 🕑 8.55am-5.23pm) whisks you in three minutes close to a shrine and the 1333m-high summit of **Myōken-dake**, from where the hike to Fugen-dake via **Kunimi-wakare** takes just under two hours return. You can also walk the 3.5km back from the shrine to Nita via the village and valley of Azami-dani. For a longer excursion (three hours), you can detour to **Kunimi-dake** (1347m). Along the way you can get a good glimpse of Japan's newest mountain, the smoking lava dome of **Mt Heisei Shinzan** (1486m; literally 'new mountain'), created in November 1990, when Fugen-dake blew its stack.

Sleeping & Eating

Unzen has numerous hotels, *minshuku* and *ryokan* with nightly rates from around ¥8500, including dinner and breakfast. A weekend surcharge usually applies.

Shirakumo-no-ike camping ground (白雲の池キャンプ場; ☎ 73-2642; campsites from ¥300; 10 Jul–31 Aug) This picturesque summer camp site next to Shirakumo Pond is about a 600m walk downhill from the post office, then a few hundred metres from the road. Tent hire is available (¥500).

Unzen Sky Hotel (雲仙スカイホテル; www.unzen-skyhotel.com, in Japanese ☎ 73-3345; r per person with/without 2 meals from ¥9000/6000; Ⓟ ⊠) Between Yunosato onsen and Manmyō-ji, this budget option has predominantly Japanese-style rooms and an attractive sulphur *rotemburo*.

Kyūshū Hotel (九州ホテル; ☎ 73-3234; www.kyushuhtl.co.jp/language/en/; r per person with 2 meals from ¥16,950; Ⓟ ⊠) A sprawling oldie, deliciously refurbished in chocolate tones, plush fabrics and with a splash of Zen. There's a variety of tempting room types (some with open-air baths and balconies) with rates sometimes lower if you just walk in.

Unzen Kankō Hotel (雲仙観光ホテル; ☎ 73-3263; www.unzenkankohotel.com, in Japanese; s/d & tw from ¥10,500/18,900; Ⓟ ⊠) This grand hotel opened in 1936 and has been beautifully maintained. A destination in itself, it has a charming library, beautiful rooms and decadent day spa.

Unzen Tabi-no-biiru-kan (雲仙旅の麦酒館; ☎ 73-3113; 🕑 10am-6pm, closed Thu) Overlooking woodsy Unzen, this brewpub pours a local favourite, *unzen yuagari biiru* (after-bath beer) and serves pizza or a beer curry with salad from ¥950.

Getting There & Away

Buses run between Nagasaki and Unzen (¥1900, two hours) but more frequently from Isahaya (¥1400, 80 minutes). Isahaya is 35 minutes by train (¥450) from Nagasaki. Onward buses from Unzen to Shimabara (¥810, 45 minutes) stop at Shimabara's port (p717) and castle before arriving at Shimabara train station.

SHIMABARA 島原

☎ 0957 / pop 49,480

The ferry port to nearby Kumamoto, Shimabara is known for its clear springs, which first appeared following the 1792 eruption of Mt Unzen. The **Tourist Information Office** (☎ 62-3986; 🕑 8.30am-5.30pm) is inside the ferry terminal–bus station. Shimabara castle (a reconstruction), a samurai street and reclining Buddha are the town's main attractions, but if time is limited head to Unzen or beyond.

Sights

Built between 1618 and 1625, **Shimabara-jō** (島原城; ☎ 62-4766; 🕑 9am-5pm) played a part in the Shimabara Rebellion and was rebuilt in 1964. The grounds have carp ponds, tangled gardens, mossy walls and picturesque pines.

The castle houses a few **museums** (☎ 62-4766; combined admission adult/child ¥520/260; 🕑 9am-5pm). The **Shimabara Cultural Hall** displays items relating to the Christian uprising, the **Fugen-dake Museum** details Fugen-dake's exploits (including the colossal explosion of 1792 in which 15,000 people died, most from the resulting tsunami) and the **Sculpture Museum** is dedicated to the artwork of Seibō

Kitamura, who sculpted the Nagasaki Peace Statue. Another small **folk museum** is stuffed with antiques.

In the Teppō-chō area, northwest of the castle, is a collection of **samurai houses** that line a pretty street. Three of the houses are open to the public, and a free rest area serves tea.

Near the Shimatetsu bus station is a **carp stream**, home to over 1500 fishy friends.

At Kōtō-ji is the beautiful **Nehan-zō** (Nirvana Statue). At 8.6m, it's the longest **reclining Buddha** in Japan.

Visitors now come to experience **Gamadas Dome Mt Unzen Disaster Memorial Hall** (がまだすドーム雲仙岳災害記念館; ☎ 65-5555; www.udmh.or.jp, in Japanese; 1-1 Heisei-machi; 9am-5pm), a hi-tech museum plonked eerily at the base of the lava flow and dedicated to those lost in the 1991 eruption. It offers patrons an insight into the science of vulcanology.

Festivals & Events

The town **water festival** is held in early August.

Sleeping & Eating

Shimabara Youth Hostel (☎ 62-4451; 7938-3 Shimokawashiri-machi; dm HI member/nonmember ¥2850/3450) A short hike north of Shimabara-Gaikō Station will lead you to what looks like a misplaced ski chalet. There are both bunk beds and futons.

Hotel & Spa Hanamizuki (☎ 62-1000; 548 Nakamachi; s/tw ¥5800/9800; P ⊠ 💻) A bright 42-room hotel with a large onsen and a good breakfast (¥840). Some English is spoken.

Shimabara's best-known dish, *guzōni*, is an acquired taste. It's a thick soup made from seafood, vegetables and *mochi* (pounded rice).

Himematsu-ya (☎ 63-7272; meals from ¥800; 10am-8pm;) Serves *guzōni* (¥980) and several types of *rāmen* (try *robuke-e soba*). The restaurant is in front of Shimabara-jō and there's a picture menu.

Drinking

There's also a cluster of *izakaya* around the castle.

Shimabara Mizuyashiki (☎ 62-8555; www.mizuyashiki.com, in Japanese; admission free; tea & sweets from ¥500; 11am-5pm) This Meiji-era tea house and museum features a delightful Japanese garden and collection of *maneki-neko* (lucky cat figurines).

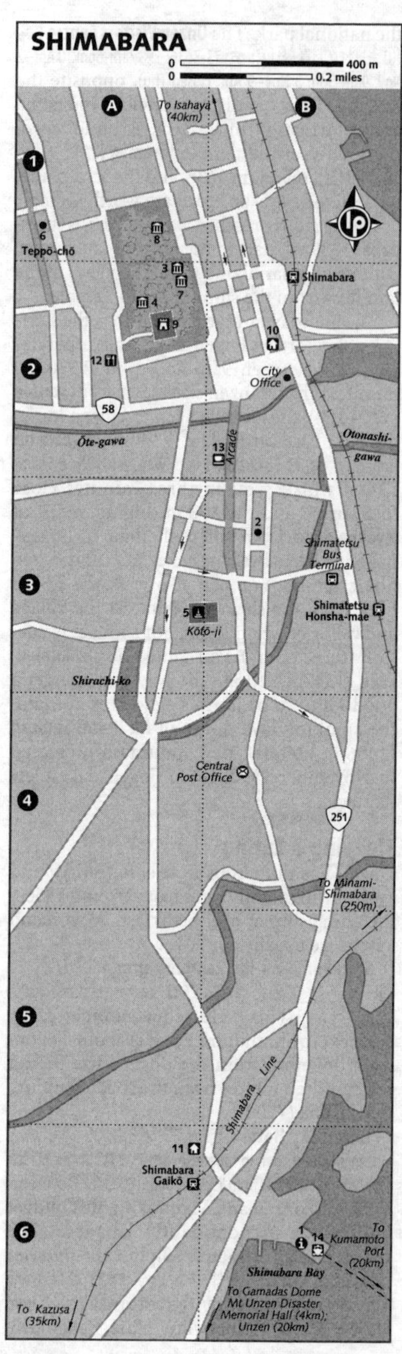

KYŪSHŪ

INFORMATION
Tourist Information Office 観光案内所 1 B6

SIGHTS & ACTIVITIES
Carp Stream 鯉の泳ぐまち 2 B3
Folk Museum 観光復興記念館 3 A2
Fugen-dake Museum 雲仙普賢岳資料館 4 A2
Nehan-zō 江東寺·ねはん像 5 A3
Samurai Houses 武家屋敷 6 A1
Sculpture Museum 北村西望記念館 7 A2
Shimabara Cultural Hall 島原文化会館 8 A1
Shimabara-jō 島原城 9 A2

SLEEPING
Hotel & Spa Hanamizuki 花みずき 10 B2
Shimabara Youth Hostel 島原ユースホステル 11 A6

EATING
Himematsu-ya 姫松屋 12 A2

DRINKING
Shimabara Mizuyashiki 島原水屋敷 13 B2

TRANSPORT
Shimabara Ferry Terminal
島原港ターミナルビル 14 B6

Getting There & Around

JR trains from Nagasaki to Isahaya (¥450, 25 minutes) connect with the private Shimabara-tetsudō line. Trains depart hourly to Shimabara (¥1450, 1¼ hours). Shimabara Station is about 350m east of the castle.

Ferries to the Kumamoto coast depart frequently from Shimabara port between 7am and 7pm. There's a jet ferry (adult/child ¥800/400, 30 minutes) and the slower car ferry (adult/child ¥680/340, one hour). All boats are bound for Kumamoto Port, a bus ride from the city (¥420, 30 minutes).

Local buses shuttle between Shimabara Station and the ferry terminal (¥100). Bikes can also be rented at the ferry terminal and at the train station (per hour ¥150).

KUMAMOTO-KEN 熊本県

KUMAMOTO 熊本

☎ 096 / pop 670,100

Kumamoto, gateway to the Aso region, and the city that brought you *kobori* (a way of swimming upright wearing a suit of samurai armour, handy for those late night commando raids) is now best known for its reconstructed castle. It has a good selection of restaurants and galleries, and has a growing population. In summer, it's one of the hottest cities in Japan, which may explain the concentration of night owls, bars and people trying to swim upright.

Orientation & Information

JR Kumamoto Station is an inconvenient few kilometres southwest of where you want to be. The area around the Shimotōri shopping arcade is where you'll find the central core, the bus centre, castle and other attractions.

On the northwest side of JR Kumamoto Station is a postal ATM. Higo Bank in central Kumamoto has currency-exchange facilities.

Cybac Café (Map p720; ☎ 24-3189; www.cybac.com; 5th & 6th fl, Carino Shimotōri, 1-2 Ansei-machi; membership fee/per 15min ¥300/100; 24hr) Has a city-centre location.

Kumamoto City International Centre (Map p720; ☎ 359-2020; 4-8 Hanabata-chō; 9am-8pm Mon-Sat, to 7pm Sun & holidays) Has free 30-minute internet use, CNN news and English-language magazines on the 2nd floor.

Tourist information desk JR Kumamoto Station (Map p718; ☎ 352-3743; 8.30am-7pm); Kumamoto Castle parking area (Map p720; ☎ 322-5060; 9am-5pm) Has English-speaking assistants and accommodation listings.

Sights

KUMAMOTO-JŌ 熊本城

Kumamoto's robust **castle** (Map p720; ☎ 352-6820; Hon-maru; admission ¥500; 8.30am-5.30pm Apr-Oct, to 4.30pm Nov-Mar) dominates the townscape. Built between 1601 and 1607, the original building was besieged and burnt during the 1877 Satsuma Rebellion, one of the final stands made by samurai against the new order. The rebels held out for 50 days before being overcome. For more on the rebellion and its leader, Saigō Takamori, see the boxed text, p733. A free tour (in English, ☎ 322-5900) of this 19th-century reconstruction is available.

Beyond the castle is the **Former Hosokawa Gyōbutei** (Map p718; ☎ 352-6522; 3-1 Kyō-machi; admission with/without castle ¥640/300; 8.30am-5.30pm Apr-Oct, to 4.30pm Nov-Mar), a large samurai villa and garden built for the Hosokawa clan, who came into power around 1632 and held sway until the Meiji Restoration.

Closer to the main road, the **Kumamoto Prefectural Museum of Art** (Map p718; ☎ 352-2111; 2 Ninomaru; admission ¥260; 9.30am-4.30pm, closed Mon & 25 Dec–4 Jan) has ancient Buddhist sculptures and modern paintings. Its **Chibajo Annexe**

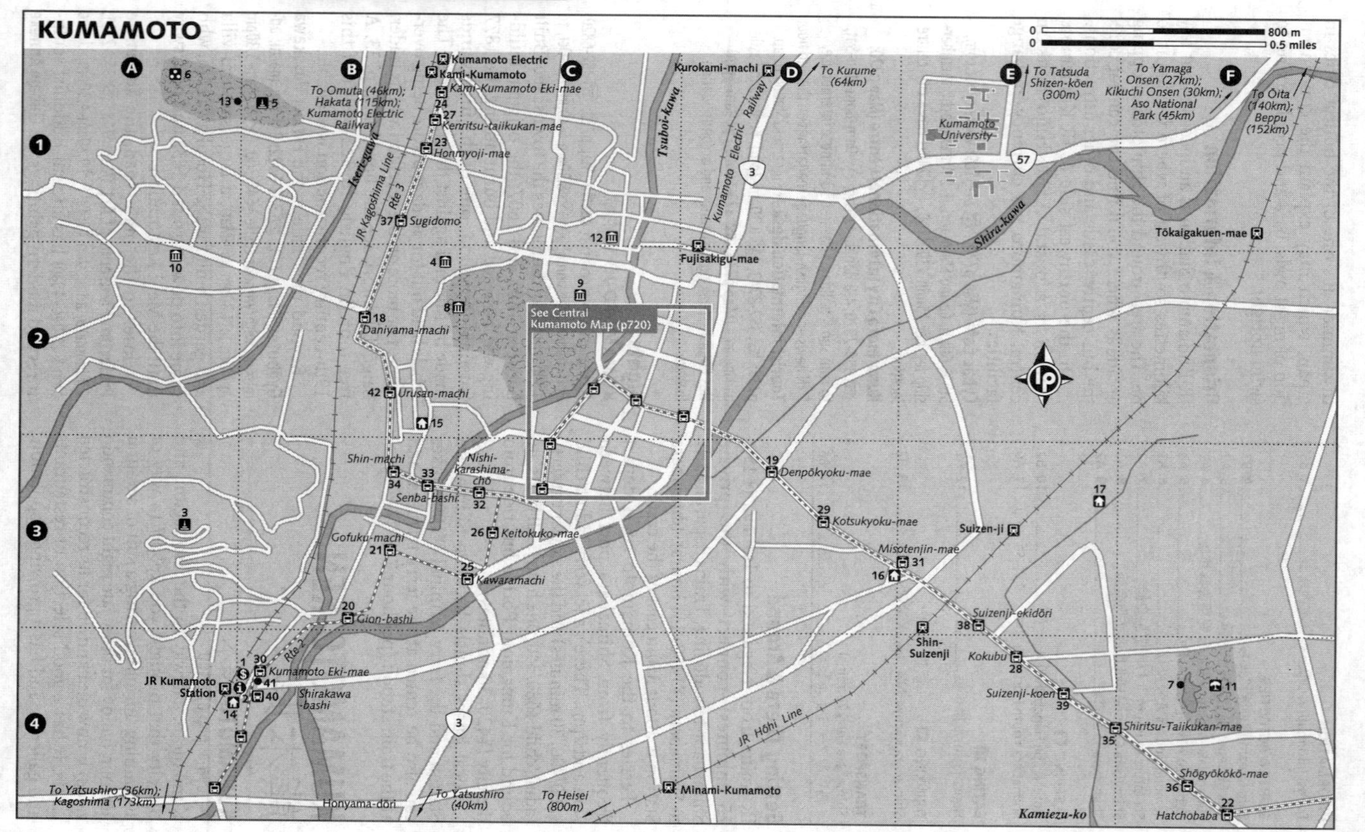
KUMAMOTO
0 800 m
0 0.5 miles
A
B
C
D
E
F
1
2
3
4
To Omuta (46km); Hakata (115km); Kumamoto Electric Railway
Kumamoto Electric
Kami-Kumamoto
Kami-Kumamoto Eki-mae
Kenritsu-taiikukan-mae
Honmyoji-mae
Iseri-gawa
JR Kagoshima Line
Rte 3
Sugidomo
Kurokami-machi
To Kurume (64km)
Tsuboi-kawa
Kumamoto Electric Railway
Fujisakigu-mae
To Tatsuda Shizen-kōen (300m)
Kumamoto University
To Yamaga Onsen (27km); Kikuchi Onsen (30km); Aso National Park (45km)
To Ōita (140km); Beppu (152km)
57
Shira-kawa
Tōkaigakuen-mae
Daniyama-machi
See Central Kumamoto Map (p720)
Urusan-machi
Shin-machi
Nishi-karashima-chō
Senba-bashi
Keitokuko-mae
Gofuku-machi
Kawaramachi
Gion-bashi
Denpōkyoku-mae
Kotsukyoku-mae
Suizen-ji
Misotenjin-mae
Suizenji-ekidōri
Shin-Suizenji
Kokubu
Suizenji-koen
Shiritsu-Taiikukan-mae
Shōgyōkōkō-mae
Hatchobaba
Kamiezu-ko
JR Kumamoto Station
Kumamoto Eki-mae
Rte 2
Shirakawa-bashi
3
JR Hōhi Line
Minami-Kumamoto
To Yatsushiro (36km); Kagoshima (173km)
Honyama-dōri
To Yatsushiro (40km)
To Heisei (800m)

INFORMATION
ATM（現金自動預け払い機）... 1 B4
Tourist Information Desk 観光案内所... 2 B4

SIGHTS & ACTIVITIES
Bussharitō 仏舎利塔... 3 A3
Former Hosokawa Gyōbutei 旧細川刑部邸... 4 B2
Honmyō-ji 本妙寺... 5 B1
Katō Kiyomasa Mausoleum 加藤清正のお墓... 6 A1
Kokin-denju-no-ma Teahouse 古今伝授の間... 7 F4
Kumamoto Prefectural Museum of Art 熊本県立美術館... 8 B2
Kumamoto Prefectural Traditional Crafts Centre 熊本県伝統工芸館... 9 C2
Shimada Art Museum 島田美術館... 10 A2
Suizenji-kōen 水前寺公園... 11 F4
Sōseki Memorial Hall 夏目漱石内坪井旧居... 12 C1
Treasure House 宝物館... 13 A1

SLEEPING
JR Kyūshū Hotel Kumamoto ＪＲホテル九州 熊本... 14 A4
Minshuku Kajita 民宿梶田... 15 B2
Suizen-ji Youth Hostel 水前寺ユースホステル... 16 D3
Youth PIA Kumamoto (Kumamoto Seinen-kaikan) ユースピア熊本（熊本青年会館）... 17 E3

TRANSPORT
Daniyama-machi 段山町... 18 B2
Denpōkyoku-mae 電報局前... 19 D3
Gion-bashi 祇園橋... 20 B3
Gofuku-machi 呉服町... 21 B3
Hatchobaba 八丁馬場... 22 F4
Honmyoji-mae 本妙寺前... 23 B1
Kami-Kumamoto Eki-mae 上熊本駅前... 24 B1
Kawaramachi 河原町... 25 C3
Keitokuko-mae 慶徳校前... 26 C3
Kenritsu-taiikukan-mae 県立体育館前... 27 B1
Kokubu 国府... 28 E4
Kotsukyoku-mae 交通局前... 29 D3
Kumamoto Eki-mae 熊本駅前... 30 B4
Misotenjin-mae 味噌天神前... 31 E3
Nishi-karashima-chō 西辛島町... 32 C3
Senba-bashi 先馬橋... 33 B3
Shin-machi 新町... 34 B3
Shiritsu-Taiikukan-mae 市立体育館前... 35 E4
Shōgyōkōkō-mae 商業高校前... 36 F4
Sugidomo 杉塘... 37 B1
Suizenji-ekidōri 水前寺駅通... 38 E3
Suizenji-koen 水前寺公園... 39 E4
Sānko Bus Stop 産交バス停... 40 B4
Toyota Renta Lease トヨタレンタリース... 41 B4
Urusan-machi 蔚山町... 42 B2

(Map p720; ☎ 351-8411; 2-18 Chibajō-machi; 9.30am-6.30pm, closed Mon & 25 Dec–4 Jan), built under the Artpolis urban reconstruction project, is recognised by architects worldwide.

Kumamoto Prefectural Traditional Crafts Centre (Map p718; ☎ 324-4930; 3-35 Chibajō-machi; admission ¥200; 9am-5pm, closed Mon & 28 Dec–4 Jan) has displays of local Higo inlay, Yamaga lanterns, porcelain and woodcarving.

SUIZENJI-KŌEN 水前寺公園

Southeast of the city centre, this strolling **garden** (☎ 383-0074; www.suizenji.or.jp, in Japanese; 8-1 Suizenji-kōen; admission ¥400; 7.30am-6pm Mar-Nov, 8.30am-5pm Dec-Feb) represents the 53 stations of the Tōkaidō (the old road that linked Tokyo and Kyoto). The miniature Mt Fuji is instantly recognisable. The **Kokindenju-no-ma Teahouse** (Map p718; tea & Hosokawa sweets ¥500-600) building was moved here from the Kyoto Imperial Palace in 1912 and now has serene views across the ornamental lake. Originally it was where the young emperor was tutored in poetry.

HONMYŌ-JI 本妙寺

Northwest of the centre, on the hills above the river, is the temple and mausoleum of **Katō Kiyomasa** (Map p718), the architect of Kumamoto's castle. A steep flight of 176 steps leads up to the mausoleum, designed to be at the same height as the castle's *donjon* (fortified central tower). There's also a **treasure house** (Map p718; ☎ 354-1411; 4-13-20 Hanazono; admission ¥300; 9am-5pm, closed Mon) next to the temple with Kiyomasa's crown and other personal items.

Shimada Art Museum (島田美術館; Map p718; ☎ 352-4597; 4-5-28 Shimazaki; admission ¥500; 9am-5pm Thu-Tue) is within walking distance of Honmyō-ji. It displays the work of Miyamoto Musashi, mainly calligraphy and scrolls.

WRITERS' HOMES

In the city centre, behind Tsuruya department store, is writer **Lafcadio Hearn's former home** (Map p720; ☎ 354-7842; 2-6 Ansei-machi; admission ¥200; 9.30am-4.30pm, closed Mon & 29 Dec–3 Jan); he was known to the Japanese as Koizumi Yakumo. Hearn also had a Japanese residence in Matsue (see p497).

The former home of famed Meiji-era novelist Sōseki Natsume is preserved as the **Sōseki Memorial Hall** (Map p718; ☎ 325-9127; 4-22 Tsubo-machi; admission ¥200; 9.30am-4.30pm, closed Mon). Sōseki lived here as an English teacher, but only for a few years. (For more on Sōseki, see p70.)

OTHER SIGHTS

Continue beyond the *minshuku* and love hotels until you reach the white **Bussharito** (a traditional stupa said to hold the Buddha's ashes; Map p718) at the top of the hill, with superb views over the town.

Tatsuda Shizen-kōen (立田自然公園; Tatsuda Nature Park; off Map p718; ☎ 344-6753; 4-610 Kurokami;

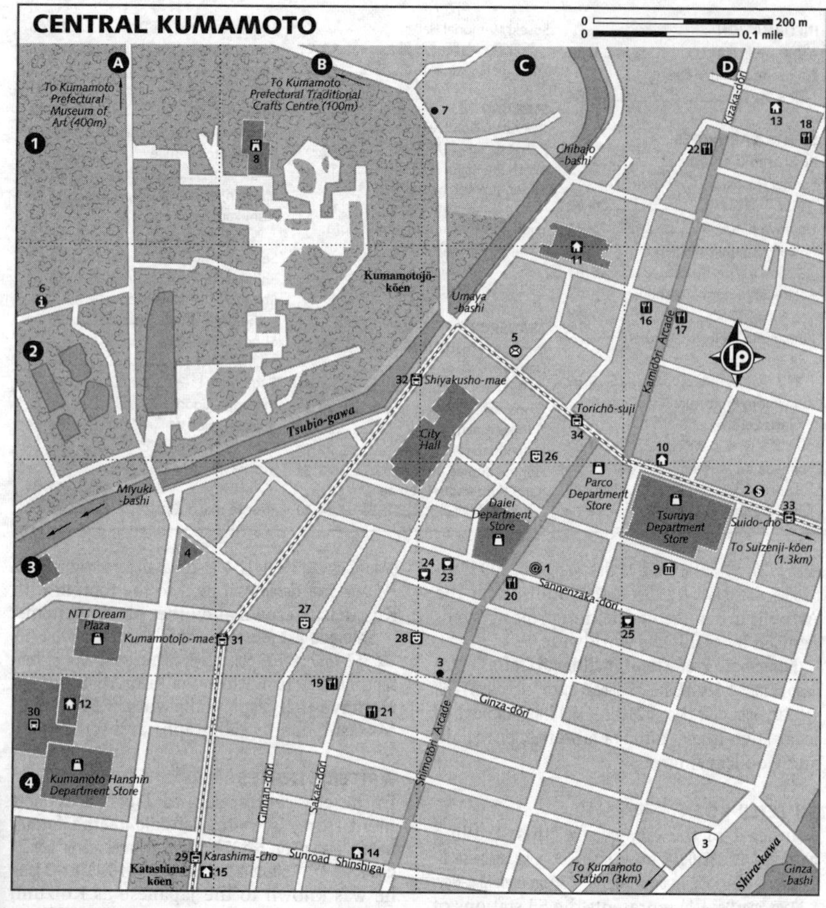

admission ¥200; 8.30am-4.30pm, closed 29–31 Dec) contains ancient trees, bamboo groves and temple ruins. To get here, take a Kusushiro Saisen line bus from Kumamoto Kōtsū bus centre, get off at Tatsuda Shizen Kōen Iriguchi stop (¥190, 15 minutes) and walk 10 minutes.

Festivals & Events

Takigi Nō (薪能) Traditional performances at Suizenji-kōen are performed by torchlight on the first Saturday in August (from 6pm), usually in Kumamoto-jō.

Hi-no-kuni Matsuri (火の国まつり; Land of Fire Festival) Lights up Kumamoto with fireworks and dancing in mid-August.

Autumn festival From mid-October to early November Kumamoto-jō has its grand festival, with *taiko* drumming and cultural events.

Sleeping

BUDGET

Suizen-ji Youth Hostel (Map p718; ☎ 371-9193; fax 371-9218; 1-2-20 Hakuzan; dm member/nonmember ¥3045/3645; ☒) This clean five-room hostel, five minutes' walk from JR Shin-Suizen-ji Station, has a 10pm curfew.

Youth PIA Kumamoto (Kumamoto Seinen-kaikan) (Map p718; ☎ 381-6221; fax 382-2715; 3-17-15 Suizenji; dm HI member ¥3045, nonmember ¥3600-4800; ☒ 💻) Ten minutes' walk from JR Shin-Suizen-ji Station, dorms and private rooms are available with an 11pm curfew.

Minshuku Kajita (Map p718; ☎/fax 353-1546; 1-2-7 Shinmachi; s/d ¥4000/7200; ☒) This small private inn with shared bathroom is clean and quiet. Look for the 'Minshuku' sign in English.

INFORMATION
- Cybac Café サイバックカフェ 1 C3
- Higo Bank 肥後銀行 2 D3
- Kinokuniya Bookstore 紀伊国屋書店 3 C3
- Kumamoto City International Centre 国際交流会館 4 A3
- Post Office 郵便局 5 C2
- Tourist Information Desk 観光案内所 6 A2

SIGHTS & ACTIVITIES
- Chibajo Annexe 熊本県立美術館分館 7 C1
- Kumamoto-jō 熊本城 8 B1
- Lafcadio Hearn House 小泉八雲熊本旧居 9 D3

SLEEPING
- Hotel Nikko Kumamoto ホテル日航熊本 10 D2
- Kumamoto Castle Hotel 熊本ホテルキャッスル 11 C2
- Kumamoto Kōtsū Center Hotel 熊本交通センターホテル 12 A4
- Maruko Hotel 丸小ホテル 13 D1
- Richmond Hotel Kumamoto Shinshigai リチモンドホテル熊本新市街 14 B4
- Toyoko Inn Karashima Kō-en 東横イン辛島公園 15 A4

EATING
- Cafe Anding カフェアンディン 16 D2
- Capricciosa カプリチョーザ 17 D2
- Izakaya Yokobachi ヨコバチ 18 D1
- Jang Jang Go ジャンジャンゴー 19 B4
- Kōran-tei 紅蘭亭 20 C3
- Okonomiyaki Arashiyama お好み焼き嵐山 21 B4
- Ramen Komurasaki 熊本ラーメンこむらさき 22 D1

DRINKING
- Jeff's World Bar ジェフズワールドバー 23 C3
- Jungle Hearts ジャングルハート 24 C3
- Shark Attack シャークアタック 25 D3

ENTERTAINMENT
- Bar Sanctuary サンクチュアリー 26 C2
- Euro Dance Bar ユーロダンスバー 27 B3
- Rock Bar Days ロックバーデイズ 28 B3

TRANSPORT
- Karashima-cho 辛島町 29 A4
- Kumamoto Kōtsū Bus Centre 熊本交通バスセンター 30 A4
- Kumamotojo-mae 熊本城前 31 B3
- Shiyakusho-mae 市役所前 32 B2
- Suido-cho 水道町 33 D3
- Torichō-suji 通町筋 34 C2

Toyoko Inn Karashima Kō-en (Map p720; ☎ 322-1045; fax 322-2045; 1-24 Kouyaima-machi; s/d ¥5145/7700) Cheap and cheerful, two tram stops from the castle and a few minutes' walk from the bus station.

MIDRANGE & TOP END

JR Kyūshū Hotel Kumamoto (Map p718; ☎ 354-8000; www.jrhotelgroup.com/eng/hotel/eng150.htm; 3-15-15 Kasuga; s/tw ¥6900/12,600) Adjacent to JR Kumamoto Station; stop here if you have luggage and aren't staying long.

Kumamoto Kōtsū Centre Hotel (Map p720; ☎ 326-8828; www.kyusanko.co.jp/hotel, in Japanese; 3-10 Sakuramachi; s/d/tr from ¥7500/16,000/19,500) A refurbished business hotel in a good location with excellent special rates online, if you can read Japanese. Rooms with LAN cable internet available.

Kumamoto Castle Hotel (Map p720; ☎ 326-3311; fax 326-3324; 4-2 Jōtō-machi; s/d/tw from ¥9345/17,850/16,800; Japanese-style r ¥31,500; P) Overlooking the castle, this upmarket hotel has formal service. Beautiful flower arrangements and artworks in the foyer make it popular with wedding parties. Make sure to request a castle-view room. Rooms have LAN cable internet facilities.

Maruko Hotel (Map p720; ☎ 353-1241; 11-10 Kamidōri-machi; s/tw with 2 meals from ¥12,600/19,600) A central, Japanese-style inn with a rooftop *o-furo* and good views. Look for the English sign inside the covered arcade.

our pick Richmond Hotel Kumamoto Shinshigai (Map p720; ☎ 312-3511; 6-16 Shinshigai; s/d/tw from ¥13,000/19,000/23,000) You can't beat the location, price and standard of this new hotel located in the heart of it all, with great-looking rooms with excellent amenities.

Hotel Nikko Kumamoto (Map p720; ☎ 211-1111; www.nikko-kumamoto.co.jp/english/en_index.html; 2-1 Kamitori-chō; s/d/tw from ¥17,325/43,890/31,185; P) Kumamoto's premier hotel is adjacent to the Contemporary Art Museum. Rooms are spacious and comfortable with big bathrooms, high ceilings and city views, but way overpriced. LAN cable internet access is available.

Eating

Adventurous diners may want to try a bite of *basashi* (raw horsemeat), *karashi-renkon* (fried lotus root with mustard) or *Higo-gyū* (Higo beef). Sometimes whale meat is also served; this may be featured on the menu as *kujira* (鯨), the Japanese word for whale.

Kōran-tei (Map p720; ☎ 352-7177; 5-26 Ansei-machi; meals from ¥735; lunch & dinner) In the Shimotōri arcade, opposite Daiei, this massive restaurant has an endless menu with a *hi-mawari* (changes daily) lunch special for ¥750.

Ramen Komurasaki (Map p720; ☎ 325-8972; 8-16 Kamidōri; meals from ¥900; lunch & dinner) This popular and fast *rāmen* joint is opposite Higo Bank in the arcade. Start with a plate of tender *gyōza* (¥400), then tuck into a bowl of king *rāmen* (¥560) with pork and fresh mushrooms.

Capricciosa (Map p720; ☎ 323-8622; 7-10 Kamidōri; pasta from ¥950, pizza from ¥1060; lunch & dinner) It's easy to spot this imitation European building with red French awnings and a corner frontage onto the arcade, housing, funnily enough, an Italian restaurant with a definite Japanese twist.

Cafe Anding (Map p720; ☎ 352-6701; 4th fl, 4-10 Kamidōri; dishes from ¥1000) Satisfy your sweet tooth at this upstairs coffee-and-pastry hang-out with English sign and menu.

Izakaya Yokobachi (Map p720; ☎ 351-4581; 11-40 Kaminoura, Kamidōri; meals with beer ¥2000-3000; dinner) The menu at this snappy eatery includes *basashi* (¥1000). Gulp. Observe the open kitchen, or sit in the shaded courtyard. The signage has a red sideways number '8'.

Jang Jang Go (Map p720; ☎ 323-1121; 12-10 Hanahata-chō; per person around ¥2500; lunch & dinner) This trendy date spot serves neo-Chinese cuisine from an open kitchen and the speciality is *taipīen* (*harusame* noodles with cuttlefish and vegetables) for ¥735. There's an extensive menu, so you can keep on ordering.

Okonomiyaki Arashiyama (Map p720; ☎ 395-2003; Sakai Bldg, 1-11-5 Shimotōri; dinner, closed Sun) This tiny hole-in-the-wall has about 10 seats and no English is spoken, but it has mastered the art of *okonomiyaki* (pancake; starting from ¥700). It's in a side street opposite Core21 department store.

Drinking

Kumamoto is a convivial and lively city after dark. The Namikizaka-dōri area at the north end of Kamidōri Arcade is particularly hip and the laneways off Shimotōri Arcade are busy.

Shark Attack (Map p720; ☎ 090-6299-1818; 8th fl, 6-3 Ansei-machi; drinks from ¥500; closed Tue) Despite the name, the mood here is mellow – a sandy floor, surfboards and tiki lamps behind the bar set the tone.

Jungle Hearts (Map p720; ☎ 356-1655; 1-5-10 Shimotōri; closed Tue) Enter another world in this ground-floor jungle-kitsch bar with all-you-can-drink specials and a mainly Japanese clientele. The beer glasses are giant.

Jeff's World Bar (Map p720; 2nd fl, 1-4-3 Shimotōri) Predominantly *gaijin* expats and local Japanese frequent this sometimes friendly, sometimes sleazy 2nd-floor pub with satellite TV, sofas and a good selection of beers. There's dancing some weekends.

Entertainment

Rock Bar Days (Map p720; ☎ 323-7110; www.rockbar-days.com, in Japanese; 3rd fl SMILE Bldg, 1-7-7 Shimotōri; drinks around ¥600) An incredible cross-genre collection of CDs adorns the wall behind the bar. Kumamoto's coolest hang-out has an awesome atmosphere that draws the best crowd. Dance if you have the space, sprawl out on sofas or make friends at the bar.

Euro Dance Bar (Map p720; ☎ 354-0803; basement, Shanse Shinagawa Bldg, 11-18 Hanabata; admission ¥400; 8pm-6am) Friday is salsa night, but you'll hear everything from disco to hip-hop at this intimate Ginza-dōri basement spot. It can be a little hit-and-miss but plenty of other options are nearby.

Bar Sanctuary (Map p720; ☎ 325-5634; 4-16 Tetorihon-machi; drinks from ¥300) This massive multi-level dance, darts and karaoke extravaganza has no cover charge and a mostly 20-something crowd. It heaves on weekends.

Getting There & Away

There are flights to Kumamoto from Tokyo (¥36,700, 1½ hours) and Osaka (¥23,500, 1¼ hours), but most visitors come by train. The JR Kagoshima line runs north to Hakata (*tokkyū;* ¥3440, 1½ hours) and south to Kagoshima-Chūō Station (*tokkyū/shinkansen;* ¥6350, 70 minutes, change at Shin-Yatsushiro), while the JR Hōhi line goes to Beppu (*tokkyū;* ¥5130, three hours) via Aso.

Highway buses depart from the Kumamoto Kōtsū bus centre. Routes include Fukuoka (¥2000, two hours), Kagoshima (¥3650, 3½ hours), Nagasaki (¥3600, 3¼ hours) and Miyazaki (¥4500, three hours).

Getting Around

TO/FROM THE AIRPORT

Buses to and from the airport (¥670, 50 minutes) stop at the Kumamoto Kōtsū bus centre and JR Kumamoto Station.

BUS

One-day tram passes are also valid for travel on green Shiei buses (but not other city buses), useful for hopping between JR Kumamoto Station and the bus centre.

The Castle Loop Bus (¥130) connects the bus centre with most sights in the castle area at least every half-hour, between 8.30am and 5pm daily. A one-day loop pass (¥300) will get you a discount at the museum and other establishments.

CAR

Renting a car is an excellent way to get from Kumamoto and onward to Aso and beyond. The service at **Toyota Renta Lease** (☎ 311-0100; http://rent.toyota.co.jp/en/index.html; 1-14-28 Haruka, Kumamoto-ekimae; 12hr from ¥5250; ⏰ 8am-8pm) is excellent, despite little English being spoken.

TRAM

Kumamoto's tram service reaches the major sights. Fares range from ¥130 to ¥200. A day pass (¥500) allows unlimited travel, and can be bought onboard.

YAMAGA & KIKUCHI ONSEN 山鹿温泉・菊池温泉

☎ 0968

The pretty hot-spring towns of Yamaga Onsen (population 57,300) and Kikuchi Onsen (population 51,620) – northeast of Kumamoto – come alive during the spectacular **Yamaga Chōchin Matsuri** held on 15 and 16 August. *Taiko* drums signal the beginning of this famous lantern festival in rustic Yamaga Onsen. For two nights the women of the town, clad in colourful summer kimonos, dance through the streets to the sound of *shamisen*, wearing *washi* (handmade paper) lanterns on their heads. **Yamaga Tourism Office** (☎ 43-2952) can help with accommodation and information.

The **Yamaga Cycling Terminal** (山鹿サイクリングターミナル; ☎ 43-1136; www.city.yamaga.kumamoto.jp/kankoh/02-shizen/02-15saikuru.html, in Japanese; r per person ¥2940; Ⓟ), situated on a scenic traffic-shielded 34km cycling route from Kumamoto via Ueki, has communal tatami rooms and baths. Meals are available.

Kikuchi Information Centre (☎ 23-1155) near the bus station has maps and brochures in English. The hot-springs ryokan, *minshuku* and a number of hotels are clustered together on a quiet maze of streets, downhill from an imposing **statue** of a lord on horseback. The delightfully rustic **Iwakura Ryokan** (☎ 27-0026; www.iwakura0026.com, in Japanese; 2224-8 Omomi, Kikuchi-shi; r with 2 meals per person from ¥17,000), also has a riverside **onsen** (¥500) for daytrippers.

Outside town, **Kikuchi Gorge** (菊池渓谷; donation ¥100; ⏰ mid-Apr–Nov), formed by Mt Aso's outer edge, has **walking trails** that follow the Kikuchi-gawa's cool waters through groves of elm and camphor.

Getting There & Around

Buses run from JR Kumamoto Station and Kumamoto Kōtsū bus centre to Yamaga Onsen (¥870, 70 minutes) and Kikuchi Onsen (¥820, 70 minutes). For a day trip to Yamaga Onsen, ask for an *ichi nichi furii joshaken* (round-trip pass ¥1200). Frequent buses run Monday to Saturday (¥430, 30 minutes) between the two onsen towns.

ASO-SAN AREA 阿蘇山

☎ 0967 / pop 29,370

In the centre of Kyūshū, halfway between Kumamoto and Beppu, lies the gigantic and very beautiful Aso-san volcano caldera. There has been a series of eruptions over the past 300,000 years, but the explosion that formed the outer crater about 90,000 years ago was monstrous. The resultant crater has a 128km circumference and now accommodates towns, villages and trainlines.

It's the largest active caldera in the world. A 1979 eruption of Naka-dake killed a woman on her honeymoon. The last major blast was in 1993, but the summit is frequently off-limits due to toxic gas emissions. Check with the Tourist Information Centre (below) for updates. The summit may close for a day or just an hour, depending on wind conditions.

Orientation & Information

It's hard at first to get a sense of the crater's shape and scale. Best explored by car, the area offers some fabulous drives, diverse scenery and peaceful retreats. Routes 57, 265 and 325 make a circuit of the outer caldera, and the JR Hōhi line runs across the northern section. If you're driving, Daikanbō Lookout is one of the best places to take it all in, but it's often crowded with tour buses. Shiroyama Tembōdai on the Yamanami Hwy is a nice alternative. Aso is the main town, but there are others, including Takamori, to the south.

Next to JR Aso Station, the helpful **Tourist Information Centre** (☎ 34-0751; ⏰ 9am-6pm) offers free road and hiking maps and local information. Coin lockers are available. A postal ATM is 100m south, across Hwy 57.

Sights

ASO-GOGAKU 阿蘇五岳

The **Five Mountains of Aso** are the five smaller mountains within the outer rim. They are

KYŪSHŪ

Eboshi-dake (1337m), Kijima-dake (1321m), Naka-dake (1506m), Neko-dake (1408m) and Taka-dake (1592m). Naka-dake is currently the active volcano in this group. Neko-dake, furthest to the east, is instantly recognisable by its craggy peak but Taka-dake is highest.

ASO VOLCANIC MUSEUM 阿蘇火山博物館

This unique **museum** (☎ 34-2111; www.asomuse.jp, in Japanese; admission with/without cable-car return ¥1480/840; 9am-5pm) has a real-time video feed from a camera mounted inside the active crater wall, which you can direct from inside the museum. There are English-language brochures and a video presentation of Aso friends showing off.

KUSASENRI & KOME-ZUKA 草千里・米塚

Opposite the volcanic museum, **Kusasenri** is a grassy meadow with two 'lakes' in the flattened crater of an ancient volcano. It's a postcard-perfect picture on a clear day, or sorely disappointing if there hasn't been any rain.

Just off the road that runs from the museum to Aso town is the perfectly shaped cone of **Kome-zuka** (954m), another extinct volcano.

NAKA-DAKE 中岳

Naka-dake (1506m) has been very active in recent years. The cable car to the summit was closed from August 1989 to March 1990 due to eruptions, and it had only been opened for a few weeks when the volcano erupted again in April 1990, spewing ash over a large area.

In 1958, after an eruption killed 12 onlookers, concrete bunkers were built around the rim to protect sightseers from such events. Nevertheless, an eruption in 1979 killed three visitors over 1km from the cone, in an area that was thought to be safe.

From the Aso Volcanic Museum (above), it's 3km up to the cable-car station. If Naka-dake is behaving, the **cable car** (ropeway; each way ¥410; 9am-5pm) whisks you up to the summit in just four minutes, or it's ¥560 in tolls and parking if driving yourself. From there, the walk to the top takes less than 30 minutes. The 100m-deep crater varies in width from 400m to 1100m and there's a walk around the southern edge of the crater rim. Arrive early in the morning to glimpse a sea of clouds hovering inside the crater, with Kujū-san (1787m) on the horizon.

Activities

From the top of the cable-car run you can walk around the crater rim to the peak of Naka-dake, on to the top of Taka-dake and then descend to Sensui Gorge (Sensui-kyō), which blooms with azaleas in mid-May, or to the road that runs between Taka-dake and Neko-dake. Either way will lead you to Miyaji, the next train station east of Aso. The direct descent to Sensui Gorge is steep, so it's easier to continue back from Taka-dake to the Naka-dake rim and then follow the old Aso-higashi cable-car route down to Sensui Gorge. Allow four to five hours from the Aso-nishi cable-car station walking uphill to Sensui Gorge, then another 1½ hours for the descent.

Shorter walks include the easy ascent of Kijima-dake from the Aso Volcanic Museum, about 25 minutes to the top. You can then return to the museum or take the branch trail to the Naka-dake ropeway in about 30 minutes. You can also climb to the top of Eboshi-dake in about 50 minutes.

Perfect after a long hike, **Yume-no-yu Onsen** (☎ 35-5777; admission ¥400; 10am-10pm), just in front of JR Aso Station, has wonderful indoor and outdoor pools and a large sauna. Family baths are available (¥1000 per hour).

INFORMATION

Tourist Information Office 観光案内所	1	C3

SIGHTS & ACTIVITIES

Aso Volcanic Museum 阿蘇火山博物館	2	B4
Aso-jinja 阿蘇神社	3	D2
Daikanbō Lookout 大観望	4	C1
Kusasenri 草千里	5	B4
Naka-dake Crater 中岳	6	C4
Shiroyama Tembōdai Lookout 城山展望台	7	D2
Uchinomaki Onsen 内牧温泉	8	B2
Yume-no-yu Onsen 夢の湯温泉	9	C3

SLEEPING

Aso YMCA 阿蘇YMCA	10	A3
Aso Youth Hostel 阿蘇ユースホステル	11	C3
Bluegrass ブルーグラス	12	D5
Bōchū Kyampu-jo 坊中キャンプ場	13	C3
Kyūkamura Minami-Aso 国民休暇村南阿蘇	14	D5
Shukubou Aso 宿房あそ	15	C3
Takamori-Murataya Ryokan Youth Hostel 村田屋旅館ユースホステル	16	D6

EATING

Bluegrass ブルーグラス	(see 12)	
Sanzoku Tabiji 山賊旅路	17	C3

TRANSPORT

Aso-nishi Cable-Car Station 阿蘇西ロープウェイ乗り場	18	C4
Eki Rent-a-Car 駅レンタカー	(see 1)	

KYŪSHŪ

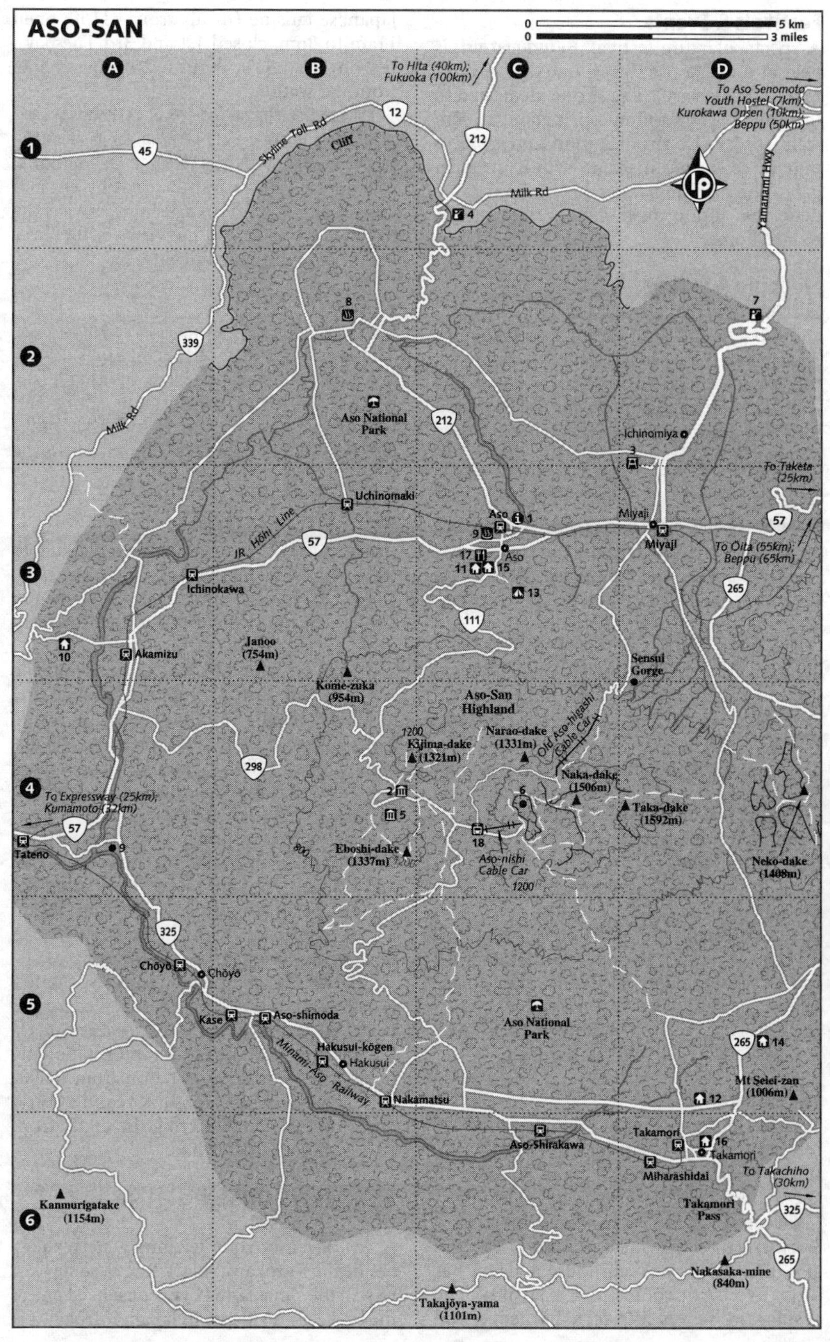
ASO-SAN
To Hita (40km); Fukuoka (100km)
To Aso Senomoto Youth Hostel (7km); Kurokawa Onsen (10km); Beppu (50km)
Skyline Toll Rd
Cliff
Milk Rd
Yamanami Hwy
Aso National Park
Ichinomiya
To Taketa (25km)
Uchinomaki
JR Hōhi Line
Aso
Miyaji
To Ōita (55km); Beppu (65km)
Ichinokawa
Akamizu
Janoo (754m)
Kome-zuka (954m)
Sensui Gorge
Aso-San Highland
Kijima-dake (1321m)
Narao-dake (1331m)
Old Aso-higashi Cable Car
Naka-dake (1506m)
Taka-dake (1592m)
To Expressway (25km); Kumamoto (32km)
Tateno
Eboshi-dake (1337m)
Aso-nishi Cable Car
Neko-dake (1408m)
Chōyō
Kase
Aso-shimoda
Hakusui-kōgen
Hakusui
Minami-Aso Railway
Nakamatsu
Mt Seiei-zan (1006m)
Aso-Shirakawa
Takamori
Miharashidai
To Takachiho (30km)
Takamori Pass
Kanmurigatake (1154m)
Nakasaka-mine (840m)
Takajōya-yama (1101m)
KYŪSHŪ

Festivals & Events

A spectacular fire festival, **Hi-furi-matsuri**, is held at **Aso-jinja** (☎ 22-0064) one day in mid-March (dates vary). The shrine, dedicated to the 12 gods of the mountain, is about a 300m walk north of JR Miyaji Station, and is one of only three shrines in Japan with its original gate. The drinking water here is said to be delicious, and at dusk visitors fill canteens to take home.

Sleeping & Eating

Finding a bed in the area is easy, with most accommodation in Aso, Akamizu or Takamori. Away from the towns, restaurants and lodgings are scattered and hard to reach by public transport. Stocking up on snacks is a good idea and there's a cluster of eateries on Hwy 57 near JR Aso Station.

ASO TOWN

Bōchū Kyampu-jo (☎ 34-0351; campsites per person ¥310; ⌚ Jun-Sep) Easiest to reach by car, this sprawling campsite off the highway en route to the mountain has a lovely position, good facilities and tent rentals (from ¥2040).

Aso Youth Hostel (☎ 34-0804; dm ¥2450; P) This small hostel with neighbouring campground is a 20-minute uphill hike from JR Aso Station, past pretty Saigenden-ji temple, which dates from AD 726. Buses to the cable-car station stop outside the hostel. A kitchen is available.

our pick **Shukubou Aso** (☎ 34-0194; fax 34-1342; r per person with/without 2 meals from ¥11,000/5000; P) This lovely rustic *minshuku* with modern touches is set in the trees, less than 500m from Aso Station, offering excellent value.

Sanzoku-Tabiji (☎ 34-2011; set meals from ¥950; ⌚ 11am-7pm; ♿ V) is known for its *dangojiru* (miso soup with dumplings) and healthy mountain-vegetable *teishoku*. It's on Hwy 57, opposite the Villa Park Hotel, 10 minutes' walk from JR Aso Station and has an English menu.

TAKAMORI

Takamori-Murataya Ryokan Youth Hostel (☎ 62-0066; dm HI member/nonmember ¥2625/3225) A tiny hostel in Takamori town, about 800m from the station. Toilets are Japanese-style only.

Bluegrass (☎ 62-3366; www.aso-bluegrass.com, in Japanese; r per person with/without 2 meals ¥7000/3500; P) This cowboy ranch house and inn has attractive clean rooms and a Jacuzzi! The restaurant serves Western barbecue and Japanese cuisine (meals from ¥1150; open 11am to 8pm, closed 1st and 3rd Tuesday). It's on Hwy 325, about a 20-minute hike from the station.

Kyūkamura Minami-Aso (☎ 62-2111; www.qkamura.or.jp/aso, in Japanese; 3219 Takamori, Takamori-machi; r per person with 2 meals from ¥8400; P) A national vacation village easiest to reach by car and crowded in July and August. Otherwise, the facilities are great and the views of the three main peaks are magnificent.

AKAMIZU

Aso YMCA (☎ 35-0124; www.kumamoto-ymca.or.jp/aso, in Japanese; dm ¥3300-4000; P) Set on a hillside with a wooded outlook, this large, inviting hostel has a main lodge, comfortable cabins and lots of facilities. It's an uphill hike about 600m west of JR Akamizu Station, across the river.

Getting There & Around

Aso is on the JR Hōhi line between Kumamoto (*tokkyū*; ¥1980, 70 minutes) and Ōita (*tokkyū*; ¥3290, 1¾ hours). Some buses from Beppu (¥3080, 2¾ hours) continue to the Aso-nishi cable-car station (an extra ¥1130).

To get to Takamori on the southern side of the crater, transfer from the JR Hōhi line at Tateno (¥360, 30 minutes) to the scenic Minami-Aso private line, which terminates at Takamori (¥470, 30 minutes). Buses from Takamori continue southeast to Takachiho (¥1280, 70 minutes, three daily).

Buses operate approximately every 90 minutes from JR Aso Station via the youth hostel and volcano museum to Aso-nishi cable-car station (¥470, 35 minutes). The first bus up leaves at 8.37am, with the last return trip down from the cable-car station at 5pm.

Bike rentals are available at JR Aso Station (¥300, two hours). Cars can be rented for the day at **Eki Rent-a-Car** (☎ 34-1001 www.ekiren.co.jp, in Japanese), opposite the tourist information office adjacent to the train station, from ¥6000.

If driving, a toll (¥560) is required on a portion of the road skirting the crater from Aso-nishi to Kato-nishi.

KUROKAWA ONSEN 黒川温泉

☎ 0967 / pop 400

A few dozen ryokan lie along a steep valley beside the Kurokawa (Black River), some 6km west of the Yamanami Hwy. Considered one of the best onsen villages in Japan, Kurokawa is everything a resort town should be. Although well known in Japan, this idyllic village is safely secluded from the rest of the world and maintains its tranquillity. It's the perfect spot to experience a ryokan.

For day-trippers, an 'onsen passport' (¥1200) from the **tourist information desk** (☎ 44-0076; 9am-6pm) allows access to three baths of your choice (8.30am to 9pm). Kurokawa is especially famous for its 23 *rotemburo*. Among local favourites are Yamamizuki, Kurokawa-sō and Shimmei-kan, with its cave baths and riverside *rotemburo*. Many places offer *konyoku* (mixed bathing).

At Ubuyama village, between Kurokawa and Senomoto near the junction of Rtes 11 (Yamanami Hwy) and 442, you'll double take at your first glance of hundreds of life-size birds and animals, meticulously pruned out of hedges over seemingly random hectares of land. There's a car park to take surreal photographs from.

Sleeping

The onsen ryokan at Kurokawa are undoubtedly worth paying for. They aren't cheap, but this isn't an experience you'll have every day.

Aso Senomoto Youth Hostel (阿蘇瀬の本ユースホステル; ☎ 44-0157; www.jyh.gr.jp/aso/next.html; dm HI member/nonmember ¥2940/3540) Between Miyaji and Kurokawa Onsen, this friendly hostel has English information about hiking Kujū-san and other high peaks in the area. Breakfast and dinner are available.

Chaya-no-hara Campground (茶屋の原キャンプ所; ☎ 44-0220; campsite per person from ¥600) A little further down the road towards the resort is this place , which is essentially a sloping lush green paddock with a truly wonderful outlook.

Sanga Ryokan (山河旅館; ☎ 44-0906; www.sanga-ryokan.com, in Japanese; r per person with 2 meals from ¥14,300; Ⓟ) Several of the 15 delightful rooms at this romantic ryokan have private onsen attached. Exquisite *kaiseki* meals, attention to detail and heartfelt service make this a place to treat yourself to the Japanese art of hospitality.

Okyakuya Ryokan (御客屋旅館; ☎ 44-0454; fax 44-0551; r per person with 2 meals from ¥12,500; Ⓟ) Nearby is another noteworthy choice, and overlooks a serene garden. English is spoken at both *ryokan*, and a station pick-up service can be arranged.

Getting There & Away

Experiencing this area is most enjoyable by car. But there are also five daily buses between JR Aso Station and Kurokawa Onsen (¥960, one hour). The last bus back to Aso departs at 5.55pm, to Kumamoto at 8.30pm (¥1430, one hour) or Beppu at 7pm (¥2350, two hours).

AMAKUSA ARCHIPELAGO 天草諸島

☎ 0969

South of the Shimabara Peninsula are the islands of the Amakusa-shotō. The islands were a stronghold of Christianity during Japan's 'Christian Century' and the grinding poverty here was a major factor in the Shimabara Rebellion of 1637–38. It's still one of the least developed regions of Japan.

Around the islands are opportunities for diving and dolphin-watching cruises. **Hondo** is the main town and has exhibition halls relating to the Christian era. **Amakusa Youth Hostel** (天草ユースホステル; ☎ 22-3085; dm HI member/nonmember ¥2783/3383) is about a 300m walk uphill from the bus terminal. Tamioka, where Nagasaki ferries berth, has castle ruins. Getting to the islands usually involves a ferry from various places in Nagasaki-ken or along the Kumamoto coast. Amakusa Five Bridges links the island directly with Misumi, southwest of Kumamoto.

KAGOSHIMA-KEN 鹿児島県

Kyūshū's southernmost prefecture has a charm of its own. Beautiful, bayside Kagoshima city lies in the shadow of a highly active volcano, whose very presence cannot be separated from the local identity. People celebrate life here, reminded daily of its fragility. The fertile coastal plains of the Satsuma Peninsula lie to the south, and to the north, striking Kirishima-Yaku National Park, also with its string of volcanoes and superb hiking opportunities.

KIRISHIMA-YAKU NATIONAL PARK 霧島屋久国立公園

The day walk from Ebino-kōgen (not to be confused with the town of Ebino down on the plains) to the summits of a string of volcanoes is one of the finest hikes in Japan. It's 15km from the summit of Karakuni-dake (1700m) to the summit of Takachiho-no-mine (1574m). If the peaks aren't being lashed by thunderstorms or shrouded in fog, common during the rainy season (mid-May through June), the vistas are superb. Shorter walks include a lake stroll on the plateau, and if hiking isn't an option, the windy mountain highways are great to drive. The area is known for its wild azaleas, hot springs and the impressive 75m waterfall, **Senriga-taki**, unimpressively dammed and shrouded by concrete reinforcements.

Orientation & Information

A centre at each end of the volcano walk has bilingual maps and hiking information.

Ebino-kōgen Eco Museum Centre (☎ 0984-33-3002; 🕑 9am-5pm) Has free information on local sleeping and eating options with topographic hiking maps for sale. There's an indoor rest area with vending machines and displays on wildlife and geology.

Takachiho-gawara Visitors Centre (☎ 0995-57-2505; 🕑 9am-5pm) Established to provide information on the local environment and wildlife.

Sights & Activities

EBINO PLATEAU WALKS

The Ebino-kōgen lake circuit is a relaxed 4km stroll around a series of volcanic lakes – **Rokkannon Mi-ike** is intensely cyan in colour. Across the road from the lake, Fudō-ike, at the base of Karakuni-dake, is a steaming *jigoku*. The stiffer climb to the 1700m summit of **Karakuni-dake** skirts the edge of the volcano's deep crater before arriving at the high point on the eastern side. The panoramic view to the south is outstanding, taking in the perfectly circular caldera lake of Ōnami-ike, rounded **Shinmoe-dake** and the perfect cone of Takachiho-no-mine. On a clear day, you can see Kagoshima and the smoking cone of Sakurajima. Naka-dake is another nice half-day walk, and in May and June it offers good views of the Miyama-Kirishima azaleas. Friendly wild deer roam freely through the town of Ebino-kōgen and are happy to be photographed.

LONGER WALKS

The long views across the lunarlike terrain of volcano summits are truly otherworldly. If you are in good shape and have six or seven hours, you can continue from Karakuni-dake to Shishiko-dake, Shinmoe-dake, Naka-dake and Takachiho-gawara, from where you can make the ascent of Takachiho-no-mine.

INFORMATION

Ebino-kogen Eco-Museum Centre えびの高原ビジターセンター	1 C2
Takachiho-gawara Visitors Centre 高千穂河原ビジターセンター	2 B3

SIGHTS & ACTIVITIES

Kirishima-jingū 霧島神宮	3 B4

SLEEPING

Ebino-kōgen Campground & Lodge えびの高原キャンプ村	4 C2
Ebino-Kōgen Onsen Hotel えびの高原荘温泉ホテル	5 C2
Karakuni-sō からくに荘	6 D2
Krishima Jingu-mae Youth Hostel 霧島神宮前ユースホステル	7 B4
Minshuku Kirishima-ji 民宿きりしま路	8 B4
Takachiho-gawara Camping Ground 高千穂河原キャンプ場	9 B3

TRANSPORT

Bus Centre バスセンター	10 C2

Close up, Takachiho is a formidable volcano with a huge, gaping crater. The whole trek goes above and below the treeline on a trail that can be muddy or dry, clear or foggy; some Kagoshima monks-in-training do this route daily!

If you miss the afternoon bus (3.49pm) from Takachiho-gawara to Kirishima-jingū, it's a 7km walk down to the village shrine area, or a ¥1200 taxi ride. A taxi up to Ebino-kōgen is about ¥3750.

KIRISHIMA-JINGŪ 霧島神宮

Picturesque, tangerine **Kirishima-jingū** (☎ 0995-57-0001) has a good vantage point. Though it dates from the 6th century, the present shrine was built in 1715. It is dedicated to Ninigi-no-mikoto, who, according to *Kojiki* (a historical book compiled in 712), made his legendary landing in Japan on the Takachiho-no-mine summit.

The shrine is accessible by bus (¥240, 15 minutes) from JR Kirishima-jingū Station. The festivals of **Saitan-sai** (1 January), **Ota-ue-sai** (mid-March) and the lantern festival of **Kontō-sai** (5 August) are worth seeing. If you're a temple fan, visit Kirishima Higashi-jinja for ancient cedars and scenic views.

Sleeping & Eating

Ebino-kōgen village has good accommodation options, but few eateries. Most village shops close by 5pm. Stock up when you can.

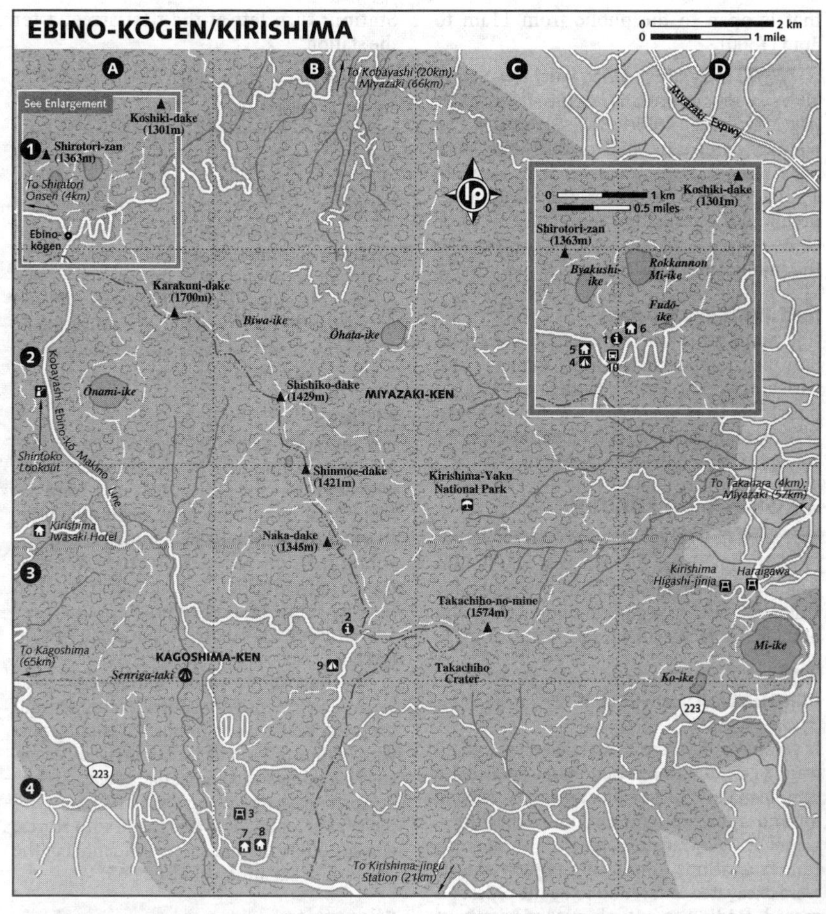

Ebino-kōgen Campground & Lodge (☎ 0984-33-0800, 0984-35-1111; campsites/tent rental/lodge cabins per person from ¥800/1100/1130; Ⓟ) A pretty stream runs through the middle of this delightful campground, 500m from the Eco-Museum Centre. It's open year-round, but in July and August the price for the lodge cabins jumps to ¥6490.

Takachiho-gawara camping ground (☎ 0995-57-0996; campsite ¥1100; 🕒 Jul & Aug; Ⓟ) Tent rental with blankets and cooking utensils for five people costs ¥2760.

Shiratori Onsen (白鳥温泉; ☎ 0984-33-1104; r per person from ¥2850; Ⓟ) There are exquisite views from this delightful hillside onsen and *rotemburo* (¥300) on Rte 30 from Ebino town towards Ebino Kōgen. In autumn the trees are ablaze with the colours of *kōyō* (turning leaves).

Kirishima Jingū-mae Youth Hostel (☎ 0995-57-1188; dm HI member/nonmember ¥3200/3800; Ⓟ) Southeast of Kirishima-jingū, this clean and comfy youth hostel maintains a midnight curfew, and offers breakfast (¥500) and dinner (¥1000).

Minshuku Kirishima-ji (☎ 0995-57-0272; r per person ¥4500) This basic but friendly six-room inn is close to the shrine and has been looking after LP readers for years. Breakfast is available (¥700) and the bathrooms are shared.

Karakuni-sō (☎ 0984-33-0650; fax 0984-33-4928; per person with 2 meals ¥8600, annexe house s/d/tr ¥5200/8200/9200) This small, attractive Ebino-kōgen ryokan has a wonderful onsen that is open to the public from 11am to 3pm (¥300).

our pick **Ebino-kōgen Onsen Hotel** (☎ 0984-33-0161; www.ebinokogenso.jp, in Japanese; s/tw per person with 2 meals from ¥9200/10,800; P ⊠ ▣) The friendly front-desk staff of this large 'people's hotel' communicate well in English. The facilities are excellent, the location superb and the restaurant makes tasty affordable meals. The lovely *rotemburo* is open to the public from 11.30am to 7.30pm (¥500).

Getting There & Away

The main train junctions are JR Kobayashi Station, northeast of Ebino Plateau, and Kirishima-jingū Station to the south, but a direct bus from Kagoshima to Ebino-kōgen (¥1570, 1¾ hours) is the best method of public transport. Schedules change often.

KIRISHIMA-SHI KOKUBU 霧島市国分

Directly north of Sakurajima you'll find Kokubu, Kagoshima's second-largest city. It's still rural, but has a growing population and branches of tech giants Kyōcera and Sony.

Sights

UENOHARA JŌMON-ERA SITE
上の原縄文遺跡

If you have an interest in archaeology, you'll want to detour to see Uenohara, once just a remote make-out spot with an empty parking lot and a few lonesome vending machines. Uenohara was transformed when during routine excavations, Jōmon-era pottery shards were excavated and found to be the oldest on record, leading to entirely new views about how civilisation developed in Japan. It now appears that the first humans may have come from the south rather than the north, via canoes or rafts along the Ryūkyū island chain. A re-created Jōmon-era village, demonstrations, tools and artefacts make this appealing **museum** (上野原縄文の森; ☎ 48-5701; admission ¥300; 🕑 9am-5pm, closed Mon) a fascinating spot.

Getting There & Around

Kokubu is easily reached by train from Kagoshima (see p737). Buses from Kokubu Station (¥400, six daily) arrive at the Uenohara Jōmon Site in 24 minutes. The last bus back departs at 5.35pm. Car rentals can be made with **Toyota Renta Lease** (☎ 0995-47-0600; 🕑 8am-8pm), three minutes' walk from Kokubu Station; turn left at the first street after the station.

KAGOSHIMA 鹿児島

☎ 099 / pop 604,480

Sunny and oddly relaxed Kagoshima, 'Naples of the Orient', is the southernmost metropolis of Japan's four main islands, set against the backdrop of a very much living volcano, *just* across the bay. Unfazed locals have been known to raise their umbrellas against the mountain's recurrent ablutions, when fine ash falls to the ground like snow, coating the landscape and obscuring the sun – creepy, yet captivating.

There's plenty to see and do here and it's worth staying for a few days.

History

For much of its history Kagoshima prefecture was dominated by the Shimazu clan, who held sway for nearly 700 years, until the Meiji Restoration took hold, beginning here. In 1865 the family helped smuggle a dozen young men into the UK to study Western technology first-hand. A statue in front of JR Kagoshima Station commemorates these adventurers who defied a national ban on foreign travel.

The Kagoshima (or Satsuma) region has long been receptive to outside contact and for many years was an important trading post with China. St Francis Xavier arrived here in 1549, making Kagoshima, like Nagasaki, one of Japan's earliest gateways to Christianity and the West. Contact was also made with Korea, whose pottery methods were influential in the creation of Satsuma-yaki (see p65).

Orientation

Kagoshima spreads north–south beside the bay and has two JR stations, the main being Kagoshima-Chūō to the south. The city centre is where the Tenmonkan-dōri shopping arcade crosses the tramlines. The garden of Sengan-en (p732), one of Kagoshima's main attractions, is north of JR Kagoshima Station (the other one) but most of the action is around Tenmonkan, north of Kōtsuki-gawa, with beloved Sakurajima often in view.

Information

Numerous places in the city (including the tourist information centre) carry an excellent English guide called *Kagoshima*. It has a host of activities and model excursions broken into three-hour, half-day and whole-day sections,

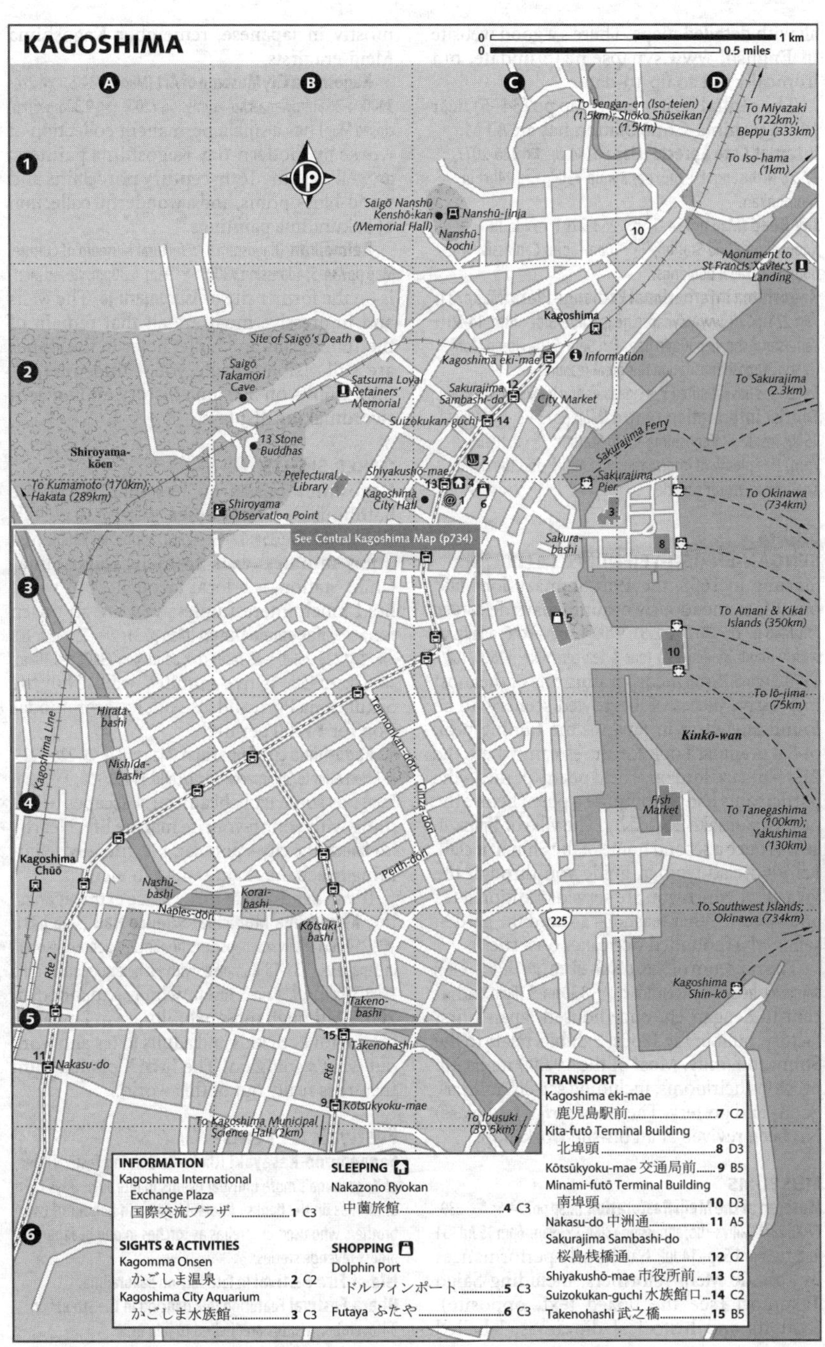
KAGOSHIMA
0 1 km
0 0.5 miles
To Sengan-en (Iso-teien) (1.5km); Shōko Shūseikan (1.5km)
To Miyazaki (122km); Beppu (333km)
To Iso-hama (1km)
Saigō Nanshū Kenshō-kan (Memorial Hall)
Nanshū-jinja
Nanshū-bochi
Monument to St Francis Xavier's Landing
Kagoshima
Site of Saigō's Death
Kagoshima eki-mae
Information
Saigō Takamori Cave
Satsuma Loyal Retainers' Memorial
Sakurajima Sambashi-do
City Market
To Sakurajima (2.3km)
Suizokukan-guchi
Sakurajima Ferry
13 Stone Buddhas
Shiroyama-kōen
Prefectural Library
Shiyakushō-mae
Sakurajima Pier
To Kumamoto (170km); Hakata (289km)
Kagoshima City Hall
To Okinawa (734km)
Shiroyama Observation Point
See Central Kagoshima Map (p734)
Sakura-bashi
To Amani & Kikai Islands (350km)
Hirata-bashi
Kagoshima Line
Tenmonkan-dōri
To Iō-jima (75km)
Kinkō-wan
Nishida-bashi
Ginza-dōri
Fish Market
To Tanegashima (100km); Yakushima (130km)
Kagoshima Chūō
Perth-dōri
Nashū-bashi
Korai-bashi
Naples-dōri
Kōtsuki-bashi
To Southwest Islands; Okinawa (734km)
Rte 2
Kagoshima Shin-kō
Takeno-bashi
Takenohashi
Nakasu-do
Rte 1
Kōtsūkyoku-mae
To Kagoshima Municipal Science Hall (2km)
To Ibusuki (39.5km)
INFORMATION
Kagoshima International Exchange Plaza 国際交流プラザ 1 C3
SIGHTS & ACTIVITIES
Kagomma Onsen かごしま温泉 2 C2
Kagoshima City Aquarium かごしま水族館 3 C3
SLEEPING
Nakazono Ryokan 中薗旅館 4 C3
SHOPPING
Dolphin Port ドルフィンポート 5 C3
Futaya ふたや 6 C3
TRANSPORT
Kagoshima eki-mae 鹿児島駅前 7 C2
Kita-futō Terminal Building 北埠頭 8 D3
Kōtsūkyoku-mae 交通局前 9 B5
Minami-futō Terminal Building 南埠頭 10 D3
Nakasu-do 中洲通 11 A5
Sakurajima Sambashi-do 桜島桟橋通 12 C2
Shiyakushō-mae 市役所前 13 C3
Suizokukan-guchi 水族館口 14 C2
Takenohashi 武之橋 15 B5
KYŪSHŪ

all with detailed maps. There's a good website in English, www.synapse.ne.jp/update, but ironically not so up-to-date.

The central post office (Map pp734–5) near JR Kagoshima-Chūō Station has an ATM.

Internet Café Aprecio (Map pp734-5; ☎ 226-2077; 17-28 Nishisengoku-chō; per 30min ¥300; 24hr) In Tenmonkan.

Joy Road (Map pp734-5; ☎ 253-2201; inside JR Kagoshima-Chūō Station; 10am-6pm) Can assist with domestic travel bookings.

Kagoshima International Exchange Plaza (Map p731; ☎ 221-6620; www.synapse.ne.jp/kia/e/index.htm; 14-50 Yamashita-chō; per 30min free; 9am-5pm, closed Mon) Near JR Kagoshima Station this great resource for foreigners has satellite TV, magazines and books for browsing.

Tourist information centre (Map pp734-5; ☎ 253-2500; inside JR Kagoshima-Chūō Station; 8.30am-7pm) Has plenty of information in English and the handy *Kagoshima* visitor's guide.

Sights

SENGAN-EN (ISO-TEIEN) 仙巌園（磯庭園）

Starting in 1658, the 19th Shimazu lord laid out this tremendously beautiful bayside **garden** (off Map p731; ☎ 274-1551; 9700-1 Yoshinochō; admission with/without guided villa tour & tea ceremony ¥1500/1000; 8.30am-5.15pm), incorporating one of the most impressive pieces of 'borrowed scenery' to be found anywhere in Japan – the fuming peak of Sakurajima. Look for the stream where the 21st Shimazu lord once held poetry parties – the participants had to compose a poem before the next cup of sake floated by. The villa of **Shimazu-ke** was once a second home of the Shimazu clan. Kimono-clad women guide you through the villa, after which you are served traditional tea and sweets. Other teashops around the garden sell *jambo* (pounded rice cakes on a stick).

The museum of **Shōko Shūseikan** (尚古集成館; admission free with garden ticket; 8.30am-5.15pm), adjacent to Sengan-en, once housed Japan's first factory, built in the 1850s. Exhibits relate to the Shimazu family. Most of the 10,000 items are precious heirlooms, including scrolls, military goods and pottery. The art of *kiriko* (cut glass) has been revived at an on-site workshop.

MUSEUMS

Museum of the Meiji Restoration (Map pp734-5; ☎ 239-7700; 23-1 Kaijiya-chō; admission ¥300; 9am-6pm 15 Jul–31 Aug, to 5pm 1 Sep–14 Jul) has hourly performances by robotic Meiji reformers, including Saigō Takamori (see the boxed text, opposite). Exhibits and historical dioramas, labelled mostly in Japanese, remember Kagoshima Meiji-era firsts.

Kagoshima City Museum of Art (Map pp734-5; ☎ 224-3400; 4-36 Shiroyama-chō; admission ¥200; 9.30am-6pm, closed Mon) has a small, permanent collection of works by modern-day Kagoshima painters, as well as some 16th-century porcelains and wood-block prints, and a wonderful collection of Sakurajima paintings.

Reimeikan (Kagoshima Prefectural Museum of Culture; Map pp734-5; admission ¥300; 9am-4.30pm, closed Mon) is on the former site of **Tsurumaru-jō**. The walls and impressive moat are all that remain of the 1602 castle, and bullet holes in the stones are still visible. Inside you'll find interesting exhibits on Satsuma history and ancient swordmaking displays.

OTHER SIGHTS

Kagoshima boasts no less than 50 public bathhouses. **Nishida Onsen** (Map pp734-5; 西田温泉; ☎ 255-6354; 12-17 Takasu; admission ¥360), just a few minutes' walk from JR Kagoshima-Chūō Station, is a local favourite, but won't hold much interest unless you are an onsen fanatic. **Kagomma Onsen** (Map p731; かごっま温泉; ☎ 226-2688; 3-28 Yasui-chō; admission ¥360; 10am-1am, closed 15th) is five minutes' walk from the Sakurajima Port, and also offers accommodation for ¥4000 per night.

Kagoshima City Aquarium (Map p731; ☎ 226-2233; 3-1 Hon Minato Shinmachi; adult/child ¥1500/750; 9am-5pm) has some truly beautiful seascapes brimming with your favourite marine life. Nearby **Iso-hama**, the city's popular, kid-friendly swimming beach, has Sakurajima in view.

It's all hands-on at this science extravaganza, the **Kagoshima Municipal Science Hall** (Map p731; ☎ 250-8511; www.synapse.ne.jp/~kmsh-science/top.html, in Japanese; 2-31-18 Kamoike; with Planetarium adult/child ¥900/350; 9.30am-5.30pm), which expanded in 2007. Although most exhibits are in Japanese, it's fun for both kids and adults to try and work out what's going on! The IMAX planetarium theatre is really out of this world.

Festivals & Events

Sogadon-no-Kasayaki (Umbrella Burning Festival) One of Kagoshima's more unusual events in late July. Boys burn umbrellas on the banks of Kōtsuki-gawa in honour of two brothers who used umbrellas as torches in one of Japan's oldest revenge stories.

Isle of Fire Festival In late July on Sakurajima.

Ohara Festival Featuring folk dancing in the streets on 3 November; visitors are invited to join in.

KYŪSHŪ

SAIGŌ TAKAMORI 西郷隆盛

Although he played a leading part in the Meiji Restoration in 1868, in 1877 Saigō Takamori had second thoughts about the curtailment of samurai power. This hesitation led to the ill-fated Satsuma Rebellion. During the rebellion, Kumamoto's magnificent castle was incinerated and when defeat became inevitable, Saigō retreated to Kagoshima and committed *seppuku* (ritual suicide by disembowelment).

Despite his mixed status as both hero and villain of the Restoration, Saigō is a towering figure in the history of Japan. His square-headed features and bulky stature are instantly recognisable, and Kagoshima, like Ueno-kōen in Tokyo, has a famous Saigō statue (Map pp734-5; see p151), as well as a memorial hall, in honour of the Samurai.

Sleeping

Kagoshima has plenty of good-value places to stay. The station is a bit far from the action, so aim to stay towards Tenmonkan if you can.

BUDGET

Kagoshima Little Asia Guesthouse (Map pp734-5; ☎ 251-8166; www.cheaphotelasia.com; Yamano Bldg, 2-20-8 Nishida; dm/s ¥1500/2500; ⊠ 💻; 🚉 JR Kagoshima) Good luck finding cheaper accommodation anywhere in Japan. It's very basic, but clean and superfriendly and a mere stone's throw from the station. There are even free bicycles (one hour), free internet and laundry facilities.

Hotel Ishihara-sō (Map pp734-5; ☎ 254-4181; 4-14 Chūō-chō; s/d ¥3990/7980; 🚉 JR Kagoshima-chuō) The clean and tidy rooms, presumably designed for patrons of the Satsuma restaurant downstairs, make for excellent cheap lodging close to the station.

Nakazono Ryokan (Map p731; ☎ 226-5125; 1-8 Yasui-chō; s/d/tr ¥4200/8400/11,970; ⊠) This friendly Japanese Inn member has been looking after LP readers for years and will give you a taste of Kagoshima hospitality. The traditional inn is central, comfortable and filled with the personality of its keeper.

Hotel Gasthof (Map pp734-5; ☎ 252-1401; www.gasthof.jp, in Japanese; 7-1 Chūō-chō; s/d/tw/tr ¥5565/8400/8925/12,600; ⊠ 💻; JR Kagoshima-chuō) Old-world Europe meets urban Japan at this unusual 48-room hotel, with good-sized rooms and chunky wooden furniture. Near the station and with triple and interconnecting rooms, it's a good choice for families.

Plaza Hotel Tenmonkan (Map pp734-5; ☎ 222-3344; fax 222-9911; 7-8 Yamanokuchi-chō; s/d/tw with breakfast from ¥5700/10,300/11,000; ⊠ 💻) Rooms are small but bright in this 224-room business hotel in an excellent location. The breakfast buffet is generous.

MIDRANGE

Sun Days Inn Kagoshima (Map p731; ☎ 227-5151; fax 227-4667; www.sundaysinn.com, in Japanese; 9-8 Yamanokuchi-chō; s/d/tw ¥6300/9300/10,300; ⊠ 💻) Slick, modern and Euro-styled, offering excellent value. The rooms are compact, but the beds, showers and warm decor make up for it. The Deluxe, an oversized room with two double beds and a sofa, is ¥25,000. Rates are cheaper booked on the homepage, if you can read Japanese.

Chisun Inn Kagoshima (Map pp734-5; ☎ 227-5611; fax 227-5612; www.solarehotels.com/english/chisun/inn-kagoshima/guestroom/detail.html; 1-3 Gofuku-chō; s/d ¥6800/12,000; ⊠ 💻) Opposite Tenmonkan-dōri tram stop, this new hotel is easy to find and perfectly located. Rooms are tiny but fresh and there are bunk rooms for travellers with children, and free internet via LAN cable.

Lexton Hotel (Map pp734-5; ☎ 222-0505; www.nisikawa.net/lexton/english; 4-20 Yamanokuchi-chō; s/d from ¥7350/11,550; Ⓟ ⊠ 💻) Popular with wedding parties, this smart hotel is a little dated but still nice. Rooms are of a good size, arranged around an open, light-filled atrium and there is an onsen on site. Check the homepage for examples of interiors.

Blue Wave Kagoshima (☎ 224-3211; fax 224-3212; www.bluewaveinn.jp/kagoshima, in Japanese; 2-7 Yamanokuchi-chō; s/tw ¥7665/15,225; ⊠ 💻) A modern, good-value business and leisure hotel, in the heart of bustling Tenmonkan. There's a Family Mart on site.

Onsen Hotel Nakahara Bessō (Map pp734-5; ☎ 225-2800; fax 226-3688; 15-19 Terukuni-chō; r per person with/without 2 meals from ¥12,600/8400; Ⓟ ⊠) This well-located, family-owned inn, opposite a lovely park, dates from 1904. Ignore its boxy exterior; inside you'll find spacious Japanese-style rooms, a modern *rotemburo*, traditional artwork and a good *Satsuma-ryōri* restaurant.

Eating

Kagoshima's climate is conducive to enjoying oneself. The JR Kagoshima-Chūō Station area and the alleys of Tenmonkan have an

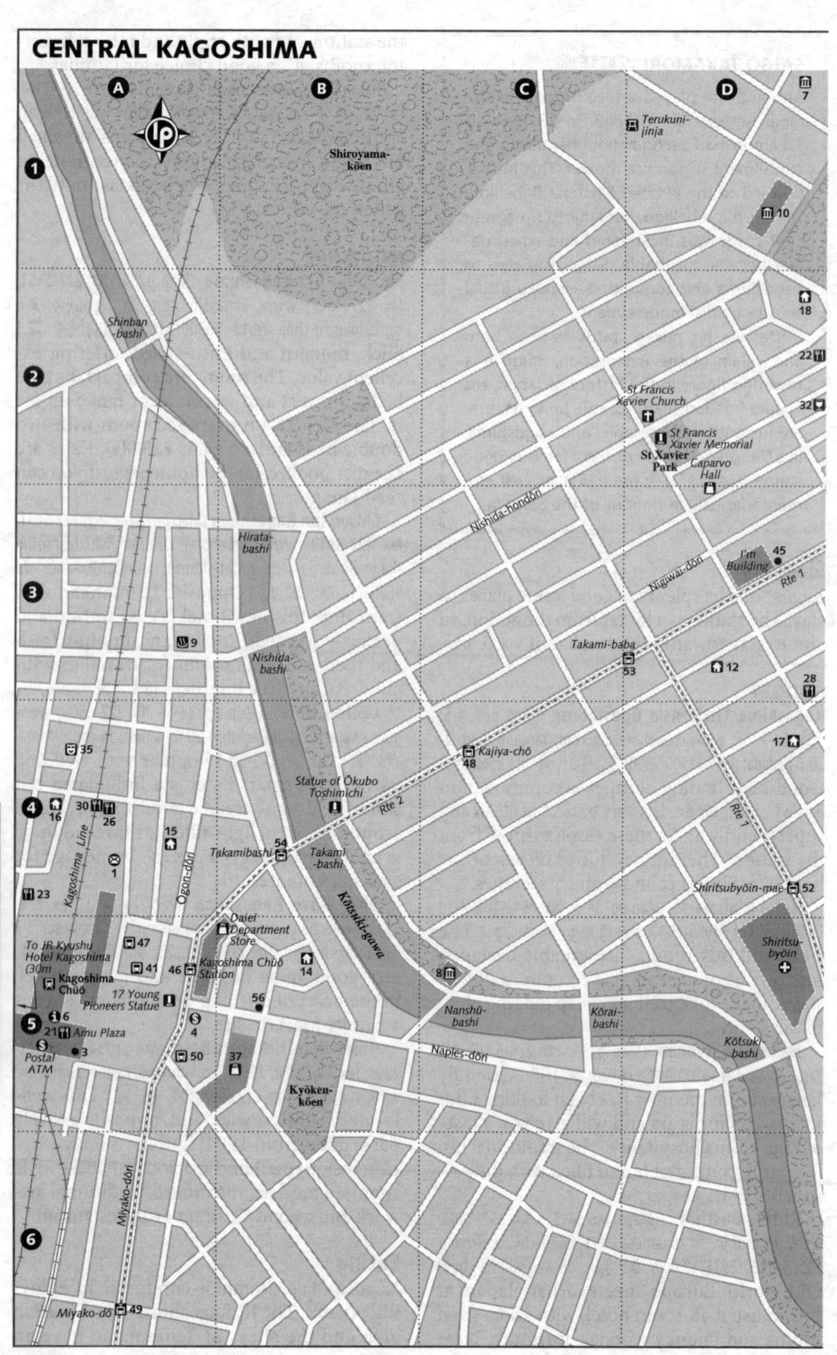
CENTRAL KAGOSHIMA
Shiroyama-kōen
Terukuni-jinja
Shinban-bashi
Hirata-bashi
Nishida-bashi
St Francis Xavier Church
St Francis Xavier Memorial
St Xavier Park
Caparvo Hall
Nishida-hondōri
Nigiwai-dōri
I'm Building
Rte 1
Rte 2
Takami-baba
Kajiya-chō
Statue of Ōkubo Toshimichi
Takamibashi
Takami-bashi
Kōtsuki-gawa
Kagoshima Line
Ogon-dōri
Daiei Department Store
Kagoshima Chūō Station
To JR Kyushu Hotel Kagoshima (30m)
Kagoshima Chūō
17 Young Pioneers Statue
Amu Plaza
Postal ATM
Nanshū-bashi
Kōrai-bashi
Kōtsuki-bashi
Naples-dōri
Kyōken-kōen
Shiritsubyōin-mae
Shiritsu-byōin
Miyako-dōri
Miyako-dō
KYŪSHŪ

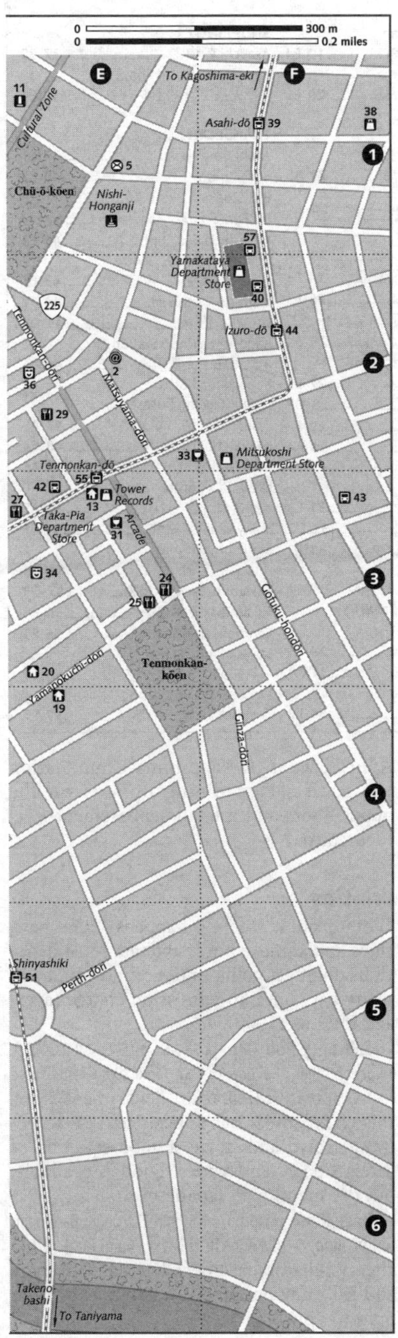

abundance of restaurants, many featuring *Satsuma-ryōri* regional cuisine. Try *tonkotsu* (pork ribs) seasoned with miso and black sugar) and *satsuma-age* (deep-fried fish cake flavoured with sake).

Ōshō (Map pp734-5; ☎ 253-4728; 1-4 Chuō-machi; dishes ¥200-570; 🕒 lunch & dinner) Just north of the station, you'll find this simple eatery with nongreasy *kara-age* (fried chicken), fried rice, *gyōza* and soups – it's tasty, fast and supercheap. Look for the picture menu board out the front.

our pick Kumatora Ikka (Map pp734-5; ☎ 219-3948; 2nd fl, Horie Bldg, 14-17 Sennichi-chō; dishes from ¥300; 🕒 dinner, closed Mon) There's a great atmosphere at this happy *izakaya,* festooned with an eclectic collection of Shōwa-period (1926–89) pop-culture memorabilia. Young Japanese come to hang out over a few rounds of beer and moreish comfort food. The bite-sized *hitokuchi-gyōza* are the best (20 pieces for ¥750!) and there's plenty of other morsels to tempt. There's no English sign, but there's a dark wooden street frontage and a staircase leading upstairs. You can see the faces in the windows from the street.

Izakaya Wakana (Map pp734-5; ☎ 286-1501; 2-21-21 Nishida-chō; dishes from ¥600; 🕒 lunch & dinner) The Kagoshima-Chūō branch of this famous local eatery is a two-minute walk from the station's West exit. For tasting, try the *kushiage moriawase* (barbeque skewer selection; five pieces ¥650) or *miso oden moriawase* (hotpot selection; four pieces, ¥700). Look for the red *noren* (doorway curtains).

Xiang Xiang (Map pp734-5; ☎ 255-0468; 1-11 Chuō-machi; dishes from ¥735; 🕒 lunch & dinner, closed Mon) Next door to Ōshō, you'll find this tidy restaurant serving flavoursome, aromatic Vietnamese cuisine. Some staff speaks English and there's an English menu.

Sunny Public Market (Map pp734-5; ☎ 219-9550; 1-30 Higashi-sengoku-chō; dishes from ¥850; 🕒 lunch & dinner) From the creators of the Wakana brand, this bright, open trattoria serves delicious European cuisine. The daily lunch special, a Western-styled *obentō (Himawari yōfū bokkusu)* is excellent value at ¥950 (¥1300 on weekends).

No No Budo (Map pp734-5; ☎ 206-7585; 5th fl, Amu Plaza; lunch/dinner buffet ¥1480/1980; 🕒 lunch & dinner; ⊠ 👪 Ⓥ) At Amu Plaza next to JR Kagoshima-Chūō Station you'll find this fun all-you-can-eat buffet with healthy choices. There's no English, but it's self-serve.

INFORMATION

Central Post Office 中央郵便局 1 A4
Internet Café Aprecio アプレシオ 2 E2
Joy Road ジョイロード 3 A5
Kagoshima Bank 鹿児島銀行 4 A5
Kagoshima East Post Office 鹿児島東郵便局 5 E1
Tourist Information Centre 観光案内所 6 A5

SIGHTS & ACTIVITIES

Kagoshima City Museum of Art 鹿児島市立美術館 7 D1
Museum of the Meiji Restoration 維新ふるさと館 8 C5
Nishida Onsen 西田温泉 9 A3
Reimeikan 黎明館 10 D1
Saigō Takamori Statue 西郷隆盛銅像 11 E1

SLEEPING

Blue Wave Kagoshima ブルーウェーブイン鹿児島 12 D3
Chisun Inn Kagoshima チサンイン鹿児島 13 E3
Hotel Gasthof ホテルガストフ 14 B5
Hotel Ishihara-sō ホテル石原荘 15 A4
Kagoshima Little Asia Guesthouse 安宿鹿児島リトルアジア 16 A4
Lexton Hotel ホテルレクストン 17 D4
Onsen Hotel Nakahara Bessō 中原別荘 18 D2
Plaza Hotel Tenmonkan プラザホテル天文館 19 E4
Sun Days Inn Kagoshima サンデイズイン鹿児島 20 E3

EATING

Amu Plaza アミュプラザ鹿児島 21 A5
Curryteria Sara カレーテリア 沙羅 22 D2
Izakaya Wakana 吾愛人中央駅店 23 A4
Kumatora Ikka 熊虎一家 24 E3
Meigetsu 明月 25 E3
No No Budo 野の葡萄 .... (see 21)
Ōshō 王将 26 A4
Sunny Public Market サニーパブリック マーケット 27 E3
Tontoro 豚とろ 28 D3
Wadaya 和田屋 29 E2
Xiang Xiang 香香 30 A4

DRINKING

Beer Reise ビアライゼ 31 E3
Kanejō かねじょう 32 D2
Salisbury Pub サリスブリパブ 33 E2

ENTERTAINMENT

Latin Dining & Sports Bar El Para エルパラ·ラテンスポーツバー 34 E3
Recife れしふえ 35 A4
Wine & Jazz Pannonica パノニカ 36 E2

SHOPPING

Asa-ichi 朝市 37 B5
Kagoshima Brand Shop 鹿児島ブランドショップ 38 F1

TRANSPORT

Asahi-dō 朝日通 39 F1
Bus Station バスセンター 40 F2
Bus Stops バスのりば 41 A5
Eki Rentacar 駅レンタカー .... (see 6)
Hayashida Bus 林田バス 42 E3
Izuro Kōsoku Bus Centre いづろ高速バスのりば 43 F3
Izuro-dō いづろ通 44 F2
JAL 日本航空 45 D3
Kagoshima Chūō Station 鹿児島中央駅前 46 A5
Kagoshima Kōtsū (Sightseeing Buses) 鹿児島交通（観光バス） 47 A5
Kajiya-chō 加治屋町 48 C4
Miyako-dō 都通 49 A6
Nissei Bus Centre バスセンター日生ビル 50 A5
Shinyashiki 新屋敷 51 E5
Shiritsubyōin-mae 市立病院前 52 D4
Takami-baba 高見馬場 53 D3
Takamibashi 高見橋 54 B4
Tenmonkan-dō 天文館通 55 E3
Toyota Renta Lease トヨタレンタリース 56 B5
Yamakataya Bus Centre バスセンター 山形屋 57 F1

Meigetsu (Map pp734-5; ☎ 225-5174; 9-1 Sennichi-chō; meat for 2 from ¥3000; ⌚ dinner) Reputedly the best *yakiniku* (Japanese do-it-yourself barbecue) in town at this bright, beery eatery in the heart of the entertainment district, off the Yamanokuchi main arcade. Look for the red-and-white 1980s styling. Ask for the *Nimei-moriawase* (500g meat selection for two, ¥3000) and barbecue away. Alternatively, sukiyaki is served upstairs.

Curryteria Sara (Map pp734-5; ☎ 223-8240; 5-26 Higashi-sengoku-chō; curries from ¥1300; ⌚ lunch & dinner, closed Mon) Delicious, vibrant black and red curries are the order of the day at this casual eatery easily spotted off Tenmonkan Arcade. Try the *Kagoshima kuro-karee* (black curry) made from black pork, local vegetables and spices (¥1350).

There's always a *rāmen* debate in Japan, but in Tenmonkan, two reliable favourites are the bustling **Tontoro** (Map pp734-5; ☎ 222-5857; 9-41 Yamanokuchi; rāmen dishes from ¥500; ⌚ until late) and **Wadaya** (Map pp734-5; ☎ 226-7773; 11-2 Higashi-sengoku-chō; bowls ¥630-800; ⌚ lunch & dinner).

Amu Plaza at JR Kagoshima-Chūō Station has good seated dining options on the upper floors and a fabulous basement-level food court.

Drinking

Tenmonkan is where it happens – shot bars, clubs and *karaoke* boxes abound. Most dance clubs don't get going until around 11pm and many bars have an admission charge (average ¥500 to ¥1000).

Salisbury Pub (Map pp734-5; ☎ 223-2389; 2nd fl, Shigenobu Bldg, 1-5 Gofuku-chō; ⌚ 6.30pm-1am, closed Tue) Opposite Mitsukoshi department store, this classy, quiet bar appeals to a 30-something crowd and stocks a good selection of foreign beers and wines. Food is available, but the menu is in Japanese.

Beer Reise (Map pp734-5; ☎ 227-0088; Basement, Hirata Bldg, 9-10 Sennichi-chō; ⌚ 6pm-1am) This cheery narrow basement bar has Guinness and Kilkenny on tap and a happy hour from 6pm to 7pm.

Kanejō (Map pp734-5; ☎ 223-0487; 2nd fl, 7-20 Higashi-sengoku-chō) Chinese tea house by day, jazz bar by night, this quaint little spot is a nice place to soothe those traveller's blues.

Entertainment

Wine & Jazz Pannonica (Map pp734-5; ☎ 216-3430; 2nd fl, 7-10 Higashi-sengoku-chō; 🕑 6pm-2am, closed Mon) The original Pannonica closed in 2000 and was replaced with this restaurant for discerning adults, with occasional live jazz on weekends.

Recife (Map pp734-5; ☎ 258-9774; 2-1-5 Takashi) Arty and cool, this mellow multipurpose bar-restaurant also has DJ decks and hosts occasional parties. It's popular with locals and expat groovers and has a strong Brazilian flavour.

Latin Dining & Sports Bar El Para (Map pp734-5; ☎ 223-3464; 2nd fl, Diamond Bldg, 11-7 Yamanokuchi-chō; 🕑 6pm-1am, closed Mon) There's an awesome menu of tapas here, including spicy buffalo chicken wings. Think cosy booths, sports on the big screen and darts.

Shopping

Regional specialities include a variation of Japanese doll, and cards printed with inks produced from Sakurajima volcanic ash. Sakurajima ash is used in the making of Sakurajima pottery, but the main ceramic wares are white and black Satsuma-yaki (a term used to describe a wide range of styles heralding from the Satsuma region). *Imo jōchū* (see the boxed text, right) is the drink of choice.

Futaya (Map p731; ☎ 222-5261; 5-20 Yasui-chō) Sells vintage kimonos and inexpensive gifts, near Nakazono Ryokan.

Asa-ichi (Morning Market; Map pp734-5; 🕑 6am-noon Mon-Sat) Kagoshima's morning market is just south of JR Kagoshima-Chūō Station.

Dolphin Port (Map p731; ☎ 226-2233; 5-4 Honminato-shinmachi) On the Kagoshima waterfront; a pleasant place for a stroll with a selection of tempting boutiques and eateries.

You can shop for traditional merchandise and local produce at Sengan-en (Iso-teien; p732) and **Kagoshima Brand Shop** (Map pp734-5; ☎ 225-6120; 1st fl, Sangyo Kaikan bldg, 9-1 Meizan-chō; 🕑 9am-5pm) in Tenmonkan.

Amu Plaza at JR Kagoshima-Chūō Station is brimming with retail opportunities.

Getting There & Away

AIR

Kagoshima airport has connections to Hong Kong, Shanghai and Seoul, and convenient domestic flights to Tokyo (¥38,900, 1½ hours), Osaka (¥26,800, one hour), Fukuoka (¥18,600, 45 minutes), Yakushima (¥13,900, 30 minutes) and Okinawa (Naha; ¥26,300, 85 minutes).

BOAT

Ferries shuttle every 10 to 30 minutes across the bay to Sakurajima (¥150, 15 minutes). Jetfoils depart from Kita-futō (north wharf) to Yakushima (from ¥7000, three hours). Regular ferries to Yakushima depart from Minami-futō (south wharf; from ¥4200, 13 hours). From Kagoshima Shin-kō (Kagoshima New Port), **Queen Coral Marix Line** (☎ 225-1551) has ferries to Naha (Okinawa) via the Amami archipelago (¥14,600, 25 hours).

BUS

Long-distance buses depart from the Express Bus Centre opposite Amu Plaza. Highway bus stops are also near Kagoshima-Chūō Station and Yamakataya (Map pp734–5) in Tenmonkan.

Routes include Miyazaki (¥2700, 2¾ hours), Fukuoka (¥5300, four hours), Oita (¥5500, six hours) and overnight to Osaka (¥12,000, 12 hours).

Hayashida buses to Ebino-kōgen (¥1550, two hours) depart from JR Kagoshima-Chūō Station.

TRAIN

Most trains arrive and depart from JR Kagoshima-Chūō Station. Additionally,

> **DRINKING SHŌCHŪ**
>
> The drink of choice throughout Kyūshū is *shōchū,* a strong distilled liquor. The island's southern region claims the highest consumption in Japan, which may well contribute to the generally relaxed vibe! Each prefecture is known for its own particular variety. In Kumamoto, it's usually made from rice; in Oita, barley. But in the *izakaya* (pub-eatery) of the south, sweet potato is the first choice: *imo-jōchū*. You can drink it straight, with soda or over ice, but the most traditional way (*oyu-wari,* ie with hot water) is to sip it from a tiny cup, after it's been heated in a stone pot over glowing coals until you begin to glow yourself.

the JR Kagoshima line heads north to Kumamoto (*shinkansen/tokkyū;* ¥6350, 70 minutes, change at Shin-Yatsushiro) and Fukuoka (*shinkansen/tokkyū;* ¥8920, 2½ hours, change at Shin-Yatsushiro). Also stopping at Kagoshima Station, the JR Nippō line goes to Miyazaki (*tokkyū;* ¥3790, two hours) and Beppu (¥9460, five hours).

Trains also run south to the popular hot-spring resort of Ibusuki (p740) and continue partway around the Satsuma Peninsula (*kaisoku,* ¥970, 55 minutes).

Getting Around

TO/FROM THE AIRPORT

Express buses to Kagoshima airport depart every 20 minutes from JR Kagoshima Chūō Station (¥1200, 40 minutes).

BICYCLE

Bikes can be rented (two hours/day ¥500/1500) at JR Kagoshima-Chūō Station and returned at a number of participating hotels (¥300). JR pass holders get a 40% discount. Ask at the tourist information office for details (p732).

BUS

There's a comprehensive city bus network, though trams are usually simpler.

The City View Bus (¥180) does a loop of all the major sights, departing every 30 minutes, from 9am to 5pm daily. You get on and off when you want. A one-day pass (¥600) is also valid on trams. Single tickets cost ¥180.

CAR

Cars can be rented for trips around Satsuma Peninsula from **Nankyu Senpaku** (☎ 422-1083) and **Kagoshima Shosen** (☎ 334-0012). For longer trips, **Eki Rent-a-Car** (Map pp734-5; ☎ 258-1412; www.ekiren.co.jp, in Japanese; 2nd fl, tourist information centre, JR Kagoshima-Chūō Station; 12hr from ¥4720; 8am-8pm) or **Toyota Renta Lease** (Map pp734-5; ☎ 268-0100; http://rent.toyota.co.jp/en/index.html; 5-46 Chūō-machi, JR Kagoshima-Chūō Station; 12hr from ¥525; 8am-8pm) are good options.

TRAM

Trams are the easiest way to get around town. Rte 1 starts from Kagoshima Station and goes through the centre into the suburbs. Rte 2 diverges at Takami-baba to JR Kagoshima-Chūō Station and terminates at Korimoto. Either pay the flat fare (¥180) or buy a one-day travel pass (¥600) from the tourist information centre or on the tram.

SAKURAJIMA 桜島

☎ 099 / pop 5800

Dominating the skyline from Kagoshima is the brooding cone of this spectacular active volcano. Since 1955 there has been an *almost continuous* stream of smoke and ash; think about that for just a second. The most violent eruption was in 1914, when the volcano poured out over three billion tonnes of lava, overwhelming numerous villages and joining the island to the mainland. If you stick around long enough, it's likely you'll experience some degree of volcano-mojo, hopefully without such devastation.

Despite its vocality, Sakurajima is at the present moment friendly enough that you can get up fairly close. Among the volcano's three peaks, only Minami-dake (1040m) is active. Visitors are not permitted to climb the mountain, but there are several good lookout points with walkways across a small corner of the immense lava flow. While some parts of Sakurajima are covered in deep volcanic ash or crumbling lava, other places have exceptionally fertile soil. Huge daikon (radishes) weighing up to 35kg and tiny *mikan* (oranges) only 3cm in diameter are locally grown.

Information

Information desk (Ferry terminal bldg; 8.30am-5pm) Has maps and timetables.

Sakurajima visitors centre (☎ 293-2443; 9am-5pm) Near the ferry terminal; has exhibits about the volcano, including a working model showing the volcano's growth.

Sights & Activities

The island is best enjoyed by car and it only takes a few hours to visit all the sights. If you're of good fitness, you could cycle all the way around, but it would take a full day. South of the visitors centre is **Karasujima Observation Point**, where the 1914 lava flow engulfed the small island that had once been 500m offshore. The same lava flow swallowed three villages, destroying over 1000 homes.

Continuing anticlockwise around the island, you'll reach the **Furusato Kankō hotel** and its special **rotemburo** (☎ 211-3111; admission

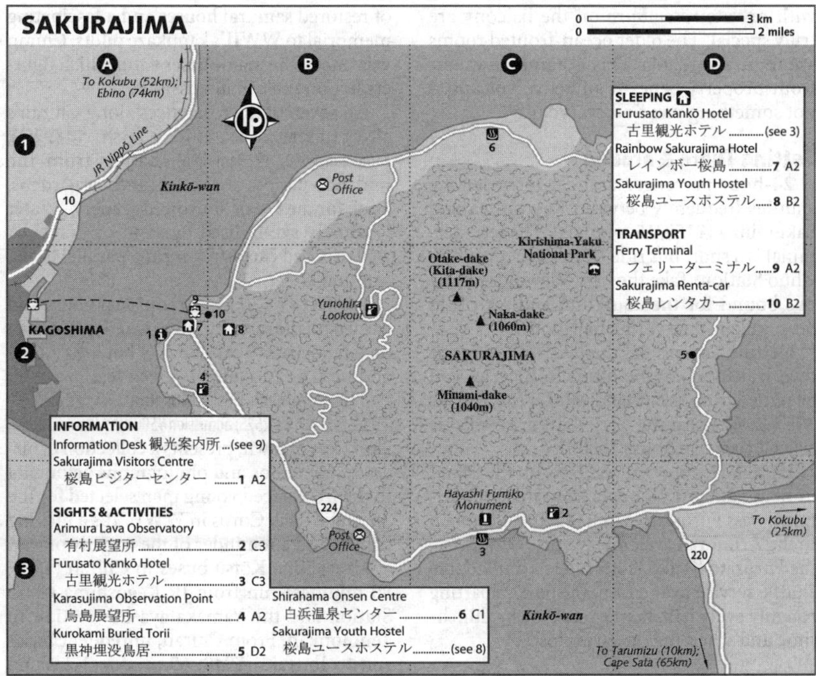

¥1050, rental locker & towel ¥410; ⏰ for hotel guests 6am-10pm, onsen-only visitors 8am-8pm, closed Mon & Thu morning), nestled among rocks by the sea. As it is also a shrine, you'll be given a *yukata* (cotton kimono) to wear in the water, allowing both men and women to bathe here. Continuing your circumnavigation you'll come to the **Arimura Lava Observatory**, one of the best places to observe the smoky cape of Minami-dake and the lava flow. Further on, only the top third of a 3m-high *torii* emerges from the volcanic ash at **Kurokami Buried Torii**. On the north coast you can soak in the hot, earthy brown waters of **Shirahama Onsen Centre** (☎ 293-4126; admission ¥300; ⏰ 10am-9pm), where you can also see a good accumulation of ashfall, most of the year.

Tours

Sightseeing bus tours of Sakurajima leave from JR Kagoshima-Chūō Station at 8.50am (adult/child ¥4000/2000, six hours). Tours are conducted in Japanese, but an English transcription is available. It's the only way to see the island if you don't have a car and are pressed for time.

Sleeping

If you're in Kagoshima for a few days, it's nice to spend a night on Sakurajima. Aside from the options below, there's a simple, seasonal camping ground opposite the visitors centre.

Sakurajima Youth Hostel (☎/fax 293-2150; dm with/without 2 meals ¥3870/2650; P ⊠ 💻) Less than 500m from the ferry terminal, this cheery hostel has an onsen for both men and women (just flip the English sign by the door to indicate your gender and it's all yours). Catch the 9pm ferry from Kagoshima to arrive before reception closes.

Rainbow Sakurajima Hotel (☎ 293-2323; www.rainbow-sakurajima.com, in Japanese; per person d & tw with 2 meals from ¥10,185) Adjacent to the ferry terminal, this lovely property faces the puffing volcano in one direction, and Kagoshima city across the bay, in the other. Most rooms are Western style and water facing. There's also an onsen open to the public (¥300; 8am to 8pm) and a bayside beer garden over summer.

Furusato Kankō Hotel (☎ 221-3111; www.furukan.co.jp, in Japanese; r per person with 2 meals from ¥10,150) This wonderful old seaside hotel is slowly being refurbished and some of the pricier new rooms with private *rotemburo* on the balcony are truly special. The older ocean-fronted rooms are more affordable. This is a unique waterfront property beneath an active volcano – not something you find everyday.

Getting There & Around

A 24-hour passenger and car ferry service shuttles frequently between Kagoshima and Sakurajima (¥150, 15 minutes). The ferry terminal is a short bus ride from JR Kagoshima-Chūō Station. Take the City View Bus or any bus bound for the aquarium and get off at Suizokukan-mae (¥180, half-hourly).

Getting around Sakurajima without your own transport can be difficult. Bicycles can be rented from **Sakurajima Renta Car** (☎ 293-2162; 1/2hr ¥400/600) near the ferry. Cars are available as well (per two hours ¥6500).

Local buses operate regularly on the island until about 8pm. JR buses from the ferry terminal pass Furusato Onsen (¥290) and run up to the Arimura Lava Observatory. Otherwise, the Furusato Kankō Hotel offers a limited free shuttle service to and from the port, departing roughly every half-hour except during lunchtime and when the onsen is closed.

SATSUMA PENINSULA 薩摩半島

The peninsula south of Kagoshima city has fine rural scenery, the pretty and contemplative town of Chiran, and Ibusuki with its sand baths. On the other side of Kinkō-wan (Kagoshima Bay) is Cape Sata, the southernmost point of the Japanese mainland.

Exploring the peninsula by train and bus is time-consuming. The JR Ibusuki-Makurazaki line operates south from Kagoshima to Ibusuki and then turns west to Makurazaki, from where you can make your way by local bus back to Kagoshima. Renting a car from Kagoshima is a smart move (see p738). The stretch of the Ibusuki Skyline road south from Chiran offers some wonderful views.

Daily bus tours to Ibusuki and Chiran depart from JR Kagoshima-Chūō Station. A daily sightseeing bus (¥4550) heads off to Chiran at 8.50am, whizzes you around the sights and then does the same thing in Ibusuki, ending the day with a soak in a hot spring.

Chiran 知覧

☎ 0993 / pop 13,453

Chiran, 34km south of Kagoshima, is a pretty village with a lovely river, a superb collection of restored samurai houses and a fascinating memorial to WWII's kamikaze pilots. Chiran was one of the major bases from which fighters left on their final missions.

All seven of the residences along Chiran's street of **samurai houses** (武家屋敷; ☎ 83-2511; admission ¥500; 🕑 9am-5pm), dating from the mid-Edo period, are noted for their gardens. Look for the use of 'borrowed scenery'. Water is usually symbolised by sand or gravel. A well-stocked carp stream runs parallel to the samurai street.

Taki-An (高城庵) is a traditional house and garden on the samurai street where you can sit on tatami mats to eat a bowl of hot *soba* (¥600) and sip Chiran's famous green tea.

The **Kamikaze Peace Museum** (知覧特攻平和会館; ☎ 83-2525; admission ¥500; 🕑 9am-4.30pm), 2km west of town, presents a collection of aircraft, mementos and photographs belonging to the fresh-faced young men selected for the Special Attack Corps in WWII. It's a moving tribute and a reminder of the tragedy of war.

Kagoshima Kōtsū buses to Chiran (¥920, 80 minutes) run from JR Kagoshima-Chūō Station and the Yamakataya bus station in Tenmonkan. From Chiran, infrequent buses run to Ibusuki (¥940, 65 minutes), leaving from stops along the highway.

Ibusuki 指宿

☎ 0993 / pop 46,250

At the southeastern end of the Satsuma Peninsula, 50km from Kagoshima, is the hot-spring resort of Ibusuki. It's quiet, especially in the low season, and more especially after dark. Ibusuki Station is about 1km from the beachfront and most accommodation, but the few eateries are near the station. The station **information desk** (☎ 22-2111; 🕑 8.30am-5pm) has basic maps and can assist with directions.

ACTIVITIES

Ibusuki's *raison d'etre,* the reputedly blood-cleansing **Tennen Sunamushi Kaikan** (天然砂蒸し会館; ☎ 23-3900; admission ¥900; 🕑 8.30am-noon & 1-9pm) sand baths, are located on the beachfront. Pay at the entrance, change into the provided *yukata* and wander down to the beach where the shovel ladies are waiting to bury you in hot volcanic sand. Reactions range from panic to euphoria. Fifteen minutes is recommended, but many stay longer. When you're through, head back up to soak in the onsen.

Yoshi-no-yu (吉の湯; ☎ 22-3556; admission ¥300; ⏲ 2pm-9pm, closed Thu) is a delightful onsen with pretty *rotemburo* set in a garden.

SLEEPING & EATING

Tamaya Youth Hostel (圭屋ユースホステル; ☎ 22-3553; dm with 2 meals/breakfast ¥4915/3970) Loves Lonely Planet readers and is the closest hostel to the sand baths. Look for the palm tree out the front.

Minshuku Marutomi (民宿丸富; ☎ 22-5579; fax 22-3993; r with 2 meals from ¥7500) A homely inn around the corner from Ryokan Ginshō serves its guests delicious fresh-seafood dinners.

Iwasaki Hotel (いわさきホテル; ☎ 22-2131; http://ibusuki.iwasakihotels.com/en; tw from ¥15,015; Ⓟ ⊠ ♿) Straight out of 1980s Hawaii, this massive, kitsch, kid-friendly resort hotel has a golf course, onsen, pools and acres of landscaped gardens. All rooms face the ocean. The beachfront summer beer garden is lots of fun.

Ryokan Ginshō (旅館吟松; ☎ 22-3231; www.ginsyou.co.jp in Japanese; r per person with 2 meals from ¥15,750; Ⓟ) The exquisite 9th-floor *rotemburo* of this upscale beachfront ryokan has lantern-lit shower stalls and a lovely relaxation garden. Ocean-facing rooms start from ¥17,850 and rooms with baths on the balcony are available.

Aoba (青葉; ☎ 22-3356; dishes from ¥480; ⏲ lunch & dinner, closed Wed) A two-minute walk to the left of the station exit you'll find this pretty grey building with white *noren* door hangings and plants out the front. The *kurobuta roosukatsu* (crumbed black pork cutlet) *teishoku* for ¥1320 will satisfy most, but a true gourmet would try the Satsuma *jidori sashimi* (raw sliced chicken) for ¥780.

GETTING THERE & AWAY

Ibusuki is less than two hours from Kagoshima by bus (¥850). A bit faster is JR's Nano-Hana Deluxe train (¥1000, 60 minutes).

AROUND SATSUMA PENINSULA

Inhabited by giant eels, **Ikeda-ko** is a volcanic caldera lake west of Ibusuki. South of the lake is **Cape Nagasaki-bana**, from where you can see offshore islands on a clear day.

The beautifully symmetrical 924m cone of **Kaimon-dake** can be climbed in two hours from the Kaimon-dake bus stop, or from JR Jamakawa Station and JR Kaimon Station. An early start may reward you with views of Sakurajima, Cape Sata, and Yakushima and Tanegashima islands.

At the southwestern end of the peninsula is **Makurazaki**, a busy port famous for *katsuo* (bonito) and the terminus for the train line from Kagoshima. Just beyond Makurazaki is **Bōnotsu**, a fishing village that was an unofficial trading link with the outside world via Okinawa during Japan's two centuries of seclusion.

ŌSUMI PENINSULA 大隅半島

Marked by the oldest lighthouse in Japan, at the tip of the Ōsumi Peninsula on the opposite side of Kagoshima Bay, **Cape Sata** is the southernmost point of Japan's four main islands. You can reach the cape from the Kagoshima side by taking the ferry (¥600, 50 minutes) from Yamakawa, a stop south of Ibusuki, to Nejime on the other side, but public transport onward is nearly impossible. It's at least an hour by car to the 8km bicycle and walking track that leads down to the end of the cape. If you're determined to get here, the best option is to rent a car (see p738).

The glass-bottomed **Sata-Day-Go** (☎ 0994-27-3355; 30min tours adult/child ¥2000/1000), offers day cruises to see the coral, sea turtles, *fugu* (pufferfish), dolphins and even sharks.

MIYAZAKI-KEN 宮崎県

The Miyazaki region is the mythical home of the sun goddess Amaterasu, who it is said took refuge in a remote cave here, plunging the world into darkness. Only after her fellow gods lured her out did light and warmth return to the land of the rising sun.

Rte 222 from Miyakonojō to Obi and Nichinan twists through the hills by the sea. Although there are train and bus services, the most rewarding way to explore this diverse prefecture is by car.

MIYAZAKI 宮崎

☎ 0985 / pop 311,098

Miyazaki has a balmy climate and some of the best surfing in Japan, particularly at Kizaki-hama and other beaches north towards Hyūga. Many areas around Miyazaki played an important part in early Japanese civilisation, and are recorded in Japan's oldest chronicle, the *Kojiki*. Interesting excavations can be seen at Saitobaru (p747).

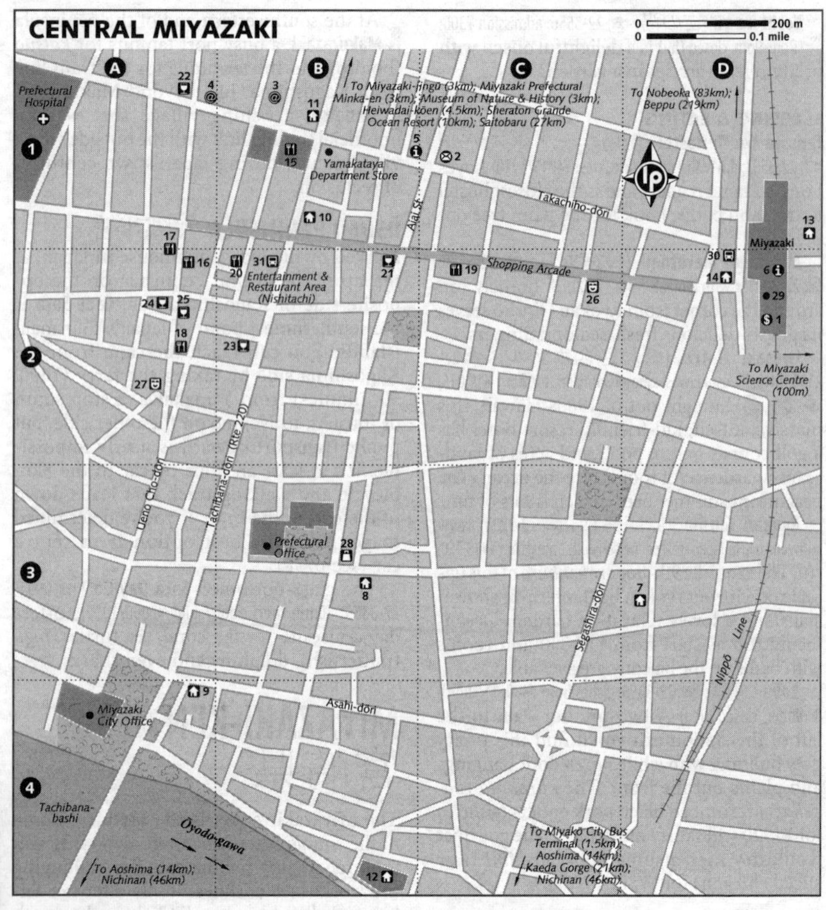

Information

Inside JR Miyazaki Station, the **tourist information centre** (☎ 22-6469; 🕑 9am-6.30pm) has maps of the city and surroundings. There's an international ATM at the southern end of the station, and at the central post office, five minutes' walk west along Takachiho-dōri. Opposite the post office, the **Miyazaki Prefectural International Plaza** (☎ 32-8457; 8th fl, Carino Bldg; 🕑 10am-7pm Mon-Sat) has satellite TV and foreign-language newspapers and magazines.

Further along Takachiho-dōri, **Emutto Internet & Comics** (☎ 28-2266; 3rd fl, Maruya Bldg, 1-2-4 Shimizu; open seating per 30min ¥180, after 9pm for 12hr in a booth ¥2000; 🕑 24hr) has internet. There's a **Cybac Café** (☎ 61-7562; 2nd fl, Drug 11 Bldg, 3-4-26 Ōhashi; access from ¥280; 🕑 24hr) in an alley before the bridge.

Sights

MIYAZAKI SCIENCE CENTRE

宮崎科学技術館

A short walk from Miyazaki Station, this interactive **science museum** (☎ 23-2700; 38-3 Miyawakichō; admission with sky show ¥730; 🕑 9am-4pm, closed Mon) boasts one of the world's largest planetariums. English-language pamphlets are available.

MIYAZAKI-JINGŪ & MUSEUM

宮崎神宮・宮崎総合博物館

This **shrine** (☎ 27-4004; 2-4-1 Jingū) honours the Emperor Jimmu, the semimythical first emperor of Japan and founder of the Yamato court. Spectacular 600-year-old wisteria vines cover the thickly forested grounds. It's a 500m walk from Miyazaki-jingū Station.

KYŪSHŪ

INFORMATION
- ATM 1 D2
- Central Post Office 中央郵便局 2 C1
- Cybac Café サイバック宮崎店 3 B1
- Emutto Internet & Comics 宮崎市のインターネットカフェえむっと 4 A1
- Miyazaki Prefectural International Plaza 宮崎県国際交流センター 5 B1
- Tourist Information Centre 観光案内所 6 D2

SLEEPING
- Business Hotel Royal ビジネスホテルロイヤル 7 D3
- Fujin-kaikan Youth Hostel 婦人会館ユースホステル 8 B3
- Green Rich Hotel Miyazaki グリーンリッチホテル 宮崎 9 A4
- Hotel Kensington ホテルケンジントン 10 B1
- Hotel Route Inn ホテルルートイン宮崎 11 B1
- Miyazaki Kankō Hotel 宮崎観光ホテル 12 B4
- Richmond Hotel Miyazaki Ekimae リチモンドホテル宮崎駅前 13 D1
- Toyoko Inn Miyazaki Ekimae 東横イン宮崎駅前 14 D2

EATING
- Bon Belta Department Store ボンベルタ 15 B1
- Don Don Ju どんどんじゅ 16 A2
- Izakaya Seoul 居酒屋ソウル 17 A1
- La Dish Gourmet & Deli ラ·ディシュグルメアンドデリ 18 A2
- Pari No Asaichi パリの朝市 19 C2
- Restaurant-Bar De-meté-r デーメテール 20 B2

DRINKING
- Bar 21 B2
- Café Lanai カフェラナイ 22 A1
- Igokochiya Anbai いごこち屋あんばい 23 B2
- One Coin Bar ワンコインバー 24 A2
- Suntory Shot Bar 4665 サントリーショットバー4665 .... 25 A2

ENTERTAINMENT
- Jazz Spot Lifetime ライフタイムジャズバー 26 C2
- Planet Café Sports プラネットカフェ 27 A2

SHOPPING
- Miyazaki Prefectural Products Promotion Exhibition Hall みやざき物産館 28 B3

TRANSPORT
- Eki Rent-a-Car 駅レンタカー 29 D2
- Miyazaki Ekimae Bus Center 宮崎交通 30 D2
- Tachibana dori 3-chome Bus Stop 橘通り三丁目バス停 31 B2

Just north of the shrine grounds, the **Miyazaki Prefectural Museum of Nature & History** (☎ 24-2071; 2-4-4 Jingū; admission free; 9am-4.30pm, closed Tue) has exhibits on local history, archaeology, festivals and folkcrafts. Behind the museum is the interesting **Minka-en** (民家園; admission free), with four traditional-style Kyūshū farmhouses.

HEIWADAI-KŌEN 平和台公園

The centrepiece of **Heiwadai-kōen** (Peace Park; ☎ 24-5027; admission free) is a 37m-high tower constructed in 1940, a time when peace in Japan was about to disappear. **Haniwa Garden**, within the park, is dotted with reproductions of the clay *haniwa* (earthenware figures found in Kōfun-period tombs) that have been excavated from the Saitobaru burial mounds (p747).

Heiwadai-kōen is about 1.5km north of Miyazaki-jingū. Frequent buses stop along Tachibana-dōri (¥270, 20 minutes).

Festivals & Events

Yabusame (samurai-style horseback archery) You can witness this at Miyazaki-jingū (opposite) on 2 and 3 April.

Fireworks show Kyūshū's largest, lighting up the summer sky over the Oyodo-gawa in early August.

Erekocha Matsuri (えれこっちゃみやざき) Miyazaki's newest festival with dancers and *taiko* drummers filling Tachibana-dōri in mid-August.

Miyazaki-jingū Grand Festival (Jimmu-Sama) In late October; brings in the autumn with horses and *mikoshi* being carried through the streets.

Sleeping

Fujin-kaikan Youth Hostel (☎ 24-5785; 1-3-10 Asahi; dm ¥3350;) A Japanese-style hostel that doubles as a recreation centre during the day, necessitating a strict 10am check-out and no check-ins before 3pm. There's a restaurant downstairs and a 10pm curfew.

Business Hotel Royal (☎ 25-5221; fax 29-1103; 2-5-20 Segashira; s/d/tw from ¥4095/5460/6300; P) Close to Miyazaki Station on a quiet side street, this dated little hotel is cheap and friendly.

Green Rich Hotel Miyazaki (☎ 27-9991; fax 27-0023; 1-5-8 Tachibana-dōri-higashi; s/d/tr ¥5000/9000/10,500; P) An imposing building near the prefectural office, flanked by palms. Inside, all of the stylish modern rooms have free LAN internet access and many have sofas or massage chairs. Oversized executive rooms are available. It's very well priced and above the standard of a business hotel.

Toyoko Inn Miyazaki Ekimae (☎ 32-1045; 2-2-31 Oimatsu; s/tw with breakfast ¥5250/7770; P) Just outside Miyazaki Station (West exit) this business hotel has wi-fi in the lobby and all of the cheap, clean rooms have free LAN internet access.

Hotel Route Inn (☎ 61-1488; fax 611-492; www.route-inn.co.jp/english; 4-1-11 Tachibana-dōri-nishi; s/d with breakfast ¥5900/9500; P) About 800m west of the station, this hotel is excellent value with a great breakfast buffet, nice interiors and free LAN internet access in all rooms.

Hotel Kensington (☎ 20-5500; www.kensington.jp, in Japanese; 3-4-4 Tachibanadōri-higashi; s/d ¥6600/11,500; P ⊠ 💻 📶) Recently renovated, this hotel has compact, nicely furnished rooms, all with free internet via LAN cable. Wi-fi access is in the lobby. The breakfast and lunch buffet is good value.

Miyazaki Kankō Hotel (☎ 32-5920; www.miyakan-h.com/english; 1-1-1 Matsuyama; s/d from ¥7500/13,000, Japanese-style r from ¥10,000; P ⊠ 💻) By the river, this international hotel is well priced for its high standard. Rooms are fittingly spacious and well furnished. All have LAN cable internet access. There's a hotel onsen and a baby grand in the lobby.

Richmond Hotel Miyazaki Ekimae (☎ 60-0055; fax 60-2000; www.richmondhotel.jp/e/miyazaki; 2-2-3 Miyazaki-ekihigashi; s/d with continental breakfast from ¥7800/13,650; P ⊠ 💻) Behind Miyazaki Station, this light-filled business hotel has nice furnishings and free LAN cable internet access in all rooms, with rental laptops available for ¥800.

Sheraton Grande Ocean Resort (☎ 21-1133; fax 21-1144; www.starwoodhotels.com; Hamayama, Yamazaki-cho; d/tw from ¥22,880; P ⊠ 💻 👪) Seriously good rates are often found online for this true five-star hotel with excellent leisure facilities. The 154m-high oceanfront tower adjoins the SeaGaia entertainment complex. Oversized rooms are well appointed, although internet access is overpriced. It's about a 20-minute drive into town, but there's a free shuttle and ample parking.

Eating

Hiya-jiru is a cold summer soup made from baked tofu, fish, miso paste and cucumbers, served over rice. Miyazaki is also known for *yuzu-kosho*, a tangy citrus spice. At Miyazaki Station, *shiitake ekiben*, a boxed lunch featuring mushrooms, is popular.

La Dish Gourmet & Deli (☎ 32-7929; 1-1 Chuōdōri; 🕑 11am-3am Mon-Sat, 6pm-1am Sun) Amid the hustle of the entertainment district, this import grocery store sells both cold and hot deli items, plus a good selection of wines, cheeses and desserts.

Don Don Ju (☎ 26-6126; 1st fl, Dai 2 Yoshino Bldg, 2-11 Chūōdōri; dishes ¥300-1950; 🕑 dinner) Two blocks south of Bon Belta department store, you'll find this bustling eatery, specialising in *Miyazaki-gyū* (beef). Cheese lovers won't go past the *butaniku-no-mottsarera-chiizu-age* (mozzarella cheese rolled in pork, crumbed and shallow fried) for ¥600. The Japanese signage is white on black and there's a picture menu.

Restaurant Bar De-meté-r (☎ 29-0017; 2nd fl, 3-8-18 Tachibana-dōri-nishi; dishes/pizzas from ¥470/750; 🕑 dinner, closed Tue) Popular for its brick-oven pizza and import-beer selection, it has a good bilingual menu and no cover charge.

Izakaya Seoul (☎ 29-8883; 1st fl, Dai 1 Yoshino Bldg, 7-26 Chūōmachi; nabe from ¥1200; 🕑 dinner) This Korean-Japanese restaurant is all about the food, has an English menu and does great *nabe* (hotpot) dishes.

Pari No Asaichi (☎ 0120-28-6137; 2nd fl, Nihonbashi Bldg, 1-6-8 Hiroshima; lunch sets from ¥1575; 🕑 lunch & dinner) This sweet little restaurant has been serving French cuisine for over 20 years and has a half-decent winelist and an English menu. There's a lovely big tree beside the brown-brick building.

Bon Belta department store (☎ 26-6126; 3-10-32 Tachibana-nishi) Has an 8th-floor restaurant arcade with lunch sets under ¥1000. The basement marketplace has a variety of takeaway treats with a wonderful *onigiri* (rice-ball snack) counter.

Drinking

Miyazaki also plays to the wee hours, especially in the summer. Hundreds of tiny bars draw a regular crowd. Most of the action is centred on the west side of Tachibana-dōri (locally known as 'Nishitachi') and the Ichibangai shopping arcade. In summer Bon Belta department store has a rooftop beer garden.

One Coin Bar (☎ 31-1152; 8-21 Chūō-dōri; 🕑 closed Tue) All drinks are ¥500 (one coin!) at this smart eight-stool hole-in-the-wall with a regular clientele who return for the conversation. The well-mannered 'master' speaks English and appreciates the custom of travellers.

Suntory Shot Bar 4665 (☎ 25-4665; 1-12 Chūōdōri; 🕑 closed Mon) Dark, quiet, art deco–styled, this is a nice spot for a quiet drink. The owner speaks some English.

Igokochiya Anbai (☎ 27-4117; 3-1-24 Tachibana-dōri-nishi; 🕑 6pm-2am, closed Mon) On Tachibana-dōri opposite Hotel Merieges, this thoroughly Japanese *izakaya* has over 350 varieties of *shōchū* and a selection of delicious appetisers.

Bar (☎ 71-0423; www.thebarmiyazaki.com; 3rd fl, Paul Smith Bldg, 3-7-15 Tachibana-dōri-higashi; 🕑 7pm-late) This hub of the expat community and its local friends draws a cheery mixed crowd who are proud of their city and keen to welcome visitors over a few cold beers. There's even a full-size billiard table.

Entertainment

Jazz Spot Lifetime (☎ 27-8451; 2nd fl, 2-3-8 Hiroshima; admission Fri ¥500; ⏰ 11.45am-2pm & 5pm-12.30am, closed Sun) Modern jazz is alive and well in Miyazaki with near-nightly jams at this upstairs bistro-bar. Drinks start at ¥600, with coffee, snacks and steaks on the menu.

Café Lanai (☎ 23-3412; 2-1-1 Shimizu; ⏰ 6pm-midnight) This mellow establishment with an island-fever vibe plays surf videos above the full bar. Dishes (from ¥700) also have a tropical twist.

Planet Café Sports (☎ 32-5064; 8-25 Kamino-machi; ⏰ 7pm-2am) Come for the sports and local *ji-dori* (grilled chicken), a perfect complement to a cold beer.

Shopping

Miyazaki Prefectural Products Promotion Exhibition Hall (☎ 22-7389; 1-6 Miyata-chō; ⏰ 9.30am-7pm Mon-Fri, 10am-6.30pm Sat & Sun) Sells distinctively coloured handwoven silk *tetsumugi* textiles, clay *haniwa* and Takachiho *kagura* masks (see p748).

Getting There & Away

AIR

Miyazaki is connected by air with Tokyo (¥36,700, 1½ hours), Osaka (¥23,500, 1½ hours), Okinawa (¥25,600, 1½ hours) and Fukuoka (¥19,700, 50 minutes).

BOAT

Ferry services link Miyazaki with Osaka (2nd class ¥11,600, 13 hours) and Kawasaki (¥14,440, 21 hours). For reservations contact **Marine Express** (☎ 22-8895).

BUS

Most long-distance buses originate at the **Miyakō City bus terminal** (☎ 52-2200) south of the river, near JR Minami-Miyazaki Station. Routes include Kagoshima (¥2700, 2¾ hours), Kumamoto (¥4500, 3¼ hours), Nagasaki (¥6500, 5½ hours) and Fukuoka (¥6000, four hours).

TRAIN

The JR Nippō line runs down to Kagoshima (*tokkyū*, ¥3790, two hours) and up to Beppu (*tokkyū*, ¥6070, three hours). The charming JR Nichinan line runs slowly along the coast south to Aoshima (¥360, 30 minutes) and Obi (¥910, 65 minutes).

Getting Around

Miyazaki's airport is connected to the city centre by bus (¥400, 30 minutes) or train (¥340, 10 minutes) from JR Miyazaki Station. Most city bus services use the **Miyazaki Ekimae Bus Centre** (☎ 53-1000) opposite the station and many run along Tachibana-dōri.

Car rental is, again, an excellent idea in this coastal area, especially if you plan to explore Aoshima and the Nichinan coast. **Eki Rent-a-Car** (☎ 24-7206; www.ekiren.co.jp, in Japanese; West exit, Miyazaki-eki; 12hr from ¥4720; ⏰ 8am-8pm) is easiest.

AOSHIMA & KAEDA 青島・加江田

☎ 0985

Aoshima is a tiny palm-covered island, fringed by unique washboard rock formations. It's connected to the mainland by a thin causeway. The name Aoshima also applies to the small town. Beneath its touristy exterior, you'll find a relaxed, alternative community here. This lovely area is the perfect spot to surrender to the summer heat, and a good alternative to staying in Miyazaki city.

The tourist information booth has local maps, though little English is spoken. It's a short walk from the station on the road leading to the shrine

Sights & Activities

On the island, just east of Aoshima Station, photogenic **Aoshima-jinja** (青島神社; ☎ 65-1262) is reputedly good for matchmaking (see Festivals & Events, below). Nearby is a **botanical garden** (青島熱帯植物園; ☎ 65-1042; admission ¥200) boasting 64 different species of fruit trees.

KAEDA GORGE 加江田渓谷

An 8km-long, well-maintained **hiking path** winds through Kaeda Gorge following the Kaeda-gawa, a refreshingly clear stream filled with boulders and excellent swimming holes. Lush foliage includes banana palms and mountain cedars. To get to the car park, turn off Rte 220 onto prefectural road 339.

Festivals & Events

Aoshima-jinja (above) is the scene of two exciting festivals. On the second Monday in January, loincloth-clad locals dive ceremoniously into the ocean. At the end of July there's more splashing as *mikoshi* are carried through the shallows to the shrine.

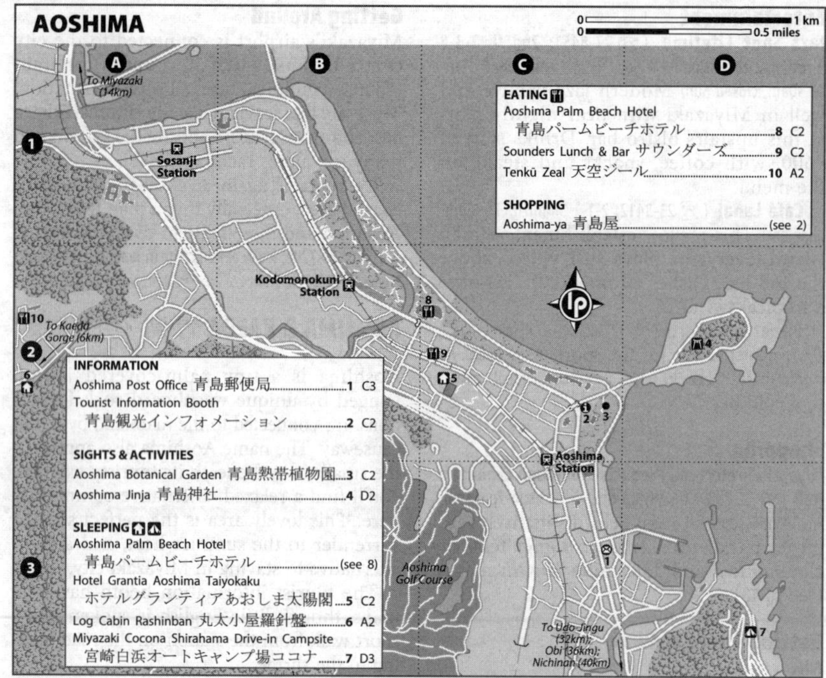

Sleeping & Eating

Miyazaki Cocona Shirahama Drive-in Campsite (宮崎白浜オートキャンプ場ココナ; ☎ 65-2020; tent hire ¥1570, campsites from ¥2940, cabins for up to 4 people ¥9970;) Opposite Shirahama beach, this modern complex has plenty of room and some nice rustic cabins set back from the main area.

ourpick **Log Cabin Rashinban** (丸太小屋羅針盤; ☎ 65-0999; dm ¥3500; P) If it's time for a tree change, head to this fascinating owner-builder chalet on the banks of a soothing stream. The closest station is Sosanji. Although there are roadside signs nearing the property, you'll need directions or a taxi from town if you don't have a rental car, at least for the first trip. When you get there, little English is spoken – but this distinctive accommodation in a tranquil setting is great if you want to get away, and even better if you're travelling with someone.

Hotel Grantia Aoshima Taiyokaku (ホテルグランティアあおしま太陽閣; ☎ 65-1531; www.route-inn.co.jp/english; s/d from ¥5500/10,000; P) Located on the hillside midway between Aoshima and Kodomo-no-kuni Stations, this property offers excellent value, with the West Wing completed in November 2008. All rooms have LAN internet access and rental laptops are available for ¥1000.

Aoshima Palm Beach Hotel (青島パームビーチホテル; ☎ 65-1555; s from ¥6000) This sparkling Florida-styled beachfront hotel is reasonably priced. Tsuki-no-shizuku, the hotel restaurant, does great tempura and sashimi straight from the ocean. Set menus start at ¥1500, but for a real treat, ask for the head chef's *omakase* course featuring a selection of the day's delicacies, at ¥3000 per person.

Sounders Lunch & Bar (☎ 65-0767; 1-6-23 Aoshima; set meals from ¥650; lunch only Sun-Mon, Wed-Fri, dinner Fri & Sat;) You'll love the relaxed vibe at this open-air surf shack serving spinach-and-bacon salads, tasty burgers and fish tacos. The menu's in English and there's live music most weekends.

Tenkū Zeal (天空ジール; ☎ 65-1508; http://tenku-zeal.jugem.jp; 6411 Kaeda; buffet adult/child ¥1300/800; lunch Sat, Sun & holidays; V) Not far from Rashinban, this wonderful hillside providore and macrobiotic lunch spot with sunny alfresco dining offers a constantly changing menu from

KYŪSHŪ

produce grown on-site. This is as delightfully hippie as it gets in Japan, English is spoken and the food couldn't be better for you.

Shopping

Aoshima-ya gift shop and restaurant is an imposing black building next door to the tourist information booth, selling local produce and souvenirs.

Getting There & Around

Aoshima is on the JR Nichinan line from Miyazaki (¥360, 30 minutes). Buses from Miyazaki train station stop at Aoshima (¥670, 40 minutes, hourly) en route to Udo-jingū.

UDO-JINGŪ 鵜戸神宮

If you walk through this brightly painted coastal **shrine** (☎ 0987-29-1001) to the end of the path, you'll find yourself in an open cavern overlooking an unusual rock formation. It's protocol to buy five *undama* (luck stones), make a wish and try to hit the shallow depression on top of one of the turtle-shaped rocks. Wishes are usually related to marriage and childbirth, because the boulders in front of the cavern are said to represent Emperor Jimmu's mother's breasts.

Hourly buses from Aoshima (¥990, 40 minutes) and Miyazaki (¥1440, 1½ hours) stop on the highway. From the bus stop, the 700m walk to the shrine will take you past interesting rock formations and picturesque fishing boats.

OBI 飫肥

From 1587 the wealthy Ito clan ruled this town from the castle for 14 generations, surviving the 'one kingdom, one castle' ruling in 1615. The clan eventually dissolved as the Meiji Restoration ended the feudal period.

Sights & Activities

Only the walls of the original castle remain, but the grounds of **Obi-jō** (飫肥城; ☎ 0987-25-4533; combined admission ¥600; 9.30am-4.30pm) contain a number of interesting buildings, including the impressive gate, **Ōte-mon**. The castle **museum** has a collection relating to the Ito clan's long rule over Obi. **Matsuo-no-maru**, the lord's private residence, has been reconstructed.

Yōshōkan, formerly the residence of the clan's chief retainer, stands just outside the castle entrance and has a large garden incorporating Atago-san as 'borrowed scenery'.

Shintōku-dō, the hall adjacent to the castle, was established as a samurai school in 1831. Up the hill behind Shintōku-dō is photogenic **Tanoue Hachiman-jinja**, shrouded by old-growth trees and reached by a steep flight of steps. On the western side of the river, **Ioshi-jinja** has a pleasant garden and the Ito family mausoleum.

Getting There & Around

The JR Nichinan line connects Obi with Miyazaki (*kaisoku;* ¥910, 65 minutes) via Aoshima. From Obi Station, it's a short bus ride (¥140) and walk to the castle. Buses from Miyazaki (¥1990, 2¼ hours, last return bus 4pm) stop below the castle entrance. Bikes are the best way to visit and can be rented (¥300 for three hours) at the train station.

NICHINAN-KAIGAN & CAPE TOI 日南海岸・都井岬

The scenic 50km stretch of coastal road from Nichinan to Miyazaki has great views. The vistas from Cape Toi are memorable, and a dramatic **fire festival** is held here on the last weekend in September. The cape is also famed for herds of wild horses, which now seem rather friendly.

Just off the coast from the beach at **Ishinami-kaigan**, the tiny island of **Kō-jima** is home to a group of monkeys that apparently rinse their food in the ocean before eating, but they're a fickle bunch, and hard to spot. Swimming at this tempting beach is prohibited. To stay overnight in the area, head to **Koigaura Beach** where the surf-*zoku* (tribe) hang out. It's about 5km from Cape Toi or 7km from Kōjima. If you need to stay in this remote spot, the very basic **Minshuku Tanaka** (☎ 0987-76-2096; per person with 2 meals from ¥6000) or **Koigaura Minshuku** (☎ 0987-76-1631; per person with 2 meals from ¥4500) are your only options. It's a bit of a disappointing trek unless you're keen to get isolated. Highway construction blights the landscape in parts.

SAITOBARU 西都原

☎ 0983

North of Miyazaki, at the **Saitobaru Burial Mounds Park**, several square kilometres of fields and forest are dotted with over 300 *kofun* (burial mounds). The mounds, dating from AD 300 to 600, range from insignificant bumps to hillocks large enough to appear as natural creations.

The small **Saitobaru Archaeological Museum** (西都原考古博物館; ☎ 41-0041; admission free; ⏲ 10am-6pm, closed Mon) has displays of archaeological finds, including ancient swords, armour, jewellery, *haniwa* and much more.

The park area is always open. Buses run frequently to Saitobaru from Miyakō City bus terminal (¥1040, one hour). You'll need your own transport if you want to explore the mound-dotted countryside, or you should plan to walk a lot.

Saitobaru is just outside the town of Saito, where the unique **Usudaiko dance festival**, with drummers wearing odd polelike headgear, takes place in early September. The equally interesting **Shiromi Kagura** performances are on 14 and 15 December, part of a harvest festival that lasts from 12 to 16 December.

TAKACHIHO 高千穂

☎ 0982 / pop 15,840

The pretty mountain town of Takachiho is midway between Aso-san and Nobeoka on the east coast. North of the Miyakō Bus Centre is the **Takachiho Tourism Association** (☎ 72-1213; ⏲ 8.30am-5pm) offering information in English about events and lodgings in and around Takachiho.

Sights

TAKACHIHO-KYŌ 高千穂峡

Takachiho's magnificent **gorge** with its waterfall, overhanging rocks and sheer walls was formed over 100,000 years ago by a double volcanic eruption. There's a 1km-long nature trail above the gorge, or view it up close from a **rowboat** (☎ 73-1213; per 30min ¥1500; ⏲ 8.30am-5pm). Depending on the season, it may be like rush hour on the water.

TAKACHIHO-JINJA 高千穂神社

Takachiho-jinja, near the bus station, is set in a grove of cryptomeria pines. See below for performances.

AMANO IWATO-JINJA 天岩戸神社

The Iwato-gawa splits **Amano Iwato-jinja** (☎ 74-8239) into two parts, Nishi Hongū (the main building) on the west bank of the river and Higashi Hongū on the east, the cave in which many believe, according to Shintō myth, sun goddess Amaterasu hid, plunging the world into darkness, until she was eventually lured out by the saucy performance of another goddess, Ama no Uzume.

A short walk beside a picturesque stream takes you to the **Amano Yasugawara** cave, where thousands of other deities allegedly conspired to find ways of luring Amaterasu from hiding. Take the Iwato bus from the Miyakō bus terminal, then walk 15 minutes. Buses leave a little over an hour apart (¥300, 20 minutes).

Festivals & Events

Important local *iwato kagura* festivals (see the boxed text, left) are held here.

From November to February, **dances** (☎ 73-2413; tickets ¥500) are performed at Takachiho-jinja (above) for an hour each evening from 8pm.

In May, September and November (dates change every year) performances are held at the Amano Iwato-jinja (above) from 10am to 10pm.

There are also all-night performances in farmhouses from November to February. Visits are arranged by enquiring at the Amano Iwato-jinja. In all, 33 dances are performed from 6pm until 9am the next morning. If you brave the cold until morning, prepare to be caught up in a wave of excitement.

Sleeping & Eating

Takachiho has over 30 hotels, ryokan, *minshuku* and pensions. Every place in town can be booked out during peak holiday periods.

Many visitors just eat at their ryokan or *minshuku*, but Takachiho also has plenty of *yakitori-ya* where you can order *kappo-zake* (local sake heated in bamboo stalks).

> **TAKACHIHO LEGENDS**
>
> In Takachiho, residents insist that Ninigi-no-mikoto, grandson of the sun goddess Amaterasu, descended to earth atop the legendary mountain Takachiho-no-mine. They also lay claim to Ama-no-Iwato, the cave in which Amaterasu, angered by her brother's misbehaviour, exiled herself, plunging the world into darkness. Eventually, the sun goddess was lured out by the bawdy antics of another goddess Ama no Uzume, and light was restored to earth.
>
> The *iwato kagura* dances performed in Takachiho today are said to be derived from the dance that lured Amaterasu from hiding and are characterised by masks with unusually long noses...

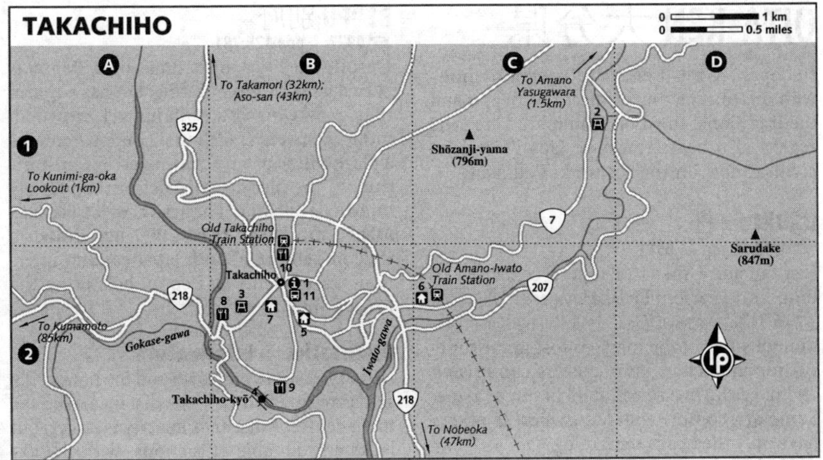

INFORMATION
Takachiho Tourism Association
高千穂町観光協会 1 B2

SIGHTS & ACTIVITIES
Amano Iwato-jinja 天岩戸神社 2 C1
Nishi Hongu 西本宮 .... (see 2)
Takachiho-jinja 高千穂神社 3 B2
Takachiho-kyō 高千穂峡 4 B2

SLEEPING
Folkcraft Ryokan Kaminoya 民芸旅館かみの家 5 B2
Takachiho Youth Hostel 高千穂ユースホステル 6 C2
Yamatoya Ryokan 大和屋旅館 7 B2

EATING
Chiho-no-ie 千穂の家 8 B2
Onokoro Chaya おのころ茶屋 9 B2
Young Echō ヤングエコー 10 B2

TRANSPORT
Miyakō Bus Centre 宮交バスセンター 11 B2

Takachiho Youth Hostel (☎ 72-3021; 5899-2 Mitai, Takachiho; dm HI member/nonmember ¥2800/3400; P) About five minutes' walk from old Amano-Iwato Station, this large hostel is clean and efficient. Breakfast is available.

Yamatoya Ryokan (☎ 72-2243; fax 72-6868; r per person with 2 meals ¥8000-15,000; P ☒) All rooms are traditional ryokan style, and there's helpful English-speaking staff. Look for the masked *iwato kagura* dancer painted on the front.

Folkcraft Ryokan Kaminoya (☎ 72-2111; www.kaminoya.jp/english.html; r with 2 meals from ¥9975; P 💻) Down from the bus station in the centre of Takachiho, this ryokan has a definite folky feel, spacious rooms and shuttered windows. Look for the woodwork and whitewashed facade.

Young Echō (☎ 72-4948; dishes from ¥600; ⏲ breakfast, lunch & dinner; 💻) This cheery eatery near the old station has an English menu, a mix of Western and Japanese foods, free internet terminal and an outdoor summer beer garden, open from 5pm to 10pm. The carbonara pasta for ¥740 is cheap and cheerful

Chiho-no-ie (千穂の家; ☎ 72-2115; meals from ¥500; ⏲ lunch) Serves seasonal regional treats and *sōmen-nagashi* (¥600) – catch tasty noodles with your chopsticks as they float by in halved bamboo rafts. It's a three-storey building on the corner with a red awning.

Onoroko Chaya (おのころ茶屋; ☎ 72-3931; meals from ¥500; ⏲ lunch & dinner). Nestled among trees, outdoor tables beneath traditional red lanterns set the scene. *Sōmen-nagashi* is ¥500 here, or try the *masu-zushi* (trout sushi) for ¥800.

Getting There & Around

Since the JR Takachiho line closed in 2008, the only way in and around is by road. You can walk to the gorge and Takachiho-jinja, but other sights are some distance from town.

The Miyakō Bus Centre is the new transport hub. Buses run to Takamori (¥1280, 1¼ hours, three daily) and Kumamoto (¥2300, 2¾ hours). Regular tours leave from here; the 'A Course' (¥2000) covers everything, while the 'B Course' (¥1500) skips Amano Iwato-jinja.

ŌITA-KEN 大分県

In Japan, Ōita prefecture is synonymous with onsen. The tourist mecca of Beppu and the traditional town of Yufuin are here. The region also bears traces of Japan's earliest civilisations, on the Kunisaki Peninsula.

USUKI 臼杵

☎0972 / pop 43,051

Just outside Usuki is a superb collection of thousand-year-old **Buddha images** (臼杵石仏; ☎65-3300; admission ¥530; ⏲8.30am-4.30pm), although some of the magic is lost in the tourist-trap ambience. Four clusters comprising 59 images lie in a series of niches in a ravine. Some are complete statues, whereas others have only the heads remaining.

Usuki has several temples and well-preserved traditional houses. On the last Saturday in August, the town hosts a **fire festival**, and other festivities are held throughout the year; ask for details at the **tourist information office** (☎64-7130; ⏲8.30am-5pm) adjacent to Usuki Station. There's free internet at **Sala de Usuki** (サーラデ臼杵; ☎64-7271).

Local restaurants boast the best *fugu* in Japan; expect to pay about ¥8000 for a dinner set, including *sake*.

The town of Usuki is 40km southeast of Beppu. Take the JR Nippō line to Usuki Station (*tokkyū;* ¥1430, 55 minutes), from where it's a 20-minute bus ride to the ravine site. Bikes can also be rented free from **Usuki Station** (☎63-8955).

KYŪSHŪ

BEPPU 別府

☎0977 / pop 126,781

Despite the hype, or because of it, Beppu is at first a little disappointing, but has a charm that grows on you. Quaint yet crowded, modern meets traditional, Beppu remains a place where people come to escape, historically to the pleasure district or the literally hundreds of baths. The arrival of **Ritsumeikan Asia Pacific University** in 2000 has drawn a welcome influx of both Japanese and international students to Beppu, bolstering the town population.

Orientation & Information

Beppu is a sprawling town and the hot-spring areas are spread over some distance from the town centre. Adjacent Ōita city is larger, but lacks any notable attractions, with the exception of its lively and colourful Tanabata Matsuri (p754). The tiny but beautiful onsen village of Myōban (p753) is a quieter place to soak.

The convenient Beppu Station **Foreign Tourist Information Office** (Map p753; ☎21-6220; 12-13 Ekimae-machi; ⏲9am-5pm) has helpful bilingual volunteers with an arsenal of local information and advice. **Beppu International Plaza** (Map p753; ☎23-1119; cnr Ekimae-dōri & Ginza Arcade; ⏲9am-5pm), the sister branch, is a five-minute walk downhill and has free internet.

International ATM machines can be found at the Kitahama post office (Map p753) and the nearby the Cosmopia shopping centre. Ōita Bank handles foreign-exchange services.

INFORMATION
Main Post Office 中央郵便局 1 D4
Post Office 郵便局 2 D2

SIGHTS & ACTIVITIES
Beppu Traditional Bamboo Crafts Centre 別府市竹細工伝統会館 3 C4
Chi-no-ike Jigoku 血の池地獄 4 B2
Hihōkan Sex Museum 別府秘宝館 5 D2
Hon Bōzu Jigoku 坊主地獄 6 A3
Hyōtan Onsen ひょうたん温泉 7 D2
Ichinoide Kaikan いちのいで会館 8 B5
Kamado Jigoku (Oven Hell) かまど地獄 9 C2
Kinryū Jigoku 金龍地獄 10 D2
Kitahama Termas Onsen 北浜温泉テルマス 11 D5
Mugen-no-sato 夢幻の里 12 A5
Mushi-yu Steam Bath むし湯 13 D2
Myōban Onsen Area 明礬温泉 14 A2
Oni-yama Jigoku 鬼山地獄 15 D2
Onsen Hoyōland 温泉保養ランド 16 A2
Shibaseki Onsen 柴石温泉 17 B2
Shira-ike Jigoku 白池地獄 18 D2
Shōnin-ga-hama Sand Bath 上人ヶ浜 19 D3
Tatsumaki Jigoku 龍巻地獄 20 B2
Umi Jigoku 海地獄 21 B2
Yama Jigoku 山地獄 22 C2

SLEEPING
Suginoi Hotel 杉乃井ホテル 23 B5

EATING
Tomonaga Panya 友永パン屋 24 D6

TRANSPORT
Ferry Port フェリーのり場 25 D3
Kamenoi Bus Station (Buses to Beppu Station) 亀の井バスターミナル (至別府駅) 26 D2
Kamenoi Bus Station (Buses to Chi-no-ike Jigoku) 亀の井バスターミナル (至血の池地獄) 27 D2
Konya Jigoku-mae Bus Stop 紺屋地獄前バス停 28 A3
Minami-baru Bus Stop 南原バス停 29 B4
Yakyū-jō-mae Bus Stop 野球場前バス停 30 C6

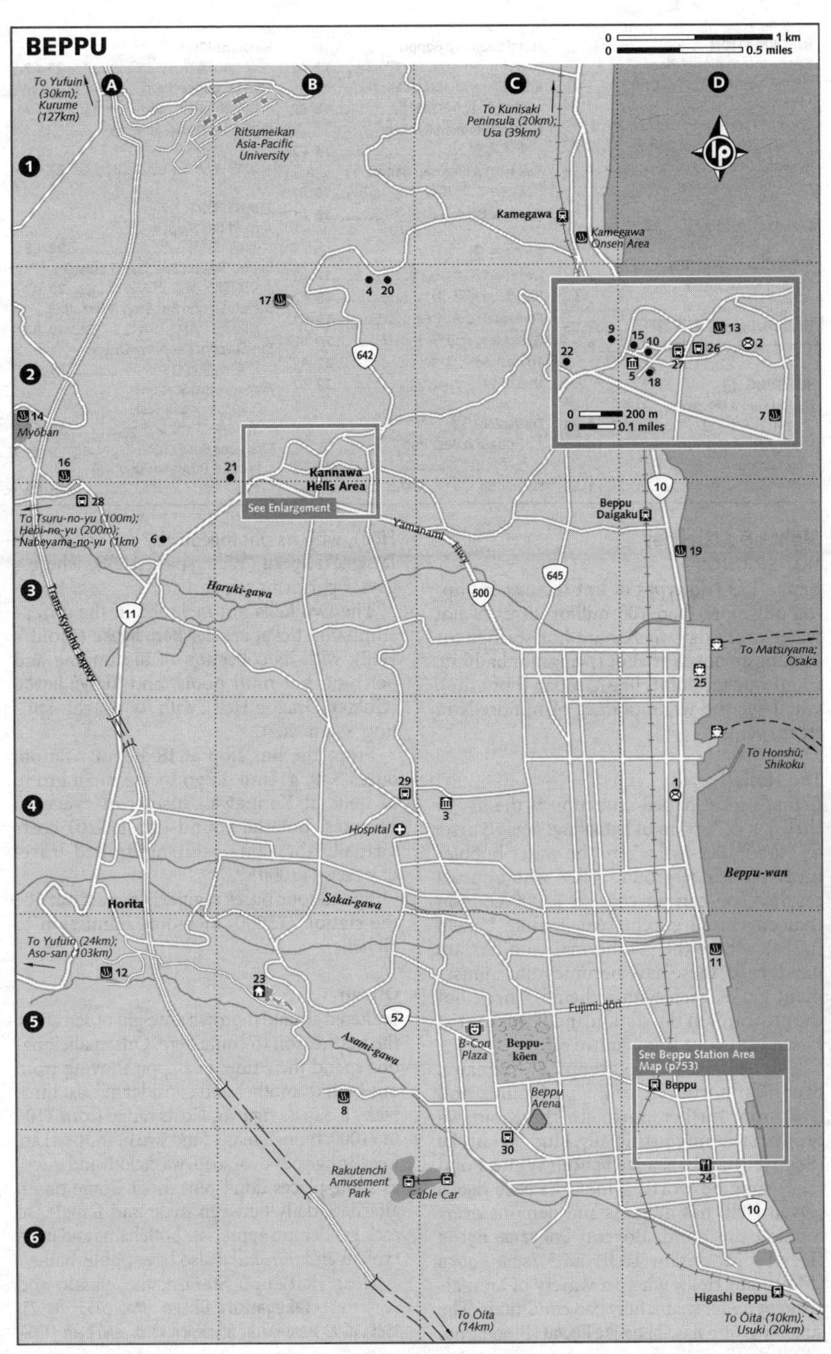
BEPPU
0 1 km
0 0.5 miles
A
B
C
D
1
2
3
4
5
6
To Yufuin (30km); Kurume (127km)
Ritsumeikan Asia-Pacific University
To Kunisaki Peninsula (20km); Usa (39km)
Kamegawa
Kamegawa Onsen Area
Myōban
To Tsuru-no-yu (100m); Hebi-no-yu (200m); Nabeyama-no-yu (1km)
Kannawa Hells Area
See Enlargement
0 200 m
0 0.1 miles
Beppu Daigaku
Yamanami Hwy
Haruki-gawa
Trans-Kyushu Expwy
To Matsuyama; Osaka
To Honshū; Shikoku
Hospital
Beppu-wan
Horita
Sakai-gawa
To Yufuin (24km); Aso-san (103km)
Fujimi-dōri
B-Con Plaza
Beppu-kōen
Asami-gawa
See Beppu Station Area Map (p753)
Beppu
Beppu Arena
Rakutenchi Amusement Park
Cable Car
Higashi Beppu
To Ōita (14km)
To Ōita (10km); Usuki (20km)

KYŪSHŪ

INFORMATION
Beppu International Plaza 別府外国人観光客案内所＆サロン 1 B2
Foreign Tourist Information Office 外国人旅行者観光案内所 2 A2
Iyo Bank 伊予銀行 3 B2
Kitahama Post Office 別府北浜郵便局 4 C2
Ōita Bank 大分銀行 5 C2

SIGHTS & ACTIVITIES
Ekimae Kōtō Onsen 駅前高等温泉 6 B2
Hirano Library 平野資料館 7 C3
Takegawara Onsen 竹瓦温泉 8 C3

SLEEPING
Beppu Guest House 別府ゲストハウス 9 B3
Hotel Aile ホテル エール 10 C2
Hotel Arthur ホテルアーサー 11 B2
Hotel Seawave Beppu ホテルシーウェーブ別府 12 A2
Kokage International Minshuku インタ-民宿こかげ 13 B2
Nogami Honkan Ryokan 野上本館 14 C2
Spa Hostel Khaosan Beppu スパホステルカオサン別府 15 B1
Yamada Bessou 山田別荘 16 B1

EATING
Dekadon デカドン 17 B2
Eki Ichiba 駅市場 18 A2
Fugu Matsu ふぐ松 19 C1
Gyōza Kogetsu 餃子湖月 20 B2
Toyotsune とよ常 21 A2
Ureshi-ya うれしや 22 B2

DRINKING
Jin Robata & Beer Pub ろばた焼仁 23 C2
Kuishinbō くいしん坊 24 B2
Natsume Kissa なつめ喫茶 25 C2
Shingai Coffee Shop しんがいコーヒーショップ 26 C3
World Sports Bar Small Eye ワールドスポーツバースモールアイ 27 C2

TRANSPORT
Airport Bus Stop 空港バス停 28 C2
Beppu Station Bus Stop (East side) 別府駅　東口バス停 29 A2
Beppu Station Bus Stop (West side) 別府駅　西口バス停 30 A2
Bus Stop for Kannawa Onsen 鉄輪温泉行きバス停 31 C2
Kamenoi Bus Station (Sightseeing Buses) 亀の井バスセンター 32 C2
Kitahama Bus Station (Sightseeing Buses & Buses to Fukuoka) 北浜バセンター 33 C2

Sights & Activities

HOT SPRINGS

Beppu has two types of hot springs, pumping out more than 100 million litres of hot water every day. *Jigoku* are hot springs for looking at; onsen are hot springs for bathing. From vantage points like Myōban (opposite), you'll see the white plumes of hundreds of steam vents.

The Hells

Beppu's most hyped attraction is the *jigoku* (hells), a collection of **hot springs** (Map p751; each hell ¥400; 8am-5pm) where the water bubbles forth from underground, often with unusual results. You can purchase a ¥2000 coupon that covers all except two. Unlike Unzen (p714), where the geothermal wonders are unadorned, these have become mini-amusement parks, each with a theme. Check out the postcards at the station and if this tourist kitsch isn't your thing, move on.

The hells are in two groups, at Kannawa, over 4km northwest of Beppu Station, and two more further north. In the Kannawa group, steaming artificially blue **Umi Jigoku** (Sea Hell) and **Shira-ike Jigoku** (White Pond Hell) may be worth a look. **Kamado Jigoku** (Oven Hell) has dragons and demons overlooking the pond. Boycott **Oni-yama Jigoku** (Devil's Mountain Hell) and **Yama Jigoku** (Mountain Hell), where a variety of animals are kept under shamefully bad conditions. The smaller group has **Chi-no-ike Jigoku** (Blood Pool Hell), with its photogenically red water, and **Tatsumaki Jigoku** (Waterspout Hell), where a geyser performs regularly.

The two hells not included in the group-admission ticket are **Hon Bōzu Jigoku** (Monk's Hell), with its collection of hiccupping and belching hot-mud pools, and **Kinryū Jigoku** (Golden Dragon Hell), with its 'dragon-spitting' steam vent.

From the bus stop at JR Beppu Station, buses 5, 9, 41 and 43 go to the main group of hells at Kannawa. Buses run every 20 minutes, but the round-trip (¥820) costs virtually the same as an unlimited-travel day pass (¥1000).

Jigoku tour buses regularly depart outside the station (¥3000, including admission to all hells).

Onsen

Scattered around the town are eight onsen areas, the best reason to come here. Onsen aficionados spend their time in Beppu moving from one bath to another and consider at least three baths a day *de rigueur*. Costs range from ¥100 to ¥1000, though many (and two of the best) are free. Bring your own soap, washcloth and towel, as some places don't rent them. Some onsen alternate daily between male and female, so each gender can appreciate both baths and most ryokan and *minshuku* also have public baths.

Near JR Beppu Station, the classic and *very* hot **Takegawara Onsen** (Map p753; ☎ 23-1585; 16-23 Moto-machi; admission ¥100, sand bath ¥1000;

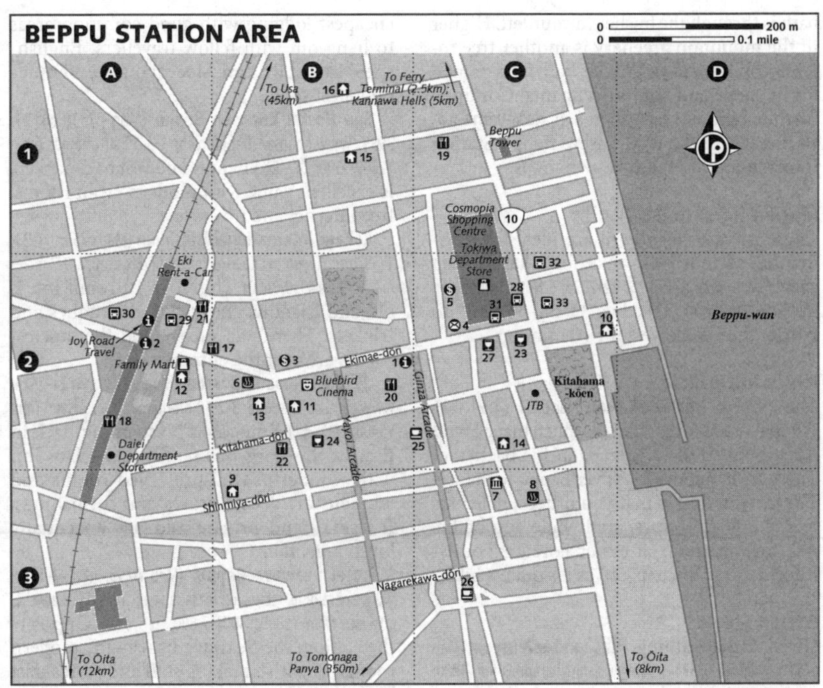

6.30am-10.30pm, sand bath 8am-9.30pm) dates from Meiji times. Bathing is simple; scoop out water with a bucket, wash yourself, then soak. There's also a sand bath where a *yukata* is provided so you can lie in a shallow trench and get buried up to your neck in hot sand. **Ekimae Kōtō Onsen** (Map p753; ☎ 21-0541; 13-14 Ekimae-machi; admission ¥300) is also basic and just a couple of minutes' walk from the station.

North of town, near the Kannawa group of hells (Map p751), is the popular **Mushi-yu steam bath** (Map p751; ☎ 67-3880; 1 Furomoto, Kannawa; admission/yukata ¥500/210; 9am-6pm). **Hyōtan Onsen** (Map p751; ☎ 66-0527; 159-2 Kannawa; admission/yukata ¥700/200; 8am-9pm) has a *rotemburo* and sand baths.

Shibaseki onsen (Map p751; ☎ 67-4100; 4 Noda; admission ¥210; 7.20am-8pm, closed 2nd Wed of each month) is near the smaller pair of hells. You can rent a private *kazoku-buro* (family bath) for ¥1570 per hour.

Between JR Beppu Station and the Kamegawa onsen area, **Shōnin-ga-hama sand bath** (Map p751; ☎ 66-5737; admission ¥1000; 8.30am-6pm Apr-Oct, 9am-5pm Nov-Mar) has a great beach location and English is spoken.

Northwest of town, the hilly **Myōban onsen area** (Map p751) is more peaceful. There are numerous baths and Edo-era replicas of the thatched-roof huts in which bath salts were made. Nearby, **Onsen Hoyōland** (Map p751; ☎ 66-2221; 5-1 Myōban; admission ¥1050; 9am-8pm) has giant mud baths, open-air and mixed-gender bathing.

For a seaside onsen experience, head to **Kitahama Termas Onsen** (Map p751; ☎ 24-4126; admission ¥500; 10am-8pm). The outside *rotemburo* mixes it up, but you'll need a bathing suit.

HIDDEN BATHS

Tsuru-no-yu, Hebi-no-yu & Nabeyama-no-yu 鶴の湯・へびん湯・鍋山の湯

For purists, the Myōban area has some wonderful, secluded baths *à la naturale*. Locals built and maintain **Tsuru-no-yu** (the easiest to reach), a lovely free *rotemburo* on the edge of Ogi-yama. In July and August, a natural stream emerges to form the milky blue bath. Take a bus to Konya Jigoku-mae bus stop (25 minutes northwest from JR Beppu Station). Walk up the small road that hugs the right side of the graveyard until the road ends. The bath is through the bushes to your left. Higher in the mountain greenery is another free *rotemburo,* **Hebi-no-yu** (Snake Bath), so named for its shape and not its occupants! Continue further (about 1km) to reach **Nabeyama-no-yu**, the last of the wild onsen. Beppu Station information has hand-drawn maps.

Mugen-no-sato 夢幻の里

These private *rotemburo* are ideal for a romantic, secluded dip. Ask for a **kazoku-buro** (private bath; Map p751; ☎ 22-2826; 6 Hotta; admission ¥600; 9am-9pm). Take bus 33, 34, 36 or 37 to Horita then walk west for 10 minutes.

Ichinoide Kaikan いちのいで会館

The owner of **Ichinoide Kaikan** (Map p751; ☎ 21-4728; 14-2 Uehara-machi) loves onsen so much that he built three pool-sized *rotemburo* in his backyard. There are fabulous views over Beppu to the sea. The general deal is that you order a delicious *teishoku* (¥1200), prepared while you bathe. Ask for directions at either Foreign Tourist Information Office (p750) as it's quite a hike.

OTHER SIGHTS

Given all that bathing, **Hihōkan Sex Museum** (Map p751; ☎ 66-8790; 338-3 Shibuyu, Kannawa; admission ¥1000; 9am-6pm) fits right in. Among the Kannawa hells, it hosts a bizarre collection of sex-related items ranging from erotic *ukiyo-e* (wood-block prints) to zany porno and kinky toys. There are plenty of souvenirs with which to disturb the customs officials on the way home.

Near Takegawara Onsen, the **Hirano Library** (Map p753; ☎ 23-4748; 11-7 Motomachi; admission free; Mon-Sun) is a private institution with historical exhibits and photographs of the Beppu area.

The hands-on **Beppu Traditional Bamboo Crafts Centre** (Map p751; ☎ 23-1072; 8-3 Higashi-sōen) displays works from the Edo period, as well as examples of what can be made with this versatile material. From Beppu Station, take Kamenoi bus 25 to Dentō Sangyō-mae, in front of the centre.

Festivals & Events

Onsen festival During the first weekend in April.

Tanabata Matsuri In adjacent Ōita city, held over three days from the first Friday in August.

Sleeping

Beppu Guest House (Map p753; ☎ 76-7811; www.beppu-g-h.net; 1-12 Ekimae-chō; dm/s ¥1500/2500; ⊠ 💻) There's a welcoming atmosphere in Beppu's cheapest lodging with good common areas to hang out with fellow travellers. English-speaking staff can steer you to Beppu's bubbliest spots.

Spa Hostel Khaosan Beppu (Map p753; ☎ 23-3939; www.khaosan-beppu.com; 3-3-10 Kitahama; dm/s ¥2500/3500; ⊠ 💻) Beppu's newest backpackers is excellent value with modern clean rooms, free internet and no curfew.

Kokage International Minshuku (Map p753; ☎ 23-1753; http://ww6.tiki.ne.jp/~kokage/index.html; 8-9 Ekimae-machi; s/d ¥4350/7650) This cosy 10-room inn is old and friendly, chock-full of antiques and trinkets. There's an onsen, and the quietest rooms are over the entrance.

our pick **Yamada Bessou** (Map p753; ☎ 21-2424; www.yamadabessou.jp; 3-2-18 Kitahama; r per person from ¥5400; P) You could be stepping back in time at this gorgeous family-run 1930s inn with wonderful well-preserved rooms and fabulous art-deco features and furnishings. It's small and private and has an equally lovely *rotemburo*.

Hotel Seawave Beppu (Map p753; ☎ 27-1311; www.coara.or.jp/seawave, in Japanese; 12-8 Ekimae-chō; s/tw/ste from ¥5800/8400/17,800; P ⊠) Opposite the station, the Seawave has smart, modern rooms, English-speaking staff and a breakfast buffet (¥600).

Hotel Aile (Map p753; ☎ 21-7272; 2-14-35 Kitahama; s/d/tw ¥6240/9540/10,590; P ⊠ 💻) The fantastic rooftop *rotemburo* and attractive, well-appointed rooms, some with great views, make this an excellent choice, just five minutes' walk from the station. LAN cable internet access is available.

Nogami Honkan Ryokan (Map p753; ☎ 22-1334; www008.upp.so-net.ne.jp/yuke-c/english.html; 1-12-1 Kitahama; r per person with/without breakfast ¥6400/5500; P ⊠ 💻) Located near Takegawara onsen, most rooms have private bathrooms. Five small baths can be reserved for private use and owner Ken is a knowledgeable and gracious host.

Hotel Arthur (Map p753; ☎ 25-2611; 1-2-5 Kitahama; s/d from ¥6700/10,000; ⊠) Less than five minutes' walk from Beppu Station, Arthur is clean and well appointed. Some rooms have LAN cable internet connectivity.

Suginoi Hotel (Map p751; ☎ 24-1141; www.suginoi-hotel.com/english; 1 Kankaiji; r per person with 2 meals from ¥15,900; P ⊠ 💻) The highest standard of accommodation and an incredible tiered rooftop *rotemburo* define this wonderful hotel. The Ceada floor is worth the splurge if you can afford the luxury.

Eating

Beppu is renowned for freshwater fish, *fugu* and wild mountain vegetables, commonly used in *dango-jiru*, a miso soup with dumplings.

Eki Ichiba (Station Market; Map p753; ⌚ 9am-5pm) You don't need much Japanese to enjoy this bustling market under the tracks out the back of Beppu Station. It's great fun to wander from stall to stall, savouring the *yobuko-ika* (squid tempura) or *futomaki sushi* (rice and seaweed roll). There's an abundance of fresh produce and ready meals perfect for a picnic on the beach at Kitahama-kōen.

Tomonaga Panya (Map p751; ☎ 23-0969; Chio-machi 2-29; ⌚ breakfast & lunch Mon-Sat) Tomonaga's oven-fresh breads and pastries are worth waking up early for, and they go fast! The walls are filled with photos going back to 1917.

Gyōza Kogetsu (Map p753; ☎ 21-8062; 3-7 Ekimae-honmachi; ⌚ 2pm-9.30pm, closed Tue) Only two things are on the menu in this tiny eatery; *gyōza* and beer. Both are ¥630 and the perfect compliment to a late afternoon soak on a warm day. Ask for directions at the Beppu International Plaza.

Dekadon (Map p753; ☎ 21-8062; 3-7 Ekimae-honmachi; dishes from ¥400; ⌚ lunch & dinner) Just down from the station on the left, this tasty *obentō* kitchen has tasty, cheap takeaway boxed meals displayed fresh in the glass counter.

Toyotsune (Map p753; ☎ 22-2083; 3-7 Ekimae-honmachi; dishes from ¥650; ⌚ lunch & dinner, closed Thu) This excellent, friendly eatery opposite Beppu Station has an English menu. The *ebi-tendon* (tempura prawns on rice) is as huge as the sashimi *teishoku* (from ¥1080) is mouthwatering.

Ureshi-ya (Map p753; ☎ 22-0767; 7-12 Ekimae-honmachi; dishes from ¥750; ⌚ dinner, closed Mon) You'll get your money's worth at this friendly and busy *shokudō* (budget all-round eatery) with *donburi* (dishes served over rice), sashimi, *oden* (hotpot) and noodle dishes. Food models are displayed in the window.

Fugu Matsu (Map p753; ☎ 21-1717; 3-6-14 Kitahama; fugu from ¥4000; ⌚ lunch & dinner) This is the place to try *fugu* in style, if you're game (diehards love it). There's an English menu.

Drinking

Jin Robata & Beer Pub (Map p753; ☎ 21-1768; 1-15-7 Kitahama) A flashing neon fish sign directs you to this welcoming, international pub. There's plenty of great food to go with your booze. Pick from the rows of fresh fish on display, then watch it being grilled behind the counter.

World Sports Bar Small Eye (Map p753; ☎ 21-3336; 2nd fl, 1-10-12 Kitahama; drinks/snacks from ¥500/400; ⌚ closed Thu). You'll find a good mix of young folk at this Yankee-styled bar with high ceilings, darts and beach umbrellas.

Natsume Kissa (Map p753; ☎ 21-5713; 1-4-23 Kitahama; ⌚ closed Wed) A good snack and dessert spot best known for its own onsen *kōhī* (¥530), coffee made with hot-springs water.

Shingai Coffee Shop (Map p753; ☎ 24-1656; 10-2 Kusu-machi; ⌚ closed Mon) A mellow place with good coffee, plus antique maps and old photos of Beppu.

Kuishinbō (Map p753; ☎ 21-0788; 1-1-12 Kitahama-dōri; ⌚ 6pm-2am) A cheerful corner *izakaya* serving unusual tofu and daikon steaks, *chawan-mushi* (savoury custard), and ¥100 *yakitori* skewers to complement the alcohol.

Getting There & Away

Flights go to Ōita airport from Tokyo Haneda (¥35,600, one hour) and Osaka (¥19,300, one hour). Flights also operate to Seoul.

The JR Nippō line runs from Hakata (Fukuoka) to Beppu (*tokkyū;* ¥5550, two hours) via Kitakyūshū, and Miyazaki (¥5770, 3¼ hours). The JR Hōhi line connects Beppu with Kumamoto (¥4830, three hours) via Aso-san (¥3440, two hours).

There's a Beppu Kyūshū Odan bus to Aso Station (¥2950, three hours).

The **Ferry Sunflower Kansai Kisen** (☎ 22-1311) makes an overnight run between Beppu and Osaka and Kōbe (¥9600, 11 hours), stopping at Matsuyama (4½ hours). The evening boat departs at 7pm to western Honshū and passes through the Inland Sea, arriving at 6am the next morning. For the port, take bus 20 or 26 from Beppu Station's west exit.

Getting Around

TO/FROM THE AIRPORT

Hovercraft (☎ 097-558-7180, 0120-81-4080) run from JR Ōita Station to Ōita airport (¥2950, 25 minutes), located on the Kunisaki Peninsula.

Beppu airport buses to Ōita-ken airport stop outside the Tokiwa department store (¥1450, 45 minutes, twice daily) and Beppu Station.

BUS

Kamenoi (☎ 23-5170) is the main bus company. An unlimited 'My Beppu Free' travel pass comes in two varieties: the 'minipass' (adult/student ¥900/700), which covers all the local attractions, including the hells, and the 'wide pass' (one/two days ¥1600/2400), which extends to Yufuin and Ritsumeikan Asia Pacific University. Passes are available from the Foreign Tourist Information Office (p750) and at various lodgings around town. Buses 5, 9 and 41 take you to Myōban (20 minutes).

KUNISAKI PENINSULA 国東半島

Immediately north of Beppu, Kunisaki-hantō bulges eastward from the Kyūshū coast. The region is noted for its early Buddhist influence, including some rock-carved images linked to more famous ones at Usuki (p750).

Sights

USA 宇佐

In the early post-WWII era, when 'Made in Japan' was no recommendation at all, it's said that companies would register in Usa so they could proclaim their goods were 'Made in USA'! **Usa-jinja** (宇佐神社; ☎ 0978-37-0001; admission to treasure hall ¥300; ⏰ closed Tue), the original of which dates back over a thousand years, is connected with the warrior-god Hachiman, a favourite deity of Japan's right wing. It's a 10-minute bus ride from Usa Station, which is on the JR Nippō line from Beppu.

OTHER SIGHTS

The 11th-century **Fuki-ji** (富貴寺; ☎ 0978-26-3189; admission ¥200) in Bungo-takada is the oldest wooden structure in Kyūshū and one of the oldest wooden temples in Japan. Ōita Kōtsū buses from Usa Station go to Bungo-takada (¥810, 35 minutes); from there, it's a 10-minute taxi ride (around ¥1000).

In the centre of the peninsula, near the summit of Futago-san (721m), is **Futago-ji** (両子寺; ☎ 0978-65-0253; admission ¥200), dedicated to Fudō-Myō-o, the ferocious, fire-enshrouded, sword-wielding deity, able to repel attacks while appearing calm.

Nearby **Taizō-ji** (☎ 0978-26-2070; admission ¥200; ⏰ 8.30am-5pm) is known for its famously uneven stone stairs. Local legend says that they are so random and haphazard that the Oni (devils) must have created them in a single night, confirming that, even in mythology, it has always been hard to get good help.

Carved into a cliff behind Taizō-ji, 2km south of **Maki Ōdō**, are two 8th-century Buddha images; a 6m figure of the Dainichi Buddha and an 8m figure of Fudō-Myō-o. Known as **Kumano Magaibutsu**, these are the largest Buddhist images of this type in Japan. There are also other stone statues, thought to be from the Heian period. Without a car, get a taxi from Fuki-ji to Bungo-Takada, then a bus to Usa (¥260).

YUFUIN 由布院

☎ 0977 / pop 36,407

About 25km inland from Beppu, delightful Yufuin sits in view of the twin peaks of Yufu-dake. Yufuin is noted for its high-quality handicrafts and has some interesting temples and shrines. Although tourism development has increased, legislation prevents further expansion, protecting the town's character. Even so, Yufuin is best avoided on holidays and weekends. If staying overnight arrive before dusk, when the day-trippers leave and wealthier Japanese retreat to the sanctuary of their ryokan.

The **tourist Information office** (☎ 84-2446; ⏰ 9am-7pm) inside the train station has some information in English, including a detailed walking map showing galleries, museums and onsen. There's a postal ATM next to the station, which also houses a small art gallery.

As in Beppu, making a pilgrimage from one onsen to another is a popular activity. **Shitan-yu** (下ん湯; admission ¥200; ⏰ 10am-9pm) is a thatched bathhouse on the northern shore of Kirin-ko, a hot spring–fed lake.

The double-peaked **Yufu-dake** (1584m) volcano overlooks Yufuin and takes about 90 minutes to climb. Some buses from Yufuin stop at the base of Yufu-dake, Yufu-tozan-guchi (由布登山口; ¥360, 16 minutes).

Sleeping & Eating

Yufuin has plenty of expensive, upscale ryokan, where most patrons return to eat. A handful of eateries by the station remain open.

our pick **Yufuin Country Road Youth Hostel** (由布院カントリーロードユースホステル; ☎ 84-3734 www4.ocn.ne.jp/~yufuinyh/, in Japanese; dm member/nonmember ¥2835/3435; P ⊠ 💻) On a forested hillside overlooking the town, this character-filled hostel with its own onsen has a beautiful outlook. The experience is completed by the personality of its English-speaking owners. It's possible they may pick you up from the station if you aren't in time for one of the infrequent buses (¥200). Two meals are available for an extra ¥1680.

Pension Yufuin (ペンション由布院; ☎ 85-3311; r with breakfast from ¥6500; P) This riverside guest house à la *Anne of Green Gables*, is

KYŪSHŪ

verging on the kitsch, but it's homey and in a lovely spot. The kind owner speaks a little English.

Makiba-no-ie (牧場の家; ☎ 84-2138; r per person with 2 meals ¥8000-13,500; P) Atmosphere aplenty in this series of thatched-roof huts around a large *rotemburo*. The antique-filled garden restaurant does chicken *jidori* and wild-boar *teishoku* meals from ¥1500. Visitors can use the *rotemburo* for ¥525.

Hanayoshi (花吉; ☎ 84-5888; 11am-4pm; V) You'll find delicious bowls of *soba* and *udon* from ¥550 here, opposite the bike shop down the first right from the station. There's a picture menu.

Aji-ichi Sugitaya (味一すぎた屋; ☎ 84-5644; lunch & dinner, closed Tue) Walk straight out of the station for 400m and you'll see the photo menu and the hanging lantern out the front. Try the generous speciality, *toriten* (chicken tempura) and *dangojiru* (miso soup with dumplings) *teishoku* for ¥1200. All of the set meals are great value.

Getting There & Away

Local trains on the JR Kyūdai line connect Beppu with Yufuin (¥1080, 1¼ hours) via Ōita. For train buffs, there's a magical 'Yufuin no Mori' express train a few times daily (¥4400, 2¼ hours).

Buses depart from JR Beppu Station (p755) for Yufuin throughout the day (¥900). Continuing beyond Yufuin is not so simple. Buses go to Aso and Kumamoto but not year-round. There are also express buses (Kyūshū Sanko) to Fukuoka (¥3100).

YUFUIN TO ASO-SAN

The picturesque Yamanami Hwy extends 63km from near Yufuin towards Aso-san. It's a wonderful drive if you have the opportunity. You'll cross a high plateau and pass numerous mountain peaks, including **Kujū-san** (1787m), the highest point in Kyūshū.

Just off the highway, the **Kokonoe 'Yume' Ōtsuribashi** (九重'夢'大吊橋; ☎ 0973-73-3800; admission ¥500; 9am-4pm) suspension bridge completed in 2006 is the largest of its kind in Japan. Hovering 173m above the Naruko-gawa (777m above sea level), it's a shaky 390m walk from one side of the gorge to the other. The views are breathtaking but not recommended for acrophobics and the bridge is often very crowded. Without a car, it's a major effort. The nearest station is Bungo-Nakamura.

Taketa 竹田

South of Yufuin, near the sleepy town of Taketa, the **Oka-jō ruins** have a ridgetop position affording lovely vistas. The ruins are over 2km from JR Bungo-Taketa Station. Taketa has some interesting reminders of the Christian period, as well as atmospheric temples and well-preserved traditional houses. **Taketa Onsen Hanamizuki** (花水月温泉; ☎ 0974-64-1126; admission ¥500; 1pm-9pm) is a short walk from the station.

From Aso-san, it takes just under an hour by train on the JR Hōhi line to Bungo-Taketa (*futsū;* ¥820); from there it's just over an hour by train to Ōita (¥1250) – just a little longer by bus.

Okinawa & the Southwest Islands 沖縄南西諸島

Japan's Southwest Islands, or Nansei-shotō, are *the other Japan:* a chain of semitropical islands that feels more like Hawaii or Southeast Asia than mainland Japan. Stretching from Kyūshū in the north to within sight of Taiwan in the south, these coral-fringed islands are sure to be a revelation to those who make the journey.

First and foremost, the islands are a nature lover's paradise: starting with the islands of Kagoshima-ken in the north, you'll find lush primeval forests hidden among the craggy peaks of Yakushima. In the same prefecture, there's the starfishlike island of Amami-Ōshima, with lots of fine beaches in its convoluted coastline. Also in the Amami-shotō, tiny Yoron-tō is basically all beach, with an airport on top for easy access.

Heading south, the first stop is Okinawa-hontō, the bustling main island of Japan's southernmost prefecture, Okinawa-ken. While the main island is great, the offshore islands are even better, including the spectacular Kerama-shotō, a group of tiny gems with white-sand beaches and crystal-clear waters. Next along is Miyako-jima, which also boasts killer beaches and a laid-back scene. And, finally, there is brilliant Yaeyama-shotō, with Japan's best coral reefs, subtropical jungles and extensive mangrove swamps, not to mention manta rays, hammerhead sharks and the mysterious sunken ruins of the 'Atlantis of the Pacific'.

Of course, spectacular nature is only the half of it: the southern islands also boast a fascinating and peculiarly 'un-Japanese' culture. Indeed, Okinawa was actually a separate country and culture for most of its history and the Ryūkyū cultural heart still beats in Japan's Southwest Islands.

HIGHLIGHTS

- Hike into the mountainous heart of **Yakushima** (p761) to commune with ancient *yaku-sugi* trees
- Dive with playful mantas off **Ishigaki-jima** (p793)
- Explore the mangrove swamps, jungles and coral reefs of Japan's last frontier, **Iriomote-jima** (p795)
- Take a ferry to a simpler time on the 'living museum' island of **Taketomi-jima** (p798)
- Soak up the sun on one of the white-sand beaches of the **Kerama-shotō** (p783)
- Seek out the traces of Ryūkyū culture in the backstreets and markets of **Naha** (p778)
- Try to keep your cool amid a school of hammerhead sharks off **Yonaguni-jima**, then check out the 'Atlantis of the Pacific' (p800)

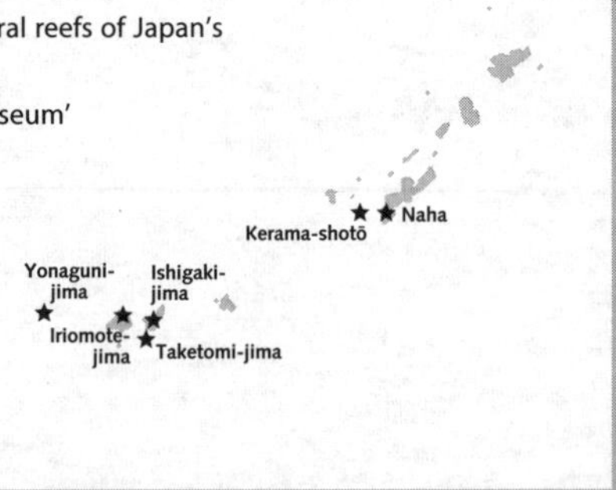

History

For centuries, Okinawa and the Southwest Islands were ruled by *aji* (local chieftains), who battled for control of small fiefs, and struggled among themselves for power and fame. In 1429, however, the islands were united by Sho Hashi of the Chūzan kingdom, which led to the establishment of the Ryūkyū dynasty. During this period Sho Hashi increased contact with China, which contributed to the flourishing of Okinawan music, dance, literature and ceramics. In this 'Golden Era' weapons were prohibited, and the islands were rewarded with peace and tranquillity.

With no weapons and little means of defence, the Ryūkyū kingdom was not prepared for war when the Shimazu clan of Satsuma (modern-day Kagoshima) invaded in 1609. The Shimazu conquered the Ryūkyū kingdom easily, and then established severe controls over its trade. While the rest of Japan closed its doors to the world prior to 1853, the Shimazu sustained trade with China under the guise of the Ryūkyū kingdom. The islands were controlled with an iron fist, and taxed and exploited greedily for the next 250 years.

With the restoration of the Meiji emperor and the abolition of the Japanese feudal system, the Ryūkyūs were annexed to Japan as Okinawa Prefecture in 1879. However, life hardly changed for the islanders as they were treated as foreign subjects by the Japanese government, just as they had been by the Shimazu. Furthermore, the Meiji government stamped out local culture by outlawing the teaching of Ryūkyū history in schools, and establishing Japanese as the official language.

In the closing days of WWII, the Japanese military made a decision to use the islands of Okinawa as a shield against the allies, hoping to slow their relentless advance across the Pacific. This decision to sacrifice Okinawa to protect the mainland cost the islanders dearly: by the time the Battle of Okinawa was over, 12,500 US soldiers and an estimated quarter of a million Japanese had died.

Following the war, Okinawa was again sacrificed by Tokyo: while the occupation of the Japanese mainland ended in 1952, Okinawa remained under US control until it was officially returned to Japan in 1972. The return, however, was contingent upon Japan agreeing to allow the Americans to maintain bases on the islands and some 30,000 American military personnel remain stationed in several bases on Okinawa-hontō. For more information on the continuing occupation of Okinawa, see p780.

Climate

The Southwest Islands have a subtropical climate and are much warmer than mainland Japan, particularly as you head further south into Okinawa-ken. With the exception of the peaks of Yakushima, which may even be snowcapped between December and February, the islands escape anything resembling a real winter. You can comfortably travel the Southwest Islands any time of year, but swimming might be uncomfortable between late October and early May, unless you're the hardy sort.

The average daily temperature on Okinawa-hontō in December is 20°C, while in July it is 30°C. The islands of Kagoshima-ken average a few degrees cooler than this, while those of Yaeyama-shotō and Miyako-shotō average a few degrees warmer. The islands are most crowded during June, July and August and during the Golden Week holiday in early May. Outside of these times, the islands are often blissfully quiet.

The main thing to keep in mind when planning a trip to the Southwest Islands is the possibility of typhoons, which can strike anytime between June and October. If you choose to visit during these months, build some flexibility into your schedule, as typhoons often cause cancellations or delays in flight and ferry departures. Be prepared to spend a few days hunkered down on an island waiting for a storm to pass. Ideally, purchase tickets that allow changes without incurring a fee. The **Japan Meteorological Agency's website** (www.jma.go.jp/en/typh) has the latest details on typhoons approaching Japan.

Language

Although the Ryūkyū islands used to have their own distinctive language, this has by and large disappeared. Standard Japanese is spoken by almost every resident of the islands. That said, travellers who speak some standard Japanese might find the local dialects and accent a little hard to catch.

Getting There & Away

The Southwest Islands are easily accessible from mainland Japan.

There are flights between major cities in mainland Japan and Amami-Ōshima,

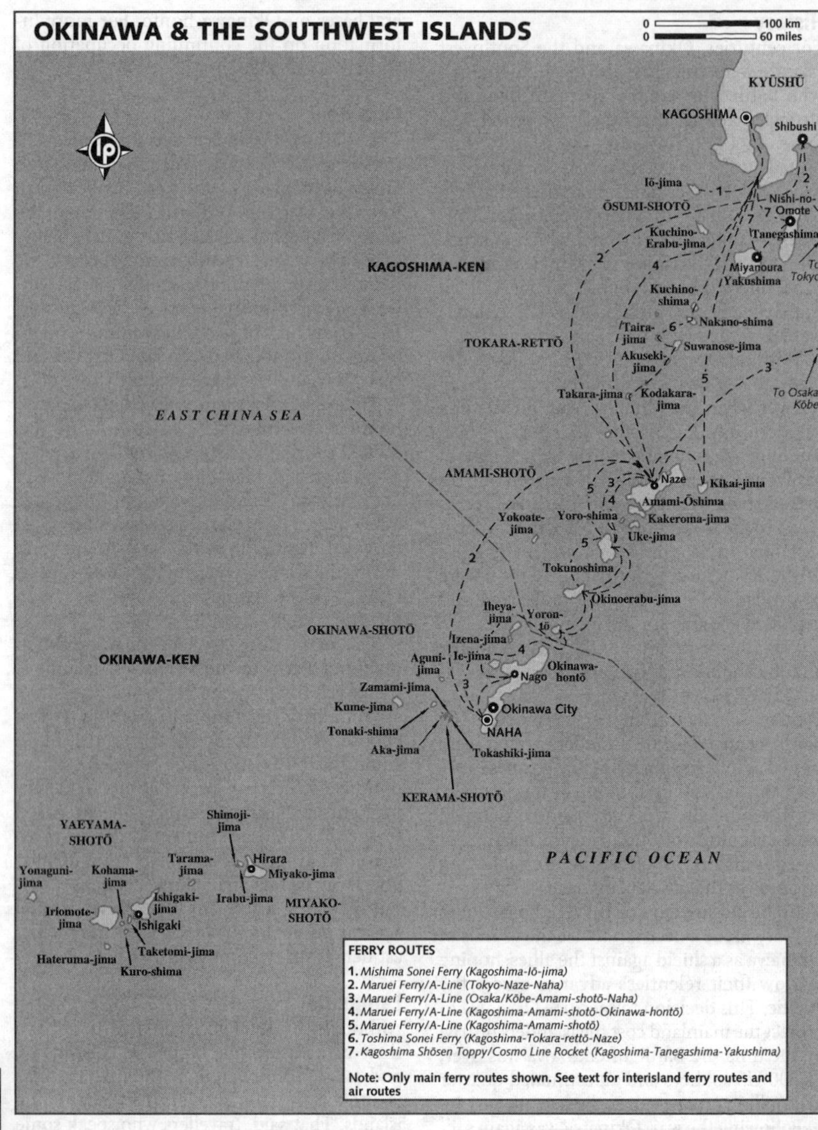

Okinawa-hontō (Naha), Miyako-jima and Ishigaki-jima (Map p832). Kagoshima, in Kyūshū, has flights to/from all these islands and many of the smaller islands as well. Other outer islands such as Yonaguni-jima, Kume-jima and Zamami-jima can be reached by air with a change of flight in Naha (or, Ishigaki, in some cases).

There are ferries between Tokyo, Osaka/Kōbe and Kagoshima to the islands of Amami-shotō and Okinawa-hontō, as well as plentiful ferries between Kagoshima and Yakushima and Tanegashima. Once you arrive in a major port like Naze on Amami-Ōshima or Naha on Okinawa-hontō, there are plenty of local ferry services to nearby islands. Unfortunately, the Arimura Sangyō ferry service that used to ply the length of the Southwest Islands between Kyūshū and Taiwan is now defunct. Thus, you cannot reach Miyako-shotō or Yaeyama-shotō by ferry from mainland Japan. A new service might start at any time, so you can always check with tourist information offices for the latest details.

If you are arriving in Japan by air, it is worth noting that JAL and ANA both offer 'visit Japan'-type airfares for domestic flights within Japan – as long as they are bought outside Japan in conjunction with a ticket to Japan. Such tickets, if used to Okinawa, are an incredible saving from standard domestic airfares bought within Japan.

Getting Around

Once you arrive in a major hub like Naha on Okinawa-hontō or Ishigaki on Ishigaki-jima, you will find plenty of ferry services to the surrounding islands. Services are plentiful and you can use cities like these as bases for island-hopping vacations. There are also reasonable air networks in Amami-shotō, Okinawa-shotō and Yaeyama-shotō, with airfields on most (but not all) islands.

Getting around the islands themselves is a little less convenient. While most islands have public bus networks, there are usually not more than a few buses per day on each route. Thus, if at all possible, we recommend bringing an International Driving Permit and renting a car or scooter, particularly on Yakushima, Ishigaki, Iriomote and Okinawa-hontō. Another solution is renting a bicycle, but rental bikes are often old creakers, so if you're serious about cycling, you may want to bring your own touring bicycle.

KAGOSHIMA-KEN 鹿児島県

The northern end of the Southwest Islands is actually part of the prefecture of Kagoshima-ken, which also includes the southern end of Kyūshū, one of the Japanese mainland islands. The Kagoshima-ken part of the Southwest Islands contains three island groups (island groups are called 'shotō' or 'rettō' in Japanese).

Northernmost is Ōsumi-shotō, which is home to the island of Yakushima, one of the most popular destinations in the Southwest Islands. These islands, around 100km south of the Kyūshū mainland, are accessible by frequent ferries from Kagoshima. There is also limited air service to two of the islands.

Next is the Tokara-rettō, consisting of 12 rarely visited volcanic islets, which is one of the most remote destinations in the region. The Tokara-rettō are served by ferries that make the run between Kagoshima and Amami-Ōshima.

Southernmost is Amami-shotō, which is home to the population centre of Amami-Ōshima as well as several more picturesque islands. Located 380km south of Kyūshū, this group has a more pronounced tropical feel than other islands in the Kagoshima-ken. This group of islands is easily accessed by frequent ferries from Kagoshima and planes from Kagoshima. There are also weekly ferries from Tokyo and Osaka/Kōbe.

ŌSUMI-SHOTŌ 大隅諸島

Ōsumi-shotō comprises the two main islands of Yakushima and Tanegashima and the seldom-visited triumvirate of islands known as Mishima-mura. The all-star attraction in the group is Yakushima, a virtual paradise for nature lovers that attracts large numbers of both domestic and international travellers. Tanegashima, which is famous as the home of Japan's space program, sees few foreign travellers, though it is a popular surfing destination for Japanese. Finally, the most commonly visited island in the Mishima-mura group is tiny Iō-jima, a rarely visited gem of a volcanic island with excellent onsen (hot springs).

Yakushima 屋久島

☎ 0997 / pop 14,000

Designated a Unesco World Heritage Site in 1993, Yakushima is one of the most rewarding islands in the Southwest Islands. The craggy mountain peaks of the island's interior are home to the world-famous *yaku-sugi* (屋久杉; *Cryptomeria japonica*), ancient cedar trees that are said to have been the inspiration for some of the scenes in Miyazaki Hayao's animation classic *Princess Mononoke*.

Hiking among the high peaks and mossy forests is the main activity on Yakushima, but the island is also home to some excellent coastal onsen and a few sandy beaches.

Keep in mind that Yakushima is a place of extremes: the mountains wring every last drop of moisture from the passing clouds and the

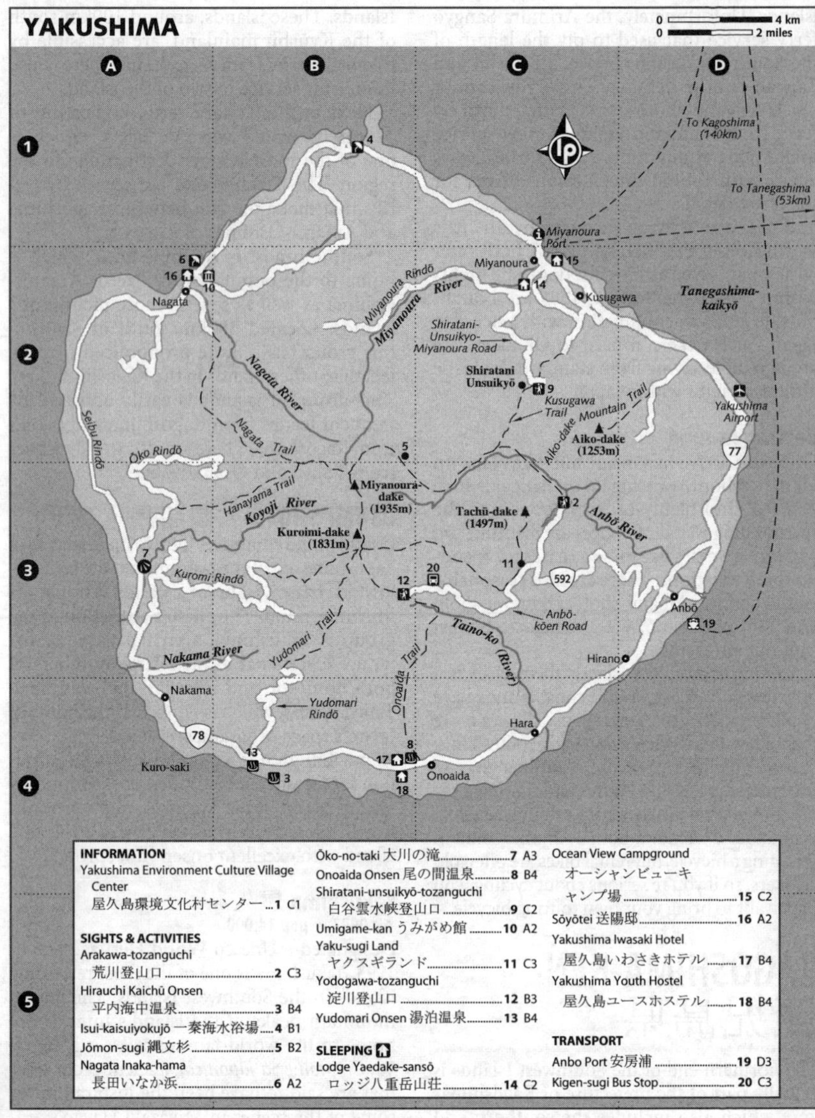

interior of the island is one of the wettest places in Japan. In the winter, the peaks may be covered in snow, while the coast is still relatively balmy. Whatever you do, come prepared and don't set off on a hike without a good map and the proper gear. An International Driving Permit will also vastly increase your enjoyment here, as buses are few and far between.

ORIENTATION

Yakushima's main port is Miyanoura (宮之浦), on the island's northeast coast. This is the most convenient place to be based, as most buses originate from here. From Miyanoura, a road runs around the perimeter of the island, passing through the secondary port of Anbō (安房) on the east coast, and then through the hot-springs town of Onoaida (尾の間) in the south. Heading north from Miyanoura, the road takes you to the town of Nagata (永田), which has a brilliant stretch of white-sand beach.

INFORMATION

Miyanoura's ferry terminal has a useful **tourist information centre** (☎ 42-1019; 🕑 8.30am-5pm) in the white building on your right as you emerge from the Toppy and Rocket ferry offices. It can help you find lodgings and can answer all your questions about the island. In Anbō there's a smaller **tourist office** (☎ 46-2333; 🕑 9am-5.30pm) on the main road just north of the river.

If you plan to get around the island by bus, we recommend buying a bus pass (see p766).

SIGHTS & ACTIVITIES

Onsen

There are several onsen around the island, the best of which are located near the village of Onoaida, on the southern coast of the island, accessible by southbound buses from Miyanoura or Anbō.

Onsen lovers will be in heaven at the **Hirauchi Kaichū Onsen** (admission ¥100; 🕑 24hr). The outdoor baths are in the rocks by the sea and can only be entered at or close to low tide (ask at the TIC or at your lodgings for times). You can walk to the baths from the Kaichū Onsen bus stop, but the next stop, Nishikaikon, is actually closer. From Nishikaikon, walk downhill towards the sea for about 200m and take a right at the bottom of the hill. Note that this is a *konyoku* onsen (mixed bath), so if you're shy, you'll just have to wait until other bathers clear off, as swimsuits are not allowed.

About 600m west is **Yudomari Onsen** (admission ¥100; 🕑 24hr), another great seaside onsen that can be entered at any tide. The small bath here has a divider that affords a bit more privacy. Get off at the Yudomari bus stop and take the road opposite the post office in the direction of the sea. Once you enter the village, the way is marked. It's a 300m walk and you pass a great banyan tree en route.

In the village of Onoaida is **Onoaida Onsen** (admission ¥200; 🕑 7am-9.30pm May-Oct, to 9pm Nov-Apr, from noon Mon), a rustic indoor bathhouse that is divided by gender. This is a great local bath and you're likely to be bathing with the village elders here. It's at the top (mountain side) of the village, a few minutes' walk uphill (about 350m) from the Onoaida Onsen bus stop.

Hiking

Hiking is the best way to experience Yakushima's beauty. If you're planning anything more than a short stroll around Yaku-sugi Land (see p764), pick up a copy of the Japanese-language *Yama-to-Kougen-no-Chizu- Yakushima* (山と高原の地図屋久島; ¥840), available at major bookshops in Japan. You'll also need proper hiking gear, including rain gear and warm clothing, especially in winter, as well as a sleeping bag and sufficient food if you intend to overnight in the *yama-goya* (mountain huts).

Before heading up into the hills, be sure to alert someone at your accommodation of your intended route and fill in a *tōzan todokede* (route plan) at the trailhead.

The most popular hiking destination on the island is the **Jōmon Sugi**, a monster of a *yaku-sugi* that is estimated to be at least 3000 years old. There are two ways to reach the tree: the 19.5km, eight-to10-hour round-trip from the **Arakawa-tozanguchi** trailhead (604m), which is served by two daily buses to/from Miyanoura (¥1380, 85 minutes, March to November), and the round-trip from the **Shiratani-unsuikyō-tozanguchi** trailhead (622m), which is served by up to eight daily buses to/from Miyanoura (¥530, 35 minutes, March to November).

Note that since Yakushima became a Unesco World Heritage Site, the Jōmon Sugi area has been besieged by visitors and those averse to crowds should visit outside the summer and Golden Week high seasons. Also note that you cannot drive a rental car to Arakawa-tozanguchi during the entire month of August (there are shuttle buses to/from Yakusugi Land, where you can park).

The granddaddy of hikes on Yakushima is the day-long outing to the 1935m summit of **Miyanoura-dake**, the highest point in southern Japan. Fit climbers should allow about seven hours return from **Yodogawa-tozanguchi** trailhead (1370m). Yodogawa-tozanguchi is about 1.5km (about 30 minutes) beyond the Kigen-sugi bus stop, which is served by two buses a day to/from Anbō (¥910, one hour). Note that the buses do not give you sufficient time to complete the round-trip in a day – an early-morning taxi from Miyanoura (around ¥10,000) will give you time to make the second bus back to Anbō.

Finally, it's possible to make a traverse of Miyanoura-dake with a stop at Jōmon Sugi en route. Do not attempt this in a day; you'll have to spend the night in one of the *yama-goya* above Jōmon Sugi. Typical routes are

SEA TURTLES

Loggerhead sea turtles and green sea turtles come ashore on the beaches of Yakushima to lay their eggs. Unfortunately, human activity can significantly interfere with the egg-laying process. Thus we recommend that you keep the following rules in mind when visiting the beaches of Yakushima (particularly those on the northwest coast):

- Never approach a sea turtle that has come ashore.
- Do not start fires on the beach as the light will confuse the chicks (who use moonlight to orient themselves). Likewise, do not shine torches (flashlights) or car headlights at or near the beach.
- Do not walk on the beach at night.
- Be extremely careful when you walk on the beach, as you might inadvertently step on a newly hatched turtle.
- If you want to observe the turtles, enquire at the **Umigame-kan** centre on Yakushima (below).

between Yodogawa and Arakawa or Yodogawa and Shiratani-unsuikyō. A full traverse of the island is described in Lonely Planet's *Hiking in Japan*.

If you're feeling a little less adventurous, consider a visit to **Yaku-sugi Land** (admission ¥300; 9am-5pm). The name screams tourist trap, but this forest preserve amid the island's peaks is well worth a trip and it's a great way to see some *yaku-sugi* without a long trek into the forest. It offers shorter hiking courses over wooden boardwalks, and longer treks deep into the ancient cedar forest. There are four walking courses here, the two shorter ones being mostly over boardwalks. There are four buses (¥720, 40 minutes) a day to/from Anbō.

Other Attractions

In Miyanoura, the **Yakushima Environment Culture Village Center** (42-2900; admission & film ¥500; 9am-5pm Tue-Sun Sep-Jun, 9am-5pm daily Jul & Aug) is at the corner of the ferry-terminal road. It has exhibits about the island's natural environment and history, with limited English signage. It screens a large-format 25-minute film in Japanese hourly (even if you don't understand Japanese, we highly recommend it).

On the northwest coast of the island in the village of Nagata is **Nagata Inaka-hama**, a beautiful stretch of yellow sand where sea turtles come to lay their eggs from May to July. It's beside the Inaka-hama bus stop, which is served by Nagata-bound buses from Miyanoura. About midway along the beach, along the main road is the **Umigame-kan** (49-6550; admission ¥200; 9am-5pm, closed Tue), which has displays and information about the turtles (mostly in Japanese).

The **Issō-kaisuiyokujō** is another fine beach, located on the north coast of the island, about midway between Miyanoura and Nagata. It's a short walk from the Yahazu bus stop (served by any Nagata-bound bus from Miyanoura).

On the west coast is **Ōko-no-taki**, which is Yakushima's highest waterfall at 88m. It's a five-minute walk from Ōko-no-taki bus stop, which is the last stop on some of the buses running south and west from Miyano-ura and Anbō (note that only two buses a day run all the way out here).

SLEEPING

The most convenient place to be based is Miyanoura, which has two hotels and lots of *minshuku* (Japanese guest houses), as well as some riverside cabins. You'll find additional lodgings in each of the island's villages and several barebones *yama-goya* in the mountains.

In July and August and the spring Golden Week holiday, it's best to try to reserve ahead, since places fill up early. And if you're staying outside Miyanoura, you'll want to phone ahead anyway in the hope that the lodge owner will meet you at the ferry pier.

Miyanoura

Ocean View Campground (Yakushima Youth Campground; 47-3751; www.yakushima-yh.net; per person ¥840) This basic camping ground is pretty much just a field for tents and a couple of showers and bathrooms, with a bit of rocky beach down the hill. It's just west of the Eneos petrol station. There are a few other camping grounds on the island, including one in Anbō and another in Yahazu.

Miyanoura Portside Youth Hostel (☎ 49-1316; www.yakushima-yh.net; dm HI member/nonmember ¥3200/3800; P 💻) About 10 minutes' walk from the pier in Miyanoura is this simple and clean youth hostel. The place doesn't offer meals, but there are several good restaurants close by. To get there from the pier, walk into the village, then follow the first main shoreline road on the left.

Lodge Yaedake-sansō (☎ 42-1551; r per person with meals ¥7800; P) This secluded accommodation features Japanese-style rooms in rustic riverside cabins connected by wooden walkways. There's a private bath where you can soak up the beauty of your surroundings and children will enjoy splashing in the river. The lodge is located inland upriver on the Miyanoura-gawa; if you make a booking, staff will pick you up in Miyanoura. There are no cooking facilities but meals are served. You'll probably need a vehicle if you're staying here.

Seaside Hotel (☎ 42-0175; www.ssh-yakushima.co.jp, in Japanese; r with 2 meals from ¥12,600; P 💻) Overlooking the ferry port in Miyanoura, this popular resort hotel is extremely convenient and quite appealing. The mostly Western-style rooms are spacious and the seaside rooms have great ocean views. There's a very nice pool and meals are available. It's a five-minute walk from the Miyanoura ferry pier (look for the access road on your right as you walk towards town).

Onoaida

Yakushima Youth Hostel (☎ 47-3751; www.yakushima-yh.net; dm with/without meals ¥4620/2940; P 💻) This well-run youth hostel is about 3km west of Onoaida. Accommodation is in Western-style dorms and the cypress wood tub in the new wing is great. Get off any southbound buses from Miyanoura at the Hirauchi-iriguchi bus stop and take the road towards the sea for about 200m.

Yakushima Iwasaki Hotel (☎ 47-3888; http://yakushima.iwasakihotels.com, in Japanese; d from ¥20,000; P 💻) The island's most luxurious hotel commands an impressive view from its hilltop location above Onoaida. Spacious Western-style rooms have either ocean or mountain views. The hotel has its own onsen bath and meals are available in two restaurants. Southbound buses from Miyanoura stop right in front of the hotel.

Nakata

Sōyōtei (☎ 45-2819; http://soyote.ftw.jp/u44579.html, in Japanese; r per person with meals ¥12,600; P) On the northwest of the island near Inaka-hama, this impressive guest house has a collection of semidetached units that boast private verandahs and ocean views. There is an outdoor bath overlooking the sea, but it's not always open. It's very close to the Inaka-hama bus stop.

EATING

There are a few restaurants in each of the island's villages, with the best selection in Miyanoura. If you're staying anywhere but Miyanoura, you should ask for the set two-meal plan at your lodgings, since it's troublesome to have to eat out. If you're going hiking, you can ask your lodging to prepare a *bentō* (boxed meal) the night before you set out.

Resutoran Yakushima (☎ 42-0091; 🕑 9.30am-4.30pm) On the 2nd floor of the Yakushima Kankō Sentaa (look for the green two-storey building on the main road, near the road to the pier), this simple restaurant serves a ¥500 morning set breakfast with eggs, toast and coffee and a tasty *tobi uo sashimi teishoku* (flying fish sashimi set meal, ¥900) for lunch. You can also access the internet on two Japanese laptops here.

Ten Ten (☎ 42-0689; 🕑 5.30pm-10pm, closed irregularly) On the main road in the middle of Miyanoura, this friendly little *izakaya* (pub-eatery) serves a mouth-watering *yakizakana teishoku* (grilled fish set meal, ¥1000). It's a little hard to spot; you might have to ask a local to point it out.

Oshokuji-dokoro Shiosai (☎ 42-2721; 🕑 11.30am-2pm & 5.30-10pm, closed Thu) Also on the main road in the middle of Miyanoura, this fine restaurant offers counter, table and tatami (woven floor matting) seating and a full range of Japanese standard dishes and great local seafood. There is no English menu, so if you're at a loss, try the *sashimi teishoku* (sashimi full set, ¥1700) or the wonderful *ebi-furai teishoku* (fried shrimp full set, ¥1400). Look for the blue and whitish building and the automatic glass doors.

Lastly, if you need to stock up on supplies for camping or hiking, you'll find Yakuden supermarket on the main street in Miyanoura, just north of the entrance to the pier area.

GETTING THERE & AWAY

Air

JAC has flights between Kagoshima and Yakushima (¥12,750, 35 minutes, five daily). Yakushima's airport is on the northeastern coast between Miyanoura and Anbō. Hourly buses stop at the airport, though you can usually phone your accommodation for a pick-up or take a taxi.

Boat

Three ferry services operate between Kagoshima (Kyūshū) and Yakushima, some of which stop at Tanegashima en route. **Kagoshima Shōsen/Toppy** (☎ 099-226-0128) and **Cosmo Line/Rocket** (☎ 099-223-1011) each run at least three hydrofoils a day between Kagoshima and Miyanoura (¥5000, one hour 50 minutes for direct sailings, two hours 50 minutes with a stop in Tanegashima). Kagoshima Shōsen/Toppy also has hydrofoil sailings between Kagoshima and Anbō Port on Yakushima.

Keep in mind that the hydrofoils stop running at the slightest hint of inclement weather. During the summer and Golden Week high seasons, you should reserve in advance by telephone or in person at the ferry offices the day before your intended departure from Kagoshima. In other seasons, you can usually just turn up and board the next sailing.

Orita Kisen (☎ 099-226-0731) runs the normal *Ferry Yakushima 2* between Kagoshima and Miyanoura (one way/return ¥5200/8500, four hours, once daily). The ferry departs from Kagoshima at 8.30am, and leaves Miyanoura at 1.30pm. Reservations aren't usually necessary for this ferry.

GETTING AROUND

Local buses travel the coastal road part way around Yakushima roughly every hour or two, though only a few head up into the interior. Buses are expensive and you'll save a lot of money by purchasing a *Furii Jōsha Kippu*, which is good for unlimited travel on island buses. One-/two-day passes cost ¥2000/3000 and are available at the Toppy Ferry Office in Miyanoura.

Hitching is also possible, but the best way to get around the island is to rent a car. **Toyota Rent-a-Car** (☎ 43-5180; up to 12hr from ¥5775; ⏲ 8am-8pm;) is located near the terminal in Miyanoura.

Tanegashima 種子島

☎ 0997 / pop 36,000

A long narrow island about 20km northeast of Yakushima, Tanegashima is a laid-back destination popular with Japanese surfers and beach lovers. Home to Japan's Space Centre, Tanegashima also has the dubious distinction of being the spot where firearms were first introduced to Japan by shipwrecked Portuguese in 1543. Good ferry connections make this island easy to pair with a trip to Yakushima. Unfortunately, the relative lack of buses makes it difficult to enjoy this island without a rental car or scooter, or, at least, a good touring bicycle.

The island's main port of **Nishi-no-Omote** (西の表) is located on the northwest coast of the island, while the airport is about halfway down the island near the west coast. The best beaches and most of the surfing breaks are on the east coast of the island, which is also home to an onsen.

There is a helpful **information office** (種子島観光案内所; ☎ 22-1146; ⏲ 8.30am-5.30pm) at the pier in Nishi-no-Omote, inside the Cosmo ferry office/waiting room.

SIGHTS & ACTIVITIES

Tanegashima's **Space Centre** (種子島宇宙センター), on the southeastern coast of the island, is a large parklike complex with rocket-launch facilities as well as a **Space Technology Museum** (宇宙科学技術館; ☎ 26-9244; ⏲ 9.30am-5.30pm, closed Mon) that details the history of Japan's space program. There are models of Japan's rockets and some of the satellites it has launched. Note that the museum is closed on launch days. The closest bus stop is Iwasaki Hotel, from where it's a 10-minute walk.

The coastline in the immediate vicinity of the Space Centre is known as the **Takesaki-kaigan** (竹崎海岸), and is home to a beautiful stretch of white sand that is immensely popular with surfers. The best spot to enjoy this area is the beach in front of the Iwasaki Hotel (closest bus stop: Iwasaki Hotel), which has some impressive rock formations on either end. The **Nagahama-kaigan** (長浜海岸) on the west coast of Tanegashima is home to a 12km stretch of beach that is equally popular with surfers.

Further up the east coast, the **Kumano-kaigan** (熊野海岸) has a long beach, a caming ground and the **Nakatanechō Onsen** (中種子町温泉; per person ¥300; ⏲ 11am-8pm Oct-Mar, to 9pm Apr-Sep, closed Thu). The closest bus stop for these is Kumano-kaisuiyokujō.

The **History & Folklore Museum** (中種子町立歴史民俗資料館; ☎ 27-2233; admission ¥160; 9am-7pm, closed Mon), near Tanegashima's airport, has displays on the history and traditional lifestyles of the islanders. The closest bus stop is Noma.

SLEEPING & EATING

Ryokan Miharu-sō (旅館美春荘; ☎ 22-1393; r per person with 2 meals ¥6300; P) This cheap and friendly surfers' hang out in Nishi-no-Omote has basic Japanese-style tatami rooms. Meals are served on the premises. Walk to the main road from the pier and take a left, then turn right at the light and walk inland (uphill).

East Coast (イーストコースト; ☎ 25-0763; www.eastcoast.jp/; bungalow for up to 3 people ¥10,500, per additional person ¥3150; P) This surf-school–restaurant has two cosy bungalows for those who want to stay near the breaks. The owner is an English-speaking Japanese surfer. The bungalows can handle small groups and families, and have cooking facilities and bathrooms. As you might guess, it's on the east coast of the island.

Mauna Village (マウナヴィレッジ; ☎ 25-0811; r per person with 2 meals from ¥6800; P) Also on the east coast of the island, this collection of cute cottages is popular with surfers and families. Some units have sea views and all have toilets, but bathing facilities are shared and meals are taken in a common dining room.

Izakaya Minshuku Sangoshō (居酒屋民宿珊瑚礁; ☎ 23-0005; r per person with 2 meals from ¥8400; P) For something totally different, try this slice of Southeast Asia transported to Japan. It's a 'guest house–pub' with tonnes of cool features, including a brilliant rock-lined bathtub and a huge banyan tree out the front. Accommodation is in simple Japanese-style rooms. It's on the northwest coast, about five minutes' drive from town.

Koryōri Shirō (小料理しろう; ☎ 23-2117; dishes from ¥1000; 5-11pm) Head to this friendly little *izakaya* in Nishi-no-Omote to sample island hospitality and tasty dishes like the *sashimi teishoku* (sashimi full set, ¥1200). There are plants out front and blue-and-white *noren* (doorway curtains). It's a short walk from the Hotel New Tanegashima (look for the tall hotel building then ask directions when you get nearby).

GETTING THERE & AWAY

Tanegashima has flights to/from Kagoshima (¥11,550, 35 minutes) and Osaka's Itami Airport (¥29,950, 90 minutes) on JAC.

There are also several daily high-speed ferries to/from Kagoshima and Yakushima; for details, see opposite. Finally, **Kashō Kaiun** (☎ 099-261-7000) operates one normal ferry a day between Kagoshima and Tanegashima (¥3000, three hours and 40 minutes).

Iō-jima 硫黄島

☎ 09913 / pop 115

Iō-jima is a tiny bamboo-covered island with a smouldering volcano and two brilliant seaside onsen. Seldom visited by foreign travellers, this island makes a good overnight trip for those who like to step off the beaten track.

The port and the only village are at the southwest end of the island. A small souvenir shop at the pier usually stocks a Japanese pamphlet about the island, with a useful map of the island.

The eastern end of the island is home to **Iō-dake** (硫黄岳; 704m), an active volcano that frequently emits clouds of sulphurous yellow smoke. Run-off from the volcano is responsible for the rust colour of the island's harbour. Note that climbing of the volcano is strictly forbidden.

There are two free onsen on the island. On the north coast, about a 4km walk from the port, is **Sakamoto Onsen** (坂本温泉), a rectangular pool built into the sea. The flow of hot water here is around 50°C; test the water with your hand before entering, and, if necessary, enter one of the adjoining pools that contain mostly seawater. The signs to this onsen are irregular; just try to work north and a little east over the waist of the island.

Higashi Onsen (東温泉), on the south coast, about a 3km walk east of the port and right below Iō-dake, is a much more appealing choice (and much easier to find). There are three rock-lined pools of varying temperatures looking out over the Pacific. The view is dominated by an offshore rock spire that looks like one of the fellows from Easter Island decided to relocate to Japan.

Tucked below the cliffs about 250m to the west of the pier, the Iō-jima **camping** area is free and open year-round, and you can use the showers at the swimming pool next door for ¥300. If you're looking for a roof over your head, **Minshuku Gajmaru** (民宿ガジュマル;

(☎ 2-2105; r per person with 2 meals from ¥6000) is a friendly, simple *minshuku*, roughly in the middle of the little village, a five-minute walk from the pier (ask anyone for directions). Be sure to have a Japanese speaker call in advance to reserve.

Mishima Sonei Ferry (☎ 099-222-3141) operates the ferry *Mishima* three times a week between Kagoshima and Iō-jima, generally leaving Kagoshima at 9.30am and arriving at Iō-jima four hours later (¥3500).

TOKARA-RETTŌ トカラ列島

pop 700

The Tokara-rettō is a group of seven inhabited and five uninhabited volcanic islands strung out between Yakushima and Amami-Ōshima. The total population of the island chain is only 550 and even for Japanese, these islands seem like the end of the world. The islands aren't really beach destinations, but they do offer hiking, fishing and plentiful onsen. There are *minshuku* on the inhabited islands and camping is also possible. Pictures of the islands and *minshuku* information can be found on the **Tokara website** (www.tokara.jp, in Japanese).

Nakagawa Unyu (Ferry Toshima; ☎ 099-219-1191) has a ferry that leaves Kagoshima on Mondays and Fridays, and stops at each inhabited island down the chain to Takara-jima (the Monday departure continues on to Naze on Amami-Ōshima). The return trip leaves Takara-jima on Wednesdays and Sundays. Check departure dates and times before turning up as they can vary and are affected by typhoons. Second-class travel between Kagoshima and Takarajima costs ¥7800 and takes about 13 hours.

Travelling from north to south, the ferry visits Kuchino-shima (口之島), Nakano-shima (中之島), Taira-jima (平島), Suwanose-jima (諏訪之瀬島), Akuseki-jima (悪石島), Kodakara-jima (小宝島) and Takara-jima (宝島). A large pod of dolphins is regularly spotted between Akuseki-jima and Kodakara-jima – stay on deck for this leg. Even if you don't see any dolphins, you will certainly see lots of flying fish.

AMAMI-SHOTŌ 奄美諸島

The southernmost island group in Kagoshima-ken is Amami-shotō. Amami-Ōshima, the largest and most popular island, lies at the northern end of the group. It serves as the main transport hub and boasts excellent beaches, as well as dense jungle. The other islands in the chain are dominated by sugarcane fields but also have some good beaches. Heading south, Tokunoshima is famous for its 'bovine sumo', Okinoerabu-jima has intriguing caves and tiny Yoron-tō is fringed with excellent beaches.

Amami-Ōshima 奄美大島

☎ 0997 / pop 70,000

Some 350km southwest of Kagoshima, Amami-Ōshima is Japan's third-largest offshore island after Okinawa-hontō and Sado-ga-shima. With a mild subtropical climate year-round, the island is home to some unusual flora and fauna, including tree ferns and mangrove forests. The coastline of the island is incredibly convoluted – a succession of bays, points and inlets, punctuated by the occasional white-sand beach – making the island an interesting alternative to islands further south. Ferry access from Tokyo, Osaka/Kōbe and Kagoshima sweetens the deal for backpackers.

ORIENTATION & INFORMATION

The main city and port, **Naze** (名瀬), is on the north coast. The island's tiny airport is 55 minutes away by bus (¥1100, almost hourly, buses are timed to meet flights) on the northeast coast. The best beaches are at the northeast end of the island. There's a small **tourist information counter** (☎ 63-2295; 🕓 8.30am-6.45pm) in the airport arrivals hall that can help with maps and bus schedules, but nothing at the ferry terminal. **Amami Nangoku Travel Service** (☎ 53-0085) in the centre of Naze, across from the Amami Sun Plaza Hotel, is a useful travel agency that can help with ferry and air bookings.

SIGHTS & ACTIVITIES

The closest beach to Naze, **Ōhama-Kaihin-kōen**, is popular for swimming, snorkelling and sea kayaking in summer. It can get crowded and it's not as nice as beaches further afield, but it's convenient. Take an Ōhama-bound bus from Naze and get off at the Ōhama stop (¥400).

For a really stunning beach, head to **Sakibaru Kaigan**, which is about 4.5km down a point of land just north of Kise (about 20km northeast of Naze). Take a Sani-bound bus from Naze and get off at Kiseura (¥950), and then walk. If you're driving, it's marked in English off the main road (be prepared for *narrow* roads).

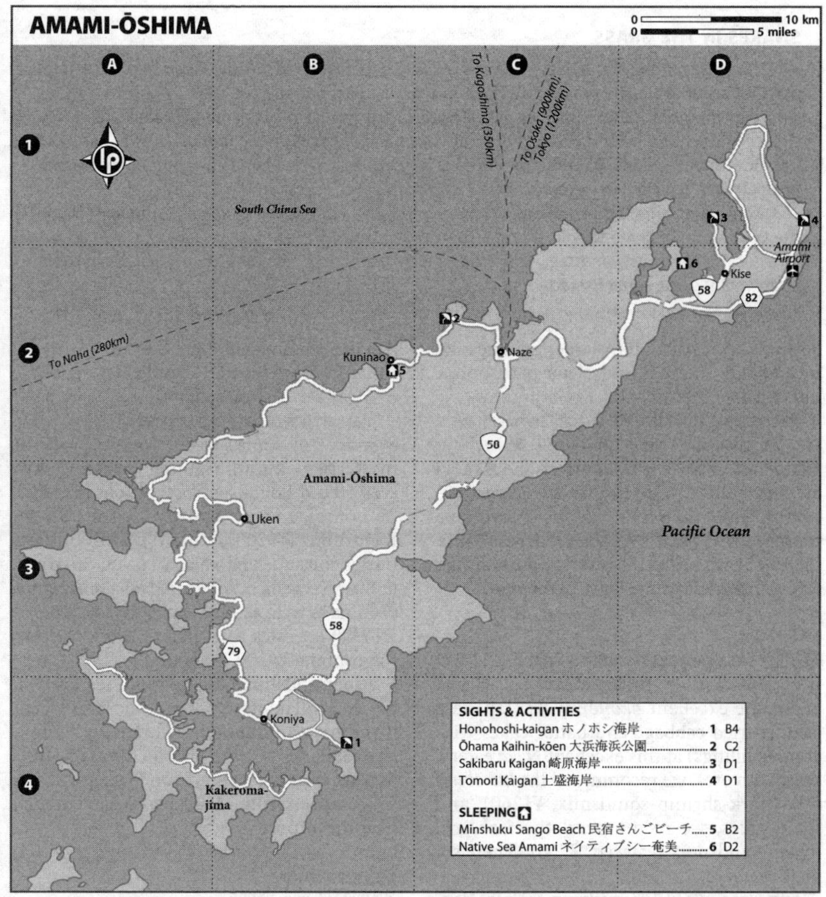

It's easier to get to **Tomori Kaigan**, which also offers brilliant white sand and some great snorkelling with a channel leading outside the reef. It's about 3km north of the airport. Take a Sani-bound bus from Naze and get off at Tomori (¥1210).

Amami-Ōshima is a great island to explore by touring bicycle or rental car. The coastal route out to **Uken** (宇検) on the west coast has some lovely stretches. Another option is to take Rte 58 south to **Koniya** (古仁屋), from where you can continue southwest to the **Honohoshi-kaigan** (ホノホシ海岸), a rocky beach with incredible coastal formations, or you can catch a ferry to **Kakeroma-jima** (加計呂麻島), a small island with a few shallow beaches.

SLEEPING

Minshuku Tatsuya Ryokan (☎ 52-0260; r per person with/without meals ¥4500/3000; Ⓟ) If you're looking for a bargain in Naze, this foreigner-friendly ryokan has simple but acceptable rooms and a kindly, informative owner. It's roughly in the centre of town, near the Hotel New Amami.

Minshuku Sango Beach (☎ 57-2580; per person with 2 meals from ¥6000) Overlooking a lovely sand beach in the village of Kuninao, this laid back *minshuku* has a vaguely Southeast Asian feeling. Guests sleep in three semidetached units and meals are taken overlooking the sea. Look for the sign that reads 'yes we speak English'.

Amami Sun Plaza Hotel (☎ 53-5151; s from ¥6500; Ⓟ) In the centre of Naze, this well-run

SNAKES IN THE GRASS

Any discussion of the Southwest Islands eventually gets around to 'deadly' habu snakes. Perhaps it's a reflection of Japan's severe shortage of real dangers, but you could easily get the impression that the poor habu, a species of pit viper, is the world's most dangerous snake, and that there's one waiting behind every tree, shrub, bush and barstool on the islands. They're hardly so prolific – the most likely place to see one is at a mongoose-versus-habu fight put on for tourists, or floating in a jar of very expensive (and slightly poisonous) sake.

Nevertheless, they are venomous! It's not a good idea to go barefoot when stomping through the bushes, though you should stomp – the vibrations will scare any snakes away. If you do get bitten, take it seriously and seek immediate medical advice as fatalities (though rare) can occur if antivenin is not administered.

business hotel has slightly larger than normal rooms and cramped but clean bathrooms. There is free internet and a restaurant.

Native Sea Amami (☎ 62-2385; www.native-sea.com; per person with 2 meals from ¥13,650; P) About 18km east of Naze (or 3km from the Akaogi bus stop), this dive centre-resort has nice accommodation in a room block perched on a promontory over a lovely bay. There is a nice shallow beach below the resort and the dining room and guest rooms have great views.

EATING

our pick **Okonomiyaki Mangetsu** (☎ 53-2052; 2-2-1F Irifune-cho, Naze; 11.30am-2.30am) Locals pile in for the excellent *okonomiyaki* (Japanese griddle-fried cabbage and batter cakes with various fillings) at this excellent Naze eatery. For carnivores, we recommend the *kurobuta* mix (pork-shrimp-squid mix, ¥1260), and for veggies, we recommend the *isobecchi* (cheese and nori seaweed, ¥750). There's a picture menu.

Burroughs (☎ 52-7306; meals from ¥800; 11am-midnight) Amami-Ōshima was the last place we expected to find a coffee shop named after American beat author William Burroughs, but Japan is always full of surprises. It doesn't serve a *Naked Lunch*, but it does have light meals and all the usual coffee drinks and you can browse its great book collection as you eat. Look for the tiny English sign above a locksmith's shop.

GETTING THERE & AWAY

Amami-Ōshima has flights to/from Tokyo (¥42,500, 2½ hours, one daily), Osaka (¥33,200, one hour 45 minutes, one daily) and Kagoshima (¥21,200, one hour, four daily) on JAL or JAC. RAC operates a daily flight between Naha and Amami-Ōshima (¥21,400, one hour). There are also flights between Amami-Ōshima and the other islands in the Amami group (see each island's Getting There & Away section for details).

Maruei Ferry/A Line (☎ in Kagoshima 099-226-4141; www.aline-ferry.com, in Japanese) operates four or five ferries a month running to/from Tokyo (¥20,500, 37 hours) and Osaka/Kobe (¥15,500, 29 hours), as well as daily ferries to/from Kagoshima (¥9200, 11 hours). Most of these ferries continue on to Naha, so you can travel in the reverse direction from Naha to Amami-Ōshima as well. **Amami Kaiun** (☎ in Kagoshima 099-222-2338) operates five ferries a week to/from Kagoshima (¥9200, 14 hours).

Amami-Ōshima has a good bus system, but you will definitely appreciate a rental car if you have an International Driving Permit. **Matsuda Renta Car** (☎ 63-0240) on the main street in Naze near the Amami Sun Plaza Hotel has subcompacts from ¥4500. It also has a branch near the airport.

Tokunoshima 徳之島

☎ 0997 / pop 28,000

Tokunoshima, the second-largest island in Amami-shotō, has some interesting coastal rock formations and a few good beaches. The island is famous for **tōgyū** (闘牛大会, bovine sumō), which has been practised on the island for more than 500 years. Other attractions include decent diving and snorkelling and views that occasionally call to mind parts of Hawaii.

On the island's east coast is the main port of **Kametoku-shinkō** (亀徳新港) and the main town of **Kametsu** (亀津). Tokunoshima's airport is on its west coast, not far from the secondary port of **Hetono** (平土野). A small **tourist information office** (徳之島観光協会; ☎ 82-0575; 9am-6pm Mon-Sat) at the ferry building has a detailed Japanese pamphlet and a simple English one about the island.

SIGHTS & ACTIVITIES

There are 13 official *tōgyu* venues on the island that stage around 20 tournaments a year. The three biggest events for the year are held in January, May and October – call the tourist office to confirm details as dates vary.

Several good beaches are dotted around the coast, including the excellent **Aze-Princess Beach** (畦プリンセスビーチ), which is near the Aze/Fruits Garden bus stop on the northeast coast.

About 9km north of the airport at the northwestern tip of the island, **Mushirose** (ムシロ瀬) is an interesting collection of wave-smoothed rocks that would make a great picnic spot. On a point on the southwest coast of the island, the **Innojō-futa** (犬の門蓋) is a collection of bizarrely eroded upthrust coral that includes a formation that resembles a giant pair of spectacles. It's hard to find and poorly marked. Look for it on the coast about 10km south of the airport.

SLEEPING

Aze Campground (畦キャンプ場; camping free; Ⓟ) This fine little camping ground at Aze Princess Beach has showers, nice grassy sites and a trail down to its own private beach.

Cōpo Shichifukujin (コーポ七福人; ☎ 82-2618; per person ¥3000) These slightly funky rooms in a converted apartment building have showers and kitchen facilities and are good for a cheap night in central Kametsu.

our pick **Kanami-sō** (金見荘; ☎ 84-9027; per person with 2 meals from ¥7350; Ⓟ) In the village of Kanami at the very northeast tip of the island, this friendly divers' lodge has a great location overlooking a good snorkelling beach. Some of the upstairs rooms have sweeping views and attached bathrooms. The place specialises in *ise ebi ryōri* (Japanese lobster cuisine).

GETTING THERE & AWAY

Tokunoshima has flights to/from Kagoshima (JAL; ¥24,600, one hour, two daily) and Amami-Ōshima (JAC; ¥12,200, 35 minutes, two daily).

Tukunoshima is served by Maruei/A Line ferries, which run between Kagoshima (some originating in Honshu) and Naha, and Amami Kaiun ferries, which run between Kagoshima and Okinoerabu-shima. See opposite for details.

There are bus stations at both ports, and a decent bus system to all parts of the island, but you'll definitely appreciate the convenience of a car, scooter or touring bicycle. **Toyota Renta Car** (トヨタレンタカー; ☎ 85-5089) is right outside Kametoku-shinkō pier. There are also car-rental places near the airport.

Okinoerabu-jima 沖永良部島

☎ 0997 / pop 15,000

About 33km southwest of Tokunoshima, Okinoerabu is a sugarcane-covered island with some excellent beaches, interesting coastal formations and a brilliant limestone cave. Perhaps the most appealing aspect of the island is the slightly retro down-at-the-heels feeling of **Wadomari** (和泊), the island's main town. You might feel like you've stepped out of a time machine as you walk the backstreets of the place.

The airport is at the eastern tip of the island, with **Wadomari-kō** (和泊港), the main port and town, 6km away on the east coast. There is a small **tourist information booth** (☎ 92-2901; ⏰ 8.30am-5pm) at Wadomari port on the 2nd floor of the terminal building, which has maps of the island (the office is next to the ferry ticket window).

SIGHTS & ACTIVITIES

There are excellent beaches all around the island, but one is worth a special mention: **Okidomari-kaigan** (沖泊海岸), at the northwest end of the island, about 3km east of Taminamisaki (see below). Backed by amphitheatre-like green cliffs, the white sand and offshore coral formations of this beach make it a must-see. You'll also find several 'secret' little beaches off of the coastal road between Fūcha (see below) and the airport.

On the southwest slopes of Ōyama (the mountain at the west end of the island), you will find the brilliant **Shōryūdō** (昇竜洞; ☎ 93-4536; admission ¥1000; ⏰ 8.30am-5pm), a limestone cave with 600m of walkways and illumination. When you come to the end, it's like emerging into a lost jungle world (lost being the operative word – follow the main asphalt road uphill for 400m to get back to the starting point). It's a few kilometres inland from the southwest coastal road.

The island's coast has many impressive geographical landforms. **Taminamisaki** (田皆崎), at the northwest tip of the island, has ancient coral that has been upthrust to form a 40m cliff. At the island's northeast tip, **Fūcha** (フーチャ) is a blowhole in the limestone rock, which shoots water 10m into the air on windy days.

A FOOD LOVER'S GUIDE TO OKINAWA

In the culinary lexicon of Japanese food, if *kansai-ryōri* (Kansai cuisine) is a different dialect, then Okinawan cuisine is a different language. Reflecting its geographic and historical isolation – Naha is closer both geographically and culturally to Taipei than Tokyo – the food of Okinawa and the Southwest Islands shares little in common with that of mainland Japan. Since it was only approximately 130 years ago that the Ryūkyū kingdom was incorporated into the country, the southern islands still have a strong sense of being caught between the two behemoth cultures of China and Japan.

Okinawan cuisine originated from the splendour of the Ryūkyū court and from the humble lives of the impoverished islanders. Healthy eating is considered to be extremely important. Indeed, island thought has long held that medicine and food are essentially one and the same. The Okinawan language actually splits foodstuffs into *kusui-mun* (medicinal foods) and *ujinīmum* (body-nutritious foods). Today the island's staple foods are pork, which is acidic and rich in protein, and *konbu* (a type of seaweed), which is alkaline and calorie free.

The humble pig often features in Okinawan food, and every part of the animal is used, from top to bottom. *Mimigā* (ミミガー), which is thinly sliced pig's ears marinated in vinegar, might not be at the top of every gourmand's must-try list. However, on a hot, sweltering night in Naha, it's the perfect accompaniment to a cold glass of Orion (オリオンビール), the extremely quaffable local lager. *Rafutē* (ラフテー), which is very similar to the mainland *buta-no-kakuni* (豚の角煮), is pork stewed with ginger, brown sugar, rice wine and soy sauce until it falls apart. If you're looking for a bit of stamina, you should also try an inky black bowl of *ikasumi-jiru* (イカスミ汁), which is stewed pork in black squid ink. Finally, try the *inamudotchi* (イナムドチ), a hearty stew of pork, fish, mushrooms, potatoes and miso that is said to be reminiscent of eating wild boar.

While stewing is common, Okinawans prefer stir-frying, and refer to the technique as *champurū* (チャンプルー). Perhaps the best known stir-fry is *gōya-champurū* (ゴーヤチャンプルー), which

SLEEPING & EATING

Okidomari Campground (沖泊キャンプ場; camping free; P) This excellent camping ground at Okidomari Kaigan beach has showers and large grassy areas with trees for shade.

Business Hotel Wadamari-kō (ビジネスホテル和泊港; ☎ 92-1189; s with breakfast ¥3500; P) A few minutes' walk from the port, this simple, cheap hotel looks more like a private house. It is on the left soon after exiting the pier area.

Kankō Hotel Azuma (観光ホテル東; ☎ 92-1283; r per person with 2 meals from ¥7300; P) In Wadomari, this friendly hotel looks a little worn, but the rooms are spacious and comfortable, and any place with a sign that reads 'We support foreign travellers' is OK by us. It's a little hard to spot: from the Menshiori Shopping Street (when coming from port), take the first right then the first left.

Mouri Mouri (☎ 92-0538; meals from ¥1500; dinner). Opposite the Kankō Hotel Azuma, this is a friendly place for dinner in Wadomari. See if you can break the local beer-chugging record (that's skolling for Australians and Kiwis).

There are two minimarkets in town for self-catering.

GETTING THERE & AWAY

Okinoerabu has flights to/from Kagoshima (¥27,050, one hour 30 minutes, three daily), Amami-Ōshima (from ¥15,400, 35 minutes, one daily) and Yoron-tō (from ¥9200, 25 minutes, one daily) on JAC.

Okinoerabu-shima is served by Maruei/A Line ferries, which run between Kagoshima (some originating in Honshu) and Naha, and Amami Kaiun ferries, which run between Kagoshima and Okinoerabu-shima. See the Amami-Ōshima section (p770) for details.

The island has a decent bus system, but you'll definitely welcome the convenience of a car, scooter or touring bicycle. You'll find **Toyata Renta Car** (トヨタレンタカー; ☎ 92-2100) right outside the airport.

Yoron-tō 与論島 ・ヨロン島

☎ 0997 / pop 6000

A mere 5km across, tiny Yoron-tō is the southernmost island in Kagoshima-ken. On a good day, Okinawa-hontō's northernmost point of Hedo-misaki is clearly visible just 23km to the southwest. Fringed with picture-perfect white-sand beaches and extensive (if fairly dull) coral reefs, Yoron-tō is one of the most appealing islands in the Southwest Islands chain.

is a mix of pork, bitter melon and the island's unique tofu, *shima-dōfu* (島豆腐). *Shima-dōfu* is distinguished from the mainland variety by its sturdy consistency, which makes it especially suited to frying. Occasionally, you will come across an unusual variant known as *tōfuyō* (豆腐痒), which is sorely fermented, violently spicy and fluorescent pink – try small amounts from the end of a toothpick and do not eat the whole block!

The Okinawan working folk's food is *okinawa-soba* (沖縄そば), which is actually udon (thick white noodles) served in a pork broth. The most common variants are *sōki-soba* (ソーキそば), which contains pork spare ribs; and *shima-tōgarashi* (島とうがらし; pickled hot peppers in sesame oil) and *yaeyama-soba* (八重山そば), which contains thin white noodles akin to *sōmen*.

Others dishes to look out for include *hirayāchi* (ヒラヤーチ), which is a thin pancake of egg, vegetables and meat that is similar to the mainland *okonomiyaki* (お好み焼き). *Yagi-jiru* (山羊汁; goat soup) is an invigorating (albeit stinky) reminder of a past era when goats were traditionally slaughtered to celebrate the construction of a new house. On the island of Miyako-jima, look for *umi-budō* (海ぶどう), literally 'sea grapes', an oddly textured seaweed that is often described as 'green caviar'. Finally, there's nothing quite like a scoop (or two) of Blue Seal (ブルーシール) ice cream, an American favourite that was introduced to the island following WWII.

Okinawans are a gregarious and cheerful bunch who love their food almost as much as their drink. While travelling through the Southwest Islands, be sure to sample the local firewater, namely *awamori* (泡盛), which is distilled from rice and has an alcohol content of 30% to 60%. Although it's usually served *mizu-wari* (水割り; diluted with water), this is seriously lethal stuff, especially the *habushu* (ハブ酒), which comes with a small habu snake (see the boxed text, p770) coiled in the bottom of the bottle. If you're hitting the *awamori* hard, take our advice and cancel your plans for the next day (or two).

The harbour is next to the airport on the western tip of the island, while the main town of **Chabana** (茶花) is 1km to the east. Beside the city office in Chabana is the useful **tourist information office** (ヨロン島観光協会; ☎ 97-5151; ⌚ 8.30am-5.30pm), which provides maps, an English pamphlet and can make accommodation bookings.

SIGHTS & ACTIVITIES

On the eastern side of the island, Yoron's best beach is the popular **Oganeku-kaigan** (大金久海岸). About 500m offshore from Oganeku-kaigan is Yurigahama (百合ヶ浜), a stunning stretch of white sand that disappears completely at high tide. Boats (¥1000 return) putter back and forth, ferrying visitors out to it. Other good beaches include **Maehama-kaigan** (前浜海岸), on the southeast coast, and **Terasaki-kaigan** (寺崎海岸), on the northeast coast.

At the island's southeastern tip, the excellent **Yoron Minzoku-mura** (与論民族村; ☎ 97-2934; admission ¥400; ⌚ 9am-6pm) is a collection of traditional thatch-roof island dwellings and storehouses that contain exhibits on the island's culture and history. If at all possible, bring along a Japanese speaker, as the owner is an incredible source of information on the island.

The **Southern Cross Center** (サザンクロスセンター; ☎ 97-3396; admission ¥300; ⌚ 9am-6pm), a short walk from the Ishini (石仁) bus stop 3km south of Chabana, is a five-storey concrete lookout that serves as a museum of Yoron and Amami history and culture. Offering good views south to Okinawa, the museum's name celebrates the fact that Yoron-tō is the northernmost island in Japan from which the Southern Cross can be seen.

SLEEPING & EATING

The following places are all in Chabana.

Minshuku Nankai-sō (民宿南海荘; ☎ 97-2145; fax 43-0888; r per person with/without meals ¥5500/3000; Ⓟ) This simple *minshuku* offers simple accommodation, shared bathrooms and a laid-back communal atmosphere. To get there from the tourist office, turn your back to the office, walk straight into the opposite street and look for it on your right. Staff will pick you up if you phone ahead.

Shiomi-sō (汐見荘; ☎ 97-2167; per person with meals from ¥5500; Ⓟ 💻) This friendly and casual *minshuku* is popular with young people. Starting from Chabana harbour, take the main road north (uphill) out of town and look for it on the left after the turn; it looks like a private house. Staff will pick you up if you phone ahead.

Hotel Seikai-sō (ホテル青海荘; ☎ 97-2046; per person with meals from ¥6300; Ⓟ) This simple hotel on the main street in Chabana is well run, clean and comfortable. It's a good choice if you want a Western-style room and privacy.

Izakaya Kayoi-bune (居酒屋かよい舟; ☎ 97-3189; meals from ¥1200; 🕑 dinner) On the main street in Chabana, just a little north of the Hotel Seikai-sō (on the same side of the street), you will find this simple *izakaya* that serves the usual fried suspects and island fish dishes. There is a picture menu. Look for the blue, red and white sign and the red lantern.

In addition, there are two minimarkets in the centre of Chabana.

GETTING THERE & AWAY

Yoron-tō has direct flights to/from Kagoshima (JAC; ¥28,400, one hour 20 minutes, one daily), Okinoerabu-shima (JAC; ¥9200, 40 minutes, one daily, with connections onward to Amami-Ōshima) and Naha (RAC; ¥13,000, 40 minutes, one daily).

Yoron-tō is served by Maruei/A Line ferries, which run between Kagoshima (some originating in Honshu) and Naha, and Amami Kaiun ferries, which run between Kagoshima and Okinoerabu-shima. See the Amami-Ōshima section (p770) for details.

Yoron-tō has a bus system, but you'll definitely appreciate the convenience of a car, scooter or touring bicycle. **Yoron-tō Kankō Rentacar** (ヨロン島観光レンタカー; ☎ 97-5075), located in Chabana, will meet car-rental clients at the airport.

OKINAWA-KEN 沖縄県

pop 1.35 million

Japan's southernmost prefecture, Okinawa-ken, makes up the southern half of the Southwest Islands. The prefecture stretches from the southern islands in Kagoshima-ken to within 110km of Taiwan. Three island groups make up the prefecture: Okinawa-shotō, Miyako-shotō and Yaeyama-shotō.

The northernmost island group is Okinawa-shotō, which contains Okinawa-hontō (meaning 'Okinawa Main Island' in Japanese). The largest island in the chain, Okinawa-hontō is home to the prefectural capital, Naha. This bustling city is Okinawa-ken's transport hub, and is easily accessed by flights and ferries to/from the mainland. Plentiful ferries run between Naha and Kerama-shotō, which lie about 30km west of Okinawa-hontō. The Kerama islands offer excellent beaches and brilliantly clear water.

Located 300km southwest of Okinawa-hontō, the middle group of islands in Okinawa-ken is Miyako-shotō, which is home to the popular beach destination of Miyako-jima. There is no ferry access to this group; you must arrive via flights from the mainland, Naha or Ishigaki.

The southernmost island group is Yaeyama-shotō, a further 100km southwest. This island group includes the coral-fringed island of Ishigaki and the nearby jungle-clad Iriomote-jima. Like Miyako-shotō, there are no ferries to this group; only flights from the mainland, Naha or Miyako-jima.

OKINAWA-HONTŌ 沖縄本島

☎ 098

Okinawa-hontō is the largest island in the Southwest Islands, and the historical seat of power of the Ryūkyū dynasty. Although its cultural differences with mainland Japan were once evident in its architecture, almost all traces were completely obliterated in WWII. Fortunately, Allied bombing wasn't powerful enough to completely stamp out other remnants of Okinawan culture, and today the island is home to a unique culinary, artistic and musical tradition.

Okinawa-hontō is a place where cultures collide: Ryūkyū, Japanese, American, Chinese and a growing number of Korean, Taiwanese and Hong Kong tourists. It is a place of delicious contrasts and juxtapositions, and the better you know Japan, the more you'll find yourself wondering, Where the heck am I?

In addition, the island is home to some excellent beaches, delicious food and friendly people, many of whom speak a little more English than their mainland counterparts. Of course, with United States Air Force jets flying overhead from time to time, it's hard to forget the reality of the continuing American military presence on the island and the history behind that presence (for more details, see the boxed text, p780).

Okinawa-hontō is home to the prefectural capital and largest city, Naha, which serves as a transportation hub for the other islands in the prefecture. War memorials are clustered in

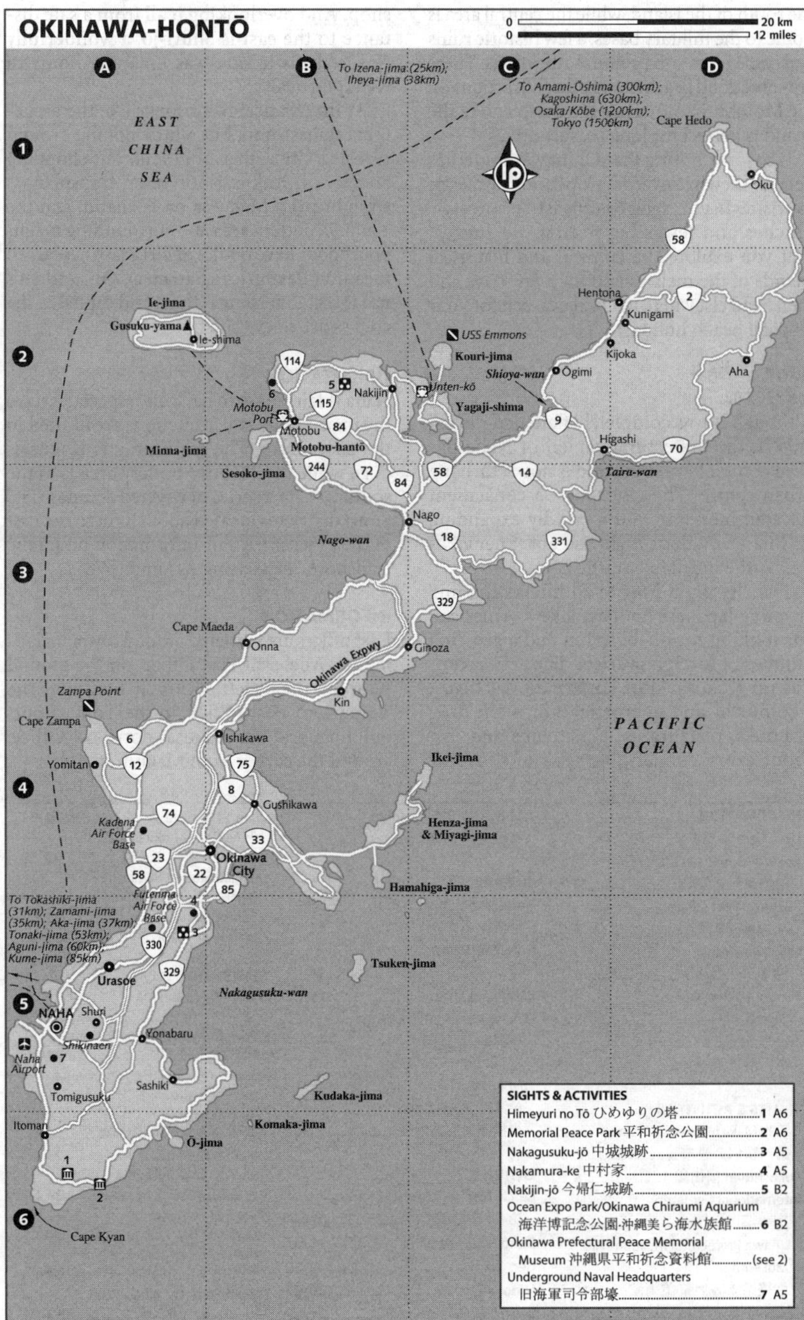

SIGHTS & ACTIVITIES

Himeyuri no Tō ひめゆりの塔 1 A6
Memorial Peace Park 平和祈念公園 2 A6
Nakagusuku-jō 中城城跡 3 A5
Nakamura-ke 中村家 4 A5
Nakijin-jō 今帰仁城跡 5 B2
Ocean Expo Park/Okinawa Chiraumi Aquarium 海洋博記念公園·沖縄美ら海水族館 6 B2
Okinawa Prefectural Peace Memorial Museum 沖縄県平和祈念資料館 (see 2)
Underground Naval Headquarters 旧海軍司令部壕 7 A5

the south of the island, while the central area is home to the military bases, a few historic ruins and some interesting cultural attractions. There are some good beaches and other attractions on the Motobu-hantō, while the north end of the island is perfect for long seaside drives.

It's worth noting that Okinawa-hontō has been somewhat overdeveloped for domestic tourism. If you seek Southeast Asian–style beaches and fewer big resorts, we suggest that you explore the cultural and historical islands of the main island for a few days and then head elsewhere in Okinawa-ken for your tropical beach holiday.

Naha 那覇

pop 320,000

Although it was completely flattened during WWII, the prefectural capital of Naha has been completely rebuilt and is now a thriving urban centre. The city sports a convenient elevated monorail and a rapidly expanding skyline of modern high-rise apartments, as well as the inevitable traffic jams.

The city plays host to an interesting mix of young Japanese holidaymakers, American GIs looking for off-base fun and a growing number of foreign tourists. The action centres on Kokusai-dōri (International Blvd), a colourful and energetic 2km main drag of hotels, restaurants, bars, clubs and just about every conceivable type of souvenir shop. And overlooking it all from a safe distance to the east is Shuri-jō, a wonderfully restored castle that was once the home of Ryūkyū royalty.

At first glance, Naha looks like the archetypal tourist trap, but a little poking around reveals a city with a lot of soul. The shopping arcades off Kokusai-dōri seem transplanted straight from Malaysia or Thailand, and the Tsuboya pottery area and surrounding neighbourhoods have oodles of *aji* (a Japanese word meaning flavour or character). Oh, and let's not forget that Naha is the world capital of the cool short-sleeve shirt.

ORIENTATION

Naha is fairly easy to navigate, especially since the main sights and attractions are located in the city centre. The main drag is Kokusai-dōri, while the Tsuboya pottery area is to the southeast via a series of covered arcades. The Shuri district is located about 3km to the east of the city centre. For information on public transport, see Getting Around (p781).

INFORMATION

Post offices are scattered around town, including the Miebashi Post Office, on the ground floor of the Palette Kumoji building, the Tomari-kō Post Office, in the Tomari port building, and the Kokusai-dōri Post Office, around the corner from Makishi station.

INFORMATION

Gera Gera ネットカフェ **1** D2
Kokusai-dōri Post Office 国際通り郵便局 **2** E2
Miebashi Post Office 美栄橋郵便局 **3** C3
Okinawa Tourist 沖縄ツーリスト **4** C3
Tomari-kō Post Office 泊港郵便局 **5** C1
Tourist Information Office 那覇観光案内所 **6** D2

SIGHTS & ACTIVITIES

Daichi Makishi Kōsetsu Ichiba 第一牧志公設市場 **7** D3
Fukushū-en 福州園 **8** B2
International Cemetery 国際墓地 **9** D1
Okinawa Prefectural Museum/Art Museum 沖縄県立博物館·美術館 **10** E1
Sōgen-ji 崇元寺 **11** E2
Tsuboya Pottery Museum 壷屋焼物博物館 **12** E3

SLEEPING

Hotel Marine West Naha ホテルマリンウエスト那覇 ... **13** B3
Hotel Sun Palace ホテルサンパレス **14** C3
Kashiwaya 柏屋 **15** D3
Okinawa International Youth Hostel 沖縄国際ユースホステル **16** B4
Tōyoko Inn Naha Asahibashi-eki-mae 東横イン旭橋駅前 **17** B3

EATING

Daichi Makishi Kōsetsu Ichiba 第一牧志公設市場 .... (see 7)
Daitō Soba 大東そば **18** D2
Gen 玄 **19** C2
Minoya みの家 **20** C3
Swan II 白鳥２ .... **21** C3
Swan 白鳥 **22** C2
Uchina Chaya Buku Buku うちなー茶屋ぶくぶく **23** E3
Yakiniku Station Bambohe 焼肉ステーション Bambohe **24** D2
Yūnangi ゆうなんぎい **25** C3

TRANSPORT

Ferries to Aguni-jima 粟国フェリー **26** C1
Ferries to Aka-jima, Zamami-jima 阿嘉島 **27** D1
Ferries to Kume-jima, Tonaki-jima, Minami-daitō-jima, Kita-daitō-jima 久米島·渡名喜島·南大東島 北大東島·フェリー **28** C1
Ferries to Tokashiki-jima 渡嘉敷島フェリー **29** D1
Naha Bus Terminal 那覇バスターミナル **30** C3
Naha-kō Ferry Terminal Building 那覇港フェリーターミナル .. **31** B3
Tomari Ferry Terminal 泊フェリー乗り場 **32** D1

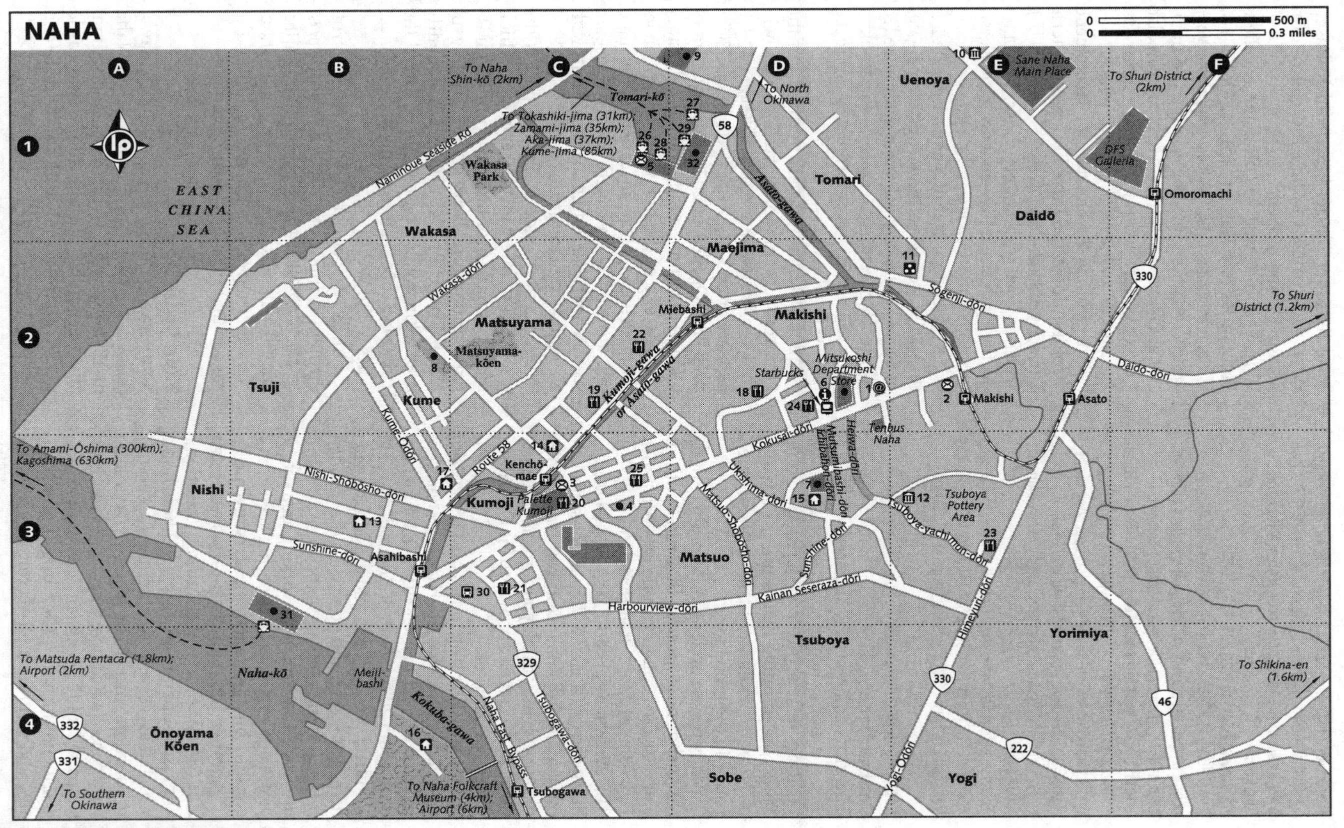

OKINAWA & THE SOUTHWEST ISLANDS

Gera Gera (☎ 863-5864; 2-4-14 Makishi; per hr ¥480; ⏲ 24hr) A convenient net cafe on Kokusai-dōri. It's just a little east of the Family Mart convenience store, on the 2nd floor.
Okinawa Tourist (☎ 862-1111; 1-2-3 Matsuo; ⏲ 9.30am-6.30pm, closed Sun) On Kokusai-dōri, a competent travel agency with English speakers who can help with all manner of ferry and flight bookings.
Tourist information counter (☎ 857-6884; Arrivals Terminal, Naha airport; ⏲ 9am-9pm) At this helpful prefectural counter, we suggest picking up a copy of the *Naha City Guide Map* before heading into town. If you plan to explore outside Naha, also grab a copy of the *Okinawa Guide Map*.
Tourist information office (☎ 868-4887; ⏲ 8.30am-8pm Mon-Fri, 10am-8pm Sat & Sun) The city office also has free maps. It's just off Kokusai-dōri (turn at Starbucks).

SIGHTS & ACTIVITIES

Central Naha 那覇中心街

The city's main artery, **Kokusai-dōri** (国際通り), is a riot of neon, noise, souvenir shops, bustling restaurants and Japanese young things out strutting their stuff. It's a festival of tat and tackiness, but it's a good time if you're in the mood for it.

Many people prefer the atmosphere of the three shopping arcades that run south off Kokusai-dōri roughly opposite Mitsukoshi Department Store: **Ichibahon-dōri** (市場本道り), **Mutsumibashi-dōri** (むつみ橋通り) and **Heiwa-dōri** (平和通り). Prepare for some serious cognitive dissonance as you explore these places: you may think you somehow stepped through a secret passageway to the Chinatown district of Bangkok.

Our favourite stop in this area is the **Daichi Makishi Kōsetsu Ichiba** (2-10-1 Matsuo; ⏲ 10am-8pm), a covered food market just off Ichibahon-dōri, about 200m south of Kokusai-dōri. The colourful variety of fish and produce on offer here is amazing, and don't miss the wonderful local restaurants upstairs. Keep in mind, however, that this is a working market, so please don't get in the way of shopkeepers and consider buying something as a souvenir.

Another highlight is the **Tsuboya pottery area** (壷屋). More than a dozen traditional kilns still operate in this neighbourhood, which has served as a centre of ceramic production since 1682, when Ryūkyū kilns were consolidated here by royal decree. Most shops sell all the popular Okinawan ceramics, including *shiisā* (lion-dog roof guardians) and containers for serving *awamori*, the local firewater. To get here from Kokusai-dōri, walk south through the Heiwa-dōri arcade for about 350m.

In Tsuboya, you will find the excellent **Tsuboya Pottery Museum** (☎ 862-3761; 1-9-32 Tsuboya; admission ¥315; ⏲ 10am-6pm, closed Mon), which contains some fine examples of traditional Okinawan pottery. Here you can also inspect potters' wheels and inspect *arayachi* (unglazed) and *jōyachi* (glazed) pieces.

After visiting the museum, we recommend strolling down the incredibly atmospheric **Tsuboya-yachimun-dōri** (壺屋やちむん通り), which is lined with pottery shops. The lanes off the main street here contain some classic crumbling old Okinawan houses.

At the eastern end of Kokusai-dōri, a left turn will take you to the reconstructed gates of **Sōgen-ji**. The original stone gates once led to the 16th-century temple of the Ryūkyū kings, though it was unfortunately destroyed in WWII.

About 15 minutes' walk northwest of the Omuromachi monorail station, you will find the **Okinawa Prefectural Museum** (☎ 941-8200; Omuromachi 3-1-1; admission ¥400; ⏲ 9am-5.30pm, closed Mon). Opened in 2007, this museum of Okinawa's history, culture and natural history is easily one of the best museums in Japan. Displays are well laid out, easy to understand and attractively presented. The art museum section holds interesting special exhibits with an emphasis on local artists.

On the north side of Tomari port is the fascinating **international cemetery**, which has a small monument commemorating Commodore Perry's 1852 landing in Naha. The US naval officer subsequently used Okinawa as a base while he forced the Tokugawa shōgunate to finally open Japanese ports to the West.

Finally, garden fans should take a stroll through Chinese-style **Fukushū-en** (Map p777; ☎ 869-5384; 2-29 Kume; admission free; ⏲ 9am-6pm Thu-Tue). All materials were brought from Fuzhou, Naha's sister city in China, including the pagoda that sits atop a small waterfall.

Shuri District 首里

Shuri was the original capital of Okinawa, though the title was surrendered to Naha in 1879 just prior to the Meiji Restoration. Shuri's temples, shrines, tombs and castle were all destroyed in WWII, but the castle and surrounding structures were rebuilt in 1992.

The reconstructed castle, **Shuri-jō** (首里城; ☎ 886-2020; admission ¥800; 🕑 9am-5.30pm), sits atop a hilltop in the centre of Shuri, overlooking the urban sprawl of modern-day Naha. It was originally built in the 14th century and served as the administrative centre and royal residence of the Ryūkyū kingdom until the 19th century.

Enter through the Kankai-mon (歓会門) and proceed up to the Hōshin-mon (奉神門), which forms the entryway to the inner sanctum of the castle, dominated by the impressive **Seiden** (正殿). Visitors can enter the Seiden, which contains exhibits on the castle and the Okinawan royals. There is also a small collection of displays in the nearby Hokuden.

While you're at the castle, be sure to visit the **Irino-Azana** (西のアザナ), a viewpoint about 200m west of the Seiden that affords great views over Naha and as far as Kerama-shotō.

To reach the complex, take the Yui-rail monorail to its eastern terminal, Shuri station. Exit to the west, go down the steps, walk straight, cross one big street, then a smaller one and go right on the opposite side, then walk about 350m and look for the signs on the left.

Around Naha 那覇周辺

Around 4km east of the city centre is the **Shikina-en** (識名園; ☎ 855-5936; admission ¥300; 🕑 9am-5pm closed Wed), a Chinese-style garden containing stone bridges, a viewing pavilion and a villa that belonged to the Ryūkyū royal family. Despite its flawless appearance, everything was painstakingly rebuilt after WWII. To reach the garden, take bus 2, 3 or 5 to the Shikinaen-mae stop (¥220, 20 minutes).

A three-minute walk from Akamine station (follow the English signs) is the **Naha Folkcraft Museum** (那覇市伝統工芸館; ☎ 868-7866; 2F Tenbusu Naha, 3-2-10 Makishi, Naha; admission ¥300; 🕑 9am-6pm, closed year-end & new-year holidays), which houses a detailed collection of traditional Okinawan crafts. Staff members are on hand to demonstrate glass-blowing, weaving and pottery-making in the workshops. Enter by 5.30pm.

FESTIVALS & EVENTS

Dragon-boat races Held in early May, particularly in Itoman and Naha. These races – called *hari* – are thought to bring luck and prosperity to the island's fishermen.

Ryūkyū-no-Saiten (琉球の祭典; end of October, three days) Brings together more than a dozen festivals and special events celebrating Okinawan culture.

Naha Ōzunahiki (那覇大綱引き) Takes place in Naha on Sunday around the national Sports Day Holiday in October, and features large teams that compete in the world's biggest tug of war, using a gigantic 1m-thick rope weighing over 40 tonnes.

SLEEPING

Naha is the most convenient base for exploring Okinawa-hontō.

Kashiwaya (☎ 869-8833; www.88smile.com/kasiwaya; 2-12-22 Wakasa; dm ¥1500, r per person ¥3000; Ⓟ 💻) Conveniently located just off Kokusai-dōri, near the Daiichi Makishi Kōsetsu Market, this funky guest house has a variety of basic accommodation for backpackers. The place has a laid-back vibe and a cool bar-restaurant downstairs that's worth a visit even if you aren't staying.

Okinawa International Youth Hostel (☎ 857-0073; www.jyh.gr.jp/okinawa/english.htm; 51 Ōnoyama; dm HI member/nonmember ¥3360/3960; Ⓟ 💻) This excellent youth hostel is located in Ōnoyama-kōen, a five-minute walk from the Asahibashi station (cross to the far side of Meiji-bashi). If you're walking from Asahibashi station, turn left at the torii (shrine gate).

Tōyoko Inn Naha Asahibashi-eki-mae (☎ 951-1045; www.toyoko-inn.com/e_hotel/00076/; 2-1-20 Kume; s/d from ¥5460/8190; Ⓟ 💻) Just a short walk north of Kokusai-dōri, the Tōyoko is a good-value business hotel with small but serviceable rooms and useful features like free internet and washing machines. It's one of the better values in this price range.

our pick **Hotel Sun Palace** (☎ 863-4181; www.palace-okinawa.com/sunpalace, in Japanese; 2-5-1 Kumoji; per person with breakfast from ¥6500; Ⓟ 💻) About 10 minutes' walk from Kokusai-dōri, the Sun Palace is a step up from a standard business hotel. The fairly spacious rooms have interesting design touches and some have balconies.

Hotel Marine West Naha (☎ 863-0055; www.marine-west.jp, in Japanese; 2-5-1 Kumoji; s/tw from ¥5040/9450; Ⓟ 💻) A short walk west of Kokusai-dōri, this converted apartment building has comfortable rooms, a pleasant breakfast nook and free internet, as well as helpful staff. It's popular with divers and there's a gear storage and drying room on the ground floor.

EATING

Naha is the perfect spot to sample the full range of Okinawan cuisine. For descriptions of the Okinawan dishes mentioned in this section, see the boxed text (p772).

AMERICAN BASES IN OKINAWA

The US officially returned Okinawa to Japanese administration in 1972, but it negotiated a Status of Forces Agreement that guaranteed the Americans the right to use large tracts of Okinawan land for military bases, most of which are on Okinawa-hontō. At present, out of a total of 85 American bases on Japanese soil, 33 are located in Okinawa. These bases are home to approximately 24,000 American servicemen.

Although the bases provide a certain amount of economic support to the island economy, they are a continual sore spot for islanders, due to occasional crimes committed by American servicemen. Antibase feelings peaked in 1996, when three American servicemen abducted and raped a 12-year-old Okinawan girl. Similar incidents in recent years have perpetuated animosity towards the Americans.

Okinawans rightly believe that by playing host to the bulk of American forces stationed in Japan, they are once again being sacrificed by Tokyo. (The original sacrifice, of course, came when Tokyo used Okinawa as a buffer to slow the American invasion of mainland Japan.) Various Okinawan governors and citizens groups have pleaded with the national government to remove the bases. So far, their pleas have gone unanswered.

At the time of writing, various plans are in the works to move some of the bases away from the most populous areas of Okinawa-hontō to less crowded areas, or to offshore bases. In addition, there are plans to move about 6000 servicemen to a base in Guam, but US military officials have said that this might not occur until as late as 2015.

Tourists to Okinawa are surprised to find that the servicemen stationed in Okinawa keep a relatively low profile. Unless one ventures to the areas north of Naha, where most are stationed, it is possible to spend a few days in Okinawa without even noticing their presence. In fact, you could almost forget that the island is under occupation, until another American fighter jet goes screaming overhead.

Daitō Soba (☎ 867-3889; 1-4-59 Makishi; 🕑 11am-9pm) This little noodle house is the perfect spot for sampling your first bowl of *okinawa-soba* (¥500, ask for *daitō-soba*). It's one block north of Kokusai-dōri; look for the yellow banner and lantern. Last order 8.30pm.

Yakiniku Station Bambohe (☎ 861-4129; 1-3-47 Makishi; 🕑 11am-11pm) If you've got a big appetite, try this place for an all-you-can-eat *yakiniku* (Korean barbecue) feast, which will only set you back ¥1860 for men and ¥1700 for women. The restaurant is just off Kokusai-dōri, across from the tourist information office.

Minoya (☎ 869-4955; 9th fl, Palette Kumoji Shopping Mall; 🕑 11am-10pm) This restaurant has zero ambience, but it serves tasty versions of all the local favourites. There's a picture menu with such standards as *sōki-soba* (¥650) and *gōya-teishoku* (set-course meal with bitter melon; ¥850). You'll see the restaurant as you emerge from the elevators; look for the black-and-yellow sign.

our pick **Gen** (☎ 861-0429; 2-6-23 Kumoji; 🕑 11.30am-2pm & 5pm-midnight) This atmospheric *yakiniku* place is one of our favourite places in Naha for a good meal. If you're a carnivore and want some excellent grilled meat washed down with great *awamori*, this is the place. Look for the English sign at the bottom of the steps. If you can't speak Japanese, ask your accommodation owner to call and order the *yakiniku* course (¥3500 per person) as it must be ordered in advance.

Swan (☎ 927-9135; Kumoji; 🕑 5pm-midnight, closed Sun) Literally a hole in the wall, this unusual little *yakitori* joint serves great grilled chicken and island pork (known as *yanbaru shima buta*). If you can't read or speak Japanese, just order a *makase* course (set course: seven sticks ¥1000, 14 sticks ¥2000). Look for the picnic tables outside. There's a bigger branch (Swan II) near the Naha bus terminal.

Yūnangi (☎ 867-3765; 3-3-3 Kumoji; 🕑 noon-3pm & 5.30pm-10pm, closed Sun & national holidays) You'll be lucky to get a seat here, but if you do, you'll be treated to some of the best Okinawan food around, served in atmospheric traditional surroundings. Try the *okinawa-soba* set (¥1400). Look for the wooden sign with white letters in Japanese and the plants.

Uchina Chaya Buku Buku (☎ 861-2950; 1-28-3 Tsuboya; 🕑 10am-4.30pm, closed Wed) This incredibly atmospheric tea house near the east end of the Tsuboya pottery area is worth a special trip. It takes its name from the traditional frothy Okinawan tea served here: *buku buku cha*. It's up a small lane just north of Tsuboya-yachimun-dōri.

Daichi Makishi Kōsetsu Ichiba (2-10-1 Matsuo; meals from ¥800; 10am-8pm) We highly recommend a meal at one of the eateries on the 2nd floor of this food market. It's pointless to make a recommendation; have a look at what the locals are eating and grab a seat.

GETTING THERE & AWAY

Air

Naha International Airport (OKA) has international air connections with Seoul, Taipei, Hong Kong and Shanghai. Connections with mainland Japan include Kagoshima (¥24,100, one hour 25 minutes), Hiroshima (¥29,400, two hours), Osaka (¥31,400, two hours 15 minutes), Nagoya (¥35,600, two hours 25 minutes), Tokyo (¥37,500, two hours 45 minutes) and Sapporo (¥54,400, three hours 40 minutes). Note that this is only a partial list; most large Japanese cities have flights (check with your travel agent).

Naha also has air connections with Kume-jima, Aka-jima, Miyako-jima Ishigaki-jima and Yoron-tō, among other Southwest Islands. See the relevant sections for details.

Ferry

Naha has regular ferry connections with ports in Honshū (Tokyo and Osaka/Kōbe) and Kyūshū (Kagoshima).

Maruei Ferry/A Line (☎ in Naha 861-1886, in Tokyo 03-5643-6170; www.aline-ferry.com, in Japanese) operates four or five ferries a month running to/from Tokyo (¥24,500, 46 hours) and Osaka/Kobe (¥19,600, 42 hours), as well as daily ferries to/from Kagoshima (¥14,600, 25 hours).

There are three ports in Naha, and this can be confusing: Kagoshima/Amami-shotō ferries operate from Naha-kō (Naha Port); Tokyo/Osaka/Kōbe ferries operate from Naha Shin-kō; and Kume-jima and Kerama-shotō ferries operate from Tomari-kō (Tomari Port).

GETTING AROUND

The Yui-rail monorail is perfect for exploring Naha. The line runs from Naha International Airport in the south to Shuri in the north. Prices range from ¥200 to ¥290. Kenchō-mae station is at the western end of Kokusai-dōri, while Makishi station is at its eastern end.

Naha-kō is a 10-minute walk southwest from Asahibashi station, while Tomari-kō is a similar distance north from Miebashi station. Bus 101 from Naha bus terminal heads further north to Naha Shin-kō (20 minutes, hourly).

When riding on local town buses, simply dump ¥200 into the slot next to the driver as you enter. For longer trips, take a ticket showing your starting point as you board and pay the appropriate fare as you disembark. Buses run from Naha to destinations all over the island.

A rental car makes everything easier when exploring Okinawa-hontō (once you escape the traffic of Naha). There's a rental-car counter in the arrivals hall of Naha International Airport, where staff can arrange for you to be taken to the offices of the main rental agencies. Normally, we like Toyota Rentacar, but its Naha office can be very crowded since it's a favourite of domestic tourists. You'll get more attentive service at **Matsuda Rentacar** (☎ 857-0802; 2-13-10 Akamine), which is near Akamine station and has a courtesy bus to/from the airport.

Southern Okinawa-hontō 沖縄本島の南部

During the closing days of the Battle of Okinawa, the southern part of Okinawa-hontō served as one of the last holdouts of the Japanese military and an evacuation point for wounded Japanese soldiers. Although southern Okinawa-hontō is now a residential area, there are some striking reminders of those terrible days. A visit to the area is highly recommended for those with an interest in the wartime history of Okinawa. The area can easily be visited as a day or half-day trip from Naha.

Okinawa's most important war memorials are clustered in the **Memorial Peace Park** (dusk-dawn), located in the city of Itoman on the southern coast of the island. The centrepiece of the park is the **Okinawa Prefectural Peace Memorial Museum** (☎ 997-3844; admission ¥300; 9am-5pm, closed Mon), which focuses on the suffering of the Okinawan people during the invasion of the island and under the subsequent American occupation. The main exhibits are on the 2nd floor. The museum strives to present a balanced picture of the Pacific War and the history that led to the invasion, but there is plenty here to stir debate.

Outside the museum is the **Cornerstone of Peace** (dusk-dawn), which is inscribed with the names of everyone – foreign, Okinawan,

Japanese, military and civilian – who died in the Battle of Okinawa. To reach the park, take bus 89 from Naha bus terminal to the Itoman bus terminal (¥500, one hour, every 20 minutes), then transfer to bus 82, which goes to Heiwa Kinen-kōen (¥400, 25 minutes, hourly).

An interesting stop en route to the Peace Park is the **Himeyuri no Tō** (Himeyuri Peace Museum; ☎ 997-2100; admission ¥300; 9am-5pm), located above a cave that served as an emergency field hospital during the closing days of the Battle of Okinawa. Here, 240 female high-school students were pressed into service as nurses for Japanese military wounded. As American forces closed in, the students were dismissed and the majority died, either in the crossfire or as the suicides encouraged by Japanese military authorities. The museum is likely to arouse conflicting emotions, particularly among those familiar with Okinawan and wartime history. Bus 82 (see preceding paragraph) stops outside.

Directly south of Naha in Kaigungo-kōen is the **Underground Naval Headquarters** (☎ 850-4055; admission ¥420; 8.30am-5pm), where 4000 men committed suicide or were killed as the battle for Okinawa drew to its bloody conclusion. Only 250m of the tunnels are open, but you can wander through the maze of corridors, see the commander's final words on the wall of his room, and inspect the holes and scars in other walls from the grenade blasts that killed many of the men. To reach the sight, take bus 33 or 46 from Naha bus terminal to the Tomigusuku-kōen-mae stop (¥230, 20 minutes, hourly). From there it's a 10-minute walk – follow the English signs (the entrance is near the top of the hill).

Central Okinawa-hontō 沖縄本島の中部

The densely populated strip to the north of Naha/Shuri is home to the American military bases and the thriving metropolis of **Okinawa City** (沖縄市; Okinawa-shi). This area is the most Americanised part of the island, and evidence of the foreign presence is visible in the form of pizzerias, drive-throughs and the odd military vehicle (not to mention all the military air traffic). It's also home to an amazing number of artificial tourist attractions aimed at domestic tourists. However, you will find some interesting cultural and historical sites scattered about, all of which are best visited as a day trip from Naha. If you plan to drive, we recommend using the expressway as local roads are slow and confusing.

On the east coast of the island and just south of Okinawa City are the castle ruins of **Nakagusuku-jō** (☎ 895-5719; admission ¥300; 8.30am-5pm). Commanding an enviable position overlooking the coast, Nakagusuku-jō predated stone construction of this type on the mainland by at least 80 years. Although the castle was destroyed in 1458, the remaining foundation hints at its former grandeur.

A 10-minute walk uphill is **Nakamura-ke** (☎ 935-3500; admission ¥300; 9am-5.30pm), which is probably the best-preserved traditional Okinawan house on the island. Although the Nakamura family's origins in the area can be traced back to the 15th century, the foundation dates from around 1720. Notice the substantial stone pigsties, the elevated storage area to deter rats and the trees grown as typhoon windbreaks. Both sights are a 10-minute taxi ride from Futenma, which can be accessed via bus 25 from Naha (¥500, one hour, hourly). If you're driving, these sites are closest to the Kita-Nakagusuku expressway exit.

Motobu-hantō 本部半島

Jutting out to the northwest of Nago, the hilly peninsula of Motobu-hantō is home to some scenic vistas and decent beaches, as well as an incredibly popular aquarium. The peninsula also serves as the jumping-off point for several nearby islets. Motobu-hantō is served by frequent loop lines from Nago – buses 66 and 65 respectively run anticlockwise and clockwise around the peninsula.

A couple of kilometres north of Motobu town is the **Ocean Expo Park**, the centrepiece of which is the wonderful **Okinawa Chiraumi Aquarium** (☎ 043-3748; admission ¥1800; 8.30am-6.30pm, later in summer, closed 1st Wed & Thu in Dec). The aquarium is built around the world's largest aquarium tank, which houses a fantastic variety of fish including two whale sharks. Unfortunately, this place is on the checklist of every single tourist to the island, and it can be packed. From Nago, bus 70 runs directly to the park (¥800, 45 minutes). Both peninsula loop lines (buses 65 and 66) also stop outside.

Set back from the peninsula's north coast and winding over a hilltop are the crumbling remains of **Nakijin-jō** (☎ 56-4400; admission ¥150; 8.30am-5.30pm), a 14th-century castle. It's not a must-see attraction, but might be of interest to history buffs. Be sure to buy your ticket at the shop beside the parking lot before heading up. From the summit of the hill, there are superb views out to sea. Both peninsula loop lines (buses 65 and 66) stop outside.

Finally, if you're after natural instead of artificial attractions and you've got your own wheels, we recommend a drive out to **Kouri-jima** (古宇利島) via **Yagaji-shima** (屋我地島). The bridge between these two islands is surrounded by picturesque turquoise water, and there's a decent beach on either side of the road as you reach Kōri-jima. The bridge to Yagaji-shima starts just north of the Motobu-hantō off Rte 58.

Northern Okinawa-hontō 沖縄本島の北部

The northern part of Okinawa-hontō is largely undeveloped and comparatively wild and rugged. Because of its hilly terrain, thousands of Okinawan families escaped the destruction in the south of the island at the end of WWII by hiding out here. Since there is limited public transport in the north, you will probably need a rental car.

Rte 58 hugs the west coast all the way up to **Cape Hedo** (辺戸岬), which marks the northern end of Okinawa. The point is an incredibly scenic spot backed by hills, with rocks rising from the dense greenery. On a good day, Yoron-tō, the southernmost island in Amami-shotō, is easily seen only 23km to the northeast.

From Cape Hedo, the road wraps around the tip of the island and heads down the east coast. For the next stretch of the drive, the road narrows and winds past one quiet bay after another – the contrast with southern Okinawa-hontō couldn't be more extreme. Keep your eyes peeled for small birds, which sometimes walk across the road, and be sure you've got enough petrol before setting out on an east-coast drive.

ISLANDS NEAR OKINAWA-HONTŌ

If you've had enough of the crowds and resorts of Okinawa-hontō, hop on a ferry to one of the nearby islands. The best of the lot are the three main islands of Kerama-shotō, which lie a mere 30km offshore from Naha. These islands are among the most attractive in the entire Southwest Islands, with crystal-clear water and excellent white-sand beaches. A little further out is the rarely visited island of Kume-jima. For those with a sense of adventure, there are several other islands that we don't cover in this guide: Ie-jima, Iheya-jima, Izena-jima, Aguni-jima, Kita-daitō-jima and Tonaki-jima.

Kerama-Shotō 慶良間諸島

The islands of Kerama-Shotō are a world away from the hustle and bustle of Okinawa-hontō, though even these islands can get crowded during the summer holiday season. The three main islands here are Zamami-jima, Aka-jima and Tokashiki-jima. You can easily visit any of these as a day trip from Naha, but we recommend a few days in a *minshuku* on one of the islands to really savour the experience.

AKA-JIMA 阿嘉島

☎ 098 / pop 310

A mere 2km in diameter, tiny Aka-jima makes up for in beauty what it lacks in size. With some of the best beaches in the Keramas and an extremely peaceful atmosphere, it's easy to get stuck here for several days. There's also some great snorkelling and diving nearby.

If you keep your eyes open around dusk you might spot a **Kerama deer** (慶良間シカ), descendants of deer that were brought by the Satsuma from Kagoshima when they conquered the Ryūkyūs in 1609. The deer are smaller and darker than their mainland cousins, and have been designated a National Treasure.

There are great beaches on every side of the island, but for sheer postcard-perfect beauty, it's hard to beat the 1km stretch of white sand on the northeast coast known as **Nishibama Beach** (ニシバマビーチ). This beach can be crowded in summer; if you want privacy, there are quieter beaches on the other sides of the island.

Dive shop–hotel **Marine House Seasir** (ペンションシーサー; ☎ 0120-10-2737; www.seasir.com, in Japanese; r per person with meals ¥7350) at the west end of the main village has good clean Western-style and Japanese rooms with attached bath. Most of the guests are divers.

Air Dolphin (☎ 858-3363) has two daily flights between Naha and Kerama airport (¥6500, 20 minutes). **Zamami Sonei Ferry** (☎ 868-4567) has two or three fast ferries a day (¥2750, 50 minutes) and one regular ferry (¥1860, 1½ hours) to/from Naha's Tomari-kō. A motorboat also makes four trips a day between Aka-jima and Zamami-jima (¥300, 15 minutes).

Due to its small size, the best way to get around the island is on foot.

IN DEEP WATER

Although it's not nearly as popular with divers as Southeast Asia, the Southwest Islands have some excellent diving. The waters surrounding the southern islands are home to an impressive variety of fish and coral species. There is also a healthy smattering of underwater wrecks, cavern systems and even the odd archaeological ruin.

Costs for diving in the Southwest Islands are higher than you might pay in Southeast Asia, but standards of equipment and guiding are fairly high. In order to dive around Okinawa and the Southwest Islands, you will need to be in possession of a valid diving certification. If you're renting equipment, you should know your weight in kilograms, your height in metres and your shoe size in centimetres.

One of the biggest deterrents for foreign divers is the fact that few operators on the islands speak English. Fortunately, there are a few operators in the islands who speak English and who welcome foreign divers. They include the following:

- **Ishigaki: Sea Friends** (☎ 0980-82-0863; 346 Ishigaki, Ishigaki-shi Aza; 1/2 dives ¥11,550/15,750, equipment rental ¥3150; 🕒 8am-8pm)
- **Ishigaki: Umicoza** (☎ 0980-88-2434; 827-15 Kabira, Ishigaki-shi; 1/2 dives ¥9450/12,600, equipment rental ¥5250; 🕒 8am-6pm)
- **Okinawa Hontō: Reef Encounters** (☎ 098-968-4442; www.reefencounters.org)
- **Yonaguni: SaWest** (☎ 0980-87-2311; 59-6 Yonaguni, Yonaguni-chō Aza, Yaeyama-gun; 1/2 dives ¥8000/12,000, equipment rental ¥5000; 🕒 8am-6pm)

ZAMAMI-JIMA 座間味島

☎ 098 / pop 610

A stone's throw from Aka-jima, Zamami-jima is *slightly* more developed, but also has some great beaches and a few rocky vistas. It's got some brilliant offshore islands and great diving and snorkelling in the surrounding waters. There is a **tourist information office** (☎ 987-2277; 🕒 9am-5pm) at the port.

Furuzamami Beach (古座間味ビーチ), approximately 1km southeast from the port (over the hill), is a stunning 700m stretch of white sand that is fronted by clear, shallow water and a bit of coral. The beach is well developed for day-trippers, and has toilets, showers and food stalls. You can also rent snorkelling gear here (¥1000).

If you fancy a little solitude, you'll find picturesque empty beaches in several of the coves on the other sides of the island. The best beaches, however, are on **Gahi-jima** (嘉比島) and **Agenashiku-jima** (安慶名敷島), which are located about a kilometre south of the port. Ringed by delightful white-sand beaches, they are perfect for a half-day *Robinson Crusoe* experience. One boat operator who can take you to these islands and arrange snorkelling trips is **Zamami Tour Operation** (☎ 987-3586). The TIC can also help arrange boat tours (pick-up/drop-off ¥1500 per person round trip).

Whale-watching is possible between the months of December and April. For more information, either enquire at the tourist information office or call the **Zamami-mura Whale-Watching Association** (座間味村ホエールウォッチング協会; ☎ 896-4141; tours ¥6000; 🕒 1-2 2hr tours daily).

Zamami-jima makes a great day trip from Naha, but an overnight stay will be more relaxing. A good spot to call home for the night is **Joy Joy** (ジョイジョイ; ☎ 0120-10-2445; http://keramajoyjoy.com/index.html; r per person with breakfast from ¥5250) in the northwest corner of the village. Accommodation is in a variety of rooms that surround a small garden. This pension also runs a dive shop.

Minshuku Summer House Yū Yū (民宿サマーハウス遊遊; ☎ 098-987-3055; www.yuyu-okinawa.jp/index.html, in Japanese; r per person with/without meals from ¥6000/3500) is a friendly *minshuku* that is just up the street from Joy Joy in the main village. Both places are an easy walk from the pier.

Zamami Sonei (☎ 868-4567) has two or three fast ferries a day (¥2750, 50 minutes) and one regular ferry (¥1860, two hours) to/from Naha's Tomari-kō. The ferries usually stop at Aka-jima en route from Naha to Zamami. A motorboat also makes four trips a day between Aka-jima and Zamami-jima (¥300, 15 minutes).

There are no buses or taxis on Zamami-jima, though nothing is too far away. Rental cars, scooters and bicycles are available near the pier (the TIC can help with arrangements).

TOKASHIKI-JIMA 渡嘉敷島

☎098 / pop 750

Tokashiki-jima, the largest island in Kerama-shotō, is a long, skinny, north-south island that has some great beaches. It's very popular with young Japanese holidaymakers, but is actually slightly less appealing than Aka-jima or Zamami-jima. Ferries arrive at the port of Tokashiki (渡嘉敷) on the east coast.

The island's most attractive beaches are **Tokashiku Beach** (とかしくビーチ) and **Aharen Beach** (阿波連ビーチ), both of which are located on the west coast. Both beaches are well developed for tourism, and have toilets, showers, food stalls and shops where you can rent snorkelling gear (¥1000).

You can easily visit Tokashiki as a day trip from Naha. If you prefer to spend the night, Aharen is the place to be. **Southern Cross** (サザンクロス; ☎987-2258; r per person with/without meals ¥6500/4000), a family-run inn with simple Western- and Japanese-style rooms, is practically on the beach. It's popular with young Japanese holidaymakers and families. A little further back in the village you'll find **Kerama-sō** (けらま荘 ☎987-2125; r per person with/without meals ¥5775/3675), a simple *minshuku* with basic Japanese-style rooms and reasonable rates. Staff will pick you up at the pier if you can get someone to reserve in advance in Japanese.

Tokashiki Sonei (☎868-7541) operates one or two fast ferries a day (¥2430, 35 minutes) and one regular ferry (¥1620, one hour 10 minutes) from Naha's Tomari-kō.

Buses run from Tokashiki Port to the beaches on the west coast. Bicycles, cars and scooters are available in Tokashiki Port.

Kume-jima 久米島

☎098 / pop 9600

The furthest flung of the outer islands, Kume-jima is a quiet island that sees fewer visitors than the Keramas. It's mostly flat and covered with sugarcane, with a few good beaches and the mother of all sandbars off its east coast.

The airport is at the western extreme of the island, while the main port of Kaneshiro (兼城) is on the southwest coast. There is a **tourist information office** (☎985-7115) at the airport that opens to meet incoming flights in summer.

The most popular beach on the island is **Ifu Beach** (イーフビーチ), on the east coast. *Ifu* means 'white' in the local Kume dialect, and not surprisingly, the beach is known for its powdery white sand. Another attractive beach is **Shinri-hama** (シンリ浜), on the west coast near the airport, which is known for its sunsets over the East China Sea.

Kume-jima's most famous attraction is **Hate-no-hama** (はての浜), a 7km sandbar that extends from the eastern point of the island, pointing back towards Okinawa-hontō. If you arrive by air, you can't miss this coral-fringed strip of white framed by the turquoise waters of the East China Sea. The best way to get there is on an excursion with **Hatenohama Kankō Service** (☎090-8292-8854), which runs a three-hour tour to the sandbar for ¥3500. If you book in advance, staff members can pick you up from your accommodation.

On tiny **Ōjima** (奥武島), which is connected to Kume-jima's east coast by a causeway, you'll find the intriguing **Tatami-ishi** (畳石), a natural formation of flat pentagonal rocks that covers the seashore.

Ifu Beach is the place to stay, and there are plenty of choices along the 1.5km waterfront. Our pick is **Minshuku Nankurunaisā** (民宿なんくるないさぁ; ☎985-7973; http://nankurunaisakume.ti-da.net, in Japanese; r per person from ¥5000; P 💻), an excellent, friendly new *minshuku* set back just a bit from the beach. It's got Japanese- and Western-style rooms with bathroom. For those with tents, there is a small camping ground on Ōjima, before the Tatami-ishi.

JTA and RAC operate five flights a day between Naha and Kume-jima (¥10,800, 35 minutes). JTA operates one daily flight from Tokyo and Kume-jima between June and September (¥46,700, 2½ hours). **Kume Shōsen** (☎098-868-2686) runs a daily ferry from Naha's Tomari-kō to/from Kume-jima (¥3000, three hours 15 minutes).

Kume-jima has an efficient bus system. **East Rentacar** (☎896-7766) has a counter at the airport.

MIYAKO-SHOTŌ 宮古諸島

Miyako-shotō lies about 270km southwest of Okinawa-hontō and 100km northeast of Yaeyama-shotō. This island group contains the main island of Miyako-jima, and the nearby islands of Ikema-jima, Irabu-jima, Shimoji-jima

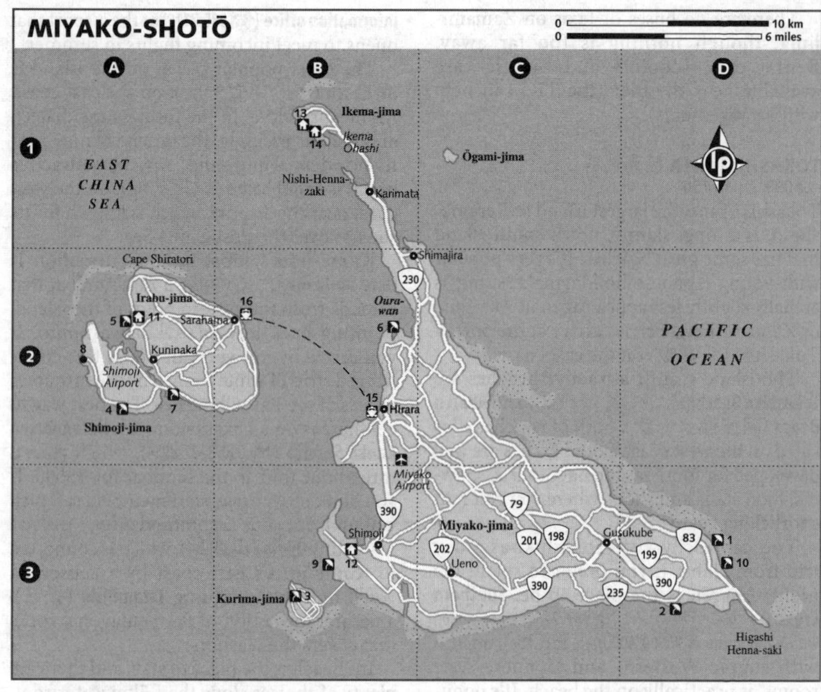

SIGHTS & ACTIVITIES
Aragusuku Beach 親城海岸 1 D3
Boraga Beach 保良川ビーチ 2 D3
Nagahama 長浜 3 B3
Nakanoshima-Kaigan 中の島海岸 4 A2
Sawada-no-hama Beach 佐和田の浜 5 A2
Sunayama Beach 砂山ビーチ 6 B2
Toguchi-no-hama 渡口の浜 7 A2
Tōri-ike 通り池 8 A2
Yoneha-Maehama Beach 与那覇前浜 9 B3
Yoshino Beach 吉野海岸 10 D3

SLEEPING
Guesthouse Birafuya びらふやー 11 A2
Guesthouse Miyako-jima ゲストハウス宮古島 12 B3
Island Terrace Neela アイランドテラス·ニーラ 13 B1
Raza Cosmica Tourist Home ラザコスミカツーリストホーム 14 B1

TRANSPORT
Hirara Port 平良湖 15 B2
Sarahama Port 佐良浜港 16 B2

and Kurima-jima, as well as a scattering of tiny islets. Located just north of the Tropic of Cancer, Miyako-shotō is the quintessential beach destination and there is good diving and snorkelling in the waters offshore.

Unfortunately, Miyako-shotō is no longer served by ferries from the mainland or Okinawa-hontō, which means that the only way to get there is to fly. Of course, this might change by the time this book is published, so it doesn't hurt to check the latest information online or at local tourist offices. Those who spring for the plane tickets will find themselves rewarded by some of the best beaches in the Southwest Islands and a friendly laid-back atmosphere.

Miyako-jima 宮古島

☎ 0980 / pop 55,200

The main island in Miyaho-shotō, Miyako-jima is a mostly flat expanse of sugarcane fringed by excellent beaches, with long fingers of land pointing out into the sea. Lying just offshore are four smaller islands, two of which are connected to the main island by bridges (another bridge is under construction that will allow road access to all the nearby islands).

First and foremost, Miyako-jima is a beach island and you can happily spend your days here hopping from one great beach to the next, with a spot of snorkelling at each one if you're so inclined. If you tire of that, a seaside drive to the various capes of the island is a great way to spend a few hours. And, finally, there are a few attractions in the main city of Hirara to keep you occupied on a rainy day.

INFORMATION

Hirara-Nishizato Post Office (Map p788; 平良に西里郵便局; Ichiba-dōri; 🕒 9am-5pm, ATMs longer, closed Sat & Sun) The ATMs here accept foreign ATM cards.

Public library (Map p788; 市立図書館; cnr McCrum-dōri & Chūō-dōri) It's possible to access the internet for free on the 2nd floor.

Tourist information desk (☎ 72-0899; 🕒 9.30am-5pm) In the arrivals hall of the airport, you can pick up a copy of the *Miyako Island Guide Map*. Japanese readers should also pick up a copy of the detailed *Guide Map Miyako*.

SIGHTS & ACTIVITIES

Just 4km north of town you will find the excellent little **Sunayama Beach** (Map p786), which lies at the bottom of a large sand dune (hence the name 'Sand Mountain Beach'). A cool stone arch at one side of the beach provides a bit of shade.

On the southwest coast, beautiful **Yonaha-Maehama** (Map p786) is a 6km stretch of white sand that attracts a lot of families and young folks due to its shallow waters. It's a lovely beach, but it can get crowded and the presence of the occasional jet-ski is a drawback. It's just before the Kurima-Ōhashi Bridge, on the north side.

If you've had a look at the crowds at Yoneha-Maehama and decided you want something quieter, head across the Kurima-Ōhashi and drive to the northwest coast of **Kurima-jima** (来間島), where you will find the brilliant (and usually uncrowded) **Nagahama** (Map p786).

On the southeast corner of Miyako-jima is **Boraga Beach** (Map p786), which is a popular spot for snorkelling and kayaking (with a hair-raisingly steep access road). Around the cape to the north, you'll find **Yoshino Beach** and **Aragusuku Beach** (both Map p786), two relatively shallow beaches with a lot of offshore coral (much of it dead).

If you've got a car, we recommend a drive out to the end of **Higashi Henna-saki** (東平安名崎), a narrow finger of land that extends 2km into the Pacific Ocean. There are picnic tables, walking trails and a lighthouse at the point for you to explore.

Another good drive is across **Ikema-Ōhashi** (池間大橋) to **Ikema-jima** (池間島; Map p786). The shallow turquoise water on either side of this 1.4km bridge is incredibly beautiful on a sunny day (just try to keep your eyes on the road). You'll find several **private pocket beaches** around the coast of Ikema-jima.

If you can pry yourself away from the beaches for a moment, there are a few sights in Hirara, including the **Miyako Traditional Arts & Crafts Centre** (Map p788; ☎ 72-8022; admission free; 🕒 9am-6pm Mon-Sat), which displays traditional island crafts – be sure to check out the *minsā* weaving looms on the 2nd floor. It's next to the small **Miyako-jinja** and across from the Daiichi Hotel (see p788).

SLEEPING

Most of the accommodation is located in the town of Hirara, but you'll also find places to stay closer to the beaches. There are free camping grounds at many beaches, including Yonaha-Maebama, Boraga and Aragusuku.

Hiraraya (Map p788; ☎ 75-3221; www.miyako-net.ne.jp/~hiraraya; dm night/week ¥2000/12,000, r per person night/week ¥3000/18,000; meals available; Ⓟ) Located in central Hirara just one block north of Miyako-jinja (look for the light blue curtain that says guest house), this laid-back spot is run by a charming young woman who will do everything to make you feel at home. Accommodation is available in

THE 'COMMUNICATION DRINK'

The friendly people of Miyako-jima have earned a reputation for drinking, and the Izato entertainment area in the town of Hirara is said to have more bars per capita than any other town in Japan.

Miyako even has its unique local drinking custom, called *otori*. This group ritual involves making a speech, filling your own glass (usually with potent *awamori*, the local liquor) and then filling the glasses of all in the room. Everyone drinks up, the leader makes a short closing speech, picks the next victim and the routine starts all over again. Miyako's *otori* is so notorious that even hard-livered Okinawans from neighbouring islands are said to fear the ritual.

If you happen to end up lured into an *otori* and want to sneak out before getting plastered, one local veteran boozer advises, 'Never say goodbye. Just head for the toilet and don't come back!'

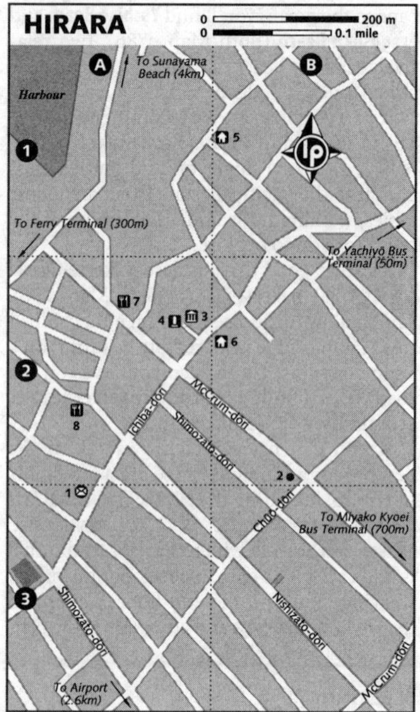

INFORMATION
Hirara-Nishizato Post Office 平良西郵便局 1 A3
Public Library 平良市立図書館 2 B2

SIGHTS & ACTIVITIES
Miyako Traditional Arts & Crafts Center 3 A2
Miyako-jinja 宮古神社 4 A2

SLEEPING
Hiraraya ひららや 5 B1
Miyako Dai-ichi Hotel 宮古第一ホテル 6 B2

EATING
Chūzan 中山 7 A2
Koja Shokudō Honten 古謝食堂本店 8 A2

dorms and Japanese-style *tatami* rooms, and there are special rates available for longer-term stays. Meals also available.

Guesthouse Miyako-jima (Map p786; ☎ 76-2330; www2.miyako-ma.jp/yonaha/index.html; dm night/week ¥2500/11,200, r per person night/week ¥4000/21,000; P) This bright and cheery guest house has a scenic location near Yoneha-Maehama beach, and is perfectly set up for budget travellers. Accommodation is in cosy Western-style dorms and private rooms with shared facilities, and there are special rates available for long-term stays. Guests can also borrow bicycles and scooters.

Miyako Dai-ichi Hotel (Map p788; ☎ 73-5522; r per person from ¥6825; P) This centrally located business hotel has comfortable and fairly spacious rooms and a friendly staff, as well as a large parking lot and an on-site restaurant.

Raza Cosmica Tourist Home (Map p786; ☎ 75-2020; www.raza-cosmica.com; r per person with breakfast from ¥8000; P) This charming South Asian–themed inn sits above a lovely secluded beach on Ikema-jima. Romantic Western-style rooms offer peace and quiet in truly lovely surroundings, which makes this the perfect destination for holidaying couples or honeymooners. Bathrooms are shared and children below 12 years of age are not permitted. Look for the Shiva eyes on the door.

Island Terrace Neela (Map p786; ☎ 74-4678; www.neela.jp; r per person with breakfast from Y30,000; P) Overlooking the same private beach as the Raza (preceding), this intimate high-end resort looks like a whitewashed Mediterranean resort airlifted to Japan. The private villas would make the perfect honeymoon destination.

EATING

There are eateries scattered here and there across the island, but you'll find the best selection in the town of Hirara.

our pick **Koja Shokudō Honten** (Map p788; ☎ 72-2139; 🕑 10am-10pm) One block northwest of the intersection between Ichiba-dōri and Nishizato-dōri, this nondescript noodle house is something of a local legend. For more than 50 years, Koja has been serving up steaming bowls of *sōki-soba* (¥650). The owner speaks English. It's across from a parking lot; look for the white tiles around the entryway.

Chūzan (中山; Map p788; ☎ 73-1959; 🕑 4pm-midnight) This popular *izakaya* is a great spot that offers a variety of locally caught seafood. You can't go wrong with the *sashimi-moriawase* (sashimi assortment; ¥1000), which washes down perfectly with a tall glass of *nama-biiru* (draught beer; ¥450). There's a limited picture menu. Service can be a little slow. Look for the red lanterns outside.

GETTING THERE & AWAY

Miyako-jima has direct flights to/from Tokyo's Haneda airport (JTA; ¥42,900, 2½ hours, one daily), Osaka's Kansai International Airport

(JTA; ¥42,900, 2½ hours, one daily), Naha (JTA/ANA; ¥16,100, 50 minutes, 12 daily) and Ishigaki (JTA/RAC; ¥10,900, 20 minutes, four daily).

GETTING AROUND

Miyako-jima has a limited bus network that operates from two bus stands in Hirara. Buses run between the airport and Hirara (¥170, 20 minutes). Buses also depart from Yachiyo bus terminal for Ikema-jima (¥460, 35 minutes), and from the Miyako Kyōei bus terminal, 700m east of town, to Yoshino/Bora (¥470, 50 minutes). Yet another line runs between Hirara and Yoneha/Kurima-jima (¥390, 30 minutes).

The island's flat terrain is perfectly suited to biking. If you want to move faster, there are rental-car counters at the airport and offices in Hirara.

Irabu-jima & Shimoji-jima 伊良部島・下地島

A 10-minute ferry ride from Hirara (Miyako-jima) brings you to Irabu-jima and Shimoji-jima, which are pleasantly rural islands covered with fields of sugar cane and linked by a series of six bridges. Like Miyako, Irabu and Shimoji are a beach lover's paradise, and there are ample opportunities for swimming, snorkelling or simply sprawling out underneath the tropical sun. The islands are best visited as a day trip from Hirara, though there are a handful of low-key guest houses on the island as well as plenty of free camping grounds.

The best swimming beach on the island is **Toguchi-no-hama** on Irabu-jima's west coast. With fine yellow sands and turquoise waters, you'd be hard-pressed to find more beautiful spot for an afternoon swim. There are some small shops here where you can rent snorkelling equipment; as well as free campsites with basic facilities.

Easily the best snorkelling beach is **Nakanoshima-kaigan**, on the west coast of Shimoji-jima. Here you can snorkel around a series of hard coral heads that are protected by a high-walled bay. Oddly, some of the best coral is fairly close to the shore, due to the unfortunate habit of local divers touching and standing on coral. Look for the sign reading 'Nakano Island The Beach'.

Another interesting sight is **Tōri-ike**, two seawater 'ponds' on the west coast of Shimoji-jima that are actually sinkholes in the coral that formed the island. Boardwalks link the 'ponds' with the parking lot off the main road. This is a great spot to walk around, though the best place to experience it is underwater. Not surprisingly, this is a popular diving destination for operators on nearby Miyako-jima.

Another 'attraction' on Shimoji-jima is **Shimoji airport**, which is used as a practise runway by Japanese airlines. Plane-spotters come here from around Japan to watch the pilots practise landings, take-offs and go-arounds.

If you'd like to stay the night on the island, the chilled-out backpackers haven of **Guesthouse Birafuya** (☎ 78-3380; www.birafuya.com, in Japanese; dm/s/d ¥2000/3000/5000; P 💻) is a few blocks inland from Sawada-no-hama beach. Birafuya has a dorm and small Western-style rooms and is a great place to meet other travellers, both Japanese and foreign. If you phone ahead, staff will pick you up at the ferry terminal. Bikes are also available for rent.

Fast ferries (¥400, 10 minutes, 11 daily) and car ferries (¥360 per walking passenger, ¥2000 per car, 25 minutes, 13 daily) run between Hirara on Miyako-jima and Sarahama Port on Irabu-jima.

The best way to explore the island is by bicycle, which can be rented in the port on Irabu-jima. Or, if you have a rental car or scooter, you can bring it over on the ferry from Hirara. Note that, at the time of writing, a bridge between Miyako-jima and Irabu-jima was under construction.

YAEYAMA-SHOTŌ 八重山諸島

At the far southwestern end of the Southwest Islands are the islands of Yaeyama-shotō, which include the main islands of Ishigaki-jima and Iriomote-jima as well as a spread of 17 isles. Located near the Tropic of Cancer, the isles of Yaeyama-shotō are renowned for their lovely beaches, superb diving and lush landscapes. The islands are also a haven for Japanese *freeters* (alternative lifestylers), which means you're bound to meet an intriguing cast of characters during your stay here.

Yaeyama-shotō is arguably the top destination in the Southwest Islands. These islands offer Japan's best snorkelling and diving, and some of Japan's last intact subtropical jungles and mangrove

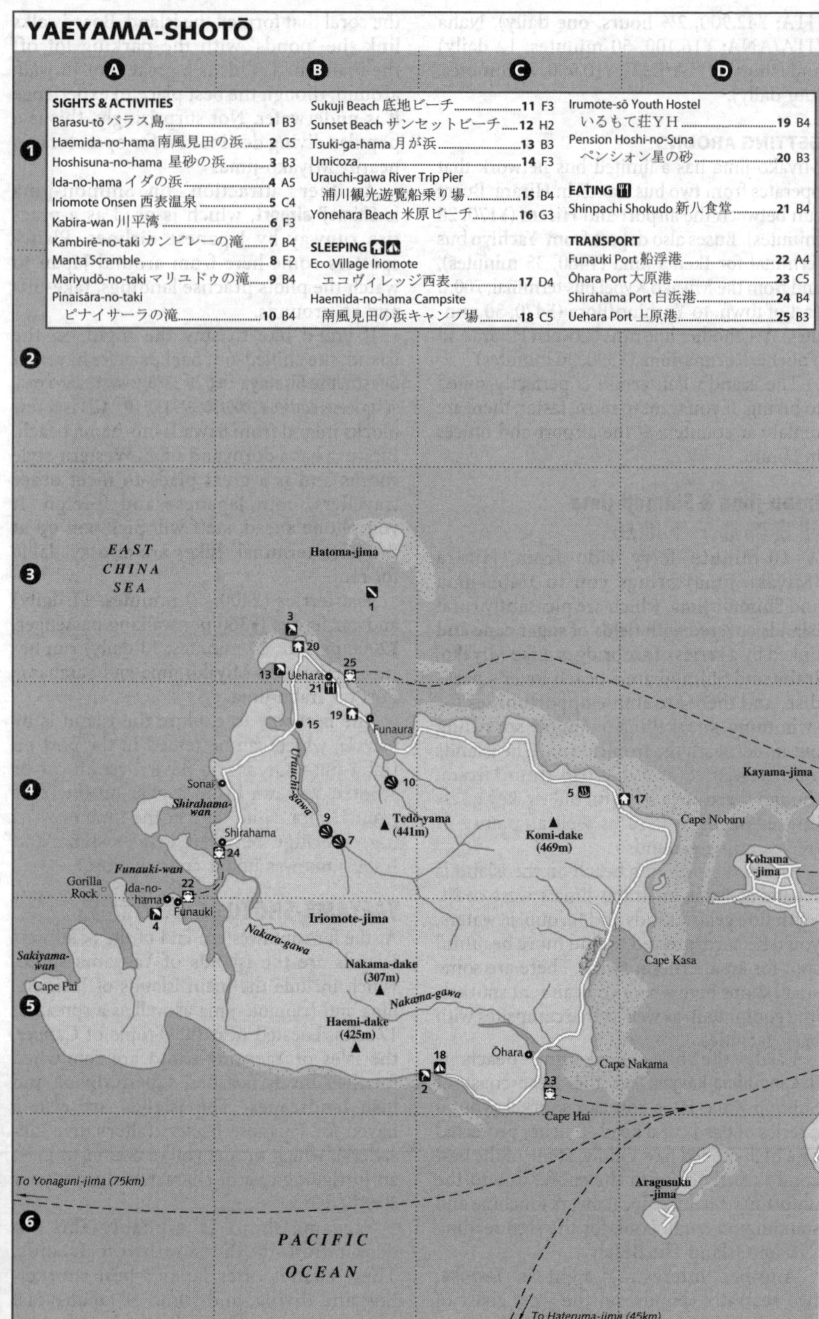
YAEYAMA-SHOTŌ
A
B
C
D
1
2
3
4
5
6
SIGHTS & ACTIVITIES
Barasu-tō バラス島 1 B3
Haemida-no-hama 南風見田の浜 2 C5
Hoshisuna-no-hama 星砂の浜 3 B3
Ida-no-hama イダの浜 4 A5
Iriomote Onsen 西表温泉 5 C4
Kabira-wan 川平湾 6 F3
Kambirē-no-taki カンビレーの滝 7 B4
Manta Scramble 8 E2
Mariyudō-no-taki マリユドゥの滝 9 B4
Pinaisāra-no-taki ピナイサーラの滝 10 B4
Sukuji Beach 底地ビーチ 11 F3
Sunset Beach サンセットビーチ 12 H2
Tsuki-ga-hama 月が浜 13 B3
Umicoza 14 F3
Urauchi-gawa River Trip Pier 浦川観光遊覧船乗り場 15 B4
Yonehara Beach 米原ビーチ 16 G3
SLEEPING
Eco Village Iriomote エコヴィレッジ西表 17 D4
Haemida-no-hama Campsite 南風見田の浜キャンプ場 18 C5
Irumote-sō Youth Hostel いるもて荘YH 19 B4
Pension Hoshi-no-Suna ペンシォン星の砂 20 B3
EATING
Shinpachi Shokudo 新八食堂 21 B4
TRANSPORT
Funauki Port 船浮港 22 A4
Ōhara Port 大原港 23 C5
Shirahama Port 白浜港 24 B4
Uehara Port 上原港 25 B3
EAST CHINA SEA
Hatoma-jima
Uehara
Funaura
Sonai
Shirahama-wan
Shirahama
Urauchi-gawa
Tedō-yama (441m)
Komi-dake (469m)
Kayama-jima
Cape Nobaru
Kohama-jima
Funauki-wan
Gorilla Rock
Ida-no-hama
Funauki
Iriomote-jima
Nakara-gawa
Sakiyama-wan
Cape Pai
Nakama-dake (307m)
Nakama-gawa
Haemi-dake (425m)
Cape Kasa
Ōhara
Cape Nakama
Cape Hai
Aragusuku-jima
To Yonaguni-jima (75km)
PACIFIC OCEAN
To Hateruma-jima (45km)

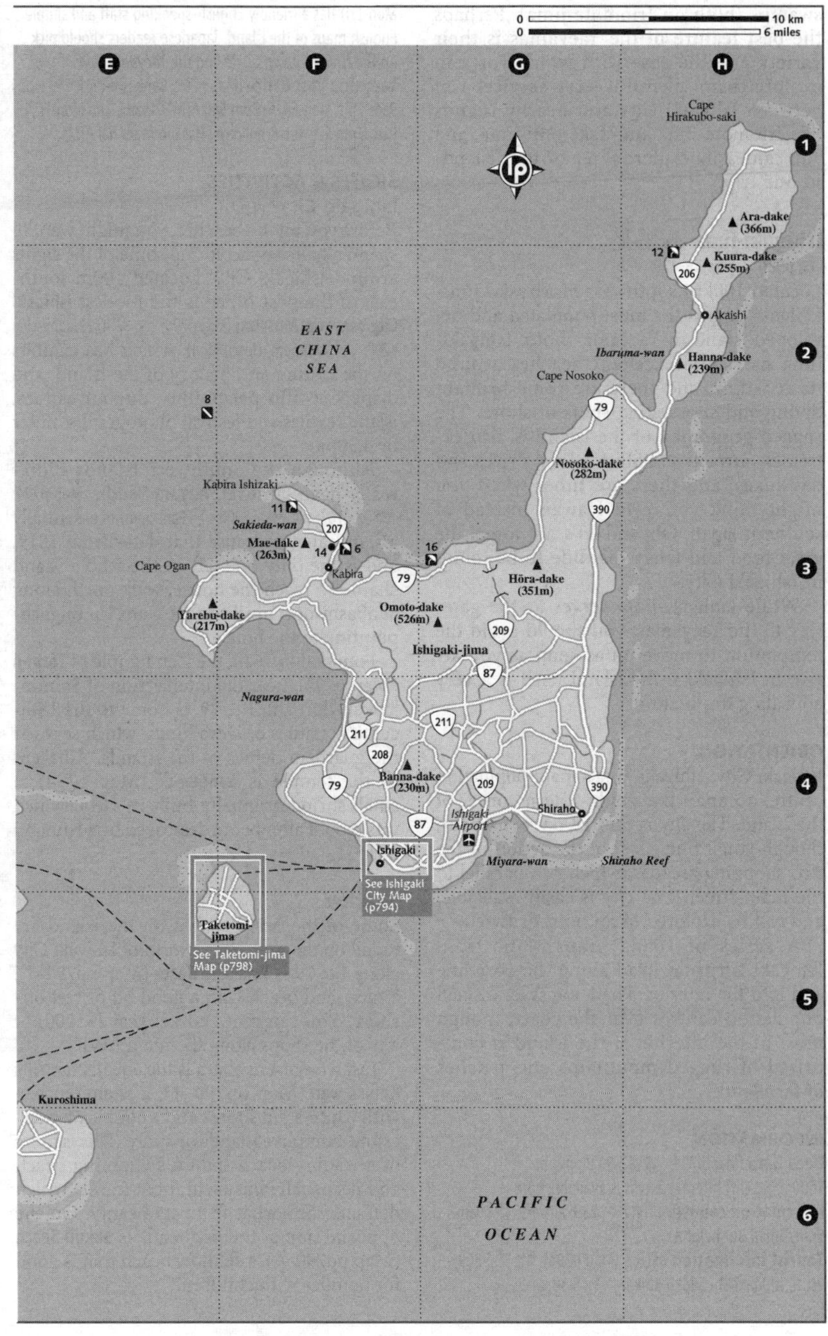
0 10 km
0 6 miles
E
F
G
H
1
2
3
4
5
6
Cape Hirakubo-saki
Ara-dake (366m)
Kuura-dake (255m)
12
206
Akaishi
Ibaruma-wan
Hanna-dake (239m)
Cape Nosoko
79
Nosoko-dake (282m)
390
EAST CHINA SEA
8
Kabira Ishizaki
11
Sakieda-wan
207
Mae-dake (263m)
14
6
Kabira
Cape Ogan
16
79
Hōra-dake (351m)
Yarebu-dake (217m)
Omoto-dake (526m)
209
Ishigaki-jima
87
Nagura-wan
211
211
208
Banna-dake (230m)
79
209
390
Shiraho
Ishigaki Airport
87
Ishigaki
See Ishigaki City Map (p794)
Miyara-wan
Shiraho Reef
Taketomi-jima
See Taketomi-jima Map (p798)
Kuroshima
PACIFIC OCEAN

swamps (both on Iriomote-jima). Perhaps the best feature of the Yaeyamas is their variety and the ease with which you can explore them: plentiful ferry services run between Ishigaki City and nearby islands like Iriomote-jima and Taketomi-jima, and you can easily explore three or four islands in one trip.

Ishigaki-jima 石垣島

☎ 0980 / pop 48,420

Located 100km southwest of Miyako-jima, Ishigaki-jima is the most populated and developed island in Yaeyama-shotō. Ishigaki-jima has some excellent beaches around its coastline, and there are some brilliant diving and snorkelling spots offshore. The rugged geography of the island is also extremely attractive, both for long drives and day hikes, and there are times when you might think you're in Hawaii instead of southern Japan. Oh, and let's not forget the great food and lively nightlife to be found in Ishigaki City.

While Ishigaki-jima serves as the gateway to the Yaeyamas, you should avoid the temptation to move on as soon as you arrive in Ishigaki – the island itself is a very appealing destination.

ORIENTATION

Ishigaki City, Ishigaki-jima's main population centre, occupies the southwestern corner of the island. The city is centred on its harbour, though you'll find most of the action in the two shopping arcades, which run parallel to the main street. The city is easily walkable, and can be explored in an hour or two.

A series of roads branch out from Ishigaki City and head along the coastline and into the interior. There are several small population centres near the coast, though most of the interior of the island is comprised of rugged mountains and patches of farmland.

INFORMATION

Gera Gera (Map p794; ☎ 82-8025; per hr ¥400; 🕑 24hr) Internet access is available here.

Information counter (☎ 88-5239; airport; 🕑 9am-5pm) Small but helpful.

Tourist information office (Map p794; ☎ 82-2809; 1st fl, Ishigaki-shi Shōkō Kaikan; 🕑 8.30am-5.30pm Mon-Fri) Has a friendly English-speaking staff and simple English maps of the island. Japanese readers should pick up the *Ishigaki Town Guide* and the *Yaeyama Nabi*.

Yaeyama Post Office (Map p794; Sanbashi-dōri; 🕑 lobby 9am-7pm Mon-Fri, to 3pm Sat, ATM 8.45am-7pm Mon-Fri, 9am-7pm Sat, Sun & holidays) Has international ATMs.

SIGHTS & ACTIVITIES

Ishigaki City 石垣市

Before you hit the beaches, you might want to spend a half-day exploring some of the sights around Ishigaki City. Located 100m southeast of the post office is the modest **Ishigaki City Yaeyama Museum** (Map p794; ☎ 82-4712; admission ¥200; 🕑 9am-5pm, closed Mon), which has exhibits on the culture and history of the island, and displays coffin palanquins, dugout canoes, island textiles and festival photographs. Enter by 4.30pm.

Although the Southwest Islands didn't really have samurai, **Miyara Dōnchi** (Map p794; ☎ 82-2767; admission ¥200; 🕑 9am-5pm) is essentially a samurai-style house that dates from 1819, and is the only one left in the whole island chain. To reach the house, walk north along Sanbashi-dōri until you see signs (in English) pointing to the house.

Founded in 1614, the Zen temple of **Tōrin-ji** (Map p794), near the intersection of Shimin-kaikan-dōri and Rte 79, is home to the 18th-century statues of Deva kings, which serve as the guardian deities of the islands. Adjacent to the temple is **Gongen-dō** (Map p794), a small shrine originally built in 1614, which was rebuilt after being destroyed by a tsunami in 1771.

Beaches

Some of the best beaches on the island are found on the west coast. North of Ishigaki City along Rte 79 is **Yonehara Beach** (Map pp790–1), a nice sand beach with a good bit of reef offshore. You can rent snorkel gear (¥1000) at any of the shops along the main road.

Just west of Yonehara is the equally famous **Kabira-wan** (Map pp790–1), a sheltered bay with white-sand shores and a couple of interesting clumplike islands offshore. This is more of a wading beach than a swimming beach and it's usually busy with boat traffic, which detracts somewhat from its beauty. On the opposite side of the peninsula is **Sukuji Beach** (Map pp790–1), a shallow beach that is good for families with children.

DIVE SITES OF OKINAWA

There is decent diving around most of the islands of the Southwest Islands, but the real action is in Okinawa-ken, and the further south you go, the better it gets. Just to whet your appetite a bit, here's a list of our favourite *daibingu-supotto;* or 'dive spots'.

- **Manta Scramble** (below) Located off the west coast of Ishigaki-jima, this popular dive spot virtually guarantees a manta ray sighting if you go in spring and summer.
- **Irizaki Point** (p801) If swimming alongside sharks doesn't absolutely terrify you, this famous spot off the coast of Yonaguni-jima is frequented by schools of hammerheads in winter.
- **Underwater Ruins** (p801) One of the most unusual dive spots in Southwest Islands is also located off the coast of Yonaguni-jima, and is home to a mysterious underwater archaeological ruin of unknown origin.

At the north end of the island, on the west coast, you will find **Sunset Beach** (Map pp790–1), another long strip of sand with a bit of offshore reef. As the name implies, this is a good spot to watch the sun set into the East China Sea.

Diving

The sea around Ishigaki-jima is famous among the Japanese diving community for its large schools of manta rays, particularly from June to October. The most popular place is **Manta Scramble**, off the coast of Kabira Ishizaki. Although it's likely that you'll be sharing with a fair number of dive boats, you're almost guaranteed to see a manta (or four).

There are a number of dive shops on Ishigaki-jima. Two shops with English-speaking dive guides are **Umicoza** (☎ 88-2434; 827-15 Kabira, Ishigaki-shi; 1/2 dives ¥9450/12,600, equipment rental ¥5250; 🕑 8am-6pm) and **Sea Friends** (☎ 82-0863; 346 Ishigaki, Ishigaki-shi Aza; 1/2 dives ¥11,550/15,750, equipment rental ¥3150; 🕑 8am-8pm).

Other Attractions

A drive to the far northern tip of the island, **Hirakubo-saki** (Map pp790–1), is highly recommended for those who have their own wheels. The view of the waves pounding in over the reefs from this high bluff is spectacular here, and the lighthouse is quite photogenic against the backdrop of the East China Sea.

SLEEPING

Ishigaki City serves as the island's principal accommodation centre – the following listings are all within walking distance of the ferry terminal.

Yashima Ryokan Youth Hostel (Map p794; ☎ 82-3157; www.jyh.or.jp/english/kyushu/yaesu/index.html; dm ¥2500 with breakfast; Ⓟ 💻) East of the Yaeyama Museum, this cosy youth hostel is in a traditional Ryūkyū-style house. Accommodation is in several communal Japanese-style tatami rooms with shared facilities.

Rakutenya (Map p794; ☎ 83-8713; www3.big.or.jp/~erm8p3gi/english/english.html; r per person ¥3000; Ⓟ 💻) This quaint guest house is two blocks north of the covered markets, and has attractive Western- and Japanese-style rooms in a rickety, old wooden house. The managers are a friendly Japanese couple who speak a little bit of English, and are a fantastic source of local information.

Pension Yaima-biyōri (Map p794; ☎ 88-5578; www.yaima-well.net/ybiyori/index.htm, in Japanese; r per person ¥3000) Two blocks northwest of the bus station, this welcoming pension offers simple but spacious Western- and Japanese-style rooms with shared facilities.

Super Hotel Ishigaki (Map p794; ☎ 83-9000; www.infinix.co.jp/sh, in Japanese; s with light breakfast ¥5800; Ⓟ 💻) Four blocks northeast of the city hall is this efficient business hotel. The rooms are what you'd expect of a business hotel and will suit if you prefer more privacy than a guest house affords.

Hotel Harbor Ishigakijima (Map p794; ☎ 88-8383; s from ¥5250; Ⓟ) You can't beat the location of this small, friendly three-storey business hotel: it looks right over the harbour and it's a one-minute walk to the ferry terminal. Rooms are fairly spacious and include massage chairs.

EATING & DRINKING

Ishigaki City has a good mix of boutique tourist restaurants, cheap but atmospheric local dives and boisterous watering holes.

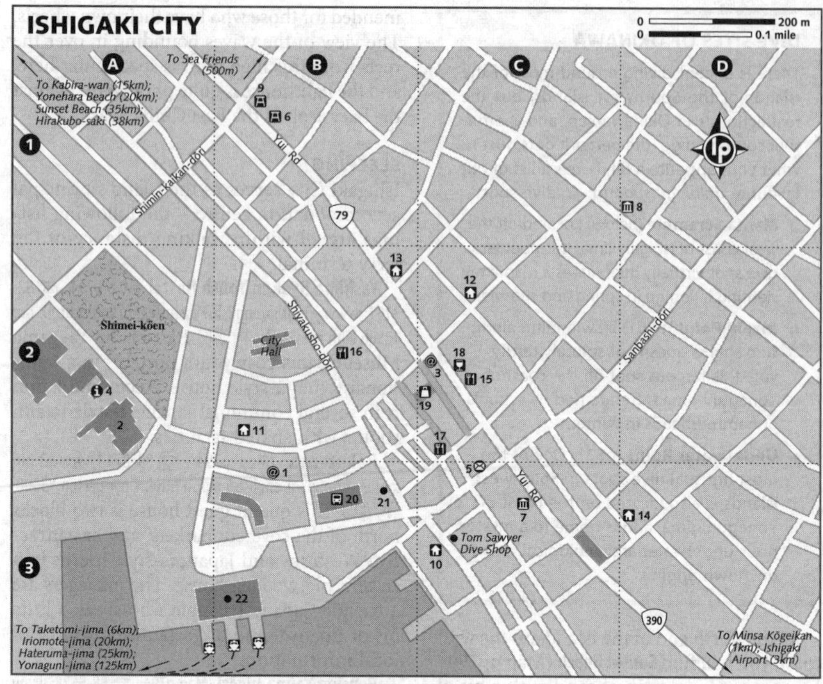

INFORMATION
Gera Gera ゲラゲラ 1 B3
Ishigaki City Library 石垣市立図書館 2 A2
Ishigaki Net Café 石垣ネットカフェ 3 C2
Tourist Information Office 観光協会案内所 4 A2
Yaeyama Post Office 八重山郵便局 5 C3

SIGHTS & ACTIVITIES
Gongen-dō 権現堂 6 B1
Ishigaki City Yaeyama Museum 石垣市立八重山博物館 7 C3
Miyara Dōnchi 宮良殿内 8 D1
Tōrin-ji 桃林寺 9 B1

SLEEPING
Hotel Harbor Ishigakijima ホテルハーバー石垣島 10 C3
Pension Yaima-biyōri ペンションやいま日和 11 B2
Rakutenya 楽天屋 12 C2
Super Hotel Ishigaki スーパーホテル石垣島 13 B2
Yashima Ryokan Youth Hostel 八洲旅館ユースホステル 14 D3

EATING
Asian Kitchen KAPI アジアンキッチンカピ 15 C2
Eifuku Shokudō 栄福食堂 16 B2
Paikaji 南風 17 C2

DRINKING
Mori-no-Kokage 森のこかげ 18 C2

SHOPPING
Ishigaki City Special Products Center 石垣市特産品販売センター 19 C2

TRANSPORT
Bus Terminal バスターミナル 20 B3
Ishigaki Rentacar 石垣島レンタカー 21 B3
Ishigaki-jima Rittō Ferry Terminal/Ferry Company Offices 石垣島離島ターミナル·フェリー事務所 22 B3

Eifuku Shokudō (Map p794; ☎ 82-5838; ⏲ 8.30am-11pm) This hole in the wall, one block northwest of the covered arcade, is easy to find: the owner has posted a write-up from an old edition of Lonely Planet in the window. Eifuku is one of the cheapest places on the island for *yaeyama-soba* (thin noodles in broth; ¥300), though we recommend the stinky (but tasty) *yagi-soba* (goat soba; ¥500).

Asian Kitchen KAPI (Map p794; ☎ 82-2026; lunch/dinner about ¥1000/3000; ⏲ 11.30am-3pm & 6.30-11pm; closed Thu) Next door to Mori-no-Kokage (look for the English sign), this trendy Pan-Asian bistro is a good choice if your Japanese is limited. In addition to the local cuisine, KAPI also offers an impressive range of Asian favourites, from Korean-style hotpots to fiery Indonesian curries.

our pick **Paikaji** (Map p794; ☎ 82-6027; ⏰ 5pm-midnight) It's worth the wait to get into this deservedly popular local restaurant that serves all the Okinawan and Yaeyama standards. Both the atmosphere and kitchen get top marks. Try the *ikasumi chahan* (squid ink fried rice; ¥650), the *gōya-champurū* (gōya stir-fry; ¥700) or the *sashimi moriawase* (sashimi assortment; ¥750/1300/1800 depending on size). There's no English sign or menu. Look for the traditional front, coral around the entryway and a red-and-white sign.

Mori-no-Kokage (Map p794; ☎ 83-7933; Yui Rd; ⏰ 5pm-midnight closed Tue) Just north of the covered arcade on Yui Rd, this fine little *izakaya* has great warmth and natural ambience. There is a generous selection of local specialities on offer, including *Ishigaki-gyuu salada* (Ishigaki beef salad; from ¥1280) and the local microbrew, Ishigaki-shimanari (¥650). Look for the plants and tree trunks outside.

SHOPPING

A good place to shop for *omiyage* (souvenirs) is the main shopping arcade, which also has a public market. Upstairs from the market is the **Ishigaki City Special Products Centre** (Map p794; ☎ 88-8633; ⏰ 11am-7pm), which lets visitors sample traditional herbal teas, and browse textiles and pearl jewellery.

Also worth a look is the **Minsā Kōgeikan** (みんさー工芸館; off Map p794; ☎ 82-3473; ⏰ 9am-6pm), which is a weaving workshop and showroom with exhibits on Yaeyama-shotō textiles. The building is located between the city centre and the airport, and can be reached via the airport bus (be sure to tell the driver you want to stop here).

GETTING THERE & AWAY

Air

Ishigaki-jima has direct flights to/from Tokyo's Haneda airport (JTA; ¥54,000, 3½ hours, two daily), Osaka's Kansai International Airport (JTA; ¥44,400 2 hours 50 minutes, one daily), Kōbe (JTA; ¥44,400, 2¼ hours, one daily), Naha (JTA/ANA; ¥21,100, one hour, 20 daily), Miyako-jima (JTA/RAC; ¥10,900, 35 minutes, three daily), Yonaguni-jima (JTA/RAC; ¥29,100, 30 minutes, one or two daily) and Hateruma-jima (Air Dolphin; ¥8500, 25 minutes, four weekly, more in summer).

Boat

Ishigaki-jima Rittō Ferry Terminal (Map p794) is located on Ishigaki-wan, a short walk southwest of the city centre. Countless daily ferries operate between here and outlying islands in Yaeyama-shotō each day. Destinations include Iriomote-jima, Kohama-jima, Taketomi-jima and Hateruma-jima (see the relevant sections for details). Departures are frequent enough that you can usually just turn up in the morning and hop on the next ferry departing for your intended destination (although you might want to stop by the day before to make reservations during the summer high season). The three main ferry operators are **Yaeyama Kankō Ferry** (☎ 82-5010), **Ishigaki Dream Kankō** (☎ 84-3178) and **Anei Kankō** (☎ 83-0055). All three have ticket offices inside the ferry terminal.

GETTING AROUND

The bus station is across the road from the ferry terminal in Ishigaki City. There are hourly buses to the airport (¥200, 20 minutes), as well as a few daily buses to Kabira-wan (¥700, 50 minutes), Yonehara Beach (¥800, one hour) and Shiraho (¥400, 30 minutes).

Rental cars, scooters and bicycles are readily available at shops throughout the city centre. If you're comfortable on a scooter, it's a scenic four- to five-hour cruise around the island, though you should plan for longer if you want to spend some time relaxing on the island's beaches. **Ishigaki Rentacar** (☎ 82-8840) is located in the city centre and has reasonable rates.

Iriomote-jima 西表島

☎ 0980 / pop 2290

Although it's just 20km west of Ishigaki-jima, Iriomote-jima could easily qualify as Japan's last frontier. Dense jungles and mangrove forest blanket more than 90% of the island, and the island is fringed by some of the most beautiful coral reefs in all Japan. If you're superlucky, you may even spot one of the island's rare *yamaneko*, a nocturnal and rarely seen wildcat.

Needless to say, Iriomote-jima is the perfect destination for outdoor enthusiasts. Several rivers penetrate far into the lush interior of the island and these can be explored by riverboat or kayak. Add to the mix sun-drenched beaches and spectacular diving and snorkelling, and it's easy to see why Iriomote-jima is one of the best destinations in Japan for nature lovers.

Most visitors to Iriomote are day-trippers from Ishigaki, but we recommend spending a night or three if you have the time. If you do so, you'll be rewarded with a glimpse of a Japan that seems worlds away from central Tokyo.

ORIENTATION & INFORMATION

Iriomote-jima has a 58km-long perimeter road that runs about halfway around the coast. No roads run into the interior, which is virtually untouched. Boats from Ishigaki-jima either dock at Uehara on the north coast, which is closer to the main points of interest, or at Ōhara on the southeast coast. Ōhara is the closest thing to a population centre on the island. At the western terminus of the main road, you will find the hamlet of Shirahama. The best beaches on the island are around its northern end, while river trips take place on the Urauchi-gawa, in the central/north part of the island.

SIGHTS & ACTIVITIES

Beaches

The majority of the island's beaches are shallow due to the extensive coral reef that surrounds the island. The best swimming beach on the island is **Tsuki-ga-hama** (Moon Beach; Map pp790–1), a crescent-shaped yellow-sand beach at the mouth of the Urauchi-gawa on the north coast.

If you're looking to do a bit of snorkelling, head to **Hoshisuna-no-hama** (Star Sand Beach; Map pp790–1) on the northwestern tip of the island. The beach is named after its star sand, which actually consists of the dried skeletons of tiny sea creatures. If you are a competent swimmer and the sea is calm, make your way with mask and snorkel to the outside of the reef – the coral and tropical fish here are spectacular.

From **Shirahama** (白浜), at the western end of the north coast road, there are four daily boats to the isolated settlement of **Funauki** (船浮; ¥410). Once there, it's a mere 10-minute walk on to the absolutely gorgeous **Ida-no-hama** (Map pp790–1), which pretty much meets all expectations of a picture-perfect tropical beach.

If you want to have a sandy beach to yourself, head to **Haemida-no-hama** (Map pp790–1), at the extreme western end of the south coast road. The seemingly never-ending beach wraps around the coast for kilometres on end, and consists of yellow sand strewn with massive boulders (and, unfortunately, a fair bit of flotsam). On a clear day, you can see the island of Hateruma-jima (p799) to the south. There is a parking lot where the asphalt ends and a sign; from here, it's a 100m walk to the beach.

Onsen

If outdoor activities are rained out, a good back-up plan is the **Iriomote Onsen** (Map pp790-1; ☎ 85-5700; admission ¥1500; ⏰ noon-10pm), which is part of the Painu Maya Resort hotel, on the east coast of the island. The onsen consists of sex-separated indoor and outdoor baths. The grounds are attractively landscaped, and there are soothing views of the nearby forest. Buy a ticket at the main counter in the lobby of the resort. The onsen-hotel is easy to miss; it's off the main road about 20km north of Ōhara.

River Trips

Iriomote's number-one attraction is a boat trip up the **Urauchi-gawa** (浦内川), a winding brown river that is reminiscent of a tiny stretch of the Amazon. From the mouth of the river, **Urauchi-gawa Kankō** (☎ 85-6154) runs boat tours 8km up the river (round-trip ¥1500, 30 minutes each way, multiple departures daily between 8.30am and 5pm). At the 8km point, the boat docks and you can walk a further 2km to reach the scenic waterfalls known as the **Mariyudō-no-taki** (マリユドウの滝; Map pp790–1), from where another 200m brings you to the **Kambiray-no-taki** (カンビレーの滝; Map pp790–1). The walk from the dock to Kambiray-no-taki and back to the dock takes around two hours. Of course, if you want, you can just take the boat trip to the dock and back. The pier for these boat trips is about 6km west of Uehara

From a pier on the south side of the river, just east of the bridge in Ōhara, **Tōbu Kōtsū** (☎ 85-5304; ⏰ 8.30am-5.30pm) runs river cruises up Iriomote's second-largest river, the **Nakama-gawa** (仲間川). The one-hour tour (¥1500) passes through lush mangroves and thick vegetation.

If you're the independent type, you can rent kayaks and canoes (¥8000 per day) near both departure points for the river tours.

Hiking

Iriomote has some great hikes, but do not head off into the jungle interior without a local guide: the trails in the interior are hard to follow and the jungle is dense – lots of people have gotten lost and required rescue in recent years. We suggest that you stick to well-marked tracks like the one listed here. If you want to try something more ambitious, your accommodation owner can help arrange a local guide.

At the back of a mangrove-lined bay called Funaura-wan a few kilometres east of Uehara, you can make out a lovely waterfall plunging 55m down the cliffs. This is **Pinaisāra-no-taki** (ピナイサーラの滝; Map pp790–1), Okinawa's highest waterfall. When the tide is right, you can paddle a kayak across the shallow lagoon and then follow the Nishida-gawa to the base of the falls. A path branches off and climbs to the top of the falls, from where there are superb views down to the coast. The walk takes less than two hours, and the river is great for a cooling dip.

Unfortunately, it is difficult to find a tour company that will rent you a kayak without requiring you to join a guided tour. If you have a foldable or inflatable kayak, we suggest bringing it. Otherwise, accommodation owners can arrange participation in a guided tour.

For another good hike, try the hikes along the Urauchi-gawa (see River Trips, opposite).

Diving

Iriomote has some brilliant coral around its shores, much of which is accessible to proficient snorkellers. Most of the offshore dive sites around Iriomote are served by dive operators based on Ishigaki; see p793 for details.

One spot worth noting is the unusual **Barasutō**, between Iriomote-jima and Hatoma-jima, which is a small island formed entirely of bits of broken coral. In addition to the island itself, the reefs nearby are in quite good condition and make for good boat-based snorkelling on a calm day.

SLEEPING

Iriomote-jima's accommodation is spread out around the island, so it's best to phone ahead and make a reservation before arriving on the island. Most places will send a car to pick you up from the ferry terminal if you let them know what time you will be arriving.

In addition to the places listed below, there is a free camping ground with showers, toilets and a cooking area at Haemida-no-hama, on the southern coast of the island, just before the beach parking lot.

Irumote-sō Youth Hostel (Map pp790-1; ☎ 85-6255; www.ishigaki.com/irumote, in Japanese; dm from ¥3600; Ⓟ 💻) If you're on a budget, a good choice is this well-run youth hostel, which is located fairly close to Uehara Port. Accommodation is in comfortable dorms and simple Japanese-style private rooms. Meals are served in the large communal dining room (breakfast/dinner ¥500/1000). It's inland and up the hill a little south from Uehara Port; we recommend calling for a pick-up before you arrive the first time, since it's not easy to find on your own.

Pension Hoshi-no-Suna (Map pp790-1; ☎ 85-6448; www.hoshinosuna.ne.jp; r per person from ¥7500; Ⓟ) Located right above Hoshinosuna-hama, this popular pension is a great choice in terms of location. Accommodation is in Western- and Japanese-style rooms with ocean views and small verandahs. There is also a small on-site bar and restaurant, as well as a dive shop.

Eco Village Iriomote (Map pp790-1; ☎ 85-5115; http://eco-village.jp, in Japanese; r per person from ¥10,000; Ⓟ) This upscale resort on the northeast coat of the island is a good choice for those who want a bit more comfort. There are several types of rooms, from simple rooms in the main building to full-detached beachfront suites. There is an on-site restaurant and kayaks are available for rent.

EATING

With few restaurants on the island, most travellers prefer to take meals at their accommodation (or self-cater). However, if you want a meal out, we recommend the following spot.

Shinpachi Shokudō (Map pp790-1; ☎ 85-6078; ⏲ lunch & dinner) Just 200m south of the port in Uehara, this no-frills noodle shop is the perfect spot for a hot bowl of *sōki-soba* (¥700) or a *gōya champuru* (¥800), washed down with a nice draught beer. Look for the blue front and the banners outside.

For those who want to self-cater, there is a supermarket in the middle of Uehara, just north of Eneos petrol station.

GETTING THERE & AROUND

Yaeyama Kankō Ferry (☎ 82-5010), **Ishigaki Dream Kankō** (☎ 84-3178) and **Anei Kankō** (☎ 83-0055) operate ferries between Ishigaki City (on Ishigaki-jima) and Iriomote-jima. Ferries from Ishigaki sail to/from two main ports on Iriomote: Uehara Port (¥2000, 40 minutes, up to 20 daily) and Ōhara Port (¥1540, 35 minutes, up to 27 daily). Note that Uehara Port is more convenient for most destinations on Iriomote.

Six buses each day ply the island's main coastal road between Ōhara and Shirahama (¥1200, 1½ hours). Due to the relative scarcity of buses, it's a good idea to rent a car or scooter if you have an International Driving Permit. **Yamaneko Rentacar** (☎ 85-5111) has offices in both Uehara and Ōhara (the Uehara office is on the main road a little south of the ferry pier). Most of the island accommodation also rents bicycles to guests. With plenty of alternative lifestylers on the island, hitching is also an option, but take the usual precautions.

Taketomi-jima 竹富島

☎ 0980 / pop 350

A mere 10-minute boat ride from Ishigaki-jima, the tiny islet of Taketomi-jima is a living museum of Ryūkyū culture. Centred on a flower-bedecked village of traditional houses complete with red *kawara* (tiled) roofs, coral walls and *shiisa* statues, Taketomi is a breath of fresh air if you're suffering from an overdose of modern Japan.

In order to preserve the island's historical ambience, residents have joined together to ban signs of modernism such as asphalt. Instead, the island is criss-crossed by a series of crushed-coral roads that are ideally explored by the humble push bike. Taketomi is also refreshingly free of other eyesores such

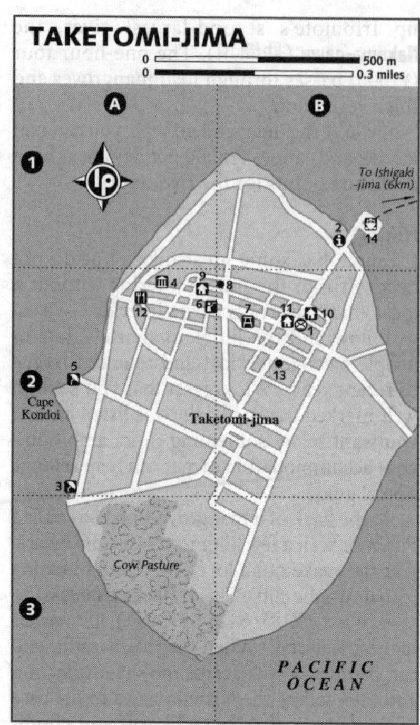

as the ubiquitous convenience store, though there are plenty of adorable 'Mum & Dad' shops scattered around the island.

While Taketomi is besieged by Japanese day-trippers in the busy summer months, the island is blissfully quiet at night, even in summer. If you have the chance, it's worth spending a night here as Taketomi truly weaves its spell after the sun dips below the horizon.

ORIENTATION & INFORMATION

Ferries arrive at the small port (竹富東港) on the northeast corner of the island, while Taketomi village is located in the centre of the island. Since the island is only 3km long and 2km wide, it is easily explored on foot or by bicycle.

There's a small **information desk** (☎ 84-5633; ⏲ 7.30am-6pm) in the port building, but for the full scoop on Taketomi-jima, head next door to the **Taketomi-jima Yugafu-kan** (竹富島ゆがふ館; ☎ 85-2488; ⏲ 8am-5pm) visitors centre, which has excellent displays and exhibits on the island.

INFORMATION
Information Desk .... (see 14)
Taketomi Post Office 竹富郵便局 1 B2
Taketomi-jima Yugafu-kan 竹富島ゆがふ館 2 B1

SIGHTS & ACTIVITIES
Gaiji-hama ガイジ浜 3 A2
Kihōin Shūshūkan 喜宝院蒐集館 4 A2
Kondoi Beach コンドイビーチ 5 A2
Nagomi-no-tō なごみの塔 6 A2
Nishitō Utaki 西塘御嶽 7 B2
Taketomi Mingei-kan 竹富民芸館 8 B2

SLEEPING
Minshuku Izumiya 民宿泉屋 9 A2
Ōhama-sō 大浜荘 10 B2
Takana Ryokan 高那旅館 11 B2

EATING
Soba Dokoro Takenoko そば処竹の子 12 A2

TRANSPORT
Maruhachi Rentals 丸八レンタサイクル 13 B2
Taketomi Port 竹富港 14 B1

SIGHTS & ACTIVITIES

There are a number of modest sights in Taketomi village, though the main attraction here is simply wandering around and soaking up the ambience.

Roughly in the centre of the village, the modest lookout tower of **Nagomi-no-tō** (admission free; 24hr) has good views over the red-tiled roofs of the pancake-flat island. Nearby, **Nishitō Utaki** is a shrine dedicated to a 16th-century ruler of Yaeyama-shotō who was born on Taketomi-jima. **Kihōin Shūshūkan** (☎ 85-2202; admission ¥300; 9am-5pm) is a private museum with a diverse collection of folk artefacts. **Taketomi Mingei-kan** (☎ 85-2302; admission free; 9am-5pm) is where the island's woven *minsā* belts and other textiles are produced.

Taketomi-jima also has some decent beaches. At **Kondoi Beach** on the west coast you'll find the best swimming on the island. Just south is **Gaiji-hama**, which is the main *hoshi-suna* (star sand) hunting ground.

SLEEPING & EATING

Many of the traditional houses around the island are Japanese-style ryokan that serve traditional Okinawan cuisine. However, don't turn up on the last ferry expecting to find accommodation; Taketomi fills up quickly in the summer, so be sure to book ahead.

Takana Ryokan (高那旅館; ☎ 85-2151; www.kit.hi-ho.ne.jp/hayasaka-my, in Japanese; dm with/without meals ¥4390/2990, r per person with meals from ¥8500) Opposite the tiny post office, Takana actually consists of a basic youth hostel and an attached upmarket ryokan. Basic Western-style dorms in the youth hostel are a great option if you're on a budget, though the charming Japanese-style tatami rooms in the ryokan are a romantic choice if you're travelling with a loved one.

Ōhama-sō (大浜荘; ☎ 85-2226; fax 85-2226; r per person with/without meals ¥5500/3500) Also beside the post office, this *minshuku* has a light and jovial atmosphere, especially when the owner starts to entertain on the *sanshin* (Okinawan three-stringed lute) after dinner. Accommodation is in simple yet comfortable Japanese-style tatami rooms with shared facilities.

Minshuku Izumiya (民宿泉屋; ☎ 85-2250; r per person with meals ¥5500) On the northwest edge of the village, this intimate *minshuku* is centred on a stunning traditional garden. Accommodation is in Japanese-style tatami rooms with shared facilities.

Soba Dokoro Takenoko (☎ 85-2251; 10.30am-4pm & 6.30-10pm) This tiny restaurant on the northwest side of the village (look for the blue banner and the umbrellas) serves *sōki-soba* (¥700) and *yaki-soba* (fried *soba*; ¥700), as well as Orion beer to wash it down with.

GETTING THERE & AROUND

Yaeyama Kankō Ferry (☎ 82-5010), **Ishigaki Dream Kankō** (☎ 84-3178) and **Anei Kankō** (☎ 83-0055) operate ferries between Ishigaki City (on Ishigaki-jima) and Taketomi-jima (¥590, 10 minutes, up to 45 daily).

Rental bicycles are great for exploring the crushed-coral roads. **Maruhachi Rentals** (丸八レンタサイクル; ☎ 85-2260; bicycles per hr ¥300; 8am-5.15pm) runs a free shuttle between its shop and the port. Another way to see the island is by taking a tour in a **water buffalo cart**. Two operators in the village offer 30-minute rides for ¥1200 per person.

Hateruma-jima 波照間島

☎ 0980 / pop 600

Forty-five kilometres south of Iriomote-jima is the tiny islet of Hateruma-jima, Japan's southernmost inhabited island. Just 15km around, Hateruma-jima has a couple of nice beaches and a seriously laid-back vibe.

Ferries arrive at the small port on the northwest corner of the island, while Hateruma village is in the centre. Slightly larger than Taketomi-jima, Hateruma-jima is easily explored by bicycle or scooter. There's a small **information desk** (☎ 82-5445; 8.30am-5pm, closed Sat, Sun & holidays) in the port building, and also in the airport, that can help you find accommodation on the island.

Just to the west of the port is **Nishihama** (ニシ浜), a perfect beach of snow-white sand with some good coral offshore. Here you will find free public showers, toilets and a camping ground. At the opposite southeast corner of the island, directly south of the airport, is the impressive **Takanasaki** (高那崎), a 1km-long cliff of Ryūkyū limestone that is pounded by the Pacific Ocean. At the western end of the cliffs is a small monument marking **Japan's southernmost point** (日本最南端の碑), which is an extremely popular photo spot for Japanese visitors.

There are several *minshuku* on the island, including the popular **Minshuku Minoru-sō** (民宿みのる荘; ☎ 85-8438; r per person with/without meals ¥5000/2500) near the town centre. The friendly owners rent out bicycles, scooters and snorkelling gear. Accommodation is in cosy Japanese-style tatami rooms. If you make a reservation, the owners can pick you up from the ferry port.

Another good choice is **Pension Sainantan** (ペンション最南端; ☎ 85-8686; r per person from ¥8500), which has both Japanese- and Western-style rooms, all with unit baths. This place is only three minutes' walk from Nihihama.

Air Dolphin has one flight a day from Ishigaki to Hateruma-jima (from ¥8500, 25 minutes). **Anei Kankō** (☎ 83-0055) and **Hateruma Kaiun** (☎ 82-7233) each have three ferries a day to Hateruma-jima from Ishigaki (¥3000 and ¥3050 respectively, one hour). There is no public transport on the island, but rental bicycles and scooters are readily available for hire.

Yonaguni-jima 与那国島

☎ 0980 / pop 1630

About 125km west of Ishigaki and 110km east of Taiwan is the islet of Yonaguni-jima, Japan's westernmost inhabited island. Renowned for its strong sake, small horses and marlin fishing, the island is also home to the jumbo-sized Yonaguni atlas moth, the largest moth in the world.

However, most visitors to the island come to see what lies beneath the waves around the island. In 1985, a diver discovered what appeared to be man-made 'ruins' off the south coast of the island. In addition, the waters off the west coast are frequented by large schools of hammerhead sharks. Needless to say, this makes the island perhaps the most famous single diving destination in Japan, and it would make a good counterpoint to a coral reefs and mantas around Ishigaki and Iriomote.

ORIENTATION & INFORMATION

The ferry port of Kubura (久部良) is at the island's western extreme. The main settlement is around the secondary port of Sonai (租内) on the north coast. In between, on the northwest coast, you'll find the airport.

There are small **information counters** (☎ 87-2402; 8.30am-5.30pm, closed Tue & Sat) in both the port building and the airport, which can help you find accommodation. Even if you can't read Japanese, it's worth picking up a copy of the Japanese-language *Yonaguni-jima* map.

SIGHTS

Just as Hateruma-jima has a monument to mark Japan's southernmost point, Yonaguni-jima has a rock to mark the country's **westernmost point** (日本最西端の碑) at **Irizaki** (西崎). If the weather is perfect, the mountains of Taiwan are visible far over the sea (this happens only about twice a year – so don't be disappointed if you can't make them out).

Yonaguni has an extremely rugged landscape, and the coastline is marked with great rock formations, much like those on the east coast of Taiwan. The most famous of these are **Tachigami-iwa** (立神岩), literally 'Standing-God Rock', **Gunkan-iwa** (軍艦岩) and **Sanninu-dai** (サンニヌ台), all of which are off the southeast coast. At the eastern tip of the island, Yonaguni horses graze in the pastures leading out to the lighthouse at **Agarizaki** (東崎).

Displays on Yonaguni's giant moths, which have a wingspan of 25cm to 30cm and are affectionately known as Yonaguni-san, can be seen at **Ayamihabiru-kan** (アヤミハビル館; ☎ 87-2440; admission ¥500; ⏰ 10am-4pm Wed-Sun), about 1km south of Sonai.

If you want to sample Hanazake, the island's infamous local brew, head to **Kokusen Awamori** (国選泡盛; ☎ 87-2315; ⏰ 8am-5pm), which is located in Sonai and offers free tastings and sales on-site.

ACTIVITIES

Diving

Local divers have long known about the thrills that await at **Irizaki Point** (西崎ポイント), off the coast of Cape Irizaki. In the winter months (January, February and March), the deep waters here are frequented by large schools of hammerhead sharks. Local diver operators say that if you dive here two days in a row during one of the winter months, you have a good chance of seeing a hammerhead school.

Even more popular than the sharks are the famous **Kaitei Iseki** (Underwater Ruins ; 海底遺跡), which were discovered by chance in 1985 by the Japanese marine explorer Kihachirou Aratake. Some claim that these ruins, which look like giant blocks or steps of a sunken pyramid, are the remains of a Pacific Atlantis, although there are equally compelling arguments that they are just the random result of geological processes. We suggest that you judge for yourself. If you don't dive, **Jack's Dolphin glass-bottomed boat** (☎ 87-2311; per person ¥6000; ⏰ sailings at 9am & noon) does two daily trips to the ruins, provided a minimum of three people are present.

There are numerous dive operators on the island. One shop with English-speaking guides is **SaWest** (☎ 87-2311; 59-6 Yonaguni, Yonaguni-chō Aza, Yaeyama-gun; 1/2 dives ¥8000/12,000, equipment rental ¥5000; ⏰ 8am-6pm).

Beaches

There are several good beaches around the island, the best of which is **Ubudomai-hama** (ウブドゥマイハマ), which is located at the east end of the island, shortly before Agarizaki (look out for the steep access road).

Fishing

In addition to diving, the seas off Yonaguni are also renowned for **marlin fishing**, and the All-Japan Billfish Tournament is held here each year in June or July. If you're interested in trolling, boats in Kubura can be chartered from ¥55,000 a day – call the **Yonaguni Fishing Co-operative** (☎ 87-2803, in Japanese) for information.

SLEEPING & EATING

Although there are several sleeping options around the island, it's best to phone ahead as Yonaguni is quite a distance to travel without a reservation. The following places will pick you up at either the airport or the ferry terminal.

Minshuku Yoshimarusō (民宿よしまる荘; ☎ 87-2658; r per person with meals ¥6825) Near the ferry terminal in Kubura, Yoshimarusō is ideal for divers, as the friendly owners also operate the on-site Yonaguni Diving Service. Simple Japanese-style tatami rooms with shared facilities have nice views of the nearby port, though the real appeal of this *minshuku* is the owners' local diving expertise. It's up the hill, overlooking the port.

Hotel Irifune (ホテル入船; ☎ 87-2311; www.yonaguni.jp, in Japanese; r per person with meals ¥6000) If you want to be based in Sonai, this simple business hotel is located near the main post office. Irifune offers fairly standard Japanese- and Western-style rooms, though it's a good option if you're looking for a little bit of privacy.

Fujimi Ryokan (ふじみ旅館; ☎ 87-2143; fax 87-2956; r per person with 2 meals from ¥5800) One block inland from the Hotel Irifune in Sonai, this basic ryokan is a good choice if you're looking for more traditional accommodation. It's roughly between the traffic light and the post office.

Ailand Resort (アイランドリゾート与那国; ☎ 87-2300; www.ailand-resort.co.jp; tw per person with 2 meals from ¥13,000; P 💻) This spiffy new hotel-resort is located on the north side of the island, between the airport and Sonai. It's got spacious, light, comfortable Western-style rooms and an on-site restaurant.

Adan (阿壇; ☎ 87-2140; ⏰ lunch & dinner, closed Sun or Mon) In the centre of Sonai, about 100m northeast of the only traffic light in town, you'll find this delightful little Okinawan-style restaurant that serves *soba*, *yaki-soba* and *gyūdon* (cooked beef over noodles), all for around ¥600. Three nights a week, it has

have live music in the evenings. Look for the English sign outside.

There is a decent camping ground on the south coast near the village of Higawa, next to Kataburu Hama (a decent beach).

If you want to self-cater, there are two simple supermarkets in the centre of Sonai.

GETTING THERE & AROUND

RAC has flights between Yonaguni and Naha (¥29,100, one hour 40 minutes, four daily). RAC or JTA operate flights between Yonaguni and Ishigaki-jima (¥18,000, 30 minutes, one or two daily).

Fukuyama Kaiun (☎ 87-2555) operates one or two ferries a week between Ishigaki-jima and Kubura Port on Yonaguni (¥3460, four hours 30 minutes).

There are public buses on Yonaguni-jima, but they make only four trips around the island per day, so the best way to get around the island is by rental car or scooter. **Yonaguni Honda** (☎ 87-2376) in central Sonai will send a car to meet you at the airport or the ferry terminal if you phone ahead. Another good car-rental operation that will also pick you up at the airport is **Ailand Rentacar** (☎ 87-2300).

Directory

CONTENTS

ACCOMMODATION

Japan offers a wide range of accommodation, from cheap guest houses to first-class hotels. In addition to the Western-style accommodation, you'll also find distinctive Japanese-style places, such as ryokan (traditional Japanese inns; see p807) and *minshuku* (inexpensive Japanese-style guest houses; see p806).

In this guide, accommodation listings have been organised by neighbourhood and price. Budget options cost ¥6000 or less; midrange rooms cost between ¥6000 and ¥15,000; and top-end rooms will cost more than ¥15,000 (per double). Room rates listed in this book include tax (ie the national 5% consumption tax is figured into the rates).

Of course, there are some regional and seasonal variations. Accommodation tends to be more expensive in big cities than in rural areas. Likewise, in resort areas like the Izu-hantō, accommodation is more expensive during the warm months. In ski areas like Hakuba and Niseko, needless to say, accommodation prices go up in winter and down in summer.

Since air conditioning is basically ubiquitous in Japan (due to its hot summers), we do not list air-con icons for accommodation options in this guide. We only note places that do not have air-con. If nothing is mentioned about air-con, you can assume a place has it.

Reservations

It can be hard to find accommodation during the following holiday periods: Shōgatsu (New Year) – 31 December to 3 January; Golden Week – 29 April to 5 May; and O-Bon – mid-August. If you plan to be in Japan during these periods, you should make reservations as far in advance as possible.

Tourist information offices at main train stations can usually help with reservations, and are often open until about 6.30pm or later. Even if you are travelling by car, the train station is a good first stop in town for information, reservations and cheap car parking.

Making phone reservations in English is usually possible at larger hotels and foreigner-friendly ryokan. Providing you speak clearly and simply, there will usually be someone around who can get the gist of what you want.

BOOK YOUR STAY ONLINE

For more accommodation reviews and recommendations by Lonely Planet authors, check out the online booking service at www.lonelyplanet.com/hotels. You'll find the true, insider low-down on the best places to stay. Reviews are thorough and independent. Best of all, you can book online.

PRACTICALITIES

- **Newspapers & Magazines** There are three main English-language daily newspapers in Japan: the *Japan Times, Daily Yomiuri* and *Asahi Shimbun/International Herald Tribune*. In the bigger cities, these are available at bookstores, convenience stores, train station kiosks and some hotels. In the countryside, you may not be able to find them anywhere. Foreign magazines are available in the major bookshops in the bigger cities.
- **Radio** Recent years have seen an increase in the number of stations aimed specifically at Japan's foreign population. InterFM (76.1FM; www.interfm.co.jp/) is a favourite of Tokyo's expat community, and the Kansai equivalent is FM Cocolo (76.5FM; www.cocolo.co.jp).
- **Electricity** The Japanese electric current is 100V AC. Tokyo and eastern Japan are on 50Hz, and western Japan, including Nagoya, Kyoto and Osaka, is on 60Hz. Most electrical items from other parts of the world will function on Japanese current. Japanese plugs are the flat two-pin type.
- **Video Systems** Japan uses the NTSC system.
- **Weights & Measures** Japan uses the international metric system.

For more information on making accommodation reservations in Japan, see Japanese Accommodation Made Easy (opposite).

The **International Tourism Center of Japan** (formerly Welcome Inn Reservation Center; www.itcj.jp/) operates five Welcome Inn Reservation Centers in Japan as well as an online booking system. It's free service includes hundreds of *minshuku*, ryokan, inns and pensions in Japan. It operates counters in the main tourist information offices in Tokyo (see p126) and Kyoto (see p328), and at the main tourist information counters in Narita and Kansai airports. You can also make reservations online through its website (which is also an excellent source of information on member hotels and inns).

The **Japanese Inn Group** (www.jpinn.com/index.html) is a collection of foreigner-friendly ryokan and guest houses. You can book member inns via its website or phone/fax. Pick up a copy of its excellent miniguide to member inns at major tourist information centres in Japan.

It is common courtesy to cancel a reservation if you change your plans and it makes things easier for those who come after you. (One reason foreigners occasionally have a hard time with accommodation is because others who have gone before them have made reservations and then pulled no-shows.)

Camping

Camping is possible at official camping grounds across Japan, some of which are only open during the summer high season of July and August. Camping is also possible year-round (when conditions permit) at camping grounds in the mountains or around certain mountain huts (p806). 'Guerrilla' or unofficial camping is also possible in many parts of rural Japan, but we recommend asking a local person about acceptable areas before setting up your tent.

Cycling Terminals

Cycling terminals *(saikuringu tāminaru)* provide low-priced accommodation of the bunk-bed or tatami-mat variety and are usually found in scenic areas suited to cycling. If you don't have your own bike, you can rent one at the terminal.

Cycling terminal prices compare favourably with those of a youth hostel: at around ¥3000 per person per night, or ¥5000 including two meals. For more information, check out the website of the **Bicycle Popularization Association of Japan** (www.cycle-info.bpaj.or.j p/english/begin/st.html).

Hostels

Japan has an extensive network of youth hostels, often located in areas of interest to travellers. The best source of information on youth hostels is the *Zenkoku Youth Hostel no Tabi* booklet, which is available for ¥1365 from **Japan Youth Hostels, Inc** (Map pp142-3; JYHA; ☎ 03-3288-1417; www.jyh.or.jp/english; 9th fl, Kanda Amerex Bldg, 3-1-16 Misaki-chō, Chiyoda-ku, Tokyo 100-0006). Many youth hostels in Japan sell this handbook.

The best way to find hostels is via the JYHA website, which has details in English on all member hostels, and allows online reservations. Another option is the *Youth Hostel Map of Japan*, which has one-line entries on each hostel. It's available for free from Japan National Tourism Organization (JNTO) and travel information centres (TICs) in Japan.

MEMBERSHIP, PRICES & REGULATIONS

You can stay at youth hostels in Japan without being a member of either the JYHA or the International Youth Hostel Federation (IYHA). You can purchase a one-year IYHA membership card at youth hostels in Japan for ¥2500.

Hostel charges currently average ¥3000 per night; some also add 5% consumption tax (see p817 for more information). Private rooms are available in some hostels from ¥3500 per night. Some hostels have introduced a special reduction – sometimes as much as ¥500 per night – for foreign hostellers.

Average prices for meals are ¥500 for breakfast and ¥900 for dinner. Almost all hostels require that you use a regulation sleeping sheet, which you can rent for ¥100 if you do not have your own. Although official regulations state that you can only stay at one hostel for three consecutive nights, this is sometimes waived outside the high season.

Hostellers are expected to check in between 3pm and 8pm to 9pm. There is usually a curfew of 10pm or 11pm. Checkout is usually before 10am and dormitories are closed between 10am and 3pm. Bath time is usually between 5pm and 9pm, dinner is between 6pm and 7.30pm, and breakfast is between 7am and 8am.

Hotels

You'll find a range of Western-style hotels in most Japanese cities and resort areas. Rates at standard midrange hotels average ¥9000 for a single and ¥12,000 for a double or twin. Rates at first-class hotels average ¥15,000 for a single and ¥20,000 for a double or twin. In addition to the 5% consumption tax that is levied on all accommodation in Japan, you may have to pay an additional 10% or more as a service charge at luxury hotels in Japan. Note that the rooms rates listed in this book include the consumption tax.

JAPANESE ACCOMMODATION MADE EASY

More than one foreign traveller has turned up unannounced in a ryokan or *minshuku* (Japanese-style guest house) and been given a distinctly cold reception, then concluded that they have been the victim of discrimination. More than likely, they simply broke one of the main rules of Japanese accommodation: don't surprise them. Unlike some countries, where it's perfectly normal to rock up at a place with no reservation, in Japan, people usually make reservations, often months in advance. With this in mind, here are a few tips to help you find a bed each night in Japan. Note that these also go for hotels, although they are generally a little more flexible than traditional accommodation.

- **Make reservations whenever possible** Even if it's a quick call a few hours before arriving, if you give the place a little warning, you'll vastly increase your chances of getting a room.
- **Fax** The Japanese are much more comfortable with written than spoken English. If you fax a room request with all your details, you will find a warm welcome. You can always follow it up with a call, once you're all on the same page.
- **The baton pass** Get your present accommodation to call ahead and reserve your next night's accommodation. This will put everyone at ease – if you're acceptable at one place, you'll be just fine at another. Remember: this is a country where introductions are everything.
- **Tourist information offices** In even the smallest hamlet or island in Japan, you'll find tourist information offices, usually right outside train stations or ferry terminals. These offices exist just to help travellers find accommodation (OK, they also give brilliant directions). They will recommend a place and call to see if a room is available, and then they will tell you exactly how to get there. This is another form of introduction.

Lastly, there will be times when you just have to slide that door open and hope for the best. Even the Japanese have to resort to this desperate expedient from time to time. The secret here is to try to minimise the shock. Smile like you're there to sell them insurance, muster your best *konbanwa* (good evening) and try to convince them that you actually prefer futons to beds, green tea to coffee, chopsticks to forks and baths to showers.

BUSINESS HOTELS

These are economical and practical places geared to the single traveller, usually local businessmen who want to stay somewhere close to the station. Rooms are clean, Western style, just big enough for you to turn around in and include a 'unit bath' (ie a bath/shower and toilet). Vending machines replace room service.

Cheap single rooms can sometimes be found for as low as ¥4500, though the average rate is around ¥8000. Most business hotels also have twin and double rooms, and usually do not have a service charge.

CAPSULE HOTELS

One of Japan's most famous forms of accommodation is the *capseru hoteru*. As the name implies, the 'rooms' in a capsule hotel consist of banks of neat white capsules stacked in rows two or three high. The capsules themselves are around 2m by 1m by 1m – about the size of a spacious coffin. Inside is a bed, a TV, a reading light, a radio and an alarm clock. Personal belongings are kept in a locker room. Most capsule hotels have the added attraction of a sauna and a large communal bath. The average price is ¥3800 per night.

Capsule hotels are common in major cities and often cater to workers who have partied too hard to make it home or have missed the last train. The majority of capsule hotels only accept male guests, but some also accept women (see Capsule Hotel Riverside, p166).

LOVE HOTELS

As their name indicates, love hotels are used by Japanese couples for discreet trysts. You can use them for this purpose as well, but they're also perfectly fine, if a little twee, for overnight accommodation.

To find a love hotel on the street, just look for flamboyant facades and signs clearly stating the rates. Love hotels are designed for maximum privacy: entrances and exits are kept separate; keys are provided through a small opening without contact between desk clerk and guest; and photos of the rooms are displayed to make the choice easy for the customer.

During the day, you can stay for a two- or three-hour 'rest' (*kyūkei* in Japanese) for about ¥4000 (rates are for the whole room, not per person). Love hotels are of more interest to foreign visitors after 10pm, when it's possible to stay the night for about ¥6500, but you should check out early enough in the morning to avoid a return to peak-hour rates. Look for the sign outside stating the rates. Even if you can't read Japanese, you should be able to figure out which rate applies to a 'rest' and which applies to an overnight stay.

Most love hotels are comfortable with foreign guests, but some travellers have reported being turned away at the odd place. Same-sex couples may have more trouble than one man and one woman.

Kokumin-shukusha

Kokumin-shukusha (people's lodges) are government-supported institutions offering affordable accommodation in scenic areas. Private Japanese-style rooms are the norm, though some places offer Western-style rooms. Prices average ¥5500 to ¥6500 per person per night, including two meals.

Minshuku

A *minshuku* is usually a family-run private guest house, rather like a Western-style B&B, except that you get both breakfast *and* dinner at a *minshuku*, making them extremely convenient for the traveller. The average price is around ¥6000 per person per night (with two meals). *Minshuku* are particularly common in rural areas and on the outer islands of Japan, where they may be the only accommodation option. For information on staying in a *minshuku*, see opposite.

Mountain Huts

Mountain huts *(yama-goya)* are common in many of Japan's hiking and mountain-climbing areas. While you'll occasionally find free emergency shelters, most huts are privately run and charge for accommodation. These places offer bed and board (two meals) at around ¥5000 to ¥8000 per person; if you prepare your own meal, that figure drops to ¥3000 to ¥5000 per person. It's best to call ahead to reserve a spot (contact numbers are available in Japanese hiking guides and maps, and in Lonely Planet's *Hiking in Japan*), but you won't be turned away if you show up without a reservation.

Pensions

Pensions are usually run by young couples offering Western-style accommodation based on the European pension concept. They are common in resort areas and around ski fields. Prices average ¥6000 per person per night, or ¥8500 including two meals.

STAYING IN A RYOKAN OR MINSHUKU

Let's face it: a hotel is a hotel wherever you go. Just as you want to try local food when you're on the road, you probably also want to try a night in traditional local accommodation. In Japan you'll find two kinds of traditional accommodation: ryokan and *minshuku.*

Ryokan (written with the Japanese characters for 'travel' and 'hall') are often fine old wooden Japanese buildings, with tatami mats, futons, gardens, deep Japanese bathtubs, traditional Japanese service and kitchens that turn out classic Japanese cuisine. Of course, much simpler ryokan also exist, and some even resemble hotels in every respect but the Japanese-style rooms.

Minshuku (written with the Japanese characters for 'people' and 'accommodation') are simpler versions of ryokan, sometimes private Japanese homes that have a few rooms given over to guests, other times purpose-built accommodation.

Due to language difficulties and unfamiliarity, staying in a ryokan or *minshuku* is not as straightforward as staying in a Western-style hotel. However, with a little education, it can be a breeze, even if you don't speak a word of Japanese.

Here's the basic drill. When you arrive, leave your shoes in the *genkan* (foyer area) and step up into the reception area. Here, you'll be asked to sign in and perhaps show your passport (you pay when you check out). You'll be shown around the place and then to your room where you will be served a cup of tea, or shown a hot-water flask and some tea cups so you can make your own. You'll note that there is no bedding to be seen in your room – your futon is in the closet and will be laid out later. You can leave your luggage anywhere except the *tokonoma* (sacred alcove), which will usually contain some flowers or a hanging scroll. If it's early enough, you can then go out to do some sightseeing.

When you return, you can change into your *yukata* (lightweight cotton Japanese robe or kimono) and be served dinner in your room or in a dining room. In a ryokan, dinner is often a multicourse feast of the finest local delicacies. In a *minshuku,* it will be simpler but still often very good. After dinner, you can take a bath. If it's a big place, you can generally bathe anytime in the evening until around 11pm. If it's a small place, you'll be given a time slot. While you're in the bath, some mysterious elves will go into your room and lay out your futon so that it will be waiting for you when you return all toasty from the bath.

In the morning, you'll be served a Japanese-style breakfast (some places these days serve a simple Western-style breakfast for those who can't stomach rice and fish in the morning). You pay on check out, which is usually around 11am.

Rider Houses

Catering mainly to touring motorcyclists, rider houses *(raidā hausu)* provide extremely basic shared accommodation from around ¥1000 per night. Some rider houses are attached to local *rāmen* (noodle) restaurants or other eateries, and may offer discounted rates if you agree to eat there. You should bring your own sleeping bag or ask to rent bedding from the owner. For bathing facilities, you will often be directed to the local *sentō* (public bath).

Rider houses are most common in Hokkaidō, but you'll also find them in places like Kyūshū and Okinawa. If you can read some Japanese, spiral-bound *Touring Mapple* maps, published by Shobunsha and available in Japan, mark almost all of the rider houses in a specific region, as well as cheap places to eat along the way. Japanese readers will also find the **Rider House Database** (www.tabizanmai.net/rider/riderdate/k_db.cgi, in Japanese) useful.

Ryokan

Ryokan are traditional Japanese lodgings. They are often interesting wooden buildings with traditional tatami-mat rooms and futons for bedding. Ryokan range from ultra-exclusive establishments to reasonably priced places with a homey atmosphere. Prices start at around ¥4000 (per person per night) for a no-frills ryokan without meals and climb right up to ¥100,000 for the best establishments. For around ¥10,000 per person, you can usually find a very good place that will serve you two excellent Japanese meals to complement your stay.

See the websites of the **International Tourism Center of Japan** (formerly Welcome Inn Reservation Center; www.itcj.jp/) and the **Japanese Inn Group** (www.jpinn.com/index.html) for information about the ryokan booking services they offer. For information on staying in a ryokan, see the boxed text (above).

Shukubō

Staying in a *shukubō* (temple lodging) is one way to experience another facet of traditional Japan. Sometimes you are allocated a simple room in the temple precincts and left to your own devices. Other times you may be asked to participate in prayers, services or *zazen* (seated meditation). At some temples, exquisite vegetarian meals *(shōjin-ryōri)* are served.

Tokyo and Kyoto TICs produce leaflets on temple lodgings in their regions. Kōya-san (p433), a renowned religious centre in the Kansai region, includes more than 50 *shukubō* and is one of the best places in Japan to try this type of accommodation. The popular pilgrimage of Shikoku's 88 sacred temples (see p656 for more information) also provides the opportunity to sample *shukubō*.

Over 70 youth hostels are located in temples or shrines – look for the reverse swastika in the JYHA handbook. The suffixes *-ji, -in* or *-dera* are also clues that the hostel is a temple.

Toho

The **Toho network** (www.toho.net/english.html) is a diverse collection of places that has banded loosely together to offer a more flexible alternative to youth hostels. Most of the network's 90 members are in Hokkaidō, although there are a few scattered around Honshū and other islands further south. Prices average ¥4000 per person for dormitory-style accommodation, or ¥5000 with two meals. Private rooms are sometimes available for about ¥1000 extra.

ACTIVITIES

Japan may be best known for its cultural attractions, but it's also a great place to ski, climb, trek, dive, snorkel and cycle. And, needless to say, it's an ideal destination to pursue martial arts, such as judo, aikido and karate.

Cycling

Bicycle touring is fairly popular in Japan, despite the fact that most of the country is quite mountainous. See p832 for more information on cycling in Japan. See also Cycling Terminals (p804) for information on places to stay.

Diving & Snorkelling

The great diving and snorkelling to be had around Japan's southern islands is one of the world's best kept underwater secrets. How many people even know that you can dive with mantas or hammerheads in the Land of the Rising Sun? Popular diving destinations include the Okinawan islands (p758), in the far southwest of Japan, and the chain of islands south of Tokyo, known as Izu-shotō (Izu Seven Islands; p240). Other dive sites in Japan include the waters around Tobi-shima (p557), off northern Honshū, and the Ogasawara-shotō (p245).

Diving in Japan can be expensive in comparison with other parts of Asia. Typical rates are ¥12,000 per day for two boat dives and lunch. Courses for beginners are available in places like Ishigaki-jima (p793) and Iriomote-jima (p797) in Okinawa, but starting costs are around ¥80,000. Instruction will usually be in Japanese.

If your plans include a trip to Okinawa or the Ogasawa-shotō, consider bringing your own mask, snorkel and fins (large-sized fins can be hard to find at dive shops). Serious divers may want to go further and bring their own regulars and even BCDs (buoyancy control devices), although these are available for rent at dive shops in country.

Hiking & Mountain Climbing

The Japanese are keen hikers, and many national parks in Japan have hiking routes. The popular hiking areas near Tokyo are around Nikkō (p197) and Izu-shotō (p240). In the Kansai region, Nara (p417), Shiga-ken (p384) and Kyoto (p324) all have pleasant hikes.

Japan comes into its own as a hiking destination in the Japan Alps National Park, particularly in Kamikōchi (p280), the Bandai plateau (p519) in northern Honshū, and Hokkaidō's national parks (p579).

While rudimentary English-language hiking maps may be available from local tourism authorities, it's better to seek out proper Japanese maps and decipher the kanji. Shobunsha's *Yama-to-Kōgen No Chizu* series covers all of Japan's most popular hiking areas in exquisite detail. The maps are available in all major bookshops in Japan.

Serious hikers will also want to pick up a copy of Lonely Planet's *Hiking in Japan,* which covers convenient one-day hikes near major cities and extended hikes in more remote areas.

Martial Arts

Japan is the home of several of the world's major martial arts: aikido, judo, karate and kendo. Less popular disciplines, such as *kyūdō* (Japanese archery) and sumō, also attract devotees from overseas. It is possible for foreigners to study all these disciplines here, although it's sometimes difficult to do so as a traveller. If you are really keen, we suggest living for a short spell near your *dōjō* (training place) of choice.

All Japan Jūdō Federation (Map pp142-3; Zen Nihon Jūdō Renmei; ☎ 03-3818-4199; www.judo.or.jp, in Japanese; c/o Kōdōkan, 1-16-30 Kasuga, Bunkyō-ku, Tokyo)

All Japan Kendō Federation (Map pp142-3; ☎ 03-3211-5804; www.kendo-fik.org/english-page/english-top-page.html; c/o Nippon Budōkan, 2-3 Kitanomaru-kōen, Chiyoda-ku, Tokyo)

All Nippon Kyūdō Federation (Map p134; ☎ 03-3481-2387; www.kyudo.jp/english/index.html; 4th fl, Kishi Memorial Hall, 1-1-1 Jinnan, Shibuya-ku, Tokyo)

International Aikidō Federation (Map pp128-9; ☎ 03-3203-9236; www.aikido-international.org; 17-18 Wakamatsu-chō, Shinjuku-ku, Tokyo)

Japan Karate Association (Map pp128-9; ☎ 03-5800-3091; www.jka.or.jp/english/e_index.html; 2-23-15 Kōraku, Bunkyō-ku, Tokyo)

Japan Karate-dō Federation (Map p138; ☎ 03-3503-6640; www.karatedo.co.jp/jkf/jkf-eng/e_index.htm; 6th fl, Nihon Zaidan Daini Bldg, 1-11-2 Toranomon, Minato-ku, Tokyo)

Nihon Sumō Kyōkai (Ryōgoku Sumō Stadium; Map pp128-9; ☎ 03-3623-5111; www.sumo.or.jp/eng; c/o Ryōgoku Kokugikan, 1-3-28 Yokoami, Sumida-ku, Tokyo)

Skiing

Japan is the best place to ski in Asia and it boasts some of the most reliable snow in the world. For more information, see the Skiing in Japan chapter (p108).

BUSINESS HOURS

Department stores usually open at 10am and close at 6.30pm or 7pm daily (with one or two days off each month). Smaller shops like food shops, stationery stores or clothing shops are open similar hours (usually 9am to 5pm Monday to Friday, to noon or 1pm Saturday) but may close on Sunday. Large companies usually work from 9am to 5pm weekdays and some also operate on Saturday morning.

Banks are open 9am to 3pm weekdays (some open until 5pm). For information on changing money, see p817. Post offices open 9am to 5pm Monday to Friday (major post offices 8am to 8pm); central post offices have after-hours/weekend windows.

Restaurants are usually open from 11am to 2pm and from 6pm to 11pm, with one day off per week, usually Monday or Tuesday. Some stay open all afternoon. Cafes are usually open 11am until 11pm, with one day off per week, usually Monday or Tuesday. Bars usually open around 5pm and stay open until the wee hours.

CHILDREN

Japan is a great place to travel with kids: it's safe and clean and there's never a shortage of places to keep them amused. Look out for *Japan for Kids* by Diane Wiltshire Kanagawa and Jeanne Huey Erickson, an excellent introduction to Japan's highlights from a child's perspective. In addition, Lonely Planet publishes *Travel with Children*, which gives the low-down on getting out and about with your children.

Practicalities

Parents will find that Japan is similar to Western countries in terms of facilities and allowances made for children, with a few notable exceptions. Cots are available in most hotels and these can be booked in advance. High chairs are available in many restaurants (although this isn't an issue in the many restaurants where everyone sits on the floor). There are nappy-changing facilities in some public places, like department stores and some larger train stations; formula and nappies are widely available, even in convenience stores. Breast feeding in public is generally not done. The one major problem concerns child seats for cars and taxis: these are generally not available. Finally, child-care agencies are available in most larger cities. The only problem is the language barrier: outside Tokyo, there are few, if any, agencies with English-speaking staff. See also Eating with Kids (p93) for some helpful tips on ordering food with children in tow.

Sights & Activities

Tokyo has the most child-friendly attractions in Japan, including Tokyo Disneyland (p159); for more information, see Tokyo for Children (p161). In Kansai, popular attractions for the young 'uns include Osaka's Universal Studios Japan (p400), Osaka Aquarium (p400) and Nara-kōen (p420) in Nara, with its resident deer population.

Children who enjoy the beach and activities like snorkelling will adore the islands of Okinawa (p758) and the Izu-shotō (p240).

CLIMATE

The combination of Japan's mountainous territory and the length of the archipelago (covering about 20° of latitude) makes for a complex climate. Most of the country is located in the northern temperate zone, which yields four distinct seasons. In addition, there are significant climatic differences between Hokkaidō in the north, which has short summers and lengthy winters with heavy snowfalls, and the southern islands, such as Okinawa in Nansei-shotō (Southwest Archipelago), which enjoy a subtropical climate.

In the winter months (December to February), cold, dry air-masses from Siberia move down over Japan, where they meet warmer, moister air-masses from the Pacific. The resulting precipitation causes huge snowfalls on the side of the country that faces the Sea of Japan. The Pacific Ocean side of Japan receives less snow but can still be quite cold, while the big cities of Honshū like Tokyo, Osaka, Nagoya and Kyoto have winters with highs in the single digits or low teens and lows temps a few degrees above zero (celsius). The odd January or February day will be colder, but these cold snaps usually don't last.

The summer months (June to August) are dominated by warm, moist air currents from the Pacific, and produce high temperatures and humidity throughout most of Japan (with the blissful exception of Hokkaidō). In the early part of summer, usually mid-May to June, there is a rainy season lasting a few weeks that starts in the south and gradually works its way northward. Although it can be inconvenient, this rainy season is not usually a significant barrier to travel. August, September and October is typhoon season, which can make travel in Okinawa, the Izu-shotō and Ogasawara-shotō difficult.

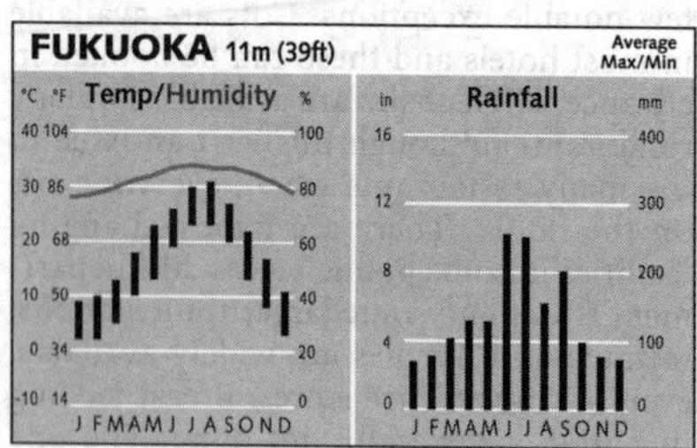

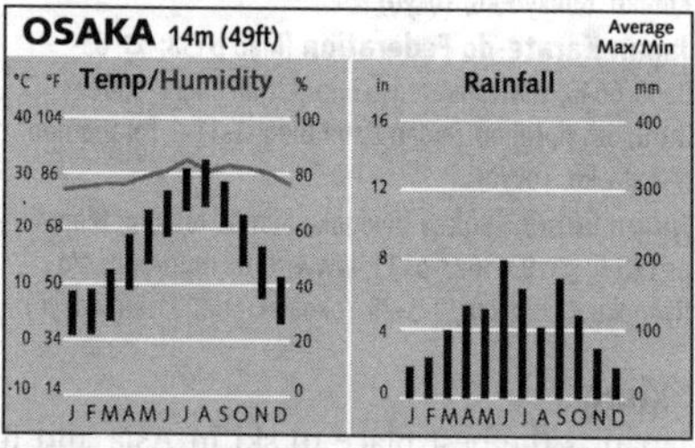

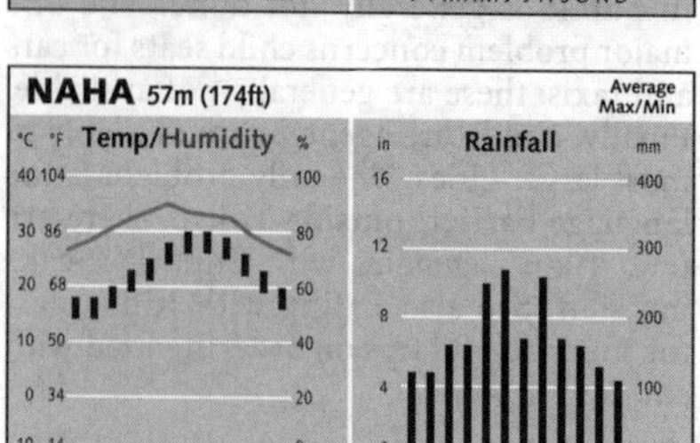

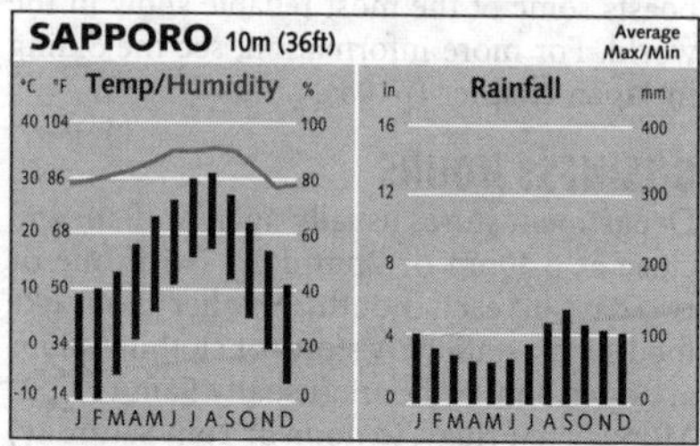

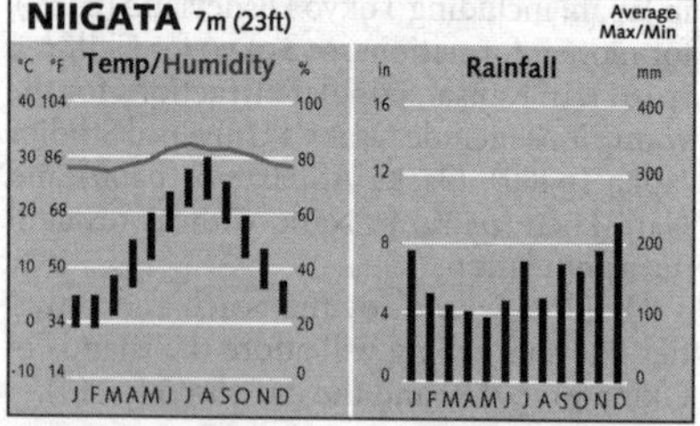

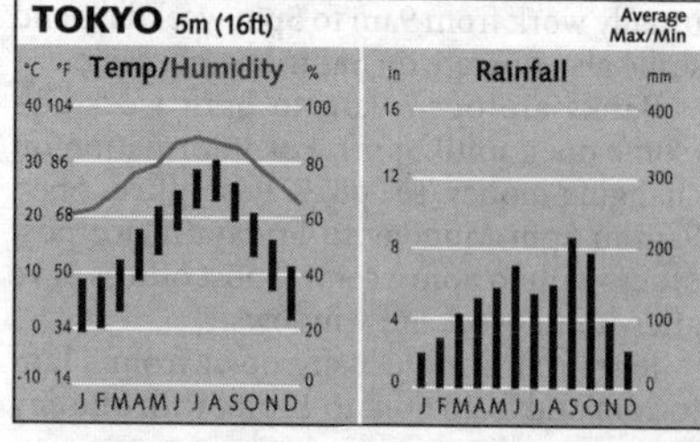

In contrast to the extremes of summer and winter, spring (March to May) and autumn (September to November) in Japan are comparatively mild. Rainfall is relatively low and the days are often clear. These are, without a doubt, the very best times to visit the country.

COURSES

A course is a great way to deepen your appreciation of Japanese culture. Kyoto and Tokyo are the best places to find courses taught in English. Cultural activities visas require applicants to attend 20 class hours per week. Those wishing to work while studying need to apply for permission to do so. For more information on cultural activities visas, visit the website of the **Ministry of Foreign Affairs of Japan** (www.mofa.go.jp/j_info /visit/visa/04.html).

For information on food and cooking courses, see p93.

Japanese Language

While you can study Japanese in most cities in Japan, you'll find the best selection of schools and courses in Tokyo, Kyoto, Nagoya, Osaka and Kōbe. In Kansai, you'll find lots of ads for language courses in *Kansai Time Out* magazine. In Tokyo, any of the many English-language magazines will have ads for courses. Alternatively, ask at any tourist information office.

Costs at full-time private Japanese language schools vary enormously depending on the school's status and facilities. There is usually an application fee of ¥5000 to ¥30,000, plus an administration charge of ¥50,000 to ¥100,000 and the annual tuition fees of ¥350,000 to ¥600,000. Add accommodation and food, and it is easy to see why it may be necessary to work while you study.

Traditional Arts

Many local cultural centres and tourist offices can arrange short courses in Japanese arts, such as ceramics, *washi* (Japanese papermaking), *aizome* (indigo dyeing), wood working, *shodō* (calligraphy), ink painting and ikebana (flower arranging). The best place to pursue these interests is Kyoto (p324), where the TIC (p328) or the International Community House (p327) can put you in touch with qualified teachers.

CUSTOMS

Customs allowances include the usual tobacco products plus three 760mL bottles of alcoholic beverages, 56mL of perfume, and gifts and souvenirs up to a value of ¥200,000 or its equivalent. You must be over the age of 20 to qualify for these allowances. Customs officers will confiscate any pornographic materials in which pubic hair is visible.

There are no limits on the importation of foreign or Japanese currency. The export of foreign currency is also unlimited but there is a ¥5 million export limit for Japanese currency.

Visit **Japan Customs** (www.customs.go.jp/english /index.htm) for more information on Japan's customs regulations.

DANGERS & ANNOYANCES

Earthquakes

Japan is an earthquake-prone country, although most quakes can only be detected by sensitive instruments. If you experience a strong earthquake, head for a doorway or supporting pillar. Small rooms, like a bathroom or cupboard, are often stronger than large rooms but even a table or desk can provide some protection from falling debris. If you're in an urban area, do not run outside as this could expose you to falling debris.

All Japanese hotels have maps indicating emergency exits, and local wards have emergency evacuation areas (fires frequently follow major earthquakes). In the event of a major earthquake, try to stay calm and follow the locals, who should be heading for a designated safe area.

For more information on what to do in the event of an earthquake in the Tokyo area, see p127.

Fire

Although modern hotels must comply with certain safety standards, traditional Japanese buildings – with their wooden construction and tightly packed surroundings – can be real firetraps. Fortunately, most old buildings are low-rise, but it's still wise to check fire exits and escape routes.

Noise

In Japanese cities the assault on the auditory senses can be overwhelming: you'll hear announcements on buses, escalators, elevators, on footpaths, in shopping malls, even at popular beaches and ski resorts. Earplugs can help, particularly when you're trying to sleep.

Size

Even medium-sized foreigners need to mind their heads in Japanese dwellings. The Western frame may make it hard to fit into some seats and those with long legs will often find themselves wedged tight. Toilets in cramped accommodation necessitate contortions and careful aim (be warned!). Bathtubs are also sometimes on the small side and require flexibility on the part of the bather.

Theft

The low incidence of theft and crime in general in Japan is frequently commented on. Of course, theft does exist and its rarity is no reason for carelessness. It's sensible to take the normal precautions in airports and on the crowded Tokyo rail network, but there's definitely no need for paranoia.

Lost-and-found services do seem to work; if you leave something behind on a train or other mode of transport, it's always worth enquiring if it has been turned in. The Japanese word for a lost item is *wasure-mono*, and lost-and-found offices usually go by the same name. In train stations, you can also enquire at the station master's *(eki-chō)* office.

DISCOUNT CARDS

Hostel Cards

See p805 about obtaining a youth hostel membership card.

Museum Discount Card

The **Grutt Pass** (www.museum.or.jp/grutto/about-e.html) is a useful ticket that allows free or discounted admission to almost 50 museums in the Tokyo area. For more information, see p126.

Senior Cards

Japan is an excellent place for senior travellers, with discounts available on entry fees to many temples, museums and cinemas. To qualify for widely available senior discounts, you have to be aged over 60 or 65, depending upon the place/company. In almost all cases a passport will be sufficient proof of age, so senior cards are rarely worth bringing.

Japanese domestic airlines (JAS, JAL and ANA) offer senior discounts of about 25% on some flights (for airline contact details, see p831). Japan Rail (JR) offers a variety of discounts and special passes, including the **Full Moon Green Pass** (http://www.japanrail.com/JR_discounttickets.html), which is good for travel in Green Car (1st-class) carriages on *shinkansen* (bullet trains), regular JR trains and sleeper trains. The pass is available to couples whose combined age exceeds 88 years (passports can prove this). The pass costs ¥80,500/99,900/124,400 per couple for five/seven/12 consecutive days of travel. They are available at major JR stations within Japan from 1 September to 31 May, and they are valid for travel between 1 October and 30 June (with the exception of 28 December to 6 January, 21 March to 5 April and 27 April to 6 May). Note that these dates may change slightly from year to year. See the Full Moon Green Pass website for details.

Student & Youth Cards

Japan is one of the few places left in Asia where a student card can be useful, though some places only offer discounts to high school students and younger, not to university and graduate students. Officially, you should be carrying an International Student Identity Card (ISIC) to qualify for a discount, but you will often find that any youth or student card will do.

EMBASSIES & CONSULATES

Japanese Embassies & Consulates

Diplomatic representation abroad:

Australia Canberra (embassy; ☎ 02-6273 3244; www.au.emb-japan.go.jp; 112 Empire Circuit, Yarralumla, Canberra, ACT 2600); Brisbane (consulate; ☎ 07-3221 5188); Melbourne (consulate; ☎ 03-9639 3244); Perth (consulate; ☎ 08-9480 1800); Sydney (consulate; ☎ 02-9231 3455)

Canada Ontario (embassy; ☎ 613-241 8541; www.ca.emb-japan.go.jp; 255 Sussex Dr, Ottawa, Ontario K1N 9E6); Calgary (consulate; ☎ 403-294 0782); Montreal (consulate; ☎ 514-866 3429); Toronto (consulate; ☎ 416-363 7038); Vancouver (consulate; ☎ 604-684 5868)

France (☎ 01 48 88 62 00; www.fr.emb-japan.go.jp; 7 ave Hoche, 75008 Paris)

Germany (☎ 493-021 09 40; www.de.emb-japan.go.jp; Hiroshimastr.6, 10785 Berlin, Bundesrepublik Deutschland)

Hong Kong (consulate; ☎ 852-2522 1184; www.hk.emb-japan.go.jp/eng; 46-47/F, One Exchange Sq, 8 Connaught Pl, Central, Hong Kong)

Ireland (☎ 01-202 8300; www.ie.emb-japan.go.jp; Nutley Bldg, Merrion Centre, Nutley Lane, Dublin 4)

Netherlands (☎ 70-346-95-44; www.nl.emb-japan.go.jp; Tobias Asserlaan 2 2517 KC, Den Haag)

New Zealand Wellington (embassy; ☎ 04-473 1540; www.nz.emb-japan.go.jp; Level 18, Majestic Centre, 100 Willis St, Wellington 1, PO Box 6340; Auckland (consulate; ☎ 09-303 4106)
South Korea (☎ 822-2170 5200; www.kr.emb-japan.go.jp; 18-11, Jhoonghak-dong, Jhongro-gu, Seoul)
UK (☎ 020-7465 6500; www.uk.emb-japan.go.jp; 101-104 Piccadilly, London, W1J 7JT)
USA Washington DC (embassy; ☎ 202-238 6700; www.us.emb-japan.go.jp; 2520 Massachusetts Ave NW, Washington DC, 20008-2869); Los Angeles (consulate; ☎ 213-617 6700); New York (consulate; ☎ 212-371 8222)

Embassies & Consulates in Japan

Diplomatic representation in Japan:
Australia Tokyo (embassy; Map pp140-1; ☎ 03-5232-4111; www.australia.or.jp/english; 2-1-14 Mita, Minato-ku, Tokyo); Fukuoka (consulate; ☎ 092-734-5055; 7th fl, Tenjin Twin Bldg, 1-6-8 Tenjin, Chūō-ku, Fukuoka); Osaka (consulate; ☎ 06-6941-9271; 16th fl, Twin 21 MID Tower, 2-1-61 Shiromi, Chūō-ku, Osaka)
Canada Tokyo (Map pp140-1; embassy; ☎ 03-5412-6200; www.canadanet.or.jp/english.shtml; 7-3-38 Akasaka, Minato-ku, Tokyo); Nagoya (consulate; ☎ 052-972-0450; Nakatō Marunouchi Bldg, 6F, 3-17-6 Marunouchi, Naka-ku, Nagoya); Sapporo (consulate; ☎ 011-281-6565; Nikko Bldg, 5F, 1, Kita 4 Nishi 4, Chūō-ku, Sapporo); Hiroshima (consulate; ☎ 082-211-0505; No 709, 5-44 Motomachi, Naka-ku, Hiroshima)
France Tokyo (embassy; Map pp128-9; ☎ 03-5798-6000; www.ambafrance-jp.org; 4-11-44 Minami Azabu, Minato-ku, Tokyo); Osaka (consulate; ☎ 06-4790-1505; 10th fl, Crystal Tower, 1-2-27 Shiromi, Chūō-ku, Osaka)
Germany Tokyo (Map pp140-1; ☎ 03-5791-7700; www.tokyo.diplo.de/Vertretung/tokyo/de/Startseite.html; 4-5-10 Minami Azabu, Minato-ku, Tokyo); Osaka (consulate; ☎ 06-6440-5070; 35th fl, Umeda Sky Bldg Tower East, 1-1-88-3501 Ōyodonaka, Kita-ku, Osaka)
Ireland Tokyo (embassy; Map pp142-3; ☎ 03-3263-0695; www.irishembassy.jp; Ireland House, 2-10-7 Kōji-machi, Chiyoda-ku, Tokyo); Osaka (honorary consulate; ☎ 06-6204-2024; c/o Takeda Pharmaceutical Company Ltd, 4-1-1,Doshō-machi, Chūō-ku, Osaka)
Netherlands Tokyo (embassy; Map pp140-1; ☎ 03-5401-0411; www.mfa.nl/tok-en/; 3-6-3 Shiba-kōen, Minato-ku, Tokyo); Osaka (consulate; ☎ 06-6944-7272; 33rd fl, Twin 21 MID Tower, 2-1-61 Shiromi, Chūō-ku, Osaka)
New Zealand Tokyo (embassy; Map pp128-9; ☎ 03-3467-2271; www.nzembassy.com/home.cfm?c=17; 20-40 Kamiyama-chō, Shibuya-ku, Tokyo); Osaka (consulate; ☎ 06-6373-4583; Umeda Centre Bldg, 2-4-12 Nakazaki-nishi Kita-ku, Osaka 530-8323)
Russia Tokyo (embassy; Map pp140-1; ☎ 03-3583-4445; www.rusconsul.jp; 2-1-1, Azabudai, Minato-ku); Sapporo (Off Mapp584; consulate; ☎ 011-064-0914; www.rusconsul.jp; Nishi 12-chōme Minami 14-jo, Chūō-ku, Sapporo)
SouthKorea Tokyo (embassy; Map pp140-1; ☎ 03-3452-7611; www.korea.net; 1-2-5 Minami Azabu, Minato-ku, Tokyo); Fukuoka (consulate; ☎ 092-771-0461; 1-1-3 Jigyōhama, Chūō-ku, Fukuoka)
UK Tokyo (embassy; Map pp142-3; ☎ 03-5211-1100; www.uknow.or.jp/index_e.htm; 1 Ichiban-chō, Chiyoda-ku, Tokyo); Osaka (consulate; ☎ 06-6120-5600; 19th fl, Epson Osaka Bldg, 3-5-1 Bakuromachi, Chūō-ku, Osaka)
USA Tokyo (embassy; Map pp140-1; ☎ 03-3224-5000; http://japan.usembassy.gov/t-main.html; 1-10-5 Akasaka, Minato-ku, Tokyo); Fukuoka (consulate; ☎ 092-751-9331; 2-5-26 Ōhori, Chūō-ku, Fukuoka); Osaka (consulate; Map p397; ☎ 06-6315-5900; 2-11-5 Nishitenma, Kita-ku, Osaka)

FESTIVALS & EVENTS

A *matsuri* (festival) is often the highlight of a trip to Japan. It is a chance to see the Japanese at their most uninhibited, and get some insight into the ancient traditions and beliefs of the country. In addition to *matsuri*, there are several important annual events, including Buddhist imports from China, and more recent imports from the West (eg Christmas).

The Japanese often welcome interested foreigners to participate in their local *matsuri*. You might help carry a portable shrine around a neighbourhood, march in a parade or just dance around a fire. If you'd like to join a local *matsuri*, the best thing to do is ask at the local tourist information office. If you happen upon a *matsuri*, you can usually ask one of the participants if it would be OK to join in. Be warned: participation in a *matsuri* usually also means participation in the drinking session that inevitably follows the festival – or is the main part of the festival!

For a list of Japan's most interesting *matsuri* and other yearly events, see the Events Calendar (p29).

FOOD

In the bigger cities, the restaurants that appear in the Eating sections of this guide are divided by neighbourhoods and either by budget or by type of cuisine (Japanese or international). Outside the bigger cities, eating options are generally presented in one section. In this guide, budget options cost ¥1000 or less; midrange eateries cost between ¥1000 and ¥4000; and top-end places will cost more than ¥4000. For more information about Japan's cuisine, see p76.

GAY & LESBIAN TRAVELLERS

With the possible exception of Thailand, Japan is Asia's most enlightened nation with regard to the sexual preferences of foreigners. Shinjuku-nichōme in Tokyo is an established scene where English is spoken and meeting men is fairly straightforward.

In provincial areas there may be one 'snack' bar, where you pay about ¥1500 for the first drink, entry and the snack. Snack bars can be found in the central entertainment districts of towns and cities. They are usually small places capable of seating only a dozen or fewer customers. They may appear like hole-in-the-wall bars. (Note that most snack bars cater to heterosexual customers. Gay-friendly snack bars are hard to locate without an inside connection.)

Staying in hotels is simple as most have twin rooms but love hotels are less accessible; if you know someone Japanese and can overcome the language barrier, a stay in a love hotel may be possible, but some are not particularly foreigner friendly (see p806). The lesbian scene is growing in Japan but is still elusive for most non-Japanese-speaking foreigners. Outside Tokyo you may find it difficult to break into the local scene unless you spend considerable time in a place or have local contacts who can show you around.

Given Japan's penchant for convenience the internet has been a boon for the gay and lesbian scene. **Utopia** (www.utopia-asia.com) is the site most commonly frequented by English-speaking gays and lesbians. For information about gay and lesbian venues in Tokyo, see p186.

There are no legal restraints to same-sex sexual activities of either gender in Japan. Public displays of affection are likely to be the only cause for concern for all visitors – gay, straight or otherwise.

HOLIDAYS

Japan has 15 national holidays. When a public holiday falls on a Sunday, the following Monday is taken as a holiday. If that Monday is already a holiday, the following day becomes a holiday as well. And, if two weekdays (say, Tuesday and Thursday) are holidays, the day in between (Wednesday) will also become a holiday.

You can expect travel and accommodation options to be fully booked during the New Year festivities (29 December to 6 January), Golden Week (29 April to 5 May) and the mid-August O-Bon festival. See p813 for more details of these festivals and events.

Japan's national holidays:

Ganjitsu (New Year's Day) 1 January
Seijin-no-hi (Coming-of-Age Day) Second Monday in January
Kenkoku Kinem-bi (National Foundation Day) 11 February
Shumbun-no-hi (Spring Equinox) 20 or 21 March
Shōwa-no-hi (Shōwa Emperor's Day) 29 April
Kempō Kinem-bi (Constitution Day) 3 May
Midori-no-hi (Green Day) 4 May
Kodomo-no-hi (Children's Day) 5 May
Umi-no-hi (Marine Day) Third Monday in July
Keirō-no-hi (Respect-for-the-Aged Day) Third Monday in September
Shūbun-no-hi (Autumn Equinox) 23 or 24 September
Taiiku-no-hi (Health-Sports Day) Second Monday in October
Bunka-no-hi (Culture Day) 3 November
Kinrō Kansha-no-hi (Labour Thanksgiving Day) 23 November
Tennō Tanjōbi (Emperor's Birthday) 23 December

INSURANCE

A travel insurance policy to cover theft, loss and medical problems is a good idea. Some policies will specifically exclude 'dangerous activities', which can include scuba diving, motorcycling and even trekking; if you plan to engage in such activities, you'll want a policy that covers them.

You may prefer a policy that pays doctors or hospitals directly rather than have you pay on the spot and claim later. If you have to claim later, make sure you keep all documentation. Some policies ask you to call (reverse charge) a centre in your home country where an immediate assessment of your problem is made. Check that the policy covers ambulances or an emergency flight home.

Some insurance policies offer lower and higher medical-expense options; choose the high-cost option for Japan. Be sure to bring your insurance card or other certificate of insurance to Japan; Japanese hospitals have been known to refuse treatment to foreign patients with no proof of medical insurance.

For information on car insurance, see p836. For information on health insurance, see p843.

INTERNET ACCESS

If you plan on bringing your laptop to Japan, first make sure that it is compatible with the Japanese current (100V AC; 50Hz in eastern Japan and 60Hz in western Japan). Most laptops function just fine on Japanese current. Second, check to see if your plug will fit Japanese wall sockets (Japanese plugs are flat two pin, identical to most ungrounded North American plugs). Both transformers and plug adaptors are readily available in electronics districts, such as Tokyo's Akihabara (p149), Osaka's Den Den Town (p406) or Kyoto's Teramachi-dōri (Map p336).

Modems and phone jacks are similar to those used in the USA (RJ11 phone jacks). Conveniently, many of the grey IDD pay phones in Japan have a standard phone jack and an infrared port so that you can log on to the internet just about anywhere in the country if your computer has an infrared port.

In this book, an internet symbol (💻) indicates that the accommodation option has at least one computer with internet for guests' use. We also note where wi-fi (📶) is available. Note that wi-fi is far less common in Japanese hotels than in their Western counterparts. It is much more common to find LAN cable internet access points in hotel rooms (the hotels can usually provide LAN cables, but you may want to bring your own to avoid having to ask for one everywhere you stay). These LAN connections usually work fine, but you may occasionally find it hard to log on due to software or hardware compatibility issues or configuration problems.

You'll find internet cafes and other access points in most major Japanese cities. Rates vary, usually ranging from ¥200 to ¥700 per hour. As a rule, internet connections are fast (DSL or ADSL) and reliable in Japan. Most accommodation options also have some way of getting online, with terminals in the lobby, wi-fi or LAN access.

See p28 for some useful websites on Japan.

LEFT LUGGAGE

Only major train stations have left-luggage facilities, but almost all stations have coin-operated storage lockers (¥100 to ¥500 per day, depending on size). The lockers are rented until midnight (not for 24 hours). After that time you have to insert more money before your key will work. If your bag is simply too large to fit in the locker, ask someone '*tenimotsu azukai wa doko desu ka*' (Where is the left-luggage office?).

LEGAL MATTERS

Japanese police have extraordinary powers. They can detain a suspect without charging them for up to three days, after which a prosecutor can decide to extend this period for another 20 days. Police can also choose whether to allow a suspect to phone their embassy or lawyer, though if you find yourself in police custody you should insist that you will not cooperate in any way until allowed to make such a call. Your embassy is the first place you should call if given the chance.

Police will speak almost no English; insist that a *tsuyakusha* (interpreter) be summoned. Police are legally bound to provide one before proceeding with any questioning. Even if you do speak Japanese, it's best to deny it and stay with your native language.

If you have a problem, call the **Japan Helpline** (☎ 0120-46-1997), a nationwide emergency number that operates 24 hours a day, seven days a week.

MAPS

If you'd like to buy a map of Japan before arriving, both Nelles and Periplus produce reasonable maps of Japan. If you want something more detailed, wait until you get to Tokyo or Kyoto, where you'll find lots of detailed maps in both English and Japanese.

The JNTO's free *Tourist Map of Japan*, available at JNTO-operated tourist information centres inside the country and JNTO offices abroad, is a reasonable English-language map that is suitable for general route planning.

The *Japan Road Atlas* (Shobunsha) is a good choice for those planning to drive around the country. Those looking for something less bulky should pick up a copy of the *Bilingual Atlas of Japan* (Kodansha). Of course, if you can read a little Japanese, you'll do much better with one of the excellent *Super Mapple* road atlases published by Shobunsha.

MONEY

The currency in Japan is the yen (¥) and banknotes and coins are easily identifiable. There are ¥1, ¥5, ¥10, ¥50, ¥100 and ¥500 coins; and ¥1000, ¥2000, ¥5000 and ¥10,000 banknotes (the ¥2000 notes are very rarely seen). The ¥1 coin is an aluminium lightweight coin, the ¥5 and ¥50 coins have a punched hole in the middle (the former is coloured bronze and the latter silver). Note that some vending

WARNING: JAPAN IS A CASH SOCIETY!

Be warned that cold hard yen (¥) is the way to pay in Japan. While credit cards are becoming more common, cash is still much more widely used, and travellers cheques are rarely accepted. Do not assume that you can pay for things with a credit card; always carry sufficient cash. The only places where you can count on paying by credit card are department stores and large hotels.

For those without credit cards, it would be a good idea to bring some travellers cheques as a back-up. As in most other countries, the US dollar is still the currency of choice in terms of exchanging cash and cashing travellers cheques.

machines do not accept older ¥500 coins (a South Korean coin of much less value was often used in its place to rip off vending machines). The Japanese pronounce yen as 'en', with no 'y' sound. The kanji for yen is: 円.

The Japanese postal system has recently linked its ATMs to the international Cirrus and Plus networks, and 7-11 convenience stores have followed suit, so getting money is no longer the issue it once was for travellers to Japan. Of course, it always makes sense to carry some foreign cash and some credit cards just to be on the safe side. For those without credit cards, it would be a good idea to bring some travellers cheques as a back-up.

For information on costs in Japan, see p25. For exchange rates, see the inside front cover of this guide.

ATMs

Automated teller machines are almost as common as vending machines in Japan. Unfortunately, most of these do not accept foreign-issued cards. Even if they display Visa and MasterCard logos, most accept only Japan-issued versions of these cards.

Fortunately, Japanese postal ATMs accept cards that belong to the following international networks: Visa, Plus, MasterCard, Maestro, Cirrus American Express and Diners Club cards. Check the sticker(s) on the back of your card to see which network(s) your card belongs to. You'll find postal ATMs in almost all post offices, and you'll find post offices in even the smallest Japanese village.

Note that postal ATMs work with bank or cash cards – you cannot use credit cards, even with a pin number, in postal ATMs. That is to say, you cannot use postal ATMs to perform a cash advance.

Most postal ATMs are open 9am to 5pm on weekdays, 9am to noon on Saturday, and are closed on Sunday and holidays. Some postal ATMs in very large central post offices are open longer hours.

Postal ATMs are relatively easy to use. Here's the drill: press 'English Guide', select 'Withdrawal', then insert your card, press 'Visitor Withdrawal', input your pin number, then hit the button marked 'Kakunin' (確認 in Japanese), then enter the amount, hit 'Yen' and 'Confirm' and you should hear the delightful sound of bills being dispensed.

In addition to postal ATMs, you will find a few international ATMs in big cities like Tokyo, Osaka and Kyoto, as well as major airports like Narita and Kansai International Airport. International cards also work in Citibank Japan ATMs. Visit www.citibank.co.jp/en/branch/index.html for a useful branch index.

Finally, 7-11 convenience stores across Japan have recently linked their ATMs to international cash networks, and these often seem to accept cards that for one reason or other will not work with postal ATMs. They are also open 24 hours. So, if you can't find an open post office or your card won't work with postal ATMs, don't give up: ask around for a 7-11 (pronounced like '*sebun erebun*' in Japanese).

Credit Cards

Except for making cash withdrawals at banks and ATMs, it is best not to rely on credit cards in Japan (see also the boxed text, left). While department stores, top-end hotels and some restaurants do accept cards, most businesses in Japan do not. Cash and carry is still very much the rule. If you do decide to bring a credit card, you'll find Visa the most useful, followed by MasterCard, Amex and Diners Club.

The main credit-card offices are in Tokyo.

Amex (☎ 0120-02-0120; 4-30-16 Ogikubo, Suginami-ku; 🕑 24hr)

MasterCard (Map p134; ☎ 03-5728-5200; 16th fl, Cerulean Tower, 26-1 Sakuragaoka-chō, Shibuya-ku)

Visa (Map pp142-3; ☎ 03-5275-7604; 7th fl, Hitotsubashi Bldg, 2-6-3 Hitotsubashi, Chiyoda-ku)

Exchanging Money

Banks, post offices and discount ticket shops will change all major currencies and travellers cheques. As with most other countries, you'll find that US dollars are the easiest to change, although you should have no problems with other major currencies. Note, however, that the currencies of neighbouring Taiwan (New Taiwan dollar) and Korea (won) are not easy to change, so you should change these into yen or US dollars before arriving in Japan.

You can change cash or travellers cheques at most banks, major post offices, discount ticket shops, some travel agents, some large hotels and most big department stores. Note that discount ticket shops (known as *kakuyasu kippu uriba* in Japanese) often have the best rates. These can be found around major train stations.

INTERNATIONAL TRANSFERS

In order to make an international transfer you'll have to find a Japanese bank associated with the bank transferring the money. Start by asking at the central branch of any major Japanese bank. If they don't have a relationship with your bank, they can usually refer you to a bank that does. Once you find a related bank in Japan, you'll have to give your home bank the exact details of where to send the money: the bank, branch and location. A credit-card cash advance is a worthwhile alternative.

Taxes

Japan has a 5% consumption tax *(shōhizei)*. If you eat at expensive restaurants and stay in top-end accommodation, you will encounter a service charge that varies from 10% to 15%.

Tipping

There is little tipping in Japan. If you want to show your gratitude to someone, give them a gift rather than a tip. If you do choose to give someone a cash gift (a staff member in a ryokan, for instance), place the money in an envelope first.

PHOTOGRAPHY

Japan is one of the world's best places to buy cameras (digital or film), photographic equipment, memory and anything else that you can possibly think of to help you record your trip. Japan's photo shops also offer a wide range of services for digital photographers, such as high-quality prints from digital files. The typical cost for printing digital photos is ¥35 per print.

For more information on buying cameras and other photographic equipment, see p819.

POST

The Japanese postal system is reliable, efficient and, for regular postcards and airmail letters, not markedly more expensive than other developed countries.

Postal Rates

The airmail rate for postcards is ¥70 to any overseas destination; aerograms cost ¥90. Letters weighing less than 25g are ¥90 to other countries within Asia, ¥110 to North America, Europe or Oceania (including Australia and New Zealand), and ¥130 to Africa and South America. One peculiarity of the Japanese postal system is that you will be charged extra if your writing runs over onto the address side (the right side) of a postcard.

Sending & Receiving Mail

The symbol for post offices is a red T with a bar across the top on a white background (〒). District post offices (the main post office in a ward) are normally very conveniently open from 9am to 7pm weekdays and 9am to 3pm Saturday, and are closed Sunday and public holidays. Local post offices are open 9am to 5pm weekdays, and are closed Saturday, Sunday and public holidays. Main post offices in the larger cities may have an after-hours window open 24 hours a day, seven days a week.

Mail can be sent to, from or within Japan when addressed in English (Roman script).

Although any post office will hold mail for collection, the poste restante concept is not well known and can cause confusion in smaller places. It is probably better to have mail addressed to you at a larger central post office. Letters are usually only held for 30 days before being returned to sender. When enquiring about mail for collection ask for *kyoku dome yūbin*.

It should be addressed as follows:

Darren O'CONNELL
Poste Restante
Central Post Office
Tokyo, JAPAN

SHOPPING

Japan is truly a shopper's paradise, and it is not as expensive as you might imagine. As well as all the electronic gadgetry available in Japan, there is a wide range of traditional crafts to choose from, all of which make great souvenirs. The big department stores often have the best selections of Japanese gift items, and they usually have English speakers on hand.

Bargain hunters will want to check out Japan's famous *hyaku-en shops* (¥100 shops) – you will be amazed what you can buy for ¥100 (about US$1). *Hyaku-en* shops can be found in the central shopping areas of medium and large cities (sometimes inside covered shopping arcades). Helpfully, they usually have the number 100 written in large letters on their signs.

Bargaining

Bargaining is largely restricted to flea markets (where anything goes) and large discount electronics shops (where a polite request will often bring the price down by around 10%).

Computer Equipment

Computers, computer accessories and software are widely available. Unfortunately for the foreign traveller, most of what's out there – operating systems, keyboards and software – is in Japanese and not of any use unless you intend to work with the Japanese language. However, if you're after hardware like peripherals, chips and the like, where language isn't a factor, you will find lots to choose from, including second-hand goods at unbelievably low prices. The world's biggest selection of computer equipment can be found in Japan's major electronics districts: Akihabara in Tokyo and Den Den Town in Osaka (see Electronics, below).

Electronics

Nowhere in the world will you find a better selection of electronics than in Tokyo's Akihabara district (p189) and Osaka's Den Den Town (p406). Keep in mind, though, that much of the electrical gadgetry on sale in Japan is designed for Japan's curious power supply (100V at 50Hz or 60Hz) and may require a transformer for use overseas. The safest bet is to go for export models – the prices may be slightly higher but, in the long run, you'll save the expense of converting the equipment to suit the conditions in your own country.

Japanese Arts & Crafts

As well as all the hi-tech knick-knacks produced by the Japanese, it is also possible to go home loaded with traditional Japanese arts and crafts. Anything from *koinobori* (carp banners) to kimono can make good souvenirs for the Japanophile.

KASA (JAPANESE UMBRELLAS)

A classic souvenir item, *kasa* (Japanese umbrellas) come in two forms: *higasa,* which are made of paper, cotton or silk and serve as a sunshade; and *bangasa,* which are made of oiled paper and keep the rain off. Department stores and tourist shops are your best bet for finding *kasa.*

KATANA (JAPANESE SWORDS)

A good *katana* (Japanese sword) could cost more than all your other travel expenses put together. The reason for their expense is both their mystique as the symbols of samurai power and the great care that goes into making them. Sword shops that sell the real thing will also stock *tsuba* (sword guards), and complete sets of samurai armour. Some department stores, on the other hand, stock realistic (to the untrained eye at least) imitations at affordable prices.

KIMONO & YUKATA

A good kimono is perhaps the ultimate souvenir of a trip to Japan, and prices for new kimono start at around ¥60,000. Keep in mind that you'll have to go for at least one fitting and wait for around a week before the finished item is ready to pick up. A used kimono is a good solution if you don't have the time or money to spend on a new one. Used-clothing shops usually stock a variety of kimono ranging in price from ¥1500 to ¥9000. Another good place to pick up a used kimono is a flea market, where you can find a huge variety of often very fine kimono for less than ¥2000.

Yukata (light cotton kimono or bathrobes) are another great souvenir and new ones can be had for as low as ¥2000. Unlike kimono, these are easy to put on and can be worn comfortably around the house. These are available from tourist shops and department stores in Japan.

KOINOBORI (CARP BANNERS)

The lovely banners that you see waving in the breeze on Kodomo-no-hi (Children's Day; 5

May) throughout Japan are called *koinobori*. The carp is much revered for its tenacity and perseverance, but you might like the banners for their simple elegance.

NINGYŌ (JAPANESE DOLLS)

Not for playing with, Japanese dolls are usually intended for display. Often quite exquisite, with coiffured hair and dressed in kimono, *ningyō* make excellent souvenirs or gifts. Also available are *gogatsu-ningyō,* dolls that are dressed in samurai suits used as gifts on Kodomo-no-hi. The most well-known dolls are made in Kyoto and are known as *kyō-ningyō*.

Ningyō can be bought in tourist shops, department stores and special doll shops. In Tokyo, Edo-dōri in Asakusa is well known for its many doll shops, such as Yoshitoku (p190).

POTTERY

Numerous pottery villages still exist in Japan; many feature pottery museums and working kilns that are open to the public. Of course, it is also possible to buy examples of stoneware and porcelain. Sources of different pottery styles abound: there's Bizen (p454), near Okayama in western Honshū, which is famed for its Bizen-yaki pottery; and Karatsu (p698), Imari (p700) and Arita (p700) in Kyūshū (the home of Japanese pottery).

Department stores are a surprisingly good place to look for Japanese pottery, and Takashimaya (see p189 for details) often has bargain bins where you can score some real deals. For even better prices try some of Japan's flea markets.

SHIKKI (LACQUERWARE)

Another exquisite Japanese craft is *shikki* (lacquerware). The lacquerware-making process, involving as many as 15 layers of lacquer, is used to create objects as diverse as dishes and furniture. As you might expect, examples of good lacquerware cannot be had for a song, but smaller items can be bought at affordable prices from department stores. Popular, easily transportable items include bowls, trays and small boxes. Department stores often have good selections of lacquerware in their housewares sections.

UKIYO-E (WOOD-BLOCK PRINTS)

Originating in the 18th century as one of Japan's earliest manifestations of mass culture, wood-block prints were used in advertising and posters. It was only later that *ukiyo-e* was considered an art form. The name (literally, 'pictures from the floating world') derives from a Buddhist term indicating the transient world of daily pleasures. *Ukiyo-e* uniquely depicts such things as street scenes, actors and courtesans.

Today, tourist shops in Japan stock modern reproductions of the work of famous *ukiyo-e* masters such as Hokusai (1760–1849), whose scenes of Fuji-san are favourites. It is also possible to come across originals by lesser-known artists at prices ranging from ¥3000 to ¥40,000.

WASHI (JAPANESE PAPER)

For more than 1000 years, *washi* (Japanese paper) has been famous as the finest handmade paper in the world. Special shops stock sheets of *washi* and products made from it, such as notebooks, wallets and so on. As they're generally inexpensive and light, *washi* products make excellent gifts and souvenirs. You'll find them in the big department stores. See p381 for suggestions on places to buy *washi*.

Pearls

The Japanese firm Mikimoto developed the technique of producing cultured pearls by artificially introducing an irritant into the pearl oyster. Pearls and pearl jewellery are still popular buys for foreign visitors. The best place in Japan to buy pearls is Mikimoto's home base: Toba (p446), in Mie-ken.

Photographic Equipment

Tokyo is an excellent hunting ground for photographic equipment. As almost all of the big-name brands in camera equipment are locally produced, prices can be very competitive. The prices for accessories, such as motor drives and flash units, can even be compared to Singapore and Hong Kong. In addition, shopping in Japan presents the traveller with none of the rip-off risks that abound in other Asian discount capitals.

Tokyo's Shinjuku area is the best place for buying camera equipment, although Ginza also has a good selection of shops (see p191 for details). Second-hand camera equipment is worth checking out. In Tokyo, both Shinjuku and Ginza have a fair number of second-hand places where camera and lens quality is usually very good and prices are around half what you would pay for new equipment. In Osaka, the area just south of Osaka station has used-camera shops as well (see p406).

Tax-Free Shopping

Shopping tax free in Japan is not necessarily the bargain that you might expect. Although tax-free shops enable foreigners to receive an exemption from the 5% consumption tax *(shōhizei)* levied on most items, these still may not be the cheapest places to shop. Shops that offer this exemption usually require that you pay the consumption tax and then go to a special counter to receive a refund. You will often need to show your passport to receive this refund. Tax-free shops will usually have a sign in English that announces their tax-free status.

Toys

Tokyo has some remarkable toy shops. See p190 for more information. Elsewhere, look out for some of the traditional wooden toys produced as regional specialities – they make good souvenirs for adults and children alike.

SOLO TRAVELLERS

Japan is an excellent place for solo travellers: it's safe, convenient and friendly. Almost all hotels in Japan have single rooms, and business-hotel singles can cost as little as ¥4000. Ryokan usually charge by the person, not the room, which keeps the price down for the single traveller. The only hitch is that some ryokan owners baulk at renting a room to a single traveller, when they might be able to rent it to two people instead. For more on accommodation, see p803.

Many restaurants in Japan have small tables or counters that are perfect for solo travellers. *Izakaya* (pub-eateries) are also generally welcoming to solo travellers, and you probably won't have to wait long before you're offered a drink and roped into a conversation, particularly if you sit at the counter. Finally, the 'gaijin bars' in the larger cities are generally friendly, convivial places; if you're after a travel partner or just an English-speaking conversation partner, these are good places to start.

TELEPHONE

Japanese telephone codes consist of an area code plus the number. You do not dial the area code when making a call in that area. When dialling Japan from abroad, dial the country code ☎ 81, followed by the area code (drop the '0') and the number. Numbers that begin with the digits ☎ 0120, ☎ 0070, ☎ 0077, ☎ 0088 and ☎ 0800 are toll-free.

Directory Assistance

For local directory assistance dial ☎ 104 (the call costs ¥105), or for assistance in English ring ☎ 0120-36-4463 from 9am to 5pm weekdays. For international directory assistance dial ☎ 0057.

International Calls

The best way to make an international phone call from Japan is to use a prepaid international phone card (see below).

Paid overseas calls can be made from grey international ISDN phones. These are usually found in phone booths marked 'International & Domestic Card/Coin Phone'. Unfortunately, these are very rare; try looking in the lobbies of top-end hotels and at airports. Some new green phones found in phone booths also allow international calls. Calls are charged by the unit, each of which is six seconds, so if you don't have much to say you could phone home for just ¥100. Reverse-charge (collect) overseas calls can be made from any pay phone.

You can save money by dialling late at night. Economy rates are available from 11pm to 8am. Note that it is also cheaper to make domestic calls by dialling outside the standard hours.

To place an international call through the operator, dial ☎ 0051 (KDDI operator; most international operators speak English). To make the call yourself, dial ☎ 001 010 (KDDI), ☎ 0041 010 (SoftBank Telecom) or ☎ 0033 010 (NTT) – there's very little difference in their rates – then the international country code, the local code and the number.

PREPAID INTERNATIONAL PHONE CARDS

Because of the lack of pay phones from which you can make international phone calls in Japan, the easiest way to make an international phone call is to buy a prepaid international phone card. Most convenience stores carry at least one of the following types of phone cards. These cards can be used with any regular pay phone in Japan.

- KDDI Superworld Card
- NTT Communications World Card
- SoftBank Telecom Comica Card

AREA CODES IN JAPAN

These are the area codes for some of Japan's main cities. When calling from overseas, drop the first 0.

Fukuoka/Hakata	☎ 092
Hiroshima	☎ 082
Kōbe	☎ 078
Kyoto	☎ 075
Matsuyama	☎ 089
Nagasaki	☎ 095
Nagoya	☎ 052
Nara	☎ 0742
Osaka	☎ 06
Sapporo	☎ 011
Sendai	☎ 022
Tokyo	☎ 03
Yokohama	☎ 045

Local Calls

The Japanese public telephone system is extremely reliable and efficient. Unfortunately, the number of pay phones is decreasing fast as more and more Japanese buy mobile phones. Local calls from pay phones cost ¥10 per minute; unused ¥10 coins are returned after the call is completed but no change is given on ¥100 coins.

In general it's much easier to buy a telephone card *(terefon kādo)* when you arrive rather than worry about always having coins on hand. Phone cards are sold in ¥500 and ¥1000 denominations (the latter earns you an extra ¥50 in calls) and can be used in most green or grey pay phones. They are available from vending machines (some of which can be found in public phone booths) and convenience stores. They come in a myriad of designs and are also a collectable item.

Mobile Phones

Japan's mobile- (cell-) phone networks use 3G (third generation) mobile-phone technology on a variety of frequencies. Thus, non-3G mobile phones cannot be used in Japan. This means that most foreign mobile phones *will not work* in Japan. Furthermore, SIM cards are not commonly available in Japan. Thus, for most people who want to use a mobile phone while in Japan, the only solution is to rent a mobile phone.

Several telecommunications companies in Japan specialise in short-term mobile-phone rentals, a good option for travellers whose own phones won't work in Japan, or whose own phones would be prohibitively expensive to use here.

The following companies provide this service:

Mobile Phone Japan (☎ 090-8523-2053; www.mobilephonejp.com) This company offers basic mobile-phone rental for as low as ¥2900 per week. Incoming calls, whether international or domestic, are free, and outgoing domestic calls are ¥90 per minute (outgoing domestic calls vary according to country and time of day). Free delivery anywhere in Japan is included and a free prepaid return envelope is also included.

Rentafone Japan (☎ 0120-74-6487; www.rentafonejapan.com) This company rents out mobile phones for ¥3900 per week and offers free delivery of the phone to your accommodation. Domestic rates are ¥35 per minute and overseas calls are ¥45 per minute.

Useful Numbers

If you're staying long term, adjusting to life in Japan can be tough; but there are places to turn to for help. **Metropolitan Government Foreign Residents' Advisory Center** (☎ 03-5320-7744; 🕑 9.30am-noon & 1-4pm Mon-Fri) is a useful service operated by the Tokyo metropolitan government. Otherwise, try the 24-hour **Japan Helpline** (☎ 0120-46-1997).

TIME

Despite the distance between Japan's east and west coasts, the country is all on the same time: nine hours ahead of Greenwich Mean Time (GMT). Sydney and Wellington are ahead of Japan (+1 and +3 hours, respectively), and most of the world's other big cities are behind Japan (New York -14, Los Angeles -17 and London -9). Japan does not have daylight savings time (also known as summer time).

TOILETS

In Japan you will come across both Western-style toilets and Asian squat toilets. When you are compelled to squat, the correct position is facing the hood, away from the door. Make sure the contents of your pockets don't spill out! Toilet paper isn't always provided, so it is best to carry tissues with you. You may be given small packets of tissue on the street in Japan, a common form of advertising.

In many bathrooms in Japan, separate toilet slippers are often provided just inside the toilet door. These are for use in the toilet only, so remember to change out of them when you leave.

It's quite common to see men urinating in public – the unspoken rule is that it's acceptable at night time if you happen to be drunk. Public toilets are free in Japan. The katakana script for 'toilet' is トイレ, and the kanji script is お手洗い.

You'll often also see these kanji:

- Female 女
- Male 男

TOURIST INFORMATION

Japan's tourist information services are first-rate. You will find information offices in most cities, towns and even some small villages. They are almost always located inside or in front of the main train station in a town or city.

A note on language difficulties: English speakers are usually available at tourist information offices in larger cities. Away from the big cities, you'll find varying degrees of English-language ability. In rural areas and small towns you may find yourself relying more on one-word communication and hand signals. Nonetheless, with a little patience and a smile you will usually get the information you need from even the smallest local tourist information office.

Japan National Tourism Organization (JNTO)

The **Japan National Tourism Organization** (JNTO; www.jnto.go.jp, www.japantravelinfo.com) is the main English-language information service for foreign travellers to Japan. JNTO produces a great deal of useful literature, which is available from both its overseas offices and its Tourist Information Center (p126) in Tokyo. Most publications are available in English and, in some cases, other European and Asian languages. JNTO's website is very useful in planning your journey.

Unfortunately for foreign travellers, JNTO is pulling out of the business of operating tourist information centres inside Japan. The sole remaining domestic office is the Tokyo office.

JNTO has a number of overseas offices:

Australia (☎ 02-9279 2177; Level 7, 36-38 Clarence St, Sydney, NSW Australia 2000)

Canada (☎ 416-366 7140; 481 University Avenue, Suite 306, Toronto, ON M5G 2E9)

France (☎ 01 42 96 20 29; 4 rue de Ventadour, 75001 Paris)

Germany (☎ 069-20353; Kaiserstrasse 11, 60311 Frankfurt am Main)

UK (☎ 020-7398-5670; H5th fl, 12/13 Nicholas Lane, London, EC4N 7BN)

USA Los Angeles (☎ 213-623 1952; 340 E 2nd St, Little Tokyo Plaza, Suite 302, Los Angeles, CA 90012); New York (☎ 212-757 5640; One Rockefeller Plaza, Suite 1250, New York, NY 10020)

Other Information Offices

There are tourist information offices (*kankō annai-sho;* 観光案内所) in or near almost all major train stations, but the further you venture into outlying regions, the less chance you have of finding English-speaking staff.

TRAVELLERS WITH DISABILITIES

Japan gets mixed marks in terms of ease of travel for those with disabilities. On the plus side, many new buildings in Japan have access ramps, traffic lights have speakers playing melodies when it is safe to cross, train platforms have raised dots and lines to provide guidance, and some ticket machines in Tokyo have Braille. Some attractions also offer free entry to disabled persons and one companion. On the negative side, many of Japan's cities are still rather difficult for disabled persons to negotiate, often due to the relative lack of normal footpaths on narrow streets.

If you are going to travel by train and need assistance, ask one of the station workers as you enter the station. Try asking: *'karada no fujiyuū no kata no sharyō wa arimasu ka?'* (Are there train carriages for disabled travellers?).

There are carriages on most lines that have areas set aside for people in wheelchairs. Those with other physical disabilities can use the seats set near the train exits, called *yūsen-zaseki*. You will also find these seats near the front of buses; usually they're a different colour from the regular seats.

The most useful information for disabled visitors is provided by the **Japanese Red Cross Language Service Volunteers** (housi-2008@lanserv.gr.jp; www.lanserv.gr.jp/index.shtml, in Japanese; c/o Volunteers Division, Japanese Red Cross Society, 1-1-3 Shiba Daimon, Minato-ku, Tokyo 105-8521, Japan). Its website has online guides for disabled travellers to Tokyo, Kyoto and Kamakura.

For information on negotiating Japan in a wheelchair, see the website for **Accessible Japan**

ADDRESSES IN JAPAN

In Japan, finding a place from its address can be difficult, even for locals. The problem is twofold: first, the address is usually given by an area rather than a street; and, second, the numbers are not necessarily consecutive, as prior to the mid-1950s numbers were assigned by date of construction.

In Tokyo very few streets have names – so addresses work by narrowing down the location of a building to a number within an area of a few blocks. In this guide, Tokyo addresses are organised as such: area number, block number and building number, followed by area and ward. For example, 1-11-2 Ginza, Chūō-ku.

In Kyoto, addresses are simplified. We either give the area (eg Higashiyama-ku, Nanzen-ji) or we give the street on which the place is located, followed by the nearest cross street (eg Karasuma-dōri-Imadegawa). In some cases, we also give additional information to show where the place lies in relation to the intersection of the two streets mentioned. In Kyoto, the land usually slopes gently to the south; thus, an address might indicate whether a place lies above or north of *(agaru)* or below or south of (*sagaru* or *kudaru*) a particular east–west road. Thus, 'Karasuma-dōri-Imadegawa' simply means the place is near the intersection of Karasuma-dōri and Imadegawa-dōri; Karasuma-dōri-Imadegawa-sagaru indicates that it's south of that intersection. An address might also indicate whether a place lies east *(higashi)* or west *(nishi)* of the north–south road.

In Sapporo, a typical address would be S17W7-2-12 Chūō-ku. The 'S17W7' is the South 17, West 7 block. The building is in the second section at number 12.

Elsewhere in this guide, addresses list area number, block number and building number, followed by area and ward. This is the more common presentation in English. For example, '1-7-2 Motomachi-dōri, Chūō-ku'. Where given, the floor number and building name are listed first.

To find an address, the usual process is to ask directions. Have your address handy. The numerous local police boxes are there largely for this purpose. Businesses often include a small map in their advertisements or on their business cards to show their location.

Most taxis and many rental cars now have satellite navigation systems, which make finding places a breeze, as long as you can program the address or phone number into the system. Needless to say, you'll have to be able to read Japanese to input the address, but phone numbers should be no problem.

(www.tesco-premium.co.jp/aj/index.htm). Also, listings throughout this book indicate with the icon ♿ if a place has wheelchair-access.

Eagle Bus Company (☎ 049-227-7611; www.new-wing.co.jp/english/english.html) has lift-equipped buses and some English-speaking drivers who are also licensed caregivers. It offers tours of Tokyo and around for travellers with disabilities. However, the number of English-speaking drivers/caregivers is limited, so it is necessary to reserve well in advance. Group bookings are possible. It also offers English-language tours of Kawagoe, a small town outside Tokyo, which is sometimes known as little Edo.

VISAS

Generally, visitors who are not planning to engage in income-producing activities while in Japan are exempt from obtaining visas and will be issued a *tanki-taizai* (temporary visitor) visa on arrival.

Stays of up to six months are permitted for citizens of Austria, Germany, Ireland, Mexico, Switzerland and the UK. Citizens of these countries will almost always be given a 90-day temporary visitor visa upon arrival, which can usually be extended for another 90 days at immigration bureaux inside Japan (for details, see p824).

Citizens of the USA, Australia and New Zealand are granted 90-day temporary visitor visas, while stays of up to three months are permitted for citizens of Argentina, Belgium, Canada, Denmark, Finland, France, Iceland, Israel, Italy, the Netherlands, Norway, Singapore, Spain, Sweden and a number of other countries.

Japanese law requires that visitors to the country entering on a temporary visitor visa possess an ongoing air or sea ticket or evidence thereof. In practice, few travellers are asked to produce such documents, but to avoid surprises it pays to be on the safe side.

For additional information on visas and regulations, contact your nearest Japanese embassy or consulate, or visit the website of the **Ministry of Foreign Affairs of Japan** (www.mofa.go.jp). Here you can find out about the different types of visas available, read about working-holiday visas and find details on the Japan Exchange & Teaching (JET) program, which sponsors native English speakers to teach in the Japanese public school system.

Note that on entering Japan, all short-term foreign visitors are required to be photographed and fingerprinted. This happens when you show your passport on arrival.

Alien Registration Card

Anyone, and this includes tourists, who stays for more than 90 days is required to obtain an Alien Registration Card (Gaikokujin Torokushō). This card can be obtained at the municipal office of the city, town or ward in which you're living or staying.

You must carry your Alien Registration Card at all times as the police can stop you and ask to see the card. If you don't have the card, you may be taken back to the station and will have to wait there until someone fetches it for you.

Visa Extensions

With the exception of those nationals whose countries have reciprocal visa exemptions and can stay for six months, the limit for most nationalities is 90 days or three months. To extend a temporary visitor visa beyond the standard 90 days or three months, apply at the nearest immigration office (for a list of immigration bureaux and regional offices visit www.immi-moj.go.jp/english/soshiki/index.html). You must provide two copies of an Application for Extension of Stay (available at the immigration office), a letter stating the reasons for the extension, supporting documentation and your passport. There is a processing fee of ¥4000.

Many long-term visitors to Japan get around the extension problem by briefly leaving the country, usually going to South Korea. Be warned, though, that immigration officials are wise to this practice and many 'tourist visa returnces' are turned back at the entry point.

Work Visas

Unless you are on a cultural visa and have been granted permission to work (see p161), or hold a working-holiday visa, you are not permitted to work in Japan without a proper work visa. If you have the proper paperwork and an employee willing to sponsor you, the process is straightforward, although it can be time-consuming.

Once you find an employer in Japan who is willing to sponsor you, it is necessary to obtain a Certificate of Eligibility from the nearest immigration office. The same office can then issue you your work visa, which is valid for either one or three years. The whole procedure usually takes two to three months.

Working-Holiday Visas

Australians, Britons, Canadians, Germans, New Zealanders and South Koreans between the ages of 18 and 25 (the age limit can be pushed up to 30 in some cases) can apply for a working-holiday visa. This visa allows a six-month stay and two six-month extensions. It is designed to enable young people to travel extensively during their stay; although employment is supposed to be part-time or temporary, in practice many people work full time.

A working-holiday visa is much easier to obtain than a work visa and is popular with Japanese employers. Single applicants must have the equivalent of US$2000 of funds, a married couple must have US$3000 and all applicants must have an onward ticket from Japan. For details, enquire at the nearest Japanese embassy or consulate (see p812).

VOLUNTEERING

Japan doesn't have as many volunteer opportunities as some other Asian countries. However, there are positions out there for those who look. One of the most popular volunteering options in Japan is provided by **Willing Workers on Organic Farms Japan** (WWOOF Japan; fax 011-780-4908; www.wwoofjapan.com/main/index.php?lang=en; 6-7 3-chōme Honchō 2jō, Higashi-ku, Sapporo 065-0042, Japan). This organisation places volunteers on organic farms around the country, where they help with the daily running of the farms and participate in family or community life. This provides a good look into Japanese rural life, the running of an organic farm and a great chance to improve your Japanese-language skills.

Alternatively, you can look for volunteer opportunities once you arrive in Japan. There are occasional ads for volunteer positions in magazines like *Kansai Time Out* in Kansai and the various English-language journals in the Tokyo area. Word of mouth is also a good way to search for jobs. Hikers, for example, are sometimes offered short-term positions in Japan's mountain huts (see p806).

WOMEN TRAVELLERS

Japan is a relatively safe country for women travellers, though perhaps not quite as safe as some might think. Women travellers are occasionally subjected to some forms of verbal harassment or prying questions. Physical attacks are very rare, but have occurred.

The best advice is to avoid being lulled into a false sense of security by Japan's image as one of the world's safest countries and to take the normal precautions you would in your home country. If a neighbourhood or establishment looks unsafe, then treat it that way. As long as you use your common sense, you will most likely find that Japan is a pleasant and rewarding place to travel as a woman.

Several train companies in Japan have recently introduced women-only cars to protect female passengers from *chikan* (men who feel up women and girls on packed trains). These cars are usually available during rush-hour periods on weekdays on busy urban lines. There are signs (usually pink in colour) on the platform indicating where to board these cars, and the cars themselves are usually labelled in both Japanese and English (again, these are often marked in pink).

If you have a problem and find the local police unhelpful, you can call the **Japan Helpline** (☎ 0120-46-1997), a nationwide emergency number that operates 24 hours a day, seven days a week.

Finally, an excellent resource available for any woman setting up in Japan is Caroline Pover's excellent book *Being A Broad in Japan*, which can be found in bookstores and can also be ordered from her website at www.being-a-broad.com.

WORK

Japan is an excellent and rewarding place to live and work and all major cities in Japan have significant populations of expats doing just that. Teaching English is still the most common job for Westerners, but bartending, hostessing, modelling and various writing/editorial jobs are also possible.

The key to success in Japan is doing your homework and presenting yourself properly. You will definitely need a sharp outfit for interviews, a stack of *meishi* (business cards) and the right attitude. If you don't have a university degree, you won't be eligible for most jobs that qualify you for a work visa. Any qualification, like an English-teaching certificate, will be a huge boost.

Finally, outside of the entertainment, construction and English-teaching industries, you can't expect a good job unless you speak good Japanese (any more than someone could expect a job in your home country without speaking the language of that country).

> **WORK WARNING**
>
> As this book went to press, the Japanese economy was suffering the effects of the worldwide recession that started with the American subprime loan crisis in 2008. Unemployment was on the rise and job opportunities were diminishing in all fields. We suggest that you research carefully the current employment conditions in the field in which you wish to work before packing your bags for Japan.

Bartending

Bartending does not qualify you for a work visa; most of the foreign bartenders in Japan are either working illegally or are on another kind of visa. Some bars in big Japanese cities hire foreign bartenders; most are strict about visas but others don't seem to care. The best places to look are 'gaijin bars', although a few Japanese-oriented places also employ foreign bartenders for 'ambience'. The pay is barely enough to survive on – usually about ¥1000 per hour. The great plus of working as a bartender (other than free drinks) is the chance to practise speaking Japanese.

English Teaching

Teaching English has always been the most popular job for native English speakers in Japan. A university degree is an absolute essential as you cannot qualify for a work visa without one (be sure to bring the actual degree with you to Japan). Teaching qualifications and some teaching experience will be a huge plus when job hunting.

Consider lining up a job before arriving in Japan. Big schools, like Nova for example, now have recruitment programs in the USA and the UK. One downside to the big 'factory schools' that recruit overseas is that working conditions are often pretty dire compared with smaller schools that recruit within Japan.

Australians, New Zealanders and Canadians, who can take advantage of the Japanese working-holiday visa (p824), are in a slightly better position. Schools are happier about taking on unqualified teachers if they don't have to bother with sponsoring a teacher for a work visa.

There is a definite hierarchy among English teachers and teaching positions in Japan. The bottom of the barrel are the big chain *eikaiwa* (private English-language schools), followed by small local *eikaiwa*, inhouse company language schools, and private lessons, with university positions and international school positions being the most sought after. As you would expect, newcomers start at the lower rungs and work their way up the ladder.

ELT News (www.eltnews.com) is an excellent website with lots of information and want ads for English teachers in Japan.

GOVERNMENT SCHOOLS

The program run by **Japan Exchange & Teaching** (JET; www.jetprogramme.org) provides 2000 teaching assistant positions for foreign teachers. The job operates on a yearly contract and must be organised in your home country. The program gets very good reports from many of its teachers.

Teachers employed by the JET program are known as Assistant Language Teachers (ALTs). Although you will have to apply in your home country in order to work as an ALT with JET, it's worth bearing in mind that many local governments in Japan are also employing ALTs for their schools. Such work can sometimes be arranged within Japan.

Visit the JET website or contact the nearest Japanese embassy or consulate (p812) for more details.

INTERNATIONAL SCHOOLS

Major cities with large foreign populations, such as Tokyo and Yokohama, have a number of international schools for the children of foreign residents. Work is available for qualified, Western-trained teachers in all disciplines; the schools will usually organise your visa.

PRIVATE SCHOOLS

Private-language schools *(eikaiwa)* are the largest employers of foreign teachers in Japan and the best bet for the job-hunting newcomer. The classifieds section of the Monday edition of the *Japan Times* is the best place to look for teaching positions. Some larger schools rely on direct enquiries from would-be teachers.

Tokyo is the easiest place to find teaching jobs; schools across Japan advertise or recruit in the capital. Heading straight to another of Japan's major population centres (say Osaka, Fukuoka, Hiroshima or Sapporo), where there are smaller numbers of competing foreigners, is also a good bet.

Proofreading, Editing & Writing

There is a huge demand for skilled editors, copywriters, proofreaders and translators (Japanese to English and, less commonly, vice versa) in Japan. And with the advent of the internet, you don't even have to be based in Japan to do this work. Unfortunately, as with many things in Japan, introductions and connections play a huge role, and it's difficult to simply show up in Tokyo or plaster your resume online and wind up with a good job.

You'll need to be persistent and do some networking to make much in this field. Experience, advanced degrees and salesmanship will all come in handy. And even if you don't intend to work as a translator, some Japanese-language ability will be a huge plus, if only for communicating with potential employers and clients. If you think you've got what it takes, check the Monday edition of the *Japan Times* for openings.

For more information about proofreading and editing in Japan, visit the website for the **Society of Writers, Editors & Translators** (SWET; www.sw et.jp).

Ski Areas

Seasonal work is available at ski areas in Japan and this is a popular option for Australian and Kiwi travellers, who want to combine a trip to Japan, a little skiing and a chance to earn a little money. A working-holiday visa (see p824) makes this easier, although occasionally people are offered jobs without visas. The jobs are typical ski town jobs – ski lift attendants, hotel workers, bartenders and, for those with the right skills (language and skiing), ski instructors. You won't earn much more than ¥1000 per hour unless you're an instructor, but you'll get lodging and lift tickets. All told, it's a fun way to spend a few months in Japan.

Transport

CONTENTS

GETTING THERE & AWAY

ENTERING THE COUNTRY

While most travellers to Japan fly via Tokyo, there are several other ways of getting into and out of the country. For a start, there are many other airports in Japan, which can make better entry points than Tokyo's somewhat inconvenient Narita International Airport. It's also possible to arrive in Japan by sea from South Korea, China and Russia.

Passport

A passport is essential. If your passport is within a few months of expiry, get a new one now – you will not be issued a visa if your passport is due to expire before the visa. For information on visas, see p823.

AIR

There are flights to Japan from all over the world, usually to Tokyo, but also to a number of other Japanese airports. Although Tokyo may seem the obvious arrival and departure point in Japan, for many visitors this may not be the case. For example, if you plan on exploring western Japan or the Kansai region, it might be more convenient to fly into Kansai International Airport near Osaka.

Airports & Airlines

There are international airports situated on the main island of Honshū (Nagoya, Niigata, Osaka/Kansai and Tokyo Narita), and on Kyūshū (Fukuoka, Kagoshima, Kumamoto and Nagasaki), Okinawa (Naha) and Hokkaidō (Sapporo).

NARITA INTERNATIONAL AIRPORT

With the exception of a handful of flights, almost all international flights to/from Tokyo use **Narita International Airport** (NRT; www.narita-airport.or.jp/airport_e). Since Narita is the most popular arrival/departure point in Japan, flights via Narita are often cheaper than those using other airports. See also p192.

KANSAI INTERNATIONAL AIRPORT

All of Osaka's international flights now go via **Kansai International Airport** (KIX; www.kansai-airport.or.jp/en/index.asp). It serves the key Kansai cities of Kyoto, Osaka, Nara and Kōbe. Airport transport to any of these cities is fast and reliable (though it can be expensive if you're going all the way to Kyoto).

CENTRAL JAPAN INTERNATIONAL AIRPORT (CENTRAIR)

Conveniently located near Nagoya, **Central Japan International Airport** (Centrair; NGO; www.centrair.jp) is Japan's newest international airport. Centrair has connections with China, Dubai, Finland, France, Germany, Guam, Hong Kong, Indonesia, the Philippines, Saipan, Singapore, South Korea, Taiwan, Thailand and the USA.

THINGS CHANGE...

The information in this chapter is particularly vulnerable to change. Check directly with the airline or a travel agent to make sure you understand how a fare (and ticket you may buy) works and be aware of the security requirements for international travel. Shop carefully. The details given in this chapter should be regarded as pointers and are not a substitute for your own careful, up-to-date research.

CLIMATE CHANGE & TRAVEL

Climate change is a serious threat to the ecosystems that humans rely upon, and air travel is the fastest-growing contributor to the problem. Lonely Planet regards travel, overall, as a global benefit, but believes we all have a responsibility to limit our personal impact on global warming.

Flying & Climate Change

Pretty much every form of motor travel generates CO_2 (the main cause of human-induced climate change) but planes are far and away the worst offenders, not just because of the sheer distances they allow us to travel, but because they release greenhouse gases high into the atmosphere. The statistics are frightening: two people taking a return flight between Europe and the US will contribute as much to climate change as an average household's gas and electricity consumption over a whole year.

Carbon Offset Schemes

Climatecare.org and other websites use 'carbon calculators' that allow jetsetters to offset the greenhouse gases they are responsible for with contributions to energy-saving projects and other climate-friendly initiatives in the developing world – including projects in India, Honduras, Kazakhstan and Uganda.

Lonely Planet, together with Rough Guides and other concerned partners in the travel industry, supports the carbon offset scheme run by climatecare.org. Lonely Planet offsets all of its staff and author travel.

For more information check out our website: lonelyplanet.com.

FUKUOKA INTERNATIONAL AIRPORT

Fukuoka, at the northern end of Kyūshū, is the main arrival point for western Japan. **Fukuoka International Airport** (FUK; www.fuk-ab.co.jp/english/frame_index.html), conveniently located near the city, has flights to/from the following cities: Bangkok, Beijing, Busan, Dalian, Guam, Guangzhou, Ho Chi Minh City, Hong Kong, Manila, Seoul, Shanghai, Singapore and Taipei.

HANEDA AIRPORT

While most international flights to/from Tokyo use Narita International Airport, five airlines (Japan Airlines, All Nippon Airways, China Eastern Airlines, Shanghai Airlines and Air China) operate a few international flights out of **Haneda airport** (HND; www.tokyo-airport-bldg.co.jp/en). This airport, a 22-minute monorail ride southwest of Tokyo, also handles the great bulk of Tokyo's domestic flights. International destinations served by Haneda are Shanghai, Seoul and Hong Kong (note that all three destinations also have flights to/from Narita).

NAHA AIRPORT

Located on Okinawa-hontō (the main island of Okinawa), **Naha airport** (OKA; www.naha-airport.co.jp, in Japanese) has flights to/from Hong Kong, Seoul, Shanghai and Taipei.

NIIGATA AIRPORT

Located north of Tokyo, **Niigata airport** (KIJ; www.niigata-airport.gr.jp, in Japanese) has flights to/from Guam, Harbin, Honolulu, Irkusk, Khabarovsk, Seoul, Shanghai, Vladivostok and Xian.

OTHER AIRPORTS

On Kyūshū, **Kagoshima airport** (KOJ; www.koj-ab.co.jp, in Japanese) has flights to/from Shanghai and Seoul; **Kumamoto airport** (KMJ; www.kmj-ab.co.jp, in Japanese) has flights to/from Seoul; and **Nagasaki airport** (NGS; www.nabic.co.jp/english) has flights to/from Shanghai.

On Hokkaidō, **New Chitose Airport** (CTS; www.new-chitose-airport.jp/language/english/index.html) has connections with Beijing, Dalien, Guam, Hong Kong, Seoul, Shanghai, Shenyang and Taipei.

At Northern Honshū's **Sendai airport** (SDJ; www.sdj-airport.com/english/index.html), 18km south of the city centre, there are international flights to various destinations in Asia, such as Beijing, Dailan, Guam, Seoul and Shanghai.

Tickets

The price of your ticket will depend to a great extent on when you fly. High-season prices are determined by two sets of holidays and popular travel times: those in the country you're flying from and those in Japan. Generally, high season for travel between Japan and Western countries is in late December (around Christmas and the New Year period) and late April to early May (around Japan's Golden Week holiday), as well as July and August. If you must fly during these periods, book well in advance.

Australia

Jetstar now operates between Australia and Japan's Narita and Kansai international airports, and it often offers the cheapest fares for Australia–Japan routes. Garuda, Malaysian Airlines and Cathay Pacific also offer competitive fares, usually with a stop somewhere in Southeast Asia en route. Direct flights to Japan with airlines such as Qantas and Japan Airlines (JAL) are more expensive but convenient if you're in a hurry.

Two well-known agencies for cheap fares are **STA Travel** (☎ 134 782; www.statravel.com.au), which has offices in all major cities, and **Flight Centre** (www.flightcentre.com.au), which has dozens of offices throughout Australia. For online bookings, try www.travel.com.au.

Canada

There are direct flights between Japan and two Canadian cities: Toronto and Vancouver. Carriers to check include JAL, All Nippon Airways (ANA) and Air Canada. If you're on a tight budget, consider flying with a Chinese, Taiwanese or Korean airline, which will involve backtracking to Japan from their Asian hubs. You might also consider flying from nearby cities in the USA on carriers like United Airlines or Northwest Airlines, which can sometimes be cheaper, even with the connecting flight from Canada.

Travel Cuts (☎ 800-667-2887; www.travelcuts.com) is Canada's national student travel agency. For online bookings, try www.expedia.ca and www.travelocity.ca.

China

There are several daily flights between Japan and Hong Kong on Cathay Pacific, as well as on JAL and ANA. In Hong Kong try **Four Seas Tours** (☎ 0852-2200-7777; www.fourseastravel.com/fs/en). There are also flights between Japan and Beijing, Dalian, Guangzhou, Harbin, Shanghai, Shenyang and Xian.

Continental Europe

Most direct flights between Europe and Japan fly into Tokyo, but there are also some flights into Kansai. The following are recommended travel agencies in continental Europe.

FRANCE

Anyway (☎ 08 92 89 38 92; www.anyway.fr, in French)
Lastminute (☎ 08 99 78 50 00; www.fr.lastminute.com, in French)
Nouvelles Frontières (☎ 08 25 00 07 47; www.nouvelles-frontieres.fr, in French)
OTU Voyages (☎ 01 55 82 32 32; www.otu.fr, in French) This agency specialises in student and youth travellers.
Voyageurs du Monde (☎ 08 92 23 56 56; www.vdm.com, in French)

GERMANY

Expedia (☎ 01805-007146; www.expedia.de, in German)
Just Travel (☎ 089-747 33 30; www.justtravel.de)
STA Travel (☎ 069-743 032 92; www.statravel.de) For travellers under the age of 26.

ITALY

CTS Viaggi (☎ 064 41 11 66; www.cts.it, in Italian)

THE NETHERLANDS

Airfair (☎ 0900-771 77 17; www.airfair.nl, in Dutch)

SPAIN

Barcelo Viajes (☎ 902 20 04 00; www.barceloviajes.com, in Spanish)

New Zealand

Airlines that fly between Japan and New Zealand (Auckland) include Malaysian Airlines, Thai International, Qantas and Air New Zealand (direct). You'll save money by taking one of the Asian airlines via an Asian city rather than flying direct.

Both **Flight Centre** (☎ 0800 243 544; www.flightcentre.co.nz) and **STA Travel** (☎ 0508 782 872; www.statravel.co.nz) have branches throughout New Zealand.

South Korea

Numerous flights link Seoul and Busan with Japan. In Seoul, try the **Korean International Student Exchange Society** (Kises; ☎ 02-733-9494; www.kises.co.kr, in Korean; 5th fl, YMCA Bldg, Chongno 2-ga).

See p831 for information on sea-travel bargains between Korea and Japan.

Taiwan

There are plentiful connections between Taipai and various airports in Japan. Flights also operate between Kaohsiung and Osaka or Tokyo.

TRANSPORT

UK

ANA and JAL offer direct flights between London and Japan. Air France is also a reliable choice for flights to Japan (usually Tokyo), but you'll have to change in Paris. You'll often save a lot of money by taking a Middle Eastern airline, but this will involve a stop somewhere en route. The following travel agencies are recommended:

Flight Centre (☎ 087-0499 0040; www.flightcentre.co.uk)

Flightbookers (☎ 087-1223 5000; www.ebookers.com)

North-South Travel (☎ 01245 608291; www.northsouthtravel.co.uk/) North-South Travel donates part of its profit to projects in the developing world.

Quest Travel (☎ 087-1423 0135; www.questtravel.com)

STA Travel (☎ 087-1230 0040; www.statravel.co.uk) For travellers under the age of 26.

Trailfinders (☎ 084-5058 5858; www.trailfinders.co.uk)

Travel Bag (☎ 080- 0082 5000; www.travelbag.co.uk)

USA

There are flights between several American cities and Japan (mostly to Narita, but also to Kansai and a few other airports). Some carriers to check include JAL, ANA, United Airlines and Northwest Airlines. If you don't mind flying via another Asian country, you can sometimes save money by flying with a Chinese, Taiwanese or Korean airline, but this will involve backtracking to Japan.

IACE Travel USA (☎ 800-872-4223, 212-972-3200; www.iace-usa.com/us/index.php) is a travel agency specialising in travel between the USA and Japan that can often dig up cheap fares. San Francisco's **Avia Travel** (☎ 800-950-2842, 510-558-2150; www.aviatravel.com) is a favourite of Japan-based English teachers and can arrange tickets originating in Japan. **STA Travel** (☎ 800-781-4040; www.statravel.com) is also a good place to check.

Other Asian Countries

There are daily flights between Japan and the following Asian countries: India (Mumbai and Delhi), Indonesia (Jakarta and Denpasar), Malaysia (Kuala Lumpur), the Philippines (Manila), Singapore, Thailand (Bangkok) and Vietnam (Ho Chi Minh City and Hanoi). There are also occasional flights to/from Nepal (Kathmandu).

Other Regions

There are flights between Japan and South America (via the USA or Europe), Africa (via Europe, South Asia or Southeast Asia) and the Middle East.

LAND

Trans-Siberian Railway

A little-used option of approaching or leaving Japan is the Trans-Siberian Railway. There are three Trans-Siberian Railway options, one of which is to travel on the railway to/from Vladivostok in Russia and take the ferry between Vladivostok and Fushiki in Toyama-ken. The cheaper options are the Chinese Trans-Mongolia and Russian Trans-Manchuria routes, which start/finish in China, from where there are ferry connections to/from Japan via Tientsin, Qingdao and Shanghai. See below for info on ferry connections between Japan, Russia and China.

More detailed information is also available in a good number of publications – see Lonely Planet's *Trans-Siberian Railway: A Classic Overland Route*. Those making their way to Japan via China (or vice versa) should pick up a copy of Lonely Planet's *China* guide, which has invaluable information on travel in China as well as information on Trans-Siberian travel.

SEA

China

The **Japan China International Ferry Company** (☎ in Japan 06-6536-6541, in China 021-6325-7642; www.shinganjin.com, in Japanese) links Shanghai and Osaka/Kōbe. A 2nd-class ticket costs around US$200. The journey takes around 48 hours. A similar service is provided by the **Shanghai Ferry Company** (☎ in Japan 06-6243-6345, in China 021-6537-5111; www.shanghai-ferry.co.jp, in Japanese). For more information on both of these, see p407.

The **China Express Line** (☎ in Japan 078-321-5791, in China 022-2420-5777; www.celkobe.co.jp, in Japanese) operates a ferry between Kōbe and Tientsin; 2nd-class tickets cost US$230. The journey takes around 48 hours. For more information, see p413.

Orient Ferry Ltd (☎ in Japan 083-232-6615, in China 0532-8387-1160; www.orientferry.co.jp, in Japanese) operates ferries between Shimonoseki and Qingdao, China, with three departures a week. The cheapest one-way tickets cost around US$130. The trip takes around 28 hours. See p486 for details.

Russia

FKK Air Service (☎ 0766-22-2212; http://fkk-air.toyama-net.com, in Japanese) operates ferries between Fushiki in Toyama-ken and Vladivostok.

One-way fares start at around US$450. The journey takes around 36 hours. The ferry operates from July until the first week of October. For more details, see p249.

An even more exotic option is the summertime route between Wakkanai (in Hokkaidō) and Korsakov (on Sakhalin Island), operated by the **Heartland Ferry** (☎ in Japan 011-233-8010, in Russia 4242-42-0917; www.heartlandferry.jp/english/index.html). One-way fares start at around ¥24,000 (around US$250) and the journey takes around 7½ hours. The ferry operates from mid-May to the end of October. For more details, see p617.

South Korea

South Korea is the closest country to Japan and has several ferry connections.

BUSAN–SHIMONOSEKI

Kampu Ferry (☎ in Japan 0832-24-3000, in Korea operating under Pukwan Ferry 051-464-2700; www.kampuferry.co.jp, in Japanese) operates the Shimonoseki–Busan ferry service. One-way fares range from around US$85 to US$180, and the journey takes around 12 hours. See p486 for more details.

BUSAN-FUKUOKA

A high-speed hydrofoil service, known as the Beetle, is run by **JR Kyūshū** (☎ in Japan 092-281-2315, in Korea 051-465-6111; www.jrbeetle.co.jp/english) and connects Fukuoka with Busan (around US$140 one way, three hours). **Camellia Line** (☎ 092-262-2323 in Japan, 051-466-7799 in Korea; www.camellia-line.co.jp, in Japanese & Korean) also has a daily ferry service between Fukuoka and Busan (around US$95, six hours from Fukuoka to Busan, six to 10 hours from Busan to Fukuoka). See p696 for more details.

Taiwan

Travellers who have been to Japan before might recall the Arimura ferry line that used to operate between Kagoshima (Kyūshū) and Taiwan, via Okinawa. Sadly, this line has ceased operating, and there are now no passenger ferries between Taiwan and Japan.

GETTING AROUND

Japan is justifiably famous for its extensive, well-organised and efficient transport network. Schedules are strictly adhered to and late or cancelled services are almost unheard of. All this convenience comes at a price, however, and you'd be well advised to look into money-saving deals whenever possible (see p840).

AIR

Air services in Japan are extensive, reliable and safe. In many cases, flying is much faster than even *shinkansen* (bullet trains) and not that much more expensive. Flying is also an efficient way to travel from the main islands to the many small islands around Japan, particularly the Nansei-shotō (the southern islands of Kagoshima-ken and Okinawa-ken).

In most of Japan's major cities there are travel agencies where English is spoken. For an idea of the latest prices in Tokyo check the travel ads in the various local English-language publications, and in Kansai check *Kansai Time Out*. In other parts of Japan check the *Japan Times*. For more details on city-based travel agencies, see the relevant sections under Tokyo (p126), Osaka (p393) and Kyoto (p328).

Airlines in Japan

Japan Airlines (JAL; ☎ 03-5460-0522, 0120-255-971; www.jal.co.jp/en) is the major international carrier and also has a domestic network linking the major cities. **All Nippon Airways** (ANA; ☎ 0570-029-709, 03-6741-1120, 0120-029-709; www.ana.co.jp/eng) is the second-largest international carrier and operates a more extensive domestic system. **Japan Trans Ocean Air** (JTA; ☎ 03-5460-0522,

> **BAGGAGE FORWARDING**
>
> If you have too much luggage to carry comfortably or just can't be bothered, you can do what many Japanese travellers do: send it to your next stop by *takkyūbin* (express shipping companies). Prices are surprisingly reasonable and overnight service is the norm. Perhaps the most convenient service is Yamato Takkyūbin, which operates from most convenience stores. Simply pack your luggage and take it to the nearest convenience store; staff will help with the paperwork and arrange for pick-up. Note that you'll need the full address of your next destination in Japanese, along with the phone number of the place. Alternatively, ask the owner of your accommodation to come and pick it up (this is usually possible but might cost extra).

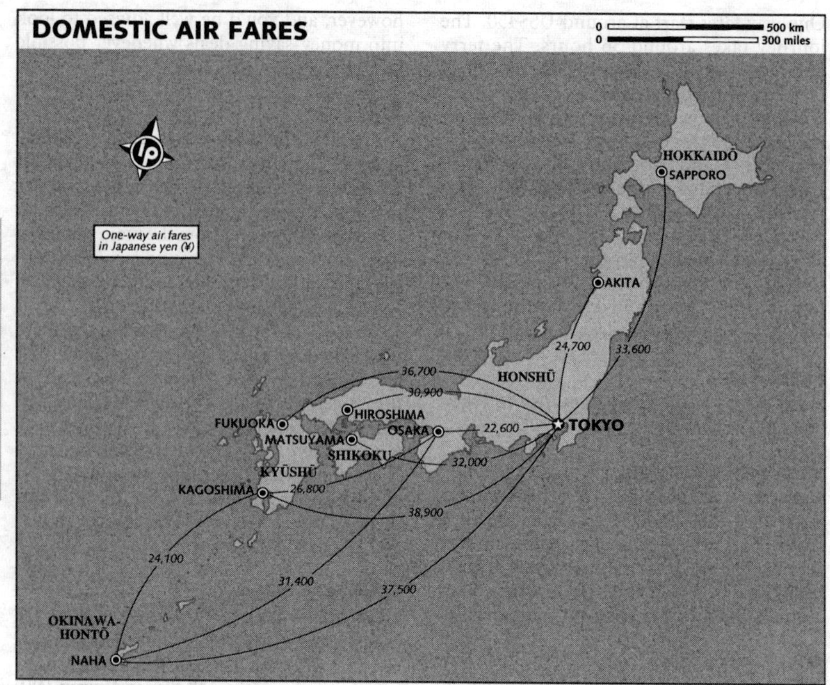

0120-255-971; www.jal.co.jp/jta, in Japanese) is a smaller domestic carrier that mostly services routes in the Nansei-shotō.

In addition to these, **Skymark Airlines** (SKY; ☎ 050-3116-7370; www.skymark.co.jp/en) is a recent start-up budget airline, and **Shinchūō Kōkū** (☎ 0422-31-4191; www.central-air.co.jp, in Japanese) has light-plane flights between Chōfu airport, outside Tokyo, and the islands of Izu-shotō.

The Domestic Air Fares map (p832) shows some of the major connections and one-way fares. Note that return fares are usually around 10% cheaper than buying two one-way tickets. The airlines also have some weird and wonderful discounts if you know what to ask for. The most useful of these are the advance-purchase reductions: both ANA and JAL offer discounts of up to 50% if you purchase your ticket a month or more in advance, with smaller discounts for purchases made one to three weeks in advance. Seniors over 65 also qualify for discounts on most Japanese airlines, but these are sometimes only available if you fly on weekdays.

ANA also offers the Star Alliance Japan Airpass for foreign travellers on ANA or Star Alliance network airlines. Provided you reside outside Japan, purchase your tickets outside Japan and carry a valid international ticket on any airline, you can fly up to five times within 60 days on any ANA domestic route for only ¥11,550 per flight (a huge saving on some routes). Visit www.ana.co.jp/wws/us/e/travelservice/reservations/special/airpass.html for more details.

BICYCLE

Japan is a good country for bicycle touring and several thousand cyclists, both Japanese and foreign, traverse the country every year. Favourite bike touring areas include Kyūshū, Shikoku, the Japan Alps (if you like steep hills!), Noto-hantō and Hokkaidō.

There's no point in fighting your way out of big cities by bicycle. Put your bike on the train or bus and get out to the country before you start pedalling. To take a bicycle on a train you may need to use a bicycle carrying bag, available from good bicycle shops.

See p836 for information on road maps of Japan. In addition to the maps mentioned in that section, a useful series of maps is the

Touring Mapple (Shobunsha) series, which is aimed at motorcyclists, but is also very useful for cyclists.

For more information on cycling in Japan, you can check out the excellent website of **KANcycling** (www.kancyc ling.com).

Guided Bicycle Tours

For information about guided bicycle tours in Kyoto, see p383. There is talk of a similar service being offered in Tokyo in the future – a web search should turn up the operator once it's up and running.

Hire

You will find bicycle rental shops outside the train or bus stations in most of Japan's popular tourist areas, as well as near the ferry piers on many of the country's smaller islands. Typical charges are around ¥200/1000 per hour/day. Kyoto, for example, is ideally suited to bicycle exploration and there are plenty of cheap hire shops to choose from.

Note that the bicycles for rent are not usually performance vehicles. More commonly they're what the Japanese call *mama chari* (literally 'mama's bicycles'): one- or three-speed shopping bikes that are murder on hills of any size. They're also usually too small for anyone over 180cm in height.

Many youth hostels also have bicycles to rent – there's a symbol identifying them in the *Japan Youth Hostel Handbook*. 'Cycling terminals' found in various locations around the country also rent out bicycles. For more on cycling terminals, see p804.

Purchase

In Japan, prices for used bikes range from a few thousand yen for an old shopping bike to several tens of thousands of yen for good mountain and road bikes. New bikes range anywhere from about ¥10,000 for a shopping bike to ¥100,000 for a flash mountain or road bike.

Touring cycles are available in Japan but prices tend to be significantly higher than you'd pay back home. If you're tall, you may not find any suitably sized bikes in stock. One solution for tall riders, or anyone who wants to save money, is to buy a used bike; in Tokyo, check the English-language publications and in Kansai check *Kansai Time Out*.

BOAT

Japan is an island nation and there are a great many ferry services both between islands and between ports on the same island. Ferries can be an excellent way of getting from one place to another and for seeing parts of Japan you might otherwise miss. Taking a ferry between Osaka (Honshū) and Beppu (Kyūshū), for example, is a good way of getting to Kyūshū and – if you choose the right departure time – seeing some of the Inland Sea (Seto-nai-kai; p471) on the way. Likewise, the ferry run up and down the Izu-shotō (p240) can be incredibly scenic.

The routes vary widely, from two-hour services between adjacent islands to 1½-day trips in what are in fact small ocean liners. The cheapest fares on the longer trips are in tatami-mat rooms where you simply unroll your futon on the floor and hope, if the ship is crowded, that your fellow passengers aren't too intent on knocking back the booze all night. In this basic class, fares are usually lower than equivalent land travel, but there are also more expensive private cabins. Bicycles can be brought along and most ferries also carry cars and motorcycles.

Information on ferry routes, schedules and fares is found in the *JR Jikokuhyō* (p842) and on information sheets from the Japan National Tourism Organization (JNTO; see p822). Some ferry services and their lowest one-way fares appear in the table, p835.

BUS

Japan has a comprehensive network of long-distance buses. These 'highway buses' are nowhere near as fast as the *shinkansen* but

> **BARGAIN BUSES**
>
> Japan Railways (JR) operates the largest network of highway buses in Japan, and we quote its prices for most long-distance bus routes in this guide. However, several budget bus companies have recently sprung up in Japan and these are gaining popularity with backpackers. One such company is **123Bus** (☎ 050-5805-0383; www.123bus.net). Some of its services include Tokyo–Osaka (¥4100), Tokyo–Nagoya (¥2900) and Tokyo–Hiroshima (¥6900). Booking is possible in English online. Check the website for the latest details and pick-up/drop-off points.

TRANSPORT

the fares are comparable with those of normal *futsū* (local) trains. The trip between Tokyo and Sendai (Northern Honshū), for example, takes about two hours by *shinkansen*, four hours by *tokkyū* (limited express) train and nearly eight hours by bus. Of course, there are many places in Japan where trains do not run and bus travel is the only public transport option.

Bookings can be made through any travel agency in Japan or at the *midori-no-madoguchi* (green counters – look for the counter with the green band across the glass) in large Japan Rail (JR) stations. The Japan Rail Pass is valid on some highway buses, but in most cases the *shinkansen* would be far preferable (it's much faster and more comfortable). Note that the storage racks on most buses are generally too small for large backpacks, but you can usually stow them in the luggage compartment underneath the bus.

Costs

Some typical long-distance fares and travel times out of Tokyo include the following.

Destination	Fare (¥; one way)	Duration (hr)
Aomori	10,000	9½
Hakata	9900	16
Hiroshima	11,600	12
Kōbe	8690	9½
Kyoto	8180	9
Nagano	4000	4
Nagoya	5100	6
Nara	8400	9½
Osaka	4300	8
Sendai	6210	5½

Night Services

Night buses are a good option for those on a tight budget without a Japan Rail Pass. They are relatively cheap, spacious (allowing room to stretch out and get some sleep) and they also save on a night's accommodation. They typically leave at around 10pm or 11pm and arrive the following day at around 6am or 7am.

CAR & MOTORCYCLE

Driving in Japan is quite feasible, even for just the mildly adventurous. The major roads are signposted in English; road rules are generally adhered to and driving is safer than in other Asian countries; and petrol, while expensive, is not prohibitively so. Indeed, in some areas of the country it can prove much more convenient than other forms of travel and, between a group of people, it can also prove quite economical.

Automobile Associations

If you're a member of an automobile association in your home country, you're eligible for reciprocal rights with the **Japan Automobile Federation** (JAF; ☎ 03-6833-9000, 0570-00-2811; www.jaf.or.jp/e/index_e.htm; 2-2-17 Shiba, Minato-ku, Tokyo 105-0014). Its office is near Onarimon Station on the Tōei Mita line. JAF produces a variety of publications, and will make up strip maps for its members.

Driving Licence

Travellers from most nations are able to drive in Japan with an International Driving Permit backed up by their own regular licence. The international permit is issued by your national automobile association and costs around US$5 in most countries. Make sure it's endorsed for cars and motorcycles if you're licensed for both.

Travellers from Switzerland, France and Germany (and others whose countries are not signatories to the Geneva Convention of 1949 concerning international drivers' licences) are not allowed to drive in Japan on a regular international permit. Rather, travellers from these countries must have their own licence backed by an authorised translation of the same licence. These translations can be made by their country's embassy or consulate in Japan or by the JAF. If you are unsure which category your country falls into, contact the nearest JNTO office (p822) for more information.

Foreign licences and International Driving Permits are only valid in Japan for six months. If you are staying longer, you will have to get a Japanese licence from the local department of motor vehicles. To do this, you will need to provide your own licence, passport photos, Alien Registration Card and the fee, and also take a simple eye test.

Expressways

The expressway system is fast, efficient and growing all the time. Unfortunately, it is rather expensive, and tolls can really add up on longer journeys. Tolls run about ¥24.6 per kilometre. Tokyo to Kyoto, for example, will cost about ¥10,050 in tolls. The speed limit on expressways is 80km/h but seems to be uniformly ignored. At a steady 100km/h, you will still find as many cars overtaking you as you overtake.

There are good rest stops and service centres at regular intervals. A prepaid highway card, available from tollbooths or at the service areas, saves you having to carry so much cash and gives you a 4% to 8% discount in the larger card denominations. You can also pay tolls with most major credit cards. Exits are usually fairly well signposted in romaji but make sure you know the name of your exit as it may not necessarily be the same as the city you're heading towards.

Fuel & Spare Parts

You'll find *gasoreen sutando* (petrol stations) in almost every town in Japan and in service stations along the country's expressways. The cost of petrol per litre ranges from ¥104 to ¥107 for regular and ¥116 to ¥118 for high-octane.

Spare parts are widely available in Japan for Japanese cars. For foreign cars, you may have to place a special order with a garage or parts store.

Hire

You'll usually find car-rental agencies clustered around train stations and ferry piers in Japan. Typical rental rates for a small car are ¥5000 to ¥7000 per day, with reductions for rentals of more than one day. On top of the rental charge, there's about a ¥1000 per day insurance cost.

It's also worth bearing in mind that car rental costs go up during high seasons (28 April to 6 May, 20 July to 31 August and 28 December to 5 January). The increase can make quite a difference to costs.

Communication can sometimes be a major problem when hiring a car. Some of the offices will have a rent-a-car phrasebook, with questions you might need to ask in English. Otherwise, just speak as slowly as possible and hope for the best. A good way to open the conversation is to say '*kokusai menkyō wo motteimasu*' (I have an international licence).

Two of the main Japanese car-rental companies and their Tokyo phone numbers are **Hertz** (☎ 0120-489-882) and **Toyota Rent-a-Lease** (☎ 0070-8000-10000).

TRANSPORT

FERRY FARES & TIMES

Hokkaidō–Honshū	Fare (¥)	Duration (hr)
Otaru–Maizuru	9600	20
Otaru–Niigata	6200	18
Tomakomai–Hachinohe	4080	7
Tomakomai–Nagoya (via Sendai)	10,500	38½
Tomakomai–Ōarai	8000	19
Tomakomai–Sendai	8100	15
Departing from Tokyo	**Fare (¥)**	**Duration (hr)**
Naha (Okinawa)	24,500	46
Shinmoji (Kitakyūshū)	14,000	34
Tokushima (Shikoku)	9900	18
Departing from Osaka/Kōbe	**Fare (¥)**	**Duration (hr)**
Beppu (Kyūshū)	10,000	11½
Matsuyama (Shikoku)	7500	9¼
Miyazaki (Kyūshū)	10,600	13
Naha (Okinawa)	19,600	42
Shibushi (Kyūshū)	11,500	14¾
Shinmoji (Kitakyūshū)	6420	12
Departing from Kyūshū	**Fare (¥)**	**Duration (hr)**
Kagoshima–Naha (Okinawa)	14,600	25

MOTORCYCLE HIRE & PURCHASE

Hiring a motorcycle for long-distance touring is not as easy as hiring a car, although small scooters are available in many places for local sightseeing.

Although Japan is famous for its large-capacity road burners, most bikes on the road are 400cc or less. This is because a special licence is required to ride a bike larger than 400cc, and few Japanese and even fewer foreigners pass the test necessary to get this licence.

The 400cc machines are the most popular large motorcycles in Japan but, for general touring, a 250cc machine is probably the best bet. Apart from being large enough for a compact country like Japan, machines up to 250cc are also exempt from the expensive *shaken* (inspections).

Smaller machines (those below 125cc) are banned from expressways and are generally less suitable for long-distance touring, but people have ridden from one end of Japan to the other on little 50cc 'step-thrus'. An advantage of these bikes is that you can ride them with just a regular driving licence, so you won't need to get a motorcycle licence.

The best place to look for motorcycles in Japan is the Korin-chō motorcycle neighbourhood in Tokyo's Ueno district. There are over 20 motorcycle shops in the area and some employ foreign salespeople who speak both Japanese and English. For used bikes in Kansai check *Kansai Time Out, Kansai Flea Market* or the message board in the Kyoto International Community House (p327).

Insurance

When you own a car, it is necessary to get compulsory third-party insurance *(jidosha songai baishō sekinin hoken)*. This is paid when your car undergoes the compulsory inspection *(shaken)*. It is also recommended that you get comprehensive vehicle insurance *(jidosha hoken)* to cover any expenses that aren't covered by the compulsory third-party insurance.

Maps & Navigation

Get yourself a copy of the *Road Atlas Japan* (Shōbunsha). It's all in romaji with enough names in kanji to make navigation possible even off the major roads. If you're really intent on making your way through the back blocks, a Japanese map will prove useful even if your knowledge of kanji is nil. The best Japanese road atlases by far are the *Super Mapple* series (Shōbunsha), which are available in bookshops and some convenience stores.

There is a reasonable amount of signposting in romaji, so getting around isn't all that difficult, especially in developed areas. If you are attempting tricky navigation, use your maps imaginatively – watch out for the railway line, the rivers, the landmarks. They're all useful ways of locating yourself when you can't read the signs. A compass will also come in handy when navigating.

These days, many rental cars come equipped with satellite car navigation systems, which can make navigation a snap, provided you can figure out how to work the system (ask the person at the rental agency to explain it and be sure to take notes). With most of these systems, you can input the phone number of your destination, which is easy, or its address, which is just about impossible if you don't read Japanese (although you can always ask for help here, too). Even without programming in your destination, with the device on the default *'genzai-chi'* (present location) setting, you will find it very useful.

Motorcycles

For citizens of most countries, your overseas driving licence and an International Driving Permit are all you need to ride a motorcycle in Japan (see p834 for details on which nationalities require additional documentation). Crash helmets are compulsory and you should also ensure your riding gear is adequate to cope with the weather, particularly rain. For much of the year the climate is ideal for motorcycle touring, but when it rains it really rains.

Touring equipment – panniers, carrier racks, straps and the like – is readily available from dealers. Remember to pack clothing in plastic bags to ensure it stays dry, even if you don't. An adequate supply of tools and a puncture repair kit can prove invaluable.

Riding in Japan is no more dangerous than anywhere else in the world, which is to say it is not very safe and great care should be taken at all times. Japan has the full range of motorcycle hazards, from single-minded taxi drivers to unexpected changes in road surface, heedless car-door openers to runaway dogs.

Parking

In most big cities, free kerbside parking spots are almost nonexistent, while in rural areas you'll be able to park your car just about wherever you want. In the cities you'll find that you usually have to pay ¥200 per hour for metred street parking, or anywhere from ¥300 to ¥600 per hour for a spot in a multistorey car park. You'll find car parks around most department stores and near some train stations. Fortunately, most hotels have free parking for guests, as do some restaurants and almost all department stores.

Road Rules

Driving in Japan is on the left. There are no real problems with driving in Japan. There are no unusual rules or interpretations of them and most signposts follow international conventions. JAF (p834) has a *Rules of the Road* book available in English and five other languages for ¥1000.

HITCHING

Hitching is never entirely safe in any country in the world, and we don't recommend it. Travellers who decide to hitch should understand that they are taking a small but potentially serious risk. In particular, Japan is a very dangerous place for solitary female hitchhikers; there have been countless cases of solitary female hitchers being attacked, molested and raped. People who do choose to hitch will be safer if they travel in pairs and let someone know where they are planning to go.

Provided you understand the risks and take appropriate precautions, Japan is known as a good country for hitchhiking. Many hitchhikers have tales of extraordinary kindness from motorists who have picked them up.

The rules for hitchhiking are similar to anywhere else in the world. Dress neatly and look for a good place to hitch – expressway on-ramps and expressway service areas are probably your best bet.

Truck drivers are particularly good for long-distance travel as they often head out on the expressways at night. If a driver is exiting before your intended destination, try to get dropped off at one of the expressway service areas. The *Service Area Parking Area* (SAPA) guide maps are excellent for hitchhikers. They're available free from expressway service areas and show full details of each interchange (IC) and rest stop. These are important orientation points if you have a limited knowledge of Japanese.

For more on hitching in Japan, pick up a copy of the excellent *Hitchhiker's Guide to Japan* by Will Ferguson. In addition to lots of general advice, this book details suggested routes and places to stay on the road. All in all, it's just about invaluable for anyone contemplating a long hitch around Japan.

LOCAL TRANSPORT

All the major cities offer a wide variety of public transport. In many cities you can get day passes for unlimited travel on bus, tram or subway systems. Such passes are usually called an *ichi-nichi-jōsha-ken*. If you're staying for an extended period in one city, commuter passes are available for regular travel.

Bus

Almost every Japanese city has an extensive bus service, but it's usually the most difficult public transport system for foreign travellers to use. The destination names are almost always written in kanji and often there are no numbers to identify which bus you want.

Fares are either paid to the driver on entering or as you leave the bus and usually operate on one of two systems. In Tokyo and some other cities, there's a flat fare regardless of distance. In the other system, you take a ticket as you board that indicates the zone number at your starting point. When you get off, an electric sign at the front of the bus indicates the fare charged at that point for each starting zone number. You simply pay the driver the fare that matches your zone number. There is often a change machine near the front of the bus that can exchange ¥100 and ¥500 coins and ¥1000 notes.

In many tourist towns there are also *teiki kankō basu* (tour buses), often run from the main train station. Tours are usually conducted in Japanese, but English-language tours are available in popular areas like Kyoto and Tokyo. In places where the attractions are widespread or hard to reach by public transport, tours can be a good bet.

Taxi

Taxis are convenient but expensive and can even be found in quite small towns; the train station is the best place to look. Fares are fairly uniform throughout the country – flagfall (posted on the taxi windows) is ¥600 to ¥660 for the first 2km, after which it's around ¥100 for each 350m (approximately). There's also a time charge if the speed drops below 10km/h. During the day, it's almost impossible to tell if a moving taxi is occupied (just wave at it and it will stop if it's free); at night, vacant taxis are distinguishable by an illuminated light on the roof – an occupied taxi will have its light turned off.

Don't whistle for a taxi; a simple wave should bring one politely to a halt. Don't open the door when it stops; the driver does that with a remote release. The driver will also shut the door when you leave the taxi.

Communication can be a problem with taxi drivers in Japan, but perhaps not as much as you fear. If you can't tell the driver where you want to go, it's useful to have the name written down in Japanese. At hotel front desks there will usually be business cards complete with name and location, which can be used for just this purpose. Of course, Japanese script is provided on map keys in this guidebook, too.

Tipping is not necessary. A 20% surcharge is added after 11pm or for taxis summoned by radio. There may also be an added charge if you summon the taxi by phone or reserve the taxi. Finally, taxis can usually take up to four adult passengers (one person can sit in the front). Drivers are sometimes willing to bend the rules for small children.

Train & Subway

Several cities, especially Osaka and Tokyo, have mass transit rail systems comprising a loop line around the city centre and radial lines into the central stations and the subway system. Subway systems operate in Fukuoka, Kōbe, Kyoto, Nagoya, Osaka, Sapporo, Sendai, Tokyo and Yokohama. They are usually the fastest and most convenient way to get around the city.

For subways and local trains, you'll most likely have to buy your ticket from a machine. They're pretty easy to understand even if you can't read kanji as there is a diagram explaining the routes; from this you can find out what your fare should be. If you can't work the fare out, a solution is to buy a ticket for the lowest fare. When you finish your trip, go to the fare-adjustment machine *(seisan-ki)* or counter before you reach the exit gate and pay the excess. JR train stations and most subway stations not only have their names posted above the platform in kanji and romaji but also the names of the preceding and following stations.

Tram

Many cities have tram lines – particularly Nagasaki, Kumamoto and Kagoshima on Kyūshū; Kōchi and Matsuyama on Shikoku; and Hakodate on Hokkaidō. These are excellent ways of getting around as they combine many of the advantages of bus travel (eg good views of the passing parade) with those of subways (it's easy to work out where you're going). Fares work on similar systems to bus travel and there are also unlimited-travel day tickets available.

TRAIN

Japanese rail services are among the best in the world: they are fast, frequent, clean and comfortable. The services range from small local lines to the *shinkansen* super-expresses or 'bullet trains', which have become a symbol of modern Japan.

The 'national' railway is **Japan Railways** (JR; www.japanrail.com), which is actually a number of separate private rail systems providing one linked service. The JR system covers the country from one end to the other and also provides local services around major cities like Tokyo and Osaka. There is more than 20,000km of railway line and about 20,000 services daily. JR operates the *shinkansen* network throughout Japan. *Shinkansen* lines operate on separate tracks from regular trains, and, in some places, the *shinkansen* stations are a fair distance from the main JR station (as is the case in Osaka). JR also operates buses and ferries, and convenient ticketing can combine more than one form of transport.

In addition to JR services, there is a huge network of private railways in Japan. Each large city usually has at least one private train line that services that city and the surrounding area, or connects that city to nearby cities.

Types of Trains

The slowest trains stopping at all stations are called *futsū* or *kaku-eki-teisha*. A step up from this is the *kyūkō* (ordinary express), which stops at only a limited number of stations. A variation on the *kyūkō* trains is the *kaisoku* (rapid) service (usually operating on JR lines). Finally, the fastest regular (non-*shinkansen*) trains are the *tokkyū* (limited express) services, which are sometimes known as *shin-kaisoku* (again, usually operating on JR lines).

Train Types

shinkansen	新幹線	bullet train
tokkyū	特急	limited express
shin-kaisoku	新快速	JR special rapid train
kyūkō	急行	ordinary express
kaisoku	快速	JR rapid or express
futsū	普通	local
kaku-eki-teisha	各駅停車	local

Other Useful Words

jiyū-seki	自由席	unreserved seat
shitei-seki	指定席	reserved seat
green-sha	グリーン車	1st-class carriage
ōfuku	往復	round trip
katamichi	片道	one way
kin'en-sha	禁煙車	nonsmoking carriage
kitsuen-sha	喫煙車	smoking carriage

SHINKANSEN

The fastest and best-known train services are JR's *shinkansen,* Japan's famed 'bullet trains'. *Shinkansen* reach speeds of up to 300km/h and some experimental models have gone significantly faster. In addition to being incredibly fast, *shinkansen* are also incredibly safe: in more than 30 years of operation, there has never been a fatality.

The service efficiency starts even before you board the train. Your ticket indicates your carriage and seat number, and platform signs indicate where you should stand for that carriage entrance. The train pulls in precisely to the scheduled minute and, sure enough, the carriage door you want is right beside where you're standing.

On most *shinkansen* routes, there are two or three types of service: faster express services stopping at a limited number of stations, and slower local services stopping at more stations. There is no difference in fare, except for the Green Car (1st-class) carriages, which cost slightly more.

There are a limited number of *kin'en-sha* (nonsmoking carriages); request one when booking or ask on the platform for the *kin'en-sha-jiyū-seki* (unreserved nonsmoking carriages). Unreserved carriages are available on all trains, but at peak holiday periods they can be very crowded and you may have to stand.

For prices on specific *shinkansen* routes, see right.

Classes

Most long-distance JR trains, including *shinkansen,* have regular and Green Car carriages. The seating is slightly more spacious in Green Car carriages, but most people will find the regular carriages perfectly acceptable.

Costs

JR fares are calculated on the basis of *futsū-unchin* (basic fare), *tokkyū-ryōkin* (an express surcharge levied only on express services) and *shinkansen-ryōkin* (a special charge for *shinkansen* services). The following are some typical fares from Tokyo or Ueno (prices given for *shinkansen* are the total price of the ticket):

Destination	Basic Fare (¥)	Shinkansen Fare (¥)
Fukushima	4620	8500
Hakata	13,440	21,520
Hiroshima	11,340	17,850
Kyoto	7980	13,020
Morioka	8190	13,640
Nagoya	6090	10,580
Niigata	5460	10,070
Okayama	10,190	16,160
Shin-Osaka	8510	13,550
Sendai	5780	10,390
Shin-Shimonoseki	12,810	20,370

SURCHARGES

Various surcharges may be added to the basic fare. These include reserved seat, Green Car, express service and *shinkansen* surcharges. You may also have to pay a surcharge for special trains to resort areas or for a seat in an observation car. The express surcharges (but not the *shinkansen* super-express surcharge) can be paid to the train conductor on board the train.

Some of the fare surcharges are slightly higher (5% to 10%) during peak travel seasons. This applies mainly to reserved seat tickets. High-season dates are 21 March to 5 April, 28 April to 6 May, 21 July to 31 August and 25 December to 10 January.

Further surcharges apply for overnight sleepers, and these vary with the berth type, from approximately ¥9800 for various types of two-tier bunks, and ¥20,000 for a standard or 'royal' compartment. Note that there are no sleepers on the *shinkansen* services as none of these run overnight. Japan Rail Pass users must still pay the sleeper surcharge (for more on the Japan Rail Pass, see p840). Sleeper services mainly operate on trains from Tokyo or Osaka to destinations in Western Honshū and Kyūshū.

The Nozomi super express has higher surcharges than other *shinkansen* services and cannot be used with a Japan Rail Pass. As a guideline, the Nozomi surcharge for Tokyo–Kyoto is ¥300; for Tokyo–Hakata it's ¥600 (seat reserve fee).

Passes & Discount Tickets

If you plan to do any extended travel in Japan, a Japan Rail Pass is almost essential. Not only will it save you lots of money, it will also spare you the hassle of buying tickets each time you want to board a train.

In addition to the Japan Rail Pass, there are various discount tickets and special fares available. The most basic is the return fare discount: if you buy a return ticket for a trip that is more than 600km each way, you qualify for a 10% discount on the return leg.

JAPAN RAIL PASS

The Japan Rail Pass is a must for anyone planning to do extensive train travel within Japan. The most important thing to note about the pass is this: the Japan Rail Pass must be purchased outside Japan. It is available to foreign tourists and Japanese overseas residents (but not foreign residents of Japan). The pass lets you use any JR service for seven days for ¥28,300, 14 days for ¥45,100 or 21 days for ¥57,700. Green Car passes are ¥37,800, ¥61,200 and ¥79,600, respectively. The pass cannot be used for the super express Nozomi *shinkansen* service, but is OK for everything else (including other *shinkansen* services).

Since a one-way reserved seat Tokyo–Kyoto *shinkansen* ticket costs ¥13,220, you only have to travel Tokyo–Kyoto–Tokyo to make a seven-day pass come close to paying off. The only surcharge levied on the Japan Rail Pass is for overnight sleepers. Note that the pass is valid only on JR services; you will still have to pay for private train services.

In order to get a pass, you must first purchase an 'exchange order' outside Japan at JAL and ANA offices or major travel agencies. Once you arrive in Japan, you must bring this order to a JR Travel Service Centre (found in most major JR stations and at Narita and Kansai international airports). When you validate your pass, you'll have to show your passport. The pass can only be used by those with a temporary visitor visa, which means it cannot be used by foreign residents of Japan (those on any visa other than the temporary visitor visa).

The clock starts to tick on the pass as soon as you validate it. So don't validate it if you're just going into Tokyo or Kyoto and intend to hang around for a few days. Instead, validate when you leave those cities to explore the rest of the country.

For more information on the pass and overseas purchase locations, visit the JR website's **Japan Rail Pass** (www.japanrailpass.net/eng/en001.html) section.

JR EAST PASS

This is a great deal for those who only want to travel in eastern Japan. The passes are good on all JR lines in eastern Japan (including Tōhoku, Yamagata, Akita, Jōetsu and Nagano *shinkansen*, but not including the Tōkaidō *shinkansen*). This includes the area around Tokyo and everything north of Tokyo to the tip of Honshū, but doesn't include Hokkaidō.

Prices for five-day passes are ¥20,000/10,000/16,000 for adults over 26/children aged six to 11/youths 12 to 25. Ten-day passes are ¥32,000/16,000/25,000 for the same age groups. Four-day 'flexible' passes are also available, which allow travel on any four consecutive or nonconsecutive days within any one-month period. These cost ¥20,000/10,000/16,000 for the same age groups. Green Car passes are available for higher prices.

As with the Japan Rail Pass, this can only be purchased outside Japan (in the same locations as the Japan Rail Pass) and can only be used by those with temporary visitor visas (you'll need to show your passport). See the preceding Japan Rail Pass section for more details on purchase places and validation procedures.

For more information on the JR East Pass, visit the JR website's **JR East Pass** (www.jreast.co.jp/e/eastpass/top.html) section.

JR WEST SAN-YŌ AREA PASS

Similar to the JR East Pass, this pass allows unlimited travel on the San-yō *shinkansen* line (including the Nozomi super express) between Osaka and Hakata, as well as local trains running between the same cities. A four-day pass costs ¥20,000 and an eight-day pass costs ¥30,000 (children's passes are half-price). These can be purchased both inside Japan (at major train stations, travel agencies and Kansai International Airport) and outside Japan (same locations as the Japan Rail Pass), but can only be used by those with a temporary visitor visa. The pass also entitles you to discounts at station car-hire offices. For more information on this pass, see the JR West website's **San-yō Area Pass** (www.westjr.co.jp/english/global.html) section.

JR WEST KANSAI AREA PASS

A great deal for those who only want to explore the Kansai area, this pass covers unlimited travel on JR lines between most major Kansai cities, such as Himeji, Kōbe, Osaka, Kyoto and Nara. It also covers JR trains to/from Kansai International Airport but does not cover any *shinkansen* lines. One- /two- /three- /four-day passes cost ¥2000/4000/5000/6000 (children's passes are half-price). These can be purchased at the same places as the San-yō Area Pass (both inside and outside Japan) and also entitle you to discounts at station car-hire offices. Like the San-yō Area Pass, this pass can only be used by those with a temporary visitor visa. For more information, see the JR West website's **Kansai Area Pass** (www.westjr.co.jp/english/global.html) section.

JR KYŪSHŪ RAIL PASS

This pass is valid on all JR lines in Kyūshū with the exception of the *shinkansen* line. A five-day pass (the only option) costs ¥16,000 (children's passes are half-price). It can be purchased both inside Japan (at Joyroad Travel Agencies in major train stations in Kyūshū) and outside Japan, at the same locations as the Japan Rail Pass (see opposite for purchase details). It can only be used by those on a temporary visitor visa. If you purchase an exchange order overseas, you can pick up your pass at major train stations in Kyūshū. For more information, visit the website of **JR Kyūshū** (www.jrkyushu.co.jp/english/kyushu_railpass.html).

SEISHUN JŪHACHI KIPPU

If you don't have a Japan Rail Pass, one of the best deals going is a five-day Seishun Jūhachi Kippu (literally a 'Youth 18 Ticket'). Despite its name, it can be used by anyone of any age. Basically, for ¥11,500 you get five one-day tickets valid for travel anywhere in Japan on JR lines. The only catches are that you can't travel on *tokkyū* or *shinkansen* trains and each ticket must be used within 24 hours. However, even if you only have to make a return trip, say, between Tokyo and Kyoto, you'll be saving a lot of money. Seishun Jūhachi Kippu can be purchased at most JR stations in Japan.

The tickets are intended to be used during Japanese university holidays. There are three periods of sale and validity: spring – which is from 20 February to 31 March and valid for use between 1 March and 10 April; summer – from 1 July to 31 August and valid for use between 20 July and 10 September; and winter – from 1 December to 10 January and valid for use between 10 December and 20 January. Note that these periods are subject to change. For more information, ask at any JR ticket window.

If you don't want to buy the whole book of five tickets, you can sometimes purchase separate tickets at the discount ticket shops around train stations.

For more on Seishun Jūhachi Kippu, see the JR East website's **Seishun Jūhachi Kippu** (www.jreast.co.jp/e/pass/seishun18.html) section.

KANSAI THRU PASS

See p326 for details on this pass, which allows unlimited travel on all non-JR private train lines and most bus lines in Kansai.

SHŪYŪ-KEN & FURII KIPPU

There are a number of excursion tickets, known as *shūyū-ken* or *furii kippu* (*furii* is Japanese for 'free'). These tickets include the return fare to your destination and give you unlimited JR local travel within the destination area. There are *shūyū-ken* available to travel from Tokyo to Hokkaidō and then around Hokkaidō for up to seven days. A Kyūshū or Shikoku *shūyū-ken* gets you to and from either island and gives you four or five days of travel around them. You can even go to Kyūshū one way by rail and one way by ferry. These tickets are available at major JR stations in Japan. For more information on these and other special ticket deals, see the JR East website's **Useful Tickets and Rail Passes for Visitors to East Japan** (www.jreast.co.jp/e/pass/index.html) section.

DISCOUNT-TICKET SHOPS

Discount-ticket shops are known as *kakuyasu-kippu-uriba* in Japanese. These shops deal in discounted tickets for trains, buses, domestic plane flights, ferries and a host of other things like cut-rate stamps and phone cards. You can typically save between 5% and 10% on *shinkansen* tickets. Discount-ticket agencies are found around train stations in medium and large cities. The best way to find one is to ask at the *kōban* (police box) outside the station.

Schedules & Information

The most complete timetables can be found in the *JR Jikokuhyō* (Book of Timetables), which is available at all Japanese bookshops but is written in Japanese. The JNTO, however, produces a handy English-language Railway Timetable booklet that explains a great deal about the services in Japan and gives timetables for the *shinkansen* services, JR *tokkyū* and major private lines. If your visit to Japan is a short one and you will not be straying far from the major tourist destinations, this booklet may well be all you need.

Major train stations all have information counters, and you can usually get your point across in simplified English.

If you need to know anything about JR, such as schedules, fares, fastest routes, lost baggage, discounts on rail travel, hotels and car hire, call the **JR East Infoline** (☎ 050-2016-1603; www.jreast.co.jp/e/info/index.html; 🕑 10am-6pm, closed during the year-end/new-year period). Information is available in English, Korean and Chinese. More information can be found on the website. The website **Hyperdia** (www.hyperdia.com) is also a useful source of online train schedules.

Tickets & Reservations

Tickets for most journeys can be bought from train station vending machines or ticket counters/reservation offices. For reservations of complicated tickets, larger train stations have *midori-no-madoguchi*. Major travel agencies in Japan also sell reserved-seat tickets, and you can buy *shinkansen* tickets through JAL offices overseas if you will be flying JAL to Japan.

On *futsū* services, there are no reserved seats. On the faster *tokkyū* and *shinkansen* services you can choose to travel reserved or unreserved. However, if you travel unreserved, there's always the risk of not getting a seat and having to stand, possibly for the entire trip. This is a particular danger at weekends, peak travel seasons and on holidays. Reserved-seat tickets can be bought any time from a month in advance to the day of departure.

Information and tickets can be obtained from travel agencies, of which there are a great number in Japan. Nearly every train station of any size will have at least one travel agency in the station building to handle all sorts of bookings in addition to train services. Japan Travel Bureau (JTB) is the big daddy of Japanese travel agencies. However, for most train tickets and long-distance bus reservations, you don't need to go through a travel agency – just go to the ticket counters or *midori-no-madoguchi* of any major train station.

Health

CONTENTS

Japan is a wealthy industrialised country with a high standard of medical care, although quality can vary, depending on where you go. Food and water sanitation is generally good, though there is a slight risk of disease transmission through eating certain raw or undercooked foods. There is a low risk of catching an insect-borne disease such as Japanese encephalitis, Lyme disease and tick-borne encephalitis in specific areas at certain times of the year. Medical care is reasonably priced, but ensure you have adequate travel insurance.

BEFORE YOU GO

Prevention is the key to staying healthy while abroad. A little planning before departure, particularly for pre-existing illnesses, will save trouble later. See your dentist before a long trip, carry a spare pair of contact lenses and glasses, and take your optical prescription with you. Bring medications in their original, clearly labelled containers. A signed and dated letter from your physician describing your medical conditions and medications, including generic names, is also a good idea. If carrying syringes or needles, be sure to have a physician's letter documenting their medical necessity. If you have a heart condition, bring a copy of a recent electrocardiogram (ECG/EKG). If you take any regular medication, carry extra supplies in case of loss or theft – it may be difficult to get exactly the same medications in Japan. In particular it can be difficult to get oral contraceptives.

Although medical care in most of Japan is quite reasonable, it is still wise to carry a basic medical kit suitable for treating minor ailments. Recommended items include simple painkillers, antiseptic and dressings for minor wounds, insect repellent, sunscreen, antihistamine tablets and adequate supplies of your personal medications.

INSURANCE

Even if you are fit and healthy, don't travel without specific travel health insurance – accidents can happen. If your health insurance does not cover you for medical expenses while abroad, get supplemental insurance. Find out in advance if your insurance plan will make payments directly to providers, or reimburse you later for overseas health expenditures. Take a higher medical expense option, because health costs in Japan are relatively high. If you are seeing a doctor as an outpatient in Japan you will usually be expected to pay up front. If you're admitted to hospital, your insurance company may be able to pay the hospital directly.

RECOMMENDED VACCINATIONS

No vaccinations are required for Japan. However, you should be aware that Japan scrupulously checks visitors who arrive from countries where there is a risk of yellow fever and other similar diseases.

The World Health Organization (WHO) recommends that all travellers be covered for diphtheria, tetanus, measles, mumps and rubella, regardless of their destination. Since most vaccines don't produce immunity until at least two weeks after they're given, visit a physician at least six weeks before departure. Specialised travel medicine clinics are your best source of information as they will be able to give you personalised information for you and your trip. The doctors will take into account factors like your medical history, past vaccination history, the length of your trip, time of year you are travelling, and any activities you may be undertaking, as any of these factors can alter general recommendations. Ensure you receive an International Certificate of Vaccination (the yellow booklet), which lists the vaccines you have received.

Adult diphtheria/tetanus/pertussis (DTP) If it is more than 10 years since your last tetanus shot you should have a booster, ideally of the vaccine that also provides protection against whooping cough (pertussis).

Measles/Mumps/Rubella (MMR) Two doses of MMR are recommended unless you have had the diseases. Many adults under the age of 35 require a booster. Occasionally a rash and flu-like illness can occur about a week after vaccination.

Varicella (Chickenpox) If you have not had chickenpox you should discuss this vaccine with your doctor. Chickenpox can be a serious disease in adults, with complications such as pneumonia and encephalitis. As an adult you require two shots, six weeks apart (usually given after a blood test to prove you have no immunity).

Under certain circumstances, or for those at special risk, the following vaccinations are recommended. These should be discussed with a doctor specialised in travel medicine.

Hepatitis A The risk in Japan is low but travellers spending extensive amounts of time in rural areas may consider vaccination. One injection gives almost 100% protection for six to 12 months; after a booster at least 20 years' protection is provided. This vaccine is commonly combined with the hepatitis B vaccine in the form of 'Twinrix'.

Hepatitis B For those staying long term or who may be exposed to body fluids by sexual contact, acupuncture, dental work etc, or for health-care workers. Three shots are required, given over six months (a rapid schedule is also available).

Influenza If you are over 50 years of age or have a chronic medical condition such as diabetes, lung disease or heart disease, you should have a flu shot annually. Side effects include a mild fever and a sore arm.

Japanese B encephalitis There is no risk in Tokyo, but there is risk in rural areas of all islands. The risk is highest in the western part of the country from July to October. Three shots are given over the course of a month, with a booster after two years. Rarely, allergic reactions can occur, so the course is best completed 10 days prior to travel.

Pneumonia (pneumococcal) Recommended for travellers over the age of 65 or with chronic lung or heart disease.

Tick-borne encephalitis This is present only in the wooded areas of Hokkaido and is transmitted from April to October. This vaccine is readily available in Europe but can be difficult or impossible to find elsewhere.

INTERNET RESOURCES

There is a wealth of travel-health advice on the internet. For further information, the Lonely Planet website, at www.lonelyplanet.com, is a good place to start. WHO publishes a superb book called *International Travel and Health,* which is revised annually and is available free online at www.who.int/ith/. Other websites of general interest are MD Travel Health at www.mdtravelhealth.com, which provides complete travel-health recommendations for every country; the Centers for Disease Control and Prevention, which has a good site at www.cdc.gov; and Fit for Travel at www.fitfortravel.scot.nhs.uk, which has up-to-date information about outbreaks and is very user-friendly.

It's also a good idea to consult your government's travel-health website before departure, if one is available.

Australia (www.dfat.gov.au/travel/)
Canada (www.travelhealth.gc.ca)
New Zealand (www.moh.govt.nz)
UK (www.dh.gov.uk)
USA (www.cdc.gov/travel/)

FURTHER READING

For those spending an extended period of time in Japan, the best book is *Japan Health Handbook* by Meredith Maruyama, Louise Picon Shimizu and Nancy Smith Tsurumaki. It gives an excellent overview of the Japanese medical system for expats. Lonely Planet's *Healthy Travel Asia & India* is a useful pocket-sized guide to travel health. *Travel with Children* from Lonely Planet is useful if you are taking children with you. Other recommended general travel-health references are *Traveller's Health* by Dr Richard Dawood and *Travelling Well* by Dr Deborah Mills – check out the website www.travellingwell.com.au for other tips.

IN TRANSIT

DEEP VEIN THROMBOSIS (DVT)

Blood clots may form in the legs during plane flights, chiefly because of prolonged immobility. The longer the flight, the greater the risk. The chief symptom of DVT is swelling or pain of the foot, ankle or calf, usually but not always on just one side. If a blood clot travels to the lungs it may cause chest pain and breathing difficulties. Travellers with any of these symptoms should seek medical attention immediately.

To prevent the development of DVT on long flights you should walk around the cabin, contract the leg muscles while sitting, drink plenty of fluids and avoid alcohol. If you have previously had DVT, speak with your doctor about preventive medications (usually given in the form of an injection just prior to travel).

JET LAG & MOTION SICKNESS

To avoid jet lag (common when crossing more than five time zones) try drinking plenty of nonalcoholic fluids and eating light meals. Upon arrival, get exposure to natural sunlight and readjust your schedule (for meals, sleep and so on) as soon as possible.

Antihistamines such as dimenhydrinate (Dramamine), prochlorperazine (Phenergan) and meclizine (Antivert, Bonine) are usually the first choice for treating motion sickness. The main side effect of these medications is drowsiness. A herbal alternative is ginger.

IN JAPAN

AVAILABILITY & COST OF HEALTH CARE

The quality of medical care can vary from place to place, but, in many cases, it is significantly better in the major cities compared to rural areas. Outside urban areas it may be difficult to access English-speaking doctors, so try to take a Japanese speaker with you to any medical facility. Japan has a national health-insurance system, but this is only available to foreigners if they have long-term visas in Japan. Be aware that medical facilities will require full payment at the time of treatment, or proof that your travel insurance will pay for any treatment that you receive.

A few handy tips:

- In general, it is better to seek care at university hospitals or other large hospitals, rather than at clinics.
- Japanese doctors are sometimes reluctant to treat foreigners. Therefore, it's important that you show proof of insurance or cash when seeking care. You have every right to insist on care.
- Most hospitals and clinics have regular hours where they will see patients (usually in the morning).
- Hotels and ryokans that cater to foreigners will usually know the best hospitals in a particular area (also, they will know hospitals with English-speaking doctors).

Dental services are widespread and of good standard; they're reasonably priced, but it's probably best to have a check-up before you leave home.

Tourist offices operated by Japan National Tourism Organization (JNTO; p822) have lists of English-speaking doctors and dentists, and hospitals where English is spoken. You can contact your insurance company or embassy to locate the nearest English-speaking facility.

Drugs that require a prescription in the West also generally require one in Japan. Ensure you bring adequate supplies of your own medications from home.

There are certain medications that are illegal to bring into Japan, including some commonly used cough and cold medications such as pseudoephedrine (found in Actifed, Sudafed etc) and codeine. Some prescription medications not allowed into Japan include narcotics, psychotropic drugs, stimulants and codeine. If you need to take more than a one-month supply of any other prescription drug, you should check with your local Japanese embassy, because you may need permission. Ensure that you have a letter from your doctor outlining your medical condition and the need for any prescription medication.

INFECTIOUS DISEASES

AIDS & STDs

There is less risk of contracting AIDS (acquired immune deficiency syndrome) and STDs (sexually transmitted diseases) by abstaining from sexual contact with new partners. Condom use in Japanese society is relatively low. HIV (human immunodeficiency virus) is still relatively uncommon in Japan, but the incidence is slowly increasing. In the year 2008, 89% of new cases were contracted via sexual contact. Condoms can help prevent some sexually transmitted infections, but not all. If you have had sexual contact with a new partner while travelling, or have any symptoms such as a rash, pain or discharge, see a doctor for a full STD check-up.

Hepatitis B

Hepatitis B is a virus spread via body fluids, eg through sexual contact, unclean medical facilities or shared needles. People who carry the virus are often unaware they are carriers. In the short term, hepatitis B can cause the typical symptoms of hepatitis – jaundice, tiredness and nausea – but in the long term it can lead to cancer of the liver and cirrhosis. Vaccination against hepatitis B is now part of most countries' routine childhood vaccination schedule and should be considered by anyone travelling for a long period of time or who may have contact with body fluids.

Hepatitis E

Hepatitis E is a virus spread via contaminated food and water. There have been a number of cases reported in Japan, linked to eating boar and deer meat, and undercooked pork liver. The disease causes jaundice (yellow skin and eyes), tiredness and nausea. There is no specific treatment, and those infected usually recover after four to six weeks. However, it can be a disaster for pregnant women, with a death rate for both mother and baby of up to 30% in the third trimester. Pregnant women should be particularly careful to avoid eating any undercooked foods. There is no vaccine yet available to prevent hepatitis E.

Influenza

Influenza is generally transmitted between November and April. Symptoms include high fever, muscle aches, runny nose, cough and sore throat. It can be a very severe illness in those aged over 65 or with underlying medical conditions such as heart disease or diabetes. Vaccination is recommended for these high-risk travellers or for anyone who wishes to reduce their risk of catching the illness. There is no specific treatment for 'the flu', just rest and paracetamol.

Japanese B Encephalitis

Japanese B encephalitis is a viral disease transmitted by mosquitoes. It is a rare disease in travellers and the vaccine is part of the routine childhood vaccination schedule in Japan. Risk exists in rural areas of all islands, but is highest in the western part of the country. In western Japan the risk season is from July to October. In the Nansei-shotō (the islands of Kagoshima-ken and Okinawa-ken) the risk season runs from April to December. Vaccination is recommended for travellers spending more than a month in rural areas during the transmission season. Other precautions include general insect avoidance measures such as using repellents and sleeping under nets (if not in screened rooms). Although this is a rare disease, it is very serious – there is no specific treatment and a third of people infected will die and a third will suffer permanent brain damage.

Lyme Disease

Lyme disease is spread via ticks and is present in the summer months in wooded areas. Symptoms include an early rash and general viral symptoms, followed weeks to months later by joint, heart or neurological problems. The disease is treated with the antibiotic doxycycline. Prevent Lyme disease by using general insect avoidance measures and checking yourself for ticks after walking in forested areas.

Tick-Borne Encephalitis

Tick-borne encephalitis occurs on the northern island of Hokkaidō only, and, as its name suggests, is a virus transmitted by ticks. The illness starts with general flu-like symptoms, which last a few days and then subside. After a period of remission (about one week) the second phase of the illness occurs with symptoms such as headache, fever and stiff neck (meningitis), or drowsiness, confusion and other neurological signs such as paralysis (encephalitis). There is no specific treatment, and about 10% to 20% of those who progress to the second phase of illness will have permanent neurological problems.

You can prevent this disease by using insect avoidance measures and checking yourself for ticks after walking in forested areas. A vaccine is available in Europe but is very difficult, if not impossible, to find elsewhere. Two doses are given four to 12 weeks apart with a third shot after nine to 12 months. Boosters are required every three years to maintain immunity.

TRAVELLER'S DIARRHOEA

There is a low risk of traveller's diarrhoea in Japan: only 10% to 20% of travellers will experience some stomach upset. If you develop diarrhoea, be sure to drink plenty of fluids, preferably an oral rehydration solution (eg Dioralyte). A few loose stools don't require treatment, but if you start having more than four or five stools a day you should start taking an antibiotic (such as norfloxacin, ciprofloxacin or azithromycin) and an antidiarrhoeal agent (such as loperamide). If diarrhoea is bloody, persists for more than 72 hours, is accompanied by fever, shaking, chills or severe abdominal pain, or doesn't respond quickly to your antibiotic, you should seek medical attention.

ENVIRONMENTAL HAZARDS

Air Pollution

If you have an underlying lung condition, air pollution can be a problem in major centres such as Tokyo. If you do have a pre-existing lung condition, speak with your doctor to ensure you have adequate medications to treat an exacerbation.

Altitude Sickness

Altitude sickness could develop in some people when climbing Mt Fuji (for more information, see p210) or on some of the higher mountains in the Japan Alps. Altitude sickness is best avoided by slowly acclimatising to higher altitudes. If this is impossible, the medication Diamox can be a helpful preventative, but it should only be taken on a doctor's recommendation. The symptoms of altitude sickness include headache, nausea and exhaustion, and the best treatment is descending to a lower altitude. We recommend that you familiarise yourself with the condition and how to prevent it before setting out on any climb over 2000m. Rick Curtis's *Outdoor Action Guide to High Altitude: Acclimatization and Illness* (www.princeton.edu/~oa/safety/altitude.html) provides a comprehensive overview.

Hypothermia

Hypothermia is possible when hiking in the Japan Alps, swimming in cold water or simply being outside in winter (December to March). It is surprisingly easy to progress from very cold to dangerously cold due to a combination of wind, wet clothing, fatigue and hunger, even if the air temperature is above freezing. It is best to dress in layers; silk, wool and some of the new artificial fibres are all good insulating materials. A hat is important, as a lot of heat is lost through the head. A strong, waterproof outer layer (and a space blanket for emergencies) is essential. Carry basic supplies, including food that contains simple sugars to generate heat quickly, and fluid to drink.

Symptoms of hypothermia are exhaustion, numb skin (particularly of the toes and fingers), shivering, slurred speech, irrational or violent behaviour, lethargy, stumbling, dizzy spells, muscle cramps and violent bursts of energy. Irrationality may take the form of sufferers claiming they are warm and trying to take off their clothes. To treat mild hypothermia, first get the person out of the wind and/or rain, then remove their clothing if it's wet, and replace it with dry, warm clothing. Give them hot liquids – not alcohol – and some high-calorie, easily digestible food. The early recognition and treatment of mild hypothermia is the only way to prevent severe hypothermia, which is a critical condition. If hypothermia has progressed from mild to severe, the person should be warmed by any means necessary, including direct physical contact with another person (in a sleeping bag, if possible). Evacuation and medical treatment should be sought if at all possible.

Insect Bites & Stings

Insect bites and stings are not a common problem in Japan. You should, however, follow general insect avoidance measures if you are hiking in the woods or are in rural areas during the summer months. These include using an insect repellent containing 20% to 30% DEET (diethyl-M-toluamide), covering up with light-coloured clothing and checking yourself for ticks after being in the forest. When removing ticks ensure you also remove their heads. Some people have an allergic reaction to ticks so it is a good idea to carry an antihistamine with you.

Water

The water in Japan is generally safe to drink.

WOMEN'S HEALTH

Supplies of sanitary products are readily available in Japan. It can be very difficult to get the oral contraceptive pill so ensure you bring adequate supplies of your own pill from home.

Pregnant women should receive specialised advice before travelling. Some vaccines are definitely not recommended; others are only prescribed after an individual risk–benefit analysis. The ideal time to travel is during the second trimester (between 15 and 28 weeks), when the risk of pregnancy-related problems are at their lowest and pregnant women generally feel at their best. During the first trimester there is a risk of miscarriage, and in the third trimester problems such as premature labour and high blood pressure are possible. Always travel with a companion, have a list of quality medical facilities available at your destination and ensure you continue your standard antenatal care while you travel. Avoid travel to rural areas that have poor transport and medical facilities. Most importantly, ensure your travel insurance covers you for pregnancy-related problems, including premature labour. See p846 for information regarding the risks of contracting hepatitis E during pregnancy.

TRAVELLING WITH CHILDREN

Japan is a safe country in which to travel with children. Prior to travel, ensure they are up to date with their basic vaccinations.

TRADITIONAL MEDICINE

The two best-known forms of traditional Japanese medicine are shiatsu and reiki.

Shiatsu is a type of massage that emerged in Japan out of traditional Chinese medicine. It is a form of manual therapy incorporating gentle manipulations and stretches derived from physiotherapy and chiropractic, combined with pressure techniques exerted through the fingers or thumbs. The philosophy underlying shiatsu is similar to many traditional Asian medical systems and involves the body's *ki* (pronounced chi; vital energy) flowing through the body in a series of channels known as meridians. If the *ki* is blocked from flowing freely, illness can occur. The technique is used to improve the flow of *ki*. In the mid-1900s Shiatsu was officially recognised by the Japanese government as a therapy in its own right.

Reiki claims to heal by charging this same life force with positive energy, thus allowing the *ki* to flow in a natural, healthy manner. In a standard treatment, reiki energy flows from the practitioner's hands into the client. The practitioner places their hands on or near the clients' body in a series of positions that are held for three to 10 minutes. People become practitioners after receiving an 'attunement' from a reiki master.

If you do decide to have any traditional medical treatments make sure you tell your practitioner whether or not you are taking any Western medicines.

Language

CONTENTS

Japanese is the language spoken across all of Japan. While the standard language, called *hyōjungo,* is understood by almost all Japanese, many people speak strong local dialects (known as *ben,* as in the famous dialect of Kansai, *Kansai-ben*). These dialects, particularly in rural areas, can be quite difficult to understand, even for Japanese from other parts of the country. Luckily, you can always get your point across in *hyōjungo.*

In this language guide you'll find a selection of useful Japanese words and phrases. For information on food and dining, including words and phrases that will help in deciphering menus and ordering food in Japanese, see p76. For information on language courses available in Japan, see p811.

GRAMMAR

To English speakers, Japanese language patterns often seem to be back to front and lacking in essential information. For example, where an English speaker would say 'I'm going to the shop' a Japanese speaker would say 'shop to going', omitting the subject pronoun (I) altogether and putting the verb at the end of the sentence. Also, some conjunctions that in English are often placed at the start of a sentence, occur at the end of a sentence in Japanese, as in the sentence 'Japan to going if' – 'if you're going to Japan'.

Fortunately for visitors to Japan, it's not all bad news. In fact, with a little effort, getting together a repertoire of travellers' phrases should be no trouble – the only problem will be understanding the replies you get.

TRYING ENGLISH IN JAPAN

Visitors to Japan should be warned that many Japanese do not speak or understand much English. Although English is a required subject in both junior high school and high school, and many students go on to study more of it in university, several factors conspire to prevent many Japanese from acquiring usable English. These include the nature of the English educational system, which uses outdated methods like translation; the extreme difference between English and Japanese pronunciation and grammar; and the typical reticence of the Japanese, who may be shy to speak a language that they haven't mastered.

There are several ways to facilitate communication with Japanese who may not have a mastery of spoken English:

- Always start with a smile to create a sense of ease.
- Speak very slowly and clearly.
- When asking for information, choose people of university age or thereabouts, as these people are most likely to speak some English. Also, Japanese women tend to speak and understand English much better than Japanese men.
- If necessary, write down your question; Japanese are often able to understand written English even when they can't understand spoken English.
- Use the sample phrases in this chapter and, if necessary, point to the Japanese phrase in question.

WRITTEN JAPANESE

Japanese has one of the most complex writing systems in the world, which uses three different scripts – four if you include the increasingly used Roman script, romaji. The most difficult of the three, for foreigners and Japanese alike, is kanji, the ideographic script developed by the Chinese. Not only do you have to learn a couple of thousand of them but, unlike in Chinese, many Japanese kanji have wildly variant pronunciations depending on context.

Due to the differences between Chinese and Japanese grammar, kanji had to be supplemented with a 'syllabary' (an alphabet of syllables), known as hiragana. And there is yet another syllabary, which is used largely for representing foreign loan-words such as *terebi* (TV) and *biiru* (beer); this script is known as katakana. If you're serious about learning to read Japanese you'll have to set aside several years.

If you're thinking of tackling the Japanese writing system before you go or while you're in Japan, your best bet would be to start with hiragana or katakana. Both these syllabaries have 48 characters each, and can be learnt within a week, although it'll take at least a month to consolidate them. Once in the country, you can practise your katakana on restaurant menus, where such things as *kōhii* (coffee) and *kēiki* (cake) are frequently found. Practise your hiragana on train journeys, as station names are usually indicated in hiragana (in addition to English and kanji).

ROMANISATION

The romaji used in this book is based on the Hepburn system of romanisation. In addition, common Japanese nouns like *ji* or *tera* (temple) and *jinja* or *jingū* (shrine) are written without an English translation.

Silent Letters

Hepburn romaji is a direct system of Romanisation that doesn't fully reflect all elements of spoken Japanese. The most obvious of these is the tendency in everyday speech to omit the vowel 'u' in many instances. In this language guide, and in Useful Words & Phrases on p93, these silent letters have been retained to provide accuracy in the written Romanisations, but they have been enclosed in square brackets to aid accurate pronunciation.

LANGUAGE BOOKS

Lonely Planet's *Japanese Phrasebook* gives you a comprehensive mix of practical and social words and phrases that should cover almost any situation confronting the traveller to Japan.

If you'd like to delve deeper into the intricacies of the language, we recommend *Japanese for Busy People* for beginners, *Introduction to Intermediate Japanese* (Mizutani Nobuko) for intermediate students, and *Kanji in Context* (Nishiguchi Koichi and Kono Tamaki) for more advanced students. One of the best guides to the written language, for both study and reference, is *Kanji & Kana* (Wolfgang Hadamizky and Mark Spahn).

PRONUNCIATION

Unlike other languages in the region with complicated tonal systems, such as Chinese, Vietnamese and Thai, Japanese pronunciation is fairly easy to master.

The following examples reflect British pronunciation:

a as in 'father'
e as in 'get'
i as in 'macaroni'
o as in 'bone'
u as in 'flu'

Vowels appearing in this book with a macron (or bar) over them (*ā, ē, ō, ū*) are pronounced in the same way as standard vowels except that the sound is held twice as long. You need to take care with this as vowel length can change the meaning of a word, eg *yuki* means 'snow', while *yūki* means 'bravery'.

It is important to make the distinction between single and double consonants (*pp, tt* etc), with a slight pause before a double. Other consonants are generally pronounced as in English, with the following exceptions:

f a softer sound – purse the lips and blow lightly when pronouncing
r halfway between an 'l' and an 'r'

ACCOMMODATION

I'm looking for a ...
…を探しています。
... o sagashite imas[u]

camping ground
キャンプ場 *kyampu-jō*
family-style inn
民宿 *minshuku*
guest house
ゲストハウス *gesuto hausu*
hotel
ホテル *hoteru*
Japanese-style inn
旅館 *ryokan*
love hotel
ラブホテル *rabu hoteru*
youth hostel
ユースホステル *yūsu hosuteru*

Do you have any vacancies?
空き部屋はありますか?
akibeya wa arimas[u] ka
I don't have a reservation.
予約はしていません。
yoyaku wa shiteimasen

single room
シングルルーム *shinguru rūmu*
double room
ダブルルーム *daburu rūmu*
twin room
ツインルーム *tsuin rūmu*
Japanese-style room
和室 *washitsu*
Western-style room
洋室 *yōshitsu*
Japanese-style bath
お風呂 *ofuro*
room with a (Western-style) bath
バス付きの部屋 *basu tsuki no heya*

How much is it (per night/per person)?
(一泊/一人)いくらですか?
(ippaku/hitori) ikura des[u] ka
Does it include breakfast/a meal?
(朝食/食事)は付いていますか?
chōshoku/shokuji wa tsuite imas[u] ka
I'm going to stay for (one night/two nights).
(一晩/二晩)泊まります。
hitoban/futaban tomarimas[u]
Can I leave my luggage here?
荷物を預かっていただけませんか?
nimotsu o azukatte itadakemasen ka

CONVERSATION & ESSENTIALS

The all-purpose title *san* is always used after a name as an honorific and is similar to saying Mr, Miss, Mrs and Ms.

Good morning.
おはようございます。
ohayō gozaimas[u]
Good afternoon.
こんにちは。
konnichiwa
Good evening.
こんばんは。
kombanwa
Goodbye.
さようなら。
sayōnara
See you later.
ではまた。
dewa mata
Please/Go ahead. (when offering)
どうぞ。
dōzo
Please. (when asking)
ください。/お願いします。
kudasai/onegai shimas[u]
Thanks. (informal)
どうも。
dōmo
Thank you.
どうもありがとう。
dōmo arigatō
Thank you very much.
どうもありがとうございます。
dōmo arigatō gozaimas[u]
Thanks for having me. (when leaving)
お世話になりました。
osewa ni narimash[i]ta
You're welcome.
どういたしまして。
dō itashimashite
No, thank you.
いいえ,けっこうです。
iie kekkō des[u]
Excuse me/Pardon.
すみません。
sumimasen
Excuse me. (when entering a room)
おじゃまします。/失礼します。
ojama shimas[u]/shitsurei shimas[u]
I'm sorry.
ごめんなさい。
gomen nasai

What's your name?
お名前は何ですか?
onamae wa nan des[u] ka
My name is …
私は…です。
watashi wa … des[u]
This is Mr/Mrs/Ms (Smith).
こちらは(スミス)さんです。
kochira wa (sumisu) san des[u]
Pleased to meet you.
どうぞよろしく。
dōzo yorosh[i]ku
Where are you from?
どちらのかたですか?
dochira no kata des[u] ka
How are you?
お元気ですか?
ogenki des[u] ka
Fine.
元気です。
genki des[u]
Is it OK to take a photo?
写真を撮ってもいいですか?
shashin o totte mo ii des[u] ka
Cheers!
乾杯!
kampai
Yes.
はい。
hai
No.
いいえ。
iie
No. (for indicating disagreement)
違います。
chigaimas[u]
No. (less emphatic)
ちょっと違います。
chotto chigaimas[u]
OK.
だいじょうぶ(です)。/オーケー。
daijōbu (des[u])/ōke

Requests

Please give me (this/that).
(これ/それ)をください。
(kore/sore) o kudasai
Please give me a (cup of tea).
(お茶)をください。
(ocha) o kudasai
Please wait (a while).
(少々)お待ちください。
(shōshō) omachi kudasai

SIGNS

Information	
案内所	*annaijo*
Open	
営業中	*eigyōchū*
Closed	
準備中	*junbichū*
Entrance	
入口	*iriguchi*
Exit	
出口	*deguchi*
Toilets	
お手洗い/トイレ	*otearai/toire*
Male	
男	*otoko*
Female	
女	*onna*

Please show me the (ticket).
(切符)を見せてください。
(kippu) o misete kudasai

DIRECTIONS

Where is the …?
…はどこですか?
… wa doko des[u] ka
How far is it to walk?
歩いてどのくらいかかりますか?
aruite dono kurai kakarimas[u] ka
How do I get to …?
…へはどのように行けばいいですか?
… e wa dono yō ni ikeba ii des[u] ka
Where is this address?
この住所はどこですか?
kono jūsho wa doko des[u] ka
Could you write down the address for me?
住所を書いていただけませんか?
jūsho o kaite itadakemasen ka
Go straight ahead.
まっすぐ行って。
massugu itte
Turn (left/right).
(左/右)へ曲がって。
(hidari/migi) e magatte
near/far
近い/遠い
chikai/tōi

HEALTH

I need a doctor.
医者が必要です。
isha ga hitsuyō des[u]

LANGUAGE

How do you feel?
気分はいかがですか?
kibun wa ikaga des[u] ka
I'm ill.
気分が悪いです。
kibun ga warui des[u]
It hurts here.
ここが痛いです。
koko ga itai des[u]
I have diarrhoea.
下痢をしています。
geri o shite imas[u]
I have a toothache.
歯が痛みます。
ha ga itamimas[u]

I'm ...
私は… *watashi wa ...*
diabetic
糖尿病です。 *tōnyōbyō des[u]*
epileptic
てんかんです。 *tenkan des[u]*
asthmatic
喘息です。 *zensoku des[u]*

I'm allergic to antibiotics.
抗生物質にアレルギーがあります。
kōsei busshitsu ni arerugii ga arimas[u]
I'm allergic to penicillin.
ペニシリンにアレルギーがあります。
penishirin ni arerugii ga arimas[u]

antiseptic
消毒薬 *shōdokuyaku*
aspirin
アスピリン *asupirin*
(a) cold
風邪 *kaze*
condoms
コンドーム *kondōmu*
contraceptive
避妊用ピル *hinin yō piru*
diarrhoea
下痢 *geri*
dentist
歯医者 *ha isha*
doctor
医者 *isha*
fever
発熱 *hatsunetsu*
hospital
病院 *byōin*
medicine
薬 *kusuri*

EMERGENCIES

Help!
助けて!
tas[u]kete
Call a doctor!
医者を呼んでください!
isha o yonde kudasai
Call the police!
警察を呼んでください!
keisatsu o yonde kudasai
I'm lost.
道に迷いました。
michi ni mayoi mash[i]ta
Go away!
離れろ!
hanarero

migraine
偏頭痛 *henzutsū*
pharmacy
薬局 *yakkyoku*
tampons
タンポン *tampon*

LANGUAGE DIFFICULTIES

Do you speak English?
英語が話せますか?
eigo ga hanasemas[u] ka
Does anyone speak English?
どなたか英語を話せますか?
donata ka eigo o hanasemas[u] ka
Do you understand (English/Japanese)?
(英語/日本語)はわかりますか?
(eigo/nihongo) wa wakarimas[u] ka
I don't understand.
わかりません。
wakarimasen
I can't speak Japanese.
日本語はできません。
nihongo wa dekimasen
How do you say ... in Japanese?
日本語で…は何といいますか?
nihongo de ... wa nan to iimas[u] ka
What does ... mean?
…はどんな意味ですか?
... wa donna imi des[u] ka
What is this called?
これは何といいますか?
kore wa nan to iimas[u] ka
Please write in (Japanese/English).
(nihongo/eigo) de kaite kudasai
(日本語/英語)で書いてください。

Please speak more slowly.
もうちょっとゆっくり言ってください。
mō chotto yukkuri itte kudasai
Please say it again more slowly.
もう一度，ゆっくり言ってください。
mō ichidō yukkuri itte kudasai

NUMBERS

0	ゼロ/零	*zero/rei*
1	一	*ichi*
2	二	*ni*
3	三	*san*
4	四	*yon/shi*
5	五	*go*
6	六	*roku*
7	七	*nana/shichi*
8	八	*hachi*
9	九	*kyū/ku*
10	十	*jū*
11	十一	*jūichi*
12	十二	*jūni*
13	十三	*jūsan*
14	十四	*jūyon*
20	二十	*nijū*
21	二十一	*nijūichi*
30	三十	*sanjū*
100	百	*hyaku*
200	二百	*nihyaku*
1000	千	*sen*
5000	五千	*gosen*
10,000	一万	*ichiman*
20,000	二万	*niman*
100,000	十万	*jūman*
one million	百万	*hyakuman*

QUESTION WORDS

What?
なに? *nani*
When?
いつ? *itsu*
Where?
どこ? *doko*
Who?
だれ? *dare*

SHOPPING & SERVICES

bank
銀行 *ginkō*
embassy
大使館 *taishikan*
market
市場 *ichiba*
post office
郵便局 *yūbin kyoku*
a public telephone
公衆電話 *kōshū denwa*
toilet
お手洗い/トイレ *otearai/toire*
the tourist office
観光案内所 *kankō annaijo*

What time does it (open/close)?
何時に(開きます/閉まります)か?
nanji ni (akimas[u]/shimarimas[u]) ka
I'd like to buy …
…を買いたいです。
… o kaitai des[u]
How much is it?
いくらですか?
ikura des[u] ka
I'm just looking.
見ているだけです。
miteiru dake des[u]
It's cheap.
安いです。
yasui des[u]
It's too expensive.
高すぎます。
taka sugimas[u]
I'll take this one.
これをください。
kore o kudasai
Can I have a receipt?
領収書をいただけませんか?
ryōshūsho o itadakemasen ka

big
大きい *ōkii*
small
小さい *chiisai*
bookshop
本屋 *hon ya*
camera shop
写真屋 *shashin ya*
department store
デパート *depāto*
shop
店 *mise*
supermarket
スーパー *sūpā*

TIME & DAYS

What time is it?
今何時ですか? *ima nanji des[u] ka*

today
今日 *kyō*
tomorrow
明日 *ash[i]ta*

yesterday
きのう *kinō*
morning/afternoon
朝/昼 *asa/hiru*

Monday
月曜日 *getsuyōbi*
Tuesday
火曜日 *kayōbi*
Wednesday
水曜日 *suiyōbi*
Thursday
木曜日 *mokuyōbi*
Friday
金曜日 *kinyōbi*
Saturday
土曜日 *doyōbi*
Sunday
日曜日 *nichiyōbi*

TRANSPORT

What time does the next ... leave?
次の…は何時に出ますか?
tsugi no ... wa nanji ni demas[u] ka
What time does the next ... arrive?
次の…は何時に着きますか?
tsugi no ... wa nanji ni tsukimas[u] ka
boat
ボート/船 *bōto/fune*
bus (city)
市バス *shibas[u]*
bus (intercity)
長距離バス *chōkyoribas[u]*
tram
路面電車 *romen densha*
train
電車 *densha*
bus stop
バス停 *basutei*
station
駅 *eki*
subway (train)
地下鉄 *chikatetsu*
ticket
切符 *kippu*
ticket office
切符売り場 *kippu uriba*
timetable
時刻表 *jikokuhyō*
taxi
タクシー *takushii*
left-luggage office
荷物預かり所 *nimotsu azukarijo*
one way
片道 *katamichi*
return
往復 *ōfuku*
nonsmoking seat
禁煙席 *kinen seki*

How much is the fare to ...?
…までいくらですか?
... made ikura des[u] ka
Does this (train, bus etc) go to ...?
これは…へ行きますか?
kore wa ... e ikimas[u] ka
Please tell me when we get to ...
…に着いたら教えてください。
... ni tsuitara oshiete kudasai
I'd like to hire a ...
…を借りたいのですが。
... o karitai no des[u] ka
I'd like to go to ...
…に行きたいです。
... ni ikitai desu
Please stop here.
ここで停めてください。
koko de tomete kudasai

LANGUAGE

Glossary

For a list of culinary terms, see p76. For useful terms and phrases when visiting an onsen, see also p106.

Ainu – indigenous people of Hokkaidō and parts of Northern Honshū
Amaterasu – sun goddess and link to the imperial throne
ANA – All Nippon Airlines
ANK – All Nippon Koku
annai-sho – information office
asa-ichi – morning market

bama – beach; see also *hama*
bangasa – rain umbrella made from oiled paper
bashō – *sumō* tournament
bonsai – the art of growing miniature trees by careful pruning of branches and roots
bugaku – dance pieces played by court orchestras in ancient Japan
buke yashiki – *samurai* residence
bunraku – classical puppet theatre using huge puppets to portray dramas similar to *kabuki*
Burakumin – traditionally outcasts associated with lowly occupations such as leather work; literally 'village people'
bushidō – a set of values followed by the *samurai;* literally 'the way of the warrior
butsudan – Buddhist altar in Japanese homes

chikan – men who feel up women and girls on packed trains
chō – city area (for large cities) between a *ku* and *chōme* in size; also a street
chōchin – paper lantern
chōme – city area of a few blocks

daibutsu – Great Buddha
daimyō – regional lords under the *shōgun*
daira/taira – plain
dake – peak; see also *take*
dani – valley; see also *tani*
danjiri – festival floats
dera – temple; see also *tera*
dō – temple/hall of a temple

eki – train station
ema – small votive plaques hung in shrine precincts as petitions for assistance from the resident deities
enka – often described as the Japanese equivalent of country and western music, these are folk ballads about love and human suffering

fu – urban prefecture
fundoshi – loincloth or breechcloth; a traditional male garment consisting of a wide belt and a cloth drawn over the genitals and between the buttocks, usually seen only at festivals or on *sumō* wrestlers
furii kippu – one-day transport pass (*furii* means 'free' and *kippu* means 'ticket')
fusuma – sliding screen door
futsū – a local train; literally 'ordinary'

gagaku – music of the imperial court
gaijin – foreigners; literally 'outside people'
gaijin house – cheap accommodation for long-term foreign residents
gaman – to endure
gasoreen sutando – petrol stations
gasshō-zukuri – an architectural style (usually thatch-roofed); literally 'hands in prayer'
gawa – river; see also *kawa*
geisha – woman versed in arts and drama who entertains guests; not a prostitute
gekijō – theatre
genkan – foyer area where shoes are removed or replaced when entering or leaving a building
geta – traditional wooden sandals
gū – shrine
gun – county

habu – a venomous snake found in Okinawa
haiku – 17-syllable poems
hama – beach; see also *bama*
hanami – blossom viewing (usually cherry blossoms)
haniwa – earthenware figures found in tombs of the Kōfun period
hantō – peninsula
hara – uncultivated field or plain
hari – dragon-boat races
hatsu-mōde – first shrine visit of the new year
heiwa – peace
henro – pilgrims on the Shikoku 88 Temple Circuit
higasa – sunshade umbrella
Hikari – the second-fastest type of *shinkansen*
hiragana – phonetic syllabary used to write Japanese words
hondō – main route or main hall
honsen – main rail line

ichi-nichi-jōsha-ken – day passes for unlimited travel on bus, tram or subway systems
ikebana – art of flower arrangement

irezumi – a tattoo or the art of tattooing
irori – hearth or fireplace

JAC – Japan Air Commuter
JAF – Japan Automobile Federation
JAL – Japan Airlines
JAS – Japan Air System
ji – temple
jigoku – boiling mineral hot springs, which are definitely not for bathing in; literally 'hells'
jikokuhyō – timetable or book of timetables
jima – island; see also *shima*
jingū – shrine; see also *jinja*
jinja – shrine
jinja – shrine; see also *jingū*
jizō – small stone statues of the Buddhist protector of travellers and children
JNTO – Japan National Tourism Organization
jō – castle
JR – Japan Railways
JTB – Japan Travel Bureau
juku – after-school 'cram' schools
JYHA – Japan Youth Hostel Association

kabuki – a form of Japanese theatre based on popular legends, which is characterised by elaborate costumes, stylised acting and the use of male actors for all roles
kaikan – hall or building
kaikyō – channel/strait
kaisoku – rapid train
kaisū-ken – a book of transport tickets
kami – Shintō gods; spirits of natural phenomena
kamikaze – typhoon that sunk Kublai Khan's 13th-century invasion fleet and the name adopted by suicide pilots in the waning days of WWII; literally 'divine wind'
kana – the two phonetic syllabaries, *hiragana* and *katakana*
kanji – Chinese ideographic script used for writing Japanese; literally 'Chinese script'
Kannon – Bodhisattva of Compassion (commonly referred to as the Buddhist Goddess of Mercy)
karakuri ningyō – mechanical puppets
karaoke – bars where you sing along with taped music; literally 'empty orchestra'
kasa – umbrella
katakana – phonetic syllabary used to write foreign words
katamichi – one-way transport ticket
katana – Japanese sword
kawa – river; see also *gawa*
ken – prefecture
kendo – oldest martial art; literally 'the way of the sword'
ki – life force, will
kimono – brightly coloured, robe-like traditional outer garment
kin'en-sha – nonsmoking train carriage
kissaten – coffee shop
ko – lake
kō – port
kōban – police box
kōen – park
kōgen – high plain (as in the mountains); plateau
koi – carp; considered to be a brave, tenacious and vigorous fish; many towns have carp ponds or channels teeming with colourful ornamental *nishiki-goi* (ornamental carp)
koinobori – carp banners and windsocks; the colourful fish pennants that are flown in honour of sons whom it is hoped will inherit a carp's virtues. These wave over countless homes in Japan in late April and early May for Boys' Day, the final holiday of Golden Week. These days, Boys' Day has become Children's Day and the windsocks don't necessarily simply fly in honour of the household's sons
kokumin-shukusha – peoples' lodges; an inexpensive form of accommodation
kokuritsu kōen – national park
kotatsu – heated table with a quilt or cover over it to keep the legs and lower body warm
koto – 13-stringed instrument derived from a Chinese zither that is played flat on the floor
ku – ward
kūkō – airport
kura – earth-walled storehouses
kyō – gorge
kyūkō – ordinary express train (faster than a *futsū*, only stopping at certain stations)

live house – nightclub or bar where live music is performed

machi – city area (for large cities) between a *ku* and *chōme* in size; also street or area
machiya – traditional Japanese townhouse or city house
maiko – apprentice *geisha*
mama-san – woman who manages a bar or club
maneki-neko – beckoning or welcoming cat figure frequently seen in restaurants and bars; it's supposed to attract customers and trade
manga – Japanese comics
matsuri – festival
meishi – business card
mikoshi – portable shrines carried during festivals
minato – harbour
minshuku – the Japanese equivalent of a B&B; family-run budget accommodation
misaki – cape
mon – gate
mura – village

N'EX – Narita Express
NHK – Nihon Hōsō Kyōkai (Japan Broadcasting Corporation)
Nihon – Japanese word for Japan; literally 'source of the sun'
nihonga – term for Japanese-style painting
ningyō – Japanese doll
ninja – practitioners of *ninjutsu*
Nippon – see *Nihon*
nō – classical Japanese drama performed on a bare stage
noren – cloth hung as a sunshade, typically carrying the name of the shop or premises; indicates that a restaurant is open for business
norikae-ken – transfer ticket (trams and buses)
NTT – Nippon Telegraph & Telephone Corporation

o- – prefix used to show respect to anything it is applied to
obi – sash or belt worn with a *kimono*
ōfuku – return ticket
o-furo – traditional Japanese bath
OL – 'office lady'; female clerical worker; pronounced 'ō-eru'
onnagata – male actor playing a woman's role (usually in *kabuki*)
onsen – hot spring; hot mineral-spa area, usually with accommodation
oshibori – hot towels provided in restaurants

pachinko – popular vertical pinball game, played in *pachinko* parlours
raidā hausu – basic shared accommodation/houses, catering mainly to those touring on motorcycles

rakugo – Japanese raconteurs, stand-up comics
rettō – island group
Rinzai – school of Zen Buddhism which places an emphasis on *kōan* (riddles)
romaji – Japanese roman script
rōnin – students who must resit university entrance exams; literally 'masterless *samurai*', sometimes referred to as 'wanderers'
ropeway – Japanese word for a cable car, tramway or funicular railway
rotemburo – open-air or outdoor baths
ryokan – traditional Japanese inn

saki – cape
sakoku – Japan's period of national seclusion prior to the Meiji Restoration
sakura – cherry blossoms
salaryman – male white-collar worker, usually of a large firm
sama – even more respectful suffix than *san*; used in instances such as *o-kyaku-sama* – the 'honoured guest'
samurai – warrior class
san – mountain
san – suffix which shows respect to the person it is applied to
san-sō – mountain hut or cottage
sentō – public baths
seppuku – ritual suicide by disembowelment
shamisen – a three-stringed traditional Japanese instrument that resembles a banjo or lute
shi – city (to distinguish cities with prefectures of the same name eg Kyoto-shi)
shikki – lacquerware
shima – island; see also *jima*
shinkaisoku – express trains or special rapid train (usually on JR lines)
shinkansen – super express trains, known in the West as 'bullet trains'
Shintō – the indigenous religion of Japan; literally 'the way of the gods'
shirabyōshi – traditional dancer
shitamachi – traditionally the low-lying, less affluent parts of Tokyo
shodō – Japanese calligraphy; literally the 'way of writing'
shōgekijō – small theatre
shōgi – a version of chess in which each player has 20 pieces and the object is to capture the opponent's king
shōgun – former military ruler of Japan; generalissimo
shōgunate – military government
shōji – sliding rice-paper screens
shōjin ryōri – Buddhist vegetarian meals (served at temple lodgings etc)
shotō – archipelago or island group
Shugendō – offbeat Buddhist school, which incorporates ancient Shamanistic rites, *Shintō* beliefs and ascetic Buddhist traditions
shūji – a lesser form of *shodō*; literally 'the practice of letters'
shukubō – temple lodgings
shunga – explicit erotic prints; literally 'spring pictures', the season of spring being a popular Chinese and Japanese euphemism for sexuality
shūyū-ken – excursion train ticket
soapland – Japanese euphemism for bathhouses that offer sexual services, eg massage parlours
Sōtō – a school of Zen Buddhism which places emphasis on *zazen*
sumi-e – black-ink brush paintings
sumō – Japanese wrestling

tabi – split-toed Japanese socks used when wearing *geta*
taiko – drum
taisha – great shrine
take – peak; see also *dake*
taki – waterfall
tani – valley; see also *dani*

tanuki – racoon or dog-like folklore character frequently represented in ceramic figures
tatami – tightly woven floor matting on which shoes are never worn. Traditionally, room size is defined by the number of tatami mats
TCAT – Tokyo City Air Terminal
teien – garden
tennō – heavenly king, the emperor
tera – temple; see also *dera*
TIC – Tourist Information Center
tō – island
to – metropolis, eg Tokyo-to
tokkyū – limited express; faster than an ordinary express *(kyūkō)* train
tokonoma – sacred alcove in a house in which flowers may be displayed or a scroll hung
torii – entrance gate to a Shintō shrine
tōsu – lavatory

uchiwa – paper fan
ukiyo-e – wood-block prints; literally 'pictures of the floating world'

wa – harmony, team spirit; also the old *kanji* used to denote Japan, and still used in Chinese and Japanese as a prefix to indicate things of Japanese origin, eg see *wafuku*
wabi – enjoyment of peace and tranquillity
wafuku – Japanese-style clothing
wan – bay
washi – Japanese handmade paper

yabusame – samurai-style horseback archery
yakimono – pottery or ceramic ware
yakuza – Japanese mafia
yama – mountain
yamabushi – mountain priests (Shugendō Buddhism practitioners)
yama-goya – mountain huts
yamato – a term of much debated origins that refers to the Japanese world
yamato-e – traditional Japanese painting
yatai – festival floats/hawker stalls
YCAT – Yokohama City Air Terminal
yukata – light cotton summer *kimono*, worn for lounging or casual use; standard issue when staying at a *ryokan*

zaibatsu – industrial conglomerates; the term arose prior to WWII but the Japanese economy is still dominated by huge firms like Mitsui, Marubeni and Mitsubishi, which are involved in many different industries
zaki – cape
zan – mountain
zazen – seated meditation emphasised in the Sōtō school of Zen Buddhism
Zen – introduced to Japan in the 12th century from China, this offshoot of Buddhism emphasises a direct, intuitive approach to enlightenment rather than rational analysis

The Authors

CHRIS ROWTHORN

Coordinating author, Kansai, Okinawa & Southwest Islands

Born in England and raised in the USA, Chris has lived in Kyoto since 1992. Soon after his arrival in Kyoto, Chris started studying the Japanese language and culture. In 1995 he became a regional correspondent for the *Japan Times*. He joined Lonely Planet in 1996 and has worked on guides to Kyoto, Tokyo, Japan and on hiking in Japan. When not on the road, he spends his time seeking out Kyoto's best restaurants, temples, hiking trails and gardens. He also conducts walking tours of Kyoto, Nara and Tokyo. For more on Chris, check out his blog at www.insidekyoto.com.

ANDREW BENDER

Central Honshū

France was closed, so after college Andy left his native New England to work in Tokyo. It ended up being a life-changing journey, as visits to Japan often are. He's since mastered chopsticks, the language, karaoke and taking his shoes off at the door, and he's worked with Japanese companies on both sides of the Pacific, from his current base of Los Angeles. His writing has appeared in *Travel + Leisure*, *Forbes*, the *Los Angeles Times* and many airline magazines, plus over a dozen Lonely Planet titles. In an effort toward even greater transoceanic harmony, Andy does cross-cultural consulting with businesses and sometimes takes tour groups to Japan. Find out more at www.andrewbender.com.

MATTHEW D FIRESTONE

Northern Honshū, Hokkaidō

Matt is a trained anthropologist and epidemiologist who should probably be in the midst of a successful academic career by now, though somehow he can't seem to pry himself away from Japan. A resident of the massive megalopolis that is Tokyo, Matt works primarily as a freelance journalist and writer, though he took a break from his urban trappings to research Japan's far north for this edition. Matt has also written more than a dozen guidebooks for Lonely Planet covering Asia, Africa and Latin America.

LONELY PLANET AUTHORS

Why is our travel information the best in the world? It's simple: our authors are passionate, dedicated travellers. They don't take freebies in exchange for positive coverage so you can be sure the advice you're given is impartial. They travel widely to all the popular spots, and off the beaten track. They don't research using just the internet or phone. They discover new places not included in any other guidebook. They personally visit thousands of hotels, restaurants, palaces, trails, galleries, temples and more. They speak with dozens of locals every day to make sure you get the kind of insider knowledge only a local could tell you. They take pride in getting all the details right, and in telling it how it is. Think you can do it? Find out how at **lonelyplanet.com**.

TIMOTHY N HORNYAK

Environment, Around Tokyo

A native of Montreal, Tim moved to Japan in 1999 and has written on Japanese culture, technology and history for publications including *Scientific American*, *Wired News* and the *Far Eastern Economic Review*. He has lectured on Japanese robots at the Kennedy Center in Washington, DC; travelled to the heart of Hokkaidō to find the remains of a forgotten theme park called Canadian World; and retraced the steps of haiku poet Matsuo Bashō in Akita-ken. He firmly believes that the greatest Japanese invention of all time is the onsen (hot spring). Having visited all 47 of Japan's prefectures, his next goal is to go to the hot springs officially listed as 'secret' by an industry group.

BENEDICT WALKER

Kyūshū

Inspired by a primary school teacher, Ben's love of Japan blossomed early and by 17 he was runner-up in the Australian finals of the Japan Foundation Japanese Speech Contest, and had made two solo trips to Japan. In 1998, with a degree in Communications under his belt, Ben hit the road in earnest. After long stints in Canada and Europe, he found himself teaching English in Osaka until his tattered Lonely Planet guide led him to the mountains of Matsumoto, where he found work as a translator and lived like a local. Currently based in Melbourne, Ben manages travel for rock stars and dreams about his next trip. This is his first assignment for Lonely Planet.

PAUL WARHAM

Western Honshū, Shikoku

Paul grew up in Lancashire, and got out as soon as he could. He came to Japan as a teenager, and after waiting tables at golf clubs in Osaka and Kōbe went on to have an undistinguished career as a student of Japanese literature at Oxford and Harvard. He is based in Tokyo, where his current research interests include drinking in old sake pubs and translating Japanese novels set in supermarkets.

WENDY YANAGIHARA

Tokyo

Wendy first toured Tokyo on her mother's hip at age two and was raised on white rice and wanderlust. Between and beyond childhood summers spent in Japan, she has woven travels through her stints as psychology and art student, bread peddler, jewellery pusher, espresso puller, graphic designer, English teacher and more recently as author for titles including *Tokyo Encounter*, *Costa Rica*, *Indonesia* and *Grand Canyon National Park*. She has spent months over the last several years eating, drinking and dancing her way across Tokyo in the name of research. She's currently based in beautiful Boulder, Colorado.

CONTRIBUTING AUTHORS

Brandon Presser wrote the Architecture chapter. He holds a degree in the history of art and architecture from Harvard University and has spent much of his professional life collaborating with Japanese architects in Tokyo and Paris. These days, Brandon is a freelance writer and has co-authored roughly a dozen Lonely Planet guides.

Dr Trish Batchelor wrote the Health chapter. Dr Batchelor is a travel medicine specialist and a medical advisor to the Travel Doctor New Zealand clinics. She teaches travel medicine through the University of Otago and is interested in underwater and high-altitude medicine, and in the impact of tourism on host countries.

Ken Henshall wrote the History chapter. He teaches Japanese Studies at the University of Canterbury, New Zealand. A Fellow of the Royal Historical Society, he is well-known for his *History of Japan: From Stone Age to Superpower*, which has been translated into numerous languages, and his other books on Japanese history, literature, society and language.

Behind the Scenes

THIS BOOK

This 11th edition of *Japan* was written by a team of authors led by Chris Rowthorn, who also coordinated the last four editions. This guidebook was commissioned in Lonely Planet's Melbourne and Oakland offices, and produced by the following:

Commissioning Editor Emily K Wolman
Coordinating Editor Gina Tsarouhas
Coordinating Cartographer Diana Duggan
Coordinating Layout Designer Aomi Hongo
Managing Editors Geoff Howard, Annelies Mertens
Managing Cartographers David Connolly, Adrian Persoglia
Managing Layout Designer Sally Darmody
Assisting Editors Carolyn Boicos, Jackey Coyle, Justin Flynn, Charlotte Harrison, Victoria Harrison, Joanne Newell, Rosie Nicholson, Kristin Odjik, Stephanie Pearson, Fionnuala Twomey, Saralinda Turner
Assisting Layout Designers Nicholas Colicchia, Kerrianne Southway
Assisting Cartographers Fatima Bašić, Alex Leung, Marc Milinkovic, Jacqueline Nguyen, Amanda Sierp, Brendan Streager, Bonnie Wintle
Language Content Laura Crawford
Project Manager Chris Love
Cover Image research provided by lonelyplanetimages.com

Thanks to Lucy Birchley, Nicole Hansen, Corey Hutchison, Carol Jackson, Craig Kilburn, Yvonne Kirk, Katie Lynch, Lauren Meijklejohn, Wayne Murphy, Jeanette Wall

THANKS

CHRIS ROWTHORN

I would like to thank the following people: Hiroe, KS and HS, Araki Toshiaki, Keiko Hagiwara, Perrin Lindelauf, Christopher Wood, Kise Erina, Mary Marjanovic, Rebecca Chau, Emily K Wolman, Chris Love, David Connolly, Andy Bender, Wendy Yanagihara, Ben Walker, Tim Hornyak, Matt Firestone and Paul Warham. I would also like to thank all the readers of Lonely Planet Japan books who sent in letters and emails with information about Japan – your input really helps and I've tried to use as much of it as possible!

ANDREW BENDER

First thanks to Yohko Scott and Naoko Marutani at the JNTO Los Angeles office for their always excellent support. Other key helpers on this project include Yamada Eri in Nagoya, Endô Akira in Matsumoto, Wani Naoko and the staff at Takayama's friendly tourist offices, Yoshie Yasuko in Fukui, Matsubara Takuya in Obama and Kita Kazuko in Noto. Inhouse, thanks to Emily K Wolman,

THE LONELY PLANET STORY

Fresh from an epic journey across Europe, Asia and Australia in 1972, Tony and Maureen Wheeler sat at their kitchen table stapling together notes. The first Lonely Planet guidebook, *Across Asia on the Cheap,* was born.

Travellers snapped up the guides. Inspired by their success, the Wheelers began publishing books to Southeast Asia, India and beyond. Demand was prodigious, and the Wheelers expanded the business rapidly to keep up. Over the years, Lonely Planet extended its coverage to every country and into the virtual world via lonelyplanet.com and the Thorn Tree message board.

As Lonely Planet became a globally loved brand, Tony and Maureen received several offers for the company. But it wasn't until 2007 that they found a partner whom they trusted to remain true to the company's principles of travelling widely, treading lightly and giving sustainably. In October of that year, BBC Worldwide acquired a 75% share in the company, pledging to uphold Lonely Planet's commitment to independent travel, trustworthy advice and editorial independence.

Today, Lonely Planet has offices in Melbourne, London and Oakland, with over 500 staff members and 300 authors. Tony and Maureen are still actively involved with Lonely Planet. They're travelling more often than ever, and they're devoting their spare time to charitable projects. And the company is still driven by the philosophy of *Across Asia on the Cheap*: 'All you've got to do is decide to go and the hardest part is over. So go!'

Chris Rowthorn, Gina Tsarouhas and Diana Duggan, while back on the home front thanks to Susan and Leonard, Elaine, Nancy and Steve.

MATTHEW D FIRESTONE

To my loving parents and wonderful sister, thank you all for always offering me nothing but your limitless support. I would also like to thank the entire Lonely Planet *Japan* team, particularly Chris, who has overseen this wonderful travel tome through so many editions. Finally, I'd like to acknowledge the cast of characters that make my life in Japan so complete. To Tac, you're a great roommate and an even better friend, and I know you're going to enjoy the view at the top of the world. To Will, you've got a big heart and a great golf swing, so follow your dreams. To Aki, thank you for sticking with me all these years, and I hope that you find nothing but happiness in life.

TIMOTHY N HORNYAK

I'd like to thank Chris Rowthorn, Matt Firestone and Lonely Planet staff, and my family (especially Alex for joining me on the road) for their patience with my wanderlust and kind support. Heartfelt thanks also go to Izu Islands JETs Tyler Roy, Robert Synovec, Rachel Turner and Michael Holdsworth; the Ide family of Fuji-Kawaguchi; John Washington of Chichi-jima; Burritt Sabin of Yokohama; Mamiko Hokari and Amal Gayed.

BENEDICT WALKER

This work is dedicated to my teachers. To the memory of my father, Tony Walker, my Nanna, Catherine Cook, my guru, Denise Crundall, and my friend Nanayo Kato-Wilder, all now deceased. Each of whom recognised my connection with Japan, encouraged me to explore it, had faith that I would make the right choices, and showed me the magic of following our dreams. My thanks to family and friends and those who helped me on the road; to John Vlahides who showed me I could do this; to Chris Rowthorn and Emily K Wolman; to Bicky, Kaori, Takashi and Purima Shimizu and my friends in Matsumoto; and the beloved gang at Stage and Screen Travel Melbourne. Without your patience, friendship and support, this journey would not have been possible. Thanks to Aunty Bonnie, a wordsmith in the truest sense, who gave me Lonely Planet *Japan* on my 11th birthday. Finally, all my love and gratitude to my Mum, Patricia Walker, who always believes in me, no matter what I do, or how far away I am.

PAUL WARHAM

Countless people helped me out while I was on the road: by suggesting a little-known local sight, recommending a restaurant or bar, or by pointing me in the right direction when I was lost. Everywhere I went in Shikoku and Western Honshū I met warm smiles and an eagerness to help. In Tokyo, I owe a debt of gratitude to Shimokawa Tokiji, for permitting me to turn his lovely apartment into an unholy mess of leaflets, notebooks, and orange peel. I owe Chris Rowthorn a large, well-chilled jug of juice for the times he bent over backwards, only to have me push him further. Thanks to my parents, for teaching me to keep my eyes open. And thanks as always to Emi, for everything.

WENDY YANAGIHARA

For their continued love and support, I am so thankful to my family: Dad, Jason, and the Maekawa, Takahashi and Yamamoto families. Many thanks also to Kenichi Anazawa, Mariko Matsumura, Meiko Fujimura, Natsuki Shigeta, Mr and Mrs Konishi, Naoya Suzuki, Midori Thiollier and Denis Taillandier for all of your help and good times, and to Mark, for surviving the whole process in such good humour.

OUR READERS

Many thanks to the travellers who used the last edition and wrote to us with helpful hints, useful advice and interesting anecdotes:

A Rita Aiello, Stephen Alldritt, Anders Andersson, Helena Andersson, Vincent Ardley **B** Valentina Baez Rizzi, Simon Baptist, Simon Bird, Kyle Bobrick, Tad Boniecki, Gwen Bouvier, Karlis Bremanis, Pierre-Yann Bridé, Nicolas Bruchet, Martin Burningham, Duncan Butland, Tammie Buxton **C** Melanie Cardew, Adolfo Carli, Marie-Hélène Cayer, Raoul Chaves, Marin Chhim, Chai Sia Chuah, Damon Churchill, Lee Collins, Steve Connor, Heather Cox, Matthew Crawford, Laura Creighton, Anna Cumming **D** Justin Dabner, Laura Daniels, Chen David, Graham Davies, Frazer Davies, Erica Dencs, Autumn Depoe, Molly Des Jardin, Sarah Katie Duggan, Jenny Dunlop, Patrick Dunne, Monique Duroux **E** Rosh Ebrahim, Sandra Elmoznino, Nate England **F** Claus Falsig, Alexander Fekete, John Fenech, Vinita Fernandes, Sue Finch, Amy-Lynn Fischer, Yvonne Fletcher, Jennifer Folkner, Eleanor Forward, Victoria Fraser, Sonal Barot, Paul Frederickson, Ichiro Fudai **G** Fiona Gainsford, Jo-Ann Gamble, Stuart Geddes, Chihiro Goddard, Peter Goltermann, Gabriel Gonzalez Maurazos, Peter Goss, Petra

Grosskinsky Jeckelmann **H** Marc Hadfield, Danny Hanse, Kathryn Harriott, Melanie Harrison, Tomoko Hayashi, Murray Hayter, Claire Hewat, Hamish Hockings, Sutton Place Hotel, Patrick Hovey, Armin Howald, Russ Howells **I** Miyoko Imanaka, Miyoko Imanaka **J** Sally Jackson, Nick Jacobs, Tanith James, Amie Jones, Stuart Jones **K** Alan Kavanagh, Simon Keller, Cam Kenalty, Nicholas Klar, Sigurd Kleiven, Jeffrey Knapp, Brian Knox, Knox Family, Kimberly Kohler, Scott Kolwitz, Christoph Kopke, Andrew Kudlick, Andreas Laimboeck **L** Donald Lee, Nicole Lees, Ali Lemer, Matthew Leonard, Frederik Lewy, Cathrine Lindblom, Louis Loke, Yew-Ming Loo, Barbara Lorenz, Fredrik Lundvall **M** Timothy Mac Neill, Jelena Macan, Dorothea Mahnke, Diane Malone, Haruko Masuo, Denise Matthews, Daniel McCall, Susan McEwan, Aneta McNally, L Melanie, Peter Merrett, Sarah Metcalfe, Stephen Meth, Scott Meyer, Joel Millwood, Daniela Miwa Kikuchi, Ada Montessoro, David Moreton, Carol Mulligan, Andy Murdock **N** Koji Nakagawa, Michael Nedoma, James Newton, Delacroix Nicolas **O** Rena Okino, Pip Oldham, Adamek Ondrej **P** Elke Parsa, Andrew Parson, Simon Partner, Ryan Paugh, Mark Paul, Colin Paul, Julie Peasley, Cyndi Pecanic, Darren Peets, Marion Penaud, Marion Penaud, Eleonora Piccolo, Ana Piris, Chris Ploegaert, Rachel Pulley **R** James Randerson, Simon Ratcliffe, Nick Raynor, Stacey Reed, Jordi Ribas Romagós, John Rigg, Peter & Yumiko Riley, Monica Riquelme, Patrick Roman, Marcus Rosenberg **S** Scott Sadler, Janice Sare, Kumiko Sasaki, Daniel Scherzer, Ellena Scheufler, Sally Scott, Andrew Smith, Al Smith, Richard Smith, Dschun Song, Jeff Stewart, Peter Stutvoet, Juni Suwa, Kyoichi Suzuki, George Swithinbank **T** Kentaro Takahashi, Jason Tam, Claire Tanaka, Hans Ter Horst, Svenja Thies, Melinda Thomas, Rob Tremewan, Nadja Turkovic, Alison Turley **V** Steven Van Vegten, Emile Vd Heide, Hans Verwegen, Bernard Vixseboxse, Kiara Vormwald **W** John Wallace, Maureen Walsh, David Watts, Vera Weiduschat, Bill Weir, Mika Weller, Kasper Wichmann, Joshua Williams, Rachel Winton

SEND US YOUR FEEDBACK

We love to hear from travellers – your comments keep us on our toes and help make our books better. Our well-travelled team reads every word on what you loved or loathed about this book. Although we cannot reply individually to postal submissions, we always guarantee that your feedback goes straight to the appropriate authors, in time for the next edition. Each person who sends us information is thanked in the next edition – and the most useful submissions are rewarded with a free book.

To send us your updates – and find out about Lonely Planet events, newsletters and travel news – visit our award-winning website: **lonelyplanet.com/contact**.

Note: we may edit, reproduce and incorporate your comments in Lonely Planet products such as guidebooks, websites and digital products, so let us know if you don't want your comments reproduced or your name acknowledged. For a copy of our privacy policy visit lonelyplanet.com/privacy.

ACKNOWLEDGMENTS

Many thanks to the following for the use of their content:

Globe on title page ©Mountain High Maps 1993 Digital Wisdom, Inc.

Tokyo metro map: © 2009 Tokyo Metro and Bureau of Transportation Tokyo Metropolitan Government. Tokyo Metro Co., Ltd. approved (Approval Number 20-A065).

Osaka Transport map: Osaka Subway System map © Osaka Municipal Transportation Bureau 2009.

Internal photographs: All other photographs by Lonely Planet Images, or as credited, and by p505 (#3), p507 (#1) John Ashburne; p505 (#2) Anthony Plummer; p505 (#3), p507 (#2) Martin Moos; p506 (#1), (#4) Oliver Strewe; p506 (#2) Greg Elms; p506 (#3) Paul Dymond; p507 (#3) John Borthwick; p508 (#1), (#3) Mason Florence; p508 (#2) Richard Cummins.

Index

INDEX

INDEX

000 Map pages
000 Photograph pages

N

INDEX

000 Map pages
000 Photograph pages

INDEX

INDEX

000 Map pages
000 Photograph pages

INDEX

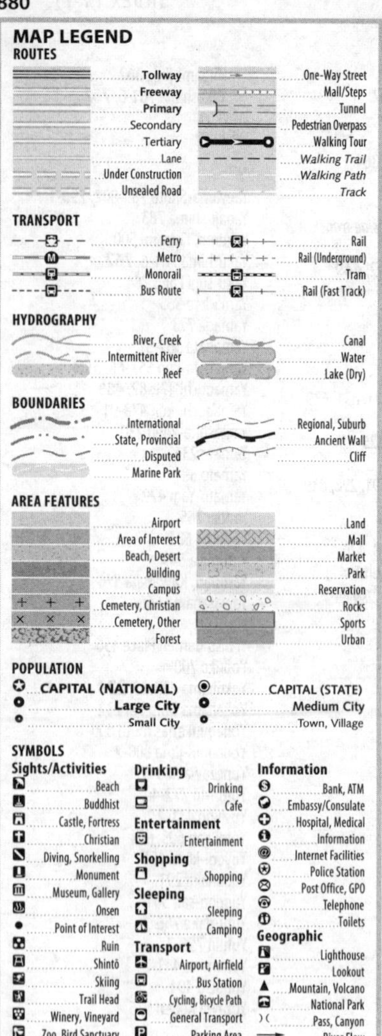

LONELY PLANET OFFICES

Australia
Head Office
Locked Bag 1, Footscray, Victoria 3011
☎ 03 8379 8000, fax 03 8379 8111
talk2us@lonelyplanet.com.au

USA
150 Linden St, Oakland, CA 94607
☎ 510 250 6400, toll free 800 275 8555
fax 510 893 8572
info@lonelyplanet.com

UK
2nd fl, 186 City Rd,
London EC1V 2NT
☎ 020 7106 2100, fax 020 7106 2101
go@lonelyplanet.co.uk

Published by Lonely Planet Publications Pty Ltd
ABN 36 005 607 983

Cover photograph: Japanese girls in kimonos overlooking a line of rowboats, off the coast of Honshū. Chad Ehlers/Nordic Photos. Many of the images in this guide are available for licensing from Lonely Planet Images: www.lonelyplanetimages.com.

Printed by Toppan Security Printing Pte. Ltd.
Printed in Singapore